# VOLUME 89

# 1985

**Argus Specialist Publications Ltd**

**Wolsey House, Wolsey Road, Hemel Hempstead, Herts HP2 4SS**

# WOODWORKER VOLUME 89
# Index

## 12 monthly copies January 1985 – December 1985

## AUTHOR INDEX

## Argus Specialist Publications, Argus Books Ltd.

# SUBJECT INDEX

# ADVERTISERS' INDEX

**On the Cover: artist-craftsman David West's 30-room model of West Wood House boasts 110 working sliding-sash windows and stands 8ft. 6in. tall!**
**(See pp 299)**
Photo: Fisher Fine Art Gallery

Published by
Argus Specialist Publications
Argus Books Ltd.,
Wolsey House, Wolsey Road,
Hemel Hempstead, Herts.

Argus Specialist Publications Ltd.
First Published 1985

Printed in Great Britain

# The magazine for the craftsman
## ~ and the aspiring craftsman!

January 1985
Vol. 89
No. 1094

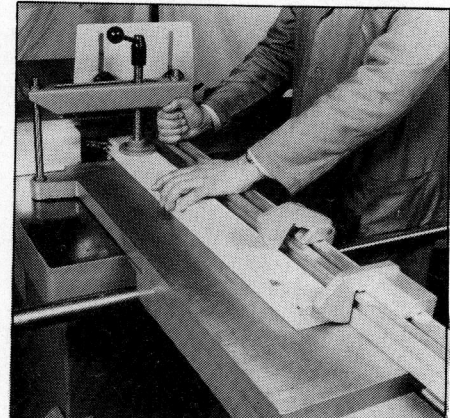

● *Using a spindle moulder: page 865 features a buyer's guide to this formidably useful machine. Shown here is a tenoning operation on the new Wadkin BEL*

**Publisher** Tony Dowdeswell
**Editor** Peter Collenette
**Deputy Editor** Aidan Walker
**Graphics** Peter Kirby
**Group Art** Nick Howell
**Guild of Woodworkers** Aidan Walker
**Publishing Director** John Foster
**Chairman and Chief Executive** Jim Connell

If you write to us, please enclose a stamped addressed envelope. Unfortunately we cannot accept responsibility for the loss of or damage to unsolicited material. Nothing published in *Woodworker* may be reproduced without permission.

**Advertisement Manager** Paul Holmes
**Advertisement production** Karyn Stewart

ABC

We reserve the right to refuse or suspend advertisements without explanation, and regret we can take no responsibility either for clerical or printing errors or for the bona fides of advertisers.

**Editorial, advertisements and Guild of Woodworkers** PO Box 35, Wolsey House, Wolsey Road, Hemel Hempstead, Herts HP2 4SS; telephone Hemel Hempstead (0442) 41221
**Subscriptions and back issues** Infonet Ltd, 10-13 Times House, 179 Marlowes, Hemel Hempstead, Herts HP1 1BB; telephone Hemel Hempstead (0442) 48434
**Subscriptions per year** UK £15; overseas outside USA (accelerated surface post) £16.50, USA (accelerated surface post) $21.50, airmail £41.50

**UK trade** SM Distribution Ltd, 16-18 Trinity Gardens, London SW9 8DX; telephone 01-274 8611
**North American trade** Eastern News Distributors, 166-41 Powells Cove Boulevard, PO Box 69, Whitestone, New York 11357 (**Postmaster**: Please send address changes to England)
**Printed in Great Britain** by Ambassador Press Ltd, St Albans, Herts
**Mono origination** Multiform Photosetting Ltd, Cardiff
© Argus Specialist Publications Ltd 1984
ISSN 0043 776X

On the cover: Sectional tables in ash from the Style 84 exhibition (page 58), designed by Gina Tajirian and Edward Richards of Planks Design Consultancy in London

# Argus Specialist Publications Ltd
**Wolsey House, Wolsey Road, Hemel Hempstead, Herts HP2 4SS (0442) 41221**

## Craft Wars

Some favourite names are to be seen at the British Crafts Centre from mid-January, not least the illustrious Fred Baier. 'Five Furniture Pieces' is an exhibition that aims to 'illustrate a current force in the field of craft furniture'. Rather than merely go in for showy displays of skill in a piece of furniture, 'there are a number of designers concerned that this should be an inherent quality in their work.' The intention, apparently, is to highlight the practical and functional considerations involved in designing furniture to commission, or for limited production; 'Perfection in execution . . . on a par with that of industrial furniture' is what we are assured the lucky exhibitors are striving for.

Remember the triangles and boxes in 'Events', *Woodworker* October? Floris van den Broecke, whose purple prose we quoted, is showing an original piece here — a multi-purpose settle, metal framed and upholstered with a specially woven and printed textile. Ralph Ball's shelving unit in steel, glass and aluminium is also to be seen, exploring structures under tension.

Never mind the question 'Is it furniture?' — if it's misguided enough to compete with the perfectly executed products of MFI or Dexion, it must be worth exhibiting . . . mustn't it?
● 'Five Furniture Pieces' is at the British Crafts Centre, 42 Earlham St, London WC2H 9LD, tel. 01-836 6993; 11 Jan-16 Feb.

## Pye-eyed

The Crafts Council, however, are exhibiting between 21 Nov and 3 Feb the work of an acknowledged craft master which

● *A box in Bombay rosewood with a screw-thread lid. The inside is turned, the outside carved (photo David Cripps)*

is original, beautiful and even practical! David Pye, Professor of Furniture at the Royal College of Art for 26 years, has lent 80 turned boxes from his own priate collection to the Crafts Council to show at their London Gallery. A selection of 60 of his carved dishes and bowls, with their distinctive spiral and organic motif, are also to be seen. A household name amongst turners — one to be mentioned in hushed tones — Mr Pye's influence as a craft teacher and practitioner extends through his books on the theory of workmanship and design. Beauty will always owe much to the beholder's eye, but who could not be bewitched by the delicacy and proportion of his work? If you want to see perfection in execution, this show is the one to choose.

Twelve pieces will be on open display so that blind people will

● *David Pye carves fine flutes in dishes and bowls with this appliance he designed himself (photo David Cripps)*

be able to appreciate for themselves Mr Pye's artistry, and a sound tape will also be running, with commentaries printed in Braille. A touching idea for the sake of those who cannot enjoy the visual experience.
● Crafts Council, 12 Waterloo Place, London SW1Y 4AU, tel. 01-930 4811.

● *The table and cabinet right and below were both made in Acklington prison. None of the men have previous experience!*

## Inside jobs

**Kevin Rowntree** writes: One of the most unusual exhibitions of handcrafted furniture ever seen in the northeast of England went on display in Northumberland recently. The men who made the award-winning pieces were nowhere to be seen, however; nor are they likely to be in evidence for some time. They are all serving sentences at HM Prison in Acklington, near Morpeth.

In charge of the activity which, year after year, leads to such fine pieces is vocational-training instructor David Duffield. His course lasts for 12 months, and covers a broad range of furniture-making skills: it includes wood machining, cabinetmaking, upholstery, french-polishing, metal work, technical drawing, design and theoretical studies, and leads to the City and Guilds 555 Furniture Craft certificate.

All the work is handmade and hand-finished. None of the inmates has had any previous experience in making furniture, and after one has viewed the incredibly high standard achieved in only one year it comes as no surprise to learn that the City and Guilds Institute repeatedly award Acklington men the highest credits.

The men start by learning how to sharpen and handle tools, and they make a simple beech frame which is then used for the seat in a mahogany stool. From these basic beginnings they develop their skills to very high standards, and produce five or six different pieces each during the 12 months. These include a variety of occasional tables, chairs, writing-tables and bureaux. Much of this is inlaid and decorated with marquetry.

It isn't always easy to assess the rehabilitative value of such a course, but prison welfare staff report that inmates show a marked improvement.

Perhaps most encouraging of all, there is considerable continuity between the course and outside employment; several of the men are known to have continued their studies in outside colleges, and others to have found employment as a direct result of qualifications obtained in prison.

## Becalmed

Richard Sarjent has been ill and consequently unable to write this month's Tradewinds. We intend to resume in February.

## Woodmen and Luna

**Gerry Baker** writes: I would like to allay any fears readers may have about Luna products bought from Woodmen of Bicester, who have officially ceased trading.

We assure everyone who has bought a Luna machine (including the 40 universal, previously known as the MIA6)

that our warranty will be fully honoured in respect of goods sold by Woodmen. Sales, service and spare-part supply will continue through our key dealers.
● Gerry Baker, Director, Luna Tools & Machinery Ltd, 20 Denbigh Hall, Bletchley, Milton Keynes, Bucks MK3 7QT, tel. (0908) 70771.

● *As pine goes by . . . these whimsical timepieces are by Surrey designer Rupert Senior, who showed them at the Chelsea Crafts Fair in October. The hanging medal is 11¾in high, the watch 24in fully extended. They're quite reasonably priced too, at £20-30*

## Correction time

Apologies, actually — to Mr R. F. Turton. His carving entries, mentioned in the Yorkshire Woodworker Show report (WW/Nov), were attributed to R. F. Turner.

● *Confused about the 'olive ash goblet in fig. 10' of Bruce Boulter's tigerwood turning project (WW/Nov)? Sorry, we missed one photo out – this is it*

● The price for Norman Reed's instrument-making courses in Totnes is £815, not £185 as quoted last month in Shoptalk.

● If you live in or around London, you'll be wondering what happened to part 2 of our A-Z supplement. There's a dispute between the distributors and trade unions who handle our London copies. We decided to leave the supplement off so you would at least get the cake, cream or no cream. We'll publicise our plan for getting the A-Z to you.

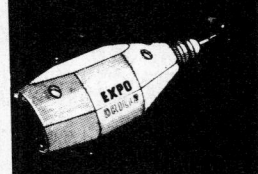
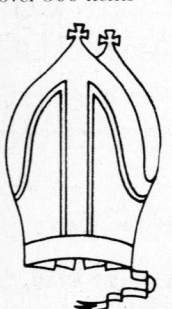

Prices quoted are those prevailing at press date and are subject to alteration due to economic conditions.

# Shoptalk

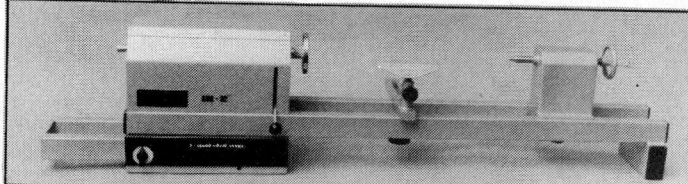

● *Apollo's new Woodstyler ¾hp lathes are imaginatively engineered and attractively priced – £345+VAT for the 800 model, 32in between centres. Design engineer Barry Beck has spring-mounted and counterbalanced the motor to keep vibration to the minimum; a friction clutch lever allows gradual engagement, giving the sort of control previously associated only with metalworking lathes. You can mount a saw table and a sanding disc – the disc on either side of the headstock – and there are seven speeds, 570-3600rpm. Apollo Products, 100 Stone Rd, Toftwood, Dereham, Norfolk NR19 1LJ, tel. (0362) 3515*

West German manufacturers **Aigner** have introduced a complete range of **aids and safety devices for wood machining,** designed to eliminate the need for a helper and save your fingers and thumbs. It's the first such range we have seen as accessories.

There is a table extension which can be fixed to any machine — bandsaw, spindle moulder, planer and bench saw are illustrated in the brochure — and a series of multi-adjustable cross-stops and fences which allow accurate and safe insertion moulding. We particularly liked the look of the 'clamping strip', an adjustable hand-guard and holder for short workpieces.

Clamps, guide wheels, deflector strips, the 'UniMould' for working small radii, and the 'BowmouldMulti', would all take the place of those bits and pieces that you have to work out for specific operations in specific jobs, often get in the way, and are devils to readjust, if they aren't junked anyway. If you're serious about costing the time that goes into these one-off jigs and aids, it could well be worth investing in some of this equipment. It would also pay to look closely at how long they take to set up, and where it would cease to be economic to use them for a small run. Leicester Wood Technique are the agents for the range, which was developed in association with the German Woodworking Safety Control Association.

● Leicester Wood Technique Ltd, Holthorpe House, Main St, Theddingworth, Lutterworth, Leics LE17 6QY, tel. (0858) 880643

**Ian Norbury** and **A. J. Charlton** write: We would like to apologise most sincerely for the absence of Ian Norbury's woodcarving demonstration from the opening exhibition of Charltons Timber Centre at Radstock, Avon, at the end of October. This was due to unforeseen events, and we hope it did not cause too much inconvenience or disappointment.

● *One of the most sensible ideas for a woodworking winter has to be the waste-burning space heater. But you need the right unit for the space; it may not be economical if you don't create enough waste. This is the MiniCal, in which a fan circulates the warmth. It costs £798×VAT from Fercell Engineering Ltd, Unit 20, Swaislands Drive, Crayford Industrial Estate, Crayford, Kent, tel.(0322) 53131*

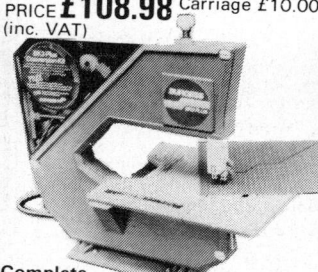

5

 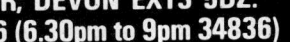
6

Prices quoted are those prevailing at press date and are subject to alteration due to economic conditions.

# Timberline

**Arthur Jones** presents the month's inside news of supplies

First find your supplier. That is a strongly held view among woodworkers who use hardwoods. In far too many areas, there are still very few merchants who can pretend to have even a model stock of hardwoods — let alone one especially designed to supply the craftsman.

The hardwood trade is now running a national campaign, involving all those firms who claim to hold hardwood stocks plus any newcomers, urging them to concentrate upon twelve species — iroko, utile, beech, oak, afrormosia, teak, sapele, African mahogany, meranti, African walnut, south American mahogany and lauan.

Not many will provide a reasonable selection in all these species, and wherever merchants have only a limited interest in hardwoods you can expect that they will be stocking only the species to be found in this list. It is, of course, a restricted selection, and any woodworker wishing to use other hardwoods will have to do some searching.

Paradoxically, the range of hardwoods on the commercial market today is actually greater than ever; this is attributable largely to the development of the tropical hardwood forests in south America and the Far East — especially in the Philippines, Indonesia and Malaysia. But don't expect to buy these other woods in small quantities, except through merchants who specialise in supplying craftsmen.

To quote the imported prices for the less usual hardwoods can be misleading, because these are available only in small quantities at much enhanced prices. It is no secret that the prices obtained by merchants for some hardwoods are a matter for amazement and jealousy among the bigger firms.

The woodworker must also remember that the markets are constantly changing, sometimes for reasons quite unconnected with supply. For example, the west African hardwoods are becoming much more popular because the producers are making larger supplies available for export, and they can be bought in sterling or other currencies not linked with the dollar. On the other hand, hardwoods from south America, Canada and the USA have to be bought in dollars, and the rate of exchange has never been so low. What is good news for the American tourist is bad news for the woodworker wanting to use hardwoods from these countries.

Not that there is much hardship in using west African hardwoods, which rightly won a high place in the hardwood market long ago — it was only internal problems in the region which put these woods into the background; there has been no change whatsoever in the value of the timbers.

One of the listed hardwoods which merchants are being urged to stock is lauan. There's plenty of this wood here at the moment because of over-production in the Far East and some frantic shipping of the timber to the UK on consignment. This situation is going to change quite rapidly, and in 1985 we shall undoubtedly see lauan selling at much higher prices.

In some areas, DIY centres have started stocking hardwoods. Sizes are often limited; the prices may appear attractive, but this is often because the shops are stocking lower-quality material. This policy is surely mistaken. The woodworker, in general, seeks a good-quality hardwood. He doesn't want his effort and skills wasted on shoddy timber.

In softwoods, there are few problems ahead. Importers have been holding back from the market and showing no enthusiasm for new contracts. Stocks are high enough to cover current sales without any desperate need for forward purchasing, and we may assume that this hesitancy is also based upon a conviction that world prices of softwood will rise only marginally in 1985. 1985.

If the importer sees no benefit in building up his stocks, the woodworker would be wise to follow his example and let the timber trade do all the stockholding — buying only as the need arises, in the fairly certain knowledge that the required stocks will be there for immediate delivery and the price will have changed little with the wait. 'Steady as she goes' seems to be the 1984 motto in the timber trade, and it can reasonably be adopted by the woodworker too. ∎

7

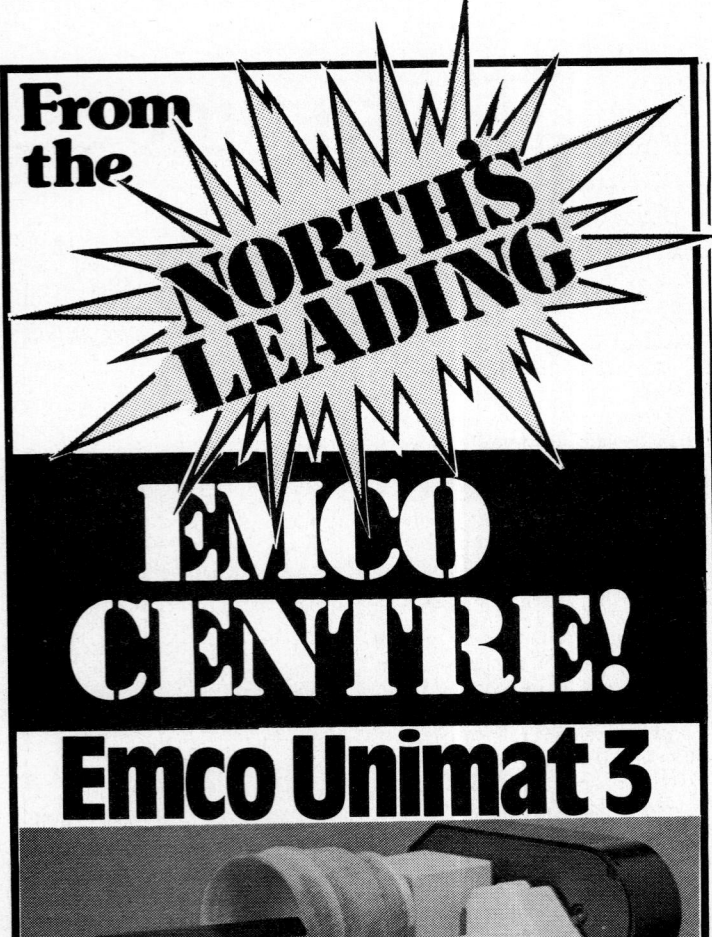
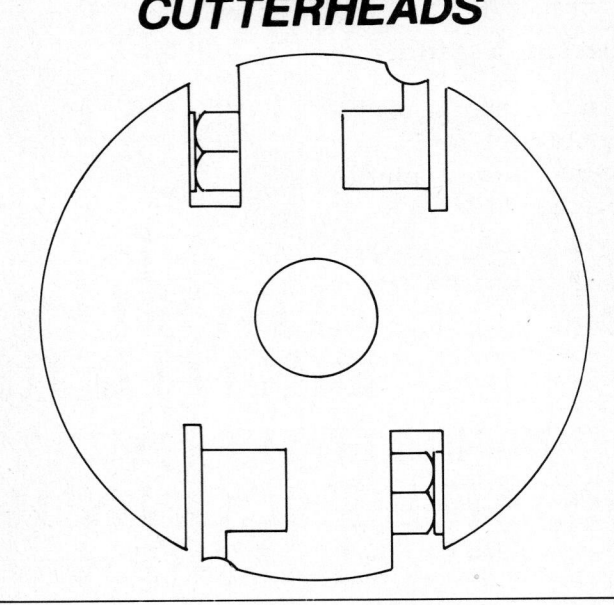

Prices quoted are those prevailing at press date and are
subject to alteration due to economic conditions.

# Shoptalk special

## Selecting a spindle

### Alan Holtham explains what to look for if you're buying a spindle moulder

**U**ntil quite recently the spindle moulder has been a machine for the professional workshop. However, following the tremendous boom in router sales over the last few years, many people have realised the potential of a shaping machine of some sort, and have then taken the next logical step and progressed to a spindle moulder in its own right.

These machines have always been treated with a certain degree of fear, which to some extent is justified. They are without doubt one of the most dangerous woodworking machines, and many professionals, as well as amateurs, have suffered hand injuries on the spindle moulder. Nevertheless, as on all machines if handled properly and with common sense, these accidents are avoidable, and with practice the versatility of this machine becomes apparent. One soon develops a healthy respect for it instead of mighty dread!

As the name suggests the spindle moulder is basically a heavy shaft on to which is bolted a cutterblock which carries the shaped cutters, usually mounted in matched pairs. Unlike the router, which works at very high rpm, the spindle-moulding block, with its much larger diameter and therefore higher peripheral speed, works at a lower rotational speed. In fact most machines have several speeds, and one should look for at least two, in the 4000-10,000rpm range. As one would expect, the higher the speed the better the finish, but make sure that the speed selected does not exceed that stamped on the block. Speeds are invariably changed by the conventional means of belt changing, but we are just beginning to see a few electronic control devices that might be worth looking at.

When selecting a spindle moulder there are several points to look for in comparing the various models. Since the actual spindle is the heart of the machine, check to see that it is of a common diameter, so that tooling will be readily available. 30mm seems to be about the

● *Wadkin's new BEL, a medium-duty four-speed machine with high safety standards. £1,695+VAT; with tenoning table, £2,295+VAT; 5hp motor*

most popular size, though some of the heavier machines use 1¼in. There should be a good amount of rise and fall on the spindle, and this adjustment should be easy to make. However, check to see that the spindle is lockable at the desired height. One otherwise excellent machine I once used had a very poor locking system, so that when you took heavy cuts the spindle gradually dropped, making a beautifully tapered mould which looked very clever, but was not always what was required!

The length of the actual spindle is important too, since it may sometimes be necessary to mount two or more cutting heads. For instance, when tenoning, the easiest way is to mount two blocks with a spacer in between to cut the two halves of the tenon simultaneously. Some spindles have a slot through them to take the 'French head', seen on the Kity machines, but these are the exception rather than the rule. Most only have provision for conventional cutterblocks.

A tilting table, although a handy luxury, is not essential, and most machines in the domestic or light industrial range only have fixed tables. The fences are the other vital feature,

as the movement of these backwards and forwards across the table controls the depth of cut, so look for a model which has some form of easy adjustment, preferably on a screw arrangement for fine setting. I have always regretted the rather crude fence on our machine, a Scheppach HF30, which is otherwise excellent. I have heard, though, that these are to be modified in the next few months, and new models will have independently ajustable fences.

I have often argued that many modern woodworking machines are so overguarded as to make them positively dangerous, since the guards continually get in the way and hamper proper controls and vision. However, on the spindle moulder adequate

guarding is absolutely essential, so make sure this looks and feels comfortable without restricting movement. Remember that, when you use a spindle moulder, you are basically performing an operation that would otherwise be regarded as foolhardy in the extreme — namely, poking a lump of wood into a fast-revolving lump of metal with projecting blades. There is inevitably going to be a bit of 'equal and opposite' reaction, so sensible guarding is vitally necessary. Usually this takes the form of hold-down springs which push the work hard down on to the table, and horizontally on to the fence. These should always be used if possible, as they help the feed remain constant and therefore aid an even surface finish. Our machine has rubber rollers which are angled towards the fence to help push the wood that way. Looking at the fences and hold-down unit, remember that the moulding operation pro-duces a lot of shavings, so see that there is adequate provision for them to escape. Usually a draught extraction point is provided.

Even if you do not anticipate using one, check that there is a sliding table available to fit the machine. These are almost essential if you anticipate tenoning, or any moulding across the grain. Similarly, for circular work a bearing ring or ring guide should be available, along with its complementary overhead guard.

This covers the main points to look out for when comparing machines. Other features are fairly obvious — basic construction, motor power, operating height, etc. You can only decide on these yourself, knowing how much work you anticipate putting through it — but bear in mind that, once set up in your workshop, the spindle moulder will probably get a lot more use than you think! ■

● *The Emco TF 65. Three speeds and 2.5hp for £390+ VAT. The tenoning table is an extra*

# Question box

Our panel of experts solve
your woodworking problems

**Q** Recently I have been given a bead plane which I have difficulty in operating. I am told that part of the cutter is not supposed to cut – yet it is still sharpened with the cutting part of the bead. I hope you will be able to enlighten me.

J. W. Davies, Llangadog, Dyfed

**A** The cutters of side-bead and astragal moulding-planes are exactly the same shape although they function rather differently. A side-bead has been described as 'a round moulding used to remove a sharp arris'. In other words, it is worked right on the edge of a board. The plane rounds off the sharp corner, and grooves out a quirk so as to leave a semicircular moulding. An astragal, on the other hand, is set slightly back from the edge and separated from it by a small rebate or fillet. The plane's cutter therefore has to perform the extra function of cutting the rebate, as well as grooving the quirk and

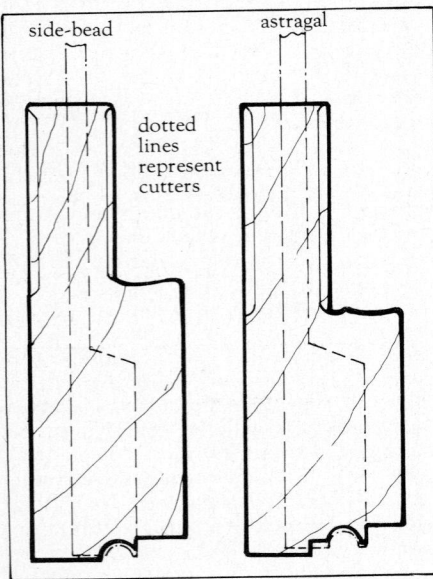

side-bead          astragal

dotted
lines
represent
cutters

rounding the bead. For this purpose its flat, left-hand (seen from behind) section has to be kept sharp, just like the arch-shaped centre section and the narrow quirk router. The flat section of a side-bead cutter has no cutting function but merely supports the cutter in its correct position in the plane.

The fact that both sorts of cutter are often found to have been sharpened in the same way has no significance. It is simply easier to sharpen a cutter straight across the bottom than to try to sharpen the little spur, or quirk router part, alone.

Two further points may help. Firstly, a bead is a semicircle in cross-section. Its sides are therefore virtually perpendicular to the surface being planed. In the nature of things the parts of the cutter that shape these sides cannot actually cut; they can only scrape. In sharpening, care must therefore be taken to maintain the correct arch shape but at the same time to relieve

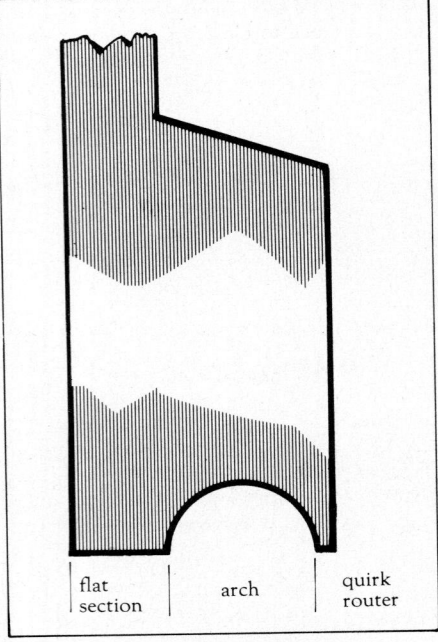

flat          arch          quirk
section                     router

the back edge slightly so that the front edge alone meets the wood. If this is not done the cutter will merely squeeze the wood to form the sides of the bead. This makes the work hard and the result misshapen.

Secondly, softwoods are easily compressible but tenacious (witness the tensile strength of the long shavings), so it is difficult to get a clean result when working mouldings. A timber like mahogany, which is crisper, drier and more friable, works much more satisfactorily.

*Philip Walker*

**Q** I plan to make the desk shown here. The sides and back will be panelled. Dimensions are 1500×600mm, height 730mm. The top will be of solid bird's-eye maple 25mm thick, the main frame and drawers of Japanese oak. The top will be made of four or five boards, edge-jointed after matching the grain for appearance. The side and back panels will be of 10mm oak, recessed into the legs and fielded. I would very much welcome your advice on the following before I set out on this formidable task:

**1** Will it suffice to join the boards for the top by a loose tongue not running the full length (for the sake of appearance), and will they have to be joined with the grain alternating as usually recommended?

**2** Would it be best to use quarter-sawn oak for the legs, drawer fronts and panels? The timber is kiln dried. I feel quarter-sawn oak will perhaps show less figure and not detract from that of the top.

**3** All joints will be mortise and tenon.

**4** What timber would you suggest for the drawer sides and bottoms? The drawers will have dovetail joints, at least at the front ends.

**5** I would prefer to leave the timber in its natural colour and finish with matt polyurethane without filling the grain.

**6** I plan to fix the top to the frame with buttons. Would these be strong enough if the desk were lifted by its top?

K. Ratib, Nottingham

**A 1** You should certainly alternate the grain on adjacent boards to minimise the effect of shrinkage, and your idea of stopped housings is a very good one.

**2** The plainest oak is that called 'through and through' because the log has been cut from end to end in parallel 'slices'. The outside 'slices' (planks) are the plainest; the others become progressively more figured as the centre of the log is reached. Quartering oak is generally reckoned to be the sawing method which gives most figure. By the way, you no doubt know that the moisture content should be in the region of 6-12%.

**3** I would be inclined to use dovetails where marked, as I feel this will make a tighter job of the framing.

**4** If you want nice dovetails on your drawer fronts, you will need to use an even grained wood with a close texture. Poplar, alder, obeche and even chestnut are often used, but are generally too soft and open grained. If you can get it, genuine yellow birch from Canada would be ideal; if not, try sycamore if you must have a plain whitish colour. Another choice could be one or other of the African pseudo-mahoganies; abura would probably be best, but you will get a light-mahogany coloured drawer.

**5** It would be best to give the whole job an initial coat of the polyurethane 50/50 with white spirit. This will seal the grain, and help to stop any endgrain soaking up the subsequent coats.

**6** Yes, turn-buttons must be used for the top. Their strength is limited by the narrow top rails, which can only carry a small rebate, so put one every 250mm.

*Vic Taylor*

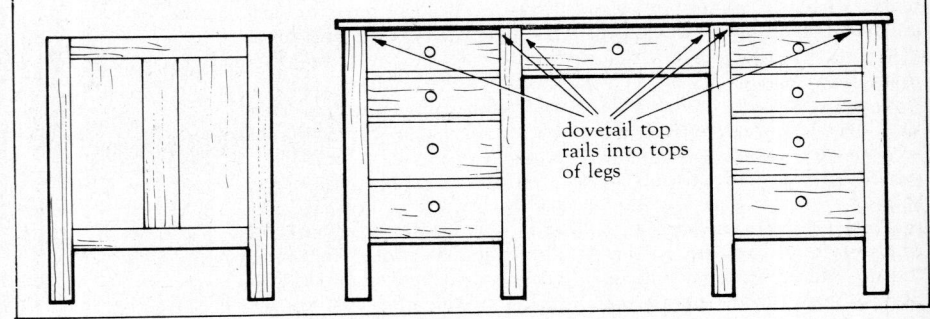

dotted top
rails into tops
of legs

# Question box

**Q** *I want to hang a pair of doors in an opening in my garden wall. The existing doors hang on $3\frac{3}{4}\times2\frac{1}{2}$in angle iron, buried in concrete and bolted to the end of the wall on each side. L-shaped hangers are welded to the angle iron. The base of the bottom hanger is 5in from the ground and the base of the top hanger 5ft 8in. These doors are of differing widths. Over the years the larger one has tended to sag badly, catching on the tarmac driveway.*

*The opening in the 5ft wall is 5ft $2\frac{3}{4}$in. I would like the doors to be 6ft high and of equal width, and I intend to paint them. Can you advise on:*
- *the best wood for the purpose, and the proportions for the various rails;*
- *method of construction, i.e. type of mortise and tenon to be used;*
- *method of buttressing to prevent sag, also wedging of joints;*
- *height above ground for lower edge of doors:*
- *whether I should re-use the T-shaped steel strips from both sides of the mid-rail (hanging side and opening side), used in the old doors with the aim of preventing sag?*

*Cyril Hayes, Glasgow*

**A** The design commonly employed for such doors is known as 'framed, ledged, braced and battened'; it employs mortise-and-tenon joints which are both wedged and dowelled, with the braces inclining upwards from the hanging edge in each case.

As the doors are to be painted, Russian red deal of joinery quality should be obtained, in not less than the following minimum sizes:
- top rails 115×60mm
- middle and bottom rails 225×35mm
- stiles 115×60mm
- braces 115×35mm
- T&G boards 25mm.

The top rails are haunch-mortised-and-tenoned to the stiles, and all are grooved to take the T&G boards. The middle and bottom rails are set flush to the back of the framework using barefaced mortise-and-tenons (a pair of tenons for the middle rail and a pair with a haunch for the bottom rails) in order that the facing boards may lie over them and come flush with the front of the structure. The inclined braces are housed into the rails some 38mm from the stiles. All tenons should be wedged and then dowelled with a hardwood pin 13mm in diameter. These should be fixed 26mm in from the tenon shoulder line to prevent the wood from splitting when driven in.

The boards should be nailed and clenched over the rails and braces to make a tight construction, and a capping piece should be fixed to the tops of the doors. Remember to paint the edges of the boards and frame members before assembly.

Your existing hinges could be used again, or you could employ Scotch T-hinges, strap hinges, or bands and gudgeon hooks — a visit to your local builder's ironmonger should satisfy you as to the best type.

The clearance under the gates depends somewhat on the driveway over which they will swing. If there is a rise behind them, they will have to clear the ground in their open position by an inch or so. If the ground is level, a $1\frac{1}{2}$in clearance when closed will suffice.

*Bob Grant DLC FRSA MSIAD*

---

**Q** *My calling is in woodturning. I urgently require advice on how to bleach bone to the whiteness of this paper. I have seen a considerable number of lace bobbins made from this material, and although I have tried boiling with domestic bleach I have not met with success yet.*

*G. Hall, Sunderland*

**A** A woodturner and ex-slaughterhouseman, Les Neal, tells us that the best bone for this purpose is a front shin of beef. The secret is to remove all the marrow first. Then either scrape it clean or give it to a dog before boiling it — in biological washing-powder, not bleach. The absence of marrow will prevent it from yellowing.

---

**Q** *I was fascinated to read the 'Question box' reply (WW/May) to Mr Dodd's enquiry on splayed bevels, since I shall shortly be faced with a similar problem on a bookcase pediment.*

*I can confirm the bevel angle of 66° for a canting angle of 26°, but for the life of me cannot confirm the butt angle, nor understand the principle on which it is based – Bob Grant seems to have taken a diagonal between the flushed-off line and the original top line, but I* can't see the relevance of this to the bevel in the thickness of the timber.

*B. Tildesley, Louth*

**A** I regret that my sketch showing the bevels needed for splayed (sometimes called hopper) work was not as clear as it might have been. I am including another sketch dealing principally with the butt cut, which relates solely to the thickness of the material being used. I suggest that the best way to increase your understanding of the problem would be to make up a model of one corner using fairly thick wood, say $1\frac{1}{4}$in. Cut the bevel angles but leave the ends square to face. Butt the two pieces firmly together; although the dihedral angle may be 90°, the true angle on plan will not. If making a splayed box, pediment, tea-tray or whatever, you will need to have the article square on plan; to achieve this, it becomes necessary to cut an angled butt on the side or end.

The sketch shows an elevation and part plan as before. The elevation has been developed by hingeing down the side at point A. The laid-flat side is shown in dotted line. The new and true plan is now projected from this, and it reveals that the thickness of the wood must be bevelled to ensure the job remains square. You could verify this by modifying your model to include the butt cut.

The geometry of splayed bevels is the same as for roofing work, and many trade manuals on carpentry have a chapter devoted to it. I can recommend Frank Hilton's book *Building Geometry and Drawing*, published by Longmans, for a detailed explanation of the problem.

*Bob Grant DLC FRSA MSIAD*

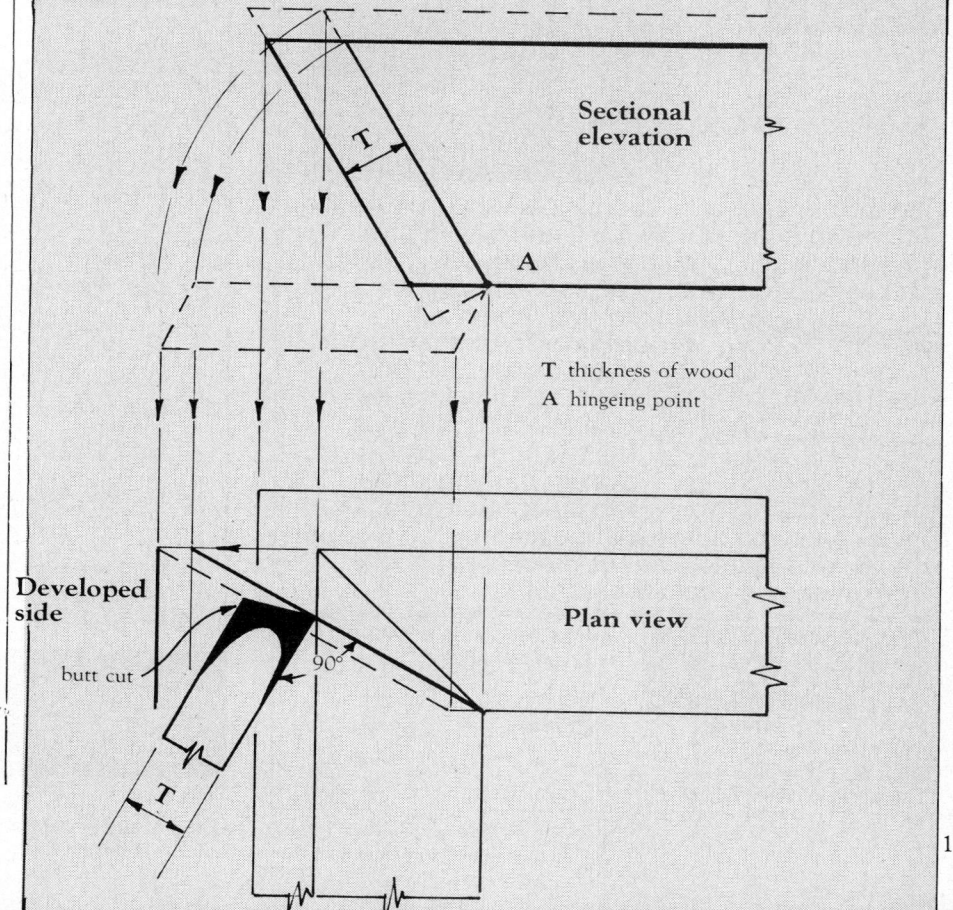

Sectional elevation

T thickness of wood
A hingeing point

Developed side

butt cut

90°

Plan view

T

# HirsH – Power Tool Partnership

## "Trust the Yanks to think of everything"

### TST-1 Saw Table

Gives the circular saw the accuracy of a sawbench

### TRST-2 Router and Jigsaw Table

Converts portable routers and jigsaws into stationary power tools.

### TWL-1 Woodlathe
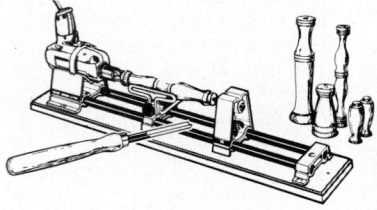

Converts your electric drill into a woodworking lathe. Base and tool included.

### TWDSG-1 Wet 'n Dry Sander/Grinder

**NEW AVAILABLE NOVEMBER**

Converts your electric drill into 7" dia disc sander. Exclusive wetting feature permits use as a wet grinder.

### TCE-96 Cutters Edge

All purpose cutting guide over 8' long for use with both power and hand tools.

### TPC-1 Frame Clamp
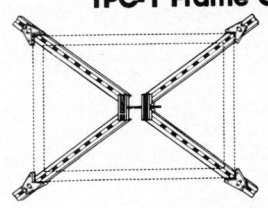

Indispensable for all woodworkers. Self-squaring . . . tighten all four corners at one time

## Now everyone can get professional results with their power tools

Or send for leaflet (State which model/s) and stockist list with SAE to Sumaco Merchandising Ltd., Suma House, Huddersfield Road, Elland HX5 9AA Telephone (0422) 79811. **SUMACO**

---

# THE BENCH YOU ALWAYS DREAMED ABOUT

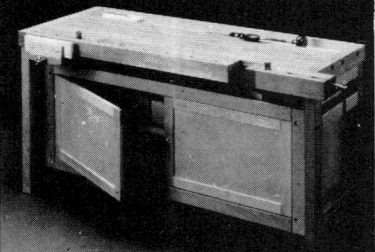

Illustrated, 6ft. Bench No. 607CU.

Lervad benches are superb pieces of furniture in their own right, sturdily built and beautifully finished in kiln dried prime Danish beech, oiled and sealed for lifelong protection against distortion. Above all, designed by craftsmen for comfortable, efficient working. Big capacity vice at *both* ends plus built-in surface clamping system running whole length of top. Optional cupboards and quick change kit for metalworking, etc. Various models to choose from in detailed colour brochure.

*SUPPLIERS TO SCHOOLS FOR 90 YEARS. TEACHERS PLEASE ASK FOR EDUCATION CATALOGUE.*

## LERVAD

Lervad (U.K.) Limited
4 Denham Parade, Denham
Uxbridge UB9 4DZ
Telephone: (0895) 833690

Please send me details of Lervad benches.

Name ..................................................

Address ..............................................

.............................................................

W.W.

---

## Elu ®

# POWER TOOLS & MACHINES

**All prices include V.A.T.**
**Post & Packing £1.50 UK & Ireland.**
*Telephone or write quoting your credit card number or enclose cheque.*

| | |
|---|---|
| **SANDERS** | |
| MVS 47 Orbit Sander | £90.92 |
| MVS 156 Orbit Sander with dust bag | £53.76 |
| MVS 156E Orbit Sander with dust bag 'Electronic' | £63.25 |
| MVS 94 Orbit Sander with dust bag | £83.02 |
| MHB 90 Belt Sander | £132.83 |
| MHB 90K Belt Sander with frame | £164.17 |
| MHB 157 Belt Sander | £75.11 |
| MHB 157E Belt Sander 'Electronic' | £83.02 |
| **SAWS** | |
| ST 142 Jigsaw Orbit Action, 2 speed | £79.06 |
| ST 142E Jigsaw Orbit Action, 'Electronic' | £86.97 |
| ST 152 Jigsaw Orbit Action, 2 speed | £79.06 |
| ST 157E Jigsaw Orbit Action 'Electronic' | £86.97 |
| MH 151 Ripsaw 50mm 2" cut c/w TC Blade | £67.21 |
| MH 182 Ripsaw 80mm 3⅛" cut c/w TC Blade | £94.88 |
| MH 65 7¼" Ripsaw 2⅜" cut with TC Blade | £79.06 |
| MH 85 9¼" Ripsaw 3⅜" cut with TC Blade | £118.60 |
| **PLANERS** | |
| MFF 80K Planer/Rabbeter Set c/w dust bag, side fence, bevel fence, carrying case, fitted TCT Blades | £94.88 |
| MFF 40 Planer/Rabbeter fitted with TCT Blades | £128.09 |
| **JOINTER/GROOVER** | |
| DS 140 Biscuit Jointer fitted with TCT grooving blade supplied in carrying case | £140.74 |
| **ROUTERS** | |
| MOF 96 Router Set, ¼" Collet | £67.21 |
| Accessory kit | £59.16 |
| Dovetail Attachment c/w TCT Cutter | £60.38 |
| MOF 98 Router Set, ½" Collet | £138.36 |
| MOF 31 Router Set, ¼" Collet | £118.60 |
| **PLASTIC TRIMMER** | |
| MKF 67 Plastic Edge Trimmer, fitted with ¼" Collet | £90.92 |
| **DOUBLE ENDED GRINDERS** | |
| EDS 163 6" dia. wheels 1 — phase | £50.60 |
| EDS 164 7" dia. wheels 1 — phase | £53.78 |
| MWA 149 Grinder/Honer 1 — phase | £59.29 |
| MWA 61 Grinder/honer 1 — phase | £99.62 |
| **MACHINES** | |
| DB 180 Woodworkers Lathe | £193.71 |
| TGS 171 Sawbench Mitre Saw | £253.00 |
| TGS 172 Sawbench Mitre Saw Tilt Arbor | £308.35 |

## asles

Vineyard Road,
Wellington,
Telford,
Shropshire.

**Telford 48054**

---

12

**Prices quoted are those prevailing at press date and are subject to alteration due to economic conditions.**

# Project 564

The City and Guilds 564 course provides a unique start in cabinetmaking. Here is Peter Collenette's report — plus a project to give you a taste of what's involved

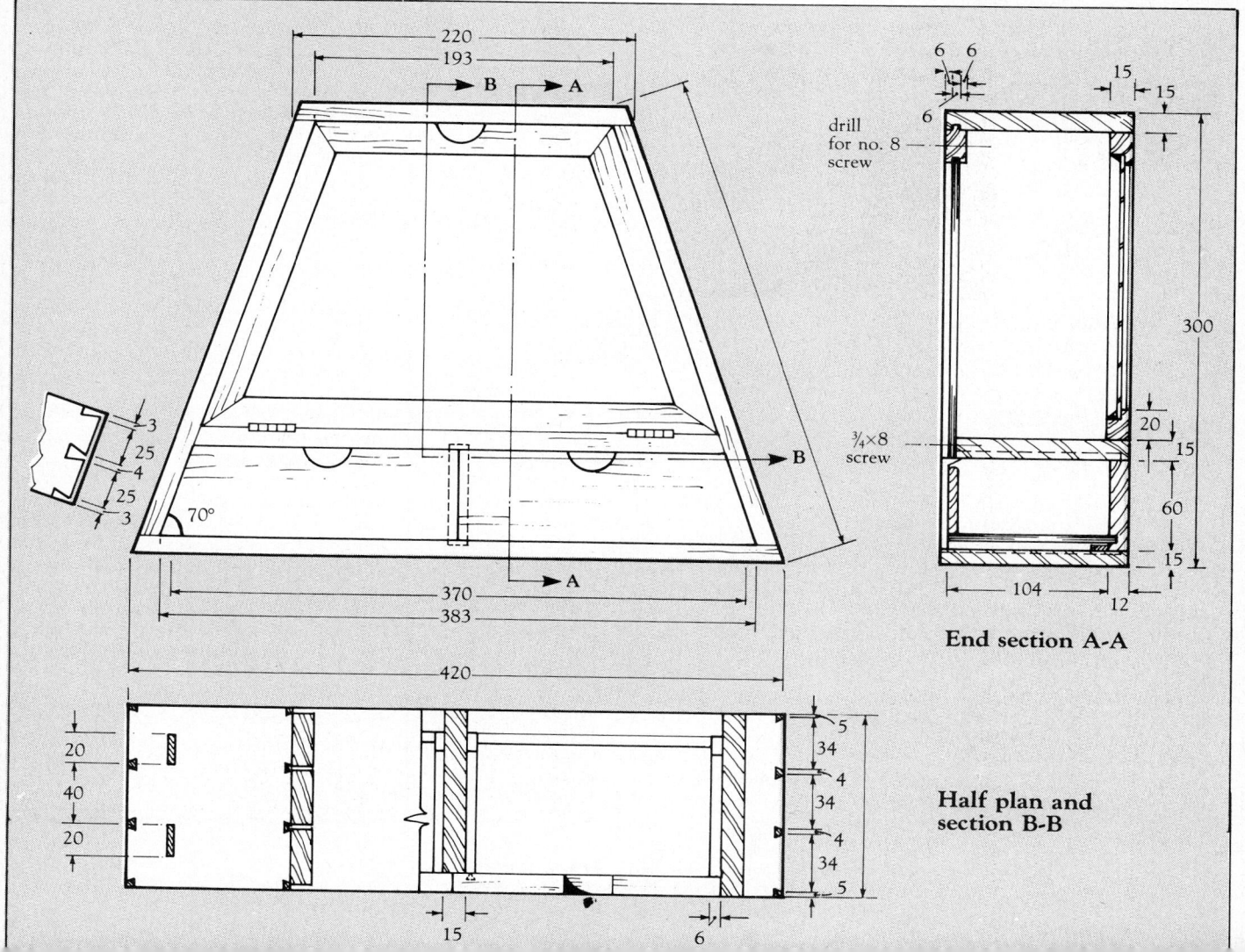

The mighty umbrella of the City and Guilds of London Institute shelters a few courses that don't quite serve the broad industrial training policies which are its main concern, yet which do valuable jobs in their own fields. Such a one is course no. 564/1: Cabinetmaking, as experienced at the London College of Furniture.

Responsible for it is Bob Thornhill, lecturer in furniture-making, himself an LCF graduate, who worked for major manufacturers Austinsuite. He took over five years ago when the 564 was a three-year evening class: 'Almost', he says, 'an old boys' club', in which students did roughly what they liked. But Bob brought with him a serious commitment to craft skill, and it wasn't long before the syllabus was re-written (after experience in teaching at Wormwood Scrubs!).

What's more, the course stopped being just an evening affair: current options (all involving the same syllabus, the same assessment procedure and sometimes the same teaching staff) allow students to attend for one year full-time, two years on one day per week, or three years on three evenings per week. The last option is still useful for those in the trade who can't get away in working hours, but it does present problems in teaching machining and finishing — subjects which require full workshop facilities.

● *This challenging display cabinet, a set project for assessment, is often made by absolute beginners within weeks of starting*

In each case the course provides an immediately specialised grounding in essentials as the more varied furniture-industry courses cannot. It was originally for 'mature students'. The present students come from several backgrounds and age groups, but Bob does assert: 'I don't think a 16-year-old should come out of school saying, "I want to be a cabinetmaker".' Though 16 is the minimum age for entry, he personally regards it as only worth applying

● *Left to right, work by course students: Sara Wilkinson's ash cabinet, a grey-stained ash projector stand by Penny Martin-Jones, and a cherry display case by Martin Vickers*

● *This unusual low table was made in English walnut by Peter Reid*

# Starters

Chris Nussbaum inaugurates a full-time student's diary from the LCF's C&G Cabinetmaking course

**B**eginning is always the hardest part. On a Monday morning in mid-September I think we were all aware of that, 16 new students meeting in the workshop for the first time. We're a motley crew really — cinema projectionist, market-gardener, geologist — all aspiring to the ranks of 'committed amateurs', as *Woodworker* recently tagged us. But that's what we each bring to this hectic one-year course. Whatever other skills we have, we bring commitment.

I'm on the course as the first stage of a joint project with my wife — to set up, in loose terms, our own furniture-making business. She's working, supporting me, while she studies for a City & Guilds upholstery certificate at evening classes. Which leaves me 1054 teaching hours to learn all I can, soak it up, pick their brains!

I can't tell you much about the course yet — it's only just begun — but I hope you'll find some interest in the trials and tribulations, even successes, of 16 would-be cabinetmakers as the year unfolds. The course is heavily workshop-biased, starting from the real basics, but progressing as quickly as we (the students) will allow it; from just planing up and making a simple cross-halving joint in the first week, to constructing a rebated frame with haunched mortise-and-tenon joints, both through and stopped, by the end of the second week. By the time Christmas arrives we will have mastered all the basic joints and constructed a job from drawings embodying what we have learnt.

A good dose of technical drawing through the year will help our appreciation of construction theory and technique where time simply does not permit hands-on experience. All this is topped off with brief sorties into polishing, metal and plastic work, veneering, wood-machining and the history of furniture-making. If I've got any time left after all that, I would like to contact some of the local cabinetmaking businesses, persuading them to let me visit them and to talk to me about just how the business runs, their design and production criteria, and so on.

The people who run the course are, I'm thankful to say, every bit as committed to us as we are to the work, if not more so; so our only real problems arise in finding the funds to buy tools and books. I suppose there's no reason to hope that we should escape the cutbacks everyone else is suffering, so we'll have to grin and bear it. Still, I bought some new chisels and a jack plane the other day, and that made me feel just fine! ∎

● Enquiries to Bob Thornhill, London College of Furniture, 41 Commercial Rd, London E1 1LA, tel. 01-247 1953.

if you're 18 or over. However, the course does not stress particular entry requirements. If you have no woodworking experience, he and his colleagues will look for some other craft interest, or even a background in design.

So what can be learnt in the time available? 'It's really a foundation course,' says Bob. Half his students go into the trade in one way or another, the other half come back to LCF for further study. All have undergone a training which is demanding and, in Bob's words, 'heavily practical'. He reckons the average full-time student's day runs from 8.30 to 8.30. Assessment requires the making of two pieces of furniture (one a set project — an example is the wall-hung display cabinet shown here

— and the other an original design); it also involves a four-hour exam in technical drawing, design and history, plus three hours on materials and processes.

Declaring 'Excellence of demonstration is the key', Bob aims for conservatism in making coupled with flexibility in design. All pieces are made by hand as one-offs in solid timber, but he tries to ensure that students' experience and knowledge go well beyond that. 21 hours of the course are devoted to metals and plastics.

His approach is summed up by his simple statement of a basic belief which every craft woodworker might well be happy to endorse. 'Skill is in your hands. Sooner or later someone will pay you to make something with those hands.' ∎

# Micro marvels

An exhibition of very small
and very beautiful furniture
was held in Birmingham
recently. Stuart King,
himself a master of the craft,
was there

Public awareness of the miniaturist's craft was first promoted
by Queen Mary in the 1920s. She
would have been delighted with the enthusiasm for the diminutive today, which
was much in evidence at the Miniatura
exhibition and Fair held at Edgbaston,
Birmingham, recently. I was invited on
behalf of *Woodworker* to go and have a look
at what three couples, all miniaturists and
living in the Midlands, had organised to
prove that not all shows have to be held in
London to be a success. Most of the work
was in ½₁₂ scale, but ½₂₄ and even smaller
were to be seen.

It is always pleasant to meet old friends
and established fellow-craftsmen, but I was
especially happy to see many new faces; not
just male ones, either. Jane Newman, for
instance, who at the age of 25 has a very
comprehensive range of simple Victorian
domestic furniture including dressers,
tables and Windsor chairs, is completely
self-taught and has a healthy mail order
business, flourishing after only two years.
Encouragement, surely, to anyone who
wonders whether there is room to be
successful in this type of work. Miniature
shows are an ideal way to meet potential
customers, and to get ideas and feedback.

Another lady miniaturist who has
established a niche for herself is Miren
Tong, who operates from Time Warp
Studio. While most miniaturists concentrate on classical or conventional styles,
Miren has turned her attention to
something very different. Her inspiration is
derived from both the Arts and Crafts
movement of the late 19th century, and Art
Nouveau, the florid art form that had short-
lived success early in this one. Although the
design and conception are Miren's, her
husband Michael helps with the assembly
after various components have been carved,
gilded, upholstered and generally prepared.
'It's the most interesting time in furniture
history, so many styles were put in the
melting pot,' said Miren. 'It started in the
Victorian era with High Gothic, then Arts
and Crafts which turned into Art Nouveau.
That died, and it ended with the more rigid
Art Deco. Don't you find that interesting?

'When you look at a piece of full-size
furniture you tend to take in the details,'
Miren continued. 'When you look at a
piece in miniature the eye takes in the whole
piece at a glance and moves on. I try to catch
the attention and treat the subject as a
painting so that the details stand out. One
way to do that is to have different texture,
which can be achieved by using carving to
produce shadow and relief. I also use inlays
of mother-of-pearl, gold, silver, etc.'

Another craftsman I much admired was

● *These pieces by Art Nouveau specialist Miren Tong are faithful reproductions from the genre –
in miniature. Top, two tables of her own design; above left, a dressing-table, stool and chair, and
right, a high-back settle in bird's-eye maple with gold inlay*

David Wadley, who in just 12 months has
mastered the art of turning in miniature —
encouraged, he told me, by a *Woodworker*
article on making small chisels from OBO
nails.

His work includes chessmen and working
spinning wheels. He started with the
Picador Pup lathe and has now progressed
to the more solid Unimat 3.

Makers of doll's-houses, room settings
and miniature furniture would find many
aspects of the work more difficult without
the DIY range of mouldings, panelling and

door and window kits produced by Alan
Borwell. Alan, who trades under the name
of Borcraft, started 3½ years ago after a
back injury forced him out of his previous
business, making fitted kitchens. He told
me that he made the transition in a month.
He has subscribed to *Woodworker* since
1953, and was first inspired by two articles
on miniatures sometime back. Then he
discovered a gap in the market — most
miniaturists were having to make their own
intricate mouldings, or give up in the
attempt. Having always made his own

● *This country kitchen in ½₁₂ scale is complete down to the eggs and pie-dishes*

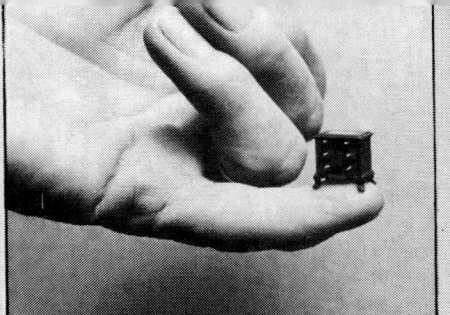

● *Above: Stephen Borwell proudly displays a window from his father Alan's range of 1/12-scale joinery. They also produce mouldings*

● *25-year-old Jane Newman has built up a flourishing mail-order business in two years, selling all kinds of furniture for the desirable Victorian miniature residence*

● *John Davenport showed this startling chest-of-drawers, inlaid tripod table – and French workboxes, complete with carving, gilding and crossbanding*

cutters for his former business, he set to and made the cutters necessary for the antique styles miniaturists need to give authenticity to their work. Stephen, Alan's young son, helps in the workshop, particularly with the range of windows. It was pleasing to meet a young woodworker at the show.

For those with a taste for perfection in very fine detail, John Hodgson and John Davenport have never been known to disappoint, and at Miniatura visitors were treated to displays of the highest quality from both craftsmen.

John Davenport was showing some of his beautifully inlaid pieces, ranging from writing-desks in the French style to lady's workboxes on stands, and the smallest chest of drawers I have ever seen. John Hodgson's favourite timber is walnut, which figures largely in his Queen Anne and other 18th century pieces. He makes the whole range of walnut furniture one would expect to find in that period including tables, cabinets, dressers and chairs. Some of the pierced and carved work in his chair backs has to be seen to be believed. His work was displayed in a large 18th century room setting complete with family portraits hanging on the walls, all to great effect. Both Johns are old hands and have long established themselves at the top as miniaturists par excellence. John Hodgson started 12 years ago, like many others I talked to, by making doll's-house furniture for his daughter; he duly sold it, and tells me that his daughter is still waiting for replacements!

Perhaps your imagination will be fired by reading and seeing something of the people and the craft at Miniatura. If you feel the attraction of the miniscule, why not have a go — you may surprise yourself with some hitherto untapped talent! ∎

● *Left: the walnut furniture in John Hodgson's early-18th-century room setting is detailed with an intricacy that would do credit to full-size work*

# WOODWORKER SHOW

## Chances for change

The 1984 Woodworker
Show drew the crowds; it
contained lots to fascinate
and delight. But could it
achieve even more? Here is
Peter Anstey's verdict

The October Woodworker Show, un-doubtedly the largest and most successful yet, left me with mixed impressions. In some years of observing these annual showcases of the woodworking scene, I cannot recall any which better illustrated not merely the whole field of tools and machines, including the latest trends and develop-ments, but also what is being achieved in craft practice by men and women in whom the distinction between amateur and professional is becoming increasingly blurred.

Yet, on one of the few occasions when the representatives of craft and industry come together and can stand back to look at where they are going, opportunities were still being missed.

On the one hand, many exhibitors gave surprisingly unclear definitions of the market to which their presence at the Show was presumably directed. Manufacturers of the growing range of combination machinery were certainly enthusiastic about its potential, but they seemed to regard their principal market as the small business rather then the home craftsman. Nor did they appear to be making undue effort to use the Show to tap this huge and growing outlet. I would like to have seen more practical demonstrations of the advantages of using universal machines in the home workshop.

Meanwhile, the impressive competition and demonstration sections of the Show suggested to me that many craftsmen (amateurs and professionals alike) continue to practise traditional craft skills without enough regard for the potential contribution to their work of advancing technology or the best modern factory techniques. Many things pointed to a persistent gap between craftsmanship *per se* and the need for its continuous rejuvenation by intelligent harnessing of appropriate elements from industrial practice — although this gap is beginning to be filled in the curricula of the best of our schools and colleges, themselves well represented at the Show.

Now for some more detailed impres-sions. First, the exhibitors. Combination, or universal, machines were an obvious highlight. They illustrate a trend which in the future can surely only accelerate. It is often assumed that the typical home crafts-man has unlimited time at his disposal. He seldom has. Only the right combination of

accurate, space-saving machinery can satisfy his need to produce quality work as quickly as possible, usually under cramped conditions. Sadly notable in this area of the Show was a virtual monopoly by continental exhibitors such as Kity, Luna, Inca and others, with Startrite as the sole UK representative. According to one distributor, it is a great pity that so few UK manufacturers are prepared to take on the task of making a good universal. One of the most impressive (if also, at over £3000, the most expensive) from the continental stable was a newcomer to the Show, the Felder BF3 universal woodworking system from Austria; as well as satisfying all the small craftsman's criteria, this has some truly outstanding technical features, including a tilting shaper spindle which substantially increases shaping versatility from a very few shaper heads. One thought in this area for future shows. It is confusing for the visitor, as well as an unnecessary dilution of expensive marketing resources, to have the same machines displayed both on manufacturers' stands and on those of their distributors. Better liaison between the two must be the message.

Woodturning equipment, notably lathes and quality turning tools, was prominent as usual, no doubt because it appeals so strongly to craft aspirations and at the same time offers such splendid opportunities for linking the products with demonstrations and teaching. In this area, at least, it was encouraging to see British manufacturers so well represented. More than one dis-tributor went out of his way to stress to me his preference for British products, given the right quality, price and suitability for the market. One outstanding example was the range of lathes displayed by Tyme Machines of Bristol. Several distributors

● *A rousing welcome to Show visitors came from this creation of Caerphilly's Lawrence Jeffreys*

agreed that theirs was a well engineered product, reasonably priced, and with useful features (such as a swivelling head) in which lateral thinking had been brought to bear and user needs borne clearly in mind.

Impressive, too, among the wood-turning-tool exhibitors were the stands of Sorby and Ashley Iles, whose represen-tatives both stressed to me what a strong continuing demand there was, particularly overseas, for high-quality, British-made specialist hand tools. According to Tony Walker of Sorby, the UK is still a world

● *Efforts are crowned as John Tiranti awards Stephen Cooper the Henry Taylor Award for woodturning. Stephen's work was featured in* Woodworker *for June*

● Above: A London greengrocer's 'turnout' by R. Bates was the appetising bronze-medal winner in its class

● Above: This intriguing rolltop desk by Bryan Chew of Wimborne is only a couple of inches high

● Above: Still in Lilliput, Tom Ellison's minuscule entry was highly commended by the judges

● An exciting innovation was the Guild of Woodworkers' first 'London gallery', open to all members for free display. Whitehead & Lightfoot's deckchairs impressed many

leader here, while I was astonished to learn from Barry Iles of Ashley Iles that with a labour force of only 10 skilled craftsmen 70% of the firm's output now goes to America — a remarkable tribute to the continuing role of craft methods in a tough industrial environment.

Impressions of the broad range of woodworking products were for me heightened by the assembly for the first time of the whole exhibition under a single roof. It seems that a great many exhibitors

take space for one of two reasons: either to increase sales of standard 'me too' products by offering special show discounts, or to promote particular lines by clever demonstrations. Such valid objectives underline the fact that the Show inevitably attracts widely differing categories of visitor —

● Fred Booth rose to his own remarkable challenge with this lidded dodecahedron box

● Maurice Lund's Falco carried off first prize in the Ashley Iles Carving Competition

differently motivated, and perhaps with a distinction between those who come during the week and those who visit at the weekend. The appeal of many stands was less to the serious craftsman than to the part-time 'do-it-yourselfer', who comes to the Show to pick up a bargain, to be impressed by gimmickry, or maybe to take a short cut to woodworking skill by watching manufacturers' demonstrations.

Which brings me to what is surely the Show's principal rationale, the link-up of machines and products to skills. The best examples were undoubtedly the woodturning stands supported by expert demonstrations; all seemed to be attracting full houses. Less effective, because by definition they did not set out to bridge the gap between traditional skills and modern machines and methods, were the stands of individual craftsmen such as Stan Thomas (traditional hand tools) and Jack Hill (chairmaking). From a historical and social point of view these were totally absorbing, but they seemed sadly irrelevant to the contemporary scene. Stan Thomas, a Welsh craftsman with more than 50 years' experience, told me that there was little demand today for his type of skill. Many of his 'customers', he said, had been housewives wanting to know how to use a chisel or a plane.

Craft competitions were, as always, a major feature, and I am left with an overwhelming impression of the dedication, imaginative skill and sheer painstaking effort displayed by those — notably in the modelmaking and wood-carving classes, who by and large do not follow such pursuits in order to make a

● Above: James Gray's immaculate toy American locomotive in Brazilian mahogany won the Richard Blizzard Cup. Below: strong grain figure in a piece by Mrs Susan Navin

● Left: The miniature lath-back Windsor armchair by David Booth which won the new Stuart King Award, a specially made trophy. Below is Rodney Smith's 'Wistman', silver-medal winner in relief work

● Above: A walnut sculpture by Pat Elmore of Faringdon. Left is one of the breathtaking tours-de-force which made up the model-horse-drawn-vehicle display

**Show photos Manny Cefai and Neil Proctor**

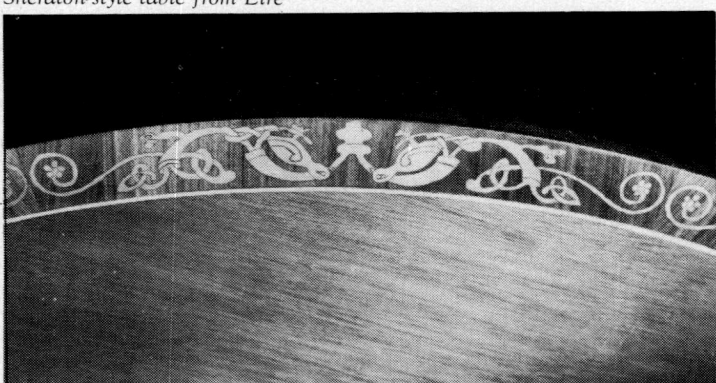

● Left: Rodney Smith's relief carving 'Fisherman's Tale', which won the Henry Taylor Tools Award for the best woodcarving at the Show: a cash prize newly upped, like the firm's woodturning award, to £250, plus a silver rose bowl. Below is the impressive Celtic marquetry edge of Ignatius Foster's Sheraton-style table from Eire

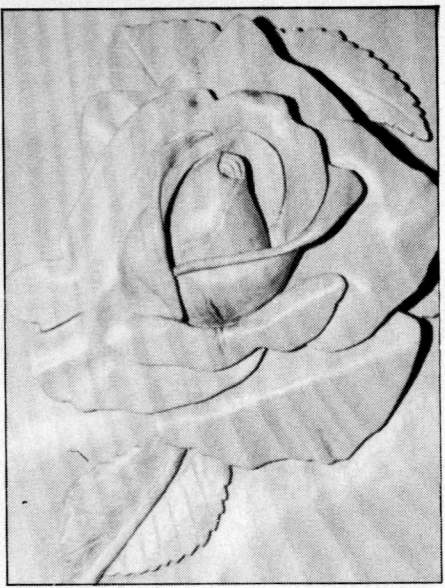

● Left: 'Precious Platinum' by W. G. Lucas is the name of the rose. Above: A. J. Gilbert's fighting fish. Above right: G. Brown's miniature spokeshave – an entry in the brand-new Sarjents Hand-Tool Making Competition, sponsored by Sarjents Tools and won by Ralph Fellows with a magnificent panel plane. Below: Hugh Storey's yogi. Below left: Christopher Bulloch's heron – very highly commended

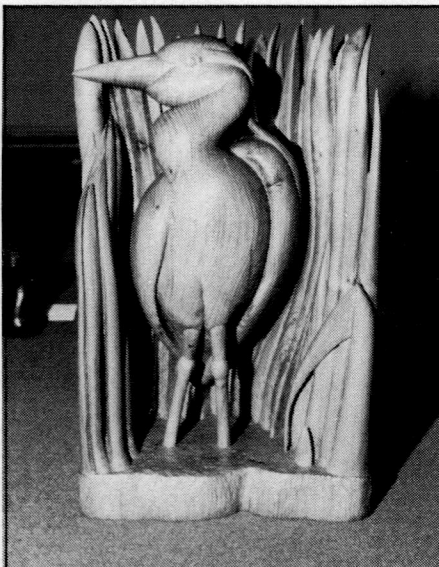

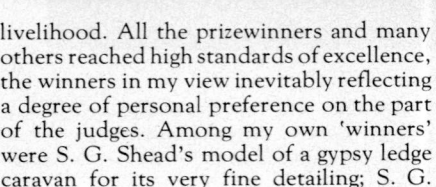

● Above: A. C. Duncan's prizewinning powder-bowl. Left: Richard Willis' delightful lady's writing-desk

Bradbury's marquetry reproduction of Uccello's painting in the National Gallery, 'The Rout of San Romano', a *tour de force* by any standard; and, above all, E. B. Graveling's starkly simple and totally convincing woodcarving in yew, simply entitled 'Refugees'.

Other competition entries, notably those in the field of cabinetmaking, made a less positive impact. There is not the slightest doubt of the talent and skill of young people coming out of the colleges, but a real sense of direction seems curiously lacking. While they can produce work to a high

livelihood. All the prizewinners and many others reached high standards of excellence, the winners in my view inevitably reflecting a degree of personal preference on the part of the judges. Among my own 'winners' were S. G. Shead's model of a gypsy ledge caravan for its very fine detailing; S. G.

standard, there is often little apparent awareness of the need to ally innovative design concepts to the constraints of industrial production. An exception for me here was P. L. Higgs' laminated table in the shape of an S. Not everyone would respond to it as a design, but it did well illustrate the application of laminating techniques to industrial furniture production. In more traditional contrast I much enjoyed, in the young professionals' class, Peter Howlett's excellently crafted writing-table in solid and veneered maple — though to what extent it was a practical proposition for factory production I do not know. More than one exhibitor commented on the inability of many craftsmen, both amateur and professional, to think in economic and industrial terms, whatever their skill at producing tools and jigs for solving one-off problems in a small craft situation.

● *Above: Simon Higgs' silver-medal-winning study in lamination. Below: An oak side cabinet by Frank Niering*

Perhaps it is here that the schools and colleges should be playing an increasing role. The Woodworker Show admirably provides free space for such institutions, though Shrewsbury College missed an opportunity by only sending photographs and information. Merton Technical College took the trouble to mount an outstanding demonstration of its two-year course on musical-instrument manufacture. According to Merton's Phil Chambers, few of the students who qualify experience real difficulty in later obtaining full-time employment in their chosen field. Central Manchester College provided another good illustration of the fact that a college's best advertisers are its own students.

I hope these somewhat random impressions will not be interpreted as generally critical of a hugely successful event. It's just that a significant opportunity — the 'interface' between the consumer/craftsman and the supplier/manufacturer — remains to be grasped. For the benefit of both sides, craft skills must be continuously updated by the best industrial technology. One postscript drives home the point. Small timber-drying equipment, surely the biggest single opportunity for the home craftsman to reduce his costs, was not represented at all. I wonder why?

# Competing views

The competition entries, as usual, made a varied and vastly appealing series of displays. But all was not quite well. The judges explain

**Bert Marsh, Ray Key, Cecil Jordan** and **John Tiranti** write: The number of woodturning entries was very low, and the standard very poor. Some high technical competence was coupled with very little thought on the design side.

The ring- and cup-chuck class attracted the most entries, and some were extremely good. The gold medal went to T. Ellison's set of miniature eggs, which must have taken many hours of delicate work — but the silver-medal-winning powder bowl by A. C. Duncan, though very well executed, was let down by the design of its lid. In the face-plate class only two entries were judges worthy of an award at all.

The overall Henry Taylor Award of £250 for the best piece of turning in the Show, generously increased to that amount for the first time this year by Henry Taylor Tools of Sheffield, went to a 'lover's wheel' by Stephen Cooper — one of only five entries in the spindle-turning class; but, when it came to the laminated and built-up work, we felt the work was so bad that fairness to past winners required us not to make any awards.

**Martin Bulger** writes: The clocks section was a disappointment. Only two entries, and one of those was the worst I've seen in the seven years I've been involved with the Show. William Watts' mahogany longcase, on the other hand, was a worthy and easy winner. Using both plain and attractively figured boards, it was well constructed — and well finished, despite some awkward grain.

**William Watts** adds: 'The piece was inspired by seeing pictures of early examples of Fromanteel's work, and also examining one at very close hand in the Victoria & Albert Museum. Fromanteel is credited with introducing the pendulum into this country from Holland in the mid-17th century, an event which heralded the so-called Golden Age of English clockmaking. It was said of Fromanteel and his case-maker Joseph Clifton that it was a marriage made in heaven! Usually the casemakers of old were anonymous, but it seems that one of Clifton's tokens was found inside an authenticated example. He worked at Bull Head Yard, Cheapside, London, and the token was dated 1663.

'The movement was handcrafted by Steven Kelly of Exeter, who has been a clockmaker for over 60 years. It was a very great privilege for me to work with Mr Kelly, who translated all my ideas into very practical form. The dial engraving, silvering and waxing, and also the cutting of the hands and tempering to the traditional blue, are very fine. Sadly, Mr Kelly's engraver Mr Crutchett died only two months ago, aged over 80, so that this quality of work has become even harder to find. The spandrels, cast in brass from a carved wooden pattern, show a quality of detail rarely seen today.

'The case includes what I believe to be Cuban mahogany (purchased from North Heigham Sawmills), very rare and choicely figured. The design is original, following the Fromanteel only in broad outline. It is also larger than the V&A example. The brasswork came from J. D. Beardmore in Bristol, and the case was french-polished to a very high mirror gloss. It is my first unaided piece of work in this genre and the award is naturally very encouraging. I now have under construction a second case, which will be a reproduction of an authentic Fromanteel dated 1660. It will incorporate the last of Mr Crutchett's dials, and of course the movement by Mr Kelly.' ■

● *Three visitors got the right answers to the Tool & Trades History Society's 'Whatsit' contest; a ballot gave the prize to Capt. Rogers of Ilminster.* **A** *is a circular cutting-gauge or circular router, for thin boards;* **B** *a barking spud, barking iron, peeling iron, wrong iron or rinding iron – for peeling bark from felled trees, usually for tanning;* **C** *A sash or scribing gouge, for use when jointing moulded window bars (the extended handle follows the template);* **D** *a pair of trammels or beam compasses;* **E** *a shipbuilder's slice or stick – a large paring chisel;* **F** *a saw-sharpening vice*

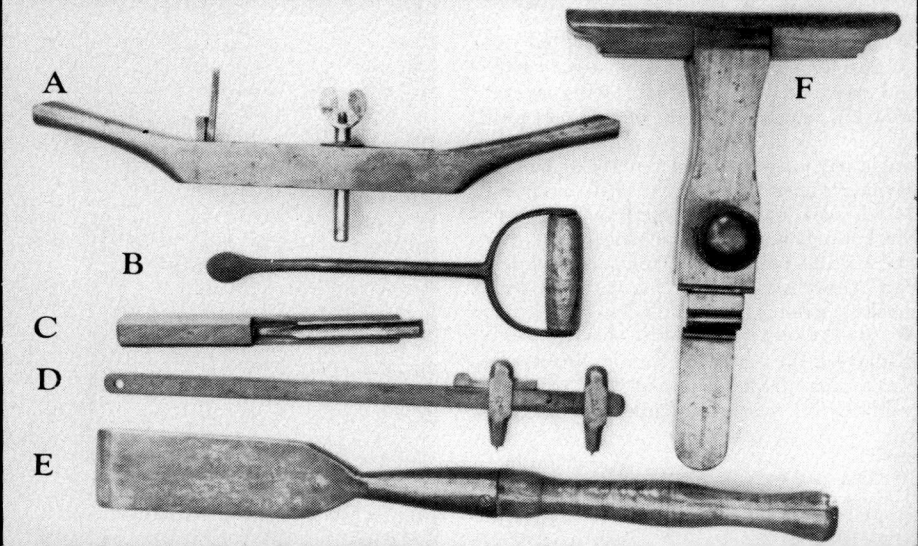

● *Malcolm Dinning of Cambridge earned his niche in history as the first winner of the new English Abrasives Award for Finishing – presented (above) by exhibition MD Gos Home. The celebrated cabinetmaker Alan Peters and equally celebrated turner Ray Key judged his untitled sculpture (left) the best-finished piece in the whole Show. It was rubbed down with Oakey glasspaper before beeswaxing. Runners-up were Stephen Cooper's prizewinning spinning-wheel, and the writing-table which gave Peter Howlett a gold medal among the young professionals. The table, with plans, is featured in* Woodworker *next month*

# Editorial encounters

**Peter Collenette** writes: It was my great pleasure as editor to spend all four full days at the Show and seize its once-yearly chance of looking and talking. Aidan Walker and I met happy readers, fulsome in their praise; we met disgruntled readers (two or three) who swore the magazine was going steadily down the tube and who couldn't think why they still bothered to read it. We met contributors who had only been voices on the phone, and lots of people whose stories and drawings and pictures we hope to show you in these pages very soon. And we saw all kinds of interesting and beautiful objects. Here are some of the things that, for me, made the Show, tickled the fancy, or simply provoked thought.

● Robert Major's visit. He came from New Hampshire with a briefcase full of Japanese tools so stunning that I was converted from the tenon saw to the *dozuki* in half a dozen sweet strokes. But then, a price of £150 (asked for this particular version) certainly should imply not less than perfection . . .

● The new location. Some like the Alexandra Pavilion; others would have the old venue back at any cost. Granted, the AP catering department's idea of a varied and wholesome menu is not mine or most other people's; the hall is a fair way from the station; and parking wasn't as effortless as some had expected. But I thought myself that most of those problems were outweighed by having everyone in one building.

● As more than one person pointed out — despite recent features in *Woodworker* and elsewhere, and despite growing general concern, health and safety were clearly well to the back of exhibitors' minds. Not a single pair of goggles, face-mask or pair of ear-muffs anywhere in sight, with (as far as I could see) the sole exception of Scan Marketing's workmanlike range. True, the Show isn't a factory; but isn't this attitude a bad example to the coming generation of machine-orientated woodworkers?

● Always one of the most sheerly useful displays in the whole exhibition, Stobart & Son's breathtaking range of woodworking publications was accompanied this time by a fat free catalogue in the form of newspaper: a near-essential for the craftsman who doesn't know everything.

● Warco's radial-arm saw — unique, to my knowledge, in being a push-across rather than a pull-across. This brings it into line with all other machines, on the sound principle that the direction of cut opposes the direction of feed. Warco's extension kit provides a second pillar to support the near end of the machine, in effect turning it into a sort of gantry: instinctively a more stable arrangement than the usual one.

● The college stands. As Peter Anstey says, most were focal points; and I have to admit that my personal favourite of all the items under that vaulting roof was John Knight's delectable satinwood side-table from Rycotewood.

● Hegner's impressive new Multicut cast-metal table jigsaws, especially the Multicut 3 with its 25in throat: £430 plus carriage plus VAT, but (but the look of it) as solid as any rock.

● The affable Andy Milne of Trimbridge, doing great business with edgebanders — items you perhaps wouldn't expect to create much interest at a 'craftsman's' show. It says something about the true interests of many of those attending; and perhaps it also has something to do with the fact that Andy's range starts with a hand-held model at only £130+VAT.

● Harold Stern, who arrived straight off a plane from South Africa, is MD of the Hardware Centre Group in Bloemfontein, Johannesburg and Cape Town, and he's anxious to help South African woodworkers communicate with one another. If you're interested, get in touch with him at PO Box 1162, Bloemfontein 9300, tel. 89761, and see what ideas can be generated for courses, exhibitions and mutual co-operation. ■

● *Left: The Warco radial-arm saw. Below: A faultless piece from John Knight of Rycotewood College (photo Royston Carss)*

# Past master: W.R.Lethaby

Idris Cleaver profiles one
of the most influential
disciplines of
William Morris

William Richard Lethaby was born in Barnstaple, Devon, in 1857. His father was a carver, gilder and picture-framer. He studies at the Barnstaple School of Art, where his architectural drawings were so good that they attracted the attention of a local architect, who took him into his office as an articled apprentice. At the age of 21 he moved to Duffield, near Derby. The editor of *Building News* was so impressed with his drawings of old buildings in and around Duffield that he published them. The drawings clearly showed the influence of Norman Shaw, one of the leading architects of the day — who, on seeing them, invited Lethaby to join him.

At about the same time, a series of meetings took place which were to have a momentous impact on furniture-making in both England and Europe. Ernest Barnsley entered into articles with the architect John Dando Sedding, and about a year later he was joined by Ernest Gimson — recommended to Sedding by William Morris. Shortly afterwards Barnsley's younger brother Sidney joined Norman Shaw's office, and there struck up a lasting friendship with Lethaby. Barnsley introduced him to his brother and Gimson, and soon all four became firm friends. Their relationship lasted the rest of their lives.

In 1890 Lethaby joined the brothers Barnsley, Gimson and two others to form Kenton & Co. They were so dissatisfied with the quality of the furniture produced at the time that they determined to have furniture made to their own designs in their own workshops, by their own workmen, from the finest materials. Lethaby was the dominant personality and driving force in this venture. Lack of finance, however, caused it to fold after about two years.

Lethaby remained in Shaw's office for about 10 years, during which time he interested himself in many organisations which were to have a great influence on his career. A number of Shaw's pupils and apprentices met monthly as a discussion group, the St George's Art Society. The Art Workers' Guild was formed from this in 1884; Lethaby was for many years a leading figure in the Guild, eventually becoming mster in 1911. Among its members were the prominent Arts and Crafts architects Mervyn Macartney and Edward Prior. The AWG was soon joined by another group know as the Fifteen, prominent among whom were Lewis F. Day and Walter Crane, subsequently well known Arts and Crafts artists. Nearly all the Fifteen were architects, artists, craftsmen and designers; they included such well-known names as C. F. A. Voysey, William Morris, Edward Lutyens and Roger Fry (of Omega Workshops). Most of them were also to play important roles in the Arts and Crafts movement too.

A logical extension of the AWG was the formation in 1889 of the Arts and Crafts Exhibition Society to provide a platform for the work of the Arts and Crafts designers. Also in 1889, Gimson introduced Lethaby to the Society for the Protection of Ancient Buildings (commonly known as Anti-Scrape); this had been set up by William Morris to prevent the destruction and alteration of old buildings, and it presented a forum for discussion on modern architecture and the crafts. Its meetings were usually presided over by Philip Webb, and it was there that Lethaby learnt from Webb that architecture was 'not designs, forms and grandeur, but buildings, honest and human, with hearts in them'.

When eventually Lethaby left Shaw's office to set up as an independent architect, his reputation was growing. Shaw passed on to him a commission to build a house for Lord Manners in the New Forest, known as Avon Tyrrell. Much of the furniture in this house was made by Kenton & Co., as in some of the other houses on which he was engaged. His growing interest in architecture and workmanship led him to writing, and in 1892 he published his first major literary work, *Architecture, Mysticism, and Myth*. He later re-wrote this as *Architecture, Nature and Magic*, and thereafter published extensively and with great authority on all aspects of architecture — particularly the importance of workmanship.

1896 saw a major change in the direction of Lethaby's career. In that year, supported by a strong recommendation from William Morris, he was appointed with the sculptor George Frampton as joint principal of the newly formed LCC's Central School of Arts and Crafts. Frampton rarely put in an appearance, so Lethaby virtually had a free hand. Up to that time, art schools had been unable to train industrial designers: the education was not practical, confirming itself almost exclusively to work on paper. Students had little or no opportunity of trying out their designs in schools or industry. Lethaby changed all that by appointing instructors who were themselves successful practitioners in the crafts, and who went back to their workshops when not actually teaching. Among the prominent artist/craftsmen of

● Right: an oak chest, inlaid with sailing ships, from Kenton & Co.'s workshops, 1890/1; below left, an inlaid oak sideboard designed by Lethaby and made by A. Mason, 1906

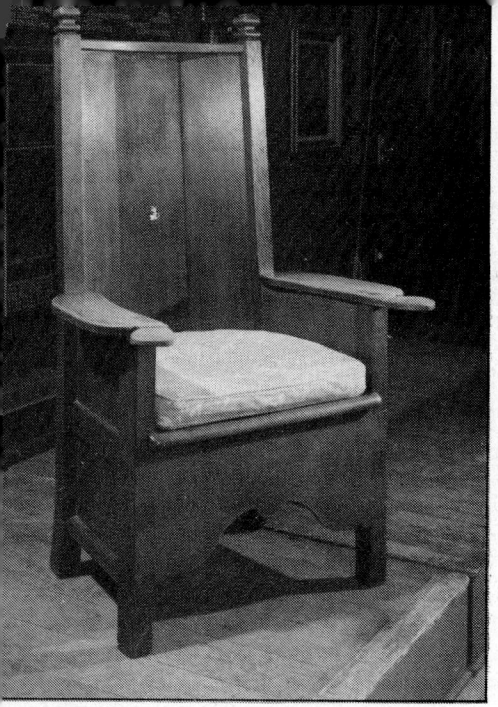

● One of two master's chairs owned by the Art Workers' Guild, which Lethaby designed in 1893

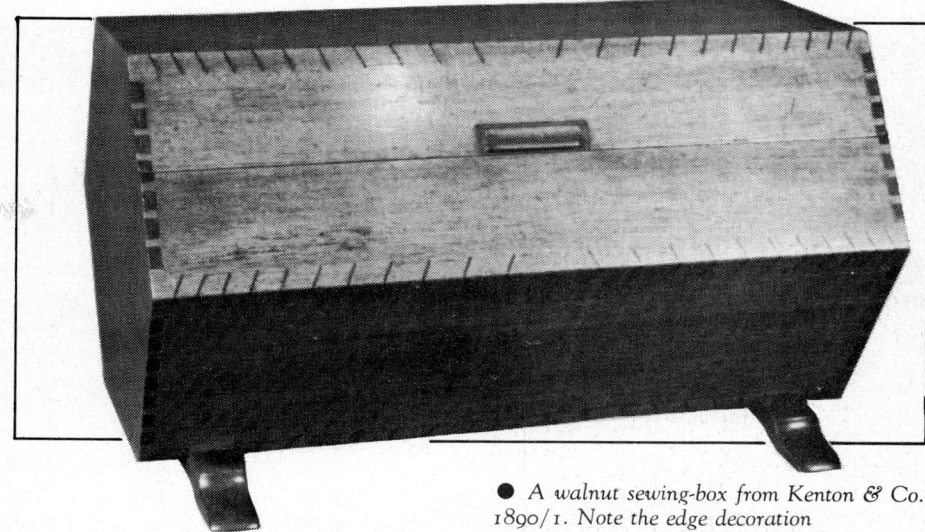

● A walnut sewing-box from Kenton & Co., 1890/1. Note the edge decoration

the day who helped were Douglas Cockerell (bookbinding), J. H. Mason (printing) and Edward Johnston, the calligrapher. The secret of the school's success was undoubtedly this employment of part-time practising artists and craftsmen, by whose involvement Lethaby created the most dynamic art school in the world. It was later to become the precursor of the famous Bauhaus.

Such was the success of the Central School at home and abroad that foreign governments sent both teachers and pupils to study there. During this time Lethaby

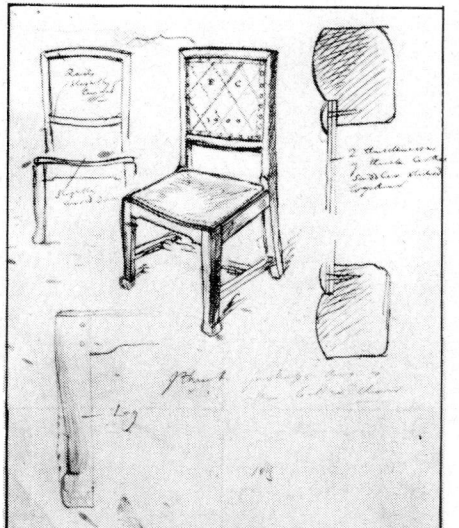

edited the 'Artistic Crafts' series of handbooks, which included Edward Johnston's *Writing & Illuminating & Lettering* and Douglas Cockerell's *Bookbinding and Care of Books*.

While still continuing as one of the leading figures in the Art Workers' guild, Lethaby also contrived to devote a great deal of time to writing. In 1906 he published a book on medieval art called *Westminster Abbey and the King's Craftsmen*, in which he gave particular recognition to the workmanship of master craftsmen such as John of Gloucester, Edmund of Westminster and Robert of Beverley. The book was so well received that Lethaby was appointed surveyor of Westminster Abbey, a post he held from 1906 to 1928 and to which was subsequently added in 1920 that of surveyor of Rochester

● Left: 'I think perhaps this is the better chair' – Lethaby's sketch for the Eagle Insurance Co.'s office furniture, 1900; below, an 1890 shot of pieces by Lethaby, Gimson, Blomfield and F. M. Brown

Cathedral. These appointments, in addition to his work for SPAB, meant that Lethaby was now recognised as the nation's supreme authority on the care of old buildings.

1911 saw a further step towards the new approach to the teaching of arts and crafts in schools and colleges. Lethaby resigned as principal of the Central School to take up a full-time appointment as the first Professor of Design — a post he had first held part-time in 1900 — at the Royal College of Art. Now he was directly involved in the training of students who would themselves become art teachers, and his experience in industry and teaching was to prove invaluable in raising the design standards of everyday articles.

The English Arts and Crafts movement had an immediate effect on continental designers and manufacturers, but upon English furniture and other trades it had no such direct impact. The superb handmade furniture of Gimson and the Barnsleys, and the best reproduction work of the time, was outside the reach of all but the rich. For ordinary people with small incomes, the work mass-produced by machine was of inferior design and workmanship. To bridge this gap was the aim of the Design and Industries Association, founded in 1915. Three of its seven founder-members were furniture designers, namely Ambrose Heal, Harry Bach (originator of Dryad cane furniture) and Hamilton Temple Smith. Soon they were joined by others, including Lethaby and Gordon Russell.

● *Above: A dresser in unpolished oak, inlaid with ebony, sycamore and bleached mahogany, designed by Lethaby for Melsetter House in the Orkneys, 1900; below, a richly decorated cabinet on a stand, another example of Lethaby's work with Kenton & Co.*

The pattern for the DIA was the German Werkbund, founded in 1917. The DIA presented a memorandum to the Board of Trade pointing out that German expansion in trade before the war was due to the untiring efforts of German industrialists to improve the quality of their work, and in this connection the Werkbund was specially mentioned. The Board of Trade responded almost immediately and organised an exhibition at Goldsmith's Hall in London of well-designed Austrian and German products. The DIA, through Lethaby, appointed Gimson to make designs for industrial production, and a lengthy correspondence followed between the two friends. Gimson felt unable to accept, saying his best contribution was to raise standards by continuing to produce quality work and training his apprentices to produce it. The correspondence brought one of Gimson's celebrated remarks — 'Let machinery be honest and make its own machine-buildings and its own machine-furniture; let it make its chairs and tables of stamped aluminium if it likes; why not?'

The public's awareness of the need for good design in everday things has developed over the years, nurtured by various national exhibitions supported by all governments. A great deal of this awareness must be attributed to the work of Lethaby, who reduced design to fundamentals by his famous sayings, such as 'Designing is right doing'. He also asserted 'Designing is not the abstract power exercised by a genius. It is simply arranging how work shall be done.' ■

The Central School of Art and Design's exhibition on William Lethaby's life and work is at the Cheltenham Art Gallery and Museum, 40 Clarence St, Cheltenham, from 27 December 1984 to 2 February 1985.

# ARUNDEL

## QUALITY BRITISH LATHES

'THE CHOICE OF THE PROFESSIONAL'

### K-600

'FOR THE SERIOUS AMATEUR'

### K-450

## NEW

'FOR THE BEGINNER'

### K-150

### A QUALITY LATHE . . . AT A REALISTIC PRICE

## £197.00 + VAT

For full details of all our lathes
send to:

## TREEBRIDGE LTD.

Mills Drive, Farndon Road,
Newark, Notts. NG24 4SN
Tel: Newark (0636) 702382

---

## NEW CRAFT & HOBBY BREAKS

### the guide to hundreds of creative holidays

### WHETHER YOU ARE 16 or 60 there is a course listed – JUST FOR YOU

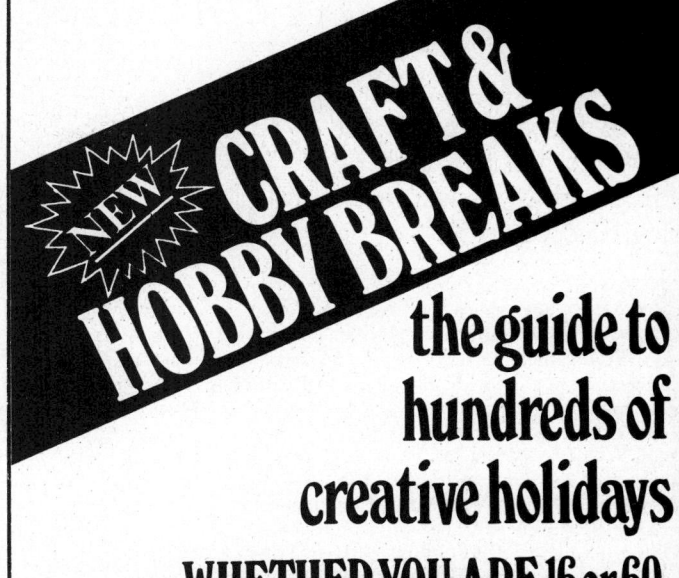

AN ARGUS SPECIALIST PUBLICATION        £2.95

**CRAFT & HOBBY BREAKS 1985**

Hundreds of Creative Holiday Breaks Listed Inside

FROM THE PUBLISHERS OF CRAFTS

Want to take up weaving? Looking for a language course? Longing to find out more about Hobby Ceramics? Or potty about Pottery? Thinking about taking up Picture Framing professionally? Or are you into Stone Walling, Computing or Yoga? Would you like to become a Wine Buff, a Wood Turner or decorate your own Wedding Cake?

All these interesting subjects and many hundreds more you may have never considered are listed in this comprehensive guide. Many of them are held in stately homes in glorious surroundings. All of them give you the opportunity to get away from dull routine and spend a week, weekend or just a few hours, immersed in the Craft or Hobby of your choice — with the added bonus of spending your time with like minded companions who share your enthusiasm.

**Craft and Hobby Breaks 1985 on sale at your news-agent now — price £2.95 or send a cheque/postal order for £2.45 (post free) to Infonet Ltd., Times House, 179 Marlowes, Hemel Hempstead HP1 1BB.**

---

# Edwardian excellence

Colin Greaves gives full instructions for making a dining-chair from an unjustly neglected period

**E**ven for those who take the dividing line between 'antique' and 'modern' as occurring only a century ago, Edwardiana has not yet come of age. Nevertheless a great deal of good furniture was made during the reign of Edward VII, better than most Victorian in concept and construction. Much of it reverts to the styles of Adam and Sheraton for its inspiration. The best of Edwardian is better than that made immediately before and immediately after; it belongs to a world that existed before the first war, and in that sense is almost as remote from ours as that of Georgian England.

Recently we were asked to complement four genuine Edwardian dining-chairs with two copies. How it was done is explained here. Short of a rather drastic demolition job it was not possible to determine how the joints had been made, so some alternatives are suggested. Neither could we be sure what lay under the 'gravy browning', except that it was pale in colour and had the

density and hardness of beech. The timber is typical of the period, so beech was chosen. Each piece has been given a two-letter identification as shown in fig. 1.

Because of the amount of shaping that has to be done to such pieces as TR and MR, it is not essential to start with them planed and squared to the dimensions given in table 1. We prefer to do so, however, because it reveals hidden faults, because marking off is simplified, and because it is easier to hold them in the vice. There is no best order in which to make the components; we decided to make all the back parts first, then make the front ones (FL, SF, FR), and make SL and SR so they united the two sections firmly.

Several templates are needed; these are shown on a grid. Except where otherwise mentioned in the text, the scale is 4mm per small square. Manilla folders, when opened up, are useful for making templates; in the case of BL/BR two or more strips will have to be joined. Rather than make a template to draw round for MS it is probably better to draw it full-size on ordinary paper, or even wallpaper, and transfer the shape to the wood using carbon paper — there is plenty of spare wood on which to pin it.

TR & MR are shown in rectangles, each of which encompasses three templates. The

**Fig. 1**

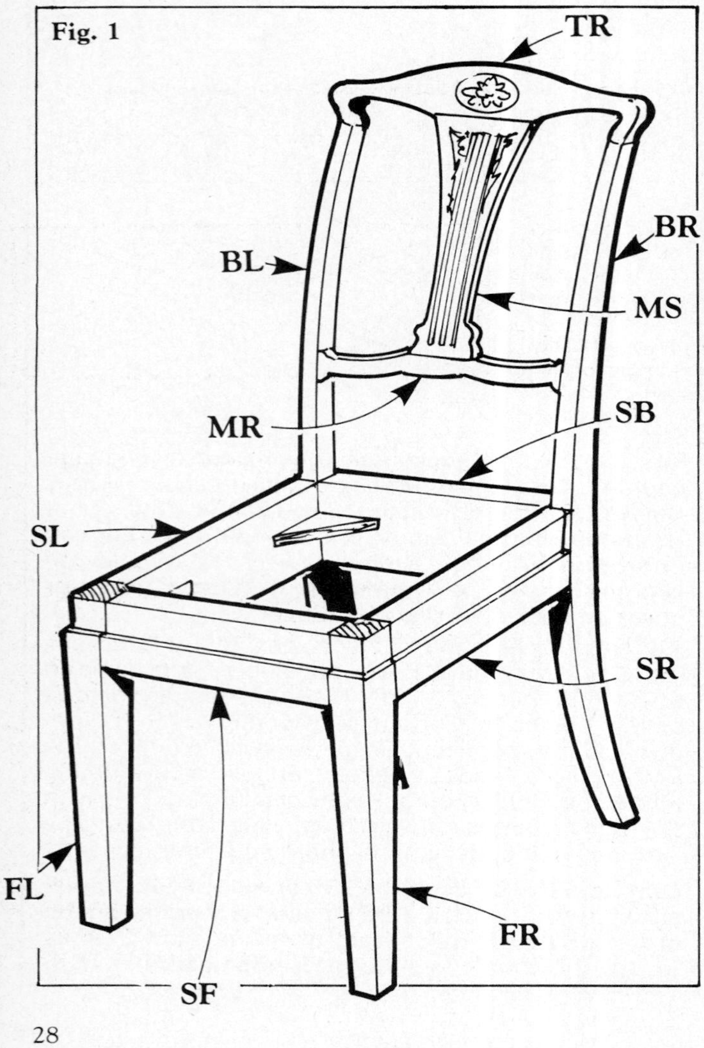

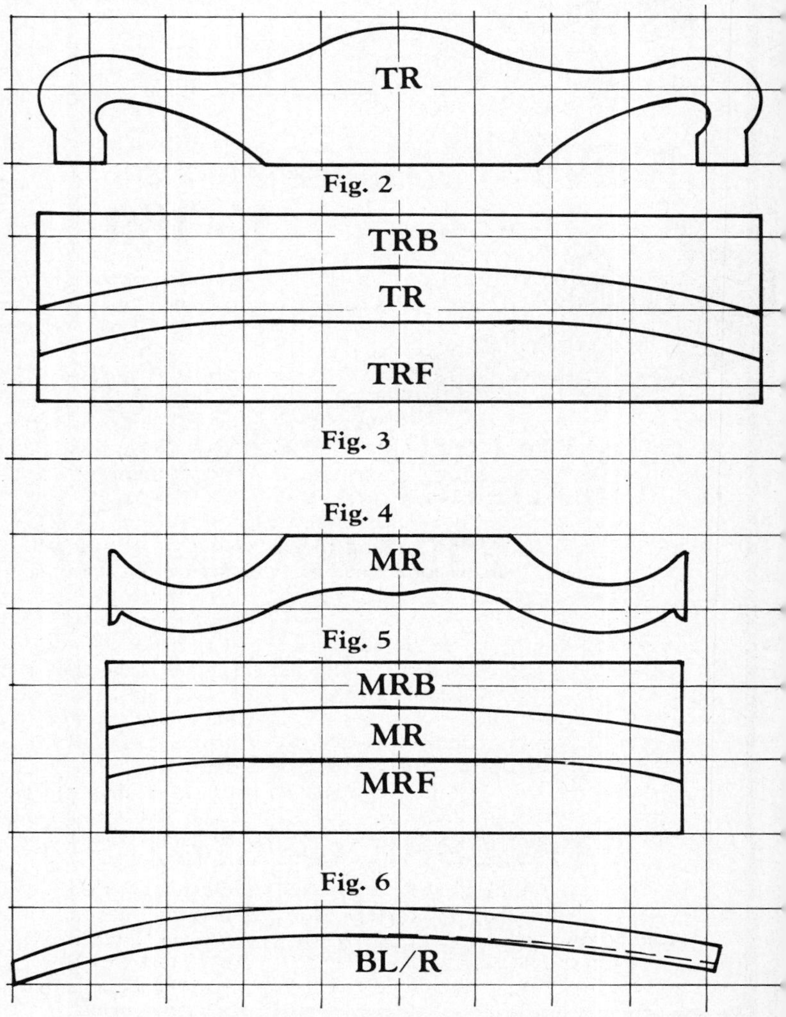

**Fig. 2**

**TR**

**Fig. 3**

**TRB**

**TR**

**TRF**

**Fig. 4**

**Fig. 5**

**MR**

**Fig. 6**

**MRB**

**MR**

**MRF**

**BL/R**

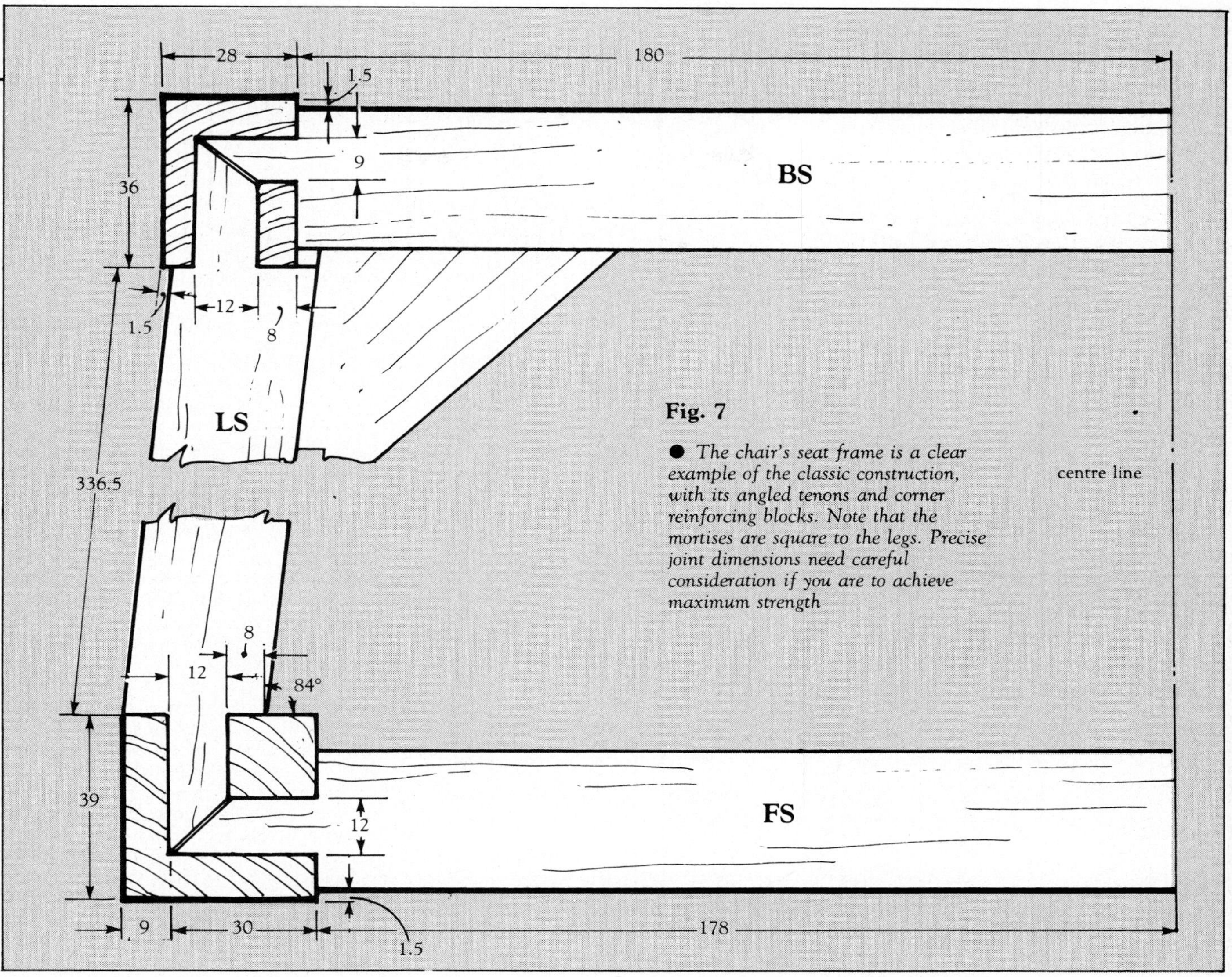

## Fig. 7

● *The chair's seat frame is a clear example of the classic construction, with its angled tenons and corner reinforcing blocks. Note that the mortises are square to the legs. Precise joint dimensions need careful consideration if you are to achieve maximum strength*

BS

LS

FS

centre line

28   180   1.5   9   36   12   8   1.5   336.5   8   12   84°   39   12   9   30   1.5   178

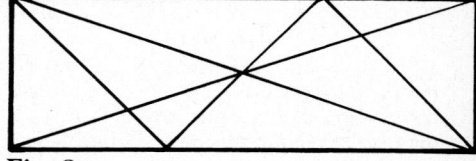

**Fig. 8**

middle one is used for marking out the blank and the other two for checking the back and front after preliminary shaping (figs. 3 & 5). Note that, although TR & MR are generally curved, the front centre portion (where MS joins) is flat — so be careful how you use the spokeshave.

To make the top rail, first plane the piece all square to the dimensions given in table 1; then trace round the template TR (fig. 3) both top and bottom, leaving a bit of spare at either end. When this has been cut out using a bandsaw (if you have one), spokeshave and scraper, trace around the TR template (fig. 2) top and bottom — but do not cut it out yet.

Before you go any further with TR, a few other parts have to be made. Firstly take MR to the same stage as TR (figs. 4 & 5), then cut out and trim to size the back legs BL/BR using the template in fig. 6 (one small square represents 10mm). The main dimensions are 30mm at the bottom, 36mm at seat level and 32mm at the top. The thickness is constant at 26mm. Up to the top of the seat level the cross-section of the legs remains rectangular, but the tops will later become parallelograms.

It is not possible accurately to shape the legs yet, but now is the time to mortise the legs for SL, SB and SR and drill the 9.5mm dowel holes for fixing TR and MR. For

maximum gluing area SL/SR have double tenons 12mm wide; the tenons for SB are single and only 9mm wide (see fig. 7). The first chair was made with mortise-and-tenon joints for MR, but for the other we used 9.5mm dowels; the latter is probably the better method. The marking of the centre for the hole in the top of BL/BR follows standard practice, i.e. using crossed diagonals. Fig. 8 should re-assure those who are concerned that the centre of a rectangle will not coincide with that of a parallelogram. (Euclid showed that the diagonals of a parallelogram bisect each other.) While making mortises, it is opportune to make those in TR and MR to take MS.

Put aside all those pieces and thickness the material for the seat (SL, SB, SR, SF). In the original it appeared that these were a composite of hardwood at the bottom and softwood at the top, but we made the whole from one piece of beech. While it is in one piece, make the 3 mm rebate shown in fig. 9 (this is not shown on fig. 7 as the cross-section has been taken below this level). This may now be cut into four, making due allowance for the tenons.

Select SB, tenon it to suit BL and BR, and insert the dowels in TR so that they may be assembled to the legs. This will reveal any minor errors in marking out the shape of

TR as seen in elevation. It is also a good time to mark the tops of the legs to show what needs to be removed from front and back so that it will blend into TR.

We are created with marvellous senses, and I never cease to wonder at the sensitivity of the human hand; by running finger and thumb along either side of a piece of wood it is possible to check simultaneously not only that the sides are parallel but also that they are smooth and flat. When you have planed the angle on front and back of the legs so that it tapers down to nothing at the seat, use the finger-and-thumb test. This will reveal a sloping ridge back and front, as shown in fig. 10a, which must be removed with a spokeshave to give a gradual helix. When it is finished, a straightedge placed across any part of the leg should neither rock nor show a gap. Keep using finger and thumb until it is correct (see fig. 10b).

While TR can still be held in the vice relatively easily, the shaping of the cross-section AA (fig 11) may be carried out. Then carve the rose, the bottom of which is 10mm up. Only three simple carving tools are needed: 5 and 12mm firmer gouges and a V-gouge. The sequence is illustrated in fig.

● *Edwardian chairs like this one often demonstrate a lightness and elegance of line which comes as a relief, if not actually a surprise, after the frequent distortions of Victorian times. In many cases Edwardian designs look back to the 18th century*

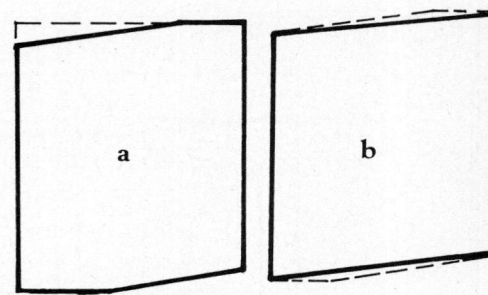

**Fig. 10**

**Fig. 9**

sure they fit TR and MR before cutting the outside shape.

Some preliminary blending may be done before gluing up where TR joins BL and BR, and where TR sweeps round into MS. Unless every joint is perfect, there will be slight movement when you clamp up which will show as a hairline difference in level, so the final blending should be delayed until the glue has set.

Fig. 10 shows that FL and FR taper from 42mm to 21mm on their insides and backs. Both tapered sides are mortised 85×12mm to accept tenons from SF and SL/SR. Take care when gluing and clamping that FL and FR are parallel to each other and SF will be parallel to the floor.

From fig. 7 it can be seen that the mortises in BL, FL are at right angles to the legs. The dimensions of the seat put SL at an angle of about 84°, so the tenons at each end of SL will be at the same inclination. Here is a point where the maxim 'measure twice, cut once' has to be rigorously applied. The junction of SR with BL/FL is a mirror-image of fig. 7. Before gluing, clamp up dry and check that the chair stands firm and level on a flat surface and the dimensions are as in fig. 9. The final woodwork is to glue (and screw if you wish) the triangles which strengthen the seat. Remember they are not 90/45° triangles.

The appropriate finish is deep walnut stain followed by french-polishing. A local upholsterer completed the chairs for us in pale blue Dralon using horsehair, three springs, and webbing. materials cost between £20 and £25 (in 1983) including professional upholstery. ■

12. Cut round the small ellipse in the middle with a knife. Then cut inwards and down towards it so that it stands up in a depression; round its edges a little. With a knife mark out the big ellipse, then follow round with the V-gouge (it is far easier to draw a knife round accurately than to push a gouge). Use the 12mm gouge to produce the pattern given in fig. 12a, and afterwards the 5mm one as in 12b. Then cut deeply round the shape shown in 12c, and cut down toward it from the outer ellipse so that the rose shape stands proud. Finally, V-gouge the lines shown in 12c.

Care should be exercised in cutting out the shape of TR as seen from the front, especially if a jigsaw is used — there is no flat surface on which to rest the sole-plate to ensure that the blade cuts at the correct angle. Proceed carefully and keep checking the other side to see if you are following the line drawn on the other side. MR may now be cut out similarly, after dowelling to fit the back legs.

Only one more piece is required to complete the back — MS. Starting with a generous rectangle of material, with due allowance for tenons top and bottom, cut out all the inside shapes with fretsaw or

jigsaw and clean up (see fig. 13, which is on a 4mm grid). Before cutting the outside shape it is as well to complete the carving, as shown in fig 14. Tenon the ends and make

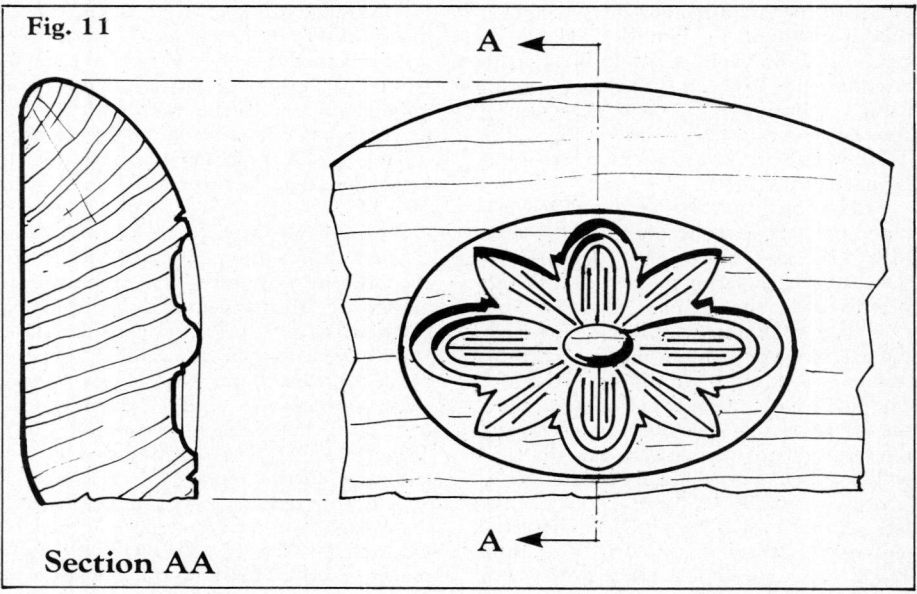

**Fig. 11**

**Section AA**

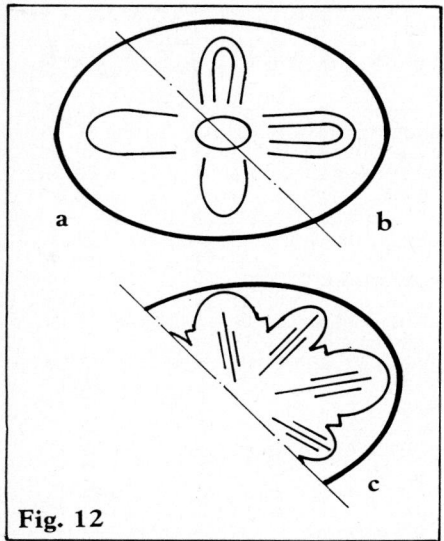

**Fig. 12**

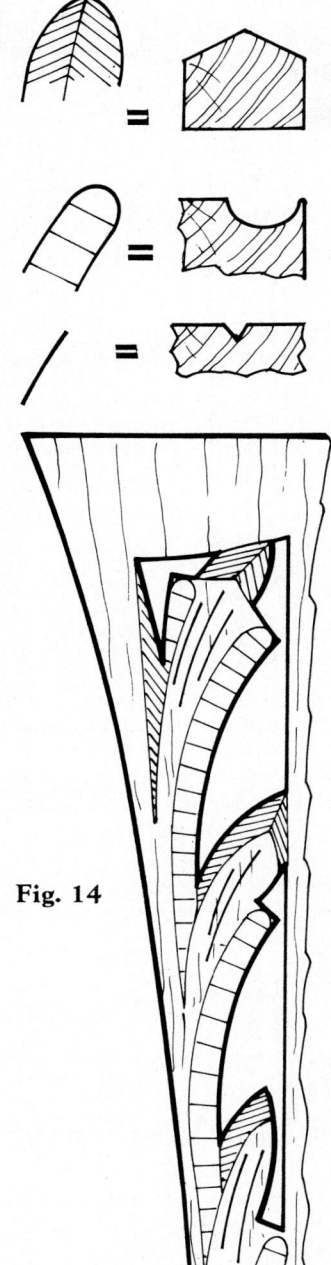

**Fig. 14**

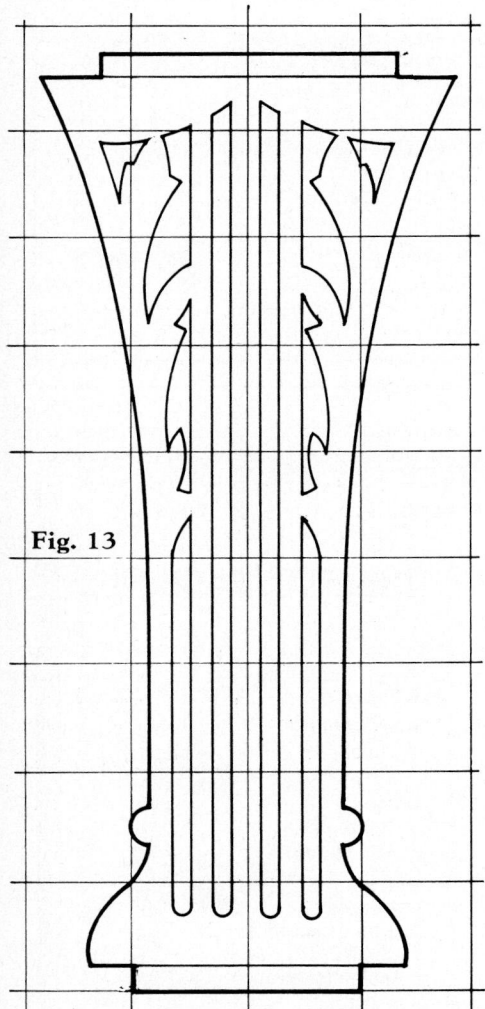

**Fig. 13**

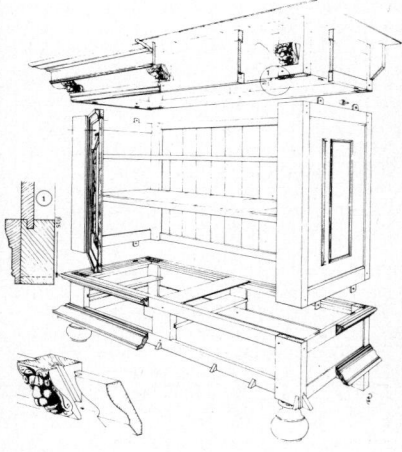
## Cutting list

Planed sizes in mm, beech

| | | | | | |
|---|---|---|---|---|---|
| SB | 350 | × 90 | × 30 | | |
| SL, SR | 400 | × 90 | × 30 | 2 off | |
| SF | 415 | × 90 | × 30 | | |
| BL, BR | 920 | × 100 | × 28 | both from one piece | |
| FL, FR | 445 | × 42 | × 42 | 2 off | |
| TR | 380 | × 75 | × 50 | | |
| MR | 330 | × 55 | × 30 | | |
| MS | 350 | × 160 | × 15 | | |

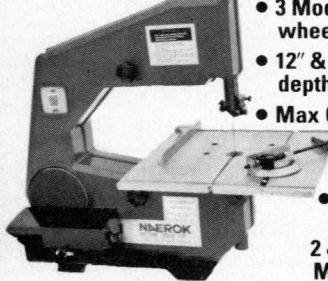
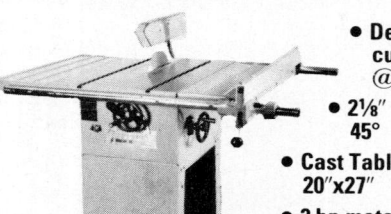
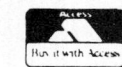

**Prices quoted are those prevailing at press date and are subject to alteration due to economic conditions.**

# Lost and sound

**Two craftsmen in music explore the fascinations and frustrations of timbers and timbres**

Paul Fischer describes his journey through the devastated forests of Brazil in search of a rosewood alternative

● *Paul Fischer deep in the Brazilian hinterland with a felled ironwood*

The classical guitar is the most important instrument using rosewood, as it is directly related to the instrument's tone. For the past ten years this wood has been extremely difficult to obtain, and so the small quantity reaching Europe has been ridiculously expensive and not very high quality. The problem has been exacerbated by the Brazilians' insistence on payment in US dollars and their own inflation of 140%.

Before the supplies of rosewood became totally exhausted it seemed an appropriate time to undertake a serious study in Brazil and establish once and for all the true situation, and while I was there seek suitable alternative woods for further study. Bearing in mind the vast range of similar species available from that region and the success of work already done with a few of the woods from Brazil, I decided to concentrate on other woods from South America.

Many guitar makers have changed to the well established alternative East Indian rosewood (*Dalbergia latifolia*), which has proved most satisfactory, but I felt it should not be considered the only alternative.

I travelled throughout Brazil, starting first in São Paulo, then on to Belem on the Equator and the Amazon region. Belem is the most important port for the export of timber from the state of Para and the Amazonas.

In the main docks in Belem, I visited two very large timber merchants both supplying mahogany (*Swietenia macrophylla*) and cedar (*Cedrela odorata*) to the U.S.A. and Europe. Directors of both companies informed me that mahogany from the Para region would be finished within three years and they were preparing to go over to plywood production. Both mahogany and cedar are woods commonly used in the manufacture of guitars.

After four days in Belem I flew to the state of Bahia. This whole region is engaged in the timber trade, felling, converting and transporting timber to the ports and cities of the south. There being no railway, all timber is transported by road and very bad roads at that. It is not uncommon for sections of the road to disappear; with very

little forest remaining, the light soil is easily washed away taking the road with it. I travelled the whole length of Bahia state and the picture was the same everywhere — vast areas of barren hillside with nothing but solitary dead burnt tree trunks, a testimony to the once flourishing forest and its fiery destruction. There were only a few small pockets of trees left, quite often on difficult ridges or terrain.

I gathered the system is to cut only the mature trees, perhaps 30% of the forest, and the remainder is burned to clear the land quickly for cattle or sugar cane. Much of the forest is owned by peasant farmers and they have a duty to re-plant three trees for each one cut down, but because of the remoteness of many of the farms and poor communications, they rarely do it; their wish is for a regular income. In all my travels I saw no indications of replanting, a failure made more urgent because of the destruction of future supplies by fire, not to mention the eco-system destroyed likewise. Burning is not confined just to Bahia; it is common practice throughout Brazil.

My study was centred in Bahia because rosewood only grows in that state, and a number of other interesting species are found there. I visited many mills and timber merchants, and it was clear rosewood had not passed their saws for a very long time. The sawyers and merchants just shook their heads at my enquiries about rosewood, and I came eventually to the conclusion that commercially at least, it is extinct.

I saw a number of very large sawmills in the throes of closing and even some of the smaller ones were short of work, a clear indication of the depletion of the forest. They are now mostly converting timber for domestic use, using any tree at all. There appears to be no selection of the most suitable tree for a specific purpose — even ebony was used for railway sleepers!

The mills are particularly primitive; there is very little lifting gear and the logs are

manhandled, even the largest of 4-5ft diameter. They move logs from truck to saw carriage with crowbars and winches, a very dangerous operation. The saws themselves are equally primitive, large belts and blades exposed and unguarded. Most common was the frame saw. Although of vintage manufacture and design, it seems particularly suitable for cutting some of the extremely hard woods, such as ironwood and pernambuco.

After nine days in the region of Itamaraju I left for Vitoria, in the state of Espirito Santo, to visit Atlantic Veneers, a veneer and plywood factory which also holds a good stock of domestic timber in log and plank form for general sale. We were shown six small logs of rosewood, each about 15cu ft, for which the price quoted was $8,000!

I found three other interesting woods in their yard, all of promising colour, weight and tonal quality. Unfortunately the company refused to sell me some for my work, only dealing, like any big merchant, in large quantities. The three woods of interest were macacouba (*Platymiscium*), cardinal wood (*Brosimum paraenses*), and sabourana (*Swartzia laevicarpae*).

On my return to São Paulo, I spent a full day studying the 2000 timber samples at the Institute de Pesquisas Technologies. I

● *What was once forest is now blasted heath, not replanted*

narrowed the possibilities for my work down to nine. They were as follows: *Casalpinia ferraea, Swartzia fasciata, Astronium fraxinifolium, Coniorrhachis marginata, Diptadenie macrocarpa, Machaeriam villosar, Astronium macrocalyz, Dalbergia frutescens,* and *Ferreira spectabilis.* Although most of the specimens selected may prove suitable for making guitars, some are, or will be shortly, as difficult as rosewood to obtain. Because of their close resemblance to rosewood, they have been sought as substitutes and used to make veneers and furniture.

As relief from the intense study in Bahia and I.P.T in São Paulo, I paid a visit to the guitar factory of Tranquillo Giannini, escorted by Sergio Abreu. He is Brazil's leading concert guitarist, and is called in by the company as a consultant to improve their instruments. They are very anxious to fill the needs of the professional guitarist, and could have chosen no better representative. My visit to the research and development department stimulated a lot of discussion, particularly on the use of new woods. The company had experimented with one or two new species with some success, but cracking had created some delays. Humidity in Brazil is extremely high, particularly in the South, and I was able to contribute from my own experience in workshop humidity control.

With the knowledge gained in Bahia and later at I.P.T., I felt confident in selecting a final seven woods to make up into guitars on my return. Although not all have the rich colour and beautiful grain pattern of the true Brazilian rosewood, the weight, density, flexibility and tone match sufficiently to give me the greatest chance of success. Keep your ears open!

● Paul Fischer is an internationally-reputed classical guitar maker, who produces about 40 instruments a year from his Chipping Norton workshop for top artistes such as Alice Artzt.

---

**Peter Collenette** writes: A public 'play-off' of Paul Fischer's seven guitars was held in London in October. John Mills performed — on the other side of an open doorway, so that his audience would not be influenced by the colours of the unfamiliar woods. The judges, seated among the throng, looked for projection, clarity, balance, sustain, response and tonal character. Each guitar had the traditional spruce soundboard and the same bracing pattern, but Fischer had used his professional skill to adjust thicknesses and other variables to produce a similar sound from all the instruments. In his estimation, the back and sides — that is, the parts fashioned here from new species — account for 20-25% of the tone colour.

The clear winner was aruda or folho de bolo (*Swartzia fasciata*), which looks a lot like Brazilian mahogany. Joint second were kingwood (*Dalbergia cearensis*) and brownheart (*Ferreira spectabilis*), and princewood (*Cordia trichotoma*) came in third. The question now must be whether the timber men will take the hint.

---

## Zach Taylor, luthier and music teacher, outlines the research in the Lignaphonics Laboratory at Haberdashers' Aske's School

If you ask a luthier what material he prefers to use for his soundboards, like as not he will tell you 'Swiss pine' — unless he happens to make pianos, in which case the reply will probably be 'Rumanian pine'. It is likely to be the same material but in fact both answers are incorrect. Take a sample to an expert for inspection, and it will undoubtedly be identified as spruce (*Picea abies*).

Anyone wishing to unravel some of the mystery shrouding the acoustics of musical instruments will realise that considering the length of time that we have enjoyed playing music, little is known about the physics involved in timbre (sound-quality). Whether one sees it as an art, a craft, or a science, and I personally see it as a blend of all three, it has not up till now been the subject of thorough research.

Although manufacturers have produced, and are producing, large quantities of instruments, most are slavish copies of existing, and in some cases redundant and obsolete, designs with more research into production techniques than the science of acoustics. Experiments are often carried out by individual makers who lack sufficient equipment or the scientific expertise to produce reliable information.

As a maker and teacher of lute and guitar for more than 25 years, I know only too well how much reference needs to be made to the work of other makers in order to get the best out of my materials and methods.

I teach the playing of classical guitar and lute, but I also have some students learning instrument-making as an ancillary subject for sixth-form General Studies.

Good resources are available at the school, and for some time I was keen to arrange co-ordination between departments for the study of science applied to musical instruments. A colleague who is both a physics teacher and a keen amateur musician put me in touch with some interested sixth-formers; I threw at them the title 'Lignaphonics' and the subject was born. (*Lignum* — Latin for wood; *phone* — Greek for sound.)

Our object is to discover what elements are responsible for the difference in timbre of wooden soundboards in stringed instruments. The guitar has been chosen for the experiments because it represents percussive stringed instruments available at every level of quality. The school has a strong tradition of guitar playing, being one of the first to offer it as a subject.

The founding of the Lignaphonics Laboratory created an immediate link between many departments at sixth-form level for musicians studying science, scientists studying music and students of acoustics as a special subject. Direct references are necessary to the departments of Biology, Computer Science, Maths, Design and Technology, Crafts, Physics and Music. In addition, frequent raids are made on Tony the chippy to purloin odd bits of wood of dubious origin and indifferent quality for obscure purposes!

In taking the soundboards as the prime component in the instrument, many variables have to be considered, including material, dimensions, grain structure, bracing, soundhole diameter and position, bridge design, varnish, and glues. In order to measure, record, analyse and compare the data from experiments, various pieces

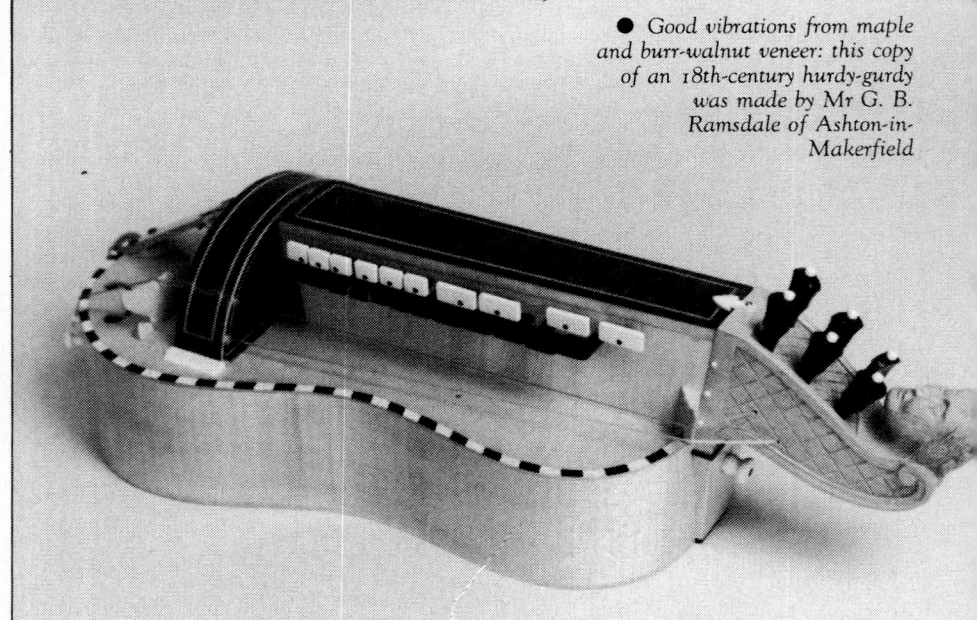

● *Good vibrations from maple and burr-walnut veneer: this copy of an 18th-century hurdy-gurdy was made by Mr G. B. Ramsdale of Ashton-in-Makerfield*

of apparatus include the following: a VELA microprocessor, a cathode ray oscilloscope, a microphone, a transducer, an amplifier, a chart recorder, a microcomputer, disk drive and printer, a TV monitor, a signal generator, and a frequency analyser.

We do not have all of these as yet and in fact the last item might be regarded as whimsical since it would cost more than all the other equipment put together! Among the essential data required from the experiments on our test pieces for comparative analysis are sound intensity, frequency of vibration and particle velocity — sound waves travelling at different speeds through different materials. We also collect sound pressure data, and details of resonance. Analysis of ADSR (Attack, Decay, Sustain, Reverberation) and the harmonic structure of tonal response make up the list.

The preparation of test rigs is essential but time-consuming, since there is little information on the subject and many false avenues have been, if misleading, at least not wasted. Merely programming the sequence of tests to avoid squandering precious materials needs careful planning, and we are about to set up a secondary schedule of experiments with existing conventional instruments to refine the analogical procedure.

We hope we can publish the results of our work to contribute greater awareness of musical instrument design, of tone quality, and the efficient exploitation of timber resources. Should anyone with an interest in one or other facet of Lignaphonics care to make contact, a welcome is assured.

● R. Z. Taylor, Haberdasher's Aske's School, Butterfly Lane, Elstree, Borehamwood, Herts WD6 3AF, tel. 01-207 4323.

● Also heavily involved in this field of research is Dr Bernard Richardson of the Dept of Physics, University College, PO Box 78, Cardiff CF1 1XL. His group has devised the holographic interferometer — 'an optical instrument which is capable of visualising vibrations on large, three-dimensional objects. It is extremely sensitive and can record movements of less than a millionth of a metre, a necessary requirement for observing the minute

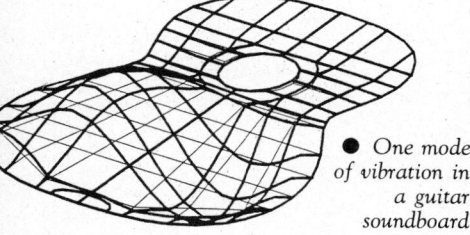

● One mode of vibration in a guitar soundboard

movements of guitar plates while they are vibrating at different frequencies.' A laser is used to make a hologram of the instrument; when this is reconstructed, the object can be seen in three dimensions.

Another useful procedure in Dr Richardson's work is 'finite-element analysis'. 'Details of the structure, its dimensions and material properties, are fed into a computer, which calculates its modes of vibration.' He hopes this may one day help instrument-makers to make difficult design decisions without having to waste valuable material on experimenting. ■

# Books

*Terry Forde*
***Easy-to-Make Wooden Toys***
*David & Charles, £7.95 hardback*
*Reviewed by Alan Bridgewater*
If you are an absolute beginner and you would like to tackle a range of very basic toy making projects, this could well be the book for you. Terry Forde sets out the projects in a simple, 'make no bones about it' way; the written instructions are short and to the point, the diagrams are clear, and the eight pages of coloured photographs are helpful.

The book includes, in all, 24 projects, from cars and garages to Noah's Arks, zoo animals, castles and dolls' furniture. The toys are colourful, practical and sturdy. There's plenty to keep the beginner interested; I particularly liked the train-making project and the soldier cut-outs, which remind me of some of the better 30s and 40s toys.

Now for the less happy news; the cover blurb describes the toys as 'imaginative' and of such wide range that they will 'keep any parent usefully employed and their children blissfully happy' . . . well, I don't really think so. The toys are basic and solid, but not imaginative or exciting.

These projects are aimed at beginners, so they need to be simple and direct, but it doesn't mean that sections on design, tools and materials should be skimped. Surely beginners need more advice rather than less? My big moan is that this book tosses off 'painting' in 100 or so throw-away words. I know from bitter experience that painting plywood is difficult — paints dribble, reject each other, bleed and bloom; wood grains swell and materials buckle. There's really no mention of these problems in this book.

This isn't a 'rip-off' book; the author has put a lot of himself into the projects, but it's a pity there are one or two gaps. This isn't for the serious, keen beginner who wants to learn about wood and make toys; rather for the 'non-wood' person who is interested in making toys, and sees the wood as just a means to an end.

*Anthony Dew*
***Making Rocking Horses***
*David & Charles, £7.95 hardback*
*Reviewed by Margaret Spencer*
This is the first book I have seen which actually explains how to make and dress rocking horses. It is aimed at the hobby woodworker who wants to try a first attempt at a useful toy for a child.

As the woodworker (and child) gains confidence, the more ambitious forms of rocking horse can be attempted; the book gives details on how to make a hobbyhorse, a toddlers' plywood rocking horse and two fully carved versions, one of average size on a swinger stand and a smaller one on rockers.

The last chapter dealing with the restoration of old rocking horses is lacking, in that Anthony Dew has under-emphasised the amount of care, skill, and above all, patience needed to undertake

● *Expert rocking-horse maker and restorer Margaret Spencer re-assures a new patient*

some of the repairs, such as re-fitting loose legs.

There are however, many tips that can be understood and followed by any practical person.

The diagrams are to scale and very simple, and there are many excellent black and white photographs showing construction to emphasise points in the text. This makes for easy reading, which so many authors on practical subjects forget is of paramount importance. I am glad to see a nicely written book on my favourite subject added to the huge choice available to the hobby woodworker.

*Christopher Proudfoot and Philip Walker*
***Woodworking Tools – A Christie's Collectors Guide***
*Phaidon/Christies, £15.00 hardback*
*Reviewed by David Savage*
People who collect old tools are a pretty motley crew. Some collect for speculation and have profited from the enormous increases in market prices over the past few years. Others collect because there are no modern equivalent tools of similar quality or because they enjoy using old tools, some of brass and rosewood, that have been through the hands of two or three generations of craftsmen.

This book is intended as a guide to the would-be collector of tools. Christopher Proudfoot has not only a thorough understanding of the subject, but also interest in and affection for the tools as objects, and some knowledge of their use. Without pretensions of craftsmanship, he has clearly attempted, sometimes without success, to use many of the tools. These descriptions of how and where to use a certain type of plane give another aspect to an otherwise rather arid pursuit.

The accent is on collecting tools rather than their history, but the chapter by Philip Walker on decorated and dated tools will provide something for the established collector from a leading authority on the subject.

Produced on good quality paper with clear typography, crisp photographs and good graphics, this is quite simply a beautiful book that makes a valuable contribution to our understanding of the subject.

# The hunter's kayak

Tim Kidman presents drawings and construction details for a design whose original was tested in Arctic waters

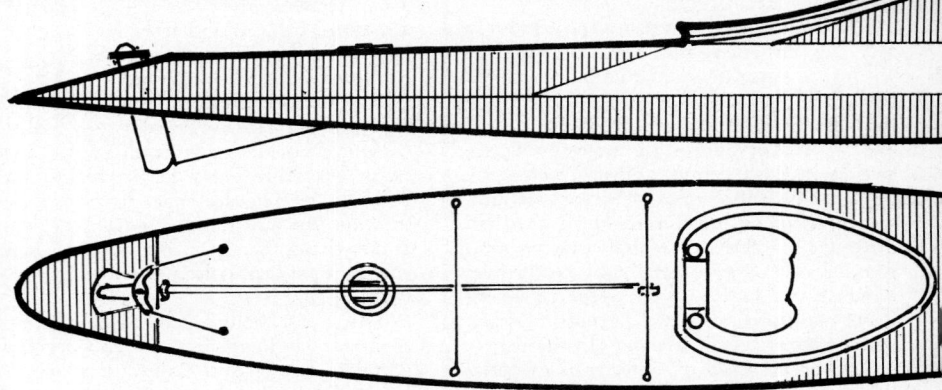

Not to be confused with dugout canoes or the birch-bark open boats of the north-American Indians, the kayaks of the Eskimos use sealskin for the hull covering. This material may make economic sense for them, but for us there's no comparison with 4mm marine ply — on grounds of humanity, price or availability!

The Pacific Eskimos call their skin boats *baidarkas*; they use them in the towering waves of the icy north Pacific, hunting whales and sea otters. More common in Europe and the US, however, is the design developed from the Eskimo caribou-hunting kayak, whose curved keel gives it great manoeuvrability. This kind of craft is used in competition — hence the name 'high-volume slalom canoe' — but I am a sea-kayakist, and I was inspired by the Eskimo designs in the Liverpool Museum to create a boat that handles well in big waves.

I started with numerous cardboard models, trying out various keel and hull forms to get an idea of what shape would be best for sea conditions. This design is the mark 3 version; faster than the mark 2, it also handles better in high waves, and has

various other improvements of detail. It needs a rudder because the chine makes it a little difficult to turn quickly.

Mark out one sheet of ply as in diagram 1, and cut it out with a Stanley knife or a jig-saw. An extra side panel with reverse transom should be marked out and cut from the second sheet of ply. If you butt the joints, cut 1in shorter and cover the join with a 2in piece. Mark the overlapping areas of the pieces carefully as shown; they will join over the piece bearing the same letter.

Prepare two pieces of 1×¾in clear spruce by cutting as in fig. 1. Steam the last 3in in a steam box, then bend to the curve of the bow side panels. Finally, pin and glue the spruce to the side panels.

Drill ¹⁄₁₆in holes at 3in intervals along the edges of the hull bottom pieces. Place 3in lengths of wire (Rytie) in the holes, and

twist it tight to pull the hull sections together.

The side pieces (with spruce pieces attached) are now joined using a similar procedure, again ¹⁄₁₆in holes 3in apart, starting aft. The bows are joined for the first six holes before pulling in the bowside sections to the hull.

After joining the hull sides to the bottom, the bottom centre seam can be taped with 2in tape and polyester resin. When it has set the first bulkhead can be fitted 3ft from the bow. It is glued and brass-pinned from the outside. The forward bulkhead (fig. 2) can be fitted with a cut-out at the top for the lifting toggle. Glue two pieces of ply either side of the cut-out, drill a ¼in hole through both pieces, and push in a piece of ¼in brass rod to which you can attach the toggle.

A piece of 1in square spruce long enough to give a total beam of 22in is pinned and

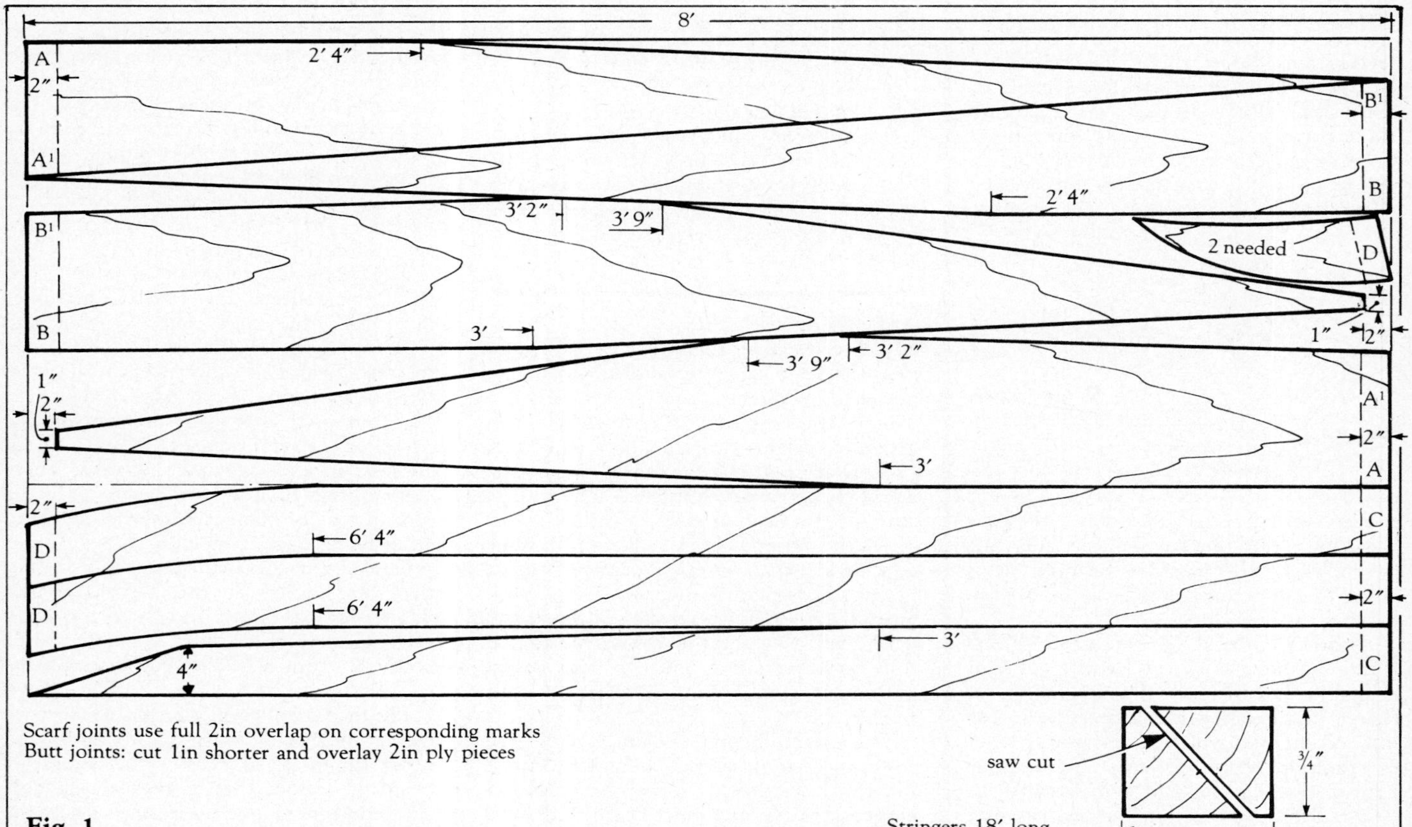

Scarf joints use full 2in overlap on corresponding marks
Butt joints: cut 1in shorter and overlay 2in ply pieces

**Fig. 1**

Stringers 18' long

saw cut

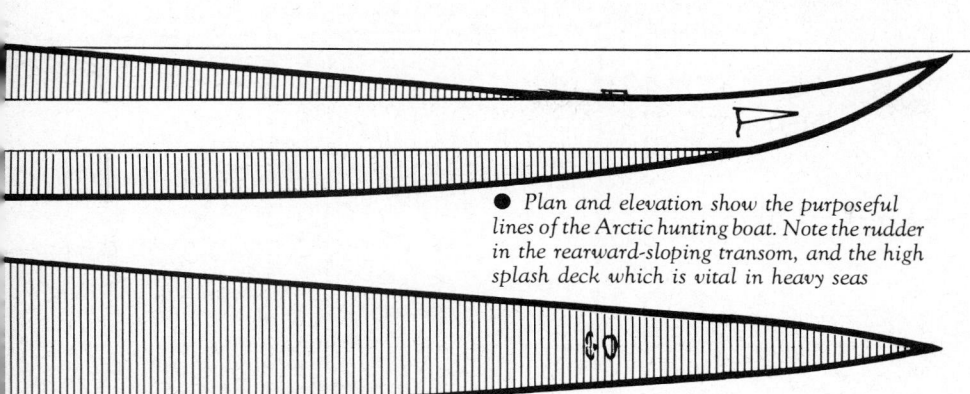

● *Plan and elevation show the purposeful lines of the Arctic hunting boat. Note the rudder in the rearward-sloping transom, and the high splash deck which is vital in heavy seas*

● *Looking forward before the decking goes on. The brace is to hold the hull in shape while the glue in the hull joints dries*

glued, 71in from the transom, into recesses made in the stringers. The rear of the cockpit bulkhead (fig. 2) can now be fitted to this piece and the hull by pinning and gluing. When the glue has set, the cockpit side is taped with resin to ensure watertightness. All the other seams can now be taped with glass tape and resin.

The forward cockpit support (fig. 2) is made by laminating pieces of 4mm ply over the mould shown. Two pieces of 1in, one piece of 1½in and one of 2in are used, the wider ply on the outside. When set the support should retain its shape on removal from the mould. It can then be screwed to the stringers 105in from the bow. The second bulkhead can also be fitted 86in from the bow, pinned and glued and taped with glass tape and resin on the cockpit side when set.

● *View into the cockpit before the coaming is fitted. The laminated forward cockpit support and spruce framework can be seen*

When the seams are finished, the transom (fig. 2) can be fitted, by gluing and nailing with copper boat nails. When this has set any pieces above deck level can be planed away so that the aft deck may be pinned and glued to it. The aft deck, cut from a piece of ply 22×60in, should be reinforced before fitting, by gluing to it smaller pieces of 4mm ply — away from the edge so as not to hit the stringers. The reinforcing is needed to stop the deck bending when you sit on it. Other fittings in the aft deck should be fixed before gluing. The foredecking can also be fitted; it is a difficult bend, so I used a piece of 3mm ply.

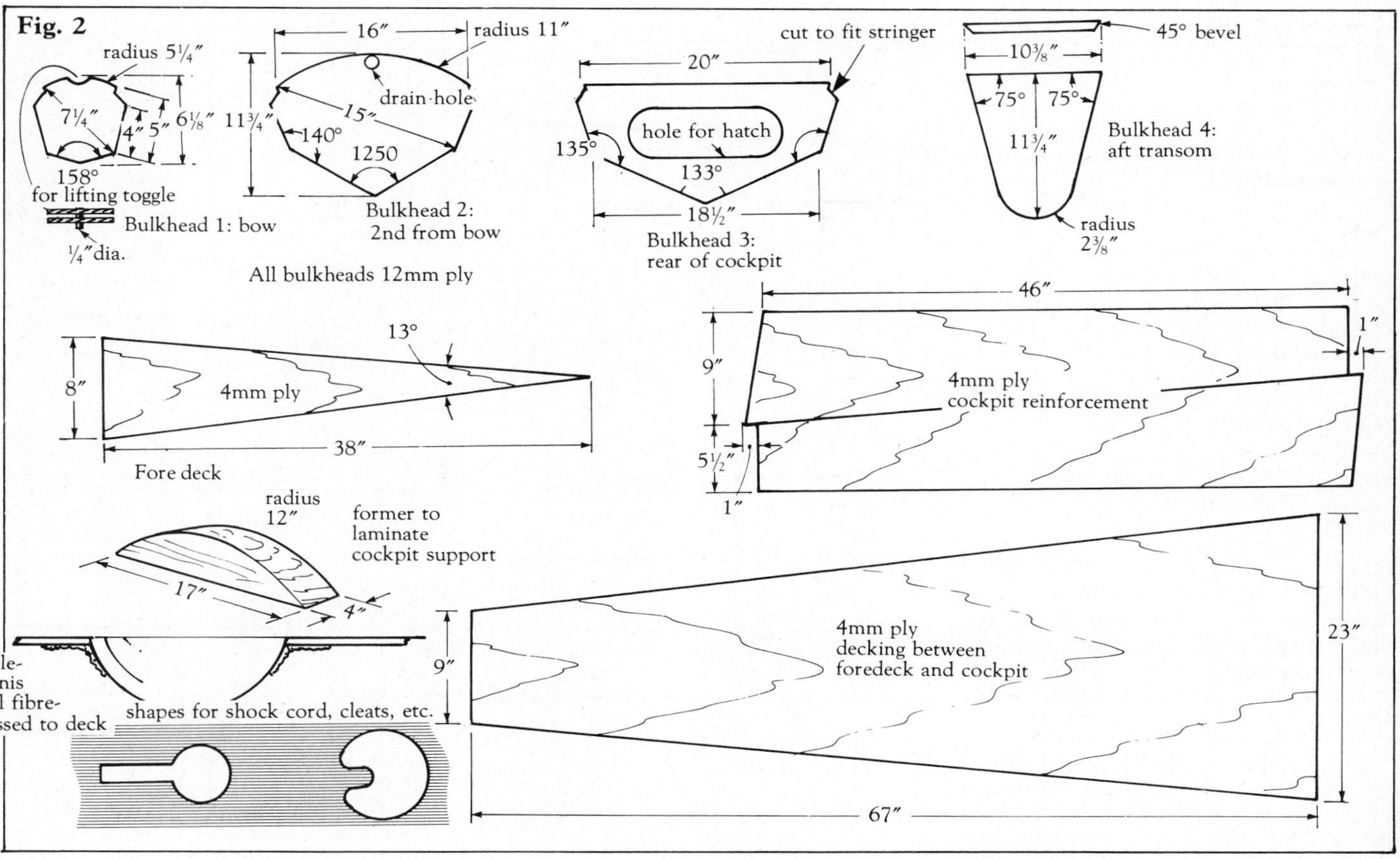

---

**Fig. 2**

radius 5¼"

7¼"   4" 5" 6⅛"   11¾"

158°
for lifting toggle

¼" dia.

**Bulkhead 1: bow**

16"   radius 11"

drain hole

15"

140°   1250

**Bulkhead 2: 2nd from bow**

All bulkheads 12mm ply

cut to fit stringer

20"

hole for hatch

135°   133°

18½"

**Bulkhead 3: rear of cockpit**

45° bevel

10⅜"

75°   75°

11¾"

radius 2⅜"

**Bulkhead 4: aft transom**

13°

8"   4mm ply

38"

**Fore deck**

46"

1"

9"

4mm ply cockpit reinforcement

5½"

1"

radius 12"   former to laminate cockpit support

17"   4"

table-tennis ball fibre-glassed to deck

shapes for shock cord, cleats, etc.

9"

4mm ply decking between foredeck and cockpit

23"

67"

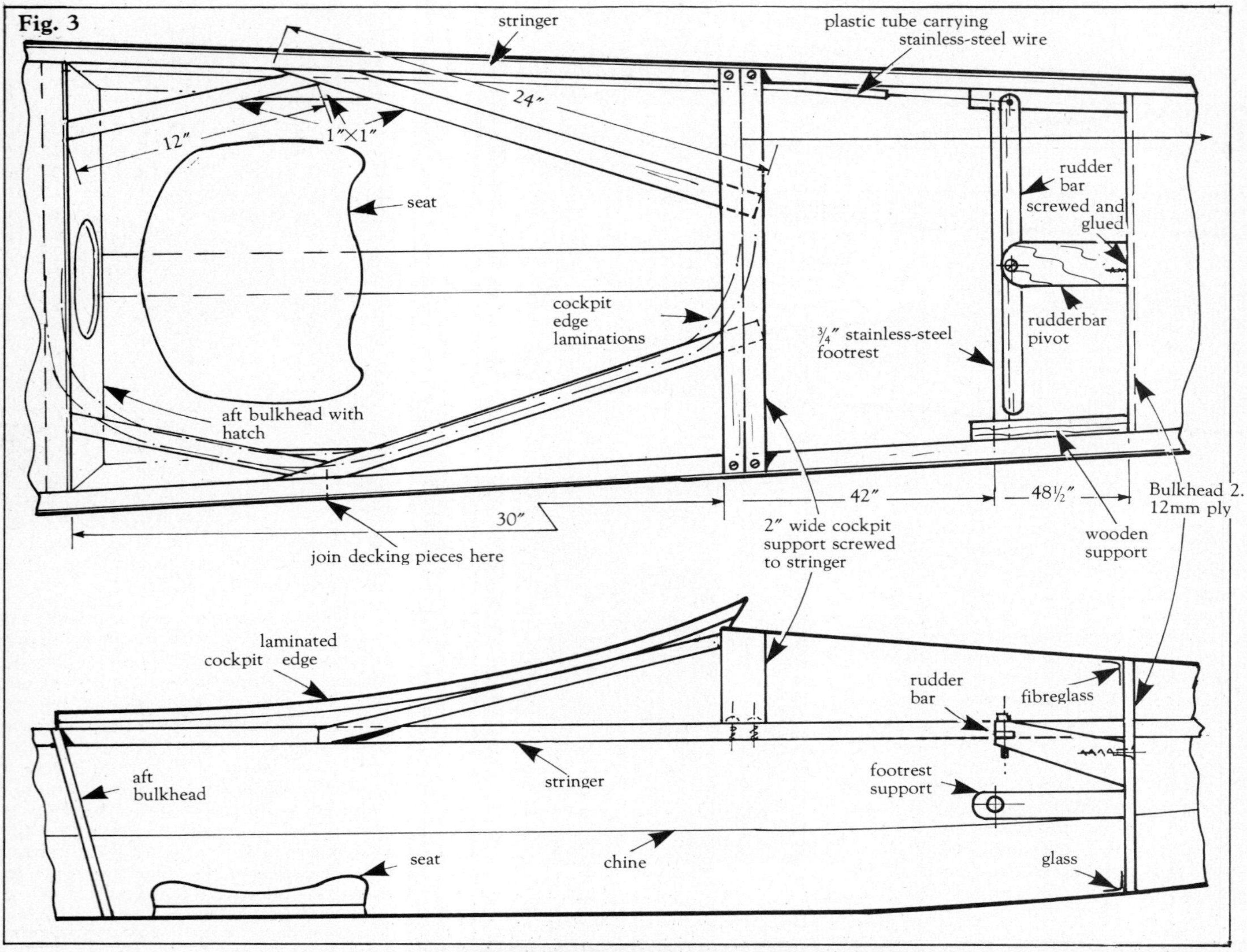

**Fig. 3**

stringer

plastic tube carrying
stainless-steel wire

24″

12″

1″×1″

seat

rudder
bar
screwed and
glued

cockpit
edge
laminations

¾″ stainless-steel
footrest

rudderbar
pivot

aft bulkhead with
hatch

Bulkhead 2.
12mm ply

30″

join decking pieces here

2″ wide cockpit
support screwed
to stringer

42″

48½″

wooden
support

laminated
cockpit edge

rudder
bar

fibreglass

aft
bulkhead

stringer

footrest
support

seat

chine

glass

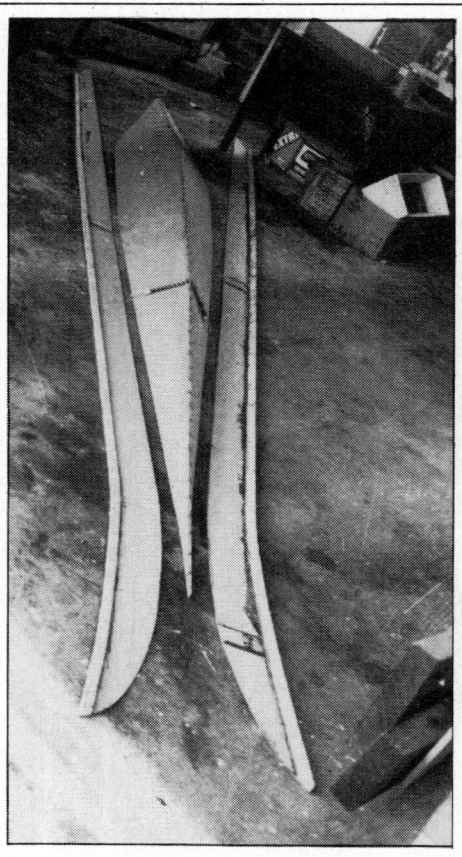

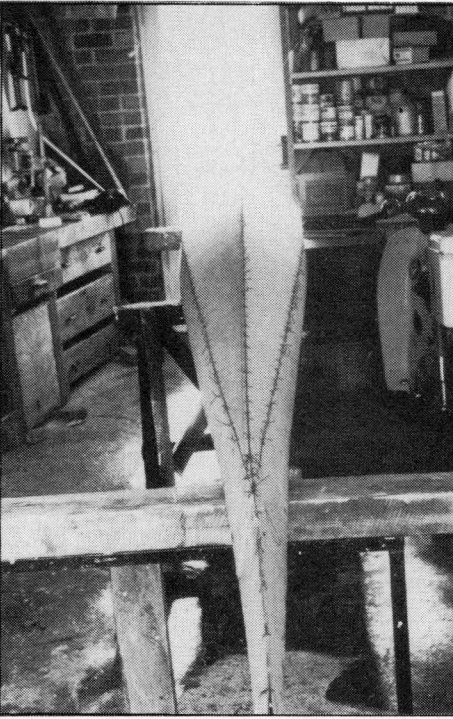

Do not forget to leave the lifting toggle free. At this point the wire pieces that pulled the hull together can be removed with side cutters and the wire centre pulled out with pliers.

The cockpit-reinforcing pieces (fig. 2) are glued to the hull bottom using polyester resin and held in position with copper boat nails.

With the fibreglass seat taped with polyester resin to the reinforcing on the hull bottom 1½in in front of the cockpit bulkhead, you can sit in the canoe and get someone to measure you for the footrest. This is a piece of stainless steel ¾in in diameter, fitted into blocks long enough to just touch the bulkhead and wide enough to take a hole for the tube, placed to transfer thrust to the bulkhead and hull sides. A rudder bar can be fitted 4in above the foot rest (fig. 3).

The cockpit is formed by a 1×1in spruce framework to support the decking. First a 2ft length is fitted; offer it up to the side 3in down from the mid-point. Shape the two pieces and glue and pin them. Pieces of spruce 1ft long are now fitted to the aft bulkhead 4in from the side to the pieces already fitted. A small piece can be fitted where the two join (fig. 3).

The decking can now be completed. Cut the rest of the foredeck from a piece of ply 67in long (fig. 2), and glue and nail it with copper boat nails to the second bulkhead,

● *Left: The cut and joined shapes of the upper hull pieces laid out ready for assembly to the bottom. Above: The assembled hull upside-down on trestles. The looped wire fixings are placed at 3in intervals*

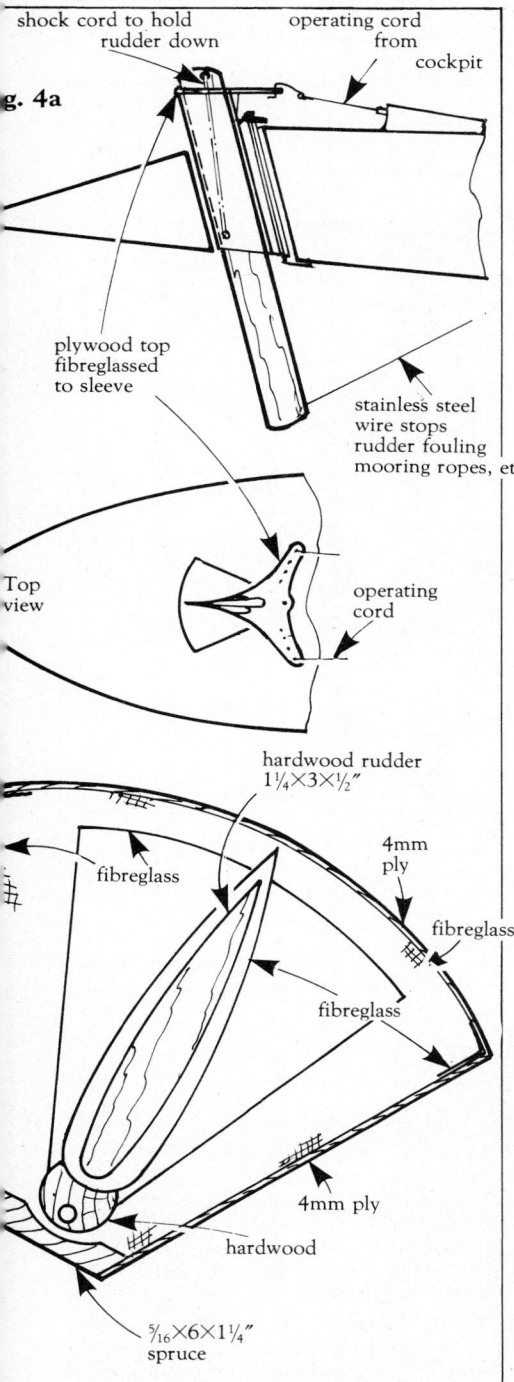

**g. 4a**

shock cord to hold rudder down

operating cord from cockpit

plywood top fibreglassed to sleeve

stainless steel wire stops rudder fouling mooring ropes, etc.

Top view

operating cord

hardwood rudder 1¼×3×½"

4mm ply

fibreglass

fibreglass

fibreglass

4mm ply

hardwood

⁵⁄₁₆×6×1¼" spruce

**Fig. 4b**

screw

studding

screw

bottom pintle plate

top pintle plate

stainless steel or brass

hole for pintle

● *The bow without its decking, showing the footrest and two forward bulkheads.*

the stringers and the cockpit support. The decking around the cockpit is fitted by offering up pieces of ply of about the right size, marking, cutting, and gluing and pinning (fig. 3).

The cockpit coaming is fitted by gluing ½in-wide pieces of ply, cut to fit, to the cockpit edge. Build it up to three pieces high and finish it with two ¾in pieces to form a lip for fastening the spray deck. If a thick spray deck is going to be used, another piece of ply 1in wide should be added.

All external seams are now taped with 1½in tape. Then the canoe can be sanded, primed, sanded, undercoated, sanded, top-coated, sanded and finished with a final top-coat.

During construction either keyholes or cleats can be cut into the plywood

panels of the fore and aft decks. They can be waterproofed by glassing in half a table-tennis ball under the deck, and are used to fit fore and aft lines and athwart-ship shock-cord retainers for charts, paddles, compass, etc.

A rudder can also be fitted to be worked from the cockpit by the feet. This is in a well fitted into the reverse slope of the transom; the control can be either by cords operating through polythene tubing from the rudder bar to the rudder control on top of the rudder sleeve, or by a solid stainless-steel wire operating on one side of the rudder control. The polythene tubes need to be incorporated in the kayak during its construction.

A triangular tube 6in long is constructed of 4mm ply, using a piece of spruce for the apex (fig. 4a). The construction is similar to

the canoe in that the ply-to-ply corners are constructed by sewing with Rytie and then taping with glass tape and polyester resin; the spruce is 1×⁵⁄₁₆×6in, with a bevel on the vertical sides (fig. 4a).

This tube is now used as a pattern to cut the hole in the reverse transom, with the spruce upright fitted at the top of the transom, just inside the aft deck, 12½in from the end of the transom. It is fixed with resin and tape at the top and bottom. Later a hole will be cut in the bottom to accommodate the rudder.

The rudder, 14×3×½in, is made from hardwood. The sleeve to hold the rudder is made by wrapping four layers of newspapers round it, then a sheet of polythene, and then moulding fibreglass round the shape using glass tape and polyester resin. When the first moulding is set it is removed from the rudder along with the polythene and newspaper. A rounded piece of hardwood 5×³⁄₈×½in is then fibre-glassed to the front of the sleeve. A stainless-steel tube 5in long and of enough internal diameter to allow 2BA or 0BA stainless-steel studding is fixed into the piece of wood for the rudder pintle.

The pintle is a 6in-long piece of stainless steel or brass 2BA or 0BA studding, brazed to a piece of stainless steel or brass shaped as in fig. 4b. This is screwed into the bottom of the hull just before the hole for the rudder, and fixed so that the rudder sleeve can be pushed down the studding and turn in the triangular hole. The top fixing is a piece of stainless steel or brass as in fig. 4b. This is wide enough to absorb the shock if the rudder grounds and re-tracks. The studding is then held in place with a nut fastened down to the piece of metal.

*Bon voyage!* ∎

## Materials

Marine plywood BS 1088
    2 sheets 8×4ft×4mm (3 sheets for two canoes)
    Odd pieces of ½in(12mm) ply also required for bulkheads
Other wood
    18ft×1×¾in clear spruce for stringers to be cut as fig. 1
    18ft×1×¾in clear spruce for pit and bulkhead supports
    18×4×2½in softwood for making forward cockpit support by laminating
Fastenings
    4oz (approx 140) ¾×14 copper boat nails
    4oz (approx 450) ¾×17 brass boat pins
Glue
    Aerolite 306 500g
    hardener GBP 500g
Glass tape
    1½in (38mm) 50m roll
Resin
    Polyester type A 1kg
Cooper wire or Rytie
Seat
    GRP obtainable from canoe suppliers or moulded
Hatches
    Hol Alan HA337 and HA 338

# Wheels for spinners

Woodturner Peter Royle has updated the spinning-wheel in scores of ingenious ways — all aimed at serving the user. Michael Sylvester reports

I t is at least 4000 years since man first invented spinning: maybe longer. At first he (or she!) used a simple hand-held spindle — a tapered stick with a weight attached to act as a flywheel; later a hand-turned drive wheel was added to drive a bobbin-flyer mechanism; finally came a foot treadle, and (although designs varied throughout the world) the spinning-wheel as we know it came into its own.

Slow but dependable, it meant that three or four hand-spinners, working from home, could keep one weaver supplied with yarn. It was the classic cottage industry. But between 1764 and 1779 Hargreaves' spinning-jenny, Arkwright's water-frame and Crompton's mule revolutionised the system. By 1812 one factory spinner could produce 200 times as much as a hand-spinner. Technology, or the Industrial Revolution, had come to stay. Every few years saw further sophistication or efficiency added. The spinning-wheel was obsolete.

That's the theory. But Peter Royle, a woodturner from Leyland in Lancashire, would disagree. He earns a living making spinning-wheels — or, as he prefers to call them, 'spinners' wheels'. The distinction is important to him because the wheels he constructs, on the lines of the traditional Saxony wheels but with many adaptations and additions of his own, are for use, not ornament: profit as well as pleasure. A practised spinner on a really good wheel now has the basis of a viable business.

Peter is quite literally helping to reverse history — re-introducing cottage industry and re-popularising a machine abandoned by serious spinners over 200 years ago. The measure of his achievement is that in 1982 his wheel won the North West Arts Three-Dimensional Design Award, and was described by Eileen Chadwick (one of

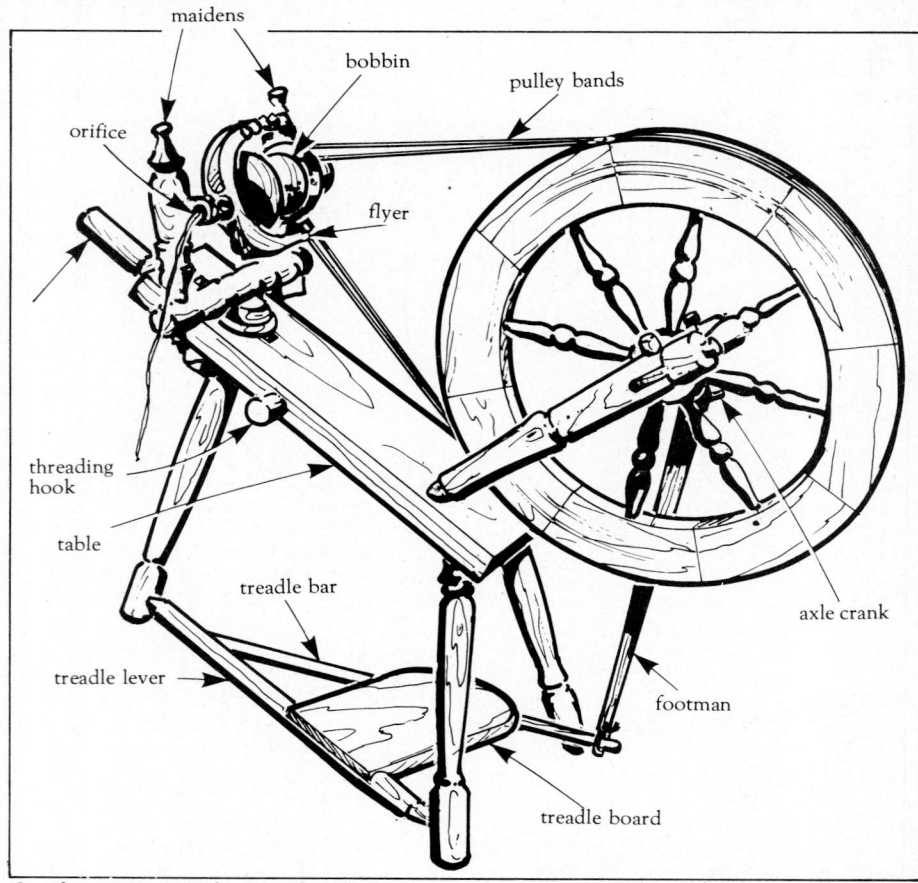

● Above: Naming of parts. The wheel imparts twist to a supply of fibre fed through the orifice, turning it into yarn which is wound on to the bobbin

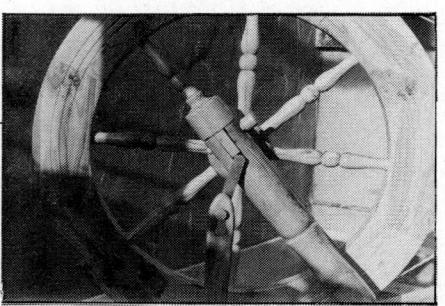

● Footman, axle and crank – an ancient concept, but the parts are now running on sealed ball bearings and phosphor-bronze bushes!

Britain's leading spinners) as 'the best to look at, and the best to use, that I have seen'.

To attain that standard Peter has combined the modern and the traditional. He does not scorn the use of metal components produced to present-day engineering tolerances, but simultaneously delights in creating an elegant, instantly recognisable example of the woodturner's craft.

'It's immensely satisfying,' he told me, 'because a wheel is the most complex example there is of composite turning skills. You're aiming for the perfect combination of beauty and efficiency.'

P eter taught himself to spin, just as years before he had taught himself to turn wood, partly from curiosity and partly as an element in the self-sufficiency which first hardship after redundancy and later conviction have made a way of life for him and his family. He so enjoyed using a wheel after his first experiments on a drop-spindle, and so appreciated the wide variety of yarns this put at his disposal, that he decided to build his own. Acquiring a set of published plans, he began work and soon had a functional instrument.

Functional to a degree, that is. In his own words: 'By this time I was a moderately competent spinner, and even at that stage I could feel the machine did not work really well.' Now, as a skilled spinner, he knows why. 'It was designed by a woodturner, not a spinner. There was none of what you

● Detail of the flyer mechanism which distributes the yarn on the bobbin. Note the hooks and precision-made metal parts

might call 'spinning technology'. I've noticed the same thing in certain woodturning lathes which have been designed by engineers and not by woodturners. You've got to ask the user what he or she wants.'

That is precisely what he did — but not before making certain alterations himself. Even as a relatively inexperienced spinner he realised that some parts would wear too quickly or need too frequent lubrication; there were also no bushes or bearings, and the orifice was too small. To rectify this he locked the pulley to the spindle with a grub screw instead of a push fit, introduced a sealed ball-bearing unit into the axle, and increased the size of the orifice. The machine was now more than just a piece of furniture; but he did not attempt to market it, instead going to the experts — in this case Judith Storey of Whalley.

Together they analysed the new wheel, their aim being to create one which beginners could manage, which professional spinners would find efficiently productive, and which was small enough to fit comfortably into a modern house. back at the drawing-board and the lathe, Peter adapted, changed and added.

First he tackled the wheel itself — increasing the diameter to 20in (significantly smaller than the Norwegian or 'double table') but compensating for this by smoother running and a truer lining-up. He also altered the wheel-rim profile to take the pulley-band better. Then the ratio of the steps on the drive pulley was increased to give greater winding-on potential, the maidens were raked back further to provide more positive drive, the orifice was enlarged again to take a wider variety of yarns, and the treadle broadened to accommodate different feet at different angles (very important, because spinning for long periods is an exhausting business).

It was still basically a Saxony wheel, but now it was indubitably the Royle Saxony — the 'Countess'. And it had the advantages lacking in wheels produced by non-spinners. For instance, Judith Storey had pointed out the importance of residual momentum. Treadled to an appropriate speed, a wheel should continue to revolve 'under its own steam' long enough to allow some respite for the spinner and to afford the beginner better control of what looks a simple activity but is in fact a highly complex one.

One major breakthrough was the invention of the Royle bobbin. As yarn accumulates on a bobbin the increased weight leads to friction and power loss. The new bobbin, combined with precision engineering and a very high degree of accuracy in turning, has overcome the problem to the extent that it will hold at least twice as much as the conventional bobbin, and more if necessary. Thus spinning becomes more efficient, as there are fewer bobbin changes yet no greater efforts from the spinner.

With all its modifications the new machine began to attract favourable attention and a growing market. But Peter Royle, a perfectionist if ever there was one, took advantage of an invitation to Quarry Bank Mill at Styal to consult Eileen Chadwick. She was impressed but inevitably made suggestions. Just as inevitably, Peter took notice. 'I've always aimed up-market in my work. I wasn't selling decorative pieces of furniture — I was selling spinning-wheels to spinners. Here was an authority.'

Her suggestions have since been adopted. Now he supplies the optional extra of a flyer assembly with narrower jaws, a slimmer bobbin, a smaller orifice, and a flyer with more and smaller hooks. This allows the spinning of very fine yarns and increases the versatility of an already versatile wheel.

One of her ideas he has not been able to implement, however, is that of a device for automatically spacing the yarn equally round the bobbin as it is spun. 'This is an on-going project,' he told me.

'Non-going,' his wife Janet corrected him gently. He reluctantly agreed. 'Some claim Leonardo da Vinci drew a plan of one in 1553, and it was certainly done by John Planta in the 1880s, but the equipment is so cumbersome that it would turn the machine into a monstrosity.'

Meanwhile production of the Countess continues. Each is made, in yew, walnut or oak, specifically for a particular client, but still with an eye open for possible improvements. Peter works with a friend skilled in model engineering, and modern metal technology is used where it will do most good; needle roller-bearings, sealed ball-bearing axle units, and graphite-impregnated phosphor-bronze bushes replace the easily worn-out wooden and leather fitments of the past. Perhaps most importantly, the inevitably crude parts traditionally supplied by the village blacksmith have been superseded, which ensures smooth running and durability.

And so a craft which should by rights be only a memory is not only preserved, but improved to the point of profitability. ■

● Above: Another view of the flyer mechanism shows how the fibre twists as it enters the orifice and is distributed as yarn over the bobbin by the hooks

● Left: Peter Royle at work on his own 'Countess' wheel. This one is in yew; oak and walnut are the other choices

# Woodworker PLANS SERVICE

## 2 plans for only £4

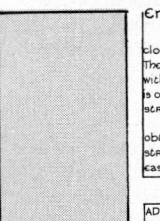

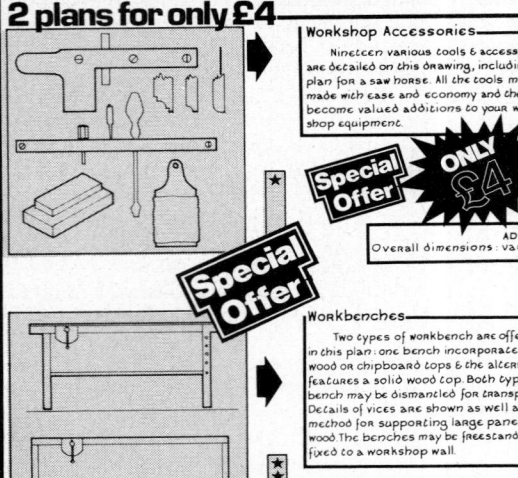

### Workshop Accessories

Nineteen various tools & accessories are detailed on this drawing, including a plan for a saw horse. All the tools may be made with ease and economy and they will become valued additions to your workshop equipment.

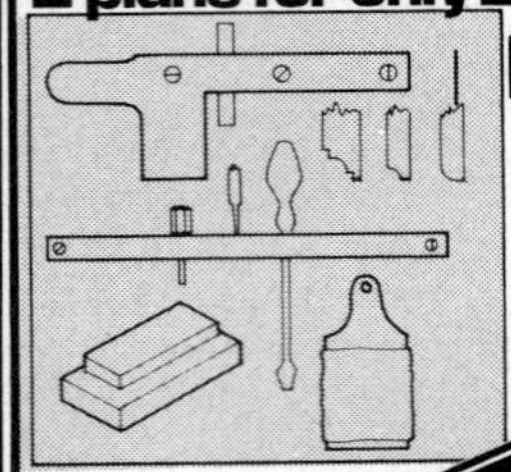

★

Special Offer ONLY £4

ADW 109
Overall dimensions: various

Special Offer

### Workbenches

Two types of workbench are offered in this plan: one bench incorporates plywood or chipboard tops & the alternative features a solid wood top. Both types of bench may be dismantled for transport. Details of vices are shown as well as a method for supporting large panels of wood. The benches may be freestanding or fixed to a workshop wall.

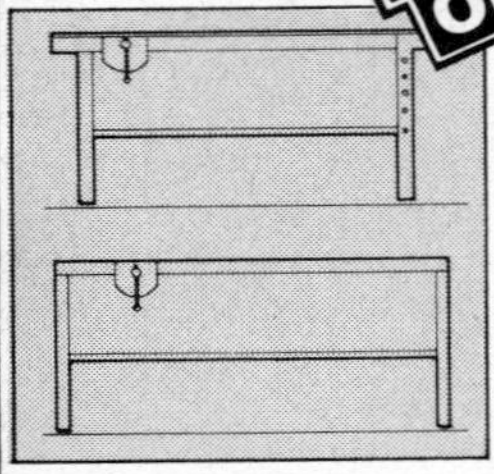

★★

ADW 108
Overall dimensions: 2020 x 908 x 800 mm.
79½" x 35¾" x 31½"

### Kitchen Accessories

Variations on simple designs for knife blocks, bread boards, notice/pin boards, kitchen-roll holders and rolling pins [rolling pin set] are detailed on this plan.

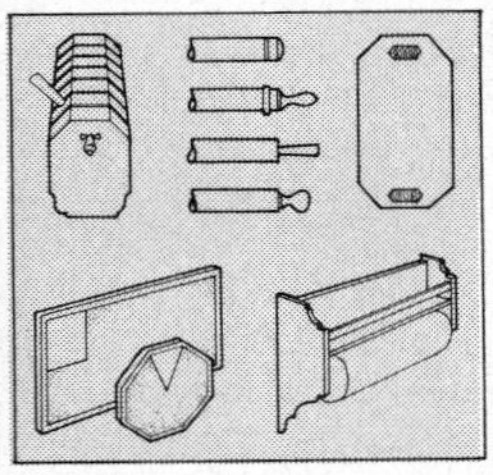

£3.25

ADW 119
Overall dimensions: various

### English Dial Clock

This plan features a pattern of wall clock popular in the first half of the 19th C. The bezel surround is of turned mahogany with solid mahogany carved ears. The trunk is of veneered mahogany with inlaid brass stringing.

The design incorporates an easy to obtain dial & bezel and the movement may striking or non-striking, mechanical or easy to fit quartz.

£3.25

ADW 130
Overall dimensions: 513 x 380 x 110mm.
20 3/16 x 14 15/16" x 4 5/16"

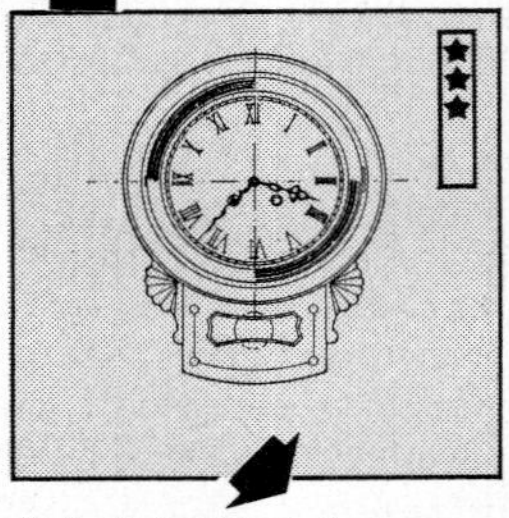

★★★

### Magazine Racks

This plan offers an open magazine rack and an alternative version with a table top. There is scope for decorative variations on both versions and suggestions are shown on the drawing. Construction incorporates simple housing joints.

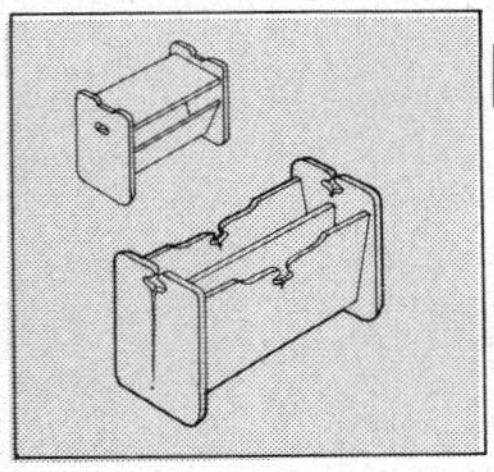

£2.75

ADW 116
Overall dimensions: 476 x 360 x 260 mm
18¾" x 14⅛" x 10¼"

### Patio Chair & Bench Seat

Build these traditional country inn seats to adorn your patio and to use in those sunny lazy days of summer. Simple construction simulates traditional pegged building methods.

ADW 122
Overall dimensions: 1017 x 678 x 405 mm
40" x 26¾" x 16"
& 560 x 678 x 405 mm
22" x 26¾" x 16"

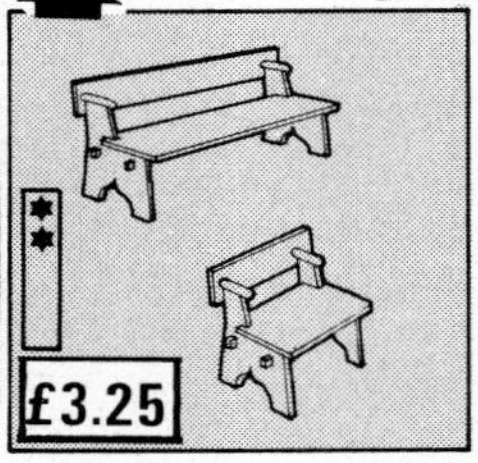

£3.25

## ashby design workshop

### 18th Century Gateleg Table

The convenience of the traditional gateleg table is admirably suited to the home of today. This design, which is based on an actual antique, features elegant turnings to a superbly designed profile. The original table was built in brown oak, but any English hardwood or fruitwood would give a most satisfactory result.

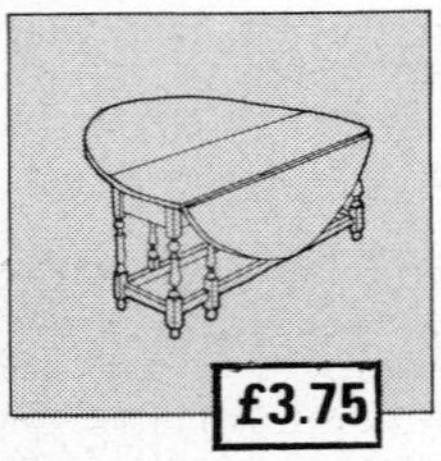

★★★

£3.75

ADW 103
Overall dimensions: 1140 x 992 x 737 mm
44⅞" x 39 1/16" x 29"

### Victorian Pedestal Sewing Box

This elegant piece of occasional furniture, featuring an hexagonal top, will not only enhance the smaller modern house, but its large storage space will be useful to the home needleworker. English walnut was used on the original antique but successful results could be obtained using other hardwoods.

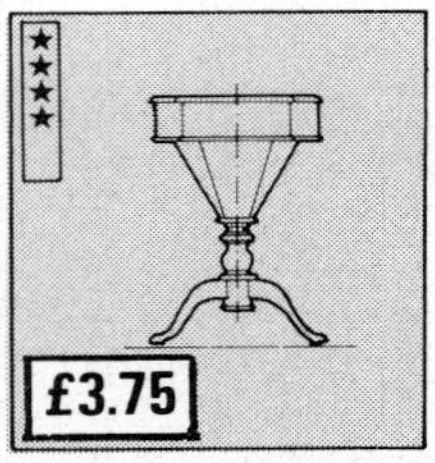

★★★★

£3.75

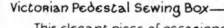

ADW 105
Overall dimensions: 735 x 462 x 520 mm
28 15/16" x 18 3/16" x 20½"

### Nursery Play Table

This versatile table has a number of features that make it ideal for the nursery. The working height of the table, which varies with the adjustable blackboard, will suit children between three and ten years old. There is storage space for large and small toys & an optional posting box may be built into the system. A simple screw & glue construction is used, needing less than 2 sheets of plywood & 4½ metres of softwood batten.

ADW 110
Overall dimensions: 1675 x 750 x 618 mm.
66" x 29½" x 24 5/16"

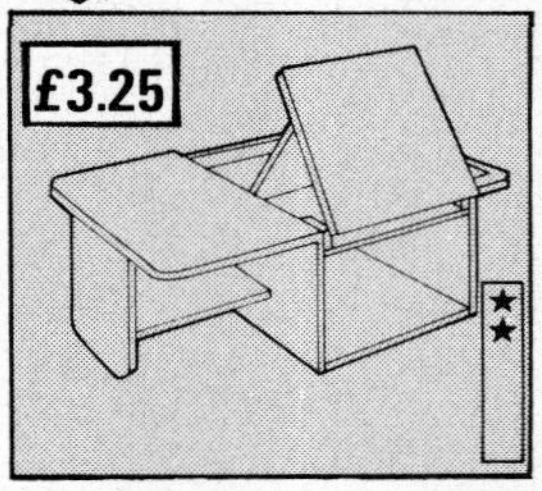

£3.25

★★

### Lap or Table Desk

This compact item will be a favourite with all the family for letter writing & homework. The basic design offers good storage for papers, pens etc. Construction may be on a simple screw & glue basis or could incorporate dovetails or comb joints as desired. Build in solid wood or use plywood and veneers.

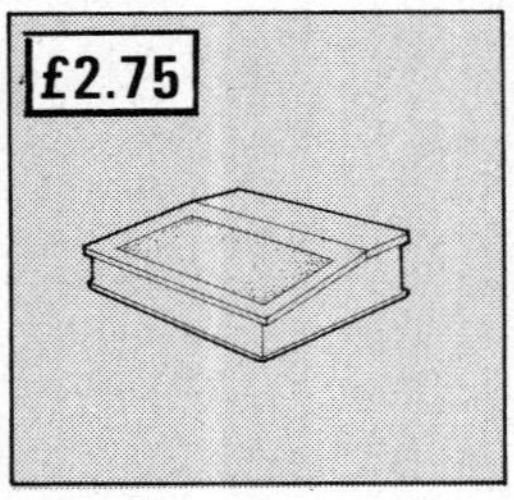

£2.75

★★

ADW 115
Overall dimensions: 394 x 470 x 115 mm
15½" x 18½" x 4½"

### Regency Davenport Desk

This design is based on a measured drawing of an actual desk. The compact size and surprisingly large storage capacity make it an ideal and useful item for the smaller homes of today. The original construction method used is fully detailed but this may easily be varied to suit modern materials and techniques.

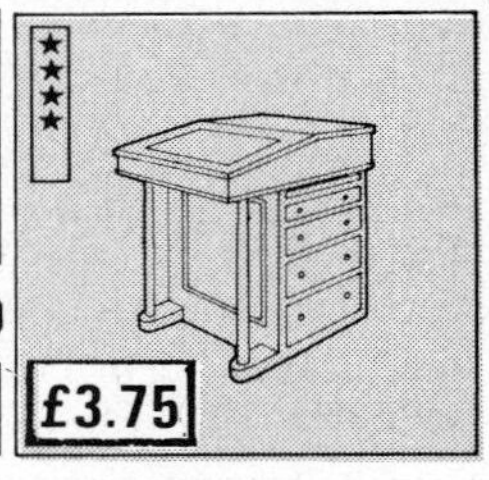

★★★★

£3.75

ADW 101 & ADW 102
Overall dimensions: 788 x 484 x 520 mm.
31" x 19 1/16" x 20½"

**PLANS SERVICE dramatically expands its range of construction plans with the ASHBY DESIGN workshop collection.**

**Beginners are recommended to start with a one or two star plan.**

**Fully detailed cutting list and operations schedule included with all plans.**

## Model & Allied Publications

JAN 85 WW

**P.O. Box 35, Wolsey House, Wolsey Road, Hemel Hempstead, Herts. HP2 4SS.**

*Please supply the following plans*

Plan No. ______ Quantity ______ Price ______

Plan No. ______ Quantity ______ Price ______

Plan No. ______ Quantity ______ Price ______

Total cash value ______

**POSTAGE: Inland — Up to £5.50 - 50p; Over £5.50 - 60p.**

**Overseas — Accelerated Surface Post: Up to £4.00 - 90p; £4.00 to £7.00 - £1.10; Over £7.00 - £1.40.**

*Name* ......................................

......................................

*Address* ......................................

......................................

......................................

......................................

......................................

***Post Code*** ......................................

# Lace bobbins: Projects and patterns

A detailed guide to the traditions and techniques involved in one of the woodturner's most delightful specialities

**N**ick Perrin writes: With the religious persecution of Protestants in Flanders and France during the reign of William III, many skilled lacemakers fled to England for safety, bringing their basic tools with them. Landing along the south coast and in the west country, they spread up the centre of England; they settled especially in the villages of Bedfordshire, Buckinghamshire and Northamptonshire, as well as the western areas of Devon, Somerset, Dorset and Wiltshire.

The cottage industry thus born flourished for about 200 years until it became uneconomic in the face of machine-made products, from Nottingham in particular. In the last 20 years, however, a new generation of lacemakers has grown steadily. These people do not seek to earn a living from such a slow-growing craft; rather to find enjoyment in making beautiful things and keeping alive old skills and traditions. New ideas and patterns, as well as new techniques, are growing out of the old ones. And, as with the lace, so too with the tools that are used.

My own interest in bobbin-making started with a wish to experiment in fine woodturning. In the past six years I have studied the work of old bobbin-makers by visiting the museums in Luton, Bedford, Olney and Honiton as well as Bruges and Tønder. I have been privileged to see and photograph treasured collections, and have developed my skills with the continuing encouragement of today's lacemakers.

In the 18th and 19th centuries bobbins were made from easily obtainable materials — bone, and woods from the hedgerow and orchard. Apple, plum, holly, hawthorn, blackthorn, box, beech and spindle were among the commonest. Nowadays we have access to beautifully coloured and grained foreign woods which extend the turner's range and make lacemakers very aware of

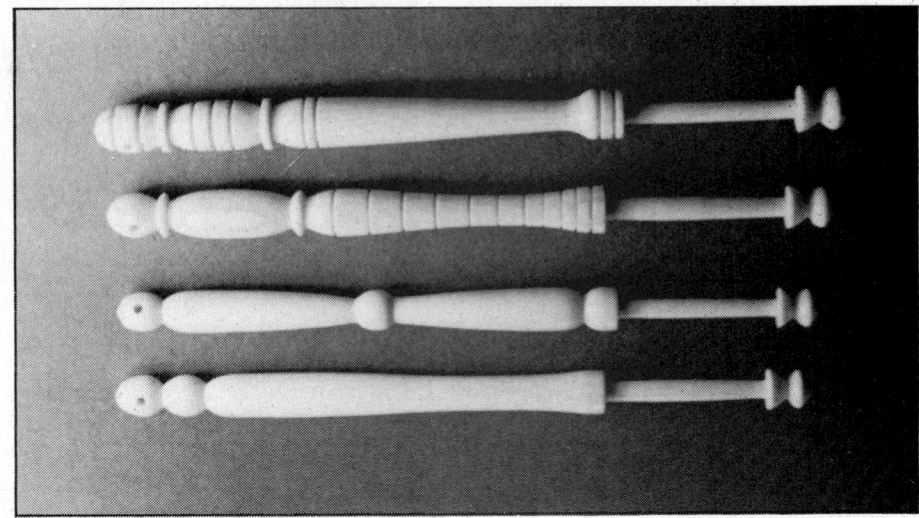

● *Four ivory bobbins of the Midland pattern turned by Nick Perrin — more common than they were, but still expensive! The grain can just be seen*

the complementary beauty of their bobbins to the lace on their pillows. While the traditionalists will spend much time and money searching out the antique pewter 'butterflies' of Archibald Abbott and the spirally inscribed bone bobbins of Bobbin Brown, the new collectors demand cocobolo, ebony, rosewood, zebrano, satinwood and many others.

There are plastic bobbins. There are even good plastic bobbins! But, although bobbin-makers do work in bone, ivory, horn and some metals, it is wood that is most in demand.

Any wood may be turned, but not all can be used for fine bobbins. The coarser-grained woods such as ash, oak and elm are difficult to use, although they often are. They tend to be weak at the point where the neck joins the shank; they often break in use, and so are not popular for the fine, slim Midland and Honiton bobbins. However, I have seen some splendid heavy German cased bobbins made in ash.

Boxwood was highly prized and used sparingly. It often formed an insert on 'bitted' bobbins of darker base colour. Being close-grained, it did not pick up the darker shade when being turned. Many of the woods available today come from equatorial areas and very slow-growing trees; this makes them equally close-grained

and ideal for miniature turning. They can be highly decorative, too, and they possess a wide colour range. Lacemakers do not take kindly to dyed woods because there is always the fear that the delicate thread will be stained. Thus it is important to get colour variation by bringing out the natural tones of the piece.

Ivory is formed in a different way from bone, and when it is cut a grain pattern becomes visible. THis is particularly marked where the cut is across the tusk, and it looks very similar to the endgrain of wood. The colour varies from a luminous white to a dead-leaf brown. In the past very few bobbins were made from ivory as it was a very expensive material and most lacemakers were very poor; only ladies of quality would have been able to afford such products. Nowadays ivory is still relatively expensive, and not available in unlimited quantities, but it is much sought after by many lacemakers.

In the past deer antlers provided the horn for bobbins. Though not used extensively it was available at the turn of the century, particularly from a firm in Cumberland. Horn bobbins feel heavier than bone or ivory bobbins of a similar size, and often show a clear grey smudge down one side where some of the spongy inner core of the antler has been included.

## Fig. 1

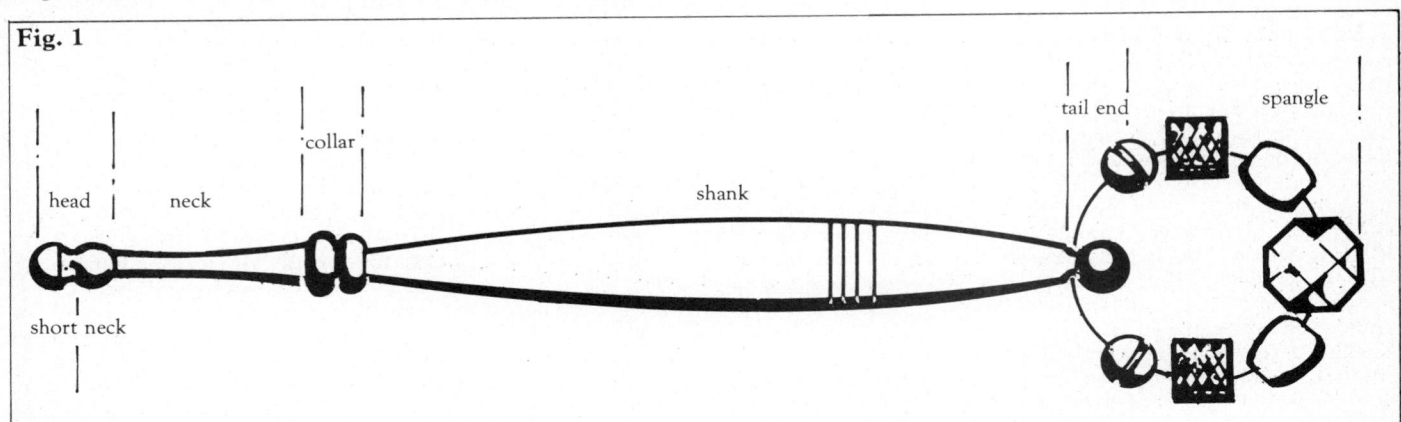

head · neck · 'collar' · shank · tail end · spangle · short neck

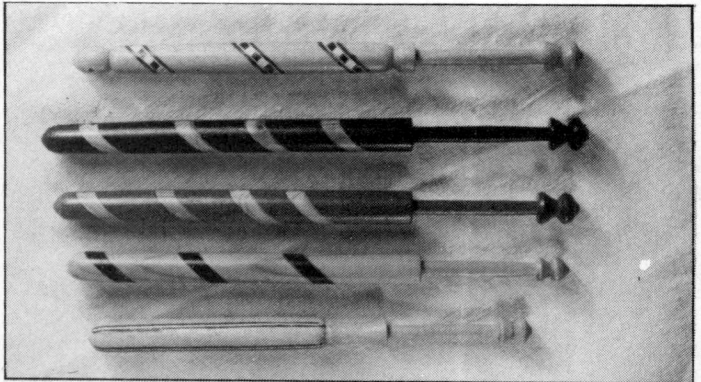

● *Bitted bobbins of the Midland pattern, inlaid with yew, rosewood and boxwood*

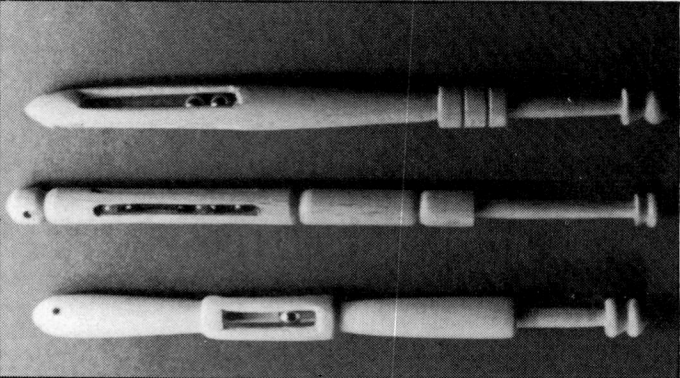

● *The traditional 'lantern' variation on the Midland pattern. These are of beech*

Today deer antler is as expensive as ivory. Far more common is water-buffalo horn. This can vary from black through grey to white. The material heats up and softens while being worked, but with care and patience it can be turned down to fine detail and given a high polish.

The bobbin acts as a spool on which to wind the thread whilst keeping the required tension.

Over the centuries bobbins have changed in shape and size from place to place; such variations are associated with the type of lace being made and the thickness of thread used. The coarsest threads today are the linen threads used in the making of torchon lace. This is sometimes combined in Belgium and Holland with machine-made braid lace. The heavy bulbous bobbins used in these countries are all of the same design on the pillow, and often of the same wood — usually box or beech. So you do not see the same variety as on the English pillow of a worker making fine Bucks point lace. The finer point laces use finer bobbins, and they need extra weight for correct tension. This is achieved by adding gaily coloured beads known as spangles (fig. 1).

Makers of Honiton lace, however, the finest and most prized of all, use very slim unbeaded bobbins which are tapered to fairly sharp points because they frequently have to join one section of a pattern to another by needling — drawing the thread on one bobbin through a fine loop on another part of the design with the aid of a fine needle, and then fixing the join by threading the bobbin and thread through the loop so made.

Some of the earliest bobbins, those of Flemish origin, were quite large — as much as 6in long and 1in in diameter. Some were very plain and others were carved rather than turned. Over the years, bobbins generally became slimmer, and by the early 19th century they had become about the thickness of a pencil and around 8-10cm long. Wide pieces of point lace, such as flounces, might take as many as 1200 bobbins on the pillow at the same time. The Midland type of bobbin, the most widely used in England today, is usually made about 10 or 12cm long; individual teachers and pupils have personal preferences as to thickness. The shank or main body of the Midland bobbin lends itself to decoration, and many traditions have emerged. These bobbins are the only ones to be spangled.

In south Bucks the most popular bobbin, and the nearest in shape to the Flemish, was the thumper, sometimes called the Huguenot. This hung well on the big straw bolster pillows common in the area. Some were decorated with loose rings of pewter known as jingles. The jingles added weight and served to identify the heavy gimp threads which outline a pattern. These bobbins, with their smooth rounded ends, were not beaded, but sometimes a skilled turner or carver would shape the end into an acorn, bell or barrel. Some charming examples of this decoration are being produced in High Wycombe today. Today's lacemakers tend to use just on or two of these heavier bobbins on their pillows at a time to hold the gimp thread.

Even bigger and heavier bobbins known as yaks were used with a coarse wool worsted thread, yak wool. The lace museum at Olney has some excellent examples. With the development of the City and Guilds Creative Textile Course, some of the students at Windsor and Maidenhead College have experimented with bobbins based on rolling-pins when creating large-scale designs with homespun woollen theads. There is also one small area of southern Spain where very large yak-type bobbins are still commonplace.

At the other end of the scale, the Honiton lacemakers demand slim, finely finished bobbins that will not snag or rub the extremely fine cotton threads they use. Since their bobbins are frequently taken on and off the pillow as the design develops and there is much joining of sections, the bobbins require a neat smooth head, a short neck (as only a small amount of thread is wound on at a time) and a fine, smoothly finished tapered point on the shank for easy threading through the work. Only about 6-8cm long, the Honiton bobbin cannot be ornately decorated and is usually left plain; decoration is limited to painting or inscribing.

The workshops of the 18th and 19th centuries were equipped very differently from those of today, but the tools were more than adequate in the hands of a skilled craftsman.

Originally the pole lathe was used. Power was later derived from a treadle, and this arrangement survived in craft workshops until very recently.

Though expensive, the modern electric miniature lathe is capable of running at speeds of 4000 or even 7000rpm. This enables fine work to be produced without any further finishing. Turning tools, however, have always been a problem for the bobbin-maker and miniature turner. Standard tools are inappropriate and it is necessary to adapt existing ones or make them yourself. There are firms which specialise in miniature turning tools, but often these are just scaled-down versions of the full-size product and still not altogether suitable.

I and other bobbin-makers generally make our own tools to individual needs. These are often re-ground or specially shaped chisels; otherwise we produce tools from tool-steel blanks set in turned wooden handles. The steel used today is much harder than that in use a 100 years ago, so the tools need less sharpening and consequently last longer.

The rest of the craftsman's tools are, in the main, conventional. His needs are to cut and roughly shape the blanks for turning and to drill the small hole in the end for the wire on which the spangles are mounted. For drilling the spangle hole and decorative spots, an Archimedian drill was traditionally used; a small, flat spear bit would have been used for the hole and a dome-ended bit for the decoration and lettering. The spots would be coloured by filling with natural pigments. I use a small powered pillar drill with a ¼in capacity.

For rough cutting of blanks before turning, the modern tool is a bandsaw. Again, because bobbin blanks are small, a modestly sized one will suffice.

Some bobbins are cut open to be fitted with a tiny bobbin inside. To do this by hand requires a skill only achieved with experience. The bobbins were held on the lathe and cut by hand with a knife, then indexed and cut again at 90° intervals. Today this can be done using a tiny circular saw — or, as I prefer, by mortise-slotting with a milling attachment on the lathe.

There are several methods for producing wooden bobbins; all rely on a rotating blank in a lathe. The most common uses a standard woodturning lathe, the various shaping tools being manipulated by hand to cut the blank to shape. Methods of chucking vary between bobbin-makers; some use a two- or four-pronged centre at the headstock, with a dead or live centre in the tailstock. Others simply use a pair of cone chucks with the tailstock running live. I use a cone at the headstock and a dead centre at the tailstock. This enables me to minimise wastage because I can use a shorter blank.

Other turners tell me they use conventional Jacobs or collet chucks, but in my experience these need the blank to be of accurate diameter before turning, and I find they always work loose during turning.

Once the blank is held firmly in the lathe it has to be revolved, and this is where the first practical problem arises. For miniature turning with these small diameters very high speeds are required to achieve a proper cutting rate. I estimate that for a workpiece of 5-7mm diameter the rotational speed should be around 15,000rpm. This is impossible on a standard woodturning lathe because of the type of bearings used, and not many engineering lathes can manage it either. The best you can do is run your lathe at its highest speed — usually around 3000-rpm — and keep your tools very sharp. Even then, with the coarser-grained woods, some papering will be needed.

To shape the square blank into a round bobbin requires four basic tools. These are: a shallow 20mm straight-ended gouge for roughing down to a round section. Next, a 13mm skew chisel; instead of the conventional bevel on both sides, this is ground with a bevel on one side only. This modification is to ease the task of smoothing the rough-turned blank — the standard tool cannot be used at the correct angle with work this size. A secondary advantage is that it is easier to use with one hand; at various stages of bobbin-making it is essential to have one hand free to support the work.

The third tool is another gouge, a 6mm round-nosed type. This is used for decorative shaping along the body of the bobbin. But the last of the four is probably the most important: a 4mm square-ended chisel, again ground on one side only. There is a further reason for this non-standard shape; it takes the place of three different tools — the parting tool, the square-end scraper, and a small chisel.

Most bobbins can be turned using these four tools, although specials (such as bobbins with loose rings on the body and bobbins with unusually shaped grooves) need special tools. I often make such tools for casual or short-run work from masonry nails set in wooden handles and ground to shape.

With a blank fixed to the lathe, you first rough it down to a cylinder of about 8mm diameter and smooth it off with the large chisel to 6 or 7mm.

Next, using the 4mm chisel, round off at the tailstock end — without removing too much wood, otherwise the tailstock centre may not hold the blank. Using the 4mm chisel on its side as a parting tool, mark out the position of the neck and body on the blank.

Working from the headstock, round off the tail of the bobbin, but take care not to cut too deeply. Later on the bobbin will be parted at this point. Going further along, the body can now be shaped to a specific design, left plain or decorated as required.

The neck has to be left last because it weakens the blank. Cutting the neck can be done in several ways; I shall describe two. Either the gouge is used to remove most of the wood and finally the corners scraped out, or the small chisel is used to cut into the ends of the neck before the waste is removed. Whilst the neck is being cut the bobbin is at its most vulnerable to breaking, so I use the second method because it leaves me with a hand free to support the workpiece from behind.

All that now remains to be done is the head. There is a wide variety of shapes for this. Many bobbin-makers use the head shape as a trade mark. However, it does need a smooth groove around it, in which the lacemaker makes a half-hitch to stop her thread from unwinding. The exception is the Honiton bobbin, whose very small head means that the half-hitch must be made on the neck.

The bobbin may need a light sanding before being burnished, polished and parted off. Polishing is much easier while the bobbin is still turning on the lathe, but this does depend on the polish. Turners use various waxes and friction polishes, or they just burnish with wood shavings. Others use french polishes, polyurethanes and recipes of their own.

Part the bobbin off and then drill the hole to hold the spangle. This hole should not be larger than 1.5mm in diameter, and is located no more than 6mm from the end of the bobbin.

---

**R**oger Holley writes: 200 years ago bobbin-making was a thriving industry practised by both individuals and firms. Many tools were improvised by the bobbin-maker — the archimedian drill, screw box, angled scraper and narrow parting tool. Each maker produced traditional patterns of bobbin, but usually incorporated a design feature of his own. Many bobbins were heavily decorated with coloured dyes, stains, brass and copper wire, tinsel, pewter, and glass beads. The bobbins used in the west country for traditional Honiton lace are quite plain compared to the more elaborate design. Many inlaid and decorated pieces were also carved, and some had inscriptions on them for good measure. Many romantic traditions became connected with bobbins. Some were given to newly-weds as love tokens, and others commemorated religious events — even historic ones, such as elections. Bobbins often acquired expressive names, too. Tigers and leopards, for instance, are bobbins with strips or spots of inlaid pewter. A butterfly has inlaid decorations on the shank, in the form of an arrowhead or butterfly (Fig. 2).

Makers contrived many other ways to elaborate on their designs. They turned bobbins with hollow shanks, which when pulled out revealed a miniature bobbin attached to the tail part — a cow and calf (fig. 3). Beside it in the illustration is a similar design with a two-part hollow shank which separates to release a loose miniature bobbin known as a jack-in-the-box. The two other examples are a Mother and Babe, which is a miniature bobbin enclosed in a pierced shank, and the church-window

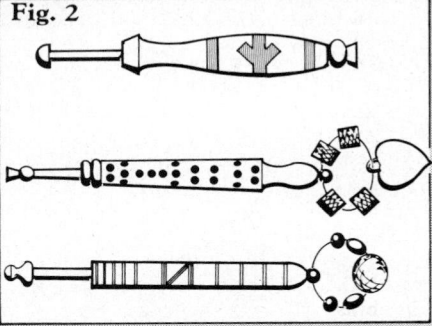

Fig. 2

type, which simply has empty pierced openings.

Another common design feature was to incorporate a loose wooden or pewter ring, turned or cast captive on the bobbin. This is known as a jingle. I'll describe the method of turning one a little later.

The tools were varied, but sometimes included a wooden block — drilled to take a bobbin — and a metal cutter. This screw-box arrangement I have used in fig. 4, to

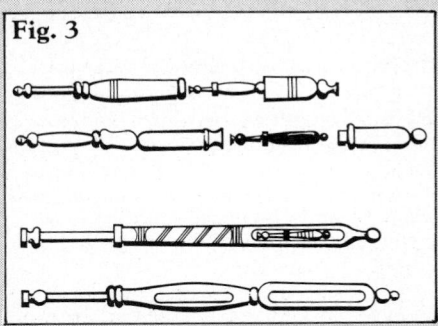

Fig. 3

produce the spiral decoration shown. The cutter I use is an old drill ground to a skew-chisel point.

Although traditional bobbin materials were box, apple, pear, holly and cherry, at the turn of this century there was mass production in beech and birch. Bone bobbins came mainly from the bigger animals such as working horses, mature fat beef cattle and mutton, which made it relatively easy to find raw material thick enough in section. For my own bobbins I asked the butcher for the largest shin from the hind leg of beef. I bandsawed the two knuckle ends off (the dog did better out of this bit than I did!), then cut the straight piece of bone into strips. Having cleaned out the marrow, I boiled them for a couple of hours and let them dry.

Wooden bobbins are easier to practise on, though, and here I am using ⅜in squares of boxwood, about 4½-5in long. They are mounted either directly into a morse-taper sleeve in the headstock of the machine or into a hardwood chuck drilled out to take the squares, slightly tapered as in fig. 5.

**S**tart turning by roughing out square to round with a ¾in gouge, as in fig. 6. This size of tool looks formidable for a delicate job but serves the purpose well. Then carefully form the 'thistle' shape on the short neck and head as in fig. 7, using a parting tool like the one I have ground from an old file. This tool serves well to shape the collar if you rock it gently from left to right and use the corners left and right to simulate the action of a chisel (fig. 8).

To shape the shank I suggest you use a

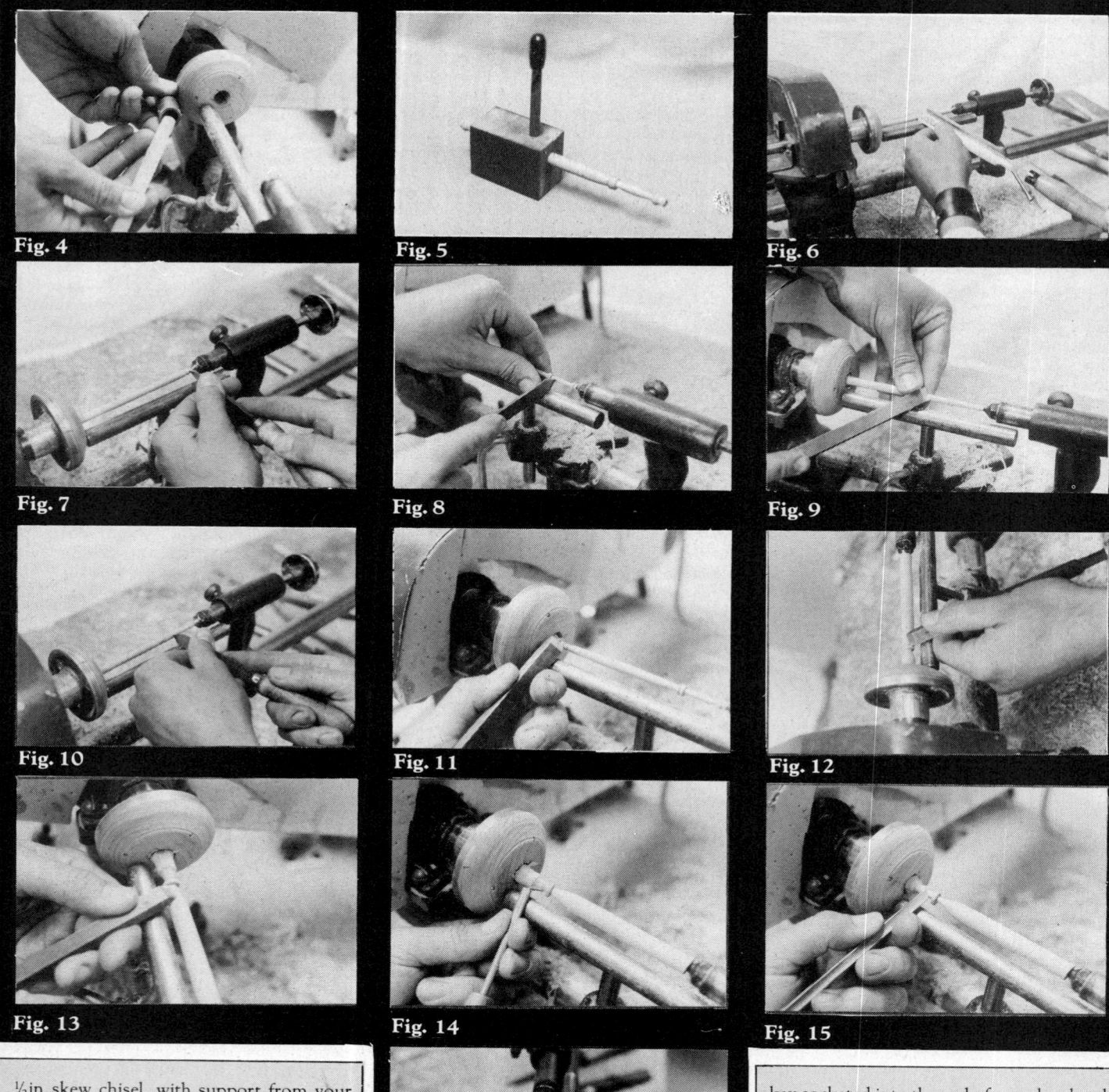

Fig. 4

Fig. 5

Fig. 6

Fig. 7

Fig. 8

Fig. 9

Fig. 10

Fig. 11

Fig. 12

Fig. 13

Fig. 14

Fig. 15

Fig. 16

½in skew chisel, with support from your hand behind the workpiece to stop vibration (fig. 9). Fig. 10 shows the narrow parting tool reducing the neck diameter. This is a delicate operation since a dig-in or vibration will snap the bobbin, so take it steadily. The final operation of parting off is best done with the long point of the ½in skew — fig. 11. If the whole process sounds and appears simple, that's because it is! The difficulties that may arise initially will probably come from getting used to working in a delicate section of wood. Don't be tempted to speed the machine above 1500rpm; it won't help. Concentrate on practice.

A jingle is initially turned as a small bead, using a skew chisel (fig. 12). The depth below the bead is then increased with a small gouge or skew chisel to allow access under the bead as in fig. 13. The special tool used in fig. 14 is simply an old small allen

● Basic procedures are clearly illustrated in these photos for the benefit of would-be bobbin turners. The blanks are ⅜in boxwood. Note the screw-box, the taper of the blank for chucking, and the ground Allen key for undercutting the jingle – all mentioned in the text

key socketed into the end of a steel rod and ground to a point. This enables the undercutting and eventual cut-off of the bead when it is used alternately left and right. The area in which the jingle floats can then be cleaned up with a gouge as in fig. 15.

For turning bone the same tools as for wood can be used, but take extra care because it can be very brittle. Fig. 16 shows the roughing gouge turning up a square of raw material.

The finished pieces can be decorated and embellished with dyes, wire and beads. The bead spangle can be made from old necklaces or even seashells; its purpose is merely to stop the bobbin turning over and undoing its thread on the lace-pillow. Bobbins can be dyed using organic materials such as tree bark and cochineal. Experiment with your own ideas and help develop a contemporary style to continue this long-established craft. ∎

KINDLY MENTION 'WOODWORKER' WHEN REPLYING TO ADVERTISEMENTS

# Joinery for profit

## Lawrence Russell shows how to lay out a machine shop for maximum efficiency

The plan depicts a small joinery-manufacturing unit which I ran very successfully between 1950 and 1970. The economic situation was very different then: it was a time of comparatively full employment and a buoyant market — but the benefits of efficient production methods never change.

I designed the shop and machine layout to operate profitably with a small workforce, and it performed very well. Competent and reliable joiners were not easy to come by, and even apprentices were a problem; I never employed more than three or four people, and often there was only myself, one man and one apprentice. But we always showed a good profit at the end of the year. My bread-and-butter line was replacement windows, which use largely standard timber sections and

production processes. I am convinced that I was able to keep quality up and price down by careful setting out of the workshop so that wastage of time, effort and timber was always at a minimum.

The timber was bought in standard lots and stacked and skidded under shed — a few yards from the main workshop sliding doors, which could be slid open for the admission of timber to each individual machine. The standard window-framing was usually produced from 6×2½in red deal. The first operation was to bring the

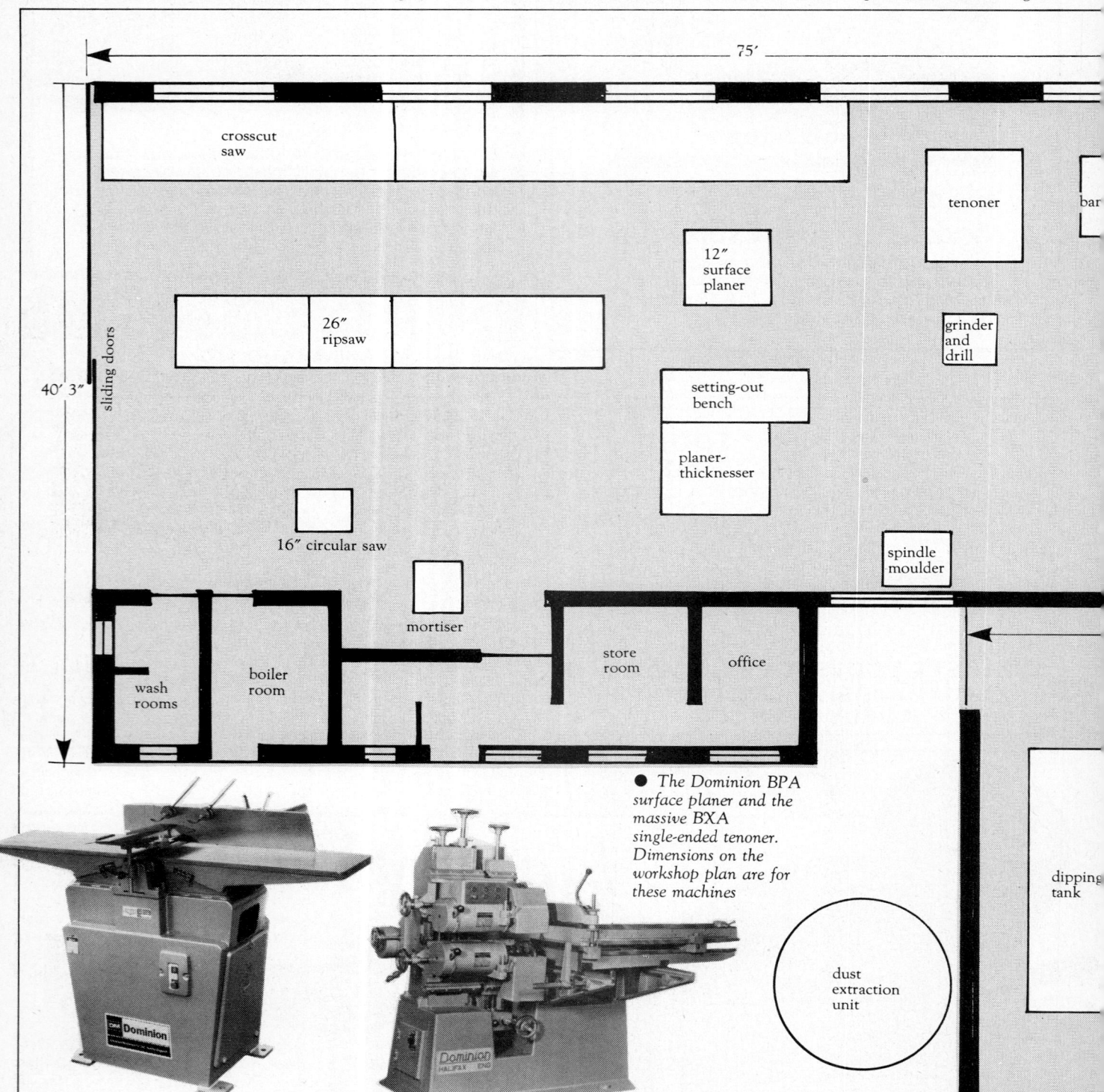

75'

40' 3"

sliding doors

crosscut saw

12" surface planer

26" ripsaw

tenoner

bar

grinder and drill

setting-out bench

planer-thicknesser

16" circular saw

spindle moulder

mortiser

store room

office

wash rooms

boiler room

dipping tank

● *The Dominion BPA surface planer and the massive BXA single-ended tenoner. Dimensions on the workshop plan are for these machines*

dust extraction unit

planks in, place them on the crosscut bench and cut them to length.

They were then handed across to the sawbench and ripped up the middle, and then back on to the top end of the crosscut sawbench behind the planer. This meant that the operator could then pick up each piece, surface one side and one edge, and hand it on to the setting-out bench close by.

The setting-out bench was, in fact, the focal point of the whole operation. From here each piece was put through the thicknesser and brought to width and thickness — then handed back to the setting-out bench, where it was marked for mortising and tenoning. From then onwards the job progressed automatically:

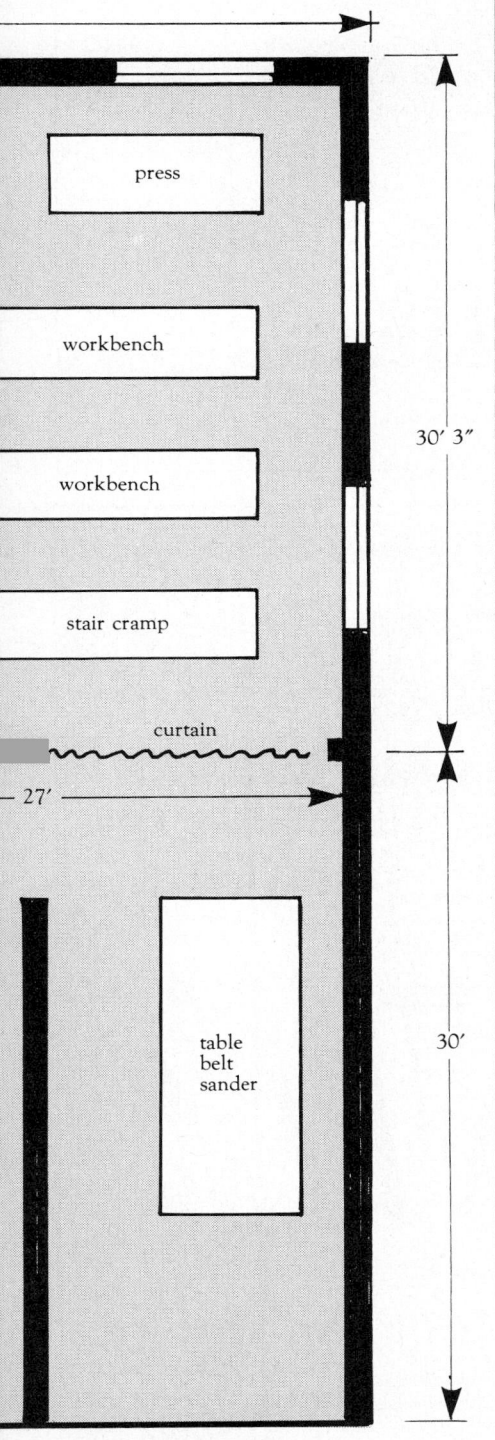

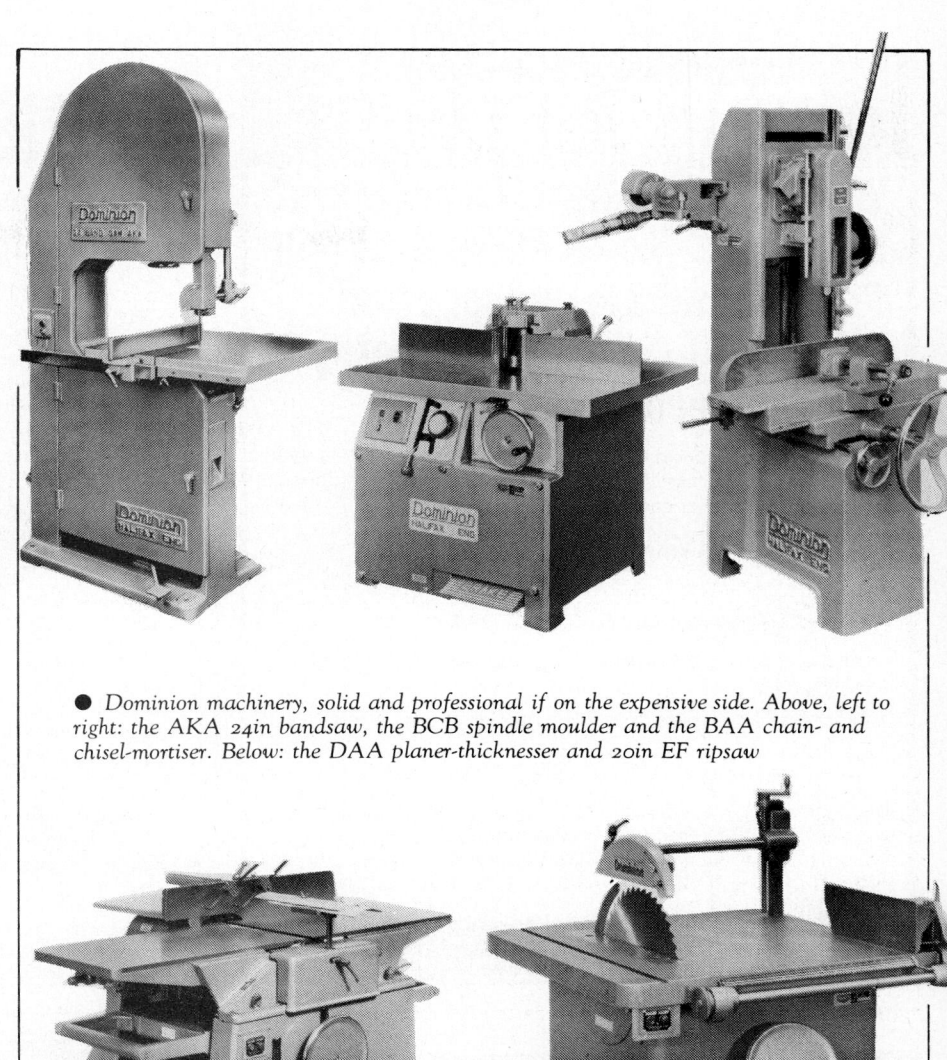

● *Dominion machinery, solid and professional if on the expensive side. Above, left to right: the AKA 24in bandsaw, the BCB spindle moulder and the BAA chain- and chisel-mortiser. Below: the DAA planer-thicknesser and 20in EF ripsaw*

across to the mortiser, then to the tenoner and the spindle moulder, and finally up to the workbenches for assembly.

The 16in sawbench was excellently placed for cutting sheet materials. The sliding doors could be opened for the sheets to be brought in, placed behind the sawbench, and cut to size at will. The saw is also well situated for the production of small beads and fillets for use with the joinery components, and for mitre cutting.

The 12in planer is well placed for surfacing timber as it leaves the sawbench, also for handing across to the thicknesser for planing to the finished thickness. The single-ended tenoner is away from the wall, to allow access to the end of the machine for cleaning and servicing.

The grinder and drill is well placed for the boring of joinery parts, although this machine must be arranged so that its top is lower than the top of the sliding table on the tenoner.

The 26in ripsaw is well placed for the deep cutting of planks up to 9in for the production of staircase materials, which are often in short supply from timber merchants.

The bandsaw is in close proximity to the workbenches. This is often useful to for cutting small pieces of material for use in the assembly of joinery components.

In today's economical turmoil there is a place for small production units of this type. With such a set-up three or four like-minded people can join forces to establish a small but profitable business. I can say from 25 years' experience that the layout I have shown takes a lot of beating.

My layout shows only machines made by Dominion, for the simple reason that when I wrote to them for information they promptly forwarded a full complement of illustrated leaflets. I found the material very useful and informative, and their products appear to be excellent value.

● Dominion Machinery Co. Ltd, Denholmgate Rd, Hipperholme, Halifax, West Yorks HX3 8JG, tel. (0422) 202258. ■

49

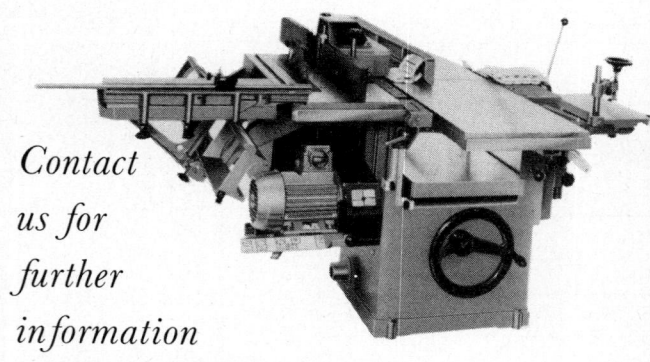
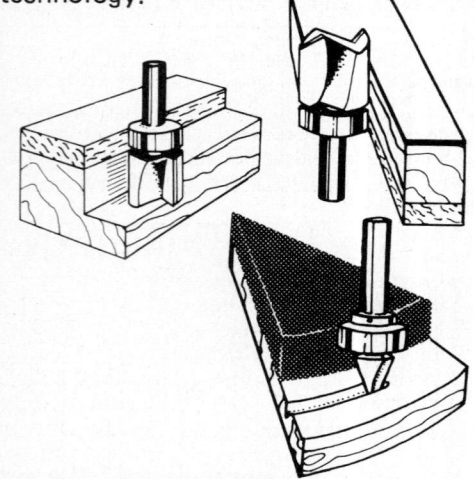
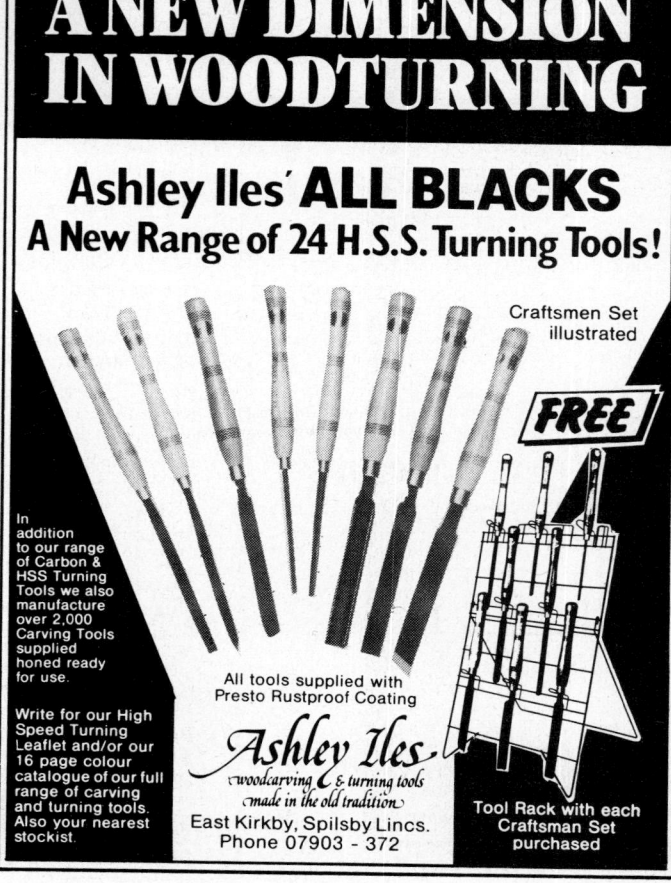
50

Prices quoted are those prevailing at press-date and are subject to alteration due to economic conditions.

# WOOD SUPPLIERS

# WOOD SUPPLIERS

52

# The soft option

Vic Taylor starts to reveal
the contents of many a
woodworker's closed book

**W**ith the possible exception of polishes and laquer finishes, probably the greatest recent advances in furniture materials have been for upholstery, particularly cushioning.

30 years ago traditional methods using webbing, cone springs and various stuffing and covering materials were still going strong, but were rapidly being superseded by spring units. These were sets of springs riveted to a framework of metal laths, which was made to specified dimensions and screwed in place. Now these have been ousted in turn by latex and plastic foams, both of which are capable of being used in several ways.

The various modern methods of support for both seat and back cushions are 1) tension (or cable) springs, 2) sinuous wire springs (also called surpentine or zigzag springs) and 3) rubber webbing. A fourth involves stretching a rubber-sheet platform on to the seat frame, but it calls for special equipment and is recommended for use by professionals only. Although it is usual to use the same method of springing for both seat and back, this is not an inviolable rule, and there is no reason why you should not mix methods and use those that serve your purpose best. For instance, you could employ tension springs for the seat and rubber webbing for the back.

Beginning, then, with tension springs. A typical specimen is shown at B, fig. 1; typical, that is, except for the fact that those you buy will almost always be fitted with plastic sleeves which prevent the metal of the spring from marking the cushion cover. If you have some springs which are bare metal you can still use them, but you will have to make a fabric cover as shown in fig. 1(A); basically this consists of a piece of calico, canvas or similar fabric with sleeves sewn at either end which are slipped over the outside springs so that the fabric is stretched tightly over the intervening ones.

There are two diameters of tension springs, ½in (13mm) for seat springs and ⅜in (10mm) for back springs. They are made in various lengths; to determine what length you will need, allow 1½-2in (38-51mm) for expansion — thus an 18in (457mm) long spring can be expanded to span a maximum of 20in (508mm). The distance from spring to spring should not be less than 2½in (64mm) centre to centre, and a useful average spacing would be about 3in (76mm).

Now we come to methods of fixing. There are three, as shown at C, D and E in fig. 1. In C the hooks of the springs engage in holes drilled in metal fixing laths which are screwed to the wooden frame. Usually you can buy these laths, ready-drilled, where you buy the springs. This is a widely used method, but the drawback is that the hooks tend to grind in their holes when any weight is put on the springs. Make sure the

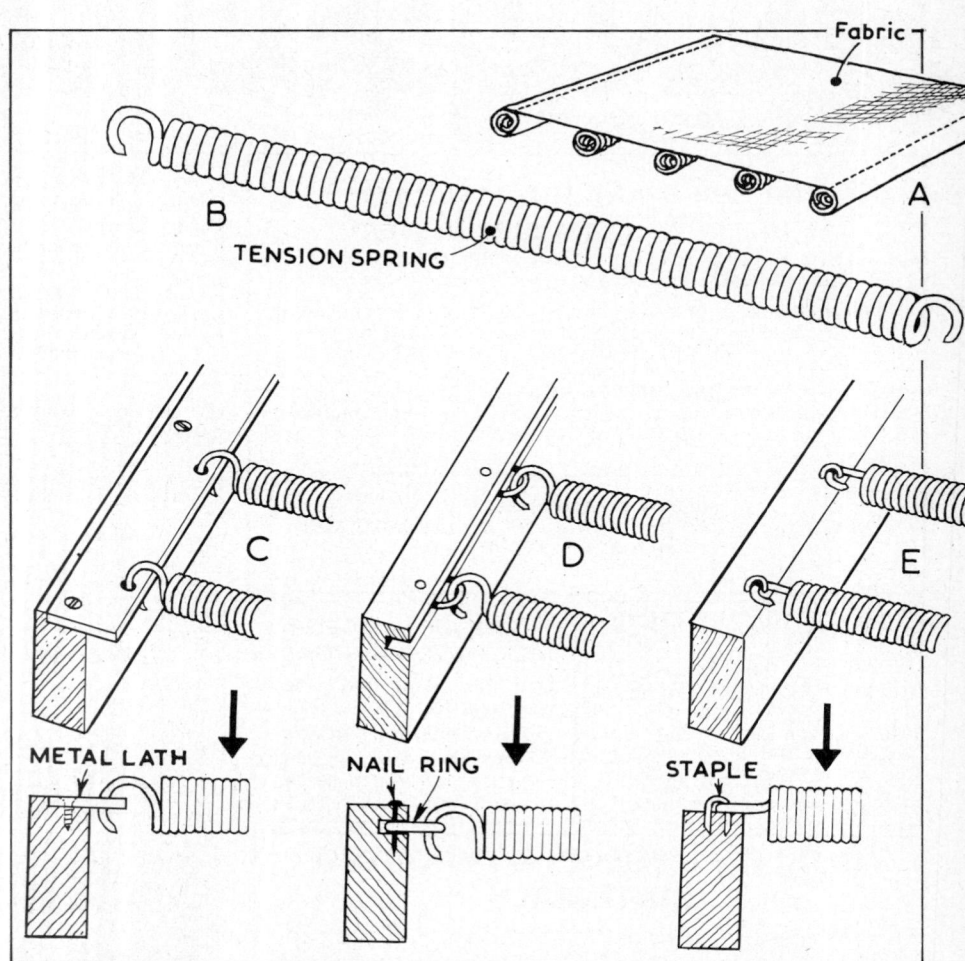

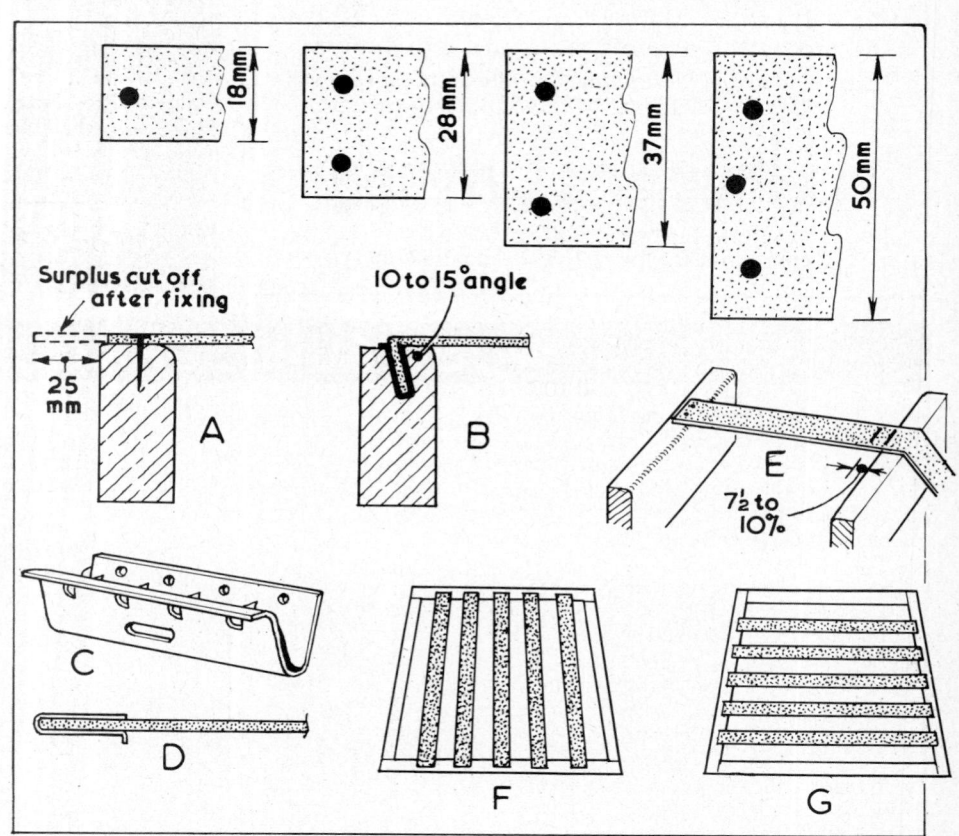

points of the hooks are pointing downwards — it's not difficult to imagine the damage the hook points can do to the cushion fabric if they are left pointing upwards. This also applies to method D.

A neat procedure is the one which entails cutting a groove on the inside edge of the rail near the top (D). Rings are inserted in this groove, one for each spring, and secured by nailing; the hooks of the springs then engage through the rings and the whole thing looks very professional. There are a couple of points to watch for, though; one is that you need strong rings which can withstand the considerable strain without breaking or distorting. The other is that the height of the springs under tension will probably be below the level of the surrounding wooden frame, which means that the underside of the cushion could be marked. It may also be possible to feel the hard edge of the frame through the cushion.

The third method (E) has the virtue of simplicity and little else. It is obvious that the points of the hooks may damage the underside of the cushion; another objection is that the constant pulling strain on the staples can cause the edge of the frame rail to be sheared off. All in all, my favourite method is the one at C, and it is also the one employed by many manufacturers.

Sinuous or serpentine springing is comparatively new and the way it is fixed is shown in fig. 2. You can buy it in cut lengths or in 100ft coils, and in various gauges — the thicker the gauge, the more suitable for heavy work. Its most common use is for dining-chair seats, although the thicker gauges may be used for armchairs, etc. The only point to note is that the fixing clip should overhang the rail by a minimum of 3mm as shown at A, fig. 2.

The third method of providing support is by using rubber webbing. This is made in four widths — 18mm (¾in), 28mm (1⅛in), 37mm (1½in) and 50mm (2in) (fig. 3). Which width you choose depends on the job you want it for; the thin 18mm webbing would be suitable for a small stool, and if 'checked' (that is, interlaced) it could be fitted to a dining-chair. Generally, however, the 28mm webbing is used for this purpose and the lengths are arranged in either of the two ways shown in fig. 3 F and G. The 37 and 50mm webbings are used for the backs and seats respectively of armchairs and settees.

You will need to consider two factors when you are fitting the webbing. One is the length each web needs to be to allow for tensioning; allow between 7½ and 10%, so that a distance of 381mm (15in) would need a webbing length of 343mm (13½in) to span it. The other factor is the distance between one web and the next; the rule of thumb here is that the distance should not be much more than the width of the webbing being used.

Finally we have to consider the various ways of fixing the webbing. The simplest way is with tacks; you will see in fig. 3 the number to use and their positioning. Don't be tempted to use more than the recommended number, as too many can cause the webbing to fray under constant flexing in use. You will see from A that it's a good idea to allow a surplus of about 25mm (1in) when fixing, cutting off after tacking

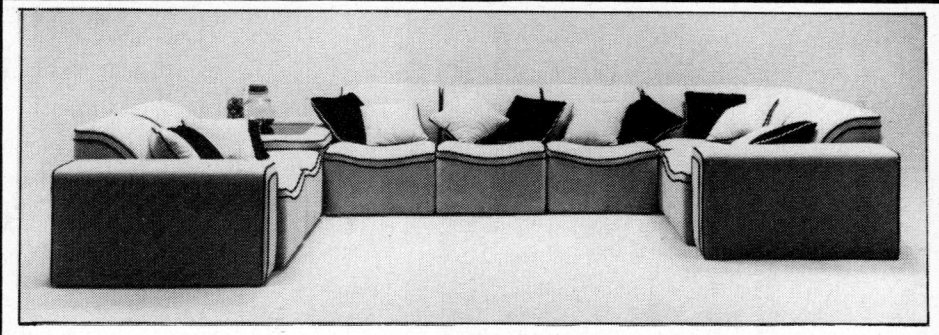

● *These two strikingly up-to-the minute designs ('Wave', above, and 'Laguna' below) come from the north London works of HK Furniture, a style-conscious medium-sized company. Their techniques typify the modern approach. Blocks of foam are bought in, already cut to shape, and given Dacron wraps to reduce friction beneath the covering. Often they are supported by springs or webbing in the ways Vic Taylor describes here. Frames are usually beech, dowelled and PVA-glued, but hardboard, plywood and chipboard also make their appearance. Coverings are fixed with staples and glue*

has been completed to prevent the webbing from splitting. Note also that the inside edge of the frame rail should be rounded off to avoid any possibility of its cutting into the webbing — this applies to both methods of fixing.

The neatest and best way to fix the webbing is shown at B and C, fig. 3. It involves cutting a groove in the rail at an angle of 10-15°; the groove size is 12mm (½in) deep by 7mm (⁵⁄₃₂in) wide, and this should accept the special clip C. These clips can be bought at the same time as the

webbing, and pressed on to the ends of the webbing in an ordinary woodworking vice.

You can experiment with the widths of webbing and the tension applied — thus, in the seat of, say, a fireside chair, the webbing can run from side to side with narrow strips at the front to give a soft edge and wider ones at the back where the weight falls. Or you can interlace the strips at the back and not the front, which gives the same effect; it is possible to work out a combination to suit most seating requirements you are likely to meet. ■

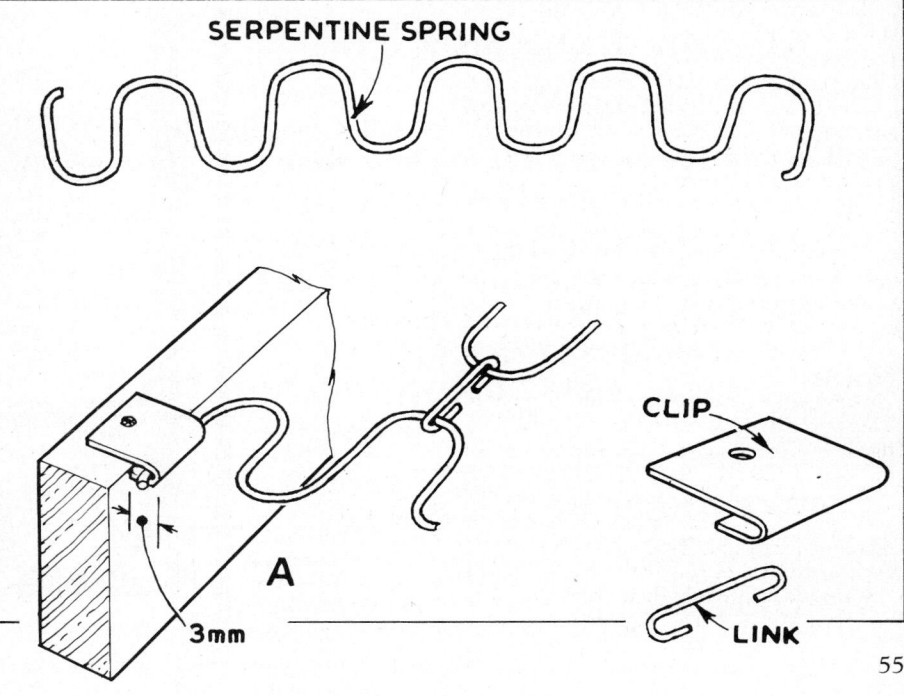

SERPENTINE SPRING

CLIP

LINK

A

3mm

Prices quoted are those prevailing at press date and are
subject to alteration due to economic conditions.

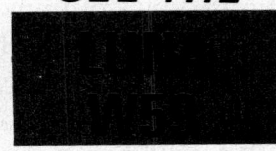
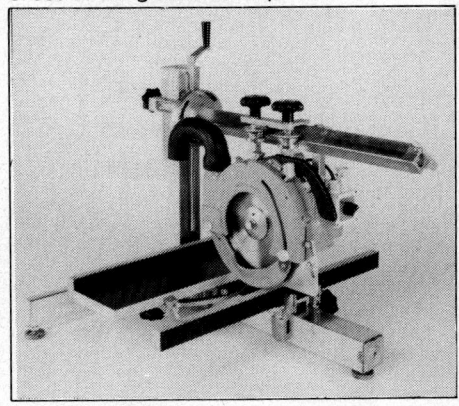
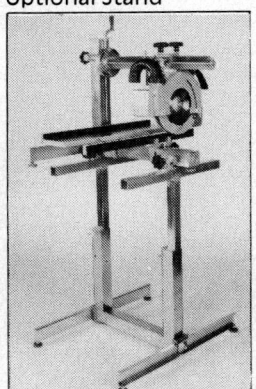
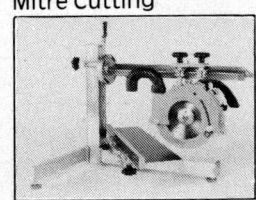

# Design takes its stand

Luke Hughes visited the furniture trade's big Style 84 exhibition — but what caught his eye were the lively student displays

What a breath of fresh air! What talent to look forward to, and how interesting to see all the furniture colleges next to each other.

The Style 84 show at Earl's Court was the first major all-British furniture exhibition ever held, and it had a special section devoted to furniture from 16 of the UK's design colleges and polytechnics. Each college displayed four or five pieces made by students in the academic year 1983/4; the occasion presented a unique opportunity to look at these colleges, their students, and the work they feel best represents them. An award in memory of Sir Gordon Russell (the design of which must have the great man's remains turning at 78rpm) was presented by Patrick Jenkin, Secretary of State for the Environment, to the college with the best display. Leicester Polytechnic have now to find somewhere to hang the wretched thing.

The show's principal exhibitors were the big brand names in furniture, but their showing unfortunately brought home how ugly and flat most British furniture is. Plasticated finishes, highlighted tints in stains, mock Tudor, Dralon, foam, mock brass hinges, Regency chairs scaled down by a third, shag-pile carpets and souvenir ashtrays . . . it's hardly surprising that, as the

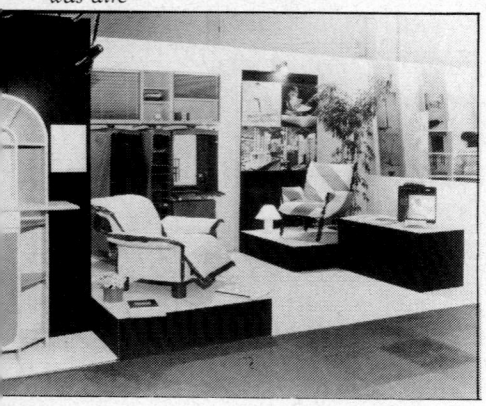

● Bucks College (above) and Leicester Poly's stands. Some of the other colleges' promotion was dire

● A laminated beech frame is the basis for this production prototype chair. Note the knockdown joint fittings

● Sinuous and sculptural, if not ergonomic – a chaise longue that pushes lamination to the limit and beyond

● Ash veneers and blue-stained beech cylinders are the elements of this geometrical cabinet. The top two panels are doors

organisers efficiently informed me, the British share of the home furniture market is declining annually by 3%, and that the 1983 deficit between imports and exports was £230m. Let's face it, the furniture-buying British public have better taste than the furniture-selling fraternity — so they buy from abroad.

So congratulations to the organisers for giving the colleges the opportunity, and congratulations to the colleges on some very commendable work. Almost without exception, the furniture was well made. The exception will know who she is; a little label on an otherwise beautiful piece bore the words 'Please do not touch — exhibition model only'. This is unlikely to instil confidence in the visitor!

Overall impression from the student scene were that pale woods with pastel-tinted details are still in; so are stripes, especially diagonals. And basic geometric shapes are still voguish too — triangles, squares, cones, cylinders, etc.; I think this comes from the current teaching that furniture should be sculptural. Sculpture in furniture and architecture really means geometry, unless you're Michelangelo, or you're going to be as bold as the Memphis exhibitors in Milan a few years ago. It's interesting to reflect that, although the Memphis display provoked heaps of abuse at the time, its influence is clear today even in some of the most delightful pieces.

The colleges whose work stood out in my mind were Kingston Poly, Rycotewood, Leicester Poly, and Parnham in Dorset. Most of the presentations were excellent (and a show like this is a chance in a million

● Kingston Poly's Jane Rawson used Colorcore for this cabinet, inspired by classical Italian façades and Tuscan colour

**Peter Collenette** writes: Aside from the colleges' remarkable spread, only two stands in the whole show impressed with their innovative spirit amid the massed grey ranks of the industry. Neither has much to offer the traditionalist — but both made up for their isolation with striking designs and a warm welcome.

The first was Flat Furniture, run by Richard Newnham. This outfit produces (from a yard in Kilburn, London) small batches which are mostly in the near-obligatory materials of the moment: medium-density fibreboard, and pale hardwoods such as sycamore and ash. Their self-assembly designs are tailored, one hopes not too optimistically, to production by computerised overhead router. But the firm's major asset is an eye-opening range of glossy, glittering, lustrous, multicoloured sprayed lacquer finishes; developed by an associate enterprise across the yard, the futuristically named Aerographic Wood Finishing, these are available to other furniture producers too.

The other stand-out was the two-person firm of Planks Design, responsible for the pleasing segmental tables grouped on this month's cover. Director Gina Tajirian convincingly explained the rather rough finish on the show model with vivid tales of last-minute production — a rush aggravated by the organisers' sudden gift of extra space equal to the area Planks had already hired. But, say Gina and her partner Edward Richards, their initial nerves were

more than overcome: not only by a heartening volume of good enquiries which kept them busy all the time, but also by the cordial interest they experienced from their fellow-exhibitors at the 'heavy end' of the industry.

Gina trained at Middlesex Poly, where Edward currently teaches. Planks, another north-London enterprise, functions from the basement car park of a Kentish Town block of flats — part converted by the council into a series of small workshops. Their only machines are a Startrite table saw (with sliding extension) and planer-thicknesser. To an even greater extent than Flat Furniture, the pair have set their sights firmly on producing designs and prototypes for production by others. They have sickened (perhaps more quickly than most other small firms) of turning out kitchens, and even such unusual commissions as the conversion of a casualty ambulance into a mobile home have failed to divert them from seeking fame and a market on the international design scene.

They devote a lot of time to refining their designs — and, significantly, to photographing them. This latter emphasis ensured that their coloured table appeared in the show catalogue and in *Cabinet Maker* magazine. In fact, their recent endeavours could hardly form a clearer example of the publicity openings available even to the tiniest firms. The media (*Woodworker* included!) will always jump at something new; so the coverage often goes to those with pluck.

● *Gina Tajirian designed and made this coffee-table in brown oak and sycamore. Extensions of the pale strips to form the rectangular pattern for the legs give it a slightly Japanese austerity*

to sell yourself, so presentation is crucial), but Leicester, Buckinghamshire College and the London College of Furniture excelled themselves. In some cases, other colleges infuriatingly gave no credits for the work on show. This is foolish. I suppose the head of department felt the work shown represented the college and not just the individual — but, if that was his logic, it is false logic. Individuals should never be dissociated from their creations.

As for individual contributions, much attention was rightly lavished on a walnut settee by Lucie McCann of Kingston. It was elegant, refined, sound, and it had a joke — three neo-classical porticos ranged along the back. Also from Kingston, Francesca Graham displayed a dressing-table in solid plane and lacewood veneer with marbled papers lining the drawers; it passed a test in being obviously modern yet functional and adaptable to most environments. Again at Kingston, Jane Rawson designed a glorified neo-classical ice-cream cupboard, most interesting for the use of Colorcore, a new plastic laminate from Formica that has colour all the way through instead of on just one surface. Something is brewing at Kingston: three women, three neo-classical pieces. Watch for next year's instalment.

Another name to watch is Jonathan Baulkwill from Ravensbourne College of Art; he submitted a gentleman's dressing-table which was very chic, and especially useful in presenting maximum clothes storage in the minimum space. He also had an extending table in sycamore which won an award at the show (apparently a spur-of-the-moment gesture by a manufacturer impressed with student efforts and achievements). From Parnham, Andrew

● *Leicester Poly were fortunate enough to win this*

Klimacki displayed a desk in English oak that doubled as a dining-table. This was one of the most ingenious and versatile designs in the show. Also from Parnham, a rocking-chair by Robin Williams was very satisfying

● *Lucie McCann's walnut settee – cheeky, but the work is first-class*

— and, it appears, has earned him many orders (but why, both of you, do you not have good photographs to give me? They'd be published by now). Another interesting piece was a carved mirror by Tessa Howes of Brighton.

It was very encouraging to see that the designers now emerging are of a completely different calibre to those producing the rubbish that makes up the statistics of the 'furniture industry'. They are slick, professional, energetic and imaginative; and, what's more, most of their work displays a good understanding of batch production. This augurs well, so long as they keep up the momentum. However, I would recommend that each student make much more individual effort to sell him-or-herself; if the college won't pay, get your own publicity organised. Have some photographs to hand, get some handouts of your own. For an investment of £100 or so you will have publicity material to see you through this and many other exhibitions.

For those who complain about seeing the same names at craft shows, I'd say: Hoist this lot aboard and give them all the help you can. To the editor of *Woodworker*, I say: Let's try to have a stand at Style 85 alongside the colleges — showing work from readers of *Woodworker* who don't have the benefit of a college behind them. There are many who have excellent ideas but lack the facilities to put them in front of buyers. Let's see new ideas, new faces, new names; because there are a lot about.

● Information on Style 85 from Amanda Clarke or Dominic Lyle, Cameron Choat & Partners, 9 Walton St, London SW3 2JD, tel. 01-589 8292. ■

# Guild notes

## Guild of WOODWORKERS

Shared information, advice and help are vital to good woodwork. They are also the basis of the **Guild of Woodworkers**: an international organisation which welcomes new members — whatever their skills. PO Box 35, Hemel Hempstead HP2 4SS (phone 0442 41221).

Guild members get
- priority on our courses
- free publicity in *Woodworker*
- 15% off Woodworker Show entry
- a free display area and meeting-point at the Show
- 15% discount on our plans
- access to and inclusion in our register of members' skills and services
- the chance to contact other members for help and advice where appropriate
- specially arranged tool inrance at low rates

Please quote your Guild number when contacting us.

*Aidan Walker*

## Taking Stock

Everybody thanked everybody else at the Show, but who thanked you? I want to say how much I enjoyed meeting you all, and how useful it was for me — and for the Guild, because getting your ideas face to face is really what it's all about. Here's where you yourselves start putting in some of the work . . .

## Local Reps

Mentioned last month, this is an idea I now want to launch officially. We are an association which can and should have a social function; the benefits of meeting are obvious. Woodcarvers' evenings, co-operative use of workshop equipment and space, turning tips picked up over a cup of coffee or a pint, the enjoyment of just meeting people who share the same interests . . . unless you all get to meet each other, how will the Guild really function as such?

We need local representatives to cover the country, whose names can be printed, prepared to act as a focus for Guild members in their area. They will have a list of members in their vicinity, and will be able to put enquirers in touch with them.

## COURSE CORNER

### Woodmachining — Ken Taylor

The Guild of Woodworkers' first-ever one-day introductory course in woodmachining will be held in London on February 9th. You will be able to get a grip on the basic techniques of the bandsaw, circular saw, radial arm saw, planer/thicknesser and spindle moulder. It will cover safety, planning the work, understanding the principles of each machine, and actually getting your hands on it and having a go. You should leave at the end of the day with a set of notes, a good idea of what proper machines will do, and solid information on how to choose them for yourself — particularly a universal.

Ken Taylor got his City and Guilds in woodmachining in the 1940s; from building Mosquito fighter aeroplanes to

An initial group meeting, which again can be advertised on this page, will lead to more; different people can host such meetings on a turn-by-turn basis. The whole point is to have real local communities of members. If you are interested in taking on this task for your area initially, please get in touch with me. Once something like this gets going, it will have its own momentum — but we need a members' representative for each area.

Now's the time to pick up that 'phone!

works manager of Wrighton Kitchens, his career in the trade speaks for itself. He now lectures in Woodmachining Technology at the London College of Furniture. Definitely of the 'what he doesn't know isn't worth knowing' variety! The course costs £25.00+VAT, and is from 9.30 to 5.30. Send a cheque, quoting your Guild number, to book your place — don't delay, numbers are limited. If you aren't a member of the Guild but want to go on the course, don't despair; enquire now, there may be some places for non-members.

### Country Chairmaking — Fred Lambert

This magnificent pile is Pull Court near Tewkesbury, the venue for the first of what we hope will be a series of Fred Lambert courses on all the aspects of this specialised and fascinating craft. Over five days, from April 1st-5th 1985, you will be introduced

to the use of the traditional timbers, ash and elm; to using developed traditional tools, the rotary planes; to understanding and using the special drawings and jigs, and to setting out the work. The course is suitable for both beginners and more experienced people, and, astonishingly, needs no woodworking knowledge. You will leave at the end of the week with a piece of country furniture that you have made yourself — and, without a doubt, you'll be itching to come back for the toolmaking and stage 2 steam bending and jig-making courses. It costs £145.00+VAT, which will include excellent lunches, and the day will also be 9.30-5.30.

● For both these, and all other Guild courses, booking is by cheque, made payable to the Guild of Woodworkers, for the full amount. The cheques are held until there are enough people, then banked — or returned if the course is full. This is for ease of administration.

## STOP PRESS
## Finishing and Polishing Course — Charles Cliffe

10th and 11th Jan are the dates for the course, cost £36.00. Closing date early because of Christmas — hurry, hurry!

## Tree People

Plant a million trees in less than four years? They did it — in America, not surprisingly, and where else but Los Angeles?

An LA City Planning Department study in 1980 stated that a million extra trees, after 20 years of growth, would be filtering 200 tons a day of 'particulate matter' from the famous air of the LA Basin — enough to bring it to within 80% of meeting their Clean Air Act standards. The cost was prohibitive — the manpower wasn't there; it would take 200m tax dollars and 20 years. Pity.

Andy Lipkis, a young man whose organisation of community volunteers, already committed to re-planting and conservation, had won the city's heart by their relief work in the floods earlier that year, took a deep breath and said 'We'll do it' — and at a fraction of the cost. By mobilising advertising agencies and huge concerns such as McDonald's (hamburgers) and General Telephone of California, they made the work a community issue; government and city agencies were persuaded to donate, and the whole 'Urban Re-Leaf' programme became one of educating and involving ordinary people.

The work of collecting seedlings, distributing them and having them planted, monumental as you may imagine, was dwarfed by the most difficult task of all: counting and confirming where and when the trees had actually been dug in. Despite an initial donation of 100,000 seedlings, delivered in milk cartons by the US Army, only 60,000 were confirmed planted in January 1984. The deadline was July — Olympic month. The saving factor was television. A local station did a week's programmes which spread the word

throughout the LA area: 'Phone 273-TREE when you've planted a seedling.' On 24 July, one million trees were officially confirmed as planted.

Only in the USA could it happen, you say — and rightly so. Nowhere else offers the right combination of ecological panic, national pride and media saturation; nowhere else do 'high-profile' companies consider it worthwhile to involve themselves with such issues. Nevertheless, Tree People are ordinary folk who took it upon themselves to act. Faced with the dreary facts of deforestation, acid rain and other forms of arboreal destruction, anyone might be forgiven for saying: yes, but what can I do? Tree People thought about it, and then went out and did it.

If you like trees, and want to see them survive so you can use them to make things from time to time, you may contact at least two organisations in the UK committed to their plantation and protection. The potential conflict between woodworker and tree protector doesn't seem to exist — rather the reverse, in fact, since those who already love wood understand how sensible policies can keep everyone happy.

● Men of the Trees: national chairman Dennis Hull, Erin, 7 Abbotsfield Crescent, Tavistock, Devon PL19 8EY, tel. (0822) 3722.

● The Tree Trust: director Paul Caton, Hermitage Rd, Upton, Long Sutton, Langport, Somerset, tel. (045 824) 567.

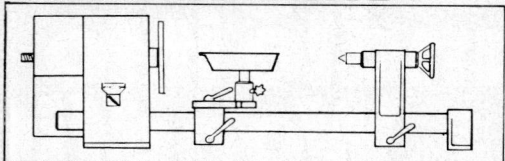

64

Prices quoted are those prevailing at press date and are
subject to alteration due to economic conditions.

# Woodworkers: making a living

Luke Hughes quizzes
professionals on their
working lives

This series is designed to present to people in the trade, and those contemplating a career in the trade, the kind of everyday problems by which woodworkers are beset — not so much how they make things as how they make a living. These things are not taught at college and can only be learned from experience. But I shall continue to present the answers I have received from many different types of woodworkers to a single set of questions. Ultimately, I hope to summarise the important points and produce a checklist for people who may think it a 'nice idea' to set up a workshop.

If you run a workshop which is unusual, or you have any interesting short cuts that might interest others, do please let me know through *Woodworker*.

## Martin Godliman and Man Sing Chan, Fulham, London

*Aged 35 and 37 respectively; run Cranstons, a small workshop where they make and repair stringed instruments, expecially violins. Martin trained at Hill's. Man Sing was born in Singapore, trained first as a musician and came to study at the Royal Academy of Music, then went to work with a violin-maker in Twickenham before joining Cranstons. Martin has made about 100 fiddles to date; Man Sing about 35. Martin does the talking.*

● *Martin assesses the finish on a violin for repair. Note the essential reading matter*

'OUR WORK is split equally between repairing, making, and buying and selling. It's quite good having a combination of all three, because I get bored doing too much of one thing — except making, which is endlessly satisfying. The repairing can be from anything as severe as a fiddle that's been sat on, to a few minor scars. Buying old fiddles, restoring them and then selling them on would bring easier money, but doing so doesn't use the extent of our abilities. Also, we're always aware that we can never fully compete with the big names in the instrument world when it comes to commanding high prices.

'Ours is perhaps one of the few branches of the woodwork trade where many people (musicians especially) are made a little uncomfortable by visiting the workshop; the sight of a treasured instrument being just a collection of bits of timber in a heap is too much for them. Not having the mahogany counters, the Bond Street manner, the glass cases, the suit, the charisma and the name in gold leaf on the window means that purchasers of valuable instruments tend not to take you too seriously. So if we offer them a superb fiddle they'll take it off to Beare's or Hill's, who turn up their noses and show them one of theirs instead. Even with modern fiddles, there's not much difference between those from the better makers, but there's quite a lot of showmanship and mystique that can be cultivated.

'We started Cranstons with three others. Unable to think of a name, we picked the least usual of our middle names. It's a limited company. The others have moved on now, so there's only Man Sing and me left. There wasn't much cash to start with, so we began by selling six fiddles at £500 each. For the workshop we bought a 20-year lease at £6000 per year, which is quite a lot to find. Our turnover is just over £60,000; we both live on about £500 per month, and value our time at £10 per hour. We have an accountant and book-keeper who tidy up the business ends once a month and see off the VAT man. I'm a greate believer in letting the right man get on with the job he's trained for, and accounts aren't really my scene.

'Quoting is done largely by experience, both for making and repairing, though I find I tend to under-quote when short of work — perhaps from anxiety about more work coming in. Doing so is always a mistake, since the moment the under-quote is made it's invariably followed by a rush of work. Most of the work comes from individual players who are recommended to us. We turn away very little, and our quotes are very rarely rejected either: only by people who haven't got enough insurance cover. Yes, there are times when a job turns up which looks very profitable to start with — usually an insurance job; but it rarely feels that way when we're finished.

'No, I don't keep the workshop very tidy, and Man Sing is worse than I am, though when I was apprenticed at Hill's the workshop was like a laboratory. Still, I can always find everything. We sweep up every

● *Man Sing Chan eyeing the result of a closely guarded secret varnishing process*

day because of the insurance conditions, and Man Sing takes the scraps home to burn.

'We very rarely have bad clients; there was one who took a fiddle away for two and a half years, but we got it back eventually. The worst mistake we tend to make is buying something for resale which turns out to need a major repair.

'The machines we use are a bandsaw, grinder, table-saw and electric drills. The most indispensable is the bandsaw. We've never had any problems with any particular makes. We use the local hardware shop for the odd hand tool, or go round the junk shops and old market stalls, but tools for fiddle-making don't wear out very easily and we've now got most of what we need.

'For stains we use anything from cold coffee to chemical products like Colron, diluted with olive oil. As for varnish, we have our own little cheat that is very effective. No, I won't say any more, but it has an oil base.

'We don't really want to employ anyone else. It's too much responsibility. They're usually too inexperienced to earn a full wage. The problem with most of the people who come out of college is that they have no concept of working quickly. The work they show is usually quite safe, but anyone can make anything if they take enough time over it. The question is whether they can make a living.

'The skill I'd most like to acquire, but never have the time for, is to play an instrument. I can't play a note, not even the penny whistle, and I now regard it as impossible. I can't even hold a decent conversation about classical music. Man Sing was a musician before he even started. As for him, the skill he'd most like is to speak English better.'

'That's not fair: I also want to fly an aeroplane, and to play more, and share more experience with other musicians. It's difficult running your own company; you have very little free time. I'd like to travel much more, too.' ■

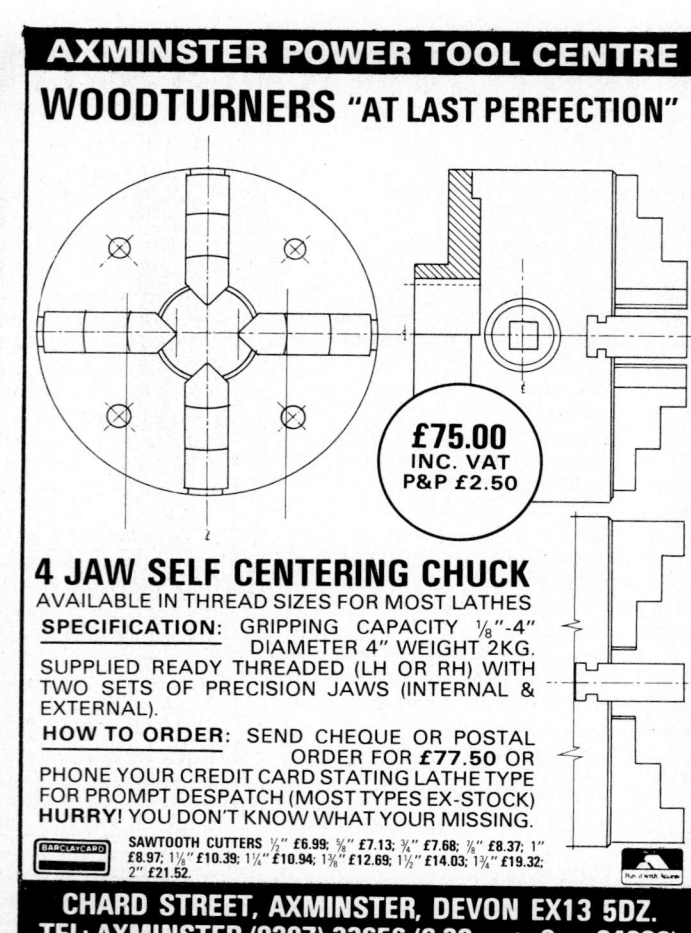
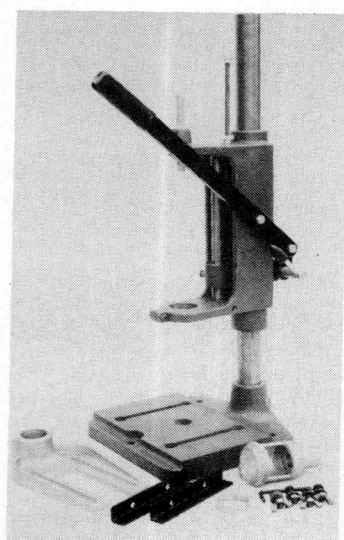

---

Prices quoted are those prevailing at press date and are subject to alteration due to economic conditions.

# shopguide

## AVON

**BATH**     Tel. Bath 64513
JOHN HALL TOOLS   ★
RAILWAY STREET

Open; Monday-Saturday
9.00 a.m.-5.30 p.m.
H.P.W.WM.D.A.BC.

**BRISTOL**    Tel. (0272) 741510
JOHN HALL TOOLS LIMITED   ★
CLIFTON DOWN SHOPPING CENTRE
WHITELADIES ROAD
Open: Monday-Saturday
9.00 a.m.-5.30 p.m.
H.P.W.WM.D.A.BC.

**BRISTOL**    Tel. (0272) 629092
TRYMWOOD SERVICES   ★
2a DOWNS PARK EAST, (off North View)
WESTBURY PARK
Open: 8.30 a.m.-5.30 p.m. Mon to Fri.
Closed for lunch 1.00-2.00 p.m.
P.W.WM.D.T.A.BC.

**BRISTOL**    Tel. (0272) 667013
FASTSET LTD
190-192 WEST STREET   ★
BEDMINSTER
Open: Mon-Fri 8.30 a.m.-5.00 p.m.
Saturday 9.00 a.m.-1.00 p.m.
H.P.W.WM.D.CS.A.BC.

## BEDFORDSHIRE

**BEDFORD**    Tel. (0234) 59808
BEDFORD SAW SERVICE
39 AMPTHILL ROAD

Open: Mon.-Fri. 8.30-5.30
Sat. 9.00-4.00
H.P.A.BC.W.CS.WM.D.

## BERKSHIRE

**COOKHAM**    Tel. (06285) 20350
CHURCH'S TIMBER
STATION HILL

Open: Mon-Sat. 8.30 a.m.-5.30 p.m.
Wed 8.30 a.m.-1.00 p.m.
H.P.W.T.CS.MF.A.

**READING**    Tel. (0734) 591361
HOME CARE CENTRE
26/30 KING'S ROAD

Open: Monday-Saturday
9.00 a.m.-5.30 p.m.
H.P.W.D.A.WM.BC.

**READING**    Tel. Littlewick Green
DAVID HUNT (TOOL    2743
MERCHANTS) LTD   ★
KNOWL HILL, NR. READING
Open: Monday-Saturday
9.00 a.m.-5.30 p.m.
H.P.W.D.A.BC.

## BUCKINGHAMSHIRE

**SLOUGH**    Tel. (06286) 5125
BRAYWOOD ESTATES LTD.
158 BURNHAM LANE

Open: 9.00 a.m.-5.30 p.m.
Mon-Sat
H.P.W.WM.CS.A.

**HIGH WYCOMBE** Tel. (0494) 22221
ISAAC LORD LTD   E
185 DESBOROUGH ROAD

Open: Mon-Fri 8.00 a.m.-5.00 p.m.
Saturday 9.00 a.m.-5.00 p.m.
H.P.W.D.A.

**HIGH WYCOMBE**   Tel: (0494)
SCOTT SAWS LTD.    24201/33788
14 BRIDGE STREET   ★

Mon.-Sat. 8.30 a.m.-6.00 p.m.

H.P.W.WM.D.T.CS.MF.A.BC.

**MILTON KEYNES**   Tel. (0908)
POLLARD' WOODWORKING    641366
CENTRE   ★
51 AYLESBURY ST., BLETCHLEY
Open: Mon-Fri 8.30-5.30
Saturday 9.00-5.00
H.P.W.WM.D.CS.A.BC.

## CAMBRIDGESHIRE

**CAMBRIDGE**    Tel. (0223) 247386
H. B. WOODWORKING
105 CHERRY HINTON ROAD
Open: 8.30 a.m.-5.30 p.m.
Monday-Friday
8.30 a.m.-1.00 p.m. Sat.
H.P.W.WM.D.CS.A.

**CAMBRIDGE**    Tel. (0223) 63132
D. MACKAY LTD.   E★
BRITANNIA WORKS, EAST ROAD

Open: Mon.-Fri. 8.30 a.m.-1 p.m./2.00-
5.00 p.m. Sat. 8.30 a.m.-1.00 p.m.
H.P.W.D.T.CS.MF.A.BC.

**PETERBOROUGH**    Tel. (0733)
WILLIAMS DISTRIBUTORS    64252
(TOOLS) LIMITED   ★
108-110 BURGHLEY ROAD
Open: Monday to Friday
8.30 a.m.-5.30 p.m.
H.P.A.W.D.WH.BC.

## CHESHIRE

**NANTWICH**    Tel. Crewe 67010
ALAN HOLTHAM   ★
THE OLD STORES TURNERY
WISTASON ROAD, WILLASTON
Open: Tues-Sat 9.00 a.m.-5.30 p.m.
Closed Monday
P.W.WM.D.T.C.CS.A.BC.

## CLEVELAND

**MIDDLESBROUGH**   Tel. (0642)
CLEVELAND WOODCRAFT    813103
(M'BRO), 38-42 CRESCENT ROAD

Open: Mon-Sat 9.15 a.m.-5.30 p.m.

H.P.T.A.BC.W.WM.CS.D.

## CORNWALL

**FALMOUTH**    Tel. (0326) 76555
WOODSTOCK (HARDWOODS) LTD.
PONSHARDEN

Open: Mon-Fri 8.30 a.m.-5.30 p.m.
Sat 9.00 a.m.-1.00 p.m.

T.

**HELSTON** Tel. Helston (03265) 4961
SOUTH WEST    Truro (0872) 71671
POWER TOOLS    Launceston
MONUMENT ROAD    (0566) 3555

H.P.W.WM.D.CS.A.
T.

**TRURO**    Tel. (0872) 71671
TRURO POWER TOOLS   E★
30 FERRIS TOWN

Open Mon.-Sat. 8.00 a.m.-12.30 p.m./
1.30 p.m.-5.00 p.m.
H.P.W.WM.D.CS.MF.A.BC.

## DERBYSHIRE

**BUXTON**    Tel. (0298) 871636
CRAFT SUPPLIES   ★
THE MILL, MILLERSDALE

Open: Mon-Sat 9.00 a.m.-5.00 p.m.

H.P.W.D.T.CS.A.BC.

**DERBY**    Tel. (0332) 41862
HAZLEHURSTS LTD.   E★
LONDON ROAD AND CANAL STREET

Open: Mon.-Sat. 8.30 a.m.-5.30 p.m. (retail)
Mon.-Fri. 8.00 a.m.-5.00 p.m. (trade)
H.P.W.MF.A.BC.

## DEVON

**BRIXHAM**    Tel. (08045) 4900
WOODCRAFT SUPPLIES   E★
4 HORSE POOL STREET

Open: Mon.-Sat. 9.00 a.m.-6.00 p.m.

H.P.W.A.D.MF.CS.BC.

**EXETER**    Tel. (0392) 73936
WRIDES TOOL CENTRE
147 FORE STREET

Open: 9.00 a.m.-5.30 p.m.
Wednesday 9.00 a.m.-1.00 p.m.
H.P.W.WM.A.

## ESSEX

**ILFORD**
CUTWELL TOOLS LTD.   ★
774-776 HIGH ROAD

Mon.-Fri. 9.00 a.m.-5.00 p.m.
and also by appointment.
P.W.WM.A.D.CS.

**LEIGH ON SEA**    Tel. (0702)
MARSHAL & PARSONS LTD.    710404
1111 LONDON ROAD

Open: 8.30 a.m.-5.30 p.m. Mon-Fri
9.00 a.m.-5.00 p.m. Sat.
H.P.W.WM.D.CS.A.

## GLOUCESTERSHIRE

**CHELTENHAM**   Tel. (0242) 39099
HAMBURY MACHINE SERVICES   E★
UNIT 14, MALMESBURY ROAD
Open: Mon.-Fri. 9.00 a.m.-5.30 p.m.
Sat. 9.30 a.m.-12.00 p.m.
W.WM.P.D.

**PLYMOUTH**    Tel. (0752) 330303
WESTWARD BUILDING SERVICES   ★
LTD., LISTER CLOSE, NEWNHAM
INDUSTRIAL ESTATE, PLYMPTON
Open: Mon-Fri 8.00 a.m.-5.30 p.m.
Sat. 8.30 a.m.-12.30 p.m.
H.P.W.D.A.BC.

KEY: H HANDTOOLS

KEY: P POWER TOOLS

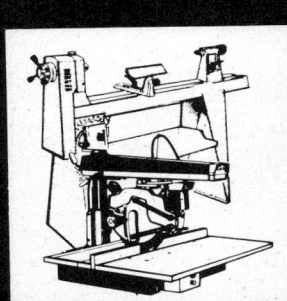

KEY: W WOODWORKING
MACHINERY

# shopguide

## HAMPSHIRE

**TEWKESBURY**    Tel. (0684)
TEWKESBURY SAW CO. LTD.    293092
TRADING ESTATE, NEWTOWN

Open: Mon-Fri 8.00 a.m.-5.00 p.m.
Saturday 9.30 a.m.-12.00 p.m.
P.W.WM.D.CS.

**ALDERSHOT**    Tel. (0252) 28088
BURCH & HILLS MACHINERY LTD
BLACKWATER WAY TRADING ESTATE

Open Mon-Fri 8.30 a.m.-5.30 p.m.
Saturday 8.30 a.m.-12.00 p.m.
H.P.W.WM.D.A.BC.

**PORTSMOUTH**    Tel. (0705)
EURO PRECISION TOOLS LTD.    667332
259/263 LONDON ROAD, NORTH END   E★

Open: Mon-Fri 9.00 a.m.-5.30 p.m.
Sat. 9.00 a.m.-1.00 p.m.
H.P.W.WM.D.A.BC.

**SOUTHAMPTON**    Tel. (0703)
H.W.M.    776222
THE WOODWORKERS
303 SHIRLEY ROAD, SHIRLEY
Open: Tues-Fri 9.30 a.m.-6.00 p.m.
Sat 9.30 a.m.-4.00 p.m.
H.P.W.WM.D.CS.A.BC.T.

## HERTFORDSHIRE

**ENFIELD**    Tel. (01-363) 2935
GILL & HOXBY LTD.
133-137 ST. MARKS ROAD EN1 1BB

Mon.-Sat. 8.30 a.m.-6.00 p.m.
Early closing Wednesday 1.00 p.m.
H.P.W.WM.T.CS.A

**HITCHIN**    Tel. (0462) 4177
ROGER'S    E
47 WALSWORTH ROAD
Open: Monday-Saturday
9.00 a.m.-5.30 p.m.
(Closed all day Wednesday)
H.P.W.WM.D.CS.MF.BC.

**WATFORD**    Tel. (0923) 48434
HOME CARE CENTRE    ★
20 MARKET STREET
WATFORD, HERTS
Open: 9.00 a.m.-5.30 p.m.
Mon-Sat
H.P.W.A.WM.BC.D.

## HUMBERSIDE

**GRIMSBY**    Tel. Grimsby (0472)
58741 Hull (0482) 26999
J. E. SIDDLE LTD. (Tool Specialists)   E★
83 VICTORIA STREET
Open: Mon-Fri 8.30 a.m.-5.30 p.m.
Sat. 8.30 a.m.-12.45 p.m. & 2 p.m.-5 p.m.
H.P.A.BC.W.WMD.

## KENT

**BIDDENDEN**    Tel. (0580) 291555/7
BRITISH GATES & TIMBER
BENENDEN ROAD    ★
Open: Mon-Fri 7.30 a.m.-5.30 p.m.
Saturday 8.30 a.m.-midday
(not Bank Holiday weekends)
H.T.CS.MF.

**MAIDSTONE**    Tel. (0622) 50177
SOUTH EASTERN SAWS (Ind) LTD   ★
COLDRED ROAD,
PARKWOOD INDUSTRIAL ESTATE
Open: Mon-Fri 8.00-5.00pm
Sat. 9.00-12.00
B.C.W.CS.WM.PH.

**MATFIELD**    Tel. Brenchley
LEISURECRAFT IN WOOD    (089272)
'ORMONDE,' MAIDSTONE RD.    2465
TN12 7JG
Open: Mon-Sun
9.00 a.m.-5.30 p.m.
W.WM.D.T.A.

**WYE**    Tel. (0233) 813144
KENT POWER TOOLS LTD.
UNIT 1, BRIAR CLOSE
WYE, Nr. ASFORD

H.P.W.WM.D.A.CS.

## LANCASHIRE

**LANCASTER**    Tel. (0524) 32886
LILE TOOL SHOP
43/45 NORTH ROAD
Open: Monday to Saturday
9.00 a.m.-5.30 p.m.
Wed 9.00 a.m.-12.30 p.m.
H.P.W.D.A.

## LEICESTERSHIRE

**PRESTON**    Tel. (0772) 52951
SPEEDWELL TOOL COMPANY    E★
62-68 MEADOW STREET PR1 1SU
Open: Mon.-Fri. 8.30 a.m.-5.30 p.m.
Sat. 8.30 a.m.-12.30 p.m.

H.P.W.WM.CS.A.MF.BC.

**HINCKLEY**    Tel. (0455) 613432
J. D. WOODWARD & CO. (POWER    ★
TOOL SPECIALISTS)
THE NARROWS, HINCKLEY
Open: Monday-Saturday
8.00 a.m.-6.00 p.m.
H.P.W.WM.D.CS.A.BC.

## LONDON

**ACTON**    Tel. (01-992) 4835
A. MILLS (ACTON) LTD    ★
32/36 CHURCHFIELD ROAD W3 6ED
Open: Mon-Fri 9.00 a.m.-5.00 p.m.
Saturdays 9.00 am-1.00 p.m.
H.P.W.WM.

**FULHAM**    Tel. (01-385) 5109
I. GRIZZARD LTD.    E
84a-b LILLIE ROAD, SW6 1TL
Open: Mon-Sat 9.00-5.30 p.m.
Half day Thursday

H.P.A.BC.W.CS.WM.D.

**LONDON**    Tel. (01-567) 2922
G. D. CLEGG & SONS    ★
83 OXBRIDGE ROAD

Mon-Sat 9.15 a.m.-5.30 p.m.
Closed for lunch 1.00-2.00p.m.
Early Closing 1.00 p.m. Wed.
H.P.A.W.WM.D.CS.

**LONDON**    Tel. (01-965) 4050)
EME LTD    E★
BEC HOUSE
VICTORIA ROAD NW10

Mon.-Thurs. 9.00 a.m.-4.30 p.m.
Fri. 9.00 a.m.-5.00 p.m.

**LONDON**    Tel. (01-263) 1536
THOMAS BROTHERS    (01-272) 2764
798-804 HOLLOWAY ROAD, N19    E
Open: Mon.-Fri. 8.30 a.m.-5.30 p.m. Thurs.
8.30 a.m.-1 p.m. Sat. 9 a.m.-5 p.m.

H.P.W.WM.CS.MF.BC.

**LONDON**    Tel. (01-858) 6444
TOOL HIRE BUY LTD
74/76 CHARLTON ROAD
LONDON SE3 8TT
Open: Mon-Fri 8.30 a.m.-5.30 p.m.
Saturday 8.30 a.m.-12.30 p.m.
H.P.W.WM.D.CS.A.BC.

**LONDON**    Tel. (01-636) 7475
BUCK & RYAN LTD    ★
101 TOTTENHAM COURT ROAD W1P ODY

Open: Mon-Fri 8.30 a.m.-5.30 p.m.
Saturday 8.30 a.m.-4.00 p.m.
H.P.W.WM.D.A.

**NORBURY**    Tel. (01-679) 6193
HERON TOOLS & HARDWARE LTD
437 STREATHAM HIGH ROAD SW16
Open: Mon-Fri 8.30 a.m.-5.00 p.m.
Wednesday 8.30 a.m.-1.00 p.m.
Sat. 9.00 a.m.-1.00 p.m.
H.P.W.A.

**WOOLWICH**    Tel. (01-854) 7767/8
A. D. SHILLMAN & SONS LTD
108-109 WOOLWICH HIGH STREET
SE18

Open: Mon-Sat
8.30 a.m.-5.30 p.m.
H.P.W.CS.A.

## GREATER MANCHESTER

**ROCHDALE**    Tel. (0706) 342123/
C.S.M. TOOLS    342322
4-6 HEYWOOD ROAD    E★
CASTLETON
Open: Mon-Sat 9.00 a.m.-6.00 p.m.
Sundays by appointment
W.D.CS.A.BC.

**MANCHESTER**    Tel: (061 789)
TIMMS TOOLS    2601
102-104 LIVERPOOL ROAD
PATRICROFT M30 0WZ    ★
Weekdays 8.00 a.m.-5.00 p.m.
Sat. 9.00 a.m.-1.00 p.m.
H.P.A.W.WM.

## MERSEYSIDE

**LIVERPOOL**    Tel. (051-207) 2967
TAYLOR BROS (LIVERPOOL) LTD
195-199 LONDON ROAD
LIVERPOOL L3 8JG
Open: Monday to Friday
8.30 a.m.-5.30 p.m.
H.P.W.WM.D.A.BC.

## MIDDLESEX

**HOUNSLOW**    Tel. (01-570)
Q.R. TOOLS LTD    2103/5135
251-253 HANWORTH ROAD

Open: Mon-Fri 8.30 a.m.-5.30 p.m.
Sat 9.00 a.m.-1.00 p.m.
P.W.WM.D.CS.A.

## NORFOLK

**RUISLIP**    Tel. (08956) 74126
ALL MODELS ENGINEERING    E★
91 MANOR WAY

Open: Mon.-Sat. 9.00 a.m.-5.30 p.m.
H.P.W.A.D.CS.MF.BC.

**GT. YARMOUTH**    Tel. (0493)
ANGLIA POWER TOOLS    850388
3 DENESIDE, NR30 2HL
Open: Monday to Saturday
8.30 a.m.-5.30 p.m.
Closed all day Thursday
H.P.W.D.CS.A.

**KINGS LYNN**    Tel. (0553) 2443
WALKER & ANDERSON (Kings Lynn) LTD
WINDSOR ROAD, KINGS LYNN
Open: Monday to Saturday
7.45 a.m.-5.30 p.m.
Wednesday 1.00 p.m. Saturday 5.00 p.m.
H.P.W.WM.D.CS.A.

**NORWICH**    Tel. (0603) 898695
NORFOLK SAW SERVICES
DOG LANE, HORSFORD
Open: Monday to Friday
8.00 a.m.-5.00 p.m.
Saturday 8.00 a.m.-12.00 p.m.
H.P.W.WM.D.CS.A.

**KEY: CS CUTTING OR SHARPENING SERVICES**

**KEY: MF MATERIAL FINISHES**

**KEY: BC BOOKS/CATALOGUES**

# shopguide

## NORTHAMPTONSHIRE

**NORWICH**   Tel. (0603) 400933
WESTGATES WOODWORKING
61 HURRICANE WAY,   975412
NORWICH AIRPORT INDUSTRIAL ESTATE
Open: 9.00 a.m.-5.00 p.m. weekdays
9.00 a.m.-12.30 Sat.
P.W.WM.D.BC.

**SWAFFHAM**   Tel: (0760) 23073
TONY WADDILOVE,
STATION HOUSE,
LITTLE DUNHAM, KINGS LYNN
Tuesday-Saturday 9.00 a.m.-6.00 p.m.
H.P.W.D.T.CS.A.BC.

**NOTTINGHAM**   Tel. (0602) 225979
POOLEWOOD   and 227064/5
EQUIPMENT LTD.  (06077) 2421 after hrs.
5a HOLLY LANE, CHILLWELL
Open: Mon-Fri 9.00 a.m.-5.30 p.m.
Sat. 9.00 a.m. to 12.30 p.m.
P.W.WM.D.CS.A.BC.

**RUSHDEN**   Tel. (0933) 56424
PETER CRISP OF RUSHDEN   E★
7 HIGH STREET NN10 9JR
Open: Mon.-Fri. 8.30 a.m.-12.30 p.m./
1.30 p.m.-5.30 p.m. Sat. 8.30 a.m.-5.30 p.m.
Early closing Thurs. 1.00 p.m.
H.P.W.MF.D.A.BC.

## OXFORDSHIRE

**CROWMARSH**   Tel. (0491) 38653
MILL HILL SUPPLIES   E★
66 THE STREET
Open: Mon.-Fri. 9.30 a.m.-5.00 p.m.
Thurs. 9.30 a.m.-7.00 p.m.
Sat. 9.30 a.m.-1.00 p.m.
P.W.D.CS.MF.A.BC.

**WITNEY**   Tel. (0993) 3885
**TARGET TOOLS**   & 72095 OXON
(Sales, Hire & Repairs)   ★
AVENUE 2, SWAIN COURT
STATION INDUSTRIAL ESTATE
Open: Mon.-Sat. 8.00 a.m.-5.00 p.m.
24 hour Answerphone
BCH.P.W.D.CS.BC.WM.A.

**TAUNTON**   Tel. Taunton 79078
KEITH MITCHELL   ★
TOOLS AND EQUIPMENT
66 PRIORY BRIDGE ROAD
Open: Mon-Fri 8.30 a.m.-5.30 p.m.
Saturday 9.00 a.m.-4.00 p.m.
H.P.W.WM.D.CS.A.BC.

## SHROPSHIRE

**TELFORD**   Tel. Telford (0952)
ASLES LTD   48054
VINEYARD ROAD, WELLINGTON   E★
Open: Mon-Fri 8.30 a.m.-5.30 p.m.
Saturday 8.30 a.m.-4.00 p.m.
H.P.W.WM.D.CS.BC.A.

## STAFFORDSHIRE

**TAMWORTH**   Tel. (0827) 56188
MATTHEWS BROTHERS LTD
KETTLEBROOK ROAD
Open: Mon-Sat 8.30 a.m.-6.00 p.m.
Demonstrations Sunday mornings by
appointment only
H.P.WM.D.T.CS.A.BC.

## SUFFOLK

**IPSWICH**   Tel. (0473) 40456
FOX WOODWORKING   E★
142-144 BRAMFORD LANE
Open: Tues., Fri. 9.00 a.m.-5.30 p.m.
Sat. 9.00 a.m.-5.00 p.m.
H.P.W.WM.D.A.BC.

## SOMERSET

**TAUNTON**   Tel. (0823) 85431
JOHN HALL TOOLS   ★
6 HIGH STREET
Open Monday-Saturday
9.00 a.m.-5.30 p.m.
H.P.W.WM.D.CS.A.

## SURREY

**FARNHAM**   Tel. (0252) 725427
A.B.E. CO. LTD. (Quick Hire)   ★
GOODS SHED
STATION APPROACH, FARNHAM
Open: Mon-Fri 8.00 a.m.-5.30 p.m.
Sat 8 a.m.-4 p.m.
H.P.W.D.CS.A.BC.

## SUSSEX

**BOGNOR REGIS** Tel. (0243) 863100
A. OLBY & SON (BOGNOR REGIS) LTD
"TOOLSHOP," BUILDER'S MERCHANT
HAWTHORN ROAD
Open: Mon-Thurs 8 a.m.-5.15 p.m. Fri.
8 a.m.-8 p.m. Sat 8 a.m.-12.45 p.m.
H.P.W.WM.D.T.C.A.BC.

**NEWCASTLE**   Tel. (0632) 320311
HENRY OSBOURNE LTD.   E★
50-54 UNION STREET
Open: Mon.-Fri. 8.30 a.m.-5.00 p.m.
H.P.W.D.CS.MF.A.BC.

## EAST SUSSEX

**ST. LEONARD'S-ON-SEA**   Tel.
DOUST & MONK (MONOSAW)  (0424)
25 CASTLEHAM ROAD   52577
Open: Mon-Fri 9.00 a.m.-5.30 p.m.
Most Saturdays 9.00 a.m.-1.00 p.m.
H.P.W.WM.D.CS.A.

## WEST MIDLANDS

**WOLVERHAMPTON**   Tel. (0902)
MANSAW SERVICES   58759
SEDGLEY STREET   ★
Open: Mon-Fri 9.00 a.m.-5.30 p.m.
H.P.W.WM.A.D.CS.

## WEST SUSSEX

**WORTHING**   Tel. (0903) 38739
W. HOSKING LTD (TOOLS &   E★
MACHINERY)
28 PORTLAND RD, BN11 1QN
Open: Mon-Sat 8.30 a.m.-5.30 p.m.
Closed Wednesday
H.P.W.WM.D.CS.A.BC.

**BIRMINGHAM**  Tel. (021-554) 5177
ROTAGRIP   E★
16 LODGE ROAD, HOCKLEY
Open: Mon.-Fri. 9.00 a.m.-5.00 p.m.
Sat. 9.00 a.m.-12.00 p.m.
H.P.W.CS.A.BC.T.MF.

## TYNE & WEAR

**NEWCASTLE UPON TYNE**  Tel.
J. W. HOYLE LTD.   (0632) 617474
CLARENCE STREET NE2 1YJ   ★
Open: Mon-Fri 8.00 a.m.-5.00 p.m.
Saturday 9.00 a.m.-4.30 p.m.
H.P.A.BC.W.CS.WM.D.

## YORKSHIRE

**BOROUGHBRIDGE**  Tel. (09012)
JOHN BODDY TIMBER LTD   2370
FINE WOOD & TOOL STORE   ★
RIVERSIDE SAWMILLS
Open: Mon-Thurs 8.00 a.m.-6.00 p.m.
Fri 8.00 a.m.-5.00 p.m. Sat 8.00-4.00 p.m.
H.P.W.WM.D.T.CS.MF.A.BC.

**CLECKHEATON**   Tel. (0274)
SKILLED CRAFTS LTD.   872861
34 BRADFORD ROAD   ★
Open 9.00 a.m.-5.00 p.m. Monday-
Saturday. Lunch: 12.00 a.m.-1.00 p.m.
H.P.A.W.CS.WM.D.

**KEIGHLEY**   Tel. (0535) 663325
EUROMAIL (TOOLS)   ★
PO BOX 13
108 EAST PARADE
Open: 9.15 a.m.-5.00 p.m.
Not Tuesday but inc. Saturday
H.P.W.A.BC.

**HARROGATE**   Tel. (0423) 66245/
MULTI-TOOLS   55328
158 KINGS ROAD   ★
Open: Monday to Saturday
8.30 a.m.-6.00 p.m.
H.P.W.WM.D.A.BC.

**HUDDERSFIELD**   Tel. (0484)
NEVILLE M. OLDHAM  641219/(0484)
UNIT 1 DAYLE ST. WORKS   42777
DAYLE STREET, LONGWOOD   ★
Open: Mon-Fri 9.00 a.m.-5.30 p.m.
Saturday 9.30 a.m.-12.00 p.m.
P.W.WM.D.A.BC.

**LEEDS**   Tel. (0532) 574736
D.B. KEIGHLEY MACHINERY LTD. ★
VICKERS PLACE, STANNINGLEY
PUDSEY LS2 86LZ
Mon.-Fri. 9.00 a.m.-5.00 p.m.
Sat. 9.00 a.m.-1.00 p.m.
P.A.W.WM.CS.BC.

**LEEDS**   Tel. (0532) 790507
GEORGE SPENCE & SONS LTD
WELLINGTON ROAD
Open: Monday to Friday
8.30 a.m.-5.30 p.m.
Saturday 9.00 a.m.-5.00 p.m.
H.P.W.WM.D.T.A.

**SHEFFIELD**   Tel. (0742) 441012
GREGORY & TAYLOR LTD   E
WORKSOP ROAD
Open: 8.30 a.m.-5.30 p.m.
Monday-Friday
8.30 a.m.-12.30 p.m. Sat.
H.P.W.WM.D.

**THIRSK**   Tel. (0845) 22770
THE WOOD SHOP   ★
TRESKE SAWMILLS LTD.
STATION WORKS
Open: Seven days a week 9.00-5.00
T.H.MF.BC.

## SCOTLAND

**EDINBURGH**   Tel. (031 337) 5555
THE SAW CENTRE   ★
38 HAYMARKET TERRACE
HAYMARKET
Open: 8.30 a.m.-5.30 p.m.
Monday-Saturday
H.P.W.WM.D.CS.A.

**GLASGOW**   Tel. (041 429) 4374/
THE SAW CENTRE   4444, Telex: 777886
600 EGLINTON STREET   ★
G5 9RR
Open: Mon-Fri 8.00 a.m.-5.30 p.m.
Saturday 9.00 a.m.-1.00 p.m.
H.P.W.WM.D.CS.A.

**EAST KILBRIDE** Tel. (035 52) 48221
EME LTD   E★
THE MACHINE TOOL CENTRE
LAW PLACE, NERSTON
Open: Mon-Thurs 9.00 a.m.-5.00 p.m.
Friday 9.00 a.m.-4.30 p.m.
W.WM.A.D.

## HUMBERSIDE

**PERTH**   Tel. (0738) 26173
WILLIAM HUME & CO
ST. JOHN'S PLACE
Open: Monday to Saturday
8.00 a.m.-5.30 p.m.
8.00 a.m.-1.00 p.m. Wednesday
H.P.A.BC.W.CS.WM.D.

## WALES

**CARDIFF**   Tel. (0222) 396039
JOHN HALL TOOLS LIMITED   ★
CENTRAL SQUARE
Open: Monday to Saturday
9.00 a.m.-5.30 p.m.
H.P.W.WM.D.A.BC.

**LONDON**   Tel. (01-636) 7475
BUCK & RYAN LTD   ★
101 TOTTENHAM COURT ROAD W1P 0DY
Open: Mon-Fri 8.30 a.m.-5.30 p.m.
Saturday 8.30 a.m.-4.00 p.m.
H.P.W.WM.D.A.

**CARDIFF**   Tel. (0222) 595710
DATAPOWER TOOLS LTD,
MICHAELSTON ROAD
CULVERHOUSE CROSS
Open: Mon-Fri 8.00 a.m.-5.00 p.m.
Sat. 9.00 a.m.-1.00 p.m.
H.P.W.WM.D.A.

**CARMARTHEN**  Tel. (0267) 237219
DO-IT-YOURSELF SUPPLY
BLUE STREET, DYFED
Open: Monday to Saturday
9.00 a.m.-5.30 p.m.
Thursday 9.00 a.m.-5.30 p.m.
H.P.W.WM.D.T.CS.A.BC.

**SWANSEA**   Tel. (0792) 55680
SWANSEA TIMBER & PLYWOOD CO LTD. ★
57-59 OXFORD STREET
Open: Mon to Fri 9.00 a.m.-5.30 p.m.
Sat 9.00 a.m.-1.00 p.m.
H.P.W.D.T.CS.A.BC.

# Classified Advertisements

All classified advertisements under £25.00 must be pre-paid: Cheques/PO made payable to A.S.P. Ltd. (WW). **Private and trade rate** 35p per word (minimum £5.25). **Display box rates** s.c.c. £7.25 (minimum 2.5×1). All advertisements are inserted in the first available issue.
**Copy to Classified Dept. (W.W.), A.S.P. Ltd., 1 Golden Square, London W.1.**
There are no re-imbursements for cancellations.

## FOR SALE

LACE BOBBIN TURNING BLANKS in unusual and exotic hardwoods and ivory. SAE for list: J. Ford, 5 Squirrels Hollow, Walsall WS7 8YS.

FOR ALL SUPPLIES
FOR THE
## Craft of Enamelling
ON METAL
Including
**LEAD-FREE ENAMELS**

PLEASE SEND 2 × 10p STAMPS
FOR FREE CATALOGUE, PRICE
LIST AND WORKING
INSTRUCTIONS

## W. G. BALL LTD.
ENAMEL MANUFACTURERS

Dept. W. LONGTON
STOKE-ON-TRENT
ST3 1JW

### Alan Holtham
The Old Stores Turnery, Wistaston Road, Willaston, Nantwich, Cheshire.
Tel: 0270 67010

**BANDSAW BLADES**
Skip tooth type with hardened teeth. Prices include VAT. P+P 1–3 Blades 90p, 4-6 Blades £1.70, Over 6 post free.

| Model | | Price inc. VAT |
|---|---|---|
| Birch | ¼" | £3.62 |
| DeWalt BS1310 | ⅜" | £3.74 |
| Kity 612 | ½" | £3.91 |
| Lazzari P32 | ⅝" | £4.77 |
| Bandit | | |
| Startrite 301 | | |
| Black & Decker | ¼" | £2.99 |
| DeWalt 100 | ⅜" | £3.11 |
| | ½" | £3.22 |
| Burgess | ¼" | £3.11 |
| | ⅜" | £3.25 |
| Inca | ¼" | £3.45 |
| | ⅜" | £3.57 |
| | ½" | £3.62 |
| | ⅝" | £4.20 |
| Startrite 352 | ¼" | £4.54 |
| | ⅜" | £4.60 |
| | ½" | £4.77 |
| | ⅝" | £5.87 |
| | ¾" | £6.15 |
| Willow | ¼" | £4.03 |
| | ⅜" | £4.08 |
| | ½" | £4.20 |

WOODTURNERS' HARDWOOD DISCS SQUARES 50lb. £9. 100lb £15. Buyers collect. Lace Bobbin Blanks 50 mixed £4, 50 yew £3 including UK. Postage or SAE for complete list. P. Rushbrook 39 Deben Avenue Martlesham, Ipswich.

CORONET CONSORT SAWBENCH with TCT blade, on wooden stand, excellent condition, 4 years old £140 ono. Berkhamsted 2404 after 7 p.m.

TRADITIONAL PATTERN GUN-METAL PLANES. Finished or kits. 17p stamp for list/photo. Bristol Design, 14 Perry Road, Bristol BS1 5BG.

### The Saw Centre Ltd
ESTABLISHED 1889
**Specialists in the Supply of Machinery and Tooling**

38 Haymarket Terrace, Edinburgh EH12 5JZ
Tel: 031-337 5555
OPEN: MON-SAT 8.30-5.30

Eglinton Tool, Glasgow G5 9RP
Tel: 041-429 4444/4374
Telex: 777886 SAWCO G
OPEN: MON-FRI 8-5.30 SAT 9-1

**Competitive prices! Large stocks.**
Elu Makita DeWALT. Scheppach.
Startrite: Griggio: Volpato: Sedgwick
Tungsten carbide tipped saw blades
Disposable bandsaw blades: tooling for machinery. *Write or phone to try us*

MORTISERS; TENNONERS; SPINDLES; PLANERS; BANDSAWS; LATHES; CROSSCUTS; ROUTERS; SANDERS; DRILLS?
YOU CAN CERTAINLY SEE ALL CLASSES AND TYPES OF MACHINES HERE.
WE ARE MAIN STOCKING AGENTS FOR: MULTICO; ELU; SEDGWICK; KITY; SCHEPPACH; INCA; CORONET; DeWALT; WARCO; DOMINION; METABO; STARTRITE; TREND; ASHLEY ILES; SORBY.
*P.S. OUR ELU PRICES COMPARE WITH ANYONES.*
*P.P.S. CALL US ABOUT WOODTURNING LESSONS WOODCARVING LESSONS (See our Swiss carving tools)*
*ALWAYS HELPFUL, KNOWLEDGEABLE, GOOD SERVICE AT:*
## CLEVELAND WOODCRAFT
**38-42 CRESCENT ROAD, MIDDLESBROUGH.**
TEL: (0642) 813103

## MUSICAL MOVEMENTS
* LOVE STORY * LARAS THEME * SPEAK SOFTLY LOVE * FUR ELISE * FEELINGS * FASCINATION * IMPOSSIBLE DREAM * MUSIC BOX DANCER * LA PALOMA * THE EMPEROR WALTZ * TRY TO REMEMBER * ROMEO AND JULIET *
Complete with screws and spring mechanism £2.50 inc. p&p. 20 or more of one tune ordered £1.50 each. Available from:
The Jewel Box Shop,
112 Pentonville Road, London N1 9JB.

## HAND CARVED
'Adam Style' Mantle motifs in Mahogany — Example 10" × 5" centre lamp and two side pieces.
Send S.A.E. for details and quotation. Your own design quoted for if required.
SAM NICHOLSON
22 Lisnagarvey Drive, Lisburn,
Co. Antrim, N. Ireland.
Phone Lisburn 3510

CRAFTSMAN QUALITY TOOLS OFFER . . .
**COMBINATION MORTICE & MARKING GAUGES**
Brass Slide R.R.P. £5.00
Polished Wood **£2.99** (+ 30p postage)
9" TRY SQUARES
Blue Spring Steel, Brass Facing, Wood Handle. RRP £8.50 **£3.99** (+£1 post)
Order Now from MIDAS MARKETING
3 River Lane, Brompton-on-Swale, Richmond, North Yorkshire, DL10 7HH.
DETAILS FREE

## SOLID OAK CHAIRS
Sanded, ready for staining and polishing. From £35 each. Also tables, tops only, kits or assembled.
Country Tables & Chairs
The Cottage, St. Nicolas,
The Cottage, St. Nicholas La., Chislehurst, Kent.
Tel: 01-467-1192

SMALL MOTORISED WOODTURNING LATHE, Japanese make. 85mm centre height, 800mm between. Two-speed. As new £75. Huddersfield 29737 late evenings.

EBAC MINOR TIMBER DRIER Unused and complete. Bargain at £600 or would consider part-exchange for 12" rise and fall saw and planer. Phone Wrexham (0978) 845260 (evenings).

## THE GREENJACKETS TOOL CENTRE
*SUPPLIERS OF HAND AND POWER TOOLS AND EQUIPMENT TO GOVT. DEPARTMENTS, LOCAL AUTHORITIES, SCHOOLS, TRADE & INDUSTRY, ETC., ETC.*

OFFICIAL MAIN STOCKISTS OF: BOSCH — HITACHI — ELU — MAKITA — A.E.G. — De WALT — BLACK & DECKER (PROFESSIONAL) ALSO STOCKISTS OF CRAFTSMAN — PEUGOT — SKIL — WOLF — RYOBI DISTRIBUTORS OF SUZUKI GENERATORS AND PUMPS — WAGNER SPRAY GUNS, POWER HAMMERS & ACCESSORIES. LOWEST PRICES ON STANLEY — MARPLES — SANDVIK — DISSTON — RECORD — ECLIPSE — ESTWING — DREMEL — ETC.
De Walt DW320 Radial Arm Saw **£199.00** + VAT; Bosch POF52 Router **£36.99** + VAT; Skil 593U Belt Sander **£44.95** + VAT.
THE GREENJACKETS LTD., 32-34 St. Mary's Road, Ealing W5 5EU.
Telephone 01-579 1188/9
*Prompt Mail Order Service.*
*Visa & Access accepted - account customers welcomed.*

Prices quoted are those prevailing at press date and are subject to alteration due to economic conditions.

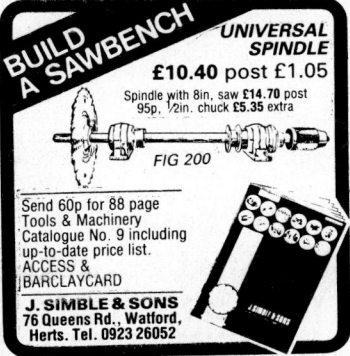
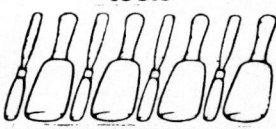

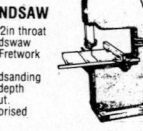
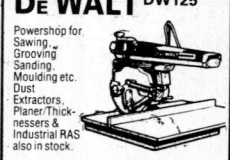

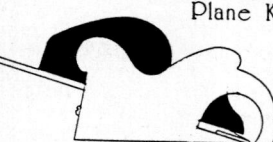
Prices quoted are those prevailing at press date and are subject to alteration due to economic conditions.

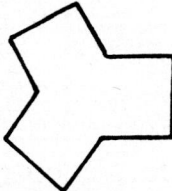

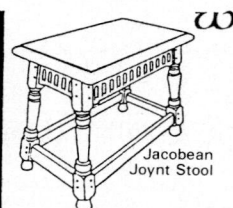
Prices quoted are those prevailing at press date and are subject to alteration due to economic conditions.

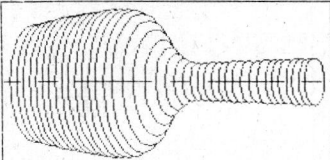

76

**Prices quoted are those prevailing at press date and are subject to alteration due to economic conditions.**

# Then...

## Max Burrough

### Continuing the absorbing tale of an old-time apprenticeship

With today's talk of tea-breaks, washing time, travelling time and every other excuse for not working, I find it difficult to realise that our work continued from 8 o'clock until 12.30, 1.30 until 5.30, and 8 o'clock to 12.30 on Saturdays with no recognised breaks. Occasionally, if there was heavy work, a slice of *home-made* cake would be carried and, around 10.30, would be eaten — but often while work was continued, and sometimes with the man resting on his tool-chest. If a man was thirsty, an ancient cup would be cleaned of sawdust, and water obtained from the tap downstairs. Never did I see tea or coffee being made in the workshop.

Had any overtime been worked recently, the single man could afford to send a boy out for a doughnut — jam at a penny each, cream at 1½d. each — or, if something a little more substantial was sought, a twopenny or threepenny slice of lardy cake. Len, whose mother kept the best café in the town, would often fall out of bed at 8 o'clock and walk across the street dressing on the way. By 9 o'clock he would be hungry, and then it would be 'Slip over to mother, please, Ben, and ask her for a drink.' The drink would be a jug of freshly made coffee and a bag of home-made cakes — all again consumed, I may add, while working.

The men's tool-chests interested me greatly, for until 10 years before I joined the firm, it was expected that each apprentice in his last year would make his own chest, the firm providing the materials and the boy making it in his own time. Fred in the top shop and Reg in the bottom were the last to follow this tradition. Bert's and Charlie's chests were the best, and after Bert's death I managed to buy his. About 37×23×23in, the carcase is of yellow pine, the outside painted flat black. Inside, half the bottom is full of Greenslades planes — hollows and rounds, beads and ogees. Above, half the space contains a sliding nest of drawers of mahogany, lined with yellow pine and crossbanded with tulipwood etc. ½in wide, each drawer having a Chippendale-rococo-style brass handle. The lid has a French-style double lock: the key has to be turned twice and then held back against the spring before the lid can be opened. The jealousy with which each man guarded and treasured his tools can be judged by the fact that Bert went to the extreme of keeping his key on the end of a chain attached to his braces, the key and chain residing in his trouser pocket.

Apart from a slight variation in the cross-banding all the tool chests were virtually identical, with the exception of Fred's, who had made his nest of drawers from solid padauk.

About a year after my arrival a number of heavy boxes about 2ft square were delivered. In due course, and after a great deal of speculation, each was found to contain a secondhand electric motor. The 8hp gas engine was removed and each machine fitted with its own motor and starter.

The acumen of the Boss was soon apparent, for a few months later the electricity board brought a 220v supply to the town, with the result that the motors were changed by the board for new ones of the correct voltage. Apparently, this was done without costing the firm a penny, and all the men thought that the Boss had been pretty smart and was to be congratulated. This affair worried me for a long time, until finally, I concluded that I would have done the same thing had I been the Boss instead.

Looking back, I can only assume it was a miracle, or a succession of miracles, that only one accident occurred while I was with the firm. The flat canvas belts, 4in wide, were completely unguarded, and joined with the Mastabar Patent Belt Fastener. Unfortunately, we did not have one of the purpose-made jigs to facilitate the joining of the two belt ends. The belt was simply placed between the barbed grips, which were then hit with a hammer, and at times the resultant mess was horrible to behold. When you consider that these unguarded belts were flapping about with jagged, rough joints, and that every man and boy wore a long white apron, it must be obvious why I talk of miracles.

The circular saw never had a guard on it; in fact, there wasn't one to put on. Yet these premises were inspected every year by a government factory inspector. One year, to the men's amazement and disbelief, the inspector was a woman! The old hands wagged their heads and said, 'What is the country coming to?' Every time, the 'tale' was told — that the guard had been removed before sharpening, or the saw had just been sharpened and the guard not yet replaced (Bert having been called out on an urgent job). As there was no continuity, a different inspector calling every time, nobody in the inspectorate realised the true situation.

Bert, incidentally, was the only man allowed to sharpen and set the saw. This he did by holding the 24in blade against the side of his bench and using a flat file for the teeth's edges and a large round one for the gullets. He counted the strokes, and it says

much for his skill when I say that I never knew the saw cut badly or wander off course. Occasionally, he would true the circumference by holding an old oilstone against the teeth with the saw at full speed.

As for the wretched chain mortiser, it was never used unless the Boss expressly ordered it. The trouble was that it was out of true, and — no matter what packing was inserted — a correction was impossible to maintain. On one never-to-be-forgotten occasion, when it was being used by the senior hand from the bottom shop, smoke was pouring from the chain and the waste was coming away jet black. When I pointed out that something must be wrong, it was discovered that the chain had been put in backwards.

With the increased use of the machines, due of course to the new 'instant' starting, came the only real accident during my time. Both the planer and the spindle, especially the latter, were running far too slowly — the reason being, I imagine, that the stiff, flat canvas belts and the manner in which they were joined made high speeds virtually impossible. Len was planing some thin oak for showcase drawer-sides, and the wood (simply held by his hands with no pressure bars of any kind on the machine) was chattering badly. The only so-called guard was a piece of curved metal above the cutter block; it was adjustable for height, but, considering the state of the machine, the short, thin pieces of oak ought never to have been put through. Unusually, only old Jim, the carpenter, and I were in the workshops, when a scream from Len made us only too conscious of the fact that the fingers of one hand had been taken in by the cutters. Poor Len, holding his hand with blood dripping everywhere, danced about, moaning and groaning with pain.

From the one and only first-aid box — it was all of 12×9×3in — Jim found a large pad of cottonwool which he quickly bandaged over the fingers. Then he said, 'Quick, Len, run up to the hospital; and you, boy, you go with him.' Before I had time to find my jacket Len was away like a greyhound. I soon followed: although he was out of sight for much of the journey, all I had to do was pursue the trail of blood. Down the stairs, through the yard, across the road, up through the alleyway beside the pub, through the churchyard and the pathfields and on to the hospital.

By the time I arrived, breathless, Len was being attended to, and for some reason I was allowed to watch. Before long, it seemed to me as the cottonwool was gently removed that we were surrounded by blood — in basins, on the table, on the floor. I took in the scene as though mesmerised. The next thing I remember is a nurse leading me outside to sit on a low brick wall and advising me to breath deeply to take in some fresh air.

After quite a while I heard the church clock chime 12.30, and I slowly walked home to my dinner. I did not stay or return to enquire after poor Len; but a few days later, heavily bandaged, he called at the workshop to report his progress and also to enquire after my own health. Although the episode did not deter me from entering hospitals in later years, it did put into me an abiding hatred of woodworking machinery, a hatred which I have never lost. ■

Prices quoted are those prevailing at press date and are subject to alteration due to economic conditions.

# Letters

I am often puzzled why manufacturers
advertise high-speed bench grinders as if
high speed were a virtue. The reverse is true,
surely — high speed is a vice when it comes
to sharpening tools. Apart from the
expensive whetstones which run in water
troughs, is there a bench grinder which runs
at about 1000rpm?

*P. Brooke, Dursley*

A year ago I was commissioned to make 11
newel-posts for a farmhouse, to match four
ancient pieces. The shape of the pommel
into which the handrails would be mortised
was a critical feature to copy.

The pommel faces were based on ellipses.
I made a template off the original newel-
posts from stiff card, cutting it fractionally smaller all round, with four integral
positioning lugs which spanned the full
width of the squared stock to be used.
Having completed most of the turning, I
established the precise location of the
pommel and marked it in with the blank
still held in the lathe. The template was then
positioned carefully on one face of the
piece, and marked all round with a red biro.

All the part of the face that had to be
removed, from the red line to the nearest
arris, was then shaded in red. To mark and
shade in this way on just two faces would be

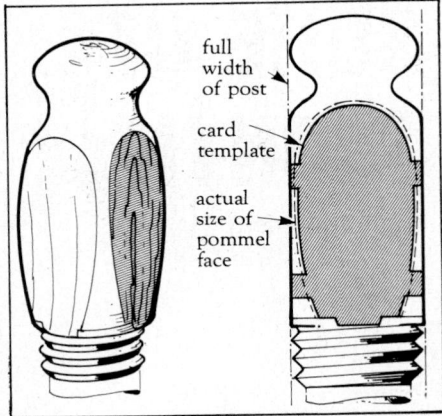

full
width
of post

card
template

actual
size of
pommel
face

enough. With the lathe switched on, a red
shadow could be clearly seen above and
below the wood-coloured blur. The
division can be seen even more accurately
with the help of a dark background and a
bright light on the work.

A sharp spindle gouge (12-18mm) was
used to remove the red area, moving from
middle to left or right, bringing the handle
up gradually through the swing of the
movement, the open face of the gouge
pointing half in the direction of the cut.

I found that, just at the point the red
shadow had disappeared from the revolving
work, a thin red line could be seen when it
was stationary. The template was smaller
than the original pommel face by half the
thickness of the Biro tip, so at the point I
could still see the line, the process was

complete. Then it only remained to remove
the line with glasspaper, the work static. I
used a sanding block to avoid dubbing over
the crisp edges.

While complimenting the editorial staff
on the continuing good quality of the
magazine, I would like to make one plea:
many of the instructional articles and
diagrams make wood resemble a feature-
less, grainless substance akin to soap or
processed cheese. Why not change the emphasis from this ideal state to deal with the
difficulties and complications of real,
present-day wood? In other words, describe
what can go wrong and how to avoid it —
and, if it's already going wrong, what to do
about it.

*Malcolm Cobb, Carnforth*

The construction of Jeremy Broun's
rocking chair (WW/May) is striking and
interesting, but I do have a criticism of the
faulty shape — particularly at the lower end
of the back. The curve here is exactly the
reverse of what the human body requires.

Anyone with disc lesions in the lumbar
spine, sitting in the chair, will experience
back pain almost immediately; in fact,
seeing the shape, they will probably avoid it
altogether! But, worse than this, anyone
with a perfectly intact back, young or old,
will experience compression and distortion
of all the lumbar discs if they sit in the chair
for any length of time. This could easily lead
to the development of a so-called 'slipped
disc' — painful, permanent and incurable.

For this reason I think the design is
dangerous and should be modified to
include some sort of lumbar support. A
look at the 'ortho-stool' featured in the
February issue will emphasise my point.
When I showed the article to my sixth-
form pupils, they spotted this defect immediately, though all liked the construction and general appearance of the design.

*Stephen Fogg, Bromley*

With reference to Richard Sarjent's
column in the November issue I would
make the following comments.

There are many versions available of the
type of door furniture mentioned,
presumably designed to avoid chopping
mortises. One must also bear in mind that
such fittings are designed not only for
entrance doors but also internal doors; as
some of the latter consist of two faces of
thin ply, the gap stuffed with corrugated
paper and a 'lock block' marked in, a drill of
any sort can be a distinct disadvantage. I
would suggest the following method:

Mark the centre, then scribe the hole
diameter with a compass. For reference
later, when the hole is worked and no centre
point visible, square horizontal and vertical
lines in soft pencil through the centre and
beyond the hole diameter. Drill a ⅜ or ½in
hole through the centre, and with a pad- or
jigsaw produce a series of 'cake-slice' kerfs,
the closer together the better. The waste can
then be easily removed and the profile
cleaned up with a rasp. The cross lines will

be appreciated when fitting the furniture.

In any case, I for one would not call a
2¼in bit 'a tool that in all probability will
never be used again'. That may be true for
the handyman, but the best way to build up
a craftsman's tool kit is to buy the tool
when it is necessary. In this instance, surely
the expansive bit is the answer.

I note also with some interest the
advertisement for the four-jaw engineer's
type chuck. These chucks have been used
by woodturners for aeons, and anyone who
has experienced their ease of operation,
positive remounting facility and general
precision will agree they are almost a must
for the wood-turner. Readers may wonder
why I have never used or encouraged the
use of such chucks. The answer is that I
consider them a **potential** danger. Such a
weight, spinning at 2000rpm plus, would
very easily take more than just the skin off a
knuckle; you would probably lose a finger
trapped between those protruding jaws and
the tool-rest.

Most of the work the chuck would be
used for, however, would keep the fingers
well away from danger, so — provided you
are not the 'it could never happen to me'
sort and are aware of the potential hazard —
you could not make a better investment.

I was intrigued with the photo of Mr
Reginald Slack on page 706 and would
make the following plea to my good friend.
Reg, you have obviously discovered the
secret of eternal youth, and the hair restorer
you are using is working a treat — how
about letting a few of us old 'uns in on it?
Alternatively, will the real Reg Slack please
stand up!

*Bruce Boulter, London SE9*

I liked the look of the 'Bedside companion'
in your October issue. For me, however, it
lacked one thing — a gallery. I've just put
quite a nice shop-made article in the
saleroom because of this lack; for those of
us who prefer to feel for the watch, for
example, and not switch the light on, that
modest strip is a must Otherwise, one can
quite easily have a valuable timepiece
clattering to the floor!

*H. H. Bridge, Southport*

I would like to make a mitre screw, and have
seen the screw part for sale separately in a
tool catalogue in the last two years. I aim to
get this part and make the wooden
components myself, but I cannot for the life
of me remember whose catalogue it was.
Does anyone know of a tool firm which
sells the steel screw part alone? I have
thought of using the part from a G-cramp
— what is the approximate length of travel
for the average mitre screw?

*J. F. Hodges, 24 Roa Island,
Barrow-in-Furness*

I would be grateful if you could help me
find the manufacturer or suppliers of the
'Centec Senior' electric router. Having
bought one at an auction, I need some
spares, but there is nothing written on the

# Letters

tool itself bar the name. Does anyone know anything about these tools?

*E. Jude, 56 Stafford Rd, Darlaston, Wednesbury WS10 8TY*

Further to recent correspondence about Arcoy cutters, I would very much appreciate it if anyone could supply me with a replacement sawblade for my Arcoy Rabbeter.

*R. M. H. Smith, 2 Observatory Rd, London SW14 7QD*

I wish to draw attention to the work of gremlins in the September issue of *Woodworker*, as I'm sure Arthur Jones knows exactly what he's talking about (Timberline). Arthur is talking about the possible sale by the Russians of a substantial quantity of timber; firstly I'm sure they wouldn't bother only offering 160,000cu in, but if they did, and got £156 per cu in for it, they would be more than satisfied! Shouldn't the printer have used an 'm'? The price of hardwoods in this country is astronomical, but it pales into complete insignificance compared to this quote on Russian softwoods!

*B. D. Crabtree, Harare, Zimbabwe*

I was delighted to read Rhys Thomas' remarkable if erroneous letter concerning my 'plagiarism' of his piece (WW/Nov). It allows me to point out something rather

obvious that a few people fail to understand: given similar problems, people are likely to roduce similar solutions. If we have come to parallel conclusions, we should congratulate each other, not get bitter about it!

I've since discovered similar pieces commercially produced in Germany, Italy and England — I don't think we're all sending spies to Wales! I might add that to bolt a piece of free-standing furniture to the wall to stop it falling over is no solution.

*Nick Turner, Shaftesbury*

With much respect to Bob Grant I regret to say that 'Turning plane tapers' (WW/June) is not so excellent. It will be apparent that one quarter of a revolution of the job in the lathe will bring the corners of the pommel

proud of the turned taper, as shown. What then?

*Hugh Blogg, Broadstairs*

**Bob Grant** replies: Mr Blogg is quite right, of course. As it stands the process seems to achieve the impossible — but the piece was intended as a 'hint' or 'tip' feature and thus did not warrant a detailed explanation of the procedures in the whole job.

The words 'rough the taper with a gouge working from the desired maximum to the minimum diameter' imply the usual practice of establishing the two diameters with a parting tool and forming the curved shoulder with a skew chisel. This should be done before the planing process described, so the problem of the plane hitting the corners does not arise.

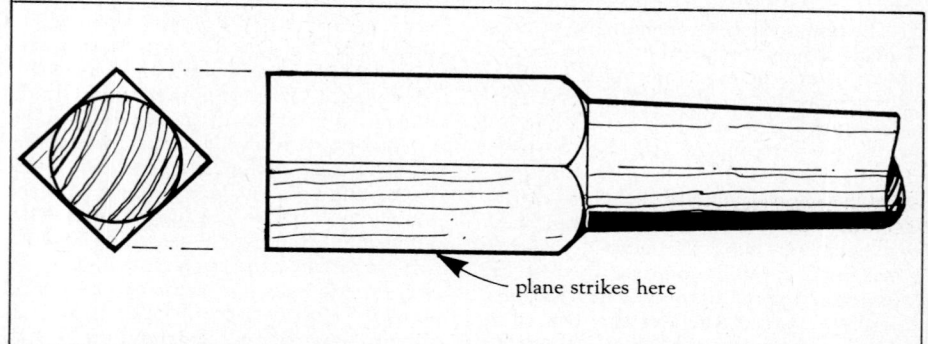

plane strikes here

# The magazine for the craftsman
## ~ and the aspiring craftsman!

February 1985
Vol. 89
No. 1095

**Publisher** Tony Dowdeswell
**Editor** Peter Collenette
**Deputy Editor** Aidan Walker
**Graphics** Peter Kirby
**Group Art** Nick Howell
**Guild of Woodworkers** Aidan Walker
**Publishing Director** John Foster
**Chairman and Chief Executive** Jim Connell

If you write to us, please enclose a stamped addressed envelope. Unfortunately we cannot accept responsibility for the loss of or damage to unsolicited material. Nothing published in *Woodworker* may be reproduced without permission.

**Advertisement Manager** Paul Holmes
**Advertisement production** Karyn Stewart

We reserve the right to refuse or suspend advertisements without explanation, and regret we can take no responsibility either for clerical or printing errors or for the bona fides of advertisers.

**Editorial, advertisements and Guild of Woodworkers** PO Box 35, Wolsey House, Wolsey Road, Hemel Hempstead, Herts HP2 4SS; telephone Hemel Hempstead (0442) 41221
**Subscriptions and back issues** Infonet Ltd, 10-13 Times House, 179 Marlowes, Hemel Hempstead, Herts HP1 1BB; telephone Hemel Hempstead (0442) 48434
**Subscriptions per year** UK £15; overseas outside USA (accelerated surface post) £16.50, USA (accelerated surface post) $21.50, airmail £41.50

**UK trade** SM Distribution Ltd, 16-18 Trinity Gardens, London SW9 8DX; telephone 01-274 8611
**North American trade** Eastern News Distributors, 166-41 Powells Cove Boulevard, PO Box 69, Whitestone, New York, 11357 (**Postmaster:** Please send address changes to England)
**Printed in Great Britain** by Ambassador Press Ltd, St Albans, Herts
**Mono origination** Multiform Photosetting Ltd, Cardiff
© Argus Specialist Publications Ltd 1985
ISSN 0043 776X

**ABC**

**On the cover:** The new board material MDF is ideal for carcase furniture — but used adventurously in this chair, where care has been taken to ensure that each component is strong enough. Details of our big MDF design competition are on pages 102-3

# Argus Specialist Publications Ltd
Wolsey House, Wolsey Road, Hemel Hempstead, Herts HP2 4SS (0442) 41221

## Lathe winner

Many congratulations to Mr P. A. Fleming of Kenilworth, Warwickshire, who will shortly be the proud owner of an Emco DB6 lathe. Our contest brought a huge number of entries, and a lot of work sorting them all out, but there was only one winner!

Mr Fleming will be presented with the machine of his dreams at the EME headquarters in London amid due festivities. We'd like to thank everyone who entered, and extend our condolences to the disappointed — keep a watch on *Woodworker* for the next competition to test your knowledge and ingenuity. Many thanks, too, to Emco for donating the machine.

For the record, the answers to the quiz were:

**1** Which of the following would be turned between centres?
*A baluster, a table leg, and a chair stretcher. A spherical ball can also be made in this way.*

**2** Which of the following are used in woodturning?
*The centre square, the steady rest, the parting-tool, the ring centre, friction polish, and the side-cutting scraper.*

**3** The swing of the lathe is:
*The maximum diameter (or radius) of the workpiece.*

**4** The bed of a lathe is:
*The part that links the headstock and tailstock.*

**5** The Emco DB6:
*Is 1000 watts or 1kw in power; is made in Austria; accessories available are copying attachment, screw chuck, cup centre, steady rest, 3- and 4-jaw chucks, 3-jaw drill chuck, tool rest, chuck guard, goggles, templates.*

**6** In what year was the Emcostar first put on sale?
*1949.*

Tricky, eh?

## Can't stick the noise?

'The Health & Safety Executive is not waving a big stick at British machinery makers,' John Rimington is anxious to emphasise. He is the director-general of the Executive, and was speaking at a London conference in November.

The real threat, he added, is from the pressures of a competitive market, which will wield that fearsome knobkerry if manufacturers don't take noise regulation into account. 'In the long term the sales potential of needlessly noisy machinery is bound to suffer.'

On the awkward subject of enforcement, Mr Rimington said that the HSE inspectors would soon be paying more attention to the need for building noise control into new machinery, and that the Executive might want to propose changes in the regulations so that they cover imported machinery too.

Meanwhile, back at the workshop, remember as you clock up your eighth hour on the trot bent over the surfacer that it's an *employee's responsibility* to wear hearing protection where noise reduction is impractical. Your employer has a duty to look for ways of reducing noise on existing plant; but as far as your own ears are concerned, it's down to you.

## Stick standard

**Polly Curds** writes: The British Stickmakers Guild, whose incorporation was reported in *Woodworker* for November, should be aware that a British Standard exists for wooden walking-sticks. Some may remember a heated debate on the subject of stick length following an article by Jack Hill!

The standard, BS 5181, was originally prepared at the request of the DHSS, and the test requirements are for the types of sticks normally used in hospital practice. They are based on the chestnut walking-sticks which have given good service over the years, and specify three grades — light, medium, and heavy — each obtainable in three nominal lengths of 915, 965 and 1015mm. The standard gives details of timber requirements, finish, and static loading tests, as well as length, diameter, and crook-handle dimensions.

On a related subject which has also been discussed in *Woodworker* recently, those interested in the anthropometric aspects of furniture design (WW/Oct) will be pleased to know that the BSI has just published a new booklet, *Anthropometrics for Schools and Colleges* by S. T. Pheasant. It is excellent for all those designing furniture and fitments, and lists all the relevant British Standards.
● British Standards Institution, 2 Park St, London W1A 2BS, tel. 01-629 9000.

## 銘日企業股份有限公司

Fitting out a restaurant or hotel lobby? You might be interested in some very quirky publicity which has found its way into the *Woodworker* office from Taipei, Taiwan, proclaiming the virtues of King Sun Mfg Co's **decorative wooden screens**. 'Improve on your living enviroment (sic) more gorgeous, elegant and broader; make you feel more comfortable', exhorts one of the numerous brochures; 'Inheritance of the art of the oriental carving culture, beautify your living enviroment (sic again) and make you feel comfortable' pronounces another. 'Enjoy the palatial magnificent residence, use the ornamental moulding of King Sun.' The patterns are distinguished with such names as Triple Angular Doughnut, Deformed Marronnier, Ruby, Lemon, Orange, Thunder and Light Show.

Their complexity and construction defy description; they are obviously in the tradition of Oriental architectural carving, and equally obviously now machine-produced. The marriage of computer-controlled production technology and ancient decorative design brings strange offspring into the world . . . stranger than this, we have yet to see. Meanwhile, you can experience 'The needful interior decoration to a noble family'.
● David Gillespie Associates Ltd, Dippenhall Crossroads, Farnham, Surrey GU10 5DW, tel. (0252) 723531

Makers of **TCT router cutters and saw blades** Carbex have a new packaging and storing idea to help shift their products in a very competitive market. The cutters come in a blister pack, firmly ensconced in a snippet of MDF which has been profiled to the shape and size of the tool. The hole in the top is good for storage, and the cut shape obviously tells you exactly which cutter it is. More for the retailer than the user, perhaps, but it's a neat idea. A ½in diameter two-flute straight bit with ¼in shank is £10.30+VAT; a roman ogee with ⅞in depth of cut, £21.20+VAT.
● Carbex Products Ltd, 66A High St, Great Missenden, Bucks HP16 0AN, tel. (02406) 2116

The only people who might not be pleased to hear about Loctite's **new PVA**, Wood Bond Rapid, are the manufacturers of cramps. You won't need so many now you can get a glue which sets in two minutes! This is their claim — you can release work from cramping pressure after the time it takes to have a cup of tea. 'Typical bonds' on pine withstood a shear load of 470lb per sq in after five minutes under test, and after 24 hours a bond strength of more than ½ ton per sq in was achieved. There has to be a catch — 125ml of this stuff will cost you £1.49 retail.
● Loctite UK, Watchmead, Welwyn Garden City, Herts AL7 1JB, tel. (903) 31277

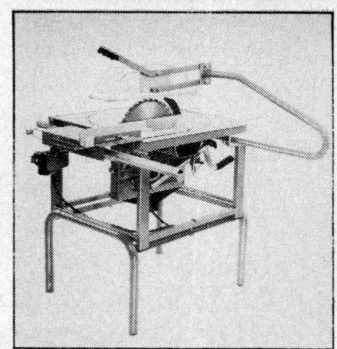

● *Sawbenches like this one form a rugged alternative to the more compact (but heavier) workshop types. It costs £495+VAT for the single-phase version (a TCT blade is thrown in); it comes from Luna, 20 Denbigh Hall, Bletchley, Milton Keynes, Bucks MK3 7QT, tel. (0908) 70771*

Craft Supplies' luxurious new **catalogue for the woodturner** provides 80 pages of mouthwatering reading, 28 of which are in full colour. Seasoned wood is now available for a range of items such as pepper mills, nutcrackers, tiles, clocks and barometers, plus, of course, all the turning tools and accessories for which the Derbyshire concern is justly famous. Essential for the serious turner, a measly quid is the price.

● Craft Supplies Ltd, The Mill, Millers Dale, Buxton, Derbyshire, tel. (0298) 871636

**Aidan Walker** writes: Well, at least the Bosch book 'Routing for the Home Craftsman' is free — and it is beautifully produced. You'd have to be a lot more than a craftsman to make sense of the projects, though.

It is admirable in addressing an 'information area' notable for its gaps. Produced as it is by a router manufacturer, it is hardly surprising that it looks like a plug for Bosch machines — there's nothing really wrong in that. The first half consists of luscious colour pics of Bosch POF52

routers and PKF25 laminate trimmers (a type of small router), plus tables and stands, cutter charts and handling tips. It is a good aspect of their design that these little machines can be mounted in the Bosch S7 drill stand, and the fence accessory is useful too.

Nevertheless, several buts. The safety pages should be at the beginning of the book, surely, not the end, where everyone's reading patience is long exhausted? As for the projects — the cutting lists are comprehensive, but the procedure dwell so much on routing that there seems no room for all the things in between. You'll find out how to cut tenons and open mortises with what is effectively an overhead router, but if you expect concise step-by-step instructions on how to build a 'Rustic style pinewood cupboard' you'll be sorely disappointed.

Still, who can complain when it's free? Just write to Bosch.

● Robert Bosch Ltd, PO Box 98, Broadwater Park, North Orbital Rd, Denham, Uxbridge, Middx UB9 5HJ

**Alan Thomas** writes: At first sight, the brightly coloured plastic components in the Cabinet Mate set of equipment look like toys for an intelligent 10-year-old. The makers do themselves a disservice, for their system is clever, effective, and potentially very useful indeed.

The basic premise is that many people want to make furniture, particularly fitted furniture, from the wide variety of laminated boards on the market. Also readily available, of course, are finished and ready-to-use cupboard doors — and it is these pre-finished doors themselves which provide the basis for Cabinet Mate. The system uses them as templates upon which furniture units are built up and assembled. It's not only doors that can be used: chests of drawers, using the fronts as templates, also come within range.

Single-door units are straightforward, but included in each kit are spacers which give working clearances in multi-door or multi-drawer fronts. With these spacers separating its several parts, each front is fitted into rigid corner-posts. These are secured with webbing cramps and, when placed correctly, provide the cutting dimensions for carcase panels. Once the panels are cut and trimmed, screw-clamps hold them in position inside the corner-posts too. When side, bottom and top panels are all in place, a drill-maker template slips into each screw-clamp and shows where the fixing-screw holes should go. It is also possible to locate fixed shelves accurately with the standard components.

Although these devices are simple, the variety of ways they

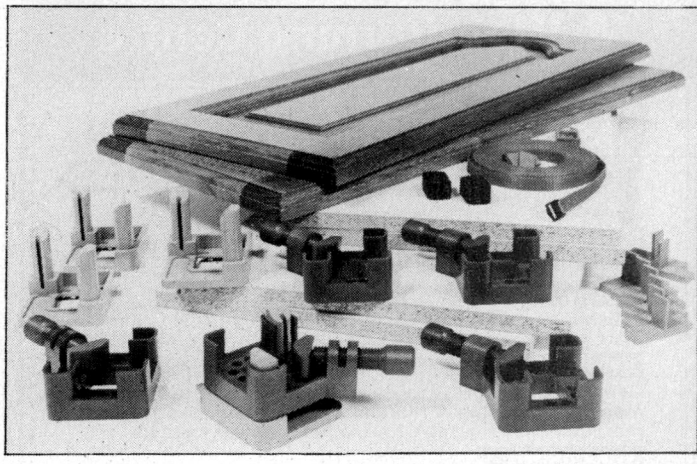

● *The Cabinet Mate kit, plus components of a simple carcase for assembly. In Alan Thomas's view the system is well-designed, robust, and a lot more useful than it may look at first sight*

can be used has prompted the makers to supply a 32-page instruction booklet which gives much useful information on designing kitchen, bedroom and other furniture. It goes into considerable detail on making drawers and the economical use of material.

No doubt some purists will take a poor view of any constructional aid which obviates nearly all the traditional cabinetmaking skills; they will also disapprove,

for that matter, of the materials it uses. Realistically, however, there is nothing wrong with the sort of furniture for which Cabinet Mate is designed — it is well suited to its purpose, easily cleaned and serviceable. Its drawback for most skilled people is that it is usually required in quantity, and the task of making it is downright boring. The less adept sort of do-it-yourselfer probably finds difficulty in producing results equal to even the cheapest flat-pack furniture. But with the Cabinet Mate (as long as you can make clean cuts at accurate right-angles) assembly should be rapid, successful and painless. And there is nothing to stop any enthusiast from using doors of his or her own design and making. It is coming into the shops now at £19.95.

● Adds Alan: 'So impressed have I become with this ingenious device that quite soon I shall use it in making up a great deal of kitchen furniture.'

● Pentabridge Ltd, 32 St Mary's St, Stamford PE9 2DS, tel. (0780) 56068

The Design Council's 1985 edition of 'Design Courses in Britain', their **comprehensive information handbook,** contains details of over 2000 courses. It offers advice on choosing a design career and the right course, and covers foundation, non-degree and higher level courses, secondary-level teacher training, and all the BTEC courses throughout Britain. It is available from bookshops for £3.75, and also by post (add 50p).

● The Design Council Bookshop, 28 Haymarket, London SW1Y 4SU.

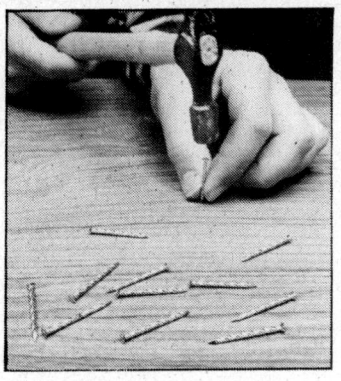

● *Drill Nails come in ¾, 1 and 1¼in lengths from SEAC Ltd, Chesterfield Rd, Leicester LE5 5LP, tel. (0533) 739501*

*Traditional Homes* magazine deals specifically with the renovation, repair and upkeep of old houses. Its publishers are now producing a *Building Trades and Services Directory*: a finder for seekers of architects, ornamental iron-mongers, builders, thatchers — anyone concerned wholly or partly with this sort of work. Contact them if you want your name and address in the directory (it costs nothing), or indeed want more details of the service.

● S. Foster, CFE Publishing Ltd, Monmouth House, 87 The Parade, High St, Watford, Herts WD1 1LN, tel. (0923) 55125

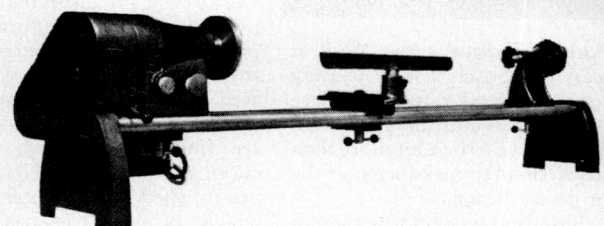

# Timberline

**Arthur Jones** presents the month's inside news of supplies

Estimating future supplies and prices can be useful for the woodworker. Once a year a chance comes to benefit from the deliberation of experts from the softwood trade in all the main European timber-importing and producing countries, as well as north America, when they meet to look at the world market.

This year has seen the creation of a major problem for the main producers — Sweden, Finland, Canada and the US. They have been producing softwood lumber way ahead of world demand. The recovery in both Europe and America did not reach the proportions expected. In the case of the US, the forecast was much too optimistic, with producers bringing mills back into full production. The result has been a heavy build-up of stocks just at a time when importers are buying less.

The Swedes acknowledge that they will have to make a massive cut in their output next year. But there are no regulations to bring this about; it will depend upon voluntary action by the sawmills across the country. Past experience suggests that the reduction will fall well below the quantity required if supply is to match falling demand.

This will put pressure on prices, and the experts do not expect timber to rise much in value in 1985; in fact, they will probably be happy if the increase can keep pace with the modest 4½% rate of UK inflation. And this sort of increase is likely to apply only to the better grades of redwood. Whitewood is still far from popular; its price has fallen steadily in the second half of 1984, with no sign that the bottom has been reached. It is doubtful whether whitewood prices will hold; certainly they are unlikely to increase.

This is all good news for the woodworker. He can now rest assured that supplies will be more than ample, giving him plenty of selection, and that prices will be highly competitive. In this sort of market there is almost always a weak seller, so there could also be quite a few bargains around — especially if the building trade continues in the doldrums as a result of the cuts in home-improvement-grant work.

The conference report on the UK market showed that importers had cut back sharply on their forward purchases for 1985 because of the relatively high stocks in the country and the weakness in sales. Stockists want to reduce their expensive holdings as fast as possible to get into line with sales. By the end of the year stocks should be falling, though they will still be 15% higher than a year earlier. This destocking is expected to continue through 1985. Sales in 1984 will probably show a fall of 3%, be followed by another 2% drop in 1985.

The UK report predicted that much of the fall in sales will have come to an end by about April, and there may be some recovery later in the year. A lot will depend on government policies, which are currently aimed at cutting expenditure; this will hit construction work.

A pointer to the 1985 market has already been given by a leading Finnish shipper, who has sold for shipment up to next summer at unchanged prices. He obviously does not expect rises.

So the outlook for the UK woodworker who uses softwood must be brighter at the moment than it has been for many a year. Having seen the cost of his raw material shoot upwards in recent years, he is now getting the benefit of a period of stability; in real terms, even lower prices.

A somewhat similar situation prevails in the plywood market. Importers who have been buying for 1985 deliveries have generally been able to secure shipments at autumn 1984 prices. The export licensing system being introduced in Indonesia should bring more stability to prices from that country, a major UK plywood supplier.

In hardwoods, stock remains generally good in the UK — though much is held by importers rather than merchants, which might mean that in some areas the woodworker is not finding the species he favours. A furniture report notes that mahogany has gained ground in furniture production and teak is still being widely used, though this wood has gone out of favour in most European countries.

As always, hardwood prices vary for a number of reasons; but ramin remains among the cheaper species, and Brazilian mahogany has encountered a lot of competition — meaning that prices are keen. ∎

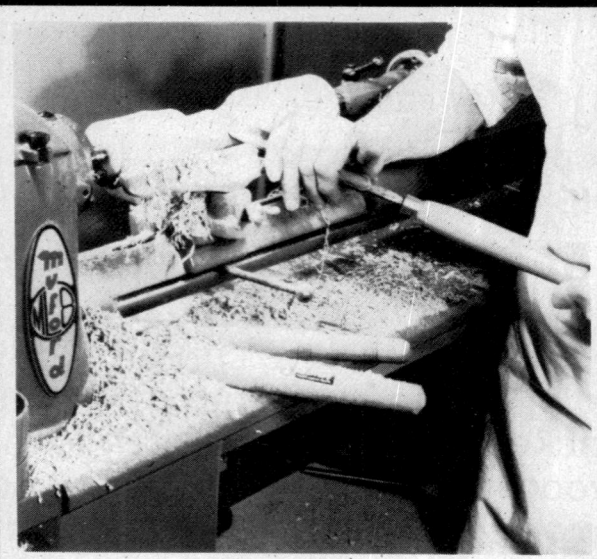
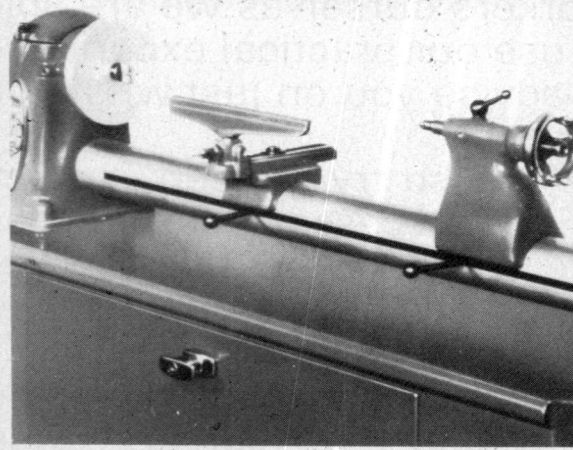

Prices quoted are those prevailing at press date and are subject to alteration due to economic conditions.

# Tradewinds

**Richard Sargent** gives a regular inside view of the tool trade

Apologies for my absence last month; due to shows, hospital and generally taking on too much, I missed Mr Editor's deadline. Smacked wrists, naughty boy, must try harder!

Belatedly, then, a comment or two on the Woodworker Show. Obviously the various sectors of the woodworking market all see the show from different viewpoints. Naturally, too, exhibitors' comments often differ from those of visitors, of the people entering the various competitions, and indeed of the organisers.

From a visitor's point of view, the standard of an exhibition depends on the organisation, the venue — and the contents of the show, in terms both of trade stands and other exhibits. The exhibitor is also concerned with the quantity and quality of visitors. All these things are down to efficient work before the doors open on the first day.

When asked for comments on something like the Woodworker Show, you tend to list complaints first rather than praise — however good the event! So perhaps I ought to say first that in general I thought it a good show, but one still capable of being bettered. From the visitor's point of view I thought the signposting could have been clearer, and the car parking was badly organised; the PA system was incomprehensible and the catering was *awful*! For an exhibitor a new venue is always difficult to adjust to, as we all get used to what we know. The main new element for us at Ally Pally was the security staff. I thought we rid this world of their kind of attitude about 40 years ago. We all have our job to do, and somebody needs to tell them next time that theirs could be done just as easily with civility and manners.

The Show looks like improving from year to year. I have no doubt certain changes will be made next time. In particular, it would be nice to see more *Woodworker* readers there; the attendance represents only a fraction of the magazine's readership. I would be most interested to hear why some people *don't* come.

One last point. As I've said before, in the woodworking trade we count our competitors as friends rather that otherwise. At events such as the Woodworker Show, most of us usually end up staying at the same hotel, which leads to useful exchanges of views and information after hours. This year there was no one obvious hotel, and we were all scattered around north London; moreover, there was no exhibitors' lounges at the Show (not that we ever find time to sit!). So there was no contact. I hope that perhaps another year this will be remedied by the show organisers' block-booking a hotel; the communication fostered certainly benefits exhibitors, and therefore (one hopes) the trade generally.

Back in July I moaned in this column about traditional hand tools that had been discontinued, bewailing the possibility that such items may well be replaced by imported tools, and cited the versatile Multi-plane as an example. I am delighted to be able to tell you that the Multi-plane is back in production in Britain, and therefore available again. It is particularly pleasing that a British company took up the challenge, and are able to supply this craftsman's tool once more. The Clifton Multi-plane is priced at £199.50 including VAT.

And it is not the only tool to re-appear. While I agree with Roger Buse's letter pointing out that saw-tooth machine centre bits, Forstner bits, plug cutters and others were still available, my original point was that they were not British-made, having been discontinued by Bahco Record Tools Ltd. Again, it is with some satisfaction that I hear we are once again able to stock and sell woodworking boring tools manufactured in Britain.

I thank Robert Jarvis of New South Wales, Australia, for his response to my piece on fools' errands that apprentices used to be sent on.

Mr Jarvis says: 'We were building the Fox Inn at Bix when I was told to go and find a "little round straight-edge". Finally, after searching the site and having become increasingly aware of the smirks, I realised the hopelessness of my quest. At 63 years of age I still feel embarrassed when I recall the incident!' ∎

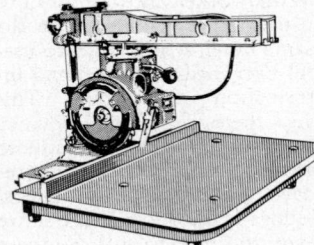
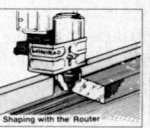

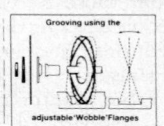

88       Prices quoted are those prevailing at press date and are
subject to alteration due to economic conditions.

# Question box

*Our panel of experts solve
your woodworking problems*

**Q** *I have recently bought some agba. Perhaps you could tell me something of this wood, and why it is not sold in the UK any more? When being worked it gives off a very strong aroma, and during machining I develop a sore throat.*

*K. Rayson, Lincoln*

**A** I am wondering if your wood is mansonia and not agba. You can soon check this because the appearances of the two species are quite different. Here are a few notes on each wood.

Agba (*Gossweilerodendron balsamiferum*) comes mainly from Nigeria, and has been imported for many years. Any falling-off is likely to be due to a preference for mahogany. Agba varies slightly in colour from a pinkish shade with a yellowish cast to a reddish-brown very much like that of light-coloured mahogany. Its grain enhances the mahogany appearance, but agba is duller, lacking the slight lustre typical of mahogany. Agba is inclined to be gummy. It is a very valuable wood for many purposes, both exterior and interior. I have never experienced a strong aroma from it, and know of no reason why it should be truly unavailable.

Mansonia (*Mansonia altissima*) also comes from west Africa. It is generally greyish or greyish-brown in colour with a purplish cast and looks like a very plain walnut (it is used as a walnut substitute). It has a pungent, peppery odour when worked. Because of its irritant nature, imports were halted some years ago, but any non-availability today is due to lack of demand. The wood can finish beautifully for furniture, cabinets, high-class joinery and the like.

Many woods contain extractives to which a person may be allergic or oversensitive. It would be wise to use a respirator or mask if the symptoms persist.

*Bill Brown FIWSc*

---

**Q** *I wish to veneer a number of panels, the largest of which is 23in×15in, with mahogany. I have received much conflicting advice – e.g.: a pressure of 30lb/psi is required; a pressure of 15lb/psi is adequate; Evostik Resin W is satisfactory (the instructions with the adhesive say 'apply light pressure'); use a glue which sets slowly to allow the veneer to adapt; do not use contact adhesive; IM904 Evostik contact adhesive is satisfactory; do not use glues soluble in water; soak the veneer in water and press between paper overnight before gluing.*

*Your help will be greatly appreciated, and accepted as the final judgement! I have a press similar to that described in your December 1983 issue.*

*B. Moss, Colwyn Bay*

**A** The groundwork must be flat and 'keyed'. Keying is best done with a toothing-plane but almost as good is S2 glasspaper used with a cork rubber or at least a wooden block. The papering is done diagonally and across the grain.

Mahogany curl veneers, when dry, are generally buckled. They must therefore be made flat before cutting and certainly before pressing. This is done by dampening (not soaking), with clean cold water from a clean rag, both sides of each leaf, and placing them together while damp in the same sequence that they have been removed. Put the whole bunch between two boards larger than the veneers and at least ¾in thick, and place some heavy weights on top. Better still, put it in your press and tighten it as hard as you can. Leave it for 3-4 hours or preferably overnight. Do not put paper between the wet leaves; this will result in a soggy mess. Do not keep the leaves damp between the boards for more than two or three days, because mould could develop.

The adhesive used for centuries for hand and press veneering was animal or Scotch glue. It has an almost immediate gel, so that hot cauls must be used when pressing. They are placed on the veneer surfaces, or between them if more than one panel at a time is done, with two layers of paper between the cauls and the veneers to prevent them from sticking together. When the pressure is applied, the glue will be reactivated and will flow.

Most of the modern synthetic adhesives are very good. Contact or impact adhesives are ideal for sticking laminated plastics, but not for veneering wood — not even edges. PVA glues such as Resin W and UniBond are very suitable for cold-pressing veneers, but cannot generally be used for laying by hand. Their advantages are an indefinite 'pot life', usage straight from the container with no preparation, a long gelling time (15-30 minutes, depending on temperature), and compatibility with damp surfaces.

The glue should be brushed evenly and fairly generously on the panel only. Place the veneer in position, tape or otherwise fix it, and cover it with several layers of newspaper. With a little experience both sides of one or more panels can be done at the same time, always with paper to separate the veneers. Tighten the press as hard as you can and forget about PSI. Wash away some of the surplus glue and leave to set overnight.

If the panels are not to be held in a solid frame then they should be veneered on the back to prevent distortion. Curls and burrs are liable, in time, to develop hair cracks where the grains coincide with that of the groundwork. It may be advisable to doubleveneer, laying the first one either diagonally or across the grain of the groundwork.

*Mark Kenning*

---

**Q** *I have a bandsaw problem which I am sure other users must encounter. The machine in question was, I am told, purchased new in 1945; it is made of cast iron; the wheels, 15in in diameter, are balanced to perfection and the bearings are running as new; the tyres are the originals – rubber, about ¼in thick and 1½in across. They are flat and in good condition.*

*When attempting to track the blade in the centre of the tyres, I back off the guides and thrust (top and bottom). The top wheel is in a sliding section held by big strips; this is moved up and down by a hand wheel below the mechanism. The canting is done by adjusting two square-headed bolts, and there is a locking bolt between them. The adjustment moves the wheel-bearing assembly in a pivoting action (somewhat like a stepladder).*

*The bottom wheel has an adjustment, but all it does is to cant the wheel slightly one way or the other. This I am sure is only intended for use from new or as an initial factory setting. I have, however, adjusted one, the other, and both together. Sometimes, when the blade is running on the front edge, I start adjustment; at first there is no movement – then, after very careful turning of the adjustment bolts, the saw shoots across the tyre and runs on the back edge. Sometimes it runs on the front of the top wheel and the back of the bottom one, and sometimes vice versa.*

*I must stress that the machine's general condition is superb. Do you think I should sand a crown on the tyres?*

*Samuel G. Walker, Wallasey*

**A** This problem even crops up occasionally with new machines. Assuming the tyres are in good condition, the answer relies on getting the bottom wheel in the right relative position before attempting to track the top one. It is unusual to have any sort of adjustment on the bottom wheel, so at least you have a head start. On the other hand, if the adjustment had not been there, someone might not have messed it up!

Start by putting a straight-edge vertically across the upper and lower wheels, and adjust both of them until the tyres are as near to 90° to the straight-edge as you can tell by eye. Put the blade on and tension up as normal, taking care not to overdo it. Then spin the wheels by hand, in the correct direction and see where the blade moves to. If it moves forward on the top wheel, tip that wheel slightly backwards with the tracking adjuster and try again. If the blade moves backwards, tip the top wheel forwards.

Keep making small adjustments until the blade tracks correctly. If it still keeps running off, make a small alteration to the bottom wheel and try the whole process all over again. In all cases, keep the adjustments small, as the correct alignment is quite precise and it is very easy to overrun it. There is no substitute for patience here, so take your time. I well remember spending a couple of hours on a machine with exactly the same problem, and I thought I would never get it right. The blade kept going off backwards and then forwards — but suddenly everything came right, and the machine is now running perfectly three years on.

I do not think that sanding a crown on the wheels would be of any benefit, even if possible.

*Alan Holtham*

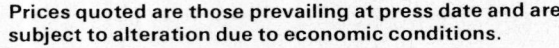
Prices quoted are those prevailing at press date and are subject to alteration due to economic conditions.

# Question box

**Q** *Can you tell me the correct type of wood to use for a flower trough? It will be fronting a timbered cottage; in size about 42×10in by 2ft in height; and therefore fairly rustic in appearance. Also, could you suggest a finish?*

*J. H. Jowitt, Warwick*

**A** I suggest you use elm, as a timber which can well stand being alternately wet and then dry. A rustic look can be achieved by using waney-edge boards. I would suggest several coats of linseed oil, both inside and out, before the trough is brought into use; the exterior could then be re-treated annually.

*Roger Woods*

**Q** *About a month ago I cut an oblique slice from a trunk of beech in order to make a 'rustic' sign. Realising that it would split if left to its own devices, I set about looking for some polyethylene glycol. In the end I had to buy from a Fisons distributor, which proved rather expensive. I suspect the laboratory grade is carefully purified and this explains the high price. Was it absolutely necessary for me to use PEG? I have seen many rustic signs of this sort and none had split. Is there another way of controlling shrinkage in this kind of cross-section work? (Not according to R. Bruce Hoadley, whose excellent book* Understanding Wood *contains an informative section on the use of PEG.) Finally, is PEG harmful to health in any way?*

*Simon Rish, Launceston*

**A** While the prevention of splits during the drying of endgrain wood discs is difficult, it is not impossible with suitable care.

Bruce Hoadley's advice is concerned with square-cut sections. The fact that tangential shrinkage (around the annual rings) is greater than radial shrinkage (across the rings) can create weaknesses which cause splits. Beech, unfortunately, has a high differential shrinkage ratio; in drying from the green state it shrinks, on average, 9.5% tangentially and 4.5% radially. However, if a disc is cut from a log obliquely this not only produces a better face for signwriting but, more importantly, places the pores and fibres at an angle and thus offers greater restraint to differential drying forces.

Polyethylene glycol is a bulking agent: when applied to wet wood it replaces the moisture held in the cell walls and thus prevents excessive shrinking. If the chemical is used, the wood must be very wet for it to be effective; it must penetrate deeply. However, a saturated solution of salt will do much the same job.

There is another alternative. Put out your sections to dry in the open air, carefully in stick, with a minimum of top cover. Watch them carefully; if the weather is dry, every couple of weeks break down the pile and dunk the pieces for a couple of hours in a bath of water, hose down the pile, or otherwise wet the wood. A couple of hours' wetting will not penetrate more than a tiny depth of the surface; the aim is to encourage the inner moisture to move rapidly to the surface, which must be kept moist until the very final stages. You should keep one piece as a control and, if possible, weigh it progressively. Even a smaller section can provide a guide. Beech at 15% MC will weigh around 45lb per cubic foot.

There is no reason to suppose that PEG is detrimental to the health of the average person.

**Q** *I have some difficulty in getting an even finish from proprietary stains, especially with softwoods. Is it an advantage to begin with a coat of filler, perhaps plaster of Paris, to which a little vandyke brown powder has been added?*

*Anthony Hewitt, Barnet*

**A** To even up the rate of absorption, make a mixture of equal parts raw linseed oil and white spirit, brush this on to the work and leave it for a few minutes. Then rub off the surplus oil with a clean rag and allow about 24 hours to dry. Use an oil stain to achieve the desired colour.

If a grain filler is to be used, choose an appropriate colour and apply it after staining.

Hardwoods should not be so difficult to stain evenly, and either water or oil stains will give excellent results. If any light patches do appear they can usually be evened up by applying a little more stain, diluted if necessary, to the areas concerned.

*Charles Cliffe*

**Q** *Old English wheelback chairs of the 18th century, which have been repaired quite a bit, are difficult to maintain in a usable, stable condition in the US climate. Can anyone recommend methods for stabilising these and not causing irreparable damage, such as may happen with epoxy glue or wedges in stretchers.*

*D. W. Kennard, St Louis, USA*

**A** St Louis has (according to my atlas) a continental climate with hot summers and cold winters, but high rainfall throughout the year. Fluctuations in humidity, i.e. the percentage of moisture in the air, would undoubtedly have an adverse effect. If the chairs are kept in a room where moisture and high summer temperatures, together perhaps with direct sunlight for part of the day, and dryness with high (central-heating) temperatures in winter are the general pattern, movement is inevitable and loose joints will result. 18th-century furniture in museums is normally kept in conditions of stable humidity and temperature to avoid this very problem. I can only recommend following the same procedure.

*Jack Hill*

# Elbow power

Aidan Walker sorts the useful
from the doubtful among
hand-held power tools

Every woodworker and most DIY-inclined householders of even average experience know something about power tools — even if it's only what they do and don't like. This is not a buyer's guide, nor an advertisement for Elu of Black & Decker, nor a list of complaints about (for example) Stanley or Wolf. It's a compendium of hints and handling ideas that have worked for me. Some you already know; some you may violently disagree with; some you may find useful.

## Safety

An attitude I have heard openly expressed more than once, and possibly the biggest danger of all, is: 'Not worth the bother — it's only the big machines that are dangerous.' With any machine, particularly those that are carried and held, the dangers to eyes and hands are manifold.
● The first principle of safety is one of attitude — this tool is designed to cut, drill or abrade material many times harder than my flesh, and should therefore always be treated with respect.
● Confidence is important, however, for smooth operation which is controlled and safe. The thing will bite you if it's treated timidly, just as much as if it's handled carelessly, impatiently, or as a means of proving how brave you are.
● Don't expect that because it's a machine it will perform any operation to which you set it as a knife performs in butter. Delicacy and sympathy are just as necessary using powered tools as they are for hand tools; you have to be aware of the way the wood is behaving and what sort of strain the machine itself is under.
● Be careful with power leads — don't swing drills from the tops of ladders by the wire; don't trail a lead across work you are belt-sanding. If you're using a number of tools in messy conditions, clear up periodically. One old coffin-maker and shopfitter I worked with swept up every 20 minutes.
● Don't put off changing or sharpening blades or drills — blunt cutting tools put too much wear on the machine, can chip or break, and may jam or burn the wood.

## Drills

Because of the DIY market, the competition in pricing drills is fiercest of all. It means that you can get a drill so cheap as to be almost disposable, and there is an argument for approaching them in this spirit. So many jobs need two or even three drills constantly available — clearance hole, countersink, pilot; masonry, wood, countersink — that it's well worth having two cheap tools as well as one of really good quality that'll last a lifetime.

The Stanley Screwsink bits are excellent, if expensive, for a hole and countersink in one; they break easily and can't always be

● *This Ryobi power plane can handle rebates up to 23mm deep*

used, but having a couple of common sizes will rationalise at least one pair of operations.

A hammer drill for masonry is indispensable, the manufacturers would have us believe, though everyone seemed to manage before they came on to the market. If you do a lot of masonry drilling, AEG or the Bosch industrials are the ones to go for. The Black & Decker industrial range is also excellent, but all these are horrifyingly expensive. Makita and Ryobi are serious Japanese contenders for this end of the market — but watch for different power ratings and accessories. Watch out, too, for the Bosch Professional DIY range; they are a lot less robust than they look.

A cheap Black & Decker hammer drill, with a reversible speed-controlled switch for screwdriving, has done me excellent service for four years — less than 20 quid and still going strong. If you fancy screeching screws into undrilled ply at eight or 10 a minute, you've got to have case-hardened, sharp-threaded items such as those Titus do, or GKN's new range of Supafast. The gremlin here is that they can often be harder than your screwdriver point, and if the fit isn't good you can throw away £5 a day in bits! Don't bother with a screwdriver facility on a drill that doesn't reverse.

Cordless tools are good for people who spend most of their days up ladders or inside heating ducts. I suspect that many cordless users have two of each, for until recently you had to charge the things for almost as long as you used them. They are getting better in this respect, and to have no wire trailing round a workshop floor is an obvious boon.

## Drill stands

Although cheap and cheerful might be OK for your second and third drills, don't skimp on the stand. Generally speaking, a cheap tool is a waste of time and money, and here you are asking for the accuracy and solidity of a proper drill-press at less than half the price. You gets what you pays for — some calibration systems are well worthwhile,

some are just decoration. Maintenance is particularly important, because grease on the column picks up dust and grit, and can do permanent damage. The more expensive stands can be turned into chisel-mortisers, for which strength and accuracy are vital. Look at the fencing arrangements — will you have to do a lot of your own modifications for setting up a repetitive drilling operation, or is the base designed for easy and quick fence adjustments? Can you take the base off to mount it in a Workmate for horizontal drilling?

## Attachments

Forget it. Difficult to set up, inaccurate to operate, attachments are the quickest and most efficient way of burning out your drill.

## Saws

If you can only afford one, it had better be a jigsaw. It can do the job of a circular saw, though not as well, and can be used where a circular saw is out of the question. Either way, it's best not to economise on this purchase.

The motor and blade fixing should be able to handle 2in-thick softwood with no trouble; have a careful look at the way the blade is mounted — does it have a supporting wheel behind it to counter forward pressure? If the blade sits deep in the mounting, the wheel may not be necessary. It can wear through quite quickly, and once there's a flat on it it won't spin. The Bosch system of fitting the blade is strong but fiddly; it depends on an extra-long narrow screwdriver which is easily lost. These Bosch tools are in the £70-100 industrial range, which like the Black & Deckers of equivalent price are well worth it.

Don't expect a perfectly vertical cut through timber of any thickness; jigsaw blades bend and wander very easily. Likewise, a tilt facility on the shoe is rather a waste of time if you need an accurately bevelled cut. For a good straight line in material up to ¾in thick, a proprietary guide or a straight-edge clamped to the work should give reasonable results, but a circular saw is better. Remember jigsaw blades cut upwards, so have the good face of the board downwards. Take care if you're cutting a complex shape to fit into an awkward corner, because you need to mark it out mirror-image so it fits the right way up.

In tight curves, see that you're not straining the blade. If it's a pocket cut-out, for a power point in a wall panel for instance, drill a clearance hole in each corner first. Otherwise cut a rounded shape and then work back into the tight corners. Try not to plan a cut-out where there's no room for the saw to come at it from all directions.

## Circular saws

Not just a site tool. With a bit of ingenuity you can set up jigs and tables to make circular saws perform with the accuracy of much

● *Right: Ideas for the home-made circular-saw table*

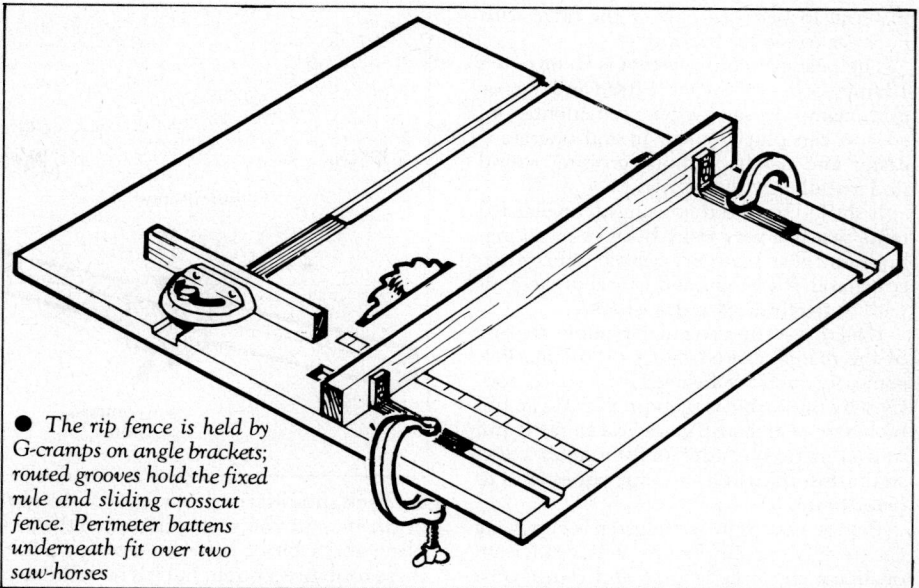

● *The rip fence is held by G-cramps on angle brackets; routed grooves hold the fixed rule and sliding crosscut fence. Perimeter battens underneath fit over two saw-horses*

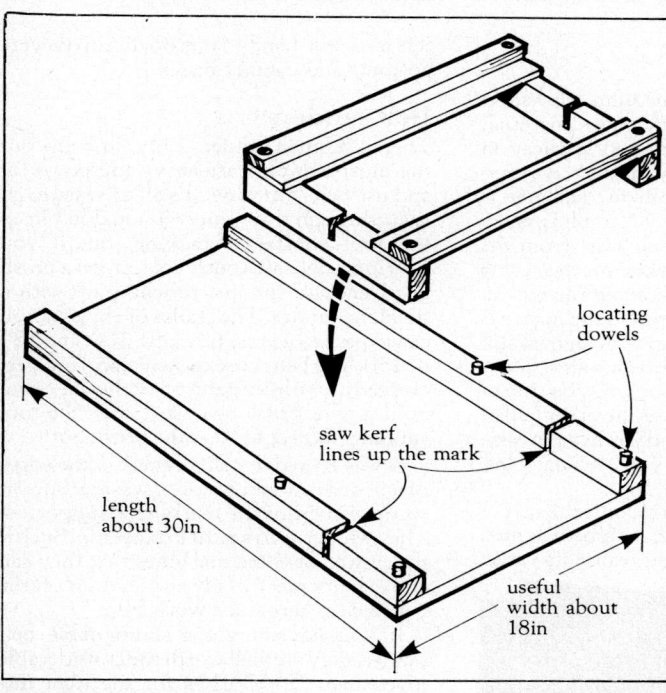

length about 30in

locating dowels

saw kerf lines up the mark

useful width about 18in

hardwood

6mm ply

● *Above: The saw plate runs against the hardwood; the ply lines up to the mark Left: This crosscut jig also works well for mitreing wide boards*

more expensive machines, yet keep the versatility of the 'take-the-tool-to-work' approach. In handling, firm and sure is safe. Again, the cut is upwards.

A 7¼in. blade is most common and most useful, but prices vary enormously. This size of blade will get you through up to about 2⅜in softwood, slightly less for hardwood; if you'll be mounting the saw in a proprietary or home-made table, reckon on losing at least another ¾in. Take long hard looks at the blade-guarding and guiding systems; some are so skinny as to be downright dangerous, some are so heavy and cumbersome as to be almost unusable. I particularly like the Skil guard, which can be moved without putting your hand anywhere near the blade.

The shoe on lightweight saws is not as strong as it should be; after dropping one a couple of times you'll have to do your own blacksmithing. The only way to be sure of accuracy, whether for angle settings or everyday perpendicular cutting, is to check with a square. Bigger models — by Elu,

Makita, and Black & Decker especially — have very solid, tough shoe-plates, but their weight makes them somewhat cumbersome. The small 6in AEG I have found very impressive, with a good fence, and even adjustable bushes for wobble-sawing grooves of different widths; expensive, though.

Guiding the cut: by and large the fences that come with the machines are inaccurate. They also mean you reproduce the line of the edge, which surprisingly often is far from straight. Far more reliable is a good straight-edge clamped or pinned the same distance from the line as the edge of the shoe from the blade. Remember which side of the line you want to go! A good solid T-square will aid crosscuts on wide boards; so will a two-piece frame jig of the type illustrated, which can take any board up to the maximum width. Remember to adjust the blade so that it cuts about 1mm into the base board, to avoid breakout on the underside. The kerf in the rails of the jig itself will be a good reference point for your first

few cuts, but the inevitable wobble in the bearings of saws like this will soon make it too wide to be reliable. A length stop is easily arranged if you need to cut many pieces to one size.

Well worth the investment of as much time and care as you can muster, a table for your hand-held saw more than doubles its usefulness. If you accurately square the board into which the machine will be mounted, and mount it equally square, you can use the edges as reference for the rip-and cross-cut fences. The more elaborate you want to be, the more accurate you can be. Rout a groove to run a proprietary or home-made crosscut/mitre fence. Mount a hardwood or metal bar at the end of the table to slide the rip fence on, and set a steel rule into the table as calibration for your ripped sizes — or, to keep it slightly simpler, a line scored down the table minutely out of parallel with the blade will give accurate reference to set the rip fence. It should travel away from the back of the blade by about ¹⁄₃₂in in 5ft.

For mounting the saw underneath, the trade-off is between strength of fixing and depth of cut. If the saw is to be taken in and out of the table, a routed recess for the sole-plate is a good idea, to re-align accurately with your reference marks. Don't make it too deep; you have to countersink machine screws into the surface of the table to line up with holes drilled in the sole-plate, so allow for that depth, plus some strength of material in between. Cover the table with Formica to reduce friction.

The best switching system is to mount a 13amp socket on the table itself and tape or mini-clamp the saw switch permanently on, so you can plug the saw in and operate it easily and safely without groping round underneath.

It should be said that using an unguarded table saw is a very risky business; a riving-knife and guard can very easily be fabricated, adjustable for height and lateral movement with butterfly-nuts and washers.

If all this seems too much trouble, try one of the manufactured tables on the market, some of which can be used for a router too. Or why not just invest about £250 in an Elu table saw, which also gives you snip-off and mitre functions? A dream for a small workshop, this, though its accuracy does tend to deteriorate.

Blades; east or west, tungsten is best. One cut in ply or chipboard will render an ordinary steel blade dull and dangerous, likely to snatch, and certain to strain the motor. Tungsten doesn't go on for ever, but it feels like it!

## Power planes

These are not substitutes for hand planes, as the Black & Decker ads would have us believe. Some say you can get a fine finish with them, but real accuracy is out of the question. The adjustment is the same as the standing machines — moveable front plate, back plate dead level with the revolving cutter; but, because you're moving the tool along the work, the back plate moves up and down with the surface irregularities. The blades are only three or four inches wide, too, which makes it well-nigh impossible to get an even surface across a board wider than that.

The notch in the front shoe for chamfering also has its drawbacks. Once you've made the first pass and knocked off the sharp corner, the notch is very difficult to register accurately for an even line. Once

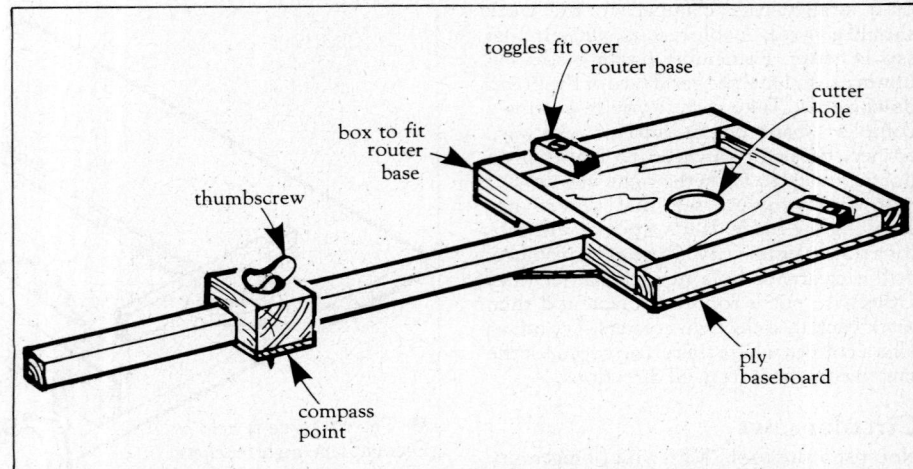

the back shoe lifts or drops, the cutters miss or dig in, and you wish you'd used the jack plane and a bit of patience. For some jobs these tools are a boon, but it's better to save enough for two and buy a small planer-thicknesser.

## Biscuiters

More for the small-to-medium workshop producing cabinets from sheet material, biscuit jointers have a limited application but perform marvellously within it. A 3mm-wide blade about 100mm in diameter is mounted vertically to pivot in a solid casing. The fence sets the distance away from the edge, the centre line marked on the casing positions it to your mark; press the button and push the handle, in which the motor is mounted, and you end up with an oval slot that takes a compressed beech wafer.

The slot in the corresponding position of the board to be joined takes the other half of the protruding biscuit, and you have an easy, accurately located and very strong joint. Glue and clamp or screw.

This tool still has to overcome the sort of market resistance which chipboard met, but once you use one you realise its value.

● *For accurate setting of the router compass, square a line round the block through the pin. If you know the distance from the edge of the baseboard to the cutter centre, the rest is easy*

It is also very handy for grooving in drawer-bottoms and cabinet backs.

## Belt sanders

There are small sanders with 3in belts, but the most common are heavy and powerful and use belts 4in wide. It's all too easy to go right through thin veneer if you don't keep the tool constantly moving, but if you develop a delicate touch you can get a finish good enough for just touching up with a finishing sander. The grades of abrasive you can expect to use are 60 or 80, 100, and 120 or 150. The belts are expensive, so if one gets clogged up with old paint or pitch-pine resin, hold a wire brush against it with the tool running. Expect to wear the brush out!

A way to avoid losing veneer at the edges of a board is to pin strips of waste around it so the weight of the machine is supported. They will serve to hold it in place too. Such is the power of these machines that they can grab a hefty piece of ply and shoot it off the bench clear across the workshop.

If you haven't got a sliding-table belt sander, they are well worth the considerable investment (£150-£200 for the right machine) — but practise on waste first. Going back and forth across the piece, sweeping the grain slightly, is the best way for the first coarse work; then go carefully in the direction of the grain. The adjustable frame on some models limits the amount you can take off in any one area, and helps towards an even finish.

## Finishing sanders

Orbital sanders operate at very high speed and can produce a very fine finish. If you are really finicky, however, you will almost always be able to see tiny circular scratches which will not come out unless you take to the scraper and cork block. They can be minimised by dusting the work off at short intervals to get rid of the grit that creates them, but you'll never eliminate them completely.

The faster the machine the better — a £40

● *Around £93+VAT buys this 7¼in circular saw from the Bosch industrial range; 1kw motor and a very heavy blade guard*

Black & Decker works at 7000rpm, an £80 Elu at 11,000. A strong motor and solid construction are always good, but really heavy ones like the bigger Elu can be very tiring to use. I have found the Elu versions surprisingly unreliable, too, perhaps because of their high speeds. The little palm-sized sanders, first introduced by Makita, are nice to use but also not very long-lived. Consider them an addition to a full-sized one, not a substitute.

## Routers

Last but definitely not least. Ten years ago, only those in specialised areas of the trade had even heard of the router; today, you're not a woodworker without one. Recessing, rebating, slotting, moulding, dovetailing, template work — the huge range of operations is limited by the power of the machine you have, and by the cutters you can or can't afford. As with saw-blades, TCT cutters are best, although HSS (carefully maintained) will do light work in softwoods.

When buying, shop around and make careful comparisons. Can you stand the tool upside-down to change the cutters? Is the switch within reach without your moving your hand from the grips? If the router is a plunge version, how smooth is the rise and fall? Is the lock mechanism likely to shake the machine if you operate it while it's running? Is there a choice of depth stops, and are they easily adjustable and unlikely to move with vibration? Also, is the fence strong and easy to fit? Does it have fine adjustment? How good are the fittings? Are removable bits easily replaced, or will you have to wait for the next shipment from Korea? How heavy is it? What's the collet size? — if it's ¼in, can you get one to fit ⅜in- or ½in-shank cutters?

If you're not going to use the tool for really heavy work, a small model such as the Bosch POF52 is fine. It only has a 500w motor — very easy to overload — but the accessories and fence are well made. Light machines like this are best for freehand work; obviously you won't be able to use them for window rebates in hardwood frames all day long, but for many jobs the bigger, heavier, more powerful machines are difficult to use.

Cutting speeds are especially critical with the router, and obviously vary according to the size of cutter as well as the rating of the machine. The rule of thumb is that you don't push it so the motor is labouring. Don't try a full-width cut deeper than the diameter of the cutter, and always feed against the direction of rotation. There shouldn't be a drop in motor speed under load of more than 20%. Feeding too slowly will cause friction and burning; feeding too fast will give a roughly finished cut, if the tool can handle it and the cutter doesn't break. Using blunt cutters will give you both sets of bad effects — a burnt, roughly finished cut, and quite likely ruined bearings as well. Pulling the machine towards you is generally the safest and most controlled way of using it, although it isn't always possible. Maintain a grip that gives you maximum control, resting the edges of your hands on the work and keeping some sideways pressure if using a guide.

Torque reaction can cause quite a heavy tool to leap from your grasp — have it running at full speed before you start feeding, and bring it in smoothly to the

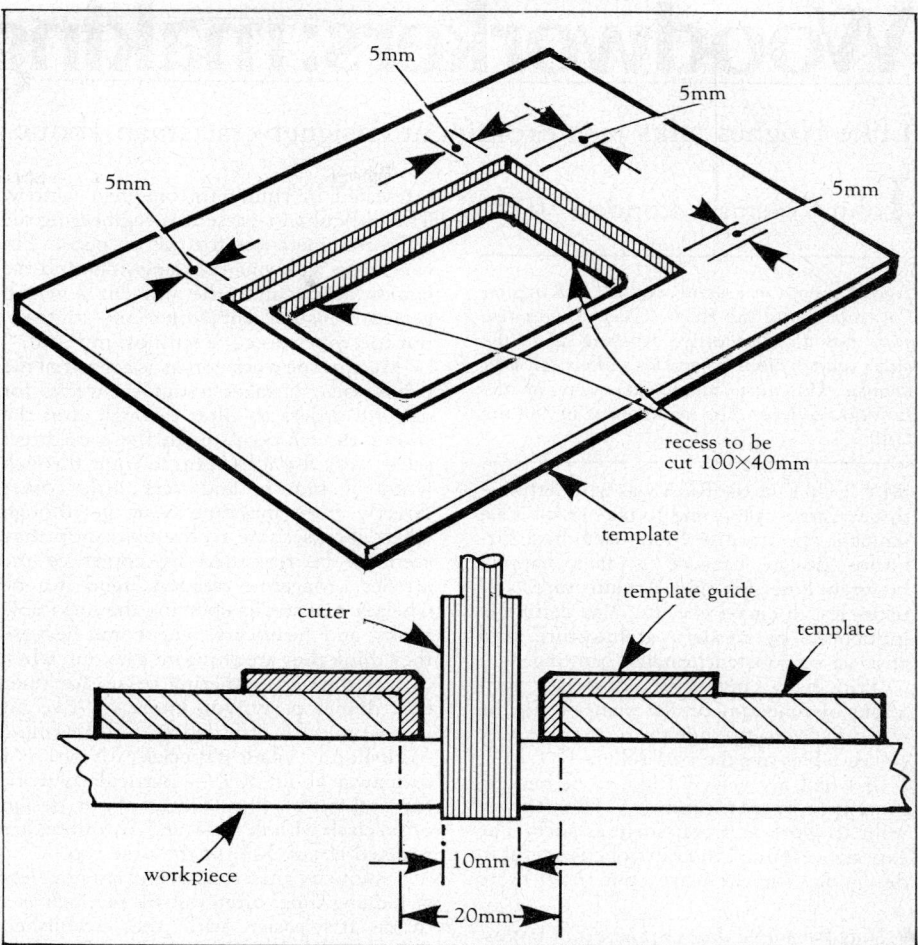

● *Getting the template right; subtract cutter diameter from template-guide diameter and add the difference to the size of the required cut. For a* 100 × 40mm *recess with a* 10mm *cutter and a* 20mm *guide, the template opening is* 110 × 50mm

work. Remember that a router is a high-speed chisel, and needs as much delicacy in use. Loose clothing and hair near the machine are obviously very risky; because you usually want to watch the cut closely, eye protectors are an absolute must.

The clamped T-square is probably the most useful routing jig for cuts across wide boards. Positioning it is easily done by subtracting half the cutter diameter from half the base-plate width.

Any shape of template can be cut, using the tool inside a ply baseboard with batten fences; elementary maths again gives you the correct size. If the template is 0.5mm out, don't try and alter it — chuck it and start again. For decorative shapes, a template guide (which should come with the machine) bolts on round the cutter. Be careful, if you aim to produce small designs, that the template isn't too small to hold the router base properly.

For circles, proprietary trammel-bars are available, but you can easily make your own adjustable 'router compass'. A box with toggles that will fit and clamp the base in place is fixed to a solid batten, on to which you slide a close-fitting ply box with a sharpened screw point projecting underneath and a butterfly-nut tightener on top. Mark the position of the point accurately so you can get the right radius. With all such

gadgets, always set up and test before you make the irrevocable cut.

Dovetails: for drawers, you need not only a dovetail cutter but a template guide and a dovetailing jig. If you plan this, make sure when you buy the machine that a jig is available for it. They aren't cheap — the Elu version will set you back £57. For dovetail housing joints, you need to mount the machine upside-down; tables are available, or you can make your own and pass (say) the drawer-side vertically over the cutter, most of which is buried in the fence. Careful setting-up and testing are needed to get the right fit into the groove.

A table is another boon, and comparatively simple to make because the fence does not need to be parallel to its edge. If you pivot a hardwood fence at one end of the table, run the machine and gently feed the fence into the cutter, it will bury itself up to the necessary depth and form a very good chipbreaker too. Rebating or moulding components before assembly is a dream with the router set up like this.

As for bearing and pin cutters, guide pins spin at the same speed as the cutter — at best leaving a mark on the edge of the work and at worst burning and digging a hole in it. Removable bearings are more expensive, but worth it; you can get different sizes to make, for example, an ovolo into a rounding-over cutter. They also collect gunge; clean them regularly with meths or thinners.

The more you use a router, the more you realise you can use it. Like a drill, it soon begins to tell you it should have a bigger (or smaller) companion in your workshop. ■

# Woodworkers: making a living

Luke Hughes talks to a prominent designer-craftsman about work and pay

## John Coleman, London W11

*Aged 31; born in London, studied at Kingston Polytechnic and the RCA. Over the last few years has had impressive exposure at all the major craft exhibitions and his work is now well known. Has also taught at many of the furniture colleges. His workshop is in Notting Hill.*

'MY TIME at the RCA was wonderful — three years to play, and to take risks; it's a fantastic opportunity. I suppose I chose furniture design because it falls happily between Fine Art and Architecture, and takes less long to execute; I'm definitely influenced by modern architecture, and abstract or constructionalist painting.

'Principally, my work comprises variations of veneering on flat planes using the wood figure to provide the decoration. My coffee-tables are the best-sellers.

'If I had my way, I'd like to be making more prototypes for industry. I don't really want to work as a craftsman as such. The experience gained in craftwork is useful in designing for industry but I'm more interested in running a one-man factory. The difficulty at present is engineering the right circumstances for this to occur. I'm caught up with small commissions and the exhibition circuit at the moment — which generates insufficient work to sub-contract, but too much to cope with on my own.

'Most of the work comes as a result of the exhibitions. It takes about six weeks for definite orders to filter through after the shows, though occasionally there are direct sales. Very few jobs seem to come through word of mouth, and very little comes directly from magazine coverage, though when clients come to the workshop they seem to be reassured by copies of the articles. Magazine readers tend to be Chelsea matriarchs sporting the inevitable husky and headscarf, who come because they think they are doing me a favour, when in fact they are gathering gossip for their next dinner party; you know — "I've got this wonderful little fellow . . . charming workshop . . . made it specially for me . . ." I turn away about 30% — particularly work for architects, whose ideas about design often clash with mine — and my quotes are rejected about 30% of the time too.

'I quote by guesstimate, and am hopeless at judging time: often out by as much as a third. It's easier with the established designs. I seldom get jobs when the potential profit looks huge, but when I do, I start to feel guilty, though I haven't got to the stage of offering a refund yet. Yes, I've had one bad client who refused to pay for some design work, which taught me to be less ambiguous about the terms of an agreement. I had to live with the loss, which was about £600. I've never had a really bad cock-up, though I've sometimes felt that the quality of work has been lower than it should be.

'I bought the workshop freehold, and I have a flat above. It was an absolute bargain. My initial investment was a Startrite 352 bandsaw but to date I have probably invested about £7500. I have a Startrite dimension saw, a planer/thicknesser, a Multico mortiser and a pillar drill. The most indispensable machine is the dimension saw, though the line on a long crosscut tends to curve slightly. The machine I've most regretted buying is a medium-sized router, and I'd recommend anyone to go for a big one. I've also got an Elu 713 belt sander which irritates me; the belt is awkward to change, especially if you have the frame on, and it tends to skew in operation. Elu make a good orbital sander, though, and on the whole I rate their products fairly highly. By contrast, all the Makita machines I've come into contact with have no guts and are clumsy to use.

'As local suppliers I use Cecil Tyzack and Barrie Irons. I buy hand tools there too. I don't lose that many each year, but I have been known to box them up in stud partitions.

'I'm meticulous about keeping the workshop tidy — or at any rate as much as one can in a dusty job, not only because of the insurance requirements but because I can't stand going into a dusty workshop in the morning. Scraps and waste I cut up for my parents to burn.

'I teach at Rycotewood for 20 days a year. In terms of pay, it's not that rewarding, but it gets me out of the workshop and into contact with others. I enjoy talking to the students.

'I don't employ anyone. I have done, but I fret too much about the quality and time taken. I'd rather subcontract totally, and put it all out of sight. I wouldn't employ ex-Rycotewood students unless they had at least a year's commercial experience. At college they gain no idea about making a living, and a year in someone else's workshop, even at a pittance, would give them that. I can't afford to give it to them, though. I did take on one person for 18 months who had been an excellent student, but his work deteriorated when confronted with the time factor. I would expect to pay £2 to £2.50 per hour.

'My preferred finish is two-part acid-catalyst lacquer. I'm desperately looking for someone else to do this.

'The skill I've always wanted to acquire but never got round to is upholstery. I did a little in 1979 which whetted my appetite, but have never found the time since.' ∎

● *Note the mitred drawer-front detail in this sycamore-and-ebony piece (photo Janet Baldwin)*

● *A blanket chest by John Coleman in walnut and sycamore*

# Guild notes

## Guild of WOODWORKERS

Shared information, advice and help are vital to good woodwork. They are also the basis of the **Guild of Woodworkers**: an international organisation which welcomes new members — whatever their skills. PO Box 35, Hemel Hempstead HP2 4SS (phone 0442 41221).

Guild members get
- priority on our courses
- free publicity in *Woodworker*
- 15% off Woodworker Show entry
- a free display area and meeting-point at the Show
- 15% discount on our plans
- access to and inclusion in our register of members' skills and services
- the chance to contact other members for help and advice where appropriate
- specially arranged tool in-rance at low rates

Please quote your Guild number when contacting us.

*Aidan Walker*

## Oz opinion

Norm Matthews writes to join the Guild, and let us know a little of what he does. He is a builder by occupation and a wood-carver/sculptor by inclination, and prefers to use reclaimed material. Finding the right piece, he says, is at least part of the pleasure; he also gets a lot out of using the beautiful Antipodean timbers for his cabinet work — blackwood, myrtle, red gum and wild cherry. He would like to correspond with other woodworkers in Australia who share his interests.
- Write to Norm at 138 Arundel St, Benalla 3672, Victoria, Australia.

## Milton Keynes Craft Guild

To be launched in early 1985, the Milton Keynes Craft Guild will cover north Bucks, south Northants, north Herts and all of Bedfordshire. It is intended to encourage interest and awareness in all crafts, to maintain the best standards of craft and design, and to promote craft work, and will mount lectures, demonstrations, exhibitions and workshops.

There will be two tiers of membership, full professional and associate, and one of the aims is to co-operate with numerous like-minded local organisations such as East Midlands Arts and the Milton Keynes Workshop Trust. The subscription has not yet been fixed; if you want to know more, write to John Gordon, 4 Waterside, Peartree Bridge, Milton Keynes, Bucks.

## Cabinetmakers' Decorative Techniques

Bob Grant's Oxford course on 1 December was valuable and interesting, all agreed at the end of the day. There was a suggestion that a **stage 2 course** be arranged to follow on where the first leaves off, and Bob is willing to teach one — but, obviously, if you haven't been on the first the second would not be so relevant. The best idea is to arrange the two in fairly close conjunction in late spring/early summer.

This is a request to gauge the reaction — **write or phone** if you'd like to spend a day with Bob learning the basic techniques of hand moulding and inlaying, and another dealing with more advanced theory and practice. Cost will be £26.50+VAT. No point in fixing it up if there aren't enough people, so let me know.

## COURSE CORNER

### Woodmachining — Ken Taylor

The Guild's first one-day introductory course on basic woodmachining techniques is in East London on 9 February, £25+VAT. Still a few places left — send your cheque immediately for a confirmed place. If it's full, you will go automatically on to the list for the next one . . .

### Woodmachining — Guild/A. Pollard

In happy association with this highly respected old-established Buckinghamshire tool merchant, the Guild is mounting the second of its introductory woodmachining courses on 16 March 1985. Ken Taylor will again be instructing from his wealth of experience; we are grateful to Bruce Pollard of Pollard & Son in Bletchley for making his well-equipped premises available for the day. He is a distributor of Luna machinery, who manufacture most of the gear you will get your hands on. Naturally — being a Guild course — this is not a puff for one type of machine over another, so you should get a good overview of what machine is best to buy, as well as acquaint yourself with the basic tricks of band- and circular-sawing, planing, thicknessing, mortising and spindle moulding. £25+VAT; full payment confirms booking.

## Finishing and Polishing — Charles Cliffe

The first of these popular courses for 1985, in January, sold out almost before it came out! For the disappointed, we have asked Charles to do another one in April, and the dates are now confirmed — 25th and 26th. Because the Guild now has to charge VAT on all its courses, the cost will be £40 inclusive; still an excellent bargain for a thorough introduction to surface preparation, staining, filling, bodying up and spiriting off, and the various sorts of finish. And who can put a price on those invaluable hints that only come from someone of Charles' experience?
- Send your cheque to book your place — if you are disappointed this time, there will be another one as soon as possible.

## Country Chairmaking

Pull Court, Tewkesbury, Gloucester — in these palatial surroundings, learn the basic techniques of making Country ('stick') furniture from Fred Lambert, the country's acknowledged master. 1-5 April, 1985; five full days' instruction, including tea, coffee, and lunch, for £145+VAT. Details of hotels, guest-houses or bed and breafast in this pretty part of the country are available if you let me know when you book — as with all courses, a place is confirmed on full payment of the fee.

According to the response we get to this course in its new venue, we hope to arrange the more advanced subjects of toolmaking, steam-bending and design, all under Fred's experienced tutelage. Bookings to me at the *Woodworker* office.

- *The craft workshops behind this stately building, which now houses Bredon School, are fully equipped for country chairmaking – a Fred Lambert course*

98

Prices quoted are those prevailing at press date and are subject to alteration due to economic conditions.

# Guild notes

## Woodland Trust

In response to the 'Splendour and Peril' article in December's *Woodworker*, Adrian Peter writes to ask me to put a word in for the Woodland Trust, a charity formed to safeguard Britain's native broad-leaved woodlands.

'As people who love to work beautiful timber,' says Adrian, 'we owe a debt of gratitude to the past which produced it, and can repay this debt by a sense of duty to the future. Not only with a view to ensuring supplies of fine timber to woodworkers as yet unborn (future *Woodworker* readers?), but to protecting our whole environment. The preservation of our broad-leaved woodlands also protects the habitats of many of the wild creatures which we enjoy depicting in our carvings.' Good point, that last one — spoken from a heart of oak, Adrian. Thank you for feeding this particular bee in my bonnet.
● Woodland Trust, Westgate, Grantham, Lincolnshire NG31 6LL, tel. (0476) 74297.

## Women's workshop

Olympic Gold Medallist Tessa Sanderson cut the tapes at the Southwark Women's Training Workshop on 16 November, to open officially a very significant institution.

The publicity material that came into the office was extremely coherent and well-produced: a good sign for any organisation that wishes to be taken seriously. Although the workshop has been operating for nearly a year, they have waited until now for the official launch, presumably to establish themselves and get a considered response from the women who have been working there.

It is for women over 25 in the London Borough of Southwark, and runs two courses a year with 24 trainees on each for 28 hours a week. All the instructors are women, all City and Guilds trained, from all areas of the trade — between them they have experience in purpose-made joinery, site work, woodmachining, shopfitting, stage carpentry and building maintenance. The courses are designed to bring trainees

● *Trainees at Southwark Women's Training Workshop get 22 hours a week practical work and 1½ hours technical drawing (photos Brenda Prince)*

to the level of the first-year City and Guilds Craft Certificate, and covers benchwork and building techniques; most go on to building college, where their first-year study is waived.

Naturally, a women's approach to a traditionally male-dominated trade also includes

advice and help on dealing with the resistance they are bound to meet. 'It is hard', one carpentry student is quoted as saying, 'because you have to be really, really sure it's what you want to do. You have to be really determined.' The workshop employs a childcare co-ordinator to minimise the factors that generally keep women out of skill training.

In 1979, of over 300,000 pupils taking craft, design and technology subjects at O and CSE levels, less than 3% were girls. In Greater London, men who make and repair things earn an average of £138 a week; women in the same category earn £54. However small a drop the workshop represents in however huge an ocean, it is certainly a healthy move for women's fulfilment, in both craft and professional terms — and it's important for woodwork too. Why should a woodworker be a he?

## Community workshop

Another enterprise worth noting is the Ormond Road Workshops in north London — set up to make woodworking facilities (among others) available to those lacking experience, equipment and space. For a nominal yearly subscription the user gets access to the workspace, a chance for instruction, and opportunity to borrow tools. The classes are funded partly by the Inner London Education Authority and partly by the workshop's own activities.

They plan a new set of buildings, for which they have already raised £210,000, and they are currently aiming to raise another £110,000 to get the scheme finished by September. The new premises are designed for use by disabled people too, and the extra money is needed mainly for specialist equipment, machinery, fixtures and fittings.

As one who has recently been suffering severe withdrawal symptoms from a professional workshop, this sort of input into a local community is what I like to see! They'd be glad of even a quid or two to help them buy some good machinery, so if you're feeling generous . . .
● Ormond Road Workshops, 25 Ormond Road, London N19, tel. 01-263 3865.

# Light reliefs

INSPIRED by the colour-impregnated wood-blocks used for textile printing, Howard Raybould sees himself as the provider of a style of embellishment appropriate to the simple, often harsh, lines of modern furniture.

With a training in sculpture and experience in an architectural woodcarving workshop, Howard moved into making mirror frames for a living — going, as he puts it, for 'a gorgeous, generous feeling' which average, restrained frames lacked.

Where do the bowls of fruit fit in? 'Look at the decoration over an Adam fireplace,' he says, 'and you will find a bowl . . .'

This is no gallery art, but every day woodcarving to be enjoyed in the home or on the street. Fading colours on boats and buildings in the bright light of the Mediterranean prompt him to plan age into his work, letting the wood's darkening and the paints' fading processes alter the feel of the piece as time advances. 'Colour is bad,' he says, 'if it obscures the feeling of the wood.'

A city-dweller, Howard does not look for the shape aching to get out of his timber blank. His material comes from timber yards, not forests; 'Relief carving suggests itself when all you can get is planks!' ∎

# The WOODV MDF Compe

## A major design contest for a major new material

If you're in the furniture trade or even at college, you'll already know about medium density fibreboard — and you'll know why it's caught on so firmly.

Arguably the first new panel product since chipboard arrived after World War II, MDF challenges its predecessor in important ways; and it's very nearly as cheap. No material will do everything — but MDF bids fair to take a well-earned place of its own alongside the established favourites. And it's now being made in the British Isles.

The funny thing is that a lot of people haven't heard of it yet. But it's widely available if you know where to look (FIDOR will tell you the names of stockists in your district), so there's no reason not to give it a try.

That's why we've organised this competition. Amateur and professional will be in with equal chances, because we're after clever, attractive, original designs — whether or not they need a lot of time and/or fancy equipment in the execution.

We also guarantee extensive national publicity for the winners and their designs — in the form of coverage in **Woodworker** magazine, nationally available each month, plus a comprehensive release to the media by FIDOR.

The closing date isn't till 30 April 1985: so please don't be shy. Go on — enter! We have no preconceptions about what's going to win: and we're longing to hear from you.

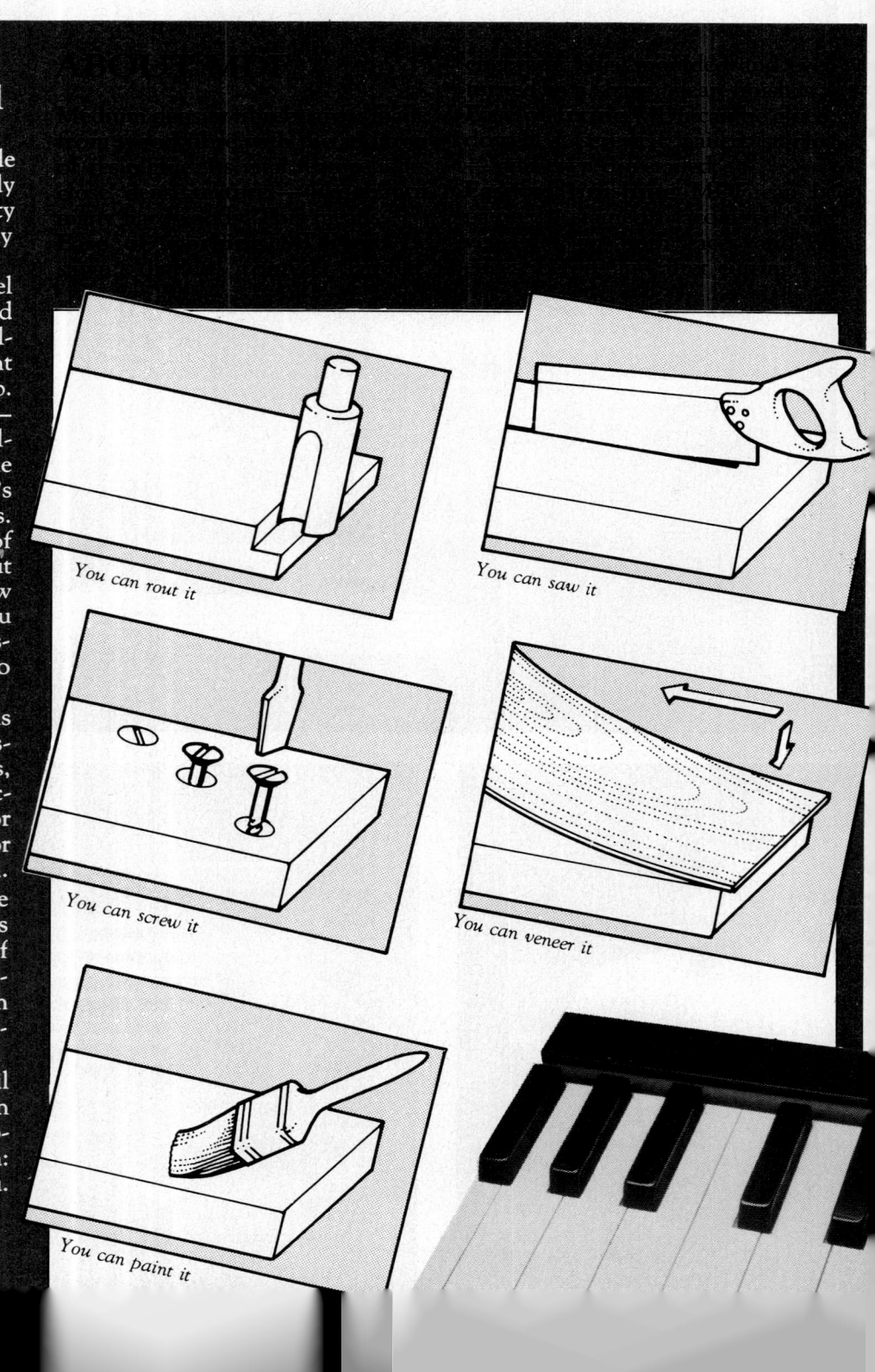

You can rout it

You can saw it

You can screw it

You can veneer it

You can paint it

# ORKER Magazine
# ion

**Sponsored by FIDOR
— the Fibre Building
Board Organisation**

*pictures Medite of Europe*

## THE RULES

**1** Each entry must be an object which has been made substantially in MDF:
*either* a free-standing piece or set of pieces of furniture *or* a fitment or decorative feature for domestic or business use.

**2** The entry must consist of a written description outlining the nature of the design and the

● *Curves and planes; the chairs on the cover are MDF, as is this triangular table by Gerry Auburn of Bucks College*

thinking behind it (this should not run to more than two sides of A4 paper); a set of dimensioned drawings; *and either* a perspective drawing *or* one or more photos *or* both.

● *The versatility of MDF: applied mouldings, piano parts and snooker tables are among the many roles it plays*

**3** All entries should be sent to FIDOR and arrive before 1 May 1985.

**4** To enter, you must live on the UK mainland.

**5** The decision of **Woodworker** magazine and FIDOR is final in all matters concerning this competition. The judges reserve the right not to make awards if they think it inappropriate.

We'll be looking for a design which is interesting in itself, and effectively uses the principal characteristics of MDF (credit being given for originality in both respects). Quality of execution will also be an important factor.

FIDOR is at 1 Hanworth Rd, Feltham, Middx TW13 5AF, tel. 01-751 6107. They will be pleased to help with all queries, no matter how simple or how technical. And anyone who asks (competition entrant or not) will be sent a comprehensive package of information about MDF — including a personalised list of MDF stockists in his or her own particular area.

**To** FIDOR, 1 Hanworth Rd, Feltham, Middx TW13 5AF

### The WOODWORKER magazine MDF Competition

**1** Please send me more information about MDF
**2** I would like to enter the competition and enclose my description, drawings, and perspective or photo
*(Please delete either 1 or 2 if inapplicable)*

Name ......................................................................................................

Address ...................................................................................................

# Outrageously subtle

Peter Howlett won the Young Professionals section at the Woodworker Show with this classy writing-table. Here he outlines his inspiration and methods

● The frame is maple and the top is bird's-eye-maple veneer. For the sitter's convenience there are only three lower rails

The primary source for this design was, believe it or not, the pure line of 19th-century Korean furniture. Unlike Chinese furniture of the same period, this has a great simplicity of both appearance and construction. My other influence was the American cabinetmaker and author James Krenov. Although at times too esoteric for my taste, he has produced some elegant pieces.

Thus inspired, I set to work at the drawing-board. I wanted a table that could be made in five hours (I have to earn a living); could exist in several forms, from occasional to dining (I have to justify the tooling, plus the time spent on producing the design and making jigs); would not look out of context in a modern setting (I do not subscribe to the modern-movement philosophies which seem intent on making things as big, bold and thoroughly impractical as possible); and yet would be individual enough to catch the eye.

I satisfied the last requirement very quickly by choosing bird's-eye maple; I love the subtle outrageousness of this timber's figuring when revealed in flat surfaces. The other points came down firmly to one consideration: money. The table could not possibly be hand-made, as I would be suffering losses the moment I picked up a mortise chisel. I used my overarm router to break away from square-sectioned legs. This is my favourite tool, and juggling with the radii was fun. Eventually I arrived at proportions I felt pleasing.

The double rail, however, was chosen for aesthetic reasons rather than economy, its visual function being to break up what would otherwise be a thick section necessary for the table's rigidity.

Finally, a veneered top eliminates the troubles associated with solid wood — and, more importantly, provides a wider and more commercially available palette of colour and texture. I do not hold with a dogmatic insistence on solid wood when a better and more efficient alternative is obtainable and within my budget.

I began to play with these three basic elements — the shaped upright, the double rail and the highly decorative flat surface; and new ideas began to flow. One of Krenov's books illustrates what he calls a 'no-glass showcase' made by him. This resembled a Korean display cabinet I knew,

pictured here. I felt that the table's elements could be combined in a similar design.

A double rail at the top would have made the piece look top-heavy, so I placed it at the bottom. Both Krenov and the Korean master had put drawers above the cupboard space, but I felt this would make the design look squat; I wanted the sense of height, though without the object's being physically tall. Besides, drawers would mean a lot of building out from the rails — clumsy construction which would detract from the simplicity of the piece as well as chiselling away at the profit margin.

I exceeded my time-limit for the making, but the design works well in production. The construction was based on the router, which is a beautiful machine not only for

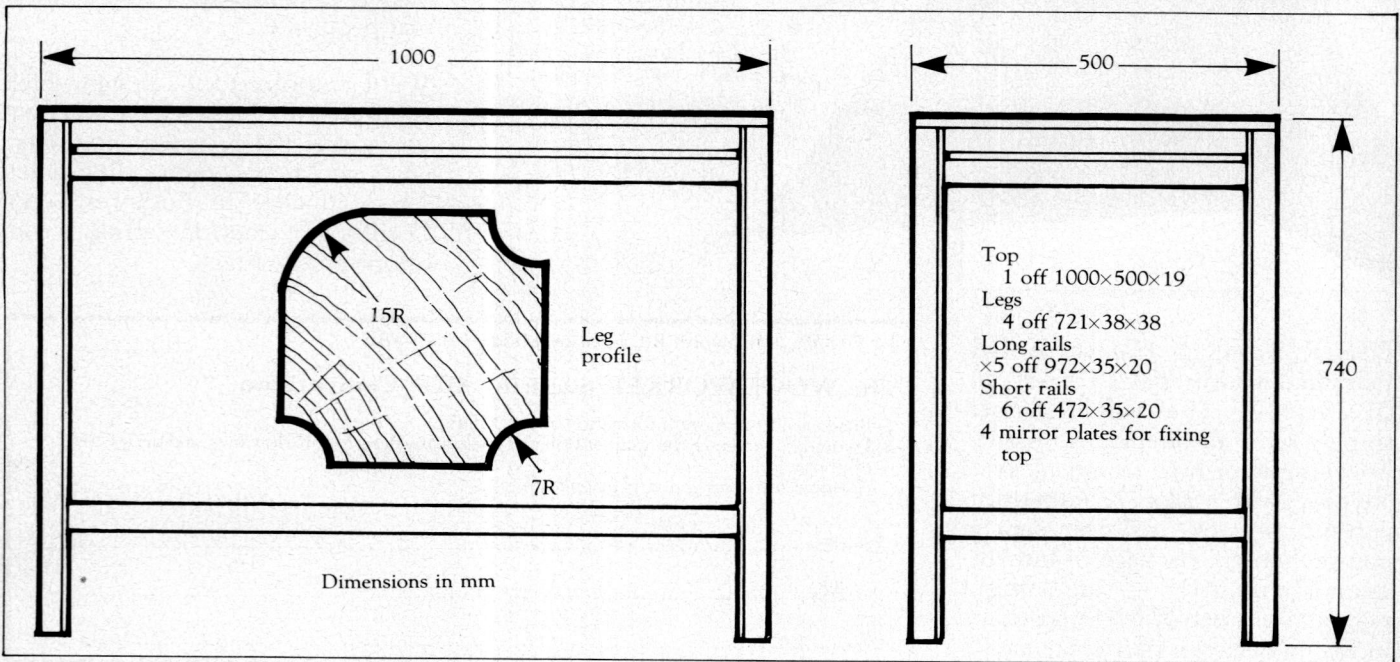

1000

15R

7R

Leg profile

Dimensions in mm

500

Top
  1 off 1000×500×19
Legs
  4 off 721×38×38
Long rails
  ×5 off 972×35×20
Short rails
  6 off 472×35×20
4 mirror plates for fixing
  top

740

● For Peter Howlett, these two antique Korean pieces possess the simple elegance he is trying to achieve in his own work

shaping but also for cutting clean mortises. Its use is far from purely mechanical: much skill is involved in setting up stops, and in 'graining-out' (feeding into the machine without tearing the grain). You can tell by feel when the wood is having a tough time.

It's a mistake for woodworkers to dismiss machines, for that is to ignore their potential. My head of department at college was a journeyman cabinetmaker whose work was beyond compare. He used to say to the technician, no less of a genius: 'There must be a better way of doing this. I'll come back in half an hour when you've worked it out.' As a result of this philosophy, the workshop was full of jigs. Nevertheless, it was only when we had learnt to hand-plane our wood face-side and edge, to gauge it and plane to thickness, that we were allowed to use the planer.

As in all things, you need a bit of luck. The lippings for the top came from a veneer cover-board which I noticed leaning against the wall in a merchant's shed. I bought it cheaply with the table in mind. The element of chance must never be overlooked, because many a wood-yard contains hidden surprises.

Afterwards, I found myself drawing screens which would complete a suite. The Oriental design was producing 20th-century clones. The double rail was now at the top, middle and bottom — but the very tight constraint of hingeing meant that the shaped upright had to go. Strong yet relatively thin members and coarsely woven silk would provide the subtle balance between form and function. Meanwhile I

have been able to keep both the leg shape and double rail for a small free-standing display cabinet, again based on the Korean model.

The finish for all these is spraygun-applied, plastic-based, and so very practical that its use in the modern workshop cannot be ignored. Since I only like matt finishes, the surfaces were flatted with wire wool — using wax as a lubricant, rather than a finish in its own right.

For me furniture must be simple, without pretension, and obviously man-made rather than contrived to look the opposite. I always rely on a careful choice of materials, more often than not juxtaposing exotic veneers with plain structural parts — not only for visual but also for practical reasons: in the early days many of my most prized timbers exploded in the planer or were chewed up by the router. Now I hand-plane what treasures I can find, reserving them for small boxes and the like.

In any project, ideas must be tested against reality. For instance, I exhausted my thinking in trying to incorporate the shaped vertical member in the screen, being squarely beaten by its impracticability in the situation. But I won hands down with the double rail, which could be used everywhere.

These pieces, of course, are speculative exhibition work. They were not made to commission and they are currently awaiting buyers. You need a little adventure between the pedestrian hours spent making for the average customer; otherwise being a self-employed woodworker would be very dull.

● Peter Howlett, 13 Cromer Close, Laindon, Basildon, Essex SS15 6HT, tel. (0268) 414975. ■

● Peter designed the showcase (below) and screen (right) as companion pieces to the prize-winning table

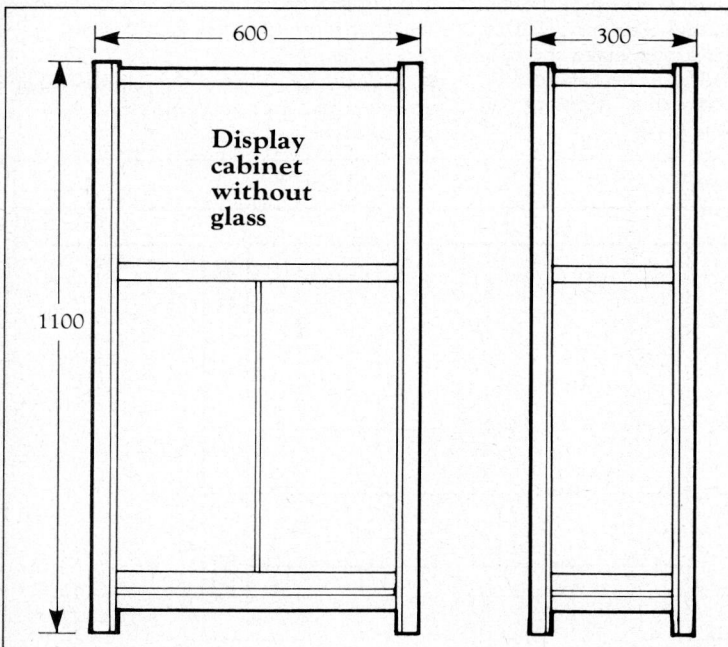

600

Display cabinet without glass

1100

300

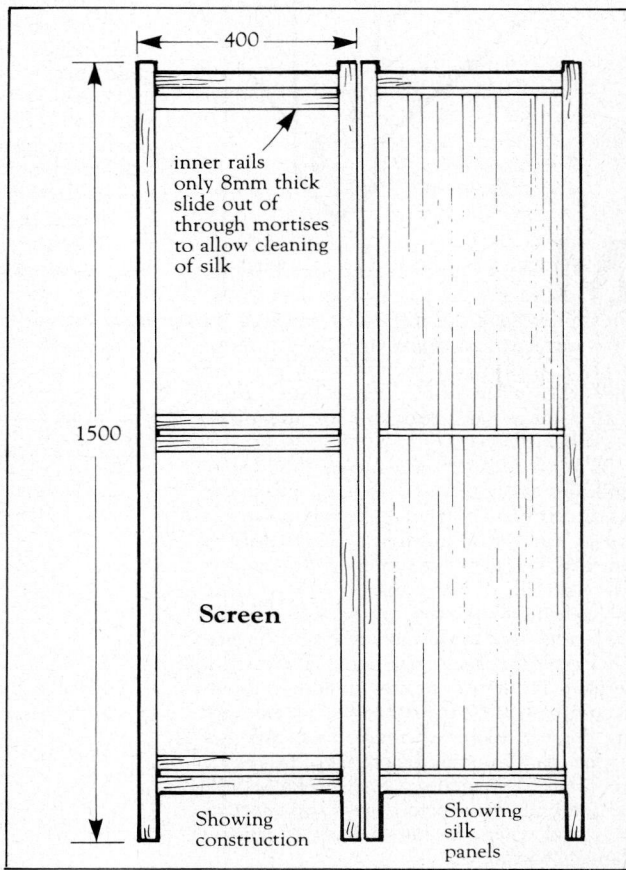

400

inner rails only 8mm thick slide out of through mortises to allow cleaning of silk

1500

Screen

Showing construction

Showing silk panels

# The craft of cabinetmaking

Benches — David Savage's
expert advice includes plans
of your next best friend

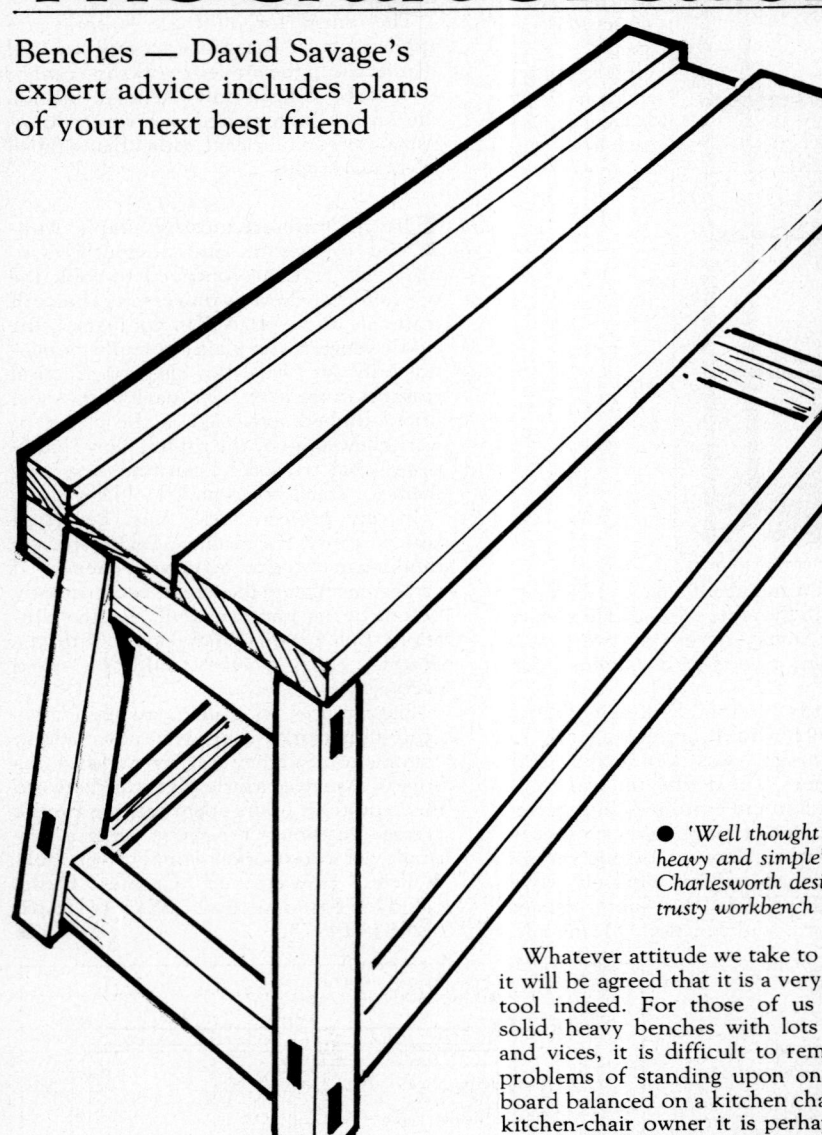

● *The removable tool-well, clearly shown
here, gives great clamping advantages*

**M**y workshop at present has two
work-benches that stand facing
each other about four feet apart.
This allows me the luxury of working on
two surfaces and four vices — or more
usually working on one surface and piling
the other with tools, cutting lists, notes,
coffee mugs and remnants of the dog's
breakfast.

When I recently considered the idea of
building an additional two benches, the
whole problem of what makes a good workbench came flooding back. This really is
one for the letters page. Every craftsman has
his own idea. For example, there's the
engineering approach, in which the flat
surface is used in the same way as a surface
plate; any damage to the bench surface is a
serious reduction in its reliability as an
accurate tool. At the other end of the scale
are those workers who regard a bench as a
surface that must in the course of fast work
become damaged. This surface will
occasionally be replaced by a top sheet of
plywood when the bench itself is causing
damage to the job.

● *'Well thought out, solid,
heavy and simple' – the
Charlesworth design for a
trusty workbench*

Whatever attitude we take to the bench,
it will be agreed that it is a very important
tool indeed. For those of us who have
solid, heavy benches with lots of clamps
and vices, it is difficult to remember the
problems of standing upon one end of a
board balanced on a kitchen chair. For the
kitchen-chair owner it is perhaps difficult
to recognise the full benefits of working in
comfort with both hands free to make the
cut. The difference is one of balance. With a
bench you are balanced to make the cut,
with the kitchen chair you are balanced to
hold the stuff still as well as trying to cut
somewhere near your mark.

The design of a work-bench must be the
result of an examination of its uses. A
cabinetmaker may consider some or all of
the following as important properties.
● To be rock-solid when in use, yet mobile
and light enough to move around. I try to
place benches beneath windows or sky-
lights so they can be moved into a stream of
daylight if a particularly exacting bit of
cutting is undertaken. This necessitates a
strong, heavy undercarriage with a broad
base that will not allow movement. Fixing
your bench to a wall may be an answer to
stability in some situations, but it robs the
bench of more facilities than it gives.

● *Alter the dimensions to suit your own height
or arm length. Note the massive rails and
wedged tenons*

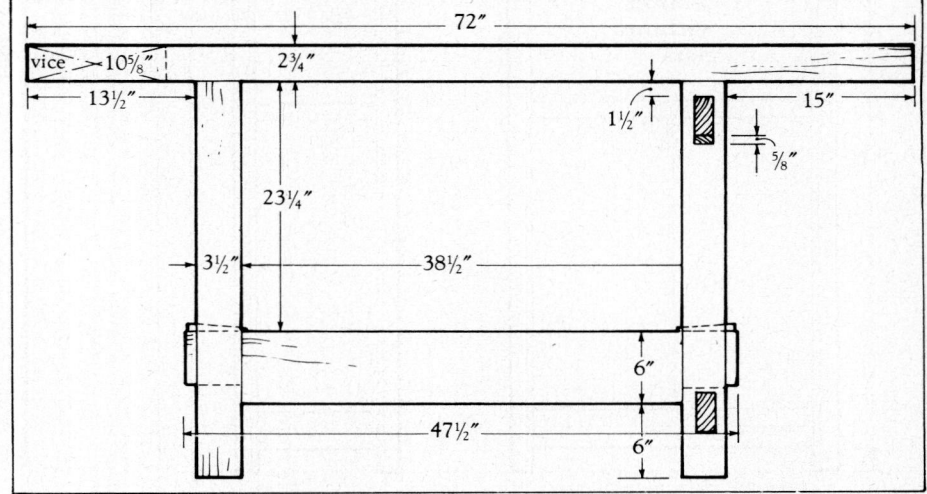

● The bench surface should be a work platform at a convenient height. This is a personal thing — one chap I know has his bench at armpit height, claiming that it helps him deal with an old back injury. The surface should be capable of taking a heavy pounding if you do any hand-mortising. This is normally done with the job clamped above one of the front legs, the worker standing at one end of the bench.

● The bench should, when it is well organised, be a work centre. Tools in constant use should be in racks, drawers or shelves on or near the bench. The place between the leg stretchers is a favourite cubby-hole — marking-gauges can go on a rack at one end of the bench, other bits and bobs in a drawer hung beneath the top; but beware — these drawers always want to be opened when there is a bench dog in the way.

● The prime functions will involve holding devices for various jobs such as sawing, marking out, and holding jigs like shooting-boards and mitre traps. The vices on a bench are in constant use so be careful to choose one that will do all you need and no more. For the main vice, the choice is between modern, metal and quick-acting, like the Record, and the home-made type found on many continental benches.

The Record 53E is strong, fast opening, wide enough to be useful, accurate, and very expensive at about £80. It has the disadvantage of requiring wooden jaws, and because of its design does not hold vertical long lengths for work on the endgrain very easily. The continental vice does this job extremely well. It is as wide as you wish it to be, slow to operate, inaccurate in a useful way (it will hold wedge-shaped jobs very well) and with a metal screw is reasonably cheap at about £20. As I have one of each of these vices on each of my two benches I can recommend both, though I do more work with the Record. One system I have seen to facilitate endgrain work with the Record is to attach a 3×3×24in block to the moving jaw. This bears against the edge of the bench and helps long pieces to clear the screws of the vice. This system can be blighted by twisting or bending timber, so select with the utmost care.

● For the other main use, that of planing, the bench must be very critically examined. Most planing these days is done by machine, with hand planing reserved for cleaning up or fitting parts together. Even

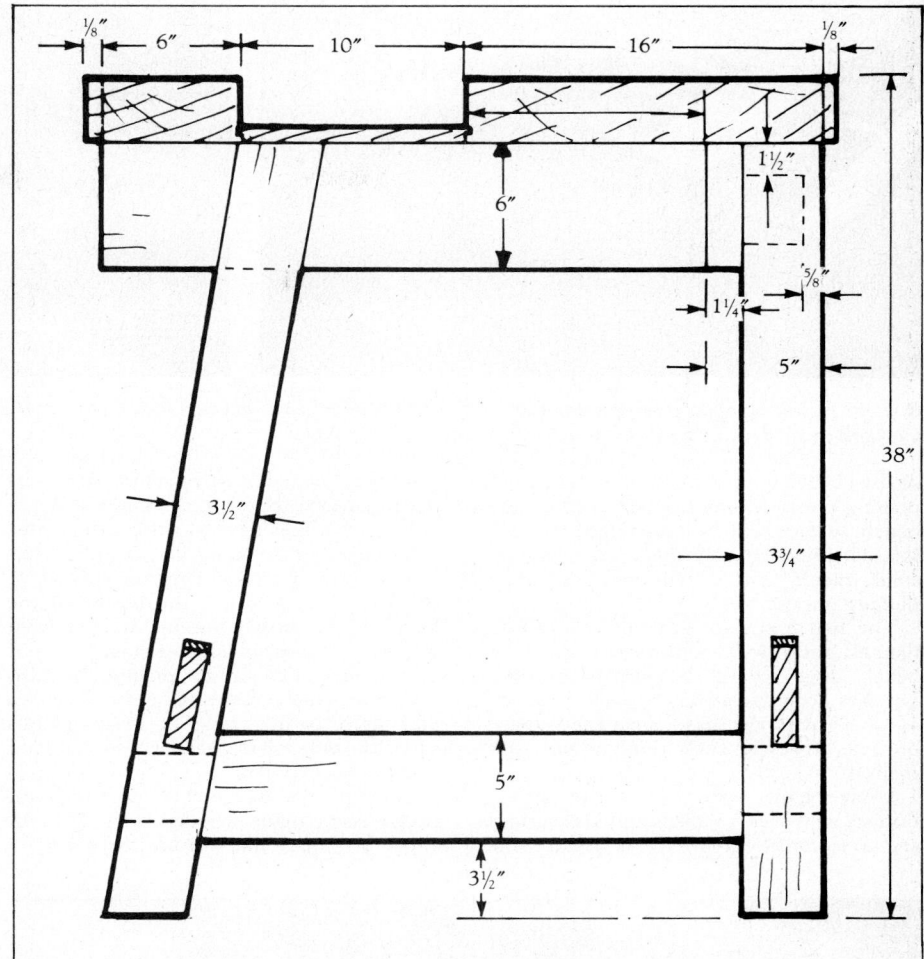

**Cutting list**
(all sizes in inches)

| | | | | |
|---|---|---|---|---|
| 2 | front legs | 35 | × 3½ | × 3½ |
| 2 | back legs | 36¼ | 3½ | 3½ |
| 1 | long rail | 46 | 6 | 3 |
| 2 | lower side rails | 31½ | 5 | 3 |
| 2 | upper side rails | 32 | 6 | 3 |

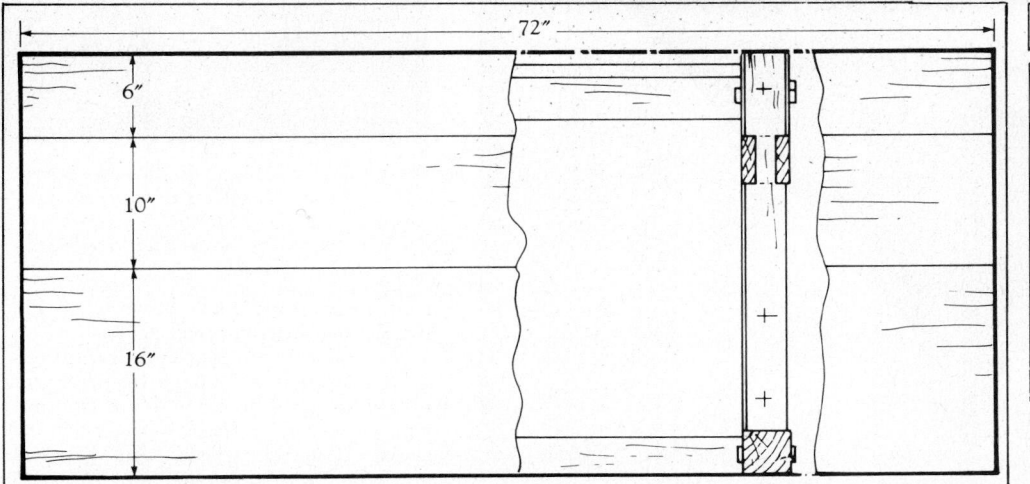

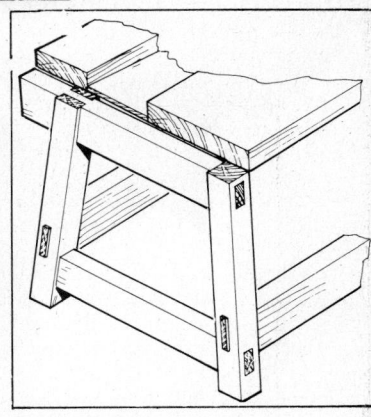

● The slope on the back legs, mainly to teach angled jointing, gives extra stability

● Left: A close-up of the continental-pattern vice, 'usefully inaccurate' and very good for holding long pieces for work on the endgrain. Right: A view of the work area, showing Englishman and Continental side-by-side

so, by placing your stuff on your bench and planing one side, any bow or twist on the bench surface will be transferred to your job. This may be only slight, especially on small pieces, but it will make accurate planing impossible.

The bench surface generally should be flat and out of wind — the area around the bench dogs should be very, very flat. Benches do move around, beech does cup and twist with the seasons, so keep an eye on it and true the whole thing up now and again.

I have great respect for those perfectionists who seek an absolutely flat surface and go to considerable expense and trouble to keep it flat and free from marks across its entire surface, but I must admit that my benches are nowhere near this ideal state.

What about a planing vice, or end vice as it is commonly called? The type with a row of pegs or dogs down the length of the bench is the most common. I am blessed with two of these invaluable aids. They not only hold boards still for planing, but also grip bench jigs as tight as can be. The end vice itself is not wide or of enormous capacity, but it has clear jaws so endgrain work is no problem.

Some people use metal bench dogs, but I prefer home-made wooden ones. A hard, slippery timber like lignum vitae with a

spring of yew and facing pad of hornbeam is ideal. I have recently installed a new set of these along the entire length of one of my benches so now I won't have to constantly

● Left: An old joiner's bench with cranked vice-handle and movable-peg leg. Top: Tail vice with dogs on the continental bench. Above: The peg leg support for long boards has a choice of heights

move dogs up and down the wretched thing for planing different-sized boards.

The construction of an end vice is not too difficult, but it will take a bit of concentration to get it to fit and run smoothly without any play. The end screw will cost about £20 and the whole set-up will need a few hours' work, but it's well worth the effort. There is a large Record vice, 52½D, with a dog on the moving jaw — this seems to do the jobs of end and side vice in one. I have never used one and I have not seen many in professional shops, probably because its position on the end of a bench is not the most stable nor the most convenient for working.

The simple alternative to the end vice is not to have one. The other answer is to have a row of dogs or stops and plane against these. Users of this system say that as you are only planing in one direction, why hold the stuff at both ends, which will only encourage it to bow up under pressure.

An advocate of this method, and designer of one of the more successful modern cabinetmaker's benches, is David Charlesworth. As it is a student project that has developed over the years, the Charlesworth bench is well thought out, solid, heavy and simple. 'This evolved from an old CoSIRA design,' says David; 'the undercarriage is perhaps unnecessarily heavy, and the back legs only slope as they do for teaching purposes. I think it is important to put the Record vice at the very end of the bench to help crosscutting, and I do not encourage people to build very wide working surfaces. More than 17 or 18in and it becomes difficult to reach with a plane unless your arms are very long.'

A novel and useful feature of this design is the removable bottom to the tool-well. The tool-well is marvellous as a collector of half-eaten biscuits and those tiny but essential tools that you spend half an hour looking for. Marking-knives have a particular affinity for tool wells. I have just bought a new plastic-handled marking-knife in brilliant orange that I can spot at twenty paces.

Not only does the whizz Charlesworth remove the ends from the tool-well, but with its sectional, removable base you can arrange clamping from this side by a mere flick of the wrist. This is a good project for a student or anyone beginning woodworking because it can be enjoyed as a gateway to further work.

Building a bench like the one shown here will leave you with little change out of £200, which is one reason my own building plans will be delayed until next spring. I shall continue to work with my elderly and solid Englishman and the rather neurotic young Continental. Do not, incidentally, make my mistake and build a bench on the continental pattern — the narrow end has not enough width for real stability.

The traditional timber for toolmaking is beech, which can be had kiln-dried for between £7.50 and £9 per cu ft. Stuff of 3in thickness can be difficult to get, but Timber Met of Oxfordshire seem to keep a good stock. An alternative would be to use discoloured stuff that was otherwise good — I was offered some at £5 per cu ft for this very purpose.

If you intend using bench dogs you can get away with a 2in-thick top if the front is lipped with a 2×3in member. This allows the dadoes for bench dogs to be cut through 3in. The dadoes are then capped with a piece of 3×1in — much simpler than chopping out damn great mortises all day.

If you should decide to make either your first or another better bench, be assured the effort spent will be well rewarded! ∎

# Books

*Patrick Spielman*
**Router Handbook**
*Sterling Publishing Co./Blandford Press,*
    *£7.50 paperback*
*Reviewed by Jim Phillips*

I found Patrick Spielman's book most absorbing. It provides an insight into the router world of the USA, and gives an excellent run-down of every conceivable router from the cheapest hobby types to the heaviest-duty ones, including stationary machines. There is a huge hobby market in the USA, not to be confused with that of serious amateurs. One minor criticism I had is that the uninitiated might not be able to sort out the wheat from the chaff, in terms of the working efficiency of some devices shown. Several of these have not come up to scratch in tests; however, a number of the jigs were impressive. The Leigh dovetailing jig, which offers variable finger spacings, I thought was excellent.

Mr Spielman is obviously an enthusiast himself, and he writes lucidly and in a manner which shows he has researched his subject very well indeed.

There is always some doubt about the usefulness of a book published in the States, particularly when technical gadgets that might not be available here are mentioned, but in the current absence of any other such encyclopaedic treatment of the subject, £7.50 is a bargain for what you get.

---

*Gordon Warr*
**Q & A: Woodwork**
*Newnes Technical Books, £2.95 paperback*
*Reviewed by Chris Nash*
There are questions you ask when you're up against real woodworking problems and questions you ask when you don't actually practise a craft but like reading technical manuals to mystify yourself. Working with timber, even at the bodge-and-codge level, isn't normally interrupted by sudden gasps

of: 'My goodness, what's a corner bracket for? I wish I had a book I could look it up in!' At the more recondite end, neither does one ruminate on 'What is meant by secondary seasoning?' The way the question pops up is more like: 'How can I stop this pine dresser coming apart at the seams like a cardboard suitcase in a monsoon the week after the missus has decked it with her best willow pattern?'

Scattered about in *Q & A: Woodwork* there is a good deal of interesting, sometimes authoritative information, as there is in the *Encyclopaedia Britannica*. But just as you're unlikely to become a polymath by reading the latter from Aardvark to Zygote, so can one not expect to get a practical reference work out of a roughly assembled hodge-podge of statements culled (at a guess) from standard texts, rephrased as questions to lend the personal touch and duly answered.

Take the section on joints. We are advised, sensibly, that a through tenon can be secured with hardwood wedges. In a book which considers it necessary to explain that a corner bracket is used for bracketing corners, neither text nor illustration indicates where to put the wedges, or that it's a good idea to make saw-cuts to take them. Further: if a through joint needs wedging, a stopped joint of similar dimensions needs it more. I hope Mr Warr knows about pre-inserted 'hidden' wedges, but if so he doesn't let on. Three sections are devoted to the uses of dowelling, including the pegging of a draw mortise-and-tenon. What about draw-boring, which is possibly the best way to get a tight, shrink-proof and self-positioning assembly? Not a word. The maintenance of edged tools can be a cause of grief and pain. 'Lock your wrists', advises the author with the blitheness of a yogi master telling a new student to get into the lotus position.

I'd have liked to be told where to get a decent honing guide — not one of those futile objects like midget roller-skates. May I add also that, unmoved by debate over the relative merits of Arkansas as against composition stones, I'd more urgently like to know where to get one that can take a plane iron square on; and if no one makes one wide enough, why not? Questions like these, rather than 'What are "identical" and "handed" components?' strike me as being top priority.

The layout Mr Warr (or his publishers?) chose is pretty good if the book is used as a preparation aid for examinations in theory with a bias toward technical nomenclature, but that's not what it professes to be. As far as the home woodworker is concerned the author has given him a dictionary where what he needed was a thesaurus. In short, he doesn't want to know the definition of winding-sticks, but how to test a piece of wood for flatness. Unfortunately, winding-sticks are in the index and flatness isn't. Redrafted along the lines implied, *Q & A: Woodwork* might present in a more usable form the many nuggets of valuable information which seem to have been carefully concealed in its pages.

# The cushion cabinet

Dutch master-craftsman
René Coolen details a historic
piece from the time when the
ancient guilds held sway

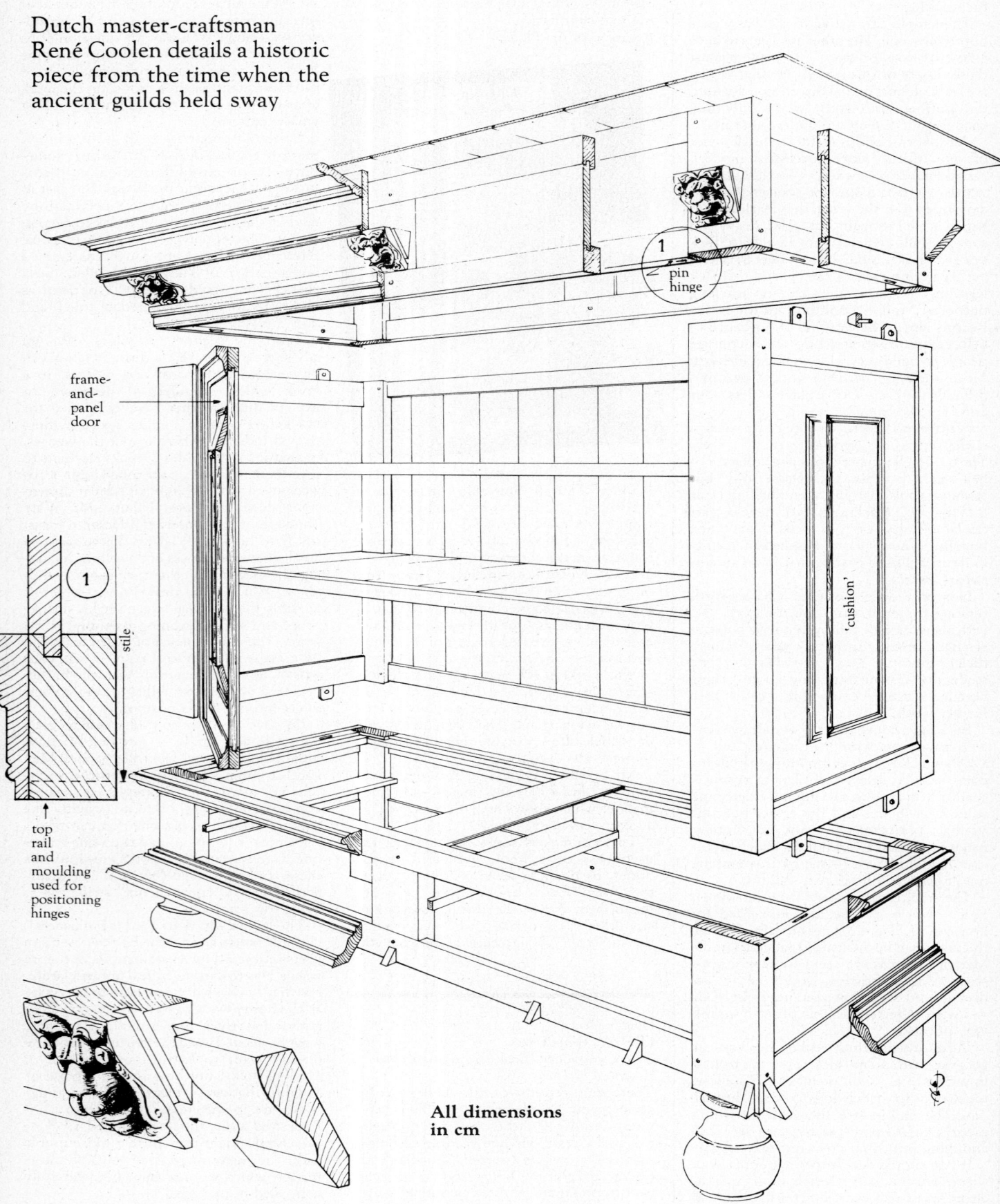

pin
hinge

frame-
and-
panel
door

'cushion'

1

stile

top
rail
and
moulding
used for
positioning
hinges

**All dimensions
in cm**

During the Renaissance and afterwards, the Netherlands played a very important role in the development of furniture design. Their styles and techniques were copied all over Europe (and exported by refugees), and the influence showed itself in Britain as elsewhere.

When, at the end of the 16th century, the country then called the Northern Lowlands liberated itself from Spanish occupation, it began to develop a very particular native style — and not only in a national sense; the individual provinces had their own distinctive tastes in cupboards and other types of cabinet. Such wide local differences resulted from the presence of the craftsmen's guilds, each of which at that period enforced very strict rules in the town where it was established.

One of the best-known regional items was the 'cushion cabinet' from the province of Holland, produced in the third quarter of the 17th century. This is so called because the raised panels on the doors were known as 'cushions'.

Many cabinets of this type were made primarily for show, and constructional excellence often took second place. In the original, the cabinet shown here — an early example — was just such a display item. The top lacked proper jointing, and the timber was too thin. The doors were so simply made (of panels without framing) that sooner or later deformation was bound to occur. The slide-work for the large drawer in the base was too light; moreover, the drawer itself included no dovetails, and its base hung loosely underneath. Lastly, the cabinet was not made up (as you might expect) from three separate components assembled on site.

In short, a good maker would have done it better. The likelihood is that the piece came not from a guild workshop in one of the towns but from the outlying countryside, where the guilds had little or no influence and the cabinetmakers were not organised.

My detail drawings show better alternatives, and the perspective depicts a completely solid construction which the modern craftsman may reproduce with absolute confidence.

The original was made entirely of oak, and decorated with Brazilian- or Rio-rosewood veneer. One of its special features is pair of secret drawers in the interior — reached by pushing upwards against a carved panel. ■

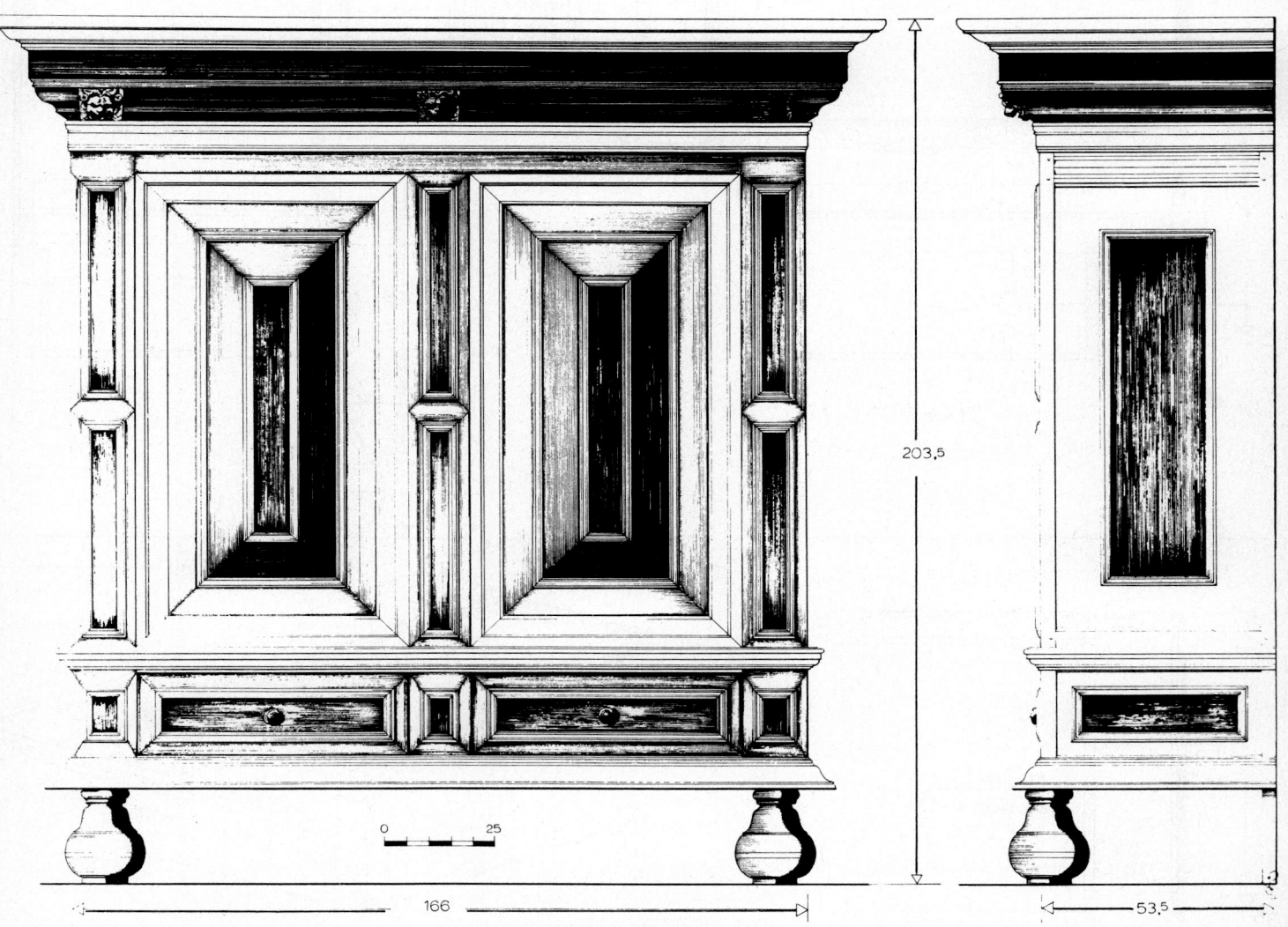

203,5

0    25

166

53,5

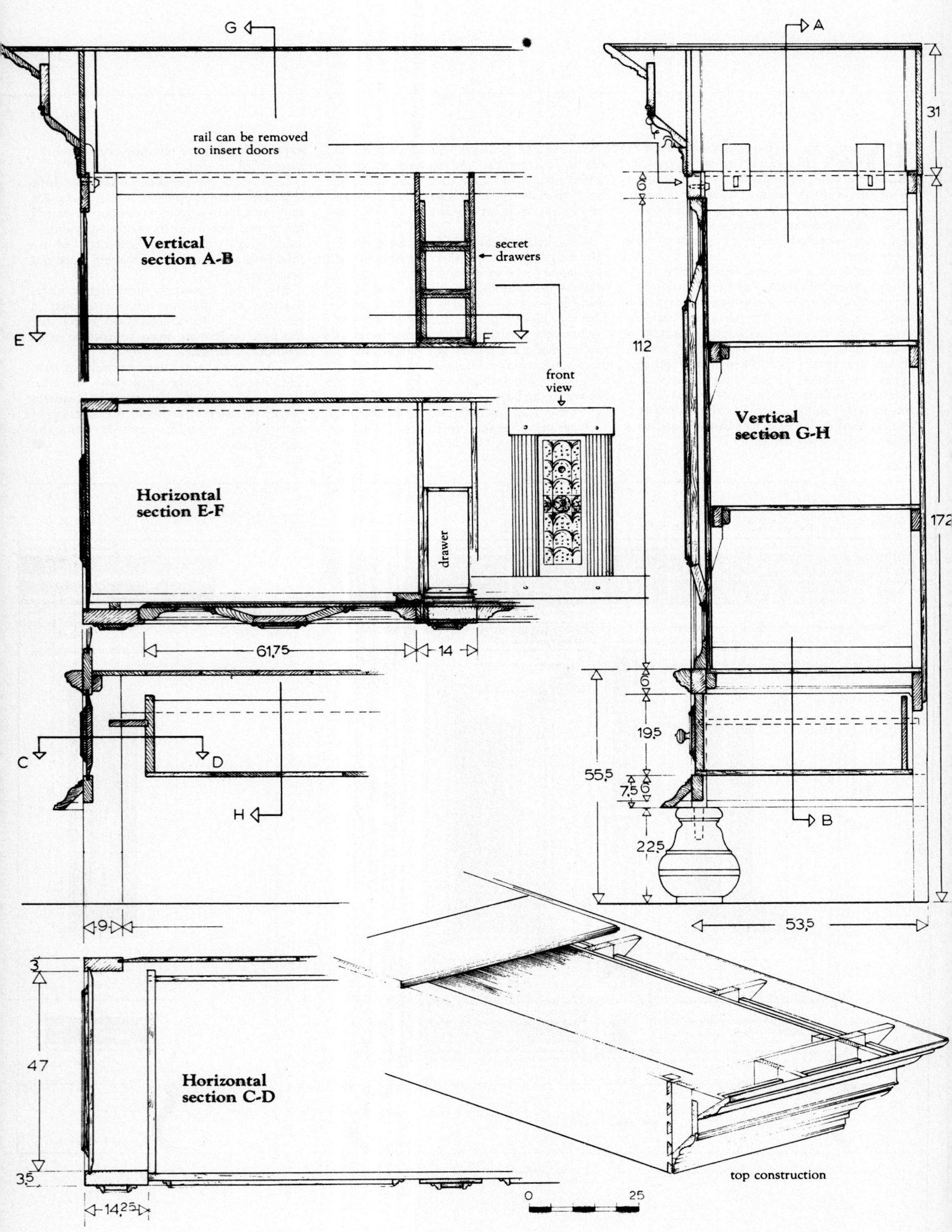

G

Vertical
section A-B

rail can be removed
to insert doors

secret
drawers

front
view

E

F

Horizontal
section E-F

drawer

A

31

6

112

Vertical
section G-H

172

61,75

14

C

D

H

6

19,5

55,5

7,5 6

22,5

B

9

Horizontal
section C-D

3

47

3,5

14,25

top construction

0        25

53,5

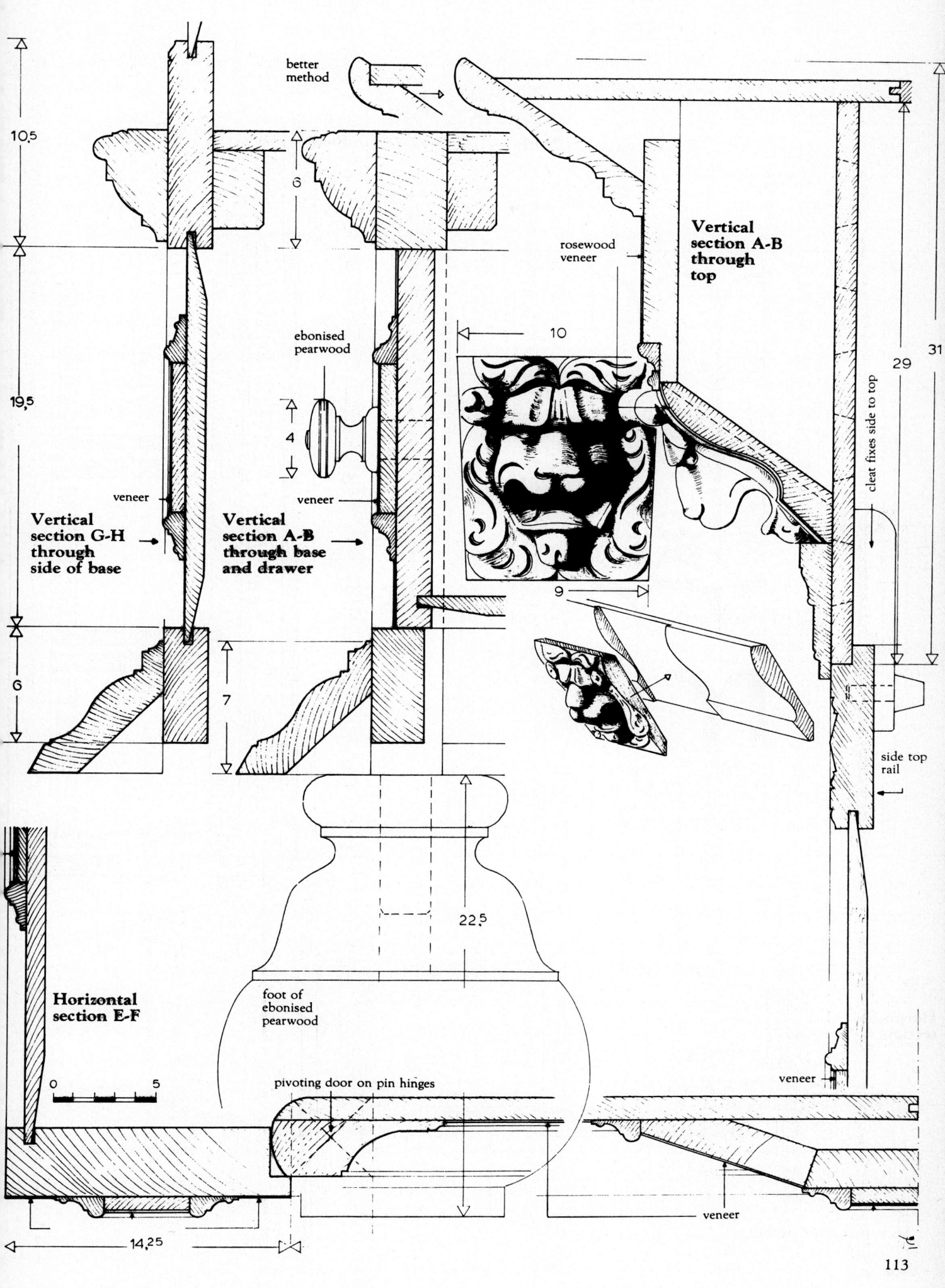

better method

10,5

6

rosewood
veneer

**Vertical
section A-B
through
top**

19,5

ebonised
pearwood

4

10

29    31

cleat fixes side to top

veneer

veneer

**Vertical
section G-H
through
side of base**

**Vertical
section A-B
through base
and drawer**

9

6    7

side top
rail

22,5

**Horizontal
section E-F**

foot of
ebonised
pearwood

pivoting door on pin hinges

veneer

0    5

14,25

veneer

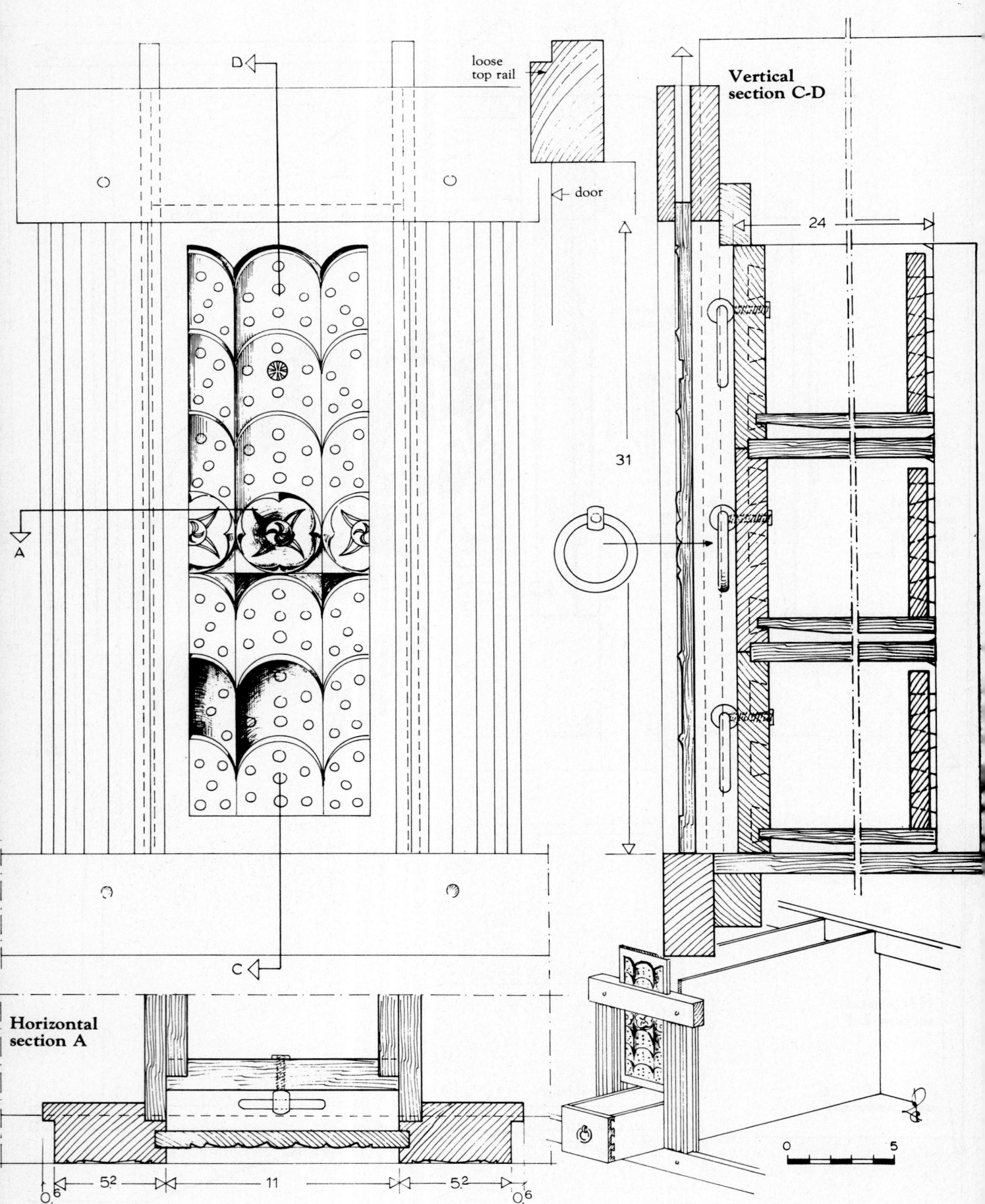

loose
top rail

◁— door

**Vertical
section C-D**

24

31

**Horizontal
section A**

5.2    11    5.2

0.6    0.6

**Secret-drawer details**

0    5

# Steering the right course

Qualifications mean skills; and skills are the woodworker's best friend. Peter Collenette explores the bountiful world of the City and Guilds

Once upon a time, it was easy. You were apprenticed. You learnt all there was to learn; and you set up in the trade.

But then the machines came along, and the machines changed everything. You can't learn the trade from a machine, and anyway the machine's arrival changed the trade's very nature — in woodworking as everywhere else. Problems arose.

'The application of scientists' discoveries to practical use in industrial production, processing, manufacture and services came as early in Britain as anywhere in the world. The application of education and training to the country's greatest single natural resource — its people — was a much slower and more difficult process.'

True enough; but the people who said that have done more than most to make up for lost time. The words come from a 1978 *Broadsheet* of the City and Guilds of London Institute.

Throughout public life — in industry, government and education — the CGLI (to use its initials) is recognised in the field of training as pre-eminent arbiter of standards, assessor and advisor. It serves the armed forces and even plays a considerable role internationally.

Yet it has reached this commanding position in a typically British way: it is not a government department, and indeed not official at all. It was set up in 1878 (at the suggestion of Gladstone) jointly by the Corporation of the City of London and some of the City Livery Companies, wealthy successors to the ancient guilds; and to this day it is entirely independent. It is not government-subsidised, except for overseas work, and nearly £7m of its £8m annual income arrives in the form of candidates' fees.

That's not to say it stands outside the Establishment — its 'instruments of governance' are authorised by the Privy Council, and the Duke of Edinburgh is its President. But in the end its own authority derives from its own achievements.

These are considerable. Since 1878 the CGLI has examined, in round figures, 10m people, and current candidates number ½m a year. Its certificates provide unarguable proof of skill and knowledge across the entire world of work.

What makes the Institute so uniquely useful is its steady emphasis on practical skill. While others attend, as a matter of high national policy, to academic education of the sort offered by universities and polytechnics, someone has to ensure that the nation's butchers, bakers and cabinetmakers learn their trades. The CGLI speaks

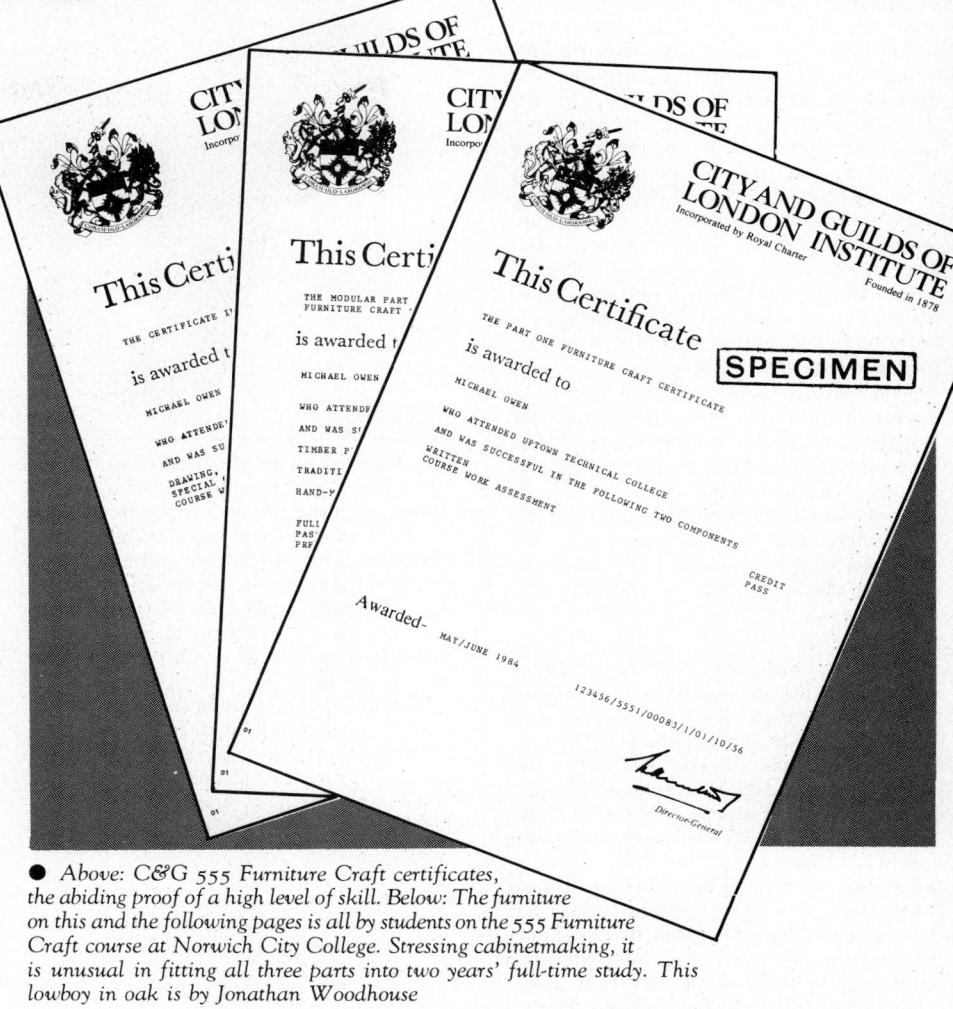

● *Above: C&G 555 Furniture Craft certificates, the abiding proof of a high level of skill. Below: The furniture on this and the following pages is all by students on the 555 Furniture Craft course at Norwich City College. Stressing cabinetmaking, it is unusual in fitting all three parts into two years' full-time study. This lowboy in oak is by Jonathan Woodhouse*

wryly of 'the continuing overall shortage of public money . . . which has resulted in some imbalance between the support given to university and other full-time students in arts, social sciences, and science and technology, and to those who become available for productive employment directly on leaving school'. And it insists that you must not only know your job but also, in the words of staff member Heather Adlam, be able to do it.

She stresses, too, that the CGLI provides tests, not teaching. However, its examination syllabuses are only put into effect after a very close look at current practise in each industry concerned, plus exhaustive discussions in what Adlam describes as 'a fairly hefty committee structure' involving management, unions and others.

The Institute's staff are not all technically expert in the fields with which they deal, but they are good at making sense of what they see and hear. The content of a City and Guilds syllabus comes from people in industry who have made it their lives' work; but ambiguities and inconsistencies are removed by people at the Institute who make it their business to ask the right questions.

**A**ll City and Guilds courses are numbered. If you want to know what's on offer, it helps if you learn the code. Woodworking courses run as follows.

**555 Furniture Craft Subjects and Advanced Studies** — probably the most important set of courses for craftspeople, and the one on which we'll be concentrating below.

**563 Stringed Keyboard Instrument Manufacture** — This includes a basic Part I, plus options in action finishing and regulating, harpsichord design and construction, piano-tuning and toning, and piano repairs and re-conditioning. There's also a 563 course in Musical Instrument Repair.

**564 Furniture Crafts** — a group of special schemes at particular establishments, such as the London College of Furniture cabinetmaking course (564-1) featured in January's *Woodworker*. Also included are LCF courses in upholstery (564-2) and soft furnishing (564-6); Rycotewood College's basic certificate, certificate and advanced certificate in fine craftsmanship (564-3, 4 and 5 respectively); and Bucks College's courses (564-8) in traditional and modern chairmaking.

**585 Carpentry and Joinery** A basic craft course, and four advanced-craft options — site practice, formwork, purpose-made joinery and maintenance work.

**586 Machine Woodworking** Again a basic craft course, in either woodworking proper or sawmilling, followed by advanced options in toolroom technology, materials technology, construction of machined components, production planning for the machine shop, plant layout and materials handling, and machine-woodworking science.

**587 Shopfitting** Craft and advanced craft.

**T**he 555 is the central syllabus for all whose business is furniture: cabinet-makers, upholsterers, polishers, even restorers.

It resulted from the National Labour Agreement for the industry, which made reference to employers' requirements for flexibility of skills and transferability from place to place — and it remains, says Heather Adlam, the best way of dealing with manufacturers' geographical dispersion. But its many components also enable committed people to reach high levels of specialised skill.

Like all City and Guilds courses, the 555 is divided and subdivided. It currently falls into three sections — 555-1, 2 and 3; these include 17 topics or modules (many of which are options) and a total of 31 different examinations and other assessments.

Parts I and II each lead to a Certificate in Furniture. Part I simply helps you to find your bearings and to distinguish the various trades, materials and procedures one from another. Part II, on the other hand, offers 12 separate modules, which fall into two groups:

**A Materials preparation**
Timber preparation

● *A Japanese dining-table in Brazilian mahogany by Nigel Howes*

Metal and plastics preparation
Upholstery and bedding preparation
Finishing preparation

**B Production technology**
Carcase and wooden frame construction
Metal and plastics construction
Modern upholstery and bedding construction
Traditional upholstery
Traditional finishing
Modern finishing
Soft furnishing
Hand-made furniture construction.

To get a Part II Certificate you must pass one module from A and two from B — but you (and/or your employer) may choose your precise options according to your precise interests or job.

Part III leads to the Advanced Craft Certificate in Furniture, to the Certificate of Advanced Industrial Studies in Furniture,

● *Jacqueline Sawyer made this coffee-table in Brazilian mahogany and afrormosia. Norwich City College is in Ipswich Rd, Norwich NR2 2LJ; contact Mr A. M. Router on (0603) 660011, ext. 225*

or to both if you study for both. The former is for people who want to attain excellent standards in a particular skill; the latter for intending supervisors and managers. Both options feature the same general test in drawing and construction, history and industrial studies; but each also includes a separate assessment in its own particular field. For craft students this means choosing one from a range of specialisms, which vary from college to college; for example, the LCF currently offers cabinet- or chairmaking, upholstery, soft furnishing, restoration, jigs and production aids, finishing, drawing-office practice, or carving and gilding. For the other students it means a paper on organisational studies.

Those who do both Part III courses and have the right industrial experience qualify for the Licentiateship of the CGLI, which confers a status equivalent to that of Master Craftsman in Europe. The exalted title is justified by the long road up.

Each module, incidentally, is examined in two ways: by a written paper and by assessment of work done during the course itself (555-3 qualifications mean two written papers besides the course-work assessment).

The 555 syllabus has seen remarkably few changes in the last 15 years. Part I has remained the same. The number of modules in Part II has dropped — industrial priorities being reflected in the loss of some modules and re-organisation of others.

Part III, however, first examined in 1979, was introduced because existing courses failed (in the words of Roger Saunders, City and Guilds Course Director at the LCF) to satisfy industry's continuing demand, even today, for craftspeople whose training goes beyond a straightforward apprenticeship. It's and intriguing hint that skill, not knowledge, is still the basic need.

Still changing, too, are the ways in which 555 courses are provided. Traditionally, the apprentice was released one day a week for a year to study for his Part I. Passing that, he spent one day a week for another two years on Part II. Now he or she can do a further year or more of one-day (and/or evening) study for Part III.

The furniture industry, though, has been dealt swingeing blows by recession. The number of apprentices coming to the LCF for 555-1 and 2 has decreased from 600 to 50 (in round figures) in about four years. A shocking drop — but the variety, flexibility, ready availability and practicality of City and Guilds courses have not lessened. They have proved themselves in other ways. Ever-growing numbers of people are seeking re-training in mid-life: after redundancy, or simply because they want a change. Attracted to the furniture crafts, such people fit naturally into relatively new full-time and three-day-a-week courses which have been established for school-leavers as alternatives to the declining day- and block-release arrangements — while the latter still offer a means of earning while you learn.

By the same token, you don't always have to go through all the hoops. Generally speaking, and depending on the college concerned, you may be admitted at any level if you have the right experience and/or other qualifications. Possession of a City and Guilds certificate from the next level down is only one possible key.

As a newcomer or near-newcomer to woodworking, you want to learn the craft under arrangements which suit you; to learn it properly; and to be able, if necessary, to prove to others that you've learn it properly; and to be able, if necessary, to prove to others that you've learnt it. Even if you have experience, you may want that turned into hard qualifications. For professional, semi-professional and even amateur, the CGLI courses amply fulfil all these requirements, and offer a ready-made challenge to every aspirant.

Most colleges will do all they can to find out your needs and then to accommodate you. You could do worse than investigate further. ∎

The following is a complete list of UK colleges now offering C&G 555 Furniture Craft, Advanced Craft and Advanced Industrial Studies courses. Not all offer all three parts; some offer only parts I and II.

Bucks College of Higher Education, High Wycombe
Cambridge College of Arts and Technology
Falmouth Technical College
Darlington College of Technology
Harlow Technical College
Southend-on-Sea College of Technology
Brunel Technical College, Bristol
Highbury College of Technology, Portsmouth
Hertfordshire College of Building, St Albans
Burnley College of Arts and Technology
Central Liverpool College of Further Education
Manchester College of Building
Halton College of Further Education, Widnes
South Fields College of Further Education, Leicester
London College of Furniture
Tottenham College of Technology
Norwich City College of Further and Higher Education
College of Arts and Technology, Newcastle
Basford Hall College, Nottingham
North Oxon Technical College and School of Art, Banbury
Rycotewood College, Thame
Shrewsbury College of Arts and Technology
West Bromwich College of Commerce and Technology
Suffolk College of Higher and Further Education
Brighton Technical College
City of Birmingham Polytechnic
Keighley Technical College
Huddersfield Technical College
Hull College of Further Education
Jacob Kramer College, Leeds
Shirecliffe College, Sheffield
Bridgend College of Technology
Telford College of Further Education, Edinburgh
Glasgow College of Building and Printing
Kirkcaldy College of Technology

# Starters

## Chris Nussbaum's diary of the London College of Furniture C&G 564 cabinetmaking course

Among the numerous shows and exhibitions going on around the country, the Woodworker Show at Alexandra Palace caught our attention, being close at hand. A group of us went along to feast our eyes on the latest hardware available, and some of the beautiful results that are being crafted with it.

The experience generated quite a lot of debate; I know several of us were particularly impressed with the carving work displayed, but everyone came away having been tempted by some particular tool or gadget — giving in, or not, according to the bank balance. It's a shame good tools cost so much; which brings me to a pet gripe. Why is it that dedicated students in a worthwhile trade get so little support from that trade? Where are the suppliers who could come to the College to offer helpful discounts?

Anyway, we all enjoyed the show. I think it just proved a bit too tantalising for some.

We don't have much time to worry about tools any more, because work is beginning in earnest. I am still surprised at how much we've learnt in the past six weeks. Last week I underwent for the very first time in my life an experience that no doubt many of you will appreciate — cutting my very first perfect joint, a secret-mitre dovetail. It was only a small exercise piece, but five weeks beforehand I didn't know what a secret-mitre dovetail was; it gave me a real thrill to look at this little thing, the product of a mere two hours at the bench!

I think we are all learning the special value of concentration when coupled with hard work. This is probably especially true for those three miserables who sawed right through between the half-pin and the mitred end on the box carcase we are all constructing. Five seconds of inattention and the air is suddenly thick with unrepeatables! This small mahogany box we are making — through-dovetailed, with a hinged lid, and solid panels grooved in top and bottom — will give an idea of how we are progressing. Within the exercise there is room for originality: perhaps a spot of carving, or some fielding on the lid panel.

I've tried a little hand-veneering, too. There are all sorts of activities going on about the place, and you only have to stick your nose in the right place at the right time to learn something new. I must add cooking to my list of acquired skills — my wife started full-time work last week, so now I must keep house. Still, you know what they say about jacks of all trades. ∎

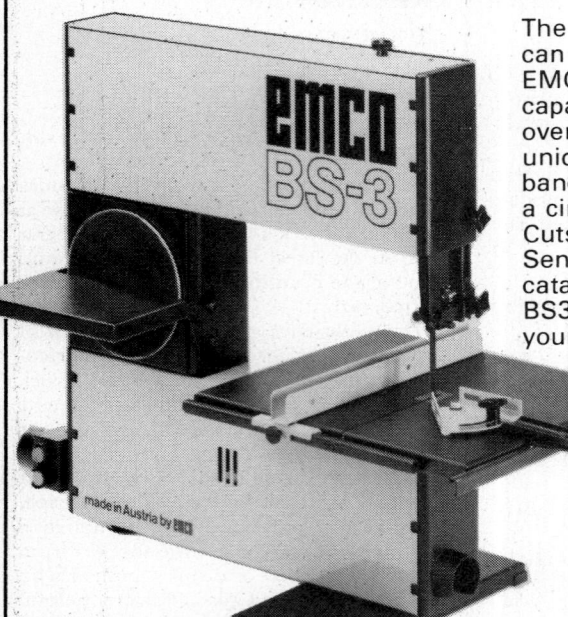
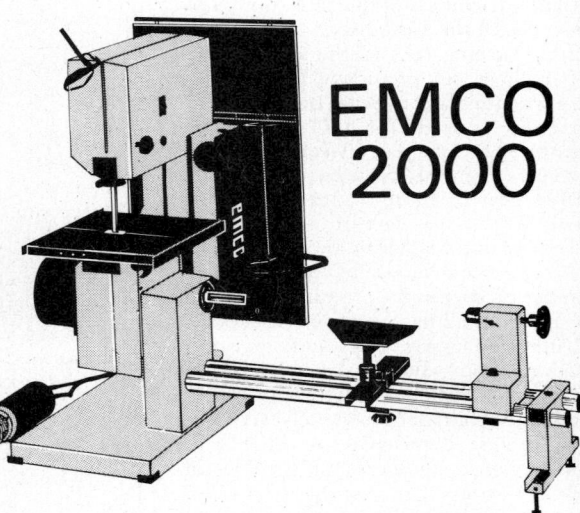
Prices quoted are those prevailing at press date and are subject to alteration due to economic conditions.

# Project turning: Coffee mill

## Roger Holley details another very practical and not-quite-simple design

**T**his project will interest the more ambitious turner who wants to practise his skills with the bandsaw and lathe. An essential element is, of course, one of the grinder mechanisms available from Craft Supplies. These are attractive reproduction-type pieces made in cast iron, aluminium and nylon (fig. 2), which can be fitted to a base of your own design. Our project will involve making a heavy turned base fitted with a drawer to hold the ground coffee; fig. 1 shows the result.

I am using a solid square of 6×6in sycamore about 8in long. This is the easiest shape to work on initially, as the square edges allow easy marking-out (fig. 3). If you have difficulty in obtaining such a large section, do not be afraid to use 3×3in, for example, or even an old table leg cut into four pieces and glued back into a 6in block as in fig. 4.

After marking out your proportions, cut the block on the bandsaw carefully across the top and bottom lines of the drawer (fig. 5). Make sure the cuts are continuous, and as straight and upright as your saw can be set. The importance of a sharp blade cannot be over-emphasised. I use a narrow 1/4in blade with 7tpi skiptooth pattern; others may prefer a wider one. Go straight through without stopping. If you stop you will leave a ridge on the joint when the pieces are re-glued.

Once the centre section has been cut out, mark all three adjacent faces to ensure that the grain of the block is matched up when re-assembling. Then, on the middle section B, mark and cut out the drawer block as shown in fig. 6. The drawer can be lightly sanded top and bottom on a disc sander to make it a sliding fit between the top and bottom slabs. All three pieces can then be glued and re-assembled with PVA, making

**Fig. 1**

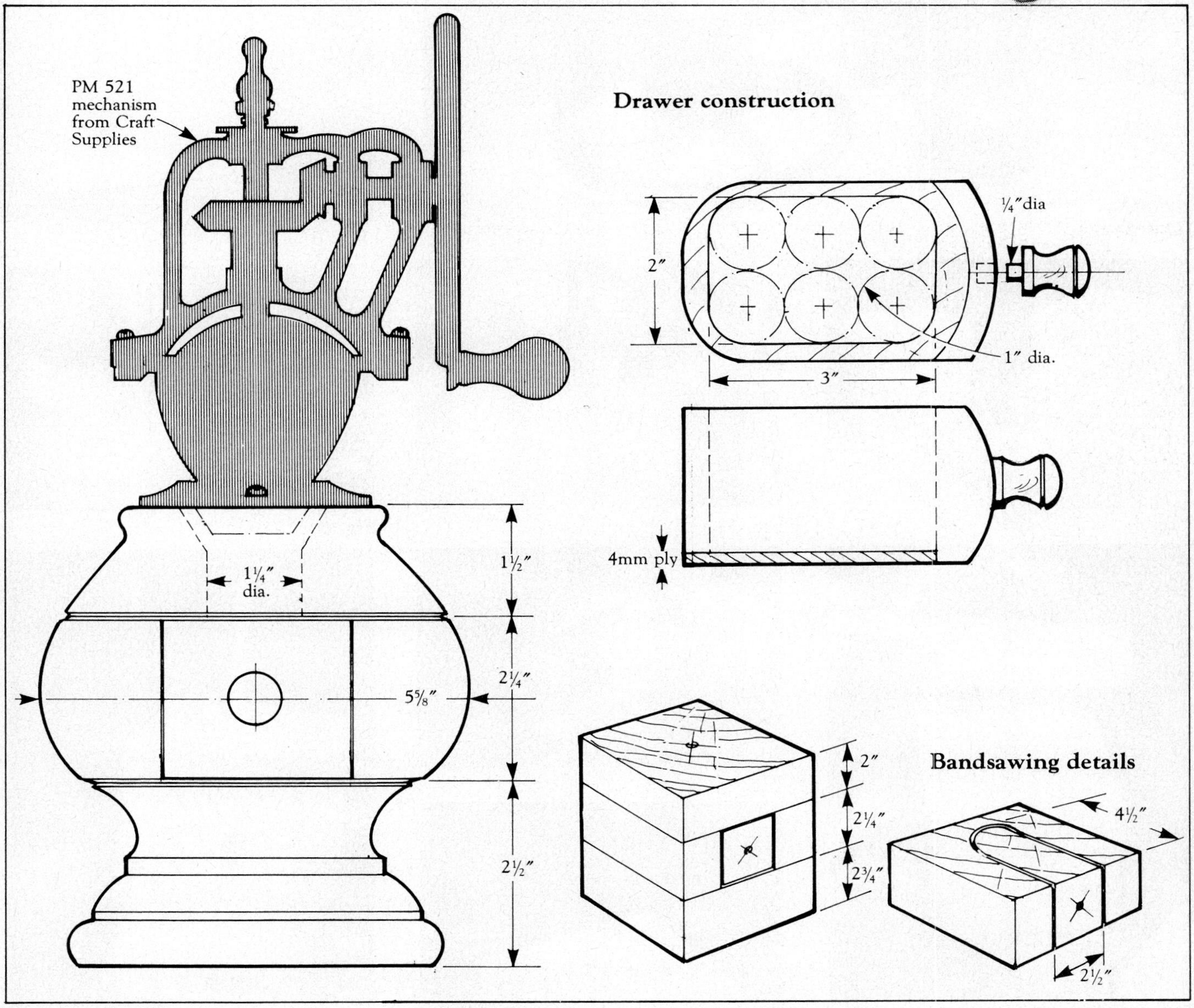

---

PM 521 mechanism from Craft Supplies

1 1/4" dia.

1 1/2"

2 1/4"

5 5/8"

2 1/2"

**Drawer construction**

1/4" dia.

2"

3"

1" dia.

4mm ply

2"

2 1/4"

2 3/4"

**Bandsawing details**

4 1/2"

2 1/2"

119

sure that the drawer area is kept free of adhesive as in fig. 7.

For the final stage of assembly, clamp the whole block in a vice and use a large G-cramp to close the gap slightly around the edges of the drawer. Put a screw in the centre of the drawer block to allow you to pull it out, and check for a good sliding fit before finally tightening up the vice (fig. 8).

To prevent centrifugal force throwing the drawer out when turning I fix it in place temporarily with ½in dowel. Mark out the centre of your block and drill a ½in hole, penetrating the drawer to a depth of about ½in (fig. 9). The dowel will lock the drawer firmly in position; fig. 10 shows the idea.

Use the dowel end as the tailstock end when mounting the block in the lathe. For machines which cannot take a full-sized square 6in block over the bed, saw or plane off the corners before mounting between centres.

Set the machine on a low speed for roughing-out until the bulk of the waste is removed as in fig. 11.

Once you have turned a satisfactory shape (as in fig. 12, for example), hollow out an undercut in the top to allow the bottom of the grinder to fit flush on top of your turned base. A tip to help hide the glue joint lines above and below the drawer is to make them more prominent! I cut a V-

groove on the lines with the point of the skew; this serves as a nice feature to exaggerate the matching drawer (fig.13).

The picture also shows the next stage in producing a good finish. I use a spirit stain such as Colron, in teak or rosewood colours, on a light timber such as sycamore. Apply it liberally with a cloth and use a small brush for the grooves and shoulders. Wipe off any runs and allow it to dry overnight.

To remove and finish the drawer, use an 1¼in flatbit set so that it just contacts the upper face of the drawer (fig. 14). This diameter also suits the base of the mill mechanism. The drawer can then be re-

**Fig. 2**

**Fig. 3**

**Fig. 4**

**Fig. 5**

**Fig. 6**

**Fig. 7**

**Fig. 8**

**Fig. 9** ▶

**Fig. 10**

moved and marked out — in this case, for six 1in-diameter holes drilled to produce a 3×2in drawer as in fig. 5. Using a sawtooth bit, drill through the block accordingly. Be careful when holding the block, because the drill tends to bind as it heats up in the deep holes. Use a drill vice or G-cramp to hold the work securely.

Once all the drilling is complete, remove the remaining waste with a coping-saw, chisel and file. Then mark off approximately a ⅛in strip from the base and bandsaw up to the front edge of the drawer as in fig. 16.

Cut out a piece of ⅛in ply to fit the base (fig. 17), glue in position and hold with elastic bands until set. Finally, sand it flush

around the edge, and stain the sides and bottom.

The last piece you need is a small knob, turned as in fig. 18 from a scrap of similar material. Finish the base of the knob with a small dowel against a shoulder that will match nicely against the face of the drawer. Drill out the hole in the drawer after removing the screw, and glue the knob in position.

The grinding mechanism simply sits on top of the base, held in position wth two black-japanned roundhead screws. Final treatment is a matter of choice, but I prefer

not to use a wax finish since frequent handling and damp conditions in the kitchen would soon spoil it. A polyurethane varnish (two coats) is my first choice. Rustins Plastic Coating would also do the job admirably; for a really professional touch, a sprayed cellulose lacquer would give an excellent, lasting finish.

Whichever you go for, I'm sure the product will prove not only most enjoyable but also (if you feel inclined) most saleable.

● Craft Supplies, The Mill, Millers Dale, Buxton, Derbyshire SK17 8SN, tel. (0298) 871636. ∎

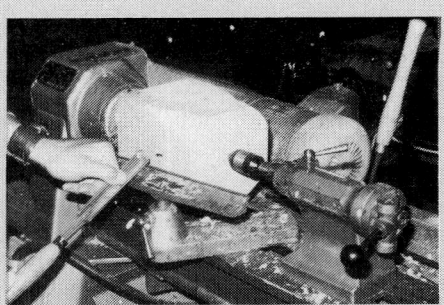

Fig. 11

Fig. 12

Fig. 13

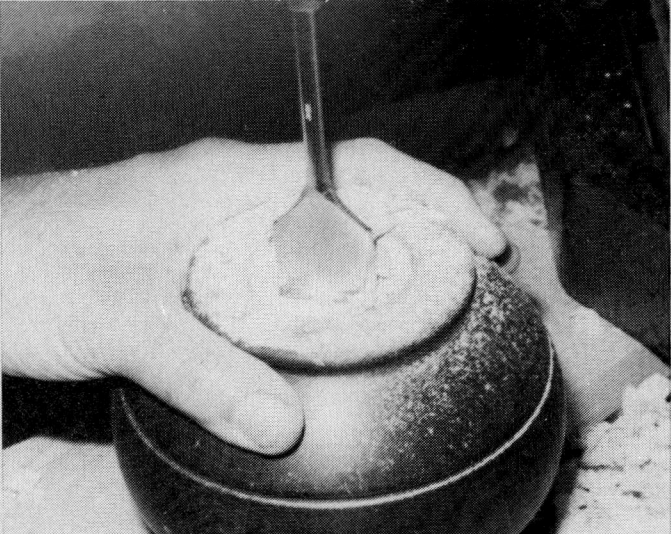

Fig. 14

Fig. 16

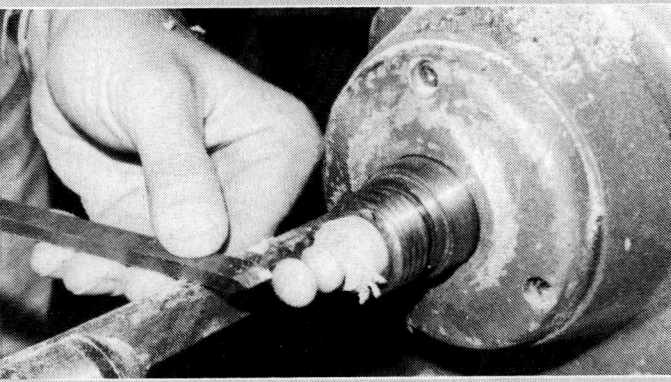

Fig. 17

Fig. 18

# English furniture:

## Dave Batten brings to an end his major series

The Arts and Crafts Movement instigated some of the most important changes in the course of British furniture design. Before that, however, there is one minor yet interesting fashion we should look at.

This was the popularity of Japanese artefacts from 1862, when they were displayed at the second Great Exhibition in London, to 1900 when the public appetite was sated. In furniture the trend manifested itself in a flood of bamboo tables, chairs, and occasional pieces. At first exquisitely made and decorated, these were soon taken up by mass-manufacturers and debased. Even so, authentic Japanese ideas proved one of the inspirations for the developing Arts and Crafts Movement. There were several exponents of the style, namely William Burges (notable, and some would say notorious, for his work at Cardiff Castle and Castell Coch); E. W. Godwin (who showed several of his most important desgins at the Paris Exhibition in 1878); Thomas Jeckyll; and Christopher Dresser. The famous painter, James McNeill Whistler, also joined the worshippers at the throne of 'Japonisme', and decorated many pieces, the most beautiful examples in the Peacock Room at no.1 Holland Park, London, when it was the home of Alexander Ionides, a well-known art collector.

The actual name of the Arts and Crafts Exhibition (which became the Movement) was suggested in 1888 by T. J. Cobden-Sanderson, a highly-accomplished bookbinder, and extended to include many different groups of similar persuasion — notably the Century Guild, founded in 1882 by A. H. Mackmurdo, C. R. Ashbee's Guild and School of Handicraft founded in 1888 in Mile End Road, London, which later moved to Chipping Camden in the Cotswolds, and the Cotswold School itself

at Sapperton (also in the Cotswolds).

But the Movement had earlier sources in the writings and philosophies of men like William Morris (1834-96), John Ruskin (1819-1900), Philip Webb (1831-1915), and a man we have mentioned already, Charles Locke Eastlake. Their common philosophy was summed up in an 1882 lecture by William Morris, in which he said: 'Our furniture should be good citizens' furniture, solid and well made in workmanship, and design should have nothing about it that is not easily defensible, no monstrosities or extravagances, not even of beauty lest we weary of it.'

William Morris is undoubtedly a giant in the history of British design, and it was his revulsion at the appalling mediocrity of most of the exhibits at the Great Exhibition of 1851 which spurred him into action. In 1861 he founded the firm of Morris, Marshall, Faulkner and Company, which included such famous names as Burne-Jones, Madox Brown, Rossetti and Philip Webb; as you will have noticed, three of them were painters, and one of the principal features of Morris's decorative style was his lavish use of painted panels.

A glance at his background and education will elicit his motivation. Born at Walthamstow in London of wealthy parents, he was educated at Marlborough and Exeter College, Oxford, where he entered a coterie of young men who like himself wished to better the social conditions of the poor, and to abolish the squalid slums caused by the Industrial Revolution. He had originally intended to be ordained, but abandoned this plan; gradually he evolved the idea of a non-industrialised society based on the practice of traditional craft work amid the brotherhood which he thought had prevailed in the old-time guilds.

The theory, like so many, contained the germ of its own destruction, in that the only people who could afford his wares were the same people whose standards he deplored. His company, however, soon realised the paradox and split its production into two distinct parts — one making custom-built pieces to indulge the taste of rich clients, and the other devoting itself to manufactur-

ing 'cottage'-style furniture for ordinary customers. Among the most popular designs in the latter class were a plain rush-seated armchair called the Sussex and an upholstered easy chair with an adjustable back; both designs were produced in large numbers from 1865 onwards. In 1870, the firm was re-organised on a more commercial basis, and a craftsman called George Jack became chief designer: from then until it ceased to exist in 1939 it was indistinguishable from several other manufacturers of good-quality furniture.

Apart from some large settles for a flat he shared with Burne-Jones, Morris does not seem to have designed any furniture, but the range of his influence was catholic indeed and embraced such diverse artifacts as stained glass, embroidery, tapestries, fabrics, metalwork, wallpaper and typography.

Morris was undoubtedly in love with medievalism, and this feeling was transmitted to all his work. When his firm showed its productions at the International Exhibition of 1862, the show-piece was the 'King Renée Cabinet' designed by the architect John Seddon; its panels showed scenes from one of Sir Walter Scott — an author who shared Morris's romantic vision of the past. This employment of painted panels was a hallmark of the firm.

Another characteristic was the use of coloured stains on furniture from 1861 onwards (Philip Webb designed several pieces which relied on the stain alone for decoration) — but generally the designs were enriched with carving and painting as well. The painting was undertaken by Burne-Jones, Rossetti, Ford Madox-Brown, Burges or even Holman Hunt. Burges deserves special mention, as his work had a jewel-like appearance with its richly coloured grounds and lavish gilding.

I have already mentioned the Cotswold School, and it is now time to take a look at the three men whose names are associated with it — Ernest Gimson (1864-1919) and the brothers Barnsley: Ernest (1863-1926) and Sidney (1865-1926). Their lives are fully documented, and a visit to Cheltenham Museum will provide you with all the details, plus a permanent exhi-

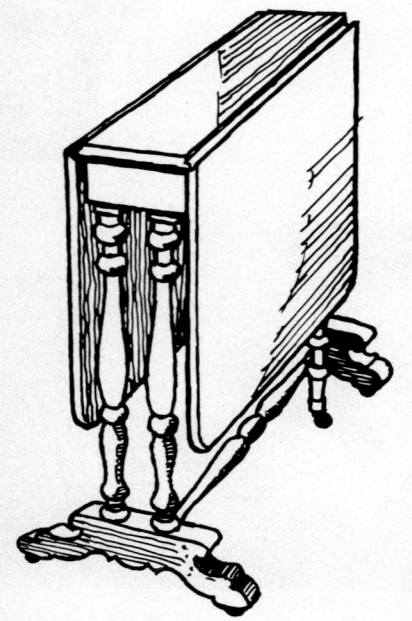

bition of their work. The three men originally met in the John Sedding's offices in 1886. Both Gimson and Sidney Barnsley travelled in Europe studying historical architecture and decoration; in 1895 they persuaded Sidney's brother Ernest to join them in the Cotswolds at Pinbury Park. In 1901 Gimson and Ernest entered into partnership and hired cabinetmakers to execute their designs, while Sidney chose to work independently. In 1905 the partnership between Gimson and Ernest was dissolved; while Ernest returned to his first love, architecture, Gimson continued at the Daneway workshops until his death.

Their furniture was characterised by its 'honesty' — they saw no reason why well-made joints should be hidden, and used them as a decorative feature; screws, however, were abhorred, and so were all finishes except for simple waxing to enhance the beauty of the wood. Such carving as there was was simple, often chip-carving, and chamfering was one of the approved forms of embellishment. But they certainly did not condemn the use of machinery. In the words of Edward Barnsley, 'It is seldom realised that Morris

● *An 1880 Arts and Crafts octagonal table, whose arched leg detail harks back to the Gothic; and a rosewood Art Nouveau folding desk by Hector Guimard*

never spoke or wrote that the machine must not be used . . . He urged that machines should not be used if their use removed from the work of making the pleasure of it. And that was the approach of the Barnsleys and Gimson.' Edward Barnsley, Sidney's son, became a master cabinetmaker in his own right, working from Froxfield, Hampshire.

Turning from rustic simplicity to sophisticated (some would say neurotic) flamboyance, we come to Art Nouveau. The style was originated and nurtured in France and Germany before it spread to England and filled the vacuum left by the gradual demise of the Arts and Crafts Movement at the end of the century.

Its ideal was to reconcile machine-made

furniture with good artistic principles and to produce goods for the masses; it was axiomatic that the designer should be in complete and unquestioned control of the mechanical processes. In Germany the concept brought forth functional designs combined with restrained decoration, but in France the themes utilised plant forms and tendril-like embellishments almost to the point of the grotesque.

In England C. A. Voysey (1857-1941), who was one of the founder-members of the Art Workers' Guild and an architect by profession, translated the Continental designs into a more restrained British style. He was accompanied by three other able designers: Charles Rennie Mackintosh, M. H. Baillie Scott and A. H. Mackmurdo.

Voysey's furniture was usually made in oak and of almost severe simplicity, which was often relieved by the spectacular use of brass for enormous hinges and mounts. Mackintosh regarded good items of furniture as visually perfect accessories to an artistically inspired interior, and in some of his chairs he was prepared to subordinate comfort to appearance. He was fond of furniture painted in soft pastel colours, often with mother-of-pearl inlay or inset panels which accorded with this principle, Scott worked mainly in mahogany or oak, which was often embellished with coloured woods, ivory, and metals such as brass and pewter. Mackmurdo followed the advice given by Owen Jones in 1856: 'Beauty of form is produced by lines going out one from the other in gradual undulations — in surface all line should flow out of a parent stem.' He frequently included, in otherwise plain and uninspired furniture, fretted panels which accorded with this principle, with some odd results; however, in other designs he used the medieval motifs and painted panels so beloved of William Morris.

The work of Voysey's Century Guild was short-lived, and was terminated by the same problem that beset Morris; namely that good furniture, beautifully decorated, prices itself out of the mass market and can only be afforded by a few rich patrons. However, the Guild was formed to bring good furniture into the reach of the masses, and it did not want to be a pale imitation of Morris's medievalism. It tried to look forward and to uphold the same tenets as the Continental Art Nouveau designers, and it therefore became one of the early advocates of the style in England. ■

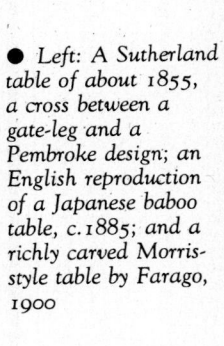

● *Left: A Sutherland table of about 1855, a cross between a gate-leg and a Pembroke design; an English reproduction of a Japanese baboo table, c.1885; and a richly carved Morris-style table by Farago, 1900*

● *Left: A Mackmurdo writing-desk, 1886; and a Sidney Barnsley oak 'hay-rake stretcher' table, 1924 (below)*

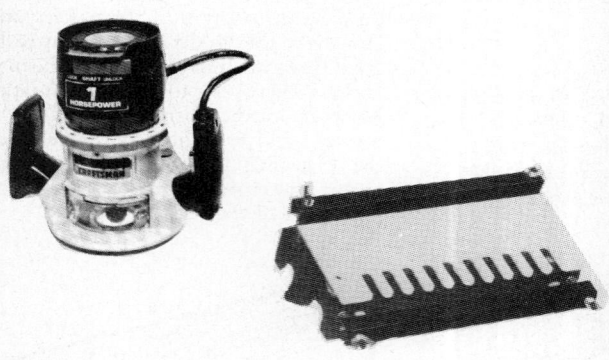

Prices quoted are those prevailing at press date and are subject to alteration due to economic conditions.

# Revolutionary circles

Will the ring gouge re-write the dictionary of the lathe? Bruce Boulter puts a brand-new tool through its paces

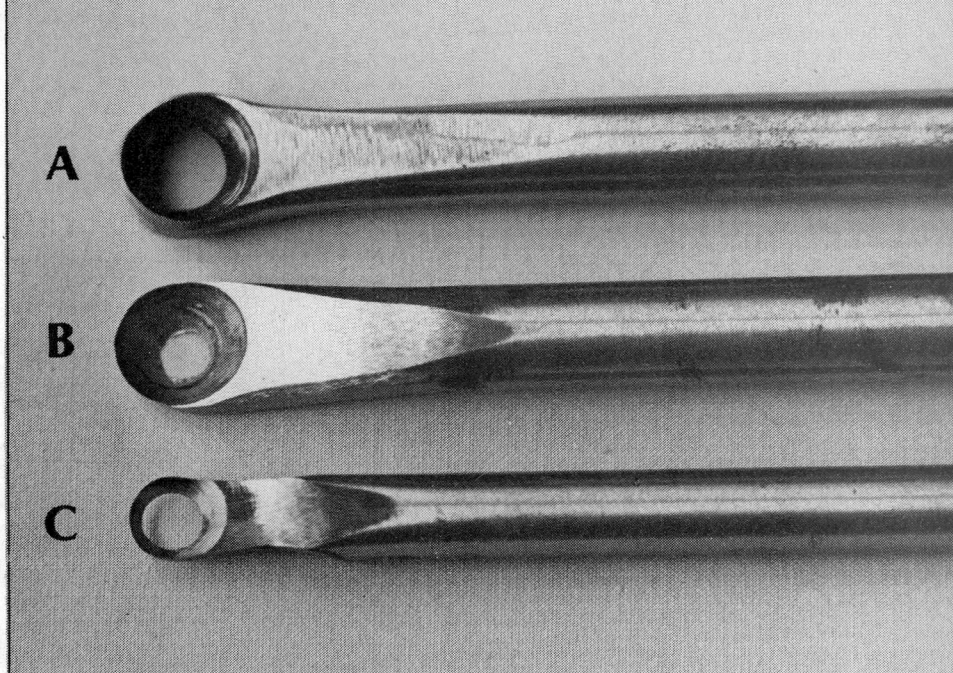

**Fig. 1**

This exciting new tool, invented by Vin Smith of Tasmania, is a natural progression from the 'turning hook' used by the treadle-lathe turners of old.

His original idea was to pursue the hook system, but after a few trials Vin thought: 'Why a hook? Why not a ring?' After a lot of work and a lot of trial and error making tools of different shape by hand, he arrived at the prototypes shown here.

'The tool-cum-idea is still in its infancy,' says Vin; 'we have established what it will do so far, and it was originated purely as a finishing tool. However, it's becoming obvious that there will be many applications.'

In fig. 1 there are three ring gouges. I would describe A as a general-purpose tool; it will work the insides of bowls (none of the tools are recommended for the outsides of faceplate work) and it also does well on work between centres.

B is a delight to use between centres in producing large coves and for general shaping.

C I did not like very much. The idea is good — the tool is only ⅜in o.d. — and being very finely made is most suitable for small work. But it is a weak design, and I managed to break it doing some tests after the photography.

In trying them out, Vin advised me to use a slow speed, and I never had reason to disagree.

I tried the first one on a disc of cocobolo, a hardish timber, and the finish straight from the tool was excellent. This was my first attempt with a ring gouge, and I found it worked with ease, with no tendency to skid. I got a very fine shaving and an un-torn surface, using only the very lightest pressure on the tool, at a speed of 500rpm. As the cuts deepened, keeping the speed at 500rpm and the tool slightly less on its side but with the same sweeping action, it behaved perfectly. The finish would not need coarser abrasive than 350 grit to get a professional result. I tried increasing the speed to 1000rpm, keeping the tool at the same angle and using the same pressure, but the finish was no better.

Some might tend to present the tool in scraper fashion — indeed that seemed its natural cutting position; but it is not.

Flushed with success, I could not wait to try the second gouge on stuff between centres, and chose a length of shreddy English walnut. Fig. 2 is a close-up as the turner would see the work; though the tool is taking a heavy cut, very little pressure from the hand is required.

As with a normal spindle gouge, the cuts are made from the high point to the centre of the cove/hollow, but the tool itself is of course angled in the opposite direction

(figs. 3 & 4). In fig. 3 the finish is obvious; it would require little abrading before polishing. I doubt the experienced turner would find this tool better than, say, a ½in or even ¾in spindle gouge, but for less experienced people, and for this type of work, B is well worth it.

My only practice had been at the tailstock end, where I found the tool completely docile and vice-free. The sharp profile was easy to work, and again there was no tendency for the gouge to skid. The toolrest is set about ½in away from the workpiece to permit a swing as the shape of the cut is followed.

It seems the obvious course to present the ring flat as you would a scraper, but I tried and did not like the results. All the work with B was done at 1000rpm.

Finally we come to C. The tool is perfect for working into small areas, though it must be used with great care and sparingly; it is so small that its life will inevitably be limited. Elm, an open-grained timber and not always the easiest to finish, was selected. Up till now I had stuck with the usual method of working from the centre outwards (I subsequently discovered the reverse is just as effective with A); so with this format, all

endgrain, it was worth a try in the opposite direction (fig. 5). The tool was so easy to use that I was becoming blasé, even euphoric — a short-lived state of mind, because almost immediately after fig. 6 was taken, the ring snapped during a heavy cut.

C is very much a finishing tool, intended for those final few gossamer-light cuts to obviate as much sanding as possible, and the finish it was going to produce is plain to see.

In practice the ring gouge can be considered as a normal tool because it cuts, rather than scraping. The essential difference is that it is much easier to present to the working area. Though it is possible to snag it, you have to be very clumsy or try very hard.

● *Sharpening:* The makers recommend the use of mounted points, or making your own mandrel in hardwood, shaped to fit on to the tool. You can maintain the edge with this and a little valve-grinding paste.
● *Length of life:* If you accept that this tool is intended for finishing, to get the last cut or two before polishing and to obviate any sanding above 350-grit garnet, it should give

**Fig. 2**

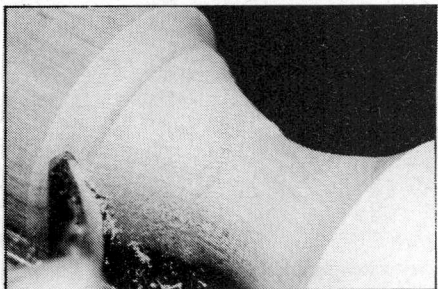

**Fig. 3**

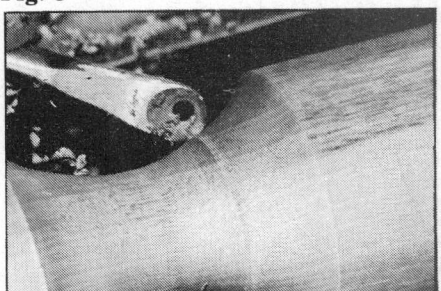

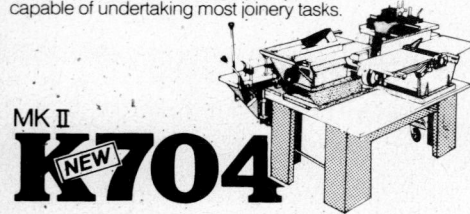
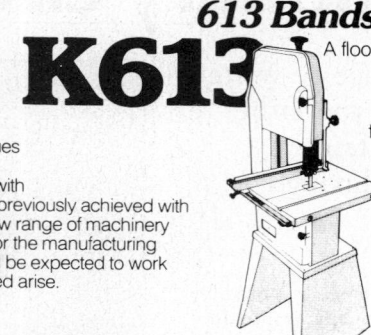
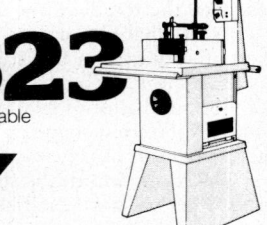

**Fig. 4** ▲

good service. It has such a clean cutting action that it will require honing less often than the average gouge. It can never be ground because it is of carbon steel. Honing with either method is positive and controlled, and the minimum of steel is removed. The gouge's longevity would certainly be on a par with that of a TCT-insert scraper.

● Other shapes and sizes are on the drawing board, which will include left and right cranked, to accommodate inboard and outboard turning. A double ended tool is also planned, for bowl work at one end and spindle turning at the other. The handle will be in the centre and it will come with a protective cap for the end not in use. All other tools will be offered unhandled.

With its benign characteristics, the ring gouge would be useful to students or beginners in woodturning, or to the worker who turns as a supplement to another speciality, such as the cabinet maker, carver or luthier. It is very safe to use, and at the low speeds recommended it is a great confidence builder; at the same time, the beginner can produce some well finished work. The tool will not replace or render obsolete any existing turning tool — that will be decided by the users.

I wish I had thought of it!

**Fig. 5** ▲    **Fig**

● **D. R. Moult** of the *Tasmania Mercury* writes: There seems little doubt that the ring gouge will be marketed by Siddons Distributors, 559 Gardeners Rd, Mascot, New South Wales, Australia.

It was designed with the novice in mind, but already professionals are using it here for commercial work. I watched one professional turning out eggcups of a commercially acceptable standard in a shade under two minutes, using no other tool.

The ring gouge has been improved since Bruce Boulter tested it — the main modification being to square the shank. With the shank on the lathe toolrest, the cutting ring is automatically presented at the correct angle to the wood, so anyone can use it successfully.

● Vin Smith, c/o Hall's Machinery, 82 Warwick St, Hobart, Tasmania, Australia. ■

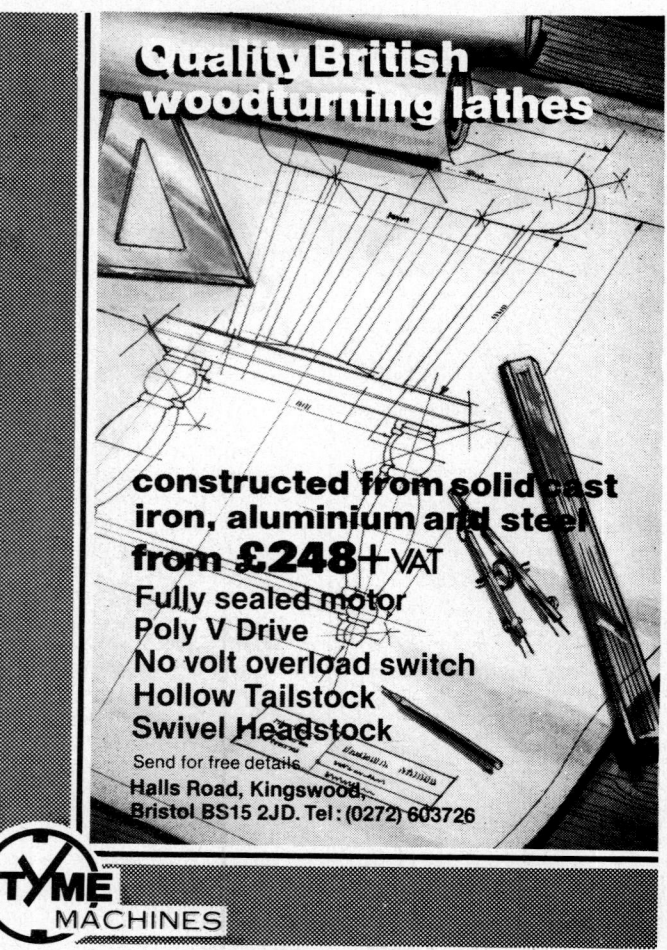
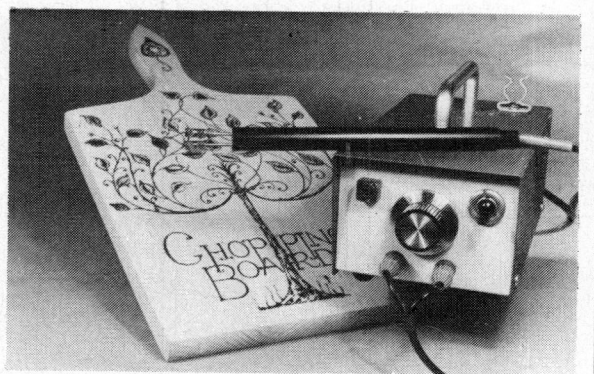
Prices quoted are those prevailing at press-date and are subject to alteration due to economic conditions.

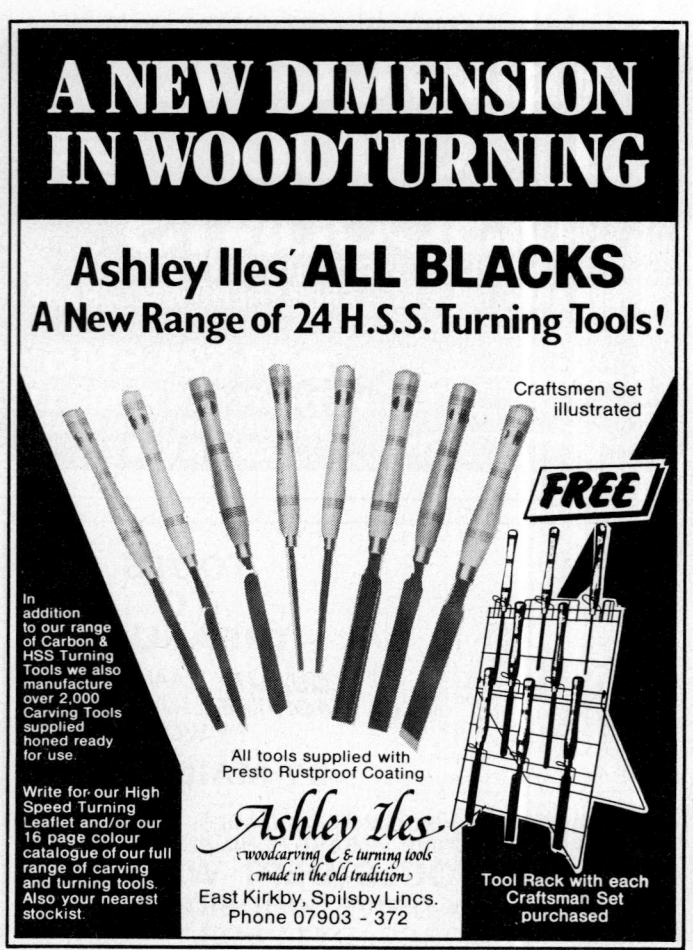

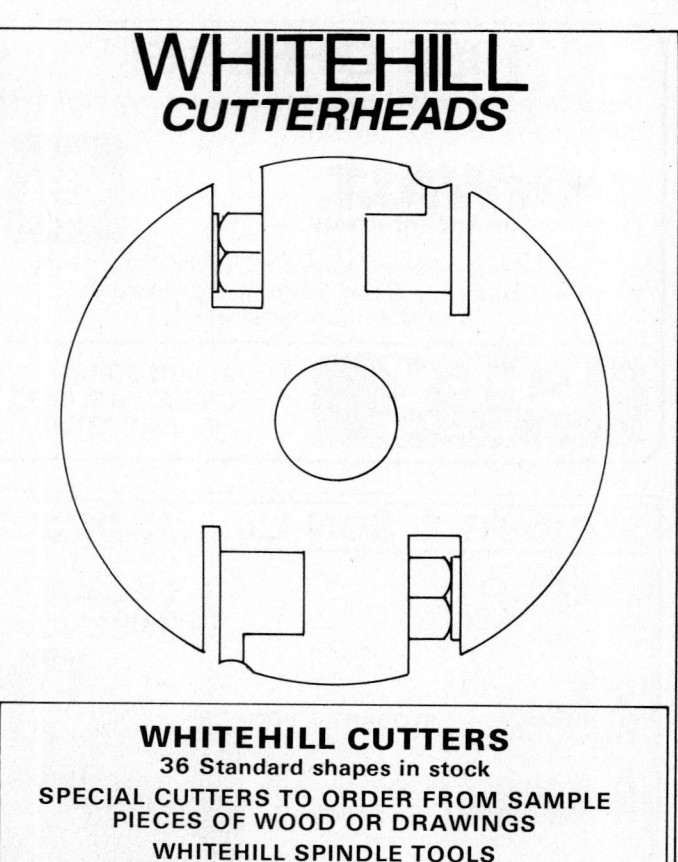
Prices quoted are those prevailing at press date and are subject to alteration due to economic conditions.

# Gauging exactly

## Bob Wearing's complete guide to the precise world of tools for measuring and marking

Usually the small professional or amateur craftsman has little money to spend. The more tools he can make, the more funds are available for power tools which he cannot make. In the case of gauges, there's a further incentive: while their number and variety is more or less limitless, only three types are generally available, so the others have to be made anyway.

Before I go into details, consider alternative methods of clamping the stock. The standard device — a wooden (nowadays plastic) screw in a threaded hole — is not generally applicable. The wood tap and die for this are expensive and of little use for anything else. Attempts to make do with an engineer's tap and die will prove unsucessful.

The nearest approach to this is shown in fig. 1. A thumbscrew passes through a clearance hole in the wood, then through a square nut which applies pressure on the stem via a shoe of brass or other metal which prevents damage. The jig for bending a number of shoes is shown in fig. 2. It is made from 25×25mm and 12×3 (or 5)mm bright mild steel with two 6mm or ¼in RH screws. The shoe is from ¾×¹⁄₁₆in brass (or 16-gauge sheet). Make the shoe first than plane the fence to fit it. I prefer this method to all others — but it is wise to anneal the brass shoe before bending.

An alternative, using a plastic knock-down fitting glued in the hole and then tapped, is shown in fig. 1A. Further clamping methods are shown in figs. 1b & 1c. In fig. 1b a ½in hole is bored through the stock. Two greased wood plugs are fitted to locate centrally a greased ¼in (6mm) screw. The hole is then filled with car-body filler. When the filler is hard, the wood plugs are removed, the lower one being sawn through first. The stock is then produced finally to shape. The finished screw is fitted, and also a ½in-dia. steel pellet to protect the stem. The plug is arranged to leave space for this. In fig. 1c the same hole can be drilled and a similar greased plug fitted. This time the hole is completely filled with body filler. When dry it is drilled and tapped. Both these threads will stand up well to reasonable use.

If manufactured thumbscrews are not available, fig. 3 shows four methods for making them. 3a is a strip soldered into the slot of a RH brass machine screw, ¼in BSW or M6. 3b is made by soldering a wing nut to a piece of screwed rod. Again brass both looks and solders best. Steel may be brazed. A small knob (c) may be turned or found and soldered on; (d) shows a soldered-on cylinder later drilled for a tommy-bar. A radio or electrical knob of suitable shape and size is a further possibility.

In earlier times craftsmen having no metalworking facilities locked their gauges

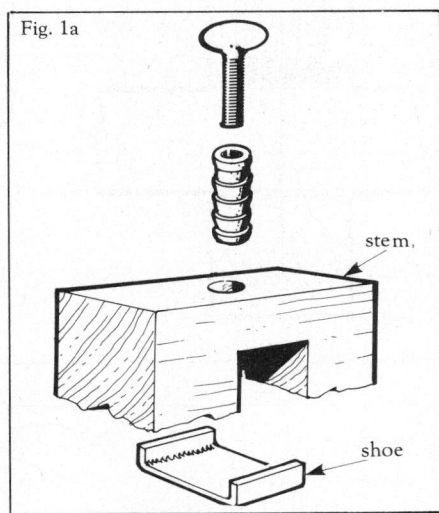

Fig. 1
thumbscrew
stock
made nut
shoe
stem

Fig. 1a
stem
shoe

with wedges. A round protrusion on the thin end prevents the wedge from falling out, fig. 4. This method remains quite successful but is not so quick to set. It can be used by the average worker without expense or the purchase of special tools.

Fig. 5 shows another method of clamping, by closing up a saw-kerf to grip on a stem. Having chopped the stem mortise, drill the small hole and make the saw-cut to it. This cut must not be too fine. The clamping can be achieved in any of three ways. In each case the 'upper jaw' has a clearance hole. Through this can pass a thumbscrew converted from a woodscrew as illustrated. An alternative is to tap the lower jaw with, say, a ¼in BSW tap and screw a similarly threaded thumbscrew into this. If the tool is to have a lot of use, a nut could also be let into the lower face. The other possibility is to thread the lower jaw using the taper tap and then only until the point emerges, giving an undersized thread. Into this a short length of threaded rod is permanently screwed.

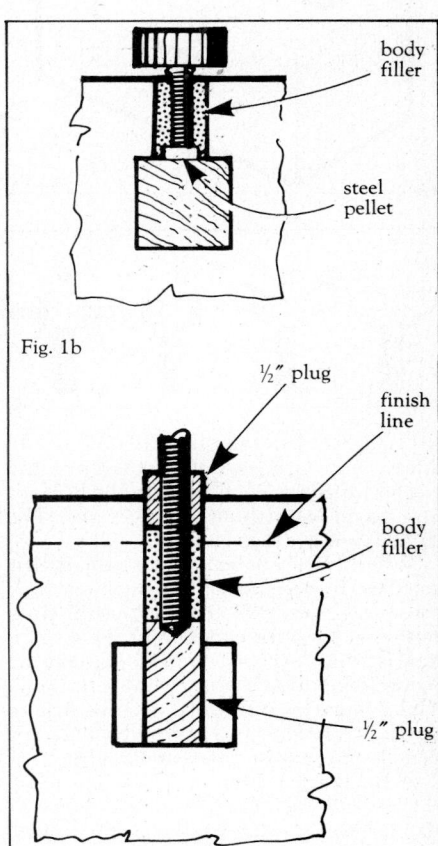

body filler
steel pellet

Fig. 1b
½″ plug
finish line
body filler
½″ plug

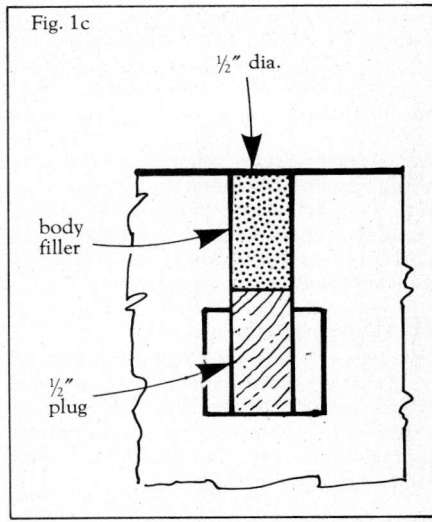

Fig. 1c
½″ dia.
body filler
½″ plug

Tightening is then done with a wing-nut and washer.

Yet another method (fig. 6) is to chop a square mortise, preferably with one cut of a machine chisel, to take a small, thick, square nut. This mortise is cut at the bottom of a deep hole drilled to the size of the nut's diagonal. A dowel is glued into the round hole and then drilled to take the locking screw with an easy fit. The top surface is finally sanded smooth. The stem is proctected from damage by the screw with the insertion of a small steel pellet, either round or square. A variation (fig. 6a) is to

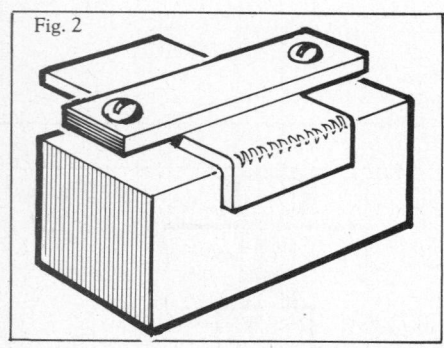

Fig. 2

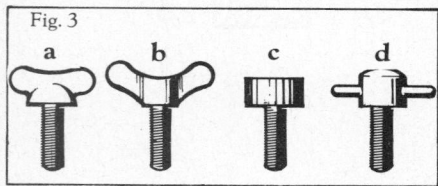

Fig. 3
a    b    c    d

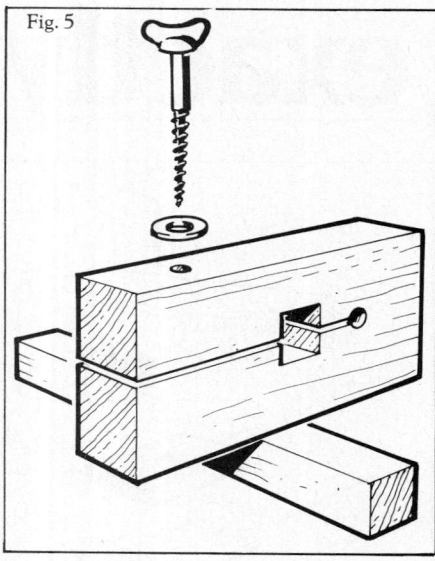

Fig. 5

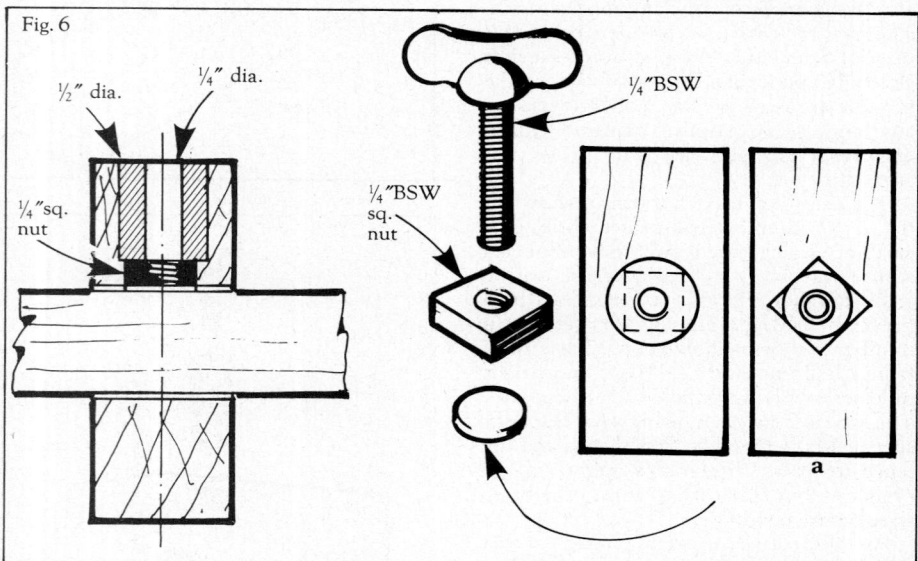

Fig. 6

½″ dia.    ¼″ dia.
¼″sq. nut
¼″BSW
¼″BSW sq. nut
a

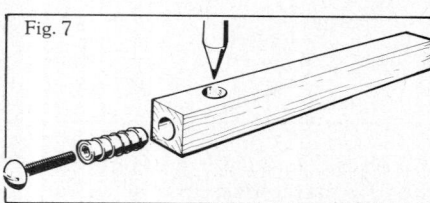

Fig. 7

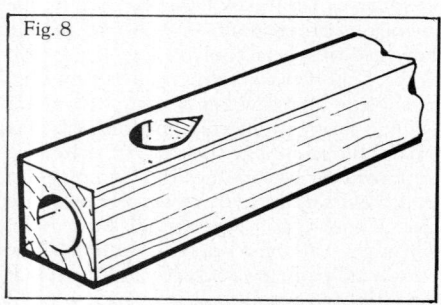

Fig. 8

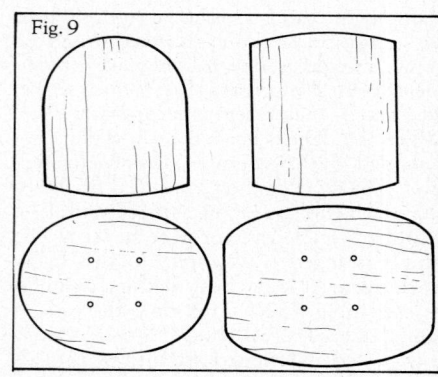

Fig. 9

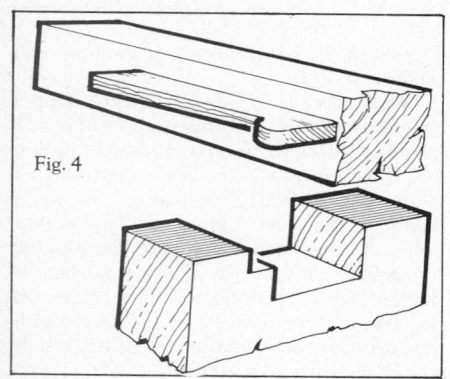

Fig. 4

drill slightly less than the diagonal of the square nut. Using a bolt and large strong washer, this nut is pulled into the hole far enough to leave room for the pellet. The drilled dowel is then glued in.

When a pencil or ballpoint is being used it can best be secured with a small machine screw, say $\frac{3}{16}$in BSW. In order that this does not soon strip the endgrain of the stem, a hole is drilled — probably $\frac{5}{16}$in — to take the nylon knock-down fitting shown in fig. 7. This is glued in. A thread cut in this is quite durable. A hole shaped as in fig. 8 will accept pencils and pens of different diameters.

A number of different stock and fence shapes have been used. Some are shown in fig. 9. There is a wide choice for the maker, who may well much prefer shapes of his own choosing. The length of the fence has a great bearing on the exact use of a gauge, so it is not wise to standardise on one shape or size throughout. Ample thickness is needed for a good rigid lock, so the figures given should not be appreciably reduced. On the other hand, stems may be thinned somewhat. The sizes shown were in some cases chosen to match up with stock metal sizes for shoes and nuts. You can of course fit the conventional rounded stems, but this complicates the work and assumes access to the two scribing-gouges needed to make the mortise.

## Marking-gauge

Of course you have one already, but a second is always very useful, and on some jobs even a third. See fig. 10. Several shapes have been suggested for the stock, but you may prefer to design your own. The sizes given make a good, comfortable gauge.

Commercially made gauges have a rounded bottom edge to the stem. This allows the pointer to trail rather than having to be stabbed in vertically. However, chopping this curve and making the stem to suit adds quite a bit to the work. If the stem is to remain square, drill the hole for the drill

point at an angle to achieve this trailing action. If you are left-handed, remember to reverse this angle. Points can be bought from a good tool merchant. Otherwise make them from $\frac{1}{16}$in-dia. silver steel, available in 13in lengths, or from an old steel knitting-needle. Harden and temper the material.

The point should not protrude more than $\frac{1}{16}$in or 2mm. In school and college workshops, gauges with $\frac{3}{8}$in of point are common, but the design is quite wrong.

The best general finish these days is three coats of polyurethane varnish, matt or satin for preference, lightly sanded with the finest paper between coats. An idea to experiment with would be a working face of Formica-type plastic laminate.

## Marking-gauge for curved work

See fig. 11 for this. When you're gauging from a curve, if it's not too sharp, the fence is modified by the addition of two hardwood strips. 'Hard' must be emphasised; small offcuts of rosewood or the like are ideal. They are suitably rounded, then glued into shallow housings. They can be put on the back of a gauge stock so that one gauge will serve two purposes.

Incidentally, it is often required that a gauge mark shall start and terminate exactly as in fig. 12a, and not overrun as in fig. 12b. If the point is stabbed in firmly on the finish line, at the end of its run it will drop decisively into the hole.

## Pencil-gauge

By the word 'pencil' I mean any writing

# The bench-mounted gauge

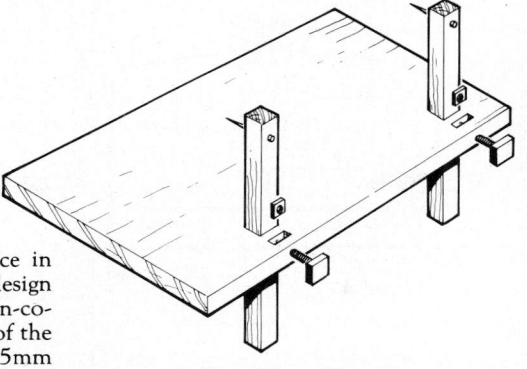

**R. J. Stephenson** writes: Experience in secondary schools prompted me to design this alternative marking-gauge for un-co-ordinated beginners. Near one edge of the 12mm flat base, two stems about 12-15mm square are a push fit in their mortises. Near the top of each stem a metal pin is pushed through. Two clearance holes for coach bolts are bored from the edge to meet the stems, and two mortises are cut — a tight fit for the nuts. These are filed flush if they protrude. For use as a marking-gauge, one stem is pushed right down and the other adjusted to give the height to be measured. The workpiece is placed on the base and pushed along so that the point marks the required line.

Two stems, gripped in the vice, hold the base much more firmly than one. They can also be set to different heights and used to mark two different sizes, for instance the width to which a piece of wood is to be planed on one point and the depth of a groove on the other; also, obviously, they make a mortise-gauge.

When setting up, the coach bolts only need to be finger-tight. Once in the vice the stems are held firmly.

Sizes: a good average would be a base of about 300mm square. The only critical size is the distance between the stems, which must be small enough for them to fit in the vice cheeks and large enough for them to straddle the bars.

A few variations may be tried . . . The pins may be replaced by pencils. More than two stems may be fitted. More than one pin may be fitted to the stems. The variations are endless. I've even used the device for marking out dovetails by placing a wedge-shaped piece of wood on the base!

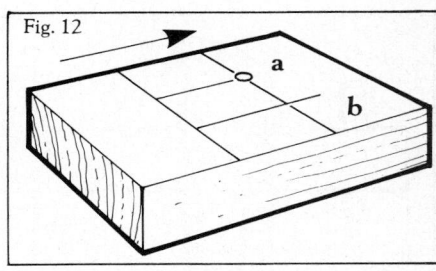

Fig. 12

variety of shapes can be used.

The plastic insert with screw holds the pencil in. Make the hole to suit the chosen implement. A wedge could be used instead, operating in a slot in the stem, but I am not keen on this method as the wedge tends to get lost if the pencil is taken out.

Such a pencil-gauge is only suitable for marking out from a straight edge. For working from a curve, a modification is necessary — fig. 14. Here the rebate is replaced by two stubby dowels which run sweetly round any smooth, regular curve.

## Cutting-gauge

This is generally mass-produced in exactly the same style as the marking-gauge. When making by hand, you can preserve this similarity if you like the shape, but there are alternatives. Again a longer stock facilitates work at the ends of components.

Not everyone wants to roll the cutting-gauge over in the manner of the marking-gauge. In this case a rebate, as in the pencil-gauge just described, might be thought convenient. If you find it a disadvantage in that narrow sizes cannot be gauged, you can easily turn the stock round.

In making an effective cutting-gauge (fig. 15) great care must be given to setting the knife. It's not enough just to chop a hole and wedge it in. An accurate square or rectangular hole must be cut; then the face nearest to the stock must be slightly angled. For a right-handed worker, cut as illustrated (fig. 15). Left-handers reverse the angle. Naturally the wedge, which may be of ebony, rosewood or brass, needs to be slightly filed off to suit this irregular shape.

Cutting-gauge knives can be bought, but I imagine that very, very few tool dealers stock them. (The same is true of marking-gauge points.) They can easily be made. Possible sources of materials are pieces of cabinet scrapers and old handsaws, power hacksaw blades, and pieces of ground flat stock (tool steel).

Workers grind a variety of shapes for cutting-gauge knives. Basically they fall into two classes — fig. 16. If a marking-gauge is used across the grain, as for dovetails, the fibres will tear and splinter, so for this job a cutting-gauge is superior. When the gauge is used for such marking, a pointed shape (a) is most suitable. For heavier work, such as cutting small rebates and when crossbanding, a firmer and more rounded shape (b) is to be preferred.

As the blade has a bevel on one side, the tiny groove it cuts has one vertical side and one sloping. The sloping side must always be in the waste piece, so the bevel must be set towards or away from the stock depending on the job in hand.

In better-quality gauges the face is protected from wear by the insertion of two

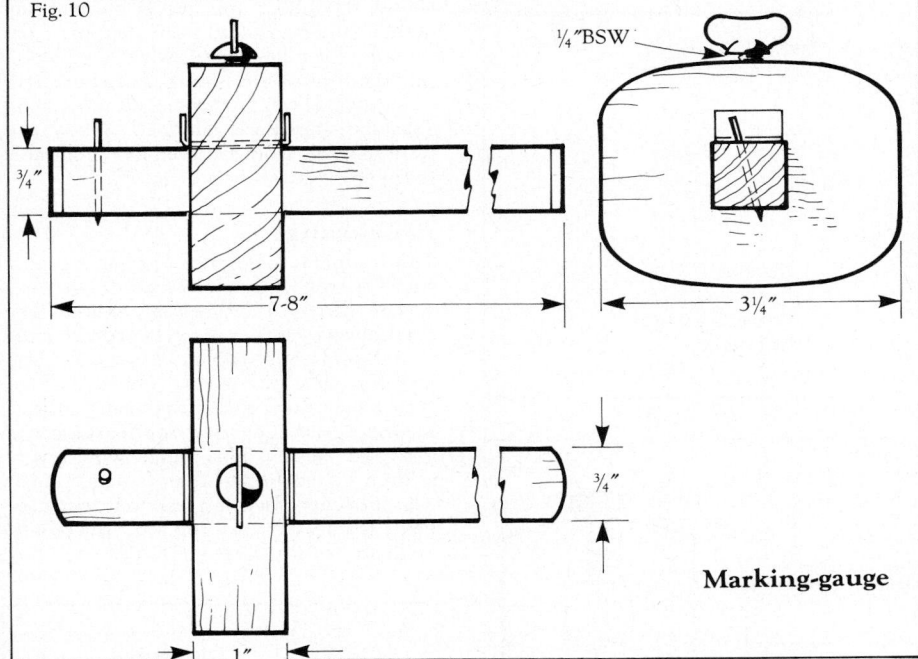

Fig. 10

¼"BSW

7-8"

3¼"

¾"

¾"

1"

**Marking-gauge**

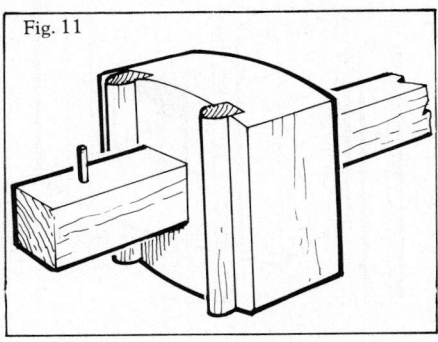

Fig. 11

appliance — pencil, ballpoint, fibre-tip, etc. Ball- and fibre-points give a fine, clear line of constant width, but be sure before using them that the ink will not harm the work. The pencil-gauge (fig. 13) is generally used for rough marking-out, so its inability to gauge very narrow widths is no inconvenience. With a fine pen the tool can sometimes be used for precise marking.

A rebate in the stock is customary for this type of gauge. The extra length of the stock facilitates gauging at each end of a board. Naturally any of the locking devices shown are applicable. Above the rebate quite a

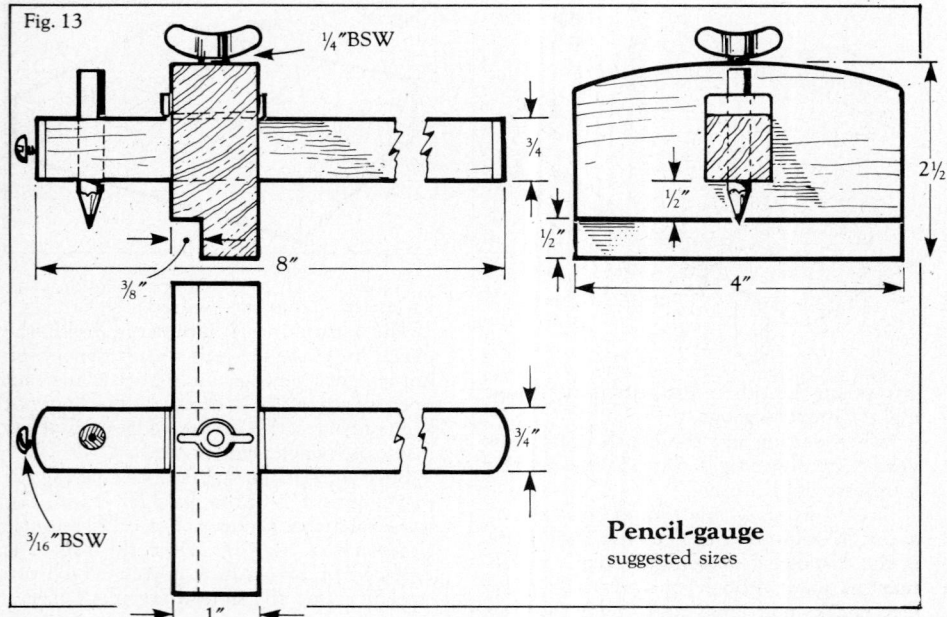

Fig. 13

¼"BSW

¾

½"

2½"

8"

4"

⅜"

³⁄₁₆"BSW

¾"

¾"

1"

**Pencil-gauge**
suggested sizes

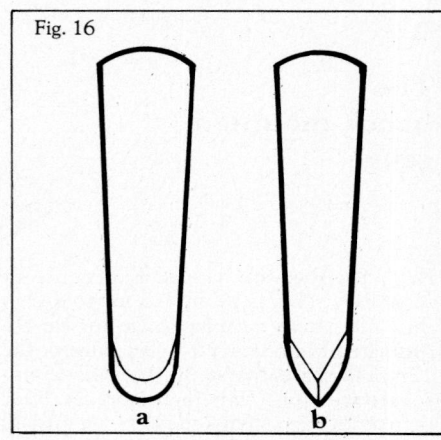

Fig. 16

**a**       **b**

brass strips (fig. 17). Some makers fix these in place with epoxy-resin glue, others with two small countersunk screws each. After fixing, the working surface must be levelled, generally by disc sanding. Also on the better gauges, the knife used to be held in place with a screw and a brass pressure plate. This is shown in the modification at fig. 15a.

## Grasshopper gauge

This gauge may be fitted either with a writing instrument or with a point. Generally the former is used. To the best of my knowledge this tool have never been manufactured. It has two distinct forms. Fig. 18 shows a marking being made across a lip; fig. 19 shows the other application — marking across an overhang: for example, the marking for a line of nails where a plywood lid, slightly oversize, is pinned to a box, later to be planed level. In this second case a small subsidiary fence (a) is added. When you want to gauge from a curved face, a suitable fence (b) is fitted — see fig. 20.

## Panel-gauge

This is similar, to the pencil-gauge, except in size. The stock is generally made longer, and a wide variety of shapes is possible. The stock always has the rebate. In order that the tool should not be too unwieldy, it's a good plan to make two stems, one somewhat longer than that of the pencil-gauge, with a second really long one for marking out plywood sheets. This gauge would very seldom be used other than from a straight edge. For curved work, a second stock can be made with two dowels replacing the rebate, as illustrated for the pencil-gauge.

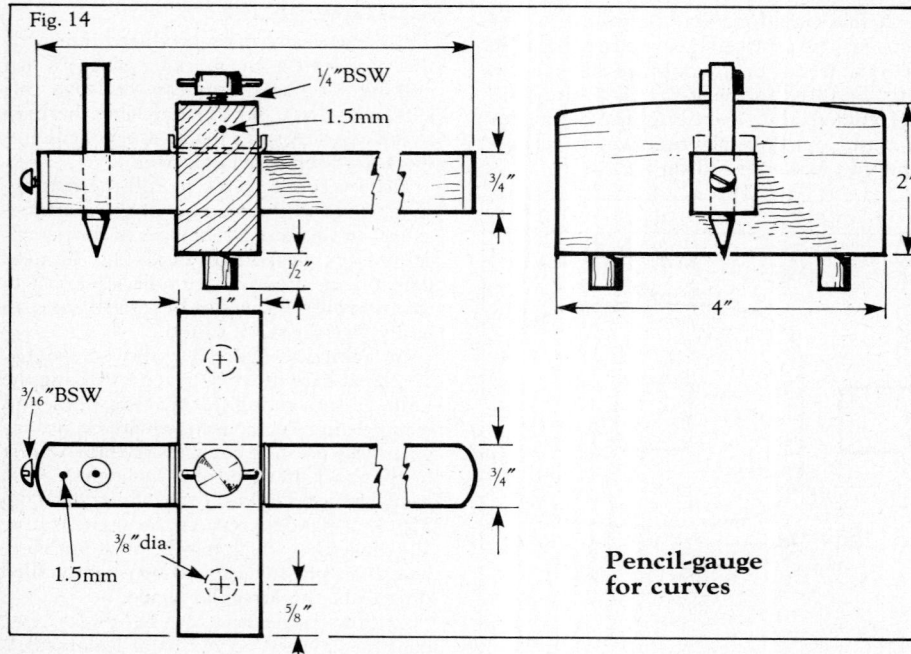

Fig. 14

¼"BSW

1.5mm

¾"

½"

1"

³⁄₁₆"BSW

¾"

⅜"dia.

1.5mm

⅝"

2"

4"

**Pencil-gauge
for curves**

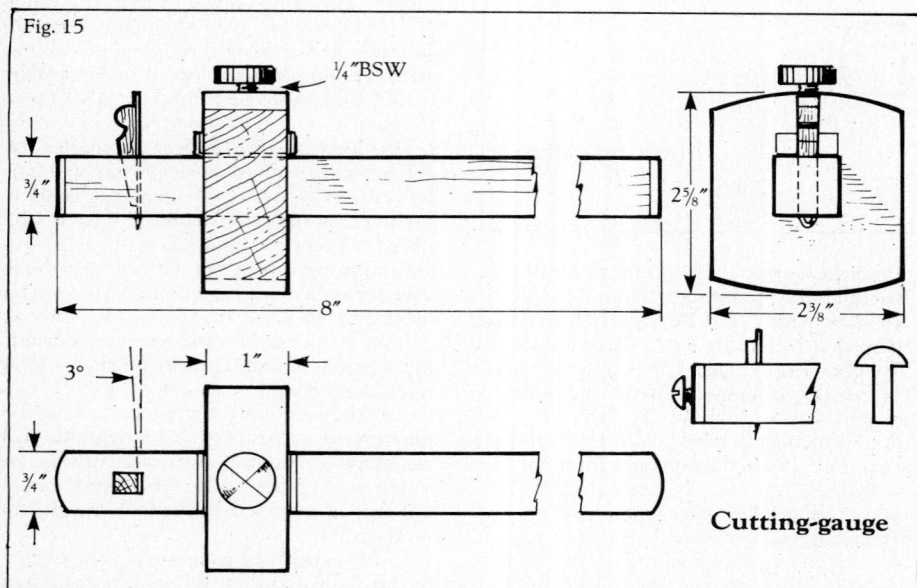

Fig. 15

¼"BSW

¾"

8"

3°

1"

¾"

2⅝"

2⅜"

**Cutting-gauge**

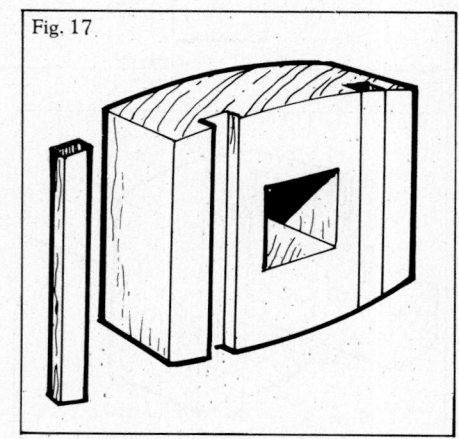

Fig. 17

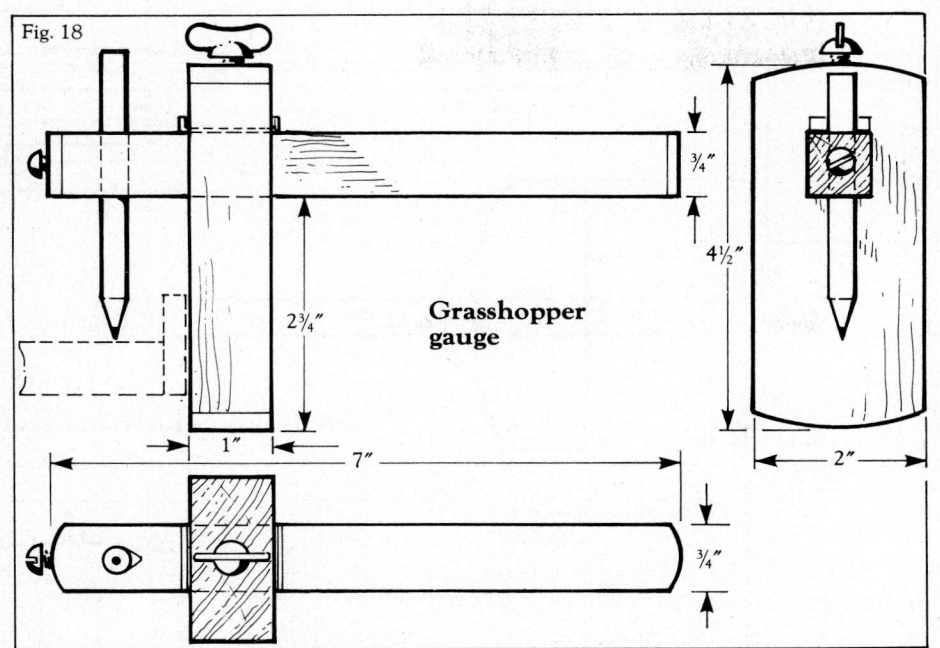

Fig. 18

**Grasshopper gauge**

wire nails. Admittedly these last cannot be hardened, but such a gauge is used only occasionally. Fig. 24 shows the shape of the points. The small spigot is first turned or filed, then the cone is produced by holding in a drill chuck in the lathe or in a bench-mounted electric drill.

The fixed point is riveted into a brass block about ½×¼×⅛in (13×6×3mm), filed flush and held into its housing with a small woodscrew. The moving point is similarly fixed into a longer block of about 1¼×¼×⅛in. (30×6×3mm). This is tapped to take a suitable round- or cheese-headed screw: 2BA, M3 or M4 are suggestions. The stem is slotted to take this, preferably with a router — which can also cut the housing for the two brass blocks. Assembly and adjustment are straightforward.

You may find it restricting to have the point's locking screw proud of the stem; so, if you intend to use the gauge close to the working edge in spite of its long stem, the locking screw can be sunk into a housing (fig. 25). In this case the brass shoe is essential for the fence-clamping screw.

This assumes that pencil, fibre-tip or the like is the marking method. If a point is preferred, allowance must be made for the essential space between the mortise and the rebate. An extra block of this thickness is glued to the stem, fig. 21a. The rebate does not permit the stem to be rotated in the manner of the marking-gauge, nor does the greater length of the stem help. The hole for the point is therefore drilled through the stem and spacing block at an angle (fig. 10). This achieves a trailing point for easier gauging. Left-handers should remember to reverse this angle.

## Combined setting-out square and gauge

This is very useful for making large full-size 'rods' on hardboard sheets. A wooden metre or 3ft rule is recommended. To make this a good fit, the mortise is built up in the stock, the two centre sections being glued to the base with the rule in place — well waxed to prevent adhesion. When the glue is dry, the drilled top is added and the stock shaped. A pressure disc is turned to a loose fit in the hole, and faced below with glasspaper. The rubber square is now glued to stock and disc. For use as a gauge with a hand-held pencil, the rule is locked to length by thumb pressure on the disc. Careful gluing-up gives a square accurate enough for this purpose: fig. 22.

## Long mortise-gauge

The mortise-gauge is generally bought, often at considerable cost, but nevertheless a simple form can be made. Fig. 23 shows the method by which adjustments of the gap between the points and the stock or fence position are made quite independently. The distance from stock to points is severely limited on the standard gauge, making long markings impossible. The same gauge, fitted with a long stem, may for example be used to mark stub mortise-and-tenon joints in the middles of a wide carcass.

Making the gauge is quite straightforward, and you can use any of the clamping methods described. The stock should be made longer than normal, for this will help when working

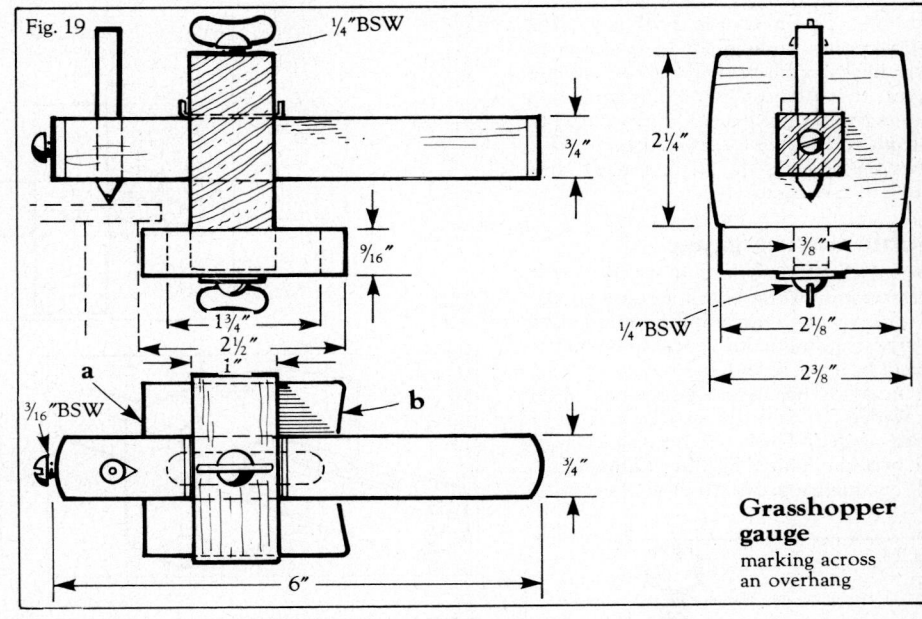

Fig. 19

**Grasshopper gauge**
marking across an overhang

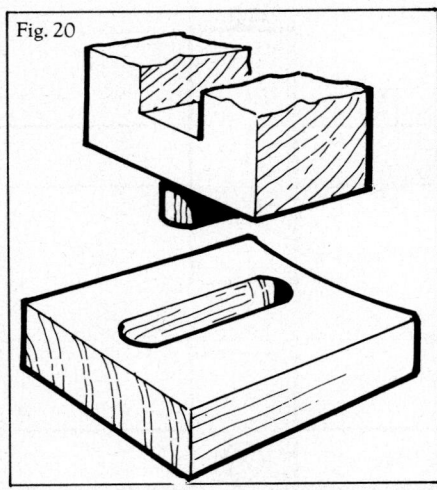

Fig. 20

at some distance from an edge. The points can be made from the most suitable material to hand — ideally tool steel or silver steel, otherwise knitting-needles or even large

## Gauge for marking and cutting plastic laminates

A small tungsten-carbide cutter of the type shown in fig. 26 is freely available in tool shops. The end is sawn off as shown and a gauge produced to take it, fig. 27. Size and shape are of course matters of personal taste. To cope with the wear from such materials as Formica the face of the stock or fence should be faced either with a similar material or with thin steel or brass. Laminate is glued on; metal will require four well countersunk woodscrews.

This tool is particularly useful for quick production of lippings for tabletops, shelf edges and the like. Scored heavily from both sides, the material snaps off easily. This gauge is shown using the clamping method of fig. 6a.

## Close-up or 'into the corner' gauge

From time to time the length of stem extending beyond the point of a standard

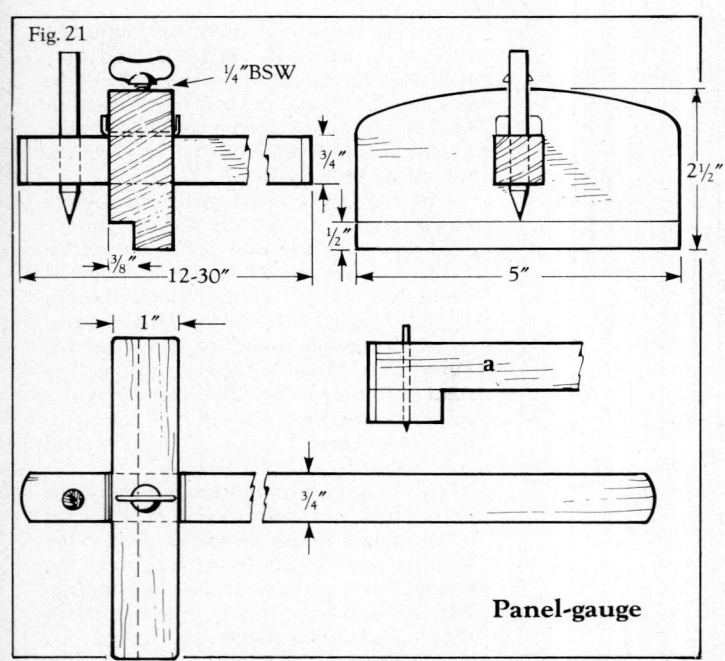

Fig. 21 ¼"BSW

**Panel-gauge**

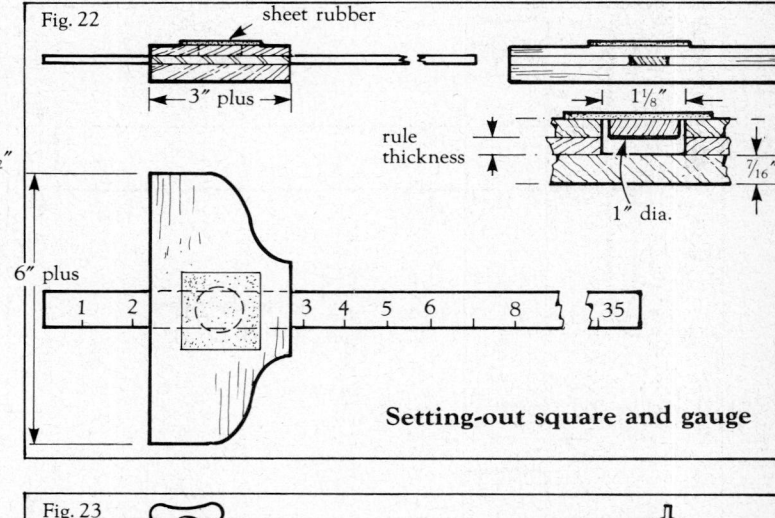

Fig. 22 sheet rubber

rule thickness

1" dia.

**Setting-out square and gauge**

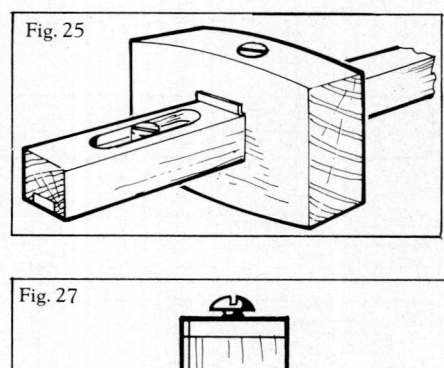

Fig. 23

**Mortise-gauge**

marking-gauge can get in the way. Fig. 28 shows a solution to the problems. The marking point can be made from a piece of power hacksaw blade, handsaw or cabinet scraper. It is filed to shape, hardened and tempered to a light brown, and secured to the stem end with a long woodscrew. Two screws are better if the stem is made large enough to take them.

## Double cutting-gauge

This is useful, particularly in reproduction and restoration work, both for cutting housings for inlay bandings and for cutting plain and crossbanding from veneer. The blades are held in place by either a screw, fig. 29a, or a brass or hardwood wedge, fig. 29b. The wedge requires the mortise end to be slightly angled. The screw needs a brass or steel pressure plate, fig 29c. (The single-blade cutting-gauge described above can use

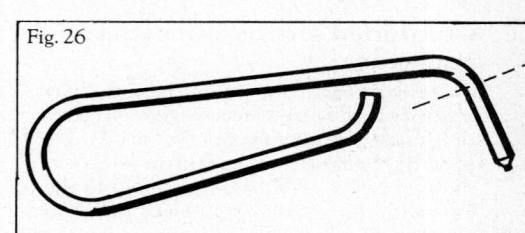

Fig. 25

Fig. 26

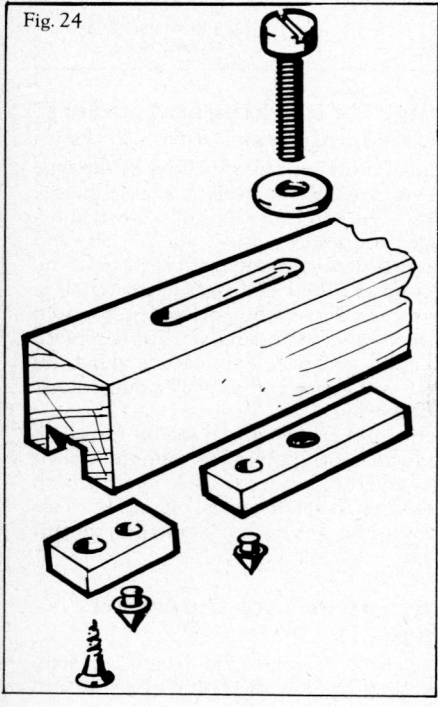

Fig. 24

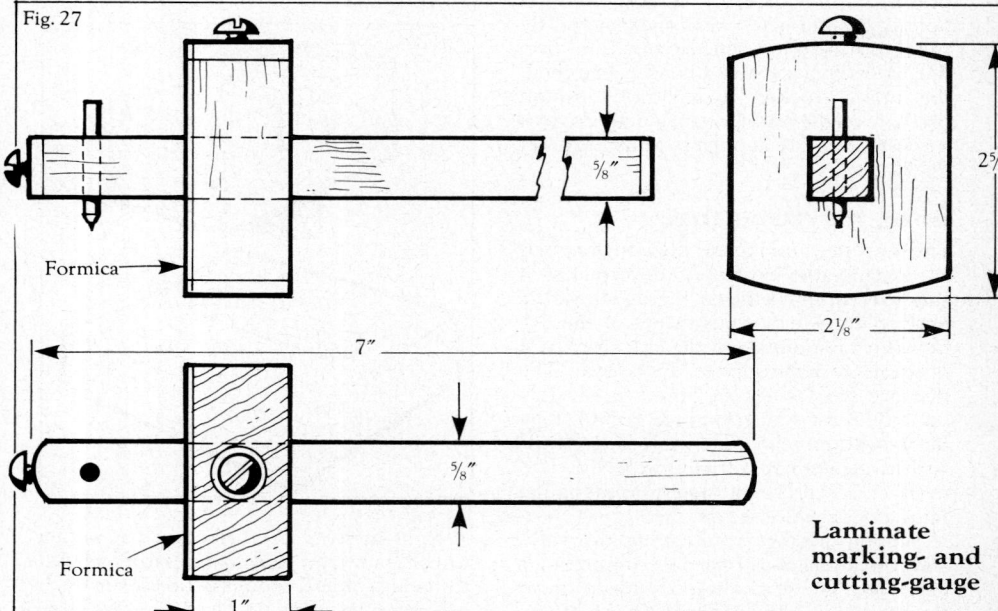

Fig. 27

Formica

Formica

**Laminate marking- and cutting-gauge**

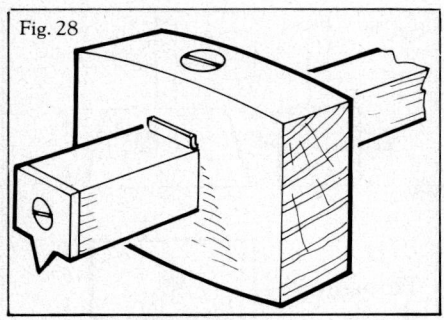

Fig. 28

recommended. For cutting housings the bevels of the knives are inwards; for cutting veneer strip they face outwards. This fence is shown clamped, using the method in fig. 6 and an old radio knob.

## Beam compasses

The most unsatisfactory means of marking large circles is a pin and a length of string. The string always stretches. The beam compasses readily available are the drawing-office type, not very large and not strong enough to stand up to rough workshop use. The model

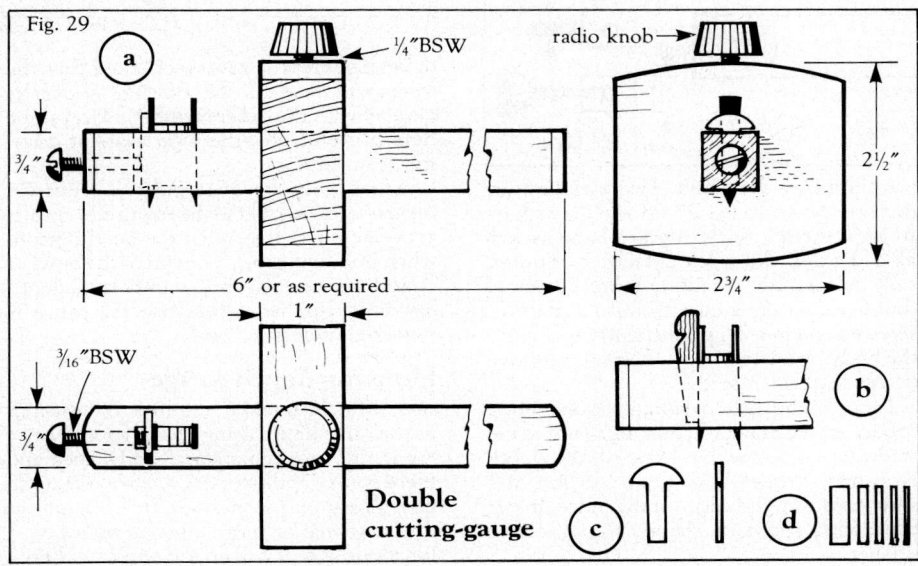

Fig. 29

a

¼"BSW
radio knob→
¾"
6" or as required
1"
2½"
2¾"

³⁄₁₆"BSW
¾"

**Double cutting-gauge**

b

c  d

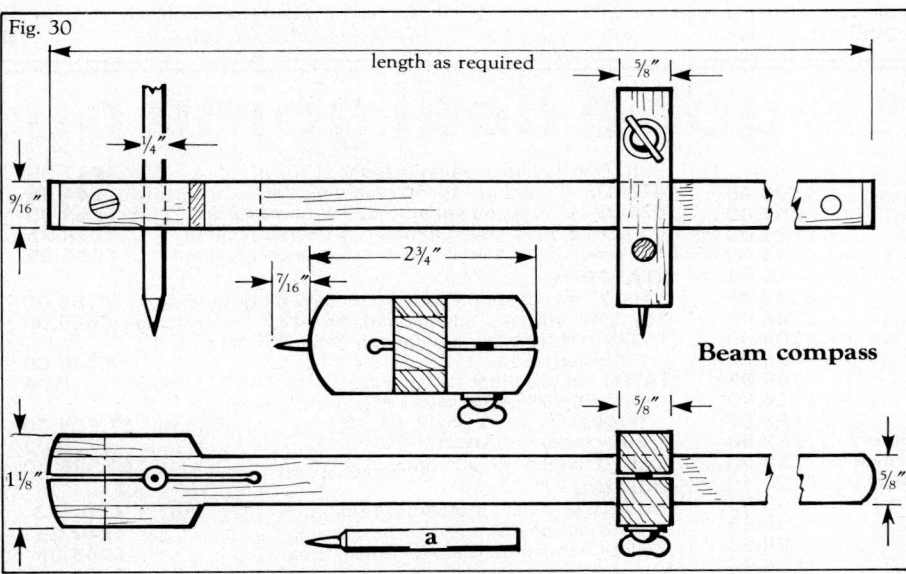

Fig. 30

length as required
⁵⁄₈"
¼"
⁹⁄₁₆"
2¾"
⁷⁄₁₆"

**Beam compass**

⁵⁄₈"

1⅛"
a
⁵⁄₈"

a similar screw-clamping method.)

The most convenient spacing method is to obtain from a jobbing printer a very small handful of printer's type-spaces. A convenient thickness size is '14-point'. Printers' spaces come in five sizes, fig. 29d. The largest, called an 'em' space, is as wide as it is thick, i.e. a square in plan view. An 'en' is half an em. A 'thick' space is a third of an em, a 'mid' is a quarter and a 'thin' is a fifth. By manipulating a few of these, very accurate and solid spacing can be obtained. Failing this, small wood blocks and slivers of veneer and card can be used — though nothing like so conveniently.

A slightly longer fence than normal is to be

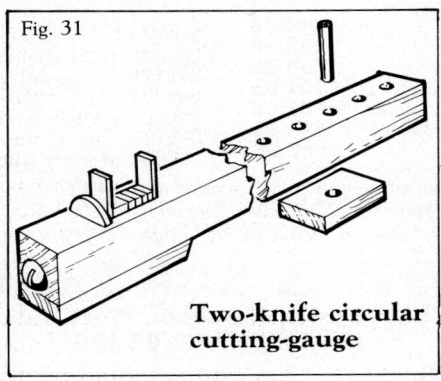

Fig. 31

**Two-knife circular cutting-gauge**

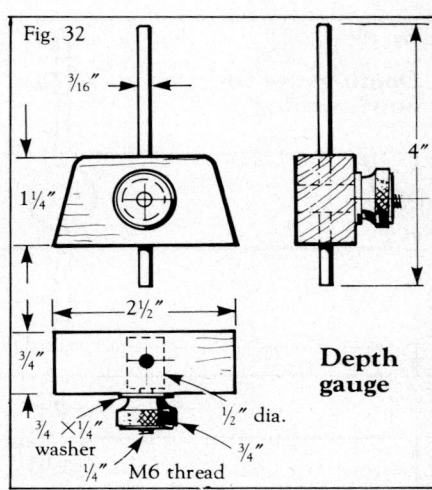

Fig. 32

³⁄₁₆"
1¼"
2½"
¾"
4"

**Depth gauge**

¾ × ¼"
washer
½" dia.
¾"
¼"  M6 thread

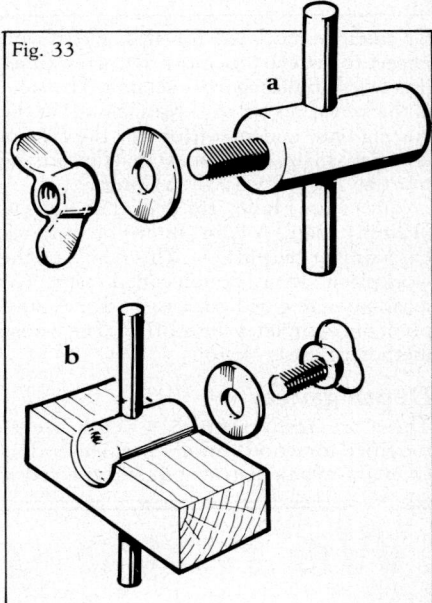

Fig. 33

a

b

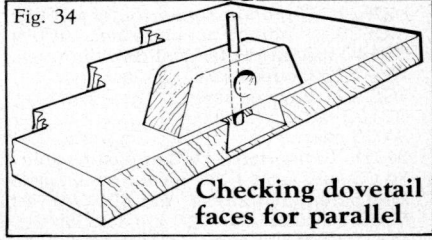

Fig. 34

**Checking dovetail faces for parallel**

shown in fig. 30 is certainly robust. Make it in two sizes, or at least make two lengths of stem. For storage, don't forget to drill a hanging hole. Any of the clamping methods previously described can be adapted to the compasses, and the drawing shows a further very suitable method. Lastly, drill the stock and glue in a dowel; this prevents the stock from cracking if the screw is excessively tightened.

The sizes given are just a guide, but for hard use in a communal workshop they should not be greatly reduced. The metal point in fig. 20a may be substituted for the pencil or ballpoint. A piece of round steel, filed to a knife point and suitably hardened, converts the tool to a circular cutting-gauge.

## Two-knife circular cutting-gauge

The stem from the beam compasses can

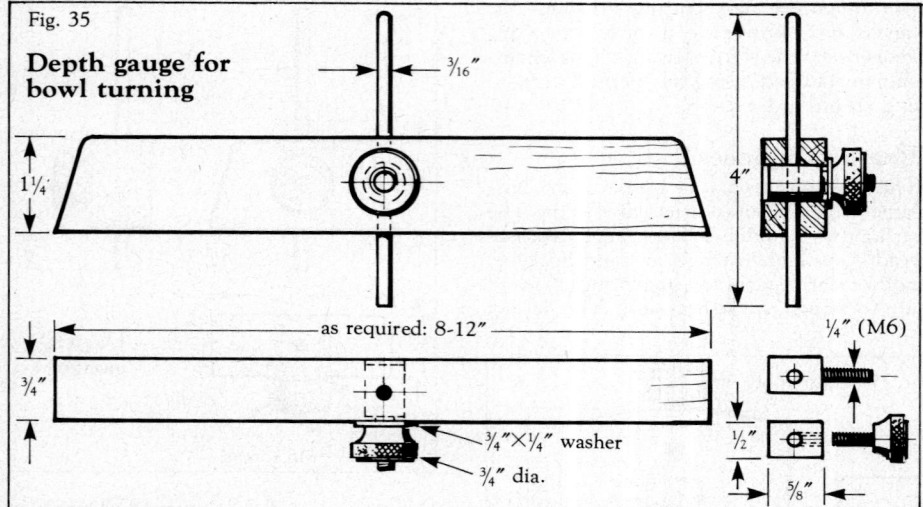

**Fig. 35**

**Depth gauge for bowl turning**

3/16"

1 1/4"

4"

3/4"

as required: 8-12"

1/4" (M6)

1/2"

5/8"

3/4"×1/4" washer
3/4" dia.

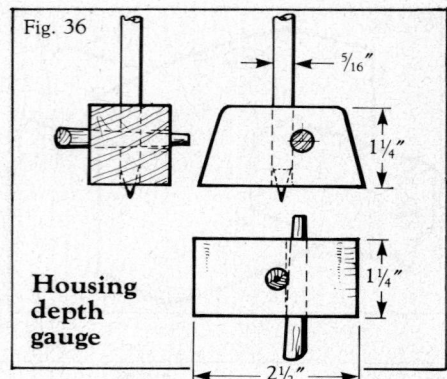

**Fig. 36**

5/16"

1 1/4"

1 1/4"

**Housing depth gauge**

2 1/2"

be suitably modified for this, but if you expect to use the tool more than a few times it is worth building from scratch. The stem is thickened up by, say, 5/16in (8mm) at the cutting end, and provision for the cutters is made as in fig. 29 — except that the mortise must be about 1/2in (13mm) longer.

1/8in (3mm) holes are drilled about 1/2in (12mm) apart. A 5/16in (8mm) pivot block has a similar central hole. This is held on the workpiece with double-sided tape (or masking-tape glued back-to-back). A steel pivot pin completes the tool (fig. 31), whose method of use is obvious.

## Depth gauges

These are really engineer's depth gauges modified for woodworkers' use. The body is of any available hardwood, and the rod is

held in it by a draw bolt. Two variations of this are shown in fig. 33. Model A, with its integral thread, really needs a lathe as well as a die and die-stock. Model B requires only a tap, but needs a more advanced thumbscrew. As a compromise a piece of screwed rod may be permanently fixed into the body by an over-tight fit, some adhesive or a spot of silver solder.

Prepare and drill a suitable wood body and insert the drawbolt, making sure that the screw face is below the surface of the wood. Now drill through both wood and bolt, and smooth off up the edges of the holes. Insert the depth rod and clamp, using a large washer.

Apart from checking mortises and drilled holes, the smaller version will be found useful when cutting lap and double-lap

dovetails. Here it can be checked that the long-grain face of the dovetail socket is parallel with the outer face (fig.34). A slope here prevents an otherwise well-cut dovetail from fitting.

A long body (fig. 35) is particularly useful in turning bowls. Set to the required depth, it prevents turning through the bowl bottom when hollowing out. The rim of the bowl of course must not be turned until total depth has been reached, otherwise the gauge is rendered useless.

## Housing depth gauge

It is difficult to make a number of housings to the same depth using a hand router, since the cutter must be gradually advanced and there is no depth stop. A gauge made up to take a ballpoint overcomes this. As long as the gauge marks, more must be cut away. A longer drawbolt will grip the pen, but here a simple cotter is shown. A dowel with a tapered flat face taps in to fix the pen. Fig. 36 needs no further explanation. ∎

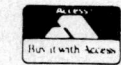
Prices quoted are those prevailing at press date and are subject to alteration due to economic conditions.

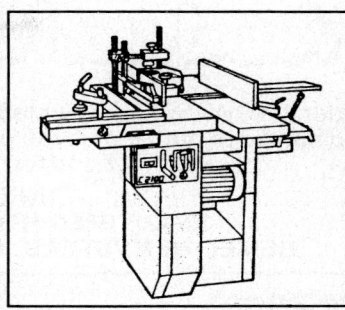

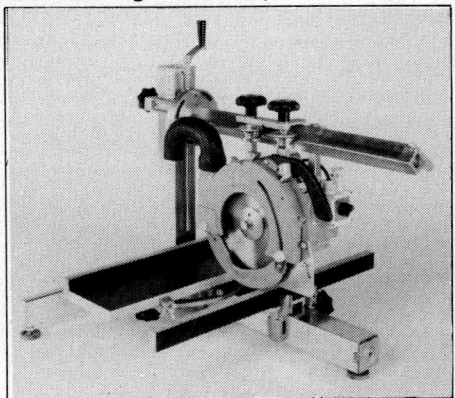
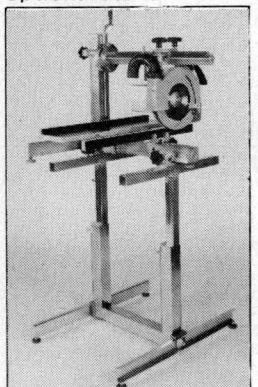
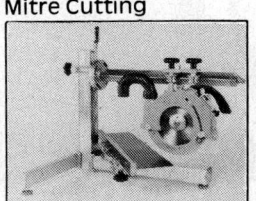

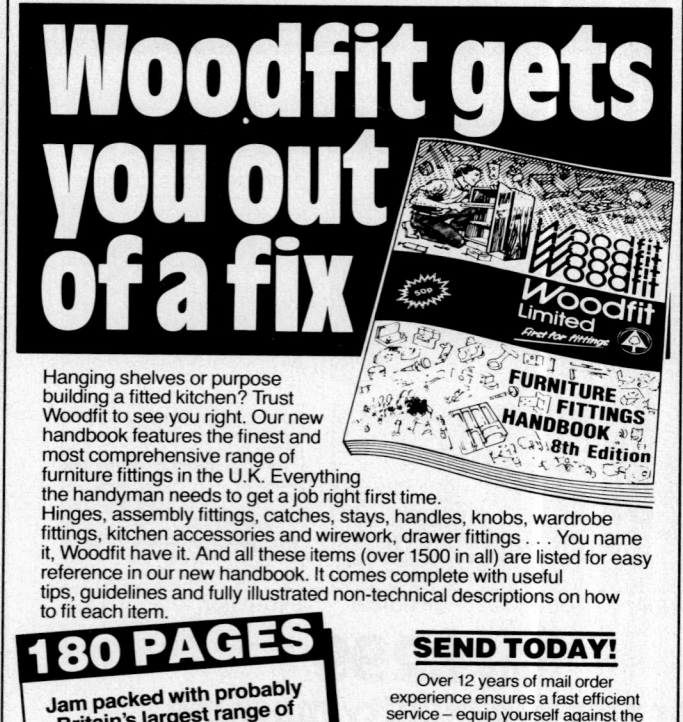
Prices quoted are those prevailing at press date and are
subject to alteration due to economic conditions

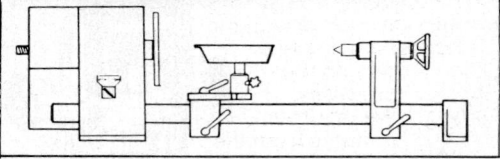

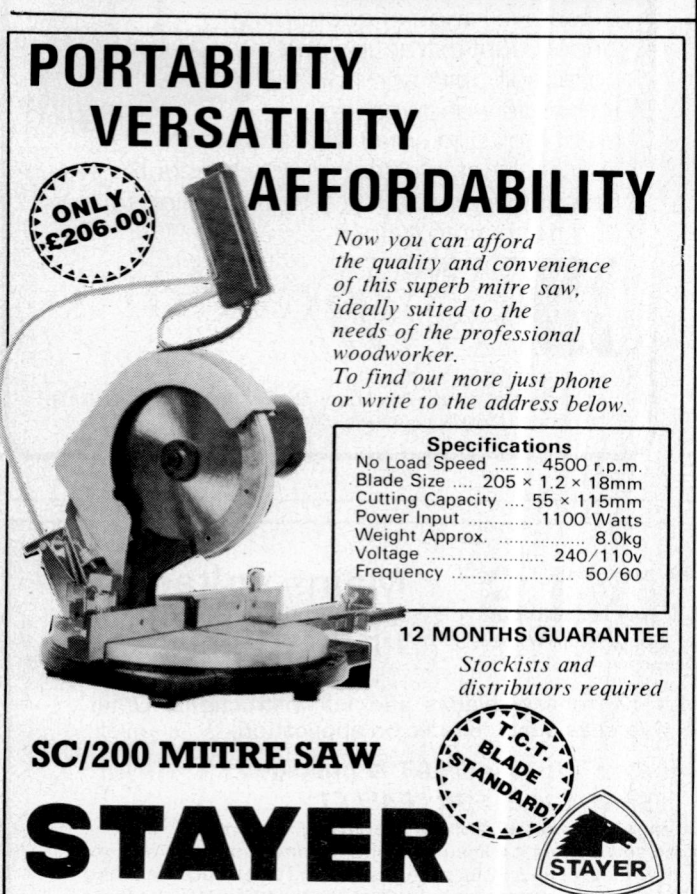
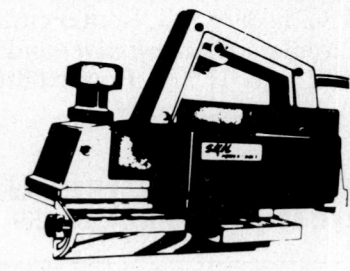
**Prices quoted are those prevailing at press date and are subject to alteration due to economic conditions**

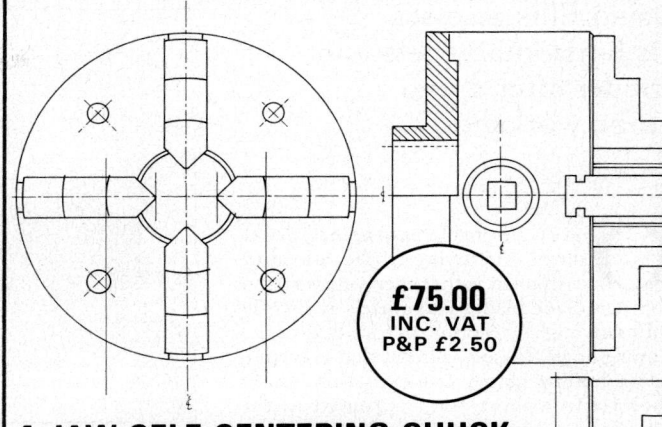
---

KINDLY MENTION 'WOODWORKER' WHEN REPLYING TO ADVERTISEMENTS

# Sharp practice

David Ellis assesses
his horizontal whetstone
grinder after a year
in the workshop

**Fig. 1**

One of the problems in a small workshop employing three or four craftsmen is that everyone tends to sharpen plane blades and chisels at slightly different angles, resulting in rounding of the honing angle. I used to insist that everyone use a honing guide, but even this wasn't foolproof; grooves soon appeared in the oilstones, so a horizontal whetstone grinder with an accurate jig appeared to be the only answer. At the 1983 Woodworker Show we had a good look at them all and settled on a model from Sarjents Tools.

Grinding and honing on a whetstone has, since the earliest times, been the most satisfactory method of obtaining a keen edge, and until the introduction of oilstones (and, much later, the high-speed rotary bench grinder) it was the only method. The modern carborundum wheel may grind quickly, but it can all too easily draw the temper from the tool.

The only drawback of the large, old-fashioned whetstone running in a water bath is the resulting hollow-ground edge. This was, of course, overcome by the introduction of a flat-surfaced stone running in the horizontal plane.

There are now several different models on the UK market, all except one imported from Japan. The exception, manufactured and now marketed by Sharpenset in this country, was until March 1983 sold under the Buckingham Tool Co. label. This is a superb machine but very much more expensive.

Our model is sold, by mutual agreement between Roger's and Sarjents tool stores, at £119.95 for the basic machine plus £39.95 for the precision honing guide. The machine comes with a 1000-grit stone as standard for general sharpening. Two other stones are available, 180 grit for coarse sharpening and re-grinding, at £25, and 6000 grit for fine honing and polishing, at

£35. All the stones should be soaked in water for about 10 minutes before initial use.

The machine consists of a vertically mounted motor driving, through gears, an 8in grinding wheel running in the horizontal plane. Water from a small tank drips at a pre-determined rate onto the wheel as it revolves at about 450rpm and this is spread by centrifugal force over the whole grinding surface. It drains via a sump and tube in the side of the casing. The motor and gearing are mounted on the underside of the plastic housing but well above the water level. Supplied with the machine is an edge-tool guide consisting of two pillars which fit into the machine casing, with a strip of pressed steel between them that can be adjusted in height and locked to various angles. This guide is rather flimsy and inadequate; but, if you can't afford the precision honing guide, a piece of 2×2in angle iron about 3in long, cut absolutely square, will make accurate grinding of chisels much easier. This device is shown in fig. 1.

The instructions that accompany the Sarjents machine are written in 'Nippon' English; they leave a great deal to be desired, but are being re-written. One thing they fail to indicate is whether blades should be sharpened on the leading or the trailing surface of the wheel. This, of course, has been a matter of controversy ever since the horizontal whetstone hit the tool shops, and

it will probably continue as such for a long time yet!

Trial and error have convinced me that it is usually more satisfactory to sharpen on the leading surface, with the stone coming towards the tool. This enables the tool to be more easily controlled; using the trailing edge, the tool tends to lift off the guide, making sharpening more difficult. However, when hand-holding small items such as knives, Stanley blades and the like, it is easier to use the trailing surface without the edge guide.

For multi-purpose, accurate sharpening the precision honing guide is essential, although I think £40 is exorbitant. It is in two parts, the fixed based and the sliding carriage, and it replaces the standard edge-tool guide. It was originally designed to facilitate accurate honing of planer blades, and is extremely useful for that purpose. As long as the blades have been set up accurately the machine will produce results equal to those of any commercial sharpening house. It is too big to hold the blades of smaller planers such as the Coronet 4½in model but a simple modification solves this problem; the holes in the upper clamping plate are elongated by 6-8mm to allow the plate to clamp lower down the blade. A more extreme measure is to grind a little off the bottom of the carriage casting itself, but only if you have access to an accurate surface-grinder.

As supplied, the precision honing guide is not suitable for holding chisels and wood-plane blades. However, with a little metalwork it will accommodate virtually any size or type of blade. These simple modifications are shown in fig. 2. With the upper clamping plate removed, 2½in in the middle of the upper section of the rib is removed flush with the surface. The cast steel is easily cut and filed, but remember that this type of casting will fracture if dropped or hammered.

At *exactly* 90° to the left-hand edge of the opening thus created, a mild steel peg is inserted ¾in from the front edge. The threaded end of a ¼in Whit. set bolt with about ¼in of the unturned section left projecting is ideal. Fig. 3 clearly shows the function of this peg — which, as long as the preliminary marking-out is accurate, will

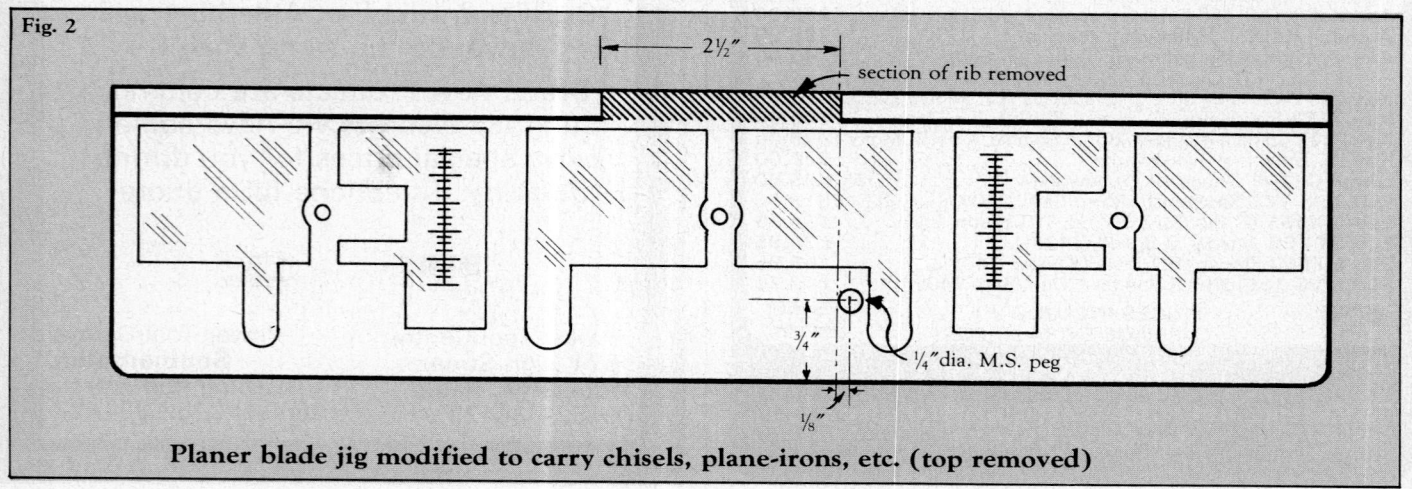

**Fig. 2**

2½"

← section of rib removed

¾"

¼"dia. M.S. peg

⅛"

**Planer blade jig modified to carry chisels, plane-irons, etc. (top removed)**

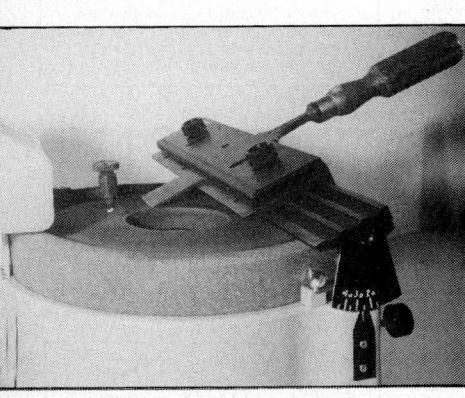

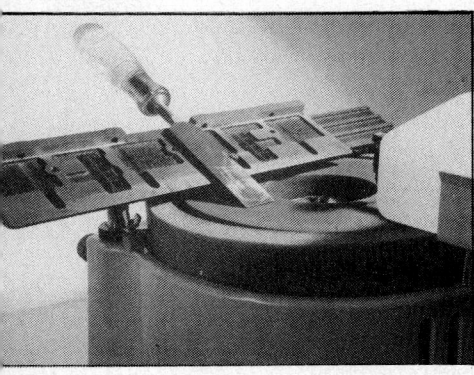

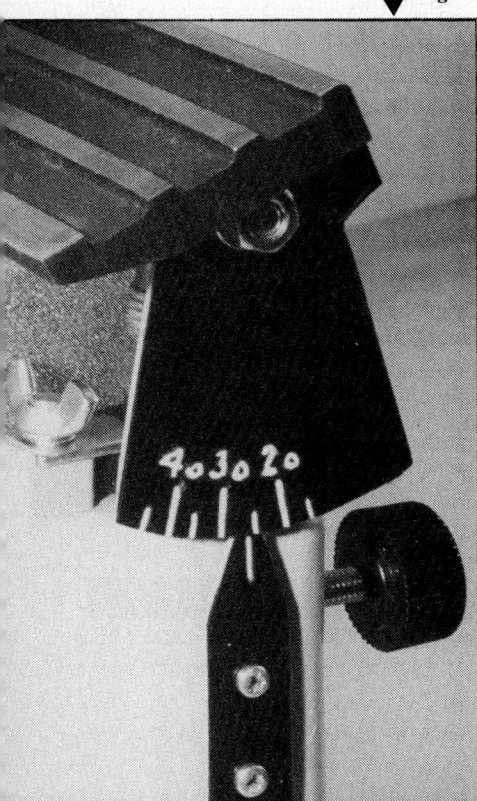

▼ **Fig. 6**

align the tools dead square to the sharpening stone. When the top clamping plate is screwed down, the tools will be held firmly in position, and with some plane blades the centre clamping screw will coincide with the slot in the blade as in fig. 4.

The precision honing guide can be adjusted to raise or lower the whole mechanism and to alter the honing angle. A fundamental omission on this machine is any means of setting this angle to a predetermined figure. On our grinder we have fitted an indicator that enables the angle to be set accurately between 15° and 45°, which is shown with a chisel mounted in it in fig. 5.

The indicator arc and pointer are made from laminated engraving plastic, but any suitable material such as brass or aluminium could be used. The pointer is mounted vertically on the body of the machine with two ½in self-tapping screws, and the arc is clamped to the underside of the lower section of the guide by the spring-tensioned axis bolt seen in fig. 6. Before any figures are marked on the arc, it should be set up with the pointer and adjusted to various angles using an adjustable bevel gauge and a protractor. When the main angles of 20°, 30° and 40° are found and checked, they can be marked on the arc and the intermediate 5° lines drawn. Fig. 7 shows the dimensions of the arc and pointer, which can be varied to suit materials available. It is important that the arc fits tightly to the underside of the guide, as movement can lead to incorrect readings and honing angles.

We have now been using this machine, with its modifications, for nearly a year, and the technique is simple. Initially, set the angle adjuster to 40° and then set the height-adjusting pillars so the lower guide is just touching the surface of the stone the whole way across. Then set the angle adjuster to just under the desired honing angle, say 29°. Slacken off the upper plate finger screws and insert the chisel until it is barely touching the stone, making sure that the chisel is hard against the guide peg and the rear shoulder. Start the grinder, adjust the water feed to a slow drip (about one drip a second is sufficient on the standard stone, although a higher rate is necessary when using the 180-grit stone) and then, using the angle adjuster, gently lower the blade on to the stone — about 1° should be enough. Move the upper slide in both directions to ensure that the whole of the right-hand side of the stone is traversed. There is enough 'float' to allow a little extra hand pressure to be applied to the blade on the stone if necessary.

After a few moments, lift the whole assembly off the slide without unclamping the chisel and check that honing is even across the blade. If it isn't, the tool is possibly not tight up to the guide peg and shoulder or, more likely, the previous honing was incorrect. Honing is complete when you have an even mirror finish right up to the front edge of the blade.

Once the machine has been set up it only takes a minute or so to put a keen edge on a chisel or plane blade — the burr may be removed by laying the tool *absolutely* flat on the *left-hand* side of the stone. A word of warning here; these stones are very soft and it is quite easy to dig into them, particularly

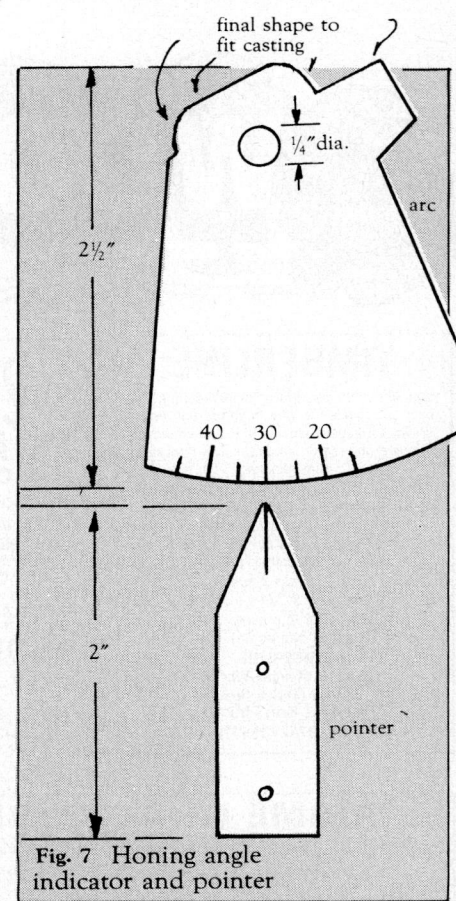

**Fig. 7** Honing angle indicator and pointer

with narrow chisels. At £25 a time, replacements are expensive! If the worst happens, don't despair; small chips can be filled with epoxy putty such as Sylmasta, which is available from most builder's merchants. This will not replace the grinding properties of the original stone, but it will enable the stone to be used without sounding — and feeling — like a chipped gramophone record.

Very little maintenance is necessary on this machine, but keep the arbor greased; a little heavy grease or Vaseline on the sliding surfaces of the honing jig will make its operation easier, too. It is also wise to clean out the water-well under the stone from time to time.

We use this machine every day of the working week, and it produces a quicker, keener and more accurate edge than anything else. However, it is vastly over-priced. This is no reflection on the retailers, who I believe are marketing it at — to them — an economic figure. But what does it cost to produce compared to other machine tools? The grinder comprises a cheap plastic moulded casing and a small electric motor driving, through noisy gears, a spindle carrying the whetstone. Compare this to, say, an Elu MOF96 router, three of which can be purchased for the price of one whetstone grinder!

The Japanese are no longer manufacturers of cheap tools, but I see absolutely no reason why they charge as much for a very simple product as they do for their superb cameras. An enterprising British manufacturer should be able to market as good or better a machine for around £75, complete with a purpose-designed precision jig. But for the moment, although it's expensive, this machine produces a superb cutting edge and we certainly wouldn't be without ours. ■

# WOOD SUPPLIERS

## TIMBERLINE

In addition to our much improved range of over 50 species of fine imported and home grown hardwoods we would like to announce that we now carry comprehensive stocks of the following:

Veneers, decorative lines and bandings, polishes, waxes, stains, adhesives, abrasives and woodwork construction plans. You are always assured of good service and a friendly welcome.

*Business hours*
*Tues.-Sat. 9.30am-5.30pm*
Please send large sae for free catalogue quoting ref. WW.

**TIMBERLINE,**
Unit 7, Munday Works,
58-66 Morley Road,
Tonbridge, Kent TN9 1RP.
Tel: (0732) 355626

---

**KW projects**
**JOINERY GRADE**
**PITCH PINE**
**0652 34985**
St. Chads, Waterside Road,
Barton-upon-Humber,
South Humberside DN18 5BG

### TO FILL
### THIS SPACE
### PHONE GILL ON
### 07-437 0699

**VENEERS,** all types. SAE list. S. Gould (Veneers) 342 Uxbridge Road, W12. Telephone: 01-743 8561. T/C

---

**18TH CENTURY** pitch pine, superb quality. Bandmilled to your requirements. Most English hardwoods stocked, air and kiln dry. Tel. Will Tyers, cabinet maker for price list — (0468) 21292 (Nr. Lancaster).

**CONVERT TIMBER YOURSELF,** with a portable chainsaw mill. Cuts a 36in. width 200 sq.ft., per hour. Keenest prices. Brochure demonstration. Philip Cole, 16 Kings Lane, Flore, Northampton. Tel: Weeden (0327) 40337 evenings. T/C

**YEW.** All shapes and sizes. Air seasoned. Any quantity. Fossebridge (Glos.) 249. T/C

**BASS** and many other hard and specialist woods, air and kiln dried. Priced stock list. Items prepared to your cutting list. Minns, 7 Westway, Oxford (0865) 247840. G-J

---

## JOHN MACFARLAN TIMBER

**ENGLISH HARDWOODS, SPECIALLY SELECTED, SAWN AND KILN-DRIED' FOR THE CRAFTSMAN**

Send sae for stock list or phone at any time.

**THE GLEN, HORNTON, BANBURY, OXON.** Tel: 029 587 492

---

## ENGLISH HARDWOODS

Oak, Ash, Sycamore, Beech etc. Air & Kiln dried
*All sizes in stock*
**HOUGHTON TIMBER**
HIGHER WALTON TRADING ESTATE
PRESTON, LANCS.
Tel: Preston 323566

---

## PRIME QUALITY BRITISH HARDWOODS

Sawn Square-edged Kilned and Air Dried
Stocks of: Ash, Beech, Cherry, Elm, Larch, Oak, Pine, Sycamore, etc.
For details and quotations apply to:
# R. E. & R. DUFFIELD & SONS LTD.
**The Boathouse Sawmills, River View Road, RIPON, North Yorks.**
## Tel: (0765) 3667
Or our Sales Depot at: Glencairn Mill, Heads Nook, nr. CARLISLE. Tel: (0228) 61800

---

**IN THE RACE TO BUY & SELL, MAKE SURE YOU'RE QUICK OFF THE MARK BY ADVERTISING IN WOODWORKER CLASSIFIED PAGES. 'PHONE GILL ON 07-437 0699 FOR DETAILS!**

---

## LIMEHOUSE TIMBER

Suppliers of quality timbers: Mahogany, Oak, Teak, Walnut, etc. Bargain here for your selection. A range of machined boards each individually priced. Open 6 days.

**MON-FRI: 9am-5pm**
**SAT: 9am-3pm**
*Send 17p stamp for stocklist.*
SPECIAL ON FINE ENGLISH
ELM £12.50cu.ft. S.T.A.
*a division of:*
**DAVEY AND COMPANY**
**5 GRENADE STREET**
LONDON E14 8HL          01-987-6289

---

# TIMBER
cut to your requirements

We cut and prepare to your cutting list

## TEAK, OAK, ROSEWOOD, MAHOGANY, BEECH, BOXWOOD, etc. —VENEERS and PLYWOODS

We carry large stocks of dry hardwoods for cabinet and joinery trade. Turning done to your drawing. Brassware and cabinet fittings available.

Open all day Saturday — early closing Thursday.
Send S.A.E. with your cutting list for quote.

# GENERAL WOODWORK SUPPLIES
Dept. W.W., 76-80 STOKE NEWINGTON HIGH STREET, LONDON N16 _____          Phone: 01-254 6052

---

# Broughton-Head Timber Ltd
**Parva Stud, Church Row,
Hinton Parva, Swindon,
Wilts. Tel: Wanborough (079379) 552**

Kiln dried and air dried stocks including English and American Oak, English Ash, Cedar, Cherry, Apple, Pear, Plum, Lacewood, Chestnut, Walnut, Elm, Sycamore, Yew, Larch and Beech, Brown Oak, Holly, Lime, American Black Walnut. **Please telephone or send stamp for details**
**We specialise in small quantities. — Minimum one plank**
**Opening hours: Anytime subject to confirmation by telephone.**

---

## OAK

*Best Quality Kiln Dried.*
*Keenest prices available.*

*Also most home grown timbers*

**IRONBRIDGE**
**(0952) 453373 EVENINGS**

---

## HEXHAMSHIRE HARDWOODS

Seasoned English hardwoods for North East England and Scotland. Hardwoods for Turning and Carving
**Telephone: (Anytime)**
**Slaley (043473) 585697**

---

**FOSS GLEN FORESTRY**
*AIR DRIED*
*ENGLISH HARDWOODS*
*FROM THE COTSWOLDS*
*Please note our new address and Telephone number as of 1st June, 1984*
Bowles Bridge, Fields Road, Chedworth, Glos. GL54 4NQ.
Tel: Fossebridge (028572) 619
For our new catalogue of our wide variety of English Hardwoods and softwoods, suitable for carving, turning, cabinet making etc. Please send 17p stamp to the above address.

---

## TIMBER SAMPLE BOARDS

Quality product for customer or user selection. 30 species on black background. Professional lettering. Information sheet. Home-grown and imported including exotics (Kingswood, Rosewood, etc.). Cheques and PO's for £18.50 (inc. P&P) to:
**M. A. CHARLES**
Wood Products, Coachman's Cottage, Albury, Oxon. OX9 2LP.
*Tel: Ickford 535*

---

selected butts of **British hardwoods,** sawn & kilned through & through;

**quality handtools,** veneers and finishes

**de meester** (the master)

54 Chalk Farm Road  London NW1  01.267 0502 (open Sat and Sun)

Prices quoted are those prevailing at press date and are subject to alteration due to economic conditions.

# WOOD SUPPLIERS

# WOOD SUPPLIERS

## NORTH HEIGHAM SAWMILLS

Good, Kiln-Dried stocks of most Home-Grown timbers, and exotic, Imported Hardwoods.

Stocks include: Apple, ash, beech, blackwood, box, cedar, cherry, cocobolo, ebony, elm, holly, lemonwood, lignum, lime, mahogany, maple, oak, padauk, pear, plane, rosewood, satinwood, sycamore, walnut, yew, zelkova.

*Please send S.A.E. for priced stock list to:*

**North Heigham Sawmills, Paddock St. (off Barker St.), NORWICH NR2 4TW. Tel: Norwich 22978.**

## TO FILL THIS SPACE 'PHONE GILL ON 01-437 0699

## ENGLISH OAK

Kiln dried 1" oak boards ¼ sawn, and through and through.

**D. M. Mumford, White Hollow, Ticknall, Derby. Telephone Melbourne (03316) 2121.**

### TREEWORK SERVICES

**Suppliers of Native Hardwoods**

MOST HOMEGROWN SPECIES IN STOCK LARGE AND SMALL QUANTITIES SUPPLIED FRESH SAWN, AIR DRIED AND KILN DRIED

Send sae for Price List to
**TREEWORK SERVICES LTD**
CHESTON COOMBE, CHURCH TOWN, BACKWELL, NR. BRISTOL. (027583) 3917
or phone JOHN EMERY on CHEW MAGNA (027589) 3222
*We also offer a tree milling service*

## Earn £200 per hour drying timber with your own kiln...

My seasoners need so little attention that your time could hardly be better spent than by drying your own timber. Can you afford to invest a few hundred pounds in order to guarantee that your work is stable in central heating and ensure that your English hardwoods will cost half as much for many years to come.

No need to keep large untidy stacks of timber slowly drying and spoiling for years and years — these machines work from green in a few weeks and cost only a few pence per cubic foot to run.

The smallest seasoner costs less than £400 and will dry enough timber to keep several people busy or make you some money selling surplus timber. It can live outside and does not usually need a box much larger than 8' × 4' × 4'. As I am the man who developed these machines, I hope that my information, prices, references etc., are second to none.

Write for details or ring me any time for answers to your questions completely without obligation.

**JOHN ARROWSMITH
74 Wilson Street, Darlington,
Co. Durham DL3 6QZ. Tel: 0325 481970**

**ZEBRANO** ¼ cut boards 1"/2" thick. Exquisite figuring. Also Ebony, Rosewoods, Paurosa, Padauk and many other exotics. CHART, Reading (0734) 695336. Evenings/Saturdays.

**ENGLISH HARDWOODS.** Oak specialists, also Ash, Beach, Cherry, Yew. Over 3000 cu.ft. Send for stock list to W. H. Mason & Son Ltd., The Sawmills, Wetmore Road, Burton-on-Trent, Staffs. Telephone 64651.

# WOOD SUPPLIERS — COUPON

FROM _____

_____

_____

I enclose remittance to the value

of £_____ to cover _____ insertions

DETAILS

**Send to: Gill,
Woodworker Classified Dept.
1 Golden Square,
London W1R 3AB.**

Rates: 35p per word, minimum £5.25, semi-display £7.25, minimum 2.5cm.

|  |  |  |  |
|---|---|---|---|
|  |  |  |  |
|  |  |  |  |
|  |  |  |  |
|  |  |  |  |
|  |  |  |  |
|  |  |  |  |

**Prices quoted are those prevailing at press date and are subject to alteration due to economic conditions**

# shopguide

## AVON

**BATH**    Tel. Bath 64513
JOHN HALL TOOLS    ★
RAILWAY STREET

Open: Monday-Saturday
9.00 a.m.-5.30 p.m.
H.P.W.WM.D.A.BC.

**BRISTOL**    Tel. (0272) 741510
JOHN HALL TOOLS LIMITED    ★
CLIFTON DOWN SHOPPING CENTRE
WHITELADIES ROAD
Open: Monday-Saturday
9.00 a.m.-5.30 p.m.
H.P.W.WM.D.A.BC.

**BRISTOL**    Tel. (0272) 629092
TRYMWOOD SERVICES
2a DOWNS PARK EAST, (off North View)
WESTBURY PARK
Open: 8.30 a.m.-5.30 p.m. Mon. to Fri.
Closed for lunch 1.00-2.00 p.m.
P.W.WM.D.T.A.BC.

**BRISTOL**    Tel. (0272) 667013
FASTSET LTD
190-192 WEST STREET
BEDMINSTER
Open: Mon.-Fri. 8.30 a.m.-5.00 p.m.
Saturday 9.00 a.m.-1.00 p.m.
H.P.W.WM.D.CS.A.BC.

## BEDFORDSHIRE

**BEDFORD**    Tel. (0234) 59808
BEDFORD SAW SERVICE    K
39 AMPTHILL ROAD

Open: Mon.-Fri. 8.30-5.30
Sat. 9.00-4.00
H.P.A.BC.W.CS.WM.D.

## BERKSHIRE

**COOKHAM**    Tel. (06285) 20350
CHURCH'S TIMBER
STATION HILL

Open: Mon-Sat 8.30 a.m.-5.30 p.m.
Wed 8.30 a.m.-1.00 p.m.
H.P.W.T.CS.MF.A.

**READING**    Tel. (0734) 591361
HOME CARE CENTRE
26/30 KING'S ROAD

Open: Monday-Saturday
9.00 a.m.-5.30 p.m.
H.P.W.D.A.WM.BC.

**READING**    Tel. Littlewick Green
DAVID HUNT (TOOL    2743
MERCHANTS) LTD    ★
KNOWL HILL, NR. READING
Open: Monday-Saturday
9.00 a.m.-5.30 p.m.
H.P.W.D.A.BC.

## BUCKINGHAMSHIRE

**SLOUGH**    Tel. (06286) 5125
BRAYWOOD ESTATES LTD
158 BURNHAM LANE

Open: 9.00 a.m.-5.30 p.m.
Monday-Saturday
H.P.W.WM.CS.A.

**HIGH WYCOMBE**    Tel. (0494)
ISAAC LORD LTD    22221
185 DESBOROUGH ROAD    KE

Open: Mon-Fri 8.00 a.m.-5.00 p.m.
Saturday 9.00 a.m.-5.00 p.m.
H.P.W.D.A.

**HIGH WYCOMBE**    Tel. (0494)
SCOTT SAWS LTD.    24201/33788
14 BRIDGE STREET    ★

Mon.-Sat. 8.30 a.m.-6.00 p.m.

H.P.W.WM.D.T.CS.MF.A.BC.

**MILTON KEYNES**    Tel. (0908)
POLLARD WOODWORKING    641366
CENTRE    ★
51 AYLESBURY ST., BLETCHLEY
Open: Mon-Fri 8.30-5.30
Saturday 9.00-5.00
H.P.W.WM.D.CS.A.BC.

## CAMBRIDGESHIRE

**CAMBRIDGE**    Tel. (0223) 247386
H. B. WOODWORKING    K
105 CHERRY HINTON ROAD
Open: 8.30 a.m.-5.30 p.m.
Monday-Friday
8.30 a.m.-1.00 p.m. Sat.
H.P.W.WM.D.CS.A.

**CAMBRIDGE**    Tel. (0223) 63132
D. MACKAY LTD.    E★
BRITANNIA WORKS, EAST ROAD

Open: Mon.-Fri. 8.30 a.m.-1 p.m./2.00-
5.00 p.m. Sat. 8.30 a.m.-1.00 p.m.
H.P.W.D.T.CS.MF.A.BC.

**PETERBOROUGH**    Tel. (0733)
WILLIAMS DISTRIBUTORS    64252
(TOOLS) LIMITED    K
108-110 BURGHLEY ROAD
Open: Monday to Friday
8.30 a.m.-5.30 p.m.
H.P.A.W.D.WH.BC.

## CHESHIRE

**NANTWICH**    Tel. Crewe 67010
ALAN HOLTHAM    K★
THE OLD STORES TURNERY
WISTASON ROAD, WILLASTON
Open: Tues.-Sat. 9.00 a.m.-5.30 p.m.
Closed Monday
P.W.WM.D.T.C.CS.A.BC.

## CLEVELAND

**MIDDLESBROUGH**    Tel. (0642)
CLEVELAND WOODCRAFT    813103
(M'BRO), 38-42 CRESCENT ROAD    K

Open: Mon-Sat 9.15 a.m.-5.30 p.m.

H.P.T.A.BC.W.WM.CS.D.

## CORNWALL

**FALMOUTH**    Tel. (0326) 76555
WOODSTOCK (HARDWOODS) LTD.
PONSHARDEN

Open: Mon-Fri 8.30 a.m.-5.30 p.m.
Sat. 9.00 a.m.-1.00 p.m.
T.

**HELSTON**  Tel. Helston (03265) 4961
SOUTH WEST    Truro (0872) 71671
POWER TOOLS    Launceston
MONUMENT ROAD    (0566) 3555
    K
H.P.W.WM.D.CS.A.

**TRURO**    Tel. (0872) 71671
TRURO POWER TOOLS    E★
30 FERRIS TOWN

Open Mon.-Sat. 8.00 a.m.-12.30 p.m./
1.30 p.m.-5.00 p.m.
H.P.W.WM.D.CS.MF.A.BC.

## DERBYSHIRE

**BUXTON**    Tel. (0298) 871636
CRAFT SUPPLIES    K★
THE MILL, MILLERSDALE

Open: Mon-Sat 9.00 a.m.-5.00 p.m.

H.P.W.D.T.CS.A.BC.

**DERBY**    Tel. (0332) 41862
HAZLEHURSTS LTD.    E★
LONDON ROAD AND CANAL STREET

Open: Mon.-Sat. 8.30 a.m.-5.30 p.m. (retail)
Mon.-Fri. 8.00 a.m.-5.00 p.m. (trade)
H.P.W.MF.A.BC.

## DEVON

**BRIXHAM**    Tel. (08045) 4900
WOODCRAFT SUPPLIES    E★
4 HORSE POOL STREET

Open: Mon.-Sat. 9.00 a.m.-6.00 p.m.

H.P.W.A.D.MF.CS.BC.

**EXETER**    Tel. (0392) 73936
WRIDES TOOL CENTRE
147 FORE STREET

Open: 9.00 a.m.-5.30 p.m.
Wednesday 9.00 a.m.-1.00 p.m.
H.P.W.WM.A.

**PLYMOUTH**    Tel. (0752) 330303
WESTWARD BUILDING SERVICES    ★
LTD., LISTER CLOSE, NEWNHAM
INDUSTRIAL ESTATE, PLYMPTON
Open: Mon-Fri 8.00 a.m.-5.30 p.m.
Sat. 8.30 a.m.-12.30 p.m.
H.P.W.WM.D.A.BC.

## ESSEX

**ILFORD**    Tel.
CUTWELL TOOLS LTD.    ★
774-776 HIGH ROAD

Mon.-Fri. 9.00 a.m.-5.00 p.m.
and also by appointment.
P.W.WM.A.D.CS.

**LEIGH ON SEA**    Tel. (0702)
MARSHAL & PARSONS LTD.    710404
1111 LONDON ROAD    K

Open: 8.30 a.m.-5.30 p.m. Mon-Fri
9.00 a.m.-5.00 p.m. Sat.
H.P.W.WM.D.CS.A.

## GLOUCESTERSHIRE

**CHELTENHAM**    Tel. (0242) 39099
HAMBURY MACHINE SERVICES    E★
UNIT 14, MALMESBURY ROAD
Open: Mon.-Fri. 9.00 a.m.-5.30 p.m.
Sat. 9.30 a.m.-12.00 noon.
W.WM.P.D.

**KEY: H HANDTOOLS**

**KEY: P POWER TOOLS**

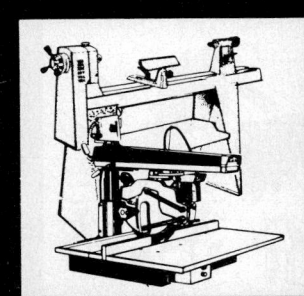

**KEY: W WOODWORKING MACHINERY**

# shop guide

## HAMPSHIRE

**TEWKESBURY** Tel. (0684)
TEWKESBURY SAW CO. LTD. 293092
TRADING ESTATE, NEWTOWN K

Open: Mon-Fri 8.00 a.m.-5.00 p.m.
Saturday 9.30 a.m.-12.00 p.m.
P.W.WM.D.CS.

**ALDERSHOT** Tel. (0252) 334422
POWER TOOL CENTRE K
374 HIGH STREET

Open Mon-Fri 8.30 a.m.-5.30 p.m.

H.P.W.WM.D.A.BC.

**PORTSMOUTH** Tel. (0705)
EURO PRECISION TOOLS LTD 667332
259/263 LONDON ROAD, NORTH END ★

Open: Mon-Fri 9.00 a.m.-5.30 p.m.
Sat. 9.00 a.m.-1.00 p.m.
H.P.W.WM.D.A.BC.

**SOUTHAMPTON** Tel. (0703)
H.W.M. 776222
THE WOODWORKERS
303 SHIRLEY ROAD, SHIRLEY
Open: Tues-Fri 9.30 a.m.-6.00 p.m.
Sat 9.30 a.m.-4.00 p.m.
H.P.W.WM.D.CS.A.BC.T.

## HERTFORDSHIRE

**ENFIELD** Tel. (01-363) 2935
GILL & HOXBY LTD. K
133-137 ST. MARKS ROAD EN1 1BB

Mon.-Sat. 8.30 a.m.-6.00 p.m.
Early closing Wednesday 1.00 p.m.
H.P.W.WM.T.CS.A

**HITCHIN** Tel. (0462) 4177
ROGER'S KE
47 WALSWORTH ROAD
Open: Monday-Saturday
9.00 a.m.-5.30 p.m.
(Closed all day Wednesday)
H.P.W.WM.D.CS.MF.BC.

**WATFORD** Tel. (0923) 48434
HOME CARE CENTRE ★
20 MARKET STREET
WATFORD, HERTS
Open: 9.00 a.m.-5.30 p.m.
Mon-Sat
H.P.W.A.WM.BC.D.

## HUMBERSIDE

**GRIMSBY** Tel. Grimsby (0472)
58741 Hull (0482) 26999
J. E. SIDDLE LTD. (Tool Specialists) E★
83 VICTORIA STREET
Open: Mon-Fri 8.30 a.m.-5.30 p.m.
Sat. 8.30 a.m.-12.45 p.m. & 2 p.m.-5 p.m.
H.P.A.BC.W.WMD.

## KENT

**BIDDENDEN** Tel. (0580) 291555/7
BRITISH GATES & TIMBER
BENENDEN ROAD ★
Open: Mon-Fri 7.30 a.m.-5.30 p.m.
Saturday 8.30 a.m.-midday
(not Bank Holiday weekends)
H.T.CS.MF.

**MAIDSTONE** Tel. (0622) 50177
SOUTH EASTERN SAWS (Ind) LTD ★
COLDRED ROAD,
PARKWOOD INDUSTRIAL ESTATE
Open: Mon-Fri 8.00-5.00pm
Sat. 9.00-12.00
B.C.W.CS.WM.PH.

**MATFIELD** Tel. Brenchley
LEISURECRAFT IN WOOD (089272)
'ORMONDE,' MAIDSTONE RD. 2465
TN12 7JG
Open: Mon-Sun
9.00 a.m.-5.30 p.m.
IW.WM.D.T.A.

**WYE** Tel. (0233) 813144
KENT POWER TOOLS LTD.
UNIT 1, BRIAR CLOSE
WYE, Nr. ASFORD

H.P.W.WM.D.A.CS.

## LANCASHIRE

**LANCASTER** Tel. (0524) 32886
LILE TOOL SHOP K
43/45 NORTH ROAD
Open: Monday to Saturday
9.00 a.m.-5.30 p.m.
Wed 9.00 a.m.-12.30 p.m.
H.P.W.D.A.

**ROCHDALE** Tel. (0706) 342123/
C.S.M. TOOLS 342322
4-6 HEYWOOD ROAD E★
CASTLETON
Open: Mon-Sat 9.00 a.m.-6.00 p.m.
Sundays by appointment
W.D.CS.A.BC.

**PRESTON** Tel. (0772) 52951
SPEEDWELL TOOL COMPANY E★
62-68 MEADOW STREET PR1 1SU
Open: Mon.-Fri. 8.30 a.m.-5.30 p.m.
Sat. 8.30 a.m.-12.30 p.m.
H.P.W.WM.CS.A.MF.BC.

## LEICESTERSHIRE

**HINCKLEY** Tel. (0455) 613432
J. D. WOODWARD & CO. (POWER ★
TOOL SPECIALISTS)
THE NARROWS, HINCKLEY
Open: Monday-Saturday
8.00 a.m.-6.00 p.m.
H.P.W.WM.D.CS.A.BC.

## LONDON

**ACTON** Tel. (01-992) 4835
A. MILLS (ACTON) LTD ★
32/36 CHURCHFIELD ROAD W3 6ED
Open: Mon-Fri 9.00 a.m.-5.00 p.m.
Saturdays 9.00 am-1.00 p.m.
H.P.W.WM.

**FULHAM** Tel. (01-385) 5109
I. GRIZZARD LTD. E
84a-b LILLIE ROAD, SW6 1TL
Open: Mon-Sat 9.00-5.30 p.m.
Half day Thursday

H.P.A.BC.W.CS.WM.D.

**LONDON** Tel. (01-567) 2922
G. D. CLEGG & SONS ★
83 UXBRIDGE ROAD, HANWELL W7 3ST
Mon-Sat 9.15 a.m.-5.30 p.m.
Closed for lunch 1.00-2.00p.m.
Early Closing 1.00 p.m. Wed.
H.P.A.W.WM.D.CS.

**K = KITY
WOODWORKING
CENTRE**

**LONDON** Tel. (01-263) 1536
THOMAS BROTHERS (01-272) 2764
798-804 HOLLOWAY ROAD, N19 E
Open: Mon.-Fri. 8.30 a.m.-5.30 p.m. Thurs.
8.30 a.m.-1 p.m. Sat. 9 a.m.-5 p.m.

H.P.W.WM.CS.MF.BC.

**LONDON** Tel. (01-858) 6444
TOOL HIRE BUY LTD
74/76 CHARLTON ROAD
LONDON SE3 8TT
Open; Mon.-Fri. 8.30 a.m.-5.30 p.m.
Saturday 8.30 a.m.-12.30 p.m.
H.P.W.WM.D.CS.A.BC.

**LONDON** Tel. (01-636) 7475
BUCK & RYAN LTD ★
101 TOTTENHAM COURT ROAD W1P ODY

Open: Mon.-Fri. 8.30 a.m.-5.30 p.m.
Saturday 8.30 a.m.-4.00 p.m.
H.P.W.WM.D.A.

**NORBURY** Tel. (01-679) 6193
HERON TOOLS & HARDWARE LTD
437 STREATHAM HIGH ROAD SW16
Open: Mon-Fri 8.30 a.m.-5.00 p.m.
Wednesday 8.30 a.m.-1.00 p.m.
Sat. 9.00 a.m.-1.00 p.m.
H.P.W.A.

## GREATER MANCHESTER MERSEYSIDE

**WOOLWICH** Tel. (01-854) 7767/8
A. D. SHILLMAN & SONS LTD
108-109 WOOLWICH HIGH STREET
SE18
Open: Mon-Sat
8.30 p.m.-5.30p.m.
H.P.W.CS.A.

**MANCHESTER** Tel. (061 789)
TIMMS TOOLS 2601
102-104 LIVERPOOL ROAD ★
PATRICROFT M30 0WZ
Weekdays 8.30 a.m.-5.00 p.m.
Sat. 9.00 a.m.-1.00 p.m.
H.P.A.W.

**LIVERPOOL** Tel. (051-207) 2967
TAYLOR BROS (LIVERPOOL) LTD K
195-199 LONDON ROAD
LIVERPOOL L3 8JG
Open: Monday to Friday
8.30 a.m.-5.30 p.m.
H.P.W.WM.D.A.BC.

## MIDDLESEX

**HOUNSLOW** Tel. (01-570)
Q.R. TOOLS LTD 2103/5135
251-253 HANWORTH ROAD

Open: Mon-Fri 8.30 a.m.-5.30 p.m.
Sat. 9.00 a.m.-1.00 p.m.
P.W.WM.D.CS.A.

## NORFOLK

**RUISLIP** Tel. (08956) 74126
ALL MODELS ENGINEER E★
91 MANOR WAY

Open: Mon-Sat 9.00 a.m.-5.30 p.m.
H.P.W.A.D.CS.MF.BC.

**GT. YARMOUTH** Tel. (0493)
ANGLIA POWER TOOLS 850388
3 DENESIDE, NR30 2HL

Open: Monday to Saturday
8.30 a.m. 5.30 p.m.
H.P.W.D.CS.A.

**KINGS LYNN** Tel. (0553) 2443
WALKER & ANDERSON (Kings Lynn) LTD.
WINDSOR ROAD, KINGS LYNN
Open: Monday to Saturday K
7.45 a.m.-5.30 p.m.
Wednesday 1.00 p.m. Saturday 5.00 p.m.
H.P.W.WM.D.CS.A.

**NORWICH** Tel. (0603) 898685
NOROLK SAW SERVICES
DOG LANE, HORSFORD
Open: Monday to Friday
8.00 a.m.-5.00 p.m.
Saturday 8.00 a.m.-12.00 p.m.
H.P.W.WM.D.CS.A.

KEY: CS CUTTING OR
SHARPENING SERVICES

KEY: MF MATERIAL FINISHES

KEY: BC BOOKS/CATALOGUES

# shopguide

## NORTHAMPTONSHIRE

**NORWICH**   Tel. (0603) 400933
WESTGATES WOODWORKING   975412
61 HURRICANE WAY,
NORWICH AIRPORT INDUSTRIAL ESTATE
Open:   9.00 a.m.-5.00 p.m. weekdays
9.00 a.m.-12.30 Sat.
P.W.WM.D.B.C.   **K**

**SWAFFHAM**   Tel: (0760) 23073
TONY WADDILOVE,   ★
STATION HOUSE,
LITTLE DUNHAM, KINGS LYNN
Tuesday-Saturday 9.00 a.m.-6.00 p.m.

H.P.W.D.T.CS.A.BC.

**NOTTINGHAM**   Tel: (0602) 225979
POOLEWOOD   and 227064/5
EQUIPMENT LTD.   (06077) 2421 after hrs
5a HOLLY LANE, CHILLWELL
Open: Mon-Fri 9.00 a.m.-5.30 p.m.
Sat. 9.00 a.m. to 12.30 p.m.
P.W.WM.D.CS.A.BC.

**RUSHDEN**   Tel. (0933) 56424
PETER CRISP OF RUSHDEN   **KE**★
7 HIGH STREET NN10 9JR
Open: Mon-Fri 8.30 a.m.-12.30 p.m./
1.30 p.m.-5.30 p.m. Sat. 8.30 a.m. 5.30 p.m.
Early closing Thurs. 1.00 p.m.
H.P.W.MF.D.A.BC.

## OXFORDSHIRE

**CROWMARSH**   Tel. (0491) 38653
MILL HILL SUPPLIES   **E**★
66 THE STREET
Open: Mon.-Fri. 9.30 a.m.-5.00 p.m.
Thurs. 9.30 a.m.-7.00 p.m.
Sat. 9.30 a.m.-1.00 p.m.
P.W.D.CS.MF.A.BC.

**WITNEY**   Tel. (0993) 3885
TARGET TOOLS (SALES,   & 72095 OXON
**TARGET TOOLS**   HIRE & REPAIRS)   ★
SWAIN COURT
STATION INDUSTRIAL ESTATE
Open: Mon.-Sat. 8.00 a.m.-5.00 p.m.
24 hour Answerphone
BC.W.M.A.

**TELFORD**   Tel. Telford (0952)
ASLES LTD.   48054
VINEYARD ROAD, WELLINGTON   **K**★

Open: Mon. Fri. 8.30 a.m.-5.30 p.m.
Saturday 8.30 a.m.-4.00 p.m.
H.P.W.WM.D.CS.BC.A.

### SHROPSHIRE

### SOMERSET

**TAUNTON**   Tel. (0823) 85431
JOHN HALL TOOLS   ★
6 HIGH STREET

Open Monday-Saturday
9.00 a.m.-5.30 p.m.

H.P.W.WM.D.CS.A.

**TAUNTON**   Tel. Taunton 79078
KEITH MITCHELL   ★
TOOLS AND EQUIPMENT
66 PRIORY BRIDGE ROAD
Open: Mon-Fri 8.30 a.m.-5.30 p.m.
Saturday 9.00 a.m.-4.00 p.m.
H.P.W.WM.D.CS.A.BC.

## STAFFORDSHIRE

**TAMWORTH**   Tel. (0827) 56188
MATTHEWS BROTHERS LTD.   **K**
KETTLEBROOK ROAD
Open: Mon-Sat 8.30 a.m.-6.00 p.m.
Demonstrations Sunday mornings by
appointment only
H.P.WM.D.T.CS.A.BC.

## SUFFOLK

**IPSWICH**   Tel. (0473) 40456
FOX WOODWORKING   **KE**★
142-144 BRAMFORD LANE
Open: Tues., Fri., 9.00 a.m.-
Sat. 9.00 a.m.-5.00 p.m.

H.P.W.WM.D.A.B.C.

## SURREY

**FARNHAM**   Tel. (0252) 725427
A.B.E. CO. LTD. (Quick Hire)   ★
GOODS SHED
STATION APPROACH, FARNHAM
Open Mon.-Fri. 8.00 a.m.-5.30 p.m.
Sat. 8.00 a.m.-5.30 p.m.
H.P.W.D.CS.A.BC.

## SUSSEX

**BOGNOR REGIS**   Tel. (0243) 863100
A. OLBY & SON (BOGNOR REGIS) LTD.
"TOOLSHOP," BUILDERS MERCHANT
HAWTHORN ROAD   **K**
Open: Mon-Thurs 8 a.m.-5.15 p.m. Fri.
8 a.m.-8 p.m. Sat 8 a.m.-12.45 p.m.
H.P.W.WM.D.T.C.A.BC.

## EAST SUSSEX

**ST. LEONARD'S-ON-SEA**   Tel.
DOUST & MONK (MONOSAW)-(0424)
25 CASTLEHAM ROAD   52577

Open: Mon.-Fri. 8.00 a.m.-5.30 p.m.
Most Saturdays 9.00 a.m.-1.00 p.m.

H.P.W.WM.D.CS.A.

## WEST SUSSEX

**WORTHING**   Tel. (0903) 38739
W. HOSKING LTD (TOOLS &   **KE**★
MACHINERY)
28 PORTLAND RD, BN11 1QN
Open: Mon.-Sat. 8.30 a.m.-5.30 p.m.
Closed Wednesday
H.P.W.WM.D.CS.A.BC.

## TYNE & WEAR

**NEWCASTLE UPON TYNE**   Tel.
J. W. HOYLE LTD.   (0632) 617474
CLARENCE STREET NE2 1YJ   **K**★
Open: Mon-Fri 8.00 a.m.-5.00 p.m.
Saturday 9.00 a.m.-4.30 p.m.

H.P.A.BC.W.CS.WM.D.

## WEST MIDLANDS

**NEWCASTLE**   Tel. (0632) 320311
HENRY OSBOURNE LTD.   **E**★
50-54 UNION STREET

Open: Mon-Fri 8.30 a.m.-5.00 p.m.

H.P.W.D.CS.MF.A.BC.

**WOLVERHAMPTON**   Tel. (0902)
MANSAW SERVICES   58759
SEDGLEY STREET   **K**★

Open: Mon.-Fri. 9.00 a.m.-5.00 p.m.

H.P.W.WM.A.D.CS.

**BIRMINGHAM**   Tel. (021-554) 5177
ROTAGRIP   **E**★
16 LODGE ROAD, HOCKLEY
Open: Mon.-Fri. 9.00 a.m.-5.00 p.m.
Sat. 9.00 a.m.-12.00 p.m.

H.P.W.CS.A.BC.T.MF.

## YORKSHIRE

**BOROUGHBRIDGE**   Tel. (09012)
JOHN BODDY TIMBER LTD   2370
FINE WOOD & TOOL STORE   ★
RIVERSIDE SAWMILLS
Open: Mon.-Thurs. 8.00 a.m.-6.00 p.m.
Fri. 8.00am-5.00pm Sat. 8.00am-4.00pm
H.P.W.WM.D.T.CS.MF.A.BC.

**CLECKHEATON**   Tel. (0274)
SKILLED CRAFTS LTD.   872861
34 BRADFORD ROAD   ★

Open: 9.00 a.m.-5.00 p.m. Monday
Saturday Lunch 12.00 a.m.-1.00 p.m.
H.P.A.W.CS.WM.D.

**KEIGHLEY**   Tel. (0535) 663325
EUROMAIL (TOOLS)   ★
PO BOX 13
108 EAST PARADE
Open 9.15 a.m.-5.00 p.m.
Not Tuesday but inc. Saturday
H.P.W.A.BC.

**HARROGATE**   Tel. (0423) 66245/
MULTI-TOOLS   55328
158 KINGS ROAD   **K**★

Open: Monday to Saturday
8.30 a.m.-6.00 p.m.

H.P.W.WM.D.A.BC.

**HUDDERSFIELD**   Tel. (0484)
NEVILLE M. OLDHAM   641219/(0484)
UNIT 1 DAYLE ST. WORKS   42777
DAYLE STREET, LONGFORD   ★
Open: Mon-Fri 9.00 a.m.-5.30 p.m.
Saturday 9.30 a.m.-12.00.
P.W.WM.D.A.BC.

**LEEDS**   Tel. (0532) 574736
D. B. KEIGHLEY MACHINERY LTD.   ★
VICKERS PLACE, STANNINGLEY
PUDSEY LS2 86LZ
Mon.-Fri. 9.00 a.m.-5.00 p.m.
Sat. 9.00 a.m.-1.00 p.m.
P.A.W.CS.BC.

**LEEDS**   Tel. (0532) 790507
GEORGE SPENCE & SONS LTD.
WELLINGTON ROAD
Open: Monday to Friday
8.30 a.m.-5.30 p.m.
Saturday 9.00 a.m.-5.00 p.m.
H.P.W.WM.D.T.A.

**SHEFFIELD**   Tel. (0742) 441012
GREGORY & TAYLOR LTD   **E**
WORKSOP ROAD
Open: 8.30 a.m.-5.30 p.m.
Monday-Friday
8.30 a.m.-12.30 p.m. Sat.
H.P.W.WM.D.

**THIRSK**   Tel. (0845) 22770
THE WOOD SHOP   ★
TRESKE SAWMILLS LTD.
STATION WORKS
Open: Seven days a week 9.00-5.00

T.H.MF.BC.

## SCOTLAND

**K = KITY
WOODWORKING
CENTRE**

**EDINBURGH**   Tel. (031 337) 5555
THE SAW CENTRE   ★
38 HAYMARKET TERRACE
HAYMARKET
Open: 8.30 a.m.-5.30 p.m.
Monday-Saturday
H.P.W.WM.D.CS.A.

**GLASGOW**   Tel. (041 429) 4374/
THE SAW CENTRE   4444, Telex: 777886
600 EGLINGTON STREET   ★
G5 9RR
Open: Mon-Fri 8.00 a.m.-5.30 p.m.
Saturday 9.00 a.m.-1.00 p.m.
H.P.W.WM.D.CS.A.

**PERTH**   Tel. (0738) 26173
WILLIAM HUME & CO   **K**
ST. JOHN'S PLACE
Open: Monday to Saturday
8.00 a.m.-5.30 p.m.
8.00 a.m.-1.00 p.m. Wednesday
H.P.A.BC.W.CS.WM.D.

## WALES

**TAYSIDE**   Tel: (05774) 293
WORKMASTER POWER TOOLS LTD.   ★
DRUM, KINROSS
Open Mon.-Sat. 8.00 a.m.-8.00 p.m.
Demonstrations throughout Scotland by
appointment
P.W.WM.D.A.BC.

**CARDIFF**   Tel. (0222) 396039
JOHN HALL TOOLS LIMITED   ★
CENTRAL SQUARE

Open: Monday to Saturday
9.00 a.m.-5.30 p.m.

H.P.W.WM.D.A.BC.

**CARDIFF**   Tel. (0222) 30831
F. W. MORGAN   & 25562
(CANTON) LTD., 129-133
COWBRIDGE RD EAST
CANTON
Mon-Sat 8.00-5.00 Sun 9.30-12.30
H.P.T.CS.A.BC.

**CARDIFF**   Tel. (0222) 595710
DATAPOWER TOOLS LTD,
MICHAELSTON ROAD,
CULVERHOUSE CROSS
Open: Mon.-Fri. 8.00 a.m.-5.00 p.m.
Sat. 9.00 a.m.-1.00 p.m.
H.P.W.WM.D.A.

**CARMARTHEN**   Tel. (0267) 237219
DO-IT-YOURSELF SUPPLY   **K**
BLUE STREET, DYFED
Open: Monday to Saturday
9.00 a.m.-5.30 p.m.
Thursday 9.00 a.m.-5.30 p.m.
H.P.W.WM.D.T.CS.A.BC.

**SWANSEA**   Tel. (0792) 55680
SWANSEA TIMBER & PLYWOOD CO. LTD.
57-59 OXFORD STREET   ★

Open: Mon to Fri 9.00 a.m.-5.30 p.m.
Sat. 9.00 a.m.-1.00 p.m.

H.P.W.D.T.CS.A.BC.

# Classified Advertisements

**FOR SALE**

## THE GREENJACKETS TOOL CENTRE

*SUPPLIERS OF HAND AND POWER TOOLS AND EQUIPMENT TO GOVT. DEPARTMENTS, LOCAL AUTHORITIES, SCHOOLS, TRADE & INDUSTRY, ETC., ETC.*

OFFICIAL MAIN STOCKISTS OF: BOSCH — HITACHI — ELU — MAKITA — A.E.G. — De WALT — BLACK & DECKER (PROFESSIONAL) ALSO STOCKISTS OF CRAFTSMAN — PEUGOT — SKIL — WOLF — RYOBI DISTRIBUTORS OF SUZUKI GENERATORS AND PUMPS — WAGNER SPRAY GUNS, POWER HAMMERS & ACCESSORIES. LOWEST PRICES ON STANLEY — MARPLES — SANDVIK — DISSTON — RECORD — ECLIPSE — ESTWING — DREMEL — ETC.
De Walt DW320 Radial Arm Saw **£199.00** + VAT; Bosch POF52 Router **£36.99** + VAT; Skil 593U Belt Sander **£44.95** + VAT.
**THE GREENJACKETS LTD., 32-34 St. Mary's Road, Ealing W5 5EU.**
**Telephone 01-579 1188/9**
*Prompt Mail Order Service.*
*Visa & Access accepted – account customers welcomed.*

MORTISERS; TENNONERS; SPINDLES; PLANERS; BANDSAWS; LATHES; CROSSCUTS; ROUTERS; SANDERS; DRILLS? YOU CAN CERTAINLY SEE ALL CLASSES AND TYPES OF MACHINES HERE.

WE ARE MAIN STOCKING AGENTS FOR: MULTICO; ELU; SEDGWICK; KITY; SCHEPPACH; INCA; CORONET; DeWALT; WARCO; DOMINION; METABO; STARTRITE; TREND; ASHLEY ILES; SORBY.
*P.S. OUR ELU PRICES COMPARE WITH ANYONES.*
*P.P.S. CALL US ABOUT WOODTURNING LESSONS WOODCARVING LESSONS (See our Swiss carving tools)*
*ALWAYS HELPFUL, KNOWLEDGEABLE, GOOD SERVICE AT:*
## CLEVELAND WOODCRAFT
**38-42 CRESCENT ROAD, MIDDLESBROUGH.**
**TEL: (0642) 813103**

**LACE BOBBIN TURNING BLANKS** in unusual and exotic hardwoods and ivory. SAE for list: J. Ford, 5 Squirrels Hollow, Walsall WS7 8YS.

### HAND CARVED
'Adam Style' Mantle motifs in Mahogany — Example 10″ × 5″ centre lamp and two side pieces.
Send S.A.E. for details and quotation. Your own design quoted for if required.
**SAM NICHOLSON**
22 Lisnagarvey Drive, Lisburn, Co. Antrim, N. Ireland.
Phone Lisburn 3510

FOR ALL SUPPLIES
FOR THE
## Craft of Enamelling
ON METAL
**Including**
## LEAD-FREE ENAMELS
PLEASE SEND 2 × 10p STAMPS
FOR FREE CATALOGUE, PRICE
LIST AND WORKING
INSTRUCTIONS
## W. G. BALL LTD.
ENAMEL MANUFACTURERS
**Dept. W. LONGTON**
**STOKE-ON-TRENT**
**ST3 1JW**

**TRADITIONAL PATTERN GUN-METAL PLANES.** Finished or kits. 17p stamp for list/photo. Bristol Design, 14 Perry Road, Bristol BS1 5BG.

### Alan Holtham
The Old Stores Turnery, Wistaston Road, Willaston, Nantwich, Cheshire.
Tel: 0270 67010

### BANDSAW BLADES
Skip tooth type with hardened teeth. Prices include VAT. P+P 1–3 Blades 90p, 4-6 Blades **£1.70**, Over 6 post free.

| Model | | Price inc. VAT |
|---|---|---|
| Birch | ¼″ | £3.62 |
| DeWalt BS1310 | ⅜″ | £3.74 |
| Kity 612 | ½″ | £3.91 |
| Lazzari P32 | ⅝″ | £4.77 |
| Bandit | | |
| Startrite 301 | | |
| Black & Decker | ¼″ | £2.99 |
| DeWalt 100 | ⅜″ | £3.11 |
| | ½″ | £3.22 |
| Burgess | ¼″ | £3.11 |
| | ⅜″ | £3.25 |
| Inca | ¼″ | £3.45 |
| | ⅜″ | £3.57 |
| | ½″ | £3.62 |
| | ⅝″ | £4.20 |
| Startrite 352 | ¼″ | £4.54 |
| | ⅜″ | £4.60 |
| | ½″ | £4.77 |
| | ⅝″ | £5.87 |
| | ¾″ | £6.15 |
| Willow | ¼″ | £4.03 |
| | ⅜″ | £4.08 |
| | ½″ | £4.20 |

### MUSICAL MOVEMENTS
* LOVE STORY * LARAS THEME * SPEAK SOFTLY LOVE * FUR ELISE * FEELINGS * FASCINATION * IMPOSSIBLE DREAM * MUSIC BOX DANCER * LA PALOMA * THE EMPEROR WALTZ * TRY TO REMEMBER * ROMEO AND JULIET *
Complete with screws and spring mechanism £2.50 inc. p&p. 20 or more of one tune ordered £1.50 each. Available from:
**The Jewel Box Shop,**
112 Pentonville Road, London N1 9JB.

## D.I.Y.
**ESTABLISHED 1889**
## THE SAW CENTRE LIMITED
### HAS THE EDGE
Hire or buy machinery or power tools from our extensive stock:
Elu  DeWALT  makita  Black & Decker
- SCHEPPACH  ■ STARTRITE  ■ GRIGGIO
- VOLPATO  ■ SEDGWICK
- TUNGSTEN CARBIDE TIPPED SAW BLADES
- DISPOSABLE BANDSAW BLADES

**SAWN OFF PRICES**

**HEAD OFFICE & MAIN WORKS:**
EGLINTON TOLL GLASGOW G5 9RP. TEL: 041-429 4444/4374 OPEN: MON - FRI 8 - 5.30 SAT 9 -1. TELEX: 777886 SAWCO G.
ALSO AT: 38 HAYMARKET TERRACE EDINBURGH EH12 5JZ. TEL: 031-337 5555. OPEN: MON - SAT 8.30 - 5.30.

### SOLID OAK CHAIRS
Sanded, ready for staining and polishing. From £35 each.
Also tables, tops only, kits or assembled.
**Country Tables & Chairs**
The Cottage, St. Nicolas, The Cottage, St. Nicholas La., Chislehurst, Kent.
Tel: 01-467-1192

**LUNA W59 UNIVERSAL MACHINE.** Good condition, many added accessories including Luna dust extractor. For more information contact Mr. J. McCarthy on (02805) 351.

**ARCOY DOVETAILER,** as new, three cutters, two unused. Record combination plane No. 050, 17 cutters. Offers: John, Solfach, Aberporth, Cardigan, Dyfed.

**MYFORD ML8 SAW TABLE** with fence, blades, etc. Recent list £220. £65 o.n.o. Tel: Cambridge 247395.

**FUNDITOR (LTD. LONDON) SUPERSAW —** 2' 0″ × 2' 3″ sliding table, micrometer slide gauge adjustment, see-thru safety guard, adjustable lighting fixture £120 o.n.o. Phone: Maidenhead (0628) 31401.

Have you seen the latest catalogue of
## Bygones
See Display advertisement

Prices quoted are those prevailing at press date and are subject to alteration due to economic conditions.

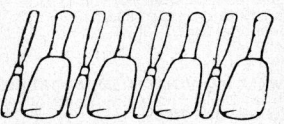

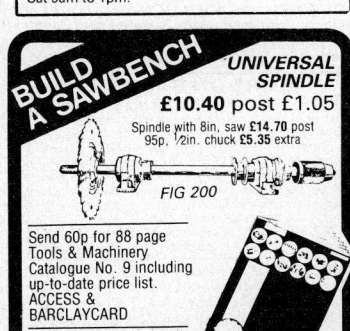

Prices quoted are those prevailing at press date and are subject to alteration due to economic conditions.

Prices quoted are those prevailing at press date and are subject to alteration due to economic conditions

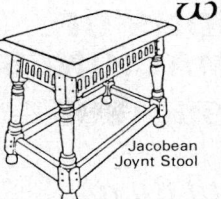

Prices quoted are those prevailing at press date and are subject to alteration due to economic conditions

# Then...

## Max Burrough

I was soon introduced to the art and mystery of saw sharpening — not a task to be undertaken lightly, it seemed. Saws were treated almost with reverence, and never left lying on the bench. As soon as sawing was finished, the saw was hung up immediately, and not one ever left the workshop without its guard being fitted on first. Every handsaw in the top shop was a 26in Disston 12 spring with six points to the inch, except Bert's, which had six and a half. They were all beautifully sharpened and maintained, and worked sweetly. Downstairs, poor Leonard's saws were horrible to behold, for he just could not sharpen them; that was why everything was such hard work and why he never achieved the standards of the others. Previously a saw doctor had called regularly, but when he died there was no one to take his place.

I soon learned why the flat of a file was run along the points first, it being necessary to maintain the line of teeth slightly convex so that when kerfing a coffin-side a cut of equal depth could be obtained right across the board. After checking the slight curvature by eye, sharpening would commence, the file always pointing towards the handle. I once owned a saw manual issued by an American manufacturer that insisted the file should point towards the toe of the saw. On reflection, it is apparent that this method leaves a ragged burr on the cutting edge of each tooth, while pointing the file towards the handle obviates this and thus ensures that the important edge is clean and sharp.

Occasionally, and if it looked as though a very good result had been achieved, a man would get a needle and prove his skill by holding the saw slightly on the slope; if properly sharpened the needle would run between the points from one end of the saw to the other. Try it the next time you sharpen your handsaw — but let me remind you first of what is often forgotten: the needle must be straight. Sometimes they are not.

There seemed to be no definite rule for setting the teeth; some men did it before sharpening, others after. Only on man had a saw-set of the pliers type, and I cannot recall this ever being used without at least one tooth being snapped off. The others scorned such contraptions and use the time-honoured method of hammer and punch, with the waw resting on a piece of even-grained wood such as American whitewood, sycamore or beech. I used this quick and easy method continually until I bought the wonderfully efficient Eclipse saw-set made by Neill. I have always considered this one of the best tools they have ever produced.

Beginners were warned to avoid 'cows and calves', the term used when teeth became large and small alternately. I can still see the first saw sharpened by Albert, the bottom-shop apprentice who started a week before I did: a tenon saw, half the teeth finished like those of a dovetail saw and the other half the size of a ripsaw's. Albert had hands like plates of ham; he later became a robust rugby forward, and in due course a policeman.

The Boss was well known for several characteristics, one being his sarcasm and another his inability to take accurate measurements. It was some years later that I stopped him being sarcastic to me, and quite early that I experienced his lack of capability with a measuring tape. Early one morning Fred was ordered to cut off two 14ft lengths of linoleum (only the very best quality was stocked). I had to help. We loaded the rolls into the back of the car and got on board ourselves, together with Fred's tool-bag. Fred sat in front beside the Boss, while I sat in the dicky seat holding on for dear life to the lino. In time we drew up, with the panache that only our boss could achieve, outside the front door of a lovely little white-painted Georgian house.

'Right,' said the Boss. 'Put the lino down in the spare bedroom, and I'll collect you at 12 o'clock. Give my regards to the Reverend.' And he drove off.

After introducing ourselves to the charming old vicar and his equally charming wife, we carried the lino and tool-bag up into the bedroom. Fred looked around and remarked that he didn't like the look of things. I asked why, and we unrolled a piece of the lino. It was three inches short. So was the other piece. A quick check showed that we had cut it to the size given on the Boss's paper. Fred said he had better go and telephone, and disappeared downstairs. I looked out of the windows: not a telegraph pole in sight. Fred returned with the news that the nearest telephone was two miles away.

We admired the view and talked of many things. Promptly at 11 o'clock, there was a tap on the door and the maid entered — black dress, white frilly apron and cap to match. Tray with cloth, silver teapot, Derby china, milk, sugar and two home-made cakes. Those were the days!

At 12 o'clock the Boss returned, and his expression when he saw the two rolls of lino standing outside the front door can be imagined. I often wondered what happened, as no one ever returned to that house with more lino.

Some readers may wonder why I tell this story. It illustrates a facet of the old apprenticeship system that many boys miss today. They go to large schools and perhaps on to technical college, polytechnic or university, and in their spare time they watch the rubbish offered on their television sets. My apprenticeship years taught me a great deal more than how to use a saw, chisel and plane.

Although at times he was absolutely infuriating, our Boss taught me a great deal — far more than he ever realised, and indeed much more than I appreciated at the time. A tall, heavy man, always impeccably dressed, his looks belied him, for a crippling disease had made his legs like matchsticks. Walking was difficult for him, though he managed to drive a motor-car.

He fell often, but such was his obstinacy that he refused to use a stick, and no one dared to help him get up. Only once did I try, when were together taking measurements in an empty house. The floors were highly polished parquet, and down he went. Instinctively I ran to help — to be met with a snarl as from a trapped tiger. One look, and I quietly left the room to watch from a partly closed doorway. Slowly and with much difficulty, he dragged himself to another door and, holding the handles, pulled himself upright.

A few minutes to regain his breath and composure, and then a shout for me. We carried on without a word. That was the pride and spirit of this man who kept his firm going throughout the depression of the 1930s, and during and after the war, until age made retirement inevitable. He was a Tory of the deepest dye; any talk of government aid or outside assistance of any other sort would have left him speechless.

His standards were the highest, and I can see him now examining, say, a chest-of-drawers brought down for his inspection. A finger and thumb — his hands were always beautifully manicured — would hold each knob or handle in turn. Every door and drawer were expected to respond to the slightest touch. Only when he approved would we fetch one of those wretched handcarts while he phoned to inform the owner of our impending arrival. Should a fault be found or a correction be needed, it would be back up those stairs for adjustment.

His greatest failing was that he never gave the customers what they wanted — always what he thought they ought to have, with the result that many a heated discussion was overheard between him and his clients.

I am quite sure that the mistakes sometimes made by outside suppliers were the result of the Boss's drawings — which often puzzled his own staff, who saw them frequently. They were always on thin paper, and the pencil was used so gently that the lines and dimensions were barely discernible. Everything made by the firm — shopfronts, fittings, fixtures and furniture — was designed by the Boss in his own office. His furniture designs either outraged or puzzled the men. ∎

# Letters

## Our open forum — where woodworkers can talk to one another

Noel Leach's advice to J. E. Coldwell (WW/Dec) on how to remove milky blotches from what I took to be a cellulose-finished table top is a bit like rowing someone out into the middle of a lake, handing them swimming instructions, pushing them overboard and rowing off. Stripping and re-polishing is the last resort, especially for someone who is in-experienced.

There is no mention of the risk of 'cissing', which is almost inevitable when re-finishing a used piece of furniture with cellulose. A dining-table top is one of the most difficult surfaces to re-finish successfully. By now Mr Coldwell will probably have handed back to his friend or customer a table with a surface like a relief map of the moon!

*E. Garratt, Bedford*

---

It was stressed in the article on the Kestrel knife (WW/Oct) that I put a lot of emphasis on keeping the tools sharp. Some woodworkers have expressed doubt at their abilities in this area. Although I feel it essential to keep the edge of the crooked knife sharp, my attitude about it differs little from my approach to any edged tool.

When a tool is hand-driven, a sharp edge means less resistance to its cutting action, cleaner cuts, less fatigue and more control. It is no more important to keep the Kestrel knife sharp than a whittling knife. The difference is that the potential of the crooked knife is so amazing. It is little more difficult to keep the Kestrel knife sharp than any properly heat-treated tool of fine high-carbon steel.

*Gregg Blomberg,*
*Kestrel Tool,*
*Lopez, Washington, USA*

---

I would like to make a mitre screw, and have seen the screw part for sale separately in a tool catalogue in the last two years. I aim to get this part and make the wooden components myself, but I cannot for the life of me remember whose catalogue it was. Does anyone know of a tool firm which sells the steel screw part alone? I have thought of using the part from a G-cramp. What is the approximate length of travel for the average mitre screw?

*J. F. Hodges, 24 Roa Island,*
*Barrow-in-Furness*

---

I would be grateful if you could help me find the manufacturer or suppliers of the Centec Senior electric router. Having bought one at an auction, I need some spares, but nothing is written on the tool itself bar the name.

*E. Jude, 56 Stafford Rd, Darlaston,*
*Wednesbury WS10 8TY*

---

Further to recent correspondence about Arcoy cutters, I would very much appreciate it if anyone could supply me with a replacement sawblade for my Arcoy rabbeter.

*R. M. H. Smith, 2 Observatory Rd,*
*London SW14 7QD*

---

I liked the look of the bedside companion in your October issue. For me, however, it lacked one thing — a gallery. I've just put quite a nice shop-made article in the sale-room because of this lack; for those of us who prefer to feel for the watch, for example, and not switch the light on, that modest strip is a must. Otherwise, one can quite easily have a valuable timepiece clattering to the floor!

*H. H. Bridge, Southport*

---

Mr Peter Davies asks for information about brasswork for old wooden cameras (WW/Nov).

Yes, a number of people make wooden cameras. Bellows can be bought from a firm in the Midlands, but for a Sanderson they

CAMERA FITTINGS of all descriptions. Special Designs can be quoted for in quantities.

are quite expensive. Why not make one? I have plans and drawings and can let him have photocopies. The illustration shows the type of brasswork concerned, of which I have quite a bit.

*Cecil W. Vanston,*
*35 Kings Court, Mount Pleasant,*
*St Albans, Herts AL3 4TH*

---

As a professional photographer and collector of old wooden cameras, I was interested to read Mr Peter Davies' letter (WW/Nov). I have made a couple of wooden cameras based on early models.

I do not know of any direct supplier of the necessary metalware, and my own answer is to cannibalise from several wrecks in my possession. I have been able to make a few focusing knobs on a metalworking lathe, but the rack-and-pinion parts are beyond my skill. It ought, however, to be possible for a reasonably good metalworker to make all the parts. If anyone does know a source for these items I would be pleased to hear about it.

Wooden cameras still have a certain application in studio and technical photography, and I know of a couple of people in production for the trade and for 'instant collector's items'; however, they do not supply parts to others. The Sanderson was among the most popular of the field cameras, as they were called, but the metal parts were more complicated than most. Over two years I have been — on and off — re-assembling a genuine Sanderson.

*Stanley Folb,*
*1 Odeon Parade,*
*London Rd, Isleworth,*
*Middx TW7 4DE, 01-560 3200*

---

I wish to draw attention to the work of gremlins in the September issue of *Woodworker*, as I'm sure Arthur Jones knows exactly what he's talking about (Timberline). Arthur is talking about the possible sale by the Russians of a substantial quantity of timber; firstly I'm sure they wouldn't bother only offering 160,000 cu in, but if they did, and got £156 per cu in for it, they would be more than satisfied! Shouldn't the printer have used an 'm'?

*B. D. Crabtree, Harare, Zimbabwe*

---

I have been quite surprised by the popularity of Arcoy products. Hoping to do a fellow woodworker a good turn, I have available the following: a standard Arcoy dovetailer complete with three cutters (two of which are in mint condition) and a cutter selection chart; an Arcoy power planer (mark II), the blades of which could do with expert re-grinding and honing. The instruction leaflet is still with this machine.

Both these tools are in very good condition and if anyone would like to make an offer for the two together and can collect, perhaps they would contact me.

*H. R. Williams,*
*42 Granville Rd, Melksham,*
*Wilts SN12 8AS*

● All future dealings in Arcoy to the classified ad department, please!

---

**By special request**
A brief message to Diana. Don't let them wear you down. Keep plugging away — you'll make it. *Paul*

# The magazine for the craftsman
## ~ and the aspiring craftsman!

March 1985
Vol. 89
No. 1096

● *Ideas blossom: one of Ted and Caroline
Vincent's intricate, original 'playpieces' –
pages 178-9*

**Publisher** Tony Dowdeswell
**Editor** Peter Collenette
**Deputy Editor** Aidan Walker
**Graphics** Peter Kirby
**Guild of Woodworkers** Aidan Walker
**Publishing Director** John Foster
**Chairman and Chief Executive** Jim Connell

It you write to us, please enclose a stamped addressed envelope. Unfortunately we cannot accept responsibility for
the loss of or damage to unsolicited material. Nothing published in *Woodworker* may be reproduced without permission.

**Advertisement Manager** Paul Holmes
**Advertisement production** Karyn Stewart

We reserve the right to refuse or suspend advertisements
without explanation, and regret we can take no responsibility either for clerical or printing errors or for the bona
fides of advertisers.

**Editorial, advertisements and Guild of Woodworkers** PO
Box 35, Wolsey House, Wolsey Road, Hemel Hempstead,
Herts HP2 4SS; telephone Hemel Hempstead (0442) 41221
**Subscriptions and back issues** Infonet Ltd, 10-13 Times
House, 179 Marlowes, Hemel Hempstead, Herts HP1 1BB;
telephone Hemel Hempstead (0442) 48434
**Subscriptions per year** UK £15; overseas outside USA (ac-
celerated surface post) £16.50, USA (accelerated surface
post) $21.50, airmail £41.50
**UK trade** SM Distribution Ltd, 16-18 Trinity Gardens,
London SW9 8DX; telephone 01-274 8611
**North American trade** Eastern News Distributors, 166-41
Powells Cove Boulevard, PO Box 69, Whitestone, New York
11357 (**Postmaster:** Please send address changes to
England)
**Printed in Great Britain** by Ambassador Press Ltd, St
Albans, Herts

**Mono origination** Multiform Photosetting Ltd, Cardiff
© Argus Specialist Publications Ltd 1985
ISSN 0043 776X

ABC

# Argus Specialist Publications Ltd

Wolsey House, Wolsey Road, Hemel Hempstead, Herts HP2 4SS (0442) 41221

**On the cover** (and we hope you like our new
look!): Peter Crutch's bathroom 'storage
tower' and Stanley Tigerman's double chair,
both in Colorcore laminate (pages 218-9) —
and Francesca Graham's delectable dressing-
table (full story and plans on pages 181-6)

## More Miniatura

Another showcase for miniature crafts, like the one reviewed by Stuart King in January's *Woodworker*, is in Birmingham on 24 March. Not just furniture but all kinds of miniature marvels will be displayed. There is free parking for 1000 cars, and the show lasts all day from 10.30-5p.m.

● Miniatura, Pavilion Suite, Warwickshire County Cricket Ground, Edgbaston Rd, Birmingham, tel. 021-382 6176 and 021-783 2070.

## Hazards — or not?

**A. R. H. Tawn** writes: I have been concerned with health and safety in the surface-coatings industries (including timber coatings, preservatives and adhesives) for over 20 years. For some years I was a member of the Health & Safety Executive working party dealing with the materials with which readers may come into contact. I was thus most interested in Peter Anstey's short article in your December issue. I suggest that more — much more — needs to be said about Health and Safety in general.

The greatest difficulty I have encountered arises from lack of appreciation of the law, and in the area of paints and timber chemicals a general confusion resulting largely from contradictory reports of hazards. Unless you happen to be a scientist your only warnings appear in the form of scare announcements selected by the press for their publicity value.

Creosote is not listed in either current enactments or the new draft regulations but, like most more or less volatile materials, it should not be used in a confined space, and appropriate precautions should be taken if it is to be sprayed. Pentachlorophenol and its water-soluble salt (PCP), however, are indeed listed. They must be labelled TOXIC and carry defined warning phrases.

The other group is more a matter for debate. Arsenicals like lead have long been excluded from most surface coatings, largely by voluntary action on the part of manufacturers who saw the writing on the wall before limits economically unattainable in industrial

practice were imposed. There remains a demand for white- and red-lead paints, but the precautions needed in handling the dry pigments have led to increased costs. The short answer is that, the more safety insurance you want, the more you have to pay for it.

Copper is the difficult one. The common component of green wood preservatives is copper naphthenate, which is not listed in any Statutory Instrument or Draft known to me. Copper is permitted in, for example, paints for toys and school materials. The only people who monitor it closely are the river and water authorities and they do this solely because of its effect on the bacteria in biological treatment plants.

Toxic hazard is a most difficult thing to assess and, unless one has the services of an expert, it is better both commercially and morally to err on the safe side. Problems arise in trading across national boundaries, and all too often one finds a scare generated for reasons of political or personal aggrandisement. What the pressure groups must realise is that as many hares (or scares) as finish the course are killed off midway. Saccharin is one example, aerosols another (though controversy still rages between the USA and Europe). I could quote dozens more; but what about the print union which effectively barred tannic acid as an ink component whilst continuing to insist on their right to tea-breaks?

## Summer School

Nice in these dark days to think of a month's course in antique restoration or upholstery in the elegant surroundings of Missenden Abbey. Brochures are now available for the Missenden Summer School, where these courses, plus wood and stone carving among others, will be running from 28 July till 24 August. Weekend courses are also running on 29-31 March, 3-5 May and 14-16 June. Full details of the summer school are still being prepared; write for brochure.

● The Summer School Secretary, Misbourne Centre, Missenden Abbey, Great Missenden, Bucks HP16 0BD, tel. (02406) 2904.

If your desire to reach a really high level of skill in cabinetmaking is fierce enough, David Savage's **courses** are obviously the ones. Any reader will have realised of late that David is one of that rare and wonderful breed — the woodworker who is also a very competent wordworker. His articles are always pored over in the office before

editorial processing, accompanied by grunts of 'Hmmm . . . never knew that.' He is running two-day courses in through-dovetailing and drawer-making in his Bideford workshops for two or three people; such limited numbers obviously mean you will get all the personal attention you can cope with!

Bideford is an old timber-importing town, so the ambience could scarcely be more appropriate. You are asked to bring a few hand tools, and instruction is based round making a single piece to carry away, usually a carcase or box. A good 8.30-5.30 working day, too. Says David: 'The courses are specific rather than general in nature as I feel this to be the only way I could teach the detailed techniques necessary **for high-quality work.**'

● David Savage Cabinetmaking, 21 Westcombe, Bideford, Devon EX39 3JQ, tel. (02372) 79202

**A. C. T. Shaddick** writes: As an antique-furniture restorer in business on my own, I have a small bandsaw. Despite trying many different blades, including the makers' own, I was for a long time unable to find a really first-class pattern.

Until, that is, a friend recommended me to Skellingthorpe Saw Services. What a wonderful discovery! Though they were unable to sharpen or set my existing blades, they sold me three — ¼, ⅜ and ½in. I have used the ⅜in one for some weeks, and its quality is outstanding. It is exceptionally thin and thus more accurate than the others I have used.

The boss is John Dexter, a saw doctor with more than 20 years' experience whose advice on anything to do with saws is of immense value. The blades, superbly welded, come in any length required.

I've also had excellent service from Williams Distributors of Peterborough, where David Burt is a reliable ally when it comes to machinery — no matter how small the order.

● Skellingthorpe Saw Services Ltd, Old Wood, Skellingthorpe, Lincoln, tel. (0522) 689369

Williams Distributors (Tools) Ltd, 108-110 Burghley Rd, Peterborough, Cambs, tel. (0733) 64252

● *Graham Garner started his own wheelwrighting business 15 years ago from his garden shed. He expanded into making and restoring horse-drawn carriages, vintage cars and lorries. His problem was small supplies of good hardwood. His solution was to do his own milling. Using a Forestor mobile bandsawmill, Graham can saw what he wants how, when and where he wants it. He is now offering a milling service for woodworkers in his area who need small amount of accurately sawn timber. Hawker Paddock, Ampfield, Romsey, Hants*

Beating your brains out looking for a 1/24-scale bog-brush? The Mulberry Bush's **catalogue** looks like the answer to all miniaturists' tortured searches for those tiny bits of atmospheric artisanship that give a **doll's house** credibility. Furniture, crockery, curtain-rails, moulded skirtings, fishing-rods . . . fishing rods? The kitchen sink is definitely included. 28 closely-printed pages of items, nearly every one illustrated. The firm make much of the furniture themselves, and they do a range of books too. Their mail-order list costs £1.95 post-free.

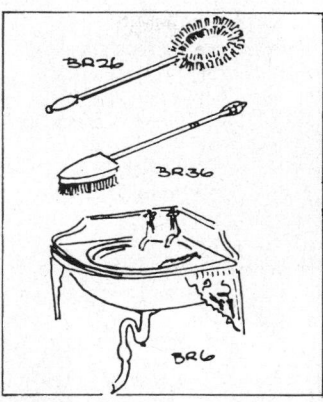

● The Mulberry Bush, 25 Trafalgar St, Brighton, Sussex BN1 4EQ, tel. (0273) 493781

The **woodworking store** is a new kind of shop — new and very welcome. One of the latest recruits is Matthews of Tamworth in Staffordshire — and one of the pluses is that the management are woodworkers like their customers.

The firm was founded in 1961 to concentrate on custom cabinet-work and Adam-style interiors. The woodworking and design business is still very much alive under the care of the two older Matthews brothers, but steady evolution has led to its coupling with a full-scale retail business run by Philip Matthews.

Starting with the sale of offcuts, this now stocks what the company call 'the very efficient smaller machines such as Kity, Scheppach, Warco, Elu, Coronet and Startrite' — plus 'a very large selection of specialised hand tools for carving, turning, veneering, cabinet work', etc. Not to mention 'veneers, inlays, marquetry work, clock movements, **the full range of Liberon**

waxes and wood finishes, sheet materials and timbers cut to your sizes, specialised hinges and brassware, many adhesives (including pearly glue), one of the best selections of Trend router cutters in the Midlands, Washita sharpening stones, Japanese Iyoroi chisels, a full range of TCT circular-saw blades, bandsaw blades', and so on.

'We're very traditional people,' say the firm, laying the accent on help and advice, 'as well as carrying a large stock of the small bits and pieces we can never find in the modern shop'. They have, they say, ample parking space, and are open six and a half days per week. They also run two large demonstrations a year for woodworking machines and craft supplies; a line from any reader up to a fortnight beforehand will guarantee him or her a personal invitation.

● Matthews Brothers (Woodworkers) Ltd, Kettlebrook Rd, Tamworth, Staffs, tel. (0827) 56188

This imposing vista is part of the German factory where Michael Weinig manufacture woodworking machinery (or *Holzbearbeitungsmaschinen* if you passed your German O-level). Here, too, is one of the mighty moulders which are their speciality.

Small doubt that the technology they offer is among the world's most advanced. At

● *One of Michael Weinig's giant planer/moulders*

least, that's what they say in the huge, fat, glistening, silver-coloured folders of press information which land on our desk almost weekly accompanied by brisk letters from the Weinig publicity staff (who are clearly earning their salaries). They've even sent a photo of one of their big-spending clients, a gentleman from Buenos Aires, riding in a balloon at a 'typical German festival' to which he was conducted by the attentive Weinig salesman. 'During the

flight he was baptised with sparkling wine by the pilot.' (It doesn't say whether his chequebook got wet.)

All great fun. The question is, do Weinig's products mean anything to any of the people who read *Woodworker*? Are any of you in the market for purchases running into the tens of thousands of pounds? Even if not, are you interested in knowing what goes on right up at the heavy end? We'd very much like the answer — and we're sure that many of our advertisers would too. Perhaps you'll tell us. After all, people like reading about spaceships!

If you've often found yourself at a loss to describe in the right words at the right time a fibreboard that is neither softboard nor hardboard, plywood nor blockboard — nor cardboard, come to that — you may find it worthwhile investing £16.20 in a BSI **glossary** that will insure you against such embarrassing verbal vacuity. For that paltry sum, a *section* of a *part* of BSI 6100 will be forwarded to you, defining all the different words you use when you talk about board.

● BSI Sales Dept, Linford Wood, Milton Keynes MK14 6LE

# Win a Woodworker Show Award

**AT BRISTOL MAY 25, 26, 27 AND LONDON OCT 24, 25, 26, 27**

SEND FOR YOUR ENTRY FORM TODAY

London entries: – £250 to be won by best of show Woodturner and Woodcarver – sponsored by Henry Taylor (Tools) Ltd., Sheffield.

There will be a Woodworker Show at **Bristol in May '85** at the Bristol Exhibition Centre, Canons Road and in **London in October '85** at the Alexandra Pavillion. There are many competition classes including cabinet-making, woodcarving, woodturning, musical instruments, marqueting, model horse drawn vehicles, toys and miniatures.

Send for your competition entry form for BRISTOL or LONDON or both to: – Woodworker Show '85, Argus Specialist Exhibitions Ltd, Park View House, Park View Road, Berkhamsted, Herts. HP4 3EY. Tel: (04427) 73291.

# Timberline

**Arthur Jones** reveals the latest supply news from the trade

Central heating in the modern home has produced warmth for the occupants and problems for the woodworker. Most projects in wood are for interior use. That means that properly dried timbers have to be used.

The art of kiln-drying has certainly been brought to the stage where it compares with the results of lengthy air-drying; but the work has to be carried out correctly. There have been complaints from the UK timber importers that some of the joinery-quality softwood reaching us from Sweden and Finland contains shakes caused by bad kilning. The producers, who nowadays mount massive kilning operations to ensure quick sales, accept that there are failures, and seminars have been held to promote higher standards. In the meantime, look closely to ensure that the wood you buy is free from kilning defects, especially shake.

Whitewood is currently on offer at exceptionally attractive prices, while redwood prices are steady at rates which applied in summer 1984. Whitewood may fall again, but the trade is confident that this trend will reverse later this year. Massive efforts are being made to cut whitewood output until the market settles.

Importers are taking an extremely quiet view of the forward market, buying only to meet known requirements in the short term, and the pattern for prices in 1985 shipments is not expected to be established firmly for some weeks. Stocks are good enough, at a time of modest domestic sales, for this policy to be safe.

On the hardwood market there has been a drop in sales of *Shorea* timbers because of the decline in home-improvement work, especially hardwood window-frames. This has led to some pressure on selling prices, from which woodworkers have benefited.

The supply situation for tropical hardwoods is generally good, and among the stocks on the high side are Brazilian mahogany and lauan. Here too, some pressure upon selling prices has inevitably developed,

again to the woodworker's advantage.

Just now there are few problems in price or supply of timber. This is a comparatively rare state of bliss — at which, some may say, it has taken a long period of rising prices to arrive, and which the woodworker has thoroughly earned!

Interest has grown not only in Brazilian mahogany, but also in plywood from Brazil. That country has an EEC allocation of duty-free plywood for the UK market; but, while Far Eastern suppliers have quickly exhausted their quotas each year, until now there has usually been some left over from the Brazilian. This has stemmed from problems with supplies. Now, however, the trade appears to be settling into a pattern — and, more importantly, the mills are offering a better and more reliable product. We should be seeing more plywood from Brazil in future, so it may pay to take a new look at the stocks available.

Incidentally, there has been a spate of complaints over sub-standard ply on the market. The user is offered plenty of protection through the standards which govern the adhesives in and manufacture of plywood, and no problems arise when these are observed. The simple answer is to insist a guarantee that the material offered meets the standards. It will be appropriately marked; do not accept the assurances of a stockist who says: 'It's as good as the stamped product.' Cheaper it may certainly be — but as good? Probably not, and you won't discover that truth before wasting much labour.

Insecticides to protect wood from the common furniture beetle have been available for many years; but, now that dieldrin has been withdrawn from use in the UK, the industry is seeking alternatives.

Tests have been made by the Building Research Establishment into the merits of cypermethrin. Most remedial treatments for the common furniture beetle have been emulsions, and the cypermethrin results so far suggest that an improvement is possible without any of the dangers or problems. The early hopes are now being tested under practical service conditions to substantiate the claims for cypermethrin. ∎

# Question box

## Our panel of experts solve your woodworking problems

**Q** *Having made some mediocre dressers the hard way, I wish to motorise my workshop for the same purpose (and to cut down on the mediocrity!) Given about £1000 to spend, would you advise going for a 'multi-machine', or for separate equipment such as a radial-arm saw plus a planer-thicknesser?*

R. Kay, Oldham
Alec Martin, Oxford

**A** This question of singles versus universals is a very common one, and in theory the answer is quite straightforward; but it always becomes complicated by basic factors such as the amount of available cash and space. If both these are unlimited, always buy independent machines. It is so much more simple to move from machine to machine without having to re-set everything and change belts every time you want to perform another operation, as is usually the case with universal machines.

Unfortunately most of us are limited by one or probably both of these factors, so we have to look at universal machines of one sort or another. The main requirements for the type of work you have mentioned are a saw, a planer with power-feed thicknesser, a mortiser, and a small spindle-moulder and/ or router.

However, with £1000 to spend you are right on the borderline between the options, and you could equally well go in either direction. A universal machine would certainly provide you with more operations per pound spent. For example, you should be able to get a combined saw, planer/ thicknesser, slot-mortiser and small spindle-moulder, and still have a little bit of change left over for a small router. But, equally, do you need all these operations at this stage? You seem to have managed quite well without any of them until now! You will probably find that the best solution is to buy a good-sized planer/thicknesser, preferably with the facility to add on a slot-mortiser at a later date, and then either a bandsaw or radial-arm saw depending on the type of work you anticipate mostly producing.

These two machines, along with a router, should do everything you need to start with, and for £1000 you will get two decent-sized machines rather than the four or five with rather limited capacity that you would get on a universal in this price range. You can then build up more machines as space and finance permit; but always buy the biggest that you can afford, since once the workshop is motorised you will soon realise the extra potential the machines give you. Then you become much more ambitious, and you will want all that extra capacity. Mediocre dressers should become things of the past — or at least a lot quicker to produce!

*Alan Holtham*

**Q** *I have recently been involved in making Windsor chairs, and would be grateful if you could suggest a method of making the tapered 'sticks' for the backs. Can you tell me if rounding-planes are available – or perhaps you could suggest another alternative to the old-fashioned way? Also, is there a drill that will make tapered holes for the stretcher-to-leg and other fixings?*

R. Kay, Oldham

**A** The problems associated with turning the thin, tapered back sticks for Windsor chairs are those inherent in turning any long, thin stock between lathe centres. Back sticks of ash or beech averaging, say, 20×½in can be exceptionally difficult because of flexing in the material under both end pressures and the pressure of the cutting tool. Many advocate the use of lathe steadies to support it, whilst some are clever enough to use the left hand for the same purposes.

The rounding-plane to which you refer is a tool of the type developed by Fred Lambert (*Woodworker*, July 1981). These produce round sticks, or dowels to be precise, in a variety of diameters depending upon the size of tool. For tapering, a slightly different version is used. Known as a trapping-plane, it literally traps the rotating stick material between its cutting edge and an adjustable, grooved block, the taper being formed by altering the pressure of the hand as the tool is moved progressively along the workpiece.

These tools are no longer available commercially. The only way they can be obtained is by attendance at one of Fred Lambert's toolmaking courses; see 'Guild notes' in this issue.

An alternative way of making back sticks is not to turn them at all but to use a spokeshave or drawknife and simply shave them to shape, finishing with a scraper. I have come across several old country-made chairs where the presence of flats along the length of back sticks bears testimony to

their having been made in this way.

To my knowledge taper drills or bits are not available new in this country. Occasionally they turn up in tool auctions, where they are usually (and regrettably) bought at high prices by tool collectors. I make parallel tenons and drill parallel holes using saw-tooth Forstner bits. If you must have a taper hole, a re-ground flatbit makes a crude substitute for the real thing.

*Jack Hill*

**Q** *I have just finished carving a pair of herons in soft pine. Is there a substance I can brush on as a base coat before getting on with final finishing? Also – what kind of finish is generally required by the judges at woodworking shows?*

J. Hartshorn, Ilkeston

**A** Yes! You can use linseed oil. Brush it on, leave it for a day or two, and if necessary add a further coat. Then leave it for a week or more — the longer the better.

Now comes the hard work. Take a mixture of beeswax and turps or a good wax polish, rub it in very thoroughly indeed, and then polish with a soft cloth and plenty of elbow grease. A brush is useful for both waxing and polishing; a toothbrush is particularly good. Hard or soft wood, it makes no difference: a good polish can be achieved — but it takes time and effort.

For exhibition purposes this finish is second to none. However, experiment with teak oil, too, and with different types of wax polish; or just apply the wax without the oil, which will give you a much quicker brilliance.

The grain can be filled before polishing. It makes things easier, but personally I don't like fillers.

The point is that a good finish demands firstly a good surface before you even think about the polishing process, and secondly hard work. I know of no brush-on substance which will give an instant finish of high quality.

*Maurice Lund*

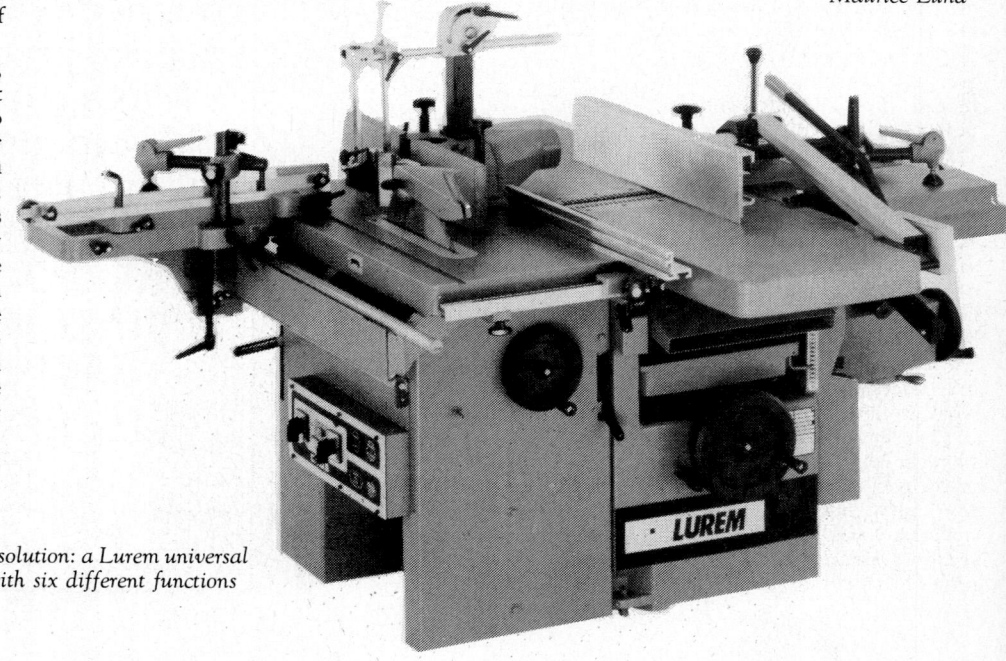

● *The heavy solution: a Lurem universal woodworker with six different functions*

# BLIZZARD'S
## WIZARD WOODWORK

COTSWOLD CLOCK

TOP & BOTTOM

SUPPORT RAIL
MAKE ONE

CLOCK SIDE
MAKE TWO

Section 'B – B'

CLOCK FRONT
MAKE ONE

CENTRES FOR DECORATIVE SPIKES

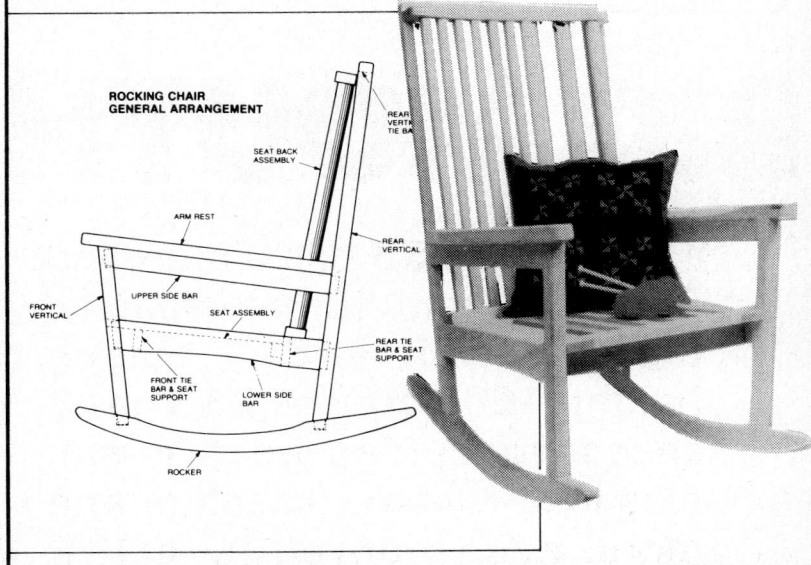

ROCKING CHAIR
GENERAL ARRANGEMENT

SEAT BACK ASSEMBLY

ARM REST

REAR VERTICAL TIE BAR

REAR VERTICAL

REAR TIE BAR & SEAT SUPPORT

FRONT VERTICAL

UPPER SIDE BAR

SEAT ASSEMBLY

FRONT TIE BAR & SEAT SUPPORT

LOWER SIDE BAR

ROCKER

Following his immensely successful book and television series on toys, Richard Blizzard now presents a range of imaginative projects for the home and garden. This new book includes many new design ideas which will be demonstrated in the BBC 1 series *Blizzard's Wizard Woodwork*.

His ideas for the house include elegant wall clocks and a combined bunk bed, storage unit and desk for a youngster's bedroom. For the garden he has designed a range of sturdy and attractive items, from a handy cart to a complete patio arrangement.

Only basic woodworking skills are needed to build these attractive and practical units. They are beautifully illustrated in colour, and clear step-by-step instructions and cutting lists are provided to help you put them together. The book also gives advice on woodworking and information on hand and power tools.

**£8.95    From Booksellers**

- Bunk bed/desk for child's bedroom
- Computer work-station
- Carving platter and cutlery
- Hi-fi/video housing
- Rocking chair
- Table loom for home weaving
- Fitted wardrobe for the bedroom
- Wooden wall clocks
- Patio arrangement
- Bonsai display rack
- Garden trolley
- Flower wagon
- Refectory table and benches
- Cloche and cold frame
- Pergola

LEG
MAKE TWO

TOOL TIDY

**BBC**
PUBLICATIONS

Prices quoted are those prevailing at press date and are
subject to alteration due to economic conditions

# Question box

**Q** In F. G. Emmison's *Elizabethan Life*, a work based on the wills of Essex tradesmen during the late 16th century, I found mention of some curious carpenter's tools. Perhaps you could explain what they were and their uses. Some of the names may, of course, be common only in East Anglia. The puzzling ones are a drawing stock, joint, twybill, holdfast, mortise wimble, draught wimble, long wimble, piercer, shave, berse and little thoyer, plus 'three pair of scrazes'.

And in 1595 a Chelmsford man's will lists his stock of timber as follows: '200 of quarters, 200 of ½″ board and 100 of mountains'. According to another source, quarters are pieces or 2×4in. Could 'mountains' be muntins?

*D. A. Truslove, Loughton*

**A** Your letter touches on a very interesting subject. Virtually no tools (other than those found in the *Mary Rose*), or even illustrations of tools, have survived from the English 16th century. So we have to rely for our knowledge of that period on wills and inventories.

These are rare, and there are two problems in understanding them. Firstly, there was not then any 'correct' spelling. The same word was spelled in many different ways. Secondly, writing was done by clerks, who wrote down what they thought was said but had little idea of what technical things actually were.

Piercers and wimbles were both tools for boring holes. They were usually the auger or gimlet type of thing, but wimble (wymbel, wombill, womble, etc.) could also mean a brace and bit. A mortise wimble would have had a fairly large diameter, say 1in, for the initial opening-up of morises. The *draught* wimble was probably ½in or so, needed for draw-bore-pinning of joints. When the clerk wrote 'berse' I imagine the carpenter had said 'pierce(r)'.

The 'joint' was almost certainly a jointer-plane.

The 'drawing stock' may have been a draw-bore pin, or a straight-edge? A holdfast then was an iron in the shape of a figure 7, about 18in long. With its leg put through a hole in the top of the bench, and hammered down, the arm will hold a workpiece just as firmly as the modern type with hinge and screw. The 'pair of scrazes' seem to have been screws — i.e. screw-jacks, useful for raising heavy timbers when building ships or bridges.

The twybill is perhaps the most interesting item, but it is tantalising. We know that it was a large, double-ended tool for chopping and paring mortises but, although there are plenty of written records of English carpenters having had them, no example of one has ever been seen. The ones used in Germany were rather like the modern pick-axe, about 2ft from flat edge (the parting chisel) to narrow edge (the mortise chisel) and with a long wooden handle in the middle. The French carpenter's twybill, on the other hand, was a straight bar about 4ft long, with only a short iron grip in the middle. Some day an English one will be found, perhaps in the roof space of an old timber building, but I

do wonder if it will be recognised for what it is!

The 'thoyer' defeats me. Perhaps a 'sawe'? Or an 'alger', or a 'nawger' (=auger)?

'Mountain' (montayne, moontan, munting, etc.) — yes, a muntin: the vertical piece between panels, or (for a carpenter) the upright beam or post in a building.

*Philip Walker, Stowmarket*

**Q** I have been offered the trunk of a cherry tree shortly to be cut down. It is 3-4ft long and 8in in diameter. I propose to have it cut into six or so boards ⁷⁄₁₆in finished, in order to make decorative shelving.

I have the use of a well ventilated car-port for stacking and drying. What precautions must I take to prevent stick marks from the spacing pieces, and generally to avoid warping and splitting? And will six months be long enough?

*D. E. F. Green, Mayfield*

**A** Cherry wood dries readily, but with a tendency to warp, so this will need to be restrained. The log is small and will probably contain grain not entirely straight; this could emphasise the warping tendency.

It would be as well to take a look at the ends of the log before sawing to see how best the pieces may be sawn out; if the heart centre, containing the pith, can be avoided, this will reduce cupping tendencies. You might also find it expedient slightly to increase the off-saw sizes, which presumably would be ⁹⁄₁₆in for a ⁷⁄₁₆in finish. If a little more wood is left on, cleaning up offers more chance of correcting any warp.

The car-port should be satisfactory. The boards should of course be kept well off the ground, and stick marks can be avoided by using offcuts of the cherry. The main thing is to ensure the sticks are the same thickness, say ¾ or ⅞in, spaced at (say) 9-12in apart, and kept in alignment; front and back sticks should be flush with the ends of the boards. Weighting down the wood as it dries is important — but do not use bricks, for example, directly on the wood, since they will hold moisture and tend to discolour it; put a few sticks first, with perhaps the outer slabs from the log on these and then something heavier on top. Six months ought to be sufficient for initial drying. Then the wood should be removed indoors to where the finished item will be used, in order to equalise.

*Bill Brown FIWSc*

**Q** I would like to know more about ornamental woodturning – in particular any information on reading matter, and on where the craft is practised and by whom.

*C. Downing, Plymouth*

**A** The definitive book on ornamental turning is *The Principles and Practice of Ornamental or Complex Turning* by John Jacob Holtzapffel, available at £14.85+£3 postage from Stobart & Son Ltd, 67-73 Worship St, London EC2A 2EL, tel. 01-247 0501. Its author gave his name to the

specialised lathes without which the craft would not exist.

It is practised by a few turners in Great Britain and abroad, notably the USA. The secretary of the Society of Ornamental Turners is Philip Holden, 17 Chichester Drive, East Saltdean, Brighton BN2 8LD, tel. (0273) 31031. The Society should certainly come up with contacts and advice.

*Roger Holley*

**Q** I have made three large flower-pedestals in oak (Japanese, with small parts of English) and am faced with the problem of how best to lime them.

I used ordinary builder's lime on the first one, and have met with disaster! The lime has turned the oak brown. I carried out the usual method for liming as per articles in previous Woodworkers, i.e. rubbing in the lime (paint consistency), cleaning off with a rag while still damp, leaving overnight, rubbing down with fine abrasive, and giving two coats of white polish. The result looks more like mahogany than oak.

*John Harvey, Looe*

**A** When finishing wood it is always sound practice to experiment with stains on pieces of scrapwood from the work in hand before staining the article itself. If there's no scrap available, experiment on an inconspicuous part.

One of your difficulties is that your pedestals are made from different varieties of oak. English oak usually responds better to liming than other oaks because of its tannic-acid content. The surface to be limed is scraped and glasspapered in the usual way, and then lightly damped with warm water to raise the grain. The work is allowed to dry completely before being smoothed with 7/0 garnet paper. All dust is removed.

Builder's lump lime is used, 2lbs being slaked in about six pints of water. Stir the lime with a stick; its consistency should be like that of thin cream. It's advisable to wear protective gloves and avoid splashing it about. Using a canvas pad and working across the grain, rub the lime well into the open pores of the grain. When it is almost dry, take a clean rag and — working now in the direction of the grain — wipe off the surplus. The work is now set aside for about 48 hours to dry completely.

With fine garnet-paper, gently smooth the surface by working in the direction of the grain. Dust off thoroughly and brush on two applications of white french polish. When that is completely hard, glasspaper lightly to remove any little nibs of polish or dust specks. The white polish seals in the lime and keeps the work clean.

Use the lightest-coloured wax polish obtainable; five or six waxings should produce a beautiful deep shine.

It may well be that your liming mixture was too strong. I would advise you to make some slaked lime in the proportions described and try it on some oak samples. If you use liming paste from a finish supplier, there should be no colour change; but, here again, try it out on some waste first.

*Charles Cliffe*

# Woodworkers: making a living

Luke Hughes talks to professionals about starting and prospering in the trade

**M**andy Campbell, Martin Merritt and Lou Leask, Phoenix Antique Furniture Restoration Ltd, south London

*Aged 25, 20 and 26 respectively; their co-operative business has risen from the ashes of their former employer's firm following his move to the country.*

PHOENIX Furniture Restoration was among the earliest co-operatives to receive financial assistance from the London Co-operative Enterprise Board. The LCEB is a limited company whose aim is to encourage worker co-operatives in the Greater London area. The GLC put up £30m in this and last financial year, and the organisation is now sufficiently independent to survive the GLC's impending abolition. It aims to provide cheap loans up to £25,000 for worker co-operatives. Repayments are re-lent to future co-ops needing finance.

Minority groups are especially encouraged, and their applications are given 'administrative priority'. To be eligible for a loan, applicants must prove they are bona fide co-operatives (for instance, by belonging to the Industrial Co-operative Ownership Movement) and submit realistic business plans. The loans are usually for five years; interest is currently at 5%. Any profit made on the side of co-operative assets is repayable to the LCEB for re-lending (this provision was introduced to prevent profiteering). No repayment need be made for the first year.

Phoenix's business plan was a work of art, and the care with which they put it together was a major factor in their being able to get their loan — plus credibility with their local bank. 'Lloyds in Elephant and Castle turned us down outright when we applied for overdrawing facilities, but after they saw the plan they couldn't have been more helpful. It's a good lesson for anyone else applying for loans or grants.' The plan was more than 40 pages long, bound together with one of those plastic sleeves available from any stationer, and it had a proper title-page bearing the proposed logo of the firm. As soon as you pick it up you know they mean business. The contents are

● *20-year-old Martin Merritt handles veneering and general work*

broken down as follows:

**General background** The reason for setting up, a little of their recent history, and a proposed outline of trading.

**Product service** What they consider to be involved in their business; definitions of basic terms and procedures spelt out for the uninitiated financier, e.g. 'Restoration — to repair furniture so that it becomes fit for use and aesthetically pleasing by using the tools, methods and skill of the originator to achieve an overall satsifying condition while attempting not to detract from its age or nature.

**Market research** They defined the types of clients they had had in the past, which were companies, private individuals and dealers, and where they had come from, i.e. from advertising in the Yellow Pages or through word of mouth. They then drew conclusions as to what business they could expect from these sources in the future, along with graphs and pie-charts to ram the point home — just the thing for those who fiddle with figures all day. The real meat in this section is the reaction Mandy experienced when she rang through the Yellow Pages and invited seven other antique restorers to come and estimate on some dilapidated furniture in her grandparents' flat. The prices varied enormously; so did the pro-

fessionalism. Mandy tabulated the results and compared them against what Phoenix would charge. Again, this was hard-headed — and very convincing to those who might turn round and ask: 'How do you know what you're charging is right, and how do you know that your work is any better than anyone else's? **Curriculum vitae** For all three, giving just the basics: schools, qualifications, previous experience, current employment, outside interests.

**Proposed internal structure** The areas of responsibility in the proposed company: Mandy for office management and general work; Martin for veneering, general work, collections and deliveries; Lou for dealing with clients and polishing.

**Financial assistance required** A list of capital items (such as tools and workshop kit) and materials (timber, polish and colours, upholstery fabric).

**Cash-flow forecasts** Projected for two years to show the viability of the scheme, giving all the foreseeable expenditure and income, plus the likely percentage efficiency in any given month (allowing for the interruptions that beset every workshop). A friend put all the relevant figures through a computer to give the likely permutations.

**Premises** The space, the location, the rent, the parking facilities.

**Letters of recommendation** From past clients, showing their intention to continue using Phoenix.

In preparing their plan, the three had much help from Paul Williams of Southwark Co-op Development Agency and from Margaret Burke at the LCEB. Most local boroughs have their own CDA, where help can be obtained. They also run 'taster' courses in business management.

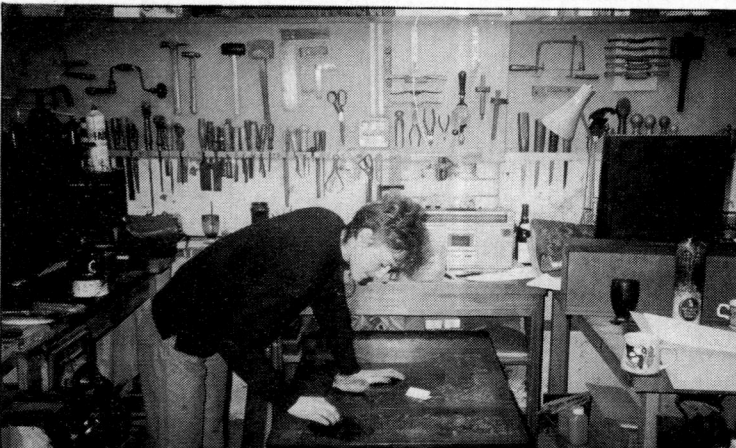

● *Lou Leask takes care of most of the polishing work. Here she is re-finishing a marquetry table*

So, armed with their plan and an advantageous loan of £14,000, Phoenix are now setting out to prove that all the forecasts are correct, and to convince their backers and themselves that they are capable of the monumental undertaking they have begun. They estimate their turnover will be about £33,000, and they are paying themselves £6,000 p.a. each. Quotations are worked out on an hourly basis (at £10.50 per hour), and they reckon to be within a couple of hours either way — surprisingly accurate. Private clients make up 60% of the work, companies 35% and dealers 5%; it comes equally from word of mouth and the Yellow Pages. Other forms of advertising are not productive.

On receiving the loan, Phoenix were in an enviable position. They had the money to go out and buy all the machines they wanted. It must have been like Christmas. They bought many portable power tools — belt sander, planer, router, etc.; Elu feature strongly. They also bought an Elu lathe which was cheaper by £100 or so than any comparable machine on the market, and has proved excellent. They invested in a Startrite 352 bandsaw, with which they are delighted, and a planer/thicknesser is on its way.

They all seem to prefer buying second-hand tools. 'They look much nicer, and the steel is so much better. Bermondsey market in Long Lane early on a Friday morning is the best hunting-ground round here, but you have to get down there by about seven a.m.

'The one thing we're still short of is sash-cramps. We never have enough. At the Woodworker Show we bought many Jet Clamps, which are all right in some respects, but you can't use them to pull joints together very easily.'

So many people tend to drift in the woodwork business. They drift from one job to the next; from bankruptcy to solvency (usually like a cork in the rapids); from times when they like to wallow in a chaotic workshop to times when they are passionate about tidiness. And there's something very endearing about this lifestyle. But it is rare indeed to see so much single-mindedness and determination as in these three. They have overcome huge difficulties in getting set up, and have come to grips with the financial problems in a way that should be an example to many. It serves to reinforce what should be in every would-be professional's mind before he or she starts: the aim to be a businessman (or woman) first, and a craftsman second, if you truly want to make a living.

● Greater London Enterprise Board and London Co-operative Enterprise Board, 63-7 Newington Causeway, London SE1 6BD, 01-403 0300;

Industrial Common Ownership Movement, 7-8 The Corn Exhange, Leeds, (0532) 461738;

National Co-operative Development Agency, 20 Albert Embankment, London SE1, 01-211 3000;

Industrial Common Ownership Finance Ltd, 4 St Giles St, Northampton NN1 1SA, (0604) 37563;

Co-operative Advisory Group, 272-6 Pentonville Rd, London N1 9JY, 01-833 3915. ■

# Books

Peter and Ann MacTaggart
**Practical Gilding**
*Mac and Me Ltd, 19 Mill Lane, Welwyn, Herts AL6 9EU, £5.95 paperback (also available from Stobarts)*
*Reviewed by David Ellis*

Till now, the average craft worker who needed to gild or re-gild parts of a piece of furniture, or perhaps a picture-frame, faced an almost complete lack of books on the subject.

Peter and Ann MacTaggart's new book changes all this. Not only does it embrace the knowledge and experience this couple have gained over many years, but that is put over in a style easily understood even by the complete beginner. One of the easiest traps for the specialist to fall into is to assume that the student knows more than he really does, but the MacTaggarts have not made this mistake.

In spite of what the professionals would have us believe, gilding (like french-polishing) is a comparatively simple procedure in itself, though it requires plenty of practice to acquire speed and a consistent standard. It is not very expensive, either (and the more efficient one becomes the cheaper it gets).

This book includes some fascinating introductory chapters on the history of gold leaf, the preparations for laying it and the tools used — few crafts can have remained virtually unaltered for 3000 years. These are followed by two distinct sections on oil-gilding and water-gilding. The differences are very often not fully realised by the uninitiated, but both the preparatory techniques and the end uses are very different.

Throughout the book there is detailed information on the various types of varnishes, gessos, sizes, etc., needed in gilding.

The chapter on special techniques is particularly welcome as it covers the different ways of marking out designs, laying out lettering on manuscripts, and the like. There is an interesting chapter on various types of protective varnishes, and the book is rounded off with details of the MacTaggarts' own speciality — the decoration of period musical instruments, a field in which they are acknowledged leaders.

The book is well illustrated throughout with clear line drawings by Ann MacTaggart. It has been a privilege to read and review this excellent volume, and for anyone interested in gilding — whether as a complete beginner or with some experience in the subject — I can unreservedly recommend it.

José Claret Rubira
**Encyclopaedia of French Period Furniture**
*Sterling, £10.95 paperback*
*Reviewed by Peter Collenette*

Nothing old, everything new; nothing borrowed — everything blue, or lilac, or stained pink, or given an outlandish tartan gloss. The work of certain craftsmen recently featured in this venerable magazine has seemed to reveal a credo of originality at any cost: one which would have left their forebears gasping.

But woodworking is, if nothing else, an infinitely various world, and those craftsmen who still believe in following, borrowing, adapting and blending may find in Sr Rubira's book an extremely valuable and perhaps unique hoard of material on which to draw.

Indeed, it presents itself mainly as a design resource. It contains no text to speak of. What you get are 411 pages of immaculate and closely packed line drawings. These are not rendered or shaded, but their very directness enhances the extraordinary detail in which they depict a vast range of first-quality pieces from the Romanesque period in the seventh century to the Second Empire in the 19th. By far the main emphasis, naturally, is on the reigns of Louis XIV, XV and XVI.

French furniture is noted above all for its ornament. That is here recorded with a precision that makes the book an inspiration as well as a magnificent reference. Mouldings, marquetry, carving, legs, plinths, cornices, and even bronze and ormolu work, are among the comprehensive range of features displayed — largely in perspective and elevation, with the occasional plan and section. There are no dimensions and no constructional details, but the book's true purpose is splendidly achieved. The only practical objection is that the style often makes it hard to distinguish between marquetry, paint, carving and other media.

Each page carries a few words of titling and brief description, and there is an index of furniture types. Some may find the food too rich; but those who relish it could not wish for a more appetising menu.

E. J. Tangerman
**Carving Birds in Wood**
*Sterling, £4.95 paperback*
*Reviewed by Alan Bridgewater*

E.J. certainly knows his subject inside-out and back-to-front; he doesn't mess around with acres of page-padding — he goes straight to the heart of woodcarving and describes just how it's done.

There are 17 chapters and over 300 illustrations, so this book really does cover the ground. Tools and materials; tails and wings; basic birds; birds of Bali; stylised birds; Korean ducks; bird mobiles; eagles; cocks; roosters; ravens — and so on. I particularly like the way the chapters are backed up with masses of enthusiastic details and 'thrown in' information.

However, the book isn't all roses. There are huge gaps when it comes to setting-out and hands-on illustrations. E.J. tends to assume that all his readers know and understand how to use a full range of woodcarving tools; consequently, although the book is packed with beautiful folk, tribal and ethnic inspiration, it's a bit thin on 'how to do'.

Besides, the publishers have taken great lumps of text and at least 50 illustrations from other post-1981 Tangerman books. If you already have *Relief Woodcarving*, *Carving the Unusual* and *Carving Animals*, don't buy this book!

**Prices quoted are those prevailing at press date and are subject to alteration due to economic conditions**

# Frank furniture

Strong lines and visible joints mark Andrew Lawton's work. He explains how to make this solid, stylish oak chest

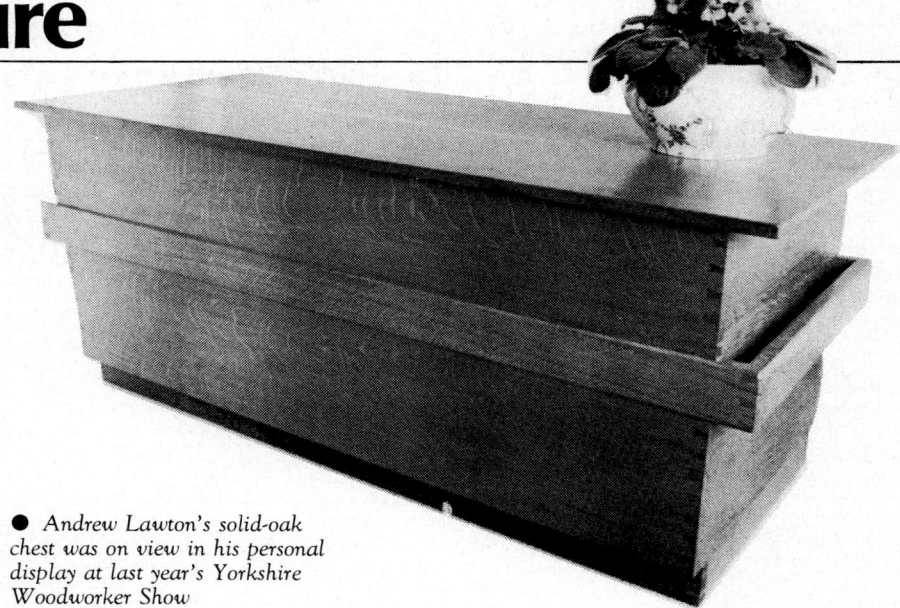

● Andrew Lawton's solid-oak chest was on view in his personal display at last year's Yorkshire Woodworker Show

I designed this chest to be robustly constructed, but not too heavy; easily portable; frank in its joints and essential structure; expressive of the timber's nature; and a testing piece of craftsmanship that was within reach of the dedicated amateur. The result is quite simple, but precisely for this reason care is needed in its making. Any errors would be only too obvious in such an unadorned piece.

To realise the full effect, straight-grained timber should be used. Mine was quarter-sawn English oak, with cedar of Lebanon for the bottom. With quarter-sawn boards you will have to use two or more pieces for the top to reach the width needed; I used two wide boards on each side, with a narrow piece in the centre the same width as the handles. The important point is to maintain the balance.

In the bottom, the grain runs from side to side; the boards were grooved into an oak frame. This arrangement was for two reasons. Firstly, short pieces would not sag as full-length boards would do — there are no cross-members. Secondly, my cedar had its usual quota of dead knots and shakes. By adopting this method I was able to eliminate them and produce clean, defect-free pieces.

The structure of the chest is shown in the drawings. Do ensure, before gluing up the three pieces for the sides, that the ends are dead square and exactly in line. Since the weight of the contents (which could be considerable) is carried by the rub-joints between pieces A, B and A1, I mortised all three and inserted loose tenons, ensuring that they were tight in the width and just a comfortable hand-fit in the thickness. The former is needed for them to function as intended, but if too tight in thickness they will simply burst the side pieces. A true surface is essential where the three pieces meet, so shoot the edges accurately with a try-plane.

The quality of the dovetails set the standard of workmanship for the finished chest. Spend time marking them out, getting a balance between joints which are strong enough to do the job yet well proportioned and pleasing to the eye. Use a sharp saw and razor-sharp chisels when paring back to the shoulder-lines. I cut the tails first and marked the pins from them.

After gluing up the main structure with PVA or urea-formaldehyde and subsequently cleaning it up, attention can be turned to the bottom. The cedar boards are

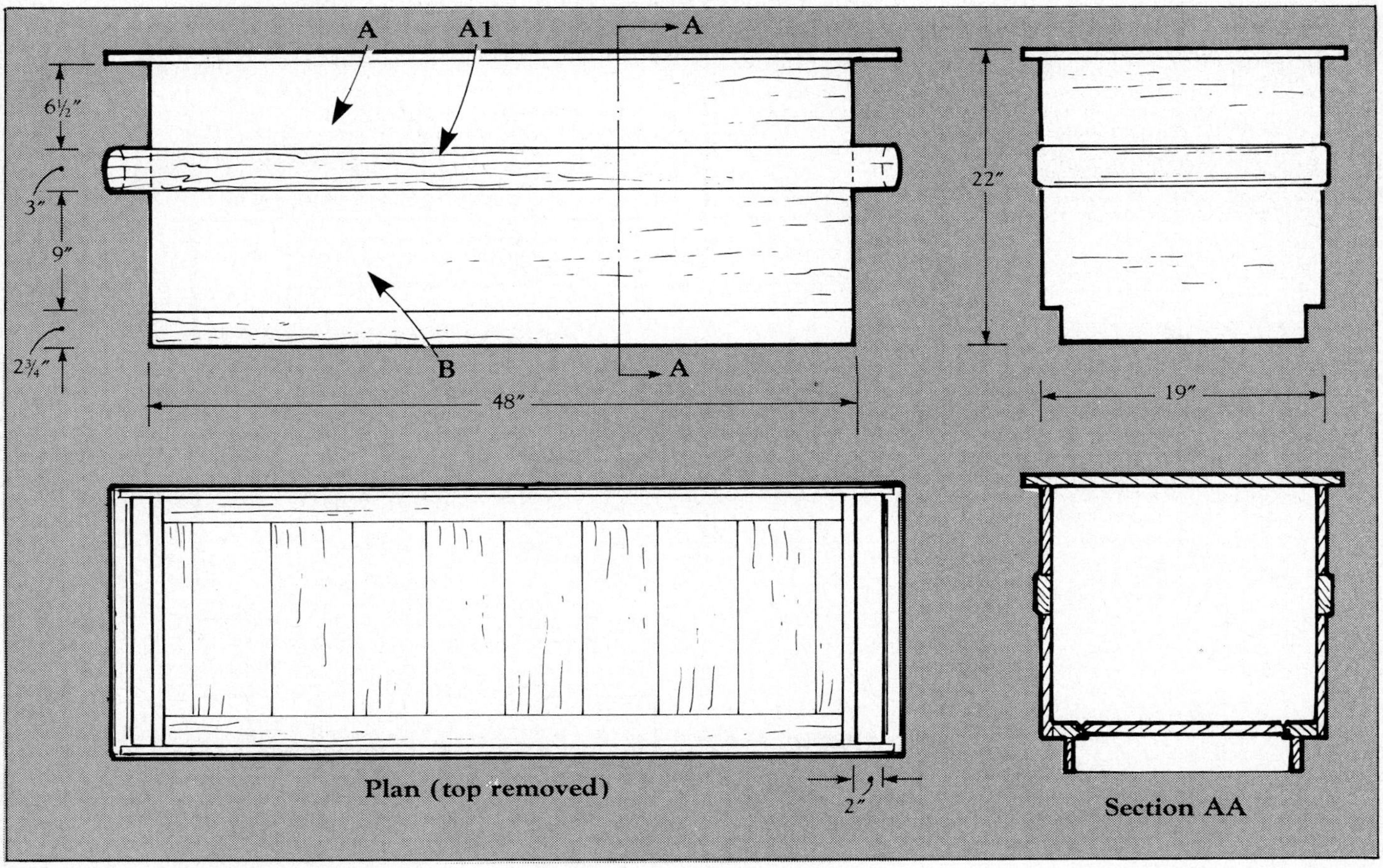

A · A1 · A

6½"

3"

9"

2¾"

48"

B · A

Plan (top removed)

2"

22"

19"

Section AA

rebated to slot together, and fit in a groove in the frame. The sectional elevation should make this clear. A small V-groove is worked where all the pieces meet. To allow for movement, each board has only its central inch glued. When the bottom has been assembled it is carefully fitted to the carcase and glued in place. You will notice that the bottom assembly gives stiffness to the whole chest, and the weight of the contents is carried by the plinth.

Construction and hingeing of the lid are straightforward. Polish the hinges with

● *Right: A closer view of the piece's unusual construction*

● *Below: The highly original sprung stay mechanism is made entirely from solid timber*

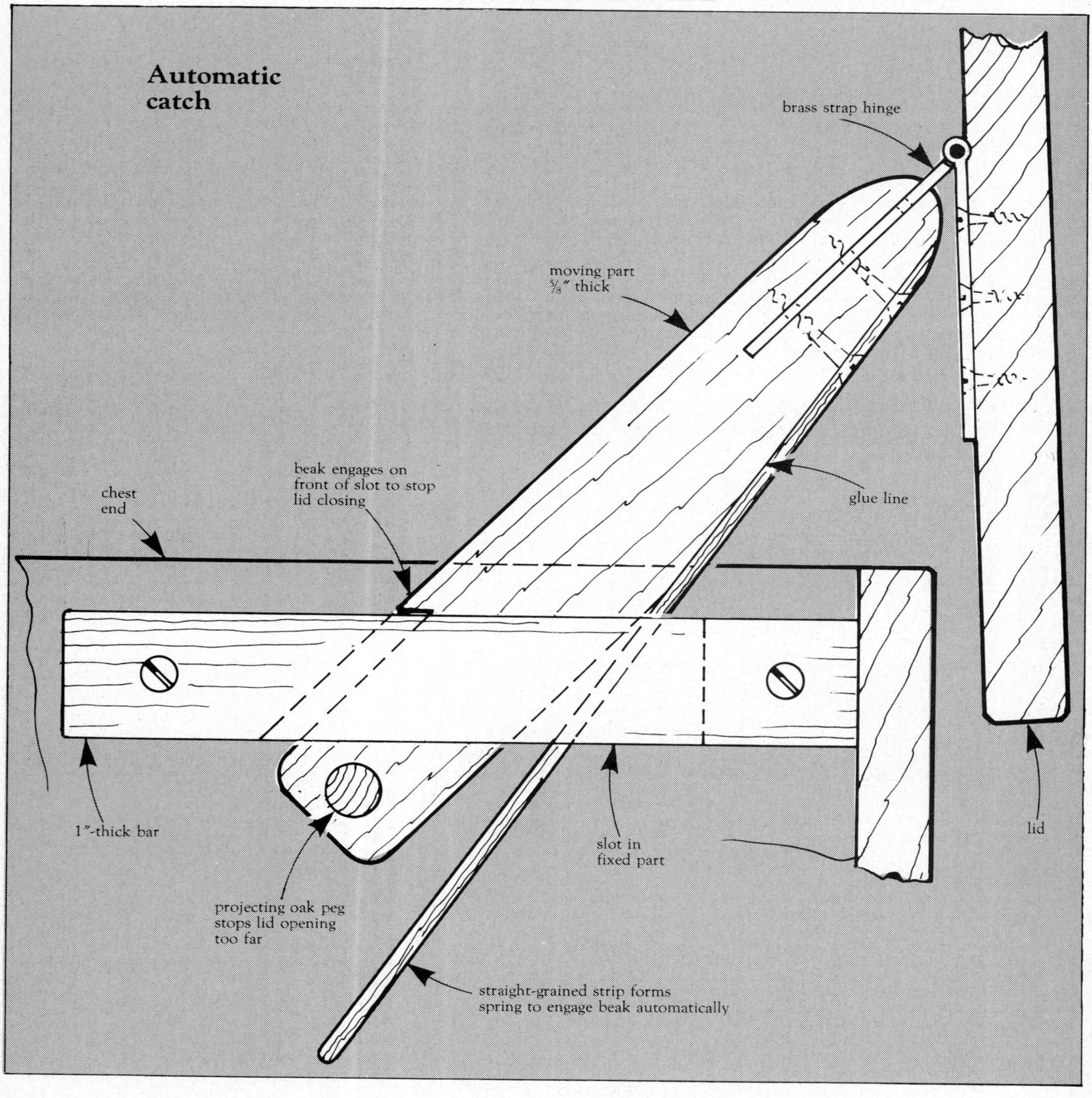

emery cloth to give them a bright finish. The automatic catch prevents the lid both from accidentally falling shut and from being pushed too far back and putting a strain on the hinges. Its main components are a brass strap-hinge and a straight-grained piece of oak for flexibility. The drawing shows its construction.

Finish the chest to preserve the character of the timber and simplicity of the design. After cleaning up with a sharp smoothing-plane, sand with fairly fine paper, but don't overdo it. The surface should be free from tool-marks and smooth to the touch, but oak looks wrong if smoothed as much as you would mahogany or walnut. Apply a coat of cellulose sanding sealer, sand lightly, rub in wax and buff up the next day.

And there you have it — a simple design whose elegance and strength should keep it in daily use for lifetimes! ■

## Automatic catch

brass strap hinge

moving part ⅝" thick

beak engages on front of slot to stop lid closing

glue line

chest end

1"-thick bar

projecting oak peg stops lid opening too far

slot in fixed part

lid

straight-grained strip forms spring to engage beak automatically

# The WOODWORKER Magazine MDF Competition

**Sponsored by FIDOR — the Fibre Building Board Organisation**

## A major design contest for a major new material

If you're in the furniture trade or even at college, you'll already know about medium density fibreboard — and you'll know why it's caught on so firmly.

Arguably the first new panel product since chipboard arrived after World War II, MDF challenges its predecessor in important ways; and it's very nearly as cheap. No material will do everything — but MDF bids fair to take a well-earned place of its own alongside the established favourites. And it's now being made in the British Isles.

The funny thing is that a lot of people haven't heard of it yet. But it's widely available if you know where to look (FIDOR will tell you the names of stockists in your district), so there's no reason not to give it a try.

That's why we've organised this competition. Amateur and professional will be in with equal chances, because we're after clever, attractive, original designs — whether or not they need a lot of time and/or fancy equipment in the execution.

We also guarantee extensive national publicity for the winners and their designs — in the form of coverage in **Woodworker** magazine, nationally available each month, plus a comprehensive release to the media by FIDOR.

The closing date isn't till 30 April 1985; so please don't be shy. Go on — enter! We have no preconceptions about what's going to win: and we're longing to hear from you.

## ABOUT MDF

Medium density fibreboard is made from wood fibre with the addition of resin glue. Its vital feature is its close, dense texture — like that of many hardwoods. This means:

**Ease of working** MDF can be sawn, drilled, routed, sanded, engraved, edge-moulded and even turned to a sharp, clean finish;

**Ease of fixing** MDF can be glued, dowelled, screwed, nailed, stapled — and even dovetailed;

**Ease of finishing** MDF can be painted, stained, lacquered and veneered on both faces and all edges, before and after cutting.

*You can saw it*

*You can veneer it*

*You can rout it*

*You can screw it*

*You can paint it*

● The versatility of MDF: applied mouldings, piano parts and smoker tables are among the many roles it plays

● Curves and planes, the chairs on the cover are MDF, as is this triangular table by Gerry Auburn of Bucks College

## THE RULES

1 Each entry must be an object which has been made substantially in MDF: *either* a free-standing piece or set of pieces of furniture or a fitment or decorative feature for domestic or business use.

2 The entry must consist of a written description outlining the nature of the design and the thinking behind it (this should not run to more than two sides of A4 paper); a set of dimensioned drawings; and *either* a perspective drawing or one or more photos or both.

3 All entries should be sent to FIDOR and arrive before 1 May 1985.

4 To enter, you must live on the UK mainland.

5 The decision of **Woodworker** magazine and FIDOR is final in all matters concerning this competition. The judges reserve the right not to make awards if they think it inappropriate.

We'll be looking for a design which is interesting in itself, and effectively uses the principal characteristics of MDF (credit being given for originality in both respects). Quality of execution will also be an important factor.

FIDOR is at 1 Hanworth Rd, Feltham, Middx TW13 5AF, tel. 01-751 6107. They will be pleased to help with all queries, no matter how simple or how technical. And anyone who asks (competition entrant or not) will be sent a comprehensive package of information about MDF — including a personalised list of MDF stockists in his or her own particular area.

*picture Medite of Europe*

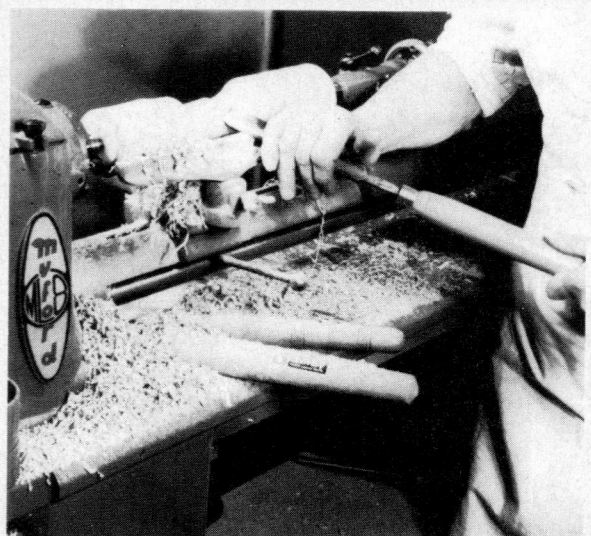
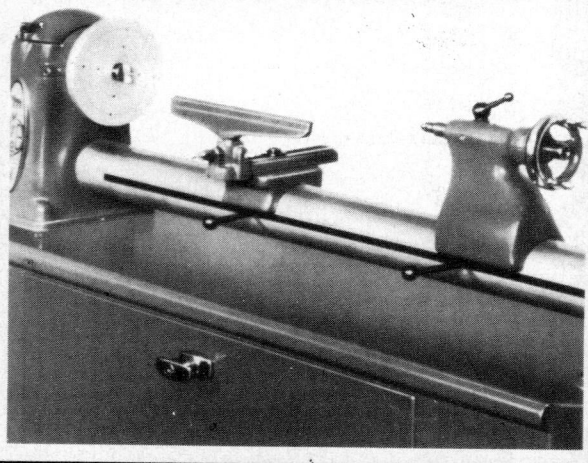

**Prices quoted are those prevailing at press date and are
subject to alteration due to economic conditions**

# Guild notes

## Guild of WOODWORKERS

Shared information, advice and help are vital to good woodwork. They are also the basis of the **Guild of Woodworkers**: an international organisation which welcomes new members — whatever their skills. PO Box 35, Hemel Hempstead HP2 4SS (phone 0442 41221).

Guild members get
- priority on our courses
- free publicity in *Woodworker*
- 15% off Woodworker Show entry
- a free display area and meeting-point at the Show
- 15% discount on our plans
- access to and inclusion in our register of members' skills and services
- the chance to contact other members for help and advice where appropriate
- specially arranged tool in-rance at low rates

Please quote your Guild number when contacting us.

*Aidan Walker*

## Golden opportunity

Pooling resources was mentioned on the Guild pages in the December issue of *Woodworker* in a list of functions that we could and should encourage. Mr. G. N. Mackie of Solihull in Warwickshire gets a full-marks Guild accolade for making this very attractive offer: **use of a well-equipped workshop in exchange for some work.**

Mr Mackie, whose wife Rosemarie's tapestry table was pictured in November's *Guild Notes*, has a 350sq ft workshop with a Sheppach sawbench, a Kombi planer/thicknesser, a DeWalt radial-arm saw, a Burgess bandsaw, and various portable power and hand tools. He envisages a mutually beneficial arrangement with someone who is looking for workshop space from which to run their own business; the details to be worked out individually, but the basis being an exchange of time for space. The 'cohabitee' would work perhas a day a week making footstools and tables for Mr and Mrs Mackie, and have the workshop facilities for his or her own business the rest of the time. There would be an initial trial period of six months, during which time either party could terminate the arrangement with due notice.

It sounds an excellent idea to me, and the sort of thing that the Guild supports and encourages to the hilt — if we aren't about mutual benefit and support for wood-workers, what are we about? Mr Mackie asks that enquiries about this arrangement be sent to me at the *Woodworker* office, and I will pass them on to him.

## Norfolk turning

Tony Waddilove's woodturning operation near King's Lynn includes a range of courses — a natural spin-off, he says, from his work as a professional turner. Tony is now also serving the turners and carvers of East Anglia, who may have fretted over difficulties in getting tools, equipment and materials, through his newly opened shop. Get in touch with him for details.
- Tony Waddilove, Station House, Little Dunham, King's Lynn, Norfolk, tel. (0760) 23073.

## Local Reps

I will keep plugging this idea, because I think it is all-round good news for the Guild. Once you have begun to meet, the actual work of arranging it will take care of itself. The obvious advantage is a social and functional focus for woodworkers in a particular area. One person takes responsibility for arranging one meeting, then another . . . it'll snowball for sure, to everyone's benefit.

News about activities and plans will naturally find their way back onto this page; the possibilities are numerous and attractive. At the moment (early January) my map on the wall has pins in Dumfries-shire, W. Yorkshire, Norfolk, Bedford-shire, Herefordshire and Surrey. Not enough! The scheme promises a lot of benefit for a little work — so write or phone to let me know if you're interested in some solid Guild input!

# Painted playthings

THESE INTRICATE and sophisticated toys are educational, decorative or diverting; as games or as sculpture, they promise to boggle the mind and fertilise the imagination. Husband-and-wife team Ted and Caroline Vincent, from fine-art and furniture-design backgrounds, have conceived and executed the pieces so they can be taken apart and put together in numerous ways. The Magic Garden becomes a castle with a moat; the round birthday cake ends up square or diamond-shaped. Even arranging the components as patterns of shape and colour on a baseboard can provide endless fun for children — old or young.

'Basically, they are sets of bricks,' says Ted; but no average building block is designed and made with such vitality and versatility.

● *Ted and
Caroline Vincent,
The Cottage, Rowston
Lowfields, Scopwick,
Lincolnshire.*

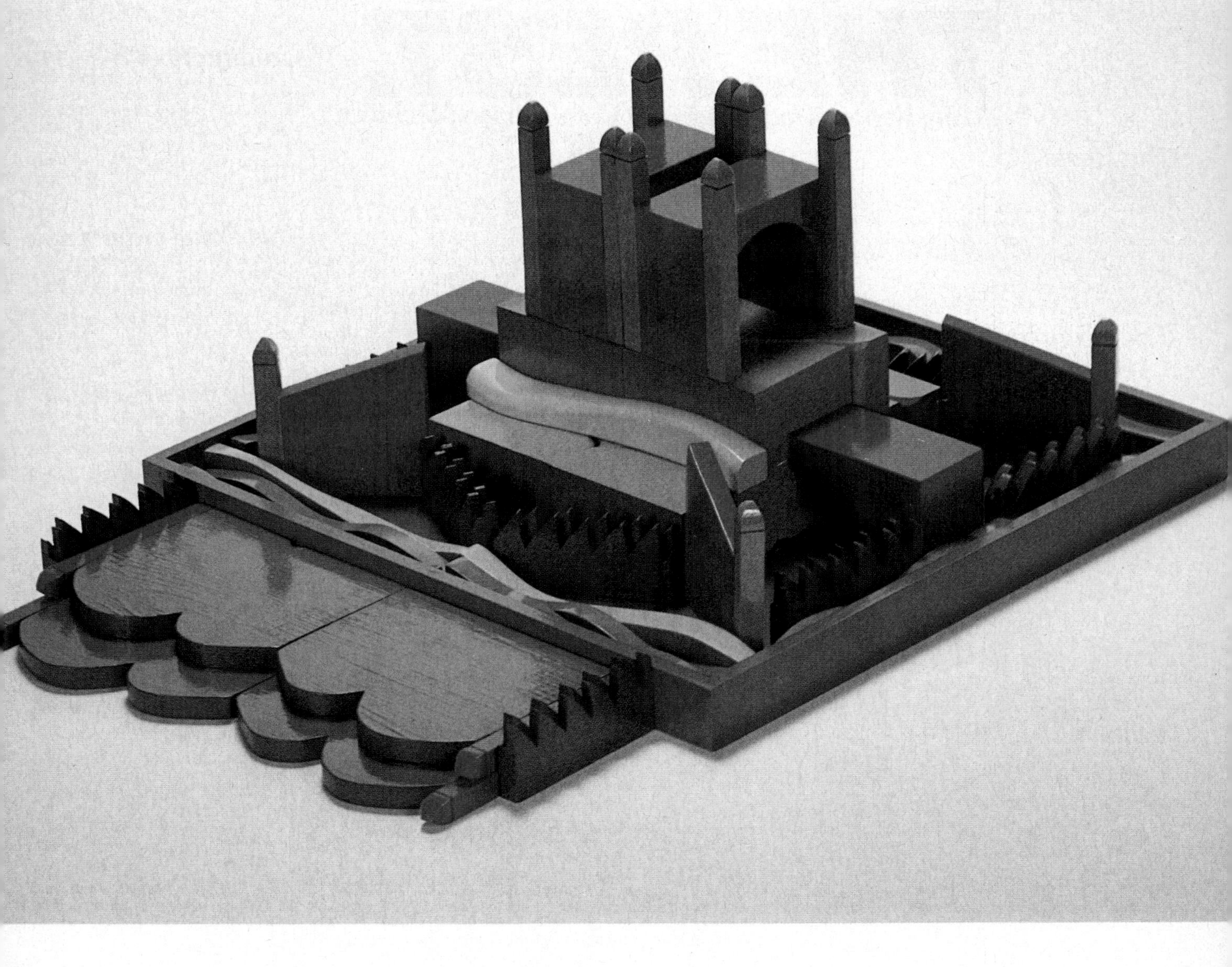

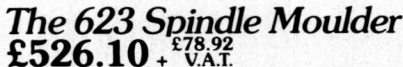
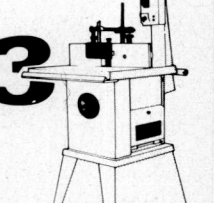
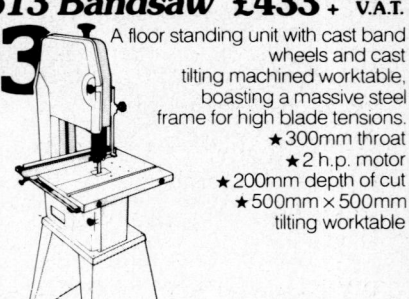
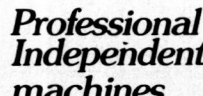

180

# Dressing in lace

Francesca Graham's design for a magnificent dressing-table — explained and exploded for the confident and ambitious

Despite widespread use of cosmetics since as early as the 14th century, dressing-tables seem not to have been designed as such until the Restoration. Wainscot tables, usually covered in fringed draperies, were used to keep powders, brushes and combs.

The walnut and japanned swing toilet-glasses on box stands that came into fashion around 1700 were placed on small tables veneered or japanned to match. They had cabriole legs and usually two or three deep drawers to hold brushes and combs. This type, and the familiar small knee-hole table with drawers at the sides, were also used as writing-desks. They remained popular throughout the first half of the 18th century, even after dressing-tables with complex fittings had become fashionable.

Inventories, bills and advertisements of about this time often mention stands in conjunction with a table and mirror, these objects together forming a set. Such sets were probably used for dressing, candlesticks being placed on the stands which stood either side of the dressing-table.

During the 1750s a small number of dressing-tables were made in the Chinese taste, using fancy lattice-work, marquetry and japanning. Dressing-tables were more practical than ever before, with pivoting or swing mirrors and separate compartments for storage. Tables with fittings for dressing began to appear in inventories: in 1743 William Hallett supplied the fourth Earl of Cardigan with 'a mahogany table on castors, the top to lift up with a glass and boxes; a shelf underneath with the sides and back cut open'. At first they were generally of knee-hole pedestal form, with the top drawer divided into compartments and a small hinged glass in the centre.

Dressing-tables with hinged mirrors on the top, set between cupboards, were also made at this time; they can be seen in Chippendale's *Director*, 1762. Such tables were often draped, and for this purpose Chippendale recommends 'silk damask with gold fringe and tassels'.

Dressing-tables with hinged-box lids, when thrown open, exposed a framed mirror with the many box compartments. The smaller and more compact specimens fitted with drawers are called shaving-tables in catalogues of the period.

Another distinct type is the 'commode dressing-table' with the top drawer containing the necessary equipment. In Hepplewhite's *Guide* of 1788 they are shown with serpentine fronts, and the book recommends that the drawers should be ornamented with inlay or painted work.

A man named Rudd, described by Hepplewhite as a 'once popular character', is said to have invented a dressing-table with two drawers in the sides to swing out, provided with mirrors on a quadrant, so that a lady could see herself from every angle. Hepplewhite says 'Rudd's table or Reflecting Dressing-table possesses every convenience which can be wanted or mechanism or ingenuity supply . . .'.

Sheraton illustrated a considerable number of dressing-tables, with the hinged box-lids on narrow tapering legs.

In designing this piece I was initially inspired by the Sheraton period. Small

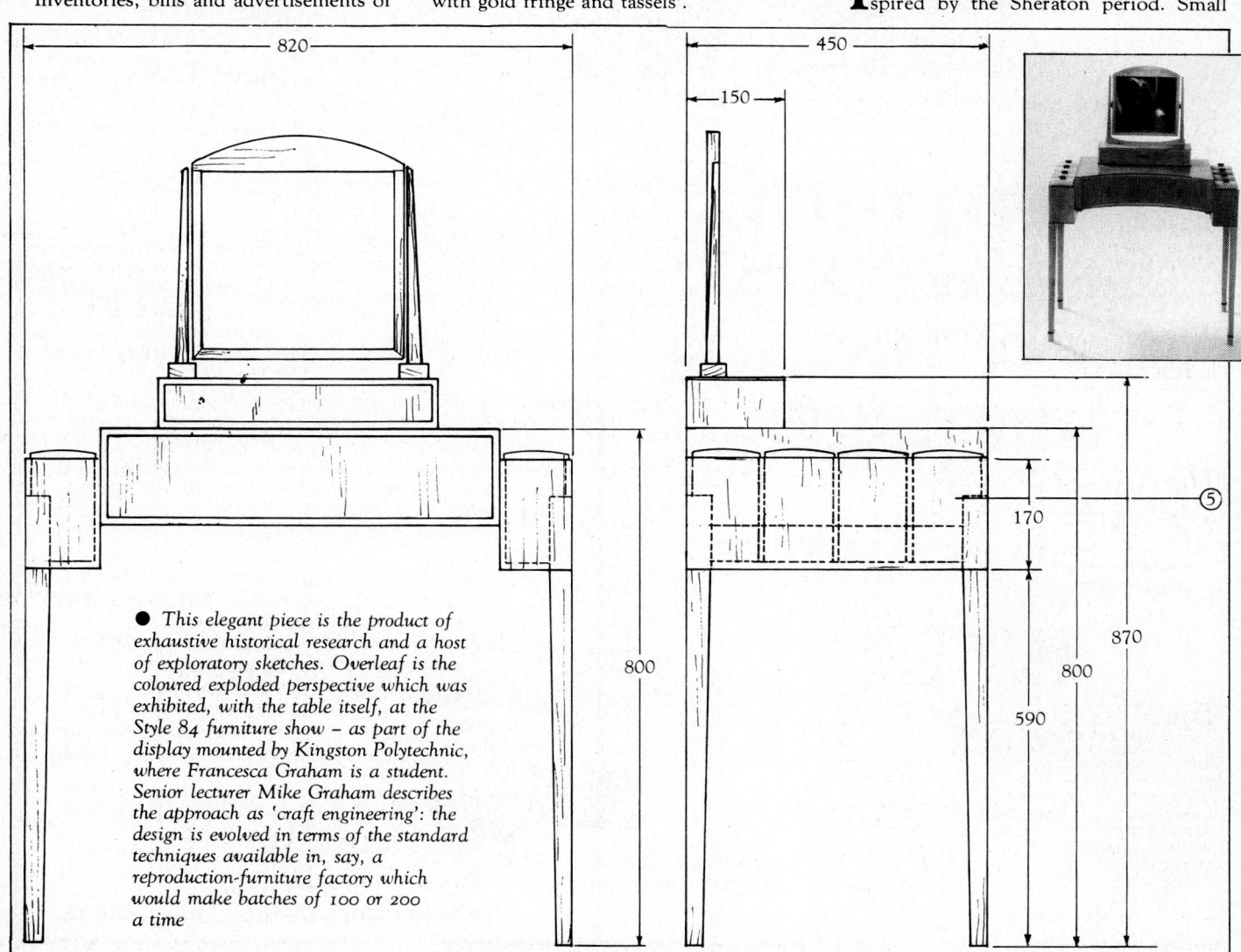

● *This elegant piece is the product of exhaustive historical research and a host of exploratory sketches. Overleaf is the coloured exploded perspective which was exhibited, with the table itself, at the Style 84 furniture show – as part of the display mounted by Kingston Polytechnic, where Francesca Graham is a student. Senior lecturer Mike Graham describes the approach as 'craft engineering': the design is evolved in terms of the standard techniques available in, say, a reproduction-furniture factory which would make batches of 100 or 200 a time*

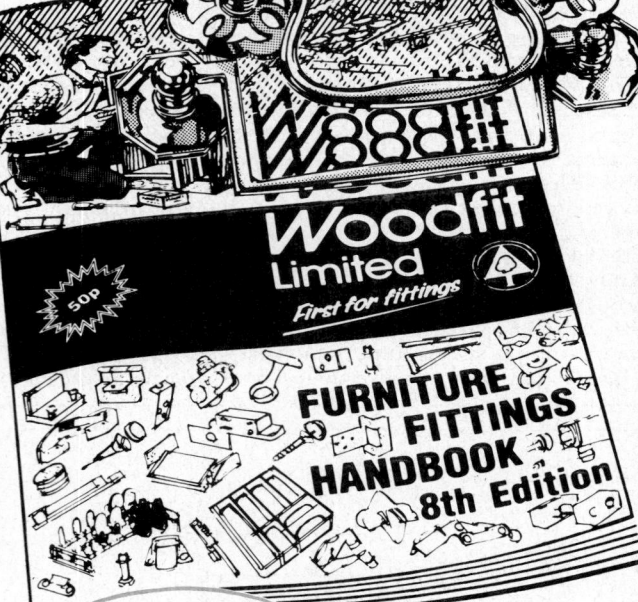

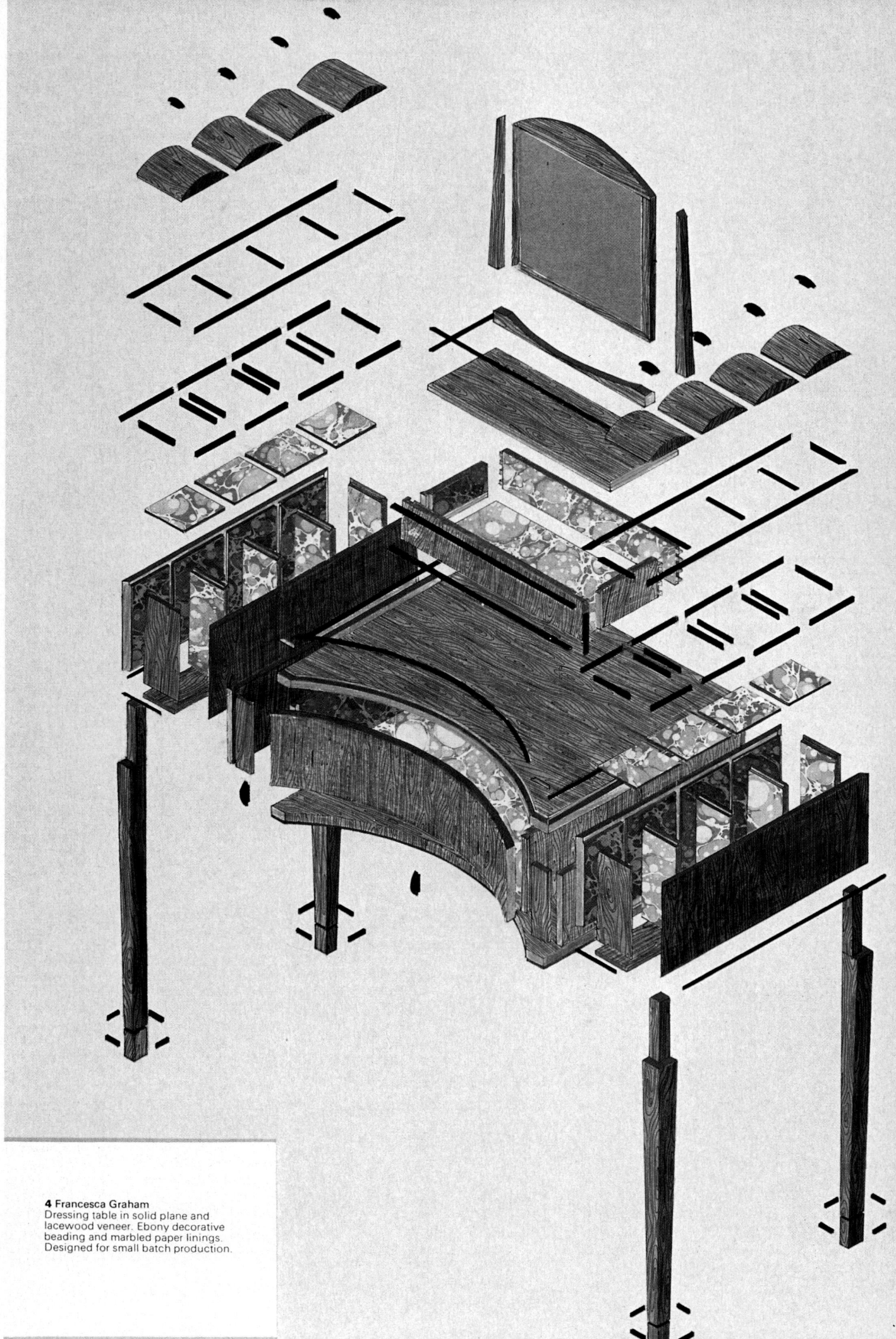

**4 Francesca Graham**
Dressing table in solid plane and
lacewood veneer. Ebony decorative
beading and marbled paper linings.
Designed for small batch production.

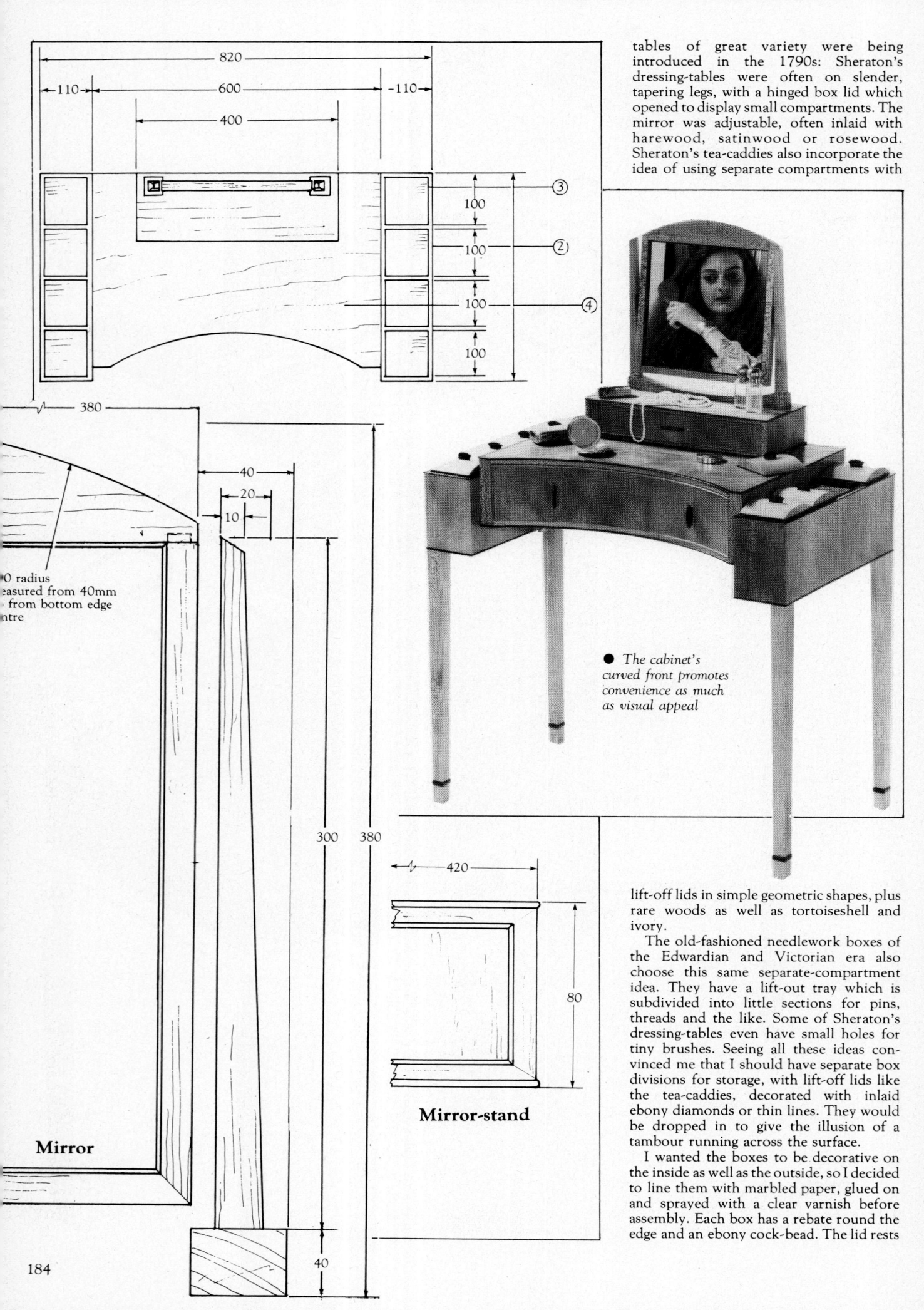

**Mirror**

820
110
600
400
110

100
100
100
100

③
②
④

380

40
20
10

0 radius
easured from 40mm
 from bottom edge
ntre

300 380

40

**Mirror-stand**

420

80

• *The cabinet's curved front promotes convenience as much as visual appeal*

tables of great variety were being introduced in the 1790s: Sheraton's dressing-tables were often on slender, tapering legs, with a hinged box lid which opened to display small compartments. The mirror was adjustable, often inlaid with harewood, satinwood or rosewood. Sheraton's tea-caddies also incorporate the idea of using separate compartments with

lift-off lids in simple geometric shapes, plus rare woods as well as tortoiseshell and ivory.

The old-fashioned needlework boxes of the Edwardian and Victorian era also choose this same separate-compartment idea. They have a lift-out tray which is subdivided into little sections for pins, threads and the like. Some of Sheraton's dressing-tables even have small holes for tiny brushes. Seeing all these ideas convinced me that I should have separate box divisions for storage, with lift-off lids like the tea-caddies, decorated with inlaid ebony diamonds or thin lines. They would be dropped in to give the illusion of a tambour running across the surface.

I wanted the boxes to be decorative on the inside as well as the outside, so I decided to line them with marbled paper, glued on and sprayed with a clear varnish before assembly. Each box has a rebate round the edge and an ebony cock-bead. The lid rests

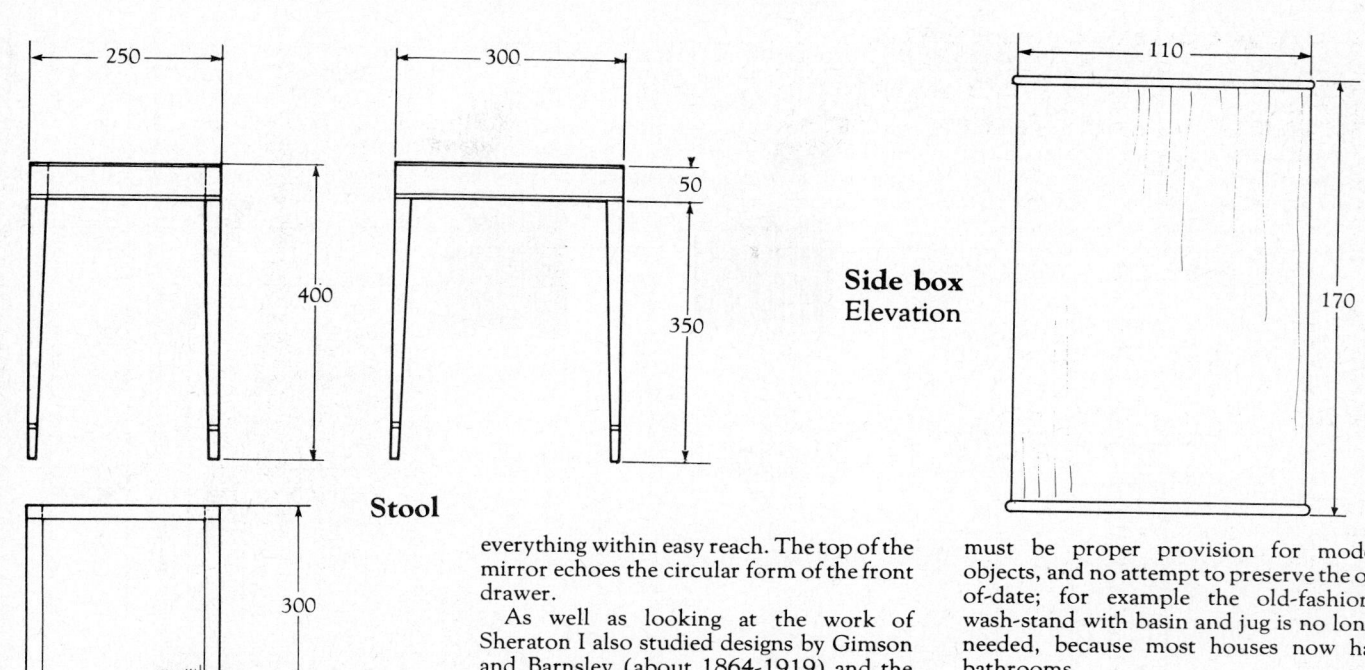

**Stool**

**Side box**
**Elevation**

on the top of the cock-bead, so that when it is on a thin black line shows round the edge of each box. The ebony cock-bead is not just decorative; it stops the marble paper from tearing.

The corner boxes on each side are shallow, to keep cosmetics and jewellery, because the leg must fit inside rather than having bracing at the bottom. The two central boxes on each side are deeper.

Originally the legs were only tapered on one inside surface, to give the illusion of kicking outwards, but I realised they looked rather heavy so I decided to put a taper on both inside faces.

I chose the shape of the front because of the need to sit close to the mirror and have

everything within easy reach. The top of the mirror echoes the circular form of the front drawer.

As well as looking at the work of Sheraton I also studied designs by Gimson and Barnsley (about 1864-1919) and the slightly later work of Peter Waals, J. H. Sellers, Serge Chermayeff and Gordon Russell. Their inspiration is taken from period pieces interpreted in a new way. The rooms of today are much smaller than those which contained the furniture of our Georgian ancestors; a modern piece must be compact and of exactly the right dimensions for present-day use. There

must be proper provision for modern objects, and no attempt to preserve the out-of-date; for example the old-fashioned wash-stand with basin and jug is no longer needed, because most houses now have bathrooms.

I chose wood from the plane-tree because, quarter-cut, it has a very decorative figure (lacewood). The legs, mirror posts and frame are worked in solid timber and the rest is veneered.

There are ebony cock-beads round the top and bottom of each carcase as well as a decorative ebony band round each of the

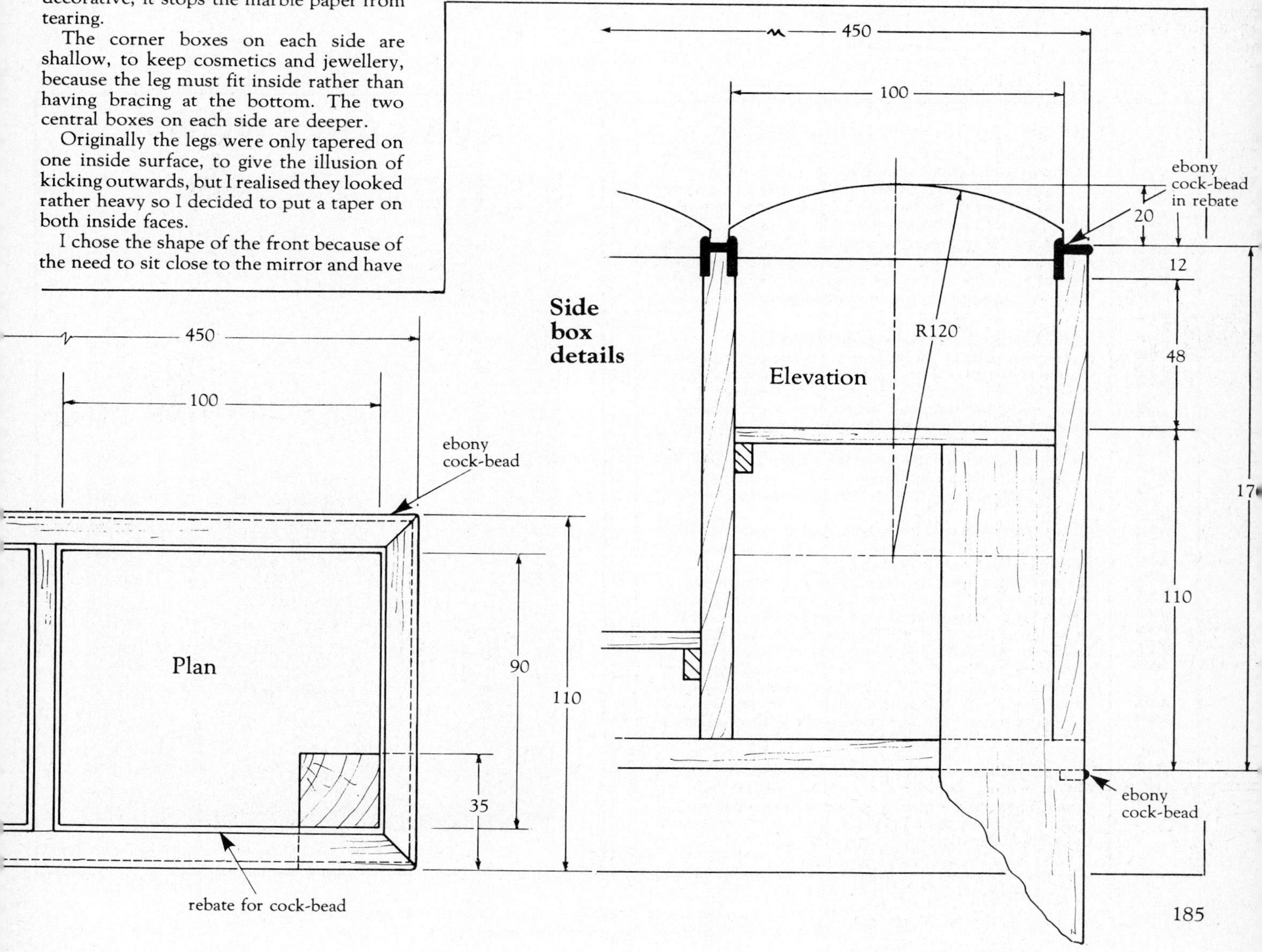

**Side box details**

Elevation

Plan

rebate for cock-bead

legs, to offset the plane. The cock-beads vary in thickness depending on where they are put.

The height of the central surface was arrived at by having a knee clearance height of 615mm on to which is placed the central drawer assembly, bringing the height up to 800mm. 615mm allows for a great deal of leg-room clearance, so that the user may sit cross-legged comfortably.

The table surface is cut away towards the mirror, and — along with the arrangement of the storage boxes down either side — this means that the storage space and mirror form an arc round the user. The mirror is part of this arc and is adjustable by touch. ∎

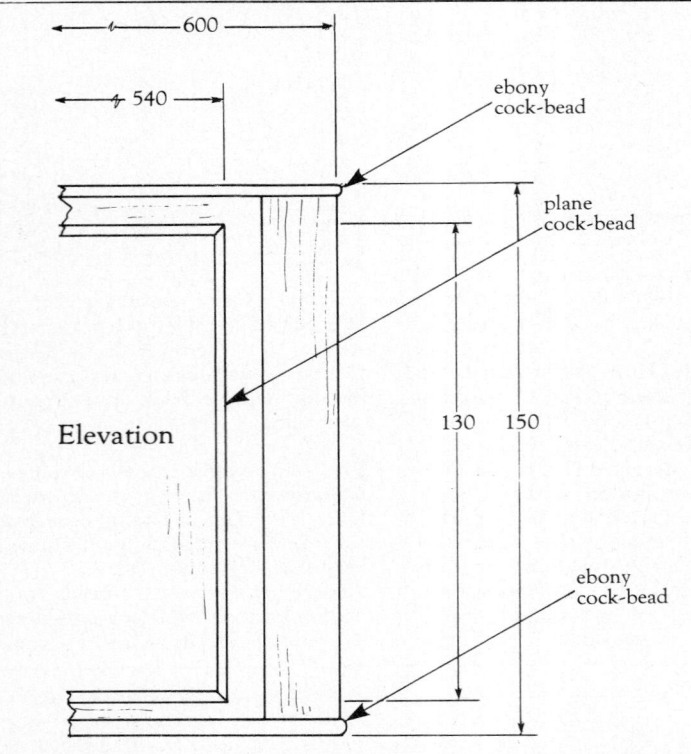

600

540

ebony cock-bead

plane cock-bead

Elevation

130  150

ebony cock-bead

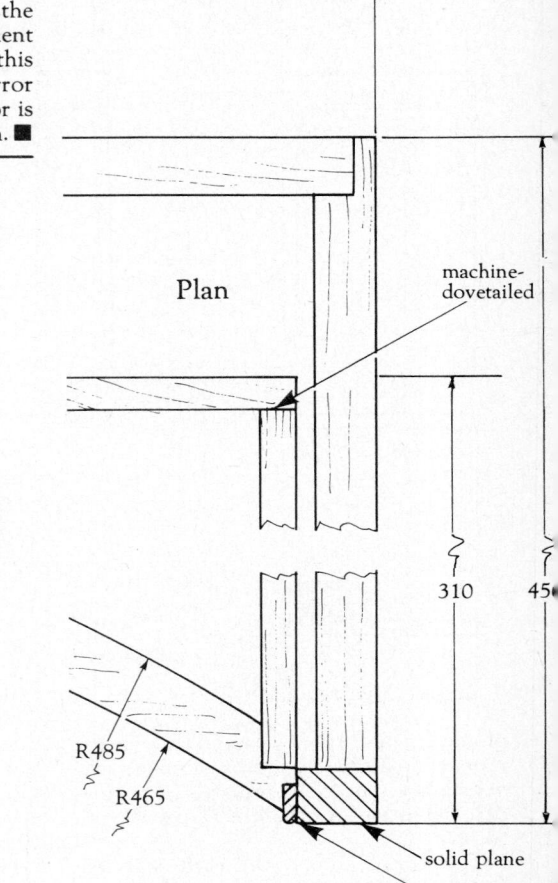

600

Plan

machine-dovetailed

Centre section and drawer

310   45(

R485

R465

solid plane

ebony cock-

# Colouring wood~complete!

Noel Leach presents everything (but *everything*) you need to know about stains and staining

Having produced a coffee-table or a staircase, why colour the wood? The various dyeing or staining agents can be used for any of the following reasons:
● To give the wood an artistic or decorative appearance.
● To show up or emphasise the graining and figuring. (Figure is a term used to describe unusual or attractive patterns in the texture and natural colour of timber. 'Ribbons' or 'burls' are revealed by skilled cutting of the log in the sawmills.)
● To match new woods to old and to blend different woods, for instance when repairing antiques and veneers.
● To make inferior woods such as pine resemble — for instance — walnut: a common practice in the furniture trade.
● Tradition — the colouring of wood has been practised for thousands of years. The ancient Egyptians covered their furniture in heavy coloured shellac and gold leaf, as relics in their excavated tombs reveal.
● To preserve the wood. Most external preservatives have colouring matter in them as well as preserving salts and chemicals, and the Cuprinol, Craftsman and Blackfriar ranges of fluid external wood preservatives include colours like red cedar, dark oak and transparent green. The faithful creosote is also now available in light golden and dark shades.

Colouring wood is an exciting adventure for both the amateur and the skilled professional. The wonderful effects that the various materials can create are innumerable, but to use them to their full potential you need to know what's available.

Wood colours fall into two main categories — pigments, and dyes or stains. (I shall not be dealing here with coloured waxes, or with coloured lacquers for spraying as finish coatings.)

## Pigments

Pigments are used when obliteration or partial obliteration of the wood is required, and consist basically of natural earth colours such as brown umber, burnt sienna, yellow ochre, titanium white, brunswick green, ultramarine blue, and so on. They are most frequently used by the professional wood-finisher, for either spray application or touching-in, and are best mixed with methylated spirits, plus a little white shellac as a binder.

A point to bear in mind is that pigments mixed in this way do not penetrate the grain but merely float 'dry' on top of the surface. They tend not to be very light-fast, but are nevertheless excellent for touching in or 'tea-wash' spray coatings over stained surfaces to blend in a colour. Pigments can be obtained from artist's shops and trade houses.

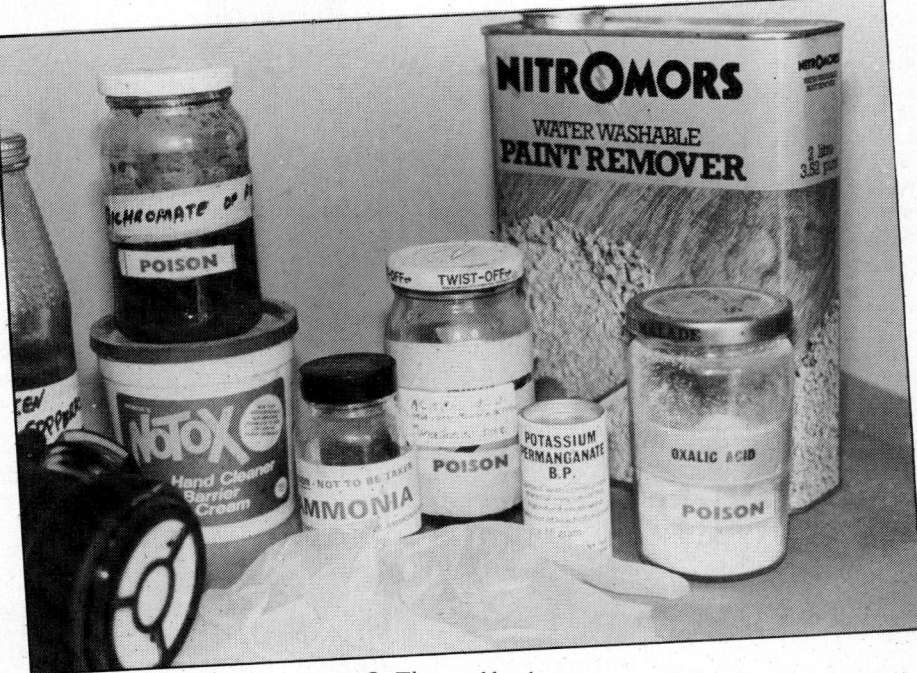

● *The woodfinisher's armoury. Only a handful of the vast range of products is pictured here*

## Dyes and stains

Produced from aniline and coal-tar sources, dyes or stains are intended to colour the wood without obliterating the grain. They do this by penetrating the fibres of the wood; because different fibres absorb varying amounts of the fluid, the effect can enhance the beauty of attractive figuring or graining. A knot in pine, for instance, will absorb very little stain, but endgrain will drink up a large amount. Dyes are soluble in spirit, water or oil, depending on their type; they must be light-fast or fade-proof — and, very importantly, must have minimum chemical reactivity with surface coatings.

Those available to the craftsman are:
● Oil stains — Colron by Sterling Roncraft, Blackfriar by E. Parsons & Sons, and Rustins;
● Spirit stains, from artist's shops and trade houses;
● Chemical stains, from various sources such as chemists, Fiddes & Co. and John Myland Ltd;
● Water stains — Furniglas;
● Varnish stains;
● Naphtha stains;
● Preservatives with added colours, mainly for external use — e.g. the Blackfriar, Cuprinol, Craftsman, Sadolin and Dulux ranges, obtainable from ironmongers and builder's merchants.

## Oil stains or dyes

These are the most common stains on the DIY market. They are ready-made and supplied in various convenient quantities ready for use. Most manufacturers produce a full selection of colours, typically light oak, medium oak, Jacobean dark oak, Spanish mahogany, mahogany, walnut, teak and cedar.

The Blackfriar range by Parsons of Bristol is spirit-based (it uses turpentine substitute) with a small amount of binder to hold the colour; drying time is from six to 10 hours according to temperature. Oil stains work on new solid wood, restored surfaces, plywood, chipboard, blockboard, MDF, veneers and hardboard; they will sink deeply into the surface and enhance the beauty of the grain.

### Application

1 Empty the contents from the manufacturer's tin into another tin with a broad open neck.
2 Apply with a fad or lint-free linen cloth, or a polisher's mop. Work in the direction of the grain — **never** across it; apply as quickly as possible and avoid overlapping.
3 Apply one coat at a time and allow to dry out thoroughly before applying the second.
4 Leave for six to 10 hours in a dry, warm place before applying a surface coating.

If you intend to use a finishing coat of varnish such as polyurethane, a thin coating of bleached shellac should first be applied over the stain, allowed to dry and lightly sanded down with 320 Lubrisil silicon-carbide abrasive paper. This will prevent the stain from 'bleeding' when the varnish is applied.

### Advantages

● Oil stains can be bought ready for use in 125ml, 250ml, 500ml and 2.5-litre tins.
● Colour charts are available, and stains in the same product range can be intermixed. (It is *not* advisable to mix stains from different manufacturers.)
● They can be ordered repeatedly without fear of any colour variation.
● They are simple to use and can be applied by brush, mop or fad.

- They penetrate very well.
- When dry, they leave the grain clear and un-obliterated.
- They artistically improve the graining.
- They do not raise the grain.
- The stain is reversible with oil solvents such as white spirit, and can therefore be easily stripped off if required.
- They are ideal for covering very large surfaces such as wall panels.
- They are light-fast or resistant to fading.

**Disadvantages**
- The shades available are limited to timber colours.
- Drying times are slow.
- Lacquers, varnishes and waxes will make the stain bleed if applied directly over it.
- Oil stains react in particular ways on certain woods. For instance, if a rosewood colour is applied to mahogany it will darken it, but on pine it will give a patchy, greasy red/brown effect. Areas around knots will absorb very little stain, showing up light, while endgrain will drink large amounts and show up dark.
- They can be somewhat expensive.
- They are not suitable for use under lacquer where a completely heat-, stain- and water-resisting finish is required. They therefore tend to reduce the lacquer's advantages.

### Spirit stains
These stains are made up from dyes such as aniline, or from pigments dissolved in methylated spirits with a little bleached shellac as a binder. This cuts down the range of colours, as not all aniline dyes are spirit-soluble. Dyes for spirit stains include bismarck brown, chrysoidine (red), purple and greens, while for pigments brown umber, yellow ochre, burnt sienna, orange chrome and black oxide are the important colours.

These stains have limitations. They are used mainly to obliterate the grain on wood, and are made as strong as possible for this purpose simply by adding more of the aniline or pigment powder colour to the spirit-and-shellac medium. For a very thin 'tea-wash', very small amounts of the colours can be used.

**Application**
Drying is rapid because of the evaporation of the spirit, so these stains must be applied quickly. Apply with a mop, brush or rag — again in the direction of the grain, never across it. Avoid overlapping, as this will cause streaks.

**Advantages**
- Very fast drying time because of spirit evaporation — two to 10 minutes.
- Very strong colours which can be intermixed for obliteration of the grain.
- These stains can be sprayed on as a 'tea-wash' to blend in a colour.
- They are excellent for touching up — applying by pencil brush for highlights and colouring over faults in wood.
- They can be used for simulating grain effects.
- They will not raise the grain of the wood.

**Disadvantages**
- They are not light-fast, and tend to fade.
- They have poor penetration, tending to 'float dry' on top of a surface.
- Because of the very short drying time, it is difficult to cover large areas and to avoid overlapping.

- They obliterate the grain whenever they are used.
- There is a limited colour range.
- They are not pre-packed and colour-controlled like oil stains, so there is no continuity in colour blending.
- Skill is required in their application.

### Chemical stains
These consist of chemicals which cause reactions in the natural chemical structure of the wood fibres, producing changes of colour. Most chemicals used by the wood finisher for staining can be found in an ordinary household, in either the kitchen or the garden shed, and can be obtained from the local chemist, hardware store or grocer. They are mainly used by antique restorers, and in other situations where mature colouring is required — for example, repairing church furniture to blend with the old colour. But there is no reason why a skilled amateur should not get good results.

Chemical stains fall into two groups, **alkalis** and **acids**; both are water-based.

- *Touching in with pigments, shellac and methylated spirit*

Alkalis consist of series of compounds called bases, which are highly soluble in water and produce a caustic or corrosive solution. Acids are composed of hydrogen and other elements, and are also corrosive. Alkalis used by the wood finisher are ammonia, caustic soda (or lye) and washing soda; among the acids used are acetic, nitric, sulphuric and tannic.

Application varies with the stain.

**Advantages**
- Colours are permanent and light-fast.
- They penetrate deep into the fibres of the wood and react with the tannic acid in the timber to become part of its structure.
- They are cheap.

**Disadvantages**
- As they are water-based, they tend to raise the grain.
- Drying times are long — approximately 24 hours.
- Great care is required in handling many of them. Protective clothing, barrier creams, gloves and goggles should be used.
- They are not available pre-packed like oil and water stains.

It is impossible to describe every stain in this group, but the following three are among the more important.

**Acetic acid or white vinegar** — obtained from the kitchen. Place a few iron nails or bolts in about a cupful of white vinegar and allow to stand overnight. Strain off and bottle, making sure that you label the bottle

correctly. Try out on a piece of oak and watch the fantastic reaction. Within seconds the oak will darken or turn black, depending on how strong you have made the mixture of vinegar and nails. This solution is used to 'weather' oak, and should be applied as quickly as possible using a rag, fad or sponge.

**Permanganate of potash** — from the chemist. This is an old favourite. Its violet-coloured crystals, dissolved in (rain) water, will produce a warm brown colour when applied to beech, ash or oak. Once again apply with a rag, fad or sponge — but use plastic gloves, or the strong violet dye will be absorbed into the skin as well as the wood!

**Bichromate of potash** — from a chemist or trade house. This chemical, produced by a French craftsman decades ago, consists of bright yellow and orange crystals. When made up to a concentrated solution with warm water it makes an excellent stain for darkening oak, ash, mahogany or any other wood which contains strong tannic acid. Apply with a rag, fad or sponge.

**Using chemical stains: general**
- Always wear protective clothing, including gloves and goggles, when handling, and make sure you have good ventilation.
- When diluting acids, add them to water *slowly* — **NEVER** the other way round.
- Alkalis and acids must be stored in cool places, in glass containers and properly labelled.
- When chemical stains are dry, other stains such as oil or spirit types can be applied over them.

The colouring qualities of these chemicals cannot be precisely predicted, and once applied they are not reversible, so:
- always mix enough for a project in one batch;
- always try out the stain on an offcut of the timber you are using before applying it to the finished piece; in the case of an existing piece, try it out in a hidden place.

### Water stains
For the professional, these are the most important stains — and they are now becoming increasingly popular in DIY. The dyes used in water stains are from aniline and coal-tar sources.

Furniglas products, made by Evode Ltd of Stafford, come in a 12-colour range — golden, light, middle, dark, black and grey oak; teak; brown and red mahogany; rich brown walnut; rosewood; and moss green. All the colours can be intermixed, so virtually any shade can be produced. They are long-lasting stains which penetrate the timber and enhance the wood because they are transparent, neither obliterating the grain nor muddying the colour. When they are dry, water stains can be finished with any surface coating — varnish, nitrocellulose or catalysed lacquers, french polish, oil or wax.

They should be applied by rag, fad or sponge, with the direction of the grain, as quickly as possible, and without over-lapping.

**Advantages**
- Any colour or shade can be produced for matching.

● They are obtainable in pre-packaged bottles or as powders.
● They will not fade in strong sunlight or from weather.
● They give a clear, transparent colour.
● They do not obliterate the grain.
● They are reasonably cheap.
● They have no 'after-coating' effect, no matter what finish is applied over them.
● They do not leave a muddy surface when they have dried.
● They are ideal for all cellulose surface coatings because there is no chemical interaction.

**Disadvantages**
● The solvent is water, which raises the grain and causes a rough surface. To avoid this the wood should be wetted and allowed to dry, then sanded down with garnet paper, before the application of water stains.
● They cannot be used on veneers fixed with water-bonded glue. Generally, trouble arises when you use water stains on veneers in any case.
● Skill is required in application to avoid streaks and overlaps.
● On certain woods such as teak, ebony and cedar they have poor penetration.
● At least 12 hours' drying time must be allowed, depending on the temperature.

**Using water stains**
● Vandyke brown crystals dissolved in water make a traditional water stain for walnut shades. A little added ammonia or detergent will help the stain to penetrate deeper into the fibres of the wood.
● Rainwater is better than tap-water for mixing water stains, particularly in very hard-water areas such as London and Gloucestershire.
● The surface must be bone-dry before any surface coating can be applied.

## Varnish stains
These offer a method of applying both a colour and a surface coating to wood in one operation. Varnish stains will greatly improve pale and uninteresting woods by simple application straight from the tin with a good varnish brush.

It is best to apply one coat and allow it to dry for about 72 hours. Sand this with Lubrisil 320-grade silicon-carbide paper, and then dust it off with a Tak rag. Finally, apply one or two coats of polyurethane gloss, semi-gloss (satin) or matt varnish — whichever you prefer.

Blackfriar make 10 stained varnish wood shades — light, medium and dark oak, deep red mahogany, Jacobean oak, sapele shade, dark Jacobean, dark mahogany, walnut, and teak. All are available in 125ml, 250ml, 500ml and 2.5-litre tins. The firm also produce a polyurethane varnish in high gloss, semi-gloss and matt which has exceptional resistance to wear, alcohol, dilute acids and abrasion.

Furniglas have a range of 18 colours, and produce an exciting moss green and a red mahogany. Other brands are available.

**Advantages**
● They are very easy to apply straight from the tin.
● Very little skill is required.
● A good choice of colours is available from most manufacturers.
● They have a reasonable drying time —

six to 12 hours.
● They will not fade.
● They are ideal for inexpensive furniture and joinery work.
● They are easily available from DIY, hardware and ironmongery shops.

**Disadvantages**
● They have very poor penetration.
● They are not suitable for antique furniture or high-class work.
● The surface finish shows a heavy build-up of varnish.
● They have a tendency to obliterate the grain.
● They require good ventilation during application, particularly the polyurethane type.

## Naphtha stains
These penetrating stains are produced mainly for the trade. They give a transparent colour to the wood, free from muddiness and reasonably light-fast. They are easy to apply by either rag or fad, and dry very quickly. Special naphtha thinners must be used — white spirit and distillates are definitely not recommended with this type of stain. Normal wood-colouring shades are produced by various manufacturers.

**Advantages**
● They have very rapid drying times — bone-dry within the hour, so work can proceed very quickly.
● They do not show a green fluorescence under cellulose, as some other stains do.
● They come as batch-controlled, ready-to-use fluids in containers.
● They are ideal for a production line.

**Disadvantages**
● They are expensive.
● They are not recommended for spraying, shading or touching in.
● Special thinners must be used as a solvent.
● Skill is required in application; because of their rapid drying and extreme penetration qualities, overlapping is a danger.

## Wood-preserving stains
These are not basically stains at all, but oils containing various active chemical ingredients such as naphthenate, which also include added colouring matter.

The two major manufacturers of these products are Cuprinol and Signpost, who both produce ranges of coloured preservative fluids. Red cedar, for instance, is specially formulated to protect and re-colour weathered western red cedar shingles, cladding and the like. Other colours produced are dark oak, light oak and green. The clear fluid, on the other hand, contains no added colour and is used where preservation but no coloration is required. The oaks are ideal for treating large floor-board areas and interior beams as well as external woodwork, whereas the green is mainly for greenhouses, seedboxes, joists and rafters. Most preservative stains have a low odour and soon dry to a satin sheen.

Application is usually by brush, but you can spray where access is difficult.

**Advantages**
● They are cheaper than paint.
● They are water-resistant.

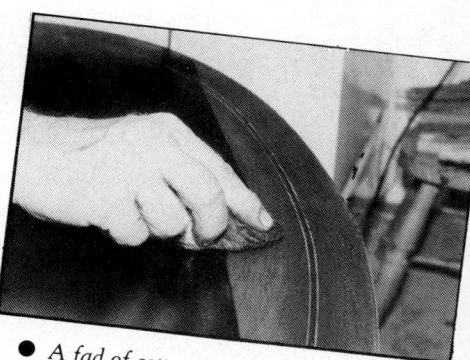
● *A fad of cotton wadding is being used here to apply stain*

● They prevent rot and insect attack.
● They have a low odour.
● They dry rapidly.
● They are colour-fast.
● They are harmless to plant life.

**Disadvantages**
● Care must be taken to provide adequate ventilation when they are used for interior work.
● Protective clothing must be worn; gloves and a hand barrier cream to prevent skin troubles or discoloration, plus a face-mask when using the fluids in confined spaces.
● Most of these fluids have fumes which are harmful to fish; animals and children, too, should be kept away from treated areas until they have dried out.

**Using wood-preservative stains**
● When treating a whole floor area, cover it with polythene when application is complete. This will prevent fumes from contaminating the whole house.
● Use a good paintbrush for application.
● Wipe off any spillages on paintwork immediately with white spirit.
● Do not smoke, drink or eat when using these fluids.
● Always apply to external surfaces when the wood is bone-dry and the grain open — a hot dry day is ideal.

## Addresses
Blackfriar — E. Parsons & Son Ltd, Blackfriars Road, Nailsea, Bristol BS19 2BU; Furniglas — Evode Ltd, Common Road, Stafford ST16 3EH; Sterling Roncraft, Chapeltown, Sheffield S30 4YP; Tak rags — Grand Chemicals International Ltd, Hayes Lane, Lye, Stourbridge, West Midlands DY9 8PJ; John Myland Ltd, 80 Norwood High Street, London SE27 9NW; Fiddes & Son, Florence Works, Brindley Road, Cardiff CF1 7TX; Cuprinol Ltd, Adderwell, Frome, Somerset BA11 1NL; Signpost Paints, Haverhill, Suffolk CB9 8PQ. ■

● *This mahogany tabletop has been stained with a water-based product, applied along the grain*

# Wood finishes: What and where?

Fine finishing materials, and the gear for applying them, can be almost as elusive as they're numerous — and vital. Here's our guide to the specialist firms who can supply the goods you're searching for

Readers' queries in *Woodworker* are just one indication that wood finishing is a major area of puzzlement for many craftspeople. The question is always: Which materials should I use for a particular job? How should I use them? And frequently: Where can I get them?

What's more, the answers are rarely straightforward, for there's no denying that fine finishing takes experience, knowledge and practice. Chemistry sees to that; and the difficulties of working with specialised and often volatile substances (which dry off, and which sometimes refuse to be compatible with one another) are compounded by their extraordinary number and variety — not to mention the number and variety of the timbers they may be used to anoint.

Timber, in fact, is finishing's main rival for first place in the bewilderment stakes. However, the perplexed craft woodworker faced with a finishing problem has one great advantage over his colleague who's faced with a problem in buying wood: namely, the attitude of the trade. Timber merchants who really enjoy helping the small user are as leaves on an oaktree in January. Finishing is different.

If you're a keen woodworker aiming for top-class results you cannot, of course, rely on a tin of something you've bought in Texas Homecare. Ronseal polyurethane varnish has its honourable place, but you cannot hope for a really good finish on every job unless you acquaint yourself with at least some of the immense range of specialised materials, both ancient and modern, and indeed of brushes, abrasives and other ancillary items.

For these you will need to go to the specialised finishing suppliers. However, as this guide shows, they are not only fairly numerous, but also (in many if not all cases) willing or even anxious to help and advise. 'We operate a full advisory service'; 'We offer full technical assistance', they say. And several provide — in addition to their product lists, which are already valuable information resources — admirable explanatory sheets, notably on french-polishing, whose detail, conciseness and practical good sense often knock spots off anything you can find in a glossy hardback book.

What we cannot do here is to mention all the products stocked. There are probably over a thousand, and there's a very considerable overlap between suppliers. Waxes, for example, are stocked by nearly all the firms listed. However, waxes alone vary greatly in colour, composition, durability and so on, and there is no easy short cut to choosing the right one for a given job. You could do worse than to circularise all these companies. In fact, a great many of them manufacture 'own-brand' products and complete ranges to their own unique formulas.

Generally speaking, products include: oils, waxes, traditional varnishes, sanding sealers, polyurethane varnishes, french polishes, shellac lacquers, cellulose lacquers, pre-catalysed lacquers, acid-catalysed lacquers; strippers, bleaches, liquid and powder stains of several types, stoppings, grain-fillers; meths, turps, and other solvents; burnishing creams, coated abrasives, steel wool, polishing brushes, artist's brushes, varnishing brushes; paints; Scotch glue and synthetic adhesives . . . Plus more.

---

**Fiddes & Son**
Brindley Rd
Cardiff
CF1 7TX
(0222) 40323
'Manufacture a complete range of wood finishes supplied to the craftsman and small user. No minimum order value exists'. Mail-order service, callers and van delivery (delivery free on orders over £80). Products include Robjo waxes. There's also a very good package of information and advice.

**Henry Flack (1860) Ltd**
PO Box 78
Beckenham
Kent
BR3 4BL
01-658 2299
Major products include Briwax, a beeswax/carnauba mixture designed for bare timber, which can also be used over a sealer; Mr Flack's Olde English French Polisher Kit, which includes stain, oil, spirit, abrasives and instructions as well as polish; Sheradale Antique wax polish; and Mel-Pol, a french polish which contains melamine to bring about a dramatic improvement in wearing qualities.

**House of Harbru**
101 Crostons Rd

**Elton**
Bury
Lancs
BL8 1AL
061-764 6769
Mail-order suppliers who are a familiar sight at the Woodworker Show. Their products, mostly bearing their own brand name, are primarily for traditional finishing.

---

**James Jackson & Co. (London) Ltd**
76-9 Alscot Rd
London
SE1 3AW
01-237 2862-3
French polishes, synthetic lacquers, a good range of shellac and other varnishes, plus sundries.

---

**W. S. Jenkins & Co. Ltd**
Tariff Rd
London
N17 0EN
01-808 2336

---

**Liberon Waxes Ltd**
6 Park St
Lydd
Kent
(0679) 20107

Another Woodworker Show stalwart — again mail-order, but also through stockists (names supplied) and to callers. Especially strong in stoppings, including wax and shellac beaumontage, and in waxes; also supply other products mainly for traditional methods, notably oil-free steel wool. 'The company runs a free consumer/user advice service'.

**Marrable & Co. Ltd**
22 Bateman's Row
London EC2
01-739 3299;
Delamare Rd
Cheshunt
Herts
EN8 9SP
(0992) 37361

---

**F. T. Morrell & Co.**
214 Acton Lane
London NW10
01-965 1782

---

**John Myland Ltd**
80 Norwood High St
London
SE27 9NW
01-670 9161
01-761 5754

A colossal range of both traditional finishes (waxes, french polishes), and modern ones which include spraying and brushing lacquers — shellac, cellulose, polyurethane, melamine: pre-cat and acid-cat. Also many other things. Full information sheets deal with many of these products in great detail, and in some cases carry step-by-step instructions.

---

---

● And, of course, there's the new breed of woodworking store which carries specialist finishes (often from makers listed here) along with tools, machines, other equipment and timber in varying combinations. These include John Boddy Timber of Boroughbridge; Charltons of Frome; Craft Supplies of Buxton; Matthews of Tamworth; The Old Stores Turnery of Willaston, Nantwich; and Sarjents Tools of Reading, Swindon and Oxford — all regular advertisers in *Woodworker*. ■

# Yesterday's wheels

*Jocelyn Bailey describes a fascinating restoration job from a Kentish wheelwright's workshop*

I thought I had got used to living in a sort of village-wheelwright's-shop time-capsule! My husband is a fourth-generation village wheelwright and carpenter — but recently even I had an eye-opener when he voluteered to re-build a pair of wheels for an old Kentish wheeled turnwrest plough. It belongs to a local man who wanted to restore it as a museum piece.

These old horse- or ox-drawn ploughs were still in use early in this century, but no one really knows just how far back they were in existence. Of course, like other agricultural implements, they were made locally by the wheelwrights and carpenters; the blacksmith made most of the iron parts apart from the cast pieces, which came from a foundry.

This pair of wheels came in with the wood eaten and rotted away but recognisable. The iron parts were in very nice condition, which made the job manageable and interesting. Here was a sight not seen in our old shop for many years — yet my husband knew and did the job as if only yesterday there had been a production line of Kent plough-wheels!

Under the old workbench there are still some unused heel-plates for Kent ploughs, and overhead lies a worm-eaten length of wood marked off as a pattern to give the measurements for plough beams.

The work on these wheels proceeded much as for ordinary waggon wheels; one difference, however, is that there are fewer spokes for such 'trent-tyred' wheels, and there are no wooden felloes. The iron trents are slim and they cut through the soil with less clogging up. They are held in place by two iron sprigs or 'calves teeth' driven into the spoke ends, each of which is protected by an iron ferrule. As with most wooden wheels the nave is made of elm and the spokes of cleft oak.

The most striking piece of historical re-enactment came with the boxing of these wheels — a procedure I never expected to see in my lifetime. Quarter-boxes like the ones on this plough only exist in old wheels which ran on wooden axles. The later boxes were in one piece and ran on iron axle-ends. The wheelwright's gouge is shown being used to prepare the centre for boxing. The two quarter-boxes for the front and back of the nave are cast iron, so must be driven into the nave carefully to avoid breakage; a really thick piece of wood is placed to even out the impact of the sledge.

When the plough is eventually fully restored by its owner, I look forward to seeing it on show at the museum. But my mind will be on the scene at our old shop. ■

● *Above: Using a wheelwright's gouge to prepare the nave for boxing*

● *Above right: Driving in one of the quarter-boxes with a sledgehammer*

● *Right: Trimming the wedges round the box*

## *on reflection . . .*

it's worth using Smith & Rodger products —
they set off your workmanship so well.

SMITH & RODGER LTD, manufacturers to the Woodfinishing Trades since 1877 still maintain the highest standards of quality and personal service. Our products include both the traditional and the latest in technical development and are always competitively priced.

# ESSAR WOODFINISHES

| | |
|---|---|
| French Polishes | — Shellac Sanding Sealer |
| Cellulose Lacquers | — Sealers — Pullover |
| Catalyst Lacquers | — Precatalysed Lacquers |
| Spirit Varnishes | — Polyurethane Varnish |
| Drawer Edge Paint | Q.D. Spirit Paints |
| Industrial Paints | Wood Bleach Soln. |
| Spirit Stains | Dry Colours |
| Oil Stain | Dry Stain |
| Water Stain | Strippers |
| Shading Stains | Wax Polishes |
| Precatalysed Stains | Wood Grain Fillers |

Linseed & Teak Oils — Stoppers — Hard Waxes
Methylated Spirit — White Spirit — Solvents
Polishing Cloths — Mutton Cloth — Staining Cloth
Abrasives — Garnet & Glass Paper — Steelwool
PVA Woodworking & Contact Adhesive — Pearl
Glue — Polishing Mops — Paint & Artists Brushes

Our Technical Representatives cover the Midlands, North of England and Scotland and will gladly call if requested. Visit or telephone Glasgow for practical advice from our experienced laboratory staff.

Package sizes to suit most needs, including popular products bottled for resale. Details on request.

Samples, leaflets, stock and price lists sent on request.

*Delivery by our own transport in many areas or by national carriers nationwide is free on orders over £50.00.*

# SMITH & RODGER LTD.
## 32-36 ELLIOT STREET, GLASGOW G3 8EA.
### TEL: 041-248 6341

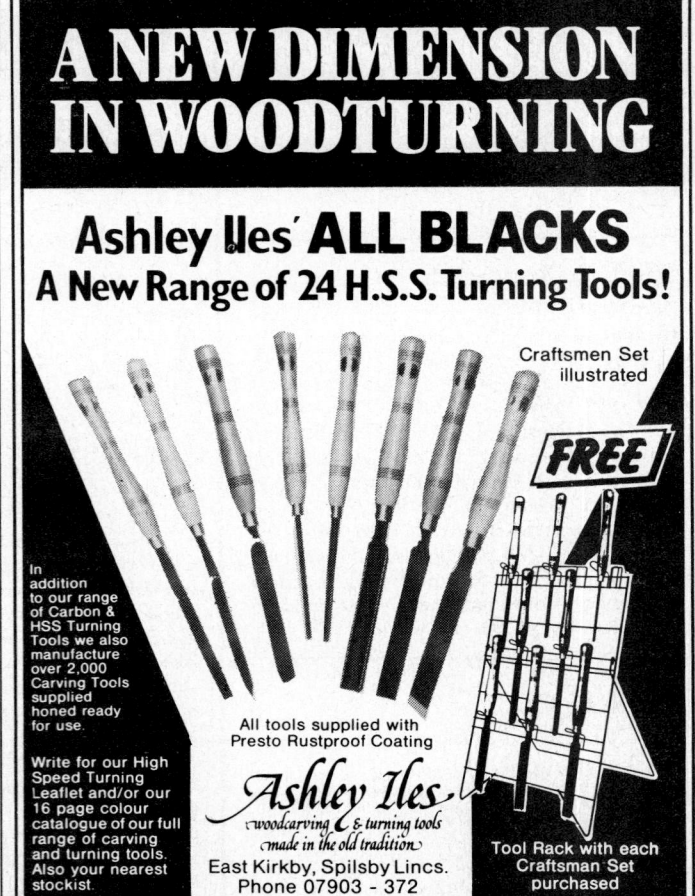

# A NEW DIMENSION IN WOODTURNING

## Ashley Iles' ALL BLACKS
### A New Range of 24 H.S.S. Turning Tools!

Craftsmen Set illustrated

**FREE**

In addition to our range of Carbon & HSS Turning Tools we also manufacture over 2,000 Carving Tools supplied honed ready for use.

Write for our High Speed Turning Leaflet and/or our 16 page colour catalogue of our full range of carving and turning tools. Also your nearest stockist.

All tools supplied with Presto Rustproof Coating

*Ashley Iles*
woodcarving & turning tools
made in the old tradition
East Kirkby, Spilsby Lincs.
Phone 07903 - 372

Tool Rack with each Craftsman Set purchased

# CHARLTONS
## TIMBER CENTRE
### OPEN TO BOTH PUBLIC AND TRADE

SPECIALISING IN HARDWOOD (HOME-GROWN & IMPORTED) ALL ON DISPLAY AND AVAILABLE FOR CUSTOMER SELECTION PLUS FULL MACHINE SERVICE SOFTWOODS — FINISHES — OFFCUTS AND TURNING BLOCKS — PORTABLE AND LIGHT WOODWORK MACHINERY — CABINET FIXTURES — FASTENINGS — TOOLS MOULDINGS

EVERYTHING FOR THE PROFESSIONAL AND AMATEUR WOODWORKER

PROBABLY THE LARGEST SELECTION OF HOME GROWN TIMBERS IN THE SOUTH WEST INCLUDING APPLE, ASH, BEECH, CEDAR, CHERRY, CHESTNUT, ELM, LIME, OAK, PEAR, SYCAMORE, WALNUT, YEW + FULL RANGE OF IMPORTED TIMBERS.

**GORDON STOKES**
Monthly Demonstrations — bring your turning problems. Sat. 16th February & Saturday 16th March. Large range of Lathes & Turning Tools.

## CHARLTONS TIMBER CENTRE, FROME ROAD, RADSTOCK, BATH. RADSTOCK 36229

# The acorn housewife

## Tobias Kaye presents an exquisite miniature project for the keen turner

As a woodturner, acorns fascinated me from early on. I attempted various sizes of simple hollow acorn, from life-size up, before hitting on this idea. The acorn-shaped body opens and holds one needle-case glued into the base; one cotton-bobbin sliding over the same needle-case, and one thimble fitting over the bobbin (fig. 6). Having made a few of these items, I discovered that the Victorians had done it all first. They called the kit a housewife (pronounced 'hussef'), and every sailor had one.

If you intend using yours you may wish to scale it up a bit, as the needles to fit this one (size 8 'betweens') are very small. One of my early ones, with larger needles, was given to a girl who found it most useful. The strap of her rucksack broke while she was hiking in upper Egypt, and it was only by sewing it up there and then with her acorn housewife that she was able to continue.

To make one you will need some small scrapers (fig. 7). Mine are HSS, made from engineer's parting-tools $\frac{1}{8}$in thick and $\frac{1}{2}$in wide. Failing that, old small files will do, though not so well. Ideally you need a chuck in your tailstock to hold drills; you can do all the work with the scrapers, but it's laborious. You will need a small quantity of close-grained hardwood. An exotic is ideal, but not necessary. I have successfully used African blackwood, tulipwood, boxwood, ebony, various rosewoods, holly, hornbeam, laburnum, sandalwood, plum, pear, ivy and ekki — to list them in order of preference.

For one acorn, cut four pieces of your chosen wood as follows:
$3\frac{1}{2}\times1\frac{1}{8}$in square for body and cap
$1\frac{1}{2}\times1\frac{11}{16}$in square for the thimble
$1\frac{1}{2}\times\frac{1}{2}$in square for the bobbin
$2\times\frac{5}{16}$in square for the needle-case.

I have always turned the pieces while holding them in a $\frac{1}{2}$in drill chuck. This has certain advantages, such as access for the tools and final delicate parting-off, but is not the most vibration-free mounting. You could also use a collet chuck or spigot chuck, or glue into waste wood for a screw-chuck. In each case, calculate the requirements for holding and clearance for final working, and alter your cutting list accordingly. (Compare with fig. 1.)

Prepare all the blanks between centres to fit whatever chucking method you're using (photo 1). Place the body-and-lid blank in the chuck at the lid end and part off the body section.

Forming the lid: drill out to $\frac{1}{2}$in with a $\frac{7}{8}$in twist bit ($\frac{3}{8}$in for a dowel bit or sawtooth bit, so as not to cut into the walls); photo 2. If you have no $\frac{7}{8}$in bit, use your largest and take out the rest with a scraper. Scraper no1 (fig. 7) is best for the lid — make it into the shape in fig. 2, complete with undercut. I find it easiest and safest to hold the scraper like a pen (photo 3); there

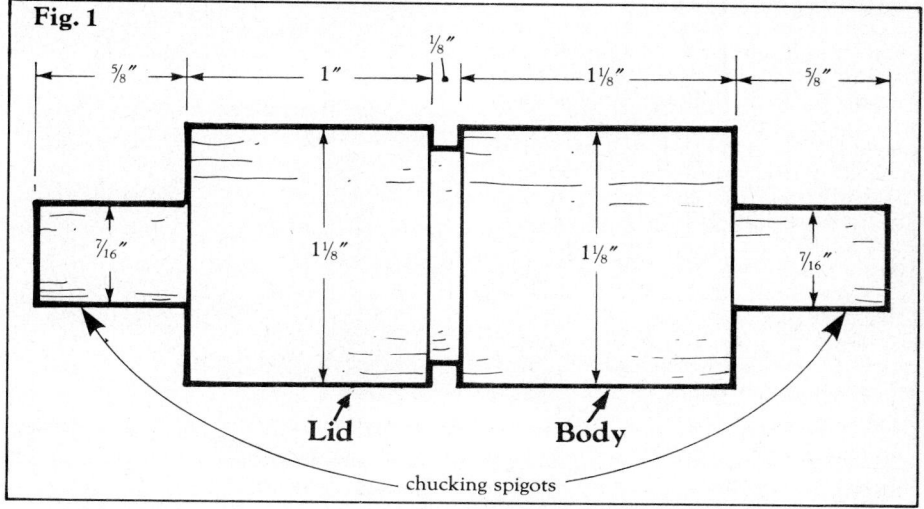

**Fig. 1**

$\frac{5}{8}$"  1"  $\frac{1}{8}$"  $1\frac{1}{8}$"  $\frac{5}{8}$"

$\frac{7}{16}$"  $1\frac{1}{8}$"  $1\frac{1}{8}$"  $\frac{7}{16}$"

**Lid**   **Body**

chucking spigots

are no handles on my scrapers. Now carefully round the leading edge slightly so that the lid will go easily on to the popper later. Sand out tooling marks with 400-grit flexible aluminium-oxide cloth.

Now cut the outside of the lid to the stage shown in photo 4. Sand as above, and polish inside and out before attempting the handle. This is perhaps the trickiest bit. I do it with the corner of a $\frac{1}{8}$in beading and parting tool — twisting while I cut, as with a skew. If you funk that, make the handle a simpler shape, such as the one shown by the dotted lines in fig. 6. No one will use it anyway.

Like the lid, the body is best begun with a drill — a $\frac{5}{8}$in twist-bit to $\frac{5}{8}$in deep (photo 5); shallower for a square-ended bit, as before. Do not cut the $\frac{7}{32}$in mortise for the needle-case yet. First shape the hollow. Tool no2 (fig. 7) is best for the job. Sand as above and polish before cutting the mortise. Cut the mortise with a $\frac{7}{32}$in drill-bit.

In photo 6 a $\frac{1}{4}$in wide bit of tape is stuck to the tailstock barrel to indicate how a depth guide for cutting this mortise should be made. Scratch the barrel slightly at the edges of this tape and take it off, as the action of the barrel will scrape it off anyway. Now line up the left-hand scratch mark at the point where it would disappear into the bore of the tailstock, with the right-hand scratch mark inside the bore. With the lathe stopped, slide the whole tailstock up till the point of the drill rests against the bottom of the hollow. Start the lathe and wind in the drill till the second mark shows.

Although in photo 6 the lid was fitted before the mortise was cut, afterwards is better to get the good pop fit. First cut the whole body down to 1in external diameter, then cut a taper $\frac{1}{8}$in long (narrowing towards the right) down to the size of the lid opening. Stop and offer up the lid. If it fits over, start the lathe and offer up the lid again. This will make a polished mark on the taper. Now cut the taper to the left of

● *The housewife's component parts. The finished ones on the right are blackwood, boxwood and holly*

193

**Photo 1**

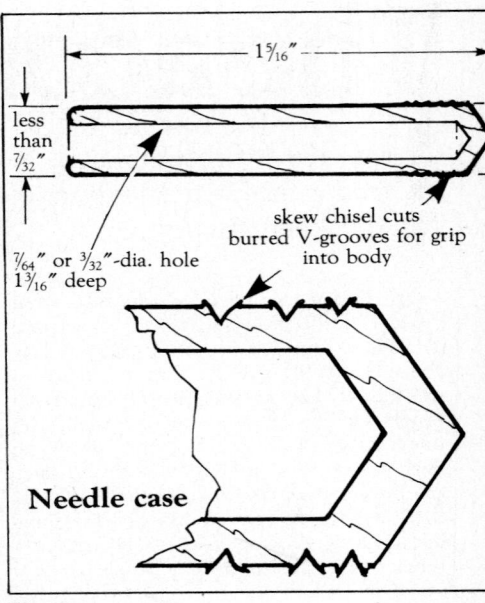

**Needle case**

1⁵⁄₁₆″

less than ⁷⁄₃₂″

⁷⁄₆₄″ or ³⁄₃₂″-dia. hole 1³⁄₁₆″ deep

skew chisel cuts burred V-grooves for grip into body

**Fig. 3**

this mark nearly flat and offer up the lid once more. It should go on no further.

Now cut to the left of the polished mark again — this time forming a very slight taper opposite to the first one, and creating a ridge (fig. 2). Burnish this ridge with the bevel of your tool, and the lid may pop on. If not, cut (scrape) off a couple of thou from the ridge and try again. If that doesn't work, burnish and try again; if no good, cut, etc., till a firm (not hard — I've split many lids) push gets the lid home. If this has been done right, the lid will not rattle around once over the slight ridge. During the whole process, bear in mind that (because of the rounded lips) the narrowest part of the lid is set slightly back from the edge. — fig. 2). Also note that the whole lid housing must not be longer than ⅛in, or the lid won't fit over the thimble (fig. 6).

Shaping the outside: as with the lid, take it down to a small neck first, sand it (except for the lid housing) and polish it before finishing the shape so that it drops off.

**Fig. 2**

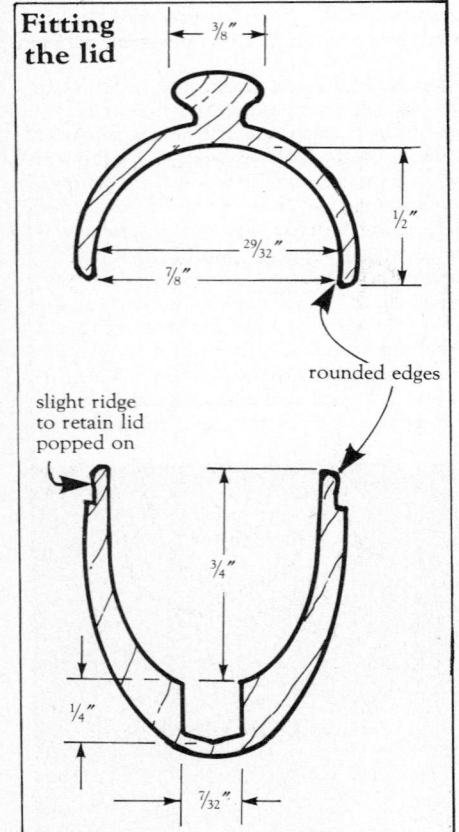

**Fitting the lid**

³⁄₈″

²⁹⁄₃₂″

⁷⁄₈″

½″

rounded edges

slight ridge to retain lid popped on

¾″

¼″

⁷⁄₃₂″

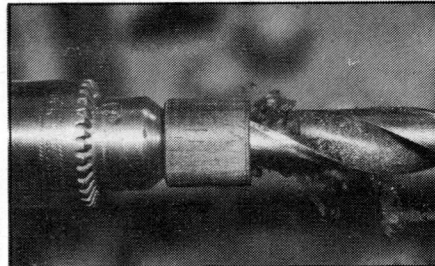

**Photo 2**

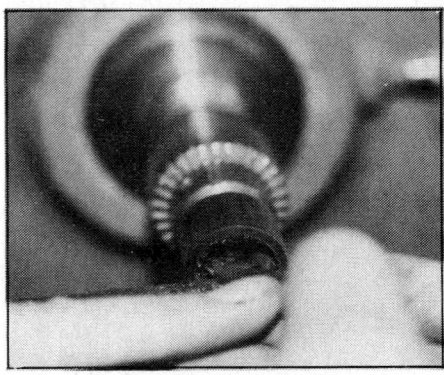

**Photo 3**

**Photo 4**

Photo 7 shows the needle-case made. Cut to ⁷⁄₃₂in, sand the main section to slightly less than this, and then raise a burr on the tenon section with the point of a skew (fig 3a). Drill the hole for the needles (photo 7) short of the bottom (fig. 3), or it will fill with glue during assembly. Open out the mouth of the needle hole with tool no3 in fig. 7 or with a twist of sandpaper. When you're assembling this part, the needle-case should go home with a few very light taps with a pin-hammer, the body resting on a piece of close-grained but softish wood. With rosewood and some others that even epoxies don't like, roughen the mortise by holding a ³⁄₁₆in drill in your hand and twisting and wiggling it in the hole.

To cut the thimble (fig. 4), I ground a drill to the shape of the inside (photo 8) after the first dozen or so, but a depth cut with a ¹⁹⁄₃₂in bit and hollowing with tool no1 is not difficult. This size fits a lot of fingers, but not all; if you're making yours as a present for someone, creep up and measure the finger when its owner isn't looking. Having got your finger size, you may find it necessary to taper your bobbin or swell your body to fit your thimble.

Photo 9 shows an offcut having been split halfway down, its length being used to sand the thimble out. Slide the end of a piece of abrasive into the crack and wind it round.

Photo 10 shows a depth check being

**Photo 5**

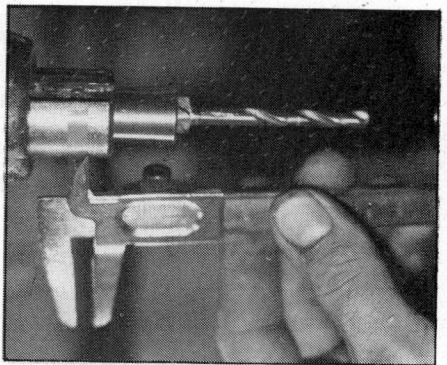

**Photo 6**

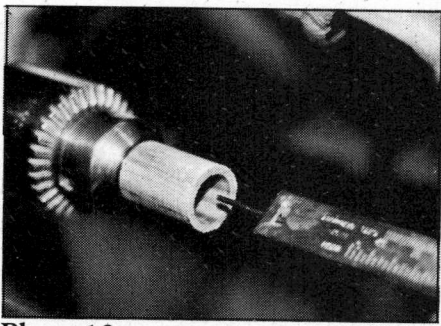

**Photo 10**

**Photo 11**

depth of the cotton recess cuts. Support the work with a revolving tailstock while cutting these (photo 15). Sand and polish.

As for winding the cottons — support the reel where it can spin freely, for example on a drill-bit held in the toolrest support (photo 16). Dampen the first 2in of cotton and wind by hand, then switch on and guide the cotton on with a clean hand; not too tight. Switch off before the reel is full, as the machine will run on. Wind the last few turns by hand up to one end of each recess, and pull the last winding tight against the wood. This will sink it in so it doesn't unwind. Cut the cotton.

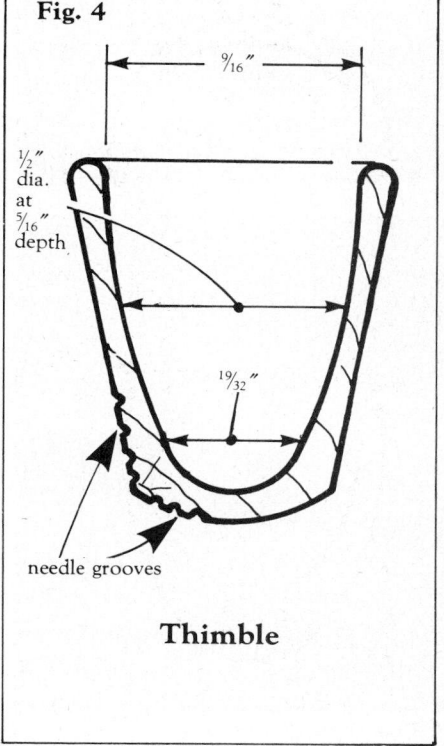

**Photo 12**

box, African black and some others will need finer still.

Please don't use friction polish. Hours of beautiful work are ruined if you paste the result with glossy plastic! I use a wax/oil blend — 50% good furniture wax (Fiddes Robjo or suchlike), 30% boiled linseed oil,

**Photo 7**

**Photo 8**

taken with the vernier to mark off the outside. Add 1/16in to the internal length to get the external length. Do the same for the body of the acorn. The thimble must not be too thick at the top or the lid won't close.

Photo 11 shows the needle-gripping grooves being cut in the side of the thimble — tool no3 in fig. 7 — for this job. Ground on two sides with the point squared off on an oilstone, this tool cuts clean grooves without raising a burr. To cut the grooves in the top of the thimble, first shape and polish the whole piece and cut off. Now make a spigot (photo 12) to match loosely but fairly accurately the inside of the thimble. Raise largish burrs on this with a skew as before; this should grip the thimble well enough for careful cutting of the grooves (photo 13).

To make the bobbin (fig. 5), drill the 7/32in hole first, as this helps to gauge the

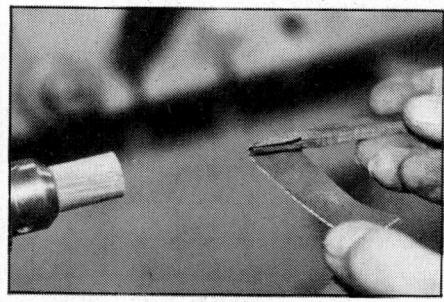

**Photo 9**

Two last words. Flexible abrasives are not easy to find. Offcuts of RB307 (the best) are available at the door from Tex Abrasives, Colchester. If you don't live there you could try a *good* wet-and-dry. Some people use Brasso on exotics; I haven't tried. 400 grit will do for most, but

**Fig. 4**

9/16"

1/2" dia. at 5/16" depth

19/32"

needle grooves

**Thimble**

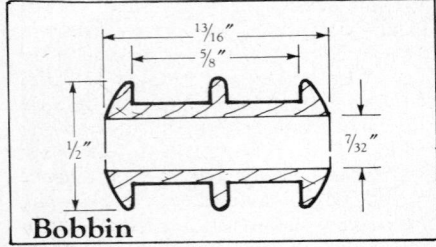

Bobbin
**Fig. 5**

alternative handle profile

**Fig. 6**

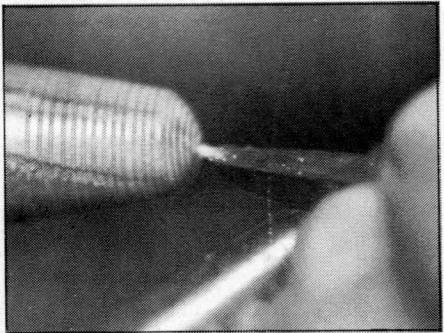

Photo 13

Photo 14

**Photo 15**

**Photo 16**

and about 20% nitro thinners. Melt the wax in a double-boiler, take it well away from the flames and add oil and thinners. Stir well. When cool, rub the mix into the stationary work by hand and burnish with a cloth until very hot. This sets the oil to seal the grain, and leaves a beautiful satin finish which is pleasing to the eye and touch. The formulation is suitable for all turning requiring a fine finish.

The acorn took me a day to make first time round, and three and a half hours last time. Writing it up took five or six times longer than making it! ■

**Fig. 7**

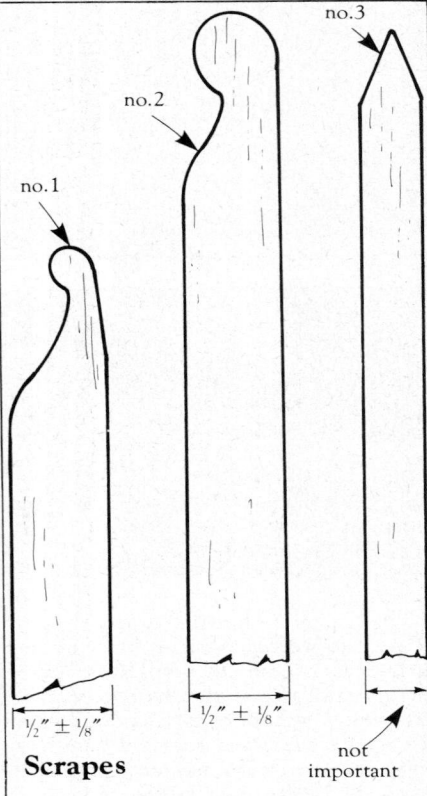

no.3

no.2

no.1

½" ± ⅛"    ½" ± ⅛"    not important

**Scrapes**

# The multifario

## Bill Brown sorts out your *Meliaceae* from your *Swietenia* (not to mention *Khaya*!)

**M**ahogany first became popular in Europe for furniture and cabinet-making during the reign of George I, and developed rapidly as a primary wood under the influence of designers like Hepplewhite and Sheraton. It had been introduced into Spain much earlier; in fact Philip II used mahogany for the library of the Escorial Palace in 1584.

This was the Spanish or Santo Domingo mahogany; African mahogany arrived on the European scene around the 1920s, during the resurgence of timber exploitation following World War I. Since it was also then that shipments of mahogany from the West Indies and Cuba were very much reduced, the increase in the supply of red woods from Africa and elsewhere took on a new significance: the botanically inappropriate name 'mahogany' was tacked on to a number of woods. There have been Gaboon 'mahogany', Philippine 'mahogany', satin 'mahogany' — and sapele 'mahogany', which is more of a misnomer than any other since the species does not even belong to the mahogany family!

Calling such woods 'mahogany' does them a disservice because it suggests special attributes which they do not possess, and sometimes obscures other, more favourable characteristics. Philippine mahogany was a popular trade name for red lauan; in disuse today, in 1932 there was a prolonged case in the American courts revolving round its legality in the marketing of lauan. Actually, the various lauans belong to a family totally unrelated to the *Meliaceae*, which produces the mahoganies.

In certain tropical areas, separate species of a particular genus are grouped under the same trade name for shipment. This is particularly so in south-east Asia, but also in other areas; some plywood is shipped from Africa under the description 'African redwoods'. This term does not imply an inferior product that looks like mahogany; it simply indicates that it conforms to BS 1455 for plywood manufactured from tropical hardwoods. Because of the many red woods available, and the difficulties in selecting the right type for the job, an attempt has been made to get some sort of order into the confusing array.

You can obtain true mahogany-faced plywood if it's essential for furniture or panelling, but for other uses any red-faced material will suit provided the glue line is appropriate. For boatbuilding, not only must the glue line be weather- and boil-proof, but the veneers must be of naturally durable species; not all the mahoganies and so-called mahogany meet this requirement.

The *Meliaceae* family contains two genera which produce mahogany — *Swietenia* and *Khaya*. *Entandrophragma* produces sapele and utile. Other genera in the family produce mahogany-type timbers, each with its own characteristics, but *Swietenia* and *Khaya* are the source of true mahogany.

# mahoganies

● *The now-familiar richness of mahogany was much less common in Britain when this chest of drawers was made in the 18th century*

## Mahoganies and their uses

| | | | |
|---|---|---|---|
| American mahogany | *Swietenia* | durable | 460 to 640 kg/m³ A to K |
| African mahoganies | *Khaya* | moderately durable | 530 to 800 kg/m³ A to K |
| sapele | *Entandrophragma cylindricum* | moderately durable | 640 kg/m³ A to K |
| utile | *Etandrophragma utile* | durable | 660 kg/m³ A to K |
| ekebergia | *Ekebergia rueppleiana* | non-durable | 545 kg/m³ A and H |
| gedu nohor | *Entandrophragma angolense* | moderately durable | 560 kg/m³ A to K |
| guarea | *Guarea* | durable | 640 to 590 kg/m³ A to I |
| omu | *Entandrophragma candollei* | moderately durable | 640 kg/m³ H and E |
| andiroba/crabwood | *Carapa guianensis* | moderately durable | 640 kg/m³ A, C, E, H, F, L |
| central American and south American 'cedar' | *Cedrela* | durable | 480 kg/m³ A to L |
| canjerana | *Cabralea cangerana* | moderately durable | 705 kg/m³ A, H and carving |
| Australian 'cedar' | *Toona australis* | moderately durable | 450 kg/m³ A, C, H, I |
| Meliaceae/rose kamala | *Aglaia* | moderately durable | 720 to 830 kg/m³ A, C, H |
| | *Amoora* | | |

A furniture and cabinets    E veneer    I Shopfitting
B panelling    F plywood    J instrument cases
C boatbuilding    G turnery    K flooring
D pattern-making    H joinery    L construction

Multiply kilos by 0.0624 to obtain pounds per cubic foot, e.g.500kg/m³ = 31.2lbs/ft³

● Durability means natural resistance to decay and refers to heartwood; sapwood is regarded as perishable. Thus, for exacting exterior use, American mahogany, utile and guarea may be expected to have long life. American 'cedar' is also durable, but its lighter weight might preclude its use in some cases, and there is a tendency for gum to exude. However, in the Caribbean and tropical American areas 'cedar' and mahogany are use for similar purposes. As a guide, in temperate climates 'durable' means a life expectancy of around 15 to 25 years for a 2×2in section (and pro rata), while 'moderately durable' means a potential life of 10 to 15 years.

Spanish, Santo Domingo and Cuban mahogany are derived from *Swietenia mahagoni*, the original much-cherished timber. The species is now more historically than commercially significant because of indiscriminate felling throughout the Caribbean in the past. In the *Cuba Review* of 1919, H. O. Neville commented: 'Many hundreds of cords of the timber, ranging from 12in in diameter down, are annually burned under the boilers of our sugar mills and locomotives; hundreds of trees of the proper sizes are annually cut down and rough-hewed into railway ties; and for posts, corralled fences, and the myriad other uses of the plantation, mahogany is utilised. There will come a day not very far distant when the waste of this valuable timber will be regretted.'

How right he was! By the early 1920s very little West Indian mahogany was on the world's markets, and by 1946 Haiti and the Dominican Republic had banned its export entirely.

Its place has been taken by *Swietenia macrophylla*, a tree with a much wider range of growth, extending from Mexico to Belize and Panama and down to Colombia and Brazil. The differences in location and conditions account for differences in colour, weight, grain and texture.

One of the mildest and most popular imports has been Honduras — now Belize — mahogany, but political unrest in Belize and increased activity in Brazil have shifted the emphasis to the latter country, which presently supplies much of Europe's mahogany. The Brazilian is darker and a little harder than the Belize wood, and about 20% heavier, often resembling Cuban in colour and weight.

It is said that the wood from the Araguaia area of Brazil is similar to central American stock in its medium texture and shallow interlocking grain, while the wood extracted from Caceras and Tocantins is generally heavier and darker-coloured, with a more marked interlocking grain and coarser texture.

Present-day African mahogany is produced mainly from *Khaya ivorensis* and *Khaya anthotheca*; in both cases the wood is moderately lightweight and paleish-red woods. *Khaya grandifoliola* generally produces a darker, heavier wood, but lighterweight specimens are frequently mixed with the other two species for shipment.

Utile is the product of *Entandrophragma utile* while sapele comes from *Entandrophragma cylindricum*; both woods have similar colouring to *Khaya* species, but they produce a ribbon figure when quartersawn. The broad ribbon stripe is usually more pronounced in utile, and more broken in sapele. Ripple and mottle figure is frequent in both these woods, but also found in *Khaya* as well as crotch and curl figure.

African mahogany, as a description, is confined to *Khaya* species. All other red woods of the *Meliaceae* are best described by their standard commercial names since although they are of the mahogany family, they have their own individual characteristics. These should be recognised because of different end-uses. ■

# The great kitchen facelift

**Bob Grant describes his approach to a popular task that gives a lot of result for (comparatively!) little work**

Fig. 1

Re-appraising my home decor, it occurred to me that the kitchen furniture, particularly the sink unit and matching wall cupboards, were exhibiting that tired look of the 60s and 70s. Doors and drawers are flat expanses of plastic-faced chipboard; I decided to apply a more contemporary and fashionable look by making replacements in solid pine. The units were originally built by a well-known commercial manufacturer and employed the conventional front- and back-frame construction with melamine-faced end panels,

**Fig. 2**

**Fig. 3    Panel types**

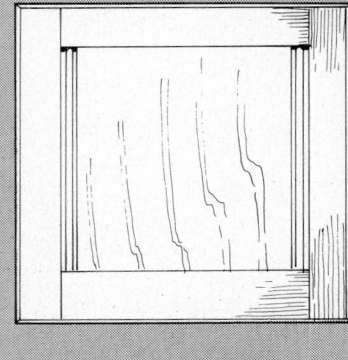

as shown in fig. 1. Such units are commonly made to a modular size; my description applies to both wall and floor cupboards.

The doors and drawers are planted on to the constructional front framework using patent hinges. It is an easy matter to remove these and save them for re-fixing later — the overall door and drawer sizes can also be taken from the originals. Fig. 2 shows the finished remodelled sink unit, featuring traditional solid wood panels. They are edged with an ovolo moulding, worked with a portable router and ½in pilot-bit.

Although a simple flush panel with bead is shown, other traditional panel types would serve equally well (figs 3B and C). They all employ a blind-mortise-and-tenon-with-groove construction. The two stiles and top rail are made from 2¾×¾in stuff, and the bottom rail is 3¼in wide. This adds visual weight to the appearance, and provides a larger tenon at the bottom stresspoint. Frame members are from straight-grained stock, and the ½in-thick panels should ideally exhibit pronounced or interesting grain. Deep-cutting a board to get the necessary width can heighten this effect by giving a matched look.

As the making of such frames is routine, no description need be given here except to point out that panels are *not* glued into the frameworks and that a tolerance is allowed in the panel-width for later expansion. If you try the overlaid panel, bear in mind that the face of the framework must be cleaned off and finished before assembly, and the panel and frame mouldings must also be worked.

The original flat doors had nasty extruded plastic grips on their top edges. I decided not to re-use them, but make up simple half-ellipse handles about 2½×⅝in, from a matching piece of scrap wood (fig. 4). These are lightly scalloped out on both sides using a firmer chisel bevel-downwards; the whole thing is then bandsawn out and cleaned up with glasspaper. Two screws from the back of the frame fix the handles, which should be set at a convenient height. set at a convenient height.

The doors can be re-hung using the

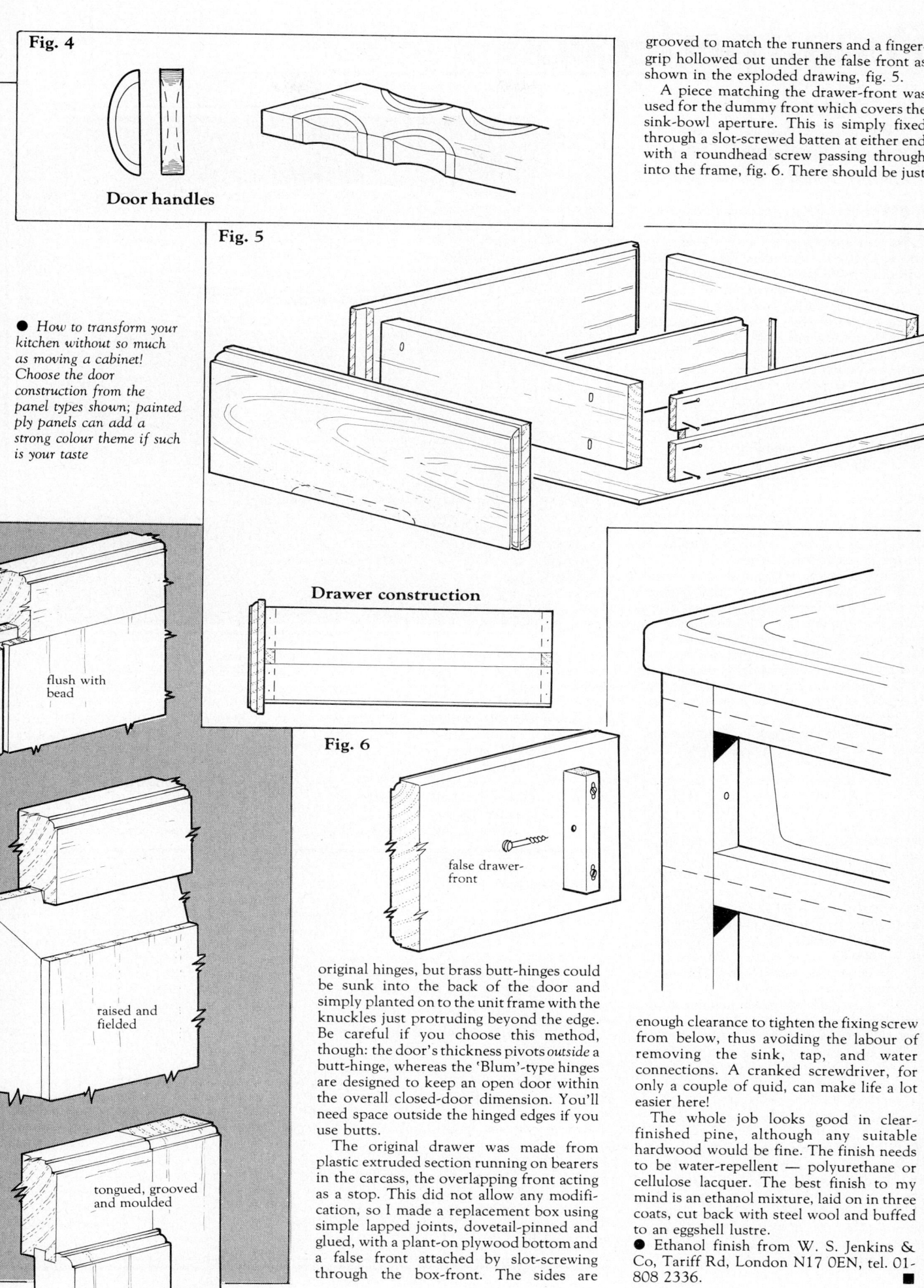

## Fig. 4

**Door handles**

grooved to match the runners and a finger-grip hollowed out under the false front as shown in the exploded drawing, fig. 5.

A piece matching the drawer-front was used for the dummy front which covers the sink-bowl aperture. This is simply fixed through a slot-screwed batten at either end with a roundhead screw passing through into the frame, fig. 6. There should be just

## Fig. 5

● *How to transform your kitchen without so much as moving a cabinet! Choose the door construction from the panel types shown; painted ply panels can add a strong colour theme if such is your taste*

flush with bead

raised and fielded

tongued, grooved and moulded

**Drawer construction**

## Fig. 6

false drawer-front

original hinges, but brass butt-hinges could be sunk into the back of the door and simply planted on to the unit frame with the knuckles just protruding beyond the edge. Be careful if you choose this method, though: the door's thickness pivots *outside* a butt-hinge, whereas the 'Blum'-type hinges are designed to keep an open door within the overall closed-door dimension. You'll need space outside the hinged edges if you use butts.

The original drawer was made from plastic extruded section running on bearers in the carcass, the overlapping front acting as a stop. This did not allow any modification, so I made a replacement box using simple lapped joints, dovetail-pinned and glued, with a plant-on plywood bottom and a false front attached by slot-screwing through the box-front. The sides are

enough clearance to tighten the fixing screw from below, thus avoiding the labour of removing the sink, tap, and water connections. A cranked screwdriver, for only a couple of quid, can make life a lot easier here!

The whole job looks good in clear-finished pine, although any suitable hardwood would be fine. The finish needs to be water-repellent — polyurethane or cellulose lacquer. The best finish to my mind is an ethanol mixture, laid on in three coats, cut back with steel wool and buffed to an eggshell lustre.

● Ethanol finish from W. S. Jenkins & Co, Tariff Rd, London N17 0EN, tel. 01-808 2336. ■

# Period perfection

Vic Taylor's detailed drawings and instructions for a real challenge — this Regency library table

Fig. 1

The heyday of circular-topped tables was the Regency period and the early years of Queen Victoria's reign — about 1810-40. One of the best known types is the rent table, which usually had 12 drawers — one for each month of the year — and often included a small till for money in the centre of the top. Another was the loo table, although this appeared at the end of the period and took its name from the game of loo which was a social craze at the time. Then there was the gueridon, a table for displaying *objets d'art* and curios.

The piece illustrated could also be called a drum or capstan table because of its appearance. It was probably used in the library, the baize-lined top allowing books to be moved about without fear of scratching or marking any polish. I have simplified the design a little; the original had carved tapering and spiralling reeds on the columns, and boldly carved acanthus leaves on the knees of the claw legs.

Solid mahogany was used for the legs and columns; also for the top and bottom blocks — in the latter case the block is deep-cut from 3½in (89mm) thick solid plank so that the grain runs vertically (fig. 2C and D). Probably this was done so that the sockets which accept the dovetails on each of the legs would be as strong as possible. Details of the dovetails are shown in fig. 3 at B and H.

The sides of the legs are routed out to a depth of about ³⁄₁₆in (5mm). You should be able to do this with a machine router, and chop the corners out by hand. However, the routed area on the knee is a different proposition because it is curved; it will almost certainly have to be done by hand. Another piece of hand work is the raised beading on the front of the legs, which is carved in the solid. I have shown a sketch of the original castors at C, fig. 3; it's highly unlikely that you will be able to find any of this design, but there are several different patterns of this kind of socket castor on the market. Don't forget you may have to alter the size of the toe (fig. 4D) to fit the castor you have chosen.

Turning up the four columns should be straightforward enough, and there is a pattern for you to follow — fig. 4A. The pins at top and bottom are for fixing into the top and bottom blocks. The top block is a plain piece of solid mahogany, 2in (51mm) thick, with two opposite edges bevelled off on the underside (fig. 2B).

Now we come to the circular case which comprises the upper and lower tops and the drawers. On the original table both tops are in pine, the upper one 45in (1143mm) diameter and the lower one 43in (1092mm). Both are ¾in (19mm) thick; the upper top has a ⅞in (22mm) crossbanding round the edge.

As you can see from fig. 2 there are four drawers, and figs 3 F and G give further details. Two parallel division rails run right across, and there are four smaller division rails at right-angles to them. This arrangement gives four drawers, and four quadrant-shaped spaces, which are left empty. Their fronts are finished in just the same way as the drawer-fronts, even to the extent of dummy handles and escutcheons. These division rails, fig. 3E, are pine except at the ends, where a piece of vertically grained oak is jointed on. The show-wood face is veneered in mahogany.

Frankly, this is not a construction that greatly appeals to me, and I think the job offers a great opportunity to try out the new MDF panel material. It would be ideal for making up the entire case, tops and all, as shown at fig. 3A. You will notice that I recommend buttoning the top down as well as gluing the stub tenons; the divisions could be tenoned right through the lower top, and the tenons wedged from beneath.

## Cutting list

| | | in | | | mm | | |
|---|---|---|---|---|---|---|---|
| 1 | upper top (grain long way) | 46 × | 45½ | ¾ | 1168×1155 × | | 19 |
| 1 | lower top (grain long way) | 46 | 43½ | ¾ | 1118 | 1105 | 19 |
| 4 | columns | 14 | 3½ | 3 | 356 | 89 | 77 |
| 4 | claw legs | 18¼ | 5½ | 2 | 464 | 140 | 51 |
| 1 | top block | 19 | 10½ | 2 | 483 | 267 | 51 |
| 1 | bottom block | 12 | 11½ | 3½ | 305 | 292 | 89 |
| 2 | top carcase rails, long | 43 | 5⅛ | ¾ | 1092 | 130 | 19 |
| 4 | top carcase rails, short | 14 | 5⅛ | ¾ | 356 | 130 | 19 |
| 2 | drawer-stops | 7⅛ | 1 | ⅝ | 182 | 25 | 16 |
| 4 | drawer-fronts | 16¾ | 3⅝ | ¾ | 425 | 93 | 19 |
| 4 | drawer-sides, long | 20⅜ | 3⅝ | ⅜ | 518 | 93 | 9 |
| 4 | drawer-sides, short | 14½ | 5⅝ | ⅜ | 368 | 93 | 9 |
| 4 | drawer-backs | 16¾ | 2¾ | ⅜ | 425 | 70 | 9 |
| 2 | drawer-bottoms, large | 19½ | 15¾ | ⅜ | 495 | 400 | 9 |
| 2 | drawer-bottoms, small | 13⅜ | 15¾ | ⅜ | 340 | 400 | 9 |
| | Drawer-slip (from one length) | 112 | 1 | ¼ | 2844 | 25 | 6 |
| | Drawer quadrant moulding (from one length) | 112 | ¾ | ¼ | 2844 | 19 | 6 |

Small drawer-stops from oddments
Working allowances for planing, cutting, etc., have been made to lengths and widths; thicknesses are net.

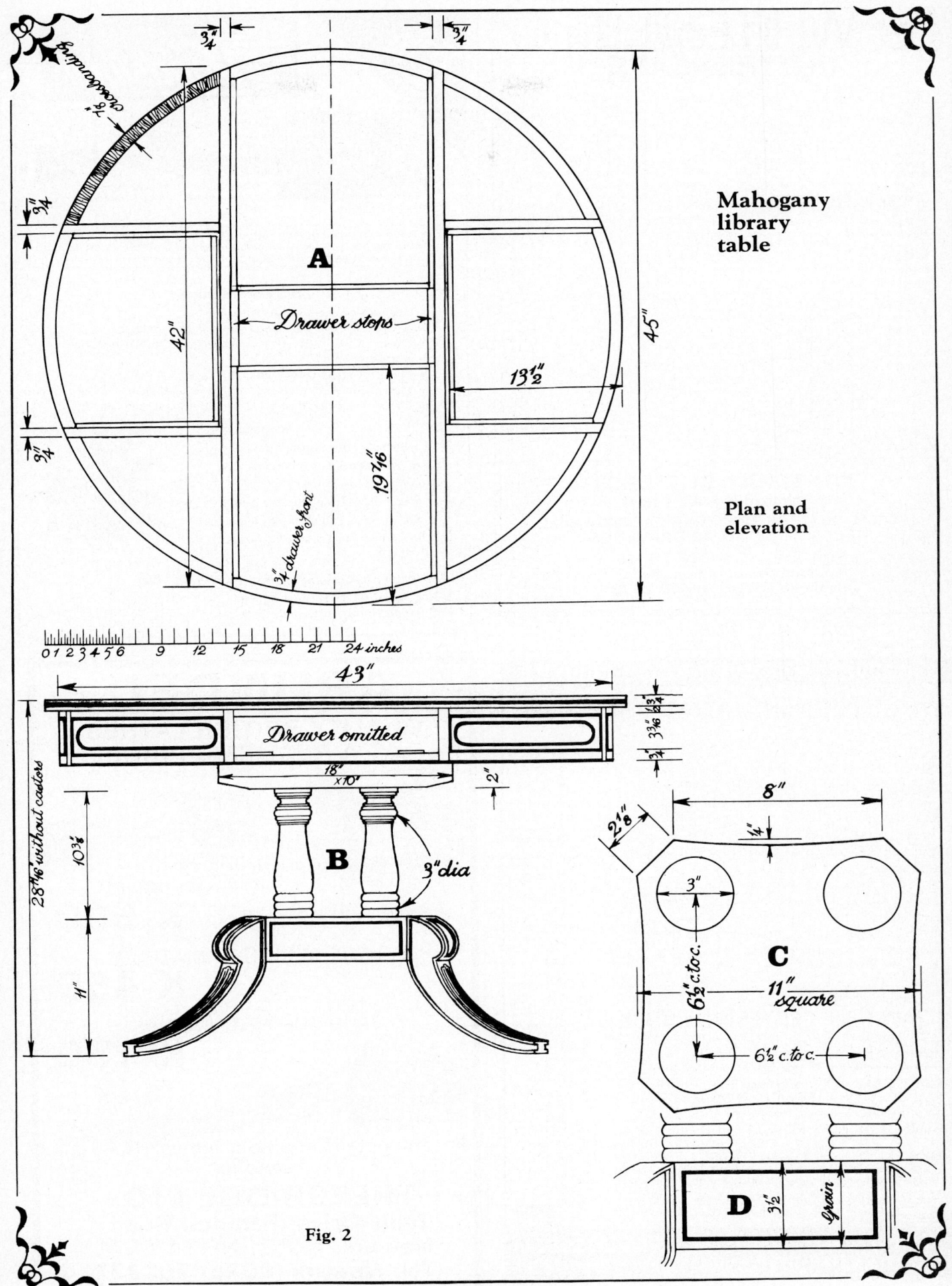

**Mahogany library table**

A

*Drawer stops*

42″

13½″

19⁷⁄₁₆″

¾″ drawer front

¾″ chamfering

¾″

¾″

45″

3″ 3″
¾″ ¾″

Plan and elevation

0 1 2 3 4 5 6   9   12   15   18   21   24 inches

43″

*Drawer omitted*

B

3″ dia

18″ x 10″

2″

28¹¹⁄₁₆″ without casters

10¾″

11″

3¾″ 3³⁄₁₆″ 2¹⁄₄″

C

8″

2⁵⁄₈″

¼″

3″

6½″ c. to c.

11″ square

6½″ c. to c.

D

3½″

*Grain*

Fig. 2

201

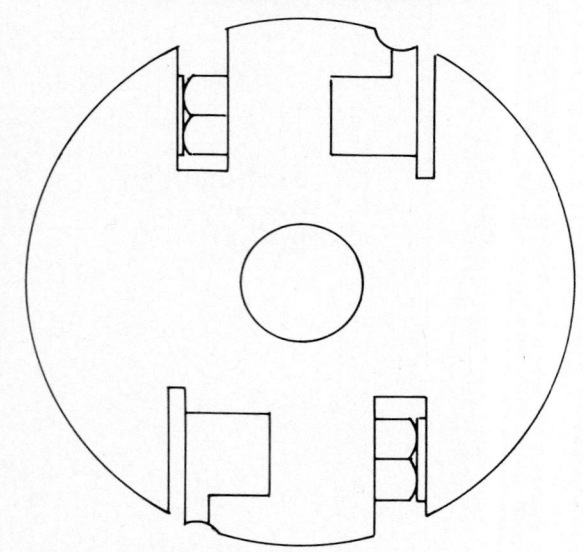

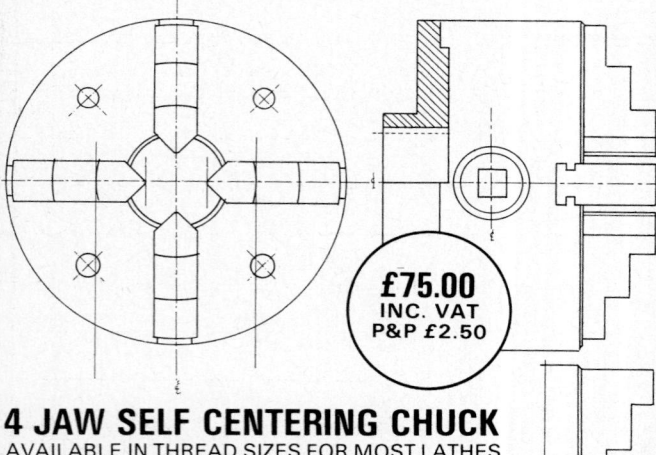
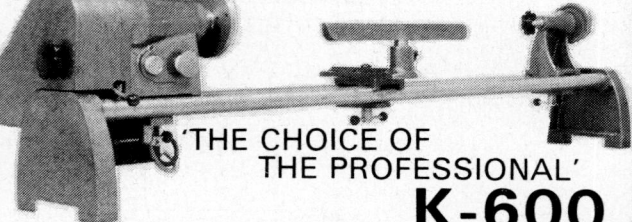
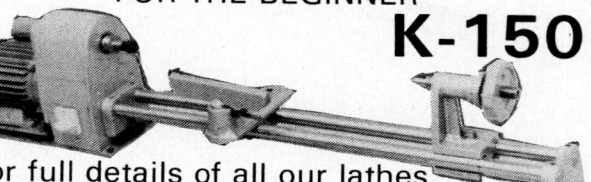
Prices quoted are those prevailing at press date and are
subject to alteration due to economic conditions

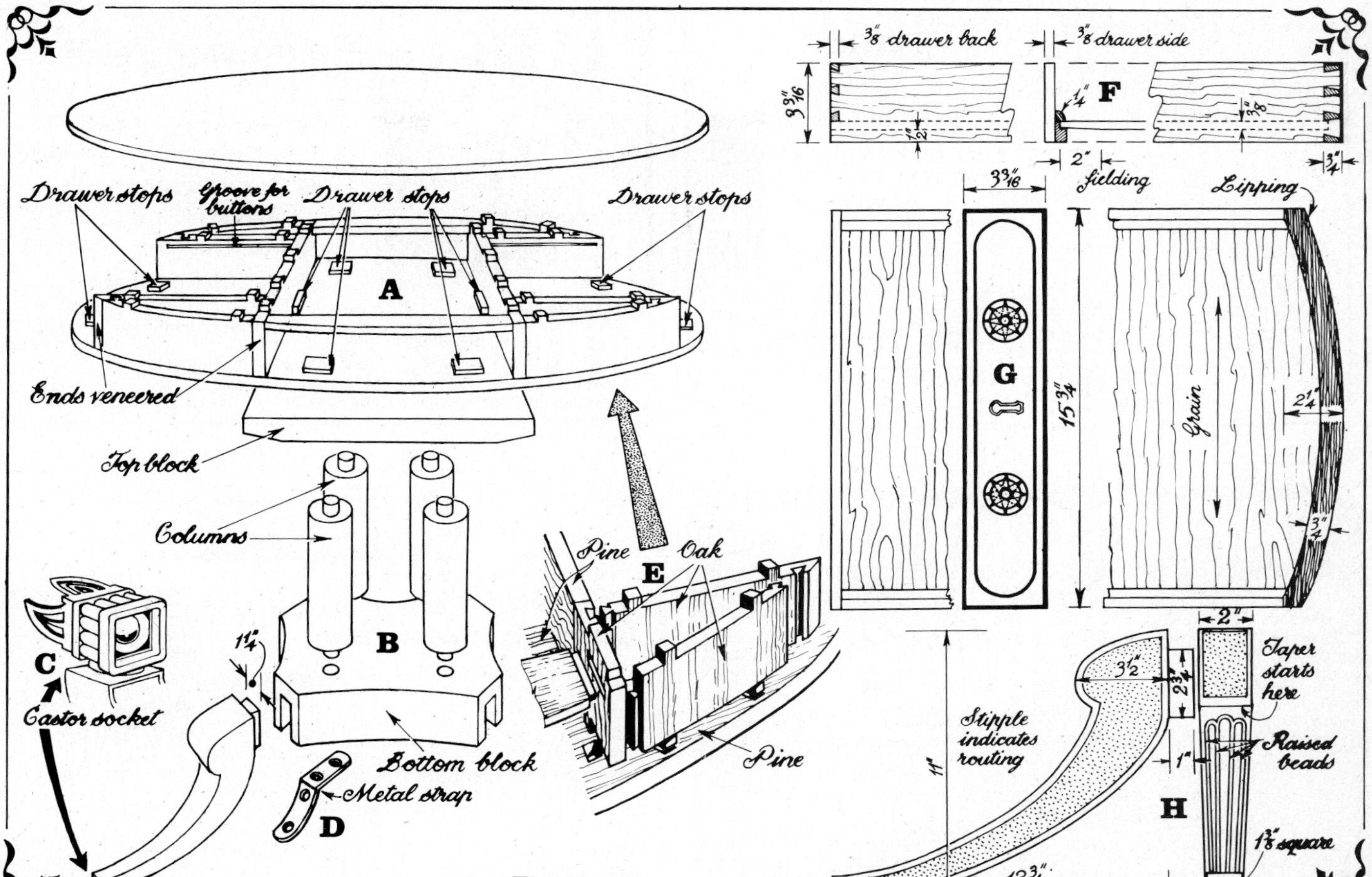

3/8" drawer back
3/8" drawer side
3 3/16"
F
1/4"
1/2"
2" fielding
Lipping
3/4"
3 3/16"
15 3/4"
G
Grain
2 1/4"
3/4"
Drawer stops
Groove for buttons
Drawer stops
Drawer stops
A
Ends veneered
Top block
Columns
B
1 1/4"
C
Castor socket
Bottom block
Metal strap
D
Pine
Oak
E
Pine
2"
3 1/2"
2 1/4"
Taper starts here
Stipple indicates routing
11"
1"
Raised beads
H
1 3/8" square
12 3/4"

Fig. 3

The edges of both tops and the ends of the rails will need to be veneered, of course. The rails should be fixed and buttoned to the upper top before gluing on the lower top, or it will be hard to get at the buttons.

Details of the drawers are shown in figs. 3F and G. They follow traditional construction, with lap-dovetails at the front corners; as the drawer-fronts are curved, a flat has to be planed off each front corner to enable the dovetail joints to be made. On the original the grain in the oak drawer-fronts runs vertically and they are veneered with horizontally grained mahogany. The method of making them depends on what timber you have available — obviously, they will almost certainly have to be deep-cut from solid stuff in order to achieve the curve. If you are using mahogany you may be able to have the grain running horizontally and dispense with the veneer. The drawer-bottoms are grooved into the back of the drawer-fronts and supported by slips along the sides; they run out at the back and the grain runs from side to side (fig. 3G). Note that a black lipping is laid on the upper edges of the drawer-fronts.

A
B
C
D
One inch squares

Fig. 4

Finally comes ornamentation, which mainly consists of inlaid black bandings. Beginning with the top, there is the cross-banding around the edge — already mentioned; in addition, a 3/8×1/16in (9×2mm) black banding is inlaid into the edge itself. On the original this is actually a carved beading, but I have substituted the banding as many readers will not have the tools or the expertise to cope with the carving. Oak, suitably ebonised, will make good bandings and lippings.

The rest of the bandings are all the same — black, and 3/16×1/16in (5×2mm); they are arranged as shown in fig. 2B and D. A profile of the knob handle is illustrated in fig. 4B, plus details of the inlaid patera which surrounds the knob. Again I have simplified this considerably, as the original was a complicated sunburst design; I suggest a dark wood such as ebony (or ebonised oak) for the centre, rosewood for the rays and the outer circle, and a light-coloured wood such as holly or sycamore for the infill.

I have deliberately left the details of decoration rather vague, because in my experience most woodworkers adapt such things to suit their own tastes, tools and expertise. ■

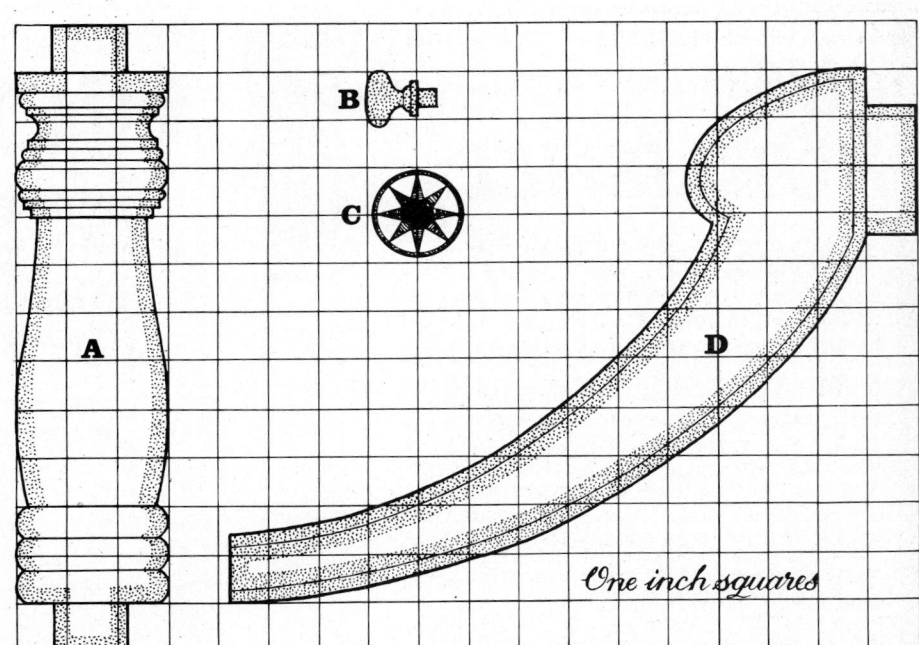

Prices quoted are those prevailing at press date and are subject to alteration due to economic conditions

# WOOD SUPPLIERS

Prices quoted are those prevailing at press date and are subject to alteration due to economic conditions.

# WOOD SUPPLIERS

KINDLY MENTION 'WOODWORKER' WHEN REPLYING TO ADVERTISEMENTS

# WOOD SUPPLIERS

## THE WOOD SHOP

Our Cabinetmaker and Woodturners sawmill specialises in **homegrown,** imported and exotic timbers for the small user.

We can **machine** to your cutting list and **deliver** to your home.

**Open 7 days a week, 9 to 5.**

Send for new brochure to Treske Sawmills, Station Works
Thirsk YO7 4NY
Tel (0845) 22770

## Treske Sawmills

**ENGLISH HARDWOODS.** Oak specialists, also Ash, Beach, Cherry, Yew. Over 3000 cu.ft. Send for stock list to W. H. Mason & Son Ltd., The Sawmills, Wetmore Road, Burton-on-Trent, Staffs. Telephone 64651.

**ZEBRANO** ¼ cut boards 1"/2" thick. Exquisite figuring. Also Ebony, Rosewoods, Paurosa, Padauk and many other exotics. CHART, Reading (0734) 695336. Evenings/Saturdays.

Rates of charge:
**35p per word
(min. £5.25)
semi-display
£1.25 per s.c. cm.
(min. 2.5cm)
'Phone 01-437 0699
for details.**

## TREEWORK SERVICES
**Suppliers of Native Hardwoods**
MOST HOMEGROWN SPECIES IN STOCK
LARGE AND SMALL QUANTITIES
SUPPLIED FRESH SAWN, AIR DRIED
AND KILN DRIED

Send sae for Price List to
**TREEWORK SERVICES LTD**
CHESTON COOMBE, CHURCH TOWN,
BACKWELL, NR. BRISTOL. (027583) 3917
or phone JOHN EMERY on CHEW MAGNA
(027589) 3222
*We also offer a tree milling service*

## Earn £200 per hour drying timber with your own kiln. . .

My seasoners need so little attention that your time could hardly be better spent than by drying your own timber. Can you afford to invest a few hundred pounds in order to guarantee your work is stable in central heating and ensure that your English hardwoods will cost half as much for many years to come.

No need to keep large untidy stacks of timber slowly drying and spoiling for years and years — these machines work from green in a few weeks and cost only a few pence per cubic foot to run.

The smallest seasoner costs less than £400 and will dry enough timber to keep several people busy or make you some money selling surplus timber. It can live outside and does not usually need a box much larger than 8' × 4' × 4'. As I am the man who developed these machines, I hope that my information, prices, references etc., are second to none.

Write for details or ring me any time for answers to your questions completely without obligation.

**JOHN ARROWSMITH
74 Wilson Street, Darlington,
Co. Durham DL3 6QZ. Tel: 0325 481970**

## ENGLISH TIMBERS
### KILN DRIED HARDWOODS FOR THE CRAFTSMAN

Please visit our new warehouse

**P. Smith, The Old Chapel, Kirkburn,
Nr. Driffield, East Yorkshire - Tel: 0377 89301**

# WOOD SUPPLIERS — COUPON

FROM _____

_____

_____

I enclose remittance to the value

of £_____ to cover _____ insertions

DETAILS

**Send to: Jason,
Woodworker Classified Dept.
1 Golden Square,
London W1R 3AB.**

Rates: 35p per word, minimum £5.25,
semi-display £7.25, minimum 2.5cm.

|  |  |  |  |  |
|---|---|---|---|---|
|  |  |  |  |  |
|  |  |  |  |  |
|  |  |  |  |  |
|  |  |  |  |  |
|  |  |  |  |  |
|  |  |  |  |  |

KINDLY MENTION 'WOODWORKER' WHEN REPLYING TO ADVERTISEMENTS

# The cannibal workshop

You needn't be hard up for new machines — if you know how to re-cycle old ones. James Paffett explains what's involved

Our civilisation buys domestic machines in large and increasing numbers. But the stream of white and gleaming boxes flowing out of the High Street stores is matched by a sorrier procession from back doors to municipal dumps as old machines are abandoned.

Some are worn out; many, though, are still usable — merely outmoded. A shrewd craftsman will not leave an old appliance for the dustman until he has gone over it for useful salvage. Half an hour's work on a dead washing-machine or dishwasher will yield a rich harvest of nuts, bolts, springs, switches and other parts suitable for post-mortem transplantation — and, above all, an electric motor.

The motors in domestic appliances are generally robust and reliable, and with care they can be used for a variety of jobs around the workshop. My own shop contains more than a dozen miscellaneous small machines powered by motors from washing-machines, spin-driers, vacuum-cleaners, etc.

However, using a motor for a purpose quite different from that for which it was designed calls for care and common sense, plus some basic background knowledge.

The FHP or fractional-horse-power motors used in domestic appliances are of two sorts: induction motors and commutator motors. It is important to be able to distinguish between them, as they have quite different characteristics.

The induction or 'squirrel-cage' motor usually appears in the larger sizes, and is commonly found in washing-machines. It runs quietly at a nearly constant speed, on or off load. The usual speeds are around 1450 and 2900rpm, depending on the type of winding. The starting torque is low, maximum torque being developed only around normal working speed. The motor speed cannot be adjusted by the ordinary electronic speed-control unit. Induction motors are suitable where a substantial torque is needed at a moderate and constant shaft speed, for example in lathes, disc sanders and buffing wheels.

The commutator or universal motor is smaller and lighter, for a given power, than the induction motor. It is commonly used in portable tools, vacuum-cleaners, spin-driers, etc. It operates at a higher speed; some types will run up to 20,000rpm or more off load. It also tends to be noisy — particularly so when gearing is used to reduce the speed, as in portable drills. The torque is at maximum on starting and falls off as speed rises, so that running speed varies with load. Speed can be controlled by an electronic speed-control unit wired into the supply. Commutator motors are suitable for applications where weight is important, and where high or variable speeds are required.

In preparing a salvaged motor for transplantation, you must first identify the type. This means looking at the rotating parts inside the motor casing. In a commutator motor the rotating part — the armature — is wound in a complex way with copper wire, and a commutator (a segmented copper cylinder) is mounted on the shaft at one end of the armature, just inside the end bearing. Two carbon 'brushes' in the motor casing bear upon the commutator; these convey current to and from the armature windings. If the wires leading to the brush

● *Below: A Hoover washing-machine provided the motor for this grinder-cum-wire-wheel. The front overhangs the table to stop it 'walking back'*

holders are accessible, it is worth noting that exchanging them brush-for-brush will reverse the direction of rotation.

In the induction motor the commutator and brushes are absent. The armature is not wound with wire; instead it carries a pattern of copper rods lying in slots — the 'squirrel cage'. Some (but not all) induction motors need to be connected to a capacitor to operate properly. The capacitor, if present, will appear as an aluminium can, square or cylindrical, mounted close to the motor or bolted on to its frame, and connected to the motor by two wires. Such a capacitor must be carefully retained and the wires, if disconnected, marked so that they can be correctly replaced. It may be possible to lift out motor and capacitor together without disturbing the interconnecting wires.

If, apart from any capacitor connections, there are only two wires coming out of a motor, you can assume that these are the mains leads and connecting up will be straightforward. If, however, there are three or more, care is called for. One wire may well be an earth lead connected to the motor frame; that can be checked easily enough by testing for continuity between each wire and the frame, using a torch battery and bulb. When identified, an earth lead should be connected through to the earth pin on the mains plug. Indeed, even if no earth wire comes with the motor it is a good idea to fit one, connecting the motor frame or chassis solidly to the mains earth.

If there are three or more leads yet none is an earth lead, detective work is needed. Some motors are reversible, the various windings being brought out separately so that external switching can be used to change direction of rotation. One type of washing-machine motor boasts no less than six leads. In such a case you can try to trace back through the machine wiring to work out the power-supply and switching circuit, or alternatively strip the motor down completely to see where the wires go inside. Either way, the job is one for an electrical specialist, and beyond the scope of this

● *Far left: A mini-saw with a tilting table whose motor came from a vacuum-cleaner. Left: A grinder-sander known in James Paffett's household as The Mills of God; here a vacuum-cleaner extracts dust. Below: An old metal lathe adapted for lace-bobbin turning, with a spin-drier motor*

article. If confronted with a motor dangling multiple leads, the non-electrician would be wise to seek advice, or to look around for another motor with only two leads.

Having decided the type and identified the mains leads, you can carry out a bench test on your motor. This involves connecting the leads to the mains. If there is still some lingering doubt about whether the leads you intend using are the right ones, it is worth connecting a 100w lamp in series with the motor for the initial trial. If there is a dead short circuit between the leads, the lamp will light up brightly while the motor stays dead — a preferable alternative to a shower of sparks and a blown fuse. If things are in order the motor will run at reduced power and the lamp will light dimly. In this event the lamp can be removed from the circuit and the trial resumed with full mains pressure on the motor.

There is a mechanical point to watch when testing a strange motor on the bench. When switched on, a motor suffers quite a jerk as the armature suddenly starts spinning. If not restrained, the body may go rolling across the bench, pulling wires loose

and sending sparks flying. It's as well to wedge the motor body securely in place before venturing to switch the power on for trial, however briefly.

A motor which has been wet may need special treatment. Moisture in the windings can allow electricity to leak into the frame, with some danger of shock and blown fuses. You can check for leakage if an electrical resistance meter is available. The insulation

● *A spin-drier motor powers this small grinder, used for putting a rough bevel on wide chisels. The shaft includes a flexible coupling of garden hose to combat inevitable misalignment*

resistance — that is, the electrical resistance between any of the windings and the frame — should be several megohms. If it is less than, say, one megohm, the whole motor should be baked for an hour or two in the domestic oven on the lowest heat setting. This treatment has effectively restored the insulation resistance in motors taken from washing-machines which had been left in the open air for several months. If a motor is of unknown or dubious origin there is no harm in baking it anyway, just in case.

Assume now that we have salvaged a motor, dried it out, determined its type, identified the leads and test-run it on the bench. The next task is to mount it up so that it can do a useful job of work. Electrically, all that is required is to fit a mains lead with a switch in the 'line' side (the brown lead). As already mentioned, the motor frame should be wired through to the earth pin (via the yellow/green lead). For some applications it may be convenient to wire a commutator motor through an electronic speed-control box. In choosing an on-off switch it's as well to err on the generous side; a rating of 5 amps or more is advisable — particularly for the larger induction motors, which take quite a heavy starting current.

A salvaged motor sometimes presents problems because it has no feet suitable for mounting it on a base-board. In such a case you can form your own feet by attaching angle lugs bent up from aluminium sheet. Most motors are held together by long bolts passing right through the motor casing from one end plate to the other; one can sometimes use these bolts for adding feet. In fastening feet, brackets or other members to the motor body, however, you should take care not to block the ventilation openings in the motor end plates; a loaded motor will overheat if the airflow is obstructed. A method of adding feet is shown in fig. 1.

Most motors have internal fans to maintain a cooling airflow, but in some types the fan rotors are mounted on the shaft externally with the blades exposed. In such cases you must fit some form of shroud or protective casing to keep fingers from getting caught in the blades.

The next problem is to find some means of leading the mechanical power away from the motor shaft. This is usually best done by V-belt and pulleys. If there is no suitable pulley already on the shaft, you need to fit one. If the shaft diameter is a neat $\frac{3}{8}$in, $\frac{1}{2}$in, $\frac{5}{8}$in or the like, you can choose from the excellent range of pulleys marketed by Picador. If, however, the shaft has some non-standard diameter and you have no matching drill to bore out a standard pulley, you can machine a pulley in place.

You first prepare a round blank of hardwood or thick plywood somewhat larger than the required pulley. The blank is drilled centrally with a hole $\frac{1}{4}$in or so larger than the shaft, countersunk at both ends. The motor is set up on end with the shaft pointing vertically upwards. The blank is positioned concentrically with the shaft and held in place with a pudding of Plasticene at the lower end, as shown in fig. 2. Liquid polyester resin (e.g. Holt's Cataloy) is then cast into the annular gap between wood and

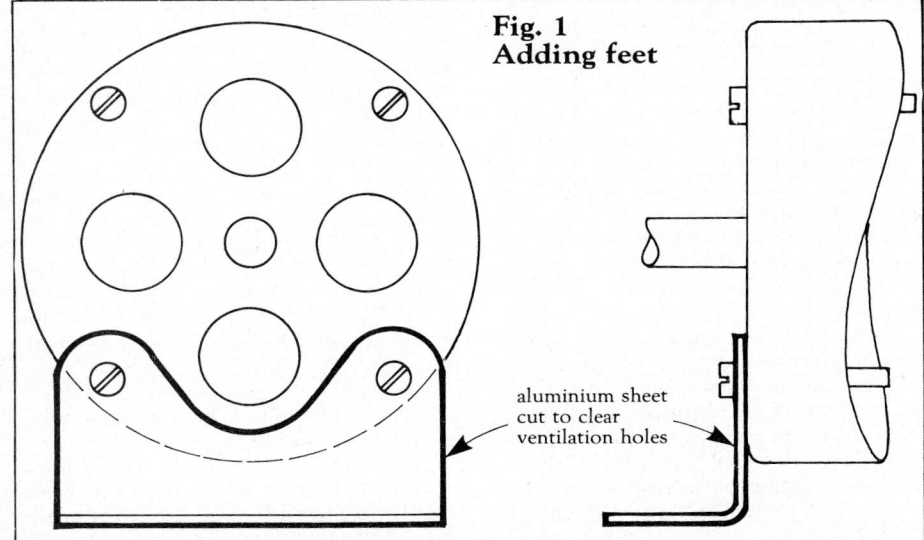

**Fig. 1
Adding feet**

aluminium sheet cut to clear ventilation holes

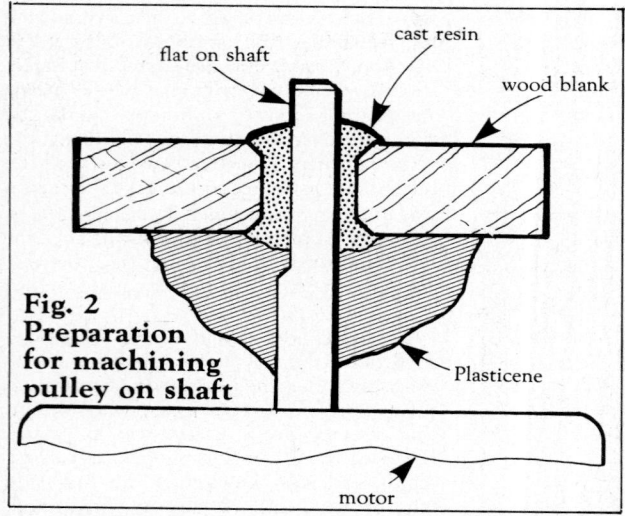

Fig. 2
Preparation
for machining
pulley on shaft

flat on shaft
cast resin
wood blank
Plasticene
motor

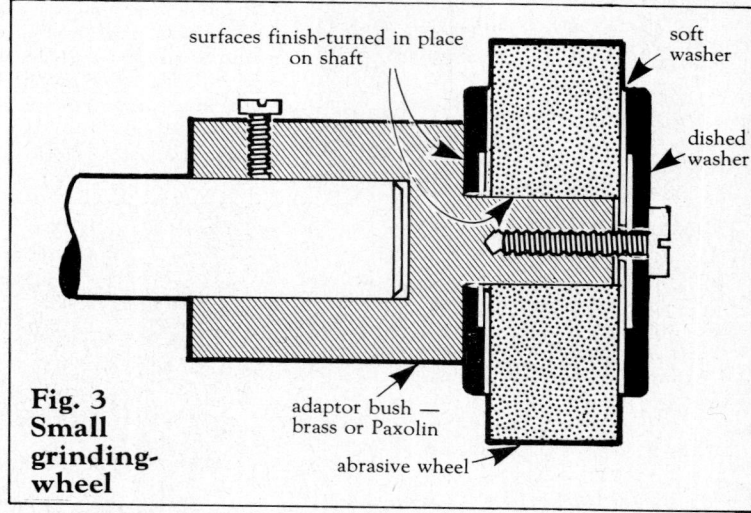

Fig. 3
Small
grinding-
wheel

surfaces finish-turned in place on shaft
soft washer
dished washer
adaptor bush — brass or Paxolin
abrasive wheel

shaft, care being taken not to let any resin dribble into the bearings or the works.

When the resin has set solid the motor is secured horizontally on the bench and a wood block is fixed close to the pulley to act as a temporary toolrest. The motor is then run; ordinary woodturning tools are used to true up the rim and faces of the pulley, and to cut the V-channel in the rim to suit the available belt. Convenient belts can be salvaged from washing-machines, or bought from domestic-machine spares dealers. The V in the pulley is machined deep enough to ensure that the belt bears upon its sides and not on the root of the V.

There may be some risk of the cast resin bush slipping round on the shaft if the shaft has no flat on it. In such cases it's advisable to make one with a file.

It may be that you have a metal pulley whose hole is too big to fit the shaft. You might hold the pulley in place and cast in a resin bush as described above, but it would be difficult to ensure exact positioning of the wheel — and errors could not be corrected by later machining, as they can with wood. Rather than put up with a wobbly pulley, it is better to proceed as follows. Cast a simple resin blob around the shaft end, using a Plasticene cup to hold the resin while liquid. When the resin has set hard, turn it down (using woodturning techniques) until it forms a concentric and parallel bush which will just accept the available pulley. Lastly, cut a radial hole in the resin to allow the pulley set-screw to pass through into the metal of the shaft.

Grinders need special thought. If you mount the abrasive wheel directly on the motor shaft there is no need for belts or pulleys. Moreover, if the shaft is screwed the wheel can be mounted easily, using bushes and packing washers as required. But mounting on a plain shaft is less straightforward.

If metal-turning facilities are available, you can make a special mounting bush as in fig. 3. Nevertheless, a word of warning is needed. Every grinding-wheel has a limiting speed above which it cannot be used safely; a 4in wheel, for example, might be limited to 4700rm. Some commutator motors under no load can run very fast indeed, so mouting a stock wheel on a salvaged commutator motor could be asking for trouble. If you're using a motor of this sort for a home-made grinder, the wheel used should be of small diameter, as with the small drum type sold on arbors for use in portable drills. Bigger wheels should be powered by induction motors, whose modest speed gives some protection.

On any grinder a metal shroud should be fitted to cover all of the wheel except the working arc.

Reverting to belt drives: what goes on the other end of the belt? If a lathe or similar machine is waiting to take the drive, the remaining problem is the choice of pulleys to give the right speeds. The Picador range includes several stepped pulleys; by using one of these at each end you can make available a wide choice of 'gear ratios'. If you have a motor but no clear idea of what

to do with it, a good scheme would be to match it through a pair of stepped pulleys to a Picador spindle — a ⅝in shaft running in bearings, whose threaded ends can be used to take sawblades, wire wheels, sanding discs, lathe face-plates, etc., to taste. A washing-machine induction motor driving a Picador spindle makes a good general-purpose tool in almost any workshop.

What other kinds of machine can be driven by salvaged motors? There seems to be no limit. Looking around, I can see a 6in saw-bench, a woodturning lathe, a sanding machine with a built-in (salvaged) vacuum-cleaner to collect the dust, a mini-planer, an air-compressor for the car tyres, a potter's wheel with electronic speed control, a minia-ture grinder for sharpening twist drills, a flexi-drive for sculpture . . . All these ma-chines have given trouble-free service for years. All the motors were salvaged — some literally from the scrapyard.

Not every salvaged motor is suitable for transplantation, and there have inevitably been some rejects, but the survivors earn their keep. Some of the machines look a bit odd, but they all work. What's more, every one has provided me with the satisfaction of having made something useful out of materials costing virtually nothing; and that's always fun.

● You can get Picador pulleys from London V Rope Drive Ltd, Clifton Terrace, London N4 3JS, tel. 01-272 4212. ■

# Starters

### Chris Nussbaum's diary of the London College of Furniture C&G 564 cabinetmaking course

This full-time course is certainly full-time! I don't think I have ever under-taken anything quite so demanding — of time, discipline, and plain hard slog; but it is still great fun. As this third month draws to a close, the group of students and staff is

rapidly cohering, adapting to each other, becoming better acquainted. A good atmos-phere has developed, conducive to progress, with perhaps an edge of competitiveness.

The past four weeks have mainly been spent on the most interesting and stimulating project to date. Originating as an exercise in hand-veneering, it developed into a brief to design and construct a clock, using 1m of 50×25mm beech, a rectangle of 6mm ply 300×150mm, a small quartz clock movement, and any veneers we chose.

What was most fascinating for me was not just that 15 people produced 15 (very nearly) different designs, but the number of unexpected facets of the project which developed to stimulate general thought and debate. Of course all sorts of odd technical points arose, but so did discussions about

(for instance) the application of commer-cial production criteria to particular designs.

Perhaps the liveliest debate in some quarters concerned aesthetics versus function, and whether there was or should be any conflict in the first place. The whole question of function in design was brought home sharply to those who designed clocks which did not display the time clearly, therefore failing in function. Unfortunately there isn't the space here to develop these interesting arguments — which will, I suspect, continue with increasing intensity as the course develops.

At the end of the day, however, I hope my little nephew will be happy with his Christmas present — a clock with his name on it, instead of numbers! ■

# The craft of cabinetmaking

## David Savage talks through an essential technique: framing and panelling

Frame-and-panelling is one of the really good techniques in cabinet work. A wide board of solid timber must be allowed to expand or contract; it is fixed not with glue or pins, but floats within a framework.

There must be dozens of different types of frame-and-panel constructions. Many are less common than they were, because of plywood and other board materials, but the technique is still widely used in top-class work, and for parts that need the visual rhythm it provides. Many kitchen-cabinet doors have frame-and-panel construction, using modern jointing systems that are quickly and accurately cut on the spindle-moulder with heavy-duty tooling.

The job in hand involves a simple raised and fielded panel with mortised-and-tenoned frame, grooved and haunched. The requirement was a pair of iroko doors in a hatchway connecting two rooms. The panels, therefore, had to be raised and fielded on both sides. On a cabinet back, it is usual to field only one side, leaving the back plain.

Experienced workers would be able to look at the opening, think out the width of the rails, make a few notes and get down to chopping up the iroko. A less heroic approach, and one I recommend for anyone who has any doubts about the procedure, is to make a very accurate drawing. Precise drawings are needed all the time, so it is worth getting a good drawing-board, or a piece of ply with one straight side, a reliable T-square, a couple of triangles and an architect's scale.

Making drawings for yourself is easier than drawing for another craftsman, where certain trade conventions have to be observed. Choose a scale that gives you what you need, and draw one half for visual appearance and the other for technical comprehension. The first purpose of the drawing is to get the proportions right; choose a width of stile bearing in mind that it will be doubled where the two doors meet. Choose a width of rail; although it is customary to have the top rail the same width as the stile, the bottom rail can be deeper. This is done for the same reason that mounts around framed prints and drawings are deeper at the bottom — it prevents the illusion that the picture or panel is dropping out of the frame. Then choose the width of fielding on the panel. All these are visual more than structural considerations; the visual rhythm of differently spaced verticals, the control of light and shade, movement and stop; all are decided here and now. You can call it designing, but what you are really doing is playing with shape, colour and light to reach an attractive conclusion.

The other half of the problem, dealt with in the other half of the drawing, is tackling

● *Mortising a two-in-one rail. Working this way saves time and emphasises the line in a pair of doors*

constructional details. Use this side to work out how the thing will be built. Assess the position of the panel in relation to the joints, making the groove 1-2mm deeper than the position the panel will take sitting in it. In deepest, dampest Devon I do not expect much timber to expand after leaving me, so I do not allow much — you must make your own assessment. Draw your tenons 1mm less in length than their mortices, and don't be tempted to cut longer tenons into the deep bottom rail. Do them all the same; it makes the job simpler.

The important thing to grasp is the function of the haunch, which is really only there to enable you to cut the grooves for the panels right through to the ends of the stiles. Making stopped grooves is a real bore; the haunches fill the gap and stiffen the upright at the same time. Make the drawing accurately and you will be able to proceed with confidence to the cutting list.

Cut out your stuff to dimension. Machine-planing and thicknessing is a dimensioning procedure that can be done with great accuracy. Cleaning up and sanding will remove only a shaving, so trust your drawing and set the machines accordingly.

Throughout this job I will describe setting up and cutting using certain machines — but it is not essential to work this way, and other ways may be better or worse. I use techniques of modern machine woodworking suitable for the small shop.

Firstly, clamp the rails together; do not separate the two doors at this stage. It is quicker to build them as one item with the rails running through both, which means the stiles will be tenoned into the rails — the opposite of the traditional method. This way the figure and colour of timber are unified, too. Mark out the mortise

positions, scribing across both top and bottom rails with a sharp marking-knife; pencil in the waste. Leave about 20mm at each end for horns, and 4mm for the kerf of the saw between the two centre stiles.

Set up the mortiser using a scrap piece. It is worth remembering beforehand to cut a square mortise bit. Once set, adjust it to the exact centre of the rail — you will see why when we come to cutting the tenons. Don't trust this, however; always gauge from the face side. All face sides should ideally have been positioned on one side of the job with face edges looking inwards, but this may not be possible if the timber's pattern and colour are to be taken into account.

Set up the mortiser using a scrap piece. It is worth remembering beforehand to cut a few scraps to the same dimensions as your rails. I must admit to having trouble with my mortiser. The Japanese mortise chisels do not seem to do the job as well as they should — perhaps the single-wing cutter is not guiding the cut accurately enough. However, as these cuts are concealed in stopped mortises, it is not too important.

Now to the tenons. With these it is very important that all the stiles are exactly, and I mean exactly, the same length. Any discrepancy will show up as gaps in the joint, so take some time here. Also cut half a dozen spare bits for setting up the saws. This may seem a lot, but it is very annoying to run out of test pieces when you are setting up the machine that is also used to cut the test pieces.

With this technique, it is only necessary to mark out tenons on the test piece, saving a lot of time marking eight tenons that are going to be cut from the same machine setting anyway. It may seem risky, but it is good workshop practice to omit unnecessary stages.

● *Be careful! Health and safety officers may flinch at this efficient tenoning method*

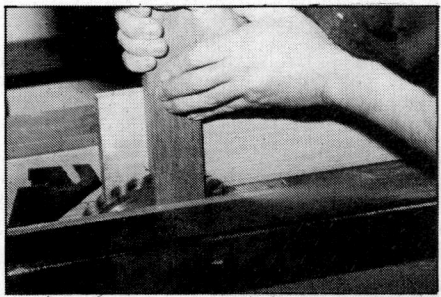

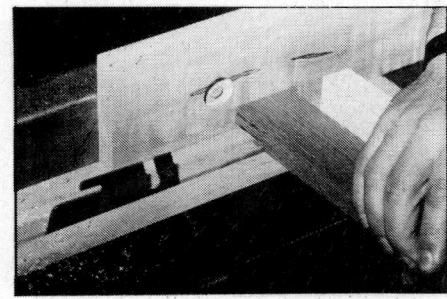

● *Cutting the shoulders with the blade re-set. Note the block on the sliding fence that prevents 'spelching'*

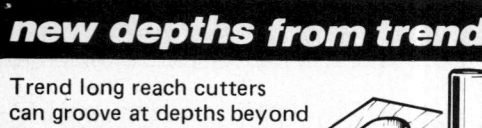
## Correction time

On p14 of the January issue we carried a picture of a rather nice display case by Chris Vickers of the London College of Furniture. Only we said it was by Martin Vickers. Sorry, Chris.

Using the same mortise-gauge setting as for the rails, mark 2 or 3 test pieces from the face side. Cutting tenons can be done very safely on the bandsaw with moderate to good results, depending upon the condition of the blade. Most small shops that I know cut tenons on the table-saw, working above the blade from a high auxiliary fence. Because the guard must be removed for this work it would not be allowed in factories, and is rightly regarded as dangerous; but it would be unrealistic to say that it were not common practice. If, along with the rest of us, you really wish to commit tenoning *hara-kiri*, set up a very, very sharp blade parallel to the high fence. The fence is seldom exactly at right-angles to the table, but it should be close. Waxing the fence and table insert helps the vitally important smooth, controlled feed across the blade. If the mortise-gauge has been set to scribe in the centre of the job, it will now be possible to cut both tenon cheeks from one machine setting.

The problem with working above the blade is that you and your wiggly bits are in close proximity to high-speed steel! 'Nuff said.

For cutting the shoulders, use the test pieces again. Set the blade height to just kiss the tenon, set the rip fence to the tenon length, and work the job from the mitre fence or sliding table. It is important always to make two passes, the first cutting off half the waste. If you cut at the shoulder line first time, the waste will jam between blade and fence and go whistling off round the shop. It is also important, when using the rip fence as a dimension stop, to run all pieces from the same point on the fence; I am assuming that the fence is correctly set about 0.5mm off square over the depth of the table. Again, the secret of a clean cut with the shoulders is check it out on a test piece until it is exactly right. Use a very sharp blade, and back the cut up to prevent spelching.

It also makes sense to cut the haunches at this stage. Check the drawing, mark each one (as it is very easy to cut haunches in the wrong places) and saw to dimension.

To cut the groove for the panels you can use a router or mini-spindle, but most people will use the table saw again, fitted with a dado head. This is a useful piece of kit which enables saw-kerfs of infinitely variable widths to be made with and across the grain. Provided you work solid wood,

● *Third stage of tenoning on the table-saw is cutting the haunches. Best to use a bandsaw to make the long cut first – be sure which edge is which!*

the tool-steel sets are adequate — for plywood or chipboard you will need to take out a second mortgage and get tungsten. The width of cut and its position are adjusted to remove the exact width of a tenon. Make sure to groove the right side of the rails and stiles or you will be proper narked.

Panels should be cut to exact dimension from the drawing. Remember that the face of the panel should be below the faces of the frame components; you will see why when you come to clean up.

Fielding the panels is best done on the spindle-moulder using a small saw, with a jig to incline the job by 5°. There are special fielding cutters, shockingly expensive. Another way is using the table saw and finishing by hand; first, cut 3mm deep grooves round the panels to delineate the raised centre. Then tilt the saw arbor 5° away from the high auxiliary fence and feed the job through. If the saw is set correctly the two cuts will meet and the waste will fall away. Do not incline the saw towards the fence. The blade may cut more sweetly, but the waste will jam against the fence and fly out very fast indeed. This technique does not leave the clean finish of the spindle-moulder or even the router with special tooling, but it can be cleaned up with the aid of a shoulder-plane, so make the sawcuts slightly over-size.

Sand down the panels, check for fit in the groove using a scrap (called a mullett), and

then knock up the frame with the panels inside. If you are confident, and an accurate machinist, it will not be strictly necessary to test-fit every time, especially if you are working a batch; if you are not so sure, or if it is one-off, it makes sense to do so.

As you will have left the horns on the rails, you will now be glad of them. They protect the job from accidental dings and are useful when knocking mortise-and-tenon joints apart. A good joint will slide together with a little stiffness. It should not require a club hammer to tap it home. Remember that glue will swell the tenons, making the joints even stiffer to assemble. Take care; if necessary, shave the cheeks of tenons with a shoulder-plane — but this should not be necessary, as the joints should be correct straight from the saw.

If all is well, first finish the panels with whatever polish you choose, as glue may seep from the joints and finish will help to keep the panels free. Assemble the job, this time with glue and cramps. I use PVA on mortise-and-tenon joints as it allows for some creeping when rails expand and contract.

Finishing the frame will need a few judicious cuts 'around the corner' with a finishing plane across the joint. As you swing your plane around the place you will see why I suggest that the panel sits below the frame surface. Follow this with a lick of finishing paper and polish of your choice. Well and truly framed! ∎

● *The pair of doors cramped up, still as one. The gap between the two central stiles can just be seen*

● *Finishing the faces of the joints 'round the corner'. Razor-sharp blade and panel surfaces below the frame level ensure success*

# Sweating and patching

Mark Kenning details some clever techniques for 'impossible' repairs

Sooner or later, most of us suffer the misfortune of having our work bruised or scratched through carelessness. On solid timber you can sometimes cure the damage with the aid of plane, scraper and glasspaper. Where the plane must not be used, for example on veneered work, turnery and mouldings, it may be possible to restore the surface by 'sweating'.

That means using heat and water to create steam which will swell the affected part level so that it can, when thoroughly dry, be cleaned up in the usual way. It involves thoroughly wetting a piece of non-linty rag (use a clean rag and clean water), folding it two or three times, and applying part of it to the damage — then pressing the point of a very hot flat-iron to it. The water will steam and sizzle and the spot will dry very quickly. Lift the rag and move it to another wet spot; re-wet the rag as often as necessary. Continue until the bruise or scratch is level, and leave to dry.

Unfortunately there is a limit to how much sweating can be done. If it is continued for too long the wood fibres will soften and darken. Only experience can guide you, since so much depends on the depth of the damage, the type of timber, the location and so on. The best plan is to stop after two or three minutes, leave the job for several hours (ideally till the following day) and continue for two or three minutes more. If the damage has not been cured after at most three attempts, leave it alone.

One serious word of warning. These days the electric iron will be used for this work (for hand-veneering, too, and the same warning applies). Water and electricity are a lethal combination, so before picking up the hot iron *switch off and remove the plug*. When inserting the plug, switch on *after* it has been inserted.

If a horizontal surface such as a tabletop is to be polished (particularly with a high-gloss finish) and is of solid timber, sweat up the damage as far as possible and re-finish the surface with plane, scraper and glasspaper until all traces of the bruise or scratch have disappeared completely; otherwise the result will be disappointing, because no matter how skilfully one fakes these spots they will inevitably show in any reflected light. It is not unknown for a top to have to be replaced entirely and the damaged one used for something else.

So much for the solids. Veneered surfaces present a somewhat different problem. They, of course, cannot be planed at all. Only the slightest of marks can be scraped and papered away. It is possible to sweat up a slight dent or scratch, provided the fibres have not been severed across the grain. On dark, wild-grained veneers such as burr walnut you may even get away with an appropriately coloured filler and the skilled

use of the colour brush during polishing. Worst of all to put right are the straight-grain veneers such as the pencil-stripe mahoganies and walnuts, straight-grain oak and lots more. If these have been severed across the grain it is physically impossible to make an invisible repair. The only certain solution is re-veneering.

However, since the option of re-veneering is always available as a last resort, it is usually well worth while to attempt patching. You have nothing to lose, except maybe a little time, and the experience is invaluable. But there are still some instances where patching is not advised. One is on sycamore. Any patch on this veneer, no matter how skilfully done, will show the joins as contrasting black lines, even if 'white' glue is used. Another is if the piece is to be exhibited; grit your teeth and re-veneer, or don't show it.

The secret of near-invisible patching is to have pieces of veneer as near as possible to the texture and grain of the section to be cut out. If you could afford to cut an identical piece from a leaf in the same bundle, that would be ideal. I always save any sizeable offcuts from the leaves I use — not only until the job is finished and finally out of the workshop, but for much longer than that. This has paid off on several occasions.

Cutting in a patch in the burrs and figured veneers is, if anything, slightly easier than repairing straight-grained ones, so let's deal with the former first.

Select a suitable piece of veneer at least ¼in (6mm) larger all round than the part to be patched. If it's at all buckled, damp it and place between two boards for a couple of hours or as long as necessary. Then offer it to the site. Move it around, turning it over if need be, until the grain patterns on the patch and the main veneer match in the best possible way. Next, turn the patch back like the leaf of a book, apply some thin glue to the face now uppermost (scotch glue is best for this sort of work) and turn it back again. Rub it down with the veneer hammer, or the pein of an ordinary hammer if it is small, and leave for 10-15 minutes. The patch must be kept damp during the whole of the operation otherwise it could buckle again.

The patch is glued in position before cutting because of the extreme difficulty of holding a small piece of veneer in place with one hand while cutting it accurately all round with the knife in the other. The fingers must not be moved for fear that the patch may move too.

A very sharp knife is essential. Do not use a chisel, which is too clumsy, nor the Stanley knife, which is not flexible enough. A veneer-preparer's knife or scalpel is ideal. They are relatively cheap and most good tool shops stock them. The cutting is done freehand, following the grain as closely as possible. Where you need to cut across the grain, work obliquely and not directly across. Try to sever both thicknesses of veneer in one pass, but without using so much force that the groundwork is penetrated to any great extent: that could cause other problems. Should a second cut be

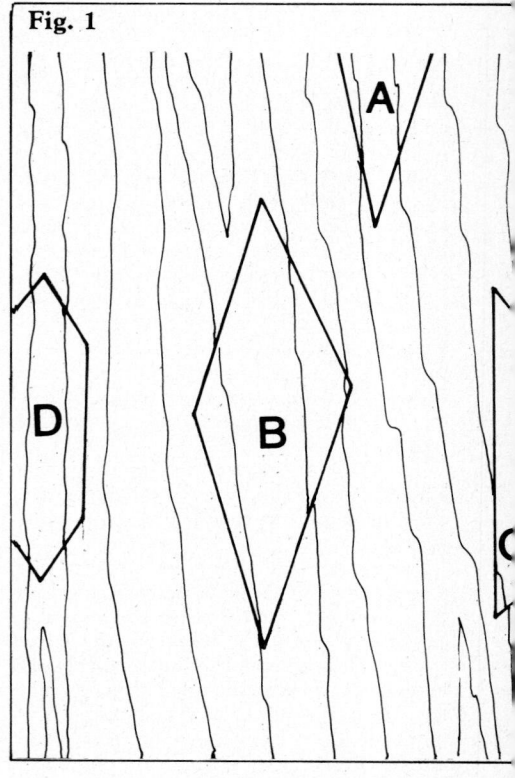

**Fig. 1**

necessary, do it a little at a time, making sure you don't damage the non-waste part of the main veneer.

When all the cutting has been completed and the waste carefully removed with the point of the knife, wet the patch and apply a warm (not hot) iron to it. Prise it up, wash off the glue from the underside and place it between two boards while still damp. Now remove the waste from the main veneer. If scotch glue was used, wetting the waste and applying the tip of the iron (hot this time) will melt it sufficiently. If not, the veneer must be nibbled away with the point of the knife.

When all the waste has been removed, check that there are no nibs of glue or veneer remaining. If scotch glue was used clean the bare section with the rag and hot water. If thermosetting glue was used you may find a gritty deposit; this must be removed by scraping with the sharp edge of the knife; the point is used close to the join — however, it will only be possible to clean down to a flat surface. A thin layer of the glue will unavoidably remain, to which scotch glue will not adhere. I will deal with this in a moment.

If scotch glue was used for veneering the main panel, brush glue liberally onto the groundwork, insert the patch, tuck the edges well in and rub it down with the hammer. Tape the join all round, then put aside to set.

When a modern non-reversible glue has been used to lay the main veneer, the patch will have to be laid by pressure and a synthetic glue used. The PVA glues — UniBond, Resin 'W' and others — I have found ideal for this purpose. The pressing may be done in a normal press, if available, or with cramps and/or handscrews via bearers, or with a strut to the ceiling. Sometimes even heavy weights like house bricks can be effective. The glue is applied to the groundwork, and the patch placed in position and taped to prevent it from slipping. Several layers of newspaper are put on it to take up any minor irregularities, and the pressure is applied. Leave to set until the following day. See fig. 1.

Straight-grained veneers present different problems. The grain cannot be followed in the width, but a very neat repair can be achieved by splicing the patch (fig. 1). Select a piece of veneer to match the part to be cut away, damp it and cut the splices at both ends a little oversize. If the damage is close to the top or bottom of the panel, only splice one end of the patch and let the other end follow through.

The actual length of the 'fingers' is not important, but (within reason) the longer the better. Their lengths should vary. The

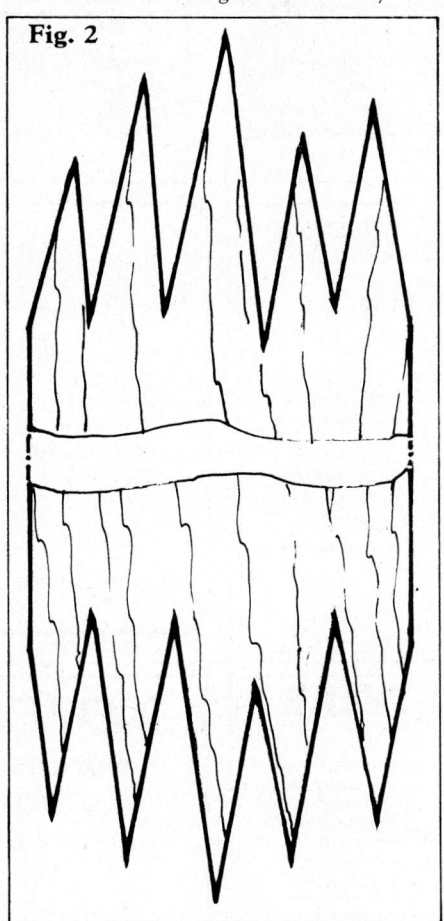

**Fig. 2**

most important feature is their width at the base — about ¼in (6mm), no more. The points must be crisp, with no flat tops.

Having prepared the patch, lay it on the affected part to check that it will cover with a little to spare, and that the grain will match. Glue it in place in the same way as for a figured patch, and leave it for 10-15 minutes. As before, the patch must be kept damp at all times while work is being done on it. For this type of patch I would suggest that a thin straight-edge be used with the knife — except where there are curly parts: these should be cut freehand.

Try to sever both thicknesses of veneer in one pass, and take care not to over-run with the knife and cause nicks in the non-waste parts of the veneers. If the straight cuts do not sever both veneers, very carefully re-cut freehand because it will be extremely difficult, if not impossible, to find the exact spot where the straight-edge should go. Remove the waste as the work proceeds, and lift the patch by dampening it, applying a warm iron and inserting the knife somewhere in the centre — never at any of the points, for fear of breaking them. Clean the glue off and place between two boards while still damp. Removing the waste, re-gluing and laying by hand or press is also done in the same way.

Cleaning up the patch is done in the same way for both figured and straight-grained veneers. Wash off the tapes and any paper that has adhered, and leave to dry thoroughly. The patch will almost certainly be proud of the main veneer. If you have used a piece of the same material, the amount by which it is proud obviously depends on how much veneer has been sanded away from the main panel. It follows that the prouder the patch the thinner the main veneer, and the more careful one needs to be in cleaning up. ∎

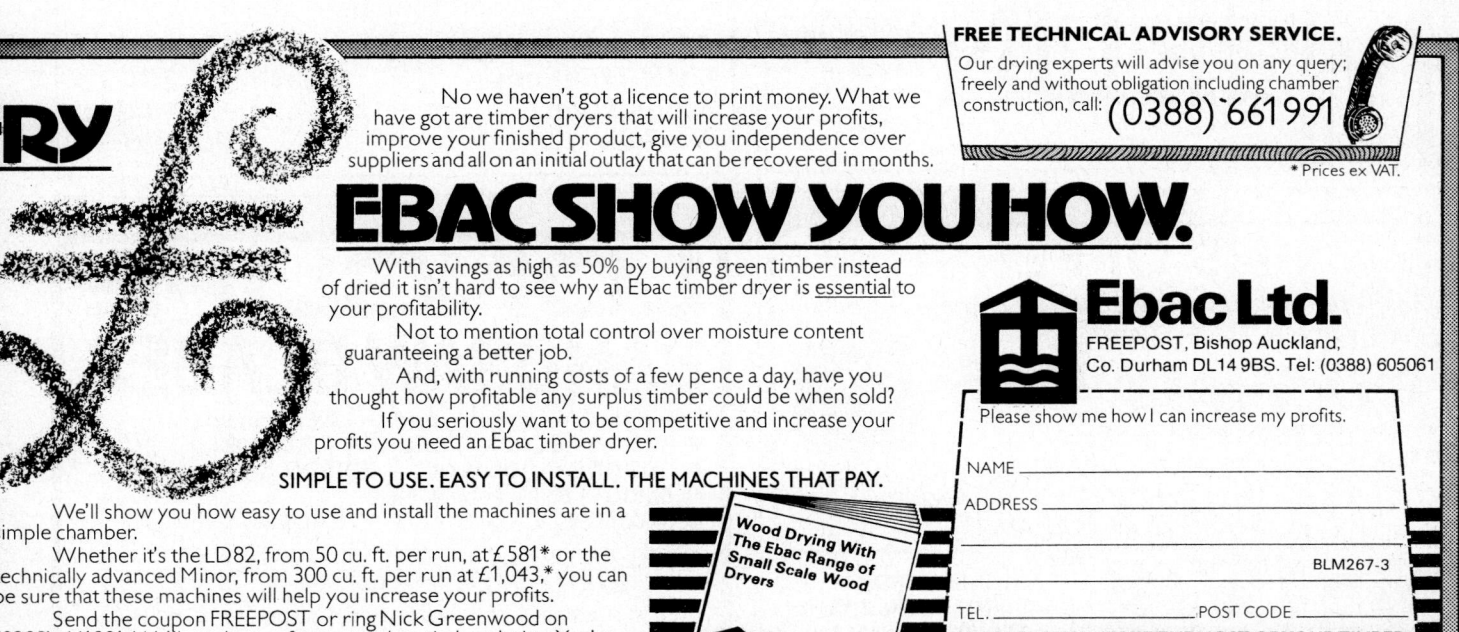

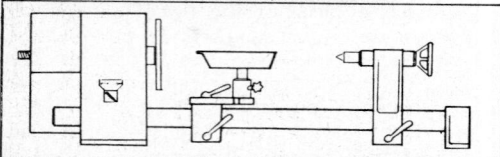

216

Prices quoted are those prevailing at press date and are subject to alteration due to economic conditions

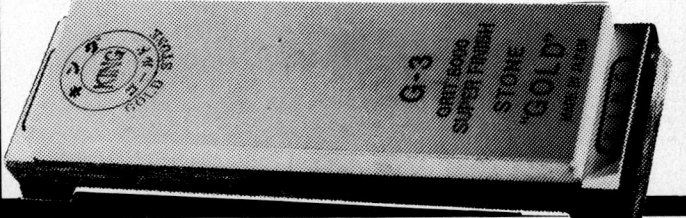

217

# Where the rainbow starts?

A new household name is born? Aidan Walker explores Formica's answer to Formica's problems

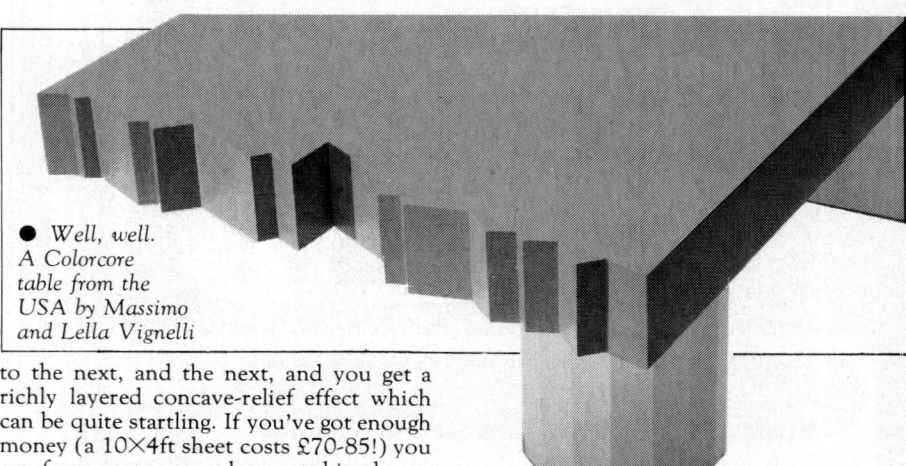

● *Well, well. A Colorcore table from the USA by Massimo and Lella Vignelli*

**W**hat has the edge over the average plastic laminate? 'Formica Ltd has taken a revolutionary step forward', proclaims their publicity. 'And called it COLORCORE.'

Their new material, a 1.3mm laminate which is 'Solid colour — all the way through' has numerous and exciting possibilities for the designer, the craftsman, even the artist, as well as the bigger commercial user. The absence of a black-line edge means that a form covered in one of the 20 subtle shades on offer gives the appearance of a solid mass of colour. Introduced in 1982, Colorcore first came into the public eye at the Chicago Neocon furniture fair in June 1983. International architects' entries in the 'Surface and Ornament' competition included a Neapolitan-icecream block table, a fish lamp sculpture (!), and a superb classical cabinet by Paul Chiasson in delicate pinks and greys.

Unlike ordinary Formica, Colorcore doesn't have to be used simply as a surface covering. Laminate a number of sheets together and then rout through one surface to the next, and the next, and you get a richly layered concave-relief effect which can be quite startling. If you've got enough money (a 10×4ft sheet costs £70-85!) you can form your own colour-combined constructional material, building it up to the thickness of ply or blockboard and using as many rainbow hues as you like. Hardness is as consistent as colour through the thickness; nor does the material yellow or fade, so wear won't bring the characteristic 'old Formica' tattiness.

For the traditional craftsman in wood, the material seems to have great inlay and edge-banding possibilities. It bends to 12in diameter, and problems of awkward, brittle grain are non-existent. Using it in ¼in strips would make one of those sheets last longer, too.

'You need a router, for a start,' says John Collier, right-hand man of designer-craftsman Michael Reed, and probably one of Britain's most experienced workers with Colorcore. John and Michael have made lighting-control desks and kitchen worktops with it, covering surfaces and then rounding over or bevelling the edges to get a beautiful mixture of flat colour and natural wood. 'All your cutting and routing tools must really be tungsten. You can plane it if the thickness isn't too great, but don't depend solely on tool steel for working it.'

They have laminated up to eight thicknesses together, and successfully moulded the material; but here's the catch — there are gluing problems. Formica's nearly black base means that the glue-line is invisible, but joining Colorcore edge-to-edge or surface-to-surface to get a 'solid' effect demands that there be no glue-line at all. Catalytic PVA seems to be most successful on porous surfaces such as that of chipboard; Formica also recommend a clear, slow-drying epoxy resin, for example Araldite 6003 — but 'It takes 24 hours to go off,' says John, 'which is a pain.' If you put too much pressure on it, the glue squeezes out and you get no bond at all.

● *Above: Again surfaced with Colorcore, this sideboard was designed by David Vickery and made by Michael Reed*

● *Left: Idol fantasies — the prizewinning Temple Chair by Lewis & Clark*

**Fabrication Guidelines**

Overhang — Edge Not Flush

RIGHT — WRONG

Allow for up to 6mm overhang when applying the first piece of COLORCORE to the substrate. This allows for machining flush with the surface for a tight joint.

Machined Flush — Rounded Edge

RIGHT — WRONG

Use sharp tools to machine COLORCORE flush with the substrate and free from chips. If sanding, always work towards the substrate using a fine (100) grit belt. Take care not to round over the edge as this will result in a wide glue line.

Tight Joint — Rounded Edge

RIGHT — WRONG

Apply the horizontal surface using a sufficient, even coating of adhesive and again allowing a slight overhang. Use bonding pressures correct for your operation that result in a tight glueline.

Tight Joint — Thick Glueline

RIGHT — WRONG

Machine the finished edge of the horizontal surface with a standard bevel or radius cutter, and file or scrape smooth.

● How to use it: part of Formica's information package

Surfacing beech with Colorcore using Araldite 6003 was a disaster. 'The wood moved like crazy, the bond broke, and the sheet just plain fell off!'

John suspects that only high-technology processes can guarantee the perfection that Formica claims is possible. 'The aircraft industry apparently sieve glass beads to 3 thou, and mix those with the glue to ensure a good bond. But that ensures a 3-thou glueline as well.' — and how many of us stock glass beads to a consistent $\frac{3}{1000}$in?

Finish? Formica call it 'a warm velour, a subtle grained texture . . . that enhances the beauty of colour and design without obscuring or "fuzzing" its detail.' Michael and John use metal polish to get a sheen consistent with a rich wood finish, and find that it ages to a soft patina — not unlike a leather desk-top, but of course infinitely more hardwearing.

An attractive material altogether. But, at that price, don't let your router slip!

● Product information from Product Applications Design & Development Dept, Formica Ltd, North Shields, NE29 8 RE, tel. (0632) 575566

● London sockist: Gunham Plastics, 40 Rivington St, London EC2, tel. 01-739 7114. ■

The Boilerhouse Project's exhibition at the Victoria & Albert Museum from 27 November to 13 January was the 'first opportunity to make international comparisons of new ideas in furniture', according to the blurb. 'Designers now feel free from constraints and are able once again to explore pattern, colour, symbolism and metaphor. It demonstrates that Post-Modernism is not one style, but many.'

Six English furniture designers were specially commissioned by Formica to make pieces for this exhibition, which included work by American and French furniture makers, previously seen in Chicago, New York and Paris. Definitely more arty than crafty — some of the pieces were more like jokes than furniture — but, as a heavily-financed opportunity for designers to let their imaginations run free, why not? There was a time when those who provided visual interest for the everyday world were dependent on the patronage of the nobility; this system now seems to have become the domain of the fabulously rich multi-national corporation. Earls and Dukes were not looking for publicity, however. The sumptuous display that the Cyanamid corporation can afford to mount underlines every hardworking designer-maker's problems.

The Americans were largely responsible for the excesses, the French for classical style, and the English came nearest to producing practical but very pretty furniture. Stanley Tigerman's variation on the love-seat theme, featured on the cover, showed first-class workmanship but doubtful anthropometrics; Peter Crutch's storage tower, also on the cover, looks as if it might actually be used in the real world, although visually it is perhaps less inspired. David Vickery's black, formal sideboard is attractive and nicely proportioned, although somewhat betrayed by hurried detail finish.

A *trompe l'oeil* chest by John Cederquist, whimsically entitled The Great Art Deco Furniture Explosion, looked from across the room as if it were a bit of cardboard leaning up against the wall. On closer inspection it turned out to be a tour-de-force of the cabinetmaker's art, using every imaginable compound angle, meticulously inlaid veneers, and drawers that ran perfectly in appallingly difficult planes. For the average living-room? Not a chance.

Lewis and Clark, South Carolina cabinet-makers, won the Surface and Ornament competition's 'Best Conceptual Design' award. One for the museums, this — a 4×4×4ft fantasy in 'Tawny blush', it 'was created for a deity who sits enthroned while tiny imaginary worshippers perform exotic rituals to their seated god'. The arms have built-in staircases, the headpiece is hollow with a model ladder for the worshippers to climb out . . . if this is anything more than an expensive joke, it needs a more subtle appreciation than mine.

John Makepeace's low table, scrubbed oak legs and characteristically leaf-derived top, deserves mention as the most successful conqueror of the glue-line problem. None of these pieces had bad workmanship, though some had detail faults, but Makepeace gave himself the most pastel shades, with long, shallow, curved bevel edges — the most difficult gluing combination of all — and it looked a treat.

Relevance to the everyday woodworker? Inspiration, discussion, envy of the freedom from market constraints that Formica's money afforded; the point is the distinction between good furniture and bad art. True excellence in a designer-maker's craft is surely embodied in a piece whose beauty matches its workmanship; in 'Post Modern Colour', the craft was (mainly) impeccable, the art disposable.

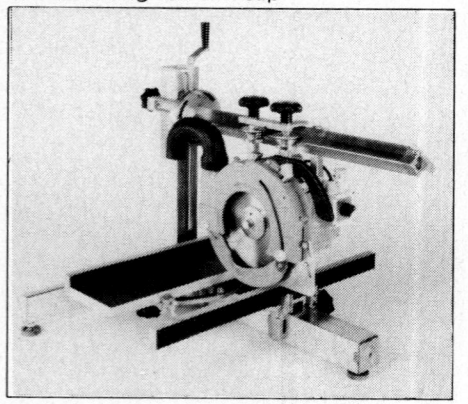
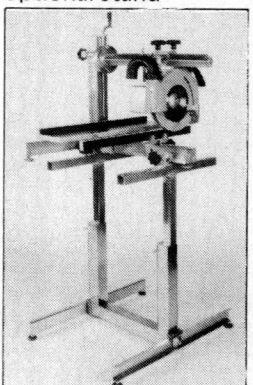
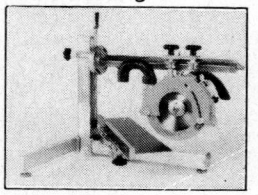

Prices quoted are those prevailing at press date and are
subject to alteration due to economic conditions.

# Paddle power

Tim Kidman follows up January's kayak project with the means of propulsion — in case you were up the creek without one

**K**ayak paddles were originally rather short, small in blade area and also unfeathered, the two blades being in the same plane. Modern slalom paddles are feathered; the large curved blades are set at right-angles, and so 'handed'. They can be over 7ft long. If you paddle with your right hand holding the shaft, allowing it to twist through your left, you are right-handed and so need a right-hand feather. If you hold the lower blade concave side towards your feet, the top blade when held vertically will face to the right.

Paddles are used for three purposes; obviously for propelling the canoe, but also as a rudder at either stern or bow — you can steer by paddling harder on one side than the other — and for support. The paddle keeps the canoeist upright, or it can bring you back topside from underneath!

The strain is in the shaft, whose flexing can often be seen in photographs of active canoeists, so it needs to be made of a tough and springy wood. I use close-grained Columbian pine, which I find gives the right paddling feel.

To make my own paddles (I am a sea kayakist and use a long paddle with long narrow blades) I select a piece of Columbian pine 8ft 4in long, planed to 1¼in square, and then add pieces of mahogany, silver spruce and iroko to give me a 6in-wide blade.

My paddle blades are constructed by cutting out the side pieces to a series of shapes that I have made in hardboard. I use these patterns to mark out two sets of each wood of the required thickness — mahogany for the first, silver spruce the next and iroko for the outside. I cut the shapes by bandsaw. The ends of the shaft are marked out using the longest pattern, a process that needs special care because this is when the paddle is handed and given the correct feather.

I glue the side pieces to the shaft with Aerolite 306 glue, clamping them tightly. When all six pieces are glued and set the blades are shaped, firstly with a bandsaw to give the overall shape — again marked from a cardboard pattern — and then with a 10in drawknife to shape the curve. The final shaping needs a smoothing-plane and spokeshave, finishing with a belt sander.

The shaft now needs to be rounded because outside the paddle blades it is still 1¼in square. This can be done by marking the square section with a spar gauge, a spar- and mast-makers' tool, before rounding it off, but I use an ordinary marking-gauge set at ⁵⁄₁₆in. Then I plane until the markings are cut away. At the blade end I use the spokeshave to carry the cut into the blade, blending with the paddle's curved edges.

At each end of the rounded shaft, about 10in from the blade, I flatten the round section of the shaft to give the paddler a feel of the position of the blade. The flat should be at right-angles to the blade — if you take about ⅛in off each side, it can easily be felt by the hand. The whole shaft can be finished off by completing the round with a spokeshave and then pulling a piece of old sanding belt along it to take out any high spots.

When the shaft is completed, the blades need balancing. This is done by measuring to find the centre of the shaft, and marking it; if you balance it on a piece of thin metal you can see which end needs wood removing. Removal is carried out from the back with a smoothing-plane and spokeshave.

When balanced and sanded, the ends of the paddle are reinforced using fibreglass tape and polyester resin. A length of 2in glass tape is pulled along the curved end of the paddle and stretched so that an equal amount comes over both sides, then it is held in place with bulldog clips. The tape is then impregnated with recently catalysed polyester resin.

After setting, excess tape is removed to the edge of the paddle and the end sanded to remove excess resin. Another piece of tape, usually 1½in wide, is now laid on and impregnated with resin, set and sanded to a smooth surface.

Finally the blades are given three coats of polyurethane varnish. ∎

● *The patterns for the separate blade components. The longest is also used to shape the ends of the shaft*

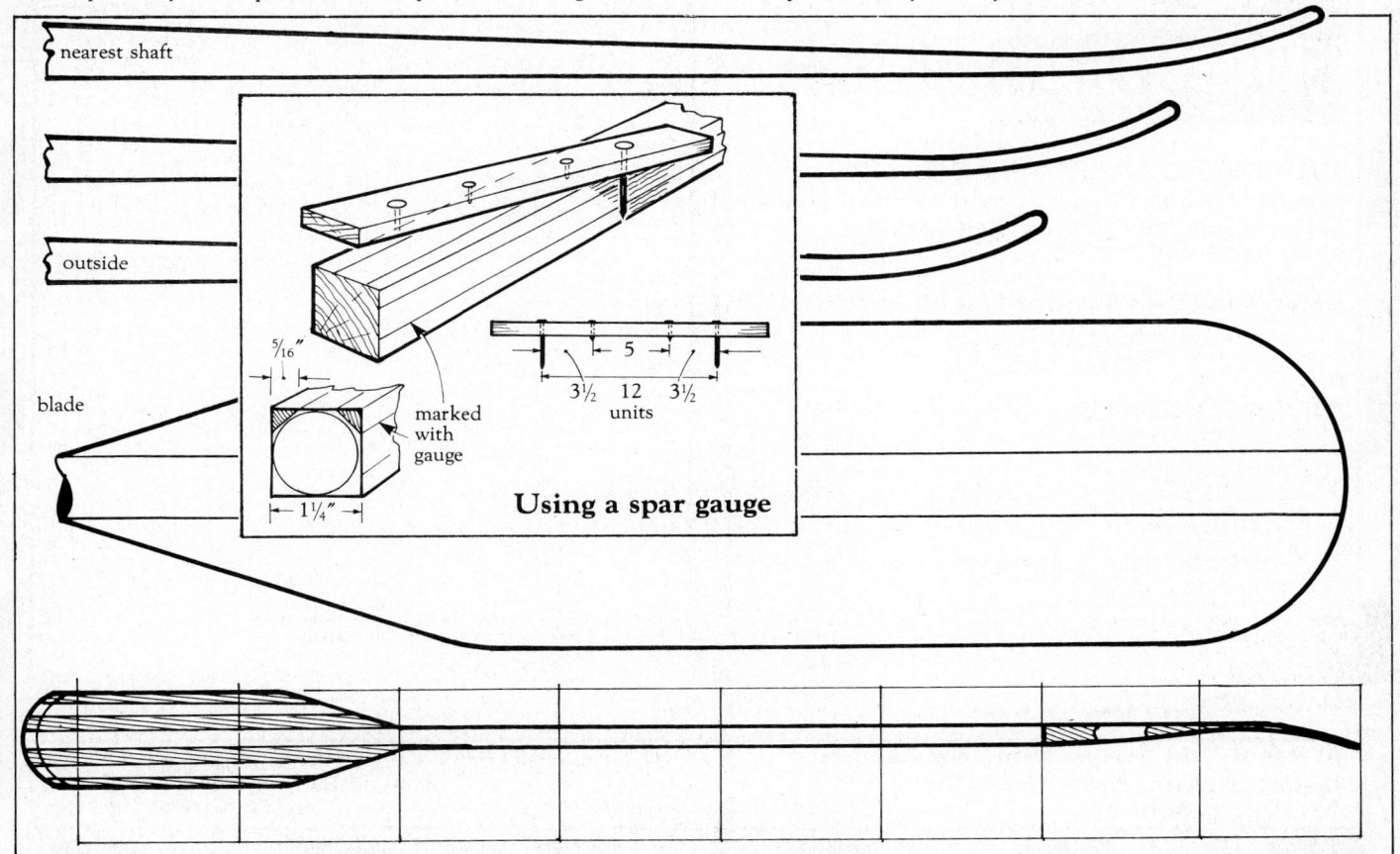

nearest shaft

outside

blade

⁵⁄₁₆″

marked with gauge

1¼″

5

3½  12  3½
units

**Using a spar gauge**

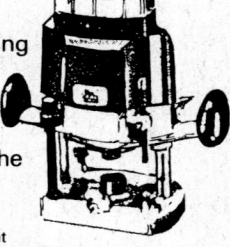

# Joinery for show

Showcases and their joints present a legendary challenge to the cabinetmaker. Stan Thomas explains

I recently designed and made a display case for my local library. This sort of job divides firmly into two parts — corresponding to the two halves of the piece itself. And one is a lot easier than the other.

The easier part is, of course, the pedestal. In my design the top rails are flush-jointed. This seems to have become the fashion, but I'm no great lover of this method; I prefer the traditional way of setting the rail faces below the leg surfaces. This case being of teak, very little shrinkage has occurred between rails and legs; but if I had used sapele, for example, I feel sure that the centrally heated conditions in which it stands would have opened out the joints very visibly. In the traditional method, with the tenons going in barefaced, shrinkage could not manifest itself at the shoulders (see fig. 1).

The tenons do not have to be the conventional ⅓ of the rail thickness, for look at the stiles into which they are going: 2½×2½in finished. Since the rails are 1½in, the tenons can be at least ¾in in thickness; there are obvious advantages in strength.

The bottom rails, being the same thickness, can be given ¾in tenons too —

with their tenons being full-width; that is, without edge shoulders. About all that is gained from edge-shouldering is a narrowing and consequent weakening of the tenons. Eyebrows will be raised here, I know; but I was brought up in a very high-class hand workshop where this was standard practice. Provided that the mortise is cut very slightly short, so that the rail is a good tight fit in its width, we have a perfect joint with maximum tenon strength: fig. 2. (Hand workshop, did I say? We even tenoned 9in rails and housed stair strings by hand!)

However, all the tenons in the pedestal are fox-wedged. I feel sure that anyone contemplating a job like this will be familiar with fox-wedging — the technique of inserting wedges in the end of the tenon before it is driven home. Of course, as with any job like this, the whole 'square' should not be glued and cramped in one operation; the ends are done first, the glue allowed to set, and then these two assemblies cleaned and each glued together as phase two. The important point is that all inner surfaces must be cleaned up before assembly.

After assembly, strengthening gussets of good-quality (not 'stoutheart') ¼in or ⅜in ply are fitted across each corner, as in fig. 3, while the shelf slats are double-notched (fig. 4). The main purpose of the shelf is to prevent the ends of the pedestal from spreading if the case should be slid too harshly over an uneven floor — hence the notchings.

Now for the hard part — the case proper. This is a job for the dovetailing enthusiast, for four types of dovetail are used here — the ordinary through dovetail, the lap, the mitre and the three-way.

Fig. 5 shows the sections and sizes of the case members. These dimensions being nominal, each would of course lose ⅛in or so in planing.

Begin, then, by jointing up the back frame; lap dovetails at its base and through dovetails at its top, with the tails being in the long members. Dovetails are vital here to withstand the stopping of the sliding doors. All jointing done, these four pieces should be cleaned up all round, but glass-papered on their inner surfaces only. This frame can now be glued up, squared (pin temporary braces in the rebates) and allowed to set.

Now we come to the bottom rails — two side (or end) rails and one front. One end of each side rail (remember to pair up) will have to be tenoned for fitting to the back frame; the other two ends, along with both ends of the front rail, will have to be mitre-dovetailed.

By the time all this jointing is done, the back frame will have set. Lay this flat upon the bench for the chopping of the mortises for the side rails, which can then be pre-fitted up. The mitre dovetails can now be assembled dry, and this bottom frame tried up into the base of the back frame.

If all fitting-up is satisfactory, clean up the surfaces of the bottom rails and glasspaper the inner one. Then the mitre dovetails can be glued up, the baseboard (¾in block-board) glued and pocket-screwed into its groove, and all this assembled and cramped into the back frame — which now, being the lighter of the two, should be the vertical one on the bench. Add squaring braces again, from back frame to base, and again leave to set while you get on with the corner bars. The vertical corner bars are stub-tenoned into the bottom frame, fig. 6, and the end top corner bars run across the corners of the back frame (fig. 7).

Now, with the verticals tenoned into place, the mitre points can be 'picked', to obtain the lengths of the top bars — front and ends. The front connection of the three is by three-way dovetail: see fig. 8.

Lastly, the bars can be glued and assembled. The 'run-across' junctions at the back frame can be G-cramped off triangular bits of wood fitted into the corners, while the stub-tenons of the verticals should be tight enough to hold these shoulders close. But the corners, if they need cramping, should be 'strung' as in fig. 10 — being pulled inwards by a longer string picking up the three points, extending to the base, and tacked.

The finished base of this case is matt-black Formica.

The case is glazed with 6mm float (¼in plate). A smaller case could be done with 4mm (32oz).

Glass should always be measured ⅛in

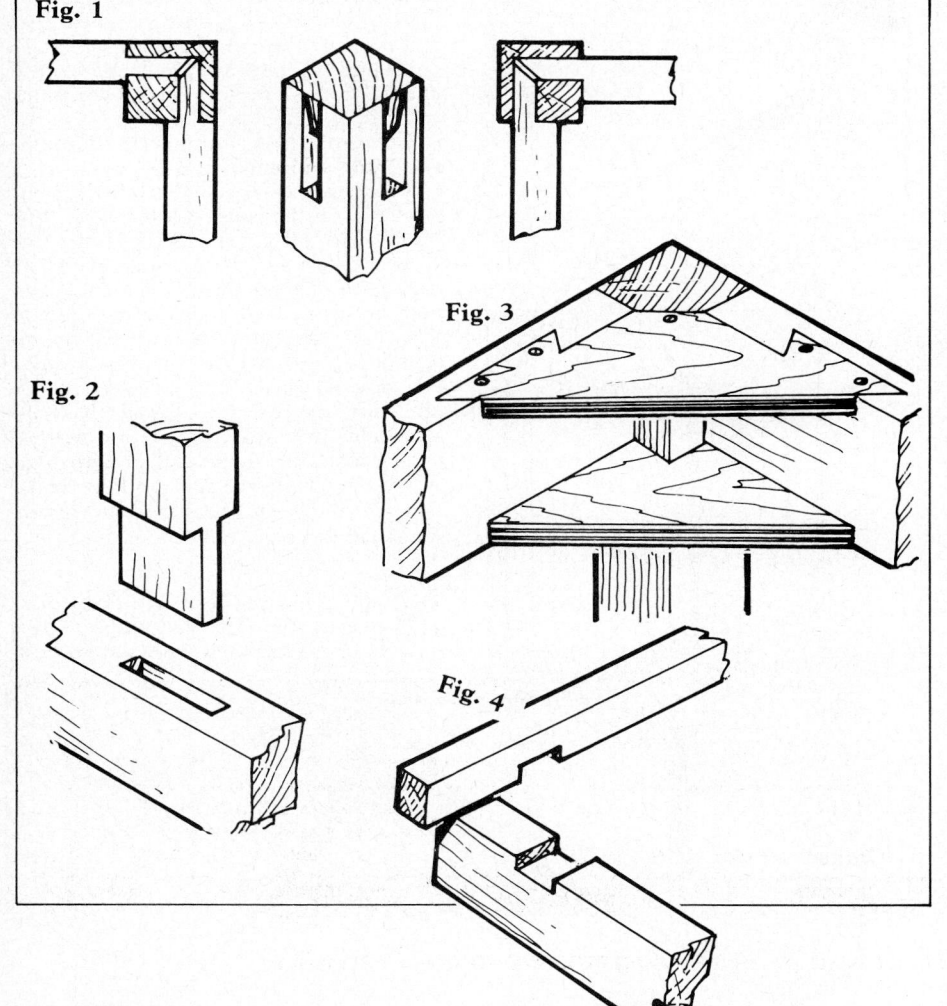

Fig. 1

Fig. 2

Fig. 3

Fig. 4

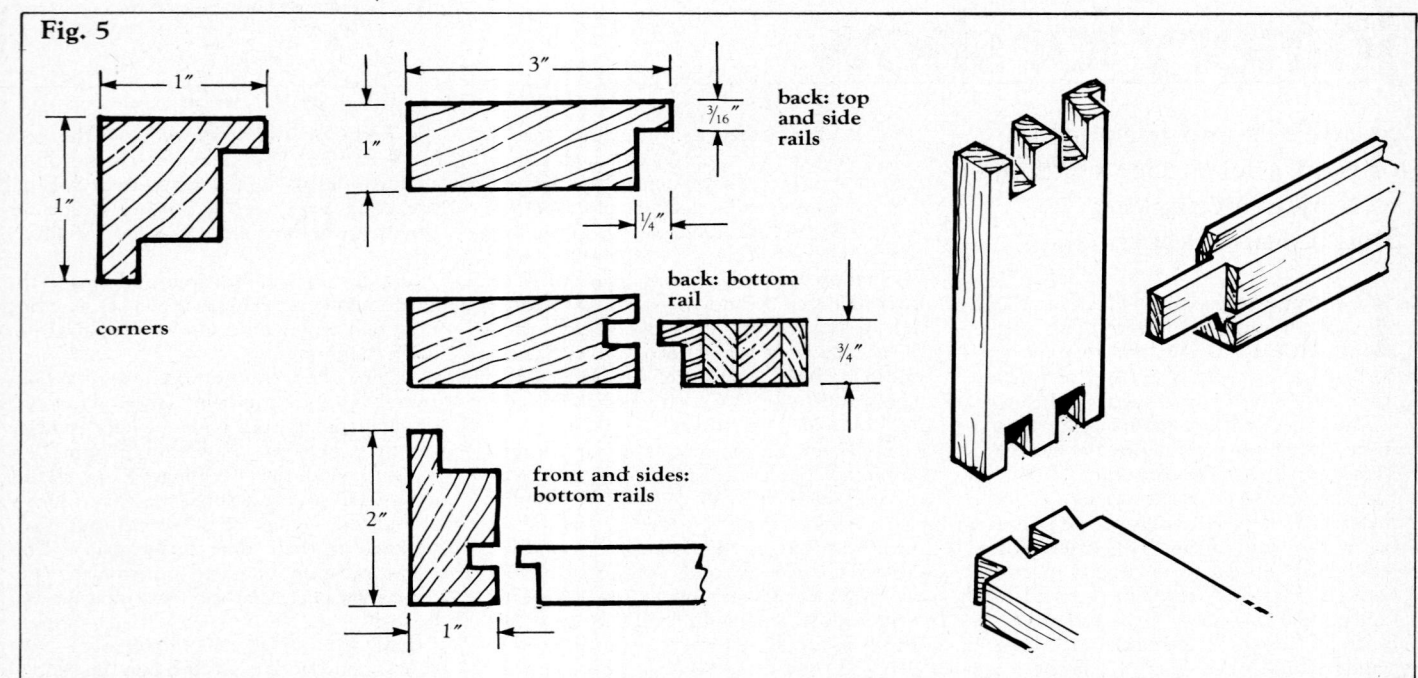

**Fig. 5**

1″

1″

corners

3″

1″

3/16″

1/4″

back: top and side rails

back: bottom rail

3/4″

front and sides: bottom rails

2″

1″

small. We have ¼in rebates here, and that will give us ⅟₁₆in clearance all round. The way to get the glass exactly right is to cut two light laths to the exact length and breadth of each glass, and to try these in position — checking each end. The laths should be clearly identified; we don't want, say, the front verticals mixed up with the top sides. Having ensured that all is OK I prefer to take the laths themselves to the glazier, rather than to measure. On the other hand, if I do have to measure, I always get someone to double-check.

Cases like this are always glazed upside-down. Put the upturned case on the bench, and tack a good straight batten along one side of the bench to buttress the top glazing bar (now on the bottom); see fig. 11. This is important both for keeping the bar straight and for resisting 'push' when inserting the corner-fillet screws.

The first glass to go in is the front. Firstly, try it in place dry; then, having ensured that it falls into place, remove it, and fill the rebates well with very soft — even sticky —

**Fig. 7**

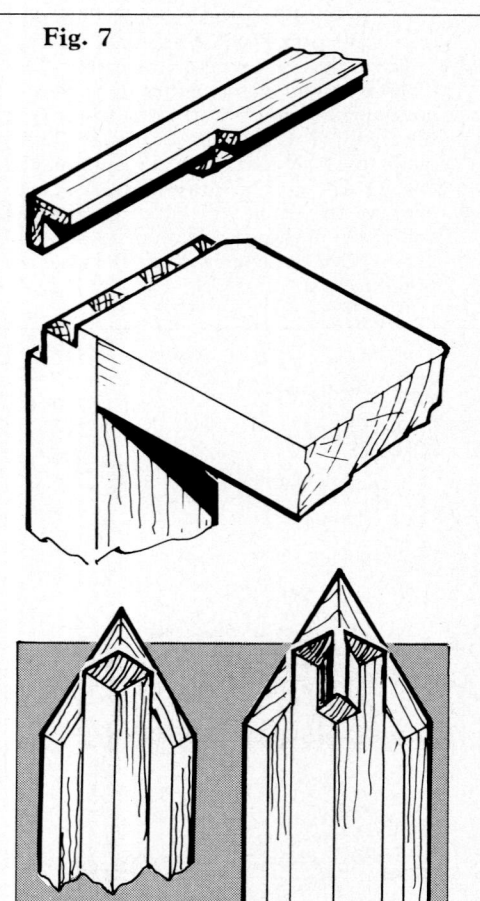

**Fig. 6**

remove corner after dovetailing

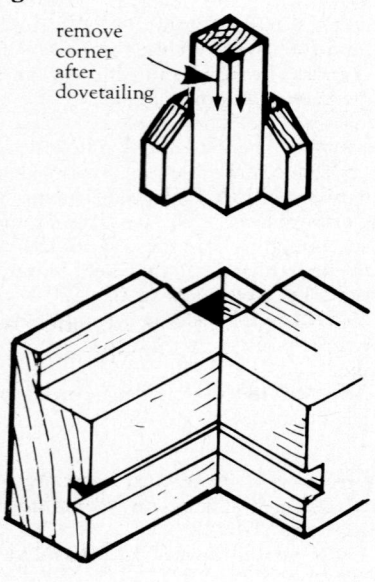

**Fig. 8**

putty, of an appropriate colour. Position the glass bottom edge first and pivot it in; then keep it in place with a small block and pin. Now repeat with the top glass.

So far, we've had the ends of the case open for manipulation. If we had done the ends second, we'd have to be extremely careful in locating the top; we'd more than likely foul one of the ends, and have a bad scratch or worse. Nor would we be able to get our hands through for locating the top.

However, with the top now resting comfortably, it's advisable to lay upon it a piece of hardboard or insulation board, so that if one of the ends slips during location no damage will be done. The ends are put in like the front — bottom edge, pivot, block and pin.

The glazing fillets can now be cut in: the back (top and ends) and the base (front and ends); see fig. 13. All that remains is the screwing of the corner fillets (fig. 14). These will of course butt against the 'square' fillets. Do the top first, and mitre them at the front corners. The verticals can now be scribed over the mitres, but in screwing the verticals we have no supporting batten to resist pressure; nor can we 'hold against' with one hand, as for the ends. So it's necessary to have an accomplice to 'hold against' the vertical corner bars while the screws are turned in. While the pins in the square fillets can be spaced at about 9in, the corner-fillet screws should be spaced at only about 3in.

Nothing has yet been said about final cleaning-up. This is because up to now the construction has been too fragile to

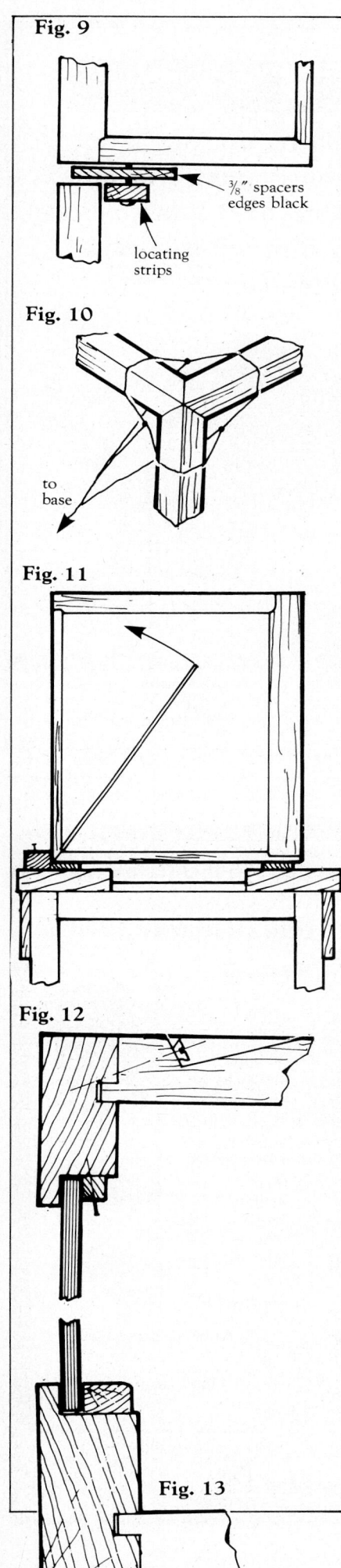

**Fig. 9**

⅜″ spacers edges black

locating strips

**Fig. 10**

to base

**Fig. 11**

**Fig. 12**

**Fig. 13**

**Fig. 14**

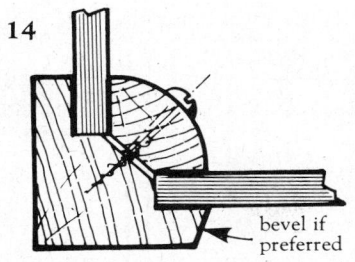

bevel if preferred

resist the forces of planing, etc. With glazing completed, however, the whole structure is rock-solid. First remove surplus putty, with a fillet cut to a chisel edge (no metal); then use a finely set sharp plane, or a scraper, for flushing off the joints, and finish with abrasive paper.

Now we come to the doors. The back top and bottom rails can of course have been double-grooved to take two ordinary pieces of glass — say 4mm (32oz). The arrises on the glass should be removed all round with a piece of carborundum stone, and these glass doors would then have to be manipulated in the palm of the hand. This is a cheap method, and good for doors that are to be used infrequently. But, for a first-class job, the frame dimensions should be given to a glazier who will then supply everything: sliding tracks, runners, lock, handle depressions, polished edges, a 'brush' dust guard at the lap of the doors, and ideally a light vertical rod to support the top rail at its centre (it would tend to sag without this). For the home-made doors, a ⅜in steel rod can be used, being sunk into shallow holes at top and bottom. The top will lift up far enough to allow you to insert this.

The display panel is made of insulation board, covered with cloth.

Incidentally, this case was all hand-made. Rebates and grooves were cut with rebate plane and plough; even the mortises were chopped by hand — though that was only because I had no access to a mortiser!

Overall dimensions are:
Pedestal — 54×24×30 (L×W×H)
   legs 2½×2½in finished
   top rails 4×1½in nominal
   bottom rails 3×1½in nominal
   shelf slats 1½×1⅛in nominal;
Height of case 30in.

The outer corners of the legs are chamfered ½×½in, running out to nothing 9in from the floor. ∎

227

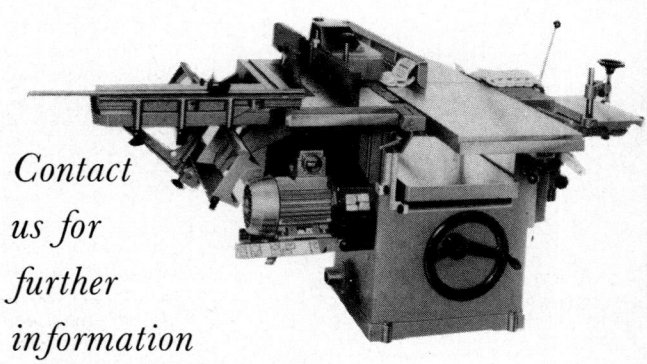
**Prices quoted are those prevailing at press date and are subject to alteration due to economic conditions**

# shopguide

## AVON

**BATH**  Tel. Bath 64513
JOHN HALL TOOLS  ★
RAILWAY STREET

Open: Monday-Saturday
9.00 a.m.-5.30 p.m.
H.P.W.WM.D.A.BC.

**BRISTOL**  Tel. (0272) 741510
JOHN HALL TOOLS LIMITED  ★
CLIFTON DOWN SHOPPING CENTRE
WHITELADIES ROAD
Open: Monday-Saturday
9.00 a.m.-5.30 p.m.
H.P.W.WM.D.A.BC.

**BRISTOL**  Tel. (0272) 629092
TRYMWOOD SERVICES
2a DOWNS PARK EAST, (off North View)
WESTBURY PARK
Open: 8.30 a.m.-5.30 p.m. Mon. to Fri.
Closed for lunch 1.00-2.00 p.m.
P.W.WM.D.T.A.BC.

**BRISTOL**  Tel. (0272) 667013
FASTSET LTD
190-192 WEST STREET
BEDMINSTER
Open: Mon.-Fri. 8.30 a.m.-5.00 p.m.
Saturday 9.00 a.m.-1.00 p.m.
H.P.W.WM.D.CS.A.BC.

## BEDFORDSHIRE

**BEDFORD**  Tel. (0234) 59808
BEDFORD SAW SERVICE  K
39 AMPTHILL ROAD

Open: Mon.-Fri. 8.30-5.30
Sat. 9.00-4.00
H.P.A.BC.W.CS.WM.D.

## BERKSHIRE

**COOKHAM**  Tel. (06285) 20350
CHURCH'S TIMBER
STATION HILL

Open: Mon-Sat 8.30 a.m.-5.30 p.m.
Wed 8.30 a.m.-1.00 p.m.
H.P.W.T.CS.MF.A.

**READING**  Tel. (0734) 591361
HOME CARE CENTRE
26/30 KING'S ROAD

Open: Monday-Saturday
9.00 a.m.-5.30 p.m.
H.P.W.D.A.WM.BC.

**READING**  Tel. Littlewick Green
DAVID HUNT (TOOL  2743
MERCHANTS) LTD  ★
KNOWL HILL, NR. READING
Open: Monday-Saturday
9.00 a.m.-5.30 p.m.
H.P.W.D.A.BC.

**READING**  Tel. Reading 661511
WOKINGHAM TOOL CO. LTD.
99 WOKINGHAM ROAD

Open: Mon-Sat 9.00 a.m.-5.30 p.m.
Closed 1.00-2.00 p.m. for lunch
H.P.W.WM.D.CS.A.BC.

## BUCKINGHAMSHIRE

**SLOUGH**  Tel. (06286) 5125
BRAYWOOD ESTATES LTD
158 BURNHAM LANE

Open: 9.00 a.m.-5.30 p.m.
Monday-Saturday
H.P.W.WM.CS.A.

**HIGH WYCOMBE**  Tel. (0494)
ISAAC LORD LTD  22221
185 DESBOROUGH ROAD  KE

Open: Mon-Fri 8.00 a.m.-5.00 p.m.
Saturday 9.00 a.m.-5.00 p.m.
H.P.W.D.A.

**HIGH WYCOMBE**  Tel. (0494)
SCOTT SAWS LTD.  24201/33788
14 BRIDGE STREET  ★

Mon.-Sat. 8.30 a.m.-6.00 p.m.

H.P.W.WM.D.T.CS.MF.A.BC.

## CAMBRIDGESHIRE

**MILTON KEYNES**  Tel. (0908)
POLLARD WOODWORKING  641366
CENTRE  ★
51 AYLESBURY ST., BLETCHLEY
Open: Mon-Fri 8.30-5.30
Saturday 9.00-5.00
H.P.W.WM.D.A.BC.

**CAMBRIDGE**  Tel. (0223) 247386
H. B. WOODWORKING  K
105 CHERRY HINTON ROAD
Open: 8.30 a.m.-5.30 p.m.
Monday-Friday
8.30 a.m.-1.00 p.m. Sat.
H.P.W.WM.D.CS.A.

**CAMBRIDGE**  Tel. (0223) 63132
D. MACKAY LTD.  E★
BRITANNIA WORKS, EAST ROAD

Open: Mon.-Fri. 8.30 a.m.-1 p.m./2.00-
5.00 p.m. Sat. 8.30 a.m.-1.00 p.m.
H.P.W.D.T.CS.MF.A.BC.

**PETERBOROUGH**  Tel. (0733)
WILLIAMS DISTRIBUTORS  64252
(TOOLS) LIMITED  K
108-110 BURGHLEY ROAD
Open: Monday to Friday
8.30 a.m.-5.30 p.m.
H.P.A.W.D.WH.BC.

## CHESHIRE

**NANTWICH**  Tel. Crewe 67010
ALAN HOLTHAM  K★
THE OLD STORES TURNERY
WISTASON ROAD, WILLASTON
Open: Tues.-Sat. 9.00 a.m.-5.30 p.m.
Closed Monday
P.W.WM.D.T.C.CS.A.BC.

## CLEVELAND

**MIDDLESBROUGH**  Tel. (0642)
CLEVELAND WOODCRAFT  813103
(M'BRO), 38-42 CRESCENT ROAD  K

Open: Mon-Sat 9.15 a.m.-5.30 p.m.

H.P.T.A.BC.W.WM.CS.D.

## CORNWALL

**FALMOUTH**  Tel. (0326) 76555
WOODSTOCK (HARDWOODS) LTD.
PONSHARDEN

Open: Mon-Fri 8.30 a.m.-5.30 p.m.
Sat. 9.00 a.m.-1.00 p.m.
T.

**HELSTON**  Tel. Helston (03265) 4961
SOUTH WEST  Truro (0872) 71671
POWER TOOLS  Launceston
MONUMENT ROAD  (0566) 3555
  K
H.P.W.WM.D.CS.A.

## DERBYSHIRE

**TRURO**  Tel. (0872) 71671
TRURO POWER TOOLS  E★
30 FERRIS TOWN

Open Mon.-Sat. 8.00 a.m.-12.30 p.m./
1.30 p.m.-5.00 p.m.
H.P.W.WM.D.CS.MF.A.BC.

**BUXTON**  Tel. (0298) 871636
CRAFT SUPPLIES  K★
THE MILL, MILLERSDALE

Open: Mon-Sat 9.00 a.m.-5.00 p.m.

H.P.W.D.T.CS.A.BC.

**DERBY**  Tel. (0332) 41862
HAZLEHURSTS LTD.  E★
LONDON ROAD AND CANAL STREET

Open: Mon.-Sat. 8.30 a.m.-5.30 p.m. (retail)
Mon.-Fri. 8.00 a.m.-5.00 p.m. (trade)
H.P.W.MF.A.BC.

## DEVON

**BRIXHAM**  Tel. (08045) 4900
WOODCRAFT SUPPLIES  E★
4 HORSE POOL STREET

Open: Mon.-Sat. 9.00 a.m.-6.00 p.m.

H.P.W.A.D.MF.CS.BC.

**EXETER**  Tel. (0392) 73936
WRIDES TOOL CENTRE
147 FORE STREET

Open: 9.00 a.m.-5.30 p.m.
Wednesday 9.00 a.m.-1.00 p.m.
H.P.W.WM.A.

**PLYMOUTH**  Tel. (0752) 330303
WESTWARD BUILDING SERVICES  ★
LTD., LISTER CLOSE, NEWNHAM
INDUSTRIAL ESTATE, PLYMPTON
Open: Mon-Fri 8.00 a.m.-5.30 p.m.
Sat. 8.30 a.m.-12.30 p.m.
H.P.W.WM.D.A.BC.

## ESSEX

**ILFORD**
CUTWELL TOOLS LTD.  ★
774-776 HIGH ROAD

Mon.-Fri. 9.00 a.m.-5.00 p.m.
and also by appointment.
P.W.WM.A.D.CS.

**LEIGH ON SEA**  Tel. (0702)
MARSHAL & PARSONS LTD.  710404
1111 LONDON ROAD  EK

Open: 8.30 a.m.-5.30 p.m. Mon-Fri
9.00 a.m.-5.00 p.m. Sat.
H.P.W.WM.D.CS.A.

**KEY: H HANDTOOLS**

**KEY: P POWER TOOLS**

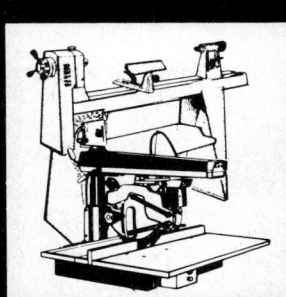

**KEY: W WOODWORKING
MACHINERY**

# shopguide

## GLOUCESTERSHIRE

**CHELTENHAM** Tel. (0242) 39099
HAMBURY MACHINE SERVICES E★
UNIT 14, MALMESBURY ROAD
Open: Mon.-Fri. 9.00 a.m.-5.30 p.m.
Sat. 9.30 a.m.-12.00 p.m.

W.WM.P.D.

**TEWKESBURY** Tel. (0684)
TEWKESBURY SAW CO. LTD. 293092
TRADING ESTATE, NEWTOWN K

Open: Mon-Fri 8.00 a.m.-5.00 p.m.
Saturday 9.30 a.m.-12.00 p.m.
P.W.WM.D.CS.

## HAMPSHIRE

**ALDERSHOT** Tel. (0252) 334422
POWER TOOL CENTRE K
374 HIGH STREET

Open Mon-Fri 8.30 a.m.-5.30 p.m.

H.P.W.WM.D.A.BC.

**PORTSMOUTH** Tel. (0705)
EURO PRECISION TOOLS LTD 667332
259/263 LONDON ROAD, NORTH END ★
E

Open: Mon-Fri 9.00 a.m.-5.30 p.m.
Sat. 9.00 a.m.-1.00 p.m.
H.P.W.WM.D.A.BC.

**SOUTHAMPTON** Tel. (0703)
H.W.M. 776222
THE WOODWORKERS
303 SHIRLEY ROAD, SHIRLEY
Open: Tues-Fri 9.30 a.m.-6.00 p.m.
Sat 9.30 a.m.-4.00 p.m.
H.P.W.WM.D.CS.A.BC.T.

## HERTFORDSHIRE

**ENFIELD** Tel. (01-363) 2935
GILL & HOXBY LTD. K
133-137 ST. MARKS ROAD EN1 1BB

Mon.-Sat. 8.30 a.m.-6.00 p.m.
Early closing Wednesday 1.00 p.m.
H.P.W.WM.T.CS.A

**HITCHIN** Tel. (0462) 4177
ROGER'S KE
47 WALSWORTH ROAD
Open: Monday-Saturday
9.00 a.m.-5.30 p.m.
(Closed all day Wednesday)
H.P.W.WM.D.CS.MF.BC.

**WATFORD** Tel. (0923) 48434
HOME CARE CENTRE ★
20 MARKET STREET
WATFORD, HERTS
Open: 9.00 a.m.-5.30 p.m.
Mon-Sat

H.P.W.A.WM.BC.D.

## HUMBERSIDE

**GRIMSBY** Tel. Grimsby (0472)
58741 Hull (0482) 26999
J. E. SIDDLE LTD. (Tool Specialists) ★
83 VICTORIA STREET
Open: Mon-Fri 8.30 a.m.-5.30 p.m.
Sat. 8.30 a.m.-12.45 p.m. & 2 p.m.-5 p.m.
H.P.A.BC.W.WMD.

## KENT

**BIDDENDEN** Tel. (0580) 291555/7
BRITISH GATES & TIMBER
BENENDEN ROAD ★
Open: Mon-Fri 7.30 a.m.-5.30 p.m.
Saturday 8.30 a.m.-midday
(not Bank Holiday weekends)
H.T.CS.MF.

**MAIDSTONE** Tel. (0622) 50177
SOUTH EASTERN SAWS (Ind) LTD ★
COLDRED ROAD,
PARKWOOD INDUSTRIAL ESTATE
Open: Mon-Fri 8.00-5.00pm
Sat. 9.00-12.00
B.C.W.CS.WM.PH.

**MATFIELD** Tel. Brenchley
LEISURECRAFT IN WOOD (089272)
'ORMONDE,' MAIDSTONE RD. 2465
TN12 7JG
Open: Mon-Sun
9.00 a.m.-5.30 p.m.

W.WM.D.T.A.

## LANCASHIRE

**WYE** Tel. (0233) 813144
KENT POWER TOOLS LTD.
UNIT 1, BRIAR CLOSE
WYE, Nr. ASFORD

H.P.W.WM.D.A.CS.

**LANCASTER** Tel. (0524) 32886
LILE TOOL SHOP K
43/45 NORTH ROAD
Open: Monday to Saturday
9.00 a.m.-5.30 p.m.
Wed 9.00 a.m.-12.30 p.m.
H.P.W.D.A.

**PRESTON** Tel. (0772) 52951
SPEEDWELL TOOL COMPANY E★
62-68 MEADOW STREET PR1 1SU
Open: Mon.-Fri. 8.30 a.m.-5.30 p.m.
Sat. 8.30 a.m.-12.30 p.m.

H.P.W.WM.CS.A.MF.BC.

## LEICESTERSHIRE

**BURY** Tel. (061 764 6769)
HOUSE OF HARBRU ★
101 CROSTONS ROAD
ELTON
Open: Mon.-Fri. 9.00 a.m.-5.00 p.m.
Send 2 × 1st class stamps for catalogue
MF.

**HINCKLEY** Tel. (0455) 613432
J. D. WOODARD & CO. (POWER ★
TOOL SPECIALISTS)
THE NARROWS; HINCKLEY
Open: Monday-Saturday
8.00 a.m.-6.00 p.m.
H.P.W.WM.D.CS.A.BC.

## LONDON

**ACTON** Tel. (01-992) 4835
A. MILLS (ACTON) LTD ★
32/36 CHURCHFIELD ROAD W3 6ED
Open: Mon-Fri 9.00 a.m.-5.00 p.m.
Saturdays 9.00 am-1.00 p.m.
H.P.W.WM.

**FULHAM** Tel. (01-385) 5109
I. GRIZZARD LTD. E
84a-b LILLIE ROAD, SW6 1TL
Open: Mon-Sat 9.00-5.30 p.m.
Half day Thursday

H.P.A.BC.W.CS.WM.D.

**LONDON** Tel. (01-567) 2922
G. D. CLEGG & SONS ★
83 UXBRIDGE ROAD, HANWELL W7 3ST
Mon-Sat 9.15 a.m.-5.30 p.m.
Closed for lunch 1.00-2.00p.m.
Early Closing 1.00 p.m. Wed.
H.P.W.A.W.WM.D.CS.

**LONDON** Tel. (01-263) 1536
THOMAS BROTHERS (01-272) 2764
798-804 HOLLOWAY ROAD, N19 E
Open: Mon.-Fri. 8.30 a.m.-5.30 p.m. Thurs.
8.30 a.m.-1 p.m. Sat. 9 a.m.-5 p.m.

H.P.W.WM.CS.MF.BC.

**LONDON** Tel. (01-858) 6444
TOOL HIRE BUY LTD
74/76 CHARLTON ROAD
LONDON SE3 8TT
Open; Mon.-Fri. 8.30 a.m.-5.30 p.m.
Saturday 8.30 a.m.-12.30 p.m.
H.P.W.WM.D.CS.A.BC.

**LONDON** Tel. (01-636) 7475
BUCK & RYAN LTD ★
101 TOTTENHAM COURT ROAD W1P 0DY
Open: Mon.-Fri. 8.30 a.m.-5.30 p.m.
Saturday 8.30 a.m.-4.00 p.m.
H.P.W.WM.D.A..

**NORBURY** Tel. (01-679) 6193
HERON TOOLS & HARDWARE LTD
437 STREATHAM HIGH ROAD SW16
Open: Mon-Fri 8.30 a.m.-5.00 p.m.
Wednesday 8.30 a.m.-1.00 p.m.
Sat. 9.00 a.m.-1.00 p.m.
H.P.W.A.

**WOOLWICH** Tel. (01-854) 7767/8
A. D. SHILLMAN & SONS LTD
108-109 WOOLWICH HIGH STREET
SE18
Open: Mon-Sat
8.30 p.m.-5.30p.m.
H.P.W.CS.A.

## GREATER MANCHESTER

**MANCHESTER** Tel. (061 789)
TIMMS TOOLS 2601
102-104 LIVERPOOL ROAD
PATRICROFT M30 0WZ ★
Weekdays 8.00 a.m.-5.00 p.m.
Sat. 9.00 a.m.-1.00 p.m.
H.P.A.W.

**ROCHDALE** Tel. (0706) 342123/
C.S.M. TOOLS 342322
4-6 HEYWOOD ROAD E★
CASTLETON
Open: Mon-Sat 9.00 a.m.-6.00 p.m.
Sundays by appointment
W.D.CS.A.BC.

## MERSEYSIDE

**LIVERPOOL** Tel. (051-207) 2967
TAYLOR BROS (LIVERPOOL) LTD K
195-199 LONDON ROAD
LIVERPOOL L3 8JG
Open: Monday to Friday
8.30 a.m.-5.30 p.m.
H.P.W.WM.D.A.BC.

## MIDDLESEX

**HOUNSLOW** Tel. (01-570)
Q.R. TOOLS LTD 2103/5135
251-253 HANWORTH ROAD

Open: Mon-Fri 8.30 a.m.-5.30 p.m.
Sat. 9.00 a.m.-1.00 p.m.
P.W.WM.D.CS.A.

**RUISLIP** Tel. (08956) 74126
ALL MODELS ENGINEER E★
91 MANOR WAY

Open: Mon-Sat 9.00 a.m.-5.30 p.m.
H.P.W.A.D.CS.MF.BC.

## NORFOLK

**GT. YARMOUTH** Tel. (0493)
ANGLIA POWER TOOLS 850388
3 DENESIDE, NR30 2HL

Open: Monday to Saturday
8.30 a.m. 5.30 p.m.

H.P.W.D.CS.A.

**KINGS LYNN** Tel. (0553) 2443
WALKER & ANDERSON (Kings Lynn) LTD.
WINDSOR ROAD, KINGS LYNN K
Open: Monday to Saturday
7.45 a.m.-5.30 p.m.
Wednesday 1.00 p.m. Saturday 5.00 p.m.
H.P.W.WM.D.CS.A.

**KEY: CS CUTTING OR SHARPENING SERVICES**

**KEY: MF MATERIAL FINISHES**

**KEY: BC BOOKS/CATALOGUES**

# shopguide

## NORTHAMPTONSHIRE

**NORWICH**    Tel. (0603) 898685
NOROLK SAW SERVICES
DOG LANE, HORSFORD
Open: Monday to Friday
8.00 a.m.-5.00 p.m.
Saturday 8.00 a.m.-12.00 p.m.
H.P.W.WM.D.CS.A.

**NORWICH**    Tel. (0603) 400933
WESTGATES WOODWORKING   Tx
61 HURRICANE WAY,   975412
NORWICH AIRPORT INDUSTRIAL ESTATE
Open: 9.00 a.m.-5.00 p.m. weekdays
9.00 a.m.-12.30 Sat.
P.W.WM.D.BC.      K

**SWAFFHAM**    Tel. (0760) 23073
TONY WADDILOVE,    ★
STATION HOUSE,
LITTLE DUNHAM, KINGS LYNN
Tuesday-Saturday 9.00 a.m.-6.00 p.m.
H.P.W.D.T.CS.A.BC.

**NOTTINGHAM**   Tel. (0602) 225979
POOLEWOOD    and 227064/5
EQUIPMENT LTD.   (06077) 2421 after hrs
5a HOLLY LANE, CHILLWELL
Open: Mon-Fri 9.00 a.m.-5.30 p.m.
Sat. 9.00 a.m. to 12.30 p.m.
P.W.WM.D.CS.A.BC.

## OXFORDSHIRE

**RUSHDEN**    Tel. (0933) 56424
PETER CRISP OF RUSHDEN   KE★
7 HIGH STREET NN10 9JR
Open: Mon-Fri 8.30 a.m.-12.30 p.m./
1.30 p.m.-5.30 p.m. Sat. 8.30 a.m. 5.30 p.m.
Early closing Thurs. 1.00 p.m.
H.P.W.MF.D.A.BC.

**CROWMARSH**    Tel. (0491) 38653
MILL HILL SUPPLIES   E★
66 THE STREET
Open: Mon.-Fri. 9.30 a.m.-5.00 p.m.
Thurs. 9.30 a.m.-7.00 p.m.
Sat. 9.30 a.m.-1.00 p.m.
P.W.D.CS.MF.A.BC.

**WITNEY**    Tel. (0993) 3885
TARGET TOOLS (SALES, & 72095 OXON
HIRE & REPAIRS)   ★
SWAIN COURT
STATION INDUSTRIAL ESTATE
Open: Mon.-Sat. 8.00 a.m.-5.00 p.m.
24 hour Answerphone
BC.W.M.A.

**TELFORD**   Tel. Telford (0952)
ASLES LTD    48054
VINEYARD ROAD, WELLINGTON   EK★
Open: Mon. Fri. 8.30 a.m.-5.30 p.m.
Saturday 8.30 a.m.-4.00 p.m.
H.P.W.WM.D.CS.BC.A.

## SHROPSHIRE

## SOMERSET

**TAUNTON**    Tel. (0823) 85431
JOHN HALL TOOLS   ★
6 HIGH STREET

Open Monday-Saturday
9.00 a.m.-5.30 p.m.
H.P.W.WM.D.CS.A.

**TAUNTON**    Tel. Taunton 79078
KEITH MITCHELL   ★
TOOLS AND EQUIPMENT
66 PRIORY BRIDGE ROAD
Open: Mon-Fri 8.30 a.m.-5.30 p.m.
Saturday 9.00 a.m.-4.00 p.m.
H.P.W.WM.D.CS.A.BC.

## STAFFORDSHIRE

**TAMWORTH**    Tel. (0827) 56188
MATTHEWS BROTHERS LTD.   K
KETTLEBROOK ROAD
Open: Mon-Sat 8.30 a.m.-6.00 p.m.
Demonstrations Sunday mornings by
appointment only
H.P.WM.D.T.CS.A.BC.

## SUFFOLK

**IPSWICH**    Tel. (0473) 40456
FOX WOODWORKING   KE★
142-144 BRAMFORD LANE
Open: Tues., Fri., 9.00 a.m.-5.30 p.m.
Sat. 9.00 a.m.-5.00 p.m.

H.P.W.WM.D.A.B.C.

## SURREY

**FARNHAM**    Tel. (0252) 725427
A.B.E. CO. LTD. (Quick Hire)   ★
GOODS SHED
STATION APPROACH, FARNHAM
Open Mon.-Fri. 8.00 a.m.-5.30 p.m.
Sat. 8.00 a.m.-5.30 p.m.
H.P.W.D.CS.A.BC.

## SUSSEX

**BOGNOR REGIS** Tel. (0243) 863100
A. OLBY & SON (BOGNOR REGIS) LTD.
"TOOLSHOP," BUILDERS MERCHANT
HAWTHORN ROAD   K
Open: Mon-Thurs 8 a.m-5.15 p.m. Fri.
8 a.m-8 p.m. Sat 8 a.m-12.45 p.m.
H.P.W.WM.D.T.C.A.BC.

## EAST SUSSEX

**ST. LEONARD'S-ON-SEA**   Tel.
DOUST & MONK (MONOSAW)-(0424)
25 CASTLEHAM ROAD    52577

Open: Mon.-Fri. 8.00 a.m.-5.30 p.m.
Most Saturdays 9.00 a.m.-1.00 p.m.
H.P.W.WM.D.CS.A.

## WEST SUSSEX

**WORTHING**    Tel. (0903) 38739
W. HOSKING LTD (TOOLS &   KE★
MACHINERY)
28 PORTLAND RD, BN11 1QN
Open: Mon.-Sat. 8.30 a.m.-5.30 p.m.
Closed Wednesday
H.P.W.WM.D.CS.A.BC.

## TYNE & WEAR

**NEWCASTLE UPON TYNE**   Tel.
J. W. HOYLE LTD.   (0632) 617474
CLARENCE STREET NE2 1YJ   K★
Open: Mon-Fri 8.00 a.m.-5.00 p.m.
Saturday 9.00 a.m.-4.30 p.m.

H.P.A.BC.W.CS.WM.D.

**NEWCASTLE**    Tel. (0632) 320311
HENRY OSBOURNE LTD.   E★
50-54 UNION STREET

Open: Mon-Fri 8.30 a.m.-5.00 p.m.

H.P.W.D.CS.MF.A.BC.

## WEST MIDLANDS

**WOLVERHAMPTON**   Tel. (0902)
MANSAW SERVICES    58759
SEDGLEY STREET   K★

Open: Mon.-Fri. 9.00 a.m.-5.00 p.m.

H.P.W.WM.A.D.CS.

**BIRMINGHAM**   Tel. (021-554) 5177
ROTAGRIP   E★
16 LODGE ROAD, HOCKLEY
Open: Mon.-Fri. 9.00 a.m.-5.00 p.m.
Sat. 9.00 a.m.-12.00 p.m.

H.P.W.CS.A.BC.T.MF.

## YORKSHIRE

**BOROUGHBRIDGE**   Tel. (09012)
JOHN BODDY TIMBER LTD   2370
FINE WOOD & TOOL STORE   ★
RIVERSIDE SAWMILLS
Open: Mon.-Thurs. 8.00 a.m.-6.00 p.m.
Fri. 8.00am-5.00pm Sat. 8.00am-4.00pm
H.P.W.WM.D.T.CS.MF.A.BC.

**CLECKHEATON**    Tel. (0274)
SKILLED CRAFTS LTD.    872861
34 BRADFORD ROAD   ★

Open: 9.00 a.m.-5.00 p.m. Monday
Saturday Lunch 12.00 a.m.-1.00 p.m.
H.P.A.W.CS.WM.D.

**KEIGHLEY**    Tel. (0535) 663325
EUROMAIL (TOOLS)   ★
PO BOX 13
108 EAST PARADE
Open 9.15 a.m.-5.00 p.m.
Not Tuesday but inc. Saturday
H.P.W.A.B.C.

**HARROGATE**   Tel. (0423) 66245/
MULTI-TOOLS    55328
158 KINGS ROAD   K★

Open: Monday to Saturday
8.30 a.m.-6.00 p.m.

H.P.W.WM.D.A.BC.

**HUDDERSFIELD**    Tel. (0484)
NEVILLE M. OLDHAM   641219/(0484)
UNIT 1 DAYLE ST. WORKS    42777
DAYLE STREET, LONGFORD   ★
Open: Mon-Fri 9.00 a.m.-5.30 p.m.
Saturday 9.30 a.m.-12.00 p.m.
P.W.WM.D.A.BC.

**LEEDS**    Tel. (0532) 574736
D. B. KEIGHLEY MACHINERY LTD.   ★
VICKERS PLACE, STANNINGLEY
PUDSEY LS2 86LZ
Mon.-Fri. 9.00 a.m.-5.00 p.m.
Sat. 9.00 a.m.-1.00 p.m.
P.A.W.WM.CS.BC.

**LEEDS**    Tel. (0532) 790507
GEORGE SPENCE & SONS LTD.
WELLINGTON ROAD
Open: Monday to Friday
8.30 a.m.-5.30 p.m.
Saturday 9.00 a.m.-5.00 p.m.
H.P.W.WM.D.T.A.

**SHEFFIELD**    Tel. (0742) 441012
GREGORY & TAYLOR LTD   E
WORKSOP ROAD
Open: 8.30 a.m.-5.30 p.m.
Monday-Friday
8.30 a.m.-12.30 p.m. Sat.
H.P.W.WM.D.

## SCOTLAND

**THIRSK**    Tel. (0845) 22770
THE WOOD SHOP
TRESKE SAWMILLS LTD.
STATION WORKS
Open: Seven days a week 9.00-5.00

T.H.MF.BC.

**EDINBURGH**    Tel. (031 337) 5555
THE SAW CENTRE   ★
38 HAYMARKET TERRACE
HAYMARKET
Open: 8.30 a.m.-5.30 p.m.
Monday-Saturday
H.P.W.WM.D.CS.A.

**GLASGOW**   Tel. (041 429) 4374/
THE SAW CENTRE   4444, Telex: 777886
600 EGLINTON STREET   E★
G5 9RR
Open: Mon-Fri 8.00 a.m.-5.30 p.m.
Saturday 9.00 a.m.-1.00 p.m.
H.P.W.WM.D.CS.A.

**PERTH**    Tel. (0738) 26173
WILLIAM HUME & CO   K
ST. JOHN'S PLACE
Open: Monday to Saturday
8.00 a.m.-5.30 p.m.
8.00 a.m.-1.00 p.m. Wednesday
H.P.A.BC.W.CS.WM.D.

## WALES

**TAYSIDE**    Tel: (05774) 293
WORKMASTER POWER TOOLS LTD.   ★
DRUM, KINROSS
Open Mon.-Sat. 8.00 a.m.-8.00 p.m.
Demonstrations throughout Scotland by
appointment
P.W.WM.D.A.BC.

**CARDIFF**    Tel. (0222) 396039
JOHN HALL TOOLS LIMITED   ★
CENTRAL SQUARE

Open: Monday to Saturday
9.00 a.m.-5.30 p.m.

H.P.W.WM.D.A.BC.

**CARDIFF**    Tel. (0222) 30831
F. W. MORGAN   & 25562
(CANTON) LTD., 129-133
COWBRIDGE RD EAST
CANTON
Mon-Sat 8.00-5.00 Sun 9.30-12.30
H.P.T.CS.A.BC.

**CARDIFF**    Tel. (0222) 595710
DATAPOWER TOOLS LTD,
MICHAELSTON ROAD,
CULVERHOUSE CROSS
Open: Mon.-Fri. 8.00 a.m.-5.00 p.m.
Sat. 9.00 a.m.-1.00 p.m.
H.P.W.WM.D.A.

**CARMARTHEN**   Tel. (0267) 237219
DO-IT-YOURSELF SUPPLY   K
BLUE STREET, DYFED
Open: Monday to Saturday
9.00 a.m.-5.30 p.m.
Thursday 9.00 a.m.-5.30 p.m.
H.P.W.WM.D.T.CS.A.BC.

**SWANSEA**    Tel. (0792) 55680
SWANSEA TIMBER & PLYWOOD CO. LTD.
57-59 OXFORD STREET   ★

Open: Mon to Fri 9.00 a.m.-5.30 p.m.
Sat. 9.00 a.m.-1.00 p.m.

H.P.W.D.T.CS.A.BC.

# Classified Advertisements

## FOR SALE

**LACE BOBBIN TURNING BLANKS** in unusual and exotic hardwoods and ivory. SAE for list: J. Ford, 5 Squirrels Hollow, Walsall WS7 8YS.

### FOR ALL SUPPLIES FOR THE
### Craft of Enamelling
### ON METAL
### Including
### LEAD-FREE ENAMELS
PLEASE SEND 2 × 10p STAMPS FOR FREE CATALOGUE, PRICE LIST AND WORKING INSTRUCTIONS

**W. G. BALL LTD.**
ENAMEL MANUFACTURERS
Dept. W. LONGTON
STOKE-ON-TRENT
ST3 1JW

---

**MUSICAL MOVEMENTS**
* LOVE STORY * LARAS THEME * SPEAK SOFTLY LOVE * FUR ELISE * FEELINGS * FASCINATION * IMPOSSIBLE DREAM * MUSIC BOX DANCER * LA POLOMA * THE EMPEROR WALTZ * TRY TO REMEMBER * ROMEO AND JULIET *
Complete with screws and spring mechanism £2.50 inc. p&p. 20 or more of one tune ordered £1.50 each. Available from:
The Jewel Box Shop,
112 Pentonville Road, London N1 9JB.

---

**STARTRITE 275** 12" Tilt Arbor Sawbench. Extension bars, single phase, TCT blades. Good condition £825.00 ono. Various hardwoods: pear, apple, box. Useful odds and ends at giveaway prices. Dorking (0306) 888456.

**MILLING AND DRYING EQUIPMENT.** Ebac Minor Seasoner, control box, 36" Sperber Mill with two Stihl 075AV chainsaws, spare chain, cutting guide. Seasoner unused £1,300 ono. Telephone London 693-0887.

**QUALITY TOOLS.** 9" Carpenters Squares (R.R.P. £8.50) £3.75 + 40p postage. Mortice/Marking Gauges £2.99 + 30p postage. Free details. Midas Marketing, 3 River Lane, Brompton-on-Swale, Richmond, N. Yorkshire, DL10 7HH.

**OVERARM ROUTER,** cast iron, 3/8"/1/4" colletts, 2000W motor, foot operated rise/fall, floor standing, new condition £395.00. 10" Radial Arm Saw, shopmate 5200AT4. TCT blade, c/w Dado cutters, 2000 rpm shaft. Takes Router cutters, 3,450 rpm. Shaft for standing etc. Floor standing, v.g.c. £220.00. Space urgently needed, hence low prices. Tel: (029668) 398.

---

**HAND CARVED**
'Adam Style' Mantle motifs in Mahogany — Example 10" × 5" centre lamp and two side pieces.
Send S.A.E. for details and quotation. Your own design quoted for if required.
**SAM NICHOLSON**
22 Lisnagarvey Drive, Lisburn,
Co. Antrim, N. Ireland.
Phone Lisburn 3510

**TRADITIONAL PATTERN GUN-METAL PLANES.** Finished or kits. 17p stamp for list/photo. Bristol Design, 14 Perry Road, Bristol BS1 5BG.

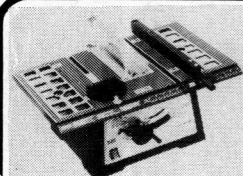

**SOLID OAK CHAIRS**
Sanded, ready for staining and polishing. From £35 each.
Also tables, tops only, kits or assembled.
Country Tables & Chairs
The Cottage, St. Nicolas, The Cottage, St. Nicholas La., Chislehurst, Kent.
Tel: 01-467-1192

---

**Portable 10"**
**£139.95**
**Sawbench**
inc. VAT/Del.
12 MONTHS GUARANTEE
40T T.C.T. BLADE £18 EXTRA
- CAST ALLOY TABLE
- NEW IMPROVED 1½HP INDUCTION MOTOR
- QUIET RUNNING — EFFICIENT
- RISE FALL/TILT ARBOR
- SAFETY GUARD & SWITCH
- HIGHLY RECOMMENDED

**BRAYWOOD ESTATES LTD.**
158 BURNHAM LANE, SLOUGH. Tel. Burnham (06286) 5125
Hours of Business: 9-5.30. Mon./Sat.

---

MORTISERS; TENNONERS; SPINDLES; PLANERS; BANDSAWS; LATHES; CROSSCUTS; ROUTERS; SANDERS; DRILLS?
YOU CAN CERTAINLY SEE ALL CLASSES AND TYPES OF MACHINES HERE.
WE ARE MAIN STOCKING AGENTS FOR: MULTICO; ELU; SEDGWICK; KITY; SCHEPPACH; INCA; CORONET; DeWALT; WARCO; DOMINION; HITACHI; STARTRITE; TREND; ASHLEY ILES; SORBY.
*P.S. OUR ELU PRICES COMPARE WITH ANYONES.*
*P.P.S. CALL US ABOUT WOODTURNING LESSONS WOODCARVING LESSONS (See our Swiss carving tools)*
*ALWAYS HELPFUL, KNOWLEDGEABLE, GOOD SERVICE AT:*
**CLEVELAND WOODCRAFT**
**38-42 CRESCENT ROAD, MIDDLESBROUGH.**
TEL: (0642) 813103

---

**D.I.Y.**
ESTABLISHED 1889
## THE SAW CENTRE
### LIMITED
### HAS THE EDGE
Hire or buy machinery or power tools from our extensive stock:
**Elu DeWALT makita Black & Decker**
- SCHEPPACH ■ STARTRITE ■ GRIGGIO
- VOLPATO ■ SEDGWICK
- TUNGSTEN CARBIDE TIPPED SAW BLADES
- DISPOSABLE BANDSAW BLADES

**SAWN OFF PRICES**

**HEAD OFFICE & MAIN WORKS:**
EGLINTON TOLL GLASGOW G5 9RP. TEL: 041-429 4444/4374
OPEN: MON - FRI 8 - 5.30 SAT 9 -1. TELEX: 777886 SAWCO G.
**ALSO AT: 38 HAYMARKET TERRACE EDINBURGH EH12 5JZ.**
TEL: 031-337 5555. OPEN: MON - SAT 8.30 - 5.30.

---

Have you seen the latest catalogue of
**Bygones**
See Display advertisement

---

**Alan Holtham**
The Old Stores Turnery, Wistaston Road,
Willaston, Nantwich, Cheshire.
Tel: 0270 67010

**BANDSAW BLADES**
Skip tooth type with hardened teeth. Prices include VAT. P+P 1—3 Blades **90p**, 4-6 Blades **£1.70.** Over 6 post free.

| Model | | Price inc. VAT |
|---|---|---|
| Birch | 1/4" | £3.62 |
| DeWalt BS1310 | 3/8" | £3.74 |
| Kity 612 | 1/2" | £3.91 |
| Lazzari P32 | 5/8" | £4.77 |
| Bandit | | |
| Startrite 301 | | |
| Black & Decker | 1/4" | £2.99 |
| DeWalt 100 | 3/8" | £3.11 |
| | 1/2" | £3.22 |
| Burgess | 1/4" | £3.11 |
| | 3/8" | £3.25 |
| Inca | 1/4" | £3.45 |
| | 3/8" | £3.57 |
| | 1/2" | £3.62 |
| | 5/8" | £4.20 |
| Startrite 352 | 1/4" | £4.54 |
| | 3/8" | £4.60 |
| | 1/2" | £4.77 |
| | 5/8" | £5.87 |
| | 3/4" | £6.15 |
| Willow | 1/4" | £4.03 |
| | 3/8" | £4.08 |
| | 1/2" | £4.20 |

Prices quoted are those prevailing at press date and are subject to alteration due to economic conditions.

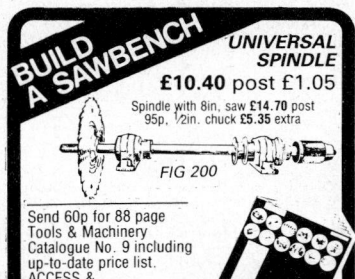
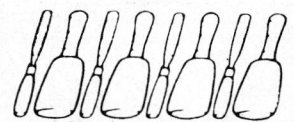

Prices quoted are those prevailing at press date and are subject to alteration due to economic conditions.

KINDLY MENTION 'WOODWORKER' WHEN REPLYING TO ADVERTISEMENTS          235

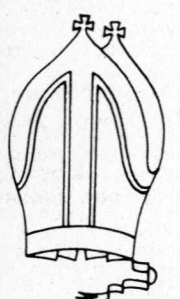
Prices quoted are those prevailing at press date and are
subject to alteration due to economic conditions

# Then...
## Max Burrough

## Continuing the absorbing tale of an old-time apprenticeship

Each man saw his job through from start to finish. He would study the drawings, make a cutting list, fetch the required timber from the yard, saw, plane, joint and assemble until completion — and then stain and polish as stipulated. For many years a polisher had been employed, but the results so offended the men that he had been sacked. They asserted that their work was ruined by too much polish looking like treacle, fine mouldings being 'lost', grain being obscured by too much colour, etc.

By the same token, it is of little use polishing carefully unless the wood is prepared properly beforehand. As I looked back on my efforts at finishing wood when at school, the quality control in this workshop was a revelation.

The smoothing-plane would be sharpened, the shape of the cutting edge being carefully checked against the brass-faced stock of the try-square, to ensure that it was practically flat with just the corners rounded off. (A carpenter's finish was held to ridicule and compared to corrugated iron; their plane irons were too rounded.) The top of a table, for example, would be smoothed over and then planed again. The second time, the plane being taken right through from one end to the other without a break in the shaving. each stroke just overlapping the last. With the cap-iron set very close and perhaps the thumbs resisting the exit of the shavings, a good finish was confidently expected. Close inspection would reveal any areas that needed to be scraped, and occasionally a surface might be scraped all over as a form of insurance.

Glasspapering was then carried out in a manner befitting such an important operation. I have seen more splendidly made amateur pieces spoiled by bad finishing than any other cause. But I find it surprising now that only three grades of glasspaper were used — strong 2, middle 2 and fine 2, plus 0 when french-polishing. A flat hardwood block was always used, each man making his own, with a piece of thick cork lino glued to the bottom. This block was also used under the shoe of the holdfast; the size, about 5×2¾in, was dictated by the size of a quarter-sheet of Oakey glasspaper. If there was any suspicion of dampness the paper would first be warmed over the gas-ring. It was folded in half, torn accurately across, and then folded again but not torn; the block was placed in the middle and the paper rolled up at the sides to fit the hand perfectly, ready for action. Glasspapering was always carried out methodically, each nook, cranny and edge being observed constantly, and when it was completed the work would be brushed off carefully with the bench brush. (No man ever bought such a brush. It was always the wife's worn-out or broken household dustbrush.)

If water stain was to be used, warm water would be applied using a clear rag; when the job was completely dry, it was lightly glasspapered again. The stains stocked were basic, but I cannot recall their ever being inadequate for the wide range of work undertaken. Vandyke brown, mahogany and black crystals were all mixed with hot water and used when cold. Bichromate and permanganate of potash were used for oak and mahogany; .880 ammonia was used for some oak colours, either applied with a brush or occasionally for fuming small articles placed in boxes. The men could recall fuming whole rooms — oak floor, skirting, doors and architraves — with the ammonia being poured into open shallow containers and the door closed and sealed for a few days. (Fred asserts that rose petals were bought by the sackful to make a stain, but I have never tried this.) Head colds were infrequent, for as soon as a man thought he might have one coming he took an occasional sniff of the ammonia bottle.

Practically every job had the grain filled with plaster of Paris, slightly tinted to match the final colour, and applied with meths to save time in drying. French-polishing I never really enjoyed, although in time I became reasonably proficient at it. The polishes stocked were brown, white, transparent, black, and dark and light Anglo-Yankee Shine from Henry Flack Ltd of PO Box 78, Beckenham, Kent. I have never seen or heard of a better polish for mahogany than Flack's Anglo-Yankee Shine. My advice to any serious amateur struggling to achieve to achieve a genuine french polish (still the best finish for some jobs) is to buy, beg or borrow some. It has no sediment, so it needs no shaking; much more importantly, less oil is needed to lubricate the wad, which means that there is less to remove when finishing off. The colour — the dark is like port wine — enhances the colour and grain of what I call real mahogany (I refuse to use the African varieties).

The white and transparent polishes, although always used on oak, were not popular — especially the latter, as they often took a long time to harden off. Later I realised this might have been because the polish was frequently old and stale. Wax-polishing was avoided if at all possible, and I cannot recall a really good wax finish being obtained while I was with the firm. I now find this difficult to understand. A round brush was used, about 5in in diameter and with very short bristles, but the work was hard and produced only a mediocre result. Today I can transform a piece of antique furniture by the judicious use of one of Flack's wax polishes — and its an ideal way to stimulate the circulation on a cold and frosty morning!

I have a feeling that amateurs often think there is a mystique about french-polishing, whereas all you require for an acceptable finish are the basic materials and an understanding of the processes involved. (Please don't misunderstand me; I am not talking of such items as pianos. To obtain a professional finish on a black grand takes skill and experience.)

Any piece of furniture in need of cleaning, especially if french-polished, was usually given to a boy with the instruction 'Give it a good going-over with fake'. 'Fake' was a simple 50-50 mixture of methylated spirits and raw linseed oil; applied with a piece of soft rag, left to stand for a few minutes and then rubbed off with a clean rag, it is more than adequate, and was often used during spring-cleaning and on furniture that had been in store for a long time. The only product I have found superior to fake on highly polished surfaces is a mixture called Liquid Glass Polish Reviver. I bought a small bottle many years ago in a London piano showroom, and have blessed the day on several occasions since.

The stains I mentioned remind me of several pieces of furniture. Although the firm did not deal extensively in antiques, there were always a few very good examples in the showrooms.

In the shop one day I was inspecting a piece I had not seen before. It was a bacon settle; although I have seen quite a few since, especially during the past ten years, I have yet to see a better one. It was slightly curved, with arms at the ends, doors to the panelled seat front, and a panelled back with doors giving access to the original iron hooks whereon would have hung the sides of bacon. The whole was that unusual red colour occasionally seen in country-made antiques; no one seemed to know what produced it. It was not the colour, however, which puzzled me. While I was gawking, I realised the Boss was behind me.

'Well, young man, and what do you think of it?'

'Very good, sir. A fine piece.'

'Yes, but can you tell me what the wood is?'

'No, sir, I can't. It looks like oak but it's not. It looks like elm but it's not. It looks like ash and it's not. It . . .'

'Huh,' in his most sarcastic manner. 'I didn't think you would know.'

I could have murdered him.

'I will tell you, m'boy. It is chestnut.' And he limped on into his office. Afterwards I studied that settle long and earnestly, and ever since have reckoned to know a piece of chestnut when I see it. ∎

# Letters

Our open forum — where woodworkers can talk to one another

I write in reply to the disgust expressed by Messrs Heaney and Sellers (WW/Dec) at the work of Mr LaTrobe Bateman. They are saying that, because the surfaces of his chests are not flat, the joints not tight, the wood split and the chests themselves large, they are rubbish. I disagree.

Why is medieval furniture so much admired? Not because every surface is flat, every joint tight or every plank perfect, but because the surfaces have texture — the tool marks and undulations caused by an adze, the irregular marks of a pit-sawn plank, and boldness of design and execution.

Mr LaTrobe Bateman's work is refreshing because he displays some of these age-old characteristics, but in his own style; he has not been tied down by our modern preoccupation with finish, which leaves woodwork perfectly flat, perfectly square and perfectly inhuman. Thousands of people can knock together timber which has been machined perfectly square and flat. How many can take a rough-sawn, waney-edged plank varying in thickness, and joint that? Mr LaTrobe Bateman may

be showing more skill in handling his chainsaw than a vast number of electric-planer-happy whizz-kids wielding dovetail jigs and biscuit-jointers.

To make a chest out of elm is (to say the least) courageous because, no matter how well seasoned the wood may be, it will always move. One answer is to try to minimise and restrain the movement; the other is to sit back and enjoy it — and I believe this is what Mr LaTrobe Bateman is doing. He is not, as Mr Heaney suggests, trying to make a fool out of anyone. I actually very much like these chests.

As for Mr Heaney's opinion that 'found wood' is a euphemism for rubbish — not at all. Woodworkers have traditionally reused materials, knowing that the wood will be well seasoned as well as cheap. Only in our own era does public opinion dictate that new work should be made from entirely new material. It is encouraging to find furniture-makers who can produce work without the enormous wastage that modern techniques and machinery encourage.

*John Milner, South Petherton*

---

When the editor asks me to reply to a question sent in by a reader of *Woodworker* on a finishing problem, I take the trouble to read it most carefully. So I studied Mr Cold-

well's letter ('Question box', WW/Feb) very closely. What Mr Garratt does not know is that the original was over 500 words long, and included a detailed drawing to show the various faults on the table-top surface. For obvious reasons, the editor condensed it. I have been a professional polisher for many decades, and I stand by every word of the 13-point workshop procedure I described. Indeed, it would have been irresponsible for me to have suggested any other.

I would also like to take issue with Mr Garrett on a particular point. '"Cissing"', he says, 'is almost inevitable when refinishing a used piece of furniture with cellulose'. This is not so if the job is carried out properly. The term 'cissing' is used to describe a spraying fault which is always associated with foreign matter either on the wood surface or within the cellulose coating. Grease, finger grease, traces of silicone, oil stains and shellac can all prevent the free flow of wet cellulose film coatings. Eliminating cissing is a simple matter of seeing that all containers and airlines are clean, and that all traces of abrasive paper or steel wool have been removed before spraying takes place.

I hope this will be of some use to Mr Garrett, and I wish him a cissing-free 1985.

*Noel Leach, Uckfield*

**Prices quoted are those prevailing at press date and are subject to alteration due to economic conditions**

# The magazine for the craftsman
## ~ and the aspiring craftsman!

April 1985
Vol. 89
No. 1097

● *Shimmering complexity in a chair by Rupert Williamson — pages 262-3*

**Publisher** Ray Lewis
**Editor** Peter Collenette
**Deputy Editor** Aidan Walker
**Advertisement Manager** Paul Holmes
**Advertisement production** Karyn Stewart
**Guild of Woodworkers** Aidan Walker
**Group Editor** Chris Adam-Smith
**Publishing Director** John Foster
**Chairman and Chief Executive** Jim Connell

Editorial, advertisements and Guild of Woodworkers
1 Golden Square, London WC1R 3AB, telephone 01-437 0626

Unfortunately we cannot accept responsibility for loss of or damage to unsolicited material. We reserve the right to refuse or suspend advertisements, and regret we cannot guarantee the bone fides of advertisers.

**Subscriptions and back issues** Infonet Ltd, 10-13 Times House, 179 Marlowes, Hemel Hempstead, Herts HP1 1BB; telephone Hemel Hempstead (0442) 48434
**Subscriptions per year** UK £15.60; overseas outside USA (accelerated surface post) £17, USA (accelerated surface post) $22.50, airmail £42
**UK trade** SM Distribution Ltd, 16-18 Trinity Gardens, London SW9 8DX; telephone 01-274 8611
**North American trade** Eastern News Distributors, 166-41 Powells Cove Boulevard, L Box 69, Whitestone, New York 11357

**Printed in Great Britain** by Ambassador Press Ltd, St Albans, Herts
**Mono origination** Multiform Photosetting Ltd, Cardiff
**Colour origination** Derek Croxson Ltd, Chesham, Bucks

© Argus Specialist Publications Ltd 1985
ISSN 0043 776X

# Argus Specialist Publications Ltd
1 Golden Square, London W1R 3AB; 01-437 0626

## Just awards

Two current competitions cover both ends of the design/craft spectrum. Both have major sponsorship.

Main drawback of The Carpenters Award 1985 is the prize: 'a specially designed and inscribed plaque . . . and certificates'. That's all. Nice in its way, but you'd have thought the combined coffers of the Worshipful Company of Carpenters, William Mallinson

& Sons and Mallinson-Denny Ltd — who have jointly endowed the scheme — could have run to, let's say, a new set of chisels. Not to mention the Royal Institute of British Architects, the Joinery Managers' Association and the British Woodworking Federation, whence come the assessors. The point, it seems clear, is to laud the work and boost the firm responsible — not primarily to reward the boys at the bench.

The recipients will have produced 'an outstanding example of joinery' in a building commissioned between 1.1.83 and 31.12.84. Entry forms from The Carpenters Award, Carpenters Company, Carpenters Hall, Throgmorton Ave, London EC2; the closing date is 30 April.

The Young Designer of the Year Award, by contrast, carries a prize of £350 in its cabinet and upholstered furniture section, as in five others — plus a showing at the IDDA Decorex trade show later in the year. It's open to final-year design and/or craft students at colleges, art schools and polys who are taking a degree, advanced or higher-diploma course. You must also have been born on or after 1 May 1955. Entry is organised through college principals and heads of department, who will probably know about the competition by now. Other enquiries to Peta Levi on 01-435 4348.

## Victorian values

**W. Cyril Brown** writes: I am president of the Queenscliff and District Woodcrafters' Guild in Victoria, Australia. We have only been in existence for a couple of years, and because of our location do not have a very large membership. Like other groups we keep beavering away doing our own thing. But we believe that belonging to a group such as this is worthwhile, otherwise it would cease to exist.

At the same time, working in a small group has its limitations because there is a limit to the variety of experience members can generate among themselves. We would therefore like to invite any of your Australian readers who belong to a woodworking guild to contact us so we can exchange news of events, activities and anything else of common interest.

Two displays our members recently attended in other cities in the area have provided ample evidence of the high standard achieved by craftsmen and craftswomen in this neck of the woods. If more groups are prepared to contact one another, the shared experience will enrich us all.
● W. Cyril Brown, 22 Kirk Rd, Point Lonsdale, Victoria 3225, Australia.

## BRISTOL WOODWORKER SHOW

Take note — it was Doncaster 84, but this year it's the West Country. Bristol is the place and early summer is the time.

The **Bristol Woodworker Show** will take place at the Bristol Exhibition Complex on 25, 26 and 27 May (the Bank Holiday weekend). It'll include all the features of the highly successful London show: plenty of trade stands, demonstrations — and competition entries (see elsewhere in this issue too).

The West is a noted stronghold of craftsmanship in wood, so we all have great hopes of the delights that'll be on view. See you there!
● Details from Argus Specialist Exhibitions Ltd, Park View House, 1 Park View Rd, Berkhamsted, Herts HP4 3EY, tel. Berkhamsted (04427) 73291.

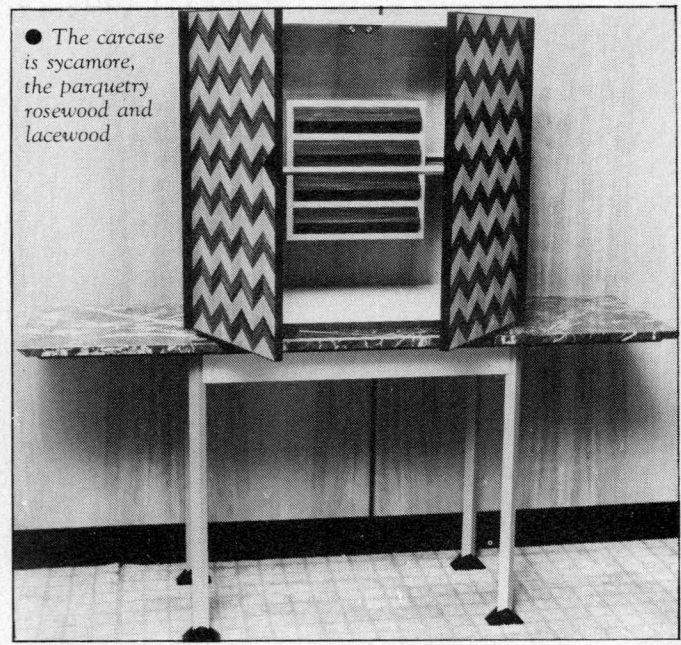

● The carcase is sycamore, the parquetry rosewood and lacewood

● Ultra-contemporary . . . and firmly traditional. Two Showpiece of the Year awards at the NEC went to Bromsgrove designer-craftsman Tony McMullen (above) and William Tillman Ltd (below). Tony exhibited under the auspices of CoSIRA

## Fine craft, high profile

**Peter Collenette** writes: Furniture trade shows are a drag. Year after year, it seems, British industry hauls out the same dead weight of tired designs, cheap materials and often tacky constructions. Like a supertanker, it delivers the goods but it takes a very long time to change direction — even assuming the desire is there in the first place.

Legging it round Birmingham's International Furniture Show late last year offered no surprises. No surprises — but one oasis. For a small group of designer-craftspeople, asserting their role in the industry despite its size and problems, had taken up the challenge such a show implies, and staked a place in the front line by mounting their own stand.

On display were individual and batch-produced pieces from nine workshops, based as far apart as Bristol and Norwich. The initiator and principal organiser was Geoff Godschalk of Ashwell in Hertfordshire; the collective effort resulted in an appealing stand and a smartly produced if not wildly exciting booklet.

What was the exhibitors' message for those, both trade and public, who came to look and talk? 'Yes, we can produce imaginative one-off creations in a number of styles. Yes, we can do small batch runs. But no, we cannot produce and are not

interested in runs of 10,000 items.'

The words come from Tim Ashby of Ashby Design Workshop in Frome, Somerset. The visitors' reaction, he says, was summed up in a typical conversation. For an international furniture show (a Danish buyer told him), exhibiting what was supposed to be the best in British furniture, 90% of the exhibits were depressingly dull and had been seen on the market in one form or another for the past 10 or 15 years. The buyer declared how refreshing it was to see the lively design and quality workmanship emerging from the small British shops — and what a pity that they could not supply him with the volumes he needed.

Antonios Nielsen, another of those on the stand, explained further. He sold one cabinet during the show — encountering a few buyers, but also meeting recurring problems with the mark-ups they require. Can the small designer-craftsman price low enough, he asks, to cope with the retailers' overheads? If you're willing to try, you may find yourself (for better or worse) becoming more of a manager and less of a designer or craftsman.

But direct sales, of course, are only part of the story. As Tim adds, the industry's argument 'that "we are only producing what the British customer likes" is negated by the fact that imports are now at an all-time high of 40%. There is a wealth of design talent in this country that can help boost demand for British furniture at home and abroad. Certainly the Continental companies have not hesitated to employ British designers'.

And he proclaims, 'We can design and build the one-off prototypes for industry to make in large volumes — one-offs are our forte!'

The Design Council recently proposed that £700,000 be spent over two years on convincing managers of design's importance. And listen to Richard Young, boss of G-Plan, speaking at the Style 84 show: 'Retailers and manufacturers together, by our collective apathy, stupidity, greed, indolence, sloth and amateurish ways, have reduced our industry to a shambles. We have now the remnant of a scruffy, dull, down-at-heel, unglamorous trade, with merchandise which appears mostly designed and almost universally presented to appeal only to those driven by absolute practical necessity to buy it.'

Faced with that, who can quibble with the brave designer-craftsmen's decision to take a stand?

● Designer-makers interested in future promotional projects may like to contact Geoff Godschalk or Ann Walsh at Cerdan Ltd, Dixies, High St, Ashwell, Herts SG7 5NT, tel. (046274) 2837.

In more distraught moments we sometimes think we might need a special monthly column to accommodate all the corrections to the various slip-ups which (you may have noticed) occasionally appear in *Woodworker*. Maybe that's going too far. It's just that when there aren't many of you in the editorial office, and your contributors aren't infallible either . . . Bruce Boulter's February article on the ring gouge included, for some reason unknown both to us and to him, on p127 the extraordinary statement that the tool cannot be ground because it is of carbon steel. That, of course, doesn't make sense. The real reason is its shape. We all apologise — until next time.

## Changes and thanks

**Peter Collenette** writes: By the time you read this, if all goes well, we shall be based in London. Our new address is 1 Golden Square, London W1R 3AB, tel. 01-437 0626. That's for the editorial office, display and classified advertising, and the Guild of Woodworkers. Only subscriptions and back numbers will remain external affairs: they're still handled by Infonet Ltd, 10-13 Times House, 179 Marlowes, Hemel Hempstead, Herts HP1 1BB.

So much for the humdrum details. But the move also means a very fond farewell to two people who have made big contributions. Mrs Pat Young has been helping to keep the Guild, plus a few other things, on the rails since last summer — while Peter Kirby, our long-time graphic designer, has been largely responsible for giving *Woodworker* the face it now wears. If you like what you see, thank Peter: our man with his fingers in the Cow Gum who can swiftly turn jumbled sheaves of photos, galley-proofs and incomprehensible drawings (handed him by an over-enthusiastic editor) into bright, interesting articles which make people want to read them. Thank you both.

# Shoptalk

The 1984 **Woodworker Annual** runs to no fewer than 856 pages and includes a complete year of features, news, reviews, plans and inspiration from Britain's premier woodworking magazine. In addition to exhaustive coverage of cabinet-making, woodturning, carving, finishing, restoration, tools, timber and machinery, there are hosts of invaluable workshop hints from expert craftsmen. And that's not

all. It also contains dozens of major projects with full working drawings – pine dressers; a bedside cabinet; double and single beds; Victorian toys; strikingly unusual desks; a traditional Davenport; blanket chests; an elegant Georgian corner cabinet; and more – to say nothing of others especially for carvers and turners.

● £17+£1.70 p&p from Argus Books, Wolsey House, Wolsey Rd, Hemel Hempstead, Herts HP2 4SS, tel. (0442) 41221.

For all those who want the cutting list for that delectable dresser, or the full

story on spraying, who have all the *Woodworkers* published since 1901 but who can't just lay their hands on the right issue — the **1984 Woodworker Index** is now available. Fully catalogued lists, by author and subject, of all the main topics and features, projects and stories covered last year, telling you in which issue each appears, and where. If, like most *Woodworker* readers, you keep all the monthly wit and wisdom of the wood world in a huge pile in the workshop or attic, you'll find this index indispensable to make proper use of your collection.

● £1.25 from Argus Specialist Publications Ltd, Sales Dept, Wolsey House, Wolsey Rd, Hemel Hempstead, Herts HP2 4SS, tel. (0442) 41221. The index is sent free to all subscribers.

R. A. Bridgewater writes: You may be interested in my experience with one of your advertisers, Axminster Power Tool Centre. Planning to equip a workshop, I wrote to a number of advertisers in *Woodworker* with a request to quote for certain specific tools. Axminster replied by return, first-class post. After checking their prices against those of local merchants and later replies to my enquiries, I sent my order to Axminster on 14 January. I received the complete order — bandsaw, cordless drill, router and router table — on 19 January. To say I was pleased would be an understatement. Their service is one I would recommend to anyone, and I will certainly be sending them further orders as my needs dictate.

● This block takes solid-carbide cutters – ground to order in 24-48 hours; Supreme Saws Ltd, Unit C1, Newton Ind. Est., 159/161 Eastern Ave West, Chadwell Heath, Romford, Essex, 01-597 7391

# Timberline

**Arthur Jones** presents the month's inside news of supplies

'**B**uy British' has once more become a theme for economic recovery, this time with the encouragement of the CBI. Woodworkers back the idea strongly with their support for British hardwoods; indeed, it is a big grumble that there is usually not enough top-quality wood available in many favoured species.

But what about softwood? The time has come for us to look more closely at the softwood available from native forests. Gone are the times when the home-grown timber mill was a ramshackle business turning out wood of indifferent quality and grading. Now there is a yearly increasing quantity of native sawn softwood on offer, and the standards set by British mills are high, so you can confidently expect quality timber. What's more, the price is often highly competitive with the corresponding imported grade. This is a market worth careful investigation.

So far as imported softwood prices are concerned, there is an uncanny steadiness in the better grades of redwood and considerable uncertainty about whether whitewood or the lower grades can hold even the present depressed levels. As a pointer to the market, the Polish state selling agency's first stock-notes for UK shipments up to the summer show that prices are unchanged from last summer.

The trade accepts that the producers overseas cannot continue to cut whitewood and sell it at present prices, but importers are unwilling to buy heavily forward even at these bargain prices. There might be further reductions — it's like seeing the value of the pound sinking against the dollar. Which reminds me; timbers, whether softwood, hardwoods or panel products, that come from dollar countries are costing more without paying the shipper a higher price, simply because of the falling pound.

Another accepted fact in the timber market-place is that there is almost no chance of increase in wood sales in the first half of this year, so stocks should be enough to give the woodworker a good choice. With prices staying steady, even in a period of continuing inflation, and stocks plentiful, there should be few softwood problems. Shop around carefully and there could also be some good bargains from time to time.

**T**erence Mallinson is a leading figure in the UK timber trade as well as being the marketing director of the major hardwood Mallinson-Denny Group. He recently claimed that woodworkers are generally reluctant to change from the single well-known hardwood and grade of their choice. There is a lot of truth in this, but we might equally say that the choice is based on experience.

However, with the considerable range of hardwoods available in Britain today, many woodworkers must be sticking to choices made long ago when something better — or at least as good, and perhaps cheaper — is on the market.

There is plenty of information available on selection from such bodies as the Timber Research and Development Association (TRADA), and there are British Standards to help. Incidentally, BS1186 is expected to be published in March; this will list hardwoods with varying durabilities. It will also include recommendations on treatments for 'less than moderately durable' hardwoods when used externally.

The current hardwood market has been upset price-wise by recent substantial consignment (speculative) shipments of lauan, seraya and Brazilian mahogany. These have created imbalance in a market already showing some signs of weakness, and the result must be some lower selling prices for these woods. Woodworkers who have these species on their list should look around and compare prices.

**A** lot is heard about quality standards these days, and TRADA has been asked to look into the possibility of producing a quality-assurance scheme covering plywoods.

Chipboard users will know of the keen price competition in this field, and now the EEC producers have lodged a complaint that eastern Europe chipboard mills are selling chipboard at dumping prices — values below production costs. These complaints are being investigated by the EEC. ■

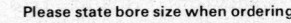 

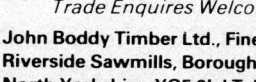

# Question box

## Our panel of experts solve your woodworking problems

**Q** *I had a large, reputable timber yard specially machine 120 T&G boards, 22×80 ×2050mm, from Scots pine, so that I could make a number of ledged doors for a cottage I am renovating.*

*I received the boards in the middle of the summer and stored them raised off a damp-proof concrete floor in a room which has a doorway open to the outside. I don't know the moisture content of the wood as supplied, but it appears (from drying a sample in the oven) to be about 15%. When I am ready to make a door, I bring a batch of boards indoors to a heated room for a couple of weeks.*

*I have now made three doors, but am finding that quite a number of the boards are in winding, some so badly that they cannot be used. Is this a natural hazard, and is there anything I can do about it? I have considered making framed-and-battened doors instead.*

*Graham Hewitt, Stirling*

**A** You have handled your timber quite correctly. The winding is caused by stress, which is indeed a natural hazard after machining. Little or nothing can be done to alleviate the situation.

A framed, ledged and braced type of door would be more rigid than a battened one, and this rigidity might keep the boards more in check. I would leave the tongues on, as this might help prevent them from moving apart. However, this construction might not solve the problem completely.

*Frank Boddy*

---

**Q** *I am making a circular box frame with sliding sashes. Could you provide some drawings?*

*H. W. Compton, Goring-by-Sea*

**A** A box window, segmental in plan — what an interesting job, and how gratifying to see that there are still those who take on such work! Presumably you have a router for the moulds on the sash rails; otherwise, you have some scratch-stock work ahead.

No work such as this should be attempted without having first made a full-size setting-out — in this case a plan section — upon a sheet of white hardboard. Only thus can correct bevels, etc., be accurately picked up and applied to the material; note (fig. 2) that even the edge bevels of the sash stiles vary from side to centre.

If the window is concave on its outside, it can be constructed with radial jambs, for sash removal is a simple matter: fig. 1. But if the window is convex on its outside, it has to be constructed with parallel jambs, so that the sashes can be removed from the inside (fig. 2). Alternatively, radials can be used, with an outer, removable stop-bead at one side of the frame. Once the bead is removed (also the parting-bead, of course), the sashes can be released and brought through the frame and into the room.

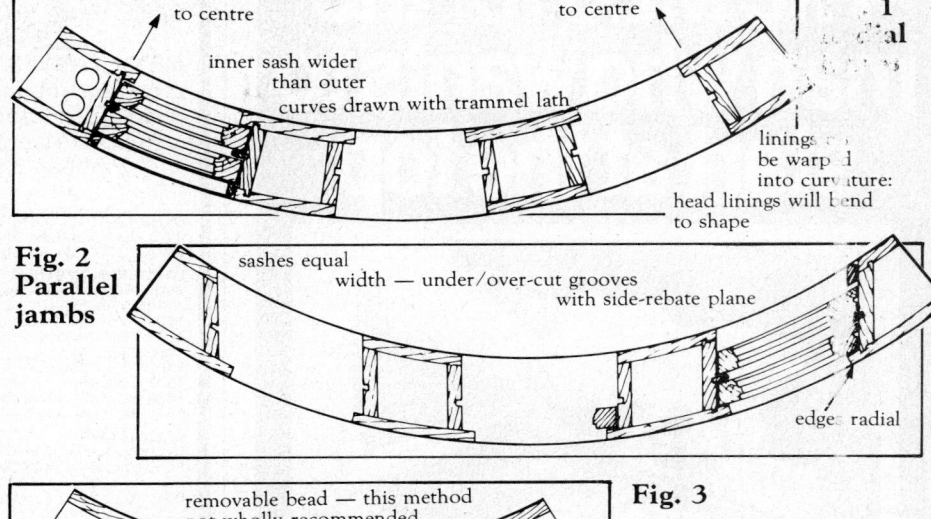

inner sash wider than outer
curves drawn with trammel lath
to centre        to centre

linings... be warped into curvature: head linings will bend to shape

**Fig. 2 Parallel jambs**

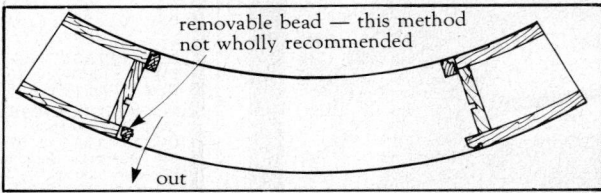

sashes equal width — under/over-cut grooves with side-rebate plane

edge radial

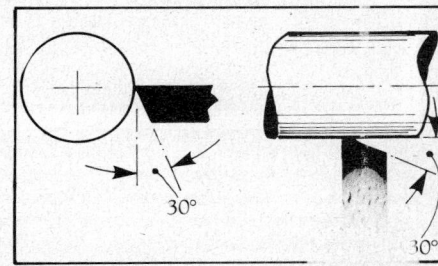

removable bead — this method not wholly recommended

**Fig. 3**

out

However, there is an obvious security risk with this method — which was mainly used for upper-floor windows; fig.3.

You can use box mullions, but they may be solid if preferred, with the outer-sash-cords running over the heads of fixed side sashes, and with grooved head-slats to cover the inner-sash-cords.

Cording is a simple matter. Open out a knot of sash-cord, tie one end to something, and give it a good pre-stretch. Now fasten the lead weight known as a 'mouse' to one end, and feed through an outer pulley. Fish out at the pocket, and pull through the whole length of cord. Now feed the mouse into the opposite outer pulley, and repeat the process. Then from pocket no.2 up to the opposite-side inner pulley, and from there up to the final (inner) pulley — fishing out at pocket 4, of course, and with the cord now forming an X in the frame.

Don't cut any cord now; just tie its extreme end to a weight, drop the weight into its pocket, and pull until the weight is right up to the pulley. Now drive a lath nail (1in wire) through the cord, just at the pulley, and into the pulley stile. Cut this cord to length, and repeat three more times — and what cord remains will be in one length.

*Stan Thomas*

---

**Q** *I was most grateful for your detailed advice on drying cherry. Can you please help on two further points?*
● *At what stage should bark be removed from the ½in boards?*
● *Should the ends of the planks be oiled before drying?*

*Donald Green, Mayfield*

**A** The bark will act as an indicator of drying progress, and first of all will start to peel from the outside. Later, the thinnish bark will begin to crack and come away easily from the wood, showing that it is very much drier. With your thin stock this should be in a few months' time.

Do not apply oil to the ends of the boards. It will only tend to creep into the wood and stain it.

*Bill Brown FIWSc*

---

**Q** *I make Irish and Northumbrian bagpipes from materials such as African blackwood and lignum vitae. Although these turn with relative ease, I would like some advice*

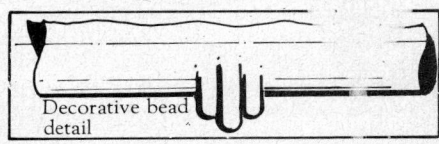

Decorative bead detail

on speeds and cutter-rake angles when using a compound tool-post and HSS cutters. At present I work with top rake and approximately 30° side and bottom rake, with the tool on the centre line. The speed is about 1000rpm for ¾in-diameter finishing and 1500rpm for ½in diameter finishing.

Another problem is in the manufacture of

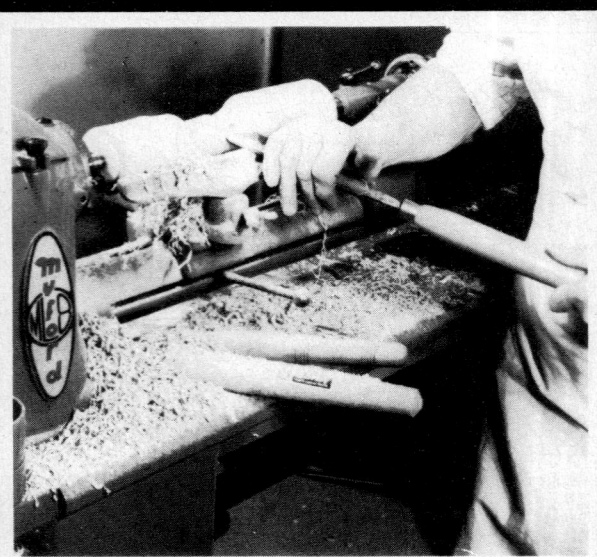
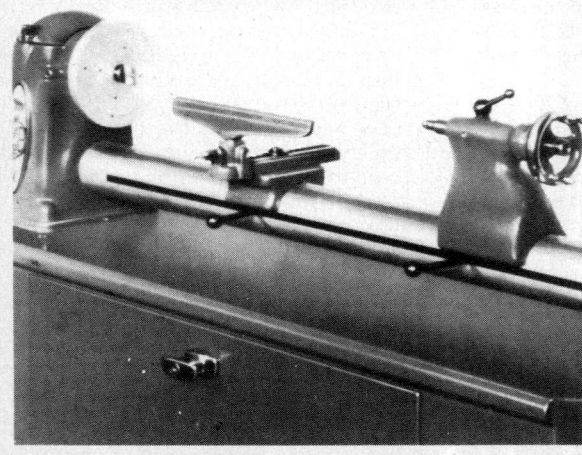

248

Prices quoted are those prevailing at press date and are subject to alteration due to economic conditions

# Question box

decorative beads as shown.

*I would like to produce form tools. Can you advise on rake angles and speeds if you feel this is possible?*

S. J. McCordick, Duffield

**A** It is not clear whether the tool angles and speeds that you are currently employing are successful. Without a top and side rake, however, I would guess that the tool is only rubbing and scraping, while the 30° clearance is excessive and is probably leading to local heating at the work point.

Accordingly I conducted some trials on your behalf, turning ebony to 1in diameter with tools ground from 7/16in toolsteel. They performed well and produced an excellent finish. They were initially ground to the compound angles shown and then finished with an oilstone slip. The angle 'point' of the roughing tool produces a clean cut and is designed to throw the swarf clear, whilst the finishing-tool nose gives a smooth, ring-free surface.

The speed was based on a notional 2500in per minute (i.e. 2500in of surface passing the tool point in every minute of time). This was easily calculated in terms of

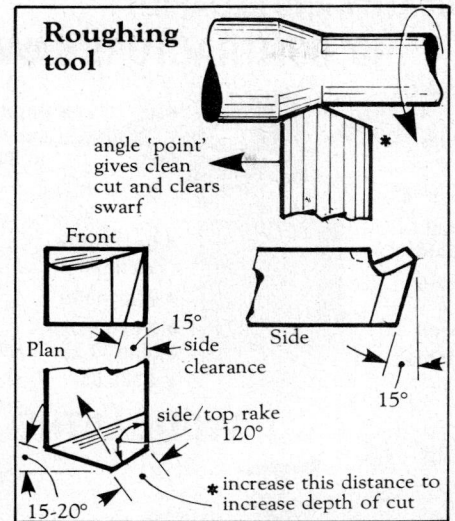

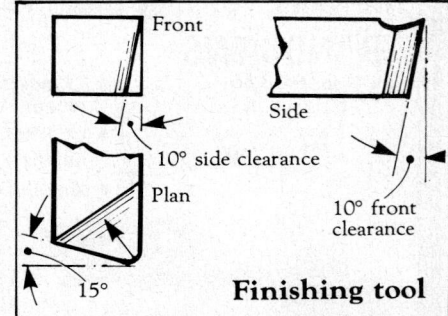

rpm by dividing the circumference of the piece being turned into the speed in inches per minute. The rate of feed is also important, as the tool should be constantly cutting new material and not given a chance to rub during hesitant feeding.

I did not make up a forming tool, but the following observations should be borne in mind. Such tools must be mounted on the centre line of the work with a front clearance of not more than 10°. Top rake should also be minimal (5° at most) if it's necessary at all, as any increase in rake will mean a distortion in the true shape of the cutter profile.

To get a semicircular bead with a tool that has a pronounced top rake, the cutter shape would have to be elliptical. The foregoing information on speed also applies to forming tools.

*Bob Grant DLC FRSA MSIAD*

# Marquetry in the USA

**Ernie Ives** writes: The first International Creative Marquetry Show, held at Wesleyan College, Virginia Beach, USA, in October 1984 was a brave attempt to get marquetry out of its sterotyped image of designs done from set patterns and copies of other people's work. To this end the work was first vetted by two artists, and the selected pieces then judged by two art experts and a practising marquetarian. The criteria for selection were creativity and originality.

Some of the work on show was excellent both as art and as fine craftsmanship, but many artistically pleasing pieces were spoiled by poor workmanship; wide gaps between the pieces, blistered and uneven surfaces. Some pieces were not even marquetry — rather overlay or collage. For me marquetry should be a marriage between art and craft, and work in which one is divorced from the other is like a hammer without a head — it doesn't fulfil its purpose. An attractive design disfigured by the scars of poor joins is offensive to the

● *Above is Ernie Ives' own 'Country Fiddler'; below left is the controversial 'Mondrian box' by Richard Foote of Virginia*

eye; the superbly cut piece with no artistry is a mere technical exercise. Together, they can be an art form which taps the rich and unique resources of the world's most beautiful veneers.

The 'Best in Show' award was taken by George Monks of California with his 'Hummingbird with Hanging Vines'. George used an unusual bleaching technique to create the blur in the bird's wing. Each feather was cut from the background and individually bleached, neutralised, sealed with a 2:1 solution of PVA glue and water, dried, and then glued back into its original position.

In my opinion the 'Burl and Stripes' box by Richard Foote wasn't really marquetry, as the fault in the burl overlaid the stripes and was not let in flush with the surface. An original idea, and one which evoked either pleasure or hatred from those who viewed it (it certainly drew some emotion from me!); but it was not marquetry.

Second place went to Gary Wright, for 'Variation 1: High Country'. Delightfully simple in concept and yet very evocative. One could really see the mountains receding miles into the distance. Two simple tree silhouettes in the foreground added to the depth. Simple in design it might be, but it's very difficult to find just the right veneers to give a picture its mood and atmosphere. Excellently cut and finished, too.

'The Narrows' by Jeff Nelson was given third place, and another of Richard Foote's boxes took an honourable mention. Again it was not 100% marquetry, as the lacewood was overlaid on to the marquetry design underneath. The design is in the style of the Dutch painter Mondrian, who used these bold, colourful, squared-up forms in some of his work. My own 'Country Fiddler' was given an honourable mention. The Show attracted a lot of attention (sales topped $1,000) and was successful enough for the organisers to plan a larger show for October this year. Early application is advisable, as time has to be allowed after the screening of entrants' slides for overseas exhibitors to get their work to the show.
● Details from Suzanne Cartwright, 1501 Mill Dam Road, Virginia Beach, Va 23454, USA. ■

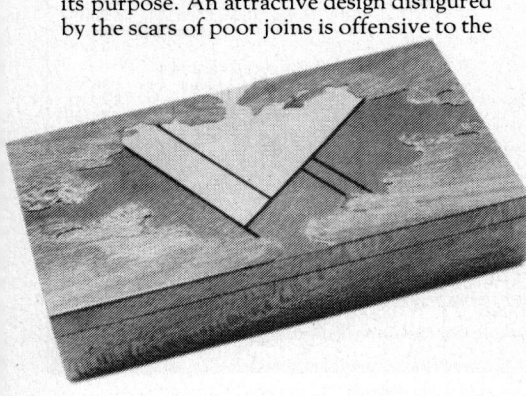

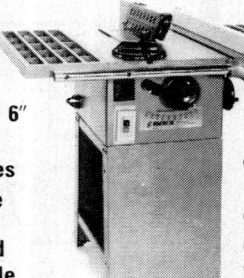

Prices quoted are those prevailing at press date and are subject to alteration due to economic conditions

# Guild notes

## Guild of WOODWORKERS

Shared information, advice and help are vital to good woodwork. They are also the basis of the **Guild of Woodworkers**: an international organisation which welcomes new members — whatever their skills. PO Box 35, Hemel Hempstead HP2 4SS (phone 0442 41221).

Guild members get
- priority on our courses
- free publicity in *Woodworker*
- 15% off Woodworker Show entry
- a free display area and meeting-point at the Show
- 15% discount on our plans
- access to and inclusion in our register of members' skills and services
- the chance to contact other members for help and advice where appropriate
- specially arranged tool in-rance at low rates

Please quote your Guild number when contacting us.
*Aidan Walker*

## Free London space!

It's already. This month we make the first announcements for the Woodworker Show in October. We will be mounting the **London Gallery** exhibit of members' work on the *Woodworker/Guild* stand again, and applications are invited in good time. If you want to show your work in woodworking's premier display-case, **write to me enclosing photographs.** The dates of the Show are 24-27 October; space will be limited, so it's first come first served. At the moment, square footage is undecided — but don't expect that we'll be able to accommodate your range of dining-tables! One or two medium-sized pieces maximum. Remember: the earlier such things are arranged, the better. Don't delay — if you want to take advantage of this astounding offer, **write today.**

## Craft village appeal

Full-time quality craftspeople are wanted to work in a new venture, opening in Derbyshire on 23 May. It is Britannia Park, a leisure complex which will include 'British Genius Pavilions', 'Small World', (a 1/25-scale panorama), a sports centre and holiday chalets, among other things. Most interesting to woodworking craftspeople is the offer of a workshop, a salary, and what looks like an excellent marketplace to sell your work. There are 32 workshops available, set in the 'Craft Village' section of the 350-acre site. It will be open all year round, and there will be a constant flow of visitors.

Britannia Park is on the A6007 Ilkeston to Heanor road, nine miles out of Derby.
● Write to Bob Neill, Craft Village Manager, 10 Long Croft, Aston-on-Trent, Derby DE7 2UH. He is available in the evenings on Derby 792036.

## COURSE CORNER

### Country chairmaking — Fred Lambert

Pull Court, Tewkesbury, Gloucester, **1-5 April**. This course is now fully booked; watch this space for the **combined chairmaking and toolmaking sequels,** which we hope to arrange for the summer holiday. Because of copy dates and forward planning, arrangement of these courses is always somewhat in the dark as far as reader response is concerned. The best way is to ring me at the office and tell me you want another of these excellent courses of Fred's, and then we can go ahead with fair certainty that no one will be disappointed. £145+VAT for five days' instruction, lunches, tea and coffee; payment in full confirms booking.

### Finishing and polishing — Charles Cliffe

**6-7 June,** Bexleyheath; full introduction to this challenging subject. Plenty of opportunity to discover the mysteries for yourself; Charles doesn't let you sit about! £40 inc. VAT. The April course sold out within about six weeks of the first mention on these pages — don't delay if you want to be sure of a place.

### Finishing and polishing in the north

It didn't take long for me to realise that finishing and polishing is a very popular subject among Guild course-goers, and not a lot longer to sympathise with dwellers in the far north who are hard put to travel all the way down to Bexleyheath. I am happy to announce that we now have a **Guild finishing and polishing course in Cheshire** in June. The final dates and venue have yet to be tied up, but we are aiming at the weekend of 29/30. It will be a two-day course, taught by Ian Hosker, a qualified teacher in schools and further education, and a professional polisher and restorer with his own business.

Ian will cover the following subjects over the weekend: the materials, surface preparation, the use of the cabinet scraper, stains and staining, grain-filling, bodying and spiriting, and restoring polished surfaces. The cost? £45, including VAT and the materials you use on the course. May's issue will carry final dates and details, but we're taking bookings — cheque for the full amount, held until the course is fully booked — from now.

## 'Fine Craft and Fine Design'

- \* Seminars and courses
- \* Comprehensive tool insurance
- \* Central skills register
- \* Information and advice
- \* Show entry discounts

Professional and amateur

write to: Guild of Woodworkers, Wolsey House, Wolsey Road, Hemel Hempstead, Hertfordshire HP2 4SS.

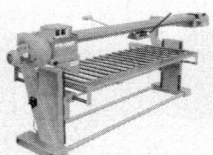

Prices quoted are those prevailing at press date and are subject to alteration due to economic conditions

# Win a Woodworker Show Award

## AT BRISTOL MAY 25, 26, 27 AND LONDON OCT 24, 25, 26, 27

SEND FOR YOUR ENTRY FORM TODAY

London entries:–
£250 to be won by best of show Woodturner and Woodcarver–sponsored by Henry Taylor (Tools) Ltd., Sheffield.

There will be a Woodworker Show at **Bristol in May '85** at the Bristol Exhibition Centre, Canons Road and in **London in October '85** at the Alexandra Pavillion. There are many competition classes including cabinet-making, woodcarving, woodturning, musical instruments, marqueting, model horse drawn vehicles, toys and miniatures.

Send for your competition entry form for BRISTOL or LONDON or both to:–
Woodworker Show '85, Argus Specialist Exhibitions Ltd, Park View House, Park View Road, Berkhamsted, Herts. HP4 3EY. Tel: (04427) 73291.

253

# Woodworker Show 1985

It's a bit early, for sure, to think about visiting this year's London **Woodworker Show** (again at Alexandra Pavilion in October, in case you're wondering).

But not too early to think about a trip to the **Bristol Woodworker Show** on 25, 26 and 27 May at the Bristol Exhibition Complex.

And certainly not too early to think about entering the **competitions** which will form a major part of the displays at *both* shows.

Cabinetmaking, turning, carving; marquetry, clocks, musical instruments; juniors and young professionals; and plenty more besides... The whole wide world of woodwork will be represented, and so should you! The door is open — and if you think your work would never stand a chance, you're probably wrong.

There's no harm in having a go. More than that: there are real benefits:

●**free entry to the show for every competition entrant *and* his or her family;**
● free display of the work throughout the show;
● if you win — a gold, silver or bronze medal, plus a certificate of merit: plus (in many cases) a cash prize.

You can hesitate, and lose vital time. Or you can wait till it's too late, and end up kicking yourself hard. Or you can enter now!

**Full details and entry forms** from Argus Specialist Exhibitions Ltd, Park View House, 1 Park View Rd, Berkhamsted, Herts HP4 3EY, tel. Berkhamsted (04427) 73291.

Go to it! ∎

# £500 cash for carvers and turners

## THE HENRY TAYLOR AWARDS

● *Below: 'The Bounty Hunter' by Wayne Holsopple*

For Barry Martin, sales and marketing manager of Henry Taylor (Tools) Ltd, the Woodworker Show raises one overwhelming question. 'Do we in manufacturing industry do enough to promote the interests of woodcarvers and woodturners in the UK?'

The old-established specialist Sheffield firm sells just as many tools in Britain as in north America, which suggests a high density of carvers and turners in the UK! Yet, says Barry, participation in shows and contests across the Atlantic is at a far higher level — in terms not only of quantity but arguably of quality too.

He cites the annual woodcarving show at the Canadian National Exhibition in Toronto, whose claimed attendance is no fewer than 80,000, and whose aims 'are to promote an interest in and an appreciation of wood carving, to unite both professionals and amateurs, to develop a high standard of craftsmanship, resulting in a first class exhibit and competition for the enjoyment

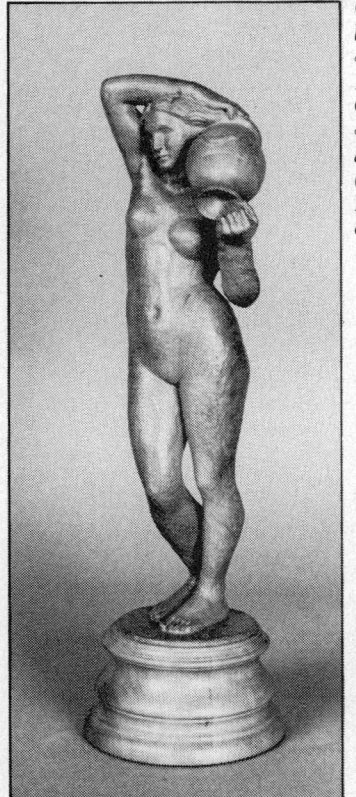

● Can the home team do better? Pictured here are six winners of the 1984 International Woodcarvers Congress in Iowa, USA, where the 'Best in Show' award from Henry Taylor (Tools) went to Wayne Holsopple for his carving opposite

of themselves and the general public'. Henry Taylor actively sponsors more than one event across the Atlantic. 'We believe much more could be done along similar lines in the UK,' says Barry.

As a first step his firm is offering two prizes to 1985 Woodworker Show entrants: **Best in Show (Carving)** and **Best in Show (Turning).** Each will consist of a full £250 in cash, plus a silver rose-bowl. This represents a remarkable advance over the amount of sponsorship available in previous years, and indeed over almost every other prize in the current Show.

With luck, the Henry Taylor Awards will reflect true excellence.

● Henry Taylor (Tools) Ltd, The Forge, Lowther Rd, Sheffield S6 2DR, tel. (0742) 340282/340321.

● Left: 'Indian', again by Frederic Cogelow

● Above, clockwise from top: 'The Swing Is Gone' by Frederic Cogelow; 'Railroad Track Laying Crew' by Ronald Hondo; 'Fighting Stallions' by Earl Saul; 'Woman with Vase' by Craig Barnes

255

# Making the carver's year
# THE ASHLEY ILES CARVING COMPETITION

Every year, a major Woodworker Show highlight is the carving competition sponsored by the celebrated toolmakers Ashley Iles of Lincolnshire.

Unlike others in the Show, the Ashley Iles awards (consisting of £75, £50 and £25 vouchers for Ashley Iles tools) are given for excellence in tackling a particular theme. Last year the subject was 'Birds of prey'. This year we're asking you to test your skills, your eye and your sharpest gouges on depicting

**Creatures of the forest.**

Interpret the subject how you like — in the knowledge that it's not only the winners whose work enchants and delights the thousands of visitors who see it. Every entry goes on display. The Show offers a stirring challenge and a unique chance to venture out against all comers: many, perhaps, no more or less experienced than yourself.

We're announcing the contest a month earlier than usual to provide plenty of time

for thought and action. Over to you!

● Details of competition arrangements from Argus Specialist Exhibitions, Park View House, 1 Park View Rd, Berkhamsted, Herts HP4 3EY, tel. Berkhamsted (04427) 73291.

● Prizes awarded by Ashley Iles (Edge Tools) Ltd, East Kirkby, Spilsby, Lincs; tel. East Kirkby (079 03) 372.

January

February

March

April

May

June

July

August

September

October

November

December

*Ivan Broadhead writes: It was probably the carvers of Ripple, Worcestershire, who in the 14th or 15th century produced these quaint depictions of a yearly round which has utterly vanished. They adorn misericords (clergy seats) at the village's parish church.*

*The* **January** *'wooding', or 'collection of dead boughs by hook or crook' was an old privilege of the villagers*

**February** *found them hedging and ditching: one man hammers a wedge to split a hedge-stake while another holds a spade handle. Between them is a bundle of untrimmed stakes*

**March** *is the month for sowing, while a horse pulls a harrow*

**April** *sees two men scaring birds – one with a flag and the other with a stick*

*Rogation-tide, and the blessing of the crops, come in* **May.** *The figure of St Mary is decked with flowers, ready to be carried round the fields*

*In* **June** *a horseman, whose left wrist once bore a hawk, rides off hunting with his dog behind him*

**July** *brings Lammas (Loaf-mass) Eve at the manorial bakery. Disputes over weight, quality and prices were frequent, so armed village police kept order. This is the only known appearance of the subject on a misericord*

**August** *is harvest-time, with a man and a woman busy reaping.*

*In* **September** *the corn is removed for malting: the figures hold partly filled sacks and long corn bins*

**October** *is the month for beating down acorns for the pigs . . .*

*. . . which are slaughtered in* **November!**

*Finally, the dark nights of* **December** *find the villagers spinning: a man and his wife sit on a curved settle by a fire, while the cat behind her licks its paws*

# The woodcarver's tale

*Vera Feldman calls herself 'an ordinary housewife', but there's nothing commonplace about her enthusiasm for wood or love for carving*

About three years ago, I felt I wanted to try my hand at woodcarving. At the same time, I heard of an old gentleman who could no longer carve and was selling his tools. They were beautiful and well kept, and came to me as a 22nd-wedding-anniversary present.

I found myself a block of pine about 6×3×3in and decided to carve a bear. I had no idea where or how to begin and looked locally for woodworking classes. I tracked one down at a nearby college of art, rang up and was told to come and spend the afternoon looking around. My piece of pine got some queer looks — it was not a wood for the professional. Since I only had a Workmate, and had never heard of 'rifflers', the teacher told me doubtfully that he didn't think this class was really for me. Anyway, he could only give me ½₂ of his time, and perhaps I ought to go home and think about it!

I did go home and think about it, and decided the class was not for me. Now, with 18 finished carvings on shelves and cupboard tops, I am very glad I made that decision. I had heard of someone called 'Spock' Morgan who did woodturning and some carving, and went along to his craft shop with my bit of pine and my tools. I was very much in awe of this man with a black beard and woolly hat but he took my piece of wood and a Stanley knife and, with magic in his hands and kindly encouragement in his words, he began shaping my bear and explaining the way of wood as he carved.

With Spock's encouragement and advice I went home and gradually shaped my little bear with utmost difficulty. At first it is very hard to think and carve in 3-D. I spent sleepless nights worrying exactly how to cut the next paw or ear; when I actually had a gouge and mallet in my hands, I found my brain wouldn't command them. Gradually, however, a shape appeared and I quickly learnt that for something to stick out or up, you needed to cut back; also that it's all too easy to remove wood, but impossible to put it back again!

Now, as 'just a housewife', I try and spend each day doing some carving, because it seems to have taken over a part of my life. It has also taken over most of our garage! I listen for the sound of a chainsaw, track it to a garden and then negotiate for a piece of the felled tree.

The things I carve are small, mostly no bigger than 8in overall, probably because I only have a Workmate vice to hold them, plus one or two other ways and means. At the beginning I tended to hold the work in my lap, but I gradually realised that this was foolish in the extreme!

To further my knowledge of carving, I have spent some time searching for books on the subject, but find that there is a very limited supply. I have only come across — and bought — nine. The last one is Ian Norbury's *Techniques of Creative Woodcarving* which is a beautiful book to hold and leaf through, although in the long run the only way to learn is pick up the gouge and mallet and do it yourself. I like to use as many types of wood as I can. Once I have made something, I know the type of wood, and hope I can learn that way.

● *Like Vera Feldman, Joe Elmore of Santa Cruz, California, taught himself. 'Sometimes at night', he says, 'I sit among my carvings. They are my friends.' Few work on such a scale: the chainsaw is his primary tool*

*Report and photos
Marie Wilson*

After I finished the little pine bear, I found a piece of left-over mahogany window-sill and so my weasel was born. A piece of sycamore from my friend Spock produced two field-mice in a tree root. The first piece of lime was only 2in thick so I used it to do my first (and only) relief carving — of a boy's head. Then I used a thin long piece of yew for a field-mouse running up an ear of corn, pine again for a penguin, and laburnum for a mother and child. The wood is very intricate, but I don't really like the subject.

Naturally, I had to try my hand at an eight-link chain when I bought E. J. Tangerman's book, and also a version of a ball-in-a-cage. On holiday in St Ives, it was pure pleasure to put the final touches to my oak comic basset-hound without having to clear up the shavings from the sandy beach! A branch from a trimmed horse-chestnut tree became a sitting bear; I was surprised that the very heavy wood took only six months to dry, turning into a very lightweight carving similar to lime. A friend's dachshund was an inspiration, and mahogany was just the right colour and texture for his curled up, nose-to-tail position.

My favourite is one of the Seven Dwarfs made from elm. He only stands 5in tall, his ample girth equally wide. To get his arms and hands right, I had my long-suffering husband posing with his hands behind his back — only the hands, I hasten to add, were used as models!

We have spent a great deal of our summer holidays tracking down woodcarvers, wherever we might be. In Cornwall we drove miles looking for one we had heard of, only to find he had gone to a show miles the other way. This year in Scotland, the Tourist Information Centre gave us addresses of three. One had already died — we met his brother, who himself was well into his eighties; the second had moved from Scotland down south, and the third had emigrated to Canada!

I had my first outing to the Woodworker Show at Alexandra Palace this year. I especially enjoyed seeing the work that other carvers do, but it isn't easy to see properly at the distance one has to stand away. It is understandable that hundreds of people cannot handle and stroke each exhibit, although this might have helped me with the great problem of finishing.

The books on the subject are very lacking in advice, mostly telling the reader either to leave the work 'as from the tool', or to work through the grades of abrasive paper till no further marks are seen. With most of my work I certainly have not done this, and looking closely I see that it would never be suitable for any competition.

This, then, is my story. Having been carving now for three years, I am rapidly running out of flat surfaces to put my work on, although even the kitchen wall has been used for a few things such as my chain, which makes it look somewhat like a dungeon. However, the joy and satisfaction is great, and although a number of people have asked whether they could buy some of the things, I would never part with them. They are 'born', or created from my hands, and give my life extra incentive and pleasure. ∎

# The fine art of success

Carvers & Gilders offer living proof of a living market for the very finest hand skills. That is, if you know where to look for it, if you're well organised — and if you're good enough.

Started in 1978, the firm is based in Wandsworth, London. None of its four partners (one male and three female) is an apprenticed craftsman or woman — they met at the City and Guilds of London Art School. Yet their skills are beyond question. They perform both high-class restoration and new commissions, and they're now finding time to work 'on spec': a move which, they hope, will enable them to interest more clients in original as opposed to traditional designs.

No doubt their location has helped — they are within easy reach of antique dealers, architects, interior designers, and the rich individuals (both in Britain and abroad) whose tastes the firm ultimately serves. But this would mean little without energy and salesmanship. It must be significant that Carvers & Gilders now employ not only two assistants but also a business manager.

● Carvers & Gilders, Unit 9, Charterhouse Works, Eltringham St, London, SW18, tel. 01-870 7047. ■

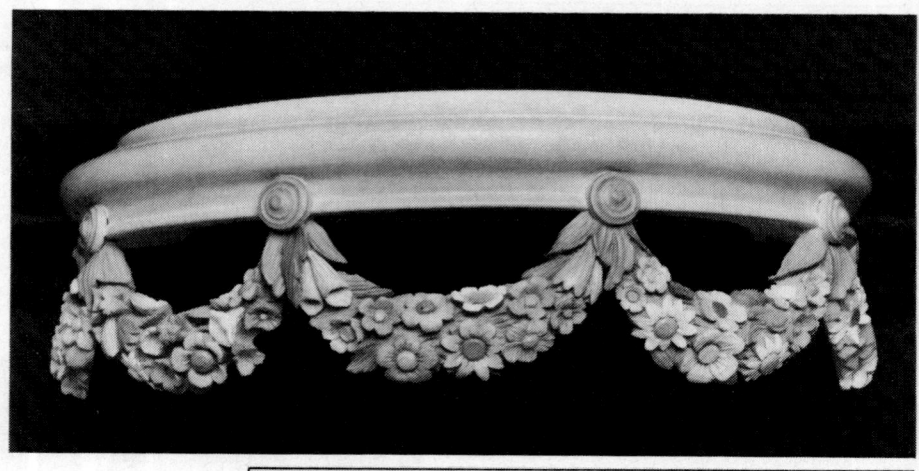

● *Above: This corona is finished in muted yet delightfully varied colours. Right: Straightforwardly traditional items such as this gilt mirror and decoration are almost routine for Carvers & Gilders*

● *Above: More lush flora – one of a pair. Left: Devoted almost entirely to hand operations, the workshop presents something of an 18th-century scene (photo Phil Sayer)*

● *Above: True rococo, re-created for the 80s – William McCombe's ho-ho birds. Left: This mirror testifies that not all the firm's interests are classical*

● *Above: A complex mirror whose slight asymmetry again gives more than a hint of the rococo*

● *Left: Also on our cover, this basket of flowers by William McCombe sums up the breathtaking skills which are the partners' stock-in-trade – impressing even London clients who thought they had seen it all*

# The craft of cabinetmaking

David Savage reveals how
to tune your machines for
a faultless performance

I do not like having to admit to being a wally. Experts who write in woodworking magazines shouldn't be wallies. But I and my mortiser are engaged in a contest; and the mortiser is making me look a right wally.

When a new machine comes into the workshop, the natural temptation is to drag it out of the crate, bolt it together and put it to work. My natural trust in human beings foolishly extends to machines, and I clasp them to my metaphorical bosom. Don't follow my example! While they are still in the box, whack them about with a big stick and show them who is boss.

If you are to get the best out of any machine — and cabinet work demands extreme precision — that precision must be instilled by you.

Setting up, fettling, tuning, call it what you will, is needed for almost every tool in the shop. Hand planes come from the makers shaped like boomerangs; chisels all need flattening and honing; marking-gauges all need attention. Machines should also have this attention, but it should be done regularly like a 10,000-mile service.

The table-saw is perhaps the best example of a suitable case for treatment. Probably the most used saw in the shop, it is capable of great precision and can be extended in versatility by the use of shop-made jigs and templates. Many small shops have two table-saws — one 1hp machine with an 8 or 9in blade, used for most jointing jobs, and a larger saw with a 2hp motor, a 10 or 12in blade and a sliding table, which deals with heavy ripping, cutting to dimension and board material. Both can be set up in a similar way. There is no distinction between light and heavy work where accuracy is concerned.

Begin at the drive belt — check for tension and wear. Clean out all dust from the tilt mechanism and put a spanner on anything that looks as if it may come loose with vibration. Carefully clean and inspect the saw arbor and blade-locating washers. Has the thread on the arbor stretched? If so, some right idiot has been using that saw. Replace the blade clean and sharp.

I find it difficult to tell when TCT blades need changing, as they hold a not-quite-sharp edge for a very long time. My answer, and it may not be the best one, is to keep a couple of trimming blades for very special work and change the general blades at the start of any major project. Good-quality blades with a heavy plate and high-quality carbide tips are usually worth the money in the long term. Cheaper items can throb and resonate, giving a variable kerf to the cut. Fit the blade carefully, but do not tighten the nut more than just tight. The saw spins against the direction of thread and you will only have to get the nut off again some time soon.

Giving support behind the job right to the blade is one of the best ways of preventing those infuriating chips of broken timber. Replace the access plate around the saw with a wooden item, clamp it in position, then wind the saw up through the plate. This will give a kerf in the tabletop of exactly the width of that blade.

The rip fence can be set by measuring from the front and back of the blade, set at full height. Some machinists like the rip fence to fall away 'just a touch' — this is really an immeasurable amount. Have the idea in your head, and it should set itself; attempt to set it to fall away, and the adjustment will be too much.

A wooden high fence can be fitted to the rip fence. Make sure this is quarter-sawn stuff, and square to the table. An alternative is a sliding box that fits over the rip fence; an American colleague gave me this idea, which seems to be a great help when working above the blade. The crosscut protractor runs in a channel across the table — check that this channel is parallel to the blade. If the protractor is at all loose in the channel, peen over the end of the steel guide bar and file to a tight sliding fit. A wooden extension fence can be fitted to the crosscut protractor. This should be longer than you need so that the saw can trim it to exact length. This also gives a locating mark when dimensioning timber, as the end of the crosscut jig is exactly where the blade will cut. Finally, it gives support behind the job right up to the blade, again helping to prevent chipping out. The crosscut wooden fence can hold home-made stops for dimension cutting. A hinged two-stage stop can do just as good a job for cutting both ends of several pieces to exactly the same length as a sliding table on a dimension saw.

The dimension saw can have the crosscut fence extended in exactly the same way as the small table-saw. But my Startrite dimension saw had a rather disturbing illness — a case of sloppy stops. As these are supposed to be the only means of controlling the position of a crosscut, it was rather serious. A couple of cut-down valve springs from a motorbike sorted it out. Whether the play was due to wear or poor design I would hate to say, but that machine was completely inaccurate and had probably been so for a long time.

With a tilt-arbor saw, it is very important that the blade should always return to 90° after the tilt has been used; set this stop very carefully. The difficulty in checking is a saw is at 90° is that the light levels have to be very high and your eyes very sharp. Another way is to measure the piece cut. Take a scrap piece 18×3×1in, crosscut one end at what you expect to be 90°, then rip the job down the centre. Now carefully clear all dust from an area of the saw-table and from the ends just crosscut. Stand the job on this crosscut end, but turn one of the two halves through 180°. If the angle of cut is really 90° both pieces will still be together at the top; if it is 89° you will see that the piece you have turned leans away from the piece you didn't.

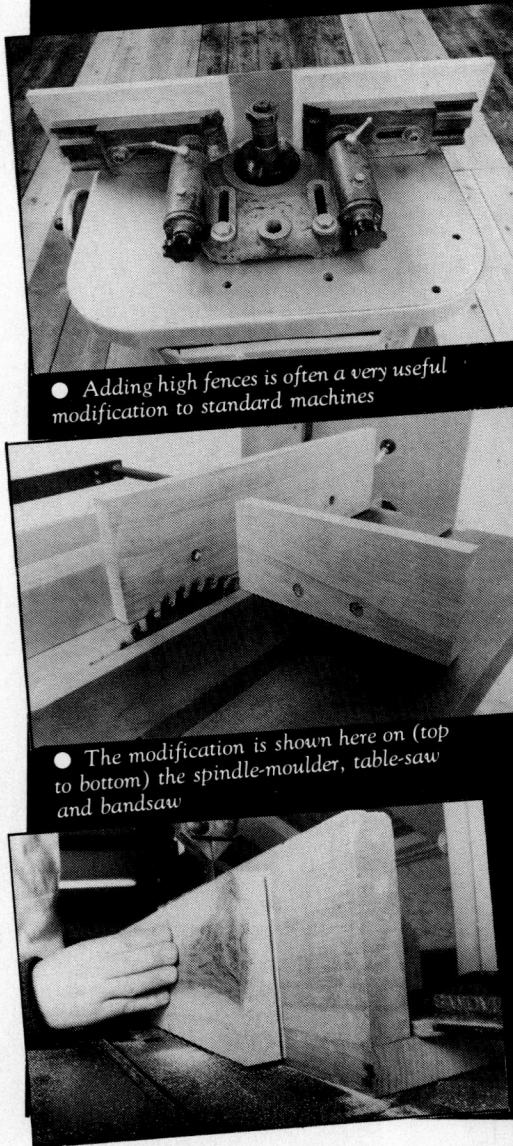

● Adding high fences is often a very useful modification to standard machines

● The modification is shown here on (top to bottom) the spindle-moulder, table-saw and bandsaw

Planers and planer-thicknessers are also candidates for periodic examination. Before getting into that, however, and thinking of my lovely Luna 17in planer thicknesser, I really must pay tribute to the lads from Axminster Power Tools. Not only did they get it to me within five working days, they also helped to install it. Putting a machine that size into a ground-floor workshop is no fun; putting it into a first-floor workshop is entertaining. Des and Ginger, who run the joinery shop next door, had already helped move in the pad-sander, the spindle-moulder and one or two other very heavy lumps, so I did not want to bother them. Axminster to the rescue. 'Of course, sir, we'll send a couple of chaps who'll get it up there in a jiffy,' said Bernie Stiles.

In due course the heavies arrived, with the Luna crated up on a trailer. Neither of them liked the look of the stone steps leading up the outside of my workshop, but to their credit they said not a word. For my part I did not like the look of the three-cubic yard crate, which had been placed on the trailer by fork-lift truck. I was right; we couldn't even lift it off.

By this time a small crowd of workers from the council yard opposite had gathered to offer advice and encouragement. After some deliberation, we saw that the only course was to take the damn thing apart. This was a brave decision, for none of us really knew how to do it, and I had not as yet paid for the machine.

The cast-iron tables of a planer this size take three people to lift them. They came off first. The carcase was then wangled off the trailer into the street. We now had a crowd of enthusiastic supporters and a traffic jam stretching into the middle of town, but without the arrival of Des the joiner I still don't think we would have got that bloody thing indoors. By heroic effort, what felt like several tons of Swedish steel was finally humped into the workshop. There it stays. I shall not move it ever again.

Before I paid the kind men from Axminster, I checked those tables for flatness. Cast iron is wonderful stuff, but if it is not properly cured before machining it

● *The dial gauge is extremely handy for checking that a planer's cutter-block is aligned exactly with the infeed and outfeed tables (photos John Gollop)*

can carry on twisting after being milled flat. The tables were acceptable — but no better than acceptable; they were flat to within ⅟₃₂in over 3ft.

Once I was left alone with the beast, I didn't have the heart to set about it with the big stick. I didn't have the energy, either. The infeed table was checked for parallel with the cutter-block. I use a dial gauge mounted in a block of steel; this sits on the table and readings are taken along the block (not the cutter). Check also that the table moves up and down with a parallel action.

The outfeed table needed more attention. It was set out of parallel with the cutter-block, and rather too low. Checking the thickness table involves feeding pieces to the left-hand and right-hand sides of the cutters, and then comparing them for thickness. The feed mechanism should also be checked: it should provide enough pressure to grip the job, but not enough to compress the fibres.

All cast-iron tables like wax, and this

machine furnished no exceptions. The black gunk that came off during the waxing process was amazing. I am still waxing that machine, and it is still absorbing the stuff.

Finally, very carefully set the planer knives parallel to each other and cutting the same arc. This may take some time, but if you use the dial gauge it is very simple. The importance of the accuracy of this adjustment cannot be stressed too heavily. Then tighten the blades up with a properly fitting socket — and do this before you do anything else. Do not get distracted on to another task. The planer is not as good at knife-throwing as the spindle-moulder, but it chucks a bigger weapon.

And as for this mortiser that I've been fooling around with . . . Sometimes it cuts wonderful, clean square mortises, and sometimes it doesn't. I must admit that I have yet to spend an afternoon sorting the thing out. Come back, Record Ridgway hollow chisels — all is forgiven! ∎

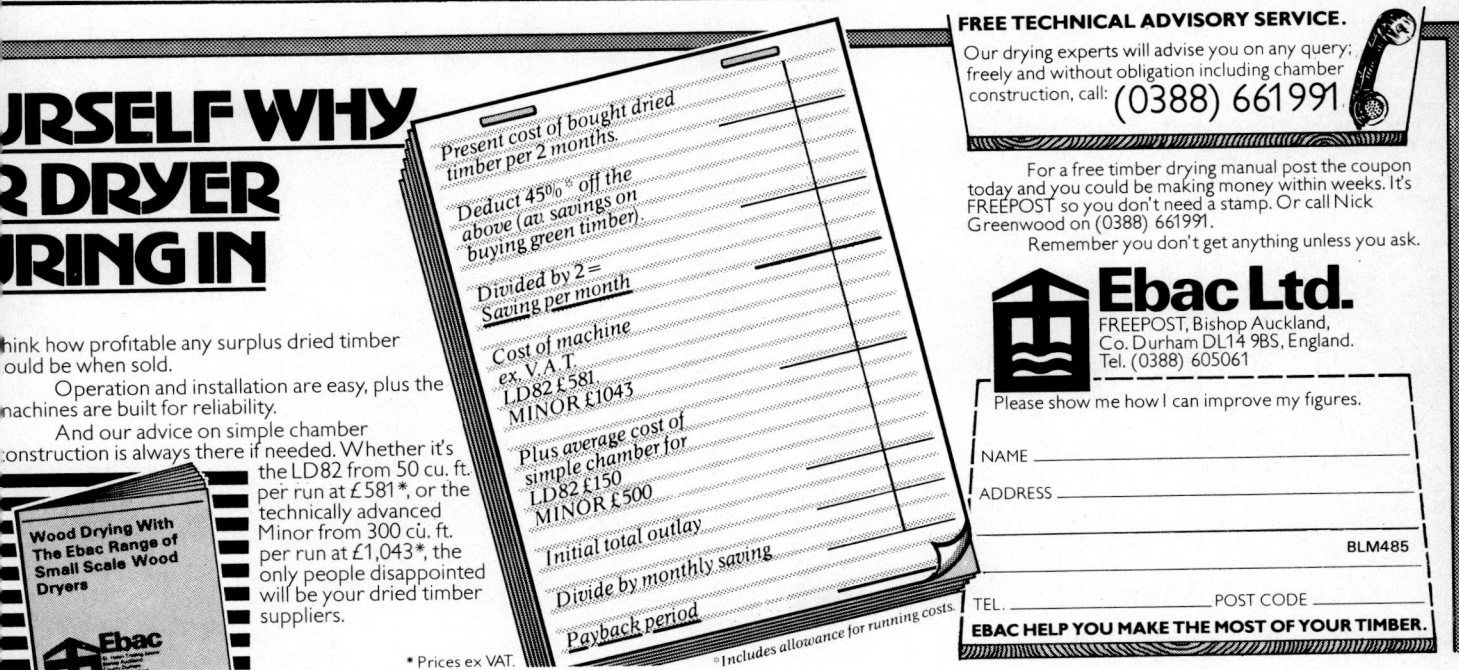

# A contemporary master

**Peter Collenette** writes: Even the still tiny profession of furniture designer-craftsman has its unknowns and its stars. Rupert Williamson must be counted among the latter.

After 11 years in the game — he started making to commission in 1974 — his work is a frequent sight at Crafts Council shows. It is currently on display in the Buckinghamshire County Museum, Milton Keynes, and has had a number of outings abroad. Few of his peers, however, can boast (as he can) the distinction of a piece in the Victoria & Albert.

Trained at the Royal College of Art and Bucks College, High Wycombe, Rupert occupies a fairly spacious and very well equipped workshop in Milton Keynes, employing one or two younger assistants at a time. Unquestionably, he caters for the top end of the market. He does not produce standard lines — though batches may be called for, particularly in the case of board-room and dining-chairs. A showcase full of models, prepared for his own use and for discussion with clients, attests to the extreme attention which he is able to accord each commission.

It also displays an unusual consistency of style. For, even in such a sophisticated field, his work stands out by reason of its highly wrought detailing. Extreme accuracy of workmanship, plus a perfect finish (he sprays a melamine lacquer), go without saying. But, while many other contemporary designer/makers in wood cling to severe plainness, and some are meticulous in preserving a 'natural' — even a primitive — appearance, Rupert clearly believes there is nothing wrong with complexity or artifice. His decorative idiom often recalls the 18th century — especially in his love for ripple figure, his intricate chair-backs and his use of stringing. A favourite ornamental device is to continue the structural lines of a piece by running inlays across adjoining surfaces.

His basic materials are solid English hardwoods, mainly cherry, sycamore and yew, but he uses fancy veneers, inlays, and even metal, as decoration. 'Antiques of the future' is an over-familiar phrase: yet there's little doubt that it describes the role Rupert's furniture is destined — and probably intended — to play.

● Rupert Williamson, New Bradwell Workspace, St James St, New Bradwell, Milton Keynes, Bucks MK13 0BW, tel. (0908) 314423. ■

● *Rupert Williamson's furniture, like his jewel-box (above right), displays a stunning richness of detail*

# Closing the deal

**Well-built and pleasingly down-to-earth: Roger Hickman presents a very attractive piece of furniture**

I made this chest of drawers in the traditional way, largely from solid deal. It came from my local supplier, who is kind enough to let me sort through the boards and select those which are sensibly flat, and have reasonable grain and not too many knots. Wide, thin planks are now no longer available, their place having been taken by man-made boards; the ⅜in-thick planks traditionally used for drawer-sides and backs, and the even thinner boards for drawer-bottoms seen in old chests-of-drawers, can now only be had at exorbitant prices.

I compromised by using thicker boards

● *Strong, simple lines and a straightforward design combined with painstaking attention to constructional detail; a challenge in the workshop and a boon in the household*

## Carcase details

- hole for top fixing
- double tenons
- tongue and groove
- drawer-stop
- stopped tenons
- shrinkage clearance
- slotted hole
- hole for plinth fixing

for drawer-sides and backs; but, even for the thickness used (¾in nominal — 15mm) I had to rub-joint the sides of all but the smallest drawers to get the depth. Rub-joints were also necessary in the carcase sides and the top. For the drawer-bottoms and carcase back I used 4mm ply.

The first operation was to build up the planks into the widths required. I have never found that deal holds glue especially well, so the joints between the planks were strengthened with dowels: 6mm for the drawer-sides and backs, and 10mm for the carcase sides and top. The dowels were grooved longitudinally to relieve the glue pressure and prevent splitting out when the boards were assembled.

Deal boards are never particularly true or of constant thickness, so I had to plane both surfaces to correct misalignment and mismatch in thickness. I used lap-dovetailed top and bottom front and rear rails for the carcase, and stop-mortise-and-tenoned intermediate rails. The central divider for the two top drawers was through-tenoned into the front rails. The inner edges of the rails were grooved to take the drawer runners, which were tongued at the ends to suit, and fitted with 3mm clearance to allow for carcase shrinkage. They were each located dry with a single central screw into the carcase side, whose rear edge was shouldered to take the ply back.

I constructed the drawers in the traditional way too, using dovetails lapped at the front and through at the back. The drawer-fronts and backs were cut and planed to a tight fit in the carcase openings, before cutting the joints. Because the sides were a little thicker than normal, I was able to dispense with drawer-slips for the bottom and groove the sides as well as the front to take the drawer-bottom. The dovetails were cut so that when the drawers were assembled the drawer-sides were

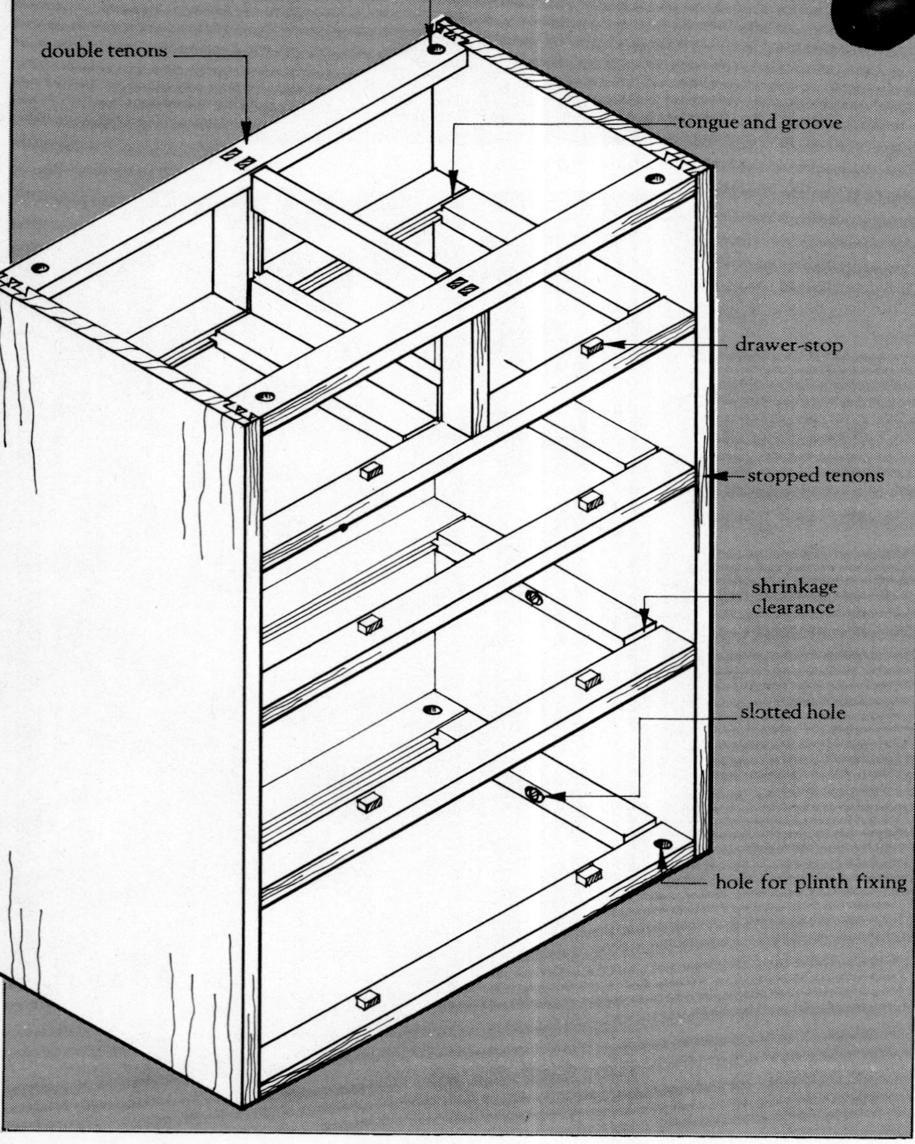

## Front elevation

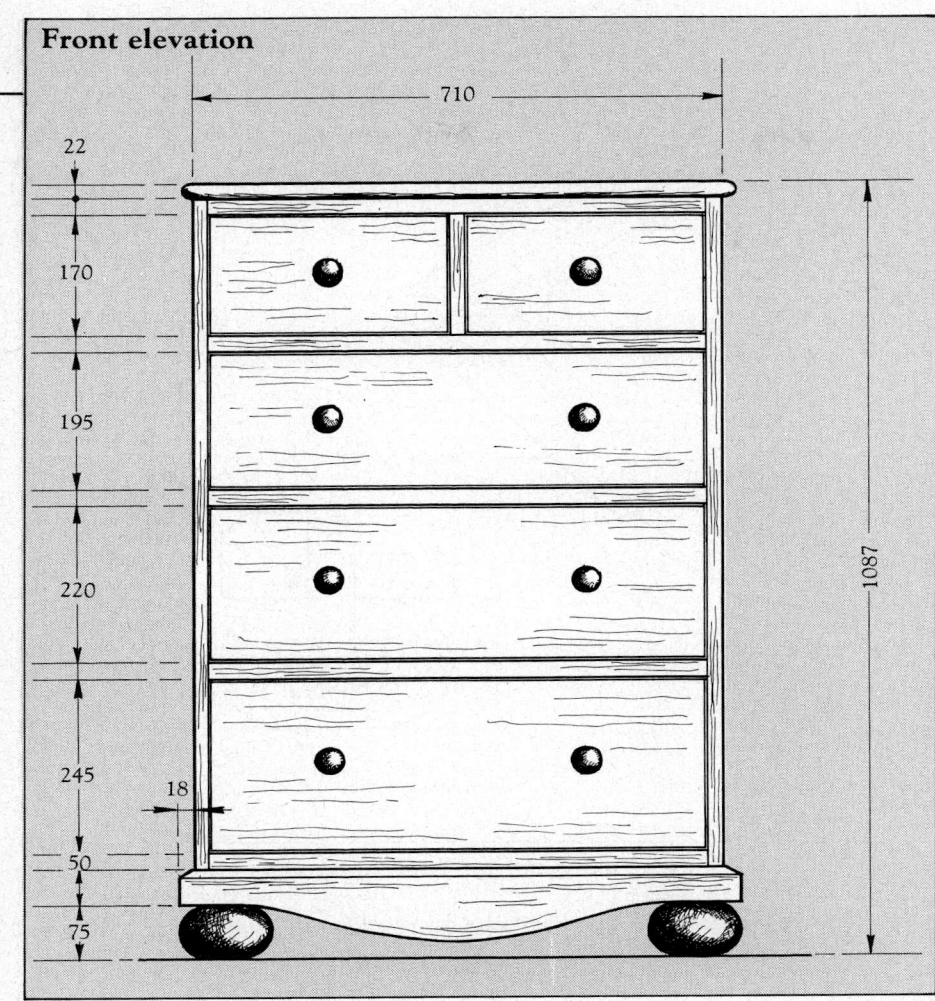

710

22
170
195
220
245
18
50
75

1087

0.5mm proud of the fronts and backs. This enabled the drawers to be cleaned up without affecting the fit of the drawer in the carcase. I bought beech handles for the drawers, but if you have a lathe you can turn your own.

The top was screwed to the carcase, four screws passing upwards through the top rails. The rear two holes were slotted to allow for differential shrinkage. The carcase stands on a plinth supported on four bun feet. The plinth sides are plain mitred to the front and stop-half-jointed to the rear rail, but all four joints were strengthened with triangular tongued corner pieces locating in grooves worked on the inside of the plinth members.

The bun feet posed a problem in construction, as I don't have a lathe, but eventually I got round it. I glued up deal offcuts to provide a blank about 150mm in diameter, sawed this into slices 75mm deep and shaped each foot individually, using a coping-saw for rough shaping. Planes, files and glasspaper all helped the final shaping. A very close inspection reveals that the feet have been made by hand, but the slight variation in shape cannot be detected at a

● *With drawers removed, the frame-and-runner details can be seen. Dividers between top drawers grooved into the hangers; shrinkage clearance allowed between rails and runner shoulders*

## Drawer details

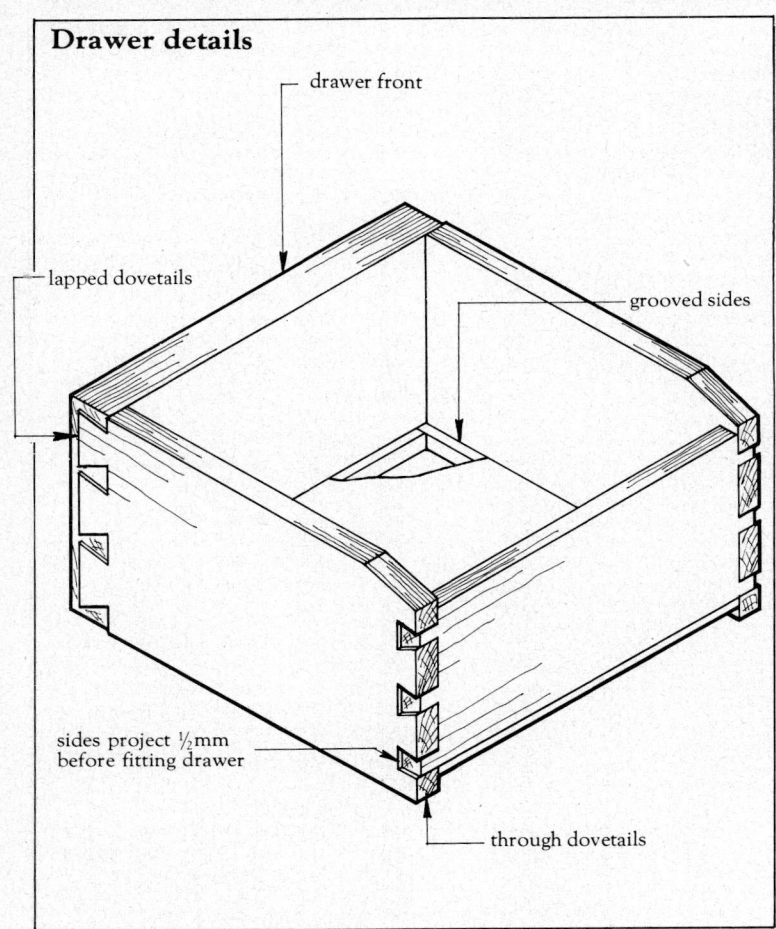

drawer front

lapped dovetails

grooved sides

sides project ½mm before fitting drawer

through dovetails

# Plinth details

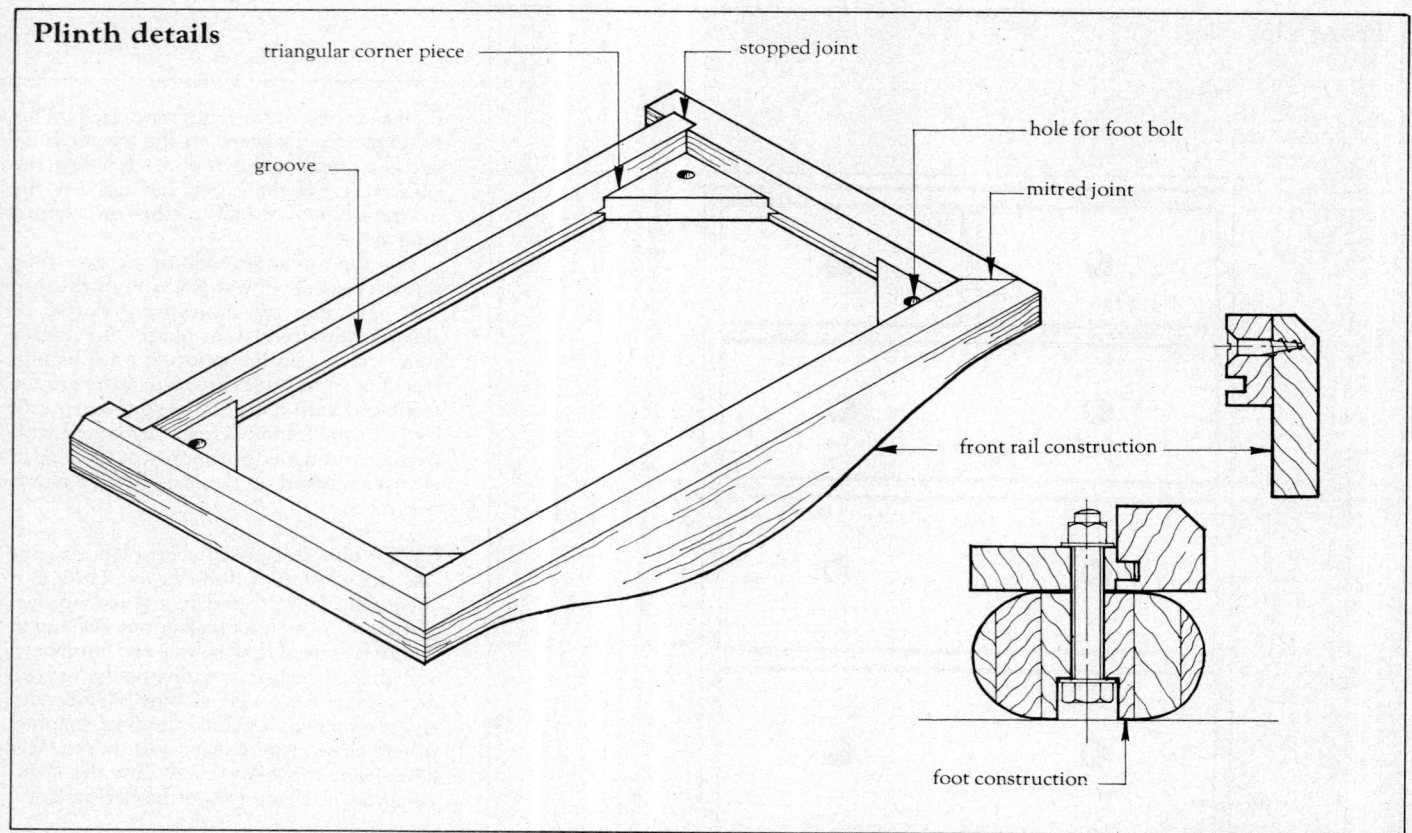

triangular corner piece — stopped joint — hole for foot bolt — groove — mitred joint — front rail construction — foot construction

normal viewing distance, and in any event the method of construction is not inappropriate for a rather rustic piece such as this. Each foot was bored and counterbored on the underside to take a substantial (10mm) steel bolt to locate it on the triangular strengthening pieces glued into the corners of the plinth.

The carcase was secured to the plinth with four screws passing through the bottom front and rear rails into the plinth members.

The various parts were separated as far as possible for final sanding, staining and finishing. The carcase, top, plinth and drawer-fronts were given the merest hint of stain to kill the very light yellow shade of new deal; then I applied a number of coats of raw linseed oil, rubbed well in with a cloth wrapped in a brick for extra weight and polishing power!

The advantage of this method is that with patience and no skill a satisfying sheen can be developed which is immune to abuse and stains from hot and cold water. The disadvantage is the time it takes — several weeks, allowing plenty of time drying out between applications of oil, and, when finally re-assembled, the piece needs to stand on polythene sheet to avoid the oil (in the early days) oozing out and staining the carpet.

The drawer-knobs and feet were finished in the same way (but without the brick). Finally the drawer-runners were lubricated with candle-grease.

As is to be expected with relatively unseasoned timber in a centrally heated house, shrinkage of the drawers has increased their vertical clearance by about 3mm, but no splitting or other movement has occurred at any of the many rub-joints. The chest looks like giving solid service in hard use for years to come. ■

## Cutting list

Where planks are built up, the overall width is given. Widths and thicknesses are prepared (i.e. not nominal).

| | | mm | | | |
|---|---|---|---|---|---|
| *Carcase* | | | | | |
| 2 sides | 950 × | 405 × | 22 | ex 9 × 1″ | boards |
| 10 rails | 710 | 45 | 22 | ex 2 × 1 | |
| 10 drawer-runners | 330 | 45 | 22 | ex 2 × 1 | |
| 2 top drawer-dividers | 330 | 45 | 22 | ex 2 × 1 | |
| 2 top drawer-runners | 330 | 45 | 22 | ex 2 × 1 | |
| 2 top drawer vertical dividers | 210 | 45 | 22 | ex 2 × 1 | |
| 1 top | 760 | 440 | 22 | ex 9 × 1 | |
| 1 back | 950 | 700 | 4 | | |
| *Plinth* | | | | | |
| 2 side rails | 450 | 45 | 45 | ex 2 × 2″ | boards |
| 1 front rail | 750 | 45 | 22 | ex 2 × 1 | |
| | 750 | 95 | 22 | ex 4 × 1 | |
| 1 rear rail | 720 | 45 | 45 | ex 2 × 2 | |
| 4 triangular corner pieces | 150 | 150 | 22 | ex 1″ | offcuts |
| 4 feet | 75 | 150 dia. | | ex 1″ | offcuts |
| *Drawers* | | | | | |
| Top drawers: | | | | | |
| 2 fronts | 340 | 170 | 22 | ex 7 × 1″ | boards |
| 4 sides | 390 | 170 | 15 | ex 7 × ¾ | |
| 2 backs | 340 | 150 | 15 | ex 7 × ¾ | |
| 2 bottoms | 390 | 340 | 4 | | |
| 3rd drawer | | | | | |
| 1 front | 680 | 195 | 22 | ex 8 × 1″ | board |
| 2 sides | 390 | 195 | 15 | ex 6 × ¾ & 4 × ¾ | |
| 1 back | 680 | 175 | 15 | ex 6 × ¾ & 4 × ¾ | |
| 1 bottom | 680 | 390 | 4 | | |
| 4th drawer | | | | | |
| 1 front | 680 | 220 | 22 | ex 9 × 1″ | board |
| 2 sides | 390 | 220 | 15 | ex 6 × ¾ & 5 × ¾ | |
| 1 back | 680 | 200 | 15 | ex 6 × ¾ & 5 × ¾ | |
| 1 bottom | 680 | 390 | 4 | | |
| 5th drawer | | | | | |
| 1 front | 680 | 245 | 22 | ex 9 × 1 & 2 × 1″ | |
| 2 sides | 390 | 245 | 15 | ex 6 × ¾ & 5 × ¾ | |
| 1 back | 680 | 225 | 15 | ex 6 × ¾ & 5 × ¾ | |
| 1 bottom | 680 | 390 | 4 | | |

# The WOODWORKER Magazine MDF Competition

**Sponsored by FIDOR — the Fibre Building Board Organisation**

*picture Mädler of Europe*

## A major design contest for a major new material

If you're in the furniture trade or even at college, you'll already know about medium density fibreboard — and you'll know why it's caught on so firmly.

Arguably the first new panel product since chipboard arrived after World War II, MDF challenges its predecessor in important ways; and it's very nearly as cheap. No material will do everything, but MDF bids fair to take a well-earned place of its own alongside the established favourites. And it's now being made in the British Isles.

The funny thing is that a lot of people haven't heard of it yet. But it's widely available if you know where to look (FIDOR will tell you the names of stockists in your district), so there's no reason not to give it a try.

That's why we've organised this competition. Amateur and professional will be in with equal chances, because we're after clever, attractive, original designs — whether or not they need a lot of time and/or fancy equipment in the execution. We also guarantee extensive national publicity for the winners and their designs — in the form of coverage in **Woodworker** magazine, nationally available each month, plus a comprehensive release to the media by FIDOR.

The closing date isn't 'till 30 April 1985: so please don't be shy. Go on — enter! We have no preconceptions about what's going to win: and we're longing to hear from you.

## ABOUT MDF

Medium density fibreboard is made from wood fibre with the addition of resin glue. Its vital feature is its close, dense texture — like that of many hardwoods. This means:
**Ease of working** MDF can be sawn, drilled, routed, sanded, engraved, edge-moulded and even turned to a sharp, clean finish;
**Ease of fixing** MDF can be glued, dowelled, screwed, nailed, stapled — and even dovetailed;
**Ease of finishing** MDF can be painted, stained, lacquered and veneered on both faces and all edges, before and after cutting.

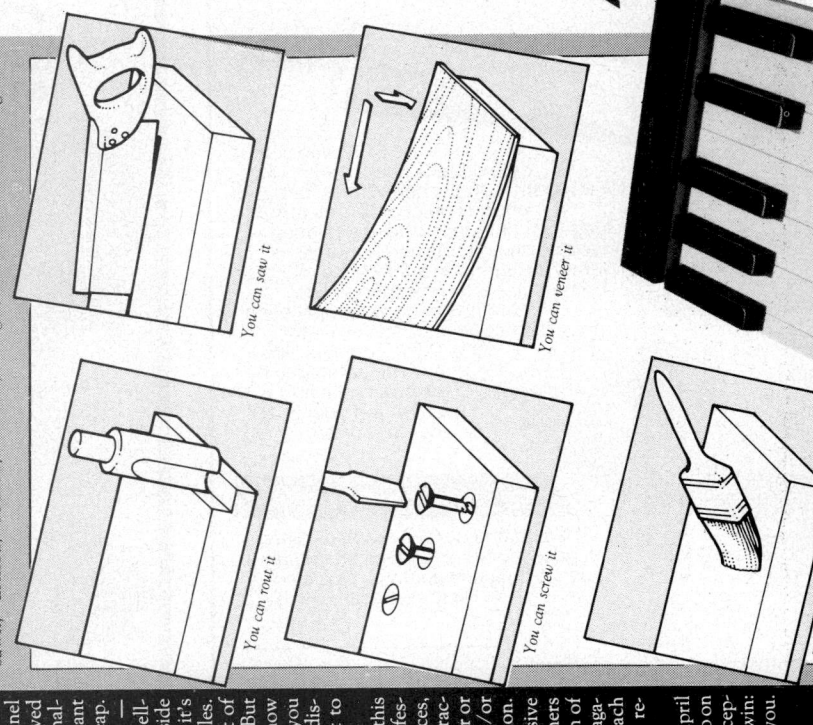

You can saw it

You can veneer it

You can rout it

You can screw it

You can paint it

## THE RULES

**1** Each entry must be an object which has been made substantially in MDF:
*either* a free-standing piece or set of pieces of furniture or a fitment or decorative feature for domestic or business use.

**2** The entry must consist of a written description outlining the nature of the design and the

- *The versatility of MDF: applied mouldings, piano parts and snooker tables are among the many roles it plays*

thinking behind it (this should not run to more than two sides of A4 paper); a set of dimensioned drawings; *and* either a perspective drawing or one or more photos or both.

- *Curves and planes; the chairs on the cover are MDF, as is this triangular table by Gerry Auburn of Bucks College*

**3** All entries should be sent to FIDOR and arrive before 1 May 1985.

**4** To enter, you must live on the UK mainland.

**5** The decision of **Woodworker** magazine and FIDOR is final in all matters concerning this competition. The judges reserve the right not to make awards if they think it inappropriate.

We'll be looking for a design which is interesting in itself, and effectively uses the principal characteristics of MDF (credit being given for originality in both respects). Quality of execution will also be an important factor.

FIDOR is at 1 Hanworth Rd. Feltham, Middx TW13 5AF, tel. 01-751 6107. They will be pleased to help with all queries, no matter how simple or how technical. And anyone who asks (competition entrant or not) will be sent a comprehensive package of information about MDF — including a personalised list of MDF stockists in his or her own particular area.

**THE PRIZES**
£250 for the winner
£150 second prize
£75 third prize
£50 fourth prize
*— plus publicity!*

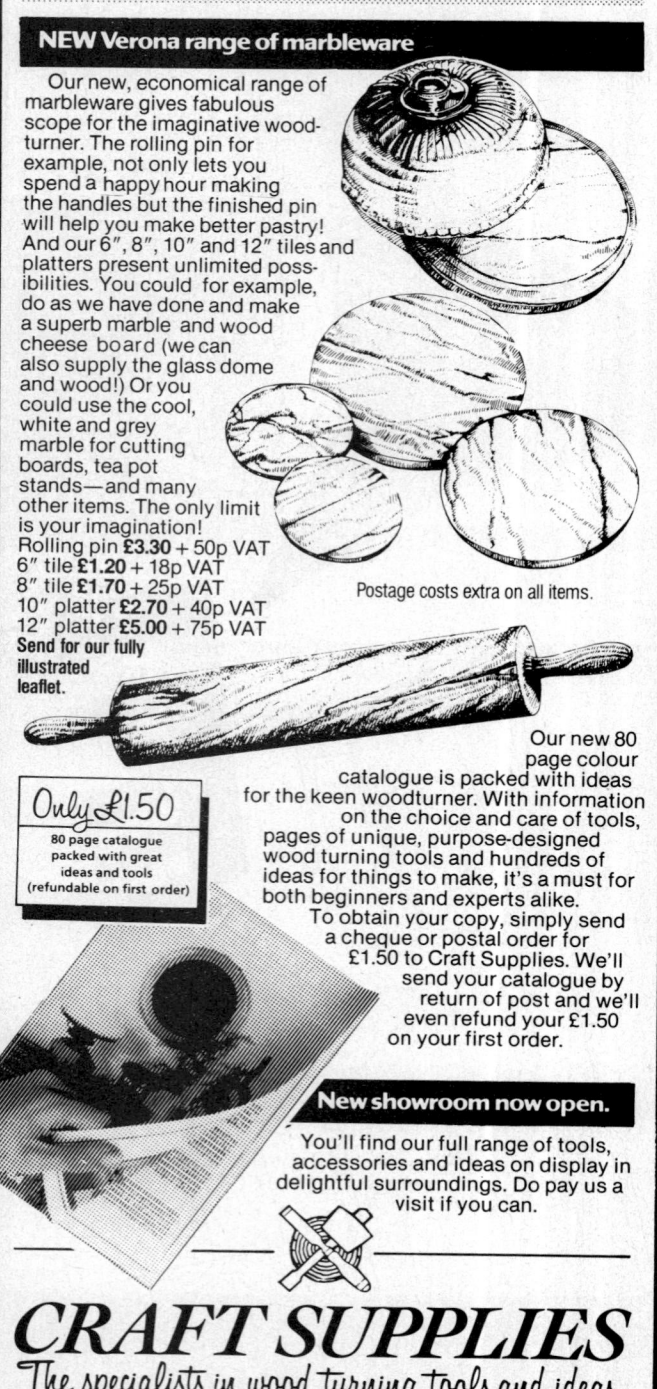
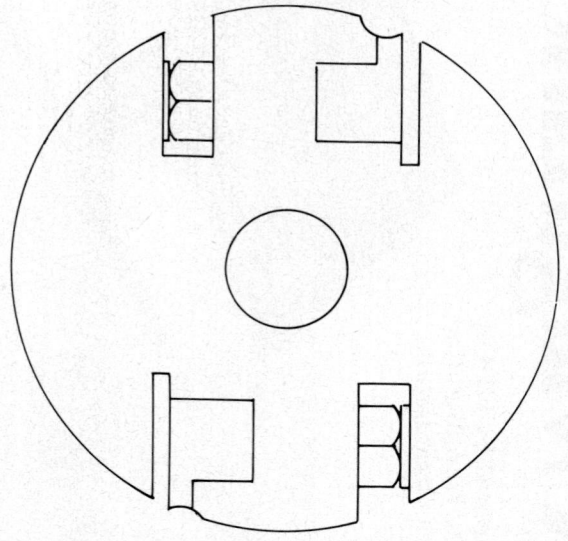

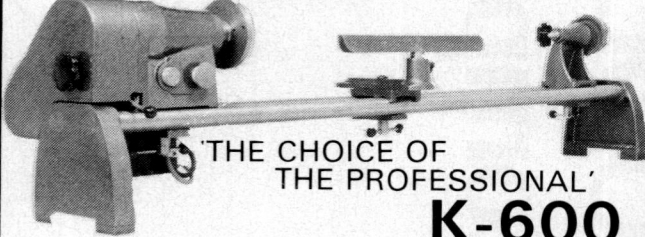

Prices quoted are those prevailing at press date and are subject to alteration due to economic conditions

# TIMBER

## The direct route

**We survey what's involved in finding, converting and seasoning your own raw material**

photo John Boddy Timber

### Alan Holtham explains why and how self-help makes sense

The increasing popularity of wood-turning and woodcarving as paying hobbies, coupled with the spiralling price of timber, has led many amateur woodworkers into the fascinating field of timber harvesting and utilisation.

Most turners and carvers use only small sections, and these logs and branchwood are well within the capacity of the enthusiastic amateur for home conversion and seasoning. Besides, they are of no interest to the commercial timber man, and as a rule they end up on a bonfire. I burnt many tons myself when clearing woodlands in my brief forestry career. This material represents a huge stock which at the moment is either wasted or not fully exploited. The vast increase in the number of wood-burning stoves must inevitably increase the competition for this 'firewood' material, so you may have to look that little bit harder, but there is a great deal of enjoyment to be had from cutting and drying yourself — despite the unavoidable failures and disappointments: because, be warned, there is more to the process than you may think.

The form in which you are most likely to be offered timber is that of small logs, usually 4-8in diameter. It is surprising how quickly a local grapevine becomes established; once people get to know that you are a woodworker they will soon be round, offering trees or branches they are removing from the garden, and these are often very unusual species, e.g. laburnum and rhododendron. But you will have to keep your eyes open as well, for some of the best finds are a question of being in the right place at the right time. Over the years we have collected timber from road-widening schemes, farms, building plots, church-yards, hedgerow clearances, and many other 'one-off' sources; so, as soon as you

hear there is likely to be any tree-felling, get down and see if anything worthwhile is available.

One of the best contacts I ever had was the superintendent of the local-authority parks and gardens department. He provided me with a vast amount of timber — some fairly common, like elm and sycamore, but at one stage about 5 tons of laburnum — all of which they had previously been dumping on the local tip. You could also try befriending the head foresters of any local private estates or gardens, as they are often thinning or felling trees and private estates often yield rare and exotic species which have been planted and grown as specimen trees. You can also try the local tree surgeons, as they are obviously involved in removing branches and limbs which may be of use to the woodworker.

Another, perhaps more obvious, source is local sawmills. Although they need the best timber for their own uses, they may be quite happy to sell off the second lengths and cordwood at reasonable prices. The list of possibilities, however, is endless, and you should soon have an enormous stock. The back-garden may come to look more and more like a shanty-town as you rig up more and more bits of plastic sheeting and corrugated tin to cover it all over. In fact, after a while you may begin to feel like the sorcerer's apprentice as the wood seems to keep on coming faster than you can use it.

When collecting timber, however, bear in mind that many of the people I have mentioned are professionals, trying to do their own jobs. In my experience, the last thing they want is hordes of dedicated wood enthusiasts, all armed to the teeth with mini-chainsaws and axes, swarming all over a 'clearfell' site with 200ft butts crashing down around them! All trees belong to someone, and except in certain circumstances you don't have any right to go out willy-nilly and hack off a branch here and there. You should have permission to take anything you find. A polite request is often all that is necessary, and once the owner knows what you are doing this often leads to a continuing friendship — and

source. You may find that a gift, in the form of a piece of your work, makes a much greater impression than a strictly cash offering.

Talking of money, it is surprising how rarely people outside the trade seem to realise that timber in the round, either standing or felled, has relatively little value, even after 150-200 years of growth. They tend to look at a timber merchant's price for the dried sawn boards and then equate this back to the standing tree, which gives a totally unrealistic value for the butt. The price of the finished timber is, in fact, determined by the large amount of work which has to be performed to bring it to a saleable state. Firstly, it has to be felled, snedded (de-branched), crosscut, lifted onto a suitable waggon and transported, possibly many miles to the mill. There it is usually sorted and graded, crosscut again and power-washed before being moved inside. All this requires a lot of handling and needs expensive lifting equipment.

Once in the mill the log has to be sawn, and this often raises its own problems. Embedded metal is the main one, and this is not at all uncommon. I have seen barbed wire, cast-iron brackets, nails, rakes and horseshoes, as well as stones and rocks, all buried deep in the butt, and no matter where they are you always seem to hit them! One momentary touch on metal is enough to ruin the cutting edge, and the sawyer will then have to stop and replace the blade — all accuracy being lost with a blunt one. Walnut seems to be particularly bad for buried metal, and I have seen one log causing two blade changes in 10 minutes before being rolled out on to the firewood pile.

After cutting, the timber is usually air-dried for a while, then re-sticked and kiln-dried. For hardwoods kilning takes weeks rather than days, and is an expensive process in terms of running costs and capital employed. When taking all these procedures into account, I often feel that timber is still quite cheap. By the same token, if you can carry any of them out for

269

yourself you can make great savings. The equipment you have defines the level at which you enter the process. Most amateurs have a small bandsaw; in conjunction with a few hand tools, such as a good bowsaw and axe, this should allow you to handle small branchwood up to about 8in in diameter. For larger logs I used to use steel timber-wedges and a sledge-hammer. It is surprising how easily and accurately you can split a butt down, provided you give a little thought to the grain orientation. Also, once it is split you will have a flat surface to put on your bandsaw table. If you have ever tried cutting round logs on the bandsaw you will probably have learnt the hard way how difficult this is; they always seem to roll and buckle the blade — usually a new one! Chopping or sawing a flat edge is always the first stage in cutting a log.

If you want to deal with larger stock, a chainsaw is going to be essential on site. This is often the only way of moving a log, by breaking it down into smaller pieces first. **Do be careful with the chainsaw.** When splitting logs with it lengthwise, do not stand it on end — rather lay it flat. Try it yourself to see the difference. Chainsawing is wasteful, as you lose about ½in on every cut, and you have to be pretty good to keep it dead straight. For the amateur, however, who has plenty of time and has probably obtained the timber for virtually nothing, it is quite effective. Be prepared for the mess it makes!

If you are only working on a small scale, a baby electric chainsaw is a tremendous asset. We recently bought one of these in order to cut up about 20 tons of timber in a very confined neighbourhood on a Sunday without disturbing the residents. Considering the machine's size and cost, its performance was amazing; we cut 30in butts with no problem, though we did use a few chains.

Perhaps the ultimate in home conversion is to buy a proper chainsaw mill, which allows accurate cutting of the butt into boards. The main advantage is that you can cut on site and then easily carry the boards away, as you cannot carry a solid log. My own experience of this operation, although limited, is that although it works very well it is noisy, very wasteful and a bit slow. In certain circumstances, however, it is the only way to begin the long job of getting the wood from the trees.

● Alan Holtham runs the Old Stores Turnery in Willaston, Cheshire, where he supplies tools, machinery and other woodworking needs, as well as timber for the small user. ■

# No trouble at mill

Philip Cole describes how a simple idea became a powerful device that could mean the end of timber troubles

'Timber conversion' conjures up the machinery of the sawmill, heavy haulage vehicles, complex lifting apparatus and enormous bandsaws. The portable chainsaw mill can change all this. Many's the time I have packed all my gear into a Morris Traveller to convert a tree on site.

The idea is incredibly simple — a powerful chainsaw with a jig to maintain a constant plank thickness. The innovation is a guide bar and chain powered by large chainsaws *each end*. This gives enough power to cut a tree up to 36in diameter (fig. 1).

The mill consists of a double-ended guide bar to which are attached large-capacity (approximately 100cc) chainsaws. Both engine units must be identical in model and capacity; both power a single chain. Vertical supports are attached to the guide bar and a roller frame is fixed above and parallel to the bar. The distance between guide bar and roller frame can be varied. Safety guards between the power units and the verticals protect the operators.

The mill is taken to the site of the felled tree. After all the branches have been removed, an aluminium ladder is fixed flat along the top of the butt. The roller frame is adjusted; during the first cut it rolls along the side of the ladder while the chain cuts along the butt (fig.2). After the first cut the ladder and the slab of timber are removed, leaving a butt with a flat extending the whole length. The roller frame is then adjusted to the thickness of the planks required and milling continues (fig. 3). It may prove necessary to raise the last few inches of the butt to clear the ground, but it will be thin enough by then for this to be easy.

The chainsaw mill has various advan-

● One of Philip Cole's chainsaw mills cutting a wide, thick board – viewed from the front

tages. Firstly, timber in the round is incredibly cheap and conversion into planks normally increases the price at least fivefold. Next, timber can be converted into the sizes required and milled to display grain to best advantage; butts can readily be quarter-sawn or converted into posts or lap boards. The plank length depends simply on the length of the initial cut with the ladder — and, of course, two ladders can be fixed end-to-end. A young man from Helsinki with a 90-foot Baltic schooner wanted long planks for hull repairs, and he got what he wanted using this mill.

Perhaps the overwhelming advantage is that conversion can be undertaken on site, and the converted timber manhandled — thus obviating the need for heavy haulage to the sawmill. Finally, I should add that a day's milling is *fun*. There is the exhilaration of an energetic stint in the open, and the sense of achievement in producing a stack of timber.

The quality of cut is comparable to that of a commercial bandsaw, both in terms of the surface achieved and the constant thickness.

The disadvantages of chainsaw milling are perhaps the thickness of the chain's cut compared to that of a band saw, and the relative slowness of operation. A speed of 5sq ft per minute is a fair average; 7sq ft is an excellent rate. When things go well it is feasible to cut 200sq ft per hour. This allows a margin for refuelling and shifting timber. However, when you consider the sort of prices paid for timber in the round, the disadvantages appear in perspective.

A milling trip does need organisation. Vaious hand tools may be needed, and I find a checklist of gear important to avoid leaving things at base. Re-sharpening is done on site with the chain on the mill, and only takes a few minutes. Care of the engines is important and, as with any machine, attention to detail pays dividends.

● Above: The mill includes two chainsaws, guards, and an ajustable roller frame

● Left: Bob Blacklow, wood-skills lecturer at the University of Hobart, Tasmania, uses a similar machine with a student

The cutting units are among the largest chainsaws made, and are potentially lethal. I regard adequate clothing for the two operators as essential, which should include forester's boots (with steel toecaps), protective over-trousers, leather gloves, goggles and ear-muffs.

Milling is an altogether fascinating business; if you consider your timber needs carefully, you may well find a portable chainsaw mill will prove a sound investment, likely to pay for itself again and again.

● Philip Cole supplies chainsaw mills from his workshops at 16 Kings Lane, Flore, Northampton NN7 4LQ, tel. (0327) 40337. ■

# Kilning with kindness

Nick Greenwood discusses the exciting new developments in small-scale drying equipment

Unlike metals and plastics, the raw material used by the small joiner or cabinetmaker is natural. As most know only too well, it requires special consideration.

When freshly felled, timber contains moisture in such quantities that the greater proportion of its weight is water and not wood fibre. As soon as the wood is sawn into manageable boards, it will begin to dry out to a level which is in equilibrium with the climatic conditions in which it is placed.

As the moisture content of the board falls, the material shrinks. While the timber is still in the form of sawn boards, shrinkage may not matter. But if it occurs after the board has become a furniture component, the results are often catastrophic. Differential shrinkage rates lead to bowed tabletops, ill-fitting joints, warps and splits.

Ensuring that his wood is thoroughly dried is vital for the cabinetmaker and his colleagues if returned pieces and customer dissatisfaction are to be avoided. Generally woodworkers consider three alternatives to the problem of finding dried material.

## Natural drying

Natural or air drying involves stacking and storage of the sawn boards in a ventilated area protected from the direct effects of rain and sun. Natural drying depends entirely on the weather; therefore drying times cannot be forecasted accurately, but they are usually measured in months and years. This unpredictable drying method wastes space, since large quantities of wood must be held. The financing of large stocks is a considerable financial burden, but a greater disadvantage is that in Britain the material will simply not dry below 16-18% moisture content. Furniture destined for use in the typical home must be made from wood dried to at least 10% if shrinkage is to be avoided.

## Buying wood ready-dried

To obtain wood that is of acceptable quality and thoroughly dried can be time-consuming and expensive.

Even when wood has been carefully dried to a low enough moisture content, if it is delivered to you on an open truck exposed to rain you run a considerable risk of disappointment. Besides, prices for dried hardwood vary considerably according to area and availability, increasing production costs and reducing profit margins. In almost every case it make financial sense to dry your own wood with a small-scale wood dryer. The savings are considerable, repaying the initial investment in just a few months.

## Small-scale wood dryers

Before considering the benefits of your own wood dryer, you must first understand how wood dries.

The rate of evaporation depends upon the difference between the vapour pressure of the wet timber and the vapour pressure of the air. When these have equalised no further drying will occur. This is the point at which the equilibrium moisture content of the wood for the surrounding air has been reached. Timber exposed to dry air will, therefore, release its moisture.

The other factor governing timber's vapour pressure is its temperature. The higher the temperature, the higher the vapour pressure and the faster the evaporation rate. It is important, however, that the rate of evaporation from the surface should not be much faster than the migration of moisture from the core of the board, otherwise too steep a drying gradient will be set up and damage will result. Higher temperatures accelerate this rate of migration from the core of the board and so allow faster drying without degrade. Experience shows that the best drying temperature to ensure reasonable drying speed yet maintain quality is approximately 45°C. Wood that has been dried in high-temparature conventional steam kilns can be prone to discoloration and other forms of degrade if excessive temperatures have been used.

Small-scale wood dryers, almost without exception, are based on specially designed de-humidifiers, equipped with additional features and controls. The dryer is placed inside an insulated box together with the wood to be dried.

Warm, dry air is blown from the dryer and encouraged to circulate around the wood. As the wood's temperature rises, its vapour pressure exceeds that of its surroundings, causing evaporation of water from the surface of the boards. The cool, damp air is drawn into the dryer by an integral fan system, where it is passed over a surface which has been refrigerated to below the dew-point temperature. The air cools, and at this lower temperature it can no longer hold as much water vapour. As a result the vapour condenses, so it can be collected and then led away to a drain.

The energy removed from the air as it was cooled is then used to re-heat the air before it is returned to the wood stack. The warm air increases the vapour pressure of the wood, causing further evaporation and so continuing the drying process. Because the dryer operates inside an enclosed, insulated area, heat loss is minimised. Because the heat energy is continuously recovered and re-cycled, a de-humidification system is energy-efficient and thus cheap to run. To ensure that the chamber temperature is maintained during cold conditions, wood-

dryer manufacturers incorporate small supplementary heaters which operate intermittently; this energy is also recovered and re-cycled by the machine.

A control system is also essential. Typically, de-humidification systems feature controls to ensure that the temperature of the wood is raised at a safe rate. A further control enables the operator to select the speed of drying he needs. De-

humidifier manufacturers publish concise drying instructions which are mastered with very little experience.

## Drying-chamber construction

Building a chamber for a small-scale wood dryer is relatively straightforward. It is likely to be one of the easiest projects encountered by a cabinetmaker. Wood-dryer manufacturers offer free advice to users on

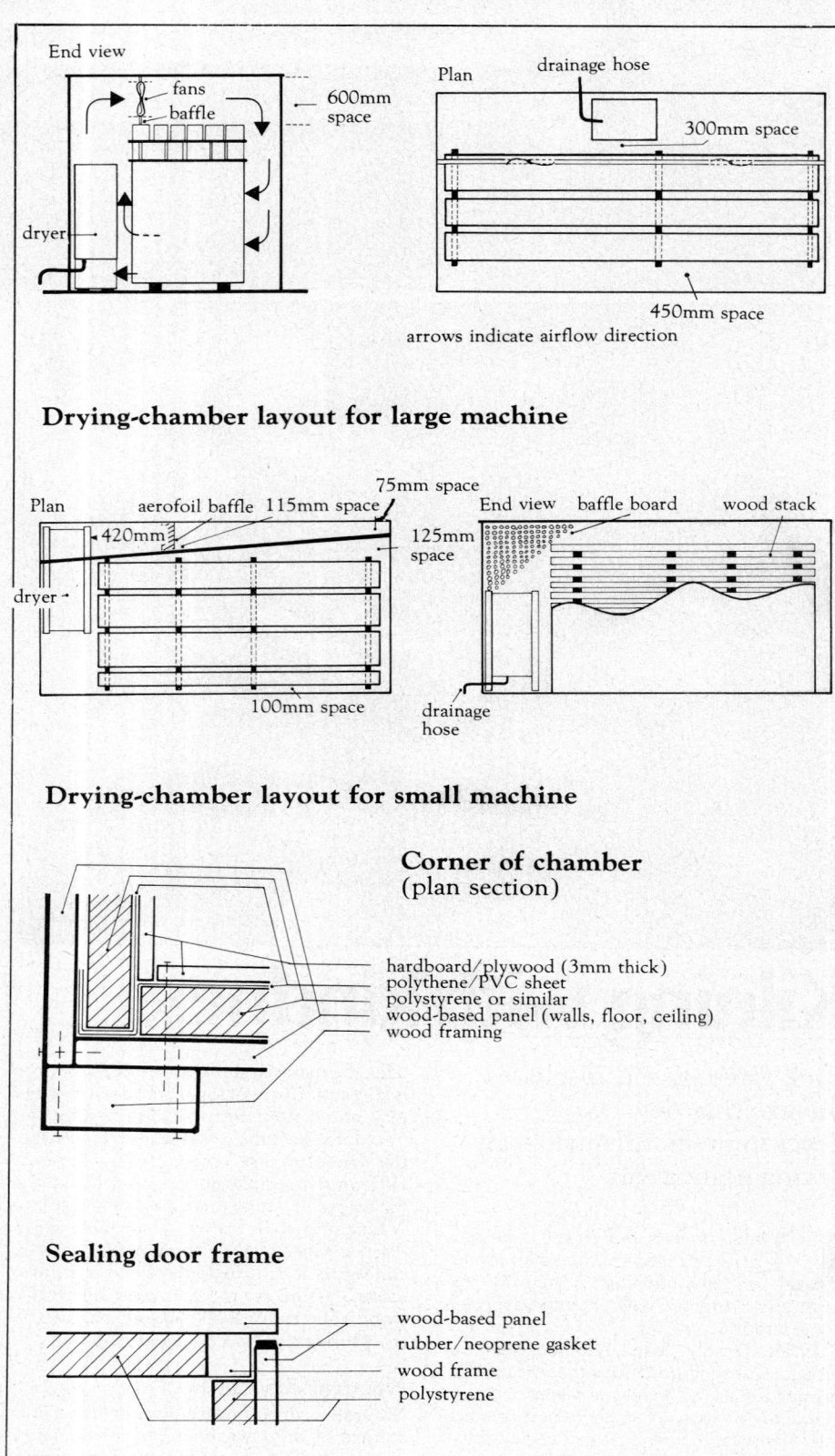

**Drying-chamber layout for large machine**

**Drying-chamber layout for small machine**

**Corner of chamber**
(plan section)

hardboard/plywood (3mm thick)
polythene/PVC sheet
polystyrene or similar
wood-based panel (walls, floor, ceiling)
wood framing

**Sealing door frame**

wood-based panel
rubber/neoprene gasket
wood frame
polystyrene

overall dimensions and layout, so that you can be assured of a system built to your individual requirements.

A small drying chamber which can hold 35cu ft of wood may measure 8ft in length, and 4ft in height and width. The walls, floor and top of the chamber should each consist of a softwood frame clad on both sides with exterior-grade plywood. The cavity should be filled with expanded-foam board for insulation. The dryer manufacturer will advise on suitable insulation thicknesses in individual cases, since these depend on the surface area of the chamber. A chamber of the dimensions given may incorporate 2in of insulation.

The walls must also incorporate a vapour seal to prevent saturation of the insulation and the ingress of moisture to the chamber. Vapour-proof paint finishes are available which can be applied to the interior of the chamber; alternatively, heavy-gauge polythene sheet should be attached over the insulation before the inner cladding is fixed in position. Take care to ensure that all joints are taped and sealed and that exposed nailheads are covered. A close-fitting removable door panel should be incorporated in the side of the chamber, through which the timber will be loaded. Fit closed-cell synthetic-foam strip around the door opening, together with retaining catches.

## Capacity and cost

De-humidification wood dryers small enough to be used by the cabinetmaker and craftsman joiner are readily available. Several thousand are currently in use today. The smallest systems will dry upwards of 20cu ft per load. Drying times depend on whether the wood was initially green or partially air-dried. The thickness of the board, as well as the density of the wood, also counts. Thick boards should be dried more slowly than thin ones, and hardwoods more slowly than softwoods. Roughly speaking 1in hardwood can be dried at a moisture content reduction of ¾% per day. Note that wood loads comprising mixed species and thicknesses can be dried simultaneously by de-humidification systems.

This account would not be complete without an analysis of the cost of running such a system. A number of variables make a rule-of-thumb guide impractical. However, a small system will consume about the same amount of energy as a home freezer.

Whether drying your own wood is worthwhile to you depends on individual circumstances. However, savings made by buying green timber and drying it yourself can be considerable, sometimes even repaying the price of the equipment within weeks. Your own drying system will certainly give you more control over the quality of the wood used in your workshop, and make you independent of wood suppliers by broadening your buying options.

If you decide that a de-humidification system is for you, take my advice and build a chamber that is more than adequate for your own requirements — because news of a source of good-quality dried hardwood travels quickly, and you might just find that you are supplying others!
● Nick Greenwood is applications engineer of Ebac Ltd. ■

# Tool-chest treasures

**R**eg Eaton writes: Once again it's time to preview my colleague Tyrone Roberts' annual auction of old and antique tools. This year there are over 1000 lots to dispose of.

When one thinks of quality in tools, the name Norris automatically springs to mind. There are 20 vintage pre-war models to select from, including the little bullnose- and chariot-planes and a rare no.31 thumb-plane which, it is estimated, will fetch over £700.

The most sought-after planes for the craftsman, however, are the dovetailed rosewood-filled smoothers with adjustment, such as the A2, A5, and A6. No less than six of these are catalogued, as well as several panel-, shoulder-, and rabbet-planes. Lot 85 will arouse some interest — a set of six unused bevel-edge chisels with boxwood handles by a maker that went out of business in 1900. Disston and Atkins saws from the USA, in fine and unused condition, are also included as well as several brass-backed Sheffield saws.

With the pound at an all-time low against the dollar (at the time of writing), the American collectors and dealers will be more keen than ever, and they will not be disappointed. More than 100 Stanley tools are offered, including one of the most rare and seemingly impractical (because it's so small) no.1 smoothing-planes. It's expected to reach around £1000, as it's in mint condition and in the original box.

Other planes in the Stanley range that will make well into three figures are the A6 aluminium fore-plane, no.9 mitre-plane, no.10¼ swivel-handle rabbet-plane, no.41 plough and fillister plane, no.51 shoot-board plane, no.55 combination plane, no.56 small core-box plane, no.62 low-angle plane, no.72½ chamfer-plane, no.97 edge-plane and no.212 scraper-plane. There are also many of the good Bedrock and other cheaper planes and gadgets that Stanley were famous for.

The successful launch of The Tool and Trades History Society in 1983 has kindled a new interest in early makers of wooden planes. How long can a situation last that makes it possible to purchase planes dateable to the 18th century for a very few pounds each? Here is a good opportunity to add to the collection. The really rare ones, though, by Robert Wooding, Loveage, Small, Phillipson, and Jennion, will make as much as £200 each, and special-purpose planes like the panel-raising tool by Madox probably £400.

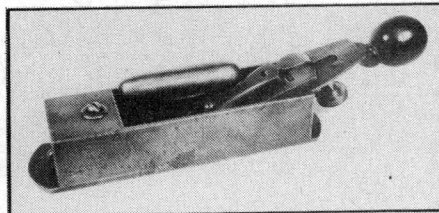
● A Stanley no. 9 mitre plane

● An early Scottish smoothing-plane with a scroll-carved front

● A fine plough-plane with boxwood screw-stems and nuts, gunmetal body, rosewood fence and handle, and brass fittings

So, if you're looking for a billiard-cue-tip-cramp and rasp, a brick cleaner's hatchet, a set of voicer's cones or only a herring-cask cooper's flencher, make it a date!
● The auction is at Kensington Town Hall, London W8, at 11.30 on 26 March. Viewing takes place beforehand and the previous afternoon. The catalogue is £2.50 and includes an estimated-prices and bidding form; from Tyrone R. Roberts, Auctioneer's Office, High Street, Heacham, Norfolk. Reg Eaton is a dealer in Heacham, and many of his own tools will be offered in the auction.■

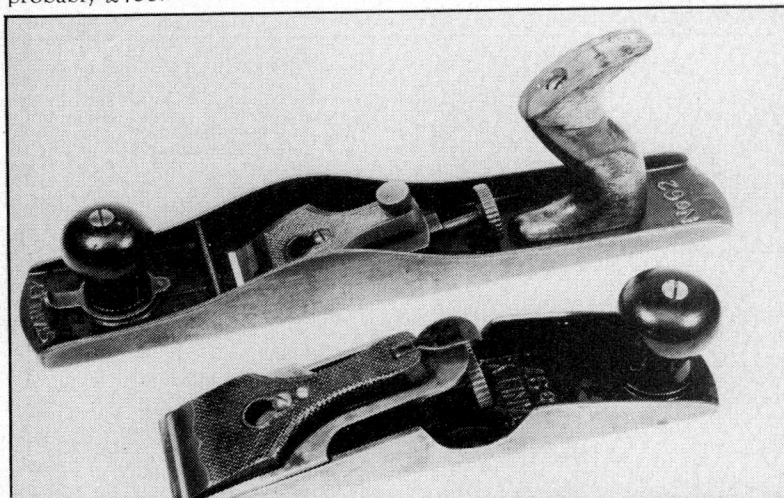
● Two Stanley low-angle planes, nos. 62 and 97

# Scheppach Sawbenches offer so much more... in more ways than one

**Elektra Beckum Kombi 2200**

**Lutz KKS 400 (315mm Dia. Model)**

NOW FITTED WITH TCT BLADE

**Scheppach TKU**

|  | Kombi 2200 | Lutz | TKU |
|---|---|---|---|
| Standard diameter of sawblade | 315mm | 315mm | 315mm |
| Depth of cut | 85mm | 90mm | 85mm |
| Table graduated for width of cut | YES | NO | YES |
| Table lip folded for extra strength and accuracy | NO | NO | YES |
| Rise and Fall and Tilt Arbor pre-factory assembled | NO | YES | YES |
| Has **handwheel** Rise and Fall | YES | NO | YES |
| Has metal table insert | NO | NO | YES |
| Will accept wobble saw and Comb jointing Att. | NO | NO | YES |
| Micro stops fitted for precise setting of Tilt Arbor at 0° and 45° | NO | NO | YES |
| Sliding table fence adjustable to 45° **both left and right.** Perfect for reverse mitres | NO | NO | YES |
| Sliding table fence has pre-set stops at every 15° | NO | NO | YES |
| Micro stop for accurate setting of dimension table fence assembly | NO | NO | YES |
| Sliding table will detach **without tooling** for transporting | NO | NO | YES |
| Panel cutting attachment **folds when not in use** or for transporting | NO | NO | YES |
| **Automatic parallel alignment** of panel cutting fence | NO | NO | YES |
| Hinged lower guard for easy sawblade access | NO | YES | YES |
| Sawguard covers teeth in lower sawblade position | YES | NO | YES |
| One piece legs for rigidity | YES | NO | YES |
| Kw of motor (**output**) | 1.76kw | 1.5kw | 1.6kw |

All information correct at time of issuing advertisement.

# Don't just ask for Scheppach – insist on it!

Send for leaflet and stockist list to
**Sumaco Ltd.**, Suma House, Huddersfield Road, Elland, West Yorkshire. Tel: 0422 79811

# Precious stones

## Specialist tool merchant Roger Buse relays the nitty-gritty on stones for the perfect edge

**M**ost woodworkers use blunt tools. A bold statement, but true. Ask yourself — could you shave with your favourite chisel or the iron out of your bench plane? This is what you are aiming for!

Customers occasionally tell me they are only amateurs so they don't need an edge that good. This is simply not true, for only with a razor edge can you do good work and do it easily. Once you have established that razor edge, a quick strop or polish on an extra-fine finish stone keeps the tool cutting crisp and clean.

The ways of producing this razor edge are as many and varied as there are craftspeople. This is a brief guide to the principal stones used and how to maintain them.

### The stones

When you are planning the purchase of new stones for sharpening edge tools, the wide range must seem daunting. What are the differences between them?

The chief characteristics to look for are the fineness of the edge produced, the speed with which the material is removed and the resistance of the stone to wear. Three variables control these characteristics: the size of the particles, their hardness, and the bonding strength of the stone. The tightness with which the particles are held together controls the rate at which they break down.

Unfortunately, there is no such thing as the ideal stone which maximises all three characteristics. As a general rule, the harder the bonding strength of the stone the slower it cuts.

There are six main categories of stone to choose from. Three are natural and three are man-made. Let's look at the properties of each.

**Arkansas** A natural stone (novaculite) estimated at 340 million years old. It is a hard, fine pure silica rock which derived its name from the Latin *'novacula'* meaning 'sharp knife'. It is only found in the Ouachita Mountains (hence 'Washita stone') around Hot Springs, Arkansas. It is very delicate, and cracks easily when quarried. This weakness and other structural faults mean that only about 2-5% finds its way into finished stones for shipment. Hence its high price.

The virtues of Arkansas stone lie in the fact that the fine particles produce an immaculate edge and the bonding is so hard that it is never likely to wear or hollow in a lifetime. On the other hand they are slow-cutting and they clog easily, so you mustn't be miserly with the honing fluid. Before putting away an Arkansas stone after use, you should sluice it down thoroughly with honing fluid. (This can get rather expensive with proprietary fluids; it's best to make your own with one part motor oil to two parts white spirit and store it conveniently

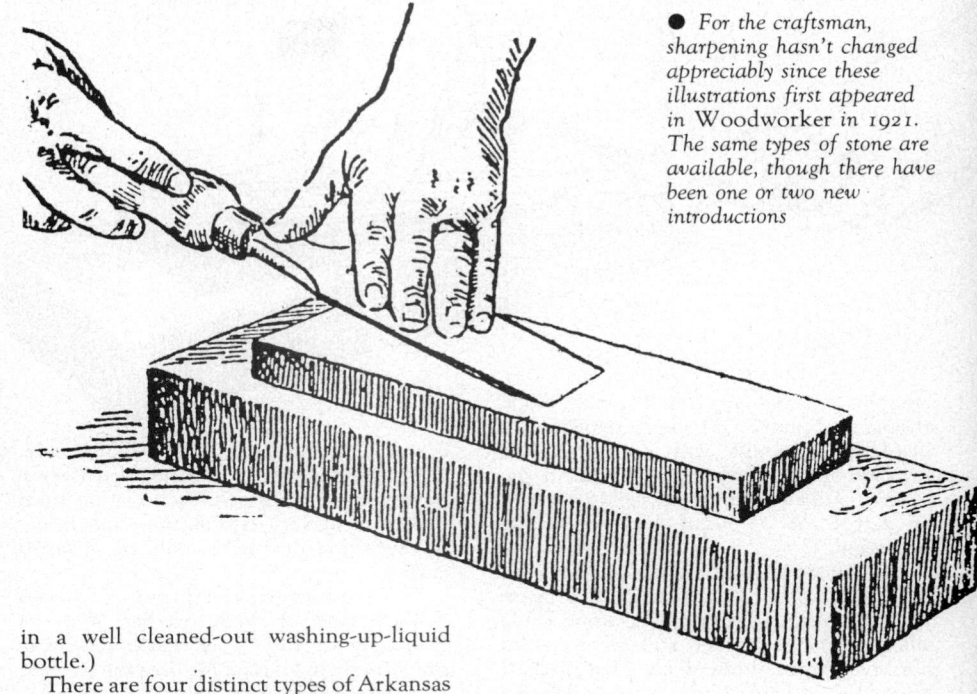

in a well cleaned-out washing-up-liquid bottle.)

There are four distinct types of Arkansas stone: *Washita* (Coarse); reasonably fast-cutting as Arkansas stones go, but only for initial honing. This grade is virtually impossible to obtain. *Soft* (Medium): a good general-purpose stone which will produce a fair edge quicker than the finer grades. *Hard* (fine): for touching up and final honing of an already sharp blade. Sharpening with this stone takes a little longer, but the exceptional polished edge is well worth it. *Black* (extra fine): Only for precision sharpening or for finishing a very sharp razor edge. This stone is extremely hard and sharpening with it takes considerable time.

**Slate** The slate stones in the UK come from the slate quarries of north Wales. Slate is a fine-grained rock formed over millenia by heat and pressure (metamorphosis) on clays or shales. The clay minerals are replaced during metamorphosis by mica, the main constituent, together with quartz, chlorite (giving it a greenish colour) and carbon (giving it a bluish to black appearance). Slate splits readily along planes of 'slaty cleavage' which occur in the rock as a result of lateral pressure.

It is easy to quarry and there is very little wastage, so it is cheap to buy. As a fine-particle stone it produces a good edge, but it wears quickly and is by no means fast-cutting. Water is used as a honing fluid but it suffers little from clogging because of its fast wear rate. Slate stone can be stored in water but make sure it doesn't go stale, or your stone will end up covered in slime. For the same reason, make sure that your stone is dry before you store it an a box.

**Sandstone** A sedimentary rock, formed on ancient shallow sea-beds and estuaries, of small grains of quartz sand (other minerals including mica may be present). Because the formation process was not high-pressure, it is very loosely bonded and the stone is delicate and soft. Sandstone is easily cut and shaped, so it became popular as building material in sandstone areas.

Because of this ease of shaping it was used extensively as an abrasive in medieval times. However, for today's woodworker sandstones have little to offer as they wear quickly because of their poor bonding strength and coarse, relatively soft grain.

Used with water as a lubricant on a motorised grinder they are reasonably fast-cutting, but they should never be used for any other purpose than primary grinding. Never leave them immersed in water, or they will literally disintegrate. If you are considering making your own motorised sandstone, it should never revolve much above 60rpm, or there is considerable danger of its breaking up.

**Silicon carbide** This man-made abrasive, marketed under the brand-names Carborundum and Crystolon, is manufactured by firing a mixture of coke, sand, sawdust and salt in a resistance-type electric furnace. The process combines the silicon in the sand with the carbon in the coke and sawdust to form silicon carbide. The crystalline result is crushed and washed with acids and alkalis to clean away impurities before grading into grit sizes for manufacture into bench stones. Sodium silicate is used as a bonding agent.

Available in coarse, medium and fine grits, all of which are on the coarse side, such stones should only be used for primary grinding and re-shaping. They are totally unsuitable for producing a fine cutting edge.

When first purchased, these stones should be immersed in a solution of paraffin and oil for 24 hours to impregnate them thoroughly with oil. Without this initial preparation, oil applied to the surface for lubrication will immediately be absorbed. After use, wipe off the stone to remove any oil and metal particles, as they

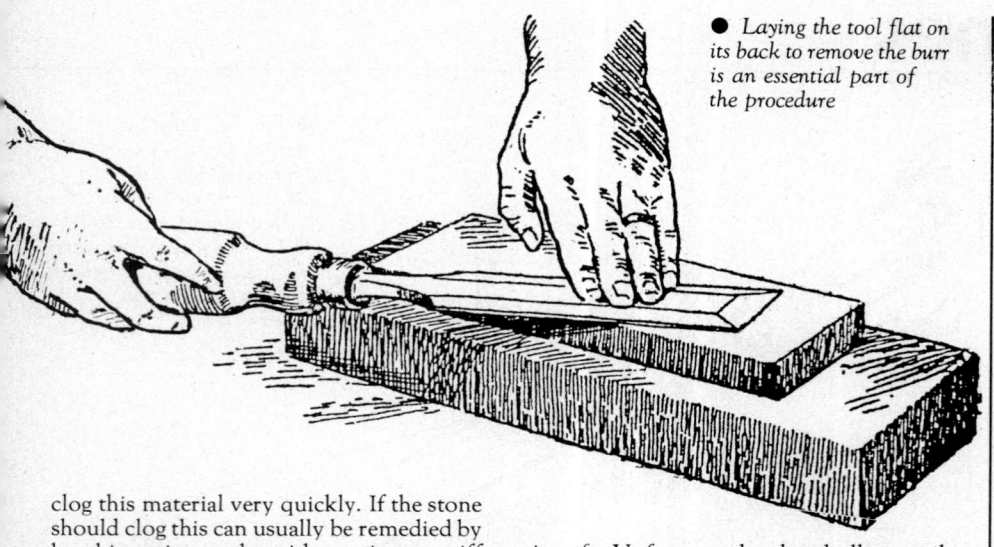

● *Laying the tool flat on its back to remove the burr is an essential part of the procedure*

# Books

John E. W. Bairstow
**Practical and Decorative Woodworking Joints**
Batsford, £7.95 hardback
Reviewed by David Savage

This book attempts to gather together all joints used in woodworking, both common and uncommon, to explain how they may be worked, and to extend the range with one or two new ideas for decorative joints.

Most things are covered, from the mundane to the ridiculously obscure — timber preparation, planing up, marking out, mortise-and-tenons, dovetails of every shape and hue. A section examines splicing joints from Europe, Japan and China. The Chinese frame-and-panel joinery of the Ming period is exploded and studied. Splined joints, carcase joints: are all clearly illustrated with line diagrams.

The technical descriptions of how to produce the joints are adequate, but in some cases misleading. Dovetails are marked using the pins as a template, but not very often — and never using a pencil, 4H or not.

The layout and design are a disaster. The diagrams and print are clear and the colour plates good; what unpleasant pieces of furniture with which to illustrate a book, though! Perhaps these are a product of the ideology; but perhaps decorative joints that advertise how clever the maker is are treading the borderline of vulgarity.

As a reference book, this is just not comprehensive enough. As a technical book, it again lacks conviction. As a source of new ideas and inspiration, it may be of some help. I do not recommend spending £7.95, but you might get your library to stock it.

clog this material very quickly. If the stone should clog this can usually be remedied by brushing vigorously with a wire or stiff brush soaked in paraffin or petrol. If the stone is still clogged, immerse it in paraffin or petrol for 24 hours and repeat the operation.

If these stones become mis-shapen with use, they may be re-surfaced by rubbing on a flat piece of marble or paving-stone, using silicon-carbide powder and water as an abrasive paste. Alternatively a flat piece of close-grained hardwood can be used with a paste made up of machine oil, paraffin and silicon-carbide powder.

**Aluminium oxide** Another man-made abrasive, sold under the brand names India and Aloxite and manufactured by firing bauxite in an arc-type electric furnace. The resulting crystalline substance is treated in the same way as silicon carbide to produce finished stones. They have very similar characteristics to silicon-carbide stones, although the particles are softer. Their care and maintenance are the same.

**Japanese water-stones (toshi)** These man-made stones use extremely sharp hard natural abrasive earth compounds which are fused together with a resin bond at low temperatures. Of fine particle grit, they produce an excellent edge in no time at all, because the particles are hard and the bond

is soft. Unfortunately, they hollow easily. This tendency is largely avoidable by using them with a light touch; their composition makes them very free-cutting, and heavy pressure does not necessarily mean faster cutting.

To keep them true, immerse two stones in water and rub them together. Water is their only lubricant — *on no account use oil*. Immerse them in water for between five and 20 minutes before use.

As the tool is worked in contact with the stone, a paste develops on the surface. This paste actually assists the fast cutting for which these stones are renowned, and should not be washed off during use. If the stone dries during use, splash a few drops of water on the surface.

After use the stone should be washed down to remove any metal particles, then allowed to dry before storing. Many users keep their stones immersed in water ready for use. No harm will be done if they are stored in this manner because, unlike sandstone, they will not disintegrate. Their softness makes it advisable when sharpening gouges to use the edges of the stone and avoid irregular wear on the face.

---

London College of Furniture
**The Woodworker's Handbook**
Pelham Books, £10.95 hardback
Reviewed by Luke Hughes

There seems to be an expanding market for this kind of book, which tries to make all the mysteries of cabinetmaking disappear with step-by-step instructions and join-the-dot pictures to convince the idle browser that he or she could make Chippendale chairs if they only bought and followed the right book.

The fact is they probably could. I've been dependent on equivalent sources for all my training and I'm sure I'm not alone. But it's not as easy as it's made to look. For this reason I question the intentions of the publishers in identifying their markets and meeting their demands. Are they looking to the complete beginner? To the young craftsman starting up who could use a reference book? Or to the know-all who buys books with good pictures, doesn't work at the trade, and invariably bores one to death with the extent of his unpractised knowledge?

*The Woodworker's Handbook* was produced by a group of lecturers from the London College of Furniture under the

| Particle size in microns | | |
|---|---|---|
| 5000-grit water | 2 | |
| black Arkansas | 5 | |
| slate | 6 | |
| hard Arkansas | 10 | |
| soft Arkansas | 13 | |
| 1200-grit water | 13 | |
| 800-grit water | 20 | |
| silicon carbide/aluminium oxide — fine | 23 | |
| thickness of human hair for reference | 50 | |
| silicon carbide/aluminium oxide — medium | 90 | |
| sandstone | 150 | |
| silicon carbide/aluminium oxide — coarse | 170 | |

**Resistance to wear** (highest first)
1 black Arkansas

2 hard Arkansas
3 soft Arkansas
4 Washita
5 fine silicon carbide/aluminium oxide
6 coarse silicon carbide/aluminium oxide
7 slate
8 Japanese water-stone
9 sandstone

**Particle hardness** (hardest first)
1 silicon carbide
2 aluminium oxide
3 Japanese water-stone
4 tungsten carbide
5 Arkansas
6 high-speed steel
7 slate
8 sandstone
9 carbon steel

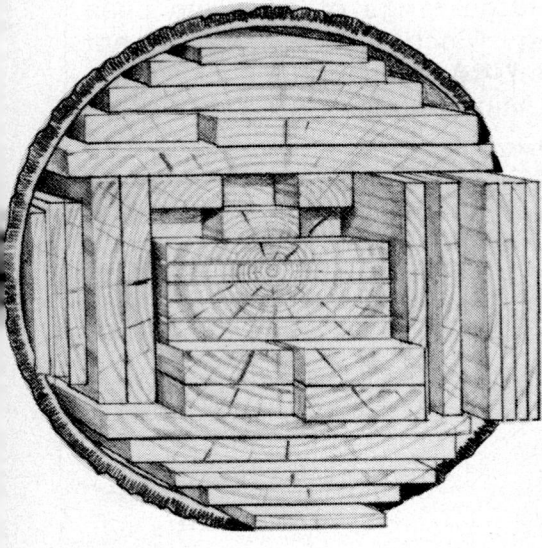

● *One of the extremely detailed illustrations from 'The Raw Material', a chapter in The Woodworker's Handbook – depicting the manifold choices open to the sawyer in converting a log*

chairmanship of Peter Metcalfe. It suffers from being the work of a committee. It is disjointed and unbalanced, and it fails miserably to achieve its aim: 'to cover every aspect of working with wood'. The jacket claims that 'If the range of coverage is exceptional, so is the authorship'. Sadly, the quality of the coverage is not.

An example of its unevenness: the first 25 pages deal with timber as a material in elaborate and faultless detail, with photographs and diagrams (including the uncredited lifting of the mouldings section of W. H. Newson's timber catalogue). But the extent of this detail is disproportionate, and likely to be incomprehensible to the occupier of a workshop who owns only the tools recommended in the second section. These amount to little more than a Workmate and an electric drill. The section on machining is disgracefully cursory.

To its credit, the book has a reasonable section on joints, though it doesn't come up with the little everyday tips designers should bear in mind when allowing for movement of timber and the subsequent effect on finish. Nor does it give some of the tips available for actually executing such joints. Another glaring omission is any mention of the biscuit-jointer, one of the few recently emerged tools to revolutionise cabinetmaking. The section on finishing is good, with some useful hints, though I wish the authors didn't have an aversion to stating the brand-names of the products they describe.

At the back is a projects section, showing principally the way elaborate furniture, both old and new, is put together. I feel the authors are a little naive in believing that these projects could be taken on by someone without considerable experience, and with only the rudimentary equipment mentioned.

*Time-Life Books*
### Repairing Furniture
*£9.50 hardback, available from W. H. Smith*
*Reviewed by Aidan Walker*
The blurb inside this straightforward book says that it is part of a series offering home-owners detailed instructions on repairs, construction and imporvement which they can undertake themselves. In other words, it's a DIY book.

Its conception and design show just where this market has been going in recent years; no longer does DIY mean simple tasks performed with an electric drill. As the services of craftspeople become more expensive, householders who wouldn't previously have considered undertaking jobs themselves are now not only going into it, but discovering that they want to do it thoroughly. This book caters admirably for such people, and indeed puts a lot of information in one place that is useful and relevant for a more serious craft approach.

Plenty of books on antique restoration and repair deal with techniques for intrinsically valuable furniture, but this book sensibly addresses the junk-shop or open-air-market buyer who finds something he or she likes that 'just needs a bit of work'. The section on duplicating pieces assumes a fairly expensively equipped workshop, but on the whole the step-by-step instructions are designed for people without either great woodworking knowledge or a full set of tools.

The illustrations are very clear and, though the information is mainly set out in 'how to' form, it is written in a no-nonsense style that manages to be both informal and un-patronising. The big difficulty in dealing with subjects like this is that general assumptions have to be made about how much the reader does or doesn't know, and you will always be talking down or up to someone. Time-Life's editors and writers — 14 people have contributed to the text — have got the balance just about right.

The sections are 'Putting the Parts Back Together', 'Surgery for Breaks and Gouges', 'From Touch-Ups to Re-finishing', and 'Re-upholstery'; they deal with specific tasks such as repairing a wobbly table, dismantling and re-assembling various chairs, drawer repairs, treatments for damaged veneers, stripping, staining and re-finishing, removing old upholstery and preparing new, using a home sewing-machine for upholstery, and putting the bounce back in springs; each section starts with general information about tools and materials, and then goes on to the particulars.

The only photographs in the book are decorative. For actually showing how, drawings are used, whose design has also been carefully thought out; halftones emphasise the focus of the job. The production is not luscious, but some very good thinking has been put into communicating what an average but enthusiastic woodworker needs to know. Without pretensions to an 'expert' treatment, *Repairing Furniture* does its job more simply and solidly than many more expensive and expansive attempts at the subject.

*Margaret K. Dodds*
### Easy to Build Wooden Chairs for Children
*Dover USA/Constable UK, £2*
*Reviewed by Alan Bridgewater*
What a tidy, well thought out, beautifully conceived little book. It contains five chairmaking projects, all with clear and easy-to-follow step-by-step instructions, plus masses of very helpful hints, tips and 'how to do' advice.

If you are a beginner woodworker and are looking for good, sensible, practical projects, this could well be the book for you. The five projects — a child's fiddle-back chair, a baby's armchair, a child's corner chair, a rocker and a side chair — all relate to the friendly, folksy, kitchen-hearth chairmaking traditions of the 18th and 19th centuries. There are turned legs, splat backs, cut-curved arms, fine-line painting, cane seats and so on, all nicely described and illustrated.

I've given this little book the 'Bridge-water test' — in other words I've shown it to the vicar, the postman, the DIY-mad lady up the road, and my two boys (who are just beginning to work with wood and upset my tidy workshop). They all agree that it's a good buy.

OK, there could have been a few more illustrations; we could have been told exactly how to paint the chairs and cane the seats; but at £2 what can you expect? All in all, it's a charming little book. Make room for it on your shelf or give it to a friend — it's good value for money.

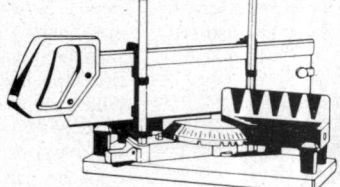

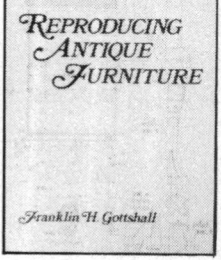
278

Prices quoted are those prevailing at press date and are
subject to alteration due to economic conditions

# The smoker's bow

Jack Hill presents a preview extract from *Making Family Heirlooms*, his brand-new book of projects

The style of low-back Windsor chair described here dates from about 1830. It is thought to have been a development from the earlier scroll-back chairs, of which there were a number of types — influenced by both the Philadelphia low-back, popular in the USA from around 1750, and the heavily built 18th-century Lancashire or Yorkshire Windsors. Characterised by sturdy construction and the continuous line of armbow and back scroll supported on a number of turned spindles, the smoker's bow, hybrid though it may be, was to become one of the most popular chairs for use in public places and offices.

It has appeared in other forms only slightly different from the original and under other names: typically the Victorian berger or bergère bow with its high curved back and pierced splats, and the so-called captain's chair popular in the pilot-houses of Mississippi steamboats. The latter has narrower arms which curve downwards and socket into the seat.

This chair is based on a traditional smoker's bow design. Elm was used for the seat and for the arm-bow because of the strength of its interlocking grain, with beech for all the turned spindles. All the material should be thoroughly dry and the beech straight-grained. Ash makes a reasonable alternative.

Shaping the elm seat is as good a place as any to begin. It is first bandsawn to the outline given in fig. 1, after which it is

● *Classic lines that never go out of style . . . the smoker's bow chair has a long history on both sides of the Atlantic*

saddled — i.e. hollowed out. This can be done using the mallet and gouge, or with the tool known as an inshave. Work across the grain — and notice that the grain in this case runs across the seat, not front-to-back.

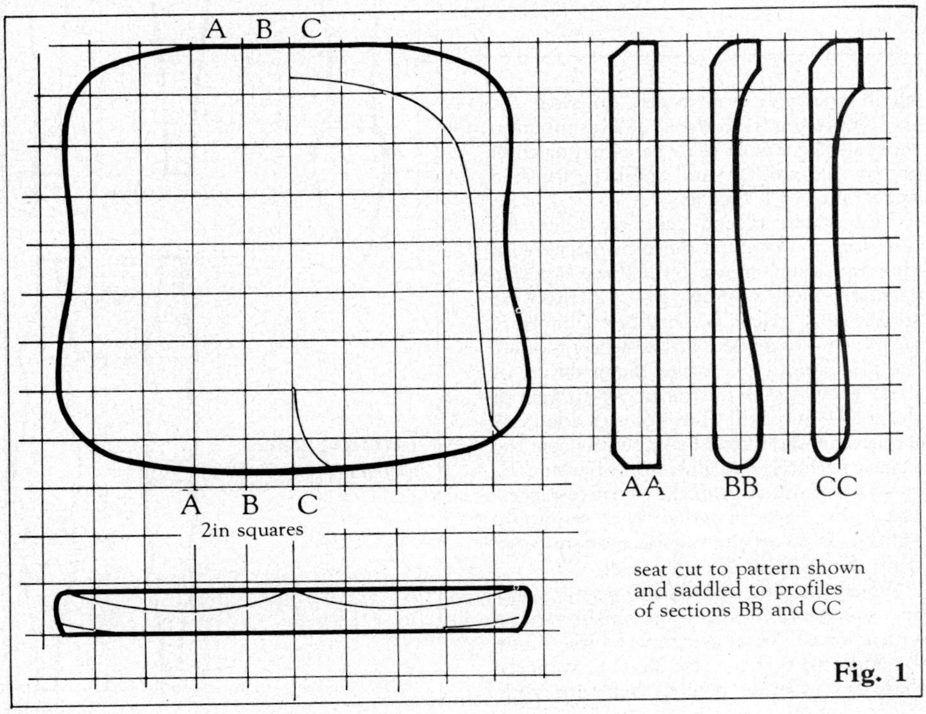

The choice of grain direction is entirely arbitrary, although some would argue differently. For me it is most often decided by the width of the board from which the seat is cut, as seats are usually wider across than they are from front to back. If I have a wide enough board I cut seats with the grain running back-to-front — it's a matter of personal choice.

Pay particular attention to getting the front edges between the so-called 'codpiece' nicely rounded over for maximum comfort. A sharp edge at these points would result in a pressure area under the sitter's thigh, which could be most uncomfortable and lead to cramping of the lower limbs.

Chamfer the edges of the seat all round, top and bottom, then finish the hollowing with a curved steel scraper and finally with glasspaper.

Still working with elm, the chair arm-bow can now be made. It is built up from three parts as shown in fig.2 and these are sawn to shape using the patterns given. The two arm-pieces come from a 1¼in-thick board; the centre piece, which is known as the scroll or crest, is made from a piece

A B C

A B C
2in squares

AA   BB   CC

seat cut to pattern shown and saddled to profiles of sections BB and CC

**Fig. 1**

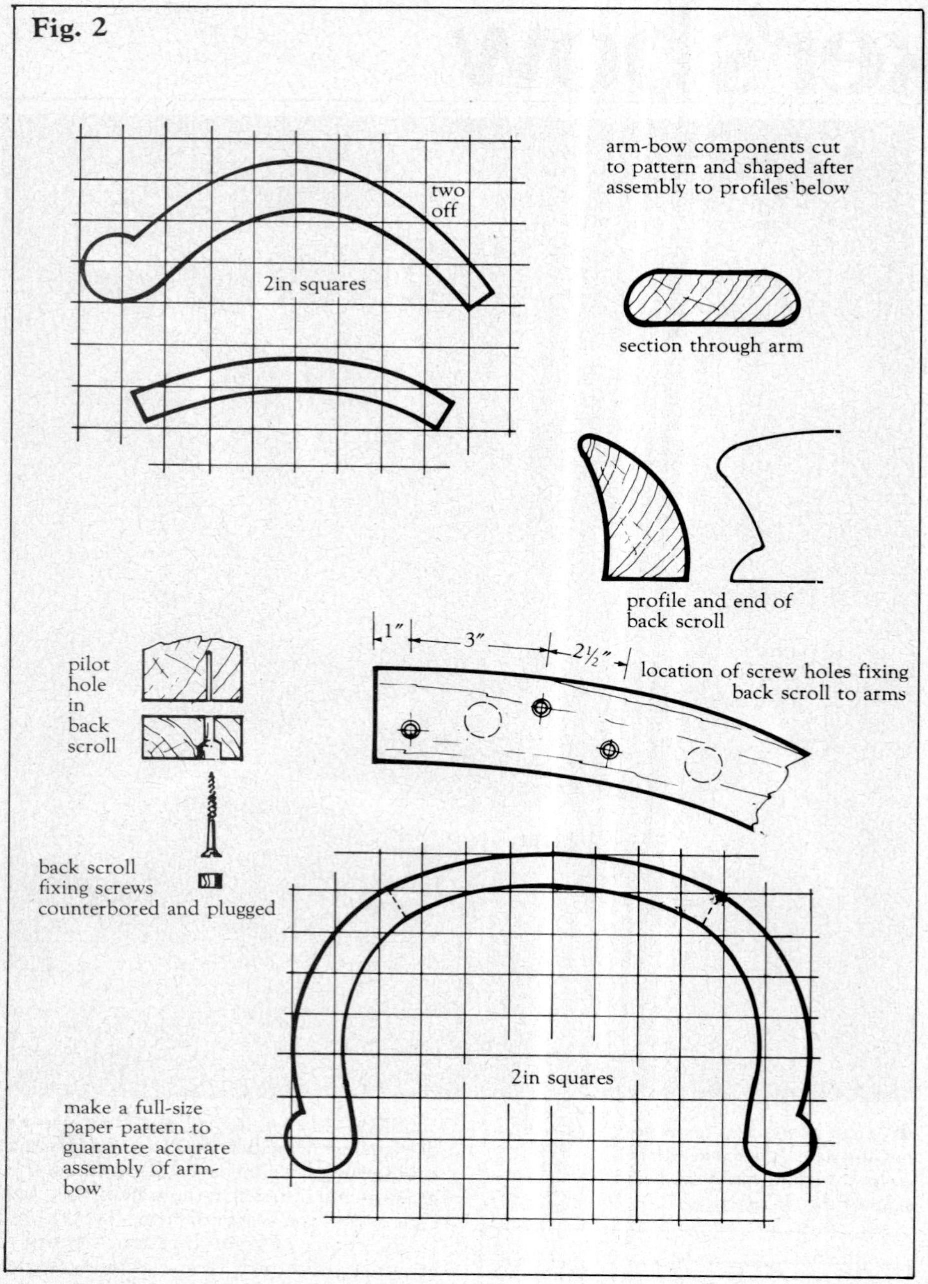

**Fig. 2**

arm-bow components cut to pattern and shaped after assembly to profiles below

two off

2in squares

section through arm

profile and end of back scroll

pilot hole in back scroll

|← 1″ →|← 3″ →|← 2½″ →| location of screw holes fixing back scroll to arms

back scroll fixing screws counterbored and plugged

make a full-size paper pattern to guarantee accurate assembly of arm-bow

2in squares

attention to top and lower surfaces. The underside remains flat, only its corners being lightly chamfered. The top surface of the arms also remains fairly flat, but their corners are more softly rounded over to give a comfortable feel. The scroll is contoured to the section given in fig. 2, the slightly concave surface at the back being made with a round-bottomed spokeshave and a curved scraper.

The remaining parts — legs, stretchers and spindles — are all made on the lathe. The legs are turned from 2½in-square material, the stretchers which form the underframing from 1¾in stuff. The type of underframing used in this chair is known as a double-H stretcher; it is stronger than the more normal H stretcher, which has only a single crosspiece. The spindles, eight in all, include six identical side and back pieces and a stronger pair of a different shape which form the front spindles or arm stumps.

The designs given for these turned parts in fig. 3 need not be strictly adhered to; there is opportunity here for some

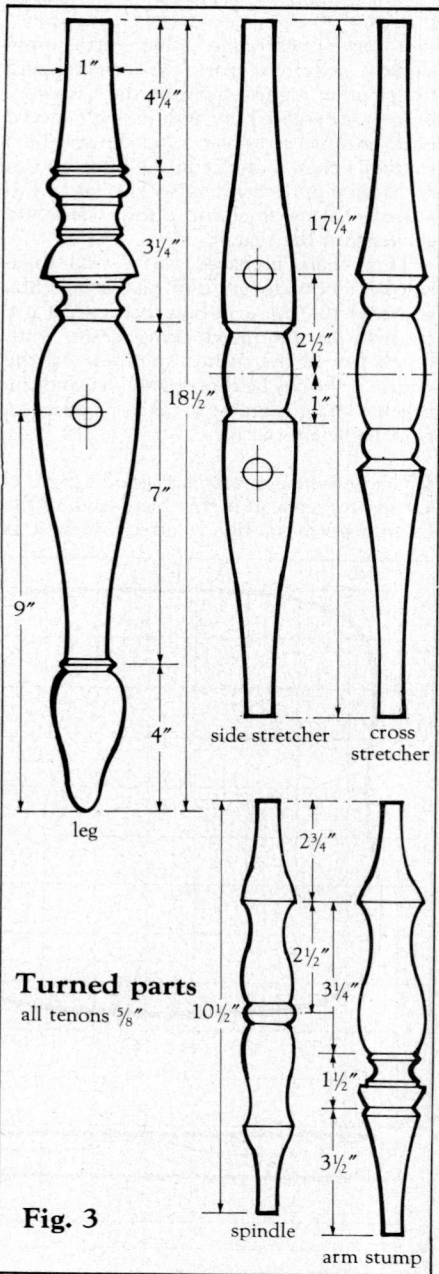

leg     side stretcher     cross stretcher

**Turned parts**
all tenons ⅝″

spindle     arm stump

**Fig. 3**

which must be 4×3in in order to obtain the required contoured shape. Note carefully the grain direction of the material used for the two arm-pieces; for maximum strength, cut these to keep the grain as straight as possible, especially through their forward ends. To ensure a close fit between arms and scroll the mating surfaces of each should be planed; this is most easily done before cutting to shape.

After planing and sawing to pattern, some preliminary shaping of the scroll may be carried out, but do not attempt a finished shape at this stage; it is achieved after the three separate parts have been joined together.

The simplest and safest way of making sure that the three parts go together right, so that you have an arm-bow of the correct size and shape, is to make a full-size paper pattern (fig. 2). Lay the parts out on this. In particular, the junction between the two ends of the separate arm-pieces must be correctly made and aligned, otherwise the arms will spread either too little or too

much and will not match up with the spindles rising from the seat. This junction must also be made a close fit, as an unsightly gap at this point would spoil the finished appearance of the chair.

The scroll, placed centrally over this junction, is fixed to the arm-pieces with glue and long screws. Drill three holes in each arm-piece as shown in fig. 2 (these are strategically placed so they don't interfere with the holes drilled later to accommodate the seat spindles), locate the position of these screw-holes on the under-surface of the scroll, and drill pilot holes of adequate diameter and depth. Then liberally coat the mating surfaces with glue, not forgetting the end-to-end junction of the two arm-pieces; place the parts together and screw up tightly. Wipe off the surplus glue squeezed from the joint, and leave to set.

When the glue is properly set the arm-bow may be fashioned to its finished shape with spokeshave and scraper. First shape the edges so that the scroll and arm-pieces all marry together nicely, then turn your

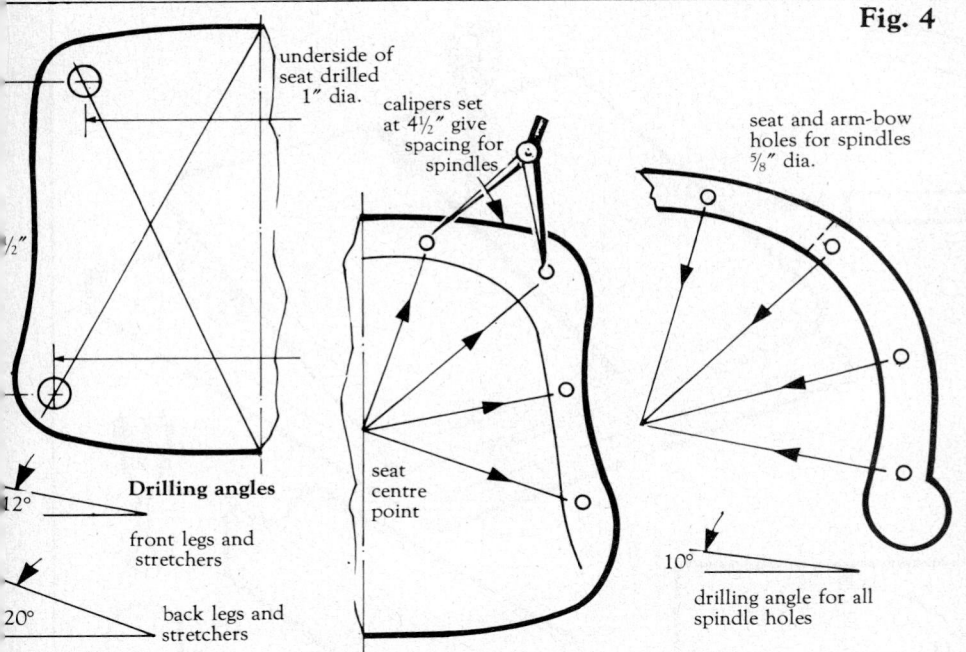

**Fig. 4**

underside of seat drilled 1" dia.

calipers set at 4½" give spacing for spindles

seat and arm-bow holes for spindles ⅝" dia.

**Drilling angles**

12°

front legs and stretchers

20°

back legs and stretchers

seat centre point

10°

drilling angle for all spindle holes

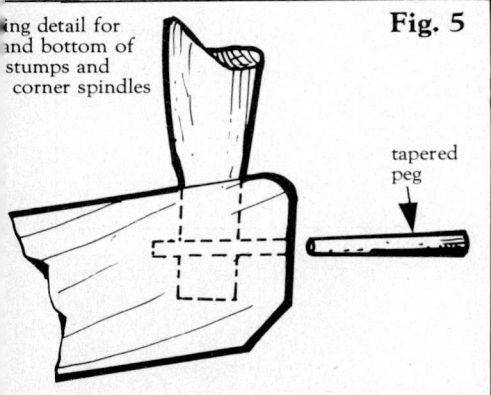

**Fig. 5**

ing detail for and bottom of stumps and corner spindles

tapered peg

● *Finishing the seat with a shaped steel scraper. 'Codpiece' shape is important!*

● *Assembling the arm-bow. Liberal glue, and screw-holes plugged from below*

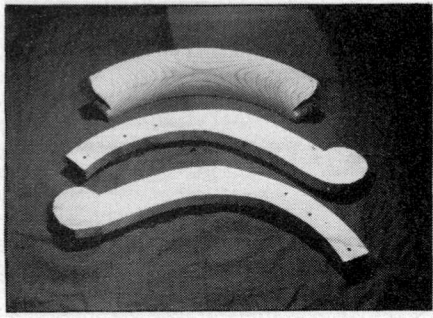

● *The arm-bow components. The scroll is finished, the arms are still rough-sawn*

● *The assembled arm-bow before glue is wiped off. Pieces are cut so the grain is longest at the tightest radius point*

individuality, but finished overall lengths and tenon sizes must be as given. It is essential that tenons be a good fit in their respective sockets. Use glue, but do not rely on it to fill gaps in loose-fitting joints. If a joint is loose because the tenon is too small or the socket hole too big, make a replacement part.

The turned parts may be polished while in the lathe. Turn each component to a smooth surface, preferably from the bevel of the turning tool, and bring to a fine finish by sanding and finally burnishing with a hand ful of shavings. Then, with the lathe running, apply a proprietary polish and burnish this with a soft cloth. Avoid getting polish on the jointing surfaces at the ends of each component, as this will seriously inhibit the adhesion of the glue used in jointing.

With all the parts of the chair made, attention can now be turned to drilling holes in most of them, each one in its proper place and at its correct angle. Traditionally, this would often have been done by hand with a brace and bit, but to simplify the task — especially in obtaining correct angles — use simple jigs in conjunction with a pillar drill, or an electric hand drill in a pillar attachment. Forstner-type toothed bits are recommended for the drilling as these produce accurate, parallel-sided, flat-bottomed holes (fig. 6).

Begin with what forms the foundation of the chair, i.e. the seat, and mark this out on its underside to locate the position and sight-lines of the leg holes (see fig. 4). Noting that the drilling angle is different for front and back legs, set the drilling jig or sloping platform to the required angle for the front legs, in this case 12°, line up sight-lines and centre lines on the jig and, after setting the depth stop on the machine, drill the front seat holes 1in in diameter. With the drilling jig at the same angle, and using the V-shaped cradle, drill two of the prepared legs as shown to take the side stretchers of the underframing. Mark these two as front legs. Now alter the drilling jig to the required angle for the back legs, 20°, line everything up and drill these holes as before. Repeat the procedure to drill stretcher holes in the two remaining legs, and mark these as back legs. The different angles of the stretcher holes will not allow front and back legs to be interchanged.

Fit the side stretchers into the legs dry, then fit the legs into the seat to make sure everything goes together correctly. While these parts are together, ascertain the position, drilling angle and actual length of the two cross-stretchers which complete the underframe; do this simply by placing them across the top of the two side stretchers and taking or marking the measurements. Dismantle the assembled parts, drill the holes for the cross-stretchers, and then have another dry assembly of the complete underframe and seat. Some minor adjustments may be required, but when all is satisfactory dismantle again so that work may be continued on the seat.

Mark out the top surface of the seat according to fig. 4 to give the positions of and the sight-lines to the spindle socket-holes. Using the drilling jig at the required angle of 10°, the spindle and arm stump holes are drilled ⅝in diameter. The two front holes are drilled as deep as possible,

281

**Fig. 6**

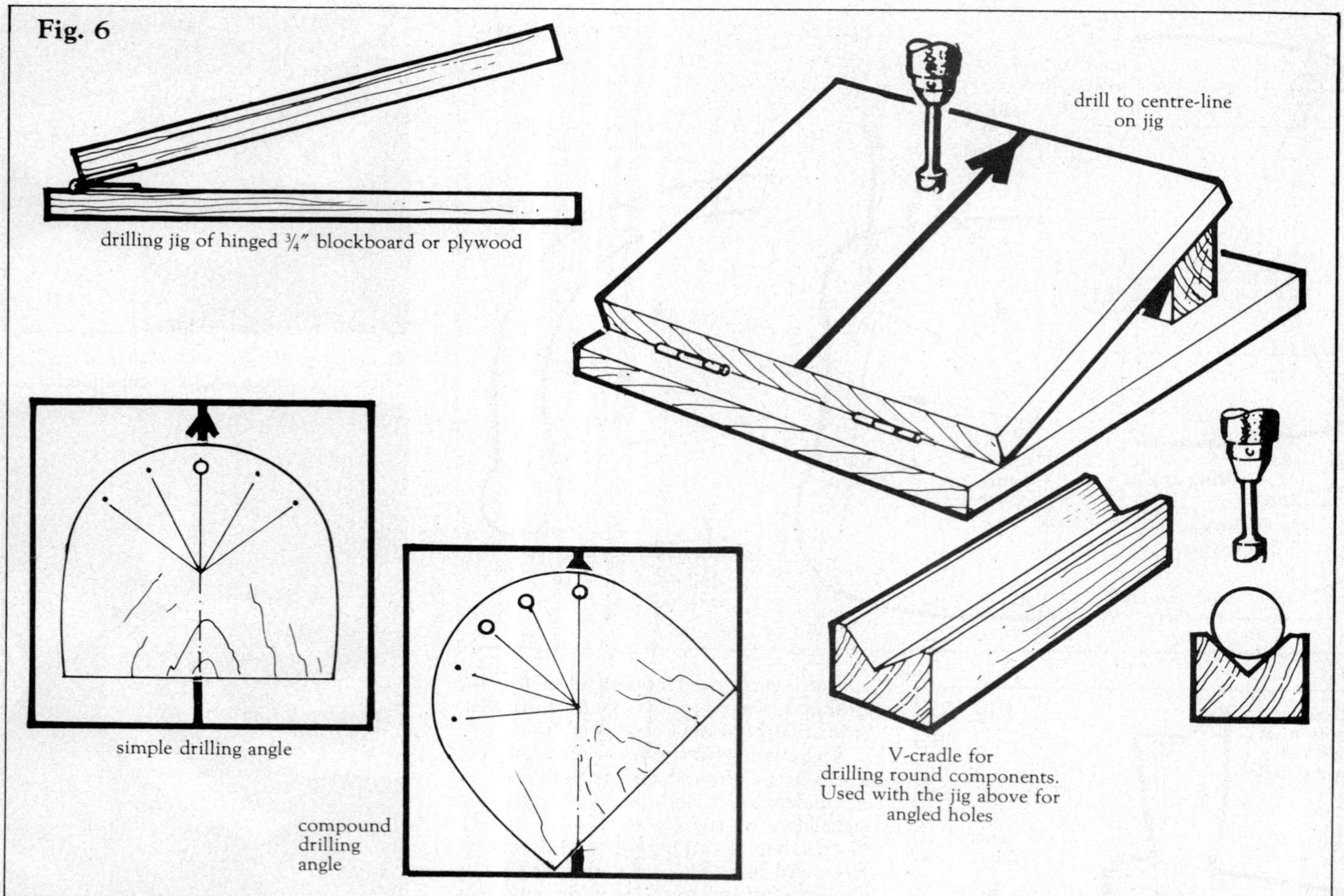

drilling jig of hinged ¾″ blockboard or plywood

drill to centre-line on jig

simple drilling angle

compound drilling angle

V-cradle for drilling round components. Used with the jig above for angled holes

somewhere betwen 1¼ and 1½in in this case, or they may be taken straight through and the spindles wedged from below. If this is done the two front components will need to be made extra long. The six spindle holes should be drilled to a depth of at least 1in.

The underside of the arm-bow should be marked out as shown in fig. 4 to give the position of the socket holes for the spindles rising from the seat. However, the bow should be put in place on the ends of the uprising spindles and the relative positions of the marks and the actual placement of the spindles checked. If any adjustments are required they are best done before drilling the holes.

All the holes in the bow are ⅝in in diameter, and they are drilled with the jig set as for the spindle holes in the seat top. Set the depth stop on the drill carefully so that the holes are not too deep; you risk breaking out the top surface of the arms. Drill only to a depth which leaves at least ¼in of solid wood remaining. The two back centre spindle holes may be made deeper, as these can go up into the scroll. A dry assembly of bow on to spindles should be made at this stage to make sure that it all goes together nicely. Make sure that all the spindles, and especially the two front ones go to or close to their full depth in the arm-bow sockets to get the maximum gluing area for maximum strength at these points.

After sanding the seat and arm-bow to remove any handling marks and all pencilled marks made during drilling and so on, the chair may be glued up and assembled. Before this is done, both the seat

● *Assembled arm-bow is shaped and smoothed with a spokeshave. A wooden one isn't vital, it just works better than metal*

and arm-bow may be given a coat of sanding sealer or varnish and rubbed down, but avoid getting sealer in the socket holes.

Begin the assembly with the underframe; put glue into socket holes and insert the cross-stretcher tenons to their full depths.

Fit stretchers to legs, put glue in the leg sockets and insert the legs into their holes in the seat; use a soft mallet, or a hammer and a block of softwood, to persuade tight joints to fit. Then set the chair up on its four legs, put glue in the spindle socket holes, and put each of the spindles and front arm stumps into their holes.

Now put glue in the holes in the arm-bow and bring this down on to the spindles, starting from the back and entering each spindle into its own hole. Press the arm-bow down into position and, if necessary, use the soft mallet to ensure that all the spindles have entered to the required depth, especially the two front ones. Check that the top of the arm-bow is at the correct height of 9½in. A slight deviation from this measurement is of little consequence; what is more important is that the arm-bow should be parallel to the top of the seat surface. Clean off any surplus glue.

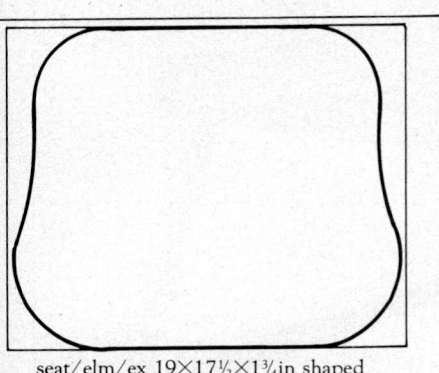

seat/elm/ex 19×17½×1¾in shaped

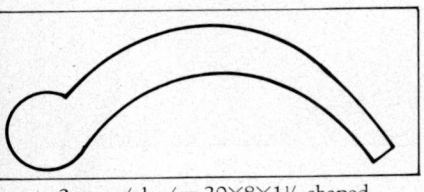

2 arms/elm/ex 20×8×1¼ shaped

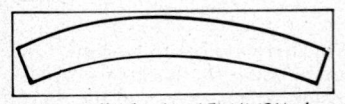

1 back scroll/elm/ex 15×4×3½ shaped

4 legs/beech/ex 19×2½×2½ turned

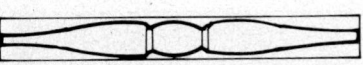

2 side stretchers/beech/ex 17½×1¾×1¾ turned

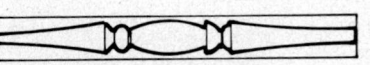

2 cross stretchers/beech/ex 17½×1¾×1¾ turned

2 arm stumps/beech/ex 11½×1¾×1¾ turned

8 spindles/beech/ex 11×1⅜×1⅜ turned

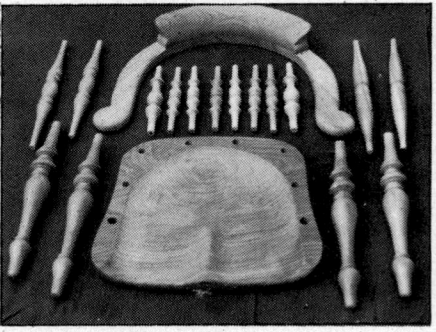

● *The parts neatly laid out before final assembly; a 'dry run' is vital for adjustments*

● *Arm stumps and spindles are checked for fit. The spindles already have a gleam of lathe finish*

● *Dry assembly of arm-bow to spindles; hide persuading-mallet in the foreground*

Some of the spindle joints are further secured by wooden pegs, as fig. 5 shows. Do this — preferably before the glue has set — by drilling ³⁄₁₆in holes at the points shown; hammer in square pegs whittled to a slightly tapered round along about two-thirds of their length. A little glue may be placed in the drilled holes before inserting the pegs. Clean off the top of the pegs flush with the surface and leave all the glued joints to set.

If the seat and arm-bow were sealed before assembly and with all the turned parts already polished, all that remains now is to give seat and arm-bow two or three applications of wax polish. The chair illustrated was finished in this way.

● *Making Family Heirlooms is published by David & Charles on 28 March at £15.* ∎

# Bending rules

Henry Rogers explains a simple — and cheap! — technique which often baffles the country-furniture novice

One of the most difficult aspects of country chairmaking is forming bent sections of timber. But wood bending does not require expensive equipment; in fact, most of it can be made out of scrap material.

The first essential is a steam generator. This can be made from a two-gallon container, such as an old paint tin, fitted with a 3kW kettle element. The lid of the generator is pierced with a hole of about 1¼in diameter, over which a 2in length of copper tube is soldered (fig. 1). Ordinary plumber's solder is quite suitable, and is probably best applied with a blowlamp. This addition to the lid ensures the steam is fed directly into the confined atmosphere of a steam-chest, in which are placed the timber sections to be bent.

The steam-chest is a long box open at both ends. It should be made from a timber which will be unaffected by heat, so don't use plywood unless it's the marine grade. The internal dimensions of the chest are not critical, but as a guide could measure 36×4×4in (fig. 2).

As well as a steam generator and steam-chest, a wooden former is required, round

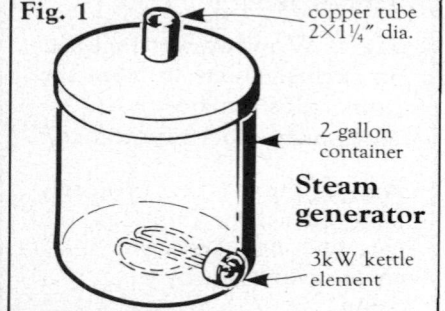

**Fig. 1**  copper tube 2×1¼″ dia.

2-gallon container

**Steam generator**

3kW kettle element

● *Many types of Windsor chair rely on bending just as much as on turning*

which the heated wood is to be bent. One suitable for bending the back of a single-bow Windsor chair is shown in fig. 3.

As the wood is bent, its fibres on the outer surface are stretched, and they will tend to rupture unless supported by a strap. Mild steel can be used for this, but stainless is better because it is less likely to stain the material. The strap is made from a 2in-wide strip of 18swg (Standard Wire Gauge)

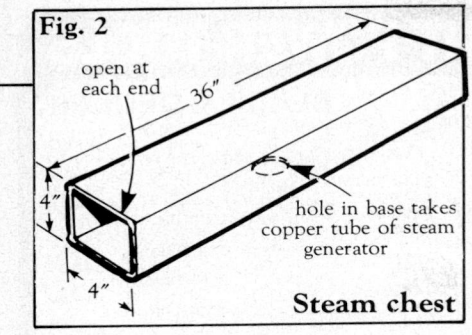

**Fig. 2**

open at each end

36"

4"

4"

hole in base takes copper tube of steam generator

**Steam chest**

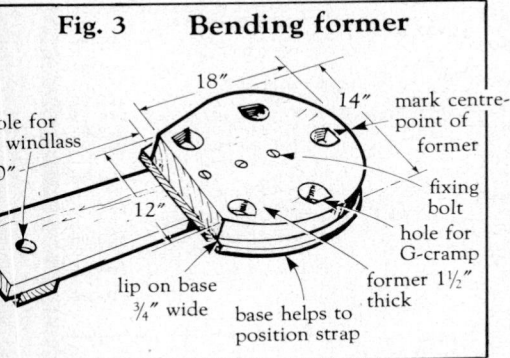

**Fig. 3    Bending former**

18"

14"

mark centre-point of former

hole for windlass

fixing bolt

12"

hole for G-cramp

lip on base ¾" wide

former 1½" thick

base helps to position strap

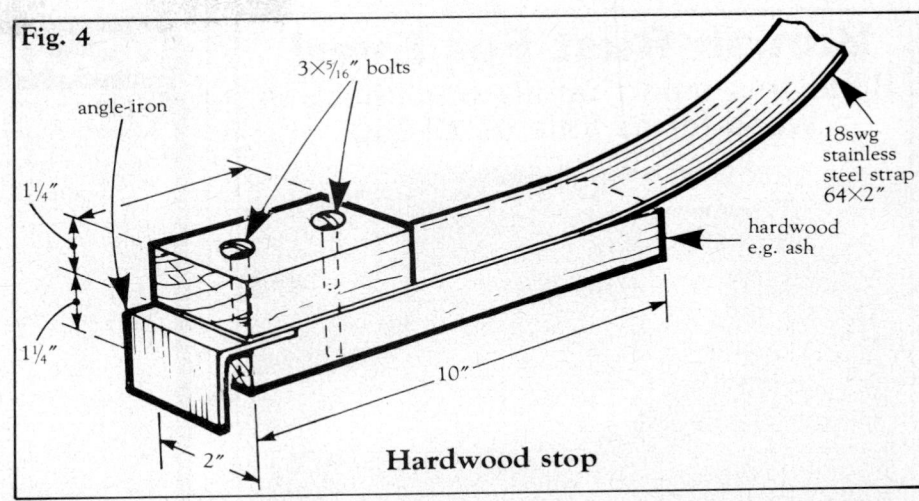

**Fig. 4**

3×⁵⁄₁₆" bolts

angle-iron

1¼"

1¼"

18swg stainless steel strap 64×2"

hardwood e.g. ash

10"

2"

**Hardwood stop**

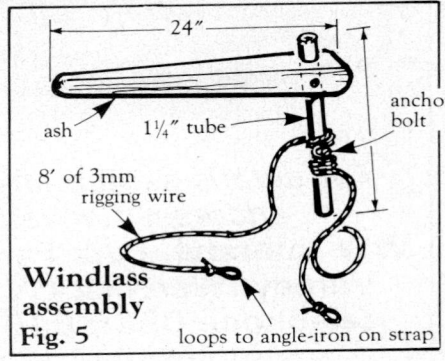

24"

ash

1¼" tube

anchor bolt

8' of 3mm rigging wire

**Windlass assembly Fig. 5**

loops to angle-iron on strap

stainless steel. Look in the Yellow Pages under 'Metal Merchants' or 'Steel Stockholders'. It is a difficult material to cut with a hacksaw, so ask the supplier for ready-prepared 2in strips.

To each end of the strap are attached hardwood stops and backing pieces (fig. 4). These help to position the workpiece and prevent any tendency for outward bending. A piece of angle-iron bored to take a hook is fitted to each stop, as steamed wood is difficult to bend unless a windlass is used (fig. 5). I was first introduced to the use of a windlass by Fred Lambert, who has been a great inspiration in my chairmaking work.

Once all the equipment has been made, you can tackle your first bent section. Select your wood carefully. Most of the home-grown hardwoods bend fairly readily, although yew is a bit troublesome. I usually bend ash. Do not use kiln-dried timber, as it is too brittle for bending and does not retain its shape. Freshly sawn (green) material is best. If your local sawmill is unable to

supply green timber, veneer mills are often a good source of supply. Air-dried timber can be bent, but is a little more difficult, as it requires a longer steaming time and greater care. Avoid material with pin knots — they cause problems out of all proportion to their size. Straight-grained material is essential until you become more familiar with the bending process. If using ash, select a piece with about eight or more annual rings per inch.

Tie the section to the metal strap with string, and make sure it is securely tied to the backing pieces of the stops. Measure its length and mark the midway point so it lines up with the former easily. For the bow of a side chair a section of planed material 1in square and 56in long is usually suitable. Shaping is done with a spokeshave after bending.

Steam the material for an hour per inch of thickness, and make sure it stays above the floor of the steam-chest, as steam rises to the top. I usually use small pieces of wood to raise it to about midway. Also, if it is a windy day pack the open ends of the steam-chest with pieces of polystyrene. The steam generator boils off water at the rate of about one gallon per hour, and therefore should not need refilling. Do not overfill the steam generator, or the water will be forced into the steam-chest.

After an hour the wood and strap can be removed from the steam-chest, and fixed to the former at the midway point with a G-

cramp (fig. 3). Do not over-tighten the cramp, as it will easily rupture the now soft and pliable wood-fibres. Connect up the wires of the windlass and quickly wind in. Cut and remove the string ties and attach the remaining G-cramps.

The whole bending operation, from removal of the workpiece from the steam-chest to getting it fully bent round the former, must be done within a minute, as the timber will quickly cool and become brittle. The strap can be removed from the former after a few minutes, but the material should be left to dry out in the strap. Allow an absolute minimum of two days in a dry atmosphere, and preferably a couple of weeks.

And then you can start on the chair! ■

● *From left: The steam generator, the steam chest (its ends packed with polystyrene to keep out draughts), and a section of timber in the strap; bending the steamed component round the former; completing the bend; and the component (still in its strap) being left to dry out*

Prices quoted are those prevailing at press date and are subject to alteration due to economic conditions

# Old planes in new hands

Any old wooden planes knocking about that you really should restore? Alan Thomas shows you how

This, frankly, is an article I have been waiting for someone else to write — someone who has used what are now old planes for a lifetime, and who knows a great deal more than I do about restoring the sick and aged to useful life. Instead, and on the assumption that there are probably other people as ignorant about the subject as I was, not so many years ago, I present some of the things I've learnt. Anyone tempted to follow the advice can at least rest assured that they will do no lasting harm.

Bench planes seem to be as good a starting place as any. Try, jack, smoother, and perhaps badger also, for although badgers are not in common use they are generally much like the jack. Sources of supply can best be described as varied, and prices likewise. I'm a hard man when it comes to prices: if a plane is in perfect condition and ready for work, then, in the opinion of most possible buyers, it is vastly inferior to its modern all-metal counterpart. And it is second-(or more)-hand into the bargain. If it is less than perfect (and they almost always are), to most people an old plane is nothing more than firewood. Set the price you are willing to pay accordingly; if the vendor has his sights on the kind of customer who is happy to hand over a tenner or more for a mantelshelf ornament, pocket your money and wish him good day.

Look carefully before you buy. Such tools don't really ever wear out, but there is little point in spending a lot of time and effort in reviving something that has seen a great deal of use when a less worn one will turn up on the next stall, or next week. Try-planes seem usually to be in good condition bodily, but often the irons are rather short. Presumably they are reflecting the need for frequent re-sharpening in a tool that leads a relatively gentle life of even tenor.

Jacks sometimes betray a hard-working past in which they have lived up to their names as jacks of all trades. Usually the signs are a tapered body and over-wide mouth. I have come across samples in which the taper from back to front must have been all of ⅜in, giving cause for reflec-

● *Three block planes, total cost £6; all set differently*

tion about the great deal of energy that someone has wasted in pressing down the front end. It is worth recalling that often a tradesman would have more than one plane: you don't particularly want his number two.

Smoothers seem to show their age in structural damage rather than wear, and the common fault is a split in the side-wall (cheek) of the mouth. The coffin shape of a typical block or smoother creates a short-grain section just here, and one careless tap of the iron sideways is enough to cause damage; to me, such damage condemns the tool. A strong invisible repair is not possible, so put the plane back and keep looking.

Typically, badgers see so little wear that damage to them is trivial.

Apart from accidents, there will more than likely be fine cracks visible on the endgrain, the result of uncaring storage in the past. Value judgement comes into play here, for how serious is serious? If you can live with them, well and good, and if they are not too bad they may respond to treatment. While looking at the endgrain, by the way, check that the medullary rays lie

more or less horizontally — the way they should lie for least wear and greatest stability. Some inferior imports had the grain running all ways.

You can hardly fail to notice if someone has used a hammer or too much gusto jarring loose the iron, and it will be impossible to disguise that splintery depression at the front. A damaged wedge is easily replaced, and a broken handle, or 'toat', should make the plane almost a gift for you. A replacement is easy enough to make.

The one certainty is that a newly acquired plane won't cut wood, so dismantle it. Tap the wedge from side to side — carefully! — until it comes free; I find that a light plastic-faced hammer is ideal for all plane adjustments. Check over the body with a straight-edge, looking for any distortions resulting from drying out, age or wear. Test the sole very carefully along its length and width, and diagonally. Then try the body for general squareness; usually they are slightly lozenged, and (while it hardly matters) if anything has got to come off the sole it may as well be from the high side. If indeed there are any cracks in the endgrain flood them now with water and leave for a few hours, watering again if you feel like it. By 'flood' I don't mean 'dunking in the bath' — a dipped fingertip is quite enough; it doesn't always work, but I have known cracks so treated to close completely.

I've yet to buy a plane with a sole so worn or distorted that it has needed more than cautious scraping, but no doubt some are so bad they would benefit from the finest of fine cuts from a perfectly sharp smoother. In any case they will probably need the scraper treatment too, and quite the best tool for the job is a narrow hook scraper of the Skarsten type — newly sharpened with great care, and kept sharp.

Provided the straight-edge is truly straight and moderately stiff, it will serve nicely to mark high spots. Rub one of its edges with a soft pencil, and then slide it along the plane sole; it will leave a pencilled witness mark on every bump it encounters. Scrape these off and repeat as often as necessary — over particularly lumpy areas a new fine-toothed file may be useful too, but

be generally careful not to round off edges. And remember that, while a straight-edge needs no help in showing up a hollow surface, if you are not careful it can conceal a slight round.

When the sole is truly flat and out of winding, turn your attention to the rest of the body. Opinions differ on cleaning up: while it would be a pity to destroy the lovingly oiled patina of years in a vain attempt to make a tool look like new, I personally don't care for the dirt and general crud that usually encrusts old planes. Some fairly fine wire wool will shift a great deal of filth, with perhaps a little scraping for the crusty bits; linseed oil, given long enough, will dry very hard indeed.

Curiously, block planes and smoothers are often found dry and un-oiled, and showing few signs of wear. My theory is that, typically, some un-handy householder found himself faced with a sticking door or window, went out to buy a plane, found wooden ones a lot cheaper than metal, bought one and did the job, and that was that. If so, his loss is our gain, and after a careful wire-woolling to get rid of the dust and spots of dark green paint (usually green: I wonder why?) oiling can begin. The traditional way of doing it was to stop the mouth with putty, fill up with linseed oil, and wait until the oil had worked its way along the grain and out at the ends. I have no doubt it worked, either; I've always found it a minor mystery that linseed oil, a viscous liquid, is readily absorbed by hard and close-grained woods.

Even on a previously oiled plane body it pays to be thorough about cleaning dirt off the endgrain, including that in the mouth: an appreciable amount of oil will then be taken up, and help prevent those water-swollen cracks from re-opening.

While the body is being allowed to drink as much oil as it wants, separate cap and iron and survey the damage. If the usual scabby rust and hardened grease are present, there is much to be said for an old file, ground square across the end, as a scraper. A brisk wire-brushing will do it all good in any case. A try-square across the cutting edge (bearing in mind that the sides of the iron may well not be parallel) will almost certainly betray long years of unthinking oilstoning, and the only cure is to re-shape on a grinding-wheel. Get it square first of all and then re-bevel, on a big, old-fashioned, proper wheel if possible; otherwise by fiddling about with a small one of the kind more generally available. It can be done!

Before honing the iron, check that its cap fits properly. It is important that the business end should be quite sharp, and bear down properly on the iron to leave no more than a hairline crack where they touch. Of course, this desirable state of affairs must obtain when the clamping screw is duly tightened.

● *Above: A now useless iron and a new, home-made cap flank an attractive antique pattern*

● *Left: The badger-plane's iron, though ground skew, must be set square to both sole and side*

Still before honing (after all, why risk more cut fingers than are strictly necessary?) get the iron and wedge to fit. Assemble them in position; a little thoughtful fingering of the wedge, this way and that, will soon indicate where the high spots are. Often, wedges have picked up some rust scale, and need no more than some judicious attention from a scraper.

From then on, for most trys, jacks and smoothers it's just a case of putting an edge on the iron, setting it carefully and planing happily ever after. For badgers, however, there is an added complication; since the blade is set at a skew the iron is skewed also. It, too, will undoubtedly have been mal-treated in the past. What I have done in two such cases is to wedge the irons firmly into what seemed the best positions; in any wooden plane there is always some sideways slack. Then I applied a free-cutting and flat oilstone to the old cutting-edge; the grit hardly marked, let alone cut, the wood, but soon took the metal down to sole level. And side level too, for the acutely angled corner of the iron sticks out at the side and must be effectively square with the sole. Then, once again dismantled, the newly generated witness mark makes it easy to back off the cutting edge in the approved manner.

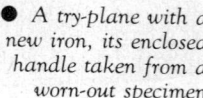

● *A try-plane with a new iron, its enclosed handle taken from a worn-out specimen*

Which leaves the problems of breakage and replacements. One of the remarkable things about these tools, largely hand-made in dozens of different factories, is the high degree of standardisation in their dimensions. No longer, of course, can you buy spare handles and irons from tool shops (although it is not so many years since such spares were generally available); nevertheless, it is certainly worth buying

● Above: The badger-plane. Below: A battered jack-plane – better ones are available

worn but suitably priced tools for the sake of the spares they contain. One jack body came to me for just 20p; granted, the handle was broken and the iron was missing, but the rest looked pretty fit. In the fulness of time arrived another — wormy but with a good and suitable blade; the handle was all right, too. Cannibalising complete, one good plane that cost 95p!

Not that open handles would be at all difficult to carve, and closed ones hardly more so — why, I wonder, are try-planes close-handled and jacks not? Irons may seem more troublesome, but they need not be. By far the majority, if not all, of the originals were made by fire-welding a piece of steel on to an iron stock, and I suppose it would be quite possible to re-steel an existing iron by cutting off the old, too short, hardened bit and electrically welding on a new length. But it hardly seems worth the trouble. What I have successfully done is to make an entirely new blade from gauge plate, or ground flat stock. This material drills and files easily and can be hardened and tempered without trouble. Just heat the business end to a thoroughgoing bright red; quench quickly in cold but not freezing water; polish; re-heat gently until the end is the palest of straw colours; and quench again.

There will be two noticeable differences between the home-made replacement and an original; the home-made will be neater and more precisely shaped, and it will also be parallel in its thickness instead of tapered. The practical effect of the latter feature is that the wedge angle will have to be slightly modified; the former has no effect at all except to illustrate the carefree attitudes of our ancestors.

If a new cap-iron is needed, all you want is a piece of ordinary mild steel. Bend the end slightly to give the characteristic spring curve before filing the whole to shape. The

nut, usually brass, will really have to be turned, and it is riveted into the plate — the thread, by the way, is $5/16$in Whitworth on all of mine. Making a new wedge hardly warrants description, but remember to allow enough clearance for the head of the blade-clamping screw.

Finally, there is the question of mouthing, and not until a plane is ready for work is it possible to be sure that the gap is too great: it is hardly likely to be too small. If it appears that something must be done (and I have yet to do it) the approved method is to let in a slip of boxwood and cautiously re-gap until satisfaction is achieved. Making a suitable shallow rebate to receive the slip would not be difficult, although it would probably pay to provide some sort of tapered keying. The body should, of course, already be saturated with oil, which won't help any glue. Perhaps a couple of punched-in brass pins might be a good idea, too. The boxwood slip might well come from an old ruler; however, I would be inclined to cut a suitable piece from a scrap body, for the repair should then be less conspicuous. In olden times bone might have been used.

And that says pretty much all that needs to be said about reviving old bench-planes. Give them an occasional oiling and all will be well for another 60, 70, or 100 years of use. It's a fair bet that any amateur using a properly set-up specimen for the first time will wonder why Bailey bothered to invent the cast-iron sort. The answer, it must be said, lies in the all-round convenience of the latter kind — they are easier both to set and to sharpen. But where time is not money, and since purchase prices permit owners to reduce the sharpening nuisance by having more than one plane of each sort — then there is a lot to be said, still, for the tactile pleasures of solid beech and the gentle aroma of linseed oil. ■

# Starters

Chris Nussbaum's diary of the London College of Furniture C&G 564 cabinetmaking course

Two particularly knotty problems have taken up most of my time this month, and the consequences will be with me for a while to come. The first concerned buying timber (do I hear sympathetic noises?); the second was a design problem.

The 'Project 564' article (*Woodworker*, January) described a wall-hung-display-cabinet exercise set to students on our course last year. This year we have been blessed with a desk-top writing-case — a real teaser, which I hope to describe in more detail later. This piece was designed in ash. The wood was to be provided by the college; short of funds as the department is, what arrived on our benches was a pile of case-hardened ash, roughly corresponding to the design cutting list, and including some excellent material for making

propellers with!

A small group of us decided to go and buy our own timber, which at the time seemed a sensible enough decision. It was my first experience of the impatience of timber merchants accustomed to selling large quantities to professionals. It took a lot of determination to convince them to spend a little time on us — the future professionals. Then there was the problem of translating in one's mind the scrappy-looking piece in its murky shed into finished boards, so as to make some judgement on the suitability thereof. And, last of all, the question of how to judge the quality of a particular plank of, say, 2in oak that is to be deeped to a 1in board, with minimum wastage yet supplying all needs. All this within half an hour, if they'll give you that much time!

We brought home two planks of kilned American oak, 6×2in, to be deeped into three. The deeped boards are, especially on the heart side, full of checks and shakes which have opened since the release of internal stresses by deeping, and we will have a lot of trouble finding enough usable material. We have learnt an expensive lesson; but perhaps the timber merchant might have been kinder, too.

There is certainly no easy answer, and now we are all confronted with the task of

buying timber for our 'final pieces' — the furniture we have been designing and must now build, upon which 60% of our bench-work assessment is based. It is this design which has been the second main concern this month. We have all spent two weeks solid at the drawing-board, most of us experiencing the 'design process' for the first time. My artistic experience is limited, and it was no easy matter to put many preconceived notions behind me and approach the new ideas of form and colour with an open mind. We had three days of 'related projects' — model-building with 'found' materials, working with colour and pattern, designing and drawing full-size on 6×6ft wall-mounted paper — before launching into seven days of designing our own pieces.

15 very different ideas, some conventional, others less so, and 15 different design techniques — some seeking inspiration from other furniture, others from architecture, others from more remotely related fields, and all of us finding inspiration and input from each other (certainly a very important factor for me). It is hard to capture in words the nature of what proved for me a very stimulating period: another of those short but enjoyable samples of something bigger, which inevitably form a large part of a relatively short course. ■

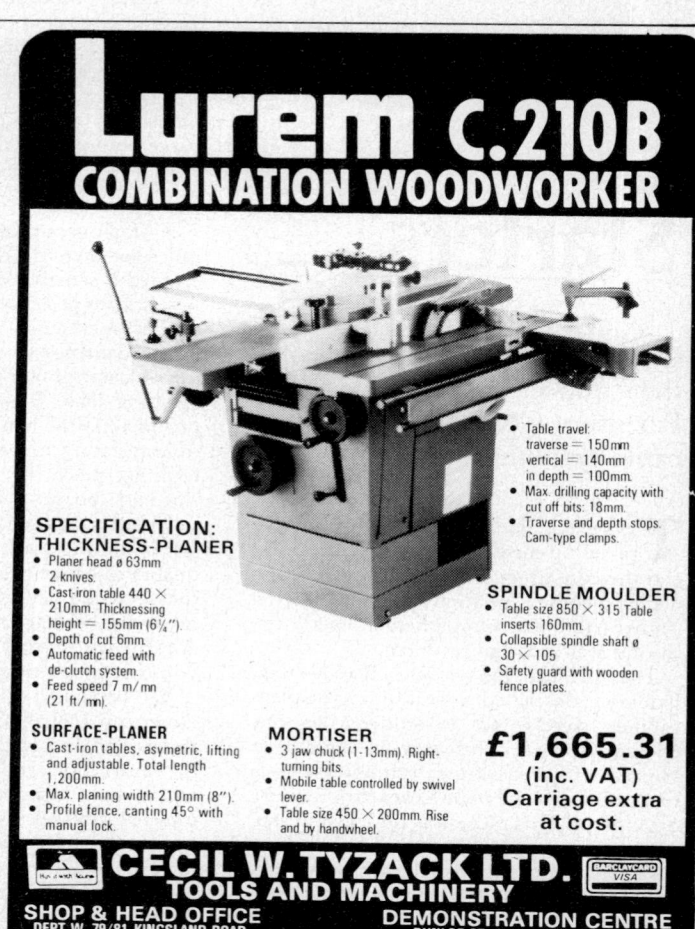

# A jewel of a chest

René Coolen introduces his meticulous drawings for a classical miniature chest from 18th-century Holland

Some particularly charming examples of the art of furniture-making are to be found among miniatures — tables, decorative boxes, clock-cases and so on. The amount of love and devotion put into these jewels of cabinetmaking is clearly visible from these drawings of a Louis XVI chest. The choice of wood alone must have been made with superb skill and care.

The marquetry on the lid is especially beautiful, and employs a special technique for shading over the colours on some of the flowers. The veneer is put in a bowl under a layer of heated fine river sand for a few minutes. Beach sand will do, as long as it's very fine. To get a deeper shadow, use a thicker layer of sand; a thinner layer for a lighter shadow.

The green on, for instance, the bird's tail was obtained by treating the veneer with copper oxide. The greenish sycamore that can sometimes be found was also used.

Working with coloured veneer demands special care; it is easy to lose the tints when you sand and finish it. Colours can run or fade when french polish is applied, too. To avoid this effect, spray two or three layers of diluted white polish over the colours, having cleaned them up with a steel scraper — and a very delicate touch! Once they're sealed, you can sand and polish safely without damage. ∎

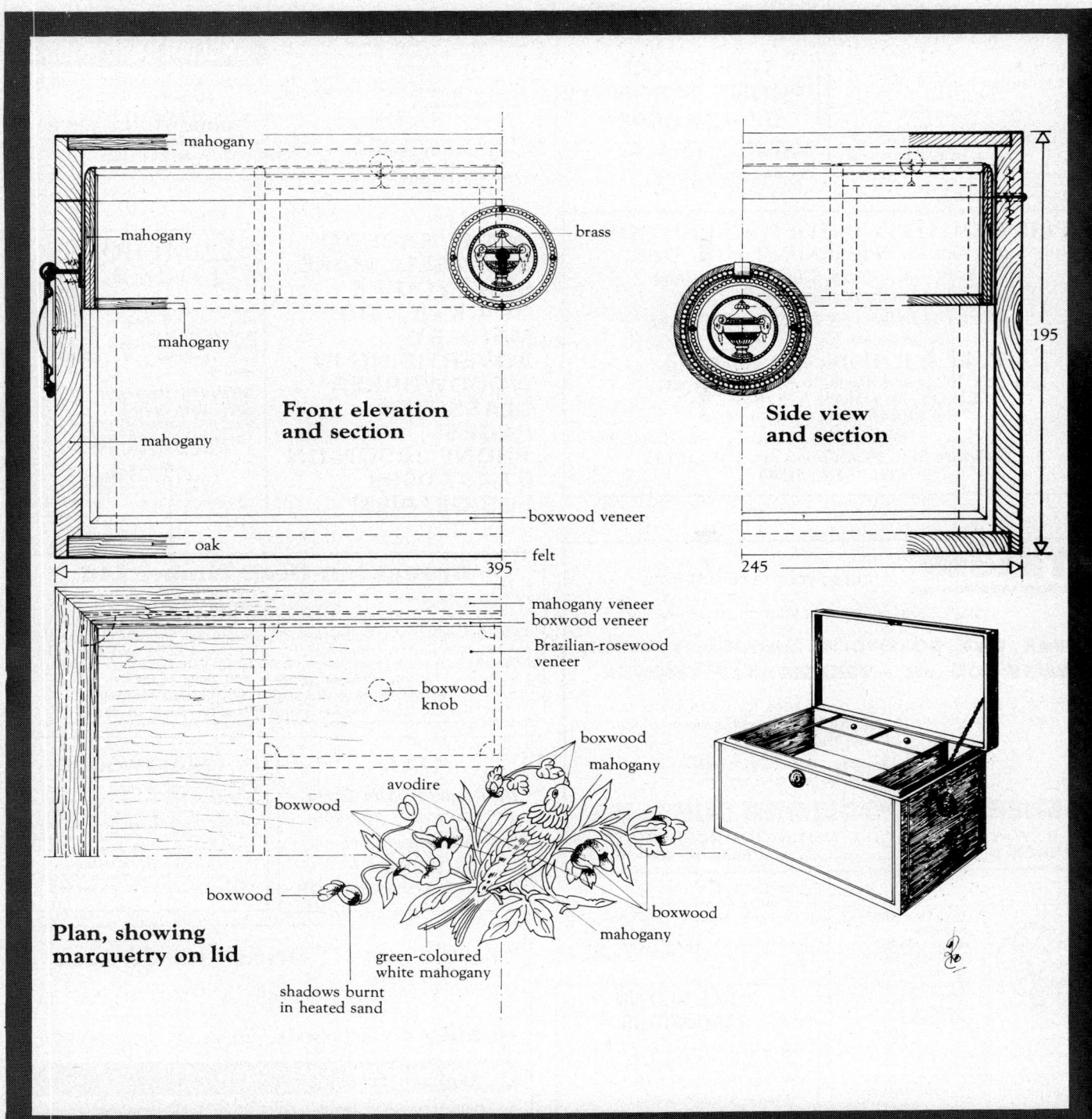

mahogany

mahogany

brass

mahogany

mahogany

**Front elevation and section**

**Side view and section**

195

boxwood veneer

oak

felt

395

245

mahogany veneer
boxwood veneer

Brazilian-rosewood veneer

boxwood knob

boxwood

avodire

boxwood

boxwood
mahogany

boxwood
mahogany

**Plan, showing marquetry on lid**

green-coloured white mahogany

shadows burnt in heated sand

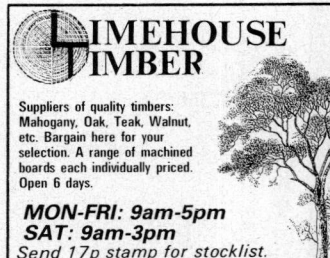

## Classified Advertisements

*From:*
.................................................................................................
.................................................................................................
.................................................................................................

I enclose remittance value ..................... to cover ...............................

Insertions under the heading:
☐ WORKSHOP EQUIPMENT
☐ COURSES
☐ CRAFT/ANTIQUE/SECONDHAND TOOLS
☐ MUSICAL INSTRUMENTS
☐ GENERAL — Classification of choice)

BUSINESS OPPORTUNITY ☐
BOOKS & PUBLICATIONS ☐
PLANS/KITS ☐
MATERIALS/FINISHES ☐
FOR SALE ☐
WOOD SUPPLIERS ☐

To: Jason, WOODWORKER
CLASSIFIED ADVERTISEMENT DEPT.
1 GOLDEN SQUARE, LONDON W1R 3AB.

★ Lineage rate 35p per word. Minimum charge £5.25.
★ Semi display single column cm = £7.25 (Minimum 2.5cm)

All Classified Advertisements under £25.00 must be pre-paid.

*Name and address if to appear must be paid for*

# Happy hours

Colin Murdoch's cocktail table promises (nearly!) as much pleasure in the making as the using

There is definitely something elegant about the basic design of a cocktail table. Unfortunately, the market is littered with cheap, shoddy models which don't do it full credit.

There are no intricate processes involved in making the piece, although patience and care are required to make a good job of the top ring. The project is fairly simple and very enjoyable to make, and does not require a lot of material. I chose four legs partly for ease of manufacture and partly for stability. I used sapele mahogany, mainly for its working qualities.

The first step is to select a piece of timber for the centre post measuring 460×60×60mm, and to mark out the four mortises using a mortise-gauge. Next, make a template for the legs as shown in fig. 1 and cut the legs out, taking note of the direction of the grain. Obviously you don't want the grain to run vertically.

The tenons can now be marked out and the joints cut and fitted. The centre post is mounted on the lathe and shaped. The legs can be finished with a spokeshave and scratch-stock. For the uninitiated, the latter is simply a cutting-gauge with the blade turned at right-angles and the stock set close to it. It can also be used to form the grooves on the legs as shown in fig. 2.

The top is made by dowelling together three pieces of timber 500×70×15mm, as shown in fig. 3. A face-plate is then mounted on it and a 500mm circle drawn on. The corners are removed before it is mounted on the lathe, flushed off at the face and turned down to round. Two grooves are then put in the edge for decoration and the recess made for the leather insert. Obviously, you will need the leather on hand to ensure that it is an exact fit.

The twelve pedestals were made two at a time, using six pieces measuring 200×25×25mm. The easiest way is first to turn the pieces of timber until round, and then mark the various lengths with a pencil and turn to shape. I used calipers to check the end sizes and visually checked the shape. Fig. 4 shows a finished version.

Finally the ring must be made. The first step is to take a piece of chipboard or blockboard and draw two circles on it, one the same size as your top and the other 25mm less (fig. 5). This will be the actual size of the wooden ring you are making. The circles are then split up into six equal parts as shown. Holes are drilled in the 12 places marked, and countersunk at the back to accept a suitable screw. Six pieces of timber measuring 270×70×20mm are then cut, mitred, and placed on the blockboard as in fig. 6. Make sure they fit tightly.

The next step is to dowel these pieces together. The easiest way is to tap a small panel pin into the end of one of the pieces and snip the end off, leaving 2mm protruding. It can then be pushed in place, where it will leave a mark on the next piece. The two pieces can then be drilled and a dowel put in place ready to mark the next piece.

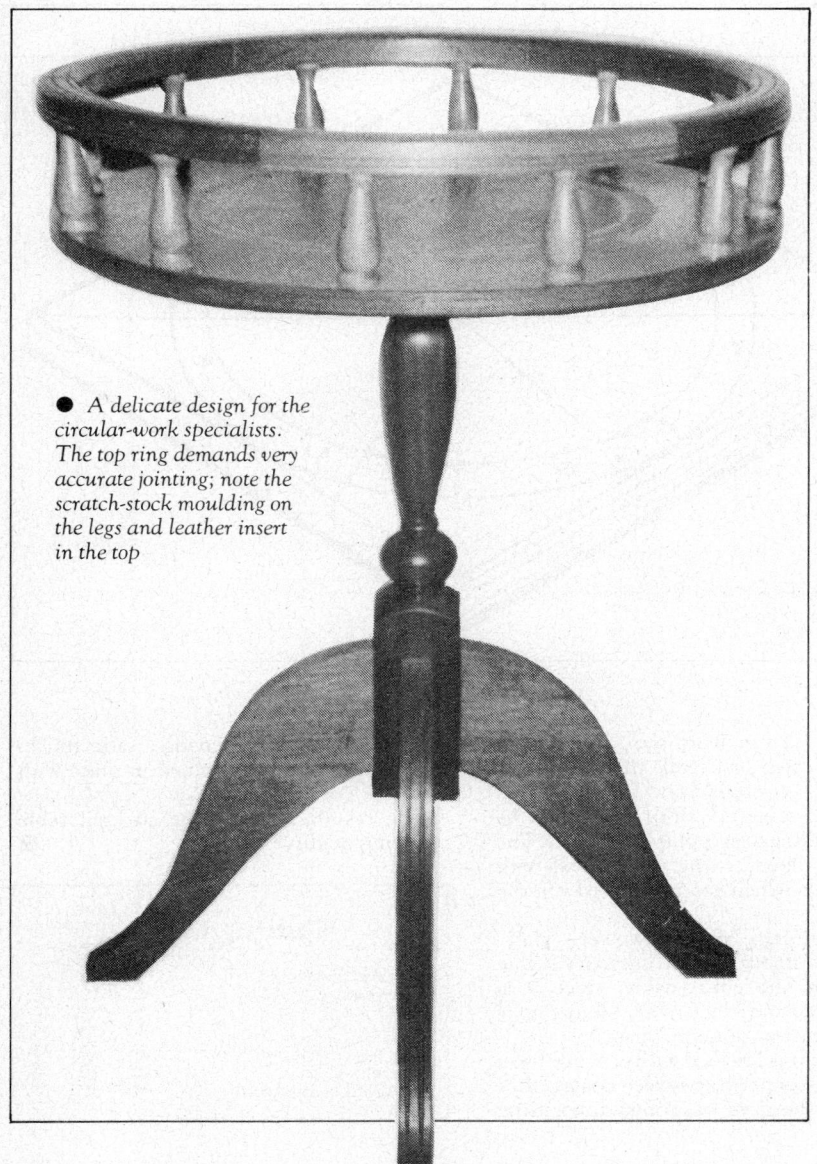

● A delicate design for the circular-work specialists. The top ring demands very accurate jointing; note the scratch-stock moulding on the legs and leather insert in the top

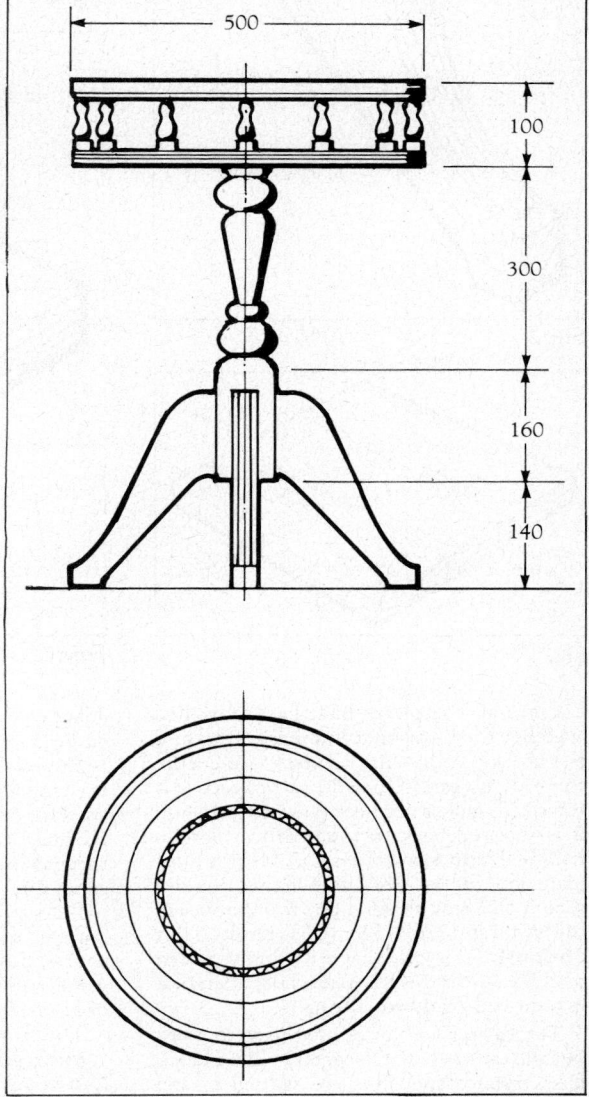

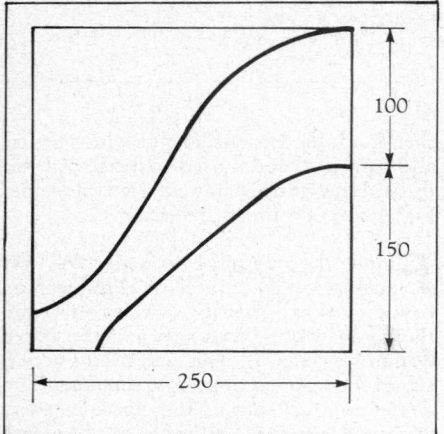

**Fig. 1**

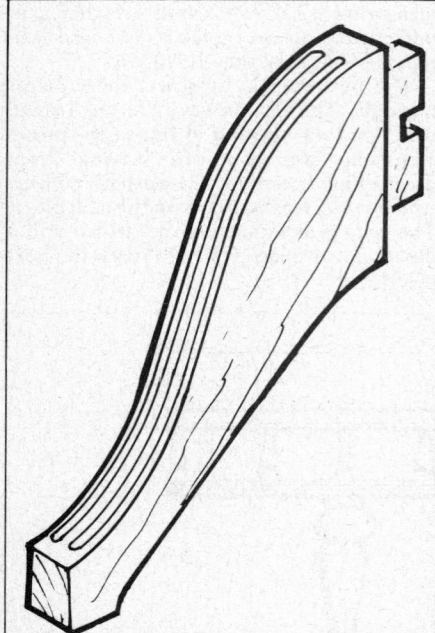

**Fig. 2**

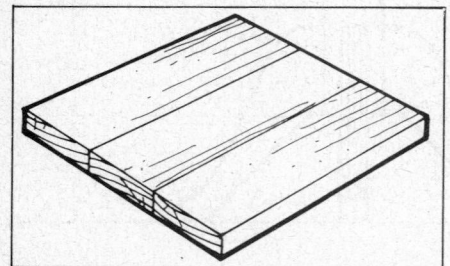

**Fig. 3**

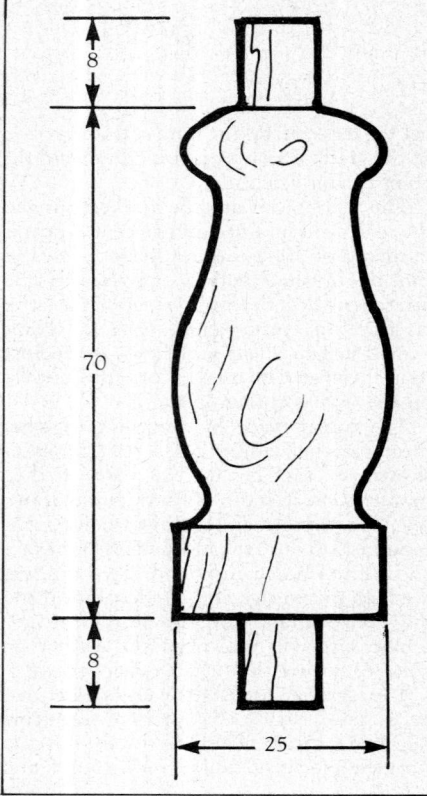

**Fig. 4**

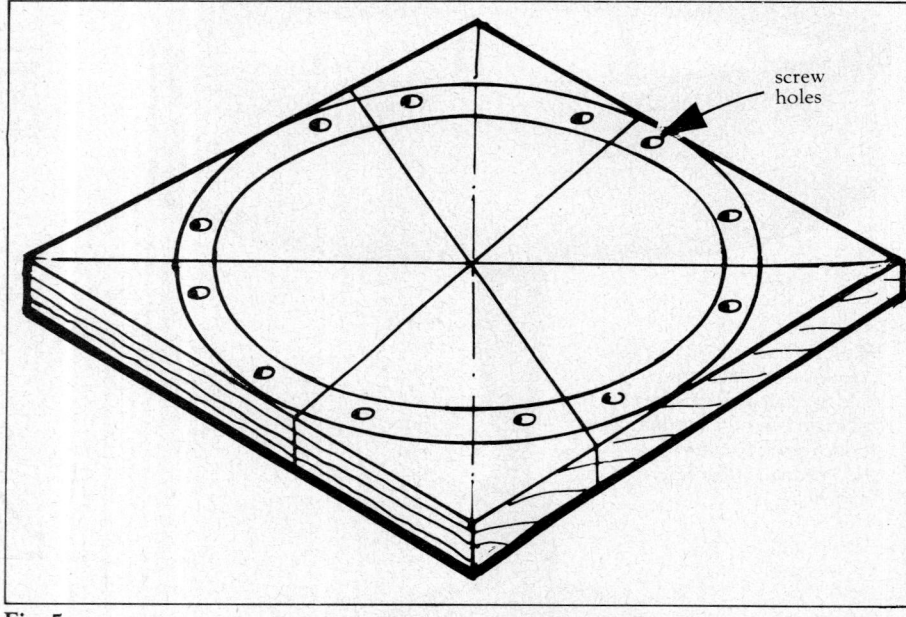

**Fig. 6**

**Fig. 7**

**Fig. 5**

Once all the pieces have been dowelled together the hexagonal frame is screwed to the blockboard — dry at first — to ensure there are no gaps. Once fitting properly it is removed, glue is applied to the dowels, and it is screwed back to the board. It is then trimmed with a saw as in fig. 7. Using a face-plate, you can now mount it in the lathe and turn it to a ring shape. I put two grooves in the top and sides on this model, but obviously you can shape it to any design you like. After this has been glasspapered, it is removed ready for fitting.

The easiest way of doing this is to mark out the tabletop in 12 segments like a clock face. Again panel pins are tapped in and

snapped off 2mm from the surface. The ring is pressed on and then carefully removed. There should now be 12 marks in the ring and tabletop, all of which may be used for drilling to accept the pedestals. The tabletop is fixed to the centre post with three dowels which can be marked out the same way.

Before gluing, all pieces were glass-papered to a smooth finish. I used PVA glue to assemble the entire table, since it is water-soluble and sets slowly. Gluing up is obviously easiest done in stages.

The table was finished with polyurethane varnish, glasspapering between coats. After four coats, the gloss was toned down using

steel wool and wax, leaving a satin finish. Finally the leather was glued in place with Evo-Stik contact adhesive.

The result: a handsome cocktail table radiating quality! ∎

## Cutting list

*Dimensions in mm*

| | | | | |
|---|---|---|---|---|
| centre post | 1 | 460× | 60× | 60 |
| legs | 4 | 250 | 250 | 20 |
| top | 3 | 500 | 70 | 15 |
| pedestals (2 from each) | 6 | 200 | 25 | 25 |
| top ring | 6 | 270 | 70 | 20 |
| blockboard or chipboard | 1 | 500 | 500 | 20 |

# An artist and his models

Peter Collenette introduces
the small and amazing worlds
of David West

You could say he made doll's-houses, but you'd be quite wrong.

It's true that David West of Lyme Regis spent about six years making West Wood House (on our cover) — a commission from Viscountess Dunluce, and currently insured for £250,000. Built on a solid-mahogany frame with veneered-plywood infill panels pierced by 110 working sliding-sash windows, it contains 30 rooms plus a cupola and a conservatory. It stands 8ft 6in tall, and is destined to house a collection of miniature furniture and porcelain.

Many of the floors are parquet, for example in mahogany and pine. There's a spiral staircase. Mahogany joinery and trim abounds: skirtings, dado rails, panel doors. Moreover, the wallpaper, with its exquisite period patterns, is entirely hand-painted — and one room is decorated as a Chinoiserie, dragons and all.

But here we approach the secret and fascination of the whole enterprise. David West is not a cabinetmaker, nor even a

● *Right: Mysteriously titled, 'The Spode Set' (about 2ft high) is a pastel Gothick pastoral – while the 'Gothic Window' (below) blends frame and picture*

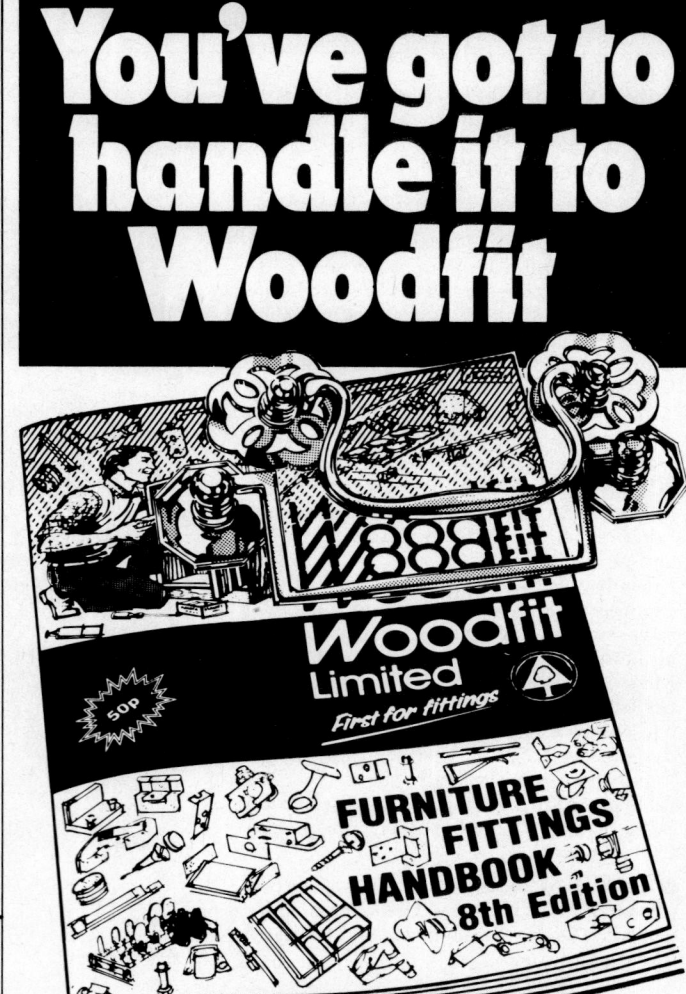

Prices quoted are those prevailing at press date and are subject to alteration due to economic conditions

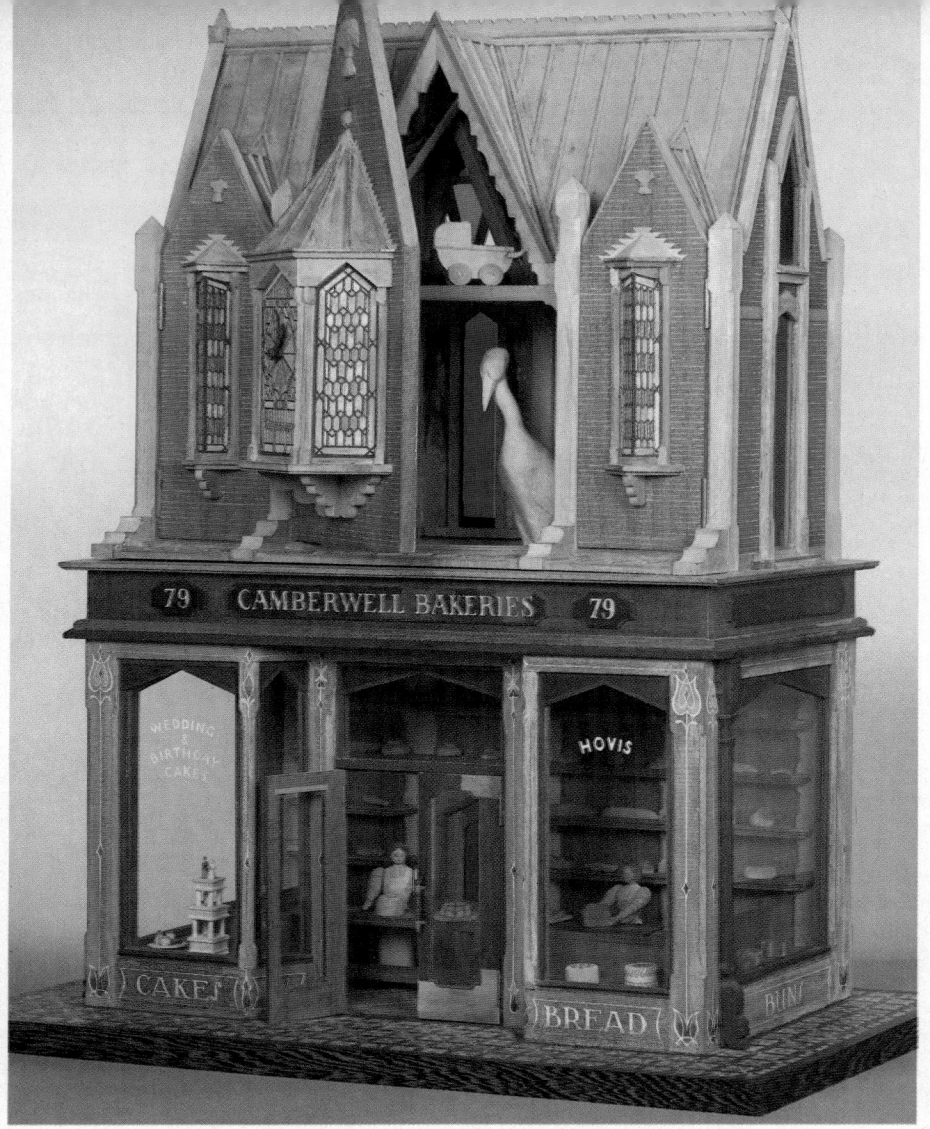

are uniformly alluring. Close to, the architecture still cannot be faulted for elegance of composition, nor the surface decoration for rightness of colour or deftness in application.

But admiration is not all his work inspires, for it must be said that he fails in tasks which the ordinary woodworker would take care to get right first. His joints are gapped, his mouldings are splintered and hairy, you can see his pencil-marks, and even the exterior of West Wood House bears unmistakable traces of an aborted window.

You would, however, be foolish to sneer

● *The 35in-high Camberwell Bakeries, despite their loving detail, are strictly a fantasy emporium. Note the crusty timber loaves and exquisite graphics*

before attempting to understand what David is up to; for his painterly eye, and his dedication, have enabled him to achieve subtle effects — succeeding where many a woodworker has never even tried. ∎

miniaturist, but an artist who has found himself inexorably drawn from two dimensions into three.

Born in 1939, he went to Sutton and Cheam School of Art and studied painting at Camberwell Art School, and much of his woodworking has taken the form of picture-frames. These are no ordinary affairs of mitred mouldings, however, but carved and even architectural pieces which on the whole display a truly sculptural approach, a superb sense of proportion and a trained eye for decorative detail. Not only that: West Wood House is only the most ambitious of a series of commissions which have established David as one of a kind — notably exact replicas of grand houses, shrunk for their owners' delight and designed as jewel-boxes, money-boxes and the like.

He is fascinated by emblems, allusions and the sense of mystery, and it's no accident that his frames tend to suggest porticos, doorways and windows into other worlds. 'The Spode Set' is a miniature stage which extends from proscenium arch right back into a landscape with a fantastical ruin. Peer into the basement of West Wood, too, and at once you're in the servants' quarters:

● *Left: The 'Westminster Barge', David West's version of British politics, is peopled when full with a crew of quirky allegorical figures ranging from the Chief Whips (hefty wrestlers – with whips) to a corgi on the throne*

'flagstones', tiled scullery, pine floorboards, long dim corridor and all. A time machine could perform no better — the impression is total.

And impressions are David West's overriding concern. From a distance, his pieces

● *The painting is called 'Cinderella, well that's who she said she was'. It displays David West's love of pattern, as its frame betokens his feel for architecture*

**All photos Fischer Fine Art**

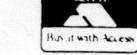
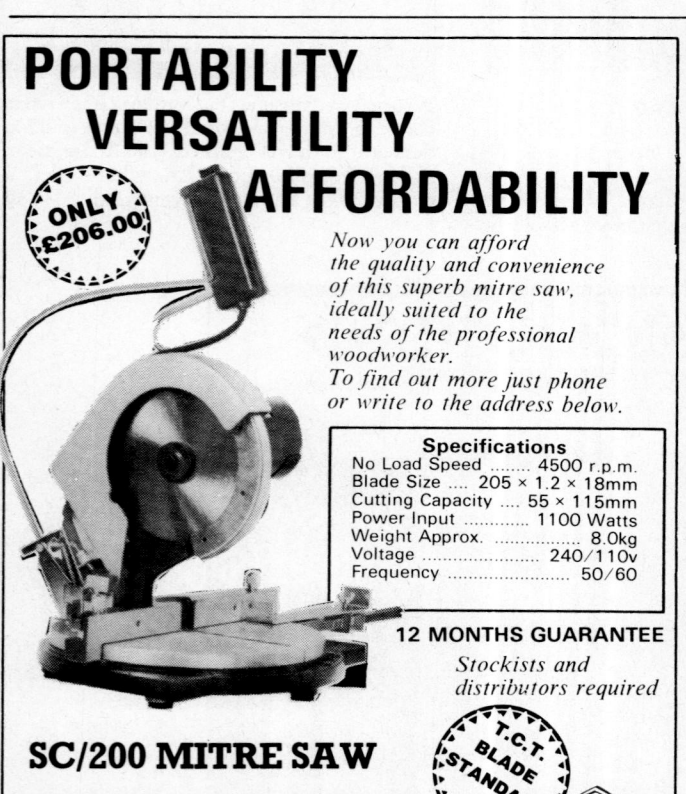

**Prices quoted are those prevailing at press date and are subject to alteration due to economic conditions**

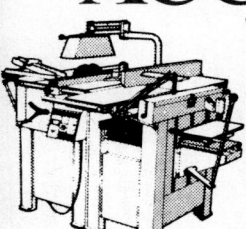

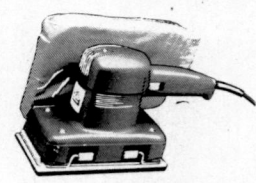
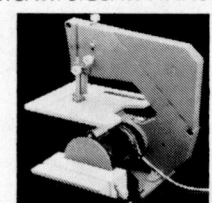

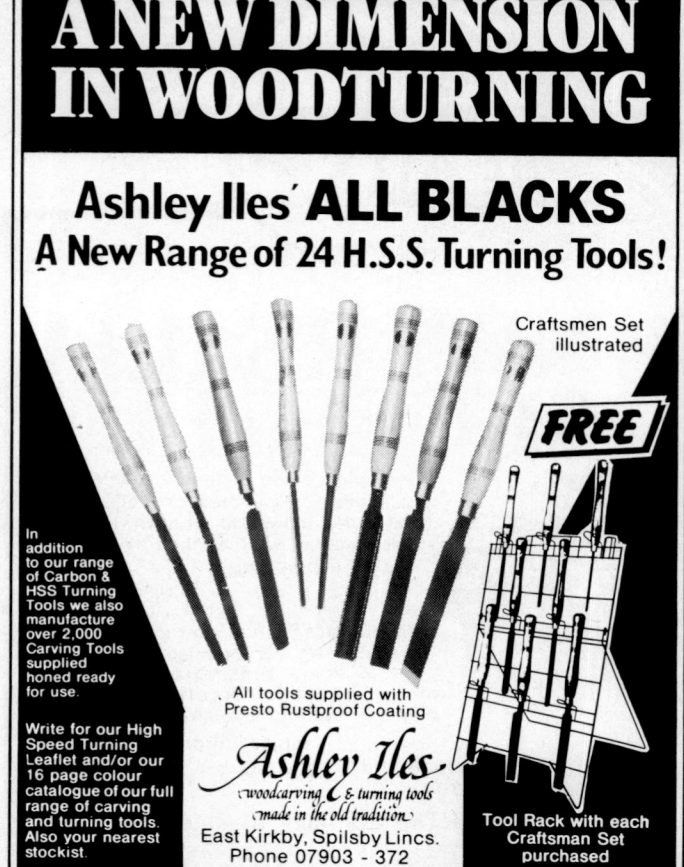
Prices quoted are those prevailing at press date and are subject to alteration due to economic conditions

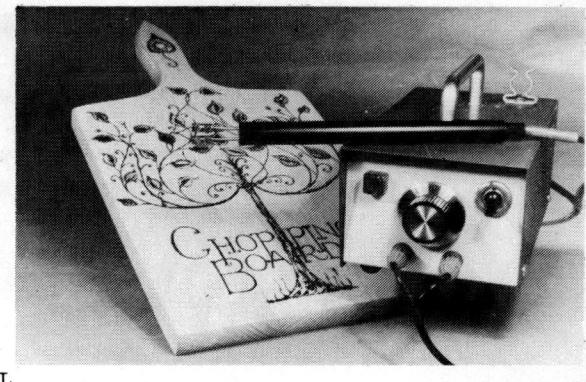

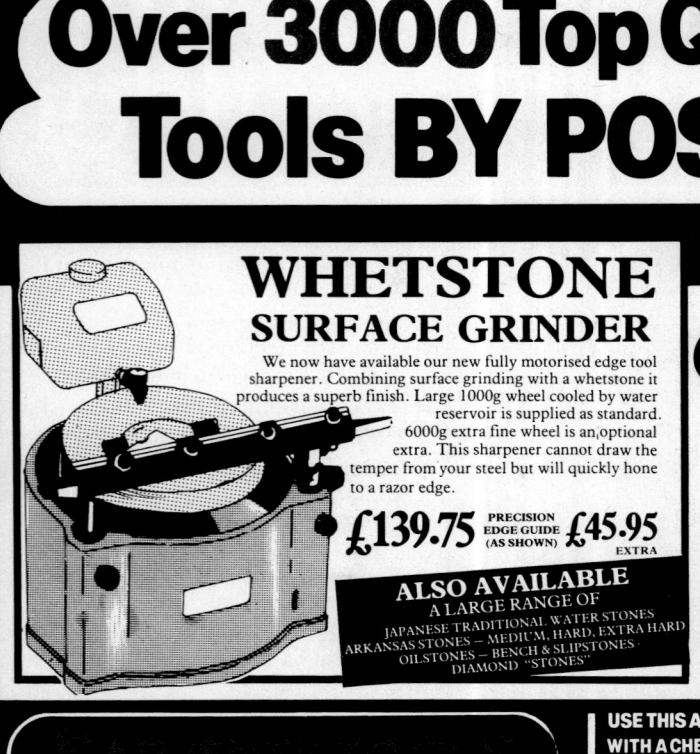

Prices quoted are those prevailing at press date and are subject to alteration due to economic conditions

# The softer option

Vic Taylor completes his guide to modern upholstery with a detailed look at working in foam

**P**olyether foam is produced on highly sophisticated equipment by reacting various chemicals together. The result is a flexible cellular material which 'breathes', and is light and very resilient.

The key to using it correctly is to choose the correct density. This is generally expressed as the weight in kilograms per cubic metre — $kg/m^3$.

Another important feature is thickness. Here you must think of the base on which the foam is to be used. On the simplest form of base — a rigid board — the foam will obviously have to provide all the comfort and resilience, so the thickest cushions will be required. Firm grades need to be at least 90mm (3½in) thick, while softer grades usually need a minimum of 120mm (4¾in) when used for seating.

On many forms of sprung or elastic-webbing supports, however, these thicknesses can be reduced. Firm grades need only be to 70 or 80mm (2¾ or 3¼in) thick,

**Fig. 1**

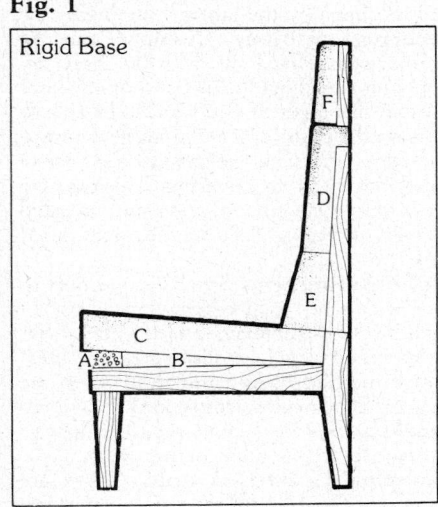

Rigid Base

and softer grades 100mm (4in) provided the frame rails are not in direct contact with the cushion. If necessary, avoid such contact by padding or modifying the base. Hessian webbing, slatted bases and shell chairs should be treated as solid bases.

## Laminating

Foam varies not only in density but also in softness — and denser does not always mean harder. Where thickness becomes a problem in relation to design, you can

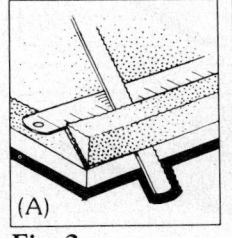

(A)　(B)

**Fig. 2**

laminate different hardnesses together. A 120mm (4¾in) cushion, for instance, can be reduced to 100mm (4in) by laminating 70mm (2¾in) of a soft grade with 30mm (1¼in) of a firmer grade. Such combinations can also be used with convertible furniture for sleeping and sitting; the soft grade provides surface comfort in the lightly loaded sleeping position, and the firmer grade prevents undue compression during use as a seat.

The wide range of different grades can be fabricated to give many combinations and overcome many upholstery problems. Cushions can be domed to prevent the effect of cover-stretch; cushion sides can be stiffened to give crisp cover lines and maintain shapes; arm pads can be designed to prevent 'bottoming' from the point of the elbow; head-rests can be made very soft but with firmer edges. Supersoft grades can be utilised as a wrapping, or for a complete cushion, when a very soft, plump look is required.

## Cutting and covering

Though thick slabs of foam are not easy to cut neatly, you should be able to achieve a satisfactory result with a fine-toothed

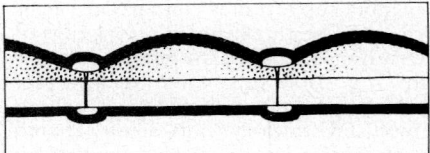

**Fig. 3**

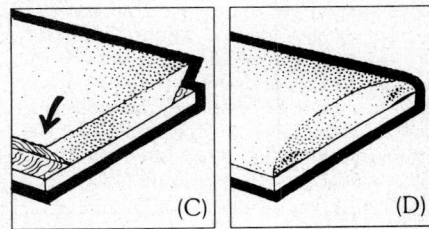

(C)　(D)

**Fig. 4**

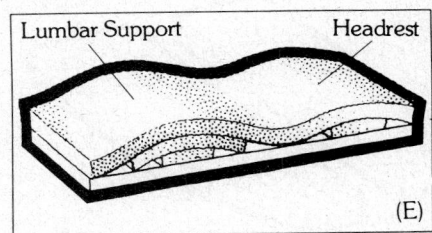

Lumbar Support　Headrest

(E)

**Fig. 5**

hacksaw blade or a really sharp, long, cook's knife. But the best tool for the job is an electric carving-knife, which will give you a professional-looking finish.

Always cut the foam slightly oversize, but make the fabric covers to exact finished dimensions. This will put the foam permanently under slight compression, ensuring clean lines and minimising wrinkles. For example, a mattress should be about 20mm (¾in) oversize in length and about 15mm (⅝in) in width, while most cushions need about 5mm (³⁄₁₆in) in both length and width.

Heavy fabrics will not give crisp lines when used on softer grades of foam, which should therefore be covered with light-weight materials. In particular, avoid foam-backed fabrics, which tend to grip the foam cushion and thus make fitting difficult.

Use a proper upholstery adhesive for

bonding foam to itself or to other surfaces — two excellent ones are Dunlop Thixofix, and Copydex. For sticking large cushions to solid bases, spread the adhesive round the edges of both surfaces in a band about 40mm (1⅝in) wide. Where two large sheets of foam are to be stuck together, reinforce the outer bands of adhesive with criss-cross strips applied at random over the area.

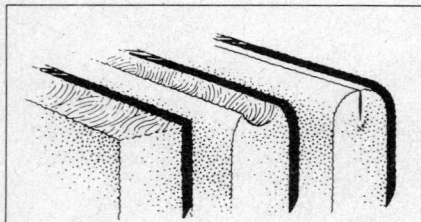

Fig. 6

## Special techniques

**Load-bearing in seating** In fig.1 you can see how various grades are used to get maximum support plus comfort on a chair with a rigid seating base. The front edge of the cushion support is the vital point to get right. If possible you should use a strip of 'chipfoam' (a reconstituted type), about 50mm (2in) thick at A; its density should be about 65kg, which is the softest grade for a chipfoam. Dunlopillo make a range of seven grades from 65kg to 230kg. The wedge-shaped piece shown at B should be a medium-density foam, about 31kg/m³. Two-thirds of the body-weight rests on the seat cushion C, and this should be about 32kg/m³; the back cushion D, however, has a much lighter load to carry, and its density could be about 18kg/m³. A lumbar support E is advisable, too; this should always be a

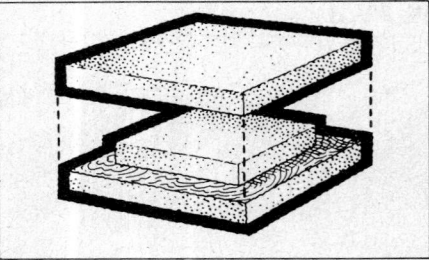

Fig. 8

little harder than the higher part of the back, and a density of about 31kg/m³ is recommended.

**Cutting squares and curves** Methods are shown in fig.2. The edge of a bench and a steel straight-edge can be used as guides when making vertical or angled cuts, as at A. To cut circles or other curved shapes, you will need two templates of hardboard or stiff cardboard. Sandwich the foam between them, secure the whole thing with a length of wire, and cut round the templates (B).

**Buttoning** For buttoned cushions or chair-backs use a layer of soft foam, 30mm

Fig. 9

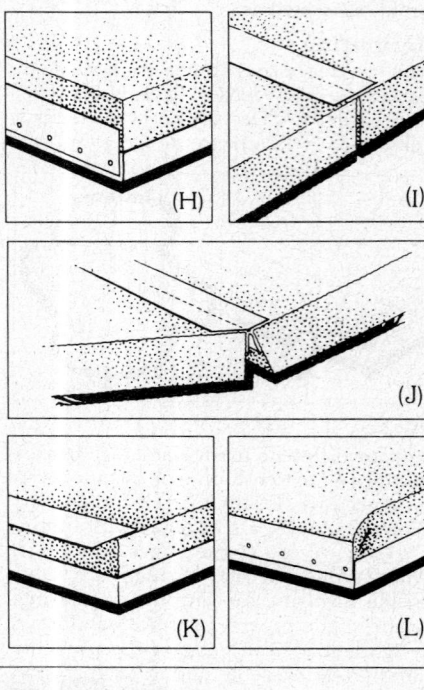

(1⅛in) thick, over the appropriate firmer grade. In the case of a bedhead, as in fig.3, a 40mm (1½in)-thick soft layer stuck to the hardboard or plywood back is all that's needed, as shown here. By the way, latex foam is unsuitable for buttoning.

**Padded backs and seats** Chamfer the edges of the foam and glue the chamfered sides to the base as at C, fig.4, and this will form the shape shown at D. Curved supports for the back and head can be created by employing the flexibility of the material. Glued together as flat slabs, pieces of foam will form the shape E when fixed into position as a frame and webbing, or on a solid panel, as in fig. 5.

**Rounded edges** Apply adhesive to the edges of the cushion, allow it to become tacky, and then pinch the edges together: see fig. 6.

**Shaped units** These should be accurately cut from a paper or card template, carefully made from the shape of the frame or base supporting them. The window seat F and

Fig. 10

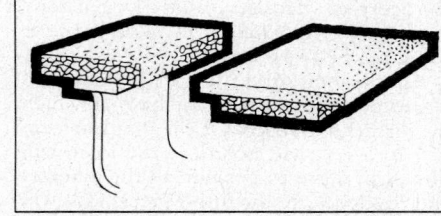

Fig. 11

the boat mattress G in fig. 7 are examples.

**Domed shapes** To make deep-domed chair cushions, use two pieces of foam, each being half the finished thickness, and sandwich between them a piece 30mm (1³⁄₁₆in) thick and 90mm (3½in) smaller all round. Glue the outer pieces around the edges, and the material will be pulled into a domes shape by the fabric covering.

**Securing cushions** Cushions can be permanently fixed to a solid base by applying a 40mm (1⅝in) band of adhesive around the edges. If you want to be able to remove the cushion at any time, glue tape to the edges and tack the tape to the base H ready for the fabric covering. Tape can also be used to form hinges I and J, and rounded edges K and L: fig. 9 shows the methods for this.

**Upholstering arms** Fig. 10 shows how to deal with a top load-bearing area; a pad of high-density foam may be used with a softer wrap-round. Fig. 11 illustrates an alternative method using lamination, as in the seat for the smaller arm type. The overlap should always be taken over the edges to protect the cover from undue wear.

**Covering firm-based units** These are shown in fig. 12, and are self-explanatory.

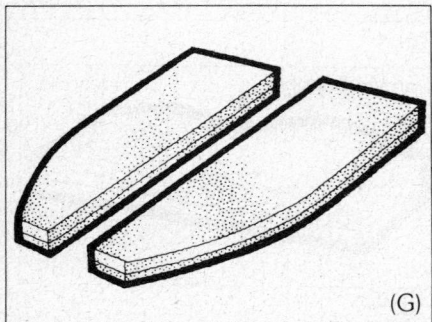

Fig. 7

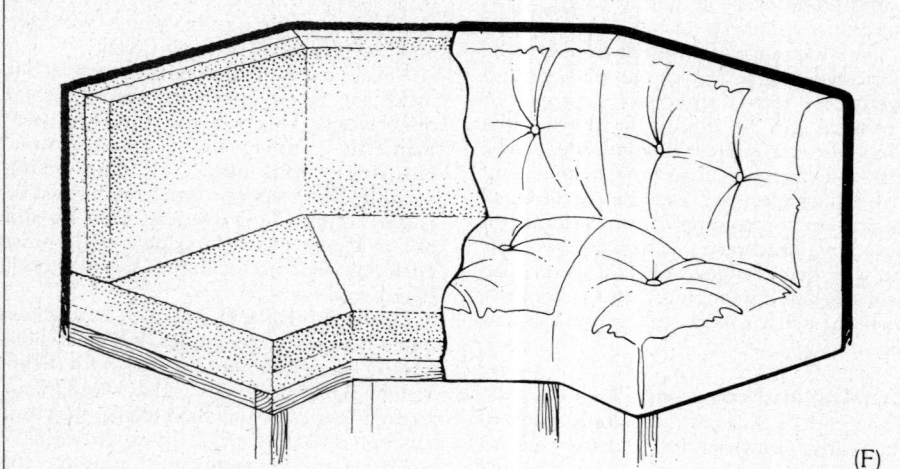

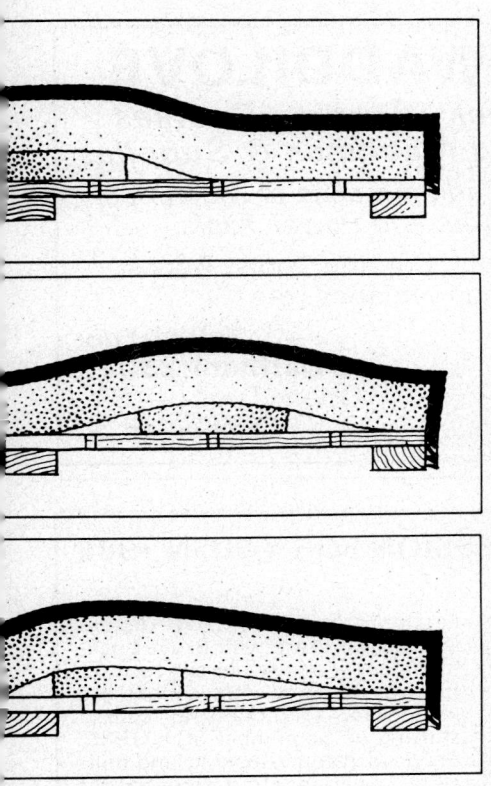

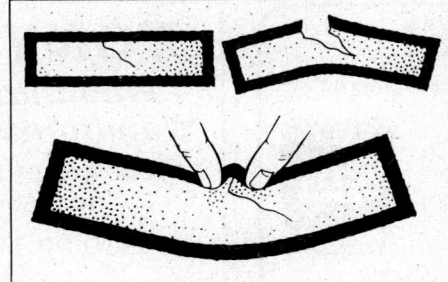

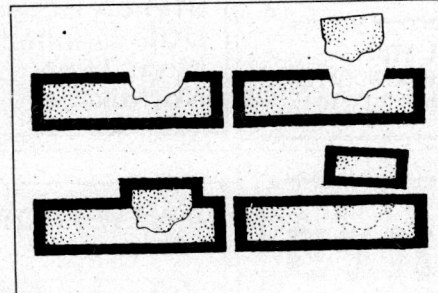

**Fig. 14**

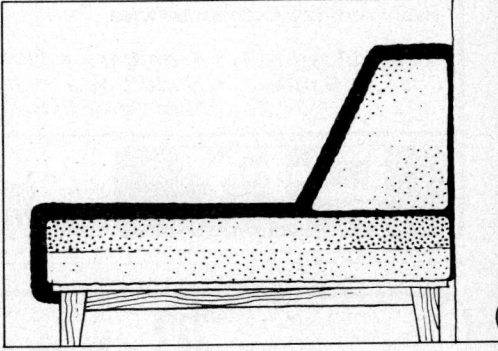

foam to the top surface of the mattress.

The mattress for a convertible bed/seating unit is shown in fig. 16. If the mattress is to be used for seating as well as sleeping, it is preferable to make the outer 40mm (1⅝in) of each edge from a firmer grade of foam (N). This will help it to keep its shape.

**Fig. 17**

(P

A loose back-rest is an easy way of turning a bed into a settee for daytime use (fig. 17). For this to be comfortable, the rest P should reduce the width of the mattress to about 500mm (19¾in), and be firm enough to offer good support to the back.

● My thanks are due to Dunlopillo Ltd for their great help with the text and illustrations for this article. Advice, information and even foam samples are readily available from their Retail Sales Dept, Pannal, Harrogate, North Yorks HG3 1JL, tel. (0423) 872411.

The British Rubber Manufacturers' Association is at 90-1 Tottenham Court Rd, London W1P 0BR. ■

**Fig. 12**

Where non-breathing material such as PVC or hide is to be used as a cover, vents are essential to permit the passage of air. Drilling holes 20mm (¾in) in diameter, spaced at 150mm (6in) centres, is a satisfactory method. On hard bases, an underpad for doming can, by positioning and thickness, give a variety of styles, as in fig. 13.

### Repairs

These are illustrated in fig. 14. To repair holes, cut the end of a piece of offcut foam roughly to shape with scissors. Glue it into the hole, leaving the spare foam projecting until the glue is dry, then cut it off flush with a sharp knife or fine saw. To repair tears, hold the tear open, apply glue, keep it open until the glue is dry, and then press together.

### Making your own bed

If you are making your own base for a foam mattress it is extremely important to

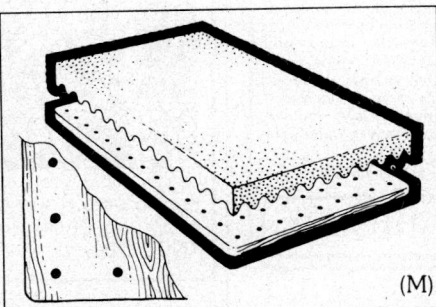

**Fig. 15**

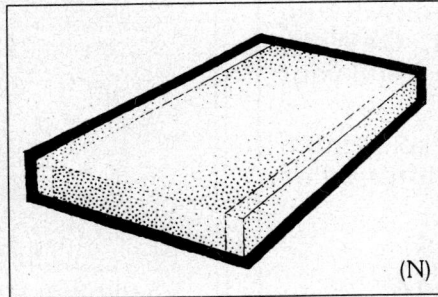

**Fig. 16**

provide proper ventilation so that the mattress can breathe. A slatted base should have a minimum of 20mm (¾in) between the slats, and a rigid board base should have 20mm (¾in)-diameter holes drilled at 150mm (6in) centres. With any type of rigid base there should ideally be a 50mm (2in) layer of profile-cut foam (the type used for camping mattresses, which has indentations on the underside giving an eggbox effect) upholstered on to the base, profiled side down as in fig. 15 (M). This helps the air to circulate properly under the mattress, and also to prevent any possibility of condensation forming on the underside. Any type of fabric can be used to cover the base as long as it is air-permeable.

For a rigid base you need a thick mattress — the minimum recommended thickness 120mm (4¾in), and the minimum density 28kg/m³. If a softer feel is preferred, this can be achieved by laminating a layer of soft

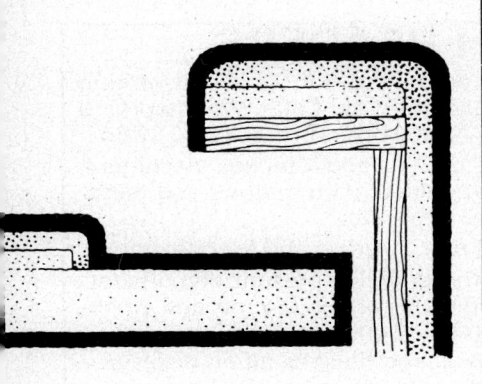

**Fig. 13**

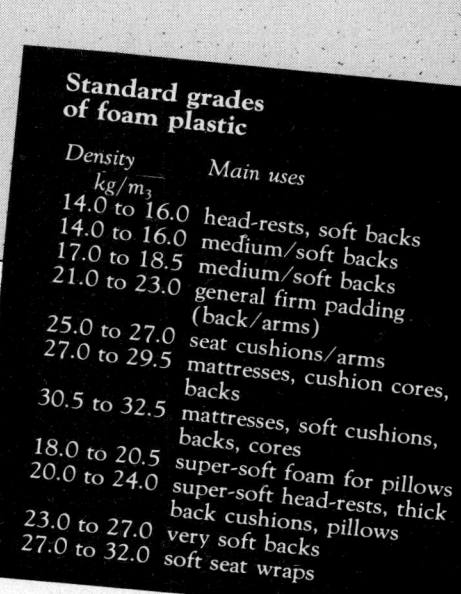

**Standard grades of foam plastic**

| Density kg/m³ | Main uses |
|---|---|
| 14.0 to 16.0 | head-rests, soft backs |
| 14.0 to 16.0 | medium/soft backs |
| 17.0 to 18.5 | medium/soft backs |
| 21.0 to 23.0 | general firm padding (back/arms) |
| 25.0 to 27.0 | seat cushions/arms |
| 27.0 to 29.5 | mattresses, cushion cores, backs |
| 30.5 to 32.5 | mattresses, soft cushions, backs, cores |
| 18.0 to 20.5 | super-soft foam for pillows |
| 20.0 to 24.0 | super-soft head-rests, thick back cushions, pillows |
| 23.0 to 27.0 | very soft backs |
| 27.0 to 32.0 | soft seat wraps |

Prices quoted are those prevailing at press date and are
subject to alteration due to economic conditions

# ·shopguide·

## EMCO DEALERS

### BUCKINGHAMSHIRE

**HIGH WYCOMBE** Tel. (0494)
ISAAC LORD LTD 22221
185 DESBOROUGH ROAD **KE**

Open: Mon-Fri 8.00 a.m.-5.00 p.m.
Saturday 9.00 a.m.-5.00 p.m.
H.P.W.D.A.

### CAMBRIDGESHIRE

**CAMBRIDGE** Tel. (0223) 63132
D. MACKAY LTD. **E★**
BRITANNIA WORKS, EAST ROAD

Open: Mon.-Fri. 8.30 a.m.-1 p.m./2.00-
5.00 p.m. Sat. 8.30 a.m.-1.00 p.m.
H.P.W.D.T.CS.MF.A.BC.

### CORNWALL

**TRURO** Tel. (0872) 71671
TRURO POWER TOOLS **E★**
30 FERRIS TOWN

Open Mon.-Sat. 8.00 a.m.-12.30 p.m./
1.30 p.m.-5.00 p.m.
H.P.W.WM.D.CS.MF.A.BC.

### DERBYSHIRE

**DERBY** Tel. (0332) 41862
HAZLEHURSTS LTD. **E★**
LONDON ROAD AND CANAL STREET

Open: Mon.-Sat. 8.30 a.m.-5.30 p.m. (retail)
Mon.-Fri. 8.00 a.m.-5.00 p.m. (trade)
H.P.W.MF.A.BC.

### DEVON

**BRIXHAM** Tel. (08045) 4900
WOODCRAFT SUPPLIES **E★**
4 HORSE POOL STREET

Open: Mon.-Sat. 9.00 a.m.-6.00 p.m.

H.P.W.A.D.MF.CS.BC.

### GLOUCESTERSHIRE

**CHELTENHAM** Tel. (0242) 39099
HAMBURY MACHINE SERVICES **E★**
UNIT 14, MALMESBURY ROAD
Open: Mon.-Fri. 9.00 a.m.-5.30 p.m.
Sat. 9.30 a.m.-12.00 p.m.

W.WM.P.D.

### HERTFORDSHIRE

**HITCHIN** Tel. (0462) 4177
ROGER'S **KE**
47 WALSWORTH ROAD
Open: Monday-Saturday
9.00 a.m.-5.30 p.m.
(Closed all day Wednesday)
H.P.W.WM.D.CS.MF.BC.

### HUMBERSIDE

**GRIMSBY** Tel. Grimsby (0472)
58741 Hull (0482) 26999
J. E. SIDDLE LTD. (Tool Specialists) ★
83 VICTORIA STREET
Open: Mon-Fri 8.30 a.m.-5.30 p.m.
Sat. 8.30 a.m.-12.45 p.m. & 2 p.m.-5 p.m.
H.P.A.BC.W.WMD.

### LANCASHIRE

**ROCHDALE** Tel. (0706) 342123/
C.S.M. TOOLS 342322
4-6 HEYWOOD ROAD **E★**
CASTLETON
Open: Mon-Sat 9.00 a.m.-6.00 p.m.
Sundays by appointment
W.D.CS.A.BC.

**PRESTON** Tel. (0772) 52951
SPEEDWELL TOOL COMPANY **E★**
62-68 MEADOW STREET PR1 1SU
Open: Mon.-Fri. 8.30 a.m.-5.30 p.m.
Sat. 8.30 a.m.-12.30 p.m.

H.P.W.WM.CS.A.MF.BC.

### LONDON

**FULHAM** Tel. (01-385) 5109
I. GRIZZARD LTD. **E**
84a-b LILLIE ROAD, SW6 1TL
Open: Mon-Sat 9.00-5.30 p.m.
Half day Thursday

H.P.A.BC.W.CS.WM.D.

**LONDON** Tel. (01-263) 1536
THOMAS BROTHERS (01-272) 2764
798-804 HOLLOWAY ROAD, N19
Open: Mon.-Fri. 8.30 a.m.-5.30 p.m. Thurs.
8.30 a.m.-1 p.m. Sat. 9 a.m.-5 p.m.

H.P.W.WM.CS.MF.BC.

### MIDDLESEX

**RUISLIP** Tel. (08956) 74126
ALLMODELS ENGINEERING LTD. **E★**
91 MANOR WAY

Open: Mon-Sat 9.00 a.m.-5.30 p.m.
H.P.W.A.D.CS.MF.BC.

### OXFORDSHIRE

**CROWMARSH** Tel. (0491) 38653
MILL HILL SUPPLIES **E★**
66 THE STREET
Open: Mon.-Fri. 9.30 a.m.-5.00 p.m.
Thurs. 9.30 a.m.-7.00 p.m.
Sat. 9.30 a.m.-1.00 p.m.
P.W.D.CS.MF.A.BC.

### SUFFOLK

**IPSWICH** Tel. (0473) 40456
FOX WOODWORKING **KE★**
142-144 BRAMFORD LANE
Open: Tues., Fri., 9.00 a.m.-5.30 p.m.
Sat. 9.00 a.m.-5.00 p.m.

H.P.W.WM.D.A.B.C.

### WEST SUSSEX

**WORTHING** Tel. (0903) 38739
W. HOSKING LTD (TOOLS & **KE★**
MACHINERY)
28 PORTLAND RD, BN11 1QN
Open: Mon.-Sat. 8.30 a.m.-5.30 p.m.
Closed Wednesday
H.P.W.WM.D.CS.A.BC.

### TYNE & WEAR

**NEWCASTLE** Tel. (0632) 320311
HENRY OSBOURNE LTD. **E★**
50-54 UNION STREET

Open: Mon-Fri 8.30 a.m.-5.00 p.m.

H.P.W.D.CS.MF.A.BC.

### WEST MIDLANDS

**BIRMINGHAM** Tel. (021-554) 5177
ROTAGRIP **E★**
16 LODGE ROAD, HOCKLEY
Open: Mon.-Fri. 9.00 a.m.-5.00 p.m.
Sat. 9.00 a.m.-12.00 p.m.

H.P.W.CS.A.BC.T.MF.

### YORKSHIRE

**SHEFFIELD** Tel. (0742) 441012
GREGORY & TAYLOR LTD **E**
WORKSOP ROAD
Open: 8.30 a.m.-5.30 p.m.
Monday-Friday
8.30 a.m.-12.30 p.m. Sat.
H.P.W.WM.D.

**GIVE YOUR BUSINESS A
BOOST — DON'T LEAVE IT
CHANCE, 'PHONE JASON
ON 01-437 0699 TO
ADVERTISE**

## ALL OTHER DEALERS

### AVON

**BATH** Tel. Bath 64513
JOHN HALL TOOLS ★
RAILWAY STREET

Open: Monday-Saturday
9.00 a.m.-5.30 p.m.
H.P.W.WM.D.A.BC.

**BRISTOL** Tel. (0272) 741510
JOHN HALL TOOLS LIMITED ★
CLIFTON DOWN SHOPPING CENTRE
WHITELADIES ROAD
Open: Monday-Saturday
9.00 a.m.-5.30 p.m.
H.P.W.WM.D.A.BC.

**BRISTOL** Tel. (0272) 629092
TRYMWOOD SERVICES
2a DOWNS PARK EAST, (off North View)
WESTBURY PARK
Open: 8.30 a.m.-5.30 p.m. Mon. to Fri.
Closed for lunch 1.00-2.00 p.m.
P.W.WM.D.T.A.BC.

**BRISTOL** Tel. (0272) 667013
FASTSET LTD
190-192 WEST STREET
BEDMINSTER
Open: Mon.-Fri. 8.30 a.m.-5.00 p.m.
Saturday 9.00 a.m.-1.00 p.m.
H.P.W.WM.D.CS.A.BC.

**KEY: H HANDTOOLS**

**KEY: P POWER TOOLS**

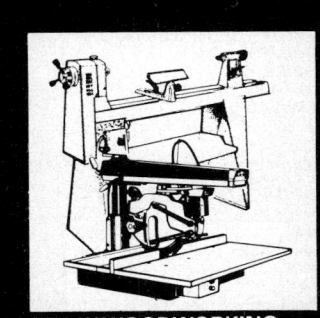

**KEY: W WOODWORKING
MACHINERY**

# shop guide

## BEDFORDSHIRE

**BEDFORD**  Tel. (0234) 59808
BEDFORD SAW SERVICE
39 AMPTHILL ROAD  **K**

Open: Mon.-Fri. 8.30-5.30
Sat. 9.00-4.00
H.P.A.BC.W.CS.WM.D.

**READING**  Tel. Reading 661511
WOKINGHAM TOOL CO. LTD.
99 WOKINGHAM ROAD

Open: Mon-Sat 9.00 a.m.-5.30 p.m.
Closed 1.00-2.00 p.m. for lunch
H.P.W.WM.D.CS.A.BC.

## BERKSHIRE

**COOKHAM**  Tel. (06285) 20350
CHURCH'S TIMBER
STATION HILL

Open: Mon-Sat 8.30 a.m.-5.30 p.m.
Wed 8.30 a.m.-1.00 p.m.
H.P.W.T.CS.MF.A.

**READING**  Tel. (0734) 591361
HOME CARE CENTRE
26/30 KING'S ROAD

Open: Monday-Saturday
9.00 a.m.-5.30 p.m.
H.P.W.D.A.WM.BC.

**READING**  Tel. Littlewick Green
DAVID HUNT (TOOL  2743
MERCHANTS) LTD  ★
KNOWL HILL, NR. READING
Open: Monday-Saturday
9.00 a.m.-5.30 p.m.
H.P.W.D.A.BC.

## BUCKINGHAMSHIRE

**SLOUGH**  Tel. (06286) 5125
BRAYWOOD ESTATES LTD  ★
158 BURNHAM LANE

Open: 9.00 a.m.-5.30 p.m.
Monday-Saturday
H.P.W.WM.CS.A.

**HIGH WYCOMBE**  Tel. (0494)
SCOTT SAWS LTD.  24201/33788
14 BRIDGE STREET  ★

Mon.-Sat. 8.30 a.m.-6.00 p.m.

H.P.W.WM.D.T.CS.MF.A.BC.

**MILTON KEYNES**  Tel. (0908)
POLLARD WOODWORKING  641366
CENTRE  ★
51 AYLESBURY ST., BLETCHLEY
Open: Mon-Fri 8.30-5.30
Saturday 9.00-5.00
H.P.W.WM.D.CS.A.BC.

## CAMBRIDGESHIRE

**CAMBRIDGE**  Tel. (0223) 247386
H. B. WOODWORKING  **K**
105 CHERRY HINTON ROAD
Open: 8.30 a.m.-5.30 p.m.
Monday-Friday
8.30 a.m.-1.00 p.m. Sat.
H.P.W.WM.D.CS.A.

**PETERBOROUGH**  Tel. (0733)
WILLIAMS DISTRIBUTORS  64252
(TOOLS) LIMITED  **K**
108-110 BURGHLEY ROAD
Open: Monday to Friday
8.30 a.m.-5.30 p.m.
IH.P.A.W.D.WH.BC.

## CHESHIRE

**NANTWICH**  Tel. Crewe 67010
ALAN HOLTHAM  **K**★
THE OLD STORES TURNERY
WISTASON ROAD, WILLASTON
Open: Tues.-Sat. 9.00 a.m.-5.30 p.m.
Closed Monday
P.W.WM.D.T.C.CS.A.BC.

## CLEVELAND

**MIDDLESBROUGH**  Tel. (0642)
CLEVELAND WOODCRAFT  813103
(M'BRO), 38-42 CRESCENT ROAD  **K**

Open: Mon-Sat 9.15 a.m.-5.30 p.m.

H.P.T.A.BC.W.WM.CS.D.

## CORNWALL

**FALMOUTH**  Tel. (0326) 76555
WOODSTOCK (HARDWOODS) LTD.
PONSHARDEN

Open: Mon-Fri 8.30 a.m.-5.30 p.m.
Sat. 9.00 a.m.-1.00 p.m.
T.

**EXETER**  Tel. (0392) 73936
WRIDES TOOL CENTRE
147 FORE STREET

Open: 9.00 a.m.-5.30 p.m.
Wednesday 9.00 a.m.-1.00 p.m.
H.P.W.WM.A.

## HELSTON

**HELSTON**  Tel. Helston (03265) 4961
SOUTH WEST  Truro (0872) 71671
POWER TOOLS  Launceston
MONUMENT ROAD  (0566) 3555
**K**
H.P.W.WM.D.CS.A.

**PLYMOUTH**  Tel. (0752) 330303
WESTWARD BUILDING SERVICES  ★
LTD., LISTER CLOSE, NEWNHAM
INDUSTRIAL ESTATE, PLYMPTON
Open: Mon-Fri 8.00 a.m.-5.30 p.m.
Sat. 8.30 a.m.-12.30 p.m.
H.P.W.WM.D.A.BC.

## CUMBRIA

**CARLISLE**  Tel. (0228) 36391
W. M. PLANT
ALLENBROOK ROAD
ROSEHILL, CA1 2UT
Open: Mon.-Fri. 8.00 a.m.-5.15 p.m.
Sat. 8.00 a.m.-12.30 noon
P.W.WM.D.CS.A.

## ESSEX

**ILFORD**  Tel. (01-
CUTWELL TOOLS LTD.  ★
774-776 HIGH ROAD

Mon.-Fri. 9.00 a.m.-5.00 p.m.
and also by appointment.
P.W.WM.A.D.CS.

## DERBYSHIRE

**BUXTON**  Tel. (0298) 871636
CRAFT SUPPLIES  **K**★
THE MILL, MILLERSDALE

Open: Mon-Sat 9.00 a.m.-5.00 p.m.

H.P.W.D.T.CS.A.BC.

**LEIGH ON SEA**  Tel. (0702)
MARSHAL & PARSONS LTD.  710404
1111 LONDON ROAD  **EK**

Open: 8.30 a.m.-5.30 p.m. Mon-Fri
9.00 a.m.-5.00 p.m. Sat.
H.P.W.WM.D.CS.A.

## GLOUCESTERSHIRE

**TEWKESBURY**  Tel. (0684)
TEWKESBURY SAW CO. LTD.  293092
TRADING ESTATE, NEWTOWN  **K**

Open: Mon-Fri 8.00 a.m.-5.00 p.m.
Saturday 9.30 a.m.-12.00 p.m.
P.W.WM.D.CS.

**SOUTHAMPTON**  Tel. (0703)
H.W.M.  776222
THE WOODWORKERS
303 SHIRLEY ROAD, SHIRLEY
Open: Tues-Fri 9.30 a.m.-6.00 p.m.
Sat 9.30 a.m.-4.00 p.m.
H.P.W.WM.D.CS.A.BC.T.

## HAMPSHIRE

**ALDERSHOT**  Tel. (0252) 334422
POWER TOOL CENTRE  **K**★
374 HIGH STREET
Open Mon-Fri 8.30 a.m.-5.30 p.m.
Sat 8.30 a.m.-4.00 p.m.

H.P.W.WM.D.A.BC.CF.MF.

**SOUTHAMPTON**  Tel. (0703)
POWER TOOL CENTRE  332288
7 BELVIDERE ROAD  **K**★
Open Mon.-Fri. 8.30-5.30

H.P.W.WM.D.A.BC.CS.MF.

**PORTSMOUTH**  Tel. (0705)
EURO PRECISION TOOLS LTD  667332
259/263 LONDON ROAD, NORTH END  ★
**E**
Open: Mon-Fri 9.00 a.m.-5.30 p.m.
Sat. 9.00 a.m.-1.00 p.m.
H.P.W.WM.D.A.BC.

## HERTFORDSHIRE

**ENFIELD**  Tel. (01-363) 2935
GILL & HOXBY LTD.  **K**
133-137 ST. MARKS ROAD EN1 1BB

Mon.-Sat. 8.30 a.m.-6.00 p.m.
Early closing Wednesday 1.00 p.m.
H.P.W.WM.T.CS.A

**WATFORD**  Tel. (0923) 48434
HOME CARE CENTRE  ★
20 MARKET STREET
WATFORD, HERTS
Open: 9.00 a.m.-5.30 p.m.
Mon-Sat
H.P.W.A.WM.BC.D.

## KENT

**BIDDENDEN**  Tel. (0580) 291555/7
BRITISH GATES & TIMBER
BENENDEN ROAD  ★
Open: Mon-Fri 7.30 a.m.-5.30 p.m.
Saturday 8.30 a.m.-midday
(not Bank Holiday weekends)
H.T.CS.MF.

**MAIDSTONE**  Tel. (0622) 50177
SOUTH EASTERN SAWS (Ind) LTD  ★
COLDRED ROAD,
PARKWOOD INDUSTRIAL ESTATE
Open: Mon-Fri 8.00-5.00pm
Sat. 9.00-12.00
B.C.W.CS.WM.PH.

**MATFIELD**  Tel. Brenchley
LEISURECRAFT IN WOOD  (089272)
'ORMONDE,' MAIDSTONE RD.  2465
TN12 7JG
Open: Mon-Sun
9.00 a.m.-5.00 p.m.
W.WM.D.T.A.

**WYE**  Tel. (0233) 813144
KENT POWER TOOLS LTD.
UNIT 1, BRIAR CLOSE
WYE, Nr. ASFORD

H.P.W.WM.D.A.CS.

## LANCASHIRE

**LANCASTER**  Tel. (0524) 32886
LILE TOOL SHOP  **K**
43/45 NORTH ROAD
Open: Monday to Saturday
9.00 a.m.-5.30 p.m.
Wed 9.00 a.m.-12.30 p.m.
H.P.W.D.A.

**BURY**  Tel. (061 764 6769)
HOUSE OF HARBRU  ★
101 CROSTONS ROAD
ELTON
Open: Mon.-Fri. 9.00 a.m.-5.00 p.m.
Send 2 × 1st class stamps for catalogue
MF.

## LEICESTERSHIRE

**HINCKLEY**  Tel. (0455) 613432
J. D. WOODWARD & CO. (POWER  ★
TOOL SPECIALISTS)
THE NARROWS, HINCKLEY
Open: Monday-Saturday
8.00 a.m.-6.00 p.m.
H.P.W.WM.D.CS.A.BC.

## LONDON

**ACTON**  Tel. (01-992) 4835
A. MILLS (ACTON) LTD  ★
32/36 CHURCHFIELD ROAD W3 6ED
Open: Mon-Fri 9.00 a.m.-5.00 p.m.
Saturdays 9.00 am.-1.00 p.m.
H.P.W.WM.

**WEMBLEY**  Tel. 904-1144
ROBERT SAMUEL LTD.  (904-1147
7, 15 & 16 COURT PARADE  after 4.00)
EAST LANE, N. WEMBLEY  ★
Open Mon.-Fri. 8.45-5.15; Sat. 9-1.00
Access, Barclaycard, AM Express, & Diners
H.P.W.CS.E.A.D.

**LONDON**  Tel. (01-567) 2922
G. D. CLEGG & SONS
83 UXBRIDGE ROAD, HANWELL W7 3ST
Mon-Sat 9.15 a.m.-5.30 p.m.
Closed for lunch 1.00-2.00p.m.
Early Closing 1.00 p.m. Wed.
H.P.A.W.WM.D.CS.

**ONLY £11 PER ISSUE TO
ADVERTISE ON THESE PAGES**

**LONDON**  Tel. (01-636) 7475
BUCK & RYAN LTD  ★
101 TOTTENHAM COURT ROAD W1P 0DY

Open: Mon.-Fri. 8.30 a.m.-5.30 p.m.
Saturday 8.30 a.m.-4.00 p.m.
H.P.W.WM.D.A.

**NORBURY**  Tel. (01-679) 6193
HERON TOOLS & HARDWARE LTD
437 STREATHAM HIGH ROAD SW16
Open: Mon-Fri 8.30 a.m.-5.30 p.m.
Wednesday 8.30 a.m.-1.00 p.m.
Sat. 9.00 a.m.-1.00 p.m.
H.P.W.A.

# shopguide

## GREATER MANCHESTER

**WOOLWICH** Tel. (01-854) 7767/8
A. D. SHILLMAN & SONS LTD
108-109 WOOLWICH HIGH STREET
SE18
Open: Mon-Sat
8.30 p.m.-5.30p.m.
H.P.W.CS.A.

**MANCHESTER** Tel. (061 789) 0909
TIMMS TOOLS ★
102-104 LIVERPOOL ROAD
PATRICROFT M30 0WZ
Weekdays 9.00 a.m.-5.30 p.m.
Sat. 9.00 a.m.-1.00 p.m.
H.P.A.W.

## MERSEYSIDE

**LIVERPOOL** Tel. (051-207) 2967
TAYLOR BROS (LIVERPOOL) LTD K
195-199 LONDON ROAD
LIVERPOOL L3 8JG
Open: Monday to Friday
8.30 a.m.-5.30 p.m.
H.P.W.WM.D.A.BC.

## MIDDLESEX

**HOUNSLOW** Tel. (01-570) 2103/5135
Q.R. TOOLS LTD
251-253 HANWORTH ROAD
Open: Mon-Fri 8.30 a.m.-5.30 p.m.
Sat. 9.00 a.m.-1.00 p.m.
P.W.WM.D.CS.A.

## NORFOLK

**GT. YARMOUTH** Tel. (0493) 850388
ANGLIA POWER TOOLS
3 DENESIDE, NR30 2HL
Open: Monday to Saturday
8.30 a.m. 5.30 p.m.
H.P.W.D.CS.A.

**KINGS LYNN** Tel. (0553) 2443
WALKER & ANDERSON (Kings Lynn) LTD. K
WINDSOR ROAD, KINGS LYNN
Open: Monday to Saturday
7.45 a.m.-5.30 p.m.
Wednesday 1.00 p.m. Saturday 5.00 p.m.
H.P.W.WM.D.CS.A.

**KINGS LYNN** Tel. (0760) 23073
TONY WADDILOVE ★
STATION HOUSE
LITTLE DUNHAM, (Nr. SWAFFHAM)
Open Tues.-Sat. 9.00 a.m.-5.30 p.m.
H.P.W.DT.CS.A.BC.

**NORWICH** Tel. (0603) 898685
NOROLK SAW SERVICES
DOG LANE, HORSFORD
Open: Monday to Friday
8.00 a.m.-5.00 p.m.
Saturday 8.00 a.m.-12.00 noon
H.P.W.WM.D.CS.A.

## NORTHAMPTONSHIRE

**NORWICH** Tel. (0603) 400933
WESTGATES WOODWORKING Tx
61 HURRICANE WAY, 975412
NORWICH AIRPORT INDUSTRIAL ESTATE
Open: 9.00 a.m.-5.00 p.m. weekdays
9.00 a.m.-12.30 Sat.
P.W.WM.D.BC. K

**SWAFFHAM** Tel. (0760) 23073
TONY WADDILOVE, ★
STATION HOUSE,
LITTLE DUNHAM, KINGS LYNN
Tuesday-Saturday 9.00 a.m.-6.00 p.m.
H.P.W.DT.CS.A.BC.

**NOTTINGHAM** Tel. (0602) 225979
POOLEWOOD and 227064/5
EQUIPMENT LTD. (06077) 2421 after hrs
5a HOLLY LANE, CHILLWELL
Open: Mon-Fri 9.00 a.m.-5.30 p.m.
Sat. 9.00 a.m. to 12.30 p.m.
P.W.WM.D.CS.A.BC.

**RUSHDEN** Tel. (0933) 56424
PETER CRISP OF RUSHDEN KE★
7 HIGH STREET NN10 9JR
Open: Mon-Fri 8.30 a.m.-12.30 p.m./
1.30 p.m.-5.30 p.m. Sat. 8.30 a.m. 5.30 p.m.
Early closing Thurs. 1.00 p.m.
H.P.W.MF.D.A.BC.

**WITNEY** Tel. (0993) 3885
TARGET TOOLS (SALES, & 72095 OXON
**TARGET TOOLS** HIRE & REPAIRS) ★
SWAIN COURT
STATION INDUSTRIAL ESTATE
Open: Mon.-Sat. 8.00 a.m.-5.00 p.m.
24 hour Answerphone
BC.W.M.A.

## SHROPSHIRE

**TELFORD** Tel. Telford (0952) 48054
ASLES LTD
VINEYARD ROAD, WELLINGTON EK★
Open: Mon. Fri. 8.30 a.m.-5.30 p.m.
Saturday 8.30 a.m.-4.00 p.m.
H.P.W.WM.D.CS.BC.A.

## SOMERSET

**TAUNTON** Tel. (0823) 85431
JOHN HALL TOOLS ★
6 HIGH STREET
Open Monday-Saturday
9.00 a.m.-5.00 p.m.
H.P.W.WM.D.CS.A.

**TAUNTON** Tel. Taunton 79078
KEITH MITCHELL ★
TOOLS AND EQUIPMENT
66 PRIORY BRIDGE ROAD
Open Mon-Fri 8.30 a.m.-5.30 p.m.
Saturday 9.00 a.m.-4.00 p.m.
H.P.W.WM.D.CS.A.BC.

## STAFFORDSHIRE

**TAMWORTH** Tel. (0827) 56188
MATTHEWS BROTHERS LTD. K
KETTLEBROOK ROAD
Open: Mon-Sat 8.30 a.m.-6.00 p.m.
Demonstrations Sunday mornings by
appointment only
H.P.WM.D.T.CS.A.BC.

## SURREY

**FARNHAM** Tel. (0252) 725427
A.B.E. CO. LTD. (Quick Hire) ★
GOODS SHED
STATION APPROACH, FARNHAM
Open Mon.-Fri. 8.00 a.m.-5.30 p.m.
Sat. 8.00 a.m.-5.30 p.m.
H.P.W.D.CS.A.BC.

## SUSSEX

**BOGNOR REGIS** Tel. (0243) 863100
A. OLBY & SON (BOGNOR REGIS) LTD.
"TOOLSHOP," BUILDERS MERCHANT K
HAWTHORN ROAD
Open: Mon-Thurs 8 a.m.-5.15 p.m. Fri.
8 a.m.-8 p.m. Sat 8 a.m.-12.45 p.m.
H.P.W.WM.D.T.C.A.BC.

## EAST SUSSEX

**ST. LEONARD'S-ON-SEA** Tel.
DOUST & MONK (MONOSAW)-(0424)
25 CASTLEHAM ROAD 52577
Open: Mon.-Fri. 8.00 a.m.-5.30 p.m.
Most Saturdays 9.00 a.m.-1.00 p.m.
H.P.W.WM.D.CS.A.

## TYNE & WEAR

**NEWCASTLE UPON TYNE** Tel.
J. W. HOYLE LTD. (0632) 617474
CLARENCE STREET NE2 1YJ K★
Open: Mon-Fri 8.00 a.m.-5.00 p.m.
Saturday 9.00 a.m.-4.30 p.m.
H.P.A.BC.W.CS.WM.D.

## WEST MIDLANDS

**WOLVERHAMPTON** Tel. (0902) 58759
MANSAW SERVICES
SEDGLEY STREET K★
Open: Mon.-Fri. 9.00 a.m.-5.00 p.m.
H.P.W.WM.A.D.CS.

## YORKSHIRE

**BOROUGHBRIDGE** Tel. (09012) 2370
JOHN BODDY TIMBER LTD.
FINE WOOD & TOOL STORE ★
RIVERSIDE SAWMILLS
Open: Mon.-Thurs. 8.00 a.m.-6.00 p.m.
Fri. 8.00am-5.00pm Sat. 8.00am-4.00pm
H.P.W.WM.D.T.CS.MF.A.BC.

**CLECKHEATON** Tel. (0274) 872861
SKILLED CRAFTS LTD. ★
34 BRADFORD ROAD
Open: 9.00 a.m.-5.00 p.m. Monday
Saturday Lunch 12.00 a.m.-1.00 p.m.
H.P.A.W.CS.WM.D.

**KEIGHLEY** Tel. (0535) 663325
EUROMAIL (TOOLS) ★
PO BOX 13
108 EAST PARADE
Open 9.15 a.m.-5.00 p.m.
Not Tuesday but inc. Saturday
H.P.W.A.BC.

**HARROGATE** Tel. (0423) 66245/
MULTI-TOOLS 55328
158 KINGS ROAD K★
Open: Monday to Saturday
8.30 a.m.-6.00 p.m.
H.P.W.WM.D.A.BC.

**HUDDERSFIELD** Tel. (0484)
NEVILLE M. OLDHAM 641219/(0484)
UNIT 1 DALE ST. MILLS 42777
DALE STREET, LONGWOOD ★
Open: Mon-Fri 8.00 a.m.-5.30 p.m.
Saturday 9.30 a.m.-12.00 noon
P.W.WM.D.A.BC.

**LEEDS** Tel. (0532) 574736
D. B. KEIGHLEY MACHINERY LTD. ★
VICKERS PLACE, STANNINGLEY
PUDSEY LS2 86LZ
Mon.-Fri. 9.00 a.m.-5.00 p.m.
Sat. 9.00 a.m.-1.00 p.m.
P.A.W.WM.CS.BC.

**LEEDS** Tel. (0532) 790507
GEORGE SPENCE & SONS LTD.
WELLINGTON ROAD
Open: Monday to Friday
8.30 a.m.-5.30 p.m.
Saturday 9.00 a.m.-5.00 p.m.
H.P.W.WM.D.T.A.

**THIRSK** Tel. (0845) 22770
THE WOOD SHOP ★
TRESKE SAWMILLS LTD.
STATION WORKS
Open: Seven days a week 9.00-5.00
T.H.MF.BC.

## SCOTLAND

**EDINBURGH** Tel. (031 337) 5555
THE SAW CENTRE ★
38 HAYMARKET TERRACE
HAYMARKET
Open: 8.30 a.m.-5.30 p.m.
Monday-Saturday
H.P.W.WM.D.CS.A.

**GLASGOW** Tel. (041 429) 4374/)
THE SAW CENTRE 4444, Telex: 777886
600 EGLINGTON STREET E★
G5 9RR
Open: Mon-Fri 8.00 a.m.-5.30 p.m.
Saturday 9.00 a.m.-1.00 p.m.
H.P.W.WM.D.CS.A.

**PERTH** Tel. (0738) 26173
WILLIAM HUME & CO K
ST. JOHN'S PLACE
Open: Monday to Saturday
8.00 a.m.-5.30 p.m.
8.00 a.m.-1.00 p.m. Wednesday
H.P.A.BC.W.CS.WM.D.

**TAYSIDE** Tel: (05774) 293
WORKMASTER POWER TOOLS LTD. ★
DRUM, KINROSS
Open Mon.-Sat. 8.00 a.m.-8.00 p.m.
Demonstrations throughout Scotland by
appointment
P.W.WM.D.A.BC.

## WALES

**CARDIFF** Tel. (0222) 396039
JOHN HALL TOOLS LIMITED ★
CENTRAL SQUARE
Open: Monday to Saturday
9.00 a.m.-5.30 p.m.
H.P.W.WM.D.A.BC.

**CARDIFF** Tel. (0222) 30831
F. W. MORGAN & 25562
(CANTON) LTD., 129-133
COWBRIDGE RD EAST
CANTON
Mon-Sat 8.00-5.00 Sun 9.30-12.30
H.P.T.CS.A.BC.

**CARDIFF** Tel. (0222) 595710
DATAPOWER TOOLS LTD,
MICHAELSTON ROAD,
CULVERHOUSE CROSS
Open: Mon.-Fri. 8.00 a.m.-5.00 p.m.
Sat. 9.00 a.m.-1.00 p.m.
H.P.W.WM.D.A.

**CARMARTHEN** Tel. (0267) 237219
DO-IT-YOURSELF SUPPLY K
BLUE STREET, DYFED
Open: Monday to Saturday
9.00 a.m.-5.30 p.m.
Thursday 9.00 a.m.-5.30 p.m.
H.P.W.WM.D.T.CS.A.BC.

**SWANSEA** Tel. (0792) 55680
SWANSEA TIMBER & PLYWOOD CO. LTD.
57-59 OXFORD STREET ★
Open: Mon to Fri 9.00 a.m.-5.30 p.m.
Sat. 9.00 a.m.-1.00 p.m.
H.P.W.D.T.CS.A.BC.

# Classified Advertisements

## FOR SALE

**LACE BOBBIN TURNING BLANKS** in unusual and exotic hardwoods and ivory. SAE for list: J. Ford, 5 Squirrels Hollow, Walsall WS7 8YS.

FOR ALL SUPPLIES
FOR THE
## Craft of Enamelling
ON METAL
Including
**LEAD-FREE ENAMELS**

PLEASE SEND 2 × 10p STAMPS
FOR FREE CATALOGUE, PRICE
LIST AND WORKING
INSTRUCTIONS

**W. G. BALL LTD.**
ENAMEL MANUFACTURERS

Dept. W. LONGTON
STOKE-ON-TRENT
ST3 1JW

### MUSICAL MOVEMENTS
• LOVE STORY • LARAS THEME • SPEAK SOFTLY LOVE • FUR ELISE • FEELINGS • FASCINATION • IMPOSSIBLE DREAM • MUSIC BOX DANCER • LA POLOMA • THE EMPEROR WALTZ • TRY TO REMEMBER • ROMEO AND JULIET •
Complete with screws and spring mechanism **£2.50** inc. p&p. 20 or more of one tune ordered **£1.50** each. Available from:
The Jewel Box Shop,
112 Pentonville Road, London N1 9JB.

**KITCHEN WORKTOPS?** Perfect butt and scribe joints using router and simple jigs. Plans £3.50 from Chris Harris, 11 The Square, Upper Cwmbran, Gwent. NP44 5AQ.

**SPERBER 52"** planking chain saw mill — £1,450. Stihl 076 motors, 2 slabbing rails 20' and 8', accessories, very good condition. Telephone Ilminster (0460) 54109 evenings.

**'MAGNOLIA'** treadle mitre machine, spare blades. Perfect condition. Backing board cutter. Selection of frame mouldings — £500 o.n.o. Hertford 550789.

**MYFORD COMBINATION CHUCK** £20. Child coil grip chuck £25 o.n.o. little used. Telephone 0326 270358.

### HAND CARVED
'Adam Style' Mantle motifs in Mahogany — Example 10" × 5" centre lamp and two side pieces.
Send S.A.E. for details and quotation. Your own design quoted for if required.
**SAM NICHOLSON**
22 Lisnagarvey Drive, Lisburn,
Co. Antrim, N. Ireland.
Phone Lisburn 3510

**QUALITY TOOLS.** 9" Carpenters Squares (R.R.P. £8.50) £3.75 + 40p postage. Mortice/Marking Gauges £2.99 + 30p postage. Free details. Midas Marketing, 3 River Lane, Brompton-on-Swale, Richmond, N. Yorkshire, DL10 7HH.

### SOLID OAK CHAIRS

Sanded, ready for staining and polishing. From **£35** each.
Also tables, tops only, kits or assembled.
Country Tables & Chairs
The Cottage, St. Nicolas,
The Cottage, St. Nicholas
La., Chislehurst, Kent.
Tel: 01-467-1192

# FOR SALE

ONE MARKETPLACE OF 30,000 POTENTIAL BUYERS IN ONE OF THE MOST SUCCESSFUL CLASSIFIED SECTIONS AVAILABLE.

**JUST LOOK**
AT WHO ADVERTISES HERE AND

**THINK**
ABOUT WHY THEY DO SO.
RING JASON ON
**01-437-0699**

MORTISERS; TENNONERS; SPINDLES; PLANERS; BANDSAWS; LATHES; CROSSCUTS; ROUTERS; SANDERS; DRILLS? YOU CAN CERTAINLY SEE ALL CLASSES AND TYPES OF MACHINES HERE.

WE ARE MAIN STOCKING AGENTS FOR:
MULTICO; ELU; SEDGWICK; KITY;
SCHEPPACH; INCA; CORONET; DeWALT;
WARCO; DOMINION; HITACHI; STARTRITE;
TREND; ASHLEY ILES; SORBY.

*2 DAY EXHIBITION OF WOODWORKING MACHINERY APRIL 12th & 13th MANUFACTURERS DEMONSTRATORS PRESENT*

*CALL US ABOUT WOODTURNING LESSONS*

*WOODCARVING LESSONS (See our Swiss carving tools)*
*ALWAYS HELPFUL, KNOWLEDGEABLE, GOOD SERVICE AT:*
## CLEVELAND WOODCRAFT
38-42 CRESCENT ROAD, MIDDLESBROUGH.
TEL: (0642) 813103

**D.I.Y.**
ESTABLISHED 1889
# THE SAW CENTRE
LIMITED

## HAS THE EDGE
Hire or buy machinery or power tools from our extensive stock:
 Elu DeWALT makita Black & Decker
- SCHEPPACH ■ STARTRITE ■ GRIGGIO
- VOLPATO ■ SEDGWICK
- TUNGSTEN CARBIDE TIPPED SAW BLADES
- DISPOSABLE BANDSAW BLADES

**SAWN OFF PRICES**

HEAD OFFICE & MAIN WORKS:
EGLINTON TOLL GLASGOW G5 9RP. TEL: 041-429 4444/4374
OPEN: MON - FRI 8 - 5.30 SAT 9 -1. TELEX: 777886 SAWCO G.

ALSO AT: 38 HAYMARKET TERRACE EDINBURGH EH12 5JZ.
TEL: 031-337 5555. OPEN: MON - SAT 8.30 - 5.30.

Have you seen the latest catalogue of
## Bygones
See Display advertisement

### Alan Holtham
The Old Stores Turnery, Wistaston Road,
Willaston, Nantwich, Cheshire.
Tel: 0270 67010

### BANDSAW BLADES
Skip tooth type with hardened teeth. Prices include VAT. P+P 1—3 Blades **90p**, 4-6 Blades **£1.70**, Over 6 post free.

| Model | | Price inc. VAT |
|---|---|---|
| Birch | 1/4" | £3.62 |
| DeWalt BS1310 | 3/8" | £3.74 |
| Kity 612 | 1/2" | £3.91 |
| Lazzari P32 | 5/8" | £4.77 |
| Bandit | | |
| Startrite 301 | | |
| Black & Decker | 1/4" | £2.99 |
| DeWalt 100 | 3/8" | £3.11 |
| | 1/2" | £3.22 |
| Burgess | 1/4" | £3.11 |
| | 3/8" | £3.25 |
| Inca | 1/4" | £3.45 |
| | 3/8" | £3.57 |
| | 1/2" | £3.62 |
| | 5/8" | £4.20 |
| Startrite 352 | 1/4" | £4.54 |
| | 3/8" | £4.60 |
| | 1/2" | £4.77 |
| | 5/8" | £5.87 |
| | 3/4" | £6.15 |
| Willow | 1/4" | £4.03 |
| | 3/8" | £4.08 |
| | 1/2" | £4.20 |

Prices quoted are those prevailing at press date and are subject to alteration due to economic conditions.

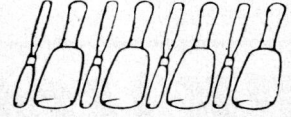
KINDLY MENTION 'WOODWORKER' WHEN REPLYING TO ADVERTISEMENTS

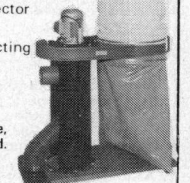

Prices quoted are those prevailing at press date and are subject to alteration due to economic conditions.

Prices quoted are those prevailing at press date and are subject to alteration due to economic conditions

# Profit from the use of Woodworking Machinery

A ONE DAY 'Wood Machining Course' to arm yourself with the necessary knowledge to enable you to:

- Make the correct choice of machine for YOUR purposes
- Use that particular machine to gain maximum efficiency, safely
- Open up new opportunities for you to profit from a small workshop

| | | |
|---|---|---|
| LEEDS/BRADFORD | Rawdon Machine Sales | 3rd April, 1985 |
| MIDDLESBROUGH | Cleveland Woodcraft | 11th April, 1985 |
| PERTH | Wm. Hume & Co. | 18th April, 1985 |
| READING | Sarjents Tools Stores | 25th April, 1985 |
| TELFORD | Asles Ltd. | 1st May, 1985 |
| CARMARTHEN | DIY Supply | 8th May, 1985 |
| HITCHIN | Roger's | 16th May, 1985 |
| TEWKESBURY | Tewkesbury Saw Co. | 23rd May 1985 |
| HELSTON | South West Power Tools | 13th June, 1985 |
| TELFORD | Asles Ltd. | 19th June, 1985 |
| CARMARTHEN | DIY Supply | 26th June, 1985 |

 Telephone now for place availability and full timetable.
Rawdon Machine Sales Ltd., 6 Acorn Park, Charlestown, Shipley, West Yorks BD17 7SW.
Telephone 0274 597826

P.S. These are NOT exhibitions or demonstrations of a particular manufacturer's machinery, but a general eight-hour 'HANDS ON' instruction course showing the techniques of using machinery. You will find your time well spent.

---

WOODCARVING, two-day courses. Residential and non-residential. Enquiries: The Knapp, Armscote, Stratford-upon-Avon. Tel: Ilmington 247 (evenings).

WOODTURNING COURSES DAY/EVENING Personal tuition by Registered Turner in well equipped workshop. Telephone John Golder, Heath Hayes 79137 (Staffs.).

CABINET MAKING: intensive two-day courses in basic bench techniques in Yorkshire dales workshop. Phone Wensleydale 22703 for details.

## KEITH ROWLEY
**(Demonstrator for Coronet tool company and member of the Guild of Master Craftsmen).**
Woodturning courses in the heart of D. H. Lawrence Country by professional turner. Weekend courses available. Coronet lathes and woodturning accessories available. 1 days tuition free if you buy your Coronet lathe through me.
S.A.E. for details or phone.
Keith Rowley, 68 Moorgreen, Newthorpe, Notts.     Tel: Langley Mill 716903

## WOODCARVING AND SCULPTURE
The best short residential courses in basic sculpture, woodcarving, modelling and sketching, etc. are taught by HENRY MOORE'S former assistant PETER HIBBARD at the OLD SCHOOL ARTS WORKSHOP, MIDDLEHAM, LEYBURN, NORTH YORKS. DL8 4QG.

Beginners welcome — S.A.E. for details.

FURNITURE MAKING, furniture renovation, woodturning. 2 day courses by professional furniture maker in country workshop. My knowledge is yours. Details: SAE Hugh A. Keegan, 12 Doves Lane, Moulton, Northants. Tel: (0604) 43706 (evenings).

---

## A VIDEO WOODTURNING COURSE
"TEACH YOURSELF TURNING" is a new tutorial video, ideal for the home craftsman, schools, colleges and other students. It presents a complete introductory course on Woodturning and includes a booklet of course notes and photographs, based on my recent series in Woodworking Crafts Magazine. The colour video runs for a full 1½ hours, during which I demonstrate and discuss the following topics:
1) The lathe and its accessories
2) Woodturning tools
3) Tool sharpening
4) Cutting techniques (spindle and bowl work)
5) Chuck work
6) Drilling boring and finishing
To order — simply send your cheque for £35.00 (including postage and package) to:
**Roger Holley, 'The Hollies' 11 Summer Leaze Park, Yeovil, Somerset BA20 2BP.**
**Tel: (0935) 25521**
giving your full name and address, in block capitals please, and state whether you require VHS or Betamax video format.
Delivery 2/3 weeks.

## REG SLACK
Practical Woodturning courses. 1-3 days duration. Max 2 students. Professional tutor backed by 30 years full time experience. Closed Thursday, Friday. Open all other days including Sunday.
*For details write or phone.*
Saracens Head Coaching House Yard, Brailford, Derbyshire (0335) 60829.
Evenings (0283) 701662.
*Also Woodturning Supplies.*

---

## DEMONSTRATIONS

# W. HOSKING
### (TOOLS, MACHINERY)

*TWO-DAY DEMONSTRATIONS*
**28 PORTLAND ROAD, WORTHING, SUSSEX.**
**Telephone: 0903 38739**

Be sure and attend on Friday & Saturday 12th and 13th April, where you can see the latest machines from **EMCO, BOSCH, DE-WALT, INCA, KITY and CORONET.**

*Refreshments available.*

*Hours: Fri. 10.30 a.m. to 5.30 p.m. Sat. 10.30 a.m. to 4.00 p.m.*

---

## RE: KERNOW GARDEN BUILDINGS LTD. (IN LIQUIDATION)

### WILSON WAY, POOL INDUSTRIAL ESTATE, REDRUTH, CORNWALL

*SALE BY AUCTION OF THE VALUABLE WOODWORKING PLANT, MACHINERY AND STOCK IN TRADE ON*

### TUESDAY, 26th MARCH, at 10.30 a.m.

*and including:*
Plant and machinery: Wadkin FB moulder with 6 heads and power feed, Stenner 48 in band re-saw, Wadkin CW 1610 cross-cut with roller feeds, Wadkin WS/12/32 cross-cut, two Wadkin Bursgreen BSW rip-saws, two De-Walt cross-cuts, Robinson chain/chisel mortiser, Wadkin Tenoner (EC335), Sedgwick 12in. planer/thicknesser, Wadkin Bursgreen BRA cross-cut, extraction plant by air-plants, Brinscombe with 9' 6" cyclone fan, Lancer-Boss side loader, 3 power chain hoists, air staplers, drills etc., saw grinders, jigs hand power tools, office furniture and equipment.
Stock: 14 various garden sheds and sectional buildings, large quantity planed timber (deal and red cedar), nails, fasteners etc., etc.

*Viewing: Monday 25th March (10am to 4pm)*
*Catalogues (£1) from the auctioneers:*

Chartered Surveyors, Alphin Brook Road, Exeter.
Tel: 0392-50441/Telex 42621

# Then...

## Max Burrough

## Continuing the absorbing tale of an old-time apprenticeship

Buying tools always caused me a great deal of anguish, the reason being that when you are earning 10 or 12s a week and giving three-quarters of it to mother there is not a lot left for tools. Also, I was terrified of asking for something and then finding that I had insufficient money. The shame and disgrace would have been unbearable.

There were three ironmongers in the town; all stocked tools, but each seemed to have his own individual interests. My oilstone came from a shop near the workshop where there was usually a good selection of stones. Unfortunately, when I called, the lugubrious individual who kept the premises did not have an India fine grade in stock and sold me a combination, i.e. a combined coarse and fine stone. When I returned to the workshop, Bert pounced on my purchase for his inspection and approval; on discovering that I had not bought according to his instructions, he practically went berserk. I returned the stone, much to my embarrassment, and waited for the new order of fine stones to arrive. (Whenever this man was caught with any item out of stock, his excuse was always the same. 'I've got the invoice, but the goods is up the station.') It is only fair to add that I have always had a small carborundum combined coarse and fine stone, $4 \times 1 \times \frac{1}{2}$in, and found it invaluable.

Eventually I made the momentous decision to order a set of chisels — a big deal for a boy in those days, and one not to be undertaken lightly, for tools were bought to last a lifetime. I walked a few hundred yards up the street to a shop owned and run by a charming old couple. For me they epitomised the Victorian age; their mode of dress complemented their quiet, precise speech and their anxiety to oblige their customers' every wish and whim. Always referred to as Tintack, the husband was well known for his ability to supply the smallest tacks, nails, screws, pins, hinges and fastenings that Birmingham had ever produced, and he and his wife seemed to delight in searching their hundreds of small boxes to find just what one required.

Proudly, I marched into Tintack's and announced that I wanted a full set of chisels. He knew me, of course, as I had been in many times before for myself and for the firm. (On one never-to-be-forgotten occasion, he had asked quietly if I would please return to my employer and say that

he would supply nothing more until his account had been settled. We both found this acutely embarrassing. I returned and told the Boss and, for once, he could have murdered me. I quite enjoyed the reversal of roles.) Yes, said Tintack, he would be delighted to order a set of chisels. Much to my surprise, he knew exactly what I required.

'A long $1\frac{1}{4}$in paring chisel, and a full set from $\frac{1}{8}$in up to $1\frac{1}{4}$in. With boxwood handles?'

'Of course,' I said. 'A good make, too. Marples?'

No, they would not be Marples; they would be from Christopher Johnson, the firm that had made all those knives — and he pointed to a showcase containing what seemed to be hundreds of pocket-knives, all different. No finer steel could be obtained anywhere, I was assured, and if at any time the chisels caused dissatisfaction I could return them and he would exchange or refund my money.

How well that man knew his trade, for the chisels have been giving pleasure and satisfaction for over 50 years.

Albert and I decided that the time had come to buy our handsaws, and when a favourable opportunity presented itself (when we knew the Boss would be away for a few hours) we walked higher up the town, to the third ironmonger, who we knew always stocked a large number of saws.

Old man Ford, as he was always called, assured us that he had just the saws we wanted, and handed us two made by Spear & Jackson of Sheffield. We said they had to be Disstons. 'Why?' He didn't have any, Spear & Jackson exported thousands of saws to America every year, and what was good enough for them was good enough for us.

Old man Ford argued, cajoled, wheedled, shouted and swore at us. What did we know about saws? He had been selling saws all his life. I thought of Bert, who had ordered me to buy a Disston and nothing else, and smiled sweetly. At last, when we had made it quite clear that we were adamant and would have nothing else, he promised to order the saws we wanted. When I asked if it were possible to get one with six and a half points to the inch, I thought the poor old man was going to have apoplexy. No, it was *not* possible.

We waited months for those saws, and I am convinced that they came over from America especially. They were worth waiting for. I still have mine now, of course; it must have been used tens of thousands of times and is as good today as the day I

bought it. I doubt whether it has been sharpened more than 10 or 12 times, and the blade is still over 7in wide.

Being a keen and powerful cyclist I thought nothing of 30 miles in an afternoon. Having decided that I must make another important purchase, one Saturday I cycled 16 miles to Exeter. After parking my bike in a friendly garage I walked to the main street and the shop I had decided to visit. When I told the salesman that I wanted a 9×2in iron smoothing-plane, he smartly placed two on the counter and said, 'There you are, young man; take your pick. One is English, the other is American.'

I compared the two planes and studied them closely, for this was a most important decision to make — and, although Record Ridgway tell me that Hamptons first made planes in 1923, this was the first Record plane I had ever seen. The two planes were alike as two peas in a pod; and, while every iron plane in the workshop was a Stanley, the posters exhorted 'Buy British'.

I took them apart while the salesman watched with tolerant amusement. They seemed identical until, on looking again at the soles, I saw that the Stanley had a step underneath the handle's projection, while the Record sloped off smoothly. I bought the Record, and have never regretted it; for some reason, planes produced later do not seem quite the same. The price was 12s 6d. I wouldn't sell that plane today for £200 — it is so good that I rarely use my Norris-type smoother by Slater.

On another visit to the same shop I bought a screwdriver that was displayed in the window, 16in long with a thick brass ferrule and an oval boxwood handle. It was just what I wanted, and I rode home with it (as I had the plane) in the saddle-bag that mother had made for me of offcuts from the Boss's car hood.

Proudly displaying and examining my new acquisition, I was dismayed and horrified to find that the price tag on the handle had been so placed as to cover a small black knot, at least $\frac{1}{4}$in in diameter. How could a firm stoop so low? This was the time of fair play, an Englishman's word was his bond, and so on. I was so annoyed at being deceived, as I thought, that I never entered that shop again until a few months ago.

I can remember, too, when Tich at last bought himself a Stanley 9×2in smoothing-plane. It was the first time anyone had seen the ridiculous tear-shaped hole in the lever cap, and all the men agreed that it seemed an absolutely pointless change. No one liked it, and I still don't. Later, when I was teaching, I bought many iron planes — but always Record, solely because of the lever-cap design. As for the handles on some of the present-day tools, I prefer not to look at them or even think about them.

In the course of time I acquired a good toolkit, buying only three cheap tools — a ratchet brace, a marking-gauge and a hand drill. The first two irritated me every time I used them, and still do. The foreign-made hand drill cost me 3s 9d and has been a lifelong friend, needing only a leather washer between handle and frame. At the time an equivalent double-pinion drill, made in England, cost 5s. In comparison, those I see on sale today are heavy and clumsy, and I wonder who on earth designs them — and for whom. ■

# Letters

## Our open forum — where woodworkers can talk to one another

May I add a little to the rather unfortunate comments of Mr. M. Bulger, who judged the Woodworker Show's clocks entries (WW/Jan)? Surely the objective is to encourage participation? If some entries fall a little short of what is hoped for, the results of the judging tell this: additional words in such a damning vein only tend to dilute the value of the competition to other participants.

● *William Watts and his winning clock (photo Bob Chisman)*

I too saw the clock in question, and feel that the exhibitor could not have intended it to be shown in the condition it presented. I believe the explanation might be that the spotlights used were very powerful, and may have sprung the glued joints. In the case of my own entry, I too was worried about the intensity of the lighting, which blistered my french polish so much that the hood had to be largely re-done on its return to my workshop.

*William Watts, Lydney*

---

I was pleased you singled out my chaise-longue for illustration in 'Design takes its stand' (WW/Jan). But my piece, it must said, is neither laminated nor lacking in ergonomic considerations.

It is in fact fabricated entirely from the humble sheet of plywood. That it should give the impression of a highly expensive laminated structure is, I think, a tribute to this neglected material, illustrating its fantastic versatility and pointing the way for a fresh look at its capabilities.

Ergonomically, it would be difficult to find a chaise-longue more suited to its purpose, tested as it was by construction of

a mock-up prior to finalisation of design. The most desirable angle for the leg-rest was selected, even though this led to considerable difficulty designing a method of joining the components — a difficulty eventually successfully overcome.

Lumbar, spine and neck regions are dealt with by a specially designed roll-down 'duvet' mattress with compartments containing differing densities of material to cater for all three, as well as the legs. This is held in position by a simple sleeve which slips over the top 3in of the chair-back and is shown in your illustration in its 'stored' position, slung from the back of the chaise-longue in its container. All who have tried this chaise-longue attest to its comfort.

*Roy Anderson, Morpeth*

---

David Savage's article on what makes a good workshop (WW/Dec) was very interesting, but unfortunately it had one glaring error. Mr Savage has been told that a no-volt release switch protects the machine in the event of overload. In fact its aim is to prevent re-starting after a power failure.

Imagine a 12in sawbench sitting quietly minding its own business when suddenly the power comes back in and the monster springs to life. The results could prove very dangerous, and even fatal. Hence the no-volt unit. Apart from that — thank you, Mr Savage, for a good series.

*N. R. Tucker, Harare, Zimbabwe*

---

When Luke Hughes extolled Mr Bateman's piled coffins I forbore from writing, confident that you would be deluged with letters from remonstrators. That you only published two leads me to suppose that reader reaction is limited. What on earth is Mr Hughes looking for? A pile of wood that any clown with a tree and a bandsaw could knock together? Doesn't he realise that Picasso wasn't the only great worker who chortled his way to the bank at the expense of his critics? I trust you will look out for more worthwhile material to review in future.

*Richard Lyon, Plymouth*

---

Mr Tildesley may find bevels for splayed work easier to understand (Question box WW/Jan) if he uses the 'direct to material' method. It is also quicker.

Fig. 1 shows a sketch of the junction of

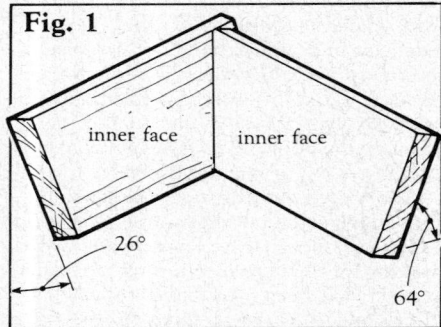

two boards sloping at 64° to the horizontal (26° to vertical). Fig. 2 shows how the face bevel is found; draw a line AB at 64° as shown. Also draw this bevel on the end of the board as at X. Along AB mark off the exact width of the board, as shown, at AC. Square this up to the top edge D. AD is the face cut.

Turn the board over as shown in fig. 3, and from A square a line across to E then down to meet the dotted line F. Draw the face bevel through F to G. Join A to G to find the edge cut.

*James Leiper, Stonehaven*

---

On the question of sharpening saws, Bill Gates was right, of course (WW/Sept). If Mr Whitrick (WW/Dec) draws the procedure over-size, he will find that only ripsaws are sharpened with a 90° angle. The teeth have a totally different action.

*Max Burrough, Colyton*

---

I have come into possession of a lathe of unknown age, and need some help. The only parts missing are the guide and motorised unit, which appears to be of the drill type. The maker's name is REVO: patent no. LO2/02/322, code no. 7/971/BA. Are these manufacturers still in business? What is their address?

*R. Drinkwater, 165 Cirencester Rd, Charlton Kings, Cheltenham, Glos. GL53 8DB*

---

I wonder if any *Woodworker* readers can help with details of how to make a clavichord?

*Richard Wilkinson, 12 Chilbolton Ave, Winchester, Hants.*

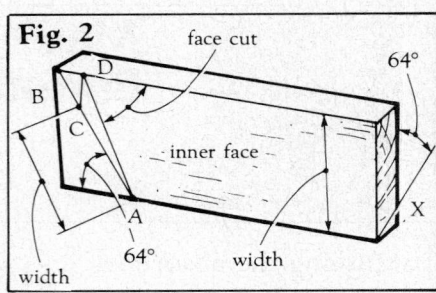

**Fig. 2**

face cut · D · B · C · inner face · A · 64° · 64° · width · width · X

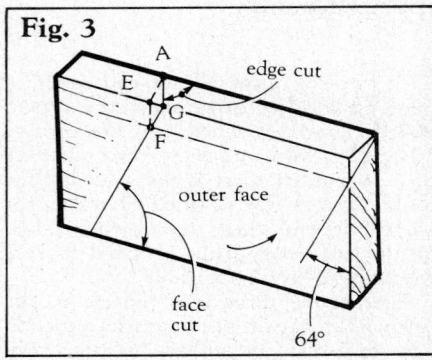

**Fig. 3**

A · edge cut · E · G · F · outer face · face cut · 64°

**Fig. 1**

inner face · inner face · 26° · 64°

# The magazine for the craftsman
## ~ and the aspiring craftsman!

May 1985
Vol. 89
No. 1098

● *A graceful table by Alan Peters (pages 347-9)*

On the cover: Herman (meet his maker on pages 336-8) presents an Alan Peters cabinet (pages 347-9); Bruce Boulter's turnings (pages 360-1) — crossgrain olive, elm with hornbeam lid, and olive again; Chris Faulkner's bureau (pages 344-6); and dominoes from Herman's home workshop

**Publisher** Ray Lewis
**Editor** Peter Collenette
**Deputy Editor** Aidan Walker
**Advertisement Manager** Paul Holmes
**Graphics** Jeff Hamblin
**Advertisement production** Karyn Stewart
**Guild of Woodworkers** Aidan Walker
**Group Editor** Chris Adam-Smith
**Publishing Director** John Foster
**Chairman and Chief Executive** Jim Connell

**Editorial, advertisements and Guild of Woodworkers**
1 Golden Square, London WC1R 3AB, telephone 01-437 0626

Unfortunately we cannot accept responsibility for loss of or damage to unsolicited material. We reserve the right to refuse or suspend advertisements, and regret we cannot guarantee the bone fides of advertisers.

**Subscriptions and back issues** Infonet Ltd, 10-13 Times House, 179 Marlowes, Hemel Hempstead, Herts HP1 1BB; telephone Hemel Hempstead (0442) 48434
**Subscriptions per year** UK £15.60; overseas outside USA (accelerated surface post) £17, USA (accelerated surface post) $22.50, airmail £42
**UK trade** SM Distribution Ltd, 16-18 Trinity Gardens, London SW9 8DX; telephone 01-274 8611
**North American trade** Eastern News Distributors, 166-41 Powells Cove Boulevard, L Box 69, Whitestone, New York 11357
**Printed in Great Britain** by Ambassador Press Ltd, St Albans, Herts
**Mono origination** Multiform Photosetting Ltd, Cardiff
**Colour origination** Derek Croxson Ltd, Chesham, Bucks
© Argus Specialist Publications Ltd 1985
ISSN 0043 776X

**Argus Specialist Publications Ltd**
1 Golden Square, London W1R 3AB; 01-437 0626

# Woodworker
# This month _____ | Shoptalk _____

## BRISTOL WOODWORKER SHOW 25-7 MAY

An Elu lathe and a DeWalt bandsaw — for free! These handsome workhorses will be given away at the Bristol Woodworker Show. Together with two professional palm-sanders from Black & Decker, they'll form prizes for all purchasers who visit our sales stand and enter our draw.

But, of course, it's only one of the attractions at a show that'll be packed with our friends in the trade, all anxious for your custom and displaying their latest and most tempting wares. An exhibition is an excellent place to look for machinery; not only will you find most if not all the different makes in one place — you'll also find that many of them are going cheap. (Well, cheaper than usual, anyway.)

What's more, there'll be plenty of actual woodwork to look at. And — especially if you live in the West Country — you can help put some of it there by entering the competition classes which will provide major exhibits for the pleasure of visitors. Remember, too, that competition entry entitles you to free show admission for yourself and one other. What have you got to lose?

● The venue is Bristol Exhibition Complex. The dates again are 25, 26 and 27 May — the Bank Holiday weekend.

## Woodworker Show, London, October

Meanwhile, there's no time like the present to get the details and to set about entering for the national competitions at the big London Woodworker Show. These cover a vast field and embrace all aspects of craft woodworking from clocks to cabinetmaking and toys to turning. In particular, the Ashley Iles Award crowns what is, to our knowledge, the UK's *only* national woodcarving contest. Its subject this year is **Creatures of the forest**. Why not enter your own interpretation, then collect your free admission to the show and see what others have made of the same challenge?

There are also, of course, the prizes . . .

**All Show details including competition entry forms are available from Argus Specialist Exhibitions Ltd, Park View House, 1 Park View Rd, Berkhamsted, Herts HP4 3EY, tel. (04427) 73291.**

## Lifestyle Furniture

The furniture trade's big shows often include talking shops (sorry, seminars) where VIPs get up and spout about the frightful problems facing the industry. There's certainly plenty to discuss.

The London International Furniture Show at Earls Court will be no exception. However, 'Lifestyle Furniture' (the title of the seminar there on 14 May) is unusual in being organised by a college: who else but the London College of Furniture? Speakers will be the chairman of Parker-Knoll, the buying director of Habitat, the director of technology at the GLC Enterprise Board, and the professor of design research at the Royal College of Art. If they can't talk sense about furniture for tomorrow's customers, no one can.

All comers are welcome at the seminar. Further details from Ray Simson at the LCF, 41 Commercial Rd, London E1 1LA, tel. 01-247 1953. Entry is £25 including show admission and lunch with wine.

## Off pat

Once upon a time . . . you could get beautiful carved wooden dies that would leave the glistening impression of a swan, a cow, a wheatsheaf, a rose, on the surface of your breakfast butter. Just another quaint adornment that's unobtainable nowadays. Or is it? If anyone still makes them, we'd love to know about it.

## Key notes

*Woodturning and Design* is the title of a book by noted turner Ray Key, soon to be published by Batsford. From 26 April to 11 May the British Crafts Centre in Earlham Street, London WC2, will be featuring an exhibition of Ray's work. The number is 01-836 6993.

A name synonymous with woodturning, the **Coronet Tool Co.**, has brought out a new **Hobby lathe** for a very reasonable £190+VAT. A ½hp motor; speeds of 2000, 1100 and 425rpm; capacities are 1000mm between centres, 133mm centre height from the bed. They are doing a 'Lathe Package' for the beginner, which includes the Hobby lathe, a bowl-turning attachment, woodscrew chuck, faceplate, woodturning book, six Ashley Iles turning tools and some friction polish — all for £294.40, including VAT. All the Coronet accessories such as collet chucks, face-plates and long-hole-boring kits fit the Hobby lathe. A sensible marketing move from a highly reputed company.

● Coronet Tool Co. (1982) Ltd, Alfreton Rd, Derby DE2 4AH, tel. (0332) 362141

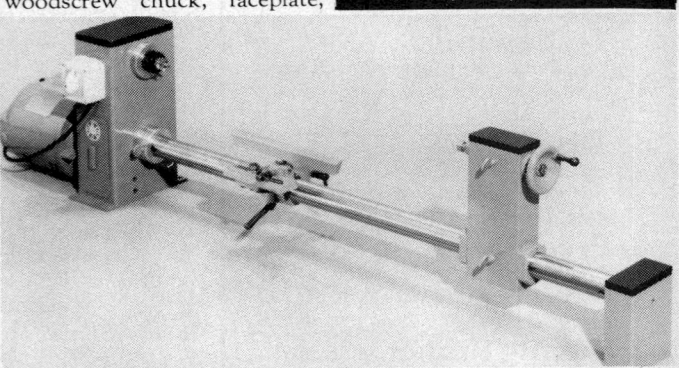

Some of Britain's most respected names in tools are wholly British again. **Bahco Record Tools Ltd's** management, with the backing of several institutional investors, have bought Record Ridgway tools back from Swedish-based AB Bahco in a £9.3m deal. The management and employees now form the largest single shareholder in what is claimed to be the UK's ninth largest successful buy-out. Chief executive Tab Taberner gives a lot of credit to the trades union's membership, who were solidly behind any management move to keep Record independent, and to Bahco themselves, with whom the company will still maintain close agency and distribution links.

Users of Record clamps and vices, Ridgway boring tools and Marples chisels will be glad to hear that the company aim to improve productivity and marketing skills, but not to compromise on the quality of their products. (The range has already been drastically altered in the last three years' tightening-up and re-structuring.) The firm employs 800 people in Britain, and notched up £25m sales last year.

● Bahco Record Tools Ltd (shortly to be known again as Record Ridgway), Parkway Works, Sheffield S9 3BL, tel. (0742) 547139.

Nitromors are close to lyrical about their new **alternative to creosote**, imaginatively entitled Nitromors Wood Protector. 'Consumer friendly', non-splash, non-flammable, non-fade, non-fuming, fungicidal, colour-stable, deep-penetrating; an all-round improvement, it would seem, on old-fashioned creosote. If Nitromors themselves weren't the biggest suppliers of creosote to the retail market, they'd be shaking in their shoes at the announcement. As it is, they're still laughing. Independent tests show this product penetrates deeper, and it's environment-friendly too! £3.50 or thereabouts for a 4-litre flagon.

The terrible Pentachlorophenol twins, Laurate and Lindane, are the active ingredients in their equally inspiringly named sister product, Nitromors Timber Preserver. Five fade-resistant colours, including red and green, come in pigments that remain on the wood surface, while the fungicidal and insecticidal chemical compounds get down deep. Low odour, too. £8.50 inc. VAT for 5 litres.

● Nitromors Ltd, Alexandra Park, Bristol BS16 2BQ, tel (0272) 656271

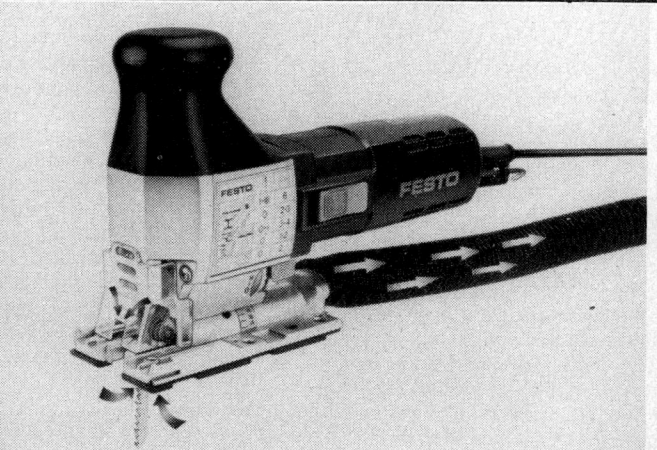

**5**00w motor . . . non-twist blade . . . three blade supports . . . cutting without break-out . . . GRP-lined shoe-plate . . . can this really be a **jigsaw**? West German tool-makers Festo, who do a huge range of heavier stuff for the motor trade as well as wood-work, are introducing the PS1E on to the British market. It looks like the proverbial bee's knees. They have obviously spent a lot of time and money on developing the design, which is a serious attempt to overcome a jigsaw's inherent problem; a twisty blade which cuts neither straight along nor straight through the material, and leaves a trail of hairs and splinters.

To a beefed-up pendulum roller guide, which supports the blade on its longitudinal axis, they have added a flat steel guide to stop twisting of the blade, and a third support which sits *in the plate* on the workpiece and guarantees that the cut is at the angle you want it. If you've ever cut through a thickish lump with a jigsaw and forgotten which way the blade bends — coming through on the wrong side of the line — you'll appreciate this feature. Not content with all this, Festo have put GRP pads on the sole-plate to stop it scratching the work, and have also devised a special guide system to produce a straight cut along a mark, irrespective of the accuracy of the edge of the board. Break-out is dealt with by a splinter guard matched to the type of blade you're using. Presumably it has to be changed with blades of different thicknesses.

Anything else? Of course — it's got a standard chip-guard, and optional dust-extraction. A Rolls-Royce (Mercedes-Benz?) of a saw, at an equivalent price — £156+VAT. Watch for their saw-table device, which is on the way; then you can turn it upside down too. The question is — does it dance and sing?

● Distributed by Minden Industrial, Newmarket Rd, Bury St Edmunds, Suffolk, tel. (0284) 3418

**A** jig designed to overcome angle difficulties when **grinding your lathe tools** is now being marketed by Tyme Machines of Bristol, the lathe manufacturers. Originally sold in Canada and the US, it comes with a clamping fixture that'll work for plane irons, carving chisels and other bench tools as well. Tyme's export/import co-operator in north America asked them to make and sell it here, and they had the renowned woodturner John Sainsbury look at it and suggest a detail improvement or two. It will retail in light-machinery stockists for around £35+VAT.

● Tyme Machines, Unit 3, Halls Rd, Kingswood, Bristol, tel. (0272) 603726

**M**odern Woodworking Machinery Ltd was modern in 1920, when it was established, but now it is one of Britain's older — and better — **machinery manufacturers.** Alistair Cook, managing director of Minirad radial-arm saw makers **Charnwood**, thinks Modern are so good, in fact, that he's gone out and bought them. Modern are thought to have been one of the first companies in Europe to make a universal woodworking machine, and three of their machines were built for Wadkin's Tradesman range; the acquisition is good news for Charnwood, who will benefit from the older company's design and production experience in heavier machinery. Watch the market for a reasonably priced, solidly built range of spindle-moulders, mortisers, planer-thicknessers, tablesaws and mitre-trimmers to be sold by Charnwood — Modern machines in modern guise.

● Charnwood, 44 Boston Rd, Beaumont Leys, Leicester LE4 1AA, tel. (0533) 350230.

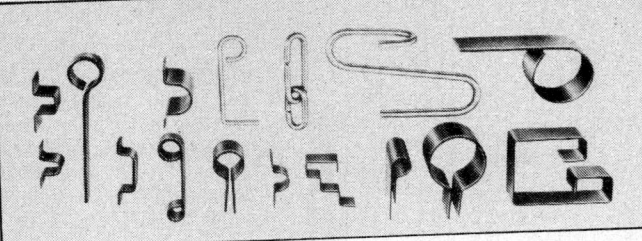

**W**hat's the Universal **metal pipe-bender** doing in *Woodworker's* pages? A question you may well ask, until you clock the weird and wonderful shapes you can make with it. If you make and mend anything of metal at home or workshop, this could be a very handy little item. Your own shelf brackets for a corner where the proprietary ones won't fit; an extra-long hasp for a padlock; it's the kind of tool you'd never really reckon you needed — until you got one and wondered what you'd do without it. It retails for about £30.

● Hobbymat Department, CZ Scientific Instruments Ltd, PO Box 43, 2 Elstree Way, Borehamwood, Herts WD6 1NH, tel. 01-953 1688

**I**f 'furniture quality' is what you've been looking for in your doors, the House of Mayfair could have the answer. Not Fablon, not Formica, 'Decordor' **transforms** your ratty old **flush doors** in seconds flat — as long as it takes to peel off the 'release paper' and stick it on. Three luxury woodgrain finishes, or a glossy white 'freshly painted look' could soon be adorning your lounge, kitchen or coal-hole door.

Decordor sports an 'easy care' surface which is scrubbable and keeps its good-looking finish for years, it says here. One door's worth, a piece 83×35in with an 83×2in strip for the edge, costs around £7 from DIY, hardware and department stores.

● House of Mayfair, Cramlington New Town, Northumberland NE23 8AQ

# Shoptalk

I would like to give a brief explanation of the approach **Treework Services** have towards our broad-leaved woodland, **writes John Emery.**

Broad-leaved woodlands used to be seen as an important resource, and were thus managed to supply the timber needs of society. This perception is no longer widespread, and is the reason why so many of our broad-leaved woodlands have disappeared — to be replaced, if at all, by conifer plantations.

Treework Services look at all aspects of a particular woodland, and attempt to devise a self-financing renovation/management scheme which is both sensitive to the environment and also ensures that the woodland will still be there for future generations. In its simplest form this means that any mature timber which is felled pays for the clearing, fencing and planting work necessary.

The ability to market timbers derived from woodland renovation schemes contributes essentially to the viability of the woodland. Thus we supply high-quality kiln-dried native hardwoods to the woodworker.

● Treework Services Ltd, Cheston Combe, Church Town, Backwell, Bristol BS19 3JQ, tel. Chew Magna 3222

● *The mitre-saw isn't a front-runner for the general woodworking shop, but it's nonetheless worth knowing about. This is the Ryobi S251, with a 1500w input. It has its own dust-bag. The table can be locked at 0°, 22½° and 45°, or any other position. It costs £269.95 +VAT (RRP). Luna Tools & Machinery Ltd, 20 Denbigh Hall, Bletchley, Milton Keynes MK3 7QT, tel. (0908) 70771*

**A**rcoy cutters lost or broken . . . expensive, highly prized dovetailers lying unused all over the country . . . These were the nightmarish visions that assailed Alan Holtham, spurring him on to track down Arcoy-compatible cutters and get a deal to distribute them. Arcoy freaks, your troubles are over; Alan now stocks Arcoy dovetailing cutters sizes 1, 2 and 3, al at £13.80+ VAT, post free.

● Alan Holtham, Old Stores Turnery, Wistaston Rd, Willaston, Nantwich, Cheshire CW5 6QJ, tel. Crewe 67010.

**T**he Mulberry Bush, makers and sellers of **doll's houses and their furniture and accessories** ('Shoptalk', WW/Mar), ask us to emphasise that all their miniatures are to ¹⁄₁₂ scale and not ¹⁄₂₄.

● The Mulberry Bush, 25 Trafalgar St, Brighton, Sussex BN1 4EQ, tel. (0273) 493781

● *Two in one – the cutter pictured here is used to trim the edges of laminates to either 45° or 90° after bonding. Trend Machinery & Cutting Tools Ltd, Unit N, Penfold Works, Imperial Way, Watford, Herts WD2 4YY, tel (0923) 49911*

**A**part from a subscription to our sister publication *Clocks*, what the timepiece enthusiast needs is a catalogue of **Craft Materials Ltd's supplies and services.** Movements mechanical and crystal, skeleton and cuckoo-clock kits, dial and case fittings, barometers, thermometers, hygrometers; brassware and fittings, wall-clock kits, finishing materials — everything you need to make clocks as well as collect them or even tell the time by them!

● Craft Materials Ltd, The Haven, Station Rd, Northiam, Rye, E. Sussex TN31 6QL, tel. (079 74) 2180

**P**eter Child writes: many years have gone since I got the idea of the world's first **two-day woodturning course.** Since then I have met and enjoyed the company of pupils of all ages, all walks of life, and many nationalities.

However, as I grow older and more tired, I feel that I am not now giving my best, so reluctantly I have decided to discontinue my teaching and use all my efforts to help my son design and improve our tools, and supply anything a turner could possibly need. I send all my guests best wishes and the hope that they have become better turners than when we first met!

**I**have been using yacht varnish for years, writes J. Fisher. It's been the best treatment for my hardwood doors and windows — but I always found the weather got under it. Now I have found **Duratec**, which I think is the winner. Sold by Crosby, the door manufacturers, it forms a tough, flexible coating with a water-repellent surface. There are different colours; it incorporates lightfast pigments, minimising the effects of sunlight, and a preservative to protect against growths of wood-staining mould. It gives lasting protection to interior and exterior doors, and has been specifically formulated for Crosby exterior doors. All Duratec colours may be intermixed.

● Crosby Doors Ltd, West St, Farnham, Surrey, tel. (0252) 722447.

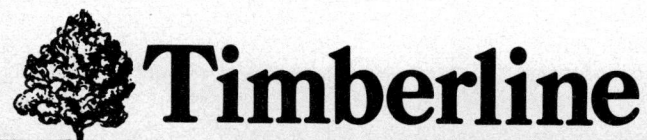

# Timberline

**Arthur Jones presents the month's inside news of supplies**

Television nightly gives prominence to the value of the pound. Everyone anxiously follows the struggle against the dollar, and we are sometimes told of the weakness of sterling against other currencies.

Woodworkers may feel this has little direct effect upon them. Nothing could be further from the truth. Many woods are bought in dollars, and not just from north America. Hardwoods from many south American sources are priced in dollars, which means that the prices in the UK go up without the overseas seller gaining an extra penny (or whatever he can buy for his money).

The same can apply to many woods bought in Europe. The Swedish krona is often used as the money base for sales, the exchange rate between the krona and the pound being agreed beforehand. For some years now the Russians have sold their softwood to the UK with prices based on the krona. This was why, in the latter part of last year, our importers had to pay the Russians more for their shipments of wood although the Soviet export agency had made no change in the selling price; it was simply because the pound had fallen against the krona.

All very complicated, but this preamble is necessary before revealing the new Soviet softwood prices for shipments to the UK for the period up to the autumn.

Woodworkers are generally interested in only the better qualities of redwood and whitewood; it is doubtful whether the craftsman would ever have a use for Russian fifths, even though for this year they have been reduced by £1 per m³ to £81. No, unsorted qualities are the most favoured, with even higher preference for the wood from the Kara Sea area (and this is the highest-priced of the Russian products).

Unsorted redwood in the first schedule is priced at £168 per m³, a rise of £12 over last year, with the Kara Sea unsorted redwood showing a bigger jump of £16 to £172 compared with the first schedule of 1984.

However, in whitewood the prices are much more attractive. Unsorted whitewood is now £102, a fall of £1 on 1984.

Having given the prices it is now important to point out that these sterling quotations are tied to an exchange rate with the krona of SKr10.25 to the pound. Because this gives sterling a much lower value than last year, in reality the value of unsorted redwood has fallen by some 4% compared with a year ago, and in the case of whitewood the fall has been over 10%.

The UK timber importers traditionally hang back until they have seen what the Russians intend to charge for their new wood, and this year they have been generally pleased with the Russian prices, which means they will buy in volume from the USSR this year.

The Scandinavian and Canadian lumbermen also await the new Russian prices anxiously, because trade comes almost to a halt until these are known. Once published, the other world shippers then pitch their prices in line with what the UK trade will accept from the Soviet Union; in other words, these prices have set the pattern for softwood prices in Britain for the rest of this year so far as the woodworker is concerned.

This is why the Soviet prices and quantities are so important (incidentally, the Russians intend to sell us at least as much wood as last year, and they may even battle for a slightly larger share of the market). A price pattern for softwood is established for months ahead, and this year the woodworker can breathe freely in the knowledge that he will still be getting his timber at a highly competitive rate and will generally be paying little, if any, more than in 1984. So three cheers for the Russians — at least for this year!

The hardwood market continues variable, and consignments of lauan — and a little Brazilian mahogany — are still being dumped at our ports by shippers who have been unable to find forward buyers. So there are many continuing opportunities to buy these woods at attractive prices, though just how much longer we shall see consignment shipping is uncertain. According to all the economic reports from overseas the practice is already senseless and unnecessary. ∎

# Win a Woodworker Show Award

## AT BRISTOL MAY 25, 26, 27 AND LONDON OCT 24, 25, 26, 27

SEND FOR YOUR ENTRY FORM TODAY

London entries:– £250 to be won by best of show Woodturner and Woodcarver–sponsored by Henry Taylor (Tools) Ltd., Sheffield.

There will be a Woodworker Show at **Bristol in May '85** at the Bristol Exhibition Centre, Canons Road and in **London in October '85** at the Alexandra Pavillion. There are many competition classes including cabinet-making, woodcarving, woodturning, musical instruments, marqueting, model horse drawn vehicles, toys and miniatures.

Send for your competition entry form for BRISTOL or LONDON or both to:– Woodworker Show '85, Argus Specialist Exhibitions Ltd, Park View House, Park View Road, Berkhamsted, Herts. HP4 3EY. Tel: (04427) 73291.

Prices quoted are those prevailing at press date and are subject to alteration due to economic conditions

# Question box

Our panel of experts solve your woodworking problems

**Q** *I am involved in finishing a Georgian-style hardwood (utile) restaurant front, which will be exposed to all weathers. We are thinking of putting on three or four coats of Fiddes shellac sealer and at least four coats of Blackfriar high-gloss polyurethane yacht varnish, rubbing down between coats with wire wool. Is this a good plan, and will the finish last?*

*Neil Richards, Barry*

**A** The professional schedule for exterior varnish is as follows:

1 Sand down the utile with 240-grade garnet paper, and wipe down with methylated spirits to remove any grease, etc.
2 If you intend to stain the wood, use a water stain, as it will not fade. Furniglas produce water-soluble dyes for light-fastness. When dry, sand down lightly again with 240 grit.
3 Now apply one liberal coating of your chosen exterior varnish. This must be thinned down by volume with 10% turpentine — far better than white spirit, because turpentine dries out. Allow this coating to dry hard.
4 Sand down this surface using 240-grade paper, and dust off.
5 Now apply a second coating of your varnish straight from the tin. Allow it to become bone-dry.
6 Using 600-grade silicon-carbide paper (wet-and-dry), employ soft water and a little soap to flat out the whole surface. Wipe down with clean water and dry off.
7 Apply a third coating of the varnish straight from the tin and allow to dry bone-hard.
8 Depending on the quality of your workmanship, a further coating may be required. The final finish should look like glass and will last for many years.

A few tips on varnishing. Always use best-quality varnish such as Blackfriars exterior varnish or Rustins yacht varnish, or in fact any branded exterior varnish of reputable name. Use best-quality varnish brushes, a good dusting brush, and Tak rags to pick up dust before applying the varnish. If any insects attach themselves to the wet film, leave them alone until the varnish is bone dry, and then simply wash off with warm water.

*Noel Leach*

---

**Q** *A friend of mine has built a porch for his new bungalow supported on four 8in-square fluted columns of native oak. The timber, which was supposed to be properly seasoned, has developed deep shakes up to ⅜in wide, and I would like your advice on a treatment to prevent the job from being a total loss.*

*William Doyle, Dublin*

**A** I feel there has been a certain amount of misunderstanding between your friend and his supplier of oak sections. I do not believe that any timber merchant would guarantee that 8×8in section of native or any other oak would be fully seasoned and would not face-shake when exposed to either internal or external atmospheric conditions.

I feel that little or nothing can be done, as filling the shakes in the summer would only cause problems when the timber closes up in the winter — which is normal in oak of this section. If this work were done in winter, the opposite would occur. This is because timber is a hygroscopic material, i.e. similar to a sponge, and will both take in and give out moisture depending on the atmospheric conditions prevailing at the time.

I can only stress that anyone wishing to use large-section oak either internally or externally should be prepared for a certain amount of both movement and face-shake.

With regard to the job being 'a total loss', I would say that shakes like those in this particular timber are part of the character of oak when used in such applications. Even if you were to use an alternative species, such as large-section softwood, primed and painted, there is no guarantee that some face-shake would not still occur. Besides, even if the oak had been totally dry, the face-shake might still have occurred on exposure to sun, wind and rain.

*Frank Boddy*

---

**Q** *Some years ago I made a boat steering-wheel 2ft in diameter of teak strips ⅛in thick, cold-bending them round a metal former. It has been very satisfactory. I would now like to make another with some seasoned yew. Can you see any reason why this should not be equally satisfactory?*

*T. Stratton, Fordingbridge*

**A** You should not experience any difficulty in cold-bending yew. Tests made to establish approximate radii of curvature are invariably based on material 1in (25mm) thick, and on this basis teak, if supported by a strap, can be bent to a radius of 18in (450mm), and if unsupported to 35in (889mm) radius. Corresponding values for yew are 8½in (215mm) and 16½in (418mm) respectively. These are again based on steam-softened wood but, taking your proposed thickness of lamination into account, there should be no real problem The only points to watch are that yew is liable to back-bend away from the strap, and inclined to check during setting.

*Bill Brown FIWSc*

---

**Q** *Please would you recommend a good durable finish for a small table I am making from yew, for outside use? Would raw or boiled linseed oil give a more suitable and long-lasting finish than, say, polyurethane varnish, or could you advise an alternative?*

*T. G. Davies, Wrexham*

**A** Yew is a most durable wood, so your table will withstand the rigours of bad weather very well. It will, however, require some protection to keep out dirt and to maintain its good appearance.

Applying linseed oil, whether raw or boiled, is not recommended. One of the drawbacks is that it takes a long time to dry, and exterior work soon becomes dirty from dust and grit sticking to the oil. Polyurethane varnish will provide a clear finish which will not hide the beauty of the wood, but if rainwater gets behind the varnish film through a minute crack, or a slightly open joint, the polyurethane will peel and lift off in a thin skin. This will leave a dirty mark which must be completely removed before re-varnishing.

Before applying any finish your table must be completely dry and glasspapered smooth so that there are no blemishes such as plane marks. If there are such marks, they will be immediately highlighted when the first application of finish is brushed on.

A good-quality oil varnish will beautify and protect your table, but yacht varnish will be even more durable. Get the clearest possible varnish so that the wood retains its light colour, and carefully follow the manufacturer's instructions about application and drying intervals.

Use a new brush when varnishing. A badly cleaned paintbrush will leave traces of paint in the varnish — usually in the most prominent position!

*Charles Cliffe*

---

**Q** *I have been using exotics for about seven years, and I was under the impression that 'grande palisander' and Mexican rosewood were the same thing. A turner I met recently was adamant that palisander is another name for Rio rosewood. Who's right?*

*T. F. Holland, Warsash*

**A** Your turner friend is correct. Brazilian or Rio rosewood is also known as palisander, and in France as *palisandre du Brazil*, a name which might correspond to your 'grande palisander' or 'palisandre'. The *Dalbergia* species produces rosewood and also highly decorative woods which are sold under other names, for example kingwood. So far as Mexico is concerned, I am fairly certain that the only *Dalbergia* growing there is *Dalbergia retusa* or cocobolo, also known locally as granadillo. I wonder if this name has become confused with your 'grande.' This species grows right along the west side of central America, whereas Rio rosewood grows in Brazil. The latter is *Dalbergia nigra*, while Honduras rosewood, *Dalbergia stevensonii*, is confined to Belize.

It is really a question of origin. If your wood came from Mexico and is cocobolo, it will look like any other *Dalbergia* but a little redder than Rio wood. Cocobolo comes from smallish trees and its uses are restricted. It is considered a turnery wood, and has been used for policemen's truncheons.

*Bill Brown FIWSc*

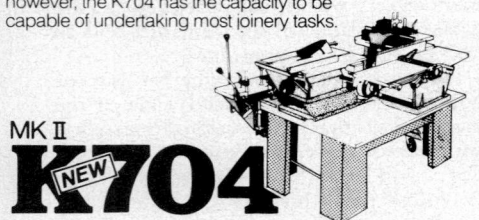

# Low-tech alternatives

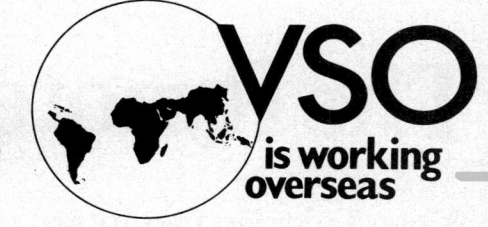

VSO is working overseas

**Aidan Walker looks into the course for VSO volunteers at the National Centre for Alternative Technology**

Tim Etheridge's draw-knife technique may well be a great deal more refined now than when his picture was taken. He has exchanged the summer sunlight of Powys for the harsh climate of Mazeras, Kenya, where since last September he has been a carpentry instructor at the village polytechnic.

An associate member of the British Institute of Certified Carpenters with full City and Guilds qualifications, until last summer Tim was working at the Ministry of Defence in Hampshire. He specialised in joinery and sawmilling, but was also doing some cabinetmaking and general building carpentry. Furniture, and moulds for carbon-fibre fabrication, also came into his job description. He contracted itchy feet, however. Combining his wish to travel with a desire to use his trade skills for some directly worthwhile task, he rang up Voluntary Service Overseas, was interviewed, and accepted their offer of a voluntary teaching post in Africa.

VSO sends skilled volunteer labour all over the world to teach trade skills, literacy and self-help techniques in the developing countries. But well-seasoned, accurately milled timber, high-quality steel and a comprehensive supply of tools are not as easy to get at in Kenya as they are in Europe; so VSO and the National Centre for Alternative Technology put their heads together to design an 'Appropriate Technology' course. The idea is to guide volunteers to a better awareness of the skills and resources to be found in developing countries. The nine-day building option for the course, held at the Centre near Machynlleth, covers brick-making, use of stabilised soil for block-making, using round-sectioned and green timber in building, ways of reducing timber degradation in tropical conditions (including termite control) and making cutting tools out of scrap metal. Old Land Rover springs, drawn and tempered over a charcoal fire, are the best bet for chisels. 'They sharpen up surprisingly well,' says Tim.

Bricklayers, plumbers and carpenters all take the same course at the same time, sharing and cross-fertilising skills and idea. The chippies spend a day and a half on ferro-cement building techniques, for grain- and water-storage tanks; in the Kenyan bush, the nearest brickie might be several days away.

The volunteers examine the theory of structures, and as a team have to design a roof-truss and a 54ft-span bridge using green-wood poles no bigger than 5in in diameter. It must be capable of carrying the weight of a Land Rover. Use and maintenance of a pitsaw, adze and draw-knife are also covered.

'To the two-by-four mind', says Rodney King, who organises the course at the Centre, 'these tools and techniques can seem simple and old-fashioned. The course gives the volunteers the confidence that they actually work.' VSO look for independent people with a feel for adventure, a spirit of service, and a great deal of self-reliance. The job description might be a year old; the priorities of the area and the work might well have changed by the time a volunteer gets there. He or she must also have a grounding in the culture of the assigned country, and be at least initially prepared for shocks to the digestive and domestic systems — let alone the socio-economic. A jar of Marmite or a pint of Guinness can take on disproportionate significance when it's just not available!

The volunteers are also briefed on sanitation and environmental health, and attend a session on development politics. One of the most important things to realise, says Rodney, is that they are going to *co-operate* in development, and return to the UK with a broader understanding of how vast numbers of people in the world live.

Going to a 'village polytechnic' with a very flexible brief, Tim must obviously be prepared for almost anything. His job is described as running a carpentry workshop, instructing students, and upgrading the other instructors' skills. The last item would surely make as much demand on your personal diplomacy as on your ability to teach pitsawing. Another essential was to understand the workings of the area into which he was going — the government departments he would have to deal with, the local contacts he would have to make, the toes on which he would have to be careful not to tread. Most of these things change from year to year, and volunteers only really know the ins and outs when they arrive.

'Every situation has its own level of perfection,' said Tim before he left. 'You're not lowering your ideals of craftsmanship — just changing them. And part of VSO's job is to make people in his country aware of what's happening. I'm not just going out there to teach — it's a matter of educational *exchange*.' A resourceful woodworker without ready-made resources, Tim sees the work as *enabling* the building carpenters of Mazeras to work out their own solutions. When he leaves after two years, he hopes he will have well and truly worked himself out of a job.

● The National Centre for Alternative Technology, Llwyngwern Quarry, Machynlleth, Powys, tel. (0654) 2400
● Voluntary Service Overseas, 9 Belgrave Sq., London SW1X 8PW, tel. (01) 235 5191.

● *Carpenter Tim Etheridge in training for a stint at Mazeras Village Polytechnic, Kenya (photo J. Hartley/VSO)*

# The Rycotewood rumble

**When Luke Hughes interviewed designer/maker John Coleman for January's *Woodworker*, he provoked strong reactions. We reproduce them here — with Luke's reply**

Parts of Luke Hughes' article give an inaccurate reflection of our work here at Rycotewood College. John himself has worked with us for over five years and he is also concerned that the impression given by some of the sentences does not reflect his true opinion.

His alleged statement that he 'would not employ ex-Rycotewood students' gives the impression that he would not recommend anyone else to do so. In fact the sentiment should be that it might not be appropriate for *him*, but he does not deny the contribution of Rycotewood graduates to other craftsmen.

His alleged statement that 'at college they gain no idea about making a living' will, I am sure, be disputed by John himself, for we at Rycotewood have always strived — more than most colleges in the art and design area — to give our students a sound commercial business sense.

When John alludes to the 'excellent student' that he employed for 18 months, I suggest that 'deterioration' and working to a 'time factor' are matters concerning the effectiveness of the employer as well as the employee.

**Chris Simpson MDes(RCA) MSIAD MSD-C NDD**
**Head of Department,**
**Department of Fine Craftsmanship and Design, Rycotewood College**

---

I felt Luke Hughes was carried away by his enthusiasm and some of my views have been somewhat misrepresented. To avoid any misunderstanding I must expand on various remarks in the article.

The work I have declined from architects in the past was usually the odd joinery or kitchen-worktop type of job. The 'ideas about design' which clashed were very often more about the construction than the appearance. Happily, now I have become more established I do not do this type of work, and can concentrate on making the furniture I have designed.

'I quote by guesstimate, and am hopeless at judging time' were rather flippant comments of mine linked together, regarding the very serious business of costing work. It is difficult to judge how long a new and untried project will take to complete, and I tend optimistically to under-estimate the time needed. Fortunately this does not happen very often, but when it does it is at my expense and not the client's, as I usually work to an agreed fee.

The comments on Rycotewood College are most misleading. I have been associated with the college for five years as a part-time lecturer, where I and other designer/craftsmen are contracted to help students with their design projects — and to bring to the studio an input on our experiences of professional life rather than just 'talking to the students'.

The remark about not employing Rycotewood students unless they have a year's experience was taken out of context. I made the general comment, for all students who leave any college, that employers very often prefer applicants to have some previous commercial experience. A college is something of a hot-house, rather different from the outside world, and it naturally takes time for a student to adjust. However, I believe that students from Rycotewood reach the highest standard of competence and slot very well into workshop situations, for example with David Field and Andy Varah. Rycotewood students also choose to establish workshops of their own, either directly from college or after a period of further studies, with great success.

The student who worked for me came directly from Rycotewood; he was conscientious in every aspect of his work and we parted most amicably. Again, I had made a general comment to Luke Hughes about having to ensure a balance between the quality of work and that of the craftsman, so that neither begins to deteriorate.

I feel that the tone of the article as a whole, particularly the sentence 'I've never had a really bad cock-up, though I've sometimes felt the quality of work has been lower than it should be' gives an uncharacteristically sour and uncaring impression. I regret if I gave it, and I do not believe it is reflected in my work.

**John Coleman**

---

As a practising furniture-maker for the past 10 years, with my own large workshops employing four young cabinetmakers, I take great exception to the article about John Coleman as it relates to Rycotewood College students.

During the past five years I have employed, straight from Rycotewood, seven students. After two or three years they have left me to set up their own workshops; every one, without exception, has proved a first-class cabinetmaker, and all are successful in their own right.

I accept that in the first six months after a student joins me there is much to teach, and it is true that students have very little commercial experience — but name me one profession where this is not the case! The techniques taught at Rycotewood are sometimes lacking in terms of the latest technology, but it is essential that students understand the old technology in order to capitalise on the new.

If a craftsman cannot afford to pay a reasonable rate, either his order book is under-filled or his costing is suspect. Certainly after 18 months my ex-students are producing excellent work very quickly.

I believe the college should encourage students to spend a month or two in a commercial environment before they leave the course, very much as teachers go on teaching practice before they qualify.

My workshop is only one of a very few in England designing and making one-off items of furniture, and, unless people like myself encourage the enormous wealth of talent in students, their prospects of becoming successful are slim indeed. At the end of the day it is not enough to cut a beautiful dovetail without being aware of the commercial pitfalls. Experience or a learning opportunity in a workshop such as mine is the only way to prevent these young hopefuls from floundering in their early endeavours. I firmly believe the few of us who have the means to encourage the next generation of craftsmen should indeed give them every possible encouragement, and your article must cause great anxiety amongst many hopeful students.

**Andrew Varah**

---

**Luke Hughes** writes: One of the curiosities about writing articles is that people are inclined to read into them what they want to see, and sometimes what they fear they might see. They often miss what is actually written. A combination of these factors seems to be in play concerning my article about John Coleman in the series 'Woodworkers making a living'.

Let me remind people of the background. The series was intended to glean as many answers as possible to the same set of questions from different part of the woodwork business. The questions were derived from the everyday anxieties I suffer, and which I know others suffer too. It is heartening to hear how others cope with them. My ultimate intention is to draw conclusions from the series that could be made into an introductory pamphlet, along with the articles themselves, for anyone who thinks it might be a 'nice idea' to start in the trade. To ensure continuity in the series, the questions must stay the same. I have a checklist.

For John to say his comments were taken out of context misses the point; he gave straight answers to straight questions, and I have written them exactly as delivered. if what he feels is that he'd rather not have said certain things, I understand his discomfort. The fact remains that he did — and in doing so revealed exactly the kind of anxiety that preoccupies someone in his position: hence its interest for anyone in a similar position. The article was not a profile of John Coleman, likely to be read by future clients; it showed how someone like John Coleman, with his experience and training in design, copes with the same everyday problems as others in the business, be they barrow-makers, spar-makers or architectural joiners.

The one remark that has prompted most reaction was about students in a working environment — it happened to refer specifically to Rycotewood, but is in fact applicable to any student from any college.

# Tradewinds

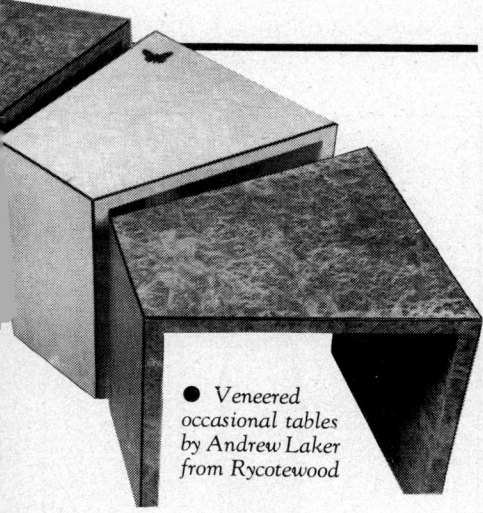

● *Veneered occasional tables by Andrew Laker from Rycotewood*

Let me add that no one has greater admiration for Rycotewood than I, and for the work that comes from it. If you look through my past articles you will find many references to this effect. The learning point in what John said, what the violin-maker said, and what I and many other potential employers in small workshops have felt, is relevant to anyone looking for a job. There is a tendency for students whilst at college to ignore the need for confidence and, most importantly, speed.

Working in a small and imaginative workshop is more fun than working in a large commercial organisation. But it is only happy when everyone works well. This means working quickly, efficiently and with minimum supervision. However good a student may be when he leaves college, he is a drain on resources unless he works well. Worse, he poisons the atmosphere. Everyone in a small workshop knows this, but the point is not always clearly expressed. John touched on this in his answers to my questions, and the strength of the reaction is revealing indeed. Andy Varah takes 'great exception', yet goes on to express on his own account exactly the point that was being made in the first place. Chris Simpson, on the other hand, fails to distinguish between giving students a 'sound commercial business sense' and making a living. Having the former does not necessarily imply that you are able to do the latter. Incidentally, Chris Simpson also writes that 'deterioration' of standards of work and confrontation with the 'time factor' involve the employer as well as the employees. How does John feel about that?

I would like to see everyone who wants to work in wood with a job. There's bags of work around. I would dearly like to employ more people myself, but I can't. My one way of helping others was to let them know what were the things they really ought to know, to provide a little insight into the potential employer's mind — and to let them know what to expect if they start on their own. It is difficult for teachers to be confronted with the natural limits of their teaching. But, if students learn from all this that 'small employers' would like to see commercial experience, 'even at a pittance', in applicants from colleges, the series is fulfilling its aim. ■

## Tool merchant Richard Sarjent gives a view from the other side of the counter

Yet another woodworking exhibition looms — this time the Bristol Woodworker Show. I and some colleagues in the trade have been comparing notes about the more unusual (and occasionally plain silly!) items we get asked for at these events. Some of the less likely included spare parts for electric drills, V-belts, spirit-level bubbles, springs, and Yankee-screwdriver components. We had to explain to the man requesting a spare vial for a spirit-level that, while we could supply him with plenty of hot air, none of it was encapsulated in glass!

It is very difficult, when preparing for a show, to decide which stock lines to take. Apart from any other consideration, most exhibitors are going from multi-thousand-square foot trading premises to temporary situations of perhaps 30×10ft — and we all know you can't get a quart into a pint pot, though it's fun trying!

We try to take the widest range possible, and to offer the visitor what he (or she) wants to see. Sounds easy, but then our display and selection has to represent us and (particularly) our mail-order catalogue; we want to be able to offer special show prices where we can; and we must be confident that we have tools of the highest quality. We try to demonstrate as much as possible, and we also try to avoid any range likely to become subject to a price war.

And so it gets more difficult. Taking the above factors into account, plus a few more like size, weight, bulk, availability and viability, one starts calling on experience. What sold last time — and why?

If I give the impression that I dislike shows, I apologise. Far from it: I enjoy shows. They're hard, frustrating work, at inconvenient times and in inconvenient places — but thoroughly enjoyable. One talks tools and woodworking with people who have an interest, with no hassle, no phone, relatively few silly questions and even fewer moans, and at the end of the day (we hope) one earns a living doing it. What more could one want? (Answers on a postcard, please . . . !)

One thing that can cause considerable work, frustration and unfortunately sometimes ill-will is the guarantee claim.

As retailers, we are the direct link between the end-user of the product, who relies on its dependability, and the manufacturer or (increasingly) importer.

If a product of a technical nature fails or breaks down in an unusually short period of usage, the producer naturally wishes to inspect the item to see whether the cause is a manufacturing fault, or something else (such as abuse or misuse) — preferably before he exchanges or repairs it.

From the user's point of view, however, tool breakdown or failure at any time is annoying and inconvenient. Under guarantee, it is even more frustrating. The customer expects the fault to be rectified in the shortest possible time, and certainly has our sympathy. Problems start occurring when suppliers will not exchange tools under warranty claims, but only repair them, and will not support us if we exchange them. Manufacturers do not seem to realise that we retailers are in the direct firing line, or that we have not only a moral but also a legal obligation to sort out faulty products *fast*.

Obviously the size of the problem varies from one maker to another. The degree of co-operation offered varies, from one manufacturer of portable power tools who backs every decision we make without quibble, to another who always repairs rather than exchanges, and has been known to take two months to do so! No names — but, when looking for the best after-sales service on power tools, buy British.

I plead with manufacturers now. You're keen to sell stock into the merchants, and you're keen for us to sell high volumes to the end-user. However, your enthusiasm needn't stop there. Be keen to provide a comprehensive after-sales service, look after the end-use of your products, and support your stockists.

## 'Wouldn't it make life simpler if everybody paid on time?'

One particularly unpleasant part of being in business nowadays is chasing payment from overdue debtors. One seems to come up against a limited selection of excuses on the phone, and I'm sure all who have had to call for money have heard the following remarks from purchase-ledger clerks:
● 'The cheque signatories are away.' They're spending it elsewhere.
● 'We're missing the invoices.' A classic delaying tactic.
● 'We're installing a computer.' Oh no! We'll not get it for months!
● 'The computer isn't working.' Try paying the maintenance bill.
● 'There's a cheque on the way.' I'll post it now.
● 'I'll post it today.' If I remember.
● 'I'll make a cheque out now.' But not post it.
● 'We'll look at your account.' But that's all we'll do.
● 'I can't pay it till I get paid.' Buck-passing.
● 'I can't pay it for six weeks — I'm broke.' Honest, at least!

Presumably there are more around; as these get well worn, somebody has to come up with new ones. Wouldn't it make life simpler if everybody paid on time? ■

# Round figures

## Richard Piner talks through the making of this classic circular table

This table is designed to stand comfortably in a pine-furnished room — but it could just as easily be made in a hardwood, and perhaps more accurately too.

The legs are made from material 2in thick, the stem from a piece 3½×4in, and the 7in-square block from more 2in stuff — all scrap roof joists. The top is from 1in shelving, cleaned up, and with one tongued-and-grooved centre joint. The two bearers below are in oak, for extra strength.

Once cramped and glued, the top was cut to 3ft diameter with a jigsaw; imperfections were taken out by mounting it in a vice and doing some careful work with a Surform. Stroking with the hand indicated raised and otherwise imperfect sections.

The stem section was reduced to a rough 3½in square, mounted in my lathe and roughed out to 3¼in plus round. The dimensions were carefully marked out, first in pencil and then with a parting-off chisel. The rest was straightforward. I left a little more than 2in in length at the top of the stem, which was useful later when gluing.

I then carefully marked out three flats at the base of the stem, each at an angle of 120°, and formed them with a width of 1¾in, the same as the width of the legs at this point. Careful marking was needed for the dovetail mortise — but not until the dovetail was formed on the legs, because I matched one to the other.

I had made an accurate template in hardboard for the legs. Having transferred its outline to the timber, I used a bandsaw to cut the legs to shape. The direction of the grain is most important. I then pencilled a centre line for each leg, top and bottom, as a guide for the even shaping of each side. Shaping was done with various Surforms and rasps or files — holding the leg in a vice and taking care to do each large section first, so giving plenty of hold for shaping the toe section. I made sure there was a smooth taper all round, and a good swelling for the toe is all-important. I included the foot pad as part of the leg, but it could be added later if that were easier.

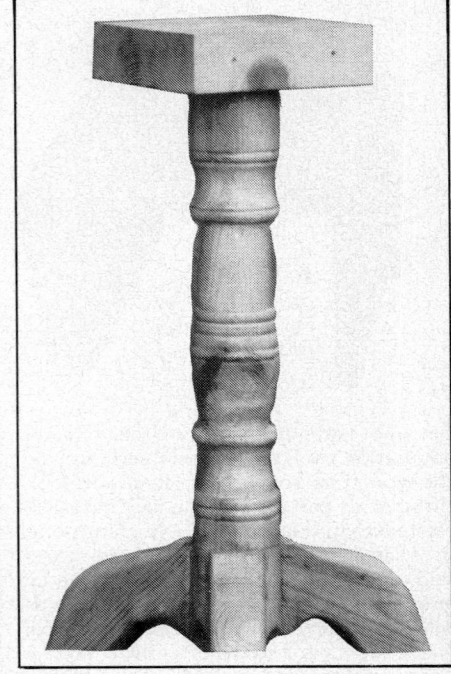

● The turned stem carries a solid square block on to which the top is fitted. A combination of turning, hand shaping and nicely dovetailed legs

The square block, 2in thick and 7in square, was carefully centred on the face-plate, and a 2in hole was turned to take the 2in section at the top of the stem. A good fit here is essential.

Two bearers were made from 1in oak, 26in long and nearly 2in thick at the centre — tapering to almost nothing at the ends, as they do not need to be seen.

Having ensured that each leg was a good fit in the stem (with room for the glue!) I mounted the stem and the legs on to a good flat surface and, using a large try-square, checked that when all was assembled the stem was vertical. In the absence of a square you could use a plumb-line.

The legs should be pushed well home against the shoulders. The lot was then glued together with Araldite. The square block was glued to the stem; again you should take care to see that it is pushed down on to its shoulder. I had previously taken the square to the underside of the top, marking the centre of both the top and the block for positioning later.

With the top still reversed, I positioned the stem and legs, and screwed one of the bearers into place. At least six screws each side are required to prevent any movement — but only insert two for the moment. The other bearer is then screwed into place, taking care to 'pinch' the block for added stiffness. The top is fastened to the block with two long screws each side; I deliberately made the table not to tilt.

I finished by careful sanding at each stage and when assembled, and I polished it with a good hard wax (leaving at least two days between applications) to provide an attractive depth of colour. ■

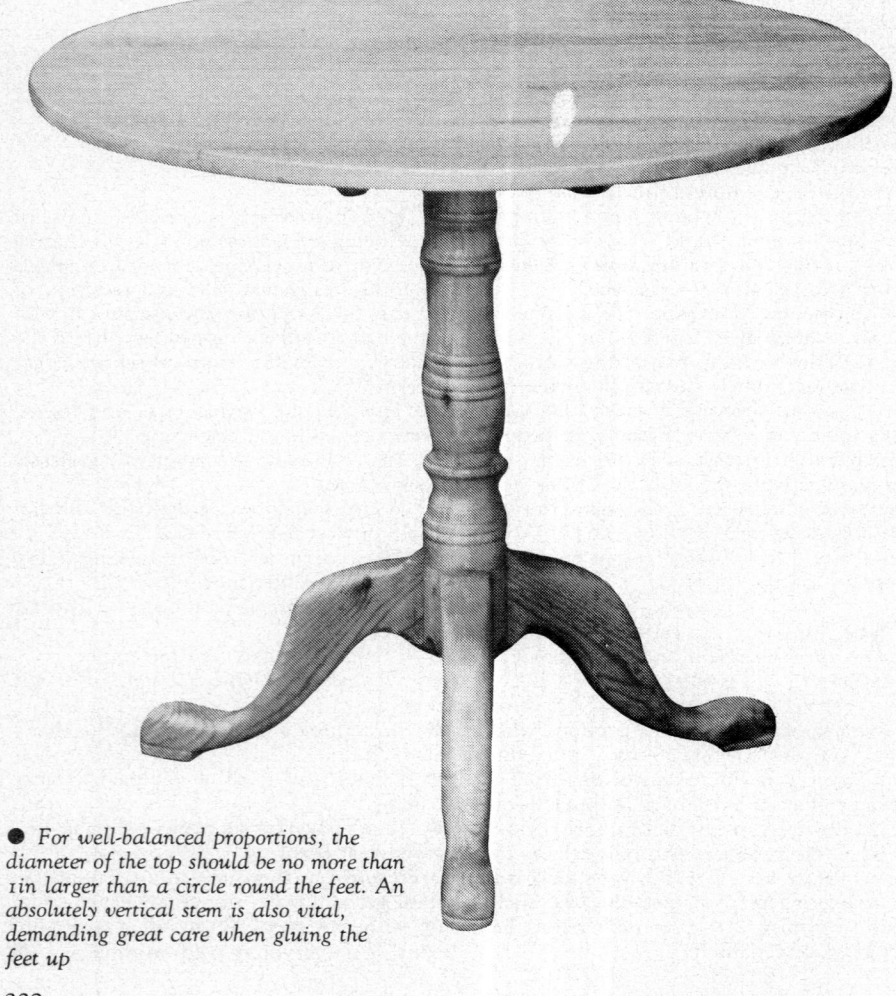

● For well-balanced proportions, the diameter of the top should be no more than 1in larger than a circle round the feet. An absolutely vertical stem is also vital, demanding great care when gluing the feet up

## Stem

2″
2¼″
2½″
5″
2″
3″
1″
4¼″

2″ dia.
top
7″ square block
3¼″ dia.
3″ dia.
3″ dia.
2¼″ dia.
2½″ dia.
3¼″ dia.
2½″ dia.
3″ dia.
3¼″ dia.

leg

dovetails

● *The legs are shaped with hardboard template and bandsaw, and jointed into the stem with long dovetails. The oak bearers for the top are screwed to the block, their ends tapering to nothing at the outer edge*

## Leg

9½″
⅝″ dovetail

centre line of stem

14⅝″
1¾″
1¼″
1¾″

## Top and bearers

1″ pine top 30″ dia.

bearers taper at outside edge

2 bearers oak 26×1″

7″ square block

stem

### Chris Nussbaum's diary of the London College of Furniture C&G 564 cabinetmaking course

Each year students on the 564 cabinetmaking course are set a relatively small piece of work to produce, embodying all or most of the practical techniques they should have acquired; our task this year is a 'correspondence cache', a portable writing/storage unit 375×330×250mm.

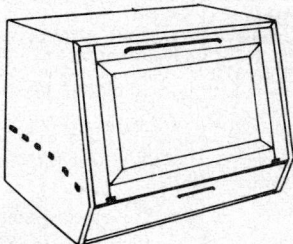

*Designed by David Starling*

Some of us have provided our own materials, so the piece is being constructed variously in ash, American oak, lacewood and English walnut. The main features are the inclined front, with forward-sloping drawer-front at the bottom, and backward-sloping flap above it which opens (pivoting along its bottom edge) to reveal a shelf, the front portion of which is canted to form a continuous sloping surface with the flap when it is fully open and resting on a table or desk.

The carcase is constructed with secret-mitre dovetails along the top edges, rails lap-dovetailed front and rear in the base, with sides and top grooved to take a veneered ply back. The shelf, which is assembled from two pieces edge-jointed at an angle, is housed and through-tenoned to show the quality (or lack of it) in the joints, which are optionally wedged. The traditional drawer construction, with its inclined front, gives us opportunity to practise our canted dovetails.

The flap is a framed fielded panel, which is simple enough, but it embodies the *pièce de résistance* of the design — the hingeing system. A rule joint is cut along the front edge of the shelf and the bottom rail of the flap with a pair of matched cutters, to give identical convex and concave surfaces. Two tiny wooden 'hinges' (rosewood reinforced with brass) are mortised into the shelf and pinned through the end of the flap to give a pivoting action. In this way the rule joint stays perfectly tight with the flap closed or open, shelf and open flap together forming a continuous sloping surface — in theory!

A break from this strenuous benchwork has been provided by a 24-hour 'work-in' in the college by a large number of students. This was organised as a protest against the Inner London Education Authority's attempt to force the college to join a new amalgamation of art and specialised colleges called the London Institute.

It was a great success — musical-instrument students producing a lute in 24 hours, other students repairing toys and equipment from a local school, and our own 564 group producing a real Rolls-Royce of a go-kart overnight, which will be donated to a local playgroup — when we've finished playing with it! ∎

# "MILLS OF ACTON"
## FOR THE BEST IN POWER TOOLS

**NEW**

**DW1251**
**"DeWALT" RADIAL ARM SAWS**
DW1251 **£385.00** carriage £20.00.
DW1370 12" Radial Arm Saw complete with leg stand **£538.00** carriage £30.00.
DW320 10" FOLD-AWAY **£235.00**. Carriage £15.00.
DW1501 with FREE leg stand **£430.00**. Carriage £20.00.

**"DeWALT" PLANER THICKNESSER**
DW1150 Our Price **£455** carr. £25
DW600 Morticing **£62.00**
DA880 Leg Stand **£28.00**

**"ELU" 3" BELT SANDER**
MHB157 with dust bag
**£86.95** p/p £1.50
MHB 157E Electronic
**£95.00** p/p £1.50

**"ELU" 4" BELT SANDER**
MHB 90 **£144.75** p/p £1.50
MHB 90K with frame **£165.50**
p/p £1.50

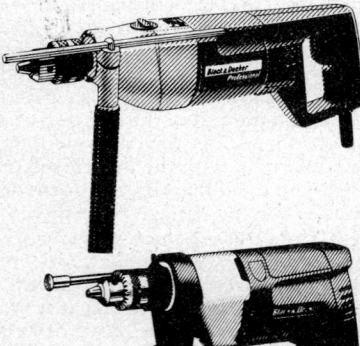

**SPECIAL OFFERS ON BLACK & DECKER PRECUSSION DRILLS**
P2162 10mm Variable Speed, Reversing Drill 450 watts 0-2200 rpm weight 2.1kg. Normally **£65** Our Price **£35.50** p/p £1.50.
P2264 13mm 2 speed General Duty 550 watts 850 dia. 1900 rpm List £73 Our Price **£44.50** p/p £1.50
P2266 13mm Variable Speed, reversing 480 watts 0 dia. 740 & 0 dia. 1650 rpm weight 2.4 kg. Normally **£96** Our Price **£54.50** p/p £1.50
P2622 13mm 2 speed Heavy Duty 720 watts 350/900 rpm Normally £121 Our Price **£74.50** p/p £1.50

**"DeWALT" BS1310 BANDSAW**
2 speeds 375 dia. 750 per min
Max: cutting height 155mm
Max: cutting width 310mm
Saw table 380 × 380mm
**£242.00** carriage £5
BS9310 VARIABLE SPEED
**£289.50** carriage £5.

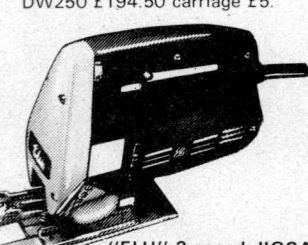

**"ELU" 2 speed JIGSAWS**
ST152 **£99** p/p £1.50
ELECTRONIC ST 152E
**£107.50** p/p £1.50

**"ELU" ORBITAL SANDER**
with dust bag
MVS 156 **£66** p/p £1.50
MVS 156E Electronic
**£78.50** p/p £1.50

**"ELU" CIRCULAR SAWS**
ALL WITH TCT BLADES
MH151 152mm blade
**£78.50** p/p £1.50
MH 65 180mm blade
**£91.00** p/p £1.50
MH182 215mm blade
**£111.75** p/p £1.50

**"DeWALT" BEVEL/MITRE SAW**
DW250 **£194.50** carriage £5.

**"ELU" FLIP-OVER SAW**
TGS/172 10" Blade **£369**
p/p £10.00.

### SPECIAL OFFER

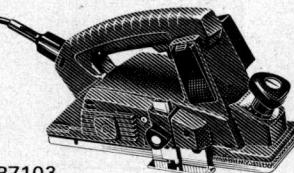

**P7103**
**BLACK & DECKER PLANES**
P7103 3¼" width of cut.
**£85.00** p/p £1.50

**"ELU" MFF 80 PLANE**
with TC blades
**£89.50** p/p £1.50
MFF 80K Planer Kit
with dust bag, all fences. Metal Case
**£107.50** p/p £1.50

**"ELU" MOF 96 ROUTER**
**£78.50** p/p £1.50
MOF 98 Router
**£144.75** p/p £1.50
MOF 31 Router
**£124.00** p/p £1.50

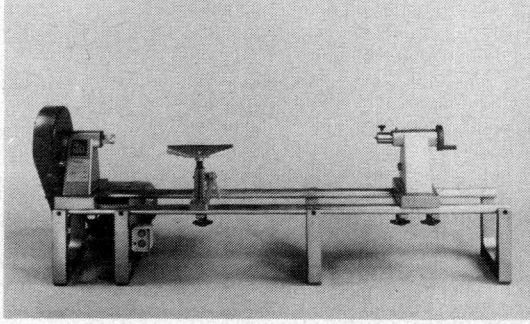

**"ELU" WOOD-TURNING LATHE DB180**
3 speeds, 1000mm between centres
**£275.00** carriage £12.00

# A MILLS (ACTON) LIMITED
*Registered Office*
**32/36 CHURCHFIELD ROAD, ACTON, LONDON W3 6ED**
Telephone 01-992-4835/6/7/8   01-993-2241/2/3
Telex 24224-305

**ACTON**

334

**Prices quoted are those prevailing at press date and are subject to alteration due to economic conditions**

# Tasmaniacs...?

**J**ohn Smith writes: Over the last 10 years, contemporary design and skilful craftsmanship have developed in Tasmanian woodcraft to professional standards, well recognised throughout Australia. A number of craftsmen have achieved national recognition for their work in wood; and many people — furniture-maker Kevin Perkins and sculptor Peter Taylor in particular — have done much to focus their enthusiasm in a degree course called 'Design in Wood', now in its fourth year at the Tasmanian School of Art, University of Tasmania.

The course began in 1982. Earlier there was a craftsman in residence, supported by the Crafts Board of the Australia Council, for which Ashley Cartwright was brought out from the UK. The first year of the course was taught by Hugh Scriven, also from England. Both Ashley and Hugh laid down firm foundations of sound design and careful craftsmanship. One student, Craig Dorrington (*Woodworker*, August 1984), who graduated just before the start of the new course, later followed Ashley to study at Rycotewood.

Hugh was followed by a visiting lecturer from the USA, Jon Brooks, who broadened the course to encompass a sculptural approach to wood. The latest lecturer to join the programme is another American, Peter Adams, who has a flair for fluid laminated forms in furniture.

The balance between English and American influences is a deliberate attempt at creating a course with breadth and variety in approaches, so that the developing Australian identity in wood design can be stimulated by attitudes from both ends of the spectrum. Other lecturers contribute technical skills in cabinet-making, drafting and business studies.

● *Below* is a display cabinet by Niall Campbell; *below right* are two of Patrick Hall's zany 'personality chairs', which incorporate silk-screened images on the canvas backs

● **Above:** A chair by Ross Straker in horizontal scrub. **Left:** This piece by Gary Rizzolo, with its huon-pine drawer, also displays the natural look!

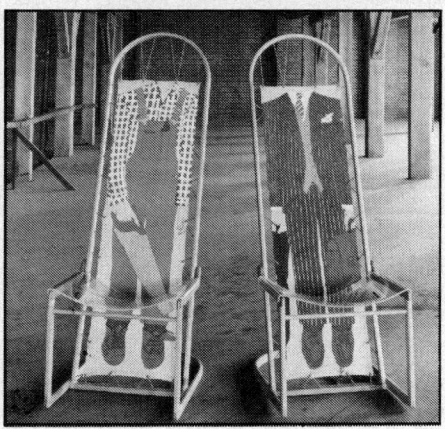

The course was the first of its kind to start in Australia, and is proving very successful. The graduates intend to become self-employed designer-makers, and the diversity of the students' work promises an interesting future for them, as for woodcrafts in Tasmania and beyond.

There is a plentiful variety of timber in the state. Some indigenous species, like huon pine and horizontal scrub, have incomparable qualities. In addition the exploration of synthetic materials — MDF, metal and leather — and use of colour are encouraged in juxtaposition with wood.

The development of original designs is central to the whole programme, and its success hinges on this factor. High craftsmanship is an automatic expectation, but skill is wasted without a personal design identity. For this combination is not only sought in the course — it is demanded of the profession.

● John Smith, a senior lecturer, is Design in Wood course co-ordinator at the Tasmanian School of Art, University of Tasmania, Box 252C, GPO, Hobart, Tasmania, Australia 7001, tel. 203274. ∎

# Precision de luxe

**Ralph Selby's approach to his craft is perfectionist by any standards. Aidan Walker went to see him at work**

Ralph Selby's Multico tenoning machine is fitted with a set of comb-jointing cutters he has had made to his own specifications. A neatly typed sticker on the sliding table catches the eye — 'For Dama tray set at 230.00 from inner base edge. Cross-cut to 252.100mm; adjust cutters to give 210.50mm b.s.'.

'I sometimes feel slightly lonely,' he admits, the merest hint of wistfulness coming through; 'I still don't know whether I'm unique.'

There is no doubt that he is not in the common run of creative woodworkers (not an ordinary breed at the best of times). He produces meticulous, almost obsessively high-quality work for a selection of corporate and private clients, who are prepared to pay the earth for the very best; and, where Ralph Selby is concerned, they get it.

Ralph (pronounced Rafe, although he's almost given up insisting on it) is an artist, a craftsman and an engineer. Most of his work is in wood, but he has taken commissions in other materials; 3D perspex models of the Lucas Industries logo, finely balanced and solidly standing at a seemingly precarious 45°, and fabricated-metal arrows for the London Docklands development complex. He took a fine-art degree at Durham University, and spent 17 years as head of the fine-art department at Derbyshire College of Art. As an educational administrator, he says, he tried to wean the teaching away from 'specialism'. His own designer/maker identity of today clearly displays the multi-faceted approach; he combines the aesthetics of an artist, the precision of an engineer, and the craftsmanship of a cabinetmaker.

Developing a collaborative relationship in the late 70s with Pentagram, a London design group, he was commissioned by Cunningham Hearst Advertising to make a relief mural for their London office's staircase. It gave him a chance, he explains, to explore the relationship between real and implied perspectives. The deceptively simple-looking arrangement of overlapping jelutong blocks is cut, machined and jointed entirely on compound angles, work in which errors increase geometrically. Fitting was an angle-drilling job for dowels that demanded absolute accuracy.

Precision is a constant keynote in his every description of every job, his quest for perfection a recurring theme. He'll re-make something to alter the proportions by 1mm or less if he's not quite satisfied, and the energy with which he speaks of the problems he encounters and overcomes tells of his own exacting standards. Higher,

● *Ralph and Herman, who adorns this month's cover, in the workshop. Full of equipment, but neatly laid out for ease and efficiency. Home-made router table in the foreground*

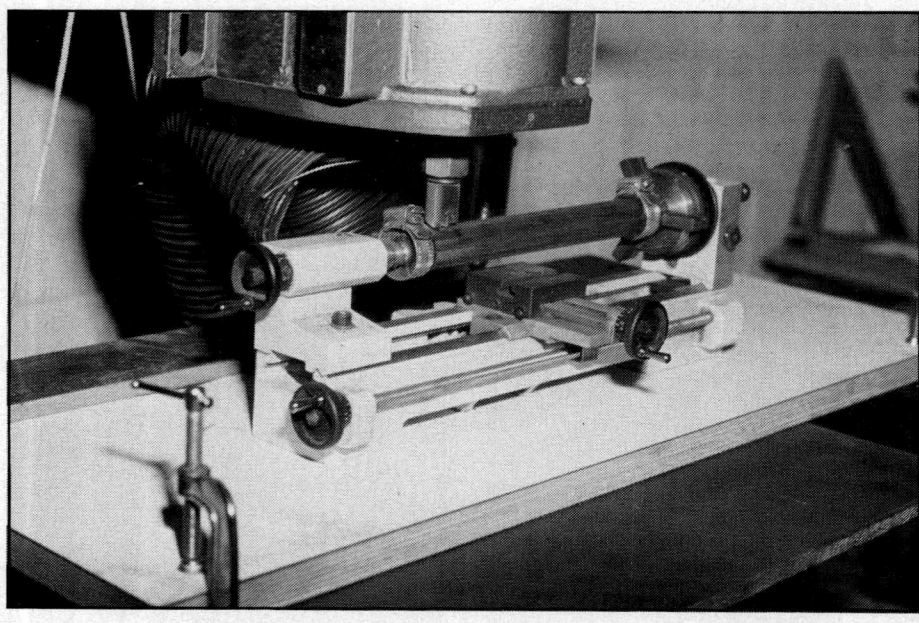

● *Mounted in a mini-lathe, the African-blackwood blank for a 12-sided pen-case can be machined under the router with absolute accuracy*

one begins to realise, than those of even the most fastidious client.

Completely blocking one end of his crammed — but not cramped — six-car-garage-sized workshop is an Ebac timber drier. Control over timber moisture con-

tent is something that Ralph just cannot allow out of his own hands; he has a digital thermometer fitted, an extra that tells you the temperature at different heights in the stack. Curiously enough, much of his timber is machined to within a fraction of a millimetre over finished size *before* drying, a quirk for which he cites lack of space as the main reason. Using small stock is another factor that reduces the risk of disastrous cupping, and is incidentally the characteristic of his work that allows two machines to fit where a joiner couldn't put one.

Pre-kilned machining has created the odd touch-and-go moment, though. 50 jigsaw maps of the Persian Gulf, a solid-gold Kuwait the tiny centre-piece, had to be on a certain plane at a certain time for shipment. No extra time. No delivery, no payment. He loaded the Ebac with a cocktail of exotic timbers, each one for a different country-shape — rosewood, padouk, chestnut, Burmese teak, voamboana, tulip-wood, lignum vitae, Brazilian freijo, yew, sycamore and maple. All were already machined to 13mm; Kuwait's arid climate being what it is, the specified moisture content was to be 7%. Finished size was to be 12.5mm, and there was no way of telling how it would all come out. The gamble paid off. A sample of the jigsaw map that Ralph still has fits together as if it had been stamped out yesterday, and it was only later that he discovered the palatial residences for which these maps were destined are often humidified!

Stamping is a cheap jigsaw production process, but these were no cheap jigsaws. The batch method for the irregular shapes meant that every piece had to fit into any example of its neighbour pieces, the pressure of time and cost prohibiting the cut-and-fit individual approach. Buying a precision bandsaw and thin, strong butcher's blades as insurance against failure, he contracted the job out as programmed laser-cutting (he shudders at the thought that he might have had to cut all those bits by hand — as would any mortal). From a drawing reproduced on film, XY co-ordinates are plotted and programmed into a computer, which then writes a punch-tape to control the movements of the table under the laser cutting-head. But time was short and the firm's programmer was in bed with flu. OK, said Ralph, I'll do it myself. And did.

**I**'m lucky enough to have had no education in woodwork at all,' he says. 'Many of my problems are solved from a light-engineering standpoint.' He is therefore not limited by thinking only in terms of wood techniques and wood processes, and two heavy testaments to this approach stand in his workshop. He uses two Emco vertical milling machines and a Maximat engineer's lathe, more often for wood than metal. The milling machines are ideal for prototyping, which makes up a lot of his bread-and-butter work, because there is no need to spend long hours devising and making holding jigs for the overhead router. What's more, once the piece is made the needs for the jig design are already established.

Every corner of his orderly production space is put to good use — there's not a

photo Malcolm Lewis

● **Above,** the map of the Gulf is made up of a tantalising selection of laser-cut exotic and English hardwoods; **left,** the catch that took so many hours' design; **below,** the Cunningham Hearst mural blocks deceive the eye and boggle the brain

# Precision de luxe

wasted inch. Unusual equipment abounds, plus more familiar gear put to very unfamiliar uses. One of the most extraordinary devices, and obviously one of his personal favourites, is an American Rockwell Delta Uniplane, bought from a New Jersey second-hand dealer, and carried back on the plane as hand luggage. It's something like a bacon-slicer: eight fly-cutters revolving round a vertical plate which is in angled alignment with the outfeed fence. The infeed is adjustable for depth of cut. Four of the cutters take off the first bulk; the other four cut finely, and add a finish on the upstroke. Before my astonished (and greedy) eyes Ralph took a $3 \times 2 \times \frac{3}{8}$in piece of jelutong and buzzed $\frac{1}{16}$in off it — just like that. The cutters' low rotating weight means that you can plane stuff of a size and thickness that you otherwise wouldn't take near a machine. It's difficult to set up, but a boon once it's done.

The more you look round the workshop, the more you see evidence of Ralph's determination, first to achieve exactitude, and then to produce. On the back wall is an old glass case of Moore and Wright's, the Sheffield precision-measuring-instrument manufacturers; it is full of dial-gauges, Vernier calipers, steel rules — and a set of digital calipers. That Multico tenoner was bought for one specific job, the production of batches of exquisitely made boards for *dama*, an Arab version of draughts. The trays were to be comb-jointed, but Ralph couldn't find cutters fine, accurate or reliable enough, so he ordered a set to be specially made. He stripped the whole machine and carefully re-built it, with a lot of much-appreciated help from Multico themselves, and when the job was done worked out the time spent on setting up against the time the machine actually ran. 18 man-days setting up; four hours' running time!

The photographs show some of the meticulous work that went into these pieces. The rosewood squares, 10mm thick, are all joined with loose tongues, and brass line inserts are laid in the length of two squares at a time to sit on the tongues. The adhesive is Araldite; the suede linings are fitted into grooves in the top, bottom and sides at the same time as the main structure is assembled. Ralph was reticent about the method he uses to keep the messy Araldite off the precious leather — one finger-mark makes one very expensive reject. The dimensioning of the squares allows no appreciable tolerance for a perfect overall size, and they're all counter-grained too. Ralph's description of working with unforgiving glue and clamping jigs displayed more than a hint of the adrenalin that flows during the assembly process.

The catches on the *dama* boards he displays with particular pride. Looking simple, working effectively, their design was the result of many hours of development, and their manufacture is a

● *The* dama *board. Holly, brass and rosewood put together in a meticulous, cunning – and secret – construction*

complex multi-step process. The recesses alone involve a three-stage jig. He pointed out to me an almost indiscernible nib in the centre of the finger-push recess. 'Look — no effective cutting speed at the centre. I've found a way round that now.'

Jigs, of course, are meat and drink in the Selby world. All use a base of ¾ or 1in Tufnel, a sort of epoxy/cloth blend for which the makers claim almost infallible dimensional stability. The dominoes, for which Ralph wanted to get 'a pneumatic fit' in their tray, are machined to length on the overhead router in a pair of jigs that took four days to make. These blackwood pieces too are cut fractionally oversize and then kilned before being given their final machining. He found that a minute inaccuracy in the positioning of the dots could quite easily be picked up by eye, so has modified a miniature lathe and a jeweller's engraving machine to guarantee perfectly consistent spacing, however hard you look. The 12-sided pen case, with its invisible polypropylene hinge (another pneumatic fit — I spent minutes working out how to open it) is machined using the miniature lathe itself as a jig under the overhead router. Precise sizing of the 12 sides needs 12 precisely indexed steps round 360°.

**H**erman, who has a special place in Ralph's affections, is a story in his own right. He is a life-size lay figure in utile, commissioned by an office-furniture manufacturer for promotional work. He was built 'inside out', Ralph explains; small lay figures were X-rayed to discover how the joints in such a construction worked. Their components were turned on a lathe; the carving part — 'relatively minor' — came last.

There is no doubt that Ralph Selby's

approach is rare, if not unique, in working wood. I doubt whether, at bottom, he'd consider himself a woodworker at all; he is certainly a businessman, and includes efficient administration and effective profitability among his creative aims. He cost his work with a computer, demonstrating that the more you can break a job down into ever-smaller units, the more accurately you can estimate. He is a first-class marketeer, and by good fortune, good salesmanship, good design and hard work has come to satisfy fabulously wealthy clients who pay according to the standards they demand. He has found buyers for his unrelenting, almost obssessive insistence on pinning the job down to ±0.01mm; but his business administration and professionalism, showing the same attention to detail, are as important to his success as the setting on his comb-jointer. What he is selling is the certainty that he won't be satisfied until the client would have been happy 100 times over, the security of his wealth of accumulated experience, and the guarantee that the work will be on time. 'Craftsmanship is a universal language,' he says, 'a sort of Esperanto that everyone understands.'

He is a modern craftsman — and commercial, as every craftsman must be. It must be said that there remains a niggling doubt. Not about his skill, his energy, or his dedication, but about that essential ingredient of a craftsman's art: warmth. In the single-minded search for perfection, could it have been mislaid along the way?

● Ralph and his wife Lu Jeffery, who took the photos, are expanding their business, and selling their charming Derbyshire stone cottage — with workshop behind it. If you're interested, their number is (0332) 880100. ∎

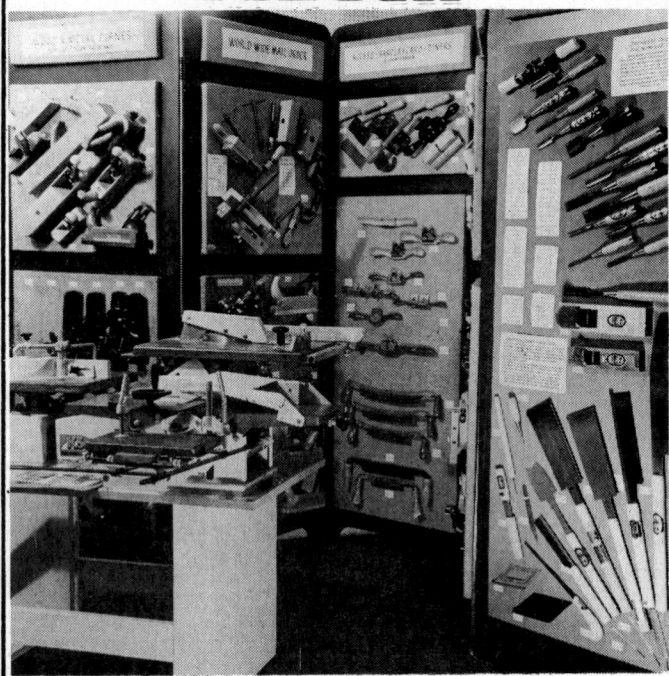

KINDLY MENTION 'WOODWORKER' WHEN REPLYING TO ADVERTISEMENTS

# The skeleton chest

## Introducing an excellent project — and its designer/maker

Noel Gaskell protests that he didn't mean to be a perpetual student. His anxiety is understandable. He has not only spent a year at Rycotewood in Oxfordshire, home of celebrated courses in fine craftsmanship and design, but also done stints at Goldsmiths College, the Royal College of Art, and Buckinghamshire College in High Wycombe.

It was all, he says, a logical journey to where he wanted to be. Namely one rather cosy unit of a well-worn GLC workshop block in Shoreditch, about the size of a smallish living-room and complete with open fire in one corner! A little studio office on a gallery platform is reached by a ladder. There's only him — no assistants; and he says he can't see himself ever wanting his operation to grow.

Keeping it securely within his two hands should, he feels, avoid the trap into which he's seen many a colleague fall — where design aspirations must be sacrificed to keep a concern going, and early ideas are buried beneath weeks and months of turning out custom kitchens.

For, although he's as well equipped as space allows, even small batches are not large in Noel's scheme of things. Instead he produces, firstly, one-offs to commission (work coming by work-of-mouth, but also through the odd magazine article, since he takes care to seize publicity wherever he can find it). Secondly, he makes prototypes, e.g. for office screens designed by himself with a view to production by the large manufacturer Intercraft.

And he spends as much time as possible at the drawing-board. He has honed his drawing skills to a level at which he can accurately visualise any design option he wants. As he points out, such development drawings can be shown to clients as hard evidence of the design work for which they will have to part with good money.

Whether a set-up like Noel's is viable must depend partly on location, on contacts, and on effective self-promotion. But there's another consideration, of course: the flair displayed in the work. In Noel's case, the project here lets you sample and judge for yourself. ∎

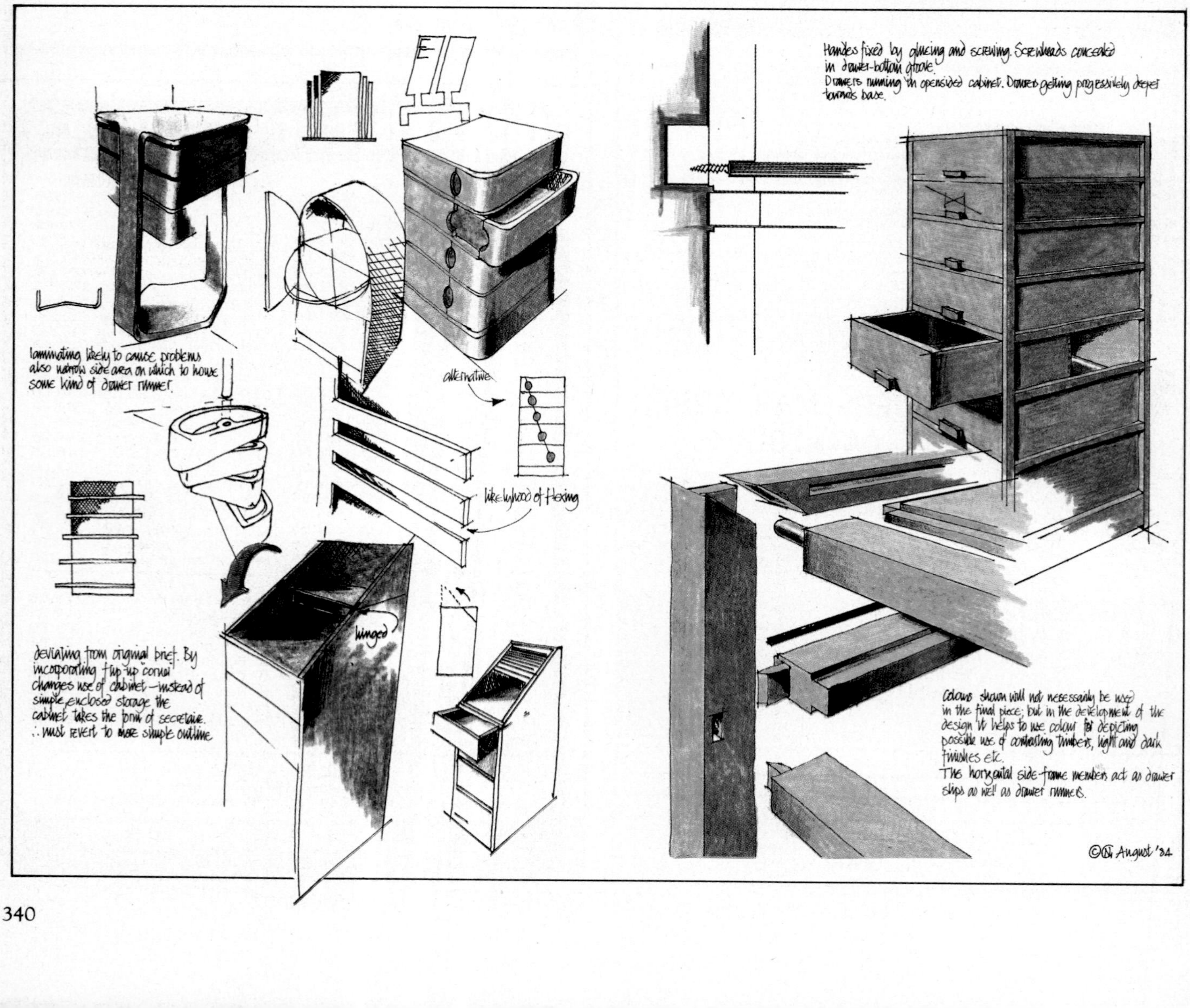

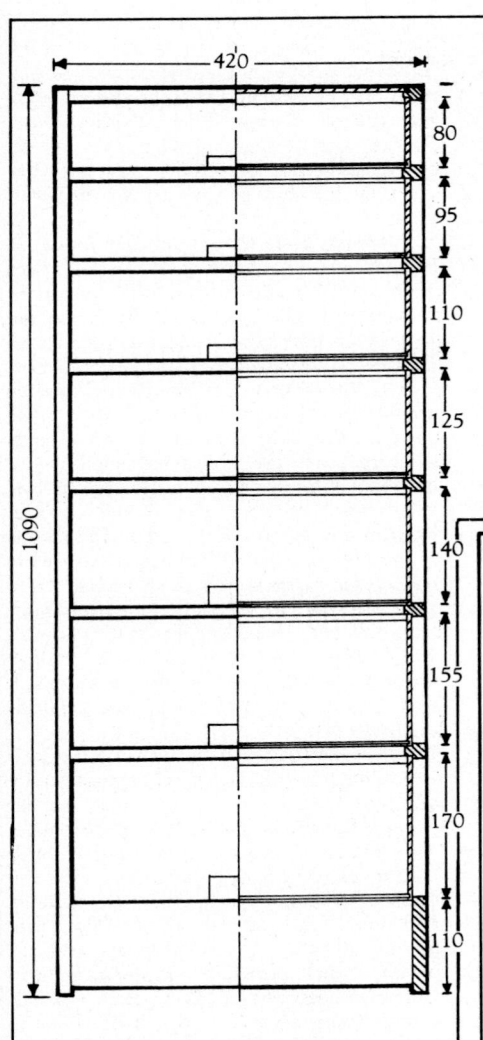

## Dimensions and details

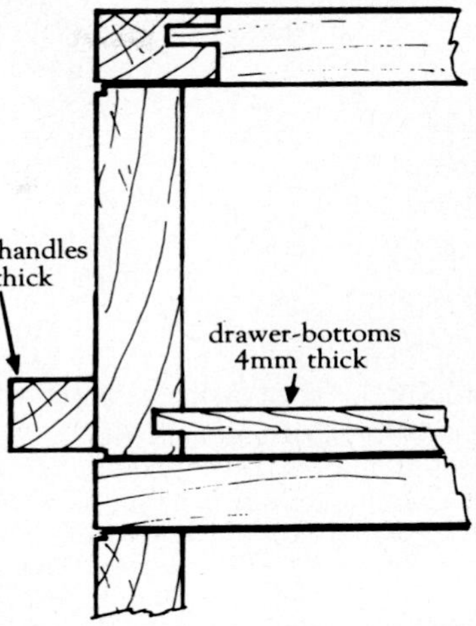

420
1090
80
95
110
125
140
155
170
110


drawer-handles 15mm thick
drawer-bottoms 4mm thick


Sizes in mm

● *The chest is made entirely in English oak, but the drawer-fronts are fumed to contrast with the frame. The drawer-sides are 8mm thick, as is the solid-oak top panel, tongued into a groove in the top frame. The drawer-bottoms are cedar of Lebanon, a popular choice for this function because of its fragrance. The handles increase in thickness proportionately to the depth of the drawer-fronts*

cabinet uses wall for support. Problem being undesireable open-topped drawers.
theme of drawers stacked vertically still prevailing; but angular, geometric shapes taking over somewhat!
10mm R
tambour
drawers
corner detail-square protruding pegs in contrasting timber.
©NG August '84.


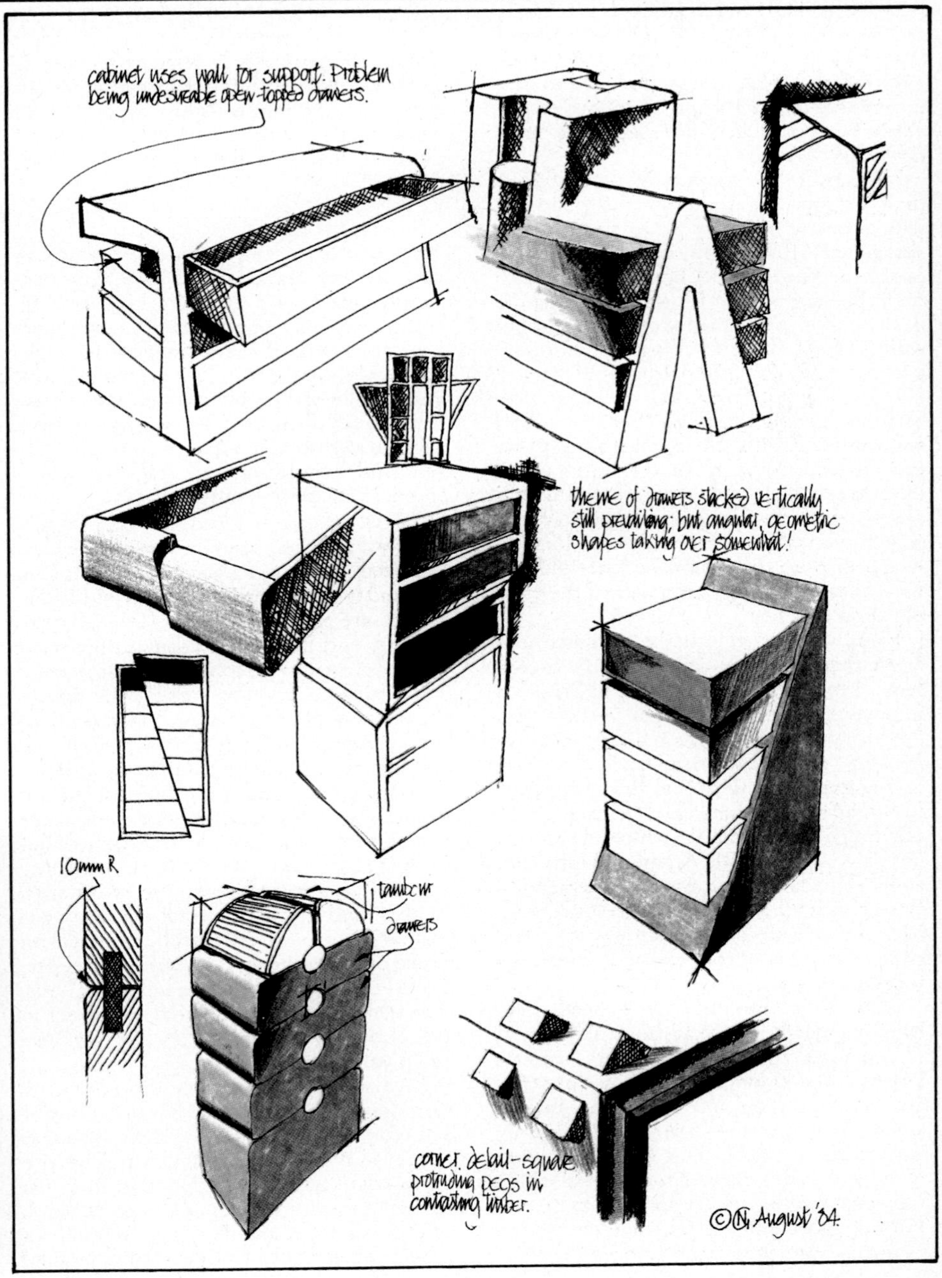

● *The working drawings* **above** *depict the final version of Noel Gaskell's handsome oak chest (***opposite top***, with a detail* **below***). The brilliantly accomplished coloured sketches,* **left** *and* **right***, show the stages on the way – and help to communicate with clients. Visualising like this can take a lot of practice*

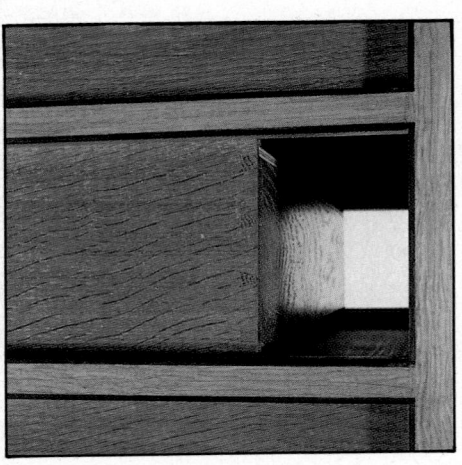

# Buying timber wisely:1

The competent woodworker is a canny buyer first. But how do you get the best from the timber trade? Alan Thomas starts with a close look at softwood

'Of course,' said the hero at the other end of the telephone, 'if we can find anything it'll cost you the thick end of thirty quid. And you'd better come and pick it up yourself — that'll save us the carriage, like.'

'It' would have been a secondhand (all right, reclaimed) oak plank about 6ft long and 8 or 9in wide for which I was expected to make a round journey of about 60 miles. And, if the price demanded sound not unreasonable, the abruptly terminated conversation took place three years ago, when £30 was worth £30.

In the event an oak gate-post superfluous to a neighbour's requirements (paid for with a bottle of white wine) and a newly sharpened ripsaw solved my immediate problem. The episode, however, served to underline a basic fact of woodworking life in Britain — the difficulty of getting timber suitable for making anything grander than a packing-case, and at an affordable price.

It was not always so. But political fortunes and misfortunes, wars won and lost, empires ditto ditto, man's insatiable greed and unconcern for the future — all have taken their toll. And anyone with a seeing eye who looks at cabinet-work, coachbuilding, or even domestic joinery, which is more than (say) 70 years old will have cause to sigh for an aspect of the good old days that has gone forever.

Even so, our grandfathers picked and chose their material; and we should do the same. Most of the timber used in Britain is imported, and much of that is softwood. For which, of course, the building industry provides the greatest demand.

The dreadful things that have happened to pound-dollar exchange rates have priced out much of the timber which used to be imported from north America. Unfortunately, Canada and the American west coast were almost the only timber resources we had which were able to supply long and wide boards sawn from trees felled in virgin forests.

Instead, Britain currently depends very heavily indeed on its traditional Baltic suppliers: Sweden, Russia, Finland, Norway, Poland. And shippers from these countries are now cutting and supplying mainly small-girth timber — that is, wood from man-planted forests. This kind of forestry is a highly industrialised business in which trees are treated as just another crop, and nothing goes to waste: even roots and branches are kept for processing into particle- and fibreboards of one kind or another. Naturally grown trees used to be felled when they were about 80 to 100 years old, but now it suits everybody connected with the trade to harvest and process when trees are no more than about 50 to 60 years old. Few are able to give more than a 3×9in board, for these butts are rarely more than 10in or so in diameter at the top, and can't produce any usefully large cross-sections in average lengths greater than about 13½ft. At least plantation trees, grown close together, have one advantage in tending to develop smaller knots.

It might be as well to outline the way in which the trade is organised. Shippers supply the sawn lumber, and sell by contract to our importers. (The shippers have an edge in these transactions, for a tree left in the forest will be worth more next year, while an importer must have something to sell this year). Most importers sell their stocks on to merchants and end-users, but some end-users are big enough to import directly themselves.

Softwood quality is judged, and paid for, usually on the basis of three grades: unsorted, fifths, and sixths — from Russia, the grades are unsorted, fourths and fifths. Sixths are really material for the case-makers, and the timber required for most joinery work will come from unsorted. There was an attempt some years ago to introduce a grading system based on end-user requirements, but the trade preferred to keep its age-old mysteries and rituals. America is understandably much preoccupied with its own enormous home demand, so mills there like to produce sizes wanted by local users rather than the dimensions acceptable here: most if not all lumber sold in the domestic US market is planed all round, even with eased edges. Some of the very nicest material, the clears, comes to Britain for use by ladder-makers, who take Douglas fir and hemlock in parcels which are graded to a high percentage of blemish-free wood.

Like sensible businessmen in any other line, people in the timber trade don't buy or sell for the fun of it. Their primary intention is to make money, so they have to be as adept at spotting trends in financial exchange rates, and fluctuations of demand, as they are at recognising the potential in a parcel of timber. It can easily happen, therefore, that there is a considerable difference between the price of stock imported in one part of the country at one time of the year and that of similar stuff brought in elsewhere at another time. Stocks, qualities and availabilities are all strictly governed by price — you get what you pay for, but getting a good deal can mean shopping around.

But what is it we are talking about? A builder buys carcassing timber; joiners want good-grade redwood; furniture-makers just call it pine. Broadly, European redwood is pine from Scandinavia or Poland. European whitewood is spruce from northern central Europe. Anyone with lingering memories of that very-high-quality Sitka spruce once used for building aeroplanes can forget it: its availability is negligible, and the same goes for once-common pitch pine. That has become almost an exotic. Maritime pine from Portugal and France is essentially packing-case material. Those big trees from Canada and the western states are Douglas fir, Californian redwood, hemlock and white spruce. Both red and white pine from the east coast, mainly Ontario, are liked for pattern-making — a useful pointer for anyone engaged in good-quality work.

Somewhat surprisingly, north American suppliers do not have a good reputation for quality. This concerns not the original timber, but the lack of care with which it is converted and seasoned. Mills there still favour band and circular saws, with the result that accurate sizing is hard to achieve and uniformity has to come from that planing all round. European frame saws are much more precise. American and Canadian seasoning methods can be casual, too: perhaps this is less important when the stuff is used locally and quickly, but for shipping overseas from the west coast all sawn material is now treated to resist staining.

WHAT EV
TIMBE
USER
SHOULD BE
GETTING
MORE OI

No user needs to be reminded that seasoning is the great unknown in all too many timber transactions. Few people, even in these days of do-it-yourself kilning, really want to buy complete butts, saw them up and season them in order to get predictable material, yet those who don't are thrown back on what the trade offers. Unfortunately theory and practice can part company when wood is being seasoned; and, while modern rapid methods can be satisfactory, sometimes they're not.

All things being equal, and where time does not matter much, time-honoured air-drying in stick produces dependable timber. However, not only do the stacks of wood take up a lot of valuable hardstanding yard space, but they also represent huge sums of money which is locked up and can't be used for anything else.

On the other hand, kilning — carefully carried out — can produce timber that is for most purposes the equal of air-dried stuff. But the economics of the trade are not geared to conscientiously grading each piece of wood and drying it for just so long and no longer. Averages are the thing, so Scandinavian timber destined for Britain is kilned down to a moisture content of about 14 or 15%, which will give acceptable stability during shipping and yard storage. The major problem caused by too-rapid kilning is that the moisture content within each piece of wood is not evenly distributed: it will be drier on the outside than it is at the centre. The snag here is that re-sawing such pieces produces sections which can be quite dry on one face and less so on the opposite one. The effects of that need no elaboration, though in fairness it should be added that just the same result could happen after a carefully kilned piece of material has been exposed to the atmosphere on a damp day!

And of course hardly anyone ever quarter-saws softwoods by making radial or near-radial cuts. The timber is usually sawn through-and-through, which adds cupping to other drying-out hazards.

Taking all in all, it does rather sound as though obtaining softwoods for any purpose is such a chancy business that it would be better to give up the whole thing and find some other occupation. And those of us who are looking, in the main, for small amounts of top-quality material are able to bring no commercial pressure to bear on our suppliers. In the circumstances it pays to be careful, calculating and cunning. Most towns of any size have at least one timber yard. Its main customers will be the building trade, and the key questions to ask its management are: 'Do you stock unsorted or joinery grades?' (the label 'joinery' is merely used to distinguish unsorted grades from fifths, which are carcassing material) and: 'Please may I sort through for myself?' If the answer to the first is yes, so much the better; but a positive reply to the latter is essential.

Unfortunately all those intriguing marks and emblems painted into the endgrain will mean nothing to most amateurs or, in all probability, to the chap who is actually helping to turn over the stock. Which is a pity, for they identify the sawmill from which the timber came. However, if the marks don't mean much, do look most carefully for knots, splits and shakes partially concealed under surface grime.

Since few logs are quarter-sawn it follows that most pieces in the stack will be flat-grained. If knots are acceptable, consider also how they can reveal, in wood from the upper part of a tree, a spiralling grain that is almost unplanable. Look carefully on any piece for the bluish staining that probably indicates poor preparation and storage, and which is both unsightly and irremovable.

Except in a few instances, craftsmen are not going to need planed-all-round material: it is merely a waste of their money, and removes much of the opportunity to adjust thicknesses and dimensions when planning a job. Something else not likely to be wanted are the pre-packs of polythene-wrapped stuff intended for Saturday morning do-it-yourselfers. My own inspections of many racks in superstores owned by several of the big retailers (names are withheld to protect the guilty) have shown that timber quality within a pack varies from barely all right to rough, and they don't even trouble to conceal the rough. Much the same is true of stock sold loose to the DIY trade — but then, supplying the high-street shops is now a distinct activity among importers and timber yards, who well know aware that handling small quantities can be made to justify price loadings of 30, 40 and even 50%.

Finally, even if the stock is well chosen and was conscientiously seasoned in the first place, its moisture content is not going to be suitable for its final role in life. Plenty has already been said in *Woodworker* about seasoning, and there is no need to repeat it all again, but with such an uncertain material it will pay every time to leave rough-sawn material for as long as possible in the place where it will ultimately come to rest, and to repeat the process when parts are shaped but still oversize. I bought a quantity of prepared tongue-and-groove matching from a reputable yard for use on a kitchen ceiling. Over three weeks' storage in the back bedroom, each nominal 4in board narrowed by an average of $\frac{1}{16}$in. Or 2in over the ceiling . . . But since it is hardly feasible to stack a pile of timber in the client's front room — or even, sometimes, in one's own — this raises the difficulty of getting constant and suitable humidity and temperature in the workshop.

Just another indication that the wise buyer is the one who knows exactly where his or her purchase is going. ∎

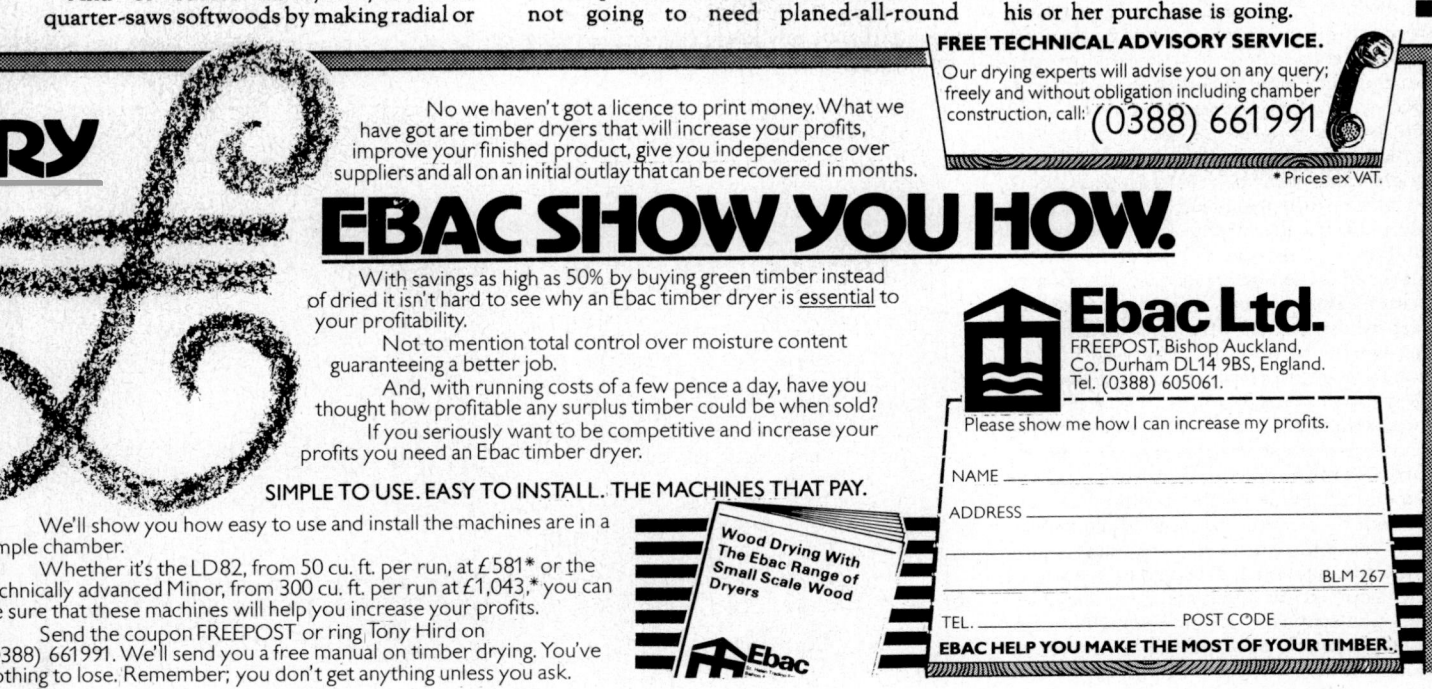

# Interior excitement

Devon designer/maker/ teacher Chris Faulkner describes the evolution, and the workshop, which produced this splendid oak writing-desk

**M**y work is mostly commissioned fine furniture in exotic and home-grown hardwoods — items such as dining-tables, chairs and writing-desks. Some pieces are traditional, such as refectory tables, and some contemporary in design. My own designs tend not to be so aggressively 'different' as some contemporary work. This is not a criticism, only my personal approach. I have survived in self-employment, I think, partly because I have made a great effort to satisfy people's particular needs. I use my experience and knowledge to produce what, from conversation with them, I think they would like, rather than what I would perhaps prefer them to like. On occasion I will gamble and make what I would like them to have, but as by then I know their idiosyncracies it is usually a safe bet.

My largest single commission was for a writing-desk, original in design, in applewood with several secret compartments. The price was a long way into four figures. I have now completed just under 200 commissions.

I hold an exhibition at my workshops every two years if possible. This consists of my own and my students' work, and I expect to generate 18 months' work from it. In my first eight years I exhibited annually with the Devon Guild of Craftsmen, and occasionally in London and travelling exhibitions. I received only three orders from exhibitions at which I was not present and available to talk to interested people; I'm not sure what this means, except that good work does not necessarily sell itself. People may buy the exhibit, but they are unlikely to place orders for other things unless they can be re-assured by conversation with the maker, there and then, while the mood is right. Two days later is too late.

I have never advertised, and word of mouth brings about 25% of my orders. I only exhibit at my workshop. An increasing number of visitors come, and — although I would reach more people if I exhibited in the public market-place — I can at least be certain that here I am spending time talking to and persuading people who are already partly committed to the idea of having something made. The reason for the limitation is that the risks involved in carrying and exhibiting my customers' work far afield are just too great. Insurance does not cover irreparable damage to someone's treasured possession. Nor can gallery owners be expected to guarantee against damage.

● *Simple in outline and sturdy, this desk opens at top and front to reveal innards that exhibit great craftsmanship*

'A home is a place for living, resting and being at peace; I don't want things to jump out and say "look at me", yet of course they must not be dull.'

**I**found while I was working in the timber-importing trade that wood held a more than normal interest for me. The company sent me on a course for wood scientists. It was fascinating — and, although I was very grateful to them it was their undoing as far as my future with them was concerned. I was off. I suddenly knew I wanted to make furniture.

I had no thought of self-employment at this stage, but after I had been introduced to Edward Baly, a founder member of the Devon Guild of Craftsmen, and had begun training with him in 1969 at Week, near Dartington, everything seemed suddenly to fall into the right order: I would survive if I worked hard enough, and was not being taken care of. The air seemed sharper; my perception of everything was brighter. Above all, the results of my labours were beyond what I had expected, and I knew after only a few weeks that I might be able to earn a living on my own. As far as I was concerned, a dream come true.

My first commission after leaving Ted was a sub-contract for eight boardroom chairs to his design. With most of the proceeds I bought my first circular saw. No more rip-sawing by hand! Next a coffee-table for a friend, and so on — in fits and starts, and also with much excitement simply because I was beginning to support myself. Independence: some like it, others don't value it. I did. Then three pieces to my own design for acceptance into the Devon Guild of Craftsmen — a proud day for me. Their summer exhibition that year was my first public platform. With my prices rather lower than they should have been, and by talking myself into the ground for the three weeks of the exhibition, I acquired 18 months' work.

Nowadays I generally arrive at a quotation by the simple addition of hours and materials, the hourly rate dictated by adding together all the overheads and the wage required. However, an order will always be secured by an adjustment. Experience provides instinct as to how best to present the package, and adjustments up or down will be made to suit different situations. A new customer should be encouraged. A simple piece will command a lower rate than a more difficult one, not because my time is suddenly worth less but because someone else could make it and be

● *Chris Faulkner made this extending dining-table in cherry. The faces of its legs are slightly curved*

happy to charge less, possibly because his overheads are lower than mine. An exhibition piece made for my own pleasure and without the constraints of another person's preferences will have been arrived at without complication, so its price will be comparatively lower than that of a commissioned piece.

**'I try to create excitement, something worth discovering, in the interiors of writing-desks, bureaux, games-tables. But for the exterior I am in search of a tranquillity to which Eastern craftsmen have come nearest.'**

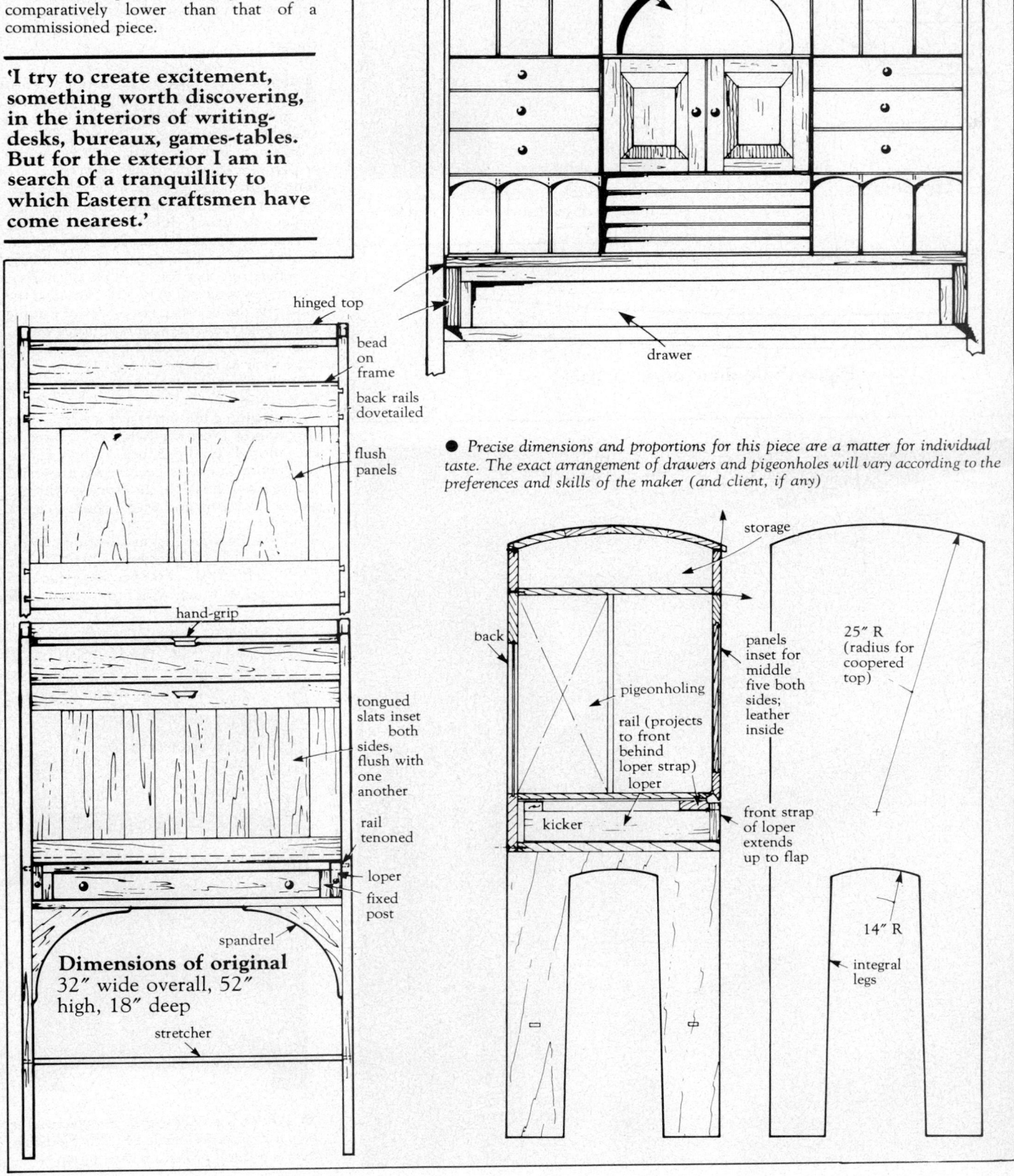

● *Precise dimensions and proportions for this piece are a matter for individual taste. The exact arrangement of drawers and pigeonholes will vary according to the preferences and skills of the maker (and client, if any)*

open front

bowed

hinged top

bead on frame

back rails dovetailed

flush panels

hand-grip

tongued slats inset both sides, flush with one another

rail tenoned

loper

fixed post

spandrel

**Dimensions of original**
32″ wide overall, 52″ high, 18″ deep

stretcher

drawer

storage

back

pigeonholing

rail (projects to front behind loper strap)

loper

kicker

panels inset for middle five both sides; leather inside

front strap of loper extends up to flap

25″ R (radius for coopered top)

14″ R

integral legs

# Interior excitement

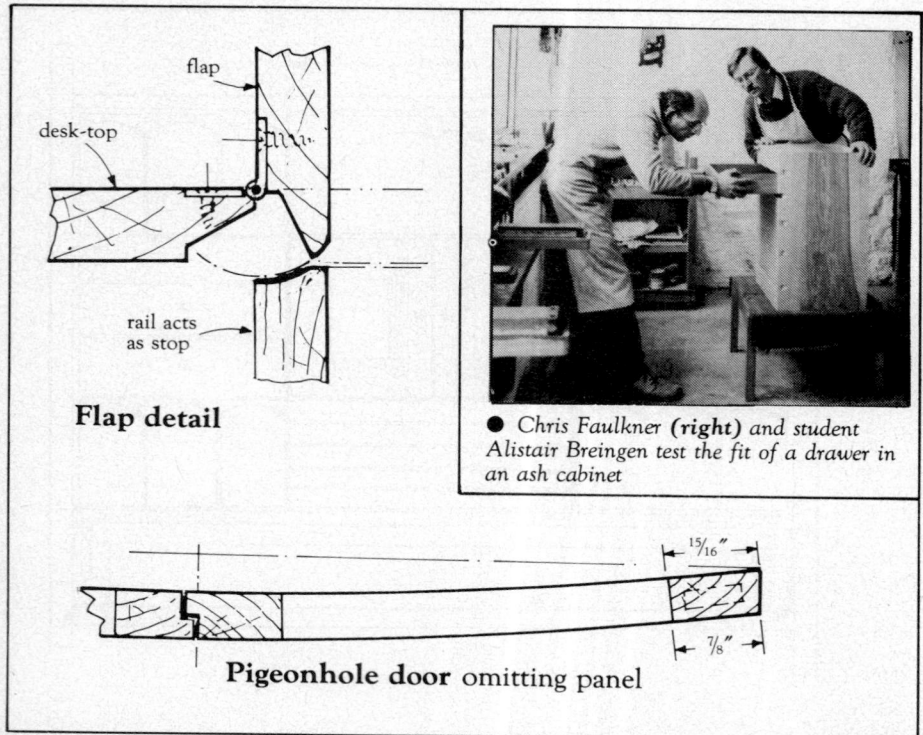

**Flap detail**

flap
desk-top
rail acts as stop

**Pigeonhole door** omitting panel

$\frac{15}{16}''$
$\frac{7}{8}''$

● *Chris Faulkner* **(right)** *and student Alistair Breingen test the fit of a drawer in an ash cabinet*

Our machines are a 10in. circular saw, planer and thicknesser, mortiser and bandsaw, plus portable power tools. No spindle, no lathe. Turning is contracted out, and we have no veneer press. We do all our veneering by the hammer process. Very little work is done with man-made boards, and I usually hold a fair stock of air-dried timber.

I don't employ anyone, but I would like to train someone who would stay with me in some sort of partnership. I teach students, usually two, full-time in my workshop, with a view to their becoming self-employed in their own right. Four are now in direct competition a few miles away. These students pay for their tuition in the same way that I did 15 years ago. The system is successful in several ways. It provides interest for all of us; it is mutually beneficial, in that the more we put into it the more we get out of it; and, provided the ability is there, it is a faster way of gaining knowledge than the other traditional way of learning, the apprenticeship. Both schemes have their advantages.

It also provides me with a second string to my bow.

Maintaining the interest is an important part of how I earn my living. If I wanted to earn more I could produce more by batch-production methods, become a factory, and before long be back in the office — which is where I came in, and what I chose to leave behind!

● Chris Faulkner is at Ashridge Barn, Dartington, Totnes, Devon TQ9 6EW, tel. (0803) 862861. Prospective students should get in touch with him there. ■

● **Above** *is a writing-desk in apple with a ripple-ash interior, made by Chris Faulkner;* **left** *is a detail of the ash chest at top*

# A cabinetmaker confesses

**With the publication of his important new book** *Cabinetmaking: The Professional Approach,* **one of Britain's most celebrated woodworking designer-craftsmen emerges as public mentor and inspiration to a whole generation of eventual successors.**

**In this first of two exclusive extracts, Alan Peters describes the personal hardships and triumphs of setting up his own workshop more than 20 years ago.**

CABINETMAKING
*the professional approach*

ALAN PETERS

I set up my first workshop in August 1962 after a brief period of teaching. It was a small beginning, in a rented corrugated-iron shed which was part of a larger builder's yard. The lease was only for 12 months, such was the difficulty then in acquiring workshop premises in the Home Counties.

My initial experience is worth recounting, for I think there may well be lessons for others in it. In that August I had some unique advantages. I had seven years' workshop experience; a teacher's certificate — my insurance against failure; a period of design training followed by some drawing-office experience; and an order book for about six months ahead. However, what I did not have was money, and my good friends, the banks, did not share my enthusiasm for good work: thus I was unable to raise any capital from that quarter.

Now, I must say that I do not consider there is any great merit in starting this way; I just had no choice. If I could have obtained a low-interest loan of £5000 at that time I would have jumped at it, but I had no security beyond what I stood up in. So I started in that shed with one secondhand bandsaw, my sole machine. My bench, the most vital tool of all, I already had, plus the good kit of hand tools acquired as an apprentice.

I soon befriended a joiner in the nearby village who would plane and thickness my timber for me, and also, having no timber stocks such as I now enjoy, I would at times get my timber pre-cut to a liberal cutting list by an excellent firm in London who sent it all down neatly packaged. It was expensive, but it was the only way without interminable travelling. Of course, this situation could not continue for long; I badly needed equipment of my own, so I began to get it in bit by bit on hire purchase — but this was, in the main, after I had

moved into my second workshop in nearby Grayshott 12 months later.

That first and bitter winter of 1962 was quite a nightmare. I had, many days, to walk the three miles over the hedge-tops to a workshop that was cold and patched to keep out the snow and the wind. I vowed then that if I was going to make furniture for the rest of my life, then I was going to do it in warmth and comfort.

Laura, just fresh out of university, went out to teach for the first five years before the birth of our children, whilst I took some part-time teaching in order to obtain the hire-purchase agreements for the machinery and later a bank loan to buy our first cottage.

During those early years I had one burning ambition, which was simply to get the business off the ground; to achieve what Gimson and the Barnsleys and many others had not been able to do at that time, which was to run a creative shop working to my own designs and to my quality, without

● *A display unit in tropical olive, strong and solid to contrast with the delicate pottery it was designed to hold*

*Cabinetmaking: The Professional Approach* by Alan Peters is published by Stobart & Son Ltd, 67-73 Worship St, London EC2A 2EL, tel. 01-247 0501. It costs £15 + £1.75 p&p.

347

# A cabinetmaker confesses

resorting to teaching or any other source of income.

I did not consider myself an artist-craftsman, but a good furniture-maker providing a design service. It seemed to me then, as it does now, that idealism and principles are nothing if the workshop cannot survive and grow; what is vital is that at the end of each year the shop is still there and has progressed in some way. One simply must balance the need for profit and money for development with the ultimate aims one has in mind. It was possible in 1962 to earn a living from making furniture, and many did, by making reproduction antiques and undertaking repair work. But I knew of less than a handful of shops who were working to their own designs and doing work of any merit, and they were not finding it at all easy.

I badly needed money to finance the business, but I was determined and made a conscious decision that I would not touch reproduction work or repairs, which would have paid better, although I was not averse to tackling high-quality joinery and built-in fitments, and my training in interior design was very useful here.

My first such job was to convert a London double-decker bus into a mobile showroom for a firm of glass importers. Laura and I worked many times into the early hours of the morning gluing on fabrics and doing much of the repetitive work that a job of this nature entails. The result, in natural pine with hand-cut dovetails and attractive fabric surfaces, was terrific. I cannot claim credit for the general design, as I was working in conjunction with a London architect, but it was an enjoyable and exciting job that paid the bills with some to spare, and — as important to me — I felt I had left my own personal stamp on that travelling bus.

Thus my work was a balance each year between one-off furniture commissions and the more profitable built-in fitments and interior work. I also did a little designing for an industrial firm in the locality and made their prototypes and exhibition models.

I think it worth saying here that interior fitments and joinery do not in any way imply inferior work. I made a good bookcase, or a good room-divider, and provided a personal design service — the difference was rather one of public attitudes, particularly in the 60s. I was competing directly with architects, interior designers and builders, but I was providing a quality and attention to detail that they could not match. Sadly, though, the same public that commissioned me was less willing to spend that money on free-standing furniture which did not add directly to the value of their property. Had there been the number of craft galleries, shops, fairs and exhibitions that there are now, I would probably have made a more serious attempt at batch production of some of my designs; as it was, I did a little, but it was mainly confined to small

items such as book-ends, lamps, stools and a few low tables and bookcases.

It took, in fact, eight years to realise my ambition totally, and it was a gradual rather than a sudden process. After five years we started a family and Laura stopped teaching; two years later I got rid of the last prop, one day a week teaching at Portsmouth College of Art. Since then we have never looked back. It was the final challenge, and by 1970 I had good, centrally heated workshops and a comfortable home, and we could even afford holidays. During that period I became involved in more complete room schemes, which at times included the entrance doors and panelling, as well as the free-standing furniture.

● A chest-of-drawers made by Alan Peters to an Edward Barnsley design just after his apprenticeship with the great man

On the surface, much has changed in the 20 odd years since that August in 1962. Workshop premises are now much easier to acquire; grants, low-interest loans, government and local-authority help and advice are now widely available. There are more opportunities to exhibit, more galleries and retail outlets through which to sell one's work, and a larger, more discerning public. On the debit side, however, one is moving into a much larger and more competitive field.

● The top of this unusual cherry table features a laminated rim

At best, all the grants and assistance you may be successful in attracting, (including any redundancy payment) will do no more than sustain you through the initial year or so. After that you are out there on your own, battling it out with a growing number of like-minded people for a market that might, for all we know, become saturated overnight.

So you, the potential self-employed furniture maker, should first ask yourself why you should succeed where so many other talented people have failed. I have experienced, this past 10 years, a steady flow of students and mature people who have expressed a strong desire to become furniture-makers; my guess is that little more than a tenth ever get started, and even fewer survive the first five years.

Why is it that, with so much now going in our favour, so few break through with any measure of success? Many, of course, are ill-prepared by training and by nature for the very demanding life that requires one individual to be so many things — from businessman to bench-hand, with a dozen more trades and professions in between. Many art-school students, in particular, have the ideas and the inspiration but not the making experience, patience or stamina to execute those ideas themselves, so they move on to more lucrative fields.

It is here that we face the real problem, namely making money. Although large sections of the population now know about and admire good work and would like to possess it, they either honestly cannot, or do not, wish to pay for the hours that quality and individual work demand. We still live in a society that generally does not reward skill in the same way that it rewards enterprise, business acumen or academic achievement. This is a fact that most of us accept and learn to live with, but it does mean that most workshops producing anything of real value operate on a financial knife-edge with little room for error or miscalculation.

I have purposely not painted a rosy picture of furniture-making as a living, as opposed to a very pleasant pastime, for it is not for the faint-hearted. My book is only a guide to the complexities of such a career. At the end of the day, you must realise that no one owes you a living; you will have to create it by your own efforts and by the quality of the work you produce. ■

## Fellow-professional David Savage assesses how far a timely book succeeds in its aims

At its best a review should be objective. But I cannot claim to be objective when describing the work of Alan Peters. My admiration for the man, his work and his ideals prevents it.

As a start, it may help to see the book in a

● *Cut from one single log, the pieces of ash in this low table are carefully colour- and grain-selected for contrast and balance. The oriental influence in the design is obvious*

historical context. During the past seven years we have seen a flood of books, encouraged by the many new small businesses, covering craft subjects in general and woodworking in particular. It is now arguably possible for a person with the right kind of bloody-mindedness to learn his or her craft and run a business entirely from book knowledge. Established craftsmen such as James Krenov have acquired a following far beyond the few that have experienced their work at first hand.

It is this turbulent publishing arena that Alan Peters has entered — with a very interesting if slightly lop-sided product.

The book begins with a very detailed, scholarly account of 'The Cotswold School and the Birth of the Craft Furniture Movement'. Peters traces the development from Ruskin and Morris, through Gimson and Barnsley, and by unspoken implication to himself. Important pieces are illustrated, and a chronology, a detailed bibliography of books and articles, and a list of sites of important collections, are given in an attempt to set down the known facts about this important period of English furniture-making. Peters also establishes, in the person of Geoffrey Lupton, the 'lost link' between the Gimson workshop at Daneway and the Edward Barnsley workshop at Froxfield.

Alan Peters' own five-year apprentice-ship is covered in a chapter full of warm recollections. The book is dedicated to Bert Upton, who was at that time the foreman of Barnsley's workshop. Now, when the crafts are so closely involved with design, art, business management and marketing, it is delightful to see the attention drawn back to the man at the point of production — the maker.

The text moves on at a brisk pace to cover the setting-up of a professional workshop, equipment, finance and business efficiency. It is the young, would-be professional cabinetmaker who will benefit most from this book, for Peters concentrates on the often neglected topic of the economis of the craft workshop. This is most important in what is a superficially uneconomical activity. The romanticism of hand-planing and hand-cutting dovetails in Devon oak, then striding home across the hillside for a well-earned tea, is tempered by a very large and necessary dose of economic realism. Peters writes exclusively of his own experience of setting up three workshops, each larger and better equipped than the last. He is rightly proud of his achievement in coming from a situation where all he had was a box of tools and a corrugated-iron shed. He gives a list of machines that he has bought either new or secondhand, and advice on showrooms, siting, layout, heating and insuring. Dust extraction is covered in some detail, as is the selection of hand tools and ancillary equipment.

The section on business management is welcome in a craft book. Although this information is available from many other sources, Peters collects together that most useful to the small furniture-maker. Job sheets, estimating sheets and proposals for record-keeping and filing systems are discussed as an essential part of professional activity — and in many ways this is just as important and enjoyable as bench work.

The third section of the book concerns Peters' thinking on design, techniques, the distinction between batch production and commission work, and training. In the design chapter, the technique of producing sketch drawings for clients and working drawings is clearly displayed. The influence of the East and its assimilation by this essentially English craftsman is shown as a

● *A chair in Indian padauk, made to match an antique bureau-desk too small for normal size*

natural process. Here Peters' advice to the young is clear and telling: take your time — forced originality will always look foolish. Back on economics, the small batch-producer of the future can cull invaluable advice from Peters' experience. For the one-off merchant, the whole business of dealing with the client is exposed, from initial enquiry to final specification and presentation drawings.

The chapter on training lists the available formal courses open to a would-be furniture-maker. It also suggests that students gain workshop experience from practising craftsmen by paying their way, either in cash or in kind.

The chapters on techniques have valuable information on timber purchase and selection, adhesives, veneering, laminating and wood finishing. Peters deliberately does not deal with any cabinet-making techniques, believing that other books have this covered quite adequately. Although I feel that his decision to not make this a technical book is correct, I can also see that many readers will regard this as a mistake. The chance to set about a description of furniture-making techniques learnt in the Barnsley workshop is still there to be taken. The omission is a historical loss, especially since it was still entirely a hand workshop with no electricity as late as 1955.

The final, and to my mind weakest section, includes plans and cutting lists for nine furniture projects. These range from a music-stool to a drop-leaf table — by no means the best designs from the Peters drawing board, but then why should he present his best-selling lines to a making public? These are adequate pieces for the person seeking designs that have been well and truly sorted out. The constructional notes are, at best, brief and to the point; less experienced woodworkers may find themselves in difficulties.

The book is well produced, with clear type and a profusion of generally rather small photographs. The line illustrations, diagrams and plans are clear and well presented.

It is very seldom that a genuinely import-ant woodworker's book comes along, but this is one. Although it is aimed at what must be a very small part of a min-ority interest, its readership will extend far outside this narrow band of lunatics. As a personal account of a successful wood-worker's career to date, it is a more con-vincing and enjoyable read than the usual technical tome.

Certainly Alan Peters is aware that he is encouraging opposition and competition in a very small market. Consequently, he does not give away everything, and one would be naive to expect him to do so. However, contained within the book are 35 years' of experience in making furniture to the highest standards. This is essential reading for anyone interested in furniture-making, amateur or professional. ■

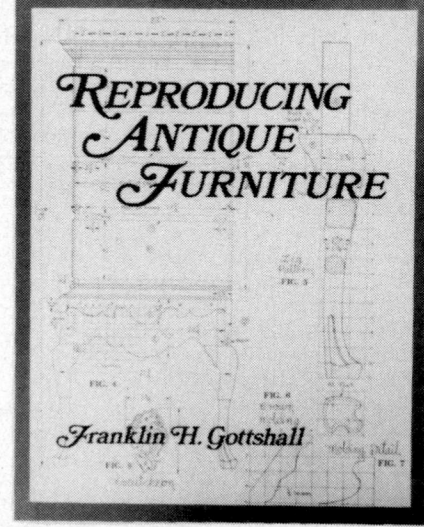
Prices quoted are those prevailing at press date and are
subject to alteration due to economic conditions

# The universal answer?

**Universal machines — versatile cure-all or awkward, unreliable curse? Alan Holtham gives his verdict**

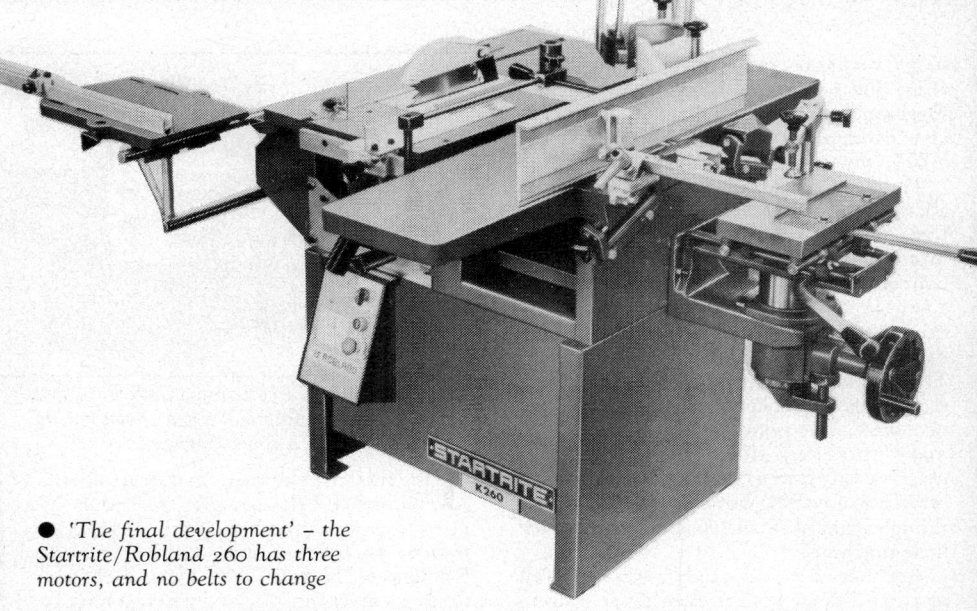

● 'The final development' – the Startrite/Robland 260 has three motors, and no belts to change

When equipping a woodworking shop, most people face one big decision: whether to buy a universal machine, a multi-function machine, or several individual machines.

I draw a distinction between the universal, which is a combination of several machines permanently assembled, and the multi-function machine, which is really a single unit on to which you add various attachments as required — usually one at a time.

I have studied the problem over a number of years: firstly in updating the machining facilities for our own woodworking business, and latterly in selling equipment to others in similar positions. What's more, I think I now know the answer.

In my opinion, you can't beat the individual-machine set-up. One machine for each job is the ideal situation. I have yet to find a universal on which you can move from one function to another without changing or altering something, and where all operations are equally accessible. The average universal machine, for example, is equipped with a very adequate planer, but you usually have to reach over something — probably the saw-bench — to get at it. Try doing that with an 8ft length of 8×3in hardwood!

However, we have to be realistic. A machine for each job requires unlimited space and plenty of cash. In the end you nearly always have to compromise and go for a universal of some sort. But make sure that the one on which you decide will minimise the compromise.

When showing machines to customers I always start by asking what they want the item to do for them, so that I can point them roughly in the right direction. It always amazes me that perhaps 80% have absolutely no idea of what they are going to produce — which makes the choice into a matter of pot luck. If you anticipate doing a lot of turning, it's no use buying a machine based on a planer-thicknesser when there are others based on the lathe.

The stock retort, of course, is that until you have the machine you don't know what you can do with it — but you really should try to sort out your basic requirements before you start looking at universals in earnest. Don't be like the customer who assured me that he was setting up a full-time joinery business and was looking for a machine to produce thousands of window-frames per week, and then stopped me dead in mid-spiel by asking, 'Er, what exactly is a spindle-moulder?'

Judging by the number of customers who buy universals and whom we never see again, there must be quite a few disappoint-ments. Perhaps they look through the glossy brochures, see wood gliding through machines without any shavings or dust in sight, and imagine that it will be like that when they get the thing home. It won't.

For many years the only universals were of the Dominion Elliot type, made of heavy cast iron and aimed principally at the professional user. Only within recent years has the market responded to the surge of interest in leisure activities — but the range of small woodworking machines, and universals in particular, is now quite amazing.

One of the faithful standards is the Coronet system — built around a lathe, and really a multi-function rather than a universal machine. It exhibits the inherent problems of this particular design. Firstly, whenever you combine a lathe with a planer there is an immediate contradiction in speed requirements. I always advise people to have a separate lathe, which needs low speeds, and combine the saw, planer and moulder, which require high ones.

Coronet overcame this by introducing the five-speed headstock, on which speed changes are very easy. Who remembers the days of the rattling gearbox and mandatory ear-defenders, or the amazing two-belt countershaft of the Minor machine? The remaining problems are that one or other of the attachments gets in the way when you are turning, and that the saw is very noisy. But there are thousands of these machines around — I have had one for about three years myself — and you soon learn to live with their limitations. What's more, they are so well built that they last for ever.

Very few other manufacturers have used the lathe-based system. The American Shopsmith Mk 5 is perhaps Coronet's only rival, but exchange-rate problems have made this machine rather expensive in the UK.

Other machines are based on either the circular saw or the planer-thicknesser. Scheppach, for example, employ the latter design. Although only of pressed steel, theirs is one of the best-performing models currently on the market in its price range. Moreover, Scheppach use a unique quick-locking system to attach the various accessories. Always take a close look at anything that requires bits to be added on. If the brochure says that 'It only takes a few minutes with the special tool provided', you'll probably have to spend five minutes on your back using two hands, plus a spanner between your teeth. In real life, you'll never bother. The Scheppach system is very simple, but a belt must also be changed to transmit the drive to the operation required. Changing belts is a necessary chore on most universals which incorporate only a single motor.

Emco's equipment is similarly based on a planer-thicknesser, adding on attachments in the same way — the most popular being a circular saw, spindle-moulder and mortiser. Just make sure that when you fit any particular attachment it doesn't interfere with the operation of your basic unit, in this case the planer.

Kity take another approach with their K5. Here a single wooden table serves as a base for three small machines, with a single motor in the middle of the group. This solution scores in that there is nothing

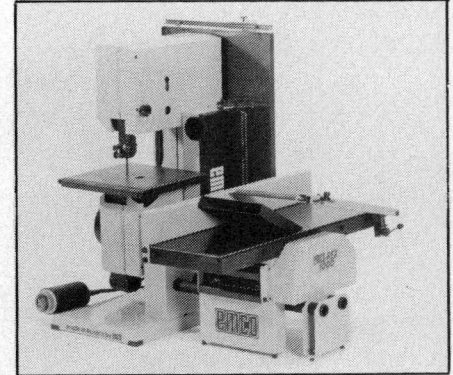

● Emcostar 2000 with Emco-Rex 1000 planer/thicknesser attachment

to add on or take off — only a belt to change from one part to another. This particular machine has a fairly small capacity, but Kity also offer a professional equivalent, the K704, which uses the same system.

The next logical development is to build all the units into one machine, as on the Luna Z40. Here again there is a single motor, but all the belts are already connected to the various operations, so it is a simple matter to change from one to the other by moving a lever on the front which operates a very ingenious sliding clutch. The clutch is so ingenious, in fact, that it is a major performance to replace a belt if necessary. The point highlights one of the major problems involved in getting a machine down to a compact size: access for service is anything but easy. Nevertheless, though again of small capacity, this is a nice little machine.

Another idea is adopted by AEG. As well as their range of conventional Lurem universals, they market a set of individual machines on to which you clip a single motor — taking the power to the machine rather than the other way round. Electra-Beckum use a very similar system. It saves expense on motors, but it doesn't save space, and it does promote the 'one more bit' syndrome. This is an extension of sod's law: when you have done, for instance, all the sawing, and set up the planer, you find one more bit that needs sawing. This, of course, is where the individual machine wins every time.

● 'Perhaps the ultimate universal'; the Felder's price and engineering make it a choice for the professional with a space problem

● The Scheppach Kombi System's basic unit is a planer/thicknesser, to which you add what you choose

The final development in universals is to eliminate belt-changing altogether by powering each function with a separate motor, as for example on the Startrite Robland K210 and K260. These each have three separate motors, and you just have to select on the starter panel the one you require. At least, that's what the brochures say, but in fact you also have to do a bit of guard-swapping as well.

The Swedish firm of Luna aim most of their machines at the more professional end of the market. They make very heavy equipment which can be separated into single units if required. Luna produce what seem to be the only universals with the planer the right way round — that is, so you don't have to lean over the saw-bench to plane long lengths; as with the others, however, there remains the distinct possibility of impaling yourself on the slot-mortiser.

Perhaps the ultimate universal is the Felder. Produced purely for the professional, Felder's two models are large and heavy, with big capacities and separate motors. But I do sometimes wonder, when you get up to this price range, whether you wouldn't do better to buy single machines.

So the universal question doesn't really have a universal answer. You have to weigh up what's on offer, after a careful assessment of your own requirements. Nonetheless, any model will certainly beat doing it by hand. ∎

● The Dominion Supreme Elliott

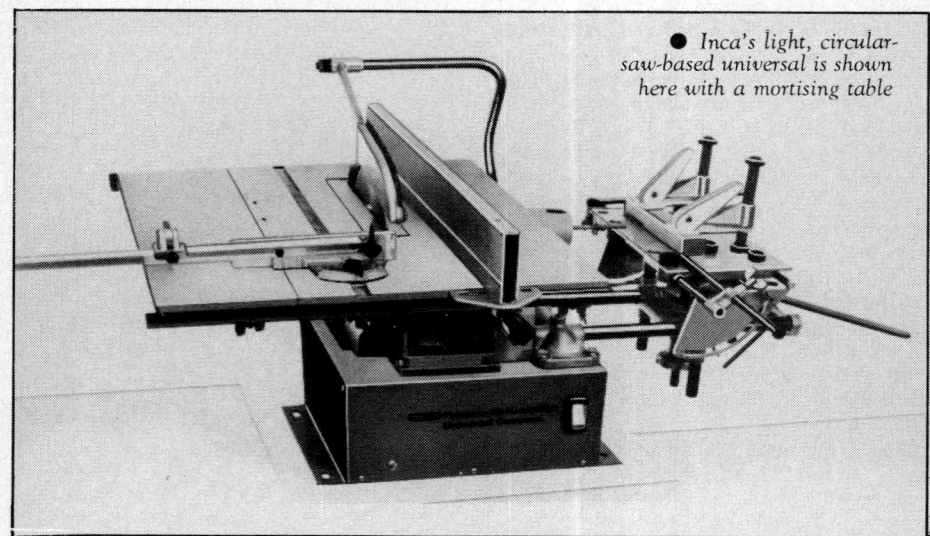

● Inca's light, circular-saw-based universal is shown here with a mortising table

## Who supplies universals?

This list includes all the UK manufacturers and importers of universal woodworking machines known to us. The range of price and capability is enormous. The basic types (lathe, single-motor and multiple-motor) give you a starting-point, but after that it's down to you, your pocket and your floor space. If you're only planning to work timber in comparatively small sizes, you might be able to fit in a bigger machine than you think.

**AEG** AEG Telefunken, 217 Bath Rd, Slough, Berks, (0753) 872101.
**Coronet** Coronet Tool. Co. (1982) Ltd, Alfreton Rd, Derby DE2 4AH, (0332) 362141.
**Dominion** Dominion Machinery Co. Ltd, Hipperholme, Halifax HX3 8JG, (0422) 202258/9.
**Emco** EME Ltd, BEC House, Victoria Rd, London NW10 6NY, 01-965 4050.
**Felder** Sanlin Leisure Marketing, 23 Church Sq., Toddington, Dunstable, Beds LU5 6AA, (05255) 2259.
**Hitachi** Hitachi Power Tools (UK) Ltd, Unit 8, Hampton Farm Industrial Estate, Bolney Way, Feltham, Middx TW13 6DB, 01-894 1236/8.
**INCA** Woodworking Machines of Switzerland Ltd, 51 Aylesbury St, Bletchley, Milton Keynes MK2 2BQ, (0908) 641492.
**Kity** Rawdon Machine Sales Ltd, 6 Acorn Park, Charlestown, Shipley, W. Yorks BD17 7SW, (0274) 597826.
**Luna** Luna Tools & Machinery Ltd, 20 Denbigh Hall, Bletchley, Milton Keynes MK3 7QT, (0908) 70771.
**Lurem** Poolewood Equipment Ltd, 5a Holly Lane, Chiswell, Beeston, Nottingham, (0602) 225979.
**Port-O-Mac** Port-O-Mac (UK) Ltd, Stanford Court, Stanford Bridge, Worcester WR6 6SR, (08865) 451.
**Sheppach** Sumaco Ltd, Suma House, Huddersfield Rd, Elland, W. Yorks HX5 9AA, (0422) 79811.
**Startrite/Robland** Startrite Machine Tool Co. Ltd, Waterside Works, Gads Hill, Gillingham, Kent ME7 2SF, (0634) 55122.
**Steton** Trymwood, 2a Downs Park East, Westbury Park, Bristol BS6 7QD, (0272) 629092.
**Titan** See Scheppach.

# Initiation test

**Mr R. B. Cannon was only a tax accountant — until he bought a Kity K5 universal. Here's his account of a stormy meeting between man and machine**

I am firmly an amateur woodworker. hand and small power tools were all I had ever used. But, when I was eventually able to escape from the demands of my profession, I began to cast covetous eyes on the universal machines.

My attitude to any purchase is, I hope, that of any good businessman — I try to buy in the best market. So I read all I could about universal machines, obtained manufacturers' pamphlets, attended exhibitions, saw demonstrations, and either asked questions or listened to those being asked by other spectators.

Unfortunately, few reviews of machines do more than report their ability to carry out the woodworking functions — perhaps telling you their limitations too. None are really critical; nor can the skilled examiner see the machine with the uncertain and probably nervous eye of the part-time enthusiast who may buy it. On the other hand, there's no substitute for experience — and I didn't have any.

Having decided on a Kity K5 and obtained what I felt was the best deal, I bought it from a merchant many miles away. He merely passed my order on to Rawdon Machine Sales, who delivered the machine direct to me. 'The monster has arrived!' said one of my sons.

● Luna's MiniMax C22, compact and quite light, major functions built in

No packing list was enclosed, so I was not immediately able to confirm that everything had been supplied. There was no instruction book, either: instead there were a number of separate sheets giving operating instructions for each of the machines. These were apparently intended to show the package contents too. Understanding them was quite a little exercise for someone who'd never handled anything bigger than a portable saw. Moreover, three specified items were missing, and there were no tools to help assemble the individual machines on the base or even to fix the saw-blade.

I telephoned the manufacturers, and was immediately asked by the warehouseman if I had received a box containing many essential parts. I had; apparently other purchasers hadn't! He seemed almost relieved to know I was only reporting three missing items. These were duly sent. He also told me that the instruction manual was in French, but that it was being translated and I would be sent a copy. Now two years have passed with no sign of it.

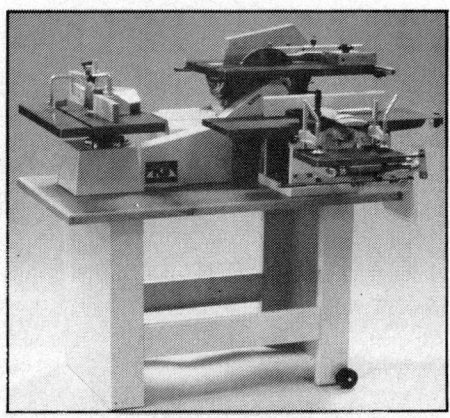

● **The Kity K5**

The saw cut well and accurately at both speeds, and I was particularly impressed by its clean cutting of Formica at the higher speed. I was less impressed by the fuss involved in moving the machine to change speeds, and was completely deceived by reports that the size of the saw-table was adequate; it wasn't. In fact, I had had a larger table as an accessory for a small power saw. I found it virtually impossible to control a 24×6in piece of timber for accurate squaring of the end. A table extension was available at a price, but I didn't feel it should have been necessary with a machine costing over £600; not for the small sizes I wanted, anyway.

The saw was advertised as having a 7in blade but taking an 8in blade for a deeper cut. It was supplied with an 8in blade which I found would not reduce to a zero cut. I

● Hitachi's U-120 uses one 2hp motor

● The AEG C2000 sports a lever function-select device

never thought to measure the minimum projection, and complained to the merchant. He changed the blade and also gave me a spanner for the saw. I got another surprise when I tried the 7in blade, the standard one for the machine. That would not cut to zero either. I had to buy a still smaller blade to get below a projection of about ½in.

I had never used a planer/thicknesser, and was delighted with the results I could produce. The thicknesser was superb. I was, however, astonished to find that — contrary to the knowledge I had acquired from constant reading of the woodworking magazines, plus many books on woodwork and the use of woodworking machines — the apparently standard method of sharpening planer blades in the machine did not work on this model. In fact, the normal simple stone was useless. In order to sharpen the blades it was necessary to buy quite an expensive accessory. Buy I did; but not without difficulty, and I was particularly disturbed when the manufacturers told me at an exhibition that they had none of these accessories in the country at the time!

The spindle-moulder was a new experience too, and quite a frightening one. Nevertheless, with its help I was able to make a replacement Georgian-type window for my house. The spindle-moulder worked most effectively, although even to cut a simple rebate I had to buy an accessory not supplied with the machine. The spring guide for keeping the timber tight against the spindle was almost impossible to adjust correctly, and that required a further special tool. At one exhibition I heard a salesman/demonstrator for a merchant tell a spectator — who could see the guides and guards were difficult to adjust — that, in the hands of a private buyer outside a regulated workshop, the awkwardness of the guards could be dispensed with simply by removing them. A horrifying suggestion.

The machine also possessed a so-called mortiser based on the planer spindle. The only part of the mortiser which even remotely appealed to me was the rise-and-fall facility in the table. There was no provision for regulating sideways movement of the timber or for perfecting accuracy. I found my old sliding table with its stops, fixed to the drill-stand, much more simple and accurate.

My attitude to the machine was not helped by the initial difficulties with and lack of interest from the manufacturer, or by the lack of a comprehensive instruction manual. Not being mechanically minded, I found bringing each separate machine into operation a tedious business. After a while I felt I was no longer taking pleasure in woodwork, even at my low level, but instead becoming a machine-setter. After about a year I sold the 'monster' to an engineer. In the frame of mind I had reached, he seemed a very appropriate buyer. ■

# Upgrading your own

**Buying a universal may plunge you into uncharted waters. Sidney Birch explains how he got round some significant snags with a Lurem**

Trying my new Lurem 7 universal in the workshop, I must admit that initially I was disappointed with a few points. When the circular saw was being used, for example, my very small workshop got covered in sawdust. And, if I wanted to rebate or deep timber, I had to remove the riving-knife and saw-guard.

Often you need to shoot the edge of the timber straight before ripping; I had to remove not only the riving-knife and saw-guard to do this, but also the dust-guard and saw-blade in order to change the belt-drive to the planer/thicknesser, and then reverse all these operations before I could rip. There is no micro-adjustment on the fence, so it was necessary to tap the fence to get the correct cut-line. As the fence is used for the spindle as well, it limited the width I could pass by the saw to about 6in.

Altogether these problems set me a challenge I couldn't resist.

Firstly I removed the saw, spindle and rear planer table (all one piece) and discarded the whole tabletop. Then I machined a piece of ½in aluminium, 24×18in, with my router, using a ⅜in carbide-tipped bit. The slot for the saw was machined large enough to enclose an oak insert through which the blade could protrude. It stops the saw from straying, and — being a good fit — it also improved the extraction of sawdust (I use a wet-and-dry vacuum).

At the same time I routed a new spindle hole, bevelled the front 6in of the edge where the planer block meets the table, and finally made an insert for a 12in steel rule.

The next part was to fit a new fence control with micro-adjustment. This was made 3in wider than the table so the fence could be turned over and out of the way if

● **Above:** *An extra 1hp motor on an aluminium plate drives the planer/thicknesser, so that lengthy belt-changing becomes unnecessary for alternate use of the planer/thicknesser and the saw. The motor is easily removed for mortising.* **Below:** *A pair of collar cutters on the new spindle, and the spaced dado-cutters set up for tenoning. Guards removed for clarity!*

sawing freehand. Once the new fence was made I found I could pass 12in by the saw, double the old width. Two holes were drilled in the new fence, and the old fence was fitted with bolts and wing-nuts so it could be bolted on to the new fence when the spindle was in use. Now it can be used on both sides of the spindle.

A 1hp motor was fitted to an aluminium plate and fixed by two Allen screws to the existing holes in the mortising table. A small pulley on a shaft was fixed to the chuck, and a V-belt was fitted. I keep it in tension at all times when the planer and thicknesser are being used, by pulling the mortise-table handle and tightening the travel lock.

Now I could shoot timber before sawing, use the saw or thicknesser without changing belts, and rebate or deep without removing the saw-guard or riving-knife (I also brought the original knife to below the top of my saws). The motor could be removed in minutes if I wanted to mortise, and the machine is now — for about £80 — far more practical than before.

I have a set of three-lip shaper-cutters, a small set of collar cutters and a dado set, all with ½in bore, and I wanted to used them on the Lurem spindle. I made up a new spindle in good-quality steel with the same thread as the bolt that holds the french cutters in the spindle. The top of this shaft was reduced to ½in and threaded for a nut and locknut. Five various spacers were made so that the cutters could be put in a combination of heights. The three-lip cutters were now, at 17,000 cuts per minute, giving a nice clean finish.

At the same time I made another spindle with a ⅜in router chuck on the end. This is not quite so useful, because of low spindle speed, but I use it for bevels, rounds and small rebates. The dado unit works very well, and I can use one of the saws to cut bevels on the sawbench.

If ¼, ⁵⁄₁₆, ⅜ and ½in spacers are made to fit the ½in shaft and put between the dado saws, tenons can be cut provided you have the slide attachment sold as an extra with the Lurem. A 5in-wide fence was made and fixed with a single wing-nut on to the fence for shooting edges of wide boards.

● Mr Birch would be only too pleased to help other Lurem 7 owners who like the look of his modifications. His address is 11a Roe Green Lane, Hatfield, Herts. ■

● Mr Birch's engineering talents are obvious from this impressive array of additions and modifications. The new tabletop, machined with a router, can be seen **above**. Also there is the new spindle opening with removable plate for wider cutters, the shorter riving-knife to allow deep cutting, and the saw-guard stretching across from the mortise-clamp spindle. Most enticing is the beautifully made micro-adjustment bar for the fence in the foreground, made extra-long so the fence can be flipped over and out of the way.

The shots at **right** and **below right** show the old spindle fence attached to either side of the new, giving a narrow table width for small pieces or a wide one for panels. New spindle shafts and spacers are shown **below left** on top of the recessed rule, with the router chuck on the right

356

Prices quoted are those prevailing at press date and are subject to alteration due to economic conditions

# The caterpillar strikes back

**In May last year we featured drawings, photographs and the complete design story for Jeremy Broun's startling yet highly evolved Caterpillar Rocker. A reader, Stephen Fogg, responded with severe criticism of the chair as a danger to health. Now Jeremy Broun replies to the charges**

The proof of this chair is in its rocking! I feel bound to respond to Mr Fogg's January letter condemning the Caterpillar Rocker I designed for readers to make, and wonder if he is suffering from clouded vision.

I asked several physiotherapists at my local hospital to try the chair and comment on its comfort. All were agreed that although it is a little low, its comfort is adequate, and when I asked specifically about the lumbar support their comments ranged from 'good' to 'very good'.

I suspect neither Mr Fogg nor his sixth-formers put the Caterpillar Rocker to the real test by making it and sitting on it, but instead made academic speculations based on what it looked like; and of course appearances are often deceptive.

I did state in my article that comfort was very much in my mind when designing this chair, and I use a 'data skeleton' based on other comfortable chairs. In this case I based the body-support data on my earlier high-backed rocking chair (*Woodworker* June 1983, p338), which has sold many times over. Having designed chairs for several years I would not dare let one leave my workshop without being *adequately* comfortable, as few people are going to pay the relatively high price for a hand-crafted chair — no matter how aesthetically interesting it is — unless it meets that requirement.

Because of my sculptural style some people are nervous about the comfort of some of my chairs, but they are pleasantly surprised when they sit on them. This is the only real test of any chair. Such visual prejudice is well illustrated by much soft furniture on the market, where the visual appeal lulls one into a state of 'mental comfort' — until you sink into the foam and find the support is either in the wrong place or non-existent.

To produce a good-looking chair which is *supremely* comfortable is a feat few designers have accomplished, myself included; and it is hardly surprising, since we all vary in body proportion, in the way we sit, and in how long we can sustain any particular sitting position when most chairs are static objects.

As for those readers who found the Caterpillar Rocker visually appealing and enough of a challenge to want to make, I hope they won't be deterred from having a go, and I very much hope the results won't be 'painful, permanent and incurable'. ■

● *This is the chair that aroused the doubts of Stephen Fogg, whose January letter we reprint* **below right**

● *Mental comfort, physical danger . . . or clouded vision? The ultimate test is the same for any chair – sit and see!*

The construction of Jeremy Broun's rocking chair (WW/May) is striking and interesting, but I do have a criticism of the faulty shape — particularly at the lower end of the back. The curve here is exactly the reverse of what the human body requires.

Anyone with disc lesions in the lumbar spine, sitting in the chair, will experience back pain almost immediately; in fact, seeing the shape, they will probably avoid it altogether! But, worse than this, anyone with a perfectly intact back, young or old, will experience compression and distortion of all the lumbar discs if they sit in the chair for any length of time. This could easily lead to the development of a so-called 'slipped disc' — painful, permanent and incurable.

For this reason I think the design is dangerous and should be modified to include some sort of lumbar support. A look at the 'ortho-stool' featured in the February issue will emphasise my point. When I showed the article to my sixth-form pupils, they spotted this defect immediately, though all liked the construction and general appearance of the design.

*Stephen Fogg, Bromley*

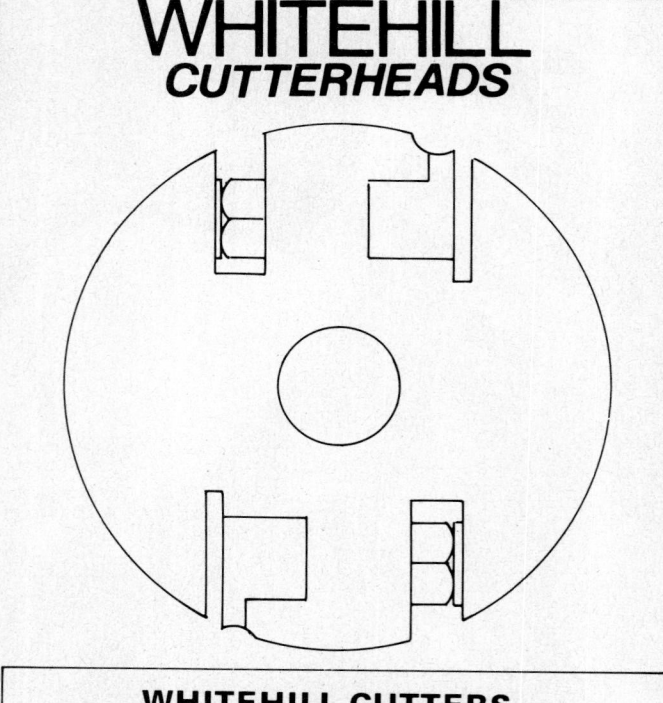
358    Prices quoted are those prevailing at press date and are
subject to alteration due to economic conditions

KINDLY MENTION 'WOODWORKER' WHEN REPLYING TO ADVERTISEMENTS

# The conservation shaker

**Bruce Boulter makes a thing of beauty from a piece of potential scrap — via a highly unusual approach**

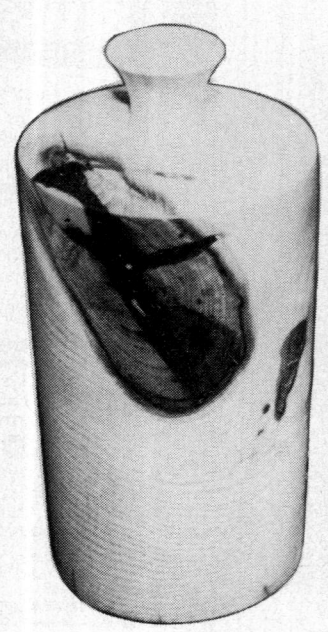

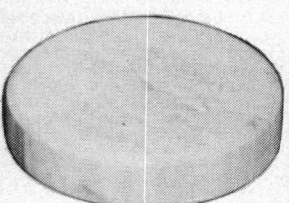

● *The unusual grain figure in the ash shaker on the left shows that a desire to conserve 'waste' can produce attractive results. Conservative to the wood, but radical when it comes to technique*

Two particular bees in my bonnet caused me to try this experiment with a piece of very flawed ash: my natural detestation, to the point of obsession, of wasting any wood at all, combined with an increasingly strong feeling about the insane devastation of the world's beautiful timbers. We should be as preservative as possible!

Another interesting dimension to the job is that it is worked in a format not often demonstrated or described; I can't understand why, as some superb effects can be achieved with this technique.

I took an odd end of English ash, cut the piece to render a square of turning stuff, and set it up between centres with the grain running *across* the bed of the lathe. Not really any different from the way in which a bowl blank would be mounted.

Then the square is reduced to a cylinder either with a roughing-gouge, or, if the timber is shreddy, with a ⅜in spindle gouge, both very sharp. In fig.1 the cylinder is worked to size with a chisel. Note the fine, polished finish you can get by using a sharp tool and taking the finest of finishing cuts. A fine finish will be obtained cutting in one direction only, which underlines the necessity of being ambidextrous with turning tools.

Fig.2 is a close-up of a real nasty; the knot is split in two directions and a section to the left has broken away. Ash is famous for its pencil-straight, uniform grain, but here the grain is vertical to the right of the knot and horizontal to the left — over a length of 3½in. Surely an advertisement for the method.

The defect must of course be filled. Araldite, coloured with poster-paint powder, is hard to better, although it is not the most economical of fillers. Most of the inside of this piece is removed to produce the shaker, and only the surface needs to be filled, so instead of wasting expensive filler I proceed as follows. In figs. 3 and 4 the fissure is filled with shavings, well tamped down to form a solid foundation, and left about ⅛in below the surface. The fast-setting Araldite is then mixed and coloured with poster-paint powder, and the crack filled up to the surface. In this case there was an area of perfect very dark brown round the periphery of the knot, so I tried to copy this colour as closely as possible.

Another technique is to allow a couple of low-filled areas to remain in the filled part and then, when the filler is almost dry after about 30 minutes, to top them up with a slightly different shade, even in some instances a different colour. The object is to get the filler to look as natural as possible, rather than having one large area of the same colour/shade.

In fig.5 the broken area has been dealt with by the simple expedient of turning it out, a remedy often used when the odd mistake occurs — i.e., change the design. A narrow parting-tool is used both to define the style and to produce a slot into which a veneer can be slipped to form a stop for the filler.

The turning is worked with a chisel to remove the excess filler and form the shape.

So far the work has been between centres. The shaker design completed, the inside waste must be removed to produce the finished workpiece. A drill-bit will remove most if not all. Alternatively, work with the largest bit you have and enlarge to the desired diameter with the long corner of a skew chisel.

I use a home-made chuck for drilling, which holds the whole job, and is tightened

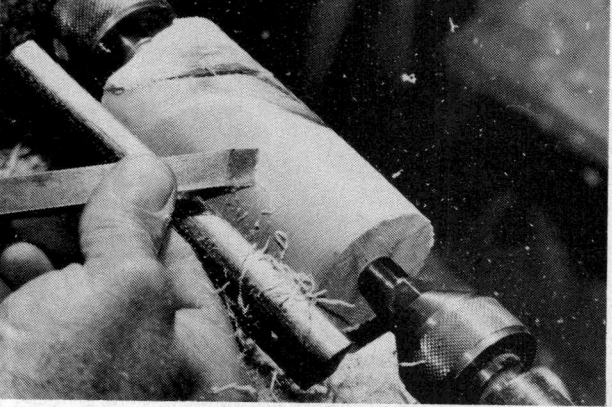

**1** *The grain running across the bed is clearly visible as the cylinder is worked to size with a skew chisel. If the timber is shreddy, use a ⅜in spindle gouge*

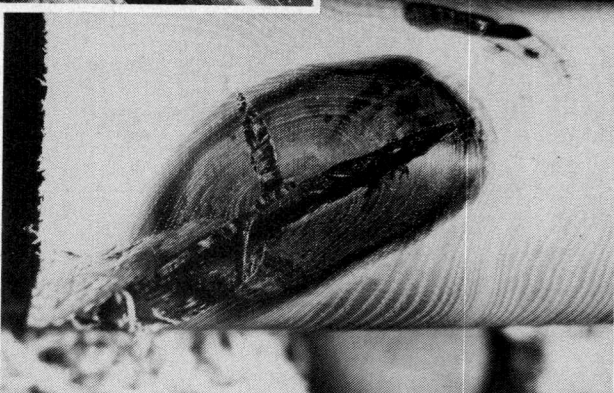

**2** *The 'real nasty'; a two-way split in a huge knot, with the grain running away in two directions and irreparable break-out towards the end*

with a hose-clip. Centring the work is aided by using the tailstock to secure it. You can also do the drilling for the contents exit in this kind of chuck.

In fig.6 the collar, in darker stuff, is made on a screw-chuck, outside diameter to suit the shaker and hole diameter to suit a proprietary rubber bung. A mandrel to fit the small hole is produced on a screw-chuck, and the whole thing can be re-mounted on the lathe for final finishing (fig. 7).

A lot of trouble to make a shaker or whatever in ash. However, if this had been a piece of exceptional, expensive or very rare and exotic timber, it would be trouble well worth taking. ■

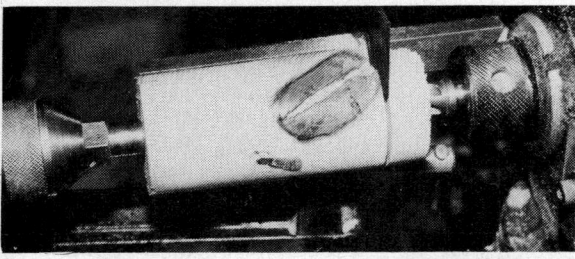

**3** The first stage in filling the knot. Shavings have been tamped hard into the fissure and left about ⅛in below the surface, ready for the Araldite

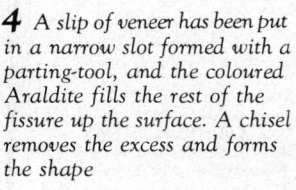

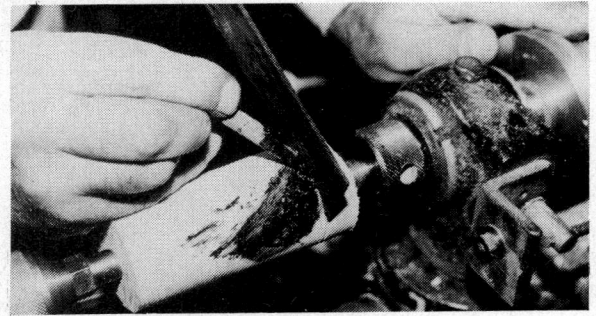

**4** A slip of veneer has been put in a narrow slot formed with a parting-tool, and the coloured Araldite fills the rest of the fissure up the surface. A chisel removes the excess and forms the shape

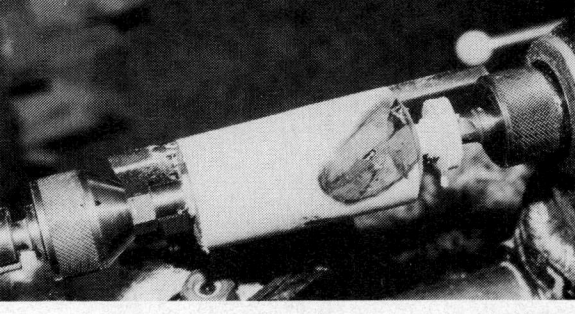

**5** Filling and shaping completed, the piece rests in the lathe ready for the knob to be turned up and drilled for the filling- and shaking-holes

**6** The darker collar has been turned to fit inside the cylinder; the fit over the mandrel, the same size as a proprietary rubber bung, is shown

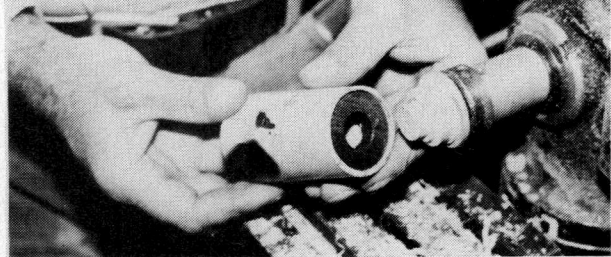

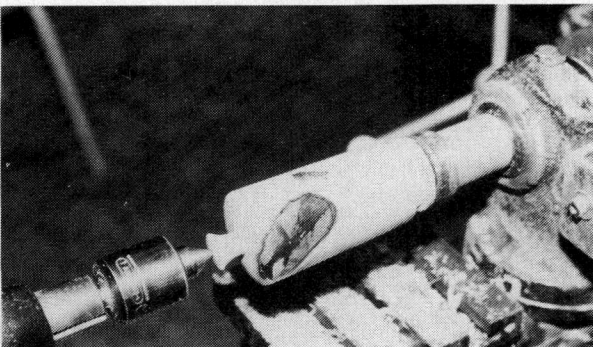

**7** Mounted on the mandrel, the tailstock centred in the hole from which the contents are shaken, the piece can be rubbed down and finished

**REMEMBER...** *Woodworker depends on woodworkers. We're willing and eager to tell the world what you're making, doing, exhibiting — even thinking. Our only aim is to produce the magazine you want to read. We're looking for photos, drawings (rough sketches will do) and words on any woodworking subject from ovolo mouldings to overhead routers. And we're on the end of the phone. We're waiting to hear from you!*
*Peter Collenette*
*Aidan Walker*

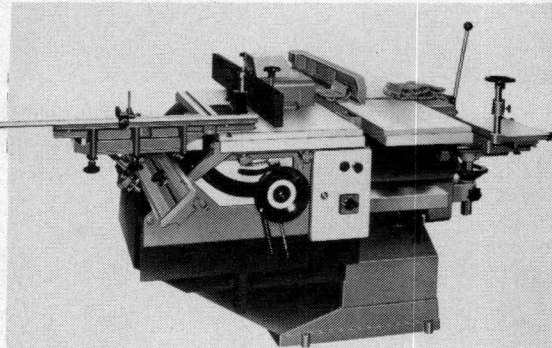

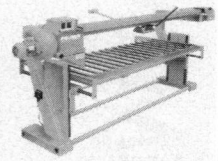

Prices quoted are those prevailing at press date and are subject to alteration due to economic conditions

# The toolmaker's tale

**Sheffield-bred Ashley Iles has been making fine carving tools for 35 years. He expounds on the craft that comes before woodworking starts**

The Sheffield tool trade is divided into sections which do not intermix. I am concerned with the light-edge-tool trade: accounting for most of this are all woodworking tools with sharpened edges. Here again, further specialisation has taken place, and since setting up on my own in 1950 I have made only tools for carving and turning.

Making carving tools is a complicated business involving considerable expertise — and the manner in which the various operations are performed is more important than the tasks themselves.

To make a carving tool, you need a 'cutting', or piece of steel cut to length. A 50-ton press usually of the 'Sheffield' type (50 tons is the force of the blow) is ideal for producing cuttings. The kinetic energy of a large flywheel is changed to potential energy by a foot-pedal which engages a vertical ram working on a cam. A bar of steel — an alloy steel of 1% carbon and 0.3% manganese is ideal for carving tools — is fed into the press and rapidly chopped to length.

The cutting then goes to the hammer, which is a forging machine giving over 600 blows per minute. Hammers vary according to the weight of the 'tup' — the lump of steel giving the blow; this ranges from ¼cwt to 2cwt. They are known as spring hammers, being vertical versions of the horizontal beam-hammers known as iron dukes.

Using the hammer, you forge the bolster and tang in one heat to produce a 'mood'. A good hammerman makes this operation look easy, but in fact it is highly skilled and needs much training. A pair of dies are fitted into the hammer, and the bolster is forged first; then the tang is drawn out, working by eye through 90°. Mooding is done in quantities.

The mood is then turned round, and with another pair of dies it is drawn out to length and width — covering all the sizes from ⅛in to 2in wide according to the size of steel used. The mood has now become a 'blade.'

In making spoon gouges and fishtail tools, drawing-out is preceded by a hammer operation to forge the rectangular stem. The next step is to prepare the blade for gouging or hollowing. This the toolsmith does by hand, on a special anvil set in a block of stone.

It is perfectly true that all these operations could be done in one go with a drop stamp. In this mass-production technique, a weight of anything up to ½ ton is hoisted to the ceiling before falling by gravity. In one almighty splat at white heat, a complete tool is formed. What happens to

● *A long bar of steel is fed into the 50 ton Sheffield press to make the cuttings. The alloy includes 1% carbon and 0.3% manganese*

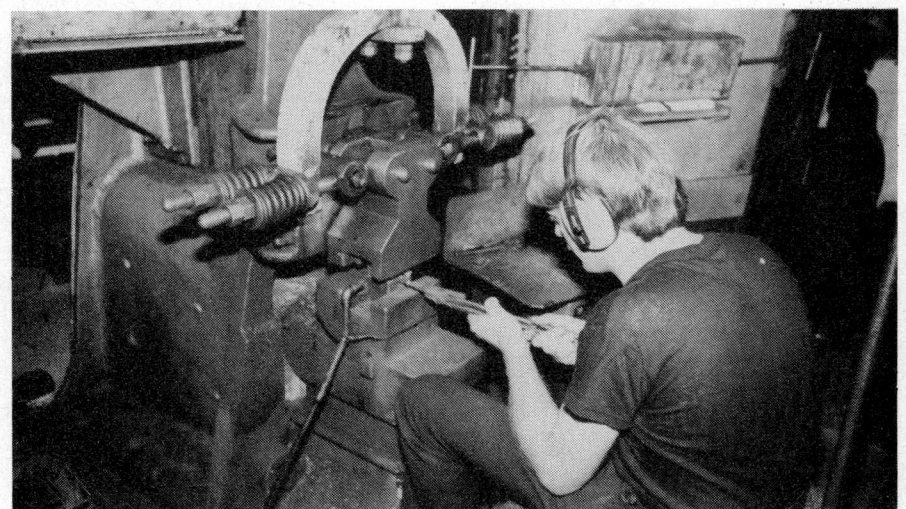

● *Quantity production of the 'moods' is done with the spring hammer, at more than 600 blows a minute. First the bolster is formed, then the tang*

● *Preparing the blade, by now drawn out to length and width, for gouging or hollowing. Despite high production volumes, every stage of the work demands great manual skill*

Prices quoted are those prevailing at press date and are subject to alteration due to economic conditions

# The toolmaker's tale

the molecular structure of the steel could well hold the answer to many present-day problems with tools.

The blade now goes to a hydraulic press fitted with one of hundreds of pairs of dies used for gouging. After 'setting' on an anvil, the forging is finished and ready for the grinding shop.

The grinding shop is completely different from the forge, and houses a separate trade. Its main feature is the wheel, a simple machine consisting of a 42×6in grinding-wheel mounted on a 4in shaft and driven by a 20hp motor. The wheel runs in a trough of water in the ground and is kept at a steady 5000ft/min. The grinder sits on a 'horsing' with the wheel between his legs running away from him. Here he grinds the forgings by hand, manipulating all the curves and flats with amazing dexterity while the water keeps the tool cool.

The inside or hollow of the tool cannot be done on the wheel. It is dealt with on a double-ender, where a grinding-wheel is mounted and then dressed to the correct shape with a 'devil-stick'. The forging is then ground on the inside by holding it against the wheel, working backwards and forwards by hand. 3000rpm is a minimum for dry grinding.

Next, the tools go back to the forge for hardening and tempering. Hardening should be done by hand. There is a critical temperature in all carbon steels — quenching below it has no effect, and quenching above it gives varying degrees of hardness. The art is to quench at a colour which produces a close-grained structure revealed by examination of the section when a test piece is broken in two. If a tool is hardened at too high a temperature, the fracture will be crystalline or sugary, and no better in use than a poor saw. The result will be the same if the properties of the steel have been lost in forging.

Steel today is better than ever it was — but it is and always has been temperamental. Only an experienced hardener knows the colours which bring out the best performance in his material.

Tempering in an oven at 375°F changes some of the hardness into toughness or 'spring'. After this the tools are black and rough, and unsuited to the skilled fingers which will use them. So it's back to the grinding shop for 'glazing' or finishing. Here, with the aid of linishers, buffs, dollies, glazing-wheels and lots of mutton fat, the tools are made ready for cannelling or grinding the edge.

The final appearance is made by the cutler, who has nothing to do with cutlery except at meal-times. His job is to finish the tool before it goes to the warehouse for despatch. He fits all the handles and then sets them straight. He also marks the name, does final inspection and hones the tool ready for use.

The rest is up to you! ■

● Ashley Iles (Edge Tools) Ltd, East Kirkby, Spilsby, Lincs PE23 4DD, tel. (07903) 372, have made a 20-minute video depicting the entire process of making carving tools, which is available free.

The firm sponsors the Ashley Iles Carving Competition every year at the London Woodworker Show, Alexandra Pavilion. Entry is open to all, and this year the subject is 'Creatures of the forest'. Details from Argus Specialist Exhibitions Ltd, Park View House, 1 Park View Rd, Berkhamsted, Herts HP4 3EY, tel. (04427) 73291. ■

● *Above: Ashley Iles at the oil vat, hardening the tools that bear his name. The correct temperature is critical in this stage, which decides the hardness of the final product – all is dependent on an experienced eye for colour*

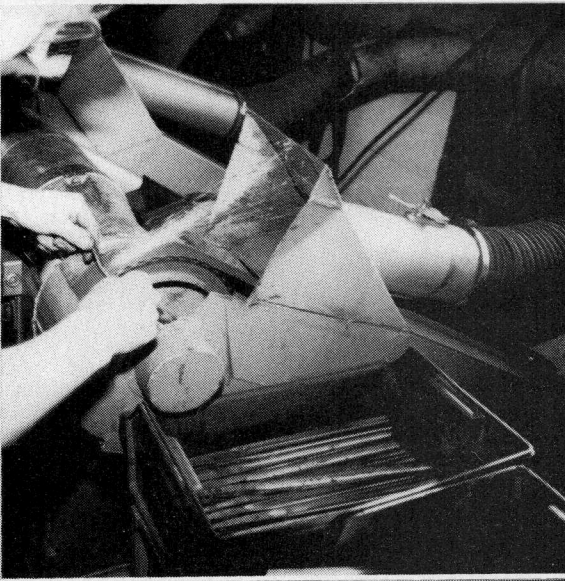

● *Right: After tempering, the tools are given the familiar finish by glazing them with various abrasive wheels, aided by quantities of mutton fat!*

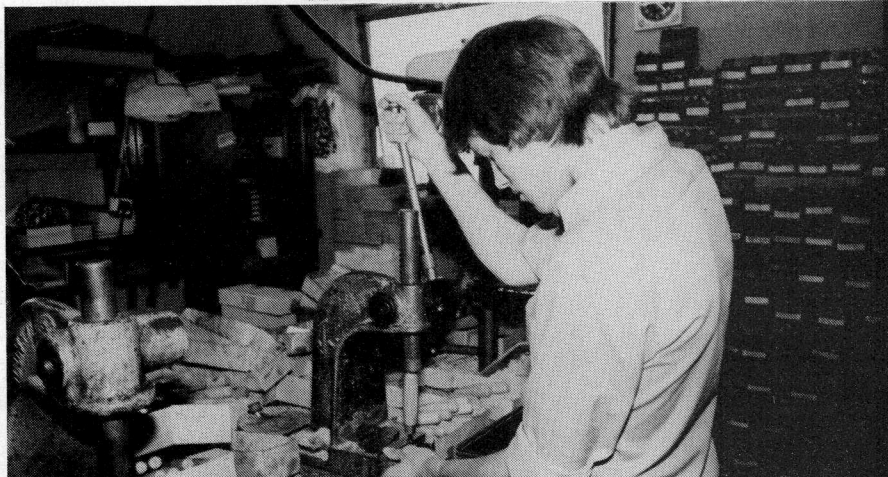

● *The cutler adds the handles, the name, and the fine edge. His sharp eye also picks out the pieces before despatch that won't meet Ashley Iles' high standards*

# BRISTOL Woodworker Show

## MAY 25 to 27 1985

Join the growing hobby, be a Craftsman in wood

**Opening Hours**
**10.00 am. to 6.00 pm.**

## BRISTOL EXHIBITION CENTRE

### Canon's Road, Centre of Bristol.

Sponsored by "Woodworker," Britain's premier magazine for the craftsman, and the aspiring craftsman.

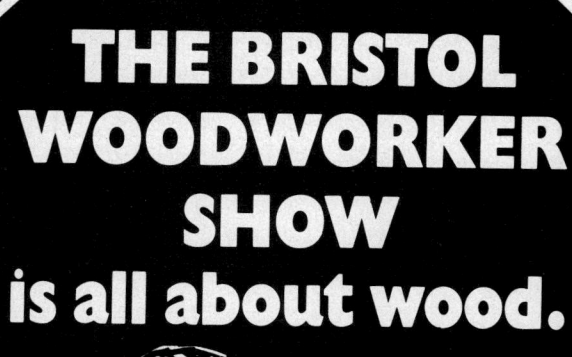

# THE BRISTOL WOODWORKER SHOW is all about wood.

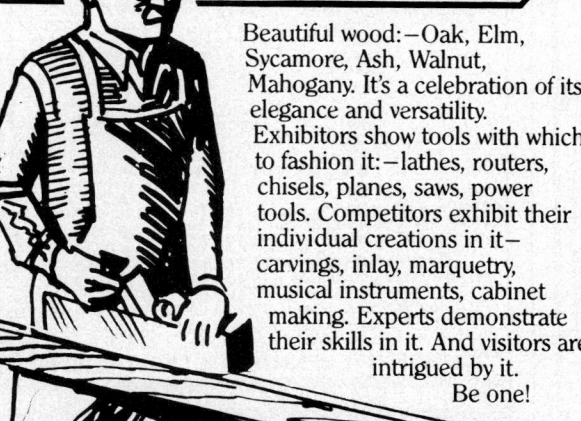

Beautiful wood:—Oak, Elm, Sycamore, Ash, Walnut, Mahogany. It's a celebration of its elegance and versatility. Exhibitors show tools with which to fashion it:—lathes, routers, chisels, planes, saws, power tools. Competitors exhibit their individual creations in it— carvings, inlay, marquetry, musical instruments, cabinet making. Experts demonstrate their skills in it. And visitors are intrigued by it.
Be one!

JOIN THE GROWING HOBBY AT THE

## BRISTOL EXHIBITION CENTRE
### CANON'S ROAD, CENTRE OF BRISTOL

# MAY 25th to 27th 1985
Opening hours: 10.00am – 6.00pm
Admission charges £2.00 Adults £1.50 OAP's and Children

*Organised by*
**ARGUS SPECIALIST EXHIBITIONS LIMITED**
Park View House, Park View Road, Berkhamsted. Tel: 04427 73291.

BRISTOL EXHIBITION CENTRE

Ample car parking facilities for the public exist in the area including surface and multi-storey car parks and street meter-parking.

The huge Canon's Marsh Car Park is situated immediately opposite the Exhibition Centre and offers all day and overnight parking.

**PARKING FACILITES**

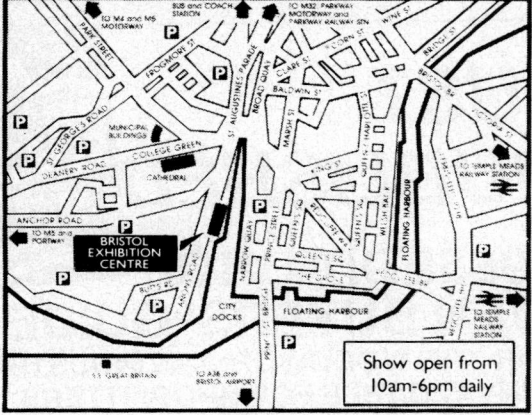

Show open from 10am-6pm daily

*A typical visitor's opinion of a past Woodworker Show.*

❝I was very impressed and considered the 350 mile round trip well worth the effort.

I particularly liked to see exhibits of actual projects and it is so easy for woodworkers to compare and purchase countless tools and machines. The exhibits provide useful inspiration to consider future projects and to measure the success of my own work. It is equally as good to see the really excellent pieces as well as the not quite so excellent. All in all a wonderful show.❞

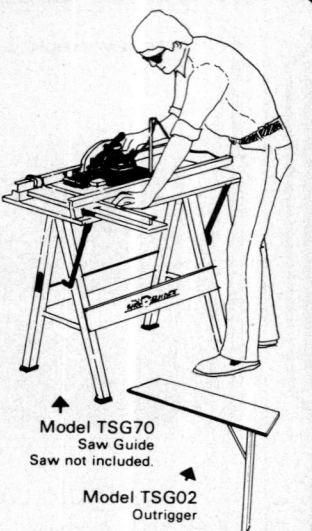

CLOCK MAKING MATERIALS AND PLANS: Mechanical and Quartz movements. Time Glasses. Brass and Alloy Dials, Chapter Rings. Bezels. Convex Glasses. Case fittings, etc.

WEATHER INSTRUMENTS: Barometers, Thermometers, Hygrometers in a range of sizes and types.

SELF-ASSEMBLY KITS: Vienna Regulator, Bracket, Longcase, Skeleton and Cuckoo Clocks. Spinning Wheel and Weighing Scales.

**Send 25p stamp for Catalogue to:**
**CRAFT MATERIALS LIMITED (WW)**
The Haven, Station Road, Northiam Rye, East Sussex.
TN31 6QL. Telephone: 079 74 2180.

---

# Bygones

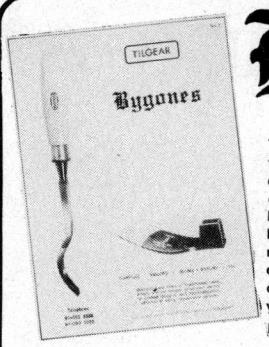

The BYGONES catalogue contains traditional hand tools for the discerning craftsman which have been discontinued and are therefore becoming increasingly difficult to obtain. It includes items such as boxwood handled chisels, plain and tee-bar sash cramps, combination planes, vices, marking gauges, squares, mallets, tool cabinets and many more. These are all offered at very reasonable prices to give you the opportunity to obtain the quality that was available in years gone by.

Please send 50p in stamps for catalogue.

TILGEAR, 20 Ladysmith Road, Enfield, Middx., EN1 3AA  Telephone: 01-363 8050/3080

**TILGEAR**

---

# WOODWORKERS SMOCKS

GUARANTEED **TOP QUALITY** - BRITISH MADE

**100% COTTON**

COMFORTABLE & HARDWEARING
RANGE OF COLOURS AND SIZES

WHEN ORDERING, PLEASE SPECIFY SIZE (M, L, XL or XXL) AND COLOUR (BROWN, NAVY or DARK GREEN), AND ENCLOSE YOUR NAME AND ADDRESS WITH REMITTANCE OF £11·99 PER GARMENT & £1·00 P&P.

Cheques & P.O's, etc, payable to:—
P. LOVELL (Workware), 3 Heol Esgyn, Cyncoed, Cardiff, South Glam. CF2 6JT.

BARGAIN! PRICE! £11·99 + £1. P&P.

---

## GUARANTEED HIGH QUALITY AT LOW! LOW PRICES!

Our quality of Machine tools and Equipment is so good that our customers include: M.O.D., British Rail, British Steel Laboratories. Our prices are so competitive that we sell to new businesses, Local Authorities etc. We supply throughout the U.K. and many countries abroad. Ask for free Catalogues. Better still, visit us to examine our products for yourself.

**EXCEL** *Machine Tools*

**Unit 1, Colliery Lane, Exhall, Coventry.**
**Telephone (0203) 365255**

---

# THE ONLY WAY TO BE SURE OF
# Woodworker EACH MONTH

Is to order it NOW through your local newsagent — simply fill in the left hand form and hand it to him — or if you prefer to become a subscriber fill in the right hand form and return to:-

**INFONET LTD**
**10/13 TIMES HOUSE, 179 MARLOWES**
**HEMEL HEMPSTEAD, HERTS  HP1 1BB, ENGLAND**

## From your Newsagent

Would you please arrange for me to receive a regular copy of **Woodworker** magazine

My Name is ........................................................................

Address ..............................................................................

..............................................................................

..............................................................................

Distributed by:
**SM Distribution Ltd**
**16-18 Trinity Gardens**
**London SW9 8DX**

**Telephone 01-274 8611**

## By Subscription

I would like to take out a subscription for one year to **Woodworker** magazine.

Remittance value .......................................... enclosed

Name ..................................................................................

Address ..............................................................................

..............................................................................

Signature ............................................................................

| | |
|---|---|
| Month to start ...................... | **SUBSCRIPTION RATES:** UK: £15.60 |
| Subscription No. ...................... | Overseas: £17.00 |
| Amount received £$ ...................... | USA: $22.50 |
| Date ...................... | All rates include postage |
| FOR OFFICE USE | |

---

# The beginner's figurine

**G**erald Dunn writes: I am nothing of a woodworker. I read this magazine because I like watching creative joy in action. My pastime is making small instruments with navigational applications, and on this occasion I was looking for a novel means of supporting a small universal ring dial I had made for one of my daughters.

I had never before done any woodcarving, though I have always kept an eye on developments in this branch of the craft. This little figurine was the product of my first attempt. It is 10in high, excluding the ring dial (in aluminium, 2½in in overall diameter). The wood is lime and the finish is oil polish.

First I made perspective drawings of the front, back and both side elevations. It is probably unnecessary to develop these as far as I did. The modelling up of the surface musculature is exaggerated without regard to aesthetics, as a substitute for making a clay maquette. This study exercise was broadened out into a third dimension by several high-reliefs which enabled me to come to grips with the body geometry, if I may use the expression. Subsequently I made scale orthographic projections before starting work on the wood. Strictly, to define a solid object a plan view should be projected as well. But this is very difficult on account of the twisting of torso and limbs.

They say that Leonardo used to pose his models in a water tank in order to measure off horizontal dimensions against a datum at different depths. I doubt it. But I don't work from a model anyway! What I did instead was to make a simple axial diagram indicating approximately the directions in which were inclined the feet, knees, hips, waist, shoulders and head. These, as you can see, are set every which way with respect to each other. You can also see that this scheme was not a complete success. For instance, in the left-hand-side elevation the head is quite incorrectly posed. It should be almost in profile instead of nearly full-face. Nor should the head be jutting forward like

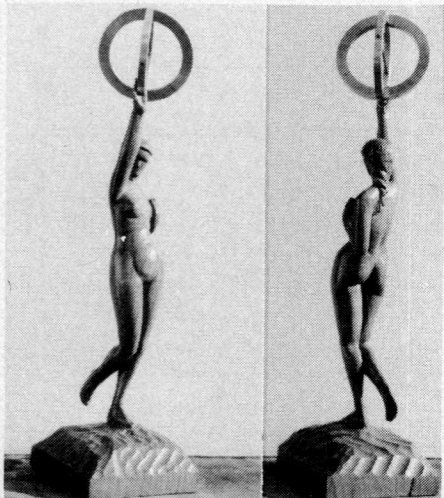

● *The little lime figurine with her nautical-style ring dial disports herself with a slightly classical air*

that of a strutting pigeon as I have sketched it; if anything it should be tilted slightly aft.

**M**y kit of tools consisted of a few gouges and rifflers. When the job was far enough advanced to be held in the hand I found great use for a set of those small Korean carving tools. They can be manipulated whilst sitting in your easy chair by the fireside — though I don't suppose experienced carvers would much approve of these toys. Nevertheless, I will go further and say that I don't despise lino-block cutters for detail. Hook gouges, draw-hooks, cranked whittling knives and scrapers I made up according to need from spent files and hacksaw blades. I think the best wood scraper in the world for sculptural surfaces is a shard of freshly broken glass, choosing curves to suit. I am not yet sufficiently confident to leave my tool-marks on the work as the masters advise!

I found it a good idea to wet the work from time to time in order to primp up any areas where the surface fibres had been compressed or bruised.

I soon gave up worrying about limbs or fragments snapped off in the course of work. If they are carefully and quickly glued back into place the fracture line is usually invisible. Obviously one should not be careless about this, but I can well imagine occasions when it might actually pay to break off a limb in order to get at an obscured area which otherwise would be difficult or impossible to reach with a tool. Caution would be needed to avoid dubbing

over the edges of the break or otherwise disfiguring the fibrous interface of the mating surfaces when the limb was re-attached.

The most important single lesson this job taught me was one seldom emphasised enough by teachers of carving. It is the importance of keeping the work on the move — never dwelling for more than a moment on any particular passage. What gives sculpture its unique particularity, and distinguishes it from all the other branches of art, is the property of 'all-round viewability'. The pleasantest part of contemplating sculpture is its ever-changing profile, and the interplay of light and shade which results from the movement of the beholder's eye round and round the exhibit. Now if it is the movement of the onlooker's eye which produces that infinity of aspects, how much more important it is for the sculptor to do likewise. The carver should be constantly turning and turning the piece of work — or, better still, rolling it over and over in his hands so that his tactile sense may come to the aid of the visual.

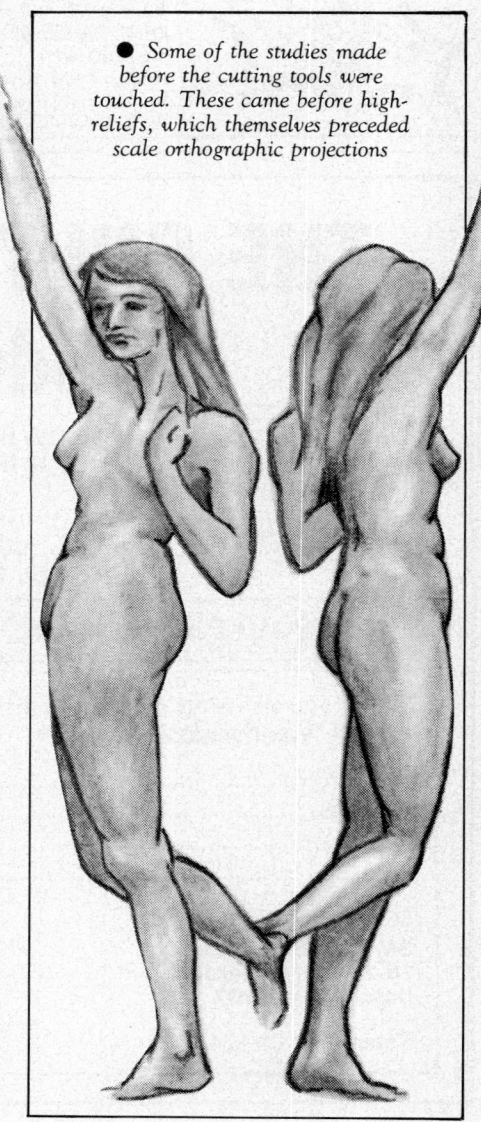

● *Some of the studies made before the cutting tools were touched. These came before high-reliefs, which themselves preceded scale orthographic projections*

Finally the plinth was hollowed out and plugged with lead. This is both to minimise internal tensions and to ballast down the structure, which is otherwise a little top-heavy.

I had better not go into details of the sundial except to explain that, if my daughter tilts the horizontal ring to suit her latitude, and aims the upright ring southwards (north in the other hemi-sphere), the shadow of the centre pin will indicate the sun time at her geographical location. She can also use the tool as a compass if she wishes — and if she doesn't know *where* she is (which heaven forbid) the instrument will find out for her. ■

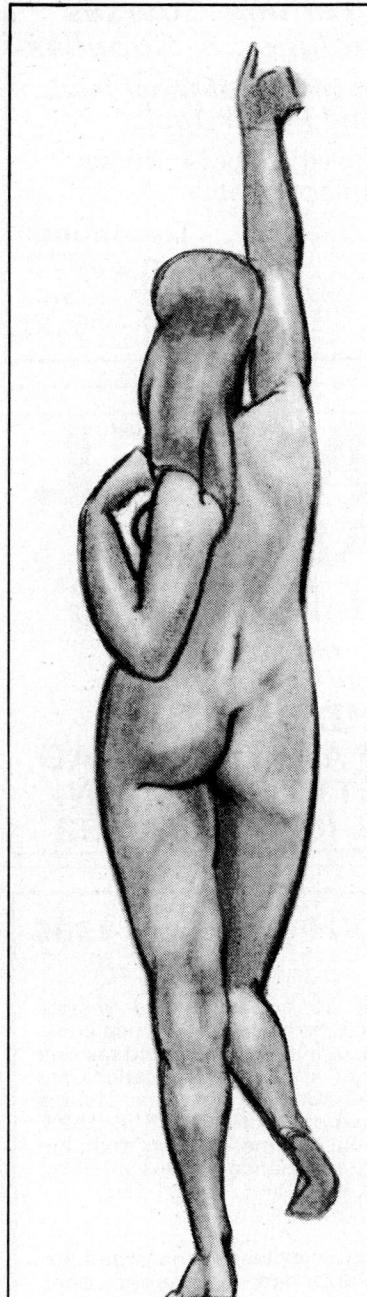

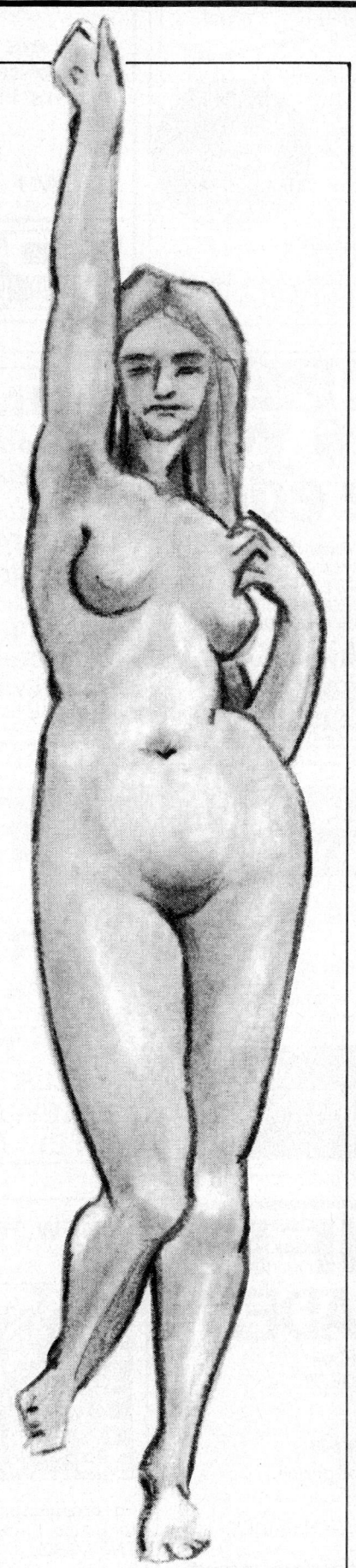

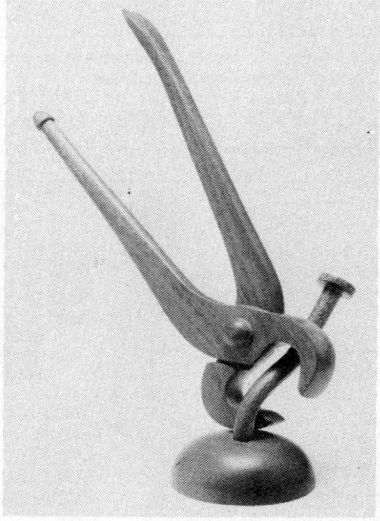

Prices quoted are those prevailing at press date and are subject to alteration due to economic conditions

KINDLY MENTION 'WOODWORKER' WHEN REPLYING TO ADVERTISEMENTS

# Working to permission

**Setting up a workshop can mean an encounter with the planning authorities. Chris Kendall DipTP MRTPI explains how to keep it legal**

Why an article about planning? Simply because many of you will come into contact with the planning process, or already have done and have found the experience painful. As a local-authority planning officer with an interest in woodwork, I hope I can give you an insight into the system and help you to avoid problems.

From the start, the best advice I can give you is this: go and talk to the local planning officer. He is there to help and, if given a chance, that is what he will do.

Let's start by thinking about woodworking at home. The law says that planning permission is not required to use your house and garden for 'purposes incidental to the enjoyment of the dwelling-house'. Basically, that means that you can use any part of your property for hobby purposes. There have been cases where it has been decided that a hobby was not 'incidental' — building hang-gliders, for example, or maintaining a racing car; but I have never yet known a purely hobby woodworker to have this problem. If you want to build a workshop (not a garage) it is likely that you won't need planning permission provided that it is used for purposes incidental to the enjoyment of the house. You can, however, forget about setting up a furniture factory in your back garden.

Your local planning department will be able to provide you with a free booklet called *Planning Permission – A Guide For Householders*. This gives details of the size limits and other restrictions.

Many of you will be forced, like me, to have to work in a garage which will also be a home for the freezer, washing-machine, etc. Again, a check will probably reveal that planning permission is not needed.

If you are only working at home as a hobby, those circumstances generally mark the limits of your involvement with the system. But if you are using an existing building, or building a new one, as a commercial workshop you will need planning permission. If you live in a residential area, that does not automatically mean that you won't get planning permission, but it is harder. If you are a one-man carving business you could be all right; if you're mass producing window-frames or roof-trusses you will have problems. A lot depends on how well you fit the legal definition of light industry — really, industry which is suitable for a residential area. If you decide to go ahead without planning permission you are not breaking the law, but watch out for the local informer who feels that you are lowering the tone of the area. In general, if you are quiet and sensible no one will notice you. If, on the other hand, you're a real nuisance, you deserve to be stopped.

For many people, working at home isn't possible or practical and they must buy or rent a workshop somewhere else. There can be problems here. Estate agents seem to use descriptions such as 'light industrial' and 'commercial' very freely. As I've said, light industry has a precise meaning in planning law, and the word commercial does not exist. So check. The old-fashioned village joiner working only with hand tools had a light-industrial shop; the modern joiner, relying heavily on machines which may be running all day, does not. Therefore, it may be that you need planning permission to use an existing joiner's workshop as a joiner's workshop. Talk to the planners before you sign up for the premises, explain what you want to do, and generally give as much information as possible.

The question is, for what sort of premises are you likely to get permission? Obviously a site on an industrial estate will not be a problem, but it may well be financially out of the question. The government, however, want the planning system to encourage small businesses, and have advised planning authorities to adopt a more flexible attitude than in the past. Disused farm buildings, old mills and old industrial premises are all places which seem to be suitable. If you can find premises which are listed as being of architectural or historic interest, or are in a conservation area, and you can convince the council that your use of them will ensure their retention, or — better still — their restoration, that should help considerably. For further advice I suggest that you look at Department of the Environment Circulars 22/80, 16/84 and to a lesser extent 23/77. Large

● *Plenty of space . . . an old building in an old country town . . . an idyllic situation. But don't bank on it until you've squared things with the planners! (photo John Gollop/David Savage)*

libraries have them, you can order them from HMSO outlets, and if you ask nicely your local planning officer will let you read his own dog-eared copies. There's also a booklet called *Planning Permission: A Guide for Industry*.

Having decided where you want to work from, ring the planning officer for the area concerned and arrange to see him. Explain clearly what you want to do, how many staff you will be employing, what machinery you will have, frequency of delivery, types of vehicle, etc. Don't assume he reads *Woodworker* and knows everything about what you want to do. Stress your good points, if you have any — e.g., mainly hand tools, little waste, restoring an interesting building. Listen to his advice. He isn't all-powerful, but he advises the elected councillors who will decide on your application.

Discuss any particular requirements that

either of you may have. What sort of hours are you likely to be working? He may feel that there should be a limit, particularly if there are houses nearby. Do you intend to store anything outside, for instance timber for air-drying? Do you intend to have a showroom or other sales outlet at the premises? What about parking and turning facilities? Talk, listen, negotiate without losing your temper. If he says something you don't understand, ask; if he looks puzzled, explain your point again.

You will now find yourself with a bundle of papers, probably multi-coloured, on which to make your application. Read through and complete them carefully. Think about sending a covering letter explaining what you want to do — planning application forms are meant to cover all types of development and are therefore not very good for any. You don't need to have the application put in for you by an estate agent, solicitor, architect or the like. There are times when such professionals are useful, but you should be able to manage on your own. If you are able to cope with VAT returns, planning forms should be a piece of cake. If you do get problems, go and ask. Planners would rather spend 10 minutes face to face than weeks in frustrating correspondence.

You must submit a plan with your application. Make sure that this covers all the buildings and land you wish to use.

Once your application is submitted, consultations will be carried out. Usually these involve the highway authority, the town or parish council (if there is one), and the neighbours. You could save a lot of misunderstanding and ill-feeling by talking to the town or parish council and your future neighbours first. Allay their fears.

Although councils can delegate functions to officers, your application will probably be considered by the planning committee. This will be made up of councillors one of whom will probably be from the area where you want to work. You could try to enlist his support before you put in the application. At the committee meeting the planning officer will tell the committee about your application, the consultation replies and anything else relevant, and then make a recommendation. After that the committee will make its decision.

If they approve, you're home and dry. If they refuse, you'll be given reasons. Can you negotiate a compromise? If not, you're faced with looking elsewhere or appealing to the Secretary of State for the Environment. But that's another story. ■

● *This model of an old joiner's and cabinetmaker's workshop appeared at a recent Woodworker Show. With nothing so hi-tech as even iron planes, a space like this would certainly need planning permission before you moved the bandsaw in*

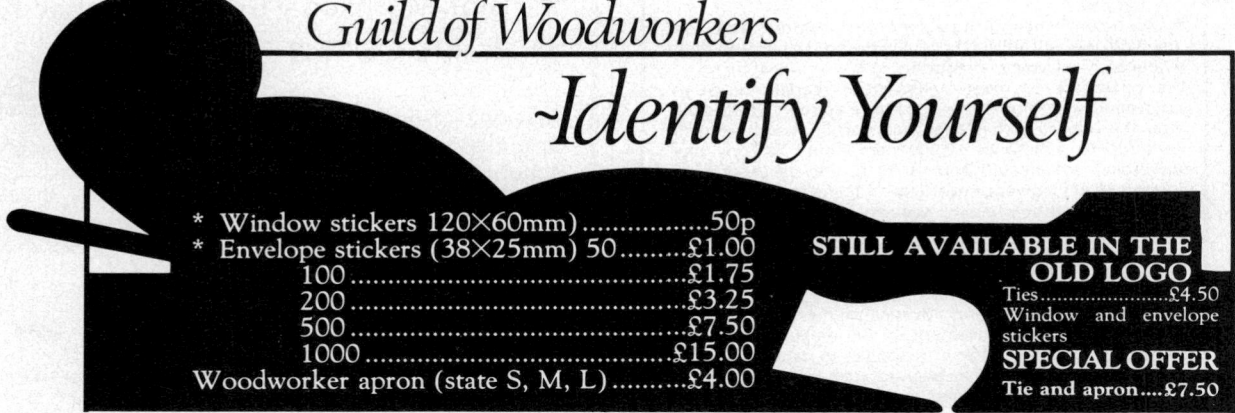

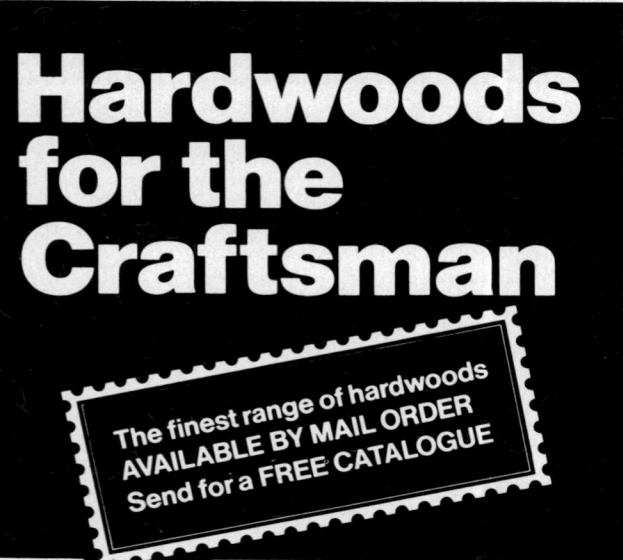

## MAIL ORDER ADVERTISING

**British Code of Advertising Practice**
Advertisements in this production are required to conform to the British Code of Advertising Practice. In respect of mail order advertisements where money is paid in advance, the code requires advertisers to fulfil orders within 28 days, unless a longer delivery period is stated. Where goods are returned undamaged within seven days, the purchaser's money must be refunded. Please retain proof of postage/despatch, as this may be needed.

**Mail Order Protection Scheme**
If you order goods from Mail Order advertisements in this magazine and pay by post in advance of delivery WOODWORKER will consider you for compensation if the Advertiser should become insolvent or bankrupt, provided:
(1) You have not received the goods or had your money returned; and
(2) You write to the Publisher of this publication, summarising the situation not earlier than 28 days from the day you sent your order and not later than two months from that day.
Please do not wait until the last moment to inform us. When you write, we will tell you how to make your claim and what evidence of payment is required.
We guarantee to meet claims from readers made in accordance with the above procedure as soon as possible after the Advertiser has been declared bankrupt or insolvent (up to a limit of £2,000 per annum for any one Advertiser so affected and up to £6,000 per annum in respect of all insolvent Advertisers. Claims may be paid for higher amounts or when the above procedure has not been complied with, at the discretion of this publication, but we do not guarantee to do so in view of the need to set some limit to this commitment and to learn quickly of readers' difficulties).
This guarantee covers only advance payment sent in direct response to an advertisement in this magazine (not, for example, payment made in response to catalogues etc., received as a result of answering such advertisements). Classification advertisements are excluded.

Prices quoted are those prevailing at press date and are subject to alteration due to economic conditions

# Clamping soundboards

WOODWORKING WHEEZE
of the month


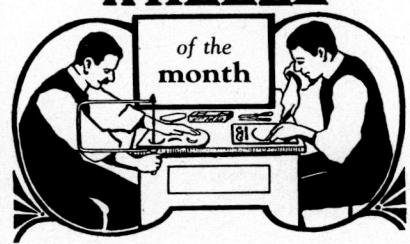

**J**ohn **Telling** writes: This time- and aggravation-saving jig makes for easy clamping of musical-instrument sound-board and back pieces of any shape, with or without a decorative strip. The version illustrated here is suitable for guitars.

The body of the jig consists of two 600×700mm pieces of 9mm ply. One piece simply forms the base-board; the other is perforated with 12 slots, each about 225×28mm, to form the top board. This top board is glued to and separated from the base-board by stock 10mm thick (shown hatched on the drawing).

Running in each of the slots is a free-sliding 'traveller' consisting of a 45mm-long piece of 25mm-diameter dowel glued into a recessed 75mm-diameter base cut from 9mm ply. All gluing needs to be firm and clean. Unwanted dollops on the travellers or inside the boards will prevent free movement. If the travellers do bind, sand their bases.

Rebate a slot about 15mm wide by 2mm deep along the centre line of the top board, and cover it with masking-tape. This slot allows excess glue to escape from the joint and creates space for placing a solid decorative strip between back pieces at the time of clamping.

The pieces to be clamped are positioned carefully on the top board, with the glued joint over the slot. Each pair of travellers is linked in turn with a 6×⅜in (or similar) rubber band. Slide two sticks under the bands, one each side of the glued joint, to provide slight downward pressure and thus prevent heaving of the jointed pieces. Add extra bands to increase the compression.

It's a simple matter to make a longer, thinner version of this jig for clamping Appalachian-dulcimer backs and fronts, and even a tiny model for head veneers.■

**We look forward to receiving readers' accounts and pictures of devices and techniques. They should be original and useful, and the text should be typed.**

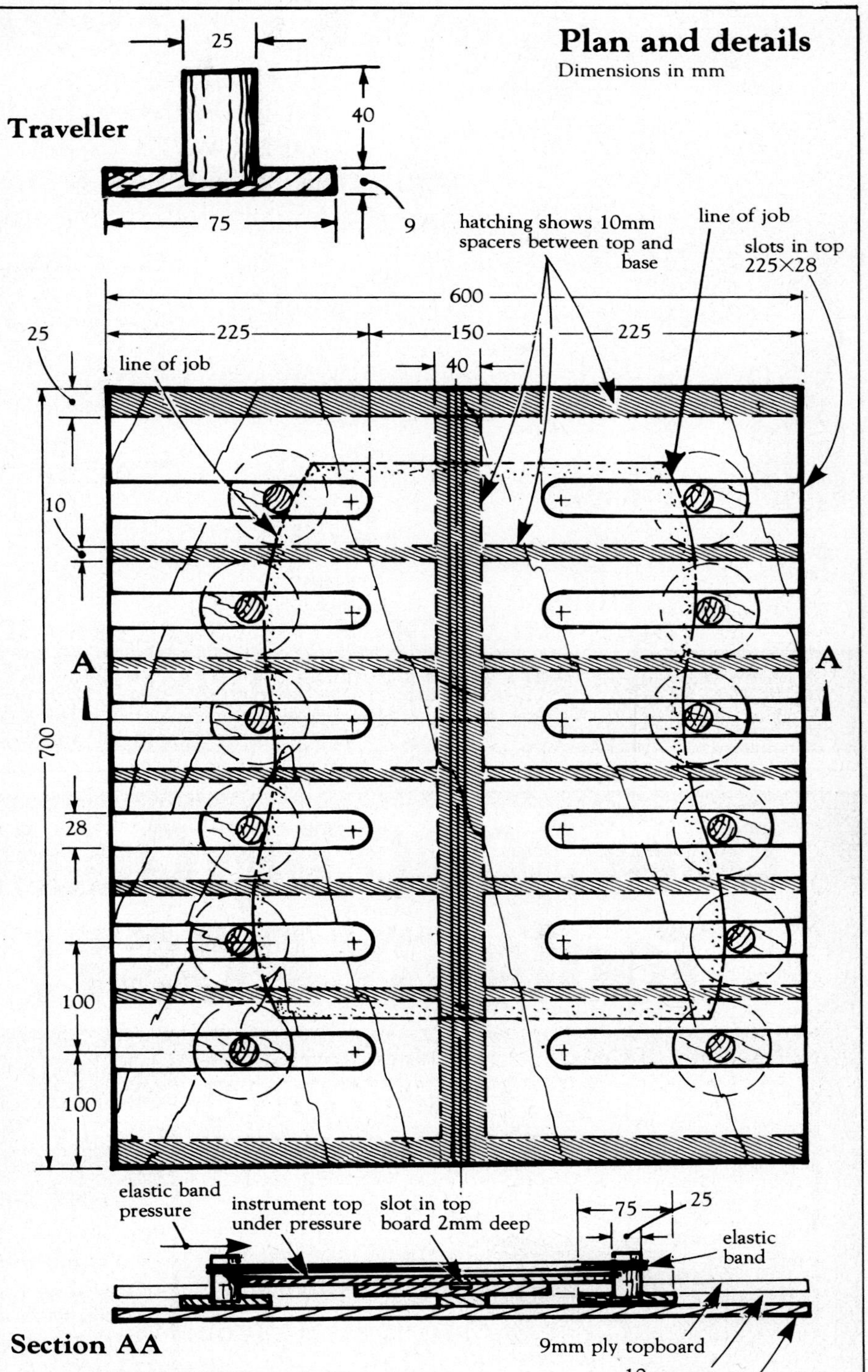

Plan and details
Dimensions in mm
Traveller
25
40
9
75
hatching shows 10mm spacers between top and base
line of job
slots in top 225×28
600
225
150
225
25
line of job
40
10
A
A
700
28
100
100
elastic band pressure
instrument top under pressure
slot in top board 2mm deep
75
25
elastic band
Section AA
9mm ply topboard
10mm gap
9mm baseboard


● *Like so many bright ideas, it looks confusing at first but the concept is very simple. The 'travellers', held together by strong rubber bands, exert pressure inwards and adjust themselves to any shape. Battens pushed under the bands hold the jointed boards flat. There's no reason why the jig should be confined to instrument-making; if you're keen on solid drawer-bottoms or jointing thin panels, the advantages of a one-piece clamping system like this are obvious. John has shown the jig to other instrument-makers, who were all impressed*

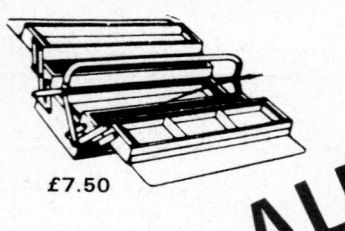

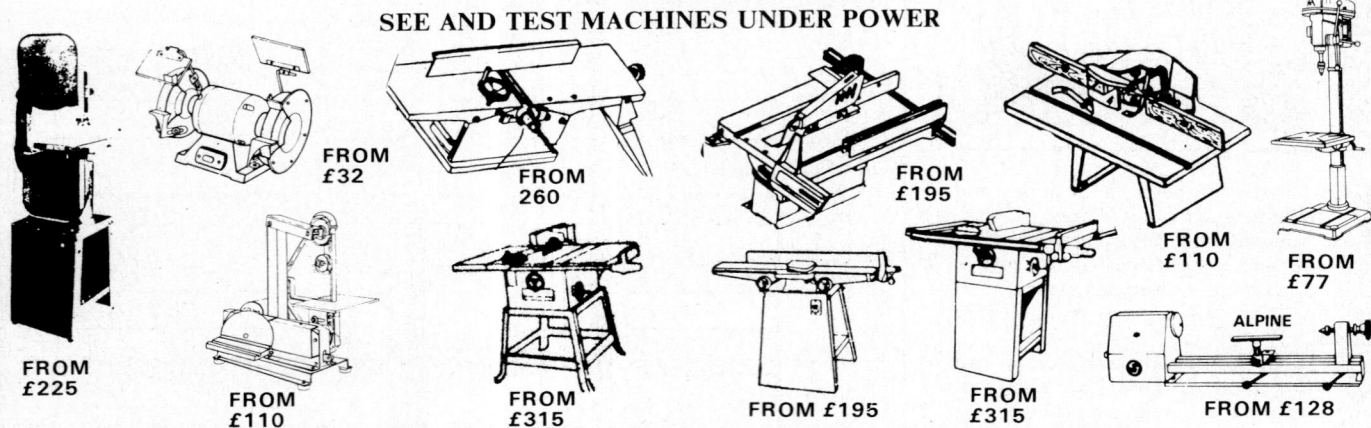

Prices quoted are those prevailing at press date and are subject to alteration due to economic conditions

# Guild notes

## Guild of WOODWORKERS

Shared information, advice and help are vital to good woodwork. They are also the basis of the **Guild of Woodworkers**: an international organisation which welcomes new members — whatever their skills. 1 Golden Sq, London W1R 3AB, tel. 01-437 0626.

Guild members get
- priority on our courses
- free publicity in *Woodworker*
- 15% off Woodworker Show entry
- a free display area and meeting-point at the Show
- 15% discount on our plans
- access to and inclusion in our register of members' skills and services
- the chance to contact other members for help and advice where appropriate
- specially arranged tool insurance at low rates

Please quote your Guild number when contacting us.

*Aidan Walker*

## New address

You'll have noticed last month's note about *Woodworker's* change of offices, but a lot of the Guild's routine administration has still been done at Hemel over the last few weeks by our trusted and valuable help Pat Young — to whom we have now said a sad goodbye, and a happy thank you. Please now address all your Guild correspondence to **1 Golden Sq., London W1R 3AB, tel. 01-437 0626.**

## Local reps

For all the mentions and enquiries I get about this, you'd think it was a great and burgeoning success. Too early yet, perhaps, to say 'Far from it', but the fact remains that there seem to be more people wanting to meet each other than wanting to be local focal points. We have about a dozen now, all eagerly waiting to spring into action, but I'm still sure there'll be more. The main thing to realise is that this *does not require an enormous input on your part*. We print your name and address, and those who want to get in touch with each other get in touch with you. If they want to be left alone, they leave you alone. Simple. I'd hate to admit this wheeze was a failure!

## Further to which

'What is it about the craft which leaves people "doing their own thing" in isolation when it might be better or more enjoyable done in company?' writes Mr H. H. Bridge of Southport. Mr Bridge, I may add, has already acted on his words and offered to be a local rep for the Guild. 'Why not Woodworker Clubs?' he asks. Why not indeed? It is unfortunately something editorial staff, much as they'd like to run around the country all week, cannot afford to put a lot of time into — but we can promote and publicise the idea, which is what, on behalf of *Woodworker* and the Guild, I'm doing here and now. Guild member or no, if you're interested in the idea I'm sure Mr Bridge would like to hear from you. His address is 2 Ashley Rd, Southport PR9 0RB.

## Handicap research

Sally Rossin, a comparatively recent addition to the Guild's ever-growing membership, is studying the design and development of wooden equipment and educational toys to aid the handicapped — physical or mental. She is researching the needs of the handicapped, designing equipment, and working on its development and construction. She emphasises that it's a comparatively new venture for her, and is at present working on a portfolio of designs; but she would, even so, be most interested to hear from anyone who is involved in similar work.
- Sally's address is 8 Moore Grove, Lymm, Cheshire WA13 9RT.

## Conservation conversation continued

Another name and address for your list of charities committed to the promotion of conservation is the **British Trust for Conservation Volunteers,** Bayfordbury House, Hertford, Herts SG13 8LD. They originally got in touch to publicise a course they were mounting in March on coppice crafts and products, to introduce the uses to which coppiced wood can be put and to demonstrate the traditional related crafts. It reached us too late for the March issue, unfortunately, but they have other things on the agenda, so you should get in touch with them if you're interested. Unusual to see such a body actually running a course — the training officer at that address is Gill Castle.

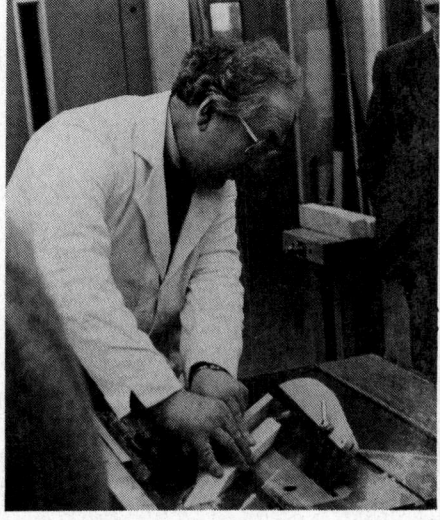

- *Ken Taylor demonstrates the intricacies of compound-mitre-cutting at the Guild's woodmachining course on 9 February*

Prices quoted are those prevailing at press date and are subject to alteration due to economic conditions

# Guild courses

May Bank Holiday and the Bristol Wood-worker Show bring summer in with a bang — and it's the season for Guild courses too. We're trying to get as full a programme as we can for you, and there are ideas I want to investigate. Basic carpentry and joinery techniques? Woodcarving introduction? Chair-caning? Write and let me know — every woodworker wants to know something, surely. It's one of the things I enjoy most about our hugely varied craft — there's always something more to learn. Let us know what you want, and we'll see what we can do.

## Finishing and polishing — Charles Cliffe

6-7 June, £40 inc. VAT. Surface prep-aration, introduction to materials, cabinet scraper, staining, filling bodying up, spiriting off. This is the third of Charles' ever-popular courses that I have been involved with, and their popularity shows what good value they are. Charles' advice on your own furniture problems is also a big attraction.

## Finishing and polishing — Ian Hosker

29-30 June; taught in the North — Chester, to be exact — by the Guild's new northern expert in this popular subject. Ian is a teacher at a technical college, and runs his own restoration business. The hours will be 10-5, with an hour for lunch; subjects covered will be materials, preparation, cabinet scraper, stains, filling, fadding, bodying and spiriting, and restoring polished surfaces. All you northerners — we're putting this one on specially for you!
● £45 for the two days, including the materials that Ian supplies. **Cheques for the full amount confirm booking.**

## Special toolmaking — Fred Lambert

15-19 July 1985, £145+VAT. After the successful and popular stage 1 course on Country Chairmaking, Fred has kindly agreed to take us one step further and teach a course on making the special tools for the job. As some chair enthusiasts already know, these rounders and trapping planes are not available on the general market, so the only way you can have your own is to make them. They are cast in aluminium alloy with brass inserts; 0151 Record or Stanley spokeshave fitting are used. Fred emphasises that there is no need to be experienced in metalwork — interest rather than skill is the most important ingredient. The five days in Tewkesbury's beautiful Pull Court will without doubt be instructive, enjoyable and productive — you'll leave with eight tools of your own, made with your own hands.
● **Cheque for full amount confirms booking** — we'll supply you with details of places to stay.

## Cabinetmaker's decorative techniques — Bob Grant

20 July 1985, St Augustine's of Canterbury School, Oxford. Bob will go into advanced techniques on this day, which has more hours in it than the one in December; he will be covering curved inlay lines, making and setting in motifs, sand shading and decorative chamfering. These are traditional processes mostly using the scratch stock; if you haven't been on the first course, don't worry, because the idea is to make it independent of previous instruction. A certain amount of experience is necessary for you to make the best of the course, naturally.
● The day is 9.30-5, and costs £27.50+VAT. **Cheque for the full amount confirms booking.**

## Hand veneering — Bob Grant

14 September 1985, also at St Augustine's School. Bob emphasises that this will be an introduction to traditional techniques. The day will include an introductory talk and looking at samples; demonstration of techniques; and then making up your own veneered panel, a centre square surrounded by a cross-veneered border with mitred corners. There'll be a balancer to put on the back as well. Added attraction to this course is the presence of **Peter Sarac**, a harpsichord maker who has worked for Robert Gable and is now running his own business. Bob and he should make a powerful combination of brains to be picked.

● Again 9.30-5, £30+VAT. If you've got a veneer hammer, bring it! As with all courses, **a cheque for full amount gets you the booking.**

## Furniture restoration and repair — Eric Burger

25-26 July, in Eric's own professional workshop in Bournemouth. A summer weekend by the sea? For the family perhaps, but you'll be working hard absorbing the mountain of information on this wide topic. The basis of the course will be very much angled to individual needs — bring your own (small!) bits of furniture — but Eric reckons to cover in a general way: repairs to furniture covering, including glues and finishes; veneers; inlaying bandings, including brass; marquetry; traditional cabinetmaking methods; preparation for french polish, and polishing itself; gilding; wax polishing and carving. Obviously all that cannot be taught in two days, but you can get a very good base for further experiments of your own. He has wide professional and teaching experience, having run his own highly reputed business in the area for many years, and also has a long-standing regular class of local people.
● £40+VAT for the two busy days, 9.30-5; this includes the cost of some basic materials like french polish. **Cheque for full amount confirms booking.**

## Woodmachining — Ken Taylor

Unhappily, we had to cancel the 16 March one-day introduction at Milton Keynes. The course will now be on **Saturday 6 July**: £25+VAT.

● *Don Coventry gets the feel of horizontal mortising at the 9 February course; see above for next woodmachining dates*

382

Prices quoted are those prevailing at press date and are subject to alteration due to economic conditions

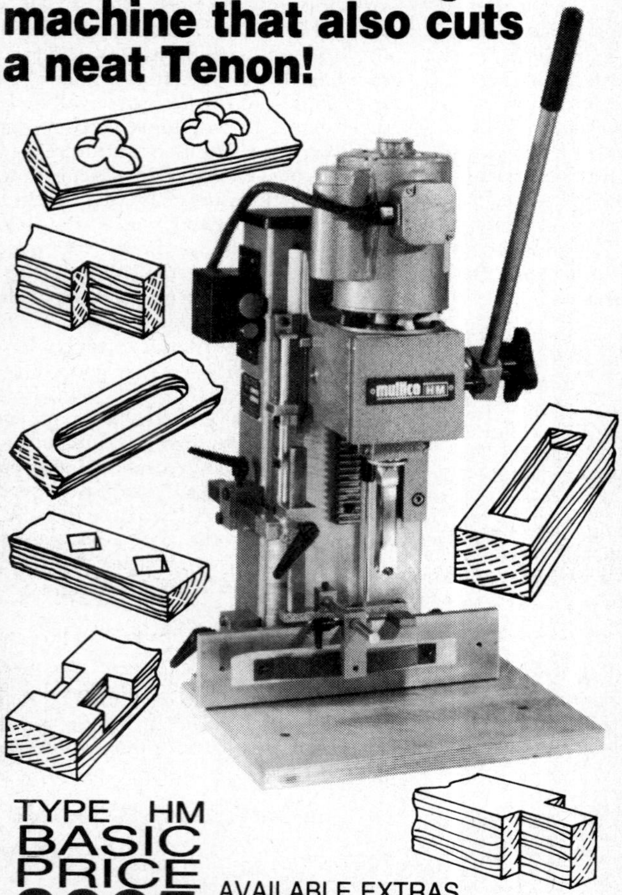

KINDLY MENTION 'WOODWORKER' WHEN REPLYING TO ADVERTISEMENTS

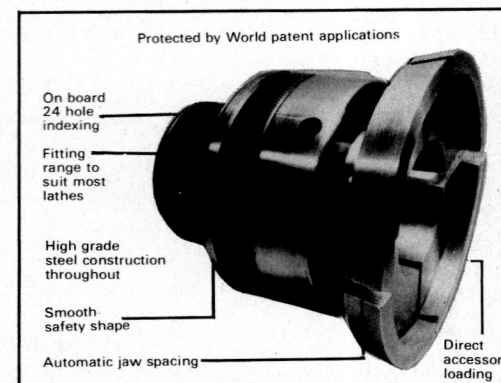

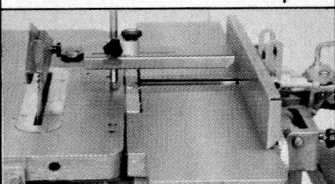

Prices quoted are those prevailing at press date and are subject to alteration due to economic conditions

# Books

*Peter Collenette*
**Woodworking School**
*Windward, £9.95 hardback*
*Reviewed by Luke Hughes*

Unlike certain other productions in the same area, this book sets itself sensible aims and succeeds in attaining them.

Geared 'as much to the experienced cabinet-maker seeking fresh approaches as to the beginner', its declared purposes are to provide a comprehensive guide to the materials and equipment used in fine cabinetmaking, to outline working methods in terms of design, basic approaches, skills and techniques, and to encourage the reader to explore new ways as well as traditional ones.

The publisher's team have also achieved an elegant presentation. There are stacks of photographs, which go further to explain how it's done than Noddy drawings.

The design-and-planning coverage is especially good. Along with structural and economic considerations in designing furniture, it includes useful advice on drawing. This section alone should sell the book — but those on tools and machines, fastening and finishing are of a comparable standard. Illustrated projects show the different techniques described, and we see Len Woodard actually putting them together.

The book ends with an acknowledgement section which includes the addresses of some suppliers, plus an index.

When Peter sent me a copy of this book to review, it arrived with a compliments slip on which were written the words 'Tread softly'. I have no need to. It is a worthy buy for anyone interested in cabinetmaking today, and even the best makers will find something here.

*José Claret Rubira*
**Encyclopedia of English Period Furniture Designs**
*Sterling, £10.95 paperback*
*Reviewed by Dave Batten*

This large book of 352 pages, was originally published in Spain in 1982. Frankly, I cannot see what purpose it serves. With some revision it could be useful, but as it stands it is a hotchpotch. The intention seems to be to illustrate typical pieces of various periods and styles; one large or two small drawings on each page, with details of mouldings, carvings, etc, plus explanatory captions. Properly done, this could be a very useful handbook: let's see now how far reality falls short of possibility.

First, the drawings. These are all line drawings — an approach of which I am in favour, as small details are difficult to see on most photographs. But the drawings are sketchy, with the details fudged; in many instances it's pretty obvious that the auther/artist is far from sure how the piece is made up, and in others the drawings are wrong — particularly those of chairs. The drawings of claw-and-ball feet are so bad that I wonder if he has ever seen one. The uncoated paper hasn't helped; it gives the impression that the artwork was drawn on blotting-paper, with the inevitable smudging of what should be clear and definite lines. Lastly, all the drawings are in outline, with no shading, and this makes it impossible for the uninitiated to visualise the modelling or sculpture of, say, a carved panel.

Now to captions. These are basic, and I mean basic. Rarely do they even mention the wood — but, worse than this, some are either unintelligible or hopelessly inadequate. What, for instance, does this mean: 'Empire 1830 — George IV Trafalgar 1837 William IV'? The facts are that the Empire (or neo-classical) style was more or less contemporaneous with Napoleon, and George IV died in 1830. Trafalgar was in 1805, and William IV ruled from 1830 to 1837. Make what you will of all this! By the way, Regency furniture seems to have been ignored.

A large slab of the book — 42 pages — is devoted to English Minorcan furniture. I must confess that I knew nothing of this; nor did the many reference books I have. Having read the section, I still don't know much. What period is covered? Presumably the time when Nelson was commander of the Mediterranean fleet. Was the furniture made in Minorca, or was it simply shipped across from England? Did it have any influence on local styles? We are told nothing, except by way of skimpy captions.

I cannot honestly recommend the book to you, particularly as I have two small books which do the same job properly and whose cost, added together, is about half the price of this one.

*Amy Zaffarano Rowland and William H. Hylton*
**Handcrafted Shelves and Cabinets**
*Century; £12.95 hardback,*
*£7.95 paperback*
*Reviewed by David Savage*

It is very pleasant to pick up a book and find it better than your initial expectations. This is a case in point — interesting and different once you get past the title, cover and general look.

It is primarily a picture-book jammed full of very-good-quality colour photographs. The work shown comes from all over the United States. By and large it is built-in furniture — kitchen cabinets, bookshelves, bathroom fittings, etc. As a general review of current work in the USA — and most American professional woodworkers are doing this type of work for 60-80% of their time — this book has a lot to offer.

The text, which is written with some warmth and insight by William Hylton, has perhaps even more to recommend it. It is built around extended interviews with five cabinetmakers of different types, ages and levels of skill. Hylton's interest in woodworking as an amateur leads him to ask questions that are pertinent and revealing. Most topics — training, workshop equipment, timber purchasing, pricing and design — are covered. The difference in attitude between the chosen woodworkers, and their different answers to Hylton's questions, give the text a bite and range that is lacking in most contemporary wood books.

I can recommend this as a good read, and good value, for any woodworker interested in American furniture-makers.

*Bruce W. Miller and Jim Widess*
**The Caner's Handbook**
*Collins, £9.95 paperback*
*Reviewed by David Ellis*

This comprehensive manual covers not only cane but nearly every other natural seating material in use today.

Many books have been written on cane seating, many on rush seating and others on wicker-work, etc., but to my knowledge none has yet been produced that deals in such depth with all these materials and the techniques for using them.

The book starts with an informative chapter on hand-woven furniture, its history and evolution, and there are some interesting photographs showing the various type of palm from which rattan, cane and bamboo are obtained.

At this stage I must make particular mention of the figure numbering and its cross-referencing to the text. Every illustration, whether a photograph or descriptive drawing, is numbered, and the numbers are boldly shown in the text so that it is quick and easy to locate the descriptive text relating to it.

The instructive part of the book starts with a chapter on machine-caning — a really informative guide to using this comparatively new innovation. The next two chapters cover in depth the subject of hand caning, from first principles to the most complex patterns — including some that I have never seen described before, such as the 'Star of David' or 'snowflake' pattern. The chapter on special techniques also covers the problems often met in curved rails, double-curved backs, blind and double caning.

The chapter on rush-work, just as explicit, covers the techniques for using both natural and fibre rush, both in the standard pattern and more specialised applications, such as deep-seated chairs and even triangular stools. Danish cord and binder cane, subjects of a later chapter, are both encountered from time to time, particularly in restoration. With the influx of lightweight furniture from Scandinavia, they should prove very useful not only for restorers but in modern furniture design.

The book is rounded off with a fascinating chapter on wicker-work. There are still plenty of antique wicker chairs around, and armed with this chapter you should have no excuse for failing to repair these lovely old pieces.

My only criticism concerns the printing of the photographs. In this UK edition they appear much darker than in the American, and some of the clarity has been lost. Nevertheless, this is not only an excellent book for the amateur chair restorer but also one that could stand, on its own merits, on many professional's shelves.

386

Prices quoted are those prevailing at press date and are subject to alteration due to economic conditions

# WOOD SUPPLIERS

## WOODSUPPLIERS COUPON

FROM _____

_____

_____

I enclose remittance to the value of _____

to cover _____ inset or retain.

Send to: Woodworker Classified, Dept. 1, Golden Square, London W1 3AB. Rates 35p per word (minimum £5.25), semi-displayed £7.25 (minimum 2.5cm).

Prices quoted are those prevailing at press date and are subject to alteration due to economic conditions

# Classified Advertisements

## FOR SALE

**LACE BOBBIN TURNING BLANKS** in unusual and exotic hardwoods and ivory. SAE for list: J. Ford, 5 Squirrels Hollow, Walsall WS7 8YS.

---

### FOR ALL SUPPLIES FOR THE
## Craft of Enamelling
### ON METAL
### Including
### LEAD-FREE ENAMELS

PLEASE SEND 2 × 10p STAMPS FOR FREE CATALOGUE, PRICE LIST AND WORKING INSTRUCTIONS

### W. G. BALL LTD.
ENAMEL MANUFACTURERS

Dept. W. LONGTON
STOKE-ON-TRENT
ST3 1JW

---

### HAND CARVED
'Adam Style' Mantle motifs in Mahogany — Example 10" × 5" centre lamp and two side pieces.
Send S.A.E. for details and quotation. Your own design quoted for if required.
**SAM NICHOLSON**
22 Lisnagarvey Drive, Lisburn,
Co. Antrim, N. Ireland.
Phone Lisburn 3510

---

Have you seen the latest catalogue of

## Bygones

See Display advertisement

---

**D.I.Y.**
## THE SAW CENTRE
LIMITED
ESTABLISHED 1889
### HAS THE EDGE

Hire or buy machinery or power tools from our extensive stock:

Elu **DeWALT** makita Black & Decker
■ SCHEPPACH ■ STARTRITE ■ GRIGGIO
■ VOLPATO ■ SEDGWICK
■ TUNGSTEN CARBIDE TIPPED SAW BLADES
■ DISPOSABLE BANDSAW BLADES

*SAWN OFF PRICES*

**HEAD OFFICE & MAIN WORKS:**
EGLINTON TOLL GLASGOW G5 9RP. TEL: 041-429 4444/4374
OPEN: MON - FRI 8 - 5.30 SAT 9 -1. TELEX: 777886 SAWCO G.
**ALSO AT: 38 HAYMARKET TERRACE EDINBURGH EH12 5JZ.**
TEL: 031-337 5555. OPEN: MON - SAT 8.30 - 5.30.

---

### MUSICAL MOVEMENTS
* LOVE STORY * LARAS THEME * SPEAK SOFTLY LOVE * FUR ELISE * FEELINGS * FASCINATION * IMPOSSIBLE DREAM * MUSIC BOX DANCER * LA POLOMA * THE EMPEROR WALTZ * TRY TO REMEMBER * ROMEO AND JULIET *
Complete with screws and spring mechanism £2.50 inc. p&p. 20 or more of one tune ordered £1.50 each. Available from:
The Jewel Box Shop,
112 Pentonville Road, London N1 9JB.

---

### PLANER FOR SALE
18" surfacer and thicknesser, "Metal Clad Ltd." 3 phase, very good working condition. Cost new would be approx. £3,500; offers, accept £1,600.
**Unit 4, Walsall Road, Norton Canes, Kannock, Staffs. Tel. Heath Hayes 79680**

---

**ELECTRA PLANER/THICKNESSER.** Latest model. Less than one hour's use. Moving, must sell now. Hence £200 (cost £450). No motor. Tring 3648.

---

**NORRIS No. 50G** smoothing plane. 2¼" iron gun metal sides, top adjustment. Excellent condition. What offers? 01-868-3853.

---

MORTISERS; TENNONERS; SPINDLES; PLANERS; BANDSAWS; LATHES; CROSSCUTS; ROUTERS; SANDERS; DRILLS?
YOU CAN CERTAINLY SEE ALL CLASSES AND TYPES OF MACHINES HERE.

WE ARE MAIN STOCKING AGENTS FOR:
MULTICO; ELU; SEDGWICK; KITY; SCHEPPACH; INCA; CORONET; DeWALT; WARCO; DOMINION; HITACHI; STARTRITE; TREND; ASHLEY ILES; SORBY.

*2 DAY EXHIBITION OF WOODWORKING MACHINERY APRIL 12th & 13th MANUFACTURERS DEMONSTRATORS PRESENT*

CALL US ABOUT WOODTURNING LESSONS
WOODCARVING LESSONS (See our Swiss carving tools)
ALWAYS HELPFUL, KNOWLEDGEABLE, GOOD SERVICE AT:
## CLEVELAND WOODCRAFT
### 38-42 CRESCENT ROAD, MIDDLESBROUGH.
### TEL: (0642) 813103

---

**BAGS, WRAPPINGS, TISSUE, BOXES, BUSINESS CARDS.** Any shape, size, amount. Comprehensive samples 86p. Terry Andrews, 53A Parsons Street, Bambury, OX16 8NB.

**SELLING** due to illness unused Watkin 12". Surface planer-thicknesser. Ring Mansfield evening 27061.

---

**MYFORD LATHE.** Motorised, reversing switch, metal cabinet stand, 30" between centres, rear turning attachment. List price £700, offered at £450 if buyer collects. Myford 36" wood bench, angle iron, braced stand, complete as above, including grinding attachments, selection of used tools. £500. Owner retiring. Peter Child, Great Yeldham 0787 237291 (Essex).

---

### Alan Holtham
The Old Stores Turnery, Wistaston Road, Willaston, Nantwich, Cheshire.
Tel: 0270 67010

#### BANDSAW BLADES
Skip tooth type with hardened teeth. Prices include VAT. P+P 1—3 Blades 90p, 4-6 Blades **£1.70**. Over 6 post free.

| Model | | Price inc. VAT |
|---|---|---|
| Birch | ¼" | £3.62 |
| DeWalt BS1310 | ⅜" | £3.74 |
| Kity 612 | ½" | £3.91 |
| Lazzari P32 | ⅝" | £4.77 |
| Bandit | | |
| Startrite 301 | | |
| Black & Decker | ¼" | £2.99 |
| DeWalt 100 | ⅜" | £3.11 |
| | ½" | £3.22 |
| Burgess | ¼" | £3.11 |
| | ⅜" | £3.25 |
| | ⅞" | |
| Inca | ¼" | £3.45 |
| | ⅜" | £3.57 |
| | ½" | £3.62 |
| | ⅝" | £4.20 |
| Startrite 352 | ¼" | £4.54 |
| | ⅜" | £4.60 |
| | ½" | £4.77 |
| | ⅝" | £5.87 |
| | ¾" | £6.15 |
| Willow | ¼" | £4.03 |
| | ⅜" | £4.08 |
| | ½" | £4.20 |

---

## WORKSHOP EQUIPMENT

**CIRCULAR AND BAND SAW BLADES** for all applications from: A. A. Smith Ltd. 63 Brighton Road, Shoreham, Sussex. Tel: 07917 61707 (24 hrs). C-N

---

### WOOD TURNERS SUPPLIES

Tudor Craft, Jung Hans clock movements, 20 different hands to choose from, barometers, weather stations, cutlery, jewellery box lids, pepper/salt/nutmeg mills, coffee grinders, ceramic tiles, new range which include hand painted tiles. Our service is extremely fast, friendly and competitive — give us a try. Send SAE for catalogue to

Tudor Craft,
100 Little Sutton Lane,
Four Oaks, Sutton Coldfield,
West Midlands B75 6PG.

---

**ARKANSAS** whetstones now readily available from importer. Large selection. SAE for lists. C. Rufino, Manor House, South Clifton, Newark, Notts. T/C

---

**ARKANSAS AND JAPANESE WHETSTONES** from main importer. Send SAE for catalogue/guide to these and other sharpening stones. Roger's, 47 Walsworth Road, Hitchin, Herts. SG4 9SU. T/C

**EBAC TIMBER SEASONERS,** Protimeter moisture meters, always good prices and advice from the man who pioneered small scale seasoning. John Arrowsmith, 74a Wilson Street, Darlington, Co. Durham. DL3 6QZ. Tel: 0325 481970. T/C

---

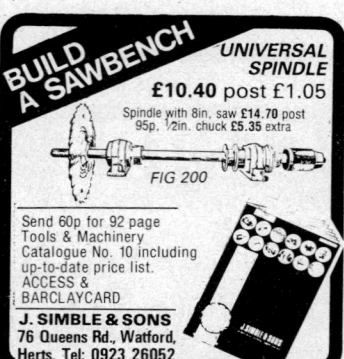

Prices quoted are those prevailing at press date and are subject to alteration due to economic conditions

392

**Prices quoted are those prevailing at press date and are subject to alteration due to economic conditions**

## WOODTURNING COURSES

2 Day courses, mid-week or weekend. Expert personal tuition in modern well equipped workshop. Comfortable accommodation available in pleasant surroundings. SAE for details to
Cliff Willetts, Gables, Frisby On The Wreake, Melton Mowbray, Leics.
Tel: Rotherby (066 475) 246

**TWO-DAY PRACTICAL WOOD TURNING COURSE IN RURAL LINCOLNSHIRE**
Comfortable accommodation arranged if required.
*S.A.E. for details to:* Peter Denniss, Cabinet Maker & Turner, The White Bungalow, South Reston, Louth, Lincolnshire. LN11 8JL or Phone: Withern 50429 S.D.T. Code 0521.

### REG SLACK

Practical Woodturning courses. 1-3 days duration. Max 2 students. Professional tutor backed by 30 years full time experience. Closed Thursday, Friday. Open all other days including Sunday.
*For details write or phone.*
Saracens Head Coaching House Yard, Brailford, Derbyshire (0335) 60829.
Evenings (0283) 701662.
*Also Woodturning Supplies.*

**WOODTURNING COURSES DAY/EVENING**
Personal tuition by Registered Turner in well equipped workshop. Telephone John Golder, Heath Hayes 79137 (Staffs.).

**CABINET MAKING:** intensive two-day courses in basic bench techniques in Yorkshire dales workshop. Phone Wensleydale 22703 for details.

## Woodturning Courses At The Mill

Spend two days under the expert guidance of Jamie Wallwin and Ray Key. We have courses for beginners and professionals alike.

Residential or non-residential.  Send SAE for further details.

### CRAFT SUPPLIES
*The specialists in wood turning tools and ideas.*
The Mill, Millers Dale 9,
── Buxton, Derbyshire. ──

**TUITION IN VIOLIN,** Viola, Cello making and restoring. The String Workshop (Putney), Phil Mienczakowski — 01-788-6744.

**ANTIQUE FURNITURE RESTORATION** and traditional upholstery courses in practical workshop. Brochure: W. Thompson, Chapel Fold, Grassington, Skipton, N. Yorks. (0756) 752463.

### London College of Furniture

The largest range of Craft Courses in WOODWORKING, FURNITURE & MUSICAL INSTRUMENT MAKING.
Write to: The SAO, Dept. WW, LONDON COLLEGE OF FURNITURE 41-71 Commercial Road, London E1 1LA.
Tel: 01 247 1953

### A VIDEO WOODTURNING COURSE

"TEACH YOURSELF TURNING" is a new tutorial video, ideal for the home craftsman, schools, colleges and other students. It presents a complete introductory course on Woodturning and includes a booklet of course notes and photographs, based on my recent series in Woodworking Crafts Magazine. The colour video runs for a full 1½ hours, during which I demonstrate and discuss the following topics:
1) The lathe and its accessories
2) Woodturning tools
3) Tool sharpening
4) Cutting techniques (spindle and bowl work)
5) Chuck work
6) Drilling boring and finishing
To order — simply send your cheque for £35.00 (including postage and package) to:
**Roger Holley, 'The Hollies' 11 Summer Leaze Park, Yeovil, Somerset BA20 2BP.
Tel: (0935) 25521**

giving your full name and address, in block capitals please, and state whether you require VHS or Betamax video format.
Delivery 2/3 weeks.

### KEITH ROWLEY
**(Demonstrator for Coronet tool company and member of the Guild of Master Craftsmen).**
Woodturning courses in the heart of D. H. Lawrence Country by professional turner. Weekend courses available. Coronet lathes and woodturning accessories available. 1 days tuition free if you buy your Coronet lathe through me.
*S.A.E. for details to:*
Keith Rowley, 68 Moorgreen, Newthorpe, Notts.         Tel: Langley Mill 716903

### WOODCARVING AND SCULPTURE

The best short residential courses in basic sculpture, woodcarving, modelling and sketching, etc. are taught by HENRY MOORE'S former assistant PETER HIBBARD at the OLD SCHOOL ARTS WORKSHOP, MIDDLEHAM, LEYBURN, NORTH YORKS. DL8 4QG.

Beginners welcome — S.A.E. for details.

### WOODMACHINING COURSES

Two-day woodmachining and one-day routing or spindle moulding courses with an experienced craftsman. For details send SAE to:
Roy Sutton, 14 St. George's Avenue, Herne Bay, Kent CT6 8JU. Tel: 0227 373297 or 0227 272136 (evenings or weekends).

Woodmachining lathe and benchwork courses well equipped workshop and qualified craft instructor. Beginners welcome. Tuition hourly or daily. Bring the family, bed & breakfast available. Private lake, fishing, birdwatching, miles of riding and walking country. Close cathedral city and coast. Timber suppliers also.
Pickelden Cottage, Mystole, Canterbury (731470)

**THOS. HARRISON & SONS.** Est. 1830.
Our four day woodturning courses are the result of many years experience and are carefully designed to give you the maximum of practical experience in the short time you spend with us. Highly recommended by students and practising professionals. Full details from Mike Law (056685) 322. The Longhouse, Maxworthy Close, North Petherwin, Cornwall.

### BE QUICK OFF THE MARK IN THE RACE TO BUY AND SELL AND USE WOODWORKER CLASSIFIEDS
### 01-437 0699

## WEST DEAN COLLEGE
## The Edward James Foundation

1 Year Course in the Restoration of Antique Furniture in conjunction with the British Antique Dealers' Association.
3 Year Apprenticeship run by West Dean College in the making of Renaissance and Baroque plucked and bowed instruments.
Commencing September 1985
**Further information from:**
The Principal, West Dean College, Chichester, West Sussex PO18 0QZ. Telephone 0243 63 301.

394    Prices quoted are those prevailing at press date and are subject to alteration due to economic conditions

# Then......

## Max Burrough

### Continuing the absorbing tale of an old-time apprenticeship

The yard, timber store and upholstery workshop provided an increasing attraction for a variety of reasons. 'Arry and 'Appy were always good for a tease, and all kinds of old timbers could be found which would jog the men's memories of jobs completed long ago, while Enoch the upholsterer proved to be an astonishing character who could talk all day, usually with a mouthful of tacks, yet continue working.

A north-countryman, Enoch for some unknown reason had travelled south, opened a small boarding-house and promptly gone bankrupt. He was lucky, for the firm's upholsterer was leaving and his job was there for the taking. He proved to be an excellent craftsman, and as he was then in his later fifties an apprentice was taken on. It did not take him long to discover that the boy's father had paid the Boss £25 for the apprenticeship, and Enoch marched down to see the Boss. He came away with £25: for, as he was going to teach the boy, he should have the money or the boy would learn nothing.

An undischarged bankrupt and a vegetarian, Enoch would eat his lunch every day, finish with an apple, and then sit back in the best armchair he was working on and enjoy a cheroot. More often than not the sun would be shining; with the south-facing double doors open and the sun streaming in, Enoch demonstrated the basics of enjoying the good life.

It transpired that he was a member of the Theosophical Society. He would talk for hours about Annie Besant, Charles Bradlaugh and Madame Blatavsky. Sid, the carpenter, loved to egg him on, and 'Arry and 'Appy would sit spellbound at all the long words they had never heard before. I became convinced that he was a charlatan, for often his sentences failed to make sense. The older men, especially Jim and Leonard, thought that much of what he said, especially about birth control and free love, was nothing short of blasphemous.

The important point, though, was that he was an excellent upholsterer of wide experience. Often he would make a chair for an individual, usually an old lady, and it would fit almost like a glove. Hair-top mattresses would be filled in the flat, not from one end like a sack, the bottom being fixed to an adjustable frame with the edges pinned up all round. The previously weighed quantity of hair would then be placed in position and carefully adjusted, and the top stitched on.

Many people considered, and still do, that a good hair mattress is far healthier to sleep on than the soft, interior-sprung type so popular today. Enoch could, if required, make a spring mattress of some quality, with every spring in its separate calico pocket, and I well remember the stage-by-stage construction being displayed in the showroom.

No one seemed to think of the fire risk, but the upholsterer's workshop was an arsonist's paradise, with dry combustible material everywhere. For one urgent shopfront job, Enoch volunteered to stain and polish a large number of sheets of mahogany three-ply and miles of mahogany capping and beading. As he used, first, a brush at least 4in wide, and then a wad the size of a tea-plate, there was polish dripping everywhere. With heating supplied by free-standing paraffin stoves, I for one did not stay long. Everyone thought that Enoch's polishing was ghastly, for he used so much polish that every tiny flaw in the plywood was accentuated.

As an apprentice I was encouraged by all the men in the top shop to do or make something in order to learn, it being made quite clear that the only real way to acquire skill was to learn by doing. Yet such is the perversity of human nature that no sooner had a boy started on a job, after receiving advice from all and sundry, than the job would disappear, having been hidden by one of the men.

It is difficult to visualise anything more infuriating, and at times it broke a boy's heart and resulted in tears; but I soon realised that it was a question of using my wits. In such a small workshop the number of hiding-places was limited, and often dictated by the size and shape of the job in hand. Often I heard the story of a boy who 'lost' a treasured, almost completed model, to find it in a wardrobe in the bedroom of the hotel where he was working. His astonishment was unbounded, and not being too bright he never did work out how it got there. Various other forms of practical joke were practised, too; although they could be irritating in the extreme, they taught a boy to control his temper, and, if he had any character at all, simple strengthened his resolve to hold his own.

The installation of shopfronts was, for some of the men, a dirty job, but it did provide experience over a wide field. When a stainless-steel front was fitted in old premises in the town, an additional support for the first floor was provided by a vertical steel stanchion about 4in in diameter, which came just inside a corner of the new window. The owner decided that it would be an ideal situation for circular plate-glass shelves, and asked if that were possible. Charlie was asked to look into the matter and, with a hand-drill and morse bits (cast steel of course), tried to drill holes wherein could be fixed chromium-plated brackets. After an abortive half-day's effort, he returned to say the job was impossible.

The 'impossible' was discussed with Bert, who went over, assessed the situation, measured the length and diameter and then returned to the workshop muttering to himself and with his moustache twitching. He obtained a piece of blind canvas, which he stretched out and fixed to a wide board; then he prepared strips of prime oak about ½in wide and 5⁄16in thick. With a small chamfer on each outside edge, the pieces were then glued side-by-side to the canvas, as if for a roll-top desk. When the glue was dry, the material was cut tight to the edge of a wood strip on one side, while about 1½in was left spare on the other. The whole was then trimmed to the length of the stanchion. With a hot pot of glue to hand, we glued the outside of the surplus 1½in, quickly wrapped the whole thing around the stanchion, and bound it tightly every few inches with thick card. After allowing a good drying time, the oak strips were glass-papered, oiled, polished and then fitted with brackets and semicircular glass shelves.

Those strips, brackets and shelves never moved until a few years ago, when a chain store bought the premises and gutted them before installing a new shop: a time lapse of at least 45 years and another tribute to Bert's ingenuity and skill. Even today, there are at least four complete shopfronts in the town that were designed by the Boss and installed in the 1930s.

In these days of specialisation it needs an effort to recall the wide variety of jobs it was then taken for granted that the workshop could and would undertake. An example was provided by a friend of the Boss. This gentleman, a local tradesman and hotel-owner, regularly competed at Bisley. One year, being dissatisfied with his scores, he bought a new rifle. This too displeased him, and he returned it to the maker — who, after twice making adjustments, said that they could do nothing more. He was still not satisfied with it, and a chance remark led to the Boss suggesting that he should 'let Bert have a look at it'.

At the appointed hour Bert was ready, his bench well padded with dust-sheets and a variety of gouges sharpened to perfection, having been told that there was vibration between the walnut stock and the mechanism. The stock being removed, the adjoining steel face was lightly smeared with dirty oil from the oilstone and an impression obtained on the walnut, so that the new high spots could be carefully eased. The procedure was repeated several times until the owner said, 'Enough' — he having sat on Bert's tool-chest all the while, watching in agonised silence.

We learned later that at the next competition he had obtained a maximum score. ■

# shop guide

## EMCO DEALERS

### BUCKINGHAMSHIRE

**HIGH WYCOMBE**    Tel. (0494)
ISAAC LORD LTD    22221
185 DESBOROUGH ROAD    **KE**

Open: Mon-Fri 8.00 a.m.-5.00 p.m.
Saturday 9.00 a.m.-5.00 p.m.
H.P.W.D.A.

### CAMBRIDGESHIRE

**CAMBRIDGE**    Tel. (0223) 63132
D. MACKAY LTD.    **E★**
BRITANNIA WORKS, EAST ROAD

Open: Mon.-Fri. 8.30 a.m.-1 p.m./2.00-
5.00 p.m. Sat. 8.30 a.m.-1.00 p.m.
H.P.W.D.T.CS.MF.A.BC.

### CORNWALL

**TRURO**    Tel. (0872) 71671
TRURO POWER TOOLS    **E★**
30 FERRIS TOWN

Open Mon.-Sat. 8.00 a.m.-12.30 p.m./
1.30 p.m.-5.00 p.m.
H.P.W.WM.D.CS.MF.A.BC.

### DERBYSHIRE

**DERBY**    Tel. (0332) 41862
HAZLEHURSTS LTD.    **E★**
LONDON ROAD AND CANAL STREET

Open: Mon.-Sat. 8.30 a.m.-5.30 p.m. (retail)
Mon.-Fri. 8.00 a.m.-5.00 p.m. (trade)
H.P.W.MF.A.BC.

### DEVON

**BRIXHAM**    Tel. (08045) 4900
WOODCRAFT SUPPLIES    **E★**
4 HORSE POOL STREET

Open: Mon.-Sat. 9.00 a.m.-6.00 p.m.

H.P.W.A.D.MF.CS.BC.

### GLOUCESTERSHIRE

**CHELTENHAM**    Tel. (0242) 39099
HAMBURY MACHINE SERVICES    **E★**
UNIT 14, MALMESBURY ROAD
Open: Mon.-Fri. 9.00 a.m.-5.30 p.m.
Sat. 9.30 a.m.-12.00 p.m.

W.WM.P.D.

**TO FILL THIS SPACE
'PHONE 01-437 0699**

### HUMBERSIDE

**GRIMSBY**    Tel. Grimsby (0472)
58741 Hull (0482) 26999
J. E. SIDDLE LTD. (Tool Specialists)    ★
83 VICTORIA STREET
Open: Mon.-Fri 8.30 a.m.-5.30 p.m.
Sat. 8.30 a.m.-12.45 p.m. & 2 p.m.-5 p.m.
H.P.A.BC.W.WMD.

### LANCASHIRE

**ROCHDALE**    Tel. (0706) 342123/
C.S.M. TOOLS    342322
4-6 HEYWOOD ROAD    **E★**
CASTLETON
Open: Mon-Sat 9.00 a.m.-6.00 p.m.
Sundays by appointment
W.D.CS.A.BC.

**PRESTON**    Tel. (0772) 52951
SPEEDWELL TOOL COMPANY    **E★**
62-68 MEADOW STREET PR1 1SU
Open: Mon.-Fri. 8.30 a.m.-5.30 p.m.
Sat. 8.30 a.m.-12.30 p.m.

H.P.W.WM.CS.A.MF.BC.

### LONDON

**FULHAM**    Tel. (01-385) 5109
I. GRIZZARD LTD.    **E**
84a-b LILLIE ROAD, SW6 1TL
Open: Mon-Sat 9.00-5.30 p.m.
Half day Thursday

H.P.A.BC.W.CS.WM.D.

**LONDON**    Tel. (01-263) 1536
THOMAS BROTHERS    (01-272) 2764
798-804 HOLLOWAY ROAD, N19    **E**
Open: Mon.-Fri. 8.30 a.m.-5.30 p.m. Thurs.
8.30 a.m.-1 p.m. Sat. 9 a.m.-5 p.m.

H.P.W.WM.CS.MF.BC.

### MIDDLESEX

**RUISLIP**    Tel. (08956) 74126
ALLMODELS ENGINEERING LTD.    **E★**
91 MANOR WAY

Open: Mon-Sat 9.00 a.m.-5.30 p.m.
H.P.W.A.D.CS.MF.BC.

### OXFORDSHIRE

**CROWMARSH**    Tel. (0491) 38653
MILL HILL SUPPLIES    **E★**
66 THE STREET
Open: Mon.-Fri. 9.30 a.m.-5.00 p.m.
Thurs. 9.30 a.m.-7.00 p.m.
Sat. 9.30 a.m.-1.00 p.m.
P.W.D.CS.MF.A.BC.

### SUFFOLK

**IPSWICH**    Tel. (0473) 40456
FOX WOODWORKING    **KE★**
142-144 BRAMFORD LANE
Open: Tues., Fri., 9.00 a.m.-5.30 p.m.
Sat. 9.00 a.m.-5.00 p.m.

H.P.W.WM.D.A.B.C.

### WEST SUSSEX

**WORTHING**    Tel. (0903) 38739
W. HOSKING LTD (TOOLS &    **KE★**
MACHINERY)
28 PORTLAND RD, BN11 1QN
Open: Mon.-Sat. 8.30 a.m.-5.30 p.m.
Closed Wednesday
H.P.W.WM.D.CS.A.BC.

### TYNE & WEAR

**NEWCASTLE**    Tel. (0632) 320311
HENRY OSBOURNE LTD.    **E★**
50-54 UNION STREET

Open: Mon-Fri 8.30 a.m.-5.00 p.m.

H.P.W.D.CS.MF.A.BC.

### WEST MIDLANDS

**BIRMINGHAM**    Tel. (021-554) 5177
ROTAGRIP    **E★**
16 LODGE ROAD, HOCKLEY
Open: Mon.-Fri. 9.00 a.m.-5.00 p.m.
Sat. 9.00 a.m.-12.00 p.m.

H.P.W.CS.A.BC.T.MF.

### YORKSHIRE

**SHEFFIELD**    Tel. (0742) 441012
GREGORY & TAYLOR LTD    **E**
WORKSOP ROAD
Open: 8.30 a.m.-5.30 p.m.
Monday-Friday
8.30 a.m.-12.30 p.m. Sat.
H.P.W.WM.D.

**GIVE YOUR BUSINESS A
BOOST — DON'T LEAVE IT
CHANCE, 'PHONE JASON
ON 01-437 0699 TO
ADVERTISE**

## ALL OTHER DEALERS

### AVON

**BATH**    Tel. Bath 64513
JOHN HALL TOOLS    ★
RAILWAY STREET

Open: Monday-Saturday
9.00 a.m.-5.30 p.m.
H.P.W.WM.D.A.BC.

**BRISTOL**    Tel. (0272) 741510
JOHN HALL TOOLS LIMITED    ★
CLIFTON DOWN SHOPPING CENTRE
WHITELADIES ROAD
Open: Monday-Saturday
9.00 a.m.-5.30 p.m.
H.P.W.WM.D.A.BC.

**BRISTOL**    Tel. (0272) 629092
TRYMWOOD SERVICES
2a DOWNS PARK EAST, (off North View)
WESTBURY PARK
Open: 8.30 a.m.-5.30 p.m. Mon. to Fri.
Closed for lunch 1.00-2.00 p.m.
P.W.WM.D.T.A.BC.

**BRISTOL**    Tel. (0272) 667013
WILLIS
157 WEST STREET
BEDMINISTER
Open Mon.-Fri. 8.30 a.m.-5.00 p.m.
No Saturday opening

**KEY: H HANDTOOLS**

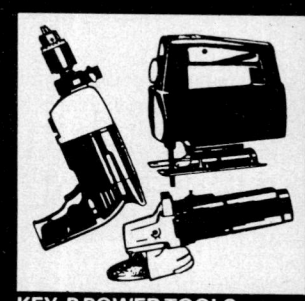

**KEY: P POWER TOOLS**

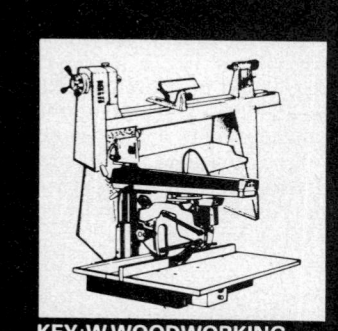

**KEY: W WOODWORKING
MACHINERY**

# shopguide

## BEDFORDSHIRE

**BEDFORD**  Tel. (0234) 59808
BEDFORD SAW SERVICE  **K**
39 AMPTHILL ROAD

Open: Mon.-Fri. 8.30-5.30
Sat. 9.00-4.00
H.P.A.BC.W.CS.WM.D.

**READING**  Tel. Reading 661511
WOKINGHAM TOOL CO. LTD.
99 WOKINGHAM ROAD

Open: Mon-Sat 9.00 a.m.-5.30 p.m.
Closed 1.00-2.00 p.m. for lunch
H.P.W.WM.D.CS.A.BC.

## BERKSHIRE

**COOKHAM**  Tel. (06285) 20350
CHURCH'S TIMBER
STATION HILL

Open: Mon-Sat 8.30 a.m.-5.30 p.m.
Wed 8.30 a.m.-1.00 p.m.
H.P.W.T.CS.MF.A.

**READING**  Tel. (0734) 591361
HOME CARE CENTRE
26/30 KING'S ROAD

Open: Monday-Saturday
9.00 a.m.-5.30 p.m.
H.P.W.D.A.WM.BC.

**READING**  Tel. Littlewick Green
DAVID HUNT (TOOL  2743
MERCHANTS) LTD  ★
KNOWL HILL, NR. READING
Open: Monday-Saturday
9.00 a.m.-5.30 p.m.
H.P.W.D.A.BC.

## BUCKINGHAMSHIRE

**SLOUGH**  Tel. (06286) 5125
BRAYWOOD ESTATES LTD  ★
158 BURNHAM LANE

Open: Mon-Sat 8.30 a.m.-5.30 p.m.
Monday-Saturday
H.P.W.WM.CS.A.

**HIGH WYCOMBE**  Tel. (0494)
SCOTT SAWS LTD.  24201/33788
14 BRIDGE STREET  ★

Mon.-Sat. 8.30 a.m.-6.00 p.m.

H.P.W.WM.D.T.CS.MF.A.BC.

**MILTON KEYNES**  Tel. (0908)
POLLARD WOODWORKING  641366
CENTRE  ★
51 AYLESBURY ST., BLETCHLEY
Open: Mon-Fri 8.30-5.30
Saturday 9.00-5.00
H.P.W.WM.D.CS.A.BC.

## CAMBRIDGESHIRE

**CAMBRIDGE**  Tel. (0223) 247386
H. B. WOODWORKING  **K**
105 CHERRY HINTON ROAD
Open: 8.30 a.m.-5.30 p.m.
Monday-Friday
8.30 a.m.-1.00 p.m. Sat.
H.P.W.WM.D.CS.A.

**PETERBOROUGH**  Tel. (0733)
WILLIAMS DISTRIBUTORS  64252
(TOOLS) LIMITED  **K**
108-110 BURGHLEY ROAD
Open: Monday to Friday
8.30 a.m.-5.30 p.m.
IH.P.A.W.D.WH.BC.

## CHESHIRE

**NANTWICH**  Tel. Crewe 67010
ALAN HOLTHAM  **K★**
THE OLD STORES TURNERY
WISTASON ROAD, WILLASTON
Open: Tues.-Sat. 9.00 a.m.-5.30 p.m.
Closed Monday
P.W.WM.D.T.C.CS.A.BC.

## CLEVELAND

**MIDDLESBROUGH**  Tel. (0642)
CLEVELAND WOODCRAFT  813103
(M'BRO), 38-42 CRESCENT ROAD  **K**

Open: Mon-Sat 9.15 a.m.-5.30 p.m.

H.P.T.A.BC.W.WM.CS.D.

## CORNWALL

**FALMOUTH**  Tel. (0326) 76555
WOODSTOCK (HARDWOODS) LTD.
PONSHARDEN

Open: Mon-Fri 8.30 a.m.-5.30 p.m.
Sat. 9.00 a.m.-1.00 p.m.

T.

**HELSTON**  Tel. Helston (03265) 4961
SOUTH WEST  Truro (0872) 71671
POWER TOOLS  Launceston
MONUMENT ROAD  (0566) 3555
 **K**

H.P.W.WM.D.CS.A.

## CUMBRIA

**CARLISLE**  Tel. (0228) 36391
W. M. PLANT
ALLENBROOK ROAD
ROSEHILL, CA1 2UT
Open: Mon.-Fri. 8.00 a.m.-5.15 p.m.
Sat. 8.00 a.m.-12.30 noon
P.W.WM.D.CS.A.

## DERBYSHIRE

**BUXTON**  Tel. (0298) 871636
CRAFT SUPPLIES  **K★**
THE MILL, MILLERSDALE

Open: Mon-Sat 9.00 a.m.-5.00 p.m.

H.P.W.D.T.CS.A.BC.

**EXETER**  Tel. (0392) 73936
WRIDES TOOL CENTRE
147 FORE STREET

Open: 9.00 a.m.-5.30 p.m.
Wednesday 9.00 a.m.-1.00 p.m.
H.P.W.WM.A.

**PLYMOUTH**  Tel. (0752) 330303
WESTWARD BUILDING SERVICES  ★
LTD., LISTER CLOSE, NEWNHAM
INDUSTRIAL ESTATE, PLYMPTON
Open: Mon-Fri 8.00 a.m.-5.30 p.m.
Sat. 8.30 a.m.-12.30 p.m.
H.P.W.WM.D.A.BC.

## ESSEX

**ILFORD**  Tel.
CUTWELL TOOLS LTD.  ★
774-776 HIGH ROAD

Mon.-Fri. 9.00 a.m.-5.00 p.m.
and also by appointment.
P.W.WM.A.D.CS.

**LEIGH ON SEA**  Tel. (0702)
MARSHAL & PARSONS LTD.  710404
1111 LONDON ROAD  **EK**

Open: 8.30 a.m.-5.30 p.m. Mon-Fri
9.00 a.m.-5.00 p.m. Sat.
H.P.W.WM.D.CS.A.

## GLOUCESTERSHIRE

**TEWKESBURY**  Tel. (0684)
TEWKESBURY SAW CO. LTD.  293092
TRADING ESTATE, NEWTOWN  **K**

Open: Mon-Fri 8.00 a.m.-5.00 p.m.
Saturday 9.30 a.m.-12.00 p.m.
P.W.WM.D.CS.

## HAMPSHIRE

**ALDERSHOT**  Tel. (0252) 334422
POWER TOOL CENTRE  **K★**
374 HIGH STREET
Open: Mon-Fri 8.30 a.m.-5.30 p.m.
Sat 8.30 a.m.-4.00 p.m.

H.P.W.WM.D.A.BC.CF.MF.

**SOUTHAMPTON**  Tel: (0703)
POWER TOOL CENTRE  332288
7 BELVIDERE ROAD  **K★**
Open Mon.-Fri. 8.30-5.30

H.P.W.WM.D.A.BC.CS.MF.

**PORTSMOUTH**  Tel. (0705)
EURO PRECISION TOOLS LTD  667332
259/263 LONDON ROAD, NORTH END  ★
 **E**
Open: Mon-Fri 9.00 a.m.-5.30 p.m.
Sat. 9.00 a.m.-1.00 p.m.
H.P.W.WM.D.A.BC.

**SOUTHAMPTON**  Tel. (0703)
H.W.M.  776222
THE WOODWORKERS
303 SHIRLEY ROAD, SHIRLEY
Open: Tues-Fri 9.30 a.m.-6.00 p.m.
Sat 9.30 a.m.-4.00 p.m.
H.P.W.WM.D.CS.A.BC.T.

## HERTFORDSHIRE

**ENFIELD**  Tel. (01-363) 2935
GILL & HOXBY LTD.  **K**
133-137 ST. MARKS ROAD EN1 1BB

Mon.-Sat. 8.30 a.m.-6.00 p.m.
Early closing Wednesday 1.00 p.m.
H.P.W.WM.T.CS.A

**WATFORD**  Tel. (0923) 48434
HOME CARE CENTRE  ★
20 MARKET STREET
WATFORD, HERTS
Open: 9.00 a.m.-5.30 p.m.
Mon-Sat
H.P.W.A.WM.BC.D.

## KENT

**BIDDENDEN**  Tel. (0580) 291555/7
BRITISH GATES & TIMBER
BENENDEN ROAD  ★
Open: Mon-Fri 7.30 a.m.-5.30 p.m.
Saturday 8.30 a.m.-midday
(not Bank Holiday weekends)
H.T.CS.MF.

**MAIDSTONE**  Tel. (0622) 50177
SOUTH EASTERN SAWS (Ind) LTD  ★
COLDRED ROAD,
PARKWOOD INDUSTRIAL ESTATE
Open: Mon-Fri 8.00-5.00pm
Sat. 9.00-12.00
B.C.W.CS.WM.PH.

**MATFIELD**  Tel. Brenchley
LEISURECRAFT IN WOOD  (089272)
'ORMONDE,' MAIDSTONE RD.  2465
TN12 7JG
Open: Mon-Sun
9.00 a.m.-5.30 p.m.
W.WM.D.T.A.

**WYE**  Tel. (0233) 813144
KENT POWER TOOLS LTD.
UNIT 1, BRIAR CLOSE
WYE, Nr. ASFORD

H.P.W.WM.D.A.CS.

## LANCASHIRE

**LANCASTER**  Tel. (0524) 32886
LILE TOOL SHOP  **K**
43/45 NORTH ROAD
Open: Monday to Saturday
9.00 a.m.-5.30 p.m.
Wed 9.00 a.m.-12.30 p.m.
H.P.W.D.A.

**BURY**  Tel. (061 764 6769)
HOUSE OF HARBRU  ★
101 CROSTONS ROAD
ELTON
Open: Mon.-Fri. 9.00 a.m.-5.00 p.m.
Send 2 × 1st class stamps for catalogue
MF.

## LONDON

**ACTON**  Tel. (01-992) 4835
A. MILLS (ACTON) LTD  ★
32/36 CHURCHFIELD ROAD W3 6ED
Open: Mon-Fri 9.00 a.m.-5.00 p.m.
Saturdays 9.00 am.-1.00 p.m.
H.P.W.WM.

**WEMBLEY**  Tel. 904-1144
ROBERT SAMUEL LTD.  (904-1147
7, 15 & 16 COURT PARADE  after 4.00)
EAST LANE, N. WEMBLEY  ★
Open Mon.-Fri. 8.45-5.15; Sat. 9-1.00
Access, Barclaycard, AM Express, & Diners
H.P.W.CS.E.A.D.

**LONDON**  Tel. (01-567) 2922
G. D. CLEGG & SONS  ★
83 UXBRIDGE ROAD, HANWELL W7 3ST
Mon-Sat 9.15 a.m.-5.30 p.m.
Closed for lunch 1.00-2.00p.m.
Early Closing 1.00 p.m. Wed.
H.P.A.W.WM.D.CS.

**LONDON**  Tel. (01-636) 7475
BUCK & RYAN LTD  ★
101 TOTTENHAM COURT ROAD W1P ODY

Open: Mon.-Fri. 8.30 a.m.-5.30 p.m.
Saturday 8.30 a.m.-4.00 p.m.
H.P.W.WM.D.A..

**NORBURY**  Tel. (01-679) 6193
HERON TOOLS & HARDWARE LTD
437 STREATHAM HIGH ROAD SW16
Open: Mon-Fri 8.30 a.m.-5.00 p.m.
Wednesday 8.30 a.m.-1.00 p.m.
Sat. 9.00 a.m.-1.00 p.m.
H.P.W.A.

# shopguide

## GREATER MANCHESTER MERSEYSIDE

### MIDDLESEX

**WOOLWICH**   Tel. (01-854) 7767/8
A. D. SHILLMAN & SONS LTD
108-109 WOOLWICH HIGH STREET
SE18
Open: Mon-Sat
8.30 p.m.-5.30p.m.
H.P.W.CS.A.

**MANCHESTER**   Tel. (061 789)
TIMMS TOOLS         0909
102-104 LIVERPOOL ROAD   ★
PATRICROFT M30 0WZ
Weekdays 9.00 a.m.-5.30 p.m.
Sat. 9.00 a.m.-1.00 p.m.
H.P.A.W.

**LIVERPOOL**   Tel. (051-207) 2967
TAYLOR BROS (LIVERPOOL) LTD  K
195-199 LONDON ROAD
LIVERPOOL L3 8JG
Open: Monday to Friday
8.30-5.30 p.m.
H.P.W.WM.D.A.BC.

**HOUNSLOW**   Tel. (01-570)
Q.R. TOOLS LTD     2103/5135
251-253 HANWORTH ROAD
Open: Mon-Fri 8.30 a.m.-5.30 p.m.
Sat. 9.00 a.m.-1.00 p.m.
P.W.WM.D.CS.A.

## NORFOLK

**GT. YARMOUTH**   Tel. (0493)
ANGLIA POWER TOOLS   850388
3 DENESIDE, NR30 2HL
Open: Monday to Saturday
8.30 a.m. 5.30 p.m.
H.P.W.D.CS.A.

**KINGS LYNN**   Tel. (0553) 2443
WALKER & ANDERSON (Kings Lynn) LTD.  K
WINDSOR ROAD, KINGS LYNN
Open: Monday to Saturday
7.45 a.m.-5.30 p.m.
Wednesday 1.00 p.m. Saturday 5.00 p.m.
H.P.W.WM.D.CS.A.

**KINGS LYNN**   Tel. (0760) 23073
TONY WADDILOVE     ★
STATION HOUSE
LITTLE DUNHAM, (Nr. SWAFFHAM)
Open Tues.-Sat. 9.00 a.m.-5.30 p.m.
H.P.W.DT.CS.A.BC.

**NORWICH**   Tel. (0603) 898695
NORFOLK SAW SERVICES
DOG LANE, HORSFORD
Open: Monday to Friday
8.00 a.m.-5.00 p.m.
Saturday 8.00 a.m.-12.00 p.m.
H.P.W.WM.D.CS.A.

## NORTHAMPTONSHIRE

**NORWICH**   Tel. (0603) 400933
WESTGATES WOODWORKING   Tx
61 HURRICANE WAY     975412
NORWICH AIRPORT INDUSTRIAL ESTATE
Open: 9.00 a.m.-5.00 p.m. weekdays
9.00 a.m.-12.30 Sat.
P.W.WM.D.BC.     K

**SWAFFHAM**   Tel. (0760) 23073
TONY WADDILOVE,     ★
STATION HOUSE,
LITTLE DUNHAM, KINGS LYNN
Tuesday-Saturday 9.00 a.m.-6.00 p.m.
H.P.W.DT.CS.A.BC.

**NOTTINGHAM**   Tel. (0602) 225979
POOLEWOOD    and 227064/5
EQUIPMENT LTD.  (06077) 2421 after hrs
5a HOLLY LANE, CHILLWELL
Open: Mon-Fri 9.00 a.m.-5.30 p.m.
Sat. 9.00 a.m. to 12.30 p.m.
P.W.WM.D.CS.A.BC.

### TO FILL THIS SPACE 'PHONE 01-437 0699

**WITNEY**   Tel. (0993) 3885
TARGET TOOLS (SALES,  & 72095 OXON
**TARGET TOOLS** HIRE & REPAIRS)
SWAIN COURT
STATION INDUSTRIAL ESTATE
Open: Mon.-Sat. 8.00 a.m.-5.00 p.m.
24 hour Answerphone
BC.W.M.A.

## SHROPSHIRE

**TELFORD**   Tel. Telford (0952)
ASLES LTD     48054
VINEYARD ROAD, WELLINGTON  EK★
Open: Mon. Fri. 8.30 a.m.-5.30 p.m.
Saturday 8.30 a.m.-4.00 p.m.
H.P.W.WM.D.CS.BC.A.

## SOMERSET

**TAUNTON**   Tel. (0823) 85431
JOHN HALL TOOLS     ★
6 HIGH STREET
Open Monday-Saturday
9.00 a.m.-5.30 p.m.
H.P.W.WM.D.CS.A.

**TAUNTON**   Tel. Taunton 79078
KEITH MITCHELL     ★
TOOLS AND EQUIPMENT
66 PRIORY BRIDGE ROAD
Open: Mon-Fri 8.30 a.m.-5.30 p.m.
Saturday 9.00 a.m.-4.00 p.m.
H.P.W.WM.D.CS.A.BC.

## STAFFORDSHIRE

**TAMWORTH**   Tel. (0827) 56188
MATTHEWS BROTHERS LTD.   K
KETTLEBROOK ROAD
Open: Mon-Sat 8.30 a.m.-6.00 p.m.
Demonstrations Sunday mornings by
appointment only
H.P.WM.D.T.CS.A.BC.

## SURREY

**FARNHAM**   Tel. (0252) 725427
A.B.E. CO. LTD. (Quick Hire)   ★
GOODS SHED
STATION APPROACH, FARNHAM
Open Mon.-Fri. 8.00 a.m.-5.30 p.m.
Sat. 8.00 a.m.-5.30 p.m.
H.P.W.D.CS.A.BC.

## SUSSEX

**BOGNOR REGIS** Tel. (0243) 863100
A. OLBY & SON (BOGNOR REGIS) LTD.
"TOOLSHOP," BUILDERS MERCHANT
HAWTHORN ROAD     K
Open: Mon-Thurs 8 a.m.-5.15 p.m. Fri.
8 a.m.-8 p.m. Sat 8 a.m.-12.45 p.m.
H.P.W.WM.D.T.CA.BC.

## EAST SUSSEX

**ST. LEONARD'S-ON-SEA**  Tel.
DOUST & MONK (MONOSAW)-(0424)
25 CASTLEHAM ROAD     52577
Open: Mon.-Fri. 8.00 a.m.-5.30 p.m.
Most Saturdays 9.00 a.m.-1.00 p.m.
H.P.W.WM.D.CS.A.

## TYNE & WEAR

**NEWCASTLE UPON TYNE**  Tel.
J. W. HOYLE LTD.     (0632) 617474
CLARENCE STREET NE2 1YJ  K★
Open: Mon-Fri 8.00 a.m.-5.00 p.m.
Saturday 9.00 a.m.-4.30 p.m.
H.P.A.BC.W.CS.WM.D.

## WEST MIDLANDS

**WOLVERHAMPTON**  Tel. (0902)
MANSAW SERVICES     58759
SEDGLEY STREET     K★
Open: Mon.-Fri. 9.00 a.m.-5.00 p.m.
H.P.W.WM.A.D.CS.

## YORKSHIRE

**BOROUGHBRIDGE**   Tel. (09012)
JOHN BODDY TIMBER LTD   2370
FINE WOOD & TOOL STORE  ★
RIVERSIDE SAWMILLS
Open: Mon.-Thurs. 8.00 a.m.-6.00 p.m.
Fri. 8.00am-5.00pm Sat. 8.00am-4.00pm
H.P.W.WM.D.T.CS.MF.A.BC.

**CLECKHEATON**   Tel. (0274)
SKILLED CRAFTS LTD.   872861
34 BRADFORD ROAD     ★
Open: 9.00 a.m.-5.00 p.m. Monday
Saturday Lunch 12.00 a.m.-1.00 p.m.
H.P.A.W.CS.WM.D.

**KEIGHLEY**   Tel. (0535) 663325
EUROMAIL (TOOLS)     ★
PO BOX 13
108 EAST PARADE
Open 9.15 a.m.-5.00 p.m.
Not Tuesday but inc. Saturday
H.P.W.A.BC.

**HARROGATE**   Tel. (0423) 66245/
MULTI-TOOLS     55328
158 KINGS ROAD     K★
Open: Monday to Saturday
8.30 a.m.-6.00 p.m.
H.P.W.WM.D.A.BC.

**HUDDERSFIELD**   Tel. (0484)
NEVILLE M. OLDHAM  641219/(0484)
UNIT 1 DALE ST. MILLS   42777
DALE STREET, LONGWOOD   ★
Open: Mon-Fri 8.00 a.m.-5.30 p.m.
Saturday 9.30 a.m.-12.00 p.m.
P.W.WM.D.A.BC.

**LEEDS**   Tel. (0532) 574736
D. B. KEIGHLEY MACHINERY LTD.  ★
VICKERS PLACE, STANNINGLEY
PUDSEY LS2 86LZ
Mon.-Fri. 9.00 a.m.-5.00 p.m.
Sat. 9.00 a.m.-1.00 p.m.
P.A.W.WM.CS.BC.

**LEEDS**   Tel. (0532) 790507
GEORGE SPENCE & SONS LTD.
WELLINGTON ROAD
Open: Monday to Friday
8.30 a.m.-5.30 p.m.
Saturday 9.00 a.m.-5.00 p.m.
H.P.W.WM.D.T.A.

**THIRSK**   Tel. (0845) 22770
THE WOOD SHOP     ★
TRESKE SAWMILLS LTD.
STATION WORKS
Open: Seven days a week 9.00-5.00
T.H.MF.BC.

## SCOTLAND

**EDINBURGH**   Tel. (031 337) 5555
THE SAW CENTRE     ★
38 HAYMARKET TERRACE
HAYMARKET
Open: 8.30 a.m.-5.30 p.m.
Monday-Saturday
H.P.W.WM.D.CS.A.

**GLASGOW**   Tel. (041 429) 4374/)
THE SAW CENTRE   4444, Telex: 777886
600 EGLINTON STREET   E★
G5 9RR
Open: Mon-Fri 8.00 a.m.-5.30 p.m.
Saturday 9.00 a.m.-1.00 p.m.
H.P.W.WM.D.CS.A.

## WALES

**PERTH**   Tel. (0738) 26173
WILLIAM HUME & CO     K
ST. JOHN'S PLACE
Open: Monday to Saturday
8.00 a.m.-5.30 p.m.
8.00 a.m.-1.00 p.m. Wednesday
H.P.A.BC.W.CS.WM.D.

**TAYSIDE**   Tel: (05774) 293
WORKMASTER POWER TOOLS LTD.  ★
DRUM, KINROSS
Open Mon.-Sat. 8.00 a.m.-8.00 p.m.
Demonstrations throughout Scotland by
appointment
P.W.WM.D.A.BC.

**CARDIFF**   Tel. (0222) 396039
JOHN HALL TOOLS LIMITED  ★
CENTRAL SQUARE
Open: Monday to Saturday
9.00 a.m.-5.30 p.m.
H.P.W.WM.D.A.BC.

### TO FILL THIS SPACE 'PHONE JASON ON 01-437 0699 NOW

**CARDIFF**   Tel. (0222) 595710
DATAPOWER TOOLS LTD,
MICHAELSTON ROAD,
CULVERHOUSE CROSS
Open: Mon.-Fri. 8.00 a.m.-5.00 p.m.
Sat. 9.00 a.m.-1.00 p.m.
H.P.W.WM.D.A.

**CARMARTHEN**  Tel. (0267) 237219
DO-IT-YOURSELF SUPPLY   K
BLUE STREET, DYFED
Open: Monday to Saturday
9.00 a.m.-5.30 p.m.
Thursday 9.00 a.m.-5.30 p.m.
H.P.W.WM.D.T.CS.A.BC.

**SWANSEA**   Tel. (0792) 55680
SWANSEA TIMBER & PLYWOOD CO. LTD.
57-59 OXFORD STREET   ★
Open: Mon to Fri 9.00 a.m.-5.30 p.m.
Sat. 9.00 a.m.-1.00 p.m.
H.P.W.D.T.CS.A.BC.

# Letters

I feel I must comment on David Savage's article in the March issue of *Woodworker*. I am a time-served joiner and now work as a lecturer in carpentry and joinery at a technical college, and I am most concerned about some of the methods depicted. The method of cutting tenons on the circular saw is particularly hazardous, especially to the inexperienced. In industry this method of tenoning is now illegal.

I know it is still practised, and it was the usual method in the workshop where I was apprenticed — I myself have cut many tenons in this way. However, my concern is for the person who has just bought a circular saw and, seeing the article, tries it out. It could easily cost a finger or two. These people cannot see the hazards of such an operation, and I think it irresponsible to encourage such practices in what is really a good magazine.

Also, although the method of construction shown is convenient, it is really second-rate. Why on earth cut tenons on stiles and mortises in rails? This shows endgrain on the rails, which looks unsightly when the doors are open; the whole thing looks wrong to the initiated when the doors are closed.

We have enough accidents in the woodworking trades without encouraging them!

*David Pinnington, Burscough*

I respect David Savage's views on benches, but I must totally disagree, firstly with his choice of material for the top, and secondly on the depth. Beech is the hard, resilient, traditional material for bench-tops. My bench, however, is made entirely from Columbian pine, which is (in relative terms) hard and resilient — with one exception; bruises and dents which may occur are not transferred from the bench on to my work. To protect the front edge I have lipped it with American oak, and it is a good 3½in deep; which, in the tool-well, has the advantage of containing my no.6 jointer without its protruding above the work-surface. Truing-up of the surface is not laborious and I find no problem with excessive wear.

I also found David Ellis' article a bit weird. No one in their right mind would want to share tools with someone else. When on site with other tradesmen I live in fear of my good nature, which often allows my tools into unknown hands.

*Peter Howlett, Basildon*

Congratulations on Bob Wearing's article on making your own gauges (WW/Feb). May I add one or two suggestions?

I have tried before to face the fence with melamine laminate, bonded with epoxy adhesive, but wood movement causes bond failure. Old-fashioned brass insert strips are probably still the best answer, although you could use any modern wear-resistant plastic

or nylon. The moisture movement doesn't arise along the grain, the direction in which the strips are fitted.

As a further suggestion for preventing the thumbscrew biting into the stem and damaging it, I recommend routing a groove along the side of the stem and bonding in a strip of harder material. I have successfully used a piece of material of the type used for printed-circuit boards and electrical insulating boards — Tufnel, SRBP, Paxolin, etc. Once again the movement problem doesn't arise along the grain.

Lastly, Bob expresses doubts about using engineer's taps and dies on wood. While I think he is right about the unsuitability of dies (they have a relatively short lead-in, and the cutting-edge rake is wrong) there is little problem with taps. To ensure success: **A** the thread form should be as coarse as possible in relation to the wood fibre; **B** the tap should be as sharp as possible, i.e. new and not previously used to cut metal; **C** a taper tap is used to give a gradual opening-out of the thread, and **D** tapping along the grain is not attempted. I'm assuming no one would try to tap into softwood!

*R. Miles, St Albans*

I produce quite a large number of turned items, including a selection of lace bobbins and accessories in wood, bone, staghorn, ivory, and ox- and buffalo-horn. I feel I must comment on some of the things Nick Perrin has to say about bobbin turning (WW/Jan).

First, he says that workpieces of 5-7mm should be turned at 15,000rpm, with which I am in complete disagreement. I turn bobbins, thimbles and other small items at 2400rpm, which is the speed of my lathe, and quite adequate. I know quite a few other bobbin-makers who turn at far slower speeds, with (for them) satisfactory results.

He goes on to say that ox- and buffalo-horn heats up and bends on him; I can turn between 30 and 40 horn bobbins a day without too much bother. As to the bobbin-turning technique he recommends: he says first rough down with a gouge, then smooth off with a one-sided skew chisel, when in fact pieces that small should be taken down to a smooth round in one operation with a skew. I've always thought a skew was meant to be used from both left to right and right to left, both over- and underhand. I find the idea of a one-sided skew amazing — it must have a very limited use!

*Geoffrey Manley, Lyme Regis*

With reference to Mr Brooke's letter in January's *Woodworker*, I know not why bench-grinder makers choose such speeds, but I can offer him a simple and inexpensive means of bringing them down to controlled, safer limits.

He can buy one of the small hand-tool motor control units available on the market, or else he can make one with a standard domestic-lamp dimmer/switch and a 13amp plug and socket, all of which are readily purchased from any electrical store.

The dimmer should be rated above 500w. I use a 630w unit, wired as shown in the sketch.

The 13amp socket and the dimmer/switch are mounted together on a simple rectangular frame roughly 3¼×6½in, made up from ¾in-square batten, with a ply or hardboard back panel. The flex to the mains plug is carried through an appropriate-sized hole drilled through the side of the frame.

I have found it convenient to mount the socket below the dimmer so that the dimmer knob and switch are not encumbered by the grinder plug and lead. I have also found it useful to fix a picture-hanger plate at the top of the frame so that the whole unit can be hung on the wall above and behind the grinder, but can be removed at will and used as a speed control for my portable electric drill and other appliances as required.

*David Kendall-Carpenter, Truro*

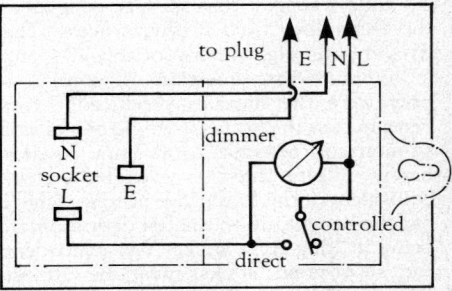

The article on stains by Noel Leach in the March issue reminded me of Mr Garrod's query concerning Tunbridge ware (WW/Dec 84). The surface-staining techniques described by Mr Leach are not really intended for the through-and-through penetration required by Mr Garrod.

When Tunbridge ware was at the height of its popularity, few synthetic dyes were on the market. It is true that spirit dyes tend to be less light-fast than some others, but they have been greatly improved, and suitable varnishing can do much to help. They also offer a wide range of hues of great brilliance, and their penetrating power is substantial. Of course, the structure of wood militates against deep penetration across the grain, and even total-immersion methods are constrained by the need to displace cellular air before dye can penetrate along the grain. Hence the technique of pressure impregnation used, for example, in the preservation of fencing timbers.

I have found a simple and relatively cheap alternative that works well. The timber spills are placed in a suitable length of pipe and most of the air is evacuated (a simple laboratory water-pump operated on mains pressure serves quite well). The dye solution is then admitted, followed by air, and the whole left to stand overnight, the wood being totally immersed. I have succeeded in penetrating ramin of 10mm section in this way using Geigy's Orasol dyes. Since the formation of the Ciba-Geigy group one should ask for Orasol; these

# Letters

spirit dyes are available in many vivid colours. There is no need to buy the stuff by the pound; a few grams will go a long way.

*A. R. H. Tawn, Petts Wood*

I was interested in Mr Garrod's letter (WW/Dec) about dyeing woods for Tunbridge-ware mosaics. I had been puzzled about a band of floral mosaic running round an antique box, because the grain was running *along* the band — not out of it, as would have been the case if it had been produced by the process described in *Woodworker*, November 1969.

I sent for the Tunbridge Museum leaflets, which confirmed the process, but also added the essential clue that Tunbridge ware used natural woods only: primarily browns, whites and freak greens. Since the roses in the antique box were still red and pink, it followed that the box was not Tunbridge but probably Sorrento ware.

Could I suggest that Mr Garrod pursue the technology used in this process? The dyes are still bright, after probably 90 years.

My immediate question, of course, is how were the mosaics produced? Most veneers I use in parquetry would be a pile of splinters if reduced to 0.7mm squares barely 0.3mm thick — even by a close equivalent of the Tunbridge process, which has the benefit, up to the last operation, of being in long-grain sticks. The equivalent for short-grain sticks must be almost unhandleable; yet the process must be by repetitive slicing, because defects are produced in each flower.

*Trevor Platt, Bristol*

I would be interested to hear if anyone might know something about my old lathe. It is very solidly constructed with a cast-iron bed, head and tailstock. The headstock carries a conical white-metal bearing with a four-step pulley designed for a flat belt. The largest pulley doubles as a dividing head, having five rows of holes round its periphery, with a detent spring mounted on the bed. The rows divide the circle into 20, 24, 96, 144 and 112. The first four sequences would provide almost any division one could want, but I cannot imagine why anyone should want to divide by 112.

The lathe will turn 8in over the bed and 27in between centres. The mandrel has a 1in Whit. thread with internal Morse taper; it carries the maker's name — W. Mellor & Co, Rainow, Macclesfield — and, I suspect, may have been use to produce bobbins and the like for the local textile industry. Any suggestions?

*John Rimmer, 429 Chester Rd, Hartford, Northwich, Cheshire CW8 2AF*

I was interested in the article in *Woodworker*, December 1984, on tipped lathe tools. Last year I made a 12in rotary sander for wood and a 10in sander for metals by cutting ⅜in-plate aluminium discs on the bandsaw and fitting them to my motor shafts. As the discs were not perfectly round they set up small

vibrations, so they needed to be balanced by turning them true on the shafts.

To make the lathe tools I turned a beech handle and used ¾in copper pipe for a ferrule and a strip of ¾×⅛in bright steel for the blade. The blade was then drilled and tapped at the end for an Allen screw to hold the carbide-tipped inserts that are usually used by engineering companies. The inserts, generally round or three-sided, are often thrown away once they are chipped or badly worn.

They turned my rotary sander-discs perfectly, and I now use them on my home-made woodturning lathe for turning brass, ebony, aluminium, nylon and even steel. The round tips are very useful because as they get blunt you only need to turn them round a fraction. When they are totally blunted I re-grind them on a soft stone grinder; however, as they cost so little they could almost be thrown away. The three-sided cutters are also very useful — you can used them with one flat to your work or on end for V-jointed working. If you have a set of Sears Craftsman moulding cutters for the saw, these could be fixed on the tool end for normal woodturning.

*S. W. Birch, Hatfield*

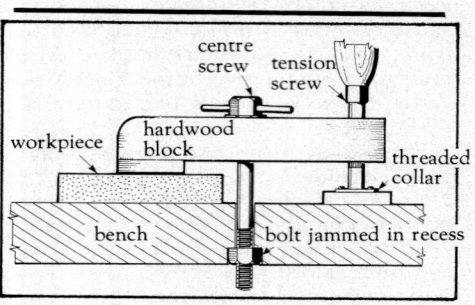

Since my article on a bench holdfast appeared (WW/Mar 84), I have received the following suggestions, which I find an improvement.

Counterbore the underside of the bench top using the same size bit or drill as the size across the flats of the chosen nut, i.e. the spanner size. For the ½in Whitworth which I used, this is ⅞in. With a hexagon-head bolt, a washer and a drilled hardwood block for protection, the nut is forced tightly into the hole, where it will stay fast.

A loose-fitting flush dowel prevents the hole from filling up with sawdust and can easily be pushed out with a pencil. To avoid lengthy screwing-up when holding thin components, I find it convenient to have both a long and a short centre screw.

If the holes in the bench are drilled at regular intervals, say 12in, a stout block similarly drilled can be used both as a further hold-down and as a fence for certain routing operations. To give a good grip, curve one of the two cramping surfaces.

*Bob Wearing, Wem*

Richard Sarjent's piece on Japanese saws (WW/Nov) brought back memories of post-war Japan, where I was in charge of the carpentry section of one of our occupation army workshops. We supplied anything

wooden that was missing or damaged from the vehicles that were being re-conditioned; there were eight Japanese carpenters, all over 40, and I was a very green 21!

My first impression of their tools was that they were very primitive, but I soon began to marvel at the speed and standard of finish. They mostly made their own planes; their chisels had very short, hollow-ground blades, and they only used water for sharpening, never oil. Although they were issued with Western-type benches, they did a lot of their work squatting on the floor or on the bench itself.

An ingenious device they used for putting a line on their work consisted of a reel of fine twine in a wooden housing, which also carried an ink-soaked pad in a well. A sharp pin on the end of the line was pushed into one end of the work to be marked, and as it was paid out a piece of shaped bamboo applied pressure to the line across the ink-pad. You pressed on to your second mark, then flicked, just as with a chalk-line. The result was a perfectly straight, very black, thin line to cut to.

Another practice I saw entailed fixing on an incline a large piece of hardwood a little smaller than a railway sleeper, with a blade set in a mouth. It worked like a long try-plane, only you pulled the timber down and towards you over the blade.

I found the planes easier to use than the saws. The main difference between our saws and theirs was that their larger ones were used with two hands. The Japanese would often hold their work with their feet when they were ripping. I think we would find sharpening them very difficult — the fine side of the saw I have has 20 teeth to the inch! They all give a super-fine cut.

*R. Edmunds, Rowlands Castle*

Mr Milner and Messrs Heaney and Sellers are both wrong — and so, if I may say so, is Mr Bateman. Hewn medieval furniture was made the way it was for only two reasons that I can see. First came a necessity: to conceal or secure household articles such as linen, crocks, jewellery and so forth. Tradesmen made up cupboards and chest to satisfy this need. They were made in the best way they could be, relative to the tools materials and tastes of the time and with regard to cost and function.

There may have been a small touch of aesthetics, but I doubt it, because the tradesman was unlikely to have been able to afford this luxury (either then or now). It is difficult nowadays, for instance, to distinguish the work styles of individual carvers of the American eagle motif which surmounted wall clocks as a feature *de rigeur*. At $8 a clock they could not afford the time to sign their work, which degenerated into crudity as a result. There is no merit in this crudity — it just about fulfilled a need of the times in the same way as plastics do today. If Mr Milner's sentiment is extrapolated into a distant future time, one may imagine collectors competing for throwaway paper cups.

*Gerald Dunn, Maldon*

# The magazine for the craftsman
## ~ and the aspiring craftsman!

June 1985
Vol. 89
No. 1099

● *Adding a violin front: the maker's tale is on pages 462-3*

**On the cover:** Chris MacDonald's mahogany can (p412), plus Francesca Graham's chest (p464); Michael Foden's goblets (see p440 for the timbers he used); applying Danish oil (p457); and a natural-edge plum bowl by Tobias Kaye (p429)

**Publisher** Ray Lewis
**Editor** Peter Collenette
**Deputy Editor** Aidan Walker
**Advertisement Manager** Paul Holmes
**Graphics** Jeff Hamblin
**Advertisement production** Karyn Stewart
**Guild of Woodworkers** Aidan Walker, Sam Jones
**Group Editor** Chris Adam-Smith
**Publishing Director** John Foster
**Chairman and Chief Executive** Jim Connell
**Editorial, advertisements and Guild of Woodworkers**
1 Golden Square, London W1R 3AB, telephone 01-437 0626

Unfortunately we cannot accept responsibility for loss of or damage to unsolicited material. We reserve the right to refuse or suspend advertisements, and regret we cannot guarantee the bone fides of advertisers.

**Subscriptions and back issues** Infonet Ltd, 10-13 Times House, 179 Marlowes, Hemel Hempstead, Herts HP1 1BB; telephone Hemel Hempstead (0442) 48434
**Subscriptions per year** UK £15.60; overseas outside USA (accelerated surface post) £17, USA (accelerated surface post) $22.50, airmail £42
**UK trade** SM Distribution Ltd, 16-18 Trinity Gardens, London SW9 8DX; telephone 01-274 8611
**North American trade** Eastern News Distributors, 166-41 Powells Cove Boulevard, PO Box 69, Whitestone, New York 11357
**Printed in Great Britain** by Ambassador Press Ltd, St Albans, Herts
**Mono origination** Multiform Photosetting Ltd, Cardiff
**Colour origination** Derek Croxson Ltd, Chesham, Bucks
© Argus Specialist Publications Ltd 1985
ISSN 0043 776X

## Argus Specialist Publications Ltd
1 Golden Square, London
W1R 3AB; 01-437 0626

# Woodworker
## This month

### Bristol Woodworker Show (right now!)

By the time you read this, there'll only be a matter of days (or even hours) to lay your plans and get down to the Bristol Woodworker Show. It takes place at Bristol Exhibition Complex, right in the centre of town yet with massive car-parking facilities, and it lasts for all three days of the Bank Holiday weekend: 25, 26 and 27 May. Roll up, see what all our friends in the trade have to offer, and feast your eyes on the woodworking talent which will be on display.

And while you're about it, come and visit our sales stand, where you can experience the chance to win an Elu lathe, a DeWalt bandsaw or one of two Black & Decker professional palm-sanders. It must be worth a whirl!

### London Show: more to win . . .

On the subject of prizes, here are two more of the meatiest going. The London Woodworker Show at Alexandra Pavilion N22, on 24-7 October, features a more or less breathtaking array of competition classes which are open for all to enter, and that includes you.

Two categories offer prizes donated by the famed specialist tool merchant **Roger's of Hitchin** — prizes which should make anyone who's eligible think twice or thrice about the wisdom of not sending for an entry form . . . For the **Juniors** there's a £100 voucher to spend in Roger's cave of treasures; and for the **Young professionals** there's a boxed set of 10 Japanese chisels — some of today's most lusted-after tools.

Over in the editorial office, by the way, we'd like to remind the young professionals (and, if it comes to that, the middle-aged and white-haired ones!) that what they do is meat and drink to the magazine. We're

always delighted to hear from anyone in the trade — in whatever branch — who'd like to talk about the possibility of an article. It might be a project with drawings, or it might be something quite different. Just telephone 01-437 0626 and ask for Peter Collenette (the editor) or Aidan Walker (his faithful deputy dawg).

Meanwhile, back in the future, another scrumptious award at the October show may descend on literally anyone who enters. That's the **English Abrasives Award for Finishing,** and it consists of a plain, unadorned cheque for £250. It goes to the entry with the best surface finish: simple as that. Last year it was won by an abstract carving, but this year it could just as easily go to a clock, a chest-of-drawers or a miniature coal-cart. Like all the other prizes, it's awarded by a team of independent judges.
- Roger's, 47 Walsworth Rd, Hitchin, Herts, SG4 9SU, tel. (0462) 34177.
- English Abrasives Ltd, Marsh Lane, London N17, tel. 01-808 4545.
- All show and competition details, plus entry forms, from Argus Specialist Exhibitions Ltd, Park View House, 1 Park View Rd, Berkhamsted, Herts HP4 3EY, tel. (04427) 73291.

### Marquetry goes national

A staggering total of between 300 and 400 pieces of marquetry will be on display at the Marquetry Society's annual national exhibition at the Town Hall, Great Yarmouth, Norfolk, from 25 May till 1 June: Sat.-Thurs. 10-6, Fri. 10-9, Sat. 1 June 10-4. Admission free. More details from Eddie Leader, Great Yarmouth (0493) 728307.

### Gluing Colorcore

The right adhesive for Formica's Colorcore laminate is Araldite 2003 — not 6003 (WW/ March).

Take a good look at International Paint's range of Woodplan **wood stains** when you see them on the shelf. They are thixotropic, which means like jelly, which means you put them on with a brush. Little or no wastage — no rags soaking it all up — and extremely good coverage: all these things are claimed; they're talking about 20 sq metres per litre! The colour will deepen with added coats; it's white-spirit-based, carrying inorganic pigments, and the penetration is 1-2mm. Mixing the seven colours in the range with one another is possible, but you'd have problems adding other oil stains to Woodplan products because of the gel consistency.

Yet another interesting point is that these stains actually leave a protective coating on the wood; not as hard as varnish, but resistant to mild acids and alkalis. Don't catch your breath too hard at the price, when you remember the coverage; £4 inc. VAT for 500ml, £2.28 inc. VAT for the 250ml can.
- International Paint, 24-30 Canute Rd, Southampton, Hants SO9 3AS, tel. (0703) 37838.

The MiniMax **table belt sander** has been well thought-out, it's obvious. One of the major arguments against installing these sanders has always been space — they're wonderful when they're being used, and a drain on precious floor area when they're not. The MiniMax L55 has a foldaway table (with electric rise and fall as well) foldaway transverse arms and detachable feet. The sanding capacity is 2500×1100×700mm, but it is only 550mm wide when it's all folded up. Just how long it takes to do that, and how convenient it is to do, is for the buyer to find out. There's also a vertical locking panel for edge-sanding doors. It comes in standard three-phase 4hp form for £1600+VAT, and 3.5hp single-phase for £1625+VAT. Extremely reasonable for what looks like a versatile and highly effective machine.

- All MiniMax machines — the bandsaws, lathes, and universals as well as the table sander — are now marketed by Luna Tools & Machinery, 20 Denbigh Hall, Bletchley, Milton Keynes, Bucks MK3 7QT, tel. (0908) 70771.

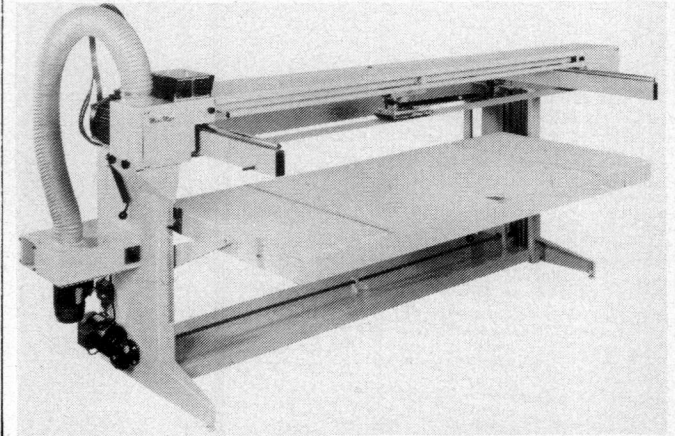

If you buy a Wolfcraft 3400 **heavy-duty drill stand,** you get £12 worth of **machine-vice free.** The stand itself has a hexagonal column and the usual calibrations, a depth stop, and a 'micro-adjustment depth scale'. £38.70+VAT buys you the stand and the machine-vice and fixing bolts, while stocks last.
- Wolfcraft, BriMarc Ltd, Kineton Rd, Southam, Leamington Spa, Warks CV33 0DR, tel. (0926 81) 2044.

If you read the article on a Norris plane in the February 1983 issue of *Woodworker*, and have been wanting to make one but can't get plans, your troubles are over. Cliff Willetts has full-scale drawings, and is offering them at £2.95 a set.
- Cliff Willetts, 'Gables', Frisby on the Wreake, Melton Mowbray, Leics LE14 2NP.

Max Burrough's story of his apprenticeship days (p479) hasn't long to run. When it ends, we'd like to give space to some of those whose stories echo his — more than one reader has said they could match his every word from their own experience. We're keen to hear from you. The only essential is double-spaced typescript.

Bruce Luckhurst, familiar to those who frequent West Dean College and its range of courses, is running a one-year **furniture-restoration course** starting 30 September. Students of either sex between 18 and 55 are invited to apply; no previous woodworking or polishing experience is necessary. Bruce aims to give a thorough grounding in the basic skills of cabinetmaking, traditional finishing, turning, carving, gilding, metalwork, marquetry and veneering. People already doing this sort of work are encouraged to bring their jobs along to help subsidise the fees, and students are actively supported in making contact with future clients while still studying.

Bruce holds a certificate in adult and further education, has been restoring furniture professionally for 20 years, and has taught at the London College of Furniture. He has worked on pieces in the Victoria & Albert Museum. Write to him for a prospectus.

● Bruce Luckhurst, Little Surrenden, Bethersden, Kent, tel. (023 382) 589.

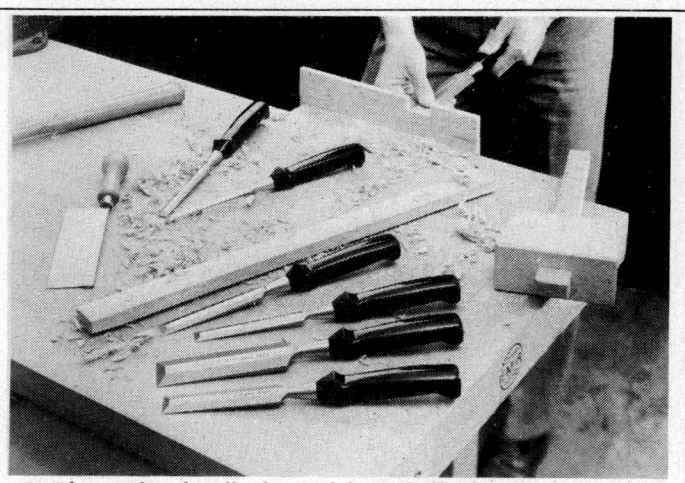

● The startling handle shape of these Sheffield-made chisels, introduced last year, is evidently what has won them inclusion in the prestige Index of London's Design Centre. All bevel-edged, they run from ¼ to 1½in. Do today's design moguls know something that makers of traditional cylindrical- and oval-handled chisels didn't? Is it just that no one's ever thought of applying to chisels the same sort of intimate hand-grip that has long been familiar on saws? Makers are The Paramo Tools Group Ltd, Hallamshire Works, Rockingham St, Sheffield S1 3NW, (0742)25262/754348-9.

● AEG's unique portable plug-in motor seen atop the AEG C260 planer-thicknesser

AEG's Multi **woodworking system** is basically three machines and one motor. The idea is that you buy your planer/thicknesser, circular saw or spindle-moulder — or all three; they all come powerless, but use an interchangeable 1.5hp single- or three-phase unit. There's a failsafe bayonet-lock system to keep the motor in place once it's hooked in, and the power unit has full safety interlocks. It's been designed for the small user with not a lot of space or initial investment capital, but one can't help wondering if the idea isn't a little misconceived. £512+VAT for a planer/thicknesser, £281+ VAT for the saw and £339+ VAT for the spindle-moulder; £147 for a single-phase motor, £136 for a three-phase. It does add up, although it isn't all going to hurt at once if you buy the system bit-by-bit (as is obviously intended). The machines have cast-alloy tables, and the floor-stands for the planer/thicknesser and spindle-moulder are also extra — £35 a time. AEG's reputation for solidity and reliability is a selling point, but heaving a motor round the workshop when you've ripped a piece and want to surface it . . . how popular will that be?
● AEG-Telefunken, 217 Bath Rd, Slough, Berks SL1 4AW, tel. Slough 872101.

Although its name is much more associated with cars than tools in the UK, **Peugeot's power-tool** presence in the French market is as big as Black & Decker's here. Quite rightly so, to judge from the specifications of some of their range. A grinder, sander and new drills made their debut in Britain in May, but the existing products seem well worth a look. Jigsaws that can cut to within 4mm of walls, into corners, or in the hollows of corrugated sheet, and mini-circular saws with a headlight to illuminate the cutting line (the jigsaws have this too). Particularly interesting is the Multiface, a general-purpose tool that can be used for cutting, grinding, sanding or polishing, with an 800w electronically controlled motor that can't be overloaded and runs at the right speed for each selected function. The mini-circular saw has a 4in blade and a 250w motor and costs £44.78+VAT; the Multifac is £69.52+VAT; and the new TE125 bench-grinder, with 5in disc and 180w motor, is £43.48+VAT.
● Peugeot Power Tools, 217 Bath Rd, Slough, Berks SL1 4AW, tel. (0753) 872500.

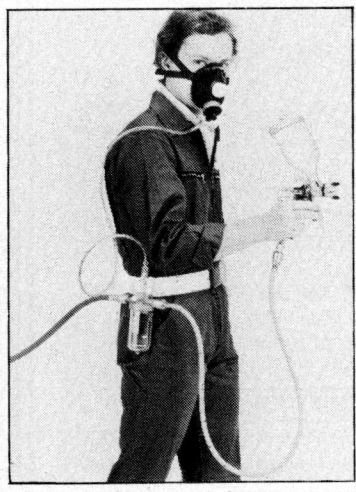

● This gent is wearing a half-mask breathing set. It appears to be a handy item of gear for spray-finishers, because the same inlet supplies air to both the mask and the spraygun itself. The mask is made of rubber, and a filter hangs from the belt (the element changes colour when it needs renewing). The set costs £99.35+VAT from Minden Industrial, Newmarket Rd, Bury St Edmunds, Suffolk IP33 3TS, (0284) 3418.

Further to A. R. H. Tawn's item in 'This month' (WW/ March) — to help both the amateur and the more professional worker, **writes D. F. Meek,** I would like to recommend an excellent book on the Health & Safety Act, which covers most chemicals and their dangers: The Hazards of Work by Patrick Kinnersley. It's published by Pluto Press, 105a Torriano Avenue, London NW5, tel. 01-482 1973, and it costs £1.95 for around 400 pages.

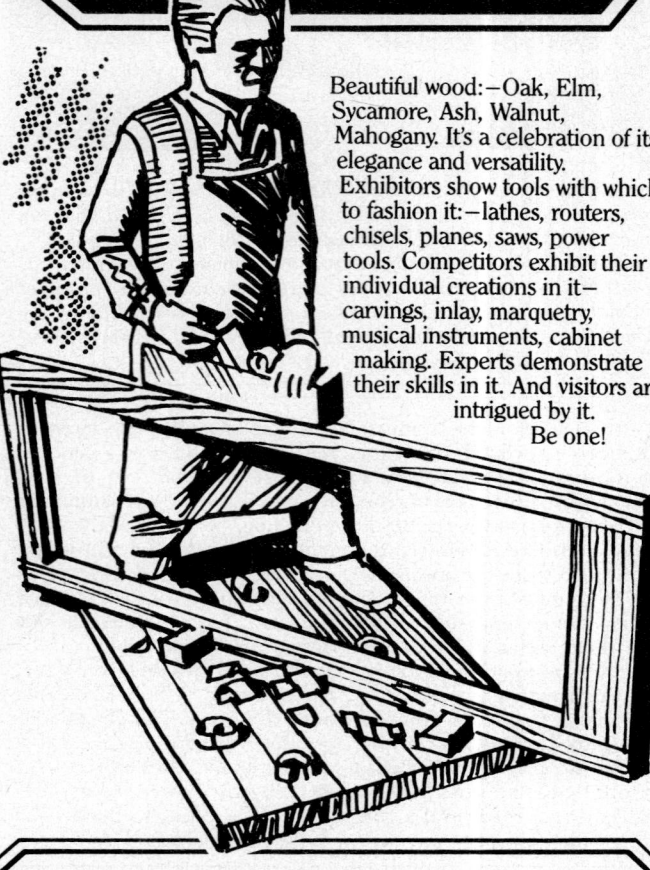

**Prices quoted are those prevailing at press date and are subject to alteration due to economic conditions.**

# Shoptalk

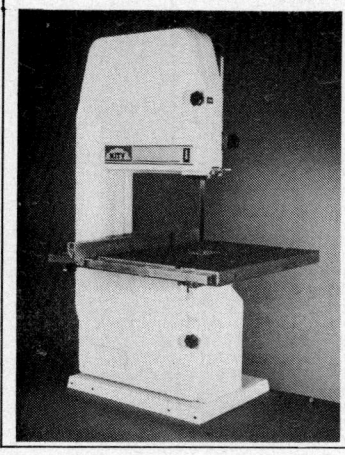

● *This is Kity's new Industrial K613 bandsaw. For £510+VAT you get an 8in depth of cut, a 12in throat, a 20×20in tilting table and a 1.5hp motor. It will accept a blade as wide as 1in under high tension because of what Kity call its 'unusual construction' incorporating 'a massive tubular steel support'. A cheaper 1hp version (the plain K613, at £383+VAT) is bench-mounted. Kity UK are at 6 Acorn Park, Charlestown, Shipley, West Yorks BD17 7SW, (0274) 597826.*

Unidoor is a flexible **self-assembly panelled-door system** for replacement of kitchen, bathroom or any other cupboard doors. A kit consists of 24×50mm solid-wood framing, ready-moulded and available in oak, beige, off-white or 'natural' finish, plus a 10mm centre panel, natural or antique oak or off-white finished. The panels have a textured pattern on the other side so you can go for a linen look if you wish. The frames are mitred together, and the only tools required for the job are a fine-tooth saw and a mitre guide (plus squares, clamps, glue, and the other bits and pieces). Measure your old doors, compute the amount of frame you need (allowing 5mm gaps between the new ones), cut it up and stick it all together. What could be simpler? 'The door or front should be assembled using a strong wood joint glue where the parts meet', it says here, to eliminate all possible confusion. Any hinge can be used with Unidoor because the frame section is a generous 24mm thick.

● Unidoor, Graham Nicholson, Beech House, 233 Queen's Rd, Beeston, Nottingham NG9 2BP, tel. (0602) 256279.

Seasoning timber is all about getting the moisture content right (and if you didn't know that already, it's time you found out!). But to get it right, you have to know it; and to know it, you have to measure it. The starkly named Mark 1 **Moisture Meter** is a little item that's ideal for the job. You stick its two prongs into the wood and read the MC off the dial. It will also deal with plaster, brick and concrete. It's powered by an ordinary 9v battery, and it weighs in at 1lb 14oz. Cost is £68+VAT.

● Channel Electronics Ltd, PO Box 58, Seaford, Sussex BN25 3JB, tel. (0323) 894961.

It's our job to look just a little askance at manufacturers' multifarious offers and gimmicks — but the current one from **Bosch** is worth a double-take. If you buy a PHO200 power plane, you get a free adjustable parallel and angle fence. If you buy a PST55-PE orbital jigsaw, you get a free table to convert it to a little bench jigsaw. If you buy a POF52 router, you get a free edge-trimming attachment. 'Free' electronic controls on an orbital sander are only a figure of speech (many fit them as standard), and the sceptical can always say none of these offers are really free at all. But why carp?

The portable Kaindle drill-grinder, say its makers, 'is small and extremely easy for even the novice to set. It will re-sharpen right hand and left hand drills (with a diamond wheel attachment it will sharpen carbide). With this grinder it is possible to form your own wood boring drills up to approximately 20mm or even sharpen Forstner bits and jobber drills to any angle.' It costs £315+VAT.

● Target Tools, Station Lane Industrial Estate, Witney, Oxon., tel. (0993) 3885.

**Prices quoted are those prevailing at press date and are subject to alteration due to economic conditions**

# Timberline

## Arthur Jones presents the month's inside news of supplies

Conservation is an emotive subject. Few people are prepared to look upon trees as a crop, a renewable resource, and there are frequent cries that we are continuing to import hardwoods from the tropical forests of the world which will soon be denuded.

If they ever are, it will certainly not be down to UK imports, for currently no less than 48% of the trees cut in tropical forests are used for fuel or energy.

So it was good to hear that timber-trade representations to Whitehall successfully prevented mahogany from being put on the list of endangered species requiring the monitoring of all imports. Incidentally, mahogany from Brazil continues to be a good buy, the wood having the greatest difficulty in holding its price in the current market.

Hardwood sales in Britain last year fell by 11%. The strong dollar meant a switch to non-dollar areas, so beech came back strongly into popularity, helped by some surplus supplies in Europe following forest windblow in Germany and France. There has also been a lot more buying from west Africa of such species as sipo, sapele, utile and iroko — all obtainable in sterling. Among our own native timbers there have been strong sales of oak and ash, so prices for both species are firm, especially in the better grades.

Visitors to the DIY stores will have noted the trend towards pre-packed wood goods, with shrink-wrapped softwood becoming increasingly common. Woodworkers usually look scornfully upon this practice. In the case of finished goods, especially panels, the packing certainly prevents transit damage; but, if you like to browse through timber and select, the practice is anathema. It is impossible to check any piece for defects (only two sides at the most can be seen) and the centre pieces have to be taken on trust.

However, shrink-wrapping is on the increase, with overseas shippers developing it at considerable pace, and the woodworking fraternity will have to live with it.

The softwood market generally continues steady and all in our favour, but Canadian wood from landed stocks is a little dearer. The Czechs have held their prices at the levels established by other east European sellers and this year they are offering LIGNA wood which has been seasoned and packaged to length. The Poles have said they are holding present prices, based on £97 per m³, until the autumn — another indicator that timber will be a good buy for months to come.

Meanwhile, in an attempt to boost parana-pine sales, Brazil is now selling the wood priced in sterling. (There was a time when it was sold as hardwood!)

The ASEAN group of plywood manufacturers have set export quotas for mills in Singapore, Malaysia, Brazil, Indonesia and the Philippines for shipments to the UK in the second quarter of this year, but the aim is really to steady the selling prices. The market is still weak and prices of plywood from Brazil continue to be the most competitive with those of Far Eastern countries.

Particleboard sales in the UK last year rose by 100,000m³ to 2,100,000m³, home-produced chipboard showing a gain of some 3%. More chipboard came from West Germany and Belgium, largely because of price. By the way, a list of the full range of particleboards sold under 20 main brand names is given in a useful leaflet, free from the Chipboard Promotion Association, Stocking Lane, Hughenden Valley, High Wycombe, Bucks HP14 4NU.

Cheap fibreboards from Portugal, Yugoslavia, Argentina and Switzerland have led to protests of dumping being made by EEC producers, and the complaints are being investigated to see whether an anti-dumping duty should be imposed. Fibreboard imports into the UK last year were up 5%, but it is interesting to note that standard plain hardboards are now being supplanted by those boards which have been subject to further processing. Such 'worked' hardboards now account for a third of all imports. ∎

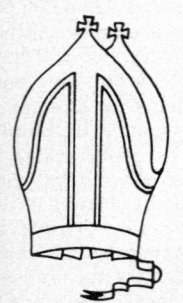

Prices quoted are those prevailing at press date and are
subject to alteration due to economic conditions.

# Question box

## Our panel of experts solve your woodworking problems

**Q** *Could you tell me how to work out the thickness of wood or multi-ply needed to build a table 50×50×80cm strong enough to hold a 3cwt refrigerator?*

J. W. Dunster, London W13

**A** A 3cwt fridge is the same weight as three sacks of cement, so you need as robust a structure as a carpenter's bench.

The sketch shows a suitable design, which has a multi-ply top rebated into the rails to avoid lipping the edges. The legs have a slight splay for extra stability; the rails are haunch-mortise-and-tenoned into the legs, and the underframe rails are stub-tenoned in. All joints are glued and dowelled. The ply top is 36mm thick, and could be made from three pieces of 12mm board glued together; the top is glued into the rebates, and could be given extra support by a bearer rail underneath, stop-dovetailed into opposite rails.

A sturdy wood like oak or beech should be used for the table members, with the following finished dimensions; legs 76×76, tapering to 70×70mm; top rails 150×30mm; underframe rails 50×25mm, set down 150mm from top rails. All the edges are radiused.

*Bob Grant DLC FRSA FSIAD*

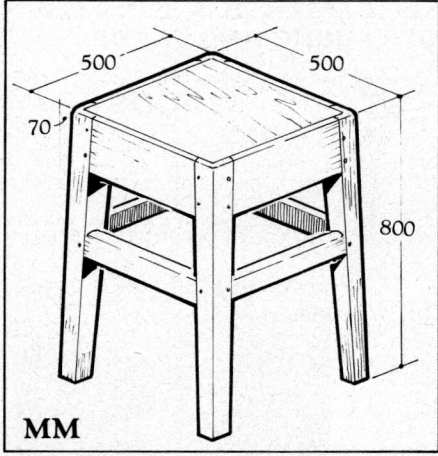

**MM**

**Q** *I am a cabinetmaker working mainly with antiques, and often have to glue up balloon-back chairs. As anyone who has done this will know, cramping the top back rail is rather difficult; I have heard the senior cabinetmakers talk of a saddle-cramp that makes the job easier, but no one knows what it looks like. Any information would be greatly appreciated.*

D. F. Burman, Great Yarmouth

**A** You are probably already familiar with the saddle-cramp, and have quite likely used it in one form or another without putting a name to it. In the case of the balloon-back chair it consists of two wood blocks shaped to fit the curve and joined by a stout leather strap. Sash-cramps put on the pressure. They pull on the seat rail, on the foot, or on a batten on which the front and rear legs stand, depending of course on the curve. In some cases the modern web-cramp has supplanted this.

The subject is well covered in *Repairing and Restoring Antique Furniture* by John Rodd, published by David & Charles in 1954 and considerably revised and extended in 1976.

*Bob Wearing DLC MCCEd*

**Q** *I had some larch trees cut down – some big enough for bowl-turning blanks – and chainsawed the blanks out either side of the centre, discarding the middle of the trunk. I turn green wood roughly to bowl shape, leave it for up to a year to season, and then finish the turning. In the larch I find pockets and long fissures, running with the grain, which ooze resin – they would make a good finished surface to a bowl impossible. Will the resin go away, dry up or all ooze out in time? If not, is there anything I can do to get over the difficulty?*

R. A. Hendrie, Norwich

**A** It is unfortunate that the particular tree in your garden happened to be a larch. I regret to say larch is not the most suitable timber for bowl-turning, with or without the resin deposits. They will definitely not go away; they may dry up, but this could make turning even more difficult.

My advice is to find some other application for this timber. I don't recommend the fire, either, as larch logs spit so badly that your hearth-rug would be soon aflame! Why couldn't it have been a walnut tree?

*Frank Boddy*

**Q** *My husband is putting up a pine ceiling in the kitchen. What is the correct procedure for sealing and protecting the wood against steam, smells and grease?*

Mrs M. Holmes, Houghton-le-Spring

**A** As you have not indicated the type of finish you want, I assume it is going to be a clear one to allow the grain of the pine to be seen. I am also assuming the ceiling will be of ½in-thick TGV boards. When fixing these boards it is best to nail them through the tongues into the joists at an angle. If nails are driven through the boards in the same way as when you lay floorboards, make sure you use non-rusting nails, e.g. copper. The steam in a kitchen soon attacks unprotected ironwork, causing unsightly stains.

A good-quality oil varnish will give both the decoration and protection you need. Polyurethane varnish is inclined to peel like a thin skin if damp gets behind it and is therefore not recommended in this situation. A reliable oil varnish which will stand up to grease and kitchen steam is Jackson's yacht varnish, obtainable from James Jackson & Co. (London) Ltd, 68-79 Alscot Rd, SE1 5SX. It is not absolutely clear, but it imparts a pleasing golden tone to pine and brings out the grain character.

When varnishing it is essential to use an absolutely clean brush; a brand-new one is recommended for this reason. Unwrap the bruch and flick the bristles between the fingers to ensure there is no dust. Buy only high-quality brushes and you will not be troubled by loose hairs being left on the varnished surface. The varnish is flowed on to the ceiling in the direction of the grain. Brush-marks will even themselves out.

Allow the varnish to harden thoroughly, and lightly smooth it with fine garnet paper to remove any little nibs. Remove the dust by wiping over with a rag moistened with white spirit, then apply a second coat of varnish.

*Charles Cliffe*

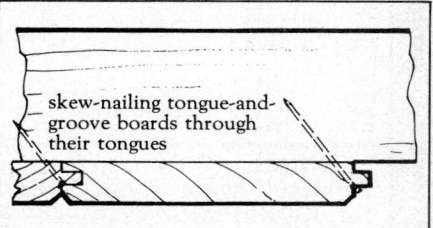

skew-nailing tongue-and-groove boards through their tongues

**Q** *I have a splendid walnut-veneered Queen Anne kneehole desk which has been badly repaired. The top face was quartered in the traditional manner, but has been spoiled by the insertion of large triangular gussets. The intention of these insertions is not wholly clear, but they could have been made to cover damage.*

*This desk was bought in the early 1920s, and no repairs have been made since then.*

*Attempts to heat and lift the present 1mm-thick veneer have apparently failed to soften the adhesive. I have assumed that scotch glue has been used and am therefore mystified at the apparent failure of the glue to soften. Perhaps my heated old-fashioned flat iron has not been hot enough? Lifting rather than destruction is wanted, so as to have material to repair the crossbanding. I have bought some new 1mm veneer.*

*Edward Akerhielm, Hadleigh*

**A** This presents several anomalies. You say that the veneered top is quartered, but your sketch shows it as halved with each half containing a triangle: this is not, in my view, historically accurate, as these tops were almost always quartered. Sometimes the quartering was ornamented with inlaid stringing, etc., but the basic pattern was still there.

Next, you mention 1mm-thick veneer. In no way can this be genuinely old stuff, as such thin veneer can only be knife-cut and until the 1880s all veneer was saw-cut. On an authentic Queen Anne piece it would have been sawn by hand. It is impossible to saw a 1mm-thick veneer by hand; saw-cut veneers are usually at least ⅛in thick and are frequently ³⁄₁₆in bare.

As to softening the glue; all wood-

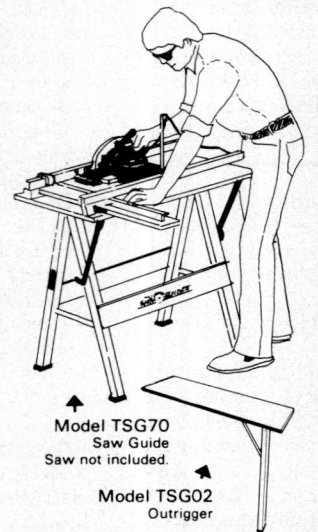

Prices quoted are those prevailing at press date and are subject to alteration due to economic conditions.

# Question box

working glue was of the animal variety until after the last war: modern adhesives were not used until the 1950s. The method you describe is roughly correct for softening the glue, but a better one is to lay a pad of damp blotting-paper on the work and leave an electric iron on it, checking progress every 10 minutes or so. The iron should be set at its lowest heat, and the purpose of the damp blotting-paper is to prevent scorching. You can also try prising up a piece of veneer and dropping in some warm vinegar with an eye-dropper, leaving it in the hope that it will soften the glue. It will probably mean up-ending the table so that the vinegar stays in the crevice.

You say that no repairs have been done since 1920: otherwise I would say that the top veneer had been removed and replaced with a modern veneer, laid with a modern adhesive (PVA or casein) for which there is no suitable solvent.

As the veneer is obviously well glued down, I would recommend removing the finish and sanding the top until you have a perfectly flat and level surface. Then lay a gaboon veneer right over it, grain lengthwise, using scotch glue, and lay out final veneers on to that once the glue has dried. Gaboon is easily obtainable and relatively cheap, being widely used as a counter-veneer. Use scotch glue for laying all veneers because it has a certain amount of flexibility to take up any movement, even when it has set; also, if you do make a mistake you can soften the glue and do the job again.

*Vic Taylor*

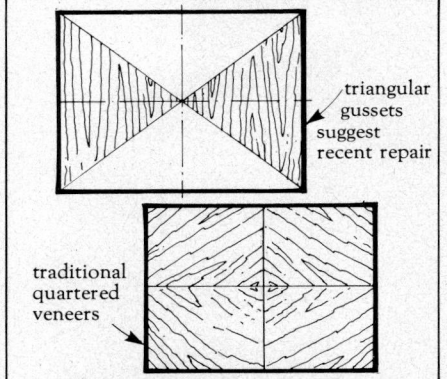

triangular gussets suggest recent repair

traditional quartered veneers

**Q** *Could you tell me how to make a long-hole-boring auger for my lathe? I have made one from a length of 7/32in steel rod, grinding a diamond-shaped point, but although it is sharp it only cuts slowly, with great effort and a lot of heat!*

*D. Greenall, Bromley*

**A** I don't think the tool you have made has enough cutting action — it would give a laborious scraping effect, which produces the heat and brings waste-removal problems.

For years I have used engineer's morse drills of the necessary diameter, attached to a suitable length of silver steel, slightly smaller in diameter so the clearance allows

waste to be removed. The lap-joint is formed by grinding and held by silver-soldering. The other end is filed to a long square pyramid to form a tang, and fitted into a file handle.

More modifications to the drill point can enhance the cutting action. Drawing A shows the cutting edge of the standard drill ground off to give a scraping action, which is suitable for very hard woods such as box and ebony (and even brass), while B shows the top of the drill ground away to make a point and wings, which improves the cutting action in most woods.

Probably the best cutting action of all comes from the shell auger (Record make one). It is best to run the lathe at about 1000rpm when deep-hole-boring, and you should withdraw the tool to empty the waste frequently so it does not overheat.

*Bob Grant DLC FRSA FSIAD*

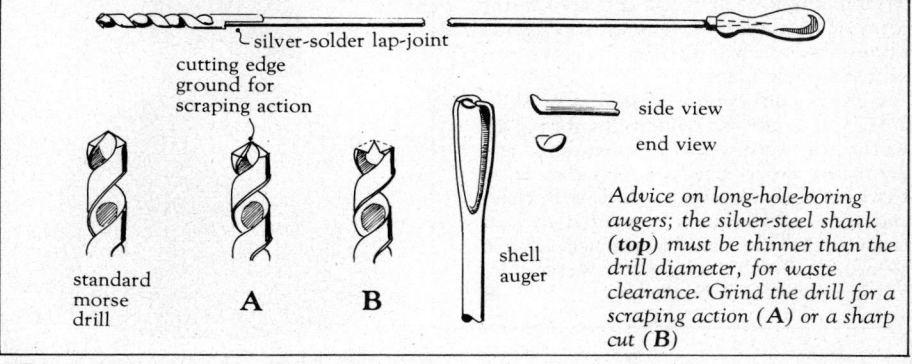

silver-solder lap-joint

cutting edge ground for scraping action

side view

end view

standard morse drill

**A**

**B**

shell auger

*Advice on long-hole-boring augers; the silver-steel shank (**top**) must be thinner than the drill diameter, for waste clearance. Grind the drill for a scraping action (**A**) or a sharp cut (**B**)*

**Q** *I would be very pleased if you could tell me where to get information on the density of home-grown hardwoods, particularly laburnum and lilac. I am using PEG (polyethylene glycol).*

*J. Stainrod, Barnsley*

**A** I know of no book that will give you the densities of the lesser-used woods, because they are not regarded as commercial timber trees. But you can easily obtain the information you need.

Weight of wood is properly assessed by weighing a sample, calculating its volume, and then dividing the weight by the volume, but this assumes the wood is conditioned to a certain degree of dryness before weighing.

You can obtain a rough idea of the weight of any wood by testing its specific gravity. Strictly speaking, if the SG is known, multiplying its value by 62.4lbs (the weight of a cubic foot of water) gives you the weight per cubic foot. For example: SG $0.6 \times 62.4 = 37$lbs per cubic foot. To do this under domestic conditions, take a small but regularly shaped cube of a given wood, place this gently in a basin or glass of water and estimate its displacement, i.e. the volume submerged below water-level. The result can be found from the following approximate table:

| | | | |
|---|---|---|---|
| Submerged volume: 25%: | SG is 0.25: | about | 16lbs/ft³ |
| 50%: | 0.50: | | 32lbs/ft³ |
| 75%: | 0.75: | | 47lbs/ft³ |
| Submerged, not sinking: | 1.0: | | 63+lbs/ft³ |
| Sinks readily: | 1.0+: | | 66+lbs/ft³ |

*Bill Brown FIWSc*

**Q** *While working in Taiwan recently, I ordered some unfinished carved wooden panels to my own design. Four of them depict the Chinese seasons with symbolic birds and flowers, and they are in carved fretwork panels about 24×15×¾in. Another four panels are relief carvings of temple and rural scenes; the maximum thickness of the relief is about ½in, and the panels are about 18in square. All the timber is very pale, and the grain gives me the idea that it's a species of mahogany. I would welcome advice on finishing the carvings, especially highlighting the deeper carved areas with dark stain.*

*P. J. Cartwright, Reading*

**A** You say your carved panels are of light mahogany, and for these I would use first a water-type stain such as Furniglas, manufactured by Evode Ltd, Common Road, Stafford ST16 3EH.

The stain can be applied by using a soft brush, a no. 6 mop or even a sponge, but care should be taken not to flood the carving as this could cause splitting. When the stain is nearly dry, use a darker shade applied with a pencil brush to the cavity sections of the carving, and leave to dry out.

When it is completely dry, a light rubbing over the high sections of the relief using 320-grade Lubrisil abrasive papers or 000 steel wool will highlight the carving.

To finish, use a liberal coating of raw linseed oil or teak oil and allow about 15 minutes for it to be absorbed before soaking up the surplus with kitchen paper. When this has dried into the wood, a further coating of the oil can be applied in the same way.

This treatment will give your carving the mature look that other finishes such as varnish or lacquer would not give, and the surface can be revived at any time by using a little oil to freshen it.

If you use teak oil, great care must be taken not to leave any swabs or cloths containing the oil in an enclosed area, or fire may result — this warning is printed on most tins of teak oil. Raw linseed oil will not present this problem.

Regular cleaning, using a soft 1½in brush to remove dust from deeper parts of the carving, will keep it in perfect condition.

*Noel Leach*

# Mr MacDonald had an idea

Chris MacDonald left teaching at Christmas 1983. Since then — helped in August 1984 by a government Enterprise Allowance — he has spent all his time developing the range of fantastical objects you see here.

At 46, he has no art or craft background except for a stint of repairing tobacco-pipes; but that taught him, he says, how to work quickly. He does not regard himself primarily as a turner: carving is his first love.

Perhaps unsurprisingly, sales and marketing are proving his biggest hurdle, and he feels that many would-be professional woodworkers must face similar difficulties to his. More than a year in the workshop, refining his creations, has been punctuated by unsuccessful attempts to find customers. Local craft fairs proved barren of sales, and it is only recently that a sizeable chink of light has appeared in the form of promised displays at two shops in London's Covent Garden — the very home of fashionable ideas.

Chris is a man whose creativity and skills are not in doubt, yet who finds entering the world of business a demanding and unsettling experience. Many readers must share his problems and hesitations. Both we and he would be very interested to hear from them. He can be reached at 206 Windmill Road, Gillingham, Kent ME7 5PE, tel. (0634) 576673. ∎

● **Above:** The brush is rosewood with horn bristles; the tube is mahogany; the paste is laminated from tulipwood and vulcanite

● A subsequent version, made by request, stands the brush and tube on a soap-dish of oak instead of the base shown here

● Mahogany scissors with a thread of basket-weaving cane

● **Right:** Recalling Chris MacDonald's training, the briar pipe sports a silver mount and vulcanite mouthpiece

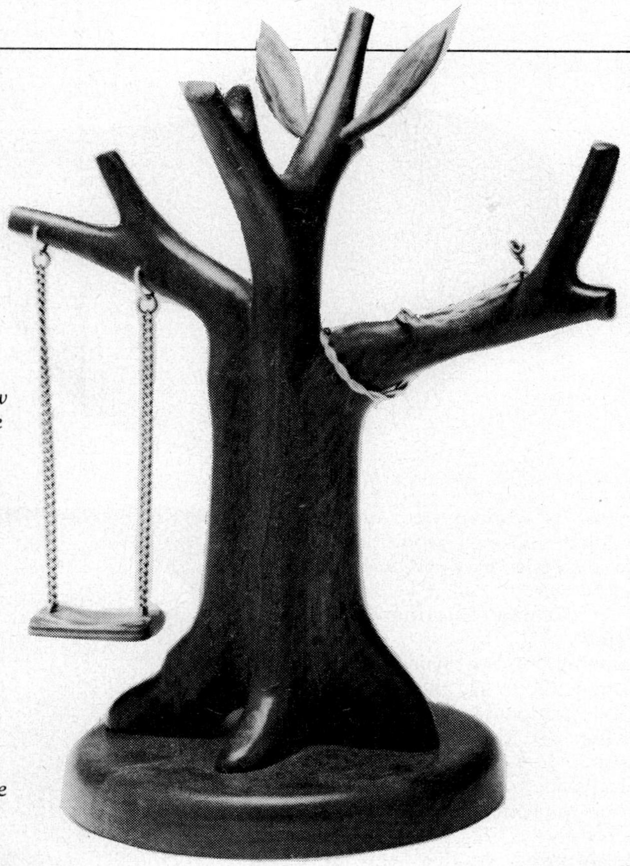

● *Made as a christening gift that the little girl would not grow out of, this jewellery tree is of mahogany with tulipwood leaves and seat; the chains and ivy are silver*

● ***Below:*** *The tap is mahogany again, but the water is horn*

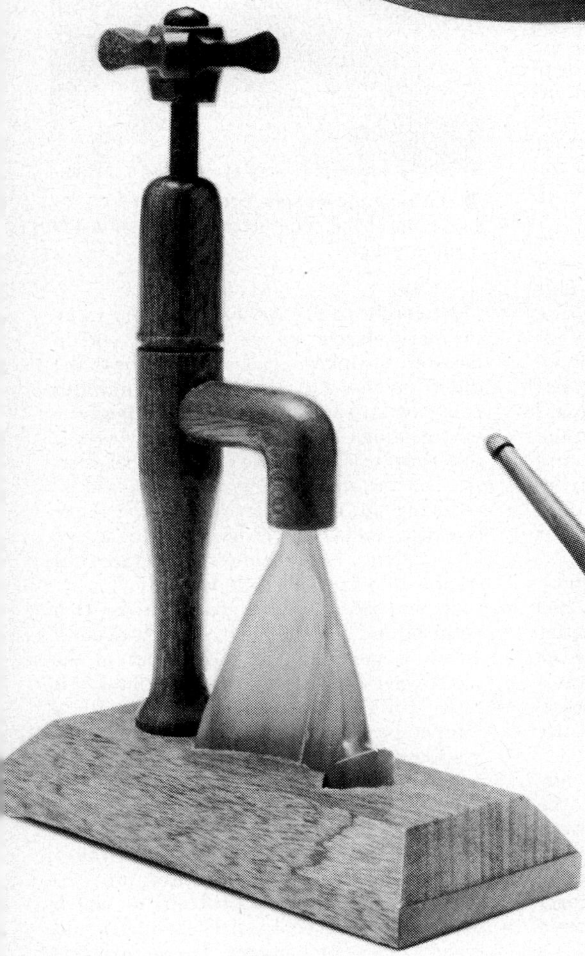

● ***Below:*** *The mahogany pincers give a final demonstration of their maker's fondness for carving. Further products include a 'quill' pen, ink-bottle and pen-knife – and a welding torch (with horn flame and vulcanite piping) and spark-plug: first shots in a campaign to interest corporate buyers who might want corporate gifts*

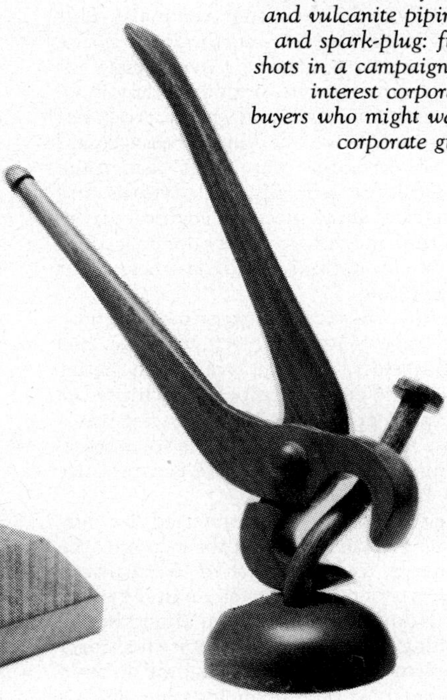

# COMING NEXT MONTH!

Could this be you? It certainly could — after you've read the July issue, with its fully detailed plans and instructions on how to make a working **pole lathe**.

Yet we'll also be featuring a whole collection of the craft's most up-to-date **chucking devices** — plus expert advice on **choosing lathe tools**.

And that's only the start. July's the month when we'll be bringing you detailed coverage of what **Scotland's woodworkers** are up to.

And there'll be a valuable survey of the woodworking **goodies you can buy through the post.**

**ON SALE 21 JUNE**

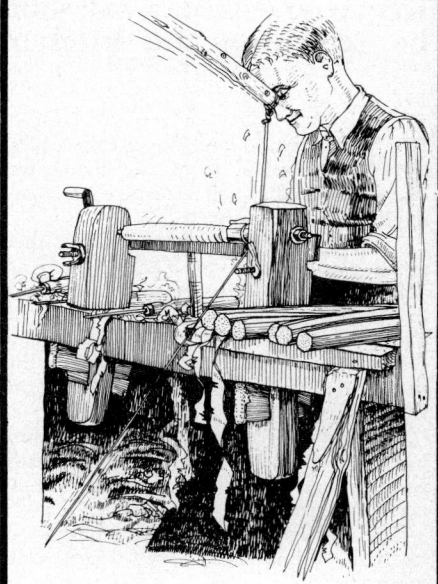

# Oven-ready timber

**Seasoning timber in 15 minutes? It's perfectly possible — in a microwave oven. Bruce Leadbeatter, the Australian behind the startling new process, tells why woodturners will soon be storming the kitchen**

● *All these pieces are micro-wave-seasoned. The cypress pine bowl was hand-shaped; the jewel box in red cedar has a two-pack polyurethane finish*

How would you like to take a piece of timber from the living tree through to the finished job in one day?

Traditionally, woodturners break their green wood down to blanks which are sealed and set aside to air-season for a year or so before turning. But it can be disappointing, after waiting all that time, to discover when you come to turn a piece that the section of burl you were contemplating is unusable because of hidden flaws.

Micro-wave seasoning makes it possible to reduce the time needed from 12 months to a few hours — or even minutes if the job is thinly turned!

The process provides a number of exciting advantages over traditional methods:
● It is very quick.
● 10 minutes in the oven softens the wood. This plasticising is similar in effect to steam-bending; a certain amount of shaping or forming is possible, which offers all sorts of design possibilities.
● The heat sterilises the wood, killing borers and fungi with no insecticide or fungicide problems.
● The usual seasoning difficulties presented by knots and pith are eliminated. The bark adheres firmly to the wood, again giving artistic possibilities.

● *The recess in the blank is made with a centreless cutter to beat shrinkage*

● Timber is worked wet, and is much softer than seasoned wood; really hard woods are easier to work, and tools stay sharper longer.
● Wet turning eliminates sawdust problems.

Seasoning timber using micro-waves seems unusual, to say the least, to people used to traditional methods of kiln- and air-drying. At the Sydney Institute of Education, however, the process is no longer considered experimental, and it has helped us to produce work of which we are very proud.

Woodworkers familiar with air-drying and its inherent problems of splitting and cracking can look forward to a new code of seasoning behaviour. For instance, in air-seasoning careful sealing of the endgrain is required to prevent checking and splitting, while with micro-wave drying this is unnecessary.

The story began when spiralling timber prices forced us to look for supplies of timber outside the usual channels. This forced us to look at unorthodox ways of doing our own seasoning. Developing a hot oil/wax process, we settled on 'cooking' green timber in a 7-litre domestic crock pot in 4 litres of olive oil, ½kg of beeswax and ½kg of carnauba wax. This was quite successful for seasoning salad forks and spoons, and small pieces of sculpture from green timber. Unfortunately the procedure has its limitations, and is messy for woodturning.

Luckily, we were also experimenting with micro-wave seasoning. At first we had mixed results, but an oven with better temperature control helped us achieve the breakthrough we needed. Our aim was a success rate at least as good as for normal seasoning. Now, happily, we can promise much better than that.

The way timber is converted for air-seasoning is fairly critical; for example, the pith needs to be eliminated. Micro-wave drying is much less restrictive. In the oven, the pith doesn't seem to know about the air-seasoning code of rules! Knots are no longer a problem — in fact they become an asset for turned work, enhancing the object's beauty.

● *Turning the outside form of a bowl on the face-plate chuck. The ribbon shaving indicates a sharp gouge*

Attempts to dry or season timber in an ordinary electric or gas oven will end in disaster. Shrinkage will simply occur in the outer layers, and within a few minutes checking and splitting will have ruined the whole thing. The secret of micro-waves is that they heat the inside of the timber first, so that the moisture is driven outwards, reducing the tension stresses in the outer layers to a much lower level than in air- or kiln-drying. Checking and splitting are thus responsible for very little waste.

Experiments do indicate, however, that splitting and checking will certainly occur if steam is generated in the timber in the microwave oven. A temperature of 80°C is best for success, and you need a temperature dial or some other system of graduating the settings. Micro-waves do not generally penetrate more than 25mm, so pre-turning gives better results and also reduces the seasoning time.

Turning the timber, micro-wave-seasoning it and then re-mounting it on the face-plate presented a problem to which traditional or even special face-plates and chucks offered no answer. The solution we developed was to make a centreless cutter

that bores a shallow recess in the base of the bowl. An expanding face-plate chuck simply locks into the recess, so that the job can be concentrically fixed or removed by turning it clockwise or counter-clockwise. When the timber shrinks during seasoning, the recess in the base is trimmed with the cutter in a drill-press. Patents have been applied for in respect of the face-plate chuck, which the Woodfast Machinery Co. (an Australian group) is planning to manufacture and export.

During early experiments, an electric moisture meter was used to measure equilibrium moisture content (EMC) so we knew when the wood was correctly seasoned. But the holes from the probes made this impractical on turned work, so we resorted to weighing the turned job until it stopped losing weight. This solution is tedious but workable. Shrinkage, of course, only occurs when moisture is evaporating from the cell walls, so it didn't take us long to work out that when normal shrinkage had happened, the timber was seasoned. In fact it is just coincidence that the time at which the recess in the bowl's base will not fit back on the chuck is the time the timber has reached EMC.

● *The face-plate chuck locks into the recess, which can be re-drilled if it has shrunk*

## Micro-wave methods

There are two distinct ways of using the microwave oven to season turning work. The first involves turning the green blank to finished size, then seasoning it; the second way is to turn the job oversize to allow for shrinkage and warping, season it, and then re-mount it and turn it to finished size.

● *Above:* A bowl in the oven – but it's not the contents cooking! 10 minutes at 'Defrost' first; the bursts of heat must be shorter after the bowl has cooled. *Below:* 'Plastic wood' takes on a new meaning; *right*, unwanted warping is corrected in a press

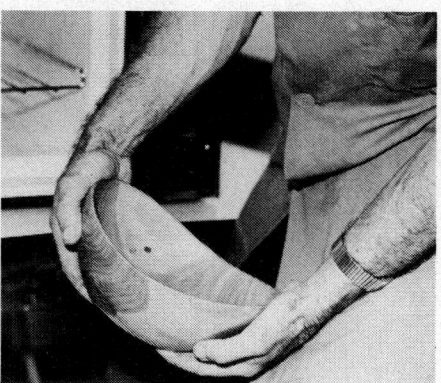

### Rapid method

1 Drill the recess in the green timber blank with the cutter supplied with the Woodfast face-plate chuck.
2 Mount the blank on the face-plate chuck and turn it to its final size, with a wall thickness of 8mm or less.
3 Place the job in the micro-wave oven and heat for 10 minutes at 'Defrost', then allow it to cool for 10 minutes.
4 Return the job to the lathe for smooth sanding. The bowl should still fit on the chuck, as long as the moisture has not been dried out of the cell walls; this is when all the shrinkage happens.
5 Return the bowl to the microwave oven; give it five minutes on 'Defrost', then allow it to cool. If the rim of the bowl warps, you can press it back into shape with your hand while the wood is still hot and relatively plastic.
6 Repeat this step three or more times until the wood is seasoned. Give it an artistic touch, if you want, by moulding the shape by hand!

7 If additional sanding, polishing or finishing is required, re-drill the recess for chucking, re-mount it on the face-plate chuck, and complete the project.

### Standard method

1 Drill the recess in the green timber with the cutter.
2 Mount the green timber on the Woodfast face-plate chuck and rough-turn it to a wall thickness of 15mm or less, depending on the anticipated shrinkage.
3 Place the semi-turned job in the microwave oven and heat for 10 minutes on 'Defrost'. Pressing or clamping the timber while it's still hot can eliminate cupping and bowing.
4 Remove the work from the oven and allow it to cool for 10 minutes.
5 Repeat the heating/cooling process — five minutes' heating, 10 minutes' cooling — until the wood is fully seasoned. If fine surface-checking occurs, the wood is too dry. A large bowl with thick walls could take two hours to dry; one with 6mm walls will take only 20 minutes.
6 The shrinkage will make it necessary to re-drill the recess in the base for re-chucking before final turning and finishing.

● Bruce Leadbeatter's address is: Sydney Institute of Education, PO Box 63, Camperdown, NSW 2050, Australia, tel. (02) 660 2855.
● The Woodfast Machinery Co. is at 912 Port Road, Woodville, South Australia 5011, Australia.

# A butterfly in the grain

## Ivan Broadhead went to visit a new maker — who's already incising his own mark!

The mouse of Kilburn and the acorn of Brandsby are well-known Yorkshire cabinetmakers' trademarks. Now there is the butterfly of Whixley.

The butterfly has been adopted by Andrew Conning, of Tancred Cottage, Whixley, near York, as he starts out in his own woodworking business.

'It took a lot of thought before I hit on the butterfly,' says 21-year-old Andrew. 'I decided I had to have an emblem that no other cabinetmaker uses — yet it also had to be comparatively easy to carve. Nothing that a child could accomplish, but something which I wouldn't have to spend too much time on.'

Andrew is a former pupil of King James School, Knaresborough, where he admits his main scene of achievement was the woodwork room. After leaving at 16 he went to Acorn Industries at Brandsby, where he served his five-year apprenticeship and continued building up the collection of woodworking tools which he had started when he was 11.

He took the plunge of independence in August 1983 and set up business in a 24×18ft shed which had been acquired a couple of years earlier. Funds for the launch of the enterprise came through the good offices of a relative who worked for an international printing firm in York. They required repairs to broken wooden pallets used for stacking paper and publications. Andrew, helped by his father (who works on a nearby estate), repaired literally thousands of pallets, and was able to purchase two sawbenches, a planer and a mortiser as well as numerous hand tools.

'I started basically by saving money, not wasting money; not boozing it, not smoking it, and generally being cautious,' says Andrew. Husbanding his cash flow like this, and with a willingness to tackle anything from furniture to joinery and barn doors to garden gates, he has built a foundation for success.

'I've succeeded for over a year and kept my head above water. I think the biggest problem with lads starting out is that they want to do furniture. They seem to want to say, "Forget anything else, I'm a cabinetmaker." You just can't do that. You

● *This oak table is headed for Germany*

have to keep money coming in. You can't say, "I'm a cabinetmaker, I won't make you a window" — because if you can make furniture you can make a window: it's a doddle!'

But Andrew's furniture-making skills were quickly recognised, and as a result he has already completed his first export order. This was an oak draw-leaf table measuring 8×3ft open and 5×3ft closed.

His first commission was for a two-piece display cabinet unit in teak with glass doors, and after that his reputation began to spread by word of mouth. 'You get a relative or a customer, they tell a friend, and so it goes on. About 80% of my business comes from personal recommendations.'

As a result he is now able to show photographs of completed work which includes an oak Welsh dresser, a refectory table, 6ft-high glass-fronted and open-fronted oak corner cupboards, coffee-tables, video and television cabinets, stools, lamps, breadboards and kitchen units.

● *Andrew Conning carves a house name-plate*

Each item is signed with the distinctive butterfly emblem, which Andrew sees as a great asset if not an essential marketing tool. 'We thought about it for months, really going through various things which I might put on,' he recalls. 'My wife wanted me to use a Siamese cat, because she's a cat-lover, but I didn't think that really went with it. So we considered a snail, but I thought that would make people think I was slow and really cause some mickey-taking. We went

## 'I don't like modern stuff — it's kids' stuff'

through literally everything — but it doesn't look right with a pig's head or a cow, does it? So you forget them straight away. But you need something to differentiate one woodworker from another.'

Just to demonstrate how devoted he is to his emblem, Andrew has now embarked on carving an oak wall light in the form of a butterfly, though at present he is only intending this for his own use.

● *The unique butterfly trade-mark*

'I don't think it's right to make a one-off, making a new design and charging the customer for me to work it out. But, if I do it for myself and get it sorted out first, I can work a price from that.'

All his designs are his own, and based on traditional styles. 'I don't like modern stuff — it's kid's stuff,' he claims.

He adds: 'You have to keep the standard high, and you'll find that customers appreciate it and are willing to pay accordingly. They're fed up with factory-built, mass-produced, self-assembly furniture.'

## 'If you can make furniture you can make a window: it's a doddle!'

Despite his undoubted success Andrew still views the future cautiously, and thinks in terms of half his business being in furniture and the remainder in joinery; but he yearns to produce furniture exclusively. With this aim in mind he is contemplating an appearance ultimately at the Great Yorkshire Show; nevertheless, he feels he must first cut his teeth on a smaller scale.

Above all, Andrew has his eye firmly fixed on excellence. 'Someone starting has to have good-quality stuff — tools, timber. I find that I can get exactly what I require from John Boddy Timber in Boroughbridge, which is only about six miles away, and Geoffrey Etherington of Hutton Sessay near Thirsk has a fantastic range of polishes, waxes and stains.

'Quotations are a big problem for the newcomer. I found it very hard working out a price for a piece of furniture. Now I work out the price of the timber to the nearest fiver and then guess how long it will take to cut out, plane, polish and so on. Then I add my hourly labour charge and end up with a good calculated guess. You can't just jump in as a nobody and charge top whack, and you get more realistic with practice.'

Practice is something of which he's getting plenty; and as for realism, he already has a head start. ■

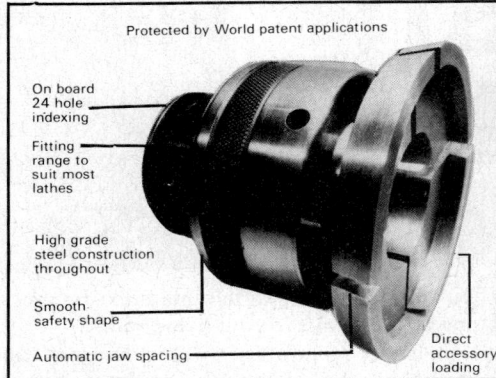

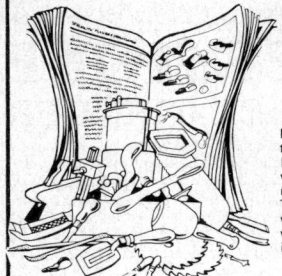

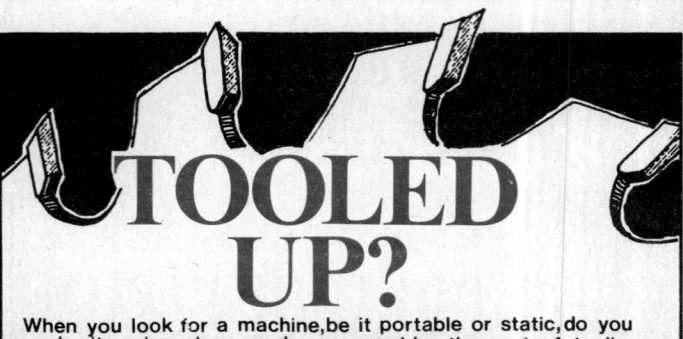

Prices quoted are those prevailing at press date and are subject to alteration due to economic conditions.

# Guild notes

## London Gallery

First news this month is members' opportunity to display their work at the Woodworker Show in October. It was mentioned last month, but just so you don't forget — we have a space about 20×8ft in which to show pieces made by members. It costs nothing to exhibit, and the area is booked on a first-come-first-served basis. Small furniture, carvings, in fact any compact woodworking creations are what we are looking for; the advantage to you need not be emphasised. Space is limited, so *act now*; send some photos of the pieces you would like to show, and we will put them before the panel of Guild-approved judges. The limit will be two or three small pieces per person.

## Antique restoration

West Dean College is inviting applications for its one-year course in furniture restoration, beginning in September. You must be over 18, be able to show you are skilled in woodwork, and have a high standard of training in cabinetmaking. On top of that, you must be keenly interested in antiques, and have the necessary dedication and patience for the work. The emphasis is on 'training at the bench', using genuine pieces from the 16th to early 19th centuries. Run in league with the British Antique Dealers' Association, the course gives you a West Dean/BADA diploma.
- Information and application forms from the principal, West Dean College, West Dean, Chichester, W. Sussex PO18 0QZ, tel. (0243 63) 301.

## Local reps

These members have offered to co-ordinate the first meeting of Guild members in their areas.

**Dumfries** Peter St D. Boddy, Valdheim, Hetland, Carrutherstown, DG1 4JX.
**West Yorks** Edgar Lawrance, Kimberley, Carr Lane, South Kirby, Pontefract.
**South Yorks** Ken Davies, 27 Ennis Crescent, Intake, Doncaster DN2 5LL.
**Sheffield** Michael Judge, 8 Haden St, Sheffield S6 4LB.
**Merseyside** H. H. Bridge, 2 Ashley Rd, Southport PR9 0RB.
**Norfolk** Steven Hurrell, 70 Decoy Cottages, Woodbastwick.
**Herefordshire** Paul Smith, Dinmaur, Hope under Dinmore, Leominster HR6 0PP.
**Bedfordshire** John Greenwell, 1 Plum Tree Lane, Leighton Buzzard.
**Middlesex** Mike Cripps, 41 The Greenway, Ickenham UB10 8LS.
**Wiltshire** David Ellis, Restorations Unlimited, Pinkney Park, Malmesbury.
**Surrey** Morrison Thomas, 3 Oak Tree Close, Knap Hill, Woking GU21 2SA.
**Essex** Doug Woolgar, 49 Ascot Gardens, Hornchurch RM12 6ST.
**Kent** Bob Holman, Copley Dene, 8 Kippington Rd, Sevenoaks.
**Sussex** P. D. Wetherill, 'Glasfryn', Colebrook Rd, Southwick, Brighton BN4 4AL.
**Cornwall** Mr Stoddern, South West Cabinetmaking, 16 Woods Browning Estate, Bodmin.
Let's hear from some more!

## COURSE CORNER
### Finishing and polishing

6-7 June, £40 inc. VAT. Surface preparation, introduction to materials, cabinet scraper, staining, filling, bodying up, spiriting off. The popularity of these courses shows what good value they are. **Charles Cliffe's** advice on your own furniture problems is also a big attraction.

### Finishing and polishing

29-30 June; in Chester, taught by the Guild's new northern expert in this popular subject. **Ian Hosker** is a teacher at a technical college, and runs his own restoration business. The hours will be 10-5, with an hour for lunch; subjects covered will be materials, preparation, cabinet scraper, stains, filling, fadding, bodying and spiriting, and restoring polished surfaces.
- £45 for the two days, including the materials that Ian supplies. Please add £8 for a 'polishing kit' which you can take away with you. **Cheques for the full amount confirm booking.**

### Special toolmaking — Fred Lambert

15-19 July 1985, £145+VAT. Country Chairmaking; a course on making the special tools for the job. These rounders and trapping planes are not available on the general market, so the only way you can have your own is to make them.

## Cabinetmaker's decorative techniques

20 July 1985, St Augustine's of Canterbury School, Oxford. **Bob Grant** will go into advanced techniques, covering curved inlay lines, making and setting in motifs, sand shading and decorative chamfering. These are traditional processes mostly using the scratch-stock, and this day's course is independent of previous instruction.
- The day is 9.30-5, and costs £27.50 + VAT. **Cheque for the full amount confirms booking.**

## Hand veneering

14 September 1985, also at St Augustine's School, an introduction to traditional techniques. **Bob Grant** will give an introductory talk, show samples and demonstrate techniques; then you make your own veneered panel, a centre square surrounded by a cross-veneered border with mitred corners, and balanced on the back. **Peter Sarac**, a harpsichord maker who has worked for Robert Gable and is now running his own business, will be there as well to advise and demonstrate.

- Again 9.30-5, £30+VAT. If you've got a veneer hammer, bring it! As with all courses, **a cheque for the full amount gets you the booking.**

## Furniture restoration

25-26 July, in **Eric Burger's** own professional workshop in Bournemouth. Eric reckons to introduce: repairs to furniture including glues and finishes; veneers; inlaying bandings, including brass; marquetry; traditional cabinetmaking methods; preparation for french polish, and polishing itself; gilding; wax polishing; and carving. Eric has wide professional and teaching experience, having run his own highly reputed business for many years.
- £40+VAT for the two busy days, 9.30-5; this includes the cost of some basic materials like french polish. **Cheque for full amount confirms booking.**

## Woodmachining — Ken Taylor

6 July, £25+VAT. Booking for the March course went slowly, so **Ken Taylor** and Bruce Pollard have kindly agreed to put the date back to a summer Saturday. I must emphasise that Bruce is letting us use his demonstration machinery at his Bletchley Woodworking Centre as a favour, and it is not a thinly disguised sales scheme — impartiality is guaranteed. Ken will take you through the basics of safety with workshop machinery, and introduce you to the table-saw, bandsaw, radial-arm saw, planer/thicknesser, mortiser and spindle moulder. The universal machine figures largely in the day too.

# The carver and his divers

**Guy Taplin carves birds for a living in the remote Essex marshes. Aidan Walker looks at his work**

'I don't really call myself a craftsman,' says Guy Taplin, the creator of these graceful wooden wildfowl. 'What I try and achieve is a theatrical effect.'

Inspired by the old American decoy-makers and long contemplations of the ducks in Regent's Park where he worked as a wildfowl keeper, Guy started carving ducks from driftwood that came up the Thames, using only a sharpened Estwing axe. He took a riverside workshop in Rotherhithe at the time work was starting on the Thames flood barrier, and baulks as big as 12in square by 20ft long would float by. 'It was as much as I could do to drag them into the workshop — I could just about put them through the bandsaw if I took the top guide off.' He uses a Startrite 352, 'a great tool', the only piece of standing machinery he has.

Moving out to Essex five years ago, he set himself up in his cottage basement where he does most of the cutting, grinding, shaping and sanding. His birds' necks are dowelled and glued on to their bodies; he likes to amass a week's work of painting, burning, waxing and finishing, and take it all down to his beach-hut workshop right on the edge of the marshes — away from children and telephone.

'I wouldn't know what to do with new wood'; all his material is picked up from the beach. Weird and wonderful shapes, abraded by sea and sand, are not really what he looks for, apart from the odd *objet trouvé* which suggests itself as a base. 6×3s and 9×4s are plentiful on this stretch of the coast, at the mouth of the river Colne. He finds unusual tropical hardwoods that Far-Eastern shippers use for packing and storing goods on deck, plus the more ordinary mahogany, oak, teak, elm and a variety of pines.

He doesn't pre-draw designs, outlining the shapes straight on to the wood and cutting from there. 'The less I think about what I'm doing the better — you don't get in the way of what's coming out. I tend to work fairly fast anyway, so I don't have much time to think.' Speed he counts as an important factor, because he's not short of work, which is why he likes the bandsaw so

> **'I don't feel I want to capture every detail. I want to capture their spirit, I suppose'**

much. He can make five or six grebes a week, for instance; many of his orders are for the US market, where interior designers looking for unusual decoration are plentiful and well-funded. An average retail price is £400, often with 100% mark-up.

'Excess wood is removed with grinders and files or contour sanders. When I arrive

at the finished shape I burn the wood, as I like the texture. I fill the holes with Tetrion — although I'm sure it's not as flexible and waterproof as they say it is. I've been meaning to ring them up and have a chat about that. Then I paint the whole thing, leaving grainy areas showing. I wire-wool or paper the paint down when it's dry, and sometimes paint again and again. I use the grain to suggest the pattern of the feathers, and keep going over the surface, bringing out the most interesting features.

'I've made ducks, swans, geese, owls, crows, ravens, rooks, shore-birds, egrets, ibis, herons, songbirds and various animals. I've always had a great love of water, particularly the sea; many of the shades and colours I see around me when I'm in my beach workshop I reproduce in my work.'

He uses a Ronson gas blowtorch for burning, and water-based emulsions for painting because oils take too long to dry and could present fire problems. His approach to self-evaluation is refreshingly straightforward. 'My techniques are terribly basic; nearly anyone making birds who really wants to can achieve a very good result in a short time. The American carvers nowadays use techniques derived from decoy-making, burning or carving literally each follicle of each feather; all I'm really after is a smooth profile. I grew up as a Jack-of-all-trades' (his CV includes messenger-boy, meat-porter, street-vendor and cook) 'and I think a lot of artists' and craftpeople's mystique is more to do with ego than talent.'

> **'The fact that my materials have knocked about for a while and already had a life before I came across them is somehow very important to me'**

For all his blunt, workmanlike attitudes, there is clearly the spirit of an artist in Guy Taplin. Encouraged to sign his work when he started exhibiting at the Portal Gallery in London, he was uneasy, feeling that it was unnatural to write his name on the birds. 'It seemed to me they'd come into being without me — I was just an instrument for making them.'

● An exhibition of Guy Taplin's work is showing from 25 May till 20 June at the Craft Shop, Victoria & Albert Museum, London SW7, tel. 01-589 5070. We would like to thank *Crafts* magazine for their help in preparing this article.

> **'I haven't yet come across anything in animal life which both inspires me and intrigues me as ducks do'**

**All photos Graham Portlock/*Crafts* magazine**

● *Guy Taplin's waterfowl seem to have swum in, literally fully fledged, from their surroundings. At **right** is a red-throated diver; **below right** are a red-breasted merganser (at right in photo) and a duck; while **below** are two whooper swans. Preening **opposite**, in black and white, are a pair of pintail ducks*

# A cabinetmaker confesses

**The second exclusive extract from Alan Peters' important new book *Cabinetmaking: The Professional Approach***

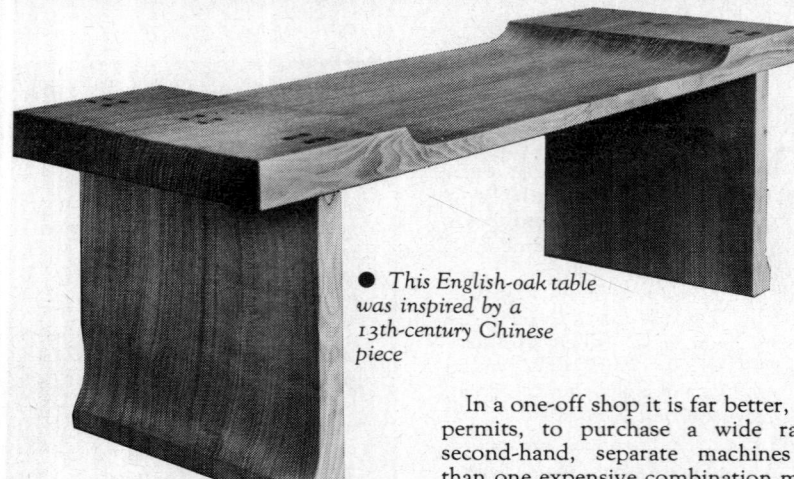

● *This English-oak table was inspired by a 13th-century Chinese piece*

My eagerness to install machinery might appear paradoxical in view of my nostalgic feelings for my pre-machine-age apprenticeship days, but I had no desire to live in poverty, and also I soon began to enjoy the challenge and scope for design that the machinery presented. During my time at the London Central School of Arts & Crafts I had used, for instance, a large overhead pad-sander of the type used frequently in industry before they were superseded by speed sanders. I had seen that it could do if operated well with a sensitive hand, and so we soon had one installed at Grayshott. That was in 1964, and it is still going strong in Devon today, having been built to last way back in 1928.

Despite some misgivings about the wider use of machinery and its implications for creative work, I know that I personally enjoy many of the machine operations. I like the speed with which the raw material can be transformed into workable sizes and components. I also like to exploit the potential for design that each new item of equipment I purchase throws up. Here I must stress that many of my designs of recent years would not have been logical, sensible or even conceived without the equipment I have at my fingertips.

Because I am chiefly engaged in working to commission, and therefore do much one-off work, machining takes up less than a fifth of my time and that of my assistants.

In order to have relative peace and quiet and a dust-free atmosphere for the remainder of our time, most of the machines are housed across the yard in a separate machine shop. Unfortunately, one item of equipment tends now to destroy this scheme, and that is the portable router. For years I resisted its intrusion into our quiet world of cabinetmaking, and never had one in the shop; eventually I relented, as its usefulness and versatility became all too apparent. I do have now an overhead table router in the machine shop, which relieves some of the problem, but the portable one still gets picked up and shatters the eardrums — simply because it is so easy to operate on the workpiece itself, rather than taking the work to the machine. Frankly, I still hate it and wish it had not been invented, although I have the quietest one on the market. One of my next projects will be to develop an adjoining store into a soundproof area just to house this monster, and the work will simply have to be carried in there. All this, of course, only becomes necessary when more than one person is using a workshop, for it is always the other guy's router which is irritating, not the one that you yourself are using.

The major decision one does have to make, however, on setting up and choosing equipment and machinery is whether you intend to concentrate on providing a service with a one-off shop (whether it be reproduction, restoration or creative work, or working for other designers, is immaterial), or whether it is a production workshop, producing in quantity either to your own or someone else's design. It is possible over the years to dabble a little in both, but I am convinced after 20 years that for success one must make this distinction and decide what one's shop is really about.

If working in the former, you may well survive for several years with very little machinery, and sub-contract work like veneering and planing quite successfully, although this may depend on the location of your workshop. Secondly, although grant aid may change one's view, second-hand machines are often quite adequate; in fact, it is often hard to justify installing expensive new equipment when most of it will be lying idle for much of the time. I have only recently replaced a second-hand panel saw that I purchased from a scrap merchant for £7.50 18 years ago with another second-hand machine.

In a one-off shop it is far better, if space permits, to purchase a wide range of second-hand, separate machines rather than one expensive combination machine, which is nothing but a nuisance in a busy workshop. These are the items of equipment I have collected over the past 20 years, predominantly to assist me and my three assistants in providing a design and making service:

● A three-screw veneer press — second-hand, 1966; sited in cabinet shop.
● A 10ft (3.05m) pad- or stroke-sander, built in 1928, bought for £100 in 1966; sited in finishing area of cabinet shop.
● A 9in (228mm) precision sawbench — new; sited in cabinet shop.
● A floor-mounted drill-press with various sanding attachments — new, 1966; sited in cabinet shop.
● A 10in (254mm)-dia. separate disc sander — new, 1968.
● A dust-collector for the pad-sander.
● Floor-to-ceiling timber racks — one to house 8×4ft (2.44×1.22m) sheets; one to store timber in constant use, e.g. ½in (12mm) oak and cedar for drawer-making.
● Timber racks for oddments, arranged by species.
● An overhead router — second-hand.
● A woodturning lathe — second-hand.
● A planer-grinder — second-hand.
● A spindle-moulder — second-hand.
● A 21×9in (534×228mm) thickness planer — bought second-hand in 1966 for £25.

● *Kirkham House, Paignton, is home to this chest in Devon oak, with letter-carving by Ronald Parsons and specially made wrought-iron hinges*

- A twin dust-collector connected to both planers, spindle-moulder and circular saw.
- A 15×72in (380×1830mm) surface planer — bought second-hand in 1980 for £150.
- A hollow-chisel mortiser — second-hand.
- A 12in (305mm) sliding-table panel saw with tilting arbor — second-hand.
- An 18in (456mm) bandsaw, new, replacing in 1981 my second-hand one bought in 1962.
- A large portable dust-collector used on the 9in (228mm) circular-saw sanding-disc, and as needed in the cabinet shop.

Portable power tools:
- Electric chainsaw — new.
- Crosscut — new.
- Small router — new.
- Small jigsaw — new.
- 3in (76mm) plane — new.

- Compressor and spraygun — second-hand.

I might add that all this, which includes two 5hp motors, operates off single-phase electricity supply, three-phase being too far away and therefore too expensive to instal. It has never caused me any problem, except that it does limit me to second-hand equipment in many instances, where the motors can simply be replaced by single-phase.

Now, all this second-hand equipment that has cost me relatively little over the years does need nursing along, but it is perfectly adequate until one starts thinking in terms of quantity production. Its weakness is readily apparent as soon as any quantity of repetitive work is undertaken, where accuracy from the machines is of the utmost importance, and where any one machine may be working solidly for many hours non-stop.

- **Right:** *The end view of a wych-elm dining-table; note that the heart side is on the top surface.*
**Below:** *is a Korean-inspired piece in white and olive ash – with a deep-blue interior!*

This is why the decision as to what your shop is really about is so important. It is pointless and expensive to install, for example, a new 36in (915mm) planer if one is going to finish up making chairs or toast-racks with a width of no more than 3 or 4in (76-100mm).

I am convinced that in cabinet work, as opposed to, say, country chairmaking, when quantity production is required one must not skimp on equipment. It must be sturdy, of the best make and preferably new, or at least comparatively so. Do-it-yourself toys and lightweight machines are fine for the amateur and useful in one-off shops, but they are completely unsuitable for any production work. Thus anyone thinking in terms of batch production must allow for considerable outlay on equipment from the outset. A very useful, simply written book on wood-machining for craftsmen is *Machine Woodworking Technology for Hand Woodworkers* by F. E. Sherlock, published by Butterworth.

- *Cabinetmaking: The Professional Approach* is published by Stobart & Son, 67-73 Worship St, London EC2A 2EL, tel. 01-247 0501, at £15 plus £1.75 p&p. ∎

# LIFE WITH THE LATHE

**Buying any machine brings its own agonies. And for the woodturner — beginner or professional — the right lathe is everything. We asked no fewer than 11 of the UK's top turners what lathes they use, and why; what modifications they have made; and what advice they can give. Here are their answers**

## CECIL JORDAN

The first turning I ever did was at school on a treadle lathe — a good exercise in co-ordination for a growing lad. The tools were awful and I was taught with more enthusiasm than expertise, but I was soon hooked. This lathe was subsequently replaced by an electrically driven screw-cutting machine, donated by a parent. It had a mass of cogs which I never understood properly, which were supposed to form something called a 'chain of gears'. It had a slide and a device for holding the cutting tool, making everything very predictable — no challenge here.

When I became a pupil in a turner's shop I was first put on a woodturning lathe mounted on something closely resembling a chest-of-drawers. Everyone started on this machine; past users eyed the newcomer with interest and compassion. It must have given rise to the now well-known saying that woodturners work to the nearest half-inch. Its unpredictability was legendary and it embodied the dispensable aspects of both ancient and modern. It had, however, one priceless legacy — if you could turn anything on that lathe you could reckon you had unknowingly developed a skill beyond the ordinary.

The prized lathe in the shop, quite rightly, was a Fenn. The only original thing about it was the machine head, a massive affair half the size of a wheelbarrow, bolted to a pair of iron H-section girders which would have held up a cathedral. These in turn were secured to two blocks of concrete which had been initially poured into tea-chests, then had bolts set in while still wet. Under normal circumstances it was, and probably still is, the most stable lathe I have ever used. There was an added delight; the motor had some fancy windings that allowed the speed to be changed without stopping the machine. With a nonchalant flick of the lever, the speed could be increased or decreased. Time had wrought changes, however, and the lever tended to be a bit 'easier' than it had been. I vividly recall an unfortunate turner swinging an elm bowl 16×5in and moving sharply from 'slow' to 'fast' (the speed for eggcups and bobbins). The effect was impressive. A high-pitched whine developed which rapidly became supersonic, audible only to domestic animals and bats. The air was filled with dust, shavings, old sandwiches and dried insects.

The concrete raft of the workshop floor showed signs of take-off, and the local colony of bats took flight in broad daylight,

assuming the Day of Reckoning was at hand. We all fought for the limited available cover, or blundered — eyes streaming — through the door. Someone reached through the window and poked the main switch off with a stick. The whine became audible again, assumed a lower register, and finally whispered to a tangible silence. There was a smell of incense and hot dustbins. Various opinions were expressed, and amid nervous laughter the survivors emerged. The bats returned. I made the same mistake myself three days later.

To set up a workshop on one's own, following such rich and varied experience, could only be a thing pale by comparison. One fact above all others I had learned; vibration is the turner's worst enemy. Massive castings, concrete blocks, impeccable bearings — these are the considerations that come first.

The house was awash with catalogues of new machines, journals offering second-hand deals, friends (and others) offering advice and lathes. I finally opted for a Harrison Graduate short-bed. I knew that I didn't want to make chairs or four-poster beds, and 14in between centres with a 19in swing looked adequate. It took up little floor-space, it was available with a single-phase motor, and you could balance an old penny on edge on the domed casing while it

● *Wormy but beautiful – a sycamore bowl by Don White (photo Tony Marsh)*

was running at full speed. I have been able to plain-turn anything I wanted to make on this lathe; I have demonstrated it dozens of times to literally thousands of people; I have changed a belt after eight years and the bearings after 10.

The snags? The mandrel is too low — it should ideally be at elbow height or slightly above, so the lathe needs blocking up or you need to dig a well to stand in. The long rest won't reach round the back of the largest bowl, and I don't like the hinge fixings on the bottom door or the top cover. I was glad not to have replaced the bearings myself the first time — Harrisons sent an engineer. It's not difficult, but you need to know the wrinkles, and have a few drifts and blocks of the right sizes.

Would I buy it again? No doubt about it.

● *Fitted with a bowl-turning attachment, the Coronet Hobby lathe will accept pieces up to 380mm in diameter. It has a ½hp motor and three speeds of 480, 1100 and 2000rpm*

## DON WHITE

Apart from the standard range of domestic ware that I produce (from small scoops up to large 19in diameter bowls), to call myself a woodturner I must be prepared to tackle anything from small knobs and finials for antique restorers to long spindles and newel-posts for builders and architects.

For large-diameter work I use a Harrison Graduate lathe, originally a bowl-turning machine, bought second-hand about seven years ago. The design meant I could only turn on the outboard end, which would have meant changing a style and technique it had taken me a long time to get right on the 'proper' side; so I decided to convert it

extended the bed on my Avon. Previously I had turned them in sections, but sometimes, when the design didn't permit that, I lost the job. A quick consultation with Tyme Machines, half a day lengthening my bench, and I was in business. I was now able to turn 7ft between centres. I must admit to having been a little apprehensive when the time came to switch on, but the rigid construction of the Avon — combined with the solid bench I had built — was more than a match for the piece of 7ft×4insq stuff that was happily whizzing round with very little vibration. I even permitted myself a bit of showing off, and balanced a 50p piece on the bed bars!

giving me the chance to learn a new trade. The extra space will allow me to improve and expand my woodturning courses. For this purpose I plan to buy a Tyme Avon mkII — plus a Tyme Cub, which I regard as an ideal lathe for the beginner.

When you are making your first purchase, look for a lathe of rigid construction that will give you a range of speeds, and that has a broad range of accessories which you can add as you become more proficient. Consider buying a machine with a little more capacity than you might need, as you can bet you will be asked to turn something bigger than you first envisaged. Another point is that if you have to stop turning, or want to dispose of your lathe to progress to something bigger and better, a good-quality machine will fetch a better price and be easier to sell on the second-hand market.

## REG SLACK

Let me start by saying that I emphatically do not suggest you rush out and buy the lathes I mention. To recommend a lathe to someone to whom I have not spoken would be like trying to forecast the weather. Each lathe has its good and bad points, so you have to buy one that suits your personal needs.

As a full-time woodturning instructor I have to have lathes that will work all day and stand being (unintentionally) misused by students who have never worked a lathe before. It's not unlike a learner driver trying to sort out the gears in a car. The handling of the lathe and the use of the tools can only come with practice, and the lathe must be within the size and price that you can afford.

My first choice must be the Coronet Elf, with the Coronet Major for the more ambitious. The second choice (which I also have in my workshop) is the Tyme Cub, with the Tyme Avon for the more ambitious. My advice to anyone buying a lathe is to go for a model for which the manufacturer makes accessories. Both Coronet and Tyme produce very wide ranges. Accessories should include such things as face-plates, woodscrew chucks, long-hole-boring kits, collet chucks with expanding jaws, and drill chucks.

Each make of lathe has a different thread on the head-stock. From the manufacturer's point of view this is good business sense, because it means that you must buy their accessories when you need them. To buy a lathe for which the manufacturer does not make accessories is asking for trouble, and could limit the possible variety of your work.

These two lathes (as far as I know) are the only ones with swivel head-stocks. Apart from taking up less space, this reduces the cost of accessories because you are always working on the same thread. Lathes with bowl-turning facilities on the left-hand end may require reverse-threaded accessories, and so increase your costs.

● *Professional Don White of Bristol is shown here using a ½hp Tyme Cub, manufactured in his home town. It forms a companion model to the ¾hp Avon*

to a short-bed version. The parts duly arrived, with an accompanying letter from Harrisons saying they would not accept responsibility for the conversion; however, I was not deterred, and by re-locating and drilling a couple of holes I very soon had it bolted together. It has been in constant use ever since and is entirely satisfactory. The pedestal body and the cross-slot bed are made of rigid iron casting, extremely robust, and free from vibration.

The only addition I have made to this lathe is to fit a reversing switch, which enables me to sand bowls in alternate directions while working my way through the various grits for a better finish.

The other lathe I use is the Tyme Avon mkI, which is made in Bristol, just a few miles from my workshop — if I need accessories in a hurry, or a particular modification carried out. On one occasion I had an order for a large number of newel-posts, which convinced me it was time I

Tyme Machines manufacture a complete range of accessories, including a long-hole-boring kit, various chucks, drive centres, revolving centres and six different-sized tool rests. All this, coupled with the fact that the head-stock swivels to allow large-diameter bowl-turning, must make this one of the most versatile lathes on the market.

I have either owned or used most of the woodturning lathes on offer today, and I am satisfied that the two lathes in my workshop represent the best value for money in their particular price range.

After long negotiations with Avon County Council it looks very probable that I and some other craft workers will be able to use a local village school for workshops. I hope to make available to youngsters in the community a lathe which belonged to my good friend the late Harry Baker — the man who introduced me to woodturning. This may in some small way repay the kindness he showed me, and recompense him for

# LIFE WITH THE LATHE

Lathes also come in various lengths, but although you might get 30in between centres, the distance will be reduced when you add fitments. If you have the space in your workshop, a lathe with 36in between centres will cover all the woodturning you are likely to do.

You will also need to change speeds fairly frequently, so buy a lathe on which this involves the least trouble. Most lathes have the motor supported on a hinged platform, and by lifting the motor the speed can be changed very easily.

If you are thinking of setting up a workshop with lathes of different sizes, the Coronet range all accept the same accessories, which means that if you buy a small Coronet and move to a larger one you will not have to replace them all.

What I would like to see on lathes generally is more space between the bed bar and the bench. I always have to block my lathes up to enable me to put my tools close to hand.

I feel, too, that the way to buy the right machine and tools for your needs is to learn about woodturning first. A good course should ensure that you buy the correct machine and tools, using your own judgement.

If this article sounds like an advertisement for certain machines I make no apologies. As I said, the choice is a personal one; I hope the points I have raised will help you make the right decision.

## NICHOLAS PERRIN

Buy the best lathe you can afford, and the one that will cope with the type of work you want to do. These have been my criteria for choosing each of the five lathes I currently use.

The first lathe I bought was a Picador Pup. Its main limitation was the size of work. It has now been adapted into a poor man's rotary-knife lathe for roughing out turning blanks.

Another is a Coronet Elf, bought for bowl-turning. Capacity for spindle work was not important at the time, but I have recently increased its bed length to 48in to take on more general turning.

Much of my work is making lace bobbins. In the search for increased productivity, one approach is to increase cutting speed in order to reduce finishing time. With this requirement I went round various manufacturers, and found that Treebridge were most helpful in adapting their standard Arundel M230 lathe to my specification.

As a general woodturner I have to be ready for a wide variety of work. When I come across a quantity of repetitive turnings, I generally dust off the largest of my lathes, which is a Luna Minimax T120 copy lathe with a 1200mm bed.

The last one is a Peatol miniature engineering lathe. I normally use this for modifying chucks and making non-standard fittings for mounting work. It has been adapted for ornamental turning, but

otherwise is not used for turning wood.

Each of my lathes was acquired for a specific task, but all are equally able to handle a wide range of work. Every lathe I own, from the massive T120 down to the Peatol, can be used for producing lace bobbins, but in the absence of a custom-built machine I would always advise using the largest available. Buying small lathes for woodturning, and miniature turning tools, will frequently result in disappointment.

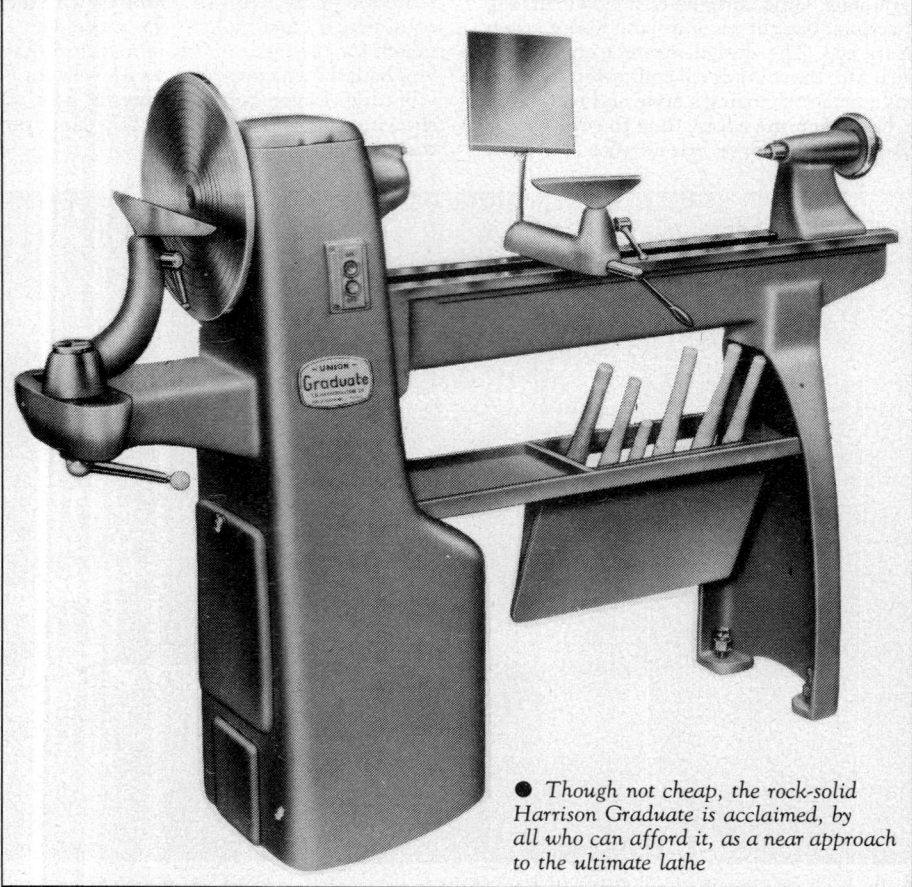

● *Though not cheap, the rock-solid Harrison Graduate is acclaimed, by all who can afford it, as a near approach to the ultimate lathe*

## BERT MARSH

I have fond memories of my apprenticeship, of which one concerns a fearsome monster of a lathe that slumbered amid a shambles of timber offcuts and wood shavings, against a window grimed with years of dust. One glance would have induced an instant heart attack in any self-respecting safety officer in 1985, but it was a beautiful giant.

The head- and tail-stocks were formed of crudely cast iron, and the wooden bed was worn into a sculpture. Alone and silent in the workshop, it looked a dilapidated old thing, but when the enormous DC motor was coaxed into life it was transformed into a furious and deafening fiend. One enormous unguarded belt rose from the motor to a ceiling shaft, from which a second belt led to the head-stock. The combination of that roaring motor, the groaning bearings and the flapping belts produced a chaotic crescendo that I shall remember with affection all my life.

Experienced hands deftly coaxed the moving belts across a couple of stepped wooden pulleys to vary the speed. No sophisticated mechanics or high-tech control panel here — just sleight of hand with the nearest length of timber.

Then came the truly magical moments as square-section timber, blurred and spinning, was transformed into subtle and undulating shapes. For months I was allowed only to watch and marvel at the union of machine and man. The great day when I was first allowed to work with the beast was a terrifying but invigorating experience. How strange — those first shapes did not appear so readily for me as they seemed to for old Harry. But since that day I have never waned in my deep affection for lathes and woodturning.

Thinking of buying a lathe? I am assuming you don't want a heavy-duty machine. There are only a limited number on today's market, as most high-production work is produced on sophisticated automatic machines. The Harrison range of lathes is very popular, and justly so in my opinion, being very substantial, soundly made, and capable of heavy work for long periods.

I would strongly advise against rushing out and buying the first unit in the shop. Analyse the type and quantity of work you intend to produce. If your interest lies in turning small pieces like lace bobbins or thimbles, you will need a compact machine with a fast spindle speed, as opposed to a large unit with heavy production capabilities.

Read all you can about lathes and woodturning; there are many good books and periodicals available. Write to manufacturers for their sales literature and lists of stockists. In many cases demonstrations can be arranged. And, if possible, seek the first-hand advice of an experienced woodturner.

The same suggestions apply to ancillary equipment and tools. Lathe manufacturers naturally recommend their own products, but often other makers produce pieces that suit individual needs better and offer better value for money. I would strongly advise against buying a 'beginner set' of turning tools with the first lathe, as many will never be used after the initial experimental period.

Manufacturers now offer woodturners a wide range of machines. Some provide spindle-turning between centres at one end of the head-stock, and bowl facilities at the other end. Alternatively, there are machines with movable head-stocks, which allow bowls to be turned on the one head-stock thread. In this case you can save on cost, as only one set of chucks is needed. One point is worth considering, though — with a right-hand thread, many turners have difficulty in adjusting to this action when turning bowls.

For a number of years I used a Myford lathe and found it very reliable indeed, but with any good machine one can always find faults. The changing of speeds was very time-consuming and awkward. The bed was made from a round hollow tube, which tended to fill up with wood chips when turning between centres, and always needed cleaning out before adjusting the tool-rest and tail-stock. The 24-point graduated dividing device was very useful indeed, but the round bed did not make for accurate drilling, because the tail-stock moved sideways. A grinding attachment is now available, but cannot be used when bowls are being turned.

Coronet produce several machines which again, like human beings, have their faults and virtues. All are fitted with a round bed made from a solid bar which is manufactured at varying lengths to suit individual needs, and the head-stock swings at right angles to the bed to allow for bowl-turning. Largest is the Coronet Major, which I have used for much of my own work. The grindstone attachment can be used at all times, but is not efficient when the lathe is working at low speeds. I have a few criticisms. The main one is the considerable time it takes to adjust or change the bearings. To be fair, I turn at very high speeds and therefore demand a lot from the machine. My starter switch proved very unreliable and, like the bearings, not very durable. The tool rests are secured in 'T'-grooves by bolts. The grooves fill up with waste and make adjustments both difficult and frustrating. Also, if the round bed is not kept scrupulously clean it is difficult to adjust the lateral

movement of the tool-rest and tail-stock.

I've heard favourable reports about Arundel and Tyme machines. Both firms produce a variety of lathes, which by all accounts have overcome some of these problems. Shavings are prevented from building up on the twin beds, and this should make for easier adjustment and more positive positioning of the rests and tail-stocks.

There are other lathes with useful and innovative features. Not infrequently, new models appear on the market for a while, then gradually disappear after the initial sales honeymoon. I have deliberately restricted my observations to a few established and experienced manufacturers, because my intention is primarily to convey the joys of woodturning and pass on a few practical hints and observations.

# WILLIAM WOOLDRIDGE

Firstly, I am not a professional turner, and secondly, I do not operate a brand-name machine!

Woodturning first caught my fancy over 30 years ago when we adapted a metal-turning lathe to produce some wooden handles urgently needed in the workshop, and the pleasure aroused by that task is re-kindled whenever the shavings start to fly.

In those days DIY was in its infancy, and lathes in New Zealand, where I lived, hard to come by; so inevitably I had a lathe made, which — although modified from time to time — is still going strong.

It has a twin-tube bed 1¾in diameter, with head- and tail-stocks formed from double ⅜in-thick plates with welded-in

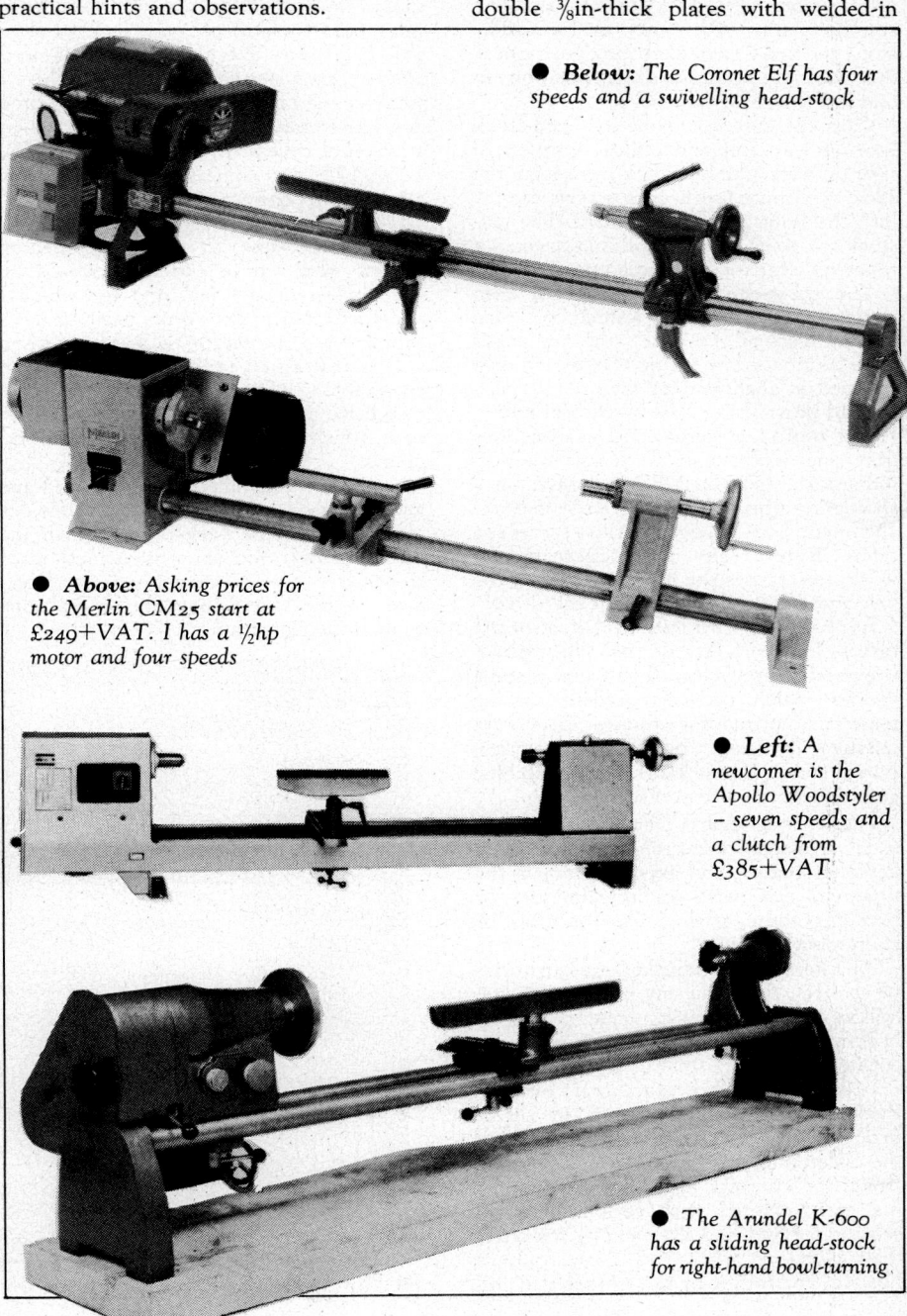

● **Below:** *The Coronet Elf has four speeds and a swivelling head-stock*

● **Above:** *Asking prices for the Merlin CM25 start at £249+VAT. I has a ½hp motor and four speeds*

● **Left:** *A newcomer is the Apollo Woodstyler – seven speeds and a clutch from £385+VAT*

● *The Arundel K-600 has a sliding head-stock for right-hand bowl-turning*

# LIFE WITH THE LATHE

tubular housings for head- and tail-stock bearings. These are phosphor bronze; at the head-stock they are split and adjustable. The mandrel is hollow, 1in in diameter and bored no. 2 Morse taper with a fitted thrust bearing. It has a 12in face-plate capacity, and carries a three-step wooden pulley with press-fit brass sleeves tapped for locking screws to the mandrel. The tail-stock poppet has a 3in projection and is also bored for no. 2 Morse taper.

The saddle is of two ½in-thick plates, machine-screwed to heavy phosphor-bronze split bushes each 3×½in, the saddle and tool-rest being locked by a lever under the bed. A spring interposed between the plates frees the saddle when the lever is released, but restrains the tool-rest in its position on the saddle. This is useful in spindle-turning when moving the saddle along the bed to a new turning position, as the tool-rest maintains its position in relation to the workpiece.

Over the course of time the head-stock bearings were split and jubilee clips fitted to take up wear; the tail-stock bushes got the same treatment, with grub-screws tapped into the housing for adjustment. The tail-stock was itself further modified to allow it to swing clear for long-hole boring.

The between-centres distance of 24in proving too short (I wanted to turn baseball-bats at the time), the bed tubes were lengthened by fitting 15in extensions, retained in alignment by long bolts which expand inner split stubs by conical nuts.

The motor, as serviceable as ever after only one overhaul in 30 years, is a ½hp induction 1450rpm GEC mounted on a sliding/rotating cradle for easy belt re-alignment. This arrangement also serves as a safety feature: any obstruction of the workpiece causes the motor to ride up the belt and effectively disconnect the drive.

So much for 'old faithful'. Most of my turning has been conventional. Picking over firewood log-piles introduced me to some species which proved excellent turning material. Outstanding amongst these were manuka (ti-tree), pohutukawa, matai, pururi and of course kauri. Australian blue gum and jarrah also served their turn.

Pepper-mills apart, I have made all the usual artefacts, trying to give each some personal quality, and experimenting at the time with new twists to old techniques, or pursuing some original idea in tools or equipment.

At intervals I produced large quantities of shakers, following my philosophy that hollow ware, to merit its name, should be hollow; wall thicknesses were always a constant ¼in.

I discovered, however, that my enthusiasm for turning waned in direct proportion to the quantity and urgency of the order, and eventually I turned only for friends or my own pleasure.

I experimented with various finishes, settling for wet and dry sanding for other than glued-up work (no dust in one's nostrils, the motor or the workshop), and

pure carnauba-wax polish on almost everything.

As a non-professional woodturner and retired engineer, I think a truly versatile lathe should have no. 2 Morse taper sockets at both head- and tail-stock. This would allow hand-turned wooden fittings to be made robust enough to withstand regular use (as do mine), and the ready interchange of metal or wood fittings, chucks, etc., between stocks. It would have a minimum between-centres length of 36in and a minimum face-plate capacity of 12in, with an optional outboard facility for the rare occasions when a coffee-table top or tray is in hand. A belt over-ride would provide added safety in all turning operations. I have always managed to turn work from ⅜ to 11½in diameter quite comfortably with the speeds my lathe provides — 750, 1150 and 1750rpm. The highest speed is used almost exclusively for grinding, so I suppose the range of seven speeds on some new lathes to be more of a selling point than a practical necessity. Four steps, say 750, 1250, 1750 and 2250, should be ample for all normal requirements.

The provision by manufacturers of an internal tool-rest to facilitate opening hollow ware up to 6in deep would be welcome: a need I felt, and for which I provided, from the very beginning. A tubular bed mounting a saddle with a spring-restrained tool-rest would be preferable to a flat bed carrying only a tool-rest. It would also be better than a boxed-in base, which is not so easily cleared of wood debris.

Lastly, although it is frowned on by some authorities on woodturning, I still consider a tool-rack at the back of the bench the most compact and convenient method of stowage; in over 30 years I have never had any trouble in reaching for or replacing tools in that position.

## RAY KEY

I make a wide range of products from fine, exotic and rare timbers; some production stuff like salad-bowls; and (the majority of my work) individual 'aesthetic' pieces such as exotic boxes, bowls and platters. I also teach an average of eight to 10 students every six weeks or so. There are six different lathes in use in the school-room, five of which are bench-mounted. The one floor-standing lathe is a Harrison Graduate — in a class of its own; the bench-mounted machines are an Arundel Treebridge K-600, a Tyme Avon, a Tyme Cub, a Coronet Major and a Myford ML8.

Interestingly, the people who use the lathes on the course consistently prefer the Arundel. This is followed by the Tyme Avon and Coronet Major; both receive criticism for their tool-rest arrangement — the Tyme for its release handle on the tool-rest and the Coronet for its spanner release of the cross-slide.

The Tyme Cub and the Myford ML8 are the least liked. The Cub, of course, is a much smaller lathe and much cheaper. The unpopularity of the Myford comes as a surprise, for it is extremely well known and well-made. However, its design is dated, in particular its double-ended spindle, and it also has a poor tool-rest design. Most feel that its small-diameter swing over the bed means larger diameters have to be turned left-handed on the outboard end. All its competitors' head-stocks either pivot or slide along the bed, enabling right-handed operation.

There are many other makes of lathe, some of which are unbelievably bad. It's best to keep away from die-cast and aluminium cheapies, of which most are imported, but there are many poor English ones around as well. Here is an extract from my book *Woodturning and Design*.

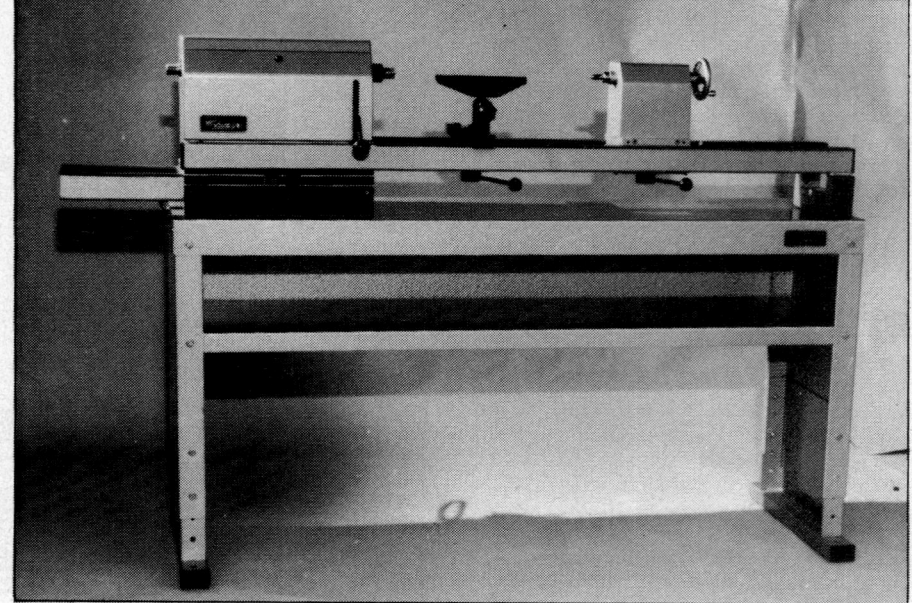

● *The Apollo Woodstyler on its stand, which costs an extra £105+VAT*

'There are many lathes on the market today, and the claims and counter-claims of each manufacturer can become quite confusing. Unfortunately, many are made with little thought for the person who is going to use them; it seems often to be a case of how easily and cheaply they can be made. Some are almost certain to put some would-be woodturners off for life.

'Bench-mounted machines are the most commonly produced. This type must be mounted on a good solid wooden base, which will help absorb vibration — not an old sideboard or prefabricated metal frame, but something like a good carpenter's bench. If you are right-handed it is always preferable to be able to turn on the inboard side of the head-stock for face-plate work. Until recently one could not often find lathes that would allow diameters of more than 300mm (12in) to be turned in this way, and in fact most capacities were less. The commonest way round this was a double-ended spindle allowing much larger diameters to be turned on the outboard end. This works, but it does mean you have to turn left-handed. When you first start learning to turn, the fewer problems you encounter the better!

'It is best to think of the bench-mounted lathes as being for occasional use. If you have plans to produce work of larger diameters regularly, buy a heavy-duty machine.

'Of the lathes that interest serious or professional turners, many are poorly designed. Many manufacturers produce poor tool-rests, tail-stock-release handles and so on, and some even still go for a spanner release. This is just not good enough. Some have solidly constructed head-stocks and beds, but are mounted on flimsy, fabricated metal cabinets that rattle and vibrate.

'However, for sheer quality one lathe is head and shoulders above the rest. The Harrison Graduate, available with short or long bed, possesses everything needed in a lathe for use every day. It has a tremendously heavy cast head-stock with excellent bearings, a good tool-rest, quick-action release handles and an excellent tail-stock. For a serious bowl-turner the short bed is a must. If spindle work is your major activity, choose the long bed.

'Having owned a short-bed since 1975, I view it as my best machinery investment. 496mm (19½in) diameter can be turned inboard, and 508mm (20in) outboard. A platter of 825mm (32½in) was once turned on mine with the arm removed for a tripod rest. I bought a bed of 1370mm (54in) capacity, and fit it when the need arises, but most of the time I use the short bed. The machine is supplied with rests, face-plates and centres; its price is about double that of the bench lathes, but its quality is superb. There is not another lathe in its class to compare with it. It will last a lifetime with the odd bearing and belt replacement along the way.'

Having lavished praise on the above

machine, I still think it could be improved if a more powerful motor were fitted and variable speed introduced. Then it would be the ultimate lathe. I regularly turn bowls weighing over ½ cwt without trouble, and in 10 years only one set of bearings and a drive belt have been fitted. The success of the design, I suggest, is largely due to the makers' consultation with a woodturner — the 'Practical Woodturner' himself, Frank Pain.

## TOBIAS KAYE

When I was choosing a lathe, I was lucky enough to have a friend — an expert bowl-turner — insist that I bought a Harrison Graduate. There are better lathes, but they cost twice as much or more.

For serious bowl-turning you are at a great disadvantage without a heavy cast lathe that bolts direct to the floor. A bench-top machine is not heavy or rigid enough, however massive the bench, for demanding bowl work to be a pleasure. The pressed-steel floor-stands of lighter machines are nothing like rigid enough to compete with a proper floor-standing cast lathe.

In addition to its massive main pedestal, the Graduate has a cast bed with two machined surfaces on which the heavy tool-rest and tail-stock units slide — easily and controllably, at the flick of a lever. This means quicker and more accurate work. The large 1½in-diameter shaft and bearings mean very smooth, silent running, with an absolute minimum of vibration.

I got mine second-hand from a dealer, and decided straight away that I needed a higher centre. About 2in below the elbow when standing with the forearm raised,

● An old 10ft engineering lathe adds a lot to the Kaye capacity

● Tobias Kaye lowered the Harrison Graduate's out-rest

elbow against one's side, is best. This meant (for me) 6in blocks under the machine.

In my present workshop I am handicapped by a wooden floor, so I put wooden blocks under the lathe with bolts right through into the joists. Even so, with a really heavy bowl up, especially if it was off-balance, the lathe tended to swing about, so I fixed cross-members from both ends of the bed to the wall. When I'm turning bowls I wedge a diagonal brace between the underside of the cast switch-housing and a block of wood glued and screwed to the floor.

Heavy off-balance lumps of wood are a frequent challenge to me, as one-off bowls are my main occupation. Often I try to incorporate as many of the natural features of the wood as possible, which can lead to a piece's being denser or even bigger on one side than the other. When it is rotating at several hundred rpm, this naturally presents problems.

These deeper bowls were not possible on the Graduate before I altered the out-rest, especially as the deep modern multi-chucks use up nearly 2in more than a face-plate. Faced one day with a piece of wood which would really suffer if I cut it down to fit the lathe, I decided to cut the lathe up to fit the bowl. I marked out on the casting, and drilled and tapped, three new bolt-holes for the out-rest, 2in lower than the existing ones. I bought longer bolts, and made up shims from dense birch five-ply to pack out from the casting. With all the packing pieces in, I gain 2¾in in bowl depth. Steel shims with machined surfaces would be better to keep vibration down, but on my budget ply still works very well. Some or all of the packing pieces have to be

429

# LIFE WITH THE LATHE

removed when I do platters, but it only takes five minutes or so, which makes this a rewarding modification.

I really enjoy the challenge of large, deep bowls, but find that the Graduate is equally well suited to intricate miniatures, its large bearings making it very smooth and quiet. The ease with which the tool-rest is re-positioned makes it a pleasure for this kind of work.

Two other modifications I have made are the addition of a reversing switch, which I picked up for a tenner, and a grindstone mounted between centres. This is held between wooden shims on a wooden shaft, with a Morse taper to fit the spindle and a hole for the live centre.

I have replaced the rather short curved bowl-rest with a 1in-section round bar bent through 70° on an 8in radius, with 2in of straight bar where it is welded on to the post. To further strengthen this, a 1½in skirt was welded to the length of the underside (see drawing). This is only used for finishing cuts in deep bowls, a straight rest being more versatile for general bowl work.

The Graduate has suited me for years and will continue to be my favourite lathe, but I do like to take on any turning I am offered, and a longer bed and travelling cross-slide would facilitate newel and pillar work immensely. To that end I have bought an old engineering lathe with a 10ft bed, power feed and power cross-feed. Simple spindle work should be much quicker with this, and the massive 16in face-plate also has a four-jaw chuck, which should prove useful for re-mounting wet-turned bowls. The power-feed facility on this machine is geared for various threads, which could be useful if I want to make little boxes; possibly it could be geared right up to cut barley-sugar twists, a router doing the cutting and the spindle turned by hand. Time will tell.

For turning as a profession, rather than to augment furniture-making or the like, I wouldn't settle for a bench- or stand-mounted lathe. Only a cast floor-standing lathe bolted to a good floor will do if you are a demanding user.

## ROGER HOLLEY

Much of my work is devoted to helping and instructing newcomers in the craft of woodturning. The main machine in my workshop is the Kity 663, which I use for both instruction and production. It is a well-designed machine with a large capacity in swing (17in maximum diameter) and length (1000mm between centres). It has a substantial head-stock and a 1hp motor, and is offered with a wide range of accessories. Its set-up and adjustments are simple and positive, and spring-loaded lock levers make altering the tool-rest position simplicity itself — far easier, for instance, than the spanner adjustments you sometimes find on other machines. The tool-rest design itself is, in my view, the best there is; I have comfortably turned lace

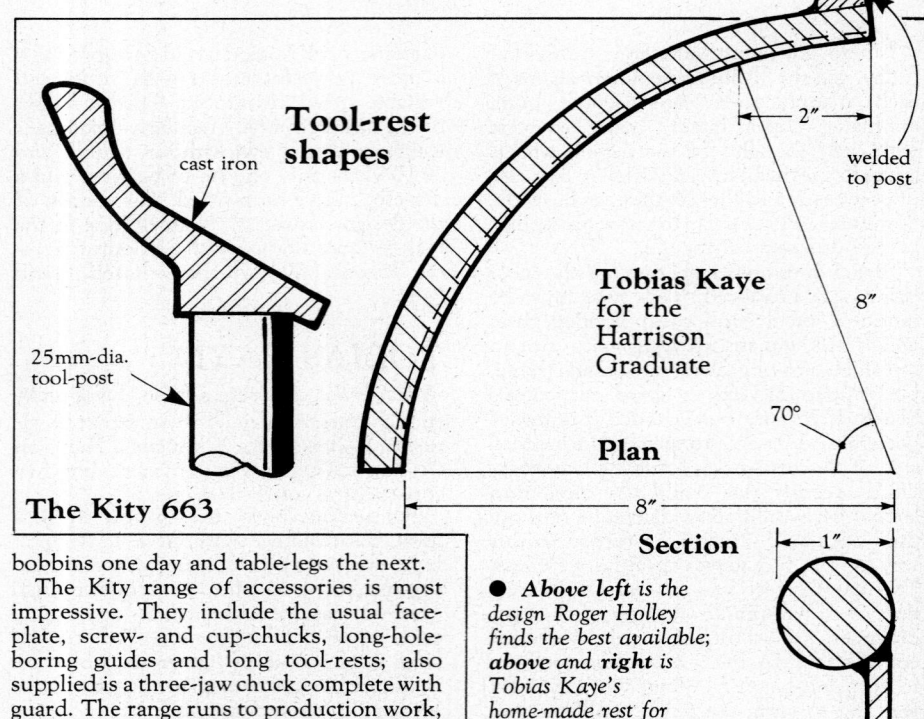

**Tool-rest shapes**

The Kity 663 — cast iron — 25mm-dia. tool-post

Tobias Kaye for the Harrison Graduate

**Plan** — 2″ — welded to post — 8″ — 70° — 8″

**Section** — 1″

● *Above left is the design Roger Holley finds the best available; above and right is Tobias Kaye's home-made rest for finishing deep bowls*

bobbins one day and table-legs the next.

The Kity range of accessories is most impressive. They include the usual face-plate, screw- and cup-chucks, long-hole-boring guides and long tool-rests; also supplied is a three-jaw chuck complete with guard. The range runs to production work, and for large batches of items such as lamps, spindles and legs I use the copy-turning attachment. This is a simple but effective device with two types of cutter, for roughing and finishing.

Many students who come on my courses and who have never used a wood lathe before have found the Kity easy both to operate and to learn on.

If I were looking for improvements to it, top of the list would be another lower speed. The bottom speed is 750rpm, which is too fast for large-diameter turning. I have made up and fitted my own stepped pulleys, which reduce the speed to about 200rpm.

Another improvement would be a starter box with push-button controls, instead of a switch. This enables the operator to use a leg to switch off and keep the hands free. But perhaps it's a little fussy to suggest this, since many makers charge extra for their starters, and Kity include the starter motor and the 13amp plug in the price.

I think these Kity machines represent excellent value for money. An investment in a machine such as this will appreciate; although the 663 is in the mid-price range, it should still be considered by first-time buyers because the initial temptation is to buy a smaller, cheaper machine which you soon outgrow.

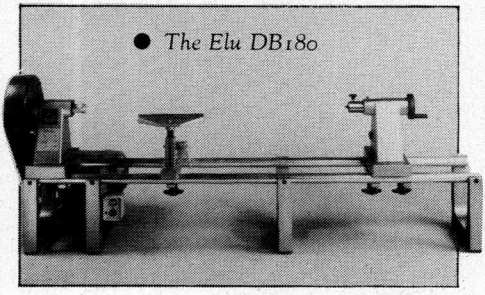

● *The Elu DB180*

## MICHAEL O'DONNELL

I bought my first lathe in 1973, a Myford ML8A because I had been learning the basics on a similar model. It is a very well engineered and sturdy machine, with solid castings for the head- and tail-stocks, and it is very easy to use. At a time when my main products were spinning-wheels, stools, lamps and so on, the machine took all I could throw at it, although I was a little concerned about the strength of the outboard tool-rest. I treated that with a little extra care, but managed to break the inboard tool-rest twice! I was surprised to find that the tool-rests were not meant to be inboard/outboard interchangeable, as it would have cost no extra to make them so. The tool-rest-adjustment lever and butterfly-nut were frustratingly fiddly to use. The tube bed regularly filled with shavings, making movement of tail-stock and tool-rest difficult; cleaning it out always seemed an unnecessary chore — but these considerations were minor compared with the overall performance of the machine.

Pieces of up to 8in diameter could be turned over the bed, and pieces up to 12in on the outboard spindle, though I did manage 19in spinning-wheel rims. Over the years I spent more on chucks and face-plates than the machine originally cost! Most of these were for the inboard side, and could not be used on the outboard end — duplication would be very expensive if necessary. Many of the new generation of small lathes eliminated this problem by having a swing head, which makes the outboard spindle redundant, although I don't think they would give the service I have had from my Myford in the last 12 years. The only part that has worn out is the belt, which is easily replaced.

In 1981 my style of turning changed dramatically and the capacity of the Myford soon became a restraint. I did try to extend it by moving the bed away from the headstock to give a 'gap bed', but it was risking serious damage so I changed it back.

Another machine became essential, and because of the specialised nature of my work — green-turned bowls — I had to be very selective in my choice. I came up with the Harrison Graduate short-bed — a real lathe. The free-standing pedestal is a solid, heavy casting, and it has all the safety features required by schools. I chose the short-bed rather than the bowl-turner because it gave a tool support on the right-hand side, much better for the flexibility of tool-rest position which I regard as essential. I also wanted to use the right side because I will be buying another Harrison later, with a long bed, and I want the chucks to be interchangeable.

I took delivery last March and felt a sudden release from previous restraints. Having used it for a year I am very pleased with the machine, and it is certainly solid enough to stand real punishment. The only disappointment is the motor size — ¾hp single-phase, the same as the Myford. I am constantly having to run at speeds slower than I would like: very frustrating when time is money! The manufacturers did offer to put in a larger motor, but the cost seemed excessive, and the power was limited by the space in the pedestal. I will probably change it myself shortly. Apart from that, I can't fault the Harrison. A really excellent machine, and incredible value for money.

## ANTHONY BRYANT

My work covers an immense range of bowls and platters in a multitude of sizes and designs from a diverse range of English hardwoods. I specialise in the use of burrs, mainly oak and elm, crotch figures, usually walnut and ash, and all other timbers possessing a ripple or similar interesting grain. I make a wide range of natural-edge bowls using timbers such as yew, laburnum, mulberry and any of the burrs — and also, through the use of greentimber, I indulge in asymmetrical pieces, usually from either holly, yew or sycamore. After they are turned very thin and immediately placed in a warm atmosphere, they adopt their own (I hope pleasing) sculptural shapes. Recently I purchased a butt of about 27cu ft of green ripple-ash boards which I turned to the Major's maximum diameter of about 22in and then heated rapidly until I was able to handle and shape each piece, into either a U or a completely folded tube. Several of these were enhanced with flower arrangements, and with a large range of other work they were quickly bought by Harrods for an in-store display.

I purchased my Coronet Major in June 1982 and have enjoyed a trouble-free time ever since. With large, heavy pieces such as 18×4in there is minimal dissipation of

power or movement in the head-stock castings. The lathe has speeds of 350, 550, 1000, 1500 and 2000 rpm, but with my work only the slowest three of these are used. These speeds are perfectly adequate for almost all needs. However, after turning full-time every day I now feel I need a lathe with greater bowl-turning capacity and speeds in the region of 100, 200, 375, 500, 775 and 1000 rpm.

I have not needed to make any modifications to the Major, but feel the cumbersome bowl-turning rest needs

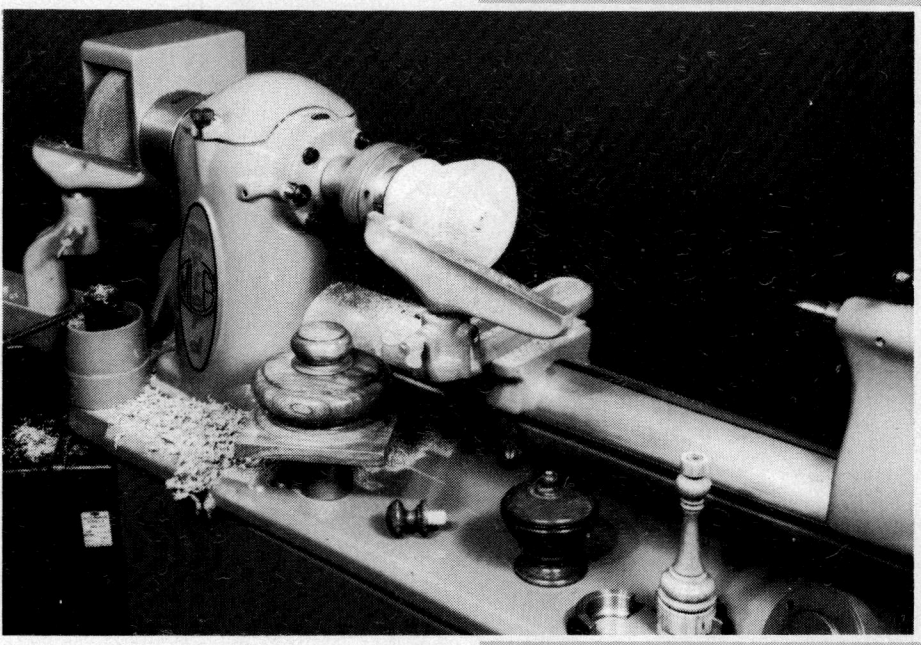

● *The Myford ML8 is a solid, well established machine whose prices start at £286+VAT. Lengths range from 30 to 42in*

improvement. I would also like to see quick-release adjusters to banish the spanner when altering the position of the rests. I believe Coronet are aware of these problems, so changes may be seen soon.

Coronet engineering is always strong, straightforward and efficient. Bearings and castings are easily maintained and adjusted. Only occasionally do I notice movement of the mandrel in the brass bearing, which is easily rectified by adjusting the two rings on the head-stock casting for a smooth, snug fit.

I use Coronet's range of accessories, including expanding and pin chucks. These are versatile, accurate and less bulky than some other makes, which I find often extend too far from the mandrel; you might have to turn a 6in-deep bowl up to 10in from the mandrel, which causes great strain on the bearing.

I have great confidence in the Coronet Major and the whole range of Coronet lathes and accessories, and feel they are perfectly suitable for amateur or professional woodturners. In the past they have been more expensive than other lathes; but in machinery, perhaps more than anything, you gets what you pays for. ■

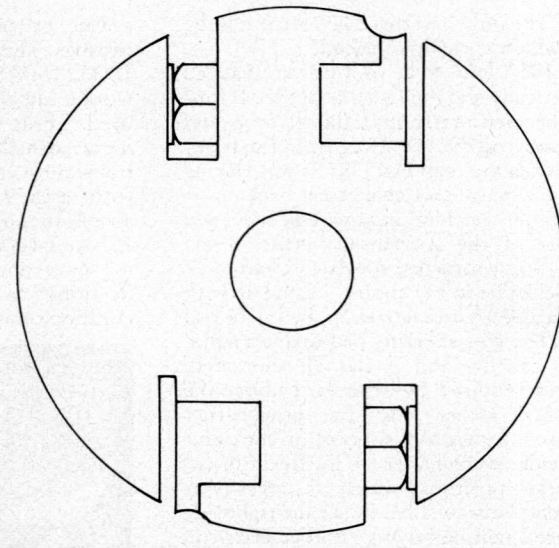
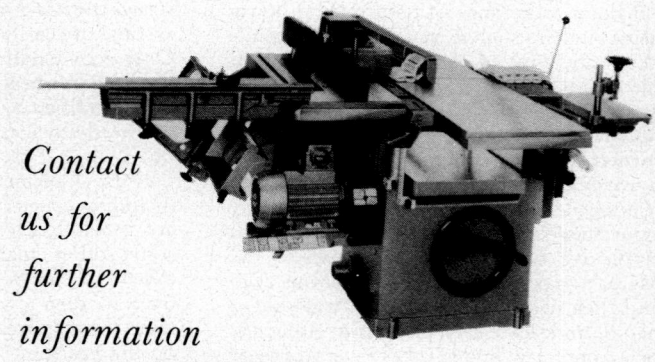
Prices quoted are those prevailing at press date and are subject to alteration due to economic conditions.

# Power-assisted waxing

**WOODWORKING WHEEZE** *of the* **month**

J ames Paffett writes: The electric hot-air paint stripper must have come as a godsend to many craftsmen. This elegant instrument emits no smoke or flame; it lifts the paint in wide strips so cleanly that they could almost be stuck down and used again. And the wood is left unscorched and looking much as it did on the day when the joiner handed it over to the first painter, pencil marks and all.

This last feature prompts the question: are there not other uses for this tool beyond stripping paint? Black & Decker perhaps anticipate such thoughts by warning purchasers that their tool is not to be used as a hair-drier. The average craftsman is hardly likely to be tempted to direct a 1kW jet on to his perhaps thinning cranium; but might he not find a more constructive use for the electric stripper around the workshop?

One such application lies in wax polishing.

The conventional way of applying wax is to use it in the form of a paste, made by mixing melted wax with white spirit. The paste is rubbed into the dry wood surface, left for a day or so for the spirit to evaporate, and the skin then burnished with a dry cloth. A number of applications are needed, particularly on an absorbent wood, to build up a smooth and glossy surface.

The polishing process can be greatly speeded up and made more thorough by the careful use of heat from the electric stripper. You first heat the surface to be polished until it is just too hot to be touched comfortably. Dry neat wax is then scattered liberally on to the wood, conveniently by using a Surform tool on a cake of wax in the manner of a nutmeg scraper. The stripper is then used again to melt the wax and to chase the puddles over the surface, aided by a stick of wood and a judicious tilt. On an absorbent material the wax may need to be topped up with fresh shavings from the cake — some timbers can soak up a surprising amount.

When the surface is uniformly wet, the hot breath is withdrawn. While the wax is congealing the surface is sandpapered *through* the waxy layer; this ensures that any open grains are filled with a mixture of wax and wood dust. Finally a quick blow-over with the stripper re-melts the wax to give a uniformly smooth surface. At this stage any obvious surpluses can be blotted off with a piece of cloth.

When the job is completely cold the surface is burnished by rubbing vigorously with a hard pad of cotton cloth, beginning with heavy pressure to make the wax run into a uniform layer without surface marks, then with decreasing force as the gloss appears.

T his technique is suitable for a flat surface such as a tabletop. However, difficulties can arise with a three-dimensional object, such as a piece of sculpture, because the dry wax shavings fall off in the air jet from the stripper. In such a case one can fall back on the paste type of polish, which will stick to the surface. Paste is applied liberally to the wood, much more thickly than with conventional cold polishing. When heat is applied from the stripper the paste melts and the spirit component rapidly and visibly boils off, leaving neat molten wax which is treated as described earlier.

By using heat in this way you can build up, in a matter of minutes, a hard and penetrating layer of wax which could only be obtained from cold paste-type polish by repeated applications over days or longer. It is fair to point out, however, that not all timbers may tolerate the heating process: some may crack or exude resin globules, so a preliminary skirmish with a piece of scrap is advisable.

The hot process works very well with plain beeswax, straight from the hive. A harder and shinier surface is given by mixing a proportion of carnauba wax with the beeswax. For conventional cold polishes a low proportion, say 10%, of carnauba is commonly used. With the use of heat this can be considerably increased; indeed, you can easily use neat carnauba. (The woodturner does this — in this case the heat comes from friction.) A pure carnauba finish, however, tends to be rather on the brittle side, and the shiny skin can sometimes be chipped off in flakes. A bee-carnauba mixture seems to be best for most purposes, the actual proportion being a matter of taste. I use a 50-50 mixture for furniture and sculptures. ∎

# Starters

**Chris Nussbaum's diary of the London College of Furniture C&G 564 cabinetmaking course**

T his month brings a change of style to the diary. I promised to describe some of the projects undertaken as 'final pieces' — the main pieces of design and construction in the course, upon which 60% of benchwork assessment is based — and have asked my fellow students each to contribute descriptions of their work.

I myself approached the design process as a complete novice, and decided that it made little difference precisely what I made — as long as I liked it; so I chose to design a grandfather clock. However, since our set piece involved conventional design and techniques, I was determined that my clock should be equally unconventional. With an otherwise open mind, I explored concepts of time and related ideas, arriving at the final form after nearly seven days of intensive work. The result is a floor-

standing pendulum clock, of 'organic' shape, with a part-solid, part-laminar structure, worked in brown and white English oak, and I think I like it!

M y colleague John writes: 'A problem with desks and writing-tables is that, no matter how large they are, they still tend to become cluttered.

'The areas to the far left and right of a conventional square table are the usual 'junk spots', but the area to the right of the centre is the most used part (for a right-handed person). This suggested to me a three-sided shape, tapering off to the left and right at the front as well as to the farthest right-hand corner. I also wanted to incorporate curves into the design for both aesthetic and practical reasons; so the front of the table curves around the person sitting at it, and the two sides curve away from the front. The radius of all the curves is 1.1m so that the rails and stretchers use the same jig.

'Choice of material was difficult. I decided on American cherry because of its

warmth in colour. However, I realised that for the top of the table anything with a straight grain would look awkward against the curves, so I opted for a burr veneer, choosing bird's-eye maple.'

Meanwhile, Gideon has chosen as his project a pair of corner cabinets, the larger being a floor-standing drinks cabinet and the smaller a wall-hung cabinet for glasses. Both are padauk and rock maple.

The cabinets have curved, coopered maple doors, the red padauk line of the door edges being their most striking feature. When the doors are opened the gentle S shape of their break-line may be seen. The larger cabinet (900mm tall) has two shelves to accommodate bottles from half-bottle to litre size, and above these three swivelling trays of diminishing depth. The top is of a polished red granite to complement the padauk and provide a place to slice lemons and impale cherries. The wall cabinet is 400mm tall, with two shelves to take most types of glasses. All shelves are veneered and lipped in padauk. ∎

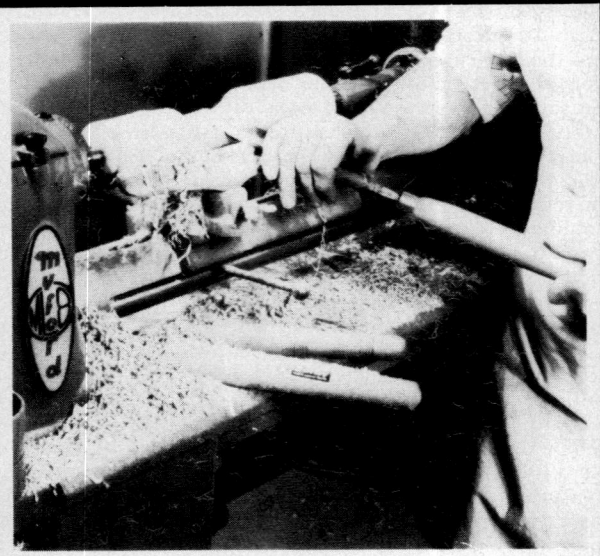
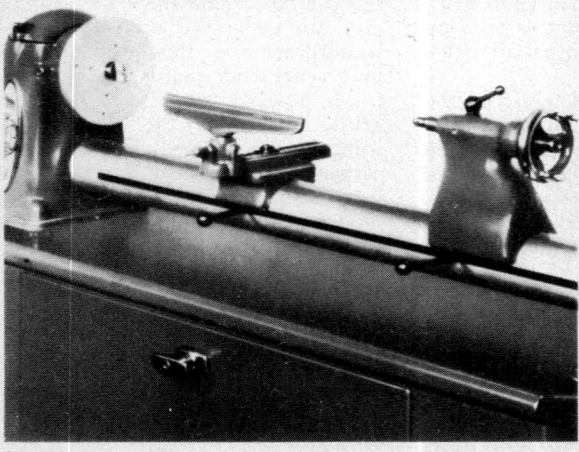

434  Prices quoted are those prevailing at press date and are subject to alteration due to economic conditions.

# Books

Michael Bennett
*Refinishing Antique Furniture*
Dryad Press, £5.95 hardback
Reviewed by David Ellis

This excellent little book first appeared in 1980.

Michael Bennett's approach to refinishing can only be described as refreshing — and different. Although much of what he says has been practised by craftsmen for many generations, he puts it over in such a delightful manner that the reader really learns afresh.

The book opens with chapters on cutting-in repairs, the use of glues and cramps, and tool sharpening. All mundane stuff to the expert, but well explained for the beginner. I was disappointed, however, to find no reference to scrapers, which play a big part in most re-finishers' work; later on the author does mention them, but only to condemn their use.

The main body of the book deals with all the basic techniques of re-finishing. It is interesting to read Mr Bennett's remarks concerning 'french polish' — as he says, there is no such thing. French-polishing is a technique used for imparting a high gloss with shellac dissolved in a solvent. This substance had been in use for 200 or 300 years before the French cabinetmakers developed a new method of applying it! Consequently he refers from then on to shellac polishing; this is, of course, more technically correct — but not appreciated by the average customer. The whole of this chapter is very explicit, and the reader who follows the author's procedures cannot fail.

Also within this section are some interesting chapters on stopping and grain-filling; but I found those on disguising repairs and on colouring and staining the most fascinating. Working in this field, I am always willing to learn something new, and I must admit that I have never used Vandyke crystals in the way that Michael Bennett describes, namely making them into a water-based 'cake'. I have since done so, with great success.

This section finishes with chapters on blemishes, distressing and cleaning and polishing — all very well described and presented. The third part deals with 'Finishing — Severe Cases'; it covers the more drastic remedies that are sometimes necessary, including stripping and bleaching. The book ends with appendixes on furniture woods and restoration materials. There are line drawings, plus black-and-white and eight colour photographs.

I am delighted to add this to my library of books on restoration, and am sure that its pages will soon be as well-thumbed as any.

Franklin H. Gottshall
*Reproducing Antique Furniture*
Stobart, £10.95 paperback
Reviewed by Dave Batten

This is a reprint of the original hardcover book published in 1971.

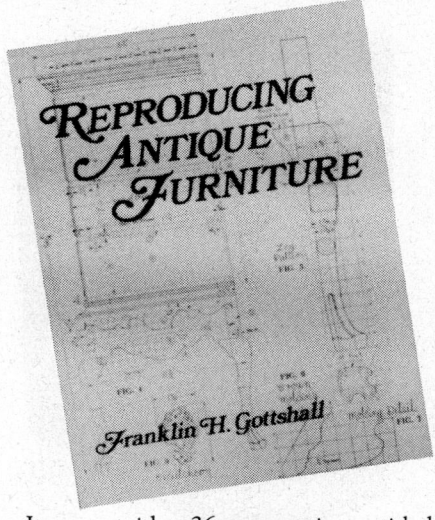

It opens with a 36-page section entitled 'Some Useful Fundamentals of Cabinet Making' which covers cabinetmaking, glues, woodturning, woodcarving, finishing and hardware; it is illustrated by photographs and line drawings. Self-evidently, such a small compass cannot possibly include all the methods and materials employed in these various techniques, and presumably the author relies on the methods of construction he describes for each design to supply any omissions.

I have my doubts about this; Mr Gottshall's designs call for cabinetmaking of the highest order, and I would have preferred more designs instead of this section — with a note recommending that only skilled craftsmen should attempt them. If the techniques cannot be dealt with adequately, in my view it's better not to try, as there are plenty of specialist books.

Now to the designs. There are 40 of these; the construction of each is explained exhaustively with copious detailed drawings, plus a bill of materials, and they are models of their kind. This no doubt helps to explain why the author has an international reputation for books of the highest standard.

He is an American and the text therefore contains the usual small differences from British practice, but these are no impediment. More crucial is the fact that when Mr Gottshall talks of a Chippendale ladder-back chair, or a Sheraton small table, he is referring to the American version — which is by no means the same as the native English product. Further, in several instances the designs have only vague affinities with the originals, and appear to be commercialised reproductions to suit a market which demands only something that looks antique without bothering too much about authenticity in the details. Examples are a 'Queen Anne Pembroke table' (the first Pembroke table was advertised in 1760 — Queen Anne died in 1714!); a 'Sheraton stool' with a saddle seat; and a 'Sheraton small table', in a chunky bedside-table style with slightly swelled reeded legs, which has none of the grace or elegance one would expect.

Nevertheless, there are some very good things to feast the eyes on. A fully upholstered Chippendale-style wing chair with cabriole legs and claw-and-ball feet; Chippendale-style ladderback chairs; a beautiful corner cupboard with a coved top and shell carving; a Dutch cupboard; an early American dresser; a Chippendale-style partners' desk with block fronts; and one of those splendid American Windsor chairs with swelled sticks and a scrolled back rail.

The book contains 240 pages, including glossary and index; page size is 305mm high by 227mm wide.

Marie Campkin
*The Technique of Marquetry*
Batsford, £4.95 hardback
Reviewed by Alan Bridgewater

If you are new to marquetry and want to know and understand the craft, this book is a must.

The author (formerly editor of *The Marquetarian*) certainly knows her subject. Everything is covered — veneers, tools, designs, mounting, pictures, fretsaw work, baseboards, glues, presses, borders, finishes, special effects, silhouettes and much, much more. It might almost be said that, if it's not in this book, it's just not worth mentioning.

However, not all is roses. This book is in fact a reprint of Marie Campkin's *Introducing Marquetry*, first published in 1969. In all truth it's a 16-year-old infant prodigy which is not wearing so well. The projects are dull, the text is cramped and the layout is less than exciting. Watch out if you're buying it for a friend who has been practising the craft for some time. He/she might have a copy of *Introducing Marquetry*.

Good old Batsford. Please keep resuscitating your old books — but just stay with the original titles; then we'll know what we're buying.

David Orchard
*Techniques of Wood Sculpture*
Batsford, £10.95
Reviewed by Maurice Lund

A quick glance through this book gives the impression that it could be very instructive. However, careful reading does not quite confirm that.

The book is interesting — but of value to a beginner? I'm not so sure. Mostly it covers, in slightly different ways, the same ground as many tool catalogues and other similar books.

The illustrations are good, and the book does attempt to tackle the subject from beginning to end. Indeed, it deals with so much in its 140-odd pages that there's no room for a lot of detail. It might prove useful in providing hints and reminders on various aspects of design and sculpture; but it won't be much use unless you already have other books on the shelf.

Incidentally, I hope that no beginner takes too seriously the hazardous example of p21, where a gouge is held in one hand and the wood in the other.

# The electronic bureau

**George Ellis wanted a writing-desk. He also wanted a TV cabinet and a video cabinet. Here's how three went into one — and very neatly, too**

I wanted my bureau to look like a bureau, and not like a cabinet adapted to house electronic gear. There was only one way to achieve that — to design it myself.

I got off to a good start by finding an excellent source of cheap timber: namely the village hall. Having bought some new tables, they were disposing of their old ones. I knew these were made of well matured oak, being ex-Air Ministry folding trestle-tables. They had been purchased by the hall committee in 1932. I bought six tables for £2 each, got them to my workshop, and started reclaiming the timber.

Generations of WI home-produce sales, Mothers' Union bazaars, children's parties and all the activities associated with a village hall had left them with an infestation of old drawing-pins, staples, nails, and even lumps of chewing-gum. They were constructed by screwing battens and hinges to the underside, so I had little to do in taking them apart. I removed about 600 screws, which left me with 60 hinges, 60 battens and 30 planks approximately 6in×5ft.

Unfortunately only about eight planks were straight. The rest were bowed because the tables had been consistently overloaded. I used the straight ones for the base frame, TV mask, shelf edging and bottom drawer-front, and part of the flap. There was quite a bit of waste, as the ends had to be cut off to avoid the screw-holes, and one or two were worm-eaten into the bargain.

I first squared and straightened the long edges. Then two planks of equal curvature were clamped back to back, which pulled them straight. I marked square lines across the edges for dowels, and drilled the dowel-holes on the slot-mortiser — clamping each board down on the table to pull out the bow and make all the holes a consistent distance from the edge. The boards were then joined edge-to-edge with the bows reversed. This procedure cancelled out the stresses, and left the boards reasonably straight. An equal amount was sawn off each edge to reduce the width and so enable the board to be machined on my 10in planer/thicknesser. This further increased the waste, but I was left with enough straight, square planed boards to complete the project.

I got the small drawer-fronts out of the boards with the least curvature, cut a little longer than required and then planed flat. This resulted in drawer-fronts being $^{11}/_{16}$in thick, with the main carcase $^3/_4$in thick.

● *The gleam of brass fittings, the strong grain of well-seasoned oak, and the classic proportions betoken a solid seven-drawer bureau . . . but is it?*

So much for the preparation. Now I could start on the construction.

The cabinet's overall dimensions were dictated by the size of the TV (26in) and the size of the video (6in high), plus the height of the writing-desk. This left no room for feet, so I took the ends right down to the floor and added a further thickness on the inside (figs 1 & 3).

The next stage was to join two of the straightened boards with dowels to form end panels. I first of all sanded these on one side to a fine finish using an Elu belt-sander and frame. They were then marked off and machined on the sanded side.

To enable the doors to swing freely, I cut a groove $^1/_{16}$in from the front edge of the panels between the writing shelf and the TV shelf, using a router with a 1in half-round bit. The shelf grooves were cut on a DeWalt crosscut using a dado head. Rebates were machined for fitting the back panels to the desk and the video sections. The back of the TV compartment was left open for ventilation. The top edges of the end panels were mitred and slotted for plywood tongues.

● *The ingenious design and modern function of the piece are revealed. Note the ventilation holes in the video drawer; for the same reason, the TV cabinet has no back*

The bottom frame, being merely a spacer, was dowelled together. The shelf for the TV was made from 1in flooring-grade chipboard. It was edged along the back and front with oak, which was joined to the chipboard with dowels. I then reduced the ends of the chipboard with the router to the thickness of the oak edging. For ventilation, eight $1^1/_4$in holes were drilled along a line in the centre of the chipboard (fig. 1).

The writing-desk shelf was made from 12mm ply, once again edged with oak; this time, however, the edging was rebated for the ply (figs 1 & 2).

The time had come to assemble the carcase. I glued and clamped the bottom frame, the TV shelf and the writing shelf first, ensuring that all was square and free from twist. The top panel was mitred and grooved to match the end frames, and (after the carcase assembly had set) I glued it in place using plywood tongues in the grooves. Clamps were applied in both directions to ensure a tight joint.

● *The details of the writing-surface, showing stay and neatly fitted flap-hinge. The head of the pivot-screw for the false drawer-doors can just be seen*

To make sure of close-fitting doors, and to locate the hinges, I adopted the following procedure. Two $^3/_{16}$in holes for hinge pins were drilled in both the writing shelf and the TV shelf. Each hole was $1^3/_8$in from the inside of the end member and $^3/_8$in from the edge (figs 1, 3 & 4). I temporarily screwed a block in each corner of the TV compartment, ensuring that the screw-holes were behind the mask position and the front of the block was $^3/_4$in from the edge (fig. 1). A piece of dead flat chipboard was cut to a tight fit in the TV aperture. It was drilled and countersunk so that the drawer-fronts and bearers could be attached (fig. 6). The chipboard was then pressed down firmly on to the blocks.

The small drawer-fronts were cut to size, allowing for the $^{13}/_{16}$in bearer and uprights to intersect them (fig. 6). They were then routed all round using a $^3/_8$in rounding-over bit (fig. 4). Then the drawer-fronts and bearers were laid on the chipboard, being once more a tight git in the aperture (fig. 6).

To keep the drawer-fronts in position, I positioned a piece of plywood to cover all of them, and clamped it on to the carcase with sash-cramps. I stood the cabinet on its feet and screwed the drawer-fronts and bearers to the chipboard, gaining access from the open rear of the cabinet. The 3/16in hinge-pin holes in the TV and writing shelves were continued into the door assembly for 1/2in (fig. 4).

The door assembly was then removed for the making and fitting of the hinge components. The hinge-pins were made from 1/4in Whit countersunk set screws 2in long. The threaded ends were gripped in the chuck of the bench drill and a plain 3/16in dia. shank was produced with a file whilst the screw was revolving (3/16in is reached when the thread is almost gone — fig. 4).

I obtained a piece of 1/2×1/8in bright mild steel for the hinge-bearing brackets, and cut and drilled it as in fig. 5. To get an accurate right-angle bend, a 3/16in drill shank was pushed through the bracket hole into the hole in the door assembly and a scribe line marked underneath. The bracket was then carefully bent. To avoid any inaccuracy the brackets were marked to re-locate in the original positions. A recess was cut in the edge of the door assembly so that the hinge bracket was slightly below the surface (fig. 4). Once more the door assembly was placed in position and clamped against the blocks. From the rear the hinge brackets were pushed in to their marked positions. The hinge-pins were then inserted, the Whitworth screws cutting their own thread in the oak. The hinge brackets were now screwed into position on the back of the chipboard (fig. 4). The result was hinges and doors which fitted with absolute accuracy (the doors still being in one piece).

The door was then cut into two. Using a router, I removed about 1/8in from the edges of the chipboard to give some clearance, and to enable iron-on veneer to be fitted. I put a 3/16in washer under the bottom hinges to take the weight of the doors and to act as a bearing. Some slight easing was necessary to enable the doors to swing sweetly and to be a snug fit.

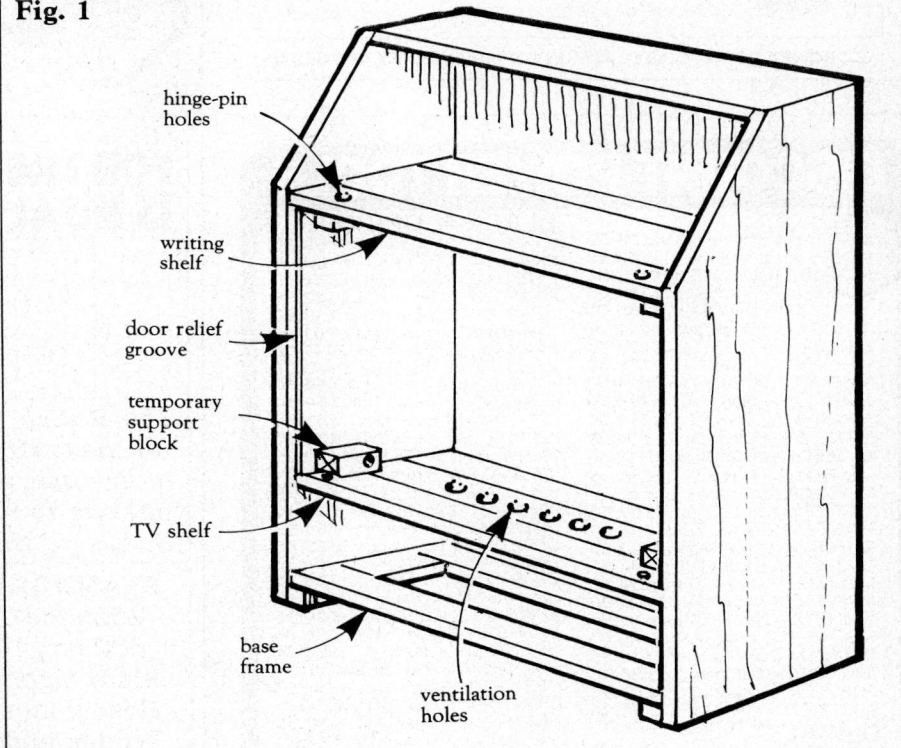

● *The bottom edge of the door, showing the pivot-hinge bracket and the TV mask that surrounds the screen. A chamfer is run round it after assembly but before fitting*

The TV mask was made to fit the TV. For ease of modification or replacement if the TV should be changed, it was assembled in four parts and screwed into the compartment (fig. 7). This assembly also gave additional stiffness to the TV and the writing shelves.

So that the bottom drawer would run smoothly whilst carrying the weight of the video, I used mechanical roller runners. The drawer was constructed from 14mm plywood, offcuts from a previous job. Traditional dovetail joints were used and the bottom was stiffened with two cross-members. Six 1 1/4in holes were cut in the centre of the bottom of the drawer to ventilate the video, and a section was removed from the front of the drawer to gain access to the video controls. The false front of the drawer was hinged and supported with a stay. It was retained in the vertical position with turn-buttons. The drawer is large enough to store a number of video cassettes, plus spare stationery.

As my workshop is part of the house building and is maintained at about the same temperature, I considered that the timber was stable, having been in the workshop for about two months. I therefore made the desk flap without allowance for movement. Two edge-joined boards were surrounded by a frame mitred at the corners. A shallow sloping recess was routed into the inside of the flap to enable the leather to finish neatly (fig. 2). To maintain the lines of the cabinet I fitted the flap inside the opening and let it protrude to match the drawer protrusion.

The pigeonhole section was constructed as a unit, screwed to the top panel and supported by two panels which formed the typewriter compartment. The small drawers were made the width of the typewriter compartment, constructed in the usual manner and side-hung. The top drawer was divided into six compartments for stamps, paper-clips, erasers, etc. The bottom drawer has one small compartment for pencils; the other compartment houses cheque-books and the like. Construction of the pigeonhole section was by the stopped-housing method, with the ends dowelled to the bearers.

I fitted brass handles and escutcheons. As the escutcheons were only decorative, I made a false key for the flap — buying a brass key, cutting it off halfway up the shank, brazing on a woodscrew at the business end and screwing the modified key into the escutcheon.

**Fig. 1**

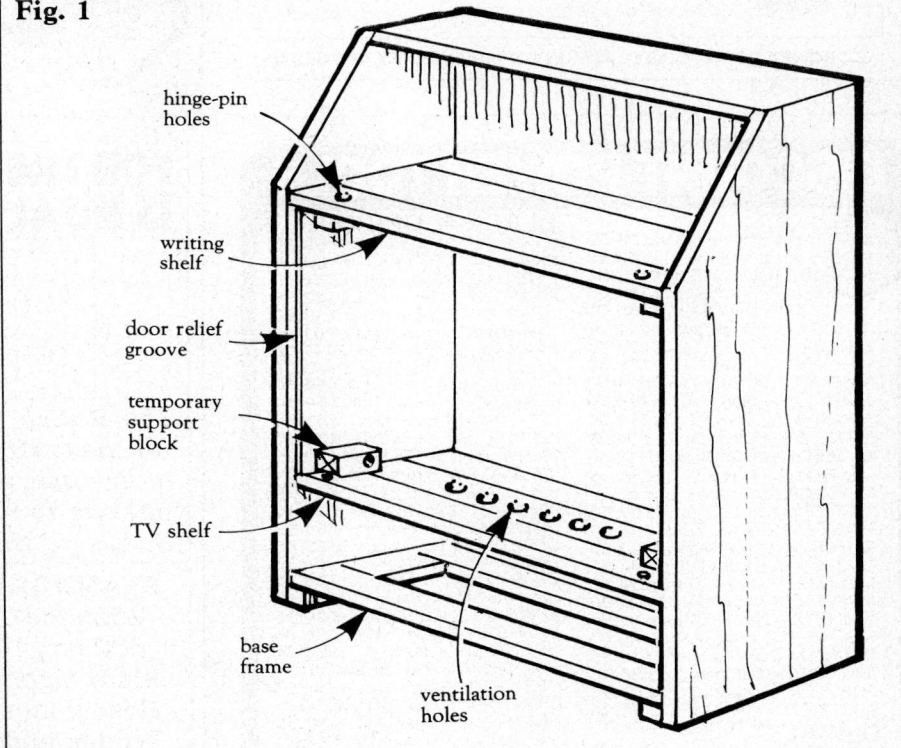

hinge-pin holes

writing shelf

door relief groove

temporary support block

TV shelf

base frame

ventilation holes

**Fig. 2**

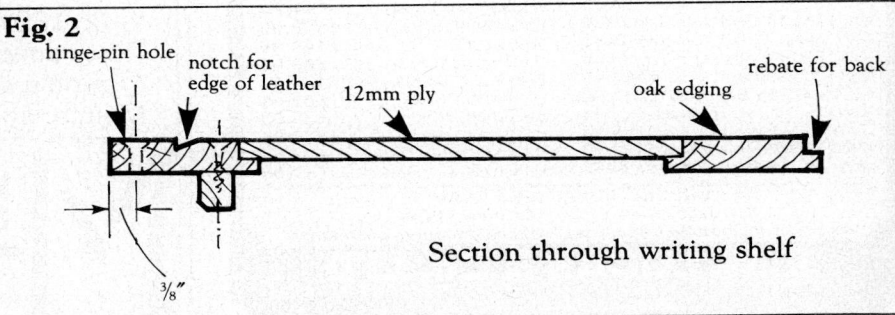

hinge-pin hole

notch for edge of leather

12mm ply

oak edging

rebate for back

3/8"

Section through writing shelf

437

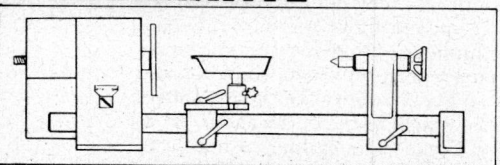
438

Prices quoted are those prevailing at press date and are
subject to alteration due to economic conditions.

# The electronic bureau

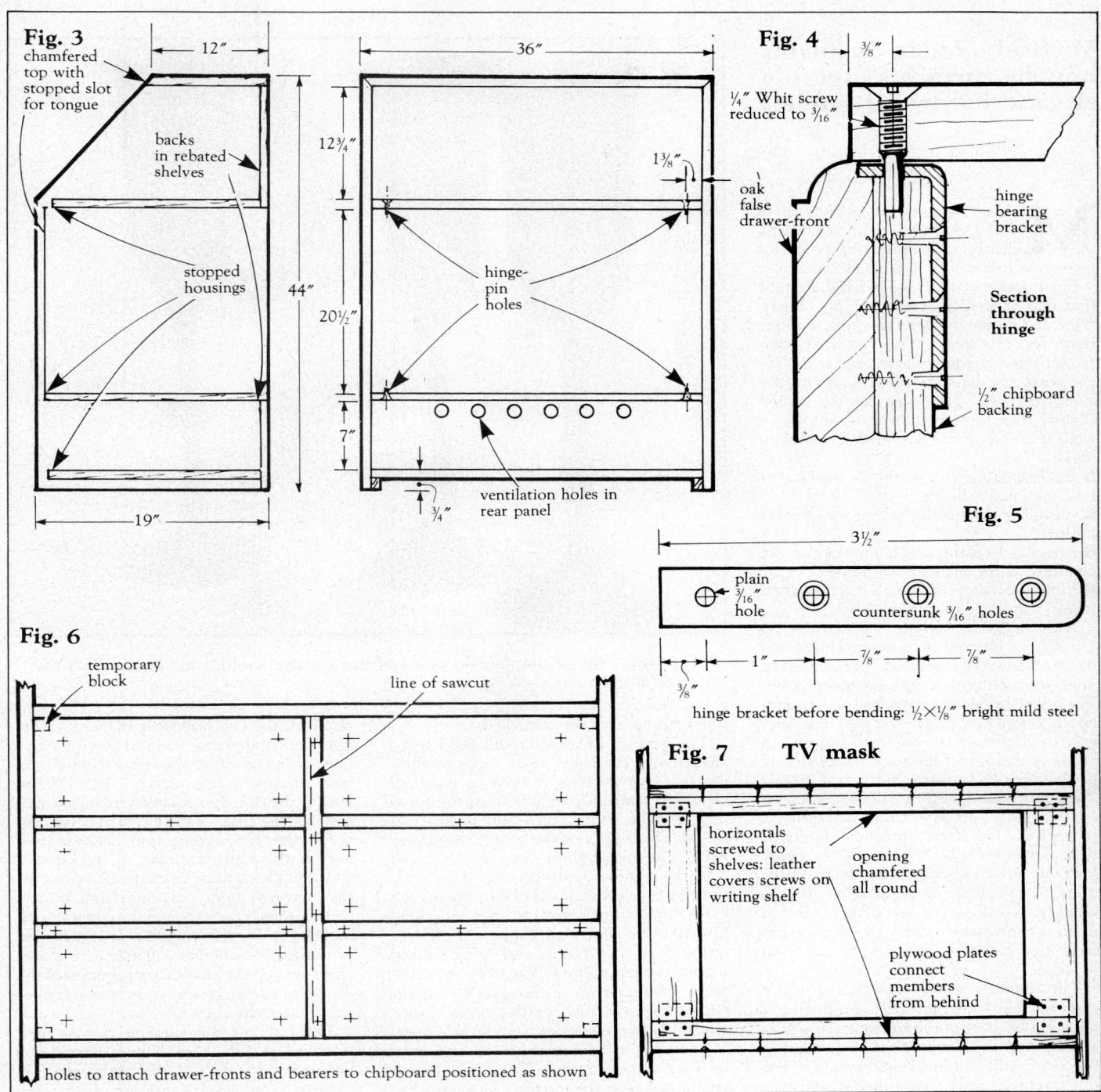

**Fig. 3**
chamfered top with stopped slot for tongue

backs in rebated shelves

stopped housings

12″

36″

12¾″

20½″

7″

44″

19″

¾″

1⅜″

hinge-pin holes

ventilation holes in rear panel

**Fig. 4**
⅜″

¼″ Whit screw reduced to ³/₁₆″

oak false drawer-front

hinge bearing bracket

**Section through hinge**

½″ chipboard backing

**Fig. 5**
3½″

plain ³/₁₆″ hole

countersunk ³/₁₆″ holes

1″   ⅞″   ⅞″

⅜″

hinge bracket before bending: ½×⅛″ bright mild steel

**Fig. 6**
temporary block

line of sawcut

holes to attach drawer-fronts and bearers to chipboard positioned as shown

**Fig. 7    TV mask**
horizontals screwed to shelves: leather covers screws on writing shelf

opening chamfered all round

plywood plates connect members from behind

After sanding down to a fine finish, I gave the piece one application of Colron stain inside and out, except for the backs of the doors. Without applying any filler, I brushed on a coat of thinned polyurethane gloss varnish inside and out, followed by a coat of satin finish outside and in the writing compartment only. This treatment brought out the fine figuring of the grain.

After I had fitted the handles, the backs of the doors were literally studded with screw heads. This necessitated veneering to give the inside surfaces an acceptable finish. The fronts, of course, were already polished.

Having had no experience whatsoever in veneering, I decided to use the modern iron-on type of veneer that can now be obtained in wide sheets. This proved almost completely successful — it produced a slight bow on the assembly, which fortunately is almost undetectable. I finished the doors matt on the inside to minimise reflections from the TV.

The cabinet is much admired. Most of those who see it seem unable to resist running their hands over it. With the doors closed it is virtually impossible to detect that this piece of furniture is anything but a seven-drawer bureau, and it surprises everyone when the secret is revealed. The doors open to 145° — wide enough to accommodate anyone who wants to view at a comfortable angle. Experience with TV cabinets shows that very often it is impossible to fold the doors right back because other furniture is in the way; the open doors do not detract from the entertainment, and look no more unsightly than doors folded round the sides of a cabinet.

There was just one more bonus. After selling my old TV cabinet for £50, and then spending £20, I had a piece of furniture that would cost not less than £500 in a shop!■

# Tall and slender

Michael Foden explains how he turns his superbly elegant hardwood goblets

● *From left to right – Brazilian rosewood, African padauk, boxwood and kingwood are the materials for these lovely goblets*

**M**aking liqueur-type goblets gives the woodturner an excellent chance to combine spindle and face-plate techniques in a single project.

Final design is up to the individual, but I find that 5½in high, with a cup opening of 1¼in and a base diameter of 1½in, is about right for this style. The cup and stem sections are of equal length, and with care the walls can be thinned to 1/20in and the stem to 3/16in. The sizes can be varied slightly, but these proportions will give a well-balanced item. There are four problem areas:

● hollowing the cup section, which has to be completed 'blind';
● thinning the outside of the cup to fine limits;
● shaping the stem, which must be cut very carefully as the diameter decreases;
● finally parting off, which requires great care because the work flexes.

A 6in length of close-grained hardwood 2in square is fixed on a screw-chuck and roughed down to a cylinder, and a 2in-deep hole is bored with a 7/8in sawtoothed bit. The hole is widened out with a small round-nosed scraper of thick section. It is very easy to alter the shape of small tools when grinding them, and the round nose should be inspected to ensure that it is correctly shaped; tiny undulations will express themselves as ridges in the work, and are difficult to remove. Great care must be exercised here, as it is very easy to end up with a badly torn interior which, because of its inaccessibility, is virtually impossible to repair. Gouges are, of course, out of the question in an opening of this size, and the scraper technique required will only come with practice.

The rim area is first widened by gently drawing the tool outwards, producing a flare. Lathe speed is a compromise: too fast, and a grab could cause a lot of damage — too slow, and the finish will be poor; but this depends on the type of timber being worked. As a general rule, a slow speed is used when working the base of the cup, where a dig-in would be difficult to mend, although the finish here should be good as it is cutting endgrain. The lathe can be speeded up to scrape the walls and improve the finish in this area.

The deeper the cup is worked, the more difficult it is to see what is happening, although it is helpful to direct an adjustable lamp into the work. It is largely a question of feel, and the lathe must be stopped frequently, the shavings cleared and the work inspected. When hollowing, the worker with outboard turning facilities or a swivel-head lathe has distinct advantages over any-one turning over the lathe bed.

The bottom of the cup will need to be shaped very carefully. The scraper is gently offered in until the bottom is reached, swivelled from side to side until the cut is felt to have commenced and drawn out slowly whilst shaping the base. Using a very narrow scraper, it should be possible to cut with the front and not the side of the tool, so there is less likelihood of its grabbing the work. Unless the turner has been extremely fortunate in choice of timber, there will probably be rough areas, and a good coat of sanding sealer can be followed by the usual range of abrasives. Although production paper (aluminium oxide) cuts more efficiently, garnet paper is preferable here, as its flexibility enables the inside curves to be worked more readily. There is only one satisfactory way to sand the inside, and that is by wrapping abrasive around a finger — ensuring that the strip is long enough to be gripped by the hand, otherwise the paper is hard to control. Incidentally, there is no danger in this method; again a slow speed is used to eliminate heat cracks and minimise scratches.

**F**rom now on scrapers are out; spindle-gouges and the skew-chisel will be used to complete the job. If the timber is very heavy, tail-stock support can be provided by a tapered wooden plug and a revolving centre, but this is not essential at this stage. A spindle-gouge is now used to shape the outside of the cup section. The depth of the cup hollow is marked on the outside, as otherwise you can end up with a napkin-ring because the taper towards the stem begins in the wrong place. When cutting the rim, the tool must travel inwards towards the base, or the wood may tear out at the edge. Good gouge control is essential, and as the walls decrease in thickness a constant check must be made. It's so easy to slice through them. All temptation to use a scraper must be resisted, as the cup walls are too fragile for this method. It is a matter of preference whether a gouge or a skew-chisel is used for final shaping, but often the design of the piece and grain of the timber will dictate the choice.

The bulk of the stem section is now removed, and the base shape is started and blended into it. As the stem girth is reduced, tail-stock support from the tapered plug will be required. The plug is gently placed in the cup and a revolving centre brought up. The lathe is started and the handwheel advanced until the centre just begins to revolve, and no more. Too much pressure will easily crack the cup. Great care will be needed as the stem gets finer, because of the considerable leverage exerted by the cup, and flexing will occur. Once again, lathe speed is a compromise, but about 1500rpm is required for a decent finish from the tool.

A skew-chisel can be used for any decoration required on the stem and at the base of the cup. You will often find that the larger tools are best for this, because they

# Open and shutter

are not so prone to vibration as lighter versions. One wrong move at this stage may ruin the work. Another problem to watch is that grain may reverse itself part-way along the stem, so that — no matter how sharp the tool — a chunk could be removed instead of a shaving. This could be fatal, as you might then have to further reduce the stem and possibly weaken it.

As the final cuts are taken on the base, there is a very real danger that the gouge will rip back and spoil the rim. There is insufficient timber at the rim to support the bevel; combined with the angle of the cut, this presents a problem. A spindle-gouge of thin section will be needed to obtain a purchase; failing that, a ¼in deep-fluted bowl gouge will complete the cut safely.

Abrasives coarser than 150 grit should not be required; in fact, coarse papers will invariably destroy the finer details. Use the slowest speed, for reasons already mentioned and also because the goblet is now very delicate. Before changing to a finer abrasive, finish off along the grain with the lathe stationary — but do not be tempted to rotate the goblet by holding the cup section or the plug, as the work will snap; hold the screw-chuck to revolve it by hand.

Only when the finish is flawless inside and out can sealer and wax be applied.

Parting off is not just a matter of pushing in a tool — this will not work, and will break the goblet. This is because there is a certain amount of flexing and movement due to the fine stem. With very gentle tailstock support, and selecting the slowest speed, a fluted parting-tool or skew-chisel is used to separate the work with the left hand whilst the right hand supports and catches it. Great care must be exercised here, and to use a conventional parting-tool is to invite trouble — although, once the work is parted off, the stem will be found to be quite strong.

Because of the slow speed, even a high-speed-steel tool will not always give a good finish on all timbers, and the base may have to be sanded before it is sealed. If the base is well undercut, a further reduction in weight is possible, and hardwood goblets of this size weighing just ¼oz are feasible.

The goblet must be finished off in this order to retain strength in the base, and all cutting on the cup section must be completed before working on the stem.

Throughout this type of work it is essential to experiment with lathe speeds and tool sizes, and different techniques will be required for different timbers. It's best to use only strong, fine-grained material, for both structural and aesthetic reasons; boxwood, kingwood and Brazilian rosewood are ideal in this respect. Don't be discouraged if the first half-dozen end up in the scrap pile — and don't think it essential to complete the work in one session. A lot of concentration is required, and there will inevitably be failures before you can regularly cut to these fine limits and feel that you have succeeded. ∎

● **Above:** A magnificent 1912 10×8in Billcliff. **Right:** A Thornton Pickard mahogany camera which takes a 6½×4¾in glass negative; the pattern was in use until the 1950s

**S**tanley Folb writes: I first got acquainted with wooden cameras when, as a young man just out of the army, I went to work for Mr Archibald Perry as general factotum in his photographic studio in London. The Guv used a wooden camera for all his work, and for banquets a 12×10in glass negative, with a tray of flash-powder to throw light on the subject.

Afterwards I went my own way, but in middle life the interest seized me again when, almost by chance, I came to possess two or three wooden cameras in rather poor condition. I wanted to renovate them, but had no skill in that area. So I took myself off to evening classes and a week's course in woodwork and metalwork, and now I suppose I could be described as a keen but perhaps not very skilful woodworker (but keen!).

Wooden cameras for photography came into being around 1839. However, they had been used for years before that by artists as drawing aids. At first they were knocked up almost by the village carpenter; then by the instrument-makers; and finally the specialist camera-makers came into existence. In Britain the firms of Lancaster, Thornton Pickard and Sanderson bring a moist eye wherever old photographers foregather — while the popular and robust Fred Gandolfi, now well into his seventies, gave up camera-making in Peckham only two or three years ago at a firm started by his grandfather in the 1880s.

I have made a couple of wooden cameras

myself based on very early models, but my main interest — and, frankly, all I get time for besides running a busy studio — is collecting pieces that interest me historically, and doing a bit of renovation. Cameras turn up in the strangest places: junk-shops anywhere, attics of old houses, and even old bakeries having a clear-out. My best piece is a 10×8in wood-and-brass camera with three lenses, found in the rubbish skip of an old carriage factory in the north of England where I was photographing. They were clearing out the old darkroom to make room for the new Xerox.

Depending on your own skill and interest, wooden cameras are not too difficult to make. What you need is a model to copy, or some very good photographs showing all the detail. The metalwork (brassware) is not generally available now, but is within the capabilities of a modelmaker. The really hard bit is the bellows.

I will not presume to tell you how to do it — but, if you do, enjoy yourself. ∎

> You can get **bellows** made to order by Camera Bellows Ltd, 2 Runcorn Rd, Birmingham B12 8RQ, 021-440 1695. For **metalware and brasswork**, ask J. Rolph (Engineering) Ltd, 2 Locksgate, Somersham, Cambs, (0487) 842845. Get **racks and pinions** from J. Smith & Sons (Clerkenwell) Ltd, 42-54 St John's Sq. EC1, 01-253 1277.

● The Billcliff unfolded. It was found crunched up in a rubbish skip

441

# Little rockers

**Two makers present their delightful designs for cradles — each offering a very different challenge**

**P**aul Davis writes: The weather was unexpectedly cold and wet, and a number of outside jobs had to be put off. I decided it was time to honour a promise to my wife to make a cradle for Anna, our month-old daughter.

The materials I had set aside were two well-seasoned through-and-through boards and a few scraps from a massive fireplace mantel, all in wild cherry. The idea was to combine a scrolled outline with the traditional dovetailed hopper construction of the French *petrin* or dough trough. Despite its apparent simplicity, this gave rise to a few posers; and then a further problem required solving — what do you do with a cradle these days once the baby has outgrown it?

After I had modified the dovetail joint to allow for the scrolling and profiling of the upper edge of the carcase, and joined a couple of pieces of beech to test the theory, I was ready to go. The answers to the other questions came as I went along.

The dimensions of the carcase were chosen so that it would fit round a 70x35cm pram mattress lying on the base 18mm from the bottom. The measurements given are the overall *inside* measurements, to take into account the 15° chamfer around the bottom.

The 27mm boards were planed down to 18mm — partly for aesthetic reasons, but also because they had spent a while propped up in a sawyer's shed and were badly warped. Unless you are lucky enough to have clean, straight boards that will allow you to cut out each of the components in a single piece, it would be advisable to cut out the scrolled parts before edge-jointing the various bits to make up the sides and ends. The offcuts from the scrolling can be used as softening and to keep the cramps in place. Note, however, that the ovals that form the handles come below the straight shoulders, and you should not attempt to cut out a single curved segment to add to straight-edged ends. In my case, the oval cut-outs also coincided nicely with a couple of unsightly knots.

The modified joint is dovetailed up to about 20mm from the top. The uppermost cuts are not raked, but made parallel to the straight edges of the board, and I mitred the two pins rather than chop one part out to take the other one entire. Thus the profiling can be done along the inside edge of the carcase as well as the outside (see the drawing). Again, be careful, as no angle in this kind of joint is square, so the mitres are not at 45°.

Making a mock-up of one of these corner joints in beech or any scrap wood can prove invaluable to get the hang of cutting at odd angles and to make sure you've got your

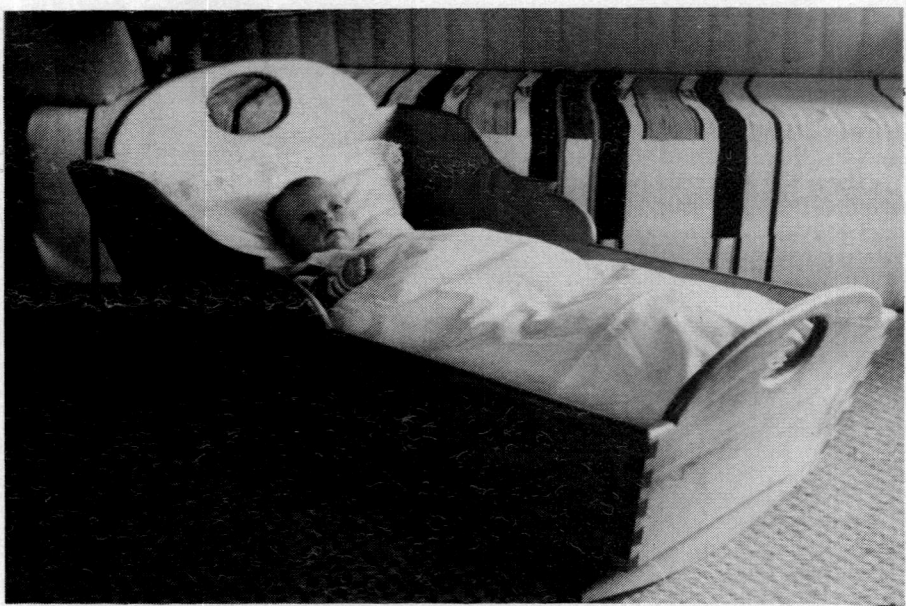

● *Wild cherry was the material for this dual-purpose cradle — the rockers are detachable so the container doesn't fall into disuse when its only or final occupant grows out of it*

geometry right before making mistakes with the real thing. A quick 'on site' way of finding the angle at which the endgrain should be cut is to take a piece of paper or plywood and draw on it two straight lines intersecting at right angles. Stand — or rather, firmly support — along one line a thickish (25mm or more) piece of wood which has been trued up and had the

bottom edge chamfered to the angle of slant you intend to use. Mark the points where the other line passes under the wood and, with a square, draw lines up both faces to the top, square edge. The line drawn across this edge which connects the two perpendiculars will give you the required angle. For a slope of 15° it should be a little under 93°.

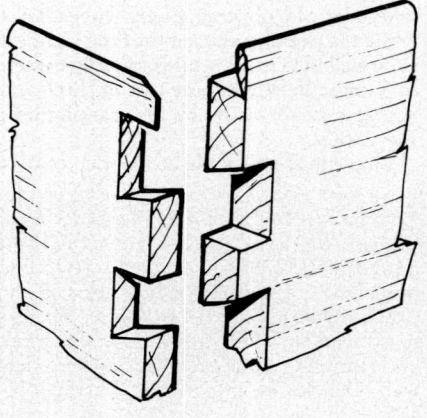

● *Taking the rockers off is a simple matter of withdrawing four screws. The box dovetails (**below**) are canted — both boards slope; Paul Davis' description tells how to set about making these joints*

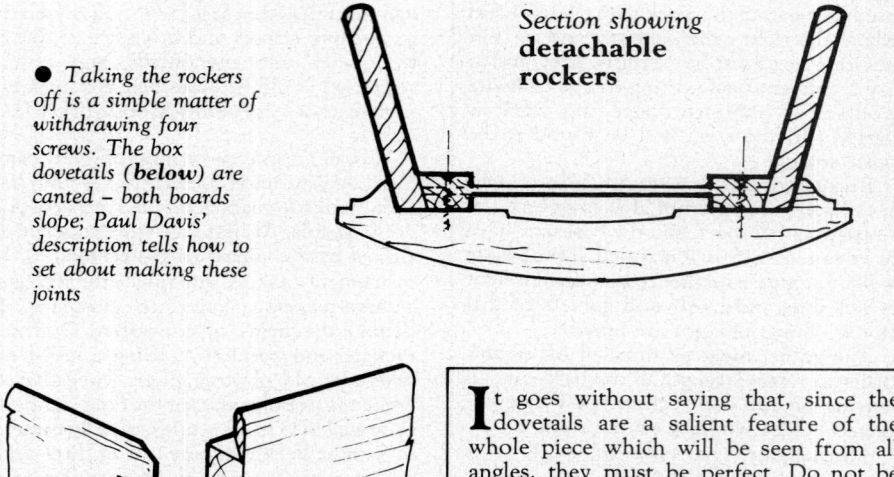

*Section showing* **detachable rockers**

**I**t goes without saying that, since the dovetails are a salient feature of the whole piece which will be seen from all angles, they must be perfect. Do not be tempted to make the fit too tight, or the arrises may crumble and break off. Should the unthinkable happen and one or two dovetails be a shade loose, it is better to use a sliver or shaving of the same wood as packing than to try and hide the fault with a mastic filler.

Before gluing, the sawn scrolls should be cleaned up with a coarse file and scraper and the edges profiled. I used a portable router and an 8mm quarter-round cutter. The 2mm flat along the middle prevents the cutter from biting into the edge on the second cut and is quickly removed afterwards during finishing. The sharp inside angles were picked out with a *very* fine modeller's-saw-kerf bisecting them, and the rounding-off was carried up to the kerf with a few strokes of a chisel. It is a good idea, too, to do most of the hard finishing work on the inside surfaces before assembly.

When the carcase is glued up — if you use cramps, have wedge-shaped softening ready to hand — the ends of the pins and tails can be gently scraped down flush and the finishing completed.

It's at this stage that you may ask yourself what is to become of your efforts once the cradle's occupant has outgrown it a few months later. I made up a base from 6mm-thick pine slats loosely through-tenoned into two narrow 'stiles' which run the length of the carcase at the bottom and have the outside edges chamfered to the same 15° slant as the sides. This rather floppy structure was fitted flush to the bottom of the carcase; then the 'stiles' were pressed hard against the sides and screwed down at the corners directly on to the rockers underneath. This procedure firmly locks the carcase into position between the base and rockers; at some later date it can be re-covered intact and adapted for more permanent use as a magazine-rack or plant-trough.

Alternatively, if no further children are forthcoming, it can be lent out as a cradle for discreet publicity purposes. But don't let your friends use it for a dog's bed or a log-bin!

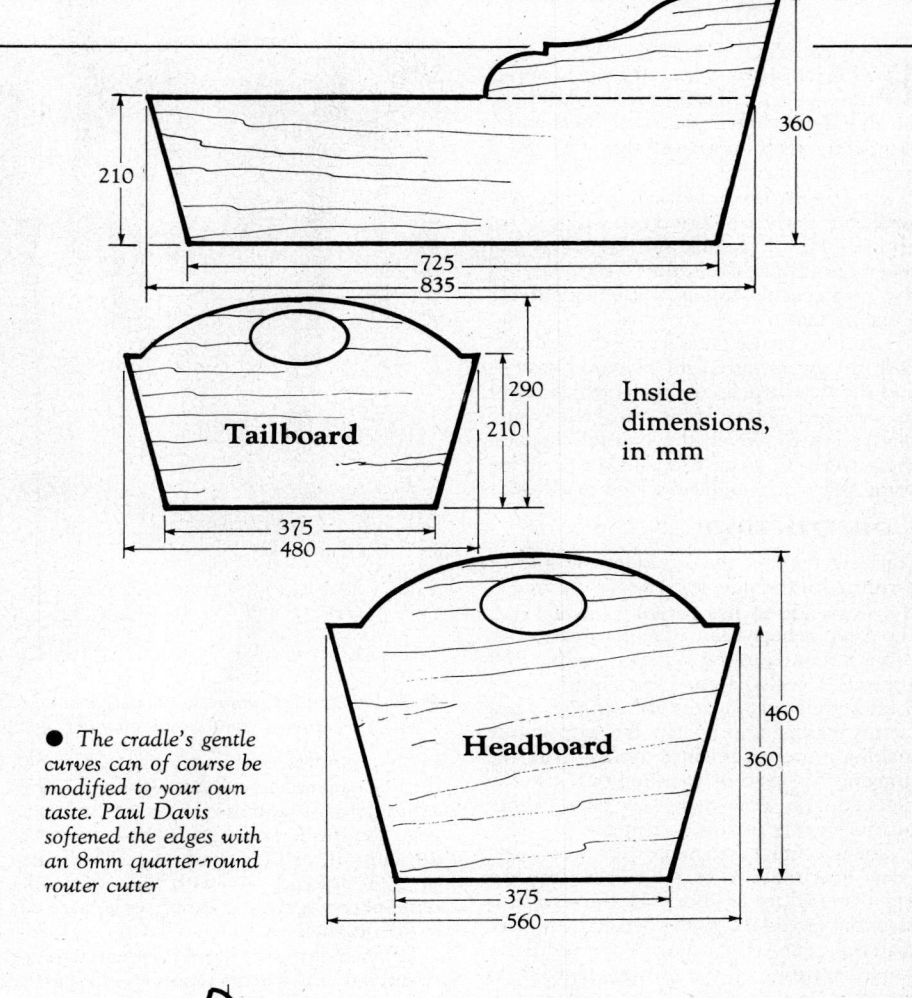

210
360
725
835
290
210
Tailboard
375
480
Inside dimensions, in mm


460
360
Headboard
375
560


● *The cradle's gentle curves can of course be modified to your own taste. Paul Davis softened the edges with an 8mm quarter-round router cutter*

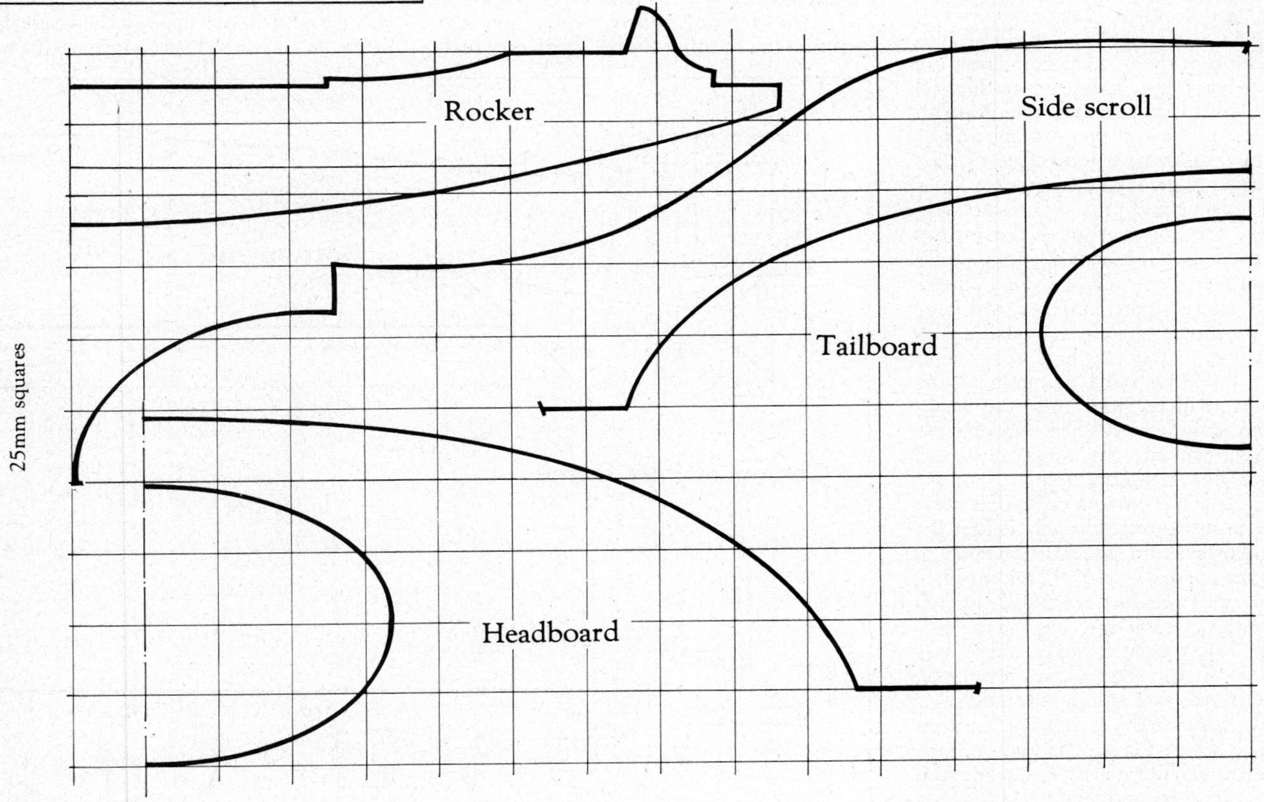

Rocker
Side scroll
Tailboard
Headboard
25mm squares

# Little rockers

**B**ill Nicholson writes: It seemed about time we had a family cradle. After all, we already have two granddaughters and a grandson, with more on the way. So I started drawing.

My 16×8ft home workshop is not very large, but fairly well fitted out with a lathe, grinder, 10 in. circular saw, bandsaw and several portable power tools. I suppose, in a way, projects like this are a way of justifying some of that!

I decided to use parana pine throughout, with the exception of the plywood base — and the two little escutcheons which cover the wedged joints, plus the two round blanks which cover the end-rail bushes; these were cut from a local ash tree, felled some years back and now well dried out.

## Construction

Start by making the 22 identical spindle turnings for the sides and ends of the cradle. If you decide to use parana pine as I did, and keep a nice keen edge on your tools, this is not as daunting a task as it may at first appear. It is also a good exercise; in fact I found, after turning about four, that I had cut my making time by half. It is worthwhile making a measurement template from the drawing for ease of marking-out; use the first spindle you make to take caliper measurements for the remainder.

The next stage is to make the four corner-posts and the two stand pillars. Use the same procedure as above. In this case it is essential to start with perfectly square material, out of winding, since there are square sections on the turning. If, while at the lathe, you decide to do the other small turning jobs, by all means go ahead — with the exception of the two spacers. These are left to the very last, after the cradle and stand are assembled. In this way you can make them to fit and take up any minor discrepancy, allowing a good, free swing.

The drawings give the diameter for holes in the knobs, stand pillars, spacers and cradle-end top rail to house the bushes which I used. But my bushes and spindles were salvaged from the paper-feed wheels of an old photocopier, and you will have to drill the holes to suit the bushes you intend using. After turning the round blanks, a hole the same diameter as the spindles is drilled 5mm into the back. When the spindle is pushed through the cradle-end bush into the blank, it is held central for gluing and cramping.

The side top and bottom rails come next. The only point to mention here is that the tenons are offset, and care must be taken to offset to the correct side. To break the plain face, two cuts 3mm deep were made by passing over the circular saw. As for the side top rails, I felt only a slight curve was required on the top edge, and achieved it by using the router as a spindle-moulder.

We now come to the end top and bottom rails. This is where the bandsaw comes into its own; although not essential, it makes the job a lot easier. I recommend a template for marking-out. Draw the radial centre-lines

● *Bill Nicholson's cradle demands care and accuracy in making several offset and angled mortises – not to mention a considerable amount of repeat spindle turning!*

of the spindles on the template; they can then be squared across the edge for midway drilling points, and drawn across the face to give the hole angles. I found no great difficulty in drilling the holes with the use of a drill-stand. As with the side rails, remember the tenons are offset and are cut at 90° to the end.

When making the legs it is essential to use a template. Ensure the tenon and foot are at 90°. The drawing shows clearly how the position is found for the mortise which

takes the stretcher support rails. However, be careful to cut them to the inside — not all the same!

The angled through mortise on the stand pillar should not cause any problem if you mark out the angle across the face and make sure your chisel is aligned before each tap of the mallet. I cut about 5mm deep from the narrow side, turned over, and worked from the wide side all the way through. I suppose you could drill out most of the waste, but I prefer to use the chisel. Once again, when

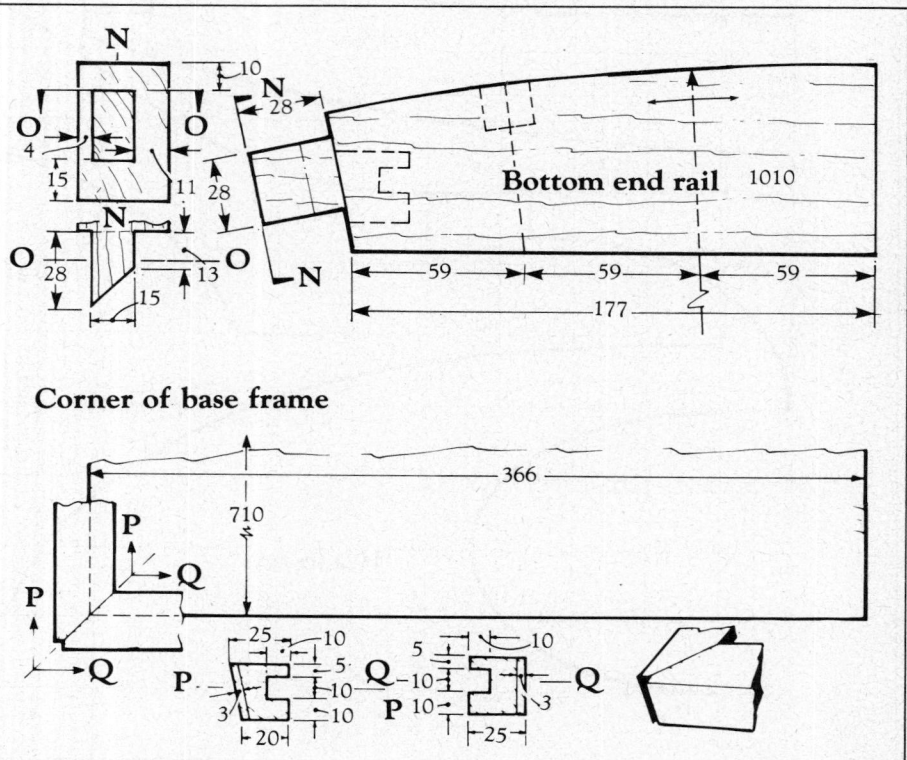

## Corner of base frame

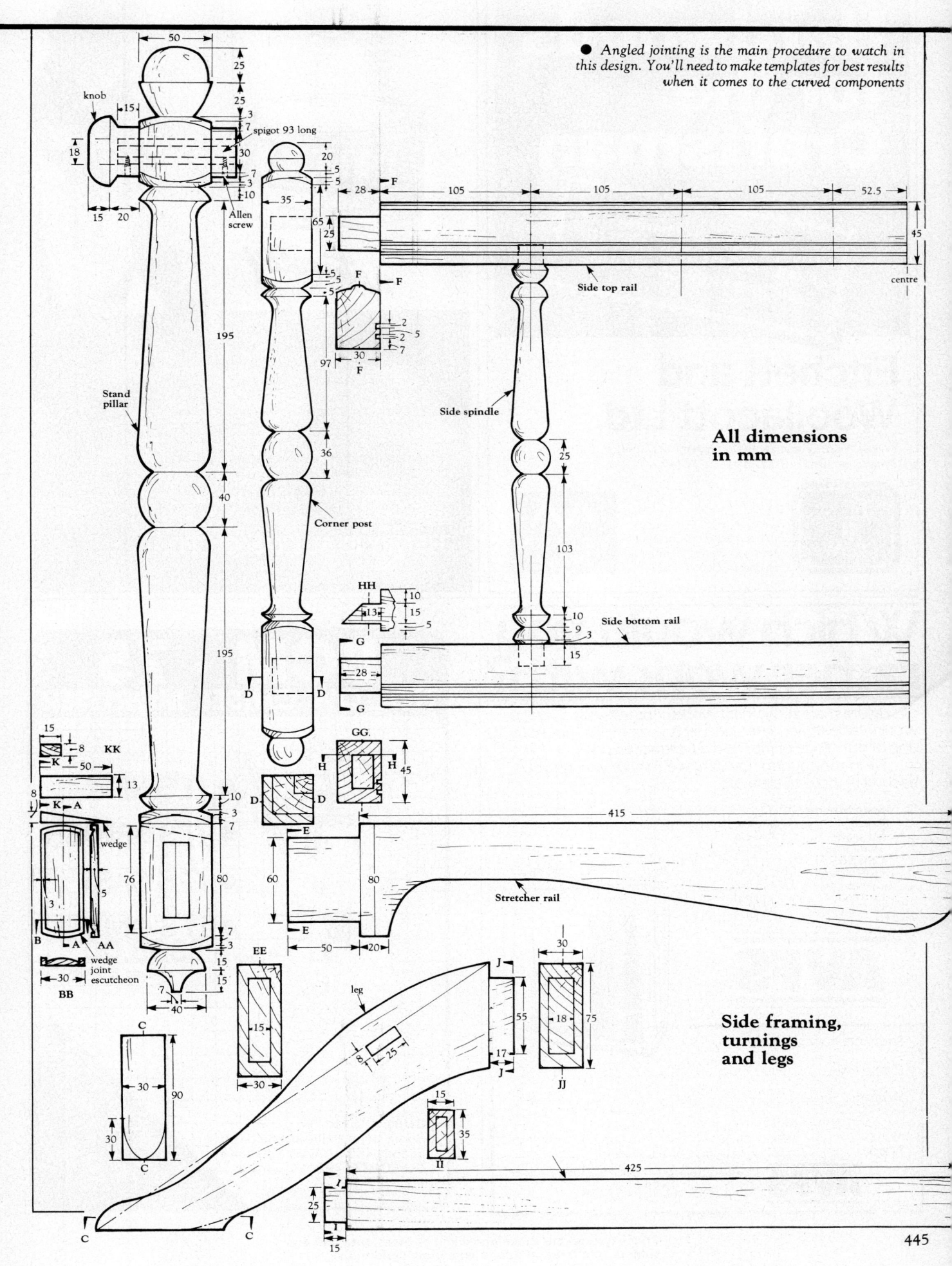

● *Angled jointing is the main procedure to watch in this design. You'll need to make templates for best results when it comes to the curved components*

knob

spigot 93 long

Allen screw

Stand pillar

50
25
25
3
7
15
18
30
7
3
10
15   20
195
40
195

35
20
5
5
28
65
25
97
36
5
5

Corner post

F
F
F
2
2   5
7
30
F

HH
10
13   15
5
G
28
G

KK
15
8
K   50
13
K   A
8
wedge
76
80
3   5
B   A   AA
wedge joint escutcheon
30
7
40
7
3
15
15

C
30
90
30
C

EE
15
30

leg
8   25

Side top rail

105   105   105   52.5
45
centre

Side spindle

25
103
10
9
3
15
10

Side bottom rail

GG.
H   H   45
D   D
E
60
80
E
50   20

415
Stretcher rail

All dimensions in mm

J
55
17
J

30
18   75
JJ

II
15
35

425

25
15

Side framing, turnings and legs

445

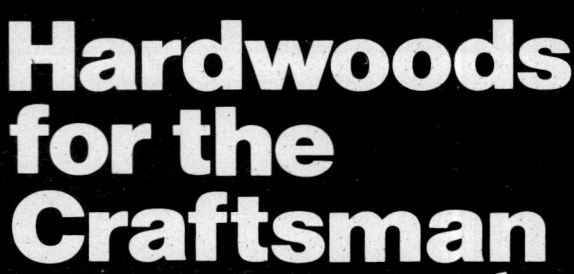

Prices quoted are those prevailing at press date and are
subject to alteration due to economic conditions.

# Little rockers

you come to the mortises on the corner posts, remember they are all offset and therefore 'handed'.

A 25mm frame is made and grooved to accept the plywood base. The only feature of any consequence is the frame corners, which are mitred. A 3mm recess is required to fit round the square section of the corner posts. It must be remembered that the sides of the cradle slope, so the sides of the frame do likewise; but the ends are vertical. This should be made clear by the sketch on the

After carving out the wedge-joint escutcheons, I found I obtained a pleasing effect with a sharp punch, filling the centre section with random marks.

I finished the cradle with antique stain varnish, after sanding it and rubbing it down with wire wool. After three coats, rubbing down between, I applied a final two coats of gloss varnish.

When mounting the cradle in the stand, put the spindle into the knob bush and tighten up the Allen screw. Sit the cradle on

the floor with the stand on its side straddling it, then push the knob spindle through the pillar bush and spacer bush, and into the end-rail bush. Repeat the operation at the other end, and finally tighten up the Allen screws in the spacer bushes.

As a final touch, I suggest a plate be made and screwed to the underside of the base, so that the names and dates of birth of the cradle's occupants may be engraved upon it. ■

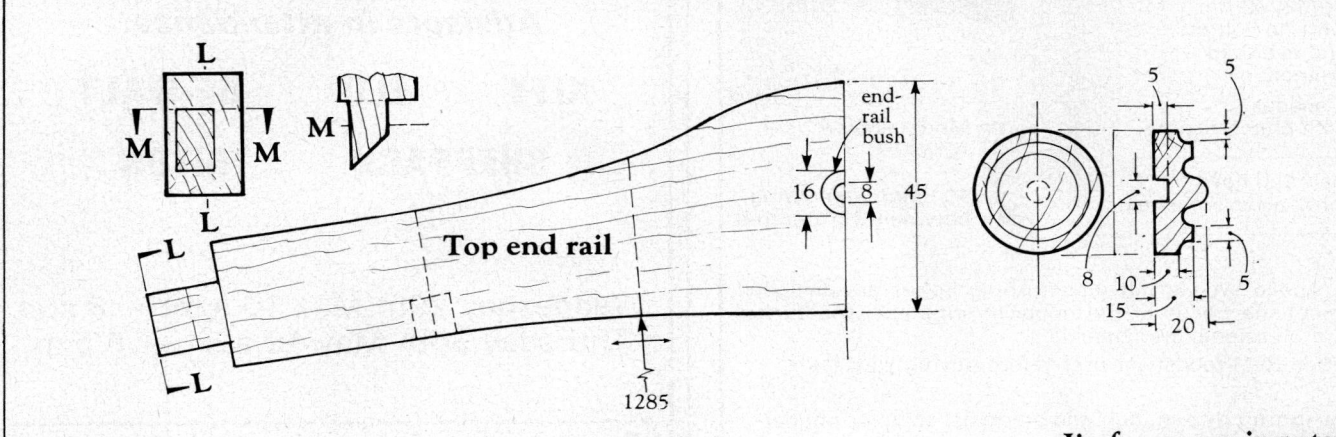

**Top end rail**

**Jig for cramping stand**

drawing. When frame and base have been assembled, the whole is inserted and glued into the cradle. The base can only drop to the designed depth, and it only requires pressure until set.

Cramping the legs required the aid of a quickly knocked-up jig. Once they were set, the stand as a whole was glued up, the wedges knocked home, and three cramps used to cramp up. Check for winding by sitting on a level surface; after all, why bother to make a swinging cradle if it's going to rock?

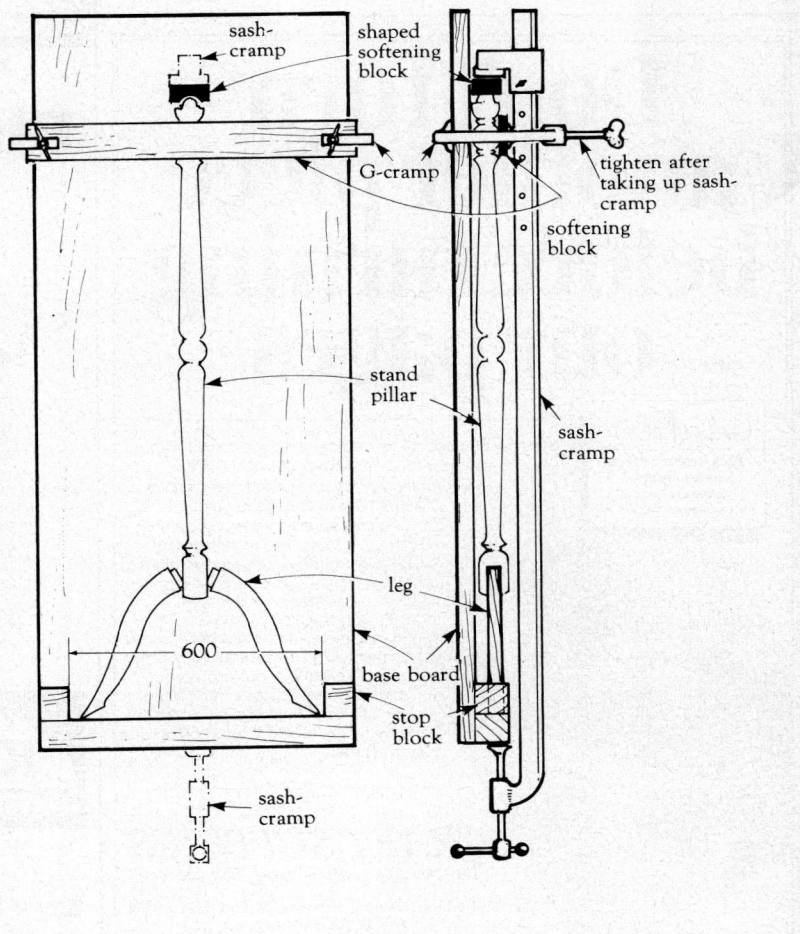

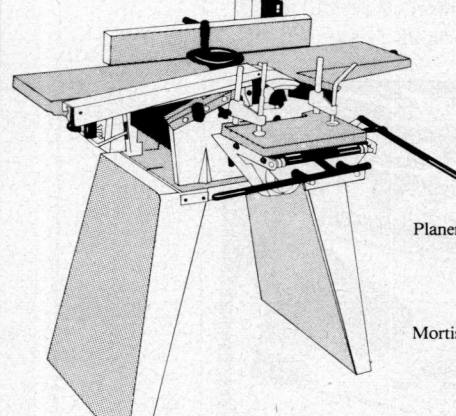

448

Prices quoted are those prevailing at press date and are subject to alteration due to economic conditions.

# Briar's market

## Jaques Cole tells the fascinating story of how roots become pipes

The briar or white heath grows in parts of the Mediterranean which enjoy a hot summer and a mild but showery winter: a belt covering Greece, Italy, Sardinia, Corsica, the south of France and Spain, Morocco, Algeria and Tunisia. The plant's large root (perhaps more accurately a growth or burl) is often partly visible above ground.

Gaining the right to exploit a certain district, the pipe-block manufacturer sends workers to dig the roots and arrange the transport to the mills. This can be on men's backs or with donkeys.

The work is quite hard. Apart from digging the roots out and getting rid of the branches, a preliminary selection must be made. Some roots may include bad parts which need to be cut out on the spot. The roots can grow quite large and heavy; it is often the practice to split them in two, initially for ease of transportation. The diggers may well have to cut their own paths on the hillsides and even build bridges over streams.

There are collecting points from which the briar is taken to the mill. There, to start with, it is covered with earth and kept damp, to avoid premature drying and therefore splitting before the roots are turned into blocks called *ébauchons*.

*Ébauchons* are produced by skilled sawyers, who have to furnish blocks of specific shapes but different sizes. They use very large saws, often without guards, which would make the most hardened British factory inspector turn white! Accidents occur — and it is not unusual for stones to be found inside a root, with dire consequences to the saw and sometimes the sawyer. Fortunately, skilled hands often recognise the signs and are able to avoid mishaps.

Once sawn, the *ébauchons* are selected in several basic qualities before being boiled in water. This boiling generally lasts for between 12 and 18 hours; its purpose is to eliminate all unwanted sap, and it is in effect a sterilising process.

Before going further, what makes briar so suitable for pipe-making? It is extremely hard, and can withstand quite high temperatures. It can be turned easily, and when fully polished it reveals a beauty of grain that enhances the final product. Briar is far less fragile than either clay or meerschaum, and far better suited for mass production and variety of shapes than even cherrywood.

Today Greek briar is considered, with good reason, to be the best; it shows a pinkish colour. Italian and Spanish wood is more likely to go towards a light yellow, and the grain may not be as interesting, perhaps showing bald patches (called branch). In

● *This old photo conveys something of the true flavour of what is still a very traditional industry. It depicts the bowl polishing and selection department of a factory, where the final touches are given in a highly labour-intensive process. Preceding stages involve specialised saws, lathes and boring machines, developed to serve the unique needs of the pipe-maker's craft*

the heyday of Algerian briar, the whole spectrum of quality could be found, but it is quite possible that most of the best briar has been used. A good briar root needs to be at least 50 years old.

Corsican (and to a lesser extent Sardinian) wood shows some very good grain, but often contains minute cracks. I have found similar cracks in both Italian and Spanish wood.

Pipe manufacturers now have to dry briar in their factories, where they can have better control than when they bought *ébauchons* ready-dried. The ideal is about 14% humidity content, but this often means stocking briar for anything up to six months. Kiln-drying was tried for a number of years. Although it had the advantage of being independent of the weather, it resulted in more cracking. Natural seasoning is now back in vogue.

The pipe manufacturers receive briar in four different basic shapes, which conform to recognised specifications:

*Plateau* This form of *ébauchon* is used only by hand-turning craftsmen. The grain radiates in comparatively straight lines from the centre of the root towards the outside; the sawyers will recognise these pieces at once and put them aside. Usually found in the best briar, they are naturals for

the production of hand-made 'straight-grains' and 'bird's-eyes'.

*Cuty* or *cutty* are the small *ébauchons* — usually referred to by their initials CP (*cuty petit*), CM (*cuty moyen*) and CMF (*cuty fort*), followed by two numbers, 1-2, 2-3 and 3-4. The latter classify them into lengths based, believe it or not, on the old French *pouce* (inch) which was done away with during the French Revolution. These *ébauchons* are never thicker than $1^5/_{16}$in, but may go up to $4^1/_2$in in length.

*Marseillaises*, M for short, also MF for the thicker ones, are similar in shape to the *cuty*, but can be thicker than $1^1/_2$in and longer than 5in. Again the numbers 1-2, 2-3, 3-4 and 4-5 classify the length.

*Relevées*, R for short, are mainly used — because of their shapes — for the turning of bents; numbers denote height, from R1 going up in $^1/_4$ins to $2^3/_4$in, although R3 has sometimes been obtainable.

The *ébauchon* supplier will have had the wood selected into qualities. Only the top grades are used by British manufacturers. Their names differ slightly from one producer to the next, but are generally recognised as 'extra-extra', 'extra', 'first' or 'prima', and 'race'. *Plateaux* represent a very top quality in their own right, and very fine extra-extra are sometimes obtainable.

Prices quoted are those prevailing at press date and are
subject to alteration due to economic conditions.

# Briar's market

The next important step is the turning of the bowls.

First, the *ébauchon* is trimmed to a standard thickness compatible with the shape to be turned. This requires a large saw not less than 12in in diameter, known as a calibrating or calibrage saw. Whereas for timber cutting the saw need only show just about the thickness of a piece of wood, the hardness of briar is such that a 'down cut' is required. The sharpening and setting of the saws are critical, and operators used to prefer doing their own.

The thick lathe spindles, with 'live' and 'dead' rings, of the original stock designs were so accurate that little maintenance was required, and even the introduction of ball-bearings did not produce any improvement in efficiency. They had been made by local craftsmen working in concert with the woodturners themselves. Improvements were made during the first 50 years of the industry, but the lathes are still basically the same. When briar bowl-turning started in England, these and other machines had to be imported from France.

The lathe drives a heavy spring chuck that holds the trimmed *ébauchon*. It has to be extremely well balanced to rotate at high speed without the slightest suspicion of vibration. The cutters are mounted on a sliding carriage to the right of the machine and include the following:
- A main cutter shaped like a thick knife, to open up the combustion hole of the bowl, just over half the eventual diameter;
- An auxiliary cutter to clear the surplus of briar round the bowl, to make way for the shaping cutter;
- The shaping cutter, which forms the model to about two-thirds or three-quarters (depending on shape) of its height. The mounting for this cutter is made in such a way as to produce in the final cut a final 'pinch' inwards that can be adjusted from a fraction to several millimetres to accommodate whatever shape is being turned.
- A last cutter to trim the top of the bowl.

Bowl-turning was improved about 20 years ago by the introduction of oil/air cylinders to actuate the movement of the carriage. The advantage was that the cutters could still 'feel' their way into the briar; a purely mechanical action would have provoked a high rate of breakage, since *ébauchons* differ in toughness.

The next operation is the turning of the stem. Here, the cutter, or a set of cutters mounted on a wheel, turns at speed, while the operator controls the movement of the bowl. The bowl is held by a chuck similar to the one used in bowl-turning, but the *ébauchon* has to be centred; hitherto this was done by hand, but now a small oil/air cylinder assists the process. A simple cam will allow the perfect marriage of the bowl and stem, and at the same time allow the cut to be made as far as possible under the bowl. Simple adjustments will permit the turning of oval or square stems.

Finally, the bottom of the bowl has to be

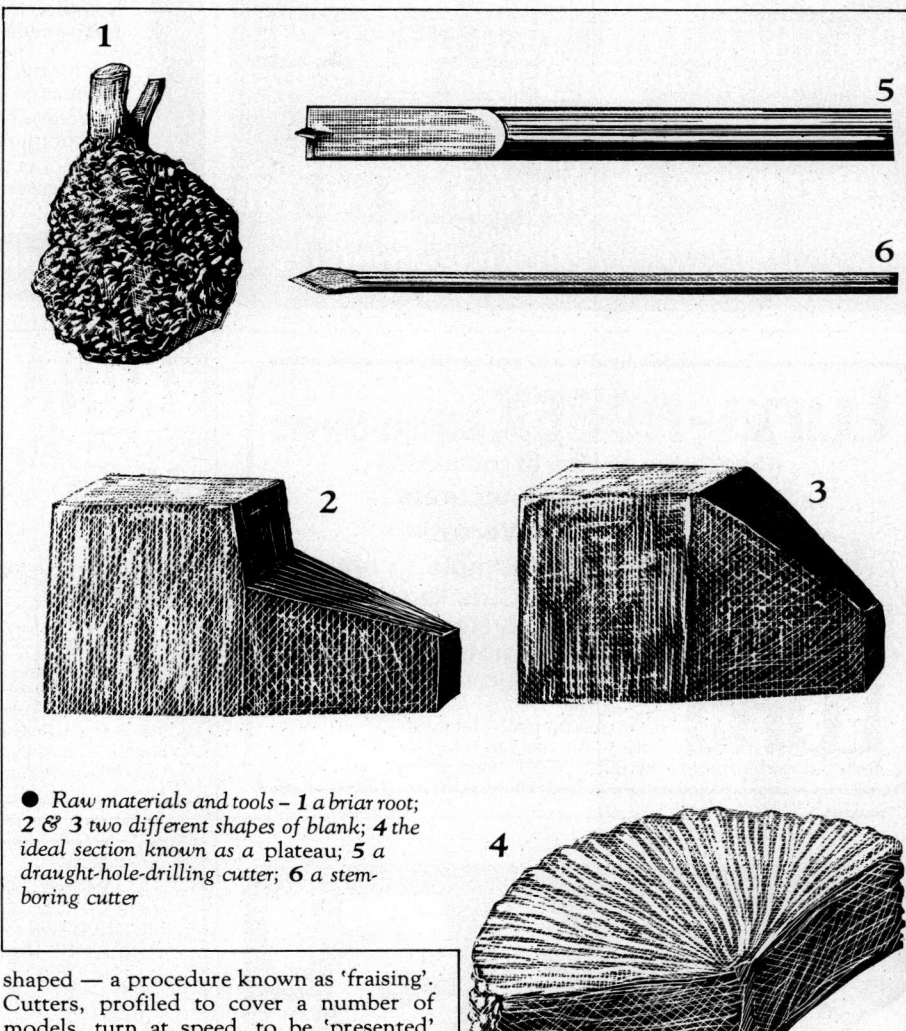

● *Raw materials and tools – 1 a briar root; 2 & 3 two different shapes of blank; 4 the ideal section known as a plateau; 5 a draught-hole-drilling cutter; 6 a stem-boring cutter*

shaped — a procedure known as 'fraising'. Cutters, profiled to cover a number of models, turn at speed, to be 'presented' with the still uncut part. The bowl can be held by a nozzle chuck, tightened by a long screw which can also be actuated by a cylinder. This is on a swivel, so that it is clear from the cutter for loading and ejects the bowl automatically afterwards.

This still leaves a small 'ear', which can be cut with a small cutter, a rasp or sandpaper.

These traditional methods are still used. But over the past decade a new machine has been introduced. Known as the Zuckerman machine, it will cut two bowls at the same time. A master form guides rotating cutters against the *ébauchons*, turning in the opposite direction. The bowl-turning machine described above must still be used, as the combustion hole is needed to hold the bowl, but the shaping cutter needs only to cut ½in from the top.

A similar machine is fitted with a papering band to complete the shaping and in effect the first papering operation.

Drilling the draught hole is simple, but twist drills normally used for wood are not satisfactory. The trade has had therefore to invent its own bits. They are in effect small cutters (the standard drill hole is 3mm). The shape of the heads differs from one factory to the other, from a 'spear' to a straight cut on an angle, but the result is the same. There must of course be enough clearance for the shavings to evacuate — and, in order to attain speed and thereby productivity, the head has to be constantly lubricated with a piece of felt soaked in oil.

For boring of the stem to take the mouthpiece (usually of vulcanite), the trade invented its own horizontal machines before vertical drills were found for the wood industry. These are still in use, although a far cry from the original equipment worked by foot treadles.

Once the pipes are fitted, the rest of the manufacturing process is more labour-intensive. Polishing is important, particularly for top-quality products. In principle, three papering operations are required, all carried out by hand — starting with an emery cloth or paper perhaps as coarse as 90 or even 80 grit, followed by 120 grit and then 240; for very good briar, an even finer grit may be used. In practice, however, the papering operations can be

452

Prices quoted are those prevailing at press date and are subject to alteration due to economic conditions.

cut down to two. For instance, in the lower qualities, when filling is used a first coarse papering is essential, whereas this will not be necessary in top qualities. On the other hand, good-quality pipes need a final pumicing operation (with a mixture of pumice powder and oil) on a felt-faced wheel; lower qualities often need only a mop with the aid of a pumicing compound.

Staining requires aniline dyes mixed with either methylated spirit or, as in France, almost pure alcohol. Each manufacturer guards his formulae and methods of application jealously. The latter include burning off the stain, letting it dry naturally, and wiping by hand with a cloth.

This will leave a sheen of varying hues. That needs to be cleaned off, an operation which at the same time ensures that the softest parts of the briar will absorb the maximum stain.

This cleaning off can be carried out in several ways:
- by a mop with a suitable compound;
- by pumicing — in effect a further polishing operation, more suitable on fine pipes where the grain needs to be shown at its best;

- by wiping off with alcohol (this often needs a light pass with the mop).

If a two-tone effect is required, a top colour will be applied on what has had to be a fairly dark initial stain.

Pipes can of course be finished natural, although the application of a very light coat of stain, particularly on top qualities, will give more life to the grain in any case.

There are two distinct ways of obtaining a final finish. Some continental manufacturers favour applying a fine coat of varnish, letting it dry and finishing the pipe on a fairly slow-turning soft mop with a wax compound. In England, the 'mop finish' is preferred. This consists of applying the required varnish directly on to the mop and, with the aid of a wax compound, working it further into the soft parts of the briar. The right way to apply both varnish and wax together is something that only experience can teach. A stiff mop is used, which is 'dressed' properly for maximum efficiency.

We have only concerned ourselves with the actual work on the briar wood itself, but almost as much has to go

into the mouthpieces, mostly vulcanite but occasionally acrylic, horn, amber (very expensive) or imitation amber such as amberine or amberoid. One operation, however, is worth noting. Once fitted, the pipe stems and the mouthpiece seldom match perfectly. They therefore require to be levelled or flushed to a continuous line. It looks simple enough, but requires attention and a feel for the round. Most trainees manage to catch their fingers on the special paper wheels, and quickly learn to avoid doing so! The really skilled operator will be able, more often than not, to do the 'double levelling' which means that however you turn the mouthpiece, it will always be seen to fit properly. For this he will use his own prepared wheel, maybe as much as 7 or 8in in diameter, whereas for normal work a 4in wheel is sufficient.

Some of the special skills appear to have gone forever or at best only to be known by a few, but it is pleasing nowadays to see young workers who are recovering some of these 'lost arts' — often guided by their elders, whereas the old hands of 70 years ago could seldom be persuaded to teach a newcomer. ∎

● *Below right* is the special lathe and sliding tool-feed used for turning pipe bowls – the timber and cutter are in the centre. The drawings show the procedures (**right**), and the cutters (**below**) in the sequence in which they are used: **1** for the combustion hole, **2** for clearing, **3** for shaping and **4** for the top of the bowl

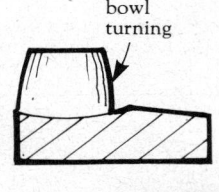

bowl turning

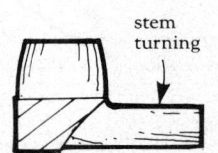

stem turning

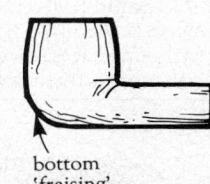

bottom 'fraising'

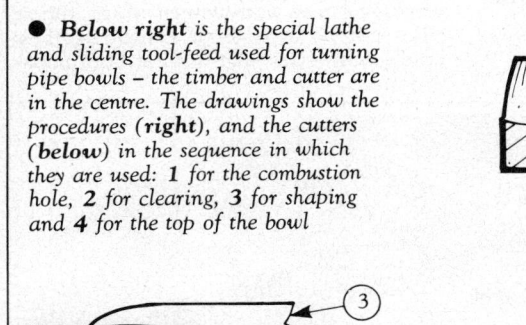

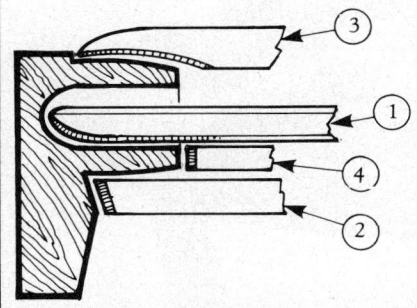

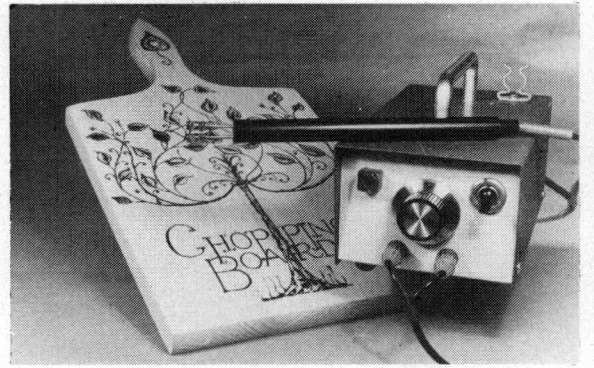

# Mainstream mentors

**Two very particular institutions show how woodworking can still be taught as an art, craft and skill in the late industrial age**

**K**enneth Lane writes: Bembridge School, Isle of Wight, was one of the first in Britain to teach arts and crafts. It began doing so at, or soon after, its foundation as early as 1919 by J. Howard Whitehouse.

A former Liberal MP, Whitehouse had always been a keen educationalist. He was a devotee of Ruskin, and amassed a large collection of his works (now housed in a library and gallery at the school, especially built for the purpose, so that Dulwich College and Bembridge probably share the distinction of being the only schools to have their own art galleries). The School buildings lie at the easternmost tip of the Isle of Wight, in a magnificent situation with the sea on two sides and long views of the Hampshire and Sussex coasts.

Whitehouse wrote a number of books, and in 1928 he published *Creative Education in an English School*. In it he wrote: 'It may not be without interest or value to attempt to set forth the creative activities of a school

● *A Bembridge schoolboy of former times uses a pole lathe – made by the boys, and still in operation*

where, without, we hope, any weakening of the literary and academic side of education, arts and crafts are regarded as instruments of spiritual and intellectual education.' The activities to which he referred included woodwork, art, pottery and printing (to this day, a termly newspaper is still printed on similar traditional presses.)

Of the woodwork room he wrote: 'A boy should be given not only hobbies for the present, but real interests in his future life.' I should add here that the school became co-educational in 1976, and girls are encouraged to include woodwork in their choices for arts and crafts. Some may well soon be opting for O-level Design and Technology.

Today the department has two aims: to participate in the modern examinations, with their concepts of technology, and yet teach all the basic skills on traditional lines. This teaching is not necessarily aimed towards higher education in craft colleges, but is formulated to give pupils a love and understanding of the natural materials with which they work; to appreciate the beauty of craftsmanship, and to develop the skilful use of tools.

We hope that at least we will succeed in producing men and women of the future who will be capable of enhancing their homes with work that has not been mass-produced.

● **Left** *are two Bembridge-made coffee-tables in mahogany, the upper one including a magazine rack and the lower with stripes of beech.* **Above** *is a marquetry-topped chess table, again in Brazilian mahogany*

**B**ob Wearing writes: The course in furniture-making at Shrewsbury College continues to grow in reputation, and attracts students from all parts of Britain — while for the second year running a Shrewsbury student has been awarded the City and Guilds silver medal as the best of the year.

This small, intimate course continues to be staffed on the woodwork side by its founder John Price, John Bennett and myself. This past year we have been joined by Dave Bennetts, recently appointed head of the school of art, who is particularly interested in the design side; his influence on the work is already visible. Each year, of course, has its fashions and fancies amongst the students: currently, there seems greater interest than usual in laminating and the vacuum-bag press.

We do not train for the furniture industry or in industrial design. Rather, we aim to produce craftsmen able to work in small individual shops — ultimately with a view to setting up on their own, which quite a number of students do immediately on completion. The failure rate seems negligible. Work is not confined merely to the City and Guilds 555 Furniture Crafts syllabus. Realism is the basis, always along with the thought of earning a successful living from the craft. In practice this means that business studies and methods are covered in detail, while additions on the craft side are wood-machining and finishing, metalwork, tool- and appliance-making, upholstery, and traditional country chairmaking based on Fred Lambert's techniques with rounding planes. Demonstrations and talks by outside practising craftsmen make welcome breaks.

Classes are limited to 16, to avoid overcrowding and to ensure personal attention. The basic course runs for two years, but selected mature students are enrolled for one year. This happy mix of older and younger students is a noticeable feature at Shrewsbury. Occasional students stay on for a third year, and there is a possibility that the course may be extended to lead to a Higher DATEC qualifications for those who achieve a higher level of work.

Pressure for places is high, and there are always people on the waiting-list — but likely candidates should not hesitate to telephone John Price.

● John Price is on Shrewsbury 51544, ext. 42. The college's annual exhibition will be held this year at the Shrewsbury Shire Hall on 20-7 June: 9-5 weekdays, 9-12.30 Saturday, closed Sunday. ■

● *This cabinet by Simon Watson, of mahogany with a sycamore interior, features curl veneers on doors and drawer-fronts*

● *The florid Victorian chair (**far left**) was a project in restoration and re-upholstery; the pieces **left** and **below** are by Flora Smith and John Deavan respectively. Two Shrewsbury students in the last five years have been appointed cabinetmakers to Her Majesty the Queen*

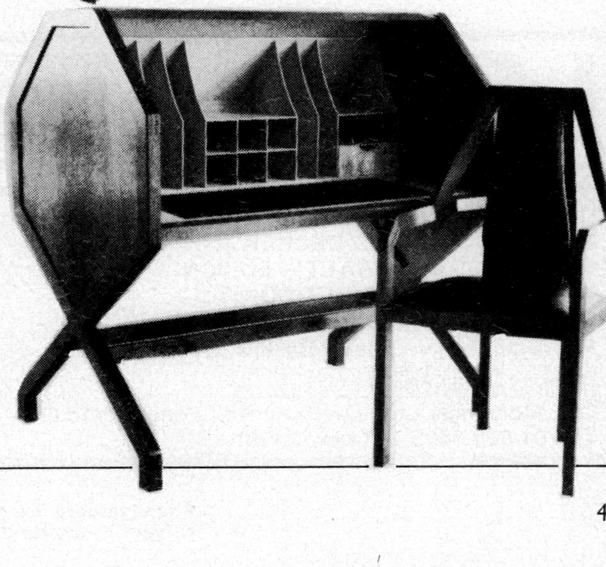

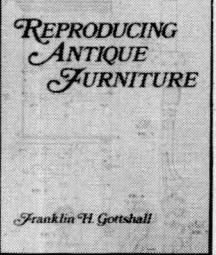
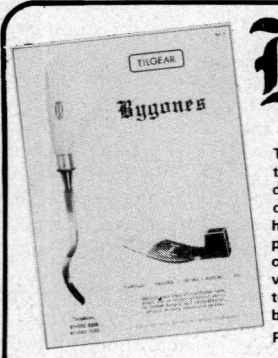

456    Prices quoted are those prevailing at press date and are subject to alteration due to economic conditions.

# The Danish finish

**Danish oil — Ronald Snell shows, in meticulous detail, how to get the best from a little-noticed finish**

Of the many types of wood finishes available, Rustins' Danish oil is one of the least often mentioned. This is a shame, because the product combines many attributes which both amateur and professional value in the final appearance of their work.

I have experimented with wax, varnish, polyurethane, shellac, lacquer and french polish, and with other oil finishes. Each had some shortcoming or drawback in final appearance, application technique required, or — in the case of oil — patience! I was tempted to sample Danish oil by chance, and I have used it exclusively for some years. I have found, moreover, that Rustins' recommendations stop short of indicating its real potential.

Danish oil appears to be compatible with most dyes and stains, water- or white-spirit-based. Choice is a personal matter, but make sure that any colouring you use has surface penetration. Some wood colours contain pigments which do not soak in, and can be rubbed off quite easily. Before beginning with the oil, ensure that the stain is absolutely dry, or it will inhibit drying of the oil. I also lightly rub out the stained surface with 0000 wire wool before applying the first coat of oil. This guarantees that any surplus colour not fully absorbed by the wood is not picked up by the applicator.

I have tried applying the oil with cloth pads, but I find brushes are by far the best method as a much better body can be built up. I cannot, however, place enough stress on the importance of brush quality. Paintbrushes will give a paintbrush finish, and I suggest the use of a Hamilton squirrel-hair 504. ½in, 1in and 2in together are adequate for most jobs.

The work can be divided into four operations: applying the oil; bodying up; rubbing out; and achieving the shine.

Before starting to apply the oil, make sure the area you work in is as free of dust as possible. Dust is the enemy of the polisher, and a corner of the joiner's shop is not the best place! Thoroughly clean the work (a tack cloth is very useful), and have the atmosphere warm — ensure fast drying and give less chance of surface contamination.

Shake the oil thoroughly before opening the tin, and allow time for bubbles to settle. Pour a quantity of oil into a small container, less than you need for the job in hand; the brush can still pick up elements of stain, which are transferred by the brush to the oil supply. If you put the surplus back in the tin when you have finished, it imparts a tint to the oil which detracts from its value.

Danish oil has a low viscosity and extremely good covering ability. The initial coat should be applied with a moderately full brush and drawn out to leave a medium film on the work. Its low viscosity gives it a tendency to run, and on vertical surfaces it is essential to check regularly. Where ridges or runs begin to appear, pull them into the surrounding area with the tip of the brush. Initial surface tack is fairly quick, but care at this stage pays dividends. Work with the grain and use as few strokes as possible. View surfaces at an angle and lightly smooth away any bubbles if they appear.

The first coat should be left for 24 hours for the oil to dry out thoroughly — not just to become surface-dry. Subsequent applications tend to dry more quickly; but, for the effort you are making, this should not be considered a cost factor.

● *A squirrel-hair brush and careful application bring out the best in the under-rated Danish oil*

The second operation is the rubbing out. After 24 hours, go over the whole workpiece with 000 wire wool. This must be done carefully; I recommend Silver Fleece wool. Cut the oil back to the wood with as little pressure as possible, and keep changing it round or renewing it to avoid clogging. Always follow the grain — if you rub out across the grain, imperfections will show in the final finish. The aim at this stage is to ensure a perfectly flat surface, but be careful of corners and edges where you can easily expose the natural colour.

The next stage is the application of a second coat of oil, but not before the whole job has been very carefully brushed off and every speck of polish and wool-dust have been cleaned away. A quick blow into corners and a wipe with a duster is just not good enough. I use a long-hair pastry-brush for corners, and finish with a tack cloth. The second coat of oil should now be applied in the same way as the first; but before this, see there is no need for retouching or enhancing the colour. This will be the last chance.

When the second coat is dry, rub it out again. Use 000 wool with even greater care, as now the aim is to remove the shine and not cut back to the wood. This process should be repeated for four coats, except that the fourth coat should be left for 48 hours to harden completely.

At this stage you must consider what quality of final finish you want. I have found a superb result can be achieved with wax polish. But, for a superior smoothness, superior abrasives are required. As a final abrasive, steel wool is too coarse to use on its own, so rub out with 0000-grade wool and wax. Great care must be taken because, once the wax is on, no further applications of oil are possible. Use small applications of wax and a very light hand. Keep changing the wool round — it quickly clogs with wax and oil — and keep as large an area of wool as possible in contact with the work to avoid localised rubbing-out. Traces of wool may work out from time to time; keep blowing these away as they are liable to scratch the surface. Keep a close eye on the work to ensure that you are only matting the surface, and not cutting the body away.

You can get a superior finish with pumice and rottenstone. Pumice is marketed in four grades, the finest being 4F. In this last stage 4F too is too coarse to be used on its own, and it requires a lubricant. A mixture of soap-ends softened in water is ideal. Apply the pumice powder direct to the workpiece — preferably with a pounce-bag, which is usually made from two thicknesses of muslin. This controls the quantity of pumice powder, but it is not essential. Rub out with a soft cloth damped in the soap mixture. Finally wash off and begin to rub out with the rottenstone. Rottenstone must be used with water as a lubricant (thin out the water/soap mixture); the result will be a mirror-like smoothness.

The last stage is waxing. Wax can be used by itself direct to the wood, or applied to many types of finishes; like all finishing materials, it is better applied in light coatings than heavy ones. When you are rubbing out with wax-lubricated wire wool, thoroughly polish off the surface with a medium coarse cloth. A short bristle brush should be used in corners to remove any excess wax. Allow some time between applications to let the solvents evaporate. The final two applications should be very thinly applied, and polished out with a soft wool cloth and soft brush to achieve a fine satiny shine.

Rustins' oil is based upon tung oil. It also contains resins and other oils, and is lead-free and non-toxic when dry — which makes it good for eating utensils and wooden bowls. The oil dries by oxidisation (absorption of oxygen), but this does not begin until the white-spirit solvent has evaporated. The final finish is very durable and is resistant to water and solvents. It should be kept in a sealed container to prevent oxidation; and, if it does thicken with age, it can be thinned back to consistency with white spirit.

● Mr Snell would like it to be emphasised that he has no connection with Rustins other than as a satisfied customer. Rustins Ltd are at Waterloo Rd, London NW2, tel. 01-450 4666.

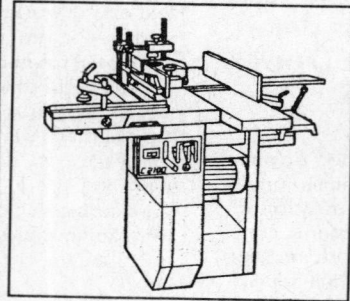
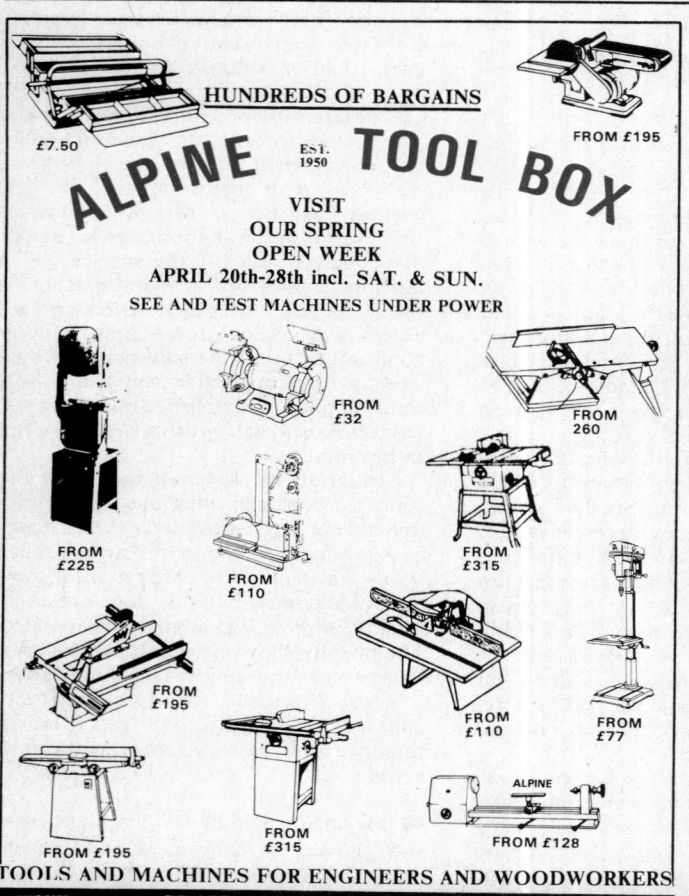

Prices quoted are those prevailing at press date and are subject to alteration due to economic conditions.

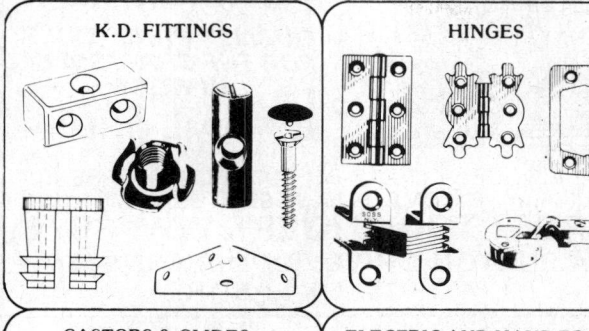
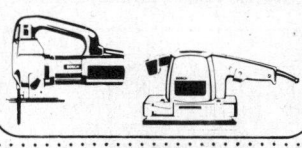

KINDLY MENTION 'WOODWORKER' WHEN REPLYING TO ADVERTISEMENTS

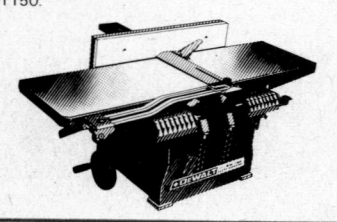

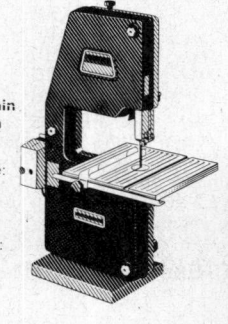

# A new dimension in small sawbenches – with scoring.

**Vadkin Better Buy – around £1100**

The new Bursgreen AGSP is an inspired development of the highly successful AGS range of sawbenches, with a big difference – a canting saw unit with scoring.

With built-in user benefits.

- ■ 2.2kW machine with cast iron table for precision work.
- ■ Caters for panels up to 1000mm x 2500mm, and deep ripping up to 100mm, using optional sliding table.
- ■ The unique foolproof, auto adjusting scoring saw gives perfect edges – no spelching or inaccuracies.
- ■ Riving knife and rip fence as standard.

Try it out at our permanent demo areas.

## Wadkin Bursgreen

### Showing the way.

Wadkin plc, Green Lane Works, Leicester LE5 4PF
Telephone: 0533 769111. Telex: 34646.

---

# Comparing notes

Once a cabinetmaker, Edward Park describes his rewarding move into the world of musical instruments

If I had been told when I left school that it would be 27 years before I started college, I wouldn't have believed it. But that's just what happened.

It was in the fifties that I left school at 15 to train as a precision woodworker, making specialised cabinets and instrument-cases for the medical industry. My job involved a lot of small precision joinery work in solid teak, which itself is virtually unheard-of nowadays because of its cost and scarcity. Surprisingly, I have fond memories of those days — despite the working conditions, which were Dickensian to say the least. No means of dust extraction meant dust everywhere: up your nose and in your ears. The noise in the small machine shop was deafening, and we endured bitter cold in the winter.

In the early sixties I moved into antiques, working as a cabinetmaker and french-polisher for a firm which was the largest antique dealer in south London at the time. In 1967 I established my own successful business restoring and making reproduction antique furniture. It lasted 15 years, and after that I was ready for a change.

By this time I had worked with furniture for 24 years. One day I was approached by a professional-musician friend who asked me to repair his guitar — and I realised that I

● Sverrier Gudmundsson, a third-year advanced student at Merton College, is watched by Tricia Mattin as he takes fine measurements for the lute he is making

lacked the technical skills to undertake such a task confidently and competently. A bad restorer, I knew, could totally ruin the tone of a musical instrument. Thinking that, I realised how much more pleasure I would gain from actually making an instrument: an object which would come to life in a way no piece of furniture ever could.

Merton Technical College seemed to offer the only course in the country which would fulfil all my needs. I was accepted after completing a small test which, to my great relief, a five-year-old could have passed. Its purpose was to test aptitude rather than skill, as the latter would be taught during the first year of the course. The student working opposite me began the course with little practical experience or skill, but with enthusiasm and encouragement she has gone on to acquire the skill to make a violin to a high standard.

This two-year full-time course, leading to the City and Guilds qualification in musical-instrument repair, covers brass and woodwind instruments, guitars, the violin family, and pipe-organ design. All these subjects are introduced in the first year, when the students concentrate on attaining a high level of hand and machine skill — including the use of a metal-turning lathe. This way, we learn to make the special tools we need. In the second year, students choose three subjects in which to develop their skills. The final examination has two written papers, plus continuous practical assessment of the second-year work.

Students come from all over the world and include ex-military bandsmen, a teacher, a social worker and a train driver, as well as school-leavers. There is a friendly,

● Edward Park finishes off the f-holes on his violin

● A trombone-slide overhaul in the capable hands of Andrew Bestwick

relaxed relationship between students and tutors, which allows individuality and self-expression. The tutors are approachable, always willing to give help and advice. We spend most of our time in the workshop, with only one morning a week in the classroom studying the theory of wood-work and metalwork. Local schools provide us with instruments to repair.

# Wind in the wood

As students discuss their future plans, one is struck by the number of areas of craft-based work for which the course has prepared us. Some intend to establish their own musical-instrument-repair business, or to work for other repairers. Others are embarking on quite different crafts — for example, those of the blacksmith or jeweller.

As for myself, I plan to set up a guitar-and-violin-making workshop, these being the two instruments in which I have enjoyed specialising. The course has been most worthwhile: I have acquired new skills, made new friends and developed my interest in music. Like many other students, I have designed and made a guitar, and I eagerly await the day when I will string it up and bring it to life. Furthermore, I am now in the middle of repairing the guitar I once had to turn away!

● All the tools and instruments made by the Merton students will be on show from 7.30pm on Wednesday 5 June at Merton College Annexe, Rutlish Rd, London SW19. Interviews for the two-year full-time course starting in September 1985 are taking place now and will continue up to the starting date in the middle of September. Part-time day courses are also offered for those who cannot study on a full-time course. Details from School of Engineering, Merton College, Morden Park, London Rd, Morden, Surrey, tel. 01-640 3001. The course tutor is Phil Chambers. ■

● *Merton final-year student Jonathan Dodd regulates a flute*

**Making wind instruments is a special challenge for the woodturner who can turn a hand to brasswork as well. Phil Kingham explains how he tackled a baroque bassoon**

When I started this project, I opted to bore it in separate joints according to standard bassoon practice. I chose as my model a four-jointed bassoon made by Proser in 1777 which is in the instrument collection of the Horniman Museum, south London. With the indulgence of the curator, and armed with a battery of plastic measuring devices, I took no less than 132 measurements from the original!

● *Chucks, centres and steadies, with a chisel for scale.* **Above right** *are 18th-century and modern bassoons, plus a modern contra-bassoon*

The main problem with the actual woodwork was the continuous tapered bore that runs the full length of the bassoon. I overcame this by making reamers for each of the five bores from redundant beech table-legs, taper-turned to diameter, gluing lengths of hacksaw blade into a routed groove and finishing the long edge on a grinder. To my surprise this worked very well if very slowly.

Reamers aside, my equipment consisted of a Woodmen KL lathe, a three-jaw chuck, a tail-stock drill chuck, two home-made lathe steadies, and the usual twist bits and turning tools.

The timber was pearwood, but any fruit-wood, beech or maple could have been substituted.

Basically, the woodturning is very similar to the method of making a standard lamp; that is, fashioning the outside after the inside hole is finished. Each section was first set up between the three-jaw chuck and steady, and the socket (where needed) bored with a flatbit in the tail-stock chuck. I

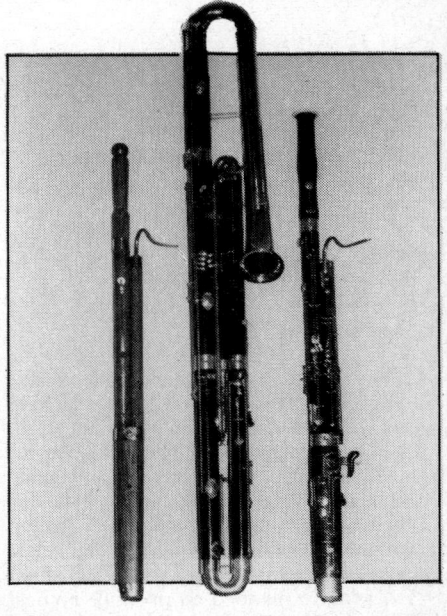

changed to a twist bit and drilled through from both ends, with the fervent prayer that the holes would eventually meet. Reaming followed, copiously lubricated with linseed oil; the sanded bore was treated to four coats of linseed to prevent condensation. The external shaping proved a great exercise in the use of the skew chisel, at which my previous proficiency was about 10%!

The top two bass joints presented no problem, but the bottom joint incorporates twin bores which converge at the bottom, so the music goes down, does a U-turn and then comes up. Here, I confess I cheated and made both bores separately, planed an edge on each and glued them together, finishing the outside dimensions by hand plane.

The first or tenor joint has a protuberance halfway, which wraps around the long joint. This was shaped mainly with gouges, taking a little off at a time and trying it.

After polishing with shellac, the tone holes were drilled in their correct positions and the appropriate brass key-work shaped, soldered and fitted. At one stage I was tempted to add extra keys in order to obtain a full chromatic scale, but decided to stay as close as possible to the original 18th-century specification.

The brass crook, which completes the outfit by joining bassoon to reed, caused many a headache. The present one is the mark 5!

It took five months of leisure (?) activity to complete the instrument, of which three were spent on the metalwork.

While involved in this project, I developed a profound admiration for the old-time craftsmen who made the original, without access to all the technology we now take for granted. ■

## Books for reference

P. Tomlin, *Woodwind for Schools*; A. Baines, *Woodwind Instruments and their History*; L. G. Langwill, *The Bassoon and Contra Bassoon*; *Woodworker*, Vols 76 & 77.

# The chest that changed its spots

**Talented newcomer Francesca Graham tells the story of the contemporary classic she designed**

The brief I set myself was to design a chest-of-drawers whose surface was both unusual, and cheap to produce.

The idea for the shape came from looking at the massive, heavy coffers made on the Continent in the late Middle Ages. These were usually constructed from solid wood, and the surfaces received no treatment other than a protective hot wax or varnish coating — which over the years, and with re-coating, acquired a glowing patina. Sometimes it was painted and/or gilded, especially when it was for use in a church.

I originally planned to produce a chest whose drawers had varied widths and depths, after the manner of a Mondrian painting — using the fronts of the drawers to create a pattern of abstract shapes. It became obvious, however, that to put such a design into even small-batch production would present too many constructional problems: not having all the drawers a standard size would be time-consuming, and the cost would be prohibitive. Therefore the only solution was to make the concept more practical. This involved using the same basic idea of varying sizes of drawers, but limiting the sizes to four only. Each drawer was carefully dimensioned to accommodate its potential contents — shirts, sweaters, socks, linen, etc.

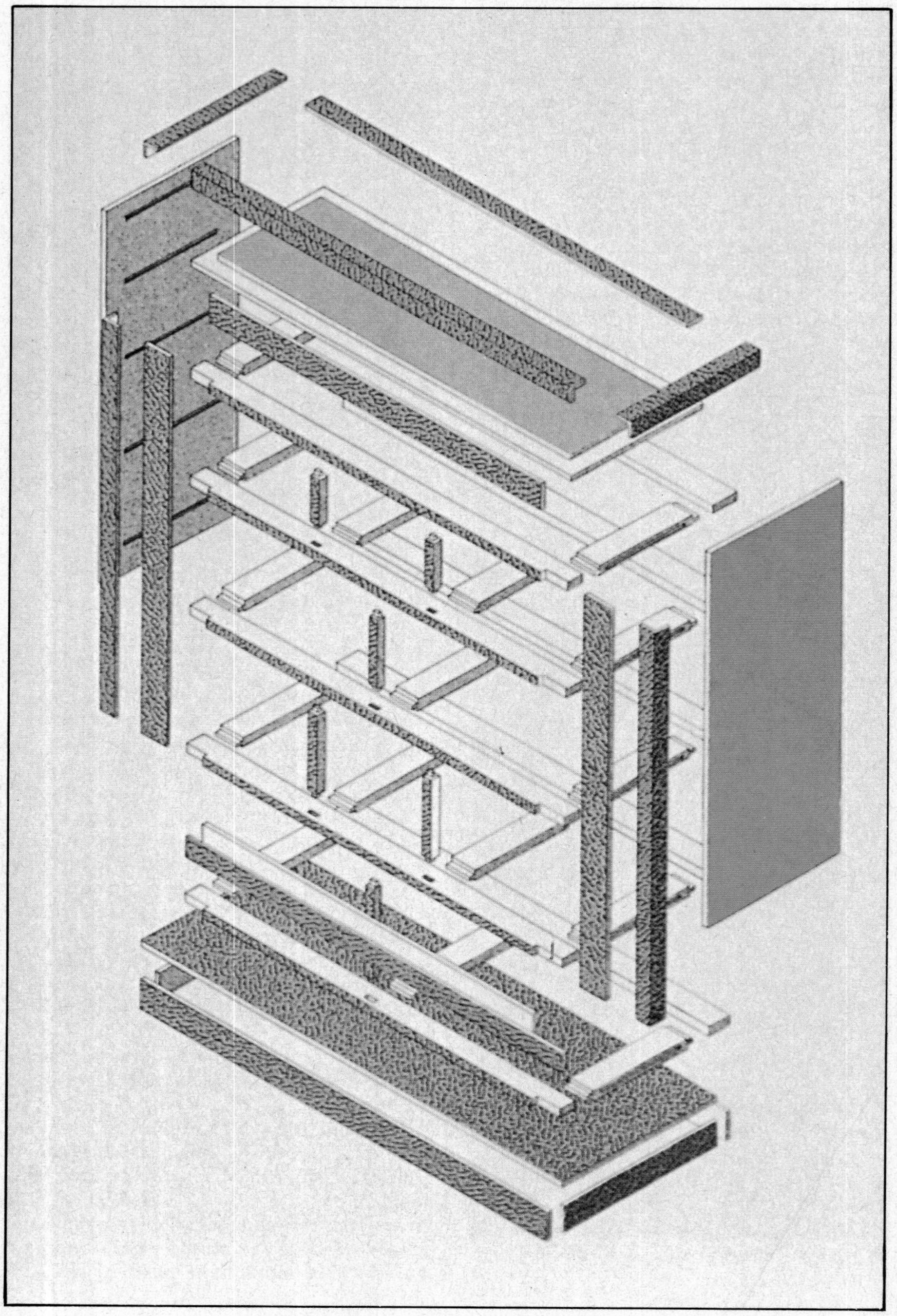

● **Right:** *Francesca Graham's exploded drawing shows how the piece goes together, while her poster **below** explores a few striking angles on her dappled creation*

I had previously designed and screen-printed my own experimental finishes on to thin plywood, but I soon realised that the eventual solution would not only be costly and take a long time to find, but also be fairly ordinary. I hope that I have short-circuited the usual techniques of dragging, sponging, splattering, etc., and produced at least an amusing and comparatively unusual effect, quickly and economically.

What I have done is to face the whole chest with two different colourways of thin plastic laminate. The edges of the drawers have been routed and picked out in dark grey paint. Ordinary plastic workshop-machinery handles, like those found on lathes, drills and so on were used. These were sand-blasted, sealed and sprayed with cellulose paint in pink. Like the drawers, they are graduated in size.

The idea of popular decorative laminates harks back to the 1950s, whose furniture is now being sought after by discriminating 'kitsch' collectors. Some people may find it overpowering — but the chest stands in my kitchen, and that hasn't happened to me yet!

● Patterned laminates and information from: Abet Ltd, Nicholas House, River Front, Enfield, Middx. EN1 3TR, tel. 01-367 3545. The range includes not only patterns both subtle and startling, but also layered laminates up to 14mm thick whose edges resemble nothing so much as liquorice allsorts. ■

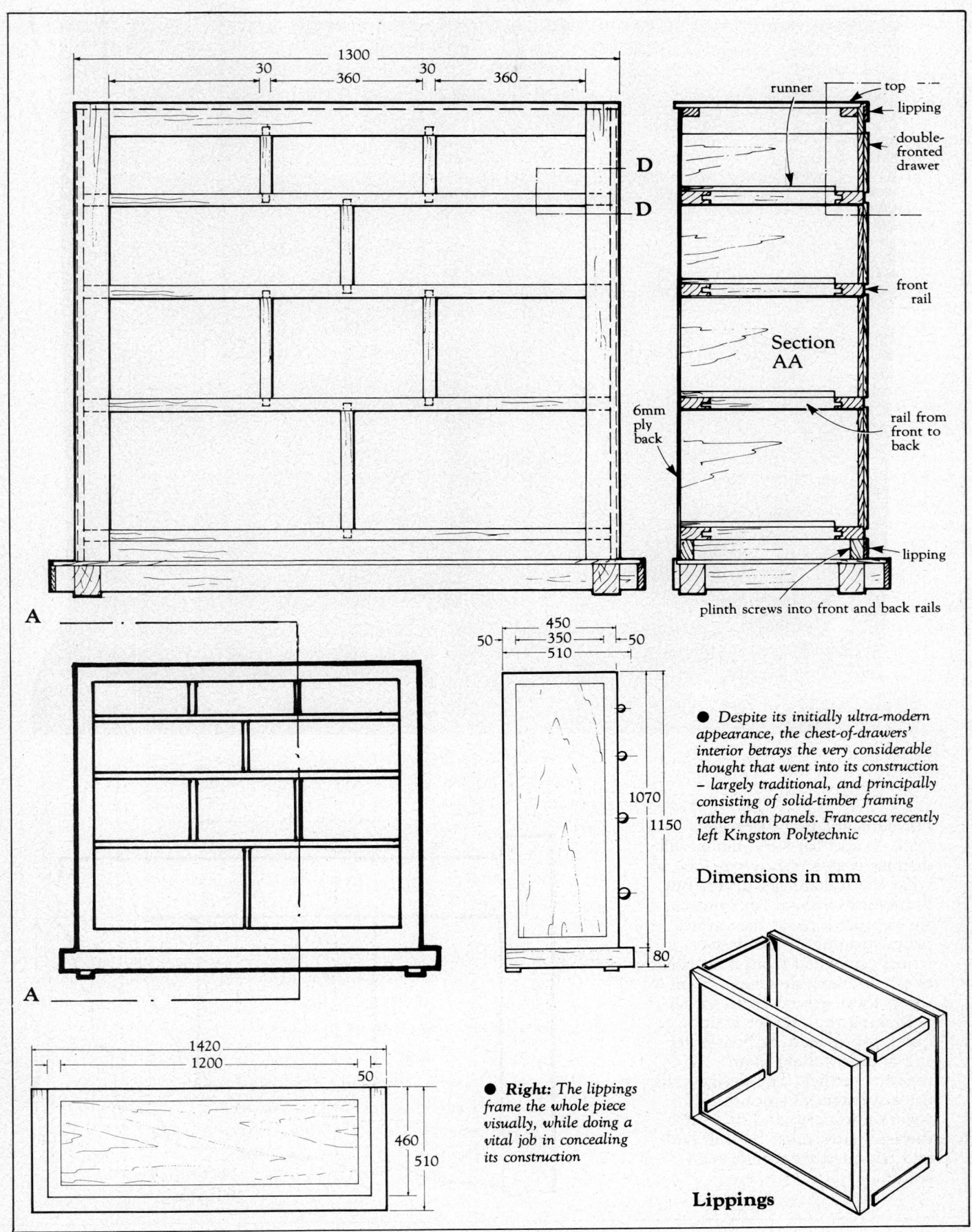

1300

30 · 360 · 30 · 360

D
D

runner · top
lipping
double-fronted drawer

Section AA

front rail

6mm ply back

rail from front to back

lipping

plinth screws into front and back rails

A

A

450
50 · 350 · 50
510

1070
1150

80

● *Despite its initially ultra-modern appearance, the chest-of-drawers' interior betrays the very considerable thought that went into its construction – largely traditional, and principally consisting of solid-timber framing rather than panels. Francesca recently left Kingston Polytechnic*

### Dimensions in mm

1420
1200
50

460
510

● ***Right:*** *The lippings frame the whole piece visually, while doing a vital job in concealing its construction*

**Lippings**

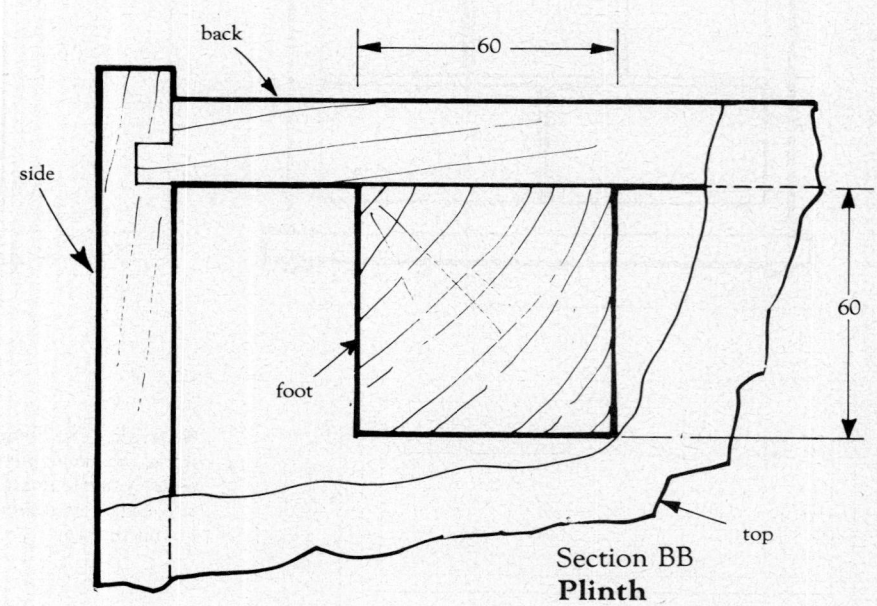

For sure, it's not everyone's taste — and for sure, many will dismiss it as a trendy pastiche of what the Italians get up to. But Francesca Graham isn't out to shock; just look at the careful proportioning of the drawer-fronts (spawned from a fat sheaf of preliminary sketches). Even the colours are far from garish.

Making the cabinet is no quick job of cutting boards to size and dowelling them together, either. The design calls for a substantial amount of accurate joinery; and of course the laminates must be well laid and trimmed for a high-class result.

back

side

60

foot

60

top

Section BB
**Plinth**

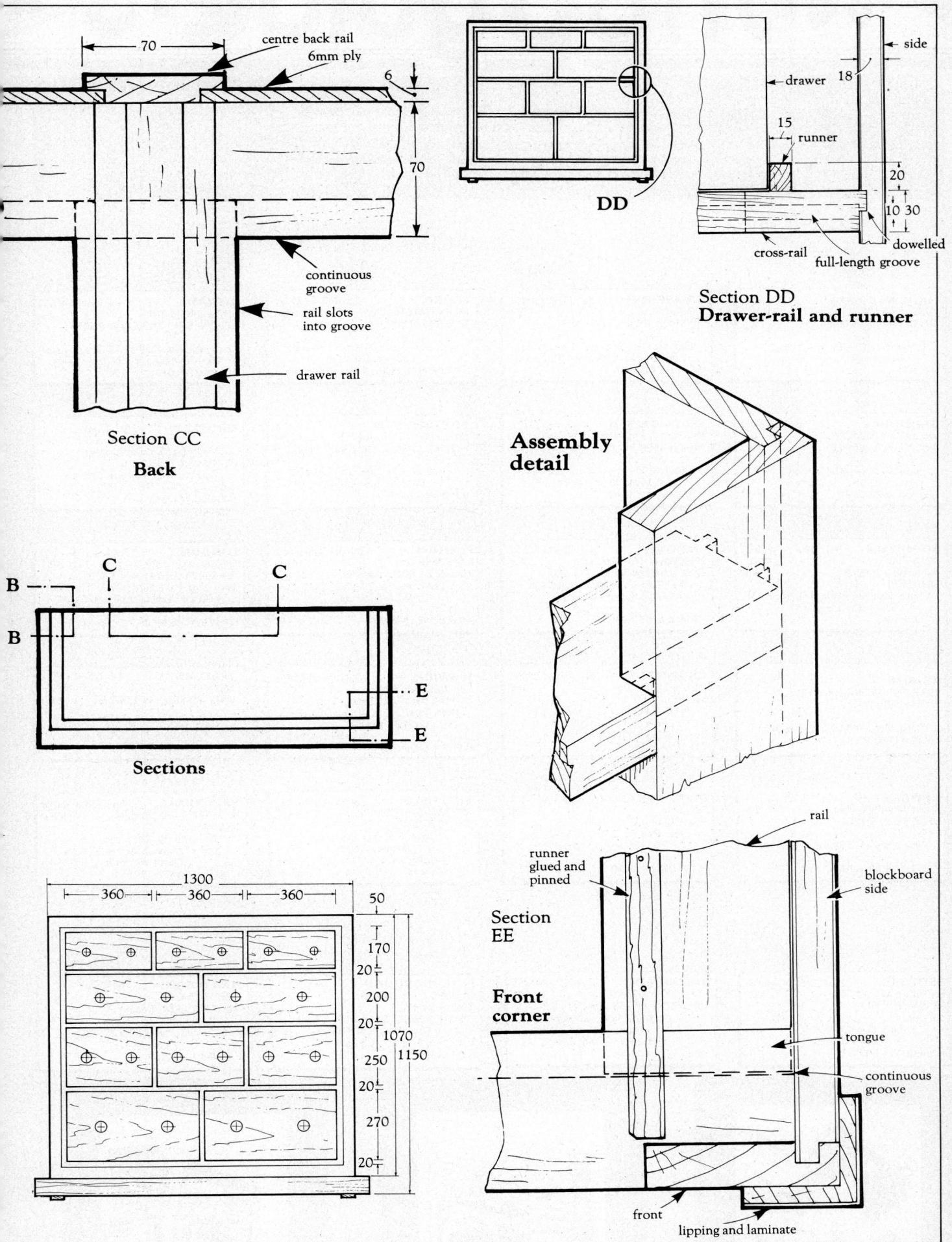

70

centre back rail
6mm ply

6

70

continuous
groove

rail slots
into groove

drawer rail

Section CC
**Back**

**DD**

side

drawer

18

15

runner

20

10 30

dowelled

cross-rail

full-length groove

Section DD
**Drawer-rail and runner**

**Assembly
detail**

B

C

C

B

E

E

**Sections**

rail

runner
glued and
pinned

blockboard
side

Section
EE

**Front
corner**

tongue

continuous
groove

1300

360    360    360

50

170

20

200

20

250

20

270

20

1070

1150

front

lipping and laminate

# shopguide

## EMCO DEALERS

**HIGH WYCOMBE**  Tel. (0494) 22221
ISAAC LORD LTD  **KE**
185 DESBOROUGH ROAD
Open: Mon-Fri 8.00 a.m.-5.00 p.m.
Saturday 9.00 a.m.-5.00 p.m.
H.P.W.D.A.

**CAMBRIDGE**  Tel. (0223) 63132
D. MACKAY LTD.  **E★**
BRITANNIA WORKS, EAST ROAD
Open: Mon.-Fri. 8.30 a.m.-1 p.m./2.00-
5.00 p.m. Sat. 8.30 a.m.-1.00 p.m.
H.P.W.D.T.CS.MF.A.B.C.

**TRURO**  Tel. (0872) 71671
TRURO POWER TOOLS  **E★**
30 FERRIS TOWN
Open Mon.-Sat. 8.00 a.m.-12.30 p.m./
1.30 p.m.-5.00 p.m.
H.P.W.WM.D.CS.MF.A.BC.

**DERBY**  Tel. (0332) 41862
HAZLEHURSTS LTD.  **E★**
LONDON ROAD AND CANAL STREET
Open: Mon.-Sat. 8.30 a.m.-5.30 p.m. (retail)
Mon.-Fri. 8.00 a.m.-5.00 p.m. (trade)
H.P.W.MF.A.BC.

**BRIXHAM**  Tel. (08045) 4900
WOODCRAFT SUPPLIES  **E★**
4 HORSE POOL STREET
Open: Mon.-Sat. 9.00 a.m.-6.00 p.m.
H.P.W.A.D.MF.CS.BC.

**LEIGH ON SEA**  Tel. (0702) 7.0404
MARSHAL & PARSONS LTD.
1111 LONDON ROAD  **EK**
Open: 8.30 a.m.-5.30 p.m. Mon-Fri
9.00 a.m.-5.00 p.m. Sat.
H.P.W.WM.D.CS.A.

**PORTSMOUTH**  Tel. (0705) 667332
EURO PRECISION TOOLS LTD
259/263 LONDON ROAD, NORTH END  ★
  **E**
Open: Mon-Fri 9.00 a.m.-5.30 p.m.
Sat. 9.00 a.m.-1.00 p.m.
H.P.W.WM.D.A.BC.

**GRIMSBY**  Tel. Grimsby (0472) 58741 Hull (0482) 26999
J. E. SIDDLE LTD. (Tool Specialists)  ★
83 VICTORIA STREET
Open: Mon-Fri 8.30 a.m.-5.30 p.m.
Sat. 8.30 a.m.-12.45 p.m. & 2 p.m.-5 p.m.
H.P.A.BC.W.WMD.

**ROCHDALE**  Tel. (0706) 342123/342322
C.S.M. TOOLS  **E★**
4-6 HEYWOOD ROAD
CASTLETON
Open: Mon-Sat 9.00 a.m.-6.00 p.m.
Sundays by appointment
W.D.CS.A.BC.

**PRESTON**  Tel. (0772) 52951
SPEEDWELL TOOL COMPANY  **E★**
62-68 MEADOW STREET PR1 1SU
Open: Mon-Fri 8.30 a.m.-5.30 p.m.
Sat. 8.30 a.m.-12.30 p.m.
H.P.W.WM.CS.A.MF.BC.

**FULHAM**  Tel. (01-385) 5109
I. GRIZZARD LTD.  **E**
84a-b LILLIE ROAD, SW6 1TL
Open: Mon-Sat 9.00-5.30 p.m.
Half day Thursday
H.P.A.BC.W.CS.WM.D.

**LONDON**  Tel. (01-263) 1536
THOMAS BROTHERS  (01-272) 2764
798-804 HOLLOWAY ROAD, N19  **E**
Open: Mon.-Fri. 8.30 a.m.-5.30 p.m. Thurs.
8.30 a.m.-1 p.m. Sat. 9 a.m.-5 p.m.
H.P.W.WM.CS.MF.BC.

**RUISLIP**  Tel. (08956) 74126
ALLMODELS ENGINEERING LTD.  **E★**
91 MANOR WAY
Open: Mon-Sat 9.00 a.m.-5.30 p.m.
H.P.W.A.D.CS.MF.BC.

**CROWMARSH**  Tel. (0491) 38653
MILL HILL SUPPLIES  **E★**
66 THE STREET
Open: Mon.-Fri. 9.30 a.m.-5.00 p.m.
Thurs. 9.30 a.m.-7.00 p.m.
Sat. 9.30 a.m.-1.00 p.m.
P.W.D.CS.MF.A.BC.

**IPSWICH**  Tel. (0473) 40456
FOX WOODWORKING  **KE★**
142-144 BRAMFORD LANE
Open: Tues., Fri., 9.00 a.m.-5.30 p.m.
Sat. 9.00 a.m.-5.00 p.m.
H.P.W.WM.D.A.B.C.

**TELFORD**  Tel. Telford (0952) 48054
ASLES LTD
VINEYARD ROAD, WELLINGTON  **EK★**
Open: Mon. Fri. 8.30 a.m.-5.30 p.m.
Saturday 8.30 a.m.-4.00 p.m.
H P.W WM.D.CS.BC.A.

**NEWCASTLE**  Tel. (0632) 320311
HENRY OSBOURNE LTD.  **E★**
50-54 UNION STREET
Open: Mon-Fri 8.30 a.m.-5.00 p.m.
H.P.W.D.CS.MF.A.BC.

**BIRMINGHAM**  Tel. (021-554) 5177
ROTAGRIP  **E★**
16 LODGE ROAD, HOCKLEY
Open: Mon.-Fri. 9.00 a.m.-5.00 p.m.
Sat. 9.00 a.m.-12.00 p.m.
H.P.W.CS.A.BC.T.MF.

**SHEFFIELD**  Tel. (0742) 441012
GREGORY & TAYLOR LTD  **KE**
WORKSOP ROAD
Open: 8.30 a.m.-5.30 p.m.
Monday-Friday
8.30 a.m.-12.30 p.m. Sat.
H.P.W.WM.D.

**WORTHING**  Tel. (0903) 38739
W. HOSKING LTD (TOOLS &  **KE★**
MACHINERY)
28 PORTLAND RD, BN11 1QN
Open: Mon.-Sat. 8.30 a.m.-5.30 p.m.
Closed Wednesday
H.P.W.WM.D.CS.A.BC.

## KITY DEALERS

**BEDFORD**  Tel. (0234) 59808
BEDFORD SAW SERVICE  **K**
39 AMPTHILL ROAD
Open: Mon.-Fri. 8.30-5.30
Sat. 9.00-4.00
H.P.A.BC.W.CS.WM.D.

**CAMBRIDGE**  Tel. (0223) 247386
H. B. WOODWORKING  **K**
105 CHERRY HINTON ROAD
Open: 8.30 a.m.-5.30 p.m.
Monday-Friday
8.30 a.m.-1.00 p.m. Sat.
H.P.W.WM.D.CS.A.

**PETERBOROUGH**  Tel. (0733) 64252
WILLIAMS DISTRIBUTORS
(TOOLS) LIMITED  **K**
108-110 BURGHLEY ROAD
Open: Monday to Friday
8.30 a.m.-5.30 p.m.
H.P.A.W.D.WH.BC.

**NANTWICH**  Tel. Crewe 67010
ALAN HOLTHAM  **K★**
THE OLD STORES TURNERY
WISTASON ROAD, WILLASTON
Open: Tues.-Sat. 9.00 a.m.-5.30 p.m.
Closed Monday
P.W.WM.D.T.C.CS.A.BC.

**KEY: CS CUTTING OR SHARPENING SERVICES**

**KEY: MF MATERIAL FINISHES**

**KEY: BC BOOKS/CATALOGUES**

# shopguide

**MIDDLESBROUGH** Tel. (0642)
CLEVELAND WOODCRAFT 813103
(M'BRO), 38-42 CRESCENT ROAD **K**

Open: Mon-Sat 9.15 a.m.-5.30 p.m.

H.P.T.A.BC.W.WM.CS.D.

---

**HELSTON** Tel. Helston (03265) 4961
SOUTH WEST Truro (0872) 71671.
POWER TOOLS Launceston
MONUMENT ROAD (0566) 3555
**K**

H.P.W.WM.D.CS.A.

---

**BUXTON** Tel. (0298) 871636
CRAFT SUPPLIES **K★**
THE MILL, MILLERSDALE

Open: Mon-Sat 9.00 a.m.-5.00 p.m.

H.P.W.D.T.CS.A.BC.

---

**TEWKESBURY** Tel. (0684)
TEWKESBURY SAW CO. LTD. 293092
TRADING ESTATE, NEWTOWN **K**

Open: Mon-Fri 8.00 a.m.-5.00 p.m.
Saturday 9.30 a.m.-12.00 p.m.
P.W.WM.D.CS.

---

**ALDERSHOT** Tel. (0252) 334422
POWER TOOL CENTRE **K★**
374 HIGH STREET
Open Mon-Fri 8.30 a.m.-5.30 p.m.
Sat 8.30 a.m.-4.00 p.m.

H.P.W.WM.D.A.BC.CF.MF.

---

**SOUTHAMPTON** Tel: (0703)
POWER TOOL CENTRE 332288
7 BELVIDERE ROAD **K★**
Open Mon.-Fri. 8.30-5.30

H.P.W.WM.D.A.BC.CS.MF.

---

**ENFIELD** Tel. (01-363) 2935
GILL & HOXBY LTD. **K**
133-137 ST. MARKS ROAD EN1 1BB

Mon.-Sat. 8.30 a.m.-6.00 p.m.
Early closing Wednesday 1.00 p.m.
H.P.W.WM.T.CS.A

---

**LANCASTER** Tel. (0524) 32886
LILE TOOL SHOP **K**
43/45 NORTH ROAD
Open: Monday to Saturday
9.00 a.m.-5.30 p.m.
Wed 9.00 a.m.-12.30 p.m.
H.P.W.D.A.

---

**LIVERPOOL** Tel. (051-207) 2967
TAYLOR BROS (LIVERPOOL) LTD **K**
195-199 LONDON ROAD
LIVERPOOL L3 8JG
Open: Monday to Friday
8.30 a.m.-5.30 p.m.
H.P.W.WM.D.A.BC.

---

**KINGS LYNN** Tel: (0760) 23073
TONY WADDILOVE **★**
STATION HOUSE
LITTLE DUNHAM, (Nr. SWAFFHAM)
Open Tues.-Sat. 9.00 a.m.-5.30 p.m.

H.P.W.DT.CS.A.BC.

---

**NORWICH** Tel. (0603) 400933
WESTGATES WOODWORKING Tx
61 HURRICANE WAY, 975412
NORWICH AIRPORT INDUSTRIAL ESTATE
Open: 9.00 a.m.-5.00 p.m. weekdays
9.00 a.m.-12.30 Sat.
P.W.WM.D.BC. **K**

---

**TAMWORTH** Tel. (0827) 56188
MATTHEWS BROTHERS LTD. **K**
KETTLEBROOK ROAD
Open: Mon-Sat 8.30 a.m.-6.00 p.m.
Demonstrations Sunday mornings by
appointment only
H.P.WM.D.T.CS.A.BC.

---

**FARNHAM** Tel. (0252) 725427
A.B.E. CO. LTD. (Quick Hire) **★**
GOODS SHED
STATION APPROACH, FARNHAM
Open Mon.-Fri. 8.00 a.m.-5.30 p.m.
Sat. 8.00 a.m.-5.30 p.m.
H.P.W.D.CS.A.BC.

---

**BOGNOR REGIS** Tel. (0243) 863100
A. OLBY & SON (BOGNOR REGIS) LTD.
"TOOLSHOP," BUILDERS MERCHANT
HAWTHORN ROAD **K**
Open: Mon-Thurs 8 a.m.-5.15 p.m. Fri.
8 a.m.-8 p.m. Sat 8 a.m.-12.45 p.m.
H.P.W.WM.D.T.C.A.BC.

---

**NEWCASTLE UPON TYNE** Tel.
J. W. HOYLE LTD.
CLARENCE STREET NE2 1YJ
**K★**
Open: Mon-Fri 8.00 a.m.-5.00 p.m.
Saturday 9.00 a.m.-4.30 p.m.
(0632) 617474
H.P.A.BC.W.CS.WM.D.

---

**WOLVERHAMPTON** Tel. (0902)
MANSAW SERVICES 58759
SEDGLEY STREET **K★**

Open: Mon.-Fri. 9.00 a.m.-5.00 p.m.

H.P.W.WM.A.D.CS.

---

**HARROGATE** Tel. (0423) 66245/
MULTI-TOOLS 55328
158 KINGS ROAD
**K★**
Open: Monday to Saturday
8.30 a.m.-6.00 p.m.
H.P.W.WM.D.A.BC.

---

**PERTH** Tel. (0738) 26173
WILLIAM HUME & CO **K**
ST. JOHN'S PLACE
Open: Monday to Saturday
8.00 a.m.-5.30 p.m.
8.00 a.m.-1.00 p.m. Wednesday
H.P.A.BC.W.CS.WM.D.

---

**CARMARTHEN** Tel. (0267) 237219
DO-IT-YOURSELF SUPPLY **K**
BLUE STREET, DYFED
Open: Monday to Saturday
9.00 a.m.-5.30 p.m.
Thursday 9.00 a.m.-5.30 p.m.
H.P.W.WM.D.T.CS.A.BC.

---

---

**NB.** See under EMCO dealers for Isaac Lord Ltd., High Wycombe, Marshal & Parsons Ltd., Leigh on Sea, Fox Woodworking, Ipswich, Asles Ltd., Telford and W. Hosking Ltd., Worthing and Gregory & Taylor Ltd., Sheffield.

## ALL OTHER DEALERS

**BATH** Tel. Bath 64513
JOHN HALL TOOLS **★**
RAILWAY STREET

Open: Monday-Saturday
9.00 a.m.-5.30 p.m.
H.P.W.WM.D.A.BC.

---

**BRISTOL** Tel. (0272) 741510
JOHN HALL TOOLS LIMITED **★**
CLIFTON DOWN SHOPPING CENTRE
WHITELADIES ROAD
Open: Monday-Saturday
9.00 a.m.-5.30 p.m.
H.P.W.WM.D.A.BC.

---

**BRISTOL** Tel. (0272) 629092
TRYMWOOD SERVICES
2a DOWNS PARK EAST, (off North View)
WESTBURY PARK
Open: 8.30 a.m.-5.30 p.m. Mon. to Fri.
Closed for lunch 1.00-2.00 p.m.
P.W.WM.D.T.A.BC.

---

**BRISTOL** Tel. (0272) 667013
WILLIS
157 WEST STREET
BEDMINISTER
Open Mon.-Fri. 8.30 a.m.-5.00 p.m.
No Saturday opening

---

**COOKHAM** Tel. (06285) 20350
CHURCH'S TIMBER
STATION HILL

Open: Mon-Sat 8.30 a.m.-5.30 p.m.
Wed 8.30 a.m.-1.00 p.m.
H.P.W.T.CS.MF.A.

---

**READING** Tel. (0734) 591361
HOME CARE CENTRE
26/30 KING'S ROAD

Open: Monday-Saturday
9.00 a.m.-5.30 p.m.
H.P.W.D.A.WM.BC.

---

**READING** Tel. Littlewick Green
DAVID HUNT (TOOL 2743
MERCHANTS) LTD **★**
KNOWL HILL, NR. READING
Open: Monday-Saturday
9.00 a.m.-5.30 p.m.
H.P.W.D.A.BC.

---

**READING** Tel. Reading 661511
WOKINGHAM TOOL CO. LTD.
99 WOKINGHAM ROAD

Open: Mon-Sat 9.00 a.m.-5.30 p.m.
Closed 1.00-2.00 p.m. for lunch
H.P.W.WM.D.CS.A.BC.

---

**SLOUGH** Tel. (06286) 5125
BRAYWOOD ESTATES LTD **★**
158 BURNHAM LANE

Open: 9.00 a.m.-5.30 p.m.
Monday-Saturday
H.P.W.WM.CS.A.

---

**HIGH WYCOMBE** Tel. (0494)
SCOTT SAWS LTD. 24201/33788
14 BRIDGE STREET **★**

Mon.-Sat. 8.30 a.m.-6.00 p.m.

H.P.W.WM.D.T.CS.MF.A.BC.

---

**MILTON KEYNES** Tel. (0908)
POLLARD WOODWORKING 641366
CENTRE **★**
51 AYLESBURY ST., BLETCHLEY
Open: Mon-Fri 8.30-5.30
Saturday 9.00-5.00
H.P.W.D.CS.A.BC.

---

**SOUTHAMPTON** Tel. (0703)
H.W.M. 776222
THE WOODWORKERS
303 SHIRLEY ROAD, SHIRLEY
Open: Tues-Fri 9.30 a.m.-6.00 p.m.
Sat 9.30 a.m.-4.00 p.m.
H.P.W.D.CS.A.BC.T.

---

**CARLISLE** Tel: (0228) 36391
W. M. PLANT
ALLENBROOK ROAD
ROSEHILL, CA1 2UT
Open: Mon.-Fri. 8.00 a.m.-5.15 p.m.
Sat. 8.00 a.m.-12.30 noon
P.W.WM.D.CS.A.

---

**PLYMOUTH** Tel. (0752) 330303
WESTWARD BUILDING SERVICES **★**
LTD., LISTER CLOSE, NEWNHAM
INDUSTRIAL ESTATE, PLYMPTON
Open: Mon-Fri 8.00 a.m.-5.30 p.m.
Sat. 8.30 a.m.-12.30 p.m.
H.P.W.WM.D.A.BC.

---

**ILFORD**
CUTWELL TOOLS LTD. **★**
774-776 HIGH ROAD

Mon.-Fri. 9.00 a.m.-5.00 p.m.
and also by appointment.
P.W.WM.A.D.CS.

---

**MATFIELD** Tel. Brenchley
LEISURECRAFT IN WOOD (089272)
'ORMONDE,' MAIDSTONE RD. 2465
TN12 7JG
Open: Mon-Sun
9.00 a.m.-5.30 p.m.
W.WM.D.T.A.

# shopguide

# WOOD SUPPLIERS

# WOOD SUPPLIERS

# Classified Advertisements

All classified advertisements under £25.00 must be pre-paid: Cheques/PO made payable to A.S.P. Ltd. (WW). **Private and trade rate** 35p per word (minimum £5.25). **Display box rates** s.c.c. £7.25 (minimum 2.5×1). All advertisements are inserted in the first available issue.

**Copy to Classified Dept. (W.W.), A.S.P. Ltd., 1 Golden Square, London W.1.** There are no re-imbursements for cancellations.

---

## FOR SALE

**LACE BOBBIN TURNING BLANKS** in unusual and exotic hardwoods and ivory. SAE for list: J. Ford, 5 Squirrels Hollow, Walsall WS7 8YS.

### FOR ALL SUPPLIES FOR THE
### Craft of Enamelling
### ON METAL
### Including
### LEAD-FREE ENAMELS

PLEASE SEND 2 × 10p STAMPS FOR FREE CATALOGUE, PRICE LIST AND WORKING INSTRUCTIONS

### W. G. BALL LTD.
ENAMEL MANUFACTURERS

Dept. W. LONGTON
STOKE-ON-TRENT
ST3 1JW

### HAND CARVED
'Adam Style' Mantle motifs in Mahogany — Example 10" × 5" centre lamp and two side pieces.
Send S.A.E. for details and quotation. Your own design quoted for if required.
**SAM NICHOLSON**
22 Lisnagarvey Drive, Lisburn, Co. Antrim, N. Ireland.
Phone Lisburn 3510

### Have you seen the latest catalogue of *Bygones*
See Display advertisement

### D.I.Y.
**THE SAW CENTRE** LIMITED
ESTABLISHED 1889

### HAS THE EDGE
Hire or buy machinery or power tools from our extensive stock:
**Elu DeWALT makita Black & Decker**
- SCHEPPACH ■ STARTRITE ■ GRIGGIO
- VOLPATO ■ SEDGWICK
- TUNGSTEN CARBIDE TIPPED SAW BLADES
- DISPOSABLE BANDSAW BLADES

SEE US AT ROYAL HIGHLAND SHOW EDINBURGH

**HEAD OFFICE & MAIN WORKS:**
EGLINTON TOLL GLASGOW G5 9RP. TEL: 041-429 4444/4374
OPEN: MON-FRI 8-5 (NO SAT) TELEX: 777886 SAWCO G.

**ALSO AT:** 38 HAYMARKET TERRACE EDINBURGH EH12 5JZ.
TEL: 031-337 5555. MON-FRI 8.30-5.30 & SAT 9-1.

### MUSICAL MOVEMENTS
*LOVE STORY ★ LARAS THEME ★ SPEAK SOFTLY LOVE ★ FUR ELISE ★ FEELINGS ★ FASCINATION ★ IMPOSSIBLE DREAM ★ MUSIC BOX DANCER ★ LA POLOMA ★ THE EMPEROR WALTZ ★ TRY TO REMEMBER ★ ROMEO AND JULIET ★*
Complete with screws and spring mechanism £2.50 inc. p&p. 20 or more of one tune ordered £1.50 each. Available from:
The Jewel Box Shop,
112 Pentonville Road, London N1 9JB.

**ARUNDEL M300 LATHE £385.** Evenwood 14" bandsaw £180. Consort sawbench £110. Myblo 6" planer with thicknessing attachment £150. Ajax bench drill £135. Hegner fretsaw £125. Sharpenset Whetstone £100. Manchester. 061-928-3877.

### BUSINESSES FOR SALE

**ESTABLISHED FURNITURE MAKING BUSINESS WITH GOOD LEASE FOR SALE YORKSHIRE DALES LOCATION**

2,500 sq.ft. of well equipped workshop space, including kiln and spray booth. T/O in excess of £16,000pa achieved on part-time basis.
As a going concern, offers in the region of £6,000.
Telephone for written details and information:
DAVE POTTS 0535 36575

MORTISERS; TENNONERS; SPINDLES; PLANERS; BANDSAWS; LATHES; CROSSCUTS; ROUTERS; SANDERS; DRILLS? YOU CAN CERTAINLY SEE ALL CLASSES AND TYPES OF MACHINES HERE.

WE ARE MAIN STOCKING AGENTS FOR: MULTICO; ELU; SEDGWICK; KITY; SCHEPPACH; INCA; CORONET; DeWALT; WARCO; DOMINION; HITACHI; STARTRITE; TREND; ASHLEY ILES; SORBY.

*CALL US ABOUT WOODTURNING LESSONS WOODCARVING LESSONS (See our Swiss carving tools) ALWAYS HELPFUL, KNOWLEDGEABLE, GOOD SERVICE AT:*
### CLEVELAND WOODCRAFT
### 38-42 CRESCENT ROAD, MIDDLESBROUGH.
### TEL: (0642) 813103

**BAGS, WRAPPINGS, TISSUE, BOXES, BUSINESS CARDS.** Any shape, size, amount. Comprehensive samples 86p. Terry Andrews, 53A Parsons Street, Banbury, OX16 8NB.

**KITY K-5** Universal Woodworking machine MkII. Only 1 year old. Price £600. Includes £200 worth of accessories. e.g. Tungston tipped tools, rebating blocks and tenon table. Tel. Cheltenham (0242) 51378/581776.

**25,000 WESTERN HEMLOCK** and Brazilian mahogany staircase spindle blanks 3' long, 1⅜" square from 30p to £1. Also wanted home turners to complete and return and sell back. Mahogany hard wood staircase timber 3' and 4' long, 10", 12" by 4": 3". All timber well under half price e.g. £15. Many more bargains including solid oak sculptured arched kitchen cabinet doors. £15 each. Also comfort range top window, frames, 500 in all e.g. 8' by 4' oblong window £160 list: £60. Phone Turton Bolton, Lancs. (0204) 852 339 any time.

**CORONET "ELF"** lathe in excellent condition. Used only for demonstration. Current price £300+. Will accept £200. Also Cowell 8" × 2" wet grinder, little used. £100. Telephone Braintree 24606.

**MINI MAX P32** Bandsaw 6' cut with Rip/Mitre fences excellent condition purchased larger machine £280 ono. Kidderminster 68599.

**BURGESS BANDSAW BBS** 20 MkII. Mortice and Planer attachments for Coronet major £75. Will separate. Maidenhead 31401.

**MIA6 COMBINATION** woodworker. £325 ono. Kity No. 700 machine. Table £30. Phone: Etwall (028 373) 2987.

### WOOD TURNERS SUPPLIES
Tudor Craft, Jung Hans clock movements, 20 different hands to choose from, barometers, weather stations, cutlery, jewellery box lids, pepper/salt/nutmeg mills, coffee grinders, ceramic tiles, new range which include hand painted tiles. Our service is extremely fast, friendly and competitive — give us a try. Send SAE for catalogue to
Tudor Craft,
100 Little Sutton Lane,
Four Oaks, Sutton Coldfield,
West Midlands B75 6PG.

415v from 230v house mains to run your 3-phase machines, the 'Maldon' Unit £66 1½ h.p.
### MALDON TRANSFORMERS
134 London Road,
Kingston-on-Thames
Tel: 546-75 34
*Access – Barclay*

**WORKBENCH** for sale 7' by 3' solid maple. 2 vices. Never used. £500. Contact Jonathan on 743 8000 Ext. 3288.

### TO FILL THIS SPACE 'PHONE PETER ON 01-437 0699

---

Prices quoted are those prevailing at press date and are subject to alteration due to economic conditions

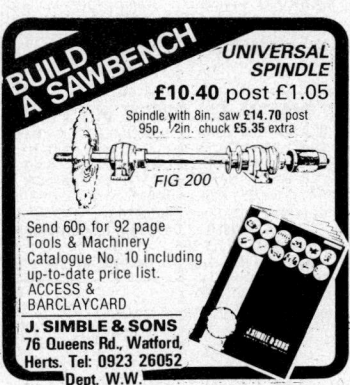

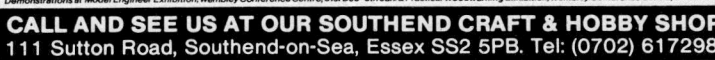

# Then......

## Max Burrough

### Continuing the absorbing tale of an old-time apprenticeship

In my fifth year all agreed that, in lieu of a large tool-chest, a miniature chest-of-drawers might be an appropriate indication of my skill and capabilities, and I embarked upon and completed this great enterprise. The piece measured about 11¼×11¼×7¼in; the oak used was all old, its colour produced by age — not the brown oak so sought after by some craftsmen. The front rails were taper-dovetailed into the ends, and I used ebony stringing.

The first chest I had made was of mahogany, oak-lined, and with a fine boxwood stringing. The drop handles being unobtainable locally, to my intense annoyance I had to go to the Boss, who could get them via a trade account from a wholesaler. The price each, I remember, was 7½d, and at that time this was considered expensive. The Boss, though, in his perverse way, would not allow me to pay for them, and he insisted that he be allowed to inspect the little masterpiece (as he called it) when finished. Expecting sarcasm, I was surprised when his comments were kind and helpful.

I was asked to display this first chest at a large arts and crafts exhibition organised by a well-to-do amateur, and it provoked so much comment that Albert and I went into partnership and made three. I managed to sell one for the magnificent sum of three guineas and we both thought we were millionaires.

I was in my early twenties when three episodes, more or less concurrent, made me wake up and decide that something must be done about my future. Definitely. One, I 'went home' with a coffin and helped to place the corpse therein, and remember very well that I spent a long time washing my hands afterwards. I did not enjoy this, and it also made me realise that one day I would be expected to wear a top hat and black frock coat and attend funerals. Having seen Tich, who was about my height, so attired, I decided that this was something I could not — would not — do.

Two, one Sunday afternoon I met a member of the firm out walking with his family, and thought: 'Great Scot, in 20 years' time that's how I shall be. Oh no, that's not for me.'

Three, I had been attending for some years the only evening classes held in the town, or indeed for many miles around. These were held twice a week, and run by Mr Brooks, the art and crafts teacher who had taught me at my grammar school. He often enquired as to my progress; and, one evening when I had said that the trade was dead and I could see no future in it, he asked, 'Why don't you try handicraft teaching?'

As far as I was concerned he could have suggested my jumping over the moon, but when he explained the set-up of the City and Guilds examinations and their craft teachers' certificates he really started me thinking.

Attempting the first hurdle with very little preparation proved my inadequacy, for I failed the first examination horribly and completely. This relatively minor setback really brought me up with a jolt. At primary school it had always been understood that I was a 'scholarship boy', and I had no trouble going through to grammar school. There, a lone ship on a lonely sea with not one real friend, I wasted my time. Now, after at least five more wasted years, I had failed, and I was absolutely furious.

My life changed. Attending the craft evening classes I plied old Brooks continually with questions. I joined the local branch of the county Library, bought books — and, most important of all, enrolled with a specialised correspondence course; and I worked. How I worked! Often until two o'clock in the morning with, from 10.30 until 12 o'clock, a background of radio broadcasts by Ambrose, Geraldo, Roy Fox, Harry Roy, Lew Stone and many other famous West End dance bands. In my spare time, as it were, I worked at what jobs were available for the firm.

As I said, jobs in customer's houses were frequent and we were expected to cope with any task thrown at us. We walked to practically every job carrying a heavy full tool-bag, dust-sheet and screw-bag. The screw-bag was made from a discarded leather chair seat. Regularly spaced holes were punched around the circumference, and a cord inserted which, when drawn tight, provided two loops for tying and carrying. In course of time a great variety of screws, nails, tacks, pins and assorted sundries were acquired and proved invaluable. I have had a screw-bag ever since, and still find it indispensable when working around the house — and often in the workshop, too. Other impedimenta often carried were slippers, a glue-pot and a polish case, the latter being made by each man according to his own ideas of 'touching up' furniture. It was made like a box, cut in half and hinged; each side was partitioned to contain four or five old Camp coffee bottles containing stains and polishes, while a shelf above held assorted brushes, rag and wadding.

I remember with considerable clarity the first job I went to on my own. Having obtained my tool-bag (with elm bottom, leather handles made by one of the local saddlers, and hair-cord and lining stitched by Stan, the junior upholsterer), I set off proudly one day after lunch. With the big hammer through the handles and the bag slung over my shoulder, I walked the half-mile to the customer's address. A red-faced individual opened the door and in the drawing-room showed me a fine walnut bureau, saying that the lock needed repairing.

Inspection showed that the screws had been 'got at', and that their slots were practically non-existent. It was then I realised that the owner was drunk. It was obvious that he had intended to do the job himself, tried, failed, fortified himself with whisky, tried and failed again — several times. I attempted to remove the screws, the owner's whisky fumes pouring over me, while he criticised me and my screwdrivers and all the rest of my precious tools. Finally I walked out and back to the shop, by which time the Boss had taken a telephone call and was waiting for me. 'The man was drunk,' I said.

'Yes, I thought so,' and he walked into his office with, for once, a smile on his face.

Jokes and pranks were plentiful but I am quite sure that the biggest joke of all, certainly in my time, was a tableau the firm entered in the town's annual carnival. Unlike today's tame and cold affairs with lorries and electric lighting, carnivals then were worth seeing, because the procession was accompanied on both sides by men and boys carrying flaming paraffin torches. These, combined with the street's gas-lamps and the reflections from the horses' polished brasses, gave a light and gaiety I find lacking now.

For a reason I never did discover, the tableau chosen was 'The Changing of the Guard'. One of the horse-drawn waggons was fitted with electric light by means of car batteries and old headlamps, and a headboard was painted to give the impression of the Tower of London. Costumes were hired; we were eight men wearing red uniforms with tall bearskins. The warder was appropriately dressed, carrying a large bunch of keys. Rifles were by courtesy of Leonard, captain of the local Church Lads' Brigade.

Grouped on the cart, with rifles at the slope, we started our journey around the town. After about a quarter of a mile someone in the crowd spotted that Hamlet had his rifle on the wrong shoulder, and he hurriedly changed it, amidst dire threats and ribald comments from the spectators. Halfway round, the lights almost failed; but what no one had foreseen was the effect that the horses' constant starting and stopping would have on a group of men trying to stand stiffly to attention and fairly close together. The scene is better imagined than described.

We did not get a prize in the historical section, and I have always thought that we might have fared better had we entered as a comic tableau. ■

# Letters

Our open forum — where woodworkers can talk to one another

SINCE 1980 I have watched in awe the clashes of correspondents in the letters page of *Woodworker*. How do you calculate the gauge of a screw to three decimal places? Is a square-recessed screw-head better than a slotted one? Do *real* woodturners hone their gouges or not?

Well, at last I have the opportunity to join in and qualify as a real woodworker — do it, read about it, and now argue about it!

Mr Tucker (WW/April) is right to say that Mr Savage is wrong to say that the purpose of a no-volt switch is to protect against overload. However, most starter switches on machines of this size offer the same protection. For that reason they have to be matched to the power of the motor. Most starter switches also contain a no-volt release; this feature is an optional extra — though, for the reasons Mr Tucker mentions, it is an option that the woodworker should take up.

*D.P. Massey, Chester*

---

I AGREE entirely with Aidan Walker's comments on the limitations of hand-held power planes (WW/Feb), but not everyone has room for a planer-thicknesser. Prompted by the threatened return of 'frozen shoulders' after planing some sawn oak, I devised a method of overcoming the limitations.

The Elu MOF80 power plane has a transverse hole at each end of the body at a centre height of 25mm from the sole plate. Through these holes I fit two 500mm lengths of 8mm-dia. screwed rod clamped to the body. These rods carry two 'depth fences', clamped one at each side of the plate body, made of two pieces of light brass angle slightly longer than the body. The lower fence member has a vertical screwed pillar attached to each end, which allows adjustment of the vertical separation of the two parts of the fence. This adjustment obviously controls the finished thickness of the planed work.

The lateral position of the fences is determined by tubular spacers which are a close fit over the 8mm screwed rods and provide added stiffness against bending. The length of the spacers is selected to suit the width of the work, since it is desirable to minimise the span. I use spacer lengths selected from the R10 series of preferred numbers; four each of lengths 63, 80, 100, 125 and 160mm, singly or in combination — these provide a suitable gradation of widths of work.

In use the work is clamped to a 'woodworkers surface table': a 6×2ft sheet of melamine-faced chipboard fastened to a rigid frame. Fitted with folding legs, this doubles as a dressmaking table for my wife, so I can justify the space occupied. To permit the plane to pass over the work

without interference the work is clamped by a simplified version of the edge clamp used on engineering planing and milling machines.

The device is not particularly elegant nor rapidly adjustable, but it saves aching shoulders; the results for flatness and parallelism are comparable with the best planer-thicknesser, and the surface finish is better than most. With the dimensions and arrangement described it is possible to plane work up to 265mm wide. Using an asymmetrical arrangement of the fences and planing each half of the work in opposite directions would permit an increase up to 350mm wide. The results would not be as good, however, due to increased vertical deflection of the plane and possible tearing of the grain.

Thank you for a stimulating and informative magazine which adds to the enjoyment of a satisfying hobby. A retired production engineer, I frequently adapt the skills and technology of engineering manufacturing to woodworking, but must constantly curb the tendency to use engineering fits for doors and drawers.

*Robert Hedley, Settle*

---

MAY I please refer to the penultimate paragraph of Chris Nash's entertaining book review (*Q & A: Woodwork*) in the February issue?

I suspect that what he is looking for is a device that does not roll the sharpening debris into the stone. I have used a Stanley 'tool and cutter grinder' (as they termed it) for the past 50 years. It was made at their New Britain, Connecticut, plant, but discontinued shortly after the war. Its catalogue number was 200 and its prewar price is 7s. The roller was behind the stone, as the illustration redrawn from the 1939 Barns catalogue shows. If Mr Nash can find one it will not be cheap; a specimen at the Hatfield auction last September fetched £40.

However, General Hardware of New York, whose products used to be — and maybe still are — imported into the UK by Markt & Co., list a similar device made in die-cast metal (the Stanley was of cast iron) under catalogue no.810. Unfortunately I have no price more up-to-date that of 1962, when it was 28s 6d.

Re Bob Wearing's article 'Gauging exactly' in the same issue, would not OBO hardened masonry nails make very good replacement points (when sharpened) for his range of marking-gauges?

Finally, I am one reader who welcomes the acerbic note of forthright criticism that is notable in several articles in this issue: Richard Sarjent on the poor catering arrangements at Ally Pally; debunking of power-plane advertising by Aidan Walker; unjustifiably high price of power whetstones by David Ellis (I've already mentioned Mr Nash's book review). If this is your doing, Mr Editor, long may it continue!

*F. Seward, London W7*

AS A TEACHER of design, craft and technology taking a modular master's degree at Salford University, I am engaged on a case-study of the development of moulding tools — from the full set of cabinetmaker's hand planes, via early mechanisation, to the industrial spindle-moulders and DIY routers of today.

I have plenty of material on the hand planes and on current equipment. I have also found books on the history of technology which deal with lathes, planers, mortising machines, etc. However, I cannot find any early references to the mechanisation of moulding production. Can you help? I would be most grateful for news of any literature sources, or collections of such machinery.

*John Jansen,*
*44 Worsborough Avenue,*
*Great Sankey, Warrington,*
*Cheshire*

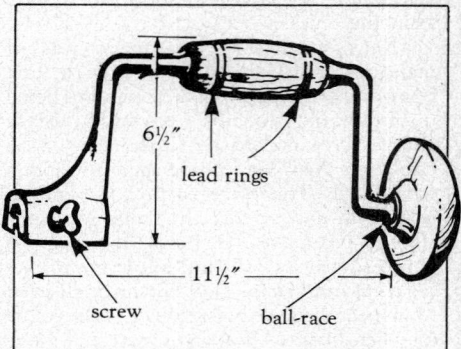

I am in the process of conserving the brace which I have sketched here. The steel is heavily pitted but otherwise it is in good condition. I seek the help of my fellow-readers in identifying its maker and the period of manufacture. I have found a trace of a manufacturer's name, which appears to be '.....LEY No. 11', stamped into the steel.

*Anthony Comben,*
*5 Mashiters Walk, Romford*
*Essex RM1 4DA*

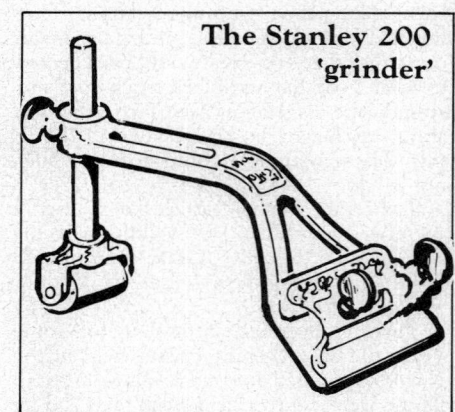

### The Stanley 200 'grinder'

# The magazine for the craftsman
## ~ and the aspiring craftsman!

July 1985
Vol. 89
No. 1100

● *You can make this pine bathroom cabinet if you follow the detailed plans on p513*

**Publisher** Ray Lewis
**Editor** Peter Collenette
**Deputy Editor** Aidan Walker
**Advertisement Manager** Paul Holmes
**Graphics** Jeff Hamblin
**Guild of Woodworkers** Aidan Walker, Sam Jones
**Group Editor** Chris Adam-Smith
**Publishing Director** John Foster
**Chairman and Chief Executive** Jim Connell
**Editorial, advertisements and Guild of Woodworkers** 1 Golden Square, London W1R 3AB, telephone 01-437 0626

Unfortunately we cannot accept responsibility for loss of or damage to unsolicited material. We reserve the right to refuse or suspend advertisements, and regret we cannot guarantee the bone fides of advertisers.

**Subscriptions and back issues** Infonet Ltd, 10-13 Times House, 179 Marlowes, Hemel Hempstead, Herts HP1 1BB; telephone Hemel Hempstead (0442) 48434
**Subscriptions per year** UK £15.60; overseas outside USA (accelerated surface post) £17, USA (accelerated surface post) $22.50, airmail £42
**UK trade** SM Distribution Ltd, 16-18 Trinity Gardens, London SW9 8DX; telephone 01-274 8611
**North American trade** Eastern News Distributors, 166-41 Powells Cove Boulevard, PO Box 69, Whitestone, New York 11357
**Printed in Great Britain** by Ambassador Press Ltd, St Albans, Herts
**Mono origination** Multiform Photosetting Ltd, Cardiff
**Colour origination** Derek Croxson Ltd, Chesham, Bucks
© Argus Specialist Publications Ltd 1985
ISSN 0043 776X

## Argus Specialist Publications Ltd
1 Golden Square, London
W1R 3AB; 01-437 0626

On the cover: Bill Childe's fabulous apple jewel-boxes (p504) are flanked by a stool and chest from fellow-Scotsman Chris Holmes (p506), plus Siberian pine as fashioned in Japan (p500)

*The wooden can on June's cover was beautifully photographed by Brent Moore*

# Woodworker
# This month

## BRISTOL SHOW — DRAW WINNERS!

Hold on to your hats — these are the winners of the prize draw held on our sales stand at the Bristol Woodworker Show:

*Mrs. J. Ashley of Droitwich (an Elu lathe); A. Brewer of Hounslow (a DeWalt radial-arm saw): E. G. Chaplin and R. Coles (each a Black & Decker palm-grip sander).*

Many congratulations to you all!

## Record times

Not long ago we went to see Record Ridgway Tools in Sheffield — newly bedecked with their old name after buying back the company from Bahco of Sweden, its owners for the last few years. We received the friendliest of welcomes, plus a concise and convincing account of Record's attempts over recent years to reverse a downward surge by fighting clever competition from the Far East and correcting its own frankly admitted sins of inefficiency in several spheres. We saw the background to the stiff catalogue cutbacks which have so annoyed craft woodworkers who believed the old style and range would go on for ever.

We saw how Marples chisels are made, we saw where vices come from, we saw how squares are squared, we saw how augers get their twist. We saw the mighty £6m automated foundry — and, on behalf of woodworkers everywhere, we seized the chance to ask its affable manager John Wharton a question we thought he was the ideal man to answer.

Many woodworkers, we said, never tire of asserting that old tools are best because steel nowadays isn't what it used to be. Old tools hold their edge longer, they say. What was his opinion?

John served his apprenticeship as a patternmaker, and told us that at home he constantly uses old chisels as well as ones made in the 1960s (in his opinion, equivalent to new ones). And, to cut a short story even shorter, he said he didn't think there was any difference.

DAVID GRAY'S article on woodworking supplies by post will appear in the August issue.

## Design for disability contest

'Quality of Life' is the surprisingly bland title of a highly interesting design contest for which entries close on 1 August.

Held in conjunction with Living with Disability Week, which takes place in Bournemouth on 9-12 September, its aim is 'to encourage new designs . . . which improve the quality of life of people suffering from any form of disability or handicap.

'It is open', add the organisers, 'to any individual or group although entries from the disabled themselves are being encouraged.'

Prizes are three microcomputer systems, and, there'll be publicity for all entries felt to have merit. Contact address is: Quality of Life Design Competition, Living With Disability Expo 1985, The Firs, Trinity Rd, Bournemouth BH1 1QJ, tel. (0202) 295777, ext. 23.

● *Mark Devany, **above,** is one of the lucky young building industry trainees who will be representing Britain in the Skill Olympics Team at Osaka in Japan in October. The mind races when the idea of a competition between skilled craftsmen is mooted – but the National Joint Council for the Building Industry didn't just moot it, they organised **Skill Build** in Leicester during April. Apprentices from all over the country tried to best each other, given 19 hours, on speed, neatness, and accuracy on some very challenging projects. Keep your ears to the ground for the results of the October Olympics!*

● *Visitors to the Royal Windsor Horse Show this year will have been fascinated to see the craft of wheelwrighting being demonstrated in spectacular fashion by young CoSIRA trainees on a special stand set up for the purpose. In conjunction with the Worshipful Company of Wheelwrights, CoSIRA are now running two-year sandwich courses; the demonstrators were the first people to finish a formal course in wheelwrighting for more than 20 years.*

*Here they are shrinking a red-hot steel tyre on to a wooden wheel.*

*The increase in enthusiasm for horse-drawn vehicles is expanding the demand for wheels and saddlery, and thus putting renewed emphasis on the making skills. If you are interested in such crafts and would like to train as a wheelwright or sadler, get in touch with CoSIRA at 141 Castle St, Salisbury, Wilts. tel. (0722) 336255*

## Shoptalk

Another woodwork-related skill for which there is great and growing demand is **upholstery**, and this time it is Sandra Rowney in Suffolk who is offering **residential weekend courses.** Full board and lodging, single or double rooms in the Rowneys' period farmhouse, and professional tuition in traditional upholstery techniques, all for £65+VAT. Complete beginners are welcome, and you can expect to complete work on a 'stuffover' dining-chair, a stool or a set of drop-in dining-seats by the end of the weekend. Bring your own pieces of furniture; non-course members are welcome to come along with partners or friends.
● Sandra Rowney Upholstery, Victoria Farmhouse, Private Rd, Earsham, Bungay, Suffolk, tel. (0986) 4360.

Fences, sheds and **exterior timbers** are coming in for **treatment** at this time of year. You want to know what you're using, and what it is and isn't going to do — to your pets and plants as well as the wood itself. The major manufacturers are falling over each other to assure us that dogs and dahlias are safer than ever before, now there are suitable alternatives to the evil destroyer creosote; mostly water-based, these new ranges of preservatives differ quite widely in price and performance.

Ronseal's Fencelife, £7.46 inc. VAT per 4lt. tub (yes, tub, which means you don't have to decant into a bucket) is OK for plants and animals, easy to use and comes in four colours — they are opaque, though, and give the wood a 'painted' thick-coloured appearance. It's highly water-repellent, and they claim greater coverage and longer fade-resistance than creosote.

'Timber Gard' from Signpost Paints is also water-based, and comes in two transparent colours; it's £2.25 for four litres, and fungicidal but not insecticidal properties are claimed. Fosroc, the parent company for Protim, is selling its DIY/small tradesman range under the 'Pro-Am' name, and offers an ordinary solvent preserver (Timber-Treat GP) at £9.40+VAT for 5lt, a solvent-based insecticide/fungicide (Timber-Treat Plus) for £10.90+VAT, and — note — a water-based (i.e., safer) insecticide/fungicide (Timber-

# Shoptalk special

Treat Non-Flam) for £6.55 +VAT. These are but a sample; other makers are trying equally hard for a slice of that £36m market.

Meanwhile, take a very good look at Ronseal's new **Exterior Wood Stain**. Apart from having a nice satin finish, it's water-repellent and highly fade-resistant, and includes wood-preservers as well. No priming or undercoating, a good range of colours, and good penetration.
● Sterling Roncraft, Chapel-town, Sheffield S30 4YP, tel. (0742) 467171;
● Signpost Paints, Haverhill, Suffolk CB9 8PQ, tel. (0440) 703611;
● Fosroc Ltd, Fieldhouse Lane, Marlow, Bucks SL17 1LS, tel. (06284) 6644.

*Another angle clamp from specialists Bessey holds workpieces together at right-angles. Could be a very useful third hand: £20.95 +VAT.*
● *Heward & Dean Ltd, 90/94 West Green Rd, London N15 3SR, tel. 01-800 3443*

**P**erfect enough for panelling . . . fashionable enough for furniture . . . these and other bold claims are being made for **hardboard** by FIDOR, the fibreboard promotion association, in a current campaign to reinstate the old friend's prominence in a competitive market. 'Don't forget your hardboard', exhorts Hardboard Harry, a specially-created if somewhat flat-faced cartoon character, 'the ever-popular and incredibly versatile board for hundreds of jobs about the home'. Interesting that FIDOR, whose

---

**May's *Woodworker* included a frank report by Mr R. B. Cannon on his past experiences with a Kity universal woodworking machine. We now publish a reply from John Farrar, managing director of Rawdon Machine Sales Ltd — the UK associate company of Kity's manufacturers — plus a letter from reader P. F. Rowe which gives a third side to the story**

**J**ohn Farrar writes: Mr Cannon, in his article 'Initiation test' in the May issue, was referring to the Kity **K5 Mark I**. Mr Cannon purchased his machine in June 1981. Since that time, the K5 Combination has undergone radical surgery to such an extent that the original model is barely recognisable. The **New Mark II K5** was launched in the UK in May 1983.

The improvements which have been made to the K5 are as follows:
● A 20% increase in the size of the saw table.
● A completely new mortiser with adjustment stops, lever control and work-mounting clamps. The new mortiser can also be retrospectively fitted to the earlier model Mark I K5.
● Simplification of the drive system to use only one belt without the need to slide the motor.
● Guarding to full industrial standard, including the spindle-moulder; this is very rare on small machines.
● The shaft diameter of the spindle-moulder has been increased to 20mm to allow the

user to purchase tooling, if desired, from sources other than Kity.
● A sturdy floor-stand with wheels is included in the cost; this again is very rare with the smaller machine.
● A 56-page comprehensive instruction book, 260-page hardback book on general machine technique and a standard adjustment toolkit are all included completely free of charge.

In order to comply with safety regulations, the planer knives are mounted in the block in a standard configuration which is exactly the same as that for all planers on the market produced by reputable manufacturers. The knives can be honed *in situ* but not sharpened.

There are probably as many different types of cutting tool for use with woodworking machinery as there are different types of wood. A considerable range of tooling is offered by Kity; in fact, some users of machines produced by other manufacturers frequently purchase Kity tooling. Our experience has shown that customers prefer to buy the basic machine at the lowest possible price, then select the tooling to suit their own particular requirements.

Mr Cannon raised some very valid points in his article relating to making the correct choice when purchasing a woodworking machine. With the approval of the editor, I hope to be able to offer some answers next month.

● **Woodworker** welcomes the opportunity to print John Farrar's views both now and in the August issue. Meanwhile we apologise to Kity UK, their customers and their potential customers for any misunderstanding that may have been

caused. It should be noted that the photo accompanying the article depicted a Kity K5 Mark II although the text does indeed refer to a Mark I machine purchased in 1981.

**A**fter having read 'Initiation test' by R. B. Cannon, I feel I must give my experience of the K5, **writes P. F. Rowe.**

A year ago I purchased a Kity Mark II universal machine. It came from my local dealer, W. Hosking of Worthing, complete in its crate, with all items and tools, and also a very comprehensive instruction manual (in English).

I have used it for a variety of cabinet and furniture projects, and although I had no previous machinery experience found it very easy to set up and use. It is very versatile and accurate.

Referring to the details of Mr Cannon's article, the guards on the spindle-moulder I have found simple to use; they give a high degree of safety to the operator. The mortiser gives great accuracy, with ample means of regulating sideways movement of the timber.

With regard to the planer knives, I have found no problem in honing them on a stone when removed from the planer. Belt changing from one machine to another takes five seconds.

I have found the importers, Rawdon Machine Sales, and my dealer most helpful, and on each occasion any item required has been received by return.

I have been so pleased with my Kity K5 that I have recently purchased one of their K712 bandsaws. This too is an excellent machine.

I hope you will find room to publish this, so as to give readers another person's view on these machines. ■

---

eggs have been recently fairly and squarely laid in an MDF basket, should now recognise the need to remind us that hardboard not only exists, but can actually be used.

'Delightful to decorate . . . fast to fix . . . wonderful to work . . .' a FIDOR-produced DIY leaflet will be on trade and DIY counters, telling you what to do with hardboard and how, and information sheets and advice are available from the Hardboard Advisory Service at FIDOR's offices.

'The advances made by newer

materials recently have pushed the benefits of hardboard into the background,' says Peter Gill, FIDOR's managing director. 'Now, with the help of Hardboard Harry, we're fighting back.' A win on points

over MDF? A straight knockout seems unlikely . . .

● FIDOR, Hardboard Advisory Service, 1 Hanworth Rd, Feltham, Middlesex TW13 5AF, tel. 01-751 6107.

---

**A WARNING.** Last month (p433) James Paffett told how to melt wax for easy application by using a hot-air paint-stripper. The trouble is, *this can be dangerous.* Alistair Robertson of wax makers Henry Flack points out that all prepared (paste) waxes have a flashpoint of only about 21°C: that's the heat at which any naked light will *explode* the vapour from the solvent. Heating dry waxes is safe — but, if you make up your own paste with white spirit, remember that has a flashpoint of 81°C. So, unless you're using solid cakes (pure beeswax, carnauba, etc.), *don't heat wax* is the safe rule.

# Shoptalk

A current favourite woodworking topic is decoys and decoy-making, but not exclusively as featured last month. Bob Ridges' highly realistic work comes from his specialist training in America, and, discovering a growing interest in it over here, he has started his own **decoy-making courses.** He has held them before at various centres of the Wildfowl Trust and some residential colleges, and now announces the opening of Britain's first School of Decorative Decoy Carving. He will be running courses for beginners, and for those wanting to improve their skills, giving 'hands on' training in all stages of carving, texturing and painting. If you see a duck in a lump of wood and want to know how to let it out, enrol without further ado.

● Bob Ridges, Decoy Art Studio, Farrington Gurney, Bristol, Avon BS18 5TX, tel. (0761) 52075.

From Guernsey, where Roger Newton has run courses at his School of Decorative Finishes for some years, comes the chance to learn **marbling, gilding,** or **graining and dragging** in the comfort of your own armchair — if you have a VHS video recorder. A natural for the video treatment, these and other techniques are offered on cassette for sale or hire in Roger's 'Master the Art' series. Like so many other finishing techniques, there has long been mystique and reticence surrounding these skills, and there must be many potential enthusiasts who have found the search for knowledge exasperatingly difficult. There could hardly be a better source of information than Roger, who has not only worked on National Trust properties and run his own business for 20 years, but has also recognised the demand for this kind of knowledge, and has gone ahead and supplied it. Tortoiseshelling, lines and decoration are in the pipeline.

The tapes cost £29.95, and there is a special hire arrangement for *Woodworker* readers; pay the full price as a deposit, and £10 a week hire is deducted from the original amount when you return the tape in good condition. If you want the full treatment, Roger's five-day residential courses in Guernsey cost £150.

● Roger Newton School of Decorative Finishes, Sausmarez Manor, St Martin, Guernsey, Channel Islands, tel. (0481) 35611.

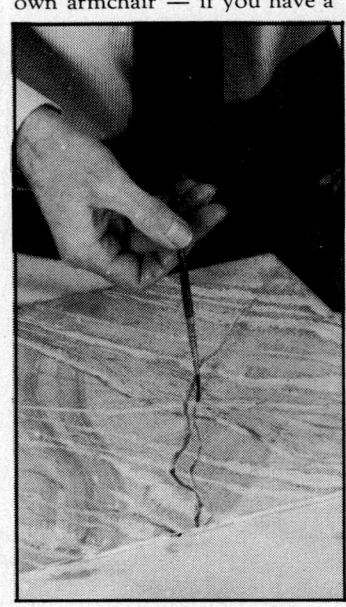

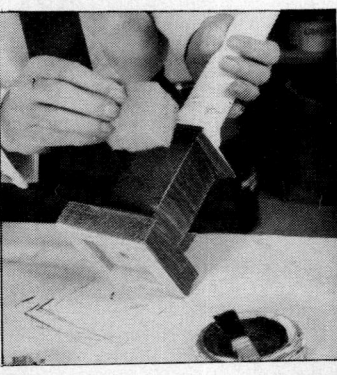

Heavy French **machinery** makes its debut on the English market in the form of Chambon's impressive range of industrial-use equipment. The more competitive the commercial atmosphere becomes, the better chance you get of a good buy, and it would surely be a mistake to overlook these machines if you are shopping round. The 234 thicknesser has no less than three separate motors — one for the four-knife 'low-noise' cutter block, one for the feed, and one for the rise and fall; the feed motor's speed is infinitely variable between 3 and 19m/min. The cutter motor is electrically braked, and there is full safety interlock of all guards. Good spec; capacity 630 x300mm, price £4515+VAT.

Chambon's 327 spindle moulder, introduced like the thicknesser at the Ligna Exhibition in Hanover, has a four-speed motor with a single control lever that allows you to change gear without stopping the motor. The complete range, which includes bandsaws, circular saws, sliding-table/scoring-cut panel saws and overhead belt sanders, looks solid and well-built, and each machine comes with a two-year guarantee.
● Chambon UK, 6 Acorn Park, Charlestown, Shipley, W. Yorks BD17 7SW, tel. (0274) 580866.

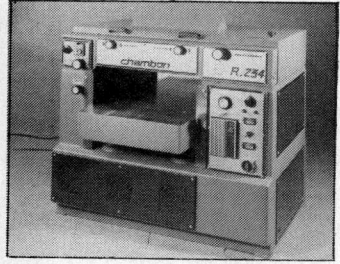

**I**f you can't trust your meter, analogue, digital or LED, then you undoubtedly need the Verus **Moisture Meter Calibrator**. Matchbox size, patented by TRADA, useful for softwoods, hardwoods, veneers, boards or finished wood products, it does the business in 20 seconds. Prototypes have been successfully tested by British Rail, among numerous likely users. £39.90+VAT.
● Verus Instruments Ltd, Ash House, Church Lane, Bledlow Ridge, High Wycombe, Bucks HP14 4AZ, tel. (024 027) 377.

**W**ith such a lot of current interest in woodmachin- for the 'small professional' or home craftsman, the market is naturally burgeoning — but not only for machinery as such. Constant desire to improve skill and capacity goes with the urge to gather information, which is where not only *Woodworker*, but also **woodworking books** come in. The Inca Woodworking Machinery Handbook is a welcome addition to this market, and (at a fairly thorough glance) looks excellent for

someone who has just invested in machinery and is now wondering what to do with it, and how. Written by an American and a Swiss — Mark Duginske and Karl Eichhorn — it is originally conceived to go with Inca's range, but the excellent, well-laid out advice, profusely illustrated, will make it very handy for owners of any machinery, and not just beginners at that.

It is divided into sections that go with the basic components of the Inca range — the circular saw, bandsaw, spindle moulder and planer-thicknesser — and deals not only with the basic functions of each machine, but also with jigs and hold-downs for all sorts of more advanced work. The circular-saw section, for instance, starts with blade theory, explains fences, kick-back, blade guards and push-sticks, pattern and taper-sawing . . . and it pays constant attention to safety, reminding you of the value of your eyes or fingers at least once a page. By no means comprehensive — what book could be? — but if you absorb every bit of know-how in this little paperback, you'll be well on the way to safe and skilled machining. It costs £9.95 inc p&p.
● Woodworking Machines of Switzerland Ltd, 49 Aylesbury St, Bletchley, Milton Keynes, Bucks MK2 2BQ, tel. (0908) 641492.

**A**rcoy continues to make the news . . . it seems that eager buyers read last month's Shoptalk news about a new source of supply — Alan Holtham's Old Stores Turnery — and wasted no time in sending off £13.80+VAT for *all three* dovetail cutters sizes 1, 2 and 3. They are £13.80+VAT *each*, Alan asks us to emphasise. Still a bargain, though, for items so rare.
● Alan Holtham, Old Stores Turnery, Wistaston Rod, Willaston, Nantwich, Cheshire CW5 6QJ, tel. Crewe 67010.

**A** pity for those keen *Woodworker* readers who like to have the whole year in one big helping, but encouraging for the purveyors of information about our ever-expanding craft: we are sorry that the **Woodworker Annual for 1984 is out of print.** You may get one for love, but you won't for money.

**REMEMBER...** *Woodworker* depends on woodworkers. We're willing and eager to tell the world what you're making, doing, exhibiting — even thinking. Our only aim is to produce the magazine you want to read. We're looking for photos, drawings (rough sketches will do) and words on any woodworking subject from ovolo mouldings to overhead routers. And we're on the end of the phone. We're waiting to hear from you!

*Peter Collenette*
*Aidan Walker*

# Timberline

## Arthur Jones presents the month's inside news of supplies

Inflation is still a bogey these days. So it's all the more pleasing to reflect on the comparatively modest price increases for most woods over the past year or two. In many cases, timber is as cheap now as it was three or four years ago — which is more than can be said for other raw materials.

This needs saying because so often people bemoan the cost of wood. Certainly there were some dramatic increases a few years back, but today it would be hard to find other materials so freely available and so competitively priced. In wood, it's a buyer's world, and the woodworker needs to keep this fact in mind despite occasional signs to the contrary. Today there is a lot of wood in the UK with a host of unwilling buyers; and, whenever such conditions prevail, there are inevitably cut prices and bargains to be found, though a little shopping around is required to get the best results.

Make the most of these competitive conditions however, because they are unlikely to be around for long. In the first place, both producers and timber traders in the UK are taking action to cut down their stocks to bring supply and demand into closer relationship. In due course they will succeed in this task, even without any recovery in the UK economy.

The softwood market continues uncertain. While the Russians have at last finished settling the details of their contracts on those first schedule prices (which were quite attractive and showing the full fall in the market), the time taken clearly shows how unwilling the importers are to buy.

Recently there have been further falls in the prices of some Scandinavian fifths, though generally the journey grades have been holding up. However, the Swedish sawmills are continuing to over-produce on a substantial scale, and this could lead to further price weakening this summer.

Hardwoods are also generally selling at weak prices. The woodworking buyer holds the reins, and importers are hesitant to place new business abroad until they can see prospects of increased demand at home.

We all know about the strength of the dollar against sterling, but this should not cloak the fact that there are good stocks of north American hardwoods available in the UK, and their prices have not changed as dramatically as the value of sterling. The woodworker can get such woods as maple, cherry, red and white oak, walnut and ash in a full range of thicknesses to satisfy most woodworking requirements.

Although the current overseas prices for most hardwoods remain weak — showing few, if any, increases over those quoted in the past six months — it is nevertheless possible to buy these same species at below the price the stockist will have to pay to replace them.

Selling below replacement cost is always a desperate measure for any timber firm, and it occurs only when the market is exceptionally depressed. Obviously, the practice can only continue for a strictly limited period before the firm goes into liquidation. So woodworkers should take full advantage of the attractive hardwood prices being quoted by those firms avid for turnover.

Among the weaker sellers which have been noted of late are keruing, lauan, nemesu, meranti and mahogany. Some of the cheaper offers in Brazilian mahogany come from mills in the south of that country, however, and there have been occasional troubles with quality and grading of the material, so the woodworker should be on guard when buying this timber.

When we talk about the fairly high cost of American oak because of the strong dollar, it's a good time to mention our own native oak, which is currently selling at about 5% lower than it was six months ago.

More west African hardwoods are coming into the country these days, and they are winning back their popularity of the immediate post-war period. There has never been anything wrong with the timbers themselves — only problems of price and delivery created by the various régimes ruling west African states. ∎

488

# Question box

**Q** *I am building a coffee-table of Brazilian mahogany. Although I am perfectly competent in the making department, my last attempt at staining and polishing was so disastrous I put the job through the bandsaw!*

*Could you tell me how to stain Brazilian mahogany to that very dark brown with a tinge of red that one sees in quality furniture? If I have any success at staining, I thought of finishing with polyurethane lacquer, brushed on. I would appreciate any information on these important parts of the job.*

*John Struthers, Greenock*

**A** Staining and polishing must be a terrible nightmare to you if your last attempt had to be sawn up for firewood. I wonder why you didn't scrape it all off and start again?

Before staining your work it is always advisable to experiment with different stains on some scraps of wood from the job in hand. In this way the unsuitable stains can be discarded, while the strength of the desirable stains can be adjusted to give the required colour without endangering the finished piece.

I think you will find water stains will suit you best. They are not expensive, they bring out the beauty of the grain and generally do not fade. The disadvantage of water stains is that they raise the grain, which results in a roughness of the surface.

Avoid this roughness by lightly sponging the work with warm water before staining. This will raise the grain. The wood is allowed to dry thoroughly before being smoothed with a new piece of fine abrasive paper such as 7/0 garnet. A new piece is used because its sharp cutting particles will remove the raised grain fibres cleanly and ensure there is no more grain-raising when the stain is applied.

A good mahogany water stain can be made by dissolving two ounces of bichromate of potash in a pint of water. The crystals are orange, but the wood will turn a pleasing brown colour which should suit your purpose very well. If, however, after the stain has dried the wood appears too red for your liking, lightly dampen it with clean water; this will show you the colour it will be when polished. If it's still too red you can increase the brown shade by brushing on a weak walnut stain. This is made with equal parts of vandyke brown and brown umber mixed into a paste with .880 ammonia and then diluted with water. When the stain is absolutely dry you can apply your polish.

In most furniture factories the work is spray-finished with lacquer, a process beyond the small user. You could certainly use a polyurethane varnish which, if carefully rubbed down between coats, will look good and stand up well to accidental spillages.

Should you require a finish that will withstand spilled water and alcohol you will find bar-top lacquer the most durable. Add up to 25% thinners to the lacquer, which is flowed on to the wood with a clean brush. Buy the thinners and the lacquer from the same source and carefully follow the manufacturer's instructions.

Normally I wouldn't recommend french polish for tabletops which may have to withstand heat and spillages, but if you do want such a finish, 'Imperva' polish (WW/Dec. 84) will give excellent results.

*Charles Cliffe*

---

**Q** *I have a problem with gluing plastic 'hockey-stick' moulding on to the edge of melamine chipboard. Originally I tried a contact adhesive. When the moulding and chipboard parted company shortly afterwards, I wrote to the company which had made the adhesive and received what I suppose is a standard reply to the effect that all surfaces must be free from grease. Since both surfaces had been thoroughly cleaned, this was not very helpful.*

*Latterly I have used a urethane adhesive which I find excellent for gluing together materials with different expansion rates. unfortunately this glue is not made in the UK, and I must obtain the small amounts I need from America. However, even this glue does not hold the moulding on permanently.*

*K. Petchell, Whitton*

**A** I have carried out some limited tests — it was clear from the greasiness of the plastic that there would have been a gluing problem. I roughened half of your sample with coarse sandpaper, and left the other half smooth. Several adhesives were tried in the first test, and in all cases the bond was stronger where the surface had been roughened. Only epoxy, however, produced a reasonably strong bond.

In the second series of tests I used a hot-melt adhesive, applied with a glue gun. This made a very good bond, and the technique is simple when only short lengths of plastic are to be glued. But hot-melts set by cooling, and there may be problems applying this adhesive on long lengths of the plastic, because some cooling would already have happened before you could get even pressure along the whole length of the join. You could possibly overcome this by pre-heating the plastic.

*Stanley Ford*

---

**Q** *I have some logs of ash, felled in early spring and stacked out of doors in the round with the ends painted. Now I find that there are large numbers of flight-holes in the bark, produced by a wood-boring insect.*

*I removed some pieces of the bark and the grubs appear to be confined to the bark itself, only furrows appearing in the timber. The holes contain white grubs and also the insects in the process of emerging. The latter are dark in colour and ⅛in or slightly less in length. Two things I find puzzling; the insects, which look like furniture beetles, emerged in the middle of October, and the timber has only been felled about seven months – I would expect that the insects would need at least a year in the grub stage (unless infestation took place before felling). The level of infestation also seems surprisingly high.*

*What are these grubs, and is the timber still likely to be usable?*

*A. Wilson, Corwen*

**A** Your logs have been attacked, probably but not necessarily in the standing tree, by the ash bark beetle, *Hylesinus fraxini*. To set your mind at rest, these beetles cause only superficial damage to wood, but they are quite serious pest in growing trees. Heavy attacks reduce the growth rate of the tree because of the damage they do to the cambium. This reduces the wood's value if it is required as 'sports ash', since fairly fast growth produces the strongest and most resilient wood.

This is because ash is ring-porous; each ring starts off with a couple of rows of open pores, followed by the denser summer-wood or 'latewood' which is the strong part of each ring. If the tree has grown slowly the rings are close together, and the weak, thin-walled cells of the springwood dominate each ring. If they are wider apart, there is a greater proportion of strong fibres. You will be able to check this when you convert the wood — but you will probably find it quite acceptable for any use.

As for the beetle, the female bores through the bark and makes a horizontal bi-armed gallery between bark and sapwood. This is called the 'parent' or 'mother' gallery. She then lays her eggs at intervals along this gallery. The larvae, when they hatch, bore at right-angles, the effect of which is to make burrows half in the inner bark and half in the sapwood edge, the larval and pupal stages taking place in each burrow. Occasionally, a slight penetration of the sapwood takes place, with one or two flight-holes visible on the face of a sawn board, but any damage is slight. Once the bark is removed the attack dies out and there is no danger whatsoever to converted wood.

The beetles probably emerged in October because of the good summer, which has left the wood warm — the bark acts as an insulator. The emerging beetles are probably dying off straight away.

*Bill Brown FIWSc*

---

**Q** *I have an Arkansas honing stone which must be about 70 years old, and not surprisingly it has hollowed over the years. Can you suggest ways of levelling it out which would work for carborundum stones as well?*

*Roger Park, Preston*

**A** A simple and very effective way of truing all kinds of oilstones uses coarse (100-grit), medium (220) and fine (400) silicon-carbide paper — wet-and-dry — on a flat surface such as a sheet of glass.

Lay a coarse sheet on the glass plate and liberally sprinkle it with water; then work the stone on the paper in a circular motion, using fairly heavy pressure. Wash the paper out frequently to stop clogging, and check the stone with a straight-edge. Continue until the stone is true, then repeat the process with the finer grades until the

490

# Question box

striations caused by the grit match the texture of the stone. With a fine stone such as Arkansas, even 400 grit may be too rough — you can rub two sheets together to reduce the cut, or try finer grades. Wet-and-dry can be bought in 1000 grit!

Oilstones should be wiped clean after use and kept in a box; a suitable standard lubricant is engineer's Tellus oil no27, which can be thinned with paraffin if you want to speed up the cut.

*Bob Grant, DLC FSIA MSIAD*

**Q** I recently had to put up a number of corner shelves, about 12in radius, to carry lamps and various pieces of bric-a-brac. I couldn't find any neat supporting brackets, so I finally built the shelves without them, using ¾in T&G floorboards.

I cut two 11×1in lengths (one grooved, the other tongued), joined them with a half-lap, and fixed the L-shaped piece into the wall corner with no8×2in screws. Then I joined three pieces of T&G, tongued the inside end-grain, radiused the other end, reeded the ends to cover the joints, and fitted the assembly into the wall-pieces. The result was quite a strong shelf.

I know there's nothing new here – but could you tell me the name of this construction, and where are the weak points?

*D. M. Williams, Cwmbrân*

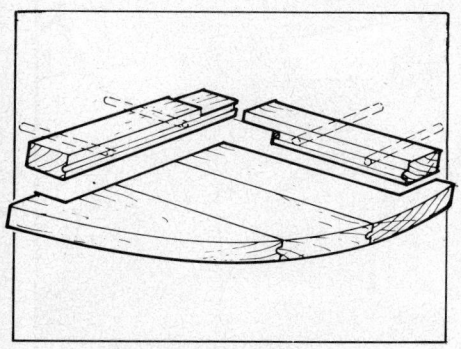

**A** I'm not aware of any particular name for your corner-shelf construction, since it appears to be your own ingenious solution. You could have overcome the non-availability of suitable brackets by making them yourself in the traditional console-corner-shelf manner, where two arms are fixed to the wall corner in an L-shape and the shelf fixed on to their top edges.

It's not clear from your description whether you glued the assembly of three T&G boards together, and whether you glued them to the back wall-pieces. If you did, problems might arise with the natural movement of the three boards across their width, which will be restrained by the glued joint on the arm which crosses the grain. Splitting could occur because of this. The other weak point in the design seems to be the board which is notched out to cover the end of the arm of the L-piece. The end-piece has no apparent support, and of course is short-grained and liable to break off if any load is put on it. A concealed dowel would

solve this, although a mitre would be neater and stronger.

*Bob Grant DLC FSIA MSIAD*

**Q** I recently acquired some very fine pieces of yew for turning, but the owner of the estate from which they came warned me that the wood was toxic and shouldn't be used for articles coming into contact with food. I knew yew leaves and berries were poisonous – but is the wood? I also, some time ago, turned a number of pepper-mills in laburnum. They were very ornamented, with fine figuring, but they didn't sell well; I suspect the reason was the same – people knew that laburnum seed was very poisonous, and assumed the wood was toxic as well. I would be grateful for your advice on both these woods, and their use as tableware.

*E. H. Minors, Skipton*

**A** Toxicity in wood is generally related to saw and sander dust — that is the irritant properties that could affect someone allergic to chemicals in the wood. There are long lists of timbers that cause nose bleeds and watering eyes, or are responsible for skin ailments like dermatitis. There are also instances where physical contact with a particular wood can cause distress — the thuyaplicenes in western red cedar give rise to one example.

Toxins in trees are concentrated more in the bark, leaves and fruit, although the wood itself is not poison-free. If you ate yew berries, you could become extremely ill, but you could probably handle and work yew wood without problems — unless of course you were allergic to it. I see no reason why laburnum and yew cannot be used for pepper-mills in the sense of customer acceptance; after all, teak, irritant to some, is used quite extensively for this purpose. The fact that complaints of ill effects are rare is probably that the finish acts as a barrier. It is unlikely in my view that ground dry pepper in contact with the bare inner surface of a mill would combine with infiltrates or inherent chemicals in the wood and do any harm.

You mention the feasibility of using these woods for tableware, and in some cases I would express a rather different view. I do not know what you have in mind, but I would not recommend wood for steak plates, for example, for several reasons: mainly hygiene, but also toxicity. Serrated-edge steak-knives would score the wood, while alkalinity in washing-up liquids tends to break down lignin, so the surface of a plate would attract microbes. Hot food and liquids could release toxins, while the alkalinity would tend to neutralise the antiseptic affect of tannic acids present in some woods.

Your friend who warned against yew wood coming in contact with food was being cautious, but food storage is a little different. For that purpose you need non-odiferous woods such as lime, poplar or willow, which do not impart odour to food. Yew is inclined to be rather oily and might tend to contaminate food, but much

depends upon what you intend to make.

If you want further advice I suggest you contact the Princes Risborough Laboratory, Aylesbury, Bucks HP17 9PX, and/or The Furniture Industry Research Association at Maxwell Rd, Stevenage, Herts.

*Bill Brown FIWSc*

**Q** I am at a loss to decide which finish to choose for a writing-desk I am making. The wood is Burmese teak, and very greasy – does this limit my choice of finish? I realise that teak oil is a finish in itself and is not restricted to use on teak only, but will I gain any advantage in highlighting the grain if I apply one coat before finishing? I seem to have a choice of: white polish sealer, finished with wax; polyurethane; french polish; and cellulose lacquer, thinned and brushed on. I think a satin finish with an open-grain effect is probably best for a piece like this. What are the relative merits of each of the options?

*David Yeo, Exeter*

**A** Most teak and teak-veneered furniture on sale today has a sprayed satin lacquer finish. A matt, satin or brilliant finish largely depends on your own preference and relative harmony with the rest of your furniture. Experiments with different finishes on offcuts will enable you to decide which you like best. As you say, Burma teak is naturally oily, and before applying any finish it is advisable to remove the surface oil by wiping it with a rag moistened with white spirit.

Teak oil is an oleo-varnish, and several applications, well rubbed-in, will give a pleasing durable finish. Any scratch-marks which come from normal use can be concealed with more oil. Wax has a lot to recommend it, giving a most attractive lustre. The first step is to brush on two coats of transparent white french polish to seal the open grain, enable a more rapid built-up of wax, and prevent any dirt which penetrates the wax from entering and staining the wood.

Allow the polish to harden thoroughly before lightly smoothing with 7/0 garnet paper. Thoroughly dust it off and, with a clean rag, evenly apply the lightest-coloured wax polish obtainable. You should be able to get it almost white. Let the work stand for about 15 minutes and then polish briskly in the direction of the grain with a clean duster. Four or five such waxings will build up a very pleasing finish. Accidental damage can be repaired by giving another good waxing.

If you intend to french-polish your table do not use white polish, which may give rise to grey streaks on your work. Instead use either transparent white polish or Imperva (WW/Dec, p781). These clear finishes will allow you to see the full beauty of the grain.

Cellulose lacquer will give a hard-wearing finish which stands up well to accidental spillages of water or alcohol. A badly-damaged or scratched lacquered surface,

# Question box

however, can be impossible to repair successfully, and often the only remedy is to strip it off and start afresh. You may therefore feel that the advantages of lacquer are to a large extent offset by this disadvantage.

Polyurethane varnish is not difficult to apply and gives a tough, hard-wearing finish. Each coat should be carefully smoothed before brushing on the next one. If you wish to give the varnish a more mellow appearance, the final coat (when thoroughly hard) can be dulled by rubbing gently with OOOO wire wool, dusted off and finally waxed.

*Charles Cliffe*

**Q** *I recently french-polished to a high gloss a small inlay-and-marquetry table of sapele veneer laid on chipboard. After three months, I put a small porcelain figure with a leather base on it, and noticed a pressure ring on the surface within a few days. I restored it and waited a year before putting another ornament on a lace mat on it. The pattern of the lace soon appeared on the surface.*

*I used a proprietary white french polish, lubricating the rubber not with linseed oil but with liquid paraffin to prevent yellowing of the inlay. An elm piece I finished in brown polish about the same time has been perfectly satisfactory. Shortly I will be finishing another piece, the result of 12 months' work, and because of the inlay I shall again be using white polish. I don't want to take any chances without exploring all the possible reasons for the poor result – what is your opinion?*

*Brian Moss, Colwyn Bay*

**A** I think you have used too much liquid paraffin — a mineral oil insoluble in methylated spirit. Its disadvantage is that it becomes plasticised with the surface film and *never dries out*. May I suggest that you strip off the offending polish and start again with a few tips in mind?

● Cut down the use of oil in the body-in process.

● Instead of using the spiriting-off technique, try the acid finish, a more positive method of removing surplus oil from the french-polish film. Briefly, you dilute one part sulphuric acid with 10 of water; remember to *add the acid slowly to the water* and allow it to cool. The weak acid kills off the superfluous oils, and then is itself absorbed by Vienna chalk, a fine magnesium powder available from trade suppliers.

● The acid solution is wiped over the bone-dry polished surface, then the chalk is dusted over and burnished off to produce a full mirror gloss.

● Leave the surface to dry out in a dry place at normal room temperature and it will be bone-hard in a month. It will not show any pressure rings or marks when things are placed on it.

This finish is used by professional polishers, and was once popular with piano-finishers.

Finally, may I suggest you use pale polish

instead of white. You may find it easier to use, and it will not obscure the grain.

*Noel Leach*

● **This question-and-answer** is a carefully combined and edited conflation of two letters from Mr Moss, separated by some weeks, and most of Noel Leach's comprehensive reply. The vital information about the use of liquid paraffin as a lubricant came after Noel had suggested a variety of reasons for the problem. Your queries can be answered with much greater accuracy and speed if you **let our experts know as much as you can** — even things that you might not consider relevant!

## When the cissing had to stop

**R**eaders with an interest in finishing materials and techniques will have been following with interest the discussion between Noel Leach and Eric Garratt, both experienced professional polishers, about the peculiar pitted effect that can occur when lacquering a surface. It started in December, with a 'Question box' query about re-finishing a cellulosed table-top; Noel gave a detailed workshop schedule, which Eric challenged in 'Letters' of February's *Woodworker*. Noel stuck to his guns on March's Letters page; here are the final two exchanges in the debate.

**E**ric Garratt writes: I would like to make it clear that I am not questioning Noel Leach's professional integrity. I read his articles in *Woodworker*, and have never been able to fault his advice. I do, however, feel strongly that his advice to Mr Coldwell (WW/Dec) was lacking, despite his subsequent letter in March.

Mr Coldwell's original problem was the removal of milky blotches from a cellulose (?) finish on a dining-table; before resorting to stripping, it is worth trying several remedies for removing this kind of mark, which is almost always caused by moisture. In my experience the safest of these is to mix any type of oil — camphorated is probably best — with tobacco ash, and rub over the affected areas with the finger or palm. It should be left an hour or so before being wiped clean, and can be repeated until either the marks are gone or it is obvious that they aren't going to go. This method may not work, but it won't leave any after-effects.

The following method is more effective, but more likely to be disastrous, and *must be done with extreme care*. Wipe the affected areas with methylated spirit, just enough to wet it, and immediately apply a lighted match. The meths must be allowed to burn for *no more than four seconds*, and any flame that lingers must be quickly blown out. This again can be repeated until successful or otherwise.

Meths alone will not affect a cellulose surface, but if the flame is left to linger, it will blister the lacquer. On a french-polished surface, the spirit will soften the polish and the flame may wrinkle and discolour the finish. If this method proves successful, any smeariness can be removed with fine wire wool.

As for cissing, Noel Leach's March letter leads me to suspect that he and I are not arguing over the same spraying fault. To me, cissing lacquer resembles at best a hammered finish and at worst a relief map of the moon.

Most domestic furniture is treated with polishes which contain silicone (the enemy!) — traces of which remain in the pores of the wood, especially if it is open-grained. This can be so even after stripping, washing with solvents and subsequent sanding. Unless surfaces are thoroughly fadded up with french polish to seal in all traces of silicone before the base-coat is sprayed on, in nine cases out of 10 the lacquer will ciss. The whole job will have to be washed off and re-started.

I should emphasise that this is exclusively a re-finishing problem, not one that occurs with new wood.

**N**oel Leach writes: At last I find out where Mr Garratt is going wrong. The sample piece that he sent is 'cissing', no doubt about that. Modern finishing products using nitrocellulose, and offshoots such as pre-catalysed, acid-catalysed, polyurethane and polyester lacquers, all have their own special solvents, fillers, bases and stains. Traditional methods must not be used with these chemically-based lacquers or the results obtained by Mr Garratt will occur.

He says 'The only sure prevention [of cissing] is by fadding [use of a piece of wadding] with french polish'. If you carry on like this, Mr Garratt, I'm not surprised you have cissing. Here is a cissing-free workshop schedule:

1 Prepare surface in normal way using 240-grade garnet paper.

2 Stain using a water or non-grain-raising (not oil) stain.

3 Fill grain if necessary with a cellulose filler.

4 Re-colour using a cellulose toner stain.

5 Apply one coat of lacquer at the correct viscosity.

6 De-nib using 600-grade silicon carbide with distilled water.

7 Apply the final coat of lacquer.

Result — no cissing. Make sure the lacquer is of the correct viscosity, and air pressure is 40-50psi: have scrupulously clean air-lines and containers, and a workshop temperature of about 60°F. Also, only use one manufacturer's products.

With regard to Mr Garratt's method of setting a lighted match to methylated spirits, I hope readers don't try this — there are easier ways of committing suicide or burning your house or workshop down! ∎

# Pole position

**Forget the Industrial Revolution when you build the original low-tech, non-polluting machine. Alan Bridgewater tried it!**

The chair-bodger is the man who — on the spot in the thick beech woods of the Chilterns — turned the legs, spars and stretchers for the cottage-type stick-and-splat Windsor chairs.

I must admit, right from the start, that I'm not what you might call a lathe man myself. I don't know much about chucks, beds, face-plates and the like. On the other hand, I've always been really interested in rural woodland crafts, and especially in the ancient craft of chair-bodging. What a beautiful notion of self-sufficiency — to work quietly in a quaint little home-made workshop deep in the woods, and there to make turned chair-legs, stretchers and spars on a simple, self-built, silent-running, tree-powered lathe. It all sounds absolutely wonderful.

To be honest, I've never met a genuine chair-bodger in the flesh, but I have seen a great many old, faded, misty photographs. Strong, hard-jawed, no-fuss, pipe-smoking men — making chair-legs at the rate of about one every five minutes: say up to 800 every week.

The chair-bodgers worked and lived in the Chiltern woods. There, in the years before the first world war, they worked the small beech-trees — selecting, thinning and clearing. The trees were sawn into workable lengths, slightly longer than chair-legs, and then split down into rough billets with axe, mallet and froe. Each of these wedge-shaped segments was then trimmed with an axe until all the hard core and bark had been removed. Old photographs show men working at tree-stumps, surrounded by four-square stacks of billets and mountains of bark and wood-chips.

The bodger next sat at his shaving-horse and worked each length of wood with a two-handed drawknife. The photographs suggest that by the time each piece of wood had been worked with the knife it was round in section, tapered at one end, and in fact more or less spar- or leg-shaped. An interesting point — the pole-lathe hut thatch was, more often than not, actually made from the shavings: not the chips and dust that spew out from modern power lathes, but long ribbons of green timber.

At this point, it might be as well to describe a traditional pole lathe in detail. Two huge upright posts are set straight in the ground about 5 or 6ft apart. Across the top of these, linking them and bridging the gap, is a massive flat beam or 'bed'. Mortised-and-tenoned and wedged into the bed, and set about 3ft apart, are two short upright posts. These are the head- and tail-stocks, or 'poppet posts'. Each of these

● *A chair bodger at work. A simple shelter, a pole-powered lathe, wet wood . . . a country idyll?*

stocks has a spiked iron mandrel or pivot, one being fixed and the other threaded and adjustable.

The whole lathe is topped by a 'see-saw' springy pole, the thin end of which hangs over the head of the bodger and is linked by means of a rope, cord or leather strap to a simple plank foot-treadle. The cord goes once or twice round the mandrel and then down to the treadle. When the bodger presses down on the treadle, the taut, pole-sprung cord spins the pivoted wood towards him; when he takes his foot off the treadle, the cord spins the wood backwards. So the working rhythm is: push down and cut with the tool — up with the foot and withdraw the tool.

With the wood all the time turning backwards and forwards, the bodger can only cut it on the down-tread. And so it goes: pushing on the treadle, working the full length of the wood with a deep gouge, smoothing up with a broad-faced round chisel, and finally cutting the traditional rings and grooves with a parting-chisel and a narrow gouge. From rough, knife-worked

billet to finished chair-leg in four or five minutes, and then on to another leg.

It's beginning to sound like hard, muscle-tearing work.

## THE PROJECT

I decided to set to and build my own. I used found materials — junk wood, and various bits and pieces.

### Frame, uprights and bed

Pole-lathe designs are many and varied. Some have two main beams and a solid plank-beam bed, while others are built into the actual fabric of the workshop and only have a single upright beam post, a couple of nailed bracers and a two-beam track or bed.

I had a good look at my concrete-floored, corrugated, asbestos-sided Nissen-hut workshop. After a lot of thought and acres of design sketches, I decided to knock up a full-size, free-standing prototype using bits and pieces I had salvaged from a massive wood-framed double bed. The material was not very beautiful, I grant you, but it fur-

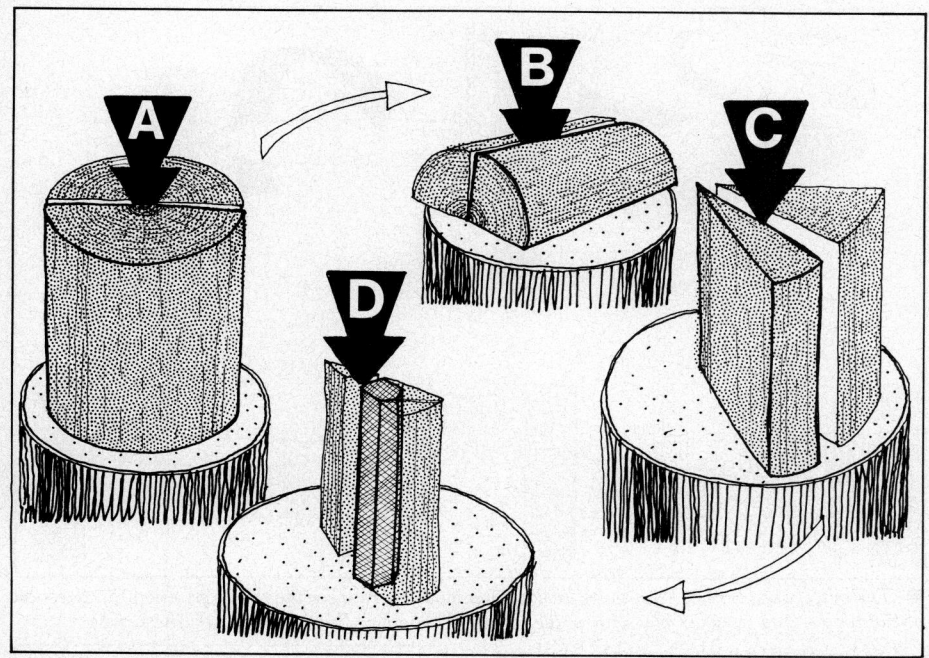

● With mallet, froe and axe, the five-sided billets were made from logs halved (A), quartered (B), cut into wedges (C), de-cored and de-barked (D)

track beams. I thought about having a complicated, fully adjustable tool-rest, but in the end I settled for a traditional, semi-fixed, wedged beam supported on two poppet-post outriggers.

### Pole, cord and treadle

The lathe has a long, springy pole which is fixed and chained at the butt end, 'see-saw'-anchored in the middle, and attached to the lathe treadle by means of a cord or leather strap. In retrospect I feel that I could have done without the pole and used a loose-coil tractor spring, or maybe a length of heavy-duty industrial rubber. However, I wanted to work within the spirit of the chair-bodger tradition.

After a bit of head-scratching and looking around, I managed to find a rather bent and ill-shaped larch that seemed to fit my needs — about 15ft long and very springy. An iron U-loop screwed to the top of the workshop door-frame, a simple frame-pivoted plank treadle, a length of natural fibre cord, and the job was done.

## USING THE POLE LATHE

I thought I'd turn a stretcher for an old

nished lots of good, solid 2½×3½in wood, a curious nut-bolt-and-beam spring-stretching arrangement, and dozens of long bolts, screws, washers and nails.

I decided to build a splayed-leg, trestle-type frame and have the poppet posts held in an adjustable vice-like track made from the bolt-and-beam bit of bed. The drawings show how I built the basic frame — no fancy joints, but plenty of screws and bolts so that I could re-design as I went along. With an experimental, trial-and-error project of this character, you need to be flexible, so don't cut or joint your material until you are absolutely sure you know what you want.

### Mandrels and poppets

The mandrels were a little bit of a problem, because I didn't want to spend a lot of money. In the end my 13-year-old son came up with a basic nut-and-bolt design. He made the mandrels at school — ⅝in threaded rod, nuts to fit, and two bent-steel-strap pockets into which the nuts are brazed; all very basic, made in a couple of hours, and very cheap. The total cost, using scrap material and (quote) 'slave labour', worked out at a little under 75p. All the metal parts of this lathe are bits of scrap salvaged from a local garage tip.

The poppet posts were measured, centred and drilled to take the threaded mandrels, which were slid home and held with a couple of screws. If, like the bodger, you only want to make (say) chair-legs and spars of a set length, the two poppet posts can be wedged fixtures. However, since I wanted the lathe to be as flexible as possible, I worked the two poppets so that they slid in a bolt-operated 'jaws' track. I measured, cut and 'necked' the two posts so that they slid between and rested on the two

● The cleft logs were split with a mallet and cleaving axe (**left**), the clefts were trimmed with an axe into rough, five-sided billets (**right**), and . . .

. . . sitting at a work-horse, the billets were further trimmed, shaped and tapered with a draw-knife

kitchen chair. I quickly set up the lathe, knocked off the corners of a bit of shop-bought timber, pivoted it between the lathe mandrels and started to pedal away.

After about an hour of standing on one leg like a stork, pedalling, sweating and pushing with the tool, I was totally exhausted; and the wood looked well and truly chewed and mangled. It all seemed a long way from the Spirit of the Old Chair Bodgers. So I had a cup of tea and thought everything out again.

Then, taking another knot-free piece of wood, and shaping it up with a draw-knife and Surform until it was well-nigh finished, I went back to the lathe. I checked that the cord was wound round in the right direction, I checked the height of the rest bar, I oiled the mandrels, and then I started pedalling.

After some 20 minutes I was just beginning to get the hang of things; but, to be honest, the wood was less round than when I had started.

# Pole position

The moral of this long and painful story is that you will get absolutely nowhere if you try working with seasoned wood; it's just too hard. You must use a soft, green, moisture-filled, sappy wood — preferably fresh-cut beech.

After a great deal of trial and error, I managed to make a chair stretcher of sorts. It isn't very beautiful, it's slightly warped, and it wouldn't win any prizes, but somehow it seems to fit my old chair just perfectly.

## Notes, hints, tips, conclusion and words of wisdom

My lathe is actually far too light in weight; even if I pin it down with sandbags, it still jumps about. I'm going to re-design the whole frame, and built a two-post lathe in the garden — the posts will be banged into the ground, and the poppet posts will be removable.

If you look at some of the very old illustrations, you will notice that the bodger has at hand a little bowl. I thought that maybe it was oil; in fact it must be water, because the drive cord needs to be dampened from time to time, otherwise it gets warm and starts to slip.

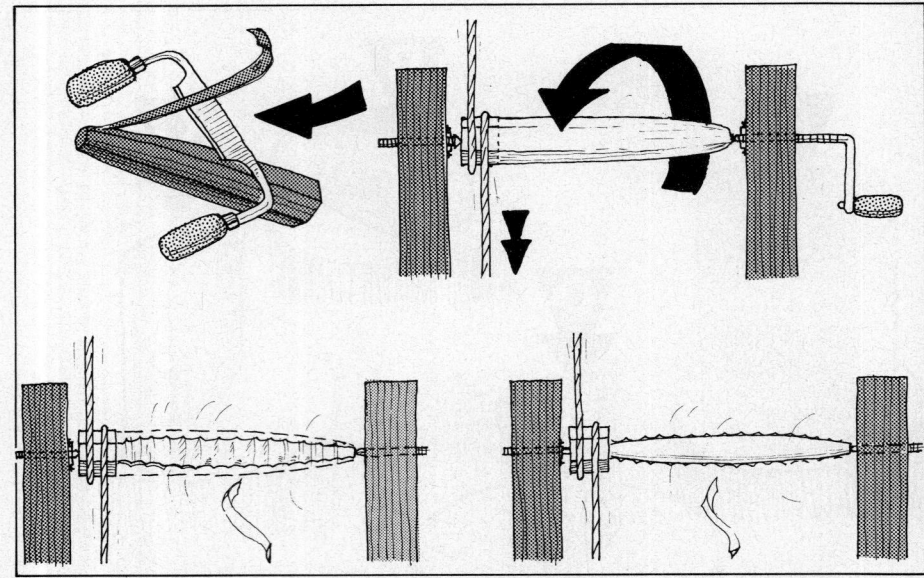

● *The billet, once worked with the draw-knife, is mounted between the mandrels – note the direction of the rope – and roughed out with a deep gouge. The drive 'lump' is cut off afterwards*

The length of the drive cord, the height of the pedal and the springiness of the pole are all critical. For example, if the pedal is too low, the cord won't pull the wood through a complete revolution, so you will finish up with an oval rather than round section.

● No doubt there are chair-bodgers or others who can fill in the gaps between trial and error when it comes to both building and using the pole lathe. If so, we'd very much like to hear from them so that we can publish their advice — and their photos and drawings, if any. ■

### Books

John D. Alexander Jr, *Make a Chair from a Tree* (Bell & Hyman, 1979)
James Arnold, *The Shell Book of Country Crafts* (John Baker, 1968)
Paul N. Hasluck, *The Handyman's Book: Woodworking* (Cassell, 1903)
Herbert Edlin, *Woodland Crafts of Britain* (David & Charles, 1973)
Norman Wymer, *English Country Crafts* (Batsford, 1946).

● The Turner *by Jan van Vliet, 1635. Note the tools, the bowl of water, and the two-beam bed*

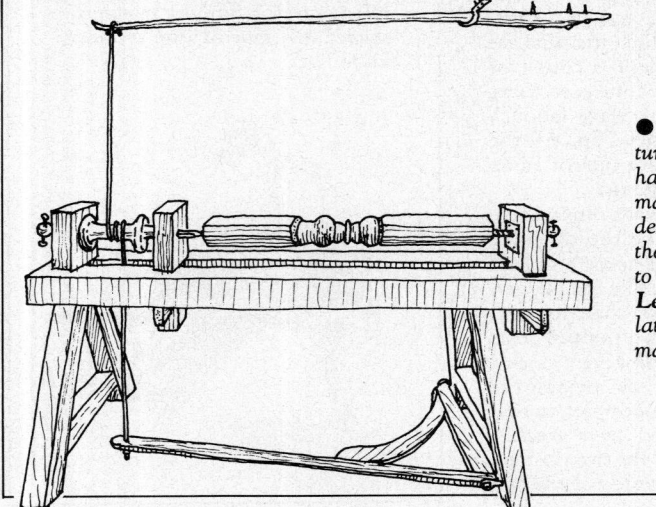

● **Above,** *a mediaeval turner at his lathe, which has a separate drive mandrel; the technical detail of which way round the rope should go appears to have escaped the artist.* **Left,** *another type of pole lathe with a separate drive mandrel and headstock*

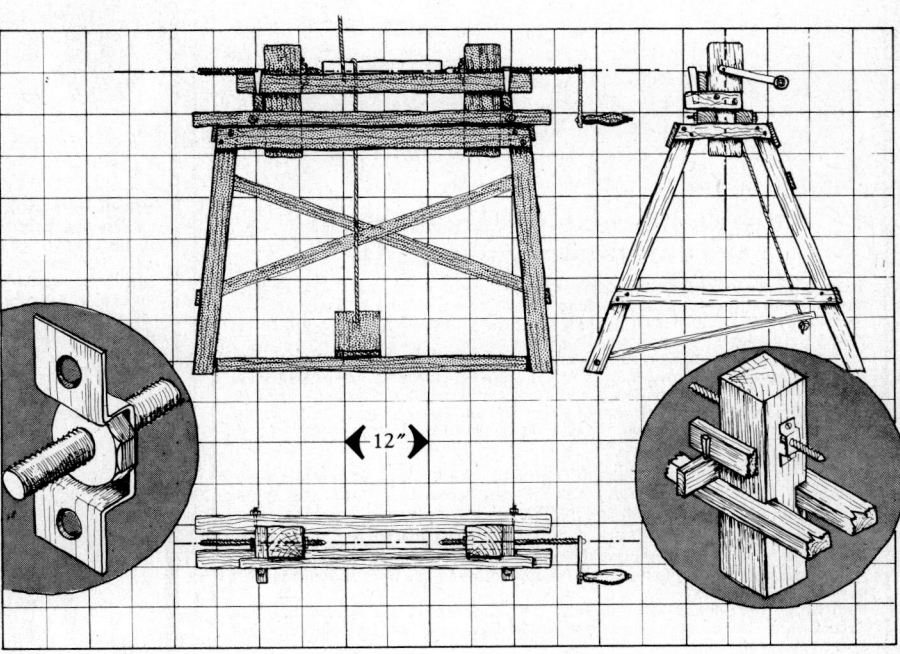

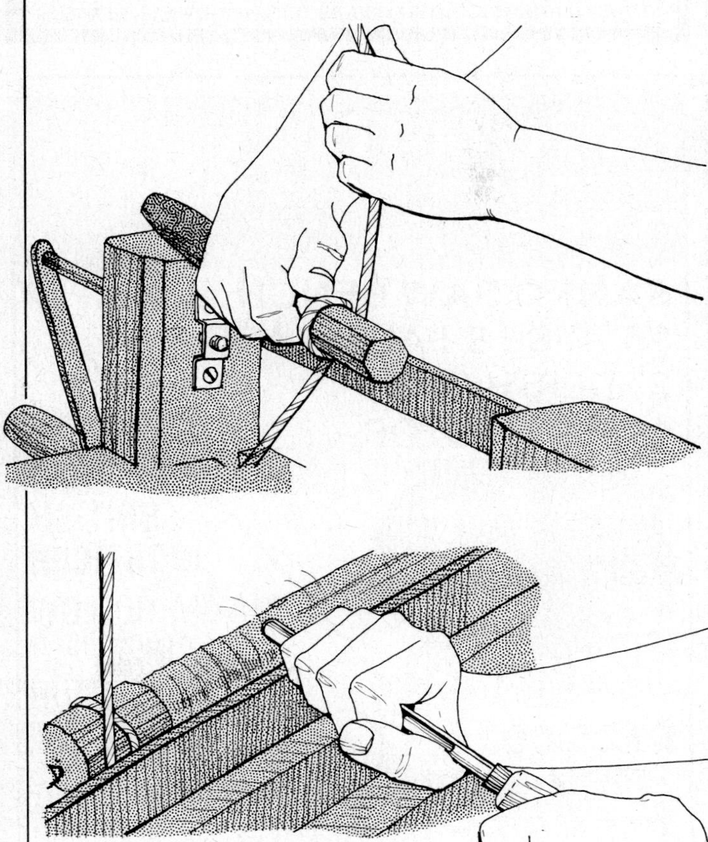

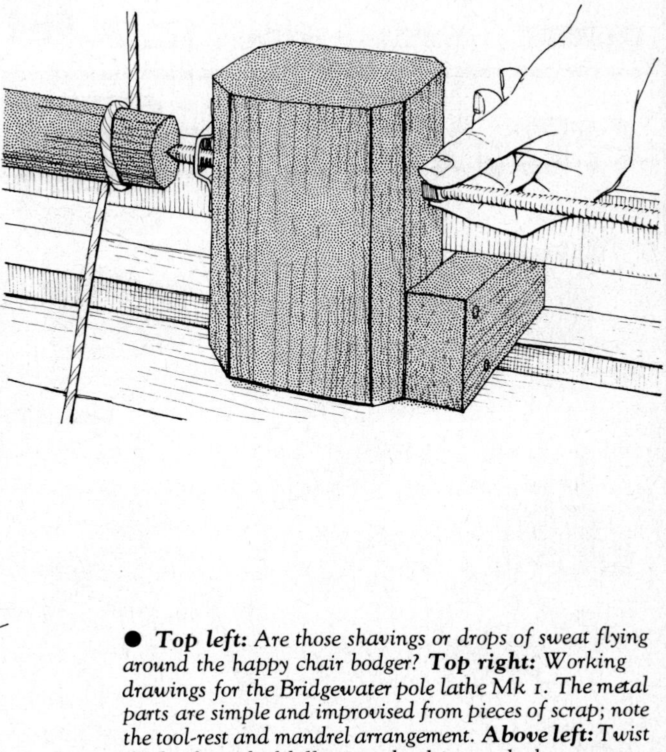

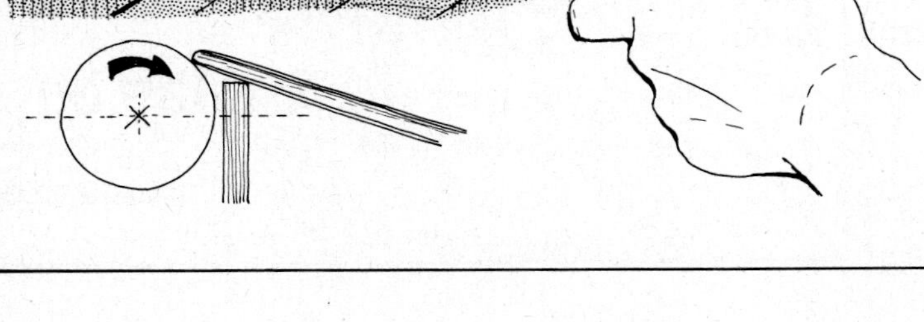

● **Top left:** *Are those shavings or drops of sweat flying around the happy chair bodger?* **Top right:** *Working drawings for the Bridgewater pole lathe Mk 1. The metal parts are simple and improvised from pieces of scrap; note the tool-rest and mandrel arrangement.* **Above left:** *Twist the knife-worked billet into the drive cord, then mount it between the mandrels, tightening and adjusting them after it is fixed (**above right**).* **Left:** *The direction of the drive cord and the height of the rest beam are critical. Use green wood, and keep the 'tread and cut' rhythm steady*

# FULL SERVICE

## If your interest is Woodworking we can satisfy your needs.

From Spaners to Spindle Moulders, Router Cutters to Planer/Thicknessers, Combination Machines to Modelling Tools. Coronet, Tyme & Warco Lathes, Sorby & Henry Taylor Turning Tools, Marples & Henry Taylor Carving Tools, Kity & Scheppach Woodworking machines.
Trend Router Cutters, Saw Tooth Cutters, Mortice Chisel & Bits, Slot Mortice Bits, Industrial TCT Saw Blades at 20% off list, large range of Bandsaw Blades, Industrial Sanding Belts for all popular machines at competitive prices. Japanese Chisels, Whet Stone Grinders. Bosch Power Tools. Drills, Vices, Stanley, Ridgway Hand Tools, Screws, Nails, Handles, Timbers etc.

**Stains/Polishes etc.**
Liberon Waxes, Stains, Polishes, Varnish, Pearl Glue, Veneers, Inlays, Bandings, Stringing, Marquetry, Clock Faces, Movements etc. Steel Wool, Garnet Paper, Books & Woodworking Plans.

**Demonstration Room**
The latest facet to our company is a large comprehensively stocked Demo/ Training Room, to enable us to teach people how to use their machines with confidence and safety.
Following the success of our woodturning courses we are extending these to cover Kity Combination machines and Radial Arm Saws, Spindle Moulders and Bandsaws.
These Courses run once a month and bookings can be taken over the 'phone.

 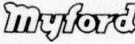  

## DeWALT

DEWALT 1501
RADIAL ARM SAW
1½ H.P.
CROSS CUT CAPACITY 18¼"
**£448.50**

ELU MHB 157 BELT SANDER
WITH DUST EXTRACTION
**£84.94**

ELU MH65
HEAVY-DUTY 180mm
CIRCULAR SAW
**£91.08**

ELU MOF 96
PLUNGING ROUTER
**£78.66**

ELU TGS 172
BENCH/BEVEL/MITRE SAW
COMP. WITH W/W KITS
**£374.00**

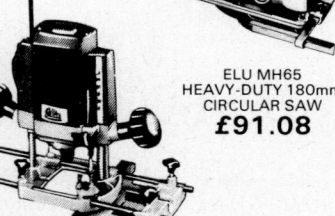  

### Unbeatable prices — Uncompromising service

## MATTHEWS

MATTHEWS BROTHERS (WOODWORKERS) LTD
Kettlebrook Road . Kettlebrook . Tamworth . Staffs
TELEPHONE TAMWORTH 56188

---

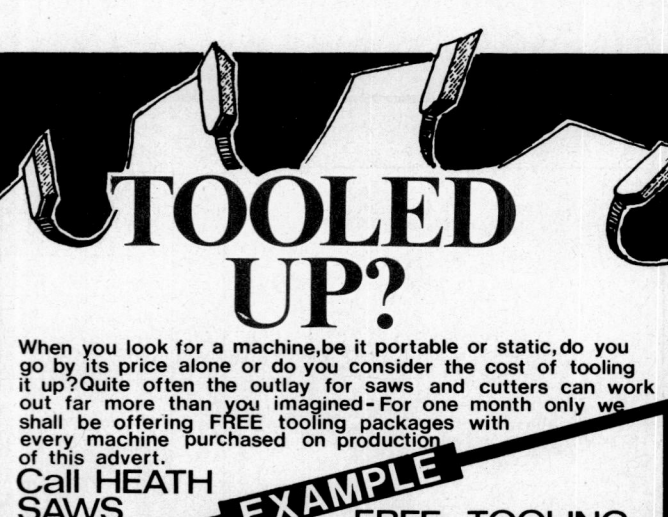

# TOOLED UP?

When you look for a machine, be it portable or static, do you go by its price alone or do you consider the cost of tooling it up? Quite often the outlay for saws and cutters can work out far more than you imagined - For one month only we shall be offering FREE tooling packages with every machine purchased on production of this advert.

**Call HEATH SAWS Now**

**EXAMPLE**

### FREE TOOLING
- TCT sawblade
- Profile cutter block
- 2prs. shaped cutters
- Drum sander
- Sanding sleeves
- 6mm and 12mm mortice bits
- Extra set of planer blades

MK II
**K704** NEW

**£1489·25 inc.vat**

TELEPHONE WARE (0920)
870230 or visit;
**HEATH SAWS,**
16, THE MALTINGS, STANSTEAD ABBOTTS, NEAR WARE, HERTS.

---

# KEITH MITCHELL TOOL AND EQUIPMENT
## 66 PRIORY BRIDGE ROAD, TAUNTON. Tel: 79078

*Distributors for: Kity, Startrite, DeWalt, Craftsman, Emco, Hitachi, Sip, Multico*

## SANKO SAW BENCH
## 10" RISE & FALL BLADE
## 3" DEPTH CUT
## 1½ H.P. MOTOR

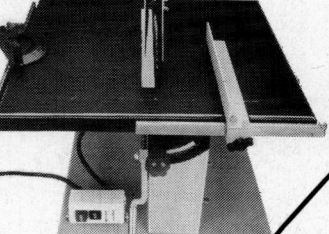

**£125.00**
INC. VAT

CARRIAGE
£5.00

### NEW BRITISH MORTICER

MAXIM HOLLOW CHISEL ¾"
¾ H.P. MOTOR
SOLID CAST

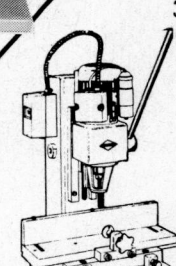

**£435.00**
INC. VAT

CARRIAGE £10.00

Chuck and Depth Stop included

---

498

# Kaki the cabinetmaker

# 粟 巣 野

**In the Japanese Alps lives a woodworker whose furniture is sturdy, handsome and a little bit English. Joanna Dale went to see him**

About 150 miles northwest of Tokyo, on the north coast of Honshu island, lies Toyama. Between the two cities are three mountain ranges — the Japan Alps, whose peaks soar to 10,000ft.

Though it's warm and pleasant during the summer, winter brings frigid Siberian air south over the Sea of Japan, depositing vast amounts of snow on the peaks and on the slopes leading down to Toyama.

In a clearing among the pine-trees of these lower slopes is a group of wooden houses. The pine from which they are built, and the wood stored between them, has taken the same route as the weather, south from Siberia to Toyama. This is where Makoto Kakitani (known as Kaki), his wife Junko (a renowned quilt-maker), his brothers and his fellow-workers live.

'The timeless beauty of solid wood' is the inscription above his name on his business card, on his labels and wherever his logo KAKI CABINET MAKER appears. His conscious appreciation of the material he works with, and the environment in which he has chosen to work, create the background for a very unusual craftsman.

Kaki was born in Toyama in 1943. He went to art college, where he learned to paint, and subsequently taught in high school. At the age of 20 Kaki decided to live in the mountains, where he could paint and ski. He picked a spot in the foothills; not having much money, he built himself a modest house of wood, and spent his time teaching painting to small groups and skiing during the winter. Occasionally he acted as mountain guide to Japanese artists.

He was shortly joined by his brother and a couple of friends, and they decided to build a lodge and open a ski-school. But the ski season lasts only four or five months of the year, and there were long periods without work. Kaki spent time making furniture for both his house and the ski lodge, confident that if he could design and build a house he must have acquired enough skill to make the furniture he wanted! Ski students arriving at the lodge saw the resulting pieces in use, and often enquired about the possibility of buying.

As the months went by, Kaki's confidence and interest in the craft grew, and he began looking at books on 17th-, 18th- and 19th-century furniture and art from Europe, north America and Canada.

● *Kaki the cabinetmaker's broad grin suggests he is well pleased with his success . . . his friends insist he is much too modest*

One day in a magazine he came across a photograph of a small, roughly made Spanish chair. Its simplicity appealed to him, and the picture proved an inspiration to him later that year when he was confined to a hospital bed for six months after breaking a leg while skiing. He was 29, and it was during this period that he made the decision to become a full-time furniture-maker.

On leaving hospital he went to Spain to look for the chair. After two months he found it in a small village near Malaga, promptly bought it, and returned to Japan.

By the end of that year his first exhibition was held in a small craft shop. Various items were sold, and three museum owners were among the buyers. At that point the commissions started, and he has since exhibited once a year all over Japan. His brothers and friends have stayed on and still

● *Kaki's own child-sized version of the Malaga chair, his original inspiration, is on the right. His design sense is rustic, timber and techniques well-nigh flawless*

work with him, and — although he has chosen not to sell through commercial outlets — the private commissions for his designs keep them busy throughout the year.

Every few months Kaki spends a day at the docks in Toyama (about an hour and a half's drive down from the mountain). There he chooses the timber himself, carefully scrutinising the latest imports of Siberian logs. 'I look for nice wood at a nice price!' he smiles. 'Siberian pine is bigger than Norwegian and therefore much more suitable for my furniture.'

The logs are sawn in Toyama and the boards taken to Kaki's home by truck. There they are kept outside for two or three years, exposed to wind and rain, and then in a ventilated storage place (under a roof to keep out direct sunlight) for a further year. After that the wood is taken into a drying room under the workshop, where it stays for one week at a temperature of 40°C in controlled humidity. Another 10 days indoors, and the material is sawn to size for the job. from then on everything is done by hand.

● *The style of this beautifully-proportioned dresser points to its mountain origins*

Kaki and his colleagues expend a great deal of time and care on maintaining and sharpening tools. Japanese blades (including those of the *samurai* swords) are made from a mixture of iron and steel. For example, the chisel combines iron for its flexibility with a steel edge for hardness. Kaki's workshop uses the tools that have been traditional for centuries all over Japan. They themselves appear to be as much works of art as the ends to which they are applied. Most are housed in purpose-built cabinets and chests, though some are wrapped in silk and stored in beautifully-made boxes. They can be worth thousands of pounds if made by well-known tool-makers.

The workshop itself is a long, New-England-style wooden building which stands within sight of the rest — the homes of Kaki and Junko and of his two brothers and family, and a show-house which holds a permanent display of the furniture. A small enamelled welcome sign, nailed to the door

● *Whatever culture inspired the low table and bench at* **right,** *their timeless simplicity spells 'classic' in any language. The dresser* **below** *exhibits some eye-catching detail variations on a typically European tradition; the wall cabinet and another dresser,* **below right,** *show minute but revealing differences from their western counterparts. The rocking chair at* **middle right** *indicates Kaki has absorbed at least some Japanese furniture history! His busy workshop is at the* **bottom**

# Kaki
# the cabinetmaker

of the workshop, greets the visitor at the top of the steps, and on entering one is welcomed again by the aroma of coffee percolating next to the burning wood-stove.

Here, in the warmth of the main workroom, surrounded by windows overlooking the 12ft-deep channels ploughed through the snow for access from house to house during the winter, Kaki answered some questions for *Woodworker*.

**Do you see yourself as being westernised?**
Yes, I'm sure I am.

**Why is that so?**
I was born in 1943, so like every Japanese child after the second world war I had an American-style education. I was 15 and at high school when I decided to become a painter. I was naturally interested in western art, since it was part of my schooling, so I followed its style. There was never a conscious decision to leave the Japanese traditions. We were never formally taught about Japanese style or art, we just absorbed the influence through the way we lived. The traditions are integral to the way of life here, even in the smaller everyday things — not necessarily in formal rules, but just in the way of doing things such as eating, bathing and so on. So I lived in this way too; but my interests were in western life-style and art.

**Have you modelled your work on anyone or anything specific in the west?**
No. But there were various influences when I began designing furniture. 25 years ago there were no furniture books here, but I knew about baroque art and Italian art, etc., and I had seen movies from the west — French, Italian and English as well as American movies.

**Do you have a fascination with English style?**
I'm not particularly interested in the latest furniture or designers in England. I don't make a point of reading about them.

**Are you part of a general trend in Japan with your designs, or are you unique?**
These days there are many young 'folk furniture designers'. Their work is influenced by early American folk art, and they are really a continuation of the west-coast hippie movement. Their work reflects that way of life.

(At this point one of Kaki's friends interrupted to say that he was being typically modest about his own success and the strength of his influence on younger furniture-makers. Kaki has a style and way of working unique in Japan, and the quality of his work plus the ensuing publicity in books and interviews have obviously inspired many less talented followers.)

**Given that there is so much western about your work, what do you feel is Japanese about it?**
About 20 years ago, when I needed to make furniture for purely practical reasons, everyone thought I was crazy, the way I went about designing and the influences I was interested in. But 50 or 100 years ago

the Japanese used solid wood to make furniture. Nowadays the people accept this style again and want to buy my furniture. Maybe it's the care, the technique, the tools and the manner in which we work that gives it some Japanese feel on closer inspection. After all, I *am* Japanese! But it also has a lot to do with the senses. The contact of skin with skin [he places his hand, palm down, on the smooth tabletop], the smell of the wood, the appeal to the eye. It's close to some Chinese and Egyptian furniture that I've seen — it's to do with being human.

**What have you studied of western techniques?**
When I first decided to make furniture I already had a style and designs that I wanted to use. I didn't know or think about the

differences between western and Japanese construction — I just wanted to make my furniture in much the same way as I had wanted to paint. So I discovered methods of construction for myself. In fact the two traditions are very similar. For example, the dovetail joint is known in Japan as the *arizashi* joint — *ari* meaning ant and *zashi* meaning joint. The shapes of the two joints are almost alike; I see them as the same thing.

**Why do you want to come to England?**
I like London a lot. It's quiet by comparison, now that it's become so popular for skiing here. I'd like a change: to work in London, to open a workshop there. There's another thing, though — I like motorcycles, and the roads in England are good! ∎

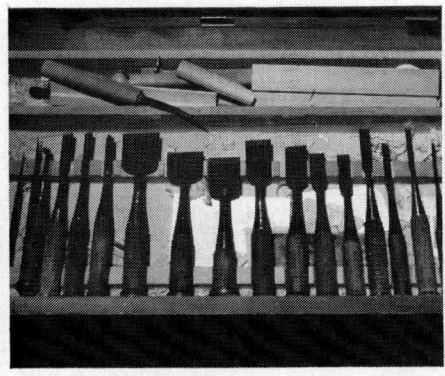

● *Tools of the trade: an array of well-used chisels in a hand-made box*

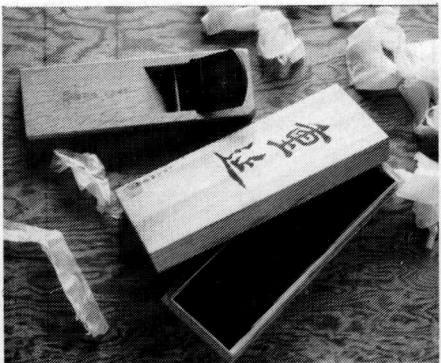

● *A plane and its case . . . someone who wraps a block-plane in silk obviously cares about his work!*

● *These two shots show Akira Deto, Kaki's chief table-maker, at work on a massive end-frame for a long table. The block-planes have a pulling action; stockinged feet ensure a bruise-free finish on the magnificent Siberian pine*

**All photos by Akira**

# MAKING IT IN SCOTLAND

Long overdue in *Woodworker* is this major report from a land where the craft currently thrives just as strongly as elsewhere

**Edinburgh furniture-maker Chris Yonge pinpoints (and advises on) the average craftsman's blind spot — marketing**

Scotland shares with few other regions of Britain its disadvantages for the furniture-maker. Remoteness from the national cultural and exhibition centres of the south, a smaller and more diffuse (though no less discriminating) market, and the need for good transport and supplies, make professional marketing essential if any small workshop or individual craftsman is to generate enough business without spending vast amounts of time or money.

It's easy enough to run a small advertisement in the local paper — but is the size you can afford going to be able to describe all you can do, and have done? Even if it does, can you handle a rush of enquiries of which only 5 or 10% may be worth the effort?

To my mind these questions virtually answer themselves. For a specialised service such as furniture-making — and particularly in Scotland, where word of mouth plays a vital role in building and maintaining this kind of business — people have to see what you do. If you want to spend money on advertising, there are really only two areas where it is worthwhile on a long-term basis.

The first, if you are fortunate enough to have a workshop with a telephone, is a listing in the Yellow Pages — it doesn't matter how small: the Pages are the one reference book everyone has and will turn to. If you have an unusual name or workshop symbol, use that in the advertisement (and, in addition, make sure it's seen in as many other places as possible).

The second way to spend your spare cash is on the highest-quality professional photography of your best pieces and yourself. Nothing so satisfactorily conveys — and enhances — the quality of fine woodworking as a glossy 6x8 or 6x10in print. It can be photocopied for handouts, sent for publication, or mounted and framed for exhibition. Be warned, though: photography is expensive. There will probably be a wide range of possible subjects, and not all will be worth a professional's time or rates. A working minimum would be half-a-dozen prints of your best pieces together with one or two portraits of yourself, both studio-shot and taken in your workshop.

Send spare prints to a few of the professional magazines with a brief note about the subject and yourself: make sure your photographer knows that some of the photographs are to be for publication, as contrast is generally less for such work. For everyday subjects like work in progress, small commissions, mock-ups, models and general woodworking, your own skills will probably suffice. Use a good 35mm reflex camera with appropriate lenses, and find a reliable printing firm to give you 4x6in prints. These can be used not only for your presentation book, but also to refresh what should be standard back-up for every craftsman — the emergency kit for the times when you can't, for whatever reason, manage to find or finish work for an exhibition to which you have been invited to contribute. If you are at all serious about finding work, *never* turn down the chance to exhibit; a little preparation by way of mounted photographs, drawings, sketches and models — or even a full size mock-up, or trial finishes — takes only a few spare hours and may even be more welcome to the organisers, as filling wall space or an awkward corner. Keep your display simple, of a high quality in design and finish, and of minimal value to eliminate last-minute insurance problems.

● *These laminated blanks will ripen into jewel-boxes*

photos: John MacGregor

● **Bill Childe's** *Edinburgh address is Candlemaker Row, but few woodworkers would be willing to hold a candle of their own to his astonishing work. He is a senior lecturer in furniture design at Edinburgh College of Art, and the apples he creates owe much in concept to an artist's eye and imagination.*

*His techniques, however, would put the average cabinetmaker into a frenzy. The shells are built up from thick sections, bandsawn and shaped for a constant inner radius (different for each level), and in the case of the dark woods the endgrain is covered with a light veneer. The organic shape is formed with sanding disc, rasp and file; the drawer-sides are laminated to their specific radius, set in a dado in the drawer-fronts (in the case of the ebony apple, again*

*laminated), and mounted to pivot on a steel pin.*

*The ones here are of voamboana, ebony and Mexican rosewood – in artistry of design and delicacy of execution this sort of jewel-box makes serious competition for the jewels themselves!*

When you do exhibit, don't forget the props that can turn a simple piece of furniture into an eloquent example of your skills and experience. Remind visitors of the time and expensive raw materials that went into making it by leaving a few design sketches (re-drawn if necessary) lying around, together with offcuts of veneer and leather, and perhaps the odd re-finished wooden plane that you don't mind losing. Look at the photography in advertisements to learn how to compose groups and to communicate the idea of quality by associating objects and materials. Keep your display simple and striking.

Make sure that you have printed or copied material ready to send out to enquirers, particularly after an exhibition or press coverage. It should include a brief CV describing your training and experience, what you can do, your major commissions and exhibitions, details of the process, charges for commissioning specially designed work (many people are very vague about how this is done), and copies of photos of your work. Send it out promptly, and keep a record so that you can follow it up a fortnight or so later if no reply is forthcoming. Make your pre-copied sheets reasonably specialised in content, and send out a suitable selection based on the nature of the enquiry; that for and architectural practice would obviously be different to that for a private client.

Keep in touch with past customers, perhaps sending them a circular or newsletter (particularly professional groups) — letting them know of any new machines, unusual commissions recently completed, extra staff, or surplus-stock bargains. In a similar vein, try your hand at writing a magazine article on a subject that interests you when you have an hour or two to spare; offer it to a likely journal and ask for comments. Many editors are too busy to be able to spare time for criticism of a potential contributor's style, but the one in 10 that will can make all the difference to your writing and its success. Use any spare moments — in the bus, the bath, or the queue at the newsagent — to think of subjects and ideas. Carry a notebook, and use it.

At the same time, when you're out, keep an eye open for unused display space. In any city or medium-sized town showcases or exhibition areas are included in buildings purely to fill a gap in the plans, and often with little or no content. Public libraries, council offices, and the windows of building societies and estate agents are the most obvious examples. Find out who's in charge of the space and make enquiries about a small, professional window display or exhibition — even of only a few photographs with a couple of old hand tools and a bagful of (clean) shavings. If you get a positive response, take it up as soon as possible, and make sure someone inside is willing to follow up any resulting interest with your card and a printed sheet. Make friends with them, explain what you're trying to do, and be sure to say thanks in some positive way when you take your display away. On similar lines, get in touch with the window-dressers of the larger local stores.

Local papers and television companies are always interested in craft-workers and their products, but remember that your pieces must be visually exciting and yourself able to put across both professionalism and enthusiasm in a clear and convincing manner. As a means to this end, make everything around you count towards the total impression; the workshop tidy, your machines smart, stores neatly labelled and racked, benches and jigs well and interestingly made. Use your workshop as a

● **Chris Yonge** *made six of these Japanese-style coffee tables – 'I suppose it should really be a tea table!' – in American ash. The tiled section also sits in the lower shelf level, or it can be removed entirely; the long grain/endgrain joints are dowelled at the outsides and held with ply slips further in to allow for movement. The chopping board on top is also ash, with rosewood inserts*

design laboratory; if you need a new chair or table, use the opportunity to try out in a simple form some new method of construction or finish. If you need a briefcase, or a sign, or a new door for your van — make a wooden one, and show it to people. If the new technique doesn't work, well and good; you'll have learnt from its failure. But, if it does, you will be able to use it in subsequent commissions with confidence and less time lost in trial pieces.

Remember that finished work, though important, is not the only thing that can be shown or promoted; as important and more unusual are such normally hidden areas as running a workshop, methods of work, design and aesthetics, and experience. People are interested in these things; use this interest to draw them into learning what a furniture-maker can do in the way of fitted, specially commissioned or batch-run furniture, or alterations. Make it clear (if you do) that you can design for others to make or manufacture others' designs. The first may be important to local manufacturers and DIY enthusiasts, the second to inventors, students and interior designers. Don't restrict yourself too much; it's easy to put people off. Make clear that you are prepared to consider and quote for almost anything. If you don't actually want some job, simply raise your price accordingly — you may still end up with a chore, but a rewarding one.

Professional groups are likely to be your best source of clients and large commissions, so go back to the Yellow Pages and work your way through. There are several ways of making contact, but wandering in un-announced off the street isn't the best of them; telephone to make an appointment with those you think particularly likely to have suitable work. Failing that, post or hand in a carefully composed and reasonably comprehensive description of your facilities, experience, training and rates. Don't overlook the chance of advertising in local professional or house journals — those for lawyers or doctors, for example. Rates are often modest, and the readership well-off and likely to be interested in something out of the ordinary run of advertisements in such publications. Conservation groups and societies also run newsletters in which it is sometimes possible to advertise, but make sure of the relevance of their circulation before committing yourself.

The entertainment media offer publicity opportunities to woodworkers in the hire of unusual pieces for sets or props; this brings useful spare cash for little work, and can lead to good contacts and commissions in a field where money is always looking for ideas.

A less exciting but more reliable way of improving your reputation is by teaching. Part-time or evening work at the local art college used to be the traditional way of financing a workshop; education cutbacks have almost killed this option, but you may still find work through local authorities. If not, go freelance; offer to lecture to clubs and voluntary groups, give demonstrations of furniture-repairing techniques, offer guided tours of your workshop. Enthusiasm is infectious; if your nature is extrovert and sociable (or even if it isn't), use every means possible to get people interested and talking about you and your work — in the pub, at your club, at work, in your street.

Become known to other woodworkers and craftsmen in your area, and get to know them. Not only can you share sources of supply and problems, but knowing a dependable sub-contractor for large jobs that have to be finished on time is a sensible precaution for any small business. The chap down the road may save your reputation for reliability one week and offer you a share in one of his own jobs the next. In addition, collaboration makes larger commissions possible for both of you, and allows you to keep 'in the family' potential clients who might otherwise have to be turned away. Joint commissions with complementary craftspeople such as fabric artists, painters, finishers and sculptors are good for both of you if standards and temperaments are well matched: those attracted by the work of one can be introduced to that of the other. Join a local association of woodworkers, no matter how amateur; the less polished your fellow-members, the more your own pieces will shine.

Sponsorship is always worth a try, beginning with your regular suppliers. Your sponsors' object will be good publicity for themselves; remember this, tailor your approach to suit their needs, and be thankful for what help and promotion you receive. But be prepared for careful investigation of your qualifications and work; no reputable company is going to spend good money to be associated with an amateur or careless woodworker.

My own experience is that people are surprisingly willing to help and offer practical advice on selling to themselves or their companies, and that a little good publicity goes a long way. So far I've not mentioned personal recommendation, crafts councils, selling to galleries, or crafts directories and slide collections; these are all reliable ways of selling your work, and well covered elsewhere.

Always keep things simple, clear and professional; look for every opportunity to put your message across. You'll be amazed at how much work there is around. ■

photo: Jack Fisher

photos: Victor Albrow

● **Chris Holmes** started his working life as a computer analyst/programmer at Edinburgh University, and built up his cabinetmaking business part-time in the years up to 1980. He acquired a disused and semi-derelict church, and with the help of grants turned it into the workshop where he built the pieces shown here. The chest of drawers (**above right**) is the latest in a seven-year evolution of designs; the display stand (**left**) was bought from an exhibition by a client who commissioned a set of the occasional tables (**below**) 'in the same style'. The chest is African walnut, the stand and tables Japanese oak and mahogany. The

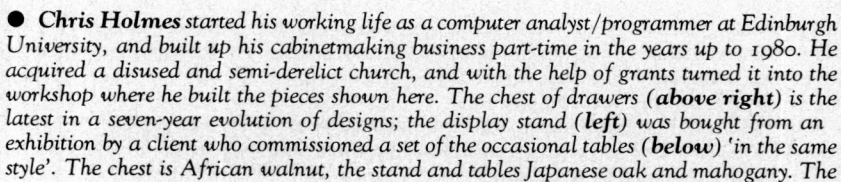

lectern (**top left**) was a commission from the City of Edinburgh – a 400th birthday present to the University. It is made in native oak, 'part laminated', and the coat of arms was carved by John Smith of Tanfield, Edinburgh. Chris is looking for a trainee on the Scottish Development Agency's craft apprenticeship three-year scheme; he wants someone young, numerate, with some woodworking experience and an interest in design. Get in touch with him at Gogar Cabinetworks, 194 Glasgow Rd, Edinburgh EH12 9BR, tel. (031) 557 2390

## Barrie Sinyard describes his business on the Borders

I have been based at Brook Cottage Workshop at Stobs, near Hawick, for two years, having moved here from industrial Tyneside. My workshop of 600sq ft started life in 1946 as a prefabricated home in the London area. It makes an ideal space, at a square-footage cost far lower than that of constructing a new building. Heating is by means of a woodburning stove, which makes sensible use of waste material.

My main work is one-off furniture, which I design to the customer's requirements and produce in a wide variety of timbers. Whenever possible I use local timber, purchased nearby and seasoned by air-drying, followed by de-humidifying and then careful storage before use. Of course, many people still want items made from the traditional imported timbers such as mahogany and afrormosia, and I make a wide range of garden furniture from iroko.

A certain amount of business involves small items sold to tourists, who are welcome to call, and at local craft fairs.

Undoubtedly, one of the benefits of moving to the Borders has been the availability of good hardwood and the opportunity of selecting to suit particular requirements. Additionally, the combining of home and business enables me to be available to potential customers over a long period seven days per week.

In order to charge realistic prices I have to make considerable use of machinery and labour-saving techniques, but all finishing is carried out by hand and all items are of solid traditional construction.

As well as being a member of the Guild of Master Craftsmen, I am also a founder-committee-member of the Border Crafts Association, which has been formed with local-council encouragement in an attempt to consolidate the numerous craft activities of the region. ■

● *A Geordie on the Borders in a pre-fab workshop from London; Barrie at the bandsaw*

photo: Northern Scottish Newspapers

photo: Alexander Caminada

● 'Wood as a medium has always spoken to me,' says **Richard Brockbank**, who makes these 'soft-shaped' boxes. He lives near Findhorn Bay, and is an associate member of the internationally-known spiritual foundation, where he realised his inspiration in a 'Hidden Talents' workshop. He has a traditional furniture-maker's training, but has worked hard to move away from constrictions of style and respond more directly to the asymmetrical shapes and patterns in the wood itself.

The drawer boxes show his cabinetmaking origins in their minute handcut dovetails; he is particularly conscious that the pieces will be touched and held, and that each one will somehow find its way to the owner for whom it is destined. 'I feel I am helping to educate people to touch wood,' he says, 'and to see its beauty.'

photos: Charles Tait

● The Norse chair (**above**) and pine corner dresser are the work of **Brian Winter,** from Harray in Orkney. His range includes alpine furniture, fitted kitchens, a Norse-inspired dining table to go with the chairs, and a traditional settle. Using mainly pine, which he imports into Orkneys from Grangemouth, he has built up quite a business in the islands themselves; 90% of his kitchens go into Orkney homes, the rest go to mainland Scotland. He exhibits twice a year, at Aberdeen's Trade and Industry Fair and the Highland Trade Fair in Aviemore.

His softwood and sheet materials come to the islands from Grangemouth, and the native hardwoods he uses are all from an estate in the north of Scotland. This far north, the influences of Scandinavian culture are as strong as British ones – witness his Norse designs. 'I find the peace and quiet in Orkney helps me to concentrate,' he says, 'especially for thinking up new designs.'

● The small chest in this group is made in olive by **Peter Davis,** a designer and cabinetmaker in Fort William, Inverness-shire. He is also perfectly at home with joinery, and takes commissions for fitting out boats. Fort William's Highland position makes it something of a metropolis for the west coast and a focus for the tourist trade, which means that Peter often gets calls for restaurant and chalet fitting work.

He uses hardwoods and pine; the chair is one of a set of six, made in beech, and the footstool is of mahogany. The chest is inlaid with various woods. From a range of designs, Peter constructs to individual specifications; his recent commissions include a mahogany chest of drawers in traditional style, some pine blanket chests, and a suite of garden furniture in mahogany. He has been in business since 1979.

## David Gray visits a Scottish professional violin-maker

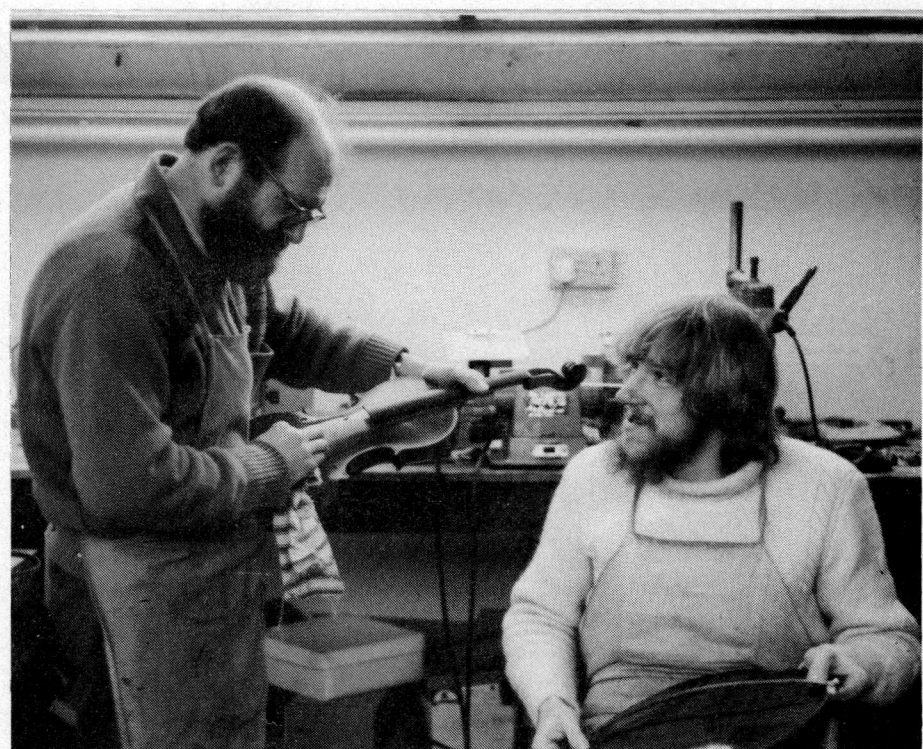

● *Derick Sanderson (**left**) and his assistant Peter Hütmannsberger discuss the advantages and disadvantages of a twelve-coat finish*

**M**any amateur woodworkers can produce high-quality musical instruments, but Scotland holds few small instrument-manufacturing businesses.

Derick Sanderson is a professional based in the small village of Alva, near Stirling. Concentrating mainly on the manufacture and repair of violins, violas and violoncellos, he employs one assistant — Peter Hütmannsberger, from Linz in Austria.

Wood for the instruments has to be mature, and is bought from tonewood dealers mainly on the Continent. The transport charges add to its already high cost. No available Scottish wood is suitable for instrument front-pieces, because of its coarse grain. Austrian sitka spruce, for example, has a finer grain than Scottish. Derick is building up a stock of Austrian wood. Wood for back pieces is not as important, and either imported or Scottish wood can be used here.

Quarter-sawn timber is stronger, is less prone to warping, looks better, and gives a better sound than slab-cut wood. Therefore fronts are often quarter-sawn while backs are usually slab-cut.

Fronts are normally of sitka spruce, and the remainder of the instrument from maple or sycamore. The ribs (sides) can be manufactured from Scottish or imported stuff: more work is needed on Scottish ribs since they are not as close to the required size.

Derick uses a standard block-plane to plane the ribs down to 1mm in thickness; they are then bent around electric heaters. Water is brushed on to the shaped ribs, and they are placed around the instrument's box mould. The ribs normally consist of six pieces of wood joined together by willow or sitka-spruce blocks. The blocks help strengthen the completed rib unit and help send vibrations from the front of the instrument to its back.

The mould, which gives the outline of the instrument's box, is made from plywood about 3.5mm thick, cut out on a bandsaw. Due to the slight overlap required where the ribs touch the front and back of the instrument, the mould for the ribs must be slightly smaller than the front and back pieces. Linings of sitka spruce or willow are mortised into the blocks and glued to the ribs, to give strength and a larger gluing surface for the front and back, then bevelled down to size.

The front and back pieces, which make up the box of the instrument along with the ribs, are derived from pieces of tonewood rub-jointed with pearl glue. This glue, says Derick, will hold its strength for around 50 years.

The shaped and jointed ribs are placed on the tonewood and their outline traced off, adding 3mm for the overlap. The front

● *Two unfinished violins and two completed violas, ready-strung, hang in the workshop. When it takes six weeks to make an instrument, you can't afford to lean it up against the wall!*

and back pieces can then be cut out on the bandsaw before producing the 'arching' — the camber-like shaping on their outer surfaces. Mr Sanderson uses five templates for the arching, which is cut initially with gouges. Violin-maker's thumb-planes are used to create the final shape, and scrapers give the final bare finish. Derick uses blunt hacksaw-blades as scrapers — not abrasive paper, which he claims removes the 'personality' of the finish.

A turned-up appearance on the lip of the

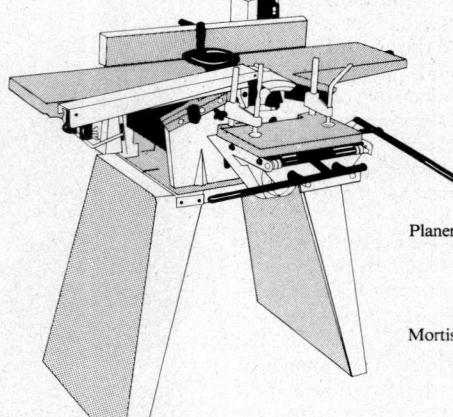

front and back pieces is then produced, using a small gouge to cut a channel 1.5mm in from the edge. Decorative purfling is inlaid within this channel — in a small, hand-cut groove of 1.2mm depth — and held in place with pearl glue. Derick uses a purfling of two strips of ebony sandwiching one of maple.

Wood must also be taken from the inner surfaces of the front and back pieces. For the front piece, a thickness of 2.4mm is used all over. For the back, a thickness of 4.5mm is created in the middle, tapering to 2.4mm at the edge. These are the thicknesses used by Stradivarius. It is often wise to use dimensions established by the 'old masters', although oscillators can be used to calculate the thickness which gives the optimum resonant quality for a given piece of wood. As Derick shapes the inner surface, he keeps a constant check on its thickness by means of a clock-dial caliper.

The F-holes (where the sound comes out of the box) are then cut in the front piece, using templates normally of plastic card or zinc. The template shapes are usually copies of those used by early masters such as the Italians Guarneri and Amati. The shape of the F-hole is traced on to the front piece, a few holes are drilled in, and a knife is used to round off the final shape. The F-holes must be very accurately placed on the front piece, as they determine the length of the strings and hence the feel of the instrument.

A base bar (27cm long and tapering along its length) is then glued to the front piece. This imparts maximum strength under the bridge (the thin, erect piece of wood which holds the strings off the box) — and down the middle, which helps to counteract the pressures from the strings.

The front, back and ribs are then glued together and held by clamps, which can be made by the craftsman. Initially the clamps are not fully tightened, so the glue can be inserted into the joints by knife.

Once the glue is dry, the instrument box is completed by rounding off the edges using scrapers and violin-maker's planes. It is said that Stradivarius used sharkskins for this task!

To make the neck of the instrument, Derick uses a quarter-cut wood block 260x45x60mm. Templates are required to shape the neck, the peg-box (the 'box' which is open on the upper surface of the neck, and into which the string pegs are inserted) and the scroll.

The neck is cut to produce a gradual taper, using the bandsaw, and the scroll is cut using a tenon-saw. Chisels and gouges are then used to finish off. Extreme care is required in keeping symmetry in the shell-like forms of the scrolls on either side of the neck. The peg-box is hollowed out initially by drilling holes, and Derick uses a registered gouge (bevelled on the upper surface only) to finish off.

The neck is inserted into the box with a mortise-and-tenon joint (Stradivarius nailed necks on!). The neck must be positioned to give the correct height of 26mm between a line projected from the fingerboard and the box in the bridge position.

Derick buys in ebony fingerboards unless he is making baroque instruments, when he manufactures his own from maple.

The pegs are also of ebony. Standard pegs are bought and shaped for each instrument, using a taper reamer. This is a very precise task, as the peg must fit the hole perfectly. A composition is applied to each peg to make it turn smoothly.

Bridges, made of maple, are bought rough-shaped. The blank is shaped for each violin by planing the edges to reduce its bulk; the front is shaped to slope backwards slightly. The feet are cut to produce the same curvature as the front of the instrument; then the top is cut to a curve which matches that of the instrument type being copied. The four notches for the strings are equally spaced.

Finishing involves, for example, linseed oil, followed by stain, and then varnish: two clear coats initially, then six to eight coats of coloured varnish, finishing with two more clear coats. Each coat is rubbed down before application of the following one. Finally the outer coat is rubbed with tripoli powder.

From start to finish, Derick and Peter take about six weeks to produce one instrument. Half of Derick's time, however, is taken up with repairs, as old instruments are often more popular than new ones. He used to advertise frequently, and received commissions from many parts of the world — especially from expatriate Scots who wanted Scottish-made instruments. Recently he has relied on word-of-mouth advertisement, which appears to be just as effective! ∎

● *Some of the material that **Robert Towers** sent us when we inquired about his work was a reprint of an article in the journal of the Norway-Orkney Friendship Association – printed in Norwegian! The obvious cultural exchange shows very clearly in Robert's Orkney chairs; here he is at work on the distinctive straw backing. His range includes chairs with drawers below the seat, and also those with the* characteristic hooded back – perhaps developed, says Robert, as a further insulation against the draughts that beset the exposed island crofts. They are a very old design, originally made by island householders with available materials – Robert offers a choice of pine or walnut. The oldest examples vary from piece to piece, indicating individual skill and access to materials; standardised designs began to appear around the 1880s. **Above right** is an astragal-glazed pine corner cabinet by **Irving Telford** of Glasgow, who was helped in the setting-up stages of his business by Glasgow district council's offer of workshop space for a probationary year. He is pleased to see Scottish publicans pulling out their plastic decor and re-furbishing in traditional style; one of Irving's biggest commissions to date is the bar of the 'Blue Blazer' in Edinburgh

# Bathroom enhancers

**T**ony Lord's neat array of bathroom fittings are all in pine, to go with a boxed-in bath, but they can just as easily be of a hardwood.

Except for the toilet-roll holder, which needs a lathe for the bar and cap, they can all be made with hand tools alone. Some dimensions are changeable; some are defined by reference to the articles held, hung or hoarded! ■

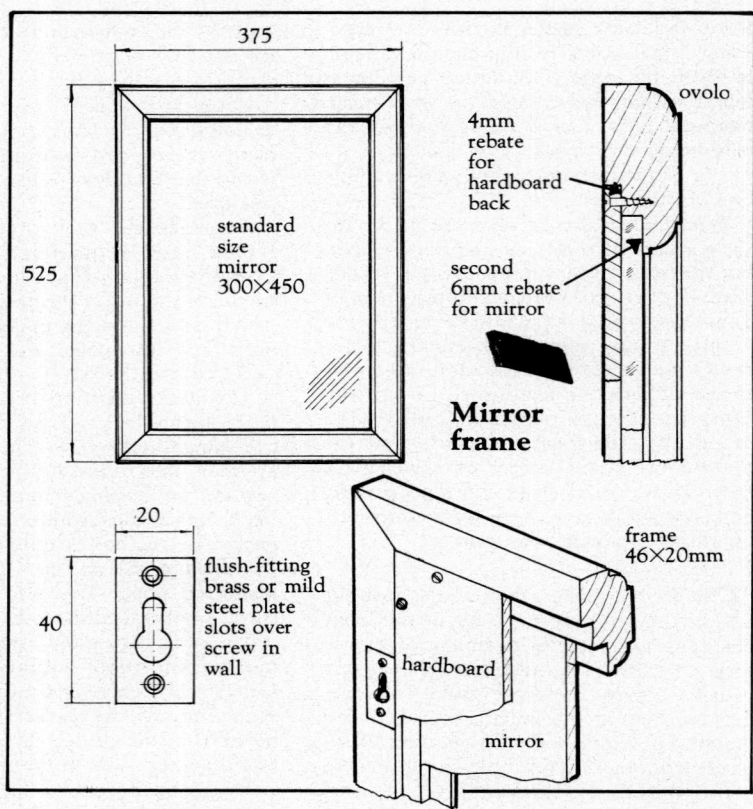

**Mirror frame**

ovolo

375

525

standard size mirror 300×450

4mm rebate for hardboard back

second 6mm rebate for mirror

20

40

flush-fitting brass or mild steel plate slots over screw in wall

frame 46×20mm

hardboard

mirror

● **Above:** The mirror is a standard size – 12×18in – held in a rebate by 4mm hardboard, fixed with no4×½in screws. Be careful to make the rebate for the back wide enough to take the screws without splitting; the frame section, ovolo-moulded by hand or router, is a hefty 46×20mm. Note the laminated construction of the mug-holder, **below left**, which avoids shrinkage and cupping; the toilet-roll holder, **below**, sports a 26mm-diameter bar with a 16mm spigot, taper-turned for a push fit into the end-cap. All dimensions are in mm

## Toothbrush- and mug-holder

76

90

220

R 150

25

rounded edges

mortise for pinned tenon

grain direction

grain

grain

5mm thick

mug-holder shaped after drilling

screw-holes countersunk or counterbored and plugged

86

80

66 dia.

40

25

84

22

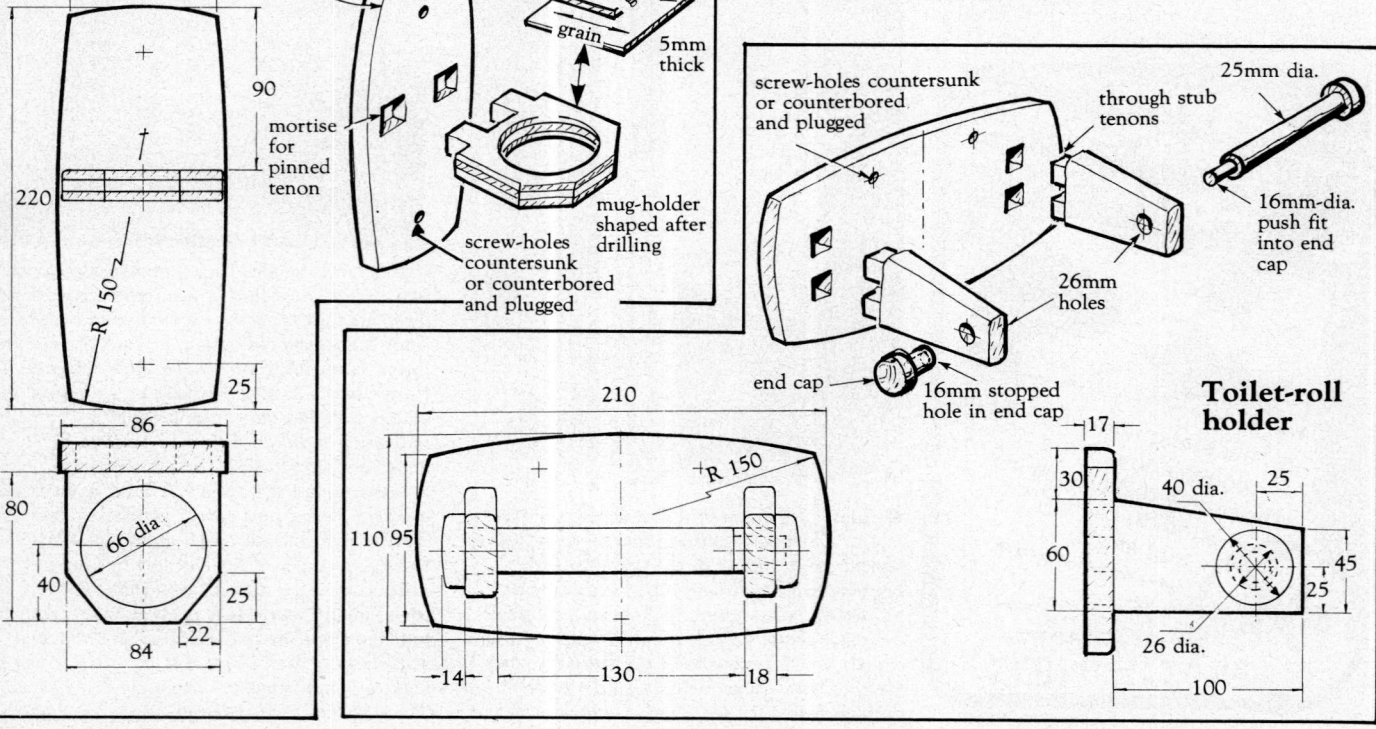

screw-holes countersunk or counterbored and plugged

through stub tenons

25mm dia.

16mm-dia. push fit into end cap

26mm holes

end cap

16mm stopped hole in end cap

210

110  95

R 150

14    130    18

**Toilet-roll holder**

17

30

60

40 dia.

25

45

25

26 dia.

100

## Shelf

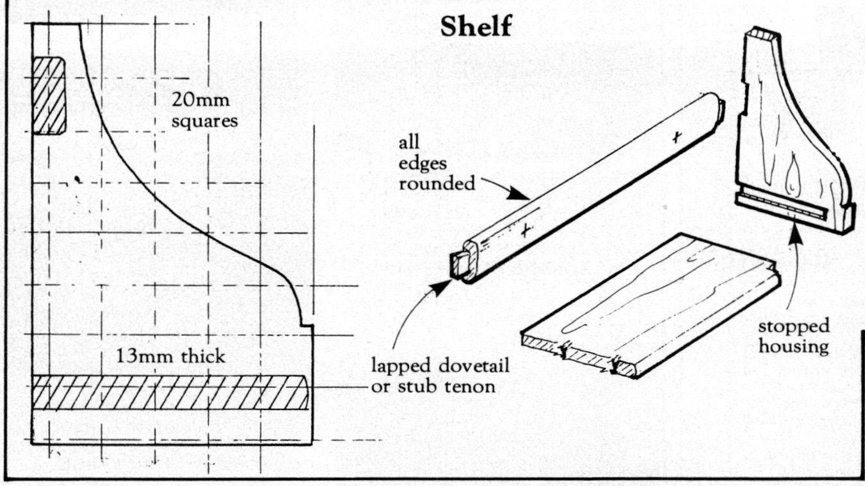

20mm squares

13mm thick

all edges rounded

lapped dovetail or stub tenon

stopped housing

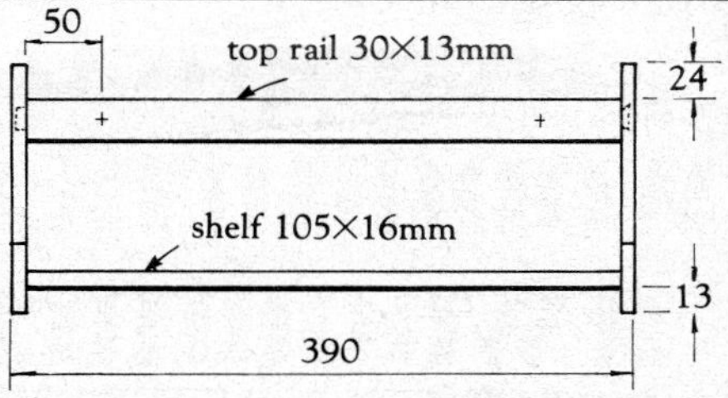

50

top rail 30×13mm

24

shelf 105×16mm

13

390

● The little shelf can be virtually any size. An extra rail across the front edge, the brackets squared off to carry it, can be a good safety feature

● The towel-rail uses stub tenons for the rail/arm joint, but a wedged tenon would give the arm/back-plate extra strength. **Below**, the cabinet is traditionally built, with shelves in stopped housings and a stub-tenoned top rail. The door panels are of 90×10mm TGV boards with an extra groove down the middle to suit the proportions.

## Towel-rail

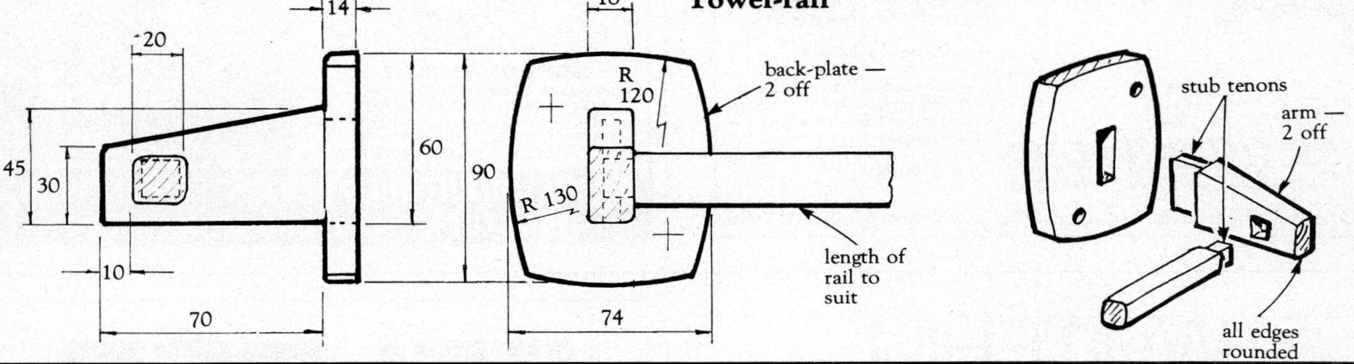

14

20

18

45

30

10

60

90

R 120

R 130

70

74

back-plate — 2 off

length of rail to suit

stub tenons

arm — 2 off

all edges rounded

## Cabinet

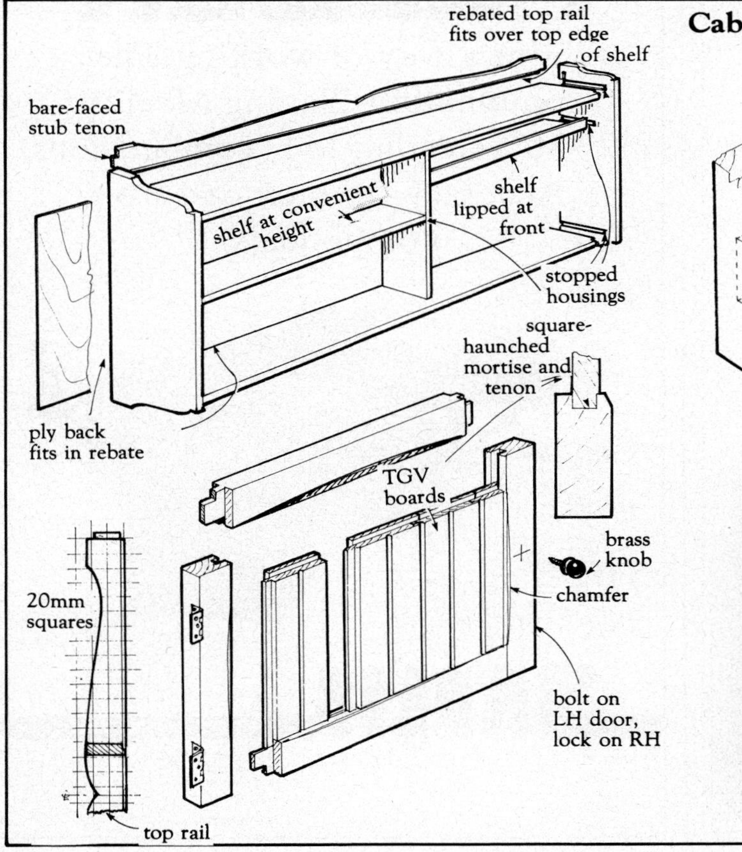

rebated top rail fits over top edge of shelf

bare-faced stub tenon

shelf at convenient height

shelf lipped at front

stopped housings

square-haunched mortise and tenon

ply back fits in rebate

TGV boards

brass knob

chamfer

bolt on LH door, lock on RH

20mm squares

top rail

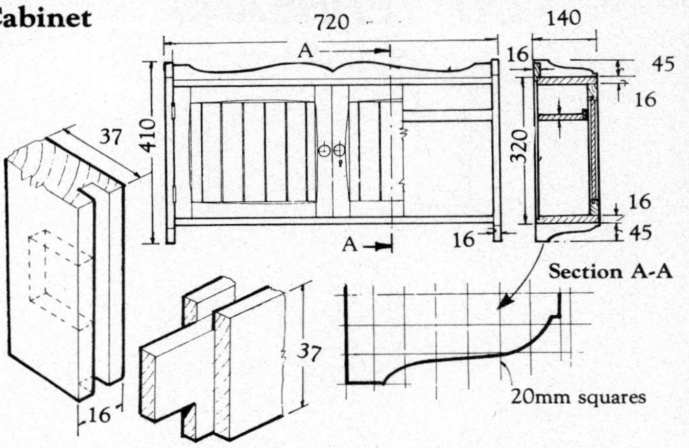

720

A

140

16

45

16

37

410

320

16

16

45

A

16

Section A-A

37

16

20mm squares

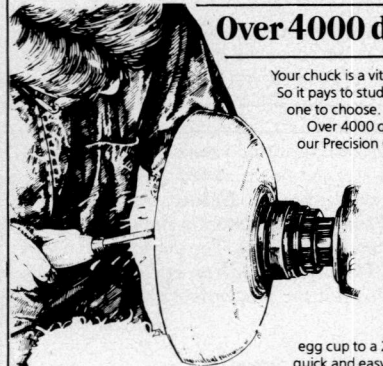

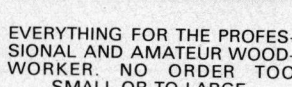

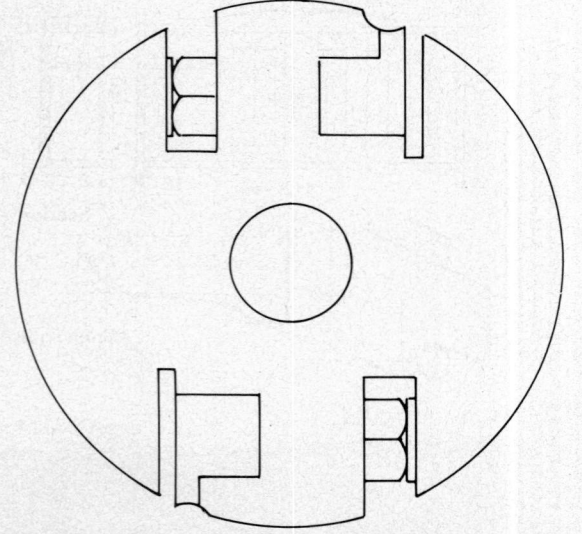
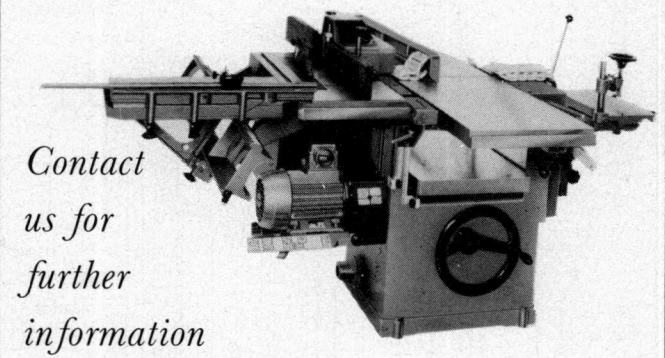
514

# The working chest

## Ian Thwaites presents his strong, simple tool-chest

I do not have a workshop but make do with a Workmate in the garage. For years I kept my tools in an assortment of cardboard boxes, and had to rummage around to find what I wanted. In the end I could stand it no longer, and built two tool-chests.

They would still be useful even if one did have a workshop, as tools still have to be carried around. With the Workmate and these chests I can take on just about any task anywhere.

I used ply of various thicknesses because this was the most practical material and the cheapest. Interestingly, the chests proved to be a fine exercise in the use of a combination plane, which I employed in almost every stage of construction. But a similar result could probably be achieved with simpler tools — or, conversely, with power tools. I just happen to have a combination plane and enjoy using it.

The first task was to weigh all my tools on a pair of bathroom scales. There is a great danger of making a chest that's too big and so heavy that it cannot be moved around without first taking out some of the tools, thus defeating its object. As it is, these chests are just as much as I can comfortably carry. It might often be better to build two small chests, for example, than one which needs two people to carry it.

## The carcase

The basic design is for a case-style drop-front chest with three tool trays. My chests measure 24×12×8in. This size was established by measuring my largest tools — the longest being the panel saw, which fits comfortably in the lid. It also enables a standard sheet of 12mm ply to be used with no waste.

Considerable thought should be given to the fitting of the lid, the various options being shown in fig. 4. The most obvious is to hinge it along the bottom edge of the chest, as in A. The disadvantage is that, for the lid to open, the chest has to be raised from the ground on feet as high as the lid is thick. But the lid has to accommodate the thickness of the saw-handles stored there. That means feet an ugly 36mm high.

The second choice, B, is to have the bottom portion of the chest fixed and the lid opening, say, a couple of inches from the bottom. This would allow full opening and avoid the need for feet. However, that would make anything such as a plane stored in the bottom particularly difficult to remove; probably one of the trays would have to be taken out first.

Therefore method C was adopted as being the most attractive and practical. The top and two sides of the chest are 165mm wide, but the bottom extends full-width to

● *Neat, sturdy and workmanlike, the craftsman's tool-chest provides some interesting constructional challenges*

the front. The edges of the lid are made from the pieces trimmed off the top and sides. The lid is attached by butt hinges to the extended base — and to the fourth edge of the lid, which is a 1×1½in hardwood strip let in between the sides. For the sake of appearance the sides of the lid extend down either side of the extended base to the bottom of the chest, being radiused to allow the lid to open.

Begin by cutting the ply into two lengths, each giving a top or bottom plus one side. Rebate a long edge on each to accept the thickness of the ply used for the back, about 7mm. On one length rebate the other long edge to the same thickness to accept the front panel; 7mm ply will also be used for this. From the second piece cut off the portion which will be the side and rebate this in similar fashion to accept the front —

but do not rebate the front edge of the base.

Now rebate across the pieces to form the lap joints. The top has its two inner edges rebated in this way, as do the bottom edges of the sides. The bottom itself is not touched. Then cut the top and two sides lengthwise so as to separate each into a piece for the carcase and a piece for the lid. Again the bottom is not touched.

It is surprising just how heavy ordinary hand tools are, and the joints of the chest must be strong. ½in square hardwood strip was used to form corner blocks. The most attractive method of fixing would be internally through the corner blocks (fig. 3). However, the ply would never be able to hold these screws, so I screwed from the outside.

The carcase can now be assembled, first gluing and screwing the corner pieces to lid

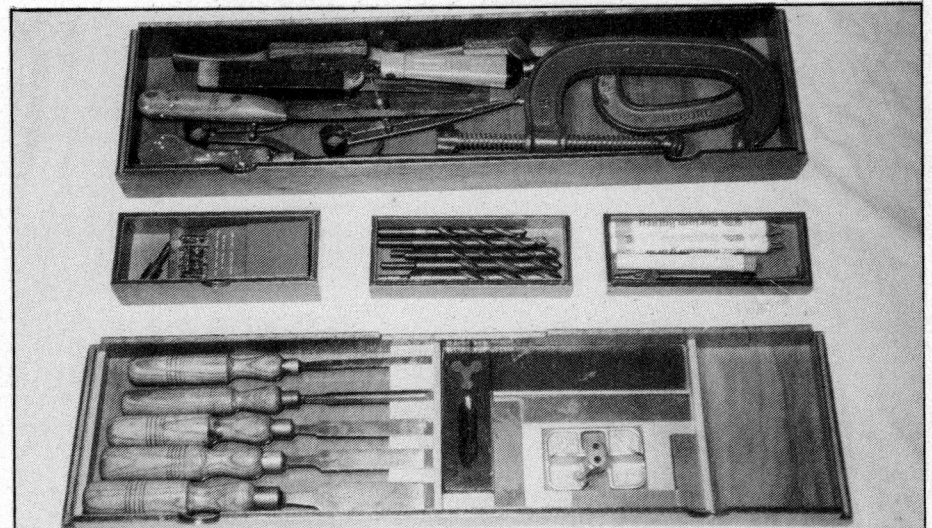

● *The various trays, showing the three-part drill-nest. It fits together in a carefully-designed arrangement of lips and rebates*

# The working chest

and sides. The base will have to be trimmed in length slightly so it fits between the sides. Then the ply back can be cut, glued and pinned.

The base can be cut out where the hinges go, and these temporarily screwed in place. I found the fitting of the hinges easier before the carcase was assembled; the same goes for the tray runners.

## The lid

Corner pieces were not used for the lid, the top being glued and screwed direct into the endgrain of the sides. The lid does not take any weight and this has proved satisfactory.

First, however, the sides have to be prepared. They have to be cut back so that the crosspiece can be let in and so that they will extend over the extended base. This requires careful work, and the result remains delicate until the lid is assembled. The crosspiece joint is glued, and secured with two screws driven into the endgrain. Before assembly, cut back the crosspiece to accept the butt hinges. Remember that, although the front panel will be let into the rebates in the top and sides, it will just fit over the full width of the crosspiece, and be glued and pinned to it. There is no rebating on the crosspiece.

Before assembly the inner corners of the sides have to be radiused, or they will foul the carcase and the chest will not open. Mark out with a pair of compasses. I rounded mine off by holding against a rigid disc-sander chucked in a power drill in a horizontal stand and fitted with a home-made sanding table.

The lid can now be assembled and tested for accuracy against the carcase. Fit the hinges next, and fix the lid.

● *To cut the half-moon finger-holes out of the tray-fronts, locate the edge of the front against the hole-saw drill, clamp firmly and proceed with care!*

## The fittings

I bought chrome handles. On their own, the screw-heads would soon pull through the ply; the best way to overcome this is to drill holes in a suitable length of steel plate and pass the screws through that before they go

through the ply and into the handle.

The chest is kept closed with a pair of matching case catches, which can now be temporarily fitted in place. They will have to be removed when the finish is applied.

I decided to make one chest for pure woodworking tools and another for general metalworking tools, my soldering iron, my decorating tools and anything else. Three saws fit into the lid of the woodworking chest, the other being loose.

Take a piece of scrap softwood about the thickness of each saw handle and mark this out to the shape of the finger-hole. Cut roughly to size, and sand to shape until the block is a good friction fit with the finger-holes, allowing for the thickness of the finish. Decide upon the most suitable position of the saws (two of mine overlap); then mark, drill and countersink the lid. The blocks are now glued and screwed into position.

**Fig. 1**

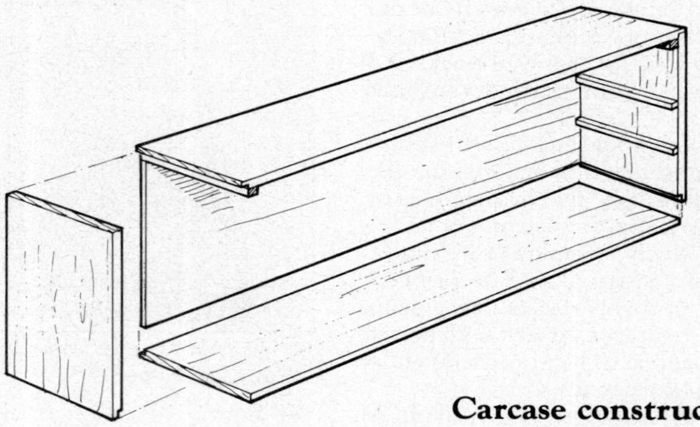

**Carcase construction**

**Fig. 2**

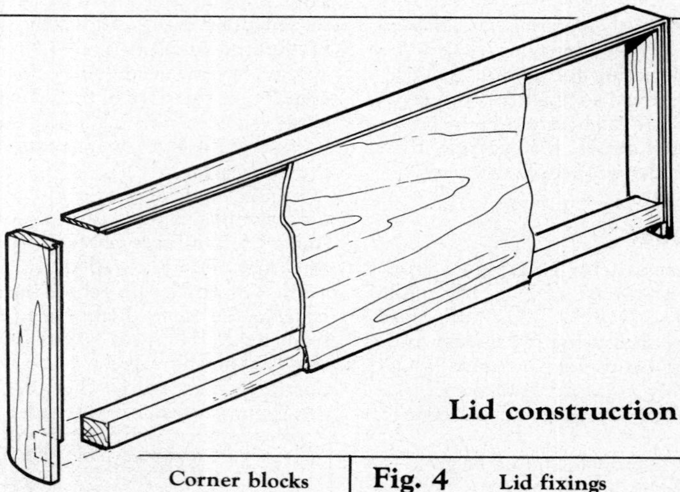

**Lid construction**

**Fig. 3**    Corner blocks

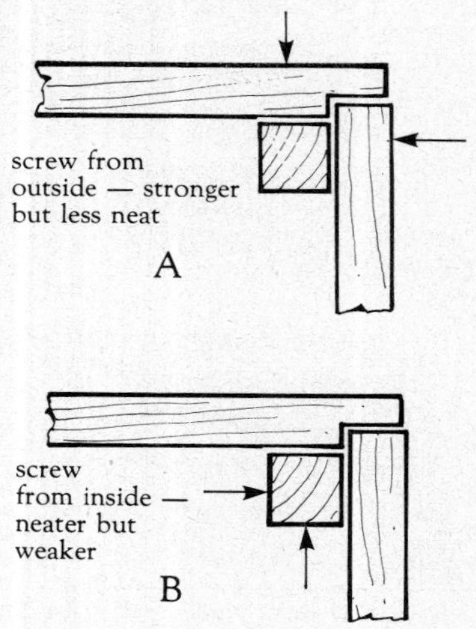

screw from outside — stronger but less neat

A

screw from inside — neater but weaker

B

**Fig. 4**    Lid fixings

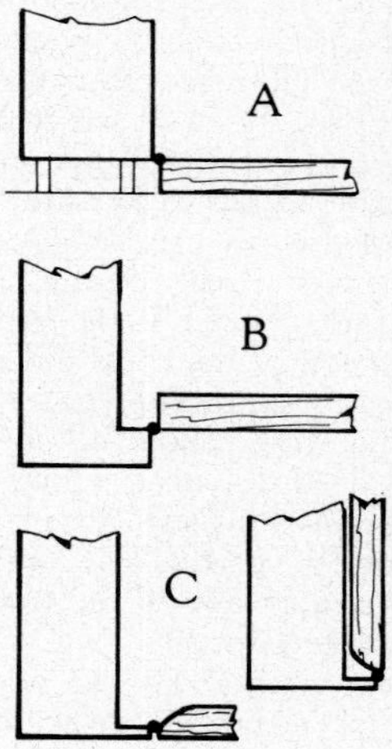

A

B

C

I also fashioned various offcuts to act as locating lugs and supports so that all the saws are firm and none touches another. The panel saw fits into a kind of socket and the others rest on blocks. Small brass catches of the tear-drop type were bent to shape and screwed to these lugs.

In the bottom of the chest I keep the two planes, because they are the heaviest and most bulky tools, together with the drill nest. It is essential that the planes are stored properly on their sides, with nothing touching the soles or blades. They must also be secured so that they do not bang into one another during transit. This was achieved by cutting ⅜in-square hardwood strip into short sections so as to make lugs.

## The trays

In all I had to make six trays, three per chest. Their construction is quite simple. The trays are made from 7mm ply for the front and back, 9mm ply for the sides and 5mm for the base. Begin by rebating the bottom edges of the fronts, backs and sides to accept the bases, which fit inside. The sides fit between the fronts and backs which are therefore cut back to form lap joints.

Half-moon cut-outs are made in the fronts to form finger-holes. These can be formed using a hole-saw. First secure a scrap piece of softwood, about 1½in thick, in the Workmate or vice. Drill a hole through it the same diameter as the pilot drill of the hole-saw. Set up the required size of cut in the hole saw. Next, release the grub screw in the hole-saw assembly and push the pilot drill until it protrudes at least an inch further forward than usual. Now place the drill in the hole in the scrap wood, with the power off. The piece of wood in which the half-moon is to be cut is placed against the pilot drill and secured firmly with a couple of G-cramps. Switch the power on, push the pilot drill into its guidance hole and apply gentle pressure. A clean half-moon will be quickly removed.

Glued and pinned together, the trays are supported on runners formed from hardwood strip about 8mm square, glued and screwed to the carcase sides. The sides of the trays have to be shallower than the fronts and backs by this amount, to clear the runner of the tray above; the top tray has to have a larger allowance because the corner blocks are stouter than the runners. The top corners of the backs have to be cut out to match the shallower sides and clear the runners — and the top corner blocks and runners should be set back by the thickness of the fronts.

The fitting-out of the trays is a matter of choice. In some cases it is undoubtedly best to make fittings for individual tools, but remember that the fittings take up room which might be better used storing an extra tool — and might also add to the weight. In my own case, I fitted out the top tray of the woodworking chest and left the other two plain to accept the more bulky tools.

The top tray contains a set of five chisels, fitments for three squares and a small router, together with a small space. Before fitting can begin, the top trays have to have cut-outs made in the tops of the backs to clear the handle fixings. The chisels fit into a rack formed from hardwood strip and softwood offcuts. The three squares are a woodworking one, a medium-sized engineer's and a small engineer's used in model-making. Each fits in a slot formed from scraps of ply, and the marking surfaces cannot become chipped. The router was fitted in a similar slot simply because there was room for it.

In the second chest I simply divided the top tray a couple of times and left the other two blank. These top trays are very shallow, and some division is needed to stop the sides warping. Use hardwood strip and glue and pin; here again there is scope for imagination.

● *Pins in the tray-fronts are punched in and filled; all the rebating was done with a combination plane*

The drill nest really is a combination-plane exercise with a vengeance! Basically it consists of three small trays which clip one on top of the other. They were made from offcuts of ply about 5mm thick, and are similar to the main trays. Size was decided by the available height in the chest, the size of the set of Dormer drills in the top tray, and the room left in the base. The top tray contains the Dormer set and a countersink bit, the middle one a further seven drills and the bottom one masonry drills and other items. The trays have to be just deep enough to take the drills and no more, otherwise space is wasted. As with the trays, the sides fit between the fronts and backs, which are cut back accordingly to form lap joints. All joints are glued and fixed with fine pins.

Fig. 6 shows a cross-section of the drill nest. Remove the shaded sections in A to achieve B. Taking the top tray first, the under-edge is rebated to accept the base plus an allowance for the lip of the second tray. The second tray is first rebated on its outer top edge to form this lip, and then on its under-edge in the same way as the top tray. The third tray has a lip cut in its top edge to fit into the middle tray, but its under-edge is only rebated for the thickness of the base. The result is a nest of three trays which neatly accept the drills, each tray fitting on each other and the whole unit sliding into the tool-chest. I also fitted locating strips to the side of the chest and the sandpaper flap in the bottom to accept the drill nest and hold it in position.

## Finishing

All the fittings were stripped off and the various items sanded. I applied two good coats of polyurethane, using a combination of clear and light-oak tones. Each item was coated inside and out, a light sanding being given to exterior surfaces between coats.

I then set the parts aside for a few weeks to allow the polyurethane to cure and harden completely.

Last of all, I added four small rubber feet.

I found this a really worthwhile project. My woodworking is more efficient now, as I now know where everything is and can grab it quickly. I found it as easy to make two chests as one, and suggest it might be worthwhile making a pair if you decide to give it a go. ∎

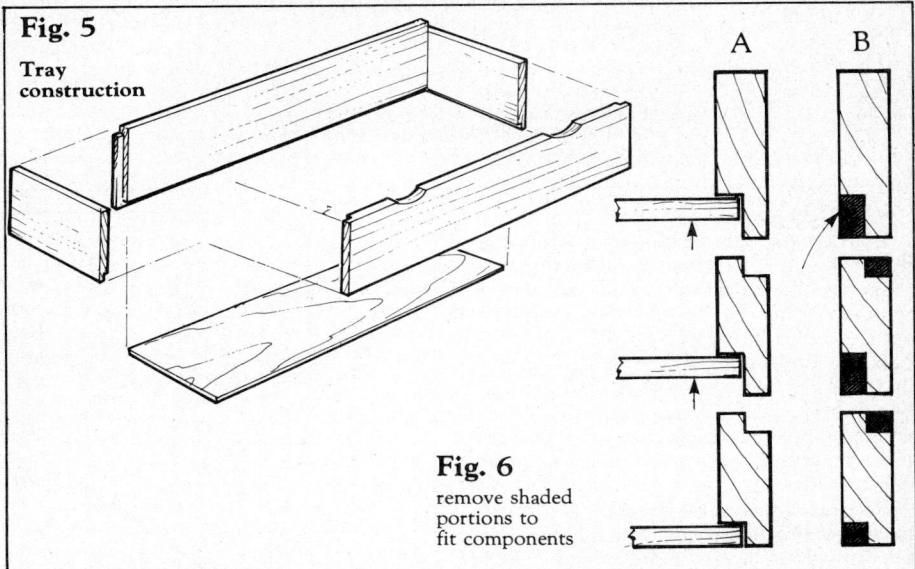

**Fig. 5**

Tray construction

**Fig. 6**

remove shaded portions to fit components

A    B

# Making equipment boxes

**B**ill Gates writes: It's often difficult to replace power tools in their original packing — particularly when a plug has been added to the cable! Yet some require protection when not in regular use. So you need to make a box.

Shown in the drawings are three possible constructions — A, B and C: rebated corners, tongued joints and dovetail joints. The top and the bottom of the two larger boxes were glued to the sides and the ends and then place under pressure until the adhesive had set, thus avoiding the use of pins. Shaped blocks and cut-outs in plywood are required to hold the articles in position; these can be made up in a number of pieces, which will make the cutting-out easier to perform. You need not fit the blocks exactly, because the thickness of the covering material must be allowed for. Softwood is quite suitable for those blocks which are to be covered; assemble them dry first and check the fit of the article — any adjustment should be made before gluing the blocks in their places.

Cabinet cloth was used for the lining, fastened with an impact adhesive.

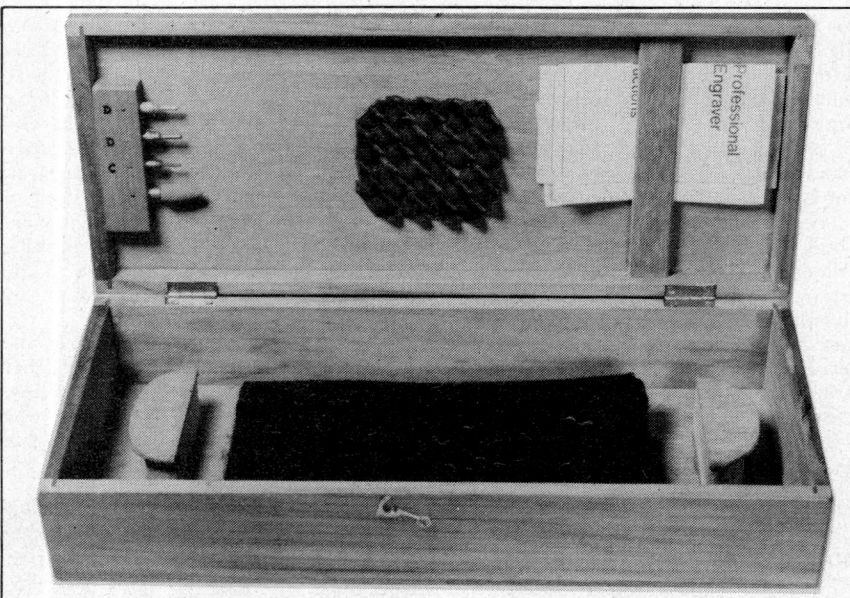

● *A neat home for your engraving tools; the shaped covered blocks hold the tool, the blocks at either end retain the cable. This is Box B*

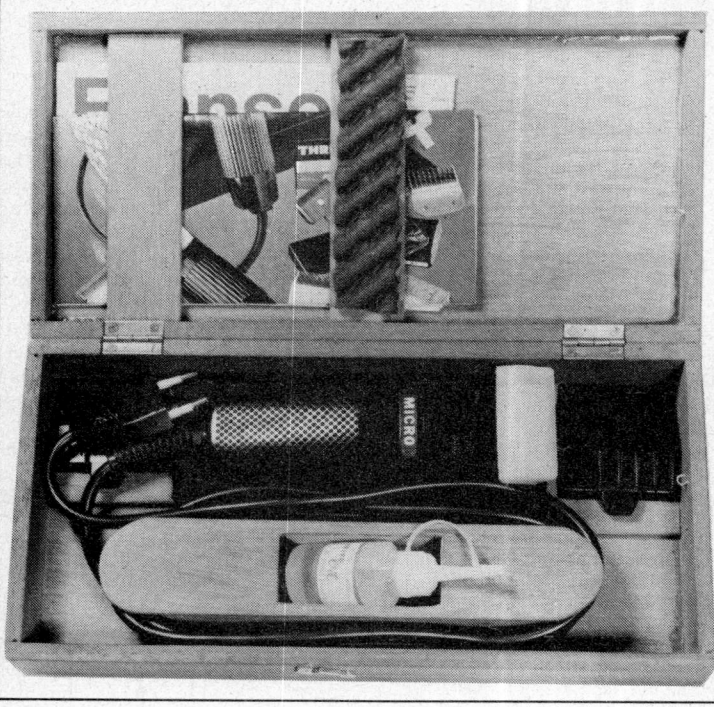

*Box A; this one, like the scalpel and the engraver box, sports a sponge cushion to keep the equipment in tightly. Provision for the leaflets to be kept in the lid is also made*

together, with the bottom only glued to the frame. 5mm plywood was prepared with cut-outs for the knives and glued to the inside of the bottom, a division being included to accommodate spare blades. The whole of the bottom is lined with cloth. To prevent the knives from moving, a piece of sponge rubber is glued to the lid to provide pressure when the box is closed. The lid is secured with a brass side hook and a screw eye.

I have made several jigs for making such boxes, which are adaptable for various operations in conjunction with a router or a plough. One consists of two parallel pieces of timber held together with screws — this makes it easier to hold and adjust before applying the cramps. The pieces of timber need to be large enough to provide a good surface bearing for the router base, and long enough to control the fence. The other is a jig for face work; waste pieces are required to support the base of the router and to prevent damage when grooving across the grain. ∎

It is best to begin with sketches, drawing the outline of the article to determine the shape of the blocks, etc., and the space required. Then make the box, complete with top and bottom. Next, clean up the box, mark the depth of the rim with a gauge line, and use a tenon-saw to cut through the box to form the lid. When dovetailed joints are employed for the corners, care must be taken to arrange their positions to suit the depth of the lid.

Rebated joints are suitable for small boxes holding lightweight articles. For box C the joints were pinned and glued

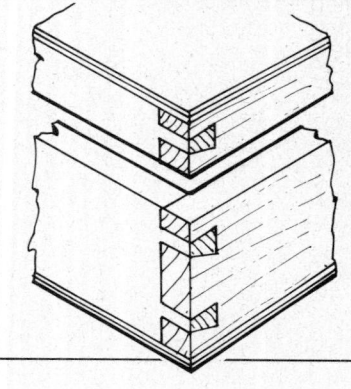

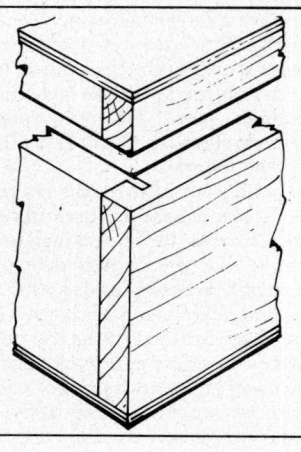

● *Alternative corner joints. Box A is on the left, Box B on the right, but you can ring the changes on these and other methods*

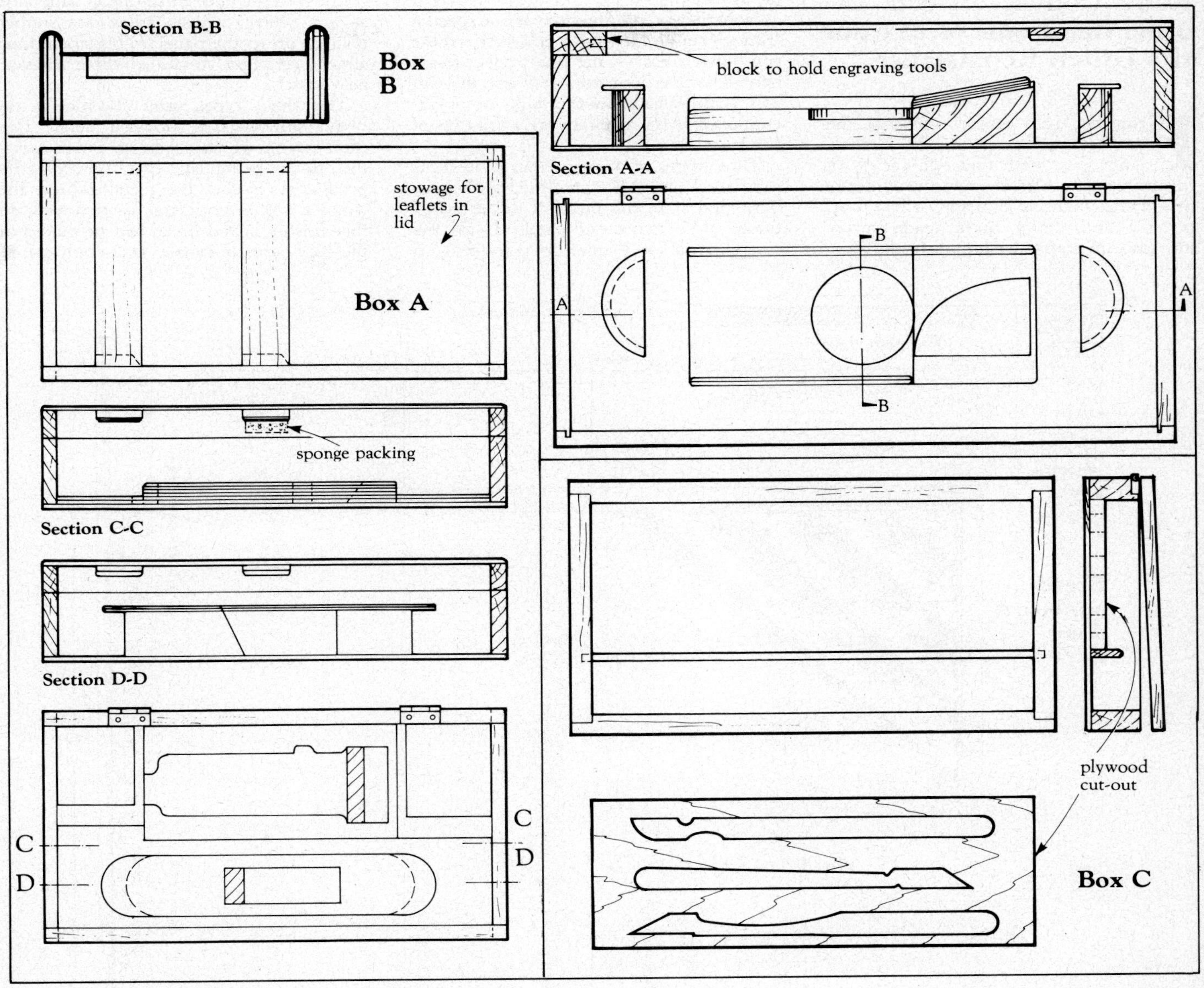

**Section B-B**

**Box B**

block to hold engraving tools

**Section A-A**

**Box A**

stowage for leaflets in lid

sponge packing

**Section C-C**

**Section D-D**

C
D
C
D

A
B
B
A

plywood cut-out

**Box C**

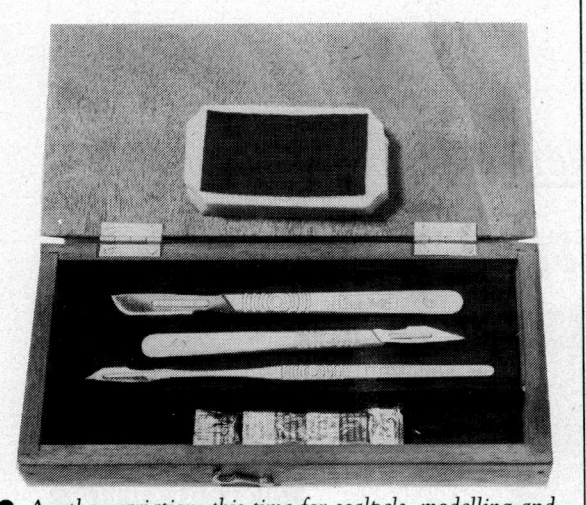

● *Another variation, this time for scalpels, modelling and artwork tools. Decide your own shapes and sizes for the precious pieces you want to keep neat and tidy*

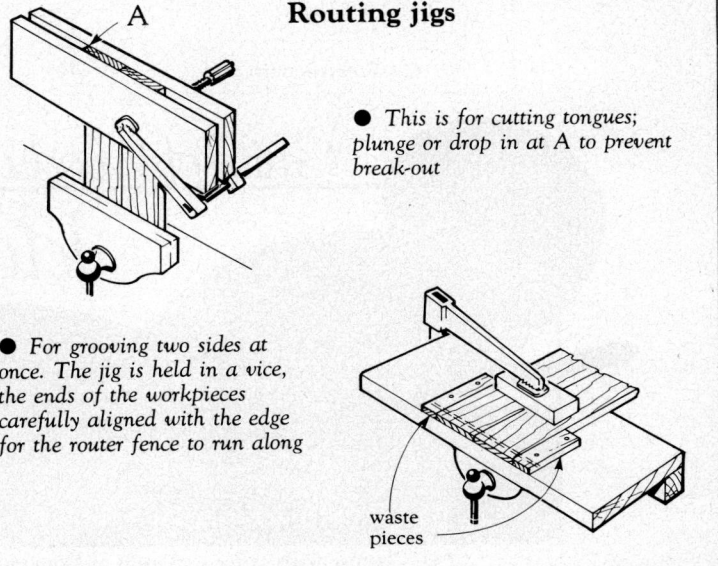

A

**Routing jigs**

● *This is for cutting tongues; plunge or drop in at A to prevent break-out*

● *For grooving two sides at once. The jig is held in a vice, the ends of the workpieces carefully aligned with the edge for the router fence to run along*

waste pieces

# The five-door cabinet

**René Coolen dissects another handsome piece from the Dutch Renaissance**

From the 16th century onwards, the northern provinces of the Netherlands gave birth to a rich variety of furniture types. Alas, the same was not true of others, such as Brabant, where war, poverty and heavy taxes made severe inroads into craftsmanship, taste and standards of living.

Nonetheless, we do know of one specific (though simple) item that emerged in these run-down areas — the one I have drawn here. The five-door cabinet is also known, just as prosaically, as the milk- or bread-cupboard. In its simplicity it is a fine item of furniture.

Three types of door are found on these cabinets. The first is exemplified by the four large doors on the piece in the drawing: these are framed-and-panelled in the conventional (and superior) manner — in contrast to the door of the small cupboard at top centre, whose 'stiles' are simply planted on to the panel. (This small door almost certainly concealed three shelves, now lost.)

The third type, used specifically on bread-cupboards, is shown in detail. The cabinet from which it came no longer exists, the door being all that remains. Its peculiarity is that the panel behind the wooden trellis-work can be removed, so that freshly baked bread can be placed in the cupboard to 'exhale' as it cools off. ■

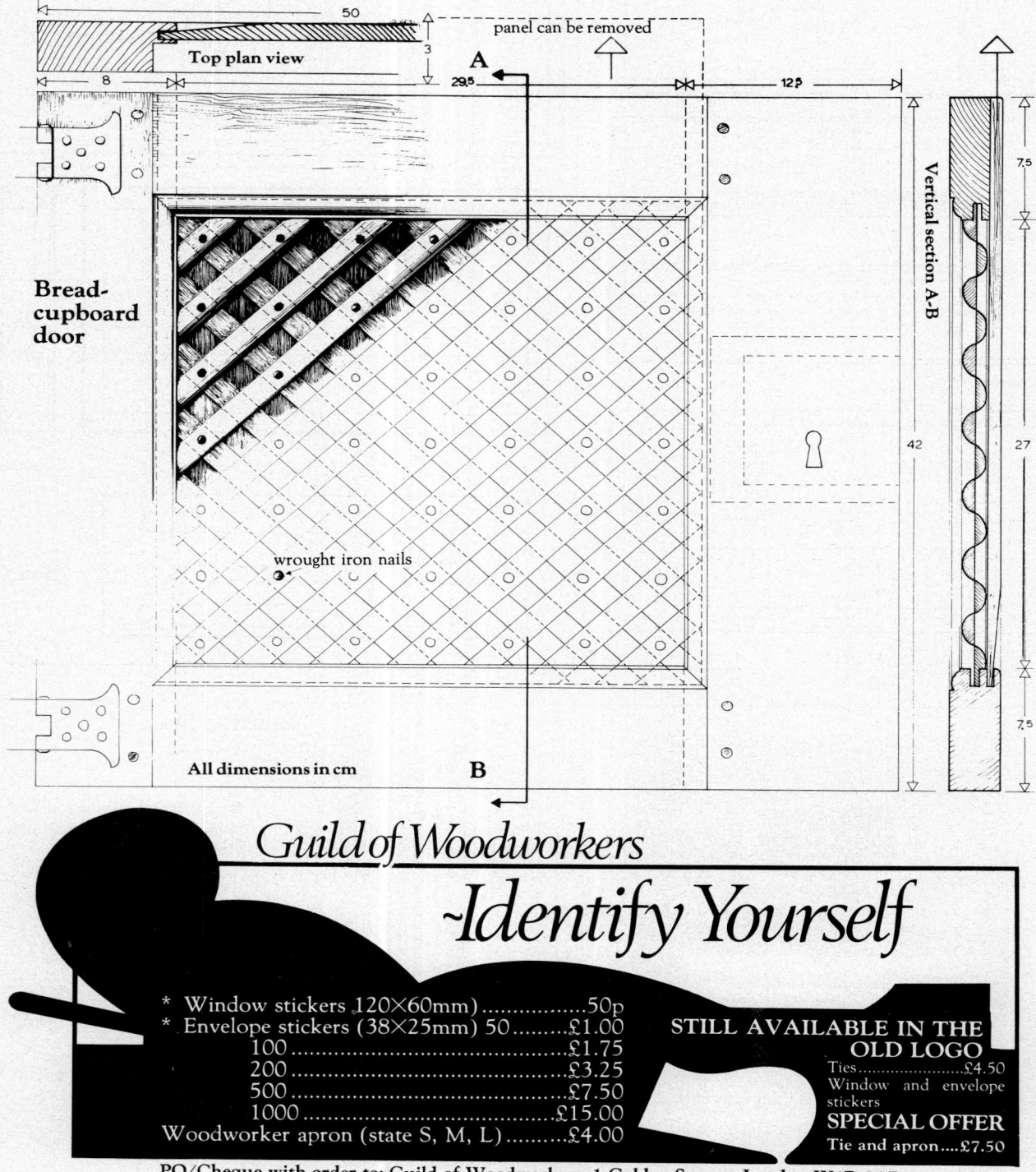

Top plan view
50
3
8
panel can be removed
A
29.5
12.5
Vertical section A-B
7.5
42
27
7.5

**Bread-cupboard door**

wrought iron nails

All dimensions in cm

B

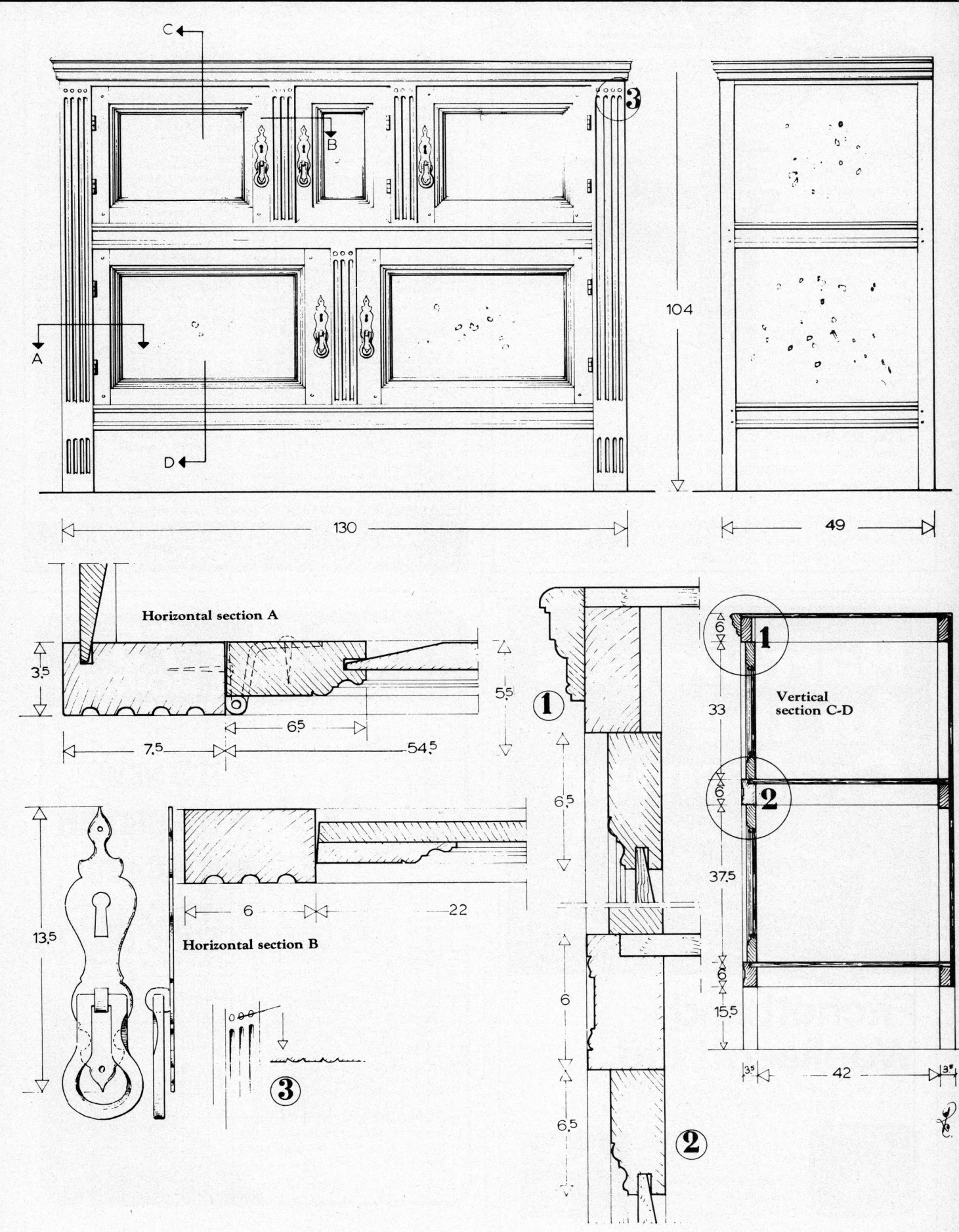

C

B

A

D

③

104

130

49

**Horizontal section A**

3,5

5,5

6,5

7,5

54,5

①

6,5

6

6,5

②

13,5

6

22

**Horizontal section B**

③

①

6

33

2

6

37,5

6

15,5

**Vertical section C-D**

3,5    42    3,5

②

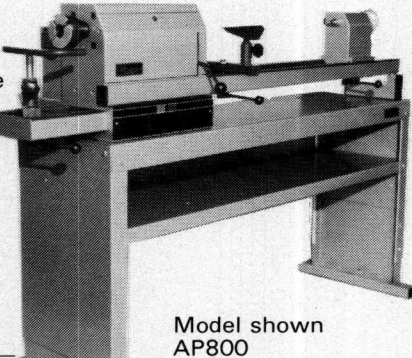

522

# The craft of cabinetmaking

## David Savage explains why he loves laminating

Steam-bending is a filthy business. Steam, hot wobbly timber and scalded hands do not a happy craftsman make.

Near my workshop is one of the few boatyards building timber-hulled ships. They have a steaming-box about 30 yards long for bending the larch planks used for the hulls. These planks, often 4in thick, emerge from this giant steamer with a life of their own, wobbling and wriggling like eels. Chairmakers I know get on with their steam-boxes very well, but I must admit that I do not share their enthusiasm. My nice dry workshop would not welcome the presence of a glorified tea-kettle; for me it's lamination every time.

Laminating is done in the comfort of the workshop. It is time-consuming and fearfully expensive, and to say that it was wasteful would be an understatement.

The idea is to achieve those bends, put into trees by nature, that we took out when we sawed and planed the timber into boards. If you take several thin pliable strips, coat them in glue and hold them together in a curve while the glue dries, that curve will remain. If the job is done properly, the curve will remain exactly as it came out of the mould, whereas steam-bent stuff can relax to a less acute curve. The curve is held by the glue because each lamination is bending to a slightly different radius from its neighbour. The compounded laminate is a solid, stable and very strong structure that has many uses in furniture-making.

Do not confuse lamination with plywood. Both use the same concept of several parts making a whole, but there the similarity ends. Lamination can be used to take apart a board of solid, figured timber and re-assemble it in curved or serpentine form. Provided you are meticulous, there will be very little evidence of your labour — no glaring glue-lines, no changes in colour or tone: just solid wood, bent. That's the good news. The bad news is that you need to make a mould or jig to hold your gluesodden laminates. In effect lamination is only really used where batch production makes this worthwhile.

I was recently asked to produce four identical oak doors for a medieval house in Devon. Because the design called for a Gothic shape, lamination was a viable technique for producing the eight stiles. No doubt the curved stiles had been and could have been produced by jointing, and it might well have been done quicker and more economically; but the result could not have been as strong or as attractive as the eventual laminated product.

First, build your mould. It would be horrible to cut your laminates, only to find them too thick to bend to the required curve — or, more likely, too short to cover the mould's full length. For a simple curve, take a substantial base material such as ¾in chipboard and carefully draw out the inner

and outer curves of your assembled lamination. Beam compasses are the best solution for curves of a diameter beyond ordinary compasses. A masonry nail with a round shank and the head removed is driven into the base-board at the curve's centre. The 'beam' is measured for the radii of inner and outer curves. A pencil is placed through a hole drilled at one end of the beam, and snug holes to accept the masonry nail are drilled at the other. In less than five minutes you have your home-made, accurate beam compasses.

● *The panels for the oak doors; laminating is probably hardest, but strongest and most attractive*

Whilst marking the base, it helps also to make thin plywood templates that can help in mould construction and in other parts of the job. A mould has two parts. The outer curve is fixed very securely to the base board; it can be made of any scrap softwood, carefully fitted to the curve and then screwed and glued down. The inner curves are made in a similar way, but not attached to the base.

The laminates are pulled up to the fixed outer curve and clamped securely between this and the inner curve of the moveable jig. Once the mould is assembled, fix it to your bench-top or a similar strong, flat structure, at a comfortable working height. Check for flatness of the mould. You will be giving the mould a fair battering when knocking down the laminates, so do not use the kitchen table. You will have to work fast, so don't put it on the floor either.

Now coat with a release agent the surfaces that will come in contact with glue; for this job I used old shellac polish to fill the grain, then several applications of wax polish. This release agent is important and should be replaced after each job. Omit this step, and the whole damn lot — laminates, glue and mould — locks up into one massive lump. I had the good fortune to see this happen to someone else. It was an entertaining spectacle watching him beat this contraption into separate bits, and a salutary lesson in not making the same error.

With the mould produced, you can measure the length of laminates required. Next, estimate what thickness will easily bend to the required curve. By easily, I mean: can you pull it up with one hand without hearing faint crackling noises? It is as well to make several test pieces at this stage.

Many craftsmen make laminates using the rip-saw, then plane both surfaces before gluing up. With high-quality tooling, I believe this is an unnecessary waste of time. Provided that you are equipped with a good table-saw, it is possible to make laminations straight from the saw. I use a Leitz 798 Rip-and-Trim carbide-tipped blade. All Leitz tooling is expensive, and this is no exception at nearly £35, but it does the job superbly well. The problem with cheap saw-blades is not only poor-quality carbide tips, but also a thin plate material that gives a vibration and resonance that result in an uneven cut. These Leitz blades, on the contrary, leave a planer-smooth surface that takes glue well and can be clamped up to leave no glue-line at all.

The essence of good rip-sawing is lateral control and a constant easy feed rate. Set up a roll-on, roll-off system if necessary, improvising bits and bobs around the workshop so that the stuff can be fed to the blade at a constant height along its entire length. Set the rip fence to the right of the blade so the laminate thickness will be produced on the free left-hand side of the blade. This is a cumbersome technique that requires the rip fence to be carefully moved each time, but it is more accurate than trapping thin laminates between fence and saw. Remember to move the fence along by the thickness of the laminate plus the 3.5mm kerf of the saw.

I mentioned wastefulness. If you end up with a 3ft pile of laminates, you will also end up with a 4ft pile of sawdust. The stuff to be laminated must be very dry — either recently kiln-dried, or shop-conditioned

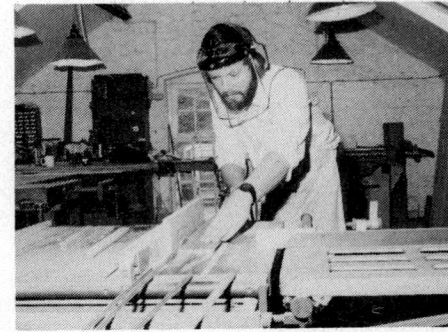

● *Cutting the long strips for the laminations. It's more accurate to dimension off the untrapped side of the blade*

for two to three months. A recommended moisture level is not more than 12%. Airdry timber straight from the yard just will not do. The stuff should be PAR to the thickness of your finished job plus a 3mm allowance for cleaning up after gluing. Mark the board with a triangle to help keep the laminates in order.

# The craft of cabinetmaking

As the laminates come off the saw, stack them in sequence. Large elastic bands help to keep them in bundle order when they are moved about the shop. Doing this job is repetitive, but it can be a relaxing change if you wear ear-defenders and a face visor, and have the protection of a dust-extraction system. Without these aids it is not a pleasant job — but then what task with modern wood machines is pleasant?

When sorting the bundles of laminates, check for lumps and bumps; most will not want attention from the hand plane, but a few will need the odd stroke here and there. Then set yourself up for the fun of gluing the whole lot together. First, the mould should be checked for stability and ease of clamping up; A dry-clamping session helps here. I use Sandvik speed-cramps for this kind of job. Although they have much less power than G-cramps, they are faster-acting and generally more versatile around the shop. For the extra power to compress about 5 glue-lines at once, a friend made me an implement that fits like a box-spanner on to the hexagonal handles of the cramps. This wonderful tool — called, for the want of a better term, the bodger — has given good service, and will always be used where cramps are clustered together and difficult to tighten. Cramps should be sited so that pressure is in the middle of the depth of the laminate. In addition, lumps may have to be lopped off the mould to enable you to position the cramps at right-angles to the glue-line.

There is a saying that you will never have enough cramps. Until I took up large-scale lamination I was reasonably confident that I did have enough clamps — in fact more than enough. But no, dear me, no: this job takes all your cramps, all your friends' cramps and the entire stock of your local tool shop in the effort to put one cramp every 8-10in. Did I tell you laminating could be costly? Pile the cramps up around the mould with the jaws open and the screws backed off, put the bodger to hand — and make a knocking-down block, as the slippery laminates may slide up under cramping pressure. Set this beside a good-sized hammer. Sort everything out now before you spread the glue.

Two trestle tables can be assembled near the mould to take the two piles of laminates. If you are only doing a small lamination that can be coated and cramped up quickly, a one-part glue like PVA is best. For anything large or complex, or where you do not want to rush too much, a two-part adhesive such as Aerolite 306 is very good indeed. Set the two piles out, using alternate laminates so that the grain graphics will be returned when the laminates are brought together in the mould. One pile will receive the adhesive, the other a formic-acid catalyst.

Rollers can be made to a convenient width by cutting up short-knap paint rollers and fitting them over Harris wallpaper-seam rollers. These put on the sticky, porridge-like adhesive with just enough

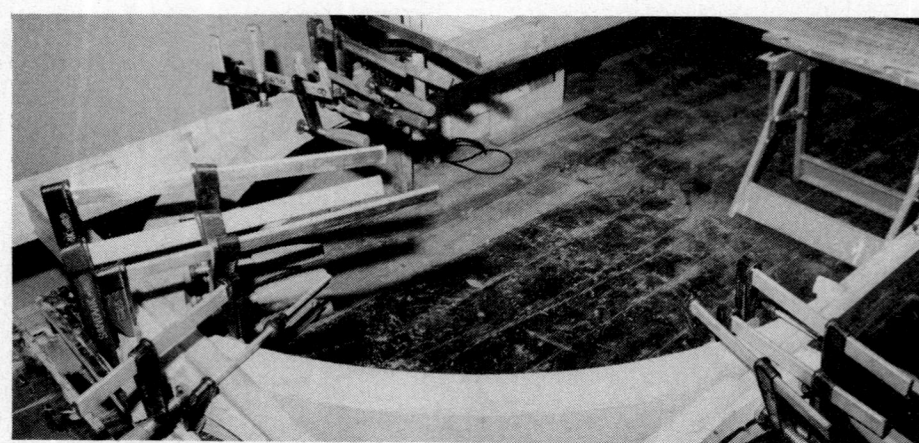

● *The door-frames in cramps; no question of laminating here. Note the blocks fixed to the outsides of the members to give proper directional pressure*

tack, evenly and quickly. Apply to both sides and pile the laminates wet to wet. Do not put adhesive on to the top face. It is possible to do this slowly and carefully so there is no excuse for missing any area of timber.

The catalyst pile must not come anywhere near the adhesive until they go together in the mould. Apply the catalyst, which is a watery clear liquid, with a similar roller; again pile wet to wet, but this time do not touch the bottom face. Wear a visor and rubber gloves for this operation, as acid splashes can be unpleasant. Start moving more quickly now, for the acid will dry on the surface, and there should be a trace of moisture for a good chemical reaction.

PBX hardener (as it is called) claims to give a clamping time of 15 minutes once the two piles are brought together. I would put it at nearer 10 minutes in a reasonably warm workshop. This, dear woodworker, explains why there is no photograph of the next stage of the operation. When attempting to pull up 15 laminates using every cramp in north Devon inside 10 minutes, a 13-stone cabinet-maker is moving at a speed too fast to be captured on film.

Put the piles together, taking one laminate from each stack. Work out a system so that the orientation is correct end-to-end and top-to-bottom. Fit it to the mould starting at one end, apply light pressure,

knock down, and then move on. As you get several cramps on, go back and tighten the earlier cramps with the bodger. Move down the mould in a controlled, methodical and calm manner, but do not hang about either. Take the telephone off the hook beforehand, and lock the door; this is not a time for visitors, reps or customers to call.

When all is tight, take a clean new cloth and wipe off any excess glue that has not already gelled. Cloths that have been sitting on the metal draining-board will react with the acid, staining the timber dark grey; the same applies to glue containers and brushes — do not allow any metal to get near this stuff.

The instructions say three hours is long enough for the glue to go off. This is a high-quality product with a clear glue line and enormous strength, but I still did not dare take my Gothic styles out of the mould in less than four hours, and more often than not I have left jobs overnight. When they come from the mould it is a good idea to leave them to cure for a few days before planing up to final dimension. A bobbin-sander can be used to clean up the inside, although I have found that a hand scraper set with a largish hook can do a first-class job.

Smaller jobs may, however, demand a different approach. I may even consider steam-bending! ∎

● *The table must be dead flat; cut notches in the inner formers if needed*

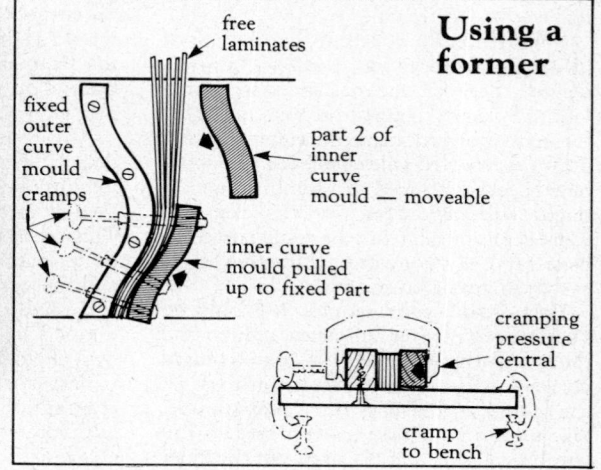

## Using a former

free laminates

fixed outer curve mould cramps

part 2 of inner curve mould — moveable

inner curve mould pulled up to fixed part

cramping pressure central

cramp to bench

# ... LOOK NO CRAMPS!

**Bill Gates** writes: Laminating is not a recent development, but it is being used more and more today — principally in large structural components for building.

Among other advantages, it allows the use of relatively low-grade timber (provided it is dense) in areas where the stress is mainly in compression. On the other hand, individual laminates can be selected with a permissible level of defects in mind, whereas large solid sections may contain defects which are hidden. Alternatively, defects in the laminates can be removed and the laminates joined in length.

For small jobs, the former or jig shown here is ideal when you don't possess (and don't feel like buying, begging, hiring or borrowing) lots of clamps.

If not too large, it can be held in a vice, with a block to keep it well clear of the bench.

The method is as follows:

**1** Put paper in the jig to prevent any squeezed-out adhesive from the joints coming into contact with it.

**2** Spread the adhesive on the laminates and place them between the radial battens.

**3** Push the pins through their holes, depressing the laminates around the jig.

**4** Drive in wedges to compress the work and hold it in place.

**5** Check that the jig is free of adhesive.

There is normally some slide between glued laminates when assembling, and an allowance must be made in the width for finishing the work to size later. To ensure that the laminations will bend without fracturing in a dry condition, the radius should not be less than 100 times the thickness of the laminates.

Where only a few items are required, a slightly thicker laminate can be used — provided the timber is treated in some way to soften the fibres, e.g. with very hot water or steam. The laminates should then be assembled on the jig without adhesive, remaining until completely dry, before the final glued assembly.

Certain factors influence the selection of timber for laminating, particularly when the curves are sharp. Straight grain, flexibility and freedom from defects are essential. Birch, elm, mahogany, beech and oak are some of the species that bend well. You can also use good-quality thin birch plywood (cut with the grain running across the width of the laminates).

The jig shown in fig. 1 is made from solid timber cut to shape; the edge must be perfectly square to the face so that pressure is applied evenly to the laminations. The holes in the radial battens need to be drilled accurately, and set in alignment when attached to the jig with glue and nails. For larger work, use the built-up method shown in fig. 2.

The thickness of the jig is controlled by the width of the lamination, and a generous clearance should be allowed. ∎

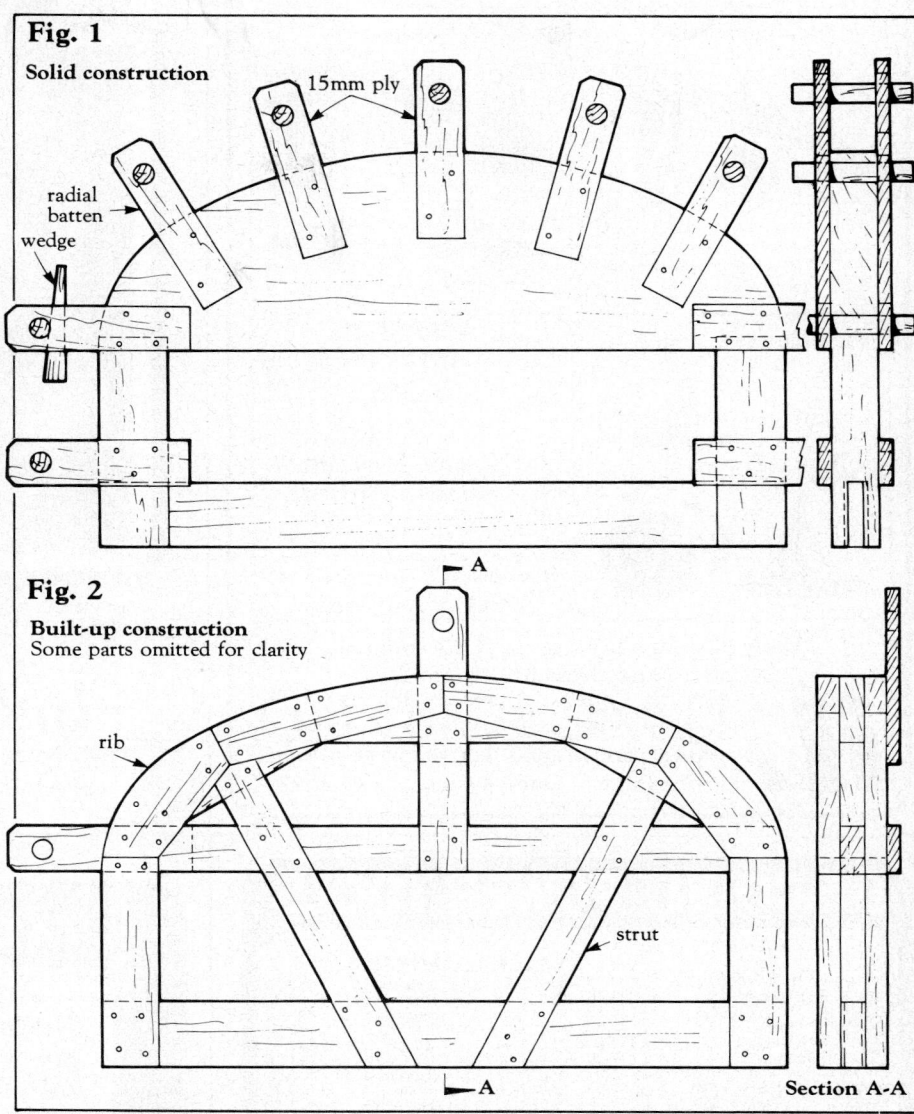

**Fig. 1**
Solid construction

15mm ply

radial batten wedge

**Fig. 2**

Built-up construction
Some parts omitted for clarity

rib

strut

A

A

Section A-A

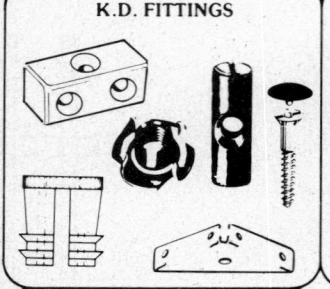
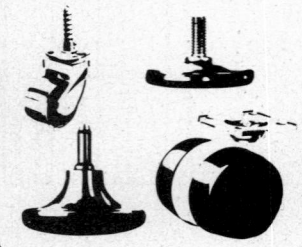

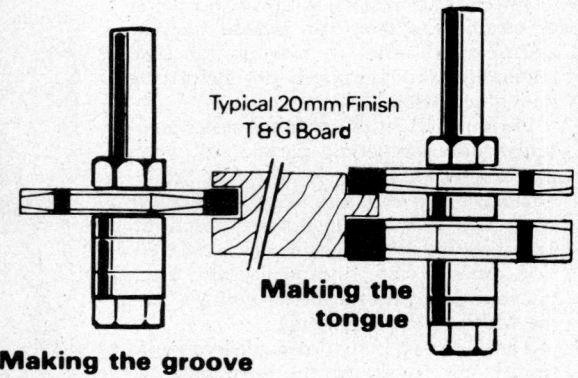

526

# Keep on chucking

A woodturner's first and often toughest problem is mounting the workpiece. Engineer/craftsman Nick Davidson leads off an expert report on the clever modern chucks which make all the difference

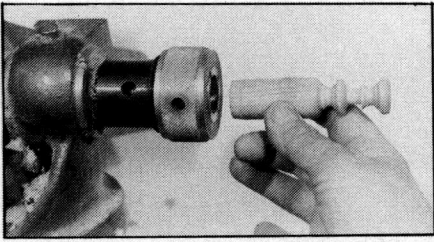

● *The collet chuck*

Over the past 15 years I have been involved in developing various ideas for woodturning. But I am reluctant to describe myself as an inventor, for to me there is no magic about inventions. Almost without exception, all the ideas I have developed have come about by discussing woodturning problems with various craftsmen — recognising a need, then 'playing around' on bits of paper until something comes up that solves the problem.

Many of the 'new' products on the market today have been around for many years. Products like the sizing tool, fluted parting-tools, collet chucks and many others can, in fact, be found in books written by Holtzapffel last century. True, the shape of these tools has changed dramatically, but the need for them was recognised many, many years ago. What has really altered is that the ideas have been developed commercially. In the past craftsmen developed special jigs and fixtures to increase their productivity, and having expended time, thought and money they were reluctant to pass on the relevant information. This habit, indeed, has not completely died out, although advanced communications and technology have certainly broken down barriers.

One aspect of turning that has indisputably advanced beyond measure since the war is chucking. Before the war the recognised means of gripping wood, other than between centres, was on a face-plate with three screws or on a screw-chuck. Without special jigs the face-plate left one with three nasty holes in the base of the finished product, and the screw-chuck (utilising the standard woodscrew) had various limitations.

The first combination chuck available was the Myford 3-in-1. This combined face-plate, screw-chuck and collar chuck. I first became involved in developing chucking when Roy and Peter Child introduced the coil grip chuck. This combined the features of the 3-in-1 with an extra unique one — the coil grip itself, in which the article to be turned is gripped on a flange by a coil spring held within the chuck as illustrated.

With this chuck also came a reducing ring to enable it to be used as a small 'collar chuck'. The limitation of any collar chuck, however, is that one has to turn the whole length of timber, with the exception of a flange at the end to enable the outer ring to be threaded over the workpiece and hence gripped within the chuck as shown. This limitation was recognised by an Irish gentleman who submitted a drawing of an interlocking ring that overcame the problem. I found that by simply cutting the ring in two I achieved the same results. Hence the introduction of the split ring.

About eight years ago I was talking to Geoff Peters, a recognised authority on woodturning. He told me that the coil-grip chuck was fine for large work, but what was needed was a small collet chuck because so few people could acquire large pieces of timber. As a result, I designed the collet chuck for gripping small items. This, however, has always been limited in usage too, in as much as tailstock support is required to maintain concentricity when initially mounting the timber. Geoff and I discussed the possibility of another chuck in which the collets expanded outwards, as we were both aware of another severe limitation: a ½in flange was required on the base of any article before the coil-grip chuck could secure it. This flange had either to become part of the article, or be cut off (which was very expensive in terms of timber).

After considerable experimentation the 6-in-1 chuck evolved. This combined the traditional methods of gripping timber, i.e. screw-chuck, face-plate and ring chuck

(collar chuck), along with the more recent split ring and the new expanding-collet feature. This last was a particularly significant step, as it made the traditional face-plate obsolete for turning bowls. Another feature developed about this time was the face-plate ring. This was particularly useful to craft turners making batches of bowls, platters and the like, and for educational establishments where there may be a dozen or so students in the process of turning a bowl might all need access to a face-plate.

At a fraction of the cost of the traditional face-plate, the face-plate ring was an attractive proposition. It can be fixed on to a block of wood and then held within the expanding collets of the 6-in-1 chuck.

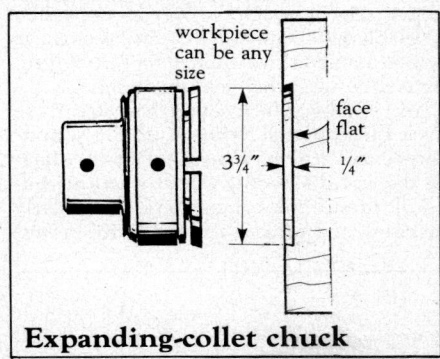

workpiece can be any size

face flat

3¾" — ¼"

## Expanding-collet chuck

A further improvement on the 6-in-1 chuck was suggested by a woodturning instructor from Vermont, USA, Russ Zimmerman. On larger pieces of turning held with the split ring, one needed to turn down the first portion to enable the split ring to be attached to the groove as shown. Russ suggested that a three-way split ring would waste far less timber, which is particularly important when using the more colourful exotic woods. This improvement was incorporated. Indeed, different sizes of three-way split ring were added to the range of accessories available for the 6-in-1 chuck.

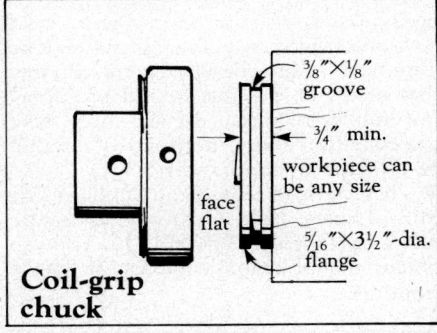

⅜"×⅛" groove

¾" min.

workpiece can be any size

face flat

⁵⁄₁₆"×3½"-dia. flange

**Coil-grip chuck**

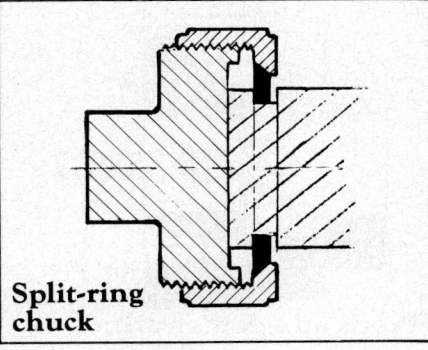

**Split-ring chuck**

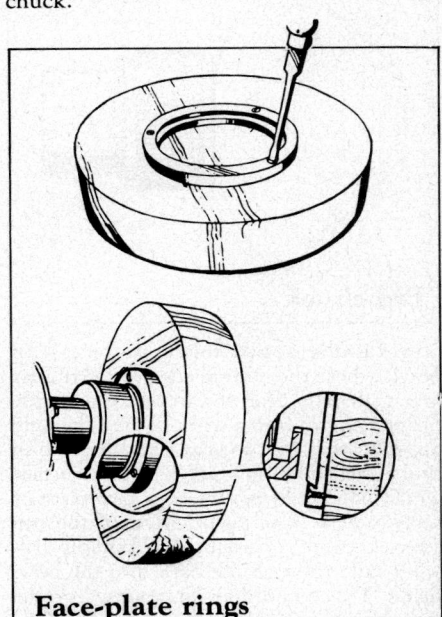

**Face-plate rings**

# Keep on chucking

The idea for the spigot chuck came after a course by Richard Raffan at our own premises, in which he was teaching students to turn decorative boxes and bowls. Richard advised me to think about a small, accurate chuck to grip boxes without wasting too much material. Richard had been using a self-centring four-jaw chuck — expensive, and considered slightly dangerous, as its gripping jaws have been known to give a nasty clout to many a turner's fingers!

The spigot chuck had the bonus of proving suitable not only for small decorative boxes, but also for small decorative bowls which we found possible to grip on a ⅛in spigot, 1½in in diameter. This facility was not available in the 6-in-1 chuck, for (although the 6-in-1 was by then available with miniature collets as small as ⅞in in diameter) we found it far safer to grip externally with the new spigot chuck.

In 1980 I was lucky enough to attend the First International Symposium for Woodturners at Parnham House in Dorset. Many of the world's leading woodturners attended. I found the atmosphere particularly inspiring, and became very interested in wet-

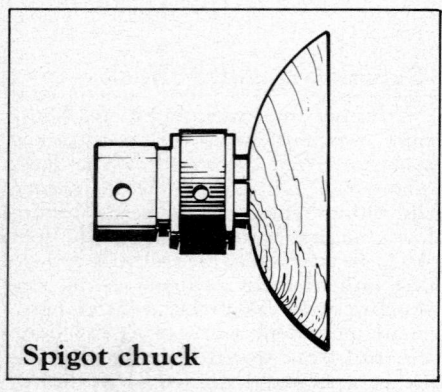

**Spigot chuck**

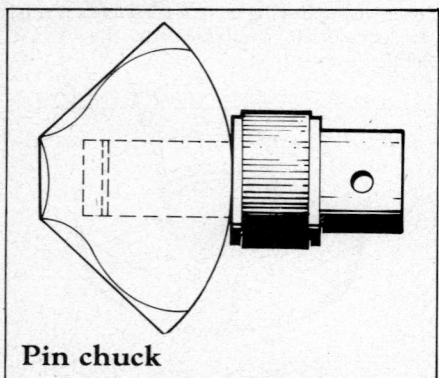

**Pin chuck**

bowl turning — particularly in the case of bowls where the natural edge of the timber is left on. This feature can turn a perfectly ordinary bowl into a work of art. The only problem was how to grip a rough piece of timber which hasn't got a rough surface which you could mount on a face-plate or screw-chuck. The significance of the pin chuck became apparent to me. I simply drilled a hole through the bark into the bowl blank. This could then be mounted on the pin chuck, its hole the same as the drilled

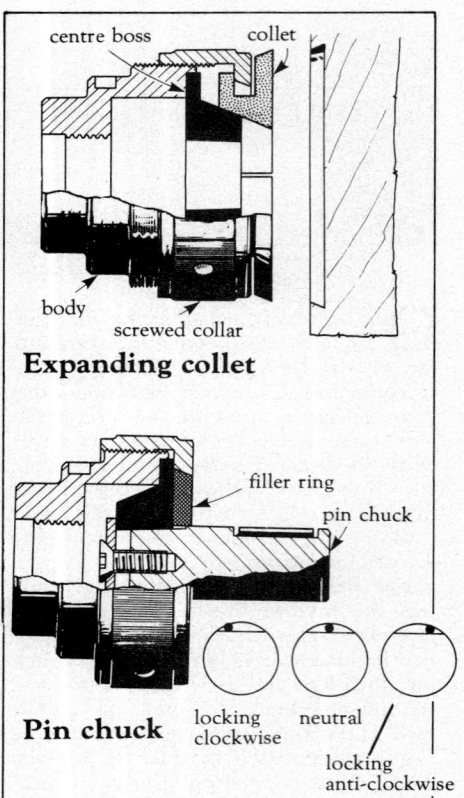

centre boss          collet

body

screwed collar

**Expanding collet**

filler ring

pin chuck

**Pin chuck**          locking clockwise   neutral

locking anti-clockwise

hole. Then you could turn the outside of the bowl, including a spigot or recess at the base, to mount on to the spigot chuck or the expanding collet chuck.

We now had three chucks on the market that I had developed, each serving entirely different functions. Many manufacturers may wish to sell as many different products as possible. I felt the need, however, for a chuck that performed all the operations of those that had come before it. So I designed the **precision combination chuck.** This combined the best features of the 6-in-1 collet chuck, the spigot chuck and others.

Furthermore, we had the chuck produced on computerised machinery to remove, where possible, human error in production.

The basic chuck is supplied with 3½in expanding collets; 1¾ and 1in three-way split rings; and a 1in pin chuck. It can also be used as a collet chuck and a cup chuck. The illustrations show the different modes of operation. As optional extras there are an additional 10 sizes of expanding collet, two

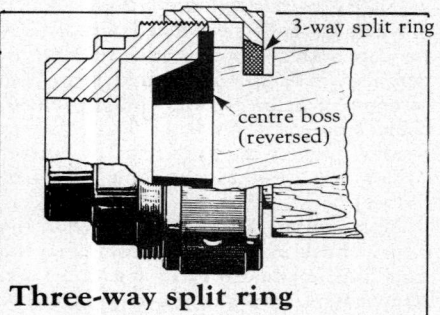

3-way split ring

centre boss (reversed)

**Three-way split ring**

sizes of 3-way split ring and four sizes of pin chuck. The various other optional extras include the much improved screw-chuck. Unlike the traditional screw-chuck, which was usually a no14 tapered woodscrew, this one is a machined parallel woodscrew fitted to the chuck body by means of a no3 stub morse taper. This ensures perfect accuracy. The screw thread is a deep, square one which bites with very little displacement of timber. As a result, a pilot hole is required for screwing the wood on to the chuck. (This principle was used initially on the American Turnmaster chuck.)

The precision combination chuck also has spigot collet chucks as illustrated. All in all, it should supply all one's chucking

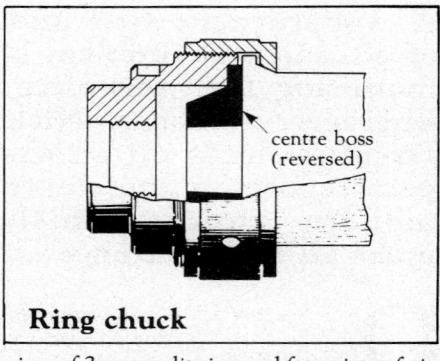

centre boss (reversed)

**Ring chuck**

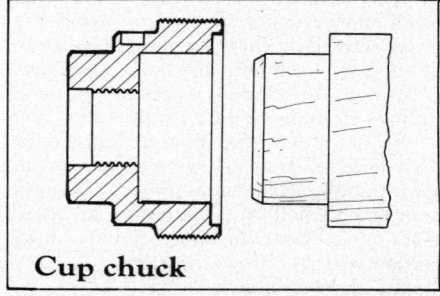

**Cup chuck**

needs with ease and accuracy. But it would be foolhardy for me to say that it cannot be improved — I have designed it in such a way that it will be possible to add additional features if required. It will only take someone to identify another need, and I'll be off again to the drawing-board.

● Nick Davidson runs Craft Supplies, The Mill, Millers Dale, Buxton, Derbyshire SK17 8SN, tel. (0298) 871636. You can obtain the precision combination chuck from there.

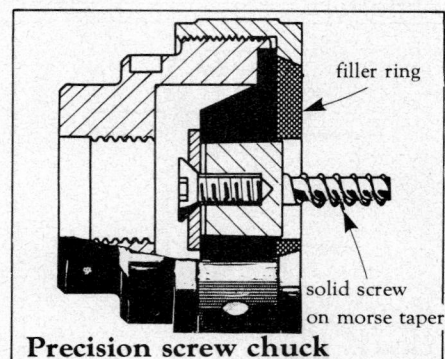

filler ring

solid screw on morse taper

**Precision screw chuck**

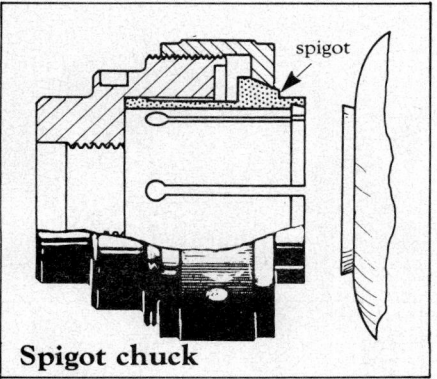

spigot

**Spigot chuck**

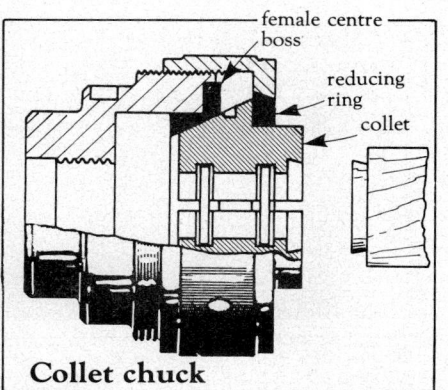

female centre boss

reducing ring

collet

**Collet chuck**

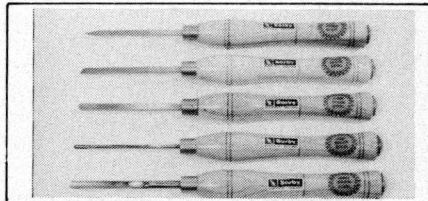

● *Robert Sorby of Sheffield, a name as familiar to woodturners as Craft Supplies, have a new range of miniature lathe tools known as the Micro-Set. They average 10in long, and are made in high-speed steel, which has previously been used only in full-size ranges. The Micro-Set costs £25.62+VAT*

# The Multistar Duplex chuck

**W**oodturning chucks have advanced greatly in recent years, **writes Bert Marsh.** Successive products have each produced new innovations and technical features, and the Multistar Duplex chuck is no exception. When it was introduced at the 1984 Woodworker Show, one could see at a glance that the makers had produced a high-quality and well designed tool. Having tested the chuck in my own workshop, I have had my initial good impressions fully confirmed.

The body fits most popular woodturning lathes with either left- or right-hand threads, and the manufacturers will produce special threads to suit individual requirements. A front ring compresses or expands the jaws when it is tightened on to the body. The jaw sets are particularly well designed, and provide a unique dual-purpose action. One set, comprising four segments secured to a retaining ring by a rubber band, is supplied with each chuck. Sets are available in five sizes, and prices vary according to size. These can be purchased at any time as both jaws and chucks are interchangeable. The two smaller sizes can be easily assembled before insertion into the front ring, but the larger jaws must be fitted inside the ring. This may seem a little difficult at first but practice soon overcomes the problem.

Each jaw segment has a small lug at its rear end which ingeniously keeps the segments equally apart while it is tightened — contributing greatly to the working and accuracy of the whole chuck unit. Two further components are necessary to expand the jaws; an inner ring fits into the centre of the jaws, expanding the segments as it is compressed, while an outer ring holds the assembly firmly within the body of the chuck.

With each unit comes a tommy-bar to hold the body of the chuck, and a C-spanner to tighten the front ring. Both are machined to a high standard and fitted with durable plastic sleeve handles. However, I think you could get more control if the tommy-bar were increased in length, or replaced with a second C-spanner.

● *The Multistar Duplex chuck*

● *The body*

● *The front ring*

The instruction booklet provides an illustrated step-by-step guide to assembly of the various parts, and a number of useful charts explaining preparation of material. Several accessories are available, which are well worth individual appraisal and comment.

**Indexing bar** An invaluable accessory for those turners who have an interest in dividing work. The bar fits into any one of the 24 holes which are accurately drilled in the body of the chuck.

**Face-plate rings** Three sizes are available, for jaws C, D and E. They are particularly useful because they enable turned work to be removed from the lathe and re-fitted quickly and accurately. Such fittings could prove invaluable in teaching. Holes are drilled in the rings for screw-fixing the material; they are not countersunk, so the screws protrude, which could be hazardous to hands. I think countersinking the holes would be a great improvement.

**Conversion ring** A very simple and effective means of securing small items. The ring fits into the chuck body, and encases a self-made hardwood collet. Coupled with the front ring, it provides equal pressure at each end of the collet. These are not difficult to make, and details are given in the instruction booklet.

**Screw-chuck, pin chuck, universal carrier** These three accessories can be used with all the jaw sets except A. The screw-chuck comes with three sizes of threads, either left- or right-handed. The unit is tightened into the chuck body by an Allen screw, but I wasn't happy with the screw-chuck I tested, finding that the screw tended to revolve in the body. The manufacturers were already aware of the problem, to their credit, and have produced a modified chuck which eliminates the fault. Using the size E jaws, large blanks can be supported against sideways movement, held only by a central screw.

Five sizes of pin chuck are available, ranging from ½ to 1½in diameter. The universal carrier is a plug with no1 or 2 morse-tapered holes. I couldn't find much use for this accessory at first, but on reflection can see its value to many users — particularly those lathe owners who do not have drilled-out headstock spindles. The carrier allows you to use various standard turning centres and a drill chuck. It can also

# Keep on chucking

● *Two jaws; note small lug keeping them apart*

● *The complete range of Duplex jaws*

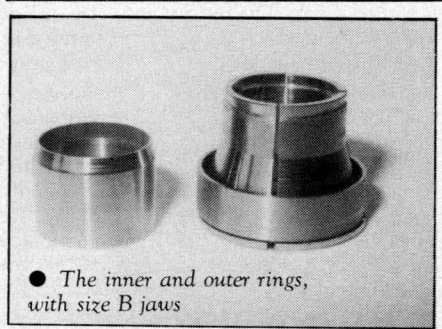

● *The inner and outer rings, with size B jaws*

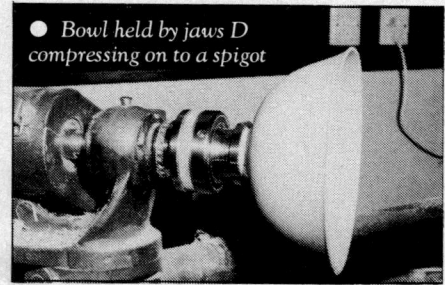

● *Bowl held by jaws D compressing on to a spigot*

● *Circular blank held by jaws A expanding into a hole*

● *The chuck with indexing bar. Note jaws equally spaced*

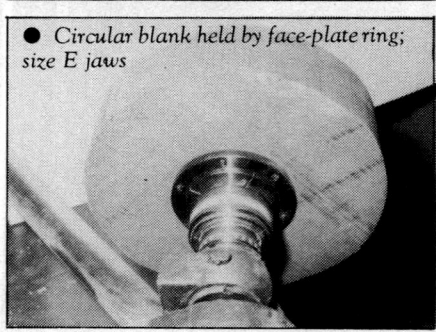

● *Circular blank held by face-plate ring; size E jaws*

● *Conversion ring and self-made hardwood collet*

● *Screw-chuck in size E jaws*

● *Complete range of pin chucks*

● *Pin chuck held in size E jaws*

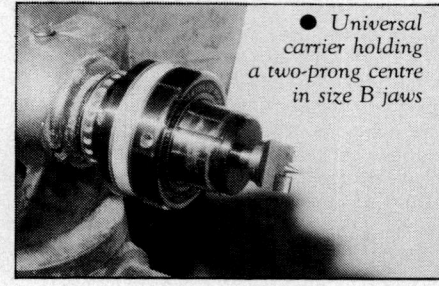

● *Universal carrier holding a two-prong centre in size B jaws*

be used with the indexing system for work between centres.

I thoroughly enjoyed putting the Multistar Duplex Chuck through its paces, and am very impressed with its quality, design and performance. All the bits and pieces are made of high-carbon steel, machined to very fine tolerances, with an excellent finish and a two-year guarantee. The man responsible for their design and production is John Lovatt, and in my opinion he can be justly proud of his achievements.

One chuck will never succeed in answering all woodturners' problems, but I am sure this product will satisfy many discerning craftsmen and become a valued part of both professional and amateur practitioners' equipment. The price is fair, bearing in mind its high quality.

I hear that John is planning the production of a woodturning lathe. If it is as well-thought-out as the chuck, then I'll be eager to see it.

● Multistar Machine & Tool Co Ltd, Ashton House, Wheatfield Rd, Stanway, Colchester, Essex CO3 5YA.

Bert Marsh's work can be seen at Hove Museum & Art Gallery, 19 New Church Rd, Hove, Sussex, tel. (0273) 770410, 4 June till 6 July, Tue-Fri 10-5, Sat 10-4.30; and Quest, Temple Court, Church St, Blackburn, Lancs, tel. (0254) 582738, during June — ring for details.

## Methods of holding work in the Multistar chuck

| Jaw size | Expanding in a circular recess | Expanding in a hole | Compressing on a round spigot | Compressing on a round dowel | Compressing on a square spigot | Compressing on a square dowel |
|---|---|---|---|---|---|---|
| A | 1¼″ | 1¼″ | 1″ | 1″ | ¾″ | ¾″ |
| B | 1¾″ | 1¾″ | 1½″ | 1½″ | 1⅛″ | 1⅛″ |
| C | 2⅜″ | | 2″ | 1½″ | 1½″ | 1⅛″ |
| D | 3″ | | 2½″ | 1½″ | 1⅞″ | 1⅛″ |
| E | 3½″ | | 3″ | 1½″ | 2¼″ | 1⅛″ |

# The four-jaw chuck

**R**oger Holley writes: The steel self-centring chuck has been used for many years, mainly by the metal-turning fraternity but also by many professional woodturners. It is normally supplied in three-jaw form, and is used to grip an infinite range of diameters, internal and external, within its limits.

The new four-jaw self-centring chuck marketed by Axminster Power Tools adds to these advantages by enabling the turner to hold square-section material as well (fig. 1). At a price comparable with those of other specialist chucks and work-holding devices on the market, it eliminates the need for precise diameters and location angles. It requires only a parallel surface area sufficient to hold the work firmly enough for the particular turning operation. Obviously heavy boring on an unsupported piece such as a goblet will need adequate 'meat' clamped in the chuck jaws (fig. 2); a useful tip here is to produce a small shoulder which can bear against the front face of the jaws to control the end thrust on the work-piece (fig. 3). Many face-plate jobs such as bowls, platters and other discs can be turned easily using this method.

Both large and small squares can be held easily, making furniture work such as square-to-round stool legs (fig. 4) and even lace-bobbin blanks (fig. 5) equally feasible. The chuck obviously shows its merits on repetitive work, since it is fast and efficient to use, and it has excellent concentricity which means minimal waste and turning up during the roughing-out part of a job.

The chuck's heavy construction means that some smaller lathes may be unsuited to the extra load on the headstock bearings. The provision of a suitable guard is also an important consideration; all lathes should be fitted with a strong guard designed to enclose the adjustable jaws as fully as possible. It's also worth noting that this tool is likely to prove safe in experienced hands, but it must be treated with utmost care and respect when used by novices — old or young.

All things considered, this new tool represents good value for money.
● Axminster Power Tool Centre, Chard St, Axminster, Devon EX13 5DZ, tel. (0297) 33656. ■

**Fig. 1**

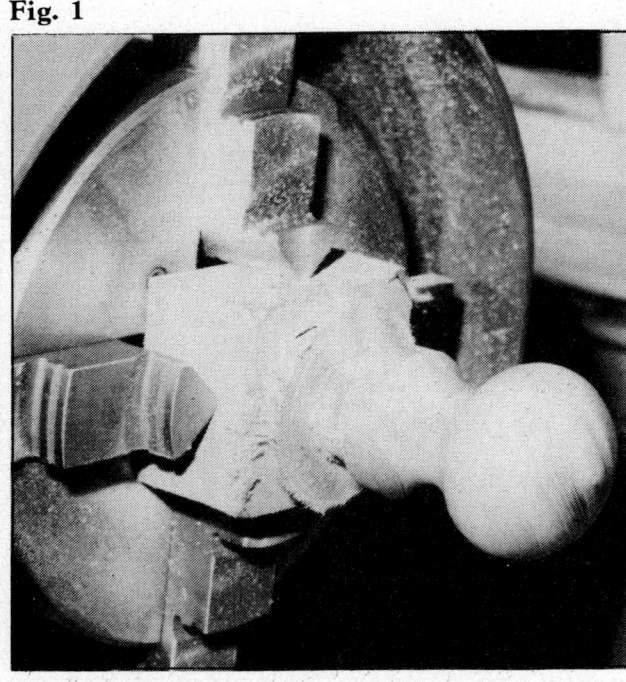

**Fig. 2**

**Fig. 3**

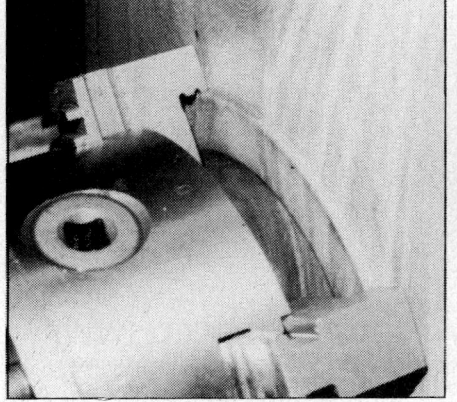

**Fig. 4**

**Fig. 5**

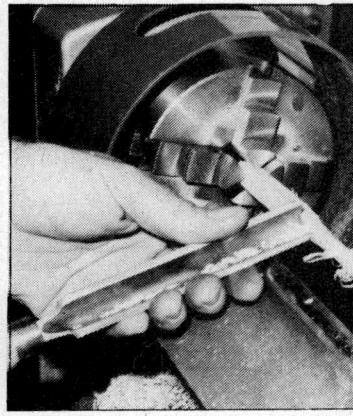

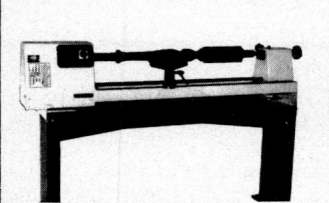

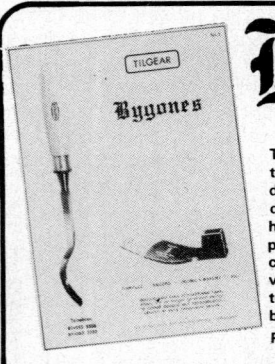

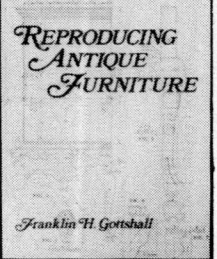

532

# The right angle

## WOODWORKING WHEEZE
### of the month

**B**ob Wearing writes: Accurate large-scale angles cannot be set out from the average protractor. 12in and larger protractors are rare and expensive. Fortunately, however, we all have the perfect tool for this job: the folding metre rule.

You simply open the rule at its centre joint, measuring off the distance between the tips until you have the angle you require — working from the table here. There is not much use for the computer in the small workshop, but for once it has come in very handy — saving an immense amount of boring calculation.

For those still loyal to the imperial measurements, the fractional calculations are much more involved. Here, however, is a simplified table for use with the folding 2ft (note — not 3ft) rule calibrated in sixteenths:

| | | | |
|---|---|---|---|
| 10°: | 2⅛″ | 40°: | 8³⁄₁₆″ |
| 15°: | 3³⁄₁₆″ | 45°: | 9⅛″ |
| 20°: | 4³⁄₁₆″ | 50°: | 10⅛″ |
| 22½°: | 4¹¹⁄₁₆″ | 60°: | 12 |
| 25°: | 5¹⁄₁₆″ | 67½°: | 13⁵⁄₁₆″ |
| 30°: | 6¼″ | 90°: | 17 |

## Distances required for given angles

| | | | | | |
|---|---|---|---|---|---|
| 1°: | 8.7mm | 46°: | 390.7mm | 26°: | 225.0mm |
| 2°: | 17.5mm | 47°: | 398.7mm | 27°: | 233.4mm |
| 3°: | 26.2mm | 48°: | 406.7mm | 28°: | 241.9mm |
| 4°: | 34.9mm | 49°: | 414.7mm | 29°: | 250.4mm |
| 5°: | 43.6mm | 50°: | 422.6mm | 30°: | 258.8mm |
| 6°: | 52.3mm | 51°: | 430.5mm | 31°: | 267.2mm |
| 7°: | 61.0mm | 52°: | 438.4mm | 32°: | 275.6mm |
| 8°: | 69.8mm | 53°: | 446.2mm | 33°: | 284.0mm |
| 9°: | 78.5mm | 54°: | 454.0mm | 34°: | 292.4mm |
| 10°: | 87.2mm | 55°: | 461.7mm | 35°: | 300.7mm |
| 11°: | 95.8mm | 56°: | 469.5mm | 36°: | 309.0mm |
| 12°: | 104.5mm | 57°: | 477.2mm | 37°: | 317.3mm |
| 13°: | 113.2mm | 58°: | 484.8mm | 38°: | 325.6mm |
| 14°: | 121.9mm | 59°: | 492.4mm | 39°: | 333.8mm |
| 15°: | 130.5mm | 60°: | 500.0mm | 40°: | 342.0mm |
| 16°: | 139.2mm | 61°: | 507.5mm | 41°: | 350.2mm |
| 17°: | 147.8mm | 62°: | 515.0mm | 42°: | 358.4mm |
| 18°: | 156.4mm | 63°: | 522.5mm | 43°: | 366.5mm |
| 19°: | 165.0mm | 64°: | 529.9mm | 44°: | 374.6mm |
| 20°: | 173.6mm | 65°: | 537.3mm | 45°: | 382.7mm |
| 21°: | 182.2mm | 66°: | 544.6mm | 71°: | 580.7mm |
| 22°: | 190.8mm | 67°: | 551.9mm | 72°: | 587.8mm |
| 23°: | 199.4mm | 68°: | 559.2mm | 73°: | 594.8mm |
| 24°: | 207.9mm | 69°: | 566.4mm | 74°: | 601.8mm |
| 25°: | 216.4mm | 70°: | 573.6mm | 75°: | 608.8mm |
| | | | | 76°: | 615.7mm |
| | | | | 77°: | 622.5mm |
| | | | | 78°: | 629.3mm |
| | | | | 79°: | 636.1mm |
| | | | | 80°: | 642.8mm |
| | | | | 81°: | 649.4mm |
| | | | | 82°: | 656.1mm |
| | | | | 83°: | 662.6mm |
| | | | | 84°: | 669.1mm |
| | | | | 85°: | 675.6mm |
| | | | | 86°: | 682.0mm |
| | | | | 87°: | 688.4mm |
| | | | | 88°: | 694.7mm |
| | | | | 89°: | 700.9mm |
| | | | | 90°: | 707.1mm |

(67.5°: 555.6mm)

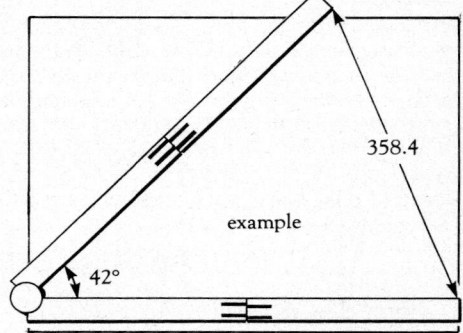

358.4

example

42°

# Starters

## Chris Nussbaum's diary of the London College of Furniture C&G 564 cabinetmaking course

**T**he more difficulty a problem will cause, the more likely it is to arise! This must be the best memorised lesson we have (painfully) learnt on this course.

Lamination, I can assure you, particularly of large pieces, is not as easy as it seems. Solid-chipboard paired moulds are expensive, and involve a great deal of work just to produce a one-off job. I have been laminating the 7ft-long sides of my grandfather clock, but am beginning to wish I had coopered and hand-veneered the thing. Rumour says that the only reason I asked my fellow-students to write about their final pieces is that I have no time myself! This is all slander — but I tend to start my working day earlier and earlier.

Steve writes: 'I began by studying the work of Ambrose Heal and Gordon Russell — furniture which relies on simple construction, straight lines and effective decoration to produce extremely functional and attractive pieces. I wanted to incorporate colour to give visual impact to a relatively simple table. The design section of the course was very short, and did not really cover the practical aspects of design, i.e. the construction of a piece of furniture. The realities became apparent after talking to our workshop tutors: some designs could not be constructed exactly as drawn, and a period of compromise began. My table ended up longer, and with stretchers, but did not lose the colour. I will use water stain on ash veneer for the top and lippings. The rest will be solid ash.

'The link between design and construction on this course has, in fact, been very weak altogether. It is important to be familiar with both aspects when designing and making furniture which is not necessarily traditional or modern, and itself an art form. Unfortunately time dictates only a short appraisal of many facets of cabinetmaking. Too often it is left too late to discover a design fault. However, I am sure we shall all succeed in making something which, a year ago, we would not have thought possible.'

And Johnny: 'I thought of my final piece long before I thought of going to the LCF, but assumed it was a nice idea that would never get off the ground. I envisaged a pillar-like cylinder that opened into two halves to reveal centrally pivoted semi-circular drawers, but I had no idea how to make it! After Christmas, however, I marched into the design studio and drew it up. I needed no advice — it was to be at least 6ft high and as slim as possible. Polite noises were made about ergonomics and tedious technical problems. I nodded in agreement, but my eyes were glazed: I had a vision!

'Then I discovered that the vacuum-bag press used to laminate the main carcase would only accept a maximum of 5½ft. I was devastated, and finally had to start accepting advice. The improved version had a foot lopped off the height, and had grown fatter. The tiny semi-circular drawers, with a 250mm diameter, would have been pretty useless, especially 5ft up in the air! I stopped the drawers at 3ft, and added a shelf, a light and a hole in the top, to enable it to double as a standing lamp. It now began to look quite feasible — except that being so tall and slim made it unstable. I thought of putting a heavy weight in the base, but have now settled for mounting it on a flat plate. Now that I have started to make the wretched thing I have reverted to my original belief — it will never fly.

'Wish me luck!'  ■

# Beam feast

If, like **Mike Rossage**, you have ugly beams spanning your best room, take a good long look at these pages. They show how Mike went about two such jobs — an African-mahogany version for his own house, and one in pine for a friend.

It's a fascinating lesson in the difficult and much-misunderstood science of site fitting; the main thing is first to establish a constant from which you can measure to quirky walls and ceilings. In this case, the bottom panels go in first. If it also looks like a lesson in wood-machining, that's no surprise; in restoring his house Mike is leaving the dining-room till last, because it houses his spindle-moulder, planer/thicknesser, and numerous other pieces of first-class equipment!

The mahogany casing was stained in potassium bichromate, grain-filled, sealed with brown shellac, given three coats of varnish, pumiced and waxed — all before assembly and fixing, leaving only some cleaning up to do in position. ■

● *This section is an assembly of the various methods that Mike used to cover his RSJ and his friend's softwood beam. All the drawings show individual measurements relating to Mike's jobs, but the systems he has used are standard; tongues machined in frame members match grooves in those that sit at right-angles so the adjoining faces come flush. Raised and fielded panels are set in rebates, overlaid with bolection mouldings. The order in which components are put together and put up is crucial; be sure to think several steps ahead if planning a job like this. Decisions at the machining stage affect the whole fitting process*

screw fix

planted bead covers joint

block infill

cut here to depth of bead

## Built-up panel and stile sections — not to scale

upper edge scribed to ceiling

top section of side piece made oversize to allow for scribing

beads cut on spindle

loose tongue

edge jointing machined on overhand planer

loose tongue

loose tongue

bead proud of lower panels

## Construction of box to encase wooden beam

● *The softwood beam casing was made in three sections to cross a 16ft span. The moulding detail at the join of the panels has the same effect as a V-grooved matchboard design, minimising the appearance of any possible shrinkage. All the grooving and rebating was done on the spindle-moulder; allowance in dimensioning the upper pieces for the side panels must be generous, to aid scribing. It pays to spend good time checking the true of the ceiling!*

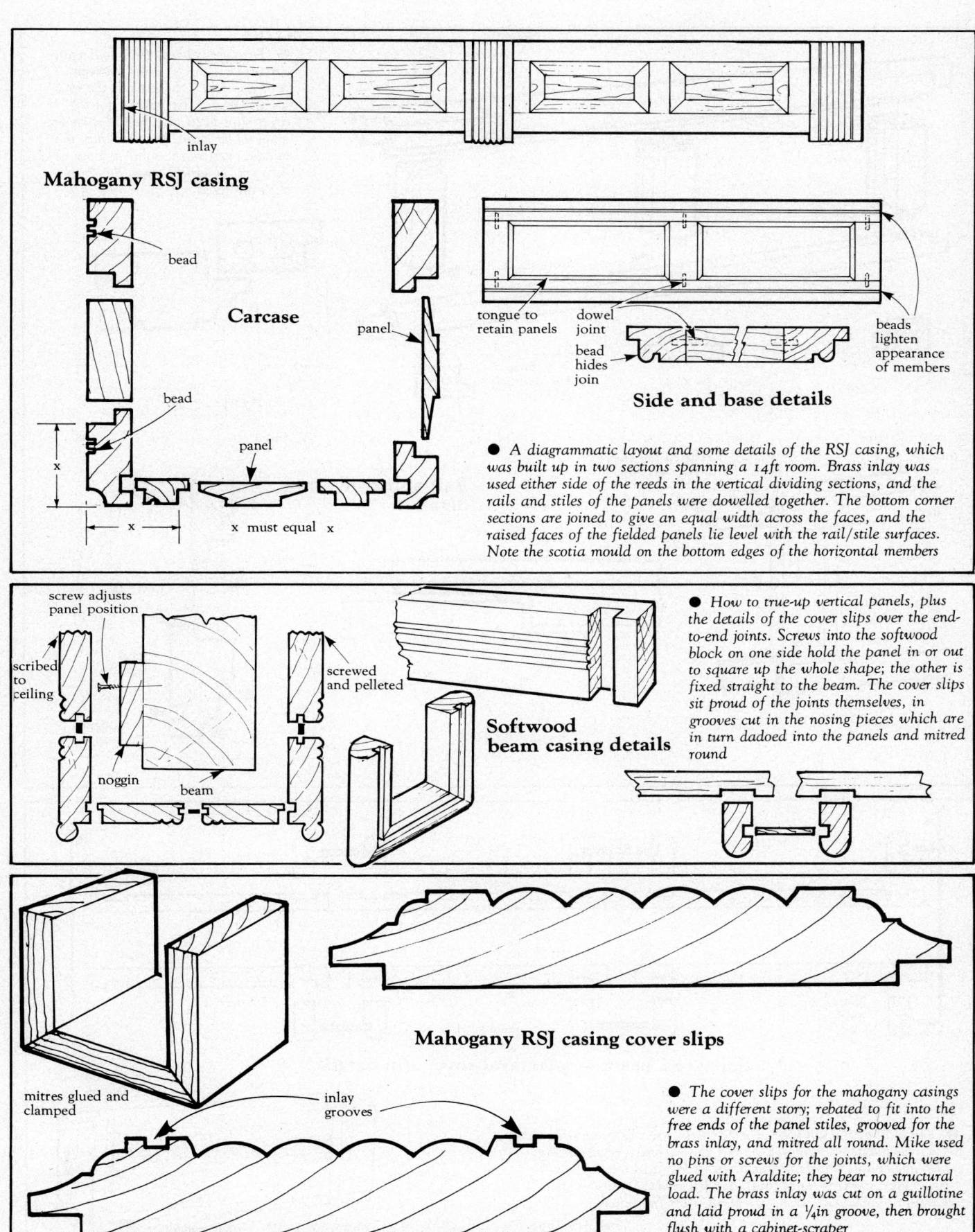

## Mahogany RSJ casing

bead

**Carcase**

panel

bead

panel

x

x

x must equal x

tongue to
retain panels

dowel
joint

bead
hides
join

beads
lighten
appearance
of members

### Side and base details

inlay

● A diagrammatic layout and some details of the RSJ casing, which was built up in two sections spanning a 14ft room. Brass inlay was used either side of the reeds in the vertical dividing sections, and the rails and stiles of the panels were dowelled together. The bottom corner sections are joined to give an equal width across the faces, and the raised faces of the fielded panels lie level with the rail/stile surfaces. Note the scotia mould on the bottom edges of the horizontal members

screw adjusts
panel position

scribed
to
ceiling

noggin

beam

screwed
and pelleted

### Softwood beam casing details

● How to true-up vertical panels, plus the details of the cover slips over the end-to-end joints. Screws into the softwood block on one side hold the panel in or out to square up the whole shape; the other is fixed straight to the beam. The cover slips sit proud of the joints themselves, in grooves cut in the nosing pieces which are in turn dadoed into the panels and mitred round

mitres glued and
clamped

inlay
grooves

### Mahogany RSJ casing cover slips

● The cover slips for the mahogany casings were a different story; rebated to fit into the free ends of the panel stiles, grooved for the brass inlay, and mitred all round. Mike used no pins or screws for the joints, which were glued with Araldite; they bear no structural load. The brass inlay was cut on a guillotine and laid proud in a ¼in groove, then brought flush with a cabinet-scraper

# Beam feast

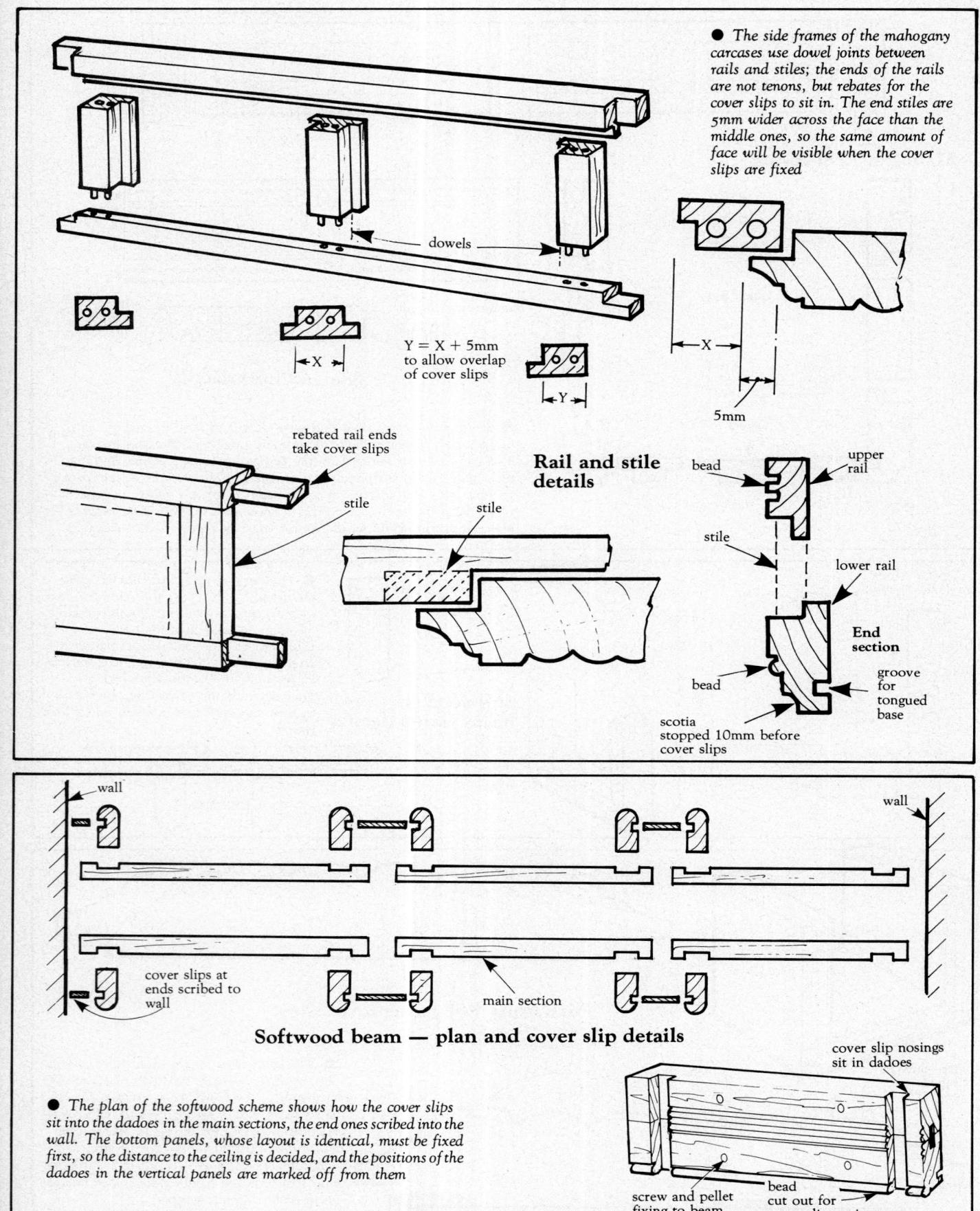

● The side frames of the mahogany carcases use dowel joints between rails and stiles; the ends of the rails are not tenons, but rebates for the cover slips to sit in. The end stiles are 5mm wider across the face than the middle ones, so the same amount of face will be visible when the cover slips are fixed

dowels

Y = X + 5mm
to allow overlap
of cover slips

X

Y

X

5mm

**Rail and stile
details**

rebated rail ends
take cover slips

stile

stile

stile

bead

upper
rail

stile

lower rail

bead

**End
section**

groove
for
tongued
base

scotia
stopped 10mm before
cover slips

wall

wall

cover slips at
ends scribed to
wall

main section

**Softwood beam — plan and cover slip details**

● The plan of the softwood scheme shows how the cover slips sit into the dadoes in the main sections, the end ones scribed into the wall. The bottom panels, whose layout is identical, must be fixed first, so the distance to the ceiling is decided, and the positions of the dadoes in the vertical panels are marked off from them

cover slip nosings
sit in dadoes

screw and pellet
fixing to beam

bead
cut out for
cover slip nosings

## Panel details

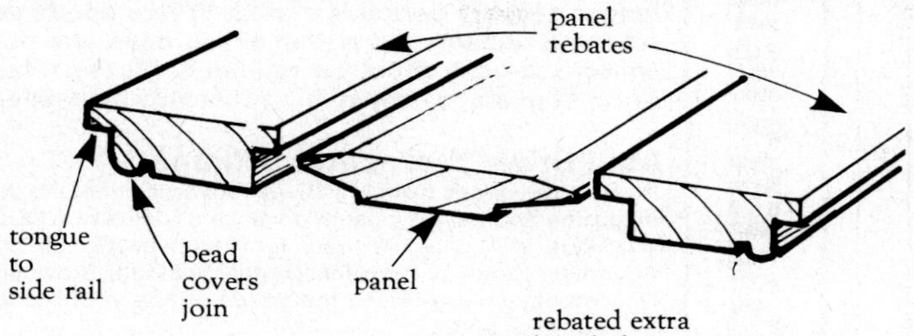

panel rebates

tongue to side rail

bead covers join

panel

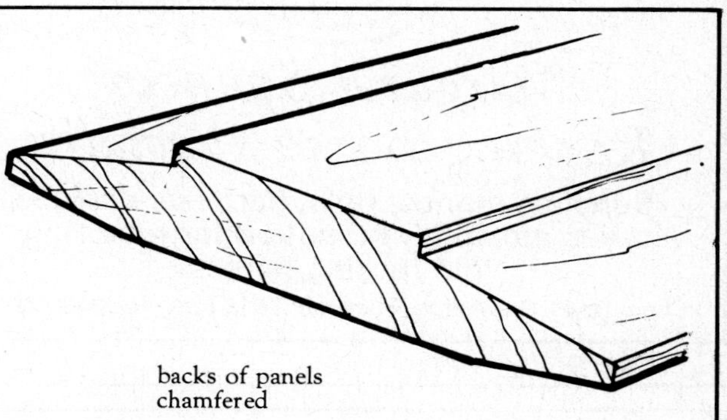

rebated extra length for cover slips

dowels

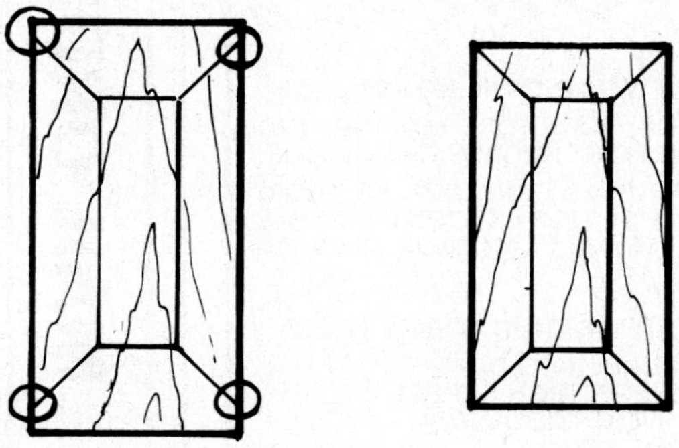

backs of panels chamfered

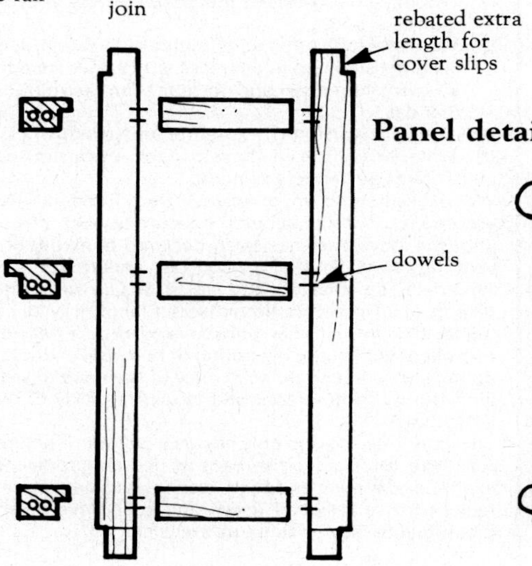

● All the middle joining rails (**far left**) were machined in long lengths to avoid pushing dangerous short pieces through the spindle-moulder; even with expensive Leitz fielding cutters, the diagonals often don't come out right and have to be cleaned up with a scraper

## Bolection moulds

squared stock

first pass

second pass

bandsaw cuts

rebate

● The bolection mouldings were all cut from the right lengths to avoid joins along a panel, machined both sides, cut and rebated. A fine-tooth carbide blade gives a 'guillotine finish'

## Fixing to the RSJ

soldier

middle stile

RSJ

screw

pellet

double thickness of plasterboard

● The middle cover slips were fixed to two carcases, the panels already in place, and the assembly fixed through plasterboard to 'soldiers' opposite the middle stiles.

## Cover slips and adjustment details

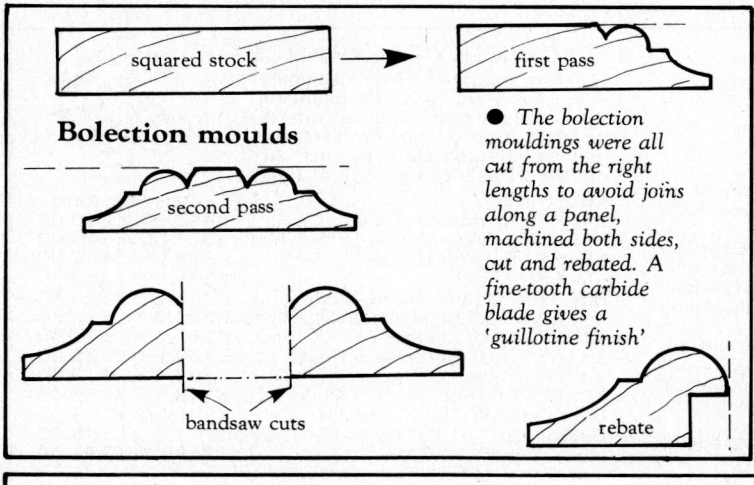

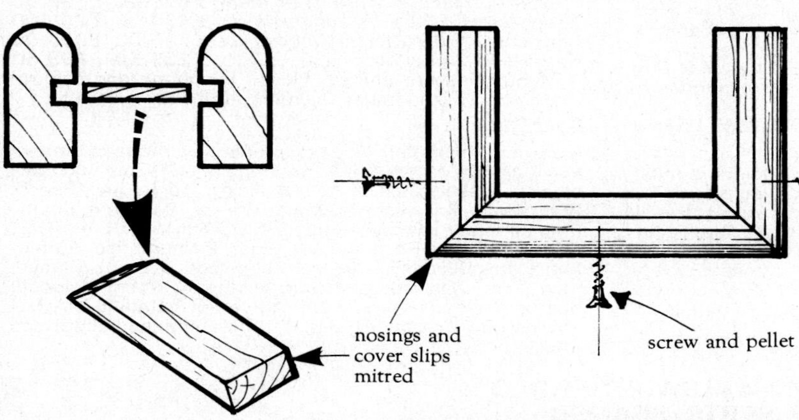

nosings and cover slips mitred

screw and pellet

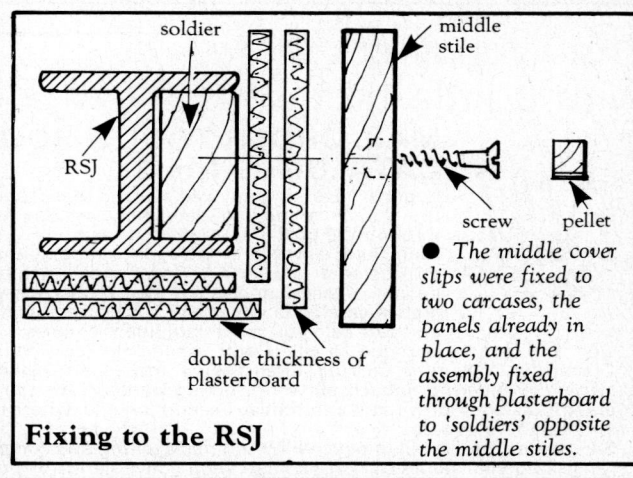

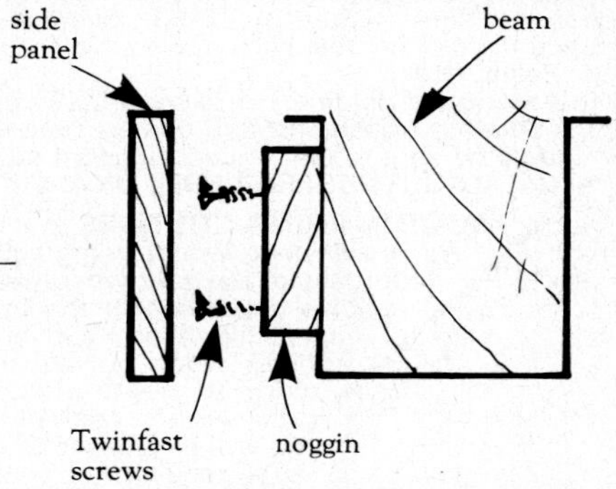

side panel

beam

Twinfast screws

noggin

● Both the nosings and the slips themselves are mitred round the joins between the panel sections. **Right**, details of the square-adjustment method; one turn of the screw gives a very accurately controlled movement either way

## Margaret Spencer
### Rocking horse specialist

Supplies manes, tails, harness, stirrups,
eyes etc and information for restoring
old rocking horses.

Chard Road, Crewkerne, Somerset TA18 8BA, Tel: 0460 72362.

---

## FURNITURE CRAFT

### WOULD YOU LIKE TO BE YOUR OWN BOSS?

WHY NOT SET UP A BUSINESS IN FURNITURE MAKING AND
RESTORATION WITH THE HELP OF WEST BROMWICH COLLEGE.

WE ARE RUNNING A ONE-YEAR FULL-TIME COURSE FROM
SEPTEMBER 1985, COVERING UPHOLSTERY, WOOD FINISHING
AND CABINET MAKING, LEADING TO A CITY AND GUILDS CERTI-
FICATE IN FURNITURE CRAFT.

FURTHER INFORMATION AND APPLICATION FORMS FROM:

MR. H. BIRKETT, ENGINEERING DEPT.
WEST BROMWICH COLLEGE, HIGH STREET,
WEST BROMWICH, WEST MIDLANDS
TEL: 021 569 2326

---

---

# The Woodwork store
# with a little bit more

### MAIL ORDER TOOL & BOOK CATALOGUE No. 3

Roger's have long enjoyed a world wide reputation for
the supply of high quality woodworking hand tools
through the post.
Alan Peter's writes in his book — Cabinetmaking: The
professional approach, "Roger's of Hitchin not only
supply excellent tools, but also produce a very informative catalogue which at £1.50 is very useful reading
and can help you make intelligent choices."
Our 160 page catalogue is filled with handtools for Cabinetmaking,
Carpentry, Coopering, Carving, Chairmaking, Instrument Making, Woodturning, Veneering, indeed all woodworking trades. Each tool is clearly
illustrated together with an informative description and, where necessary,
and outline of it's use.
Send today and our Catalogue will bring this exciting and comprehensive
range into your home so that you can shop conveniently by post.
U.K. Customers send £1.50, Eire IR£3, Outside Europe £3, Outside Europe (with the
exception of North America) £6.50. Overseas Customers may send
remittance in cash in local currency equivalent or in Sterling by Bankers
Draft or Postal Order.
North American Customers may send US$5 by Cash or Cheque to Box
213, Sedona, Arizona, 86336. Please note all other correspondance
should be sent to our United Kingdom address.
CATALOGUE COST REFUNDED ON ALL ORDERS OVER £30, US$50.

### WOODTURNING COURSES
We run daylong woodturning courses for beginners most
Saturdays of the year where we can give you a comprehensive grounding in the art of woodturning. Initial
courses like these can help you make intelligent
choices when buying a lathe and give you the
ability to progress with confidence as a woodturner. The courses cost just £39.50 and we
will be pleased to send you more details on
request.

*Roger's, please send me a copy of your Tool & Book Catalogue No. 3 by return of post.*

*Name* .................................

*address* .................................
.................................

*I enclose* .................................
*in payment* .................................

DEPT. W, 47 WALSWORTH ROAD
HITCHIN, HERTS. SG4 9SU
TEL. (0462) 34177

---

### MACHINERY CLEARANCE

**OPEN 6 DAYS MON.-SAT. FROM JULY 1ST**

Due to overstocking in our machinery
department we have the following
machines for sale. All prices are for
collection from our shop and delivery
will be charged extra at cost. All
quoted prices include V.A.T. at 15%.

| MACHINE | List | Clearance |
|---|---|---|
| Kity 627 Spindle Moulder | £357.00 | £280.00 |
| Kity 7229 Spindle Moulder, Stand, Motor | £561.00 | £448.00 |
| Kity 623 Spindle Moulder | £635.25 | £495.00 |
| Kity 636 Planer | £565.47 | £450.00 |
| Kity 7136 Planer, Stand, Motor | £766.40 | £575.00 |
| Kity K704 Mk1 Combination Machine | £1,322.50 | £1,090 |
| Kity K704 Mk2 Combination Machine | £1,563.00 | £1,190 |
| Kity 699 Dust Extractor & Hoses | £439.95 | £335.00 |
| Kity 700 Table | £93.40 | £70.00 |
| Kity 6863 D/End Motor & Pulleys | £149.60 | £115.00 |
| DeWalt DW30 Dust Extractor | £299.00 | £199.00 |
| DeWalt DW110 10" Radial (Secondhand) | | £195.00 |
| Inca Compact Saw | £369.15 | £295.00 |
| Inca Compact Saw Complete with extension table & morticer (ex-dem) | £529.00 | £395.00 |
| Sheppach HBS32 on Stand (ex-dem) | £439.30 | £295.00 |
| Emcostar 2000 Universal Woodworker | £736.00 | £625.00 |
| Burgess BK3 plus Mk1 | £139.50 | £99.50 |

N.B. Supplies are limited. Please telephone and confirm
reservation of the machine you require.

### TIMBER
Our timber yard carries a comprehensive range of timbers
available in boards, billets, squares, dimensions and bowl
blanks. Timbers include Acacia, Anjan, Apple, Ash, Beech,
Blackwood, Boxwood, Bubinga, Cherry, Cocobolo, Ebony,
Elm, Elm Burr, Hyedua, Kingwood, Lignum Vitae, Lime, Oak,
Olivewood, Pao Rosa, Padauk, Pear, Pernambuco, Purpleheart, Rosewood, Sycamore, Tulipwood, Walnut, Wenge,
Yew. Come and browse at your leisure all timber including
boards is clearly marked with the price including V.A.T. If
you require a price list please send a stamped addressed
envelope.

# Roger's
## The friendly store

538

# Buying timber wisely:2

**Alan Thomas continues his major series with a good look at hardwoods — the serious craftsman's staple**

Unlike the softwood family, where a handful of species with similar appearances and working characteristics supply virtually all our wants, the hardwoods sold in Britain display great variety. But not all are readily available in quantity, and even those are all expensive by the standards of craftsmen in home and small workshops.

If that is the bad news, the good tidings are that hardwoods offered for sale are usually of sound quality, and are unlikely to contain nasty surprises.

The days are gone when huge logs of Honduras mahogany were imported into the UK before conversion for the delectation of Chippendale, Hepplewhite, and even Waring & Gillow, and their clients. Modern supplies are of material suited to mass-production machining, and often land already cut into boards and wrapped in polythene.

The woods have changed too. Teak still comes from Burma, but Brazil is now the main source of timber labelled mahogany. Another bearing the mahogany name originates in the Philippines. West African states supply their own mahogany, plus afrormosia, iroko, utile, sapele, and also samba, which equates to the obeche we used to buy. Quantity supplies of oak and ash probably come from America; Japanese oak, a nice wood to work, is too expensive to import in quantity.

Then there are south American greenheart, Malayan keruing, west African opepe, and Australian jarrah. These are imported for such purposes as wharf piling, floors in lorries, and railway sleepers: only the brave would try to use them for ordinary bench work — they are too coarse, too hard and too tough. If any oddments came to hand, though, it might be interesting to try them on a lathe, where cutting edges can be restored quickly.

Most of the hardwood imported into Britain comes from virgin forests, although in many cases the prime trees went 15 or 20 years ago and it is the second or even third choice material that is being cut now. If that sounds a bit gloomy (and west African quality has dropped somewhat in recent years), it is comforting to learn that replanting is taking place almost everywhere, so there is a fair chance that commercially valuable species, at least, will continue to be available.

Provided, of course, that political and economic conditions allow. Our present sources of supply are not among the most stable places in the world. In addition, violent fluctuations in international exchange rates can do horrid things to forward buying and selling prices.

British importers almost invariably buy through agents, middlemen who know what materials shippers are bringing forward and who can also make a pretty good guess at what end-users are going to want. Typically, two to four months elapse between ordering and arrival.

There are some distinct advantages in importing the timber ready-milled: not only is the valueless outer waste one expects to come from a large tree left behind instead of being shipped here at great cost, but the often decaying heart found in large trees of uncertain age won't have to be paid for either. Another bonus is that wood can be graded to standards by the shipper: therefore agents and importers know what they are buying.

Lumber is bought by the cubic metre of specified thicknesses, and most parcels comprise random-sized boards with a fair selection of dimensions. Individual pieces will be at least 6ft long and 6in wide, but the average is probably nearer to 9 or 10ft long by 9 or 10in wide. At the top end, pieces go up to 20ft by 20in, and Brazilian mahogany can reach widths of 32in.

Teak, however, is so costly that wise importers buy the sizes they know they can sell readily, even down to specifying 2 x ¾in strips. (Why would anyone want to ship quantities of 2x¾in halfway round the world? Just think of all that teak garden furniture!) Generally there are no supply shortages among the popular hardwoods.

Incidentally, a great deal of the Philippines 'mahogany' comes here as ready-to-use finished joinery — typically, those cupboard doors in a pale purple wood that are stocked by giant do-it-yourself warehouses.

Currently the big sellers in Britain are beech and Brazilian mahogany, the latter aided no doubt by its popularity with suppliers of replacement double-glazing systems. Oak and ash are both coming into fashion again, but elm seems sadly to have run its course. What remains is probably earmarked for the construction industry, although some nice parcels for furniture-making are known to be tucked away up and down the country. Elm could come from Japan but, like Japanese oak, it would not be worth the trouble commercially.

Until about 20 years ago hardwoods were air-dried in stick in the time-honoured way, but few importers can afford to do that now. In self-defence the trade insists that kilned timber is just as good anyway — if kilning is done properly. Increasingly lumber is dried in its country of origin and wrapped for protection against damp while on its travels. Otherwise the wood is brought here 'shipping-dry' — that is wet, by end-user standards — for kilning by the importer. When it is done here, they say, results are always very good.

Kilning brings the moisture content down to about 12½-15%, which is fine for storage, and big joinery manufacturers use the wood at that level. For domestic use the recommendation must again be to store rough-cut material for as long as possible — at least a fortnight — in the atmosphere in which the finished product is going to live.

For customers buying in small quantities the advice is — find a yard willing to deal in small quantities! And choose pieces of wood that you like the look of: by this stage in the marketing cycle your opinion will be as good as that of anyone else. The price will not be low, because retailers must put a mark-up on the prices they pay to importers, and not many importers are willing to take orders for small quantities. Averages don't mean much here, but it can be assumed that hardwoods are going to cost between two and four times more than good-quality softwood.

When hunting out a retail supplier, bear in mind that often a yard concentrates on one range of prices: it may prefer to hold all top-quality, or middling, or — well, the rest. It should all be good stuff, but some stocks will certainly be noticeably better than others. The only real imponderable is moisture content, but again it is a fair assumption that material would not be in stock if it weren't fit for use.

In any case, a user who wants maximum value for his money really must take the trouble to work out a detailed cutting list. It is particularly important to settle the minimum cross-sectional dimensions. If the job calls for four pieces of 2x4in, 4ft long, ask for just that. Don't be tempted to 'help' the merchant by ordering one piece 8ft long of 2x8in: do so and you will certainly be helping him — but not in the way you meant to.

The total hardwood trade constitutes no more, probably, than 10% of the British timber-supply industry — and is itself almost entirely preoccupied with the relatively few 'commercial' woods: the ones that are handled in quantity. But a considerable variety of woods (apart from the home-grown ones) are also imported. Stock lines include rosewood, ebony, laurel, cedar of Lebanon, African blackwood, acacia, hornbeam, kingwood, and even such apparently native species as pear and apple. But the available quantities are usually limited, too much so to interest big importers, so supplies are not cheap.

The position is further complicated in the case of some rare woods, by governments in the growing countries, who are well aware of the value of what they have got, and are inclined to control prices by controlling supplies.

Finally, the more immediate problem of finding any good quality timber that is for sale in Britain can in large part be overcome by studying the small ads in *Woodworker*. But in future issues we intend to visit some typical retail hardwood suppliers, talk about their stocks, say what's available, and give useful alternatives to scarce or over-expensive species. If you can help — as a buyer or seller — we'd like to hear from you. ∎

# Guild notes_____

## Guild of WOODWORKERS

Shared information, advice and help are vital to good woodwork. They are also the basis of the **Guild of Woodworkers**: an international organisation which welcomes new members — whatever their skills. 1 Golden Sq, London W1R 3AB, tel. 01-437 0626.

Guild members get
- priority on our courses
- free publicity in *Woodworker*
- 15% off Woodworker Show entry
- a free display area and meeting-point at the Show
- 15% discount on our plans
- access to and inclusion in our register of members' skills and services
- the chance to contact other members for help and advice where appropriate
- specially arranged tool insurance at low rates

Please quote your Guild number when contacting us.

*Aidan Walker*

## Wandering members

On the odd occasion, a subscription-renewal reminder comes back to us with the cryptic inscription 'Gone away'. When you change your address, remember the Guild wants to know where you are — if your subscription isn't paid, obviously your membership will lapse.

## London Gallery

Another Woodworker Show reminder; there is space at the Alexandra Pavilion on 24-7 October, ready and waiting for any member with work to exhibit. We'd like to make this a regular feature of the Show — and it is potentially very good publicity for the Guild itself, as well as the obvious benefits for you, the individual. We can't accommodate too many pieces, and we can't accommodate big ones, but we'd like to get a representative spread of work, so write in and send photos of what you do. That's all there is to it — nothing to pay except your yearly subscription! It's first come, first served, so don't put it off any longer; these things take time to set up.

## Future plans

This current spate of summer courses will soon be through, and then we concentrate on the Show again — but we are now planning the autumn schedule. Another cry for member feedback goes out: please let me know if you have a burning desire to learn chair-caning or upholstery, steel-square roofing or secret-mitre dovetailing. Or anything else that comes under the encyclopaedic heading of woodworking, come to that. Every course we arrange is a cliffhanger (unless it is already tried and tested), because we arrange the tutor and the venue, finalise the details of the programme, advertise it, and then sit and hope for the bookings. Make our life a lot easier and yours more educational: write and let us know what courses the Guild should be running for you.

## Local reps

*Pour encourager* whatever others there might be . . . the latest member who wants to meet, talk with and pick the brains of other like-minded folk in his area is C. J. Allen, 3 Oakhurst Close, Hastings, E. Sussex TN34 2SE. Get in touch with him if you are keen to meet your co-members in the Hastings area.

# Guild cours

## Please note!

Occasional misunderstandings arise about the booking system for the Guild's courses. Guild members get priority, but non-members are welcome to apply on a first-refusal basis; the only sure way of booking a place is to *send in your cheque for the full amount when you first apply.*

We don't invest your money in the interim and pocket the profits — this is the most efficient and least time-consuming way of making definite bookings. We hold the cheques in the office until the course is over, which means that, if by some mischance you are unable to attend, there is no delay and no problem in refunding your money. When the course is fully booked, we confirm your place and send you all the details of times, places, bed-and-breakfast, schedule and anything else relevant. That's the business.

## Woodmachining — Ken Taylor

6 July, Milton Keynes, £25+VAT. Ken's experience is massive in this popular field — he is ex-works manager of Wrighton Kitchens, and teaches the subject part-time at the London College of Furniture. A solid introduction to the basic machines and techniques, which will equip you to buy and use the right gear in the right way. Apart from circular saws, bandsaws, planer/thicknessers and spindle-moulders, universal machines will be dealt with. Plus of course, all aspects of safety!

## Finishing and polishing — Ian Hosker

This course, I am happy to say, booked up quite quickly, which just shows that northern woodworkers are as thirsty for knowledge as any. It is full, but we shall be arranging another one with Ian in the autumn, so don't despair. Both this and **Charles Cliffe's** finishing and polishing courses are centred on french polishing, with the necessary adjuncts of preparation and staining.

## *'Fine Craft and Fine Design'*

- \* Seminars and courses
- \* Comprehensive tool insurance
- \* Central skills register
- \* Information and advice
- \* Show entry discounts

Professional and amateur

Write for application forms to: Guild of Woodworkers, 1 Golden Sq. London W1R 3AB

## Special toolmaking — Fred Lambert

15-19 July, Tewkesbury, Glos, £145+VAT. Fred is the acknowledged national authority on the making of country furniture, using steam-bending techniques, and special tools not available on the retail market. If you are serious about making Windsor chairs to any of Fred's numerous designs — or your own variations — you need these tools, and you don't need metalworking skills to make them. The elegant surroundings of Pull Court, the mansion that houses Bredon School (whose workshops the course uses), are an added bonus to a hard-working but productive week.

## Cabinetmaker's decorative techniques — Bob Grant

20 July, St Augustine's School, Oxford, £27.50+VAT. An advanced treatment of the traditional decorative hand-tool techniques such as curved inlay lines, making and setting in motifs, sand-shading and decorative chamfering. For the slightly more experienced; if you have a scratch-stock of your own, bring it along.

## Hand-veneering — Bob Grant

14 September, St Augustine's School, Oxford, £30+VAT. An attempt to meet the oft-voiced demand for an introduction to laying veneers by hand, using scotch glue and hammer. Few readers have huge presses or indeed want to learn how to use them, but many want to master the process of cutting, matching and successfully laying comparatively small leaves. Bob is your man; Peter Sarac, a local harpsichord-maker, will also be on hand with tips and advice. Bring (small!) pieces of your own to get some advice, and perhaps do some work on them while you're there.

## Furniture restoration and repair — Eric Burger

25-26 July, Bournemouth, £40+VAT. Eric himself writes: 'I have worked for 25 years in this trade, experiencing all its aspects on some of the finest pieces of antique furniture in the country. It is now possible to look after your antiques in the most professional way — the correct way. Central heating has proved to be a killer of antiques; wood warps, veneers come loose, tabletops crack in half with a sound like a shotgun — all because of lack of moisture in the air. I'd like to feel that those of us who are lucky enough to have antiques can be sure that future generations will enjoy them as much as we do — and restored antiques, of course, are worth much more!

Eric will be introducing veneering, inlaying, marquetry repairs, tool sharpening and maintenance, french polishing, gilding, even carving and upholstery if there's time.

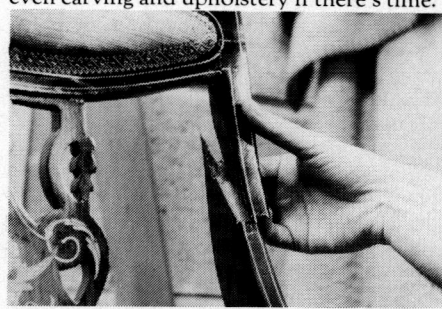

● *No need for broken hearts over broken parts – Eric Burger provides the solution*

## French polishing — Charles Cliffe

10-11 October, Bexleyheath, £40 inc. VAT. Numerous inquiries and the odd trace of confusion lead us to emphasise that Charles' courses, like Ian Hosker's in Cheshire, are specifically staining, preparation and french polishing. Mention is, however, made of other finishes.

---

# CLASSIFIED COUPON

FROM _____

_____

I enclose remittance to the value of _____

to cover _____ inset or retain.

Send to: Woodworker Classified, Dept. 1, Golden Square, London W1 3AB. Rates 35p per word (minimum £5.25), semi-displayed £7.25 (minimum 2.5cm).

| | | | |
|---|---|---|---|
| | | | |
| | | | |
| | | | |
| | | | |
| | | | |
| | | | |

# Books

*Fred Sherlock*
**A-Z Guide to Home Woodworking**
*Constable, £6.95 hardback*
*Reviewed by Peter Anstey*

While acknowledging the author's authority, I have to confess that I find the format and editorial approach of this book at best unsatisfactory.

Its alphabetical, 'potted' treatment of a subject as large and as specialised as woodworking falls into a trap: it is neither all things to all men, nor does it meet the needs of one particular group. It is never clear whether the target reader is a complete moron who does not even know the meaning of basic terms (garden gates, for example, are 'to close an entrance', while a chuck is 'the part of a hand brace, wheel brace or electric drill that holds the bit or drill'), or someone who can cope with quite specialist work needing a lot of technique and experience.

The book's subject treatment according to alphabetical headlines seems to me arbitrary and confusing. I would have thought the whole theme better tackled within a more homogeneous framework, for example, by techniques, tools, etc., rather than by a hodge-podge of disparate main headlines which places 'Removing nails' adjacent to 'Repairs — carpentry'. The method used calls for sub-headings which frequently extend over many pages and make it more difficult for the reader to find quickly the particular information he may be seeking. At the same time, I find the introduction of specific woodworking projects tiresomely inappropriate — while the overlapping of the woodworking theme into the area of house-building adds a further confusing element to the editorial scheme.

I have to add that the book does contain a wealth of useful and practical information which — provided that it can be found! — will no doubt assure it a place on library bookshelves and on those of woodworking *aficionados*.

*Phil Reardon*
**The Woodturner's Pocket Book**
*John Boddy Timber Ltd, Riverside Sawmills, Boroughbridge, N. Yorks YO5 9LJ, £5 incl. p&p, paperback*
*Reviewed by Gordon Stokes*

The growth of woodturning as a leisure craft has produced the inevitable crop of books. Some are very worthwhile; others are misleading, and unlikely to help beginners in making real progress. Some, indeed, seem to be no more than a *pot-pourri* of rehashed information from other books.

In my view, Phil Reardon's little gem is better value by far than numerous publications costing more than twice as much. To anyone who thoroughly understands the craft it is obvious that the author knows his woodturning; even more importantly, he is able to explain the fundamentals in a clear and straightforward manner for the novice. He does not make the all-too-common mistake of patronising his readers — he keeps to the point; and the

book owes no small amount of its charm to the excellent little humorous sketches provided by his wife.

This is a small book, and it does not set out to teach woodturning. It is, however, the best approach I have seen to an explanation of what is involved in taking up the craft. The light-hearted and at times jocular style may irritate a few readers, but woodturning is good fun for the hobbyist, and I felt that Phil had struck just the right note — midway between jollity and pomposity.

The reader is taken through discussions of design, setting up with a lathe and tools, sharpening methods (giving an account with which, for once, I was able to agree entirely), individual turning tools and how to use them, and much more. Phil Reardon has covered a lot of ground in a small book, and he has done his job well. I strongly recommend the result to all beginners. At its price it is an excellent investment.

*Elizabeth and Robert Williams*
**Building with Salvaged Lumber**
*Tab Books, $10.25 paperback*
*Reviewed by David Savage*

As the title suggests, this is an American book, and its value will be immediately apparent to anyone who has driven through small-town USA. There the urban landscape is filled with often decaying or derelict timber houses. Many have been restored as examples of period architecture, but most have been left to the termites, the wreckage crew — and the salvage enthusiast.

This book explains in sometimes painful detail how to take apart a house and re-use often valuable timber. It strikes a sympathetic chord in describing people avoiding mortgage repayments entirely by building houses for themselves from materials acquired for next to nothing. Unfortunately, however, its main market will be restricted to those countries, unlike Britain, that have similar timber buildings.

For UK readers, the most useful part of the book covers using the chainsaw, where techniques are discussed for low-cost one-man timber milling. Construction projects are also detailed for all aspects of home-building, and the photographs show fascinating modern homes, furniture and fittings, designed and built by people with considerable character and individuality.

It is heartwarming to find the pioneer cheapskate is alive and well in the US of A!

*John Seymour*
**The Forgotten Arts**
*Dorling Kindersley/National Trust, £9.95 hardback*
*Reviewed by Peter Collenette*

With its good paper cleverly printed to resemble a heavy, yellowing stock of greater age and even higher quality, its meticulously old-fashioned typography, its woodcut illustrations, its 'black-and-white' photos tinted brown (and in many cases deliberately faded away at the edges), this

masterpiece of book design falls headlong into some deep ironies of 1980s culture.

It appeals, of course, to nostalgia for bygone ways of life, despite the fact that its readers have never experienced those ways — and it appeals to the notion, if not the reality, of at least dabbling in a few of the crafts that supported them. The irony lies in the fact that such completely practical skills should receive such highly wrought and sentimental presentation.

That said (as it must be), John Seymour writes compellingly, in a style that is attractively plain and even racy. The information, though limited, is nonetheless extremely pithy, full of anecdote, clear and very well presented. If you're prepared to put up with two pages on oak-basket-making, two pages on boot- and shoemaking, a page on 'cotton crafts' and seven pages on boatbuilding (among a total of 61 subjects), step right in. Covered are woodland crafts (e.g. rake-making, clog-sole cutting), building crafts, 'crafts of the field', workshop crafts (e.g. coopering, sailmaking, potting), and 'textiles and homecrafts'.

It's not a woodworker's book, a potter's book, a weaver's book, or indeed a book for anyone who knows much already. It won't suffice if you actually want to start practising a craft. Moreover, it's easy to snigger as John Seymour pronounces: 'It was in search of wholeness that this book was written.' But, for all that, it's enjoyable.

*John Sainsbury*
**Planecraft**
*Guild of Master Craftsmen Publications, paperback*
*Reviewed by Roger Buse*

The preface to this book informs the reader that it is largely a re-write of *Planecraft* by Charles Hampton and E. Clifford, first published in 1934. Although it contains a large amount of material from the original, John Sainsbury has done a considerable amount of work to bring it up to date.

The history of planes is covered extensively, together with the lineage and development of the metal plane through Bailey, Warren and Traut. The development of infill planes of exceptional quality by Spears and Norris in the mid-19th century, together with their modern imitators, is fully documented.

The book covers every aspect of 'planecraft' from blade sharpening and adjusting to techniques of use, and every type of plane from bench plane to multiplane. I found the chapter on the multiplane most informative for its clear illustration of how to use this potentially difficult tool. An interesting item mentioned in the section on bench planes is the Stayset cap-iron, developed by Record but unfortunately now a thing of the past — discarded in the interests of economy.

This is altogether a thoroughly enjoyable and informative book which will delight any dedicated woodworker who enjoys using hand tools — a real credit to its authors both past and present.

# shop guide

## AVON

**BATH**    Tel. Bath 64513
JOHN HALL TOOLS   ★
RAILWAY STREET

Open: Monday-Saturday
9.00 a.m.-5.30 p.m.
H.P.W.WM.D.A.BC.

**BRISTOL**   Tel. (0272) 741510
JOHN HALL TOOLS LIMITED   ★
CLIFTON DOWN SHOPPING CENTRE
WHITELADIES ROAD
Open: Monday-Saturday
9.00 a.m.-5.30 p.m.
H.P.W.WM.D.A.BC.

**BRISTOL**   Tel. (0272) 629092
TRYMWOOD SERVICES
2a DOWNS PARK EAST, (off North View)
WESTBURY PARK
Open: 8.30 a.m.-5.30 p.m. Mon. to Fri.
Closed for lunch 1.00-2.00 p.m.
P.W.WM.D.T.A.BC.

**BRISTOL**   Tel. (0272) 667013
WILLIS
157 WEST STREET
BEDMINISTER
Open Mon.-Fri. 8.30 a.m.-5.00 p.m.
No Saturday opening

## BEDFORDSHIRE

**BEDFORD**   Tel. (0234) 59808
BEDFORD SAW SERVICE   K
39 AMPTHILL ROAD

Open: Mon.-Fri. 8.30-5.30
Sat. 9.00-4.00
H.P.A.BC.W.CS.WM.D.

## BERKSHIRE

**COOKHAM**   Tel. (06285) 20350
CHURCH'S TIMBER
STATION HILL

Open: Mon-Sat 8.30 a.m.-5.30 p.m.
Wed 8.30 a.m.-1.00 p.m.
H.P.W.T.CS.MF.A.

**HIGH WYCOMBE**   Tel. (0494)
ISAAC LORD LTD   22221
185 DESBOROUGH ROAD   KE

Open: Mon-Fri 8.00 a.m.-5.00 p.m.
Saturday 9.00 a.m.-5.00 p.m.
H.P.W.D.A.

**READING**   Tel. (0734) 591361
HOME CARE CENTRE
26/30 KING'S ROAD

Open: Monday-Saturday
9.00 a.m.-5.30 p.m.
H.P.W.D.A.WM.BC.

**READING**   Tel. Littlewick Green
DAVID HUNT (TOOL   2743
MERCHANTS) LTD   ★
KNOWL HILL, NR. READING
Open: Monday-Saturday
9.00 a.m.-5.30 p.m.
H.P.W.D.A.BC.

**READING**   Tel. Reading 661511
WOKINGHAM TOOL CO. LTD.
99 WOKINGHAM ROAD

Open: Mon-Sat 9.00 a.m.-5.30 p.m.
Closed 1.00-2.00 p.m. for lunch
H.P.W.WM.D.CS.A.BC.

## BUCKINGHAMSHIRE

**SLOUGH**   Tel. (06286) 5125
BRAYWOOD ESTATES LTD   ★
158 BURNHAM LANE

Open: 9.00 a.m.-5.30 p.m.
Monday-Saturday
H.P.W.WM.CS.A.

**MILTON KEYNES**   Tel. (0908)
POLLARD WOODWORKING   641366
CENTRE   ★
51 AYLESBURY ST., BLETCHLEY
Open: Mon-Fri 8.30-5.30
Saturday 9.00-5.00
H.P.W.WM.D.CS.A.BC.

**HIGH WYCOMBE**   Tel. (0494)
SCOTT SAWS LTD.   24201/33788
14 BRIDGE STREET   ★

Mon.-Sat. 8.30 a.m.-6.00 p.m.

H.P.W.WM.D.T.CS.MF.A.BC.

## CAMBRIDGESHIRE

**CAMBRIDGE**   Tel. (0223) 63132
D. MACKAY LTD.   E★
BRITANNIA WORKS, EAST ROAD

Open: Mon.-Fri. 8.30 a.m.-1 p.m./2.00-
5.00 p.m. Sat. 8.30 a.m.-1.00 p.m.
H.P.W.D.T.CS.MF.A.BC.

**CAMBRIDGE**   Tel. (0223) 247386
H. B. WOODWORKING   K
105 CHERRY HINTON ROAD
Open: 8.30 a.m.-5.30 p.m.
Monday-Friday
8.30 a.m.-1.00 p.m. Sat.
H.P.W.WM.D.CS.A.

## CHESHIRE

**NANTWICH**   Tel. Crewe 67010
ALAN HOLTHAM   K★
THE OLD STORES TURNERY
WISTASON ROAD, WILLASTON
Open: Tues.-Sat. 9.00 a.m.-5.30 p.m.
Closed Monday
P.W.WM.D.T.C.CS.A.BC.

## CLEVELAND

**MIDDLESBROUGH**   Tel. (0642)
CLEVELAND WOODCRAFT   813103
(M'BRO), 38-42 CRESCENT ROAD   K

Open: Mon-Sat 9.15 a.m.-5.30 p.m.

H.P.T.A.BC.W.WM.CS.D.

## CORNWALL

**HELSTON**   Tel. Helston (03265) 4961
SOUTH WEST   Truro (0872) 71671
POWER TOOLS   Launceston
MONUMENT ROAD   (0566) 3555
  K
H.P.W.WM.D.CS.A.

**TRURO**   Tel. (0872) 71671
TRURO POWER TOOLS   E★
30 FERRIS TOWN

Open Mon.-Sat. 8.00 a.m.-12.30 p.m./
1.30 p.m.-5.00 p.m.
H.P.W.WM.D.CS.MF.A.BC.

## DERBYSHIRE

**DERBY**   Tel. (0332) 41862
HAZLEHURSTS LTD.   E★
LONDON ROAD AND CANAL STREET

Open: Mon.-Sat. 8.30 a.m.-5.30 p.m. (retail)
Mon.-Fri. 8.00 a.m.-5.00 p.m. (trade)
H.P.W.MF.A.BC.

**BUXTON**   Tel. (0298) 871636
CRAFT SUPPLIES   K★
THE MILL, MILLERSDALE

Open: Mon-Sat 9.00 a.m.-5.00 p.m.

H.P.W.D.T.CS.A.BC.

## DEVON

**BRIXHAM**   Tel. (08045) 4900
WOODCRAFT SUPPLIES   E★
4 HORSE POOL STREET

Open: Mon.-Sat. 9.00 a.m.-6.00 p.m.

H.P.W.A.D.MF.CS.BC.

**PLYMOUTH**   Tel. (0752) 330303
WESTWARD BUILDING SERVICES   ★
LTD., LISTER CLOSE, NEWNHAM
INDUSTRIAL ESTATE, PLYMPTON
Open: Mon-Fri 8.00 a.m.-5.30 p.m.
Sat. 8.30 a.m.-12.30 p.m.
H.P.W.WM.D.A.BC.

## ESSEX

**LEIGH ON SEA**   Tel. (0702)
MARSHAL & PARSONS LTD.   7.0404
1111 LONDON ROAD   EK

Open: 8.30 a.m.-5.30 p.m. Mon-Fri
9.00 a.m.-5.00 p.m. Sat.
H.P.W.WM.D.CS.A.

**ILFORD**   
CUTWELL TOOLS LTD.   ★
774-776 HIGH ROAD

Mon.-Fri. 9.00 a.m.-5.00 p.m.
and also by appointment.
P.W.WM.A.D.CS.

**SOUTHAMPTON**   Tel. (0703)
H.W.M.   776222
THE WOODWORKERS
303 SHIRLEY ROAD, SHIRLEY
Open: Tues-Fri 9.30 a.m.-6.00 p.m.
Sat 9.30 a.m.-4.00 p.m.
H.P.W.WM.D.CS.A.BC.T.

**ALDERSHOT**   Tel. (0252) 334422
POWER TOOL CENTRE   K★
374 HIGH STREET
Open Mon-Fri 8.30 a.m.-5.30 p.m.
Sat 8.30 a.m.-4.00 p.m.

H.P.W.WM.D.A.BC.CF.MF.

**SOUTHAMPTON**   Tel. (0703)
POWER TOOL CENTRE   332288
7 BELVIDERE ROAD   K★
Open Mon.-Fri. 8.30-5.30

H.P.W.WM.D.A.BC.CS.MF.

**KEY: CS CUTTING OR SHARPENING SERVICES**

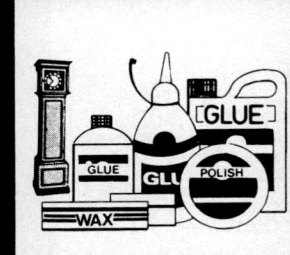
**KEY: MF MATERIAL FINISHES**

**KEY: BC BOOKS/CATALOGUES**

# shopguide

KEY·H HANDTOOLS

KEY·MF MATERIAL FINISHES

KEY·P POWER TOOLS

# shopguide

**SWAFFHAM** Tel: (0760) 23073
TONY WADDILOVE, ★
STATION HOUSE,
LITTLE DUNHAM, KINGS LYNN
Tuesday-Saturday 9.00 a.m.-6.00 p.m.

H.P.W.D.T.CS.A.BC.

## TYNE & WEAR

**NEWCASTLE UPON TYNE** Tel.
J. W. HOYLE LTD. (0632) 617474
CLARENCE STREET NE2 1YJ K★
Open: Mon-Fri 8.00 a.m.-5.00 p.m.
Saturday 9.00 a.m.-4.30 p.m.

H.P.A.BC.W.CS.WM.D.

**CLECKHEATON** Tel. (0274)
SKILLED CRAFTS LTD. 872861
34 BRADFORD ROAD ★

Open: 9.00 a.m.-5.00 p.m. Monday
Saturday Lunch 12.00 a.m.-1.00 p.m.
H.P.A.W.CS.WM.D.

## WALES

**CARDIFF** Tel. (0222) 595710
DATAPOWER TOOLS LTD,
MICHAELSTON ROAD,
CULVERHOUSE CROSS
Open: Mon.-Fri. 8.00 a.m.-5.00 p.m.
Sat. 9.00 a.m.-1.00 p.m.

H.P.W.WM.D.A.

**GT. YARMOUTH** Tel. (0493)
ANGLIA POWER TOOLS 850388
3 DENESIDE, NR30 2HL

Open: Monday to Saturday
8.30 a.m. 5.30 p.m.
H.P.W.D.CS.A.

**NEWCASTLE** Tel. (0632) 320311
HENRY OSBOURNE LTD. E★
50-54 UNION STREET

Open: Mon-Fri 8.30 a.m.-5.00 p.m.

H.P.W.D.CS.MF.A.BC.

**LEEDS** Tel. (0532) 790507
GEORGE SPENCE & SONS LTD.
WELLINGTON ROAD
Open: Monday to Friday
8.30 a.m.-5.30 p.m.
Saturday 9.00 a.m.-5.00 p.m.
H.P.W.WM.D.T.A.

**CARMARTHEN** Tel. (0267) 237219
DO-IT-YOURSELF SUPPLY K
BLUE STREET, DYFED
Open: Monday to Saturday
9.00 a.m.-5.30 p.m.
Thursday 9.00 a.m.-5.30 p.m.
H.P.W.WM.D.T.CS.A.BC.

## NOTTINGHAMSHIRE WEST MIDLANDS

**NOTTINGHAM** Tel. (0602) 225979
POOLEWOOD and 227064/5
EQUIPMENT LTD. (06077) 2421 after hrs
5a HOLLY LANE, CHILLWELL
Open: Mon-Fri 9.00 a.m.-5.30 p.m.
Sat. 9.00 a.m. to 12.30 p.m.
P.W.WM.D.CS.A.BC.

**BIRMINGHAM** Tel. (021-554) 5177
ROTAGRIP E★
16 LODGE ROAD, HOCKLEY
Open: Mon.-Fri. 9.00 a.m.-5.00 p.m.
Sat. 9.00 a.m.-12.00 p.m.

H.P.W.CS.A.BC.T.MF.

## SCOTLAND

**EDINBURGH** Tel. (031 337) 5555
THE SAW CENTRE ★
38 HAYMARKET TERRACE
HAYMARKET
Open: 8.30 a.m.-5.30 p.m.
Monday-Saturday
H.P.W.WM.D.CS.A.

**CARDIFF** Tel. (0222) 396039
JOHN HALL TOOLS LIMITED ★
CENTRAL SQUARE

Open: Monday to Saturday
9.00 a.m.-5.30 p.m.
H.P.W.WM.D.A.BC.

**WITNEY** Tel. (0993) 3885
TARGET TOOLS (SALES, & 72095 OXON
HIRE & REPAIRS) ★
SWAIN COURT
STATION INDUSTRIAL ESTATE
Open: Mon.-Sat. 8.00 a.m.-5.00 p.m.
24 hour Answerphone
BC.W.M.A.

**WOLVERHAMPTON** Tel. (0902)
MANSAW SERVICES 58759
SEDGLEY STREET K★

Open: Mon.-Fri. 9.00 a.m.-5.00 p.m.

H.P.W.WM.A.D.CS.

**PERTH** Tel. (0738) 26173
WILLIAM HUME & CO K
ST. JOHN'S PLACE
Open: Monday to Saturday
8.00 a.m.-5.30 p.m.
8.00 a.m.-1.00 p.m. Wednesday
H.P.A.BC.W.CS.WM.D.

**SWANSEA** Tel. (0792) 55680
SWANSEA TIMBER & PLYWOOD CO. LTD.
57-59 OXFORD STREET ★

Open: Mon to Fri 9.00 a.m.-5.30 p.m.
Sat. 9.00 a.m.-1.00 p.m.
H.P.W.D.T.CS.A.BC.

## SOMERSET

**TAUNTON** Tel. (0823) 85431
JOHN HALL TOOLS ★
6 HIGH STREET

Open Monday-Saturday
9.00 a.m.-5.30 p.m.
H.P.W.WM.D.CS.A.

## YORKSHIRE

**SHEFFIELD** Tel. (0742) 441012
GREGORY & TAYLOR LTD KE
WORKSOP ROAD
Open: 8.30 a.m.-5.30 p.m.
Monday-Friday
8.30 a.m.-12.30 p.m. Sat.
H.P.W.WM.D.

**CARLISLE** Tel. (0228) 36391
W. M. PLANT
ALLENBROOK ROAD
ROSEHILL, CA1 2UT
Open: Mon.-Fri. 8.00 a.m.-5.15 p.m.
Sat. 8.00 a.m.-12.30 noon
P.W.WM.D.CS.A.

**LIVERPOOL** Tel. (051-207) 2967
TAYLOR BROS (LIVERPOOL) LTD K
195-199 LONDON ROAD
LIVERPOOL L3 8JG
Open: Monday to Friday
8.30 a.m.-5.30 p.m.
H.P.W.WM.D.A.BC.

**TAUNTON** Tel. Taunton 79078
KEITH MITCHELL ★
TOOLS AND EQUIPMENT
66 PRIORY BRIDGE ROAD
Open: Mon-Fri 8.30 a.m.-5.30 p.m.
Saturday 9.00 a.m.-4.00 p.m.
H.P.W.WM.D.CS.A.BC.

**HARROGATE** Tel. (0423) 66245/
MULTI-TOOLS 55328
158 KINGS ROAD K★

Open: Monday to Saturday
8.30 a.m.-6.00 p.m.
H.P.W.WM.D.A.BC.

**CULLEN** Tel. (0542) 40563
GRAMPIAN WOODTURNING SUPPLIES AT
BAYVIEW CRAFTS
Open Mon.-Sat. 9.00 a.m.-5.30 p.m. Sunday
10.00 a.m.-5.30 p.m. Open later July/Aug.
Sept: Demonstrations SAT/SUN or by
H.W.D.MF.BC. appointment

**BOURNEMOUTH** Tel: (0202) 420583
POWER TOOL SERVICES
(Sales, spares, repairs)
849-851 CHRISTCHURCH ROAD
BOSCOMBE
Open: Mon.-Fri. 9.00 a.m.-5.30 p.m.
Sat: 9.00 a.m.-5.00 p.m.
H.P.W.CS.K.A.

**ST. LEONARD'S-ON-SEA** Tel.
DOUST & MONK (MONOSAW)-(0424)
25 CASTLEHAM ROAD 52577

Open: Mon.-Fri. 8.00 a.m.-5.30 p.m.
Most Saturdays 9.00 a.m.-1.00 p.m.
H.P.W.WM.D.CS.A.

**LEEDS** Tel. (0532) 574736
D. B. KEIGHLEY MACHINERY LTD. ★
VICKERS PLACE, STANNINGLEY
PUDSEY LS2 86LZ
Mon.-Fri. 9.00 a.m.-5.00 p.m.
Sat. 9.00 a.m.-1.00 p.m.
P.A.W.WM.CS.BC.

**TAYSIDE** Tel. (05774) 293
WORKMASTER POWER TOOLS LTD. ★
DRUM, KINROSS
Open Mon.-Sat. 8.00 a.m.-8.00 p.m.
Demonstrations throughout Scotland by
appointment
P.W.WM.D.A.BC.

**BOROUGHBRIDGE** Tel. (09012)
JOHN BODDY TIMBER LTD 2370
FINE WOOD & TOOL STORE ★
RIVERSIDE SAWMILLS
Open: Mon.-Thurs. 8.00 a.m.-6.00 p.m.
Fri. 8.00am-5.00pm Sat. 8.00am-4.00pm
H.P.W.WM.D.T.CS.MF.A.BC.

## STAFFORDSHIRE

**TAMWORTH** Tel. (0827) 56188
MATTHEWS BROTHERS LTD. K
KETTLEBROOK ROAD
Open: Mon-Sat 8.30 a.m.-6.00 p.m.
Demonstrations Sunday mornings by
appointment only
H.P.WM.D.T.CS.A.BC.

**HUDDERSFIELD** Tel. (0484)
NEVILLE M. OLDHAM 641219/(0484)
UNIT 1 DALE ST. MILLS 42777
DALE STREET, LONGWOOD ★
Open: Mon-Fri 8.00 a.m.-5.30 p.m.
Saturday 9.30 a.m.-12.00 p.m.
P.W.WM.D.A.BC.

**GLASGOW** Tel. (041 429) 4374/
THE SAW CENTRE 4444, Telex: 777886
600 EGLINTON STREET E★
G5 9RR
Open: Mon-Fri 9.00 a.m.-5.00 p.m.
Saturday 9.00 a.m.-1.00 p.m.
H.P.W.WM.D.CS.A.

GIVE YOUR BUSINESS A
BOOST — DON'T LEAVE IT
TO CHANCE, 'PHONE PETER
ON 01-437 0699 TO
ADVERTISE

## SUFFOLK

**PETERBOROUGH** Tel. (0733)
WILLIAMS DISTRIBUTORS 64252
(TOOLS) LIMITED K
108-110 BURGHLEY ROAD
Open: Monday to Friday
8.30 a.m.-5.30 p.m.
H.P.A.W.D.WH.BC.

**THIRSK** Tel. (0845) 22770
THE WOOD SHOP ★
TRESKE SAWMILLS LTD.
STATION WORKS
Open: Seven days a week 9.00-5.00

T.H.MF.BC.

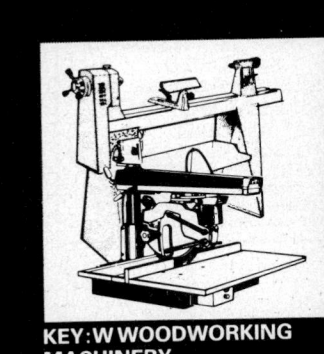

**WORTHING** Tel. (0903) 38739
W. HOSKING LTD (TOOLS & KE★
MACHINERY)
28 PORTLAND RD, BN11 1QN
Open: Mon.-Sat. 8.30 a.m.-5.30 p.m.
Closed Wednesday
H.P.W.WM.D.CS.A.BC.

**KEIGHLEY** Tel. (0535) 663325
EUROMAIL (TOOLS) ★
PO BOX 13
108 EAST PARADE
Open 9.15 a.m.-5.00 p.m.
Not Tuesday but inc. Saturday
H.P.W.A.BC.

KEY: W WOODWORKING
MACHINERY

# WOOD SUPPLIERS

548

# WOOD SUPPLIERS

549

# Classified Advertisements

## FOR SALE

**LACE BOBBIN TURNING BLANKS** in unusual and exotic hardwoods and ivory. SAE for list: J. Ford, 5 Squirrels Hollow, Walsall WS7 8YS.

---

FOR ALL SUPPLIES FOR THE

# Craft of Enamelling

## ON METAL

Including

# LEAD-FREE ENAMELS

PLEASE SEND 2 × 10p STAMPS FOR FREE CATALOGUE, PRICE LIST AND WORKING INSTRUCTIONS

## W. G. BALL LTD.

ENAMEL MANUFACTURERS

Dept. W. LONGTON
STOKE-ON-TRENT
ST3 1JW

---

### MUSICAL MOVEMENTS

★ LOVE STORY ★ LARAS THEME ★ SPEAK SOFTLY LOVE ★ FUR ELISE ★ FEELINGS ★ FASCINATION ★ IMPOSSIBLE DREAM ★ MUSIC BOX DANCER ★ LA POLOMA ★ THE EMPEROR WALTZ ★ TRY TO REMEMBER ★ ROMEO AND JULIET ★
Complete with screws and spring mechanism **£2.50** inc. p&p. 20 or more of one tune ordered **£1.50** each. Available from:
**The Jewel Box Shop,**
112 Pentonville Road, London N1 9JB.

---

### HAND CARVED

'Adam Style' Mantle motifs in Mahogany — Example 10" × 5" centre lamp and two side pieces.
Send S.A.E. for details and quotation. Your own design quoted for if required.
**SAM NICHOLSON**
22 Lisnagarvey Drive, Lisburn,
Co. Antrim, N. Ireland.
Phone Lisburn 3510

---

Have you seen the latest catalogue of

# Bygones

See Display advertisement

---

## D.I.Y. ESTABLISHED 1889

# THE SAW CENTRE LIMITED

## HAS THE EDGE

Hire or buy machinery or power tools from our extensive stock:

**Elu DeWALT makita Black & Decker**
- SCHEPPACH ■ STARTRITE ■ GRIGGIO
- VOLPATO ■ SEDGWICK
- TUNGSTEN CARBIDE TIPPED SAW BLADES
- DISPOSABLE BANDSAW BLADES

*SEE US AT ROYAL HIGHLAND SHOW EDINBURGH*

**HEAD OFFICE & MAIN WORKS:**
EGLINTON TOLL GLASGOW G5 9RP. TEL: 041-429 4444/4374
OPEN: MON-FRI 8-5 (NO SAT) TELEX: 777886 SAWCO G.

ALSO AT: 38 HAYMARKET TERRACE EDINBURGH EH12 5JZ.
TEL: 031-337 5555. MON-FRI 8.30-5.30 & SAT 9-1.

---

MORTISERS; TENNONERS; SPINDLES; PLANERS; BANDSAWS; LATHES; CROSSCUTS; ROUTERS; SANDERS; DRILLS? YOU CAN CERTAINLY SEE ALL CLASSES AND TYPES OF MACHINES HERE.

WE ARE MAIN STOCKING AGENTS FOR:
MULTICO; ELU; SEDGWICK; KITY; SCHEPPACH; INCA; CORONET; DeWALT; WARCO; DOMINION; HITACHI; STARTRITE; TREND; ASHLEY ILES; SORBY.

*CALL US ABOUT WOODTURNING LESSONS*
*WOODCARVING LESSONS (See our Swiss carving tools)*
*ALWAYS HELPFUL, KNOWLEDGEABLE, GOOD SERVICE AT:*

## CLEVELAND WOODCRAFT

### 38-42 CRESCENT ROAD, MIDDLESBROUGH.
### TEL: (0642) 813103

**CORONET "ELF"** lathe in excellent condition. Used only for demonstration. Current price £300+. Will accept £200. Also Cowell 8" × 2" wet grinder, little used. £100. Telephone Braintree 24606.

**KITY K-5** Universal Woodworking machine MkII. Only 1 year old. Price £600. Includes £200 worth of accessories. e.g. Tungston tipped tools, rebating blocks and tenon table. Tel. Cheltenham (0242) 51378/581776.

---

## SITUATIONS VACANT

# JOINER/ADMINISTRATOR

We require an enterprising skilled woodworker to help establish our new shopfitting and joinery company in Cambridge. The applicant must be qualified and prepared to assemble units and assist with the administration. There is no limit to the scope within this company. Salary will be negotiable based on experience plus a profit sharing benefit. Apply in writing to:

**Mr. P. M. Green, c/o Kerridge Ltd.,**
**11-21 Sturton Street,**
**Cambridge, CB1 2QB.**

---

**ZYLISS** vice, in new condition £30. Telephone 01-995-3342.

**PLANER THICKNESSER.** Sedgewick. Single phase 12" by 8". Good condition £1,100 ono. Telephone 0460 34272 or 0460 54109.

**MINI MAX P32** Bandsaw 6' cut with Rip/Mitre fences excellent condition purchased larger machine £280 ono. Kidderminster 68599.

**LUNA W59** combination machine. 10" planer/thicknesser 12" Tc saw spindler moulder. Single phase £1,700. Phone Saundersfoot (0834) 811266.

**PURE BEESWAX BLOCKS** ideal for woodturning. 5 for £2.50 including postage. Discount for larger orders. Sample pack available for 65p. Waxwood, Dowhills, Croesawbach, Oswestry, Shropshire SY10 9BQ.

**CORONET** longbed 'Elf' perfect cord. Two years old, extra banjo saddle rests £225. Southend 553312.

**KITY K-S** woodworking centre. Unwanted present used only once. £550. Ring 09073 77313 after 6pm.

**LACE BOBBIN PLANKS,** over 90 different woods, lists free, 50 exotic £4.50. 35 veneer samples. £1. P. Rushbrook, 39 Deben Avenue, Martleshom, Ipswich.

**GLASS CUTTERS** ideal for handyman. Used in our own glass works. Instructions. P&P. £6.50 each. F. Sherwood, Dept. W. 54 The Burroughs, Hendon NW4 4AN.

**LACE BOBBIN PLANKS.** Over 90 different woods, lists free. P. Rushbrook, 39 Deben Avenue, Martlesham, Ipswich.

**BAGS, WRAPPINGS, TISSUE, BOXES, BUSINESS CARDS.** Any shape, size, amount. Comprehensive samples. 90p. Terry Andrews, 53A Parsons St., Banbury OX16 8NB.

**MARKING STAMPS** — name stamps branding irons supplied to your requirements SAE for details. Davey, 37 Marina Drive, Brixham, Devon TQ5 8BB.　T/C

**PRECISION COMBINATION CHUCK.** Fits Coronet major (blue). Only used once. Excellent value. £40.00 ono. Tel. 0736 763275.

**CONTAX 137** M-D Quartz camera single lens reflex. Fully automatic 35mm lens and 200mm lens plus teleconverter and wide angle lens. Complete kit for any woodworking pictures Will exchange for radial armsaw or like. Telephone Wetherby (0937) 64054. Evenings only.

**25,000 WESTERN HEMLOCK** and Brazilian Mahogany staircase spindle blanks (before turning). 3' long, 1⅜" × 1⅜" sq. To be sold in large or small quantities, from 30p to £2 each. Also wanted home DIY turners to complete and return and sell back finished turned spindles. Also solid oak supreme quality kitchen cabinet arched top doors all metric. List price £50 each. To clear from £5, £8, £18 each. 300 new comfort arch top sashed red deal, window frames. Full range primed not polished, all to be sold at 65% off list price e.g. 8 × 4 metric oblong 4 arches list £165 — £65 4 × 4 £30 etc. All enquiries Turton 0204 Bolton Lancashire area 852339 any time.

551

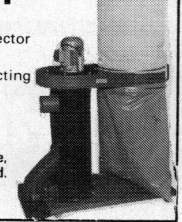

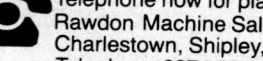

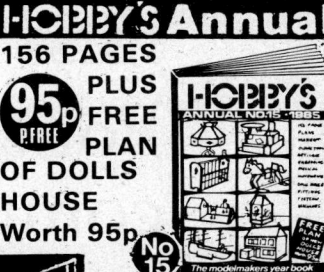
555

# Then......

## Max Burrough

**The final part of Max Burrough's evocative, informative tale of his pre-war apprenticeship**

Of the wide variety of activities we undertook I loathed coffins, auctions and removals most. But, no matter how I tried to wangle the right jobs, it was impossible to be lucky all the time. I hated coffin-making for many reasons. There was usually some uncertainty because, with a competitor a few hundred yards up the street, it was almost evens as to who would get the job. Not quite, though, for we charged £15 and £13 for oak and elm coffins respectively, while they charged almost £2 less. (These charges were inclusive and covered practically everything, including the hearse.) Firms were always anxious to obtain undertaking work, for it was the only work that was always paid for — and promptly. Quite often we would hear the church bell tolling to announce a death, and then speculation would break out. Who was ill? Had anyone seen old so-and-so lately? If it were him, would we get the job? And so on.

In due course Old Will would arrive with the sizes, having been out to measure the corpse, and usually three men were allocated to the job. Benches would be cleared, work in hand stood back against the wall, and — if it was a rush job — often all hands would set to. It was the sense of urgency I hated, for the even tenor of the work in hand and the smooth running of the workshop were rudely interrupted.

Two men, or a man and a boy, would be off to the yard selecting the boards, trying to find those that would cut with the minimum of waste and, if elm, with a reasonable grain while not being too dry. Wet elm planes easily, whereas really dry, knotty elm can be the very devil. With oak there was no problem, for American and Japanese — plain-cut with a good straight grain — was always available. (A few months ago I was somewhat astonished to read in an antique journal an article by a young man described as 'one of the country's leading restorers.' He asserted that, should a piece of oak be found that would not take stain easily, it must be Japanese; and that, in any case, such oak was not imported into the country until after the second world war. He is wrong in both assertions. Japanese oak takes stain extremely well, and hundreds of thousands of feet were imported into the country between the two world wars.) When boards came into the shop, the bottoms would be marked out, and cut and planed to size while the sides would be run through the

planing machine. This contraption was, of course, too small to take the width of a top, which had to be planed by hand — a wooden smoother usually being used for the first going-over.

The sides having been brought to width, with a reduction from the head at 14in to the foot at 12in, they were then marked for kerfing, an operation that had to be carried out very carefully if an easy smooth curve was to be obtained. The kerfing showed the efficiency of the saws and their sharpening; in the top shop each man performed the task without trouble, but down below it was a different story. Leonard, especially, made really hard work of it, scratching across 'like an old hen scratching afore daylight' as the saying has it. The head and foot went on first, with a ¾in and 1½in slope respectively, and then the sides, hot water being applied to the kerfed area. Cut clasp 1½in nails were used. If you have a few minutes to spare, I suggest that you try driving such a nail through a piece of ⅞in elm and into another piece of elm.

A simple thumb moulding was worked by hand for the top edge and a commercially made plinth fixed to the bottom; handles were fitted, and then the inside was pitched. Bought in cardboard-cased cakes, the pitch was heated in a shallow pan about 15in across and 6in deep, with a knob of tallow added to help it flow more easily.

Before polishing, the grain was filled with a mixture of whitening and a little colouring — the surplus being rubbed off with a piece of scrim, working across the grain. I can recall one occasion when the elm was so green and wet with sap that a plumber was sent for; he judiciously applied some heat from his blowlamp, so getting the wood dry enough to take the polish. It always seemed to me absurd to spend so much time french-polishing something that would be seen only for a few hours and then hidden underground. The handles and beautifully painted name-plate were screwed on. It's worth mentioning that no one in the firm had a spiral pump-action screwdriver. These tools were considered too dangerous to use on polished wood — one slip and a job could be ruined. It was suggested, at times with some sarcasm, that they might be useful to men fixing rows of cinema or theatre seating.

It was the final stage, the lining of the coffin with flannelette, that always caused me trepidation. The loose top sheets had to be pinked, using a semi-circular pinking iron against the straight-edge held in place by two of the old-fashioned type of hold-fast, i.e. that without an adjusting screw. The iron was hit with an old mallet kept for the purpose — but the trouble was that, at

the head, the loose sheets were folded in a peculiar manner; I never could get the hang of it. Over every coffin I was involved with, Fred used to watch me struggling. Finally, in desperation, he would come over and say, 'Look, like this. How many more times do I have to show you?' Poor Fred — I often marvelled at his patience and tolerance.

The trouble was that I was neither strong enough to make these 'boxes' nor tall enough to carry them at funerals; and, as I had no intention of doing either, I had no interest in the work. When made, the coffin had to be carried down the stairs, round the turn at the bottom, up the high step in the carpenter's shop, a few yards more, then two steps up to the doorway, out on to the open wood landing, across and down the open wood staircase. It might be pouring with rain, or the landing and stairs could be wet or frost-covered; for the man in front, walking backwards carrying a heavy oak coffin, this could be called hard work by any standards. On the stairs a man would walk in front, backwards, with a hand between the shoulder-blades of the man carrying — acting as a support for him and ensuring that he did not slip and fall backwards.

Is it any wonder that I dreaded hearing the tolling of the church bell?

When the end of our five-year apprenticeship was in sight, Albert and I were invited into the holy of holies. Yes, the Boss had realised that our time was up. Things being what the were, he would pay us 6½d. an hour. In our last year we had been paid 17s. 6d. a week, so the proposed new rate (with a 44-hour week) meant that we would be getting £1 3s. 10d. — less, of course, the insurance deductions.

So, almost hand-in-hand, we tapped on the office door and were invited into the holy of holies. Yes, the Boss had realised that our time was up. Things being what they were, he would pay us 6½d. an hour. In our last year we had been paid 17s. 6d. a week, so the proposed new rate (with a 44-hour week) meant that we would be getting £1 3s. 10d. — less, of course, the insurance deductions.

It was what I had expected. Albert was flabbergasted; but he could not tell me how much he had hoped to get. The year was 1933, something called a depression was really beginning to have an effect in the provinces, and I knew that the firm could not afford to pay us any more. In fact, it didn't want us at all, and the Boss knew only too well that, had we left or been sacked, there was not one firm in the town that would or could offer us a job.

That knowledge was to be tested all too soon. The depression dragged on and two men were sacked. Everyone knew that six cabinetmakers had to be kept on to enable the firm to continue its undertaking business. But, despite that, we worked fewer and fewer hours per week; and eventually the time came when Albert and I were indeed told we would have to go.

The Boss found us a job in a big firm near Cheltenham. But that very shortly turned out to be a disaster, and in truth an epoch had ended when we left the small business where we had learnt almost all we knew.

**The end**

558

# Letters

IT IS COMMONPLACE nowadays to encourage groups of people in conflict to get round the negotiating table. I am writing to suggest that we, the woodworkers and cabinetmakers, may have let the nation down. Our fellow-citizens show no reluctance to get round the dining-table. So what must be done to make the negotiating table (or tables) irresistibly attractive?

Certain features seem to me essential. It should, of course, be strong enough not to collapse under the weight of discussion. It would have a central pole or mast to which colours could be nailed; at its head would be a windsock, so that delegates would be in no doubt about which way the wind was blowing.

The timber itself would require careful selection. It should have no knotty problems, and no cracks that need papering over. Pronounced annual growth rings would be unacceptable, because they would be seen as inflationary. And no individual negotiator should find him- or herself having to go against the grain.

If a drawer is required, it should have equal numbers of dovetails and hawktails. But perhaps the only applied decoration should be a white line to indicate the middle of the road.

*Malcolm Cobb, Carnforth*

THE LETTER from S. J. McCordick ('Question box', April) prompts me to ask if anyone can recommend a book or other publication on making Northumbrian pipes. Indeed, I'd be grateful for any information on the subject.

*G.E. Boyce, The Firs,*
*Staunton Road, Monmouth,*
*Gwent NP5 3SA*

IN 'SHOPTALK' (March) you ask if readers are interested in such products as the giant Weinig moulders. I am not, and doubt if many other readers are. The *Timber Trades Journal* regularly reviews new industrial woodworking machinery, while *Forestry and British Timber* covers the forestry and home sawmilling trade — I see both of these magazines in my work as a state forest officer. I look forward to *Woodworker* for my hobby interests, and expect it to deal with light machinery and hand-tool methods of woodworking.

My own interests are in traditional techniques and projects, in solid wood; I am not attracted to the use of panel products or to modern designs. I am also a woodturner, and enjoy any articles on turning projects which have good designs. Perhaps you can tell me why the plethora of turning books are so strong on techniques but never explain the traditional spindle-turning design patterns to be seen on any antique furniture. I would welcome an article on turning design from first principles.

I also look forward to articles by Jack Hill on chairmaking, etc., or any work with draw-knife, side-axe, adze or froe. Maybe I'm not a typical woodworker, but these are my interests, and as far as I know no other

magazine caters for them. Let the other magazines deal with DIY projects.

The format of your magazine has improved in recent issues and I wish it well in the future.

*P. R. Quelch, Ardrishaig*

IN HIS ANSWER to R. Kay (WW/March, 'Question box'), Jack Hill says that, to his knowledge, taper bits are not available. Roger's of Hitchin can supply sets of chairmaker's spoon bits, including the taper bit. Their address is 47 Walsworth Rd, Hitchin, Herts SG4 9SU, tel. (0462) 34177.

As for the first part of Mr Kay's question — I tried turning Windsor-chair back sticks, but found they took too long. So I cut square strips on the saw-bench, and plane them to a taper either end by sitting them in a slot in a piece of wood with either end raised slightly — say $\frac{1}{16}$in. Press fairly hard on the plane, and the result is shown (exaggerated) in the drawing. Turn over with double the packing, and that's the other side. Modify the jig a little with V-holders, and you get an octagonal spindle. Then sandpaper while holding the piece in your hand: it's quite quick.

*David Faulkner, Christchurch, New Zealand*

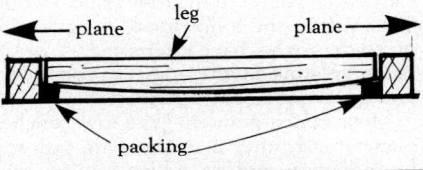

RECENTLY I visited a store to try and sell my furniture. The buyer looked at my photographs and said that my designs weren't in keeping with those on display (LaTrobe Bateman, Makepeace and one or two others). I asked if he minded if I made a comment, and the reply was to welcome it.

I let fly (I had lost anyway). One couldn't sit at the ends of the long dining-table in the corner, as the bars were too low; the stools had too-small seats; the chest-of-drawers had so many drawers, all the same size and shape, that unless each one were labelled it would be impossible to remember what was in them; etc., etc.

I went on to say that many people thought these impractical designs were all that was available, and so instead bought mass-produced items from the chain-stores. What a lot of damage it did to the small furniture-makers in this country; and so on.

I got up to go. But I was asked to sit down again, and the buyer went through my albums and ordered about six different items. When I quoted a price, he called them cheap.

So please, please, let's see more conventional, practical furniture in your magazine. Point out that complicated mouldings need a paint-scraper to clean out; that sharp edges get damaged very

easily; that sharp corners on a table can do nasty damage to a toddler's eye or an adult's thigh; that legs sticking out can trip people; that chairs need to be comfortable; that a tough, heat-resistant, water-resistant surface is a good idea. And let's see more of that at the Crafts Council exhibitions — or are they only meant for the few artists, and not as furniture displays at all?

*B. Sömme, Appledore*

I WAS INTRIGUED to read the review of *The Woodworker's Handbook* in your April issue. While, as one of the authors, I must declare a vested interest, I would like to refute the suggestion that its coverage of this vast and complex subject is minimal. Specifically, the review suggests that the book recommends 'little more than a Workmate and an electric drill' are required to 'make Chippendale chairs'.

In actual fact the book gives details of 56 tools as a basic minimum for cabinetmaking work, and describes in depth the use of many more. No less than five different types of workbench are described, and advice is given on how to build three of these. I could go on to refute each of Luke Hughes' claims in detail, with the exception of one. The biscuit-jointer was omitted, after some deliberation, since it was felt that this machine was more suited to shopfitting and display work than to bona fide cabinet-making.

All in all we feel that this book offers exceptional coverage, and 50,000 buyers have as yet failed to produce one complaint to ourselves or the publishers.

I trust that the editor will give his own recent book *Woodworking School* to Luke Hughes to review. If he fears a similar attack, I would be delighted — in the interests of bias-free reporting — to review it myself.

*Alan Smith, London College of Furniture*
● Luke Hughes' review of *Woodworking School* appeared in the May issue.

ERNIE IVES' article on 'Marquetry in the USA' (WW/April) took my attention immediately with his 'own "Country fiddler"', and his opening remarks about getting marquetry away from designs of set patterns and copies of other people's work.

Perhaps the latter remark does not refer to his copying of John Holder's wonderful drawing of a fiddler in an old chair, but a mention of this artist would have been appreciated by many who know his work.

*Robin Humphreys, St. Neots*
**Ernie Ives** writes: My apologies to John Holder if indeed he was the original artist of the picture. My marquetry picture was actually adapted from a tiny illustration clipped from a Norwegian newspaper!

I WAS SURPRISED to read in your May issue the reply Charles Cliffe gave to the question of finishing a yew table for outside use. I can see his point about linseed oil collecting dust when drying, but surely it would be far easier to clean the dirt and dust

# Letters

off oil than to sand down and re-varnish every few years.

As a buyer for a specialist woodwork shop in Bristol, I have yet to find a varnish of any kind that does not crack and peel when used outside. Another point to be taken into consideration is that yew wood can move about, especially if only air-dried, and this is what causes varnish to crack; the rest is up to the English weather.

I think Mr Davies has got to think again, and perhaps revert to his original idea — protect it with an oil or preservative. One quick-drying oil on the market, produced by Rustins (Danish oil), has a drying time of four to eight hours; or perhaps he should take a leaf out of the Swedish books and used one of their preservatives (e.g. Sadolin). None of these will crack or peel, and they are far easier to maintain.

*M. S. Potter, Bristol*

---

THE DIMMER DEVICE mentioned by Mr Kendall-Carpenter — or, indeed, any of the speed-control units supplied by DIY shops — can ONLY be used on motors of the universal (series-wound) type, typical of electric drills, routers and the like. If one is connected to the normal engineer's bench-grinder (usually equipped with an induction motor) the result will be at best disappointment, and at worst destruction of the motor. There is *no way* in which the speed of an induction motor can be varied from near-synchronisation to the mains frequency.

It is, perhaps, also worth reminding readers that universal motors should not really be used for grinding-wheel drives. Unless they are specially designed for the purpose, their no-load speed is far too fast for safety, and in addition the speed will fall dramatically as cut is put on. I have used one such on very small (3in) wheels, but it had a ventilating fan which limited the runaway speed to safe limits.

The solution to the problem for woodworkers (most double-ended bench-grinders are for metalworkers) is to use a geared motor — or, as I do, a 100-year-old treadle wet grindstone!

*Tubal Cain, Kendall*

---

MY SHARP REVIEW of Gordon Warr's *Q & A: Woodwork* (WW/Feb) led to a 'full and frank exchange of views' between the author and myself. Although in no way at his suggestion, I feel I ought to put the record straight.

Mr Warr didn't advise using *hardwood* wedges in tenons; my subconscious slipped them in. He thinks softwood better in many ways, and I see his logic. His diagram did, in fact, show where to put them. It seemed, too, as if I were saying he liked honing-guides, which in fact it turns out he doesn't — but that was a quite unintentional ambiguity of mine. I wasn't quite accurate about his comments on the use of dowel pegs in joints, either.

Perhaps more serious was a suggestion of plagiarism. Well, the worst that can be said here is that if Mr Warr had in truth had to

draw on material already in print, his own compendious writings over the years would have been a more-than-adequate source. My guess was ironic rather than serious, but in any case was amiss.

Mr Warr knows a vast deal more about woodwork than I do (though I still cling to one or two differences of opinion). I'll go further: I've learned a lot from his letters to me, not least where to get hold of a good wide sharpening stone! His comments have been rigorous (what else could I expect?) — but friendly, considering the context.

Why, then, did I seem to slight his book in my review? Not from a desire to indulge in smart-Alecry for its own sake, but from a self-confessed bodge-and-codger's desire to find at last the handbook which will get him off the hook when his saw is jammed, so to speak. I won't repeat the reasons why I still feel *Q&A: Woodwork* is something of a disappointment in this respect. Mr Warr says his choice of topics had to be random; I'd have liked to see a selection with the average woodworker's priorities in mind. But, as the author pointed out to me, no one ever knows what the average anyone really is.

*Chris Nash, Worcester*

---

WITH REFERENCE to Mr Kendall-Carpenter's letter in the May issue, I would like to draw the following to the attention of readers who have attempted — or are contemplating an attempt — to control the speeds of their bench-grinders.

Most bench-grinders (like saw-benches, planers and other machines) are powered by induction motors, which rely for their speed on the frequency of the supply rather than the voltage, and on the number of poles; hence they are effectively constant-speed devices. The speed may be determined by dividing the mains frequency by the number of pole pairs. Thus a two-pole machine will run at 50Hz (cycles or revs per second) or 3000rpm, a four-pole at 1500rpm, and so on. In practice the actual rotational speed will be somewhat less than these theoretical values (i.e. 2800, 1450 and 950rpm respectively).

Dimmer switches reduce voltage and have no effect on frequency, and therefore would be of no use in the situation suggested. These devices may, however, be used to control the speeds of most portable power-tools, which utilise entirely different types of motor — characterised by the fact that they have carbon brushes. These motors are often termed 'universal' because they will run on either DC or AC supplies. They give much higher speeds (from 20,000rpm), and they are more compact — though noisier — than the equivalent induction motors. But they are much less efficient, so induction motors tend to be used where size and weight are not a problem. Mr Kendall-Carpenter perhaps has a grinder with a universal motor — but other readers, please beware.

As far as safety is concerned, I feel that grinders (treated with reasonable care) are

no less safe than circular saws, planers or spindle-moulders — and that, used with a little practice and a delicate touch, they can work quite effectively. The reason for their high speeds must surely be that they work best: try slowing a router down to 7-8000 rpm, and see what that does to the quality of the machined surface!

*David Harrison BSc Eng, Bolton*

---

CONCERNING the question of grinding-wheel speed, or more correctly rpm control, Mr Kendall-Carpenter's suggestion in the May issue of using a commercial lamp-dimmer will frequently *not* work, and hence may incur an unnecessary and disappointing expense.

Many grinder motors are of the synchronous type, the speed being controlled purely by the frequency of the supply voltage and not by its level. Only if the motor is a brush/commutator type may the speed be controlled as Mr Kendall-Carpenter suggests.

How do you find out? A synchronous motor may have the bulge of the starter capacitor on the outside, like most single-phase bandsaws, circular saws, planers, etc., or the capacitor may be hidden within the grinder base. With the motor *not* running or switched on, press your ear against the casing. Now listen carefully as you turn or spin the wheel by hand, first in the usual and then in the opposite direction. The ticking or burring of the brushes as they go from segment to segment of the commutator is quite different from the smooth purr of the ball- or roller-races on the shaft of a synchronous machine.

Another clue or hint is the presence or absence of the plastic caps which allow brush renewal — they are almost certainly absent on your grinder, which is therefore a synchronous-motor type.

To compound the misery, I must point out that drills, sanders, routers and so on are invariably series-wound, AC/DC, brush/commutator types of machine giving a high starting torque. They may suffer damaged armatures from the method of average-voltage control employed by light-dimmers. Most light-dimmers will specify 'filament-lamp loading only'; this rules out fluorescent lamps and, by inference, inductive loads such as those of motors.

If you wish to experiment, do so while your machine is under guarantee, and practise the look of surprised innocence needed when you tell the dealer that the smelly and smoking portion of your machine 'came to bits in me 'and as I was shaping balsa-wood'. To control speed successfully you need to spend a little more on a suitable *motor-speed* controller suited to AC/DC machines. This was indeed stated in Mr Kendall-Carpenter's letter, but needs emphasising.

As a professional electronics engineer and a keen woodworker I have learnt a lot through bitter and practical experience — and I still remember looking innocent!

*D. H. E. King, Bury St Edmunds*

# The magazine for the craftsman
## ~ and the aspiring craftsman!

August 1985
Vol. 89
No. 1101

● *Star of the show . . . Rebecca Myram's steam-bent chairs are among the exhibits on p596*

**On the cover:** The fruits of Alan Dixon's efforts were prominently displayed at the Bristol Woodworker Show (p577), as were A. Mikuz' Dalmatian dancers and T. E. Moss's lifelike baboon. The table is by Neil Wyn Jones (p580)

**Publisher** Ray Lewis
**Editor** Peter Collenette
**Deputy Editor** Aidan Walker
**Advertisement Manager** Paul Holmes
**Graphics** Jeff Hamblin
**Guild of Woodworkers** Aidan Walker, Sam Jones
**Group Editor** Chris Adam-Smith
**Publishing Director** John Foster
**Chairman and Chief Executive** Jim Connell
**Editorial, advertisements and Guild of Woodworkers**
1 Golden Square, London W1R 3AB, telephone 01-437 0626

**Subscriptions and back issues** Infonet Ltd, 10-13 Times House, 179 Marlowes, Hemel Hempstead, Herts HP1 1BB; telephone Hemel Hempstead (0442) 48434
**Subscriptions per year** UK £15.60; overseas outside USA (accelerated surface post) £17, USA (accelerated surface post) $22.50, airmail £42
**UK trade** SM Distribution Ltd, 16-18 Trinity Gardens, London SW9 8DX; telephone 01-274 8611
**North American trade** Eastern News Distributors, 166-41 Powells Cove Boulevard, PO Box 69, Whitestone, New York 11357
**Printed in Great Britain** by Ambassador Press Ltd, St Albans, Herts
**Mono origination** Multiform Photosetting Ltd, Cardiff
**Colour origination** Derek Croxson Ltd, Chesham, Bucks
© Argus Specialist Publications Ltd 1985
ISSN 0043 776X

## Argus Specialist Publications Ltd
1 Golden Square, London W1R 3AB; 01-437 0626

# Woodworker
## This month

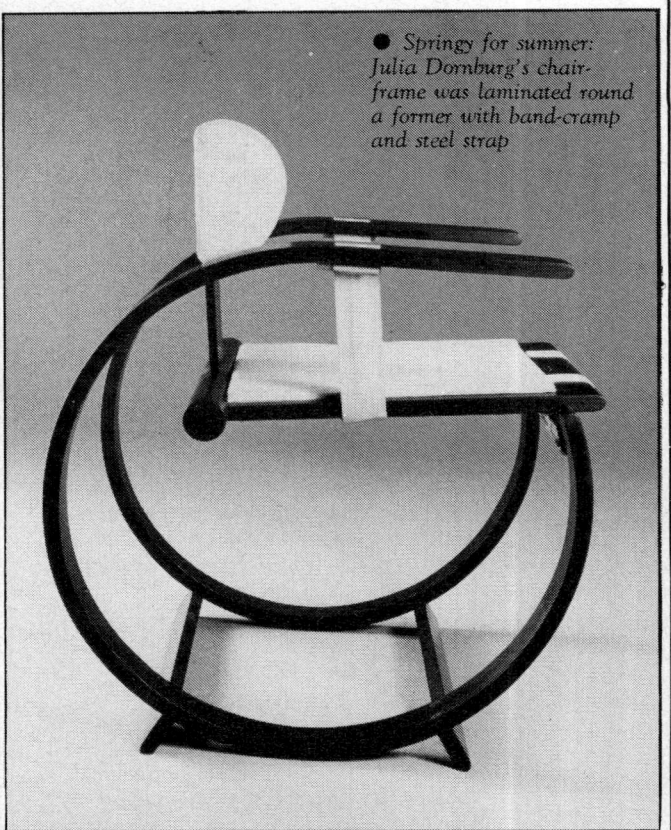

● *Springy for summer: Julia Dornburg's chair-frame was laminated round a former with band-cramp and steel strap*

● *Both in ash, both inky black, both from this year's student harvest, both from Dorset's prestigious Parnham House School. Giles Charlton's table sports a folding top; the laminated supports swivel on bright-red turned laminated bosses with PTFE bearings*

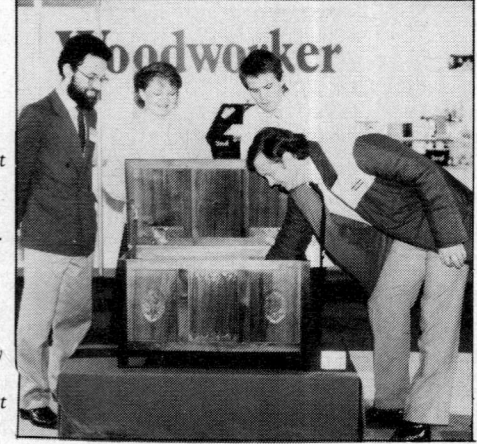

● *Extracting the good news for Judith Ashley, who won an Elu lathe at our Bristol show in May, is Black & Decker's Bill Derry. Grinning approval are editor Peter Collenette and Woodworker salespeople Lindsay Bishop and Peter Smith. Carved chest by J. S. Mansfield!*

## Shoptalk

We're always ready to blow a fanfare for a **woodworking store** — that is, the newish kind of shop that's not a timber merchant, hardware store, tool dealer or finish supplier, but a bit of each. So... trumpets for Robbins of Bristol.

Originally and still primarily a timber business stocking 'traditional' (largely homegrown) hardwoods plus parana pine, Douglas fir, sitka spruce and western red cedar, together with mouldings, boards and joinery, they will, they say, 'cut and plane to your exact requirements'.

But, while the mill's sorting out your cutting list, you can also browse over stains and other finishing materials, adhesives, hardware (including brass fittings), tools, and even books. There's a veneer showroom, too, where you'll find over 40 species plus stringings, bandings and marquetry inlays.

'This is a paradise for every lover of wood,' they claim. They might even be right.

● Robbins Ltd, Merrywood Mills, Bedminster, Bristol BS3 1DX, (0272) 633022.

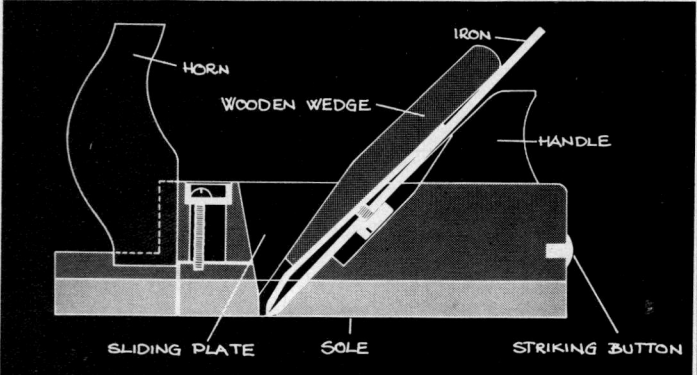

Wooden planes were once at every woodworker's right hand. Now they're as rare as a piece of solid timber in a furniture shop. Stranger still, those available come from across the Channel. But you might as well swallow national pride and investigate the very handsome range by Jack of Denmark.

It runs from a rebate plane at £8.45 to a plough with three irons at £49.95, and includes six smoothers, two try-planes and a 'rough plane'. Most are made of red beech, though one of the smoothers is of white beech and one has a white-beech sole. Two

others have soles of 'pockwood' (?), while the Reform smoothing-plane combines a pockwood sole with a fruit-wood body. At £42 the Reform is the only model to feature an adjustable mouth and screw-cap; all the others employ wedges, and some have only single irons.

All those prices exclude VAT.

● Contact Saxon Tools Ltd, Old Bush St, Level St, Brierley Hill, West Midlands DY5 1UB, (0384) 262424, for fuller details, including information about stockists. Saxon don't supply direct to users.

Roger Woods writes: In answer to readers who want a 'stripped pine' look on new pine, a product just on the market will provide exactly that. Staining waxes have been available for a long while, but Liberon have just added an 'antique pine' to their range — and it is very good.

The procedure is first to sand the surface and then to apply a couple of coats of sanding sealer. When this has dried the stain wax can be applied, preferably with 0000 wire wool.

Although you could use a rag, I prefer wire wool as it cuts back the sealer at the same time. Do not, in general, use wire wool to apply wax to oak, as there will eventually be a reaction between the steel and the tannin in the wood; this will result in staining.

When the wax has had time to harden a little, you should burnish it with a coarse cloth — although I would be reluctant to use hessian or sacking on pine for fear of scoring the surface.

● Liberon Waxes Ltd, 6 Park St, Lydd, Kent, (0679) 20107.

Anyone who has visited Jersey will have seen **walking-stick cabbages** being grown in the fields and even many a cottage back garden, **writes Alan Major.** For some 200 years they have been cultivated so that fine sticks can be made from the stalks. Most of those now grown end up with woodcarvers at L'Etacq, where they find a ready sale to tourists, although islanders still make their own. The cabbage is easy to grow and the seed very fertile, so there's no reason why creators of walking-sticks cannot grow their own supplies. Seed is obtainable from Thompson & Morgan of Ipswich at 55p a packet, plus postage, and as each packet contains approximately 55 seeds there is plenty to get you started.

Like any other cabbage, the plant does well on ordinary, well-drained soil. If planting on clay, however, it is best to put the seeds in trays first and then, when the plants are about 8in high, transplant into the clay, putting some other soil and compost around the roots if available. Space the plants 18-24in apart. If allowed to, they will reach 5-7ft in height. As they grow, the side leaves usually drop; if they don't, remove them to leave only those at the top.

Wind can be a problem because on exposed sites it causes the plants to lean, so you may need to support them with rows of wire or by staking each one with a cane. If a plant does get bent, put it upright immediately, as it will soon start to grow again and the straightness of the stalk can easily be spoilt.

When at the required height for sticks they should be pulled up. The leaf crown should be cut off and, after knocking the dirt from the roots, the plants hung up so they can slowly dry out. When ready the stalks have a woody appearance — yellow-brown, and light in weight but strong. They have knobby extrusions where the leaves were. The stalks can be lightly sandpapered, and then given one or two coats of clear varnish or Danish oil. To protect the end that touches the ground I have found black plastic or metal thimbles are easily fitted and do the job required. At the grip end the stalk can be rounded and kept natural, or fitted with other carved grips created separately.

To continue the supply of plants for the following year, seed can be sown in August and the plants will survive in a normal winter — particularly in southern England; in other areas it is better to wait until spring. The plants will get to walking-stick length in a season anyway. To obtain extra-long stalks (for crooks, for instance) do not pull up but allow them to grow for a second year. It is also a good idea to allow one or two plants to run to seed, bearing crowded heads of pale yellow flowers. After drying, their seeds can of course be used to maintain supplies year after year.
● Thompson & Morgan, London Rd, Copdock, Ipswich, Suffolk, (0473) 214226.

**B**eeswax is the business of Past-Masters Ltd. Beeswax, beeswax leather cream, beeswax pine polish, beeswax teak cream, beeswax filler sticks. Indeed, they say they make 'the only British commercially produced natural beeswax polish on the market that has not been manufactured by any high-technology process and is free of chemical additives'. They're the latest of such invaluable specialist suppliers to announce themselves to the craft woodworker.

● Past-Masters Ltd, 1257 Pershore Rd, Stirchley, Birmingham B30 2YT, 021-459 2385.

**Y**ou can't hear or read enough about **safety and health** — especially if you're in the trade. Two booklets published by the British Woodworking Federation should be a considerable help.

The shorter and slightly snappier is called *Safety & Health: Handbook for Operatives in the Woodworking Industry*, and costs 50p. You'll gather from the subtitle that it's aimed at staff. Unfortunately marred by infantile cartoons, it nevertheless makes all or most of the relevant points in quite readable fashion. Its companion volume, similarly and confusingly titled *A Simple Guide to Health & Safety for the Woodworking Industry*, is fatter and less digestible and costs £1. If you're setting up shop it could prove invaluable, because it refers to all the factory law you need to know — not just the Woodworking Machines Regulations — and does so in some detail. Both prices include postage.

● Administrative Officer, British Woodworking Federation, 82 New Cavendish St, London W1M 8AD, 01-580 5588.

**T**he **chainsaw mill** is the tool which enables do-it-yourself log conversion. Stihl, who make chainsaws, have produced an attachment which allows their models 048, 056 and 076 to be used for obtaining waney-edged planks of pre-determined thickness. It consists of a frame of slide rods supported by guide posts, with vertical adjustment via crank-handles. The bases of the posts locate and fix in holes in the guide-bar of the saw. Heavy-duty rollers are mounted on the underside of the guide-bar to control lateral movement.

It costs £145+VAT. The catch is, of course, that you need the chainsaw too. Nonetheless — subject to its capacity of 16½in width, and thickness ranging from ½in to a monster 12in — it could open up new worlds.
● Andreas Stihl Ltd, Stihl House, Goldsworth Pk Industrial Estate, Woking, Surrey GU21 3BA, (04862) 20222.

**D**avid Savage writes: Mark Charles, who describes himself as a 'Designer and Maker of Fine Furniture and Wood Products', has produced a range of rather superior **timber sample boards.** They run from a nine-sample board of British timbers at £16.50, with a sample size of 115x70mm, to a 20-sample board of exotic timbers for £21.50. The latter, like the other 20 in the range, has smaller 115x35mm examples affixed to a black base-board. The prices include VAT and postage.

I recently bought two boards as a convenient way to show prospective clients the timbers that would be available to them. Mr Charles prepared the boards to my specification and delivered a well-packed product inside the twinkling of an eye. Such service deserves comment and appreciation.
● Mark Charles, Coachman's Cottage, The Rectory, Albury, Tiddington, Oxon.

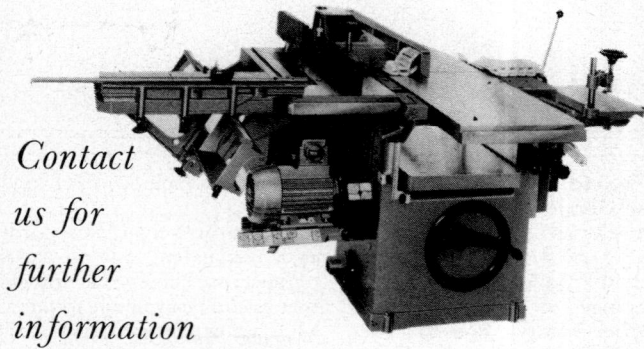
# Shoptalk

If you use British hardwoods (stand up, 90% of our readers), and even specialised home-grown softwoods, you'll know the problems of getting what you want when you want it. So the **Buyers Guide to the British Timber Industry** is well worth acquiring. Published by the British Timber Merchants Association, it includes interesting comments on all the main species, plus a complete listing of Association members (with maps). Each entry indicates the markets served by the firm, the services provided, and — in the case of hardwoods — the species sold. The main drawback is that quite a few firms don't belong to the BTMA and thus aren't included. The booklet costs £1 all-in.

THE BRITISH TIMBER MERCHANTS ASSOCIATION
**BUYERS GUIDE TO THE BRITISH TIMBER INDUSTRY**

● Secretary, BTMA, 6 Ridgeway Rd, Long Ashton, Bristol BS18 9EU, (0272) 394022.

Readers may be misled, writes **Piers Raymond**, by the details of the Mark I **Moisture Meter** from Channel Electronics given in 'Shoptalk' for June. This machine is in fact designed for the building trade, and only measures moisture content in timber down to 14% for hardwood and 16% for softwood. Thus it is of very little use to cabinetmakers. Until recently Channel marketed a Mark II specially designed for woodworkers, about 40% dearer, but this is no longer available. They tell me, however, that in the latter half of this year they will be launching a new Mark II which will be digital and will again fulfil woodworkers' needs.

● Channel Electronics Ltd, PO Box 58, Seaford, Sussex BN25 3JB, tel. (0323) 894961.

*A new name in machinery, Cowells, are marketing this all-British* **whetstone grinder.** *List price is £115+VAT, for which you get cast-aluminium and fabricated-steel construction – no plastic – a continuously-rated induction motor, and a zinc-plated adjustable tool-rest. The aluminium-oxide wheel is 10x1¾in, running on self-lubricating bush bearings, and the tank, which is fitted with a drain-plug, is epoxy-powder-coated to ward off the demon rust. Cowells are also doing 15 and 20in-throat jigsaws with blades that travel, not vibrate; they sell for £115 and £125+VAT respectively.*
● Cowells Machines Ltd, 310/312 Dallow Rd, Luton, Beds LU1 1SS, tel. (0582) 420455

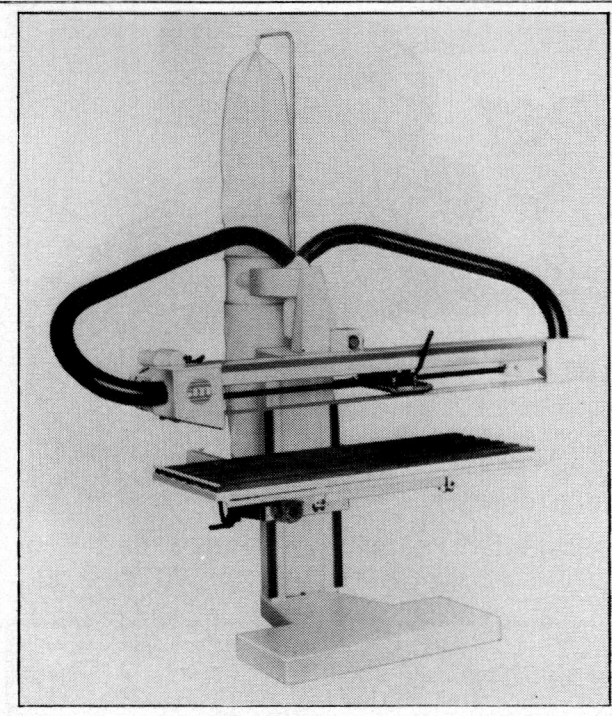

*C*harnwood are adding this **belt sander** – the P12 – to their range. The table measures 1500x600mm and you can handle edge-work as well as flat panels, the distance between table and belt stretching to 600mm. Automatic rise-and-fall and the neat dust extractor are extras. A £50 reduction is offered on the list price of £975+VAT until 31 August; dust extraction costs £199+VAT, automatic rise-and-fall £123+VAT.
● Charnwood, 44 Boston Rd, Beaumont Leys, Leicester LE4 1AA, tel. (0533) 351735

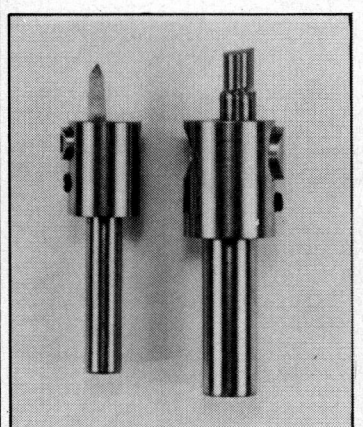

'*W*e have all taken a .015in cutter and ground it to .062in and then an hour later reground it to .010in,' says Frank Green, the inventor of the Vari-Cut **offset tool holder**. Well, maybe not all Woodworker readers share his experience – but the Vari-Cut has obvious potential for the overhead-router owner. You can adjust the offset of the cutter in the holder, giving a vast range of widths of cut. £49.50+VAT.
● Versatile Engineering Ltd, 9 Forward Drive, Wealdstone, Harrow, Middx, tel. 01-863 7818

*P*neumatic and rotary power from a single source ... spraying, drilling, polishing – BIF's **Power Centre** allows all these and more. For £299+VAT you get the unit, a tacker, spray-gun, hose, drive shaft and fixings.

● British Industrial Fastenings, Gatehouse Rd, Aylesbury, Bucks HP19 3DS, tel. (0296) 81341

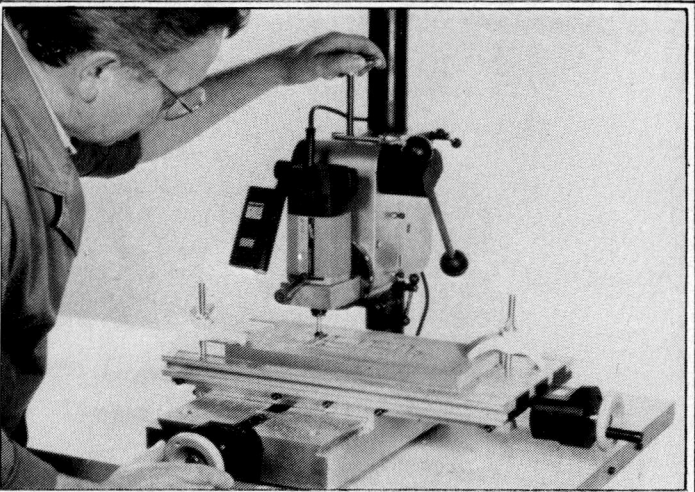

*E*lectronic measuring for the smaller budget; the precision once available only for those with £1000 is now possible with Wolfcraft's new **machining centres and drilling jigs.** This top-of-the range 5005 (around £290 inc. VAT) has a 180° compass-action, double-swivel head; the digital read-out gives you accuracy of depth to 0.5mm. Any 43mm-collar drill or router motor will fit.
● BriMarc Ltd, Kineton Rd, Southam, Warwickshire CV33 0DR, tel. (092681) 2044

*E*ssential for picture-framers and a highly prized piece of equipment in any workshop is the **mitre guillotine**. This model is by Oreteguil of Spain – the ORC 55, which retails for £210+VAT. 'Probably the world's largest manufacturer of twin-bladed guillotines,' Oretguil have recently been expanding and up-rating their production facilities, and have formed a UK sales and distribution outfit to cope with demand.

Notice the heavy twin blades on the unit's travelling block are themselves set at 45° to the fence; the fences are also adjustable for non-standard angles.

● Oreteguil (UK) Ltd, PO Box 2, Disley, Cheshire SK12 2NN, tel. (06632) 2187

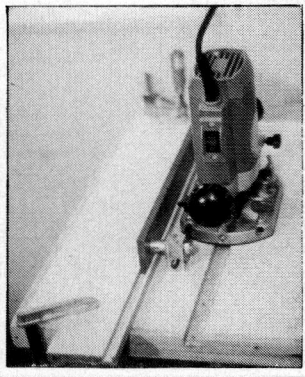

*E*ver-imaginative routing engineers Trend have come up with this **on-track routing guide** to ensure you don't veer off line and ruin your dado or housing work. The guide, which attaches with supplied fittings to any router, travels in a pre-cut groove in a board which is clamped to the work at the right setting. £12.50+VAT, or £17.80+VAT with an additional 'sub-base'.
● Trend Machinery and Cutting Tools Ltd, Unit N, Penfold Works, Imperial Way, Watford, Herts WD2 4YY, tel. (0923) 49911

**LONDON Wood Worker Show '85**

## Alexandra Palace 24th-27th October

# THE NATIONAL SHOW THAT IS ALL ABOUT WOOD

Beautiful wood:- Oak, Elm, Sycamore, Ash, Walnut, Mahogany. It's a celebration of its elegance and versatility. Exhibitors show tools with which to fashion it: lathes, routers, chisels, planes, saws, power tools. Competitors exhibit their individual creations in it—carvings, inlay, marquetry, musical instruments, cabinet making. Experts demonstrate their skills In it. And visitors are intrigued by it. Be one!

Open 10am-6pm each day—Sunday 10am-5pm
Admission: Adults £3.00 Children/OAP's £2.00.

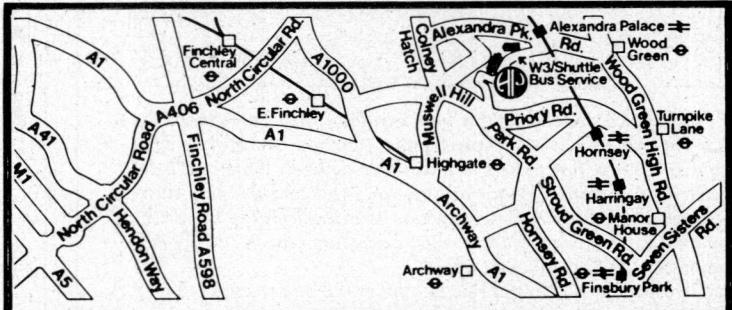

**How to get to Alexandra Pavilion**

**By Underground and bus service:**
Victoria line to Highbury and Islington and change to B.R. suburban line to Alexandra Palace. Piccadilly line to Wood Green and change to London Transport W.3 bus service.

**By British Rail:** B.R. Alexandra Palace is on the main line from King's Cross and Moorgate and a free bus shuttle operates to the Pavilion.

**By Car:** Alexandra Palace is a few minutes off the North Circular Road and there is AMPLE FREE PARKING.

# Alexandra Palace & Park, Wood Green, London N22

### *Organised by Argus Specialist Exhibitions Ltd. Telephone 0442 41221*

*Sponsored by "Woodworker" magazine.*

# Timberline

## Arthur Jones presents the month's inside news of supplies

Prices of timber and panel products change frequently. In softwoods and hardwoods they can take place overnight and occur weekly, while in panel products they usually take place once or twice a year except in times of rapid inflation.

Spring is usually the time for price changes in panel products, with perhaps a further change in the autumn if business has not progressed along forecast lines or inflation has made some increase necessary just to stand still. Some of the panel distributors issue stock and price guides, covering all the sheet materials from this country and overseas, and a free copy of the one that has just been issued by the Nevill Long Group (North Hyde Wharf, Hayes Rd, Southall, Middx UB2 5NL) is well worth getting. Not only is it a storehouse of information on sizes and prices, but the explanatory notes on different products can be helpful.

This particular guide has been issued following the introduction of new spring prices by main suppliers, but you will find that quite a number of the quoted prices are out of date by the time you come to buy. Its real value is as a guide. If you get the next issue in the autumn it is easy to make a quick comparison and see how prices have changed, as well as to keep a check on new lines introduced and old ones dropped.

For example, the list has up-to-date chipboard prices, which have risen of late. The gains seem to have been held, in spite of claims by the distributors that perhaps the manufacturers had been too hasty — especially as the output from British chipboard factories has risen this year by 30%. The Common Market authorities are even now in the middle of investigating a complaint that some European producers have been selling at below true production costs, thus dumping their chipboard in EEC markets.

There has not been a lot of movement in the other panel products. The coniferous plywood quota for this year has been exhausted, so future imports will carry a heavy duty, but woodworkers need not fear that prices for softwood plywood (mainly from Canada and the US) will rise sharply. This is really a book-balancing problem faced each year by the trade, and we can fairly safely forecast there will be adequate stocks in the country and price changes over the next few months will be marginal. Certainly there will be no big buying of this plywood when the duty has to be paid.

Producers around the world are taking dramatic action to reduce output so it comes more into line with world demand for softwood and hardwood. When this happens there will be more chance of selling at better prices (for the producer!), because for the past two years the value of timber on the world market has been falling at a time when there has been inflation everywhere. The business of sawmilling and exporting wood has been getting less and less profitable.

In softwood there has been a reduction of over 20% in Finland, and the Swedish mills are also cutting back, reducing the large stocks in these countries. Their export sales have slumped and prices are still struggling to achieve stability. The better unsorted grades of redwood are firm, and whitewood seems to be holding its own at last after falling in value steadily for a long time — but the lower grades of both continue at low prices.

The same sort of story applies to hardwoods. Stocks of meranti, seraya, lauan and Brazilian mahogany, for example, are quite high overall in the UK, and there are inevitably cheap offers from time to time.

The producing countries recognise that drastic action is needed to stop this price weakness. In Sabah, for example, the mills closed for a month, and in Sarawak production has been slashed by almost a third. It is always difficult to get agreement on prices and production, but progress is undoubtedly being made. In due course, when output comes closer to demand, this will mean that prices begin to rise again. Should there be even a small economic recovery among the importing countries, they could rise rapidly. ∎

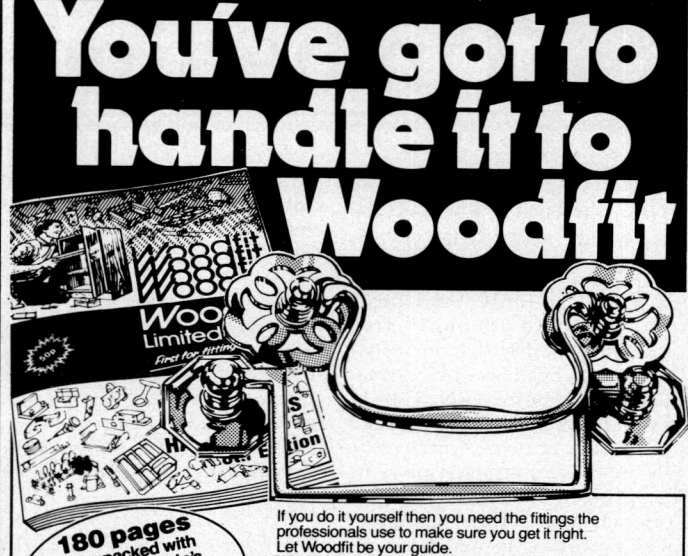

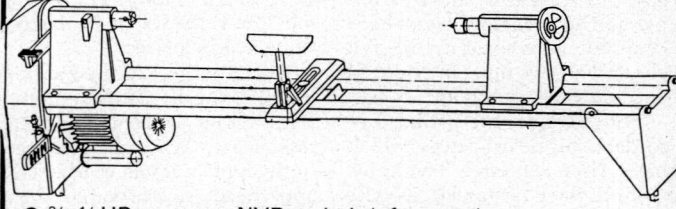
568

# Question box

## Our panel of experts solve your woodworking problems

**Q** *I have recently made an oak refectory table in mid-17th-century style, adhering strictly to the characteristics of the period. It is 8ft long and has six turned legs, and the 4in deep top rail is carved all round in lunettes. To go with it I intended making a set of eight farthingale chairs of the type contemporaneous with the table, but repairs at the V&A museum prevent me from taking measurements from their example.*

*The chairs are in oak, very plain and simple; the seat and the top half of the back of the one in the V&A are covered in 'Turkey work'. They are 37in high and 19in wide. I would like to know as many construction details as you can supply, and where there are any similar chairs I could look at.*

A. W. Pink, Fakenham

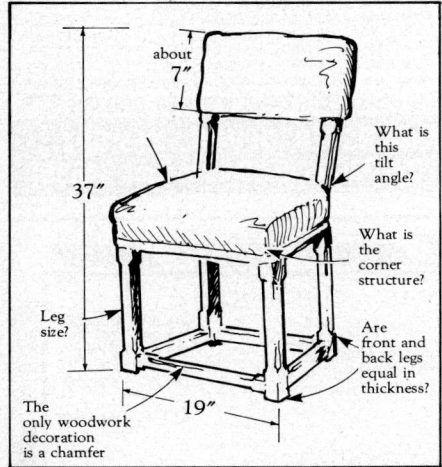

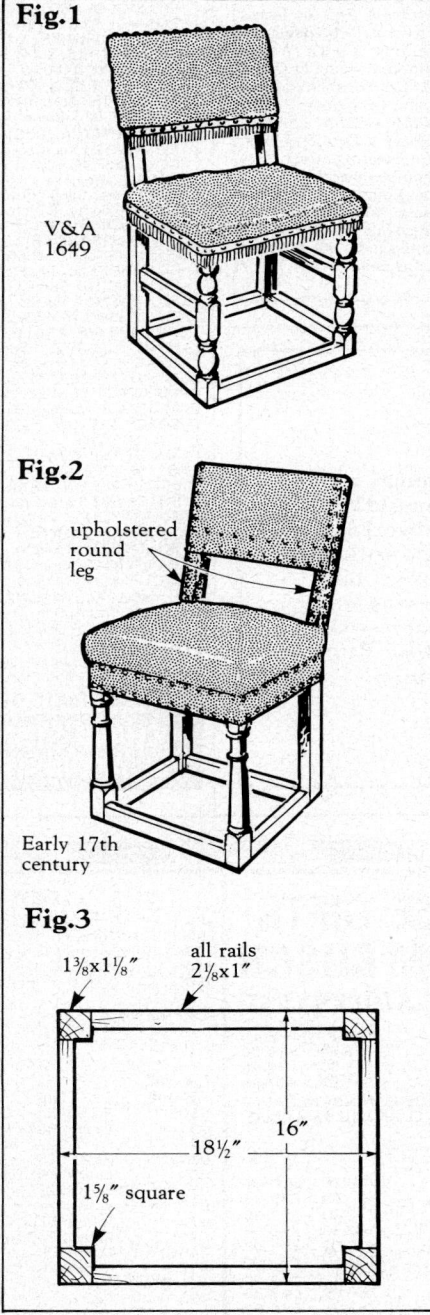

Fig.1
V&A 1649

Fig.2
upholstered round leg
Early 17th century

Fig.3
1⅜x1⅛"  all rails 2⅛x1"
18½"  16"
1⅝" square

**A** First of all, may I congratulate you on completing what must have been a mammoth task in building the table, and wish you every success in the chair project.

Before about 1600 all chairs had arms, not so much for comfort as to emphasise the status of the occupant. Any form of seat which had a back but no arms was called a 'back stool', and it was from this that the farthingale chair developed.

Its period ran from about 1580 to 1700; the absence of arms and the gap between the seat and the top rail allowed ladies wearing farthingale skirts to sit down more or less comfortably. The skirt's characteristic feature was the enormous whalebone hoop which supported it, and although by 1660 the fashion had died in England, the chairs continued to be made. They were called 'upholsterer's' or 'imbrauderer's chairs', no doubt because they were often upholstered in 'Turkey work', whose knotted pile imitated Turkish carpets. The term 'farthingale' seems to have originated in Victorian times.

I have sketched a couple of alternative designs in figs 1 & 2; fig. 3 is a sketch-plan of the seat which is rectangular.

One point to remember is that the seat was higher than is normal today, presumably to accommodate the large skirt, and can be 20-22in high.

I was rather doubtful about the type of base used for the seat stuffing, as all the examples I have seen have been re-upholstered with a webbing base — efficient, but not historically correct. Usually the top of the seat had a piece of stout canvas nailed to it, taken over the top edges and nailed round the sides. The stuffing material — wool or hair — was then laid on this and covered with the fabric, which was nailed down with brass-headed nails, spaced or clustered (fig. 5).

An alternative base for the stuffing was a mat of interlaced cords (fig.4), and in this case the top edges of the seat rails were probably given shallow rabbetts to house the nail-heads so they did not work through and tear the fabric.

Fig. 6 shows the rake of the back, although no doubt this would vary a little from one design to another; the back leg up to the seat height is vertical. One historically intriguing feature would be to upholster around the leg itself (fig. 2).

I believe there is a set of five chairs at Knole, Sevenoaks, Kent, dating back to 1610; the frames are painted birch, the legs are simple columns, and the upholstery is crimson velvet. I understand there are also some good examples at Aston Hall, Birmingham, which is administered by the Birmingham City Museum and Art Gallery.

Vic Taylor

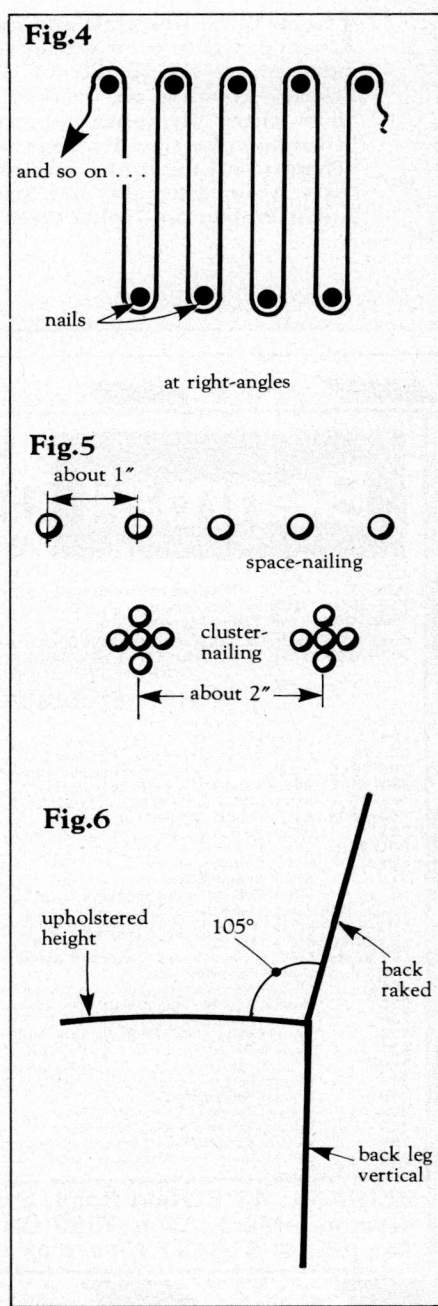

Fig.4
and so on . . .
nails
at right-angles

Fig.5
about 1"
space-nailing
cluster-nailing
about 2"

Fig.6
upholstered height
105°
back raked
back leg vertical

# Question box

Q *We would like to add a decoration to our lace bobbins, basically a uniform, very fine groove turned in spiral along the bobbin's length, about 1/16 in wide. The groove could be decorated in various ways.*

*Is there a way you could suggest of cutting this groove, perhaps with a small jig? I think it would have to be done after the bobbins were removed from the lathe, which is too simple to have screw attachments. The bobbins are wood, bone and ivory.*

G. Hall, Sunderland

A You are obviously wanting to make the traditional bound bobbins. The simplest way I have found for cutting a spiral groove is the traditional hand method with the bobbin still held in the lathe but not turning.

A fine-toothed saw is held at an angle to the bobbin and a cut made whilst the lathe is slowly turned by hand. Several light cuts will produce an accurate spiral groove whose pitch can be adjusted by varying the angle of the saw to the workpiece. .

This cut will suffice for bobbins to be bound with brass wire, but if a wider groove is needed — for wire and beads or wire and tinsel — it may be opened up with a needle-file of suitable cross-section.

Nick Perrin

---

Q *I am laying a tongue-and-groove oak kitchen floor, and would like to know the best way to achieve a resilient finish. The boards are 50x19mm; I don't want to stain the oak, but I will sand it, and thought of applying several coats of polyurethane varnish. Is this the best method?*

J. Porter, Glastonbury

A The floor can be finished with two or three coats of clear polyurethane, but as the drying time between coats is 6-8 hours it might be better to use a two-part cold-cure lacquer, such as Rustins Plastic Coating F. This type of finish is mixed with a hardener before use and then must be used within 24 hours. The curing time is 1-1½ hours at a temperature of 60°F and above, and the floor can be used two hours after the second coat has been applied.

For the first seven days, wipe any spilt water or solvent off as quickly as possible, since maximum resistance to solvents and water is not achieved for about a week.

If you choose polyurethane, use the largest brush possible, preferably 6in. This will cover the floor more quickly and show fewer brush-marks than a smaller one. You can spread the cold-cure lacquer with a brush, a roller, or a sponge-mop such as a Minit Mop.

A polyurethane finish dries by oxidation, and must not be applied so thickly as to prolong the drying time. Cold-cure lacquers, however, dry by catalytic reaction and can therefore be applied much more liberally, which is why you can use something like a mop.

Polyurethanes are usually pale to dark amber, and will darken the oak more than will cold-cure lacquers; the colour of the

wood when damped with water is a good guide to the darkening that these products cause. Oak will show very little change in colour; woods such as mahogany or teak will darken considerably, even if you use a completely colourless finish.

Whichever type of finish you use, make sure you have adequate ventilation, as a lot of solvent vapour will be released when you are working on a large area.

One litre of either finish will cover (one coat) approximately 150sq ft.

Ronald E. Rustin

---

Q *I am making a Regency bookcase in Brazilian mahogany; could you tell me how to get as near an antique finish as possible? I'm not a french polisher!*

Geoff Poppett, Rugeley

A I suggest the following procedure for an antique finish on Brazilian mahogany:

1 Damp down all surfaces with warm water to raise the grain, but don't soak them. Sand down with 240-grit garnet paper.
2 Apply a water stain if you want to colour the wood, and allow it to dry.
3 Lightly sand and apply a coloured filler if required. Sand down again using the garnet paper.
4 Colour in if necessary using the same water stain, and allow to dry.
5 Now apply a liberal coating of pale french polish, either by fad (a piece of used wadding with no cotton covering) or mop (polisher's brush). Apply numerous coats until the wood is covered, and allow to dry out for 24 hours.
6 Flat down all the surfaces with 400-grade silicon-carbide (wet-and-dry) paper, using raw linseed oil as a lubricant.
7 Using 0000 steel wool lubricated with wax, burnish the whole surface until you achieve a fine, smooth, semi-dull finish. This is your antique finish. Make sure the wax polish contains no silicones.
8 Finish with a clean piece of stockinette to remove all traces of wax polish.

In the preparation stage you could slightly distress the wood, but don't make the very common mistake of overdoing it!

Noel J. Leach

---

Q *I would like to make a spatula of wood, which would have to withstand immersion in hot fat or oil and be used for general cooking. Please could you recommend a type or types of wood?*

A.F.M., York

A Wooden spatulas could be made from non-odoriferous species such as birch, poplar, aspen, sycamore and willow, but the problem is relatively short life-expectancy. The acidity of cooking-oils and the alkalinity of washing-up liquids would progressively break down the cellulose and lignin in the wood, and the surface would gradually deteriorate. The high temperature of cooking-oil or fat would increase acidity; and, while acid absorbed into the wood

would tend to neutralise the alkalinity caused by washing-up, it would not do so completely. The thin section of the blade could thus roughen up and badly discolour. Wooden spoons (beech and maple) are frequently used in jam-making, but their immersion in hot fruit-juice is comparatively infrequent, whereas a spatula would presumably be in day-to-day use. Even so, wooden spoons do not retain their initial quality over a long period. I think this is one case where a plastic utensil is likely to outlive a wooden one.

Bill Brown FIWSc

---

Q *Coming fresh from an encounter with the wily woodworm – Anobium punctatum, I think you call him – I have yet more problems.*

*Last year a stack of 1in oak boards in my workshop was attacked, and this year the beetle – ignoring other supposedly more palatable types of timber – moved into a stack of 2in oak. Are there strains of woodworm specific to particular species of wood, as fleas are said to be to particular animals?*

*I carried outside the boards in which the wormholes were visible, and beneath which the piles of powder had accumulated, and stripped off the infected wood with a draw-knife. This revealed tunnels leading from the holes in the sapwood at the edges quite deep into the wood, but turning back from the heartwood. From time to time small white grubs appeared in the holes. I painted Cuprinol woodworm fluid on the exposed surfaces – quite unnecessarily, I suspect. If, as I understand, the familiar little holes are flight-holes made as the mature insects depart, is there any means of detecting a fresh attack before the holes appear?*

*Finally: as the second stack of oak has been drying since 1980, how can any animal sustain itself on such moisture-less material? Beetles in certain deserts, apparently, collect essential moisture from sea mists condensing on their bodies. There are no such mists in my workshop!*

John Crossley, Oakham

A It is obvious from what you say that the beetle in your oak is Lyctus, not Anobium (furniture beetle). Although there are superficial similarities in the appearance of the grubs, beetles and holes, there are a good many actual differences, of which the type of frass (bore dust) is one. If you rub a little of the frass from the oak between finger and thumb, you will find it has the consistency of talcum powder. Anobium dust is much coarser, and when seen through a hand-lens displays lemon-shaped pellets.

You ask whether wood-boring beetles have preferences; the answer is yes, very much so. In the case of Lyctus beetle, the first requirement is a wood whose pores are large enough to accept the female ovipositor during egg-laying, so host timbers are those like oak, ash, Spanish chestnut and walnut, elm and many more. The grubs also require starch as a food reserve, which is plentiful in sapwood, so the attack tends to be limited to these areas. Eggs can be laid to a depth of 7mm, so

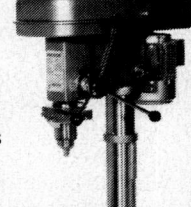

572

# Question box

superficial dousing with fluid may not have an immediate effect. The real answer is to saw the sapwood off all the boards and burn it. If quantity merits, it could go to a kiln to be sterilised by high-temperature/high-humidity treatment. *Lyctus* is generally a pest of timber yards, but it can initiate from dead tree-stumps or dead branches. If you leave *Lyctus*, or 'powder-post beetle', alone it will eventually reduce the sapwood to a powdery mass under a thin veneer of outer wood. The main period of activity is June to August, but depending on the weather it can start in May and continue till September. Beetles emerge through the flight-holes in the summer and start laying eggs in any nearby suitable wood; they can fly, but sluggishly and only for short distances, so the wind could blow them from your workshop into domestic premises. My advice is to act promptly and get rid of your oak sapwood.

This may appear drastic and expensive, but the risk of loss of customer goodwill from using *apparently* clean wood in your products ought to be more valuable than the loss of some sapwood.

Is there any way to detect a fresh attack? I can only say no, none; but while there is active attack in some of your wood, all the other sorts of timber mentioned are at risk. Untreated, the attack can go on for years. Fluids will only catch beetles emerging, and then only if the treatment is liberal; the arguments against are the odour of the insecticide and the fire risk from the fumes if you smoke. Your best bet is to remove the sapwood and burn it now, and do the same again if other woods show signs of attack later on.

*Bill Brown FIWSc*

**Q** *I own a DeWalt BS1310 bandsaw, and find a weakness in the material of the blade-guides. The originals were some sort of plastic, which wore out in no time at all, and since then I have tried several species of timber (not lignum vitae!) without much success.*

*I suspect metal is the best solution, but my knowledge in this field (like that of most woodworkers?) is limited, to put it mildly. I am reluctant to trade in for a new machine, but my wandering blades are driving me mad – can you help?*

*D. S. Cotter, Weybridge*

**A** I have had a BS1310 in service for 10 years or so, and have not so far had to replace any of the side-guides. Though not one of my main machines, it has had a lot of use, ranging from converting ebony from the log to profiling in plywood — and, on occasion, cutting up firewood! Perhaps 3000 hours of use overall.

The guides on my machine appear to be of semi-hard carbon steel — possibly hardened, quenched, and tempered to dark blue. There is some wear, but I would expect the horizontal guides to last another five years and the diagonal ones another 10. I would make two suggestions. First, write to the makers, asking if they can supply the

same type of guide as mine. Second, if this fails, obtain a piece of silver steel from your local engineer's tool dealer and, after cutting and filing to shape, heat each piece separately in a blowlamp until it reaches a cherry-red colour. Keep it at that temperature for about 10 minutes and then quench it in cold water in a bucket. Clean off the scale with emery, and then set it in a tin-lid full of dry sand. Heat from below and watch the colour change on the metal; it will pass from pale to dark straw, then purple, and then dark blue. At this point quench it again. It will now have the hardness of spring steel — about the same as that of the saw-blade.

It is, of course, vital that the guides run clear of the blade by a small amount — say 1mm — and especially that they are well clear of the teeth. I have twice found that properly adjusted guides fouled the weld on the saw-blade; both times the blade was replaced by the suppliers free of charge.

I find the machine well up to its work — it spends most of its time on hardwoods 4-6in thick — and my only serious criticism is that the die-cast degree markings are not as precise as I could wish. If you have difficulty getting silver steel locally, try K. R. Whiston, New Mills, Stockport, Lancs.

*Tubal Cain*

**Q** *I would like to know the procedure for making badminton rackets. I understand they incorporate ash and beech laminations; are the veneers steamed first – if so, how long for? and are they glued immediately, or left to dry? What glue is used? How is the work clamped? And lastly, what wood is used for the fillet in the neck?*

*D. Hasleham, Ashford*

**A** I should point out that wooden rackets are very much in decline and we no longer feature one in our badminton range. These notes relate to rackets as we used to make them, and may not be accurate as far as current producers are concerned.

Wooden badminton rackets are made from a variety of different woods — ash, beech, hickory, sycamore, mahogany and obeche. Bamboo is also used. The timber is received in either rough trunks or sawn planks. The uncut logs are first steam-soaked to make them easier to cut and trim, then peeled into veneers. Sawn planks aren't soaked before being cut into veneers, which are then selected according to the straightness of the grain.

The insert in the throat of the racket is specially machined from either solid sycamore or solid mahogany, and the shoulders of the racket are reinforced on the inside curved surface and the outside facing surfaces. For both these purposes the wood is steam-soaked and then bent to shape. The soaked and shaped blocks are machine-sawn into smooth slices of the required thickness.

The individual components are brought together to form a laminated structure known as a 'bend'. Lamination has a dual purpose; it places the appropriate wood in a

position where best use is made of its properties — for example, hickory is used as an outer veneer because of its superior resistance to impact and abrasive wear. It also enables best use to be made of grain effect. Thin strips of wood can be bent and glued together into shape, so the grain always follows the curves of the frame. This prevents cross-grain weakness and fracture of the frame under impact.

All the components except the handle- and shoulder-facings are glued with synthetic resin glue (urea-formaldehyde), and assembled in their relative positions in a clamping-frame. Hydraulic pressure is applied to the strips of wood by a metal strap and an inner head former.

After assembly, the bend is left in a controlled atmosphere to stabilise to a moisture content of 10%. The bend is then cut and finished with holes, countersinking, crescents, bevelled edges, shaft and handle before being electrostatically sprayed, gripped and strung.

*Mike Mullaney,*
*Dunlop Slazenger International*

**Q** *I am just completing a blanket box made from secondhand teak which I intend to oil. Can you advise if teak oil would be suitable for the interior, bearing in mind the box's purpose? Would the oil sweat or cause the linen to smell over a period of time?*

*Cleaning up this teak, I noticed white chalk-like lines. Could you say what this might be? – I feel it may be resin. They appear to go right through the timber; what's the best treatment for this problem?*

*R. Eaton, York*

**A** Although teak oil contains oxidising agents which make it durable and therefore suitable and attractive for the outside of your blanket chest, I don't recommend it for the inside. Normally all that's required for interior work such as on wardrobes and bookcases is to apply enough polish to prevent dust and grime from soiling the wood. A high gloss is not needed.

A suitable finish would be transparent white french polish, which has a pale yellow colour and will not significantly darken the wood. Do not use ordinary white polish as this may produce a greyish appearance on teak.

Remove the lid from the chest and wipe off all traces of dust. Work in a warm room (about 65°F) and brush a coat of transparent white polish all over the interior of the chest and lid with a soft brush. Two applications should be enough, but you can put on a third if you wish. Next day, when the polish has thoroughly hardened, any little nibs or roughnesses can be lightly eased down with fine glasspaper or 0000 wire wool.

The white chalk lines are probably secretions of apatite or calcium phosphate. They will quickly take the edge off your plane irons and chisels but will not harm your polish.

*Charles Cliffe*

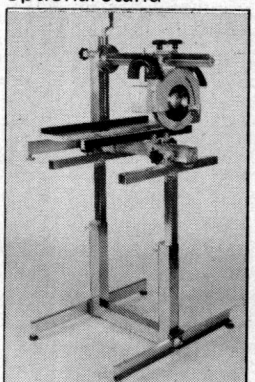
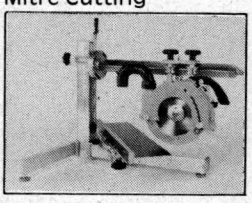

# Books

*Ray Key*
**Woodturning and Design**
*Batsford, £10.95 hardback*
*Reviewed by Cecil Jordan*

Ray Key has been turning wood for a living for a dozen years or so, and has taught turning for some of them. One would have expected him to tackle the subject in a down-to-earth fashion, and that is just what he has done. No frills here. He deals with machines, tools, chucks, sharpening, techniques and finishes in a straightforward, mainly orthodox way — adding a few of his views to accepted methods.

He acknowledges some of those turners who have influenced his own work. The illustrations and examples tend towards the derivative rather than the innovative, but the basic approach is sound enough.

The final chapters discuss shapes. Ray Key attempts to analyse the factors which make for good design, and to present shapes which he thinks typify the opposite. I found this section weak and not very convincing. The poor shapes, yes. But what of the shapes that we all want to pick up and handle? Some potters and some turners have a flair and instinct for these, and — apart from a few really basic considerations — this area does not lend itself to the kind of treatment Ray Key gives it.

I found the constant duplication of metric and imperial measurements irritating, and there is a mistake on p57 which could lead to a misunderstanding: for clockwise, read anti-clockwise in line 4 of the right-hand column.

The book is written for the amateur, and there is nothing much here for the professional.

*A. B. Emary*
**Site Carpentry and Advanced Joinery**
*Macmillan, £9.95 paperback*
*Reviewed by Bob Grant*

The author, like other modern luminaries in this specialised field of professional woodworking (such as Frank Hilton and W. B. McKay), succeeds to a long line of technical writers and illustrators stretching back to the worthy Joseph Moxon. It was Moxon who in 1677 published *Mechanick Exercises or the Doctrine of Hand Works* as the first attempt to teach the artisan the intricacies of his craft other than by time-honoured oral instruction.

Mr Emary's books for the wood tradesman are held in high esteem for their accuracy and authority, and this one is the last in a trilogy written principally for the advanced student aiming at the exams set by the Institute of Carpenters, the City and Guilds, and the Technician Education Council. The subject is timber construction of the highest and most complicated order as related to building. Hammer-beam roofs, domes, turrets, bridges, handrailing, stair-work and so forth are all here.

They are illustrated by the author's own drawings, which are characteristically clear

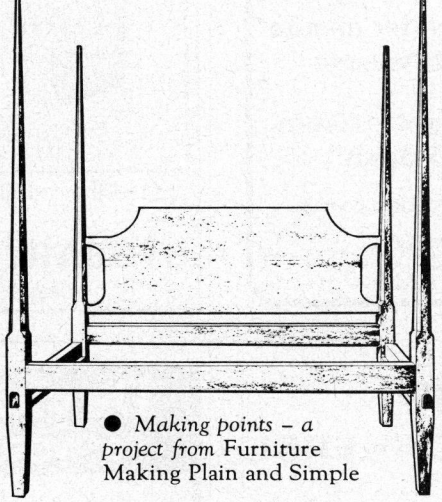

● *Making points – a project from* Furniture Making Plain and Simple

and forthright. However, he emphasises in his introduction that these must be studied in conjunction with the text. He is now retired from teaching, but knows from long experience that the tyro will always try to get away with just looking at the drawings and ignoring the rest of the page.

Unfortunately, the photographs have not reproduced well, and tend to look like the occasional snapshot. But this is a mere quibble over what is otherwise an excellent production.

Although written for the professional end of the woodworking spectrum, the book may nevertheless prove of interest to the amateur and building enthusiast. For instance, the delightful sweeping eyebrow window on p37 is now rarely seen in new work, and is regrettably one of a host of vanishing vernacular forms. Recorded here, however, it is not altogether lost.

*Aldren Watson and Theodora Poulos*
**Furniture Making Plain and Simple**
*Norton, hardback*
*Reviewed by Luke Hughes*

This excellent book claims to be designed for both the experienced and the new woodworker who want to build furniture but are frustrated by lack of construction directions, and mystified by technical drawings, plans and illustrations.

The author writes: 'I feel an affinity with all woodworkers before me undertaking for the first time to build a good and useful piece of furniture; who began at the same place with similar tools and equal trepidation; who I see now are obliged to make the very mistakes that were mine and who no less frequently despaired of ever getting things right.'

There are chapters on different woods, the buying of lumber (the Americanisms in no way detract from the relevance of the information), woodwork practices, fastenings, all the different joints, drawer construction, the hanging of doors, finishing, and at the back (as is common with such books) 11 projects of furniture. But, unlike those in many similar many books, these have a simplicity and elegance

about them which is irresistible — based, I imagine, on Shaker design principles.

An additional treat is the quality of Aldren Watson's pencil drawings. These, combined with the excellent presentation of the volume as a whole, make it one of the more attractive woodwork books to have emerged recently — quite on a par with some of the cabinetmaker's manuals of the 1920s and 1930s.

It is undoubtedly a must for schools and colleges — and for anyone who thinks that, because he doesn't have the machinery, he is wasting time making elegant furniture at weekends: for all the projects and supporting information are geared entirely to hand tools. There is a wealth of detail about setting out, and even about making turned legs without a lathe, which would not go wasted in the workshops of those of us now dominated by machinery.

*Ian Punter*
**Making Furniture for the Home**
*Batsford, £9.95 hardback*
*Reviewed by Roger Woods*

This third book by Mr Punter contains both a series of chapters on materials and techniques, and a section of design projects including working drawings and details of construction. Together these make it very interesting and useful.

A few points, however:
● In the section on planing timber, minor errors make understanding more difficult than it need be for those to whom the subject is new. When 'gauging to thickness' the gauge lines will be on the edge of the board — not the sides as stated; the sides are the broad faces. But the chapter is useful, and the techniques well described.

● I would take issue with the suggestion that the reason for cutting a thread path with a steel screw before replacing it with a brass one is only to avoid damage to the slot in the head of the brass screw. The brass screw usually shears off at the shank if the path for its screw part has not been sufficiently well prepared.

The chapter on acrylic has good suggestions on working practice, not often found in popular publications. The section on working designs includes a good summary of the design process. The island storage unit is an ingenious idea, well detailed, (save for the dimensional error where a radius of 100mm is meant but 10 is given).

All in all a very good book, with a commendable quality of drawings and a clear text. The designed objects could benefit from a sophistication of line to make them a little more elegant, but are cleverly conceived and detailed.

John Sainsbury's book *Planecraft: A Woodworker's Handbook* is published by Sterling at £14.95 hardback and £7.50 paperback — not by the Guild of Master Craftsmen Publications as we said last month.

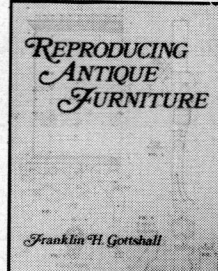
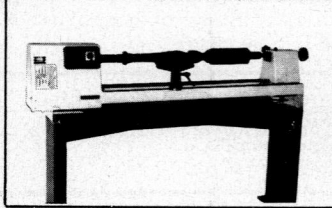

# Bristol Woodworker Show

● 'Nuts' is the title. Rodney Smith carved it from a single piece and carried off a gold metal

● Very highly commended – K. Gould's marquetry picture of Cow Lane, Guernsey

● Paul Rathkey's superb writing unit in padauk fought off two junior competitors for a gold medal

**P**eter Collenette writes: It promised to be good, and it was good. Bristol on a sunny Bank Holiday weekend made a first-class venue for the first West Country Woodworker Show.

There was lots to see and snap up in the merchandise line, and the entries for the competitions were mostly refreshingly good. The feeling was lively and I, for one, enjoyed myself. As a chance to meet and talk with future contributors, it proved more fruitful than I could have hoped.

Unquestioned stand-out of the competition classes was Robert Coles' mighty sideboard, occupying a bay all to itself at one end of the upper hall. Built in ash, elm and walnut to a very demanding design involving lots of framing-and-panelling and a scarfed beam, it was valued at £5000 and may even fetch that some day. There were some extremely attractive carvings, too (I liked the baboon myself), and the turnings were better than those at last year's London Show. The judges departed happy at what they'd seen.

Most of the suppliers, who by all accounts were doing brisk business, were familiar from previous shows and indeed from this magazine — but none the worse for that. Tools, machines, timber, finishes ... they're the specialists, and between them they can sell you almost anything you'll ever want. An interesting and welcome newcomer was Charles Stirling of Bristol Design, who deals in antique and reproduction tools. His alluring stand doubled as HQ for the Tool and Trades History Society. ∎

● Prizewinners' parade! Gold medallists, every one

From left: A. Smith, Alan Dixon, Robert Coles, prize-giver Zach Taylor, R. Hamley, Geoffrey Winnacott, Paul Rathkey, D. Smith; front – M. Henderson, Rodney Smith, Richard Shellard

# Guild notes

## Cornish craft

**Duncan Askew**, who specialises in woodturning, also makes a special range of educational toys. More or less complicated jigsaws, the pieces with or without handles, are cut out of pine or ply; with his wife Anne, he also produces clocks, a 'Harbour play puzzle', and devices designed to teach colour awareness to children. They also sell giftware, and do production runs for local firms; Duncan does a bit of teaching too. 'I am always interested in meeting fellow woodturners', he says, 'especially in the summer months when they bring their families to Cornwall.' Look him up at 31 Station Rd, St Newlyn East, Newquay, Cornwall TR8 5NE.

## Going east . . .

**John Chambers** from Carlisle, who is keen enough on his craft to have come to Oxford for a one-day cabinetmaker's-decorative-techniques course last December, is going a lot further afield — to Madras, where he'll be working with a Christian mission in a carpentry/cabinetmaking training workshop for orphans. 'For three months or possibly longer.' Best of luck, John; I've asked for news from him, so watch these pages for woodworking stories from India.

## Gramophone-phile

Apart from knocking up the occasional perfect reproduction tilt-top, crossbanded, inlaid oval table like this one, new London member **Fred Ivimey** restores acoustic gramophones. 'A slightly odd minor skill', he calls it; if he puts into his acoustic soundboxes anything like the craftsmanship the table displays, they must be a delight to the eye as well as the ear. Fred is interested in developing more modern designs, and also restores antiques. The first-class photo was taken by his son Philip, who is a professional photographer, and obviously knows what to do with furniture in front of the lens. Fred would like to meet other members; his address is 727 Lordship Lane, Wood Green, London N22 5JN.

## Bristol bouquet

Our thanks to **David Ellis**, of Restorations Unlimited, who demonstrated his skills on a special stand at the Bristol Show, and talked long and hard to members and potential members about the Guild and its future. David is a local rep, so if you're in his area, get in touch with him at Pinkney Park, Malmesbury, Wilts.

## Travelling journeyman

**Christoph Henrichsen** is a 22-year-old qualified cabinetmaker who finished his apprenticeship in Germany last year. He is interested in learning cabinetmaking in England, and would like to work for a year for someone — 'as a joiner', he says, but there might be a translation hiccup here. If you would be interested in taking on an obviously enthusiastic and determined worker, and getting into some cultural exchange into the bargain, write to Christoph at Kirchstrasse 2, 7800 Freiburg, West Germany.

● *Letters piling up . . . **Janet Maxwell** gets her head down at a demonstration.*

● *Fred Ivimey's superb reproduction table. The top is made of three edge-jointed pieces; note the brass claw feet and delicate scratch-stock work on the legs*

## Pegmen problem

**John Johnson** is another toymaker, this time in Stourbridge in the West Midlands. He has recently set up in business and is looking for someone to produce pegmen for him, preferably of beech, with a detachable head. If you think you can help him, write to him at Prospect Hill, Stourbridge, West Midlands DY8 1PN, tel. (0384) 378725.

## Guild Gallery

Remember, members — you have the opportunity to display your work on the Guild/Editorial stand at the Woodworker Show, Alexandra Palace, 24-7 October. One year's subscription has to make this the exhibition bargain of the century. One or two small pieces each — first come, first served; please send photos of your work for vetting.

## Local rep

**Birmingham:** latest enthusiastic response to the idea of meeting, talking to, and working with members in his area is from **Bill Ferguson**, 40 Quinton Lane, Quinton, Birmingham. Get directly in touch with him.

## Carving in company

New member **Janet Maxwell** is a medical artist in a medical school, but is interested in woodcarving in all its forms — particularly woodcut letters for signs. She is at a loss to find others who share her interest, so get in touch with her at 44 Wells House Rd, London NW10 6EE.

# Guild courses

### Furniture restoration — Eric Burger

25-6 July, Bournemouth, £40+VAT. This is the first course that Eric has run specifically for the Guild, and I hope by no means the last. He offers a very full programme including furniture repairs, working with glues and finishes, veneering, inlaying and marquetry, french polishing, gilding and waxing. We will be arranging more dates later in the year.

### Hand veneering — Bob Grant

14 September, St Augustine's of Canterbury School, Oxford, £30+VAT; an introduction to traditional techniques. Bob opens the subject with samples and demonstrations; then you veneer a small panel of your own with a cross-veneered border and mitred corners, and a balancer on the back. **Peter Sarac,** a local harpsichord maker, will be there as well.

● *Above, Charles Cliffe and Andrew Gowans, the works manager of John Myland, conduct an animated discussion on the refinishing of a Windsor chair. Stanley Folb took the photo. Left, this magnificent ebony and gilt table was revived in Eric Burger's workshop*

### French polishing — Charles Cliffe

10-11 October, Bexleyheath, £35+VAT. Surface preparation, stains and staining, introduction to shellac polishes and other finishes; using the cabinet-scraper, grain-filling, bodying up, spiriting off. Charles is only too happy to answer polishing queries; bring your own small pieces of furniture to work on.

# The balancing act

Neil Wyn Jones is a young Merseyside designer-maker who's searching, like many others, for the balance between creativity and commerce. He tells his own story

I started my woodworking career at home. As you can imagine, a small universal machine and a bench in the garage, a lathe in the spare bedroom upstairs and piles of timber on the landing caused a continuous stream of shavings and dust up and down stairs.

After a year at home doing a great deal of woodturning and attending numerous craft fairs, I moved into my first real workshop in the Liverpool Craft Centre in Mathew Street. With fewer distractions and more room, I developed a better attitude to work. I started producing small items of furniture at first — coffee-tables and wall-hanging corner cupboards — and through craft fairs and exhibitions in local libraries I received my first commissions.

Among these were an adjustable lectern for a local church and a hi-fi unit in oak to match an almost-black Tudor-style dining-room suite. 24 hours after it was delivered, the hi-fi unit was returned on the grounds that the colour and finish were not up to standard. I was very defensive and indignant at this, my first major setback, but I have grown to endorse the original client's opinion — particularly as the piece has taken up residence in my bedroom. The experience has put me off staining for life! I am still reluctant to stain anything, and I try to use timbers with enough character and interest of their own.

After nearly two years in my first workshop I moved into larger premises. At the same time I invested in a Startrite K260 universal and a Sears radial-arm saw. These, plus an Arundel M300 lathe and a DeWalt bandsaw bought with a grant from the Prince's Trust, make up my current collection of machines. Among my power tools I have 3in and 4in Elu belt-sanders, which have been invaluable, withstanding use and misuse for over three problem-free years.

More recently I have been fortunate to be able to concentrate full-time on making furniture, which I find more rewarding than turning. I feel I can get my teeth into larger pieces, and — to be a little optimistic — it is good to think your work may still be alive and kicking in a couple of hundred years. I still enjoy turning very much, though, and find it a pleasant change to settle down with a chunk of timber on the face-plate and see what comes out.

I work mainly in British hardwoods because I love the variety of figure to be found in, for instance, a hedgerow elm. I like to be able to identify with the tree that provides the timber, rather than using something bland and imported, and I think

● *Much of Neil's work takes advantage of ash as a complement to darker timbers. The delicate detailing of this bow-fronted desk and chair is in teak*

clients react in the same way. Most people have seen a sycamore or an ash tree and thus can have more respect for the raw materials.

As well as commission work I have made many pieces on spec, some of which have ended up in our lounge. This has enabled me to develop my own style of work, and I find it very rewarding when someone commissions me to produce a piece to certain specifications but whose design is down to me. This is a happy compromise because when I'm making on spec I'm always conscious that there's no guarantee of any money!

Paradoxically enough I find the need to make money is the most frustrating part of being in business. So far I have not managed to come to terms with the apparently never-ending conflict between commercial success and creativity. If the truth be known, I stumbled into business because it seemed the next relevant step to take after leaving college. In some ways I have surprised myself by being able not only to support myself (with the backing of my family, who are my best customers, and especially my mother who helps me with business and marketing), but also to employ Gillian, a very competent young cabinetmaker. She has done the same two-year Liverpool Central College course in

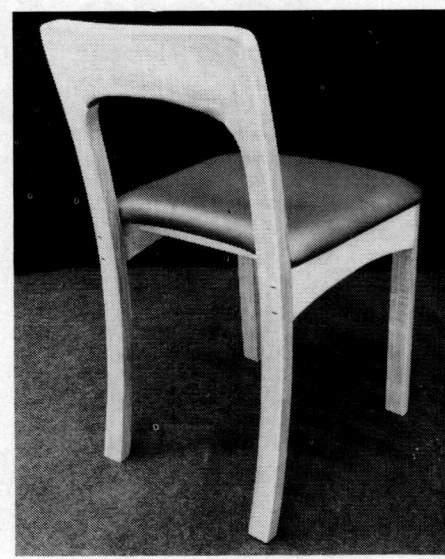

● *A low-backed dining chair to go with a solid ash pedestal dining-table*

Furniture Design and Craftsmanship as myself and came to me on a training scheme for 12 months. For the past five I have been able to employ her myself.

Most of the work I produce is contemporary, simply because I enjoy the challenge of designing. I get most satisfaction from a piece which I have taken from design to finished article, and which perhaps has just a little character of its own. In June's *Woodworker* Andrew Conning was quoted as saying modern furniture was 'kid's stuff'. In some ways I can understand that opinion, but there is far more merit in a simple modern piece than meets the eye. I try to use designs that will bring out the best in the timber, and also to create functional, well-built items that will last and be identifiable with the time and spirit in which they were made. I find this a great challenge, and hope that future generations will appreciate a genuine 20th-century piece as much as we appreciate 18th-century furniture today.

One of my most unfortunate experiences concerned a small corner cupboard which had been with me a few months. I was very pleased when someone decided to buy it, but not so happy when the client phoned me a couple of weeks later, sounding very distressed. The glass bottom had fallen out, dumping his valuable cut glass on the sideboard below and leaving his wife in tears. This was entirely my fault: I had forgotten to put a screw in a supporting stay, and the glue had finally given way. Fortunately the broken items were replaceable, but this mistake left me with a bill for £140 — almost the cost of the cupboard. To my great surprise the cupboard was still wanted, and after a quick repair job the

● *The semi-elliptical hall table* **above** *is an effective modern treatment of a characteristic traditional shape. It is also in ash, with teak edging.* **Below** *are a distinctive telephone-seat and selections from Neil's range of occasional tables. The contrast here is between brown oak and sycamore*

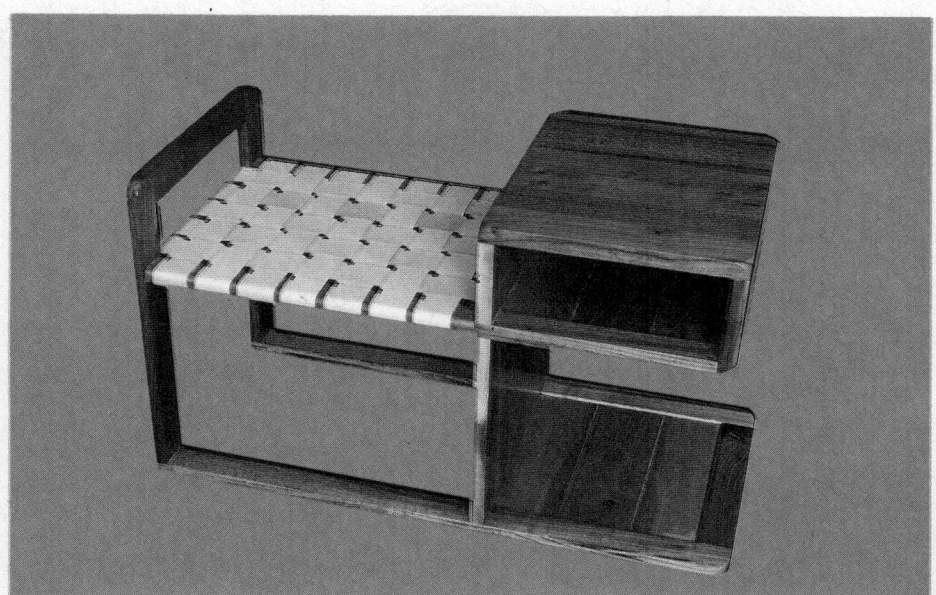

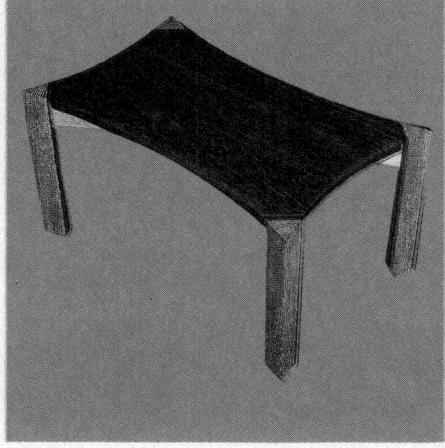

client was quite happy to try again.

Ideally I would like my own display area attached to the workshop, where I could show my work in the right surroundings. Suitable premises are always difficult to find; purpose-built workshops, as well as being very expensive, don't seem the right environment for the type of work I produce. The closure of the Liverpool Centre Craft Shop, where I did have a display, was something of a blow that has made this need even more pressing, but I show my work in galleries in Lancaster and Manchester. One of the obvious aims is to exhibit in London, and I won awards at the Woodworker Show in 1982 and 1983 — my yew goblets on an ash tray and a pierced sycamore bowl won a bronze in the faceplate woodturning class. I am hoping for even higher fortune in 1985! ∎

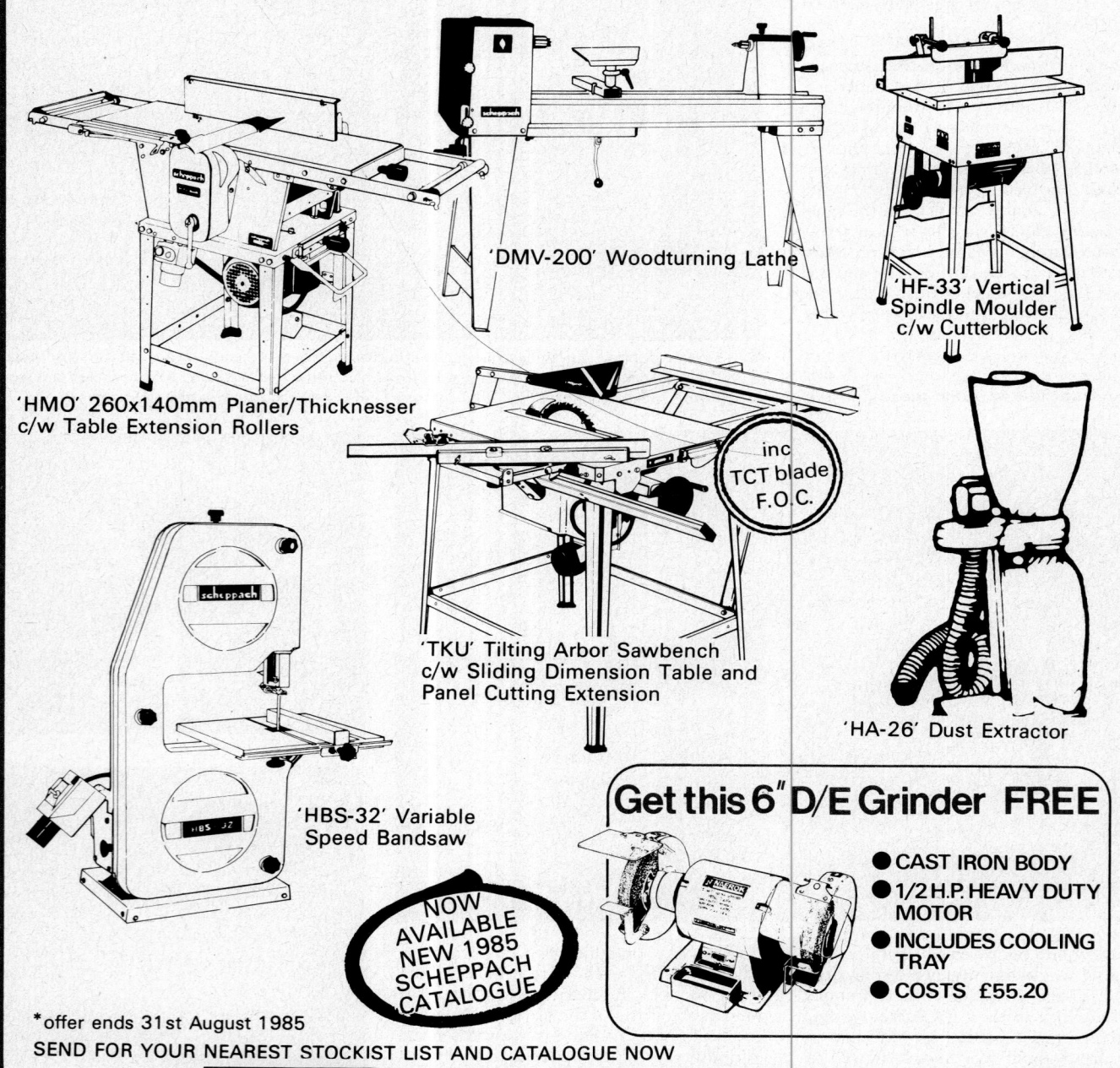

# Turning tools: On test

**Experience teaches what tools to buy — but you need the tools to get the experience. Tobias Kaye eases the dilemma by testing some major makes**

Choosing tools for woodturning is not easy. A proper study of all the brands available could involve a lot of travelling! The best solution is a trip to the Woodworker Show (or a similar exhibition). But even there you'll be faced with differences in design and handles — quite apart from the choice between carbon and high-speed steel (HSS).

So I've attempted to define what makes a good tool, and to beat a path through the advertising and salesmen's claims.

## CHARACTERISTICS

How well a gouge holds an edge is determined by its steel, but how well it cuts is determined by its shape. The shape dictates how it feels, too — how easy it is to steer and control. This is because, in use, there are three important points of contact:
● the cutting edge;
● the back of the bevel, where it touches the wood;
● the shank, which is supported by the tool-rest.

A constant or even relationship between these makes a gouge pleasant to handle and predictable in its behaviour. An uneven relationship, resulting from a sudden change in steel thickness or flute shape, or from ridges on the shank, makes a gouge tricky and less satisfying to use.

With the forged carbon-steel deep-U type of bowl gouge still available from Henry Taylor, Ashley Iles and Stormont Archer, each sample is slightly different, so you need to select carefully. Choose one which has a deep flute, even flute curvature and uniform thickness. For me, a good example of this type is far nicer to handle than the later type made from round bar. However, these forged gouges are not available in HSS, because HSS cannot be forged. And a telephone poll of five leading woodturners elicited one 'No comment' and three in favour of the round-bar type.

With spindle gouges there is again a choice between round bar in HSS and — from Iles, Archer and Taylor — forged radius-curve patterns. Again it's a matter of preference, especially since Iles now do the radius-curve gouge in HSS. Every round-bar gouge is the same as its brother, but with radius-curve gouges there are sometimes differences. Look for a smooth flute, an even curve outside, and the minimum of extra steel on either side of the flute. The less bulk on either side, the easier it is to cut up to beads, pummels and sheer edges.

With skew and square-ended chisels, the design is uncomplicated. Iles provide theirs with domed edges. This gives them a nice feel and marginally more control. But all four manufacturers (including Robert Sorby) leave the four edges a bit sharp. If you smooth these down slightly on a belt-or drum-sander, tool control will be much easier.

For scrapers the main criterion is hardness. A smooth finish on top is desirable, but at the cutting edge this can be obtained on a stone. Iles provide domed edges here too — but this is a great disadvantage with straight-edged scrapers, as it means you can't run the cutting corner tight up against its cut when, for example, forming a spigot or hollowing out. However, Iles say they will make flat-sided scrapers to order.

Parting tools are a matter of taste. Some people like flat-sided ones, some like a diamond section, some like fluted-base tools. Iles and Archer do a swaged (flare-tip) parting tool, which is fast and light to use but leaves a rough finish. The new 'de luxe' parting tool does give a good finish, but it needs careful sharpening — and it digs into the tool-rest, which is sometimes awkward and leaves ridges on the rest; these ridges catch chisels just when you're trying for a smooth shape.

Personally, my favourite parting tool is the flat-sided type. If kept sharp it gives a very good finish, is useful for fine beads, and costs little.

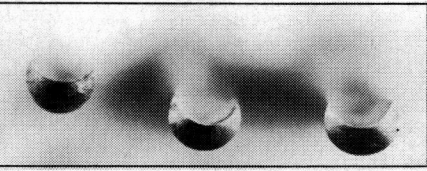

● *HSS spindle gouges: left to right – ⅜in Iles, 10mm Taylor and Sorby*

## THE TEST

The tools I tested came from Ashley Iles, Henry Taylor, Robert Sorby and Stormont Archer. Almost all were very good. I couldn't pick any one manufacturer as the best — each made one or two tools better than all the others.

Each, however, did have general strong points and general shortcomings. Iles' tools, I found, were generally longest. Taylor took the most care to polish out grinding marks, making it easier to obtain a good edge. Sorby used the hardest steel. Archer make very deep bowl gouges, but unfortunately their steel is not as hard as it should be.

I had one or two sample tools from each range tested for hardness at Stroud Technical College (my thanks go to Mr Portlock, and also to Mr Wilkinson for his kind assistance). The results were obtained on a Vickers diamond-point machine, and have been converted to their Rockwell equivalents; they appear in the table.

## Bowl gouges

Being a bowl turner, I was keen to try out the bowl gouges first. A close look showed that, of the three HSS gouges made from round bar, the Taylor Diamic Superflute gouge had the deepest, largest flute, though all three were made from the same size of bar. Sorby's flute was the smallest — definitely too small, in my opinion. Iles' flute was nice and deep but not wide enough, and it had too sudden a change of curvature at its deepest point.

Over the next three months I compared the gouges on bowl after bowl in many different woods, and these impressions were fully confirmed. The small flute in the Sorby means that basically it is a smaller gouge, cutting less than the Superflute. In addition, the resulting extra thickness of steel gives it a heavier feel than the others. The Iles cuts well but does not have the fine control of the remaining two, especially on delicate cuts. The sudden tight curve at the bottom of its flute makes it a bit unpredictable, and even sometimes a little vicious. The Superflute is definitely my favourite, coming close to (if not upsetting) my old ½in deep-V forged gouge for really pleasant handling. It is also the longest tool and the one with the nicest handle. A pity it's not made from such hard steel as the others.

Of the carbon-steel bowl gouges, Sorby's is the same shape as its HSS counterpart. The Iles is the traditional shape and very long, but not deep enough in the flute. The Taylor is a good gouge, especially if hand-picked.

From the samples I have, the Archer gouges seem to vary tremendously. The ⅜ one is a beautiful shape — very deep, with a very smooth curve and a fairly even steel thickness. But it is not very long, and the handle is too thin and too short. The ¼in one is very deep, but the flute is almost square — very difficult to control indeed. I do not know whether this disparity arises between samples or between sizes. If the former, hand-picking could furnish you with some very nice shapes. A pity the steel isn't very hard.

## Spindle gouges

The shapes of Taylor's and Sorby's HSS spindle gouges are almost identical. The Taylor is much better finished, particularly in the flute (where it matters), and I prefer the handle shape. The Sorby is of harder steel.

The Iles HSS gouges are smaller in diameter than the other two. You may find this useful if you do delicate work, but it does mean that they are not as strong. The smallest one, in particular, is very long for its size. I was ham-fisted enough to break mine. HSS breaks like file steel, and several small, sharp pieces went singing across my workshop. Personally, however, I find it very useful to have the Iles sizes in addition to the Sorby and Taylor ones.

If you want round-bar gouges, buy HSS ones. There is no advantage in having carbon-steel gouges unless you want the special shapes.

Sorby only do round-bar gouges now, except for their ¾in bowl gouge, which is still forged. Taylor and Iles both do very

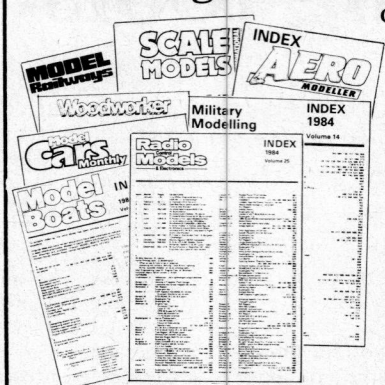

584

# Turning tools: On test

good traditionally forged radius-curve spindle gouges. It seems to me that Iles gouges have slightly less 'overhang' steel at the edges of their flutes, but both makes vary from sample to sample. Again, hand-picking for evenness of steel will give you the best results.

Iles sent me a sample of their radius-curve spindle gouge in HSS. I'm glad they're making it, as the choice between good steel and a good shape is not easy. If they would just grind the edges back a bit to reduce the overhang, it would be the best spindle gouge available.

## Roughing gouges

I have a rather motley group of sample roughing gouges — ¾in ones from Iles and ¼in from Taylor. Of the two ¾in ones the Iles is significantly larger than the Sorby, being nearly ⅞in against barely ¾in. It's a better shape, having an even 170° radius curve, where the Sorby has slight angles and flats — not so important for roughing, I admit, but many people use a ¾in roughing gouge for large curves too, and I even use mine on the outsides of bowls for roughing or finish cuts, depending on the wood. The ¾in Iles is also longer, of thicker steel, and with a wider tang — all bonus points for a roughing gouge.

Judging by the immense 1½in size of their so-called 1¼in roughing gouge, Taylor's ¾in one may be even bigger than Iles'. A gouge as large as this 1½in one is a definite bonus to the professional, to whom speed is important. It is also amusing, as countless people coming into the workshop comment on its size — asking, for instance, whether it's not perhaps used for digging graves. It smooth finish, inside and out, makes it surprisingly easy to use.

## Parting tools

What do you want out of a parting tool? Obviously hard steel is important, and Archer — whose swaged parting tool is otherwise very good — fail in this respect. Iles are the only other manufacturer offering a swaged tool; it is very long, and nice to handle in deep cuts. Sorby do a diamond-section tool, but my favourite is the Sorby flat-sided ⅛in HSS. Of very hard steel, it holds a very good edge and is nicely balanced. I use it for cutting beads as much as for parting.

## Chisels

I do like the rounded edges of the Iles tools, and their length. The ½in one has become one of my favourite tools. Archer's ½in chisel also has a nice balance and action — a pity it's not as hard as the others. It cuts well, but it needs sharpening often.

## Scrapers

Now that HSS is available, carbon-steel scrapers are not worth considering.

Look, too, for finish — on the top surface particularly, but also on the bottom, for ease of sliding on the tool-rest. A radiused bottom would be an advantage

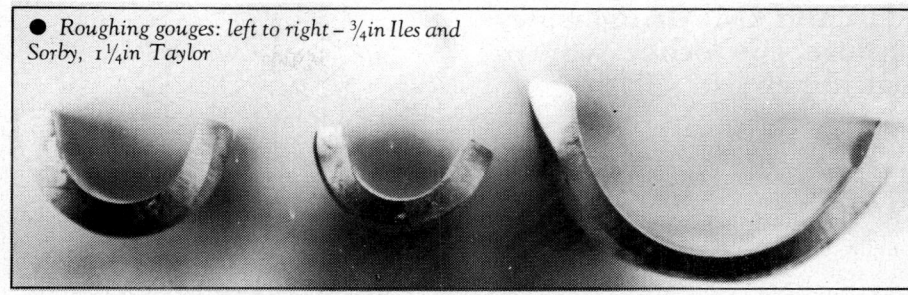

● *Roughing gouges: left to right – ¾in Iles and Sorby, 1¼in Taylor*

here, though a radiused top would obviously interfere with the cut. Iles' scrapers, with domed edges to their bases, are not good tools. Taylor's are the best finished, with smooth surfaces all round; but I would go for a Sorby, as being the hardest. I would use an oilstone to smooth the top next to the cutting edge.

### Finish

The whole Taylor range comes out best for finish. I'm not sure if the Presto black coating on Iles' All Black range covers a poor finish or highlights one, but a bit of work with a slipstone is required to get a really smooth tip in the flutes.

### Handles

It is easy to make your own handles, but not always necessary. I liked the rounded shape of Taylor's handles best, but the finish is a bit plastic — smooth to the touch, but insulting to the woodturner's eye. On that count Sorby emerge best, though I must say it beats me why they stick overgrown drawing-pins into their handles' upper ends. I liked most of Iles' handles, but the one on their big bowl gouge was too fat even for my big hands. Archer's handles are too short and too thin, except possibly for small hands.

## STAR TOOLS

After I'd worked with these tools for three months, three stood out. Others may respond differently, but I found myself reaching for these all the time. They are:
● Henry Taylor's Diamic Superflute. This is a really nice gouge. Nice length, nice handle shape, nice balance; even the rubber bung in the end is more than the gimmick I first thought it was.
● Ashley Iles' All Black ½in skew chisel. Elegant and balanced, in keeping with the fine work for which one uses a skew, this is a fine tool.
● Robert Sorby's ⅛in HSS parting tool. I used this for making fine beads in tight corners, as well as for careful parting with a minimum of wastage. Nice size, nice steel, nice handle.

I would have liked to have included

Stormont Archer's ⅜in deep-U bowl gouge, as it is an excellent shape and cuts very nicely at first, but the steel is such that it very quickly loses its edge.

Do bear in mind that, for obvious reasons, I haven't tested all the tools available, and many people will have their own selections to make.

## IN CONCLUSION

All the firms involved were friendly and helpful, but Ashley Iles the most so. They very quickly sent me everything I needed, and more: when I opened the parcel, I discovered the packing department had sent me their favourite bone-handled knife!

Sorby range me up to say that, if their carbon-steel gouges tested out softer than other people's, it was because they have switched to a special low-carbon steel, with fancy ingredients which (they assured me) give it better edge-holding properties. The sample I tested was one I bought 10 months ago, and was forged rather than round-bar; so we have not hardness-tested a round-bar carbon-steel tool from Sorby. ■

---

### SUGGESTED BEGINNER'S KITS

#### Spindle turning
*Basic necessities*
● ½in skew, Iles HSS
● 10mm spindle gouge, Taylor or Sorby HSS
● ⅛in flat-sided parting tool, Sorby HSS

*Likely to be useful*
● 7mm spindle gouge, Taylor or Sorby HSS
● ⅜in spindle gouge, Iles HSS
● ¾in roughing gouge, Taylor HSS
● 1in skew chisel, Iles HSS

#### Bowl turning
● ½in Superflute, Taylor HSS
● ½in scraper, Taylor solid HSS
● ¾in forged bowl gouge, Taylor or Sorby (ground less acutely, for the bottoms of deep bowls).

---

## Comparative hardness

On Rockwell scale

| | Average carbon-steel hardness | Average HSS hardness | ½in HSS bowl gouge hardness |
|---|---|---|---|
| Ashley Iles | 60 | 66 | 65.5 |
| Henry Taylor | 60 | 64.5 | 63 |
| Robert Sorby | 63.5 | 67.5 | 64 |
| Stormont Archer | 53 | — | — |

# Peg-legs and sgabelle

## Alan and Gill Bridgewater explore the other way of making chairs

When is a chair not a chair? And when is a stool not a stool? When it's a peg-leg, sgabelle, spindle, stick, spinning, Orkney or slab-back seat.

If you're still no wiser, picture the simple, traditional milkmaid's stool — three- or four-legged, it makes no matter. Add an upright plank back, a handful of wedges and a bit of shallow relief carving. Before you can say 'rustic and belonging to the peasant tradition', you have the basic, archetypal cottage chair.

Chairs of this type and character can't be described as belonging to specific countries or periods. All we can say for sure is that they are found wherever there is a peasant, folk-primitive, 'kitchen hearth' furniture-making tradition. In colonial New England there were beautiful plank-seated, stick-legged, wedge-tenoned chairs known as 'peg-legs'; in Renaissance Italy there were somewhat over-carved, three-legged, scroll-backed seats known as 'sgabelle'; closer to home, in Scotland and northern Europe, there were plank-backed chairs known variously as 'Orkney', 'spinning' and 'spindle' stools — and so we could go on, with examples from Russia, Scandinavia, Switzerland and Germany.

Peg-legs and plank-backs are essentially humble, rustic and home-made, and therein lies their naive and honest charm. What's more, of course, you don't need a fancy tool-kit, and there aren't any high-tech joints, screws, nails, glues or suchlike: just slab wood and simple, direct, easy-to-manage techniques. You won't finish up with a gesso-encrusted baroque cabriole-legged carver (or even, for that matter, a particularly comfortable chair); but you will be able to let rip with your own idiosyncratic design ideas, and get to grips with some honest-to-goodness making and carving.

We reckon that this project can be undertaken by the keen beginner in a couple of weekends.

## Tools and materials

Before you start, throw away most of your pre-conceived ideas on how a chair ought to be made, and try to feel yourself into the shoes of a never-done-it-before pioneer or peasant woodworker. You're using 'in-the-rough' or found wood; you only have a few basic tools; and you are seeking, to the best of your ability, to make a simple, strong, serviceable and decorative chair.

Get yourself a slab of rough-sawn 1½in half-seasoned oak, and make sure that it's reasonably straight-grained and free from warps, splits, shakes and dead knots. A board 42in long, 12in wide and 1-2in thick will do just fine. Our chair, as illustrated in the gridded working drawings, has a seat

● She had a spinning-wheel – did the Queen have a plank-back stool as well?

12x13in; the plank back is 27in long including the tenon, and tapers from 6-8in wide at the top to about 4in wide at the tenon shoulders; and there are four tapered, octagonal-sectioned legs.

As for tools, you need a large coping- or bow-saw, a mallet, a brace or hand-drill, a spokeshave or draw-knife, a straight chisel, a straight gouge, a V-section tool, a spoon-bit chisel, a spoon-bit gouge, and of course such 'around the workshop' items as pencils, a measure, a compass, a square, a cramp and rough working-out paper.

## First steps and marking out

Have a good look at our working drawings and inspirational ideas, give your wood a last check, and then with the compass, measure and pencil start to set out the design, as illustrated.

Measure and mark the eight-sided seat slab, the four legs, the plank back and the set. When you're sure that all is correct, clearly label the blanks. If you like the overall design but would prefer a taller back, a wider seat or whatever, now's the time to adjust the chair to suit your needs.

Finally, cut out the blanks with a fine-toothed straight saw.

## Setting out and carving

Before you start setting out the areas to be carved, take each piece, secure it to the

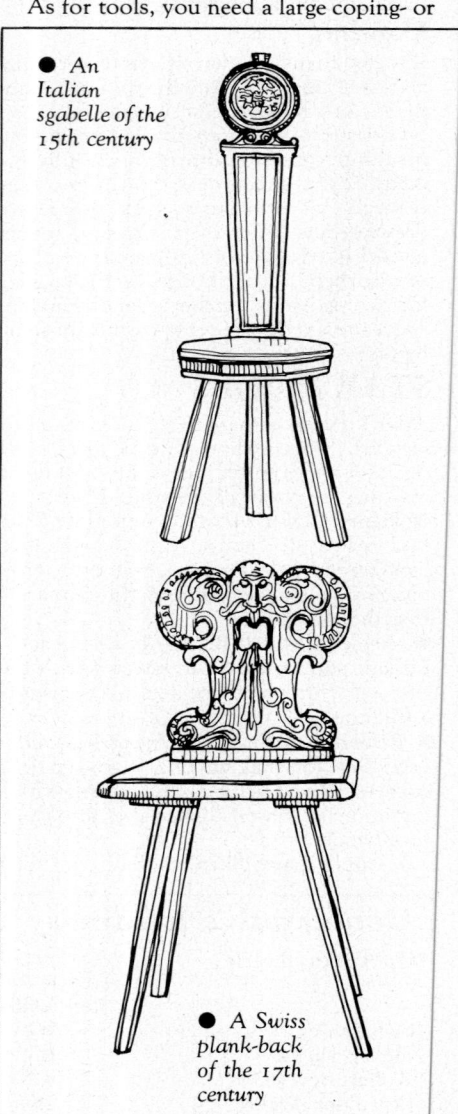

● An Italian sgabelle of the 15th century

● A Swiss plank-back of the 17th century

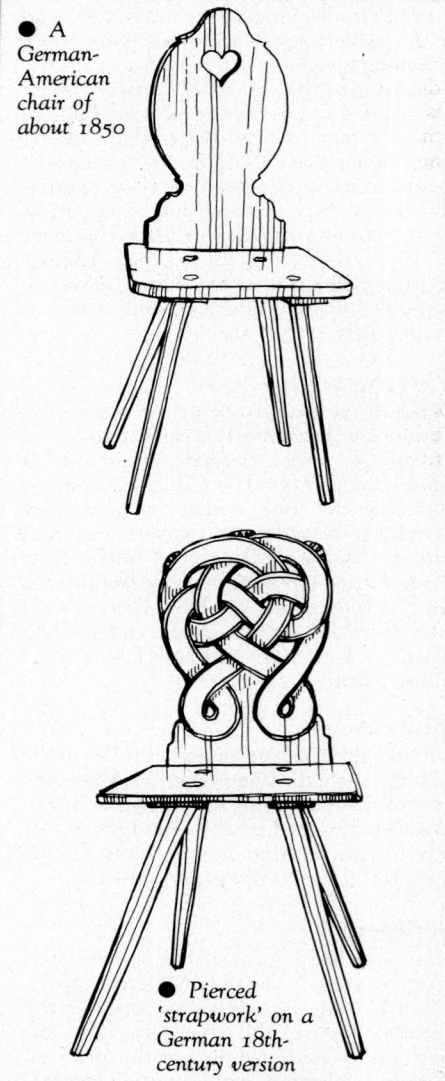

● A German-American chair of about 1850

● Pierced 'strapwork' on a German 18th-century version

● *The project's central feature gives it life . . .*

bench with the cramp, and with a shallow gouge bring its surface to a slightly rippled finish. Don't aim for a characterless 'plastic' smoothness — rather a soft, dappled and gently scalloped tooled texture.

Next, with a compass and straight-edge, set out the areas for carving. Have a good look at the gridded drawings and see how the design of the 9in-diameter seat roundel is quartered, and set back about 1¼in from the front edge of the seat slab. Notice also how the plank-back design is organised, pierced and contained within a border.

## The plank back

Once you have drawn out the design you can start to work the back. With the wood secure in the vice, take the coping-saw and hand-drill and work the pierced heart motif. Drill a starter hole, and then (with the coping-saw blade at 90° to the working surface) cut out the heart. Work with an even and steady stroke, manoeuvring and turning the saw as you go.

Then clamp the wood flat and square on the workbench and arrange your chisels and gouges so that they are comfortably to hand. Re-check the design, and with a pencil re-establish its lines and black in the areas that need to be lowered.

Now take the V-section tool and start to outline the whole of the design — all the time working on the waste or ground side, and cutting into the wood about ¼in outside the drawn lines. As you work the V-section incised trench you will be cutting both with and across the grain, so hold the tool with both hands, one guiding and one pushing; work with short, shallow, controlled strokes, and be ready to stop short if you feel the tool running into the grain or skidding out of control. At this stage you shouldn't need to use a mallet; just put your shoulder behind the tool and try to cut a smooth V-section trench, not too deep.

When you've outlined the design, go round the drawn lines and 'set in' with the straight chisel and gouge. Hold the tool in

● *A little inspiration: some seats and backs in the European folk tradition*

one hand so that the handle is leaning slightly over the design, and cut into the lines of the motif with short lively taps of the mallet. Try all the time to keep the depth of cut constant, say ⅛-¼in, and aim to establish a clean, sharp-edged design. The setting-in should follow the V-trench and the edge of the design in a single, smooth and continuous line.

Some carvers lower or 'waste' the unwanted 'ground' of the design before they set in. Otherwise, you can do this now.

Take the spoon-bit gouge, cut a broad trench on the ground side of the V-section cut, and — when you have established the depth of the lowered ground — chop out the whole area. Try to leave the lowered ground smooth and even, but not so overworked that you can't see the tool marks. Finally, work round the now raised motifs and make sure the angles are free from bits and burrs.

Look at the acorns-and-oak-leaves design, as illustrated, and see how the forms

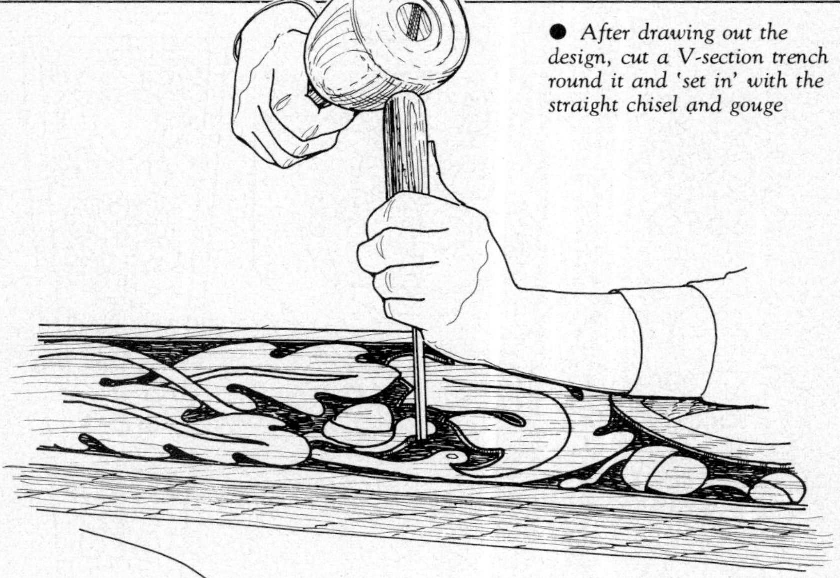

# Peg-legs and sgabelle

● *After drawing out the design, cut a V-section trench round it and 'set in' with the straight chisel and gouge*

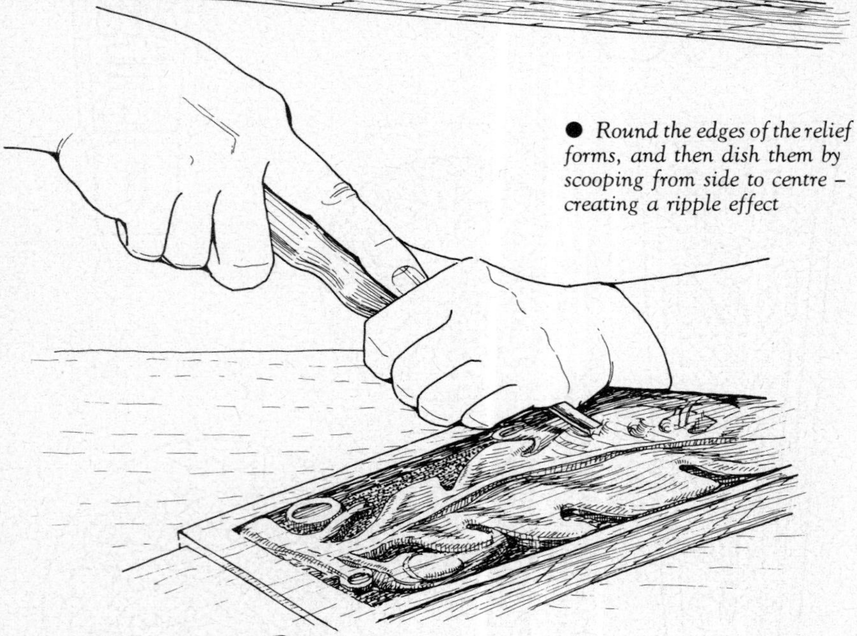

● *Round the edges of the relief forms, and then dish them by scooping from side to centre – creating a ripple effect*

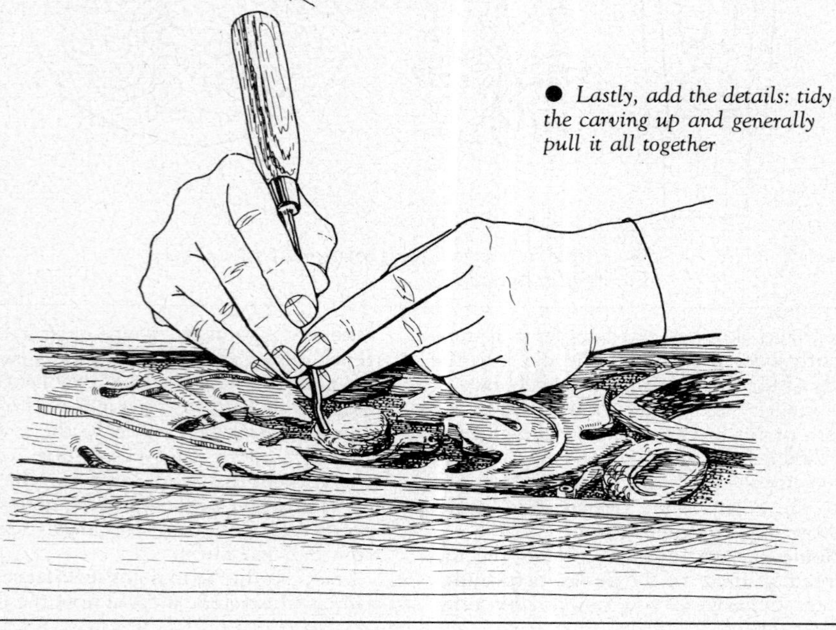

● *Lastly, add the details: tidy the carving up and generally pull it all together*

have been worked in rather a formal and mechanical manner. Take the straight gouge and work round the raised design, all the while cutting away and rounding the sharp edges. Don't even attempt to carve subtle realism and complex undercuts; rather go for swift and direct stylisation. When you have rounded the edges of the motifs, dish them gently — scoop out the wood from side to centre, all the time taking care that you don't damage short-grain areas or cut into the raised-leaf veining.

And so you continue to work: cutting and running the tools across the grain, and over and around the forms, until you feel that you have taken the carving as far as you want it to go. Don't fuss and worry the design; try to keep it simple and bold. When you have worked the plank back, work the seat roundel in like manner.

## The mortises and tenons

If you look closely at the plank-back-to-seat joint, you will see that the tapered plank is tenoned and rebated so that it enters the seat mortise at an oblique angle of about 100-110°. Once the plank tenon and seat mortise have been cut and worked to fit, the rebated shoulders of the tenon need to be pared and bevelled until they strike the seat smooth and clean.

This done, cut a mortise in the plank-back tenon, at an angle parallel to the seat, and then cut and fit a wedge as illustrated.

## Cutting and fixing the legs

Take the 14in-long leg blanks, a stick at a time, secure them in the vice and then shape

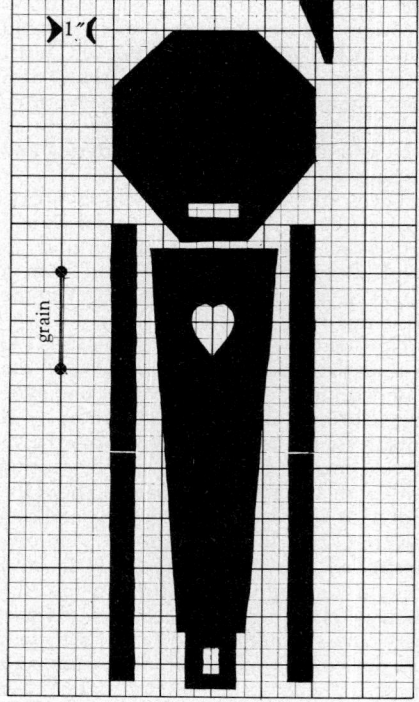

● *This cutting diagram provides a well-proportioned layout for all the components of the chair*

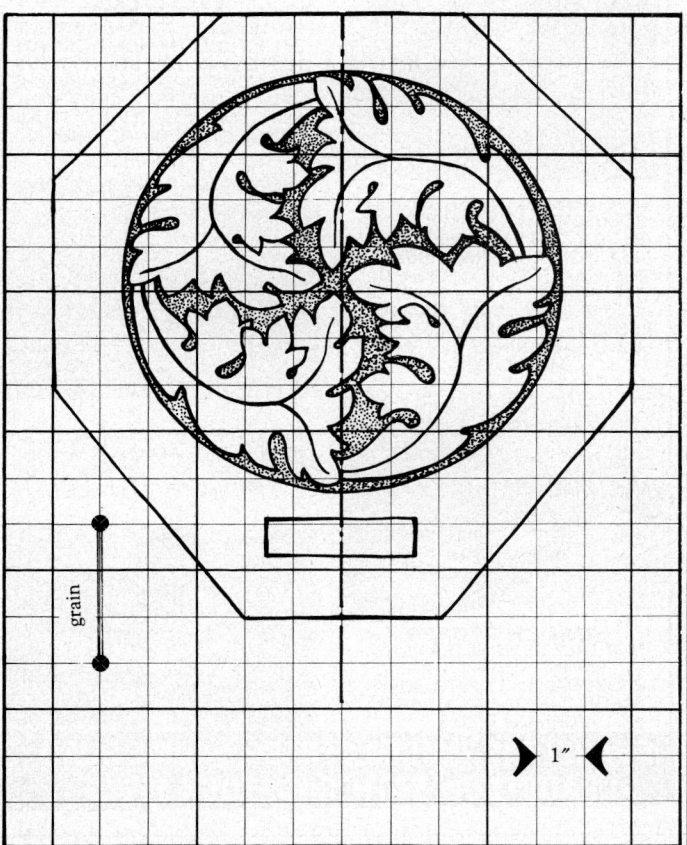

● Here is the seat design we evolved for this particular project. Again the secret of accurate setting-out is to use a grid. Apart from anything else, this ensures symmetry if the design calls for it

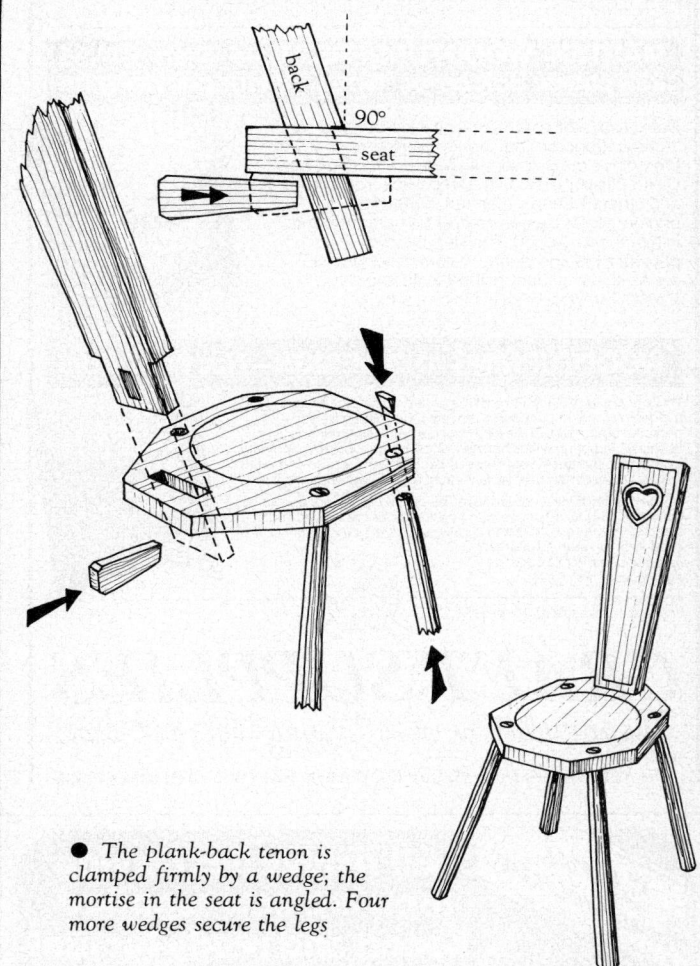

● The plank-back tenon is clamped firmly by a wedge; the mortise in the seat is angled. Four more wedges secure the legs

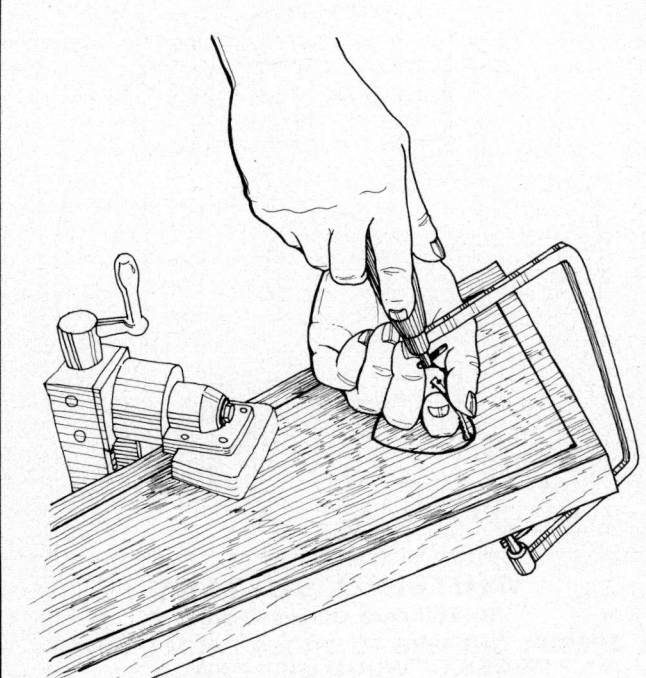

● Setting up the coping-saw for open-heart surgery on the plank back. The bow-saw is an alternative tool

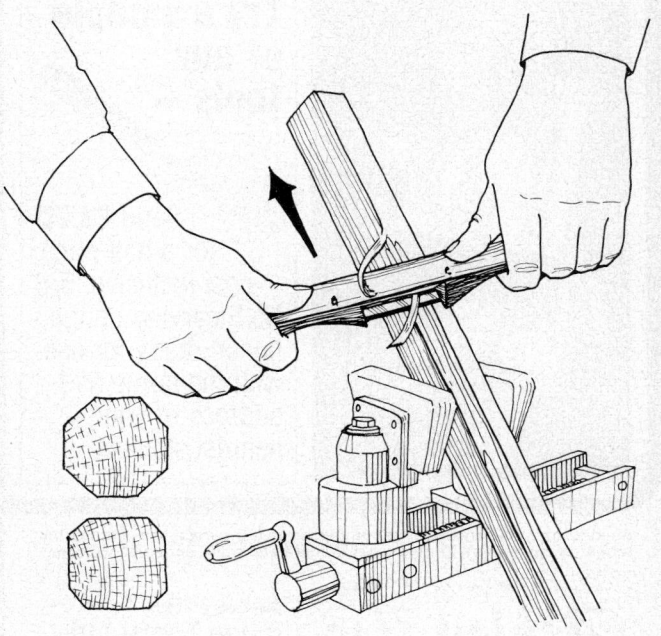

● A spokeshave, draw-knife or plane tapers the legs and takes them down to an octagonal section – regular or otherwise

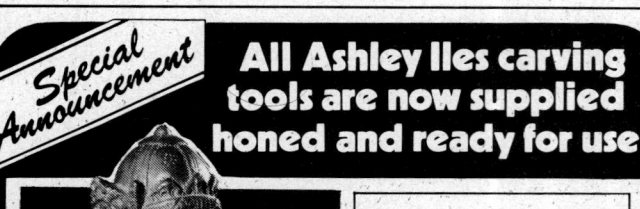

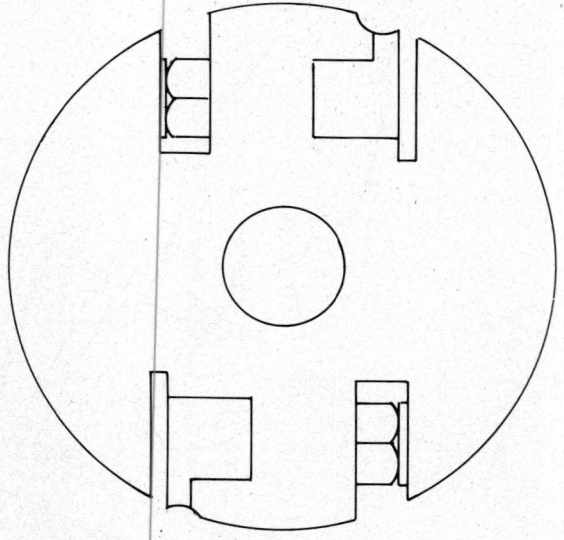

# Peg-legs and sgabelle

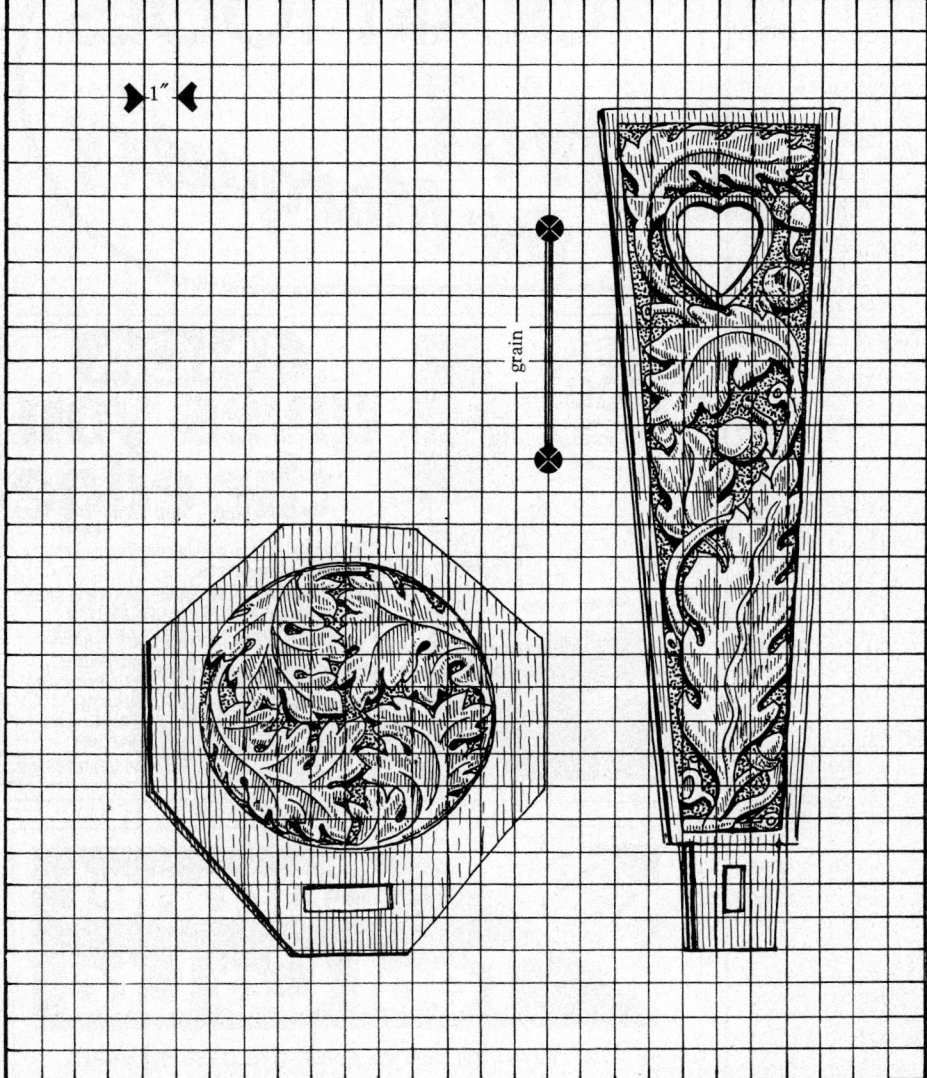

1″

grain

● *Here the seat roundel is drawn out next to its accompanying plank back. We went for an oak-tree theme, but don't let that stop you from casting as far and wide for inspiration as you like. The world's folk art offers a vast treasure-house of inspiration, and a great deal of that has found its way into books*

them with the spokeshave or draw-knife until they are gently tapered and octagonal in section. Aim to take the taper from about 1½in at the bottom to about 1¼in at the top.

When you've done four legs, place the carved seat slab face-down on the workbench and bore four angled holes. Then continue to work the tapered ends of the legs until they are a good stiff fit in the bored seat holes.

Finally, when the legs fit flush with the seat, make the joints as shown.

## Getting it all together

When the legs have been wedge-tenoned into the seat and the plank-back tenon inserted into the seat mortise, its holding wedge can be banged home. Adjust the chair so that it sits firm and four-square, and go over your work with a small gouge tidying up sharp edges and making sure all

the surfaces have a dappled, tooled texture.

Finally, remove all the dust and wood fragments with a stiff brush, give it a couple of coats of beeswax, and the job is done.

On traditional peg-leg chairs of this character the carving is usually incised or shallow-relief, but of course there's no reason why the chair shouldn't be painted, chip-carved or whatever takes your fancy.

Some other points:
● When you come to fixing the leg wedge-tenons, make sure the little wedges are cut in so that they run across the grain of the seat, as illustrated.
● If you think the 1½in-thick slab seat looks a little on the heavy side, bevel the under-edge with a gouge so that edge-on the seat looks to be about ¾in thick.
● When you bore the leg holes in the seat slab, watch out that you don't split or damage the wood. It's a good idea to drill from both sides. ∎

## REMEMBER...

*Woodworker* depends on woodworkers. We're willing and eager to tell the world what you're making, doing, exhibiting — even thinking. Our only aim is to produce the magazine you want to read. We're looking for photos, drawings (rough sketches will do) and words on any woodworking subject from ovolo mouldings to overhead routers. And we're on the end of the phone. We're waiting to hear from you!

*Peter Collenette*
*Aidan Walker*

# Machine made for man

**Stepping into a battlefield, John Farrar mediates between human and hardware with this clear step-by-step account of how to produce a cabinet door**

Recent issues of *Woodworker* (May and July) have carried wood-machining items with specific reference to the Kity K5. However, there's a lot more to be said.

Mr Cannon ('Initiation test', WW/May) comments: 'After a while I felt I was no longer taking pleasure in woodwork, even at my low level, but instead becoming a machine-setter' — a statement which highlights the very real difference between working with machines and using hand tools. To amplify the point further, I'll set out a detailed description of how to make a 500mm antique-style door using a combination machine. Its construction illustrates the main advantages and disadvantages of machine woodworking.

I encourage the use of test-runs with scrap timber. Take time to ensure that the machine is correctly adjusted *before* working with the actual components; this encourages disciplined organisation. It's essential to think out — and stick to — a logical sequence of cuts which minimises the amount of time you take to change the machine functions.

You will notice how little time is spent actually cutting timber! Machines are fast, and (if you buy from a reputable manufacturer) accurate. In fact, it takes very little more time to make 10 doors than to make one. This, of course, is the major advantage of owning machines. The normally boring and repetitive tasks, like mortising, can be handled accurately and quickly, allowing you time to apply your skills to the more interesting areas of design and finishing.

Machinery is not for all woodworkers. If your objective is carefully to produce one cabinet over a long time, each component considerately cut with love, sweat and hand tools, you are indulging in an art: a love affair with wood, where every caress of a sharp blade exposes new grain, changes of texture and invigorating fragrances. This is one very satisfying branch of the craft.

If however, you are building a boat, replacing window-frames, building fitted wardrobes in the children's bedroom, adding a conservatory, replacing glazing bars in a greenhouse, fitting a new kitchen, building garden furniture, or even just making bookshelves, a good set of machinery will pay for itself in no time at all. Your projects will be finished with real professionalism, and you will add value to your property; but above all, when you disappear into your workshop for a little peace and quiet, your family will not complain, as they will have evidence of your output. You'll be able to sit and read

● *Don't let the machine dictate the way you work; confidence grows with experience, enabling you to develop effective – and enjoyable – working methods. Using a well-set-up machine can be as satisfying as wielding a razor-sharp smoothing-plane, but you must plan the work logically. Here, tenons are being cut with spaced discs and a sliding table*

*Woodworker*, knowing it'll only take a couple of hours to produce a garden chair with your combination machine!

This door could be used as part of any cabinetmaking project, but its most obvious use is in a fitted kitchen. The instructions are useful for any machine, not just the Kity range.

## Cutting and planing

**1** Set the combination machine as a saw with the blade at maximum height and the extension tables fitted.
**2** Convert to a surface planer by moving the belt and swinging the spindle-moulder to one side.

All seven components must now be surface-planed to create a reference face, then planed with the reference face flat against the planer fence. Each component will now have two reference faces at 90° to each other.

**3** Convert the surface planer to a thicknesser by removing the fence and swinging over the chip-guard.

Start thickness-planing with the widest component, reference surface downwards on the thicknesser table. Pass each piece through the machine before adjusting the thickness height, measuring after each run; repeat this process with the other reference edges downwards on the thicknesser table.
**4** Convert to a saw bench by moving the belt, and cut to the correct finished length using the mitre guide.

## Tongue-and-grooving the centre panel (fig. 2)

**5** Convert back to a spindle-moulder by changing the belt. Mount the groove cutter of a tongue-and-grooving set and make a test cut on a piece of 19mm scrap, adjusting the fence and spindle height until the groove is central and the depth 5mm.

# Machine made for man

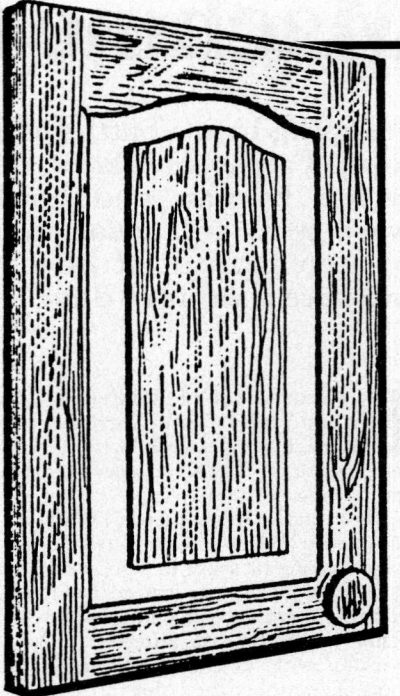

**6** Select the panel pieces (B) and match the colour and grain by placing them side-by-side, as these three components will make up the panel. Cut a groove in two of them along the butt-joint edge.

**7** Replace the groove cutter with the tongue cutter from the set, taking care *not* to adjust the fence position or the spindle height. Cut the matching tongue in the panel components, 3mm wide. Glue and cramp.

## Marking out (figs 1 & 3)

**8** Make a template from 25mm ply of the exact curve of the top door rail and the matching panel.

**9** Mark the mortises and tenons on all the components, and the other cuts (fig. 1). Also trace out the curve from the template on to the panel and the top rail.

**10** Cut out the curve on the panel (fig. 5) and the door top rail with a bandsaw, taking care to keep the cut on the waste side.

**11** Remove the cutter and straight fence from the spindle-moulder and fit a drum-sander and ring fence; finish the curve on the panel and the top bar with the drum-sander to match up to the traced line.

## Mortising

**12** Move the belt to the planer, and insert a 6mm mortise cutter in the mortiser. Mark out a standard mortise and a centre-line on the end of a scrap piece of 19mm timber, clamp it to the mortiser table, and adjust the table height until the cutter and the marked centre line match. Set the horizontal-movement stops to match the length of the mortise. Measure the setting of the depth stop to 37mm. Mark a reference line on the table at the end of the timber, and make test cuts until it's correct. Each mortise may now be cut by placing the ends of each component against the reference, clamping up, and cutting.

## Tenoning (fig. 4)

**13** Move the belt to the spindle-moulder, and stack two 100mm-dia.x10mm discs, separated by a 6mm spacer. Fit the standard fence.

**14** Using a scrap piece of 19mm timber, scribe a centre line and adjust the spindle height to leave a 6mm tenon; adjust the spindle fence to 35mm depth of cut. Make a test cut by clamping the timber in the tenoning guide. When you are completely satisfied with the adjustment, repeat-cut all the tenons.

## Fielding the panel (figs 7 & 8)

**15** Mount a fielding tool as low as possible on the spindle-moulder shaft, with the ring-fence below the disc and the ring-fence guard above and completely covering the disc.

**16** Working with scrap 19mm timber, adjust the depth of cut to give a 50mm depth of fielding with a 6mm thickness. When satisfied with the adjustment, field the panel, working across the endgrains first so that any grain break-out will be removed when you cut along the grain.

## Grooving and moulding the frame (fig. 6)

**17** Mount a 6mm grooving disc with the ring-fence, and adjust it to give a 20mm-deep groove.

**18** Test with 19mm-thick timber until the position of the groove is correct, before cutting the groove in the rails and stiles A, C and D.

**19** Mount a moulding cutter with the ring-fence. I would suggest a quarter-round or something similar.

**20** Test with scrap until correctly adjusted before cutting components A, C and D.

## Finishing the tenons (figs. 9, 10, 11 & 12)

**21** Cut the tenons to the correct width with a bandsaw, and round off with a coarse file. Cut the moulded sections at 45°, taking care to match the mouldings.

**22** Glue and cramp. When dry, lightly sand in preparation for finishing. ∎

**John Farrar** is managing director of Kity UK. The plans for the door are Kity's copyright.

● *The kitchen-cabinet door; dimensions are for upper units, so proportions will alter for base cupboards*

| Cutting list | | | |
|---|---|---|---|
| **Rough-sawn** | | | **Finished size** |
| A  620 x  66 x 23mm | 2 stiles | | 600 x  60 x 19mm |
| B  540 x 426 x 23mm | 3 centre panels | | 520 x 420 x 19mm |
| C  520 x  66 x 23mm | 1 bottom rail | | 480 x  60 x 19mm |
| D  520 x  96 x 23mm | 1 top rail | | 480 x  90 x 19mm |

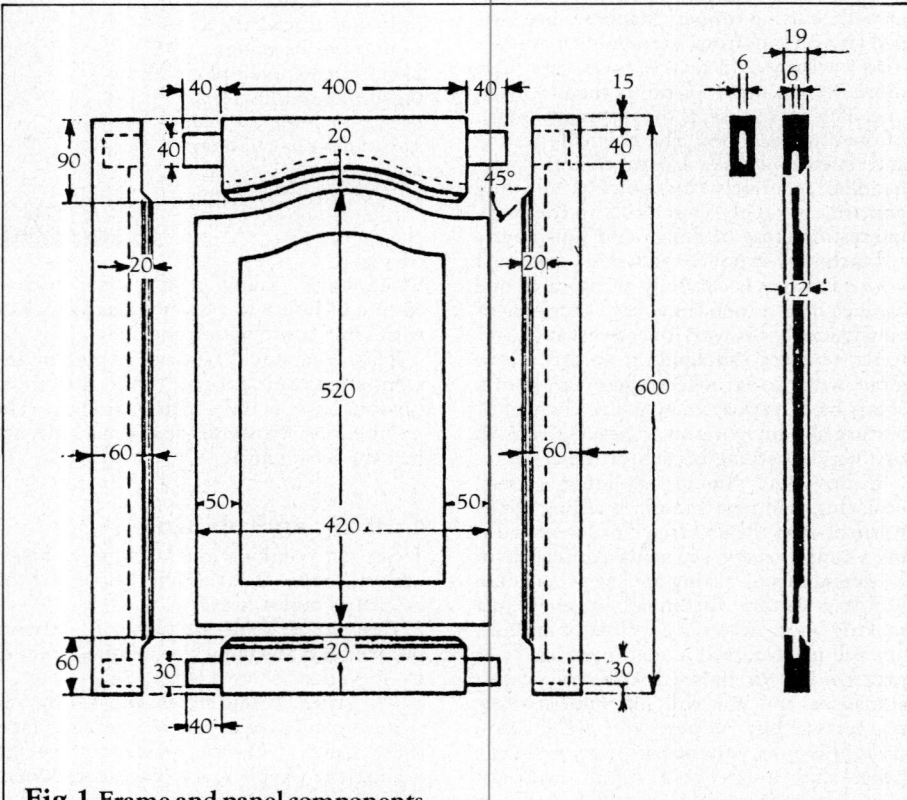

**Fig. 1 Frame and panel components**

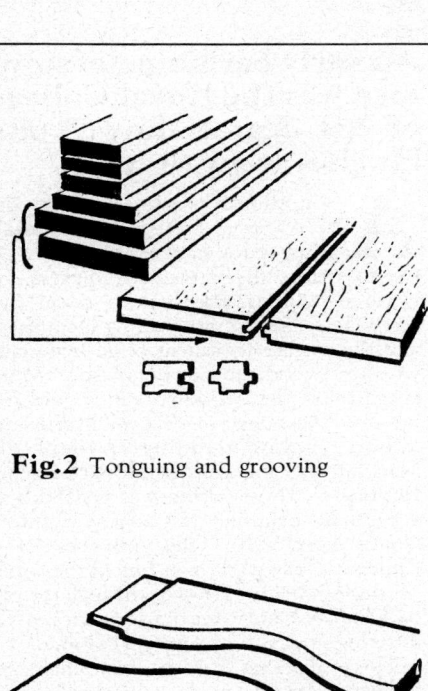

**Fig.2** Tonguing and grooving

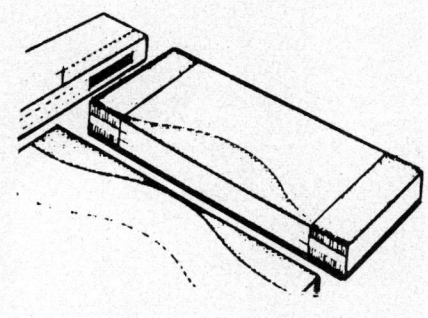

**Fig.3** Marking out the curves

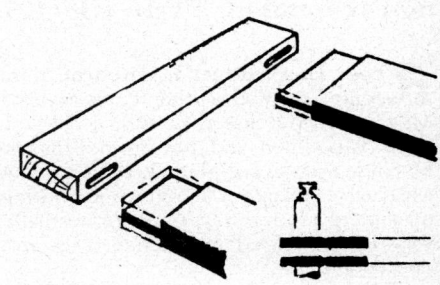

**Fig.4** Tenoning

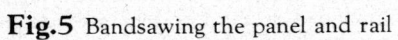

**Fig.5** Bandsawing the panel and rail

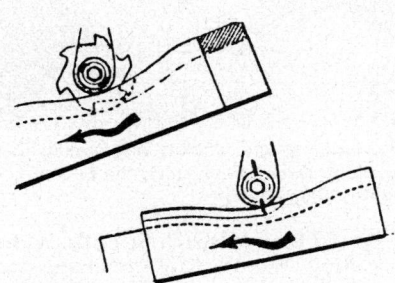

**Fig. 6** Grooving and moulding

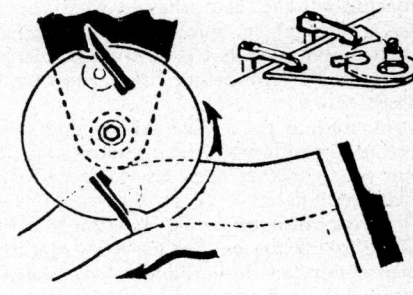

**Fig.7** Fielding the panel

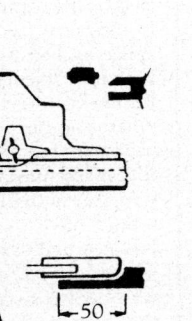

**Fig.8** Slotting and moulding the frame: fielding the panels

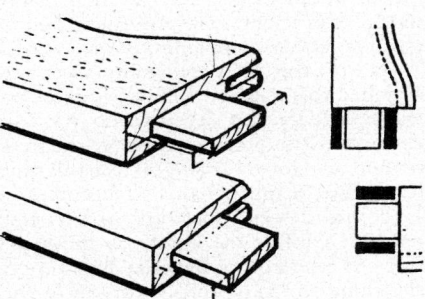

**Fig.9** Tenoning

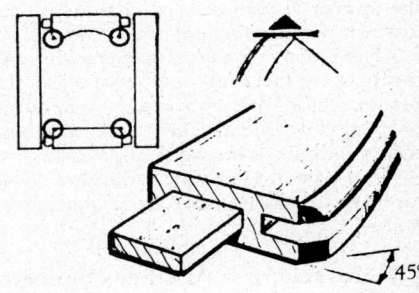

**Fig.10** Mitreing the curved mouldings

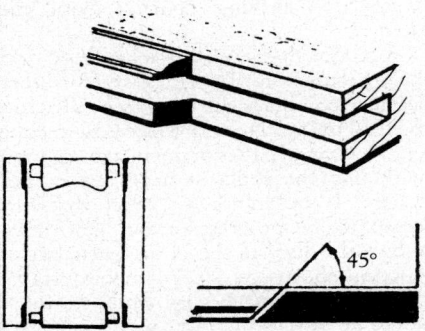

**Fig.11** Simple mitres

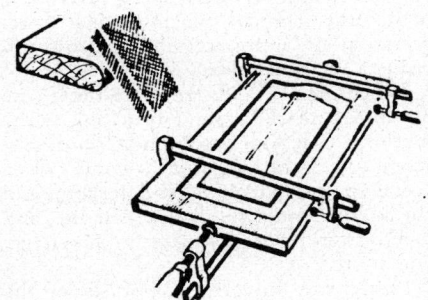

**Fig.12** Rounding off tenons and cramping

● *The machining steps, from rough-sawn boards to a finished door, are planned to avoid too many changes of function. The plans will work for any set of machines, but with a universal it is especially important to get all the work done at one stage before re-setting the machine and moving on to the next. Mouldings and mitres need less cleaning up if the cutters and blades are in tip-top condition (though for final finishing there is no substitute for a sharp plane or scraper and hand sanding)*

# Machine made for man

# RCA 85

## Some well-known suppliers had bones to pick over R. B. Cannon's comments on the Kity K5

**R**oger Buse, Roger's, Hitchin: quite apart from the fact that it now appears Mr Cannon purchased an early K5 Mk 1 from Woodmen and not from Rawdon Machine Sales as stated in the article, in my experience people buying woodworking machinery for the first time are normally very inexperienced in machine uses and operations.

90% of customers look for the dealer offering the cheapest price rather than one who will give them advice and all the educational back-up they need. Obviously the latter is hardly likely to be the cheapest. Many times I have spent evenings with customers who have cursed their new machinery and said they wished they'd never bought it, but after an evening's instruction (which I gave free of charge) were fully competent and thoroughly satisfied.

Further, a good 75% of my guarantee call-outs result from the operator's lack of knowledge rather than any fault with the machine.

It was unfortunate for Rawdon that Mr Cannon purchased a Kity K5. I get the impression that he would have had the same problems with any combination machine he purchased.

To emphasise that I have no interest here, I'll say that as a company we have decided to withdraw from the woodworking machinery market. To join the discounters would compromise our dedication to giving the utmost in service — something we are just not prepared to do.

I have many, many customers who will testify to the fact that the K5 was one of the best purchases they ever made — one of my professional clients uses his machine continually six days a week, and has done so for the past three years without a single moment of down-time from machinery faults.

**P**hilip Matthews, Matthews Brothers, Tamworth: I am in full favour of reports that inform the potential customer of the advantages and pitfalls of any range of machinery, but I do feel that Mr Cannon's should have been updated because it so obviously applies to the K5 Mk 1, and not the greatly improved Mk 2.

We sell both the K5 and its big brother the K704 with complete confidence that the customer is getting value for money in an excellently engineered machine, a comprehensive range of tooling and accessories, and strong back-up from both ourselves and Rawdon Machine Sales.

As the founder-members of this company have had more than 30 years in joinery and cabinetmaking and have used a wide range of machines, we feel we have some justification for our evaluation of Kity machines for their particular niche in the marketplace.

● *Moulding and rebating a softwood sill profile in large-section stock can be done before ripping*

**D**avid Lloyd, Burch & Hills, Aldershot: We are Kity distributors and proud of it. Kity machines account for a significant part of our sales, and we must therefore answer some specific points of Mr Cannon's from our experience.

The assertion of poor back-up by Rawdon Machine Sales Ltd is simply untrue in our experience. We find them a model of efficiency with a pleasant, helpful attitude. Other companies, please copy!

As for the K5's reliability, we have supplied this machine (and its predecessor the Mini Kity) for seven years. We have changed two motors, one planer-thicknesser and one slot-mortising table in this time, from sales of more than 130 machines.

It might seem that possession of a machine confers the ability to produce a piece of Sheraton or Barnsley furniture by switching on the motor. Nothing is further from the truth. Machines such as the K5 require continuous practice for their full potential to be realised — bear in mind that industry still requires a three- or four-year apprenticeship. Woodworking machinery in no way destroys the individual interpretation of a project, and it positively reduces the time taken.

When you decide to investigate the machinery market, don't just look at the machines. Put your dealer under the microscope too. Is he prepared to come out to you if you are in trouble? Will he come and check the machine over, run it, and demonstrate safe working techniques to get you started?

Lastly, are *you* giving your dealer the fullest information about your requirements so he can help you list appropriate accessories and work out the overall cost and the machine's capabilities? ∎

## An early harbinger of summer was the Royal College of Art degree show. Luke Hughes went to it

**A** sumptuous presentation at the RCA this year stresses the college's prime status amongst its fellows. Of the furniture, the immediate impressions were meticulous attention to detail (no screw-head burred, no sanding blemishes) and the surface treatment of all materials, whether wood, metal or plastic. More specifically the woodworker would be interested in a chair in olive ash by Eleanor Wood (acknowledging a debt to Mackintosh), and a folding stool by Rachel Heritage — whose outline was as striking as a Futurist painting, but whose comfort would have suited the purposes of a Chinese torturer (though I liked the detail of routing shallow grooves through the ply back and seat and using the porosities of the differing grains to accentuate colours.)

There was a set of steam-bent chairs by Rebecca Myram (made with the help of Andy 'Wizard' Whateley, the college's resident cabinetmaker, who has at least a hand in every piece of making); these were elegant, ingenious, and comfortable in the extreme. Rebecca's *garderobe* for gentlemen also caught the imagination.

Of interest, too, was a desk by Gavin Lindsay which had already been highly commended at the London International Furniture Show. Made of ebony veneer on mahogany and ply with solid ebony lippings, it was slim, occupied minimal space and shut up to a size and shape that forbade objects to be stacked on it. You know how useless a piece of furniture is when you have to remove clutter (souvenir ashtray, telephone directories, piles of discarded magazines and a pot plant) before you can actually get to it. Some designers would have us live without clutter. Gavin has stopped us letting it gather on his piece. This showed some understanding of the way people actually do live, as opposed to the way a designer thinks they should. There were lovely details, too; the black-chromed brass hinges and pencil-rack were masterly, and the black hide used for the desk surface and seat-covering made a particularly striking contrast with the ebony.

In one of the lavish press handouts was the proclamation: 'The successful furniture designer combines the need to be progressive and innovative with the ability to cope with the complexities of manufacturing and marketing the skills to make his or her design.' I couldn't help reflect that this 'need' to be progressive and innovative frequently distorts the comprehension of function and usage. Hence uncomfortable chairs and useless beauty trolleys, which would be thrown out in 18 months. It is by adapting to new functions when they arise that a designer will be truly innovative — not by constantly re-defining well established principles. ∎

● Rachel Heritage's folding stools combine a beech underframe with a plywood seat and back

● Ash is the timber, and the seat is leather. The designer was Eleanor Wood

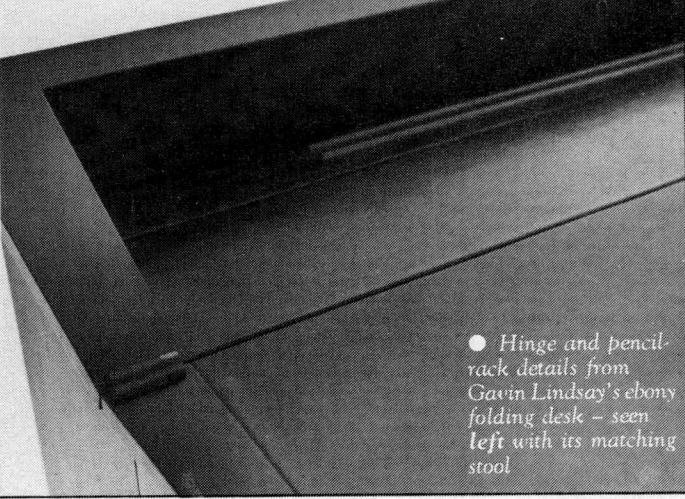

● Hinge and pencil-rack details from Gavin Lindsay's ebony folding desk – seen *left* with its matching stool

● **Below:** Rebecca Myram's dining-chairs in steam-bent English ash are 'comfortable in the extreme'

● **Below:** Also by Rebecca Myram, this 'gentleman's cabinet' in avodire is meant for wall-hanging

Photos by Tim Imrie

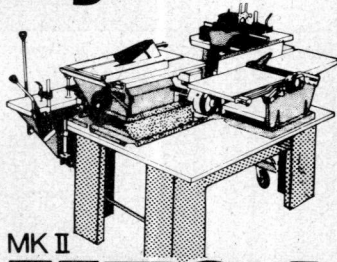

# MAINLY ON THE PLANES

## Combination cutting

**Planes must be the most cherished of all tools. Ian Thwaites opens a diverse display by defending one much-loved species**

Every woodworker has a 'special tool' — a tool which is used more often than most and which gives considerable pleasure. For me it is a combination plane. To some extent modern power tools have eclipsed the use of these planes, but they still have a great deal to offer.

My own combination plane is a Record 050A and, as near as I can guess, was made in the mid-1930s. It is beautifully crafted and still in its original wooden box. It is little different from combination planes available today, the chief changes being slight alterations in shape and less decoration.

What makes it so useful is its versatility —ploughing, rabbeting, beading, dadoing, tonguing and grooving are all possible with one tool. It takes a certain amount of practice before best advantage can be made of it; you need to get to know the tool, its parts and how it handles. Initial setting-up can take quite a while, but once it's done the actual ploughing and beading can be carried out quite quickly.

I use my combination plane mainly when making joints between ply sheets, something to which it's particularly suited. To make a lap joint in this way, first select a cutter equal to the thickness of the sheet to be joined and set it in the plane. Now cut a rebate by setting the plane's adjustable fence right up against the edge of the cutter and then holding this against the edge of the board to be cut. A clean rebate will result; and, if the same thickness of ply is being used throughout the whole job, there will be no need to make any more adjustments.

Use the depth gauge to ensure a consistent cutting depth. When cutting rebates or grooves in ply it is a good idea to ensure that the depth of cut coincides with one of the glue-lines. If the sheet is five-ply, make the rebate equal to the depth of the first two plies; this gives much the cleaner cut. Remember that the depth of cut is not the distance between the gauge and the bottom of the plane body but that between the gauge and the very tip of the blade — it is easy to make a mistake here.

Most combination planes incorporate knife-edged spur cutters, one in the main body of the plane and the other in the section which holds the blade. They are used to score the workpiece ahead of the blade in a cross-grain cut, and are essential to achieve a clean result. I use them all the time for working in ply.

To plough a groove, mark the cut on the workpiece, then position the plane and

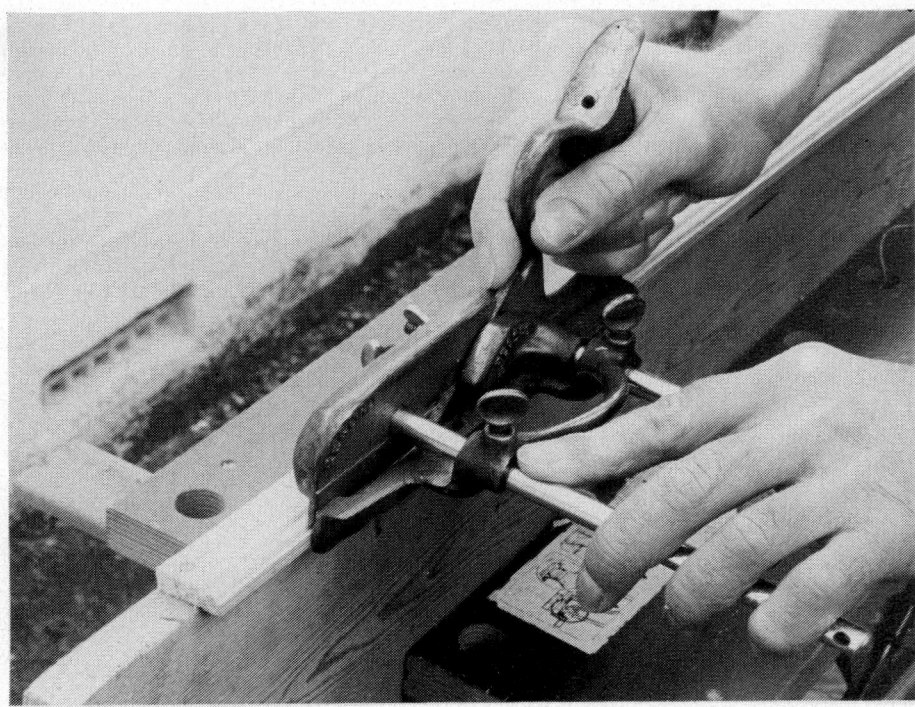

● *Ian's handsome Record 050A works as well as it did 50 years ago when it was made. The small blades are retained by an accessory clamp, not the more usual screw-adjuster*

adjust the sliding fence to rub along the timber's edge. Again use the depth gauge and spur cutters as necessary. It is essential that the sliding fence doesn't shift on the guide rails, and I still take the precaution of giving the thumbscrew tighteners a slight twist with a pair of pliers.

With any combination or plough plane the action is to push and pull backwards and forwards across the workpiece, using the left hand (assuming you're right-handed) to push the fence against the timber's edge. This double action can take a little while to master, but it is the key to really successful working — if the fence is allowed to wander from the timber even for one stroke, the cut will lose its clean, square edge. I find it is at the far edge that the fence is most likely to wander, so take particular care here. To cut a groove further in from

the edge of the timber than the sliding fence-rods allow, remove the fence entirely and clamp a lath across the workpiece. Use this to guide the plane like a traditional rebate plane.

To use a combination plane only for rebating and grooving is to waste much of its potential — it really comes into its own in decorative applications such as beading, dados and mouldings. At the moment I am making a highly decorated Victorian kitchen, where the plane not only saves the cost of manufactured beading but also allows me to work to my own non-standard designs. There is also the satisfaction of producing almost everything myself; the limits are in one's imagination, not the tool.

Some of the different types of cutter available are shown in fig. 1. I would avoid the multiple-bead cutters — not only does

### Fig.1 Cutters and profile patterns

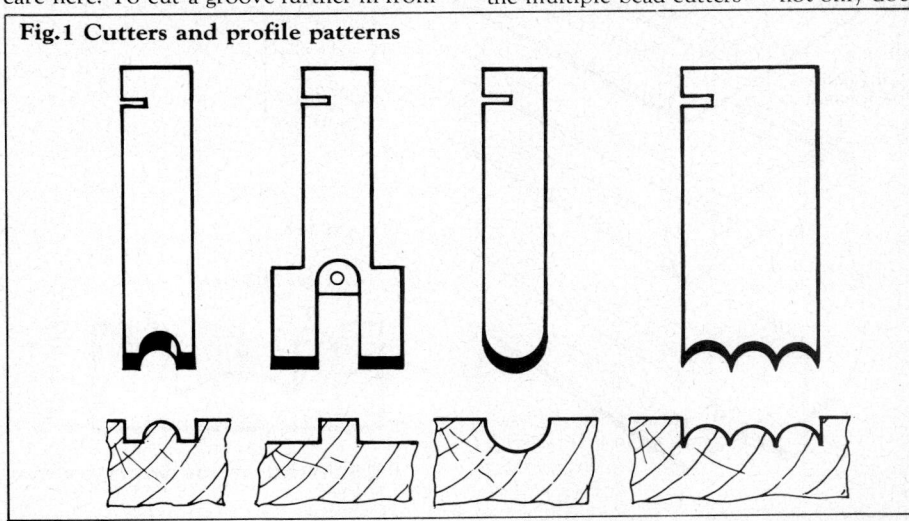

# MAINLY ON THE PLANES

it require more effort to cut two or three beads at once, it doesn't take very much longer to cut each bead individually and adjust the fence for the next one.

One of the difficulties with these planes is securing thin workpieces, because as the cutter works deeper into the wood the fence goes deeper with it. It is impossible to clamp a workpiece thinner than about 1½in between the vice-jaws and still leave room for the fence. My solution is shown in fig. 2 and the photograph. I keep a length of 9x1, which I clamp to the bench, flat or end-on according to the work, and then nail the workpiece to it. When making a moulding like this, the work should be cut a couple of inches too long to give a fixing for the nails, and then cut to length when the moulding is finished. It's a good idea to do this anyway, as inaccuracies with the moulding always show at the ends, which can be trimmed away. Some of the mouldings which can be made with a combination plane are illustrated. I have found the astragal most useful, particularly when decorating the ends of timber. The torus bead (fig. 4) illustrates what is achieved by working with two, three or more cutters in sequence. I have made quite a few architraves to this design, which is also a good one for glazing bars and picture-frames.

Fig. 3 shows the sequence of cuts to make a plate-rack. First a narrow groove is ploughed to accept the edges of the plates, then the outer edge is given a decorative astragal.

The other edge is torus-beaded using two cutters; then a section is cut off as illustrated, reversed and used as a support for the rack. This also illustrates the need to think ahead when doing moulding work — had the plate groove been cut after the astragal, the fence would have rubbed and damaged the edge. Similarly, the torus bead is cut off *after* being moulded, as otherwise you'd be left with an awkward narrow workpiece. Remember the adage of all planing — two thin shavings are better than one thick one — and that the cutters will only give good results if they are kept really sharp. Many woodworkers view this plane as an unnecessarily complicated combination of screws, cutters and accessories; but for me it is a favourite which has proved one of the most useful tools in the workshop.

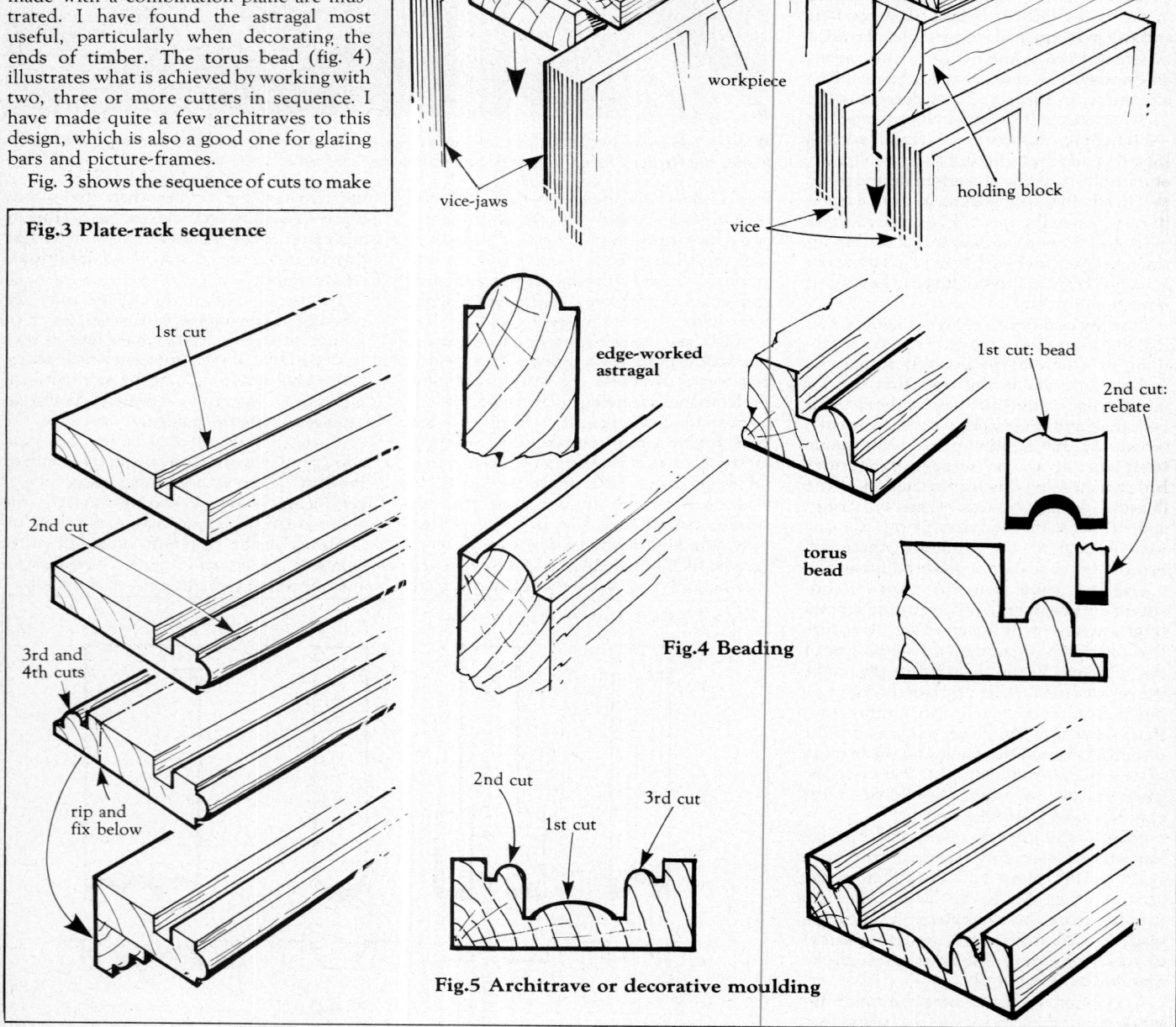

**Fig.2 Holding jigs for thin pieces**

block · over-length piece fixed here · workpiece · fix here · workpiece · holding block · vice-jaws · vice

**Fig.3 Plate-rack sequence**

1st cut · 2nd cut · 3rd and 4th cuts · rip and fix below

edge-worked astragal

torus bead

**Fig.4 Beading**

1st cut: bead · 2nd cut: rebate

**Fig.5 Architrave or decorative moulding**

2nd cut · 1st cut · 3rd cut

# Planes: making history

**Tony Murland is a fanatical collector of wooden moulding planes. He examines the growth and decline of their manufacture in Britain**

There can't be many regular readers of Woodworker who haven't heard of TATHS – the Tool and Trades History Society, writes **Polly Curds**. Membership (which has grown rapidly over the past two years) provides opportunities to meet others interested in historical hand tools and the skills and techniques of their use. Four newsletters are published each year, giving members information about meetings, exhibitions, and matters of topical interest; but members also receive an annual journal (**left**) which includes weightier articles and relevant book reviews. Volume 2 of Tools and Trades is now published and available to non-members at £5 from the Editor, Winston Grange, Stowmarket, Suffolk IP14 6LE.

Application forms and details from the Secretary, TATHS, 275 Sandridge Lane, Bromham, Chippenham, Wilts SN15 2JW.

**M**ost people know that old woodworking tools are much sought-after and have an intrinsic value. Few, however, know much of their history, or of the subtle difference between a tool that is interesting to a collector and one that is valueless. Of all woodworking tools, the plane has the most varieties, and for that reason is the most popular to collect. Its history gives some clues to its fascination.

The plane has been with us for at least 2000 years. No planes have been found among Greek or Egyptian remains, and the earliest known examples were used by Roman joiners at the beginning of the Christian era. They either had a wooden stock or were made up as an iron sole with side-plates and a wooden core. The cutting iron was fixed by a wedge driven tight against a bar across the mouth. 13 Roman planes have been discovered, all over Europe. The most renowned English find, known as the Silchester plane, can be seen in Reading museum.

The basic form of the plane changed very little between Roman times and the early 17th century. As the tool evolved, different materials were used, such as horn, bone and bronze, but no major design breakthroughs occurred. It was only in the middle of the century that fundamental changes began to happen. In this era the plough-plane is thought to have been developed. Nevertheless, even by the end of the century it is likely that planes were still being made by the craftsmen as and when they needed them. The turn of the century almost certainly saw the dawn of commercial plane-making in Britain; and the credit for being the first professional plane-maker goes to Robert Wooding, formerly a London joiner.

It is not exactly clear when Wooding made the transition from joiner to plane-maker, but by 1725 he was actively making and selling planes. He took eight apprentices in all, but none of the first four appear to have had any connection with plane-making. The last four all became professional plane-makers. William Cogdell worked from 1730 to 1752; John Jennion from 1732 to 1757; Thomas Phillipson was active between 1740 and 1760, and Robert Fitkin started in 1750 and went on till 1778. From these small beginnings plane-making mushroomed out to the provinces as the demand for the product grew.

It is worth trying to understand exactly why demand expanded, and appreciate the factors that persuaded Wooding he would be better off making planes than being a joiner. Changes in style resulted in increased use of mouldings for decoration, and, when the easier-working mahogany became available, it brought with it more moulding designs, and more call for planes to make them.

Whereas making a bench-plane would have been straightforward for a joiner, making moulding-planes would be very time-consuming and require special equipment. The influence of Renaissance architecture was also increasing the demand for profiles, so it was much more practical for the working joiner to buy moulding-planes ready-made rather than spend valuable time making them himself. A new industry was the result.

The number of plane-makers grew until 1850, when it reached a peak of over 140. By this time family businesses of plane-makers were established in main centres throughout the country: Griffith of Norwich, Varill of York, Greenslade of Bristol, Stothert of Bath, Moseley and Buck of London, King of Hull, and Moss and Darby of Preston and Birmingham.

After 1850, the industry went into a steady decline that was due mainly to mechanisation. By the 1950s the manufacture of wooden planes had virtually died out.

The collectability of planes is easy to understand, 880 manufacturers having spanned 280 years. There is a wealth of wooden (and metal) planes, an enormous variety designed for specific jobs and thus differing in form and size. Collectors must be grateful for the fact that nearly all plane-makers stamped their names on the toe end of their planes, so they are readily identifiable.

British metal planes are also very collectable. Whereas wooden planes tend to be collected for their age or because they have an interesting use, metal planes are sought for their aesthetic qualities. Few people would not appreciate the beauty of a gunmetal chariot-plane with a polished ebony wedge, a tribute to 19th-century British workmanship. Even more recent planes made by Norris, Spiers and Slater display a quality of toolmaking hard to match today.

Finely made metal planes had to survive because of their basic appeal and also because they are still very usable. It is the early wooden ones that have not survived so well and are in danger. Many joiners are guilty of having thrown away a box of old planes — wormy perhaps, but who knows how many rare 18th-century tools have been lost in this way? Yet they need to be preserved as the heritage of a once flourishing British industry.

## Books

W. L. Goodman, *British Planemakers from 1700*
W. L. Goodman, *The History of Woodworking Tools*
H. L. Mercer, *Ancient Carpenter's Tools*
R. A. Salaman, *A Dictionary of Tools*

## Chamfer plane

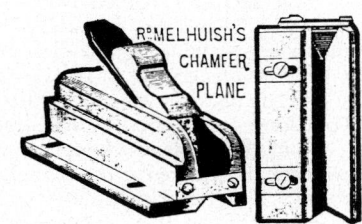

**Bob Wearing** writes: This advertisement appeared at the back of the book *Woodturner* in a series *Handy Books for Handicraft*. It was written by Paul Hasluck in 1887 and published by Crosby Lockwood at 2/-. In the days before technical education really existed, enterprising craftsmen educated themselves through books like this. Listed in this volume are no fewer than 289 others by this one publisher, ranging from dentistry to sailmaking, marine steam engines to organ-building.

Although the designs are outdated and are of interest only to students of craft and design history, the technology sections are still interesting. Tools common in the days of handwork have fallen out of use and so have ceased to be made, but the amateur and the individual craftsman will find a number of them of interest and possibly worth reviving.

## Toothing wisdom

### Bob Wearing presents his design for a toothing plane

Sad to say, no British manufacturer now makes a toothing plane, so if you want one you must give yourself the pleasure of making before that of using. The body presents no difficulty, but the toothing blade, on the other hand, is virtually unobtainable. None are manufactured in this country and second-hand ones rarely come on to the market, so this model has been devised to take throwaway blades of different degrees of coarseness.

The rear block is most conveniently made up from three pieces, making a total thickness of 2⅛in. The handle and the curves on the outer members should be completely finished before gluing together. The bed is planed accurately to an angle of 85° and a ⅛in pilot hole is drilled for the wedge-securing screw, a no12x2in, which is screwed in at this stage and then removed, to be replaced just before the front knob is glued in place. The front of the mouth is finished to an angle of 30°. Before the sides are glued on, a small housing is cut at the bottom of the bed to take the slight protrusion of the blade clamping-screw.

Cut out the sides just over 5⁄16in thick, gauge round them, then glue the plane together on an assembly board. Plane the sides down to thickness and finish off the curves. The shape near the handle can be easily made using an edge- or laminate-trimming cutter in a power router, the roller running on the curves already formed. Level up the sole and screw in the wedge-retaining screw. Turn and fit the knob but delay the gluing until later.

The wedge may be an alloy or brass casting (the pattern for this is very simple), cut from the solid or made from dense hardwood with a sunk-in metal nut. A clamping screw with knob completes this component.

The cutting unit consists of a carrier-plate (A), a clamping-plate (B), and the actual cutter (C), which is made from a hacksaw blade. Naturally a high-speed-steel blade will last longer. Several degrees of coarseness are available; broken but little-used blades are the ideal source, the teeth near the handle having generally had but little use.

The required length can be snapped off in the vice and then ground to size, leaving clean edges and corners. The type and width of blade chosen will decide the exact position of the locating pins and the blade clamping-screw.

● Small quantities of suitable metal can always be obtained from R. H. Whiston, New Mills, Stockport, Cheshire.

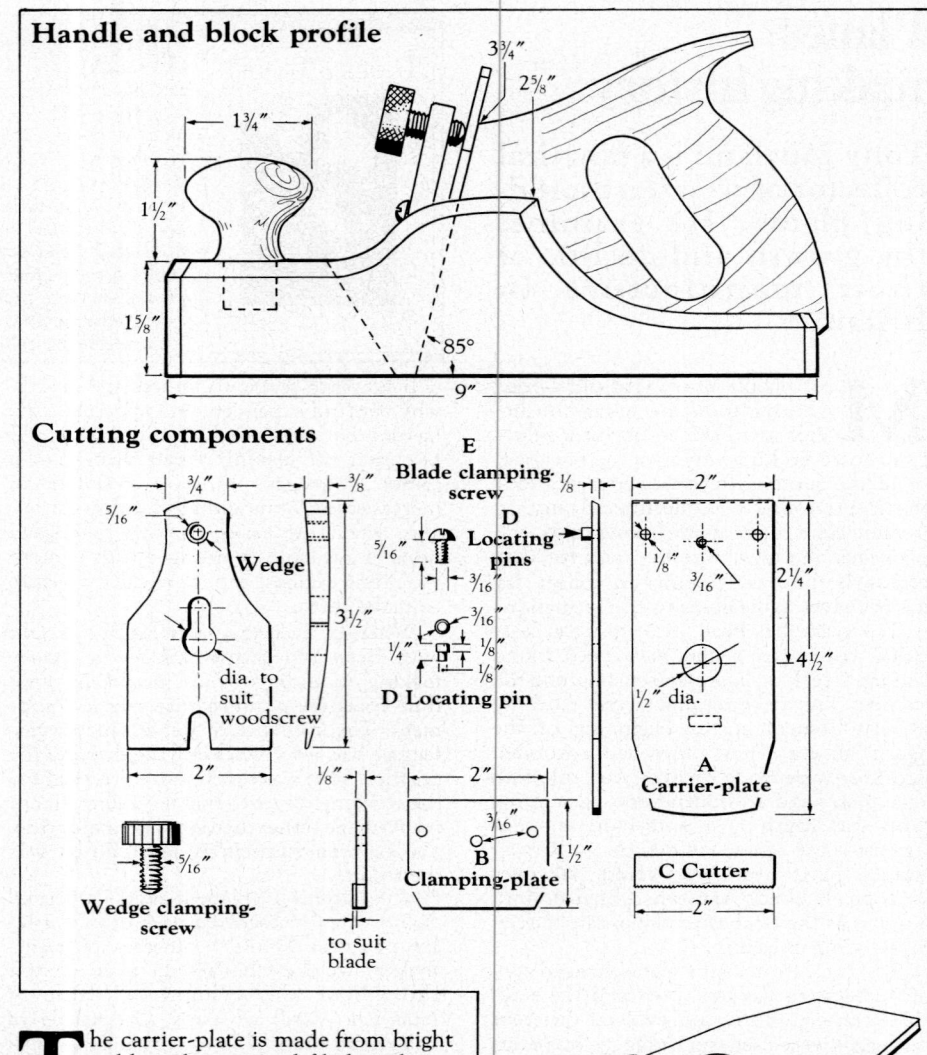

### Handle and block profile

### Cutting components

● The blade is best held between clamping- and carrier-plates by the addition of a metal slip

The carrier-plate is made from bright mild steel, sawn and filed to shape. The two small locating pins (D) can be fitted in several ways, dependent upon preference or resources. They can be tightly screwed in, then filed flush and to length, given a tiny shoulder and riveted, or silver soldered/brazed. I am always reluctant to use heat if it can be avoided because of the cleaning up afterwards. Since the carrier-plate is to be drilled and tapped anyway for the blade-clamping screw (E), you will probably opt for the first alternative. The clamping-plate is made from the same material as the carrier-plate and the two are gripped together and drilled with the tapping drill. Then the holes in the clamping plate are enlarged to clearance size. A large hole is drilled in the carrier-plate to give adequate movement round the large woodscrew in the body. A thin slip of metal, about the same thickness as the hacksaw blade, is soldered to the clamping-plate to give a better gripping action. As there is no strain on this, soft solder is strong enough. When fitting together, cut a gap from the wedge to accommodate the head of the blade-clamping screw.

I don't think an adjusting mechanism in a toothing plane is worth the effort. However, if you feel strongly enough that you want this feature, you can easily fit a mechanism along the lines of the one illustrated. The necessary slot is sketched in dotted lines on the carrier-plate drawing. You may find it necessary to lower the position of the large woodscrew slightly and raise the handle block in order to make room for the mechanism. No lateral adjustment is fitted.

I strongly recommend that you make a full-size working drawing for yourself from which you can sort out sizes and details. Note also the importance of a hemispherical end to the clamping-screw of the wedge. If this is left square, the tightening action will move the cutting unit sideways.

This will prove a most useful tool, not only for traditional veneering, but also for laying pictorial marquetry and plastic laminates like Formica. ■

# A headache in the attic

**A low-ceilinged loft room can be an excellent site for large fitted cupboards . . . but Aidan Walker recalls some nasty moments on the job**

'Three days in the workshop', said the top man blithely, 'and two on site. There's a rounding-over detail on the inside edges of the door rails and stiles, but the rails are 4½mill thinner, so we won't have to scribe the mortise-and-tenons. Have a look at the drawings, get some Douglas fir out of the top rack, and go for it. We're on a tight price, so don't hang about.'

This attic bedroom in a Victorian London house has a steep angled ceiling at one end, which drops to about 14in above the floor before it turns to the vertical. There was no proper floor, and the rough rafters and joists had to be lined with ply to make a neat storage space of one entire end of the room. The frame and five doors were to span the 8ft width, with a set of adjustable shelves behind the right-hand pair of doors and a large drawer below them.

It all looked very tidy on paper — an attractive and efficient way of turning dead space into capacious, flexible storage. The idea was to put suitcases and large items in the narrow angle of the roof, which you could reach merely by pushing through the clothes hanging on the rail to be fixed in the left-hand end.

There was a 6x4in beam running along the ceiling where the plaster ended (fig.2), to which battens would be fixed and a blockboard fascia screwed; from the bottom edge of that, a horizontal piece would go back to the angle of the ceiling — and forward to butt up to the back of the door-frame, giving it mid-height support. The small exposed space would form a handy shelf for jars, bottles, and bedroom bits and bobs.

No problems in the workshop; the beautiful straight-grained Doug-fir for the doors — 4x4in stock retrieved from an ice warehouse — was perfectly seasoned. Its comparatively wide grain did demand careful feeding through the thicknesser (a superb digital-read-out item with mechanised rise-and-fall which still appears in my daydreams), and all the cleaning-up had to be done with a scraper; even with my bench plane at its sharpest and finest set, you couldn't guarantee the grain wouldn't cut up rough. Birch-ply panels were grain-filled and given a light coat of white pre-cat lacquer for the natural pattern to show through before they were set in grooves in the rails and stiles.

In a set of doors like this, discrepancies in the gaps between door and frame will be clearly noticeable. The frame had to be made up, dry-assembled and then dismantled so it would go up the three flights of narrow stairs before gluing up on site,

but the doors had to be a perfect fit before we left the workshop. I spent a couple of absorbing hours with strips of Formica between the doors and frame members, laid out flat so I could adjust the gaps with a jack-plane and get the exact position of the hinge recesses for unbroken top and bottom lines.

● *The problems concerned tidying up awkward roof corners and making useful storage into the bargain. Clues are the heavily scribed top rail and bottom fillet. The house had subsided only a little, but the effect on the top floor was very marked. The inner cupboard, with its ornament shelf, is seen right*

The cupboard unit for the right-hand end was made of 18mm melamine-faced chipboard, Doug-fir-lipped, biscuit-jointed and screwed; the central vertical member stopped on top of a full-width horizontal shelf, which was given extra-deep and thick lipping back and front for strength. It left space below for the 300mm-deep drawer.

It's always the case with fitting jobs that you can't measure and cut one piece till the one before it is in place, whose size and shape is decided by a third, which has to fit round the first . . . and so on. The front edge of the floor, which was laid on carefully scribed 3x2s to get some semblance of a level, flat surface, had to butt to the back bottom edge of the front frame, lying on a batten screwed at the same level as the false joists. The existing floor dropped 1¼in over the 8ft span; the ply lining for the left-hand wall similarly had to butt to the vertical tie on the wall itself, which was scribed vertical and sized so the door-frame

could overlap it and be screwed from behind. The right-hand wall didn't need such tight fitting, as it was to be hidden behind the wall of the inner cupboard; but that cupboard wall, in its turn, had to tie in to the scribing piece, to which again the door-frame was fixed.

We could cope with the plummeting

floor; the walls were out of true by ⅞in over a 6ft height, and made of aerated mud to boot, but we even coped with them. The ceiling was worse than a nightmare — at least you always wake up from them. I sweated over dry-assembling the 8x6ft frame, offering it up, marking the ceiling member to scribe in two directions (a

# A headache in the attic

varying angle and an obscene bulge), dismantling it again, planing some more off, re-assembling, re-offering . . .

The tenons, long since exposed by the angle at the back, were getting shorter and weaker; the more I planed, the more I could see had to come off. Consumed with hatred and frustration, I became convinced the whole thing was made of straw, and somewhere in there was the last one. Wattle-and-daub was like reinforced concrete by comparison; the whole affair was literally held together by the lining-paper.

Fixing through the top member to the joists was no problem — at least, it was easy to establish where the joists were. The best part of a day's work carving a 60mm rail down to as little as 37mm in parts inevitably means there will be other parts which don't fit the lumps and bumps; screwing up tight was going to pull the slacker parts — on a

surface that was anyway about as rigid as blancmange — well out of true. On top of that, the frame had of course to be perfectly plumb and square, with not a trace of the winding that five doors in a row would have painfully highlighted. I took yet more off the top rail, leaving it just clear of the ceiling all along its length, and chiselled wedges for a perfect fit just where the screws would go. I put them in from the back of the rail, cutting extra space in the angle so they were concealed from the front.

The thing was just about to go in for good when I remembered the fascia-and-shelf arrangement to cover the beam. This could only be dimensioned when I knew exactly where the frame was going to stand, since the shelf had to butt to the back of the frame; the same applied to the floor, but fitting was easier because we left the front panel till last and scribed it in tight when the

frame was positioned.

The beam, unsurprisingly, was on a gradient of about 1 in 3. I had to get the bottom of the fascia absolutely level, because the shelf which attached to it formed the top of the inner cupboard. More scribing, more angles and curves at the same time; cut oversize, the fascia was pinned close to the angled ceiling, marked off with a pair of compasses set to the widest gap, and cut along the wavy line with a jigsaw set at a steep angle. Then I pinned it up higher to fit into the curves I'd cut, and got a line along the bottom with a level.

The beam needed packing more than an inch thick at one end — and some drastic shaving off at the other, for which sort of work I keep a ratty chisel and some small Surforms. The shelf-piece was now subjected to the same pin/offer/scribe/offer/mark treatment. I got the line for the

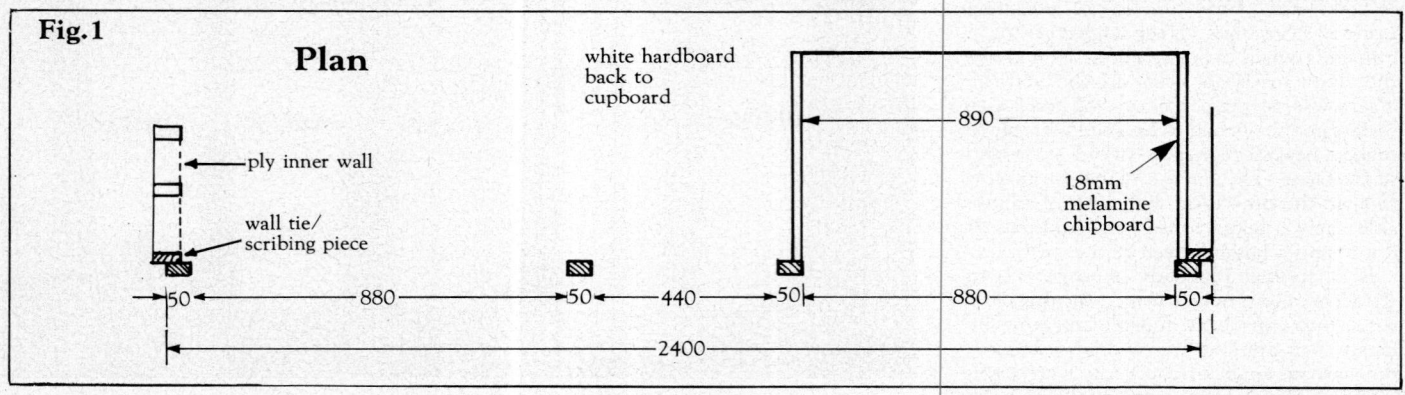

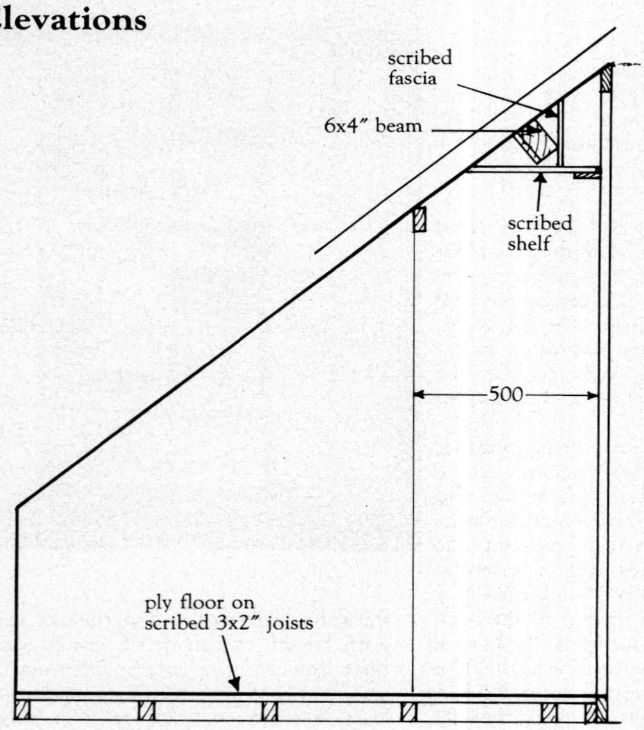

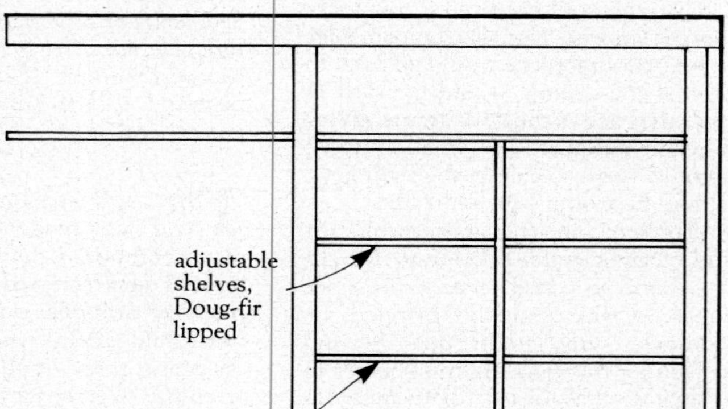

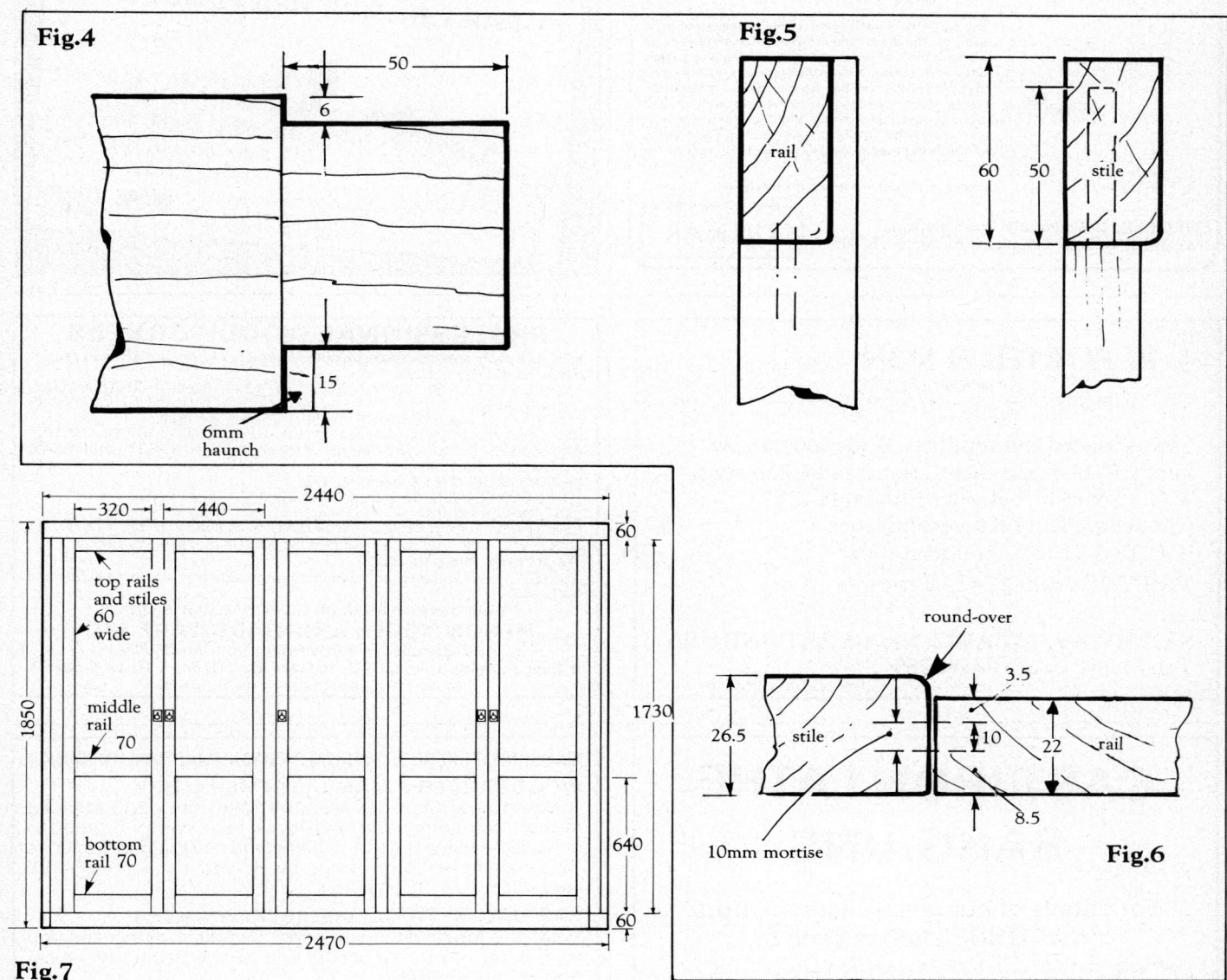

**Fig.4**

50
6
15
6mm haunch

**Fig.5**

rail

60 50 stile

**Fig.7**

2440
320 440
60
top rails
and stiles
60 wide

1850

middle rail 70

1730

bottom rail 70

640

60
2470

**Fig.6**

round-over

26.5 stile
3.5
10
22 rail
8.5

10mm mortise

front edge from the back of the wall pieces to which the frame was to be fixed, then cut back from that by the thickness of the Doug-fir lipping.

The frame finally in place, attention turned to the inner shelf/cupboard unit. Had I forgotten anything? The width of the opening was greater than that of the door-opening, so the front edges of the chipboard uprights would butt straight to the back of the frame; the cupboard components had been cut and dry-assembled in the workshops and carried on site separately — again because we would only know the height of the verticals, and the amount by which their back corners had to be angle-cut for the ceiling, when the ply linings were in place. Lots of measuring along a spirit-level with one end waving in the air; the odd wedge under the back corners to bring the lower shelf level and the cupboard itself square, and lots of grunting and groaning trying to drill and screw upwards and round corners lying on my back in a triangular hole. I could

hardly believe it finally fitted.

The doors went on and worked a treat, with the help of some mighty magnetic catches; now for the big heavy drawer. It was of 12mm ply, running on three-part metal slides, with a false front made up of loose-tongued and rub-jointed pine planks. I slot-screwed it from the inside of the front for insurance against movement, although the timber was dry as a bone.

I have made and repeated many mistakes *ad nauseam* and beyond, but the famous drawer-behind-doors trick is among the few I have made only once. A drawer inside a cupboard has to be slightly narrower than the minimum opening of the doors, measured when the two doors are open at 90° . . . Our designer was obviously not familiar with this principle, and the drawer had been made in the shop to the full internal width of the cupboard, less the allowance for the slides. The right-hand door only opened to 90° anyway since it (like me, by now) was up against the wall.

Irate phone-calls to the workshop — this

wasn't my blunder, after all: someone else had made the drawer — were unavailing. No, you should have been out of there last week, you can't come back and make another drawer; use your initiative. Much raising of eyes to the heavens (or in this case the diabolical ceiling) later, I found myself doing a 'saw the lady in half' trick with a hand-held Skilsaw; I took 35mm out of the drawer-width, screwed and glued full-width ply plates back and front, cut down the bottom and the false front, and added a packing piece for the slide to clear the door. It worked and is still working, and it is only now that the full, dreadful truth is revealed to the client.

She is very happy with the whole installation, which still looks good and works well after two years; although the doors have moved a bit . . .

● My thanks to Merle Marcuson and David Lightfoot, who provided the raw material for this cautionary tale. ■

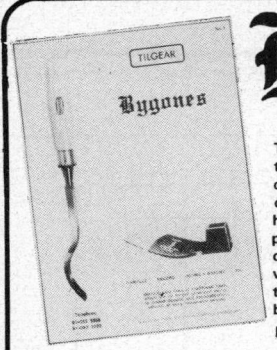

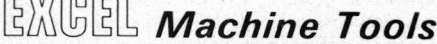

# Technical trio

**Charles Cliffe explains three time-honoured techniques from traditional furniture and carpentry**

## The knuckle joint

The knuckle joint is found on Pembroke and other tables where a flap is supported by hinge bearers. The bearer in fig. 1 is intended to be opened through 90°; sometimes a bearer is required to open 180° or more, and to achieve this the knuckles are shaped as in fig. 2.

We all take for granted the smooth working of metal hinges, but not until it comes to making a wooden hinge — which is what a knuckle joint is — do we appreciate the hinge-maker's art.

Sound straight-grained material should be selected and planed up square and out of winding. The ends where the knuckles will be cut should be shot true on a shooting-board. To mark out the joint in fig. 2b a gauge is set to the thickness of the wood and the faces of both pieces gauged at their ends. Diagonals are drawn across the edges of the resultant squares. Compasses are set to half the thickness and used to draw circles with the intersection of the diagonals as centre (fig. 3).

The gauge is now set to the distance from the knuckle end to where the diagonal meets the circle, and both sides are marked. This gives the position where the dovetail-saw is used to cut down until it meets the circle (fig. 4).

With a sharp 1in chisel the corners of the knuckles are removed, working from both edges to avoid splintering out. Most of the waste wood can be pared away in this

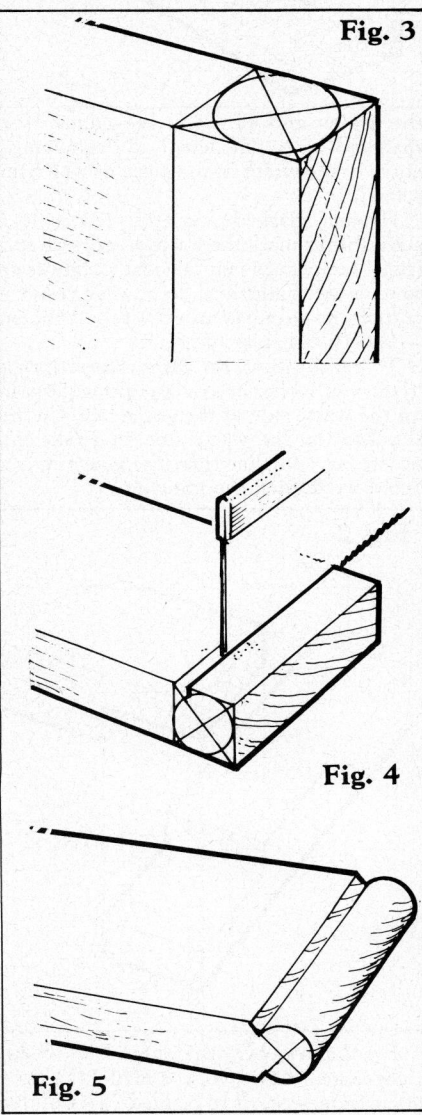

**Fig. 3**

**Fig. 4**

**Fig. 5**

manner. A metal block- or shoulder-plane will be invaluable in finishing off so the knuckles are shaped as fig. 5. Any little ridges left behind from the plane are sanded away with a shaped block.

To mark the individual knuckles, the gauge is set to one-fifth, then two-fifths, three-fifths and finally four-fifths of the

width of the bearers (fig. 6). The waste wood is clearly marked with a cross, and a tenon-saw is used to saw just within the line. A coping-saw cuts out most of the waste between the knuckles but the outer pieces can be removed with the tenon-saw.

A scribing-gouge is used to cut the hollows of these two outside pieces, but the hollows between the knuckles will have to be chiselled away with a scooping action. A slight amount of easing and adjusting will probably be required before the joint fits together properly.

When it does, you're ready to bore the hole to accommodate the metal hinge pin — a piece of 1/4in round mild-steel rod is fine. The two components of the joint are securely held between two straight battens

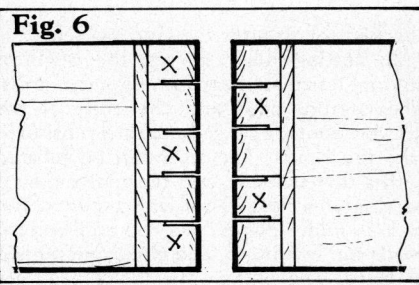

**Fig. 6**

while a sash cramp holds them longitudinally. The pivoting hole is drilled with a brace and 1/4in auger bit, working halfway in from each edge to avoid splintering out. A try-square placed near the bit will be a great help in ensuring the hole is drilled true.

The cramps can now be removed and the hinge pin lubricated by rubbing a small amount of candle grease on to it before tapping it home.

## Cock beading

A cock-bead is a traditional and attractive finishing touch for a drawer-front. It is a simple form of decoration, but fitting it — whether on new or repair work — is not quite so straightforward as it might appear.

Fig. 1 presents a side view of a cock-beaded drawer. The drawer-rails are marked R, the top cock-bead C, the side beads S and the lower bead L. The dotted line F is the drawer-front, which is in line with the front edges of the drawer-rails. You can see that the top bead C extends the full thickness of the drawer-front, whereas the bottom bead is the same width as the side beads which butt against the fronts of the dovetails. The difference in width between the top and side beads means the mitre cut at the ends of the top bead must be stopped at the width of the side bead (fig. 2).

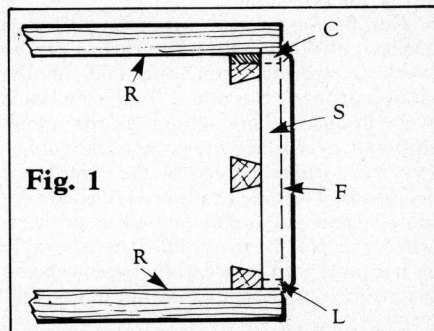

**Fig. 1**

The bottom edge of the drawer-front is fitted to the lower rail and the two ends are also trimmed to fit the opening. The beads are planed to a thickness of 1/8in, and their front edges rendered semi-circular. The top edge of the drawer-front is now planed down to allow for fitting the top bead. By taking fine shavings and testing with a length of bead there should be no difficulty in getting a slightly tight fit. This will allow for a fine shaving to be removed when making the final fitting adjustments. The drawer can now be glued together and checked for fit after the glue has set.

A cutting-gauge is set the slightest amount less than the thickness of the beads. The bottom edge and the ends of the drawer-front are gauged and then rebated to take the beads. The ends can be rebated with a dovetail-saw, and the rebate may if necessary be cleaned out with a sharp chisel or a shoulder-plane. The top and bottom beads can be mitred, and glued and pinned in place. The pins in the lower bead are driven home and punched in. The pins in the top bead are not driven home, so they can be withdrawn after the glue has set. The side beads can be mitred and tested for fit. When they are a perfect fit both they and their rebates should be given mating marks to ensure they are glued in their correct

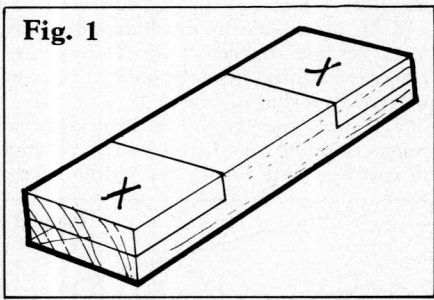

**Fig. 2**

mitre on top bead stops at width of side bead

positions. If a lock is to be fitted, the job should be done now.

Sanding with progressively finer grades of paper is followed by staining. When the stain has dried the holes left by the pins in the top bead are stopped with beaumontage. The grain is filled with a grain-filler ready for polishing.

Not fitting the side beads at this stage makes polishing easier. The rubber can be worked straight from one end of the drawer-front to the other. If the side beads were in place there would be the added difficulty of working the point of the rubber into the corners formed by the meeting of the beads. The side beads are polished separately, and glued and pinned in position when the polish has dried. It is advisable to use pins, well punched in, because being glued alone to endgrain may not be enough.

## The halving joint

One of the most straightforward and commonly used woodworking joints is the halving. It is for frame corners where speed is more important than strength, and it is also good for lengthening timbers such as wallplates. It has many other applications and variations.

The pieces to be joined are planed accurately to size and out of winding: any faults here will result in a completed framing which is twisted. The marking-gauge is set exactly to half the thickness of

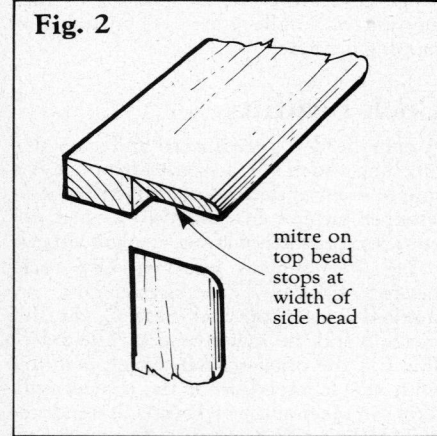

**Fig. 1**

the timber and all pieces are gauged from their face sides. The length of the halving is equal to the width of the piece to which it is joined.

Having marked out the joints it is advisable to mark the waste wood with an X (fig. 1) to ensure that the correct halves are sawn away. Failure to do so may result in cutting the wrong piece out of the right end — a very sad state of affairs.

To cut the joint, the work is held upright in the vice while the saw cuts along the grain on the waste side of the gauge line. Cut the shoulder on the waste side, and take care not to saw further than the gauge line to avoid weakening the joint.

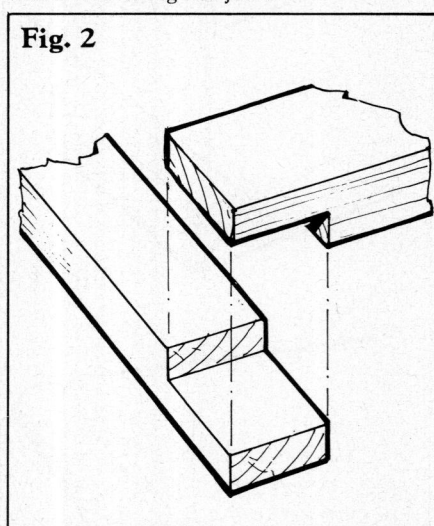

**Fig. 2**

Fig. 2 shows how the joint is cut when a right-angled framework is made. If a triangular framework is to be made the oblique-angle halving-joint (fig. 3) will be used.

If the frame is a large one it may be advisable to fit a reinforcing member across

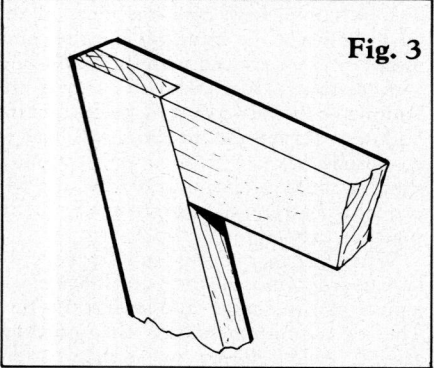

**Fig. 3**

the centre. If so, a T-halving (fig. 4) is needed. Should two such members from adjacent sides cross in the centre of the frame, a cross-halving (fig. 5) would be cut at the intersection.

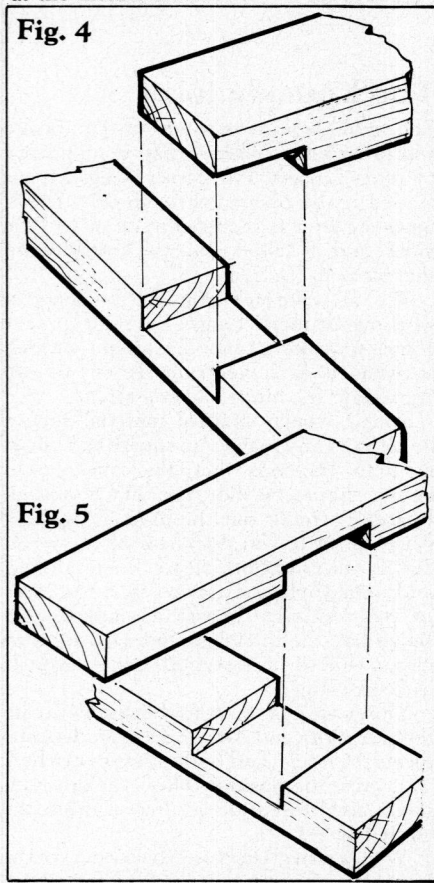

**Fig. 4**

**Fig. 5**

Where the corners of a framework are to have a mitred appearance, make a mitred halving (fig. 6). This is particularly useful when the face of the frame is moulded.

Dovetailed T-halvings make strong joints; the joint in fig. 7 resists sideways pull — but has the disadvantage of showing endgrain on the edge of the frame. To overcome this, use the stopped dovetail T-halving (fig. 8). Cut the pin first as in the usual halving joint. Next, saw the shoulders, and finally pare the dovetail carefully with a sharp chisel. The pin is then held over the piece for the socket and the sinking accurately marked with an awl. Lines are squared across the edge, which is gauged for depth. Saw just within the line for a good fit and chisel out the waste. Where the halving is to resist an upward pull, the joint should be cut as in fig. 9.

A puzzle halving joint dovetailed both ways is shown in fig. 10. It follows the same pattern as fig. 7 except that the joint is separated by a sloping downward pull. This produces the dovetail shape on face B. To make the joint, gauge the edge halfway down and on this line mark the width W. The dovetail is then marked on faces A and B. The bevel X is transferred to the opposite edge and the width W is squared over to the same edge. The work is gauged down at the

**Fig. 6**

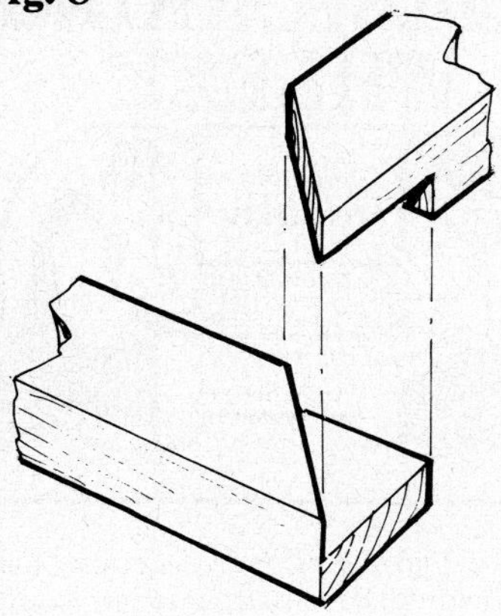

**Fig. 7**

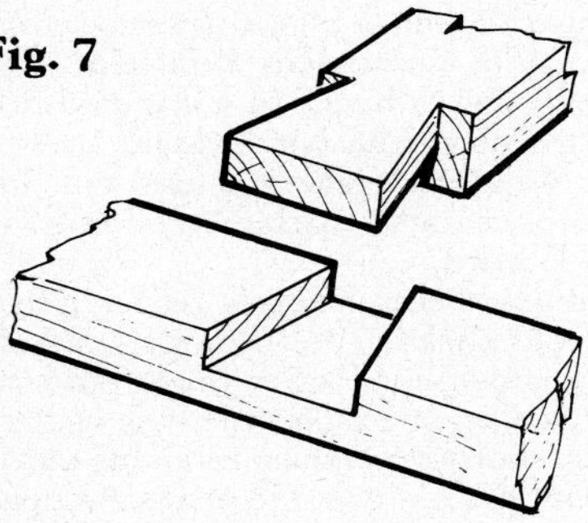

**Fig. 8**

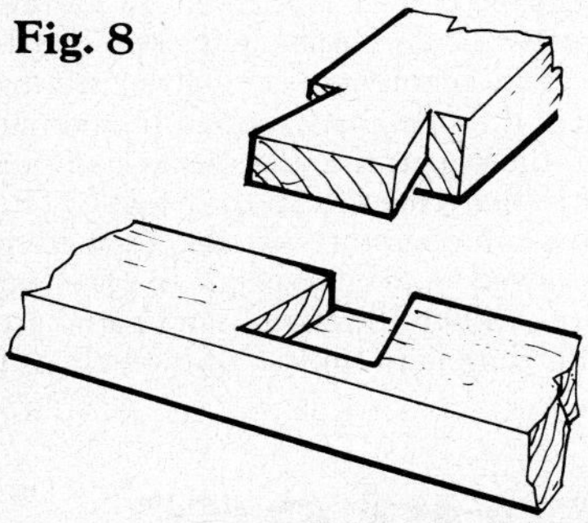

**Fig. 9**

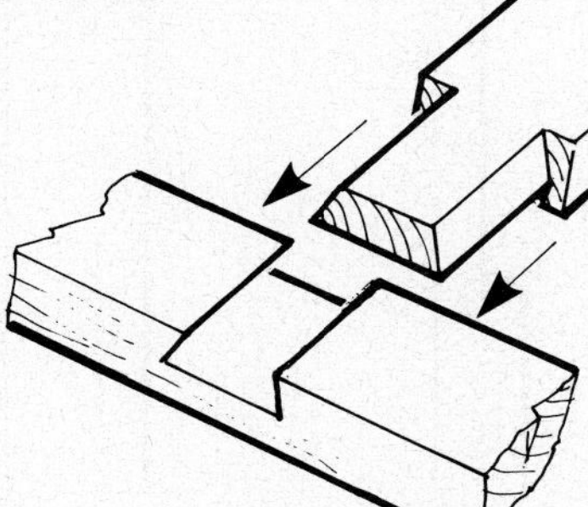

**Fig. 10**

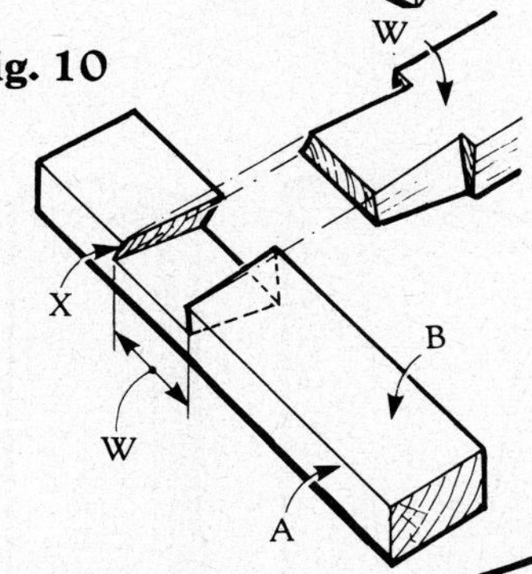

**Fig. 11**

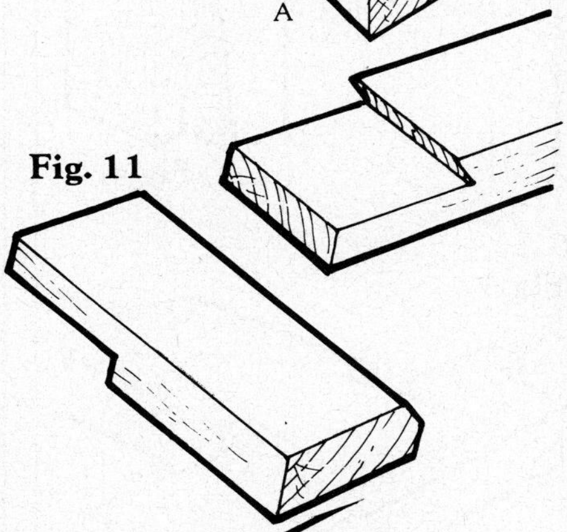

**Fig. 12**

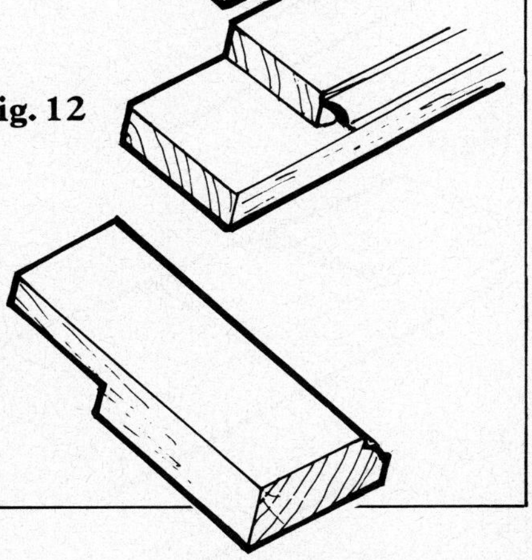

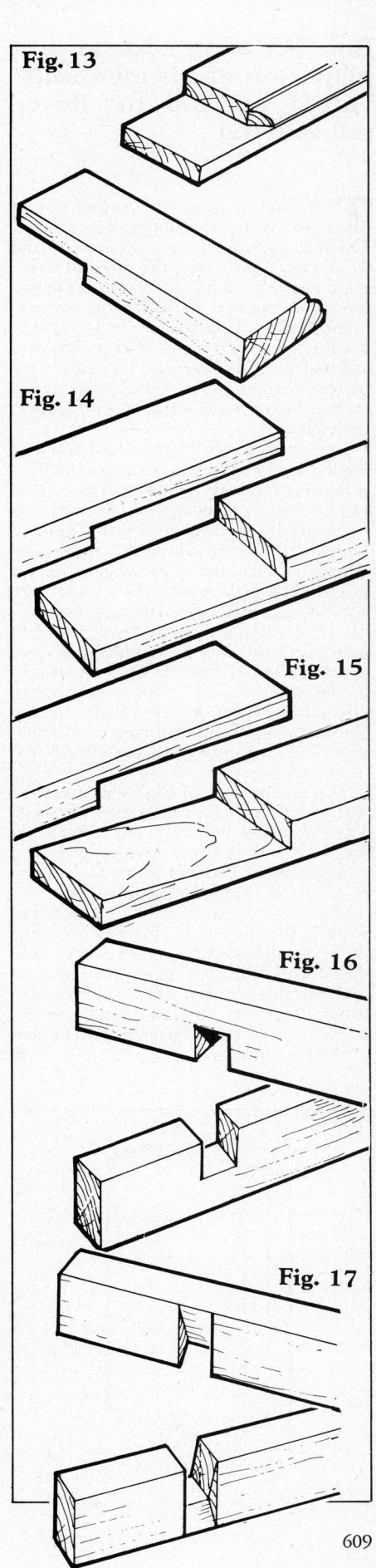

**Fig. 13**

**Fig. 14**

**Fig. 15**

**Fig. 16**

**Fig. 17**

point where the bevel and square lines intersect. Saw down within the lines and chisel out the waste. The pin is then marked and sawn slightly full to allow for fitting.

Chamfered and moulded halvings are shown in figs 11, 12, & 13. In figs 11 & 12 the joints are scribed, whereas in fig 13 the moulding is mitred. Where the moulding is on the inner edge of the frame the halving width is less than the overall width by the width of the moulding.

The straight half-lap joint (fig. 14) is used for lengthening posts, rails and wall-plates. Marking out is done with the marking-gauge and marking-knife or pencil. Where the joint has to withstand a pulling force the straight bevelled halving (fig. 15) is useful; instead of marking along the grain with the marking-gauge it is more usual to mark the slope with a template of plywood. The gauge is, of course, used to mark across the endgrain of the two pieces to ensure that the two tapers are not sawn out of square.

The cross-edged halving (fig. 16) is frequently used for divisions in drawers and pigeonholes in desks. It is also found in the construction of the infill in interior-grade plywood-faced doors. The disadvantage is that as the moisture content of the wood changes the cutaway parts can move sideways, but if the strengthened cross-edged halving (fig. 17) is used, no movement can take place. ∎

# Technical trio

## Bob Wearing adds an explanation of his own individual method for dovetail halving

This joint is generally marked out as shown in fig. 1 with the waste shaded. The first cutting removes the bulk of the waste (fig. 2). Clearly, the dovetail waste cannot now be simply sawn out, as the saw cannot start at zero on the two top corners. Some workers would chisel a little and then saw the bulk; others would saw the shoulders and then pare the dovetail. This is not a very perfect method at the best of times; if the grain curls and is awkward, the paring cut is very difficult.

The saw is a very accurate tool in skilled hands, and I like to do it all by sawing. This means setting back the dovetail as in fig. 3 just enough to allow the saw to start. I do not go to a lot of trouble shooting the ends. I prefer merely to saw them a little over-length and plane off after the glue-up. For marking the angle, a sliding bevel is not very accurate, mainly because there is not much of a bearing surface. I have found it worthwhile making the unorthodox little dovetail marker shown in fig. 4. A strip of hardwood about $3 \times \frac{3}{4} \times \frac{1}{2}$in is grooved to take a thin metal or Formica blade, which is glued and/or pinned with a few brass panel-pins. The slope is to taste, but I find 1 in 6 quite satisfactory.

The second half of the joint is scribed with a knife from the first as shown in fig. 5. The two pieces may be cramped for extra accuracy; if the knifing is heavy, a shallow groove may be pared in which the saw can be accurately started (fig. 6).

A number of other saw-cuts are made to weaken the waste (fig. 7), which is then pared out almost to the gauge mark. I would then finish with that nowadays neglected tool, the hand router, which I always keep handy. The very fine adjustment on the router makes it easy to get perfect alignment of the flat surfaces. ∎

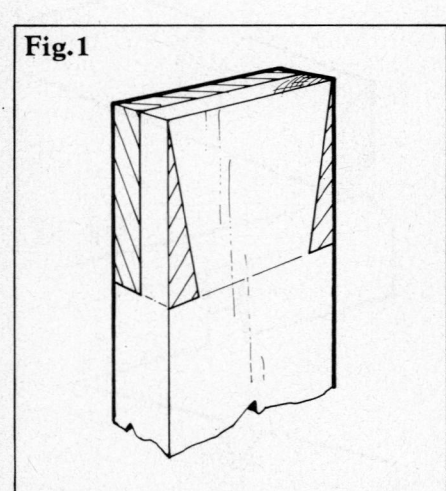

Fig.1

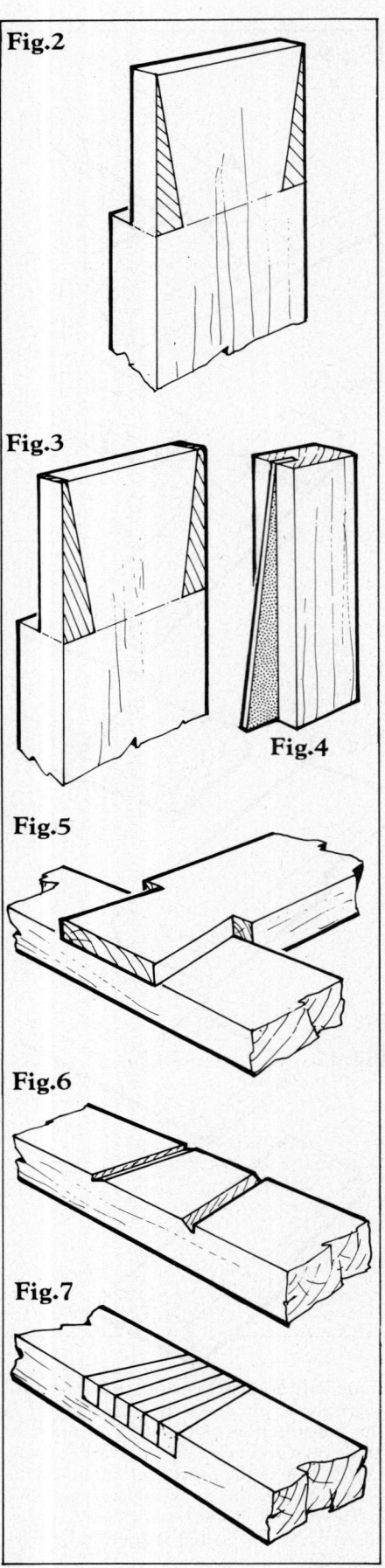

Fig.2

Fig.3

Fig.4

Fig.5

Fig.6

Fig.7

# The Planem

## WOODWORKING WHEEZE
### of the month

The problems of accurate hand-planing of small wooden components, producing true parallels and accurate squares, and holding small items to plane them true, can all be overcome by making this simple planer-thicknesser and squaring jig, **writes Roy Benfield.**

My design is based on a standard no.5 Stanley Bailey plane, but obviously sizes can vary. Whatever plane you use, the sides must be accurately machined and true with the sole-plate.

I used well-seasoned oak, retrieved from some old desks. True up a pair of side-pieces, about 24in long, with perfectly true square edges, and a flat true base which is slightly shorter than the sides and as wide as the plane plus the two side-pieces. An open-bottom plane carrier is formed by joining the matched side-pieces with two hard-wood cross-members; to give sliding clearance, the plane is wrapped in a single sheet of thin paper, the side-pieces clamped to it with their edges flush to the sole. The two cross-members are fitted one at each end, screwed and dowelled to prevent distortion. When the clamps and paper are removed, the plane should slide freely but

# Starters

**Chris Nussbaum concludes his diary of the London College of Furniture C&G 564 cabinet-making course**

It hardly seems possible that this course is nearly over, amid the hectic rush to complete outstanding work. Having been squeezed into such a short time-span, it seems only yesterday I was listening to a lecture on tool sharpening on the third day of the course!

With assessment, examinations and the end-of-year exhibition a matter of days away, everyone is becoming a little blinkered in their attempts to get projects finished — with predictable results: one person trying to polish a job next to someone else using a disc-sander (an interesting new finish perhaps?); four people gluing up at once, with only enough cramps for three! But on the whole tempers remain cool, we

firmly between the pieces.

Fit metal guide-plates to the lower edges of the box for the plane to slide on. I used ¾x⅛in brass strip, projecting into the box by about ⅛in — enough to run along the sides of the mouth, but not to touch the iron. I made six hinge members from ¾x³⁄₁₆in brass; the dimensions are not important, but the accuracy of the hole-drilling is vitally so. The holes should be a good running fit on the shanks of the fixing screws, and the distance between the hole centres is crucial. To make sure that all six pieces are the same, use one member as a drilling jig for the other five.

The next operation is most important for the final accuracy of the device. Drill six equally spaced holes, three on each side of the box; use a small clamp as a side-stop on one metal hinge-piece to ensure all six holes are equidistant from the base runners. Then screw the six hinges to the main box with a

thin spacer washer between each hinge and box. Clamp the base-plate in place; set a bevel gauge to locate and drill the other six hinge holes accurately. Fit the other six screws and spacer-washers, and you have a hinged box that can be raised and lowered with the sole and base-plate constantly parallel.

Two thickness-adjusting screws with locknuts are fitted at one end, and a third lowering screw is fitted so it will clear the vice. Also screw a strong wooden block to the underside of the base-board for holding in the vice.

A metal cross-end-stop is fitted to the upper-side of the base-board against which the workpiece may rest, and the planing frame is now complete — apart from the device to hold the workpiece itself.

Drill the base-board with a matrix of equally-spaced dowel holes, so you can make and position eccentric dowel clamps

as and where you need them. You can also use these holes to fit dowelled squaring-guides.

The 'Planemate' should be ideal for the modelmaker who wants to prepare home-made stock rather than buy expensive prepared timber, and the miniaturists would find a smaller version with a low-angle block very useful. ∎

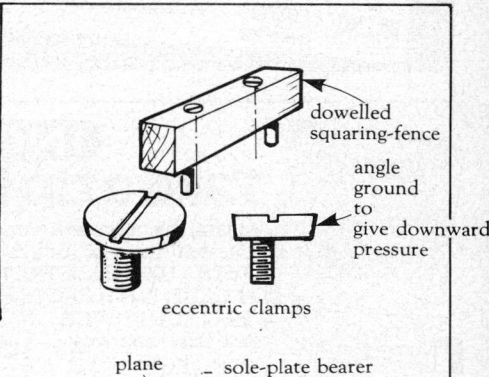

dowelled squaring-fence

angle ground to give downward pressure

eccentric clamps

## The Planemate in operation

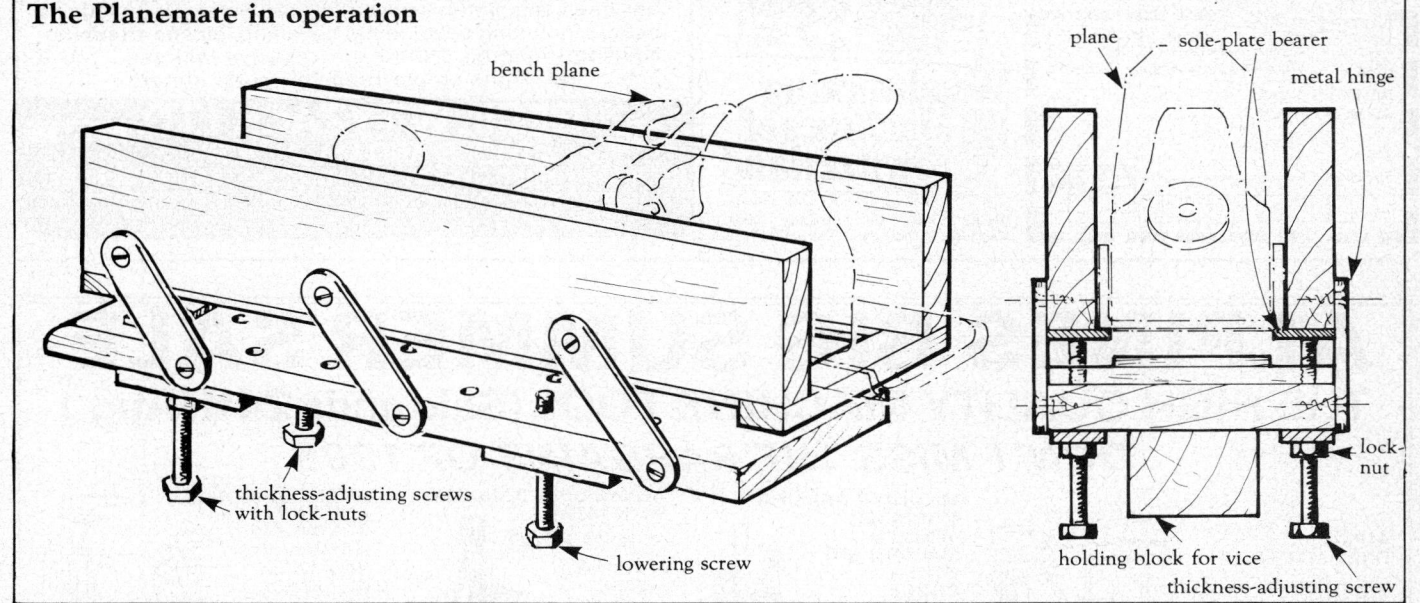

bench plane

plane — sole-plate bearer

metal hinge

thickness-adjusting screws with lock-nuts

lowering screw

lock-nut

holding block for vice

thickness-adjusting screw

retain the all-important ability to laugh (especially at ourselves), and everyone is ready to help their colleagues.

I suppose it should be the time to look back, assess the course and judge one's progress, but I have been largely preoccupied with the future: trying to decide on the best way forward for someone in my position, with a basic training in cabinet-making but next to no commercial experience. One or two of my colleagues will be trying to set up in their own workshops, but I am wary of making a commitment to earning a living on my own without gaining more business experience first. There seem to be so many facets to the successful operation of a small business that I think it would put too much strain on my limited cabinetmaking experience.

I feel that I still need to be learning alongside more experienced craftspeople — so I don't wish to become self-employed and go

jobbing either, since one learns very slowly that way. I have opted to go and work in a small workshop established a couple of years ago: big enough to be able to afford to employ me, but small enough for me to be in daily contact with all sides of the business and learn as much as possible as quickly as possible. I was lucky enough to come across the company just at the time they needed me, and I hope that we'll soon come to a final agreement about my employment!

So that's that, isn't it? You've seen my year from start to finish. I hope that, by the time you read this, many of you will have visited the college exhibition — I have admired, criticised and even been inspired! I look back with great pleasure on a period of rapid learning. I cannot count all the new little gems of knowledge I now possess.

Many things about the course did not suit me personally — decisions and structure sometimes caused by lack of funds, and

occasionally just by the way the director wanted it to be. But there again, who could expect to find something perfect? I suppose my main regret is to have spent so much time making a single piece of furniture designed by myself. Not many people agree with me, but I did not find I learnt as much as I did in smaller, more specific projects. Although one gains a great sense of personal satisfaction and achievement, I wonder if that is the right aim for a short course? One would have to be much more disciplined and organised to follow a different path, but perhaps mature students would be able to cope with that.

In the end, the proof of the pudding is that the course is successful, and continues to attract the attention of highly skilled students. Some of us will be back next year on the Advanced Furniture Studies part-time course. Who knows, we may well see some of *you* here! ∎

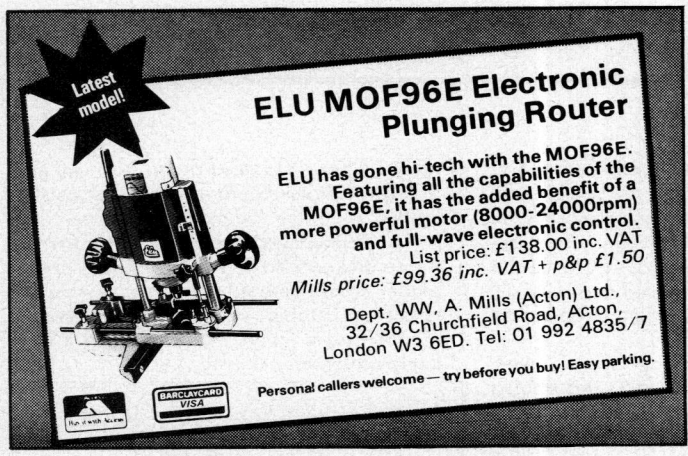

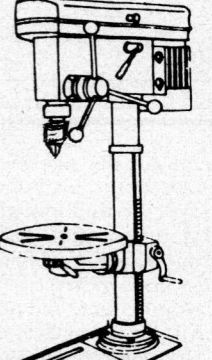
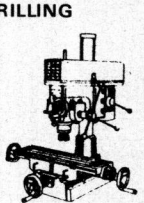

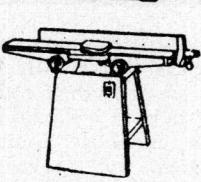 

# WOODWORKING BY POST

**Timber, tools, fittings, finishes — even machines — are as accessible as your nearest post-box. David Gray presents a personal guide to getting supplied by mail**

Whether you want button polish, bubinga, beaumontage or a bowl-turning gouge, finding and obtaining exactly what you need is seldom straightforward for the serious woodworker.

It's a safe bet that you can get almost anything somewhere. But what if the nearest 'somewhere' is 300 miles away? The answer may be unexpectedly simple. There are firms that offer mail-order supply of even small orders for both everyday and hard-to-find items under all the obvious headings — and several specialised ones. Many firms are active in more than one field.

Of necessity, the following guide is my own personal selection from the companies in the market. I have aimed for as wide a geographical spread as possible, because you may want to pick the supplier nearest home if the size or bulk of the goods would otherwise mean high delivery charges.

In addition, of course, it's quite impossible to list every item available, let alone the constantly changing prices. Most of the firms listed publish catalogues, and these (if not free) are almost invariably a good investment.

Lastly — just because a product is listed for one firm, don't conclude that no one else stocks it. The reverse may be true!

## FINISHING MATERIALS

### Craft Supplies Ltd
*Address* See under 'Hardware and fittings'.
*Ordering and delivery* See under 'Hardware and fittings'.
Baize, cork discs, garnet paper, garnet-paper rolls, Mirox papers/rolls, wet-and-dry paper, wire wool, Brummer stopping, stopping sticks, stains, quick-drying polyurethane, cellulose thinners, Craftlac standard cellulose, Craftlac melamine, beeswax, carnauba wax, plastic coating, teak oil, Danish oil, grain-filler, abrasive pads, sanding sealer, general-purpose wax, paste wax (petroleum-based), polyethylene glycol (PEG — available in several grades), paraffin wax, end seal.

### Eric Tomkinson
*Address* See under 'Hardware and fittings'.
*Ordering and delivery* See under 'Hardware and fittings'.
Cellulose sanding sealer, white friction polish, pure beeswax, carnauba wax, carnauba/beeswax mixture, french polish, white polish, button polish, plastic coating, brush cleaner, burnishing cream, Danish oil, teak oil, pure turpentine, paint remover, linseed oil, matt stains, shellac stopping sticks, wax filler sticks, grain-filler, wire wool, polishing cloth, aluminium-oxide abrasive paper, flexible tile adhesive, self-adhesive baize.

### John Boddy Timber Ltd
*Address* See under 'Timber'.
*Ordering and delivery* See under 'Timber'.
Polyethylene glycol (PEG), wood food, furniture cleaner, teak oil, wax polish, pine wax, polishing cloth, Mr Flack's Olde English polish kit, liquid end seal, wood stain with water base, spirit stain (methylated), wax filler sticks, shellac filler sticks, quick-drying wax, pure beeswax, carnauba wax, paraffin wax, furniture polish with beeswax, unbleached cotton, spirit sanding sealer, clear spirit sealer, french polish (standard, transparent, white, button, ebony, garnet), french polish kit (standard, white, dark), burnisher for french polishing, friction polish, white oil for french polishing, Rustins' wood dye, wood stopping, grain-filler, clear polyurethane varnish (matt, satin, gloss), gloss polyurethane varnish stains, clear plastic coating, black plastic coating, knotting, pure linseed-oil putty, Rynedor stains (oil-based), orange french polish, raw linseed oil, Liberon waxes, palette wood dye (water-based acrylic), re-touch crayons, Black Bison staining wax, Rapid Lak beeswax polish, aniline spirit and water crystals, powders, pigments, fine artist's brushes, seam rollers, varnish brushes, glue brushes, tallow, abrasive papers, steel wool, adhesives (pearl glue, non-drip contact adhesive, PVA, impact adhesive, flooring adhesive, powdered resin wood glue (waterproof), resorcinol resin glue with powder hardener).

### John Myland Ltd
80 Norwood High St, London SE27 9NW.
01-670 9161 and 01-761 5754.
*Ordering and delivery* Order from price list. Payment by cheque or postal order. Free van delivery service for London and its suburbs, to the south and east coasts as far as and including Dorset. For orders from further afield, a carrier service is used and the customer is charged the exact cost. The service normally takes seven to 10 days.
Polish (french, pure button, heavy button, transparent button, Stockwell shine, superfine white, heavy white, transparent white, white, special pale, special dark, transparent dark, special floor, pure shellac, white brush, pale brush, brush, super brush, etc.), dipping lacquer, french-polishing kit, exterior french polish, knotting, spirit varnish, shellac sanding sealer, shellac spray polish, oil varnish and floor sealer, solvents and oils (methylated spirits, white spirit, linseed oil (raw and boiled), white oil, teak oil, creosote, wood preservative), paints and strippers, Gedge cellulose wood lacquers and J. M. trade range, burnishing preparations, wax polishes, masking tape, paint, cellulose lacquer, solvent oils and liquid sundries, chemical sundries (liquid and solid), bleaches, abrasive papers and cloths, brushes, adhesives including pearl glue, rags, wipers, wadding, gums and waxes, pigments, dyes, stains, sundries (rosin, pumice powder, blonde lac).

### Sarjents Tools Ltd
*Address* See under 'Tools and machinery'.
*Ordering and delivery* See under 'Tools and machinery'.
Polish (transparent, white, standard, button, garnet, ebony, friction, french, traditional wax, dark oak wax, loose shellac), spirit sealer, pumice powder, steel wool, varnish (Ronseal, outdoor, Helmsman, Translac, polyurethane), Ronseal woodshades, Colron wood lightener, wood dyes, hard-finish remover, restorer and cleaner, interior varnish, coloured varnish, wood filler, scratch touch-up, knot sealer, teak oil, woodworm killer.

### Fiddes & Son
Brindley Rd, Cardiff CF1 7TX.
(0222) 40323.
*Ordering and delivery* Orders are taken on mail-order forms. Price lists are available. Payment by cheque or postal order. Delivery free on orders over £80. Insurance is provided by the carrier. Goods are despatched within one to two days of receiving order.

### James Jackson & Co. (London) Ltd
76-9 Alscot Rd, London SE1 3AW.
01-237 2862/3.
*Ordering and delivery* Orders taken by telephone or letter. Price list available. Pro-forma invoice can be provided. Payment by cheque or postal order. Insurance provided during transit of goods. Goods despatched within one day of receiving order.

### Liberon Waxes Ltd
6 Park St, Lydd, Kent.
(0679) 20107.
*Ordering and delivery* Orders taken by telephone or letter. Price list available. Payment by cheque or postal order. Delivery by post. Goods despatched within one day of receiving order.

**D. Mackay Ltd,** Britannia Works, East Rd, Cambridge, (0223) 63132.

**House of Harbru,** 101 Crostons Rd, Elton, Bury, Lancs, 061-764 6769.

**Speedwell Tool Co.,** 62-68 Meadow St, Preston PR1 1SU, (0772) 52951.

**Truro Power Tools,** 30 Ferris Town, Truro, Cornwall, (0872) 71671.

**The Wood Shop,** Treske Sawmills Ltd, Station Works, Thirsk, Yorks, (0845) 22770.

## TIMBER

### A. J. Charlton & Sons
Charlton's Timber Centre, Frome Rd, Radstock, Bath, Avon BA3 3PT.
(0761) 36229.
*Ordering and delivery* Orders are accepted by letter or telephone, but written confirmation of sizes is required from the customer. Payment with order. Delivery by post or carrier, charged at cost plus packing.
Kiln-dried timbers including a range of English hardwoods — ash, beech, cherry, elm, oak, sycamore; also cedar of Lebanon, joinery softwood, Brazilian mahogany, iroko, sapele, afrormosia, seraya.
Timber can be cut, planed, jointed and moulded to the customer's requirements.

### John Boddy Timber Ltd
Riverside Sawmills, Boroughbridge, North Yorks YO5 9LJ.
(09012) 2370.
*Ordering and delivery* Orders are taken on mail-order forms. On receipt of the order, the supplier will send a pro-forma sales invoice giving full details of total cost including postage and packing, and insurance if required. Goods will be despatched immediately on receipt of payment. For parcel post the maximum length is 1.5m. The maximum weight of parcels is 25kg. Delivery of parcels outside these restrictions is by carrier. Payment can be made by cheque, postal order, credit card or Girobank Transcash. Minimum order £5.
Kiln-dried solid boards (all boards are rough-sawn through-and-through with two waney edges and/or with one square edge and one waney edge — indicated by S/E): acacia, apple, native ash, American white ash S/E, German white beech, bubinga, cedar of Lebanon, American cherry S/E, Spanish sweet chestnut, English elm, wych elm, Dutch elm, elm burr, holly, hornbeam, hyedua, larch, lime, Brazilian mahogany S/E, oak, brown oak S/E, African padauk, pear, steamed pear, plane, Scandinavian redwood, sycamore, figured sycamore, ripple sycamore, native walnut, black American walnut S/E, wenge, yew.
Air-dried/part-seasoned solid boards: acacia, apple, native beech, native cherry, horse-chestnut, elm, holly, hornbeam, lime, sycamore (may be weathered), walnut.
Fresh-sawn stock: acacia, apple, white ash, brown-heart ash, cedar of Lebanon, cherry, sweet chestnut, Dutch elm, English elm, wych elm, hawthorn, holly, hornbeam, larch (furniture), larch (boatskin), oak, burr oak, pippy oak, brown oak, tiger oak, pear, plane (lacewood), plum, sycamore, figured sycamore, rippled sycamore, walnut, yew.

Exotic (native and imported) timbers (boards, squares and billets): acacia, afrormosia, Brazilian rosewood, amarello, anjan, apple, native ash, American white ash, German white beech, African blackwood, boxwood, bubinga, cocobolo, cedar of Lebanon, American cherry, Spanish chestnut, sweet chestnut, black ebony, marbled ebony, mottled ebony, Dutch elm, English elm, wych elm, burr elm, holly, hornbeam, hyedua, iroko, kingwood, laburnum, larch, Indian laurel, lignum vitae, lime, Brazilian mahogany, mahogany curl, oak, brown oak, olive, African padauk, pao rosa, partridge wood, pear, steamed pear, pernambuco, plane, plum, Scandinavian redwood, Amazon rosewood, Brazilian rosewood, Honduras rosewood, Indian rosewood, Madagascar rosewood, Mexican rosewood, Santos rosewood, satinwood, sycamore, figured sycamore, rippled sycamore, teak, tulipwood, native walnut, American black walnut, wenge, yew.

Bowl and platter blanks, carving blanks, musical-instrument parts in solid timber, carved hardwood mouldings, embossed mouldings, compressed wood-fibre ornaments and standard mouldings are also available.

## Robbins Ltd

Merrywood Mills, Bedminster, Bristol BS3 1DZ.
(0272) 633022.
*Ordering and delivery* Orders are taken on mail-order forms. Terms are remittance with order. Where customers are not certain of the exact overall cost, remittance of the nearest possible estimated cost is

asked for, with a balance cost to be repaid on completion. Customers requiring prompt despatch are welcome to telephone, giving Access or Barclaycard number, when goods can normally be despatched immediately. Postal delivery charges (timber only) are: under 1kg, £1.50; 1-2.5kg, £2.50; 2.5-5kg, £3.50; 5-10kg, £4.50. Timber posted cannot exceed 3ft in length. Quantity discounts are available. Consignments of 10kg and over are despatched by road. Full details of charges are available on request.

## Abrams and Mundy Ltd

286-8 High Rd, London N15.
01-808 8384.
*Ordering and delivery* Orders taken by telephone or letter. Stock list available. Payment by cheque or postal order. Insurance provided during transit. Goods delivered within one week of receiving order.

## Craftwoods, Thatchways, Thurlestone, Kingsbridge, South Devon TQ7 3NJ, (0548) 560721.

## General Woodwork Supplies

76-80 Stoke Newington High St, London N16.
01-254 6052.
*Ordering and delivery* Orders taken by telephone or letter. Payment by cheque or postal order. A quotation

can be given for the order requested. Insurance provided during transit. Following-day or three-day service.

## Wheelers Ltd

Chilton, Sudbury, Suffolk CO10 6XH.
(0787) 73391.
*Ordering and delivery* Orders taken by telephone or letter. Payment by cheque, postal order or credit card. Delivery by Wheelers' own fleet of vehicles.

## British Gates and Timber, Benenden Rd, Biddenden, Kent, (0580) 291555/7.

## Scott Saws Ltd, 14 Bridge St, High Wycombe, Bucks, (0494) 24201/33788.

## Swansea Timber and Plywood Co. Ltd, 57-9 Oxford St, Swansea, (0792) 55680.

## Timberline

Unit 7, Munday Works, 58-66 Morley Rd, Tonbridge, Kent TN9 1RP.
(0732) 355626.

## Tony Waddilove, Station House, Little Dunham, King's Lynn, Norfolk, (0760) 23073.

## Wessex Timber, Epney Road, Longney, Glos. GL2 6SJ, (0452) 740610.

# WOODTURNING TOOLS

The following firms (all listed under other sections) supply full ranges of woodturning tools and accessories:
Ashley Iles (Edge Tools) Ltd
Craft Supplies Ltd
Eric Tomkinson

John Boddy Timber Ltd
Roger's
Sarjents Tools.
Robert Sorby & Sons Ltd, Kangaroo Works, 817 Chesterfield Rd, Sheffield S8 0SR, is another manufacturer with a comprehensive catalogue.

Also in the field are:
Fylde Woodturning Supplies, 222

Horby Rd, Blackpool FY1 4HY, (0253) 24299.

Peter Child, The Old Hyde, Little Yeldham, Halstead, Essex CO9 4QT, (0787 237) 291.

Tony Waddilove, Station House, Little Dunham, King's Lynn, Norfolk, (0761) 23073.

# VENEERS AND MARQUETRY SUPPLIES

## John Boddy Timber Ltd

*Address* See under 'Timber'.
*Ordering and delivery arrangements* See under 'Timber'.
The following veneers are available at an average thickness of 0.6mm unless otherwise stated: afrormosia, anegre, ash burr, figured ash, olive ash, plain crown ash, quartered plain ash, aspen, beech, bubinga, birch masur burr, American cherry, cedar of Lebanon, macassar ebony, elm, elm 1.4mm, elm burr, iroko, koto, louro preto, Indian laurel, madrona burr, Brazilian mahogany, Brazilian mahogany 2.8mm, mahogany curl, figured makore, bird's-eye maple, oak (bog, fen, brown, brown burr, crown, quartered, red), padauk, pine (crown Carolina, knotty, quartered Carolina), purpleheart, rosewood (Madagascar, Indian, Santos, Rio), sapele (crown, figured, stripey), satinwood, sycamore, blister-figured sycamore, teak 2.8mm, figured teak, walnut (African, American, American burr, curl American, American stripe, Australian, claro burr, English), wenge, yew, zebrano. Dyed veneers are available in purple, grey, blue, red, yellow and green.

Special-thickness veneers are available for antique restoration in kingwood, tulipwood and native walnut.

The following lines and bandings are available: boxwood, black, dentil inlays, ebony lines, feather inlays, kingwood inlays, line inlays, rope inlays, rosewood lines, satinwood inlays, sycamore lines, tulipwood inlays, walnut feather. Also marquetry

florals, shells, fans, paterae, marquetry art sets, special-purpose veneer packs, and veneer selection sets.

## Robbins Ltd

*Address* See under 'Timber'.
*Ordering and delivery* See under 'Timber'. Postal charges on application.

Decorative veneers 0.6mm thick: afrormosia, crown ash, white and steamed beech, masur birch, bubinga, cerejeira, cherry, Macassar ebony, elm, bird's-eye maple, Brazilian mahogany, oak (American white and English), obeche, padauk, crown pear, pine (Oregon and South African), rosewood (Bombay, Madagascar and Santos), crown and striped sapele, east Indian satinwood, sycamore, teak, violette, walnut (African, American black and European), yew, zebrano. Burrs in elm, madrona, maple, myrtle, vavona, walnut. Dyed veneers in black, bright blue, crimson, grey, olive-brown, pea-green, puce, purple. Inlay bandings (satinwood, kingwood, tulipwood, walnut feather) boxwood lines, brass inlay strips, marquetry inlays.

## R. Aaronson (Veneers) Ltd

45 Redchurch St, London E2 7DJ.
01-739 3107.
*Ordering and delivery* Payment with order. For veneer orders, postage and packing is £3 (£1.50 for banding and £1 for marquetry). Minimum order £5. Delivery is by post or road transport. Most veneers are rolled and then boxed for transit. Exceptions are large curl and burr veneers, which are flat-packed.

Most of the following veneers are provided in 0.5 to

0.7mm thickness: ash, olive ash, ash burr, aspen, birch (masur burr), boxwood, beech, American and European cherry, elm burr, eucalyptus, kingwood, Indian laurel, mahogany (straight-grain and crown-cut sapele and Honduras, straight-grain *Khaya*, makore figured and plain, curl mahogany from Africa (*Khaya*) or Honduras), figured and plain maple, fiddleback makore, maidon, minzu, macassar ebony, paldao, padauk, pine, poplar burr, plane-tree burr, oak, oak burr, bird's-eye maple, rosewood (Santos, Rio, Madagascar, Bombay, San Domingo, satinwood, teak, tulipwood, silky oak, sycamore, tropical olive), walnut (African; Australian; American — straight-grain, crown, burr, curl; European — straight-grain, crown, butt, burry butt, burr), yew, straight or figured zebrano. Dyed veneers are available in red, dark green, light green, mauve, silver-grey, black and yellow. Thicker veneers: plain walnut 1mm, teak 1.5 and 2.8mm, beech 1.5mm, *Khaya* 2.8mm. Bandings, 0.7mm thick, are priced in 1m lengths. Marquetry inlays.

## S. Gould (Veneers)

22 Spencer Rd, North Wembley, Middx HA0 3SF.
01-904 7954.
*Ordering and delivery* Payment with order (postal only). Minimum order is 25sq ft. Postage and packing is £2.50 per 25sq ft. Delivery seven to 10 days. Any quantity supplied. Postage and packing for lines, strings and bandings is £2. Special discount for large orders.

Ash (straight and crown), afrormosia, avodire, BC pine, bubinga, cedar, cherry, macassar ebony, elm,

Indian laurel, mahogany (Honduras figured and plain, sapele), figured makore, bird's-eye maple, oak, obeche, olive, padauk, Bombay and Rio rosewood, satinwood, figured and plain sycamore, Burma teak, tulipwood, walnut (African, American, Australian), zebrano. Burr veneers (elm, madrona, myrtle, walnut), lines, strings, bandings, inlays. Marquetry parcels containing 10 leaves of assorted veneers, burrs, curls, exotics.

## Terry Mills
23 Maplestead Avenue, Wilford, Nottingham NG11 7AS.
(0602) 818850.

*Ordering and delivery* Cash with order. Minimum order £3, including postage and packing. Postage and packing charges: for orders under £3.10, 50p; £3.10-4.99, 80p; £5-9.99, £1.25; £10-24.99, £1.60. Orders of £25 and over post free. By-return service.
Terry Mills specialise in mixture packs. Packs are taken from a stock of over 40 veneer types. 'Large mixture': minimum 5sq ft. At least six types. Pack size 12x6in. Exotic and British veneers. 'Rosapak': 5.5 assorted leaves of rosewood. Pack size 8x3in. 'Melange

Ten': 10 leaves, all different types. Pack size 6x4in. 'Tinypak': mixture of small pieces. 'Bounty Pack': one of each of the above packs. Special terms for 10 packs or more of one type.

## The Art Veneer Co. Ltd
Industrial Estate, Mildenhall, Suffolk IP28 7AY.
(0638) 712550.

*Ordering and delivery* Orders are taken on mail-order forms. Payment by cheque, postal order or credit card. Insurance provided on goods valued at more than £40. Goods delivered within three days of receiving order.

## Timberline
Unit 7, Munday Works, 58-66 Morley Rd, Tonbridge, Kent TN9 1RP.
(0732) 355626.

*Ordering and delivery* Orders are taken by telephone or letter. A pro forma invoice can be provided. Payment by cheques postal order or credit card. Insurance at customer's request. Delivery within 10 days of despatch.

**CB Veneers Ltd,** River Pinn Works, Yiewsley High St, West Drayton, Middx UB7 7TA, (0895) 441986.

**General Woodwork Supplies,** 76-80 Stoke Newington High St, London N16, 01-254 6052.

**Craftwoods,** Thatchways, Thurlestone, Kingsbridge, South Devon TQ7 3NJ, (0548) 560721.

# HARDWARE AND FITTINGS

## Craft Supplies Ltd
The Mill, Millers Dale, Buxton, Derbys SK17 8SN.
(0298) 871636.

*Ordering and delivery* Orders are taken on mail-order forms. Payment by cheque, postal order or credit card. Credit-card customers can order by telephone. If total order before addition of VAT is under £40, £2 postage and packing charge must be added. Pro-forma invoices can be provided to show customer exact amount to be sent. Minimum order £5.
Whetstone grinder, Japanese waterstones, Arkansas stones, pyrography apparatus, cast-iron scraping rest, adjustable bowl-rest, fabricated steel bowl-rest, sanding-table attachment, calipers, long flexi-drive shaft, leather strop, buffing compound, Welsh slate stones, oilstones, brass walking-stick parts, clock hands, brass weights and chains, brass labels, adhesive numerals, digital clock (fits into 1¼in recess), opening brass bezels/faces combined, chapter rings, ceramic-tile faces, ceramic clock-faces, long-case movements and faces, bracket-clock movements and faces, condiment fittings and inserts (steel shaker tops, plastic bungs, cork bungs, optic corks), gemstone inserts, Perspex discs and backing plates, lazy-Susan bearings, grinder mechanisms, glass domes, brass fittings (picture-frame clips, heavy picture turns, triangular hangers, eyes, hooks, solid brass knobs), brass hanging plates, abrasive pads, cutlery blanks.

## Eric Tomkinson
86 Stockport Rd, Cheadle, Cheshire SK8 2AJ.
061-491 1726 and 061-428 3740.

*Ordering and delivery* Orders are taken on mail-order forms. Payment by cheque, postal order, cash or credit card. If the net value of the order is less than £35 there is a charge of £2 to cover postage and packing. Net cost plus postage is subject to VAT. Parcels are sent by parcel post unless otherwise requested. All parcels are fully insured while in transit. Credit-card customers can order by telephone.
Circular hanging plates, switched lamp-holders, brass nipples for lamp-holders, pepper- and salt-mill mechanisms, hour-glasses, egg-timer glass, corkscrew blanks, quartz slimline movements, quartz melody movements, quartz pendulum movements, clock hands, opening brass bezels/faces combined, brass chapter rings, brass bezels and glasses, ceramic-tile clock-faces, barometers, barometer/thermometer combinations, barometer/thermometer/hygrometer combinations, thermometers, hygrometers, self-adhesive numerals and discs, brass finials, ceramic tiles, ceramic-clock faces, brass ferrules.

## Isaac Lord Ltd
Desborough Rd, High Wycombe, Bucks HP11 2QN.
(0494) 22221.

*Ordering and delivery* Wholesale and retail trade both catered for. Payment by cheque, postal order or credit card. Credit-card customers have immediate despatch by post or carrier to all parts of the country — delivery is normally within three days. Non-account customers are sent a pro-forma invoice and the goods are despatched on receipt of remittance.
Cabinet fittings, KD fittings, hinges, handles, castors and glides, fasteners, abrasives, adhesives, upholstery fittings.

## John Boddy Timber Ltd
*Address* See under 'Timber'.
*Ordering and delivery* See under 'Timber'.
Hinges (polished brass), locks and key blanks, castors (polished brass), chest fittings (polished brass), table fittings and catches (polished brass), plate and oval antique-finish handles, escutcheons and inserts, ring handles, cabinet handles (antique finish), brass inlays and gallery rail, knobs and drops, jewel-box and fancy fittings (brass ring-screw, brass clasp-pin, gilt tiny hinge, brass hinge-pin, brass hinge, jewel-box lock, brass-plated claw-foot, black rubber foot, brass picture-frame clips, brass picture-hooks), hand-made forged iron cabinet fittings in black rustic finish, wooden beads (also knobs, wheels and balls), wood pellets and buttons, upholstery requisites (pins, fasteners, webbing, springs, linings, backings, upholstery needles), sharpening stones (Japanese waterstones, India and Arkansas oilstones), sharpening accessories, electric grinders, quartz clock movements, metal clock hands, clock numerals, clock bezels, clock-faces, chapter rings, marine clock sets, marine barometer sets, barometers, thermometers, hygrometers, cutlery blanks, condiment mechanisms and accessories, musical-box movements, glazed ceramic tiles, lazy-Susan bearings.

## Robbins Ltd
*Address* See under 'Timber'.
*Ordering and delivery* See under 'Timber'. Postal charges on application.
Beech and mahogany knobs, beech wooden balls, afrormosia inset drawer-pulls, gallery pegs, oak spindles, pine knobs, cross-grained pellets (teak, oak, ash, iroko, mahogany, pine), beech divan legs, beech plain legs, woodscrews including silicon-bronze and stainless-steel, brass- and stainless-steel surface screwcups, brass turned screw-cups, boatbuilder's fastenings.

## Woodcraft Supply (UK) Ltd
4 Horsepool Street, St Mary's Square, Brixham, Devon TQ5 9LD.
(08045) 4900.

*Ordering and delivery* Orders are taken on mail-order forms. Catalogue available. Payment by cheque, postal order or credit card. Postage and packing is free on orders over £30. On orders under £30, postage and packing is £1.75. Minimum order £5. Goods normally despatched within two days of receiving order.

## Woodfit Ltd
10 Kem Mill, Chorley, Lancs PR6 7EA.
(02572) 66421.

*Ordering and delivery* Orders taken by telephone or letter. Catalogue available. Payment by cheque, postal order or credit card. Postage and packing is free on orders over £15. On orders under £15, postage and packing is £1.50. Insurance is provided by the carrier. Goods despatched within two days of receiving order.

## W. Hobby Ltd
Knights Hill Square, London SE27 0HH.
01-761 4244.

*Ordering and delivery* Orders taken by telephone or letter. Payment by cheque, postal order or credit card. Postage and packing as follows: orders up to £2, add 45p; £2-4, add 70p; £4-10, add £1.25; £10-20, add £1.45; over £20, add £1.95. Catalogue available. Delivery within seven days of receiving order.

**David Hunt (Tool Merchants) Ltd,** Knowl Hill, Reading, Berks RG10 9UR, (062 882) 2743.

**Home Care Centre,** 20 Market St, Watford, Herts, (0923) 48434.

**John Hall Tools Ltd,** Central Square, Cardiff, (0222) 396039.

**Keith Mitchell Tools & Equipment,** 66 Priory Bridge Rd, Taunton, Somerset, (0823) 79078.

**Skilled Crafts Ltd,** 34 Bradford Rd, Cleckheaton, Yorks, (0274) 872861.

## TOOLS AND MACHINERY

Details of machines have not been included, because of continually changing stocks.

### John Boddy Timber Ltd

*Address* See under 'Timber'.
*Telephone number* See under 'Timber'.
*Ordering and delivery* See under 'Timber'.
Hand-saws: Tyzack, Eclipse, Sandvik, Footprint, Salmens, Marples. A saw-sharpening service is provided. Squares, gauges and levels: Sorby, Marples, Rabone, Vitrex, Eclipse, Maun, Stanley, Blackedge. Knives and blades: Stanley, Xcelite. Screwdrivers and bradawls: Marples, Stanley. Hammers and axes: Stanley, Spiralux, Eclipse, Sorby, Marples. Clamps and cramps: Record, Stanley, Maun, Monninger. Drill-bits: Stanley, Record, Marples, Sandvik, Ridgway, Salmens. Shaping tools: Stanley, Sandvik. Planes: Record, Primus. Chisels: Swan, Salmens, Marples, Eclipse, Sorby. Workbenches by Sjöberg.

### Roger's

47 Walsworth Rd, Hitchin, Herts SG4 9SU.
(0462) 34177.
*Ordering and delivery* Orders are taken on mail-order forms. Payment by cheque, postal order or credit card. Postal charges for Great Britain and Eire are as follows: for orders up to the value of £25, add £1.30; to £30, add £1.70; to £38, add £2.10; to £48, add £2.40; to £55, add £2.80; to £65, add £3.30; to £75, add £3.60; to £85, add £3.90; to £95, add £4.10. Orders over £95, carriage free. Most orders are fulfilled within two working days of receipt.
Adzes, awls, axes, bench-dogs, bench holdfasts, bench-hooks, bench-screws, bench-stops, bit-rolls, braces, bradawls, carving tools, cramps, dowelling equipment, draw-knives, Dremel tools (Moto-lathe, table-saw, drill-press, router attachment, Moto-tool burrs), drills, drill-stand mortisers, Elu routers, files, hammers, Japanese tools, knives, mallets, marking-gauges, squares, mitreing equipment, mortise-chisels and bits, mortise drill-stands, pincers, pinch and joint dogs, planes (bench, block, circular, combination, electric, multi-, palm, plough, rebate, router, shoulder, speciality, wooden), rasps, tapes, rules (folding, steel), saws (board, bow, coping, dovetail, fret, gents, hand, Japanese, jeweller's, pad-, piercing, power, precision, mitre, tenon, veneer), saw-blades, scrapers, screw-drivers, sculpture tools, sharpening tools, sliding bevels, speciality tools (violin-makers' knives, brass pull planes, violin-makers' gouges, wood-testing tools, gunstock-maker's tools), spokeshaves, Surforms, trammel heads, veneering tools, vices.

### Sarjents Tools Ltd

44-52 Oxford Rd, Reading RG1 7LH.
(0734) 586522.
*Ordering and delivery* Orders are taken on mail-order forms. Payment by cheque, postal order or credit card (if sending cash, use registered post). Credit-card holders may order by telephone. Orders placed by credit-card holders can only be despatched to the registered cardholder's address. All prices given in price list include VAT, carriage, packing and insurance for

delivery to the UK. All orders will be despatched within 24 hours of receipt whenever possible; 28 days should be allowed for delivery. Most goods will be sent by post, except where (because of weight or bulk) a national carrier is employed.
Adzes, augers, awls, bandsaws, bandsaw blades, benches, bench dogs, bench-screws, bevels, bradawls, carving accessories (carver's mallets, carver's punches, carver's adzes, carpenter's adzes, wood rasps, needle rasps, rifflers, file handles, needle-file handles, rasp-awls), carving chisels, carving knives, chisels, circular saws, circular-saw blades, cramps, dovetail-gauges, dowels, dowel drills, dowel jigs, draw-knives, drill-bits, drilling machines, drill-stands, engravers, files, fretsaws, gimlets, hammers, hand-saws, inshaves, Japanese tools. Kity K5 woodworker. Knives, Lion mitre trimmers, mallets, marking tools, mitre tools, mortise-chisels, Nobex saws, pincers, planers, planes (brass, com-bination, metal, wooden), punches, rasps, routers, rules, sanders, saws (including Japanese), saw-blades, saw-sets, scrapers, scratch-stocks, screwdrivers, screw-sinks, shooting boards, spokeshaves, tapes, tool-rolls, trammels, veneering tools (veneer inlay cutter, combined veneer-strip and joint cutter, veneer-trimming chisel, veneer-punches, veneer-saw, veneer knife, veneer pins, veneer hammer), vices, whetstone grinders.

### Ashley Iles (Edge Tools) Ltd

East Kirkby, Spilsby, Lincs.
(07903) 372.
*Ordering and delivery* Orders are taken on mail-order forms. Payment by cheque, postal order or credit card. Orders are despatched with 48 hours. All tools are insured in transit. Postage and packing is as follows: up to £10, 95p. Up to £20, £1.30. Up to £30, £1.67. Over £30, post free. It is Ashley Iles' policy to distribute their products through tool merchants; however, because of the multiplicity of products, the company has difficulty in finding tool dealers who can carry the complete range — hence the mail-order service.

### Asles

Vineyard Rd, Wellington, Telford, Shropshire TF1 1HB.
(0952) 48054.
*Ordering and delivery* Cheques are allowed to clear before despatch of goods. Customers ordering by credit card are guaranteed despatch by working day following receipt of order (subject to availability). Power tools and machines under 50kg are despatched by Securicor, guaranteed to be delivered within three working days. Heavier items are despatched by carrier, and normal delivery time is three to seven days.

### Axminster Power Tool Centre

Chard St, Axminster, Devon EX13 5DZ.
(0297) 33656.
*Ordering and delivery* Payment can be made either by cheque with order, or credit card by letter or telephone. All despatches are made by return post using either the Post Office (receipted parcel service or contract parcel post) or local road haulier. Axminster endeavour to answer all enquiries by return first-class post. There is no general catalogue covering their complete range, but standard leaflets are forwarded with an accompanying letter quoting prices, VAT, specific carriage charges and delivery times.

### Cecil W. Tyzack Ltd

79-81 Kingsland Rd, London E2 8AG.
01-739 7126/2630.
*Ordering and delivery* Payment by cheque with order, or by Visa or Access cards by telephone. Postage and packing variable depending on item and distance of transit.

### The Saw Centre Ltd

600 Eglinton St, Glasgow G5 9RR.
041-429 4374/4444.
*Ordering and delivery* Orders are taken on mail-order forms. Payment by cheque, postal order or credit card. Packing and delivery extra unless otherwise stated. Orders are despatched on the day received.

### Cleveland Woodcraft

38-42 Crescent Rd, Middlesbrough.
(0642) 813103.
*Ordering and delivery* Orders taken by telephone or letter. Payment by cheque or postal order. Insurance provided during transit. Heavy goods despatched on the day following receipt of order. Smaller goods are delivered by post.

### The Greenjackets Ltd

33-4 St Mary's Rd, London W5 5EU.
01-579 1188/9.
*Ordering and delivery* Orders taken by telephone or letter. Payment by cheque, postal order or credit card. Goods despatched within one day of receiving order.

### Scotspan

195-7 Balgreen Rd, Edinburgh.
031-337 7788.
*Ordering and delivery* Orders taken by telephone or letter. Payment by cheque or postal order. Insurance provided during transit. Delivery up to two weeks depending on location.

### Taylor Brothers (Liverpool) Ltd

195-9 London Rd, Liverpool L3 8JG.
051-207 3577.
*Ordering and delivery* Orders taken by telephone or letter. Payment by cheque, postal order or credit card. Goods delivered by parcel post (Taylor Brothers will replace lost or damaged goods). Goods despatched within three days of receiving order.

### John Hall Tools, 6 High St, Taunton, Somerset, (0823) 85431, and Clifton Down Shopping Centre, Whiteladies Rd, Bristol, (0272) 741510.

### Power Tool Centre

374 High St, Aldershot, Hants, (0252) 334422.

### Westward Building Services Ltd, Lister Close, Newnham Industrial Estate, Plympton, Plymouth, (0752) 330303.

### Workmaster Power Tools Ltd, Drum, Kinross, Tayside, (05774) 293.

# Wood finishing: the risks

**Fine finishes involve some nasty chemicals. Noel Leach explains how to stay safe and healthy**

Even DIY finishing products present quite a number of latent hazards. For professional users, of course, the law has plenty to say on the subject. The Health and Safety at Work Act 1974 places a duty on manufacturers and suppliers as well as those actually doing the job. It covers not only usage but also handling, storage and transport.

But the amateur is restricted by no such provisions — and thus not protected from the consequences of lack of knowledge, training or thought.

The risks fall into two main groups: those of fire and explosion, and those of toxicity — while spray finishing manages to combine the two problems! Lastly, skin trouble calls for particular precautions.

## Fire and explosion

All cans containing flammable liquids carry a flashpoint label. A flashpoint is the lowest temperature at which the vapour or fumes, mixed with air, will be ignited by a naked flame or even a spark. These liquids are classified in three main groups:

1 Flashpoint below 32°C (89.5°F):
2 Flashpoint 22-32°C (71.5-89.5°F);
3 Flashpoint below 22°C (71.5°F); this type of liquid will be labelled or marked 'Petroleum mixture giving off an inflammable heavy vapour' or 'Highly flammable'.

The higher the flashpoint, the lower the risk; the lower the flashpoint, the higher the risk. Nitrocellulose products, for example, have a low flashpoint, while boiled oil has a high flashpoint.

### Precautions

● *Never* at any time smoke in or near your working area, whether indoors or outdoors.
● Never eat or drink in a working area.
● Do not use electrical equipment which electrically sparks, such as power tools, whilst working with low-flashpoint liquids.
● Have handy a powder-type fire extinguisher and also a bucket of sand or a fire blanket.
● Keep first-aid equipment including basic materials for burns — an eye-bath, plasters, bandages, etc.
● Make sure that other people know of the hazards, and display a NO SMOKING notice if necessary.

### Storage

● All bulk stores, such as 5-litre cans of cellulose lacquers, thinners, turpentine, etc., should be kept in a separate outside store away from the house or workshop — a cool place out of the sun. You could use a metal or concrete container such as a coal bunker, or a metal dustbin with a metal lid. Every item should be clearly labelled. This is far safer than keeping potential risks on shelves in or around the home or shed.
● Only keep in the work area sufficient materials for the job in hand. There is no need to have a 5-litre can of turps around if you only require 5 fluid oz for brush-cleaning: instead, put the liquid in a small glass bottle with a cap, properly labelled.
● Do not keep your normal working supplies of white spirit, methylated spirits, pullover, etc., on shelves exposed to the sun. Keep them in a cool place, or in the shadiest area available.
● All waste such as chemical-stripper swabs and teak-oil swabs or cloths should be removed from the work area each day, and either damped down with water or burned outside in an incinerator — *never* on a fire in the house. Teak-oil waste will ignite in a container: read the instructions on each tin of teak oil.
● Label all containers, bottles and tins properly and clearly. A clear liquid could be water, cellulose thinners, white spirit, pullover or alcohol spirit.

## Toxicity: fumes and dust

Many products give off fumes or dust. Some are toxic (poisonous), others just a harmful nuisance.

### Toxic-fume producers

● Cellulose-based fluids, thinners, nitro-cellulose lacquers — and their offspring, pre-catalysed and acid-catalysed lacquers; pullover fluids, etc.
● Methylene chloride, found in most non-caustic paint and varnish removers.
● Some polyurethane varnishes and lacquers — those which give off isocyanate fumes.
● Acids and alkalis such as sulphuric acid and caustic soda, used in acid finishes in french polishing, and (in the case of caustic soda) for stripping wood. These materials must be treated with great care; always remember that, when diluting acids and alkalis, you must add the concentrate to the water — not the other way round, or a mild explosion and spitting will occur.

### Irritant-fume producers

'Irritant' fumes are unpleasant to the senses and can injure health. They dehydrate the membranes of the nose, throat and pulmonary system. Turpentine, shellac compounded with methylated spirits (although shellac by itself is harmless), french polishes, oil stains, creosote products, and some wood preservatives and woodworm fluids, all give off such fumes.

### Precautions to be taken:

● See that there is adequate fresh air and ventilation — either through open doors or windows, or (better still) via extractor fans.
● Wear protective clothing and face- or nose-and-mouth masks.
● When stripping wood with fluids, wear goggles as well.
● Have a bowl of water handy in case you accidentally get harmful fluids on your skin.
● After working with these materials, drink plenty of fluids such as tea, milk, cocoa and the like.

### Dust

Dust is more and more seen as a major hazard. It comes not only from timber and boards but from sealers, fillers, abrasive papers, steel wool and of course the normal workshop and on-site debris. As precautions:
● Wear a face-mask;
● Wear goggles or a face shield;
● Provide plenty of ventilation or use a fan;
● Keep the area of work continuously clean, preferably by using suction cleaners;
● If using power sanding tools, use the type with a dust-collecting bag.

## Hazards in spraying

Sprayguns are becoming more and more popular, particularly in the DIY market, yet they conceal many risks for the unwary, and demand great care. Main safety rules are:
● Never smoke while using a spraygun.
● Never spray with a naked flame nearby.
● Always wear masks, goggles and protective clothing.
● Never fool around with a spraygun or aim it at any part of the body.
● Never place a hand in front of a spraygun — particularly the electric airless type, which works at high velocity.
● Always have plenty of fresh ventilation while using a gun.
● Do not spray chemical stripper from a spraygun; certain chemicals react with aluminium, galvanised and zinc-coated parts, and can cause an explosion. Such chemicals, e.g. trichloroethane and methylene chloride, must never be used in a spraygun.
● Always follow the manufacturer's instructions to the letter.

## Dermatitis

The commonest skin complaint in wood finishing is dermatitis. Unpleasant for the sufferer and accounting for a great many lost working hours, it is a superficial, non-contagious inflammation or breaking-out of the skin which may be due to any one or more of a number of causes. It may be sudden, acute or chronic (long-lasting), and may be accompanied by various types of skin lesions. Numerous external irritants may cause it — strippers, turpentine, thinners, french polish, detergents, dyes and many other things. Industrial causes include rubber and oil.

If you have what looks and/or feels like dermatitis, go to a doctor. If you don't want to find yourself in that position, take precautions:
● Use a hand barrier cream;
● Wear protective gloves;
● Wash hands, arms and face after working, preferably with a coal-tar soap;
● Use a good-quality conditioner or medicated hand cream;
● Stick to a high standard of personal hygiene. ■

617

# Making games people play

We present three surprisingly tricky board-game projects for profit in the making and pleasure in the playing

---

## Martin Bulger recounts how and why he made his solitaire board triangular ...

I had two aims in designing this game. To ease the boredom of long car journeys, and to destroy the belief (widely held among my school pupils) that all boxes should have four sides.

As a table game, triangular solitaire is quite common, and it is reasonably simple in design, but as a travel game it must obviously be compact and self-contained; perhaps even small enough to go into a coat pocket!

The grid is best marked out with a 60° set-square, or perhaps a protractor. Divide a base line into eight units, the size decided by the size of the pegs you will be using (fig. 1a); I used ⅝in (15mm) spaces for pegs made from ⅛in-diameter dowels. Reverse the set-square and draw more lines from the same points (fig. 1b); then the pattern of the holes and the shape of the base can be picked out (fig. 1c).

Drill the holes, then cut away the waste. Sand the playing surface and carefully plane the edges to size — the sides are best glued on one at a time so you can cut them long and trim them to size when the glue has set.

They can be held for gluing with a G-cramp and cramping block (fig. 2), or just held with masking-tape. Cut the sides about ⅛in deeper than finished height, because the top is glued on and the whole lid then sawn off; which makes certain that lid and base are the same size. When gluing the top, make sure the grain is in line with the grain of base.

The biggest difficulty with this design was securing the hinged lid. Fixing a block or catch to one side looked distinctly lop-sided, so I decided it had to be something fitted at the leading corner.

My solution was the sliding hinge, which I produced by filing slots in one of the leaves of each of the pair (fig. 3) so I got a closing and locking action in one movement. It may break a few hinging rules, but it works!

● *Traveller's triangle ... open the box for a neat, portable game. Exact size, construction and ornamentation are up to you*

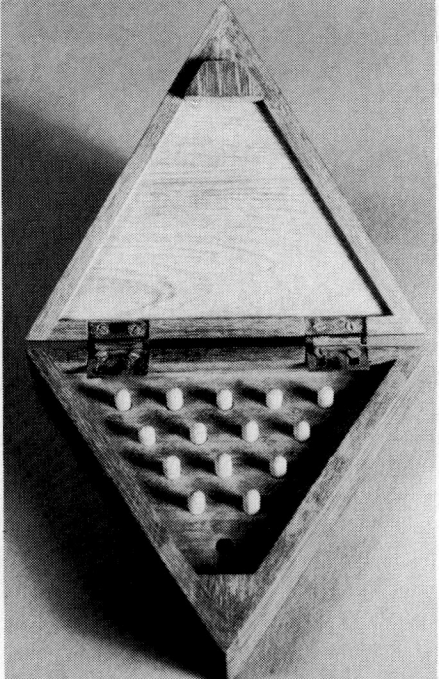

● *This version, about 5in along each side, is a solid triangular base with facings, plus a solid top*

four screws omitted to show hinge slots

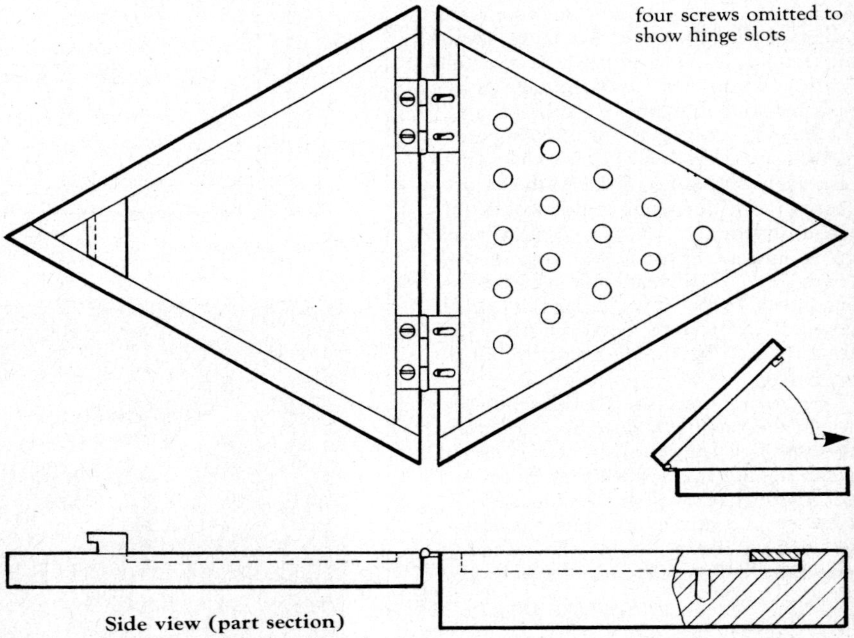

**Side view (part section)**

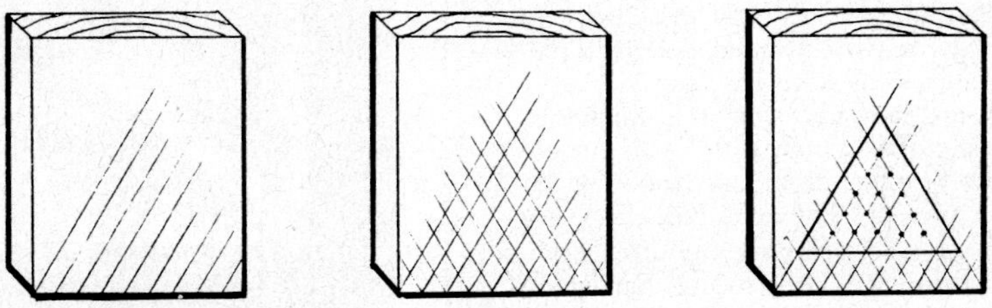

**Fig. 1a**   **Fig. 1b**   **Fig. 1c**

⅛" marked for lid/base separation (avoids destroying base by mistake!)

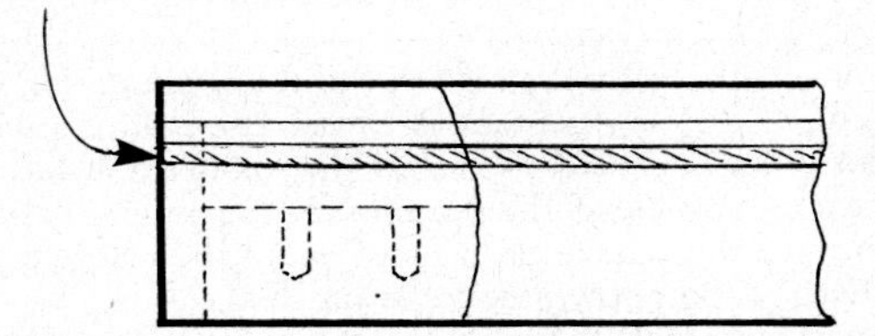

**Fig. 2** Cramping block

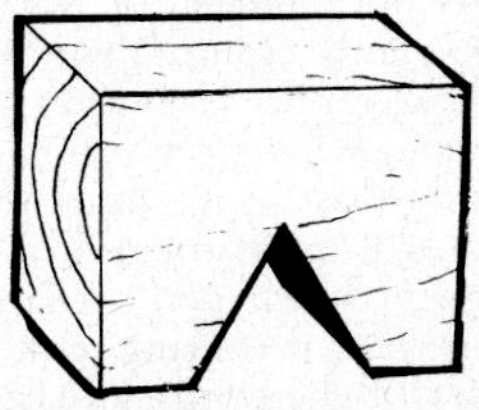

# Making games people play

## . . . and Michael Sylvester tells the secrets of nine men's morris

Nine men's morris is absorbing to play; the rules are easy enough for a young child to learn, but my own set has witnessed many a titanic and protracted struggle between adults. If you choose your timber well, and make the board carefully, you will also have a simple yet elegant ornament.

Many people will recognise the name without knowing much about the game. It was played in medieval England by country folk, the commonest board or 'pound' being that cut in any convenient piece of turf. This rustic outdoor image is, however, only part of the truth. The game translates very pleasingly into wood, and has the double merit of being a simple construction for the inexperienced woodworker and a source of endless possibilities for the more skilled and ambitious. The construction details that follow can be seen as complete or as a basis for something more elaborate.

Nine men's morris is one of those games that has stood the test of time. Although it was widely played up till the 19th century, it has in fact a much longer and more distinguished history. It was played 4000 years ago in ancient Egypt, 2000 years ago in Ceylon, and 1000 years ago in Ireland — long indeed before it was carved in English cathedral cloisters by bored choristers or cut on the Sussex Downs by lonely shepherds.

Even today there are periodic revivals, though the English Village Sports Society say it is not played 'seriously' now — except by families like my own who have their own boards: I hesitate to call our sessions 'serious'! Elsewhere it continues in similar fashion — the Germans playing *Muhle*, the Icelanders *mylla* and the Poles *siegen wulf myll*.

## Materials and construction

You will need a sheet of good-quality faced ply 16x16⅛in; 17ft of matching or contrasting hardwood strips, ½x⅝in; a pair of card-table hinges; and a clasp.

The board is made up in two mirroring hinged sections which fold together to produce a compartmentalised box for the pieces or 'merels'. The extra ⅛in allows for the saw-cut and cleaning up after completion; thus the contrasting hardwood strips are all mitred and glued in place before the base is sawn and the hinges and clasp fitted. The central strips (D) are separated by ⅛in for the saw.

Prepare and mitre the surrounds (A) first; glue and cramp them in position. Next, mark two more concentric squares of appropriate proportions, together with two diagonals. Measure and mitre the diagonals (B), cutting to meet the centre square, and allowing for the shaped corners. Glue and cramp before preparing and fitting the remainder of the centre square (C). Treat

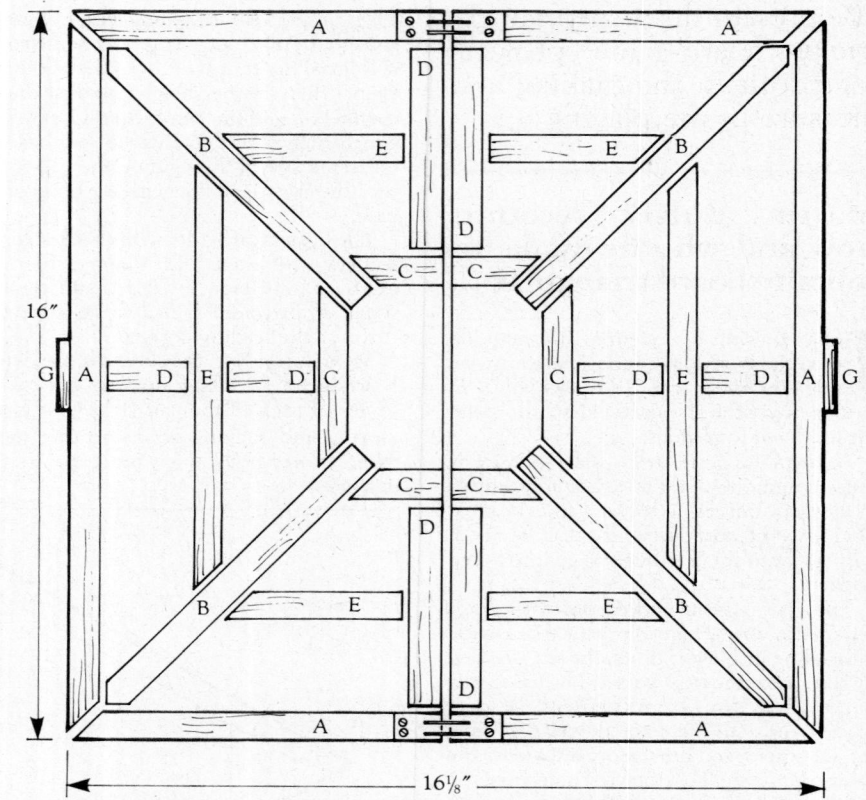

● *To make the nine-men's-morris board,* **1** *glue the strips in order A-E,* **2** *saw in half,* **3** *fit the hinges F, and* **4** *fit the clasp G*

the central strips (D) and (E) similarly.

The next task is to saw the board down the centre, clean up the exposed surfaces and chisel the recesses for the hinges. After these have been fitted, skim the whole top and apply a suitable finish.

Ideally, veneer — again either matching or contrasting — should be laid on the exposed edges of the box. Finally, fit a clasp and (if you want) a handle.

The box completed, all that remains is the making of the pieces. These can be shaped to taste. My own nine men's morris has both square and round pieces, but if contrasting woods — say rosewood and holly, or walnut and sycamore — are chosen, they can all be the same shape. There are nine of each, though it is sensible to make spares while you are at it. They should be an inch or a little more in diameter, and can be left plain or decorated as preferred.

For complete protection, the edges of the box may be rebated and strings of contrasting hardwood glued and cramped in place; but, since this project is essentially about making a lasting and elegant piece with the minimum of difficulty, any embellishment is up to you.

All that is required in construction is care, precision and a little patience. If you exercise these essential woodworking virtues, you will have a game which will never need hiding away in the toy cupboard.

## Rules of the game

There are 24 points of intersection on the board, on to which the two players, who each have nine pieces, place them alternately. The object is to make three in a row on any line. Doing this is called 'making a mill', and allows a player to remove one of the opponent's pieces, the winner being the last one with pieces still on the board.

Once all the pieces are in play, players may move any one to an empty adjacent point, breaking and re-making mills if they wish. A mill may not be made on the diagonals, in order to lessen the advantage to the first player. The ideal placement allows a player to move a piece from one mill straight into another, thus enabling him to take an opponent's piece every move instead of every other. A piece can only be removed from an opponent's mill if he has no other pieces left.

## Harold Shenker introduces the traditional round solitaire board

The traditional game of solitaire, played on a board with glass marbles, is an absorbing occupation for a single player. You cover all the holes except the centre one with glass marbles and then take them out by leapfrogging one over the other draughts-fashion. You reduce the number of marbles, putting the discarded ones in the outer groove, and ultimately (you hope!) are left with just one in the centre hole.

I made the board from parana pine, which comes in unblemished boards with a nice grain, and polishes well.

First, of course, you must buy the marbles, which you can get at any good toyshop in various sizes. The sizes of the board and the holes are both decided by the size of the marbles you buy.

I started with a piece of parana pine 10x¾in, and cut out a circle. I marked the centre panel out to a diameter of 7½in and

the outer channel to a width of ⅞in; I cut it with a bowl gouge. It needs to be deep enough to accommodate the marbles, the actual measurement depending on their sizes. Afterwards the decorative edge was cut, but of course this can take any shape you feel like.

The next operation is to mark out the centres for the blind holes. For my marbles I used a ¾in saw-toothed bit, the centres exactly 1in apart. The holes had to be

marked out starting from the centre, and were done while the board was still on the lathe. After sanding and polishing, the base can be covered with self-adhesive Fablon Velour.

Since I made the first board, all my friends have been clamouring for one, and currently I am on my fifth. They get simpler to make. As for playing, we have managed to get down to two marbles, but no one has yet achieved the magic solitaire! ■

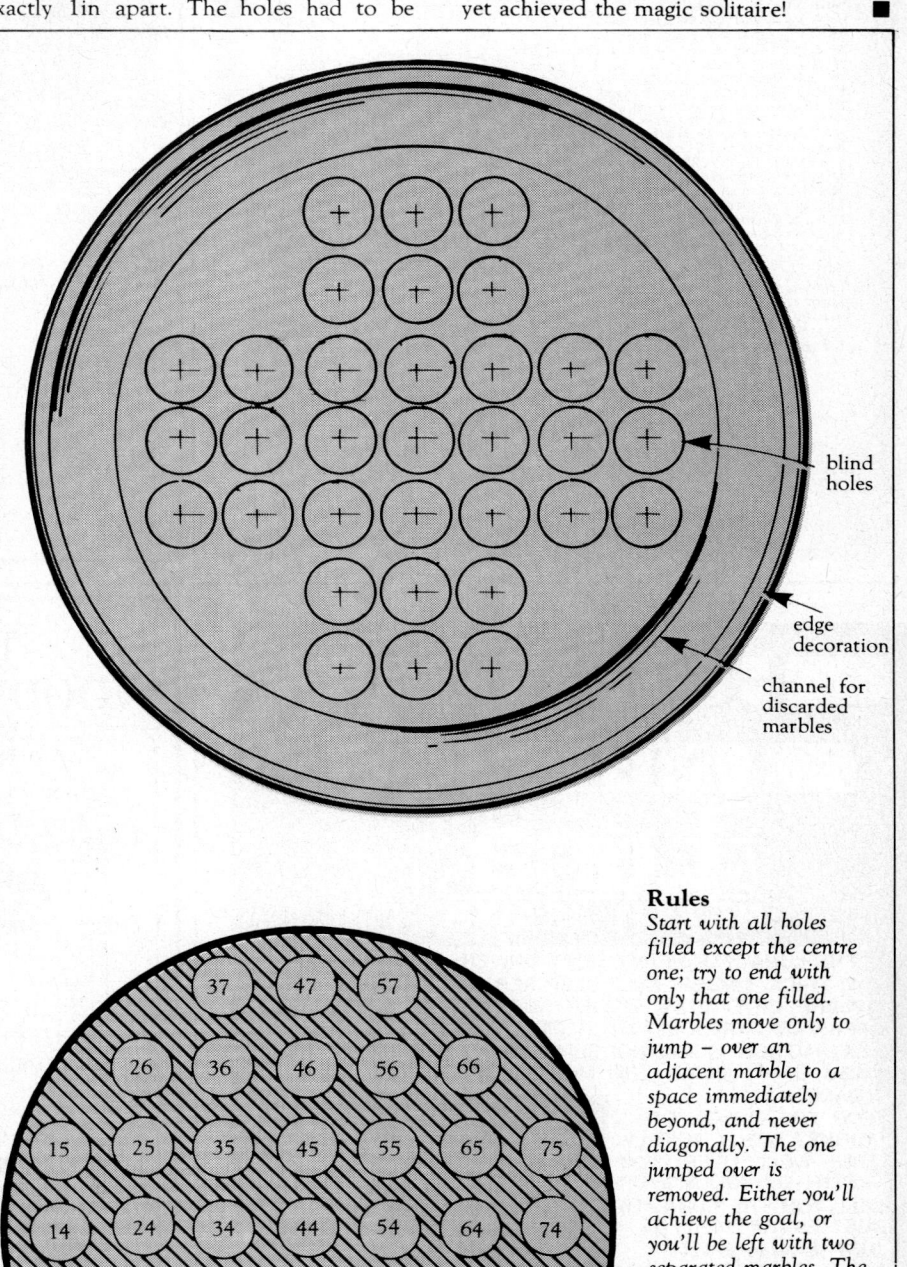

blind holes

edge decoration

channel for discarded marbles

## Rules

*Start with all holes filled except the centre one; try to end with only that one filled. Marbles move only to jump – over an adjacent marble to a space immediately beyond, and never diagonally. The one jumped over is removed. Either you'll achieve the goal, or you'll be left with two separated marbles. The shortest solution takes 18 moves: 46-44, 65-45, 57-55, 54-56, 52-54, 73-53, 43-63, 75-73-53, 35-55, 15-35, 23-43-63-65-45-25, 37-57-55-53, 31-33, 34-32, 51-31-33, 13-15-35, 36-34-32-52-54-34, 24-44*

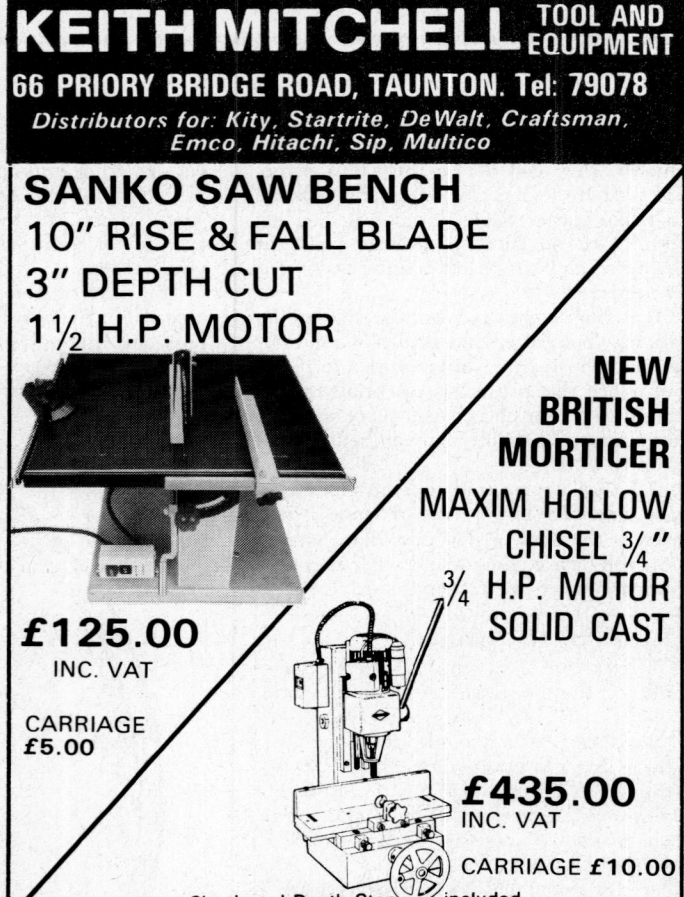

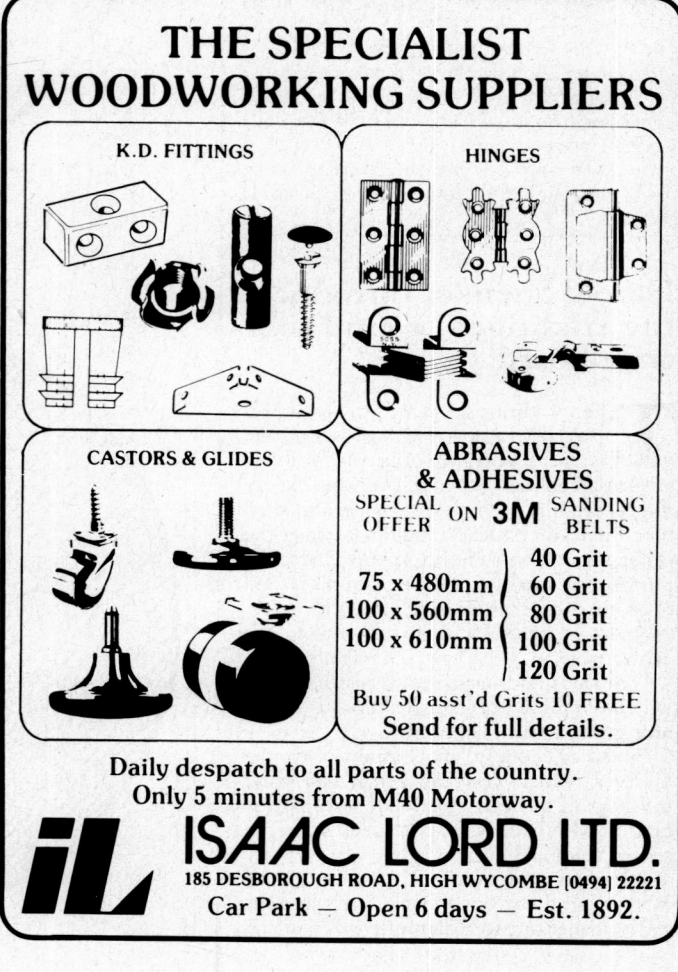

# CHISEL MORTISING

## The professional Chisel Mortiser and Drilling machine that also cuts a neat Tenon!

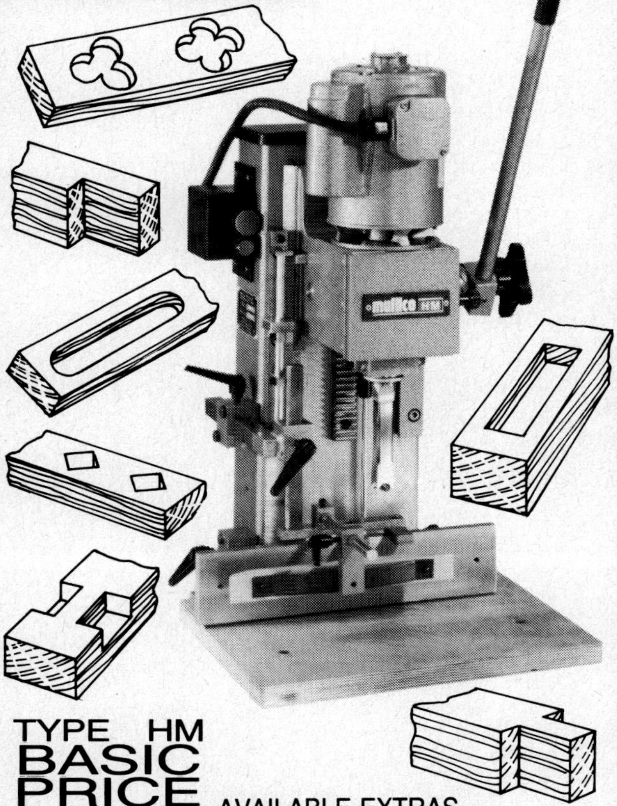

TYPE HM BASIC PRICE
**£335**
EX WORKS
SINGLE PHASE ONLY

AVAILABLE EXTRAS

| | |
|---|---|
| DRILLING CHUCK AND ARBOR ADAPTOR | £26.20 |
| DRILLING CHUCK GUARD | £25.00 |

* Maximum distance from fence to centre of chisel 115mm
* Half h.p. motor with thermal overload protection
* Depth stop with haunching facility
* Plugs straight into a 13 amp socket
* Maximum timber height 150mm
* Taking chisels up to 14mm
* No volt release starter
* Packed complete in a carton
* *Write for address of nearest dealer to:*

# multico

MULTICO LIMITED · BRIGHTON RD · SALFORDS · REDHILL
SURREY · ENGLAND RH1 5ER · TEL HORLEY (0293) 782444

# FULL SERVICE

**If your interest is Woodworking we can satisfy your needs.**

From Spaners to Spindle Moulders, Router Cutters to Planer/Thicknessers, Combination Machines to Modelling Tools. Coronet, Tyme & Warco Lathes, Sorby & Henry Taylor Turning Tools, Marples & Henry Taylor Carving Tools, Kity & Scheppach Woodworking machines.
Trend Router Cutters, Saw Tooth Cutters, Mortice Chisel & Bits, Slot Mortice Bits, Industrial TCT Saw Blades at 20% off list, large range of Bandsaw Blades, Industrial Sanding Belts for all popular machines at competitive prices. Japanese Chisels, Whet Stone Grinders. Bosch Power Tools. Drills, Vices, Stanley, Ridgway Hand Tools, Screws, Nails, Handles, Timbers etc.

**Stains/Polishes etc.**
Liberon Waxes, Stains, Polishes, Varnish, Pearl Glue, Veneers, Inlays, Bandings, Stringing, Marquetry, Clock Faces, Movements etc. Steel Wool, Garnet Paper, Books & Woodworking Plans.

**Demonstration Room**
The latest facet to our company is a large comprehensively stocked Demo/Training Room, to enable us to teach people how to use their machines with confidence and safety.
Following the success of our woodturning courses we are extending these to cover Kity Combination machines and Radial Arm Saws, Spindle Moulders and Bandsaws.
These Courses run once a month and bookings can be taken over the 'phone.

Myford · BOSCH · trend cutters · Wadkin · Elu · CORONET · scheppach · KITY · Wolf

## DEWALT · Elu

DEWALT 1501
RADIAL ARM SAW
1½H.P.
CROSS CUT CAPACITY 18¼"
**£448.50**

ELU MHB 157 BELT SANDER
WITH DUST EXTRACTION
**£84.94**

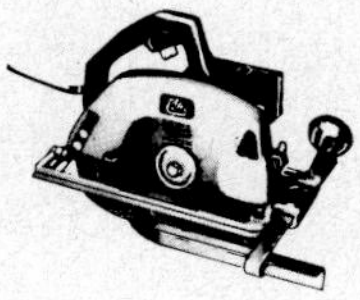

ELU MH65
HEAVY-DUTY 180mm
CIRCULAR SAW
**£91.08**

ELU MOF 96
PLUNGING ROUTER
**£78.66**

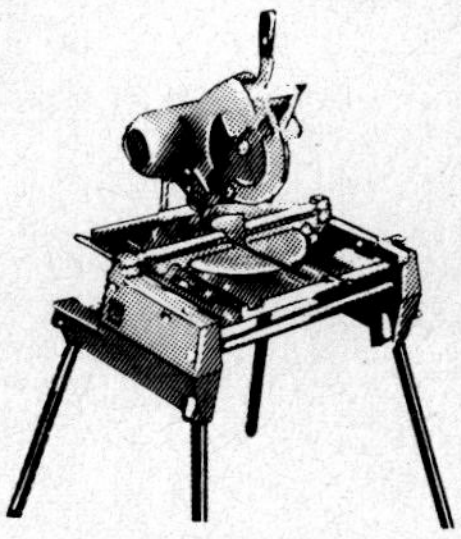

ELU TGS 172
BENCH/BEVEL/MITRE SAW
COMP. WITH W/W KITS
**£374.00**

**Unbeatable prices — Uncompromising service**

# MATTHEWS

MATTHEWS BROTHERS (WOODWORKERS) LTD
Kettlebrook Road . Kettlebrook . Tamworth . Staffs
TELEPHONE TAMWORTH 56188

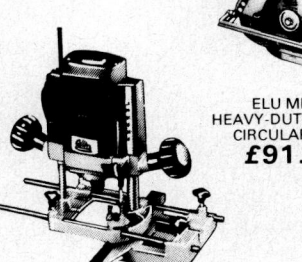

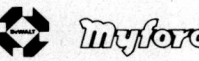

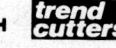

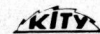

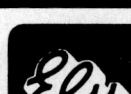

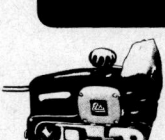

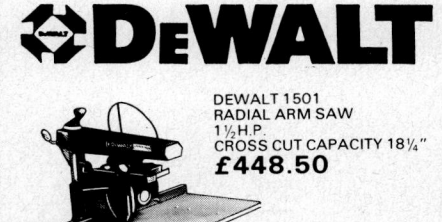

# Forthcoming fancies

Two months ahead is a fair way for a preview — but we thought you'd like to see these handsome pictures anyway. The pieces will all be on show at the Chelsea Crafts Fair in London in October.

We went last year and found it fun. It's rather like a giant church bazaar but a great deal trendier. Several of the country's best makers take stands there (or, at least, those who like to keep in the public eye), but there's none of the stifling, reverential atmosphere you often find in galleries. What's more, all the craftspeople are actually there, so you can talk to them. It's very crowded and really quite convivial.

Apart from woodwork (including furniture, turning, toys and other things) you'll find ceramics, jewellery, metalwork, glass, leather, felt, weaving, tapestry, knitting, embroidery and paper. The fair takes place on 16-22 October — 10-9 on the first three days, 10-6 on the last three; entry is £2, pensioners ad children 90p. More information from 01-373 8620. ■

● **Right:** *A rocking beauty in lime and ash by Tony and Marc Stevenson of Bethersden, Kent – carved and coated with plaster before finishing. Beech ash and oak go into the stand. Stevenson Bros are on (023382) 363*

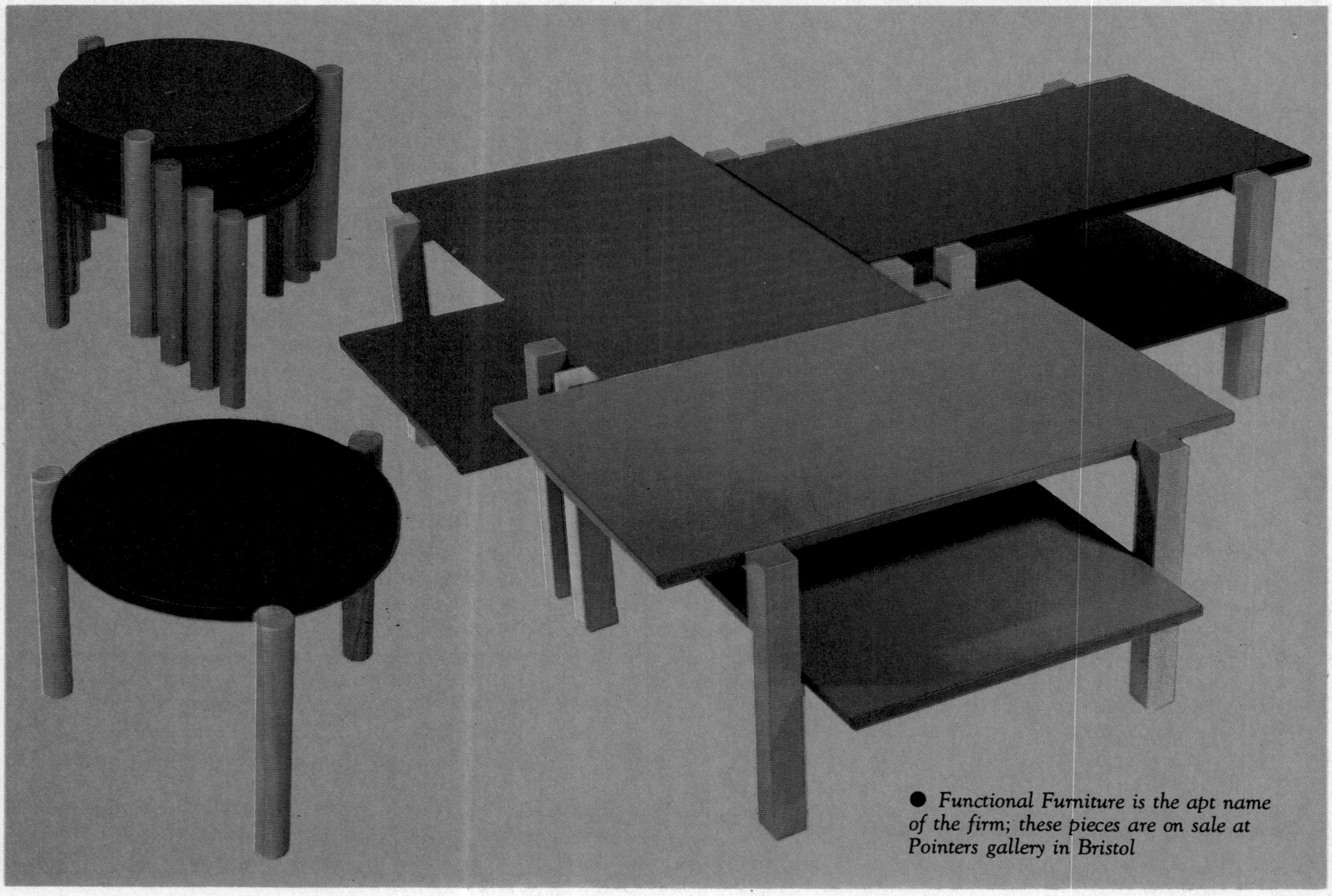

● *Functional Furniture is the apt name of the firm; these pieces are on sale at Pointers gallery in Bristol*

● Bowls (**above**) by Bert Marsh and (**right**) by Michael O'Donnell. The ark is by Cornishman David Plagerson, the folding stools by Adrian Reid of Princes workshop, Rotherhithe

# COMING NEXT MONTH!

Look closely and see if you can work out how many storage combinations Simon Hughes' **'Stack store' cabinets** will give — if you can't make 43 different permutations, September's *Woodworker* will help!

We also present beautifully crafted drawings for a superb **library table** in traditional style; an extract from Ray Key's new book, ***Woodturning and Design***; and much, much more. Like every other, September's *Woodworker* is an issue you just can't afford to miss!

ON SALE 16 AUGUST

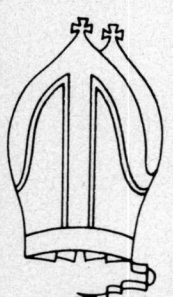

626

# WOOD SUPPLIERS

## COURSES

# WOOD SUPPLIERS

628

# shop guide

## AVON

**BATH**  Tel. Bath 64513
JOHN HALL TOOLS
RAILWAY STREET  ★

Open: Monday-Saturday
9.00 a.m.-5.30 p.m.
H.P.W.WM.D.A.BC.

**BRISTOL**  Tel. (0272) 741510
JOHN HALL TOOLS LIMITED  ★
CLIFTON DOWN SHOPPING CENTRE
WHITELADIES ROAD
Open: Monday-Saturday
9.00 a.m.-5.30 p.m.
H.P.W.WM.D.A.BC.

**BRISTOL**  Tel. (0272) 629092
TRYMWOOD SERVICES
2a DOWNS PARK EAST, (off North View)
WESTBURY PARK
Open: 8.30 a.m.-5.30 p.m. Mon. to Fri.
Closed for lunch 1.00-2.00 p.m.
P.W.WM.D.T.A.BC.

**BRISTOL**  Tel. (0272) 667013
WILLIS
157 WEST STREET
BEDMINISTER
Open Mon.-Fri. 8.30 a.m.-5.00 p.m.
No Saturday opening

## BEDFORDSHIRE

**BEDFORD**  Tel. (0234) 59808
BEDFORD SAW SERVICE  K
39 AMPTHILL ROAD

Open: Mon.-Fri. 8.30-5.30
Sat. 9.00-4.00
H.P.A.BC.W.CS.WM.D.

## BERKSHIRE

**COOKHAM**  Tel. (06285) 20350
CHURCH'S TIMBER
STATION HILL

Open: Mon-Sat 8.30 a.m.-5.30 p.m.
Wed 8.30 a.m.-1.00 p.m.
H.P.W.T.CS.MF.A.

**HIGH WYCOMBE**  Tel. (0494)
ISAAC LORD LTD  22221
185 DESBOROUGH ROAD  KE

Open: Mon-Fri 8.00 a.m.-5.00 p.m.
Saturday 9.00 a.m.-5.00 p.m.
H.P.W.D.A.

---

**READING**  Tel. (0734) 591361
HOME CARE CENTRE
26/30 KING'S ROAD

Open: Monday-Saturday
9.00 a.m.-5.30 p.m.
H.P.W.D.A.WM.BC.

**READING**  Tel. Littlewick Green
DAVID HUNT (TOOL  2743
MERCHANTS) LTD  ★
KNOWL HILL, NR. READING
Open: Monday-Saturday
9.00 a.m.-5.30 p.m.
H.P.W.D.A.BC.

**READING**  Tel. Reading 661511
WOKINGHAM TOOL CO. LTD
99 WOKINGHAM ROAD

Open: Mon-Sat 9.00 a.m.-5.30 p.m.
Closed 1.00-2.00 p.m. for lunch
H.P.W.WM.D.CS.A.BC.

## BUCKINGHAMSHIRE

**SLOUGH**  Tel. (06286) 5125
BRAYWOOD ESTATES LTD  ★
158 BURNHAM LANE

Open: 9.00 a.m.-5.30 p.m.
Monday-Saturday
H.P.W.WM.CS.A.

**MILTON KEYNES**  Tel. (0908)
POLLARD WOODWORKING  641366
CENTRE  ★
51 AYLESBURY ST., BLETCHLEY
Open: Mon-Fri 8.30-5.30
Saturday 9.00-5.00
H.P.W.WM.D.CS.A.BC.

**HIGH WYCOMBE**  Tel. (0494)
SCOTT SAWS LTD  24201/33788
14 BRIDGE STREET  ★

Mon.-Sat. 8.30 a.m.-6.00 p.m.

H.P.W.WM.D.T.CS.MF.A.BC.

## CAMBRIDGESHIRE

**CAMBRIDGE**  Tel. (0223) 63132
D. MACKAY LTD.  E★
BRITANNIA WORKS, EAST ROAD

Open: Mon.-Fri. 8.30 a.m.-1 p.m./2.00-
5.00 p.m. Sat. 8.30 a.m.-1.00 p.m.
H.P.W.D.T.CS.MF.A.BC.

---

**CAMBRIDGE**  Tel. (0223) 247386
H. B. WOODWORKING  K
105 CHERRY HINTON ROAD
Open: 8.30 a.m.-5.30 p.m.
Monday-Friday
8.30 a.m.-1.00 p.m. Sat.
H.P.W.WM.D.CS.A.

## CHESHIRE

**NANTWICH**  Tel. Crewe 67010
ALAN HOLTHAM  K★
THE OLD STORES TURNERY
WISTASON ROAD, WILLASTON
Open: Tues.-Sat. 9.00 a.m.-5.30 p.m.
Closed Monday
P.W.WM.D.T.C.CS.A.BC.

## CLEVELAND

**MIDDLESBROUGH**  Tel. (0642)
CLEVELAND WOODCRAFT  813103
(M'BRO), 38-42 CRESCENT ROAD  K

Open: Mon-Sat 9.15 a.m.-5.30 p.m.

H.P.T.A.BC.W.WM.CS.D.

## CORNWALL

**HELSTON**  Tel. Helston (03265) 4961
SOUTH WEST  Truro (0872) 71671
POWER TOOLS  Launceston
MONUMENT ROAD  (0566) 3555
K
H.P.W.WM.D.CS.A.

**TRURO**  Tel. (0872) 71671
TRURO POWER TOOLS  E★
30 FERRIS TOWN

Open Mon.-Sat. 8.00 a.m.-12.30 p.m./
1.30 p.m.-5.00 p.m.
H.P.W.WM.D.CS.MF.A.BC.

## DERBYSHIRE

**DERBY**  Tel. (0332) 41862
HAZLEHURSTS LTD.  E★
LONDON ROAD AND CANAL STREET

Open: Mon.-Sat. 8.30 a.m.-5.30 p.m. (retail)
Mon.-Fri. 8.00 a.m.-5.00 p.m. (trade)
H.P.W.MF.A.BC.

**BUXTON**  Tel. (0298) 871636
CRAFT SUPPLIES  K★
THE MILL, MILLERSDALE

Open: Mon-Sat 9.00 a.m.-5.00 p.m.

H.P.W.D.T.CS.A.BC.

---

## DEVON

**BRIXHAM**  Tel. (08045) 4900
WOODCRAFT SUPPLIES  E★
4 HORSE POOL STREET

Open: Mon.-Sat. 9.00 a.m.-6.00 p.m.

H.P.W.A.D.MF.CS.BC.

**PLYMOUTH**  Tel. (0752) 330303
WESTWARD BUILDING SERVICES  ★
LTD., LISTER CLOSE, NEWNHAM
INDUSTRIAL ESTATE, PLYMPTON
Open: Mon-Fri 8.00 a.m.-5.30 p.m.
Sat. 8.30 a.m.-12.30 p.m.
H.P.W.WM.D.A.BC.

**BOURNEMOUTH**  Tel: (0202) 420583
POWER TOOL SERVICES
(Sales, spares, repairs)
849-851 CHRISTCHURCH ROAD
BOSCOMBE
Open: Mon.-Fri. 9.00 a.m.-5.30 p.m.
Sat: 9.00 a.m.-5.00 p.m.
H.P.W.CS.K.A.

## ESSEX

**LEIGH ON SEA**  Tel. (0702)
MARSHAL & PARSONS LTD.  7.0404
1111 LONDON ROAD  EK

Open: 8.30 a.m.-5.30 p.m. Mon-Fri
9.00 a.m.-5.00 p.m. Sat.
H.P.W.WM.D.CS.A.

**ILFORD**
CUTWELL TOOLS LTD.  ★
774-776 HIGH ROAD

Mon.-Fri. 9.00 a.m.-5.00 p.m.
and also by appointment.
P.W.WM.A.D.CS.

**ALDERSHOT**  Tel. (0252) 334422
POWER TOOL CENTRE  K★
374 HIGH STREET
Open Mon-Fri 8.30 a.m.-5.30 p.m.
Sat 8.30 a.m.-4.00 p.m.

H.P.W.WM.D.A.BC.CF.MF.

## HAMPSHIRE

**SOUTHAMPTON**  Tel. (0703)
H.W.M.  776222
THE WOODWORKERS
303 SHIRLEY ROAD, SHIRLEY
Open: Tues-Fri 9.30 a.m.-6.00 p.m.
Sat 9.30 a.m.-4.00 p.m.
H.P.W.WM.D.CS.A.BC.T.

**KEY: CS CUTTING OR SHARPENING SERVICES**

**KEY: MF MATERIAL FINISHES**

**KEY: BC BOOKS/CATALOGUES**

# shop guide

| | | | |
|---|---|---|---|
| **SOUTHAMPTON** Tel. (0703) 332288<br>POWER TOOL CENTRE<br>7 BELVIDERE ROAD<br>Open: Mon.-Fri. 8.30-5.30<br>K★<br>H.P.W.WM.D.A.BC.CS.MF. | **ROCHDALE** Tel. (0706) 342123/ 342322<br>C.S.M. TOOLS<br>4-6 HEYWOOD ROAD<br>CASTLETON E★<br>Open: Mon-Sat 9.00 a.m.-6.00 p.m.<br>Sundays by appointment<br>W.D.CS.A.BC. | **NORBURY** Tel. (01-679) 6193<br>HERON TOOLS & HARDWARE LTD<br>437 STREATHAM HIGH ROAD SW16<br>Open: Mon-Fri 8.30 a.m.-5.00 p.m.<br>Wednesday 8.30 a.m.-1.00 p.m.<br>Sat. 9.00 a.m.-1.00 p.m.<br>H.P.W.A. | **LIVERPOOL** Tel. (051-207) 2967<br>TAYLOR BROS (LIVERPOOL) LTD K<br>195-199 LONDON ROAD<br>LIVERPOOL L3 8JG<br>Open: Monday to Friday<br>8.30 a.m.-5.30 p.m.<br>H.P.W.WM.D.A.BC. |

| | | | **MIDDLESEX** |
|---|---|---|---|
| **PORTSMOUTH** Tel. (0705) 667332<br>EURO PRECISION TOOLS LTD<br>259/263 LONDON ROAD, NORTH END ★<br>E<br>Open: Mon-Fri 9.00 a.m.-5.30 p.m.<br>Sat. 9.00 a.m.-1.00 p.m.<br>H.P.W.WM.D.A.BC. | **CHEADLE** Tel. 061491 1726<br>ERIC TOMKINSON ★<br>86 STOCKPORT ROAD<br>Open: Mon.-Fri. 9.00 a.m.-4.00 p.m.<br>Saturday 9.00 a.m.-1.00 p.m.<br>H.P.W.D.MF.A.BC. | **LONDON** Tel. (01-636) 7475<br>BUCK & RYAN LTD<br>101 TOTTENHAM COURT ROAD W1P ODY<br>Open: Mon.-Fri. 8.30 a.m.-5.30 p.m.<br>Saturday 8.30 a.m.-4.00 p.m.<br>H.P.W.WM.D.A.. | **RUISLIP** Tel. (08956) 74126<br>ALLMODELS ENGINEERING LTD. E★<br>91 MANOR WAY<br>Open: Mon-Sat 9.00 a.m.-5.30 p.m.<br>H.P.W.A.D.CS.MF.BC. |

| | | | |
|---|---|---|---|
| **TEWKESBURY** Tel. (0684) 293092<br>TEWKESBURY SAW CO. LTD.<br>TRADING ESTATE, NEWTOWN K<br>Open: Mon-Fri 8.00 a.m.-5.00 p.m.<br>Saturday 9.30 a.m.-12.00 p.m.<br>P.W.WM.D.CS. | **LANCASTER** Tel. (0524) 32886<br>LILE TOOL SHOP K<br>43/45 NORTH ROAD<br>Open: Monday to Saturday<br>9.00 a.m.-5.30 p.m.<br>Wed 9.00 a.m.-12.30 p.m.<br>H.P.W.D.A. | **WEMBLEY** Tel. 904-1144<br>ROBERT SAMUEL LTD. (904-1147<br>7, 15 & 16 COURT PARADE after 4.00)<br>EAST LANE, N. WEMBLEY ★<br>Open Mon.-Fri. 8.45-5.15; Sat. 9-1.00<br>Access, Barclaycard, AM Express, & Diners<br>H.P.W.CS.E.A.D. | **CROWMARSH** Tel. (0491) 38653<br>MILL HILL SUPPLIES E★<br>66 THE STREET<br>Open: Mon.-Fri. 9.30 a.m.-5.00 p.m.<br>Thurs. 9.30 a.m.-7.00 p.m.<br>Sat. 9.30 a.m.-1.00 p.m.<br>P.W.D.CS.MF.A.BC. |

## HERTFORDSHIRE

| | | | |
|---|---|---|---|
| **ENFIELD** Tel. (01-363) 2935<br>GILL & HOXBY LTD. K<br>133-137 ST. MARKS ROAD EN1 1BB<br>Mon.-Sat. 8.30 a.m.-6.00 p.m.<br>Early closing Wednesday 1.00 p.m.<br>H.P.W.WM.T.CS.A | **BURY** Tel. (061 764 6769<br>HOUSE OF HARBRU ★<br>101 CROSTONS ROAD<br>ELTON<br>Open: Mon.-Fri. 9.00 a.m.-5.00 p.m.<br>Send 2 × 1st class stamps for catalogue<br>MF. | **WOOLWICH** Tel. (01-854) 7767/8<br>A. D. SHILLMAN & SONS LTD<br>108-109 WOOLWICH HIGH STREET<br>SE18<br>Open: Mon-Sat<br>8.30 p.m.-5.30p.m.<br>H.P.W.CS.A. | **FARNHAM** Tel. (0252) 725427<br>A.B.E. CO. LTD. (Quick Hire) ★<br>GOODS SHED<br>STATION APPROACH, FARNHAM<br>Open Mon.-Fri. 8.00 a.m.-5.30 p.m.<br>Sat. 8.00 a.m.-5.30 p.m.<br>H.P.W.D.CS.A.BC. |

## HUMBERSIDE

| | | | **NORFOLK** |
|---|---|---|---|
| **GRIMSBY** Tel. Grimsby (0472)<br>58741 Hull (0482) 26999<br>J. E. SIDDLE LTD. (Tool Specialists) ★<br>83 VICTORIA STREET<br>Open: Mon-Fri 8.30 a.m.-5.30 p.m.<br>Sat. 8.30 a.m.-12.45 p.m. & 2 p.m.-5 p.m.<br>H.P.A.BC.W.WMD. | **MANCHESTER** Tel. (061 789)<br>0909<br>TIMMS TOOLS<br>102-104 LIVERPOOL ROAD<br>PATRICROFT M30 0WZ ★<br>Weekdays 9.00 a.m.-5.30 p.m.<br>Sat. 9.00 a.m.-1.00 p.m.<br>H.P.A.W. | **HOUNSLOW** Tel. (01-570)<br>2103/5135<br>Q.R. TOOLS LTD<br>251-253 HANWORTH ROAD<br>Open: Mon-Fri 8.30 a.m.-5.30 p.m.<br>Sat. 9.00 a.m.-1.00 p.m.<br>P.W.WM.D.CS.A. | **IPSWICH** Tel. (0473) 40456<br>FOX WOODWORKING KE★<br>142-144 BRAMFORD LANE<br>Open: Tues., Fri., 9.00 a.m.-5.30 p.m.<br>Sat. 9.00 a.m.-5.00 p.m.<br>H.P.W.WM.D.A.B.C. |

## KENT                  ## LONDON

| | | | |
|---|---|---|---|
| **WYE** Tel. (0233) 813144<br>KENT POWER TOOLS LTD.<br>UNIT 1, BRIAR CLOSE<br>WYE, Nr. ASFORD<br>H.P.W.WM.D.A.CS. | **ACTON** Tel. (01-992) 4835<br>A. MILLS (ACTON) LTD ★<br>32/36 CHURCHFIELD ROAD W3 6ED<br>Open: Mon-Fri 9.00 a.m.-5.00 p.m.<br>Saturdays 9.00 am.-1.00 p.m.<br>H.P.W.WM. | **LONDON** Tel. (01-263) 1536<br>THOMAS BROTHERS (01-272) 2764<br>798-804 HOLLOWAY ROAD, N19 E<br>Open: Mon.-Fri. 8.30 a.m.-5.30 p.m. Thurs.<br>8.30 a.m.-1 p.m. Sat. 9 a.m.-5 p.m.<br>H.P.W.WM.CS.MF.BC. | **NORWICH** Tel. (0603) 898695<br>NORFOLK SAW SERVICES<br>DOG LANE, HORSFORD<br>Open: Monday to Friday<br>8.00 a.m.-5.00 p.m.<br>Saturday 8.00 a.m.-12.00 p.m.<br>H.P.W.WM.D.CS.A. |

| | | | |
|---|---|---|---|
| **MATFIELD** Tel. Brenchley<br>LEISURECRAFT IN WOOD (089272)<br>'ORMONDE,' MAIDSTONE RD. 2465<br>TN12 7JG<br>Open: Mon-Sun<br>9.00 a.m.-5.30 p.m.<br>W.WM.D.T.A. | **LONDON** Tel. 01-723 2295-6-7<br>LANGHAM TOOLS LIMITED<br>13 NORFOLK PLACE<br>LONDON W2 1QJ | **FULHAM** Tel. (01-385) 5109<br>I. GRIZZARD LTD. E<br>84a-b LILLIE ROAD, SW6 1TL<br>Open: Mon-Sat 9.00-5.30 p.m.<br>Half day Thursday<br>H.P.A.BC.W.CS.WM.D. | **KINGS LYNN** Tel. (0553) 2443<br>WALKER & ANDERSON (Kings Lynn) LTD.<br>WINDSOR ROAD, KINGS LYNN K<br>Open: Monday to Saturday<br>7.45 a.m.-5.30 p.m.<br>Wednesday 1.00 p.m. Saturday 5.00 p.m.<br>H.P.W.WM.D.CS.A. |

## LANCASHIRE

| | | | |
|---|---|---|---|
| **PRESTON** Tel. (0772) 52951<br>SPEEDWELL TOOL COMPANY E★<br>62-68 MEADOW STREET PR1 1SU<br>Open: Mon.-Fri. 8.30 a.m.-5.30 p.m.<br>Sat. 8.30 a.m.-12.30 p.m.<br>H.P.W.WM.CS.A.MF.BC. | **LONDON** Tel. (01-567) 2922<br>G. D. CLEGG & SONS ★<br>83 UXBRIDGE ROAD, HANWELL W7 3ST<br>Mon-Sat 9.15 a.m.-5.30 p.m.<br>Closed for lunch 1.00-2.00p.m.<br>Early Closing 1.00 p.m. Wed.<br>H.P.A.W.WM.D.CS. | **TELFORD** Tel. Telford (0952)<br>48054<br>ASLES LTD<br>VINEYARD ROAD, WELLINGTON EK★<br>Open: Mon. Fri. 8.30 a.m.-5.30 p.m.<br>Saturday 8.30 a.m.-4.00 p.m.<br>H.P.W.WM.D.CS.BC.A. | **NORWICH** Tel. (0603) 400933<br>WESTGATES WOODWORKING Tx<br>61 HURRICANE WAY, 975412<br>NORWICH AIRPORT INDUSTRIAL ESTATE<br>Open: 9.00 a.m.-5.00 p.m. weekdays<br>9.00 a.m.-12.30 Sat.<br>P.W.WM.D.BC. K |

**KEY·H·HAND TOOLS**

**KEY·MF·MATERIAL FINISHES**

**KEY·P·POWER TOOLS**

# shopguide

## SUFFOLK

**KINGS LYNN** Tel: (0760) 23073
TONY WADDILOVE ★
STATION HOUSE
LITTLE DUNHAM, (Nr. SWAFFHAM)
Open Tues.-Sat. 9.00 a.m.-5.30 p.m.
H.P.W.DT.CS.A.BC.

**PETERBOROUGH** Tel. (0733)
WILLIAMS DISTRIBUTORS 64252
(TOOLS) LIMITED **K**
108-110 BURGHLEY ROAD
Open: Monday to Friday
8.30 a.m.-5.30 p.m.
H.P.A.W.D.WH.BC.

**HUDDERSFIELD** Tel. (0484)
NEVILLE M. OLDHAM 641219/(0484)
UNIT 1 DALE ST. MILLS 42777
DALE STREET, LONGWOOD ★
Open: Mon-Fri 8.00 a.m.-5.30 p.m.
Saturday 9.30 a.m.-12.00 p.m.
P.W.WM.D.A.BC.

**CULLEN** Tel: (0542) 40563
GRAMPIAN WOODTURNING SUPPLIES AT
BAYVIEW CRAFTS
Open Mon.-Sat. 9.00 a.m.-5.30 p.m. Sunday
10.00 a.m.-5.30 p.m. Open later July/Aug.
Sept. Demonstrations SAT/SUN or by
H.W.D.MF.BC. appointment

**BOGNOR REGIS** Tel. (0243) 863100
A. OLBY & SON (BOGNOR REGIS) LTD.
"TOOLSHOP," BUILDERS MERCHANT
HAWTHORN ROAD **K**
Open: Mon-Thurs 8 a.m.-5.15 p.m. Fri.
8 a.m.-8 p.m. Sat 8 a.m.-12.45 p.m.
H.P.W.WM.D.T.C.A.BC.

**WORTHING** Tel. (0903) 38739
W. HOSKING LTD (TOOLS & **KE★**
MACHINERY)
28 PORTLAND RD, BN11 1QN
Open: Mon.-Sat. 8.30 a.m.-5.30 p.m.
Closed Wednesday
H.P.W.WM.D.CS.A.BC.

**THIRSK** Tel. (0845) 22770
THE WOOD SHOP ★
TRESKE SAWMILLS LTD.
STATION WORKS
Open: Seven days a week 9.00-5.00

T.H.MF.BC.

**TAYSIDE** Tel: (05774) 293
WORKMASTER POWER TOOLS LTD. ★
DRUM, KINROSS
Open Mon.-Sat. 8.00 a.m.-8.00 p.m.
Demonstrations throughout Scotland by
appointment
P.W.WM.D.A.BC.

**SWAFFHAM** Tel: (0760) 23073
TONY WADDILOVE, ★
STATION HOUSE,
LITTLE DUNHAM, KINGS LYNN
Tuesday-Saturday 9.00 a.m.-6.00 p.m.

H.P.W.DT.CS.A.BC.

## TYNE & WEAR

**NEWCASTLE UPON TYNE** Tel.
J. W. HOYLE LTD. (0632) 617474
CLARENCE STREET NE2 1YJ **K★**
Open: Mon-Fri 8.00 a.m.-5.00 p.m.
Saturday 9.00 a.m.-4.30 p.m.
H.P.A.BC.W.CS.WM.D.

**KEIGHLEY** Tel. (0535) 663325
EUROMAIL (TOOLS) ★
PO BOX 13
108 EAST PARADE
Open 9.15 a.m.-5.00 p.m.
Not Tuesday but inc. Saturday
H.P.W.A.BC.

**GLASGOW** Tel. (041 429) 4374/
THE SAW CENTRE 4444, Telex: 777886
600 EGLINTON STREET **E★**
G5 9RR
Open: Mon-Fri 8.00 a.m.-5.30 p.m.
Saturday 9.00 a.m.-1.00 p.m.
H.P.W.WM.D.CS.A.

## WALES

**GT. YARMOUTH** Tel. (0493)
ANGLIA POWER TOOLS 850388
3 DENESIDE, NR30 2HL

Open: Monday to Saturday
8.30 a.m. 5.30 p.m.
H.P.W.D.CS.A.

**NEWCASTLE** Tel. (0632) 320311
HENRY OSBOURNE LTD. **E★**
50-54 UNION STREET

Open: Mon-Fri 8.30 a.m.-5.00 p.m.

H.P.W.D.CS.MF.A.BC.

**CLECKHEATON** Tel. (0274)
SKILLED CRAFTS LTD. 872861
34 BRADFORD ROAD ★

Open: 9.00 a.m.-5.00 p.m. Monday
Saturday Lunch 12.00 a.m.-1.00 p.m.
H.P.A W CS.WM.D.

**CARDIFF** Tel. (0222) 595710
DATAPOWER TOOLS LTD,
MICHAELSTON ROAD,
CULVERHOUSE CROSS
Open: Mon.-Fri. 8.00 a.m.-5.00 p.m.
Sat. 9.00 a.m.-1.00 p.m.
H.P.W.WM.D.A.

## NOTTINGHAMSHIRE

## WEST MIDLANDS

**NOTTINGHAM** Tel: (0602) 225979
POOLEWOOD and 227064/5
EQUIPMENT LTD. (06077) 2421 after hrs
5a HOLLY LANE, CHILLWELL
Open: Mon-Fri 9.00 a.m.-5.30 p.m.
Sat. 9.00 a.m. to 12.30 p.m.
P.W.WM.D.CS.A.BC.

**BIRMINGHAM** Tel. (021-554) 5177
ROTAGRIP **E★**
16 LODGE ROAD, HOCKLEY
Open: Mon.-Fri. 9.00 a.m.-5.00 p.m.
Sat. 9.00 a.m.-12.00 p.m.

H.P.W.CS.A.BC.T.MF.

**LEEDS** Tel. (0532) 790507
GEORGE SPENCE & SONS LTD.
WELLINGTON ROAD
Open: Monday to Friday
8.30 a.m.-5.30 p.m.
Saturday 9.00 a.m.-5.00 p.m.
H.P.W.WM.D.T.A.

**CARMARTHEN** Tel. (0267) 237219
DO-IT-YOURSELF SUPPLY **K**
BLUE STREET, DYFED
Open: Monday to Saturday
9.00 a.m.-5.30 p.m.
Thursday 9.00 a.m.-5.30 p.m.
H.P.W.WM.D.T.CS.A.BC.

**WITNEY** Tel. (0993) 3885
TARGET TOOLS (SALES, & 72095 OXON
**TARGET** HIRE & REPAIRS) ★
**TOOLS** SWAIN COURT
STATION INDUSTRIAL ESTATE
Open: Mon.-Sat. 8.00 a.m.-5.00 p.m.
24 hour Answerphone
BC.W.M.A.

**WOLVERHAMPTON** Tel. (0902)
MANSAW SERVICES 58759
SEDGLEY STREET **K★**

Open: Mon.-Fri. 9.00 a.m.-5.00 p.m.

H.P.W.WM.A.D.CS.

**EDINBURGH** Tel. (031 337) 5555
THE SAW CENTRE ★
38 HAYMARKET TERRACE
HAYMARKET
Open: 8.30 a.m.-5.30 p.m.
Monday-Saturday
H.P.W.WM.D.CS.A.

**CARDIFF** Tel. (0222) 396039
JOHN HALL TOOLS LIMITED ★
CENTRAL SQUARE

Open: Monday to Saturday
9.00 a.m.-5.30 p.m.

H.P.W.WM.D.A.BC.

## SCOTLAND

## SOMERSET

## YORKSHIRE

**TAUNTON** Tel. (0823) 85431
JOHN HALL TOOLS ★
6 HIGH STREET

Open Monday-Saturday
9.00 a.m.-5.30 p.m.
H.P.W.WM.D.CS.A.

**BOROUGHBRIDGE** Tel. (09012)
JOHN BODDY TIMBER LTD 2370
FINE WOOD & TOOL STORE ★
RIVERSIDE SAWMILLS
Open: Mon.-Thurs. 8.00 a.m.-6.00 p.m.
Fri. 8.00am-5.00pm Sat. 8.00am-4.00pm
H.P.W.WM.D.T.CS.MF.A.BC.

**PERTH** Tel. (0738) 26173
WILLIAM HUME & CO **K**
ST. JOHN'S PLACE
Open: Monday to Saturday
8.00 a.m.-5.30 p.m.
8.00 a.m.-1.00 p.m. Wednesday
H.P.A.BC.W.CS.WM.D.

**SWANSEA** Tel. (0792) 55680
SWANSEA TIMBER & PLYWOOD CO. LTD.
57-59 OXFORD STREET ★

Open: Mon to Fri 9.00 a.m.-5.30 p.m.
Sat. 9.00 a.m.-1.00 p.m.

H.P.W.D.T.CS.A.BC.

**TAUNTON** Tel. Taunton 79078
KEITH MITCHELL ★
TOOLS AND EQUIPMENT
66 PRIORY BRIDGE ROAD
Open: Mon-Fri 8.30 a.m.-5.30 p.m.
Saturday 9.00 a.m.-4.00 p.m.
H.P.W.WM.D.CS.A.BC.

**SHEFFIELD** Tel. (0742) 441012
GREGORY & TAYLOR LTD **KE**
WORKSOP ROAD
Open: 8.30 a.m.-5.30 p.m.
Monday-Friday
8.30 a.m.-12.30 p.m. Sat.
H.P.W.WM.D.

**CARLISLE** Tel. (0228) 36391
W. M. PLANT
ALLENBROOK ROAD
ROSEHILL, CA1 2UT
Open: Mon.-Fri. 8.00 a.m.-5.15 p.m.
Sat. 8.00 a.m.-12.30 noon
P.W.WM.D.CS.A.

**ST. LEONARD'S-ON-SEA** Tel.
DOUST & MONK (MONOSAW)-(0424)
25 CASTLEHAM ROAD 52577

Open: Mon.-Fri. 8.00 a.m.-5.30 p.m.
Most Saturdays 9.00 a.m.-1.00 p.m.
H.P.W.WM.D.CS.A.

**HARROGATE** Tel. (0423) 66245/
MULTI-TOOLS 55328
158 KINGS ROAD **K★**

Open: Monday to Saturday
8.30 a.m.-6.00 p.m.
H.P.W.WM.D.A.BC.

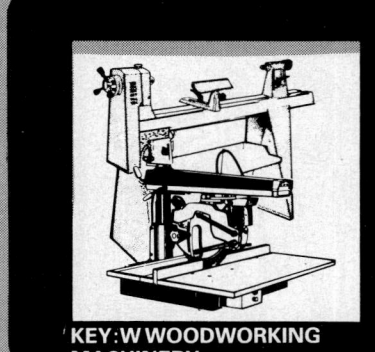

## STAFFORDSHIRE

**TAMWORTH** Tel. (0827) 56188
MATTHEWS BROTHERS LTD. **K**
KETTLEBROOK ROAD
Open: Mon-Sat 8.30 a.m.-6.00 p.m.
Demonstrations Sunday mornings by
appointment only
H.P.WM.D.T.CS.A.BC.

**LEEDS** Tel. (0532) 574736
D. B. KEIGHLEY MACHINERY LTD. ★
VICKERS PLACE, STANNINGLEY
PUDSEY LS2 86LZ
Mon.-Fri. 9.00 a.m.-5.00 p.m.
Sat. 9.00 a.m.-1.00 p.m.
P.A.WM.CS.BC.

**KEY: W WOODWORKING MACHINERY**

# Classified Advertisements

## FOR SALE

FOR ALL SUPPLIES FOR THE

### Craft of Enamelling

ON METAL

### Including LEAD-FREE ENAMELS

PLEASE SEND 2 × 10p STAMPS FOR FREE CATALOGUE, PRICE LIST AND WORKING INSTRUCTIONS

### W. G. BALL LTD.

ENAMEL MANUFACTURERS

Dept. W. LONGTON
STOKE-ON-TRENT
ST3 1JW

---

**LACE BOBBIN TURNING BLANKS** in unusual and exotic hardwoods and ivory. SAE for list: J. Ford, 5 Squirrels Hollow, Walsall WS7 8YS.

**LACE BOBBIN PLANKS,** over 90 different woods, lists free, 50 exotic £4.50. 35 veneer samples. £1. P. Rushbrook, 39 Deben Avenue, Martlesham, Ipswich.

**GLASS CUTTERS** ideal for handyman. Used in our own glass works. Instructions. P&P. £6.50 each. F. Sherwood, Dept. W. 54 The Burroughs, Hendon NW4 4AN.

**LACE BOBBIN PLANKS.** Over 90 different woods, lists free. P. Rushbrook, 39 Deben Avenue, Martlesham, Ipswich.

**BAGS, WRAPPINGS, TISSUE, BOXES, BUSINESS CARDS.** Any shape, size, amount. Comprehensive samples. 90p. Terry Andrews, 53A Parsons St., Banbury OX16 8NB.

**MARKING STAMPS** — name stamps branding irons supplied to your requirements SAE for details. Davey, 37 Marina Drive, Brixham, Devon TQ5 8BB.  T/C

**SINGLE TO THREE PHASE** converters up to 20HP 18 and 21 throat bandsaws. Illustrated details HAB Engineering Unit 24, 16-20 George St., Balsall Heath, Birmingham, B12 9RG.

---

MORTISERS; TENNONERS; SPINDLES; PLANERS; BANDSAWS; LATHES; CROSSCUTS; ROUTERS; SANDERS; DRILLS? YOU CAN CERTAINLY SEE ALL CLASSES AND TYPES OF MACHINES HERE.

WE ARE MAIN STOCKING AGENTS FOR: MULTICO; ELU; SEDGWICK; KITY; SCHEPPACH; INCA; CORONET; DeWALT; WARCO; DOMINION; HITACHI; STARTRITE; TREND; ASHLEY ILES; SORBY.

*CALL US ABOUT WOODTURNING LESSONS*

*WOODCARVING LESSONS (See our Swiss carving tools)*

*ALWAYS HELPFUL, KNOWLEDGEABLE, GOOD SERVICE AT:*

### CLEVELAND WOODCRAFT

**38-42 CRESCENT ROAD, MIDDLESBROUGH.**

TEL: (0642) 813103

---

**25,000 WESTERN HEMLOCK** and Brazilian Mahogany staircase spindle blanks (before turning). 3′ long, 1⅜″ × 1⅜″ sq. To be sold in large or small quantities, from 30p to £2 each. Also wanted home DIY turners to complete and return and sell back finished turned spindles. Also solid oak supreme quality kitchen cabinet arched top doors all metric. List price £50 each. To clear from £5, £8, £18 each. 300 new comfort arch top sashed red deal, window frames. Full range primed (not polished, all to be sold at 65% off list price e.g. 8 × 4 metric oblong 4 arches list £165 — £65 4 × 4 £30 etc. All enquiries Turton 0204 Bolton Lancashire area 852339 any time.

**CORONET MAJOR** 48″ bed planer, saw, mortiser, bandsaw, sander, drill-chucks, mobile stand. £600 ono. Newcastle on Tyne 2652792.

---

### MUSICAL MOVEMENTS

★ LOVE STORY ★ LARAS THEME ★ SPEAK SOFTLY LOVE ★ FUR ELISE ★ FEELINGS ★ FASCINATION ★ IMPOSSIBLE DREAM ★ MUSIC BOX DANCER ★ LA PALOMA ★ THE EMPEROR WALTZ ★ TRY TO REMEMBER ★ ROMEO AND JULIET ★

Complete with screws and spring mechanism £2.50 inc. p&p. 20 or more of one tune ordered £1.50 each. Available from: The Jewel Box Shop, 112 Pentonville Road, London N1 9JB.

---

**THE FINEST SELECTION ON DISPLAY IN SCOTLAND!**

WOODWORKING & METALWORKING MACHINERY POWER TOOLS HAND TOOLS

HIRE OR BUY.

**THE SAW CENTRE**

**OPEN** Mon - Fri 8am - 5pm Sat 9am - 1pm

*Visit our* NEW SHOWROOM at EGLINTON TOLL GLASGOW

Tel: 041-429 4444/4374, Telex: 777886 SAWCO G Also at, 38 Haymarket Terrace, Edinburgh EH12 5JZ. Tel: 031-337 5555

---

### AUCTIONS

500 lots of antique and modern woodworking tools. The Griffin Inn, Swithland, near Loughborough, Leicestershire on Tuesday 13th August 1985 at 12 noon. View Monday 6.30-8.30pm Tuesday from 9am. Catalogues £1 from: **David Stanley Auctions, Osgathorpe, Leicestershire.**

---

### HAND CARVED

'Adam Style' Mantle motifs in Mahogany — Example 10″ × 5″ centre lamp and two side pieces. Send S.A.E. for details and quotation. Your own design quoted for if required. **SAM NICHOLSON** 22 Lisnagarvey Drive, Lisburn, Co. Antrim, N. Ireland. Phone Lisburn 3510

---

Have you seen the latest catalogue of

### Bygones

See Display advertisement

---

## WORKSHOP EQUIPMENT

**FOR SALE.** Coronet Imp bandsaw and Capitol 7″ planer with thicknessing attachment. Telephone Godalming (04868) 28150.

**LUREM 210B** combination woodworking machine. Virtually unused. Spare planer & molder blades. £1600 ovno. Telephone Nottingham (0602) 233805.

**SJOBERG MODEL 142** de luxe workbench. Virtually unused, stored for 10 years. Best offer over £100. Kingham (Oxford) 060-871-462.

**STOCK CLEARANCE.** De Walt DW50. Combined planers/thicknessers single & 3 phase. **KNOCK-OUT PRICES.** Calder woodworking Machinery Ltd., Station Rd., Sowerby Bridge, W. Yorkshire, HX6 3LA. Tel: Halifax (0422) 831861.

---

### Braywood Estates

*Stockists of:*

B&D ★ DeWALT ★ ELECTRA ★ ELU HITACHI ★ NOBEX ★ NUTOOLS SKIL ★ STARTRITE & WADKIN

*All at Discount Prices*

**BRAYWOOD ESTATES LTD.**
158 Burnham Lane, Slough.
Tel: Burnham (06286) 5125

---

**CIRCULAR AND BAND SAW BLADES** for all applications from: A. A. Smith Ltd. 63 Brighton Road, Shoreham, Sussex. Tel: 07917 61707 (24 hrs).  C-N

---

**BUILD A SAWBENCH**

**UNIVERSAL SPINDLE**

**£11.90** post £1.05

Spindle with 8in. saw £17.20 post 95p. ½in. chuck £6.35 extra

FIG 200

Send 60p for 92 page Tools & Machinery Catalogue No. 10 including up-to-date price list. ACCESS & BARCLAYCARD

**J. SIMBLE & SONS** 76 Queens Rd., Watford, Herts. Tel: 0923 26052 Dept. W.W.

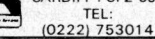

# Letters

REFERENCE your article 'Life with the lathe' in the June issue.

What an appalling article this is. At best it may be identified as little more than an ego-trip for some top (your description, not mine) UK woodturners. A few of the woodturners give advice, but in the main the needs of the amateur turner have been ignored.

It is obvious that most of the contributors fail to understand that the vast majority of the amateur market simply cannot afford a Harrison, good machine though it is. They also do not know that often the space available to the hobbyist is very limited and that lathes therefore are purchased after settling on several compromises.

Much of the so-called advice given is wholly out-of-date and must reflect the standards and attitudes of the contributors that you selected. Certainly, if I gave this standard of advice to my customers, my students or myself, I would feel that I had failed in all respects.

In the article you have done a great disservice to the amateur turner and to the many woodturning-lathe makers. It is hoped that you will try to improve your standards — a development which would be welcomed by readers and advertisers alike.

*Tony Waddilove, King's Lynn*

● *This oak panel forms part of the Stations of the Cross, carved by Nick Barberton for St Martin's Church in Salisbury. The commission took him two years of part-time work – as well as making furniture, including kitchens, and windows, he also teaches woodwork as occupational therapy in a psychiatric hospital. The panels are only 15×12×1½in*

I WAS most disappointed to read Arthur Jones' comments on timber and forest conservation in your June issue.

While I appreciate that it would be out of character for one whose main aim in life is to sell timber to try to dissuade some of his potential customers from buying his most profitable product, I do think that you, as editor, would have been wise to omit Mr Jones' indictment of the Third World poor as usurpers of our luxury goods — although I accept that there are those who would give Brazilian-mahogany chairs (upon which one may not sit) priority over cooking fires for obscure Amerindian families in remote and sweaty Amazon jungles.

It would be folly to suggest that woodworkers should consider boycotting such admirable materials, or that we could make any significant gesture to the conservationist. But we could keep the problem in mind, and at the same time save money, by considering other materials more practical than hardwoods.

Failing that, please spare a thought for the poor misguided Indian doggedly cooking his meals over wood fires, blissfully unaware of the wrong he does to Arthur Jones.

*John Otway, Windsor*

MY WIFE is an avid bobbin-lace-maker, and I make all her bobbins. She asked me if I could use a heavier wood and keep the bobbins the same size so that she could do away with the beads, because they can be a nuisance when she is using a large number.

I tried several timbers, but they were not heavy enough to hang satisfactorily. So I came up with the idea of drilling a ⅛in-diameter hole up the base of the bobbin and inserting about 1⅛in of lead, rounded up to fit in the hole. I then seal off the hole with plastic wood stained to match the timber.

*K. Brakenridge, Port Pirie, South Australia*

I WRITE with concern about Mr Kendall-Carpenter's letter in the May issue — on two counts. Firstly, most grinders nowadays are driven by single-phase induction motors. The dimmer control he uses could seriously overheat when used with such motors, besides being relatively ineffective as a speed controller. Secondly, he has made no provision for clamping the cord where it leaves the box. This is vital for safety if he uses the device in the highly portable form proposed.

*R. F. Howard BScEng FIEE, Pocklington*

CAN ANYONE tell me where to get a dowel-saw? The tool consists of a flat, unbacked, double-edged blade, fastened with countersunk or flush rivets to a wooden handle. It looks something like a cross between a tenon-saw and a Japanese ryoba. The teeth have no set, to facilitate the removal of surplus lengths of dowels and loose tongues by cutting flush with the surface of the work.

*Paul Dickie, 21 Davenport Park Rd, Davenport Park, Stockport, Cheshire SK2 6JU*

THE CORONET MAJOR came under fire ('Life with the lathe', WW/June) from several woodturners for the spanner adjustment of its tool-rest. The remedy is effective, cheap and quick!

I made a very simple modification whereby the split collars on the tool saddles are tightened by locking levers, and the banjo (which holds the actual rest) by a nut on a separate T-bolt.

To combine the two movements:
**1** Obtain two 4½x⁷⁄₁₆in Whit coach-bolts — one for each saddle;
**2** Release the grub-screw in the split collar which holds the bolt, and remove the bolt;
**3** Remove the nut, washer and T-bolt which hold the banjo to the saddle;
**4** Put one of the 4½x⁷⁄₁₆in bolts through the banjo and the saddle, and re-assemble the lever handle on the bottom. Do not tighten the grub-screw.

By tightening the lever the banjo is fixed and the split collar closed in one movement (no spanner is needed), and adjustment is only required to the rest itself.

Total cost was 50p for the pair of bolts, plus the time required to fit — about one minute for each saddle! Later cosmetic improvements were the draw-filing of the top edges of the banjo slots, which allowed them to slide more easily, and the polishing of the bolt-heads.

The square under the bolt-head fits into the banjo slot and can be positioned to give the required placing of the lever handle.

I have found this method of adjustment much easier to use for the work I do. If you try it and prefer to reach for a spanner instead, re-conversion to the standard adjustment only takes a minute.

*Frank Slack, Loughborough*

● Incidentally, the lathe we captioned as an Apollo Woodstyler on p427 of the June issue is actually a Luna SP1000 (though the Apollo details are correct as printed). Our apologies to both firms.

IN JUNE'S 'QUESTION BOX' Noel Leach says that raw linseed oil does not carry the risk of spontaneous combustion when used swabs are left in enclosed areas.

The fact is that rags, swabs and cloths soaked in linseed oil should not be left lying around under any circumstances, particularly if they are likely to be covered by other materials.

To quote from *Fire and Explosion Risks* by Dr von Schwartz: 'Should the oil be imperfectly oxidised . . . the process of oxidation will continue, a considerable amount of heat being formed. So long as this heat can be dissipated into the air danger is less imminent, though not entirely absent; it will, however, become so if the articles be kept, stored, or packed in such a manner that the heat is prevented from escaping. Under these circumstances the retained heat will produce charring, and, finally, the spontaneous ignition of the articles in question.'

*Maurice Lund, Welling*

639

# Letters

IN ROGER HICKMAN'S description of a deal chest (WW/April), the figure illustrating the drawer details shows a common error — a chamfer on the top of the drawer-sides to give a lead-in when inserting the drawer. I maintain that this chamfer should be at the bottom. In this I am supported by D. J. Gough, sometime with Gordon Russell Ltd, who wrote a very informative article on drawer-making published in *Woodworker* in August 1956.

The sketches (exaggerated) show a drawer withdrawn to its full extent. The forces exerted on it by the carcase are shown by the arrows; these prevent the drawer from tipping and falling on the floor. In A, the chamfer on the top has removed material just where it is needed. As a result the distance X between the forces has been reduced compared with that in B (both for a given drawer opening), so that the forces are correspondingly greater. Also — given that there must be some clearance, however slight — the drawer chamfered on the top will sag more than one chamfered on the bottom.

Chamfering on the bottom removes no material where it is needed, and assists the sliding action on closing the drawer.

*Malcolm Ward, Bromley*

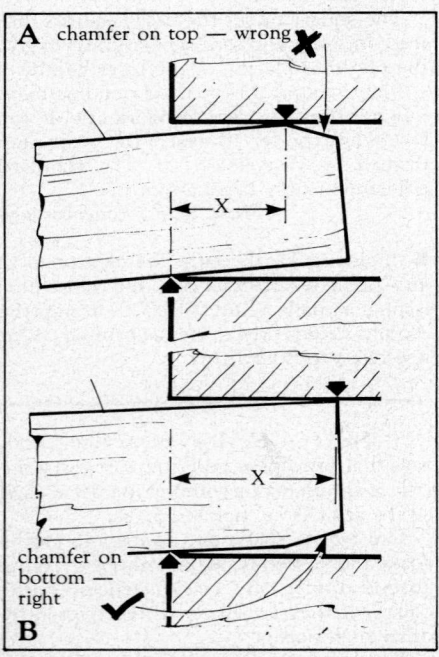

MAX BURROUGH'S comment (WW/ April), suggesting that Bill Gates was right about the implications of his home made saw-vice mount, is also quite wrong. Mr Burrough has missed the point of my correction.

May I re-state, more clearly, the facts of the matter?

● Whatever the hand-saw, be it rip, cross-cut, tenon, dovetail or gent's, the file should always be held at 90° to the blade's cross-sectional depth.

● For its chisel-type cutting action, the rip-saw has its teeth sharpened with the file held at 90° to the saw's cross-sectional depth, and 90° across the blade. Often the pitch or rake of tooth is also 90° to the line of cut.

● A crosscut saw is sharpened at 90° to the saw's cross-sectional depth — and usually 60° across the blade, although this angle may vary to suit different timbers (as may also the angle of pitch). The resulting bevel and outer point of each tooth are direct consequences of this 60° angle. These are the points which I believe both Mr Gates and Mr Burroughs failed to appreciate.

Furthermore, may I also say that in order to understand the actions of crosscut and rip-saws I do not need to 'draw the procedure oversize' as Mr Burrough suggests!

*G. Whitrick, Harrogate*

IN HIS APRIL ARTICLE Roger Buse wonders where the Washita oilstones have 'disappeared' to. I think I can tell him: they are currently being passed off (to use an old-time trade expression) as Arkansas.

Years ago, Arkansas (soft and hard) were distinctly different (and much higher priced) than Washita; both were quarried in Arkansas. On the UK market, pre-war, there were two main grades — No1 being the less expensive, and Lily White the top. My 1938 S. Tyzack catalogue shows the former costing 4s. 4d. for the 8x2x1in and 5s. 9d. for the top grade. Arkansas, not quoted, were probably five or six times as much.

In a rash moment a few years ago I bought a stone of this size, marked 'Hard Arkansas', and I also have a couple of pen-knife pieces. All have that semi-translucent, marble-like appearance, quite different from the stones I have seen of late; these are of much coarser texture and are opaque.

No woodworker need spend the large sums these stones are evidently fetching. That Rolls-Royce of stones, the medium India, will give my plane-irons and chisels an edge that, after stropping, will shave hairs off the back of my hand (though if the fancy takes me I sometimes finish off on a carborundum (genuine) extra-hard and fine).

*F. Seward, London*

THE QUESTION from Terry Holland in the May issue concerning Mexican rosewood / grande palisander deserves a little more clarification.

First, Mexican 'rosewood' is *Cordia eleagnoides*, and not a *Dalbergia* (true rosewood). The timber trade has never been slow to attach a false descriptive tag to any timber which superficially resembles another (usually extinct from commerce). 'Rosewood' has deservedly enjoyed a certain *cachet*, and it is not surprising that shippers and merchants have used this soubriquet to enhance an otherwise attractive timber which happens to be a non-*Dalbergia*.

Mexican 'rosewood' is commonly known as bocote these days, and it is not clear how the name 'Grande palisander' came into use. Palisander is often synonymous with rosewood, but anyone who researches into the numerous varieties of *Dalbergia* in Brazil and central America will soon find himself lost in a forest of 'palisanders' and 'jacarandas' (another favourite of Brazilian shippers). The only solid ground is the good old Latin names. Kingwood, tulipwood, African blackwood, cocobolo and many other well established woods are all *Dalbergias*. Confused?

Interested readers will find a wealth of reliable information in *Timbers of the New World* by Record and Hess — published by Arno in the US but currently out of print.

*Peter Lang, Timberline, Tonbridge*

I THANK YOU for publishing my query about dyeing woods for Tunbridge ware. Spirit dyes would seem to be the best answer to the dyeing problem, though I agree that natural woods should be used if possible. Jamaican mahoe gives good greens and blacks and is easy to work through the draw-plate in finishing the sticks.

The answer to Mr Platt's question about how thin the veneers can be is in the finishing. I have made up a banding pattern which, when glued to the ground, can be sanded to paper-thinness without breaking up. I use UniBond or EvoStik white woodworking adhesive, and a bandsaw with a simple jig for cutting the pieces to size. The jig prevents the pieces from falling through the blade slot in a Startrite 362 bandsaw.

*Donald Garrod, Ipswich*

APRIL'S *WOODWORKER* carried an article on steam-bending. I have done a lot of experimenting with this as a means of making chair-bows. The essential thing is perfectly straight-grained timber, preferably riven or split from the solid trunk so there are no cut fibres to start a break.

The metal strap is a good thing, as it prevents too much stretching on the outside of the bent wood — but it can cause crushing of the fibres on the inside, so some experimenting is necessary. A much cheaper alternative to stainless steel, and also easier to drill and cut, is galvanised steel (say 18 or 16swg). It is obtainable from the sort of firm that does plumbing, guttering, ducting and suchlike — and, for that size of offcut, usually for nothing.

To re-emphasise the point, I would say that good timber is more important than the steam generator. Green is best, air-dried is second-best, kiln-dried a bad third.

Some other small hints and tips:

● Oven-cleaner is very good for getting the accumulated gum off circular-saw blades.

● A piece of crêpe rubber (an old shoe-sole) held against sanding-belts while running will clean them. Some types of crêpe work better than others.

● Router cutters with pilot pins which rub along the timber are inclined to burn. Rub the edge with a candle beforehand (but be sure to remove the wax before finishing).

*David Faulkner, Christchurch,*
*New Zealand*

# The magazine for the craftsman
## ~ and the aspiring craftsman!

September 1985
Vol. 89
No. 1102

● *Keith Sealey's imposing and imaginative desk is the deserving winner of the great MDF competition. Have a closer look on p660*

On the cover: Pear bowls by Ray Key (p669) return to the log whence they came — while Shrewsbury students Nigel Bulkeley and Will Price bring in the summer show season (p664) with a mahogany desk and spalted-beech blanket-chest respectively

## PROJECTS

All with fully detailed working drawings

## REGULARS

**Publisher** Ray Lewis
**Editor** Peter Collenette
**Deputy Editor** Aidan Walker
**Advertisement Manager** Paul Holmes
**Graphics** Argus Design
**Guild of Woodworkers** Aidan Walker
**Publishing Director** John Foster
**Editorial, advertisements and Guild of Woodworkers** 1 Golden Square, London W1R 3AB, telephone 01-437 0626

**Subscriptions and back issues** Infonet Ltd, 10-13 Times House, 179 Marlowes, Hemel Hempstead, Herts HP1 1BB; telephone Hemel Hempstead (0442) 48434
**Subscriptions per year** UK £15.60; overseas outside USA (accelerated surface post) £17, USA (accelerated surface post) $22.50, airmail £42
**UK trade** SM Distribution Ltd, 16-18 Trinity Gardens, London SW9 8DX; telephone 01-274 8611
**North American trade** Bill Dean Books Ltd, 151-49 7th Avenue, PO Box 69, Whitestone, New York 11357; telephone 1-718-767-6632
**Printed in Great Britain** by Ambassador Press Ltd, St Albans, Herts
**Mono origination** Multiform Photosetting Ltd, Cardiff
**Colour origination** Derek Croxson Ltd, Chesham, Bucks
© Argus Specialist Publications Ltd 1985
ISSN 0043 776X

**Argus Specialist Publications Ltd**
1 Golden Square, London W1R 3AB; 01-437 0626

# Woodworker
# This month

## Miniatura September

Many readers were fascinated by Stuart King's report on the Miniatura show in Birmingham a few months back. Few woodworking crafts provoke such instant admiration as the tiny furniture, joinery and houses of the miniature makers. So it's good news that the exhibition is planned as a six-monthly event. It comes round again on Saturday 28 September from 10.30 to 5, at the County Cricket Ground in Edgbaston, Birmingham as before. Admission is £1.25 (50p for children, who must be accompanied), and there's free parking.

## Lead astray

Lead in petrol has been the focus of a long-running campaign; now the government is at war with the lead on your windows and doors. Modern paints, of course, are largely lead-free, but stripping old ones can easily release the nasty stuff — invisibly and slowly poisonous. The official advice is:
● Don't use a blowlamp.
● Don't dry-sand.
● Use either a hot-air stripper or chemicals, or wet-sand.
● Vacuum well; wash your skin, hair and clothes thoroughly; remove carpets (they hold dust); and don't eat or drink where you're stripping.
● But ideally, leave it untouched and decorate over it.

It will be interesting to see whether this is just the first shot in a battle like those over asbestos and creosote, to name but two examples.

## A house for show

For any woodworking professional in the Monmouth area, an intriguing promotional idea is on offer. A local builder, Highmeadow Homes, is making available a house on their new site at Wyesham, Monmouth, for the display of craft products — either for sale or in order to generate commissions. The idea is to intrigue their own buyers while giving other firms a boost into the bargain. If you'd like to get some of your own products on show, contact Dionne Johnson at 2 Duchess Rd, Monmouth, Gwent NP5 3HT, tel. Monmouth (0600) 2637.

*Mrs J. Ashley, winner of the Elu lathe in our draw at the Bristol show is congratulated by John Costello of Black & Decker, who provided the prizes. AEG and Warren Machine Tools have both generously offered to put up prizes at the October Show; a bandsaw, jigsaw, cordless screwdriver/drill and radial-arm saw await lucky winners*

## Bridgend restoring

A specialised restoring course for the unemployed aged 18-25 starts in Mid-Glamorgan this September. You need to have some hand skills already. Cabinetmaking and carving, upholstery, veneering, polishing, and the evolution of furniture are the 'modules'. No fees!
● Apply to Roy Williams, Dept of Construction, Bridgend College of Technology, Cowbridge Rd, Bridgend, Mid-Glamorgan CF31 3DF.

# Shoptalk

When you've been going since 1901 like us, it's embarrassing when people ring up with a simple question you can't answer. When it comes to shaming the editorial staff in this way, the hot favourite runs as follows: 'I'm thinking of setting up in business as a picture-framer. Where can I get mouldings and equipment?'

So we accord a heartfelt welcome to a new book called **Framing & Art Buyer's Guide.** We haven't seen a copy yet, but it apparently runs to 180 pages and lists over 600 companies supplying more than 5000 framing accessories and other things (including pictures!). 'Most leading picture-frame-moulding and equipment suppliers have taken advertisement space', say the publishers. It costs £14+1.50p&p.
● Framing & Art Buyer's Guide, 83-7 Bridge Rd, East Molesey, Surrey KT8 9HH.

*Richard Kell announces this beautiful brass **bevel-gauge** for checking the grinding angle on all your cutting tools. The apex cutaways mean you don't damage the sharp edge; it's 2in in diameter, and costs £2.95.*
● *Richard Kell, 67 Newbiggin Rd, Ashington, Northumberland NE6 0TB*

*A shock for those who thought matchstick models were the last outpost of individualism. This one comes as a kit – with the wheels, lamp and chimneys ready-made. At least it saves striking your own.*
● *W. Hobby Ltd, Knight's Hill Sq, London SE27 0HH, tel. 01-761 4244*

Solve your copying problems with Trend's **set of 12 guide bushes**, ranging from 10 to 32mm in diameter. They fit the Elu MOF96 direct, and will fit any router with the extra sub-base shown; £27.50+VAT the set, £38+VAT including the sub-base.
● *Trend, Unit N, Penfold Works, Imperial Way, Watford, Herts WD2 4YY, tel (0923) 49911*

'Life with the lathe' (WW/June) interested me greatly with its advice on choosing machines, **writes W. T. Odd.** At the age of 74, I had been wondering whether I dared take up woodturning. But nothing ventured, nothing gained — so I'd asked your opinion, got two books on the subject, and sent for every catalogue and brochure I could find announced in the magazine. I'd decided most of the makes I subsequently saw mentioned in the article were too expensive; after all, I might fail to accomplish very much. So I bought something more modest. I avoided the temptation of a Taiwanese tin can, and settled for a **Sherwood lathe** made by James Inns of Nottingham. This has proved a good buy for the price, with inexpensive accessories. It will take up to 36in between centres and bowls of up to 14in, and it has enabled me — without instruction — to produce very satisfactory items.

● James Inns, 68-70 Main St, Bulwell, Nottingham, (0602) 271317.

This here is the **Universal Clamp Rack** all the way from Poughkeepsie, New York. It lets you simultaneously clamp and stack a quantity of edge-glued panels; that includes lipped boards and doubtless other assemblies too. The clamps can be lifted out, and their design provides for automatic centring on the panel thickness. They can be arranged in all sorts of configurations to accommodate different sizes of job. 32in clamps are standard, but 44in are available; jaws may be 2½ or 3½in high. The rack itself is 6, 8 or 12ft long, 65in high and 5ft deep. 'Optional rocker plates', say the makers, mean the rack ' can also be used to produce high-quality laminated beams and turnings'. As an example, a 6ft frame with 12 clamps costs £1500; but the clamps account for most of the price, and you can start with fewer (or more!).

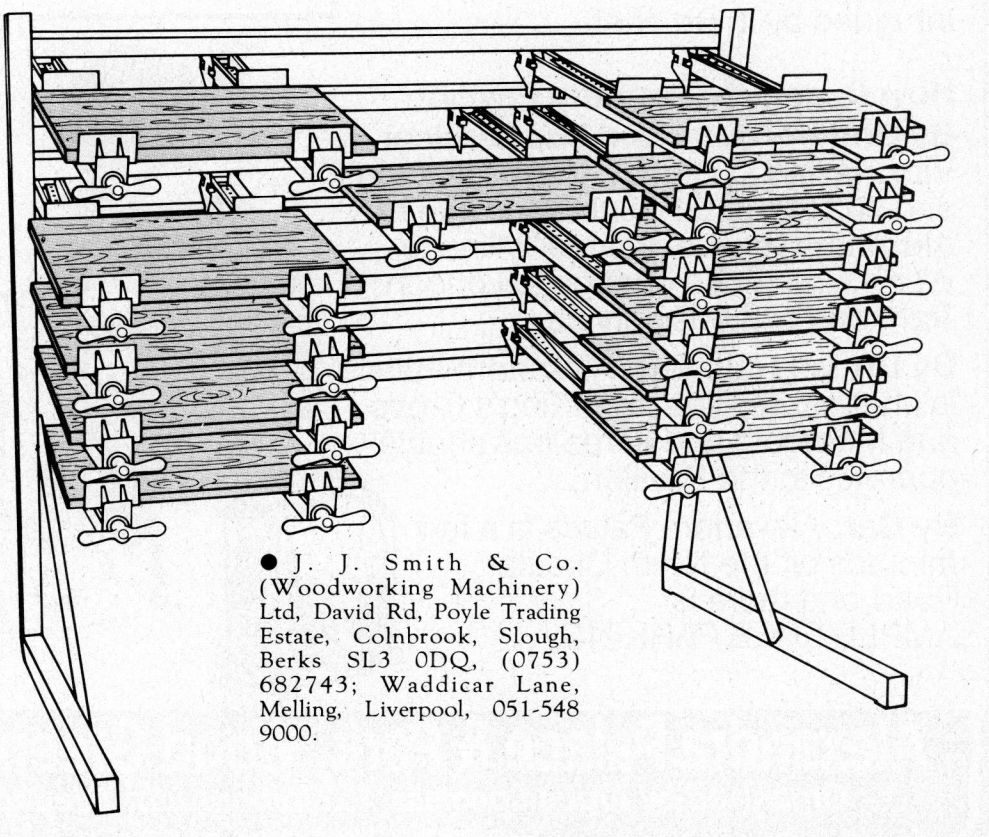

● J. J. Smith & Co. (Woodworking Machinery) Ltd, David Rd, Poyle Trading Estate, Colnbrook, Slough, Berks SL3 0DQ, (0753) 682743; Waddicar Lane, Melling, Liverpool, 051-548 9000.

# LONDON wood worker show '85

## Alexandra Palace 24th-27th October

# THE NATIONAL SHOW THAT IS ALL ABOUT WOOD

Beautiful wood:- Oak, Elm, Sycamore, Ash, Walnut, Mahogany. It's a celebration of its elegance and versatility. Exhibitors show tools with which to fashion it: lathes, routers, chisels, planes, saws, power tools. Competitors exhibit their individual creations in it—carvings, inlay, marquetry, musical instruments, cabinet making. Experts demonstrate their skills In it. And visitors are intrigued by it. Be one!

Open 10am-6pm each day—Sunday 10am-5pm
Admission: Adults £3.00 Children/OAP's £2.00.

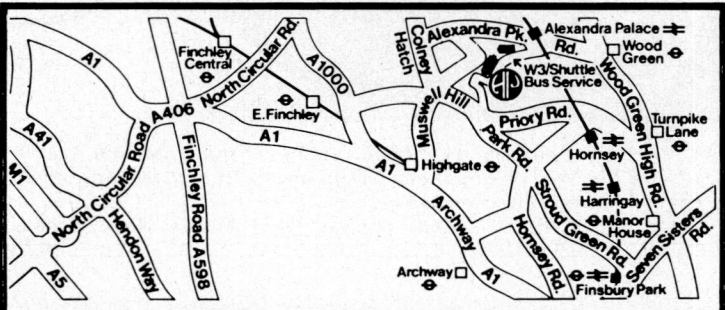

## How to get to Alexandra Pavilion

**By Underground and bus service:** Victoria line to Highbury and Islington and change to B.R. suburban line to Alexandra Palace. Piccadilly line to Wood Green and change to London Transport W.3 bus service.

**By British Rail:** B.R. Alexandra Palace is on the main line from King's Cross and Moorgate and a free bus shuttle operates to the Pavilion.

**By Car:** Alexandra Palace is a few minutes off the North Circular Road and there is AMPLE FREE PARKING.

# Alexandra Palace & Park, Wood Green, London N22

*Organised by Argus Specialist Exhibitions Ltd. Telephone 0442 41221*

*Sponsored by "Woodworker" magazine.*

# Shoptalk

*This is the Hobbymat Variant, a woodworking version of the Hobbymat MD65 metalworking **lathe**. It has a 350mm extension, 120mm centre height and 160mm bowl capacity; for the £185+VAT retail price you get chucks, chisels and a face-plate thrown in. The three-speed motor uses 370w.*
● *CZ Scientific Instruments Ltd, 2 Elstree Way, Borehamwood, Herts WD6 1NH, tel. 01-953 1688*

When you need animal glue, you really need it: hand-veneering and restoration are two jobs where its qualities of fast setting and easy re-melting (not to mention appropriateness for traditional work) are as much in demand as they were before polyvinyl acetate was even a gleam in a mad chemist's eye.

Nevertheless, even the staunchest reactionary might concede that the double-boiler and the little stove in the workshop, hitherto indispensable for heating the stuff up so you can use it, are a bit of a palaver. That's why piano-maker Geoffrey

Winter may have a winner in his Winstick adhesive. It's a **bone glue** which comes in a pot and liquefies straight away if you merely stand it in hot water.

He says it tacks and sticks well as soon as it's applied, and cures to 'immense strength' in 24 hours. It's a pale colour, it contains preservatives to stop it going funny in storage, and it incorporates no solvents except water. It's still water-soluble after setting. It conforms to BS745, and Geoffrey Winter has sent us a little sample which resembles an abstract sculpture and proves that it will stick

wood, baize, leather, and even metal in the form of a small spring. He points out that it's especially handy for craftsmen who work on site, such as piano repairers.

It costs £1.50+40p(p&p) for 4oz/114g, and £3+80p(p&p) for 120oz/340g. You can also get a leaflet explaining how to use it in hand-veneering.

● Geoffrey Winter, The Old Forge, Britway Rd, Dinas Powis, South Glamorgan, (0222) 512394.

*This AEG power-feed, with its variable rate (3-7m per min.), would be well worth £185+VAT in anyone's book. It makes for accuracy and safety in all machining where you're dealing with big bits, and a lot of them – better, in many respects, than another pair of hands. But there's more. If you buy a Lurem C210B or an AEG C2600 Universal, you'll get one of these desirable items free – that's over £200 (inc. VAT) they're giving away. What are you waiting for?*
● *AEG-Telefunken, 217 Bath Rd, Slough, Berks SL1 4AW, tel. (0753) 872553*

June's 'Shoptalk' carried an item about the **AEG Multi woodworking system,** with its single interchangeable motor. 'In general', **writes Herbert Klostermann** of AEG-Telefunken, 'the article does the system justice. However, we believe that a couple of statements will both mislead and confuse readers, and we would like to put the record straight.

'The item said the system "has been designed for the small user with not a lot of space or initial investment capital, but one can't help wondering if the idea isn't a little misconceived". The system was designed as a high-quality product which enabled the user to start off gradually and then, as his needs alter, to expand without the need to buy additional motors. The advantages are considerable; in particular, each machine within the range may be left set up (ideal for repetition work), whereas some other combination systems require adjustment when changing from one function to another.

'If the purchaser expands his activities into a professional woodworking business employing more than one person, a motor may be bought for each machine. This avoids delays in production, as each operator can work on his own machine and is not kept waiting for the use of one machine that has several functions.

'The question was also asked: "Heaving a motor round the workshop when you've ripped a piece and want to surface it . . . how popular will that be?" Very popular, we like to think! The advantages of changing a motor virtually in seconds far outweigh the additional costs. The motor only weighs 12.5kg/ 27.5lbs, and it has two convenient carrying/locating handles. A bayonet-type fitting means that the operation can be compared to changing a lightbulb. A nylon drive spline makes for smooth and easy engagement.

'The alternative to the interchangeable motorised system is to purchase individual motorised machines from the start. In most cases this will prove more expensive, as the motor is included in the cost of the unit.'

# AXMINSTER POWER TOOL CENTRE

## WOODWORKING LATHES — *OUR PRICE INC. VAT*

NEW CORONET HOBBY LATHE 36" centres 12" Bowl Turning 3 Speeds .......... **£189**
CORONET HOBBY KIT with many useful accessories .......... **£256**
HARRISON GRADUATE 30" BC .......... **£1093** 42" BC .......... **£1146**
CORONET LONG BED 'ELF' 30" centres .......... **£288**
CORONET Mk. III MAJOR CMB500 .......... **£499** CMB600 .......... **£490**
MYFORD ML8 36" centres excluding rear turning facility .......... **£359**
MYFORD ML8B 36" crs. .......... **£412** ML8C 42" crs. .......... **£445**
ELU DB180 38" crs. 15" dia. swing. Fully motorised .......... **£274**
KITY 663 4 speed .......... **£470** KITY 664 variable speed .......... **£590**
MINIMAX T90 .......... **£363** T100 .......... **£412** T120 .......... **£433**
**SPECIAL OFFER — 10% off all Coronet Wood Turning Aids & Fitments.**

## RADIAL ARM SAWS

EUMENIA 9" 1½HP Radial Saw 15" Crosscut .......... **£276** 24" Crosscut .......... **£330**
NEW DeWALT 1251 10" 1½HP 15" Crosscut .......... **POA**
NEW DeWALT DW 1501 10" Crosscut .......... **POA**
DeWALT DW1370 12" Radial saw, 2HP motor, with leg stand .......... **POA**
NEW DeWALT 12" RADIAL SAWS 2HP 18" and 24" crosscut .......... **POA**
DeWALT DW1600S 14" saw Max op cap 36" 2½HP 1PH .......... **£979** 4HP 3PH .......... **£940**
WADKIN BRA 14", crosscut. .......... from **£1,360**

## SAW BENCHES

MAKITA 2708 8" Saw (will accept router and jigsaw) .......... **£189**
STARTRITE TA255. 10" tilt arbor. TCT blade. Cast table with extensions 1PH .......... **£690**
WADKIN AGSP Scoring Panel Saw 10"/12" 3PH .......... **£1,639** 1PH .......... **£1,741**
STARTRITE TA300 PS Scoring Saw 1PH .......... **£1,377**
ELU TGS 172 Saw Bench/Mitre Saw with free wood kit .......... **£355** ELU TGS 171 .......... **£299**
LUNA L18 12" TCT Panel Saw with sliding table .......... **£980**
SCHEPPACH new TKH 12" Pressed steel bench .. **£179** New TKU as TKH with tilt .. **£199**
SLIDING TABLE for TKU-TKH .......... **£69** Panel Cutting Extension .......... **55**
WADKIN AGS 250/300 10"-12" Tilt Arbor Saw 3HP 3PH .... **£1,052** 3HP 1PH .... **£1,137**

## BANDSAWS (excellent stocks of all longlife blades)

BURGESS BK3+ MkII with FREE fretsaw and jigsaw attachment .......... **£108**
DeWALT DW100 2 speed. 13" throat 4" cut. With mitre fence & disc sander .......... **POA**
DeWALT BS1310. 2 speed. 12" throat. 6" cut .......... **POA**
KITY K613 8" cut 12" throat bench mounting .......... **£399** Floor standing .......... **£433**
STARTRITE 301. 12" throat. 6" cut. Steel table. Floor standing .......... **£395**
STARTRITE 352. 2 speed. 14" throat. 12" cut. Floor standing 1-ph. .......... **£669**
LUNA BS320 6" depth of cut. Cast table .......... **£298**
MINIMAX P32 6" cut 14" throat Cast Tables .......... **£357**
MINIMAX S45 10" cut 17" throat. Very solid construction. Cast Tables .......... **£575**

## PLANER/THICKNESSER

KITY 7136 10" × 6" 2 Speed Power Feed 1½HP Motor Floor Standing .......... **£540**
DeWALT DW1150 10" × 6" 2 Speed power feed 2HP Motor .......... **POA**
DeWALT DW600 Slot Morticer for DW1150 .......... **£65** Stand for DW1150 **£25**
STARTRITE PT260. 10" × 6" Steel tables. ⅝" rebate .......... **£820**
WADKIN M300 12" × 8" Planer/Thicknesser Power Feed Cast Construction ..... **£1380**
SHEPPACH HMO SOLO. 10" × 6". Steel tables. 2HP motor. Floor standing .......... **£480**
STARTRITE SD310. 12" × 7". ⅝" rebate. Cast iron 3PH .......... **£1,226** 1PH .......... **£1,280**
WADKIN BAOS 12" × 7" Solid Cast. Heavy Duty 3PH .......... **£2,757** 1PH .......... **£2,930**

## DRILLING AND MORTISING MACHINES

WOLF Mortice Drill Stand Attachment c/w ½" chisel. Accepts most power drills **£129**
FOBCO 'STAR'. ½" capacity. 4-speed. British made precision machine .......... **£305**
MORTICING ATTACHMENT for FOBCO M/Cs. With clamp & ⅜" chisel .......... **£57**
WARCO 'HOBBY'. ½" capacity. 5-speed, tilting table .......... **£125**
WARCO 2B ⅝" capacity 2MT tilt table bench mounting .... **£199** 2F12 floor standing **£222**
STARTRITE SP250 5 speed ½" bench drill .......... **£339** Floor standing .......... **£379**
WADKIN MORTICER 1" capacity. 1PH or 3PH .......... **£586**
Mortice Chisels & Bits ¼" **£14.50** ⅜" **£16.00** ½" **£19.00** ⅝" **£23.00** ¾" **£36.00**
**Ridgeway chisel** + bits ¼" **£19.00** ⅜" **£21.16** ½" **£23.88** ⅝" **£35.00** ¾" **£37.00**
RYOBI Chain Morticer 240v Portable Morticer .......... **£344**
BCM75 Bench Top Morticer c/w chuck and ½" chisel 240v .......... **£399**

## SPINDLE MOULDERS

KITY 623 30mm Spindle 3-speed 2HP 1PH .......... **£526**
LUNA L28 30mm spindle 3-speed 5" rise 3HP 240v .......... **POA**
STARTRITE T30 1¼" spindle with sliding table 1PH .......... **£889**
SCHEPPACH HF33 2 Speed 2HP 30mm .......... **£485** HF30 (old model) .......... **£340**
WADKIN BEL 4 Speed 5HP Spindle Moulder (3PH Only) .......... **POA**

## COMBINATION MACHINES

KITY K5 Combination Complete Spindle, Saw, Planer, Slot Morticer .......... **£725**
KITY K5 (A) as above but less spindle moulder .......... **£575**
KITY K5 (A) as above but less spindle moulder & slot morticer .......... **£499**
LUNA Z40 (ex Mia 6) with TCT blade .......... **£690**
NEW KITY 704 MkII with 30mm Spindle .......... **£1,290**
STARTRITE K260 Combination, 'FREE CUTTER SET' 3PH .......... **£1,911** 1PH **£1,999**
STARTRITE K210 Combination 'FREE CUTTER SET' 1PH .......... **£1,825**
LUNA COMBINATIONS W49. W59. W69 available 2HP or 3HP .......... **POA**
SCHEPPACH COMBI 10" × 6" Planer, 12" Saw 30m Spindle .......... **£860**

## MISCELLANEOUS MACHINES & EQUIPMENT

DeWALT DW250. 10" Bevel/Mitre saw. 1HP motor .......... **£194**
LUNA YK1500 Pad Sander 1PH .......... **£1,327** 3PH .......... **£1,300**
LUNA FAVORITE Flat Bed Sander .......... **£230**
DREMEL D576 15" FRETSAW. 12" throat. Tilt table. With disc sander .......... **£70**
HOBBY LUX fretsaw 12" throat tilt table .......... **£69**
NOBEX 202 Mitre Saw .......... **£65** NOBEX 303 Mitre Saw .......... **£41**
DeWALT DW60 Twin bag dust extractor .......... **£248** DW30 single bag .......... **£210**
LUNA SPS400 Dust Extractor 240v Portable Unit .......... **£215.00**
LUNA W178 Dust Extractor Fir, Mtg. .......... **£292**
LUNA NF259 Large Capacity Dust Extractor 1PH .......... **£422**
LION MITRE TRIMMER excellent for accurate mitre cuts .......... **£249**
LUNA Support Roller .......... **£27** Delux Combi Support roller .......... **£38**
SPRAY GUN & COMPRESSOR KIT SLIP AIRMATE 240v .......... **£105**

## SPINDLE MOULDER TOOLING

LEITZ 488 Cutter Blocks 30mm or 1¼" 92mm dia. **£44** 100mm dia. **£51** 120mm dia. **£55**
LUNA 92mm Cutter Block 30mm or 1¼" .......... **£43** Set c/w 10 profile knives .......... **£115**
WOBBLE SAWS for Spindle Moulders 6" 3mm-21mm **£76** 10" dia. 3mm-30mm **£88**

### INDUSTRIAL QUALITY T.C.T SAWBLADES

ALL PRICES INCLUDE V.A.T. AND P&P

GENERAL DUTY (MADE IN SHEFFIELD) PREMIUM QUALITY FOR CONTINUOUS USE (MADE IN W. GERMANY)

| BLADE DIAMETER | 6" | | | | 7"-7 1/4" | | | | 8" | | | | 9"-9 1/4" | | | |
|---|---|---|---|---|---|---|---|---|---|---|---|---|---|---|---|---|
| NO OF TEETH | 16 | 24 | 36 | 48 | 18 | 30 | 42 | 56 | 20 | 36 | 48 | 64 | 24 | 40 | 54 | 72 |
| GENERAL DUTY | £16 | £17 | £20 | £26 | £16 | £17 | £21 | £26 | £20 | £25 | £27 | £32 | £18 | £23 | £27 | £30 |
| PREMIUM QUALITY | - | £24 | - | £31 | - | - | - | - | - | - | - | - | - | £36 | £40 | - |
| BLADE DIAMETER | 10" | | | | 12" | | | | 14" | | | | 16" | | | |
| NO OF TEETH | 24 | 40 | 60 | 80 | 32 | 48 | 72 | 96 | 36 | 60 | 84 | 108 | 28 | 36 | 60 | 96 |
| GENERAL DUTY | £23 | £26 | £35 | £38 | £25 | £31 | £35 | £44 | £34 | £42 | £50 | £57 | - | - | - | - |
| PREMIUM QUALITY | £29 | £33 | £38 | £46 | £33 | £39 | £47 | £55 | £38 | £44 | £54 | £62 | £43 | £46 | £55 | £64 |

PLEASE STATE BORE SIZE WHEN ORDERING

## ROUTERS — OUR PRICE INC. VAT

ELU MOF 96 600w ¼" .......... **£77.95**
ELU MOF 96E 750w ¼" .......... **£98.95**
ELU MOF 31 1200w ¼" ⅜" ½" **£123.95**
ELU MOF 77 variable speed ... **£195.00**
ELU MOF 98 1500 ¼" ⅜" ½" **£144.95**
ELU MOF 112 2000w ½" ....... **£340.00**
HITACHI TR8 730w ¼" .......... **£65.00**
HITACHI TR12 1300w ¼", ⅜", ½" **£120.00**
MAKITA 3600 1500w ¼" ⅜" ½" **£141.00**
BOSCH POF52 ¼" 500w .......... **£43.95**
HITACHI TR6 Trimmer .......... **£71.00**
ELU MKF 67 Trimmer ¼" .......... **£94.95**

### ROUTER ACCESSORIES

ELU MOF 96 Accessory Kit ...... **£58.00**
DOVETAIL JIG c/w TCT Cutter **£58.00**
STAIR Routing Jig .......... **£69.00**
ELU Router Combi Bench .......... **£77.00**
MAKITA Router Bench .......... **£35.00**
ELU Router Bracket for DeWalt **£33.00**

### BELT SANDER

ELU MHB 157 3" 600w .......... **£85.95**
ELU MHB 157E 3" Variable Speed **£94.95**
ELU MHB 157 Stand .......... **£21.00**
ELU MHB 157 Frame .......... **£28.00**
ELU MHB 90 4" 850w .......... **£143.95**
ELU MHB 90K 4" with frame . **£164.95**
HITACHI SB-75 3" 950w .......... **£99.00**
HITACHI SB-110 4" 950w .......... **£129.00**
MAKITA 1" 9030 Multi Purpose **£88.00**
MAKITA 3" 9924DB 850w .......... **£98.50**
MAKITA 4" 1040w .......... **£141.50**
BOSCH 3" 620w .......... **£67.00**

### JIGSAWS

ELU ST 152 420w .......... **£98.95**
ELU ST 152E 420w .......... **£106.95**
BOSCH PST 50E 350w .......... **£32.95**
BOSCH PST 55PE 380w .......... **£54.95**
BOSCH 1581/7 Var. Speed .......... **£93.00**

### DRILL STANDS

BOSCH S7 Drill Stand .......... **£46.00**
WOLFCRAFT Compass Drill Stand **£44.00**
WOLF Morticer Stand .......... **£129.00**

### MISCELLANEOUS POWER TOOLS

ELU DS 140 Biscuit Jointer .... **£156.95**
BOSCH Wet 'n' Dry Cleaner .... **£83.00**
HITACHI Sabre Saw CF10v ..... **£120.00**
HITACHI 9" Grinder 2000w .......... **£89.00**
HITACHI 4" Grinder 430w .......... **£41.00**

### CIRCULAR SAWS

ELU MH 151 TCT 850w .......... **£77.95**
ELU MH65 7¼" TCT 1200w ..... **£90.95**
ELU MH 85 9¼" TCT 1600w .. **£143.95**
HITACHI PSU-6 6" 1050w .......... **£59.00**
HITACHI PSU-7 7¼" 1600w ..... **£87.00**
HITACHI PSU-9 9¼" 1759w ... **£103.00**
HITACHI PSM-7 7¼" TCT 1200w **£119.00**
HITACHI PSM-9 9¼" TCT 1600w **£125.00**
WOLF 9 ¼" Circular Saw .......... **£134**

### BENCH GRINDERS — OUR PRICE INC. VAT

ELU EDS 163 6" DE .......... **£56.95**
ELU EDS 164 7" DE .......... **£61.95**
ELU MWA 149 Honer Grinder .. **£73.95**
LEROY SOMER 5" DE .......... **£29.00**
LEROY SOMER 6" DE .......... **£39.00**
LEROY SOMER 7" DE .......... **£49.00**
LEROY SOMER Wetstone .......... **£73.00**
HANNING WETSTONE Grinder . **£99.00**
HITACHI NTG 150 6" DE .......... **£68.00**

### CORDLESS DRILLS

HITACHI Cordless DTC10 .......... **£59.00**
HITACHI DV10D Hammer Drill . **£87.00**
MAKITA 6012DE 2 Speed .......... **£78.00**
MAKITA Hammer Drill 8400DW **£94.50**

### HAMMER DRILL

BOSCH 400-2 400w .......... **£31.00**
BOSCH 500-2E 500w .......... **£58.00**
BOSCH 7002 RLE 700w .......... **£75.95**
HITACHI VTP13K ½" 460w .......... **£74.00**
HITACHI VTP16AK ⅝" 800w .. **£103.00**
B&D P2162 ⅜" Var. Speed Rev. **£42.00**
B&D P2264 ½" Var. Speed .......... **£47.00**
B&D P2266 ½" Var. Speed Rev. **£59.00**

### FINISHING SANDERS

ELU MVS 156 1/3 Sheet .......... **£65.95**
ELU MVS 156E Electronic .......... **£77.95**
ELU MVS 94 Heavy Duty .......... **£90.95**
ELU MVS 47 Heavy Duty .......... **£98.95**
HITACHI Palm Sander .......... **£39.00**
MAKITA Palm Sander .......... **£42.00**
B&D P6303 1/2 Sheet Ind. .......... **£47.00**
Bosch PSS230 1/3 Sheet .......... **£24.95**

### POWER PLANERS

ELU MFF80 850w .......... **£77.00**
ELU MFF80K 850w .......... **£93.00**
HITACHI FU-20 720w .......... **74.00**
HITACHI P20SA 720w .......... **£84.00**
BLACK & DECKER P7103 600w **£84.95**

### DREMEL POWER TOOLS

Disc/Belt Sander .......... **£90.00**
15" Scroll Saw Sander .......... **£71.00**
Delux Scroll Saw Sander .......... **£95.00**
4" Table Saw .......... **£98.95**
284 Woodcarvers Kit .......... **£65.00**
384 Var. Speed Carvers Kit .......... **£79.00**
258 Const. Speed Moto Tool .......... **£39.00**
358 Var. Speed Moto Tool .......... **£52.50**
359 as 358 with 35 Accs. .......... **£66.00**
Router Base for Moto Tool .......... **£11.00**
Drill Stand for Moto Tool .......... **£23.50**
238 Moto Flex Tool .......... **£71.00**
338 Var. Speed Flex Tool .......... **£79.00**

## WOODTURNERS "AT LAST PERFECTION"

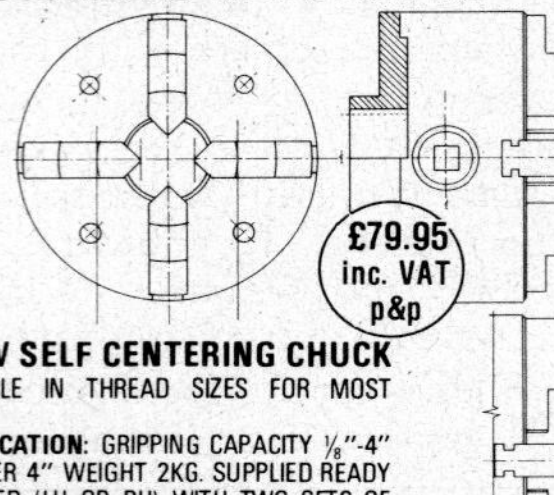


**4 JAW SELF CENTERING CHUCK**
AVAILABLE IN THREAD SIZES FOR MOST LATHES.
**SPECIFICATION:** GRIPPING CAPACITY ⅛"-4" DIAMETER 4" WEIGHT 2KG. SUPPLIED READY THREADED (LH OR RH) WITH TWO SETS OF PRECISION JAWS (INTERNAL & EXTERNAL).
**HOW TO ORDER:** TO CHEQUE OR POSTAL ORDER FOR **£79.95** OR PHONE YOUR CREDIT CARD STATING LATHE TYPE FOR PROMPT DESPATCH (MOST TYPES EX-STOCK)
**HURRY!** YOU DON'T KNOW WHAT YOUR MISSING.

## ROUTER CUTTERS

**20-25% OFF LEADING BRANDS**

**EXCELLENT STOCKS OF HSS & TCT ROUTER CUTTERS OVER 500 PROFILES IN STOCK. SEND NOW FOR FREE CUTTER CHART:-**

## BANDSAW BLADES

**MONINGER LONGLIFE QUALITY BLADES. OVER 4000 BLADES IN STOCK SEND NOW FOR CURRENT — PRICE LIST —**

## SASH CRAMPS (P&P £2.00 per order) May be mixed for quantity

RECORD 135-24" 1 off £19 5 off £17
135-36" 1 off £20 5 off £18
135-42" 1 off £21 5 off £19
135-48" 1 off £22 5 off £20
DRAPER 18" 1 off £13.50 5 off £11.50
30" 1 off £17.25 5 off £14.95
40" 1 off £18.40 5 off £16.00
60" 1 off £28.00 5 off £26.00

## G CRAMPS (P&P £1.50 per order) May be mixed for quantity

4" Record 120 .......... 1 off £6 5 off £5
6" Record 120 .......... 1 off £9 5 off £8
8" Record 120 .......... 1 off £13 5 off £11
10" Record 120 .......... 1 off £18 5 off £16
Paramo 4" .......... 1 off £6 5 off £5
Paramo 6" .......... 1 off £8 5 off £7
Paramo 8" .......... 1 off £12 5 off £11
Paramo 10" .......... 1 off £17 5 off £15

## HAND TOOLS (P&P £1.50 per order)

STANLEY 04 Smooth Plane ....... **£17.50**
STANLEY 04½ Smooth Plane .... **£19.00**
STANLEY 05 Jack Plane .......... **£26.00**
STANLEY 05½ Jack Plane .......... **£28.00**
STANLEY 06 Fore Plane .......... **£34.00**
STANLEY 07 Fore Plane .......... **£38.00**
STANLEY 10 Rebate Plane .......... **£38.00**
STANLEY 60½ Block Plane .......... **£17.00**
STANLEY RECORD 778 Rebate Pl. **£29.50**
RECORD 146 Hold Fast .......... **£14.00**
Extra Collars for 146 .......... **£3.00**
RECORD Cramp Heads .......... **£12.00**
RECORD 52½E 9" Wood Vice .... **£62.00**
LIP & SPUR DRILL 1-13mm Set **£54.00**
RECORD 04 Smooth Plane .......... **£18.00**
RECORD 04½ Smooth Plane .......... **£19.00**
RECORD 05 Jack Plane .......... **£28.00**
RECORD 05½ Jack Plane .......... **£29.00**
RECORD 06 Fore Plane .......... **£34.00**
RECORD 07 Jointer Plane .......... **£38.50**
RECORD 010 Rebate Plane .......... **£38.00**
RECORD 060½ Block Plane .......... **£15.50**
RECORD 020C Circular Plane .... **£66.00**
RECORD Dowelling Jig .......... **£31.00**
RECORD 141 Corner Cramps ..... **£21.00**
PARAMO Cramp Heads .......... **£10.00**
RECORD 53E 10½" Wood Vice .. **£71.00**
LIP & SPUR DRILL 1/16-½ Set ..... **£39.00**

## SAWTOOTH CUTTERS (inc. VAT P&P) 6" long with ½" shank

**Finest quality steel**
⅜" ..... **£7.30**; ½" ..... **£7.60**; ⅝ ..... **£7.70**; ¾" ..... **£8.35**; ⅞" ..... **£9.10**; 1" ..... **£9.75**; 1⅛" ..... **£11.30**; 1¼" ..... **£11.90**; 1⅜" ..... **£13.80**; 1½" ..... **£15.25**; 1⅝" ..... **£17.80**; 1¾" ..... **£20.20**; 1⅞" ..... **£21.80**; 2" ..... **£23.40**

**CHARD STREET AXMINSTER DEVON EX13 5DZ 0297 33656 6.30-9pm 34836**

BARCLAYCARD VISA

IMMEDIATE DESPATCH ON CREDIT CARD PHONED ORDERS — CREDIT TERMS AVAILABLE OVER £120

# Timberline

## Arthur Jones presents the month's inside news of supplies

This column deals primarily with timber and panel-product supplies and prices.

However, a letter from a reader (WW/Aug), taking me to task for failing to appreciate the needs of the third-world countries which produce so many of our tropical hardwoods, comes at a time when the Friends of the Earth have launched a strong campaign to obtain agreement among UK and European timber traders to a code of conduct. They threaten that failure to accept the code will lead to a campaign urging the public (and presumably woodworkers in particular) not to use or buy timber products from tropical rainforests.

This comes dramatically into our realm. If there is no timber to market there can be no woodworking of any kind. Far from being uninterested in the future of timber supplies, the trader is most concerned.

Emotions ride high when people talk about trees, and they ignore the simple fact that a tree is just like any other crop springing from a seed; it grows, reaches maturity and then dies. So the sensible course is to harvest the tree before it falls into decay.

Equally, because the tree is a crop, there must be a proper management system of thinning and replanting, otherwise whole areas are denuded and disaster on a vast scale can follow.

As a result, the Forestry Commission has produced a plan to increase the stock of broadleaved trees in Britain. There are proposals that felling licences be more strictly controlled and that replanting should be of hardwoods; also for new grants to encourage the planting of more hardwoods. These conservation measures, if adopted by the Government, would mean less native hardwood timber on the market in the short term.

The Friends of the Earth code requires that every tropical concession should have an approved management plan which would limit logging damage; the cut, they say, should not exceed the annual sustainable yield. New plantations should be established only on downgraded land and not primary tropical forest.

Hardwood importers should label their tropical hardwood products with the country of origin, the code suggests, and retailers should not sell unlabelled wood. The hardwood industry should set aside 1% of profits for a fund to ensure the future of rainforests. The industry should diversify the types and promote the widest range of tropical hardwoods for trade purposes.

The whole emphasis of the code, unfortunately, is placed in the wrong area. The labelling idea poses probably insurmountable problems; the controls must be made in the countries of origin, where the pressure is most needed.

It remains a fact that a large percentage of timber from the forest is used as fuel. Quite a proper use, but there is an obvious need to control the felling for this purpose, in European as well as tropical countries. For example, all homes in Austria have neat stacks of small logs for winter fuel, while the larger logs go to the sawmill.

There is a lot of sympathy in the timber trade with the basic aims of the Friends of the Earth and talks are being held with the Timber Trade Federation to see how far the two bodies can co-operate. It must be confessed, too, that the early operations of big UK timber importers in the tropical forests were disastrous in environmental terms; vast tracts were devastated merely to extract a few trees per acre.

Since those days there has been tremendous research into the properties of lesser-known species, and more of these are being used commercially.

A study on tropical forests has just been published by a respected timber expert, Dr Peter Hansom, who is an industrial consultant to the Timber Research & Development Association. He found that agriculture contributes far more than logging to tropical deforestation, and concluded that a reduction of international hardwood trading would not bring ecological benefits. He did find, however, that some selective logging practices opened up forest areas for local farmers to exploit, and here, presumably, there is a need for local legislation. ∎

# Question box

## Our panel of experts solve your woodworking problems

**Q** *I am aware of the effect of oak on steel screws, hence the use of brass; but would stainless-steel screws or bolts be similarly affected, or is it safer to stick to brass all the time?*

*D. Bowker, South Humberside*

**A** Stainless-steel screws or bolts should produce no visible staining or deterioration in oak timber for internal uses. Such screws are likely to be a little more expensive than brass, but they are stronger and therefore less likely to shear. Specially coloured stainless-steel screws are produced by GKN which match the colour of wood.

A number of woods produce staining when in contact with iron or iron compounds under damp conditions, oak and sweet chestnut being the most important of the home-grown species. The staining is usually blue/black in colour and is unsightly. It results from a chemical reaction between the iron (or iron compounds, e.g. rust) and substances inherent in the wood, such as tannins and related compounds. In addition, such timbers are liable to cause corrosion of iron and steel because of the acetic acid within the wood.

*Sue Newton, London College of Furniture*

**Q** *Can you describe the correct way to use ammonia as a means of staining oak? I would like to know the right strength and method of application, and also how the action takes place chemically.*

*J. M. G. Crossley, Oakham*

**A** Where oak has been used in stables it assumes an attractive brown colour over the years. The ammonia in the horses' urine acts on the tannic acid in the oak and causes the wood to change colour. Mahogany, which also contains tannic acid, can be fumed, but the procedure is usually reserved for oak.

Fuming does not raise the grain, and the resultant colour is not liable to fade. English oak responds very well to fuming; American white oak fumes fairly well, but red oak may prove a little difficult. The ammonia required for fuming can be obtained from most polish suppliers and is known as .880 ('point eight-eighty'). This number refers to its specific gravity, which is the strongest available. Be careful when using ammonia because the fumes are dangerous if inhaled. *Charles Cliffe*

**Q** *I'm a welder by trade, but I've made a few guitars. The reception these have received encourages me to try a modest production batch. But here's the problem.*

*A guitar finger-board needs a camber on it. This camber has to be very accurate or the instrument won't play at all; my sketch shows what is needed. Planing by hand does the job, but it's very slow – not good news on a production run. I'm thinking of spending some money on equipment such as a planer-thicknesser. Can I get a suitable cutter made to fit a planer? More importantly, would this be the right tool for the job?*

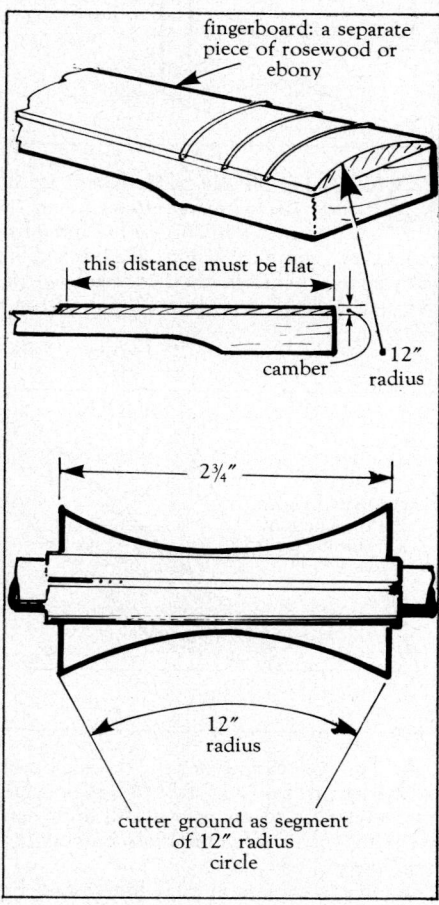

fingerboard: a separate piece of rosewood or ebony

this distance must be flat

camber

12" radius

2¾"

12" radius

cutter ground as segment of 12" radius circle

*My sketch shows my idea for a cutter: is it feasible? If necessary I'll make the thing myself (I'm a welder, remember. But I'm fed up with being a welder – I'd much rather work with wood!).*

*Tony Blunt, Gillingham, Dorset*

**A** You are quite right that a steel-strung acoustic or electric guitar (you don't say which you're making) has a cambered finger-board. But the 12in radius you give assumes that the camber follows the arc of a circle; in fact it does not — and, if it did, 12in would be too tight. In addition, the finger-board is tapered in width from the nut to the twelfth or fourteenth fret to body, depending on the instrument and scale length. Even if the curvature of your proposed cutter were correct for one end of the finger-board, it would be incorrect for part of the length.

Compared with the other tasks involved in making a steel-strung acoustic guitar, cambering the finger-board by hand takes very little time in the hands of a skilled maker.

**1** Thickness the fingerboard exactly. It must be perfectly flat and not in winding.
**2** Taper it in the width.
**3** Cut the fret slots.
**4** Pencil a centre-line along the top face.
**5** Pencil a line along each edge, about 2mm from the upper face (the exact distance depends on the camber required).
**6** Without removing any of the lines, plane the camber on each side.
**7** Increase the depth of the fret slots to follow the camber.

I cannot see that you would recoup your outlay on cutters unless and until your production reached full factory proportions!

Incidentally, holding the tapered fingerboard may present a problem when it comes to cutting the fret slots and cambering. The answer is to prepare a piece of wood flat and straight, taper it like the finger-board at one end, grip it in the vice and fix the finger-board to it with double-sided tape. When you need to remove it, work slowly and carefully by inserting a thin-bladed knife.

*Phil Chambers, Merton College*

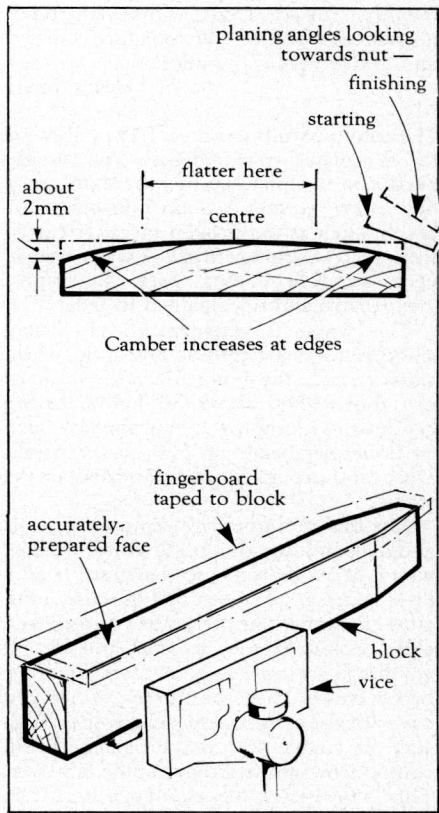

planing angles looking towards nut — finishing

starting

flatter here

centre

about 2mm

Camber increases at edges

fingerboard taped to block

accurately-prepared face

block

vice

**Q** *I am making eight dining-chairs, based on the single-bow Windsor, out of imbuia; the bows are bent in 1in square beech. I am using equipment described by Henry Rogers ('Bending rules', WW/April); I steamed the first piece of beech for an hour as he says, and it bent without any trouble. The second piece – also steamed for an hour – broke*

# Question box

*in four places to either side of the central G-cramp, and the third, which I left in the box for 1½ hours, broke just off-centre. Should I use a heavier-gauge steel strap?*

*Can you also suggest a method of staining the beech bow down to the colour of imbuia?*

*Barry Crabtree, Zimbabwe*

---

**A** I advise you to check that your steam generator is fitted with a 3Kw element, as 2Kw doesn't give a sufficient head of steam. Assuming that the generator has been correctly constructed, the problem must lie with the wood, not the strap. A heavier-gauge strap would lack flexibility.

The material to be bent must have a high moisture content, and I suspect your wood has become too dry. Freshly felled small sections of ash and beech become surprisingly dry in a matter of weeks, especially in a dry atmosphere. Dry timber can be soaked for a few days before steaming, but this is not always satisfactory, so I suggest you select some fresh material.

I achieve a 95% success rate by riving (splitting) my own bending stock from freshly felled logs. This approach guarantees wood of high moisture content, and is also very economical.

*Henry Rogers*

The colour of imbuia ranges from yellowish to chocolate-brown. Before you finally decide on the make-up of your stain, carry out a few experiments on odd scraps of beech, such as the broken pieces left over from your steaming efforts. A water stain is very suitable, being easy to apply, inexpensive and not inclined to fade.

The wood is glasspapered absolutely smooth and then lightly sponged with warm water to raise the grain. Allow the wood to dry thoroughly, about 24 hours, before gently smoothing with a fine abrasive such as flour glasspaper or 7/0 garnet paper. Dust off thoroughly before brushing on the stain.

Mix brown umber with vandyke crystals and make it into a thin paste with ammonia, which helps the stain to penetrate. Add a little water at a time to this mixture, until after experimenting on scraps you achieve a close colour-match to the imbuia. If anything, err on the side of making the beech darker than the imbuia. Once you have arrived at the colour, make up enough stain to enable you to stain all the beech components and still have some left over. This is far better than running out of stain and trying to make up a second batch of the same colour.

Brush on the stain evenly and allow plenty of time (at least 24 hours) for it to dry completely before applying any polish. Imbuia polishes very well and should make you a handsome set of chairs.

It's probable that you can't obtain brown umber and vandyke crystals locally, but many British specialist suppliers export all over the world.

*Charles Cliffe*

---

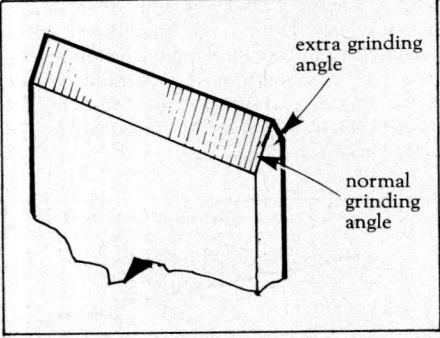

extra grinding angle

normal grinding angle

**Q** *Examining the disposable blades for a Stanley RB10 multi-purpose plane, I was interested to discover one specially ground for cutting chipboard. The method of sharpening differed from the conventional in that it was bevelled on both sides as shown. Why?*

*P. Haggett, Derby*

---

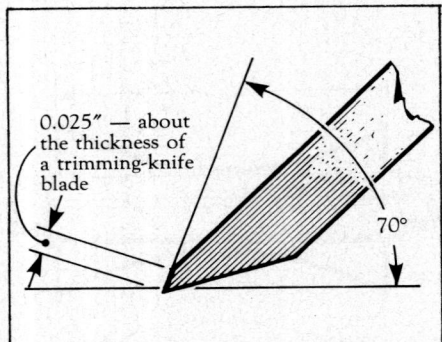

0.025″ — about the thickness of a trimming-knife blade

70°

**A** The sole purpose of the double bevel formed on our RB109 disposable plane-blade is to increase useful life when working man-made materials embodying aggressive constituents.

Similar increases in edge life should be gained if this secondary bevel is added to conventional plane irons used on the same materials, although restoration of normal geometry at the end of a job may well take longer than the re-sharpening time saved.

Attached is a sketch defining a general-purpose double bevel for planes.

*David Scott, Stanley Tools*

---

**Q** *I intend to build a bookcase which will be grafted on to and match a side-board manufactured by Ercol in elm.*

*The complete unit is intended for a wall niche which has radiused top corners and flat top. The general construction will use solid elm for the glazed doors, façade and visible side sections. The material for the bookcase has been rendered from a baulk of elm which was purchased for buffer boards to be used on cranes and similar machinery. When obtained, it was rough-sawn and had been stored in a dry, warm environment for at least 10 years.*

*The timber has been rendered down into sawn and rough-planed sections with the exception of the radius segments needed for the top corners. These will be cut from 9x9x5in*

*portions of the original; when finished, their radii will be 7in external and 6¼ internal, with a final width of 2in.*

*My queries are as follows:*

*1 Is it likely that the sections will be prone to distortion when finished?*

*2 Is there a method which can be used in the final machining and preparation to eliminate or significantly reduce such distortion?*

*3 If, in your opinion, there is a fair risk of the wood's twisting and so on, can I obtain commercially elm which has been selected, processed and prepared, so that an amateur can use it with impunity? In this event, can you tell me a suitable specification which I could use when ordering?*

*G. Farr, Billericay*

---

**A** Ercol's success in using elm, with its superb grain patterns, for furniture has encouraged quite a few others to try — with varying success. Ercol render their elm stable by 'sticking' it outside for about two years before kilning. They then kiln in steam-kilns, and the cycle that they have developed includes bringing the elm right back to almost 100% moisture content before finally drying down to about 11%.

From this you can see that trying to prepare elm is no easy matter. The second problem you may have is that elm used for chock and buffer work is likely to be of questionable quality. If it is free of check you may well be all right, but just check that the planks cut from it are not short-grained — i.e. that the grain does not run across from one face of the plank to the other. If it does this at an angle of more than 10° I would advise not using the plank.

Now to answer your specific questions:

1 Yes, there is always the likelihood that the elm will move after manufacture. Minimise this by ensuring it is entirely dry, i.e. 11% or less; choose pieces where the grain is least convoluted; and seal the work thoroughly as quickly as you can after completion.

2 Here are one or two hints that might help keep warping to a minimum.

● Rip down wide boards so that no piece is wider than 100mm when used, and reverse alternate strips.

● Avoid putting even one piece of short-grained or turbulent timber into a panel.

● It is often helpful, for example on table-tops, to run grooves along the grain underneath, spaced about 75mm apart, that penetrate to ⅔ of the thickness.

3 On the whole wych elm tends to move less than the other three varieties of elm on the market — Dutch elm, small-leaved elm and even Huntingdon elm. The wych has a lighter colour but is straighter-grained. Some people don't like it because of the green stripes that occasionally run through it.

Perhaps I should add, rather cheekily, that if you want a supply of good wych elm or any other variety properly air- or kiln-dried, the Wood Shop at Thirsk Sawmills can provide and deliver.

*John Gormley, Thirsk Sawmills*

# Announcing a Brand New Bargain Service

*The* best books on all aspects of woodworking, factually described in a free quarterly newsletter and offered at bargain prices exclusively to members.

That is what the new **Craftsman Book Society** offers you – to keep you sharp. It gives you the opportunity to pick the best books of ideas and inspiration, facts and figures, drawings and plans ... books that really help increase your skills and get more enjoyment and satisfaction from the projects you tackle (and probably save you money along the way too).

## YOUR INVITATION

*Here is your invitation to become a founder member*, enjoying a special selection of books on woodturning, woodcarving, furniture making, traditional woodcrafts, practical projects of every kind ... almost certainly some titles you would otherwise never have heard of.

Study our introductory offer without obligation. If you decide to retain it, your only commitment to our straightforward service will be to remain a member for a year and to buy four books during that time. *Every* title is substantially discounted, usually at least 25 per cent off publishers' prices. Of course we are *not* offering cheap reprints, but books identical in quality and content to the first copy off the press.

We are part of David & Charles, renowned for enterprise and fair dealing, and Jack Hill's publisher. Our Readers Union Book Clubs for enthusiasts cover many subjects, and we have often been asked to serve woodworkers. We promise to do so to the best of our ability ... *try us today!*

## MAKING FAMILY HEIRLOOMS

**What could be more exciting and rewarding than creating your own family heirlooms? Classic pieces of furniture – beautifully hand-made and designed with timeless elegance – that will be treasured and admired not only today, but for generations to come.**

Now, Jack Hill – one of Britain's best-known woodworking craftsmen – brings together 23 practical projects for you to tackle yourself, ranging from a *Doll's House* and a *Rocking Horse* to a *Welsh Dresser*, a *Dining Table*, a *Four-poster Bed*, and a *Long Case Clock*.

Each project is illustrated, with step-by-step procedures using traditional techniques and materials to preserve the standards of the past.

MAKING FAMILY HEIRLOOMS

Jack Hill

*23 Classic Projects for the Home Woodworker*

Published at £12.95

YOURS FOR JUST 95P +p&p*

when you join the Craftsman Book Society

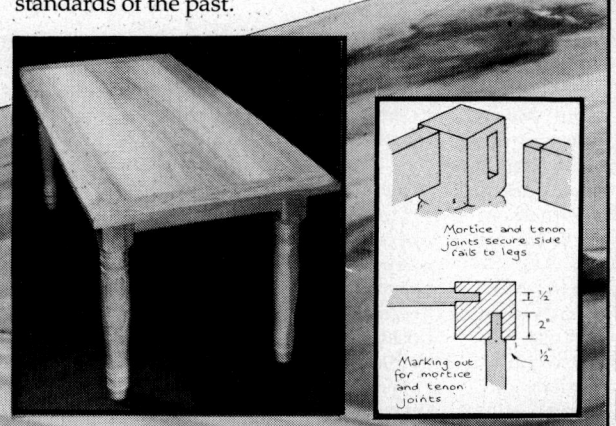

Mortice and tenon joints secure side rails to legs

Marking out for mortice and tenon joints

ESTABLISHED 1937     Readers Union, Brunel House, Newton Abbot, Devon. Reg. in England No. 843946

# At home in the business

**Andy Varah is one of Britain's best-established modern designer-craftsmen. Peter Collenette went to see him**

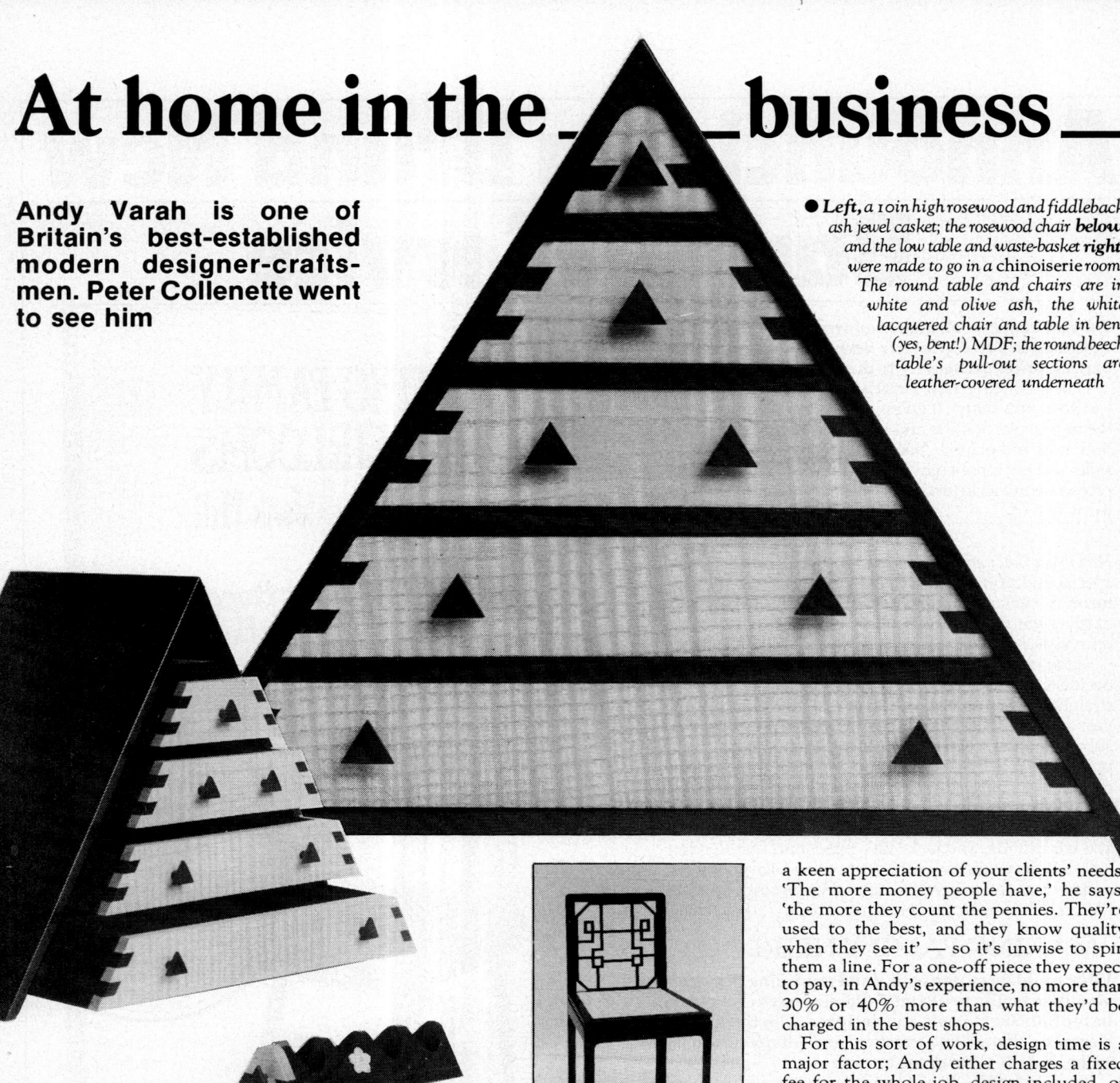

● *Left, a 10in high rosewood and fiddleback ash jewel casket; the rosewood chair below, and the low table and waste-basket right, were made to go in a chinoiserie room. The round table and chairs are in white and olive ash, the white lacquered chair and table in bent (yes, bent!) MDF; the round beech table's pull-out sections are leather-covered underneath*

V isiting Andy Varah is a pleasant experience. Especially so when the sun is shining over the Warwickshire fields as you stroll across from his ancient red-brick home, past the lawn and the summer flowers, to his equally picturesque yet very large workshop — and survey the horde of machinery which includes a Wadkin ripsaw, bandsaw, planer-thicknesser, spindle-moulder, chisel-mortiser and pad-sander, a Multico thicknesser, a Shopmate crosscut saw and even a Dominion single-end tenoner. Not to mention the dust extraction.

Chatting with him is pleasant, too; and not only pleasant, but instructive. For it soon becomes clear that Andy's relaxed approach, like his attractive, ordered and well-equipped set-up, is a sign of absolute professionalism. Indeed, his affable demeanor is almost a tool of the trade. He

agrees that the contemporary designer-craftsman must treat public relations as an essential skill. Success in this business, he asserts, requires the ability to mix with people.

'My workshop is only one of a very few in England designing and making one-off items of furniture,' he wrote in May's *Woodworker*. His clients, almost by definition, want something special. Discovering and reflecting their needs means very close involvement with them and their life-styles — 'You become almost one of the family,' says Andy. And he notes, unexpectedly, that tact is often very necessary to overcome the client's own embarrassment at explaining what can be a very personal commission; this, he finds, can be more of an obstacle than any diffidence on the part of the maker.

You don't reach Andy's position without

a keen appreciation of your clients' needs. 'The more money people have,' he says, 'the more they count the pennies. They're used to the best, and they know quality when they see it' — so it's unwise to spin them a line. For a one-off piece they expect to pay, in Andy's experience, no more than 30% or 40% more than what they'd be charged in the best shops.

For this sort of work, design time is a major factor; Andy either charges a fixed fee for the whole job, design included, or charges for design by the hour and agrees the total price later. At the other end of the process, he is unequivocal about the after-sales service he must and does offer. If anything is amiss on a Varah piece, no matter how long ago it left the workshop, a phone-call will summon Andy to the spot within hours.

H e trained at Shoreditch College in London, then spent two years teaching in London and a further two teaching in central Africa. He stayed in Africa for seven more years to manage a furniture factory before returning home and buying his present place near Rugby.

During his four years there as a one-man operation, he worked till 10pm seven days a week. Although he now employs four people, the seven-day week remains — but he admits to working fewer hours. He can boast six months' orders, which is the level he likes and maintains.

Asked how he gets the business, he answers in the same way as most other top-notch craftspeople: 'Word of mouth'. But

such mouths! . . . His furniture goes to Los Angeles, Saudi Arabia, Greece; clients include David Puttnam the cinema grandee. Naturally, installation often requires that craftsmen go too, and on big jobs he often becomes a jet commuter. He is pleased that his young staff get this unique chance to widen their outlooks, but he has refused offers to set up abroad. A full-scale operation and semi-residence in Jeddah hold fewer charms than England, home and beauty: 'I don't like money that much.'

The workshop tackles everything except upholstery, and Andy declares himself always willing to try something new. Passing through when I called were some very unusual Egyptian-style stools in black lacquer; their gilded lotus-leaf ornaments, in fibreglass where the Regency craftsmen would have used bronze, were all made in the shop. Their destination, Athens, dictated the use of solid timber for their startling up-swept curves; laminates, explained Andy, could have left the glue-lines proud on shrinking.

Resourcefulness is everything. Andy's hand-operated Interwood press bears a simple modification which must add noughts to its practical value. The problem was that special platens for heating were extras which cost a four-figure sum — yet the measly two pressings it could tackle in a day, allowing for setting time, were causing traffic-jams on big veneering jobs. So Andy bought some greenhouse cable (it comes in 80ft lengths), some MDF, some tinfoil and some aluminium sheet. Back and forth across the MDF he routed a continuous half-round groove, curving it through 180° for each return and allowing 1½in between the parallel straight stretches. He lined the groove with tinfoil, laid the cable in it, and screwed the aluminium sheet on top to cover the MDF completely. Now he can do a pressing every 15 minutes. (The shop-made platens take 15 minutes to heat up for the day's work, but only five minutes to re-heat after each subsequent switching-on.)

Andy has made a definite decision not to expand the business further, considering that he's reached a level at which he can prosper and gain satisfaction. Nevertheless, because the profession of designer-craftsman is small yet much aspired to, his survival and success have already and inevitably given him the status of mentor to a second generation.

Luckily, he likes having young blood around. He frequently employs students straight from college (finding that he can fill all his vacancies, like his order book, by word of mouth). A very high proportion have gone on to establish successful businesses in their own right — although he is encouraged to see more than one of his current employees going so far as to buy a house locally!

He makes it clear from the start that none of his staff need be shy of leaving when they feel it's time to move on to the next step, and he does this so that they feel free to ask questions and acquire as much knowledge as they can. He points out clear areas in which students can benefit from a spell in a workshop like his before setting up on their own: notably sensible buying.

On the machinery side, his recommendation is to buy second-hand — but to make sure the equipment is of cast steel construction, and then to pay for as much re-conditioning as you can afford. Always ask for help, he pleads; and that goes for timber too. He has seen too many young craftspeople fobbed off with parcels which include a treacherous mixture of air- and kiln-dried boards, or only crown boards from near the outside of the log, or wasteful sizes which the merchant finds hard to sell.

Without a doubt, businesses such as Andy's form a unique source of knowledge and experience on the craft side of the furniture trade. An hour or two with him provides proof that it's not easy — but also gives a clue to the professional attitude which can make it all happen. ∎

● Andrew Varah Ltd, Little Walton, Pailton, Rugby, Warwickshire CV23 0QL, tel. (0788) 833000.

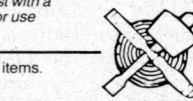

654

# The wages of wood

**What do professional woodworkers get paid? We asked Paul Greer to find out**

Y ou'd think it were a simple enough question . . . but it's not. And the first problem is that very few people who work wood for a living are even prepared to offer an estimate of wage levels.

Perhaps the main reason for their reticence is that many woodworkers are either completely independent or employed in small firms, where wage rates may well not be governed by any union agreement or parent body. Besides, some jobs are limited in scope and performed within large companies, so that organisational rather than nationally agreed levels hold sway — although this does not mean that the workers concerned are likely to be the losers; in fact, larger companies are often able to pay craftsmen more than many smaller concerns.

But sheer size is only one factor. The trade as a whole has recently seen considerable changes in the apprenticeship system, certain jobs being given over to machines and the worker becoming an 'operative' rather than a craftsman. This makes for shorter training and lowers the chance that an individual will remain in one type of work for a long time. Both results seem to have had a depressant effect on wages.

In fact, as many woodworkers will have exclaimed by now, this is not the trade to enter if money is your primary objective. Qualified craftsmen who can do overtime are often able to top up their earnings quite handsomely — but even they are on a comparatively modest basic wage; and, because the promotion structure is usually only a shallow pyramid, they are unlikely to jump up to much higher scales.

E nough of general impressions. Let's look at some figures.

In June this year the National Joint Council for the Building Industry amended the industry's wage guarantees for carpenters, joiners, bench joiners and wood machinists. The basic rate for a 'craft operative' is now £93.01½ (and for a labourer £79.36½). The respective guaranteed minimum bonuses are £14.82 and £12.48. These rates assume a 39-hour week — but it's not uncommon for a qualified joiner working overtime to reach a weekly pre-tax pay of £140.50; a top joiner may reach £200.

If you start as a trainee, weekly earnings increase at six-monthly intervals from £43.29 to £87.16½, with a guaranteed bonus of £13.84½ at the top end. The Youth Training Scheme has supplanted the first year of most formal apprenticeships; as YTS trainees, young people can expect to get £26.25 a week plus allowances for travel and equipment.

Shopfitters' rates are sometimes agreed at £2.50/2.60 an hour, and in other cases vary with the employer. The small size of many firms plays its part here — as with shuttering and formwork, where employers are often sub-contractors whose rates depend on the amount they can afford to charge main contractors.

Most timber used in Britain is imported, so that the nation contains relatively few plants for basic processing. The sawmills that do exist, however, are in general sizeable, and the rates they pay are set by the Timber Trade Federation. Again for a 39-hour week, hourly pay is currently £2.62½ for a qualified machinist and £2.29½ for others (labourers). Machinists are paid 50, 70 and 90% of their full rate during the successive years of their apprenticeships.

Also vital to the timber trade are saw doctors — so vital, in fact, that they have traditionally been paid more than machinists. Interestingly, those who service wide bandsaws earn rather less (£110-130) than those whose patients are circular saws (up to £200).

F urniture employers, or at least the major ones, are governed by the National Agreement, annually updated every year since 1946 by the British Furniture Trade Joint Industrial Council. Again, small firms stray considerably from this norm. Qualified adults — journeymen and journeywomen — currently receive £102.75 for a 39-hour week. Apprentices start at 47½%

of this rate, with increases to 50, 60½, 75 and 90%. (The rate for packers is £90.02 and for labourers £87.34.)

Most really big boats, including yachts, are built abroad, but Britain does a healthy trade in vessels up to about 60-70ft long. Skilled boatbuilders — unless they own or are otherwise heavily committed to a single firm — often travel in pursuit of available jobs. Success in this line of work depends largely on reputation, and respected craftsmen are likely to receive what they're worth. That, however, is unlikely to exceed £150 a week, and may well be less. Qualifications are not obligatory, although most boatbuilders are qualified joiners.

Musical-instrument making offers fewer opportunities than you might think. A great deal of competition comes from Japan and the USA, both of which produce large numbers of low-to-medium-priced instruments suitable for the beginner and intermediate player. Britain tends to specialise in good (and consequently expensive) instruments for the good amateur or the professional, and each firm usually confines itself to one instrument or at most a narrow range. By the same token, however, skilled craftspeople can earn £9-10,000 a year.

● *Not a grindstone for your nose, but it might as well have been; this US-made self-feed saw of 1903 is hand-and-foot-powered!*

If these rates don't inspire you, you might well consider joining the armed forces. But don't expect too much. You can be trained as a woodworker in the Army and RAF, though not the Navy. The Army pay rate, for a seven-day week, varies according to whether the recruit signs on for three, six or nine years. The sums involved are £12.87, £13.40 and £13.70 per day respectively.

Lastly, there's always teaching. Many teachers of woodwork have professional craft experience, especially those in colleges of further education and specialist craft and building colleges. The salaries are standardised nationally, with an extra allowance for London-based staff, and they are augmented by set amounts corresponding to 'points' awarded in recognition of qualifications or service. The basic

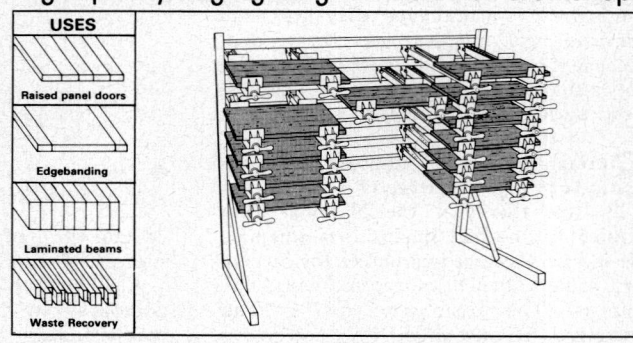

# The wages of wood

teacher's rate therefore ranges from £5442 to £8556 annually, and the lecturer's from £5910 to £10,512. Earnings above these depend on promotion.

So — don't go into it for the money. There are only three main provisos to a picture which is not, in general, encouraging.

Firstly, supervisory and managerial posts in industry tend to carry rates very different from those paid to craftsmen.

Secondly, a skill is a skill, and you can always use it to earn money in your spare time.

And thirdly, do remember that this survey is only a general guide; the firm round the corner may be paying more (or quite possibly less) than the amounts mentioned here. ∎

## Useful addresses

**British Wood Turners Association,** 89 London Rd, Enfield, Middx, 01-366 8683
**Building Industry Careers Service,** 82 New Cavendish St, London W1M 8AD, 01-580 2553
**Council for Small Industries in Rural Areas,** 141 Castle St, Salisbury, Wilts SP1 3TP, (0722) 336255
**Master Carvers' Association,** Stanhope Lodge, Arundel Rd, Clapham, Worthing, Sussex BN13 3UA, (0903) 64207
**National Association of Shopfitters,** 411 Limpsfield Rd, Warlingham, Surrey CR3 9HA, (08832) 4961
**Timber Trade Federation,** 47 Whitcomb St, London WC2H 7DL, 01-839 1891

## Craftsman's contract

Standard wage agreements and across-the-board settlements are all very well, **writes Aidan Walker,** but for many highly skilled woodworkers they are irrelevant. A huge number of us experience the mixed blessings of an employment practice widespread in all forms of woodwork — the sub-contract.

From the worker's point of view, there is little to recommend this relationship with those who are, in all but name (and some far more important things), your employers. Skilled people will often be working as sub-contractors for a governor who, because of an unpredictable workload and low profit-margins in a highly labour- and capital-intensive operation, just cannot afford to guarantee the sick-pay, the holidays, or even the job itself. Here are some extracts from a fairly typical set of terms and conditions for the engagement of sub-contractors in a high-quality joinery and cabinetmaking firm:

❛ *The sub-contractor will . . . afford services involving the execution of operations previously specified and agreed between the parties for the benefit of the contractor. The contract so made is intended to be . . . for services, and not give rise to the relationship of master and servant between the contractor and sub-contractor. In particular the sub-contractor understands that the contractor has no liability for sickness, holiday or redundancy pay.* ❜

❛ *At the convenience of the contractor . . . the sub-contractor may avail himself of certain machinery and workspace on the premises of the contractor. In such event the sub-contractor will be deemed a licensee at will in respect of the use of such machinery and space, such license terminable without notice by the contractor.* ❜

❛ *The sub-contractor is responsible for his own safety, whether working at the contractor's premises or other premises as directed by the contractor. The sub-contractor is responsible for damage by his negligence to the works, the contractor's goods, machinery or premises. In relation to the above the sub-contractor would be well advised to take out adequate insurance.* ❜

It's not as bad as it sounds, obviously; even Mr Gradgrind himself would stop short of charging you for a sawblade which you'd bent in the process of cutting off your hand. The point is that your responsibilities to the boss and the work are set out in black and white, while any return responsibilities from which you might benefit are entirely discretionary.

Most small employers prefer this way of using labour, not least because it minimises PAYE book-work. If you don't have a self-employed tax-exemption certificate, a basic 30% deduction will be made from your wages, re-assessed (and perhaps rebated) when you file your own tax return. Really, the only advantage of sub-contracting is that, as you are technically self-employed, you can claim expenses against tax.

In terms of your relationship to the employer/contractor, however, there is rarely any hint of self-determination. You are responsible for the standard of your work; demands have been known for mistakes to be rectified in unpaid time with timber bought from the hapless worker's own pocket.

All well and good, many will say; this is the traditional system, and it ensures careful and conscientious work. What is worrying about it, however, is precisely that it does rely on the skilled person's conscience. Anyone who wants to be a top-class woodworker will have a desire to do the best possible job — a motivation and commitment on which the employer/con-

tractor absolutely relies, and perforce must demand. The practical reality of a small shop (rather than a building site), where even the apprentice's labour is vital to production, is that the job is master. You'll be bawled out (at least) for a mistake that costs time and money, asked to work extra hours and even weekends to get a job out on time, and told to start at the same time as everyone else. It's even quite usual to be offered no overtime rate for your evening or weekend work.

Many such outfits have a friendly atmosphere in which you may be working alongside a boss who puts in more hours — and takes home more worries — than you do. It's difficult to ask, in this situation, for what you know you're worth; no one wants to be seen as unwilling, lazy and greedy. If you don't stand up for yourself, however, no one else will do it for you. The employer/employee relationship gives both parties certain safeguards against exploitation either way — while the one of contractor/sub-contractor, relying equally heavily on the 'right attitude' to the work, specifically excludes the pluses of paternalism and intrinsically includes the minuses. It doesn't mean you won't get a bonus at Christmas, or when the firm is doing well (many governors realise the personal and managerial importance of 'looking after' the people who work for them); but if, say, you twist your ankle getting timber from a high rack and can't work — that's it. Your money stops from that moment.

The other harsh reality, of course, is that if you get the chance of a nice job in a small workshop, producing the work you want to do, this way of selling your labour is unlikely to put you off. Nor, indeed, should it. But just be warned; take out your own medical, accident and long-term life insurances. You can always claim them against tax! ∎

# Guild notes

● *'I certify that these woodcarvings are the work of* **Eric Ingham**', *writes Christine Heatley of Lytham St Annes. Eric sent this picture as part of his application for membership – every applicant sends photographic evidence of craftsmanship. We need some carving on the Guild stand at the Show in October – any offers?*

## Show update

There's still some space available at the London Show in October for members who want to take the opportunity to display their work on their very own stand. One or two small pieces, please; send me some photos for appraisal.

## Local rep(etition)

If you keep meaning to write to the Guild rep in your area but haven't got round to it yet, you can pick up the phone instead. The general consensus is that numbers should be published; I didn't want to do this at first, for the reps' sakes, but most of them would like to be more easily available. There are still some who would prefer you to make initial contact by letter, which is why this isn't a complete list.

**Dumfries** Peter St D Boddy (038784) 640
**Norfolk** Steven Hurrell (0953) 850088
**Herefordshire** Paul Smith (0586) 611786
**Bedfordshire** John Greenwell (0525) 732689
**Middlesex** Mike Cripps (71) 75070
**Wiltshire** David Ellis (0666) 840888
**Essex** Doug Woolgar (04024) 56661
**Kent** Sevenoaks: Bob Holman (0732) 450408; Herne Bay: Roy Sutton (0227) 272136
**East Sussex** C. J. Allen (0424) 752566
**Birmingham** Bill Ferguson 021-427 4571
**Cornwall** Mr Stoddern (0208) 77649.

## Local rep(artee)

Note this time, date and place: 4.30pm, Alexandra Pavilion, north London, Saturday 26 October. As many local reps as we can gather together, and as many Guild members as possible, will be at the Woodworker/Guild stand at the Show; everyone gets the chance to meet everyone else, and put faces to names. Be there!

## Teaching opportunity

The Carlton Centre, a community centre in north London, has a vacancy for a part-time woodwork teacher from September. The hours are 7-9.30, one or perhaps two evenings a week; the class is fairly basic, and involves introducing wood and its ways to people who are completely new to it.

Technical qualifications are not as important as a love for woodwork, a liking for people, endless patience, and good communication skills. The money is quite good! If you think you are the right person, get in touch with **Jenny Watts** or **Norma Vince** at the Carlton Centre, Granville Rd, London NW6, tel. 01-624 5996.

## Teaching for the Guild

The popularity of **Ian Hosker's** french-polishing course in Cheshire emphasises what is obvious to many northern members with a thirst for information: we need more courses in the north and the Midlands. Basic woodworking skills, advanced cabinetmaking techniques, woodcarving, chair-caning, picture-framing, routing . . . the list is endless, and the requests for more continue to flood in. If you would like to teach for the Guild (and you think your qualifications and experience befit you for such a prestigious task!) please write to me, telling me of your experience, specialities and preferences.

## Design Focus . . .

. . . is the name of **Jane** and **Rob Stuart's** retail craft business in Chichester. They include in their high-quality range pieces by Guy Taplin (WW/June), Bert Marsh (WW/July) and other well-reputed woodworkers, and are looking for more people to supply them with first-class items. If you are interested in selling through such an outlet, get in touch with them at 1/15 St Peters Market, West St, Chichester, tel. (0243) 775495.

## Material benefit

Weston-super-Mare is a difficult place, apparently, for the supply of craft materials such as finishes and polishes, ceramic tiles, clock parts, glass liners and pepper-mill mechanisms. **Eddie Weston** is doing his best to solve the problem by opening a retail shop in Weston to supply exactly these things to frustrated craftspeople; he would be pleased to hear from any manufacturers or wholesalers who could supply him with such accessories for trade. Please contact him at 2A Swiss Rd, Weston-super-Mare, Avon BS23 3AU.

## COURSE CORNER

● **Please note:** our tutors teach these courses for the Guild; they are set up by the Guild, and administered by it. You will only delay your booking if you write direct to the tutors via the office. Cheques should be made payable to the **Guild of Woodworkers.**

## Hand veneering — Bob Grant

14 September, St Augustine's of Canterbury School Oxford, 9.30-5, £30+VAT. After his very successful advanced-decorative-techniques day in July, Bob is steering enthusiasts into the fascinating world of traditional hand veneering. You will be laying a panel with a veneer, crossbanding it and putting a balancer on the back; **Peter Sarac**, a local harpsichord maker, will be adding his expert advice to Bob's. Bring a veneer hammer if you have one.

## French polishing — Charles Cliffe

10-11 October, Bexleyheath, 10-5, £35+VAT. The emphasis is on the fine traditional finish, including preparation, stains and staining, grain-filling, and using the cabinet-scraper; bodying up, spiriting off, acid and eggshell finishes, and a look at varnishes and lacquers. Bring your own small piece to work on.

## Furniture finishing and restoration — Ian Hosker

9-10 November, Chester, 10-5 both days, £40+VAT. A slightly different and wider emphasis marks the second course that Ian, a teacher and restorer, is running for us; this time he will be introducing repair and restoration techniques as well as dealing with stripping and re-finishing. French polish, staining and preparation; recognising, dealing with and applying other finishes; dealing with loose joints; repairing broken components; lifting, patching and replacing veneers; marquetry and inlay repairs; all these and more are subjects you will tackle under his expert guidance.

Materials will be supplied by Ian, but he stresses that you *must tell us your needs when you book*, so we can pass the details on to him and he will have the right stuff ready. Bring your own piece to work on — and your hand tools as well, if you possess such!

● *Charles Cliffe (left) explains his bottles and brews to* **Ron Kulka (centre)** *and* **Derek Page** *at the polishing course in June. Book now for October! Photo by* **Stanley Folb**

# MDF : The winners

**It was a gamble — and we didn't even know how many runners there would be, let alone their names, colours or riders. But the results have made us more than happy.**

When FIDOR (that's the Fibre Building Board Organisation) asked if we'd like to join them in running a design competition for medium density fibreboard — MDF to its friends — we were keen. It's a new material which, used rightly, has no equal; and we like to think we have a role to play in encouraging innovation and excellence among amateurs, professionals and students alike as we've done since 1901.

But we didn't know if you'd agree. So it gives us very great pleasure to report a total of about 50 entries; four absolutely worthy winners; and around 1000 enquiries to FIDOR — living proof of a healthy desire to try something new and judge it on its merits.

The judges were David Field, a lecturer at the Royal College of Art and celebrated designer-craftsman in his own right; Jack Moses, the deputy director of the Furniture Industry Research Association; Doug Patterson of Buckinghamshire College of Higher Education, High Wycombe; Peter Gill, FIDOR's MD; and your editor Peter Collenette.

The final selection was pleasingly unanimous and unequivocal. We were delighted, too, that it included a representative mixture of one professional, one woodworker from the academic world, one semi-professional and one amateur — all being picked entirely on the merits of their entries, rather than for an artificial 'balance'.

We looked for attractive and original use of MDF, naturally; but, most importantly, for sheer good design in terms of looks, practicality and ease of production. And we found all these things.

● *Left to right:* Peter Gill, MD of FIDOR, *Alan Fell (4th prize), Keith Sealey (1st prize), Bob Hemming (3rd prize), and* Woodworker *Editor Peter Collenette*

● **Keith Sealey** was the natural winner of the £250 first prize, plus as much national publicity as FIDOR and we can ensure. His **desk** was, by common consent, outstanding. Its legs, laminated from several thicknesses of MDF, use the material to overcome what in solid timber would be horrific problems of short grain — and they use the lamination as a visual feature. The hollow-box top incorporates inset compartments whose lids rise via neat radial grooves. The half-round edgings were made from MDF, laminated, turned and

● *The colour shot of Keith's desk clearly shows the striking legs and the drawer-front moulding.* **Above** *and* **left** *are views of the clean lines when everything is folded flat, and the leg and lid details*

**2nd**

● **Right:** *Michael claims some inspiration from the manta ray for the shape of his desk-and-chair corner unit; the triangular theme is picked up in the chair-seat and angled rails*

**3rd**

● *MDF's consistency of texture is an advantage for Bob Hemmings' decorative routing. His screen is at **left**, while **below** Alan Fell's TV/video cabinet combines a coloured motif with careful ergonomics.*

**4th**

split. Perhaps the ultimate refinement — sophisticated because it's so simple — is the straightforward recess in the left-hand drawer which actually holds a telephone!

Keith is a full-time furniture-maker who works at 33 High St, Lutterworth, Leics, tel. (045 55) 56403. He now finds himself doing mainly office commissions — and that includes free-standing pieces like the winning desk, which he made on spec.

● Second came **Michael Anderson** from the furniture department at Edinburgh College of Art. His cleverly triangular **corner desk and matching chair** are superbly neat and functional; they go together beautifully as a pair; and they display a first-class finish. In solid timber, the chair's flat legs would inevitably curve with changing humidity; not so in MDF. And, as Michael points out, the fact 'that the edge of MDF can be moulded and sanded to a finish and strength equalling the face' means that no edging is required 'whose joint line would always interfere with the eye as it looks across the surfaces. With the thickness needed for a 25mm-diameter round, even under a paint finish the edge could shrink or expand, splitting the paintwork and exposing the joint'.

● **Bob Hemming's screen,** which came in third, makes perfect maximum use of MDF's excellent machining qualities. The panels are decoratively routed, using a special jig, through slightly more than half the thickness on both sides, to produce a lattice which has a distinctly Oriental or north-African look; in any other material, the procedure would be likely to result in 'hairy' grooves and consequently a lot of arduous and impractical cleaning-up. The panels are jointed into their frames.

Bob is first and foremost a trumpet-player, but he makes pine furniture when he's not on the road.

● Fourthly, **Alan Fell**'s natural-finish **video cabinet,** with its decoration in coloured inks, was acclaimed as the work of a highly practical and resourceful designer. The positioning of the recorder above the screen makes for much easier access than usual, and the box-type structural columns neatly accommodate cassettes.

Cunning touches include the rotating of the rear supports through 90° to enable access for further storage; the doors which fold right back through 270° on home-made hinges; the echoing of the panel-moulding in the bottoms of the sides; the MDF handles; and the Arts and Crafts air of the finished piece. Our only doubts concerned the decoration.

As the judges said, 'He's identified a need and fulfilled it sensibly.' Just, you might say, like MDF itself.

● If you want to know more, FIDOR are at 1 Hanworth Rd, Feltham, Middx TW13 5AF, tel 01-751 6107, and they'll be happy to help. ■

662

# The student statement: 1

**It's crazy but it's crucial: it's foolish, but it's fun. Summer's arrived and the colleges are showing — so enrol here for the graduation ball!**

## SHREWSBURY COLLEGE

A furniture show is as revealing about the philosophy of a college's teaching as about the students themselves, **writes Aidan Walker**. A warm and enthusiastic atmosphere is immediately apparent at Shrewsbury; judging by the display, it generates hard work to the highest standards.

Shrewsbury College of Art and Technology includes the original school of art, founded in 1856. The furniture department is strongly tied to the art side of the teaching — yet the primary emphasis seems to be on craftsmanship, and originality of design is left to the individual. Shrewsbury's growing reputation is illustrated by the recent appointment of 20-year-old graduate David Weigh as cabinet-maker to the Queen at Windsor Castle.

The teaching is generally oriented to the needs of the individual craftsman designing and making in his or her own workshop, but employers try to pounce on those who

are looking for work. All the final-year students have something arranged. 'We get more requests than we can cope with,' says John Price, whose modest title of 'course tutor' disguises the fact that the courses are devised almost exclusively by him.

● *Darren Smith's iroko, walnut and ash flat-pack table design; the waisted top supports itself perfectly on the lean-to legs*

Preparation for the City and Guilds furniture-craft certificates is their basis, but they go much further than that. 'The student will be expected to use his own initiative,' says the prospectus, ' and develop an independence necessary for those wishing to become self-employed craftsman designers.'

One such is Fred Perry, a mature student who got into furniture via building carpentry. His massive avodire-veneered (on MDF) dining table with robinia frame and jarrah inlay was exhibited at the London International Furniture Show earlier in the year.

All the second-year students do a business project, which this year was a design for a low table based on flat frames — the kind of thing for which you'd use offcuts. The construction had to be knockdown to pack flat; the project also involves costing, estimating and marketing, producing a business analysis, and prototyping. Particularly impressive were two designs by Darren Smith which used their own weight for triangular support. Beautifully detailed and finished in mahogany inlaid with afrormosia, and iroko with walnut and ash, they are simple, elegant, easy to pack, easy to make, and easy on the eye — a first-class solution. Darren's ash and bird's-eye-maple drinks cabinet was a bit fussier, and the tambour lid needed some sorting out; I liked his TV/video cabinet in African mahogany and padauk far better, with its spare, slightly oriental look, geometrical-block door panels, and pivoting storage drawer. The sliding-pivot doors are a good idea for an unhindered TV screen, but again the size

● *John Ericsson's charming walnut writing desk, with pull-out tilting writing surface and fold-back top, was one of the few pieces that showed a touch of the Orient*

and proportion made the mechanism work rather too hard for easy use.

John Ericsson, an architect by training, had also produced a clever solution to the flat-pack problem; the underside of his low table had dovetail sockets into which the shaped ends of the laminated legs slid and locked. He hadn't got round to the finish. His small writing-desk had obviously taken a lot more time; the mechanism of the slide-and-tilt surface must have swallowed a good few hours. The legs turn out at the bottom, another faint hint at the oriental style that seems to have lost its erstwhile popularity amongst college students.

Desks abounded, it seemed. Nigel Bulkeley's curved-front mahogany design was a favourite, its graceful line unspoilt by catch or handle. His concealed catch under

● Smooth curves in mahogany by Nigel Bulkeley

the drawers was, unusually, both effective and simple. Ronnie Salisbury's utile and padauk creation was finely detailed, but failed to catch the elegance I think he was seeking; the curves of the end-frame members confused and overtaxed their polyhedron layout, and worked against the striking form of the main body.

Ash was almost everywhere, colour (apart from black or natural wood-tones) almost nowhere. The preponderance of ash, I discovered, was not unconnected with John Price's canny buying — he gets it for £4 a cu ft, but wouldn't say where! Especially noteworthy about the exhibition

● The block-panel doors of Darren Smith's padauk TV/video cabinet showed evidence of careful grain selection

overall was that it was non-selective: everything that was finished was displayed.

Shrewsbury's name in the world of craftsmanship is well-established, and work like this is bound to strengthen that reputation. John Price asserts that it is not producing, or attempting to produce, designers. But it's a pity that colleges must still fall into either the 'design' or 'craftsmanship' category. I'm no lover of punk furniture, but I would like to see a college of such obvious craft excellence going for more daring colours and shapes.

## LEICESTER POLYTECHNIC

The Poly is grim and grey on a wet afternoon — but the student show proved a riot of colour, form and texture, **writes Robert Payn.** I lost no time in talking to those involved.

Christine Haddon won the Young Designer of the Year award in 1984, and her professional approach left me unsurprised that she already had a job to go to. Her vanity screen, conceived as an alternative to the dressing-table, is imaginative and well-

made. It features lighting, mirrors, and storage accessible from both sides; the material is cherry — solid, and veneered on to chipboard. Fabric-covered panels, variable to match surrounding decor, should enhance its attractions for Christine's target market of hotels and cruise liners.

● The fabric on one side of Christine Haddon's screen can be chosen to suit the decor

● Christine's screen from the functional side. Note the lighting, the drawer-handles, and the foldaway stool which sits neatly in the circular cut-out

# The student statement: 1

● Angus McNabe just about to demonstrate the way two surfaces of his oak serving-table turn into one. But the mechanism still had teething problems

Jeremy Heeler, Kevin Rees and Richard Addison had something in common — they'd all made laminated chairs. Jeremy and Kevin had used ash; though comfortable, their chairs looked rather severe in their natural finish. Richard's elm dining-chair, in contrast, is a pleasant honey shade and much more inviting. He has already taken some orders and is seeking a manufacturer.

Another interesting piece was Angus McNabe's oak serving-table. It functions as a compact unit with top and lower shelf; in addition, however (and in theory), a lever re-positions both top and shelf to make a single large surface. Unfortunately, Angus wasn't around, and I couldn't make it work convincingly. I think this was because the metal brackets were flimsy — they allowed too much movement in all the wrong directions; consequently the locking pins did not locate with the requisite clunk. Still, it's a good idea, and no doubt Angus will work on until it's perfected.

Angus' companion pieces are a dining-table and chairs, which echo the wide

chamfers and the shapes of the rails. Despite one or two shrinkage problems, the table looks absolutely right in oak, and I found its design impressive.

I'd have liked to have seen more imaginative shapes in the show — and more varied timbers: it's a shame not to explore fully the possibilities of colour and texture. Nonetheless, I enjoyed my visit.
● Robert Payn is course director of the Newark School of Violin Making.

● Angus' dining-table and chair

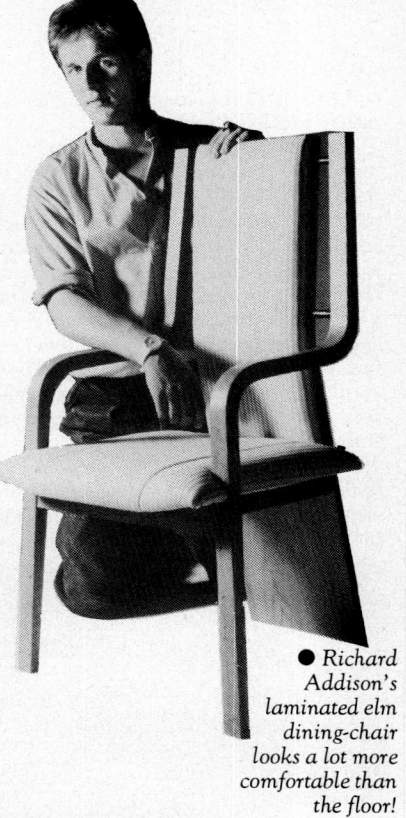

● Richard Addison's laminated elm dining-chair looks a lot more comfortable than the floor!

## BIRMINGHAM POLYTECHNIC

I have long suspected that reviewing an exhibition of students' work (particularly the final-year show — the culmination of so much toil) must be nearly as nerve-wracking for the reviewer as for the exhibitors themselves. And so it proved, **writes Keith Nurcombe.**

In the hurly-burly of the small wood-working shop, the headlong rush to stay ahead of the bills and to catch up with the schedule that's at least two weeks behindhand, it is possible to lose sight of the fact that furniture can actually be designed. I know I'm not the only one who designs as he works. When I once presented a new employee with a dimensioned drawing he expressed surprise, saying that he was normally expected to work from a rough sketch on the back of a fag-packet. So many fine woodworkers are hidden away in their jobbing shops, working from experience and with only instinct as their guide.

Clearly, though, someone intending to design furniture for someone else to produce cannot work like that. Marketability, and indeed the very economics of production must be to the fore in the designer's mind, quite apart from the shape and structure. And perhaps it was this very intensity — the knowledge that every item, successful or not, was the result of a deliberate effort to be that bit cleverer or different — that filled me with trepidation as I arrived at Birmingham Poly.

So it was with considerable relief that I found some items of real value.

After an initial cast around, it was clear

that the hi-fi cabinet in ash was the star item. Delightfully sized and well wrought by C. L. Robinson, it was an excellent illustration of the over-riding importance of proportion. Elegant enough to grace any room, its clean, simple styling needed no gimmicks to show its designer's talent.

The standard of construction of all of the exhibits was commendably high, but several failed to reach that essential balance

criticised, both in this magazine and elsewhere, for nurturing a strong tendency to irrelevance, if not frivolity. I am delighted to report that there was no evidence of either on display here. However, I was disappointed to note the total absence of any vernacular thread running through the displays. This was particularly noticeable in the joint project for furnishing Upton-on-Severn church,

which I found — sadly — almost without merit. Much modern church architecture (at least at parish level) strikes me as particularly poverty-stricken from both an artistic and a constructional viewpoint; and this is in a country which has a history of church architecture stretching back nearly 1000 years.

Asking a student to design furniture without first showing him what has been achieved since, at the latest, AD1600 is rather like asking a music student to write a symphony after teaching him how to play the penny whistle. Most good music is composed following a thorough classical training. The designer, like the composer, needs to know how to plagiarise. Life is too short, and the sum of knowledge too great, for each generation to start from scratch. New materials, new finishes, new techniques, new fastenings will all influence the designer, but his understanding of structures and techniques must surely be underpinned by a knowledge of the history of his art. ■

**College shows, unfortunately, aren't arranged around *Woodworker's* deadlines. Watch this space next month for The student statement: 2!**

● *The ash hi-fi cabinet by C.L. Robinson demonstrates a fine sense of poportion*

of proportion. Two that did, but which I thought wanting in other respects were a nicely constructed tea-trolley by D. T. Morrison and the beautifully styled magenta chair by Sue Connolly. Both were made from sycamore; the trolley with well-made keyed mitres to all of its many right-angled joints, and the chair with deliberately ostentatious finger-joints and through-tenons. I found the square, angular styling of the trolley inappropriate for the material, or should it be *vice versa*. Each time I came back to it I couldn't help feeling that the design would have worked better in powder-coated square steel section.

The magenta chair, by contrast, was delightfully appropriate for the material. It was clearly made by a budding craftswoman/artist of considerable talent — but I concluded, reluctantly, that it was structurally unsound. I could see her quandary: to brace the legs would have destroyed that simplicity which is almost achieved. Alas, the result will not do. Chairs are for people to sit upon.

An enigmatic drinks trolley by Hugh Parsons is also worthy of mention: a striking piece featuring cabinet doors on each side divided diagonally, and with the cabinet partitioned by a mirror. I have little doubt that both of these features would soon cure an addiction to drink. Nevertheless, it was a nicely worked and finished demonstration item.

The colleges have recently been

● *The magenta chair in sycamore by Sue Connolly is much stronger visually than structurally. Can a designer renounce rigidity for the sake of The Look?*

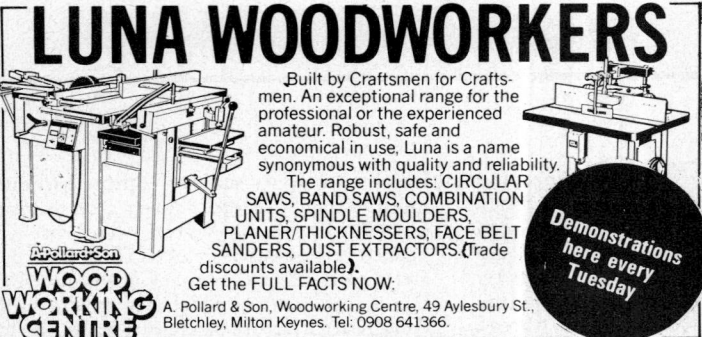

# The bowl of the tree

Fig.1

**Ray Key's new book *Wood-turning and Design* will spread his already high reputation even further. We present some of his thoughts on bowls**

Individual bowl-making gives the turner one of the greatest areas of freedom to express individual thoughts on shape and design, with the chance to use timbers of all sorts and sizes. From decayed wood that wouldn't make a good fire, to small, wet logs that are usually burnt, the opportunities are infinite, limited only by the maker's imagination and ability.

I intend to emphasise here the question of aesthetic form and the making of increasingly difficult objects, incorporating nature's beauty. Several of the principles that apply to making bowls of function are disregarded, particularly the base-to-diameter ratio. My own objectives when working in this area are to produce items that make a strong visual impact. This approach usually produces objects which are not functional, apart from giving great pleasure when touched or visually admired, but which display a strong artistic content. This is an area which always provokes heated discussions amongst craftsmen. The

Fig.2

● *Choose your own figure: these two elegant bowls were turned from the cherry log at* **top**, *marked out and cut in two different ways as shown*

majority seem to feel the craft objects ought to be functional, yet where some of the leading exponents of crafts have chosen to produce art objects, the result has often been a far greater acceptance and credence from the public. This has given many craftsmen confidence to try new ideas so that the overall standard of the craft is raised, although many objects of extremely poor quality are still being produced in all craft areas. My concern is for the craft of woodturning to be accorded a much higher level of appreciation, and I feel the increased emphasis on artistry will help to achieve this.

The first move in creating a bowl that has aesthetic appeal is normally to turn something much thinner than would be practical for use, and frequently with a small foot or base. The combination of these two factors starts to give life to any bowl form. If the choice of wood and the way it is cut are also taken into account, and the shape is designed to complement these factors, a pleasing decorative bowl should be achieved.

The structure of the wood and the size of bowl have a considerable influence on the shape and design. If you are dealing with small bowls, say up to 203mm (8in) maximum diameter and around 102mm (4in) deep, really bold-grained timbers with wide growth-rings can overpower the shape, for the size doesn't allow enough room for the

# The bowl of the tree

**Fig. 3** *A look inside the two bowls from the previous page shows even more graphically how you can vary the figure*

**Fig. 4** *Two bowls cut at different angles from an olive ash tree; again, varying patterns result*

**Fig. 5** *Inside story on the two bowls in fig. 4*

**Fig. 6** *Side-grain on the left-hand bowl from fig. 3*

feature to show to advantage. The size of log and the place where the timber is cut from within it make a tremendous difference in visual impact with bowls of similar shapes.

The bowls in figs 10-13 show exactly this, but the best economic use of the material has not been made. They have been made purposely in this instance to achieve the effect shown. The bowls in fig. 10 are made from a small cherry log some 165-178mm (6½-7in) in diameter. Cut in this way, it will yield two bowls 152(6in)x76mm(3in) deep with the pith core boxed out, which is always preferable. Users of PEG will get away with leaving it in. The end visual effect of fig. 6 is less attractive to my eyes than the one achieved in fig. 11. The problem here is that there is far greater wastage. Three bowls will be possible, but they become much smaller; 114(4½in)x63mm (2½in) deep is about the best you can hope for. But the visual effect is more pleasing, as the grain figure gives an 'ovalling' effect because of the cut through the growth rings.

You will note in both bowls that the sapwood has been incorporated. In a timber such as cherry it has little distinction in colour from the heartwood. This is true of most light-coloured timbers. In dark woods the contrast is much more pronounced, which can give added interest, and particularly in exotics it can be very dramatic. Logs of the size used here will not work with a great many timbers. In pine, for instance,

**Fig. 7** *The small bowl from fig. 3 is given its final shape on a large sanding drum. The curve is selected to follow the grain*

the sapwood could make up as much as 80-90% of the log. At the other end of the scale, oak would be equally unsuccessful, although 70% or more may be heartwood. Thoughts of using the sapwood here should be dismissed. Neither of these timbers are really turners' woods, especially for the type of items described. Also, if you intend to turn from seasoned timber, it would be a major achievement in itself to dry this type of wood without mass radial checking, even in our climate. Sapwood, by and large, is much softer than heartwood, and for this reason it is normally removed, as attacks by worm and decay are more likely. For this type of work it is no major problem. The

● *Heavy gloves mean fingers of a constant length!*

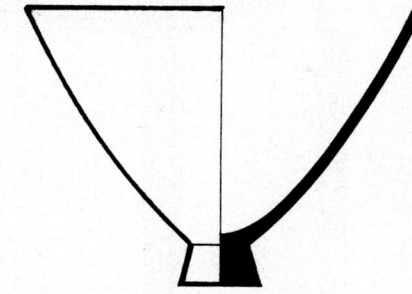

**Fig. 8** *A thin-walled bowl can have a small base . . .*

**Fig. 9** *. . . or a delicate foot*

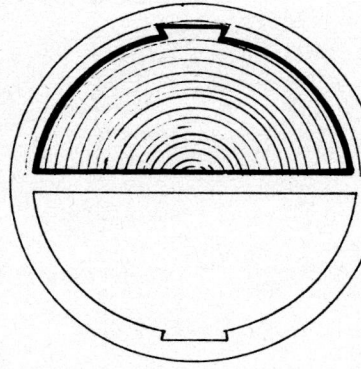

**Fig. 10** *Marking out bowls of maximum size (see also fig. 1)*

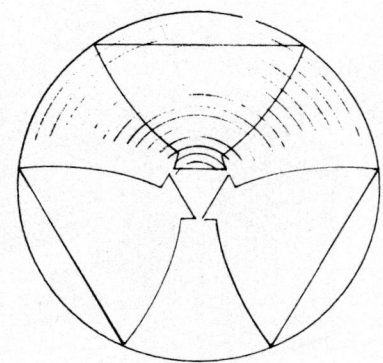

**Fig. 11** *More wastage here, but a more decorative result*

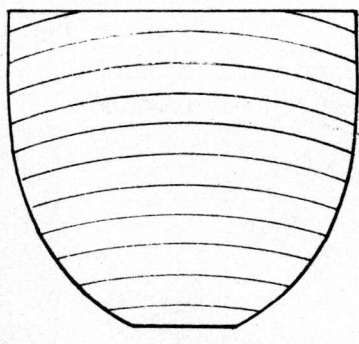

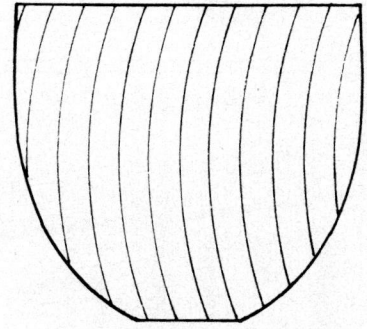

**Figs. 12 & 13** *Bowls from a large log: through-sawn (left) and quarter-sawn (right)*

sapwood in exotic timbers is often just as hard as the heartwood; even if it is softer, it is still normally harder than most northern-grown temperate hardwoods.

The bowls shown in figs 4 and 5 are made from a rippled olive ash tree some 610mm (24in) in diameter. The bowl in fig.4 was cut relative to the heart like the other one in fig. 7, but the effect is dramatically different. The size of the log results in an almost horizontal, tiered-layer effect of growth-rings, like a cut made through laminated veneers. The result is a constant reflection of the outside shape of ever-increasing and decreasing diameters, depending on the way you look at it. A totally different effect is created in fig. 13 — turned, as it were, in the quarter-sawn manner. The growth-rings give a laminated veneer effect but this time vertically. For me, this is a far less pleasing effect, but the rippled figure of the material is a saving grace.

Any item made from quarter-sawn timber will, in general, be much less prone to distortion, but it is less visually satisfying. There are a few exceptions, such as oak or plane, but bowls of this nature would destroy their attractive characteristics. Flat surfaces make best use of their ray-fleck figure. ■

● *Woodturning and Design* is published by Batsford at £10.95 hardback. We are grateful for permission to reproduce this extract.

# Authenticated excellence

## Chippendale designed the table; Vic Taylor examined and drew it. Now he explains it

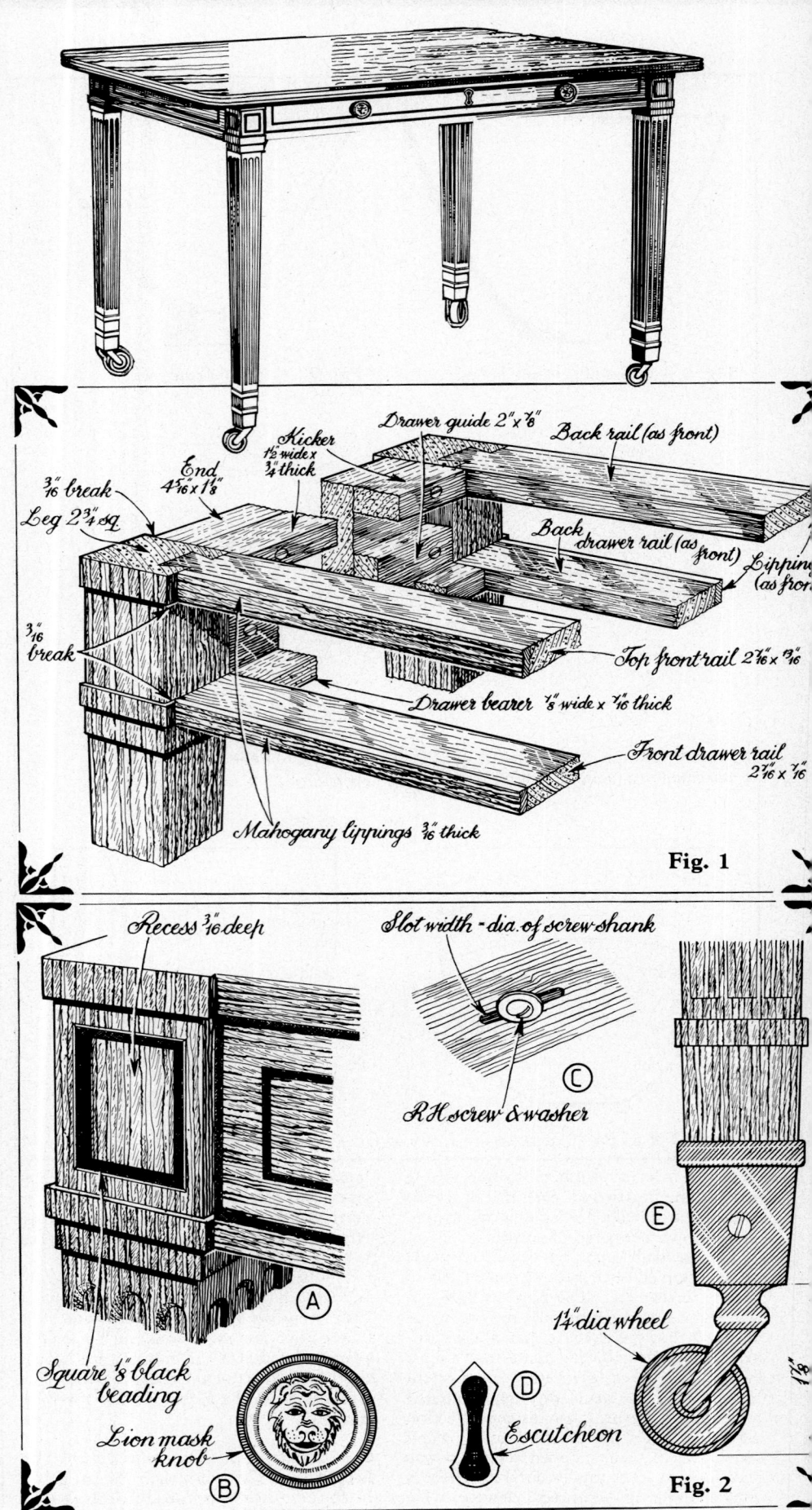

This table stands in the library at the great house of Stourhead, Wiltshire, and it could be used for writing, display or occasional purposes.

Stourhead is one of the few great houses with more or less complete accounts for the furnishings. To quote from the official handbook: 'Preserved in the Library are the bills Chippendale sent Colt Hoare for the period 1795 to 1820. Although an incomplete sequence, they show that he virtually refurnished the house as well as equipping the Library and Picture Gallery; the total payment recorded is over £3,500. After his father's death in 1779, Chippendale took over [his firm's] premises in St Martin's lane and continued in partnership with Thomas Haig until the latter retired in 1796. Haig died in 1803, by which time Chippendale's finances had become unsteady . . . Thanks in large measure to the loyalty of a few clients, such as Colt Hoare, Chippendale rebuilt the business and continued until his death in 1822 . . . The Library furniture is itemised in the accounts of 1804 and 1805.'

Our table has a mahogany top and legs. Unusually, the top is quite plain and bears no inlays or marquetry, its only decoration consisting of a triple-beaded edge (see detail, fig. 4). The frame and drawer-rails are in oak, the latter having mahogany lippings on the edges. To my mind, the drawer is too wide (40⅜in/1022mm) — even when empty, quite an effort is needed to span it and withdraw it. Further, the drawer-bottom is all in one piece without a central muntin. If I may make so bold as to criticise the late Mr Chippendale, I think it would have been more practical to have fitted twin drawers side-by-side.

The table was obviously intended to be free-standing because the back is a dummy replica of the front, exactly the same except that there is no lock and no escutcheon.

The drawer-frame construction is conventional, except that the kickers (which are softwood) are screwed and presumably glued to the ends. As far as I can see, the top is held down by screws driven up through the kickers. Whether this was original or a later addition I do not know — certainly, the woodscrews appear to be modern; but, in any event, it does not allow for any shrinkage of the top. This could be corrected by slot-screwing the screws in the kickers to allow for shrinkage in the width (C, fig. 2), and pocket-screwing along the top rails.

I have shown details of the brassware in fig. 2 at B, D and E; it's not likely that you will be able to get identical fittings, but at least you will have an idea of the kind of things to look for. ∎

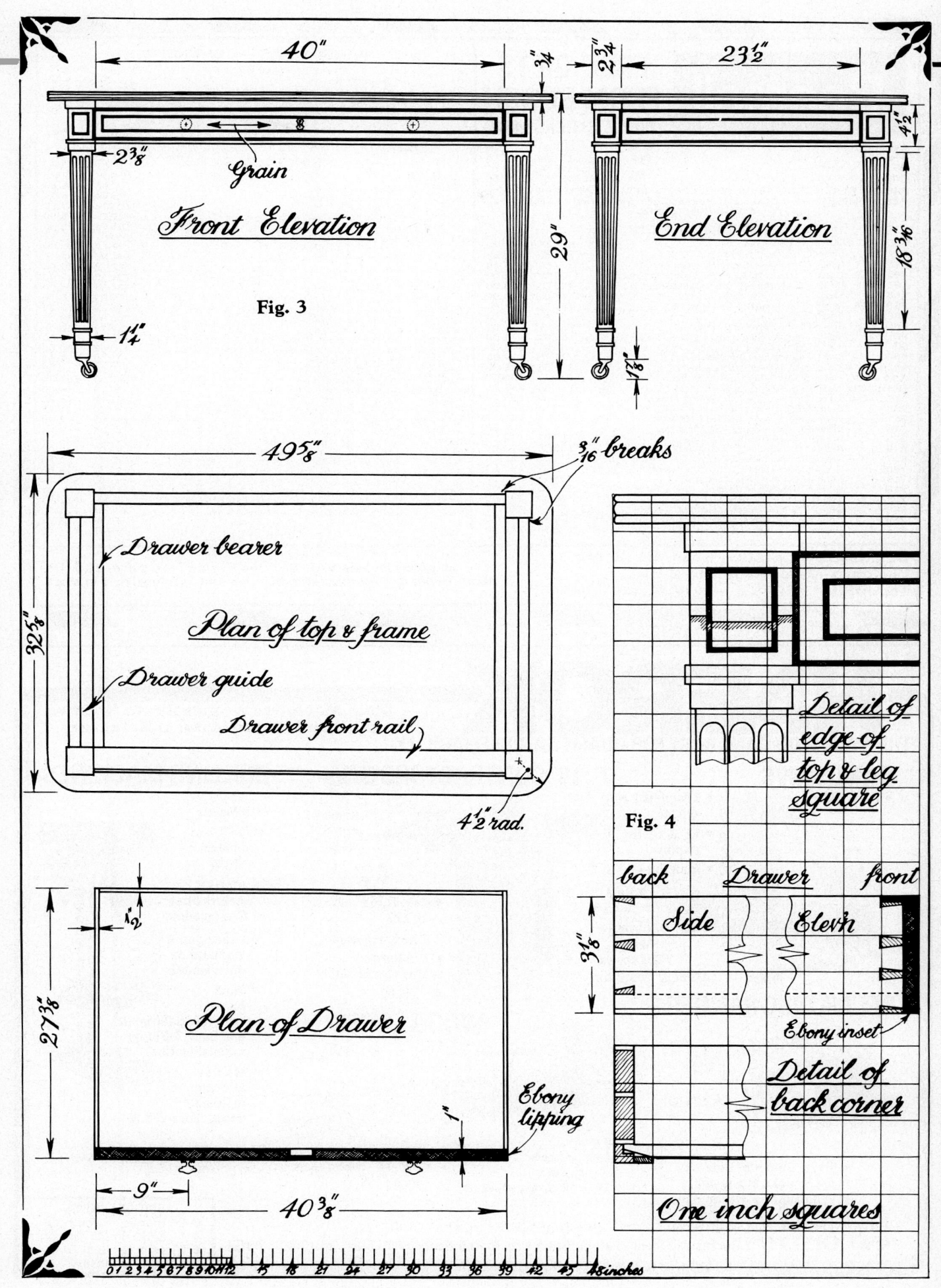

40"  3/4"  2 3/4"  23 1/2"

2 3/8"

Grain

8

Front Elevation

End Elevation

Fig. 3

29"

4 1/2"

18 3/16"

1 1/4"

1 7/8"

49 5/8"  3/16" breaks

Drawer bearer

Plan of top & frame

Drawer guide

Drawer front rail

32 5/8"

4 1/2" rad.

Detail of edge of top & leg square

Fig. 4

back  Drawer  front

Side  Elev'n

3 1/8"

Ebony inset

Detail of back corner

1 1/2"

27 3/8"

Plan of Drawer

1"

Ebony lipping

9"

40 3/8"

One inch squares

0 1 2 3 4 5 6 7 8 9 10 11 12  15  18  21  24  27  30  33  36  39  42  45  48 inches

# Buying timber wisely : 3

● *A lump of softwood encounters the power feed at Limehouse*

The experts are all right. They know just the best places to go; they recognise unerringly, under the dust of ages, the precise piece of wood they want. They know exactly what it is worth — to themselves, and to the chap who is selling it. In short, the experts can be left to look after themselves. By contrast, the rest of us poor punters are all too often left with a sense of inferiority, of ignorance, and of having been rooked.

But in honesty it must be admitted that the cause of our discomfiture is indeed ignorance — and that is a pity, for a great deal of help and information about wood and its uses is ready and waiting for anyone who cares to request it.

Among the many thousands of people in recent years who have set up businesses of their own, a number have seen a commercial future in becoming suppliers of specialist timbers, or (not quite the same thing) specialist suppliers of timber. If they weren't genuinely interested in their businesses they wouldn't be running them, and like most enthusiasts they are more than willing to share their passion. Talk to such people and a wealth of knowledge becomes available. So too, in my experience, does a fair deal and good service.

Typically untypical of suppliers who depend on cultivating small purchasers and keeping them happy is Limehouse Timber, of 5 Grenade Street, London E14 (01-987 6289). It is like many of its kind: the external appearance of the premises is unprepossessing, the stock rich in variety, and the welcome warm. The firm is actually an offshoot of an old-established ship's chandler and marine-supplies business: in step with the gradual departure of that trade, the timber yard has increased. Now it stands at about 4500sq ft of shed space, with another 4000sq ft of yard for the more robust stock. The business took its present form about three years ago, setting its sights on small trade workshops, amateurs and, not surprisingly, boatbuilders and finishers. While seeing opportunities in supplying out-of-the-run material, Limehouse boss Tim James sees his business as a bit more workaday than some of its competitors and adjusts its stocks accordingly. Brazilian mahogany, teak, iroko, and oak are held in quantity, and so is high-quality selected Russian pine in boards up to 10 or 11in wide. A limited and casual passing trade from the neighbourhood is met with some distinctly down-market softwood.

Currently about 60% of the business is supplying selected hardwoods to small cabinetmakers and design studios. This trade, says Tim James, has concentrated the firm's mind on getting exactly what these people want, and getting it to them when they want it. A further 20% is with builders and joiners who want high-quality stuff for special jobs, and the remainder is spread between woodturners, boatbuilders and home users. Vintage-car re-builders, shopfitters and schools feature among specific users.

Selling timber is one thing, but it has to be bought first. In addition to its staple lines Limehouse has recently been making considerable efforts to stock good American timber — maple, cherry, ash, oak. They've found that maple works up into, for example, hard-wearing and cheerfully light-coloured kitchen furniture, and comes at a price very competitive with that of Brazilian mahogany. But supplies are never constant or consistent: presently west Africa, once seemingly able to send us exactly what was wanted, is (in Limehouse's experience) unable to produce consistency of cross-sectional dimensions or lengths to satisfy the volume business. For the time being, however, Brazilian mahogany is scooping the pool with wide — up to 18 or 19in — boards 12-13ft long, in thicknesses of 1, 1¼ and 2in.

The current price list includes apple and hawthorn; laburnum and Indian laurel, ebony, mulberry, and plane; three kinds of rosewood and three of walnut, and much

more beside. The catalogue of veneers ranges from afrormosia to zebrano by way of beech, chestnut, mahogany, kingwood, satinwood and wenge, and is reinforced by many trays of inlays and bandings.

On the home-grown front, the company make a speciality of kiln-dried lime 3 and 4in thick; 'the ultimate carving wood'. They deal in oak, elm and sycamore, but point out to the uninitiated that, since English hardwood is not generally produced as square-edged boards, there can be a lot of expensive wastage in the unpredictable process of converting from the log-sawn state. 'A lot' can be up to 100% for yew and oak, compared with an accepted proportion of 25% in conversion generally.

Tim James is also willing to buy adventitiously, and takes in parcels of unusual material provided there is a responsible prospect of selling them again within a reasonable time. Recently a large quantity of yaka was imported by another firm for a special bank-fitting job: Limehouse took the surplus and found homes for it all. Luckily, changes in fashion are not major concerns at the retail end of the timber market.

When quantities required are small, selection and transport rapidly become the dominant factors in total costs. Because it can rely to some extent on delivery routes run by its parent, Limehouse can economically supply a surprisingly wide area although basically it is a London-and-home-counties company. A customer in Gateshead yearly takes three consignments of about £200

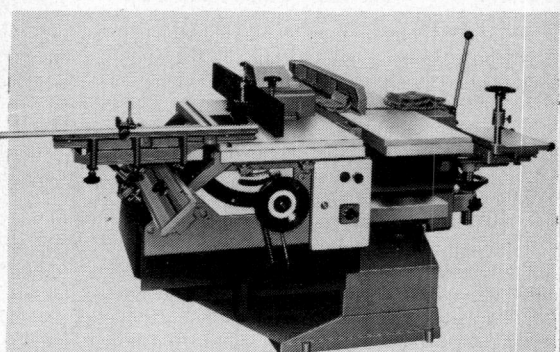

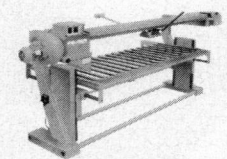

676

# Buying timber wisely : 3

each, paying a 10% transport charge. And, when three teak logs were urgently wanted in the south of France, Limehouse delivered within 72 hours.

Personal callers are welcomed, but it clearly wouldn't pay many long-distance customers to turn up in person to select and carry away material for smallish jobs. In such circumstances Limehouse is willing, if properly briefed, to use its own judgement in selecting and preparing timber to be bought on approval. Indeed, like most retailers at this end of the timber trade, Tim James and his manager Alan Parish almost insist that customers tell them exactly what the wood is wanted for. Too often interested buyers think they are being helpful by consolidating an order comprised of small sizes into a few pieces of large size — yet the customer will pay more for a single large prime piece than he would for smaller sections, and the yard is always pleased to have an opportunity to clear oddments from its racks. That does not imply third-rate stuff that is waiting for a mug to come along: parcels of timber bought by retailers always include shorter lengths of first quality. In Brazilian mahogany, for instance, 5ft lengths up to 14in wide may be 10% cheaper per cubic foot than longer, wider pieces.

Limehouse will also supply timber sawn to the customer's cutting list, and now it is toying with the idea of marketing packs of sawn material to match designs published in magazines — or even perhaps commissioned by the company. Another interesting project is to convert a small self-contained shed into a kind of studio showroom, featuring pieces of individual work or projects from colleges: the aim would be not to show only *tours de force* but the kinds of things that would encourage novices and catch the imagination of anyone looking for inspiration. The business, Tim James is certain, is as much about education and public relations as anything else, and he finds that getting buyers to enter into conversation about their projects often introduces them to woods they like better than their original choices, but which they have not previously met. And the chances are that fellow-customers will also join a conversation, adding more helpful ideas.

Limehouse Timber is open daily from nine to five — to 3p.m. on Saturdays. Callers are welcome at any time, though Saturday has developed into 'club day'. Local parking is easy at all times, and so is access by public transport.

A conversation with Timberline is rather like a cross-talk act. The firm is a partnership, with both partners fully involved.

Peter Lang and Bob Smith decided to become retailers of exotic woods in the middle of 1981. They met as commercially unsuccessful musical-instrument makers who had acquired more timber than they really needed; selling the surplus was, they found, a better living than making lutes. At the beginning of this year Timberline moved to Unit 7, Munday Works, 58 Morley Road — a large (3000sq ft), anonymous and frankly unattractive warehouse on an industrial estate outside Tonbridge in Kent. But what the building lacks in external charm it more than makes up to those who step inside; for the initiated, it is an Aladdin's cave of delights.

'Material for musical instruments is specialist rather than exotic, I would say,' remarks Bob.

'So we started with ebony, rosewood and similar stuff,' adds Peter. 'Then we started getting turners coming to us, and musical instruments got rather overlooked.'

'We get a lot of our strange ones by importing directly from south America,' says Bob, 'and we get very little in England. We have to buy from the Continent instead.'

● *In the yard at Timberline*

'That's because the fancy-goods trades here have fizzled out,' explains Peter. 'Knife-handles and tools aren't made in fine woods any more: there are hardly any industrial users left in this country.'

'Maybe the Continentals are more wood-aware than us,' concludes Bob.

Many of the woods held by Timberline are so rare that a single log comprises the entire stock (perhaps in Britain). Almost by definition, they will be required in relatively small quantities. This makes it possible to serve a very wide area without ruinous transport costs. An added factor is the amount of labour and skill that will go into work made with these kinds of woods, which makes it prudent for customers to call and select material themselves. And they come over long distances: Wolverhampton, Devon and Cornwall featured in the addresses given by recent callers.

Peter: 'We always try to get buyers to come and see for themselves rather than just getting us to send out boards. Wood is so subjective.'

Bob: 'We try to get out of 'em on the telephone what they want the stuff for, but some are surprisingly secretive.'

Peter: 'Sometimes we have to actively discourage a buyer from choosing a piece . . . '

Bob: ' . . . But it will be dead right for somebody else.'

Peter: 'No problems with our turning-bowl blanks. They are chosen to be perfect.'

Bob: 'Have to be very careful about English hardwoods, though; there's no quality control there at all.'

Because of the often very small lots that are available for Timberline to purchase, and because some of the woods are not in a real sense commercial propositions ('We found just one ton of satinoe Surinam — and that was the lot!'), the partners carry out some conversion from the log themselves. Not only does the saw kerf cost money; the very sawdust has value! Some is sold for dye-making, while sandalwood dust finds takers for its perfume.

The list of woods more or less permanently in stock reads like a litany of fine craftsmanship. The catalogue of lace-bobbin blanks lists more than 100 species, and there can be few people in the country who could readily identify even most of them. Sarabidan, platymiscium, mphane, flooded gum, wamara (heartwood or sapwood), guarea — the roll-call goes on and on. And the significance of the $5x\frac{3}{8}x\frac{3}{8}$in bobbin blanks is more real than apparent: a nigh-incredible total of 80,000 or so are sold each year.

At the other end of the scale, the warehouse floor is a maze of logs large and small, many sawn through and waiting the critical inspection of potential buyers. Two or three stacks of riven sycamore, destined to become fiddle backs, stand beside a small heap of box logs — and behind those are just three highly prized logs of snakewood. What might, for all the world, be a lump of rock is actually a thuya-burr root, waiting to be converted into turning blanks. As it stands it is worth more than £200. Not far away a stack of olivewood boards, prime stuff but full of natural faults, shows clearly why wastage — and price — can be high among the rarities.

Because of its history the company has not had a great deal to do with cabinet-makers ('Where are the cabinetmakers these days who want solid timber?'), and the partners don't really want to stock manufactured sheet materials. Peter reckons: 'Veneer is phasing out, and I hope it phases back in again. It's an ideal way to use beautiful timber.' So about 40 species are kept on the veneer shelves, some dyed ones among them, and mostly in panel lengths. Some extra-thick material is stocked especially for antique-restorers.

On the whole the partners are more interested in up-market customers than bulk purchasers. Yet Timberline's clientèle still divides a little awkwardly between

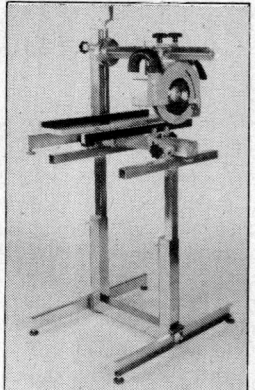
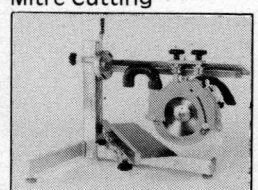

those to whom dusty logs and boards spell magic, and people who feel more at home in carefully swept studios. A new mezzanine showroom floor will, it is planned, appeal to the latter.

Like several other retail timber specialists, Timberline have diversified into finishes, steel wool, pearl and hide glue, inlays and bandings, and a few tools. They even stock mother-of-pearl, buffalo horn and elephant ivory. (The partners emphasise that all their ivory is trophy material — the last lot they converted had been adorning someone's walls since 1898.)

The 12-page Timberline catalogue is a model of its kind, clearly laid out and containing considerable information about the stock and its range of uses. Callers are welcomed between 9.30 and 5.30, Tuesday to Saturday; Monday is a day of rest; but anyone contemplating a visit is enjoined to telephone Peter Lang or Bob Smith first. The number is (0732) 355626. An adequate map is included in the catalogue, and the warehouse is within comfortable walking distance of Tonbridge railway station. ■

## The offcut trail

For a part-time woodworker (especially a carver), **writes R. B. Cannon**, buying timber is almost invariably hazardous. Quality and price vary wildly — and travel expenses, like hours of searching, soon mount up.

If you don't need much, however, and if you're prepared to buy when you can (as opposed to when you need), you can often find a bargain.

When I first started carving a few years ago, I found suitable material very hard to get. I live on the south coast, and the timber ads in woodworking journals seem mainly to cover the northern part of England. Some of my first purchases of carving timber were made 200 miles away when on holiday in Derbyshire.

Later, however, I found locally a small country sawmill which could offer lime, but in a minimum quantity. I bought a piece 8ftx8x2in for £14. The quality was good, but it was much more than I required immediately; still, I found it very nice to have a bit of stock. A little later one of my neighbours decided to cut down his cherry tree. I'd spent each autumn sweeping up the leaves which fell in my garden, so it was a pleasure to offer to take the trunk (and the offer was gratefully accepted, since it saved a journey to the tip!). The timber is drying very nicely now.

Last year, wishing to cap the newel-posts on our balustrade, I purchased a very small quantity of prime mahogany from a local merchant for £6. Later in the year, however, from an advertisement in a local newspaper, I found a window-frame manufacturer who sold offcuts at very low prices; there, £6 bought me enough mahogany board to make some expensive-looking shelves for our refurbished kitchen — and leave a surplus for stock which included one piece 36x9x2in!

Earlier this year, a few miles from home, I passed a small country pallet-making

● *Limehouse: browsing country*

sawmill which displayed a small notice offering yew for sale. I was able to buy a beautiful 12x8x8in block, plus a similar block of beech, at £2 each. These lovely pieces were described on my receipt as firewood. Later I chanced by the same sawmill, and couldn't resist a further visit. For £2 I acquired two slabs of yew each 18x18x3in, again described as firewood. Less than a fifth of this has had to be cut away as waste, and its quality compares favourably with that of a 15x15x5in block sold to me by weight for £4.60 at a craft show last year.

Last summer I looked for some elm boards for a cabinet. None of the large local timber merchants had any elm, but two of them referred me to the sawmill where I had bought the lime. Yes, the yard foreman said, they could supply my needs, but there would be an extra charge for surfacing the boards to size. After delivery I found that the surfaces were ridged from the planer — but they refunded the planing charge. In a way it did me a good turn, for I advertised

locally for a planer/thicknesser and bought an efficient if neglected 8in Kity machine for £200 from another replacement-window merchant. He also gave me a quantity of mahogany offcuts. What sort of business can afford to throw away 4ftx2x2in mahogany, not to mention several 5x1in boards of about 3ft each and a beautiful piece 18x5x1¾in of enormous dry weight and density?

I now have a nice stock of lime, cherry, yew and mahogany, plus a bit of beech, for a very modest outlay.

In his 'Timberline' column some time ago Arthur Jones mentioned that there was a bit of envy in the timber trade over the high prices some dealers are able to obtain. This is not confined to the DIY side of the business. At a recent craft show I noticed a mahogany board at £8 which represented only part of the quantity I had obtained for £6 as offcuts. Clearly, if you're in search of hardwoods but you only need small quantities, it pays to look around. ■

## Introducing kauvula

**Bill Brown** writes: A relatively new arrival on the UK market is a hardwood from Fiji called kauvula (*Endospermum medullosum*). The woodworker looking for a general-purpose timber for interior use could find it an attractive proposition. It possesses some of the best properties that can be desired of a lightweight wood; it is clean-looking and easy to work, with low shrinkage values and very good stability in service. It takes glues, nails, screws and the usual run of finishing media very well, and requires only light grain-filling.

Kauvula is creamy-white to pale yellow in colour, tending to darken slightly on exposure. It weighs about 25-30lbs/ft³ (400-480kg/m³) when dry; not much different from softwoods like European redwood and whitewood. It has a fine, even

texture and a generally straight grain. Comparatively speaking, it is something of a cross between ramin and obeche — that is to say, by superficial appearance; it has about the same hardness as ramin, and shares the slight woolliness in machining sometimes associated with obeche. All data that have come out of Australia from tests carried out on the species, which also grows in Papua New Guinea, suggest that kauvula is suitable for a wide range of uses, including flooring despite its light weight.

Hardwood importers are frequently persuaded to take in a small sample parcel of a new wood. Often these parcels 'stick', simply because the larger buyers are generally reluctant to introduce an alternative timber into well-established production runs using a familiar timber range. It will pay the small wood user to enquire into such 'odd parcels', since they often represent very good bargains.

# Old-shop curiosities

Reginald Norris tours the
tool shops of pre-war
London

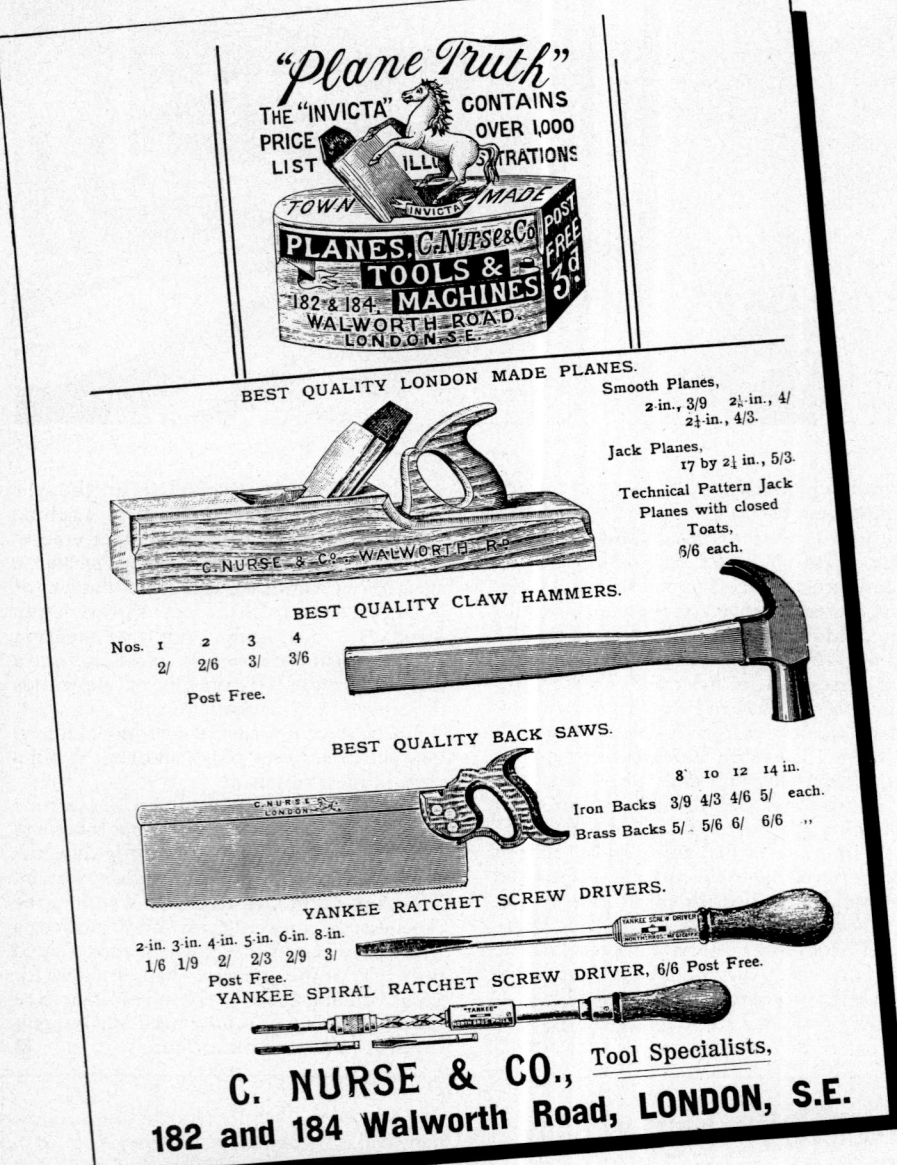

"Plane Truth"

THE "INVICTA"
PRICE
LIST

CONTAINS
OVER 1,000
ILLUSTRATIONS

TOWN MADE

PLANES, C. Nurse & Co
TOOLS &
182 & 184. MACHINES
WALWORTH ROAD,
LONDON.S.E.

POST
FREE
3d.

BEST QUALITY LONDON MADE PLANES.

Smooth Planes,
2-in., 3/9  2½-in., 4/
2¼-in., 4/3.

Jack Planes,
17 by 2½ in., 5/3.

Technical Pattern Jack
Planes with closed
Toats,
6/6 each.

C. NURSE & Co., WALWORTH Rᴰ

BEST QUALITY CLAW HAMMERS.

Nos.  1    2    3    4
      2/  2/6  3/  3/6

Post Free.

BEST QUALITY BACK SAWS.

                              8  10  12  14 in.
Iron Backs 3/9 4/3 4/6 5/ each.
Brass Backs 5/ 5/6 6/ 6/6 ,,

YANKEE RATCHET SCREW DRIVERS.

2-in. 3-in. 4-in. 5-in. 6-in. 8-in.
1/6  1/9  2/  2/3  2/9  3/

Post Free.

YANKEE SPIRAL RATCHET SCREW DRIVER, 6/6 Post Free.

C. NURSE & CO., Tool Specialists,
182 and 184 Walworth Road, LONDON, S.E.

If you leaf through old *Woodworker* annuals, you will find in most of them an advert for an old tool-making firm; 'Messrs C. Nurse & Co., Plane-makers and General Tool-makers and Suppliers. Walworth Rd, London SE.' My family home was in Camberwell in south-east London, and I well remember in 1929 being taken by my aunt along the Walworth Rd to Nurse's to buy a tool for her brother. It was a micrometer which cost then £2 10s, and was made in America by Starrett, Athol, Mass. Nurse's must have been a great firm in their day; they carried a great stock of tools.

When I started in the organ trade in 1934, I had left Camberwell at the age of 11

and moved to Norbury, in south-west London. At the age of 14 I became a tuner's boy for a well-known form of organ-builders, and after my first year I started to collect the tools I could afford. Some of the retail tool firms I bought items from over the years are still in business. I would go to Collier's in Electric Avenue, Brixton, and Valley Rd, Streatham; Turtle's of Crown Hill, in Croydon; Clegg Bros, in the Uxbridge Rd, Shepherds' Bush, Hanwell Broadway and St James' St, Walthamstow, and G. Buck's in Goodge St, off the Tottenham Court Rd.

Bucks made tools for the musical-instrument trade — organ-builders, pianoforte makers and so on. This place

brings me memories of my first visit to purchase two spindle screwdrivers — one 10in, the other 12in. The assistant opened a rack on the end of the counter, exposing various blades from 6in to 3ft. They were of die-cast steel, hand-forged and polished, engraved with the name 'Buck, Goodge St'. I chose my two blades, and then was asked what pattern octagonal box handle I wanted. There were two types — a straight box octagon with a knob on top and a brass ferrule, or a tapered octagon box, with a brass ferrule but no knob. Once the handles were agreed, the assistant retired to the back room to warm up the tangs of the blades and drive the handles on with resin sealer. The complete screwdrivers cost 4/6d and 5/6d each in 1934 — I still have them today.

If any young journeyman were sent to

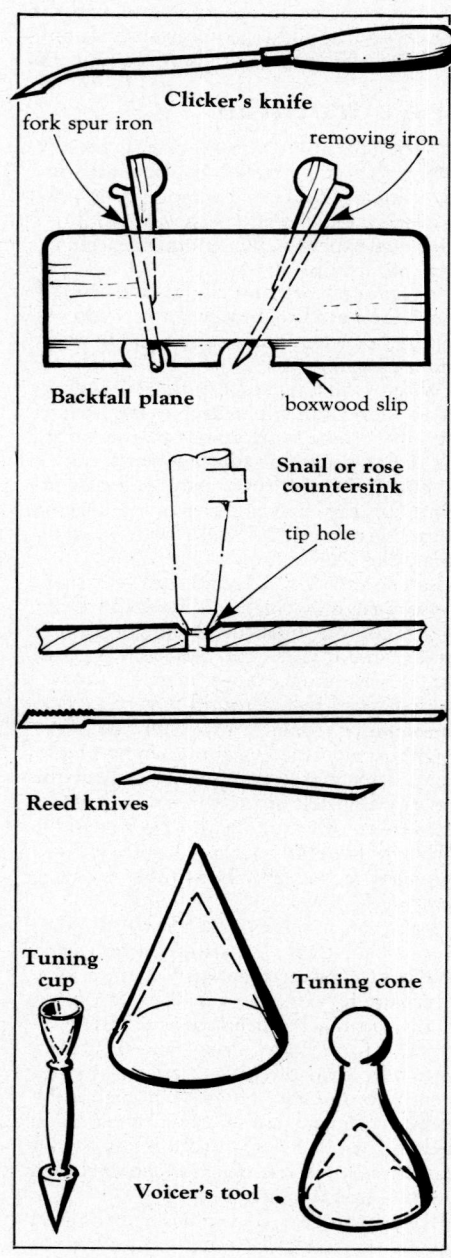

Clicker's knife

fork spur iron                    removing iron

Backfall plane                    boxwood slip

Snail or rose
countersink

tip hole

Reed knives

Tuning
cup                                Tuning cone

Voicer's tool

London from our branches they always visited Buck's in Goodge St for tools. A certain type of knife, known as a 'clicker's knife', was always bought; the 'clicker' was the person in the boot and shoe trade who cut the uppers from soft leather with this good, pointed knife. It cost 2/6d. Buck's also made organ-builder's backfall planes in beech, with a boxwood sole centre ridge. They were used for cutting grooves across a sandwich timber of mahogany on pine at various cross-grained angles, and had irons of 3/16, 1/4, 5/16 and 3/8in. Backfalls are the pivoted wooden levers in tracker-action pipe organs. The firm also supplied tuning cones, cups, reed knives and voicer's tools, which these days we get from Germany unless we can get a turner to make them from brass. Sometimes we have them specially cast and machined.

Buck & Ryan's in the Euston Rd (now Tottenham Court Rd) also had a branch in the Edgware Rd, near Praed St. It was an excellent tool house for all artisans. I bought all my Forstner bits there over a long period, 1/4-2in diameter in 1/16in sizes. In 1935 a 3/4in Forstner with a tapered brace-shank cost 25s. A set of Russell Jennings winged auger-bits, made of steel and sterling-silver alloy in a small oak chest with trays-would cost about £5. A set of 13 bits by Irwin, Gedge and Whitehouse would be less costly; a Clarks expansion bit, which went from 7/8 to 3in, came in a hardwood box and cost around £3 15s (some patterns even had a worm gear adjustment!). A Norris 14 1/2in panel plane would cost £9 15s, a 17 1/2in model £15 17s 6d. A 24in no08 Record jointer cost me £5 15s 6d in 1942. My Norris smooth coffin-shape, bought in 1947 near Tooting Broadway, cost £8 15s. I was wise at the time — I bought spare irons as well. It has the usual Norris feature of double-thread

adjustment. The large snail or rose countersink (1 1/4-1 1/2in-dia.) was only obtainable at Buck & Ryan — in the organ trade, we used them to countersink the tip holes for organ pipes before the burning iron, which gave the nice black effect.

Buck & Hickman of Whitechapel, who only sold wholesale, were agents for a well-known Sheffield firm who used the Toga trade mark. I had all my saddle and wad punches from this source, via the retail firm, Reddings of Norbury.

Then there was Matthews, ironmongers and tool dealers, of Charing Cross Rd. I never bought much here but obviously the men at Henry Bevington's, organ builders, of Manette St, Soho, used them a lot. Bevington's lasted from 1794 to 1934. My old foreman at the Great Piano House, Chalcot Rd, Camden Town, had much of his kit from Matthews, having been a Bevington journeyman. After 1914 he was an apprentice to J. W. Walker of Francis St, Tottenham Court Rd, so I reckon Bucks came into it as well. These were the days when men started at 7 and had their breakfast in the works at 8am.

Wailes, in the Euston Rd and at Tooting Broadway, had good tools, and not as expensive as the West End firms. They carried many pairs of pliers — some new, others second-hand; some were made by Lindstrom, the Swedish firm.

Reddings of Norbury were a good old family firm who carried a big stock of well-known Sheffield tools and who would order specials from larger tool suppliers if they were needed. This is how I got my punches and some bevel-edge paring chisels by Marples, Brades, Sorby, Ward and Payne.

Boshers of Falcon Rd, Clapham Junction, were pawnbrokers who devoted one window to new and second-hand tools, the other to the usual jewellery, china, watches,

fishing tackle and so on. I bought an American Estwing clawhammer here in 1947 for 25/-, with a 12oz all-steel head and shaft and a leather-bound handle. One could pick up bargains here in 1936-38.

Taborns of Clapham Junction were a shop-and-pavement-stall outfit, the latter showing good second-hand stuff at reasonable prices for 1935-38. The establishment was very near an overhead railway bridge. If my memory is correct I had a mahogany chamfer plane here, a very nice and well-made tool of the Victorian era which cost 4/- second-hand. I still have it.

Last of all come John Hall & Co. of Cardiff, Swansea and Newport, Monmouthshire. I had a few things here. They have merged into Buck & Hickman since I used them. ∎

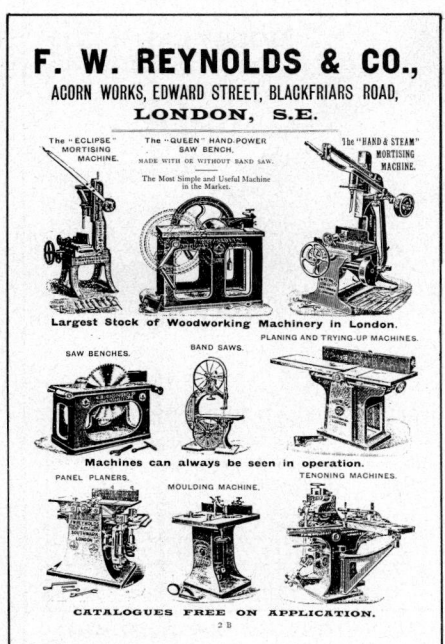

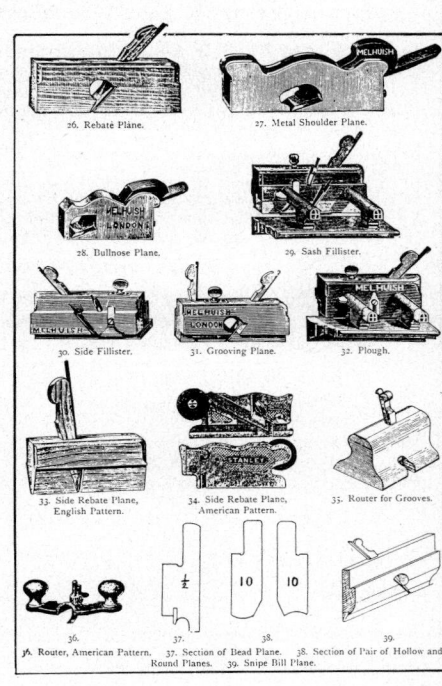

26. Rebate Plane.    27. Metal Shoulder Plane.
28. Bullnose Plane.    29. Sash Fillister.
30. Side Fillister.    31. Grooving Plane.    32. Plough.
33. Side Rebate Plane, English Pattern.    34. Side Rebate Plane, American Pattern.    35. Router for Grooves.
36. Router, American Pattern.    37. Section of Bead Plane.    38. Section of Pair of Hollow and Round Planes.    39. Snipe Bill Plane.

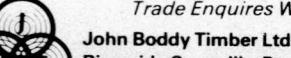
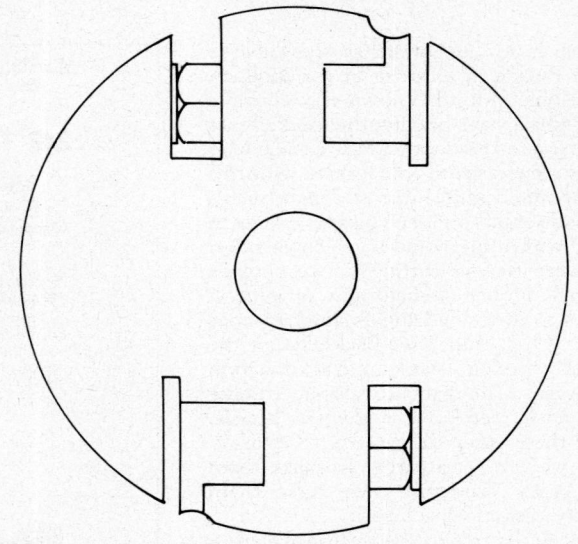

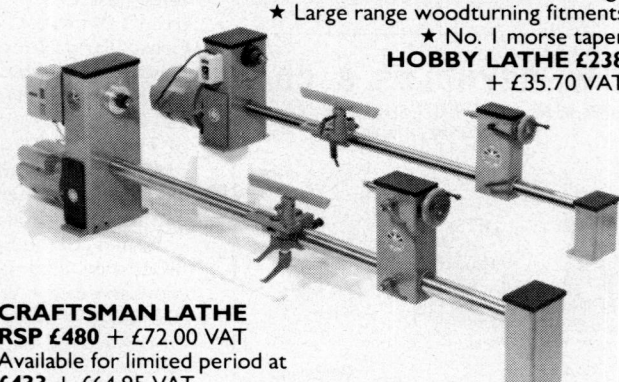

# Modest vanity

**This sensible vanity unit is an excellent project if, like Graham Hewitt, you are comparatively new to wood machining**

Having posted an arm and a leg to a machinery retailer, I was looking forward to the arrival of the universal woodworker which I'd sold myself and with which I would be able, if not to perform miracles, then at least make well-fitting mortise-and-tenons.

This investment, I hoped, would provide the answer to my dilemma, which was how to obtain good-quality and reasonably priced doors and windows for the renovation and extension of our cottage. The answer was to make our own; but the snag was me, or more precisely my limited skills. I cannot be the only one who has come late to the working of wood, with no formal training and having developed only a few basic skills through reading and trial and error.

How many of us late developers can afford to spend hours of our free time planing away at planks to produce squared-up boards, or chop dozens of mortises and saw tens of tenons until they show signs of fitting reasonably squarely? If power tools can be used to speed the work, increase accuracy, improve the finish or reduce the effort, it seems sensible to use them if you can afford them.

However, there eventually comes a time when your woodworking ambitions reach beyond what can be achieved with hand-held power tools. Then you can, if funds allow, invest in stationary woodworking equipment.

Having read and re-read dozens of brochures I was not really much further forward, and indeed there seemed to be even more unanswered questions than before. Why did some manufacturers make a virtue of cast tables while others talked of pressed steel? I knew that long planer tables were a 'good thing', but were the differences between tables of 800, 1000 and 1200mm really important? Why did some combinations need three motors while others made do with one — and what were the practical effects of different hp ratings? Could a radial-arm saw really crosscut, rip *and* mould, rout and even plane? These sorts of questions spun around in my head until eventually I succumbed to brochures syndrome, an affliction in which the victim spends countless valuable hours gazing vacantly at catalogues, incapable of rational conversation or decision-making, this trance-like state occasionally punctuated by cries of 'Depth of cut 2⅞in!' or 'Feed-rate of seven metres per minute!'

Having identified the actual functions I required, the next problem was the inevitable choice between independent and combination machines. This is a perennial question to which the answer is straight-forward if you have unlimited money and space: buy the biggest and best independent machines available. But, after looking at my needs, the capacities required, and the money and space available, a combination seemed the best compromise.

## The project

My first project was a vanity unit. Our tastes tend to the traditional, and since we aren't keen on pedestal washbasins we felt that a vanity basin housed in a pine unit would be appropriate. The two doors in the room are ledged-and-battened red pine, so a pine vanity unit would match them, and offer the bonus of cupboard space.

The design was simple, in keeping with my woodworking intellect: a framed front, housing two flush-fitting doors; a framed end-panel of T&G boards, and a chipboard or plywood top, all fixed to an internal framework which was firmly screwed to the wall. The chipboard top was to be tiled to match the walls, while inside there would be two shelves, one at the bottom acting as a false floor, the other more central and making provision for doorstops. My unit fitted into a corner, but it would be a simple matter to add a second end-panel for one placed in the middle of a wall.

When designing and installing such a unit, account must be taken of how it is secured to the wall. Leaving it free-standing might encourage the untutored to believe it could be moved around the room, and inadvertently convert it into a shower! As I had built the room from the foundations up I was able to plan ahead and incorporate battens at suitable positions.

However, if you don't have such fore-knowledge, you may have to sound the wall to locate the studs, or use special fixings depending on the type of wall. The plumbing itself is very straightforward.

The size of the unit will of course depend on the dimensions of the vanity basin, but in locating the basin try to ensure that there will be some space between the rim and the rear wall for cleaning the counter-top. Height tends to be a standard 820mm, but can be varied to suit those who will be using it; and before construction, check the floor and wall(s) for squareness so you can plan to compensate for irregularities.

The making of this unit would provide my first opportunity to use my new

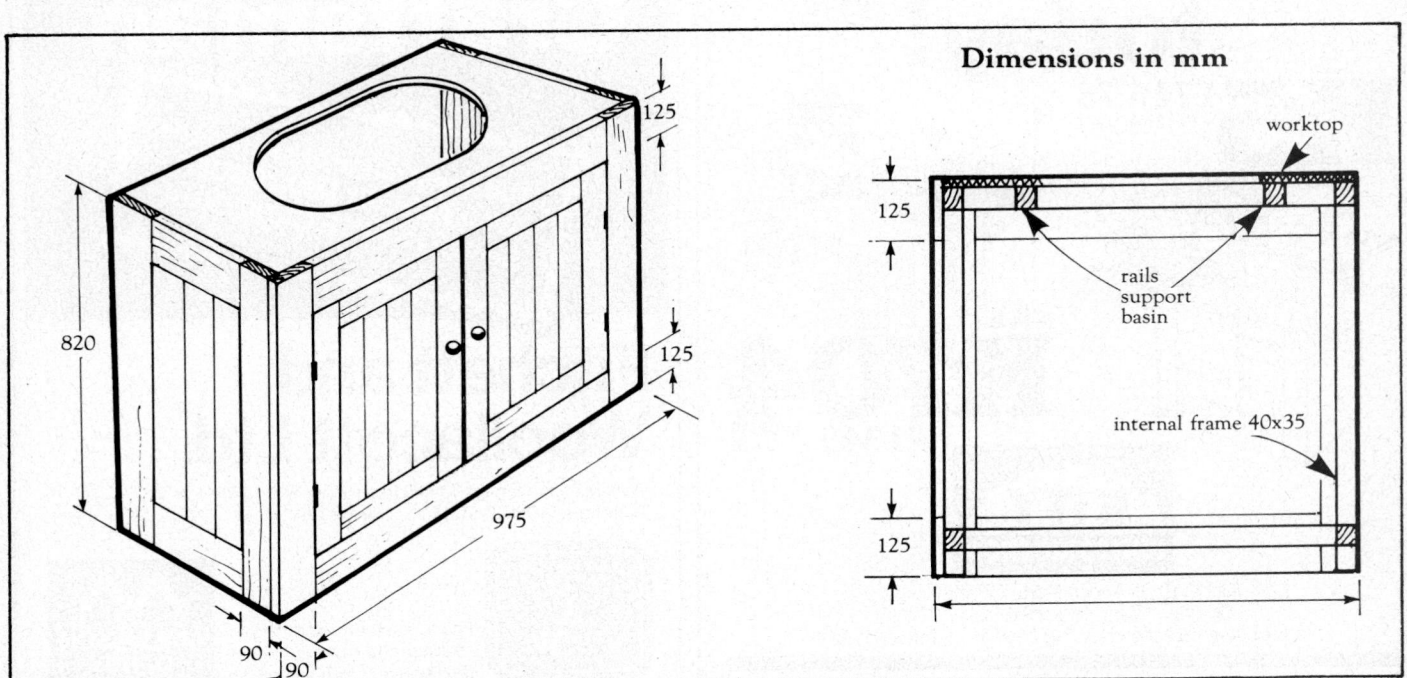

Dimensions in mm

worktop

rails support basin

internal frame 40x35

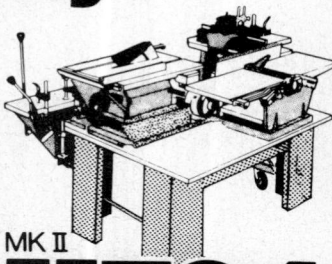

# Modest vanity

machinery, which I had spent the previous week setting up, and would require all the basic functions: planing, thicknessing, sawing, mortising and tenoning, plus tonguing-and-grooving.

I had some red pine planks from a builders' merchant, PAR, nicely warped, and complete with the distinctive ridges of slapdash planing. The width of the boards was about right, but they were more than twice as thick as I needed so I deep-cut them on the table saw, using the rip-fence and flipping them over to get the depth of cut. Lesson one: remember to place the same side against the fence for both passes and the cuts will meet nicely in the middle.

I never realised quite what a draught these saws produced and, working as I was in an air temperature below zero, I found it quite cooling. Luckily, however, I had a pair of gloves for just such an occasion — the kind without fingertips, I think in the expectation that my fingers would soon be trimmed to match!

Moving to the planer I began by surfacing one face. Gradually the ridges and warps began to disappear, until, holding the board up to the light, I could almost see my face in it. Next I surfaced the face edges, using the fence which I had carefully set at right-angles to the table. Checking the boards with a square, I was pleased to find they were true. I marked them with an 'f' and set them aside to be thicknessed. I picked up the first board and worked on it until it was reduced to the finished dimensions; having congratulated myself on producing a perfect board, I realised it would be quicker and more accurate to work on all the boards at the same time, passing them through at the same setting: lesson two.

I re-set the machine to the greatest thickness and passed all the boards through; then, reducing the setting and passing one of the boards through, I discovered my 'f' had disappeared. Lesson three: stack the work systematically so that the correct face is machined and you don't thickness your reference face.

Having dimensioned the boards on the planer I returned to the table saw, cross-cutting them to the lengths of the individual components, and remembering to make an allowance for the tenons. I cut off as waste the slight scalloped end which the thicknesser leaves. I found that a piece of squared wood fixed to the fence of the sliding mitre-square not only prevents the piece being cut from splintering, but also enables accurate alignment of the mark on your work — if you fix the fence-piece over-long, your first cut will trim it to exact length.

The next job was to cut the mortises on the slot-mortiser, but before doing so I marked out their positions in the usual way, setting the mortise gauge to the width of the bit. While I was at it I marked the tenons. Although David Savage says it is only necessary to mark one and set the machine to that, then all the others will be identical, I didn't feel confident enough to take the

risk. Having done the job I can see how doing so would be more efficient.

The rails and stiles for the end-panel were to be grooved to receive the tongues of the T&G boards and so I used the slot-mortiser to cut these as well, although a router would have been just as good had it been set up.

The blind mortises cut, I then made the tenons on the spindle moulder, using the sliding carriage and a slotting disc. If you can afford it two slotting discs will cut the tenon in one pass; otherwise you will have to turn each piece over to make a second pass, re-setting the spindle. Again, of course, it is more efficient and more accurate to make first passes on all the pieces in one run.

The completion of these operations gave me rails whose tenons fitted into the mortises of their respective stiles with a minimum of trimming and produced a joint more like the surface of a billiard table than a front-doorstep — well, almost!

● *The choice was to make it by machine, or not make it at all. For Graham Hewitt, there was no contest*

The next job was to prepare the T&G boards to fit in the end-panel and door-frames. According to Sod's Law, it is extremely unlikely that the width of boards you have will go evenly into the frame, so you will have to reduce one or more boards in width and either put tongues on them or make loose tongues to fit in grooves. However, the method I prefer, which offers several benefits, is to reduce the central board where there is an odd number, or the outer two where there is an even.

What I normally do is calculate the finished width, excluding tongues, of the board required to make up the total width of T&G panel to fit the frame, assuming the remaining boards are full-width (100mm). Say the finished width of board is 60mm, I then divide this by two and gauge 30mm plus the width of the tongue from the tongued edge of two boards of the right length. These two are then ripped just on the waste side to give two 30mm-wide pieces, each with a tongue. I then shoot the edges and join them with PVA adhesive. After cleaning up the glue-line I have a board of the correct width to make up the difference, with a tongue on each edge. This means, if you work out from the centre, that each outer board also has a tongue ready to fit into the grooves of the frame-stiles, and that both these boards are full-

width. Therefore the eye hardly notices the narrow board in the centre. When alternatively you reduce the two outer boards, once again you hardly notice the discrepancy because they are the same width.

The final job in preparing the T&G panel was to put tongues on the top and bottom edges. I began this on the spindle moulder using a slotting disc, but found that the wood tended to splinter on the chamfer at the end of each cut. As I didn't have a piece counter-profiled to support the weak endgrain I decided to make the tongues on the router mounted in a stand, where I could enter the wood at both ends and avoid splintering.

I next assembled the internal framework, all mortise-and-tenon jointed. However, since I had only two sash-cramps I used screws to secure the joints — well, if they're good enough for Sam Maloof (WW/March 82) they're good enough for me. Rigidity was further increased by the chipboard top and by screwing solidly to the wall, checking square and levels before final fixing. The basin was supplied with a template for marking the cut-out in the counter top and the piece was removed with the router, as I don't have a jig-saw. The chipboard was screwed down on to the internal frame, whereas the end-panel and front frame to take the doors were screwed from the inside after making final adjustments with the plane.

The final woodworking job was to glue up the door frames, fitting the T&G panels loose, and of course checking for winding in the usual way, which I've yet to discover. Something to do with two sticks and a boy scout? I can usually tell, when I remember, by sighting along a door on a horizontal surface and checking that both rails are in exactly the same plane. If you forget, you may get away with shaving some of the thickness off the protruding corner(s), and although you'll have a tapered door, at least it will look right.

Final thoughts: self-tutoring has its drawbacks. The graduate of an educational process, be it an apprenticeship, professional training or advanced study, will have followed a course of *systematic* training from first principles onwards. If you are a novice working alone, you have to discover for yourself the knowledge passed on by the craftsman as a matter of course to the apprentice, either by example or by instruction. And, as any teacher knows, it is often that which is most obvious to the expert which seems least obvious to the learner, but which, once grasped, makes the task much easier.

Therefore, although many of the lessons I have learned in this exercise, such as keeping the same face to the rip-fence when doing a double cut, or making trial cuts, or setting the planer for optimum speed and finish, may seem obvious and elementary, they aren't always so to the solitary beginner. I'm sure there are many more points equally simple-seeming, but essential to good, efficient and safe practice. ■

# Through the golden gate

**The classical (some say divine) rules of proportion are as valid as ever — and just as practical. Vic Taylor explains**

Over the past six months I have had several enquiries from woodworkers, in both Britain and the USA, who have encountered the problem of designing mouldings to suit furniture they have made. Their greatest worry is to achieve true proportions and a correct profile. On the face of it, that doesn't seem to be too difficult; but in fact the deeper we investigate the more intriguing the ramifications become.

As soon as we begin, we plunge into history, for there are two distinct methods of plotting curves for mouldings — the Roman and the Greek. It's generally accepted that the five principal mouldings, namely the ovolo, the scotia, the cavetto, the cyma recta and the cyma reversa, derive from the Greek and Roman orders of architecture.

Dealing first with the Roman style, we find that their mouldings were based on the square, and I have drawn them in fig. 1; the contain the profile; next we double the size of the parallelogram by extending BA to F

● *Apply the rules to this Empire mahogany chest, and you will see just how closely they were followed by the classical cabinetmakers*

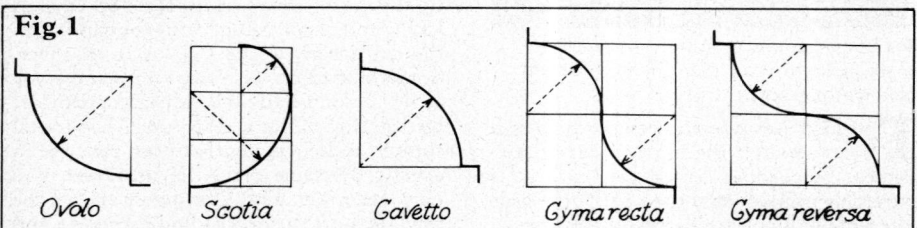

**Fig. 1** Ovolo  Scotia  Cavetto  Cyma recta  Cyma reversa

methods are so simple that they are self-explanatory. The Greeks, on the other hand, were enthusiastic geometricians who delighted in exploring the relationships between squares, parallelograms, triangles, etc. Accordingly the profiles of their mouldings were based on conic sections (fig. 2A), either elliptical or parabolic.

The ovolo and the cavetto are mirror-images of each other, so the same method can be used for drawing both, as in fig. 2B. Here, each side of the rectangle ABCD is divided first into two and then into four. Additionally, one of the shorter sides, AD, is extended to E so that AD is equal to DE. Then the point E is used as a centre for a set of radiating lines drawn through the points on the longer side DC; another set of radiating lines is centred on A and joined to the points on the shorter side CB. The intersections of these lines provide the plotting points for the curve.

Plotting the curve of the scotia mouldings, fig. 2C, is a similar procedure but a little more complicated. First of all, we have to draw a parallelogram ABCD which will

so that BA is equal to AF, and CD to E so that CD is equal to DE. Then join E to F, mark off the halfway point G, and draw the bisecting line GH. Next, divide the lines DC, AB and EF as shown, and draw in the radiating lines from G and H; the intersections of these lines provide the plotting points for the curve.

The remaining two mouldings, the cyma recta and cyma reversa, are shown in fig. 2D, and are plotted in a similar way to those already described.

So far, so good. However, we can see that a rectangle forms the basis for the diagrams (except in the case of the scotia), and it's obvious that the proportions of the rectangle (or the parallelogram, for the scotia) radically determine the shape of the curve — as we can see from fig. 2E, where I have deliberately accentuated the difference between the height and width of a cavetto moulding. What, therefore, is the ideal relationship between the two dimensions of a rectangle — the one which will yield the perfect profile? Does one even exist?

There is such a relationship, and it is called by several names: the divine proportion, the section, the golden section, the golden cut, the golden mean and the golden rule. Although its invention or discovery

has been credited to the Greek philosopher and geometer Pythagoras, many artifacts from ancient Egypt, such as vases and urns, were designed to incorporate the principle. It does not merely ensure that the proportions are visually satisfying (after all, what looks pleasing to one person can appear unspeakably ugly to another); it is a definite mathematical ratio which may be expanded to form a geometric progression. This progression can and often does act as a base for a scale of measurements for architects and designers.

The relationship, or principle, is that the first part is to the second part as the second is to the whole or sum of the two parts. This needs to be read or repeated two or three times, I find, to let it sink in! It's probably easier to understand if illustrated diagrammatically as in fig. 3A; if you want to work it out for yourself, fig. 3B shows you how.

You will see that the ratio between the two parts of the line is 1:1.618. This ratio holds good, of course, whether the line is 1cm long or a kilometre. It's worth drawing up a rectangle on a piece of tracing-paper so that the longer sides are, say, 16.18cm, and the shorter sides 10cm: an ordinary millimetre rule will allow you to approximate to the 16.18cm pretty accurately. I have drawn such a rectangle ABCD at fig. 3C, and you will see that I have drawn a diagonal AC from corner to corner. If you mark off any dimension along AB and draw a vertical up to intersect the diagonal, the length of that vertical will the proportionately shorter dimension. Similarly, if you know the measurement of the shorter side and you want to find the longer dimension, mark off the shorter length along AD and draw a vertical to the diagonal: this will be the required measurement.

# Restorer's report

## David Ellis gives a day-to-day view from the work-bench

● *Unlimited restorer – David is at ease restoring ceramics and clocks as well as fine furniture*

The range of antiques passing through our workshops for restoration covers all periods of furniture, clocks, light metalwork, ceramics, oil paintings and many other *objets d'art*. Often I am asked about the ethics of restoration — and, more practically, how restoration affects the value.

In my opinion there is no reason not to restore any item in any category. Quite illogically, some authorities on ceramics try to persuade collectors not to buy anything that has been restored; but how many clock collectors would turn away a Tompion because at some time in its life it had had a repaired escapement or a new spring? How many paintings, changing hands through reputable auction houses, have never been cleaned, repaired or re-varnished? If they were not restored they would, after 100 years of smoke and dirt, be nothing more than grey-black masses acceptable to no one. A Chippendale chair with a broken splat is worth little; but, when the broken area has been repaired (if possible with contemporary wood) and re-carved to match the original, it will lose very little value compared with a perfect piece — particularly if it is part of a set.

So why should the ceramic world take such a superior line? Of course the perfect item is preferable, if it is available, but to a genuine collector an item that has been well restored must be preferable to none at all.

Honesty is a very different matter. We all have a moral duty to declare if a piece has been restored. A good restorer's ultimate goal is always to restore a piece so perfectly that the work is virtually undetectable, but an unscrupulous dealer will often take advantage of such craftsmanship to pass it on as 'perfect'. On one occasion, at a provincial antique fair, I was standing behind a dealer who was endeavouring to pass off a piece of porcelain as perfect when I recognised it as one I had restored some months earlier. I interrupted to point this out. The business came to an abrupt end! Though the prospective buyer was grateful, the dealer was furious, and (needless to say) I did no more work for her. But such dishonesty cannot be tolerated in our dealings with one another.

So we very rarely colour and re-glaze the back of a plate that has been restored — even for a private customer. This is partly pride, for, when a badly smashed plate has been so well restored that the damage is undetectable from the front, the quality of the work is enhanced by appreciating the complexity of the break from the back. Besides, of course, colouring and re-glazing the back obscures the manufacturer's marks, dates, etc.

As far as furniture is concerned — and it constitutes the major part of our work —

we naturally blend in all restoration so that it is virtually impossible to see; but every single piece leaving our workshops carries a small sticker stating that it has been restored by us (and giving our address and telephone number).

The ethics of restoration will always be contentious, but the paradox remains: if the antique trade frowns on restoration, why are there so many restorers, many of whom work almost exclusively for the trade? My own fervent belief is that antiques are the legacy of our forefathers which we are holding in trust for future generations. While they are in our care, it is our responsibility to preserve them.

I never cease to be amazed at the variety of jobs we are called upon to tackle, but of course one must never let this surprise be seen by the customer! In the last few weeks we have been asked to make a dashboard in walnut for a vintage Alvis; reproduce 10ft of bead moulding for an 18th-century lacquered mirror; and make a coat-hanger for a turtle. Yes, honestly. When the customer, a titled lady, rang up to ask if we could make one, it was extremely difficult to confine my reply to 'Of course we can; what size would you like?'. She had just returned from a stay in the Seychelles and had brought back (as cabin baggage) a superb turtle-shell some 3ft long and 2ft wide. She just wanted a frame made so that the shell could hang on the wall alongside her other holiday souvenirs. The main criteria were that the frame must not be visible, and must be absolutely secure without any fixings into the shell. Not a difficult job, really, but one which needed a quiet session just thinking it out.

Much the same sort of quiet contemplation went into solving the problem of replacing the 'dot-dash' moulding round

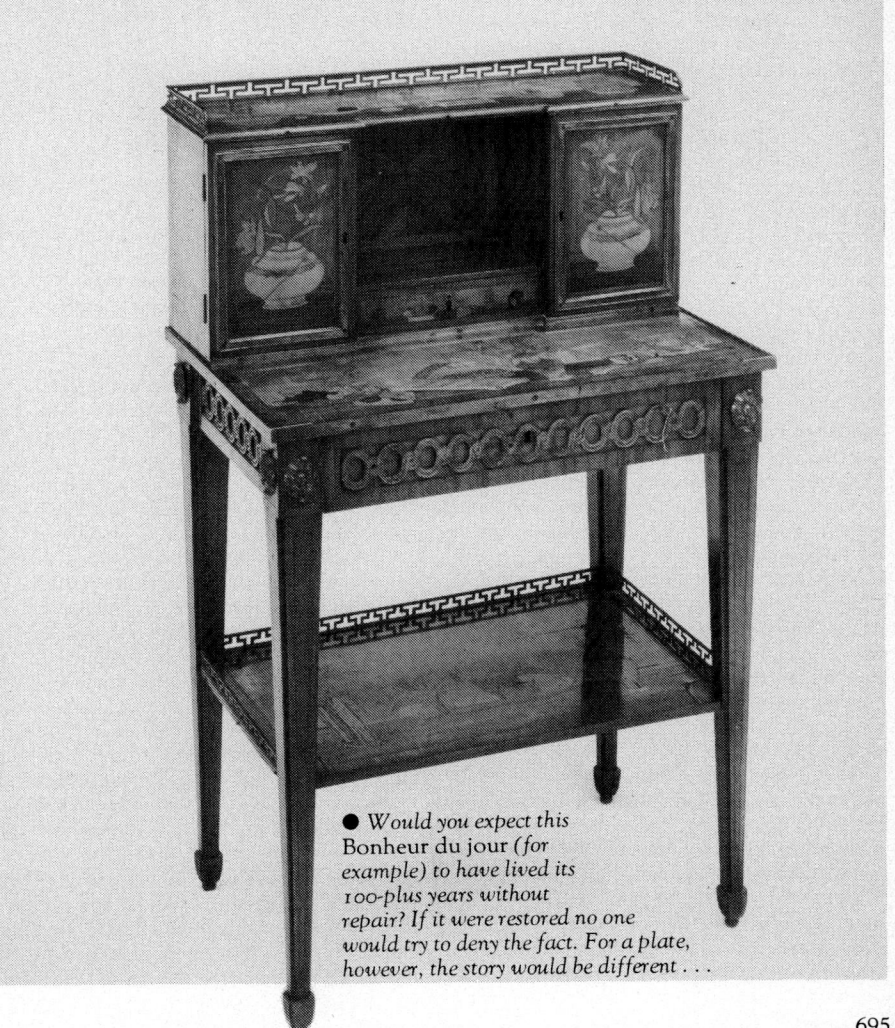

● *Would you expect this Bonheur du jour (for example) to have lived its 100-plus years without repair? If it were restored no one would try to deny the fact. For a plate, however, the story would be different . . .*

# Restorer's report

the edge of the lacquered and gilt mirror. This was originally moulded in gesso and finished in black lacquer. Some three-quarters of it were missing when the job came in. We tried various methods of making moulds from the remaining sections using wax, gelatine, latex, etc., and then casting in plaster, but none of these was really acceptable.

My quiet thinking suddenly resulted in an obvious answer — make it in wood! The finished result can stand the closest scrutiny from the expert. The finished moulding approximates to a semi-circular section of ¼in diameter. Several 2ft lengths of ⅜in softwood dowelling were accurately cut up the middle. The two halves were then stuck together again, using animal glue, with a piece of newspaper between them, and bound at intervals with masking-tape until dry. With one end in the Jacobs chuck and the other secured by the point of the revolving tail-stock, lengths of about 6-8in were turned to ¼in diameter and then bead-turned to a pattern of ¾in length with three ¼in beads.

Removed from the lathe, the pieces were momentarily steamed apart, and a perfect half-round bead moulding was ready to be stuck to the cleaned and prepared mirror using Resin W adhesive. Two coats of black enamel, followed by black french polish, completed the job, which then only needed a little touching-in with gold paint where this was missing. A delighted customer, and another problem solved and recorded for future use.

So often the appearance of an otherwise sound antique bureau bookcase is marred by cracked or broken panels in an astragal glass front. (I've never discovered why this term is used, since my dictionary defines 'astragal' as 'small moulding of semi-circular section round the top or bottom of columns'.) Replacement of these is not difficult, but it calls for a little care in measurement, plus correct preparation of the moulding.

Remove the door from the carcase. It is virtually impossible to do the job *in situ*, as adequate support is necessary if further panes are not to be broken or loosened. Lay the door face-down, with plenty of support around and under the problem area and general protection for the front surface. Remove any remaining pieces of broken glass. Then, with an old but reasonably sharp chisel, gently chip out the remaining putty. This can sometimes be rock-hard, so shaving it away is often the only method. At the intersections of the moulding you will sometimes find that there is additional fabric reinforcement, which should also be removed.

When the frame is completely clear of all old putty, replace the fabric. Strips of linen (from an old sheet or the like), about ⅜in wide and 1½in long, are stuck across each joint. White glue is ideal. On acute angles, for example at the bottom of diamonds, make sure that the fabric is pushed well into the intersection — without wrinkling. Smooth the fabric with a wet finger and

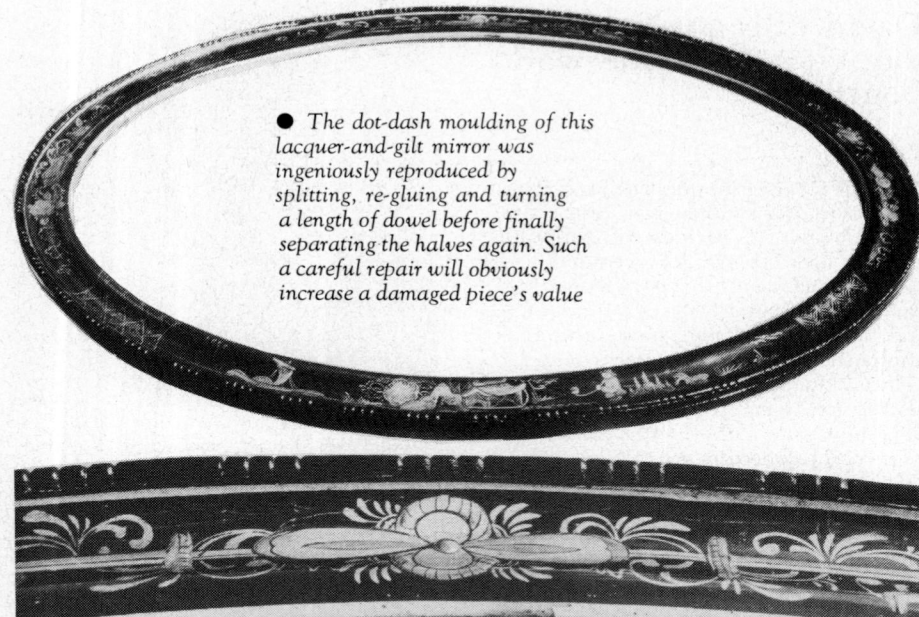

● *The dot-dash moulding of this lacquer-and-gilt mirror was ingeniously reproduced by splitting, re-gluing and turning a length of dowel before finally separating the halves again. Such a careful repair will obviously increase a damaged piece's value*

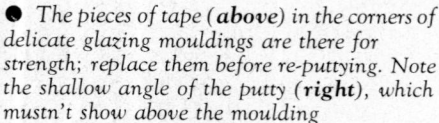

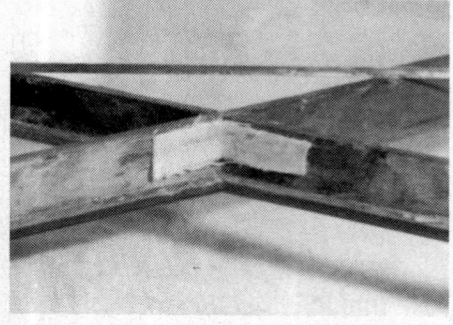

● *The pieces of tape (**above**) in the corners of delicate glazing mouldings are there for strength; replace them before re-puttying. Note the shallow angle of the putty (**right**), which mustn't show above the moulding*

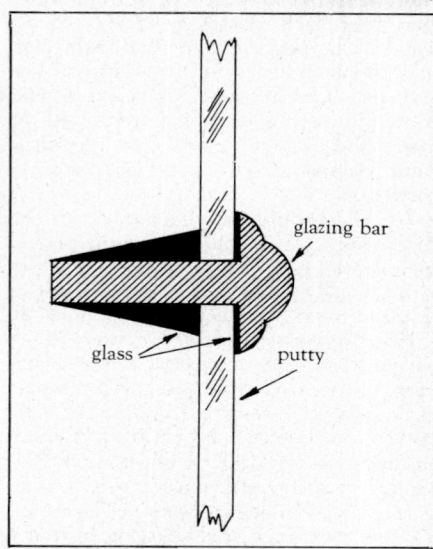

leave the area to dry out completely.

If the piece of furniture is of an early period such as the mid-18th-century, the glass used for replacement should, if possible, be of the same age; modern glass is too perfect, and will stand out against the slightly rippled original. However, the difference is slight, and modern picture-frame glass is a reasonable substitute. Cut a template of thin card to fit exactly, with the minimum of clearance (remembering that the fabric pieces will reduce the size slightly). On a perfectly flat surface, lay the new glass on top of the template and cut it to shape. If you have difficulty in cutting glass, take the template to any good glass merchant or, better still, a picture-framer, and ask him to cut the shape for you in 1mm or 1.5mm glass; but emphasise the importance of cutting it exactly to size.

Take some fresh glazing putty, worked soft and warm in the hands, and put a very thin film on the inside of the front edge of the glazing bars. Place the glass in position and apply even pressure all round to squeeze out any surplus. Then apply putty to the back (or inside) of the frame. The angle of the putty to the glass is much shallower than in normal window glazing, and the putty must not on any account be further on to the glass than at the front. If it is, it will always be visible.

Finish off the putty surface smoothly and leave to dry for a few days. After that the putty can be painted, using an enamel such as Humbrol to match the adjoining frames. We keep a small range of colours — dark red, browns and black — which can be blended. If necessary, touch in the white line of putty at the front. Replace the doors, and no one should be any the wiser!

● David Ellis runs Restorations Unlimited, Pinkney Park, Malmesbury, Wilts, tel. (0666) 840888. A local representative for the Guild of Woodworkers, he demonstrated at the Bristol Woodworker Show. ∎

698

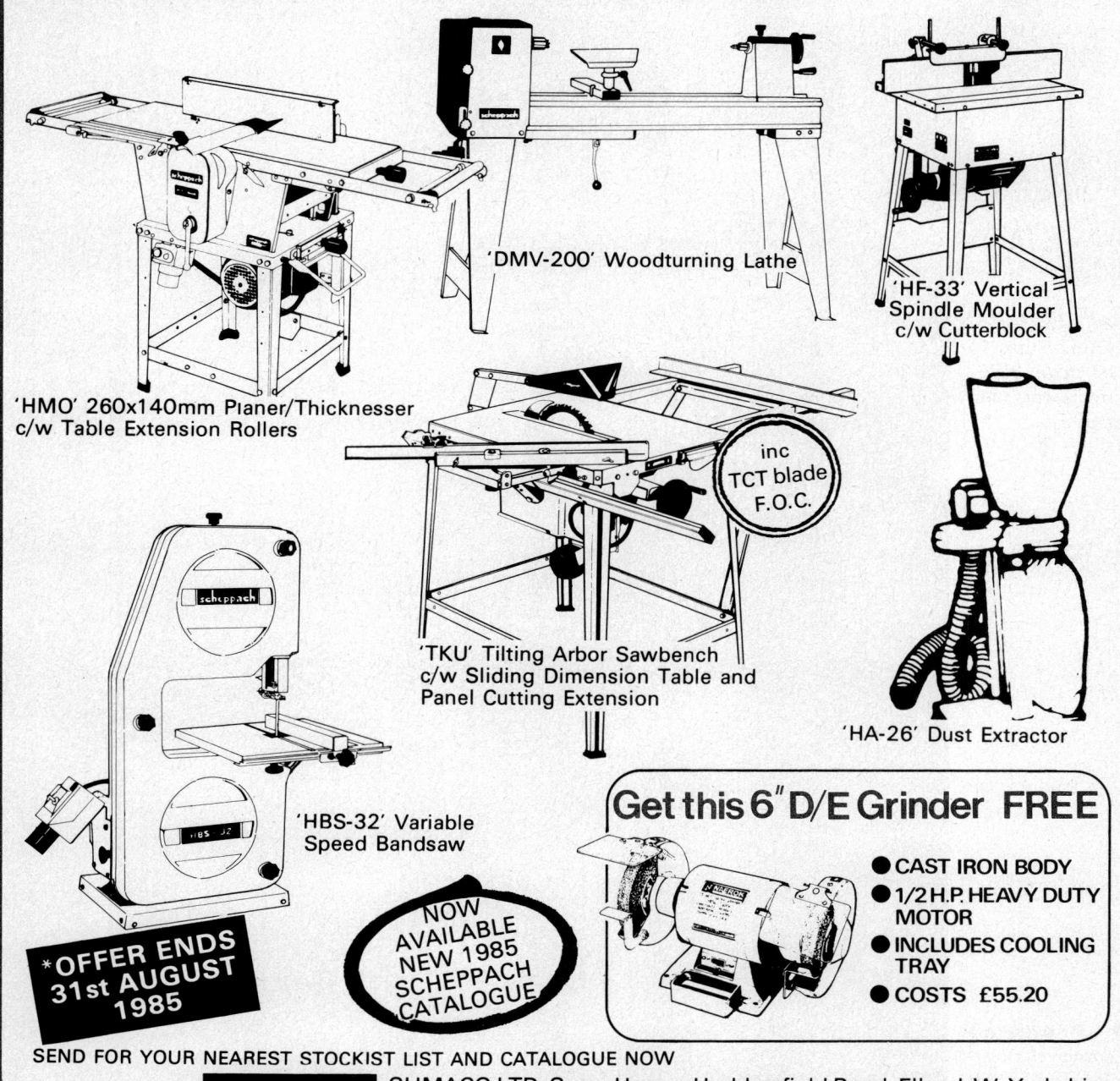

# Don't ring us...

**Meet Neil Clarke — a designer with new ideas (and an old dilemma)**

● *Neil's English-oak dining-chair, with its steam-bent slats, represents one aspect of his work . . .*

● *. . . while his corner chest-of-drawers represents another! The question is, which (if either) will sell?*

● The sideboard and table, like the chair and chest, are in oak, ash and elm. They carry more than a hint of the solid English Arts & Crafts tradition; but as for whether their character will tempt the customers – that's still a matter for conjecture

I've only recently started in business, but I already know what a daunting task it is to get people to purchase my designs!

Sometimes I feel I'm standing on an island that's getting smaller and smaller. Sales are especially difficult in Derbyshire, where I want to base myself; my exhibits at local craft shows arouse only passive interest. At the moment I'm still trying to make ends meet in my father's garage — which makes it impossible to produce goods in large quantities.

As a matter of fact it was the feature on Chris MacDonald (WW/June) which stirred me to share my experience, since I find myself in the same situation as him.

My real interest in making furniture was sparked off back in my schooldays under the expert guidance of an inspiring tutor. I studied woodwork at O-level, after which I could only develop my skills during the long summer vacations in years spent away at art college studying graphic design. Graduating successfully last year (aged 22), I returned to Derbyshire and worked for a short time in a busy studio as an illustrator. At the same time, though, I felt destined to become self-employed (especially after gaining some invaluable down-to-earth bench-work experience helping a friend who luckily has a workshop in the Peak District Park).

I would like to be able to carry on and develop ideas that I formulated whilst at college — notably the novel concept of a telephone box as a corner chest-of-drawers, which I've registered at the Patent Office and have plans to maybe batch-produce myself or possibly find a manufacturer to mass-produce, depending on demand. Other items include a scaled-down version

● A thoroughly medieval blanket-chest stands in massive contrast to what Neil calls the 'pop furniture' elsewhere in his repertoire. Yet both ranges share the same attention to detail

of Abraham Darby's famous Iron Bridge at Telford, used this time as a desk; a Morris Minor car-door cupboard; and the Chrysler Building from New York as another chest-of-drawers.

As well as my 'pop furniture', however, I've designed a range of traditional solid-wood pieces taking their inspiration from the works of Charles Rennie Mackintosh,

Hans Hoffman — and Ernest Gimson, whose work I greatly admire. My chair design in English oak (yet another idea initially conceived at college) consists of steam-bent inter-splicing seat and back slats designed to make people sit properly upright when eating, as well as to give comfort through flexibility of the wood — an idea I plan to develop further. Features

701

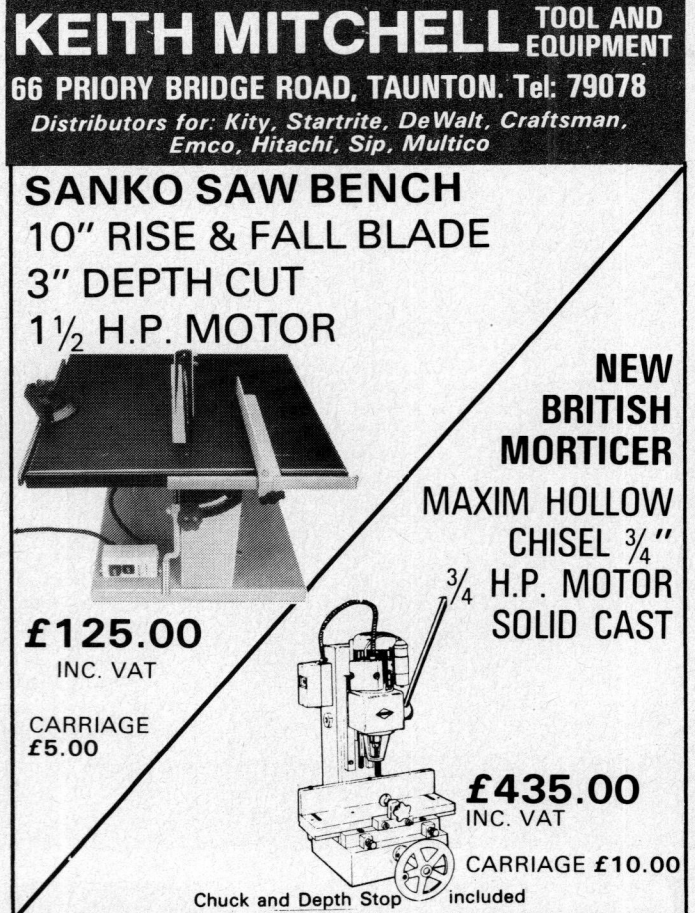

# Don't ring us...

● *Grouped together, the hardwood range displays its family links*

of the chair can be found in the legs of my table designs and in the panelling of chests and cupboards, which also incorporate elm and ash.

After studying design for four years, of course I feel it is essential to develop new ideas, no matter how subtle, within the financial boundaries imposed by making a living. At the same time, when I'm using solid wood (as opposed to plywood) I try to let the natural beauty of the grain speak for itself. Ultimately I would like to do some design work, from rough idea to prototype, for larger companies on a freelance basis.

Like many other budding professionals, I'm finding it difficult to get commissions — for either style of furniture. What's more, I'm starting from scratch. Meanwhile, I'm learning to take any work that comes along! ∎

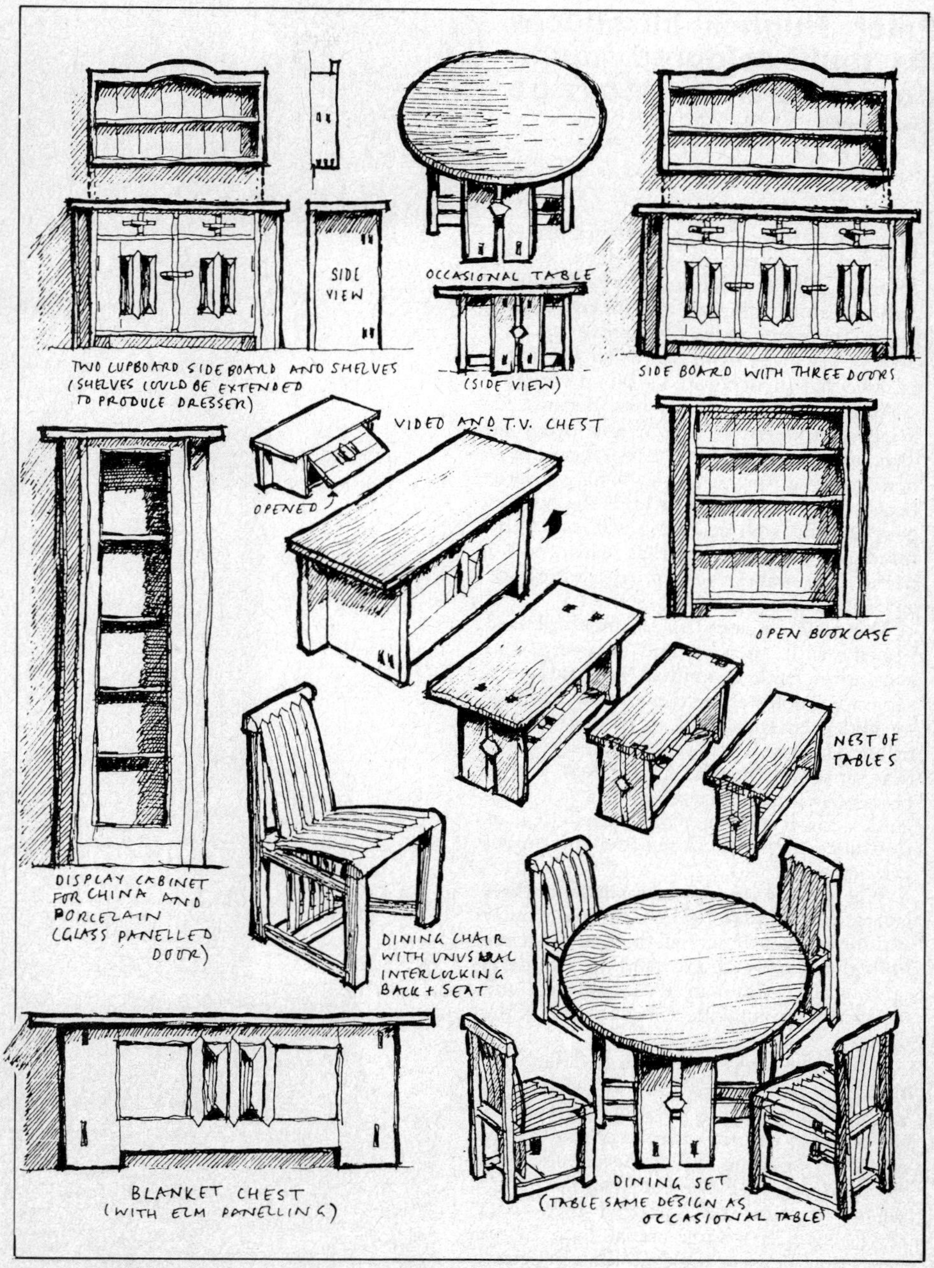

● *Neil's graphic skills are an important design tool – and a potential sales aid to sales*

TWO CUPBOARD SIDEBOARD AND SHELVES (SHELVES COULD BE EXTENDED TO PRODUCE DRESSER)

SIDE VIEW

OCCASIONAL TABLE

(SIDE VIEW)

SIDE BOARD WITH THREE DOORS

VIDEO AND T.V. CHEST

OPENED

OPEN BOOKCASE

NEST OF TABLES

DISPLAY CABINET FOR CHINA AND PORCELAIN (GLASS PANELLED DOOR)

DINING CHAIR WITH UNUSUAL INTERLOCKING BACK + SEAT

BLANKET CHEST (WITH ELM PANELLING)

DINING SET (TABLE SAME DESIGN AS OCCASIONAL TABLE)

# The 43-way stretch

## Peter Hughes introduces his multi-coloured, multi-combination storage system

In the average lounge, the ever-present space problem is nowadays solved mainly by the familiar sideboard unit, display cabinet or wall system in various forms. In designing my Stackstore system I tried to get away from this by producing a cabinet that incorporated a bit of variety.

And variety it certainly has. Because its three components stack in any order or direction, they can be put together in any one of 43 different ways. What's more, because they open at both ends the cabinet goes equally well against a wall or in the middle of the floor. For that reason, too, I decided to make a feature of the interior since it can be so readily seen.

The main carcases use 15mm chipboard lipped with maple and veneered in sycamore. Each individual box sits on a separate stool, being screwed into the legs — and each stool will sit on top of any other. This last feature created a problem in that any movement in the legs would prevent location. My solution was a brass guide dowel in the top of each leg; as insurance, however, I selected the timber very carefully too.

The laminated arch was made from three layers of constructional veneer plus an outer and inner layer of normal thickness. I made both the right- and left-hand pieces on the same single mould in a vacuum-bag, and tenoned them into the rail at the top of the carcase.

As for the interiors, I reckoned that what they needed was colour. I wanted to experiment with dyes anyway, as a means of introducing colour without obscuring the grain by painting or lacquering. For the inside surfaces I pre-cut lengths of ash veneer to size and coloured them with textile dye in a large metal bath before veneering. Because the dye didn't penetrate the veneer fully, I was then able to scrape off the top surface, to leave colour in the grain only.

The dyeing itself was straightforward, but the scraping was hard work. I learned many ways of holding a scraper and suffered numerous blisters in the process. Another problem did arise, however, from my having used an acid dye. I discovered the hard way that if you dry the panels on a steel rack you will end up with a purple-black stain around the points of contact between wood and metal. Unlike the original dye, this does penetrate all the way through! ■

● Peter Hughes has just left Loughborough College of Art and Design. His Stackstore cabinet was at the London International Furniture Show in May.

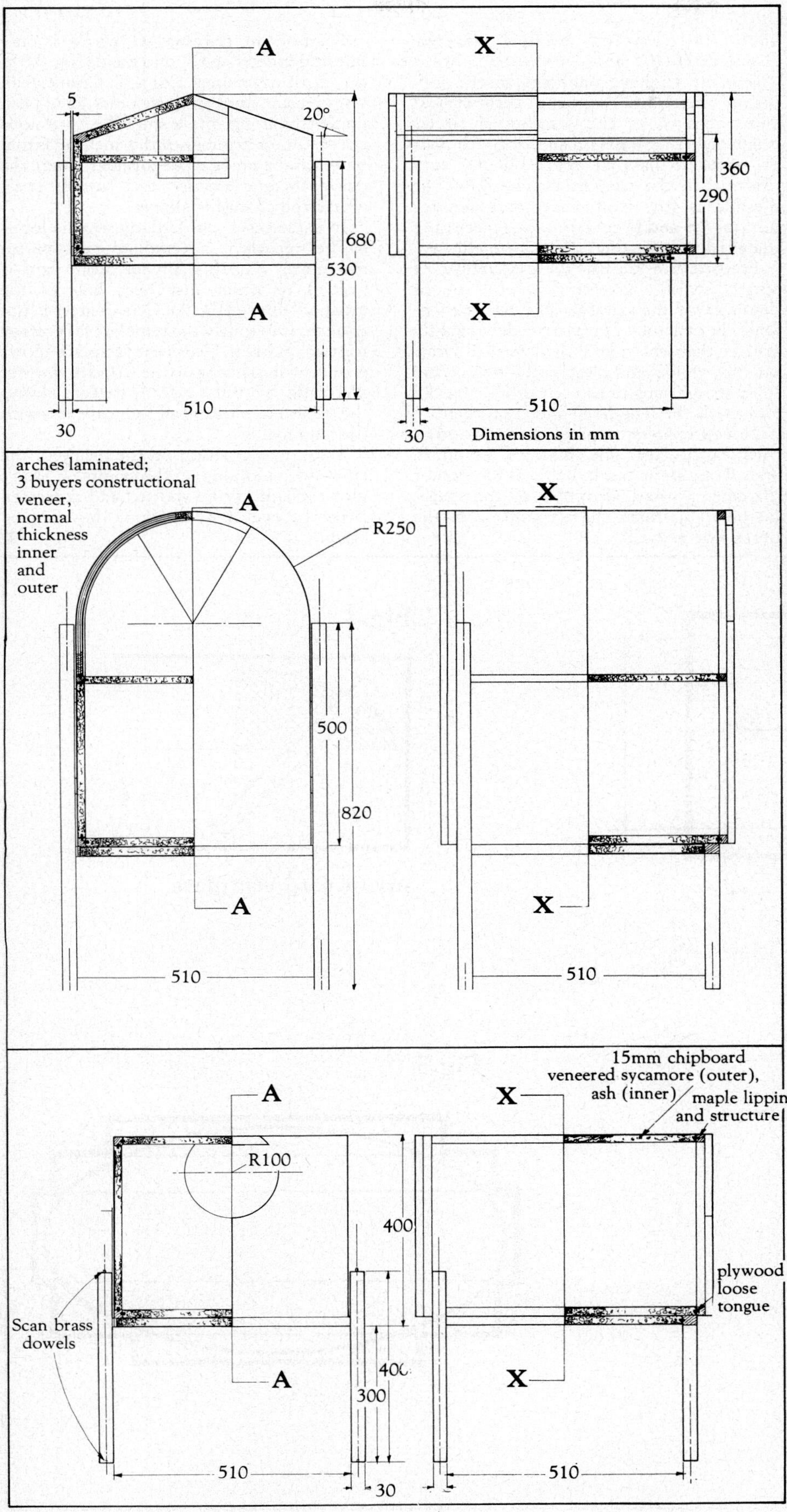

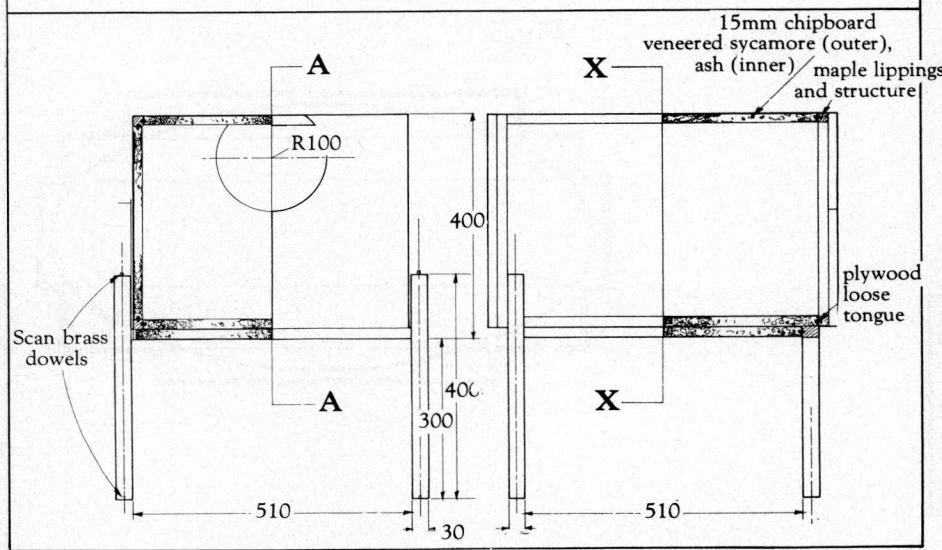

5

20°

680

530

A

A

30

510

X

X

360

290

510

30

Dimensions in mm

arches laminated;
3 buyers constructional
veneer,
normal
thickness
inner
and
outer

A

R250

500

820

A

510

X

X

510

A

A

15mm chipboard
veneered sycamore (outer),
ash (inner)

maple lippings
and structure

R100

400

Scan brass
dowels

400

300

510

30

X

X

plywood
loose
tongue

510

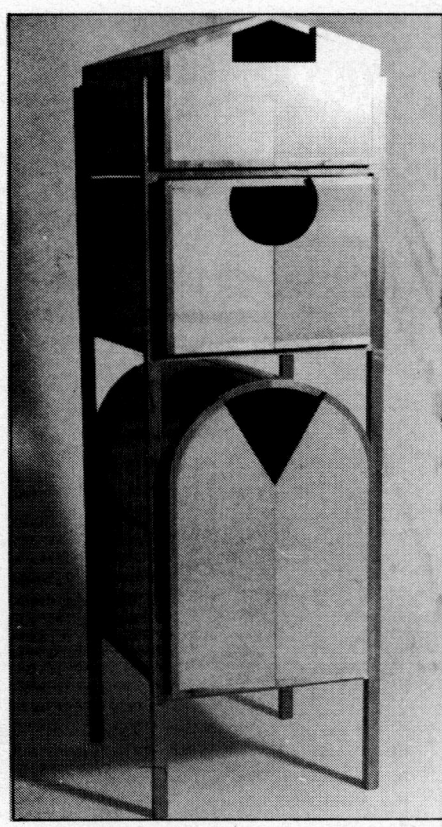

● *Peter Hughes has hit on a suggestive theme with his almost-infinitely-variable trio of cabinets*

● *Each will stand on top of (or beside) any other as the room or the mood requires*

# The elliptical plot

**E**veryone knows you can draw an ellipse with two nails and a bit of string, but few are sure just how it's done, **writes Bob Wearing.** Moreover, this is an excellent method for plotting out a garden flower-bed, but as a method for cabinetmakers it leaves much to be desired. The string invariably stretches, producing something like an elliptical spiral. The knot jolts past each nail, giving bumps on the circumference, and it's not always acceptable to have nailholes in the job. Other methods require geometrical constructions, or the drawing of circles much bigger than the finished job. All right on paper to pass an exam, but not very practical in the workshop. The following method is free from snags and requires jointing-up and preparation of a piece only marginally larger than the chosen ellipse.

Prepare the timber to a rectangle of length slightly greater than the major diameter of the ellipse. This can conveniently be called D. The width will be slightly greater than the minor diameter, d. Draw on this, thinly and clearly, the two centre lines at right-angles to each other, (fig. 1), and mark the lengths D and d on them.

Now prepare a trammel of thin wood or card (fig.2). Near one end mark a point P, and from here mark half of the minor diameter $\frac{d}{2}$ and also half of the major diameter $\frac{D}{2}$. Mark these round on to the other side as well.

Position the trammel so that $\frac{D}{2}$ is on a minor diameter and $\frac{d}{2}$ on a major (fig. 3). In this position make a plot at P. Continue in one quarter until enough plots have been made to join up into a smooth continuous curve. One advantage of this method is that plots can be made close together where the curve changes rapidly, and further apart where the change is slower.

In some cases, particularly when a job is to be repeated, a template may be an advantage. For this, ply or stout card is needed to cover just over half of the finished ellipse (fig. 4). One quarter is not enough. Obviously the template is reversed for two quarters. Use of the template allows economy in jointing up the wood in the first place (fig. 5), but naturally there is always the option of plotting all four quarters with the trammel.

Take up a position on the inside of the curve when joining up the points. A faulty plot can quickly be spotted and corrected either by eye or by applying the trammel again. ∎

**Fig.1**

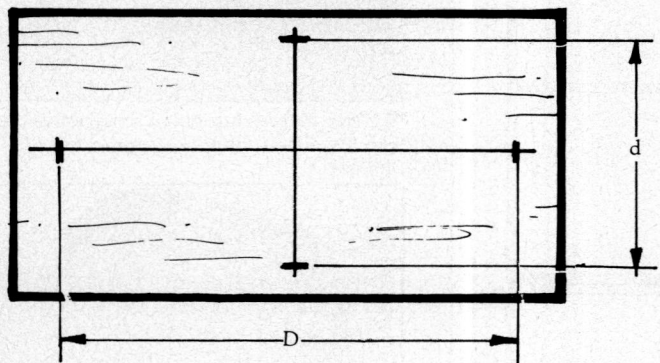

**Fig.4**

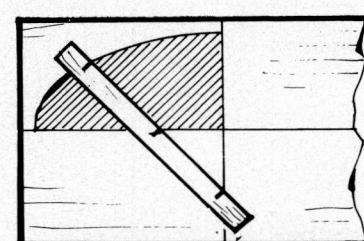

ply or card template

**Fig.2 Trammel**

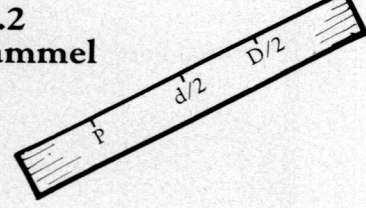

**Fig.3**

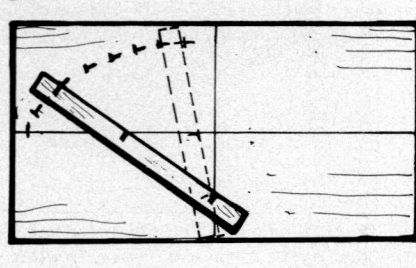

**Fig.5**

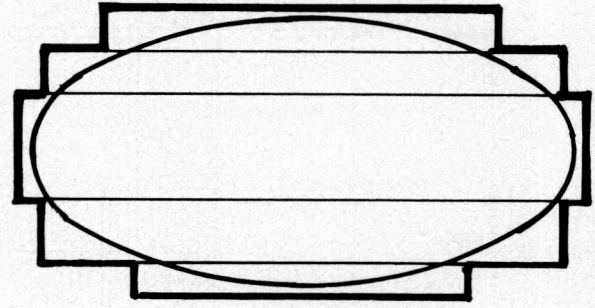

# WOOD SUPPLIERS

**ENGLISH HARDWOODS.** Oak specialists, also Ash, Beach, Cherry, Yew. Over 3000 cu.ft. Send for stock list to W. H. Mason & Son Ltd., The Sawmills, Wetmore Road, Burton-on-Trent, Staffs. Telephone 64651.

**YEW, CHERRY,** walnut, cedar, quarter-sawn oak, lime, elm, ash. Air-dried 1"-4". Flint, The Needles, Hirdon. Telephone (074789) 237.

**50 LACE BOBBIN TURNING BLANKS.** 15-20 different closed grained English and exotic species £7.50 including p&p. Send SAE for lists which include bowl blanks and turning/carving blank prices. Peregrine Crafts, 118 Moore Road, Mapperley, Nottingham.

## THE WOODSTORE
### Suppliers of Native Hardwoods
MOST HOMEGROWN SPECIES IN STOCK
LARGE AND SMALL QUANTITIES
SUPPLIED FRESH SAWN, AIR DRIED
AND KILN DRIED
**MACHINING FACILITIES AVAILABLE**
Send sae for Price List to
**TREEWORK SERVICES LTD**
CHESTON COOMBE, CHURCH TOWN,
BACKWELL, Nr. BRISTOL
OR PHONE FLAX BOURTON
(027583) 3917 OR 3078
*We also offer a tree milling service*

## QUALITY HARDWOODS
### British - Imported - Exotic

Over 50 species available ex stock, in boards, squares and blanks.

*Please call in and see for yourself.*
Open Mon-Thurs: 8am-6pm, Fri: 8am-5pm, Sat: 8am-4pm.
Or use our **MAIL ORDER** service.

Our second edition Fine Wood and Tool Store catalogue is now available - over 100 pages of 'Everything for the Woodworking Craftsman'.

*Please send £1 for a value for money copy to:-*

**JOHN BODDY TIMBER LTD.,**
**FINE WOOD & TOOL STORE, RIVERSIDE SAWMILLS,**
**BOROUGHBRIDGE, N. YORKS. YO5 9LJ. TEL. (09012) 2370**

---

## HOME GROWN HARDWOODS

Most species available. Air dry or fresh sawn. Large or small quantities. Mon.-Fri. 9am-5pm. Sat. 9am-12 noon.

Tiverton Sawmills, Blundells Road, Tiverton, Devon. Tel: (0884) 253102

## SPECIAL "OFFCUTS PACKAGE"

A random selection of English and foreign seasoned hardwood blocks for turning — for bowls, lamps, etc. **ONLY £12.00** plus VAT (£1.80) includes delivery. (UK Mainland).
CASTLETON'S OAK SAWMILLS (TURNING), Biddenden, Nr. Ashford, Kent.

## THE WOOD SHOP

Our Cabinetmaker and Woodturners sawmill specialises in **homegrown**, imported and exotic timbers for the small user.
We can **machine** to your cutting list and **deliver** to your home.
**Open 7 days a week, 9 to 5.**
Send for new brochure to Treske Sawmills, Station Works
Thirsk YO7 4NY
Tel (0845) 22770
**Treske Sawmills**

## QUALITY ENGLISH & IMPORTED MATERIALS

From one of the finest stocks in the UK we can offer high quality English Oak, Sweet Chestnut; Elm, Brazilian Mahogany, Softwoods, Sheet Materials and a whole range of sundry items.

*Telephone or call in Monday to Friday between 8am to 5pm or 8.30am to 12.30pm Saturdays.*

# Wheelers Limited

**Chilton, Sudbury, Suffolk CO10 6XH**
**Telephone: Sudbury 73391 Telex: 987893**

---

## TIMBER SAMPLE BOARDS

For customer or user selection. Home grown, foreign and exotic timbers. Professional lettering, black background, board size 610 × 380 × 9. Sample sizes:
30 samples 55 × 25 × 10
20 samples 115 × 35 × 10
9 samples (imported or home grown) 115 × 75 × 10
Please state whether samples bare or varnished. All boards £20 (inc. p&p to UK).

M. A. Charles, Wood Products, Coachman's Cottage, Albury, Oxon, OX9 2LP. Tel: Ickford 535

**OPEPE — LIMITED QUANTITY** 44" x 1½" square sawn. Pack of 15 pcs. — £10.30 D/d C.W.O. or £5.50 collected. American Red Oak 10 fts. x 3" x 1" kiln dried £3.75 each, collected ex-works: T. T. Smith Ltd., Portersfield Road, Cradley Heath, West Midlands. 0384-69581.

## SEASONED NORTH AMERICAN LONG LEAF PITCH PINE AVAILABLE

Converted from timber beams to your specification or in our standard sizes. From timber originally imported circa 1880.

Traditional and modern mouldings available.

Largest sixes section 14" × 12".

Architraving and Skirting all in stock
*FOR A LIMITED PERIOD SPECIAL SUPPLY WITCH ELM.*

**J. R. NELSON & CO**

"The Saw Mill,"
Wills Farm,
Newchurch, Kent.
**Tel: Hamstreet (023373) 3361**

## ALL ENGLISH TIMBERS, HARDWOOD & SOFTWOOD AIR DRIED & FRESH SAWN

Walnut £15, Brown Oak £15, Oak £12, Cherry & Yew £9, S/Chestnut £8, Ash & Elm £7.50, Maple, Service, Sycamore & Plane £6.50, Lime & Hornbeam £6.00, Beech £5 per cubic foot. Approximate prices, plus carriage & VAT. We welcome you to call and inspect our large stocks.

**HARRY ADCOCK**
**SAW MILLS, CORBY GLEN,**
**GRANTHAM, LINCS.**
**TEL. CORBY GLEN 231**

---

## CRAFTWOODS

Craftwoods has moved to Sunny Devon. Over 50 species in stock, plus books and veneers. Turning squares and carving blanks a speciality. We specialise in Mail Order. Send S.A.E. for catalogue to:

Thatchways, Thurlestone, Kingsbridge, South Devon TQ7 3NJ. Callers welcome. Tel: (0548) 560721

## MACKINTOSH
### CRAFT WOODS
HOMEGROWN, IMPORTED, EXOTICS
**A**MAZIQUE TO **Z**EBRANO
**A**SH TO **Y**EW
Sold by the Plank or Cut and Machined to your specification.
Polishes and Accessories.
SAE for Price List. Open 9-5 except Wednesdays.
Unit 7, Fort Fareham Industrial Estate (Nr. HMS Collingwood), Newgate Lane, Fareham, Hants. PO14 1AH
Tel: Fareham (0329) 221925

# ENGLISH TIMBERS
## KILN DRIED HARDWOODS FOR *THE CRAFTSMAN*

Please visit our new warehouse

**P. Smith, The Old Chapel, Kirkburn,**
**Nr. Driffield, East Yorkshire - Tel: 0377 89301**

# WOOD SUPPLIERS

## NORTH HEIGHAM SAWMILLS

**Good, Kiln-Dried stocks of most Home-Grown timbers, and exotic, Imported Hardwoods.**
Stocks include: Apple, ash, beech, blackwood, box, cedar, cherry, cocobolo, ebony, elm, holly, lemonwood, lignum, lime, mahogany, maple, oak, padauk, pear, plane, rosewood, satinwood, sycamore, walnut, yew, zelkova.

*Please send S.A.E. for priced stock list to:*

**North Heigham Sawmills, Paddock St. (off Barker St.), NORWICH NR2 4TW. Tel: Norwich 622978.**

## SEASONED ENGLISH OAK
### BEST QUALITY AT SENSIBLE PRICES
Carefully dried to 10-12% moisture by dehumidifying process, then graded. Square and waney edged, any quantity. Craig MacDonald (S.C.O.P.E. Products), Fair Meadow, Upper Farringdon, Alton, Hants. Haslemere (0428) 52751 (office hours) or Tisted (042058) 357 (other times)

## OAK AND ELM
Prime oak and elm kiln dried, also other British hardwoods. Cutting and Planing Service. Large or small quantities. Table tops and work tops made to measure.
NEW HALL TIMBER, Duddleston, Ellesmere, Shropshire.
Tel: (0691) 75244

## HEXHAMSHIRE HARDWOODS
Seasoned English hardwoods for North East England and Scotland. Hardwoods for Turning and Carving
**Telephone: (Anytime)
Slaley (043473) 585**

## OAK
*Best Quality Kiln Dried.
Keenest prices available.*

*Also most home grown timbers*
**IRONBRIDGE
(0952) 453373 EVENINGS**

**AIR DRIED** Oak, Ash and Buch. Good quality. Please ring Christow (0647) 52423. Evenings are best.

**HARDWOODS OF KENT:** yew, oak, lime, elm, etc. Large stock bowl blanks. Weekends and evenings phone Canterbury (0227) 731470.

---

## ENGLISH HARDWOODS
Oak, Ash, Sycamore, Beech etc. Air & Kiln dried
*All sizes in stock*
**HOUGHTON TIMBER**
HIGHER WALTON TRADING ESTATE
PRESTON, LANCS.
Tel: Preston 323566

## LIMEHOUSE TIMBER
**Suppliers of quality timbers:** Mahogany, Oak, Teak, Walnut, etc. Bargain here for your selection. A range of machined boards each individually priced. Open 6 days.

**MON-FRI: 9am-5pm
SAT: 9am-3pm**
*Send 17p stamp for stocklist.*
SPECIAL ON FINE ENGLISH ELM £12.50cu.ft. S.T.A
*a division of:*
**DAVEY AND COMPANY
5 GRENADE STREET
LONDON E14 8HL     01-987-6289**

## TIMBERLINE
In addition to our much improved range of over 50 species of fine imported and home grown hardwoods we would like to announce that we now carry comprehensive stocks of the following:
Veneers, decorative lines and bandings, polishes, waxes, stains, adhesives, abrasives and woodwork construction plans. You are always assured of good service and a friendly welcome.
*Business hours*
*Tues.-Sat. 9.30am-5.30pm*
Please send large sae for free catalogue quoting ref. WW.
**TIMBERLINE,
Unit 7, Munday Works,
58-66 Morley Road,
Tonbridge, Kent TN9 1RP.
Tel: (0732) 355626**

## William Garvey
**English Hardwoods for Cabinet & Joinery work**
*Kiln or Air Dried - Machining capacity available.*
Leyhill, Payhembury, Honiton, Devon.
**Tel: Broadhembury (040 484) 430**
Opening hours: Monday-Thursday 8am-5pm unless by appointment.

**AMERICAN OAK** floor boarding, 80 square feet, 2¼" wide, second hand £65.00 the lot. Telephone Rugeley (088 94) 2706.

---

# IMPORTED HARDWOODS
We are the name for Quality Hardwoods. We stock the most comprehensive range of Imported Hardwoods in practically every thickness.
*DON'T BUY
BEFORE YOU TRY US!!*
## ABRAMS AND MUNDY LTD.
**286-288 THE HIGH ROAD, TOTTENHAM, LONDON N15. Tel: 808-8384.**
*and at:*
**THE ELEY TRADING ESTATE, EDMONTON, LONDON N18**

## Broughton-Head Timber Ltd
Parva Stud, Church Row,
Hinton Parva, Swindon,
Wilts. Tel: Walborough (079379) 552

Kiln dried and air dried stocks including Acacia, Amazakoue, Apple, Ash, Beech, Bubringa, Cedar, Cherry, Chestnut, Burr Elm and Oak, Mahogany, English Oak, Pau Rosa, Pear, Sycamore, English and American Black Walnut, Wenge.

Please telephone or send stamp for details
We specialise in small quantities — Minimum one plank
Opening hours: Anytime subject to confirmation by telephone.

---

selected butts of **British hardwoods,**
sawn & kilned through & through:
**quality handtools,** veneers and finishes
**de meester** (the master)
54 Chalk Farm Road  London NW1  01.267 0502  (open Sat and Sun)

---

## Earn £200 per hour drying timber with your own kiln...

My seasoners need so little attention that your time could hardly be better spent than by drying your own timber. Can you afford to invest a few hundred pounds in order to guarantee your work is stable in central heating and ensure that your English hardwoods will cost half as much for many years to come.

No need to keep large untidy stacks of timber slowly drying and spoiling for years and years — these machines work from green in a few weeks and cost only a few pence per cubic foot to run.

The smallest seasoner costs less than £400 and will dry enough timber to keep several people busy or make you some money selling surplus timber. It can live outside and does not usually need a box much larger than 8' × 4' × 4'. As I am the man who developed these machines, I hope that my information, prices, references etc., are second to none.

Write for details or ring me any time for answers to your questions completely without obligation.

**JOHN ARROWSMITH
74 Wilson Street, Darlington,
Co. Durham DL3 6QZ. Tel: 0325 481970**

---

## KiLN WOOD
1a Wickenden Road, Sevenoaks,
Kent TN13 3PJ
Tel: Sevenoaks (0732) 452059
Prime Quality British Hardwoods and Softwoods Fresh Sawn, Air Dried, or Kiln Dried in most thicknesses from ½" to 3".
**A machining service is available**

## ENGLISH OAK
Kiln dried 1" oak boards ¼ sawn, and through and through.
**D. M. Mumford, White Hollow, Ticknall, Derby. Telephone Melbourne (03316) 2121.**

# WOOD SUPPLIERS

---

## DEMONSTRATIONS OF WOODWORKING MACHINES

### SEPTEMBER 19th/20th 1985

*From 10 a.m. until 8 p.m.*

*Demonstrations from the following:*

★KITY                    ★TIME LATHES
★MAKITA              ★INCA
★TREND

# WALKER AND ANDERSON

## WINDSOR ROAD, KINGS LYNN, NORFOLK.

Telephone: (0553) 2443

---

## H. G. MILDENHALL AND SONS JOINERY AND TIMBER

Over sixty species of timber available, small quantities our speciality. From Bobbin blanks, Turning and Carving blanks. Full machining facilities available. Send s.a.e. with cutting list for quote by return. To:

H. G. Mildenhall and Sons,
Joinery and Timber, 11 Oxford Street,
Lambourn, Nr. Newbury, Berks. RG16 7XS. Tel. 0488 71481

**HAMPSHIRE HARDWOODS,** wide range of English and exotic timber in many shapes and sizes for turning, carving, etc. Most air-dried. Ring: Liss 892750 evenings/weekends.

**HARD & SPECIALIST WOODS,** air and kiln dried. Priced stock list. Items prepared to your cutting list. Minns, Unit 5, West Way, Oxford (0865) 247840.

### HARDWOODS

For furniture turning/carving etc. Supplied waney edged or machined to your cutting list. English hardwoods our speciality. No minimum order. Write or phone or price list — quotation.
*Home Address:*
**Counties Hardwoods, Unit F, The Old School House, Station Approach, Woking, Surrey. Tel: Woking (04862) 65860.**
*Please phone before calling.*

### TIMBER SAMPLE BOARDS

For education or customer user selection. Professional lettering, information sheet, black background. Board size 610 × 380. 4 selections available:
9 British 115 × 70 ............ **£16.50**
20 British 115 × 35 ......... **£18.50**
12 British 8 Exours 115 × 35 **£19.50**
20 Imported and Exotics
      115 × 35 ........................ **£21.50**
*Please state whether samples bare or varnished.*
**M.A. Charles, Wood Products, Coachmans Cottage, Albany, Oxon OX9 2LQ. Tel: Ickford 535**

---

# shop guide

The quickest and easiest method of reaching all Woodworkers is to advertise in SHOP GUIDE.
Telephone **Ian 01-437 0699** Rate: **£11.00 per unit.**
Minimum of 6 months

**Key: H** — Hand tools, **P** — Power tools, **W** — Woodworking machinery up to £1,000, **WM** — Woodworking machinery over £1,000, **D** — Demonstration available on selected machines, **T** — Timber, **CS** — Cutting or sharpening services, **MF** — Material Finishes, **A** — Attachments **BC** — Books/catalogues, ★ — Mail order, **E** — EMCO Leisure Centre. **K** — Kity Woodworking Centre.

## AVON

**BATH**                    Tel. Bath 64513
JOHN HALL TOOLS                        ★
RAILWAY STREET

Open: Monday-Saturday
9.00 a.m.-5.30 p.m.
H.P.W.WM.D.A.BC.

**BRISTOL**        Tel. (0272) 741510
JOHN HALL TOOLS LIMITED            ★
CLIFTON DOWN SHOPPING CENTRE
WHITELADIES ROAD
Open: Monday-Saturday
9.00 a.m.-5.30 p.m.
H.P.W.WM.D.A.BC.

**READING**        Tel. (0734) 591361
HOME CARE CENTRE
26/30 KING'S ROAD

Open: Monday-Saturday
9.00 a.m.-5.30 p.m.
H.P.W.D.A.WM.BC.

**READING**        Tel. Littlewick Green
DAVID HUNT (TOOL            2743
MERCHANTS) LTD                      ★
KNOWL HILL, NR. READING
Open: Monday-Saturday
9.00 a.m.-5.30 p.m.
H.P.W.D.A.BC.

**CAMBRIDGE**    Tel. (0223) 247386
H. B. WOODWORKING                    K
105 CHERRY HINTON ROAD
Open: 8.30 a.m.-5.30 p.m.
Monday-Friday
8.30 a.m.-1.00 p.m. Sat.
H.P.W.WM.D.CS.A.

## CHESHIRE

**NANTWICH**        Tel. Crewe 67010
ALAN HOLTHAM                          K★
THE OLD STORES TURNERY
WISTASON ROAD, WILLASTON
Open: Tues.-Sat. 9.00 a.m.-5.30 p.m.
Closed Monday
P.W.WM.D.T.C.CS.A.BC.

## DEVON

**BRIXHAM**        Tel. (08045) 4900
WOODCRAFT SUPPLIES              E★
4 HORSE POOL STREET

Open: Mon.-Sat. 9.00 a.m.-6.00 p.m.

H.P.W.A.D.MF.CS.BC.

**PLYMOUTH**        Tel. (0752) 330303
WESTWARD BUILDING SERVICES        ★
LTD., LISTER CLOSE, NEWNHAM
INDUSTRIAL ESTATE, PLYMPTON
Open: Mon-Fri 8.00 a.m.-5.30 p.m.
Sat. 8.30 a.m.-12.30 p.m.
H.P.W.WM.D.A.BC.

709

## CLEVELAND

---

**BRISTOL**　　Tel. (0272) 629092
TRYMWOOD SERVICES
2a DOWNS PARK EAST, (off North View)
WESTBURY PARK
Open: 8.30 a.m.-5.30 p.m. Mon. to Fri.
Closed for lunch 1.00-2.00 p.m.
P.W.WM.D.T.A.BC.

---

**READING**　　Tel. Reading 661511
WOKINGHAM TOOL CO. LTD.
99 WOKINGHAM ROAD

Open: Mon-Sat 9.00 a.m.-5.30 p.m.
Closed 1.00-2.00 p.m. for lunch
H.P.W.WM.D.CS.A.BC.

---

**MIDDLESBROUGH**　　Tel. (0642)
CLEVELAND WOODCRAFT　　813103
(M'BRO), 38-42 CRESCENT ROAD　　K

Open: Mon-Sat 9.15 a.m.-5.30 p.m.

H.P.T.A.BC.W.W.M.CS.D.

---

**BOURNEMOUTH** Tel. (0202) 420583
POWER TOOL SERVICES
(Sales, spares, repairs)
849-851 CHRISTCHURCH ROAD
BOSCOMBE
Open: Mon.-Fri. 9.00 a.m.-5.30 p.m.
Sat. 9.00 a.m.-5.00 p.m.
H.P.W.CS.K.A.

---

**BRISTOL**　　Tel. (0272) 667013
WILLIS
157 WEST STREET
BEDMINSTER
Open Mon.-Fri. 8.30 a.m.-5.00 p.m.
No Saturday opening

## BUCKINGHAMSHIRE

## CORNWALL

## ESSEX

---

**SLOUGH**　　Tel. (06286) 5125
BRAYWOOD ESTATES LTD.　　★
158 BURNHAM LANE

Open: 9.00 a.m.-5.30 p.m.
Monday-Saturday

H.P.W.WM.CS.A.

---

**HELSTON**　Tel. Helston (03265) 4961
SOUTH WEST　　Truro (0872) 71671
POWER TOOLS　　Launceston
MONUMENT ROAD　　(0566) 3555
　　　　　　　　　　K
H.P.W.WM.D.CS.A.

---

**LEIGH ON SEA**　　Tel. (0702)
MARSHAL & PARSONS LTD.　　710404
1111 LONDON ROAD　　EK

Open: 8.30 a.m.-5.30 p.m. Mon-Fri
9.00 a.m.-5.00 p.m. Sat.
H.P.W.WM.D.CS.A.

## BEDFORDSHIRE

---

**BEDFORD**　　Tel. (0234) 59808
BEDFORD SAW SERVICE　　K
39 AMPTHILL ROAD

Open: Mon.-Fri. 8.30-5.30
Sat. 9.00-4.00
H.P.A.BC.W.CS.WM.D.

---

**MILTON KEYNES**　　Tel. (0908)
POLLARD WOODWORKING　　641366
CENTRE　　★
51 AYLESBURY ST., BLETCHLEY
Open: Mon-Fri 8.30-5.30
Saturday 9.00-5.00
H.P.W.WM.D.CS.A.BC.

---

**TRURO**　　Tel. (0872) 71671
TRURO POWER TOOLS　　E★
30 FERRIS TOWN

Open Mon.-Sat. 8.00 a.m.-12.30 p.m./
1.30 p.m.-5.00 p.m.
H.P.W.WM.D.CS.MF.A.BC.

---

**ILFORD**　　★
CUTWELL TOOLS LTD.
774-776 HIGH ROAD

Mon.-Fri. 9.00 a.m.-5.00 p.m.
and also by appointment.
P.W.WM.A.D.CS.

## BERKSHIRE

---

**COOKHAM**　　Tel. (06285) 20350
CHURCH'S TIMBER
STATION HILL

Open: Mon-Sat 8.30 a.m.-5.30 p.m.
Wed 8.30 a.m.-1.00 p.m.
H.P.W.T.CS.MF.A.

---

**HIGH WYCOMBE**　Tel. (0494)
SCOTT SAWS LTD.　　24201/33788
14 BRIDGE STREET　　★

Mon.-Sat. 8.30 a.m.-6.00 p.m.

H.P.W.WM.D.T.CS.MF.A.BC.

## DERBYSHIRE

---

**DERBY**　　Tel. (0332) 41862
HAZLEHURSTS LTD.　　E★
LONDON ROAD AND CANAL STREET

Open: Mon.-Sat. 8.30 a.m.-5.30 p.m. (retail)
Mon.-Fri. 8.00 a.m.-5.00 p.m. (trade)
H.P.W.MF.A.BC.

---

**ALDERSHOT**　　Tel. (0252) 334422
POWER TOOL CENTRE　　K★
374 HIGH STREET
Open Mon-Fri 8.30 a.m.-5.30 p.m.
Sat 8.30 a.m.-4.00 p.m.

H.P.W.WM.D.A.BC.CF.MF.

## CAMBRIDGESHIRE

## HAMPSHIRE

---

**HIGH WYCOMBE**　　Tel. (0494)
ISAAC LORD LTD.　　22221
185 DESBOROUGH ROAD　　KE

Open: Mon-Fri 8.00 a.m.-5.00 p.m.
Saturday 9.00 a.m.-5.00 p.m.
H.P.W.D.A.

---

**CAMBRIDGE**　　Tel. (0223) 63132
D. MACKAY LTD.　　E★
BRITANNIA WORKS, EAST ROAD

Open: Mon.-Fri. 8.30 a.m.-1 p.m./2.00-
5.00 p.m. Sat. 8.30 a.m.-1.00 p.m.
H.P.W.D.T.CS.MF.A.BC.

---

**BUXTON**　　Tel. (0298) 871636
CRAFT SUPPLIES　　K★
THE MILL, MILLERSDALE

Open: Mon-Sat 9.00 a.m.-5.00 p.m.

H.P.W.D.T.CS.A.BC.

---

**SOUTHAMPTON**　　Tel. (0703)
H.W.M.　　776222
THE WOODWORKERS
303 SHIRLEY ROAD, SHIRLEY
Open: Tues-Fri 9.30 a.m.-6.00 p.m.
Sat 9.30 a.m.-4.00 p.m.
H.P.W.WM.D.CS.A.BC.T.

## GLOUCESTERSHIRE

## HAMPSHIRE

---

**CHELTENHAM**　　Tel. (0242) 39099
HAMBURY MACHINE SERVICES　　E★
UNIT 14, MALMESBURY ROAD

Open: Mon.-Fri. 9.00 a.m.-5.30 p.m.
Sat. 9.30 a.m.-12.00 a.m.
W.WM.P.D.

---

**ALDERSHOT**　　Tel. (0252) 334422
POWER TOOL CENTRE　　K
374 HIGH STREET

Open Mon-Fri. 8.30 a.m.-5.30 p.m.

H.P.W.WM.D.A.BC.

---

**SOUTHAMPTON**　　Tel: (0703)
POWER TOOL CENTRE　　332288
7 BELVIDERE ROAD　　K★
Open Mon-Fri. 8.30-5.30

H.P.W.WM.D.A.BC.CS.MF.

---

**ROCHDALE**　　Tel. (0706) 342123/
C.S.M. TOOLS　　342322
4-6 HEYWOOD ROAD　　E★
CASTLETON
Open: Mon-Sat 9.00 a.m.-6.00 p.m.
Sundays by appointment
W.D.CS.A.BC.

## HERTFORDSHIRE

## KENT

## LANCASHIRE

---

**PORTSMOUTH**　　Tel. (0705)
EURO PRECISION TOOLS LTD　　667332
259/263 LONDON ROAD, NORTH END　　★
　　　　　　　　　　E
Open: Mon-Fri 9.00 a.m.-5.30 p.m.
Sat. 9.00 a.m.-1.00 p.m.
H.P.W.WM.D.A.BC.

---

**ENFIELD**　　Tel. (01-363) 2935
GILL & HOXBY LTD.　　K
133-137 ST. MARKS ROAD EN1 1BB

Mon.-Sat. 8.30 a.m.-6.00 p.m.
Early closing Wednesday 1.00 p.m.
H.P.W.WM.T.CS.A

---

**MAIDSTONE**　　Tel. (0622) 50177
SOUTH EASTERN SAWS (Ind) LTD　　★
COLDRED ROAD,
PARKWOOD INDUSTRIAL ESTATE
Open: Mon.-Fri. 8.00 a.m.-6.00 p.m.
Sat. 9.00 a.m.-12.00 a.m.
B.C.W.CS.WM.PH.

---

**CHEADLE**　　Tel: 061491 1726
ERIC TOMKINSON　　★
86 STOCKPORT ROAD
Open: Mon.-Fri. 9.00 a.m.-4.00 p.m.
Saturday 9.00 a.m.-1.00 p.m.
H.P.W.D.MF.A.BC.

## HUMBERSIDE

---

**TEWKESBURY**　　Tel. (0684)
TEWKESBURY SAW CO. LTD.　　293092
TRADING ESTATE, NEWTOWN　　K

Open: Mon-Fri 8.00 a.m.-5.00 p.m.
Saturday 9.30 a.m.-12.00 p.m.
P.W.WM.D.CS.

---

**GRIMSBY**　　Tel. Grimsby (0472)
　　58741 Hull (0482) 26999
J. E. SIDDLE LTD. (Tool Specialists)　　★
83 VICTORIA STREET
Open: Mon-Fri 8.30 a.m.-5.30 p.m.
Sat. 8.30 a.m.-12.45 p.m. & 2 p.m.-5 p.m.
H.P.A.BC.W.WMD.

---

**MATFIELD**　　Tel. Brenchley
LEISURECRAFT IN WOOD　　(089272)
'ORMONDE,' MAIDSTONE RD.　　2465
TN12 7JG
Open: Mon-Sun
9.00 a.m.-5.30 p.m.
W.WM.D.T.A.

---

**LANCASTER**　　Tel. (0524) 32886
LILE TOOL SHOP　　K
43/45 NORTH ROAD
Open: Monday to Saturday
9.00 a.m.-5.30 p.m.
Wed 9.00 a.m.-12.30 p.m.
H.P.W.D.A.

## KENT

## LANCASHIRE

---

---

**WYE**　　Tel. (0233) 813144
KENT POWER TOOLS LTD.
UNIT 1, BRIAR CLOSE
WYE, Nr. ASFORD

H.P.W.W.M.D.A.CS.

---

**PRESTON**　　Tel. (0772) 52951
SPEEDWELL TOOL COMPANY　　E★
62-68 MEADOW STREET PR1 1SU
Open: Mon.-Fri. 8.30 a.m.-5.30 p.m.
Sat. 8.30 a.m.-12.30 p.m.

H.P.W.WM.CS.A.MF.BC.

---

**BURY**　　Tel. (061 764 6769)
HOUSE OF HARBRU　　★
101 CROSTONS ROAD
ELTON
Open: Mon.-Fri. 9.00 a.m.-5.00 p.m.
Send 2 × 1st class stamps for catalogue
MF.

# shop guide

**MANCHESTER** Tel. (061 789)
TIMMS TOOLS 0909
102-104 LIVERPOOL ROAD ★
PATRICROFT M30 0WZ
Weekdays 9.00 a.m.-5.30 p.m.
Sat. 9.00 a.m.-1.00 p.m.
H.P.A.W.

## LONDON

**ACTON** Tel. (01-992) 4835
A. MILLS (ACTON) LTD ★
32/36 CHURCHFIELD ROAD W3 6ED
Open: Mon-Fri 9.00 a.m.-5.00 p.m.
Saturdays 9.00 am-1.00 p.m.
H.P.W.WM.

**LONDON** Tel. 01-723 2295-6-7
LANGHAM TOOLS LIMITED
13 NORFOLK PLACE
LONDON W2 1QJ

**LONDON** Tel. (01-567) 2922
G. D. CLEGG & SONS ★
83 UXBRIDGE ROAD, HANWELL W7 3ST
Mon-Sat 9.15 a.m.-5.30 p.m.
Closed for lunch 1.00-2.00p.m.
Early Closing 1.00 p.m. Wed.
H.P.A.W.WM.D.CS.

**NORBURY** Tel. (01-679) 6193
HERON TOOLS & HARDWARE LTD
437 STREATHAM HIGH ROAD SW16
Open: Mon-Fri 8.30 a.m.-5.00 p.m.
Wednesday 8.30 a.m.-1.00 p.m.
Sat. 9.00 a.m.-1.00 p.m.
H.P.W.A.

**LONDON** Tel. (01-636) 7475
BUCK & RYAN LTD
101 TOTTENHAM COURT ROAD W1P ODY

Open: Mon.-Fri. 8.30 a.m.-5.30 p.m.
Saturday 8.30 a.m.-4.00 p.m.
H.P.W.WM.D.A..

**WEMBLEY** Tel. 904-1144
ROBERT SAMUEL LTD. (904-1147
7, 15 & 16 COURT PARADE after 4.00)
EAST LANE, N. WEMBLEY ★
Open Mon.-Fri. 8.45-5.15; Sat. 9-1.00
Access, Barclaycard, AM Express, & Diners
H.P.W.CS.E.A.D.

**LIVERPOOL** Tel. (051-207) 2967
TAYLOR BROS (LIVERPOOL) LTD K
195-199 LONDON ROAD
LIVERPOOL L3 8JG
Open: Monday to Friday
8.30 a.m.-5.30 p.m.
H.P.W.WM.D.A.BC.

## MIDDLESEX

**RUISLIP** Tel. (08956) 74126
ALLMODELS ENGINEERING LTD. E★
91 MANOR WAY

Open: Mon-Sat 9.00 a.m.-5.30 p.m.
H.P.W.A.D.CS.MF.BC.

**CROWMARSH** Tel. (0491) 38653
MILL HILL SUPPLIES E★
66 THE STREET
Open: Mon.-Fri. 9.30 a.m.-5.00 p.m.
Thurs. 9.30 a.m.-7.00 p.m.
Sat. 9.30 a.m.-1.00 p.m.
P.W.D.CS.MF.A.BC.

**WOOLWICH** Tel. (01-854) 7767/8
A. D. SHILLMAN & SONS LTD
108-109 WOOLWICH HIGH STREET
SE18
Open: Mon-Sat
8.30 p.m.-5.30p.m.
H.P.W.CS.A.

**HOUNSLOW** Tel. (01-570)
Q.R. TOOLS LTD 2103/5135
251-253 HANWORTH ROAD

Open: Mon-Fri 8.30 a.m.-5.30 p.m.
Sat. 9.00 a.m.-1.00 p.m.
P.W.WM.D.CS.A.

**LONDON** Tel. (01-263) 1536
THOMAS BROTHERS (01-272) 2764
798-804 HOLLOWAY ROAD, N19 E
Open: Mon.-Fri. 8.30 a.m.-5.30 p.m. Thurs.
8.30 a.m.-1 p.m. Sat. 9 a.m.-5 p.m.
H.P.W.WM.CS.MF.BC.

**FULHAM** Tel. (01-385) 5109
I. GRIZZARD LTD. E
84a-b LILLIE ROAD, SW6 1TL
Open: Mon-Sat 9.00-5.30 p.m.
Half day Thursday

H.P.A.BC.W.CS.WM.D.

**TELFORD** Tel. Telford (0952)
ASLES LTD 48054
VINEYARD ROAD, WELLINGTON EK★

Open: Mon. Fri. 8.30 a.m.-5.30 p.m.
Saturday 8.30 a.m.-4.00 p.m.
H.P.W.WM.D.CS.BC.A.

**FARNHAM** Tel. (0252) 725427
A.B.E. CO. LTD. (Quick Hire) ★
GOODS SHED
STATION APPROACH, FARNHAM ★
Open: Mon-Fri. 8.00 a.m.-5.30 p.m.
Sat. 8.00 a.m.-5.30 p.m.
H.P.W.D.CS.A.BC.

### NORFOLK

**IPSWICH** Tel. (0473) 40456
FOX WOODWORKING KE★
142-144 BRAMFORD LANE
Open: Tues., Fri., 9.00 a.m.-5.30 p.m.
Sat. 9.00 a.m.-5.00 p.m.

H.P.W.WM.D.A.B.C.

**NORWICH** Tel. (0603) 898695
NORFOLK SAW SERVICES
DOG LANE, HORSFORD
Open: Monday to Friday
8.00 a.m.-5.00 p.m.
Saturday 8.00 a.m.-12.00 noon.
H.P.W.WM.D.CS.A.

**KINGS LYNN** Tel. (0553) 2443
WALKER & ANDERSON (Kings Lynn) LTD.
WINDSOR ROAD, KINGS LYNN K
Open: Monday to Saturday
7.45 a.m.-5.30 p.m.
Wednesday 1.00 p.m. Saturday 5.00 p.m.
H.P.W.WM.D.CS.A.

**NORWICH** Tel. (0603) 400933
WESTGATES WOODWORKING Tx
61 HURRICANE WAY, 975412
NORWICH AIRPORT INDUSTRIAL ESTATE
Open: 9.00 a.m.-5.00 p.m. weekdays
9.00 a.m.-12.30 Sat.
P.W.WM.D.BC. K

**KINGS LYNN** Tel. (0760) 23073
TONY WADDILOVE ★
STATION HOUSE
LITTLE DUNHAM, (Nr. SWAFFHAM)
Open Tues.-Sat. 9.00 a.m.-5.30 p.m.
H.P.W.DT.CS.A.BC.

**BOGNOR REGIS** Tel. (0243) 863100
A. OLBY & SON (BOGNOR REGIS) LTD.
"TOOLSHOP," BUILDERS MERCHANT
HAWTHORN ROAD K
Open: Mon-Thurs 8 a.m.-5.15 p.m. Fri.
8 a.m.-8 p.m. Sat 8 a.m.-12.45 p.m.
H.P.W.WM.D.T.C.A.BC.

**SWAFFHAM** Tel. (0760) 23073
TONY WADDILOVE,
STATION HOUSE,
LITTLE DUNHAM, KINGS LYNN
Tuesday-Saturday 9.00 a.m.-6.00 p.m.
H.P.W.DT.CS.A.BC.

**GT. YARMOUTH** Tel. (0493)
ANGLIA POWER TOOLS 850388
3 DENESIDE, NR30 2HL

Open: Monday to Saturday
8.30 a.m. 5.30 p.m.
H.P.W.D.CS.A.

## NOTTINGHAMSHIRE

**NOTTINGHAM** Tel: (0602) 225979
POOLEWOOD and 227064/5
EQUIPMENT LTD. (06077) 2421 after hrs
5a HOLLY LANE, CHILLWELL
Open: Mon-Fri 9.00 a.m.-5.30 p.m.
Sat. 9.00 a.m. to 12.30 p.m.
P.W.WM.D.CS.A.BC.

**WITNEY** Tel. (0993) 3885
TARGET TOOLS (SALES, & 72095 OXON
TARGET HIRE & REPAIRS)
TOOLS SWAIN COURT
STATION INDUSTRIAL ESTATE
Open: Mon.-Sat. 8.00 a.m.-5.00 p.m.
24 hour Answerphone
BC.W.M.A.

## SOMERSET

**TAUNTON** Tel. (0823) 85431
JOHN HALL TOOLS ★
6 HIGH STREET

Open Monday-Saturday
9.00 a.m.-5.30 p.m.
H.P.W.WM.D.CS.A.

**TAUNTON** Tel. Taunton 79078
KEITH MITCHELL ★
TOOLS AND EQUIPMENT
66 PRIORY BRIDGE ROAD
Open: Mon-Fri 8.30 a.m.-5.30 p.m.
Saturday 9.00 a.m.-4.00 p.m.
H.P.W.WM.D.CS.A.BC.

**ST. LEONARD'S-ON-SEA** Tel.
DOUST & MONK (MONOSAW)-(0424)
25 CASTLEHAM ROAD 52577

Open: Mon.-Fri. 8.00 a.m.-5.30 p.m.
Most Saturdays 9.00 a.m.-1.00 p.m.
H.P.W.WM.D.CS.A.

## STAFFORDSHIRE

**TAMWORTH** Tel. (0827) 56188
MATTHEWS BROTHERS LTD. K
KETTLEBROOK ROAD
Open: Mon-Sat 8.30 a.m.-6.00 p.m.
Demonstrations Sunday mornings by
appointment only
H.P.WM.D.T.CS.A.BC.

**PETERBOROUGH** Tel. (0733)
WILLIAMS DISTRIBUTORS 64252
(TOOLS) LIMITED K
108-110 BURGHLEY ROAD
Open: Monday to Friday
8.30 a.m.-5.30 p.m.
H.P.A.W.D.WH.BC.

## SUFFOLK

**WORTHING** Tel. (0903) 38739
W. HOSKING LTD (TOOLS & KE★
MACHINERY)
28 PORTLAND RD, BN11 1QN
Open: Mon.-Sat. 8.30 a.m.-5.30 p.m.
Closed Wednesday
H.P.W.WM.D.CS.A.BC.

## TYNE & WEAR

**NEWCASTLE UPON TYNE** Tel.
J. W. HOYLE LTD. (0632) 617474
CLARENCE STREET NE2 1YJ K★
Open: Mon-Fri 8.00 a.m.-5.00 p.m.
Saturday 9.00 a.m.-4.30 p.m.

H.P.A.BC.W.CS.WM.D.

**NEWCASTLE** Tel. (0632) 320311
HENRY OSBOURNE LTD. E★
50-54 UNION STREET

Open: Mon-Fri 8.30 a.m.-5.00 p.m.

H.P.W.D.CS.MF.A.BC.

## WEST MIDLANDS

**BIRMINGHAM** Tel. (021-554) 5177
ROTAGRIP E★
16 LODGE ROAD, HOCKLEY
Open: Mon.-Fri. 9.00 a.m.-5.00 p.m.
Sat. 9.00 a.m.-12.00 p.m.

H.P.W.CS.A.BC.T.MF.

**WOLVERHAMPTON** Tel. (0902)
MANSAW SERVICES 58759
SEDGLEY STREET K★

Open: Mon.-Fri. 9.00 a.m.-5.00 p.m.

H.P.W.WM.A.D.CS.

# shop guide

## YORKSHIRE

**BOROUGHBRIDGE**   Tel. (09012)
JOHN BODDY TIMBER LTD   2370
FINE WOOD & TOOL STORE   ★
RIVERSIDE SAWMILLS
  Open: Mon.-Thurs. 8.00 a.m.-6.00 p.m.
  Fri. 8.00am-5.00pm Sat. 8.00am-4.00pm
H.P.W.WM.D.T.CS.MF.A.BC.

**SHEFFIELD**   Tel. (0742) 441012
GREGORY & TAYLOR LTD   KE
WORKSOP ROAD
  Open: 8.30 a.m.-5.30 p.m.
  Monday-Friday
  8.30 a.m.-12.30 p.m. Sat.
H.P.W.WM.D.

**HARROGATE**   Tel. (0423) 66245/
MULTI-TOOLS   55328
158 KINGS ROAD   K★
  Open: Monday to Saturday
  8.30 a.m.-6.00 p.m.
H.P.W.WM.D.A.BC.

**LEEDS**   Tel. (0532) 574736
D. B. KEIGHLEY MACHINERY LTD.   ★
VICKERS PLACE, STANNINGLEY
PUDSEY LS2 86LZ
  Mon.-Fri. 9.00 a.m.-5.00 p.m.
  Sat. 9.00 a.m.-1.00 p.m.
P.A.W.WM.CS.BC.

**HUDDERSFIELD**   Tel. (0484)
NEVILLE M. OLDHAM   641219/(0484)
UNIT 1 DALE ST. MILLS   42777
DALE STREET, LONGWOOD   ★
  Open: Mon-Fri 8.00 a.m.-5.30 p.m.
  Saturday 9.30 a.m.-12.00 p.m.
P.W.WM.D.A.BC.

**THIRSK**   Tel. (0845) 22770
THE WOOD SHOP   ★
TRESKE SAWMILLS LTD.
STATION WORKS
  Open: Seven days a week 9.00-5.00

T.H.MF.BC.

**KEIGHLEY**   Tel. (0535) 663325
EUROMAIL (TOOLS)   ★
PO BOX 13
108 EAST PARADE
  Open 9.15 a.m.-5.00 p.m.
  Not Tuesday but inc. Saturday
H.P.W.A.BC.

**CLECKHEATON**   Tel. (0274)
SKILLED CRAFTS LTD.   872861
34 BRADFORD ROAD   ★
  Open: 9.00 a.m.-5.00 p.m. Monday
  Saturday Lunch 12.00 a.m.-1.00 p.m.
H.P.A.W.CS.WM.D.

**LEEDS**   Tel. (0532) 790507
GEORGE SPENCE & SONS LTD.
WELLINGTON ROAD
  Open: Monday to Friday
  8.30 a.m.-5.30 p.m.
  Saturday 9.00 a.m.-5.00 p.m.
H.P.W.WM.D.T.A.

### SCOTLAND

**EDINBURGH**   Tel. (031 337) 5555
THE SAW CENTRE   ★
38 HAYMARKET TERRACE
HAYMARKET
  Open: 8.30 a.m.-5.30 p.m.
  Monday-Saturday
H.P.W.WM.D.CS.A.

**PERTH**   Tel. (0738) 26173
WILLIAM HUME & CO   K
ST. JOHN'S PLACE
  Open: Monday to Saturday
  8.00 a.m.-5.30 p.m.
  8.00 a.m.-1.00 p.m. Wednesday
H.P.A.BC.W.CS.WM.D.

**CARLISLE**   Tel: (0228) 36391
W. M. PLANT
ALLENBROOK ROAD
ROSEHILL, CA1 2UT
  Open: Mon.-Fri. 8.00 a.m.-5.15 p.m.
  Sat. 8.00 a.m.-12.30 noon
P.W.WM.D.CS.A.

**CULLEN**   Tel: (0542) 40563
GRAMPIAN WOODTURNING SUPPLIES AT
BAYVIEW CRAFTS
Open Mon.-Sat. 9.00 a.m.-5.30 p.m. Sunday
10.00 a.m.-5.30 p.m. Open later July/Aug.
Sept. Demonstrations SAT/SUN or by
H.W.D.MF.BC. appointment

**TAYSIDE**   Tel: (05774) 293
WORKMASTER POWER TOOLS LTD.   ★
DRUM, KINROSS
  Open Mon.-Sat. 8.00 a.m.-8.00 p.m.
  Demonstrations throughout Scotland by
  appointment
P.W.WM.D.A.BC.

**GLASGOW**   Tel. (041 429) 4374/
THE SAW CENTRE   4444, Telex: 777886
600 EGLINGTON STREET   E★
G5 9RR
  Open: Mon-Fri 8.00 a.m.-5.30 p.m.
  Saturday 9.00 a.m.-1.00 p.m.
H.P.W.WM.D.CS.A.

## WALES

**CARDIFF**   Tel. (0222) 595710
DATAPOWER TOOLS LTD,
MICHAELSTON ROAD,
CULVERHOUSE CROSS
  Open: Mon.-Fri. 8.00 a.m.-5.00 p.m.
  Sat. 9.00 a.m.-1.00 p.m.
H.P.W.WM.D.A.

**CARMARTHEN**   Tel. (0267) 237219
DO-IT-YOURSELF SUPPLY   K
BLUE STREET, DYFED
  Open: Monday to Saturday
  9.00 a.m.-5.30 p.m.
  Thursday 9.00 a.m.-5.30 p.m.
H.P.W.WM.D.T.CS.A.BC.

**CARDIFF**   Tel. (0222) 396039
JOHN HALL TOOLS LIMITED   ★
CENTRAL SQUARE
  Open: Monday to Saturday
  9.00 a.m.-5.30 p.m.
H.P.W.WM.D.A.BC.

**SWANSEA**   Tel. (0792) 55680
SWANSEA TIMBER & PLYWOOD CO. LTD.
57-59 OXFORD STREET   ★
  Open: Mon to Fri 9.00 a.m.-5.30 p.m.
  Sat. 9.00 a.m.-1.00 p.m.
H.P.W.D.T.CS.A.BC.

# Classified Advertisements

## FOR SALE

FOR ALL SUPPLIES
FOR THE

### Craft of Enamelling

ON METAL
**Including**
**LEAD-FREE ENAMELS**

PLEASE SEND 2 × 10p STAMPS
FOR FREE CATALOGUE, PRICE
LIST AND WORKING
INSTRUCTIONS

**W. G. BALL LTD.**
ENAMEL MANUFACTURERS

Dept. W. LONGTON
STOKE-ON-TRENT
ST3 1JW

---

**MUSICAL MOVEMENTS**
★ LOVE STORY ★ LARAS THEME ★ SPEAK SOFTLY LOVE ★ FUR ELISE ★ FEELINGS ★ FASCINATION ★ IMPOSSIBLE DREAM ★ MUSIC BOX DANCER ★ LA POLOMA ★ THE EMPEROR WALTZ ★ TRY TO REMEMBER ★ ROMEO AND JULIET ★
Complete with screws and spring mechanism £2.50 inc. p&p. 20 or more of one tune ordered £1.50 each. Available from:
**The Jewel Box Shop,**
112 Pentonville Road, London N1 9JB.

---

---

**LACE BOBBIN TURNING BLANKS** in unusual and exotic hardwoods and ivory. SAE for list: J. Ford, 5 Squirrels Hollow, Walsall WS7 8YS.

**LACE BOBBIN PLANKS**, over 90 different woods, lists free, 50 exotic £4.50. 35 veneer samples. £1. P. Rushbrook, 39 Deben Avenue, Martleshom, Ipswich.

**GLASS CUTTERS** ideal for handyman. Used in our own glass works. Instructions. P&P. £6.50 each. F. Sherwood, Dept. W. 54 The Burroughs, Hendon NW4 4AN.

**LACE BOBBIN PLANKS.** Over 90 different woods, lists free. P. Rushbrook, 39 Deben Avenue, Martlesham, Ipswich.

**BAGS, WRAPPINGS, TISSUE, BOXES, BUSINESS CARDS.** Any shape, size, amount. Comprehensive samples. 90p. Terry Andrews, 53A Parsons St., Banbury OX16 8NB.

**MARKING STAMPS** — name stamps branding irons supplied to your requirements SAE for details. Davey, 37 Marina Drive, Brixham, Devon TQ5 8BB. T/C

**25,000 WESTERN HEMLOCK** and Brazilian Mahogany staircase spindle blanks (before turning). 3' long, 1⅜" × 1⅜" sq. To be sold in large or small quantities, from 30p to £2 each. Also wanted home DIY turners to complete and return and sell back finished turned spindles. Also solid oak supreme quality kitchen cabinet arched top doors all metric. List price £50 each. To clear from £5, £8, £18 each. 300 new comfort arch top sashed red deal, window frames. Full range primed (not polished, all to be sold at 65% off list price e.g. 8 × 4 metric oblong 4 arches list £165 — £65 4 × 4 £30 etc. All enquiries Turton 0204 Bolton Lancashire area 852339 any time.

---

**HAND CARVED**
'Adam Style' Mantle motifs in Mahogany — Example 10" × 5" centre lamp and two side pieces.
Send S.A.E. for details and quotation. Your own design quoted for if required.
**SAM NICHOLSON**
22 Lisnagarvey Drive, Lisburn,
Co. Antrim, N. Ireland.
Phone Lisburn 3510

---

**30 CUBIC FEET** of air dried unprepared mixed hardwoods. Oak, Beech, Elm and Yew £250. K. A. Collis 0633 400609.

---

**SHOPSMITH MARK 5 WOODWORKING MACHINE**
Planer, saw, lathe, drill press, shaper, router and sander. Solid, reliable and compact. Quick change function £2,200.
**Telephone: 01-747-0187 or 01-995-9944**

---

MORTISERS; TENNONERS; SPINDLES; PLANERS; BANDSAWS; LATHES; CROSSCUTS; ROUTERS; SANDERS; DRILLS? YOU CAN CERTAINLY SEE ALL CLASSES AND TYPES OF MACHINES HERE.

WE ARE MAIN STOCKING AGENTS FOR:
MULTICO; ELU; SEDGWICK; KITY; SCHEPPACH; INCA; CORONET; DeWALT; WARCO; DOMINION; HITACHI; STARTRITE; TREND; ASHLEY ILES; SORBY.

*CALL US ABOUT WOODTURNING LESSONS*
*WOODCARVING LESSONS (See our Swiss carving tools)*
**ALWAYS HELPFUL, KNOWLEDGEABLE, GOOD SERVICE AT:**
## CLEVELAND WOODCRAFT
**38-42 CRESCENT ROAD, MIDDLESBROUGH.
TEL: (0642) 813103**

---

THE FINEST SELECTION ON DISPLAY IN SCOTLAND!
WOODWORKING & METALWORKING MACHINERY POWER TOOLS HAND TOOLS
**THE SAW CENTRE**
HIRE OR BUY!
*Visit our* NEW SHOWROOM at EGLINTON TOLL GLASGOW
Tel: 041-429 4444/4374, Telex: 777886 SAWCO G
Also at, 38 Haymarket Terrace, Edinburgh EH12 5JZ. Tel: 031-337 5555
**OPEN** Mon - Fri 8am - 5pm Sat 9am - 1pm

---

### 𝕭𝖞𝖌𝖔𝖓𝖊𝖘

Just one item from our catalogue

**MARPLES PARING GOUGES**
Boxwood handles
1/4" – 6" radius
Straight or Cranked

*WHILE STOCKS LAST*

Special rates for quantities

Please send 50p in stamps for catalogue

**TILGEAR**, 20 Ladysmith Road, Enfield, Middx., EN1 3AA  Tel: 01-363 8050/3080

---

**ELECTRA** Dust Extractor Spa 1000 unused. Attaches to machines or used separately £150 Dalgety Bay (0383) 822289.

---

**ARCOY DOVETAIL JIG** complete with 3 cutters. Never used, Boxed £60.00. London 01-677 2955.

**ELU MFF80K** planer/rabbeter, case and accessories, used once £75. BK2 bandsaw, jig/fretsaw & circle cutting attachments, £55. 01-845 4153.

**WORKING** antique morticing m/c by Powis James, London. Includes chisels. £120 o.n.o. Also other machinery. Owner moving. Tel: (Wilts.) 321.

**CORONET IMP** bandsaw motorised. Excellent condition £275. Contact K.G. Thorp, 71 Oaklands Park, Buckfast Leigh, Devon. Tel: Buckfast Leigh (0364) 42609.

**HEGNER MULTICUT 2**, as new, would suit person contemplating purchasing new machine £215.00, no offers. Telephone Formby (07048) 76914.

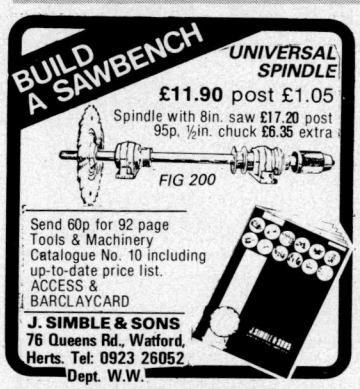

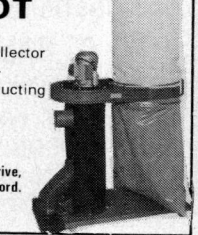

714

715

# Letters

I WAS ABOUT halfway through the May *Woodworker* when I stopped reading and thought to myself, 'This is terrific! This is an incredible issue. What are they going to do for an encore in the next and future issues?' I finished the issue and continued to feel the same way about the magazine.

I've been a subscriber for about 11 years and have enjoyed the magazine under each of the editors, as it seemed to me each put his own personality into the contents. You and your associates have put together a new kind of *Woodworker*.

As I now look back on the issue it is more difficult to put my finger on just what it is. No matter. I still like it.

I will add that what I've liked most is Max Burrough's 'Then'. It's always been great fun to end up with that.

Best wishes for future fine issues.

*Russ Zimmerman, Putney,
Vermont, USA*

---

SOME 12 MONTHS AGO, at the age of 58, I lost my sight completely as a result of retina problems.

At the start of my working life I was apprenticed as a carpenter and joiner, going on to become a foreman and later a contracts manager in the building industry. Although I did not have to use tools in my employment, I continued to make many things over the years in my spare time, including furniture for the home. The last item I made before losing my sight was a longcase clock, including all the works with the exception of the chapter ring.

After the initial period of shock at losing my sight, I have started to interest myself again in the workshop. It is obvious from the start that a re-think on many operations is necessary. The first thing I attempted was to construct two shooting-boards, one for a metal jack-plane and one for a block-plane, based on an article in *Woodworker*, February 1983, by Bob Wearing. These have proved excellent in use.

Many jigs will be required. One difficulty is in marking out. One can obviously use a pointed awl, but it is difficult to find the centres of cross-lines. Cutting freehand also presents problems relating to square ends and so on. To overcome this I have recently purchased a Nobex mitre saw, which I find excellent for cutting timber square up to its maximum capacity. I am also considering buying a plunge router, which I think may help me with many operations. I would appreciate any views on this.

I recently also bought a Braille rule, inches being marked with a large dot, with two dots at the 6 and 12in lengths; the edges are notched — the first inch in sixteenths and the remainder in eighths, the opposite edge being in metric. However, the transfer of sizes to gauges has been made easier by having wood blocks made accurately (by a relative), ranging in size from 4x2x1in, and decreasing in thickness down to $\frac{1}{16}$in — the width and length also varying. Threaded on a length of string they can be used quite quickly, and put together to form various combinations.

Patience is definitely needed in view of the length of time needed to carry out operations. I would welcome an exchange of views and ideas with anyone in the same circumstances as myself (I hope a sighted person will read this to them). Ideas or suggestions from sighted people would be more than welcome, too.

I still continue with *Woodworker* and find it very interesting, although of course it now has to be read to me.

*I. L. Styles, 74 Purlewent Drive,
Weston, Bath, Avon BA1 4BA*

---

POTENTIAL BUYERS of the four-jaw self-centring chuck (WW/July, p531) would be well advised to think carefully before investing in what is presumably a fairly expensive piece of equipment.

The drawbacks in use are obvious: total accuracy in manufacture is impossible, so

four jaws cannot be expected to exert equal pressure on a perfect circle. Moreover, before they can grip a four-sided object, the four sides must match, across flats, any inaccuracy in the chuck jaws. Moreover, the inaccuracies will change according to the size of workpiece held, since no chuck scroll is or remains constant in its errors.

Four-jaw self-centring chucks are not common: I can find only one in my catalogues, and that was offered with soft jaws (to be machined locally for special purposes) for use in production-engineering shops. In short, the type is about as generally useful to an amateur as the three-jaw independent it was once my misfortune to use! An overall disadvantage of any self-centring chuck, three or four-jaw, is its great weight. And cost.

Better by far, in my judgment, would be a four-jaw independent. Anyone with a repetition job, balusters or the like, need only slacken off two adjacent jaws to obtain all the 'benefits' of a self-centring unit while, at the same time, getting the most versatile and reliable work-holding device possible.

*Alan Thomas, London SE3*

---

THANK YOU and David Ellis for the kind words about my book *Refinishing Antique Furniture* in the June edition of your magazine. I feel that I must comment on Mr Ellis' disappointment at finding no reference to scrapers.

I do, indeed, condemn their use in any process of finishing antique furniture. The complete removal of patina and natural faded colour from an antique surface, which can so easily result from the over-enthusiastic use of a scraper, will present a daunting problem for the beginner to rectify. Hence my plea, in the chapter on stripping, for the reader never to plane, scrape or sand down a surface which appears to be too far gone.

Better a piece of furniture which shows a few signs of generations of use than one which looks as though it came from the cabinetmaker's yesterday!

*Michael Bennett, Wirral*

---

PROFESSIONALS doubtless scorn the use of honing guides for tool sharpening, but for me as an amateur they turn sharpening from a chore into a pleasure. I have tried most types.

The honing guide referred to by Mr Seward (WW/June) was certainly in production in 1983 in the USA — it appears in the Garrett Wade catalogue for that year with a price of $15.90 (Cat. No. 99MO1.01) and is presumably still available by mail order. I have one of these but I find it less useful than other, cheaper devices. Its accuracy depends upon the bench being perfectly flat and the stone being completely uniform in thickness throughout its length. More importantly, there is no automatic alignment of the tool

with respect to the stone, and I find it fiddly to locate the tool in the clamp to give both the correct honing angle and a square edge. The Japanese honing guides, which have a roller running on the stone but across its full width, are also not self-aligning. Mine also has the disadvantage that the bearing surface of the casting on which the tool rests is curved. The result is that a wide plane iron clamped in the guide is bent to a slight 'belly' by the clamping pressure and hones to a concave edge — the worst possible! This is probably not a problem with the much thicker irons of Japanese planes for which these guides are intended.

After much experimenting I always return to the Eclipse honing guide, despite its small roller. Chisels and plane irons are located firmly and perfectly square to the stone by the screw clamp, and the required angle can easily be set accurately. I usually use a rule across the roller and the tool bevel to reproduce the existing bevel angle, and find this gives perfect results. My ideal would be the clamping method of the Eclipse combined with the full-width roller of the Japanese guide to reduce hollowing of the stone. Until someone makes the perfect guide, the Eclipse remains the closest approximation to this ideal.

I do all my sharpening on Japanese waterstones and find them superb. It is true that the coarser stones wear hollow very easily, particularly when used with a honing guide, but the advice of Roger Buse (WW/April) to flatten them by rubbing two together sounds like a ploy for the sale of stones! They are easily flattened by a few seconds' rubbing on a sheet of wet-and-dry paper, used wet and supported on a sheet of plate glass.

The reason that almost all small bench-grinders run at high speeds is because they are designed for the sharpening of high-speed-steel lathe tools in engineering workshops. The method of speed control advocated by Mr Kendall-Carpenter (WW/May) will only work with the type of motor which has a coil-wound commutator, such as are used in electric drills and other portable power tools.

*N. C. Billingham, Brighton*

---

THANK YOU for June's interesting symposium 'Life with the lathe'. As usual, the expert commentary was rich with that mixture of rational principle and personal foible that distinguishes the artist-craftsman from the pure technologist on the one hand and the creative dreamer on the other. The feature reminded me of the bewildering contrasts of advice I received as a young apprentice joiner.

The almost universal approval given to the Harrison could hardly be disputed. No one who has witnessed the persistent abuse of the Harrisons in schools could doubt the inspired brilliance of its robust design. The machines just grind on regardless, with that mechanical neutrality that seems to bear little relationship to the degree of super-

vision or skill of the operator. Nevertheless, I concur with one or two of the experts who believe even the Harrison could be improved for adult comfort and convenience. That could be said, of course, of every machine on the market.

One might well turn up one's nose at the flimsy boxed tinplate hurdy-gurdy machines designed fairly obviously for no more admirable reason than to persuade Dad to part with a week's wages and get him out of the house for the odd creative hour in the shed. But I found Ray Key's sideways indictment of the Elu a trifle summary. For sure, it hovers a little uncertainly on the boundaries between fast-buck DIY and the bespoke professional market. I bought one for use at home three years ago after holding a technical debate with myself about those hollow die-cast parts in head-stock, tail-stock, bed-yokes and saddle, which initially risked analogy with the throwaway razor. but I have been pleasantly surprised by the performance — though I did have to file the scalloped bases of the tail-stock to get initially true centres lined-up on the tubular bed when I first unpacked the machine, and I made my own saddle and rests to replace the rather puny originals. But I agree with what William Wooldridge has to say about his own version of the twin-tube bedded lathe, for the Elu bed is surprisingly stiff. Nor is there a shortage of driving power. Three speeds are less adequate than four, but the DB speed options are sensible, and the ease and safety of speed-changing at least ensure that one uses all three rather than opting not to bother.

Despite my own particularly heavy cabinet I have had my Elu dancing slightly only on a couple of notable occasions. I have often used the full bed length, and close to full swing often on the head-stock end. I cannot say that I have been sold a sick pup for the £170 I paid for my DB180 in 1982 from Daving Hung Tools in Reading. I appreciate the unusually lofty bed, which enables me to fit removable horizontal tool-racks on the bench-top beneath the lathe, and to lay out all the tools I need for any particular job ready for grabbing in the right plane for instant use — and for replacement again. The wide span of the tubular bed enables a small portable too tray to be set across it to hold calipers unaltered by being stuffed in smock pockets, and expensive open bottles of sealer to be preserved from the usual fate of being knocked over on the bench or topped up with flying shavings. The Craft Supplies 4-in-1 chuck series effectively supplements the rather pricey (and rather old-fashioned?) Elu accessory range, some items of which are nevertheless quite well-made and functional. Unlike that on the more élite Myford, the DB180's bed does not fill up with shavings, and its adjustment arrangements are straightforward. Unlike those of some Avon owners, my knuckles remain unscarred by coy tightening screws, funny flaps and wayward tommy-bars.

*John Bull, Frecheville Campus, Sheffield*

# The magazine for the craftsman
## ~ and the aspiring craftsman!

October 1985
Vol. 89
No. 1103

● Pat Biddulph's charming piece from the LCF recalls summer with its carved frieze of moths and plants. Complete plans and information start on p736

On the cover: A low table by renowned designer and teacher David Field, plus student work from (left to right) Mathew Preddy of Suffolk College, Warren Bailey of Rycotewood and Juliet Whitaker of the LCF. Extracts from David's book *Projects in Wood* start on p774; our college reports start on p740

**Publisher** Ray Lewis
**Editor** Peter Collenette
**Deputy Editor** Aidan Walker
**Advertisement Manager** Paul Holmes
**Graphics** Jeff Hamblin
**Guild of Woodworkers** Aidan Walker
**Publishing Director** John Foster
Editorial, advertisements and Guild of Woodworkers
1 Golden Square, London W1R 3AB, telephone 01-437 0626

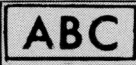

**Subscriptions and back issues** Infonet Ltd, 10-13 Times House, 179 Marlowes, Hemel Hempstead, Herts HP1 1BB; telephone Hemel Hempstead (0442) 48434
**Subscriptions per year** UK £16.95; overseas outside USA (accelerated surface post) £19.20, USA (accelerated surface post) $24.90, airmail £46.20
**UK trade** SM Distribution Ltd, 16-18 Trinity Gardens, London SW9 8DX; telephone 01-274 8611
**North American trade** Bill Dean Books Ltd, 151-49 7th Avenue, PO Box 69, Whitestone, New York 11357; telephone 1-718-767-6632
**Printed in Great Britain** by Ambassador Press Ltd, St Albans, Herts
**Mono origination** Multiform Photosetting Ltd, Cardiff
**Colour origination** Derek Croxson Ltd, Chesham, Bucks
© Argus Specialist Publications Ltd 1985
ISSN 0043 776X

## Argus Specialist Publications Ltd
1 Golden Square, London W1R 3AB; 01-437 0626

# Woodworker
# This month

## Initial initiative

IDF is the latest letter-combination to hit a design world which already resembles alphabet soup. The good news is that it stands for something potentially most useful.

The Independent Designers Federation is a new 70-strong grouping whose name describes it well. Small designers and designer-makers often have plenty of ideas and energy, but they face familiar problems when they come to market their talents. IDF aims to crack the nut by providing a contact for clients (retailers, contract specifiers, interior designers, architects and the like) who seek high-quality wares.

This, says IDF press officer Gina Tajirian, will take the form of 'premises housing exhibitions space for trade visitors to view a selection of products which will change regularly' — but there'll also be 'office facilities with basic business functions, plus a database containing market information, technical information, and details of manufacturing sub-contractors and suppliers'.

Indeed, the group also hope to generate links with larger manufacturers and so boost small firms' designs and prototypes into batch or mass-production. Currently, as Gina points out, much of the very best work reaches only and exclusive clientele.

Also planned is a group presence at trade shows, starting with Style 86 at Olympia on 27-31 October. Gina's own business, Planks Design Consultancy, was featured in *Woodworker*'s review this January of last year's Style 84 exhibition (there hasn't been a Style 85), where they took a pioneering and successful stand. A two-handed partnership operating from a small unit in the bowels of a council block in London's Kentish Town, they typify the hand-to-mouth yet resourceful firms which IDF aims to help.

● Details of IDF from Gina Tajirian at Planks Design Consultancy, Unit 14, Burmarsh, Marsden St, London NW5, tel. 01-482 1078.

● Details of Style 86 from Philbeach Events Ltd, Earls Court Exhibition Centre, Warwick Rd, London SW5 9TA, tel. 01-385 1200.

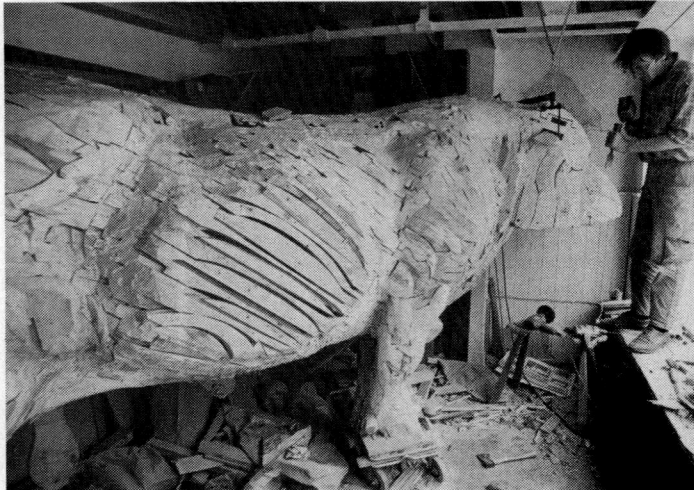

● *Woodturners who have £70 and can't get to the Woodworker Show (which is at London's Alexandra Pavilion, N22, on 24-7 October; details on (0442) 41221) will no doubt be going to the annual* **seminar** *of the* **Irish Woodturners Guild.** *This event, now attracting worldwide prestige, is at Letterfrack, Co. Galway, on 26 and 27 October. Says Guild secretary Michael Dickson, 'This year our principal demonstrator will be Del Stubbs from Chico, California, who is* amongst the top woodturners in the world and follows previous demonstrators David Ellsworth, Mick O'Donnell, Ray Key and Richard Raffan. A full supportive programme has been planned which will include a number of full-time professionals who are household names in this country and beyond.'

The £70 or $100 fee includes, says Michael, 'a good lunch on both days', and the Guild can arrange accommodation. If you want more details, write to Michael at Moylinny Mill, 9 Nursery Park, Antrim, N. Ireland BT41 1QR, and enclose 50p in stamps.

The two bowls pictured here were wet-turned by Guild member Gerry Roche of Mulhuddart, Co. Dublin. Membership costs £13.

● *A fine appreciation of grain and colour is not the hallmark of Nick Johnson's sculpture* (**left**). *Yet it demands a second look – which it receives from startled passers-by in Lewes, where he works. His menagerie has included pigs, a chicken and (seen here) a greyhound and a life-size bull. A door will have to come off to let the bull out, for sale through a London gallery.*

*Nick's raw material is secondhand softwood from pallets and packing-cases. He builds a spine, cuts the pieces to rough shape, and glues and cramps them into position. Then he 'attacks' (his word) the structure until he gets what he wants. Tools include an axe, a drill-mounted disc-sander, and a mallet and chisels. The finish is wax.*

*Nick teaches at an art college in Eastbourne, and says that it was the wood sculpture of Nigeria that triggered his zoological style.* **Story and photos by Stanley Folb**

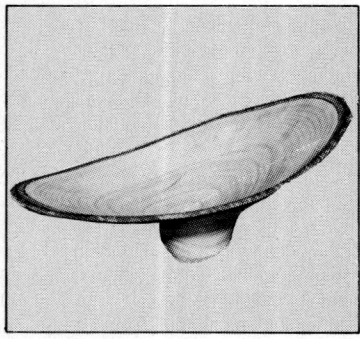

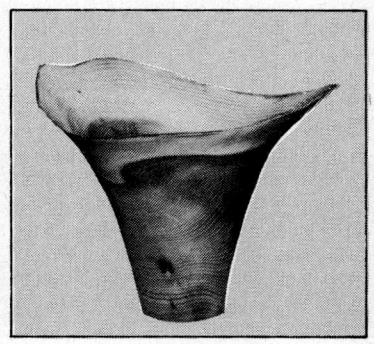

# Shoptalk

A misty moisty morning in the early 1920s, and Mr F. V. Charlton (second from left) supervises timber haulage from an estate near Frome, Somerset, where his family firm still operates. Articulated trucks don't look, smell or sound the same as those mighty shire horses – but the timber hasn't changed much, and Charltons still sell it. On 3-5 October inclusive they'll be having a three-day exhibition featuring various demonstrations, notably of woodturning. It must be worth a look-in.
● Charltons Timber Centre, Frome Rd, Radstock, Bath, Avon; tel. Radstock 36229

Testing turning tools for the August *Woodworker*, Tobias Kaye picked Ashley Iles' ⅜in high-speed-steel **spindle gouge** as a front-runner for inclusion in his suggested beginner's kit of first-class equipment.

So it's not quite a coincidence that Iles have picked the self-same tool for a half-price offer. You can get it for £3.50 including postage and VAT — unhandled, but with a brass ferrule. Ashley Iles points out that the ferrule is chamfered on the inside to give it a lead on to the handle which you'll be turning up to suit yourself.

Into the bargain (into a different bargain, actually), Ashley says his range of London-pattern carving tools, up to 1in, is now available with 'hand-polished' handles in lovely bubinga instead of workaday beech, for 25p extra each.

● Ashley Iles (Edge Tools) Ltd, East Kirkby, Spilsby, Lincs, (07903) 372.

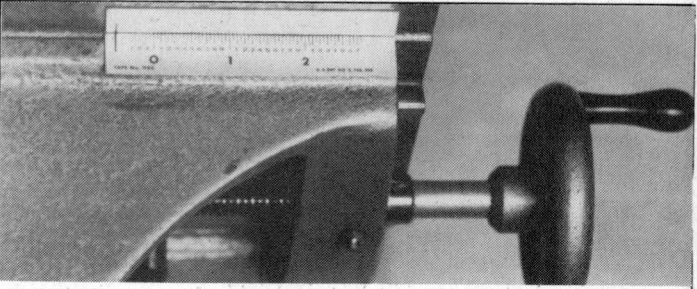

This precision Vernier scale is on self-adhesive paper, specially presented so you can stick it on to your machine fences, tables, etc., with 100% accuracy. A cheap and absurdly simple answer to a daunting-looking problem? £2.50 for a pack of three.
● J.H. Equipment Ltd, PO Box 347, 91 Redbrook Rd, Timperley, Trafford, Lancs, 061-904 9384

It's very true, as Kontoor Abrasives say, that a lot of **sandpaper** is wasted — particularly in hand work, where it often happens that only part of a sheet gives its full mileage. Kontoor's products may not be a panacea, but a sample demonstrates certain virtues.

The point is that they're double-sided: two abrasive sheets are laminated back-to-back with a woven fabric between them. The result is a lot stiffer than the usual paper or cloth abrasive, but still flexible. The stiffness means the pads won't crack, or curl when used wet. It also makes the edge quite tough — which could be handy when you're trying to get right into the corner of a rebate, for example.

It's certainly not true that, as Kontoor claim, their pads make a sanding-block unnecessary; that would be the way to rounded edges and undulating misery. But their materials are worth a second look. On offer are 'industrial wetway' (black), i.e. silicon carbide; 'heavy-duty wetway' (maroon) — aluminium oxide; 'special-purpose' (grey) — coated with zinc stearate as a lubricant, and primarily for cutting back finishes; 'heavy-duty dryway' (yellow) — aluminium oxide again; and 'industrial dryway' (brown), which is garnet.

Available formats vary from type to type, but include orbital pads and discs, ⅜x10in 'Gemstrips', full sheets, half sheets and 3½x4in pads.
● Kontoor Abrasives Ltd, Cold Norton, Essex CM3 6UA, (0621) 828882.

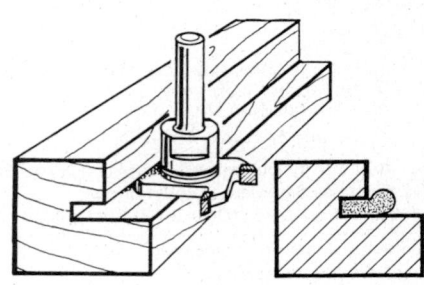

If you're making or restoring windows, you may well have a use for this **router cutter**. It enables easy insertion of plastic weatherstrips by cutting a groove flush with the bottom of the rebate. Threading on to a special arbor, it's tungsten-carbide-tipped and it comes with optional bearing guides. A typical set, say Trend (who distribute it), costs under £35.

● Trend Machinery & Cutting Tools Ltd, Unit N, Penfold Works, Imperial Way, Watford, Herts WD2 4YY, (0923) 49911.

# Shoptalk

With a name like **Horological Solvents,** you need all the friends you can get. But the Bury firm should make plenty with their **open weekend** on 12/13 October. Basically it's a very well-stocked shop-window which should prove alluring to others besides clocksters. They say there'll be 'woodturning lathes, carving and turning tools, exotic woods, veneers, stains and polishes, clocks, clock parts, model engineer's tools, books and lots of demonstrations'. Participating will be Coronet, Ashley Isles, G. K. Hadfield, Nathan Shestopal, Richards of Burton, John Myland and Restoration Materials. Admission is free; 10-6 daily.
● Horological Solvents Ltd, Proctor St, Bury, Lancs BL8 2NY, 061-764 2741.

SORRY, Robbins of Bristol ('Shoptalk', August). We said their 'traditional' hardwoods were mostly home-grown. In fact their beech comes from Europe and their ash, cherry, elm and oak from north America. None the worse for that, we're sure.

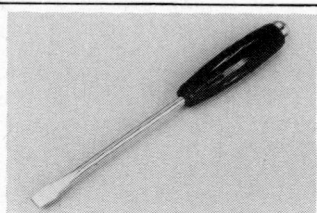

*Everybody does it, though few will admit it: that is, use screwdrivers to open tins. But the makers say this 'chisel driver' is actually designed for the purpose – and even for cutting and scraping. It costs £3.47 + VAT.*
● *Thuscan, Victoria Way, Burgess Hill RH15 9NF, (04446) 5701*

*£43.48+VAT buys this light-weight bench-grinder from Peugeot Power Tools.*
● *AEG-Telefunken (UK) Ltd, 217 Bath Rd, Slough SL1 4AW, (0753) 872500*

'At The Wood Shop we find that well over half our customers aren't sure about the projects they've embarked on and how best to start.'

No doubt many other timber traders could say the same. But John Gormley has gone further. Behind his counter is John Land — 'an accomplished cabinetmaker who not only prepares the timber to your exact specification but would be glad to talk over any making problems you may have'.

The Wood Shop (part of John Gormley's Treske Sawmills, itself an offshoot of the Treske furniture business) holds, he adds, considerable stocks of air-dried acacia, apple, ash, beech, cherry, chestnut, elm, hornbeam, lime, oak, pear, plane, poplar, sycamore, walnut, yew, cedar of Lebanon, European larch and Scots pine, in thicknesses from ½in to 3 and 4in.

Typically of the new breed of **timber suppliers to craftspeople** (but most untypically of the trade as a whole!), John adds: 'We particularly like to hear from our customers as to how they want their orders sawn: quarter-sawn, crown-cut, crotch-cut, matching boards, boards selected for colour, butt, sap, etc.'

Exotics include amazaque, beli, bubinga, padauk, pau rosa, thin win, wenge, African blackwood, boxwood, cocobolo, ebony, kingwood, laurel, lignum vitae, lemonwood, olive, pernambuco, partridge-wood, padauk, rosewood, satinwood, tulipwood and zebrano. Not unnaturally, too, Treske stocks major imported timbers — kilned rather than air-dried: afrormosia, iroko, jelutong, mahogany, teak, walnut, utile. These also run from ½in to 3 and 4in.

John is proud of his service to carvers, for whom he will laminate and even bandsaw blanks to order in lime and other woods — life-size if required!

The Wood Shop will deliver or post, wherever you are: send a cutting list (if necessary) and ask for a quote, which should arrive by return.
● Treske Sawmills Ltd, Station Works, Thirsk, N. Yorks YO7 4NY, (0845) 22770, will be at the Woodworker Show.

# Timberline

## Arthur Jones presents the month's inside news of supplies

Exchange rates are something most woodworkers are content to leave to the economists. But it is a big mistake to think that what happens on the world foreign exchanges leaves us unaffected — far from it.

This is very clearly shown in the latest offer of Russian softwood for shipment to the UK for the period up to next spring. There has been no change in the prices issued last February, but they are now based on an exchange rate of 12.75 Swedish krona to the $, compared with the previous rate of 10.25. The Russians switched to selling in Swedish krona after one year in which the value of the £ fell dramatically.

Obviously this change offers some protection to the UK softwood importers, who are far from certain about the future of currency rates; there are even strong rumours that the krona might be devalued in the autumn.

However, the reason for the painfully slow progress of sales is not connected with the assessment of the offer. The real trouble rests with the low demand for softwood in the UK and the quite considerable stocks around the country.

The price of whitewood seems to have steadied at a remarkably low level, but now the uncertainty has switched to redwood, even the better grades. Fifths have been weak for some time, but unsorted redwood has been holding its own. Even the top grades are not safe from price cuts these days, and part of the blame must rest with the Swedes, who, unlike their Finnish neighbours, have not cut back their production to match reduced world demand.

Woodworkers can expect the price of wood to stay highly competitive for some months and there should be little problem with supplies. It is worth shopping around to get the best price, but always be sure you are getting your quotations for comparable qualities and specifications.

There is also a lot more UK softwood coming on to the market from native forests. Generally well graded and prepared for the marketplace, it is certainly streets ahead of the material which used to be offered and which earned such a terrible name for native softwood. Take a second look at what is offered — but don't expect to get it at prices much different from the imported wood.

Home-grown hardwoods are quite a different matter. These have always figured prominently in the woodworker's buying list, so there will be plenty of interest in the proposals by the Forestry Commission to safeguard future hardwood stocks in the UK, with a shift towards conservation in the broadleaved woodlands. There will be stricter regulations controlling the felling of hardwoods, and an insistence upon re-stocking felled broad-leaved areas with hardwood species, but there will also be the encouragement of a new-style grant to those growers who plant hardwoods.

For the lifetime of most of us, such a policy would mean some limitation on the supplies of native hardwoods and the probability of higher prices.

Of course there is plenty of competition from imported hardwoods, and close attention to exchange rates must again be given in the recent review of supplies and prices. For example, the strength of the £ against the German mark has affected the price of beech from that country, a hardwood attractively priced for the UK.

On the other hand, American oak has continued to sell here in spite of the strong dollar, and now that sterling has risen against the $ woodworkers can expect to see more attractive offers of both red and white oak from the States, together with such species as ash, walnut and cherry.

Most of the price movements in international hardwoods over the past couple of months have been in our favour. Mahogany from south America has been helped not only by some Brazilian mills' reductions in prices, but also by a lowering of freight rates from that part of the world. Ramin has been a good buy, and keruing has been dropping steadily in value. Most of the west African hardwoods seem to be holding their own. ∎

# FOLLOW THE STAR

## EMCO
INTRODUCED THE WORLDS FIRST UNIVERSAL WOODWORKER IN 1946

## EMCO STAR
THE ORIGINAL UNIVERSAL WOODWORKING MACHINE

**emcostar 2000**

**THE NEW GENERATION**

**AND STILL No. 1**

*AVAILABLE FROM EMCO WOODWORKING STOCKISTS*

PLEASE WRITE OR PHONE FOR DETAILS

SOLE U.K. DISTRIBUTORS
## SOLENT TOOLS LTD.
### 267 LONDON ROAD, PORTSMOUTH PO2 9HA
### 0705 — 667652/3
*TRADE ENQUIRIES WELCOME*

**emco**

# Question box

## Our panel of experts solve your woodworking problems

**Q** *I have a small mahogany cabinet with a traditional 13-pane glazed door. The door is basically sound and the glazing-bars are intact, but some of the glass panes are cracked and broken and need replacing. The piece has suffered at the hands of a previous 'restorer', and the glass is held in with clumsily applied putty, stained red and now rock-hard. Can you suggest a method of removing the putty without damaging the small-section glazing-bars? Some means of softening the putty would be useful.*

*John Rimmer, Northwich*

**A** There's no easy way, I'm afraid, to remove old rock-hard putty. All you can do is chisel away very carefully so that the delicate moulding isn't damaged. The red in the putty was traditionally obtained by mixing lead oxide into it, but this is now considered unsafe. You can get the same effect by adding aniline powder.

*Gordon Hall*

**Q** *I recently made some garden furniture from douglas fir, which had been cut for less than six months and was stacked in the open when I bought it. The planks are 50mm thick and average 250mm wide, with one waney edge; I made the seats and table from 1.25m lengths, and planed the sitting and leaning surfaces smooth.*

*I treated it all with Ronseal Wood Preservative, which specifies (in words and pictures) that it can be used on garden furniture. The finish went on fine – two coats – and nothing untoward occurred until some very hot weather, when the timber seemed to sweat resin. It made the preservative come off when I drew my hand across the surface; not enough to cause patchiness, but enough to be a nuisance. In the cooler weather, out of direct sunlight – no problem.*

*After about a month I decided to coat the sitting and leaning surfaces with Furniglas All Weather varnish; again no problem until it came into direct sunlight, when the small resin bubbles appeared under the film, and the surface developed tacky patches. I can't see that longer drying would get rid of the resin – and I didn't want to seal the surface originally, preferring to let it breathe. Where did I go wrong?*

*K. G. Harding, Gillingham*

**A** It would appear your problem is insufficient seasoning of the timber, or an unduly high resin content.

When the ambient temperature rises, the resin softens and exudes from the timber, creating pressure which forces off the preservative and any surface coating. Unfortunately, there's no coating you can now apply that will prevent the exudation occurring again. The only remedy I can suggest is to heat the surface carefully with a blowlamp and scrape off the resin, as it exudes, with a flat scraper. Take care not to heat the surface so much that it chars. A hot-air stripper would be less likely to damage the surface than a blowlamp.

When no more resin exudes, your furniture can be re-treated with a wood preservative and a finish, if you wish. There's no guarantee, however, that more resin deep in the timber won't exude again in a long, hot spell.

I would also suggest you take this up with the timber merchant from whom you purchased the wood.

*Ronald E. Rustin*

**Q** *I'd like to make miniature furniture as a retirement hobby. Can you tell me: what is the usual scale? Where can I purchase plans? What is the best way to buy timber? What advice do you have about tools?*

*A. Brown, Harrow*

**A** The internationally recognised scale for doll's-house miniatures is $\frac{1}{12}$, a size which allows you to furnish a miniature room or house that doesn't take up too much display space. Because it's a standard scale there is a large selection of accessories available from specialist suppliers — fittings (hinges, handles, mouldings, etc.) and also the knick-knacks that make a setting complete but which the woodworker might not like to attempt (china, animals, carpets — you name it!).

You don't mention the doll's-house size specifically, and may have something larger in mind — perhaps specimen pieces. If this is so, $\frac{1}{8}$, $\frac{1}{6}$ and $\frac{1}{4}$ scales all offer a challenge.

Most miniaturists I know draw their own plans: from a museum, from home, or perhaps from a friendly antique shop.

Suitable timber comes from a number of sources; the original will obviously dictate the type. Oak, walnut, mahogany and so on can be salvaged from broken furniture, jumble-sales or the local tip. You would need to saw and plane to thickness yourself, or get someone with the right machinery to do it for you. Sometimes paler timbers are used already prepared, and stained to match.

X-acto produce quite a good selection of special tools suitable for both beginner and expert. I've used their razor saw for years and would be lost without it. Masonry nails and broken or worn-out carving chisels can be converted to make very useful tools, especially for fine turning. Miniature scratch-stocks are useful for making mouldings.

Finally, I suggest you subscribe to a miniaturists' magazine which will give you useful addresses and show you what others are doing; it will also tell you where all the shows are, so you can go and ask at first-hand all the questions I have left unanswered!

These are some books, publications and addresses I find useful, though this is of course by no means a complete list:

**Books** Charles Hayward, *Period Furniture Designs*, Bell & Hyman; Verna Cook Salomonsky, *Masterpieces of Furniture*, Dover; Lester Margon, *American Furniture Treasures*, Dover. *International Doll's-House News*, 56 Lincoln Wood, Haywards Heath, Sussex RH16 1LH.

**Suppliers** Borcraft Miniatures, 8 Fairfax View, Scotland Lane, Horsforth, Leeds (samples and price list £1.50); The Mulberry Bush, 25 Trafalgar St, Brighton, Sussex BN1 4EQ, tel. (0273) 493781 (mail-order catalogue and price list £1.95).

*Stuart King*

**Q** *I am making some ledged-and-battened internal oak doors for a converted barn. My intention was to fix them with clench nails, but I've been unable to locate a supplier. Could you tell me if they can still be found, and if not, what alternatives there are? The battens are 15mm and the ledges 24mm thick, so I suspect that countersunk screws covered with buttons would be too weak.*

*E. Minost, Lymington*

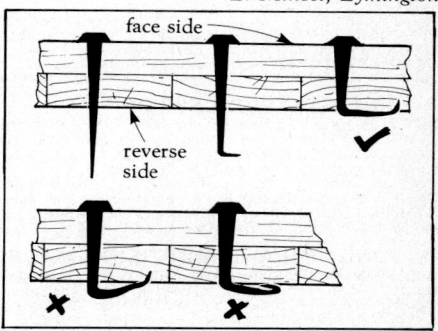

● *Even the humble clench nail needs hidden qualities. It must bend in the right places or the result will be a bodge*

**A** Clench nails were simply hand-made nails 'clenched over' — in other words, a nail long enough to protrude 2-3in through the other side of the work is bent twice and hammered back into the work to produce a stapling effect (fig. 1). I get my local blacksmith to make mine, as the nail has to bend fairly easily at the point it emerges from the back of the work, and not too easily at the tip, otherwise it will double up on itself (fig. 2). It's expensive to get them specially made, however, so cut nails (flooring brads) are a good alternative because they're tapered and grip well; but the heads aren't so attractive.

It may be necessary — depending on the grip of the nail — to have an accomplice hold a metal weight against the nail-head while you are round the back banging the long end over and in, because you can find the head loosening again.

It's a simple process, and an attractive one if done well. I think the screw method you suggest would be strong enough, but I doubt whether it would be in character with your barn.

*John Milner*

**Q** *I have recently acquired a hand-powered chisel-mortiser – which is something I have up till now only heard about, never seen. The chisels are shaped as in the sketch, and fitted to the machine by a sort of 'grub bolt'. This has a counterbalance weight to lift the chisel arm for another blow to the work, which is clamped in the same way as with electrically powered machines. It has almost*

# Question box

Who made these machines? What is their history – when did they come into use and when did they cease to be used? What sources of spare parts can you suggest?

*Kevin Smeaton, Leigh-on-Sea*

**A** These simple and sturdy machines, in which the workpiece is firmly clamped on to a cast-iron stand while the chisel is forced down by pulling on a long lever, have been in widespread use for at least 150 years. They are said to have been invented by a General Bentham, and described in his specification dated 1793. They were in use by British Admiralty dockyards by 1830.

Their great advantage over traditional hand-mortising with chisel and mallet, apart from their speed of operation, is that absolute verticality of cut is ensured — those who have chopped mortises by hand will know how easy it is to undercut one side and leave the other at an angle, with the result (after it has been corrected) that the tenon is a very loose fit.

Moreover, since the sides of the workpiece are firmly held by the screw-clamp, there is no danger of its splitting as a result of the wedging effect of the chisel. Nevertheless, a preliminary hole should first be bored to the full depth of the intended mortise to allow room for the first slice of waste. Various special chisel forms — with corners, lipped sides, or barbs — were available, and were supposed to remove the waste automatically as they were withdrawn.

Many of these machines can still be found in small joinery shops and country builder's yards, where they continue to give good service. The simplest type, with plain chisels, seems to have been most popular, although a 1912 Melhuish catalogue offered a range, with various refinements, at prices from £8 to £20 10s.

Your best chances of chisels and bits and pieces are: David Stanley Tool Auctions, (0530) 222320; Old Woodworking Tools, 288 Upper St, London N1, tel. 01-359 9313; or a street market such as the Bermondsey market, Tower Bridge Rd, London SE1, which starts at the crack of dawn on Fridays.

*Philip Walker*

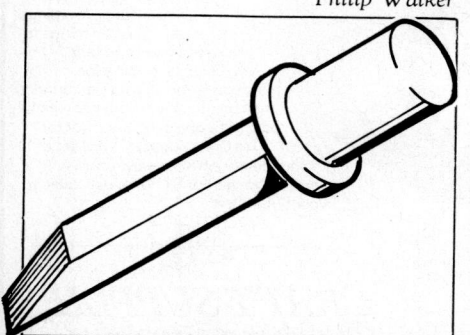

● *The simplest of many different chisels which were once available for the hand mortising machine*

● *£8 won't buy you a machine nowadays – but many of these workhorses are still in service*

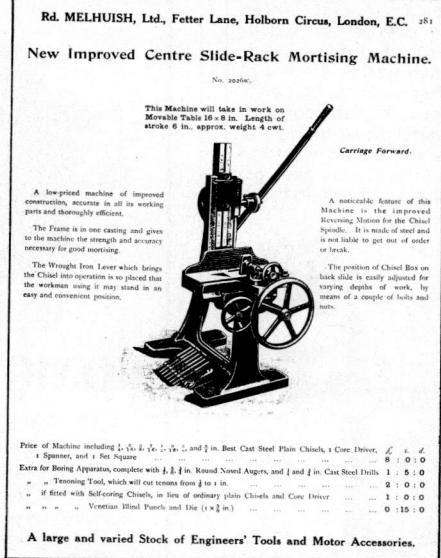

**Q** What treatment should I give solid brass handles to get rid of the 'brassy' look and obtain an oxidised or rubbed antique effect?

*W. H. Bullus, Torquay*

**A** A popular method of achieving this dulled effect to simulate old age on brass is to put the metal in mahogany shavings or sawdust to which ammonium chloride (sal ammonia, as it was known in the trade) has been added. Add enough of the chemical to make the shavings just damp, and leave the brass in them for as long as it takes to get the colour you want.

With any colouring method you use, it's important to make sure that all the lacquer has been removed from the surface before you treat it. A good book on the subject is *Colouring Metal* by Richard Hughes and Michael Rowe, published by the Crafts Council, 12 Waterloo Place, London SW1Y 4AU, tel. 01-930 4811.

*Gordon Hall*

**Q** I have a defunct Arcoy dovetailer, which, it occurs to me, I might be able to use with my power router. The Arcoy cutter holder fits the collet of the router, which would take the place of a drill; I assume that the router's high speed would produce a cleaner cut. Any comments?

*A. T. Williams, Keighley*

**A** Theoretically you should be able to use the router instead of a drill, and — as you suggest — the higher speed would undoubtedly result in a better finish. The one problem is that the bearings are designed for use with a power source of about 3000rpm max, and if you use a 20,000rpm router to drive it I suspect that they will at best overheat — and, more likely, rapidly seize solid. If you particularly want to use your Arcoy, the answer would be to modify it on the lines of the proper

dovetailer, using a template follower on the router to run round the comb, rather than use the cutter-head. It might be easier to purchase the real thing. Of course, Arcoy dovetail cutters are now available again!

*Alan Holtham*

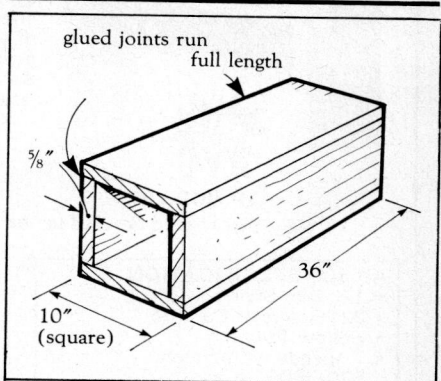

**Q** I am making a grand-daughter clock, and would like some advice on gluing and cramping the trunk – a box section 10in square and 3ft long, made of ⅝in mahogany. I'm a beginner, and propose to use ordinary PVA glue because it's convenient. How many cramps should I use along the trunk when gluing? How do I make sure the box section remains square under the pressure of the cramps? I propose to stain it with water stain (I want a brownish rather than reddish colour), then apply two coats of sanding sealer and wax-polish it; or I'm thinking of staining it and then finishing with Danish oil. Have you any tips?

*W. R. Windsor, Egham*

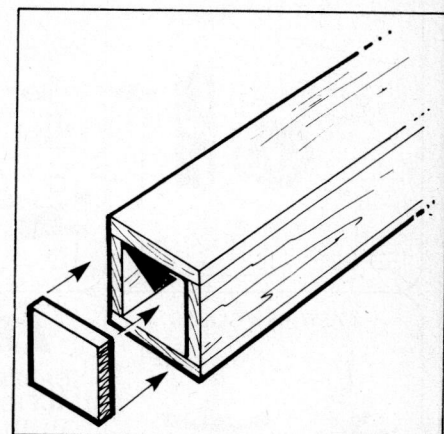

**A** I see the waist of your clock is to be solid mahogany, but you don't mention the species — Honduras, Brazilian, African, etc. This could have a bearing on staining and finishing.

Before gluing up it's essential that all four pieces of the waist are planed true and out of winding, with all edges absolutely square. Any inaccuracies will reveal themselves in gaping joints and a mis-shapen waist.

The interior measurement will be 8¾in. If you cut two pieces of blockboard or multi-ply 8¾in square and insert them into the ends of the waist while the glue is

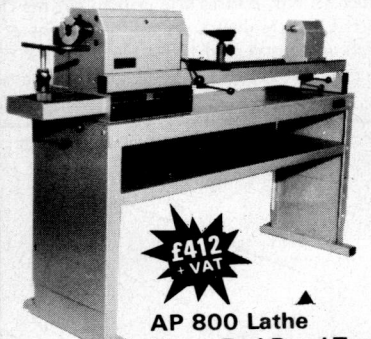
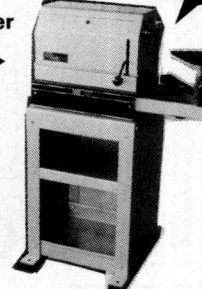

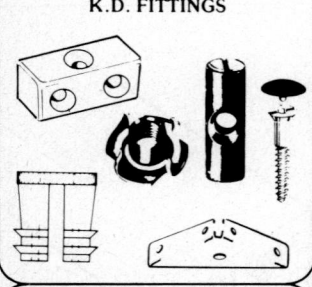
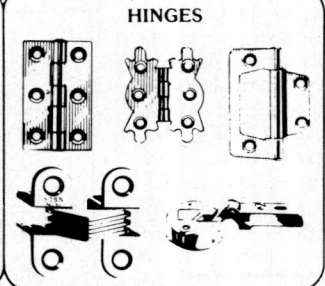
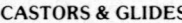
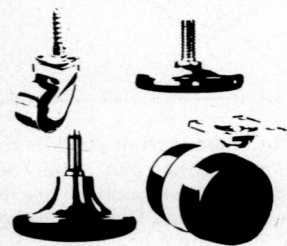

730

# Question box

setting, they will maintain the section truly square. The diagrams shows how the square block is positioned; PVA is quite satisfactory.

Three pairs of cramps will hold the work securely until the glue has set. Remember to place wooden softening blocks between the work and the cramp-heads to avoid bruising the mahogany.

Allow enough time for the glue to set, then remove the cramps in readiness for thorough glasspapering before staining. The wood must be perfectly smooth, because if there are any blemishes they will be highlighted when the work is polished. Use some of the waste wood for experimenting with stains. A good water-stain for mahogany can be made by dissolving 2oz bichromate of potash in water. If the stain is too strong it can be diluted by adding water, and if the colour is not quite dark enough you can apply more coats. This will give you the brown shade you want, although some of the African mahoganies may have a reddish tinge. Before staining, the work should be lightly sponged over with warm water to raise the grain. Allow the work to dry thoroughly and naturally before smoothing it with a new piece of flourpaper or 7/0 garnet. Dust off and brush on the stain, which will not now raise the grain. If you wish to apply Danish oil as a finish, make sure that the water-stain has dried completely; 24 hours should suffice.

Although wax-polishing is more common on oak, there is no reason why mahogany should not be waxed. After the stain has dried you can seal the open pores of the grain by brushing on two coats of french polish or sanding sealer. When this is hard, lightly rub it with fine abrasive paper to remove any slight roughnesses. Dust off and then apply an even coating of wax polish with a clean rag. Let the wax sink in for about 15 minutes before briskly polishing with a soft duster. Four or five such waxings will produce a most attractive finish.

Suppliers of good-quality polishes are listed in *Woodworker*, March 1985. Do not use polishes containing silicones.

*Charles Cliffe*

**Q** *As a non-professional woodturner I am frequently uncertain about the most appropriate lathe speed for various types and sizes of wood and work. Can you help?*
G. D. Jordan, Sheffield

**A** I usually turn at the maximum safe speed — in other words, if the lathe shakes about or the wood threatens to tear itself from the centres or screws, I slow it down. If the wood is abrasive — that is, if it has calcium deposits in the grain (elm and many African and Asian hardwoods are sometimes like this) I often find the tools go less blunt at lower speeds. Otherwise I turn hardwoods just as fast as softwoods.

The other consideration is skill. Working at higher speeds is smoother and easier, but if you catch the tool everything happens very fast and it's more difficult to

see the problem. Some lathes turn very fast indeed — about 6000rpm. If they are well bolted to a sturdy table, and can carry a workpiece at this speed, go ahead.

There is generally no need to alter speeds for sanding. If, as is the case with yew, small surface cracks appear, try pressing less hard; this also works with pitchy timbers which clog the paper. If the problem persists, try a slower speed, but generally it shouldn't be necessary. This table gives a rough guide.

|  | dia. | rpm |
|---|---|---|
| Spindle turning | 0-1in | 1500-6000 |
|  | 1-3in | 800-4000 |
|  | 3-6in | 600-3000 |
| Bowl turning | 0-2in | 1000-6000 |
|  | 2-6in | 1000-4000 |
|  | 6-12in | 800-2000 |

*Tobias Kaye*

**Q** *I have recently been given an old wooden shove-ha'penny board which I'd like to renovate. The surface must be not only smooth, but also 'predictable' over the playing area; the existing surface was greasy as well as worn. I have removed it by belt- and hand-sanding, and it's now fairly smooth, but patchy. For the next step, do I dampen the surface and fill the grain or just carry on sanding and leave the surface untreated? I'd hate to experiment and spoil it. The board is teak.*
D. H. Grout, Soberton Heath, Hants

**A** I'm not sure whether 'predictability' is a pre-requisite of a shove-ha'penny board — if it were, no one would play! Nevertheless, it is essential that the whole surface is as level as possible and completely consistent. When I checked the board in my own local, however, I found a slight hollow had been worn up the length.

You say that the existing surface was not only worn but greasy, and you have removed this grease by belt- and hand-sanding. I think this action may have been a bit drastic, but the important thing now is to get it *absolutely* flat. Unless the belt-sander you refer to was very large and of the hard-bed type, I doubt whether the surface is truly flat. Get hold of a piece of plate glass (it must be plate!) slightly larger than the board, clean it thoroughly with methylated spirit and, when it is dry, sprinkle a little french chalk evenly over it (you'll need this later anyway). Blow off the surplus and then, very gently, lower the board, face down, on to the glass. The high spots will pick up chalk from the glass, leaving the lower areas untouched. Note these high spots and remove them with a finely sharpened scraper.

Many shove-ha'penny boards were mahogany, but you say yours is teak. Finish the surface with finest garnet-paper, using a cork sanding-block and going with the grain. Assuming the colour is acceptable, I would recommend that you apply two or three thin coats of sanding sealer or french polish, leaving each coat to dry well before removing any nibs with the finest wire wool or garnet-paper. If any filling is necessary, this can be done between the coats of sealer. Follow this with a good wax polish and buff

it until all surplus wax has been removed.

The board should be lightly rubbed over with french chalk before use. This burnishes the surface and removes grease. You don't mention the grooves on the board or whether you have the brasses to go in them. Some people think these were fixed in the grooves; in fact they should be a nice fit but loose enough to be lifted, as their main purpose is to check whether or not a ha'penny is 'on the line'.

*David Ellis*

**Q** *I have a 5ft oval gate-leg mahogany table many years old, originally french-polished a dark colour. It has lived much of its life with one flap down, which has retained its colour because it has been in shadow. The rest of the table has faded from being in the sunlight. It is about to start a new lease of life with both flaps up, and I much prefer the lighter shade to the original dark colour; is there any way of hastening the fading of the dark flap?*
K. D. E. Oakley

**A** There is no form of artificial lighting you can employ to hasten the fading process; you will have to bleach out the colour by chemical means.

The first operation is to remove the french polish from the leaf to be bleached. Old french polish can be softened and washed off using methylated spirits, or you can use a chemical stripper. Alternatively, a flat surface such as a table leaf can be 'flashed'. The leaf is stood upright and wiped all over with a meths-soaked rag, then set alight at the bottom. The polish is burnt off to leave a clean, dry surface. This operation *must* be carried out where there is no danger of starting a fire!

Having stripped the old finish, you can bleach the dark leaf. A solution of oxalic acid is often used for this; but you will probably find it easier to use a proprietary two-part bleach. Carefully follow the manufacturer's instructions.

When the wood has dried thoroughly it is smoothed with fine garnet-paper, ready for staining to match the rest of the tabletop. A weak stain of bichromate of potash dissolved in water (about 1oz to a pint) should give you enough colour. Don't use a strong solution or the colour may be too deep. When the colour is a good match the leaf is put aside for 24 hours to dry thoroughly. Lightly glasspaper; and, if the grain is at all open, fill it with a mahogany grain-filler. French polish in the usual manner and spirit off.

The newly polished leaf will be brighter than the rest of the table and must be slightly dulled to match. Allow the polish to harden for two or three days and then sprinkle a little pumice-powder on to the face of a damp felt pad. Gently rub this on the polished surface in the direction of the grain until the surface is evenly matted. Wipe clean with a chamois leather and then polish with a light-coloured antique wax polish. Use the same wax to polish the rest of the table.

*Charles Cliffe*

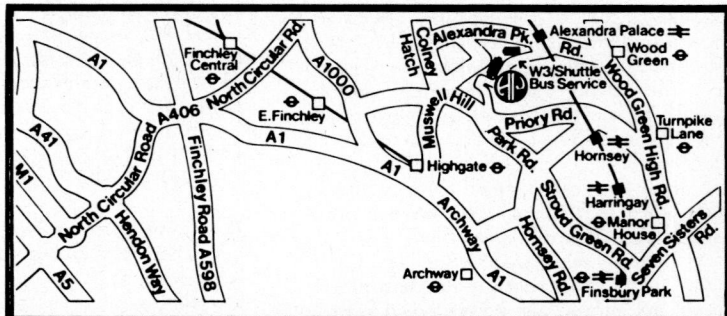

# A taste of whats to come

In just one months time the door's will open for the London Woodworker Show. As you read this the signs are that the 1985 Show will be bigger, better and even more enthralling.

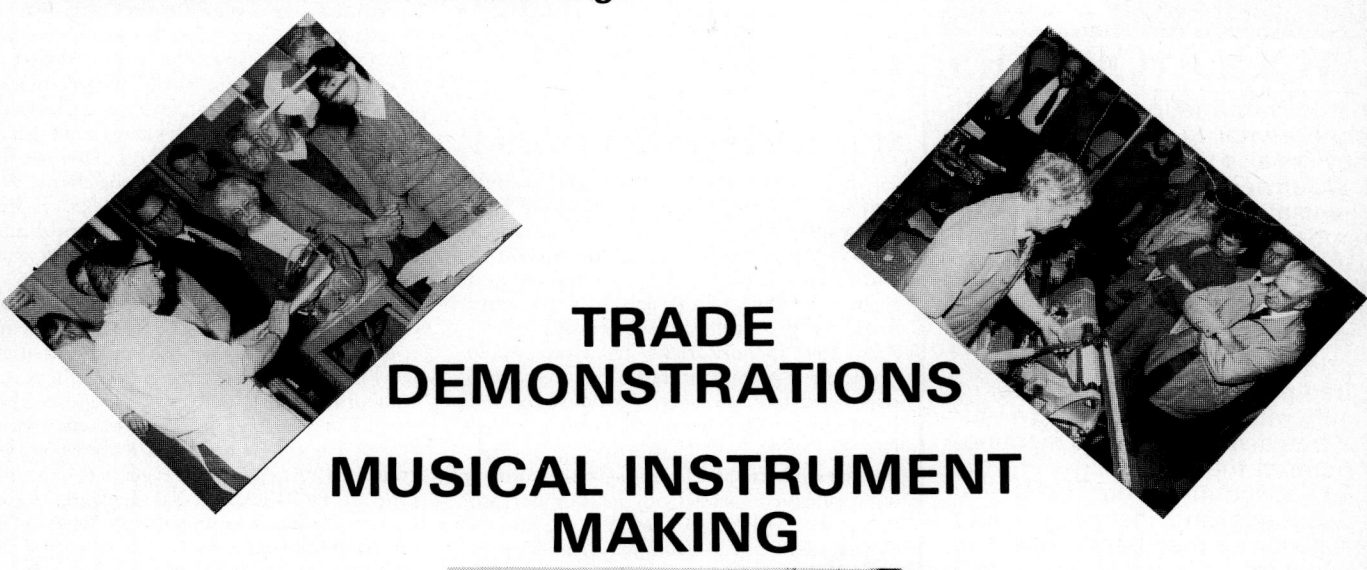

## TRADE DEMONSTRATIONS

## MUSICAL INSTRUMENT MAKING

# DON'T MISS THIS OPPORTUNITY TO SEE ON DISPLAY, THE COMPETITION EXHIBITS CREATED BY THE SKILLS OF DEDICATED CRAFTSMEN

# Come to the biggest show yet

# Guild notes

## Guild of WOODWORKERS

Shared information, advice and help are vital to good woodwork. They are also the basis of the **Guild of Woodworkers**: an international organisation which welcomes new members — whatever their skills. 1 Golden Sq, London W1R 3AB, tel. 01-437 0626.

Guild members get
- priority on our courses
- free publicity in *Woodworker*
- 15% off Woodworker Show entry
- a free display area and meeting-point at the Show
- 15% discount on our plans
- access to and inclusion in our register of members' skills and services
- the chance to contact other members for help and advice where appropriate
- specially arranged tool insurance at low rates

Please quote your Guild number when contacting us.

*Aidan Walker*

## Tool insurance!

Time to renew if you are already a part of the scheme, and time to clock the wonderful deal you can get if you'd only join the Guild. The comprehensive tool-insurance scheme is an annual group policy, which means that everyone renews at the same time — 15 October. No information about hikes in rates as yet, but they didn't go up last year — when members got £500 worth of insurance for a measly fiver, £1000 for £12.50, £1500 for £18.50 and £2000 for £30.

Your tools are insured against fire and theft wherever they are — that means in the van or on site, which is something I myself beat my brains out looking for before I knew the Guild of Woodworkers could have sorted me out.

## Milton Keynes Craft Guild

. . . Is open to people in many and various crafts, including basketry, bookbinding, calligraphy, jewellery, and of course woodworking; it aims to encourage interest in and awareness of all crafts, to develop and maintain high standards of work, and promote the crafts and members' work. Activities include talks by craftspeople on their work, running a business, and other matters of note; workshops, and exhibitions. Membership is two-tier, for people who can demonstrate a high standard of skill and for those who aspire to it. Application forms from the Membership Secretary, Milton Keynes Craft Guild, 4 Waterside, Peartree Bridge, Milton Keynes MK6 3DG.

## Land of opportunity

'Gentlemen', begins a letter from America, 'We are custom cabinet manufacturers looking for highly-skilled craftsmen. We notice people wish to relocate, and would be interested in hearing from anyone who would consider coming to the United States, if only for two or three years. We would particularly like to hear from cabinetmakers and french polishers.'

From my experience, the US is one of those countries that gives skilled people what they're worth, both financially and socially. Anyone who wants to pursue this interesting chance should write to Dantomuro Furniture Inc., 616 Merrick Rd, Lynbrook, New York 11563, USA, tel. 010-1-516-593 9437.

● **Herefordshire** local rep **Paul Smith's** phone number was unfortunately misprinted last month. It is (0568) 611786.

## More work for members

One woodworker, at least, has upped and gone to the US — to build boats. His former contractor has written asking if anyone wants to take his place. **John Stannard** has a pine furniture shop near Reading; 'We specialise in country-style "antique" furniture,' he says. 'When a client is interested in having a piece made, we take full details and attempt a diagram, send a copy to the workshop, and get a quote back in a couple of days. Then we do our sums and give a price to the client. We like to deliver in six to eight weeks; we aim to keep our service friendly, helpful and efficient, and need to find a workshop that will fit in with our spirit and approach.'

He would be very interested to hear from any members, particularly those living round Reading, either full-time craftsmen working from home or a workshop, or someone with enough spare time to be able to do a reasonable amount of work. Another good chance to turn your beloved craft into a moneyspinner; get in touch with John at 15 Wickham Rd, Badgers Walk, Lower Earley, Reading, Berks RG6 3TE, tel. (0734) 666872.

## Craft exhibition

The National Traditional Crafts Exhibition is being held at the Wembley Conference Centre, 16-17 November. 'This prestigious venue', writes **Brenda Ross,** 'offers not only fine exhibition space but also excellent catering facilities and bars. The exhibition wil be widely publicised through advertisements and press releases sent to magazines and national and local newspapers; local radio, and leaflets in craft galleries and shops. I believe I can offer a well-run, professional exhibition reaching a wide audience that will bring craftspeople the interest and business they welcome.'

If you fancy showing your work (and by the sound of it, selling it like hot cakes) at Wembley, get in touch with Brenda at 6 Franklin Close, Colney Heath, Herts AL4 0QL, tel. Bowmansgreen 23176.

● Beds and Bucks rep John Greenwell is on Leighton Buzzard 372689 (home) and Aylesbury 688905 (workshop) — not as we said.

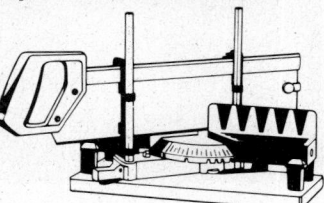

# COURSE CORNER

## French polishing — Charles Cliffe

10-11 October, Bexleyheath, £35+VAT. *Woodworker*'s expert treats you to the benefit of his wisdom in this popular field. Surface preparation, the cabinet scraper, stains and staining, an introduction to shellac finishes and other materials; grain-filling, bodying up, spiriting off. Bring an apron and a cabinet scraper if you have one, and a small piece of furniture to work on if you wish — and bring your problems too. Charles's advice is a bonus.

## Furniture repair and refinishing — Ian Hosker

9-10 November, Chester, £40+VAT. Our teacher and professional restorer in the north offers another course with a slightly different bias from his first, highly successful, french-polishing weekend. Ian will deal with repairing and replacing all kinds of joints, mending broken components and splicing in new wood, lifting and replacing veneers and marquetry, stripping, staining, re-polishing and distressing. Bring a small piece of furniture to work on, and some (sharp!) hand tools; **let us know what you want to do when you book, please.**

## Woodmachining — Ken Taylor

7 December, Bletchley, £25+VAT. A full day with a woodworker of many years' experience; Ken used to be works manager of Wrighton Kitchens, and now lectures at the London College of Furniture. He will let you into secrets of the table-saw, bandsaw, planer, thicknesser and spindle-moulder, and of mortising on both floor-standing and universal machines; there's a strong emphasis on safe workshop practice, and lots of helpful information on cutter theory, using jigs, and ingenious techniques.

## Furniture restoration — Eric Burger

17-19 January 1986, Bournemouth, £70+VAT. A three-day course, this time, from a highly reputed and experienced professional; the longer programme gives you time to repair and re-finish a piece of your own, which you must bring with you. A small selection of hand tools will be a help; Eric will provide materials like veneers and finishes on the spot. Let us know your plans when you book, so Eric will be ready for you!

● *Learn with a laugh; Benedict Critchley (**right**) discovers that french polishing can be a cause for amusement at **Charles Cliffe**'s course in June. Photo: **Stan Folb***

Meet Eric on the Guild stand at the Show; he will be there on Saturday and Sunday 26-7 October, demonstrating his skills.

● Don't forget you also have the chance to solve any knotty joinery or cabinetmaking problems with **Stan Thomas,** who has his own stand.

## Cane and rush seating — Betty Fowler

6-8 December, Longdon, Gloucestershire, £70+VAT. We're proud to announce yet another string to the Guild's educational bow — subject of many heartfelt requests, chair-caning has been something I've been hoping to arrange for a long time. A busy three days will include an introduction to the different styles and patterns of either cane or rush — Betty picks the rushes from the River Avon herself! — and making up a seat in one or the other under her expert guidance. You have to bring your own chair, already de-caned and repaired; if it's less than 12in across the front of the seat, bring two and you might be able to cane one and rush the other (without hurrying!). You need a J-cloth, scissors, a Stanley knife and a hammer. Betty appears at craft shows, gives talks and demonstrations, and is a teacher of 11 years' experience.

● *Left: **Betty Fowler**, hard at work amongst a selection of her commissions. **Below:** safe and accurate spindle moulding under **Ken Taylor**'s expert eye*

# Summer frieze

**Pat Biddulph's delightful side cabinet comes complete with its own carved garden. Read all about it**

As I approached my recent graduation from the London College of Furniture (with the BTEC Higher Diploma in furniture design/craft), I discovered an interest and skill that not all my contemporaries share: namely, carving. At the same time I became fascinated by natural, organic forms, and they began to influence all my designing. Though my studies have included work in other materials such as metal, plastic and fabric, I feel I use timber best. The result has been this side cabinet or table.

This year I spent each Friday of the spring term in St Bartholomew's Church, London, drawing and painting with one of my fellow-students. A tutor from the college's 'visual research' department kindly agreed to oversee our work and advise us, although he was not being paid for the hours involved. Drawing is very important, particularly in the run-up to a design project.

The carving represents, in slightly stylised fashion, buddleia flowers and foliage (on the front and back) and tobacco plants on the two sides. The moths include garden tigers, puss moths, fox moths, leopard moths and jersey tiger moths.

I sketched out what I wanted. The next stage was to build an accurate 1:5-scale model of the piece. This I made from the materials I envisaged for the final piece. It helped me to visualise the piece, and I changed several measurements before making the full-size cabinet. In particular, I'd always planned to paint the carved frieze in flat colour to represent faithfully each different sort of moth, but the model showed me that that effect might not be satisfactory. The frieze might look like plaster and not carved wood.

Next I produced a full set of working drawings. Reproduced here, these consisted of a full-scale front elevation, a full-size side elevation, and full-size sections through the side and front of the cabinet. These drawings were equivalent to workshop 'rods'. I also drew a full-size plan and a 1:3-scale model-making information sheet in orthographic projection.

## Construction

Apart from the colouring of the frieze, the model had shown me that my choice of materials was satisfactory. I bought a plank of maple from a local timber merchant. Although it had been kilned, I cut it oversize on the bandsaw, and left it in stick in my college studio for a fortnight. For the carving, I chose lime but with such fine detail I had to think hard about the technical considerations. To have used a sold piece would have resulted in too much short grain, liable to break. Accordingly, I decided to manufacture a plywood of lime, using three layers — two with long grain and the middle one with short grain. I pressed these in a hot-platen press using urea-formaldehyde adhesive, and a sample offcut seemed to carve well. Before I carved the four panels I rebated the backs to leave tongues, as they are grooved into the frame (like the veneered panels).

Having transferred the design to the limewood panels using graphite paper, I removed most of the waste using a router with a 3mm ($\frac{1}{4}$in)-shank cutter. This resulted in a fretwork. The next stage was to model in the detail of moths and leaves with carving gouges. Only a few tools are needed; these include a $\frac{7}{16}$in no. 9 gouge (maid of all work) for removing large areas of waste, a $\frac{5}{8}$in no. 4 gouge, a $\frac{3}{8}$in no. 5 fishtail gouge, useful for curved surfaces and especially for convex curves using the inside bevel, a $\frac{1}{2}$in no. 1 flat chisel, a $\frac{5}{32}$in no. 10 gouge for deep detail, a $\frac{1}{4}$in no. 6 gouge, and finally a $\frac{5}{16}$in no. 41 parting tool to put in final detail on foliage and moths.

The carving is time-consuming because each panel has to be worked from the back as well as the front in order to achieve a fully three-dimensional effect.

If no carving tools are available, the panels could be left at their basic fretwork stage. Like this they will be less fragile, and the effect is still very pleasing.

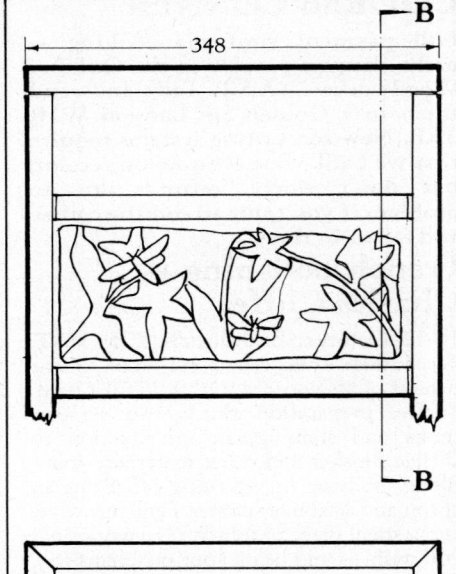

**Half plan**

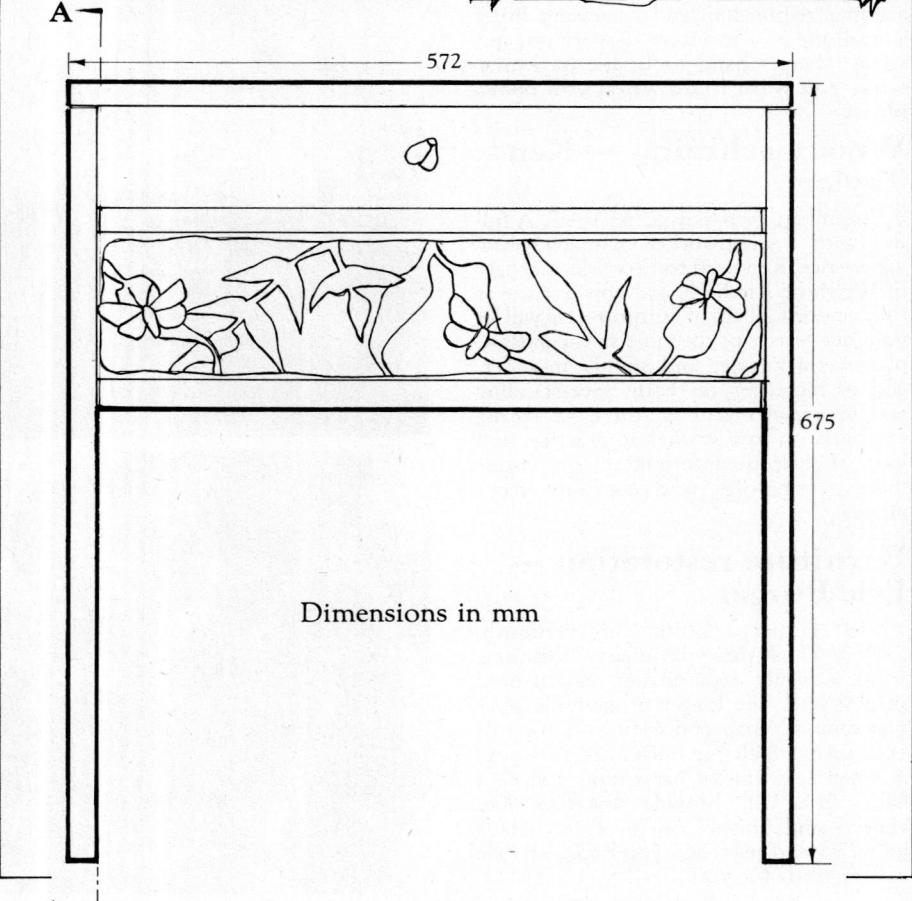

Dimensions in mm

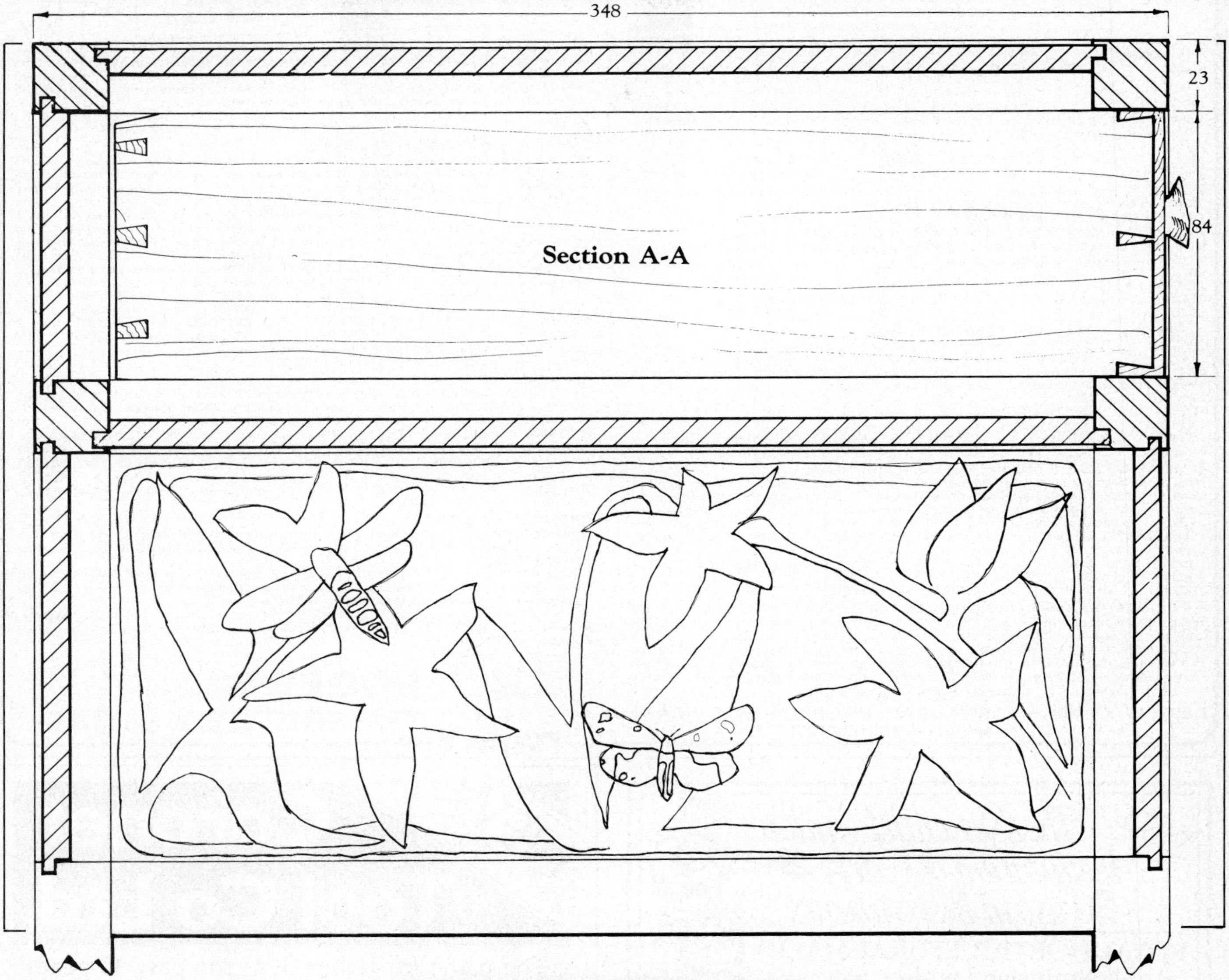

## Section A-A

348

23

84

The rest of the cabinet is made in relatively orthodox fashion. The top and side panels are of bird's-eye maple, with a balancing veneer of sycamore. The maple frame finishes at 23mm square, and is joined with mortise-and-tenon joints. The top panel is mitred and glued as a sub-assembly. I cut the grooves for the veneered and carved panels using the overhead router. I included shadow gaps at all the jointing points on the cabinet, to add interest to a slightly bland frame.

I assembled both side frames first, then put in the front and back rails to glue up the whole cabinet. The carved panels racked a little as the job was cramped up, and one detail broke and had to be re-glued. The top was glued in position along the tongues of the veneered top panels. All components were extensively scraped and sanded before assembly so that only minimal finishing was required later. The drawer is fairly traditional. It runs on the two mid-rails, which are 80mm wide and to which the drawer-stops are attached. The front is straight maple veneered in bird's-eye maple. Sides and back are sapele, and the bottom is 4mm birch plywood veneered both sides in bird's-

● *Delicate colours, light construction and elegant proportions give the cabinet its distinctive charm*

eye maple. I worked the solid-maple drawer-slips with a scratch-stock.

Originally I'd intended to cast a moth in solid silver to act as a drawer-pull. However, in the end I decided to mirror the frieze by carving a moth in lime, as though it had just alighted on the front.

### Finishing

After much deliberation I decided to tint the frieze in subtle washes of watercolour, though I needed some encouragement from my tutor. I find the carving and its colour complement the delicacy of the plain and bird's-eye maple. The carving was then sealed with two coats of shellac that soaks in and will, I hope, stop too much dirt being picked up, especially on the drawer-pull.

The panels of veneer, the drawer-front and the frame are finished in matt polyurethane diluted with white spirit. I applied it with a cloth, and it is (I find) a most satisfactory finish for both ease of application and durability. Finally the job was wire-wool-and-waxed to leave a slightly silky smooth finish.

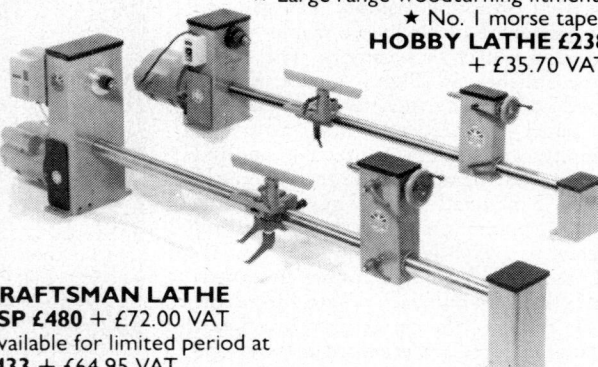

# Summer frieze

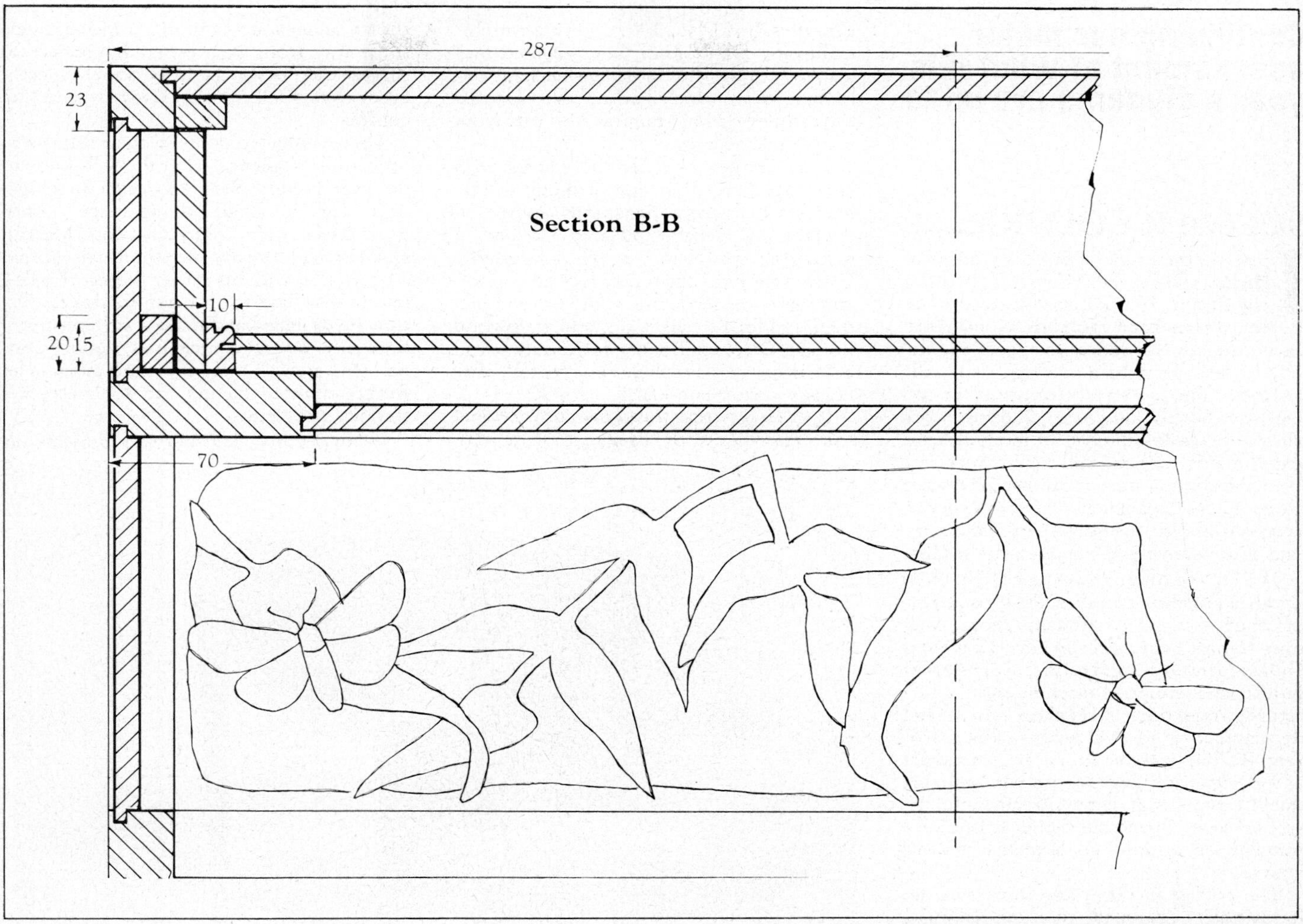

**Section B-B**

287

23

10

20 15

70

## Points

The cabinet was intended for a hallway or bedroom, and it is going to stand on the upstairs landing of my brother's house, with a carved and gilt mirror (an earlier project) above it.

Overall measurements: length 572mm, depth 348mm, height 675mm. Material cost, between £40 and £60 depending on suppliers. Making time, about two to three weeks. ∎

● In September, Pat is voyaging to Africa as a volunteer with the Church Missionary Society to help set up a craft training programme.

● *The stages in which Pat made the carved panels included constructing his own lime ply and rebating the inserts before tracing the design through graphite paper (**left**), removing for bulk waste with a router (**above,** at left) and finishing the detail by hand (**above,** at right). The panels were worked from both sides*

# The student statement: 2

**Continuing our major assessment of what this year's students are up to**

## SUFFOLK COLLEGE

Ipswich, the home of Suffolk College of Higher and Further Education, boasts a significant reproduction-furniture industry, **writes Fred Holtum.** Not surprisingly, the courses reflect the needs of local employers. Furniture-making, especially reproduction, is a strong feature at the college, but not the only one; students' work shows increasing interest in modern, even experimental design, and new courses are bringing about a close relationship between three main departments — construction (responsible for furniture), art and design, and professional and management studies.

The college offers a two-year Diploma in advanced furniture studies, the second year of which is open to students (some well over teenage) who already have a City and Guilds furniture craft certificate or relevant industrially-equipped machine shop, a furniture-production workshop for hand department of art and design offers a two-year BTEC diploma course in general art and design, and again those with suitable qualifications may enter directly into the second year. Furniture design is one of a number of options to students on this course.

The college facilities are impressive: an industrially equipped machine shop, a furniture-production workshop for hand work, polishing and upholstery, and a spray workshop with equipment for all types of spray work. There are drawing offices, design studios, a computer centre, a micro-computer lab and a large library which stays open in vacations.

Most of the college staff have an industrial background. They combine a cheerful enthusiasm with a practical understanding of the difficulties that young people have in finding work. They listen to their students and adapt courses to changing needs. This is apparent in the advanced furniture course, which is geared not only to students hoping to go to one of the local firms, but also to those who are planning to set up as independent design-craftworkers or restorers. Students like the style of the college's teaching; applicants from all over the country are being attracted to Ipswich.

Work on show this year reflected both the reproduction and modern aspects of the courses. There was a beautiful Pembroke table in curl mahogany with satinwood crossbanding made by John Landymore, a part-time student. John has already won a City and Guilds bronze medal for his work. A mahogany chair by another part-time student, Matthew Preddy, gave evidence of some very careful workmanship — even if its back and front were of different styles!

Timothy Buckle stuck to tradition with his mahogany piano stool, but ventured into his own thing with a somewhat nautical-looking desk which had an ash-veneered top cantilevered by stainless steel wire from matt-black pedestals.

James Barker's kitchen table in ash with green dyed sycamore was striking, and he had worked some ingenious mitres in overcoming what appeared to be a measuring problem; a white-lacquered beech sofa by Robert Day looked elegant, and there was some fine craftwork in Jonathan Ashford's mahogany and satinwood bureau, Stephen Bond's mahogany kneehole desk, and Stephen Paternoster's mahogany corner cupboard.

It was a pity that this more conventional work and that of the design students were shown at separate exhibitions in buildings some way from each other. It seemed to suggest that 'never the twain should meet', event though all other evidence was to the contrary.

Three design students in their final year took up a challenge from the well-known designer Freddie Baier to design a storage unit for a small living-space. And horizontals were definitely out! Martin Howells had already met the needs of the attic dweller with his earlier project of a demountable base for a futon mattress; this time he designed and made a storage-unit/bookcase/magazine-rack in sycamore and oak veneer with steel rods and fabric. He freely admitted having had to overcome stability problems.

Andy Bodily also had two projects on

● *The modernists don't have it all their own way. This mahogany Pembroke table with its satinwood crossbanding is by City and Guilds bronze-medal winner John Landymore, a part-timer from the trade; Stephen Bond made the kneehole desk*

view — a table he had completed in his first year, and the storage unit for his final year. The latter was of birch ply with painted tubular-steel legs held by some neatly worked half-egg shapes in ash. Andy had had some difficulty turning these.

Hilary Green's cone-shaped storage-unit in birch ply had given some headaches, too, and tested the resources of the furniture-making shop as well. They dusted down an almost-forgotten vacuum-former to give her the segments she required after she had made a mould on a dimension-saw.

Both Hilary and Andy had intended to dye their cabinets, but had not been happy with the results of tests made on scraps of birch ply. They saw the exhibition as an opportunity to get views, advice and encouragement from visitors, a pleasingly humble attitude from young students who — in the words of their head of department — were not only setting out to make their own careers but would, with luck, create work for others.

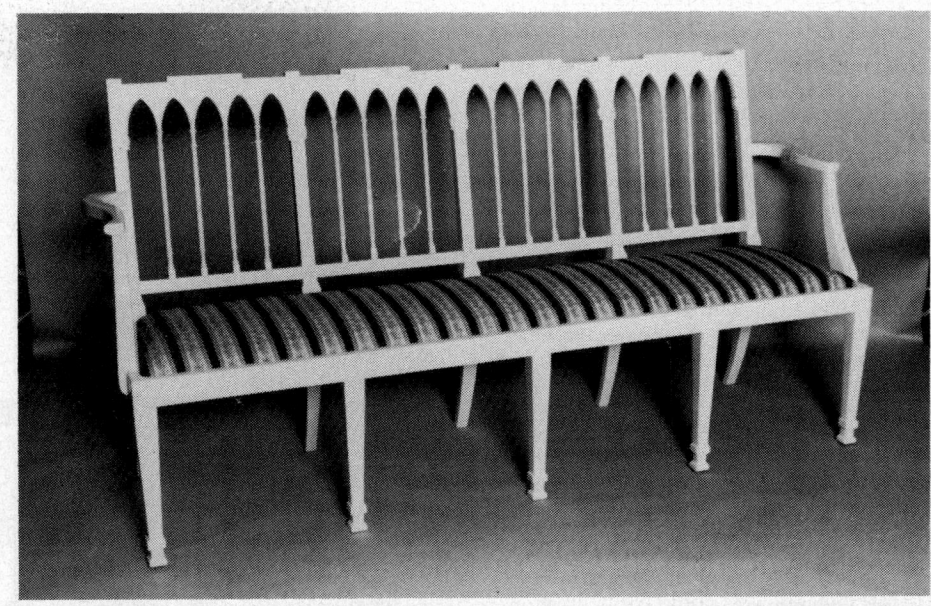

*More from Ipswich.* **Top** *is Robert Day's white-lacquered Sheraton-style settee; Andrew Bodily's cabinet and table (**above left and right**) and Hilary Green's extraordinary storage cone (**left**) betray their origins in the design course. The mahogany/satinwood bureau (**right**) is by Jonathan Ashford*

**Photos
David Burns**

741

# The student statement: 2

## BUCKINGHAMSHIRE COLLEGE

**B**uckinghamshire College stands, of course, in the centre of High Wycombe, a town which for centuries has been famous for top-quality furniture manufacture, **writes Jim Brophy.** The college's School of Art and Design, Furniture and Timber has an undisputed reputation in three-dimensional design and associated technology, borne out by some excellent work.

There was tradition, displayed in many fine pieces, but there were innovative ideas too. And their were lots of nice touches . . .

Malcolm Thomas's dry-jointed coffee-table in sycamore, with its Japanese-style low-slung look and ebony wedges, conveyed more than a hint of eastern promise. Its overall 'low polish' effect gave it considerable distinction. Also eye-catching were the circular table and chairs by Alistair Horn — in beech throughout, with black and red staining. The chairs were comfortable, and one could easily imagine oneself sitting with a couple of tankards of a foaming brew . . . Fantasy aside, the workmanship was superb and the effect exciting.

A sophisticated storage cabinet by Chris Baily was a complex item on a metal frame, designed so that it could be wheeled about — presumably to any point in the office. Made of sycamore and ebony with a double top which opened to provide additional layout space, this was a utilitarian workhorse that would do sterling service in any office or study; yet nothing had been sacrificed — the quality was again excellent. The college's involvement and close association with the furniture industry was much in evidence overall, and it was especially nice to see the style and good taste with which students had responded to the challenge of producing something that might ultimately result in production-line manufacture.

For the visitor who is also a woodworker there is always the added pleasure of knowing how things have been done. This was at its highest with the chairs that were on show. One expects to find chairs at High Wycombe, and one was not disappointed. Chair-lovers (and there are plenty of us about) would have been delighted with the simple yet elegant ladderback in ash by Adrian Moxon. Those who have been tempted to try our hand at a chair (or chairs) know the sorts of problems that can arise, and to see one such as this — with its subtle curves and fine workmanship — made by a young craftsman can only fill one with admiration. The same was true of the high-back version by Anthony Thornber. Again made of ash, with laminated arms and stays, it displayed an interesting approach to the problem of making a ceremonial chair. It was also quite comfortable, which would please any dignitary who had to endure an overlong ceremony!

Without doubt, however, the star piece of the show was a magnificent display

*Part of the year's harvest from Bucks: Malcolm Thomas's dry-jointed sycamore table with ebony wedges (**top**), Alistair Horn's chunky table and chairs in black-and-red-stained beech, and Adrian Moxon's airy ladderback in ash. The Bucks courses range from City and Guilds to full-blown BSc and MA studies*

cabinet by K. M. Krause. Its subtle elegance cannot be captured in a photograph, and it was definitely in a class of its own. The burnished black lacquer finish gave it a regal touch — and this was another piece with more than a touch of the far east about it.

Two desks, the first a neat design on a satinised steel frame in rosewood and cherry veneer by Alistair Horn and the second a draughtsman's worktable by Tony Harking, rounded off my visit. Both demonstrated the way in which students were rising to the challenge of specific furniture problems.

Good design, then, and tip-top workmanship: what better theme could there be for an exhibition?

# YTS: Genuine chances

Apart from the high-profile designs in the degree and diploma shows, **writes Peter Anstey,** Bucks College supplied something else worth seeing: an impressive reminder of the major part played by the furniture industry, the college and the trade unions in getting the government's Youth Training Scheme off the ground.

In 1981 the college was asked, in view of its traditionally close links with both employers and the unions, to take part with both sides in organising a pilot training scheme. This has since contributed substantially to the pattern for industry throughout the UK. The agreed essentials of the scheme, which remains unaltered today, were three: first, that a furniture-industry YTS must lead to a recognised qualification; second, that it must offer young people a genuinely broadening experience; and third, that it must provide them with transferable skills leading to a long-term career qualification. Outstandingly, perhaps, among many less successful YTS schemes across the country, the Wycombe scheme fulfils the third objective; all its YTS trainees, subject to successful completion of the training, are guaranted a permanent job in the industry.

Dr Hew Reid, director of studies for furniture technology at the college, stresses that the scheme is an extension of existing block-release apprentice training arrangements between the college and the furniture industry, based on the City and Guilds syllabus for furniture craft studies. In its first year, it aims to provide a practical introduction to all the craft skills associated with modern furniture production, the ground being principally covered by practical exercises in basic tool handling, cabinetmaking, wood-machining, industrial finishing, upholstery, plastics and metal work, and drawing-office practice. The scheme offers places for up to 120 trainees each year (90 were recruited in 1984-5), drawn mainly from the High Wycombe area but to an extent also from the wider catchment of the High Wycombe Furniture Manufacturers Society, which covers Bucks, Berks, Beds and Oxfordshire as well as Hampshire, the Isle of Wight and parts of Dorset.

According to Joe Hickmott, senior training advisor for the Society, which administers the scheme, one of the major factors in its success has been that no distinction in training is made between YTS trainees and those already accepted by firms under apprenticeship agreements. Subject to satisfactory progress in the first year, a trainee is guaranteed a place with a firm under a formal apprenticeship, and this is automatically backdated to the start of the course.

The craft students' exhibition at Bucks was certainly an excellent shop-window for the philosophy behind YTS. Not only did it clearly demonstrate the broad foundation of furniture craft skills which is the scheme's initial priority, but its more advanced exhibits — a beautifully designed and finished drawing-table was an outstanding example — showed how, from this essential base, students are naturally developing along the lines of particular industrial specialisms which best suit each one individually. From the items on display it seems clear that Wycombe's YTS students will provide a full share of the industry's future managers and designers.

And Dr Reid makes the further point that, whereas many industries have contracted and are still contracting the training on which their own futures are based, in this respect the furniture industry is already committed to its expansion requirements for 1990 and beyond.

● *Topping the bill was this cabinet by K. M. Krause, in beech lacquered black and burnished to a high gloss. The bevelled glass is a subtly unusual detail*

# The student statement: 2

## RYCOTEWOOD COLLEGE

I didn't see one piece of sub-standard workmanship at Rycotewood's summer show, **writes Aidan Walker;** and you'd better believe 'standard' in Rycotewood language means the very highest. Every single piece on show, from the first year to the last, was produced at a level of manual skill which many professionals would envy. Whether they were produced at the speed a professional needs to stay alive, of course, is a different matter, but the college is entirely successful in its expressed aim to 'inculcate the highest standards of workmanship to produce top-quality work'.

Other matters that you can judge objectively, like how practical the design is, and whether it does the job right, led to a few question-marks, however. First-year Christine Wood's beautiful padauk marking-gauge, exhibited with her shoulder-plane and veneer-hammer, had a cam-type locking action that I suspected would have been awkward to adjust finely. She's finding out the down-to-earth aspects of design — should the teachers have discouraged her from the start, or let her go ahead and discover the problems? I plump for the latter; it's a good way to learn if you have the time. Simon Buckley's cherry drinks chest was another case in point; again superbly made and finished — but an idea, with its lift-off-and-turn-over lid, upholstered underneath as a seat, that would certainly have been annoying to use. Should he have spent weeks working on a mechanism to make the concept more practical, or should he have abandoned the idea and made something else instead? How much had he thought about sitting on top of his liquor store, and getting up every time someone wanted a Martini?

It's easy for an outsider to ask these questions, of course; nevertheless, each designer-maker must be able to justify his or her work. That's why the college's third-year Higher Certificate course puts heavy emphasis on batch production, marketing and all the business-like skills. The prospectus says: 'Design is seen as being not only the aesthetic requirement of a particular piece, but an organisational tool to enable craftsmen efficiently to produce technically correct and aesthetically pleasing work.'

Yet that raises another question. How (apart from plugging basic rules of relationship and proportion) can you teach someone to produce something that's 'aesthetically pleasing'? Teachers can only go so far in drawing out a talent that, I believe, is either there or not.

All of which goes to say that a reviewer has a right to say 'The drawers didn't fit', but no right at all to say 'It's downright ugly'; yet our initial response to any furniture designed with aesthetics in mind is always based on what it looks like. The two 'designed' pieces I liked most were Warren Bailey's cantilever chair in bird's-eye maple veneer with rosewood stringing, and Keith Roberts' hydua and sycamore vanity mirror unit. Warren — a first-year student! — had obviously put an enormous amount of work into a staggeringly well-crafted piece, meticulously laminating and veneering the shapes, and showing his natural feel for both pleasing overall form and delicacy of detail. I couldn't try the comfort, but the springiness that the cantilever construction would give looked as if it would suit a sitter very well. The asymmetrical symmetry of Keith's mirror piece is very much to my taste — a hint of the oriental which, with spare lines and carefully contrasted timbers, makes a harmony that provokes, not lulls, the eye.

Colour and 'Japanesey' influences are obviously stale news for these students. There were a couple of witty wall-cabinets in brightly hued MDF (the Higher Certificate third year includes an all-MDF project which produced several entries for the *Woodworker*/FIDOR competition), and a pink and grey punk chair that is already dated, I fear. Alan Eldridge's 'open wardrobe', in Hammerite-painted MDF, should surely have been done in metal.

Jane Lowther and Andrew Paul had both tried hard to put colour and natural wood-

● *Symmetrically asymmetrical – Keith Roberts' mirror unit used hydua and sycamore. Sycamore appears again **below** in Andrew Paul's desk: all veneered on MDF and stained, with the addition of ebony details (photos John E. Pearson)*

tones together. Jane's olive-ash and pink-veneer table showed a better sense of inter-relating shapes and structures than of using colour to both blend and highlight at the same time; Andrew's blue-grey and pale sycamore desk, all veneers on MDF with ebony details, got it right, though the feet are a bit fussy. The colours complement the shape, and the shape is both elegant and functional.

The reproduction furniture was superb, and displayed Rycotewood's traditional excellence in this field. The history of the work is thoroughly researched; visits to museums and galleries are made, and in many cases a specific existing piece is reproduced. Anthony Spilsbury's curved-front mahogany vanity mirror was out-standing, a tribute to the love and care so evident in its painstaking construction; Brian Reeves' 'Chippendale' folding card-table also deeply impressed me, not least because it was his first job at the college! The Cotswold school had quite a few followers — Sally James and Andrew Paul were both obviously Gimson fans, Sally going for the famous curved-top exposed-dovetail oak chest, and Andrew for a lattice-back dining-chair. Stephen Hallam's tribute to Stanley Davies took the form of a reproduction of one of his walnut cabinets.

Two outrageous, uncompromising and startling designs caught my eye. Something familiar about that zig-zag chair . . . yes, it originates from 1934, a Rietveld design reproduced by Adrian Lees. Kit Benwell had chosen an equally stark wenge arm-chair, upholstered in canvas, which was designed by Marcel Breuer of the Bauhaus in 1924 and still looks avant-garde.

It's definitely love it or hate it with such furniture. Some of the Bauhaus designers produced unforgiveably uncomfortable stuff, but no one could doubt the time-lessness of their inspiration. Rycotewood's traditions of finest craftsmanship were everywhere in evidence, but that elusive combination of beauty, utility, skilful making and outright originality remains as rare as ever. It's hardly surprising. Why should we expect a genius in every bunch?

● *John Kershaw's walnut Canterbury (**above**) is almost as startling, in its Victorian way, as David Holdworth's coffee-table. Clearly David (or his tutor at Jacob Kramer) has no saucers or glasses less than about 4in across*

# JACOB KRAMER COLLEGE

**M**y first reactions to the end-of-year show at Jacob Kramer College, Leeds, were mixed, **writes Peter Nash**. It was clear that the course had stimulated creativity, and some impressive pieces were displayed, but they did not always attain the standard that might be expected. A college is special, after all; facilities are considerable, and the finan-cial constraints of covering overheads and earning a living are absent.

It's necessary to put the work into a fuller context. The Furniture Design and Con-struction course lasts only two years, and leads to a National DATEC certificate. In that short time it tries to create and develop design comprehension and ability, as well as practical skills of working in a wide variety of materials. The work shouldn't therefore be looked at merely for its own merits, but also as a product of the educative process, and indeed as a part of it.

Any review of a student show is a review of the college course. The major emphasis at Jacob Kramer is on practical work, and much time is spent in the workshops. Students are by and large responsible for building their own projects. Obviously this direct involve-ment with materials and related processes is vital to the development of knowledge and skill; but, because of the wide range the col-lege tries to give, depth is limited. This was evident in the way that some students' de-sign work, developed principally on the drawing-board and through model-making, left them with tricky technical problems in actual construction. Drawing and model-making do seem to encourage concen-tration on form and function at the expense of a complete consideration of all design aspects, including construction. But it is to the credit of both students and staff that these difficulties were overcome so well.

Most of the students join the course from school at 16; talking with them clearly revealed not only that they had enjoyed their time at the college, but also that the course had in general lived up to their expectations.

Jacob Kramer also run a number of day- and block-release City and Guilds courses which emphasise mastery of materials and techniques. The students do indeed produce some very well-crafted traditional pieces.

# The student statement: 2

## LEEDS POLYTECHNIC

The school of creative art and design at Leeds Polytechnic, **writes Peter Nash,** offers a three-year degree course in furniture design. I was immediately impressed by the thorough professionalism of the work and its presentation.

In contrast to Jacob Kramer, the emphasis here is very much on design. The students aren't expected to be able to make anything themselves, only to be able to communicate their wishes to others and in particular to the department's excellent technical staff.

All the final-year students complete a major project which they choose with their tutors. The brief is a 'realistic' design problem, and all the students showed remarkable competence and imagination in solving it. In fact one of the designs, by Andrew Slicer, won the Royal Society of Arts major award for 1985. The concept is undoubtedly very clever, an octagonal table that extends to a larger octagon by unfolding four pairs of hinged leaves. Making it work is a more impressive achievement still, but I do have reservations about its appearance.

One aspect common to both shows, though more pronounced at the Poly, was that wood was not finding much favour. Great slices of primary colour were in, MDF of course being the favoured base. I couldn't help but speculate about possible reasons for this. Fashion? Economics? Prejudices of the staff? It's interesting to see such different approaches to furniture designing and making as the two colleges' shows showed! ■

● *Tension structures (****below****) are seldom seen in woodwork, but Dawn Scoltock's bookshelves are an interesting exception. Julia Wainman's sycamore unit (****right****) is more conventional, but invites speculation as to what you can store on a diagonal shelf*

● *Andrew Slicer's dining-table is not much of a woodworker's piece (its top is MDF and its underframe is metal), but its extension method merits a closer look. And it did win £1500*

## EDINBURGH COLLEGE OF ART

Edinburgh College of Art's 1985 degree show included a furniture section displaying work by seven students. The rather cramped exhibition space on the second floor of a local chainstore presented this department, in particular, with what appeared an unnecessary challenge! **writes Chris Yonge.** Presentation was acceptable, but left one wondering what the students might have been able to achieve given better facilities.

It's always difficult to comment on individual standards of workmanship in situations like this. Those pieces apparently least well made may be the result of a student's determination to do all the work himself rather than accept technical help. The furniture was certainly solid and well-dimensioned, though I would have liked to see more attention paid to the shaping and height of the backs on several chairs, and some account taken of the need to distribute pressure away from the spine. There was a restrained and appropriate use of industrial components in the prototype production designs, and all the pieces showed attention to detail and to overall proportioning.

In some cases, however (and this is may be evidence of an over-emphasis on technical drawing — not necessarily a bad thing), not enough care had been taken to ensure that the standard of three-quarter views matched that of elevations and plans. Furniture is seen almost entirely from the former angles, and it is those details that essentially determine the user's response to a piece. Dimensioned drawings, though necessary to record and communicate specifications, are one of the least suitable ways of refining designs or describing the finished concept to a layman: often that which looks flat and uninteresting in orthogonal views develops the most elegant arrangement of planes, edges and oblique proportion when seen in three dimensions. Without much experience this is best visualised by models or sketching; the sketchbooks shown varied widely in quality and content, with only Ewen McCarthy showing evidence of consistently thinking about the appearance and function of his work from all aspects.

This was very much a designer's show, and the influence of the post-modern and Memphis schools was evident in several students' displays. The character of both styles is so strong as to swamp any originality and subtlety of detail, producing something of an Identikit result which one either likes or doesn't. Moreover, this visual exuberance was marred for me by what appeared a misunderstanding of the causes of both styles. As a reaction to and remedy for what was seen as the dead-end rationalism of late-1970s industrial design, these styles used historical and fifties-American detail and materials — magnified, distorted

and deliberately irrational — to re-assert the designer's control over appearance and function rather than let these be pre-determined by manufacturing and practical considerations. But, though this furniture's appearance reflected the styles, it is a measure of how deeply the old habits are embedded — even in art colleges — that the Edinburgh students showed little of the underlying questioning, experimentation and inventiveness that produced these highly emotive schools of design.

Where the students produced a rich and original range of objects and sketches — in their secondary subjects: jewellery, photography, ceramics and painting — these appeared curiously remote from the furniture next to them, and one looked in vain to see any cross-fertilisation of skills. Fran Malloy's ceramic lights were the closest approach to this, but one could reasonably have expected some pieces with specially made fittings and hardware — or for the marvellous colour, textures and lighting captured in the photography to be reflected by that of the furniture. Finishes in fact presented a uniformity of texture, being restricted to sprayed paint on MDF, plain laminates, and gloss sealers. The most striking in this context were Graeme Ewart's raw-steel-plate hammock and Andrew Glidden's

pink upholstered car seat complete with headlights and stereo: both outside the scope of this journal!

A designer's show has a natural tendency to concentrate on production furniture, and all that exhibited was practical and attractive. I particularly liked Ewen McCarthy's monumental conference table in MDF and Fran Malloy's triangular chairs. Doubtless because of current employment prospects, several of the students expressed their intention of setting up small design and manufacturing businesses; only one had decided to continue making furniture for a living. Others mentioned the possibility of working on prototypes; but the realities of business make it an unlikely prospect.

Professional craftsmen and designers need an awareness of their inherent strengths and weaknesses, with an appropriate technique to take maximum advantage of this knowledge. Part of a college's function is to accelerate this process — but, for whatever reason, I felt that the Edinburgh students had not been subjected to the criticism or analysis they will encounter outside. Nevertheless, all have the talent and professionalism to succeed in what promise to be widely differing careers.

● Chris Yonge designs and makes furniture in Edinburgh.

● *Flying a lonely flag here for the* **London College of Furniture** *is Juliet Whitaker's table with its solid-sycamore legs and lipping. The 18mm ply top is faced with 16 sections of fiddleback sycamore veneer, segmented into eight with diagonal black sycamore inlays, spirit-stained, and finished with a satin AC lacquer plus beeswax and turps. In January Juliet will be in business with two colleagues at The Dower House, Chawton, Alton, Hants GU34 1SB, tel. (0420) 84211.*

*We'd have like to shown you other pieces, most notably Sara Wilkinson's delightful cherry desk (a rare modern echo of classic perfection). But we rely on the college's staff and students for such things, and they all went on hols with barely a thought for us inky-fingered lads or our readers. It was the same last year. Pity.*

748

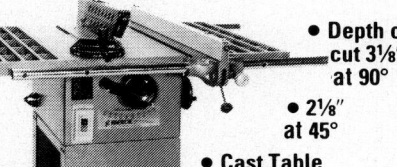

749

# Renaissance arches

**Master-craftsman Réné Coolen introduces his spectacular drawings for a challenging period project**

This graceful cabinet, dating from the Dutch Renaissance, was first made in the mid-17th century. Its simple construction uses two doors with a flat panel over the whole length; the 'blind arch' is an applied decoration at the top.

Although it is known as a Utrecht *toogkast* (*toog* means 'arch' in Dutch), this is a general name for the type of construction, and doesn't mean that it is typical only of Utrecht, nor even that it was made there. It is virtually square in elevation, but the fluted decoration gives heavy emphasis to the verticals of the door-stiles and dividers.

An excellent timber traditionally used for the flat door-panels is wainscot oak; the darker figure in the medullary rays forms a surface ornament.

The decoration in the spandrels of the arches varies widely among individual pieces and areas of manufacture, but the type illustrated here is quite simple. To get the arches on the doors corresponding exactly with the ones on the cabinet sides, the cabinetmakers would make a two-centred three-dimensional arch, known as a 'basket-' or 'hamper-arch' — a difficult combination of ellipses and arcs.

The top of the cabinet is removable, and the pin-hinged doors can also be taken out when the top carcase-rail is lifted. The carcase is an integral construction, and no other sections are removable.

A good method for carving the heads is to fix them all close together for working on. This way you can get them well-nigh identical, and it makes the work go quicker too. The same applies to the lions' heads on the doors. The bulbous feet are turned from pear-wood and varnished black, as was customary. I have indicated ebony for the turned-and-split spindles on the stiles, although pear would be just as good.

The cabinet will be familiar to those who know the work of the Dutch painter Pieter de Hooch, in whose pictures an arched cupboard appears at least three times; best-known of all is his 'The Linen Cupboard', which is in the Rijksmuseum in Amsterdam. Other variants of this construction include those made to the Renaissance system, with separable top, carcase and stand; there is also the Friesian arched cupboard, which looks different again.

## Carving and motifs

All the illustrated types of decorative carvings in the spandrels appear on southern Netherlands cabinets. The style in fig. 7d has been seen on three different cabinets, hinting at how the old guilds kept the skills of carving and cabinetmaking apart. The same carver had obviously worked for three different cabinetmakers on their own versions of the design. The braided-band or *guilloche* style (fig. 8) was well-used in Greek and Roman times, but fell into oblivion in the Middle Ages; the Renaissance reinstated it, reviving as it did an interest in classicism, but the Louis XIV and XV periods saw the shell-motif and its elaborations gain ascendance. During Louis XVI's reign, however, the excavations in Pompeii and Herculaneum renewed inspiration from the ancient world, and the so-called *guilloche* style of ornament became popular again. ∎

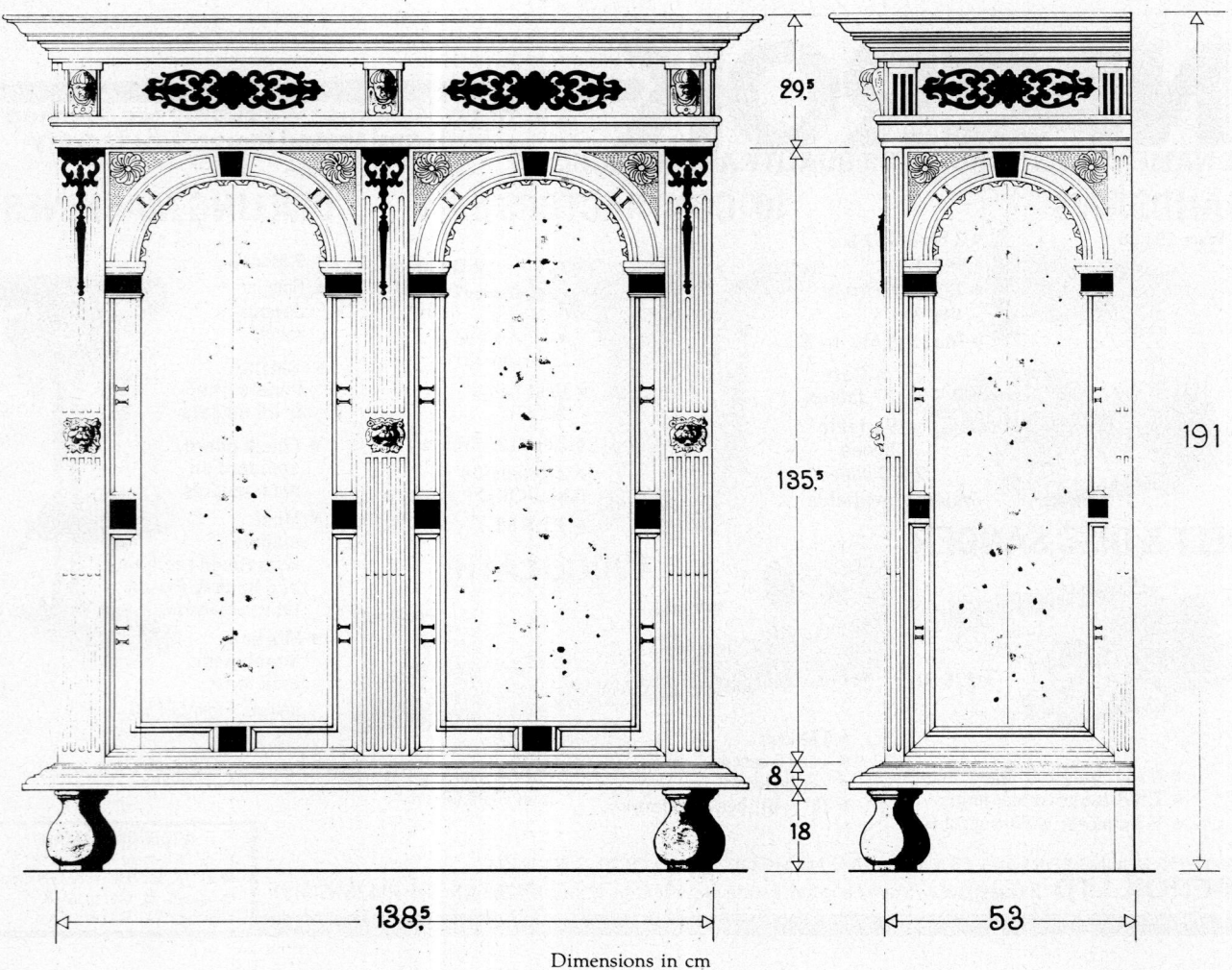

Dimensions in cm

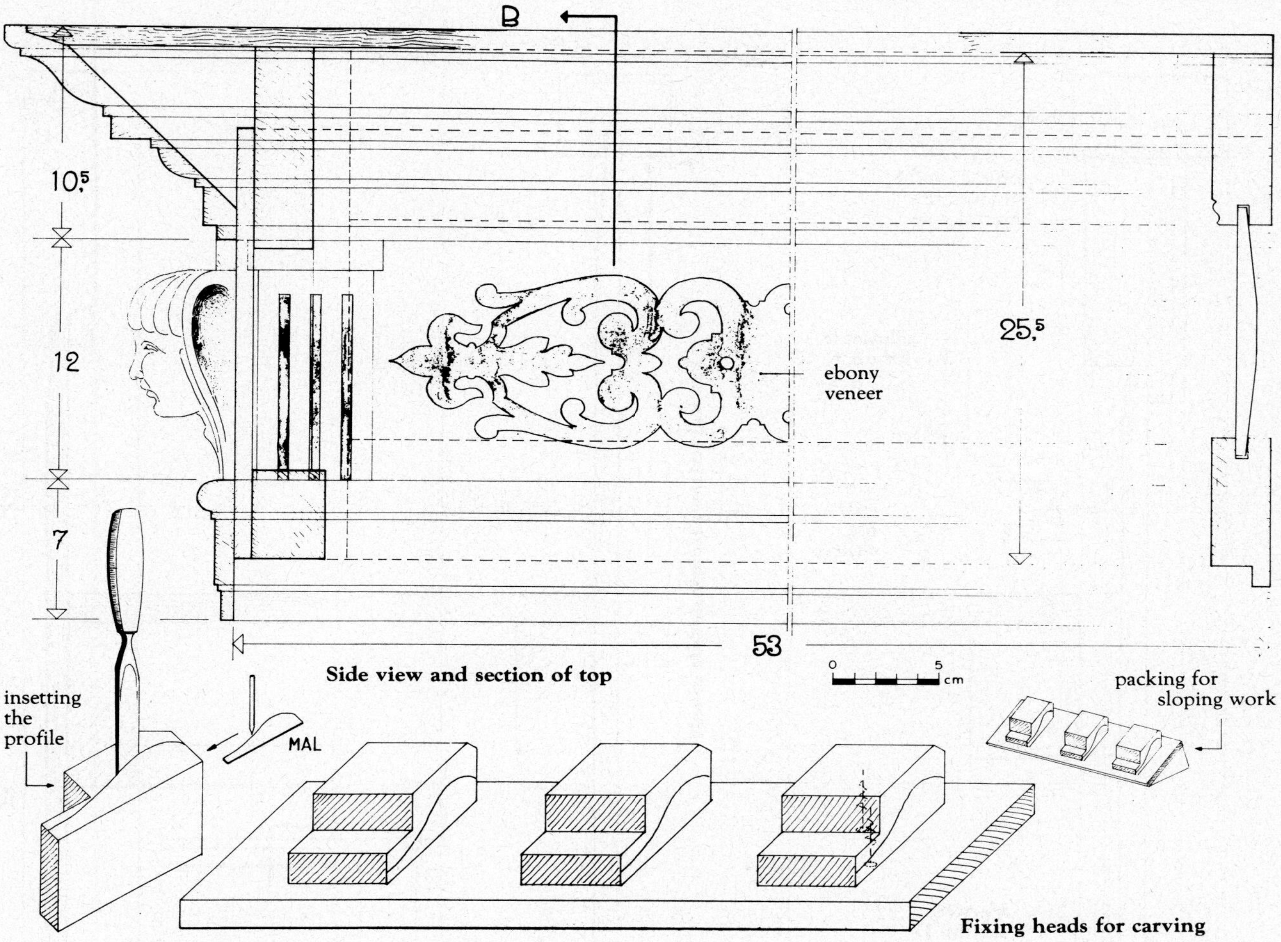

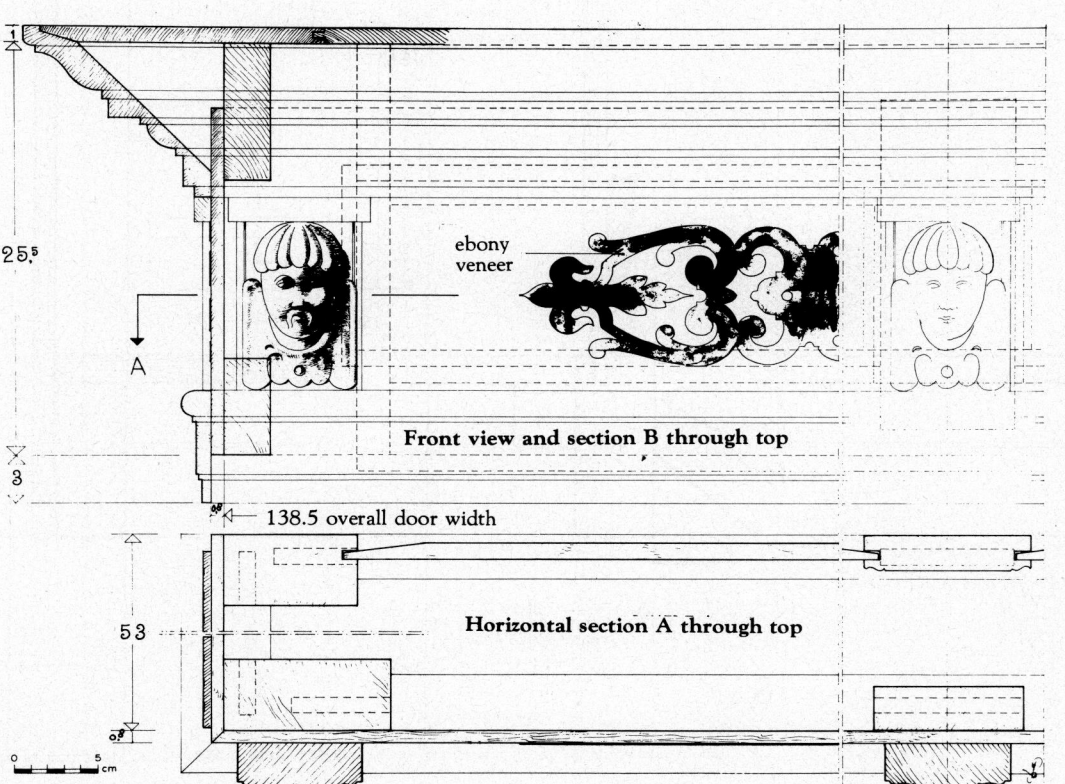

**10.⁵**

**12**

**7**

**B**

ebony
veneer

**25.⁵**

**53**

**Side view and section of top**

0    5
cm

insetting
the
profile

MAL

**Fixing heads for carving**

packing for
sloping work

**25.⁵**

**3**

A

ebony
veneer

**Front view and section B through top**

← **138.5 overall door width**

**53**

**Horizontal section A through top**

0    5
cm

● *Massively
built, cupboards
like this feature
in the work of
several famous
Dutch painters.
Despite its
somewhat
forbidding aspect,
it's a showcase
for several kinds
of decoration –
moulding,
turning, inlaying
and veneer work
as well as
prominent
carving*

# Renaissance arches

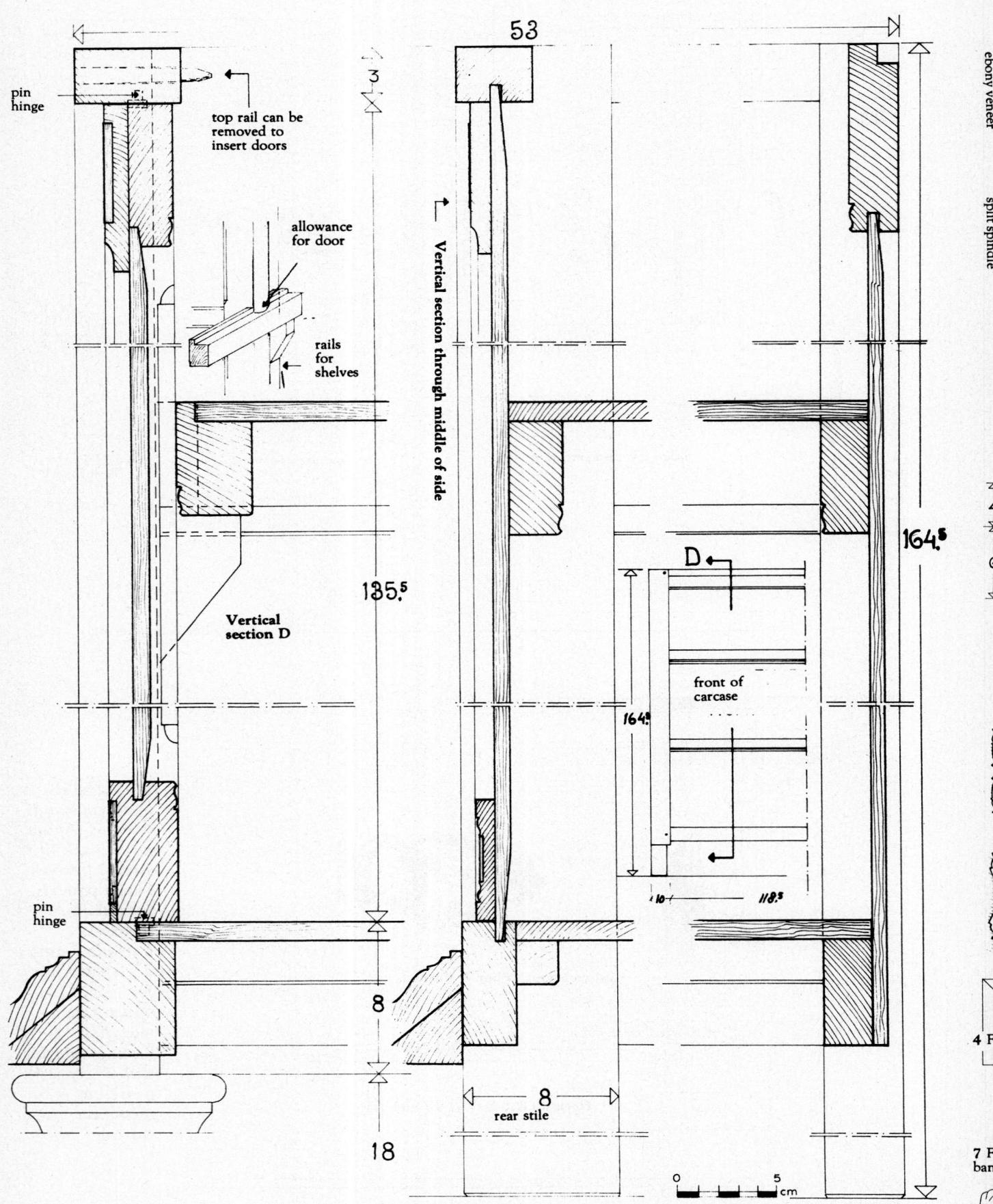

pin
hinge

top rail can be
removed to
insert doors

allowance
for door

rails
for
shelves

**Vertical
section D**

pin
hinge

3

Vertical section through middle of side

135.⁵

8

18

53

164.⁵

D

front of
carcase

164.⁵

10

118.⁵

8
rear stile

ebony veneer

split spindle

164.⁵

4 F

7 F
ban

0        5
▬▬ ▬ ▬ ▬
cm

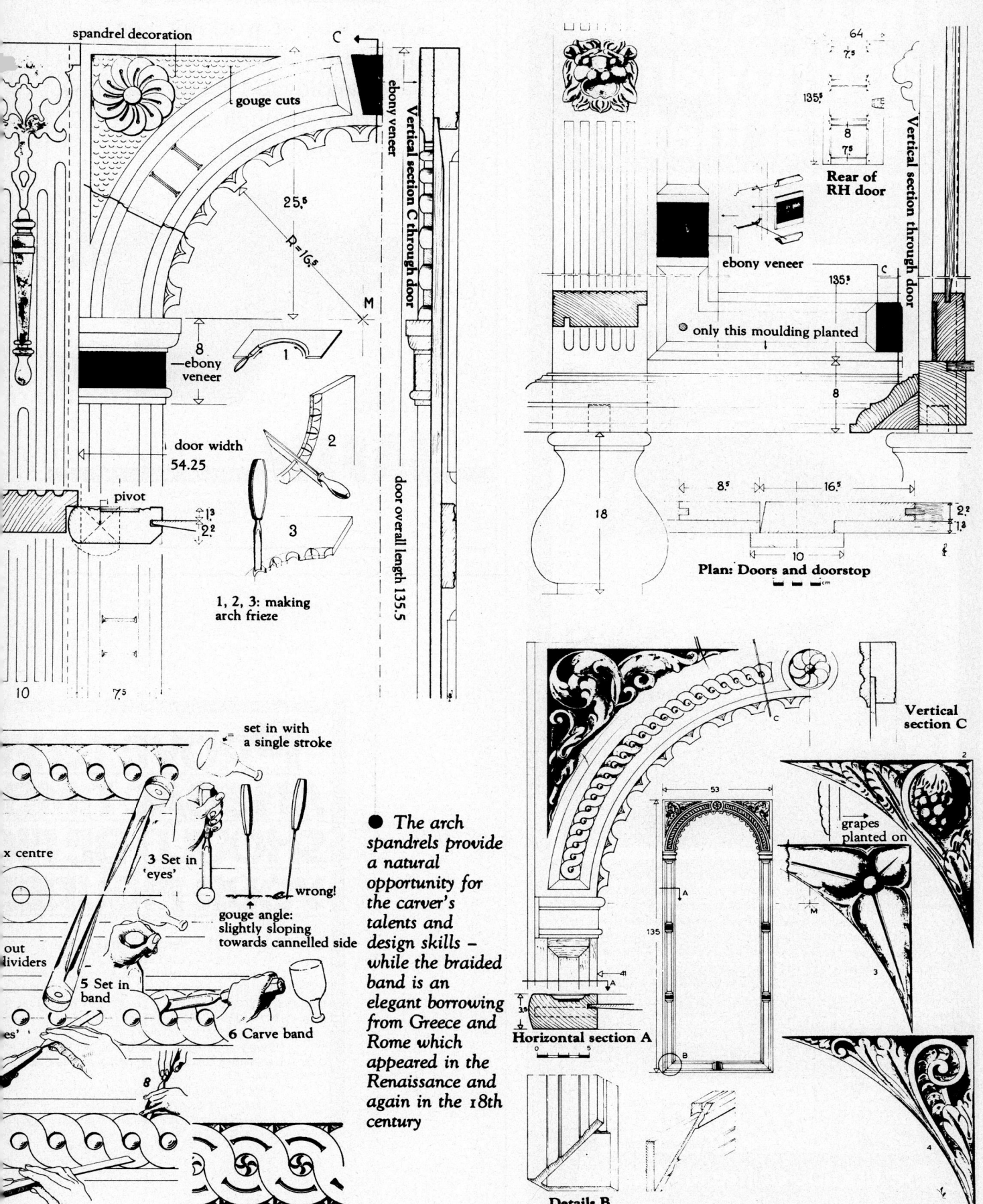

spandrel decoration

gouge cuts

ebony veneer

Vertical section C through door

25.5

R = 16.5

M

8
—ebony
veneer

door width
54.25

pivot

1

2

3

1, 2, 3: making
arch frieze

10

7.5

door overall length 135.5

64
7.5

135.5

8
7.5

**Rear of
RH door**

ebony veneer

Vertical section through door

135.5

C

only this moulding planted

8

18

8.5

16.5

2.2
1.3

10

**Plan: Doors and doorstop**

cm

set in with
a single stroke

x centre

**3 Set in
'eyes'**

wrong!

gouge angle:
slightly sloping
towards cannelled side

out
dividers

**5 Set in
band**

**6 Carve band**

es'

8

● *The arch
spandrels provide
a natural
opportunity for
the carver's
talents and
design skills –
while the braided
band is an
elegant borrowing
from Greece and
Rome which
appeared in the
Renaissance and
again in the 18th
century*

**Vertical
section C**

53

135

41

1.5

**Horizontal section A**

0

**Details B**

A

A

B

grapes
planted on

2

M

3

4

753

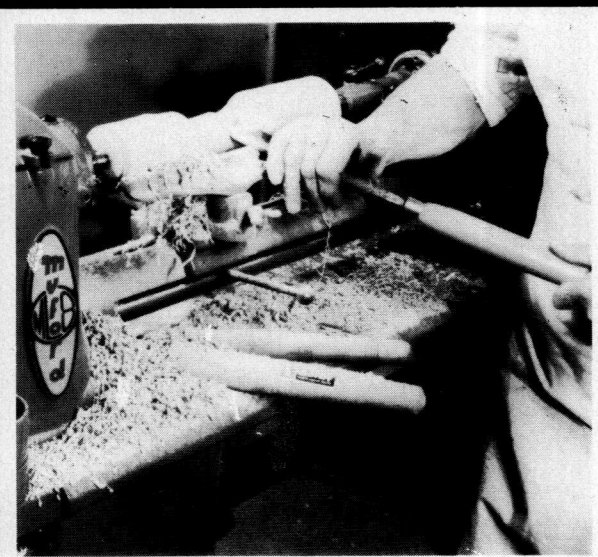
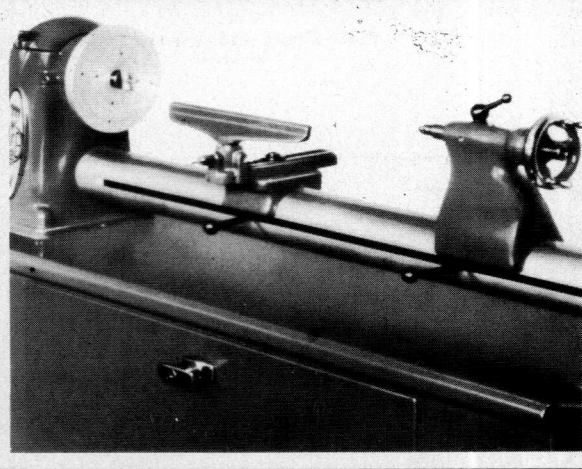

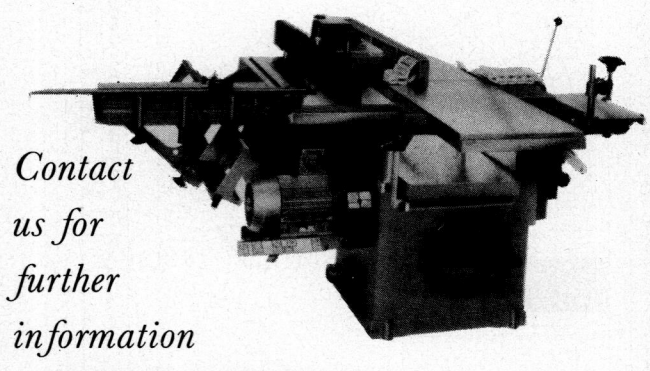

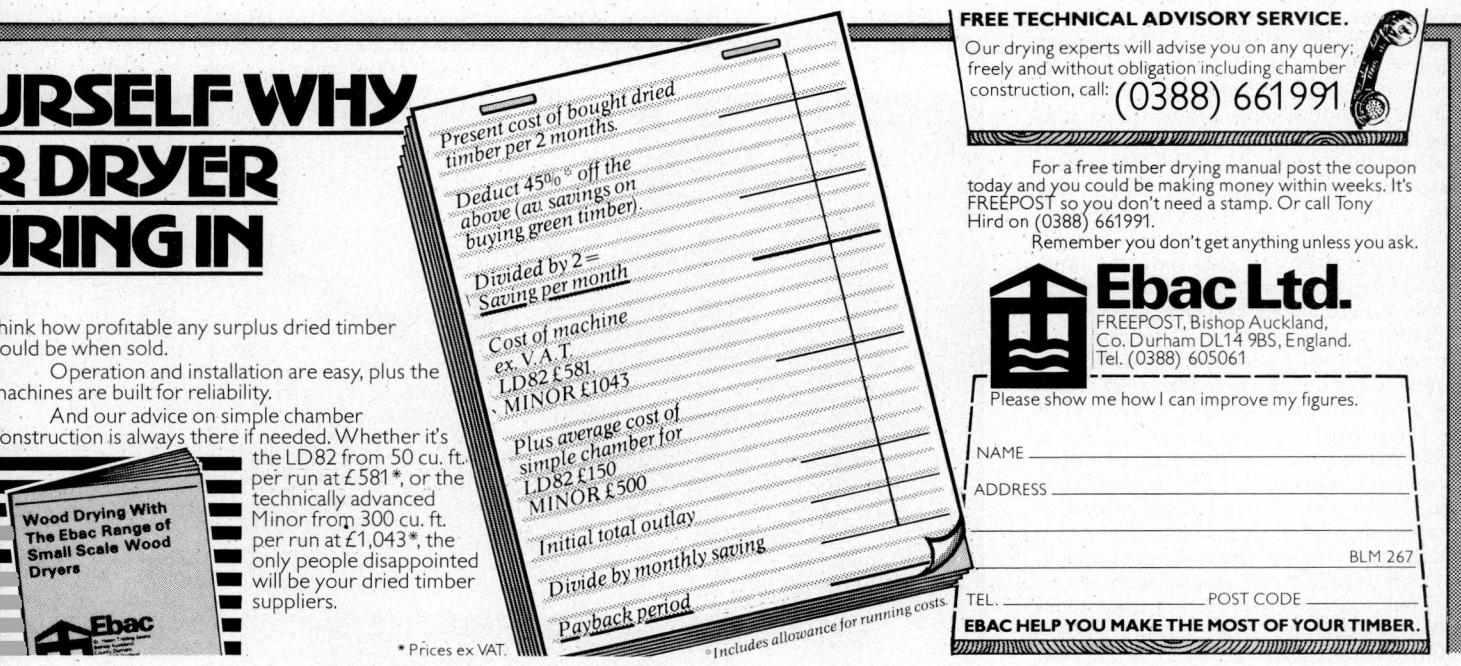

# Olden oak

## Make your own ancient throne with the help of Frank Coates' drawings and splendidly detailed explanation

I took the measurements for this project from an original wainscot chair in our living-room. Before starting work, I think it's worth making a scale drawing to keep for the future. I also made notes of the type of carving, and tried doing some brass-rubbings (I guess you'd call them wood-rubbings!), which worked very well. It gives you full-size details of the carving, and helps greatly in marking out, especially the centre panel and crown (the top decorative piece).

These measurements were needed to make a full-size working rod, which allows you to lay the components down so you can pick off the positions of the mortises and tenons, angled shoulders, and so on, with a pencil. Do a plan and side elevation as well. The rod is drawn on 6mm white vinyl hardboard — but, if you only have plain, a coat of white emulsion does the job. Make sure the edges of the board are straight and square so that all your marking-out will be dead accurate.

Make up the cutting list, adding 50-100mm to the finished length of each member to get sawn sizes and an extra 3mm on the widths and thicknesses to lose in planing. I use millimetres because I'm used to the system, but obviously the original was measured in 'feet'n'inches'.

It's wise to store the cut (sawn) pieces in a warm room to get the moisture content down so the finished chair won't twist or split as a result of more drying. Leave it as long as possible — at least five or six weeks.

After the cutting and this secondary seasoning, start planing up. I haven't any machinery yet, so I did all the dimensioning by hand, with a little help from my hand-held power planer. If you have the time, hand-planing can be very enjoyable as long as the plane is lovely and sharp!

Before you pick up the plane, cast your eye over the piece and select the two faces nearest to (or on) the heartwood (fig. 3), so you keep more of the solid heartwood in the final shape after thicknessing. This is ideal, of course, but if knots or other defects say otherwise, pick an alternative side. Check your chosen face for twist with winding-strips. If it's difficult to see whether the edges of the strips are parallel, put a bit of yellow tape along the top of one of them and have that further away from you.

Once you have the face side trued up you can square the face edge, then gauge up width and thickness and plane to dimension. Don't forget to re-write the identification marks on the pieces after planing up, or you'll find yourself in a pickle.

● *The finished chair, a handsome reminder of the days when your seat showed your status*

Templates can be made from the rod; they are invaluable for making the chairs, and even more so if you are making a quantity. They are all made of 6mm hardboard, but ply would do just as well. I made a template for the back leg (fig. 4) because it goes back at an angle up from the seat rail; the one for the crown piece was done simply by holding a piece of board behind the original and drawing round it, which is

how the one for the ears was also done. I also made two angled templates to get the angles when chopping the mortises (fig. 5a), and aid final adjustment when gluing up (fig. 5); I got the angles from the rod. Label all the templates so you know what they are. You can also use them to help select the pieces from which you will make shaped components, avoiding knots and defects.

There is no specific order for marking out. I started with the legs, front ones first. Put one leg on the rod and mark off with a pencil on the actual piece the positions of rails, arm joint and bottom end. Pair the legs off and square the marks across both, going round on to other faces where necessary. The back leg blanks were prepared and the template positioned as in fig. 4. They were then bandsawn to shape, and marked out in the same way as the front legs. I set up a mortise-gauge and marked out the tenons on the horizontal rails for an appropriate-sized chisel; all the leg mortises and tenons were marked out while the gauge was set up — from the face side and edge, of course!

Gauge the mortises in the back legs for the arms, and also mark out the tenons on top of the front legs for the arms, and on top of the back legs for the crown piece. Mark the mortises for the central panel-frame too. Remember the old adage 'check twice, cut once', and double-check all your marking out. I left the joints on the arms themselves until the whole frame was together, then made the arms to fit the completed frame. This makes sure the joints are a good snug fit.

The front frame was dry-assembled so the angled template could be used to give a guide for the chisel when I was chopping the side-rail mortises (fig. 5); the same goes for the rear frame, using the other template.

● *The templates for the angled mortises come in useful when lining up the chisel as well as marking out*

The panel-frame rails have stopped 10x10mm grooves for the panel to sit in, and the stiles have stub tenons. The grooves were cut with a power router with a straight fluted cutter, the ones in the stiles going right through. The tongue all the way round the panel was also cut with the router — be careful with your settings to get fractionally less than 10mm.

Chop the mortises for the top rail in the back legs before cutting the tenons on top that hold the crown. These are set back, off-centre of the legs, because the carving on the crown would otherwise weaken their hold. The front faces of both rails are flush with the front faces of the legs.

The mortises in the crown itself are chopped out before it is shaped (fig. 7a) so you can hold the regular oblong more easily in the vice for working. Five or six dowels are positioned along the top edge of the top rail between the top two tenons (fig. 7) — I drilled the holes with a plunge router, and used dowel poppets in the holes in the rail to mark the centres in the crown, which I fitted over the tenons and tapped down. The ears are also fixed in this way, and you need to be specially careful to get a tight fit to the leg and the overhang of the crown when marking the dowel centres on them. The only way this whole assembly will go together, obviously, is for the crown to go down on top of its tenons and the ears, which have already been fixed.

All the mortises and tenons are draw-bored (figs 8 & 9), and the tenons in the seat and lower rails mitred to get the biggest possible gluing area. Draw-boring is an excellent way of tightening a joint without using cramps; you have to make sure you bore the hole in the tenon off-centre to the one in the mortise — but 1-2mm nearer the shoulder for the tenon hole, not 1-2mm further, or you'll get a draw-opening effect, not a drawing-up-tight! Don't stagger the holes too much, or you may split something. Drill the sides of the mortise 8-10mm from the shoulder; you might think it'll split between there and the edge, but the effect is, in fact, that it gets stronger as the tenon shoulders are drawn up.

After the various bits of carving have been done and the whole framework dry-assembled and checked for square and winding, start the gluing. First comes the front frame, the easiest part; if your draw-boring hasn't quite tightened the joints or if it's out of square, use one or two sash-cramps (with softwood pads to avoid bruising) to correct the discrepancy. Don't forget to wipe excess glue away very thoroughly with a damp cloth and a chisel to get it out of the grain — there's nothing more annoying than white patches round the joints where the glue has stopped the stain absorbing.

The back frame assembly goes together next. The centre panel isn't glued in the grooves in chair-rails and panel-stiles, to allow for inevitable movement; the stub tenons on the stiles should have a touch of

glue. Then lay one back leg down, glue the appropriate ends of the various rails and fit them, and manoeuvre the other leg on to its set of tenons. Gentle persuasion with a mallet and softwood block may be necessary. Then put the dowels in the drilled joints. Again use sash-cramps to pull everything up if it isn't as tight as it should be; the crown and ears go on when the glue has set on the frame, and here you have to use sash-cramps.

When both front and back frames are dry you can join them with the side rails, but check first that no dowels have found their way into the relevant mortises. A minute with a chisel will fix them if they have. Dry-assemble, as always, and also before you put it together cut three legs to length and leave the last overlong so you can cut it to adjust the finished chair's stability on a flat surface.

When the whole frame is glued up the draw-boring effect may need a little help from the sash cramps again, but this time you must use angle padding blocks (fig. 10)

to equalise cramping pressure on both sides of the tenon shoulders in the angle frame. If you are doing the job on your own it's a good idea to tape the angled blocks on to the legs to keep them where they should be, and keep your temper where that should be too.

Now you have the basic frame glued up, all carved, minus the arms and seat with its decorative radiused border-pieces. The seat must be cut to shape and fitted before the arms go on, otherwise you'll never get it in. On the original chair it was one complete piece, but boards this width aren't easy to get, and I chose to joint mine up from smaller widths for the added reason that this method reduces warping and cupping. Place the heartwood uppermost alternately to minimise the effect of movement (fig. 11). A rubbed edge joint would be OK, but I dowelled mine as well. After I'd cleaned it up and cut it to fit the frame, I rounded over the edges with a small-diameter cutter in the router.

The radiused borders were fitted to the

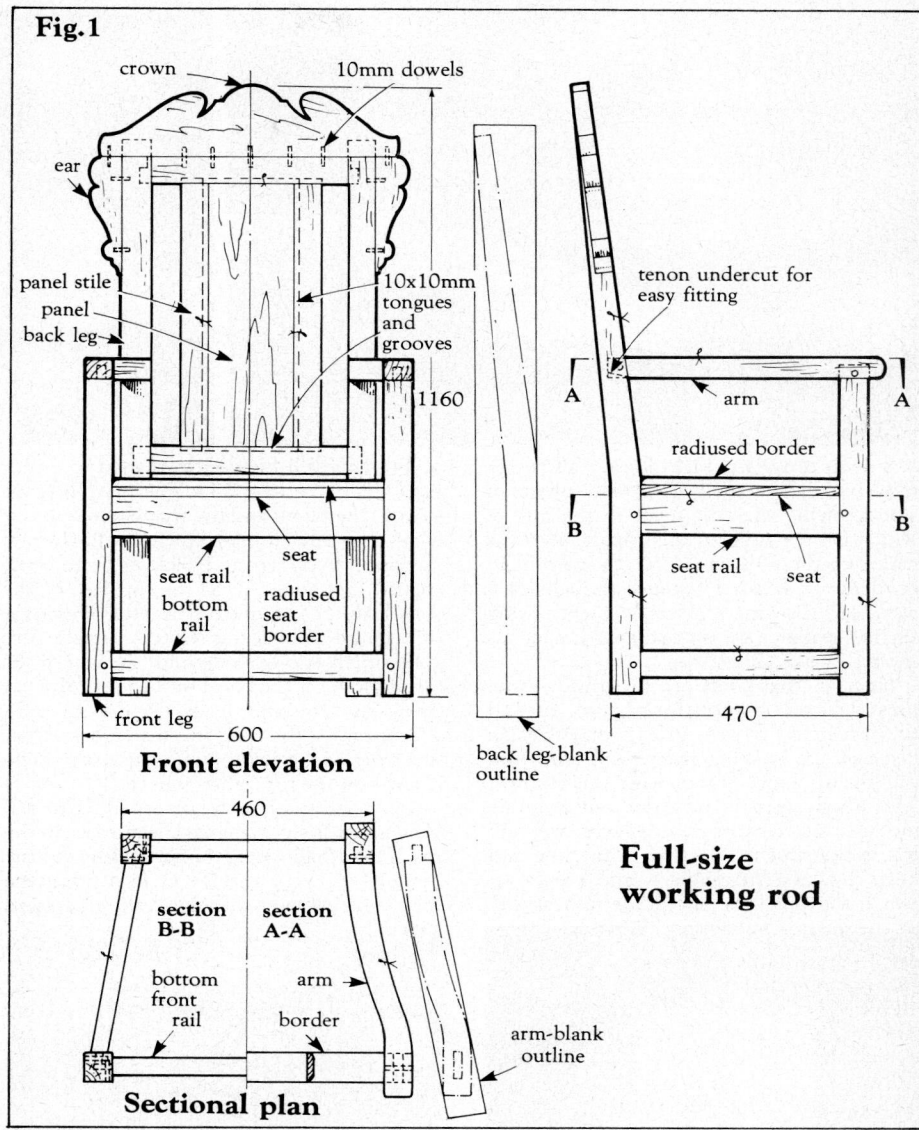

**Fig.1**

crown    10mm dowels

ear

panel stile
panel
back leg

10x10mm tongues and grooves

1160

seat rail
bottom rail

seat

radiused seat border

front leg

600

**Front elevation**

tenon undercut for easy fitting

A          A

arm

radiused border

B          B

seat rail          seat

470

back leg-blank outline

460

section B-B    section A-A

bottom front rail

arm

border

arm-blank outline

**Sectional plan**

**Full-size working rod**

# Olden oak

seat with dowels, which doesn't allow for movement and actually defeats the object of slot-screwing the seat itself to the rail — which is how I did it; the original seat was nailed to the rails, and I can't see how the borders are fixed. I've since thought of a way of allowing for movement using shrinkage plates and slot-screwing, which is shown in fig. 12.

Now all that's left are the arms — the most difficult components to mark out and fit. Either they fit or you're stuck with gaps, because the existing frame will stop you pulling up loose joints with the cramps. This is why careful and absolutely accurate measuring of lengths and angles is essential. It's tricky, but if you take your time and keep checking the maths — and keep your pencil sharp — you should get a neat job.

Start with a blank arm planed to width and thickness (fig. 14). The plan in fig. 1 shows the blank and the shape to be cut out of it. Set your sliding-bevel to the horizontal angle between arm and back leg on the rod; pencil this angle on to the top face of the blank about 75mm from the end. This is for the tenon plus some waste — make sure you've left enough length for the rest of the arm! Now set the bevel to the vertical angle between arm· and back leg on the side elevation on the rod, and mark this off on the sides of the arms, joining up to the angle drawn on the top. Then join the two angles on the sides with a line across underneath. The gauge is set to match the mortise in the back leg which takes the arm. Now cut the tenons. Be very careful in measuring the distances between the angled shoulders and

● *Above left: The line of the crown is marked out using a card template, the shape taken from the original.* **Above,** *the shaped crown, as yet uncarved, is fitted over the top tenons and dowel poppets to mark for dowel drilling*

the mortise for the front leg tenon — the rod is the guide, but work as accurately as you can from the actual chair to check. A steel folding rule is best for measuring this kind of thing, but if you use a tape make sure it's taut. Round off the underside of the tenon on the back of the arm a little to make it easier to fit.

Once the arm joints are a good fit, they

● *The carving of the centre panel in progress. A certain roughness adds authenticity*

● *The finished panel in the chair-back. It will age and darken with repeated waxing*

● *The back frame, ready for the side members to go into the angled mortises. The centre panel is already stained*

can be shaped. I use a jigsaw to get rid of the bulk, then a good sharp spokeshave to clean it up and go round the front and top edges for the 'hundreds of years of use' look. It's all too easy to overdo this ageing — stand back every so often to see the effect. Carve the arms, draw-bore the joints, and glue them in position.

That's it, woodworking-wise. The next stage is making the chair look ancient. The front bottom rail of the original had been scuffed and worn by thousands of feet, and I copied that effect (fig. 15) with a Surform and spokeshave. Again, don't overdo it, just round it over a little, like the arms. All the corners and edges most likely to get wear and abrasion should be rounded off subtly. Have a look at some old furni-

ture and see where parts have been burnished by clothing — the arms, seat and back. There's generally a fair bit of bruising round the bottoms of legs from accidental kicks and knocks, which is best simulated by a bit of firm but gentle bashing with a square-edged block. Draw the corner of this 'distressing tool' across an area where you think there ought to be a scratch; smaller, more general scratches can be done with a bit of sharp knobbly stone. Again, seat, arms and the outward lower faces of the front legs would come in for most of this ill-treatment.

The dowels can be cut off after the glue has set. They protrude a couple of mm on the original, the timber having shrunk where the dowels don't, so if you want authenticity, leave them sticking out a little.

Give the whole thing a light sanding,

using the grades of paper you're used to. I only went down to 180 grit, which I'm sure is enough for this kind of chair — remember, original wainscot chairs would have been unlikely to see such treatment!

Now to the staining. I used water-based stain, vandyke brown crystals. You need to experiment to get the right shade of typical Jacobean dark brown; soft water, slightly warmed, is best for mixing. Add a little ammonia to help penetration, and apply it with a rag on the smooth surfaces and a clean brush in the fiddly carvings. Avoid leaving excess on the surface, and drips in the details of the carving; mop it over with a clean rag after a few minutes to help get an even spread of colour. Lighten it a little, in places which would be worn, with a clean wet rag, but experiment first on offcuts.

● *Fitting the arms is perhaps the most difficult job. The mortises and angled shoulders should be marked out and cut before shaping; take measurements from the rod, but be sure to make final adjustments by fitting to the frame itself*

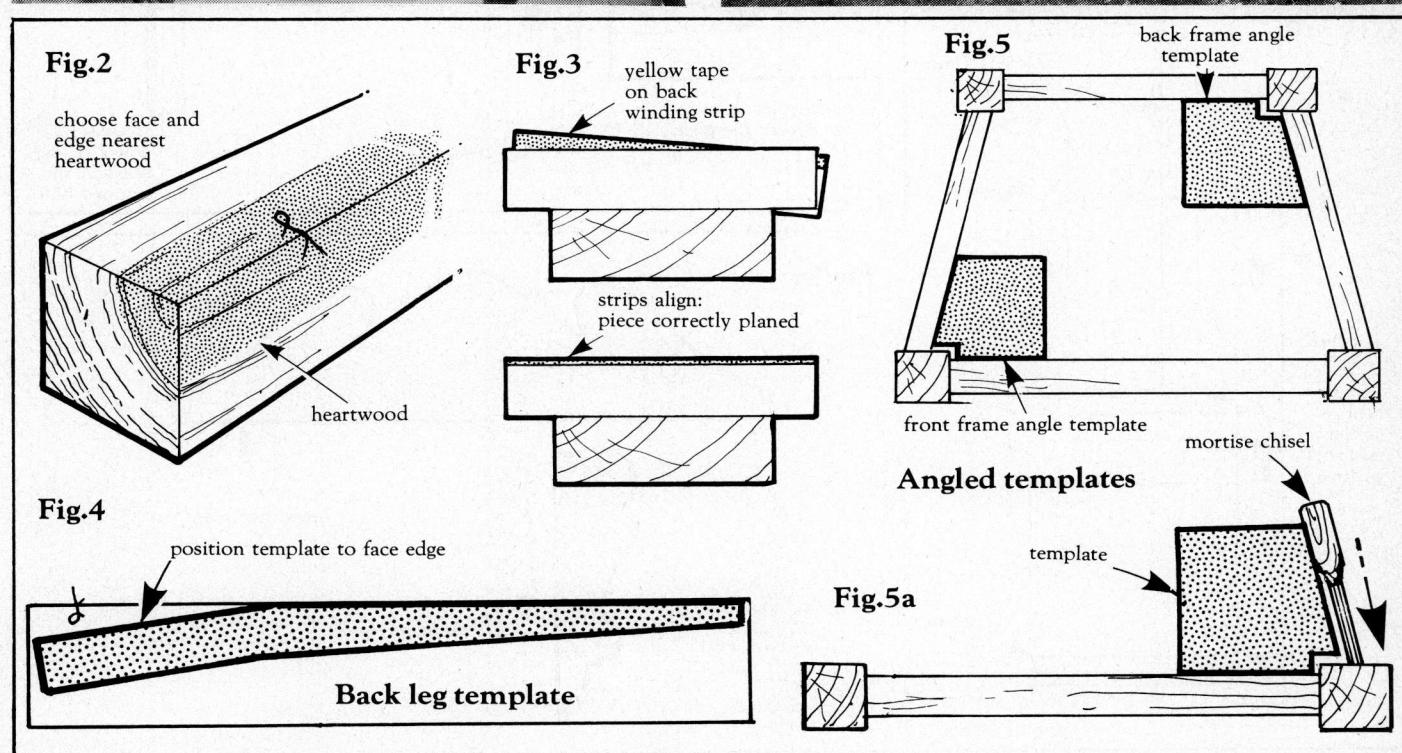

**Fig.2**
choose face and edge nearest heartwood

heartwood

**Fig.3**
yellow tape on back winding strip

strips align: piece correctly planed

**Fig.4**
position template to face edge

**Back leg template**

**Fig.5**
back frame angle template

front frame angle template

**Angled templates**

**Fig.5a**
mortise chisel

template

# Olden oak

This sort of stain raises the grain — it's usual to damp the piece before staining, let it dry and sand back the raised fibres, but I didn't do this because I wire-wool-and-waxed it. Dark oak staining wax was applied with OOOO wire wool and a brush in the nooks and crannies of the carvings; three or four coats will give you about the right colour, each one buffed before you put on the next. Polish it underneath as well, since it's supposed to look the same age all over.

I enjoyed making my pair of wainscot chairs, and I hope someone else is inspired to try. It's like having your own personal throne in your living-room! ∎

## Cutting list — sawn sizes

All dimensions in mm; widths and thicknesses reduce by 3mm to finished size; lengths include waste allowance.

| | | length | | width | thickness |
|---|---|---|---|---|---|
| A | top (crown) | 1 600 | x | 136 | x 37 (shaped width) |
| B | arms | 2 600 | | 62 | 43 (shaped width) |
| C | seat rails | 4 650 | | 78 | 33 |
| D | bottom rails | 4 650 | | 53 | 33 |
| E | front legs | 2 740 | | 55 | 55 |
| F | back legs | 2 1150 | | 120 | 50 (shaped width) |
| G | top and bottom panel rails | 2 500 | | 53 | 32 |
| H | side panel stiles | 2 600 | | 53 | 32 |
| I | panel | 1 580 | | 181 | 22 |
| J | seat | 5 650 | | 97 | 22 |
| K | ears | 2 280 | | 68 | 37 (shaped width) |
| L | seat borders | 3 600 | | 53 | 18 |
| M | dowel | 1800 | | | 10 dia.; cut to length |

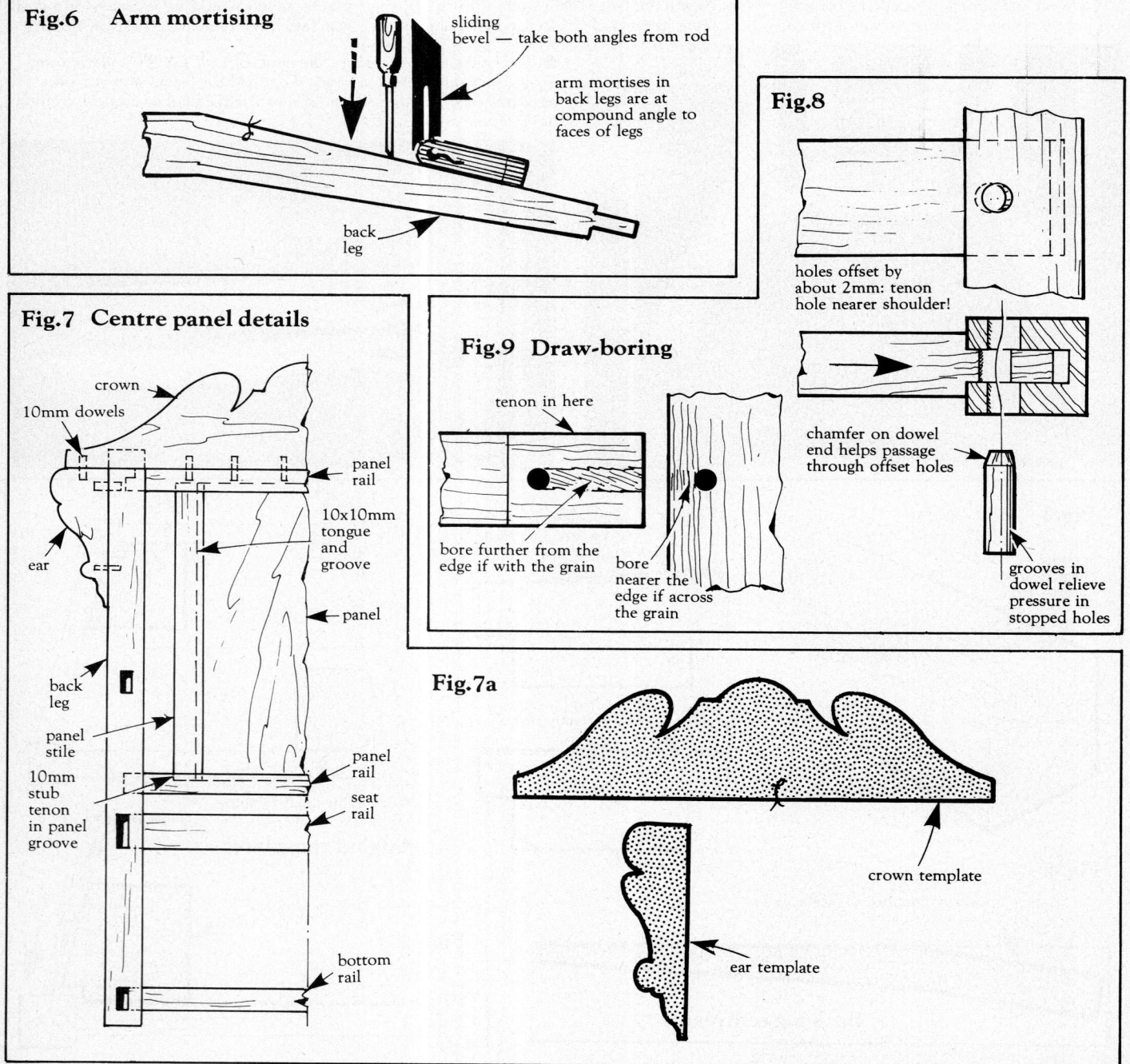

**Fig.6  Arm mortising**

sliding bevel — take both angles from rod

arm mortises in back legs are at compound angle to faces of legs

back leg

**Fig.8**

holes offset by about 2mm: tenon hole nearer shoulder!

chamfer on dowel end helps passage through offset holes

grooves in dowel relieve pressure in stopped holes

**Fig.7  Centre panel details**

crown

10mm dowels

panel rail

10x10mm tongue and groove

ear

panel

back leg

panel stile

10mm stub tenon in panel groove

panel rail

seat rail

bottom rail

**Fig.9  Draw-boring**

tenon in here

bore further from the edge if with the grain

bore nearer the edge if across the grain

**Fig.7a**

crown template

ear template

760

## Fig.10 Cramping angled frames

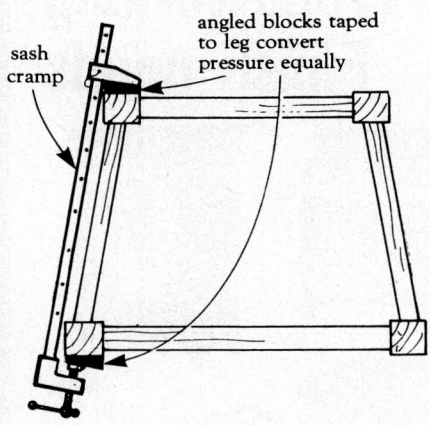

sash cramp

angled blocks taped to leg convert pressure equally

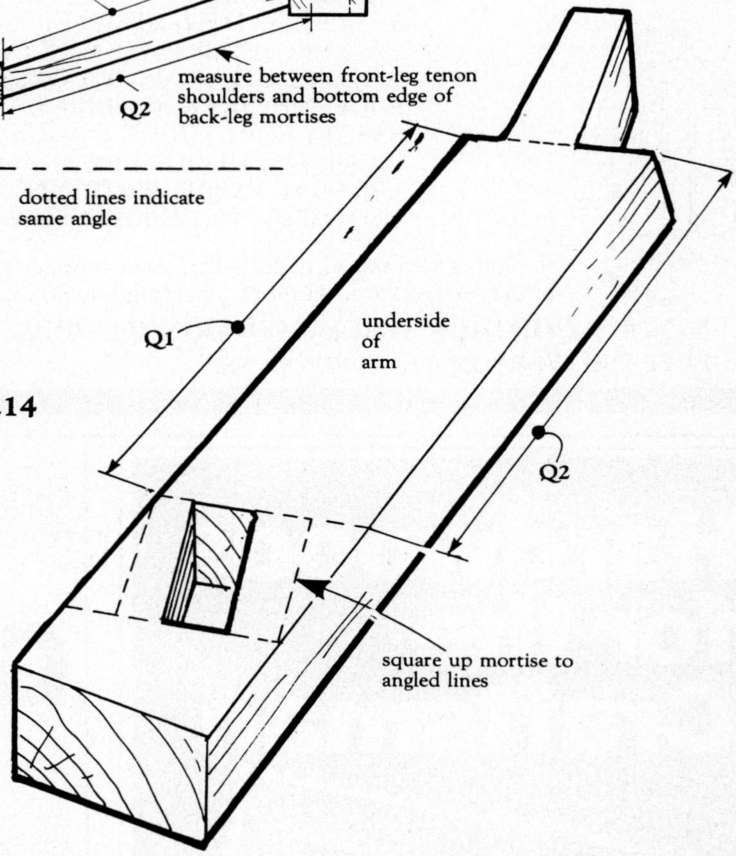

## Fig.11 Making and fixing the seat

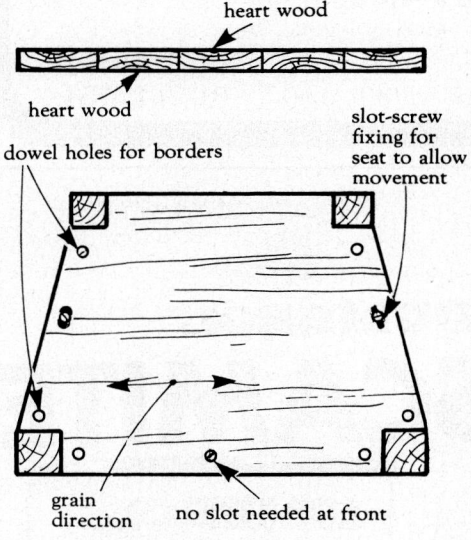

heart wood

heart wood

dowel holes for borders

slot-screw fixing for seat to allow movement

grain direction

no slot needed at front

## Fig.12 Alternative border and seat fixing

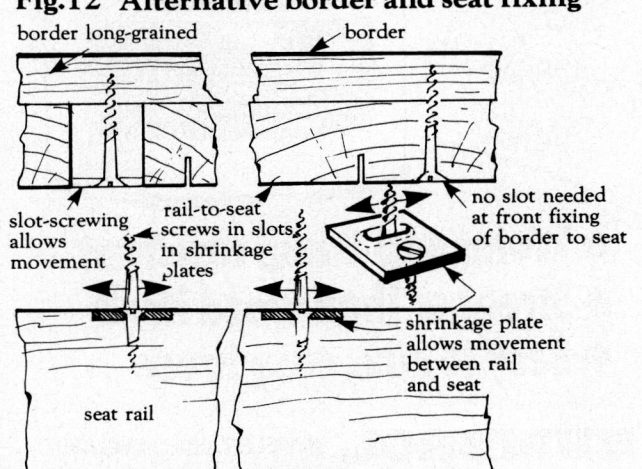

border long-grained

border

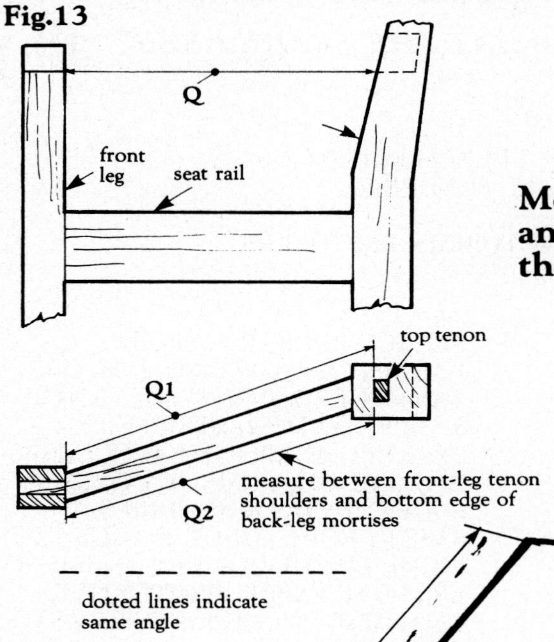

slot-screwing allows movement

rail-to-seat screws in slots in shrinkage plates

no slot needed at front fixing of border to seat

shrinkage plate allows movement between rail and seat

seat rail

### Fig.13

front leg

seat rail

Q

## Measuring and fitting the arms

top tenon

Q1

Q2

measure between front-leg tenon shoulders and bottom edge of back-leg mortises

dotted lines indicate same angle

### Fig.14

Q1

Q2

underside of arm

square up mortise to angled lines

## Fig.15 Ageing the foot rail

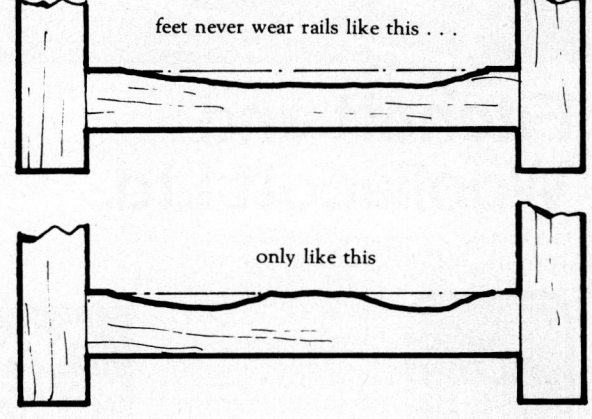

feet never wear rails like this . . .

only like this

762

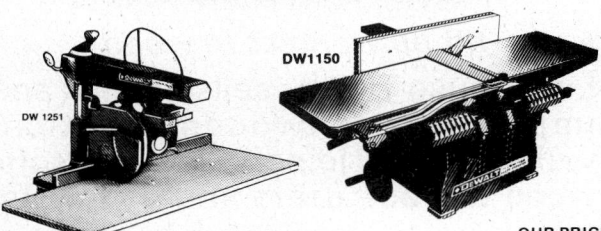

763

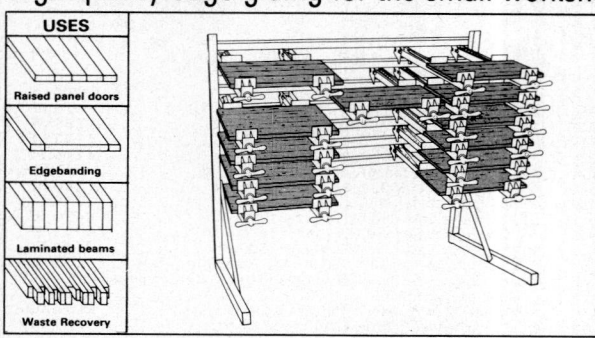
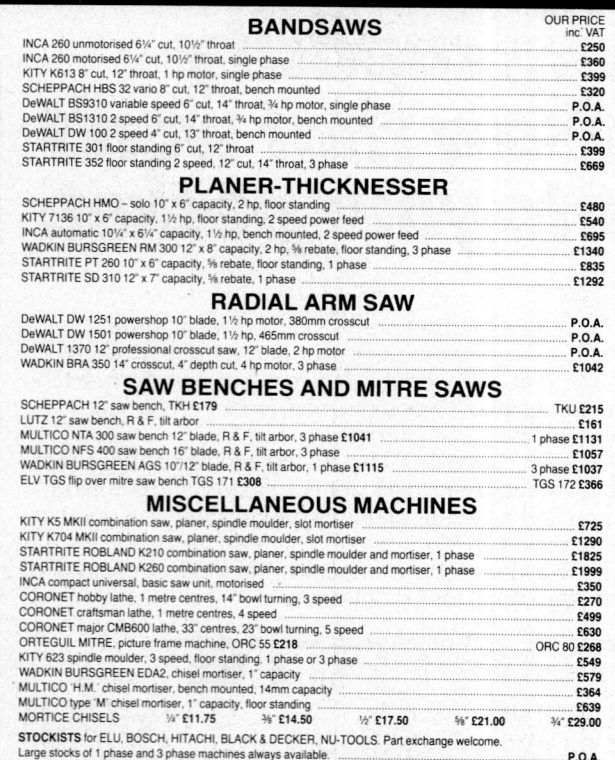

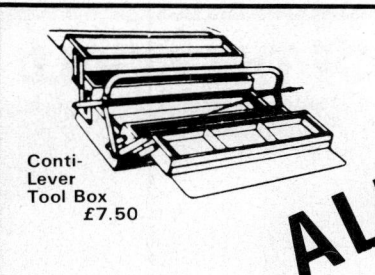

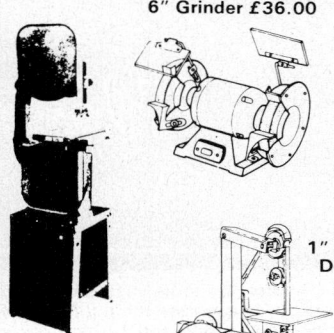

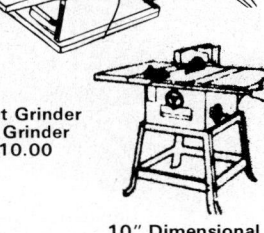
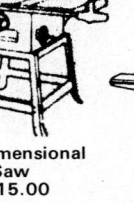
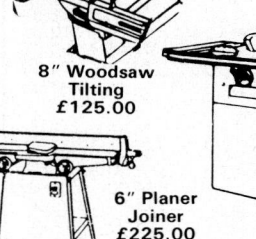

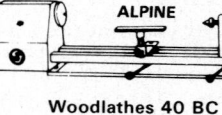
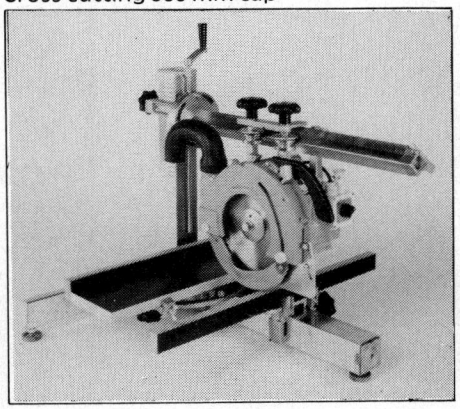
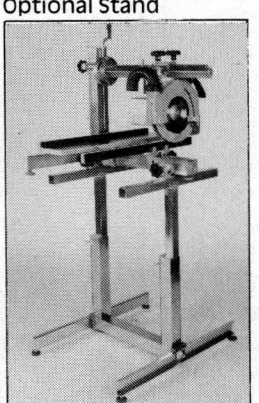
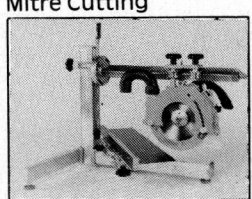

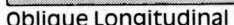

766

# The shovel-makers of Chesham

## How Stuart King discovered a living record of a dying craft

Mention Tunbridge Wells, and many a woodworker will think of Tunbridge ware. Sussex means trug baskets, and for High Wycombe it has to be chairs.

But Chesham? Beer, brushes, boots and Baptists, asserts a local saying. Yet the town, buried deep in a Chiltern valley, has been for centuries another woodware centre.

I use the term 'woodware' for an enormous range of goods — wheelbarrows, yokes, rakes, spoons, butcher's blocks, bowls of all sizes, and a string of miscellanea such as vegetable-mashers and darning mushrooms. The list is almost endless, so here I'll only talk about one item: shovels, which have been made in Chesham for over 400 years.

As an avid collector and historian of old tools and treen, I'd picked up a few pieces of Chesham ware over the years from local sheds and workshops. But late last year I heard of the imminent death of a long-established firm, and with the kind permission of its proprietor set about to make a photographic record before the demolition gang moved in.

The establishment consisted of a hotch-potch of workshops, some brick, some wooden and some a mixture of both — varying in age, and set roughly in an L-shape. A large shelter, open on two sides, had once given cover to the wagons and the steam-driven racksaw. Enclosed by the buildings was a large yard in which, years ago, timber had been stacked as high as a house.

In their modest way, these workshops were a time capsule. Old samples, patterns and templates hung on every wall. Beside them hung old tools — also to be found under benches, where they'd been left when last used, or perhaps abandoned when new methods had made them obsolete.

Wearing my worst rags in preparation for rummaging in the many odd corners that had lain undisturbed for decades, I made many visits to the old firm. I found plenty of unique tools and pieces of equipment. The purposes of some were a matter for conjecture — their day, like most of their users, being long gone.

Shaves of all kinds were by far the most numerous tools. They ranged from the universally useful straight drawshave, of various lengths, to hollow-profiled types. The medium hollow shaves were used for rounding the shovel-handles' shanks. Round shaves without wooden handles, known as scorps, were an interesting discovery, being more usually associated with coopering.

The craftsmen seem to have found spokeshaves very handy, too. Again these came in many shapes and sizes; some had steel plates let into their soles to prevent wear. There were long, thin ones, straight

● *The aged workshops told their own unique story*

ones, and some curved 'shovel-maker's shaves'. These last were used for finishing the blades of the shovels and scoops once they had been roughed out with a short-handled round adze.

Most of the tools had been made from old files by the local smith; his name, J. Nash, is stamped into some of them. He is said to have been a very competent toolmaker who enjoyed the challenge of making special items to order. Often his customer would pay several visits to the forge, each time taking the tool back to the workshop to try it out on the new job for which it was destined, and returning for an alteration to the shape or maybe the angle.

The timber for making shovels included black poplar, ash and beech. Only the best and largest wood, fault-free, was used;

of course, it was bought at a premium. The boss had to be on good terms with the agents from the large local estates, because he would walk through the wood with these men and point out the trees he wanted. Understanding the needs of local industry, the agents gave the shovel-makers first choice.

The firm had three timber wagons with double horses and two 'bob trucks' with single horses. 30 men were employed, and they worked as a family. Except for the turners, who formed a class of their own and usually concentrated solely on their turning, the employees generally were expected to help out where the need was greatest. Whether that meant felling giant beeches or crosscutting logs in the yard, they accepted it as all being part of a day's work.

● *Once upon a time, a shovel was not just a shovel*

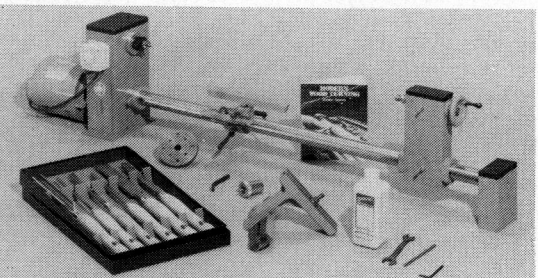

# The shovel-makers of Chesham

At the turn of the century the men were working 60-70 hours a week for about 4d an hour. No wages book was kept. 'There was more trust — men were more honest in those days. They worked honestly and didn't waste time,' one retired boss told me.

Shovels were made only from quartered timber; in other words, plank was sawn from the log radially. 'If they were cut on the flitch (through and through),' explained my retired friend, 'the shovels would split; cut on the quarter, they wouldn't. I've seen my grandfather show a customer how strong the shovels were by throwing them into the air and letting them fall to the ground.'

Some shovel-blades were 16in across; as each log yielded two shovels across its width, the logs needed to be very large — in many cases, over 4ft. Once the butts had been crosscut to the appropriate lengths, they were split into quarters with a large froe and wedges and then sliced into feather-edged planks on the steam-driven circular saw. Sawing needed up to six men. This saw was also used to convert small butts from the round. The shovel-maker himself supervised every operation, and —

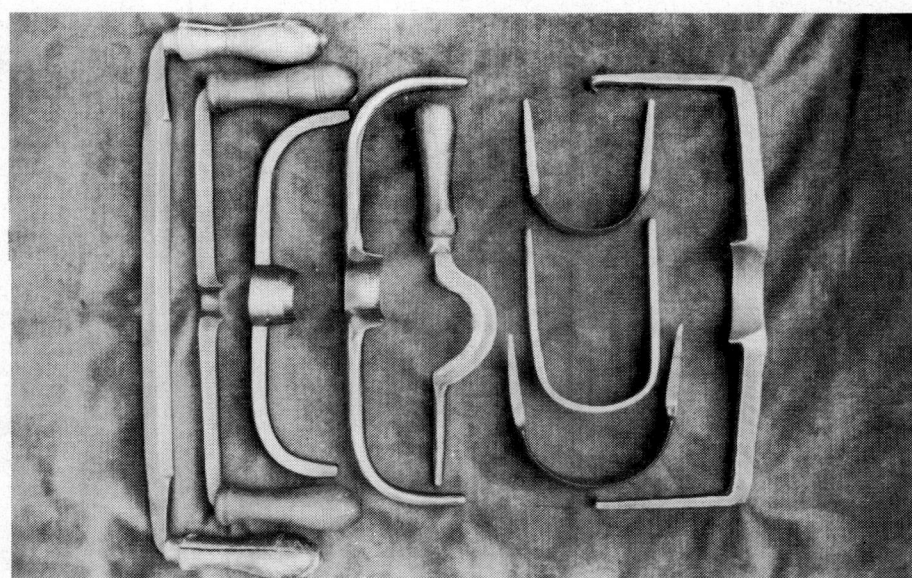

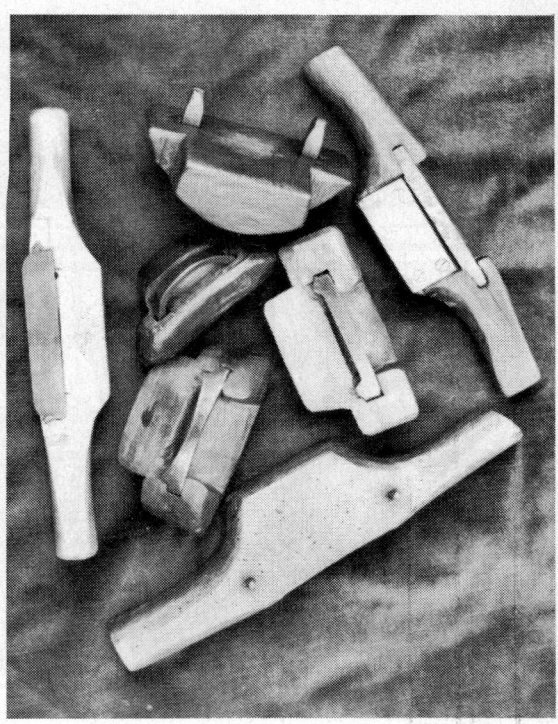

● *Shovel-making is all about shaving (**below right**). The old workshops yielded untold varieties of shaves (**top**) and spokeshaves (**right**; the curved spokeshaves in the centre are for shovel-blades). The curved adze also had its uses (**above**)*

if he happened to be in the appropriate felling gang — could see a shovel right through from tree to finished article.

The various types of shovel were marked out on the plank, using the patterns that were hung up and 'fetched out' when needed. You had to 'use your gimmick' a bit when marking out if you were to get the most from your material. The blanks were cut on the bandsaw ready for final shaping. Some small handles were turned on the lathe, but most seem to have been shaped up with the shaves. Some shovels were made from single pieces; others had separate handles, usually fixed with bolts.

The different varieties of shovel are, of course, a subject on their own. There were barn shovels, mud scoops, malt shovels (beech for wet grain, poplar for dry malt)

and so on. My favourite is the 8ft-long baker's peel of beech with its D handle, riven from the log in one piece and used, of course, for reaching those crusty loaves at the back of the long oven. If you want to know more, come to the Woodworker Show! ■

**This year's Woodworker Show will feature Stuart's live reconstruction of a Chesham woodware shop. Alexandra Pavilion, London N22, 24-7 October; details on (0422) 41221.**

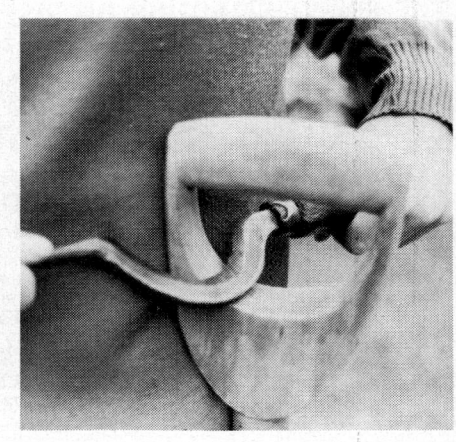

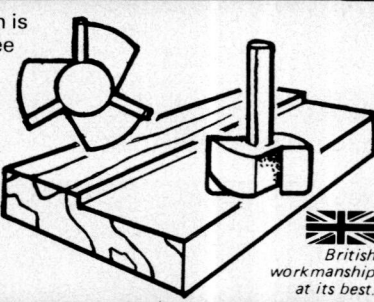

## AVON

**BATH**    Tel. Bath 64513
JOHN HALL TOOLS
RAILWAY STREET   ★

Open: Monday-Saturday
9.00 a.m.-5.30 p.m.
H.P.W.WM.D.A.BC.

**BRISTOL**    Tel. (0272) 741510
JOHN HALL TOOLS LIMITED   ★
CLIFTON DOWN SHOPPING CENTRE
WHITELADIES ROAD
Open: Monday-Saturday
9.00 a.m.-5.30 p.m.
H.P.W.WM.D.A.BC.

**BRISTOL**    Tel. (0272) 629092
TRYMWOOD SERVICES
2a DOWNS PARK EAST, (off North View)
WESTBURY PARK
Open: 8.30 a.m.-5.30 p.m. Mon. to Fri.
Closed for lunch 1.00-2.00 p.m.
P.W.WM.D.T.A.BC.

**BRISTOL**    Tel. (0272) 667013
WILLIS
157 WEST STREET
BEDMINSTER
Open Mon.-Fri. 8.30 a.m.-5.00 p.m.
No Saturday opening

## BEDFORDSHIRE

**BEDFORD**    Tel. (0234) 59808
BEDFORD SAW SERVICE   K
39 AMPTHILL ROAD

Open: Mon.-Fri. 8.30-5.30
Sat. 9.00-4.00
H.P.A.ABC.W.CS.WM.D.

## BERKSHIRE

**COOKHAM**    Tel. (06285) 20350
CHURCH'S TIMBER
STATION HILL

Open: Mon-Sat 8.30 a.m.-5.30 p.m.
Wed 8.30 a.m.-1.00 p.m.
H.P.W.T.CS.MF.A.

**READING**    Tel. (0734) 591361
HOME CARE CENTRE
26/30 KING'S ROAD

Open: Monday-Saturday
9.00 a.m.-5.30 p.m.
H.P.W.D.A.WM.BC.

**READING**    Tel. Littlewick Green
DAVID HUNT (TOOL    2743
MERCHANTS) LTD   ★
KNOWL HILL, NR. READING
Open: Monday-Saturday
9.00 a.m.-5.30 p.m.
H.P.W.D.A.BC.

## BERKSHIRE

**READING**    Tel. Reading 661511
WOKINGHAM TOOL CO. LTD.
99 WOKINGHAM ROAD

Open: Mon-Sat 9.00 a.m.-5.30 p.m.
Closed 1.00-2.00 p.m. for lunch
H.P.W.WM.D.CS.A.BC.

## BUCKINGHAMSHIRE

**SLOUGH**    Tel. (06286) 5125
BRAYWOOD ESTATES LTD   ★
158 BURNHAM LANE

Open: 9.00 a.m.-5.30 p.m.
Monday-Saturday
H.P.W.WM.CS.A.

**MILTON KEYNES**    Tel. (0908)
POLLARD WOODWORKING    641366
CENTRE   ★
51 AYLESBURY ST., BLETCHLEY
Open: Mon-Fri 8.30-5.30
Saturday 9.00-5.00
H.P.W.WM.D.CS.A.BC.

**HIGH WYCOMBE**    Tel. (0494)
SCOTT SAWS LTD.    24201/33788
14 BRIDGE STREET   ★

Mon.-Sat. 8.30 a.m.-6.00 p.m.

H.P.W.WM.D.T.CS.MF.A.BC.

**HIGH WYCOMBE**    Tel. (0494)
ISAAC LORD LTD    22221
185 DESBOROUGH ROAD   KE

Open: Mon-Fri 8.00 a.m.-5.00 p.m.
Saturday 9.00 a.m.-5.00 p.m.
H.P.W.D.A.

**TO FILL THIS SPACE**
**PHONE**
**PETER MAGNANI**
**ON**
**01 437 0699**

## CAMBRIDGESHIRE

**CAMBRIDGE**    Tel. (0223) 63132
D. MACKAY LTD.   E★
BRITANNIA WORKS, EAST ROAD

Open: Mon.-Fri. 8.30 a.m.-1 p.m./2.00-
5.00 p.m. Sat. 8.30 a.m.-1.00 p.m.
H.P.W.D.T.CS.MF.A.BC.

**CAMBRIDGE**    Tel. (0223) 247386
H. B. WOODWORKING   K
105 CHERRY HINTON ROAD
Open: 8.30 a.m.-5.30 p.m.
Monday-Friday
8.30 a.m.-1.00 p.m. Sat.
H.P.W.WM.D.CS.A.

**PETERBOROUGH**    Tel. (0733)
WILLIAMS DISTRIBUTORS    64252
(TOOLS) LIMITED   K
108-110 BURGHLEY ROAD
Open: Monday to Friday
8.30 a.m.-5.30 p.m.
H.P.A.W.D.WH.BC.

## CHESHIRE

**NANTWICH**    Tel. Crewe 67010
ALAN HOLTHAM   K★
THE OLD STORES TURNERY
WISTASON ROAD, WILLASTON
Open: Tues.-Sat. 9.00 a.m.-5.30 p.m.
Closed Monday
P.W.WM.D.T.C.CS.A.BC.

**CHEADLE**    Tel: 061491 1726
ERIC TOMKINSON   ★
86 STOCKPORT ROAD
Open: Mon.-Fri. 9.00 a.m.-4.00 p.m.
Saturday 9.00 a.m.-1.00 p.m.
H.P.W.D.MF.A.BC.

## CLEVELAND

**MIDDLESBROUGH**    Tel. (0642)
CLEVELAND WOODCRAFT    813103
(M'BRO), 38-42 CRESCENT ROAD   K

Open: Mon-Sat 9.15 a.m.-5.30 p.m.

H.P.T.A.BC.W.WM.CS.D.

## CORNWALL

**HELSTON**   Tel. Helston (03265) 4961
SOUTH WEST    Truro (0872) 71671
POWER TOOLS    Launceston
MONUMENT ROAD    (0566) 3555
  K
H.P.W.WM.D.CS.A.

**TRURO**    Tel. (0872) 71671
TRURO POWER TOOLS   E★
30 FERRIS TOWN

Open Mon.-Sat. 8.00 a.m.-12.30 p.m./
1.30 p.m.-5.00 p.m.
H.P.W.WM.D.CS.MF.A.BC.

## CUMBRIA

**CARLISLE**    Tel. (0228) 36391
W. M. PLANT
ALLENBROOK ROAD
ROSEHILL, CA1 2UT
Open: Mon.-Fri. 8.00 a.m.-5.15 p.m.
Sat. 8.00 a.m.-12.30 noon
P.W.WM.D.CS.A.

## DERBYSHIRE

**DERBY**    Tel. (0332) 41862
HAZLEHURSTS LTD.   E★
LONDON ROAD AND CANAL STREET

Open: Mon.-Sat. 8.30 a.m.-5.30 p.m. (retail)
Mon.-Fri. 8.00 a.m.-5.00 p.m. (trade)
H.P.W.MF.A.BC.

## BUXTON

**BUXTON**    Tel. (0298) 871636
CRAFT SUPPLIES   K★
THE MILL, MILLERSDALE

Open: Mon-Sat 9.00 a.m.-5.00 p.m.

H.P.W.D.T.CS.A.BC.

## DEVON

**BRIXHAM**    Tel. (08045) 4900
WOODCRAFT SUPPLIES   E★
4 HORSE POOL STREET

Open: Mon.-Sat. 9.00 a.m.-6.00 p.m.

H.P.W.A.D.MF.CS.BC.

**PLYMOUTH**    Tel. (0752) 330303
WESTWARD BUILDING SERVICES   ★
LTD., LISTER CLOSE, NEWNHAM
INDUSTRIAL ESTATE, PLYMPTON
Open: Mon-Fri 8.00 a.m.-5.30 p.m.
Sat. 8.30 a.m.-12.30 p.m.
H.P.W.WM.D.A.BC.

## DORSET

**BOURNEMOUTH**   Tel: (0202) 420583
POWER TOOL SERVICES
(Sales, spares, repairs)
849-851 CHRISTCHURCH ROAD
BOSCOMBE
Open: Mon.-Fri. 9.00 a.m.-5.30 p.m.
Sat: 9.00 a.m.-5.00 p.m.
H.P.W.CS.K.A.

## ESSEX

**LEIGH ON SEA**    Tel. (0702)
MARSHAL & PARSONS LTD.    710404
1111 LONDON ROAD   EK

Open: 8.30 a.m.-5.30 p.m. Mon-Fri
9.00 a.m.-5.00 p.m. Sat.
H.P.W.WM.D.CS.A.

**ILFORD**
CUTWELL TOOLS LTD.   ★
774-776 HIGH ROAD

Mon.-Fri. 9.00 a.m.-5.00 p.m.
and also by appointment.
P.W.WM.A.D.CS.

## GLOUCESTER

**TEWKESBURY**    Tel. (0684)
TEWKESBURY SAW CO. LTD.    293092
TRADING ESTATE, NEWTOWN   K

Open: Mon-Fri 8.00 a.m.-5.00 p.m.
Saturday 9.30 a.m.-12.00 p.m.
P.W.WM.D.CS.

## HAMPSHIRE

**SOUTHAMPTON**    Tel. (0703)
H.W.M.    776222
THE WOODWORKERS
303 SHIRLEY ROAD, SHIRLEY
Open: Tues-Fri 9.30 a.m.-6.00 p.m.
Sat 9.30 a.m.-4.00 p.m.
H.P.W.WM.D.CS.A.BC.T.

# shopguide

## HAMPSHIRE

**ALDERSHOT**    Tel. (0252) 334422
POWER TOOL CENTRE    **K**
374 HIGH STREET

Open Mon-Fri. 8.30 a.m.-5.30 p.m.

H.P.W.WM.D.A.BC.

**PORTSMOUTH**    Tel. (0705)
EURO PRECISION TOOLS LTD    667332
259/263 LONDON ROAD, NORTH END    ★
   **E**
Open: Mon-Fri 9.00 a.m.-5.30 p.m.
Sat. 9.00 a.m.-1.00 p.m.
H.P.W.WM.D.A.BC.

**SOUTHAMPTON**    Tel: (0703)
POWER TOOL CENTRE    332288
7 BELVIDERE ROAD    **K**★
Open Mon.-Fri. 8.30-5.30

H.P.W.WM.D.A.BC.CS.MF.

## HUMBERSIDE

**GRIMSBY**    Tel. Grimsby (0472)
   58741 Hull (0482) 26999
J. E. SIDDLE LTD. (Tool Specialists)    ★
83 VICTORIA STREET
Open: Mon-Fri 8.30 a.m.-5.30 p.m.
Sat. 8.30 a.m.-12.45 p.m. & 2 p.m.-5 p.m.
H.P.A.BC.W.WMD.

## KENT

**WYE**    Tel. (0233) 813144
KENT POWER TOOLS LTD.
UNIT 1, BRIAR CLOSE
WYE, Nr. ASFORD

H.P.W.WM.D.A.CS.

**MATFIELD**    Tel. Brenchley
LEISURECRAFT IN WOOD    (089272)
'ORMONDE,' MAIDSTONE RD.    2465
TN12 7JG
Open: Mon-Sun
9.00 a.m.-5.30 p.m.
W.WM.D.T.A.

## LANCASHIRE

**PRESTON**    Tel. (0772) 52951
SPEEDWELL TOOL COMPANY    **E**★
62-68 MEADOW STREET PR1 1SU
Open: Mon.-Fri. 8.30 a.m.-5.30 p.m.
Sat. 8.30 a.m.-12.30 p.m.

H.P.W.WM.CS.A.MF.BC.

**ROCHDALE**    Tel. (0706) 342123/
C.S.M. TOOLS    342322
4-6 HEYWOOD ROAD    **E**★
CASTLETON
Open: Mon-Sat 9.00 a.m.-6.00 p.m.
Sundays by appointment
W.D.CS.A.BC.

**LANCASTER**    Tel. (0524) 32886
LILE TOOL SHOP    **K**
43/45 NORTH ROAD
Open: Monday to Saturday
9.00 a.m.-5.30 p.m.
Wed 9.00 a.m.-12.30 p.m.
H.P.W.D.A.

## LANCASHIRE

**BURY**    Tel. (061 764 6769)
HOUSE OF HARBRU    ★
101 CROSTONS ROAD
ELTON
Open: Mon.-Fri. 9.00 a.m.-5.00 p.m.
Send 2 × 1st class stamps for catalogue
MF.

**MANCHESTER**    Tel. (061 789)
TIMMS TOOLS    0909
102-104 LIVERPOOL ROAD    ★
PATRICROFT M30 0WZ
Weekdays 9.00 a.m.-5.30 p.m.
Sat. 9.00 a.m.-1.00 p.m.
H.P.A.W.

## LINCOLNSHIRE

**LINCOLN**    Tel. (0522) 689369
SKELLINGTHORPE SAW SERVICES LTD.
OLD WOOD, SKELLINGTHORPE
Open: Mon to Fri 8 a.m.-5 p.m.
Sat 8 a.m.-12 pm
H.P.W.WM.D.CS.A.*.BC.
Access/Barclaycard

## LONDON

**ACTON**    Tel. (01-992) 4835
A. MILLS (ACTON) LTD
32/36 CHURCHFIELD ROAD W3 6ED
Open: Mon-Fri 9.00 a.m.-5.00 p.m.
Saturdays 9.00 am-1.00 p.m.
H.P.W.WM.

**LONDON**    Tel. 01-723 2295-6-7
LANGHAM TOOLS LIMITED
13 NORFOLK PLACE
LONDON W2 1QJ

**LONDON**    Tel. (01-567) 2922
G. D. CLEGG & SONS    ★
83 UXBRIDGE ROAD, HANWELL W7 3ST
Mon-Sat 9.15 a.m.-5.30 p.m.
Closed for lunch 1.00-2.00p.m.
Early Closing 1.00 p.m. Wed.
H.P.A.W.WM.D.CS.

**NORBURY**    Tel. (01-679) 6193
HERON TOOLS & HARDWARE LTD.
437 STREATHAM HIGH ROAD SW16
Open Mon-Fri 8.30 a.m.-5.00 p.m.
Wednesday 8.30 a.m.-1.00 p.m.
Sat. 9.00 a.m.-1.00 p.m.
H.P.W.A.

**LONDON**    Tel. (01-636) 7475
BUCK & RYAN LTD
101 TOTTENHAM COURT ROAD W1P 0DY
   ★
Open: Mon.-Fri. 8.30 a.m.-5.30 p.m.
Saturday 8.30 a.m.-4.00 p.m.
H.P.W.WM.D.A..

**WEMBLEY**    Tel. 904-1144
ROBERT SAMUEL LTD.    (904-1147
7, 15 & 16 COURT PARADE    after 4.00)
EAST LANE, N. WEMBLEY
Open Mon.-Fri. 8.45-5.15; Sat. 9-1.00
Access, Barclaycard, AM Express, & Diners
H.P.W.CS.E.A.D.

## LONDON

**WOOLWICH**    Tel. (01-854) 7767/8
A. D. SHILLMAN & SONS LTD    ★
108-109 WOOLWICH HIGH STREET
SE18
Open: Mon-Sat
8.30 a.m.-5.30p.m.
H.P.W.CS.A.

**HOUNSLOW**    Tel. (01-570)
Q.R. TOOLS LTD    2103/5135
251-253 HANWORTH ROAD
Open: Mon-Fri 8.30 a.m.-5.30 p.m.
Sat. 9.00 a.m.-1.00 p.m.
P.W.WM.D.CS.A.

**LONDON**    Tel. (01-263) 1536
THOMAS BROTHERS    (01-272) 2764
798-804 HOLLOWAY ROAD, N19    **E**
Open: Mon.-Fri. 8.30 a.m.-5.30 p.m. Thurs.
8.30 a.m.-1 p.m. Sat. 9 a.m.-5 p.m.
H.P.W.WM.CS.MF.BC.

**FULHAM**    Tel. (01-385) 5109
I. GRIZZARD LTD.    **E**
84a-b LILLIE ROAD, SW6 1TL
Open: Mon-Sat 9.00-5.30 p.m.
Half day Thursday
H.P.A.BC.W.CS.WM.D.

## MERSEYSIDE

**LIVERPOOL**    Tel. (051-207) 2967
TAYLOR BROS (LIVERPOOL) LTD    **K**
195-199 LONDON ROAD
LIVERPOOL L3 8JG
Open: Monday to Friday
8.30 a.m.-5.30 p.m.
H.P.W.WM.D.A.BC.

## MIDDLESEX

**ENFIELD**    Tel. (01-363) 2935
GILL & HOXBY LTD.    **K**
133-137 ST. MARKS ROAD EN1 1BB

Mon.-Sat. 8.30 a.m.-6.00 p.m.
Early closing Wednesday 1.00 p.m.
H.P.W.WM.T.CS.A

**RUISLIP**    Tel. (08956) 74126
ALLMODELS ENGINEERING LTD.    **E**★
91 MANOR WAY

Open: Mon-Sat 9.00 a.m.-5.30 p.m.
H.P.W.A.D.CS.MF.BC.

**CROWMARSH**    Tel. (0491) 38653
MILL HILL SUPPLIES    **E**★
66 THE STREET
Open: Mon.-Fri. 9.30 a.m.-5.00 p.m.
Thurs. 9.30 a.m.-7.00 p.m.
Sat. 9.30 a.m.-1.00 p.m.
P.W.D.CS.MF.A.BC.

**FARNHAM**    Tel. (0252) 725427
A.B.E. CO. LTD. (Quick Hire)    ★
GOODS SHED
STATION APPROACH, FARNHAM
Open Mon.-Fri. 8.00 a.m.-5.30 p.m.
Sat. 8.00 a.m.-5.30 p.m.
H.P.W.D.CS.A.BC.

## NORFOLK

**NORWICH**    Tel. (0603) 898695
NORFOLK SAW SERVICES
DOG LANE, HORSFORD
Open: Monday to Friday
8.00 a.m.-5.00 p.m.
Saturday 8.00 a.m.-12.00 p.m.
H.P.W.WM.D.CS.A.

**KINGS LYNN**    Tel. (0553) 2443
WALKER & ANDERSON (Kings Lynn) LTD.
WINDSOR ROAD, KINGS LYNN    **K**
Open: Monday to Saturday
7.45 a.m.-5.30 p.m.
Wednesday 1.00 p.m. Saturday 5.00 p.m.
H.P.W.WM.D.CS.A.

**NORWICH**    Tel. (0603) 400933
WESTGATES WOODWORKING    Tx
61 HURRICANE WAY,    975412
NORWICH AIRPORT INDUSTRIAL ESTATE
Open: 9.00 a.m.-5.00 p.m. weekdays
9.00 a.m.-12.30 Sat.
P.W.WM.D.BC.    **K**

**KING'S LYNN**    Tel: 07605 674
TONY WADDILOVE, UNIT A    ★
HILL FARM WORKSHOPS
GREAT DUNHAM, (Nr. Swaffham)
Open: Tues. — Fri. 10.00 a.m. to 5.30 p.m.
Sat. 9.00 a.m. to 5.00 p.m.
H.P.W.D.T.MF.A.BC.*

**GT. YARMOUTH**    Tel. (0493)
ANGLIA POWER TOOLS    850388
3 DENESIDE, NR30 2HL

Open: Monday to Saturday
8.30 a.m. 5.30 p.m.
H.P.W.D.CS.A.

## NOTTINGHAMSHIRE

**NOTTINGHAM**    Tel: (0602) 225979
POOLEWOOD    and 227064/5
EQUIPMENT LTD.    (06077) 2421 after hrs
5a HOLLY LANE, CHILLWELL
Open: Mon-Fri 9.00 a.m.-5.30 p.m.
Sat. 9.00 a.m. to 12.30 p.m.
P.W.WM.D.CS.A.BC.

## OXON

**WITNEY**    Tel. (0993) 3885
TARGET TOOLS (SALES,    & 72095 OXON
**TARGET** HIRE & REPAIRS)    ★
**TOOLS** SWAIN COURT
STATION INDUSTRIAL ESTATE
Open: Mon.-Sat. 9.00 a.m.-5.00 p.m.
24 hour Answerphone
BC.W.M.A.

## SHROPSHIRE

**TELFORD**    Tel. Telford (0952)
ASLES LTD    48054
VINEYARD ROAD, WELLINGTON    **EK**★
Open: Mon. Fri. 8.30 a.m.-5.30 p.m.
Saturday 8.30 a.m.-4.00 p.m.
H.P.W.WM.D.CS.BC.A.

## SOMERSET

**TAUNTON**    Tel. (0823) 85431
JOHN HALL TOOLS    ★
6 HIGH STREET

Open Monday-Saturday
9.00 a.m.-5.30 p.m.
H.P.W.WM.D.CS.A.

# shopguide

## SOMERSET

**TAUNTON**  Tel. Taunton 79078
KEITH MITCHELL  ★
TOOLS AND EQUIPMENT
66 PRIORY BRIDGE ROAD
Open: Mon-Fri 8.30 a.m.-5.30 p.m.
Saturday 9.00 a.m.-4.00 p.m.
H.P.W.WM.D.CS.A.BC.

## STAFFORDSHIRE

**TAMWORTH**  Tel. (0827) 56188
MATTHEWS BROTHERS LTD.  K
KETTLEBROOK ROAD
Open: Mon-Sat 8.30 a.m.-6.00 p.m.
Demonstrations Sunday mornings by
appointment only
H.P.WM.D.T.CS.A.BC.

## SUFFOLK

**IPSWICH**  Tel. (0473) 40456
FOX WOODWORKING  KE★
142-144 BRAMFORD LANE
Open: Tues., Fri., 9.00 a.m.-5.30 p.m.
Sat. 9.00 a.m.-5.00 p.m.

H.P.W.WM.D.A.B.C.

## SUSSEX

**ST. LEONARD'S-ON-SEA**  Tel.
DOUST & MONK (MONOSAW)-(0424)
25 CASTLEHAM ROAD  52577

Open: Mon.-Fri. 8.00 a.m.-5.30 p.m.
Most Saturdays 9.00 a.m.-1.00 p.m.
H.P.W.WM.D.CS.A.

**BOGNOR REGIS** Tel. (0243) 863100
A. OLBY & SON (BOGNOR REGIS) LTD.
"TOOLSHOP," BUILDERS MERCHANT
HAWTHORN ROAD  K
Open: Mon-Thurs 8 a.m.-5.15 p.m. Fri.
8 a.m.-8 p.m. Sat 8 a.m.-12.45 p.m.
H.P.W.WM.D.T.C.A.BC.

**WORTHING**  Tel. (0903) 38739
W. HOSKING LTD (TOOLS &  KE★
MACHINERY)
28 PORTLAND RD, BN11 1QN
Open: Mon.-Sat. 8.30 a.m.-5.30 p.m.
Closed Wednesday
H.P.W.WM.D.CS.A.BC.

## TYNE & WEAR

**NEWCASTLE UPON TYNE**  Tel.
J. W. HOYLE LTD.  (0632) 617474
CLARENCE STREET NE2 1YJ  K★
Open: Mon-Fri 8.00 a.m.-5.00 p.m.
Saturday 9.00 a.m.-4.30 p.m.

H.P.A.BC.W.CS.WM.D.

## TYNE & WEAR

**NEWCASTLE**  Tel. (0632) 320311
HENRY OSBOURNE LTD.  E★
50-54 UNION STREET

Open: Mon-Fri 8.30 a.m.-5.00 p.m.

H.P.W.D.CS.MF.A.BC.

## WEST MIDLANDS

**BIRMINGHAM**  Tel. (021-554) 5177
ROTAGRIP  E★
16 LODGE ROAD, HOCKLEY
Open: Mon.-Fri. 9.00 a.m.-5.00 p.m.
Sat. 9.00 a.m.-12.00 p.m.

H.P.W.CS.A.BC.T.MF.

**WOLVERHAMPTON**  Tel. (0902)
MANSAW SERVICES  58759
SEDGLEY STREET  K★

Open: Mon.-Fri. 9.00 a.m.-5.00 p.m.

H.P.W.WM.A.D.CS.

## YORKSHIRE

**BOROUGHBRIDGE**  Tel. (09012)
JOHN BODDY TIMBER LTD  2370
FINE WOOD & TOOL STORE  ★
RIVERSIDE SAWMILLS
Open: Mon.-Thurs. 8.00 a.m.-6.00 p.m.
Fri. 8.00am-5.00pm Sat. 8.00am-4.00pm
H.P.W.WM.D.T.CS.MF.A.BC.

**SHEFFIELD**  Tel. (0742) 441012
GREGORY & TAYLOR LTD  KE
WORKSOP ROAD
Open: 8.30 a.m.-5.30 p.m.
Monday-Friday
8.30 a.m.-12.30 p.m. Sat.
H.P.W.WM.D.

**HARROGATE**  Tel. (0423) 66245/
MULTI-TOOLS  55328
158 KINGS ROAD  K★

Open: Monday to Saturday
8.30 a.m.-6.00 p.m.
H.P.W.WM.D.A.BC.

**LEEDS**  Tel. (0532) 574736
D. B. KEIGHLEY MACHINERY LTD.  ★
VICKERS PLACE, STANNINGLEY
PUDSEY LS2 86LZ
Mon.-Fri. 9.00 a.m.-5.00 p.m.
Sat. 9.00 a.m.-1.00 p.m.
P.A.W.WM.CS.BC.

## YORKSHIRE

**HUDDERSFIELD**  Tel. (0484)
NEVILLE M. OLDHAM  641219/(0484)
UNIT 1 DALE ST. MILLS  42777
DALE STREET, LONGWOOD  ★
Open: Mon-Fri 8.00 a.m.-5.00 p.m.
Saturday 9.30 a.m.-12.00 p.m.
P.W.WM.D.A.BC.

## YORKSHIRE

**THIRSK**  Tel. (0845) 22770
THE WOOD SHOP  ★
TRESKE SAWMILLS LTD.
STATION WORKS
Open: Seven days a week 9.00-5.00

T.H.MF.BC.

**KEIGHLEY**  Tel. (0535) 663325
EUROMAIL (TOOLS)  ★
PO BOX 13
108 EAST PARADE
Open 9.15 a.m.-5.00 p.m.
Not Tuesday but inc. Saturday
H.P.W.A.BC.

**CLECKHEATON**  Tel. (0274)
SKILLED CRAFTS LTD.  872861
34 BRADFORD ROAD  ★

Open: 9.00 a.m.-5.00 p.m. Monday
Saturday Lunch 12.00 a.m.-1.00 p.m.
H.P.A.W.CS.WM.D.

**LEEDS**  Tel. (0532) 790507
GEORGE SPENCE & SONS LTD.
WELLINGTON ROAD
Open: Monday to Friday
8.30 a.m.-5.30 p.m.
Saturday 9.00 a.m.-5.00 p.m.
H.P.W.WM.D.T.A.

## SCOTLAND

**EDINBURGH**  Tel. 031-337-5555
THE SAW CENTRE  ★
38 HAYMARKET EH12 5JZ
Mon.-Fri. 8.30 a.m.-5.30 p.m.
Sat. 9.00 a.m.-1.00 p.m.
H.P.W.WM.D.CS.A.

**PERTH**  Tel. (0738) 26173
WILLIAM HUME & CO  K
ST. JOHN'S PLACE
Open: Monday to Saturday
8.00 a.m.-5.30 p.m.
8.00 a.m.-1.00 p.m. Wednesday
H.P.A.BC.W.CS.WM.D.

## SCOTLAND

**CULLEN**  Tel. (0542) 40563
GRAMPIAN WOODTURNING SUPPLIES AT
BAYVIEW CRAFTS
Open Mon.-Sat. 9.00 a.m.-5.30 p.m. Sunday
10.00 a.m.-5.30 p.m. Open later July/Aug.
Sept. Demonstrations SAT/SUN or by
H.W.D.MF.BC.  appointment

**TAYSIDE**  Tel. (05774) 293
WORKMASTER POWER TOOLS LTD. .  ★
DRUM, KINROSS
Open Mon.-Sat. 8.00 a.m.-8.00 p.m.
Demonstrations throughout Scotland by
appointment
P.W.WM.D.A.BC.

**GLASGOW**  Tel. 041-429-4444/
THE SAW CENTRE  4374 Telex: 777886
650 EGLINTON STREET  E★
GLASGOW G5 9RP
Mon.-Fri. 9.00 a.m.-5.00 p.m.
Sat. 9.00 a.m.-1.00 p.m.
H.P.W.WM.D.CS.A.

## WALES

**CARDIFF**  Tel. (0222) 595710
DATAPOWER TOOLS LTD,
MICHAELSTON ROAD,
CULVERHOUSE CROSS
Open: Mon.-Fri. 8.00 a.m.-5.00 p.m.
Sat. 9.00 a.m.-1.00 p.m.
H.P.W.WM.D.A.

**CARMARTHEN** Tel. (0267) 237219
DO-IT-YOURSELF SUPPLY  K
BLUE STREET, DYFED
Open: Monday to Saturday
9.00 a.m.-5.30 p.m.
Thursday 9.00 a.m.-5.30 p.m.
H.P.W.WM.D.T.CS.A.BC.

**CARDIFF**  Tel. (0222) 396039
JOHN HALL TOOLS LIMITED  ★
CENTRAL SQUARE

Open: Monday to Saturday
9.00 a.m.-5.30 p.m.
H.P.W.WM.D.A.BC.

**SWANSEA**  Tel. (0792) 55680
SWANSEA TIMBER & PLYWOOD CO. LTD.
57-59 OXFORD STREET  ★

Open: Mon to Fri 9.00 a.m.-5.30 p.m.
Sat. 9.00 a.m.-1.00 p.m.
H.P.W.D.T.CS.A.BC.

KEY: CS CUTTING OR SHARPENING SERVICES

KEY: MF MATERIAL FINISHES

KEY: BC BOOKS / CATALOGUES

# Designer workman: David Field

**David Field is not only a celebrated London furniture designer with his own top-class workshop. Scores of younger professionals have also experienced in him, as students and assistants, a priceless commitment to design as an all-important skill.**

---

**His new book *Projects in Wood* sets out his own insights; supports them with a wealth of practical information on designing and making; and illustrates them with photos, profiles and live projects from many of today's best talents – including himself.**

---

**Woodworker is proud to publish these extracts – including a full-scale project – from a book which is a milestone for the craftsman designer.**

David Field approaches the design of furniture with the passionate commitment of a vocation.

His academic and work experience have given a sophistication to his work and a worldliness to his thinking. He is persuaded that the profession of designer entails specific moral and social responsibilities, which require designers to be participating members of society. To that end he has been teaching furniture design since 1973, and he is a dedicated teacher.

Field began his design work as a mechanical engineer, working from the age of 16 in 1963 as an apprentice for the electronics firm, Marconi Ltd. 'I dropped naturally into an apprenticeship,' he says, 'because I'd shown a particular bent for technical subjects and mathematics, and I had an ability to draw.'

In 1966 he entered the Central School of Art in London to study industrial design. 'They had recently amalgamated the furniture and industrial-design departments. And as time went by, I found I was far more interested in furniture than in designing kettles and refrigerators.'

In 1969 he was accepted at the Royal College of Art, in the furniture school, because 'I knew that David Pye was there, and that he was an aesthete and a discerning academic — the stuff good professors are made of.' Pye, a cabinetmaker and designer whom Field describes as 'the authority on design theory and practice in Britain today, a person with a no-nonsense approach to dispelling myths about design', was to be a powerful influence on Field's thinking.

Field says, 'I was firmly put down in my first week at the RCA. I said that I wanted to produce "non-status" furniture, only to be rebuffed by the comment "Impossible!". I was stunned that anybody could be so emphatic in matters of art and design. But the explanation from Pye was clear. "If you project your furniture as being non-status, you are immediately affording it status." 'From that moment', Field says, 'I could

see that design was not an act of divine inspiration held together by esoteric jargon, and that some aspects of the subject could be taught.' He adds, 'I have taught ever since, through every conceivable medium,' including 'through the work — furniture for industry, individuals, public bodies and private collections'.

Field's design philosophy is partly derived from Pye and Ron Carter, he says. Pye emphasised the notion of workmanship, as distinct from 'craftsmanship', which 'has the connotations of corncob dolls and large hairy things hanging on the wall'. The best work is a synthesis of the highest levels of design thinking and workmanship. 'There are qualities that a skilled maker can bring to bear that enhance the object he is making so that it falls firmly into the realm of Art, with a capital A,' he explains. 'These are qualities that can't be planned on a designer's drawing-board.'

## 'Craftsmanship . . . means that you make well because the idea demands it'

Field says Carter showed him that 'craftsmanship is an attitude of mind, a response to all materials. It means that you make well because the idea demands it — the idea simply won't come off if the object isn't made well — and not just because you have a preoccupation with perfection.' There can be the highly regulated craftsmanship of the cabinetmaker, with flawless joints and finish. Or there can be free craftsmanship, rougher and less refined, such as might be used by a boatbuilder. Both types are valid under the appropriate circumstances, Field says, and it is a measure of the designer's sensitivity to the circumstances that he chooses the craftsmanship correctly — just as it is a measure of his sensitivity to the user of the object he is making. 'It's a choice, to use a highly polished finish. It's simply a technical option and in the end a matter of style.'

Field says he has been fortunate in his teachers. 'Their support was of value because of their work and the way they presented an argument. For example, David Pye could judge the merit of things he didn't personally like.'

It seems appropriate, then, that Field should find teaching so rewarding. From 1976 to 1979 he taught at the London College of Furniture, and since then has been a tutor at the RCA. He says, 'I think of it as people of more experience and people of less experience getting together and tackling problems. And to be able to discuss what I'm doing is an enormous advantage. If you're going to develop in your work, dialogue is essential. I don't have to consciously seek it because teaching is a two-way street and I get a lot from my students.'

But Field says he is often vulnerable as a teacher and consequently takes it very seriously. 'Teachers expose themselves to criticism. Very few designers can take that. These kids are incredibly bright and you can't fob them off with palliatives. You must be active, not passive.'

In his work, Field is amassing a collection of impressive clients, and his pieces have been shown in galleries and museums every year since 1976. In 1978 he lived in Hong Kong, advising the Hong Kong Trade Association on how to re-structure their furniture industry for trade with the West. He says that their industry was composed of small workshops, equipped with adaptable woodworking machinery and handmade jigs. 'They did the most amazing things with a radial-arm saw and a mortiser,' he says. 'They made double-locking three-way mitred mortise-and-tenon joints that were rather like a Chinese puzzle, using no hand tools.'

He finished his stay there by making a series of designs based on Ming-dynasty furniture. Because of the small cross-sections that were needed, the pieces were more stable in the high humidity, and were better suited for workshops with restricted space and no capacity for flowline production. And the style appealed to Western taste.

Today he has a flourishing workshop in Chiswick, London. He finds he needs to stay a step ahead of his clients, who tend to request designs based on what he has already done. 'I did metal inlay, and then lacquered things. Now I'm finding myself working in solid timber much more, and doing an enormous number of boardroom tables.'

His ideas for designs come from other sources than furniture. The metal inlay came from looking at steel straps on packing-cases; the lacquered finish was inspired by the way British fishing-boats are painted. Architecture had always influenced him. 'It's so prominent and visible, you can't really miss it.'

'I keep a sketchbook,' he says, 'which is a storehouse of information, a visual notebook with addresses, drawings, references to parts and materials. I take it on holidays rather than a camera because it makes me sit and look, rather than snap and not look.'

In the future he would like to reduce the amount of furniture made at his workshop, and only make prototypes for manufacture. 'I would like to form an association with a new generation of graduates who are superb makers. I'm a reluctant maker in many ways,' he says.

He says, as many designers do, that he is never satisfied with his work. 'I realised the other day that I'd made perhaps 400 or 500 designs in my career so far. And out of those, I only thought two or three were any good. But later I thought, Mies van der Rohe or Charles Eames probably only started getting it right in their mid-50s. So there's hope.'

## David Field on decoration:

By definition, decoration is regarded as an addition or an afterthought to serve as adornment, or more specifically to elaborate and ornament; to add richness, gaudiness, gilt, ostentation, enhancement and embellishment. But in reality it has even wider implications than that.

Decoration is present in all designers' work, but what are they doing when they decorate something? One purpose might be to 'invest the object with order': another definition which gives us a clue. Decoration in this sense unifies the visible elements of an object and satisfies a basic human craving for order. In decorating — that is, giving order to the objects that are used and seen by people — we are injecting an order

**Projects in Wood will be published on 28 October by Mitchell Beazley at £9.95.**

into the way we live our lives. The decoration of Aztec temples and Gothic cathedrals is a prime example of how humans have used visual symbolism to support the very fabric of their civilisations. Realistic symbols were used as 'reminders' on everyday objects as well as religious artefacts, as a stamp of the person who made the objects and perhaps as a way of infusing the object with the spirit of the symbol.

Abstract adornment provides balance, harmony or symmetry, and emphasises an object's shape, the grace of a curve or the regularity of a line. Abstract patterns such as geometric repeats are common because they so effectively achieve visual harmony. Although there is some direct symbolism in certain patterns, especially those using realistic images such as leaves or acorns, the power of a pattern is really in its repetitiveness; and, if used properly, it is very powerful indeed. The extreme sense of order and discipline evoked by Islamic and Celtic decoration is testimony to this.

This ability of decoration to instil order in a whole is as important today as it was in primitive times. The decorative styles of prominent buildings — centres of culture'

● *Clean and simple, David Field's dining-table opens to reveal a grey laminate surface whose two leaves are joined with brass butterfly hinges*

such as churches and theatres — are directly determined by the need to symbolise these values. They capture the spirit of an age.

Historically, the decoration of furniture often had a more prosaic purpose. It resulted from the need for a tolerance in manufacture. Before the introduction of powered machinery or abrasive papers, flat surfaces and accurate fitting were extremely difficult to achieve. Decoration served to disguise this fact by covering surfaces and panels with texture. Light is broken up and diffused by a textured surface rather than being reflected, so imperfections are not easily noticed.

The decoration that craftsmen used to disguise their work slowly evolved as their technique developed. Planed mouldings, linenfold panels, punched backgrounds, egg-and-dart mouldings, ball-and-claw feet, are all decorative motifs developed from a strict and economic procedure with hand tools. The craftsman worked in a carefully planned sequence to gain the maximum effect from the minimum number of cuts. Even so, there were bound to be inaccuracies. If you look closely at the cabriole legs of some Chippendale chairs you will discover a considerable difference in their shapes and dimensions. Normally this escapes notice because the surface decoration and the shape of the legs distracts us from comparing them. If the legs were straight and unadorned, we would notice immediately if one were larger or slightly curved more than the other.

Further evidence of the early craftsmen's reliance on decoration to mask limited techniques can be found by comparing the sophisticated work of town workshops supported by wealthy patrons with the country equivalents of the same period. The country workshops, whose clients were of more limited means, produced pieces that followed the basic shape of the style but omitted the customary decoration for which their clients could not pay. In these pieces inaccuracies are exposed for all to see. But the furniture from these workshops does not suffer in its simplicity; just the opposite, because those pieces tell an

honest story of the values and background in their manufacture.

When techniques improved in the 19th century, and flat unadorned surfaces became more easily possible with machines, decoration was still an important stylistic ingredient because it was still needed for its symbolic value. It represented tradition — enabling Victorian furniture designers, for example, to evoke the spirit of heroic ages, principally Greek and Roman, in the 'revival' pieces of the time.

## 'I could see that design was not . . . divine inspiration held together by esoteric jargon'

Decoration is still used that way even today, to symbolise traditional and therefore known and un-threatening values. Known quantities, familiar images, are the ones most people feel happy with. They demonstrate this need by buying enormous amounts of reproduced antique furniture.

During an economic boom period a cultural confidence emerges, and people will buy modern furniture (and abstract paintings). In recession, however, uncertainty and insecurity pervade their lives and they opt for the known styles of former times (and realist painting). Mass-marketed furniture, while not attempting to mimic antiques, draws upon a traditional aesthetic and is successful as a result. Many designers resent this because they do not understand the reasons for it. It is simply that much modern furniture is too threatening or demanding in its symbolism. It rejects traditional values, including decorating, rather than *extending* them.

However, if we can begin to see decoration in a wider context — as the very act of sorting and ordering all the elements of a piece of furniture, of unifying it and affording it an individual character which is not alienating to people — decoration can be seen to be of as much value to designers ❜ now as it has been in the past.

# Designer workman: David Field

## The table project

**D**avid Field's folding table is elegant enough for a dining-room and hard-working enough to use as a kitchen surface. The whole table is made of ash; the top is plywood veneered with ash on one side and laminated on the other with Formica.

It is easy to make. The bottom consists simply of two interlocking frames which support the hinged top. The top is held in place by a metal pin around which it pivots. There is a simple formula for properly locating the pin so that the top will be exactly centred over the frame whether it is opened or closed.

The legs and frame are made from solid maple 38x63mm (1½x2½in). Four pieces 685mm (27in) long will be needed for the tall legs, and four 610x81mm (24x3¼in) for the short legs. These are butt-jointed, in David Field's original, with biscuits (flat dowels), for which job you will of course need an Elu or Lamello biscuit-jointer.

The frame is mortised and tenoned into the legs, with a third top rail 800x25x100mm (31½x1x4in) to brace it and house a pivoting pin. This is tenoned into the long rails. The main rails are two 1448mm (57in) and two 800mm (31½in).

The top is made of 18mm (¾in) plywood in two sections, each 750x1000mm (29½x59in). They are held together with three brass dovetail hinges, inset in the laminated surface. The underside is counter-veneered to prevent the laminate from lifting if the plywood bows.

A brass pin 10mm (⅜in) in diameter and 20mm (¾in) long is set into the bracing rail and fitted into a corresponding hole in the laminated surface. A strip of baize runs along the supporting edge of the frame to protect the top from scratches and allow it to pivot smoothly.

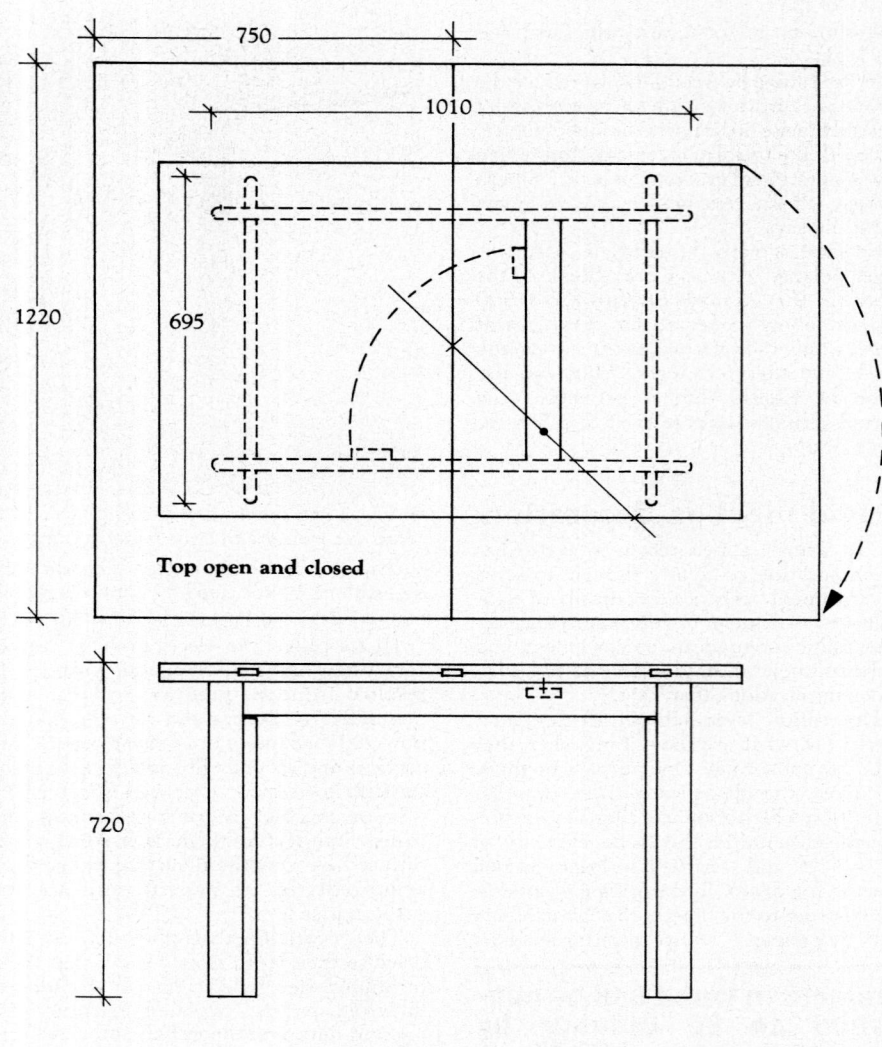

**Top open and closed**

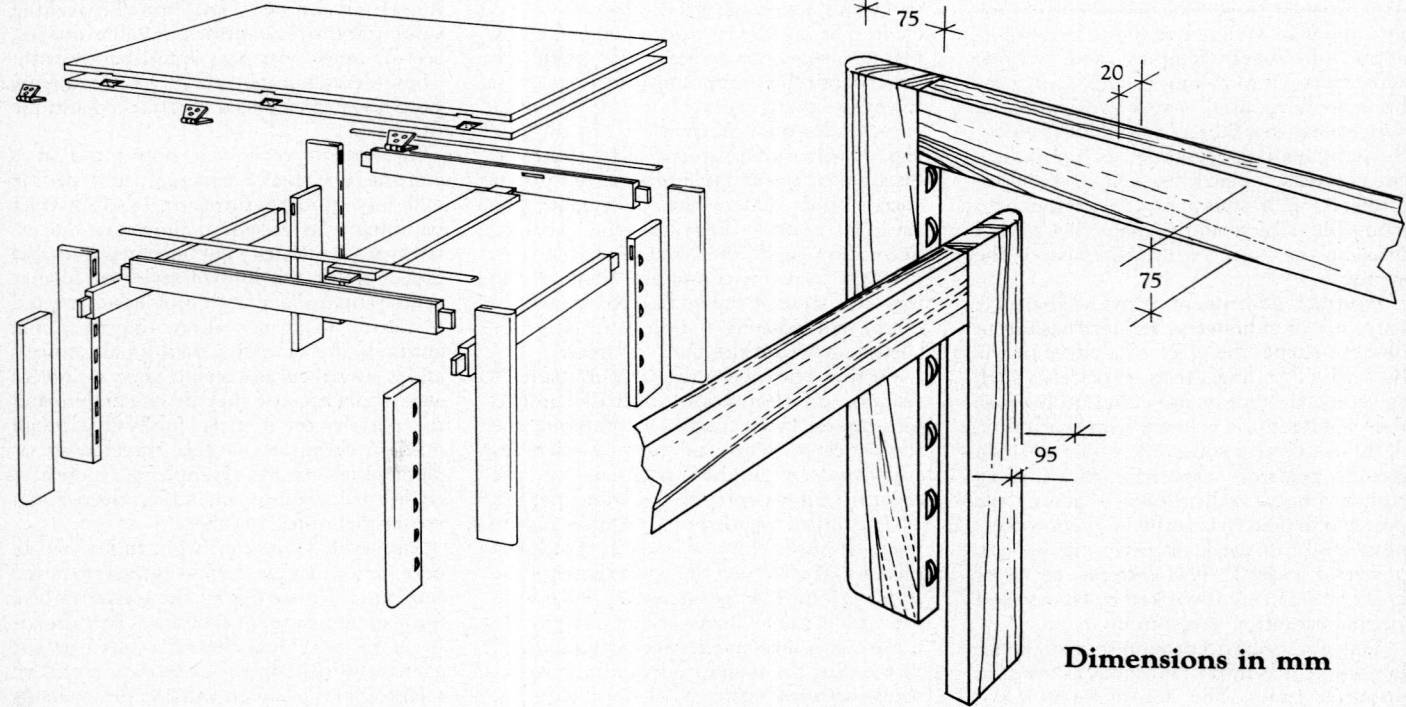

**Dimensions in mm**

## Step-by-step

First make up the legs and frame, mortise-and-tenoning the corner joints. Round off and smooth the outside corners of the frame.

Make the top by cutting out the sections in plywood, laminating one side and veneering the other. The edges should be lipped with ash. Hinge the two sections together.

To calculate the exact positions of the third rail, the pivot pin and the pinhole, place a rod (full-size template) of the opened tabletop on the floor and centre a rod of the top closed and of the table frame over it, as shown here.

Draw the two diagonals of the large rectangle (the open top) to find the centre. Draw a line along the centre line to the edge of the small rectangle (the folded top) and another line at 45° to the same edge. The mid-point of the second line is the pivot point of the top.

Having calculated this, you can assemble the frame. Simultaneously biscuit-join the sub-frames, placing the shorter frames *within* the larger ones (as shown here) and mortise-and-tenoning the third rail in position so that the pivot point centres on its width. Glue and G-cramp the sections and let them set. Then finish with two coats of lacquer.

Drill a hole at the pivot point to take the pivot pin, and glue it in place. Then cover the pin, and the two support rails, with baize stripping. Finally, set the top in position by drilling a hole in the laminated surface for the pin. Screw two 50mm (2in) stop blocks under the table to restrict the arc of the pivoting top. ■

● *The pivoting and folding arrangement is straightforward if you follow the drawings opposite. The ash veneer makes the job as neat when closed as when open*

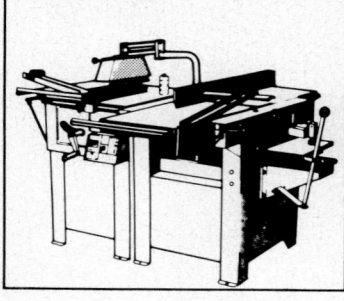 

778

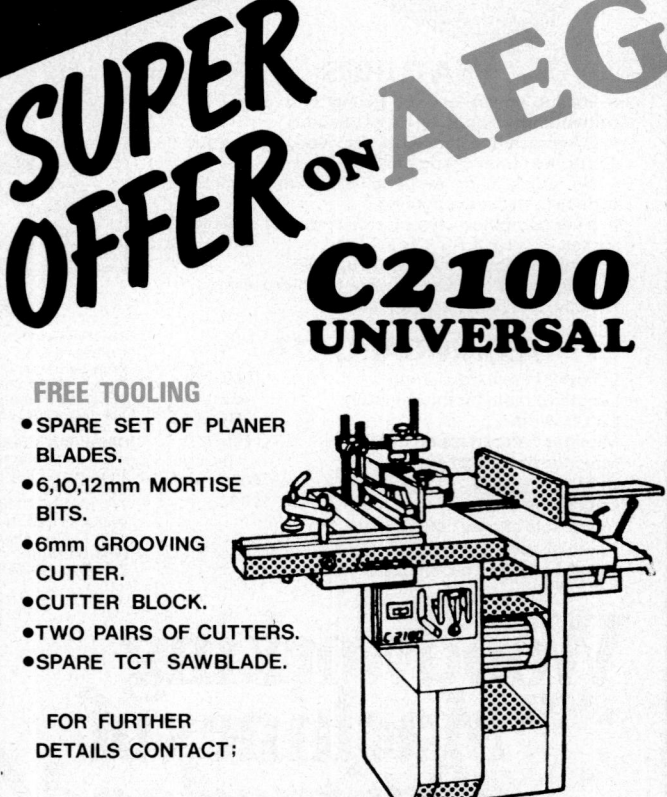

# Woodturning Tools & Hardware

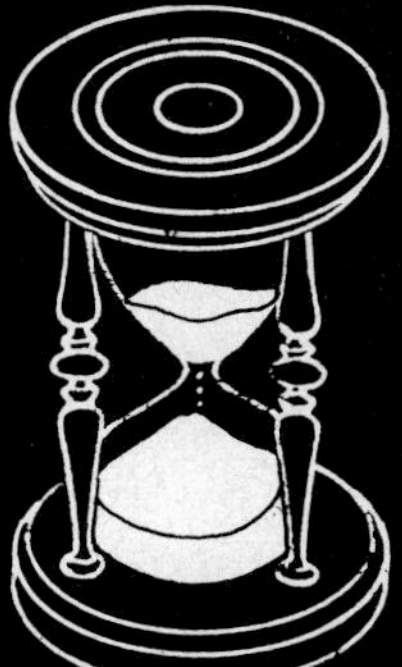

**TOOLS.** Range of 35 High Speed Steel tools plus 25 traditional tools.

**HARDWARE.** Barometers. Clocks. Lighters. Peppermill inserts. Cutlery blades. Glass dishes. Cheese domes. Tiles. Waxes and polishes.

**LATHES.** Myford lathes. Chucks and equipment. Measuring tools, etc.

**BOOK** — The Craftsman Woodturner — New Fully Revised Edition Detailing Modern Methods and New Tools. £13.50 post free worldwide.

Overseas catalogue send $1 or equivalent. Tel: (0787) 237 291.

**PETER CHILD** Send S.A.E for mail order catalogue. The Old Hyde, Little Yeldham, Halstead, Essex, CO9 4QT.

---

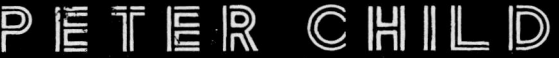

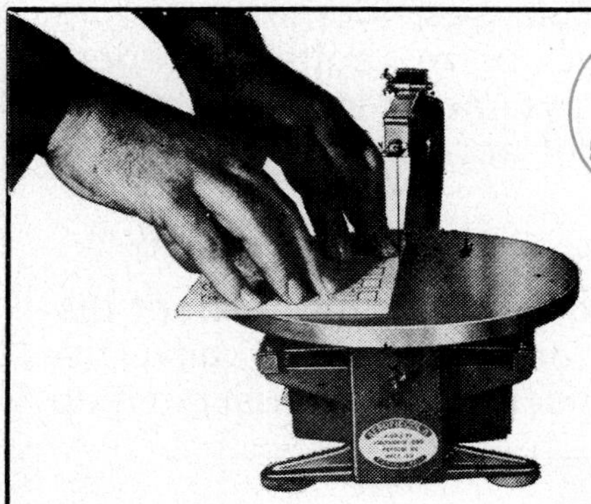

Aeropiccola 240V

## EURO MODELS

35 Crown Road, St. Margarets, Twickenham TW1 3EJ
Telephone (01) 891 0342

## Mains voltage FRETSAW

Tool complete with 12 fret-saw blades and full instructions. Other voltages available. Overseas postage rates on application.

Price £77.00 inc VAT & postage.

*SEND S.A.E. FOR LEAFLET*

Low noise cutting tool which will cut almost everything **except** your fingers. Using fret and piercing saw blades it will cut any shape **continuously** in all light metals, brass, alloy, **all** woods (even 1/32 in. sheet balsa), and all plastics including perspex. There are no rotating parts to wear – no maintenance. It **cuts** not **tears** the work – even 90° turns.

**MAIL ORDER: 35 CROWN RD, ST MARGARETS, TWICKENHAM. 01-891 0342**

---

# TOOL UP WITH MILLS OF ACTION!

SPECIALISTS TOOLS & MACHINERY — MILLS OF ACTON

**TGS 172**
**VERSATILE, TRANSPORTABLE BENCH/BEVEL/MITRE SAW**
Sawblade dia. 250mm.
Cutting capacity as 90° crosscut/45° mitre saw: 54 x 135/54 x 95mm.
Cutting capacity as 90° sawbench: 0-70mm
Cutting capacity in 45° bevel position as sawbench/crosscut saw: 38/50 x 155mm.
1,650 watts, 2,750 rpm.
Weight 33kg.
Available in 115v and 220v AC.

List price: £521.90 inc. VAT
**Mills price: £368.95 inc. VAT**
p&p: £10.00

- Unique ELU design.
- Detachable legs for easy transportation to and around the site.
- Robust all-metal construction.
- Factory-adjusted for accurate operation.
- "Flips over" to convert from bench saw to mitre saw in seconds.
- TCT blade, parallel and mitre fences standard equipment for wood cutting.
- No volt release switch.
- Non-ferrous metal — cutting accessory kit also available.
- Optional sliding tables to convert into panel saw.

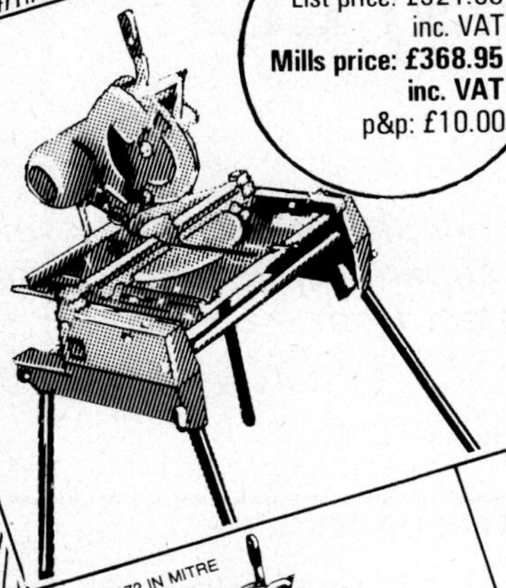

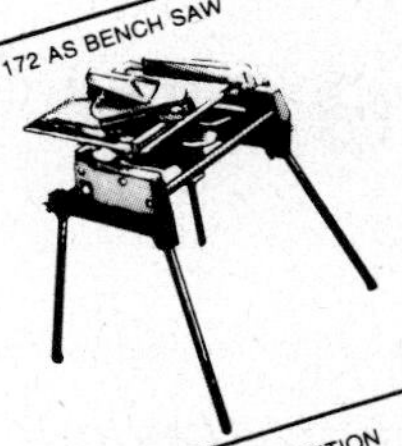

TGS 172 AS BENCH SAW

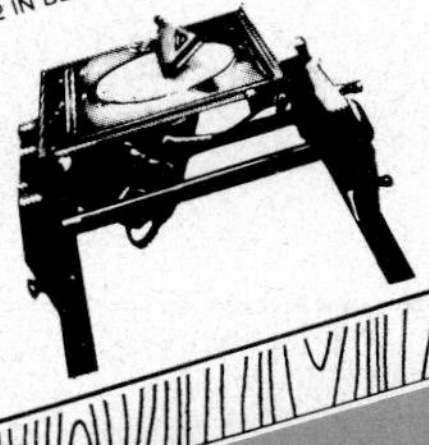

TGS 172 IN BENCH/BEVEL POSITION

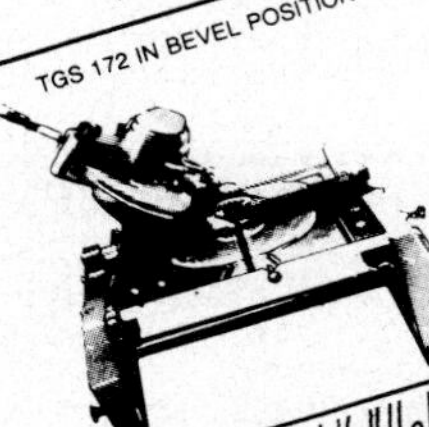

TGS 172 IN BEVEL POSITION

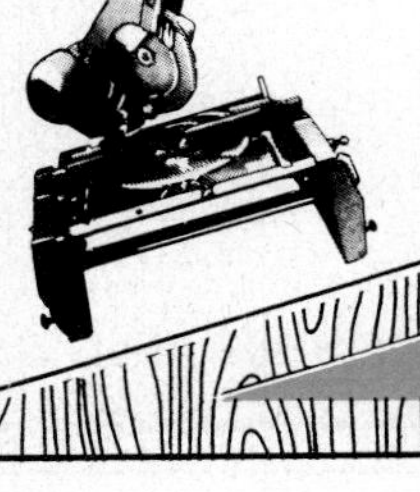

TGS 172 IN MITRE POSITION

15,000 different lines of woodworking tools and machinery in stock! Ring for immediate quote or why not visit our 4,000 square foot showroom? Open daily 8.30am-6.00pm, Saturdays 9.00am-1.00pm. Easy parking.

A. MILLS (ACTON) LIMITED, Dept WW, 32/36 Churchfield Road, Acton, London W3 6ED. Tel: 01-992 4835 (7 lines)

782

# *now* Over 3000 Top Quality Tools BY POST!

## SARJENTS TOOLS

Our Woodworking Catalogue is like having one of our shops in your living room. It NOW contains over 3000 "hard to find" tools giving you a much wider range to choose from. Here is just a sample of the vast range of items and special offers available to order from your armchair!

## SARJENTS INTRODUCE "THE ULTIMATE CRAFTSMANS TOOL" TO OUR RANGE!....

### THE CLIFTON MULTIPLANE

The multi-plane will perform a wide range of cuts including all those covered by the combination plane and the plough plane. Additional cutters and bases are also available extending the range still further. Ploughing, rebating, housing, tonguing, fillistering, beading (edge and centre), sash moulding and slitting can all be carried out. In addition, it can be fitted with special bases and matching cutters for hollows, rounds and nosings. Using the spurs fitted in the body and sliding section, cuts can be made across the grain. The plane is fitted with an adjustable fence and depth gauge, two sets of fence arms (long and short), beading stop, slitting cutter, sliding section depth gauge, cam steady and spurs for cross grain work.

Twenty-four cutters are supplied (including 4, 6, 9 and 12mm) with the plane as standard equipment, all being fully adjustable except for the ⅛", 3mm and ³/₁₆". The cutter set is packed in a protective wallet, and the plane is supplied in a polished wooden case.

**SARJENTS ARE THE SOLE UK AGENTS**
● TRADE ENQUIRIES WELCOME.

ONLY £199·50 INCLUDING VAT AND CARRIAGE

## ORDER ANY OF THESE TOOLS OR YOUR CATALOGUE NOW!

Once you are on our special mailing list you will be entitled to:–
**REGULAR EXCLUSIVE OFFERS: FAST PERSONAL SERVICE: UP TO DATE INFORMATION**

## SARJENTS TOOLS

### PERSONAL CALLERS WELCOME AT :-

44-52 Oxford Rd.,
READING.
Tel:(0734)586522

62-64 Fleet St.,
SWINDON.
Tel:(0793)31361

150 Cowley Rd.,
OXFORD
Tel:(0865)245118

USE THIS ADDRESS TO PLACE YOUR ORDERS, OR SEND YOUR NAME & ADDRESS WITH A CHEQUE/P.O. FOR £1·50 FOR YOUR COPY OF THE 'WOODWORKING CATALOGUE'

**SARJENTS TOOLS W W. 1**
**44-52 Oxford Rd., READING . RG1 7LH**

Barclaycard & Access Accepted. Ring order through & quote card No.

# Exotic tastes

## Those lovely, fancy, pricy woods lure many a turner. Michael Foden tells what to expect if you find yourself smitten

Sooner or later, you'll probably want to experiment with exotics — partly through curiosity, and partly perhaps through over-familiarity with home-grown timbers. A well turned item in yew or one of the fruitwoods can certainly look splendid; but for fine turnery, especially on smaller items, a piece of rosewood or ebony will often command most attention.

First, a word about design. Do not attempt to execute an elaborate design in highly figured wood (lace bobbins excepted). A box with intricate detail on the lid and knob will look far better in boxwood than in cocobolo, because very fine detail is obscured by the colours and the grain of such timber. Practise turning items with thin walls, too, as there is nothing more disappointing than lifting a delicate-looking item only to find it like lead. Turnings having close-fitting lids should be made a little more sturdy to ensure a good fit — but, even so, a wall thickness of ⅛in is ample.

Where boxes are concerned, in fact, the main problem that confronts the turner is making a lid that fits and stays fitted. I have known lids, perfect when made, within a short while become very loose. Even though your timber is completely dry, this phenomenon will probably occur. The movement is caused by the release of stresses with the removal of wood. The rate varies with the species of timber, the style of box and the grain direction of the finished item.

Generally speaking, lidded items are more stable if the grain is vertical. A spigot lid will ensure a good fit every time, but limit your choice of design. Otherwise it's best to hollow out the box and lid section, leaving the lid too large to fit. This procedure should result in a lid that will not loosen.

Another important detail is the shape of the recess that will accommodate the lid. This should be entirely parallel. If it slopes inward, a good fit is impossible.

What about the timbers themselves? Amongst the rosewoods, East Indian is probably the most widely available, and reasonably priced. It cuts well; the quality is usually good; and, although the timber is somewhat open-grained, a good finish is easily achieved on the lathe. There is a tremendous range of colour within this species, although wide boards are now scarce. Plantation-grown timber is available in wide sections, but at twice the price.

Honduras rosewood is capable of taking a fine finish, but even in small-diameter discs vibration is a problem because of its

● *A box by any shape . . . this one in kingwood measures 3½x2in and has a spigot lid*

very hard and brittle nature. A good deal of scraper work both inside and outside a bowl will be necessary; whatever the lathe speed, it is often difficult to hold a gouge against the wood for the final cuts.

Santos rosewood cuts, scrapes and finishes well, but in my experience it is exceptionally brittle, and subject to splits when cut thinly.

Brazilian rosewood is a personal favourite of mine. It is stable, cuts and scrapes well, and takes a superb finish. It need not be too expensive if used wisely, and I have turned from 50p-worth of this timber small items which sell for £5. (But do not assume that there is a large element

of profit here — a lot of time, hard work and know-how go into each product.)

Once you feel confident working exotics, don't be tempted into buying small pre-planed pieces of these timbers; although there may be no waste, their price is often exceedingly high. It is well worth spending £20 on a billet of timber rather than £10 on a few small prepared pieces. You will end up with four times as much timber, and with careful planning there will be very little waste from your billet (assuming you have not purchased a load of sapwood). It is surprising what tiny pieces the turner can use when making knobs, chessmen and so on.

Kingwood is another classic, though turners are sometimes dissuaded by its high price. It is subject to great colour variations, but always very attractive; as long as first-quality pieces are chosen, it is a top class timber to work and finish. (But again, a work of warning: do not be misled into believing that the exotics will all be good-quality because of the high prices; I have turned kingwood that behaved like cotton-wool.)

African blackwood does not cut well except for the endgrain; it's filthy stuff to work, and very pricy. Scrapers will be needed. On the credit side, however, it allows ridges to be sanded away easily, unlike many other exotics, and a glass-like finish is soon produced.

If very fine detailed turnings are required, European boxwood is outstanding. It is rare to find even short lengths that are not full of splits, but Joseph Gardner of Ellesmere Port stocks what is probably the finest boxwood available in the UK, and you can often obtain long straight lengths completely free of splits from this source.

Amongst the other exotics I have worked, African padauk is worthy of consideration. It has an even density which

● *The unmistakable glow of fresh padauk; 3in high, and again with a spigot lid*

● *The sapwood smiles out from this little 2in-wide bowl in cocobolo*

# Bicycle lathe

means no vibration on the lathe, and it cuts readily in all directions. Sadly, the vivid red colour does not last, and after a few months' exposure to light it assumes a dirty brown tone. In compensation, though, it is probably the cheapest of the exotics, currently averaging around £18 per cubic foot.

Finally, cocobolo deserves a mention, as being one of the most striking species when freshly cut. But its colour is usually short-lived and it quickly darkens until all grain patterns disappear. It cuts well and scrapes cleanly, calling for very little abrasive work — which is fortunate, as cocobolo is one of the worst offenders for clogging all grades of abrasive papers.

It's best to choose your own timber, and only experience will tell you how to choose good stuff by its appearance. Always take a penknife to the merchants, because it's often difficult to ascertain quality if the pieces are rough-sawn. By gently scraping the surface with the knife, the grain will be exposed: the turner should ensure the colour and quality match the high price he will invariably have to pay!

If, however, a personal visit to a merchant is impossible, I would unreservedly recommend North Heigham Sawmills in Norwich as an excellent source of exotic timbers. I have regularly dealt with this firm for many years by parcel post, and can honestly say that the prices, service and quality of timber are outstanding.

Remember that most of these timbers are very dense and heavy, and normal cutting techniques are not always successful. Some of the species will not tolerate any mistakes in tool handling, and vibration between tool and timber sometimes precludes the use of gouges at certain stages of the work — in which case the turner will have to resort to scrapers. Nevertheless, scrapers should only be required when hollowing endgrain or in bowl work, and rarely on work held between centres.

Most of the timbers can be worked successfully as long as tailstock support is used on larger pieces to counteract vibration. Because they are so abrasive, some varieties will require the use of high-speed-steel tools in order to produce the best finish. I would also recommend HSS scrapers; although the finish will not be improved by their use, the burr edge will far outlast the edge on the conventional scraper, which often has a very limited life when used on exotics, and needs frequent re-grinding.

So don't expect to turn these tropical beauties as you would a piece of beech or mahogany. Just exercise patience, on the other hand, and you'll find new continents opening up.

● Joseph Gardner (Hardwoods) Ltd, Rosscliffe Rd, Rossmore Industrial Estate, Ellesmere Port, Cheshire L65 3AS, tel. 051-355 1308. Be sure to write or telephone before placing an order.

● North Heigham Sawmills, Paddock St, off Barker St, Norwich NR2 4TW, tel. (0603) 22978. ∎

## WOODWORKING WHEEZE
### of the month

**I** have recently made a lathe, **writes Tony Bryant,** on the same lines as Alan Bridgewater's (*Woodworker*, July). The only real difference is that the treadle return uses a luggage elastic instead of a pole.

It has occurred to me, however, that the to-and-fro motion could be converted to rotary motion with the aid of a bicycle free-wheel. The drawing explains what I have in mind.

Pushing down on the treadle pulls the cord, attached to a length of cycle chain, over the sprocket which rotates the wheel. The wheel is filled with concrete so that it acts as a flywheel. When the treadle is fully depressed, the elastic releases it and pulls it back to the raised position.

The drive belt is round-section leather from a sewing-machine shop, and it turns the headstock via a small pulley. A cycle front hub is used as a headstock, to which the Black & Decker centre is attached via a piece of threaded tube. ∎

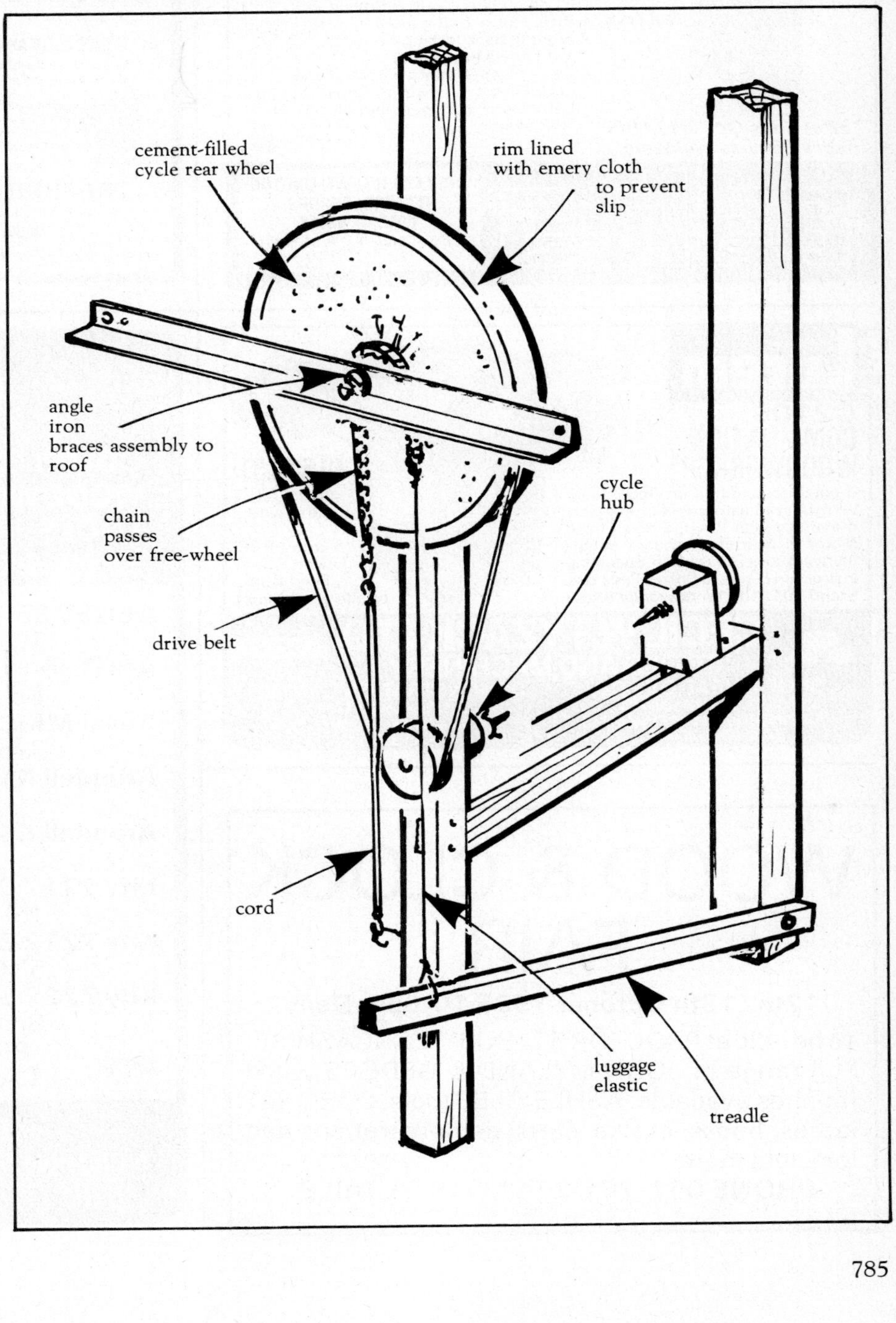

cement-filled cycle rear wheel

rim lined with emery cloth to prevent slip

angle iron braces assembly to roof

chain passes over free-wheel

drive belt

cycle hub

cord

luggage elastic

treadle

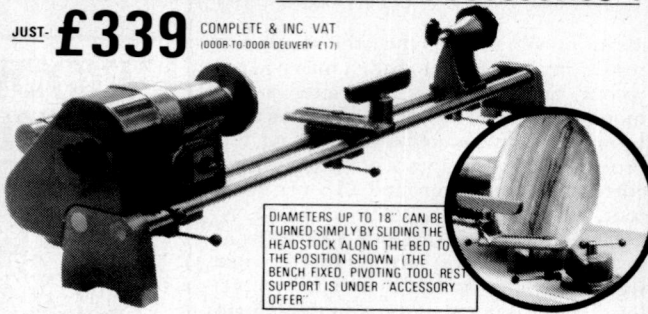

786

# Classified Advertisements

## FOR SALE

FOR ALL SUPPLIES FOR THE

## Craft of Enamelling
ON METAL

**Including**

**LEAD-FREE ENAMELS**

PLEASE SEND 2 × 10p STAMPS FOR FREE CATALOGUE, PRICE LIST AND WORKING INSTRUCTIONS

## W. G. BALL LTD.
ENAMEL MANUFACTURERS

Dept. W. LONGTON
STOKE-ON-TRENT
ST3 1JW

---

**HAND CARVED**
'Adam Style' Mantle motifs in Mahogany — Example 10" × 5" centre lamp and two side pieces.
Send S.A.E. for details and quotation. Your own design quoted for if required.
SAM NICHOLSON
22 Lisnagarvey Drive, Lisburn,
Co. Antrim, N. Ireland.
Phone Lisburn 3510

---

**BACK ISSUES** of Woodworker 1952 to 1978, mainly complete volumes. As new, offers. Droitwich 772866.

**CORONET MAJOR,** Universal Woodworking machine plus some accessories, £350. Telephone Tonbridge (0732) 360014.

**LACE BOBBIN PLANKS,** over 90 different woods, lists free, 50 exotic £4.50. 35 veneer samples. £1. P. Rushbrook, 39 Deben Avenue, Martlesham, Ipswich.

**BAGS, WRAPPINGS, TISSUE, BOXES, BUSINESS CARDS.** Any shape, size, amount. Comprehensive samples. 90p. Terry Andrews, 53A Parsons St., Banbury OX16 8NB.

**EUMENIA RADIAL ARM SAW.** Excellent condition £195. Telephone 01-660 1611 (Croydon area).

**VICTORIAN BRACE** (Marples) and eight bits. Excellent order. Offers in writing only. Futcher, Buch House, Sutton-on-the-Forest, York, YO6 1DY.

---

### Bygones
Just one item from our catalogue

MARPLES PARING GOUGES
Boxwood handles
1/4" – 6" radius
Straight or Cranked

*WHILE STOCKS LAST*
Special rates for quantities
Please send 50p in stamps for catalogue
TILGEAR, 20 Ladysmith Road, Enfield, Middx., EN1 3AA Tel: 01-363 8050/3080

---

**MINIATURE COACH BOLTS Etc.**
**LIFELIKE CHINA HORSES**
**individually hand made**
**Authentic scale harness kits**
For new illustrated brochure and price lists send £1 in stamps or 2 × 1st class stamps for one price list (state materials, horse or harness) to:

Lenham Pottery (WW)
215 Wroxham Road
Norwich, Norfolk
NR7 8AQ

---

**LACE BOBBIN** turning blanks. Extensive range of exotics, Ivory, lathes, miniature tools, sundries, lace supplies. SAE J. Ford, 5 Squirrels Hollow, Walsall WS7 8YS.

---

**LET PETER MAGNANI PUT YOU ON THE MAP ON 01-437 0699 ext. 217**

---

**OLD STONE BARNS,** quiet, near Castle Combe converted into Studio Workshops suitable for arts and crafts. Sizes flexible 600 — 2000 sq.ft. long leases reasonable prices. Contact Defty Fosse Farm Barns, Nettleton, Wilts.

**CORONET MAJOR 10"** saw 4½" Planer Thicknesser. Morticing attachment, combination table. Ply — Vee Bench Stand £600. Briscombe 0453 883245. (Stroud, Glos.).

---

MORTISERS; TENNONERS; SPINDLES; PLANERS; BANDSAWS; LATHES; CROSSCUTS; ROUTERS; SANDERS; DRILLS?
YOU CAN CERTAINLY SEE ALL CLASSES AND TYPES OF MACHINES HERE.

WE ARE MAIN STOCKING AGENTS FOR:
MULTICO; ELU; SEDGWICK; KITY; SCHEPPACH; INCA; CORONET; DeWALT; WARCO; DOMINION; HITACHI; STARTRITE; TREND; ASHLEY ILES; SORBY.

*CALL US ABOUT WOODTURNING LESSONS*
*WOODCARVING LESSONS (See our Swiss carving tools)*
*ALWAYS HELPFUL, KNOWLEDGEABLE, GOOD SERVICE AT:*
## CLEVELAND WOODCRAFT
38-42 CRESCENT ROAD, MIDDLESBROUGH.
TEL: (0642) 813103

**THE FINEST SELECTION ON DISPLAY IN SCOTLAND!**
WOODWORKING & METALWORKING MACHINERY POWER TOOLS HAND TOOLS
HIRE OR BUY!
**THE SAW CENTRE**
*Visit our* NEW SHOWROOM at EGLINTON TOLL GLASGOW
Tel: 041-429 4444/4374, Telex: 777886 SAWCO G
Also at, 38 Haymarket Terrace, Edinburgh EH12 5JZ. Tel: 031-337 5555
**OPEN**
Mon - Fri 8am - 5pm
Sat 9am - 1pm

---

**SHOPSMITH MARK V.** Fine Basic Functions, plus many useful accessories £800 o.n.o. 01-0272 8341.

**USERS AND COLLECTORS** tools for sale at the Old Craft Tool Shop, 15 High Street, Whillon Middx. Telephone 01-755 0441.

**SPIERS 15"** panel plane, mint condition Buck 15" panel plane, very nice condition Offers. Telephone 0736 753018. (Cornwall).

**CONVERTED WOOLEN** mill near Carmarthen, SW Wales. 4 bedroom 1st floor accommodation, large workshop and sales area. Car park. Trout stream at rear £44.950. Telephone Llanpumsaint 026 784 486.

---

**WOOD TURNERS SUPPLIES**

Tudor Craft, Jung Hans clock movements, 20 different hands to choose from, barometers, weather stations, cutlery, jewellery box lids, pepper/salt/nutmeg mills, coffee grinders, ceramic tiles, new range which include hand painted tiles. Our service is extremely fast, friendly and competitive — give us a try. Send SAE for catalogue to

**TUDORCRAFT,**
c/o Wentworth, Talbot Avenue, Little Ashton, Sutton Coalfield, West Midlands B74 3DD.

---

**ELEGANT LAMPS** and bowls chequered design to turn on your lathe. S.A.E. to Cabin Craft, CPA Laird St., Depot Greenock.

788

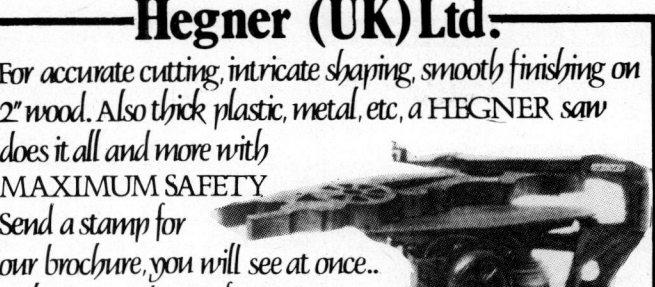

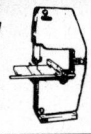

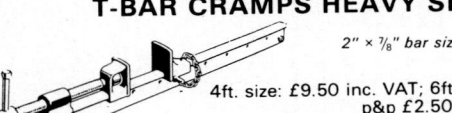 

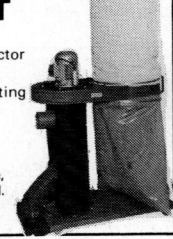

790

792

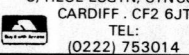

# WOOD SUPPLIERS

# Letters

I'M THE WOODWORK TEACHER for Camden Haven Learning Exchange in New South Wales. Our classes meet every Friday night between 7 and 9pm, and we'd be more than pleased to have a mention in *Woodworker*.

The brush box timber from the Camden Haven area (Kendall, Kew, Comboyne, Wauchope) was used, laminated, in the floor and the lower part of the walls in the Sydney Opera House. Alex Don and I made the table shown here from the same timber in a very similar way. Alex glued together 2ft-wide pieces ¾x1½in, and to make the 6ft-long top we glued two of these together. The legs are 2ft wide and 2ft 6in high. I bought the Norris plane in 1950 for £15!

Roger Clinton of the Herons Creek Timber Mill looks after us very well with brush box, but we don't think this will last. More timber has been cut from this part of the country than anywhere else in Australia. I first came here in 1938: there was no tap-water and no electricity, and paddle-wheel punts used to bring the timber down-river to the mills. Even before that, Cobb & Co. used to go north from Sydney. More recently Yarras Timber Mill (which supplied a lot of the Opera House timber) provided us with coachwood, rosewood and many others while it was still operating.

*Keith Hudson, Laurieton, NSW, Australia*

---

CHARLES CLIFFE'S 'Technical trio' (WW/Aug) missed a vital point about cutting halvings.

He says that 'to cut the joint, the work is held upright in the vice'. But surely the correct method for a true vertical cut is first to set the work at an angle, so that the saw can travel along both the horizontal and the vertical gauge-lines. The work is then reversed and a similar cut made on the other side. Only lastly is it set upright and the cut made down to the shoulder — the saw being guided by the triangular cuts already made.

*D. C. Marchant, Ashtead*

---

I'D LIKE to make some suggestions on gluing plastic hockey-stick moulding to the edge of melamine chipboard ('Question box', WW/July).

Firstly, I'd remove the melamine edging. This can be done with a chisel, with a plane or sometimes by heating with an iron. Because the exposed edge of the board is porous, first spread some ordinary PVA adhesive along it — forcing it into the 'grain' — and allow it to set. This acts as a sealer and filler. Then sandpaper the edge. If the edge is sized in this way first, I've always found that contact adhesive will bond the moulding very well.

Stanley Ford's answer mentioned hot-melt glue-guns. Unfortunately these are not suitable for long lengths, or for any gluing that takes more than 30 seconds (and that isn't as long as it sounds!)

Keep up the magazine's excellent standard.

*Michael Edwards, Aylesbury*

---

JOHN FARRAR'S 'Machine made for man' (WW/Aug) was informative. But the photos show the machine operator wearing a ring and bracelet. Surely you do not condone this dangerous working practice?

*John Race, Stamford*

● No, we don't, and we're sorry. We didn't take the photos, but that's no excuse. Rings and bracelets can get caught on and in things, and should therefore stay outside the machine-shop door.

---

MAY I SAY that *Woodworker* is now just about the best it has ever been? I should be able to judge — my first volume is 1919!

● *It may not look like the Sydney Opera House – but don't be fooled! Not only the timber (brush box from New South Wales) but also the laminated construction were used in the opera house's showpiece joinery. The table was made by Keith Hudson and Alex Don*

I am writing about Chris MacDonald's article in the June issue and his difficulty in disposing of his craftwork. For many years I have made miniature furniture to one-fifth scale — what people mistakenly call apprentice pieces. They were featured in *Woodworker* for March 1975. The only outlet I have ever found was the better-class London sale-rooms, and the prices they got would never have earned one a living!

In this country at any rate, Mr MacDonald is on a losing wicket. I am now 70, and still work an 8½-hour day as a joiner (stairs, fitted kitchens, the occasional church job in oak). I am convinced that, to be employed fully in woodworking, you have to be connected with the building industry in some way. You simply must produce what people want and not what you personally would like to do.

For instance: sashes go rotten. Recently I had to make 15 new ones for the same house — no two the same. It's an attitude of mind. One can take as much pride in making a good sash as in the finest piece of cabinet work. When you've been on run-of-the-mill stuff for a time and nice work eventually comes along, it's all the nicer.

*J. W. Lane, Burgess Hill*

---

I READ with great interest Cecil Jordan's review of Ray Key's book on turning, and felt that it displayed a very negative and somewhat carping view of what is quite an informative work. Jordan also reviewed Bruce Boulter's book with the same curt attitude, which displays a professional arrogance and not much sympathy for those trying to open the way for amateurs who want to emulate the professionals.

In praise of Ray Key's book, it is very much a 'this is how I do it' account which displays humility in a man making a living at his craft and still learning. As a professional working in the 'wooden object art field' I too have still a lot to learn, and actively seek out those who can teach me it. We await Cecil Jordan's retrospect of his abilities!

I also read with interest the eulogies which praise the great names and their books. I have bought Alan Peters' book but do not find in it a great deal to recommend its purchase; it seems to me that reviewers are intimidated by the stature of these established craftsmen, who sometimes produce some very dubious work (as do we all). John Makepeace's ability to produce almost 'driftwood' furniture alongside some very traditional work is evidence of the enormous design vocabulary that we have to cope with. It is wrong to feel dwarfed by the achievements of such men, great though they are. Instead, reviewers (I feel) must assess relevance, not indulgence, within the context of the modern movement, and not be intimidated by the craft and perfection found in such work.

We all make mistakes (a close look at one of Peters' pieces on public exhibition last year revealed a slip of the chisel which was very nicely repaired), so would it be possible to be more objective? Or am I being far too critical and carping?

*Peter Howlett, Basildon*

798

# Letters

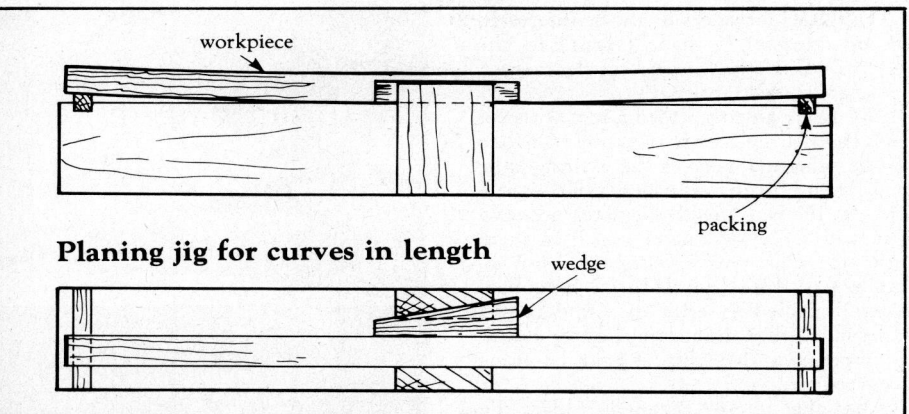

## Planing jig for curves in length

● *From a 1920s piano factory comes this beautifully simple device for tackling a difficult job*

THE DRAWING in David Faulkner's letter (WW/July) reminded me of a device used for a similar purpose in a small piano factory where I worked for a time some 60 years ago. No machinery of any kind was used in the workshop; holes for wrest- and bridge-pins were drilled with a drill-stock and bow. (Of course, all major components such as actions, keys, iron frames and soundboards were supplied by specialist firms.)

The jig was used in the formation of a large radius lengthwise on belly-bars, which are the supporting bars made from about 1in-square spruce and glued at intervals across the grain on the rear side of the soundboard or belly to resist the downward pressure of the strings via the bridges.

The sketch **above** shows the jig as far as I can remember, although the radius was much larger than I have shown.

The stuff was rested on the outer blocks, pressed down at the centre and secured by knocking home the wedge and tapping the bar down firmly. The consequent hollowed upper surface was then planed flat; when it was released from the jig by knocking out the wedge, a uniformly curved bar resulted.

I was not for long in the piano trade; the depression, coupled with the competition from gramophone and radio, was beginning to take effect, and the firm closed in 1928.

*L. C. Ducat, London N12*

MAKING BAGPIPES (Letters, July) involves many crafts. No book covers them all in depth. However, the Northumbrian and the *uilleann* (Irish) pipers' societies have each published excellent works on their individual instruments. These give the basic information required to make bagpipes.

In case you're unfamiliar with the instrument, here is a photo of a half-set of *uilleann* pipes I've recently made. These use bellows to supply the bag with air. The pipes themselves are of African blackwood, the stock of African padauk, the bellow-cheeks of oak and the bag of hand-sewn leather covered with velvet. The metalwork is stainless steel, although brass is more commonly used.

*Steve McCordick, Duffield*

CAN ANYONE provide instructions or an information leaflet for a sharpening machine / electric tool called the Wuidart, which is about 6in long and 3in in diameter, made in England, 220/250V, 0.3amp, 2800rpm? I presume this machine was for sharpening plane blades, but am not sure if the unit is complete.

*Peter Boddy, Valdheim,*
*Hetland, Carrutherstown*
*DG1 4JX*

---

AS FAR AS I'M AWARE there is only one publication on the manufacture of Northumbrian bagpipes. This is *The Northumbrian Bagpipes* by W. A. Cocks and J. F. Bryan, published by the Northumbrian Pipers Society, Newcastle-upon-Tyne. My copy is the limp-bound second edition (ISBN 0 902510 05 3), which cost £4 from Hobgoblin Music some four years ago. [The hardcover SBN is 0 902510 06 1.] This is an excellent example of a 'how to do it' publication and I can thoroughly recommend it. Incidentally, I believe the first edition included details of the half-long pipes, which has been omitted in the second edition in favour of another variant of the small pipe.

*Roderick Jenkins, Basingstoke*

● **Above** is famed Irish piper Paddy Conneely; **right** is a set of uillean *pipes by Steve McCordick. Na Píobairí Uillean (the pipers' society) is at 15 Henrietta St, Dublin 1*

SOMETIMES it's necessary to clamp a panel to lie flat on a Workmate, using the plastic stops supplied, when it's too long or too wide even to be held diagonally. A simple solution is to cut a triangular piece of plywood or chipboard and use it as illustrated **below.**

By this means you can easily hold panels up to 20in wide, and with suitable packing the piece will form a useful extra clamp for many jobs. It can be made to work more efficiently if the two shorter sides are covered with a hard plastic edging to assist the sliding movement against the stops.

*David Hodge, London E11*

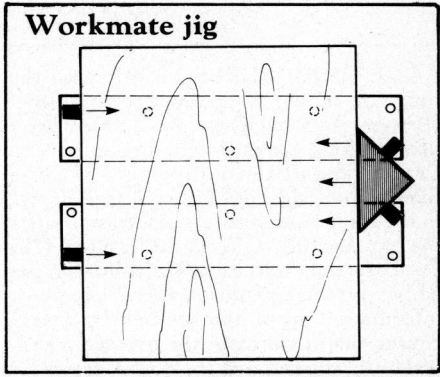

## Workmate jig

RETAILERS, importers and distributors of woodworking products have always alarmed me with the shocking lack of knowledge they sometimes display about the goods they are handling. Sometimes they make classic *faux pas* in their ignorance.

A good example was in 'Shoptalk' for August. In reading of the Jack planes from Denmark, I am sure many people puzzled over the timber referred to as pockwood. I must admit it had me in hysterics! What the distributors have done is to make a literal translation from the Danish instead of looking to see what the English equivalent is. This mysterious timber is in fact lignum vitae.

*Roger Buse, Roger's of Hitchin*

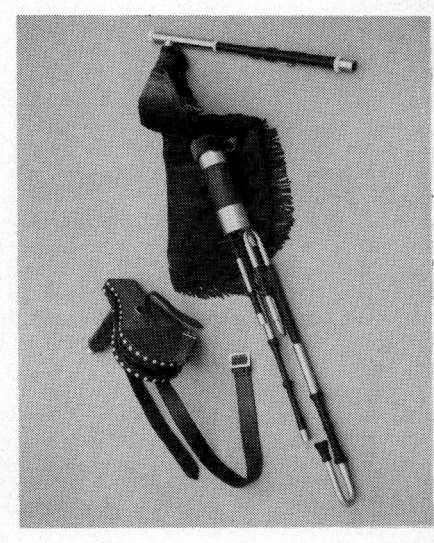

# Letters

ALAN THOMAS (WW/April) was probably not brought up in a shop where wooden planes were in frequent use, otherwise he would know that the medullary rays of a bench plane must be at right-angles to the sole. The sole wears evenly and requires less truing with vertical rays, and the plane slides more easily if the grain runs from the toe to the heel.

If the sole is not true, it should not be trued with a smoothing-plane as Mr Thomas recommends. Draw the iron back and tap the wedge firmly home. Then true the sole with a finely set trying-plane by planing from toe to heel.

*Charles Cliffe, Bexleyheath*

---

I COULDN'T AGREE MORE with the tone of Tony Waddilove's comments (Letters, August). There was a time when I used to look forward with anticipation to forthcoming articles of the type to which he refers; I no longer do! Tobias Kaye's article in the same issue stands in contrast: more's the pity that others do not find it possible to compare and contrast as Kaye did. On the whole I pick up more general pieces of information from the articles by David Savage than I do from the average grand-scale 'the experts will show you' type.

*T. G. J. Dyer, Mevagissey*

---

I HAD a startling experience this early spring in my garage workshop. Keen to start turning once more after a long winter, I began work on a face-plate job with the frost still nipping my ears. I left it on the face-plate for a couple of days, and suddenly the temperature rose. Because the co-efficients of expansion of aluminium and steel are so different, the face-plate had locked solid. I had to resort to a club-hammer and re-drill the mutilated C-spanner hole.

The moral is 'Keep your face-plate cosy'.
*Roy Benfield, Walton-on-Thames*

---

I USE a lot of fine panel and veneer pins, and have found that they often bend when driven — either because rust has formed on them in storage, or because of the nature of the ramin substitutes currently used for picture-frame and other small mouldings.

Grease, tallow and the like do help, but they pick up on the fingers, marking the timber. So I now direct a short, sharp spray of WD40 into the carton of pins before use. I find this reduces all my troubles considerably.

*J. E. Todman, Wickford, Essex*

---

WHEN A BANDSAW BLADE BREAKS it seems a pity to discard a good useful length. I find old ones provide replacements for junior-hacksaw and bowsaw blades, with a far longer life than the originals. In my experience, all blades are very easy to drill, and in the case of the junior hacksaw you only need a $\frac{1}{16}$in hole about 1in in from each end. I have made retaining pins from $\frac{1}{16}$in welding rod.

*Stephen Elford, Coventry*

---

I THOUGHT readers might be interested in an extension I made (**right**) to the Myford ML8 lathe to turn a consignment of balusters to 40in in length.

Not being able to afford a Myford 42in bed, I turned a piece of hardwood 18in long to the same diameter as the existing lathe bed. Then I turned a 6in length of the same piece to the bed's inside diameter, securing this with a $\frac{1}{2}$in-diameter coach-bolt 1in from the end, plus a washer and nut — having first drilled a hole through the bed. Next, I drilled a series of $\frac{1}{2}$in-diameter holes in line with the existing bed top slot. It is imperative that this should be done accurately.

After that it only remains to place the tailstock on the extension and secure it with another $\frac{1}{2}$in coach-bolt. It can be positioned at any one of the holes according to the length being turned; the difference is taken up with the tailstock screw.

I may add that I think the 12in overhang is about as much as you can have without causing too much pressure. However, you could turn any length of extension, provided that you bolt a Myford tailstock bed support to it.

I have turned several hundred pieces using this extension, and have had no movement or inaccuracy in my work.

*Leonard Wortley, Great Yarmouth*

---

AS A NEWCOMER to woodturning, I advance with diffidence my solution to the problem of honing turning tools. It is so simple that either it really will help other novices, or everyone has already discovered it anyway!

I have not, at least so far, achieved good results by using tools straight from the grinder. My first attempts to hone on an oilstone were disappointing, the difficulty being to maintain a constant angle of bevel. My answer is as follows.

Fit a small screw-eye to each tool at the end of the handle. A screw-hook is fitted to a batten about 18in long, which is held vertically in the bench vice. The screw-eye is engaged in the hook and the business end of the tool rested on the stone. The bevel angle is adjusted by raising or lowering the batten in the vice. Honing is carried out either by manipulating the tool on the stone or by holding the tool still and moving the stone with a reciprocating action on the bench. I use a combination of the two methods, depending on which tool is being honed.

I have found that the small screw-eye does not interfere at all with the turning process, for example by catching in clothes. The results I've achieved have been most encouraging. The bevel angle is far more accurate that I could achieve by hand and eye alone; the bevel has a smooth appearance and the edge is sharp, after removing the 'wire edge' with a slipstone. Best of all, the tools now remove satisfactorily long shavings from the workpiece.

*R. C. Southall, Inverurie*

---

● *Fitting and construction of Leonard Wortley's self-made extension for the Myford ML8 lathe*

SOME BRIEF COMMENTS on 'Buying timber wisely: 2' (WW/July).

The timber industry's changeover to metric is more than 10 years old now. The reluctance remains, I'm sure, but sizes in imperial units must retard the process.

On kiln-drying, two thoughts about the statement 'Kilning brings the moisture content down to $12\frac{1}{2}$-15%'. I would have thought that what the moisture content was brought down to would be what was specified for the particular end-use in mind. Secondly, I always feel uneasy where fractions are used in indicating MC levels. Things aren't that precise. After all, if 12% is specified, this is only an average derived from a spread of figures.

*C. G. Cable, Peterborough*

---

MAY I THANK the firm of Record Ridgway Tools, and in particular their commercial manager Mr P. J. Peck, for supplying me with a replacement block for my Preston 3-in-1 plane? Some years ago I was given a Preston bullnose/chisel plane (or that's what I thought it was). A few weeks ago I came by the nose section of a Preston plane. I tried it on mine, and it fitted — so I was the owner of a Preston 3-in-1 minus the block. It was then that Mr Peck came up trumps and saved a perfectly good plane from the scrap-heap.

*Alan Biggs, Cheltenham*

# The magazine for the craftsman
## ~ and the aspiring craftsman!

November 1985
Vol. 89
No. 1104

● *Delightful dressers . . . Find out their history and features on pp838-9; discover how to make one (plans and all) on pp880-5*

**On the cover: David O'Connor's elegant wall cabinet – full plans start on p832**

**Editor** Peter Collenette
**Deputy Editor** Aidan Walker
**Advertisement Manager** Paul Holmes
**Graphics** Jeff Hamblin
**Guild of Woodworkers** Aidan Walker
Editorial, advertisements and Guild of Woodworkers
1 Golden Square, London W1R 3AB, telephone 01-437 0626

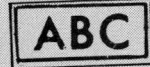
**Subscriptions and back issues** Infonet Ltd, 10-13 Times House, 179 Marlowes, Hemel Hempstead, Herts HP1 1BB; telephone Hemel Hempstead (0442) 48434
**Subscriptions per year** UK £16.95; overseas outside USA (accelerated surface post) £19.20, USA (accelerated surface post) $24.90, airmail £46.20
**UK trade** SM Distribution Ltd, 16-18 Trinity Gardens, London SW9 8DX; telephone 01-274 8611
**North American trade** Bill Dean Books Ltd, 151-49 7th Avenue, PO Box 69, Whitestone, New York 11357; telephone 1-718-767-6632
**Printed in Great Britain** by Ambassador Press Ltd, St Albans, Herts
**Mono origination** Multiform Photosetting Ltd, Cardiff
**Colour origination** Derek Croxson Ltd, Chesham, Bucks
© Argus Specialist Publications Ltd 1985
ISSN 0043 776X

## Argus Specialist Publications Ltd
1 Golden Square, London W1R 3AB; 01-437 0626

# Woodworker
# This month

## Dust dilemmas

Can yew dust cause permanent lung damage?

'You could probably handle and work yew wood without problems — unless of course you were allergic to it,' timber expert Bill Brown told a questioner in the July issue. He explained, 'There are long lists of timbers that cause nose bleeds and watering eyes, or are responsible for skin ailments like dermatitis. There are also instances where physical contact with a particular wood can cause distress.'

But a reader went further. 'I am a retired clinical biochemist . . . and from practical experience I can assure you that yew dust has a seriously destructive effect on the lining of the respiratory tract.

'I was turning a particularly difficult piece of knotty wood and, failing to get an acceptable finish with chisel or scraper, I finally resorted to abrasive paper. After some time in a heavily dusty atmosphere I experienced discomfort in the chest, and this continued — with varying sypmtoms — for a very uncomfortable and worrying six months, when some improvement began. I am now, after about two years, still

suffering some discomfort, and am affected by smoke and dust to a considerable extent.

'This is *not* an allergy, but a permanent chemical damage to the respiratory epithelium from the nose downward. Over the years the many comments in the correspondence columns on the effects of wood dust have always given the impression that, while a few exotic woods may have an irritant effect, any respiratory troubles are due to an allergic response. This is clearly not the case. Other people have obviously suffered similar damage.

'The effect of the dust is proportional to the size of the particles, and the finer the abrasive, the further the dust will reach.'

Says Bill Brown in reply: 'In giving advice, I've stressed the possibility of a health hazard only when it seems likely. The fact remains that, while literally thousands of different woods possess irritant properties, not everyone is affected by them. The Furniture Industry Research Association say that yew can cause quite severe but infrequent bronchial asthma and dermatitis, and note that the dust as a cause of dermatitis has been clinically identified. You'll

● *Startling enough on a page, but you'd get more of a shock if you were standing in front of Jan Zalud's 'Animated Head' – it's got cogs and levers which give it expression and movement; we know not what or how. It's part of Parnham House's 'Rough Wood' Exhibition, 1 September to 30 October, which includes work by Jan, Andrew Darke, Stephen Hogbin and the ubiquitous Richard La Trobe Bateman.*
● *Parnham, Beaminster, Dorset DT8 3NA, tel. (0308) 862204*

see from this that, while extreme care ought to be taken when working the wood, distress to the user doesn't occur all that regularly.'

He adds: 'I agree that the term "allergy" can often be a means of writing such problems off. I know only too well that individuals not normally sensitive to certain constituents in many woods are by no means immune.'

What's very clear is that no one knows all or even most of the answers — or that, if they do, they haven't bothered to let the average woodworker know. With something as familiar as timber, there's always a danger that real hazards will be discounted or go unrecognised.
● Perhaps other readers (especially medical professionals) can tell us what they know?

● *A launching party for a bookcase? 'We try to have one party a year,' says Charles Wheeler-Carmichael (on the right), who designed and made this piece in American black walnut with Rupert Senior.*

*It's 15ft long, slightly bow-fronted, and the pediments are carved from the solid in a total of five sections. The commission came from a London publisher who wanted to store 1000 books. The pair hired a journalist to write an information sheet – sent with photo and invitation to 75 newspapers and magazines. 'The largest hand-crafted bookcase in the world' says the heading. 'We know for certain*

# Shoptalk

You've no doubt unfolded the Planposter free with this issue. We hope you like it, and we hope you find it useful. Woodworking is fine and fancy craft: but it's also quick, sturdy storage when you or your family need it. Our thanks go to GKN for joining us in the project – and for making such good screws.

What's more, NEXT MONTH'S issue will include a very special offer enabling you to buy a special trial set of GKN Mastascrews, plus wallplugs, plus a GKN ratchet Mastadriva to put them in with – in their own box, for a 40% saving. Stand by for the December *Woodworker!*

● *Below:* The seal of the Hanseatic League was painstakingly carved by John Walterson of Scalloway, Shetland. It was commissioned to decorate the outside of the restored 'Hamburg Booth' – an ancient stone building in Symbister on the Shetland isle of Whalsay, built by 16th-century traders from north German ports. The 'Bremen Booth' is still used as a dwelling; the refurbished Hamburg booth will display the original cargo-lifting wheel and an exhibition of the Hanseatic League's and Whalsay's life and traditions. Members of the restoration trust were so impressed with John's carving that they decided to preserve that as well, and keep it inside – out of the stormy Shetland weather. They are having a replica cast in fibreglass for the outside position.

It's difficult to understand why no one has put linseed oil and urethane in the same can before. Evode have done it, called the result 'Natural Wood Finish', and put a little sponge applicator on top for good measure (and good gimmick-value) as well.

It's an attractive flat finish with the penetration of oil and the protection of urethane, and it comes (as Evo-Stik Natural Wood Tones) in seven colours. One of the deputy-editorial house doors has been given the treatment, and the news is that the spongey pad works fine (though not in corners, because the shape doesn't let you get there), and the plastic cone on which it's fixed doesn't completely disintegrate at the sight of white spirit, though it does get messy. More applications add gloss. It retails at about £3 for 220ml.

Apart from ordinary varnishes (the Furniglas range re-packaged), Evo-Stik are also doing an exterior micro-porous one that claims flexibility, and a new quick-dry 'super-hard' Floor and Stair Varnish.
● Evode Building and Consumer Products Division, Common Rd, Stafford ST16 3EH, (0785) 57755.

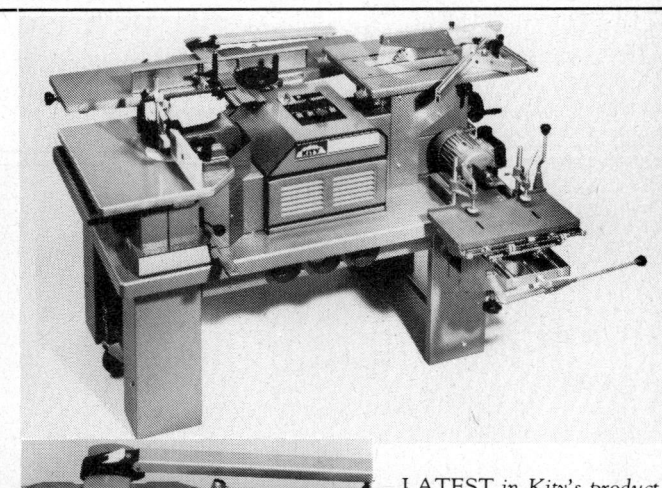

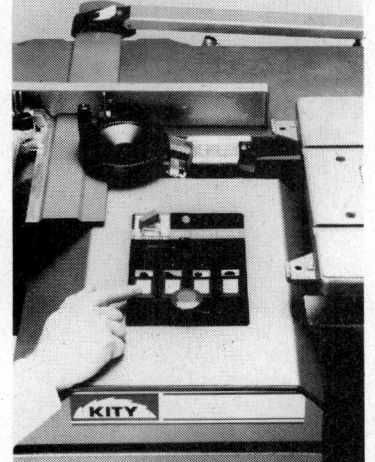

LATEST in Kity's product line-up is the new 704 Direct Drive, a combination based on the 704. All its five functions bar the mortiser are permanently connected via a belt and clutch to a single central 3hp motor; the mortiser has a .75hp motor of its own. Select the function you need with a rotary switch, and fret no more about having to alter set-ups, guards and tables; £1799+VAT.
● Kity UK, 6 Acorn Park, Charlestown, Shipley, W. Yorks BD17 7SW, (0274) 597826

*that it isn't,'* says Charles.

But publicity is publicity. And once you've stopped scoffing at the audacity of it all, and at how it's all very well for woodworkers with a head start in life (both trained at prestigious and pricey Parnham House), ask yourself whether a lot more equally competent craftspeople might not do well to borrow the attitude that fine, handsome, expensive furniture can become just as much a 'media event' as a new book or film. An attitude that has already ensured Charles and Rupert a free mention in the Daily Telegraph (circulation 1,200,000). How many customer enquiries will that bring?

WE'RE SORRY that some of you had to wait for your copy of *Woodworker* last month. The extra work of producing our special machine supplement blew a fuse or two at the printers. But we've recklessly pressed on — with the result that you're looking at what we think is the first ever **100-page issue** in our 85-year history. Happy reading!

TALKING of October's *Machine Guide*, the Apollo lathe (p19) has a ¾hp motor. No less.

BLACK & DECKER's new DN820 table-top bench saw for £120, the proverbial 'handy little item', has a 7¼in blade, a 500x400mm table – and a tilt-arbor mechanism, unusual on a machine of this size.
● Black & Decker, Westpoint, The Grove, Slough, Berks SL1 1QQ, Slough 74277

# Shoptalk

**H**aunters of newsagents may already have seen a copy of **Idealogue**. Its advance publicity (all we've been able to see at press time) makes it look a good idea indeed: an enticing, handsome-looking full-colour magazine which consists almost entirely of advertisements and listings placed by (in the publishers' words) 'designers, makers, small craft businesses and innovators'.

If it works, it might do an awful lot to crack the marketing problems — and redress the marketing faults — of small woodworking firms. If you buy an ad, you get your product(s) photographed in the magazine's own studio, and your own description appears in print. That costs £172.50 for a quarter-page, £345 for a half-page and £690 for a full page, all including VAT. An index listing costs £23 and consists of your name, address and telephone number plus 'a line that states your area of specialisation'. The magazine is divided into sections — furniture, clothing, jewellery, etc.

Whether it works (and whether it's worth your cash) depends, of course, on whether enough browsers are happy to pay the magazine's £1.50 price so they can take it home and ogle your products. But the basic plan, which is to provide craft work with the slick national exposure that the Habitat catalogue and magazines like *In Store* afford other wares, deserves a hefty cheer.

● The Idealogue Ltd, Waterside, 99 Rotherhithe St, London SE16 4NF; telephone Tim Darbey, 01-232 0978. Issue no. 2 is due out in April. The publishers provide very clear and sensible advice and instructions for advertisers.

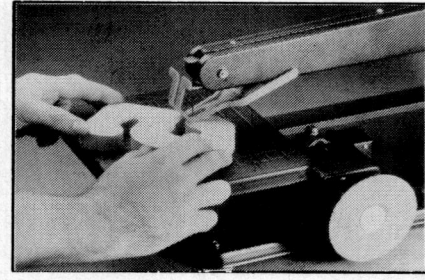

DREMEL *have brought out a scroll-saw/sander called the Moto Shop. The 205mm-square table tilts to 45°, the throat is 15in, the disc is 5in and it costs £89 inc. VAT.*
● *Dremel Tools Ltd, Fairacres Industrial Estate, Dedworth Rd, Windsor, Berks*

**A**s a specialist film-maker, writes Ken Cooper, I have always had a secret yearning to try to capture on film or **videotape** that other love of my life — the art of fine woodwork. So I viewed Ernie Ives' new tape **Marquetry for Beginners** with alacrity, because here at last was an opportunity to see the master in action and maybe learn a few of the secrets which distinguish his work from the relatively crude efforts of such fumblers as myself.

The video is basically a demonstration of the 'window' method of marquetry using a commercial kit. It lists at some length the tools and materials required, based on those supplied with the kit. Then, after a demonstration with a simple leaf design in sycamore and walnut veneers, Ernie Ives tells how to build up a very pleasing picture of a harbour scene. He explains a great deal about the art of cutting, and warns of snags and how they may be overcome. He touches on sand-shading (though I found this part a little glib), and deals in great detail with finishing and mounting.

The cassette provides an hour and 25 minutes of tuition from an acknowledged expert. But I'd have been a lot happier if the standard of the film had matched that of the marquetry. One should use the camera to emphasise things which would be difficult to see in a normal demonstration — yet here, some of the close-ups were more obscure than the long shots because of the wrong camera angle. Some scenes were too long and repetitive. In fact, competent planning, editing and camera work would have improved the programme tremendously. The colour and definition were acceptable, but here too there were problems — for instance, over-loud sound effects and barely legible captions.

The tape would be very useful to a beginner. But it would have been more effective if the visual side had been more professionally handled.

● *Marquetry for Beginners* by Ernie Ives, VHS and Betamax, £27+VAT from Breakaway Tackle Film Productions, 376 Bramford Rd, Ipswich, Suffolk IP1 5AY; Ipswich 41393. A hire facility is also planned.

CHUCK *specialists Multistar have (perhaps unsurprisingly) gone into lathe production. Already developing a reputation among woodturners, they claim some sharp ideas for the new machine: a headstock that swings through 360° for the best working position, toolrest and tailstock that 'will work from either end', and a wide speed range – 200-3500rpm. All the fittings are universal; no need to duplicate chucks and face-plates when* the headstock turns right round.

*The headstock spindle is 40mm, the construction 'decidedly heavyweight'; it also sports 'deepgroove' bearings. It has automatic belt-tension/clutch-control, and can handle 18in-diameter workpieces over the bed.*

● *Multistar Machine & Tool Co. Ltd, Ashton House, Wheatfield Rd, Stanway, Colchester, Essex CO3 5YA, tel. (0206) 549944*

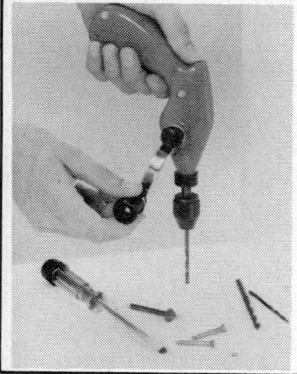

THIS IS *the Mini-Drill, made of plastic and 8in long. It has nylon gears and a ¼in (6mm) chuck; the handle includes a drill storage compartment for bits. Equally compact is the price at £6.50, which must recommend it highly if you want something to reach for when it's not worth plugging in a power drill.*
● *Vitrex, 457-63 Caledonian Rd, London N7 9BB, 01-609 0011*

'MY PASSION *is for* **veneers** *and things made from veneers,' declares Ron Aaronson. His unassuming shop in London's Shoreditch, the historic heart of the furniture trade, houses an eye-opening stock of veneers, marquetry and bandings. 'Our customers keep us on our toes, and only by being a really specialist supplier can we satisfy the most demanding!' He points out that marquetry and banding production have always been specialised skills, bought in by* even the top makers; his own suppliers, he says, still guard their secrets closely.

*Encouragingly, he says: 'Some of my best customers started by buying just enough for their first project, yet have now developed into highly successful furniture manufacturers and antique restorers.'*

*If you love those exquisite fans, shells, vases and complex patterned bands – or just want veneers (plain, exotic, curl, burr, through-and-through-dyed, the lot) – catch Aaronsons at the Woodworker Show, or call on them. An SAE brings you their picture sheet and price list.*
● *R. Aaronson (Veneers) Ltd, 45 Redchurch St, London E2 7DJ, 01-739 3107*

If pyrography (once known as poker-work) is your passion, you'll be glad to know that there's a new edition of Stewart Grainger's *Introduction to Pyrography*. This handy little manual now has four pages in colour; it costs £1.25 from the publishers, who make pyrographs. It also contains extensive plugs for their products — but fair's fair.
● Janik Wood Crafts, Brickfield Lane, Denbigh Rd, Ruthin, Clwyd LL15 2TN, (082 42) 2096.

## All about GKN's Supascrews and Mastascrews – focus of the Planposter free with this issue

Everybody knows the familiar woodscrew that's been around for years. At GKN they call it 'article one', and they still sell millions. But you get the clear impression that they'd like to stop making altogether. That's because they've invented something they think is a great deal better.

Namely, the Supascrew and its companion the Mastascrew. The Supascrew has a recessed head, i.e. one of the type that people still call Phillips — though it's got nothing to do with Phillips any longer, and anyway the design's been changed. The Mastascrew has an ordinary slot for those who still hate recesses. Both of them supersede the Pozidriv (though you can still get Pozidriv screwdrivers). They even supersede earlier versions of themselves.

The GKN screw factory at Wednesbury makes 100,000,000 screws a week 'with a following wind', and the necessary gear cost something like £5,000,000. So it's not surprising that a lot of research lies behind the current product.

Required, say GKN, were 'four major features: the means of driving — slot or recess — must be mechanically efficient and virtually indestructible; the screw must be easy to locate and start; installation must be fast; and it must be "universal" — that is, capable of fastening a wide range of natural and composite materials'.

'In physical terms,' they explain, 'these criteria dictated: heat treatment of the head/drive feature to toughen it against possible breakage or scoring; a sharp point and fast thread pick-up;' and threads which are twin-start, widely spaced, deep, sharp, hardened to cut well in different materials — and heat-treated to provide high strength and durability.

'GKN's design team worked on many permutations of pitch angle and thread form before a selection of possible forms was established. It was the sharp point, considered imperative in the new design, which proved especially difficult.'

The new screws supersede chipboard screws because they're designed to hold well in any timber, any man-made board and even thin sheet metal. The Supascrew's recess offers what a GKN sales engineer deliciously called 'a stick-fit situation': in other words, if you use the right size of screwdriver and don't wave it around too much, the screw will stay attached to its tip. Case-hardening means the recess is hard to damage.

The sharp point aids accuracy. But probably the most startling difference is that the screws really do go in a lot faster — and we've tried them. GKN say this is partly because the shank or core of the screw is parallel and not tapered, and partly because of the deep, widely spaced thread. A 2in no. 10 Supascrew has 11 ridges; an 'article one' of the same length and gauge has 26.

In fact, in soft materials the screws go in almost too easily. Be careful, when drilling pilot holes, that you don't make them too large and reduce the holding power. GKN themselves say that in softwoods and low-density boards you don't always need a pilot hole anyway. They publish a good technical data sheet (ref. 001/1) which gives recommended sizes and depths for drilling in the various materials, plus exact dimensions of the screws themselves — which come countersunk, raised-headed and round-headed.

● GKN Fasteners, Woden Rd West, Kings Hill, Wednesbury, West Midlands WS10 7TT, tel. 021-556 1991.

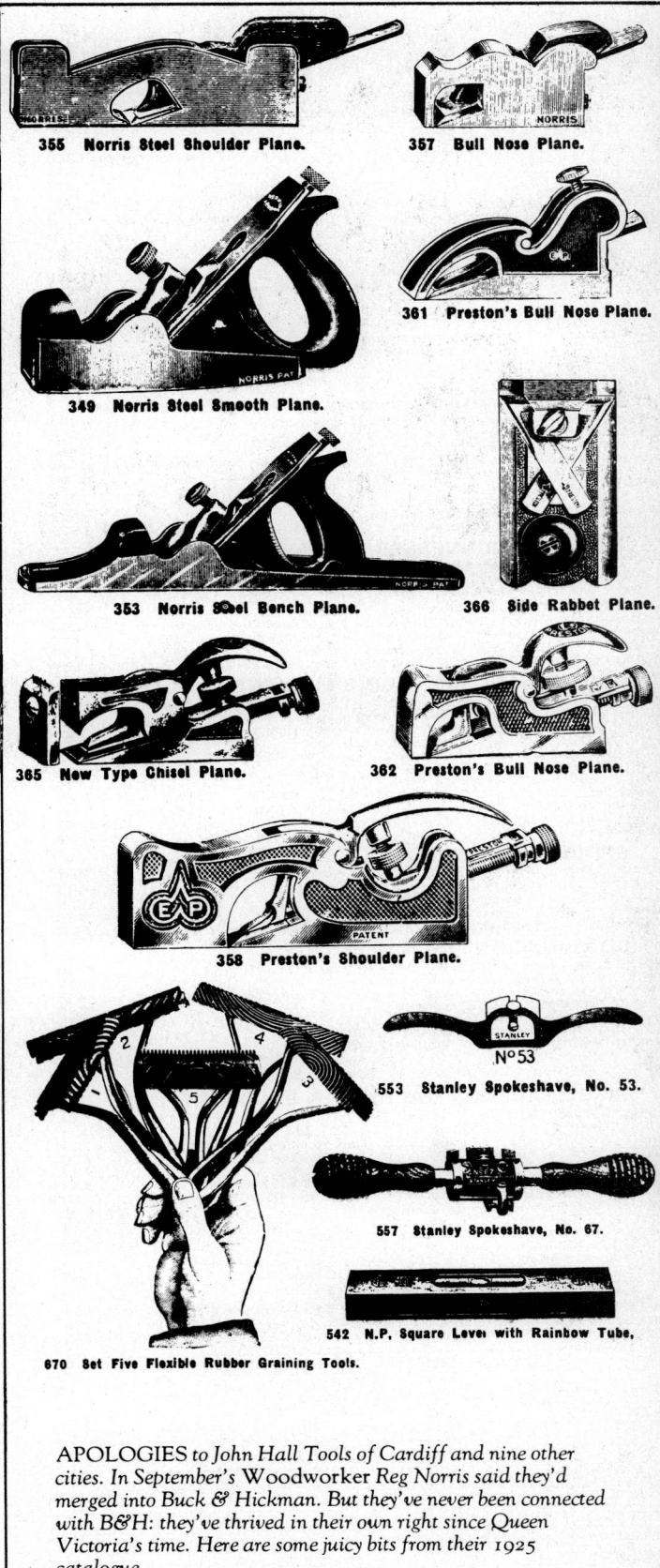

355 Norris Steel Shoulder Plane.

357 Bull Nose Plane.

349 Norris Steel Smooth Plane.

361 Preston's Bull Nose Plane.

353 Norris Steel Bench Plane.

366 Side Rabbet Plane.

365 New Type Chisel Plane.

362 Preston's Bull Nose Plane.

358 Preston's Shoulder Plane.

553 Stanley Spokeshave, No. 53.

557 Stanley Spokeshave, No. 67.

542 N.P. Square Level with Rainbow Tube.

670 Set Five Flexible Rubber Graining Tools.

APOLOGIES to John Hall Tools of Cardiff and nine other cities. In September's Woodworker Reg Norris said they'd merged into Buck & Hickman. But they've never been connected with B&H: they've thrived in their own right since Queen Victoria's time. Here are some juicy bits from their 1925 catalogue.
● John Hall (Tools) Ltd, 73 North Road, Cardiff CF1 3TF, (0222) 382242

# Timberline

## Arthur Jones presents the month's inside news of supplies

Little happens during a holiday period, except in time of boom, and the UK can hardly be said to be enjoying bumper business. So this year summer buying of timber supplies was down to a trickle. Most timbermen were safely able to leave their desks and go away, knowing that little would change in their absence.

The main difference they have discovered on their return is a drop in the value of their stockholdings — through no fault of theirs. Most of the wood in the timber yards today was bought many months ago when the pound was at a low point, nudging close to the $ pound, so the importers had to pay more for their supplies. Now the value of sterling has strengthened quite sharply, with the result that new buying can be done at lower prices because the pound buys more overseas.

Although this movement takes time to work through to new stocks in the yards, the influence upon existing stocks is almost immediate. Some easing of prices can be anticipated, which is good news for the woodworker, and horrifying for the timber trade. However, in most years the reverse movement occurs, with replacement costs rising all the time and the stockist making a useful profit: so woodworkers need shed few tears!

This question of time-lag affects plywood importers at the moment, too. Placing contracts in September with Far Eastern producers (such as in Malaysia and Indonesia) means that the plywood will be reaching our ports probably in December, when the quota allocation for duty-free imports has run out. If the importer takes delivery of the cargo, he will have to meet an extra duty charge amounting to some 13%. But what will actually happen will be the transfer of the plywood into bond — to be released in January, when the new duty-free quotas will apply.

This should not lead the woodworker to assume there will be plywood shortages towards the end of the year. This game of putting plywood into bond when the duty-free quota is exhausted is played every year, and the importers make sure they have stocks available to cover demand throughout the year. There will be no scarcity of plywood come December.

Still on the subject of plywood, most of the shippers in the Far East seem to be sticking to the price agreement set earlier this year of not selling below a certain list price less 26% for the B/BB grade often used by woodworkers.

Softwood is now pouring into the yards from purchases made this year, and stocks are on the increase. This is seasonal, but it means an excellent choice for the woodworker.

Prices have barely moved at all. The recent Russian offer of softwood has been selling slowly, and there has not been much activity in softwood buying from Sweden, Finland or Canada. The holiday is given as the excuse, but in reality the lack of interest has been due more to an uncertainty over demand.

An interesting development for the woodworker has been the decision of Magnet & Southerns, one of the biggest UK timber companies, to publish a new catalogue whose prices are available to all buyers. At first glance it seems to show big reductions on rates which woodworkers might have been paying — but the company has eliminated trade discounts, which could be as high as 40%. They claim that they now compete on price with the most competitive of the DIY superstores.

Recently I devoted a lot of space to the controversy between Friends of the Earth and the UK hardwood trade. There followed talks between the Friends and the Timber Trade Federation. As a result, the Friends will withdraw their threat to launch a campaign urging users of hardwoods to stop using species imported from the tropics, and the Federation and the Friends are to combine forces to present a common case to the Government urging measures to encourage international bodies to take all possible steps to conserve the world's rainforests — this being in the interests of both the Friends and the UK hardwood trade. ∎

807

808

# Question box

## Our panel of experts solve your woodworking problems

**Q** *I have been asked to repair a pierced carving in English oak on a pulpit designed by W. R. Lethaby in about 1887. The design of the damaged vertical section consists of a sinuous stem supporting flower-heads along its length in a repeating pattern. Four of the flowers have been broken off and only one has survived. Since the design is repeated above and below the damaged areas, what I need to do is to copy the pattern and re-create it in new wood. It is not possible to get behind the carving, so all the work must be carried out in situ from the front.*

*I have tried to make a 'brass-rubbing' impression of the pattern, but the carvings have too much depth for any useful drawing to be reconstructed. Can you suggest a way of approaching the problem, please? Perhaps a cast of a complete section could be made for copying in the workshop. If so, how should I go about it without risk of damage to what is an historically valuable piece of furniture?*

Jim Pilbeam, Macclesfield

**A** There are many considerations here. The central one is, of course, the difficulty of copying the pattern. Many years ago carvers' workshops were festooned with plaster-casts of jobs done, taken for future reference. The casts were often produced by what I believe was known as 'taking a squeeze'. Essentially, all that is required to get a working replica is to use a suitable material (I use Plasticene). With a little forethought, by squeezing the Plasticene on to the job a mould can be easily and effectively made. A surprising amount of detail is transferred, including grain configuration, and of course dimension can be gauged very accurately from the ensuing cast. Undercutting can be a problem, but this can be assessed by eye and by measurement. I acquired some dental casting plaster recently, which sets to a very hard and very fine finish. No release agent is required, the loss of the mould being the only disadvantage of this method. To my knowledge Plasticene will cause no damage; however, it is always prudent to test on an inconspicuous area that the procedure will work.

A number of other factors come in: choice of wood; grain direction; colouring; whether the repair can be reversed — how will you tie the new to the old? Choice of adhesive/fixing is important. The major concern, however, is the actual carving. First, 'read' the original carving, remembering that the craftsman who executed the job will have followed the fundamental carver's axiom 'Fit the job to the tools'. By observing the gouge cuts, you can work out the tools used and, with some practice, can identify the procedure gone through, particularly for repetition jobs. Second, there is inevitably only so much that can be done on the workbench; the rest must follow in situ. Extra material must be left, when in doubt, so judicious paring can be done to blend in the job. Great care and constant anticipation is involved to avoid damage to the original, or indeed to your own work.

In short, restoration requires ingenuity and fortitude — much of it *before* the tools are picked up!

Jim Donaldson

---

**Q** *I live near a large NATO air base on which many American servicemen and their families live. Quite a few have their own furniture shipped over, and I get called upon to give estimates for the repair of damage which has occurred in transit. Much of the furniture is finished in what appears to be a medium-dark lacquer under which are small spots of dark brown, which look as if they have been applied by flicking a brush at the item. I would be grateful if you could give me any information on this finish, how it is applied and how best to repair small areas.*

R. Hessian, Bicester

**A** This finish is a 'distressed' one called 'splattering'. It is one of a number of ways of simulating age on a new surface, and is common in reproduction furniture. If properly carried out, it gives a very pleasing effect and helps to tone down and mellow machine-made furniture. The method can also be used in antique restoration, but it has to be done very carefully as one can easily get carried away and over-do the spots.

There are three main ways of spattering; it's best to try them out on a spare piece of hardboard until you achieve the effect you want. In all three cases, start by mixing up your chosen pigment to a creamy consistency with cellulose thinners and a little matt lacquer as a binder, and strain the mixture through a metal sieve or nylon stocking.

The first method is to take a piece of wood about 10x2x1in and put it on the piece, close to the area which you wish to spatter, then dip a 1in long-haired used bristle paintbrush into the pigment mixture and knock the ferrule of the brush on to the wood — making the pigmented mixture spot or spit on to the surface.

The second method is simply to take the paintbrush loaded with the mixture and flick the tips of the bristles, making the mixture spatter across the surface. This is a little messy, so remember to warn anyone in the work area to stand well clear!

The best and easiest method is to use a quality spraygun with an inbuilt attachment to give a fully-controlled spatter effect — including the frequency of the spots!

Some very interesting effects can be obtained by experimenting with various pigments in combination — brown umber, green and metallic gold, for instance.

When you have finished the spattering to blend in with the existing finish, allow it to dry, lightly sand down with Lubrisil 320-grade paper or 0000 steel wool; then spray two coats of clear cellulose lacquer over it, allowing it to dry between coats, to seal it completely. Use either gloss or semi-gloss; complete the job in the normal way.

I have found it useful when repairing small areas of damage on site to finish with a clear cellulose aerosol lacquer, obtainable either from Sonneborn & Rieck Ltd, 91-95 Peregrine Rd, Hainault, Middx, or W. S. Jenkins & Co Ltd, Tariff Rd, London N17.

Noel Leach

---

**Q** *I have an outside stair made with soft-wood posts and stringers and hardwood treads. I have had much trouble with the softwood rotting, and I now plan to re-build the stair – replacing all the softwood with oak while keeping the existing treads.*

*Asking for a quotation, I've been told that 12ft posts in 4x4in oak are not obtainable. I believe that it is not good practice to splice posts. Can you please tell me:*

● *Whether I can get oak posts of this size?*

● *Whether I should be considering some other timber?*

● *If I splice the posts, what sort of joint I should use? And would it matter where the splice was? My instinct would be to splice above the landing level so that the main downward thrust is on unjoined timber, but I know nothing about stress. Does the length of post above the landing, tied by handrails, give any structural strength?*

R. M. H. Smith, London SW14

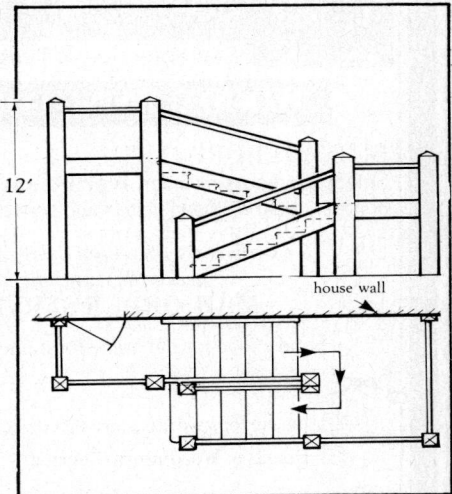

house wall

12'

**A** Constructionally, there is no objection to splicing these newel-posts. The only force applied to them would be in compression, so plain butt-splices would be the ones to use, with a couple of bolts through each — and it wouldn't matter whether above or below the landing.

However, any such joint used externally will 'catch the weather', and long before it has time to dry out the rain will come along again, so that it will be perpetually wet. This of course will prove detrimental to any

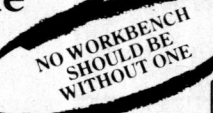

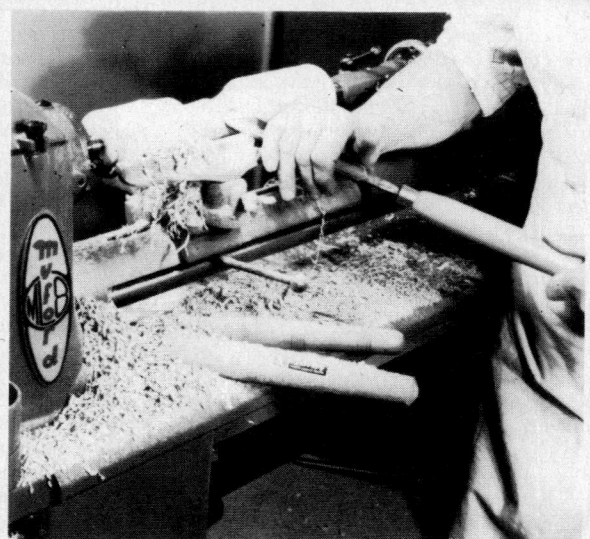
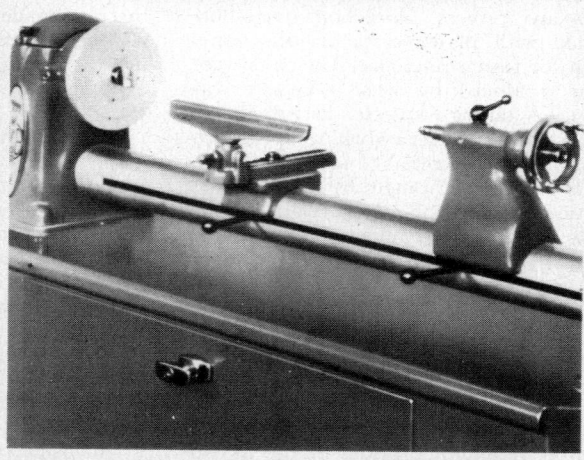

# Question box

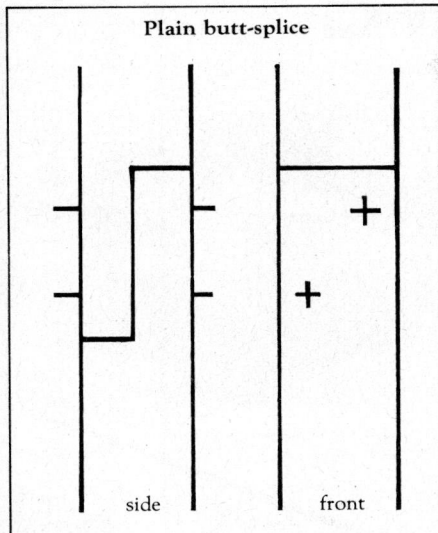

**Plain butt-splice**

side         front

ironwork — the bolts will rust, and this will induce rot around them. This would apply to any timber except teak; particularly oak, as this has a natural tendency to rust iron even under normal conditions. Splicing, therefore, should be ruled out in this situation.

There is a not uncommon belief that, if timber is hard, it is also durable; but this is not necessarily so. Beech, for example, is as hard as oak, but it is totally unsuitable for any work that is to be exposed to the weather; as also is parana pine.

It is not surprising that you are having difficulty in obtaining 12ft lengths of 4x4in oak. Why should this be so? The oak hammer-beams of Westminster Hall are each 22ft long and 22x22in in section. But the sad fact remains; oak of these dimensions is indeed virtually unobtainable. If it were available, you'd need, together with the material for the strings, about 8cu ft, at about £20 per cube. As an alternative hardwood, I would suggest iroko, with a full-width tie-rod under every fourth tread or so.

However, were I doing this job for myself, I'd go for good-quality red deal, well pre-soaked in preservative. The thing to watch here is 'blue stain'; this is a fungus that grows in the sapwood, which is also the part of 'red' that always rots. It attracts woodworm, too. If you could get selected red deal, free from sapwood, and soak it in preservative, I feel that your problem would be solved. After all, most railway sleepers were made of it; and you don't have to use creosote nowadays.

What are the objections, I wonder, to covering-in the stairs — a light structure with sheets of plastic? A staircase has so many joints to soak up water. Concerning the handrails above the landing: yes, these do of course give structural strength to the newels.

*Stan Thomas*

**Q** *At 54 I am taking early retirement from teaching woodwork. To supplement my pension, and for the sake of interest, I would like to set up on my own. Would a shed make a suitable workshop for woodwork and french-polishing?*

*I have been quoted £5000 for a brick, wood and glass garage/workshop 22x15ft, and it's more than I can afford. So I'm considering a large shed on a concrete base with a damp-proof course. Perhaps it could be insulated on the inside, and then panelled with hardboard. Would such a structure be warm enough for polishing and to keep upholstery material dry? My plan would be to section off one part for polishing and the other for bench and machinery.*

*I'm looking for something purpose-built, but I don't feel I could do the job myself as it might take for ever!*

*Jack Barratt, Woldingham, Surrey*

**A** Congratulations on your retirement, and best wishes for the future. Your intentions raise a need for careful thought and planning. *Running a Workshop*, published by the Crafts Council (12 Waterloo Place, London SW1Y 4AU) at £3.95 excl. p&p, will repay detailed study, as will the *Guide to Self-Employment* published by the Cornmarket Careers Centre (42-3 Conduit St, London W1R 0NL).

As for your premises, the cost of a traditional brick building is certainly prohibitive; moreover, it would probably need planning permission and add to your rateable value. Your alternative proposal is sound and should fulfil your requirements. Unfortunately there isn't enough space here to give you a detailed specification; but a simple sectional lean-to design can be found in Charles Hayward's *Carpentry* (Hodder & Stoughton).

However, I know from experience that it's difficult to match the commercial manufacturers' prices and if you want something ready-made you should search the Yellow Pages under 'Buildings, Sectional and Prefabricated'. A point to note is that many manufacturers do not include the floor in the basic price; nonetheless, you would be well advised to instal a timber or ¾in-T&G-chipboard floor laid on mastic or a plastic-sheet membrane over your concrete base. This will eliminate the dust that arises from concrete floors, prevent the penetration of damp, improve insulation and also save those accidentally dropped tools.

*Bob Grant DLC FSIA MSIAD*

**Q** *I bought a Coronet Major woodworking machine about 25 years ago. It has given me excellent service and been in almost constant use.*

*One of its accessories is an 8in wobble-saw. I have used this wobble-saw on numerous occasions, for cutting both wide, deep grooves up to about ⅞in wide by 1½in deep, and shallow, narrow grooves down to about ⅛in wide by 1/16in deep, both with and across the* grain, in hardwoods and softwoods; always with first-class results.

Recently, however, I had occasion to groove some chipboard along its edge, the groove being about ⅛in wide and ¼in deep. It coped with this quite well. As might have been expected, it became dull fairly quickly; the total length of material grooved was about 20ft, but during the last few feet the saw gave every indication that it needed re-sharpening. I set the saw at right-angles, topped the teeth in the usual manner and filed out the marks, keeping the tooth angle the same as it had been originally.

The next time I set the saw up to cut a groove ⅛in wide by 3/16in deep, cutting with the grain, the first few inches were fine – but then the wood started to drift away from the fence, to slide over the saw and to vibrate. Each fault got worse as the cut proceeded. I found the groove was burnt on both inside edges, and tended to narrow.

I have tried setting the teeth slightly and also increasing the angle on the top of them, but the fault persists. It's the same for all sizes of groove, with and across the grain in both hardwood and soft. What have I done to cause this problem? And what do I have to do to cure it?

*M. Nicklin, Wolverhampton*

**A** My first reaction was that you had mounted the saw backwards. However, if we dismiss this rather improbable explanation, the next thing to examine is the condition of the teeth.

Chipboard, being very abrasive, would not only blunt their tops but also round their fronts, and stoning and filing the tops would not be enough to restore a sharp point. The fronts of the teeth must be filed or ground to remove any rounding and restore a sharp, square edge. Also, if the saw has been sharpened many times the teeth may have lost any forward rake they once had. This would reduce efficiency, particularly when cutting along the grain.

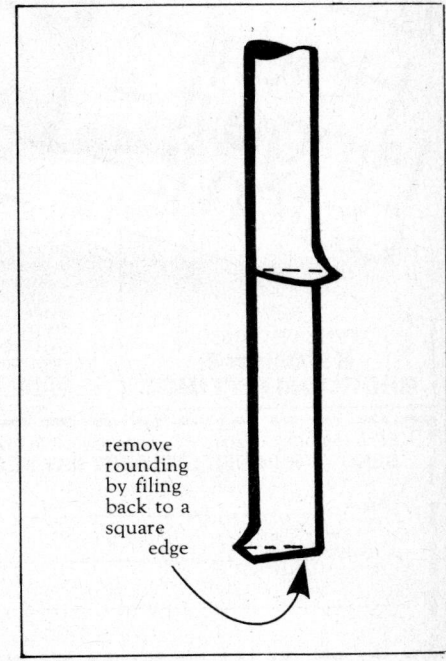

remove rounding by filing back to a square edge

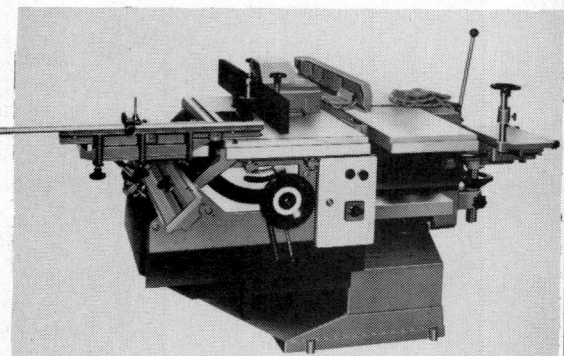

812

# Question box

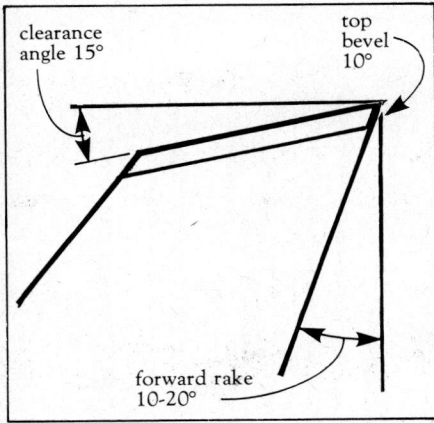

clearance angle 15°

top bevel 10°

forward rake 10-20°

Other factors which might be contributing are:
- A slipping drive belt;
- Loose pulleys on the motor shaft;
- Looseness of the saw on the arbor because build-up of resin or dust on the securing-nut threads is preventing them from being tightened properly;
- Loss of tension in the saw caused by overheating if it has been forced when cutting chipboard;
- Lack of alignment in the fence (too much toe-in), which would cause the material to bind at the back of the saw.

*Ken Taylor*

- We also asked saw specialists A. A. Smith of 63 Brighton Rd, Shoreham, Sussex BN4 6RE, for their comments. They said: 'Mr Nicklin's remarks lead us to think that the set is uneven, and that in sharpening he has taken more off some teeth than others. It is vital to maintain the same height and angle on every tooth. We can only suggest he takes his blade to a saw doctor's and gets them to re-sharpen and set it.'

**Q** *We have an elliptical-topped Victorian loo table (at least, that's what I think it is). It has four heavily fluted and moulded legs, and a centre pillar with deep gadrooning. It has been left in a shed for a year or two and the top has come unstuck. On one side, movement in the ground has ripped the burr-walnut veneer, and the veneer in one quarter has buckled, come unstuck and broken up into small pieces. Following this sad demise*
- *Is it possible to patch in the parts which have broken up, and how can I be sure of a good match?*
- *What's the best way to get the veneer off?*
- *I'm inclined to remove the veneer completely, re-glue the ground and lay new veneer – but would this devalue the piece?*

*Frank Coates, Bewdley*

**A** If it is a loo table (these were usually round, not oval) it's probably about 3ft in diameter. The problem you describe is very common and one which we often encounter in our workshops.

At the moment, the table is worth very little. Restored really well, it should regain about two-thirds of its worth in 'perfect condition'. If you're going to keep the table its value is immaterial, but its present condition doesn't make it an attractive piece of furniture in any case. So obviously the main problem in either case is the most suitable way of restoring it.

Most tables of this type and period have a groundwork of inexpensive whitewood, usually pine. Shrinkage means that the rubbed butt joints tend to break down and, of course, ruin the veneer on top. This problem is greatly exacerbated by central heating. It is very difficult to repair the split with the veneer still over it, to re-lay the area that has broken up, and to match new veneer to the existing in either figuring or thickness. So I agree that you would do well to lift the remaining veneer to give yourself a clear field.

This is not difficult and may be done in several ways, but I suggest you use steam. Assuming the surface is polished in some way, you'll speed the job up by cutting the polish back with a sharp cabinet-scraper. Lay two or three thicknesses of old sheet or similar material, well soaked and squeezed out, on the area to be tackled first. With a domestic iron set at a medium temperature, start at one edge, pressing the iron down to generate plenty of steam into the veneer. (If the iron has a steam setting, so much the better.) Once the veneer is really hot and wet, carefully ease it up with the point of a knife, and follow this up with a 1 or 2in paint scraper. As long as the generation of steam is kept up, the veneer should lift quite easily. (If the figuring is particularly good and you can use it on something in the future, try and lift the veneer in as large a sheet or sheets as possible. To store it, press it for 24 hours between two sheets of wood, with plastic on the surfaces to prevent the veneer sticking to the wood — and don't leave it longer, as mould may develop.)

Once all the veneer has been lifted, go over the surface with a damp cloth and a scraper to remove any scraps of veneer and remnants of glue.

The broken joints in the groundwork can now be repaired — using, of course, a compatible adhesive such as pearl glue; do not, on any account, use a PVA or other modern adhesive unless all the joint surfaces are cleaned off completely down to bare wood. To strengthen the repair you might consider letting in a couple of butterfly joints on the underside.

It is obvious that you are capable of quarter-veneering the top with new veneer in the accepted manner, but again I would stress the importance of using animal glue. The old surface should need little preparation other than cleaning off and light sanding — old glue remaining in the wood will help to key in the new work.

The new surface should be stained to match the original colour and the rest of the table, and french-polished. After that the job should be looking very much better than it does at the moment!

*David Ellis*

**Here it comes – and we hope you're coming! Show organiser Mary White previews the big, beautiful event of the year**

Last autumn's Woodworker Show doesn't seem a year ago. It drew the crowds, it offered masses to intrigue and delight, it was the largest and most successful yet — and it displayed not just the **tools, machines and materials** available but also the skills achieved by the craftsmen and women who entered the **competitions.**

Yet the signs are that the 1985 Show is going to be bigger, better and even more fascinating. The very heart of the exhibition, the competition classes, promises to be a show that will hold you spellbound, leaving you with an overwhelming feeling of admiration at the skills, dedication and effort of those who create such pieces of work in the pursuit of excellence rather than (in most cases) money.

For the prizewinners — whose selection the judges find more difficult each year — there are medals, cups and sponsored awards. To encourage and promote woodturners and woodcarvers, Henry Taylor Tools Ltd are sponsoring both the turning and carving classes. Each winner will receive £250 in cash, plus a silver rose bowl. Roger's of Hitchin have donated a £100 voucher for the junior winner and a set of 10 chisels for the best young professional. £250 again is the prize collected, in any class, by the entry with the best finish — with the compliments of English Abrasives. The annual Ashley Iles Competition, whose subject this year is 'Creatures of the Forest', will provide vouchers for £75, £50 and £25 to be spent with the Lincolnshire-based company, who have sponsored the award.

In the past, competition entries have been exhibited on trestle tables. This year a more attractive display will ensure that all of them, prizewinners or not, will be presented in a more attractive way — to the high standard such work deserves.

The show's **demonstrators**, together with several **colleges** and **societies**, will be more than delighted to answer your questions on their particular subjects. Musical-instrument making by the charismatic Zach Taylor, advice on joinery and on sharpening and renovating tools by Stan Thomas, and the skills of Windsor chairmaker and well-known author of many craft books Jack Hill, are all offerings not to be missed. And, if you'd like to see woodcarving demonstrated, Maurice Lund — a past winner at the show — will be very pleased to show you expert techniques. Your questions on restoration will willingly be answered by Charles Cliffe, who takes courses for the **Guild of Woodworkers.**

The Guild itself will be running a stand where you can find out exactly why and how you should join — while inspecting a stunning display of members' work. The Tool and Trades History Society will be

● *Buoyed by success last year, Bill Watts has entered this bracket clock in bubinga*

available to discuss hand tools and their uses (old and new) and will be demonstrating traditional woodworking methods. The Institute of Carpenters, Buckinghamshire College and Shrewsbury College will also be represented. Students from Merton Technical College and Central Manchester College will actually be demonstrating what their courses offer.

Ever significant name on the **retail** and **manufacturing** side of woodworking will be represented amongst the trade stands. With so many of them demonstrating too, there's no better place than the Woodworker Show to see, in use, the particular tool or machine you're thinking of buying. So many companies are exhibiting that I can't mention them all; showing for the first time, however, will be timbermen Abrams & Mundy, Apollo Products with their lathes, Brimarc Ltd, CZ Scientific (UK), Clico (Sheffield) Tooling Ltd, Chronos Ltd, Quality Tools & Machinery Ltd, and Scott & Sargeant.

In addition, your **editors** (esteemed or otherwise) will be very happy to meet and talk with you if you can catch them as they whizz around — trying to chat with all the people they haven't seen since last year. To get hold of Peter or Aidan, stop in at the Guild stand — or at the *Woodworker* **magazine stand**, which is worth a call in itself. It'll be offering the enticement of a

● *Among the furniture displayed for your critical (likely) approving gaze will be this oak Windsor c Michael Perryman of Redhill, Surrey*

**WHAT E TIMBE USER SHOULD BE GETTING MORE OI**

**prize draw** open to all who buy any of its wares: that includes a host of related books and, of course, present and back issues of this very publication.

The winners will be getting an AEG SAR320 bandsaw worth no less than £430+VAT; an AEG FSTE60 jigsaw worth £99+VAT; an AEG ABS10RL cordless drill/screwdriver worth £89+VAT; an AEG SBE420RL electronic reversible drill worth £54.95+VAT — and a Eumenia radial-arm saw from Warren Machine Tools, complete with a stand and extension which brings its value to £458+VAT. That makes a stunning total of £1300 in prizes... You owe it to yourself to pay *Woodworker* a call! ∎

**Alexandra Pavilion, London N22, Thursday 24 October to Sunday 27 October incl.; 10-6 (till 5 on Sunday). Admission £3, children and OAPs £2. Enquiries to Argus Specialist Exhibitions Ltd, Wolsey House, Wolsey Rd, Hemel Hempstead, Herts, tel. (0442) 41221**

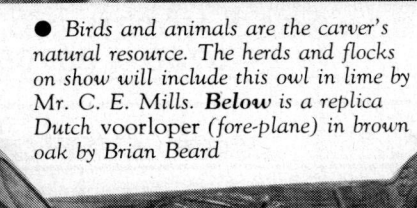

● *Birds and animals are the carver's natural resource. The herds and flocks on show will include this owl in lime by Mr. C. E. Mills.* **Below** *is a replica Dutch* voorloper *(fore-plane) in brown oak by Brian Beard*

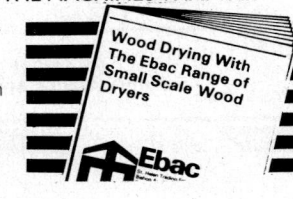

816

# Carved life styles!

'I like organic shapes,' says **Stefan Bruggisser**, 'inspired by nature or the nature of feelings in relationships and personal situations.' Stefan's interpretation of 'The Kiss' in mountain spruce (*right*) conveys a personal closeness much more spiritual than physical, *writes Aidan Walker*. Stefan sees himself as a sculptor, and wood is his favourite medium. He has a background in molecular biology and boatbuilding, among other things.

**Vera Feldman** from Birmingham describes herself as 'just an ordinary house-wife'. Her spiral form (*bottom right*) is the result of a suggestion of her car-enthusiast son's — 'Why don't you carve a car-spring?' She described her introduction to woodcarving in April's *Woodworker*, with engagingly fresh modesty and enthusiasm. She uses photos and drawings from nature books as guides; her obvious feel for wood and wildlife have needed no formal schooling, though she does cite 'Spock' Morgan as a respected mentor. The bear, sycamore mice and mahogany weasel are also hers.

Different lives (Stefan is a Swiss living in New South Wales); different styles. But there is no question that these widely disparate characters share a common love; for wood, for working it, and for finding life in it that really lives! ∎

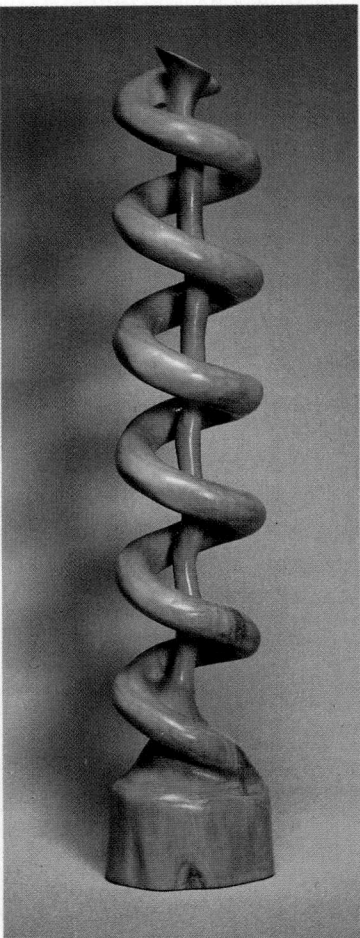

# Guild notes

## Guild of WOODWORKERS

Shared information, advice and help are vital to good woodwork. They are also the basis of the **Guild of Woodworkers**: an international organisation which welcomes new members — whatever their skills. 1 Golden Sq, London W1R 3AB, tel. 01-437 0626.

Guild members get
- priority on our courses
- free publicity in *Woodworker*
- 15% off Woodworker Show entry
- a free display area and meeting-point at the Show
- 15% discount on our plans
- access to and inclusion in our register of members' skills and services
- the chance to contact other members for help and advice where appropriate
- specially arranged tool insurance at low rates

Please quote your Guild number when contacting us.

*Aidan Walker*

## Show up!

If you're reading this on the day the magazine comes out, and so far have failed to notice the fact, the Woodworker Show is next week (24-7 October). Why not plan to be there? Look at the wonderful range of members' work on the Guild/*Woodworker*

● *This eye- and mind-boggling piece of carving is by* **Stanley Kimm** *of Harrow. It's 3½in in diameter and consists of no less than* **six** *balls, carved from a single piece of lime. Ogle it for yourself on the Guild stand at the Woodworker Show, where this and other wonderful work by members will be on display*

stand, and eat your heart out that you didn't take the chance to show your stuff free . . . Meet the man who could be your local rep at 4.30pm on Saturday 26 October at the stand . . . Gawp at the wonders **Eric Burger** performs on fine old furniture (he'll be demonstrating on the stand on Saturday and Sunday) . . . And take the chance to bend my ear about what the Guild is and isn't doing, and what it should and shouldn't be doing. Other prominent members, names familiar to regular readers, can be met at the Show too, and are ready to have their brains picked about their respective specialities; **Charles Cliffe** will be demonstrating french polishing, and **Stan Thomas** will be there to set you right on insoluble brain-teasers of joinery, cabinetmaking and tool care.

## Timber treat

'I have a friend', writes **Giles Washbourn**, 'who has collected bog oak from the Fens. He has had it cut and has a very limited supply, some of which he is prepared to sell. It is still not fully air-dried, so it can be worked. There are sections 2in sq x 24in, and ¼in planks about 24x6in. The price will have to be fixed according to each individual piece's quality. I have turned a few pieces and it's a treat to work at the moment. It's good for inlay, and small pieces will do for necklaces or something similar.'

Drooling? Phone 0638 78 854 to make a deal.

## Insure for sure

The Guild's tool insurance scheme is due for renewal the week *Woodworker* comes out (18 October). Comprehensive cover for tools, wherever they may be — does that not sound attractive? As good a reason as any for joining, I'd say. If you want to benefit from this scheme, please note it's renewed *in toto* once a year — if you joined in July, you'd still have to pay a year's premium for just a couple of months' insurance. So do the sensible thing: write for a proposal form now!

## Spring fancy

Nice to think of spring before we plummet into the depths of winter . . . the Winter Gardens in Blackpool are mounting the Spring Gifts and Fancy Goods Exhibition in February, the time when we really need that hint of lambs and daffodils. If you fancy selling your work through such an event (which, the organisers promise, will be distinguished by enticements like free exhibitors' lunches and evening buffet dances), spring into action and write to Lesley Hall, Winter Gardens, Church St, Blackpool, Lancs FY1 3PL, tel. (0253) 25252.

## Furniture repair and refinishing — Ian Hosker

9-10 November, Chester, £40+VAT. A different emphasis from Ian's first french-polishing course; bring your own piece to work on this time, and let us know what it is and what you want to do with it before you book. Don't worry if you haven't got something you want to repair, Ian will have a selection of pieces to demonstrate techniques and let you have a go. You'll be repairing and replacing all kinds of joints, mending and splicing broken bits, lifting and replacing veneers and marquetry, stripping, staining, re-polishing and distressing. Bring your hand tools, especially G-cramps if you have them.

## Power routing — Roy Sutton

8 February 1986, Herne Bay, £25+VAT. If everything you wanted or needed to know about routing could be taught in one day, Roy would undoubtedly be your man. We're very pleased to add his massive experience and skill to the Guild's re-sources. Instruction is from first principles and will include housing, grooving, rebat-ing, mortising, tenoning, circular work, templates, followers, jigs and other tech-niques too numerous to mention. The price covers a buffet lunch and materials for a small project you make to take away.

## Wood-machining — Ken Taylor

7 December, Bletchley, £25+VAT. Apart from illustrious qualifications and experience that include making Mosquitoes during the war and managing the works at Wrighton Kitchens, Ken also lectures in this subject at the London College of Furniture and has acted as our consultant on *Machining Wood*, the extensive series that begins this month. Spend a day with him circular-sawing, bandsawing, planing and thicknessing, spindle-moulding and mortising; get to grips with safe workshop practice, uses and construction of jigs, and the relative merits of different kinds of machinery.

## Cane and rush seating — Betty Fowler

6-8 December, Longdon, Gloucestershire, £70+VAT. A busy three days in which to cover the different styles and patterns of cane and rush work, and make up a seat of your own, guided by Betty's expertise. She is a teacher of 11 years' experience, and takes on numerous seating commissions from round about and far afield; when I first met her she'd just spent some days standing in the River Avon with her husband Henry picking the season's raw material! Bring your own chair, de-caned and repaired, sturdy and ready for seating; if it's small (less than 12in across the front) bring two and you might get both done.

We have the chance on this course to enjoy some **luscious catering** — chicken à la king and syllabub served during a chair-caning course? No kidding; but the only way is to do it for everyone or no one, so **tell me when you book** whether you're prepared to spend an extra £15 for three days' worth of morning coffee and biscuits, mouthwatering lunches, afternoon tea and cakes. There'll also be time to do some work, of course!

● *Betty Fowler (right) starts work on yet another commission; all the rushes she uses are locally grown and picked. Take advantage of her skills, plus a bonus of first-class food, in Gloucestershire – 6-8 December*

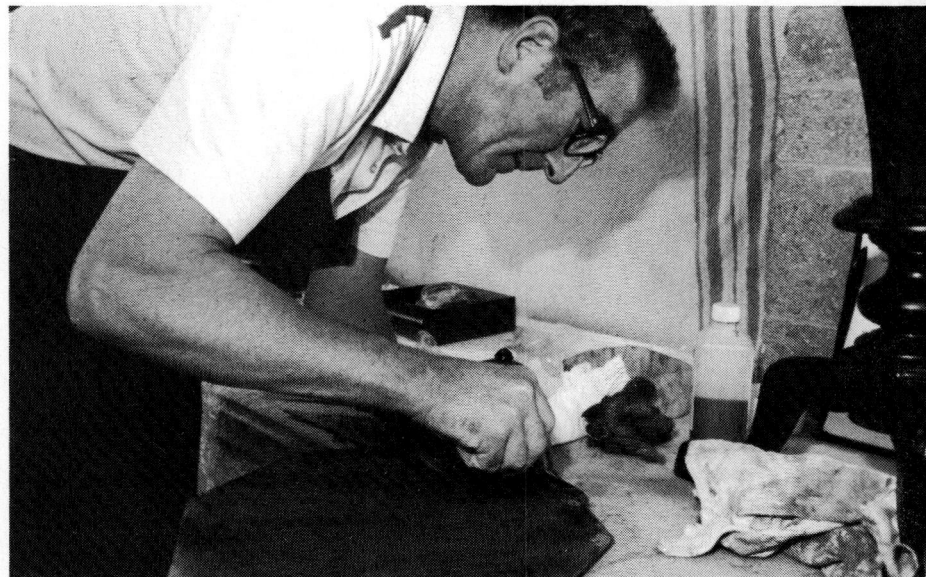

● *Stripping, wire-wooling, filling, touching in, re-staining and polishing; all these and other tricks and techniques are there for the learning in Bournemouth, 17-19 January. Bring your own piece with its own problems!*

## Furniture restoration — Eric Burger

17-19 January 1986, Bournemouth, £70+VAT. Three days' worth of meticulous work and detailed instruction from this highly-respected professional, who also teaches evening classes in Bourne-mouth. The extra day allows time for repairing and re-finishing your own piece, delving the while into the mysteries of veneering, repairing joints and components, veneers and carvings, staining, colouring-in and matching, french polish-ing and even a little bit of gilding. The scope is wide, and there's unlikely to be a problem that'll stump Eric.

# Bench marks

**Adrian Booth went to see a young rural craftsman with an old-time passion for perfection**

'I decided to set up my business in the country away from London,' says David Salisbury 'and I began looking for the ideal place — minimum mortgage, space for a workshop on the premises to keep overheads down, and not stuck in the middle of nowhere. In the end I forced the pace by giving in my notice and devoting all my time to the search.'

Throwing in a job to set up a rural woodworking business is no light decision for a young man with a growing family, but taking the plunge — for David, at least — seems to have worked. He found a house with land and out-houses in the picturesque medieval city of Wells in Somerset, and set himself to the first task: building a workshop.

'When we moved here this was the goat shed.' David surveys his workspace; 'My future workshop was dark, damp and full of soggy manure. It was so damp after I'd cleaned it out that a chisel would go rusty in six hours!'

For the first couple of months the space was unusable. The earth outside was higher than the floor level, a major cause of damp which David remedied by digging a trench and draining the water into a field behind. He cured leaks in the roof and insulated it.

Luckily the 50-year-old shed had a damp-proof course, so David painted bitumen on the inside wall up to that level to hold back the damp. Although the process was very labour-intensive, it only cost about £300. And then the waiting game began. Drying out can take a long time, but there was one thing in his favour; the drought of '84 was not welcomed by his farming neighbours, but it did speed up the drying!

The workshop is still damper than he would like, and there are plans to insulate the floor and instal two stoves. One will burn sawdust and shavings, the other off-cuts and logs — much cheaper heat than the dreaded electricity. 'Last year I used an electric fire to heat the workshop, and that proved very expensive.'

But how can you earn a living when you're waiting for your workshop to dry out? 'I went out and bought a very cheap cupboard, and made it airtight with very tight-fitting strips of thin batten round all the seals. I put silica-gel crystals in it, and it became my tool-cupboard. It worked very well. It meant I could keep my tools — which I sprayed with WD40 — in the workshop before it dried out, and that meant I could use the space. Timber had to be stored in the house, though, and gluing-up had to be done there too.'

● *David's intent expression shows how seriously he takes the sharpness of his tools. This hand-cranked grindstone is after a Krenov idea; he has a device of his own for machine planer irons*

The David Salisbury bench idea grew from his own need for a solid workbench. The result made him think there may well be a market for high-quality benches among dedicated craftsmen or professional people with discerning tastes and a woodworking hobby. That first bench was made almost exclusively by hand, planing great lumps of beech on a Workmate! Later ones came easier; he is now making as many as four a month as well as his other commissions, and at £500 apiece that's no mean feat.

The materials for each bench cost over £200, and woodworkers appreciate their sturdy construction and raw-linseed-oil finish. The beech is kiln-dried; joints are wedged mortises, dovetails and strategically-placed bolts. Cascamite is the main glue, but PVA is used on the legs, which must be able to take movement.

As soon as David had a bench to work on he was ready for business. He advertised in a local free-sheet, and got a commission almost immediately to make an odd-sized door. It's quite a common task in the area, as his rural neighbours rarely seem able to buy doors of obscure dimensions off the shelf. 'The first job was totally underpriced — I only made about 50p on it! I've kept the local ad running since then, and I've had more than enough work since. Now I'm beginning to be able to choose the work I want to do, I want to separate the more lucrative jobs from those that will give me the greatest personal satisfaction.'

David had turned his hand to a number of occupations before discovering his passion for fine carpentry. He has a degree

● *The original airtight tool cupboard, displaying a loving attention to detail that belies its outward appearance!*

in particle physics and has been a deep-sea diver in the Arabian Gulf, but it was when he was working with mentally handicapped people in a residential hostel that he was first gripped with carpentry's possibilities.

'It was my job to interest the people in the hostel in something, and carpentry was introduced as therapy. I'm a bit of a perfectionist really, and I suppose I wasn't that impressed with their efforts. So I built a small cupboard, and was very pleased with the results. I began reading all I could on the subject.

'From then on I became somewhat obsessed. I used all my spare time to learn more, and then I got to know Michael Reed, who runs a high-class cabinetmaking business in Notting Hill. He put me to work in my spare time. For two years I was doing a shift at the hostel and half a shift for Michael, and in the end things came to a head. I was enjoying the cabinetmaking more than the social work.' The period was very useful, says David, for learning workshop practice and the way to use machines.

When he set up the workshop, David already had a Kity 10in planer/thicknesser, an Elu MOF96 router and a Black & Decker hand-held circular saw that cost about £35 and is still in use. Now he has added a 12-speed heavy-duty Eastern drill-press which he is very pleased with. 'The same basic machine comes under lots of different names . . . I suppose it's much more heavy-duty than I need just for drilling holes, but it's surprisingly accurate.'

He also has a Craftsman 10in radial-arm saw. 'It's often not as accurate as I'd like it to be,' he comments. 'Not that I'm saying anything against the machine, it's just the way a radial-arm saw works — hanging off an extended arm, you're bound to get some play from side to side. But the great thing is you can adjust everything on it. You're *intended* to adjust everything, which I think is good.'

He has now added a heavier router, a Hitachi TR12, which he uses mounted in a table he built with its own dust-extractor. David has a crafty method of using the router for awkward squaring jobs like the bottoms of doors. 'I use my router with a 2in bit. As long as you have an accurately clamped guide you can't go wrong. It's particularly useful on a door because you often don't have the space for a blade to run true.' An Elektra-Beckum dust extractor ('The cheapest I could get!') completes his machinery.

'The first thing I had to do was to customise the Kity,' he says. 'I wasn't happy with the trueness of the table, so I had to grind it flat. I didn't really know what I needed when I bought the Kity; I find it a bit light for the heavy benches I make. What I really need is a planer that can machine a whole benchtop at a time.'

I particularly liked the simple roller-stands that David knocked up from deal and plywood, with wing-nuts, roller bearings and light-alloy tubing. They extend the planer/thicknesser and allow him to handle longer lengths. 'Now I have the rollers I can come straight off the planer to glue. That's a step forward — before I had them I had to plane the edges again.'

Nor was the planer the only tool he's modified to meet his own sense of perfec-

● *How many people 'just knock up' a stand with the roller set in a dovetail channel for height adjustment?*

tion. He's also ground flat the soles of all his hand-planes. It's a laborious process involving a sheet of plate glass and carborundum powders; 'I start with 150, and take it down to 400,' he says, adding that a no. 6 fore-plane takes him about six hours to grind. But the difference is quite remarkable; planing becomes a joy, provided of course that the blade itself is sharp.

'Keeping my tools sharp is something of an obsession,' he admits. For sharpening chisels and hand-plane blades, he has adapted a method of Krenov's. He uses a hand-cranked grindstone, so there's no chance of burning the metal; a block of wood is cut to a 30° angle for chisels, but a wedge can be inserted beneath it to make that 35° for planes.

'This system takes just 30 seconds. I've modified the design to include a sliding tool guide, which I find very useful. Then you just have to touch it up on the India stone.'

David proceeded to show me just how sharp his tools are. Taking his favourite 2in beveled chisel, he demonstrated how easily he could pare a piece of beech. Substantial shavings came away from the cutting edge, much as a knife might slice the local cheddar. 'Many people think when you're

planing endgrain, you either have to clamp the edges with a block of wood or chamfer them to stop break-out. You don't need to do that if your tools are sharp enough.' Lubricating the sole of the plane with a little oil ('Wax would do'), David shaved the endgrain of a piece of rough-sawn beech. Announcing that you could even use the plane to polish the endgrain, he took the blade finer and finer until the surface was smooth and shiny. After close inspection I had to admit that the sides of the timber showed no split grain at all.

I found David's method of sharpening his planer blades fascinating. 'This is my own invention,' he said, moving to the radial-arm saw. He removed the saw blade, replacing it with a cup grinding-wheel with spacers to take up the difference in bore. He produced a beech block with angled slots in it, into which he inserted the planer blades. 'It's set at 40°,' he said, turning the radial arm through 90° so the cup grinding-wheel met the blades. 'You push the block through against the guide like any piece of timber, and then give the blades a rub on the India stone. I've just bought a set of tungsten-carbide irons. Machining great quantities of beech means you spend a lot of time changing blades — one set for every bench for me. The tungsten irons will help there.'

Ornate gates for a country estate, free-standing bookcases, cupboards, built-in shelf units, and lots of odd-shaped doors; the Salisbury workshop has plenty of work. I asked him frankly if he is surviving and whether the move has been worthwhile. 'I'm working 70 hours a week and we haven't had a holiday for a long time, but yes, I am surviving. If things don't get better it won't have been worthwhile, but I feel reasonably confident that I'll be able to get more and more commissions I want to do. I don't always want to have to compete on a price basis. I want people to come to me because my work is of a high standard, not because I'm the cheapest. I'm confident that the future holds a steady increase in the quality of my commissions, while sales of the benches continue to pick up; then I may have to think about expanding.'

● David's address is Twinyards, Worth, Wells, Somerset BA5 1LW, tel. (0749) 72139. ∎

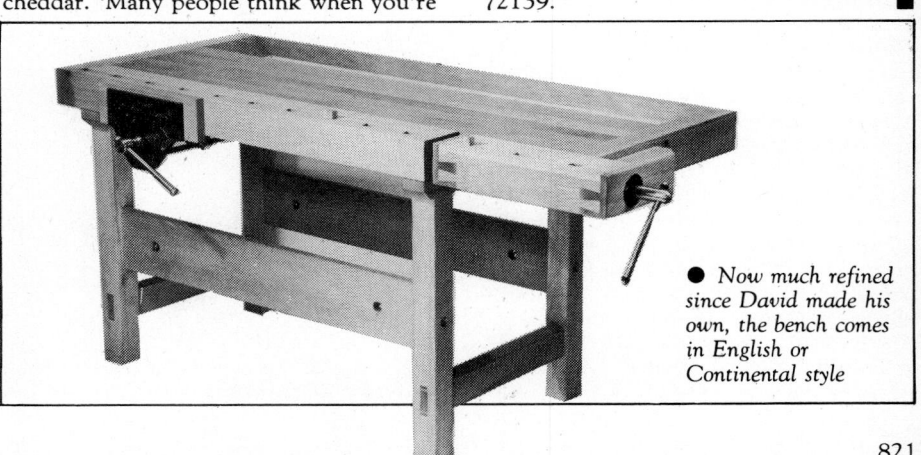

● *Now much refined since David made his own, the bench comes in English or Continental style*

# Nothing to show

**Editor Peter Collenette went to the Middlesex Poly exhibition. Here's his reluctant report**

● *The cover of the students' booklet reveals a certain attitude towards furniture . . .*

I've nothing against Daniel Reynolds. It's his 'wardrobe' that horrifies me.

The Middlesex Poly degree show was, in fact, a very unpleasant experience altogether. From spiky, spidery metal things to flimsy Wendy houses in cloth and gaudily painted plywood, the 18 students exhibiting offered almost nothing at all for the visitor's pleasure or comfort.

Well, all right. That depends on the visitor. Pleasure and even comfort are in the eyes and the life-style of the beholder and user — so I'm breaking a principle in making these criticisms and giving you my own impression. *Woodworker*'s main job is to show you what today's woodworkers are designing and making, and leave the judgements to you.

But that, of course, would make it a matter of statistics. Hands up all those who like the wardrobe.

I said, 'Hands up' . . .

No? Well, that raises the most provoking question: why do the people from Middlesex Poly (and there are quite a few like them) spend their time in making things that most other people hate?

A clue lies in the strange words with which the students announce themselves in their exhibition booklet. 'My work expresses my interest in interrelating geometric shapes. Geometry measures space and defines form both within my designs and around human beings.' 'My ideas derive from observations of natural phenomena which translate into functional, but unexpected, furniture.' Thus Jonathan Cross and Pip Brook respectively.

And, perhaps most revealingly, Stephen Horner: 'I approach each design anew, divorced from preconceptions.' That's an extraordinary thing to say. The idea that it's possible, let alone desirable, deliberately to make something without reference to the past is a peculiar product of the last mad 100 years or so.

Design, and design education, used mostly to consist of refining and combining the styles and patterns the age had inherited. On the face of it, a sensible way to ensure that furniture remained appealing and usable. Not a foolproof way, for success is never guaranteed and real talent is never common; but a working approach, and indeed one that's still in use.

Not at Middlesex Poly. Divorcing your preconceptions, like any divorce, means arguments, recriminations and trying to prove you're independent. It means trying to be different. And that's where conscious thought and fancy verbiage make their seductive entry. From then on, anything can happen.

Daniel's Neanderthal wardrobe, however, is perhaps even more than the worst of a bad bunch. It indicates a newly disturbing trend. Until now, good workmanship has been valued whatever the upheavals in design. That is, there's been little disagreement on what it involves, or on its desirability in theory. Any cheap work has resulted from tight prices, not funny ideas. But today's nihilism (that's nothing-ism) in design is infecting workmanship itself.

Daniel asserts: 'I have acknowledged the fact of human fallibility and used it as a definite tool, to help determine an aesthetic. The repetition of a basic geometric form by a human hand will inevitably produce variation. I have allowed wood to warp and split. Wood is wood.' Yes, and every step forward since the plank chests of the Middle Ages has helped to perfect the use of wood in ways that mean it need never split and never cause problems by warping. Those ways — framing-and-panelling, veneering, sophisticated carcase design — are taught to all serious woodworkers from school onwards. Now they're to be abandoned: not even to save money or time, but because of an idea.

Yet you can't sleep on an idea; you can't sit on it or keep your clothes in it. It won't furnish a room. And, if I had to choose between the idea of a square meal and a real plate of roast chicken, I know which I'd prefer. ■

● *. . . which is borne out by several of the pieces on show*

● *Daniel Reynolds' wardrobe doors are 'glazed' with kidney beans on wires. The cabinet below in yellow Perspex and ash by Briony Blyth (37 Dorset Rd SW8 1EH, 01-735 0298) talks a rather different language*

● **Left:** *Racked by geometry – Stephen Horner's drawing gives relaxation a new meaning*

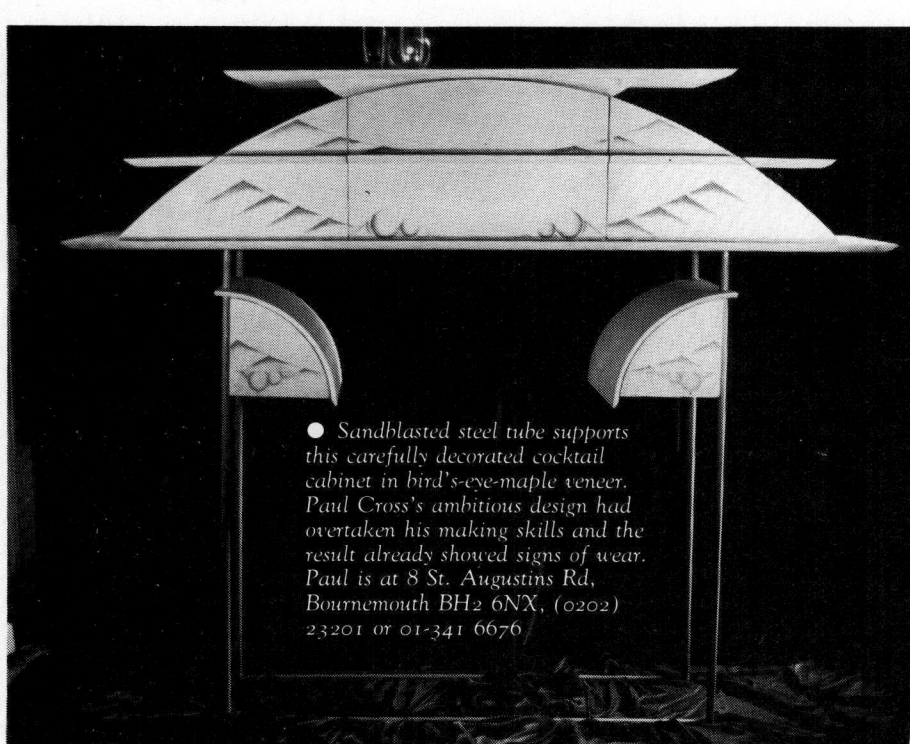

● *Sandblasted steel tube supports this carefully decorated cocktail cabinet in bird's-eye-maple veneer. Paul Cross's ambitious design had overtaken his making skills and the result already showed signs of wear. Paul is at 8 St. Augustins Rd, Bournemouth BH2 6NX, (0202) 23201 or 01-341 6676*

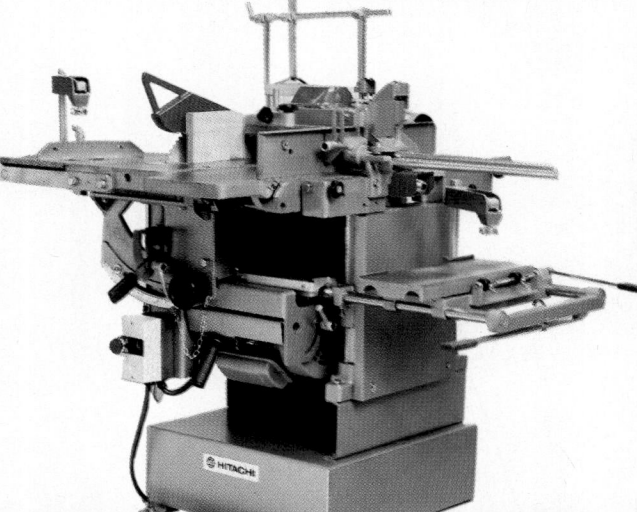
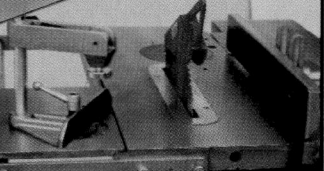

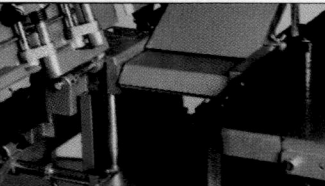

# Sliding peg-board

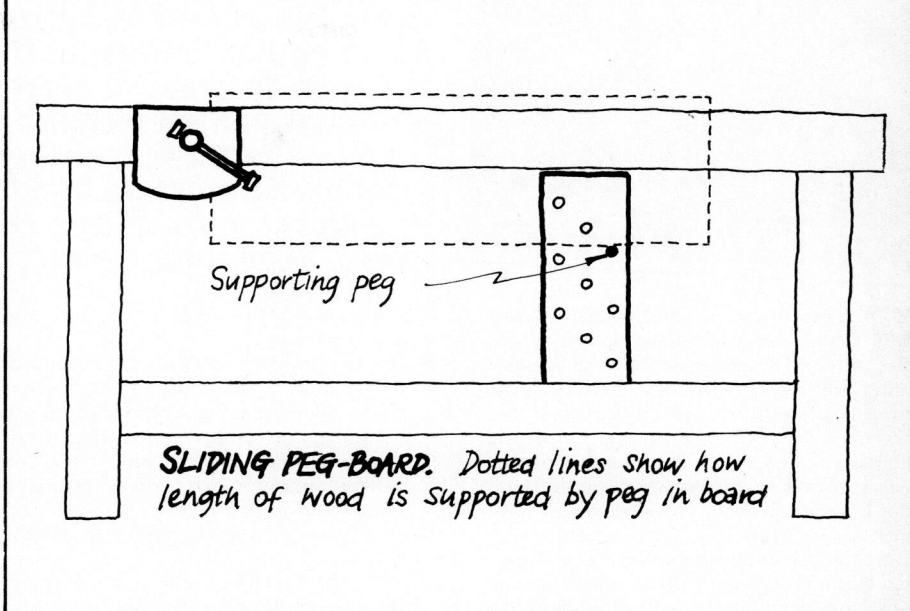

**SLIDING PEG-BOARD.** Dotted lines show how length of wood is supported by peg in board

I t frequently happens, writes **Charles Cliffe,** that a long board has to be gripped in the vice while you plane the edge. But unless both ends of the work are adequately supported it is impossible to plane the edge square and true. You can often provide such support simply yet effectively by fitting a sliding peg-board (fig. 1) between the upper and lower rails of the bench.

Grooves to accommodate tongues formed on the ends of the peg-board are worked on the lower edge of the bench top rail and on the upper edge of the lower rail. This will allow the board to slide the distance between the front legs of the bench, to support timbers of varying lengths.

If the upper groove is deeper than the lower, and the length of the peg-board slightly less than the distance between the grooves, you'll be able to remove the board if required. Holes are bored diagonally as shown, and a hardwood peg fitted into the appropriate hole supports the free end of the work. ∎

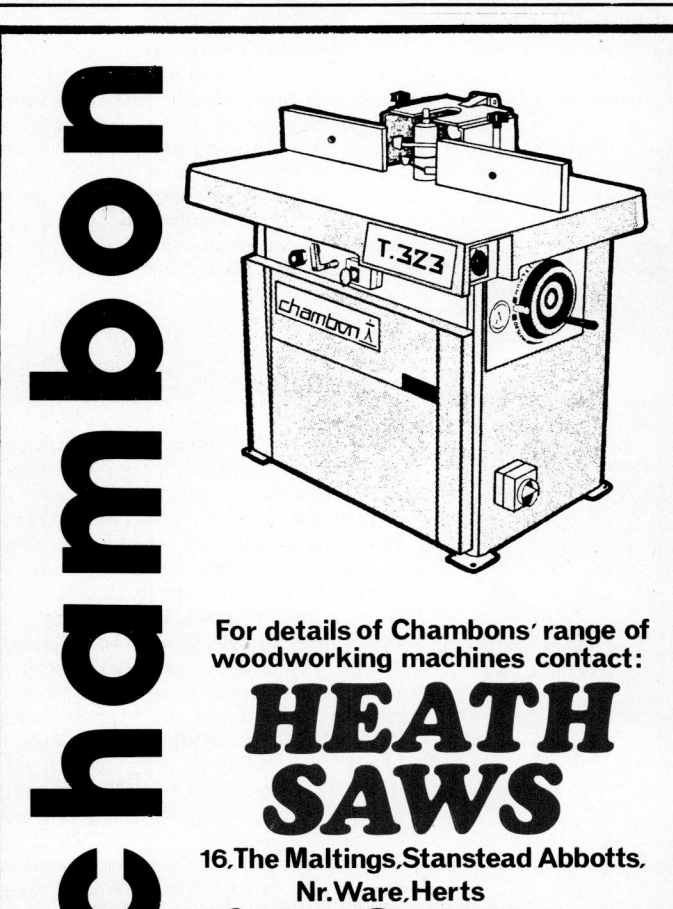
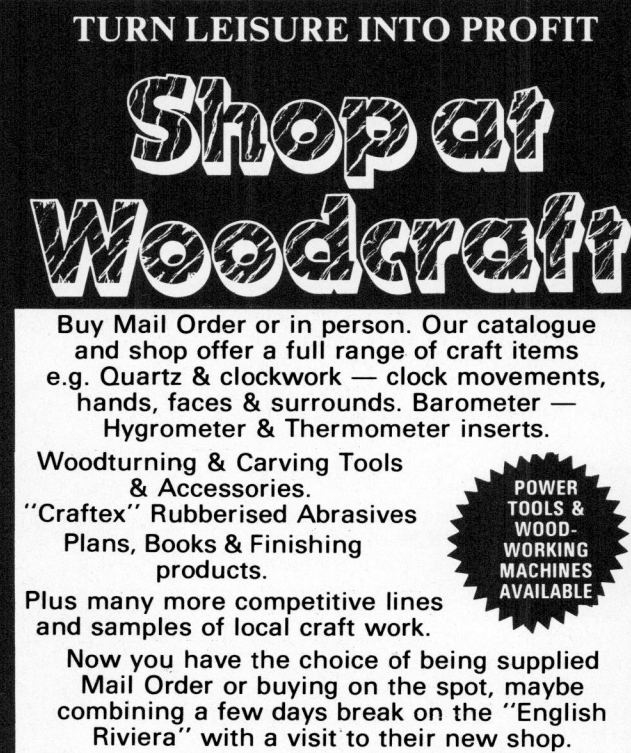

# MACHINING WOOD

## YOUR EXPERT GUIDE

# PART 1

Here it is at last: all you need to know about the basic equipment, what it does, how to use it safely and how to make it work for you – explained with plenty of pictures and in words you can understand. If you collect the monthly parts, you'll end up with your own complete handbook. We start with safety in general, plus a first encounter with circular saws. Here goes . . .

For centuries, men and women all over the world have been working in wood, either for enjoyment or to make a living. But never before has there been the same opportunity and incentive for Britain's woodworkers to combine business and pleasure. The harsh realities of recession and unemployment, coupled with rapid technological development, have created a unique situation where many competent woodworkers, fearing or suffering from redundancy from their normal jobs, are deciding to put their skills to commercial use.

Those who are turning their hobby into a profession recognise the need for machinery. Today's woodworking machines do boring, repetitive jobs quickly and easily, allowing the woodworker time to concentrate his or her energy on the tasks which call for creative skill; more than that, they open up possibilities and potential for your work that simply don't exist when you do everything by hand.

The prospective purchaser of a machine can be overcome with confusion in the fast-growing market, which is why *Woodworker* provides its readers with regular updates on machinery. But far more important even than buying the right machine is knowing how to use it best.

*Woodworker* is proud to present a series of articles on wood-machining. With photographs of demonstrations at Luna Tools and Machinery Ltd, these articles will explore the range of uses of the main types of woodworking machines, and offer advice on getting the most from machinery *safely*.

## Safety — the first priority

Statistics from the Health & Safety Executive show that some 90% of accidents at woodworking machines happen to the hands, and nearly one-third of them involve circular saws.

Although your hands are your first safety priority, don't under-estimate the value of your eyes and ears. Protect them whenever damage could be inflicted. Goggles or safety spectacles should *always* be worn while woodworking machines are in operation. You may be able to walk with a wooden leg, but you can't see with a glass eye! Always wear ear protectors too when noise levels prevent normal conversation. Some machines are worse than others, planers generally taking first prize for decibels, so use your common sense.

Some safety rules apply to any machine in any workshop.

● Avoid using machinery when you're tired;
● Never look or walk away from the machine when the blade and cutters are spinning, even after you've turned it off;
● Always isolate the machine from the power supply when you're changing blades and cutters;
● Always switch off when adjusting guards or fences;
● Always take a firm stance at the machine, usually one foot forward and one back, and try to position yourself so you won't be in the way if bits and pieces fly;
● Don't let rubbish accumulate on the floor round your feet;
● Always wear neatly fitting overalls without loose bits, and put your wristwatch, rings, ties, flowing scarves and so on to one side; make sure that long hair is suitably secured to prevent its getting caught in moving mechanisms. In this case, 'moving' can mean anything from 4000 to 17,000rpm!
● More specifically, it is vital to reduce fire risks to a minimum. 'No smoking' is a rule which should always be respected;

● Dust extraction should also be a major priority because, apart from the risks of lung damage, wood shavings and dust are highly combustible;
● Fire prevention also depends on the highest standards of electrical safety. For example, powerful machines like the circular saw, planer and spindle-moulder, if they are on a single-phase supply, should always be wired directly into a 15amp fused mains outlet by a qualified electrician — a 13amp plug will not do!
Safety with woodworking machinery depends in the first instance on careful assembly and installation and, after that, on **regular cleaning and maintenance** according to the manufacturer's instructions. When you first instal your machine, apart from checking it carefully you should read the instruction manual from cover to cover.

Reliable manufacturers place great emphasis on safe operation of their machines, and many of them include safety checks in their manuals. Some firms provide customers with a spare-parts list as well as an instruction manual which explains assembly, operation methods, maintenance procedures, safety regulations, space requirements and trouble-shooting checks for each machine. Like all high-speed indus-

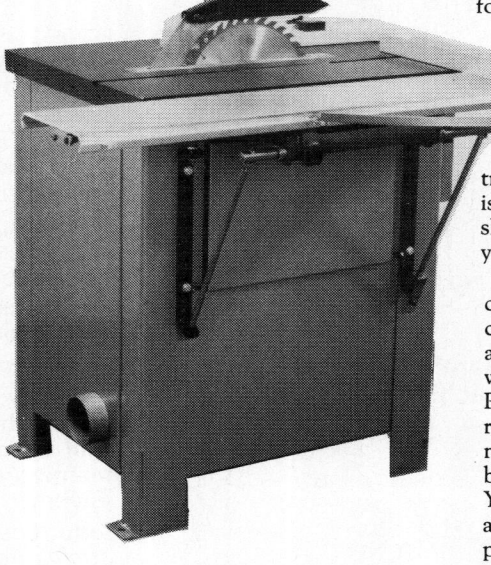

● *A circular sawbench has to be the first machine you go for if you're serious about your workshop; get the biggest blade-size and most powerful motor you can afford. Note the dust-extraction outlet and sliding crosscut table*

trial equipment, woodworking machinery is subject to stringent safety regulations and should be supplied with suitable guards for your protection. It's up to you to use them.

But above all, safe wood-machining depends on the **right mental attitude.** A consistent, methodical approach will create and instil the good working practices on which safety in the workshop depends. Powerful machinery demands a healthy respect — but not fear. The wood-machinist must adopt an attitude finely balanced between confidence and caution. You need confidence to hold wood firmly and feed it smoothly through machining processes, and caution to avoid dubious short cuts.

The best short cut for woodworkers is to **spend some time thinking and preparing** before each machining task: working out exactly how the job can be done, whether you need jigs, the right settings on the machine, and the safety problems and their solutions.

One final safety requirement is to be **sensitive to the sound and performance** of individual machines when they are functioning correctly. Sparks and smoke are obvious signs that all is not well; the woodworker should also appreciate lesser evidence of malfunction. So it's useful and cost-saving to have a certain level of mechanical knowledge, plus a basic tool kit which includes sockets, spanners, screwdrivers and Allen keys. Adjusting a drive belt, for example, is easily done, and can have a dramatic effect on machine performance.

## THE CIRCULAR SAW

No one ever got anywhere in woodwork without sawing a straight cut. The priority in any workshop must be the circular saw, which makes light work of straight-line sawing and, at the same time, is versatile enough to accomplish certain intricate tasks with great precision.

The numerous applications of the circular saw need a variety of saw-blades. In general terms, the different blades are each designed for a specific type of work:
● Ripsawing (cutting along the grain of the wood) requires a blade which has relatively few teeth, with coarse pitch (the distance between the teeth) and positive hook;
● Crosscutting (cutting across the grain of the wood) needs a blade with more teeth, of medium pitch and negative hook;
● Dimension-sawing (cutting panels of solid timber or man-made boards) usually needs blades with many teeth (at least 72 on a 12in blade) and fine pitch — often tungsten-carbide-tipped (TCT);
● Abrasive materials and those which contain glue — plastic laminates, plywood, particleboards and MDF, for instance, should be cut with hard-wearing TCT blades.

TCT blades are becoming increasingly popular because of their high resistance to wear (they need far fewer sharpenings than steel). However, tungsten carbide is extremely brittle, and the teeth can chip, crack and fall (or fly) off if the blade is handled carelessly or used to cut through nails!

Saw-blades have other important features which govern their applications. Usually, teeth of steel blades are 'set' (i.e. set alternately left and right) so that the cut is slightly wider than the body (technically known as the web) of the blade; this enables it to pass easily through the cut without jamming or burning. The teeth of TCT blades are not set, but they are wider than the web, and so still provide the required clearance.

Saw-blades can also have different body profiles. For normal ripsawing or cross-cutting, the body of the blade has the same thickness throughout and the blade is know as a plate saw. But, for dimension-sawing, the body of the blade is ground thinner towards the centre; because these hollow-

● *All tungsten-carbide-tipped ripping blades, except the HSS 10in (**top left**) and ultra-fine 96-tooth 12in panel blade (**bottom right**). The fewer the teeth, the coarser the finish*

ground saws are thickest at the rim, the teeth need not be set. (When ripsawing, this means they shouldn't be used on material more than 20mm thick.) Thin-rim saws are also available, and there are many other variations in blade profile and thickness which are designed for specific types of cutting.

If all this seems too baffling and academic, you can always seek the advice of your local saw specialist when trying to decide what type of blade to use for a particular job. Indeed, you should see him regularly anyway, in order to keep your saw-blades well maintained; achieving the best results from your circular saw will depend to a very large extent on blade condition as well as blade selection.

pitch
negative hook
clearance angle
5° front bevel, 10° top bevel
gullet
**Crosscut saw**

pitch
clearance angle
no bevel on front of teeth
**Ripsaw**
positive hook — hardwood 10° softwood 30°

● *The top of the riving-knife should never be more than 25mm below the blade's highest point, and the curve as near to the blade as possible. It should always be thicker than the blade.*

It is essential to check the sharpness of the saw teeth regularly. They can often be sharpened by hand filing in the workshop, but most woodworkers prefer to leave the job to the experts. Bluntness causes ridged or burnt surfaces, jamming of the blade, and numerous other horrors. Apart from anything else, a blunt blade puts undue strain on the machine's motor and bearings.

The finish of the cut is also determined by the feed speed. If you try to feed the wood into the blade too quickly, the saw will labour unnecessarily and give a poor cut. So work hard at developing a sympathetic

relationship with your circular saw; gentle persuasion, rather than force, will produce the best results!

### Ripping

Ripsawing can be unexpectedly dangerous. **Look at the wood.** The danger is that the saw will snatch and toss the wood back at your stomach — at about 100mph. When ripping bowed material, always place the rounded (convex) side against the fence to prevent chattering and possible throwback. The action of the saw keeps the wood down on the table; but look at the grain as well as

the shape of the piece. If the grain is unduly wild, the workpiece might lift and make the cut difficult to control; have **two push-sticks**, one to hold it down, the other to push the last 12in past the blade.

Apart from looking at the grain, make a note of splits or knots. If the cut goes across a split diagonally, you might find the blade cutting a wedge, catching it, and throwing it back and up — to about eye height. For that reason if no other . . .

**Take the correct stance.** Apart from standing to one side of the saw-blade and the workpiece, you should also be in a good position to feed the wood firmly and smoothly into the machine, ideally with the left foot forward and the left hand (well back from the blade) holding the wood against the rip-fence while the right hand pushes the workpiece towards the saw-blade. Always have your push-sticks to hand — you can't leave a piece of wood half-cut with the blade spinning while you walk over to the bench and pick them up!

**Set the machine carefully and use all the guards.** Setting the machine presents a classic case for the methodical approach. Mentally number each adjustment; and, when they have all been made, check them again by number to ensure that everything is *securely* in the right place. Let someone else answer the telephone while you concentrate on the setting procedure — a distraction could be costly and harmful.

**Blade height** is important. The saw-blade should be set so that the gullet of the teeth (the maximum depth between them) is level with the top of the wood to be cut. This ensures that the maximum number of teeth are working through the wood, reducing surface friction and consequent heating of the saw-blade, plus its tendency to snatch. At least one tooth should be in contact with the material at any moment, to regulate the rate of hand feed. A small pitch is essential for thin material, so that it is not fed too far forward into the gullet before the next tooth cuts; this prevents snatching.

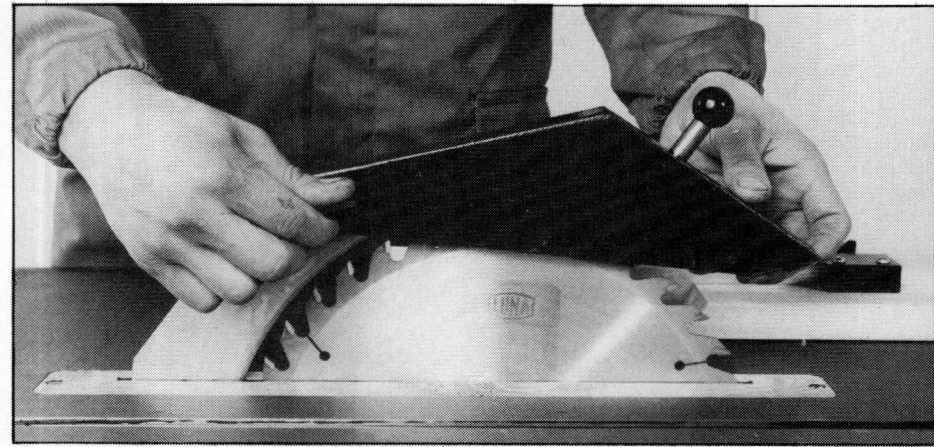

● *Top-guard adjustments vary from saw to saw; does the tightening knob maddeningly crank up to a position where it fouls the wood? 'No higher than 12mm above the work' is the rule for guards. You can see the auxiliary fence behind the blade*

**The riving-knife** is a vital safety feature of the circular saw, especially when ripping, since it acts as a wedge and prevents the saw-cut from closing behind the blade. This stops the wood kicking back at you. The riving-knife should be set as close to the saw-blade as possible — not more than 25mm below its highest point, and not more than 12mm away from the back of the blade.

When you're ripping long, wide, boards, the riving-knife will not stop the cut closing and possibly jamming, so you might need **wedges** placed in the cut; obviously you need someone else at the other end for this. In any case, the riving-knife must always be two gauges thicker than the blade.

**The top guard** should be set as close to the wood as possible, and never more than 12mm above it. This guard prevents the wood from lifting up if it snatches, and covers the maximum amount of saw-blade to reduce the risk of injury.

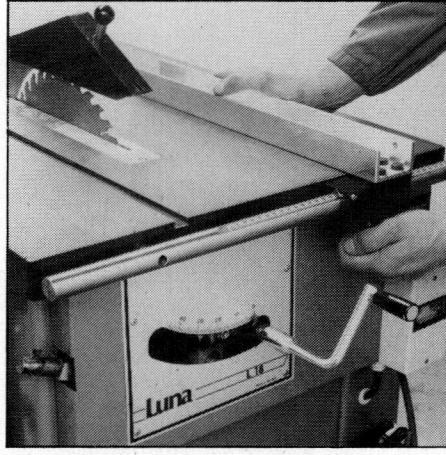

● *On some saws the calibrations on the rip fence (shown here without an auxiliary fence) can be adjusted – you can just see the screw to allow movement of the pointer against the scale*

We say again — use **push-sticks** rather than fingers to feed the wood through, certainly the last 12in; one to guide the piece through the machine and one to push against the rip-fence. Don't take offcuts and dust off the saw — or any machine, for that matter — with your fingers!

## The fences

The two basic surfaces, the table and the rip-fence, must be true and correctly set. A first-class straight-edge will tell you whether the table surface is true. Inspect the alignment of the rip-fence and the saw-blade — they should be fractionally out of parallel, something like $\frac{1}{32}$in in 5ft further apart at the back of the table. A good machine will have adjustment mechanisms on its fences.

When you're setting up a cut, be very fussy about getting the rip-fence right. Remember to measure the cutting width, depending on which side of the saw-blade you are working. Don't forget that the blade will remove 3 or 4mm of the wood (this 'width of cut' is known as the kerf) — so

● *The right stance for ripping; keep your body out of line with the back of the blade as much as you can. The left hand presses the timber in to the fence; the push-stick is at the ready (though out of sight here) to deal with the last 12in of the cut*

make sure it won't be removed from the piece you are measuring! Some saws have fine adjusters on the faces for accurate setting; the calibration should be adjustable, too. The rip-fence will slide back and forth; for 'coarse' ripping (of unplaned timber) the forward edge should line up with the gullets on the front of the blade. Ripping panels needs the fence further forward.

Rip-fences are generally supplied with holes which enable you to bolt or screw to them a variety of **auxiliary or false fences** when safety and/or the job calls for them. You will find yourself making various shapes and sizes of auxiliary fences and guards for specific tasks.

The auxiliary fence is particularly useful when crosscutting or ripping small pieces of wood and when cutting thin strips and

● *Always have the push-stick just to hand before you start the cut, and always use it for the last 12in. Sometimes you'll need two sticks. The angle of the notch is important for positive location on the workpiece*

veneers. Small pieces of wood are inclined to jam between blade and fence, so the auxiliary fence should be set to allow the cut pieces to move away from the blade after cutting.

## Final points

When ripping very long or very wide boards, you will need the help of an assistant, an adjustable **roller stand** or both. You can buy roller stands, some with a choice of 'roll-along' or 'roll-across'; stands can also be made in the workshop, adjustable with butterfly nuts. Whichever type you use, the stand should be adjusted so that it is slightly below the level of the saw-table, since the wood falls a little as it comes off the saw, and it's important that it shouldn't catch on the stand as it is fed through the machine.

Don't forget to wear goggles or safety spectacles to protect your eyes, and do attach the saw to a dust-extraction facility. Don't despair if you can't afford a proprietary one — vacuum-cleaners work very well on small machines.

**Keep watching the saw-blade until it stops moving.** Some machines have a brake on the motor to stop the saw quickly, a design feature required by safety regulations in other countries. It's not statutory in Britain yet, but most new equipment incorporates the brake as standard. ∎

**NEXT MONTH — don't miss the second episode of the circular saw!**

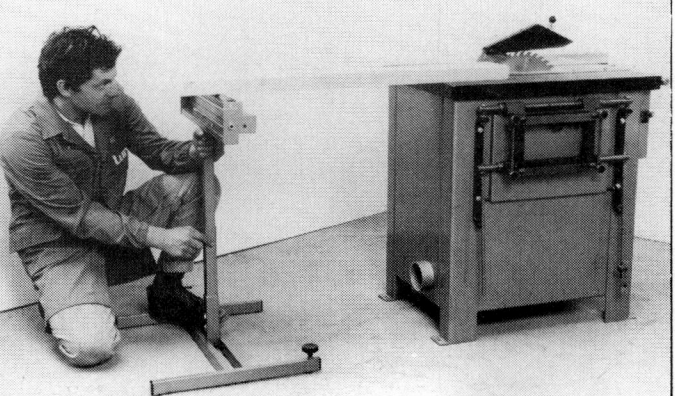

● *Set your roller stand (bought or home-made) according to the length you're cutting. The wood should drop on to the stand ever so slightly, so you avoid embarrassing and dangerous push-overs!*

● *The auxiliary fence is essential if you are cutting thin strips off a wide piece, to stop them jamming between blade and fence. You should have a number of extra fences for various jobs, each designed for versatility, strength and safety*

This series was written by Judith Barker. Ken Taylor of the London College of Furniture checked it for completeness and accuracy. Aidan Walker planned it and demonstrated the techniques. Derek Wales took the pictures. But Luna Tools and Machinery made it possible. They provided vital financial support – and for photography and demonstration they lent their machines, their space, and the help and advice of staff member Joe Wickens. So we give our warmest thanks to Luna's MD Gerry Baker for his unhesitating and generous co-operation. Luna are at 20 Denbigh Hall, Bletchley, Milton Keynes, Bucks MK3 7QT, tel. Milton Keynes (0908) 70771.

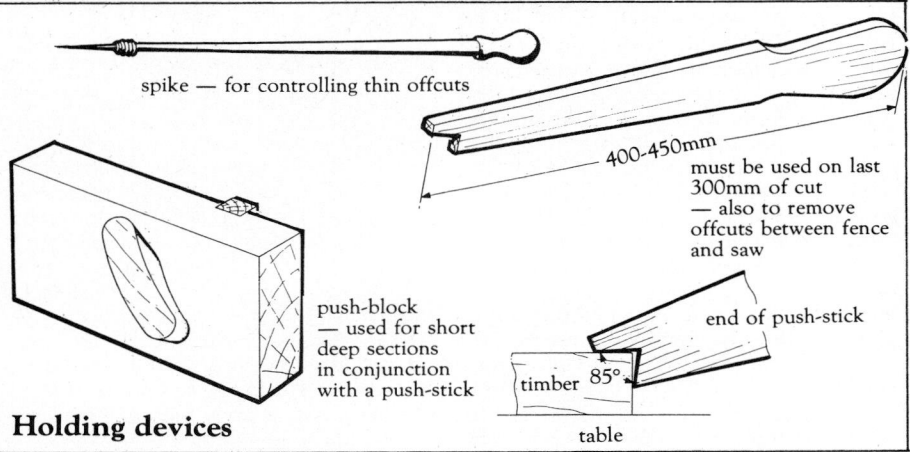

spike — for controlling thin offcuts

400-450mm

must be used on last 300mm of cut — also to remove offcuts between fence and saw

push-block — used for short deep sections in conjunction with a push-stick

timber 85°

end of push-stick

table

**Holding devices**

# Complete Anglians

## Steven Hurrell checked out two appealing recent shows

August saw the discerning Norfolk furniture-lover being treated to two notable exhibitions by neighbouring designer/craftspeople. One featured the work of the Corpusty Six, the other that of Charles Matts.

It's always difficult to distinguish the prospective client from the one sheltering (in mid-August) from the rain. It can easily turn out that the casual visitor is so taken by a certain exhibit that he gets hooked on quality furniture and comes back for more of the same. The patrons of handmade furniture are not just the very rich. The average 'person in the street' is slowly beginning to recognise that there is an alternative to the very uninteresting offerings of the larger furniture manufacturers and outlets.

Rob Corbett's Corbett Woodwork was the setting for furniture by Nigel Flower, Robert Smith and Rob himself, plus a display from three local artists. The space available was put to good use in showing a nice balance of fresh ideas — all in a style that, unlike that of the 'Is it a chair? Is it a table? Could it be a bookcase?' items so often seen, still identifies the work as functional furniture.

The central figure is undoubtedly Rob Corbett, who has established himself over 21 years of furniture-making. He employs a nephew and exhibits the work of his daughters (Kay being a cabinetmaker). The pieces are predominantly of English hardwoods. I liked the cleanliness that the exhibits displayed. It would be difficult to single out a star item, though I'm told that the green-stained folding ash chairs by Robert Smith had generated a lot of interest and discussion. For me his cedar chest was worth at least a second glance.

● For further information, contact Rob Corbett, The Street, Corpusty, Norfolk, tel. Saxthorpe 268; Nigel Flower, Brickfield Barn, Stibbard, Norfolk, tel. Gt Ryburgh 410; Robert Smith, Riverside Row, Corpusty, Norfolk, tel. Melton Constable 861032.

Alby Crafts in Erpingham attracts no less than 100,000 visitors each year. Eight small workshops housing a silversmith, weaver, potter, sculptor, artist, woodcarver, silk-painter and stained-glass worker accompany a gallery that, it is claimed, offers the very best from over 300 of Britain's best artist-craftsmen. However, you can't visit Alby without being influenced by the permanent exhibition of Charles Matts' furniture — which indeed, as a central feature, must contribute largely to Alby's popularity.

So what made Matts' August exhibition special? On show were recently completed commissions destined for the homes of clients in Harlow, Cambridge, Surrey,

● The ash table **above,** by Nigel Flower, and the oak sideboard **below** – Rob Corbett's work – were on show with other furniture and paintings in the homely setting of Corbett Woodwork, Corpusty

Leicester and Norwich. Dining suites, chests, desks, cabinets and occasional tables, exploiting locally grown and workshop-conditioned hardwoods — a wealth of grain characteristics and colour.

Charles Matts' varied career has seen him merchant-banking, selling bread and doing a stint in New Zealand — re-treading tyres, galvanising dustbins, labouring, and running his own building business. A year after he returned to the UK in 1966, the joinery firm for which he worked collapsed, and he decided to become self-employed. Graduating from joinery to furniture, he has moved from his garden shed to the present workshop premises at Manor Farm, Thurgarton — the once derelict 17th-century farm buildings restored to provide living accommodation and a workshop that employs five Matts-trained craftsmen.

The 'Please touch wood' slogan he uses is strongly emphasised, and at the very least visitors go away having experienced the feel of cherry, oak, ash, elm or yew at its most inviting.

● Contact Marianne Matts at Alby Crafts, Cromer Rd, Erpingham, Norfolk, or Manor Farm, School Rd, Thurgarton, Norfolk, tel. (0263)761422/768060. Alby Crafts is open from March to Christmas, Tues-Sun. 10-5. ■

● Both the kneehole desk (**top**) and the chest (**above**) were made in the Charles Matts workshops, where up to five cabinetmakers are kept busy

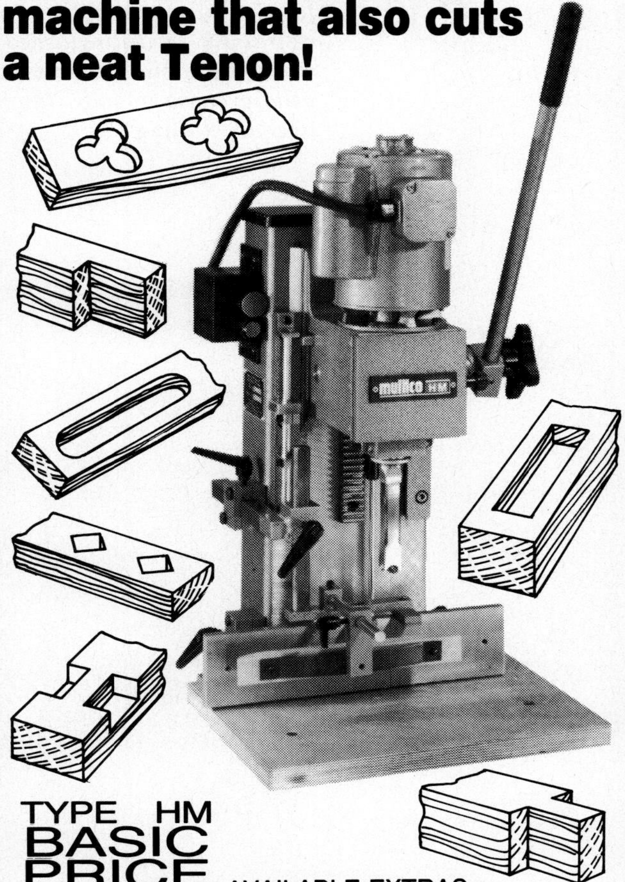

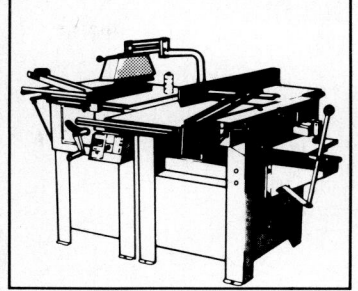

# Glazed cherry

**David O'Connor explains in detail how to make his slender, elegant wall cabinet**

**1** Plane and cut all the timber to size from the cutting list. Square the ends, but leave the two door-stiles 20mm over-length at each end.

**2** Cut grooves 10mm wide and 6mm deep at the back of the four ash carcase pieces to take the 6mm back panel.

**3** Line up the two carcase sides and mark off eight equidistant lines across both of them — it is essential that these are level. With a marking-gauge, mark off a point 36mm from the back and 20mm from the front on each line. Drill 6mm holes at these 32 points, 15mm deep, to take shelf supports.

**4** Mark out and cut dovetail pins on the carcase sides. Align the pins over the corresponding pieces and clamp them in position. Mark out the tails from the pins with a sharp scriber, and cut out the tails.

**5** Clean up the inside faces of the carcase and plywood back with a cabinet-scraper, and finish off with 0000 wire wool. Polish the cherry with three coats of teak oil or Danish oil. Polish the ash with two coats of sanding sealer or white polish and rub down; then coat with beeswax (oil doesn't work well on white woods as it tend to look dirty).

**6** Glue up the carcase.

**7** Cut 5x5mm rebates in the cherry top and plinth — in the front and sides only. Drill dowel holes, polish with oil as before, and glue the top and bottom to the carcase.

**8** There are two ways of cutting the rebated mortises and tenons on a glazed door. The first, by hand, uses long- and short-shouldered tenons with the rebate cut before gluing up. The machine method uses simple stub tenons, the rebate being cut, after gluing up, with a rebate cutter in a router. On this job, either way is possible.

**9** Polish the inside faces of the door. Before gluing up, ensure that the frame is perfectly flat, and that off-square tenons will not cause it to go in winding. If there are problems, make adjustments. Then glue and cramp.

**10** Square up the door to the carcase and trim to fit. Lay the carcase face-up on the bench, and lay the door in the open position next to the left-hand front of the carcase. Cramp both in place, and mark off the positions of the Soss hinges. Remove the door, and cut recesses for the hinges on door and carcase.

**11** Fit the cylinder magnetic catch into the carcase side and the corresponding striking-plate on the door.

● *The carcase is ash, with a cherry-veneered back; it's extended by a top and base of cherry, which match the door. The colour of the cherry enhances the plainness of the ash without overwhelming it, for a total effect that's restrained yet distinguished — while the cabinet doubles as a good exercise in both framing and dovetailing*

**12** Cut the keyhole (hanging) plates from 3mm-thick brass or mild steel. Mark out the two recesses for them on the back of the carcase, and cut out with router and chisel. Cut deeper recesses to accept the screw-heads.

**13** Clean up the outside of the cabinet and door with scraper and wire wool as before. Fit the glass in the door, drill the beading and pin it in place. Fill the pin-heads with beaumontage and hang the door.

**14** Cut 20 6mm-diameter brass bars, 25mm long, and file a 45° bevel on one end of each. Finish with wet-and-dry paper. Tap these into the holes inside the cabinet as required for shelves.

**15** Mark two points on the wall which exactly correspond to the centres of the large holes in the keyhole brackets, and drill and plug. Use no.8 screws, leaving about 5mm proud of the wall. Offer the cabinet to the wall and slot the plates over the screw-heads. ■

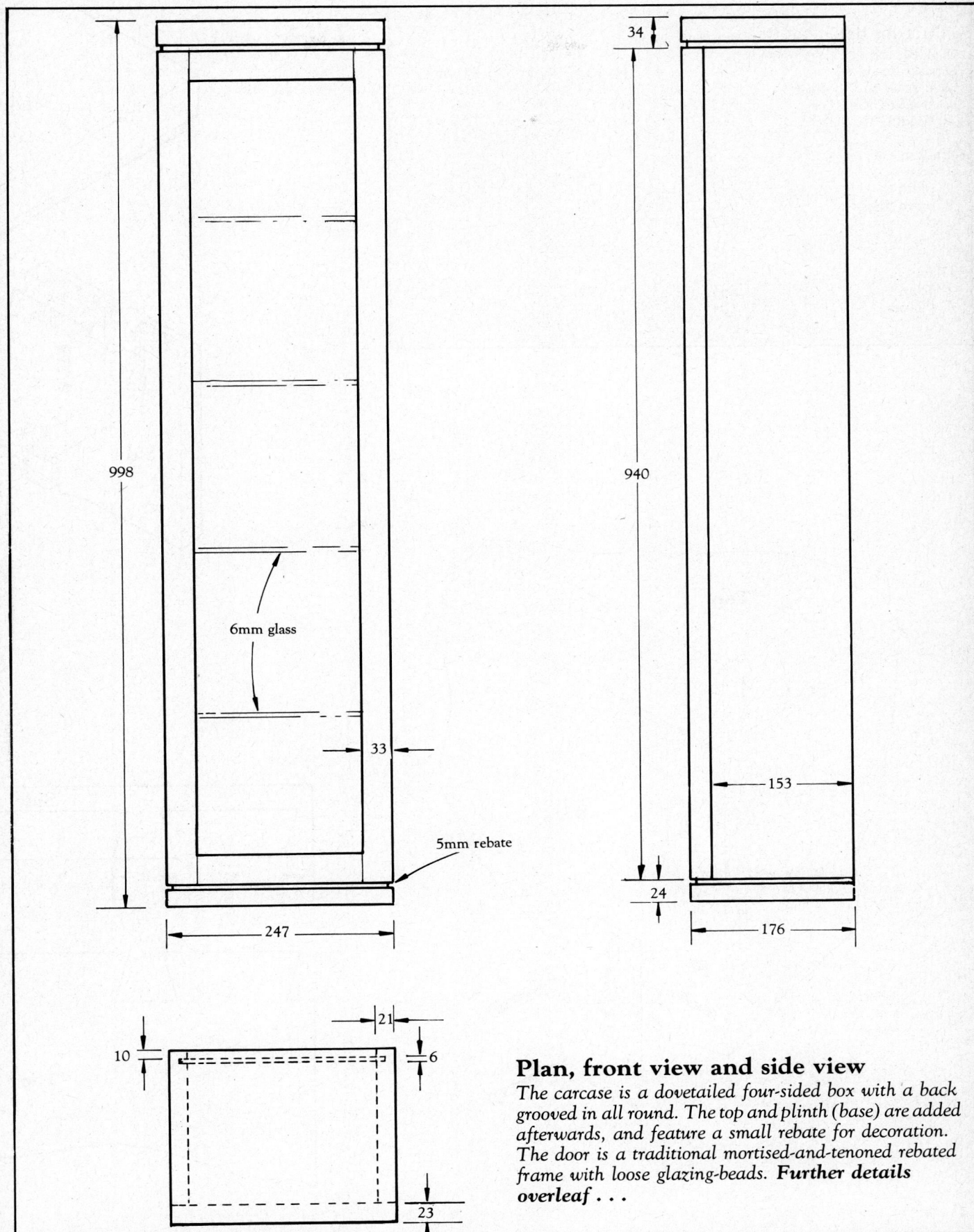

6mm glass

33

5mm rebate

998

247

940

34

153

24

176

21

10

6

23

## Plan, front view and side view

The carcase is a dovetailed four-sided box with a back grooved in all round. The top and plinth (base) are added afterwards, and feature a small rebate for decoration. The door is a traditional mortised-and-tenoned rebated frame with loose glazing-beads. **Further details overleaf . . .**

# Glazed cherry

## Cutting list

English ash:

| | | | | | | |
|---|---|---|---|---|---|---|
| 2 carcase sides | 940 | x | 153 | x | 21mm |
| 2 carcase top/bottom | 233 | | 153 | | 21 |
| 2 beading for stiles | 885 | | 11 | | 6 |
| 2 beading for rails | 180 | | 11 | | 6 |

English cherry:

| | | | |
|---|---|---|---|
| 1 top | 247 | 176 | 34 |
| 1 plinth | 247 | 176 | 24 |
| 2 door-stiles | 940 | 33 | 23 |
| 2 door-rails | 247 | 33 | 23 |
| 1 back (veneered ply) | 916 | 223 | 6 |

Glass:

| | | | |
|---|---|---|---|
| 1 door | 885 | 192 | 3 |
| 4 shelves | 204 | 127 | 6 |

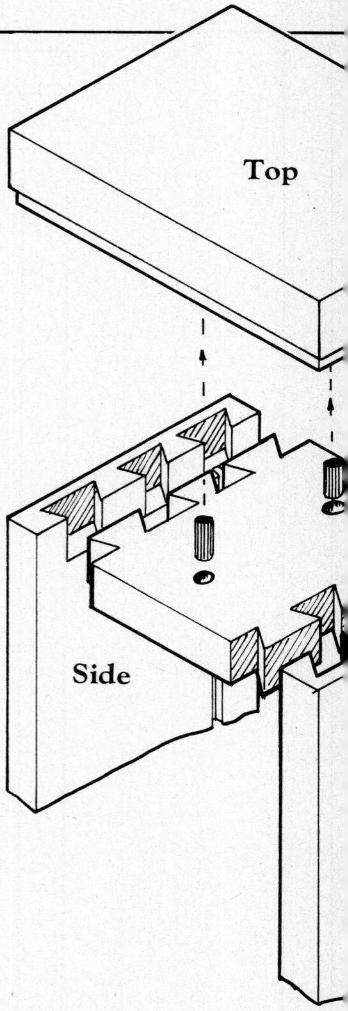

Top

Side

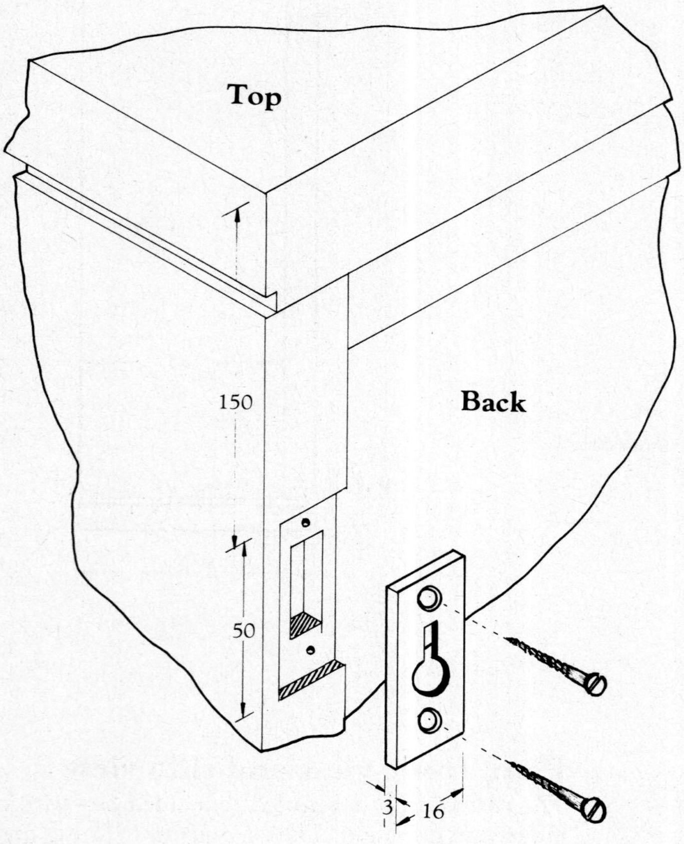

Top

Back

150

50

3 16

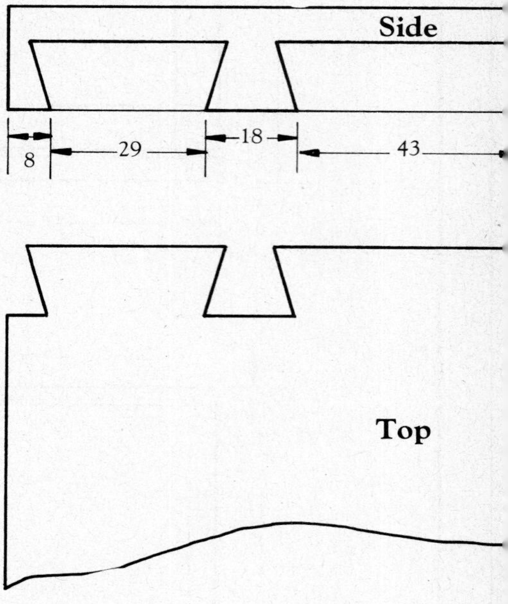

Side

8   29   18   43

Top

834

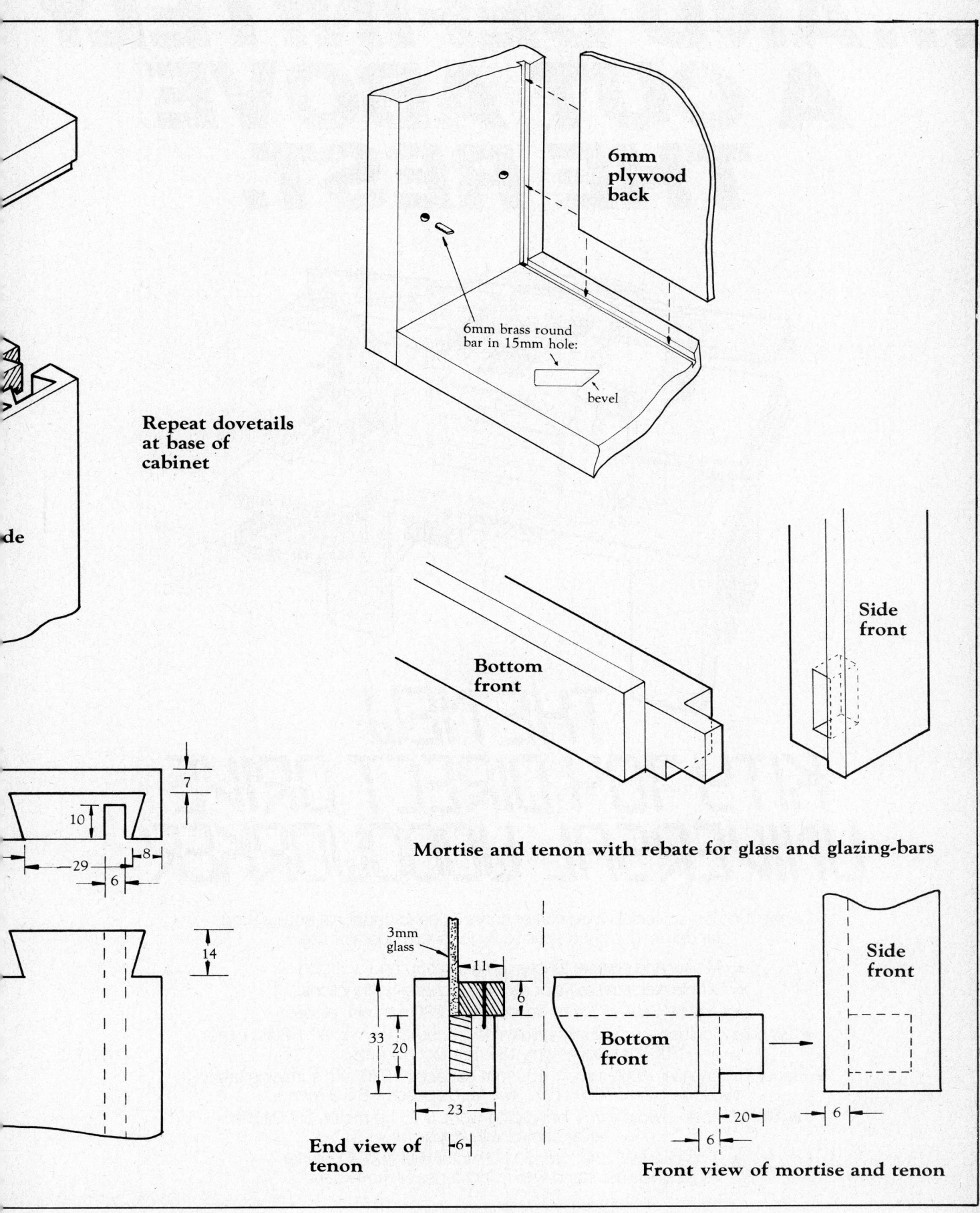

**Repeat dovetails at base of cabinet**

6mm plywood back

6mm brass round bar in 15mm hole:

bevel

Bottom front

Side front

**Mortise and tenon with rebate for glass and glazing-bars**

7

10

29    8

6

14

3mm glass

11

6

33

20

23

**End view of tenon**   6

Bottom front

Side front

20

6

6

**Front view of mortise and tenon**

# The K5 Combination Woodworker

A compact unit suitable for use in a small workshop. The K5 is a Universal Woodworker of the "complete" type with the advantage of individual worktables mounted at different heights to ensure the minimum of adjustment is required when changing functions, and the free running of timber. There is a vast range of tooling available for the K5, allowing the maximum flexibility in methods of working.

## The Basic 'K5'

### £515 + £77.85 V.A.T.

★ 65mm depth of cut saw with rise/fall and tilt
★ 150mm surface planer, 700mm cast table
★ 150mm × 100mm power feed thicknesser
★ 1 h.p. dust sealed motor with full safety protection  ★ Steel floor stand with wheels.
You may purchase at a later date the K5/Spindle Moulder and the K5/Slot Mortiser to add to your K5.

## The K5 Spindle Moulder

### £165 + £24.75 V.A.T.

★ 20mm shaft diameter, 75mm maximum tool height
★ 100mm tooling gap with 120mm maximum tool diameter
★ Full safety guarding

## The K5 Slot Mortiser

### £77.25 + £11.59 V.A.T.

★ 150mm × 150mm × 110mm adjustment
★ Full lever control with adjustment stops  ★ Double pillar type timber clamp

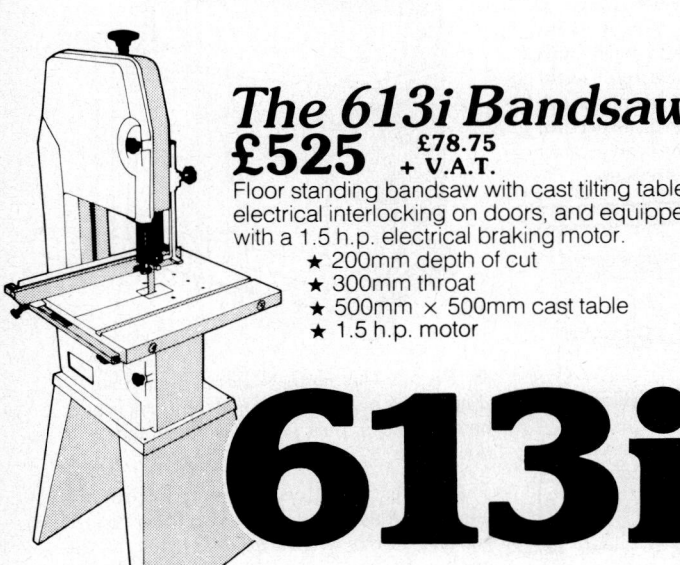

## The 613i Bandsaw

### £525 + £78.75 V.A.T.

Floor standing bandsaw with cast tilting table, electrical interlocking on doors, and equipped with a 1.5 h.p. electrical braking motor.
★ 200mm depth of cut
★ 300mm throat
★ 500mm × 500mm cast table
★ 1.5 h.p. motor

# 613i

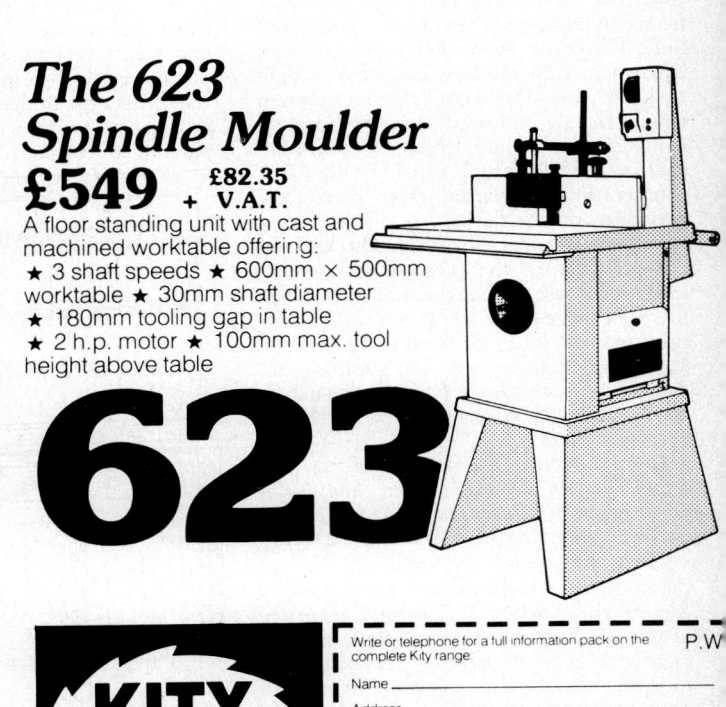

## The 623 Spindle Moulder

### £549 + £82.35 V.A.T.

A floor standing unit with cast and machined worktable offering:
★ 3 shaft speeds ★ 600mm × 500mm worktable ★ 30mm shaft diameter
★ 180mm tooling gap in table
★ 2 h.p. motor ★ 100mm max. tool height above table

# 623

# Natty dressers

## First in a guide to furniture types: Vic Taylor explores a not-always-Welsh national design

The dresser, of course, has nothing to do with dressing.

The word probably derives from the Norman-French *dressoir*, which was a side-table on and from which food was prepared and served. In the 15th century the serving-hatches in the refectory of a monastery were also called 'dressers', but it was not until the late 17th and early 18th centuries that the dresser as we know it developed from the long side-table of Stuart days, which had drawers fitted under the top. The whole thing was supported on turned legs, or legs shaped to the silhouette of a turned leg; both kinds used a stretcher underframe.

The first step was to add a small, low gallery to the top of the side table. This gallery had returned ends and moulded top edges; it was soon accompanied by a set of separate shelves fastened to the wall with iron pegs. Their purpose was to display ornamental plates, dishes and jugs. There was no backboard in the early examples, and the shelves would have either a bead fixed along the front edges, or a groove for plates to sit in which stopped them sliding forwards while they rested against the wall. In most cases the shelf assembly is separate from the lower sections, with the exception of the Bridgwater dresser, in which the end stiles ran from top to bottom.

This basic kind of dresser was not confined to Wales. There are examples from other parts of the country, a design of Suffolk dresser from 1725 for instance, which had cabriole legs and plain straight shelf uprights. There is a Yorkshire pattern which closely followed the early designs from north Wales, while Devon, Lancashire, Shropshire and Bridgwater (Somerset) all boasted their own local variations on the theme.

However, it was the Welsh who took up the design with the greatest enthusiasm. Little is known of the craftsmen who made them, because many were undoubtedly the products of local carpenters or joiners. Most were made in oak, but some of ash, elm or pine, and local fruitwoods such as apple, cherry or pear were used for the ornamental parts.

John Loudon, the author of the *Encyclopaedia of Cottage, Farm and Villa Architecture and Furniture* (1833), said that dressers were 'fixtures essential to every kitchen, but more especially to that of the cottager, to whom they serve both as dresser and sideboard. They are generally made of deal by joiners, and seldom painted, it being the pride of housewives... to keep the boards of which they are composed as white as snow, by frequently scouring them with fine white sand'.

● **Fig. 1** A 'knee-hole' or 'dog-kennel' dresser from south-west Wales. The small cupboards are probably for spices

There are two basic designs of Welsh dresser; the cupboarded dresser generally associated with north Wales, and the pot-boarded type from the south. There are, however, several local variations. One that is easy to identify is the 'dog-kennel' design from Carmarthenshire in south Wales, shown in fig. 1; as you can see it is a knee-hole pattern. The corner dresser design in fig. 7 came from the same area; it is interesting because one wing had been built into a cottage wall, and extricating it without doing damage must have been a headache! It is now in the Welsh Folk Museum, St Fagans, Cardiff, where there is an incomparable collection of Welsh dressers.

● **Fig. 2** This north-Wales design, from around 1710, boasts terminal pendant bosses on the canopy, plus fielded drawer- and door-fronts

Another variation originated from the island of Anglesey. The design followed the general north Wales style in that it was enclosed (that is, it had no pot-board), but the lower part had a break-front which protruded by about 3in and always contained four or five drawers. It appears to have been a late-18th- or early-19th-century innovation, and as you can see from fig. 3 it is a most impressive piece of furniture.

Dating Welsh dressers is a tricky business as, in common with other locally pro-

● **Fig. 3** An Anglesey break-front design from the mid-19th century

● **Fig. 4** *A magnificent tridarn from Llanberis, Caernarvonshire, dated 1695 (photo Welsh Folk Museum)*

duced woodwork such as Windsor chairs and longcase clock cases, a design which proved both useful and ornamental might well be repeated over a century or more in one locality. There are several pointers that may help. Dressers with turned drop terminals on the shelf-canopy (fig. 2) usually indicate an early piece of about 1700 to 1730, as they are vestigial reminders of the dresser's ancestor, the livery cupboard. These early specimens usually have fielded-panel doors which are often shaped at the top, and the frieze is also frequently shaped and cusped; it is unusual for them to have spice-cupboards built into the shelving, a feature more common in later examples.

Early dressers of the pot-boarded kind sometimes had turned and shaped legs terminating in a continuous stretcher which supported the pot-board, but it's more likely either that the legs were shaped to

resemble a turned pattern in silhouette, or that they were heavily chamfered. The aprons under the drawers were almost always shaped, frequently in an ornamental ogee, or with a series of cusped curves. The example in fig. 5 is rare and dates back to about 1720; note the baluster shape of the legs and the very unusual vertical slats in the ends of the lower part. As it is virtually unique it is difficult to say where it originated, but according to expert opinion it was probably central Wales. Another example is illustrated in fig. 6, an early piece with an open-backed shelf section and an apron pierced in a typical design of hearts; it is dated about 1740.

Fig. 4 is a photograph of a *tridarn* which developed in the latter half of the 17th century from the earlier *cwpwrdd deuddarn*, popular in the 16th century. The *deuddarn* was a two-piece cupboard surmounted by an upper cupboard and a heavy canopy with pendant terminal turned bosses or knobs; the *tridarn* went further and incorporated open shelves in the top section for the display of china, pewter and ornaments. I know of a Breton *tridarn* in Somerset which follows the same design although it is much cruder; and it also differs in that it has an aumbry with a pierced front for food. Unfortunately, it has been 'truncated' — cut down in height to get it into the cottage room.

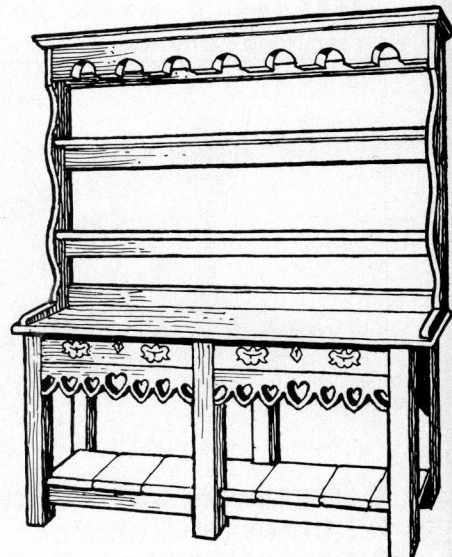

● **Fig. 6** *An open-backed dresser with a pierced apron, dated about 1740*

Dressers made at a later date, say during the closing years of the 18th and the early 19th century, often included such refinements as cock beading, mahogany cross-bandings around the drawer- and door-fronts, inlaid sunburst motifs in mahogany and sycamore, and knobs inlaid with ivory or mother-of-pearl. ■

● **Fig. 5, above:** *An early (1720) pot-boarded design with baluster-silhouette legs.* **Fig. 7, right:** *This oak corner dresser was built into a wall (photo Welsh Folk Museum)*

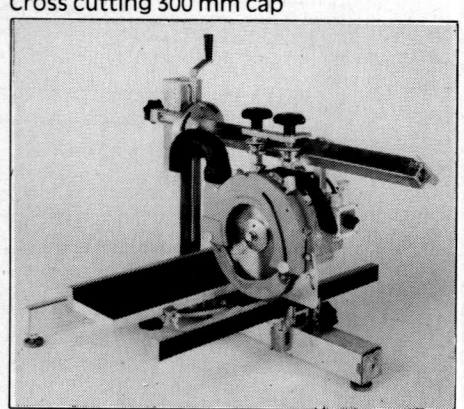
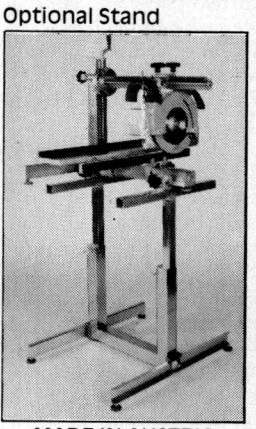
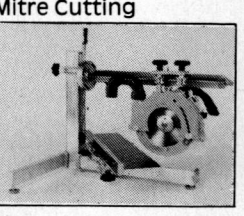

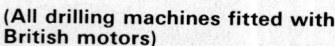
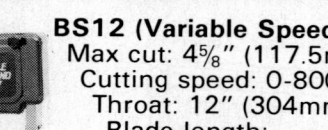

840

# The craft of cabinetmaking

## Delightful but dangerous: David Savage gives guidance on the spindle moulder

I f I could lay my hands on the ingenious gentleman who invented the plunge router, I would cheerfully throttle him. This is such a useful tool, so versatile, so clean-cutting and so accurate, that we tend to reach for it at the slightest opportunity. It is, however, probably the most unpleasant device that I shall ever lay hands on. The noise from even the smallest cabinetmaker's router is a teeth-loosening screech, and the muck and dust it throws out gets absolutely everywhere. Gone are the days of peace and concentration at the bench. Whoever designs a quiet air-powered router with built-in dust extraction will make an absolute fortune. The router relies upon high speed and low cutter-weight for its cutting action — the spindle moulder relies on the opposite.

I am besotted with my spindle moulder. It is a small and rather elderly Wadkin that still spins as smoothly as the day it was new. Buying such a machine was an act of faith that I have never regretted. Daltons of Nottingham sold it to me, unseen, in 'checked and tested' condition. Not having dealt with them before I didn't really know what to expect, but the machine arrived with new bearings, all-new adjustment bolts and drive belt. A very good service — not the cheapest, but then you wouldn't expect it to be.

The spindle moulder should be a substantial implement with a heavy cast table and a spindle of not less than 30mm diameter. Tooling of industrial quality is available in 30mm and 1¼in bore. Don't buy a scaled-down spindle moulder with a small-diameter shaft, as it won't have the power or weight to do the job. Routers whizz and scream; spindle moulders cut at

● *For short or thin pieces which want to nose-dive into the gap between the wings of the standard fence, an auxiliary fence is essential*

lower speeds, using high torque and power to spin a heavy block. A motor of 2hp is the smallest I would advise. The spindle should be interchangeable, either the whole lot coming out or the top piece being removable. This makes for speedy changes of tooling and enables you to choose between English and French heads. Concentric rings in the table-top round the spindle can be removed to give different apertures for small or large cutter-blocks.

A spindle brake may be provided and a locking device is useful when changing tooling, but neither are essential features of what is basically a very straightforward machine. A sliding table may be a useful addition when producing machine tenons in batches; otherwise jigs can be devised to perform this function.

The spindle moulder has been described as the most under-used machine in the workshop. Only perhaps in the furniture industry is it employed to its fullest capacity; clever use of jigs and guidance systems, and different methods of presenting the job to the tool, extend even further an already bewildering number of operating methods. Rebate heads, tenoning heads, groovers, French-head cutters, Whitehill blocks, safety cutter-blocks, slotted collars, solid-profile cutters, template moulding, shaping against collars or ring-fences; all these and more are tooling and techniques that extend the capacity of a small workshop. It would be easy to witter on about all of these and fill several magazines, but I will concentrate here on making simple mouldings using the universal or safety cutter-block.

T he safety blocks are those sets you often see at trade shows, displayed in nice wooden boxes with a multitude of cutters. They all look pretty much the same, but some conceal beneath their dark-blue

● *Heavy-duty, in more than one sense. The spindle moulder inspires awe, respect and affection – in that order, as experience grows*

surfaces the fact that they are aluminium, not steel. The principle of most cutter-blocks is to hold either one or two cutters at a suitable cutting angle and provide mass and weight behind the cut. The spindle is not revolving at more than 8,000rpm, so this weight is important. Buy the largest, heaviest block that will suit your machine. Luna make an aluminium block, Leitz and Wadkin make steel blocks and charge accordingly. They call them safety cutter-blocks, a term which should be examined critically. The spindle moulder and the circus knife-thrower are closely related, and in a duel at dawn I would put my money on the spindle moulder. This so-and-so can kill at 20 paces in the winking of an eye. Cutter-blocks sit at just above groin level, which explains why most wood-machinists take cover when first switching on with a newly set-up piece of spindle tooling.

The cutters are located in the block by wedges inserted from the top. There is theoretically no way that the knife can be thrown from a safety cutter-block — at least, mine looks that way; but I shall go on taking cover with the rest of the unmutilated wood-machining population. *The spindle moulder is a potentially dangerous weapon* and you really should take some kind of tuition before using one.

Safety or universal blocks come with a multitude of different cutters. For moulding softwood or rough work, one cutter is enough, but one cutter puts the block out of balance, so a cutter of similar size is usually installed in a non-cutting position. For a much better finish, one that needs no further attention, it is important to have both cutters of the same profile and both cutting. As they come from the maker these cutters will be approximately identical. Spend a bit of time on the grinder making them truly identical, especially in the small details of the moulding. Fitting to

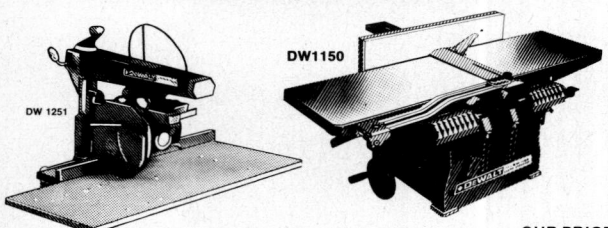

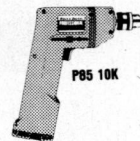 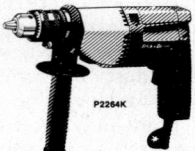

842

# The craft of cabinetmaking

● *A safety block, a selection of cutters and collars, and the top nut.*

the block can take a bit of time, but it will take a lot longer if the block is choked up with dust. Strip it down and clean it with petrol or meths. Install the cutters in what looks like the right attitude with equal projection, then check this with the block on the spindle. An engineer's dial-gauge or pointer mounted on a magnetic stand will tell you exactly what's what. A block of wood moved in until one or the other cutter scrapes it will do the same task. Then it is a matter of fiddling about until both cutters are projecting the same amount. By taking a little pressure off one locating wedge and tapping with a soft-faced hammer, it's possible to make the necessary minute adjustments. Needless to say, the machine is stationary and electrically isolated while all this is going on.

Each cutter may have only one mould on it or it may have two or three, depending on how much projection you have above the table. The spindle should be easily adjustable for height — 4in of movement is common. As with many machines, the direction of rotation tightens the nut down on the cutter block. There's no need to do more than squeeze the nut down on an 'English' head — the French head is different, but that's another story.

The horseshoe fence is the common one for this type of work. Each side will have its own micro-adjustment, and the whole lot can be positioned in the most appropriate place on the table. The sides will also have a lateral movement to bring the fence closer to the cutter if necessary. A wooden high fence is a standard feature, to which an auxiliary fence can be pinned.

First set the block up just above the working height and bolt the fence in an approximate position in front of the cutter. Check that the block is free to revolve, and check what will happen when the fence is pulled back to the point where the cutter projects through the thin auxiliary fence. With the block spinning, re-position the fence on the micro-adjustment, but *be careful*; don't pull the fence too far back, making contact between cutter and metal fence. Lower the block to working height and try a test cut.

Setting up the moulder may seem an enormous fuss. Certainly, it is more time-consuming than plugging in a router and selecting a suitable moulding bit. But using the moulder is so much better. It's noisy,

but it doesn't emit that nerve-jangling scream, and it produces chips of timber with very little dust and a good-quality clean cut. Routers burn if there is any pause in the feed rate, and TCT cutters in particular leave clear cutter-marks. A moulder has these problems, but much less acutely.

So the block is set up to make mould for, say, glazing-strips. The answer is *not* to feed thin strips of stuff to the cutter, bringing fingers perilously close in an effort to control thin, wriggly material. Plane up a board (or several) to the thickness required and plane a face edge and width, for you can work two moulds on the same piece, one down each edge. Run the moulds through. Hold-down units and 'finger boards' may be made up and used to locate the job against the fence, leaving you to concentrate on feeding the job through. Cutting the mould off the board involves a trip to the table saw.

Rip-sawing long slender pieces is another potentially hazardous pastime, as the number of one-eyed machinists bears out. Always, *always*, **always** wear a full-face visor when ripping thin pieces — they are potential arrows that the blade picks up and spits out at fearful speed. One technique that has proved safe so far is to feed the board through, pushing the mould past the arc of the teeth with a push-stick of similar width to the moulding. Carry the waste board past the cutting edge, but don't stop just as the mould is separated from the board; push the free mould through with the next moulded board. You may end up with a log-jam of moulds in the roll-off area, but you can sort them out every two or three passes.

So much for spindle-moulding — what about that mortiser I mentioned in a previous article (WW/April)? The problems facing the user of the hollow-square-chisel mortiser are many and various, but a good many of them concern the tooling. Straight from the box, these implements cut a far-from-square mortise. Record Ridgway

used to dominate this field, but they are now being seriously challenged by Japanese products imported by Draper. These are very well finished and quicker cutting, and (when properly fettled) do the job very well. Ridgway products are by comparison less well-finished and slower cutting, but they are probably of a higher-grade steel. All these tools need serious attention to detail to sharpen the chisel properly and make the auger cut inside the four walls of the chisel. This usually means spending time grinding the outside corner of the auger bit down very carefully.

The chisels imported by Draper, believe it or not, cannot be sharpened — at least not by a Draper product. The manufacturers of Record Ridgway chisels now make an adaptation of their sharpening system to fit Draper tools, which is kind of them. These are notorious for getting lost in the post, and don't work too well when they do arrive. To add to the whole sorry mess, the supply of Record Ridgway chisel sets is, to put it politely, erratic. When I didn't have room in my London workshop for a mortiser, I didn't have any of these problems. I cut my mortises with a router and got on with the job.

Having finally got the system sorted out, however, I'm delighted with the results. It has taken some sorting out. A bench mortising machine by Startrite did the job well enough, but lacked the horizontal travelling bed. This adaptation of a pillar-drill would be the best solution for the serious amateur seeking an economical square-chisel mortiser. The Startrite adaptation is in many ways superior to the £20 Taiwanese adaptors, but it's about four times the price. All these pillar-drill adaptations are capable of fine work, but they're very slow to operate. This is why I replaced the Startrite machine with a real mortiser by Sedgwick.

Children that visit my workshop always have a great time taking the place apart. Now there's a new attraction — a toy mortiser with a steering wheel at just the right height! ■

● *The horseshoe fence from the back, with high wooden fences and an auxiliary attached. The black knobs in the foreground are for individual micro-adjustments. Guards and extraction removed for clarity!*

# LEISURE LIFE EXHIBITION

## 25 January 2 February 86

Leisure Life is the exhibition you cannot afford to miss. We have left no stone unturned in our endeavours to ensure that Leisure Life will be the most important exhibition ever staged in the UK for the leisure industry.

By virtue of careful planning, arduous research and meticulous care we are confident that Leisure Life will become **the ultimate Leisure Exhibition.**

So if you are a manufacturer, supplier or retailer of leisure related products there is only one place to exhibit; Leisure Life at the new Scottish Exhibition & Conference Centre, Glasgow.

As a bonus Scots spend 20% more on leisure activities than any other Region in the UK–and 4 million of them live within just an hour of the Centre.

Never before has there been such a sales opportunity.

Leisure Life will be promoted by a full scale multi-media publicity campaign–TV, Press, Radio, Posters and PR.

Already many major organisations have booked their exhibition space. To reserve your space contact:

**Frank Boiteux, Leisure Life Exhibition, SEC Exhibitions Ltd., Scottish Exhibition & Conference Centre, Glasgow G3 8YW. Or telephone on 041-221 1769.**

Exhibits will include: ● Arts & Crafts ● Camping ● Caravanning ● Cycling ● DIY ● Fishing ● Gardening ● Golf ● Hobbies ● Motoring ● Photography ● Riding ● Shooting ● Skiing ● Sub-aqua ● Travel ● Water sports.

844

# How to make mortise chisels

**Bob Wearing's Workshop**

**All readers have glimpsed the truly encyclopedic knowledge of Bob Wearing DLC MCCEd, tutor at Shrewsbury College. Realising there was no end to it, we decided to give him a regular column in which to air it!**

As students immediately after the war we were quite unable to buy the true mortise-chisels we needed for our hand-work. None were being made. Now, 40 years on, my own students find the position repeated.

Fortunately these tools can be made with the minimum of metalworking skill or equipment. It might be asked, 'Why make them at all?' No ⅛in or 3/16in machine mortise-chisels are made; and, even with the bigger sizes, situations arise where the machine is unsuitable — for example mortising for stub tenons in the middle of a wide carcase, and in chairmaking.

The width of the chisel brings other advantages (I use the word width to distinguish from thickness, i.e. the nominal size). In the smaller sizes the risk of snapping off the chisel when levering is totally obviated. Besides, the wide blade prevents the chisel from twisting, thus producing a very straight and accurate mortise. This is particularly so in the case of the smaller sizes, where workers sometimes have no alternative but to mortise with a thin bevel-edged chisel. To my mind, this advantage alone makes it worthwhile to make some of the larger sizes too.

The blade is made from tool steel, known as ground flat stock or gauge plate. Good engineer's suppliers will stock it. Readers away from the main towns can obtain it from K. R. Whiston Ltd, New Mills, Stockport, Cheshire SK12 4PT. Two 9in chisels can be made from one 18in length. Imperial dimensions are shown in the diagram but metric stock is now available too.

None of the dimensions shown are critical apart from the rectangular slot in the steel washer. They can be varied to suit personal preference and available materials.

First saw the blade to length; with a new hacksaw blade this material saws reasonably easily. Then file it up nicely. The tang merits less attention, but take note of the two small steps on to which the bolster/washer fits. Do not yet bring the bevel to a thin edge, or it will heat up too quickly and destroy the tempering. The mild-steel bolster or thick washer is made next. De-grease and make sure that the parts are bright and clean, then join the two components by silver-soldering or brazing. Clean up.

The handle is quite massive; sizes and shape are to taste. Beech is traditional but other dense, close-grained hardwoods can be used. A pilot-hole is first drilled; then the tang is heated to red, pushed in most of the way and withdrawn. A leather shock-absorbing washer is made but not finally fitted.

The blade is now ready for hardening and tempering. Full instructions are supplied with the steel. A local firm might undertake the job in a hardening furnace, working by time and temperature; otherwise, work by observation of the colours appearing when the blade is heated.

The method is this. Heat, say, 4in at the cutting end to bright red, then rapidly quench in oil or water — preferably oil. The tool is now too hard and needs to be tempered. Brighten up the heated area using emery-cloth. Apply the heat generally, watching the colours appearing. When the area reaches a dark straw or pale brown colour, quench instantly. If the colour is missed, a second attempt can be made. Too light a colour leaves the tool too hard; too dark a colour means it is too soft.

Clean the tool up generally with fine emery-cloth, thread on the leather washer and drive on the handle. This can now be finally cleaned up and varnished — though traditionally these handles were left untreated: they are made apparently rather crudely in order to stand up to the heavy malleting they will receive, and to give a particularly good grip which prevents the chisel from turning in the mortise (as might be the case with a round handle).

Finally, grind to the correct bevel and hone. In view of the battering the tool is going to get, a thin keen edge will just crumble. So, in subsequent grinding and honing, keep it substantial.

These sizes, which are only suggestions, will generally suit chisels up to ½in in thickness with corresponding adjustments to the sizes of the bolster. The lengths will suit cabinetmaking. In the past some of these chisels were made unnecessarily and inconveniently long. ∎

**Bob Grant** writes: A small mortising tip. You can produce wedges for through tenons by sawing them from the waste piece of the haunch. This will ensure that they match the tenon thickness. Note that the tenon must be made slightly larger than is necessary to get an adequate length of wedge.

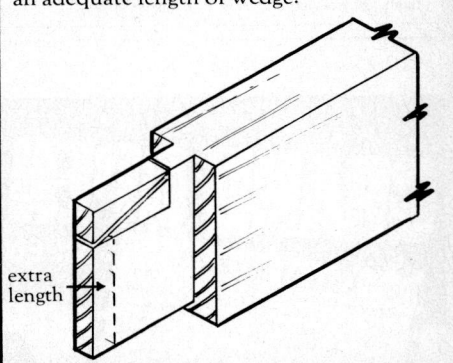

extra length

## Suggested dimensions for a ¼in mortise chisel

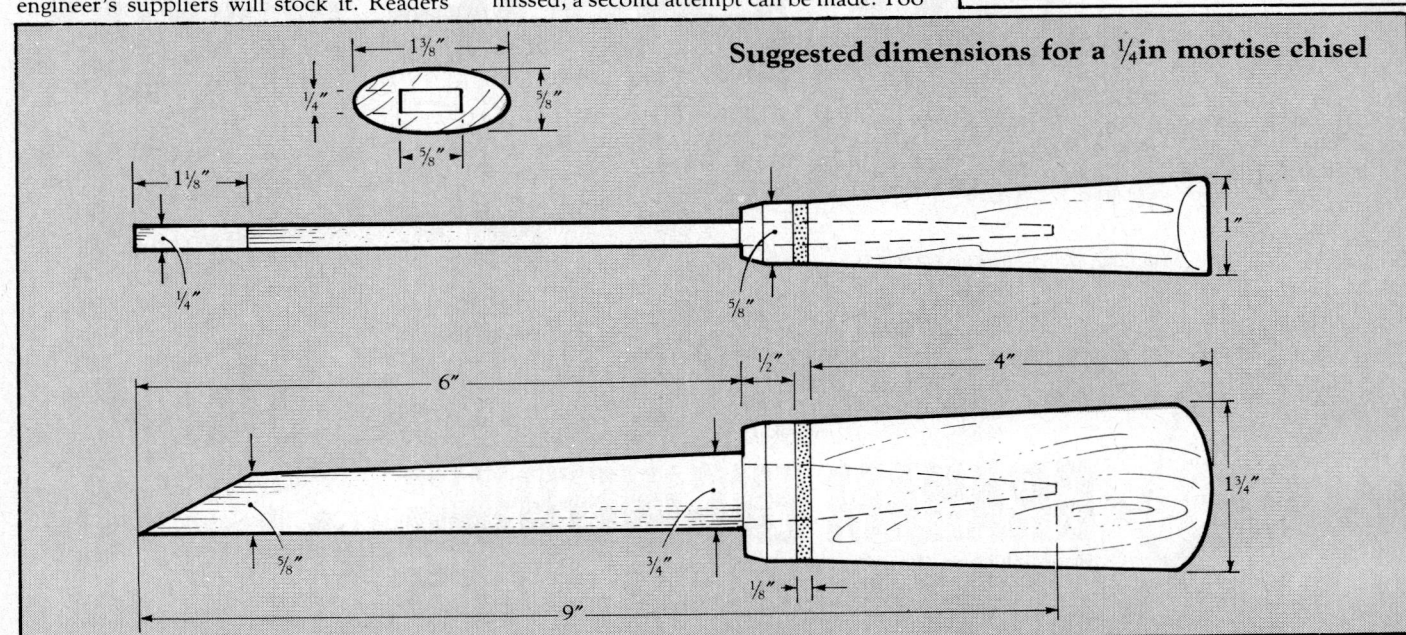

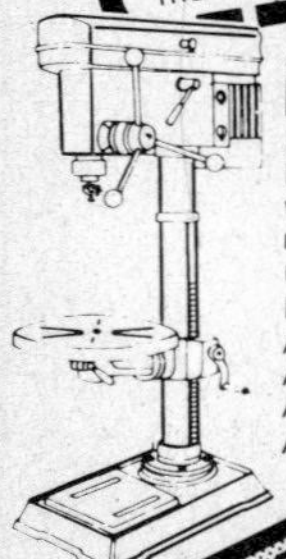

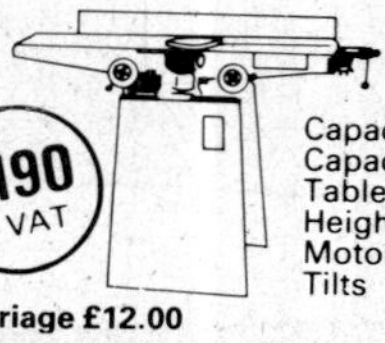

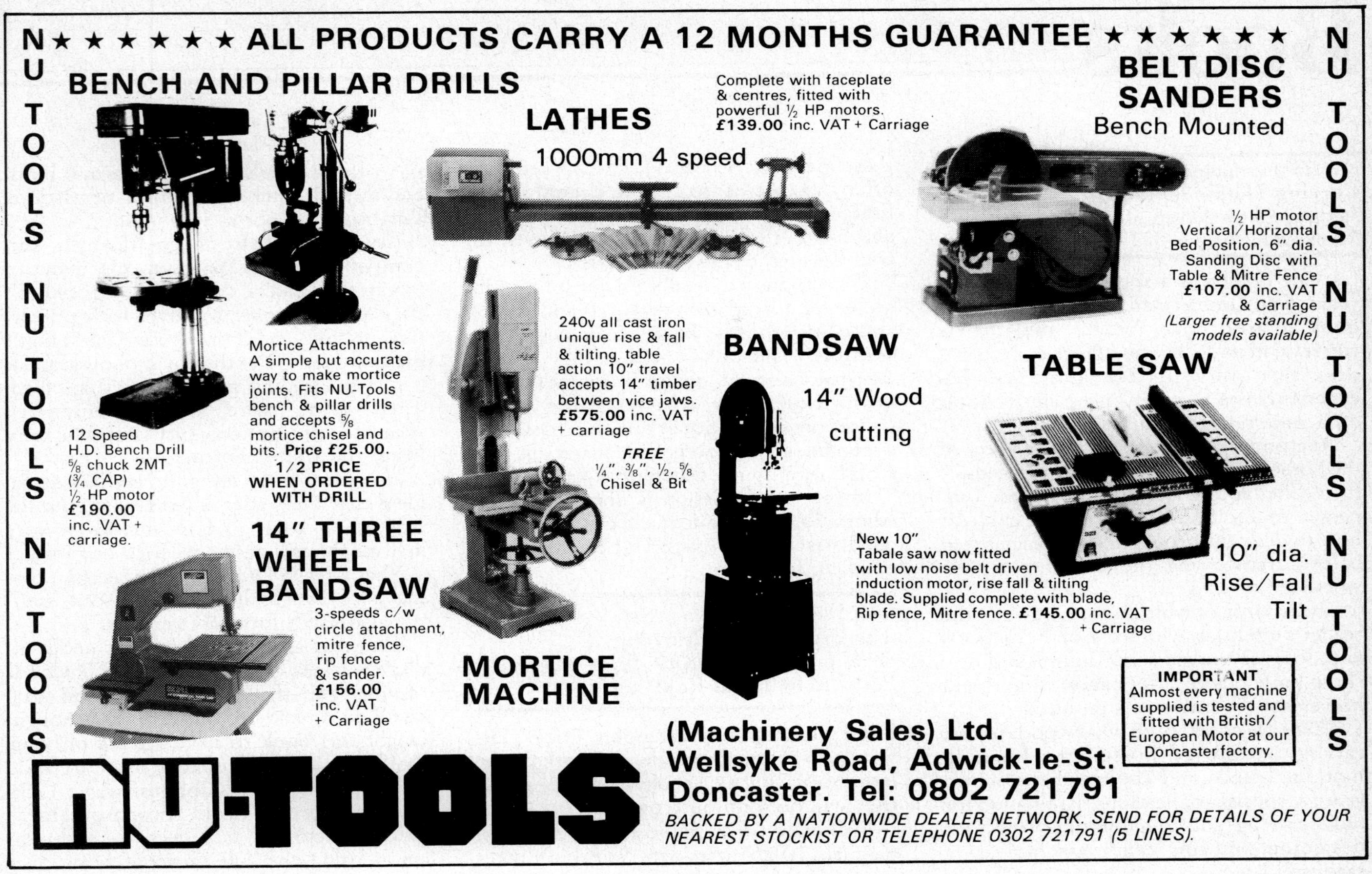
★ ★ ★ ★ ★ ★ ★ ALL PRODUCTS CARRY A 12 MONTHS GUARANTEE ★ ★ ★ ★ ★ ★ ★
NU TOOLS NU TOOLS NU TOOLS
BENCH AND PILLAR DRILLS
12 Speed H.D. Bench Drill 5/8 chuck 2MT (3/4 CAP) 1/2 HP motor £190.00 inc. VAT + carriage.
Mortice Attachments. A simple but accurate way to make mortice joints. Fits NU-Tools bench & pillar drills and accepts 5/8 mortice chisel and bits. Price £25.00.
1/2 PRICE WHEN ORDERED WITH DRILL
LATHES
1000mm 4 speed
Complete with faceplate & centres, fitted with powerful 1/2 HP motors. £139.00 inc. VAT + Carriage
BELT DISC SANDERS
Bench Mounted
1/2 HP motor Vertical/Horizontal Bed Position, 6" dia. Sanding Disc with Table & Mitre Fence £107.00 inc. VAT & Carriage
(Larger free standing models available)
240v all cast iron unique rise & fall & tilting table action 10" travel accepts 14" timber between vice jaws. £575.00 inc. VAT + carriage
FREE 1/4", 3/8", 1/2, 5/8 Chisel & Bit
MORTICE MACHINE
BANDSAW
14" Wood cutting
TABLE SAW
10" dia. Rise/Fall Tilt
New 10" Tabale saw now fitted with low noise belt driven induction motor, rise fall & tilting blade. Supplied complete with blade, Rip fence, Mitre fence. £145.00 inc. VAT + Carriage
14" THREE WHEEL BANDSAW
3-speeds c/w circle attachment, mitre fence, rip fence & sander. £156.00 inc. VAT + Carriage
IMPORTANT
Almost every machine supplied is tested and fitted with British/European Motor at our Doncaster factory.
NU-TOOLS
(Machinery Sales) Ltd.
Wellsyke Road, Adwick-le-St.
Doncaster. Tel: 0802 721791
BACKED BY A NATIONWIDE DEALER NETWORK. SEND FOR DETAILS OF YOUR NEAREST STOCKIST OR TELEPHONE 0302 721791 (5 LINES).

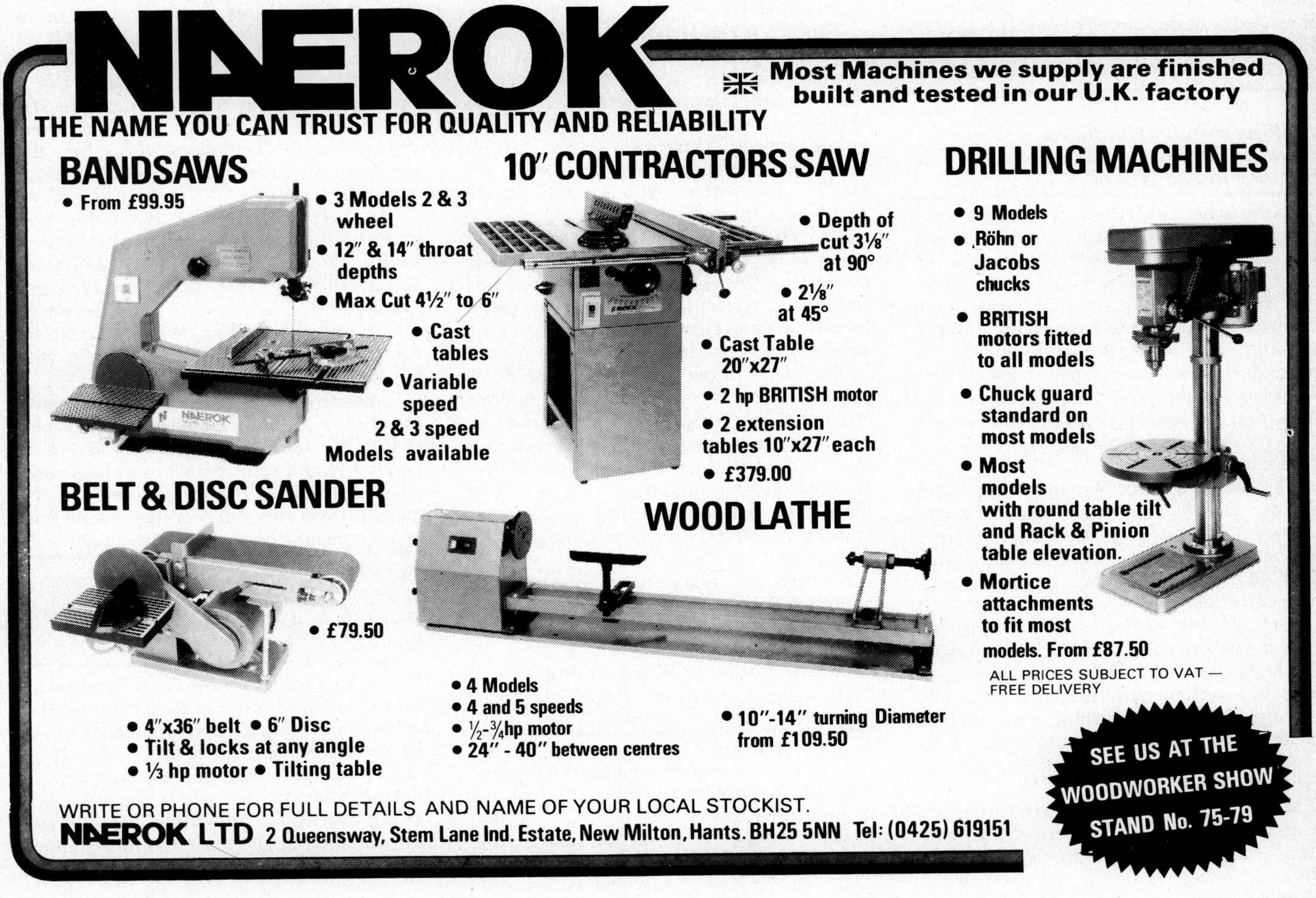
NAEROK
Most Machines we supply are finished built and tested in our U.K. factory
THE NAME YOU CAN TRUST FOR QUALITY AND RELIABILITY
BANDSAWS
• From £99.95
• 3 Models 2 & 3 wheel
• 12" & 14" throat depths
• Max Cut 4½" to 6"
• Cast tables
• Variable speed 2 & 3 speed Models available
10" CONTRACTORS SAW
• Depth of cut 3⅛" at 90°
• 2⅛" at 45°
• Cast Table 20"x27"
• 2 hp BRITISH motor
• 2 extension tables 10"x27" each
• £379.00
DRILLING MACHINES
• 9 Models
• Röhn or Jacobs chucks
• BRITISH motors fitted to all models
• Chuck guard standard on most models
• Most models with round table tilt and Rack & Pinion table elevation.
• Mortice attachments to fit most models. From £87.50
ALL PRICES SUBJECT TO VAT — FREE DELIVERY
BELT & DISC SANDER
• £79.50
• 4"x36" belt • 6" Disc
• Tilt & locks at any angle
• ⅓ hp motor • Tilting table
WOOD LATHE
• 4 Models
• 4 and 5 speeds
• ½-¾hp motor
• 24" - 40" between centres
• 10"-14" turning Diameter from £109.50
SEE US AT THE WOODWORKER SHOW STAND No. 75-79
WRITE OR PHONE FOR FULL DETAILS AND NAME OF YOUR LOCAL STOCKIST.
NAEROK LTD 2 Queensway, Stem Lane Ind. Estate, New Milton, Hants. BH25 5NN Tel: (0425) 619151

# Books

Eric Zimmerman
**Carving Horses in Wood**
*Sterling, £4.95 paperback*
*Reviewed by Sid Lye*

Carving horses as a speciality for over 20 years, Eric Zimmerman has brought to this book a great love for his subject. He conveys, in its 128 pages of text, superb line drawings and plates, some of his experiences as a carver, using simple tools on a wide range of timbers.

Anatomical sketches show the parts of the horse, and depict the different breeds — from Shetland to Shire and Morgan Tennessee to Lipizzaner. The author explains how to draw the proportions for each breed before transferring the drawings to the wood for cutting.

The hazards of whittling are drawn to the reader's attention with some of the author's anecdotes about badly cut thumbs and very sharp knife blades; after bandsawing, 'hand knives are the only tools required'.

There are chapters on what woods to use, carving a team of horses, the horse in motion, breeds and carving them, mixed groups, special applications/lamination for relief carving, and an ambitious project for designing, cutting and assembling a carousel.

Containing as it does many useful tips and techniques for carving the horse, this book is not for the absolute beginner, but rather for the person with a good basic knowledge of the carver's craft. It is a lot of horse sense for its cover price; the author and publishers are to be commended.

Jack Hill
**Making Family Heirlooms**
*David & Charles, £15 hardback*
*Reviewed by Zach Taylor*

Anyone who has visited a Woodworker Show in recent years is likely to have seen Jack Hill demonstrating furniture-making — and to have noted not only his skill, and the consummate ease with which he lovingly coaxes shapes from wood, but the humour and integrity with which he presents his work. His new book is just what one might expect from this talented man, and possession of a copy will enable you to capture a little of his magic for yourself.

The title is a trigger for inspiration, and the contents live up to it. The 272 pages include studies of classical design in terms of background and development, plus detailed descriptions of working, construction and finishing.

Each of the projects is illustrated by colour photography of a superb standard depicting the finished piece. Separate chapters deal with materials, joints, methods, carving, fitting and finishing; they supplement the projects, while being useful references in their own right for the not-so-experienced craftsman.

In some cases Jack Hill has turned to craftsman friends to present their own pieces where special skills are called for, but most are his own work. The 23 projects offer a choice of items both beautiful and functional, ranging from simple shelving and boxes, through cabinets and chests, to sophisticated chairs and dressers.

Constructional details are given for each piece, reinforced with drawings and black-and-white photos. Each project carries a sensibly laid-out cutting list whose dimensions are in imperial measure (as one might expect for what is, after all, a collection of traditional British pieces). An appendix, giving sources for materials, and a bibliography are thoughtfully added.

My recommendation is unreserved, my admiration unbounded; and my thanks and good wishes go to Jack Hill for this most excellent book.

John Sainsbury
**The Craft of Woodturning**
*Sterling; £13.95 hardback, £7.95 paperback*
*Reviewed by Tobias Kaye*

I did not enjoy reading this book. The standards it sets for producing work on the lathe may suit an absolute beginner, but they will be soon outgrown.

In common with the authors of technical manuals 10-25 years ago, Sainsbury takes pages to explain details that become obvious as soon as one lays hands on the machine or tool described. The drawings are excellent and clear, but even they are occasionally superfluous too.

This is not a small book, and on finishing it one is surprised not to have been led on to projects more demanding or adventurous than the simple work illustrated. The items shown do not have the flair or style that one would expect. Moreover, several exhibit faults, for example in the finish, that are readily discernible even in the poorly reproduced photos.

The chapter on sharpening may offer some clues to this. I do not know any professional who uses the methods described; nor could I, for one, easily handle tools so sharpened — let alone get a satisfactory finish from them.

The final chapter on 'Work by Contemporary Turners', though it does not represent an original idea, would be excellent were it not for the gulf between the standard of the work it shows and that attained in the preceding chapters. The jump is so marked that reading the book could give one no idea how some of these final pieces were made.

I would not recommend this book to anyone seriously interested in woodturning.

E. J. Tangerman
**Complete Guide to Woodcarving**
*Sterling; £14.95 hardback, £9.95 paperback*
*Reviewed by Alan Bridgewater*

E. J. Tangerman rides again . . . what a book! What value for money, what a page-by-page treasure-chest of world-wide woodcarving inspirational ideas!

With acres of very exciting and detailed illustrations and photos (over 700), stacks of working details, heaps of tips and hints, and untold numbers of words of wisdom, this book just about says it all.

Or does it? Let's go through this compendium and play that old game of 'good and bad'. It's a big fat book, it's packed from cover to cover with punchy information, and it only costs £9.95; that's got to be good. But the cover photograph is a real misleading mess-up — that's bad. Then again, there are so many well presented illustrations; pity about the fuzzy black-and-white photos.

However, there are so many wonderful ideas that the reader is left reeling. But the section on tools and techniques is very lightweight and only covers 20 or so pages — that's really bad. It's a shame, too, that the book has so little to say about traditional western furniture carving.

But then again, E.J. says just about all there is to say on the subject of folk woodcarving, and that's very good. And so I could go on and on; but enough's enough. Ought this book to have a place on your shelf? If you are interested in western classic carving — Grinling Gibbons swags, 17th-century cherubs, florid rococo ornamentation, Victorian table-legs — and you enjoy using the full range of traditional gouges, chisels and spoon-bits, this book is certainly not for you. If, on the other hand, your big passion is folk art (ethnic and tribal work, knife carving, whittled animals, stylised folk figures, faces, flowers, fishes and foliage), without doubt this book is the best of the best.

It isn't a 'how-to' book in the sense that it takes you blow-by-blow through specific projects, nor is it really aimed at never-done-it-before beginners. It's for the experienced carver with specific areas of interest.

My big moan is that the work is a compendium of E.J.'s other books, *Carving Birds in Wood*, *Carving Figures and Faces in Wood* and at least seven other titles published by Sterling since 1980. So watch out if you are thinking of buying this one for a woodcarver who already has a well stocked library.

Tangerman is a carver of over 50 years' experience. Although maybe his style is just a little dry and gruff, he comes across as very witty and totally sincere — he knows what he's talking about! I'm sure that for many carvers this will become a useful tool and a constant inspirational companion.

The Editors of Time-Life Books
**Working with Wood**
*Time-Life Books, hardback*
*Reviewed by Chris Nash*

This is an excellent book. It is handsome, but not so decorative as to end up on the coffee-table. It is a hoard of sensible and detailed information, but not of that grim kind which loses sight of the enjoyment of making things in the quest for strict accuracy. Its black-and-white photos are few but high-quality; its line illustrations contrive to be both life-like and schematic, developing film-style from 'general shots' to close-ups showing particular aspects of an operation from the most appropriate angles.

The whole is always visible in the parts. In a typical double-page spread the reader will find, say, clearly illustrated instructions for two manoeuvres with the radial-arm saw, for setting up a jig and work-surface described on the page before, and for use of a pair of sawhorses for which full plans and instructions are given a few pages later. Other layouts give bonuses in the form of box-displayed safety tips or even brief advice on the physical stresses involved in some operations.

What this means in practice is that one can have the book open while working and know that all essential information is to hand in front of one, or at the turn of a page or two. No back-tracking to contents page or index, since essential cross-referencing (kept to a minimum because of the superbly managed layout) is invariably given on the page being used.

*Working with Wood* isn't about furniture-making, though even in this area its sensible, thorough treatment of tools and techniques is of some incidental use. It sets out to offer 'home owners detailed instructions on repairs, construction and improvements which they can undertake themselves'. A sober and unpretentious version of what some more lavish productions would style 'secrets of the professionals' or sell exorbitantly in 'weekly encyclopaedia' versions of great bulk and dubious practicality. A moderately but not meanly sized volume, it displays a great deal of knowledge, not least about where to stop.

Choosing, checking, storing and assessing the usefulness of various timbers are dealt with in a brisk four pages. 'Sawing' takes in manual plus portable and workshop-centred machine procedures; drilling and mortising are refreshingly combined as 'making holes'. As each theme is developed, associated topics are integrated as appropriate, so that one learns about marking-out methods, commercial and home-made jigs, guides and work-aids as one goes along — in considerable but never bewildering variety. Particularly pleasing is the lead-in to each section, where typically the text moves from, say, a historical/mythological background to modern mechanised techniques within a single page. A style which thus manages to be selective but not superficial, enthusiastic but not rhapsodic and businesslike but not boring is a model of its kind.

Two quibbles: pp82-3 describe and show a hammer being used on a chisel — viewers of a nervous disposition are warned to avoid these; also the picture and caption on end-planing (p75) omit to indicate that it helps to scribe the workpiece all round first. Otherwise, one has here a book armed with which the ordinary handyman should feel confident enough to embark on most of his own house-carpentry, and maybe some for his friends and neighbours.

John Trussell
***Making Furniture***
*Dryad, £4.95*
*Reviewed by Luke Hughes*

This book, first published in 1970 and just now re-published, is written for the express purpose of helping those who have acquired a basic knowledge of woodworking techniques and who now want to progress to designing and making their own furniture. Or such is the claim in the introduction.

It has chapters on most of the usual techniques required in cabinetmaking, among which are some very good tips. And there is a chapter on design approaches which repeats some truths too frequently forgotten by furniture designers — or at least that would have been true 15 years ago when this book was first published, but standards have risen dramatically in the last few years and I can't help feeling that the text is rather out-of-date.

As to design, the book is badly presented — it doesn't make you want to go on reading and digesting the information, and the design projects are hideous in the extreme. This is a shame, since the author has collated a great deal of information which is useful to professionals and amateurs alike. This book is rather like a piece of furniture made by an expert craftsman, using first-rate material but an atrocious design; the result detracts from the quality of the work, spoils the material, and gives little pleasure in use.

Keith Bridenhagen and Patrick Spielman
***Realistic Decoys***
*Sterling, £11.95*
*Reviewed by Ian Norbury*

It is difficult for someone accustomed to the European tradition of woodcarving to look at a book like this without a certain scepticism. The idea of painting a carving to look realistic is rather startling — yet it is of course a far older tradition than the natural wood finish. The glass eyes used on these ducks horrify me personally, but inlays of metal, glass, enamel and precious stone were the norm on ancient Greek sculpture and on later European woodcarvings.

Perhaps what disturbs me most is the total lack of interpretation. These birds are completely realistic — not a shred of the artist's personality is put into them; or so it seems.

All that aside, if you are interested in caving decoy ducks this seems an excellent book. Every conceivable aspect of the visible duck (it appears there is no interest whatever in what happens underneath the eathers) is dealt with in minute detail. The characteristic expressions are illustrated, and there are close-up photographs of feathers from various parts of the body, plus bill, feet, etc., for the many varieties of duck. The business of producing the actual wooden shape is a minor part of the process, it would seem; most of the work consisting of burning in the hairs of the feathers with a kind of pyrograph and then painting them in a painstaking replication of the original. Carving gouges do not really figure in the equipment of the decoy carver. He works with rotary burrs, tiny grindstones, knives and sandpaper.

The last chapter, of 30 pages, concerns making ducks with a natural finish, and very nice they are too. The standard of photography and printing is fine, and there are several pages of colour plates. Finally, the appendixes deal with decoy contests and shows, explaining the rules and giving addresses and dates. Also covered are tools, equipment, and suppliers' addresses for everything you could possibly need, even magazines. I was amazed to find that plastic moulds of different types of bills. Ready-made plywood feather-tips and cast metal feet are all readily available.

It appears that decoy ducks are really big business in America. Howeer, I think this is an excellent book for anyone interested. The authors have included working drawings in another book, and also produced a book for beginners — although I think most people could manage with this one. I certainly learnt quite a lot from it which can be applied to any form of carving; but I'm not sure the painted variety will import very well.

James Lawton
***A Master Carver's Trade Secrets***
*Mansard Press (UK) Ltd, 15 Princes Rd,*
*   London W13 9AS, £5 post free*
*Reviewed by Howard Raybould*

This book is part of a series published by Mansard, designed to focus upon individual craftsmen by persuading them to write in their own words about their work in an uninhibited fashion — thus bringing the reader an invaluable insight into the world of the creative maker in the 20th century. James Lawton is not afraid to describe the small and often very amusing deceptions which are occasionally perpetrated, but he also tells us about the great commissions which are provided by private collectors, and the organisation and running of a small carving shop in London.

With his sleeves rolled up Lawton opens the book by describing a contented man of 50 or 60, carving away in his garden shed. 16 chapters later, after a rip-roaring journey in and out of the workshop, the author rolls down his sleeves as he concludes with the predicament of the present-day carver who only works in the classical style.

Not only is this the perfect bedside book, but its serious guidelines and advice make it sensible reading in colleges and schools. And for once, thank God, we have a book that brings the subject alive — not just a conglomeration of previous books, full of dogmatic nonsense, duplicated technical information and out-of-focus photos of hands holding tools. If you want a penetrating view of the predicament of the modern classical carver, or just useful and interesting information, this book is very worthwhile.

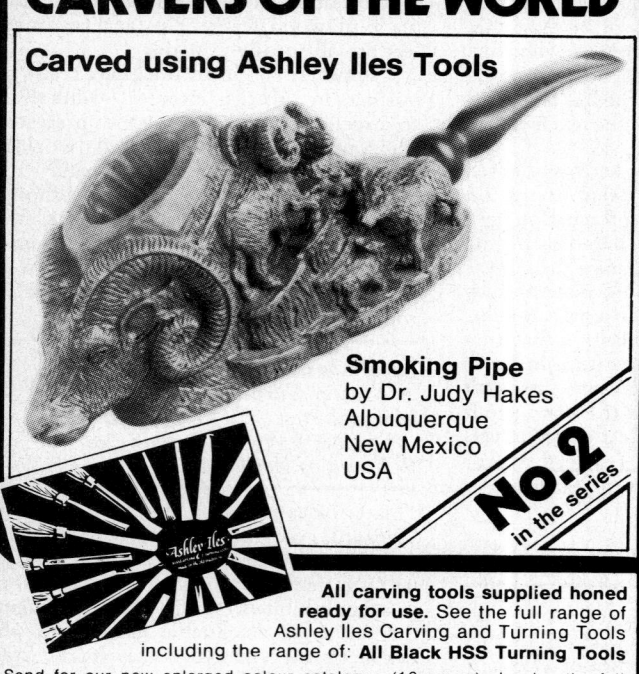

850

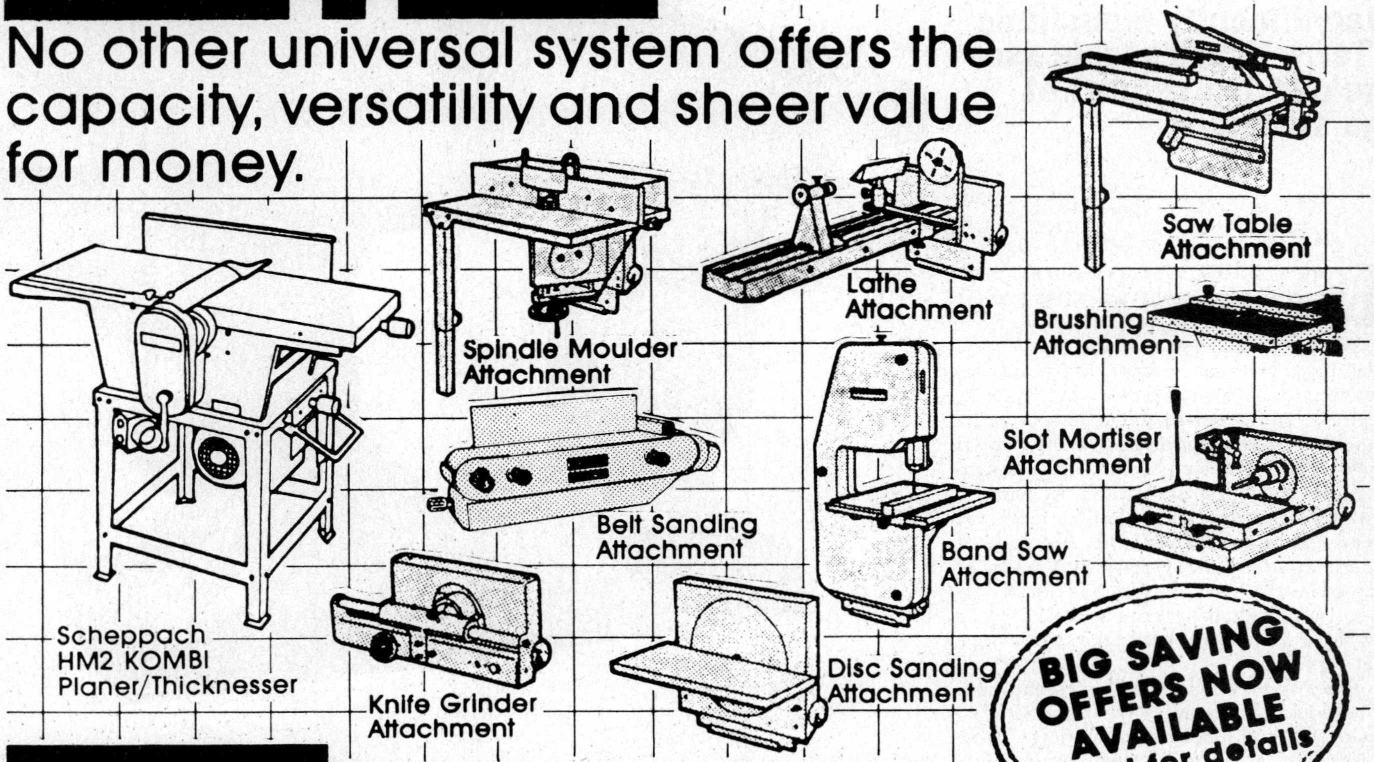

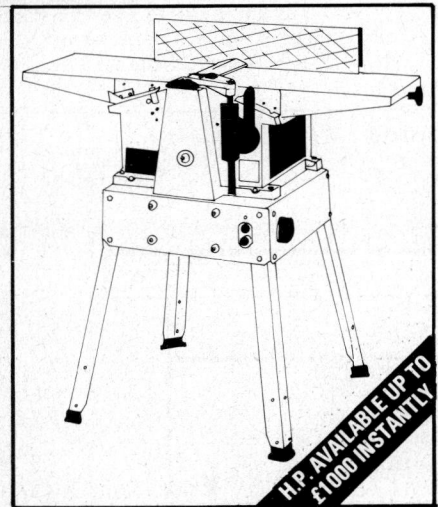

# Low overheads

## Magnificently monolithic – Terry Hoare's table uses the carving as part of the structure

I work wood just for the pleasure it gives. That feeling is really what this project is all about.

What I needed (as so often) was a good idea for a birthday present. My mind was running on coffee-tables; but that, in itself, seemed hardly out-of-the-ordinary, and I quickly realised that any originality would have to be introduced by way of the design.

So I went for something unusual. I wanted a piece that didn't look modern, yet would suit a modern setting. A couple of hours' doodling, and I arrived at the idea of carved heads. The hoods suggest the Middle Ages, and the hats (or crowns) on each one fulfil the constructional requirement for a flat top.

The wood I used was Brazilian mahogany. The blocks for the heads were laminated to make up the required thickness, using Cascamite glue and several G-cramps. When the glue was set they were cut to finished length.

Then I drilled the legs, together with the head and base crosspieces, ready for screwing into position. It's easier to do this before carving than afterwards. In addition, you can screw extra blocks on to top or bottom of the legs for clamping to the bench or holding in the vice.

I made the tabletop from three separate pieces of wood — thicknessed, edge-planed square and glued up with Cascamite. Because I had no sash-cramps, I used the procedure shown in fig. 1. I screwed a piece of 3x2 to the back of my bench, and laid some paper down in case of glue seepage. I cramped another piece to the front and yet another piece of wood against the tabletop. Then I used four pairs of wedges to apply pressure, and left the whole thing for 24 hours.

When the glue was dry, the top was squared up using plane, Surform and files, and finally sanded down. To give the table extra rigidity the stretcher was fixed to the base crosspieces with half-lap dovetail joints (fig. 2).

All that remained was the carving of the four heads. Firstly I drew the design on paper in front view and profile. Then I divided it into squares and transferred it on to the wood using the squares as a guide.

To remove the waste I used a bandsaw. Alternately you could use a coping-saw or indeed a tenon saw, making a series of cuts down to the line and chiselling out the waste (fig. 3). If you do use a bandsaw or coping saw a complete profile can be cut in one piece — which may then be taped back into position. Because the design is drawn on it,

this enables you to cut the adjacent profiles. You should be left with a rather squarish head. Now, by referring to your original drawing, re-draw the front, side and rear profiles. You can also screw holding blocks to the top/bottom of each head (fig. 4).

If you now lay the head on the bench face-upwards, placing underneath it the waste piece that was cut from the back, it will be well supported. The work should then be secured to the bench by a G-cramp, a holdfast or something similar. Mark out the oval of the face with a suitably curved gouge. The waste on the outside of this line can now be removed down to the line of the cloth on the side profile.

Cut out the waste either side of the nose, leaving a wedge shape. Then round off the edges of the face. The eyes are formed by first cutting down from the eyebrow to the bottom lid, cutting into the head. Next, cut upwards from the cheek to the same cut, and you have the rough shape of the eye-socket (fig. 5). When you have done this on both sides, cut in the top eyelids using the inside curve of a suitable gouge, and do like-wise with the bottom lids. At this point I found it easier to use a scalpel to refine the shape of the actual eyes.

You'll find it useful to refer constantly to a real face (in a mirror, if necessary!). Go on to refine the shape of the nose and mouth

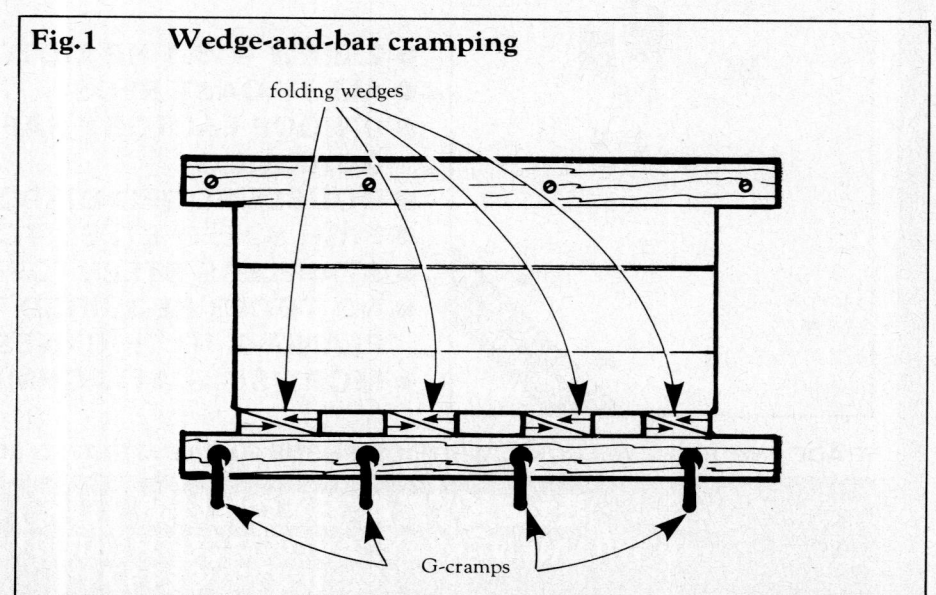

**Fig.1    Wedge-and-bar cramping**

folding wedges

G-cramps

with whatever tools you have available. I used gouges, straight and skew chisels, scalpels and various files. When you are satisfied with the shape of the face, round off the crown and front and rear of the cloth hood, mark in the folds with pencil or felt pen, and cut out using gouges and knives. Use riffler files and abrasive paper to finish off and round over sharp edges.

Lastly, shape the 'crowns'. I kept them simple, using a small riffler to mark in the lines.

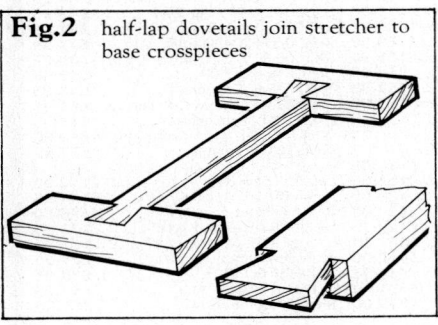

**Fig.2** half-lap dovetails join stretcher to base crosspieces

If you're satisfied with the shape of the carving as a whole, smooth down with abrasives, taking out all tool marks. I use engineer's emery cloth, which I find very good. Then dowse the whole thing in water and leave it to dry. This will raise the grain and make the carving feel as rough as a pineapple, so you now have to rub it down all over again. That's one leg done; just three more to do!

When all the carving is finished the heads can be screwed into position, and the top can be screwed on from underneath.

At this point in the job something didn't look quite right. The piece seemed too angular; so I rounded off the corners of the top cross-members. This seemed to soften the appearance that little bit.

I stained the whole table to a dark oak colour and left it for a few days to dry. Then I applied copious amounts of linseed oil by brush and left it for a week before wiping off the excess with a dry cloth. After a further few days I polished it with Colron wax.

From my mother's reaction to her birthday present, and from things she has said subsequently both to myself and other people, I knew those long though enjoyable hours of work were well worth it. Now, almost a year later and after much polishing from Mum, the table seems to have mellowed and taken on a patina that just cannot be achieved without the passing of time.

Obviously this basic design is open to many modifications, but I feel I achieved my aims. If you'd like to have a go at a similar project, but feel you don't have the necessary tools, don't let that stop you. Use whatever you have, and improvise where necessary! ∎

## Cutting list

| | | | | | |
|---|---|---|---|---|---|
| top | 1 off | 8 | x | 2 | x 45in |
| | 2 | 6 | | | 45 |
| top rails | 2 | 5 | . | 2 | 16½ |
| bottom rails | 2 | 5 | | 2 | 20 |
| stretcher | 1 | 5 | | 2 | 40 |
| legs (laminated) | 4 | 5½ | | 5 | 10 |

### Carving the profile

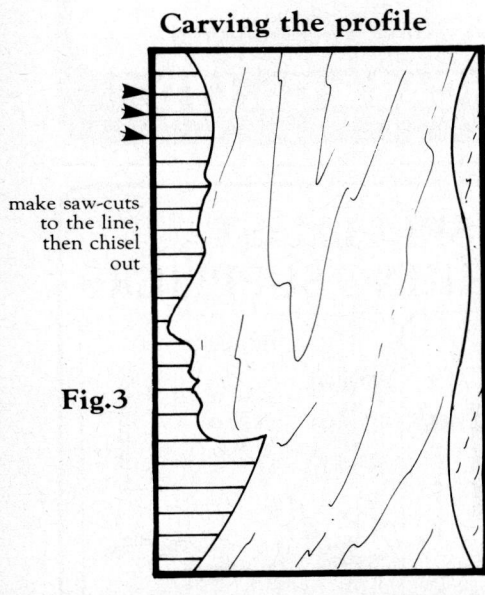

make saw-cuts to the line, then chisel out

**Fig.3**

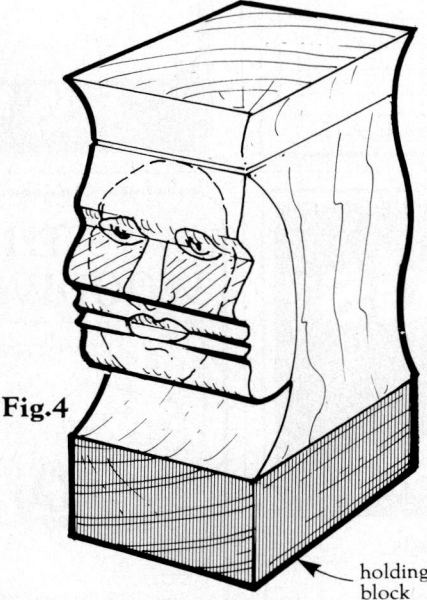

**Fig.4**

holding block

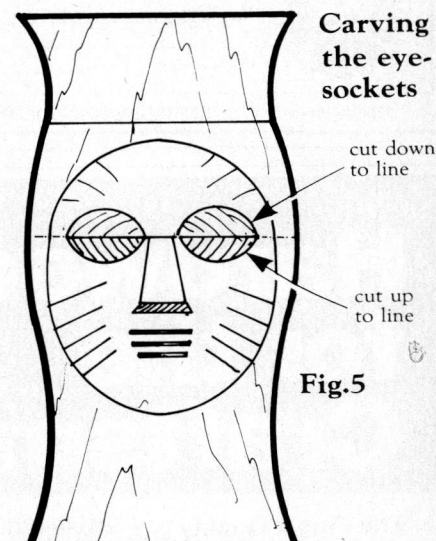

### Carving the eye-sockets

cut down to line

cut up to line

**Fig.5**

● *This view of two heads emphasises their statuesque solidity – a bit like Easter Island in your living room!*

● *Constant reference to a face (your own?) helps the life-carving*

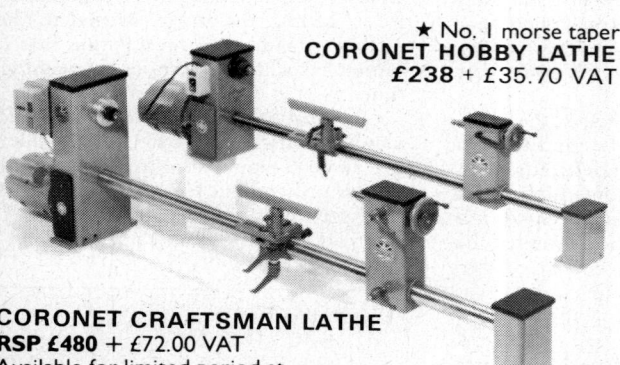

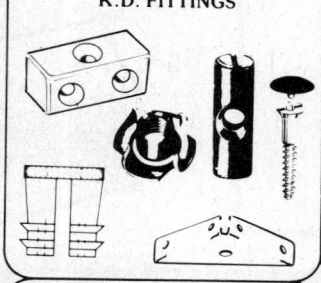
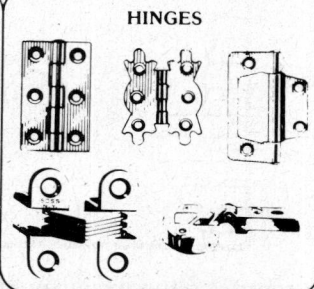
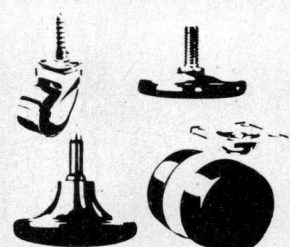

854

# A sharp idea

**James Paffett improves pencil-sharpening technology with this device that's (almost) as easy to make as it is to use**

W hat can you do with a broken Surform blade? Make a pencil-sharpener specially for the workshop.

It consists basically of a shallow box of any convenient hardwood, and a lid made from a piece of Surform blade, suitably squared off on the grinder. To sharpen a pencil you simply draw the point backwards across the surface of the steel blade, much as you would grate a nutmeg. The shavings of wood and graphite fall into the box and stay there.

It is convenient to set the blade in grooves in the box sides, and to make the box ½in or so longer than the blade, which is free to slide up and down this much. When the blade is 'down' in its normal working position, the gap at the top is covered by a strip of wood which stops the shavings from falling out. To empty out the shavings you slide the blade up to open the ½in gap at the bottom. The layout is shown in the diagram. The dimensions are not critical; the width is dictated by the blade.

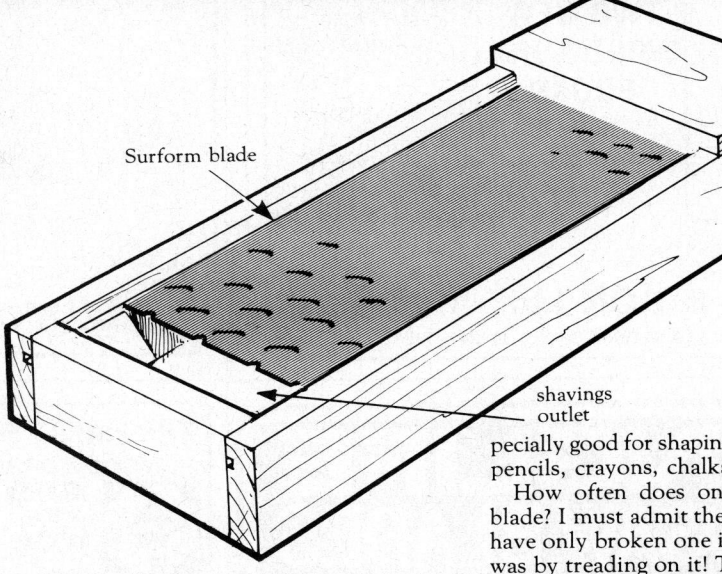

Surform blade

shavings outlet

Why, you might ask, both to make a contraption of this sort when the little twiddle-round sharpeners, much used by schoolchildren, are so cheap and effective? The Surform sharpener, I would claim, is a much more flexible instrument. It will give you a sharp or a blunt point, an ordinary conical one or a draughtsman's chisel shape as desired. It will handle any size of pencil, including the wide flat carpenter's type, and those with artistic leanings will find that it is es-

pecially good for shaping points on coloured pencils, crayons, chalks and pastels.

How often does one break a Surform blade? I must admit they're pretty robust; I have only broken one in 20 years, and that was by treading on it! The Mk 1 sharpener employed the largest surviving fragment, suitably squared off. For later models made in response to family demands, I have actually had to buy blades — the short version used in the Surform plane is suitable and needs no modification.

Perhaps the manufacturers of Surform and similar cutting blades would consider marketing a plastic-bodied sharpener along the lines described — I shouldn't look for very much in the way of royalties . . . ∎

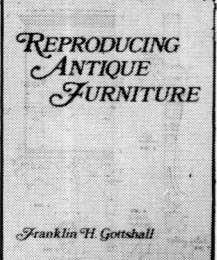
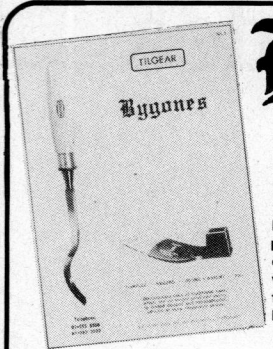

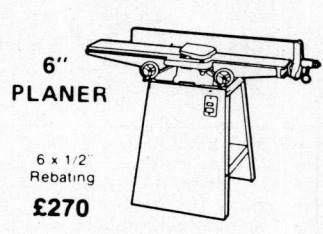
856

# Bidding for bargains

**Factory auctions can be sources of delight or despair in equipment-buying. Richard Gaskin tells the tale**

I like auctions. I was first hooked several years ago when I bought four carved stone heads for a pound, so when I saw a clearance sale 'Of interest to builders, joiners, D.I.Y; Clearance Auction of Woodworking Machinery, Power Tools, Timber Stock etc. etc.' advertised in the local paper I decided to go along and see if there was anything interesting.

One piece of advice, which I pass on to anyone who has never been to an auction, has saved me from making bigger fool of myself than I usually do. Go to the view, or at the least get to the sale early enough to have a good look round, and make a note in your catalogue of how much you are prepared to spend on any of the lots that interest you. Then try to stick to those amounts. Keep in mind that it's the auctioneer's job to get the best price for each and every lot, so he will always encourage the punters to go just one more bid. Resist the temptation. It's your job to buy at the right price, not to pay the full retail price for a piece of clapped-out junk.

Enough of the lecture; on with the sale. The first 60-odd lots were all stains and finishes that did not really interest me, though £3 for 5 litres of Jaxa dark mahogany stain seemed reasonable.

Then we got on to the contents of one of the workshops. Four sheets of plywood for £6 was cheap, but £30 for a big air-powered 12-station drill was silly. There were a number of circular saw-blades, ranging from 11¾ to 19½in diameter, both HSS and carbide-tipped. The most expensive fetched £12, which for a 19½in tipped blade in 'as new' condition seemed a snip.

A steel platform and steps, a giant Meccano 5ft high, 12ft long and 8ft wide, was very cheap at £30; 5.5kg Chubb dry-powder fire-extinguishers at £12 and £14 were good value. Then came the first aberration, when someone enthusiastically paid £15 for a dilapidated sack-truck that could be bought new for £25 or less. Sanity returned when a number of wooden trucks that were ideal for any workshop, 22x40in and all fitted with four heavy-duty castors, went for £1 each. There were no takers for 'three bags of sawdust'; I suppose everyone had enough of that at home.

On to another workshop that had once been the upholstery cutting-room. Someone bought 25kg of PVA adhesive for £12, and another buyer got 6000 hardwood dowels for £9. Several people snapped up 12x24ft dust-sheets at £3 or £4. Then an interesting lot, a no.53 Record vice, was an excellent buy at £16. Three packs of 50 sheets of silicon-carbide abrasive paper fetched £8, and a number of B&A air-operated staple guns £22-26.

In the main assembly shop, the site of the 'small and power tools', the buyers underwent a subtle change. Up to this point most of them had obviously been 'trade', and now the majority were obviously 'private'. The prices reflected this — what makes a man pay £47.50 (plus £7.13 VAT!) for a well-used (this was after all a furniture factory!) Elu MOF96 router, when he could buy a new one for £77.95 including VAT and carriage? The saving of £23.32 wouldn't really seem to make it much of a bargain, especially when you bear in mind that everything at auction is bought 'as seen', with no warranty of any sort.

The next lot, an Elu DS 140 biscuit-jointer, was a much better buy for £40. This is in my opinion a most useful tool, the best thing for cutting up sheets of ply, chip or blockboard really easily and accurately as well as joining panels. 4ft Record sash-cramps found ready buyers at £15, and so did a nearly-new bench — 7x3ft complete with no. 53 Record vice — at £70.

A Protim Timbermaster was reasonable at £47.50 and so was a pair of 10in G-cramps at £10; but it was the main machinery that provided the lucky buyers with the real bargains. A complete spray-booth about 20ft long, 12ft deep and 10ft high fetched £60, a Workrite Model 4000 wood-welder £140 and a Harrison 12in surface planer with 6ft table £175. An even bigger bargain (in both senses of the word) was a Hydrovane 66PUM compressor and receiver which was obviously relatively new yet went for only £140. An old but very solid Dominion saw, complete with a 22in tipped blade, went for £55 and a Wadkin 18x9in planer/thicknesser fetched £1700.

Conclusions to be drawn? Well, you do need to know the normal price of whatever it is you propose to bid for, otherwise you can easily pay too much, or just as easily miss a bargain. But do bear in mind that much of the machinery is three-phase, so you need to add on the cost of a phase converter or new motor if, like me, you are restricted to a single-phase supply in your workshop. There is also the problem of transporting your bargain home — most of the industrial machinery was too big and heavy to pop it into the boot!

What did I buy? A Chubb CO$_2$ extinguisher for £10, a nest of 12 drawers for £1, an 8x3ft bench with no.53 Record vice for £60, a timber trolley for £1 and a box of 1000 biscuit joiners for £1. But some of that machinery was really tempting. Perhaps there'll be another sale soon. ■

● *An 8x3ft joiner's bench, complete with no.53 Record vice – gone to that gentleman from the magazine for £60! Could it have been cheaper?*

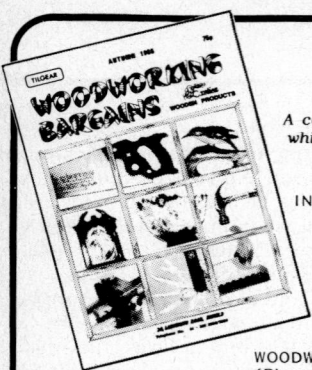

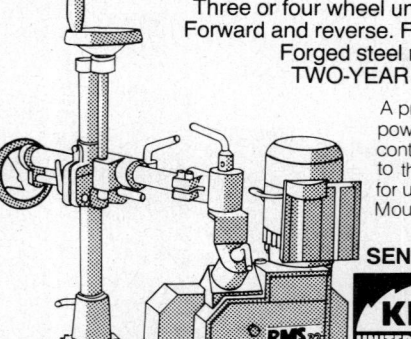

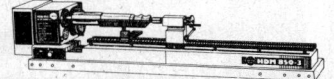

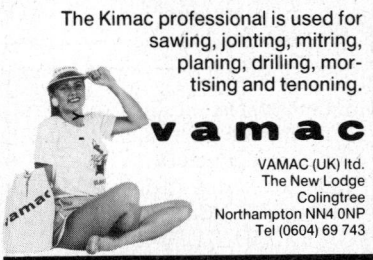

859

860

# Making the grade

## Timber expert Bill Brown shows the way through the (hard) woods

● FAS or Comsels? Waney-edged boards are prepared for the kiln (photo John Boddy Timber)

When you select your imported square-edged hardwoods from a yard, you naturally look at the cleanliness and condition of the stock, the dimensions, and the cost related to potential waste. But do you look at the commercial grading of the wood?

Shipping marks will always tell you something, but they are less important in selection than the commercial quality, mainly because the importers have already learned their best overseas suppliers. An importer pays for wood before it is seen, so obviously he will have established the mills who provide exactly what he wants — material of a consistent quality arriving in good condition after a long voyage. Irrespective of the shipping mark, it is the commercial grading and accepted quality within it which generally governs the sale.

Up to about 1930, America exported enormous quantities of square-edged hardwoods world-wide and particularly to this country and Europe. Other countries like Japan and West Africa have more or less followed their system; the two grades which generally concern us are FAS (Firsts And Seconds) and no. 1 Common and Selects (no. 1 C&S, or Comsels). There are of course grades lower than these, but not of much interest to the average woodworker. The grading rules lay down the size, number, and type of defect permitted in each grade, but essentially an FAS graded board is practically free from defect on one side. A few flaws are permitted on the reverse, so within very fine limits the wood is really top quality. A no. 1 C&S grade contains slightly more permitted defects — but, where there is a choice, don't dismiss it without good examination, since there is a price advantage. No. 1 C&S Japanese oak, for example, is often downgraded from FAS because of a higher proportion of sapwood, sometimes with a little brownish discolouration. Where you can select small quantities you can make a good buy. Apart from this, the general run of the trade is usually quite high — particularly Jap oak shorts, which tend to be wider than the longer specifications.

Square-edged mahogany boards need different consideration. While FAS will stand up to grade, colour won't necessarily be uniform because of variation betwen trees; you can usually select for colour on small quantities, but if matching is important then through-and-through log-sawn is a better bet. It's not always easy, though, when only a few boards are required, since no merchant likes to be left with a part-log.

Square-edged mahogany in no. 1 C&S requires more careful selection, not because of basic quality, but because it generally comes from very large trees and is usually produced from top lengths of the bole and from large limbs. This means there is a tendency in some boards for the grain to run off at one end, or the texture to be a little woolly. There is a price advantage, however, and these parcels should always be considered — but give forward eye to the appearance of the work you are planning. It's possible to turn deviated grain to your advantage, in solid panels for instance, if there are corresponding features in two or three boards.

The south-east Asian square-edged hardwoods meranti and keruing are generally graded Selects & Better and Standard & Better respectively. Both grades are excellent for the intended uses, and are applicable to other species from the area; they correspond to the Export grade for lauan and other Philippine woods.

Prime grade refers to top quality Yugoslavian beech in square-edged stock, while Export 1B Rumanian refers to waney-edged beech of similar quality. There is a slight difference in texture — the latter is usually a little milder than the former — but the waste from trimming the waney edges should be taken into account against cost.

In some timber stock-lists certain items are marked WHND. This means 'worm-hole, no defect', and is considered acceptable within the grading rules. It usually refers to harmless pinworm-hole, which is easily distinguished from more pernicious beetle damage by the absence of bore dust (frass). There is blackening in and around the holes, and if any very short tunnels do appear on the surface, they run across the grain. If the wood is suitable, which it invariably is, it can be used with confidence since there is no danger of re-production of the beetle which caused the initial damage. The only problem is that even filled holes, if they are still noticeable, might cause unfavourable customer reaction. There aren' a lot of these parcels about, but the do come in.

Unlike softwoods, which are invariably imported as 'dimension stock' (all one width), square-edged hardwoods come in random widths — except teak and keruing, which are usually available in dimension stock. The normal length specification for square-edged hardwoods is 1.8m and up (6ft and up), with shorts falling from 1.7m to .9m. Normal widths are 150mm (6in) and up, with strips and narrows 50mm (2in) and up. Shorts and narrows are cheaper than the normal specifications and should be sought out, bearing in mind the general quality of grading.

Hardwood logs from West Africa generally run from 3.6m to 5.4m (12-18ft); anything longer is separately imported at a higher price. They are generally visually graded before shipment into A, B and C qualities, the ratio per load roughly 40-40-20. It's not unusual, though, for a shipment to have a higher proportion of A and B, nor is it unusual for a C quality to turn out extremely good on conversion.

If you are contemplating the purchase of a complete log or logs the yard can advise you on the imported grade of any log in stock, giving a guide to the external visual quality before any decision is made to turn down a few boards. Obviously, this can only be done with a few easily reached logs. Usually, if a log is converted into boards and stacked relatively straight and well-sticked, the ends reveal much of what the general run of the wood will be like. A large, spongey area of heart and/or badly split centres are not good signs, nor are signs along the side of some of the more central boards of rusty-looking holes where metal pegs have been driven in to hold chains. This indicates that the log has been floated, and some water-marking could result. Although importers pay for their goods before taking title, it's not to say they have no redress on the odd sub-standard parcel. Claims are often made and agreed, but the wood is usually severely down-graded and priced accordingly, so you may get a chance to examine the occasional small parcel or log which could prove a worthwhile proposition. Always remember, though, that waste must be offset against basic price. ■

# shopguide

**The quickest and easiest method of reaching all Woodworkers is to advertise in SHOP GUIDE.**
**Telephone Peter Magnani 01-437 0699 Rate: £11.00 per unit.**
**Minimum of 6 months**

**Key: H** — Hand tools, **P** — Power tools, **W** — Woodworking machinery up to £1,000, **WM** — Woodworking machinery over £1,000, **D** — Demonstration available on selected machines, **T** — Timber, **CS** — Cutting or sharpening services, **MF** — Material Finishes, **A** — Attachments **BC** — Books/catalogues, ⋆ — Mail order, **E** — EMCO Leisure Centre. **K** — Kity Woodworking Centre.

## AVON

**BATH** Tel. Bath 64513
JOHN HALL TOOLS ⋆
RAILWAY STREET
Open: Monday-Saturday
9.00 a.m.-5.30 p.m.
H.P.W.WM.D.A.BC.

**BRISTOL** Tel. (0272) 741510
JOHN HALL TOOLS LIMITED ⋆
CLIFTON DOWN SHOPPING CENTRE
WHITELADIES ROAD
Open: Monday-Saturday
9.00 a.m.-5.30 p.m.
H.P.W.WM.D.A.BC.

**BRISTOL** Tel. (0272) 629092
TRYMWOOD SERVICES
2a DOWNS PARK EAST, (off North View)
WESTBURY PARK
Open: 8.30 a.m.-5.30 p.m. Mon. to Fri.
Closed for lunch 1.00-2.00 p.m.
P.W.WM.D.T.A.BC.

**BRISTOL** Tel. (0272) 667013
WILLIS
157 WEST STREET
BEDMINISTER
Open Mon.-Fri. 8.30 a.m.-5.00 p.m.
No Saturday opening

## BEDFORDSHIRE

**BEDFORD** Tel. (0234) 59808
BEDFORD SAW SERVICE K
39 AMPTHILL ROAD
Open: Mon.-Fri. 8.30-5.30
Sat. 9.00-4.00
H.P.A.BC.W.CS.WM.D.

## BERKSHIRE

**COOKHAM** Tel. (06285) 20350
CHURCH'S TIMBER
STATION HILL
Open: Mon-Sat 8.30 a.m.-5.30 p.m.
Wed 8.30 a.m.-1.00 p.m.
H.P.W.T.CS.MF.A.

**READING** Tel. (0734) 591361
HOME CARE CENTRE
26/30 KING'S ROAD
Open: Monday-Saturday
9.00 a.m.-5.30 p.m.
H.P.W.D.A.WM.BC.

**READING** Tel. Littlewick Green 2743
DAVID HUNT (TOOL MERCHANTS) LTD ⋆
KNOWL HILL, NR. READING
Open: Monday-Saturday
9.00 a.m.-5.30 p.m.
H.P.W.D.A.BC.

## BERKSHIRE

**READING** Tel. Reading 661511
WOKINGHAM TOOL CO. LTD.
99 WOKINGHAM ROAD
Open: Mon-Sat 9.00 a.m.-5.30 p.m.
Closed 1.00-2.00 p.m. for lunch
H.P.W.WM.D.CS.A.BC.

## BUCKINGHAMSHIRE

**SLOUGH** Tel. (06286) 5125
BRAYWOOD ESTATES LTD ⋆
158 BURNHAM LANE
Open: 9.00 a.m.-5.30 p.m.
Monday-Saturday
H.P.W.WM.CS.A.

**MILTON KEYNES** Tel. (0908) 641366
POLLARD WOODWORKING CENTRE ⋆
51 AYLESBURY ST., BLETCHLEY
Open: Mon-Fri 8.30-5.30
Saturday 9.00-5.00
H.P.W.WM.D.CS.A.BC.

**HIGH WYCOMBE** Tel. (0494) 24201/33788
SCOTT SAWS LTD.
14 BRIDGE STREET ⋆
Mon.-Sat. 8.30 a.m.-6.00 p.m.
H.P.W.WM.D.T.CS.MF.A.BC.

**HIGH WYCOMBE** Tel. (0494) 22221
ISAAC LORD LTD
185 DESBOROUGH ROAD KE
Open: Mon-Fri 8.00 a.m.-5.00 p.m.
Saturday 9.00 a.m.-5.00 p.m.
H.P.W.D.A.

**TO FILL THIS SPACE PHONE PETER MAGNANI ON 01 437 0699**

## CAMBRIDGESHIRE

**CAMBRIDGE** Tel. (0223) 63132
D. MACKAY LTD. E⋆
BRITANNIA WORKS, EAST ROAD
Open: Mon.-Fri. 8.30 a.m.-1 p.m./2.00-5.00 p.m. Sat. 8.30 a.m.-1.00 p.m.
H.P.W.D.T.CS.MF.A.BC.

**CAMBRIDGE** Tel. (0223) 247386
H. B. WOODWORKING K
105 CHERRY HINTON ROAD
Open: 8.30 a.m.-5.30 p.m.
Monday-Friday
8.30 a.m.-1.00 p.m. Sat.
H.P.W.WM.D.CS.A.

**PETERBOROUGH** Tel. (0733) 64252
WILLIAMS DISTRIBUTORS (TOOLS) LIMITED K
108-110 BURGHLEY ROAD
Open: Monday to Friday
8.30 a.m.-5.30 p.m.
H.P.A.W.D.WH.BC.

## CHESHIRE

**NANTWICH** Tel. Crewe 67010
ALAN HOLTHAM K⋆
THE OLD STORES TURNERY
WISTASON ROAD, WILLASTON
Open: Tues.-Sat. 9.00 a.m.-5.30 p.m.
Closed Monday
P.W.WM.D.T.C.CS.A.BC.

**CHEADLE** Tel: 061491 1726
ERIC TOMKINSON ⋆
86 STOCKPORT ROAD
Open: Mon.-Fri. 9.00 a.m.-4.00 p.m.
Saturday 9.00 a.m.-1.00 p.m.
H.P.W.D.MF.A.BC.

## CLEVELAND

**MIDDLESBROUGH** Tel. (0642) 813103
CLEVELAND WOODCRAFT
(M'BRO), 38-42 CRESCENT ROAD K
Open: Mon-Sat 9.15 a.m.-5.30 p.m.
H.P.T.A.BC.W.WM.CS.D.

## CORNWALL

**HELSTON** Tel. Helston (03265) 4961
SOUTH WEST Truro (0872) 71671
POWER TOOLS Launceston
MONUMENT ROAD (0566) 3555
K
H.P.W.WM.D.CS.A.

**TRURO** Tel. (0872) 71671
TRURO POWER TOOLS E⋆
30 FERRIS TOWN
Open Mon.-Sat. 8.00 a.m.-12.30 p.m./1.30 p.m.-5.00 p.m.
H.P.W.WM.D.CS.MF.A.BC.

## CUMBRIA

**CARLISLE** Tel: (0228) 36391
W. M. PLANT
ALLENBROOK ROAD
ROSEHILL, CA1 2UT
Open: Mon.-Fri. 8.00 a.m.-5.15 p.m.
Sat. 8.00 a.m.-12.30 noon
P.W.WM.D.CS.A.

## DERBYSHIRE

**DERBY** Tel. (0332) 41862
HAZLEHURSTS LTD. E⋆
LONDON ROAD AND CANAL STREET
Open: Mon.-Sat. 8.30 a.m.-5.30 p.m. (retail)
Mon.-Fri. 8.00 a.m.-5.00 p.m. (trade)
H.P.W.MF.A.BC.

**BUXTON** Tel. (0298) 871636
CRAFT SUPPLIES K⋆
THE MILL, MILLERSDALE
Open: Mon-Sat 9.00 a.m.-5.00 p.m.
H.P.W.D.T.CS.A.BC.

## DEVON

**BRIXHAM** Tel. (08045) 4900
WOODCRAFT SUPPLIES E⋆
4 HORSE POOL STREET
Open: Mon.-Sat. 9.00 a.m.-6.00 p.m.
H.P.W.A.D.MF.CS.BC.

**PLYMOUTH** Tel. (0752) 330303
WESTWARD BUILDING SERVICES ⋆
LTD., LISTER CLOSE, NEWNHAM
INDUSTRIAL ESTATE, PLYMPTON
Open: Mon-Fri 8.00 a.m.-5.30 p.m.
Sat. 8.30 a.m.-12.30 p.m.
H.P.W.WM.D.A.BC.

## DORSET

**BOURNEMOUTH** Tel: (0202) 420583
POWER TOOL SERVICES
(Sales, spares, repairs)
849-851 CHRISTCHURCH ROAD
BOSCOMBE
Open: Mon.-Fri. 9.00 a.m.-5.30 p.m.
Sat: 9.00 a.m.-5.00 p.m.
H.P.W.CS.K.A.

## ESSEX

**LEIGH ON SEA** Tel. (0702) 710404
MARSHAL & PARSONS LTD.
1111 LONDON ROAD EK
Open: 8.30 a.m.-5.30 p.m. Mon-Fri
9.00 a.m.-5.00 p.m. Sat.
H.P.W.WM.D.CS.A.

**ILFORD**
CUTWELL TOOLS LTD. ⋆
774-776 HIGH ROAD
Mon.-Fri. 9.00 a.m.-5.00 p.m.
and also by appointment.
P.W.WM.A.D.CS.

## GLOUCESTER

**TEWKESBURY** Tel. (0684) 293092
TEWKESBURY SAW CO. LTD.
TRADING ESTATE, NEWTOWN K
Open: Mon-Fri 8.00 a.m.-5.00 p.m.
Saturday 9.30 a.m.-12.00 p.m.
P.W.WM.D.CS.

## HAMPSHIRE

**SOUTHAMPTON** Tel. (0703) 776222
H.W.M.
THE WOODWORKERS
303 SHIRLEY ROAD, SHIRLEY
Open: Tues-Fri 9.30 a.m.-6.00 p.m.
Sat 9.30 a.m.-4.00 p.m.
H.P.W.WM.D.CS.A.BC.T.

## HAMPSHIRE

**ALDERSHOT**    Tel. (0252) 334422
POWER TOOL CENTRE    **K**
374 HIGH STREET

Open Mon.-Fri. 8.30 a.m.-5.30 p.m.

H.P.W.WM.D.A.BC.

**PORTSMOUTH**    Tel. (0705)
EURO PRECISION TOOLS LTD    667332
259/263 LONDON ROAD, NORTH END    ★
   **E**
Open: Mon-Fri 9.00 a.m.-5.30 p.m.
Sat. 9.00 a.m.-1.00 p.m.
H.P.W.WM.D.A.BC.

**SOUTHAMPTON**    Tel. (0703)
POWER TOOL CENTRE    332288
7 BELVIDERE ROAD    **K★**
Open Mon.-Fri. 8.30-5.30

H.P.W.WM.D.A.BC.CS.MF.

## HUMBERSIDE

**GRIMSBY**    Tel. Grimsby (0472)
   58741 Hull (0482) 26999
J. E. SIDDLE LTD. (Tool Specialists)    ★
83 VICTORIA STREET
Open: Mon-Fri 8.30 a.m.-5.30 p.m.
Sat. 8.30 a.m.-12.45 p.m. & 2 p.m.-5 p.m.
H.P.A.BC.W.WMD.

## KENT

**WYE**    Tel. (0233) 813144
KENT POWER TOOLS LTD.
UNIT 1, BRIAR CLOSE
WYE, Nr. ASFORD

H.P.W.WM.D.A.CS.

**MATFIELD**    Tel. Brenchley
LEISURECRAFT IN WOOD    (089272)
'ORMONDE,' MAIDSTONE RD.    2465
TN12 7JG

Open: Mon-Sun
9.00 a.m.-5.30 p.m.
W.WM.D.T.A.

## LANCASHIRE

**PRESTON**    Tel. (0772) 52951
SPEEDWELL TOOL COMPANY    **E★**
62-68 MEADOW STREET PR1 1SU
Open: Mon.-Fri. 8.30 a.m.-5.30 p.m.
Sat. 8.30 a.m.-12.30 p.m.

H.P.W.WM.CS.A.MF.BC.

**ROCHDALE**    Tel. (0706) 342123/
C.S.M. TOOLS    342322
4-6 HEYWOOD ROAD    **E★**
CASTLETON
Open: Mon-Sat 9.00 a.m.-6.00 p.m.
Sundays by appointment
W.D.CS.A.BC.

**LANCASTER**    Tel. (0524) 32886
LILE TOOL SHOP    **K**
43/45 NORTH ROAD
Open: Monday to Saturday
9.00 a.m.-5.30 p.m.
Wed 9.00 a.m.-12.30 p.m.
H.P.W.D.A.

## LANCASHIRE

**BURY**    Tel. (061 764 6769)
HOUSE OF HARBRU    ★
101 CROSTONS ROAD
ELTON
Open: Mon.-Fri. 9.00 a.m.-5.00 p.m.
Send 2 × 1st class stamps for catalogue
MF.

**MANCHESTER**    Tel. (061 789)
TIMMS TOOLS    0909
102-104 LIVERPOOL ROAD    ★
PATRICROFT M30 0WZ
Weekdays 9.00 a.m.-5.30 p.m.
Sat. 9.00 a.m.-1.00 p.m.
H.P.A.W.

## LINCOLNSHIRE

**LINCOLN**    Tel. (0522) 689369
SKELLINGTHORPE SAW SERVICES LTD.
OLD WOOD, SKELLINGTHORPE
Open: Mon to Fri 8 a.m.-5 p.m.
Sat 8 a.m.-12 p.m.
H.P.W.WM.D.CS.A.*.BC.
Access/Barclaycard

## LONDON

**ACTON**    Tel. (01-992) 4835
A. MILLS (ACTON) LTD    ★
32/36 CHURCHFIELD ROAD W3 6ED
Open: Mon-Fri 9.00 a.m.-5.00 p.m.
Saturdays 9.00 am.-1.00 p.m.

H.P.W.WM.

**LONDON**    Tel. 01-723 2295-6-7
LANGHAM TOOLS LIMITED
13 NORFOLK PLACE
LONDON W2 1QJ

**LONDON**    Tel. (01-567) 2922
G. D. CLEGG & SONS    ★
83 UXBRIDGE ROAD, HANWELL W7 3ST
Mon-Sat 9.15 a.m.-5.30 p.m.
Closed for lunch 1.00-2.00p.m.
Early Closing 1.00 p.m. Wed.
H.P.A.W.WM.D.CS.

**NORBURY**    Tel. (01-679) 6193
HERON TOOLS & HARDWARE LTD.
437 STREATHAM HIGH ROAD SW16
Open Mon-Fri 8.30 a.m.-5.00 p.m.
Wednesday 8.30 a.m.-1.00 p.m.
Sat. 9.00 a.m.-1.00 p.m.
H.P.W.A.

**LONDON**    Tel. (01-636) 7475
BUCK & RYAN LTD    ★
101 TOTTENHAM COURT ROAD W1P 0DY
Open: Mon.-Fri. 8.30 a.m.-5.30 p.m.
Saturday 8.30 a.m.-4.00 p.m.
H.P.W.WM.D.A..

**WEMBLEY**    Tel. 904-1144
ROBERT SAMUEL LTD.    (904-1147)
7, 15 & 16 COURT PARADE    after 4.00)
EAST LANE, N. WEMBLEY    ★
Open Mon.-Fri. 8.45-5.15; Sat. 9-1.00
Access, Barclaycard, AM Express, & Diners
H.P.W.CS.E.A.D

## LONDON

**WOOLWICH**    Tel. (01-854) 7767/8
A. D. SHILLMAN & SONS LTD
108-109 WOOLWICH HIGH STREET
SE18
Open: Mon-Sat
8.30 p.m.-5.30p.m.
H.P.W.CS.A.

**HOUNSLOW**    Tel. (01-570)
Q.R. TOOLS LTD    2103/5135
251-253 HANWORTH ROAD

Open: Mon-Fri 8.30 a.m.-5.30 p.m.
Sat. 9.00 a.m.-1.00 p.m.
P.W.WM.D.CS.A.

**LONDON**    Tel. (01-263) 1536
THOMAS BROTHERS    (01-272) 2764
798-804 HOLLOWAY ROAD, N19    **E**
Open: Mon.-Fri. 8.30 a.m.-5.30 p.m. Thurs.
8.30 a.m.-1 p.m. Sat. 9 a.m.-5 p.m
H.P.W.WM.CS.MF.BC.

**FULHAM**    Tel. (01-385) 5109
I. GRIZZARD LTD.    **E**
84a-b LILLIE ROAD, SW6 1TL
Open: Mon-Sat 9.00-5.30 p.m.
Half day Thursday

H.P.A.BC.W.CS.WM.D.

## MERSEYSIDE

**LIVERPOOL**    Tel. (051-207) 2967
TAYLOR BROS (LIVERPOOL) LTD    **K**
195-199 LONDON ROAD
LIVERPOOL L3 8JG
Open: Monday to Friday
8.30 a.m.-5.30 p.m.
H.P.W.WM.D.A.BC.

## MIDDLESEX

**ENFIELD**    Tel. (01-363) 2935
GILL & HOXBY LTD.    **K**
133-137 ST. MARKS ROAD EN1 1BB

Mon.-Sat. 8.30 a.m.-6.00 p.m.
Early closing Wednesday 1.00 p.m.
H.P.W.WM.T.CS.A

**RUISLIP**    Tel. (08956) 74126
ALLMODELS ENGINEERING LTD.    **E★**
91 MANOR WAY

Open: Mon-Sat 9.00 a.m.-5.30 p.m.

H.P.W.A.D.CS.MF.BC.

**CROWMARSH**    Tel. (0491) 38653
MILL HILL SUPPLIES    **E★**
66 THE STREET
Open: Mon.-Fri. 9.30 a.m.-5.00 p.m.
Thurs. 9.30 a.m.-7.00 p.m.
Sat. 9.30 a.m.-1.00 p.m.
P.W.D.CS.MF.A.BC.

**FARNHAM**    Tel. (0252) 725427
A.B.E. CO. LTD. (Quick Hire)    ★
GOODS SHED
STATION APPROACH, FARNHAM
Open Mon.-Fri. 8.00 a.m.-5.30 p.m.
Sat. 8.00 a.m.-5.30 p.m.
H.P.W.D.CS.A.BC.

## NORFOLK

**NORWICH**    Tel. (0603) 898695
NORFOLK SAW SERVICES
DOG LANE, HORSFORD
Open: Monday to Friday
8.00 a.m.-5.00 p.m.
Saturday 8.00 a.m.-12.00 p.m.
H.P.W.WM.D.CS.A.

**KINGS LYNN**    Tel. (0553) 2443
WALKER & ANDERSON (Kings Lynn) LTD.
WINDSOR ROAD, KINGS LYNN    **K**
Open: Monday to Saturday
7.45 a.m.-5.30 p.m.
Wednesday 1.00 p.m. Saturday 5.00 p.m.
H.P.W.WM.D.CS.A.

**NORWICH**    Tel. (0603) 400933
WESTGATES WOODWORKING    Tx
61 HURRICANE WAY,    975412
NORWICH AIRPORT INDUSTRIAL ESTATE
Open: 9.00 a.m.-5.00 p.m. weekdays
9.00 a.m.-12.30 Sat.
P.W.WM.D.BC.    **K**

**KING'S LYNN**    Tel: 07605 674
TONY WADDILOVE, UNIT A    ★
HILL FARM WORKSHOPS
GREAT DUNHAM, (Nr. Swaffham)
Open: Tues. — Fri. 10.00 a.m. to 5.30 p.m.
Sat. 9.00 a.m. to 5.00 p.m.
H.P.W.D.T.MF.A.BC.*

**GT. YARMOUTH**    Tel. (0493)
ANGLIA POWER TOOLS    850388
3 DENESIDE, NR30 2HL

Open: Monday to Saturday
8.30 a.m. 5.30 p.m.
H.P.W.D.CS.A.

## NOTTINGHAMSHIRE

**NOTTINGHAM**    Tel. (0602) 225979
POOLEWOOD    and 227064/5
EQUIPMENT LTD.    (06077) 2421 after hrs
5a HOLLY LANE, CHILLWELL
Open: Mon-Fri 9.00 a.m.-5.30 p.m.
Sat. 9.00 a.m. to 12.30 p.m.
P.W.WM.D.CS.A.BC.

## OXON

**WITNEY**    Tel. (0993) 3885.
TARGET TOOLS (SALES,    & 72095 OXON
   HIRE & REPAIRS)    ★
SWAIN COURT
STATION INDUSTRIAL ESTATE
Open: Mon.-Sat. 8.00 a.m.-5.00 p.m.
24 hour Answerphone
BC.W.M.A.

## SHROPSHIRE

**TELFORD**    Tel. Telford (0952)
ASLES LTD    48054
VINEYARD ROAD, WELLINGTON    **EK★**

Open: Mon. Fri. 8.30 a.m.-5.30 p.m.
Saturday 8.30 a.m.-4.00 p.m.
H.P.W.WM.D.CS.BC.A.

## SOMERSET

**TAUNTON**    Tel. (0823) 85431
JOHN HALL TOOLS    ★
6 HIGH STREET

Open Monday-Saturday
9.00 a.m.-5.30 p.m.
H.P.W.WM.D.CS.A.

863

# shop guide

## SOMERSET

**TAUNTON**    Tel. Taunton 79078
KEITH MITCHELL    ★
TOOLS AND EQUIPMENT
66 PRIORY BRIDGE ROAD
  Open: Mon-Fri 8.30 a.m.-5.30 p.m.
Saturday 9.00 a.m.-4.00 p.m.
H.P.W.WM.D.CS.A.BC.

## STAFFORDSHIRE

**TAMWORTH**    Tel. (0827) 56188
MATTHEWS BROTHERS LTD.    K
KETTLEBROOK ROAD
  Open: Mon-Sat 8.30 a.m.-6.00 p.m.
Demonstrations Sunday mornings by
appointment only
H.P.WM.D.T.CS.A.BC.

## SUFFOLK

**IPSWICH**    Tel. (0473) 40456
FOX WOODWORKING    KE★
142-144 BRAMFORD LANE
  Open: Tues., Fri., 9.00 a.m.-5.30 p.m.
   Sat. 9.00 a.m.-5.00 p.m.

H.P.W.WM.D.A.B.C.

## SUSSEX

**ST. LEONARD'S-ON-SEA**    Tel.
DOUST & MONK (MONOSAW)-(0424)
25 CASTLEHAM ROAD    52577

  Open: Mon.-Fri. 8.00 a.m.-5.30 p.m.
Most Saturdays 9.00 a.m.-1.00 p.m.
H.P.W.WM.D.CS.A.

**BOGNOR REGIS** Tel. (0243) 863100
A. OLBY & SON (BOGNOR REGIS) LTD.
"TOOLSHOP," BUILDERS MERCHANT
HAWTHORN ROAD    K
  Open: Mon-Thurs 8 a.m.-5.15 p.m. Fri.
  8 a.m.-8 p.m. Sat 8 a.m.-12.45 p.m.
H.P.W.WM.D.T.C.A.BC.

**WORTHING**    Tel. (0903) 38739
W. HOSKING LTD (TOOLS &    KE★
MACHINERY)
28 PORTLAND RD, BN11 1QN
  Open: Mon.-Sat. 8.30 a.m.-5.30 p.m.
   Closed Wednesday
H.P.W.WM.D.CS.A.BC.

## TYNE & WEAR

**NEWCASTLE UPON TYNE**    Tel.
J. W. HOYLE LTD.    (0632) 617474
CLARENCE STREET NE2 1YJ    K★
  Open: Mon-Fri 8.00 a.m.-5.00 p.m.
  Saturday 9.00 a.m.-4.30 p.m.

H.P.A.BC.W.CS.WM.D.

## TYNE & WEAR

**NEWCASTLE**    Tel. (0632) 320311
HENRY OSBOURNE LTD.    E★
50-54 UNION STREET

  Open: Mon-Fri 8.30 a.m.-5.00 p.m.

H.P.W.D.CS.MF.A.BC.

## WEST MIDLANDS

**BIRMINGHAM** Tel. (021-554) 5177
ROTAGRIP    E★
16 LODGE ROAD, HOCKLEY
  Open: Mon.-Fri. 9.00 a.m.-5.00 p.m.
  Sat. 9.00 a.m.-12.00 p.m.

H.P.W.CS.A.BC.T.MF.

**WOLVERHAMPTON**    Tel. (0902)
MANSAW SERVICES    58759
SEDGLEY STREET    K★

  Open: Mon.-Fri. 9.00 a.m.-5.00 p.m.

H.P.W.WM.A.D.CS.

## YORKSHIRE

**BOROUGHBRIDGE**    Tel. (09012)
JOHN BODDY TIMBER LTD    2370
FINE WOOD & TOOL STORE    ★
RIVERSIDE SAWMILLS
  Open: Mon.-Thurs. 8.00 a.m.-6.00 p.m.
Fri. 8.00am-5.00pm Sat. 8.00am-4.00pm
H.P.W.WM.D.T.CS.MF.A.BC.

**SHEFFIELD**    Tel. (0742) 441012
GREGORY & TAYLOR LTD    KE
WORKSOP ROAD
  Open: 8.30 a.m.-5.30 p.m.
   Monday-Friday
  8.30 a.m.-12.30 p.m. Sat.
H.P.W.WM.D.

**HARROGATE**    Tel. (0423) 66245/
MULTI-TOOLS    55328
158 KINGS ROAD    K★

  Open: Monday to Saturday
   8.30 a.m.-6.00 p.m.
H.P.W.WM.D.A.BC.

**LEEDS**    Tel. (0532) 574736
D. B. KEIGHLEY MACHINERY LTD.    ★
VICKERS PLACE, STANNINGLEY
PUDSEY LS2 86LZ
  Mon.-Fri. 9.00 a.m.-5.00 p.m.
  Sat. 9.00 a.m.-1.00 p.m.
P.A.W.WM.CS.BC.

## YORKSHIRE

**HUDDERSFIELD**    Tel. (0484)
NEVILLE M. OLDHAM    641219/(0484)
UNIT 1 DALE ST. MILLS    42777
DALE STREET, LONGWOOD    ★
  Open: Mon-Fri 8.00 a.m.-5.30 p.m.
  Saturday 9.30 a.m.-12.00 p.m.
P.W.WM.D.A.BC.

## YORKSHIRE

**THIRSK**    Tel. (0845) 22770
THE WOOD SHOP    ★
TRESKE SAWMILLS LTD.
STATION WORKS
  Open: Seven days a week 9.00-5.00

T.H.MF.BC.

**KEIGHLEY**    Tel. (0535) 663325
EUROMAIL (TOOLS)    ★
PO BOX 13
108 EAST PARADE
  Open 9.15 a.m.-5.00 p.m.
  Not Tuesday but inc. Saturday
H.P.W.A.BC.

**CLECKHEATON**    Tel. (0274)
SKILLED CRAFTS LTD.    872861
34 BRADFORD ROAD    ★

  Open: 9.00 a.m.-5.00 p.m. Monday
Saturday Lunch 12.00 a.m.-1.00 p.m.
H.P.A.W.CS.WM.D.

**LEEDS**    Tel. (0532) 790507
GEORGE SPENCE & SONS LTD
WELLINGTON ROAD
  Open: Monday to Friday
   8.30 a.m.-5.30 p.m.
  Saturday 9.00 a.m.-5.00 p.m.
H.P.W.WM.D.T.A.

## SCOTLAND

**EDINBURGH**    Tel. 031-337-5555
THE SAW CENTRE    ★
38 HAYMARKET EH12 5JZ
  Mon.-Fri. 8.30 a.m.-5.30 p.m.
  Sat. 9.00 a.m.-1.00 p.m.
H.P.W.WM.D.CS.A.

**PERTH**    Tel. (0738) 26173
WILLIAM HUME & CO    K
ST. JOHN'S PLACE
  Open: Monday to Saturday
  8.00 a.m.-5.30 p.m.
  8.00 a.m.-1.00 p.m. Wednesday
H.P.A.BC.W.CS.WM.D.

## SCOTLAND

**CULLEN**    Tel. (0542) 40563
GRAMPIAN WOODTURNING SUPPLIES AT
BAYVIEW CRAFTS
Open: Mon.-Sat. 9.00 a.m.-5.30 p.m. Sunday
10.00 a.m.-5.30 p.m. Open later July/Aug.
Sept. Demonstrations SAT/SUN or by
H.W.D.MF.BC. appointment

**TAYSIDE**    Tel. (05774) 293
WORKMASTER POWER TOOLS LTD.    ★
DRUM, KINROSS
Open Mon.-Sat. 8.00 a.m.-8.00 p.m.
Demonstrations throughout Scotland by
appointment
P.W.WM.D.A.BC.

**GLASGOW**    Tel. 041-429-4444/
THE SAW CENTRE    4374 Telex: 777886
650 EGLINTON STREET    E★
GLASGOW G5 9RP
  Mon.-Fri. 8.00 a.m.-5.00 p.m.
  Sat. 9.00 a.m.-1.00 p.m.
H.P.W.WM.D.CS.A.

## WALES

**CARDIFF**    Tel. (0222) 595710
DATAPOWER TOOLS LTD,
MICHAELSTON ROAD,
CULVERHOUSE CROSS
  Open: Mon.-Fri. 8.00 a.m.-5.00 p.m.
  Sat. 9.00 a.m.-1.00 p.m.
H.P.W.WM.D.A.

**CARMARTHEN** Tel. (0267) 237219
DO-IT-YOURSELF SUPPLY
BLUE STREET, DYFED    K
  Open: Monday to Saturday
  9.00 a.m.-5.30 p.m.
  Thursday 9.00 a.m.-5.30 p.m.
H.P.W.WM.D.T.CS.A.BC.

**CARDIFF**    Tel. (0222) 396039
JOHN HALL TOOLS LIMITED    ★
CENTRAL SQUARE

  Open: Monday to Saturday
  9.00 a.m.-5.30 p.m.
H.P.W.WM.D.A.BC.

**SWANSEA**    Tel. (0792) 55680
SWANSEA TIMBER & PLYWOOD CO. LTD.
57-59 OXFORD STREET    ★

  Open: Mon to Fri 9.00 a.m.-5.30 p.m.
  Sat. 9.00 a.m.-1.00 p.m.
H.P.W.D.T.CS.A.BC.

KEY: CS CUTTING OR
SHARPENING SERVICES

KEY: MF MATERIAL FINISHES

KEY: BC BOOKS/CATALOGUES

# 2 short cuts to the perfect finish from INCA

## Short cut No 1.

The INCA Bandsaw – Europe's top precision bandsaw cuts virtually anything, wood, non–ferrous metals and plastics. 10½" throat with tilting table up to 45° Dovetail slotted for optional mitre guide. Professional blade tracking control ensures perfect accuracy cut after cut. Optional extras – mitre guide, fret saw and sanding attachment. Available complete with motor or suitable for the customer's own motor at a considerable saving.

**SAVE OVER £100 BY USING YOUR OWN MOTOR**

**Use the coupon on the opposite page for full details of all INCA PRODUCTS.**

**5 YEAR WARRANTY**

## Short cut No 2.

The **INCA GUIDE** cuts time, effort and spoilt work by explaining and illustrating almost every woodworking detail from simple cross cutting to perfect blind–wedged tenon joints.

## Woodworking ✠ Machines of Switzerland LIMITED

Sole U.K. Agents for INCA Woodworking Machinery

### OVER 500 ILLUSTRATIONS ON 156 PAGES of FACTS AND HELPFUL ADVICE.

To Woodworking Machines of Switzerland Ltd., 49 Aylesbury Street, Bletchley, Milton Keynes, MK2 2BQ.

Cut this coupon for your copy of the **INCA GUIDE** at our **SPECIAL INTRODUCTORY PRICE** of **£9.95 incl. p & p.** (also available through our dealer network)

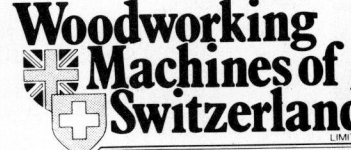

**The INCA Woodworking Machinery Handbook**
With useful tips and jigs for everyone

Mark Duginske, Karl Eichhorn

Edited by INCA L

**Makes a super gift idea**

| Please send me.........copies of the INCA GUIDE. |
| NAME ....................................... |
| ADDRESS ................................... |
| ............................................ |
| WWC1 |
| Tel: ....................................... |

Access  VISA

867

# The floater copier

Metalworking for turners:
Roderick Jenkins'
surprisingly simple
lathe copying attachment

There is no doubt that turning wood is a most satisfying pastime. Subtle movements of the hand, controlled only by the eye, ensure that no two turned objects are ever quite the same — which is something of a problem when one is trying to make 13 identical tuning-pegs for a lute. Some say minute variations in size and shape add character and show that an item has been craftsman-produced, but unfortunately my variations are not so minute. So I built a copying attachment for my lathe.

I had no previous experience of metalworking, but with some guidance I managed this construction with remarkably few problems. The attachment was built with a minimum of tools; the only items I had to add to a normal household tool-set were a tap wrench, two taps and a drill bit. It was fabricated mostly from bright drawn mild steel (BMS) flats, which are available from model-engineer suppliers. I used Whitworth (BSW) threads but any similar-diameter fasteners will do.

Fig. 1 shows a general view of the copier. It consists of a bed set up parallel to the lathe axis; along it slides a tool that can also move perpendicular to the axis. The travel of the tool towards the lathe axis is restricted by a rod that moves against a template. My copier is only 12 in long, but there is no reason why it should not stretch the whole length of the lathe bed if you wish to turn, for example, chair legs or balusters. The method of fastening the copying attachment to the lathe depends very much on the lathe itself. Mine is a Coronet Minor, which has two saddles. When the banjos are removed from these saddles a stud is left protruding upwards, to which I have bolted 1 in-wide sections of angle, which in turn are bolted to the angle on the base of the copier bed. All the bolts pass through slots to enable adjustment of copier height and distance from the lathe axis. An alternative method, which should work with most lathes, is to purchase a length of steel rod the same diameter as the leg of the tool-rest. The top of this can be fastened to the copier bed angle by filing away half the diameter at one end and drilling and bolting. Adjustments can then be made in the same way as with the normal tool-rest.

The bed of the copier is made from 2x½in BMS to which is bolted 40x6mm steel angle. For some reason BMS flats are available in every conceivable imperial dimension but angle is available only in metric sizes. The copying template is held to the underside of the bed by ¼in Whitworth screws that fasten into tapped holes in the angle supporting the bed. Another method, that does not involve buying a ¼in BSW tap, is to fasten the template with nuts that fasten to screws that protrude down from the angle. These screws have to be inserted before the bed is fastened to the angle. Drill a series of ¼in holes ¼in from one edge at 3in intervals. Countersink these on the outside of the angle so that the inserted screws lie flush with the surface, and glue the screws in place with epoxy resin.

Before joining the bed to the angle, go round the bed bar with a file, smoothing any faults or bruises and slightly radiusing all the arrises. This will enable the slide to

● The copying attachment set up to reproduce a tuning-peg shape, whose ply template is fixed below the copier bed

● The tuning-peg **below** (plum in this case) is ready to be parted off. The side view **inset** shows the toolholder housing and adjustment screws

move freely. The bed flat is fastened to the angle with 1x¼in Whitworth countersunk screws. Scribe a line 5mm in from one edge of the flat and another down the centre of the long axis of the other face. It is very much easier to see a scribed line if the surface is first painted with a blue or black spirit-based felt-tip. Using a couple of G-cramps, fasten the angle 5mm in from the edge (using the scribed line) and drill ¼in holes 1in from the end at 5in intervals through the centre line of the flat and the

angle. The holes should be deeply countersunk from the top so the screws don't protrude above the surface of the bed.

The slide is fabricated from ¼in BMS plate. From a length of 2x¼in cut a piece 2¾in long. This will be the top plate of the slide. Now cut two 2in lengths of ½x¼in for the front and back pieces. The front piece bears on the front of the bed; so that it will not rock, file a slight hollow vertically in the middle of the bed side of the front plate so it slides on the two ends. This can be checked by marking the front piece with a felt pen and rubbing it along the bed — the ink will be rubbed off where it bears on the bed. A quick look at the drawings will show that the front plate has to be screwed to the top plate. The screws pass through clearance holes in the top plate and screw into threaded holes in the front plate. Consultation of a set of thread tables will show that a ⅛in BSW screw needs a size 30 clearance hole and a 3/32in tapping drill, neither of which I used. My experience is that a ⅛in screw goes quite nicely into a hole drilled with an ⅛in bit, and also that a ⅛in BSW tap will break off in a 3/32 hole! So,

# The floater copier

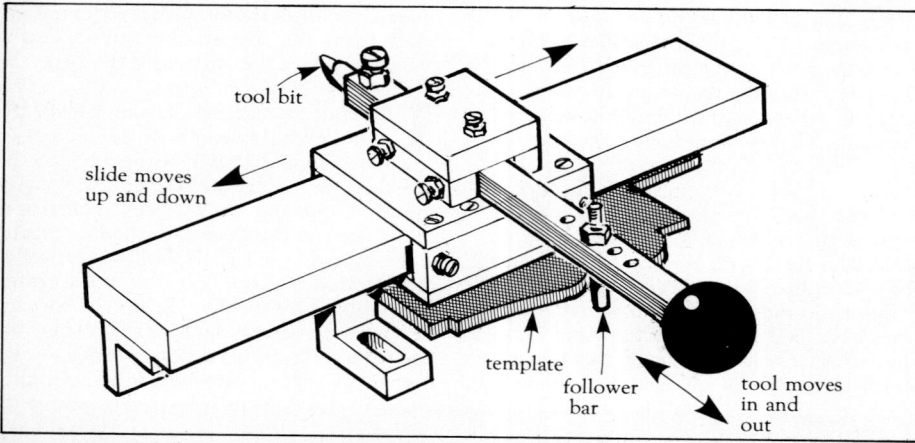

tool bit

slide moves
up and down

template

follower
bar

tool moves
in and out

using a pair of G-cramps, fasten the side plate to the top plate and drill four evenly spaced ⅛in holes ⅛in in from the edge of the top plate so they go through the top and make a shallow mark in the side plate. The clearance holes should be countersunk.

Slightly closer scrutiny of thread tables will show that a figure called '% depth of engagement' is usually quoted. For our purposes 80% is more than adequate and has the decided advantage that the tap is a looser fit in the hole, with a consequently reduced risk of breakage. Go for a 2.55mm drill, then, and (using the marks made by the clearance drill through the top plate as a guide) drill four tapping holes just under ¼in deep. Taps are sold as taper, second and plug. Taper taps are easy to start, but only cut a full thread for the top third or so of their length, which makes them useless for short, blind holes. Plug taps, on the other hand, cut a full thread over their whole length, but are almost impossible to start. The best compromise is to buy both a second and a plug. You will also need to hold the tap, and there really is no alternative to a tap-wrench. It might just be possible to manage by holding the tap in the chuck in a pillar drill and turning it by hand, but the tap is likely to slip in the chuck. Various potions are sold for application to the tap to ease thread-cutting, but we can manage with a light machine oil.

Put the second tap in the wrench, apply a few drops of oil and, keeping the tap square to the hole, give half a turn clockwise with firm pressure. Now give the tap a quarter of a turn anticlockwise. Proceed like this, half forward and quarter back, until the tap reaches the bottom of the hole. If the tap sticks, ease gently backwards and forwards. Be careful when you approach the bottom of the hole — ⅛in carbon-steel taps are very fragile and a broken tap is almost always impossible to remove from a hole. Repeat the process with a plug tap.

The back plate is attached to the top plate in similar fashion, but there is no need to relieve the middle of the bearing surface, because a 'gib strip' is used to enable the movement of the slide to be adjusted. The gib is a 2in length of ¼x¼in BMS filed down to ¼x³⁄₁₆in. Two holes are drilled and tapped for ⅛in screws toward

the ends of the centre-line of the back plate, but avoiding the screws fastening the top to the back. The gib is placed between the bed and the back plate and two shallow depressions are drilled for location of the adjusting screws.

The bottom plates are made to overlap the bed by ⅛in, so the front one is ⅜in wide and the rear ⅝in. Mine were made from ³⁄₃₂in material because I happened to have a piece but there is no reason why they shouldn't be made from a piece of the ¼in plate (filed down to ³⁄₁₆in so as not to interfere with the template). The bottom plates are fastened to the sides in similar fashion to the top. When finally assembling the slide, one or two thicknesses of shim (paper) may have to be inserted between side and bottom plates to ensure easy sliding along the bed.

The toolholder is made from ¼x¼in bar and moves in a housing fastened to the top of the slide. A hole ⅛in diameter and about 1in long needs to be drilled along the axis of the holder for the tool bit. This hole should be placed towards the lower side of the holder to leave as much meat as possible for the threaded hole of the locking-screw, which is drilled ⅛in from the end. A series of ⅛in holes should be drilled in the vertical plane of the toolholder for the template-follower. Drill these at about ½in centres. The tool bit can be moved in and out for fine adjustment. The follower is simply made from a long ⅛in screw or a length of ⅛in studding, fastened with a nut on either side of the toolholder.

The housing for the toolholder is a loose fit around the holder so that any play may be taken up by the adjustment screws in the top and one side. In this case the ends of the screws act directly on the toolholder and there are no gib strips. File the ends of the screws so that they are slightly convex. The sides of the housing are made from ¼x¼x½in BMS. These are fastened to the slide with two screws each and are ⁵⁄₁₆in apart. The side without the adusting screws should be slightly hollowed in a similar fashion to the front of the slide. Ensure that the sides are positioned so that the toolholder will move at right-angles to the bed. Make the top from a piece of ¼in plate 2x1³⁄₁₆in, and screw it to the side pieces, making sure that the screws don't interfere

with those holding the sides of the housing to the slide.

The holes for the adjustment-screws for the gib strip and the slide and also the tool locking-screw will all be ⅛in tapping size (2.55mm). Each pair should be drilled as far apart as possible without fouling any of the constructional screws. The adjustment-screws are locked in position by tightening a nut against the slide body. Care should be taken in positioning the side adjustment-screws for the toolholder so that the locking nuts can be turned without fouling the top plate of the slide.

Two items remain to be made; the knob for the end of the toolholder, and the tool bit. This former item should be turned up from a suitable piece of hardwood and be large enough to be comfortable in the hand. The tool bit is made from ⅛in diameter high-speed steel and can be bought as drill-rod or as a boring-bar insert. It will be supplied hardened and ground to diameter. The business end will have to be ground to shape. First grind the end so that it is hemispherical and then grind a flat to one half the diameter. If the rod is too long, probably the easiest way to trim it to length is to place it in a vice with the surplus end protruding, cover with a cloth and give it a sharp clout with a hammer.

The copying attachment is now ready for assembly on the lathe. The top of the flat on the tool bit should be exactly at centre height. I adjust this by putting a centre in both head- and tailstock and sliding the supporting legs until the tool bit is at the correct height at both ends of the copier bed. The bed must also be set up parallel to the lathe axis; this can be achieved with the aid of a rule and square, again using the centres. The distance of the copier bed from the lathe axis depends on the diameter of the items turned and should be adjusted to minimise tool overhang.

I make my tuning-peg templates from 4mm ply. The shape of half the plan of the peg is cut out of the ply — I like to cut both ends of the template away at the centre-line for a distance on either side of the pattern. This makes adjustment of the tool easier, since the following-peg in the toolholder should be so positioned that the tool bit is at the lathe axis when the follower bears against these ends. Slots are cut into the template, perpendicular to the axis, for fastening to the screws on the underside of the bed.

Trial and error have shown me that the best action when using the attachment is to hold the slide in my left hand (I am right-handed) and move the tool with my right hand. The tool should be fed in to take a ⅛in cut, withdrawn and then fed in again slightly further along. The final cuts can be taken by pushing the follower against the template and moving the slide back and forth along the bed. It seems to be easier to work so that the tool is moving downhill.

If you decide to have a go at constructing this device, you'll find it really isn't half as difficult as I've made it seem! ∎

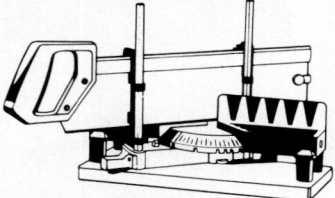
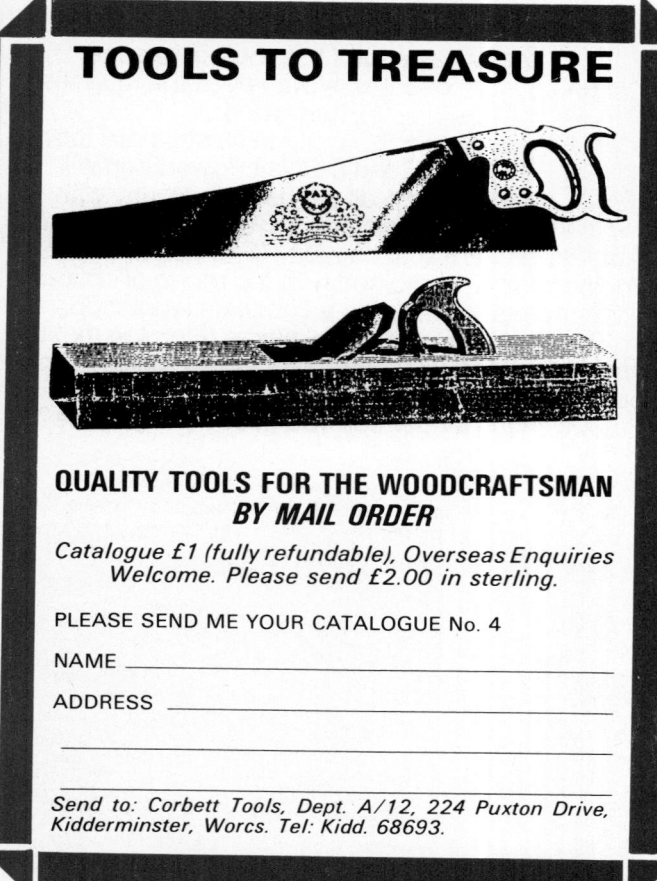

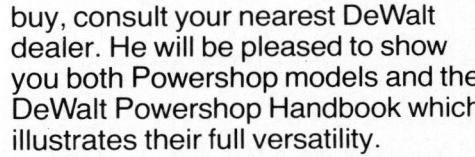

873

# New life for old tools

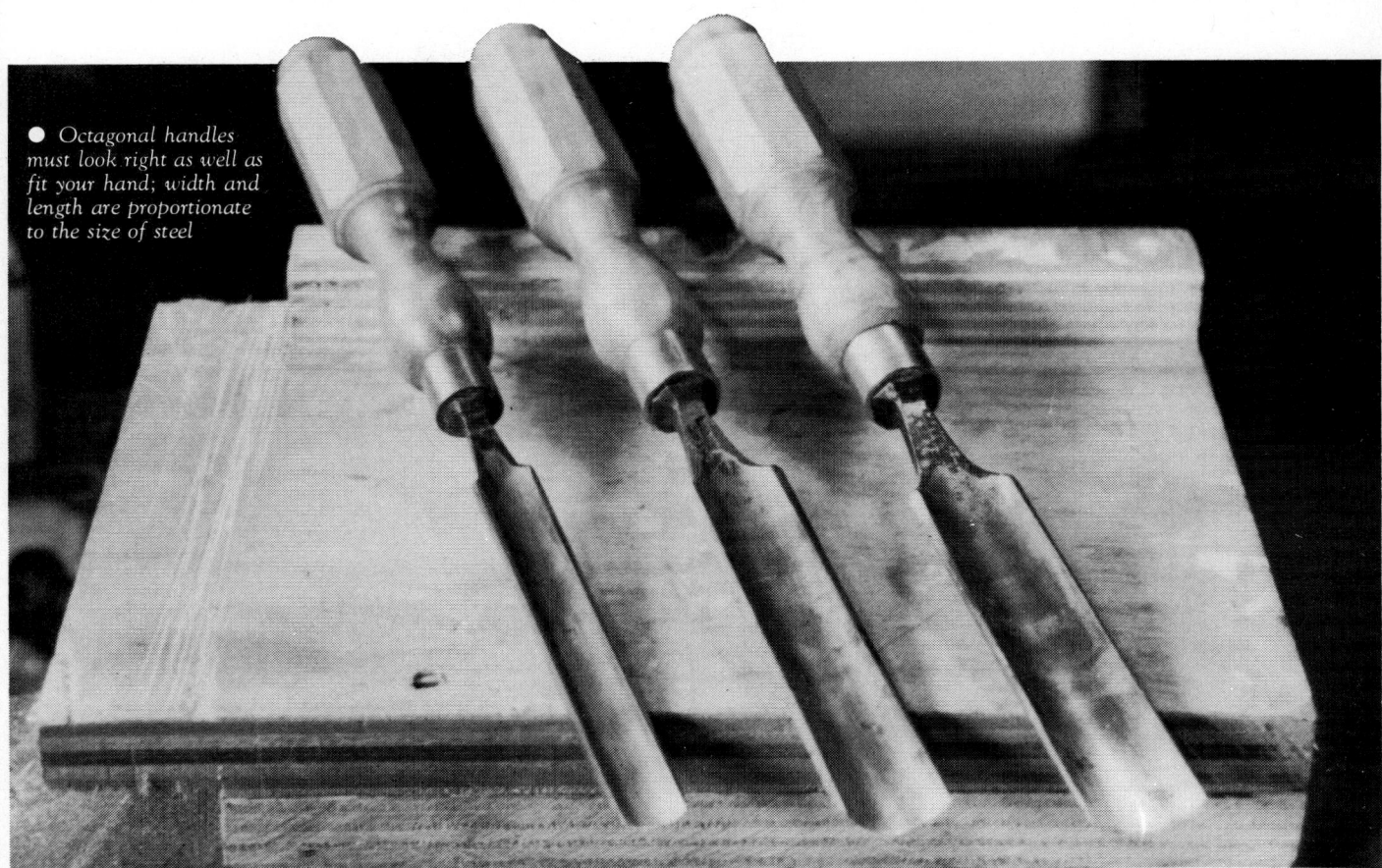

● *Octagonal handles must look right as well as fit your hand; width and length are proportionate to the size of steel*

## Show your chisels you care: give them pleasing octagonal handles. Alan Thomas tells how

At first, this was going to be an exercise in jigs and fixtures, with much machining and hardly any handwork. It didn't turn out that way.

I was surprised at the amount of interest stirred by my description of ordinary round chisel handles and how to make them (*Woodworker*, October 1982). Among the letters were a couple asking about octagonal, or carver, handles. This set a train of thought in motion. Such handles certainly look nice, and their production might raise interesting problems.

The over-riding consideration is undoubtedly that of getting perfectly even flats for the octagons. Anything less than truly parallel, sharp arrises, any hint of variation in the widths of the flats, and the result would look terrible. Therefore, it seemed to me, each one would best be essentially a plain turned-all-over handle. Then some sort of indexing device would be needed to obtain the eight circumferential divisions, and then perhaps a milling head to machine the flats.

All that would be easy on almost any engineering lathe, and owners of such equipment will need no further advice from me. But woodturning lathes are more primitive in their design and accessories.

Apart from that — precisely what shape should this sort of handle be? Most woodworkers have a broad idea of the sort of thing I mean, and no doubt could make a recognisable sketch of one. But overall proportions are important, and so is the positioning of decorative details. No attractive original was within reach, but in a 1912 tool catalogue I found a large-scale line engraving of the very thing. Re-drawn full-size, it looked right. Just to be sure, I quickly turned up a sample in a bit of softwood; the result felt right too, fitting nicely into each of three volunteer hands — all of different sizes.

### Handle sizes

| Chisel width | Gouge width | Plain handle diameter | Carver across corners | Ferrule outside dia. |
|---|---|---|---|---|
| ⅛in | | 25mm | | ⅝in |
| ¼ | ¼in | 26 | | ⅝ |
| ⅜ | ⅜ | 27 | 28mm | ⅝ |
| ½ | ½ | 28 | 29 | ⅝ |
| | 9/16 | | 29½ | ¾ |
| ¾ | ¾ | 29 | 30 | ¾ |
| | 13/16 | | 30½ | ¾ |
| ⅞ | ⅞ | 30 | 31 | ¾ |
| 1 | | 31 | 32 | ¾ |
| 1¼ | | 32 | | ⅞ |
| 1½ | | 33 | | ⅞ |
| 2 | | 34 | | ⅞ |

These dimensions are based on tools that have actually been measured. They came from several different makers, which no doubt explains the erratic progression in sizes. Longitudinal dimensions remain uniform.

Now, one of the readers who wrote after that article back in 1982 wanted more information about diameters of handles. This is something which, in the 'real' world, is trivial — who cares? Buy a handle, hammer it on, and get back to work. However, those of us who do this sort of thing largely for the satisfaction it offers might as well get it just right. That, at any rate, is my excuse, and the results of my thoughts are shown in the table. Millimetres were chosen for no other reason than that they make an easy progression; observe that the octagons are 1mm larger across the flats than the diameters of their circular fellows.

Having got something like a full set of handled chisels already, I had no need for any more, so instead I moved on to gouges. Deciding what is the width of a gouge is not quite so obvious as with chisels, but the sketch shows my way of doing it.

Now to material. In the days when such things were within the reach of ordinary mortals, box would have been the choice. Close-grained beech might do; ash is too coarse. One correspondent suggested walnut, which sounded rather dark: by chance a second-hand paring-gouge with what might well be a walnut handle has come into my possession and, indeed, somehow it doesn't look quite right. The wood should be light in colour, I think. Fortunately there is still some hawthorn under my bench, and the only drawback of this pale, close-grained, hard, box-like wood is the unpredictability that results from its erratic manner of growth. There is

875

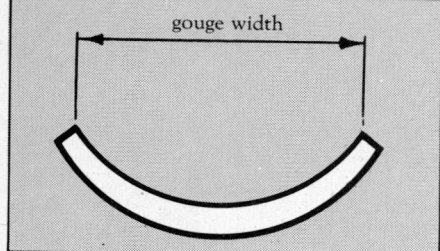
gouge width

no guessing what lies inside an apparently homogeneous piece.

However — on to the job. Using a catch-plate and carrier, not the usual woodturning 'knife' centre, turn between centres to parallel and well over-size. Drill for the chisel tang while holding the piece in a three-jaw chuck: check against the tang, for it will probably pay to counterbore the hole. Between centres again, reduce the diameter for the ferrule: about $^{10}/_{1000}$ in over-size seems about right — or, if you prefer, call it a force-on fit, using the vice. Ferrule duly fitted, put the blank back between centres and finish turning the rest, leaving a long enough pip at the top end to permit, at a later stage, cutting away all trace of the centre indentation.

I used a gouge — what else? — to shape my handles from rough to finish, knifing in the decoration, and gave them a thorough sanding right down to flour-paper while they were still revolving. Guidance for those graceful curves came from a Metco multi-needle profile-gauge, mainly because I was too idle to cut proper templates from zinc or card. In making a range of sizes you will find that, since the diameters of each body and ferrule reduce more or less together, the profile of those curves remains substantially uniform from large to small, and needs very little adjusting in order to maintain pleasing curves and a steady progression.

If no proper catch-plate and carrier are available for the lathe, excellent substitutes are a bolt projecting from the standard face-plate — and a jubilee clip!

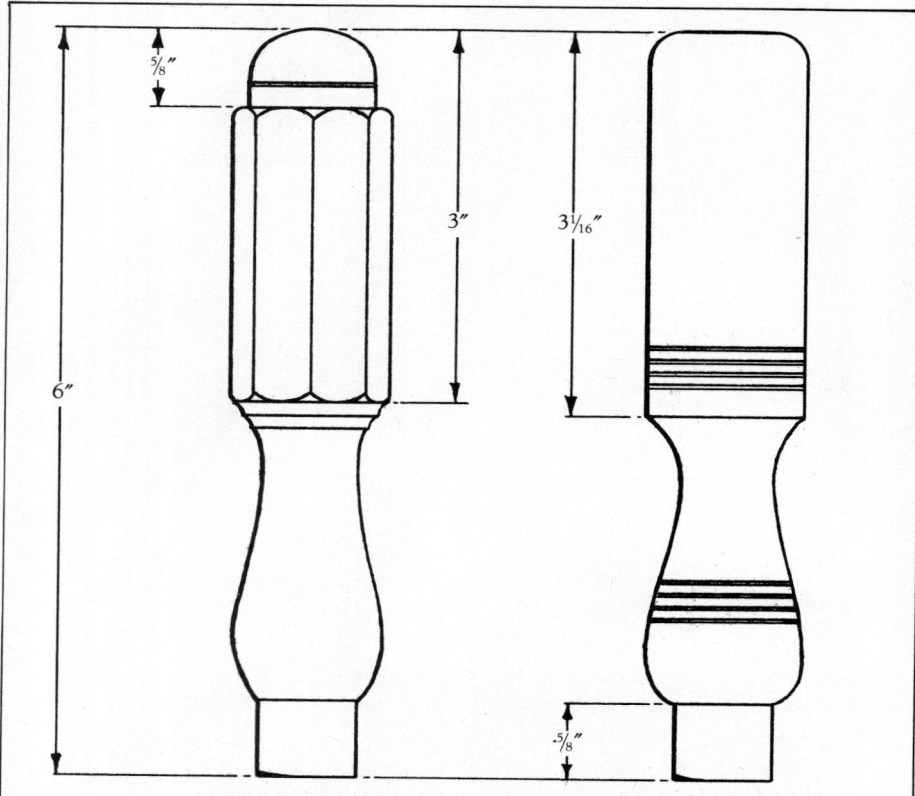

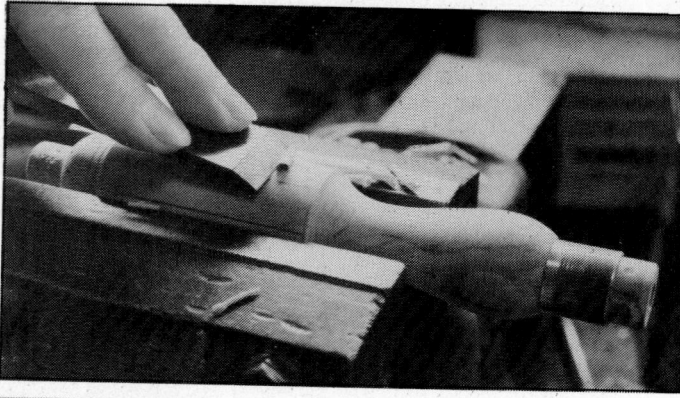

● *Having turned the handle-body blank absolutely parallel (below), set out and mark with an indexing device the eight parallel shoulder-lines; pare the flats with a chisel sharp enough to avoid the need for further finishing*

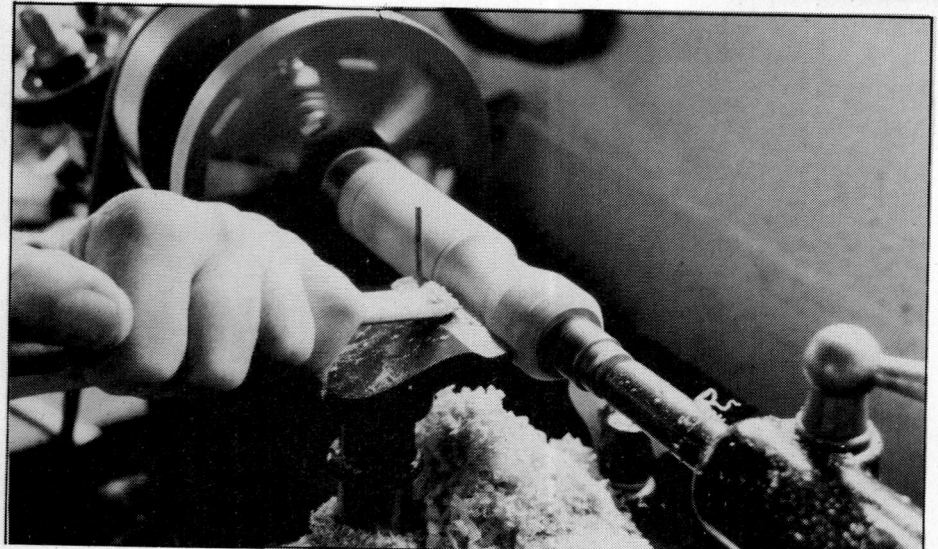

Incidentally, the lathe I prefer to use for such jobs is more than 80 years old, and foot-powered. This apparently perverse choice — after all, why work so hard when fractional-horsepower motors are available? — has developed with practice. It takes a while to get the knack of treadling steadily and automatically while concentrating on the job in hand; but, once that's acquired, the infinity of mandrel speeds that are available at will, and the total controllability, become blessings indeed. And the exercise is probably as valuable as jogging, while being rather more productive.

Whatever the machinery you use, be sure that the handle-body blanks are turned truly parallel. Spare no pains to make each one so. Then, with dividers and set-square, draw out on a bit of tinplate or zinc a circle of the same diameter as the body, and divide it into eight. Re-set the dividers to one chord and step carefully around the body circumference. Should first and last dots not come together perfectly, adjust the dividers and try again.

Back between centres, use the T-rest as a straight-edge and project the finest of pencil lines along the body from each dot. Put the handle in the vice, and with a broad sharp chisel pare down each embryo flat; make sure the grain doesn't tear, that each pencil line is left complete — just — and that no further finishing will be required. Glass-paper would undoubtedly blur the result.

Fit the handle carefully to its blade. Personally I like to use the tang as a reamer, boring out the hole until there is about ½in to go. With all the dust cleaned out, try a few tentative taps with a mallet. There is no way of determining precisely when 'tight enough' verges on too tight — but, since there is no advantage in being too tight, make sure your nerve cracks before the handle does.

A less obvious point is the desirability of making sure the chisel flat (or gouge curve) is accurately aligned with a handle flat. In the first fine flush of enthusiasm this thought never crossed my mind; the result looked horrid, and that first handle had to come off again.

Courage while hitting things is required also in connection with the tang. Quite possibly that will be out of alignment with its own blade, and unless something is done about it your new handle will end up lopsided. Fortunately chisels are not usually hardened beyond the maker's stamp, but to be as safe as possible put the blade in a vice and support it fully right up to the collar. Use hardwood packing if need be. Then tap the tang sideways very cautiously: and, as soon as it is right — desist. Check the alignment with a short straight-edge and ruler: tangs are rarely truly symmetrical, and it is not always easy to be certain that an individual is properly central.

Ah yes. Ferrules. Suitable brass tube is readily available at any non-ferrous-metal stockist. If possible, turn the ends of each piece in a lathe: if not, careful filing is quite good enough. Don't use a plumber's pipe-cutter! Remove internal burrs at the business end before pressing it on to the wood.

Finally, for polishing my handles I've relied once again on a good soaking in boiled linseed oil, four or five applications at least. Then a quick rub, and a handsome piece of work is ready to adorn your bench for a lifetime — and quite possibly that of someone else, when you are finished with it.

> If you have old tools that perplex you because you don't know what they are or how to make them work, bring them to the Woodworker Show. Stan Thomas and the Tool and Trades History Society will solve your problems.

## R. R. Gillies gives tired chisels a pick-me-up

There is no doubt that the golden age for buying good-quality new hand-tools has passed. For a lucky few, however, leisure time presents the opportunity of either making new tools or improving those we already own. A splendid example of making from scratch is the superb Norris-type panel plane which deservedly won a first prize in last year's Woodworker Show. What a pity it was chained to the stand!

Sources of inspiration for more modest attempts include back numbers of *Woodworker*, old tool catalogues and attendance at antique tool auctions. The latter, in particular, are helpful because they offer an opportunity to handle quality.

The first thing I realised is that one needs to use metal as well as wood. I found that disconcerting at first, because the idea of metalwork conjured up visions of welding, brazing, surface-grinding and other processes of which I had little experience. But these difficulties can be overcome, and it is surprising what can be achieved with a hacksaw, a file, emery paper and a soldering iron. Metal supplies were a problem at first, but a search through the Yellow Pages soon solved it. You can always send for a catalogue from K. R. Whiston Ltd of Stockport. It contains details of many useful items including brass and mild steel flats, rounds, hexagons, sheet and tubing; also ground tool-steel flat for cutting tools such as plane blades.

A wide range of projects can be tackled. For readers with a lathe there are opportunities to replace and upgrade the handles of existing tools by making replacement handles from quality hardwoods. An examination of my chisels, screwdrivers and fret- and coping-saws, not to mention woodturning chisels, revealed not only a lack of quality in the wood but similarly cheap design and finish. The fault, I think, is that of the accountants and efficiency experts who are constantly trying to reduce the cost of materials, employment of expen-

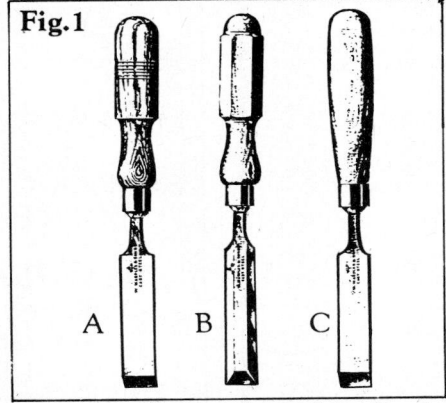

● *A choice of patterns for chisel handles; the octagonal flat-sided variety seems to suit the bevel*

sive skilled labour, and time spent on the manufacturing process.

I started with the chisels. For these there are three traditional shapes on which it is hard to improve, illustrated in fig. 1. Of the three, B has considerable eye-appeal and used to be a common choice for paring chisels. Unfortunately no tool merchant in my area still sells this pattern. Nevertheless it is a great favourite and quite easy to make. Start with a piece of square stock and plane it to an octagonal shape. Now centre it in the lathe to complete the turning to shape. If the octagon shape is a little out of true (or if the wood has not been centred accurately in the lathe) it is a simple matter to correct the fault by taking a shaving or two off one or more of the flats of the octagon with a plane when the handle has been removed from the lathe. This type of handle is also suitable for other tools, of course.

A traditional and practical shape for woodturning tools is shown in fig. 2. Widening the handle at the rear (Shaker coat-peg fashion) serves two purposes. First, it provides a good handling shape, and secondly it allows the tool to be hung from the tool rack.

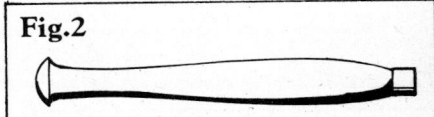

● *The 'Shaker coat-peg' style, often seen in turning tools; again the proportion of curve and length must be just right to both eye and hand*

Can you buy the necessary brass ferrules locally? If not, buy a length of brass (or copper) tubing and cut off the lengths required. A useful tool for this is a small plumber's pipe cutter which guarantees a 90° cut. Clean up the burr on the inside of the tubing and, if the diameter is large enough, slip the ferrule over the centre in the tailstock so that you can gauge the fit without removing the work from the lathe. A slide fit is sufficient because the ferrule will tighten on the handle when the tang of the chisel is driven home.

The wood used for the handles is a matter of personal choice and suitability. Ash and beech are traditional; so, too, is box. But there are other possibilities such as rosewood, mahogany, teak and yew. The last-mentioned is most attractive and turns beautifully, and I often wonder why more use is not made of it. Avoid oak: it has a corrosive effect on ferrous metal.

Some of the best sources of suitable wood are the timber merchants' stands at the Woodworker Show which have good stocks in suitable sizes. I managed to buy a cylinder of lignum vitae 5x4in for £1.75 last year, which has now been made into a wood-carver's mallet with an ash handle. Try buying one of these for less than £10-15!

Finishes for the handles include linseed or Danish oil, polyurethane or varnish. A word of warning — polyurethane does not always dry out on rosewood. ∎

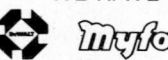  

878

879

# The universal dresser

**Steven Hurrell's splendid Welsh dresser is a powerful argument for the universal machine. He explains exactly how to build it**

The combination (or universal) could easily be called the machine of the 80s. The current market offers a wide choice to tempt the ambitious amateur with an urge to spend his bank balance.

Although the combination woodworker is often aimed at the person starting up on his or her own, it is more likely to find a home in the garage of the enthusiastic spare-time woodworker — one of a growing army. Investing in a machine that offers sawing, planing, moulding and mortising opens a bright new door that can only mean better work.

It's a misconception, by the way, that the multi-purpose machine is a recent invention. Its attractiveness was realised long enough ago for the combination to be celebrating its 127th anniversary. In 1858 a man by the name of Whines designed the first 'general joiner' — manufactured by Samuel Worssam of London and aimed, as its name suggests, at the builder's-yard set-up.

For the craftsman woodworker, the point of machinery is to supplement our hand work and allow us to charge our customers realistic prices. For the amateur, it means that the almost unattainable comes well within reach. I hope this chestnut dresser, with its traditional construction, proves that.

## Tooling

The machine I used for this project was the Startrite-Robland K260, which consists of a 10x7in planer-thicknesser, 9in circular saw, spindle-moulder and slot-mortiser. It's important to remember, of course, that buying a machine is only half the story. Proper tooling is of the essence.

The planer is fitted with a pair of high-speed-steel knives, which are set ready for use. Provided they're not nicked by offensive objects, they should give long use, benefiting from occasional honing before specialist re-grinding is necessary.

The standard tungsten-tipped 24-tooth saw-blade is best suited to ripping and requires care when used for crosscutting (especially tenon shoulders) to avoid break-out. For furniture, where a good finish from the saw is essential, it's worth investing in a general-purpose TCT blade with at least 40 teeth.

Quite rightly, Startrite leave the choice of spindle-moulder tooling to personal requirements. For the average user the Startrite/Omas tiger-head package makes an ideal complement to the K260. A large range of profiled cutters is available, plus hardened blanks with which the more ambitious can develop their own moulding ideas. Grooving is done by adding a pair of saw segments (3, 4 or 8mm). Moulding cutters and saw segments can be combined to allow moulding and grooving in one operation, e.g. for window sections.

## Breaking out

For efficiency in any project, the first task is to break out the individual components from a carefully prepared cutting list, combining judicious selection of timber with economic conversion.

After first crosscutting the boards with hand- or jigsaw, clear the machine of all fences to give a clear area for freehand ripping, removing sapwood and splitting the boards. Label each piece as it emerges, and tick it off on the cutting list: the idea is to end up with all the items on the cutting list crossed off, and a pile of components in some sort of order!

● *There are as many ways to build a dresser as there are woodworkers who can tackle the job. Steven Hurrell's way calls for a universal machine and little else – but it sacrifices nothing to technology. His material was solid chestnut, to which he applied a fairly weak brown stain before polishing*

It sounds obvious, but when breaking out material you do need to remember the capacity of the planer — in this case 10in. If you need, say, an 18in top or panels 12in wide, they cannot be got out whole even if the timber itself is wide enough.

You pass each piece over the surfacer, flattening one side and straightening the edge or edges. It's a good idea to lower the thicknessing table to its maximum to allow the chips to escape. Then, before thicknessing, the surfacing tables are hinged back and a cutter-guard/dust-chute is fitted. Clear the thicknessing table of chips — a few strokes of a candle over it will make for a smoother feed. An assistant will be useful too, and save a lot of footwork.

When using such machinery it's handy to be able to gauge the depth of cut without relying on the scale. On the K260, one complete turn of the rise-and-fall handle equals ⅛in.

## Tenoning

One of the luxuries of machine woodworking is the ability to produce tenons accurately and efficiently.

Whether you choose to do your tenoning on the saw or on the spindle-moulder, the sliding table makes an excellent tenoning carriage. The saw is handy when only a couple of rails are involved, as it requires minimal setting; but, where quantity, speed and accuracy matter, the spindle meets all the requirements.

Using the tiger head fitted with rebating cutters, tenons can be cut in two passes — the rails being held against the turnover stop to determine shoulder length. Working with the cutters below, absolute accuracy can be achieved by finely tuning the spindle height.

Rails are initially cut to length, including an allowance for tenons: these are about 1¼in long, though the design of the tiger head allows much longer ones to be cut. The stop is set at a distance equal to the shoulder length plus one tenon length from the maximum projection of the cutting circle. Because of the cutting action of the spindle, it's essential to back up the rail with another piece to avoid break-out. Any haunching can be carried out on the saw, working against the rip fence and ideally finishing off by removing the waste on the bandsaw.

Having formed a perfect tenon, you need a mortise of equal accuracy! The K260's mortising tool is mounted in a chuck that is an extension of the planer block. It's utterly essential to guard the planer's cutter-block when using the mortiser, because the planer will still be running even though it's not needed.

The rounded ends of the slot mortises require either that the tenons be rounded to match, or — more neatly — that the mortises be squared up by hand.

## Plywood

Just as much of the best old furniture employed 'inferior' wood for groundwork and interiors, I used plywood in the construction of this piece. Conservation of solid timber provides a good enough reason, but plywood is, in addition, an excellent material in its own right for unseen and seldom seen parts such as cabinet bottoms, backs, divisions, shelves and drawer-bottoms; edges can be lipped where necessary.

A facility for sizing large panels will be appreciated by anyone who has had to struggle with inadequate equipment, and one of the best features of the K260 is the useful little dimension saw with its excellent crosscut facility. This allows panels to be cut quickly and accurately.

**Fig.1** *Ripping a board freehand on the Startrite K260. Cuts should be arranged to remove sapwood and defects*

## Fielded panels

The most attractive decoration for a panel is fielding, which I have employed on the doors (the end panels are a little narrow for this detail, so I've left them plain). I carried it out on the spindle-moulder using a Whitehill-type cutter-head with a straight-forward square cutter angled about 2° (fig. 4). Working with the cutter-head below the panel, the spindle height can be finely adjusted until you have formed on the panel a tongue that fits snugly in the groove of the corresponding frame.

This type of operation uses a large cutting circle and therefore a wide opening between the fences. This is always a source of danger. When it's unavoidable, and/or when short pieces are being machined, a cover board or false fence should be used. This is a thin piece of material (¼in ply is ideal) tacked to the existing fences. Minimum cutter exposure is achieved by actually cutting into the cover board from behind, just above the desired height, and then backing off to give a slight clearance.

When fielding a panel, start with the endgrain and work clockwise around the panel, so that any break-out when you machine the endgrain will be removed when you do the long grain. This practice is common to all similar moulding operations (figs 5 & 6).

The panels are dimensioned so that they are 'lost' ⅜in into each stile or rail. This will allow for the most severe shrinkage (care must be taken during assembly that no glue accidentally gets into the groove and grips the panel).

## Assembly

The base-cabinet top employs three pieces to make up the width, wood being carefully chosen to achieve a matching grain pattern. Each joint was first straightened and squared on the surfacer, the length of whose table is more than adequate for this type of work. You need to hold the boards firmly against the fence, with a slow and steady feed for best results. Then, moving over to the bench, I shot each joint by hand, creating a hollow over the length to compensate for movement at the ends. PVA and overnight pressure brought the boards together.

Because of the width of the top (18¼in), I used the surfacing fence as a guide for ripping, the sliding table again making it easy to finish off the dimensioning. The moulded detail (fig. 8) was achieved in two operations on the spindle-moulder (the bottom edge is finished off by hand). The sliding-table-and-clamp arrangement comes into use when an extra pair of hands is not available to steady a piece of this size.

The top is finally fixed to the carcase by screwing through the top rails, the kickers and the odd batten (remember to enlarge the screw-holes to allow movement of the timber).

The bracket base has an ovolo machined on its top edge, spindled in one operation, and is fixed by gluing and screwing. The mitred corners are cut with the saw-blade canted to 45°; using the sliding table again,

**Fig.2** *Each board is thicknessed after surfacing. Two pairs of hands make the work easier and safer*

# The universal dresser

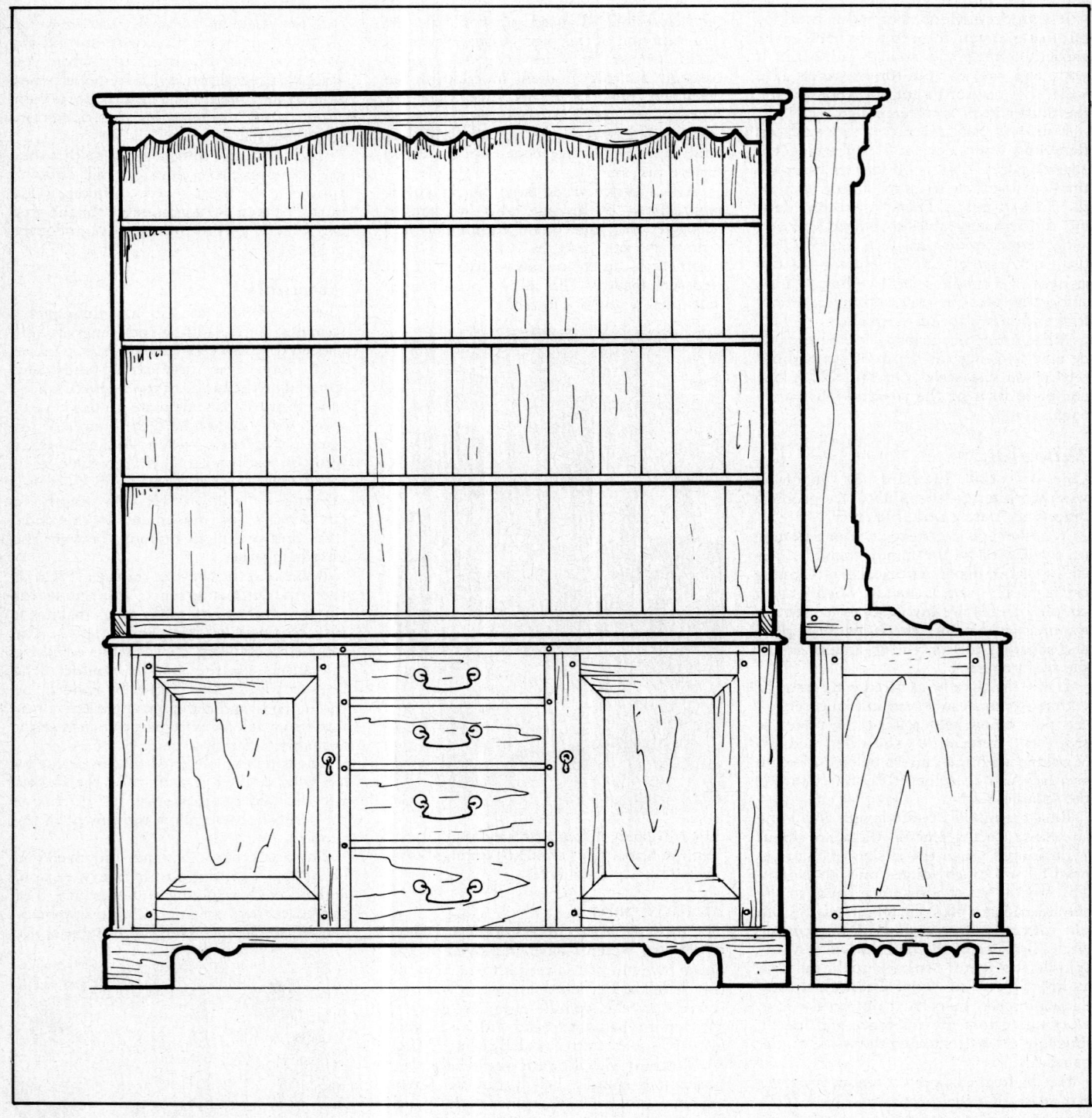

you can get them perfect. You can shape the base on the bandsaw before fixing, or afterwards using a jigsaw — whichever is the easiest.

## Drawers

The drawer construction emphasises handcut dovetails. One of the secrets of successful dovetailing is careful preparation all the way from the initial choice of wood, through machining, to accurate gauging.

Drawer-slips are used to hold the ¼in ply

bottoms in place, these being easily grooved and rounded on the spindle.

The good fitting and working of the drawers depends on the care taken to ensure that the drawer compartment is square, parallel and of equal width front and back.

## Handles

So as not to distract from the overall mellow tone of the dresser, I kept the brass handles simple, with tear-drops on the

doors and swan-necks on the drawers. Most brassware bought today is coated in a sterile-looking protective lacquer, which I removed by soaking in cellulose thinners overnight. Then I wire-wooled the fittings to produce an effective dull finish that complemented the colour of the wood.

## Dresser top

As the dresser top is a separate unit it can be made after the base cupboard is completed. Most of the work involved is in the shaped ends, feet and frieze rail, and here the K260 had to sit back and watch as attention was switched to the bandsaw. If you discreetly pin the two ends together, they can be cut out and cleaned up as one, to give a perfect match and a worthwhile time saving.

The horizontal shelves and rails can be fixed via housings, tenons or dowels. On many old dressers, shelves were tenoned right through the ends and wedged; provided this is done neatly, it can be an attractive form of exposed jointing.

The shelves have a single bead machined on their front edges, and a plate groove is also a useful addition for possible display purposes.

## Boarded back

The back of the dresser section is made up of random-width V-jointed boards, which are fixed in the rebate by nailing.

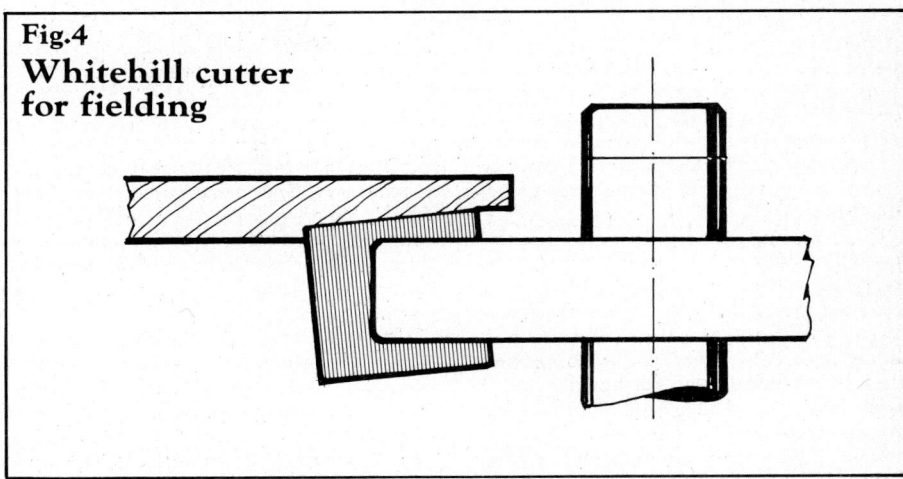

**Fig.4**
**Whitehill cutter for fielding**

Enough wood is got out (ex ½in) to cover the width of the piece. This is then ripped at random — with economy in mind — into widths varying from 2¼ to 4½in (remember that ⅜in of each board will be lost in the join). Planing and thicknessing the boards to around ⅜in, you should then straighten each edge to provide a starting-point for accurate machine-jointing.

Moving to the spindle, with the rebating knives in the tiger head, you then rebate each board on diagonally opposing edges to ⅜in deep and exactly half the thickness. After picking the best face and marking thus, the V is formed in two operations (one side needs more depth to clear the rebate), with a pair of 45° cutters in the tiger (fig. 10).

When fitting the back, an even balance is desirable among the various widths of board. Also, polishing of the top section is easier if the back is left out and fitted after final waxing.

## Cornice

Adding a good cornice makes all the difference to the overall effect of the piece. For this a length of ex-3x2in stuff is sectioned to 2½x1¾in, ready for moulding to shape.

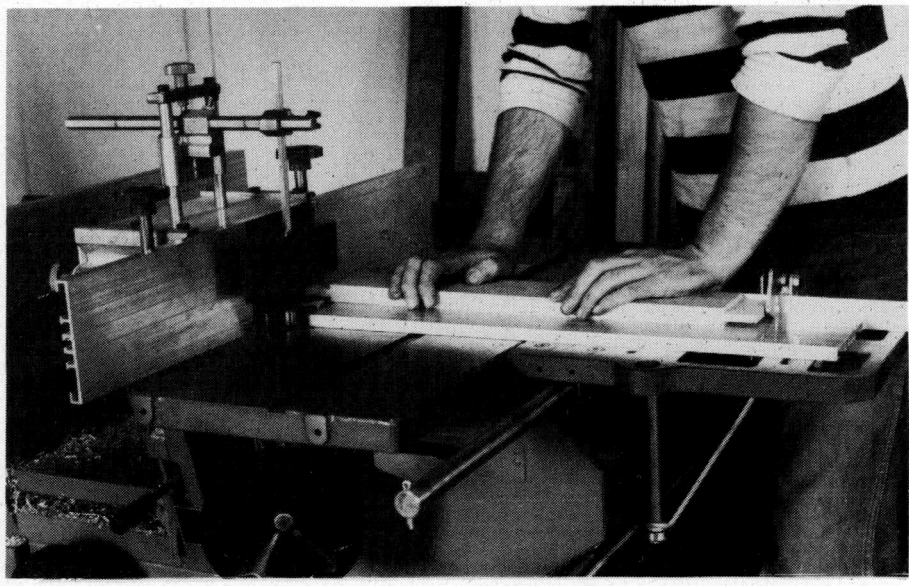

**Fig.3** *Tenons can be cut either on the saw or (as here) the spindle-moulder. A sliding carriage like this one is ideal for the job, keeping the workpiece square and ensuring a controlled feed*

**Fig.5** *Fielding a solid panel on the spindle-moulder, using a false fence for safety and a smooth cut*

**Fig.6** *The completed fielding displays the finish straight from the spindle cutter*

# The universal dresser

Assuming that your funds don't allow you to splash out on fancy tooling, this type of moulding will need to be machined in several bites using different cutter profiles (each cutter picking out a specific detail). For this particular design three shapes of cutters are needed, requiring four passes (fig. 11).

Triangulating the section on the circular saw will reduce the amount of waste to be removed, and improve safety. With heavily moulded pieces such as this, some planning is essential if you're to arrive at the best sequence of cuts. When you're doing complicated mouldings and further demand is likely, it's a good idea to run off several lengths while the operation is set up.

Your ability to produce classic moulded details depends on the profiled cutters you possess. You'll build up a selection over time, but for the newcomer it's often a matter of compromise. You may even have to supplement the spindle with hand-moulding to produce the required detail.

## Polishing

As chestnut is naturaly pale, I gave it some colour and warmth with a light wash of stain (Vandyke brown at about half normal strength). Then I used Jenkins' 'pale outside' polish to seal the piece, brushing it on and then cutting down with 240 paper. Depth was achieved by padding on a further three or four coats. After leaving these to harden for 24 hours, I dulled the surface with wire wool and then waxed it.

This finish produces a fairly durable result that requires little attention except for an occasional waxing, and brings out the beauty of the grain without obliterating it.

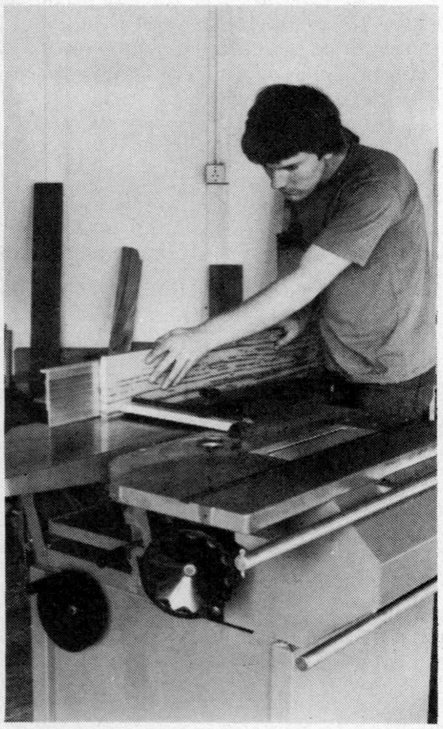

**Fig.7** *Squaring an edge on the surfacer, after first planing up a face side, is a basic wood-machining job*

## All in all . . .

Before this, I'd always been in the fortunate position of being able to use single-purpose machinery. Somewhat unfairly, I now think, I'd dismissed the combination as nothing more than a toy. Making this dresser with the help of the Startrite K260 certainly changed my views. I was impressed.

The resale value of these machines is very high — the single-phase version obviously attracting the larger market. The power difference between single- and three-phase is negligible; the machine I used was single-phase, and certainly did not suffer from any lack of muscle. Even with 415v on tap, single-phase (although initially more expensive) is worth considering. So, if you possess ambition, a love of wood, a 12x10ft space and a 13amp socket, the combination awaits your command.

● My thanks go to the Startrite Machine Tool Co, and Bill Conroy in particular, for encouragement, co-operation and the loan of the K260. Polish manufacturers W. S. Jenkins & Co. Ltd are at Tariff Rd, London N17 0EN, tel. 01-808 2336. ■

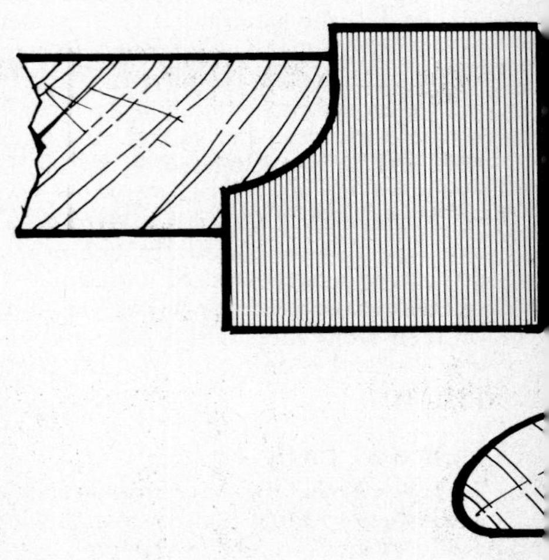

**Fig.8** **Spindling edge detail for top**

## Cutting list

**Base cabinet**

| | | | | |
|---|---|---|---|---|
| 4 corner posts | 32 3/16 x | 2 1/2 x | 1 5/8in | |
| 2 top rails | 14 | 4 | 13/16 | incl. 1 1/4in tenons |
| 2 bottom rails | 14 | 4 | 13/16 | ditto |
| 2 panels | 20 3/4 | 12 1/4 | 9/16 | |
| 1 top | 60 | 18 1/4 | 13/16 | |
| 4 rails | 57 | 2 1/2 | 13/16 | incl. 1in tenons |
| 2 divisions | 27 | 2 1/2 | 13/16 | incl. 1/2in tenons |
| 3 drawer-rails | 18 | 2 1/2 | 13/16 | ditto |
| 1 base | 60 | 5 1/4 | 3/4 | |
| 2 base returns | 18 | 5 1/4 | 3/4 | |
| 4 stiles | 26 | 1 3/4 | 13/16 | |
| 2 top rails | 16 3/4 | 1 3/4 | 13/16 | incl. 1 1/4in tenons |
| 2 bottom rails | 16 3/4 | 2 1/2 | 13/16 | ditto |
| 2 panels | 22 3/8 | 15 | 9/16 | |
| 1 drawer-front | 17 1/2 | 4 3/8 | 11/16 | |
| 1 back | 17 1/2 | 3 1/2 | 5/16 | |
| 2 sides | 15 3/8 | 4 3/8 | 5/16 | |
| 1 drawer-front | 17 1/2 | 5 3/8 | 11/16 | |
| 1 back | 17 1/2 | 4 1/2 | 5/16 | |
| 2 sides | 15 3/8 | 5 3/8 | 5/16 | |
| 1 drawer-front | 17 1/2 | 6 3/8 | 11/16 | |
| 1 back | 17 1/2 | 5 1/2 | 5/16 | |
| 2 sides | 15 3/8 | 6 3/8 | 5/16 | |
| 1 drawer-front | 17 1/2 | 7 3/8 | 11/16 | |
| 1 back | 17 1/2 | 6 1/2 | 5/16 | |
| 2 sides | 15 3/8 | 7 3/8 | 5/16 | |
| 4 drawer-bottoms | 16 7/8 | 15 3/8 | 1/4 | ply |
| 1 cabinet bottom | 57 | 11 1/2 | 3/4 | ply |
| 2 divisions | 26 13/16 | 14 | 3/4 | ply |
| 1 back | 57 | 27 | 1/4 | ply |

**Top section**

| | | | | |
|---|---|---|---|---|
| 2 ends | 51 | 6 | 13/16 | incl. 2 1/4in tenons |
| 2 feet | 14 | 2 1/4 | 1 1/16 | |
| 3 shelves | 55 3/4 | 3 3/4 | 13/16 | |
| 1 top | 55 3/4 | 5 1/2 | 13/16 | |
| 1 frieze | 55 3/4 | 5 | 13/16 | |
| 1 bottom rail | 55 1/2 | 2 1/4 | 13/16 | |
| 1 cornice | 80 | 2 1/2 | 1 3/4 | |
| Back boards to cover | 50 | 57 | 3/8 | |

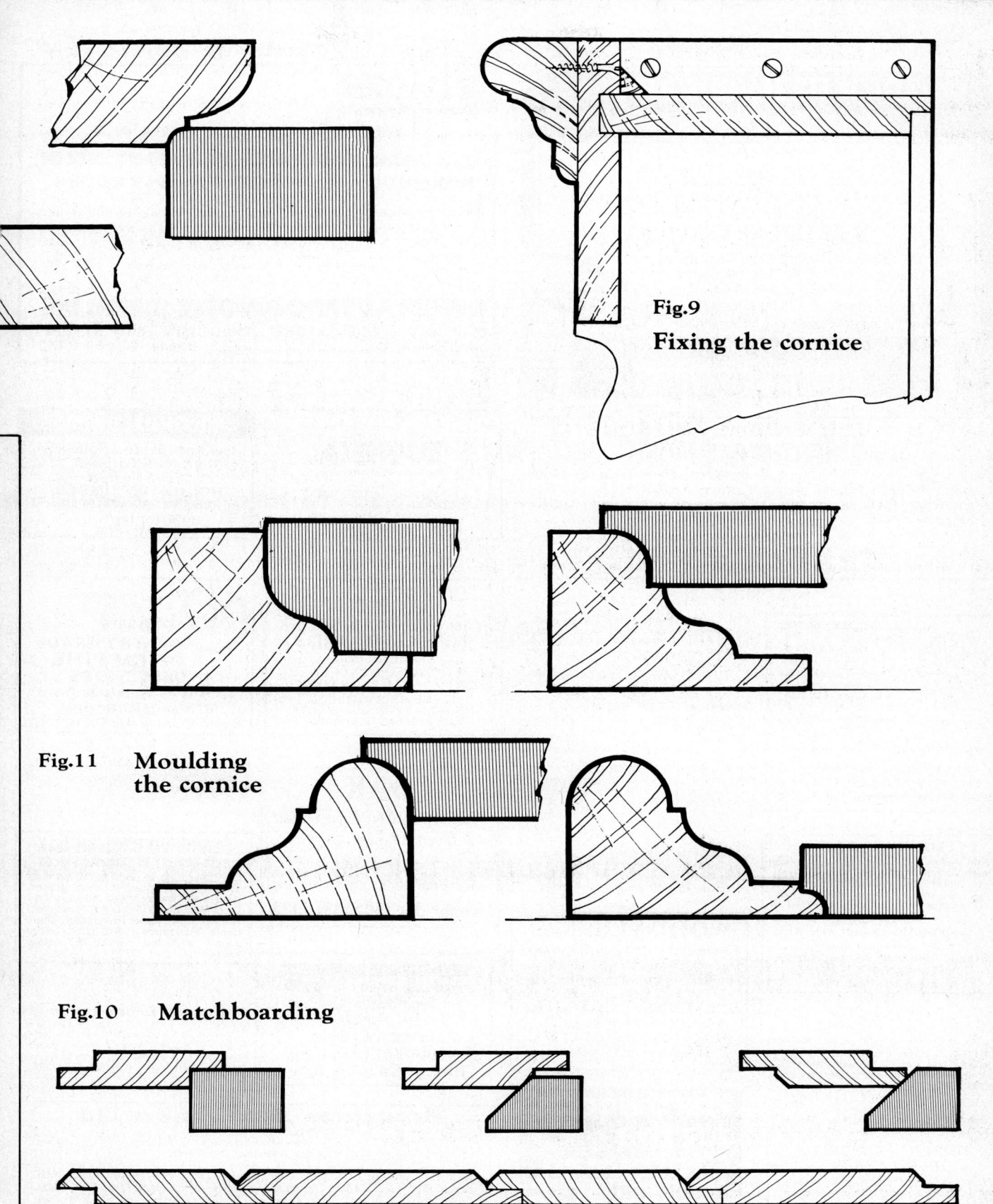

Fig.9

**Fixing the cornice**

**Fig.11** **Moulding the cornice**

**Fig.10** **Matchboarding**

# WOOD SUPPLIERS

886

# WOOD SUPPLIERS

## QUALITY ENGLISH & IMPORTED MATERIALS

From one of the finest stocks in the UK we can offer high quality English Oak, Sweet Chestnut, Elm, Brazilian Mahogany, Softwoods, Sheet Materials and a whole range of sundry items.

*Telephone or call in Monday to Friday between 8am to 5pm or 8.30am to 12.30pm Saturdays.*

## Wheelers Limited

**Chilton, Sudbury, Suffolk CO10 6XH**
**Telephone: Sudbury 73391 Telex: 987893**

## ENGLISH TIMBERS

### KILN DRIED HARDWOODS FOR *THE CRAFTSMAN*

Please visit our new warehouse

**P. Smith, The Old Chapel, Kirkburn, Nr. Driffield, East Yorkshire - Tel: 0377 89301**

---

**COUNTY HARDWOODS OF TAUNTON**
*PRIME QUALITY*
**Kiln Dried English Oak**
Competitive prices, machining service available.
Contact Nick Smyth (0823) 412405
Other kiln and air dried hardwoods in stock.

**ENGLISH HARDWOODS.** Most species available. Air dried and fresh sawn J.B. Atkinson & Son, 2 Wolfveton Road, Anlaby. Tel: Hull (0482) 658170.

## ENGLISH OAK

Kiln dried 1″ oak boards ¼ sawn and through and through.

**D. M. Mumford, White Hollow, Ticknall, Derby. Telephone Melbourne (03316) 2121.**

## THE WOODSTORE
**Suppliers of Native Hardwoods**
MOST HOMEGROWN SPECIES IN STOCK
LARGE AND SMALL QUANTITIES
SUPPLIED FRESH SAWN, AIR DRIED
AND KILN DRIED
**MACHINING FACILITIES AVAILABLE**
Send sae for Price List to
**TREEWORK SERVICES LTD**
CHESTON COOMBE, CHURCH TOWN, BACKWELL, Nr. BRISTOL
OR PHONE FLAX BOURTON
(027583) 3917 OR 3078
*We also offer a tree milling service*

### SEASONED NORTH AMERICAN LONG LEAF PITCH PINE AVAILABLE

Converted from timber beams to your specification or in our standard sizes. From timber originally imported circa 1880.

Traditional and modern mouldings available.

Largest sixes section 14″ × 12″.

Architraving and Skirting all in stock

*FOR A LIMITED PERIOD SPECIAL SUPPLY WITCH ELM.*

**J. R. NELSON & CO**

''The Saw Mill,''
Wills Farm,
Newchurch, Kent.

Tel: Hamstreet (023373) 3361

---

# Classified Advertisements

### FOR SALE

# Classified Advertisements

## FOR SALE

**THE FINEST SELECTION ON DISPLAY IN SCOTLAND!**

WOODWORKING & METALWORKING MACHINERY POWER TOOLS HAND TOOLS

**THE SAW CENTRE**

HIRE or BUY.

Visit our NEW SHOWROOM at EGLINTON TOLL GLASGOW
Tel: 041-429 4444/4374, Telex: 777886 SAWCO G
Also at, 38 Haymarket Terrace, Edinburgh EH12 5JZ. Tel: 031-337 5555

**OPEN**
Mon - Fri 8am - 5pm
Sat 9am - 1pm

---

MORTISERS; TENNONERS; SPINDLES; PLANERS; BANDSAWS; LATHES; CROSSCUTS; ROUTERS; SANDERS; DRILLS? YOU CAN CERTAINLY SEE ALL CLASSES AND TYPES OF MACHINES HERE.

WE ARE MAIN STOCKING AGENTS FOR:
MULTICO; ELU; SEDGWICK; KITY; SCHEPPACH; INCA; CORONET; DeWALT; WARCO; DOMINION; HITACHI; STARTRITE; TREND; ASHLEY ILES; SORBY.

*CALL US ABOUT WOODTURNING LESSONS*

*WOODCARVING LESSONS (See our Swiss carving tools)*
*ALWAYS HELPFUL, KNOWLEDGEABLE, GOOD SERVICE AT:*
## CLEVELAND WOODCRAFT
**38-42 CRESCENT ROAD, MIDDLESBROUGH.**
**TEL: (0642) 813103**

---

FOR ALL SUPPLIES FOR THE

## Craft of Enamelling

ON METAL

Including

## LEAD-FREE ENAMELS

PLEASE SEND 2 × 10p STAMPS FOR FREE CATALOGUE, PRICE LIST AND WORKING INSTRUCTIONS

## W. G. BALL LTD.

ENAMEL MANUFACTURERS

Dept. W. LONGTON
STOKE-ON-TRENT
ST3 1JW

---

**(FRESH SAWN HOLLY)** Limited supply variety & sizes. Reasonable rates details 02607 282. Evenings and Weekends.

**MYFORD ML8** 36" complete with motor and stand, rear turning attachment, rear sanding disc and table also other accessories and quality tools. Offers write Pearson, 33 Seekford Street, Woodbridge, Suffolk.

**CORONET MAJOR** (Red) Lathe saw-table planer, thicknesser, slot morticer. Table plus attachments on Bench £650 o.n.o. Tel: 06285 25230.

**WADKIN EVENWOOD** Universal, single phase, planer/thicknesser, saw, spindle, morticer. Excellent condition, £950. Workshop (0909) 485635.

**CORONET MAJOR LATHE** combination including c/saw planer £650 old hand morticer £20. Wallingford 38351 6-7pm.

**A SOLID WOODEN** bench 25" × 72", Height 34". Fixed vice with 10" jaw. Offers: Call 01-648-5031.

### WORKSHOP EQUIPMENT

**┌DEMONSTRATIONS┐**
**Practical Woodturning**
Kity Machinery, Ryobi, Wolf, Tyme. Saw tooth bits, whitehill blocks, router cutters and Inca bandsaws.
**Friday 8th Nov. 9am-9pm**
**Saturday 9th Nov. 9am-4pm**
**Burch & Hills, Power Tool Centre, 7 Belvidere Road, Southampton (0703) 332288**
*Special prices for visitors!*
(Only a small surcharge for Isle-of-Wight deliveries).

---

## IRISH WOODTURNERS & WOODWORKERS

We have extensive range of new and secondhand machines available for demonstration.
For friendly service and practical advice contact Bob or Chris.
**Celtic Woodworking Machinery Ltd.,**
**Old Creamery, Bennetts Bridge,**
**Co. Kilkenny, Eire.**
**Tel: 056 27401**

---

## THE CLEAN AIR SPOT

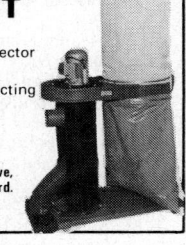

★ Mobile Dust Collector for under £240.
★ Cash & Carry Ducting
★ Free Advice
**Fercell Engineering Ltd.**
Unit 60, Swaislands Drive, Crayford Ind. Est., Crayford. DA1 4HU.
Tel: Crayford 53131/2

---

**MULTI-PURPOSE MACHINE.** Shopsmith Mark V, features; 10in. blade saw table, 34in. lathe, 16in. drill press with mortiser, 12in. disc sander, many extras. A superb machine in excellent condition £699. Great Missenden, Bucks. 02406 — 3158.

**YEW** blocks, blanks, billets, spindles. All sizes from £9 cu.ft. R. Fowler, Meopham, Kent (0474) 814468.

**BOXED SET** of Luna spindle moulding block and 10 cutter profile sets hardly used, £60 plus VAT. Telephone 0685 814111.

**EBAC MINI D** — Humidifier, fire damaged, but repairable. Timer not damaged, £73 plus VAT. Telephone 0685 814111.

**CORONET MAJOR** (Red) Lathe saw-table planer, thicknesser, slot morticer. Table plus attachments on Bench £650 o.n.o. Tel: 06285 25230.

---

**415v from 230v house mains to run your 3-phase machines, the 'Maldon' Unit £66 1½ h.p.**
**MALDON TRANSFORMERS**
**134 London Road,**
**Kingston-on-Thames**
**Tel: 546-75 34**
Access - Barclay

---

### WORKSHOP EQUIPMENT

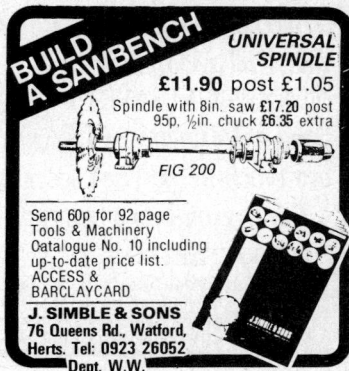

**BUILD A SAWBENCH**

**UNIVERSAL SPINDLE**
**£11.90** post £1.05
Spindle with 8in. saw £17.20 post 95p, ½in. chuck £6.35 extra

FIG 200

Send 60p for 92 page Tools & Machinery Catalogue No. 10 including up-to-date price list. ACCESS & BARCLAYCARD
**J. SIMBLE & SONS**
76 Queens Rd., Watford, Herts. Tel: 0923 26052
Dept. W.W.

---

## SHERWOOD WOODWORKING MACHINES

All cast constructed, lathes from £93.19. Bowl Turning Heads £60.81; Motors etc. 8" Saw Benches £59.50; Pulley's Belts; 8" + 10" DIY Saw Benches from £28.50.
*Send stamp for leaflets.*
**JAMES INNS (Engineers),**
**Unit 3, Welbeck Workshops,**
**Alfred Close,**
**Nottingham, NG3 1AD.**

---

## Braywood Estates

*Stockists of:*
B&D ★ DeWALT ★ ELECTRA ★ ELU HITACHI ★ NOBEX ★ NUTOOLS SKIL ★ STARTRITE & WADKIN
*All at Discount Prices*
**BRAYWOOD ESTATES LTD.**
158 Burnham Lane, Slough.
Tel: Burnham (06286) 5125

---

**EBAC TIMBER SEASONERS,** Protimeter moisture meters, always good prices and advice from the man who pioneered small scale seasoning. John Arrowsmith, 74a Wilson Street, Darlington, Co. Durham. DL3 6QZ. Tel: 0325 481970.    T/C

**ARKANSAS** whetstones now readily available from importer. Large selection. SAE for lists. C. Rufino, Manor House, South Clifton, Newark, Notts.    T/C

**SINGLE** to 3 phase converters up to 20HP 18 and 21 throat bandsaws. Illustrated details. HAB Engineering Unit 24, 16-20 George St., Balsall Heath, Birmingham B12 9RG. Telephone 021-440-6266.

**MARKING STAMPS** — name stamps branding irons supplied to your requirements SAE for details. Davey, 37 Marina Drive, Brixham, Devon TQ5 8BB.    T/C

---

## Braywood Estates

*Main stockists*
**TREND ROUTER CUTTERS, AUGERS, FORSTNER BITS**
All at discount prices
Braywood Estates Ltd., Dept WW, 158 Burnham Lane, Slough SL1 6LE.
Tel. Burnham (06286) 5125.
Hrs. Mon-Sat 9am-5.30pm

---

**MOTOR POWERED**
## FRETSAW KITS

All Components for Home Construction. Full 12" Throat. Uses Standard Blades. Free sanding hub. **Kit only £29.90** inc. P&P (Standard kit requires 1400-1500rpm motor) Suitable ex-Equipment **Motor — £11.95** inc. P&P.
(Kit excluding base mounting board).
S.A.E. or Phone 0292 — 62252
**KIT PROJECTS**
Dept. W, The Workshop, Gt. Washbourne, Nr. Tewkesbury, Glos. GL20 7AR.

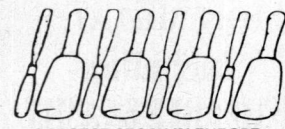

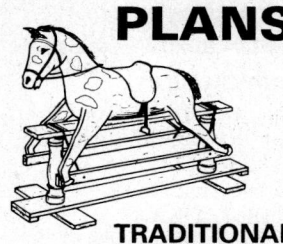

**TRESKE** is looking for skilled cabinet makers to help service their customers in the south. Own vehicle, approx. ten hours per month, easing drawers etc. Write John Gormley, Station Works, Thirsk YO7 4NY, or visit the Woodshop stand at the Woodworker Show.

894

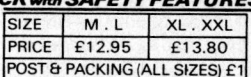

# Letters

CONGRATULATIONS on the brilliant article and carving under the heading 'The beginner's figurine' in your May issue. Such ideas, with good drawings from several angles, are especially welcome.

I don't know if I'm the farthest-flung Englishman to take your magazine, but certainly I've been flung a long way. My town (population 340) is on the Pacific coast of New Zealand. The magazine takes two months to come here and I travel 10 miles to the supermarket to buy it. Good ideas for carving are hard to obtain in such rural surroundings.

The author and carver Gerald Dunn may be interested to know that I have made a mahogany copy of his work. The aluminium navigation instrument carried by the figurine in the original is well beyond my ability or comprehension. However, I have made a tambourine instead, and am telling people that the model was in the Salvation Army.

*A. C. Danson, Mangawhai, New Zealand*

---

I'D LIKE TO THANK YOU for the source of endless information which is your magazine. I am a self-taught professional woodworker, and most of what I know has been learnt from *Woodworker* and the publications of Charles Hayward — and of course practical experience.

Having read in *Woodworker* several articles on old dovetailed planes, and having used one or two of these delightful tools, I decided to make an attempt at producing one myself, and I have since been infected by a desire to make and use more. The photograph shows two planes I have made — my first (the one on the right) and my most recent. Both are about 7in long overall, and were designed for use with either one or both hands.

My first has a mild-steel body with a brass bridge; the sole is ¼in thick, dovetailed to ⅛in sides, and the timber is black walnut. The other was an experiment, the sole being ¼in mild steel and the sides ⅜in brass — hence the visible dovetails. The timber in this one is a beautiful local species with the unlikely name of raspberry jam (*Acacia acuminata*): it resembles Indian

rosewood but is even harder and heavier. The name derives from the fact that it gives off a strong, distinctive smell of raspberry jam when freshly cut.

I'm sure many readers will be pleased to know that these planes were made entirely with hand tools (my workshop has no electricity supply) — mainly files of various sizes and shapes, a jeweller's piercing-saw, a hand-drill and steel scrapers, plus the usual woodworking tools. The most important ingredients are patience and careful, accurate hand work.

The joy in using these planes is well worth the effort; once a craftsman has experienced it, it's difficult to be satisfied with mediocre modern tools.

*Matthew Aylward, Mount Hawthorn, Western Australia*

---

I FEEL I MUST take issue with Mr Whitrick's remarks on saw sharpening (Letters, December 1984 and August 1985, plus others).

I too, like Max Burrough of Colyton, served my time with the old school; in fact his and my training were as alike as two peas in a pod. In my experience, and that of many others, Bill Gates' views on sharpening are quite correct, and his idea for an adjustable support for the metal saw-vice is very sound and eminently practical.

We were taught, shown and drilled by experts of the old school of tradesmen, and those experts were similarly trained by experts of an older school still. Their way of sharpening the various types of saw was as follows.

**Full ripsaws** (4-4½TPI): at 90° to the cutting line, 90° across the blade and 90° to the flat of the blade. The set varied according to the timber to be cut. These saws produced chips, not dust. Not many full rips were used, but there were plenty of half-rips.

**Half-ripsaws** (5-5½TPI): at 70° to the cutting line, 90° across the blade and 80° to the flat.

**Hand-saws, panel saws, tenon saws, bowsaws, dovetail saws** (6-7 and more TPI): 60° to the cutting line, 70° or 75° across the blade, and 70° to the flat of the

blade. The set varied to suit the timber and work in hand. Crosscut saws scratch-cut dust, rather than producing chips.

I wonder if Mr Whitrick has tried the ultimate test for a correctly sharpened crosscut saw? That is, to stand it on its back edge on the bench, place a fine sewing-needle in the V formed by the sharpening angle, and watch it slide down to the toe. This cannot happen on a full or half-rip.

I would be interested to know if any reader has seen, used or sharpened a lance-tooth saw from Scandinavia. It is like a normal hand-saw, but sharpened from one side only, with the tool laid flat on a 'saw board'. The file is held at 90° to the tooth line and about 30° to the blade. The saw produced a very fine cut and was made for both right- and left-hand use.

On an entirely different matter — Malcolm Ward's letter (WW/Aug). I was instructed to knock off both top and bottom edges of all drawer-sides to allow easy entry of the drawer into its home.

*L. E. Jenner, Bexhill-on-Sea*

---

IN 'QUESTION BOX' (WW/Sept) double-sided adhesive tape was recommended for holding a workpiece, and a thin knife for releasing it.

I've had a couple of disasters using this technique with thin, delicate carvings, and I've found that methylated spirit applied round the edges is a quicker, easier and safer method of release.

I still find your magazine a delight after more than 35 years in the trade.

*W. H. Harris, Redditch*

---

I WOULD LIKE to comment on the knuckle joint in the interesting article by Charles Cliffe entitled 'Technical Trio' (WW/Aug).

The metal pin could be a problem if the hinge is operated frequently. He says 'a piece of ¼in mild-steel rod is fine'. In theory, yes, but in practice it will be found that with use the pin, especially if lubricated — which it should be — will, by force of gravity, work its way down. If not hammered back, it could eventually drop below the interlocking sections, with possible disastrous results for the hinge. It may even fall out entirely. This effect can be seen quite often on piano hinges that have been cut, even if fitted horizontally.

There are two ways to overcome this problem. The first is to pin or screw a circular plate in wood or metal to the bottom of the knuckle. The second, and the method I favour — provided the hinge is no more than 6in deep — is to use a 4-6in nail. These are easy to come by, and they can be relied upon to be straight. Drill a hole to suit the nail thickness being used, recess the top to accommodate the head slightly below the wood, lubricate the metal and drive it home — from the top, of course. Cut away the bit projecting from the bottom and file it flush.

Simple, safe and cheap. The nail head will not show as it is always covered by the top of the piece of furniture.

*Mark Kenning, Evesham*

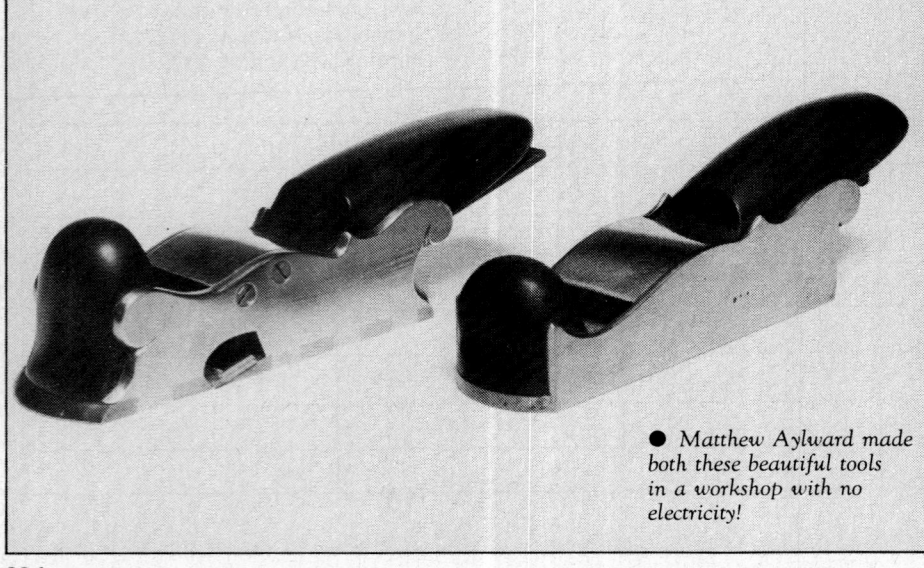

● *Matthew Aylward made both these beautiful tools in a workshop with no electricity!*

# The magazine for the craftsman
## ~ and the aspiring craftsman!

December 1985
Vol. 89
No. 1105

● *Playful but skilful – turn to p968 for more mixing of joinery and artistry*

**Editor** Peter Collenette
**Deputy Editor** Aidan Walker
**Advertisement Manager** Paul Holmes
**Graphics** Jeff Hamblin
**Guild of Woodworkers** Aidan Walker
**Editorial, advertisements and Guild of Woodworkers**
1 Golden Square, London W1R 3AB, telephone 01-437 0626

Unfortunately we cannot accept responsibility for loss of or damage to unsolicited material. We reserve the right to refuse or suspend advertisements, and regret we cannot guarantee the bone fides of advertisers.

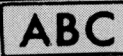

**Subscriptions and back issues** Infonet Ltd, 10-13 Times House, 179 Marlowes, Hemel Hempstead, Herts HP1 1BB; telephone Hemel Hempstead (0442) 48434
**Subscriptions per year** UK £16.90; overseas outside USA (accelerated surface post) £21.00, USA (accelerated surface post) $28, airmail £48
**UK trade** SM Distribution Ltd, 16-18 Trinity Gardens, London SW9 8DX; telephone 01-274 8611
**North American trade** Bill Dean Books Ltd, 151-49 7th Avenue, PO Box 69, Whitestone, New York 11357; telephone 1-718-767-6632
**Printed in Great Britain** by Ambassador Press Ltd, St Albans, Herts
**Mono origination** Multiform Photosetting Ltd, Cardiff
**Colour origination** Derek Croxson Ltd, Chesham, Bucks
© Argus Specialist Publications Ltd 1985
ISSN 0043 776X

# Argus Specialist Publications Ltd

1 Golden Square, London
W1R 3AB; 01-437 0626

**On the cover:** Lunar tunes from our toymaking project (pp906-7); amazing adornments (pp920-1); and our splendid special offer – GKN's magnificent Mastascrews, plus a ratchet Mastadriva to put them in with, at nearly half-price (full details on p913)

# Woodworker
# This month

## Makers for music

Returning (however temporarily) from the wilder shores of trendy furniture, the Crafts Council is devoting its 1986 Open Exhibition to musical instruments. It's part, they say, 'of an ongoing series which seeks to showcase makers reaching exceptionally high standards in a particular field'. The call to submit entries goes out to all concerned, no matter what their speciality may be: classical, early, folk, avant-garde or innovatory.

However, the notice is short. Entry forms are required back by 6 December this year. If you want one, get on to Nick Arber, Crafts Council, 12 Waterloo Place, London SW1Y 4AU, or ring Pamela Monkman there on 01-930 4811. You'll have to come up with the actual instrument(s) for selection by 12 March 1986.

● **Above:** A 'rose' for a lute soundboard by Zach Taylor

When **Michael Foden** wrote about turning boxes from exotic woods in the October issue (p784) we missed out a sentence. The correct version makes it plain. Unless you use a spigot lid, 'it is best to hollow out the box and lid section, leaving the lid too large to fit. Both items can be kept overnight and the final cuts made the following day. This procedure should result in a lid that will not move once fitted.'

● *This mythical fanfare heralds a new book – Projects for Creative Woodcarving by Ian Norbury, whose challenging designs meet a clear demand. It's published in December by Stobart & Son Ltd, 67-73 Worship St, London EC2A 2EL, 01-247 0501, at £15. If you want to meet Ian, get a copy signed, see him work, and even have a go yourself, visit his home base of the White Knight Gallery, 28 Painswick Rd, Cheltenham, Glos., on 6, 7 or 8 December between 10 and 6*

● *A bird-table is a bird-table ... is a pagoda, cathedral, Tudor cottage or Dutch barn. Raymond Miller's creations do not involve fine cabinetmaking – and why should they? They score instead with a playful, questing approach: architectural follies for woodworkers whose time, money, space or skills won't run to a full-size summerhouse. And look again; the spire is removable. Other designs replace it monthly or seasonally for a constantly changing skyline*

# Shoptalk

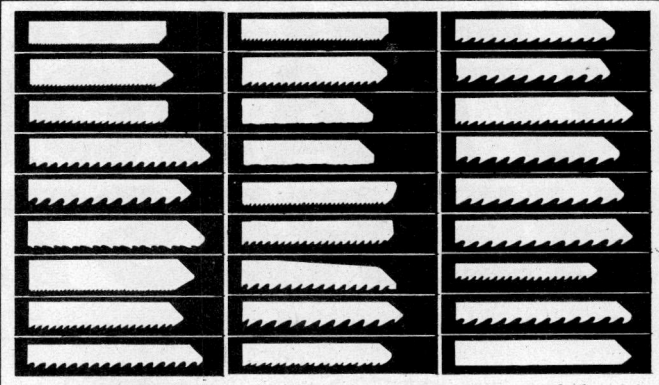

FROM HIGH-SPEED-STEEL *wavy-set to tungsten-carbide coarse-grain, this is the range of no fewer than 27 jigsaw blades just launched by AEG. Each does a specific job, and the right choice means a better finish. AEG's excellent leaflet gives the details plus some good general information. You can even get blades with teeth on both sides! And the range fits Black & Decker, Bosch, Craftsman, Elu, Hitachi, Holz-Her, Makita, Metabo, Skil, Stanley, Stayer and Ryobi jigsaws as well as AEG's own.*
- AEG, 217 Bath Rd, Slough, Berks SL1 4AW, Slough 872101

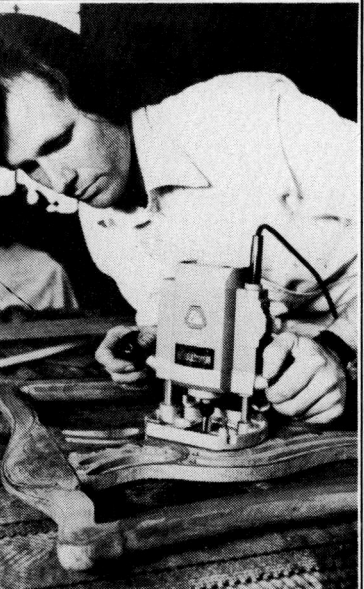

IF YOUR WORKSHOP IS SMALL *but dust is a pressing problem, you could check out Fercell's little A01 extractor with its 0.34hp single-phase motor. Its price-tag of £149+VAT is an intriguing start. The firm also do larger models, a woodburning space-heater (the GX15) at £699+VAT, and all sorts of ducting components for extraction systems.*
- *Fercell Engineering Ltd, Unit 60, Swaislands Drive, Crayford Industrial Estate, Crayford, Kent DA1 4HU, (0322) 53131/2*

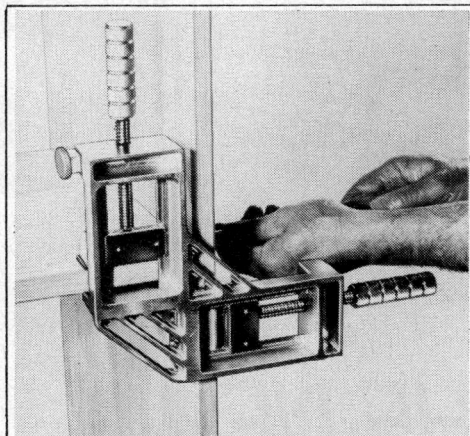

WOLFCRAFT'S *new Clamping Mobile features push-buttons for quick adjustment and a saw-guide for 45° cuts. It costs £29.50+VAT.*
- *BriMarc Ltd, Kineton Rd, Southam, Leamington Spa, Warwicks CV33 0DR, (0926 81) 2044; they'll tell you who stocks the device*

THOSE LITTLE BROWN CIRCLES *at the bottoms of recesses and rebates are familiar to users of the power router. If the cut will be exposed to view in the finished product, you've got problems cleaning up. The new 'surfacing cutters' marketed by Trend are said to obviate the difficulty because of the relief angle formed on their projecting carbide tips.*
- *Trend Machinery & Cutting Tools Ltd, Unit N, Penfold Works, Imperial Way, Watford, Herts WD2 4YY, (0923) 49911*

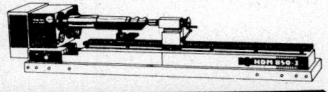

# Timberline

## Arthur Jones presents the month's inside news of supplies

Modest stocks of timber are all that woodworkers hold at the best of times; just now, they're minimal. The reasons which can warrant stockholding are almost completely absent from the marketplace.

The main reason why you might want a stock of timber on hand is the fear that, when you want to buy, the specification and species you require will be unobtainable, with a waiting period of perhaps months. Another reason, often closely linked with the first, is that the price of the wood may rise sharply, so that holding a stock can save a lot of money.

But — while no woodworker will agree that the price of wood is low — it has been in his favour for quite a long time, with the occasional drop in value and the competition on the re-sale side quite intense. Over the past couple of years price changes have often failed to cover the rate of inflation. So there has been no prospect of seeing any stockholding rise dramatically in value.

Is this situation likely to change in the near future? Not if current world trends continue. Admittedly the producers have made progress in bringing production down to the level of demand, but there is no indication that demand will recover. UK stockists have certainly had much more success, but there are probably still too many timber firms chasing the business and their main competitive drive is almost always based on price. In softwood, the fast movement of wood between Scandinavia and the UK means that any stock gaps can be filled almost overnight.

The fall in whitewood prices seems to have been halted, but those woodworkers using whitewood have made substantial gains; and the current prices being asked for unsorted whitewood, seen against the price of redwood fifths, offer a lot of encouragement to move up a grade and buy the whitewood.

But the availability of whitewood in the UK is patchy. It is much favoured in Scotland, the north-west and south Wales, but timber merchants say that in some other regions it is almost impossible to sell.

A wood much favoured by some is Parana pine, whose price has been reduced recently by around 10%. It gained favour immediately after the war, partly because it could be imported outside the softwood licensing controls, and it has been much used in quality joinery work.

From the same part of the world — Brazil — mahogany has actually strengthened a little in price, but when compared with the popular tropical hardwoods on the market it still represents good value for most woodworkers.

A great deal of fuss has been made of the fact that American hardwoods — oak, ash, walnut, cherry, maple, etc. — can be bought much more cheaply than six months ago, entirely because the dollar has weakened against the pound. But in reality the dollar is still strong, and earlier hardwood buying had to be done when the dollar had achieved almost parity with the pound — making north American hardwoods extremely expensive.

There is every probability that production in the Far East will be maintained at a high level in spite of the somewhat depressed prices. For example, in Indonesia (where there is close government control over hardwood log production and a ban on log exports) it is planned that next year production will be increased by 25%. Admittedly the emphasis will be on the use of these logs for added-value products, such as plywood, but the pressure on the market will be strong.

Woodworkers are using more hardwoods from west Africa, with shipments improving — helped by the fact that prices are not quoted in dollars. Political problems in west African countries can interrupt the smooth flow of shipments, but hardwood importers are being highly successful in regenerating this trade. ∎

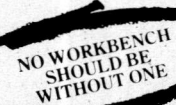

902

# Question box

## Our panel of experts solve your woodworking problems

**Q** *I have invested in a small antique and bric-a-brac business, and would like to acquire the skills to take furniture restoring/repairing seriously. Can you recommend what woodworking machinery I should acquire? I have a large barn which I plan to use as a workshop, plus the usual collection of hand tools, and I can afford good small-scale equipment. I'm a reasonably competent home handyman.*

*Peter Anzacot, Falmouth*

**A** To begin with, I'll deal with your main question of machinery. A great deal depends on the nature and range of work you intend to undertake. But I'm sure it's safe to say you wouldn't require the variety or capacity of equipment encountered in a cabinet or joinery shop. This is because the work is generally small-scale and often very intricate, so that any machinery will be grossly under-utilised.

In my view a bandsaw and lathe would be the most useful fixed machines. The bandsaw will, among many other things, produce veneers of the thickness found on very early pieces, especially if fitted with a high rip-fence (see David Savage's excellent article in April's *Woodworker*). So we're talking about a 6in depth of cut. If you don't intend to do much veneering, the capacity can of course be smaller. For the restorer, however, the bandsaw will also do many jobs otherwise carried out on the circular saw. There is, of course, no substitute for a lathe.

I find my 600w router very useful for some roughing-out work, but I certainly couldn't justify a planer/thicknesser or spindle-moulder for restoring.

You should concentrate on building up your hand-tool collection, plus a library. The skills you need to become a good restorer are not inconsiderable, so a range of definitive books on staining, polishing, restoring and the like are invaluable. No matter how experienced you are, another craftsman's advice is always worth having. A knowledge of styles, methods of construction, and materials and their correct uses, is also important, so you'll need books on furniture history.

You should also think of acquiring skills which pass beyond woodworking, such as upholstering and french polishing. Check with your local Adult Education Organiser what courses are available (and see what the Guild of Woodworkers offers).

Your barn, I confess, conjures up unpleasant images as well as pleasant ones — chief among the former being the thought of very nasty winters. You have a lot of space to heat; and, if polishing is to be part of your repertoire, heat it you must. A piece for polishing stays in my shop for about a week, and during that time (if in winter) the place is heated night and day. I use a butane-gas fire, and with a single element burning the temperature stays at about 65-70°F. This costs about £8. The workshop is draught-proofed.

I don't know whether you intend to restore your own stock or other people's. In either case you must have insurance to cover its value and your public liability. If it belongs to other people, your responsibilities are rather like those of a physician or surgeon. Poor craftsmanship destroys value and quality. Before undertaking the repair of someone else's property you must be quite sure your skills are up to it.

*Ian Hosker*

**Q** *This photo shows an old treadle lathe I've restored. I'd be glad if you could tell me its likely age, maker and approximate value.*

*Kevin Hallett, Evesham*

**A** Your lathe is a basic treadle design, but it has interesting features.

Firstly, the driving pulley is turned from a pair of cranks and rods connected to the treadle board, whereas most woodturning lathes of this period only incorporate a single crank and rod or chain. The double action was designed for heavy work.

Secondly, the tool-rest and tailstock are locked in position on the bed by levers rather than the more common cast loops or discs and nuts. The levers allow much quicker adjustment.

Finally, the tailstock centre is moved by a cranked handle rather than the usual wheel. I've been unable to find this feature on any other lathe.

These three points lead me to think that your machine is probably a brass-turning lathe made between 1850 and 1860. It will fetch whatever people are prepared to offer — which is very difficult to gauge!

*John Wilson*

**Q** *Can you tell me where to get hard balsa wood (or another lightweight timber that cuts and works reasonably cleanly) in 18-24in widths and ¼-1in thicknesses? By 'hard' I mean dense enough to cut apertures on the band- and fretsaw without tearing. Which species do you think would be suitable?*

*Glyn Williams, Cardiff*

**A** Balsa trees do not reach large diameters, and to get the widths you are seeking you would have to joint two or more pieces. To avoid grain tearing it is essential to use sharp, thin-edged tools because of the very soft nature of the wood.

You do not say what you wish to make, or how important the weight is to the product. There is no close match in terms of weight, and the best alternative would probably be to use obeche. Although twice the weight of balsa, it is pale yellow, soft and easily worked, and you could get the dimensions you require. If you do go for this wood, examine the face of the board closely for small cross-checks. In the larger logs there is a tendency for brittle-heart to occur; this results in what are sometimes referred to as thunder shakes, which make the wood liable to crumble when machined.

Another alternative is ceiba, used for plywood core stock, which weighs a little less than obeche. It is not a particularly attractive-looking timber, being variable and often streaky in colour, from grey to pinkish-brown. Both these woods are in quite good supply. Jelutong too could be considered, but it frequently contains latex canals which might mar the appearance. Jelutong is kind to work and is used, when selected, for pattern-making and drawing-boards.

*Bill Brown FIWSc*

**Q** *Can you please tell me the best timber to use for an exterior house name-board? I'd prefer one of the British hardwoods. The sign will be cut mostly by router, with a little work by hand, and finished with yacht varnish. Timbers I'm considering include English oak, ash, elm, sweet chestnut, beech, sycamore, acacia, bubinga, American cherry, hyedua/amazaque, and Brazilian mahogany.*

*Thomas Thomson, Castle Douglas*

**A** You have two primary factors to consider: weathering and durability. Both depend on exposure. If the name-board is to be fully exposed, I would place English oak last on the list — together with beech; simply because the large rays in these woods encourage severe checking, and under long-term exposure this means you'll have to spend a lot of time maintaining the varnish finish.

Sweet chestnut would be one of the best woods for the purpose, since it's easy to work and naturally durable. But it does contain a lot of tannin, and any fixings used should non-ferrous — say brass, or at least hot-dip-galvanised — in order to avoid 'ink-staining' of the wood.

Elm, and especially wych elm, would be reasonably satisfactory, but it does tend to distort; buying quarter-sawn material would lessen this possibility. Ash and sycamore would also behave quite well. Acacia (robina of false acacia), on the other hand, is hard to work to a good finish and tends to warp badly.

If available, alder, lime and selected fruit-woods, such as pear and cherry, could all be satisfactory, as could the foreign woods you mention.

Varnish is only a water-shedder, though if regularly maintained it will generally keep wood in good trim. A name-board is invariably fixed vertically, so rainwater is shed rapidly, but if holes bored to take fixings are slightly oversize and, as might be the case with your routed profiles, there is some exposed endgrain, timbers such as alder, ash, lime, fruitwoods and sycamore, and to a slightly lesser extent elm, could develop localised wet rot.

There are a number of organic wood preservatives on the market that can be varnished over once they are dry, e.g. clear Cuprinol and transparent Solignum. These might do the job. But you must remember that, if your routed edges are sharp, they offer no proper adhesion for the varnish, and the film would therefore have to be maintained especially carefully. A small 'pencil round' moulding to the edges would help considerably; if the film does tend to curl away from a sharp arris, water can soon get behind the rest of it — causing unsightly staining of the wood and premature breakdown of the whole finish.

Personally, I would attempt to find a good piece of yew. Though a softwood, it is naturally durable and would not need preservation. It is also attractive. Failing that, I would use sweet chestnut (quarter-sawn if possible) with brass fixings. If these were unavailable I would turn to one or other of the alternatives mentioned, but I would avoid oak and beech because of their weathering characteristics.

*Bill Brown FIWSc*

---

**Q** *I intend making a set of rush-seated ladderback chairs, but I have two problems.*

*1 How is the assembled seat frame attached to the legs?*

*2 Since the distance between centres of my lathe is only 30in I cannot turn the back legs, so I intend using a rectangular section – pencil-rounded and tapered from seat level to top. For various reasons I intend using pine (good-quality, with small knots only). Do you consider a section 1⅛x1⅜in finished sizes at seat level strong enough for the job? There will be six or eight stretchers below the seat.*

*D. A. Truslove, Loughton, Essex*

**A** The traditional rush-seated chair is normally constructed as shown in the illustration, the rush being woven directly on to the seat rails. The problem of attaching the 'assembled seat frame' to the legs therefore does not arise.

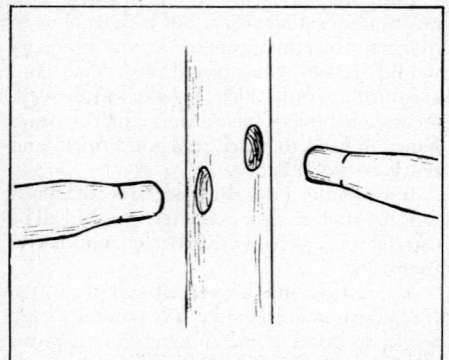

Back legs made from square or rectangular materials shaped and tapered from seat level to top are quite acceptable. However, I would not choose pine for this type of work. Ash or beech is much more suitable. Yes, I know pine is popular, and no doubt the chairs are required to match other pine furniture. But, while it may be suitable in a table or a dresser, pine lacks the resilience required in a chair subjected to the stresses of normal — to say nothing of abnormal — use. For chairs of this type I use 1⅜in square.

If you must use pine, rectangular-sectioned seat rails would make for a stronger construction.

*Jack Hill*

---

**Q** *I intend to build a cartwheel 30in in diameter. Since it's for decoration only, it will require no metalwork.*

*I'm a woodturner, so there should be no problem in turning the hub. But I wonder if you can advise me on how to go about actually making the wheel? I've been to the library, but couldn't find any useful information there.*

*B. Hayles, St Anne's*

**A** I agree that books tend not to be much help with making wheels. Authors are very good at eulogising about the wheelwright and his craft, but they never get around to explaining how to make a wheel. For a step-by-step run-down, see my article 'Turning cartwheels', published in *Woodworker* in six monthly parts starting in September 1983. It compared model with full-sized wheelmaking and covered both aspects of the subject equally.

You will probably need to make a couple of tools to assist you. Firstly you'll need to clamp the turned hub firmly whilst you chop out the spoke mortises. Wheelwrights had a special bench called a 'horse', but for a 30in wheel you should be able to use a Workmate and a couple of shaped clamps to hold the hub across the open jaws. The same arrangement will be useful when driving the spokes home.

I would suggest that you make a wheel with 12 spokes, and that the spoke tenons should be not tapered but stepped. Wheelwrights had a special chisel called a 'bruzz' for chopping out the spoke mortises, but if you stick to parallel-sided mortises an ordinary firmer chisel will be OK. When fitting the spokes you will need a 'spoke set': a simple thing, but make sure that the pivot is central and not at all floppy.

You'll also need to make a template for the felloe shape, best done in ply or hardboard. You will have to draw the full circle, to both inside and outside diameters, and accurately divide it into six.

An excellent source of information on the detail of individual cart- and waggon-wheels is John Thompson's range of plans of horse-drawn vehicles (1 Fieldway, Fleet, Hants). There are about 80 to choose from, but for a conventional iron-axled wheel I would suggest plan no. 2a, for a farm tip cart once held in the Weald and Downland

Museum in Sussex. For the older wooden-axled wheel, I would recommend the only plan of John's which was not drawn from life, but is a recreation of the tip carts described by George Sturt in his classic book *The Wheelwright's Shop*: plan no. 12a.

*Barré Funnell*

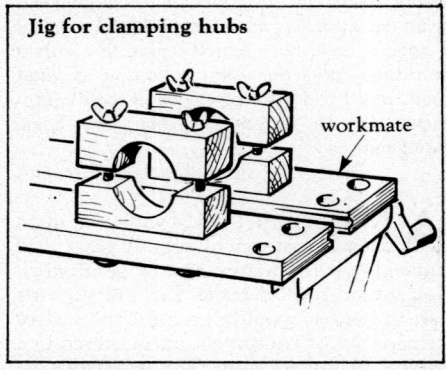

**Jig for clamping hubs**

workmate

---

**Q** *I am involved in restoring a water-powered sawmill in Norfolk. An 1835 map of the site shows four rectangular ponds – used, it is said locally, for immersing timber. Now, I know that wood can be stored in water for long periods without rotting, and that spar timber for the Victory is still floating about in Portsmouth dockyard. I also understand that imported timber which has been floated down rivers and into salt water needs further soaking in fresh water to get the salt out. But why should a small estate sawmill in the middle of rural Norfolk, presumably dealing only with local species, wish to throw their produce into a pond?*

*Barré Funnell, Norwich*

**A** I doubt whether it can be said for certain what the ponds were for. Possibly an archaeological investigation of the bottom, after draining, might throw some light on the matter. It might, for instance, indicate that the ponds were older than the earliest recorded sawmill on the site.

However, it certainly seems possible that they were used for treating timber after it had been sawn. John Evelyn, in his *Silva* (a discourse originally delivered in 1662) gives two reasons for immersing timber. Firstly: 'being put ten Days in Water it will exceedingly resist the Worm'. Then, in relation to seasoning, after describing the conventional sticking of boards in a dry, airy place, he says: 'Some there are yet, who keep their Timber . . . by submerging it in Water . . . Lay therefore your Boards a Fortnight in the Water (if running, the better, as at some Mill-pond Head) and then setting them upright in the Sun and Wind . . . Thus treated, even newly sawn Boards will Floor far better than a many Years dry Seasoning, as they call it.'

I was told by an old country wheelwright that he liked to bore the pilot bearing-hole through his roughed-out elm stocks (hubs) and then leave them for two or three years in a running stream before finishing them up for a wheel.

*Philip Walker*

**Q** I've fitted to my bench an old woodworking vice which belonged to my father. It has a quick-release lever. When I grip a workpiece in its left-hand side, all is well, but when I use the right-hand side the lever eases up and the vice springs open. To use it I need three hands – one to hold the workpiece, one to hold the lever down and one to turn the handle. It's very irritating. What's the reason for the difficulty, and how do I overcome it?

*George Young, Bedford*

**A** The problem has two possible causes: incorrect adjustment, and wear on components.

For correct operation it's essential to have enough tension on the trigger spring to keep the half nut fully engaged in mesh with the main screw. Our repair and maintenance leaflet RE9/11 details the adjustment procedure in full.

Since the vice is old, however, wear could well be the real trouble, and the symptoms you describe seem to suggest it. Gripping in the left-hand side would tend to position the main-screw and nut thread helix angles in sympathy; gripping on the right may tend to position the main screw and nut out of alignment, so that the helix angles act against each other and subsequently cause forces which allow disengagement.

If your vice is a Record product, I suggest you dismantle it, inspect for wear and re-assemble it according to the instructions in our leaflet. The instructions may also be relevant if the vice was made by another manufacturer to a similar design.

*Mike Lander, Record Ridgway Tools Ltd*

**Q** I'm refurbishing a rocking-horse which is about 60 years old. Its body is built up from blocks of wood which have then been carved to shape. The surface appears to have been treated with a substance like plaster before being painted. Can you tell me how to deal with it – and also where I can get leatherwork for the horse?

*R. A. C. Round-Turner*
*Bures, Suffolk*

**A** The plaster on your rocking-horse is gesso. If in bad condition, it is best carefully sanded off so you can start afresh.

Gesso, and the rabbit-skin glue that goes with it, can be obtained from a good art-materials shop. Make up the 400g tin according to the instructions, leave overnight, and apply one-third of the mixture with a small sponge — smoothing it over with light touches of the hand. Leave overnight again to dry out, lightly sand your work smooth, and apply another third. Repeat the process one more time. The rocking-horse is now ready for its undercoat and top coats.

If the paintwork is only chipped, use the same method, but with just a small amount of gesso on the affected areas. Clean down all the paintwork with a cleaner such as Flash, lightly sand all over with a fine paper, and re-apply the undercoat and top coats.

I supply all types of leather goods for rocking-horses.

*Margaret Spencer*
*Chard Rd, Crewkerne*
*Somerset TA18 8BA*

**Q** I have made a large hutch for my rabbits, and I'm thinking of using yacht varnish for the bottom to prevent the urine from sinking through. Can you tell me whether it will be safe for the job?

*Therese Weiss, Lincoln*

**A** I've consulted a veterinary surgeon, and this reply places the accent more on the health of the rabbits than the protection of the wood. I am pleased that you suggested a yacht-type varnish; but, even so, I don't recommend using any surface finish on a rabbit-hutch — on the floor or anywhere else — simply because rabbits would soon chew and scratch into it.

I suggest that a non-ferrous-metal floor be fitted instead — something like a bird-cage bottom, with a lip like a shallow tray so that it can be removed for cleaning easily, would be ideal. This would be harmless and indeed beneficial to your rabbits.

*Noel Leach*

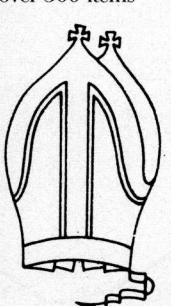

# Under a carver's moon

## Anthony and Judy Peduzzi explain how to make a celestial pedestrian dance

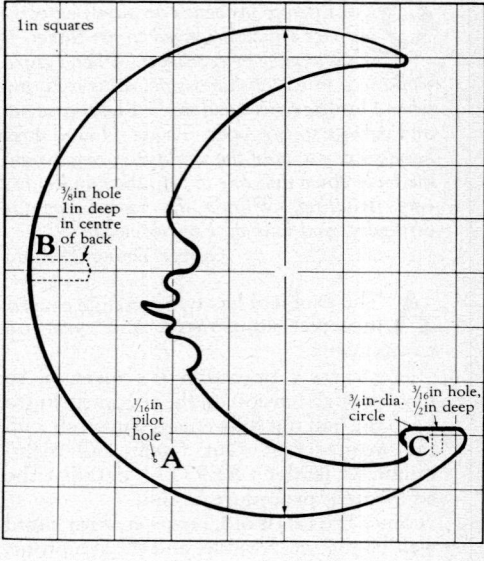

Since last century at least, serenading the moon has been a common pastime among pierrots — toy and otherwise. Our first version of this piece, many years ago, used only one piece of birch plywood, one blunt chisel, two rasp blades, various files, a craft knife and one sharpened screwdriver. Our techniques have advanced since then, but it's still an easy one.

Here's how to set about it.

**1** The first thing you'll need is eight pieces of moon. Take your piece of ¼in plywood, 9½in x 48in. Starting from one end, draw yourself a grid, with each square representing 1in. Then, following the illustration in fig. 1, draw your moon to scale. Next, cut out the moon, using a fretsaw. Using your cut-out moon as a pattern, mark out and cut your remaining seven shapes, using your fretsaw.

Now take two sections of your moon, and on one piece spread a little glue over the whole of the top surface; then glue and cramp the two sections together. Make sure you keep all your edges level. When these are dry, glue your third section into place, leave to dry, and continue until all the sections are glued together.

**2** Before you start to carve the moon, drill the ¹⁄₁₆in pilot holes for your woodscrews on each side, at the positions shown in fig. 1A, about ½in deep. Next, drill a ⅜in hole to a depth of 1in, as shown in fig. 1B, into the back of the moon.

**3** The half-round rasp was used to form the shapes of the moon, and also the platform for Pierrot. For smoothing I used the flat rasp blade and the files. The chisel I used mainly for shaping the face. Naturally, proper carving tools will give you more scope for accuracy and variety.

The shape and style of the face we leave entirely in your capable hands, for carving is a very personal craft. Just take your time. Only remove a small amount of wood each step of the way. Keep checking both sides of the face to ensure that they look alike.

**i** File or plane the back of the moon smooth and flat.

**ii** As in fig. 2, draw a centre-line from the top of the crescent right down through to the platform at the lower end. Then measure the width of the nose, 1in at the lower end to ½in at the bridge. Mark the position and design of the eyes, with top and bottom lids. Mark out a ¾in-diameter circle on the top of the platform for Pierrot to sit upon, and here drill a ³⁄₁₆in hole centrally to a depth of ½in. Draw a curve on each side as shown in fig. 2 — starting with the top of the crescent, ¼in each side of your centre-line, and finishing with the line above the eye. Then do the same with the lower crescent, measuring ½in each side of

your centre-line below the platform and finishing just below the chin.

**iii** First cut out the curves that you have just marked. Then shape these. Shape the top and lower crescents, shown in fig. 3, and also the platform. When doing this, start from just below the chin, working downwards towards your platform, and from just above the eyes upwards — always filing towards the centre-line.

This stage can be completed before you begin on the actual face.

**iv** Round and shape the chin and lower lip.

**v** Carve the nose, down to the cheeks.

**vi** Shape the upper lip and cheeks.

**vii** Carefully cut out the shape of the eyes. (If you take too much wood away on one eye you can, as a last resort, always fit an eye-patch!) Also cut the eyelids, top and bottom. If you want to put bags under his eyes, do so — after all, he does stay out all night.

And that's that. Just keep on until you're completely satisfied with the shape of the face. Then stop immediately.

Lastly, make sure that every part of the moon is absolutely smooth. Use plenty of sandpaper for this, and finish him off with a very fine papering.

**4** Now paint the eyes, slowly and steadily, and the lips. Remember that the eyes are on a sloping surface, and work carefully: otherwise the moon will appear cross-eyed or even a little tipsy. Varnish the moon.

**5** Take your tracing-paper for the last time, and draw yourself a 5½in x 3½in box. Trace the outline of Pierrot, shown in fig. 4; keep within the lines. Cut out your box, place it squarely on your piece of ¼in plywood, 5½in x 3½in, and tape both together. Transfer the outline on to your plywood.

**6** Cut out the figure. Next, drill a ³⁄₁₆in hole, ½in deep, at the position shown in fig. 4A. Put a little glue inside the hole, and push in your length of ³⁄₁₆in dowelling, 1in

long. This is the peg that holds Pierrot on to the platform. Now you can sandpaper Perrot and paint him, playing his mandolin. If you cannot manage to paint him well, showing his hands holding the instrument, you can always change his mandolin into an oar, so that he appears to be paddling a canoe. When you have finished painting him, varnish the figure.

**7** Now for the legs. Take your four lengths of ⅝in dowelling, 2in long, for the legs; two lengths of ⁵⁄₁₆in dowelling, 1¼in long, for the ankles; one piece of hardwood 2¼in x 2½in x 1in to make the boots; and your two ¹⁄₁₆in brass rods for the hinge pins.

**8** Now see fig. 5. Trace out the top view of the boots and transfer the outline to the hardwood. Drill a ⁵⁄₁₆in hole in each boot to a depth of ⅜in, and then cut out the shape. Then mark out the side view, cut that out too, and sandpaper the whole thing.

**9** Glue the lengths of ⁵⁄₁₆in dowelling into the holes in the boots.

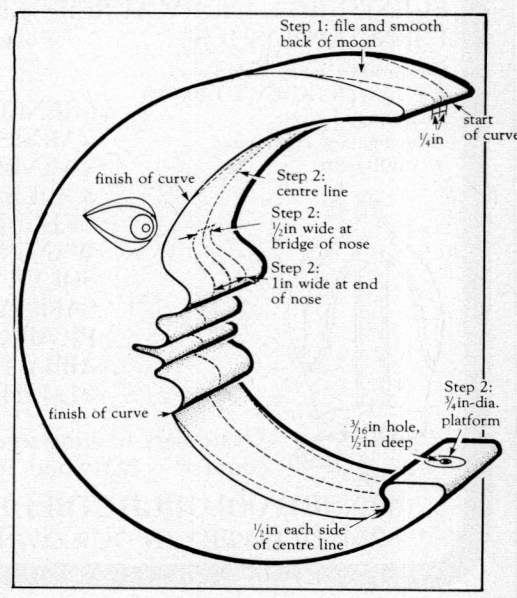

**10** Make the loose bridle-joints for the knees in the ⅝in dowelling as shown — radiusing the ends of the pieces to allow movement.

**11** Mark out the 1/16in hinge-pin holes in the bottoms of the upper pieces as shown, and drill centrally through the joint and out the other side. Assemble the joints and mark on the lower pieces the centres of the holes in the upper pieces. Then dismantle the joints and drill a 3/32in hole through each lower piece immediately above the mark. This will allow plenty of clearance for movement.

**12** Re-assemble the joints, knock in your lengths of brass rod and flush them off with a hacksaw and file.

**13** Drill ⅛in clearance holes in the tops of the legs — plus 5/16in counterbores, ⅛in deep.

**14** Glue the ankles into the lower legs.

**15** Paint the legs and varnish them; then screw them to the moon. Plug the counterbores with 5/16in pellets, and flush them off before painting and varnishing them too.

**16** Glue Pierrot to the platform.

**17** Chamfer the ends of your 16in piece of ⅜in dowelling, and push it into the moon's back.

**18** Cut the dancing-board from the 30x8in piece of plywood to the shape shown in fig. 6, and finish it as you like. ∎

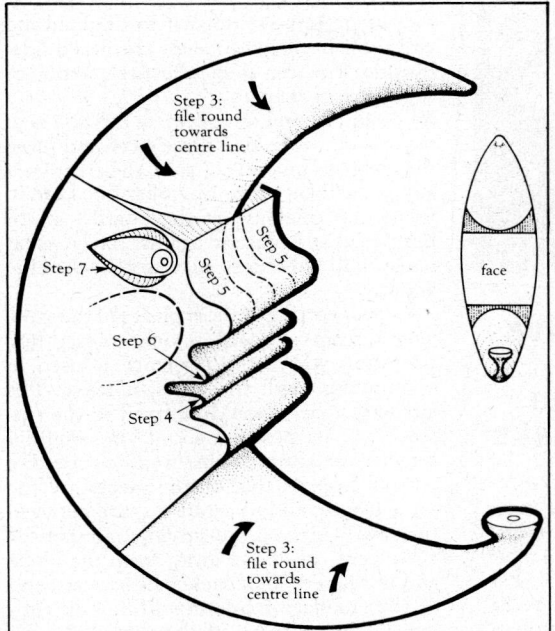

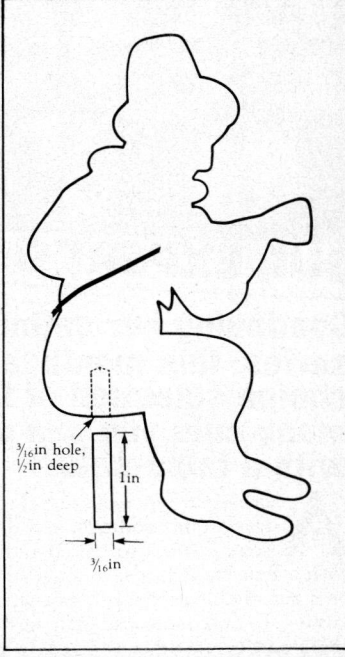

● This is an extract from *Making Moving Wooden Toys*, published by David & Charles, Brunel House, Newton Abbot, Devon TQ12 4PU, (0626) 61121, at £8.95: available from any bookshop or direct from the publisher.

## Cutting list

| | | | | | |
|---|---|---|---|---|---|
| plywood | 1 off | 48 | x 9½ | x | ¼in |
| | 1 | 30 | 8 | | ¼ |
| | 1 | 5½ | 3½ | | ¼ |
| dowelling | 4 | 2 | ⅝dia. | | |
| | 1 | 16 | ⅜dia. | | |
| | 2 | 1¼ | 5/16dia. | | |
| | 1 | 1 | 3/16dia. | | |
| hardwood | 1 | 2¼ | 2½ | | 1 |
| brass rod | 2 | ⅝ | 1/16dia. | | |
| plus brass screws and hardwood pellets | | | | | |

## MOONDANCING

What's being made here is a jig-dancing toy. Others like it have been used for hundreds of years by the travelling entertainers of Europe. Many jig-dancers emigrated to America with their owners and became 'clapboard dancers' — wooden at first, but their descendants included metal dolls that danced on phonographs as the record revolved. Among topical jig-dancing double acts was a chase between Uncle Sam and the renegade Pancho Villa — while relatives include the knee-britch marionette, secured to your knee and made to dance on your foot.

## How it works

Sit on one end of the dancing-board on a hard chair. Hold the stick so that the moon's legs dangle about ⅛in above the far end of the board. Now all you need's a lively tune: tap the board in rhythm so it springs up and down — and the moon will dance!

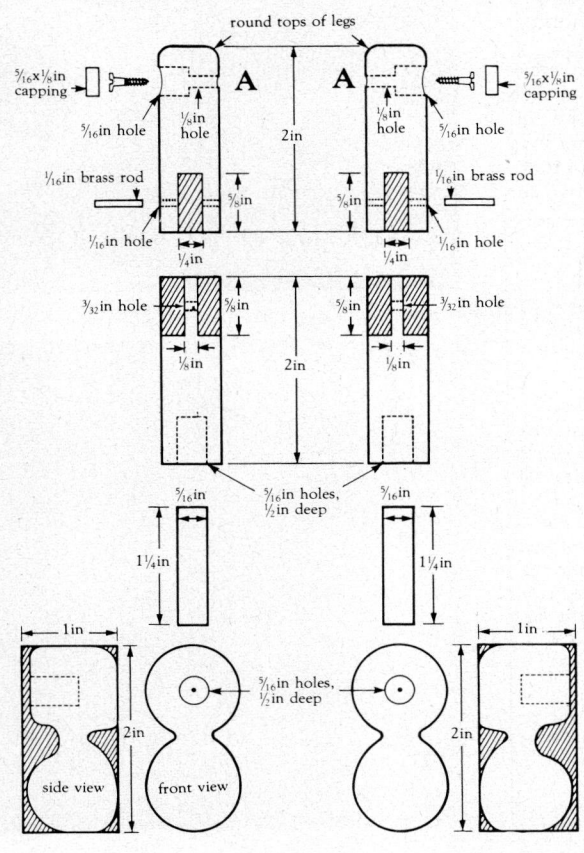

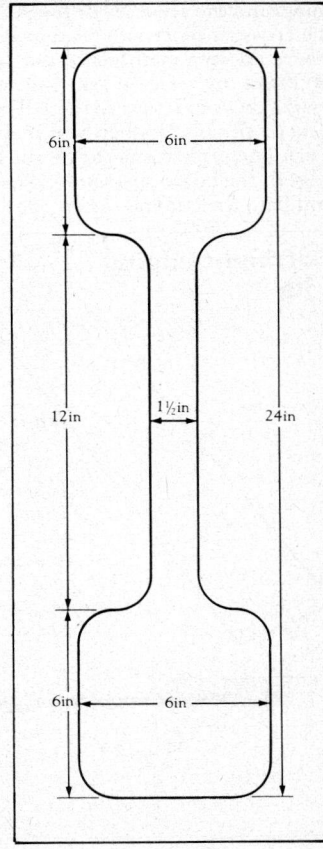

# MACHINING WOOD
## PART 2
### YOUR EXPERT GUIDE

**Continuing our definitive series: this month, a choice selection of the many cuts you can make with a table-saw**

A crosscut fence is the single most important addition to the table-saw. From a full-sized sliding table with a fence and stops, to a detachable bar on a detachable carriage, the function is the same — to make sure you get a perfect right-angle cut, every time.

### Crosscutting

When you are crosscutting (cutting across the grain of the wood) the rip-fence can be removed and the crosscut fence and sliding table will provide reference surfaces and support for the work. For safety, always move small pieces of wood away from the blade with a push-stick.

Assume that the end of a bought board is never perfectly square — it will need trimming, and the accuracy of the 90° setting of the crosscut fence will need to be checked. There are two methods of doing this:
● Make two face-marks and two edge-marks on your board so there'll be one each side of the blade when you make the cut. Turn one piece round to get the other long edge of the board against the crosscut fence and trim the cut end. Then put the two cut

ends together, face- and edge-marks in line. Any error in the setting will be doubled and will show up as the cut ends are placed side-by-side. You can then adjust the setting of the crosscut fence.
● A simpler but less accurate method is to make a cut, turn one piece over and place the cut ends together. Again, the error — if any — will be more obvious; but bear in mind that one side of the board has not been used as a 'datum' against the crosscut fence, and the edges may not be parallel anyway.

Repeat cutting of short pieces of the same length from a board is one crosscutting operation where the rip-fence is used in conjunction with the crosscut fence. The auxiliary fence should be fixed to the rip-fence and its position should be carefully set with two purposes in mind: to provide a cut-off stop so that all the pieces are the same length, and to create a space between the saw-blade and the rip-fence so that the cut pieces can move away from the blade and not jam or kick back. The forward end of the auxiliary fence should line up with the gullets or front of the saw-blade. An extra fence on the crosscut fence will help push the cut pieces well clear of blade and auxiliary rip-fence, as well as minimise

break-out or 'spelch'. Hold the board firmly against the crosscut fence and the auxiliary fence as you move it towards the blade. As you move the crosscut fence back after the cut is completed, move the wood slightly away from the blade so you don't back-cut the endgrain. This also prevents the blade catching and throwing the wood off the table.

### The mitre guide

To check the accuracy of your mitre guide, set the angle at 45° and make a cut; turn one piece over, put the cut ends together and use a try-square to test the right-angle. Any error in the setting will be doubled and will therefore show up readily. Adjust the mitre guide setting for error, and you can cut angled pieces with confidence.

Compound mitres are used in cabinet pediments, tapered boxes or any other construction where angled pieces meet with a neat join. These involve tilting the saw-blade (or, on some machines, the saw-table) as well as setting the mitre guide. On most decent table-saws, the maximum angle of tilt on the saw-blade is 45°. With safety and accuracy as the priorities, several points should be checked before cutting a compound mitre:

### Straight-edging jig

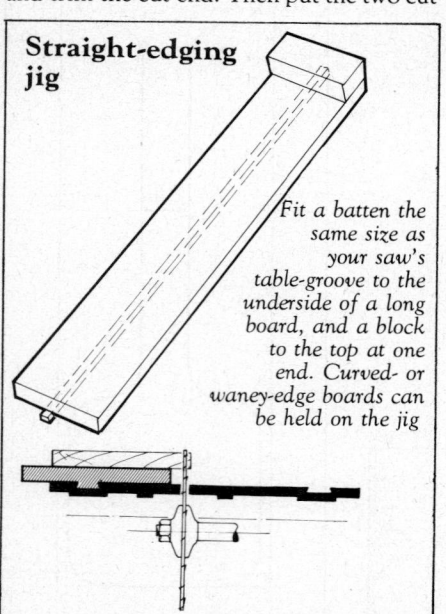

*Fit a batten the same size as your saw's table-groove to the underside of a long board, and a block to the top at one end. Curved- or waney-edge boards can be held on the jig*

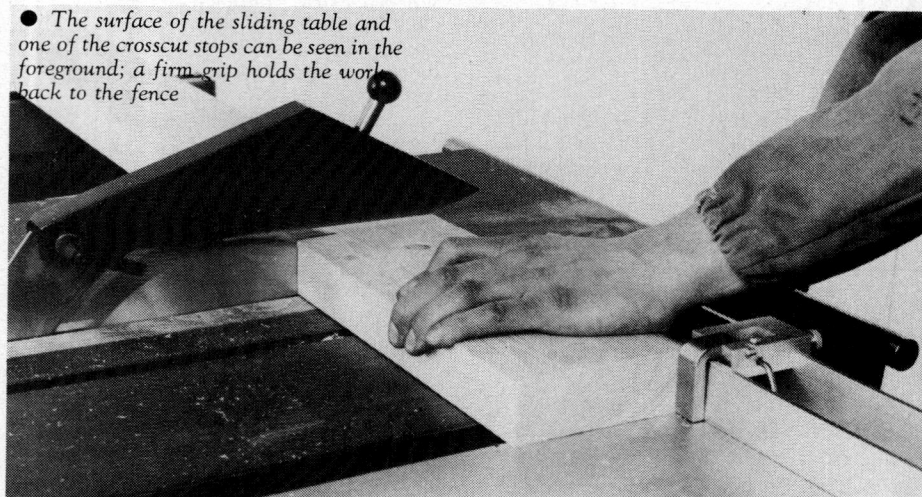

● *The surface of the sliding table and one of the crosscut stops can be seen in the foreground; a firm grip holds the work back to the fence*

● *Either the crosscut fence needs adjustment, or the two edges of the timber aren't parallel! A doubled error makes correction easier*

● Will the wood pass under the *lower* edge of the blade guard, since the guard tilts with the blade and one edge will be lower than the other?

● As the blade tilts, the saw teeth get closer to the table, so you may have to raise the blade to ensure that the saw teeth are set correctly for the thickness of the wood.

● Remember that with a tilted saw-blade the length of the cut on the top of the workpiece will be different from the length on the bottom, so allow extra length when preparing the board, and measure very carefully when setting the machine.

Our table of angles for correct setting of the saw-blade and mitre guide is for making tapered boxes; but obviously the '4-sided box' column will apply when you want the cut pieces to join at 90° in plan view.

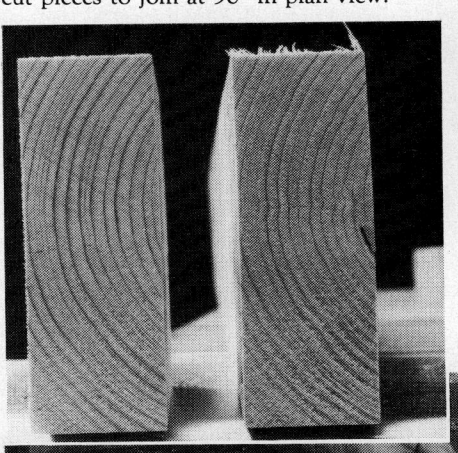

● **Above:** The rip-fence and auxiliary fence help to give a constant length for repeat cuts. The auxiliary fence should be set in line with the forward gullets. **Left:** Avoid spelch – the furry finish on the cut at **right** – by backing up the work with scraps for the blade to cut into. **Below left:** check the accuracy of your mitre guide by making one cut and seeing if the two pieces make a perfect right-angle

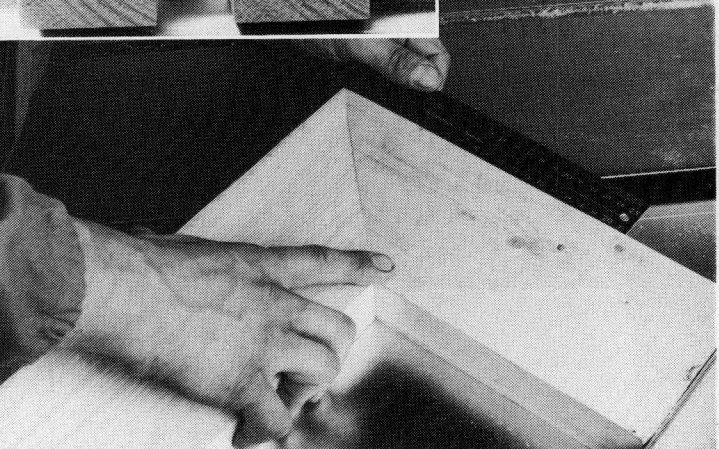

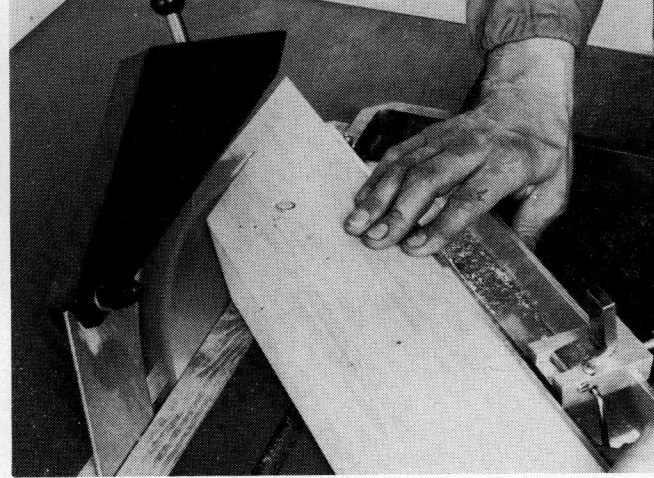

● **Above right:** The blade (or table) at one angle and the fence at another give compound mitres like the one **below**. It takes a long time to get it right by trial and error!

## Compound mitre chart

| Slope | 4-sided box | | 6-sided box | | 8-sided box | |
|---|---|---|---|---|---|---|
| | Table angle | Mitre guide | Table angle | Mitre guide | Table angle | Mitre guide |
| 5° | 44¾° | 85° | 29¾° | 87½° | 22¼° | 88° |
| 10° | 44¼° | 80¼° | 29½° | 84½° | 22° | 86° |
| 15° | 43¼° | 75½° | 29° | 81¾° | 21½° | 84° |
| 20° | 41¾° | 71¼° | 28¼° | 79° | 21° | 82° |
| 25° | 40° | 67° | 27¼° | 76½° | 20¼° | 80° |
| 30° | 37¾° | 63½° | 26° | 74° | 19½° | 78¼° |
| 35° | 35½° | 60¼° | 24½° | 71¾° | 18¼° | 76¾° |
| 40° | 32½° | 57¼° | 22¾° | 69¾° | 17° | 75° |
| 45° | 30° | 54¾° | 21° | 67¾° | 15¾° | 73¾° |
| 50° | 27° | 52½° | 19° | 66¼° | 14¼° | 72½° |
| 55° | 24° | 50¾° | 16¾° | 64¾° | 12½° | 71¼° |
| 60° | 21° | 49° | 14½° | 63½° | 11° | 70¼° |

**For example:** If you want to cut a box with the sides inclined 20°, set the blade or table at 41¾° and the mitre guide at 71¼°.

## Cutting tapers

Cutting tapers on, for instance, chair legs involves the preparation of a jig, either an adjustable taper jig (the hinged type can be bought) or a step jig. With the step jig, the width of the step should be the same as the maximum width of the cut-away section, and remember that for double-sided tapers you will need *two* steps on your jig.

To cut tapers, hold the workpiece against the upper step of the jig for the first cut and push the wood and jig through the saw together with the jig sliding along the rip-fence. Then turn the workpiece over and cut again with the newly cut taper against the lower step.

Cutting double-sided tapers with the adjustable jig involves doubling the angle between the hinged sides of the jig after the first taper has been cut.

## Cutting wedges

A simple jig is also needed for wedges, easily made from a piece of scrap wood with notches cut in the side; wedges must be cut from a wide piece of short-grained wood. The width of the piece is the length of the wedge: cut two or three notches in your jig for wedges of different length. The notches in the jig will present the grain of the work-piece to the blade at an angle, which will give you strong wedges with the grain running down their length. If you cut them with the grain running across, they will snap as soon as you tap them because the fibres will be so short. Adjust the rip-fence so the feather-end of the jig nearly touches the back, place the wood in the notch of the jig and hold both firmly as you slide the jig along the rip-fence to cut. After each cut, turn the wood over to make the next wedge. Stop before your blank gets too short and brings your fingers perilously close to the edge! A false table of 4 or 6mm ply, clamped over the blade which is then wound up through it while spinning, will stop thin wedges jamming between the blade and the mouth of the table insert.

## Cutting an odd-shaped pattern

The success and safety of this operation, like every wood-machining process, depend entirely on preparation. First, make your pattern from a piece of scrap wood so that it is *exactly* the size and shape that you want, and mount it with panel pins on top of the board to be cut. Remove the blade guard and riving-knife, and mount a wooden guide-fence on the rip-fence, or on to a high false fence attached to it. Set the guide-fence carefully so that it is just high enough to allow the board being cut to pass underneath, and line the left edge of the guide-fence, the workpiece passes underneath the guide-fence and the blade will cut exactly below the edge of the pattern. It is particularly important with this technique to move small offcuts away from the blade with a push-stick rather than fingers!

You can now cut along the sides of the pattern, using your left hand (if the piece is big enough) or a push-stick to press the

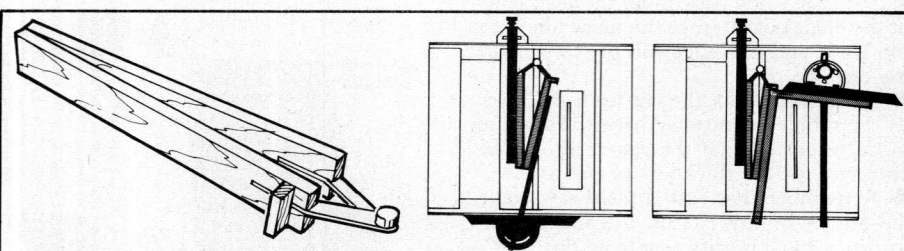

● *The adjustable taper jig, and two ways of setting the angle. First find the angle you're working to; then set it on the protractor of the mitre guide (**left**) which you then turn over and set against the back of the saw. The table acts as a datum surface. Alternatively (**right**) you can set the mitre guide protractor and square off that straight on to the jig*

● *A simple single-step taper jig, ready to roll. Any workpiece must be cut over-length, of course, because cutting from a wide blank like this will mean a feather-edge on the front of the taper*

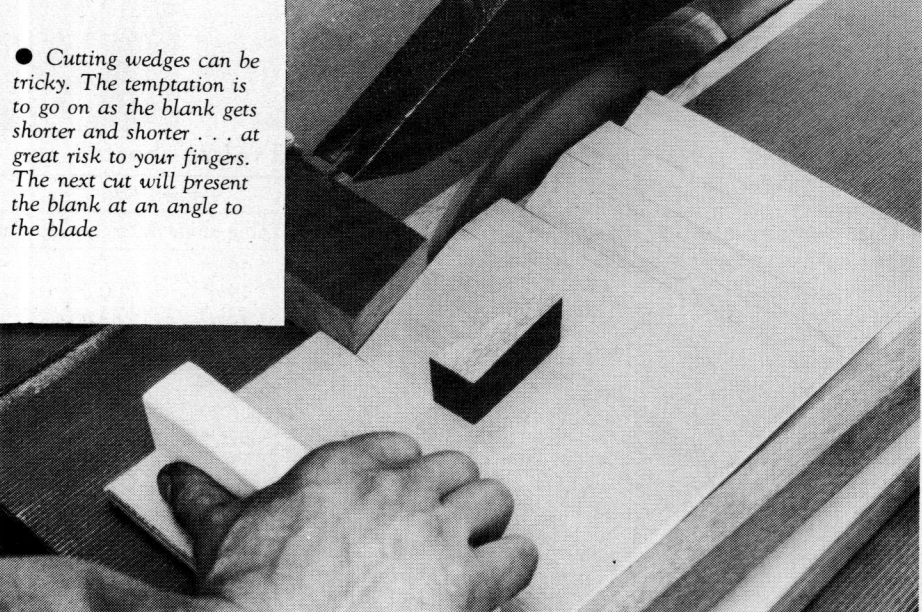

● *Cutting wedges can be tricky. The temptation is to go on as the blank gets shorter and shorter . . . at great risk to your fingers. The next cut will present the blank at an angle to the blade*

wood towards the guide fence; use a push-stick to feed the work toward the blade. As each edge of the pattern slides along the guide-fence, the workpiece passes underneath the guide-fence and the blade will cut exactly below the edge of the pattern. It is particularly important with this technique to move small offcuts away from the blade with a push-stick.

## Rebating and grooving

Cutting rebates (steps along the edge of a board) and grooves are operations which again call for the removal of the blade-guard and riving-knife, which is illegal in a professional shop. Safety and careful preparation must be prime considerations. Short-cuts will result in loss of accuracy, injury to fingers or offcuts jamming and kicking back, so always use *two* push-sticks for these operations.

A rebate is formed by making two cuts, one horizontal and one vertical, along the edge of the board. Since one of the cuts will be made with the board standing on a narrow edge, mount a high false fence on the rip-fence to act as a support. The high false fence should be made and mounted carefully so that it is perfectly square and vertical; if not, the work will be inaccurate. The best way of keeping legal and safe is to make a 'tunnel-guard' for this job — an upside-down L-shaped box which overhangs the blade and comes hard up to the board, held vertically as you cut. Otherwise clamp feather-boards — pieces of ply with long curved cuts that form springy anti-kickback teeth — to table and fence to keep the board in and down.

When making the second cut to form the rebate, keep the offcut piece on the *outside* of the blade to prevent it jamming against the fence and kicking back. And remind yourself not to stand directly behind the work!

Grooves can be cut in two ways; either in a series of passes over the blade, or in one pass over a blade tilted with wobble-washers. Two of these large wedge-shaped washers can be fitted to the blade spindle, causing the blade to move left and right as it rotates and thus make a wider-than-usual cut.

## Dropped-in work

Perhaps the most dangerous operation on the circular saw is dropped-in (or set-in) work, where a groove or slot begins or ends (or both) away from the edges of the board. It is for shallow grooves *only*, we emphasise. A featherboard, the special anti-kickback fence, should be bolted to the rip-fence. For cuts which start in the middle of the board and run off the end , you will need one stop on the end nearest you; for cuts that begin and end inside the edges of the board, two stops are needed, one at each end of the fence.

The safest way of doing this is to experiment with the rise-and-fall of the blade, and work out exactly how many turns will bring the blade up to the height you need.

● **Above:** *Cutting odd-shaped patterns needs careful setting of the blade directly below the guide-fence, which is in turn mounted to the rip-fence. Use two push-sticks if possible, or make sure the piece is big and your grip firm!*

The featherboard and stops should be positioned carefully. With the workpiece held firmly down on the table by push-stick, featherboard and hand, its back edge against the stop, start the saw and wind the blade up to the pre-determined height. Push it through to make the cut; if the groove is stopped both ends, the position of the far stop will be dictated by the length of cut. If the cut finishes before the edge of the board, push it to the far stop, turn the machine off while you hold it, wait till you are sure the blade has stopped, then wind the blade down and lift the workpiece away. You should use push-sticks wherever possible for dropped-in work.

## Raised and fielded panels

The technique of raising and fielding panels, though best done on a spindle-moulder, can be performed quite adequately on the circular saw. The main limitation is that the saw can only do straight cuts, while the spindle-moulder can produce a wide variety of interesting curved and moulded designs.

The shoulders of the panel are made first by cutting grooves round the edge of the panel section, using the stop on the crosscut fence to locate the short-side shoulders. Then the saw-blade should be tilted to the required angle to cut the cheeks of the panel. You need a high fence to support the workpiece while it rests on its narrow edges, and a spring system of holding the panel to the fence while you push it. The blades of most table-saws tilt in only one direction, so the high fence must be bolted to the right-hand side of the rip-fence. Then move the fence to the left of the saw-blade, and feed the panel smoothly through the angled cut, supported and secured by the tension guards. You can buy 'Shaw guards' which fit on most machines, or make your own adaptable featherboards.

● **Above:** *Rebating a high board; sprung guards keep the workpiece safely against the fence. Don't trap the small offcut between blade and fence*

● *The blank for the raised and fielded panel (above) has had grooves ripped and crosscut to the depth of the shoulder; the next step is below*

● *Set the rip fence to the left of the blade (right) so the angled teeth will cut just to the grooves. All guards removed for clarity*

## Tenoning

There are several ways of making one half of woodworking's favourite joint on the circular saw:

● Make the shoulders first by cutting grooves at the full depth of the tenon; then make the cheeks with a series of passes over the blade (at the same setting), working from the edge inwards towards the groove. This method is quick and fairly safe but when the workpiece is not completely square the series of passes leaves a rough finish and possibly a twisted tenon.

● Cut the shoulders first, as before, and then insert a tenoning jig (bought or made) in the table slot. Clamp the workpiece vertically to the jig so that both will slide smoothly towards the blade to cut the cheeks in one pass. This method is also safe since your fingers need push only the jig. There is a disadvantage with this method — tear-out ('spelch') as the blade emerges from the back of the workpiece. This can be prevented by inserting a small piece of scrap wood between the clamp and the workpiece on the side nearest you.

● With the workpiece held vertically in a tenoning jig, use wobble washers on the blade spindle to tilt the saw-blade and make a wider-than-usual cut along the edge of the workpiece. This technique has the disadvantage of leaving a slight curve at the top of the cut, which in this case is the shoulders of the tenon, but the tenon is cut in one operation.

● In the absence of a tenoning jig, the tenon cheeks can be cut by clamping the workpiece vertically in a sliding frame which you make and fit over the high false fence. With a bit of ingenuity you can design something that covers the blade too.

● *Below: The safest, if most laborious, way of tenoning on the circular saw is to cut the shoulders first and then pass the cheeks back and forth over the blade. Set an auxiliary fence to the centre of the workpiece's height – both sides are cut away*

## Panel cutting

Panel products such as hardboard and chipboard usually come in large sheets — and not necessarily with straight edges! Cutting large boards will mean using all the available table extensions for the machine in order to support the workpieces. The blade should be set so that one tooth's height shows above the panel.

Panel products often suffer from spelch problems. To avoid whiskered edges, get

the best saw-blade for the job (WW/Nov) and, if possible, use a false table to minimise the gap between blade, table and work. One rather laborious way of overcoming the problem is set the blade to half the thickness of the board, and cut through from both sides. Some machines have little scoring saws in front of the blade, which cut a preliminary line and ensure a clean edge.

## *Next month: The radial-arm saw*

● *Left: A proprietary tenoning jig holds the workpiece firmly. A home-made box- or tunnel-guard would be a good idea here.*

● *Below: Ripping a sheet of hardboard with a comparatively coarse blade. Laminated chipboard or thin plies will need many more teeth and finer pitch. The size of your sliding table will limit the size of board you can handle comfortably*

**T**his series was written by Judith Barker. Ken Taylor of the London College of Furniture checked it for completeness and accuracy. Aidan Walker planned it and demonstrated the techniques. Derek Wales took the pictures. But Luna Tools and Machinery made it possible. They provided vital financial support – and for photography and demonstration they lent their machines, their space, and the help and advice of staff member Joe Wickens. So we give our warmest thanks to Luna's MD Gerry Baker for his unhesitating and generous co-operation. Luna are at 20 Denbigh Hall, Bletchley, Milton Keynes, Bucks MK3 7QT, tel. Milton Keynes (0908) 70771.

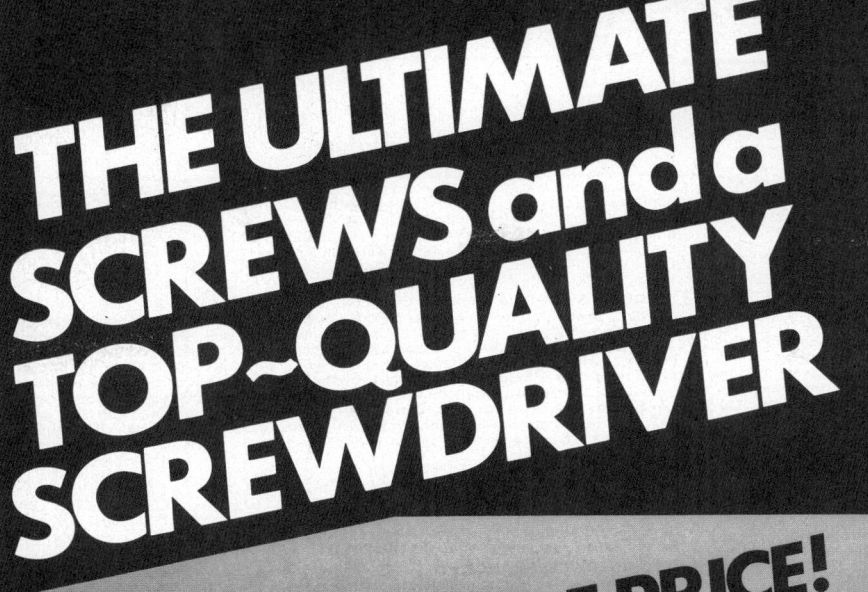

# THE WOODWORK STORE
# WITH A LITTLE BIT MORE

**PRIMUS PLANES**
These German Wooden Planes have a fine reputation for quality in manufacture and excellent results in use. Made of either Pearwood or Steamed Beech Bodies fitted with a harder sole of Lignum Vitae or Hornbeam by a Unique castellated Joint they will give years of use to the discerning craftsman. The Smoothing Plane is fitted with an adjustable mouth for the finest finishing cuts.

| Cat. No. | Type | U.K. Price | Aust & N.Z. | U.S. Price |
|---|---|---|---|---|
| 103803 | Smoothing (Pear/L.V.) | £64.95 | A$143.00 | $99.50 |
| 103802 | Jointer (Beech/Horn.) | £65.95 | A$145.00 | $101.00 |
| 103815 | Jointer (Beech/L.V.) | £75.95 | A$167.00 | $117.00 |

**CHIYOZURU SADAHIDE "EVENING CALM" PLANE**
Chiyozuru Sadahide is renowned throughout Japan for the quality of his plane blades and such is his mastery of the art that the Emperor of Japan has awarded him the title of "Living Treasure of Japan". Of all his blades his finest are enscribed with the legend "Evening Calm on Awaji Island" a place of great spiritual significance to the Japanese. We have obtained a limited number of these truly excellent blades which we asked the master to have fitted into Red Oak Bodies by a body maker of his choice. Each plane comes conditioned and ready for use in a Kiri Wood Box inscribed with the seals of this master planemaker.

| Cat. No. | Blade Size | U.K. Price | Aust & N.Z. | U.S. Price |
|---|---|---|---|---|
| 150400 | 70mm | £995.00 | A$1,780.00 | $1,250.00 |

**PRECISION SCRAPER PLANES**

Beautifully made scraper planes with a core of selected hardwood fitted with heavy brass side plates permanently bonded and riveted to the core. These fine instruments produce perfect smoothness and will never mar or score the surface. Ideal for small cabinet work or instrument making.

| Cat. No. | Size | U.K. Price | Aust. & N.Z. | U.S. Price |
|---|---|---|---|---|
| 103924 | 2½" long | £26.35 | A$56.00 | |
| 103925 | Square Iron | £5.95 | A$12.80 | US$49.50 |
| 103926 | 4" long | £34.50 | A$74.00 | |
| 103927 | Square Iron | £8.05 | A$17.50 | US$11.50 |

**LAMINATED PLANE IRONS (for Record & Stanley Planes)**
Most of the best quality planes sold before World War II were fitted with laminated plane irons. As all users of Japanese Chisels have discovered, this gives the tool the property of a good durable cutting edge that will outlast conventional blades. We have commissioned in Japan replacement blades 2" and 2⅜" to fit Record & Stanley Planes. Sold under our "Samurai" (R) Label we guarantee that these blades will outperform any conventional plane blade.

| Cat. No. | Size | U.K. Price | Aust. & N.Z. | U.S. Price |
|---|---|---|---|---|
| 150240 | 2" | £17.95 | A$34.50 | US$19.00 |
| 150241 | 2⅜" | £18.95 | A$36.50 | US$20.00 |

**ROGER PEERLESS PLANE**
We have taken delivery, of the first batch of our own brand No. 4 Smoothing planes. These are being manufactured in our own very exacting standards. *Sole:* Casting weathered for at least one year before machining to allow casting to settle. Machine ground to a tolerance of ± .0015" for perfect accuracy and clean shavings. Sides machine ground to ± 5 minutes of 90 of the sole for high quality shooting. *Blade Adjustment:* A solid brass

OPEN MON.-SAT. 9-5.30
DEPT. W, 47 WALSWORTH ROAD, HITCHIN, HERTS. SG4 9SU.
Telephone (0462) 34177

# HAVE YOU VISITED OUR TIMBER YARD YET?
## Wide range of native imported and exotic timbers.

adjustment knob is guaranteed to have less than ¼ turn of lost motion to give fast positive adjustment of the blade. *Handles:* Of larger section than those commonly available to fit the hand better and give a more positive grip. *Blade:* High quality laminated steel plane blade to give a long lasting clean cut. You will be truly amazed at the quality of edge obtainable and the length of time these blades will go between sharpening.

| Cat. No. | U.K. Price | Aust. & N.Z. | U.S. Price |
|---|---|---|---|
| 500300 | £75.95 | A$159.00 | US$99.50 |

**"IYOROI" SWORD LAMINATED CHISELS**
Of the high quality Japanese Chisel Makers, Mr Iyoroi is possibly the best known outside Japan. He has worked hard to copy the sword laminated chisels which are to be found in Japanese Museums, and has at last perfected the technique. The backing steel which takes the edge is manufactured from highest quality high carbon blue steel, reserved only for the finest tools. This is forged to multiple layers of folded high and low carbon steels to give a chisel body of immense strength and spectacular beauty. Each blade is personally hand engraved by Mr Iyoroi. Each Chisel comes in its own Kiri Wood Box decorated with Mr Iyoroi's Seal. The blades are finally fitted with a striking sandlewood handle. These chisels have been advertised in the United States at $124.00 each; at our price they are a bargain.

| Cat. No. | Size | U.K. Price | Aust & N.Z. | U.S. Price |
|---|---|---|---|---|
| 150251 | 6mm | £45.95 | A$99.00 | US$67.50 |
| 150253 | 12mm | £49.00 | A$105.00 | US$70.00 |
| 150255 | 18mm | £51.50 | A$110.00 | US$73.00 |
| 150257 | 24mm | £57.75 | A$120.00 | US$83.00 |

Save £10.00 All four of the above chisels £194.20
For our export customers A$410.00; US$275.00

**MACHINERY CLEARANCE**
Due to overstocking in our machinery department we have the following machines for sale. All prices are for collection from our shop and delivery will be charged extra at cost. All quoted prices include V.A.T. at 15%. (Offers apply U.K. Mainland only).

| MACHINE | LIST | CLEARANCE |
|---|---|---|
| Emcostar 2000 Universal Woodworker | 736.00 | 625.00 |
| Emcostar DB-6 Lathe plus Stand | 569.25 | 425.00 |
| Major CMB 600 lathe plus grinder kit | 619.28 | 450.00 |

**N.B.** Supplies are limited. Please telephone and confirm reservation of the machine you require.

**ROGER'S CATALOGUE**
These and many more of the wide range of woodworking handtools which we glean from all parts of the globe are listed in our 160 page TOOL & BOOK CATALOGUE NO. 3. Send for your copy today!
U.K. Customers send £1.50, Eire IR£3, Europe £3, Outside Europe (with the exception of North America) £6.50. Overseas Customers may send remittance in cash in local currency equivalent or in Sterling by Bankers Draft or Postal Order.
North American Customers may send US$5 by Cash or Cheque to Box 213, Sedona, Arizona, 86336. Please note all other correspondence should be sent to our United Kingdom address.

## CARRIAGE BY AIRMAIL IS INCLUDED
### IN ALL A$ OR US$ PRICES.
# ROGER'S
## roger's THE FRIENDLY STORE

---

---

915

# Working over

## Few craftspeople use the overhead router. Jim Phillips explains why it's worth a good look

Every woodworker today knows the portable electric router. But there's another kind, just as useful in its own way: the fixed-head or stationary type known as the overhead router.

It cuts in exactly the same way as the portable version, but its set-up includes one vital difference: you move the workpiece instead of the tool. The cutting head is fixed vertically, cutter downwards, in a stand which incorporates a table across which the work can be passed under the cutter. The expression 'fixed-head' is a little misleading, because a foot-pedal lowers the business end into the work for the cutting operation. This leaves both hands free to manipulate the workpiece itself.

Naturally, both portable and overhead routers have all sorts of pros and cons. It depends on the work you do — and on the cost! Industrial overhead models cost many thousands of pounds, and even the unique Trend machine for the small workshop (pictured here) costs over £1000. However, it comes into its own for repetitive jobs, where the right jigging and clamping techniques can make it cost-effective in certain situations.

### Straight machining

The overhead router can equal the spindle-moulder for many jobs which involve rebating or profiling straight edges. You simply attach to the table with clamps or bolts an adjustable side-fence, either factory- or home-made. The main limitation here is the table's relatively small size, which means that long workpieces are inclined to tip; this can be partly overcome by adding an extension table.

Moreover, the head itself can be canted by up to 45°, which offers an easy way of producing shapes not otherwise readily available.

### Copy-routing

Copy-routing involves reproducing the shape of a master template which you fix to the base of each workpiece. The template engages on a guide pin, projecting up from the centre of the table, which aligns exactly with the cutter above.

This arrangement means you can produce variations on the original pattern simply by varying the size of the cutter, its shape, its depth adjustment, the diameter of the pin, or any combination of these elements. An exact replica demands identical diameters for cutter and pin.

The maximum depth of plunge reached via the foot-pedal can be set by means of an adjustable stop which works on the same principle as the turret-stop on most modern portable routers. Once the head has

● *Jim Phillips demonstrates how the overhead router will cut circles and arcs with the aid of an adjustable trammel. Here, an Elu router is fitted*

● *If you fit a guide-fence to the table, the machine is ideal for straight moulding, grooving and rebating*

reached its full depth, you move a lever to lock it there; then, after machining, you release the lever and the head springs back up to its starting position.

In moving the workpiece across the table, remember to follow the general machining principle that the direction of feed should always oppose the rotation of the cutter.

### Using a carrier

Sometimes you can fix the workpiece directly to the template — e.g. with double-sided tape, or pins protruding upwards. Usually, however, a carrier is more practical and safer. This is a holder designed to secure the work and also allow a firm and comfortable hand grip that keeps fingers well away from the cutter. You fix the template to the carrier's underside, e.g. with tape or pins. Your third option is to enlarge and adapt the template itself so it functions as a carrier.

In all three cases, possible methods of fixing the workpiece involve tape (which will roll off easily with thumb pressure after use), pins, toggle clamps especially made for jigs, wedges (for long workpieces), and vacuum-clamping. In the USA electric spot-gluing is commonly used, but you can damage both workpiece and template or carrier when you have to remove any residue.

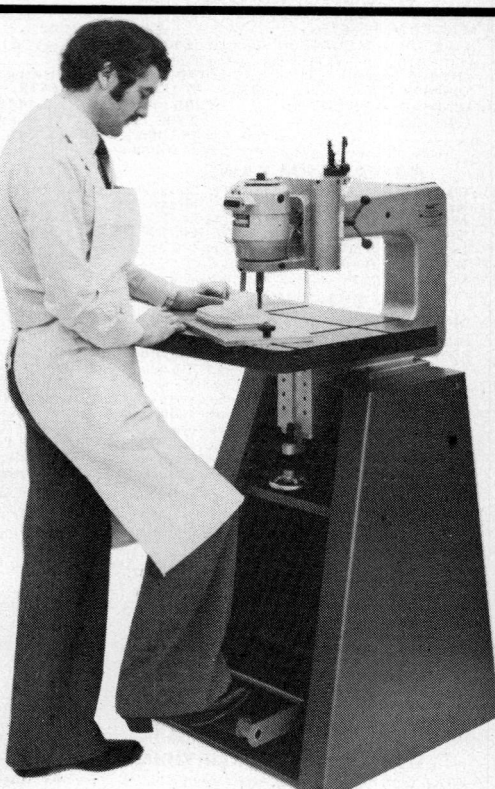

● *The complete machine. A pedal lowers the head to pre-set depths for cutting*

### Vacuum-chucking

Clamping by vacuum is a grossly under-estimated technique which deserves special mention. Its main advantage is that the working area can be kept completely free of obstructions; toggle-clamping can often restrict vision and movement — while easy fixing and removal is an area in which vacuum-clamping generally scores over pinning and screwing.

The idea is that you induce a vacuum in the carrier itself, so that the workpiece sticks to it — thereby converting the carrier to a 'vacuum-chuck'. For industrial applications the technique requires a special vacuum-pump, but the small user can work very happily with a vacuum-cleaner.

The holding power of such a device can be quite astonishing: a chuck 1ft square will hold a workpiece down so firmly that it can only be prised off with considerable difficulty. Naturally enough, a larger area means a firmer grip. The illustrations clearly show how you can make your own vacuum-chuck.

### Circular work

The overhead router is ideal for producing many types of circular shape — for plaques, breadboards, picture-frames and so on. The workpiece rotates on a pin protruding either directly into it (if it's thick enough) or into a false base fitted for the purpose. The pin stands at one end of a sliding trammel fixed to the carrier, so you can adjust and lock the distance between pin and cutter. ■

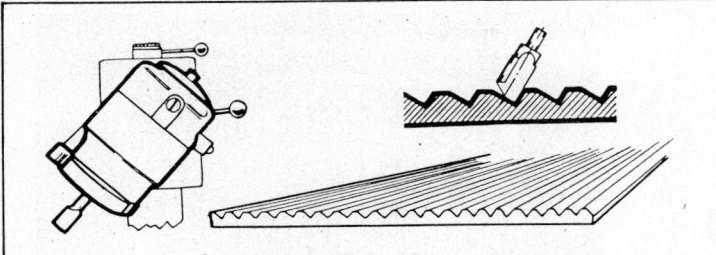

● *Tilting the head multiplies the machine's potential*

## Typical cutting techniques

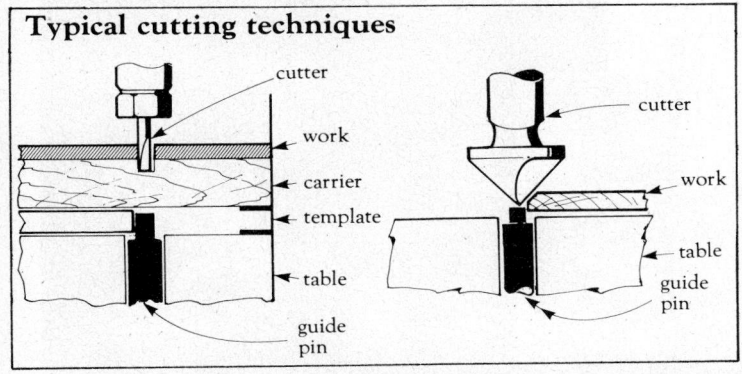

## Guide-pins and bushes available

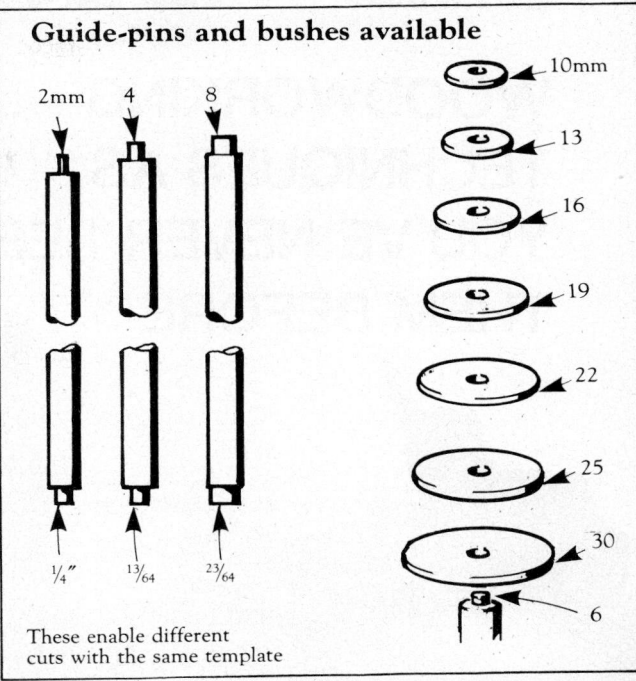

These enable different
cuts with the same template

● **Right:** *A vacuum-chuck is ideal for many copy-routing jobs on a fixed machine. It carries the work and keeps your hands away from the cutter. It's made (**far right**) in two layers, glued together: two ¼in holes through the upper layer align with the groove in the lower, which vents through a hose-connector and plastic tube to the pump. The edges are sealed with a self-adhesive strip of dense (closed-cell) neoprene, 1.5-2.5mm thick, which bears against the guide-pin.*

*For overhead routing, a template can be fixed to the jig's underside. One template may serve for a whole job, especially with varying pins and cutters*

● *A carrier (**above**) is the safe way to hold work for copy-routing. The diagram **above right** shows the carrier doubling as a vacuum-chuck; **below** are right and wrong vacuum-chuck designs*

**Vacuum problems**

✗ Not enough support    ✗ Not enough seal    ✓ Correct!

● *Left is a recessed tray (right) and the template used to make it; cutters below*

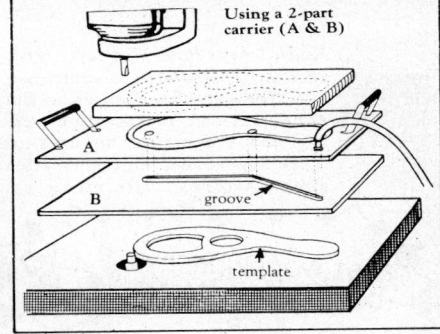

1 Square cutting
2 Inner radius
3 Outer profile
4 Base surfacing

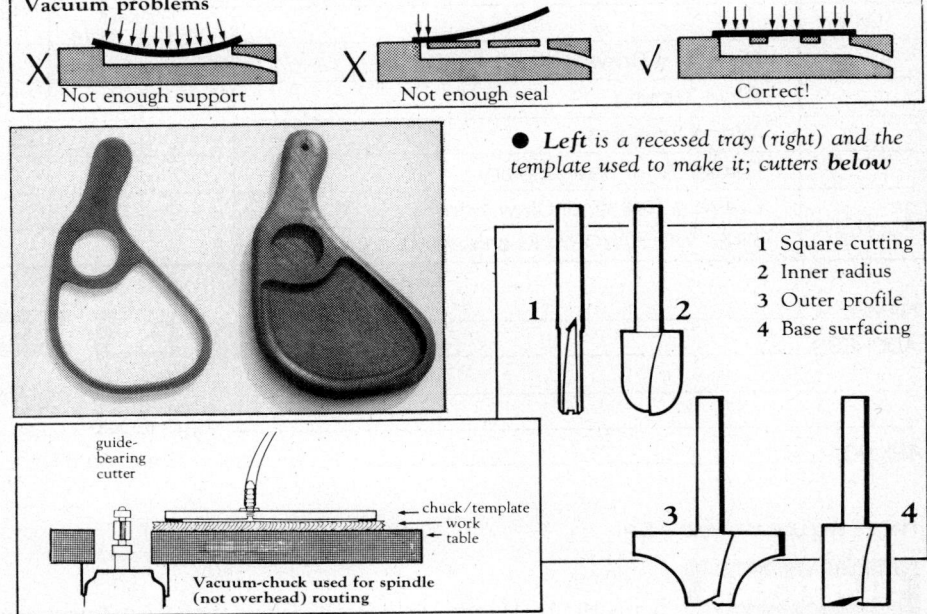

Vacuum-chuck used for spindle
(not overhead) routing

THE MACHINE shown here is marketed by Jim Phillips' company Trend — see p899. The stand (11/30 STA) costs £785+VAT and comes with a bracket to suit whichever portable router you possess; or it's available as the 11/30 1PH for £975+VAT, complete with a single-phase Elu router. The three-phase production model 11/30 3PH costs a hefty £1825+VAT but includes a high-frequency motor and converter.

# HOME VIDEO WORKSHOPS

## WOODWORKING TECHNIQUES AS YOU'VE NEVER SEEN THEM BEFORE

 **Radial-Arm-Saw Joinery with Curtis Erpelding.** The craftsman who's brought fine joinery to the radial-arm saw demonstrates the jigs and techniques he uses to make impeccable joints time after time. *Approx. 110 minutes.*

**BEST WOODWORKERS CHRISTMAS PRESENT EVER**

 **Wood Finishing with Frank Klauss.** Calling on 20 years of finishing experience, Klausz shows you how to stain, oil, varnish, lacquer and French polish your work, and how to refinish older pieces. *Approx. 110 minutes.*

 **Carve a Ball-and-Claw Foot with Phil Lowe.** A specialist in period woodworking, Lowe shows you everything you need to know to design and make that hallmark of 18th-century furniture, the cabriole leg with a ball-and-claw foot. *Approx. 115 minutes.*

 **Dovetail a Drawer with Frank Klauss.** Cabinetmaker Frank Klausz demonstrates and explains each step in making a clean, easy-to-use drawer, from preparing the stock to gluing-up and fitting the drawer. *Approx. 60 minutes.*

 **Bowl-Turning with Del Stubbs.** Learn bowl turning from one of today's leading woodturners. Stubbs demonstrates and explains all the basic equipment, tools and techniques you need to turn a chunk of wood into a handsome bowl. *Approx. 120 minutes.*

## VIDEO WORKSHOP ORDER FORM

| QTY | TITLE | FORMAT VHS | BETA | PURCHASE PRICE | 15 DAY RENTAL PRICE | AMOUNT |
|---|---|---|---|---|---|---|
| | Dovetail a Drawer | | | £42.50 | £12.50 plus £35.00 Deposit refundable on return of tape | |
| | Bowl Turning | | | £49.50 | | |
| | Wood Finishing | | | £49.50 | | |
| | Radial–Arm–Saw Joinery | | | £49.50 | | |
| | Carve a Ball–and–Claw Foot | | | £49.50 | | |
| | FINE WOODWORKING annual subscription usual £21 | | | | | FOC with 2 tapes |

**TOTAL**

NAME_____

ADDRESS_____

_____

_____

TEL.NO._____

Access  **VISA**

Method of payment:

CHEQUE ☐   ACCESS ☐   VISA ☐

Credit Card No._____

**INTRODUCTORY OFFER** BUY TWO TAPES AND GET ONE YEARS SUBSCRIPTION TO FINE WOODWORKING **FREE** SAVE £21

PRICES INCLUDE VAT AND P & P

 **sumaco** Suma House, Huddersfield Road, Elland HX5 9AA Telephone (0422) 79811

918

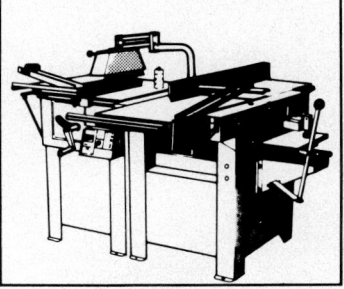
919

# Laminated jewels

## Peter Chatwin and Pamela Martin tell how they make and sell their extraordinary adornments

For many woodworkers, timber is much more than a means to an end. We, on the other hand, first used it just to add colour and texture to our jewellery.

But now that we've boiled it, dyed it, soaked finished pieces under the tap to make unfixed dye run, and in general subjected it to terrible treatment, we've ended up true converts — admirers of what it is, what it can do and what it can endure.

Our irreverent view came from our art-college training: Peter studied silversmithing at Birmingham, Pamela studied jewellery at Loughborough with the emphasis very much on metal. Since we formed our partnership, though, we've come to rely primarily on small-scale woodturning as a means of making 'production' jewellery to earn a living. This in turn has bought us time to experiment with one-off pieces which display an individual and specialised approach. That way, we feel we're not stagnating. Besides, the production work benefits from the ideas that spill over — and each helps to sell the other.

So far we've only worked with wood in laminated form. We use dyed veneer, cramped in two old-fashioned iron book presses which we've acquired from antiques fairs. For production jewellery, we then cut the resultant blocks of stripes at angles on the bandsaw and re-assemble them to create more intricate patterns. We measure and cut sections of these second blocks before turning them on a small engineer's lathe. Finally, after the silver 'findings' are in place, the work is finished with several coats of polyurethane varnish to protect it from discoloration. Perfume and sweat are especially harmful!

Our early work laid most stress on the obvious striped effects obtainable by straightforward lamination. But we moved on to assembling more complicated patterns in the way we've just described — until we were recently offered the chance of an exhibition at the Victoria & Albert Museum Craft Shop in London. For the occasion we decided to abandon the lathe altogether in favour of a new disc- and belt-sander. All the work for this show was made by assembling flat or bent pieces of laminated veneer into three-dimensional form, and then sanding them to produce shapes quite different from those obtainable on the lathe.

With each new piece of equipment we buy, more and more possibilities arise. For example, our latest pieces are far bigger than the ones we've been able to make before. In the meantime, hand work has allowed random surface decoration in contrast to the controlled patterns of earlier products.

Preparing the material is the most important and time-consuming part of making a new piece. First we mix and select colours, and dye the wood. Then we make up a few sample blocks to explore arrangements of colour and form which might prove interesting in three dimensions. At this stage we do preliminary drawings, but we make final decisions during construction. There are always surprises — fortunately good ones, on the whole; these can be incorporated in the next piece, which might well carry a surprise of its own.

Working together has proved mutually advantageous in terms not only of developing ideas, but also of making and marketing the work.

Over the past few years we have supplied our production jewellery to a number of small craft shops and galleries. We made contact early on via personal visits, and we followed up a generally favourable response. We remain in personal touch with our established outlets — and we meet new ones, mostly on our annual visit to the British Crafts Trade Fair in Harrogate. This provides enough orders for us to survive.

We find great advantage in having a range of about 40 items at under £16 each wholesale, since the price keeps it within the reach of many buyers. A simple catalogue — consisting merely of photocopied line-drawings — has been invaluable in providing prospective buyers with a reference.

Where our one-off work is concerned, inclusion on the Crafts Council slide index has counted for a lot, especially when it comes to making contacts overseas.

Our plans involve more of the same! Working in the way we do is often frantic but never dull. And, while we continue to appreciate and explore the qualities of sycamore veneer, our metalworking tools gather dust. Wood dust. ■

● Peter's and Pamela's work can be seen in the exhibition 'Carved and Coloured Wood' at the Oxford Gallery, 23 High St, Oxford, which runs from 18 November 1985 until 2 January 1986.

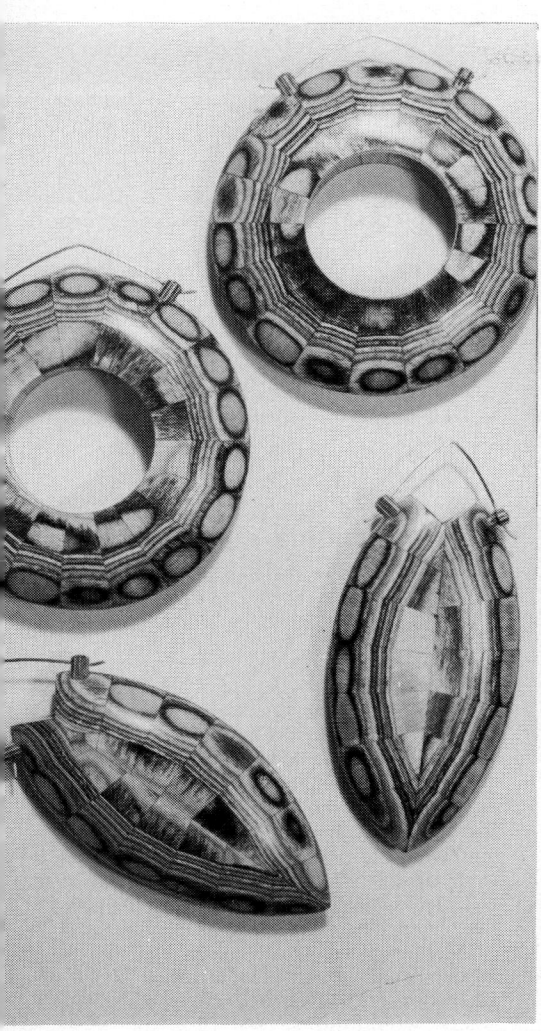

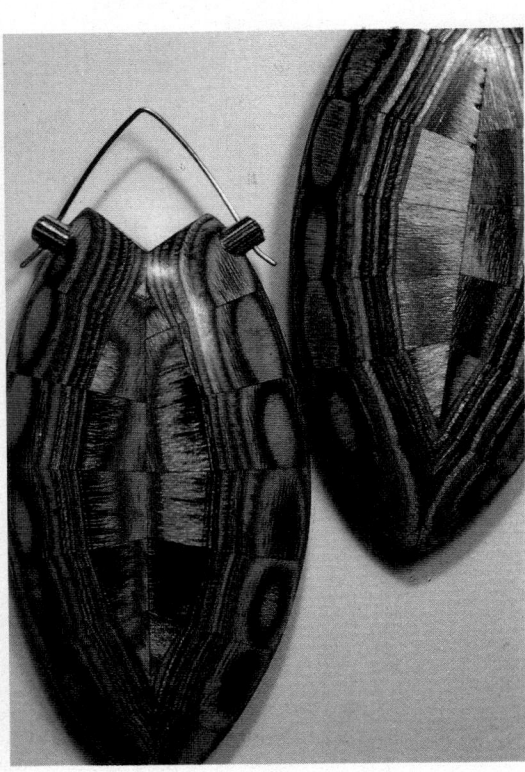

● *Like tropical fruit or painted gourds, Peter Chatwin's and Pamela Martin's earrings, bowls and boxes owe nothing to tradition. Yet they spring from ingenuity and hours of experiment in dyeing, laminating and shaping the sycamore veneers which are their staple material. Mounts are solid gold, solid silver, and gold leaf. They also make bangles. The pair of earrings at* **extreme left** *represents an earlier stage of their work*

**Many thanks to the Crafts Council for help with this feature**

# Tales out of steel

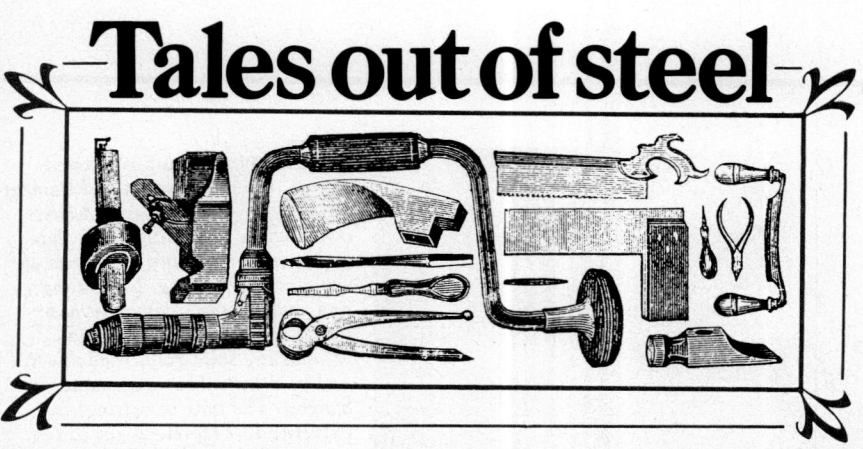

**Real history – but stranger and funnier than fiction: master toolmaker Ashley Iles recalls the amazing men and methods of Sheffield's vanished prime**

In the primitive solitude of my Lincolnshire farm, life drifts happily by. The factory runs like clockwork under a team of dedicated men and women who borrow my money and bring me all their troubles. My two dynamic sons allow me to help them run the business, and visitors hear that 'He's useful if anything goes wrong.'

It's all very different from when I started. In writing of the Sheffield tool trade in 1950, when I became a manufacturer, I have one problem: not whether you'll enjoy it, but whether you'll believe it.

Away from the city centre, whole sections of Sheffield were vast rabbit-warrens of outworkers and small manufacturers ('little mesters'). Imagine going through a dark archway into a tenement block of workshops, through a door and up one, two or even three flights of almost vertical wooden stairs. Your lungs would be assailed by the pungent mixture of a century of dust, rancid mutton-fat, powdered emery and the soot from pot-bellied stoves. Sometimes your journey would take you on to an outside platform, or a bridge in mid-air reminiscent of the rope bridges binding Tibetan ravines. At the end you would be greeted by a world-famous manufacturer in a leather apron.

There were hundreds of them, all in similar circumstances. The secret was specialisation; all the trades were divided into definite sections, and did not mix except in pubs. In addition to woodworking tools there were cutlery, pen- and pocket-knives, butcher's knives, scissors, painter's cutlery, surgical instruments, and so on and on. You name it, Sheffield made it.

Even further specialisation was evident. A man would spend his whole life buffing the handles of art-soldered table-knives with pumice-powder. I had one, Danny Spencer, near me in Solly St; he lived entirely on steak, Guinness and Woodbines. Many specialists were very highly esteemed. I was once in The Saddle, a pub in West St, with a friend — a 'pen and pocket' forger — when 'Little Billy' walked in. In a reverent tone my friend told me that Little Billy was a puttertogetherer: the man who assembled anything, such as scissors or pocket-knives. Puttertogetherers were highly skilled and respected for it. If you think I'm kidding, go to the Western Park Museum and see the pocket-knife with 150 blades.

In woodworking tools, methods of production fostered sharp demarcation lines. First came the outworkers — hardworking, hard-playing individualists, every one a complete master of his or her section of the trade. They seldom worked Mondays (the day was known as 'Saint Monday': why?); instead they could be found in pubs, usually Stones' houses, recovering from a hard weekend's drinking.

Next came the little mesters, who employed small teams of men and women and performed processes or produced finished tools. They too were fond of the ale, but because of a rigid class structure did not drink with the outworkers in the tap-room; they drank in the lounge or 'best side', where the beer was a penny a pint dearer.

Finally there were the manufacturers — making tools under their own names, or more often making tools for larger manufacturers and marking the larger manufacturers' names on them. Protocol dictated that a manufacturer was a Mester (Mr So-and-so), hence 'little mester'. Being a manufacturer was quite something in those days.

## 'You could be a full-blown manufacturer with nothing more than a name-stamp and a tiny office'

Although no one new ever came into the tool trade, to my surprise I was not only accepted but also given a great deal of help and advice. Footprint Tools in the next street opened all their doors to me, right to the top. A talk I had with Mr Baxter, their export manager, quickly got me exporting to the USA. At the other extreme, however, I remember one day when I was struggling to make a gas furnace with angle-iron, firebricks, a venturi and a vacuum-cleaner reversed to blow. Two gas-fitters walked in, and one said, 'We've come to connect thee up.'

'I'm not ready yet,' I replied. The older of the two sized me up, and the dilemma I was in, and suggested I go for a pint. There are times when I do as I'm told, and when I returned two hours later I found my furnace purring away like the Cheshire Cat. The vac, by the way, cost me £2 10s and blew for four years before needing new brushes.

But my technical training was not always appreciated. I tried to explain to a machinist that I wanted a die with a 60° groove to make V-tools. After the blank stare he spoke the immortal words: 'Trouble wi' me is, I'm all balls and no brains.'

## 'Steel is as good as it ever was . . . but temper does not arrive in rolling-mills'

The amazing thing was that you could be a full-blown manufacturer with nothing more than a name-stamp and a tiny office (perhaps a room in your house). Let's say you wanted a gross of 1in bevel-edged firmer chisels. First you would go to the mark-maker, who would make your name-stamp for you. The mark-makers were interesting chaps, but to the best of my knowledge there's only one left working on his own. Using a leg-vice, a magnifying-glass and hand steel-cutting chisels, he would cut the letters expertly by hand and then harden the stamp. He could also do you any trademark or other design or engraving. The mark would do several thousand tools before it needed re-cutting. Unfortunately mark-makers are very honest; the chances of getting a Norris mark are remote.

Equipped with your stamp, you would go to a forger or hammerman, who would make the blades for you. Hammermen were always on the ground floor of a building, and the hammer was their centre-piece. It was usually of 1cwt capacity — the weight of the 'tup' which gave the blow. The hammer is a forging machine otherwise known as a Goff hammer, a vertical version of the horizontal beam-hammer or iron duke. The tup reciprocates between two powerful springs, the downward stroke being adjustable for the force and speed of the blows. Up to 600 blows per minute are common. The tremendous advantage is that the steel is gently nursed into shape, retaining its molecular structure. A home-made coke- or gas-fired furnace provided the heat, and in two operations — with amazing speed and dexterity — the hammerman would make your blades: meanwhile not missing anything that passed the window, especially pretty girls.

Hammermen were versatile; they could, of course hand-forge equally well, and they would make their own dies. Just before 'snap time' (lunch) a black kettle would be seen boiling away on top of the furnace: in fact, a deceptive air of effortless grace pervaded the hammer shop in spite of the noise. They made it look easy, as all experts do.

Power hammers have been the curse of my life. If you are working on one, the noise is almost agreeable, but if you try to write or think within 100 yards it will drive you mad. (This was eventually a good reason for moving to Lincolnshire.) When I wanted to instal my first hammer, however, noise was not my problem. The Sheffield Corporation inspector refused permission on the grounds that the building wasn't safe. This was eyewash, as two 18inx12ft girders ran across my 13ft-square roof. I prepared for a lengthy siege — but I didn't have long to wait. A few weeks later my eldest son came back from an errand waving the evening paper. 'Dad, dad, dad! You know that man who stopped us having a hammer? He's dropped down dead in the street!'

That evening we left the cement setting around four rag-bolts in the floor, and went to bed convinced that our future was in divine hands.

Hand-forgers were all over the place and any one of them could have taught the time-and-motion men at Ford a thing or two. Albert Turner, a pen- and pocket-knife forger, had a tiny workshop in Hollis Croft, where he had four anvils in a square. Taking a piece of steel on tongs from a coke fire worked by hand bellows, he would work round four anvils and put down a finished pocket-knife-blade forging, complete with thumb nick, in one heat — and keep it up gross after gross. The contempt he had for 'engine-turned' blades was out of this world.

Across the yard from me in Solly St was Tommy Merrill, a famous forger of surgical instruments. He was peculiar in that he actually cultivated the hair on his ears. Rumours said he had a special watering-can for the job. Anyway, in making the gruesome instruments of his trade he had developed a droll sense of humour. He would explain in great detail how the human brain was inspected by first taking the top off with a brain-surgeon's saw, and he would put the saw in your hands at the same time. When he got to amputation knives and saws it was best to remember an urgent appointment. However, he also did all the forging of knives for royal wedding-cakes during his lifetime. His authentic workshop can be seen at the Abbeydale Museum, Sheffield.

**B**ack to those firmer chisels. With the blades in the boot of you car you would proceed to the hardener, who — in an exact replica of Dante's Inferno — would harden and temper the blades for you, spot on to one degree of Rockwell by colour, and at the same time overcome any problems of distortion in the steel. Hardeners were very versatile, and could change from wafer-thin palette-knives to 2in chisels without hesitation. Imagine the humility a metallurgy graduate would acquire in a place

like that. Tools were hardened in the soft Sheffield water or in whale oil, depending on the size and specification of the steel, and then tempered on a shelf over the coke fire.

At the hardener's your gross would sometimes be 143 because he would use one for a test-piece. He would harden it and smash it to bits on the anvil, and from examination of the fractures would learn all he wanted to know. Hardeners were fundamentalists. You sank or swam on your hardener; his reputation was always on the line, and he knew it — people didn't put up with things as they do today. A firm in Spital Hill sent out one batch of soft chisels. Three months later I went to the auction where they were sold up.

## 'Dust-extractors, factory inspectors? Never 'eard of 'em. "Ale washes the dust down"'

The worst thing you could do would be to walk into a hardener's with the hardening instructions from the steel manufacturers. You would learn that 'It dun't do to teck any notice o' them silly buggers'. But strange it is that the steel manufacturer gets the credit. People talk of good steel; steel is as good as it ever was, if not better, but temper does not arrive in rolling-mills. Hardening is a vast and complicated subject too involved to go into here, and after over 30 years of professional hardening I still approach the 'bosh' (quenching-tank) as a film director approaches a temperamental actress.

Next, with some trepidation and perhaps fortified by a pint of Stones yourself, you would go to the grinder's. Here you were in a world of organised chaos quite distinct from that of any of the other trades. Entering the grinding shop, you would say, 'Bevel-edge firmers.' Without looking at you or stopping work, he would shout above the din, 'Purremdarntheer — si thi on Friday.' And that was that. Grinders were to be found in single or multiple shops. I remember the Union Wheel, a building on the bank of the river Don over 100 yards long and 15ft wide. Branching off a full-length corridor were entrances to dozens of separate grinding shops no more than 15ft wide each, with what the grinder ground chalked up on the door.

The grinding shop was a masterpiece of maintenance-free engineering. Behind the grinder as he worked was a 6ft-diameter wooden wheel built up in segments, and rotating all the time from the main source of the power (in this case an electric motor; before that it had been a gas engine, and before that a water-wheel). A 2in-wide leather belt hung loose. It was connected by a flick of the wrist to a small pulley on the grindstone shaft, and off the wheel would go at an alarming speed. (The large drive pulley also drove the buffing-wheels for finishing after wet-grinding.) A peripheral speed of 5000ft/min. was the minimum.

The *Machinery Handbook* of the day gave the safe speeds for grinding-wheels, and then covered itself by saying that Sheffield grinders worked at twice the speeds.

The whole thing was called 'the wheel'. Below it was a water trough about 6x2ft, let into the floor. Bolted on either side of the trough were the 'games'. Into the games, held by wooden wedges, went the cast-iron bolsters or bearings for the 9cwt grinding-wheel and axle. The bolster was 4in square and about 14in high; in the top was an open 90° V into which the axle dropped and ran. This arrangement provided all the danger and excitement any young man could wish for, as I found out when I made one myself. The main thing was to keep the wooden wedge wet — and a big blob of mutton-fat had to go on top of the bolster to keep the bearing cool. The bearing end seated itself into the V and never needed any attention; and even then bolsters were only 25s a pair. However, if the bolster came loose, the wheel and axle would go through anything in their path, including brick walls. The kinetic energy was tremendous, and the grinding shop was not exactly a place for people of nervous disposition.

The grinder, of course, did everything by hand. He sat on a horsing with the wheel running between his legs. Protruding from the horsing and almost touching the wheel was the 'robbin', a bar of steel the width of the stone, and much use was made of it. The arse-board — a gadget on which he sat to get extra pressure — had a hook at the front, and was held behind him by a rope from the ceiling. To do the bevels of bevel-edge chisels he would put the blade across the wheel in front of the robbin, clip on the arse-board and, working from left to right, take off a perfect bevel, using the weight of his body. At 4s 6d a dozen ground and glazed, he could make a good living.

Dust-extractors, factory inspectors?

## 'No rubbish was made in the tool trade. It all came from Germany and Japan'

Never 'eard of 'em. 'Ale washes the dust down', I was told. With all the vices of Hades these men lived to ripe old ages and were outstanding characters in their own right.

Finally there was the cutler, the man who would finish the tools up to warehousing. He worked on a cutler's frame — a heavy wooden stand like a lathe bed on which were mounted pairs of puppets, between which ran glazing and buffing wheels of an infinite variety driven by a whirligig running along the floor. For our purpose he would grind the eight-sided bolsters of the chisels and fit the handles.

**O**n Friday you would go round your outworkers and 'reckon'. You would also be liable for 4% ''oliday money' in the

924

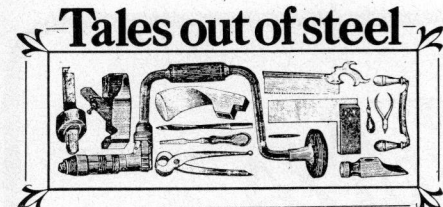
last week of July. All the prices were piece-work and fixed by the Trade Federation. So, without doing anything at all except drive, you could be a manufacturer. No wonder we hear of famous manufacturers disappearing without trace.

Don't get the idea that all manufacturers were like this, though. I seldom made use of outworkers myself; in fact, I did out-work myself at times when my wife's weekly visit to Lipton's was in jeopardy. Hundreds of small manufacturers made tools all the way through, with their own plant, workshops and men. There were many whose tools were really superb and deserved the acclaim enjoyed. I remember the firm of Josiah Cooper making Jennings-pattern twist-bits that made all the others, including those of Russell Jennings himself, look like corkscrews. A Sheffield tool dealer named G. P. Preston cornered the market and called them 'Preston's Exact Size': got any? Old man Preston couldn't knock a nail in straight, but he knew where to buy. Selling to him was a nightmare. He had a notice in the shop: WE SHOOT EVERY SECOND SALESMAN AND THE FIRST HAS JUST LEFT. International selling has its hazards, but the Yankee isn't born who could hold a candle to him.

Then there was Joseph Marples (no relation), on the top floor of the building I was in, making squares, mitre-squares, bevels, mortise-, marking-, and cutting-gauges, etc. He would come into my workshop and talk tools for hours. He was a true gentleman, and had alternatives for all the usual swear-words; his conver-sation was an engaging flow of ballys and flippin's. His set-up for making marking-gauges was a sight to see. About 40 marking-gauge heads were fixed on a steel bar with a screw at each end, and everything was done to them in that position — even the varnishing. His son still carries on the business in John St, Sheffield.

I could go on for ever about 'little men', but I'll close with Albert Seedhouse. He and his son ran a business in Rockingham St under the name of Seedland Bros. He told me that the original Seedland Bros had had, as outworkers, one of the great names in the tool business. He had no speciality; if it was made of steel and cut wood, he made it. One day he would be sweating the bit of high-speed steel on to the ends of plane-irons; the next he would be forging socket chisels (and, if you want an interesting problem in a blacksmith's shop, try thinking out how to forge the cone that the handle fits in). His workshop had the misfortune to stand in the path of a new road that Sheffield Cor-poration had in mind. One day he was there, the next day he was gone; it gave me another very good reason to move to Lincolnshire.

It is singular that no rubbish was made in the tool trade. It all came from Germany and Japan. Every Sheffield tool was a first-class professional item made to last a lifetime. A glance at the top-flight auction catalogue of David Stanley or Tyrone Roberts reveals the market to be very soph-isticated indeed, and it is quite common for single tools to fetch well into four figures. In the history of tools, Britain's role assumes massive proportions. Outstanding for sheer beauty and craftsmanship are the cast and dovetailed planes with rosewood infills, the brass-framed braces, the brass-stemmed mortise-gauges, etc. — together with an incredible range of hand-forged edge-tools for the woodworking trades.

## 'LAST OUT OF SHEFFIELD, KNOCK OUT THE LIGHTS'

In 1950 the trade as I have described it was in full swing; but the second Indus-trial Revolution was under way. All things come to an end, and nothing can stop the march of technology once it has started. Very soon I became aware of tremendous changes. Following the technical advances of the war years, machines were being developed to take the place of skilled men. The drop-stamp, previously used almost exclusively for cutlery, was not only used in the tool business but in a short time automated by Pattinson, the forging-machine people of Sheffield. Morgan Fairest, also of Sheffield, developed the hydraulic double-action chisel-grinding machine. These two new methods alone very quickly threw thousands of skilled men out of work. Some were absorbed by larger firms — others took what work they could get.

The firms that mechanised survived; those which did not, or could not raise the capital, went to the wall. As today, the auctioneers were very busy. I was not involved, because fortunately my task was to maintain the old traditions in my own products. But the demand for tools actually increased, particularly with the coming of do-it-yourself; and Sheffield held its own against world competition. That is, until recent years. The competition from the Far East, particularly Taiwan, was grossly under-estimated, and it is having a disas-trous effect on the Sheffield tool trade. The latest graffiti say LAST OUT OF SHEFFIELD, KNOCK OUT THE LIGHTS.

Signs of recovery are in the wind, and we must not overlook the antics of the phoenix. Odd corners of old Sheffield still exist meanwhile, and the whole scene is preserved in the Kelham Island Museum. But, by and large, it's all gone — and the expertise of 1000 years has gone with it. For better or for worse, the Golden Age of Tools has come to an end. ∎

**Ashley Iles' story will feature in Woodworker each month.**

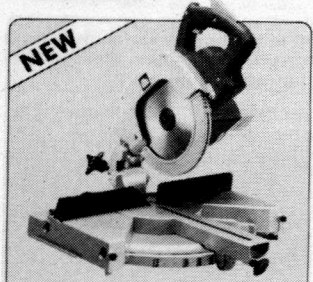

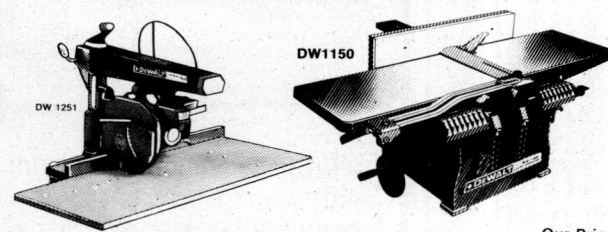
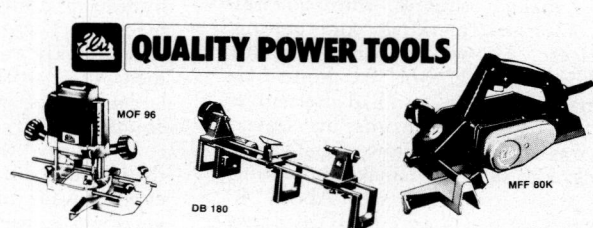

926

927

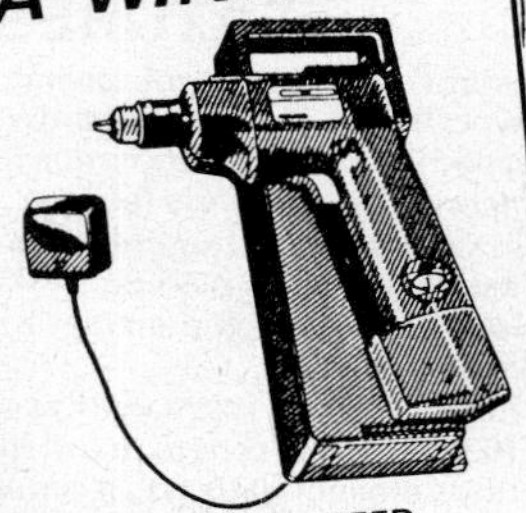

# Softly softly

## John Golder tells how to turn beautiful showpieces without inviting bankruptcy

When I demonstrate, I'm often asked, 'Can you turn softwood?' and 'Is it OK to practise on softwood?' Of course it is, and you can get great pleasure from such timbers. There is also, I may add, not so much dust and dirt. And, if you are unfortunate enough to make a mistake which means scrapping a piece, you have only lost a few pennies rather than the pounds which might disappear with a ruined piece of exotic hardwood.

Softwood is especially suitable for goblets because — despite their ostensible purpose — they are often kept on the shelf as ornaments.

To turn a goblet in European redwood, first choose a fairly close-grained piece. Normally unsorted (U/S) or fifths grade will provide what you need. Notice the fairly close rings in the endgrain (fig. 1): a fair sign that the piece will stand up to being turned thin. The size you want is 3x3x10in.

I always turn goblets using a ring-chuck of the Craft Supplies type, and I find that a tailstock is not necessary even for a goblet with a 10½in stem ³⁄₁₆in in diameter. For those of you who work with a screw-type chuck, I suggest that (as screws tend to pull out of endgrain) you drill a ½in-diameter hole through the blank about ½in from the end before turning it to a cylinder. Now push-fit a ½in dowel into the hole and turn your blank to a cylinder between centres, making the end nearest the dowel slightly concave. When you screw this end on to your screw-chuck, see that the screw enters the dowel and you should get a good tight fit. The screw is unlikely to come out.

If you own one of the various ring-chucks on the market, all you need to do (as you no doubt know) is to turn a cylinder with a flange on to suit your chuck ring; that should give you a rock-steady fixing.

I presume you've mounted your cylinder blank on to the headstock shaft's right-hand side.

**Fig.1**

**Fig.2**

**Fig.3**

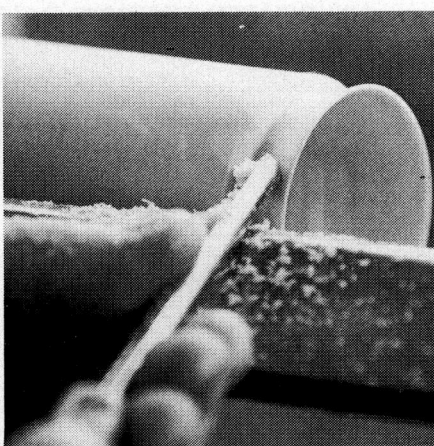

**Fig.4**

**Fig.5**

● John's goblets are a test for any turner's delicacy of touch. It's not as difficult as it looks!

**1** Set your rest at centre height or a little below, and true your blank with a ³⁄₄in roughing-gauge just to ensure it runs nicely.

**2** Set your rest across the end of your cylinder as in fig. 1, about ³⁄₁₆in below centre, and line up the nose of a small spindle-gouge (¼in) with the centre of the rotating blank. By gently turning the gouge clockwise you should be able to drill a hole to the depth of the goblet's bowl — say about 1³⁄₄in: the choice is yours, but anything up to 2in should be fine.

**3** Start removing the waste material in the bowl using the same ¼in gouge (fig. 2). With the tool on its side and your thumb supporting it, you should be able to cut neatly and cleanly right to the base of the bowl.

Fig. 3 shows the finished bowl, which has been gently sanded with 380 and 320 grit paper. The rim has been slightly rolled over.

**4** Fig. 4 shows the outer edge of the cup turned. Fig. 5 shows the operation completed — still using the same ¼in gouge.

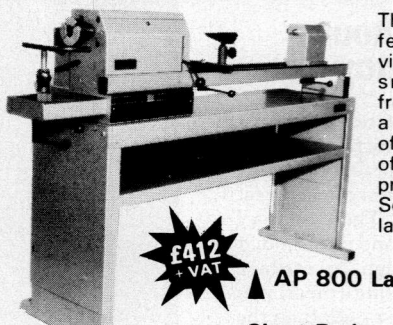

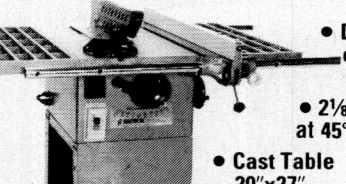
930

# Softly softly

The two pencil lines mark the bottom of the goblet and show where to begin removing wood from the outer core of the cup body.

**5** Figs 6 and 7 clearly show the method of working. Fig. 8 shows the method of checking; do this constantly — cut and check, cut and check — and you'll soon get the feel of the wall thickness. Another method is to shine a light directly into the bowl; you'll see it begin to penetrate at about ³/₃₂in wall thickness. It's normally around this time that Sod's Law creeps in. Shall I get another shaving off, or will the piece just shear? If it's your first one, my advice is: 'Don't. Just be satisfied, and try going thinner on the next one.'

**6** Fig. 9 shows the cup complete and sanded with 320 grit in preparation for that long, thin stem. Don't worry, you're doing just fine. Fig. 10 shows some of the bulk removed — working from the left towards the base using very fine cuts. For this photo the rest was lowered purely for clarity.

**7** Fig. 11 shows the cutting action of that small gouge, and fig. 12 shows the final cut being taken along that stem. Finger and thumb are supporting the now thinned-down section, and you're going great. If you've been unlucky at all, you've only lost a few pennyworth of wood; just start again and you'll get it right.

Now gently sandpaper that stem with a piece of 280 or 320 grit. Don't wrap the paper round the stem — just support the cup with one hand, and sand with the other.

**8** Finally, the base. If you've been making those cuts from left to right correctly, you'll already have had a lot of practice, and finishing the base should be no problem.

And so to parting off. A ⅛in parting tool is ideal; get the handle well down, as in fig. 13, and cut in about ½in. Then back out and widen the cut on the waste side. Now very slightly move the handle to the left and cut the base through to the centre, supporting the stem with your other hand as in fig. 14.

If you've managed up to this stage you should have the smile of success on your face. Now get the next piece in the lathe and don't hang about.

You'll need a speed of about 700-850rpm to reduce your square blank to a cylinder, and 1200-1500 (depending on your machine) to do all the work on your goblet bowl and stem. ∎

● John Golder demonstrates regularly at Matthews Bros, Kettlebrook Rd, Kettlebrook, Tamworth, Staffs, tel. Tamworth 56188.

**Fig.6**

**Fig.9**

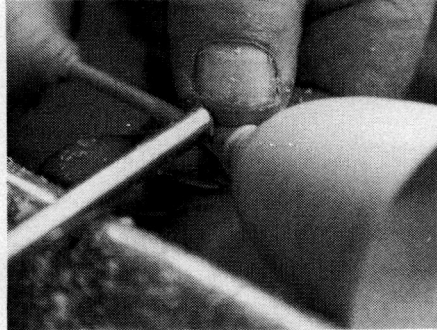

**Fig.12**

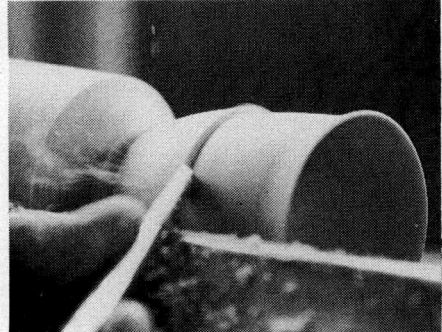

**Fig.7**

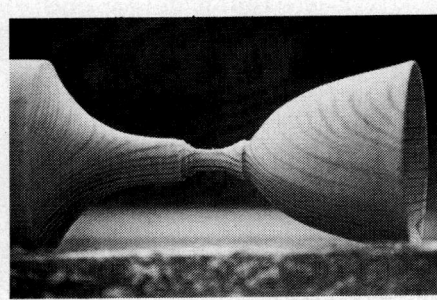

**Fig.10**

**Fig.13**

**Fig.8**

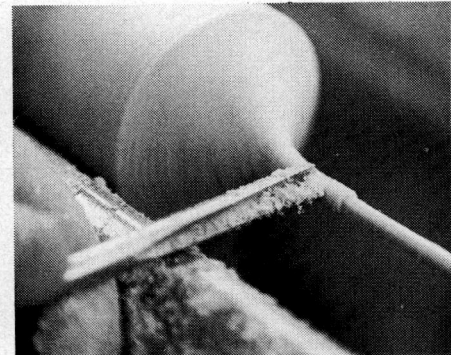

**Fig.11**

**Fig.14**

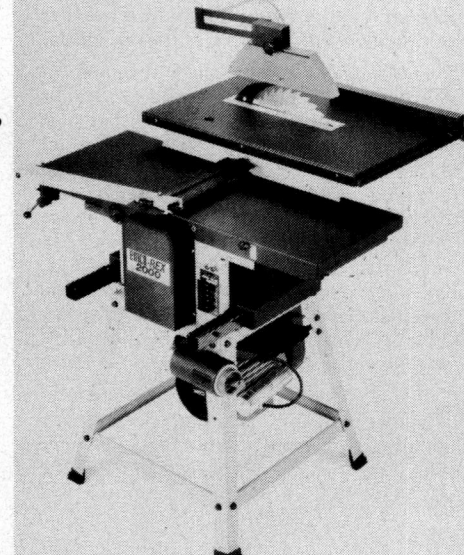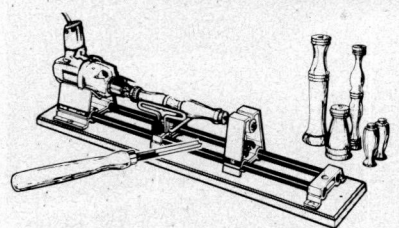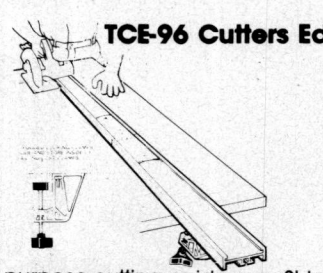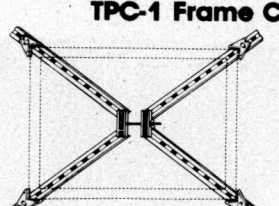
932

# PATTERNCRAFT

**Pattern-making is the unknown skill. Few woodworkers have ever encountered it. Yet it's super-accurate and very demanding. Here's what's involved . . .**

**Friedbert Meinert explains the idea and visits two pattern-shops**

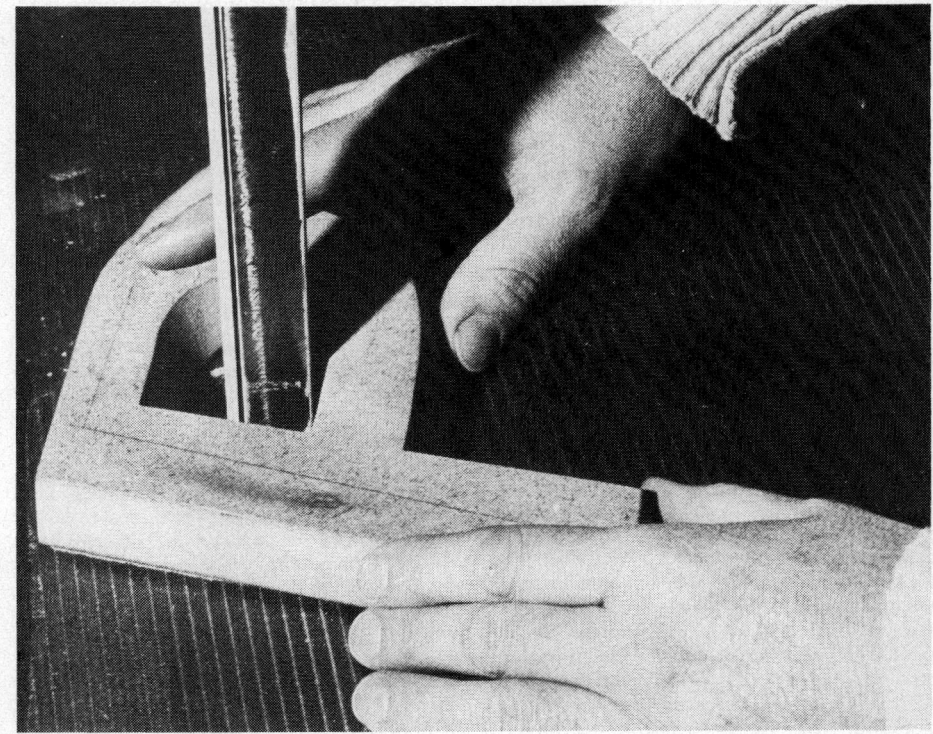

● *P for patternmaking? A specialised profile sander gets in the sharp corners and guarantees accuracy in section*

So what does the patternmaker actually do? Patternmaking is almost unknown to the average woodworker, and rarely included in the list of woodworking trades. But it has firm roots in the various woodworking traditions as well as engineering, and is probably less well known in the south of England because of the absence of heavy industry. In the industrial north it was an integral part of foundry and engineering work; but industry has changed, and patternmaking has had to respond.

The need for a pattern usually arises when something is to be cast. A wooden pattern is the original mock-up for a metal object which cannot be made easily or economically in any other way. There are also metallurgical reasons for using a pattern, which itself becomes obsolete once the casting is completed.

The time of the Industrial Revolution was probably the heyday of patternmaking and heavy manufacturing industries. Most machinery parts were ferrous castings, often unbelievably heavy — anyone who possesses a woodworking machine from the earlier part of this century will know what I mean! Any part of a machine designed as a casting was first made as a wooden pattern, from the wheels and push-rod of a steam engine to the tiny components of a sewing-machine. During the Victorian era particularly, decorative castings such as railings, fireplaces and so on were popular and fashionable too, which meant a great variety of patterns and lots of work.

The patternmaker adjusts the quality of the work (choice of material, method of construction) according to how many castings are needed. For a one-off or maybe just a dozen castings, jelutong or pine would be fine; for larger numbers, hardwoods such as maple are needed, and occasionally walnut for top quality. Cheap red beech is used for battening on core-boxes (explained later). Maple is especially preferred for its density and regular figure. I was trained in Germany and practices vary, but the general idea is the same.

The main source for the production of a pattern is an orthographically projected drawing with at least three views. There

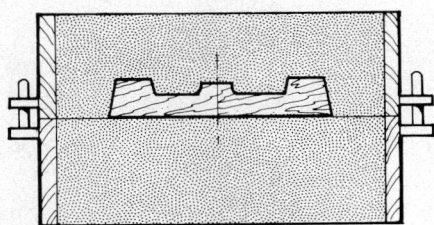

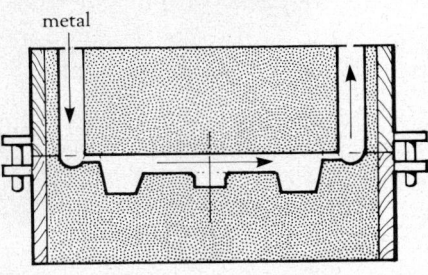

● *A simple pattern goes into the case (**top**), which is then turned over before the metal is poured (**above**)*

might be more, depending on the pattern's complexity. The drawing of say, a gearbox would have many views and detailed sections. This is in fact the engineering drawing, which is passed to the machinist once the casting has been produced. Some drawings take considerable practice and skill to read — an isometric drawing is rarely made.

Many traditional woodworking techniques are used in making a pattern. An apprentice had to practise mortise-and-tenons, dovetails, and the use of all the hand tools, just like any carpenter or joiner, while the techniques of the woodturner are needed for gluing circular blocks in segments. To these conventional practices, the patternmaker adds many more; at times the work is quite sculptural, and demands skilful handling of the chisel and a variety of rasps and rifflers. The often unorthodox application of techniques with hand and machine tools characterises the diversity of this trade, and may yet be a factor in its continued survival.

To understand the function of the pattern, it's useful to have a brief look at the casting process. Once the pattern is made and mounted on a base-plate, the foundry takes over. A metal frame (case) is set over the pattern and filled with special casting sand. It is then turned upside-down; a top case is added and also filled with sand; holes are cut in this one for pouring the metal. The cases can be separated to remove the pattern and then joined again for casting. When the metal has cooled, the sand can be knocked off and the process repeated. The pattern has to be withdrawn without disturbing the sand, which means that there should be no undercut on the pattern, but this sort of problem can be overcome with core-boxes and special forming techniques.

Patterns for casting are by no means the only type. The motor industry uses them for prototype panels, copy-milling, and such jobs as vacuum-forming moulds for dashboard coverings, these and many others are up-to-date requirements from the pattern-shop. Although wood and woodworking techniques are used it is probably true to say that the patternmaker regards the craft as engineering in wood, where a thorough knowledge of timber and its

# PATTERNCRAFT

correct use is necessary but precision is of the utmost importance.

A pattern-shop looks fairly similar to any joinery workshop equipped with a band-saw, circular saw and a planer. Additional gear for the production of precision patterns is a lathe like an engineering lathe, an overhead milling machine, and a disc-sander (a most versatile piece of machinery!). Machines manufactured specifically for the patternmaker now include quite sophisticated equipment such as oscillating-cylinder and vertical flat band-sanders, copy-millers, and a variety of adaptors and accessories for the machines.

It is still possible, however, to continue the craft with less sophisticated equipment and still make quality patterns. Graham Smith's workshop in Newbury, Berks, is a good example. Patternmaking is a sideline to Graham, but he himself is a fifth-generation patternmaker. His great-grandfather built the steering-wheel for the *Cutty Sark*, in the days when men in this trade were called pattern-model and steering-wheel makers. The Smiths' skill, passed from father to son, has been in the tradition of patterns for ferrous and non-ferrous casting. Because of declining demand for heavy casting, Graham switched to other ways of making a living.

The workshop, on the edge of Newbury, is on an old farm with masses of workshop and storage space. Graham takes on the occasional furniture commission, but his main activity is now the restoration of old commercial vehicles. Lorries from the 1920s are revived from heaps of scrap to their original splendour. If a casting is missing or beyond repair, a new one has to be drawn up and built. The gearbox, for instance, on one of the vehicles is too far gone, covered in mud and eaten away by corrosion. One of Graham's next jobs will be to make a new pattern for that particular part.

Any other vehicle work is also undertaken in the workshops, from joinery for the coachwork to mechanical restoration and assembly. Graham employs a mechanic and one other woodworker. His methods are extremely traditional; he uses no specialist patternmaking machinery except some hand tools he has made himself and an impressive selection of wooden planes and carving gouges handed down from his father and grandfather. The patterns, mainly for one-off castings, are usually fairly simple, and jelutong is the timber he uses most.

His versatility means that Graham has few worries. The restoration of one vehicle usually means work for a whole year or more, and he still receives orders for patterns from engineering firms and foundries. He doesn't shy away from any kind of work.

What does he think about the future of patternmaking? As far as he's concerned it's in decline, heavy engineering having vanished or moved north. He prefers to concentrate on the restoration work, and

hopes his son will continue the business.

Alan Brooks practises a more up-to-date, specialised version of the craft in a workshop on a small industrial estate in north London. Alma Patterns employs one other patternmaker and produces a variety of small patterns for precision-engineering casting, from complicated housing work to bases for industrial steam-irons. Brazilian mahogany is the timber Alan likes, for its lightness and ease of working. Patternmaking's most drastic changes have been in materials, and it has been important for those who want to stay in business to keep up with changing technology. The arrival of plastics and plastic products has meant new and better ways of making patterns as well as new market and type of customer.

Liquid epoxy resin is now frequently used to cast the final patterns from the wooden original. It is longer-lasting, and multiples can easily be produced to cater for mass-production. Resin patterns very often replace the grade-one high-quality hardwood variety.

Vacuum-forming is an addition to, and sometimes a replacement for, injection-moulding techniques in the plastics

industry, and moulds can now be made largely by the patternmaker rather than the toolmaker. Precision is not quite so crucial, and the work can be handled on pattern-making machinery. Is patternmaking, then, still a woodworking craft? Alan definitely thinks so. 'Your first pattern is always in wood, and that will hardly change.' It does worry him, however, that too many people are leaving the craft and not enough new blood is coming in. One of his apprentices has given up; he thinks the training system is partly to blame.

Apprentices now go on a 46-week training course at technical college, sponsored by a pattern-shop or engineering firm. It's a long time to be away from the working environment, and may allow them to lose interest, but at least apprentices go to college now!

During my journey through the craft of patternmaking I have come across some resignation, but mainly I've found positive thinking, a general agreement that pattern-makers will remain in the woodworkers' fraternity, and enough reasons to look hopeful for the future.

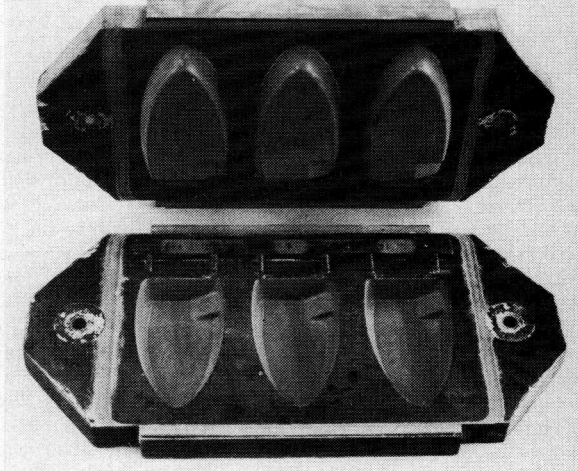

● **Above:** *A pattern and finished castings for a brass furniture fitting. The core gives the inside shape, the core-print locates it.*
**Right:** *A multiple pattern for industrial steam-iron bases – from Alma Patterns*

**Photographs: Roger Barnard**

934

## Bill Page remembers a wartime apprenticeship and expounds the finer points

I began work the very week that war was declared, in September 1939. I had shown an interest in wood since I was a small lad at my father's workbench, so he managed to get me into a pattern-shop as a learner apprentice.

Patterns? I had never heard the like, and — except for the woodwork bit — had no knowledge of what was entailed. My father knew precious little more, except that it was a good trade to be in, and 'What with the war on . . .'.

A pattern is usually a shape made in wood, though it can be in other materials, that has a casting made from it in a foundry. The pattern is put into a moulding box or boxes; the impression it leaves in special sand, with which the box is filled, is 'poured' with molten metal, and there's your casting. The industrial patterns in the engineering firm I worked in were a far cry from my concept of woodwork!

There were six men in the shop plus the gaffer, a man of about 60, and another lad besides myself. The machinery then consisted of a 10in overhand planer, a pillar drill, a bandsaw, a circular saw for ripping, a big sander with two discs (which we lads had to change once a week), and an old bone-shaker of a lathe. Later on we got a planer-thicknesser and a Wadkin lathe with its own motor, but the original machines were belt-driven from one long shaft. The belts were often breaking at the pins, or slipping, which meant one of us lads had to take a handful of resin powder and throw it on to the belt as it clunked round, a highly risky operation.

The timber we used was yellow pine and Honduras mahogany. The pine was lovely stuff, silky and straight-grained with a faint yellow sheen; the mahogany came in random widths up to about 24in — waney-edged, but nice to work with sharp tools. It was the lads' job to help unload the lorry when timber arrived and put it to store in stick under cover. Some of the mahogany was so heavy it had to be got inside on rollers! The pine came in various thicknesses up to 3in and was 10 or 12in wide.

The first two years were spent mixing varnish, rubbing patterns down after varnishing, helping to hold timber on machining jobs, learning how to plane face and side dead flat and square, studying blueprints till our heads ached, and sweeping up the shop on a Saturday morning. One other job was keeping the glue-pot going, and didn't a lad catch it if it was allowed to boil dry! I don't believe there's any nicer-smelling glue than Scotch.

We worked a 50-hour week, and my first week's wage was 11s 8d — out of which I kept five bob, half for pocket money and the other half for tools. The thrill of going into town on the old tramcar to stand gazing into tool-shop windows, preparing to buy some small tool, was worth the long hours. At 18 I made my toolbox with stuff that had lain under the bench for quite a year. The usual patternmaker's box had a drop-front with four drawers, then a space for planes, then a removable piece under which were kept the bulky things. We had no power tools then. The carcase of the box was dovetailed and the back and door panels were in mortised frames; it was all in pine except for the mahogany drawer-fronts, which had finger-holes for easy opening. The toolbox contained, beside the many edge tools, a variety of marking-out tools (some bought, some made) and the patternmaker's rules.

These are 'contraction rules', and several are needed to allow for contraction of the various metals. Cast iron contracts at $\frac{1}{100}$in per in or $\frac{1}{10}$in per ft, so all the measurements would be proportionally larger. You would need different rules for aluminium, brass, and so on.

Several of the men at our shop had open-top toolboxes, which showed the changes that were taking place even then. The inner carcase was stepped down twice to allow for two layers of lift-out trays which held all the cutting edges and small tools. Underneath lay wooden planes — jacks and smoothers; one fellow had a lovely shooter for edges. Then there were breast drills, braces, cramps, all rattling about below, and the saws buttoned inside the lid. We lads were saving hard, but not for so many of the bulky tools. My only wooden plane was a jack, though I made several radius planes later on. We often made small turning tools from old files, turned our own handles and made ferrules from brass tubing.

Accuracy in patternmaking is essential, for a casting would be useless if it did not come up to size. Where a casting was to be machined to fine limits a machine allowance was added to the pattern, usually $\frac{1}{8}$in but this could vary. Any pattern in our shop except the simplest had to be set up on the iron table, a machined surface about

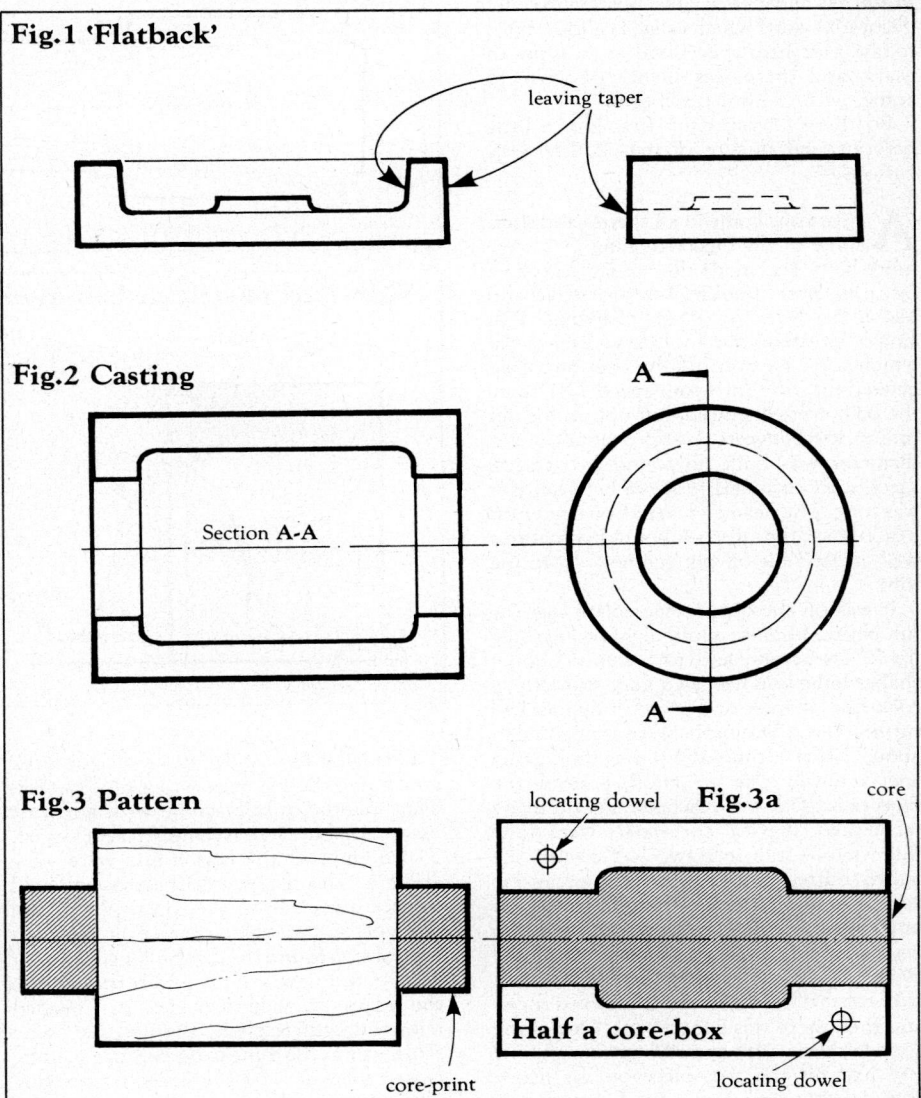

Fig.1 'Flatback'

leaving taper

Fig.2 Casting

Section A-A

Fig.3 Pattern

core-print

Fig.3a

locating dowel

core

Half a core-box

locating dowel

8x5ft. This was to ensure all verticals were square with the base-line and centres could be marked off both vertically and horizontally. When the casting went into the factory for drilling and boring or whatever, it was set up in exactly the same way.

All vertical faces were made with a minimum taper, to ensure the pattern left the mould cleanly (fig. 1). Any overhanging pieces either had to be made loose or were formed with a core-box; a 'core-print' was used to position the core, the internal shape — and a core-box made for that, producing a sand core of the extra (locating) part of the shape. This was then fitted into the mould, filling up the space made by the core-print.

Ally castings were sometimes a problem. The metal tends to sink on top surfaces after casting and this must be considered when deciding which way a job will be moulded. 'Risers' eliminate the spongy top metal — lumps that come above the casting and are sawn off in the factory before machining, leaving nice close-grained metal.

Besides our shops, there were of course many others doing domestic work such as fire-backs and grates, lamp-posts, and other decorative stuff which (alas) is almost gone today. Our firm specialised in all types of gears, and there was plenty of work to come, with the war just begun.

So there I was in my first job, a little nervous and unsure of myself, but very curious.

As patterns come in all shapes and sizes, some of the bigger turning jobs were quite hefty and made the old lathe groan a bit. Our later Wadkin was rock-solid and had a big lever for speed-changing. You simply pressed your foot down on a pedal which took tension off the belt, and then clicked the lever into your speed. Of course the belts were enclosed, but not on the old one. A job between centres over about 6in diameter was built up round an octagon piece each end, and more in between if it was long. The head end was always fixed on a face-plate, the tailstock point driven into a well-greased bit of oak screwed on to the job.

It was on the outside face-plate that the fun began, because a job might be anything up to 3ft across, and with the old bone-shaker lathe you needed a very firm grip, a rock-like stance and very long-handled turning tools. Deep jobs were segmented to about 3in at a time, the pieces then glued and screwed one to another until the required depth was reached. A good many segmented rings for core-boxes were done this way — split into two half-circles, the halves butted and then turned, because a core-box had to come apart. I remember once when an urgent job was segmented up and left to harden, but not for long enough. When old Wally pushed the wooden arm over to start her up she slowly gained speed and then there was a loud bang. One of the segments was a bit proud of its neighbour and had hit the crosspiece on the heavy tripod rest, which had crept forward with

the vibration. Segments shot in all directions, and one stayed forever after lodged up in the girders above our heads.

As we had no foundry of our own, patterns were collected by van, but sometimes a job might be urgent and the van not available. Since no one had a car, one of us lads would take it on the tram as soon as ever the varnish was dry. This gave us a chance to see what happened in the foundry, and skilled work it could be too. I sped off one time when I realised the job had a core-box and I hadn't got it. I was given the expected rollicking, but still delivered the goods, if a trifle late. As I later found, it was much easier if the foundry and pattern-shop were together; problems could be resolved quickly, and a tricky job sorted out even before the timber had been cut. Every pattern came back to us after use and was stored until it was needed again. We had literally thousands, which we lads had to number and index.

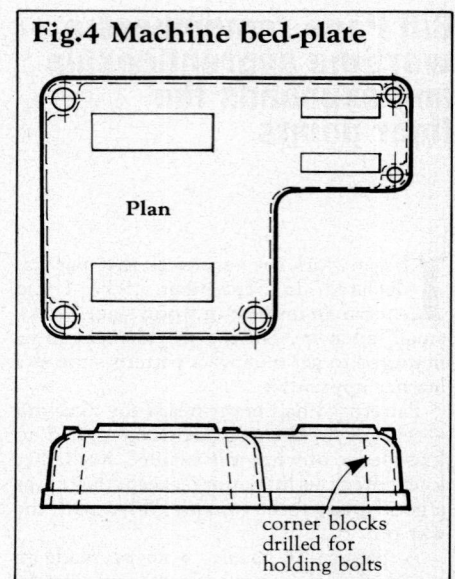

**Fig.4 Machine bed-plate**

Plan

corner blocks drilled for holding bolts

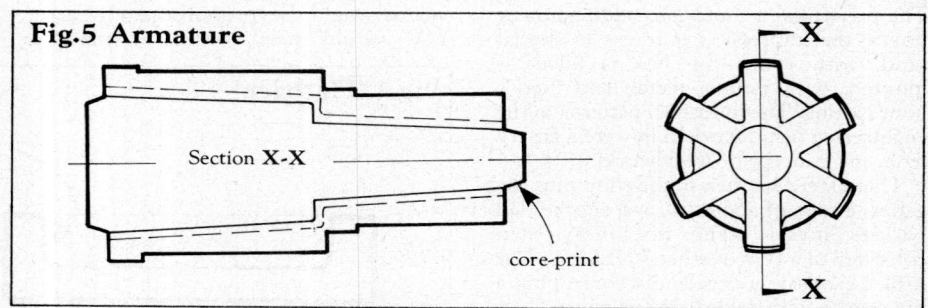

**Fig.5 Armature**

Section X-X

core-print

X

X

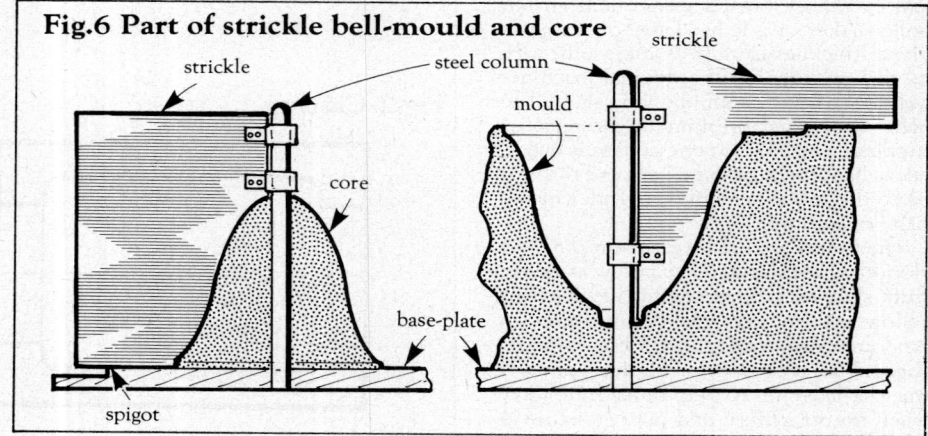

**Fig.6 Part of strickle bell-mould and core**

strickle

steel column

strickle

mould

core

base-plate

spigot

Changing the sander discs once a week and oiling the machine was a mucky task. This was the only machine with any dust extraction but it still seemed to get clogged, so we emptied the bags while were were about it. The discs were 3ft across and held by iron rims bolted over on to the plates, and you had to tighten each bolt a little in turn or you found the disc bulging. Segment jobs were quickly built up on the sander; the edges of wide segments still needed trimming with a plane, though, and some said this was the thing to do because sanding closed the grain and prevented proper glue penetration.

Our bandsaw blades were about ¾in wide and 10tpi, and we changed them fairly frequently. If one broke in use, a length of wood would be jammed against the top solid wheel to stop it, and the saw changed pronto. Both we lads used to try to be the first one into the gaffer's office to fetch a fresh saw and change it. Folding a brazed saw into three ready to go away was something an apprentice learned by trial and error; no one ever showed him how, and it was quite funny to see it sometimes — though the knack, once learned, was never forgotten. If you didn't do it right it could spring all over the place.

Another saw, out of bounds to us, was the Carp's, a big circular rip. He had a little corner of the same shop, and one of his regular jobs was to make packing-cases for the factory, mostly in elm. Some of it was so wet it sprayed out as it was sawn and used to bind like mad, but Jack the Carp was its master. He used to say he'd sooner knock a case together in wet elm than dry, because at least it lay flat while you were 'attending to it'. On occasion Carp might have a rush job on, several cases to make in an afternoon. Our gaffer might then volunteer us lads to help, and knocking nails in at the double was great fun — a welcome change for an hour or two.

'Characters' abounded in those days, as no doubt they do today, but I believe craftsmen then had a much tighter rein on their apprentices, who often inherited their set ways. One chap I remember would sort out all the quarter-sawn timber he could find that would safely fit under his bench, and curse the poor fellow that used to tidy the shavings away for disturbing any of it. Another man, if he had a big segment-turning job, would cut every segment first and lay them on edge to twist and shrink while he got on with something else. This was all very fine, but it meant his spending hours on the bandsaw when you might be wanting to use it.

Another place was a bit cold in winter (as a good many were), and old Harry had to make a rubbed joint with large boards. We always 'dogged' the ends of boards when jointing, so he would lay dogs and a hammer each end of a piece — holding it in the vice, with the other piece alongside flat on the bench. Then, making sure no one would open the door and cause a draught, he laid shavings along the top edge of the timber in the vice, got the glue-pot and set the shavings alight. After hurriedly brushing the remains away he brushed on the glue, and he and I rubbed the joint and dogged it. The joint was lovely and warm and the glue ran fine!

With my apprenticeship over, I left the firm where I'd started and got a job with one of the big electrical groups. In this shop there were two floors with about 40 men all told, and a big foundry attached. There were no apprentices; every man was his own man, and all the jobs we lads used to do were done here by unskilled hands. Other places followed, for in those days work was plentiful and a man was able to gain experience in many sides of the trade just by moving about.

The little jobbing foundries, for instance, took on any sort of work they could handle, which meant a patternmaker would spend some of his time in the foundry with the gaffer, working out the cheapest and best way of doing a job. The big shops, on the other hand, had more machinery. The first big router I ever saw had a big table and a head that would go any way you wanted it. It was a great day in the little shop when that long-awaited saw, or whatever, arrived to ease the work (and cut the price on a job).

## Fig.7 Straight-sided pattern: simplified view

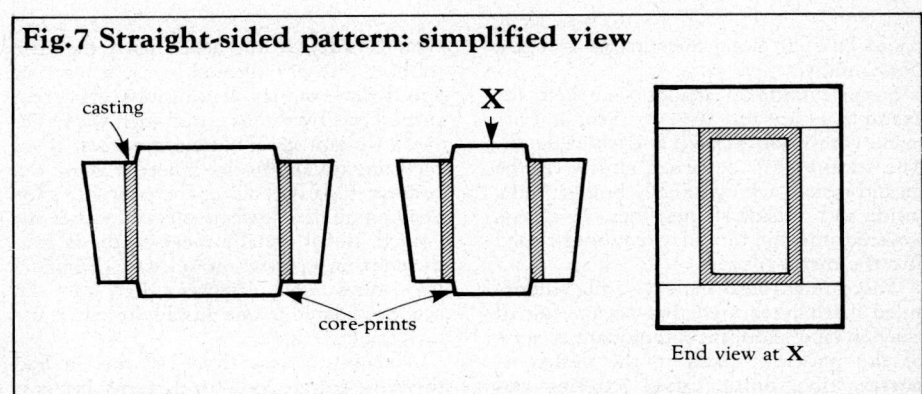

casting

X

core-prints

End view at X

## Fig.8 Pattern on a board

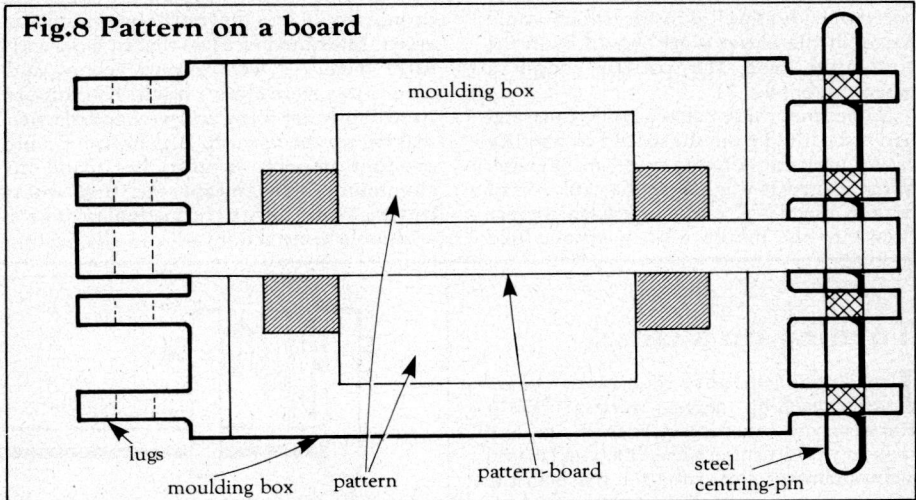

moulding box

lugs

moulding box     pattern     pattern-board     steel centring-pin

'**A** far cry from my concept of woodwork'. And so it is too; patternmaking isn't woodwork in the aesthetic sense — it's not there to look at and enjoy.

A pattern is an intermediate stage between a design and a casting, be it decorative or utilitarian. It's not the end product and therefore makes no call for joints that will show, or veneers, or pleasing grain. The finish on a pattern must be good, but this is merely to ensure a clean sand mould for the insidious molten metal that will find its way into every blemish. Even a pattern or model for a bronze statue is only a means to an end — and in the 'lost wax' process, in which the wax shape of the piece is melted out of the mould before casting, there is no pattern left at all.

The two prime requirements of a pattern are that it should leave the mould cleanly, and that it should be made with a good close-grained casting in mind, free from any structural fault. Stress is particularly important to avoid, for instance in an aircraft casting. This second point often determines which way up a job might be moulded, which in turn might alter the method of construction. There are castings with, say, thin and thick wall sections coming together, others with thin curved sections with tiny strengthening ribs in the design, and castings which, because of their peculiar shape, confound all attempts to find a joint line where the job can be safely split for top and bottom moulds.

If you yearn to be a Sheraton, a Chippendale or a Grinling Gibbons, patternmaking is not for you. Pattern work is good, solid and exacting — but unglamorous.

Let me describe a simple pattern, a flatback. As the name suggests, a flatback is flat on one face, so if necessary several can be fitted on a board if lots of castings are required. One large pattern can be done in the same way.

A 'loose' pattern was usually a one-off casting. Fig. 1 shows a typical flatback, but fig. 2, which is a casting, could also be done on a board by splitting the pattern into halves. Fig. 3 shows the pattern for that casting; as it has an inside as well as an outside shape, core-prints are added to the pattern. Fig. 3a shows a half core-box; this core is simply the inside of the pattern plus the core-prints. Fig. 8 is the pattern on its board with the moulding boxes in place; there are holes in both board and boxes into which steel pins slide to keep the job in line.

After the mould and core are made, runners for the flow of metal are cut in by the moulder, or can be put on in the pattern-shop. The core is put into the bottom mould, and the top mould closed over it. The gap left between core and mould is the thickness of metal of the casting. Some patterns were long and cylindrical and had to be cast on end because of their design (fig. 5 shows a big electrical armature), while other cylinders could be split along their length and cast horizontally.

Some cylindrical shapes — a bell, for example — are too large to turn, and are made with what is called a strickle (fig. 6). The strickle arm is turned slowly by the mould maker, who gradually builds up the inside and outside shapes; then the core is lowered into the mould, the mould closed and the metal poured.

There might also be, say, a big square-sided casting required that no amount of 'leaving taper' could accommodate because of the undercut parts in the design — bosses, ribs, holes, raised lettering and other bits and pieces. This would have to be cored outside as well as inside, which would mean all the clever work would be in the core-boxes, and the pattern simply a tapered box (fig. 7).

Sometimes these patterns were huge and had to be lifted from the mould by a gantry crane, and the cores lowered in likewise. What a sight it was to see the cauldron of molten metal tip, and the golden torrent flow into the mould while everyone held their breath. On the other hand, the little jobbing foundry seemed to me a place of speedy little money-making jobs on boards, turned out by the hundred each week. Do you own any small brass ornaments? If so, pick one up and notice where it is jointed (unless it's a flatback). The procedure for arriving at the finished piece is rather involved, but it usually means a die is produced from a plaster mould; and, of course, the more little figures that can be accommodated in one mould the better, for dies are expensive.

All shops, at least those I worked in, had the same colour code for patterns. For cast iron they would be orange, while phosphor bronze would be a dull red. Aluminium was green. Machined faces — that is, faces with extra metal — were always yellow, and core-prints were always black. The colours were in powder form, and were added when making up the varnish. A pattern for a big production run would be made in aluminium. This meant the first wood pattern would have to be made allowing for a 'double contraction' so the ally casting which was to become the pattern would be in a single contraction size when it shrank on cooling. These patterns for ally went to the foundry a nice green with yellow stripes. When it came back to us, the casting was filed, scraped and emeried until it shone, and great care taken to ensure that the leaving taper was still as it should be.

So, whether the design of the casting is in the pattern or in the core-box, it still has to be made, and it can involve all the cutting and carving anyone with a love of wood could want. Yet there's a difference. No crisp original cuts, no undercut parts — but to the blueprint, and dead accurate.

Talking of accuracy, I remember one cold day when Harold, my bench-mate, came in from the foundry with a 2ft steel rule in his hand, having done some checking. 'What's up, Harold?' I asked.

He scowled blackly. He was cold. 'How', he growled, 'am I expected to work to a sixty-fourth when I'm shivering a thirty-second?'

## Turning up a lathe!

I am studying in the second year of a three-year teaching degree, **writes Philip Barnes,** and my project is to design and make a woodturning lathe. It's based round a 3in-diameter steel tube for the bed; the project is in two parts, the first of which involves designing the main parts and casting them in aluminium. In the second stage I will be machining the castings, fitting the bearings and motor, and generally finishing the job.

The photos show the completed castings, which I have made using patterns in MDF (medium-density fibreboard); next year I'll be buying the sealed bearings, motor, switch and so on to make the whole thing work!

One interesting thing I have found is that the MDF machined so well that the finish was actually better if the surface was just sealed than if I painted it in the approved patternmaking fashion. I did end up painting some of the patterns, though. The MDF laminated shapes were bandsawn, and then filed, rasped and sanded to absolutely accurate size; the pattern for the stepped pulley was made by turning the sections separately and then laminating them together. The back of the pattern was then removed on a metalworking lathe, using a boring bar, to reduce the final weight of the pulleys. All the laminating was done with PVA.

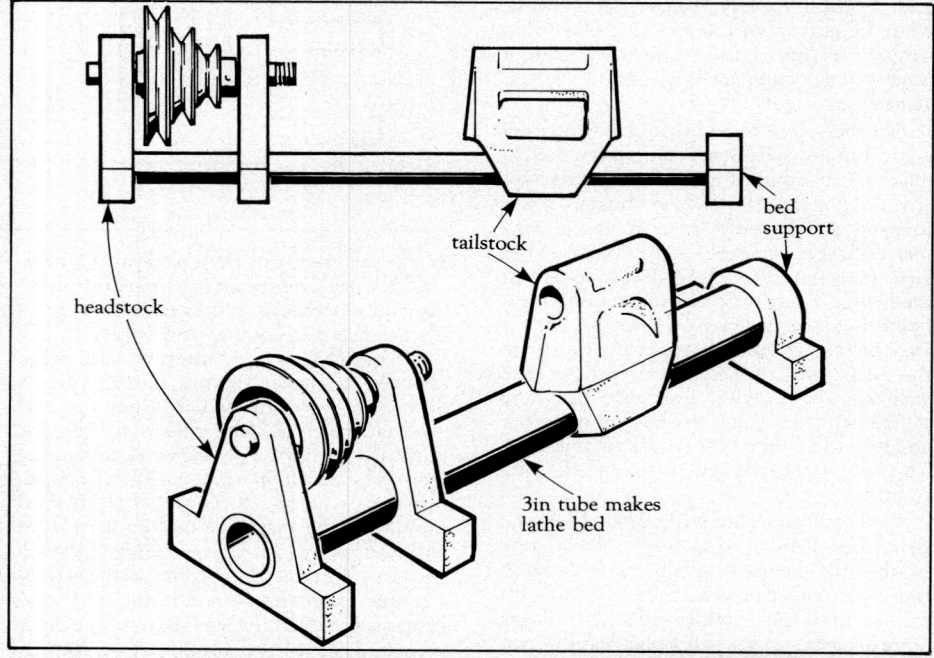

headstock

tailstock

bed support

3in tube makes lathe bed

● *The split pattern for the tailstock. All Philip Barnes' patterns were made in MDF and sealed, rather than painted; the core-prints were turned laminated sections, allowing a sand core to form the tunnel section for the tubular bed*

## Making a propeller

This is a project which not only serves its purpose as a pattern but would also make an interesting carving exercise for the non-patternmaker, **writes Patrick Spatchett.** You can always use it as an ornament!

Mahogany is the best material for the job, widely used as it is in patternmaking.

The propeller is laminated. The seven pieces of mahogany of which it is made are known as 'cants'. The patternmaker would only make a single-bladed propeller, but when it went into the foundry the moulder would produce a mould for a double-bladed one simply by moulding the pattern of one blade, rotating it on its centre shaft and moulding again, giving two blades.

Since accuracy is the most important factor in patternmaking, set-out or layout is usually necessary before starting construction. It's not essential for the non-patternmaker who only wants an ornament, so I won't go into the details of the set-out — except to say the job takes longer to set out than to make! ∎

● *If you look at these three pictures . . .*

*. . . quickly enough, you might see . . .*

*. . . the propeller begin to turn!*

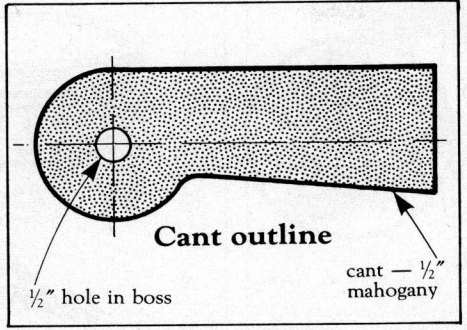

**Cant outline**

½" hole in boss

cant — ½" mahogany

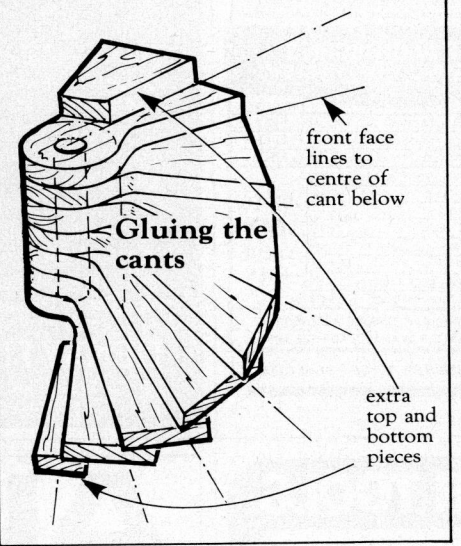

**Gluing the cants**

front face lines to centre of cant below

extra top and bottom pieces

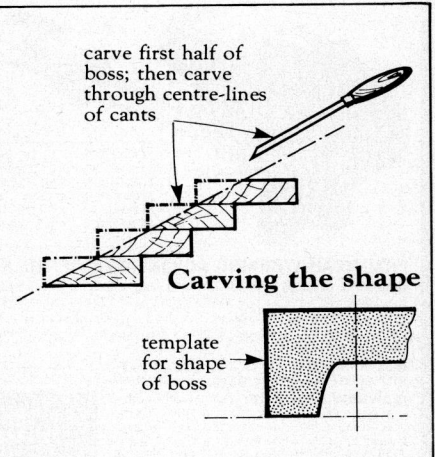

carve first half of boss; then carve through centre-lines of cants

**Carving the shape**

template for shape of boss

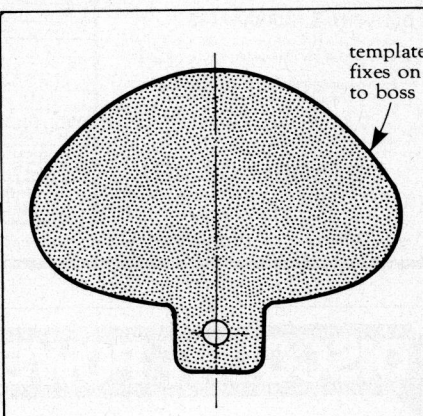

template fixes on to boss

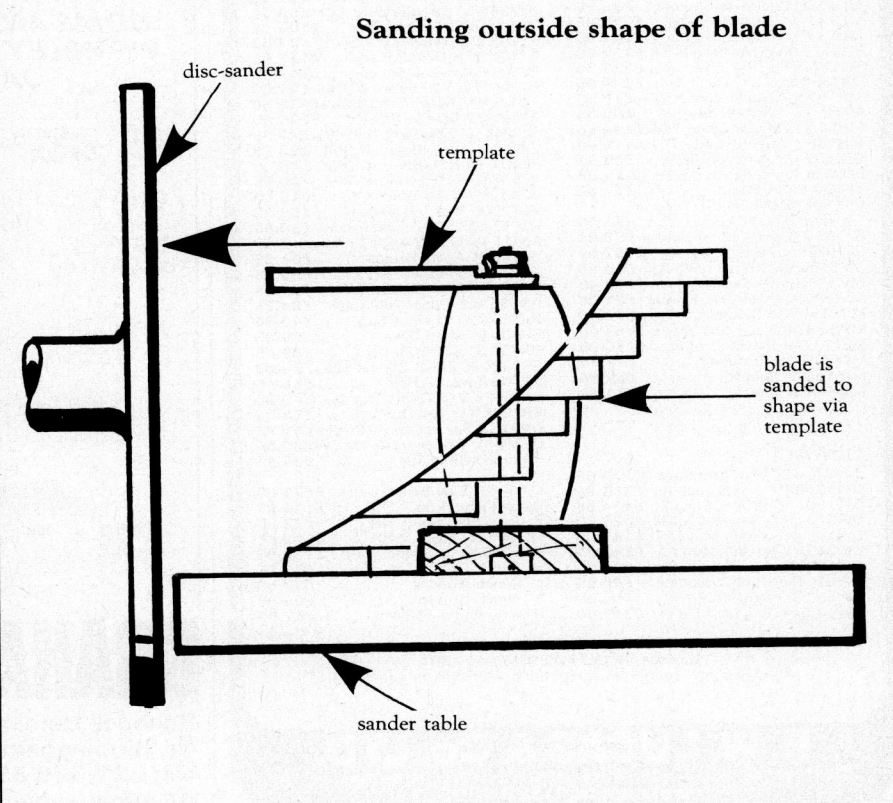

**Sanding outside shape of blade**

disc-sander

template

blade is sanded to shape via template

sander table

939

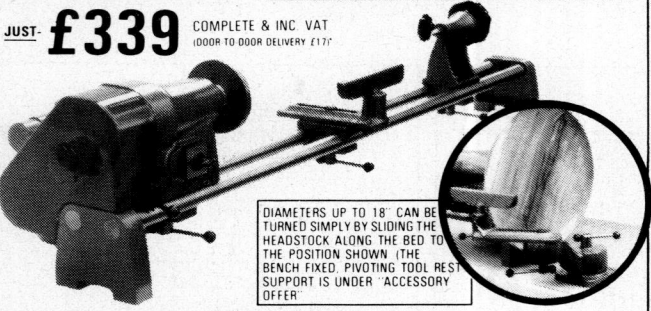

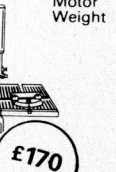

# Routing by hand

**Hand routing is rapidly and sadly disappearing in the face of electricity. Bob presents some designs to stop the rot and keep your toolmaking in trim**

The power router has come to stay. Of that there is no doubt, and it must be most readers' ambition to own one if they don't already. Nevertheless, there's still a place for the hand router. Small operations and corrections can be done by hand in less time than it takes to sort out the spanners and cutters and fit up that extension lead for the power router.

In the great days of hand work, Record, Stanley, Marples and other firms each made several patterns of router. Now, alas, apart from two Stanley models these have all gone, and long ago the wooden 'old woman's tooth' router was reduced to an illustration in obsolete textbooks. The cost of a new hand router at the time of writing is about £30, very nearly the cost of a small power router, so it's not surprising that this tool is none too common in the tool-boxes of the younger generation.

However, the hand router's great usefulness makes its construction well worth while, particularly as the methods are quick and easy and the components are cheap. Before examining the models suggested here, it's worth considering the two distinct cutting actions used. That shown in fig. 1A is the normal plane action of the traditional wooden router. As with moulding planes, the pitch is rather high — 60° was common; but of course it could be made lower.

Fig. 1B shows the cranked cutter which came in with the metal routers. Bearing in mind that a great deal of routing is done across the grain, its shearing cut is probably better than the more scraping action of fig. 1A. It is pointed, to give more of a slicing action on difficult wood and also to get into corners on inlay work. Obviously this shape needs its lower face to have no clearance at all but to be parallel to the base of the router.

The cranked cutter's vertical stem made it easy to devise and fit an adjusting mechanism. However, the design has one major disadvantage. It cannot operate in a cavity much smaller than three times its length, because of the uncut area which must remain in the centre. Fig. 1B shows this. It is for this reason that I have included the small wooden router as well.

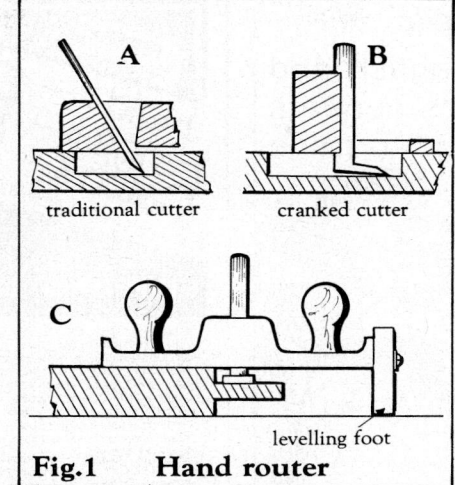

**Fig.1    Hand router**

## Small wooden router

The tricky part of making this tool — cutting the hole, tapered at 60° and 78° — is avoided in the early stages. Prepare a suitable block of any dense, close-grained hardwood slightly oversize and saw through it at 60°. Plane up for a good joint, then in the front section saw and cut out the main hole and in the rear section cut a shallow housing to take the cutter. If thick enough cutters are made, two shallow housings can be made to take cutters of ½in (12mm) and ¼in (6mm).

Glue together, true up the sole and remove the shallow escapement in front of the blade. The whole of the shaping can now be done and the wedge made. As a finish, I favour a number of coats of raw linseed oil. Some readers may prefer polyurethane varnish. The cutters are made from tool steel, sold as 'ground flat stock' or 'gauge plate'. The hardening and tempering process is described later. The sizes shown can be scaled up to make a traditional type of full-sized router.

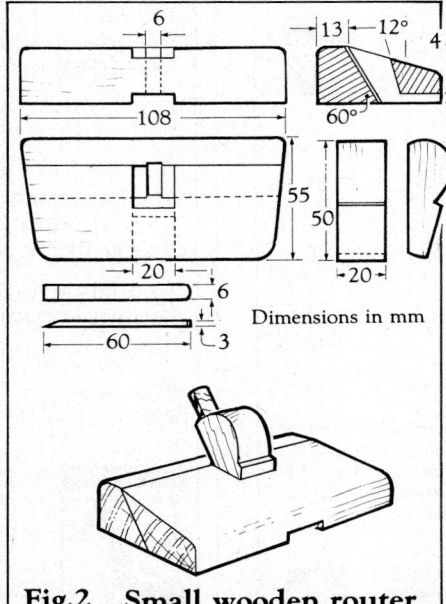

Dimensions in mm

**Fig.2    Small wooden router**

## Small metal router

This drawing needs little explanation. Either the two pieces of the body, having been filed to shape, are joined by two rectangular tenons taken through and riveted, or else the vertical member is drilled and tapped to take two or four small studs which are similarly riveted over into countersunk holes. The whole length of the joint is then silver-soldered or brazed. After this the body is filed up, and then cleaned and polished with successively finer grades of emery or wet-and-dry paper. The sole is trued on emery cloth fixed to a truly flat surface.

The draw-bolt is like the one for the router described later, except that, to give adequate strength where the thread begins, a special washer is fitted. Any suitable clamping nut may be used.

**Fig.3**    Small metal router

## Improved router

Again a good dense hardwood should be used for the body of this tool. Beech or a fruitwood are obvious choices. As a refinement for a de luxe model, a thin face of ebony or rosewood can be added. Multiply has successfully been used, with a sole of plastic laminate. This latter may warp the body, so a balancing layer needs to be applied to the top. For this I find Aerolite, with its special laminate hardener, preferable to the rubber-based adhesives. But most readers will, I imagine, want to stick with solid wood in any case.

Bore and saw out the escapement and produce the outline shape. For convenience, the body may be sawn through and jointed after the cutter block has been glued on and worked. The body can now be sanded to its final finish. Drill for the cylindrical nuts, fig. 5G, and for the handles. Drill and tap for the adjusting screw E. Then turn, sand, polish and glue in the

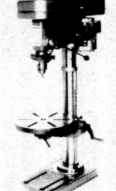

# Routing by hand

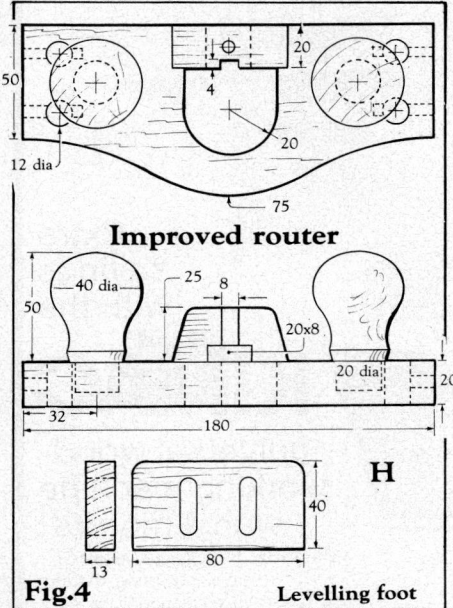

**Improved router**

**H**

**Fig.4**      Levelling foot

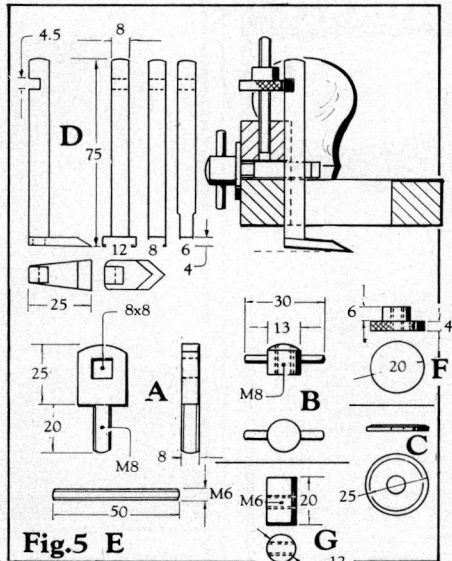

**Fig.5** **E**

knobs. They are shaped to individual taste.

Now for the metal parts. The four cylindrical nuts G are produced and pushed into place. They should be a tight fit. Drill a 5mm tapping hole through both the body and the nut. Remove and tap the nuts and drill out the body at 6mm, taking the drill a little way beyond the 12mm hole. Replace the nuts, if loose, with a touch of epoxy-resin glue (Araldite). The nuts should be turned or filed to a length just a little less than the body thickness to avoid scoring the work.

The cutters D are quite straightforward. The stem is from mild steel, notched to take the adjusting nut. The cutting end is made from ground flat stock secured to the stem with a small round tenon, riveted over and then silver-soldered. (Silver-soldering is generally neater than brazing, but you can do either.)

The clamp or draw-bolt A is simply made. File the shank round, trying it with a washer, and then cut the thread. The square hole can conveniently be a bit sloppy. A nut and washer apply the pressure. This nut will take whichever form is handiest — it may be a knurled metal knob, a plastic commercial component or even a wing-nut.

The adjusting wheel F needs to be nicely made, and I see no alternative, short-cut or potential improvisation. In brass, of course, it can be worked with hand tools in a wood-turning lathe. Otherwise you will have to cultivate an engineering friend.

The great innovation in this router is its levelling foot, fig. 4H, which when fitted at either end permits the router to be used with one side unsupported by the work. One such application, illustrated at fig. 1C, is the accurate thinning-down of an over-thick tenon. The reader will discover many others. Place the work on a level surface with the cutter withdrawn, fit the levelling foot, allow it to drop to the surface, and screw tightly.

Always adjust the cut with the blade in the housing. Unlock, increase the cut, and

then lock. If the tool is held in the air when unlocked, the cutter will drop by the amount of slack in the mechanism, giving an increase of cut greater than intended.

## Depth stop

Unlike those of the plough and filister, the cutter of the router cannot be pre-set to the finished depth, but must be advanced for each cut. If many housings are to be made, the same cut must be taken on all, then the cutter advanced and all the housings worked again. This is tedious and may require a lot of space in which to spread out all the components. This depth stop, however, permits the finished dept to be repeated at will.

It consists merely of a very thick square or circular washer with a square hole to take the cutter. It is drilled and tapped for an M4 or M5 screw, preferably with a socket head (an Allen screw). Cut the first housing to depth, drop the depth stop down to the tool body, and lock it there. Now withdraw the cutter and start on the second housing, gradually increasing the cut until the depth stop again touches the body.

20x20x8
or
20 dia x 8

M4 or 5

**Depth stop**

**Fig.6**

## Depth gauge

Fig. 7 clearly shows this simple tool. It takes a pencil or, better still, a ballpoint pen. This is set to the required depth. While it continues to mark in the housing, more wood is to be removed. The last router adjustments must be very fine; once the pen ceases to mark, the finished depth has been reached.

The sizes for the wooden block are only suggestions. The draw-bolt and nut are as previously described, drilled to suit the pen or pencil. The reader will no doubt find other uses for this little tool.

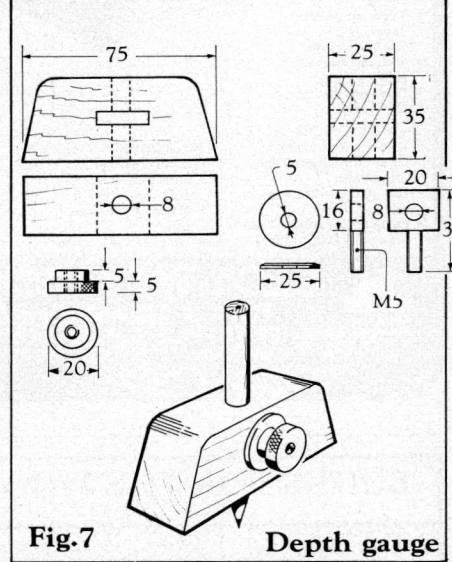

**Fig.7**      Depth gauge

## Hardening cutters

After the cutter has been brazed or forged to shape, it is cleaned up to a bright finish and the bevel part filed. A very thin edge is to be avoided. Now heat the business end to a bright red, but not hot enough to melt the brazing. Rapidly quench the tool in oil, which is preferable to water. Brighten up the cutting area with emery cloth and then heat again, playing the heat mainly on the stem behind the cutting edge. Watch the colours appear and creep towards the cutting edge. When the area round the cutting edge reaches a light brown colour, quench again. The required hardness has been obtained. Clean off any scale, and emery up to a bright finish. Grind and sharpen in the usual way.

● A useful source for small quantities of metal is K. R. Whiston, New Mills, Stockport SK12 4PT. ■

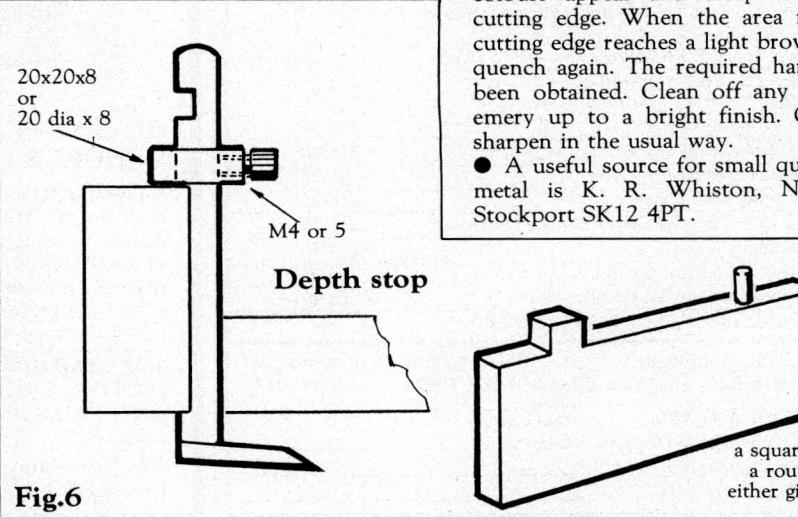

a square tenon or
a round stud —
either gives a joint
in metal

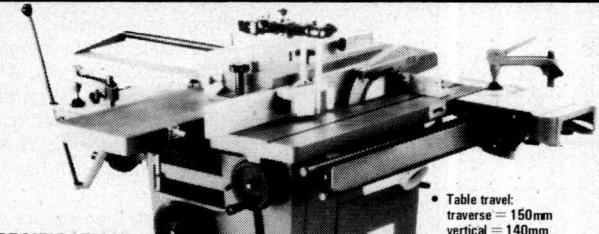

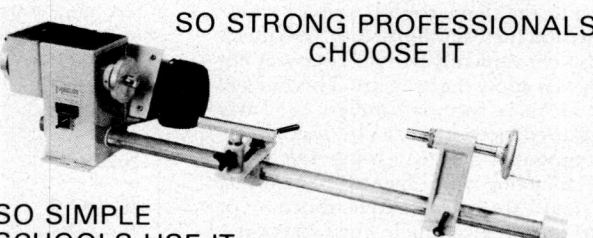

# Books

*Marion Millett*
**Working Wooden Toys**
*Sterling, £4.95*
*Reviewed by R. B. Coombes*

Beset as I am by grandchildren constantly requiring toys that are 'different', it was with great pleasure that I came across Marion Millett's second book.

Illustrated in colour and black-and-white and running to 126 pages, it details dozens of toys that can be made by the amateur woodworker, using only basic equipment except for — perhaps — a bit of riveting (and I would suggest that a jigsaw is a necessity). The scraps of wood that we all keep on one side really come into their own (such a saving, with wood the price it is!) Only for a few of the projects would one have to purchase a piece or two of plywood.

The current trend seems to be for expensive toys that paradoxically last a short time — but Marion Millett seems to have provided the answer. Movement is the keynote of these toys; and movement and colour fascinate children. So I would say the popularity of this book is assured.

**Running a Workshop**
*Crafts Council, 12 Waterloo Place, London SW1Y 4AU, £4.95 incl. p&p, paperback*
*Reviewed by David Woodnutt*

Running a workshop means being an entrepreneur, manager, salesperson and public-relations officer rolled into one. Dealing with everything from obtaining finance to arranging publicity and the implications of expanding, *Running a Workshop* takes us through the problems, offering much sound advice and many helpful suggestions. It replaces the Council's earlier book *Setting up a Workshop*, and manages a consistency of style and a well-ordered approach which make for easy reading and belie its corporate origins.

The Crafts Council is a major grant-giving body, so its advice on how best to present grant applications is well worth noting. Another useful suggestion, if you are looking for money, is to send a properly documented proposal to your bank manager before visiting him. This looks more professional and allows time for your case to be properly considered. A persistent will and plenty of determination are necessary to survive in business, and the need for professionalism is emphasised throughout the book.

For people intending to work together, various legal frameworks are discussed — though the authors are dismissive of the whole subject of co-operatives, which in my view is a grave misjudgement.

The excellent advice on costing illustrates how to take account of all the time spent in activities other than actually making things. The tremendous investment of human resources swallowed by setting up and running any small business cannot really be accounted for, but at least this book helps to ensure that such efforts are effective.

There is a host of good suggestions in the section on selling, and the chapter on publicity demonstrates the many different forms that good public relations can take: promotional material, editorial coverage, press releases — all perhaps more cost-effective than simply buying advertising space. The business of exhibiting is treated in a chapter of its own.

You can, of course, skip the cautionary words and motherly advice in the brief chapter on health and turn to the one dealing with expanding. Expanding means more costs and the red tape of employing other people; all these are dealt with. There is even a sensible word or two about computers — though unfortunately, while the authors point out the need for specialist advice, this is one case where they fail to suggest where it might be found.

An information section gives useful names and addresses, together with notes on the roles of the major agencies and institutions concerned with the development of crafts in Britain. A proper index rounds off a very user-friendly book which I shall certainly keep within easy reach.

*Ron Roszkiewicz*
**The Woodturner's Companion**
*Sterling, £9.95*
*Reviewed by Anthony Bryant*

This is one companion not recommended for woodturners — beginners or otherwise.

The last thing woodturning needs is another book written by someone who has only the merest superficial knowledge of, and ability in, basic techniques. I am disillusioned by the apparent ease with which someone can obtain the backing and promotion of publishing companies, on both sides of the Atlantic, in producing a book which contains dangerously inept and incorrect advice. It seems the author is another in the growing line of Americans who, after receiving very poor tuition in this country, return home and immediately set themselves up as authorities — without ever producing one piece of quality work, let alone spending many years mastering techniques, gaining knowledge of the large and interesting range of available timbers, and constantly refining shape and form.

Ultimately, woodturning suffers because beginners have to persevere for years before realising the worthlessness of such bad advice. Perhaps, indeed, they never gain insight into correct technique or good aesthetic form.

Chapter 2 sets the tone. With clever editing (the only good thing about the book) padding out the author's limited knowledge, we waste pages rambling on about how to make a nice tool-chest and other irrelevancies. The beginner is advised that all he requires are two scrapers, two spindle-gouges, two skew-chisels and a roughing-out gouge; and, further, that 'These tools will make any cut normally encountered in spindle and bowl turning.' I must have been wasting time for at least five

of the last 10 years — or perhaps I learnt from the wrong person?

Any lingering hope that the author has had some experience of repetition work is dashed when he talks about tailstock centres. He states that revolving centres do not last unless 'you turn a few hours a week and no more' (he has worn out a couple already). I don't know whether this is because of the poor standard of American accessories or ham-fisted over-tightening of the tailstock. The author gives credence to the latter explanation when he illustrates the cutting of two grooves with a saw on the end of a piece of wood which the tailstock centre would grip more happily.

The bowl-turning section does not fail to surprise in continuing the low level of advice. After explaining that a bowl gouge is the main tool for the job, he adds: 'It is possible to obtain the same result with a spindle-gouge if the same techniques are followed.' This advice is dangerous, and anyone who has spent some time perfecting bowl-turning techniques does not use such a gouge. Again we are the mercy of someone who is merely passing on the bad advice he has been given by people who have not produced work of the highest standard. In order to find the correct speed when using a variable-speed pulley, he counsels, 'Simply dial the speed lever as high as it will go without causing too much vibration'! High speeds do not result in quick and efficient work; quite the opposite. The whole chapter exposes the author's inability to use the bowl gouge; he relegates it to a roughing-out role, mainly because he has not ground it correctly and hence it has such a long bevel that it cannot follow the outside shape of the bowl; it follows a path from the rim straight to the centre, the rest of the turning being done with a scraper.

The author's lathe is so basic that he has to turn a bowl between centres, so the outside is turned by cutting from left to right (from rim to base). By stating 'The constantly rubbing bevel produces a lot of friction heat, which can burn the hand on the tool rest as it is drawn up the blade. Some turners wear a leather glove for protection', he tells us he has little idea of how to cut correctly. Obviously some heat is produced — but he has clearly been using a blunt tool, using the tool wrongly, or both.

The section on sanding and finishing continues the farce as we are presented with the sight of rubber-backed sanding-discs which appear to be at least 4in in diameter — almost as big as the bowl illustrated.

This book has been written by a man ill-equipped to pass on advice. He should be thinking in terms of meeting someone who can help him refine this techniques, then of replacing his lathe with one offering more scope for bowl turning and spending another couple of years perfecting his shapes. *The Woodturner's Companion* will help teach no one.

*More books overleaf . . .*

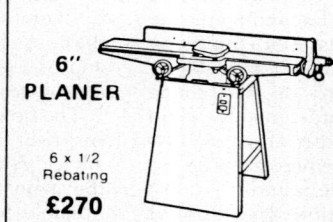

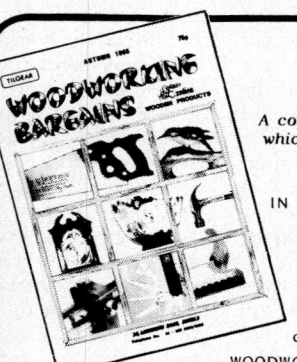
946

# Books

*David Francis*
**Turning a Bobbin**
*David Francis, 33 Charlecote Drive,*
*Wollaston, Notts NG8 2SD, £1.50*
*paperback*
*Reviewed by Nick Perrin*

This booklet by a skilled engineer and turner gives a personal account of the techniques he employs in making lace bobbins.

His particular aim has been to help the beginner, which he does simply and clearly. In turn he discusses safety, machinery and woods. When describing tools he gives excellent advice on choosing and sharpening them.

The use of each tool is described with particular reference to the fine work required for bobbin-making, and each stage is accompanied by clear line drawings. He describes in detail decorations such as beads, coves and tapers. He pays particular attention to the making of a good 'long neck' — perhaps the most difficult operation for a beginner — and sets out clearly the two most satisfactory methods.

Filling a need at a time when lace-making is enjoying a huge revival, this booklet should provide many keen woodworkers with sound advice and re-assurance.

*Margaret Gill*
**Tunbridge Ware**
*Shire Publications, Cromwell House,*
*Church St, Princes Risborough, Aylesbury,*
*Bucks HP17 9AJ, £1.25, paperback*
*Reviewed by Stuart King*

Collectors and woodworkers alike should relish this well-illustrated book, written in an easy style. It will inform both parties a great deal, and much inspire the latter.

In the last 300 years the term 'Tunbridge ware' has been used to describe a wide range of wooden objects, but since early last century it has been closely associated with mosaic and inlaid decoration. This very specialised form of woodwork originated, as its name implies, in Kent. It seems, for the most part, that the makers aimed their wares at the up-market tourist trade.

The amount of craftsmanship and artistry involved has to be seen to be believed, and even then it can often only be appreciated with the aid of a magnifying-glass. Castles, birds, landscapes and flowers were among the many subjects that, together with parquetry, decorated such items as stamp-boxes, tea-caddies and needlework accessories — and even full-size furniture. The makers' imagination was endless; so too, therefore, is the scope for those who collect these intriguing treen.

A very informative chapter describes the method of making mosaic decoration — perhaps to stir a few of us into having a go.

*Wayne Barton*
**Chip Carving**
*Sterling, £6.95, paperback*
*Reviewed by John Donaldson*

In the course of demonstrations I'm often approached by woodworkers — both the aspiring and the accomplished — who hold a set view about carving: 'I'd love to carve, but I'm not artistic.' My response is always to ask them to consider the Celtic art of Scotland: decorative designs cut in low relief, whose execution requires skills, patience and craftsmanship — but not necessarily artistic training.

This intriguing and useful book is my point of reference from now on. Full of excellent illustrations plus step-by-step 'how to do it' designs, it stimulates and motivates, providing material which is of use through all levels of woodworking. It will benefit the crafts and design class in school, the hobbyist, and carvers both novice and experienced. Finally, it is an excellent source of surface-decoration motifs for the cabinetmaker.

The techniques are those of *Kerbschnitzen* — using knives to cut the design into the wood. Although Mr Barton is American, his work is distinctively mid-European. The photographs bear testimony to its effectiveness and appeal. A cautionary note, however, with regard to the blurb on the back cover: 'Anyone can do it . . . You can create fantastic gifts — or start a profitable home business.' Work of this kind requires

a particular temperament; it can be both physically demanding and time-consuming. Such statements contrast with the honesty and humility of the book itself. Indeed, Mr Barton's personal statements provide an appealing sincerity and humanity.

The book is carefully organised, detailed and concise. The penurious buyer might perhaps be inclined to return it to the shelf. Don't. It has a lot to offer.

*Roger Cliffe*
**Table Saw Techniques**
*Sterling, £14.95, paperback*
*Reviewed by Edward Richards*

Attempts to be totally inclusive are invariably defeated by time and space. The back-cover notes on this book, which claim total coverage of all known table-saw techniques, equipment and accessories, are patently ill-advised. I feel sure that Roger Cliffe would not make such a claim himself.

Add to this the facts that the book shows equipment of US origin and that all of us who use these saws have our own ways of working, and you have to think carefully about the contents before buying.

However, the claim inside the book that it addresses a core of generally applicable basic knowledge is far more realistic. It illustrates the appearance and functioning of basic machines and accessories, followed by operating procedures in cutting, shaping and jointing wood. It also deals in general with the condition and accuracy of the machine itself. It is rounded off with a series of projects involving jig-making and the use of aids — e.g., a bedside cabinet, a hall-stand and a wall clock. A wide range of techniques is featured and safety consciousness is very evident.

The main problem is the presentation. The large number of photographs are mostly washed out and poor in detail. The freehand sketching is dreadful, and only the simple working drawings of the projects show enough clarity and technical ability.

As a general account the book contains much of interest, but its cost and quality will make it a questionable investment — especially for the more experienced.

# WOODWORKING WHEEZE
### of the month

'**D**ead Man' is a title given to many things, **writes Charles Cliffe,** notably empty liquor bottles! In this instance it is applied to two pieces of wood. One is a piece of 4x2in with a tapered

notch cut into the top edge at one end, and the other is a wedge which fits into the notch.

This device is invaluable when you're shooting the edge of a door, cutting hinge rebates or chopping the mortise for a lock.

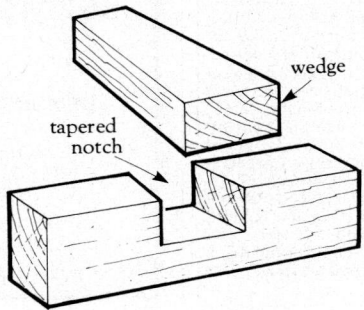

wedge

tapered
notch

The door is held vertically with its lower edge in the notch of the 4x2, a lot easier than standing astride it and holding it with your knees while you plane up to a wall. The wedge is driven into the tapered side of the notch to hold the door securely in position, and you can cut, chop, plane or trim to your heart's content — comfortably and without the door wobbling about. ∎

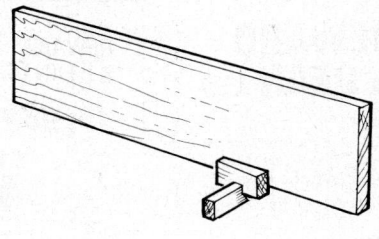

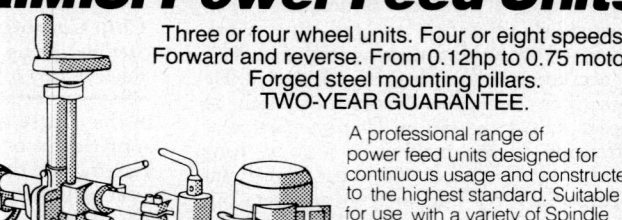

# Gracefully glazed

**Fraser Budd uses this delicate delight of a coffee-table to illustrate his thoughts on the design process**

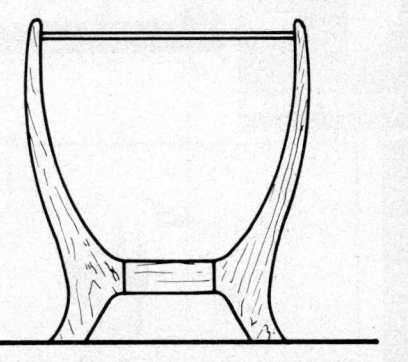

I often look at contemporary furniture which fails to perform its basic function well, yet is noted for its unusual (sometimes bizarre!) appearance.

I can't help thinking a designer should balance form and function so a piece is not just regarded as original, but is also valid because it fulfils the need for which it was produced. There's no doubt that the aesthetics of a piece must work, and it's stimulating when they're new rather than repetitive, but surely it isn't right for how it looks to be more important than how it works?

I look at the designing and making of furniture as a four-stage process that begins with the definition of a need, which itself outlines the problem. The need may emphasise the aesthetic or the functional qualities of the product, and formal furniture projects usually amalgamate the two.

The second stage is the development of the design in a literal form, which involves analysis and synthesis of all the information you can amass about the need, and results in a multitude of sketches and drawings. They should depict varying levels of detail, and models and mock-ups are often required, especially if there is something mechanical to be worked out. The third stage is actually making the thing, and the fourth is an evaluation; how successfully has it fulfilled the need?

The first stage often presents as big a problem as the other three put together, because if the need is not defined precisely it's difficult to proceed with any real direction. If you get the definition precise, you identify constraints that both limit and guide you, the designer, in the search for a satisfactory solution.

Fortunately for the professional designer, this stage is usually simplified when a customer comes with a commission, presenting a need which the two people then discuss and define. The constraints may be ones of size, shape, and material as well as the style and character of the place the piece is to occupy. If discussion is

● *The glass came first – but the client insisted it shouldn't be framed. So Fraser Budd designed a table whose structure is all in the stretchers*

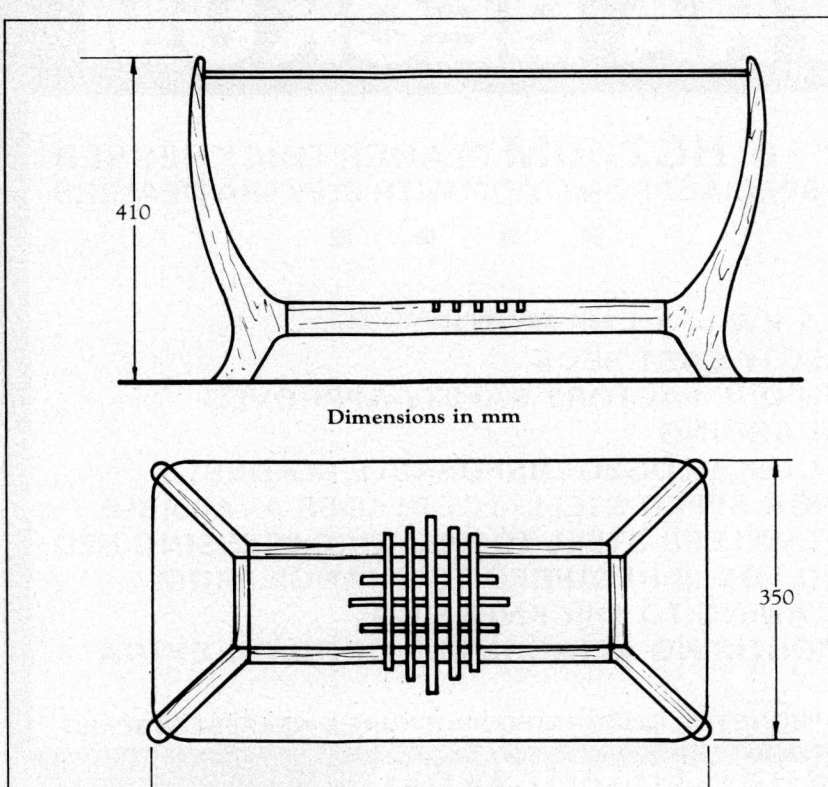

**Dimensions in mm**

410

350

760

thorough, the designer stands a far better chance of submitting something suitable and acceptable to the customer.

Reviewing such constraints in relation to a stated need, the designer can evolve something totally new and unique — a much more directed way of creating new designs which work and are not just artistic fancies. Luke Hughes comments in August's *Woodworker*: 'I couldn't help reflect that this need to be progressive and innovative frequently distorts the comprehension of function and usage . . . It is by adapting to new functions when they arise that a designer will be truly innovative.' If you want to be an innovative designer, you should create a new design brief, even for old problems, state a genuine need and

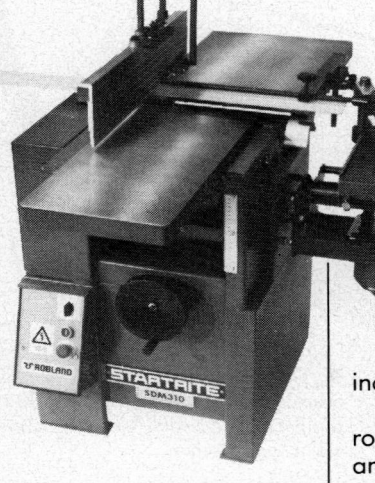

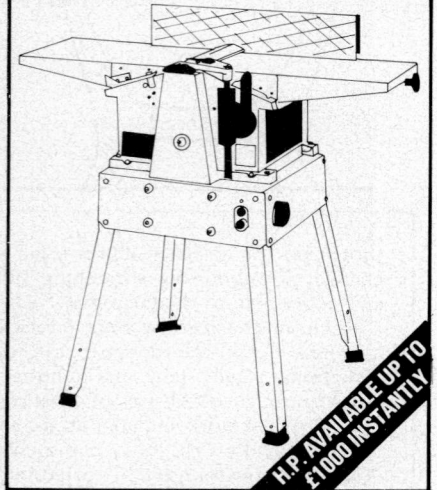

# Gracefully glazed

identify a more detailed list of constraints to give you scope to develop your ideas with guidance.

When a design is not commissioned, establishing the need and constraints may be difficult, but this should emphasise rather than reduce the importance of the process.

This small glass-topped coffee-table is a simple example of a fairly tightly constrained project suggested by a customer. The brief was along these line: 'I have a piece of plate glass 35x76cm, the remains of a larger table-top cracked by accident. The corners are curved (radiused to about 50mm). I need a low table for my sitting-room to display flowers and ornaments as well put cups and things on. The table should be of light appearance, and in particular the top shouldn't be fitted into any sort of frame.'

I felt this was a very well-defined brief for such a small project. Both I and my customer were pleased with the solution offered here, but I realise of course that the brief could be solved in many different but equally appropriate ways.

I began by writing out clearly what my customer required. I thought about the scope offered by the quite narrow piece of glass with its two rounded corners on the unbroken end, and decided to use it as large as possible. I simply squared off the end and duplicated the curved corners. I could now give attention to the design of the table itself.

My thoughts diverged in two directions, always keeping in mind the customer's need and the constraints we had identified; at this point it would be all too easy to sail off at full steam in total disregard of these guidelines! One aspect was the configuration of the table itself, the other the attachment of the glass simply and unobtrusively. I tend to tackle this kind of design on paper, putting down all the ideas I can think of in quick, rough-sketch form, and frequently stopping one avenue of thought to try to discover a completely different one. In the final analysis, it means I

have explored as many ideas as possible, and then I can select and develop the best. I look for shapes and forms created by the constructional members, whether straight or curved, which seem to go together with some kind of overall harmony. In this particular project I found the glass top, which couldn't be framed or edged, difficult to fit in with the construction beneath.

Gradually some ideas stood out as having potential, and eventually the final design emerged, along with a simple idea for fixing the glass (which had no holes).

Then I drew out my ideas more carefully and looked at the form in more detail, paying attention to the overall appearance and the achievement of the original brief. I decided to increase the scope for displaying flowers and ornaments by including a small platform in the stretcher framework so that things could be seen through the top and from the side. I could have developed this idea more, but decided against it; it would have been all too easy to over-killed it.

The next stage was to produce the true shapes of the legs on the drawing-board. I

needed to work out how they would flow into the horizontal rails, to which they are dowelled. I also had to calculate exactly the length that these rails would need to be if the glass was to fit using the method I had in mind; the design relies on the springiness of the legs to grip the corners of the glass firmly, as it rests in a small notch in the leg. For safety I included a small brass peg directly beneath the notch to give added support to the glass. To fit the glass you merely have to position it on the legs and press down — a click confirms that it's locked firmly in, with no unsightly fixings. This fixes the glass so firmly that the whole table can be lifted by its top.

After some thought about the display platform, I discarded the idea of a flat or turned piece of wood, and chose to make a grid of thin strips. It uses halving joints, and fits flush into the stretchers.

The frame was easily assembled using a single web-cramp to hold it while the adhesive set. Finally the curves were blended into the straight members using a small spokeshave, and the whole glasspapered and polished. The finish was wax. ■

**Angles on a joint: understanding in 3D is vital before you start making**

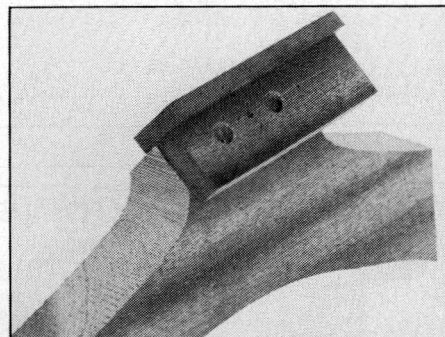

● *After bandsawing, a simple dowelling jig ensures accuracy on the 45° faces. A web-cramp held it all together, and shaping was the final step*

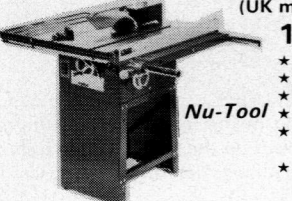
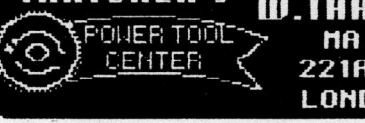

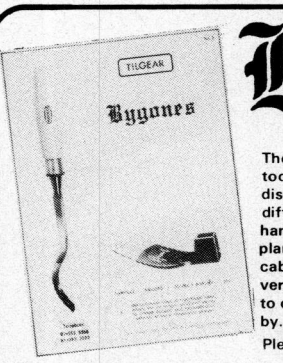
952

# The O'Connor clast

## David O'Connor takes a quirky look at setting up a one-man design-and-craft outfit

● *A lattice back that Chippendale never thought of. David O'Connor's designs are always thoughtful but sometimes startling; they range from the restrained to the definitely bold*

I grew up surrounded by woodworking. My father was a keen amateur woodworker and modelmaker, and in his eyes being ham-fisted or impractical was a cardinal sin. Probably because of this, my eight brothers and myself are almost all involved in making and design of one sort or another — most of them are engineers.

I went to a typical comprehensive school, which excelled in the creation of mediocrity in its students, with a few notable exceptions. I think they were grooming everybody to go into the civil service or become bank clerks. The school did, however, have an excellent and under-used craft department where I really learned to enjoy making. I took woodwork at A-level — I was the only pupil — and was taught by a superb craftsman/teacher, Mike Butterworth. He had an undeserved reputation for being mean because he used to 'lend' nails and tacks to fresh first-years running errands for other teachers. As they left with their 'borrowed' nails he would shout: 'And don't forget to bring them back'!

I left college in 1982 with a good — if esoteric — training in sculpture, which I thoroughly enjoyed. I am still practising, but I had to find a way to make money fast to lose a huge overdraft, which has now grown even bigger. There must be a moral there! I wanted to make furniture, a long-held ambition, so I touted around for work from people I knew, building kitchens, wardrobes and so on and buying my tools as I went along. I must point out that this way of setting up (with little formal training) was the only way to start for me, but if I were giving advice I would definitely suggest a degree course with business training. Go to a college like Rycotewood or the London College of Furniture, then get experience as an assistant with an established designer/craftsman. The way I started — no money, no experience, no tools and no workshop — isn't recommended for the faint-hearted; but you could say I had nothing to lose! I got most of my knowledge from handbooks and magazines such as *Woodworker*, working with a chisel in one hand and a book in the other.

I had a lot of problems early on with polishing — a very difficult craft, and there's a scarcity of useful literature. I also had difficulty with timber yards; sorting out the villains from the rest was tricky. One time I visited a yard, having phoned to arrange to look at 10cu ft of ash, which the yard foreman duly showed me. Then I went into the office, paid the manager, arranged the delivery and went to browse through the yard — where I was again approached by the yard foreman, who told me he could halve the boss's cost if I pulled a van up to the back yard at 3pm. He assured me no one would see us. Talk about cowboys: it was

the spurs that gave him away! The manager found us talking, and the ridiculous trio was complete: me, the boss — and the foreman behind him, halving everything in sight. Needless to say, I don't visit that yard very often. I now use North Heigham Sawmills in Norwich, which is good and the staff are friendly.

One of the most useful sources of help has been the Prince's Trust (a charity set up to assist young business-people), who awarded me a setting-up grant. Probably even more useful, they go out of their way to put you in touch with experienced people like financial advisors, and in my case an experienced furniture designer. I must admit that I haven't given as much attention to the business side as I should have done.

The two organisations which can help designer/makers are the Design Council and the Crafts Council, where I've seen many excellent exhibitions. I've been frustrated at some recent exhibitions by the Crafts Council, though; the work of Andy the Furniture Maker, for instance, appears to me to be both bad sculpture and bad furniture, fit for neither contemplation nor backside. I saw his work at the Institute of Contemporary Arts — he was using waste material: admittedly an admirable approach in other ways, although I'd like to see the skip that yielded a 2x4ft piece of iroko! The problem probably lies in the Crafts Council's attempt to gain artistic credibility: a vain effort to compete with artists at the Arts Council, which can only result in gimmickry. I don't propose to distinguish between art and craft, but I am sure that two essentials of good craft are fitness for purpose and quality of making. The work of, for instance, Martin Grierson and Alan Peters provides examples; not Andy's. I also find it puzzling that the British Crafts Centre gives wall space to incredibly bland 'international nondescript' abstract paintings — no doubt to the annoyance of many weavers and makers of lights, hangings and so on, who are eager to gain wall space in the country's few craft galleries.

My aim now is to concentrate on design and to market myself as a designer, which will solve the problem of not having the time to complete larger jobs single-handed.

I suppose it's inevitable that you either get people to make pieces from your designs, or employ assistants; there are only so many hours in the day, and no matter how hard you work you can only do so much.

I'm looking forward to working solely as a designer; it'll be a challenge. But I'll probably suffer withdrawal symptoms from giving up making. You'll probably find me chewing chair-legs in Heals! ■

---

● There is an exhibition of David's work at the Craft Gallery, Playhouse Theatre, Harlow, Essex, during December.
● Prince's Trust, 8 Buckingham St, London WC2, tel. 01-930 5932; Design Council, Design Centre, 28 Haymarket, London SW1Y 4SU, tel. 01-839 8000; Crafts Council, 12 Waterloo Pl., London SW1Y 4AU, tel. 01-930 4811; British Crafts Centre, 43 Earlham St, London WC2H 9LD, tel. 01-836 6993

● *This fashionably black cabinet would look at home in the most modern company*

# Guild notes

## Associate members!

For all you aspiring craftspeople (and which of us doesn't aspire?) who have longingly perused the Guild pages, wishing you could join but fearing your skills are not yet up to it, fear no more.

We are introducing an Associate membership level for those whose main interest is improving their woodworking capabilities. It will mean you can come on any of our courses without having to demonstrate a high level of skill; the criterion for selection is mainly an enthusiasm for learning, and the subscription is highly affordable. Pick up a pen or phone, give the word and we'll rush the forms to you.

## Outreach — South Africa

A letter from **Mr B. E. Walton** bemoans the lack of woodworking guilds in South Africa, and asks how he can start up his own. Why not, I replied, join ours and be an outreach local rep for those members in S.A. who must also be feeling isolated? If you are near enough to Durban to mull over your mutual interest with Mr Walton, get in touch with him at 2 Highview Rd, Overport, Durban 4001, Republic of South Africa.

## Crafty Christmas — Berkshire

This is naturally the best time of year for craftspeople to sell their work, and if you are in the Home Counties you should take a good look at what South Hill Park's seventh Christmas Craft Fair in Bracknell has to offer. It is on 30 November and 1 December; 6000 people came last year, and this year the space they have is even bigger. They want quality; an application to take a stand there should include photos of your work, your promotional material and an SAE for return. Send it all to Susan Foster, Assistant Head of Visual Arts, South Hill Park Arts Centre, Bracknell, Berks RG12 4PA, tel. (0344) 427272.

## Chairmaking

Our star teacher, nationally known **Fred Lambert,** has finally retired from teaching this popular subject, and we are working hard to set up a replacement course. We wish Fred all the best and a well-deserved rest! Meanwhile, if you can't wait for another Guild course, **Jack Hill** is running one at West Dean College on 16-21 February 1986. Get in touch with the college direct — at West Dean, Chichester, W. Sussex PO18 0QZ, tel. (0243 63) 301.

## Crafty Christmas — Staffordshire

'British Craftsmanship at Work '85' is the title of a show at Bingley Hall, Staffs, where you will be able to examine and/or exhibit not only 'the very best in both traditional and modern . . . craftsmanship', but also business advisory services, materials and equipment, training and career information, specialist courses and craft holidays. It runs from 29 November to 1 December and is being extensively promoted — even advertised on TV. 'Skills that provide the functional necessities,' write the organisers, 'the decorative, or maybe the entertaining elements in our lives, have never been more important in today's man-made world. The demand for such crafted goods is immense . . .' And so say all of us. Judging from the promotional material, it looks like an extremely well-conceived and organised affair, and is centrally situated in the Midlands. If you're interested in exhibiting, contact Francis Gordon Exhibitions Ltd, The Granary, Chequers Lane, Pitstone, Leighton Buzzard, Beds LU7 9AG, tel. (0296) 661092 or (044282) 6577 — or just go along to see.

## Sapele appeal

How does a figured sapele plank, 7ftx28in sawn, that should finish at 1½in planed, sound to you? How would you like to own it and fashion something monumental out of it? It's yours for free if you collect if from **George Cansdale,** who will be glad to give it to anyone who can suggest a suitable use for it. Sounds like he's going to have a job deciding on the winning application — he also has two pieces 6ftx12x2in to go with it. 'It would make a beautiful table-top for some ceremonial building,' he says. 'No chance, George,' you may think — 'that would move all over the place.' But wait a minute; this plank was cut in 1942, and has been stored inside ever since! Stable enough for you?

George brought it back from Ghana, where he worked as a forestry officer during the war. 'We found *Woodworker* very useful in those far-off days,' he recalls; 'I had up to 1000 carpenters working for me making furniture for the armed forces as a purely emergency measure, because as a forest officer I was mainly concerned with conservation. As war work fell off, we helped the better craftsmen produce furniture for soldiers to take home, and *Woodworker* helped us with ideas. They made a 6x3ft refectory table for under £3, plus £1 for a mahogany crate! Sawn over the pit, hardwoods cost 2s. 6d. a cubic ft.'

If you're after that sapele, write to George with your idea for its use at Dove Cottage, Great Chesterford, Saffron Walden, Essex CB10 1PL. If he gives it to you, send us a photo of what you make!

## Birmingham meet

The inaugural meeting of the Guild's West Midlands Branch was held on Sunday 1 September, **writes Bill Ferguson,** our local rep for that area.

Five enthusiasts managed to understand my directions, and, as not all were members of the Guild, application forms were soon handed out.

Talk about a small world! Four of them knew each other — two from recent contacts, and two had worked for the same organisation many years ago. So the ice was broken quickly and everyone was soon chatting over coffee.

There were two turners, three woodworkers/turners and one carver, which provided quite a background for discussion; two had brought samples of work, one turning and the other carving. I also produced some of my own turned work.

Then we went to see my set-up — one ex-garage, laughingly known as the wood-store, and another ex-garage which houses the machinery. (The car of course copes with the elements.)

Everyone thought the get-together was a good idea and all agreed we should do more in the future — but what? We decided to compile suggestions for future activities, meetings and visits, and let me act as a clearing-house.

Having once made the contact, it will be a great pity to lose the momentum, and we were all determined that there would be a good future for the Guild in the West Midlands. With that aim in mind, I'd like woodworkers in the West Midlands — members of the Guild or not — to write to me, and we'll see the section grow quickly and produce local benefits for local members.

● Bill Ferguson, 40 Quinton Lane, Quinton, Birmingham B32 2TS.

## Routing around

I'd like to let members know of a recent routing problem I encountered, **writes Chris Storey,** and how I overcame it. I bought an Elu MOF98 router, which I was going to use to make cupboard doors with profile-scribed tenons and a fielded central panel. But, having bought the fielding cutter, I found it was too big to go through the hole in the base of the router. I went on a course with **Roy Sutton** (*see our course list*), and with his help I designed a plate to let into a work surface with a hole big enough for the cutter; the router and a fence could also be attached to it. The sketch shows how it's worked out.

The other photo shows a recent commission, a Victorian-style vanity basin whose door was made with the cutter. It's mainly in pine; I'd like to get more work like this, and am taking advantage of the Guild's free publicity.

● Chris's plate was made for less than £20 by 602 Precision Engineering, 602 Purley Way, Croydon, Surrey, tel. 01-688 5877.

● Chris Storey, 1 Woodcote Grove Rd, Coulsdon, Surrey, tel. 01-660 8691.

● **Remember, members** — your membership gives you access to these pages! Get your wheezes and work published — just write, enclosing photos and drawings. Only good-quality b/w pix, please.

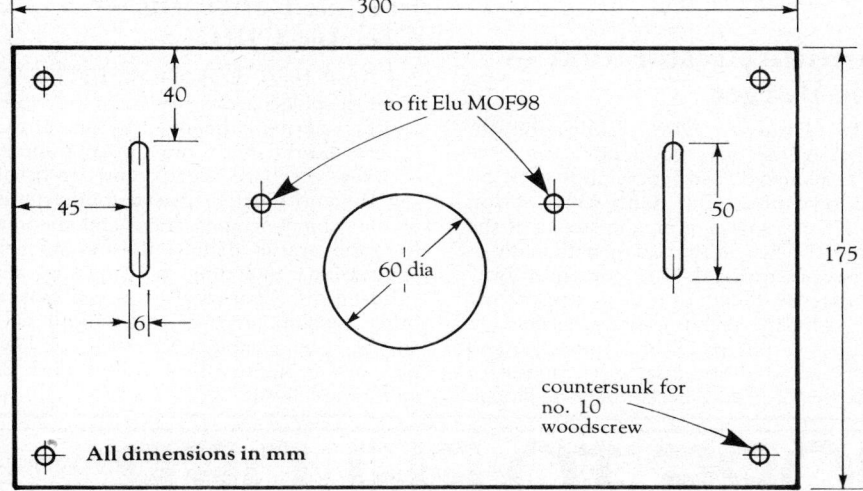

*All dimensions in mm*

● *Ever bought a nice cutter for your router, only to find it won't go through the base?* **Chris Storey** *designed the plate (left), with* **Roy Sutton's** *help, that solved the problem. Chris makes basin-stands like the one* **above**

# Guild courses

● **Booking is in advance, and can only be taken on receipt of a cheque for the full amount made payable to Guild of Woodworkers/ASP Ltd. Cancellation fee is 50% if you cancel less than two weeks before the course, other than in exceptional circumstances.**

## Cane and rush seating — Betty Fowler

6-8 December, Longdon, Gloucestershire, £70+VAT. Another three days' hard work, on one or possibly two of your own chairs, repaired and prepared for its brand-new seat. Betty will be showing patterns and processes for both cane and rush — she picks the raw material herself from the nearby river Avon — and overseeing your growing skills. She's been teaching locally for 11 years, and is a well-known demonstrator at craft shows. Bring your own J-cloth, scissors, Stanley knife and hammer as well as your chair; if the seat is less than 12in across at the front, bring two. Also

● *However elegant and valuable (or humble) your chair,* **Betty Fowler** *will teach you to reseat it. Make sure it's repaired and clean first*

please let us know when you book if you want to eat royally — we have a chance to arrange some really good catering, but we need everyone to book it to make it worthwhile. It's £15 extra for all the coffee, tea, biscuits and cake you can eat and drink, plus excellent hot lunches served in style!

## Survival metalwork — Bob Grant

15 March 1986, Oxford, £25+VAT. Despite his range of capabilities, Bob is first and foremost a woodworker, so there's no danger of someone talking at you in engineering language. This sort of knowledge is vital for building up and maintaining your own workshop — grinding and sharpening tool steel, hardening and tempering, repairing broken bandsaw blades (silver-soldering), brazing repairs to plane bodies and the like, drilling and tapping holes, turning brass and aluminium. Equip yourself with basic know-how in this important subject, and who knows if you mightn't be the next Mr Norris?

# Guild courses

### Hand veneering — Bob Grant

12 April 1986, Oxford, £35+VAT. Another date for this popular subject, in which a sound basis is essential if you want to develop in cabinet- or clock-making, restoration and many other skills besides. You will be laying a panel with veneer, mitreing a crossbanding, inlaying lines, and putting a balancer on the back; Bob will also be demonstrating more advanced inlay techniques, and will have samples of cartouches to show. Local harpsichord maker **Peter Sarac** will offer help and advice.

### Design and workshop drawing — Bob Grant

22 February 1986, Oxford, £25+VAT. At last! The beginning of our **Woodworking basics** series, which we're working hard to expand and set up all over the country so that everyone will get a chance. Head of Craft Design and Technology at a large Oxford comprehensive school, and regular contributor to these pages, Bob will get you into freehand sketching, the use of grid paper and drawing-boards, useful and accurate workshop geometry (setting out ellipses, for instance), making and using setting-out rods and templates, and a battery of other skills without which your work will just never get off the ground.

### Power routing — Roy Sutton

8 February 1986, Herne Bay, £25+VAT. We're very glad to offer a course from this well-known and popular expert on the subject. Chris Storey's story (see 'Routing around') provides a good indication of the help and instruction Roy gives. He starts from first principles (the best place) and goes through numerous operations, including housing, grooving, rebating, straight and circular moulding, tenoning, mortising, and rule-joint and template work; plus, of course, designing and setting up your own jigs. He hasn't worked out how to make a router dance and sing yet, but it shouldn't be long.

### Furniture restoration — Eric Burger

17-19 January 1986, Bournemouth, £70+VAT. A very good price for three day's intensive instruction and work on your own piece. But don't worry if you haven't got anything on the stocks at the moment; Eric will set you up with many of the basic restoring skills so you can go away and practise. Plenty of time to strip, repair and re-finish; mend joints, veneers and marquetry; fill, patch and touch in, and glean many of the time-saving techniques of an experienced and successful professional.

### Woodmachining — Ken Taylor

7 December, Bletchley, £25+VAT. If 'Machining Wood' has sharpened your appetite, spend a day with our technical consultant — Ken's experience is wide and deep. He'll show you the techniques of circular, radial-arm and bandsawing, planing and thicknessing, spindle-moulding, and mortising on both horizontal and vertical machines. There are good-quality universal machines there too, and you'll be able not only to see them in action but get your hands on one. Ken is particularly good on safety and on jigs.

### French Polishing — Charles Cliffe

3-4 April 1986, Bexleyheath, £35+VAT. After the polisher's nightmare of the winter weather, spring is heralded by one of our longest-established and most popular courses. Prepare, strip and re-finish surfaces; introduce yourself to the mysteries of the cabinet scraper, stains and staining; learn the vagaries of shellac finishes and their application, including bodying up and spiriting off. Charles also takes a look at other finishes, and is extra-helpful with advice. Bring a cabinet scraper if you have one, and a piece of furniture to work on and/or ask about.

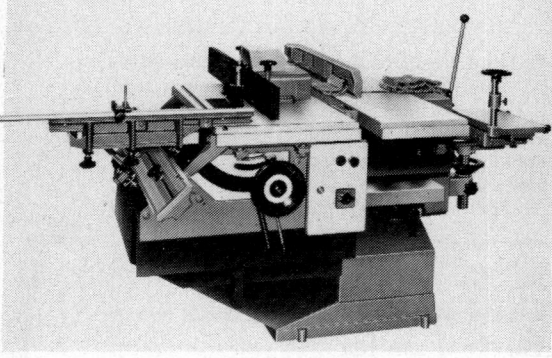

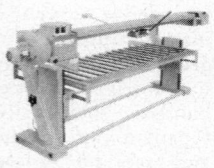

# Caravan roots

## Who better than a gipsy to restore the dwellings his forebears made? Ivan Broadhead reports

Thirty years in the open would put paid to most fine antiques. Happily, Eddie Morton's caravan is made to the standards of 1897, and it's survived.

After a full working life it spent about 16 years on its axles behind a farm, followed by another 16 years in an orchard in Otley, Yorkshire, where Eddie found it. The design is known as a Reading, because it's based on that of the straight-sided caravans originally built by Duttons of Reading; but no two were exactly alike.

They were made entirely of mahogany, and were consequently very heavy — a factor which was no cause for concern to travelling folk in the flat countryside of the Thames valley. However, when William Wright of Rothwell Haigh, near Leeds, copied the style in 1897 he had to keep in mind the hills of Yorkshire; so he used canary whitewood, which is also completely knot-free. This caravan is the only one of its kind built by Wright, because he went bankrupt after creating it, but its sister — a Ledge style which he built in the same year — is now in the Castle Museum at York.

The Reading caravan weighs about 1½ tons, is some 14ft long by 7ft wide and stands 10ft 6in high on its wheels. If that seems small for a family, Eddie reminds doubters that his grandparents raised 12 children in theirs!

A Romany himself, Eddie expects to spend something like £10,000 on materials alone. He'll use at least 500 books of gold leaf, each costing £15, and the van needs new wheels and a new roof.

Basically all the carved decorative bits and the side wings are of ash. There are also six carved lion's heads mounted on the roof, which are each fitted with a lead flash through the mouth to act as a rainwater spout.

'We think of a lion today as being like the ones we see in films,' says Eddie; 'but lions in those days were ugly. As horses in old oil paintings have long bodies, so the lions were as grotesque as the gargoyles on York Minster. Modern heads on this van would look like modern furniture in an old cottage; so I copy off the originals, and I've been very fortunate to get much of the old timber.'

He is using skills, such as carving and painting, learned from years of watching members of his family at work. Chisels, rasps, spokeshaves and a 'peg-knife' (an old cobbler's knife) are among the tools which he's been handed down.

'There were no nails whatsoever on this van,' he remarks. 'All the pieces are jointed and glued, and I've used pegs and dowels to secure rebuilt bits.' He adds: 'You couldn't do this work if you didn't love it. Working on this caravan makes me feel closer to past generations of my family, wondering whether they've ever lived in it or worked on it.

'I don't class myself as a tradesman because I never went to school hardly, but I know how to do things. I've had joiners here, painters and decorators, people in those trades, and they say, "We can't do that, it's impossible."'

Eddie applies seven coats of vivid red, greens, maroon and gold paint, and three coats of varnish. One particularly striking feature of the decoration is the giant sunflower motif on the door, which was the symbol of William Wright.

'There are very few people restoring these caravans, and I've had offers for this one from all over the world. Numerous British people have approached me, and I've had offers equal to the price of two good houses from Sweden and America. But these things are part of old England, and I'd like it to go to an English museum.'

Eddie has restored nine caravans which are now in use, and has even built small ones from scratch. He already has his eyes firmly set on caravan number 11. This is a smaller Ledge model — 10ft long by 6ft wide — also by William Wright: a dilapidated specimen owned by a Leeds businessman who bought it for £12, 30 years ago as it was about to be burned. After serving as a garden shed for many years, it now awaits its turn for a new life. ∎

● *Eddie Morton tries the fit of the fully restored rear door and window. The sunflower motif was a speciality of maker William Wright*

● *The frame-and-circle draw-gear of the Reading caravan is in ash; it leans against Eddie's next job, the 1897 Ledge model*

● *Each edge of the ventilation slats is individually carved, chamfered and finished in bright colours*

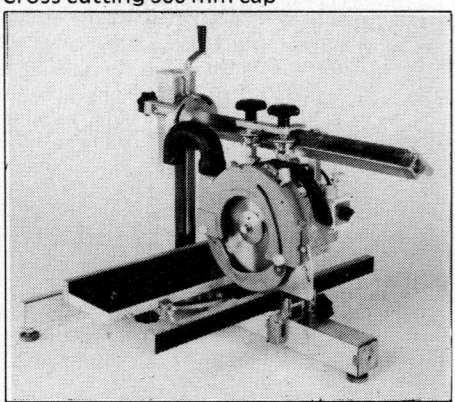

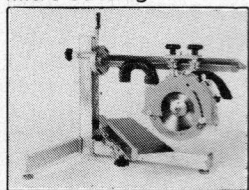

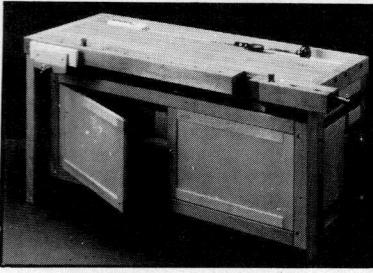

# The grand furniture saga:1

**The true history of the world's furniture involves an epic voyage across time and the globe. Fortified with a lifetime's expertise, Vic Taylor embarks**

● *The influence of Egypt never dies: Andrew Pinborough made this marquetry panel at the London College of Furniture earlier this year*

**W**oodworker recently concluded a series entitled 'English Furniture'. It ran to 11 parts — yet, in essence, it was describing only the merest local manifestation of something much deeper and very widespread.

This 'something' is the gradual development of furniture from its beginnings. At the back of our minds, many of us vaguely recognise such a process. What very few appreciate is the magnitude of the influences at work — nor the crucial importance among them of factors such as trading links, religious belief and military conquest.

To clear my mind on this subject, I attempted to draw a 'family tree' which would outline the full evolution of modern furniture styles. But the tree quickly became such an intricate tracery of boughs and twigs depicting styles and their inter-relationships that I gave up before reaching even one root! So I was thrown back to the excellent advice given by the King to Alice (in Wonderland): 'Begin at the beginning; go on until you come to the end; then stop'.

**W**e have to go back to the days of ancient Egypt, Assyria, Greece and Rome for our beginnings. The earliest surviving furniture has been found mainly in the tombs of the kings, Pharaohs and high-ranking officials. Some of the best-known finds have come from the tomb of Tutankhamun, who died about 1350BC. We can glean some knowledge, too, from depictions in wall paintings, vase paintings and the like.

Figs 1-12 show some typical examples from these ancient civilisations. One characteristic is common to all — they show furniture as used by the ruling classes; there is no sign of that used by the mass of people. The same can, in fact, be said of any period anywhere in the world before, say, AD1200. Any furniture belonging to the ordinary people must have been crude, for it has perished long ago, while only that which was the property of the nobility (or, later, the church) was considered worthy of embellishment and enrichment.

The items used by these ancient peoples seem to have been restricted to couches, chests, stools, small tables, and chairs. At meal-times the nobility reclined on couches and ate their food from small tables; the large communal dining-table was unknown. Thrones or throne-chairs were reserved for the highest-ranking dignitary present, and almost always had an accompanying footstool so that the chair itself could be made

larger and more impressive. There do not appear to have been any cupboards, and what could not be put into chests was hung from hooks in the walls (this practice could well have originated the groups of 'trophies', bows, arrows, musical instruments and the like, produced by woodcarvers in the 16th and 17th centuries).

**I**ntriguingly, the furniture was framed up with joints very similar to those we use today, such as the mortise and tenon, the dovetail and the mitre; some were pegged, while others were fixed with metal nails. Yet this method of framed construction vanished from western Europe and did not re-appear until the 14th and 15th centuries

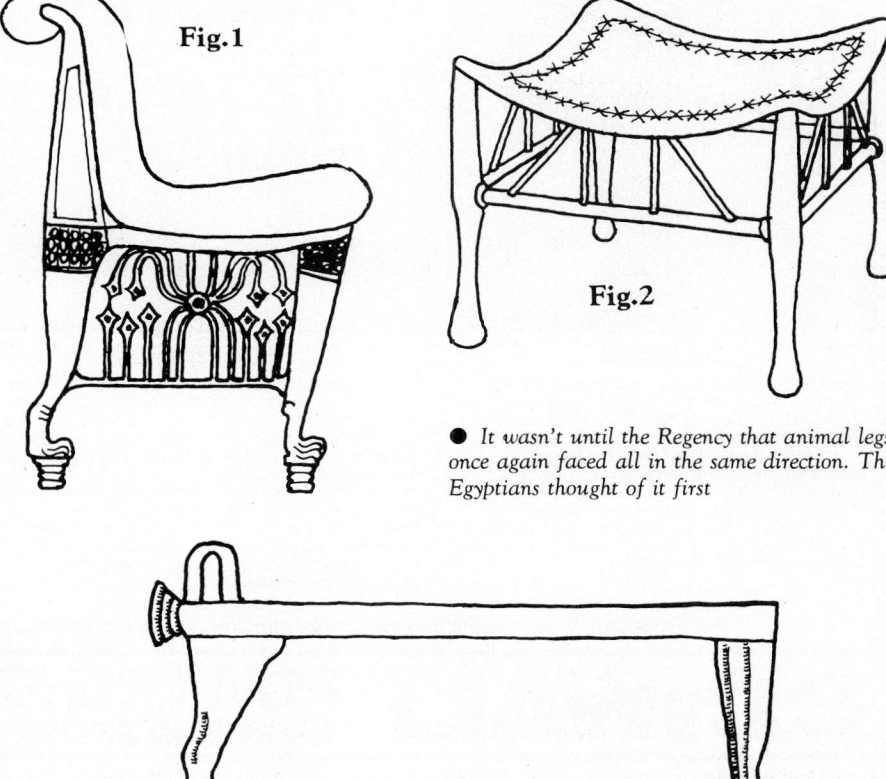

**Fig.1**

**Fig.2**

● *It wasn't until the Regency that animal legs once again faced all in the same direction. The Egyptians thought of it first*

**Fig.3**

961

# You never saw better!

The DeWalt Powershop will transform your woodworking capability. Its unique combination of precision, versatility and ease of use, long appreciated by professionals, is increasingly convincing the home woodworker and tradesman to make the DeWalt Powershop the centre-piece in his workshop.

The quiet, maintenance-free induction motor has a full 1½hp output to cope effortlessly with even the toughest hardwood.

In its standard form, the DeWalt Powershop will perform all the basic sawcuts, with the two models offering a choice of 380mm or 465mm crosscut capacity (640/730mm max. ripping width). Combined with the range of optional attachments, it becomes a complete workshop.

The DeWalt Powershop makes even the most demanding woodworking project easier, quicker and more accurate.

How much longer can you get by without one?

## SPECIAL OFFER

Free starter set of attachments when you buy a DW1251 or DW1501/3 Powershop this Autumn/Winter from participating dealers (subject to availability). Set consists of:-

- DA2000 Dado Head for grooving, rebating and tenoning.
- DA220 Drum Sander for contour and internal sanding.
- DA2073 Extra sanding sheets for DA220.
- DA231 200mm Disc Sander for general sanding.
- DA2090 Powershop handbook – packed with hints on how to make the most of your DeWalt Powershop.

Total list value **£69.00** *including VAT.*

*Price guide for DW1251 Powershop around £395.00 inc. VAT. (DW1501=£459.00 inc. VAT).*

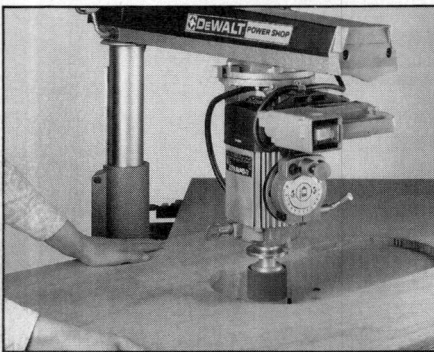

### PRECISION

The cast iron arm and substantial steel support column complement the clamping levers and machined locations for the most common cutting angles to ensure superb rigidity.

Calibrated scales are provided for setting accurately the cutting angle required. Once set, the robust Powershop will hold in that position for repeated cuts to produce identical workpieces.

Consistent accuracy is the hallmark of DeWalt, and the Powershop is fully adjustable to maintain accuracy throughout its long life.

### VERSATILITY

The Powershop's standard equipment provides for crosscutting, bevels, mitres and ripcuts, as well as dishing, hollowing and circle-cutting, while the optional attachments enable grooving, tenoning, rebating, edge-moulding, curved and straight sanding and even drilling.

With the special mounting bracket, most Elu plunging routers can also be secured to the Powershop, giving enormous scope for accurate decorative work. With all this versatility you can tackle even the most ambitious woodworking projects with confidence.

### EASE OF USE

Despite its versatility, the Powershop needs access only on three sides (unlike a traditional sawbench) so it can be positioned conveniently on an existing bench or on its optional legstand against the wall of your workshop, leaving more space free for other activity.

All operations with the Powershop are conducted with ease, accuracy and safety. Simple, yet positive controls enable quick adjustment of the depth and angle of cut.

Even the most complicated woodworking joints can be easily mastered with the DeWalt Powershop.

*For a free copy of the Powershop Colour Wallchart and the name of your nearest participating dealer, write to:-*

## ◆ DeWALT POWERSHOP ® THERE'S NO BETTER WAY TO WORK WITH WOOD

DeWalt Powershop Offer, Dept. ·      , Black & Decker Professional Products Division, Westpoint, The Grove, Slough, Berkshire SL1 1QQ. or Telephone (0753) 74277 and ask for "Service & Information Centre".

962

# The grand furniture saga:1

— although it continued to be used in the Byzantine culture.

Most of the ancient world had little in the way of timber resources, and very few sizeable trees which could be converted into wide planks. This meant that flat surfaces and cladding had to be built up with comparatively narrow strips joined edge-to-edge with a kind of tongue-and-groove joint. To hide these joints several expedients were employed: gesso was one — painted or gilded, or overlaid with silver foil. Any goldsmith will tell you that the techniques of gold-leafing have changed very little. Fig. 13 shows Egyptian gilders at work about 1380BC.

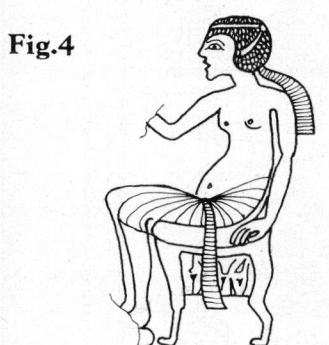

**Fig.4**

● **Above:** An Egyptian chair in use. **Below** is a couch from ancient Assyria

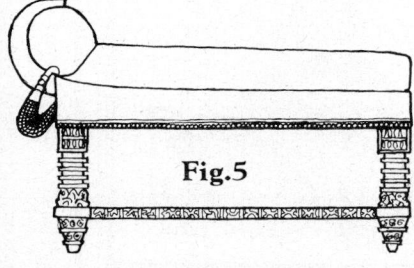

**Fig.5**

Marquetry was also used, employing thin sheets of both wood and ivory, and the patterns often included precious stones.

You will notice that some of the pieces illustrated have turned parts, and indeed the lathe seems to have been widely employed in all the ancient civilisations. Although nothing can be proven, it was probably invented in the Orient. The early lathes seem to have consisted of two convenient trees with a spike inserted into the inward-facing side of each to act as head-stock and tail-stock. The blank was mounted between them, able to rotate freely, and the rotary motion was probably imparted by a treadle. It would have been a to-and-fro rotation like that of a pole-lathe. The Egyptians and Greeks brought turning up to a fine art — so fine, in fact, that the Greeks sometimes overdid it and produced work which was very delicate and too fragile. You can see from figs 5, 6 & 7 that turning was also used in the time of the Assyrian kings, as the drawing is based on wall paintings of about 900BC.

Materials other than wood, ivory and

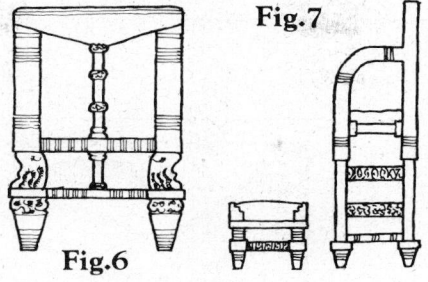

**Fig.6** **Fig.7**

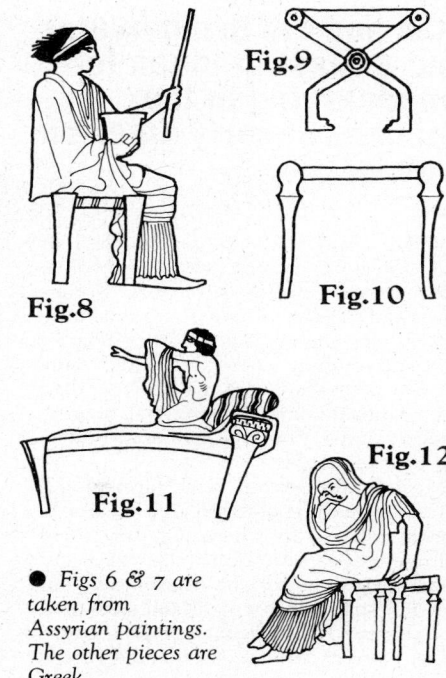

**Fig.8** **Fig.9** **Fig.10** **Fig.11** **Fig.12**

● *Figs 6 & 7 are taken from Assyrian paintings. The other pieces are Greek*

jewels were widely used, the chief being stone, bronze and silver. The little folding tripod table in silver in fig. 15 is a particularly beautiful example. The Etruscans made many of their tables and chests in bronze. They also created a kind of forerunner of the modern tub-chair, with a drum-shaped base which was carried up to form a back and curved arms. It may have been this which inspired the Romans to make their version of what we would call a hall porter's chair in the first centuries AD: it was made in wickerwork, and the back was extended up and over to form a kind of hood. It seems that this was frequently of British origin, and was exported to Rome!

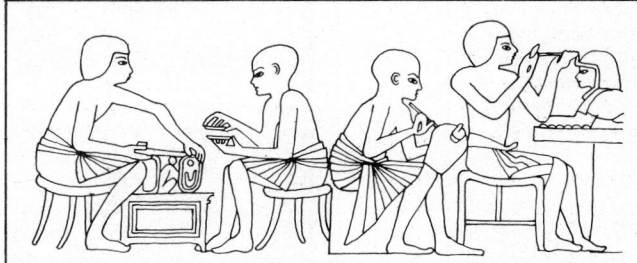

**Fig.13**

● *Gilding, like inlay and veneer work, was much used in ancient Egypt*

Ancient designs, of course, have often inspired modern ones, and it's worth noting the use of animal motifs for the arms and legs of chairs and tables; the Egyptians, in particular, were fond of lion's paws as feet and bird's heads as terminals. This usage was revived in the latter half of the 18th century in the French Empire and the English neo-classical styles. In passing, it is pretty obvious that the cabriole leg was inspired by the style of the legs shown in figs 1, 2 & 4. ('Cabriole', by the way, used to be spelt 'capriole' and means 'leap or caper like a horse without advancing'; its origins relate to the 'capra' or she-goat —

also capering, no doubt.) We cannot include the claw-and-ball foot, however, as it is definitely Oriental in origin and represents a dragon's claw clasping the pearl of wisdom.

The sacking of Rome in the fifth century AD led to a cultural parting of the ways. The western and northwestern parts of the Empire became embroiled in the bloody and barbaric strife of the Dark Ages, while the eastern — based on Byzantium — became the repository of the classical cultures. The story of how these two divergent movements came eventually to blend with and cross-fertilise each other belongs to the remainder of this series. ∎

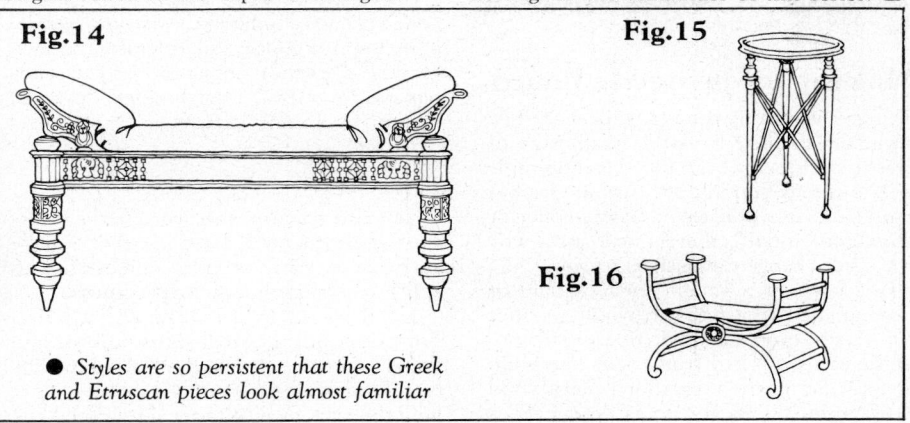

**Fig.14** **Fig.15** **Fig.16**

● *Styles are so persistent that these Greek and Etruscan pieces look almost familiar*

# Bakery making

**Alan and Gill Bridgewater find a feast of ideas for woodcarving in the kitchens of early America**

The American Colonial kitchen or 'keeping room' was an absolute treasury of fine woodwork. Butter-bowls and salt-trays; Bible-boxes and knife-racks; pipe-shelves and cutting-boards; cribs and spinning-wheels; tables and chairs . . . But best of all were the finely worked and beautifully carved *Springerle* boards, cookie-stamps, dough-rollers, and butter- and biscuit-moulds.

Most of the settlers were farmers and tradespeople who possessed very few wood-working skills. So where did they start? With crosscut saw, drawknife, adze and gouge they went for the nearest tree, cut it down, split it into boards and slabs, and then started work while the wood was green. As for patterns and designs, no doubt some had brought small items of woodware from the Old World; these could well have included shortbread moulds from Scotland, breadboards from Sweden, and *Springerle* boards from Germany (used for baking the little celebration biscuits known as *Springerle* cookies). But mostly the pioneer wood-workers had to improvise.

Initially there were no definable art or craft styles — there was just a coming together of various Old World folk traditions and designs. The approach that developed is direct, basic and honest. If an idea worked, it was valid.

For me the kitchenware captures the whole scene, with its delicate, fanciful, naively conceived motifs and its child-like interpretations of small birds and animals. And, of all these delightful 'mother-country' woodcarved items, the *Springerle* boards are the most interesting.

In early Pennsylvania German homes, every *Hausfrau* needed a set. The biscuit dough was rolled thin and pressed on to the carved hardwood boards, and the whole thing was popped into the oven. When the biscuits were taken out they were turned off the boards and then placed so that the little raised motifs and designs complemented the table arrangement.

## Making a *Springerle* board

In many ways this project is ideal for raw beginners because it uses a small piece of prepared timber, a basic tool-kit and simple techniques. If you like the overall idea but would rather work, say, a pastry-roller or shortbread-mould, there's no reason why you can't change the designs to suit.

Get yourself a small 1in-thick slab of close-grained knot-free hardwood — about 5in wide by 8in long will do fine. Go for one of the easily worked fruitwoods like plum or apple, or maybe a traditional dairy wood like sycamore. As for tools, you need a

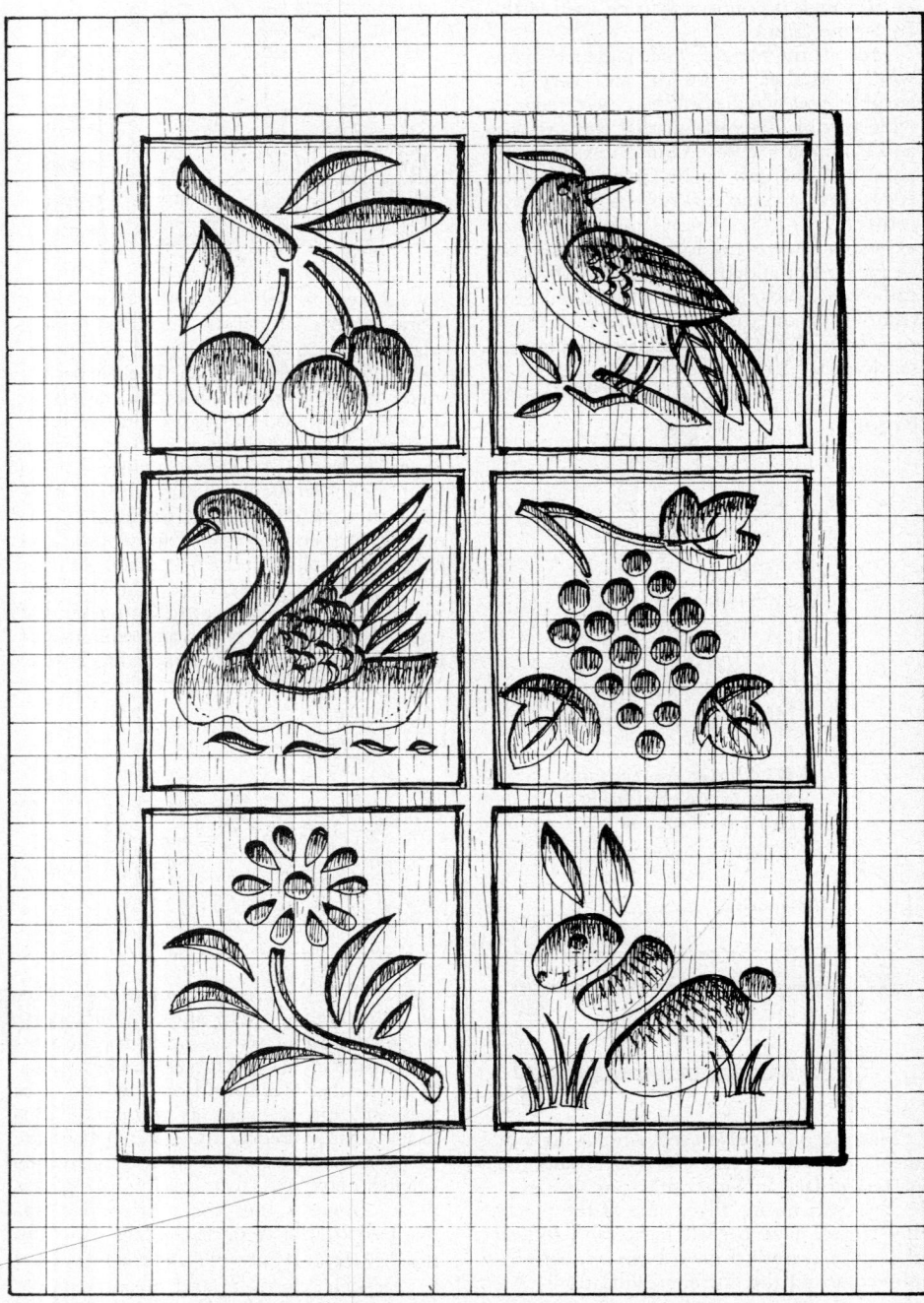

● *Finished drawing for a carved biscuit-mould: the shading helps to give the feeling*

bench clamp or holdfast; a V-section gouge; a small spoon gouge; a sharp knife; and such general workshop items as graded sand-papers, a metal straight-edge, pencils, layout paper and Plasticene.

### First steps

When you get your wood back to the work-shop, give it a good looking-over to make sure that it's clear of bark, grain twists, end splits, stains, mould and dead knots.

Now have a long look at the working drawings, inspirational illustrations and 'hand-and-tool' details, and see how the board is designed, set out and worked. Note how the various motifs are set within little

frames about 2¼in square, and how all the incised and detail is shallowly scoop-cut.

Then take the layout paper and start to rough out your own designs. Try not to copy slavishly every detail and stroke as illustrated; bring in your own ideas and whimsies, and maybe adjust the overall designs and proportions along the way. Perhaps you could personalise the project and have initials, puns on surnames, dates of christenings and weddings, or whatever.

Sketch and plan until you come up with a good, workable design. Finally, when you've achieved a well-considered master pattern, use carbon-paper or rub over the back of your drawing to transfer the design to the working face of your wood.

## Initial cuts

Secure the piece with G-cramps, holdfast or the like, take the knife and straight-edge, and score in the six frames that indicate the cutting or break-lines between the biscuits. Work each frame with a single, clean, ⅛in-deep cut.

This done, take the small V-section tool and, using the initial knife-incised lines as guides, trench out the frames. Try to keep the V-cuts straight and crisp, and be careful that your tool doesn't dig too deeply into

the grain or skid across the wood. Work with a considered, controlled action — guiding the tool in one hand, and pushing and manoeuvring with the other. Work on until your piece is nicely set out with six frames, as illustrated.

## Working the motifs

Have another good look at your master design, pencil in and re-establish the lines of the motifs, and then start cutting again. With the wood still cramped, take up the spoon gouge and tackle the design frame by frame.

Scoop out the deepest part of each motif — say, the hollows of the cherries, the body of the swan and the little hollows that go to make up the shape of the rabbit. Aim to get the little dips and scoops about ¼in deep. Don't dig the tool straight down into the grain or try to force or lever it; work the little concavities with a delicate scooping and paring action.

Cut across the grain wherever possible. Only remove small curls of wood, and try all the while to keep the carving crisp and controlled. If you feel at any time that your tool is cutting up rough, either approach the grain from another angle or maybe give the tool edge a couple of strokes on the stone and leather. Bear in mind that each carved motif needs to be smoothly cut — no undercuts, deep holes or rough surfaces.

From time to time, make a trial pressing with the Plasticene — warming it, and then rolling or pressing it into the cut shapes. See how the pressed form lifts clear of the mould, and then carefully consider your progress. Could the hollows be deeper? Do the scooped depressions produce nicely rounded, plump shapes? And so on. Be super-critical, and adjust your work accordingly.

● *Left:* A 19th-century biscuit-mould. *Below:* This 'working drawing' uses thick lines for surface cuts and thin lines for incised detail in the hollows

grain

1″

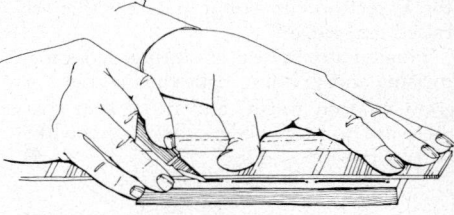

● *Above: The carved 'frames' are set in with a knife against a steel straight-edge. Then a V-tool is used (below) to cut the grooves, about ⅛in deep*

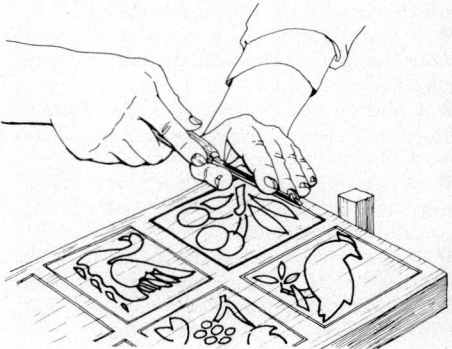

# Bakery making

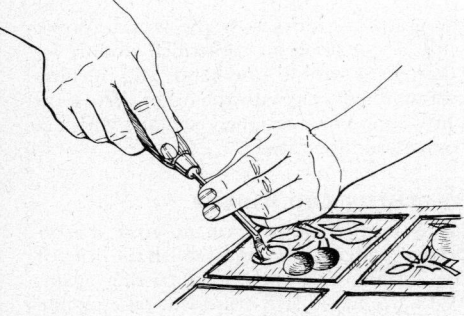

● *Scooping out with the spoon-bit gouge (above) demands a watchful eye for short grain. Working at the wrong angle can result in tearing*

● **Above:** *This sectional drawing shows the simplicity of the shapes, which can be worked with very few tools*

## Final cuts

When the main part of each motif has been scoop-cut with the spoon gouge and you're pleased with the overall design, you need to cut in the final details and textures.

Take your V-section tool or your knife, and start to work in all the little chip and sliver cuts. Add in the wing patterns, the various stalks and leaves, and all the other little details that go to make the total of the designs and motifs. Along the way, stop and take more Plasticene impressions: see how the V-section cuts result in details that are raised and ridged.

Finally, after a deal of cutting, scooping, incising and pressing, take the carving to a good smooth finish, and make sure that there are no ragged edges, burrs or the like — and the job is done. ■

● **Above:** *A set of pastry rollers.* **Below** *is a two-piece butter-mould – note the locating pegs*

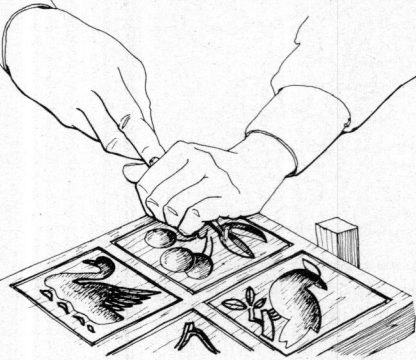

● **Above:** *A piece of Plasticene will show how you're progressing. It may be wise to cut a motif on scrap wood before starting*

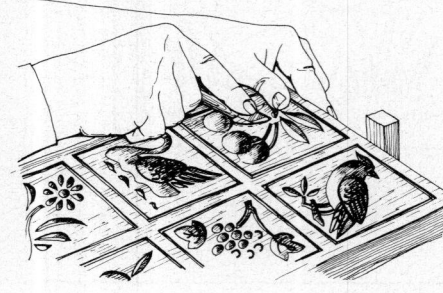

● *The leaves and stalks call for simple chip-cuts (above). The pointed ends are formed by pairs of angled cuts.* **Below:** *All the fine detail is worked with careful strokes of a knife or V-tool*

### Notes and afterthoughts

● This board is going to be used for cooking, so it can't be sealed or waxed. Just wipe it over with a damp cloth and then rub a little cooking oil into the grain.
● If your carving is a success, maybe you could hang it on the wall, or perhaps even take a plaster cast.
● Children love playing with pastry, Plasticene and clay; maybe you could re-work this project to make a toy?
● When you're finishing the board, take a rasp or sandpaper and knock off all the corners and sharp edges.
● If you decide to make a board with initials, letters, dates, names or the like, remember that they need to be cut and worked in reverse or mirror-image!

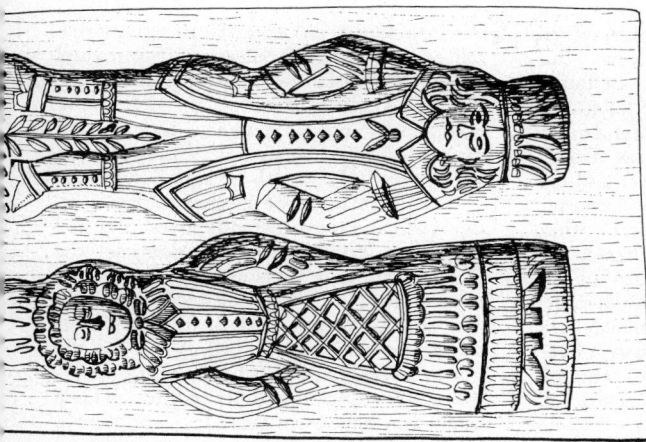

● *The cookie-mould **above** is typical of colonial America; at **right** is a Pennsylvania German Springerle board of 1843, measuring 8x6in. Inspiration enough!*

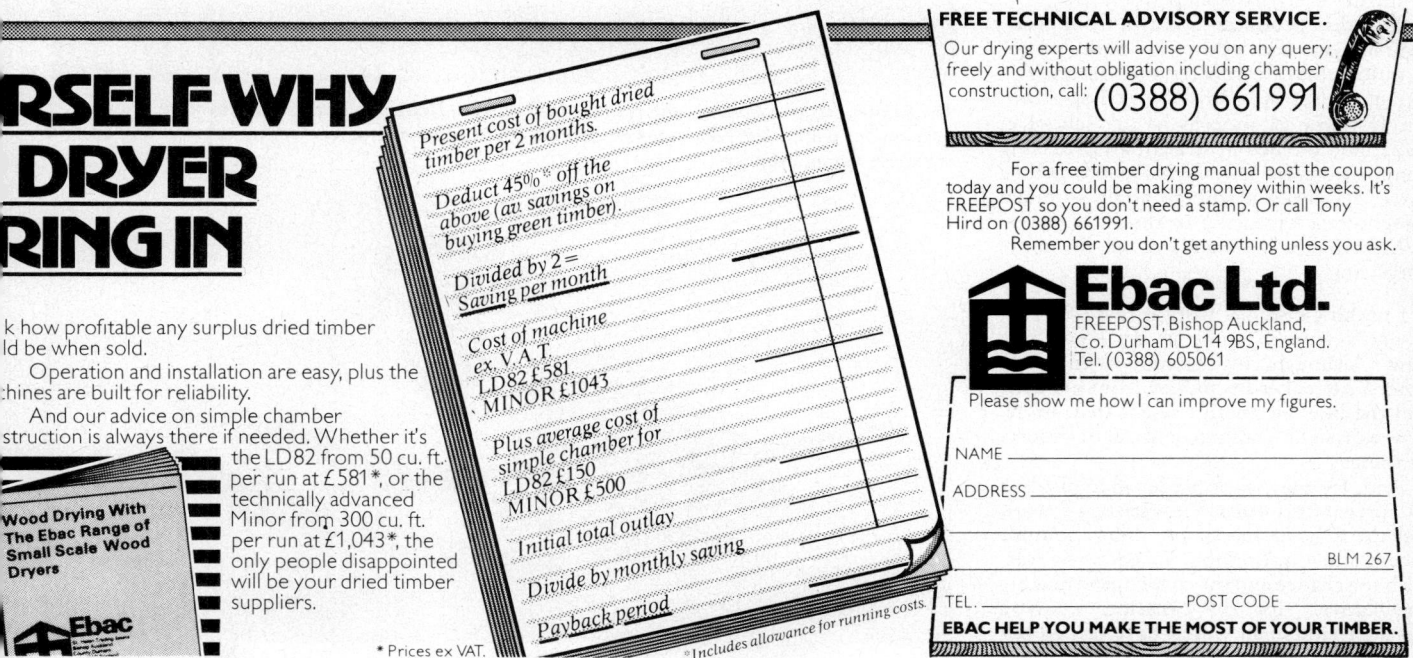

# Uncommon sensual

## Jonathan Hawkes is a designer-maker of remarkable range and accomplishment. Peter Collenette saw his work

The school woodworking prize at Eton is an award, I'd guess, to which mighty few cabinetmakers can lay claim. Especially professional ones.

But Jonathan Hawkes' real claim to distinction lies in a body of work whose sheer quality and variety would do enormous credit to any time-served tradesman — let alone a 30-year-old whose father is a chartered surveyor.

He currently runs two small companies. Professional Woodworkers, based in Pewsey, Wiltshire, concentrates on specialised commissions and small production runs of specific pieces; the London Alcove Company does shopfitting, cupboards and shelving, including a standard pattern of alcove unit. Ancillary products include some very idiosyncratic chopping-boards and other kitchen accessories.

The no-nonsense names Jonathan has chosen for his concerns stand in sharp contrast to those of the other enterprises with which he's previously been involved. These include Looner Landskates, which made skateboards and wheels, and a company called Hurricane Toke which numbered among its commissions the 8ft boardroom table, reception furniture and logo for a firm of City accountants. His current set-up dates from 1983, and employs an old friend and fellow-craftsman named Steve Pawsey plus two other workers and a YTS trainee. The London Alcove Company is a partnership.

His other products have run from backgammon sets and 'odd pieces of sculpture' to quite a bit of carpentry and joinery. Although he set up a small workshop at the family home as soon as he left school in 1972, and pitched in straight away making commissions for friends, his woodworking career has been a stop-go affair — much interrupted, especially in the early stages. Which makes his standards all the more surprising.

If nothing else, his story is that of a man who's always ready to try something new. Although, in common with many others, he makes his money from kitchens and the like, he doesn't resent that. In his own words, he 'dips into and out of all sorts of things'.

And, for the visitor hardened to displays of current furniture, the variety of work was the most extraordinary thing about his recent show in London. Faced, as he was, with the chance and the challenge of making speculatively for the occasion, many a designer-craftsman would have turned out a batch of related work in pursuit of personal themes or obsessions. But Jonathan's range includes a nest of tables copied from an Edward Barnsley design, the lovely Chinese table pictured here and taken direct from the pages of Gustav Ecke's classic *Chinese Domestic Furniture*, and the remarkable Art Deco 'honeymoon chaise', as well as the individualistic spiral coffee-tables and sculptures which represent his own explorations. The very idea of the artist-maker is, after all, not much older than this century; conventionally, the working cabinetmaker has always been something of a chameleon — adapting his skills to whatever styles his customers appreciate.

Nonetheless, Jonathan's liking for fancy timbers and embellishments is clearly apparent. The Barnsley tables are in macassar ebony and kingwood, while tulipwood, purpleheart, avodire and gonçalo alves also make their appearance. Not content with that, he and Steve Pawsey have inlaid the top of an otherwise unremarkable pillar-table with 578 pieces of abalone shell (I say 'unremarkable', but the table is made of a wood called siricote with which you're no doubt familiar!). Steve also designed and made a low table, again very Chinese, whose top sports £400-worth of lapis lazuli.

'Furniture must be elegant and easy to live with, and it must stand the test of time,' proclaims Jonathan. But he also uses the words 'fun' and 'sensual' to describe his current output. 'Pricey' is another epithet that springs to mind, at £2400+VAT for the pillar-table and £3700+VAT for the honeymoon chaise. At that level, top workmanship is the only option. 'Although Eton might not have been geared to woodworking,' says Jonathan with charming obliqueness, 'they had a friendly workshop and a very good woodworking teacher.' Since then, clearly, he has never looked back.

● Jonathan Hawkes, 1 Church St, Pewsey, Wilts SN9 5DL, tel. (0672) 62878.

● *Above,* 'tiger' *sycamore, taffeta and lush curves.* **Below,** *black walnut, avodire – and a geometrical teaser: but how many modernists could equal the veneer-work and moulding on that strangely frozen cylinder?*

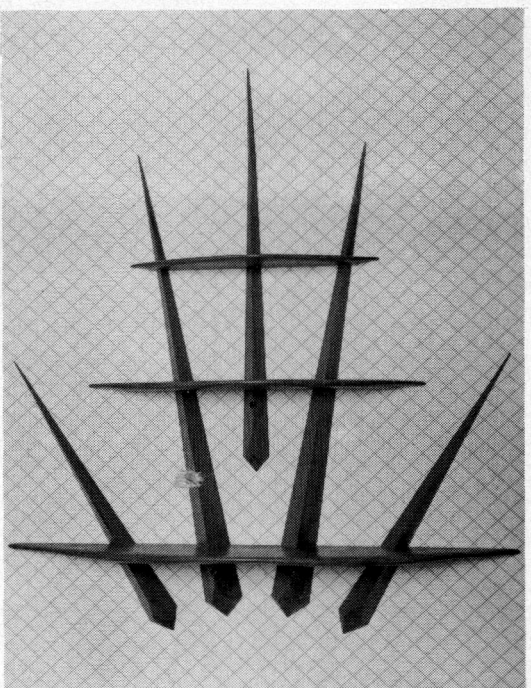

● *Fancy, to be sure – but too good to be self-indulgent. Ebony, siricote and abalone shell have found their way into the subtly startling pillar-table **above**. **Below:** The marvels of Chinese Ming design have worked their magic on many; Jonathan's reproduction uses Indian rosewood*

● **Top:** *The Hawkes approach to shelving is nothing if not eye-catching.* **Below:** *Spiral coffee-tables are something of a stock line, having put in appearances at several shows. They come in different sizes and different timbers, and a pigmented-lacquer finish is also an option*

## AVON

**BATH**  Tel. Bath 64513
JOHN HALL TOOLS  ★
RAILWAY STREET

Open: Monday-Saturday
9.00 a.m.-5.30 p.m.
H.P.W.WM.D.A.BC.

**BRISTOL**  Tel. (0272) 741510
JOHN HALL TOOLS LIMITED  ★
CLIFTON DOWN SHOPPING CENTRE
WHITELADIES ROAD
Open: Monday-Saturday
9.00 a.m.-5.30 p.m.
H.P.W.WM.D.A.BC.

**BRISTOL**  Tel. (0272) 629092
TRYMWOOD SERVICES
2a DOWNS PARK EAST, (off North View)
WESTBURY PARK
Open: 8.30 a.m.-5.30 p.m. Mon. to Fri.
Closed for lunch 1.00-2.00 p.m.
P.W.WM.D.T.A.BC.

**BRISTOL**  Tel. (0272) 667013
WILLIS
157 WEST STREET
BEDMINISTER
Open Mon.-Fri. 8.30 a.m.-5.00 p.m.
No Saturday opening

## BEDFORDSHIRE

**BEDFORD**  Tel. (0234) 59808
BEDFORD SAW SERVICE  K
39 AMPTHILL ROAD

Open: Mon.-Fri. 8.30-5.30
Sat. 9.00-4.00
H.P.A.BC.W.CS.WM.D.

## BERKSHIRE

**COOKHAM**  Tel. (06285) 20350
CHURCH'S TIMBER
STATION HILL

Open: Mon-Sat 8.30 a.m.-5.30 p.m.
Wed 8.30 a.m.-1.00 p.m.
H.P.W.T.CS.MF.A.

**READING**  Tel. (0734) 591361
HOME CARE CENTRE
26/30 KING'S ROAD

Open: Monday-Saturday
9.00 a.m.-5.30 p.m.
H.P.W.D.A.WM.BC.

**READING**  Tel. Littlewick Green
DAVID HUNT (TOOL  2743
MERCHANTS) LTD  ★
KNOWL HILL, NR. READING
Open: Monday-Saturday
9.00 a.m.-5.30 p.m.
H.P.W.D.A.BC.

## BERKSHIRE

**READING**  Tel. Reading 661511
WOKINGHAM TOOL CO. LTD.
99 WOKINGHAM ROAD

Open: Mon-Sat 9.00 a.m.-5.30 p.m.
Closed 1.00-2.00 p.m. for lunch
H.P.W.WM.D.CS.A.BC.

## BUCKINGHAMSHIRE

**SLOUGH**  Tel. (06286) 5125
BRAYWOOD ESTATES LTD  ★
158 BURNHAM LANE

Open: 9.00 a.m.-5.30 p.m.
Monday-Saturday
H.P.W.WM.CS.A.

**MILTON KEYNES**  Tel. (0908)
POLLARD WOODWORKING  641366
CENTRE  ★
51 AYLESBURY ST., BLETCHLEY
Open: Mon-Fri 8.30-5.30
Saturday 9.00-5.00
H.P.W.WM.D.CS.A.BC.

**HIGH WYCOMBE**  Tel. (0494)
SCOTT SAWS LTD.  24201/33788
14 BRIDGE STREET  ★

Mon.-Sat. 8.30 a.m.-6.00 p.m.

H.P.W.WM.D.T.CS.MF.A.BC.

**HIGH WYCOMBE**  Tel. (0494)
ISAAC LORD LTD  22221
185 DESBOROUGH ROAD  KE

Open: Mon-Fri 8.00 a.m.-5.00 p.m.
Saturday 9.00 a.m.-5.00 p.m.
H.P.W.D.A.

## CAMBRIDGESHIRE

**CAMBRIDGE**  Tel. (0223) 63132
D. MACKAY LTD.  E★
BRITANNIA WORKS, EAST ROAD

Open: Mon.-Fri. 8.30 a.m.-1 p.m./2.00-
5.00 p.m. Sat. 8.30 a.m.-1.00 p.m.
H.P.W.D.T.CS.MF.A.BC.

**CAMBRIDGE**  Tel. (0223) 247386
H. B. WOODWORKING  K
105 CHERRY HINTON ROAD
Open: 8.30 a.m.-5.30 p.m.
Monday-Friday
8.30 a.m.-1.00 p.m. Sat.
H.P.W.WM.D.CS.A.

**PETERBOROUGH**  Tel. (0733)
WILLIAMS DISTRIBUTORS  64252
(TOOLS) LIMITED  K
108-110 BURGHLEY ROAD
Open: Monday to Friday
8.30 a.m.-5.30 p.m.
H.P.A.W.D.WH.BC.

## CHESHIRE

**NANTWICH**  Tel. Crewe 67010
ALAN HOLTHAM  K★
THE OLD STORES TURNERY
WISTASON ROAD, WILLASTON
Open: Tues.-Sat. 9.00 a.m.-5.30 p.m.
Closed Monday
P.W.WM.D.T.C.CS.A.BC.

**CHEADLE**  Tel: 061491 1726
ERIC TOMKINSON  ★
86 STOCKPORT ROAD
Open: Mon.-Fri. 9.00 a.m.-4.00 p.m.
Saturday 9.00 a.m.-1.00 p.m.
H.P.W.D.MF.A.BC.

## CLEVELAND

**MIDDLESBROUGH**  Tel. (0642)
CLEVELAND WOODCRAFT  813103
(M'BRO), 38-42 CRESCENT ROAD  K

Open: Mon-Sat 9.15 a.m.-5.30 p.m.

H.P.T.A.BC.W.WM.CS.D.

## CORNWALL

**HELSTON**  Tel. Helston (03265) 4961
SOUTH WEST  Truro (0872) 71671
POWER TOOLS  Launceston
MONUMENT ROAD  (0566) 3555
  K
H.P.W.WM.D.CS.A.

**TRURO**  Tel. (0872) 71671
TRURO POWER TOOLS  E★
30 FERRIS TOWN

Open Mon.-Sat. 8.00 a.m.-12.30 p.m./
1.30 p.m.-5.00 p.m.
H.P.W.WM.D.CS.MF.A.BC.

## CUMBRIA

**CARLISLE**  Tel: (0228) 36391
W. M. PLANT
ALLENBROOK ROAD
ROSEHILL, CA1 2UT
Open: Mon.-Fri. 8.00 a.m.-5.15 p.m.
Sat. 8.00 a.m.-12.30 noon
P.W.WM.D.CS.A.

## DERBYSHIRE

**DERBY**  Tel. (0332) 41862
HAZLEHURSTS LTD.  E★
LONDON ROAD AND CANAL STREET

Open: Mon.-Sat. 8.30 a.m.-5.30 p.m. (retail)
Mon.-Fri. 8.00 a.m.-5.00 p.m. (trade)
H.P.W.MF.A.BC.

**BUXTON**  Tel. (0298) 871636
CRAFT SUPPLIES  K★
THE MILL, MILLERSDALE

Open: Mon-Sat 9.00 a.m.-5.00 p.m.

H.P.W.D.T.CS.A.BC.

## DEVON

**BRIXHAM**  Tel. (08045) 4900
WOODCRAFT SUPPLIES  E★
4 HORSE POOL STREET

Open: Mon.-Sat. 9.00 a.m.-6.00 p.m.

H.P.W.A.D.MF.CS.BC.

**PLYMOUTH**  Tel. (0752) 330303
WESTWARD BUILDING SERVICES  ★
LTD., LISTER CLOSE, NEWNHAM
INDUSTRIAL ESTATE, PLYMPTON
Open: Mon-Fri 8.00 a.m.-5.30 p.m.
Sat. 8.30 a.m.-12.30 p.m.
H.P.W.WM.D.A.BC.

## DORSET

**BOURNEMOUTH**  Tel: (0202) 420583
POWER TOOL SERVICES
(Sales, spares, repairs)
849-851 CHRISTCHURCH ROAD
BOSCOMBE
Open: Mon.-Fri. 9.00 a.m.-5.30 p.m.
Sat. 9.00 a.m.-5.00 p.m.
H.P.W.CS.K.A.

## ESSEX

**LEIGH ON SEA**  Tel. (0702)
MARSHAL & PARSONS LTD.  710404
1111 LONDON ROAD  EK

Open: 8.30 a.m.-5.30 p.m. Mon-Fri
9.00 a.m.-5.00 p.m. Sat.
H.P.W.WM.D.CS.A.

**ILFORD**
CUTWELL TOOLS LTD.  ★
774-776 HIGH ROAD

Mon.-Fri. 9.00 a.m.-5.00 p.m.
and also by appointment.
P.W.WM.A.D.CS.

## GLOUCESTER

**TEWKESBURY**  Tel. (0684)
TEWKESBURY SAW CO. LTD.  293092
TRADING ESTATE, NEWTOWN  K

Open: Mon-Fri 8.00 a.m.-5.00 p.m.
Saturday 9.30 a.m.-12.00 noon.
P.W.WM.D.CS.

## HAMPSHIRE

**SOUTHAMPTON**  Tel. (0703)
H.W.M.  776222
THE WOODWORKERS
303 SHIRLEY ROAD, SHIRLEY
Open: Tues-Fri 9.30 a.m.-6.00 p.m.
Sat 9.30 a.m.-4.00 p.m.
H.P.W.WM.D.CS.A.BC.T.

# shopguide

## HAMPSHIRE

**ALDERSHOT**    Tel. (0252) 334422
POWER TOOL CENTRE    **K**
374 HIGH STREET

Open: Mon.-Fri. 8.30 a.m.-5.30 p.m.
Sat. 8.30 a.m.-12.30 p.m.

H.P.W.WM.D.A.BC.

**PORTSMOUTH**    Tel. (0705)
EURO PRECISION TOOLS LTD    667332
259/263 LONDON ROAD, NORTH END    ★
     **E**

Open: Mon-Fri 9.00 a.m.-5.30 p.m.
Sat. 9.00 a.m.-1.00 p.m.

H.P.W.WM.D.A.BC.

**SOUTHAMPTON**    Tel. (0703)
POWER TOOL CENTRE    332288
7 BELVIDERE ROAD    **K★**
Open Mon.-Fri. 8.30-5.30

H.P.W.WM.D.A.BC.CS.MF.

## HUMBERSIDE

**GRIMSBY**    Tel. Grimsby (0472)
   58741 Hull (0482) 26999
J. E. SIDDLE LTD. (Tool Specialists)    ★
83 VICTORIA STREET
Open: Mon-Fri 8.30 a.m.-5.30 p.m.
Sat. 8.30 a.m.-12.45 p.m. & 2 p.m.-5 p.m.

H.P.A.BC.W.WMD.

## KENT

**WYE**    Tel. (0233) 813144
KENT POWER TOOLS LTD.
UNIT 1, BRIAR CLOSE
WYE, Nr. ASFORD

H.P.W.WM.D.A.CS.

**MATFIELD**    Tel. Brenchley
LEISURECRAFT IN WOOD    (089272)
'ORMONDE,' MAIDSTONE RD.    2465
TN12 7JG
Open: Mon-Sun
9.00 a.m.-5.30 p.m.

W.WM,D.T.A.

## LANCASHIRE

**PRESTON**    Tel. (0772) 52951
SPEEDWELL TOOL COMPANY    **E★**
62-68 MEADOW STREET PR1 1SU
Open: Mon.-Fri. 8.30 a.m.-5.30 p.m.
Sat. 8.30 a.m.-12.30 p.m.

H.P.W.WM.CS.A.MF.BC.

**ROCHDALE**    Tel. (0706) 342123/
C.S.M. TOOLS    342322
4-6 HEYWOOD ROAD    **E★**
CASTLETON
Open: Mon-Sat 9.00 a.m.-6.00 p.m.
Sundays by appointment

W.D.CS.A.BC.

**LANCASTER**    Tel. (0524) 32886
LILE TOOL SHOP    **K**
43/45 NORTH ROAD
Open: Monday to Saturday
9.00 a.m.-5.30 p.m.
Wed 9.00 a.m.-12.30 p.m.

H.P.W.D.A.

## LANCASHIRE

**BURY**    Tel. (061 764 6769)
HOUSE OF HARBRU    ★
101 CROSTONS ROAD
ELTON
Open: Mon.-Fri. 9.00 a.m.-5.00 p.m.
Send 2 × 1st class stamps for catalogue
MF.

**MANCHESTER**    Tel. (061 789)
TIMMS TOOLS    0909
102-104 LIVERPOOL ROAD    ★
PATRICROFT M30 0WZ
Weekdays 9.00 a.m.-5.30 p.m.
Sat. 9.00 a.m.-1.00 p.m.

H.P.A.W.

## LINCOLNSHIRE

**LINCOLN**    Tel. (0522) 689369
SKELLINGTHORPE SAW SERVICES LTD.
OLD WOOD, SKELLINGTHORPE
Open: Mon to Fri 8 a.m.-5 p.m.
Sat 8 a.m.-12 p.m.

H.P.W.WM.D.CS.A.*.BC.
     Access/Barclaycard

## LONDON

**ACTON**    Tel. (01-992) 4835
A. MILLS (ACTON) LTD    ★
32/36 CHURCHFIELD ROAD W3 6ED
Open: Mon-Fri 9.00 a.m.-5.00 p.m.
Saturdays 9.00 am-1.00 p.m.

H.P.W.WM.

**LONDON**    Tel. 01-723 2295-6-7
LANGHAM TOOLS LIMITED
13 NORFOLK PLACE
LONDON W2 1QJ

**LONDON**    Tel. (01-567) 2922
G. D. CLEGG & SONS    ★
83 UXBRIDGE ROAD, HANWELL W7 3ST
Mon-Sat 9.00 a.m.-5.30 p.m.
Closed for lunch 1.00-2.00p.m.
Early Closing 1.00 p.m. Wed.

H.P.A.W.WM.D.CS.

**NORBURY**    Tel. (01-679) 6193
HERON TOOLS & HARDWARE LTD.
437 STREATHAM HIGH ROAD SW16
Open Mon-Fri 8.30 a.m.-5.00 p.m.
Wednesday 8.30 a.m.-1.00 p.m.
Sat. 9.00 a.m.-1.00 p.m.

H.P.W.A.

**LONDON**    Tel. (01-636) 7475
BUCK & RYAN LTD
101 TOTTENHAM COURT ROAD W1P 0DY

Open: Mon.-Fri. 8.30 a.m.-5.30 p.m.
Saturday 8.30 a.m.-4.00 p.m.

H.P.W.WM.D.A..

**WEMBLEY**    Tel. 904-1144
ROBERT SAMUEL LTD.    (904-1147
7, 15 & 16 COURT PARADE    after 4.00)
EAST LANE, N. WEMBLEY    ★
Open Mon.-Fri. 8.45-5.15; Sat. 9-1.00
Access, Barclaycard, AM Express, & Diners

H.P.W.CS.E.A.D.

## LONDON

**WOOLWICH**    Tel. (01-854) 7767/8
A. D. SHILLMAN & SONS LTD
108-109 WOOLWICH HIGH STREET
SE18
Open: Mon-Sat
8.30 p.m.-5.30p.m.

H.P.W.CS.A.

**HOUNSLOW**    Tel. (01-570)
Q.R. TOOLS LTD    2103/5135
251-253 HANWORTH ROAD

Open: Mon-Fri 8.30 a.m.-5.30 p.m.
Sat. 9.00 a.m.-1.00 p.m.

P.W.WM.D.CS.A.

**FULHAM**    Tel. (01-385) 5109
I. GRIZZARD LTD.    **E**
84a-b LILLIE ROAD, SW6 1TL
Open: Mon-Sat 9.00-5.30 p.m.
Half day Thursday

H.P.A.BC.W.CS.WM.D.

## MERSEYSIDE

**LIVERPOOL**    Tel. (051-207) 2967
TAYLOR BROS (LIVERPOOL) LTD    **K**
195-199 LONDON ROAD
LIVERPOOL L3 8JG
Open: Monday to Friday
8.30 a.m.-5.30 p.m.

H.P.W.WM.D.A.BC.

## MIDDLESEX

**ENFIELD**    Tel. (01-363) 2935
GILL & HOXBY LTD.    **K**
133-137 ST. MARKS ROAD EN1 1BB

Mon.-Sat. 8.30 a.m.-6.00 p.m.
Early closing Wednesday 1.00 p.m.

H.P.W.WM.T.CS.A

**RUISLIP**    Tel. (08956) 74126
ALLMODELS ENGINEERING LTD.    **E★**
91 MANOR WAY

Open: Mon-Sat 9.00 a.m.-5.30 p.m.

H.P.W.A.D.CS.MF.BC.

**CROWMARSH**    Tel. (0491) 38653
MILL HILL SUPPLIES    **E★**
66 THE STREET
Open: Mon.-Fri. 9.30 a.m.-5.00 p.m.
Thurs. 9.30 a.m.-7.00 p.m.
Sat. 9.30 a.m.-1.00 p.m.

P.W.D.CS.MF.A.BC.

**FARNHAM**    Tel. (0252) 725427
A.B.E. CO. LTD. (Quick Hire)    ★
GOODS SHED
STATION APPROACH, FARNHAM
Open: Mon.-Fri. 8.00 a.m.-5.30 p.m.
Sat. 8.00 a.m.-5.30 p.m.

H.P.W.D.CS.A.BC.

> **An Asterisk \* denotes a Mail Order Service.**

## NORFOLK

**NORWICH**    Tel. (0603) 898695
NORFOLK SAW SERVICES
DOG LANE, HORSFORD
Open: Monday to Friday
8.00 a.m.-5.00 p.m.
Saturday 8.00 a.m.-12.00 p.m.

H.P.W.WM.D.CS.A.

**KINGS LYNN**    Tel. (0553) 2443
WALKER & ANDERSON (Kings Lynn) LTD.
WINDSOR ROAD, KINGS LYNN    **K**
Open: Monday to Saturday
7.45 a.m.-5.30 p.m.
Wednesday 1.00 p.m. Saturday 5.00 p.m.

H.P.W.WM.D.CS.A.

**NORWICH**    Tel. (0603) 400933
WESTGATES WOODWORKING    Tx
61 HURRICANE WAY,    975412
NORWICH AIRPORT INDUSTRIAL ESTATE
Open: 9.00 a.m.-5.00 p.m. weekdays
9.00 a.m.-12.30 Sat.

P.W.WM.D.BC.    **K**

**KING'S LYNN**    Tel: 07605 674
TONY WADDILOVE, UNIT A    ★
HILL FARM WORKSHOPS
GREAT DUNHAM, (Nr. Swaffham)
Open: Tues. — Fri. 10.00 a.m. to 5.30 p.m.
Sat. 9.00 a.m. to 5.00 p.m.

H.P.W.D.T.MF.A.BC.*

**GT. YARMOUTH**    Tel. (0493)
ANGLIA POWER TOOLS    850388
3 DENESIDE, NR30 2HL

Open: Monday to Saturday
8.30 a.m.-5.30 p.m.

H.P.W.D.CS.A.

## NOTTINGHAMSHIRE

**NOTTINGHAM**   Tel. (0602) 225979
POOLEWOOD    and 227064/5
EQUIPMENT LTD.    (06077) 2421 after hrs
5a HOLLY LANE, CHILLWELL
Open: Mon-Fri 9.00 a.m.-5.30 p.m.
Sat. 9.00 a.m. to 12.30 p.m.

P.W.WM.D.CS.A.BC.

## OXON

**WITNEY**    Tel. (0993) 3885.
TARGET TOOLS (SALES,    & 72095 OXON
**TARGET**    HIRE & REPAIRS)    ★
**TOOLS**    SWAIN COURT
     STATION INDUSTRIAL ESTATE
Open: Mon.-Sat. 8.00 a.m.-5.00 p.m.
24 hour Answerphone
BC.W.M.A.

## SHROPSHIRE

**TELFORD**    Tel. Telford (0952)
ASLES LTD    48054
VINEYARD ROAD, WELLINGTON    **EK★**

Open: Mon. Fri. 8.30 a.m.-5.30 p.m.
Saturday 8.30 a.m.-4.00 p.m.

H.P.W.WM.D.CS.BC.A.

## SOMERSET

**TAUNTON**    Tel. (0823) 85431
JOHN HALL TOOLS    ★
6 HIGH STREET

Open Monday-Saturday
9.00 a.m.-5.30 p.m.

H.P.W.WM.D.CS.A.

# shopguide

## SOMERSET

**TAUNTON**     Tel. Taunton 79078
KEITH MITCHELL     ★
TOOLS AND EQUIPMENT
66 PRIORY BRIDGE ROAD
    Open: Mon-Fri 8.30 a.m.-5.30 p.m.
Saturday 9.00 a.m.-4.00 p.m.
H.P.W.WM.D.CS.A.BC.

## STAFFORDSHIRE

**TAMWORTH**     Tel. (0827) 56188
MATTHEWS BROTHERS LTD.     K
KETTLEBROOK ROAD
    Open: Mon-Sat 8.30 a.m.-6.00 p.m.
Demonstrations Sunday mornings by
appointment only
H.P.WM.D.T.CS.A.BC.

## SUFFOLK

**IPSWICH**     Tel. (0473) 40456
FOX WOODWORKING     KE★
142-144 BRAMFORD LANE
    Open: Tues., Fri., 9.00 a.m.-5.30 p.m.
Sat. 9.00 a.m.-5.00 p.m.

H.P.W.WM.D.A.B.C.

## SUSSEX

**ST. LEONARD'S-ON-SEA**     Tel.
DOUST & MONK (MONOSAW)-(0424)
25 CASTLEHAM ROAD     52577

    Open: Mon.-Fri. 8.00 a.m.-5.30 p.m.
Most Saturdays 9.00 a.m.-1.00 p.m.
H.P.W.WM.D.CS.A.

**BOGNOR REGIS** Tel. (0243) 863100
A. OLBY & SON (BOGNOR REGIS) LTD.
"TOOLSHOP," BUILDERS MERCHANT
HAWTHORN ROAD     K
    Open: Mon-Thurs 8 a.m.-5.15 p.m. Fri.
8 a.m.-8 p.m. Sat 8 a.m.-12.45 p.m.
H.P.W.WM.D.T.C.A.BC.

**WORTHING**     Tel. (0903) 38739
W. HOSKING LTD (TOOLS &     KE★
MACHINERY)
28 PORTLAND RD, BN11 1QN
    Open: Mon.-Sat. 8.30 a.m.-5.30 p.m.
Closed Wednesday
H.P.W.WM.D.CS.A.BC.

## TYNE & WEAR

**NEWCASTLE UPON TYNE**     Tel.
J. W. HOYLE LTD.     (0632) 617474
CLARENCE STREET NE2 1YJ     K★
    Open: Mon-Fri 8.00 a.m.-5.00 p.m.
Saturday 9.00 a.m.-4.30 p.m.

H.P.A.BC.W.CS.WM.D.

## TYNE & WEAR

**NEWCASTLE**     Tel. (0632) 320311
HENRY OSBOURNE LTD.     E★
50-54 UNION STREET

    Open: Mon-Fri 8.30 a.m.-5.00 p.m.

H.P.W.D.CS.MF.A.BC.

## WEST MIDLANDS

**BIRMINGHAM** Tel. (021-554) 5177
ROTAGRIP     E★
16 LODGE ROAD, HOCKLEY
    Open:- Mon.-Fri. 9.00 a.m.-5.00 p.m.
Sat. 9.00 a.m.-12.00 p.m.

H.P.W.CS.A.BC.T.MF.

**WOLVERHAMPTON**     Tel. (0902)
MANSAW SERVICES     58759
SEDGLEY STREET     K★

    Open: Mon.-Fri. 9.00 a.m.-5.00 p.m.

H.P.W.WM.A.D.CS.

## YORKSHIRE

**BOROUGHBRIDGE**     Tel. (09012)
JOHN BODDY TIMBER LTD.     2370
FINE WOOD & TOOL STORE     ★
RIVERSIDE SAWMILLS
    Open: Mon.-Thurs. 8.00 a.m.-6.00 p.m.
Fri. 8.00am-5.00pm Sat. 8.00am-4.00pm
H.P.W.WM.D.T.CS.MF.A.BC.

**SHEFFIELD**     Tel. (0742) 441012
GREGORY & TAYLOR LTD     KE
WORKSOP ROAD
    Open: 8.30 a.m.-5.30 p.m.
Monday-Friday
8.30 a.m.-12.30 p.m. Sat.
H.P.W.WM.D.

**HARROGATE**     Tel. (0423) 66245/
MULTI-TOOLS     55328
158 KINGS ROAD     K★

    Open: Monday to Saturday
8.30 a.m.-6.00 p.m.
H.P.W.WM.D.A.BC.

**LEEDS**     Tel. (0532) 574736
D. B. KEIGHLEY MACHINERY LTD.     ★
VICKERS PLACE, STANNINGLEY
PUDSEY LS2 86LZ
    Mon.-Fri. 9.00 a.m.-5.00 p.m.
Sat. 9.00 a.m.-1.00 p.m.
P.A.W.WM.CS.BC.

## YORKSHIRE

**HUDDERSFIELD**     Tel. (0484)
NEVILLE M. OLDHAM     641219/(0484)
UNIT 1 DALE ST. MILLS     42777
DALE STREET, LONGWOOD     ★
    Open: Mon-Fri 8.00 a.m.-5.30 p.m.
Saturday 9.30 a.m.-12.00 p.m.
P.W.WM.D.A.BC.

## YORKSHIRE

**THIRSK**     Tel. (0845) 22770
THE WOOD SHOP     ★
TRESKE SAWMILLS LTD.
STATION WORKS
    Open: Seven days a week 9.00-5.00

T.H.MF.BC.

**KEIGHLEY**     Tel. (0535) 663325
EUROMAIL (TOOLS)     ★
PO BOX 13
108 EAST PARADE
    Open 9.15 a.m.-5.00 p.m.
Not Tuesday but inc. Saturday
H.P.W.A.BC.

**CLECKHEATON**     Tel. (0274)
SKILLED CRAFTS LTD.     872861
34 BRADFORD ROAD     ★

    Open: 9.00 a.m.-5.00 p.m. Monday
Saturday Lunch 12.00 a.m.-1.00 p.m.
H.P.A.W.CS.WM.D.

**LEEDS**     Tel. (0532) 790507
GEORGE SPENCE & SONS LTD.
WELLINGTON ROAD
    Open: Monday to Friday
8.30 a.m.-5.30 p.m.
Saturday 9.00 a.m.-5.00 p.m.
H.P.W.WM.D.T.A.

## SCOTLAND

**EDINBURGH**     Tel. 031-337-5555
THE SAW CENTRE     ★
38 HAYMARKET EH12 5JZ
    Mon.-Fri. 8.30 a.m.-5.30 p.m.
Sat. 9.00 a.m.-1.00 p.m.
H.P.W.WM.D.CS.A.

**PERTH**     Tel. (0738) 26173
WILLIAM HUME & CO     K
ST. JOHN'S PLACE
    Open: Monday to Saturday
8.00 a.m.-5.30 p.m.
8.00 a.m.-1.00 p.m. Wednesday
H.P.A.BC.W.CS.WM.D.

## SCOTLAND

**CULLEN**     Tel: (0542) 40563
GRAMPIAN WOODTURNING SUPPLIES AT
BAYVIEW CRAFTS
Open Mon.-Sat. 9.00 a.m.-5.30 p.m. Sunday
10.00 a.m.-5.30 p.m. Open later July/Aug.
Sept. Demonstrations SAT/SUN or by
H.W.D.MF.BC. appointment

**TAYSIDE**     Tel: (05774) 293
WORKMASTER POWER TOOLS LTD.     ★
DRUM, KINROSS
    Open Mon.-Sat. 8.00 a.m.-8.00 p.m.
Demonstrations throughout Scotland by
appointment
P.W.WM.D.A.BC.

**GLASGOW**     Tel. 041-429-4444/
THE SAW CENTRE     4374 Telex: 777886
650 EGLINTON STREET     E★
GLASGOW G5 9RP
    Mon.-Fri. 8.00 a.m.-5.00 p.m.
Sat. 9.00 a.m.-1.00 p.m.
H.P.W.WM.D.CS.A.

## WALES

**CARDIFF**     Tel. (0222) 595710
DATAPOWER TOOLS LTD,
MICHAELSTON ROAD,
CULVERHOUSE CROSS
    Open: Mon.-Fri. 8.00 a.m.-5.00 p.m.
Sat. 9.00 a.m.-1.00 p.m.
H.P.W.WM.D.A.

**CARMARTHEN**     Tel. (0267) 237219
DO-IT-YOURSELF SUPPLY     K
BLUE STREET, DYFED
    Open: Monday to Saturday
9.00 a.m.-5.30 p.m.
Thursday 9.00 a.m.-5.30 p.m.
H.P.W.WM.D.T.CS.A.BC.

**CARDIFF**     Tel. (0222) 396039
JOHN HALL TOOLS LIMITED     ★
CENTRAL SQUARE

    Open: Monday to Saturday
9.00 a.m.-5.30 p.m.
H.P.W.WM.D.A.BC.

**SWANSEA**     Tel. (0792) 55680
SWANSEA TIMBER & PLYWOOD CO. LTD.
57-59 OXFORD STREET     ★

    Open: Mon to Fri 9.00 a.m.-5.30 p.m.
Sat. 9.00 a.m.-1.00 p.m.
H.P.W.D.T.CS.A.BC.

**KEY: CS CUTTING OR SHARPENING SERVICES**

**KEY: MF MATERIAL FINISHES**

**KEY: BC BOOKS/CATALOGUES**

972

973

974

# WOOD SUPPLIERS

# Classified Advertisements

All classified advertisements under £25.00 must be pre-paid: Cheques/PO made payable to A.S.P. Ltd. (WW). **Private and trade rate** *46p per word (VAT inclusive) minimum £6.90.* **Display box rates s.c.c.** *£8 (minimum 2.5×1). All advertisements are inserted in the first available issue.*
**Copy to Classified Dept. (W.W.), A.S.P. Ltd., 1 Golden Square, London W.1.**
There are no re-imbursements for cancellations.

**Telephone
Peter Magnani
01-4370699**

## FOR SALE

**THE FINEST SELECTION ON DISPLAY IN SCOTLAND!**
WOODWORKING & METALWORKING MACHINERY POWER TOOLS HAND TOOLS
**THE SAW CENTRE**
HIRE OR BUY.
*Visit our* NEW SHOWROOM at EGLINTON TOLL GLASGOW
Tel: 041-429 4444/4374, Telex: 777886 SAWCO G
Also at, 38 Haymarket Terrace, Edinburgh EH12 5JZ. Tel: 031-337 5555

**OPEN**
Mon - Fri
8am - 5pm
Sat 9am - 1pm

---

MORTISERS; TENNONERS; SPINDLES; PLANERS; BANDSAWS; LATHES; CROSSCUTS; ROUTERS; SANDERS; DRILLS?
YOU CAN CERTAINLY SEE ALL CLASSES AND TYPES OF MACHINES HERE.

WE ARE MAIN STOCKING AGENTS FOR:
MULTICO; ELU; SEDGWICK; KITY; SCHEPPACH; INCA; CORONET; DeWALT; WARCO; DOMINION; HITACHI; STARTRITE; TREND; ASHLEY ILES; SORBY.

*CALL US ABOUT WOODTURNING LESSONS*

*WOODCARVING LESSONS (See our Swiss carving tools)*
*ALWAYS HELPFUL, KNOWLEDGEABLE, GOOD SERVICE AT:*
**CLEVELAND WOODCRAFT**
**38-42 CRESCENT ROAD, MIDDLESBROUGH.**
**TEL: (0642) 813103**

---

**Bygones**
Just one item from our catalogue

**MARPLES PARING GOUGES**
Boxwood handles
1/4" – 6" radius
Straight or Cranked

*WHILE STOCKS LAST*
Special rates for quantities

Please send 50p in stamps for catalogue

TILGEAR, 20 Ladysmith Road, Enfield, Middx., EN1 3AA Tel:01-363 8050/3080

---

**WOOD TURNERS SUPPLIES**
Tudor Craft, Jung Hans clock movements, 20 different hands to choose from, barometers, weather stations, cutlery, jewellery box lids, pepper/salt/nutmeg mills, coffee grinders, ceramic tiles, new range which include hand painted tiles. Our service is extremely fast, friendly and competitive — give us a try. Send SAE for catalogue to

**TUDORCRAFT,**
c/o Wentworth, Talbot Avenue, Little Ashton, Sutton Coalfield, West Midlands B74 3DD.

---

**CUBAN MAHOGANY** for sale, 1" thick boards. For details ring 0532 623269.

---

**BAGS, WRAPPINGS, TISSUE, BOXES, BUSINESS CARDS.** Any shape, size, amount. Comprehensive samples. 90p. Terry Andrews, 53A Parsons St., Banbury OX16 8NB.

---

FOR ALL SUPPLIES FOR THE
**Craft of Enamelling**
ON METAL
Including
**LEAD-FREE ENAMELS**

PLEASE SEND 2 × 10p STAMPS FOR FREE CATALOGUE, PRICE LIST AND WORKING INSTRUCTIONS

**W. G. BALL LTD.**
ENAMEL MANUFACTURERS

Dept. W. LONGTON
STOKE-ON-TRENT
ST3 1JW

---

**HAND CARVED**
'Adam Style' Mantle motifs in Mahogany — Example 10" × 5" centre lamp and two side pieces.
Send S.A.E. for details and quotation. Your own design quoted for if required.
**SAM NICHOLSON**
22 Lisnagarvey Drive, Lisburn, Co. Antrim, N. Ireland.
Phone Lisburn 3510

---

415v from 230v house mains to run your 3-phase machines, the 'Maldon' Unit £66 1½ h.p.
**MALDON TRANSFORMERS**
**134 London Road, Kingston-on-Thames**
Tel: 546-75 34
Access - Barclay

---

**LACE BOBBIN** turning blanks. Extensive range of exotics, Ivory, lathes, miniature tools, sundries, lace supplies. SAE J. Ford, 5 Squirrels Hollow, Walsall WS7 8YS.

---

**USERS AND COLLECTORS** tools for sale at the Old Craft Tool Shop, 15 High Street, Whillon Middx. Telephone 01-755 0441.

---

**ANTIQUE HAND OPERATED** mortising machine 1898 (similar Question Box, October) with chisels £130. Sevenoaks (0732) 450408.

**OLD WOODWORKING PLANES.** Spiers smoothing £75. Stanley rule and level compass plane £45. Sheffield (0742) 362852.

**CORONET HOBBY LATHE** 48" BC 5" swing overbed. One revolving centre, 2 butterfly centres, 4" face plate, ½ Jacobs chuck, little used. Cost new £320 will accept £250. Also 8 cu.ft. of Yew £50. Circular saw bench £30. Chisels and G-Clamps, B&D 3" planer. Drills and other small tools. Scarborough (0723) 515560.

**YEW** blocks, blanks, billets, spindles. All sizes from £9 cu.ft. R. Fowler, Meopham, Kent (0474) 814468.

**(FRESH SAWN HOLLY)** Limited supply variety & sizes. Reasonable rates details 02607 282. Evenings and Weekends.

**WOODWORKER** annuals 1948-55, 1957-59, 11 Volumes £88. Excellent condition. Pontefract 704083 Postage extra.

## WORKSHOP EQUIPMENT

**EBAC TIMBER SEASONERS,** Protimeter moisture meters, always good prices and advice from the man who pioneered small scale seasoning. John Arrowsmith, 74a Wilson Street, Darlington, Co. Durham. DL3 6QZ. Tel: 0325 481970. T/C

**ARKANSAS** whetstones now readily available from importer. Large selection. SAE for lists. C. Rufino, Manor House, South Clifton, Newark, Notts. T/C

**SINGLE** to 3 phase converters up to 20HP 18 and 21 throat bandsaws. Illustrated details. HAB Engineering Unit 24, 16-20 George St., Balsall Heath, Birmingham B12 9RG. Telephone 021-440-6266.

**MARKING STAMPS** — name stamps branding irons supplied to your requirements SAE for details. Davey, 37 Marina Drive, Brixham, Devon TQ5 8BB. T/C

**CORONET MAJOR** (Red) Lathe saw-table planer, thicknesser, slot morticer. Table plus attachments on Bench £650 o.n.o. Tel: 06285 25230.